NATIONAL GEOGRAPHIC | **U.S. HISTORY**

AMERICA
THROUGH THE LENS

Clockwise from center:

- American aviator Amelia Earhart poses in the cockpit of her autogyro in 1931 after setting an altitude record for female pilots.

- Completed in 1909, the Manhattan Bridge spans the East River in New York City, connecting Lower Manhattan to Brooklyn.

- Frederick Douglass was born around 1818, escaped from slavery, sought an education, and became an abolitionist and activist.

- A drone hovers mid-air, capturing footage of rain clouds with its camera.

- Rock art, or petroglyphs, carved by the ancestral Puebloans cover a rock formation near Blanding, Utah.

- An American icon—a bison—enjoys the safety of the Maxwell Wildlife Refuge in Canton, Kansas.

- The work of artist Rosalia Torres-Weiner is part of an exhibition called *Gateways/Portales,* which explores the experiences of Latino immigrants and migrants in four U.S. cities with growing Latino populations.

- The vinyl record player evolved from the phonograph, which was invented by Thomas Edison in the 1870s.

- Alfalfa, a hay crop commonly used to feed cattle, is harvested by a farmer in Kansas.

Back Cover (not shown):

American company SpaceX successfully launches the Falcon Heavy rocket into deep space on February 6, 2018 from Cape Canaveral in Florida.

Acknowledgments

Grateful acknowledgment is given to the authors, artists, photographers, museums, publishers, and agents for permission to reprint copyrighted material. Every effort has been made to secure the appropriate permission. If any omissions have been made or if corrections are required, please contact the Publisher.

LEXILE®, LEXILE® FRAMEWORK, LEXILE ANALYZER®, LEXILE ANALYZER® EDITOR ASSISTANT™, LEXILE TITLES DATABASE™, LEXILE CAREER DATABASE™, LEXILE GROWTH PLANNER™, the LEXILE® logo and POWERV™ are trademarks of MetaMetrics, Inc., and are registered in the United States and abroad. The trademarks and names of other companies and products mentioned herein are the property of their respective owners. Copyright © 2017 MetaMetrics, Inc. All rights reserved.

Pre-AP™ is a registered trademark of The College Board and used under agreement.

Credits
Front Cover: (tl) Tetra Images/Getty Images. (tr) Andy Sacks/Getty Images. (cl) ©Rosalia Torres/Brandon Torres-Weiner. (c) ©Bettmann/Getty Images. (cr) pidjoe/Getty Images. (bl1) Joel Sartore/National Geographic Creative. (bl2) David Hiser/National Geographic Creative. (bc) Amos Chapple/Getty Images. (br) Library of Congress, LC-DIG-ds-07422.

Back Cover: SpaceX.

Acknowledgments and credits continue on page R93.

Printed in the United States of America.
Print Number: 03
Print Year: 2023

For product information and technology assistance, contact us at Customer & Sales Support, 888-915-3276

For permission to use material from this text or product, submit all requests online at **www.cengage.com/permissions**

Further permissions questions can be emailed to **permissionrequest@cengage.com**

National Geographic Learning | Cengage
1 N. State Street, Suite 900
Chicago, IL 60602

Cengage is a leading provider of customized learning solutions with office locations around the globe, including Singapore, the United Kingdom, Australia, Mexico, Brazil, and Japan. Locate your local office at **www.cengage.com/global.**

Visit National Geographic Learning online at **NGL.Cengage.com/school**
Visit our corporate website at **www.cengage.com**

ISBN: 978-133-738-7149

SENIOR CONSULTANTS

FREDRIK HIEBERT

Fred Hiebert is National Geographic's Archaeologist-in-Residence. He has led archaeological expeditions at ancient Silk Roads sites across Asia. Hiebert was curator of National Geographic's exhibition "Afghanistan: Hidden Treasures from the National Museum, Kabul," and its more recent exhibition, "The Greeks: Agamemnon to Alexander the Great."

PEGGY ALTOFF

Peggy Altoff's career includes teaching middle school and high school students, supervising teachers, and serving as adjunct university faculty. Altoff served as a state social studies specialist in Maryland and as a K–12 coordinator in Colorado Springs. She is a past president of the National Council for the Social Studies (NCSS) and served on the task force for the 2012 NCSS National Curriculum Standards.

FRITZ FISCHER

Fritz Fischer is a professor and Director of History Education at the University of Northern Colorado, where he teaches U.S. History and Social Studies Education courses. Fischer is also Chair Emeritus of the Board of Trustees of the National Council for History Education (NCHE), the largest national membership organization focusing on history education at the K–12 level.

NATIONAL GEOGRAPHIC

PROGRAM CONSULTANTS

KATHRYN KEANE
Vice President, National Geographic
Exhibitions

ROBERT REID
Travel Writer
National Geographic Digital Nomad

WILLIAM PARKINSON
Associate Curator of Anthropology,
Field Museum of Natural History
National Geographic Explorer

ANDRÉS RUZO
Geothermal Scientist
National Geographic Explorer

NATIONAL GEOGRAPHIC TEACHER REVIEWERS

National Geographic works with teachers at all grade levels from across the country. The following teachers reviewed
chapters in *U.S. History: America Through the Lens.*

CRYSTAL CULP
McCracken Regional School
Paducah, KY

NICOLE ESHELMAN
Manheim Township High School
Lancaster, PA

MARY JANZEN
Duncan High School
Fresno, CA

NATALIE WOJINSKI
West Contra Costa USD
Richmond, CA

KAREN DAVIS
St. Joseph School
Conway, AR

KIMBERLY HENDRICKS
Park Hill South High School
Kansas City, MO

SYLVIA MCBRIDE
Castle Park High School
Chula Vista, CA

NATIONAL GEOGRAPHIC SOCIETY

The National Geographic Society contributed significantly to *U.S. History: America Through the Lens.*
Our collaboration with each of the following has been a pleasure and a privilege: National Geographic
Maps, National Geographic Education and Children's Media, and National Geographic Missions programs.
We thank the Society for its guidance and support.

NATIONAL GEOGRAPHIC EXPLORATION

National Geographic supports the work of a host of anthropologists, archaeologists, adventurers, biologists, educators, writers, and photographers across the world. The individuals below each contributed substantially to *U.S. History: America Through the Lens.*

SAM ABELL
National Geographic
Photographer

ROBERT BALLARD
National Geographic
Explorer-in-Residence

ARI BESER
Fulbright–National
Geographic Fellow

KEVIN CRISMAN
National Geographic
Explorer

JASON DE LEÓN
National Geographic
Explorer

LESLIE DEWAN
National Geographic
Explorer

KEVIN HAND
National Geographic
Explorer

BILL KELSO
National Geographic
Explorer

SARAH PARCAK
National Geographic
Fellow

SANDRA POSTEL
National Geographic
Freshwater Fellow
(2009-2015)

TRISTRAM STUART
National Geographic
Explorer

THROUGH THE LENS PHOTOGRAPHERS

The work of the National Geographic photographers below helps tell the story of America in striking, image-focused lessons.

LYNSEY ADDARIO

JIMMY CHIN

JEFFREY GUSKY

DAVID GUTTENFELDER

MICHAEL NICHOLS

PAUL NICKLEN

THE NATIONAL GEOGRAPHIC APPROACH

Most of us recognize that familiar magazine with the yellow border on newsstands and library shelves. You've probably come to expect from *National Geographic* engaging stories on historical and global topics, with interesting photographs. But did you know that the magazine is only one part of an institution that dates back more than 128 years—and today plays an important role in world events?

OUR PURPOSE: The National Geographic Society pushes the boundaries of exploration to further our understanding of our planet and empower us all to generate solutions for a healthier and more sustainable future.

SCIENCE AND EXPLORATION

National Geographic has become one of the largest nonprofit scientific and educational institutions in the world. NatGeo supports thousands of scientists, archaeologists, marine biologists, divers, climbers, photographers, researchers, teachers, oceanographers, geologists, adventurers, physicists, artists, curators, and writers who work on projects that add to the scientific and human record.

THE NATIONAL GEOGRAPHIC LEARNING FRAMEWORK

The Learning Framework defines and shapes National Geographic's philosophy about teaching and learning. The framework is based on the **Attitudes**, **Skills**, and **Knowledge** that embody the Explorer mindset. It covers diverse fields of knowledge and recognizes the core principles established at National Geographic, as well as the values held by families, communities, and cultures. You will see National Geographic Learning Framework activities in each unit of this text.

The chart on the next page outlines the Attitudes, Skills, and Knowledge (A.S.K.) dimensions of the National Geographic Learning Framework as it applies to *American Stories*.

ATTITUDES

Curiosity. An explorer remains curious about how the world works. An explorer is adventurous, seeking out new and challenging experiences.

Responsibility. An explorer has concern for other people, cultures, and the planet. An explorer considers multiple perspectives and respects others regardless of differences.

Empowerment. An explorer acts on curiosity, respect, responsibility, and adventurousness and persists in the face of challenges.

SKILLS

Observation. An explorer notices and documents the world and is able to make sense of those observations.

Communication. An explorer is a storyteller, communicating experiences and ideas effectively through language and media. An explorer has literacy skills, interpreting and creating new understanding from spoken language, writing, and a wide variety of visual and audio media.

Collaboration. An explorer works effectively with others to achieve goals.

NG Learning Framework: Attitudes, Skills, and Knowledge

ATTITUDES Feelings we want students to express and experience during the activity	SKILLS What we want students to do during the activity	KNOWLDEGE The type of content the activity pertains to
Curiosity	Observation	Our Human Story
Responsibility	Communication	Our Living Planet
Empowerment	Collaboration	Critical Species
	Problem Solving	New Frontiers

Problem Solving. An explorer is able to generate, evaluate, and implement solutions to problems. An explorer is a capable decision-maker—able to identify alternatives and weigh trade-offs to make a well-reasoned decision.

KNOWLEDGE

In addition to the skills and attitudes of an explorer, people need a certain knowledge set to understand how the world works. National Geographic expresses this critical knowledge through our key focus areas:

Our Human Story. Exploring where we came from, how we live today, and where we may find ourselves tomorrow.

Our Living Planet. Understanding the amazing, intricate, and interconnected systems of the changing planet we live on.

Critical Species. Revealing, celebrating, and helping to protect the amazing and diverse creatures we share our world with.

New Frontiers. Searching every day for the "new" and the "next," using the latest technology and science to go places no one has ever been and find answers no one has ever found.

A Note on National Geographic Style

Throughout the text, you will see the abbreviations B.C. and A.D. As you know, a date followed by B.C. refers to the number of years the date occurred before the birth of Christ. A date preceded by A.D. refers to the number of years the date occurred after the birth of Christ. Many historians use the abbreviations B.C.E. and C.E. for these time periods. B.C.E. stands for "Before the Common Era," and C.E. stands for "Common Era." The National Geographic Society adheres to the practice of using B.C. and A.D., and that is what is used in this text.

NATIONAL GEOGRAPHIC LEARNING
SOCIAL STUDIES CREDO

National Geographic Learning wants students to think about the impact of their choices on themselves and others, to think critically and carefully about ideas and actions, to become lifelong learners and teachers, and to advocate for the greater good as leaders in their communities. NGL follows these guidelines:

1 Our goal is to establish relevance by connecting the physical environment and historical events to students' lives.

2 We view history as the study of identity.

3 We foster the development of empathy, tolerance, and understanding for diverse peoples, cultures, traditions, and ideas.

4 We empower students to explore their interests and strengths, find their own voices, and speak out on their beliefs.

5 We encourage students to become active and responsible citizens on local and national levels and to become global citizens.

6 We believe in the beauty and endurance of the human record and the need to preserve it.

7 We affirm the critical need to care for the planet and all of its inhabitants.

PLANNING A MUSEUM VISIT

As they study history, students learn how and where civilizations developed through the centuries. They learn how to think about the world and discover the ways in which cultures and civilizations are similar—and how they are unique. They come to understand that knowing why a civilization developed can help them interpret the past, analyze the present, and anticipate the future.

By Kathryn Keane, Vice President, Exhibitions, National Geographic Society

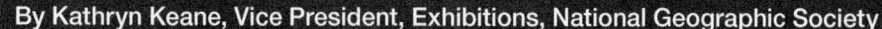

To help your students take a trip into the past, to actually immerse themselves in history, take them to a museum. Museums are like time machines. They are the keepers of our shared and collective history. Museums were created to keep track of the most special examples of human-made objects, or **material culture**. Paintings, sculpture, pottery, jewelry, clothing, furniture, cars, toys, weapons, tools, fishing lures—just about anything that humans make is a remarkable historical record of the way we live.

Some examples of material culture are featured in the Curating History lessons in this program. Each lesson features objects drawn from the collection of an important U.S. museum. But what do we learn from this stuff? Why are some things in a museum and others are not?

Generally, museums look for the best artifacts for their collections, the ones that helped define a people or culture. Egyptian sarcophagi, Peruvian face pots, African ceremonial masks, Native American pottery, or Cycladic figurines from the Greek islands are all examples of artifacts that help us better understand those who made them. People from thousands of miles away and hundreds of years ago feel more familiar when you observe that even in the distant past people ate on plates and drank from cups, had rugs on their floors and keys for their doors, and rocked their babies to sleep in wooden cradles. **Material culture** refers to what humans make—but also what makes us human. There is no better way to see this than in a museum. Use the following tips to ensure a positive museum visit for your class.

1. Plan ahead.

Before you visit, talk about the museum and its collection. Most museums have great websites, and many even have their entire collections online. Identify the must-see artifacts and works of art—the more students know ahead of time, the better. Contact the museum to see if a docent or museum educator can accompany your group. Plan travel logistics carefully, building in frequent small breaks, snacks, and so forth.

2. Let the museum help.

Once you arrive, check in with the information desk. Get maps and brochures for your students. If you haven't arranged for a docent or tour guide, ask if one might be available to accompany your class on a tour.

3. Encourage students to read, listen, and learn—and to use their imaginations.

Point out that labels, maps, time lines, videos, and audio tours will give students all the information they need as "context" for the objects. Audio tours are usually narrated by a curator, or expert, and are almost like getting a private tour. Remind students to use an artifact analysis form similar to the one shown in their History Notebook to help them analyze an artifact. Model how to think about the meaning of the objects. Ask students to imagine what it was like to live a long time ago or in a faraway place—or even in the mind of a creative artist. **ASK:** What will students 100 years from now learn about our society in a museum?

4. Dos and don'ts

Remind students to keep their voices down and leave their phones turned off and out of sight. Most important: Don't touch artifacts or lean on cases. Don't take photos unless expressly allowed, and make sure students are careful around fragile or delicate objects.

5. Back in the classroom

Spend some class time reviewing the visit and eliciting students' reactions to what they saw. **ASK:** What did you like best about the museum? What was your favorite artifact? What surprised you the most?

Encourage students to explore the museums in their community and to check out museums when they travel. Museums can become familiar and exciting companions in studying history.

SUPPORTING YOUNG PHOTOGRAPHERS

Photography as storytelling. For 40 years, I have made photographs for *National Geographic* magazine. Do you have students who are interested in photography? Here are some ideas to discuss with them.

By Kenneth Garrett, National Geographic Photographer

Help students understand how to know their subject thoroughly.

To photograph or illustrate a story, they need to think about what they want to communicate. Explain that they can follow the work of key scientists or historians in the field. It is all about being ready to photograph the moment of discovery and then to publish it in the popular media for everyone to see. Without media coverage, many great discoveries lie silent on shelves in storerooms around the world. The process is always the same. Research the subject. Know the people. Know how to be in the right place at the right time.

Help students practice their photographic and storytelling skills.

I have held this advice close to my heart throughout my career—always working to make sure that my photographs have something to say. Assignments that can be accompanied by photographs will give students practice at explaining something with visuals. Obviously, the more practice, the better.

Explain the importance of crafting each image with intent and being prepared.

I was in Guatemala working on a story about remote imaging of Maya cities, and my editor knew there was going to be a planetary alignment of Venus, Jupiter, and Mars directly over a temple in Tikal and that it would not happen again for 200 years. Of course he wanted me to get a photograph of it. I brought a portable spotlight to "paint" the temple with light and made a wonderful photo with the planets aligned over the temple. This is what I call making your own luck—being prepared and ready for what's about to happen.

Talk about customizing lighting and how to make the subject "pop."

If my subject is an artifact in a museum, I study it with a flashlight until I find an angle where it "speaks" to me. Then I create a lighting setup to bring out the personality that I identified with the flashlight. Sometimes I even make the photo by painting the object with the light from the flashlight. Photographs are made up of light, so lighting the subject, whether it is an object, a landscape, or an architectural feature, is most important. The image must pop, and readers must say "wow," or they won't stop to learn. There is simply too much visual competition out there.

Emphasize that students should be adaptable but at the same time unafraid to develop their own vision.

I was trained to be a generalist, flexible, able to adapt to any situation. I was identified as the photographer to send if there was nothing to photograph because I would *find* something to photograph. In today's world, I still believe it is important to be adaptable, but the market is often looking for photographers with an unusual specialty—a way of seeing that translates into your own unique style.

Help students develop a portfolio.

Encourage students to work for the school newspaper or yearbook. Once they have built a portfolio, they can approach local newspapers. Today, with Instagram, Facebook, and other platforms, they can have their photos "out there" as soon as they shoot them. Remind students that the ownership of their photos can be compromised if they are posted online.

Remind students to follow the new technology in photography.

Today's cameras have eliminated much of the technical difficulty of capturing an image. With this new technology come exciting new opportunities to push the envelope— for example, to shoot in virtual darkness, shoot remotely, shoot from a drone, or shoot underwater from a remotely operated submersible. Constantly following the new technology is a requirement of today's photography business.

Caution students to be prepared for the lifestyle of a photographer.

An established photographer has to be prepared to be away from home for weeks or months at a time, living with a subject until just the right situation presents itself: until a rapport is established that allows special access to an event, until a discovery is made, or until a polar bear walks up to the camera!

NatGeo's Digital Nomad Takes on U.S. History

What does a so-called Digital Nomad do? Based on what we see of Robert Reid in the *Reid on the Road* video series that accompanies *America Through The Lens*, just about anything! Here, Robert shares his thoughts on how travel helps to make history come alive—and connect to students' lives today.

By Robert Reid, National Geographic's Digital Nomad

Every time I travel to a place as National Geographic's Digital Nomad, my first questions are the same: What happened here, what books and movies talk about it, and how can I add an angle to the ongoing story, something that adds to the existing conversation? In short, my focus is looking backward to look forward. I do that by putting history into travel. It's fun and informative. Working on this textbook is the same, but in reverse direction—in trying to show how history is alive and accessible, I'm putting it through the filter of travel.

For each of the videos that accompany *America Through The Lens*, we talk with local experts—including those impersonating George Washington, overseeing Motown Records, and digging gold mines—and go up close and personal.

The goal is to bring a question or two that, I hope, will resonate with students: Why is the Statue of Liberty the greatest gift of all time? Why did Pilgrims wear funny hats? What's a hippie? Then I use travel to answer those questions.

And in some cases, I wear three layers of wool to do so. (Watch the videos—you'll get it!)

Perhaps my favorite story about developing the *Reid on the Road* video series was visiting Angel Island in San Francisco Bay. I lived in the city several years ago and had never made it there, nor did I realize that it was, in effect, the Ellis Island of the West Coast. Going there, I interviewed a Chinese American whose father entered the country through Angel Island, and I heard the stories of how immigrants entering the country from the west didn't exactly get the same reception as those entering through New York. I'll not forget it.

The goal, again, is to make a difference in students' understanding of this country—and to show that history isn't relegated to the past but is indeed alive. It moves, it changes. And how we use it is how we go through life. This may sound serious, but it's the first step in our personal chase of understanding. Which means that, like travel itself, it's about as much fun as you can have.

Robert Reid, NG's Digital Nomad, interviews a modern-day George Washington on the banks of the Delaware River.

INQUIRY AND THE HISTORY NOTEBOOK

The History Notebook that accompanies *America Through The Lens* is the student's space to comment on ideas raised in the lessons in each chapter. Many lessons in the Student Edition are supported by History Notebook pages that foster inquiry by providing critical-thinking questions and writing prompts. These features and lessons include the following:

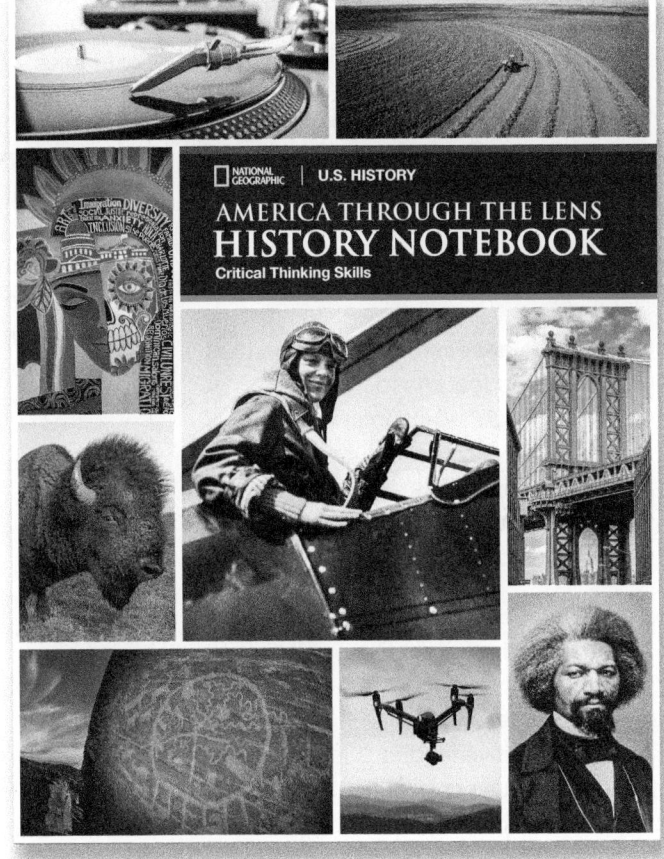

- **Archaeology in U.S. History**, a look at how the study of artifacts adds to our understanding of U.S. history

- **American Stories** at the beginning of each chapter, in print or digital format

- **Curating History**, museum lessons featuring a collection of artifacts

- **American Places**, iconic places around the United States

- **Through the Lens**, a closer look at the work of National Geographic Photographers

- **National Geographic Explorer lessons** featuring men and women doing critical research and exploration in the United States

- **American Voices**, contemporary commentary on key history-makers

- **American Galleries**, digital collections of images around one of the chapter's themes

- **Reid on the Road** video series that accompanies the program

EXAMPLE

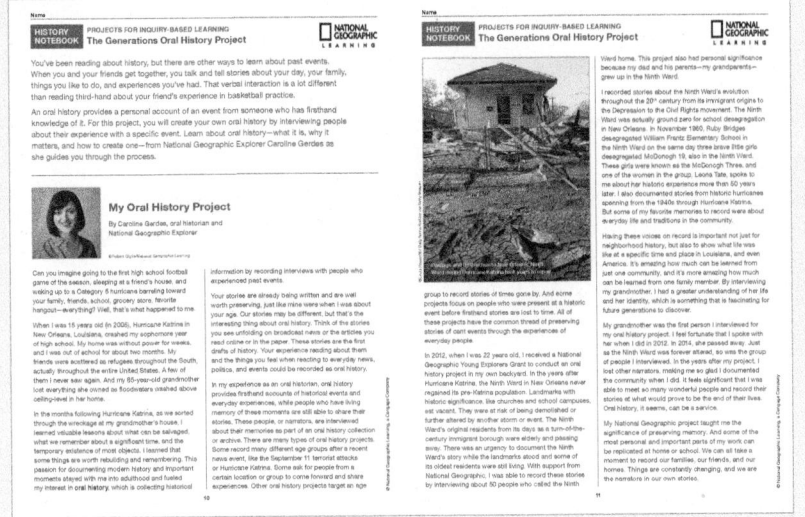

The Generations Oral History Project Students interview people about their experience with a specific event and create an oral history.

Not all students can memorize and recite the numerous dates and facts in a U.S. history program. However, all students are capable of reacting to events and ideas and forming solid opinions. All students can learn to use evidence to support their opinions, and all students can come to realize that their opinions count. The History Notebook is their partner in that endeavor.

Students can record their thoughts about how they see themselves fitting into the larger picture of American life and culture today. The Notebook also provides a format for raising questions they want to answer as they study American history and options for student projects, such as oral history projects. The History Notebook is a key to helping students explore what it means to be an American.

ASSESSMENT IN AMERICA THROUGH THE LENS

America Through The Lens provides opportunities for two main types of assessment: formative and summative.

- **Formative assessment** is assessment *for* learning. Its focus is to assist in immediate learning, it is delivered from teacher to individual students, and it takes place during instruction or in the sequence of lessons.

- **Summative assessment** is assessment *of* learning. Its focus is to measure students' progress and inform future teaching or to evaluate educational programs. Summative assessment takes place at the end of a unit, semester, or course.

Some tests or projects may serve both a formative and a summative purpose. Effective use of both formative and summative assessment enables you to create a positive feedback loop in which you can use assessment results to differentiate instruction or determine which content or skills need to be retaught and then customize future assessments to gauge learning of new and retaught material.

It is important, too, to engage in a variety of assessment modes. Some students may better demonstrate their understanding through performance assessments, such as discussions, debates, or presentations. Others may be more accurately assessed using pencil-and-paper tests and writing assignments. Students should have chances to demonstrate their knowledge through both individual and cooperative assessments.

The activities and tests in *America Through The Lens* offer a generous variety of opportunities for both formative and summative assessment in numerous modes. The following assessments, with examples, will enable you to support and measure learning at the lesson, chapter, and unit levels.

Historical Thinking Each lesson in the Student Edition ends with questions that assess students' understanding of the lesson's content and their ability to analyze it. You can use this quick formative assessment to help students develop their critical thinking skills and to determine whether any concepts need to be reinforced or retaught.

The skill head on each question reflects the support for historical thinking offered in *America Through The Lens*. Practice with these social studies skills supports student comprehension and enables students to improve their writing about history.

EXAMPLE
HISTORICAL THINKING

1. **READING CHECK** What steps did the U.S. government take to prepare for war?

2. **ANALYZE CAUSE AND EFFECT** How did entering the war affect the organization of the economy of the United States?

3. **DRAW CONCLUSIONS** How did the government's actions both unite and divide Americans?

4. **INTERPRET VISUALS** Select one of the propaganda posters (right) and consider its purpose. Who was its intended audience and what techniques were used to make the poster effective?

Guided Discussions and Active Options For each lesson, this Teacher's Edition provides Guided Discussion questions and an On Your Feet activity that requires students to engage physically by moving in the classroom and to perform collaborative activities, such as fishbowl conversations, interviews, and inside-outside circles. By observing students and providing feedback, you can use these activities for formative assessment of content mastery, critical thinking skills, and discussion skills.

EXAMPLE

GUIDED DISCUSSION

1. **Make Inferences** Considering the context of when World War I began, why would Germany expect their new weapon, the U-boat, to be more successful in combating the British blockade? *(U-boats could travel under water, which would have made them difficult for ships of that era to detect.)*

2. **Form and Support Opinions** Was Germany justified in attacking U.S. merchant and passenger ships? Support your answer with evidence from the chapter. *(Answers will vary. Possible responses: No, because Germany and the United States were not at war; yes, because the United States was exporting war supplies to aid the Allies, Germany's enemies.)*

Guided Discussion questions like those above provide additional material for classroom interaction. These questions can be discussed as a whole class, used for small group work, or assigned as homework.

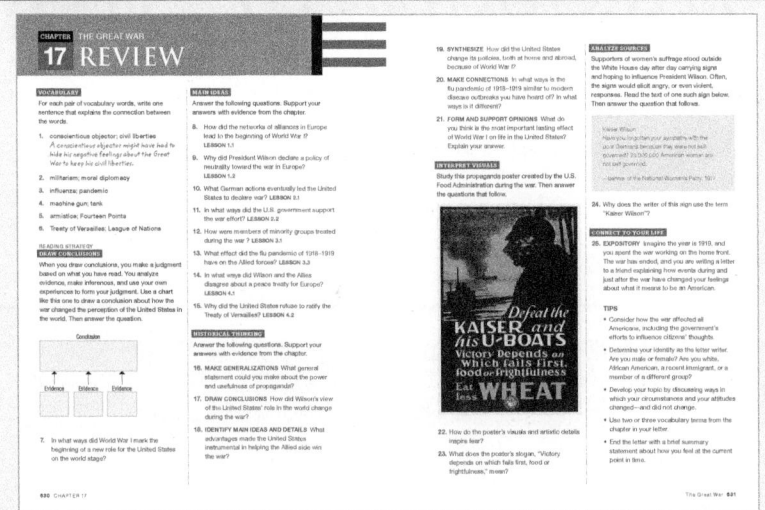

Chapter Review Each chapter concludes with a review that includes a short vocabulary test and a series of constructed response items that require students to restate the main ideas in the chapter, engage in historical thinking, interpret a visual, analyze a primary source, and write a brief essay connecting the chapter topic to their lives. This summative assessment allows you to measure students' progress and give feedback in the form of a chapter grade.

Unit Test At the end of each unit, a summative assessment evaluates students' grasp of the main ideas and overarching themes of the unit. As in the chapter review, students answer historical thinking questions, interpret visuals, and analyze a primary source. In the extended response, students engage in comparative thinking as they compare two eras or themes in history.

Gradebook The electronic Gradebook function in MindTap allows teachers to track and analyze an individual student's progress with ease. You can view the class's grades for each activity, click on a grade to view assignment details such as score and student answers, view the scores for each individual student, and categorize assignments for purposes such as applying weighting for different assessments. Students may also view their assignments, due dates, and scores. This accurate and flexible grading tool helps teachers create the assessment feedback loop that benefits all students.

Projects At the end of each unit, a Unit Inquiry and two National Geographic Learning Framework activities can be used as summative performance assessments. Teachers may use these projects to assess students' research and presentation skills as well as their content knowledge. In addition, four Projects for Inquiry-Based Learning in the History Notebook can be used for both formative and summative assessment. Over the course of these long-term projects, you will have frequent opportunities to provide ongoing assessment and feedback to students, and the end products can be assessed to measure student learning.

EXAMPLES

Write a Conflict Negotiator Profile

ATTITUDE Curiosity

KNOWLEDGE Our Human Story

Choose a historical figure you read about in this unit who demonstrated good conflict resolution skills. Research primary and secondary sources to gather evidence about his or her role in negotiating a resolution to a conflict. Note discrepancies among sources. Then write a profile for this individual or create something more visual, such as a poster or digital presentation. Your profile should include information such as birth and death dates, where the person lived, and the work she or he did. Your profile must also highlight a specific resolution to a conflict this person helped negotiate. Consider exploring what you think might have happened if she or he had not taken proactive action in negotiating a resolution.

Settle a Dispute

ATTITUDES Empowerment, Responsibility

SKILLS Collaboration, Problem Solving

Collaborate with a small group to research a dispute in your school or community. Assign roles to group members, such as researcher, interviewer, writer, and presenter. Scan the news and other diverse sources to gather evidence about the dispute, including people or groups on both (or all) sides of the conflict and important dates or events. Then, as a group, create a document or set up a poster or whiteboard on which you can chart the evidence you gather. Hold a meeting to discuss how your group might settle the dispute. Use the evidence you have gathered to put together a viable proposal. Once your group has settled on a solution, present both the dispute and your solution to the class.

The National Geographic Learning Framework activities help students understand the attitudes, skills, and knowledge that are involved in living the life of an Explorer. You will find additional explanation about the Learning Framework with your online teacher's materials and at the National Geographic website under "Education."

MINDTAP FOR *AMERICA THROUGH THE LENS*

MindTap is a personalized learning experience with relevant assignments that guide students to analyze, apply, and improve thinking. Teachers can measure skills and impact outcomes with ease.

EXAMPLE MINDTAP HOME PAGE

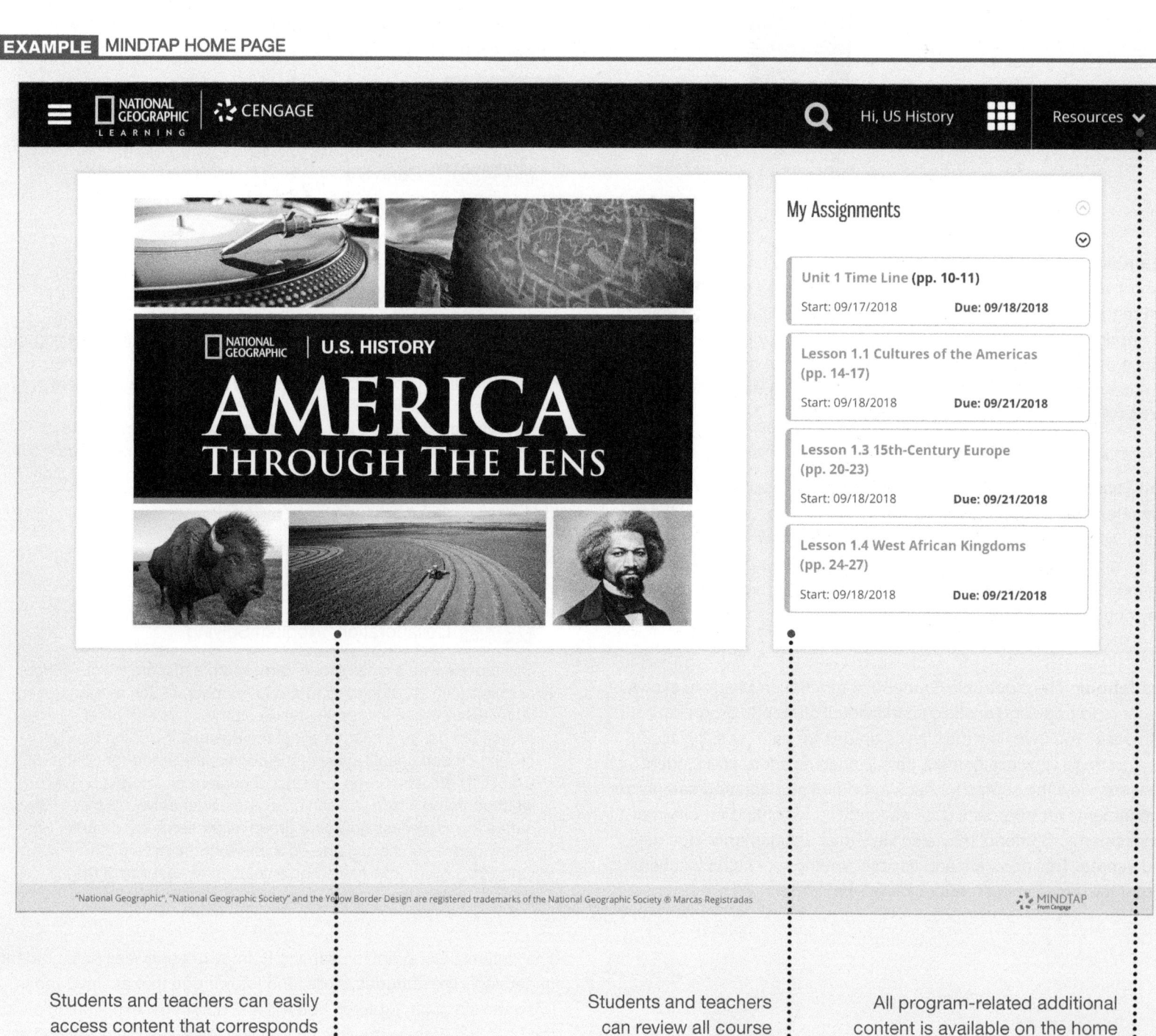

Students and teachers can easily access content that corresponds to weekly assignments.

Students and teachers can review all course assignments at a glance.

All program-related additional content is available on the home page and at point of use.

Digital Experience

The Student and Teacher eEditions provide enhancements and extra features not found in the print editions.

eReader

- The responsive page layout adjusts to students' screen or browser size.

- Clickable vocabulary words link to definition pop-ups.

- The Modified Text feature provides lesson content at a lower reading level.

- Additional features allow students to take notes, highlight text, and bookmark important content.

Student Tools

- Resources appear at the book, unit, chapter, and lesson level.

- Students can bookmark useful resources for easy access.

- eAssessment provides immediate feedback.

EXAMPLE STUDENT AND TEACHER eEDITIONS

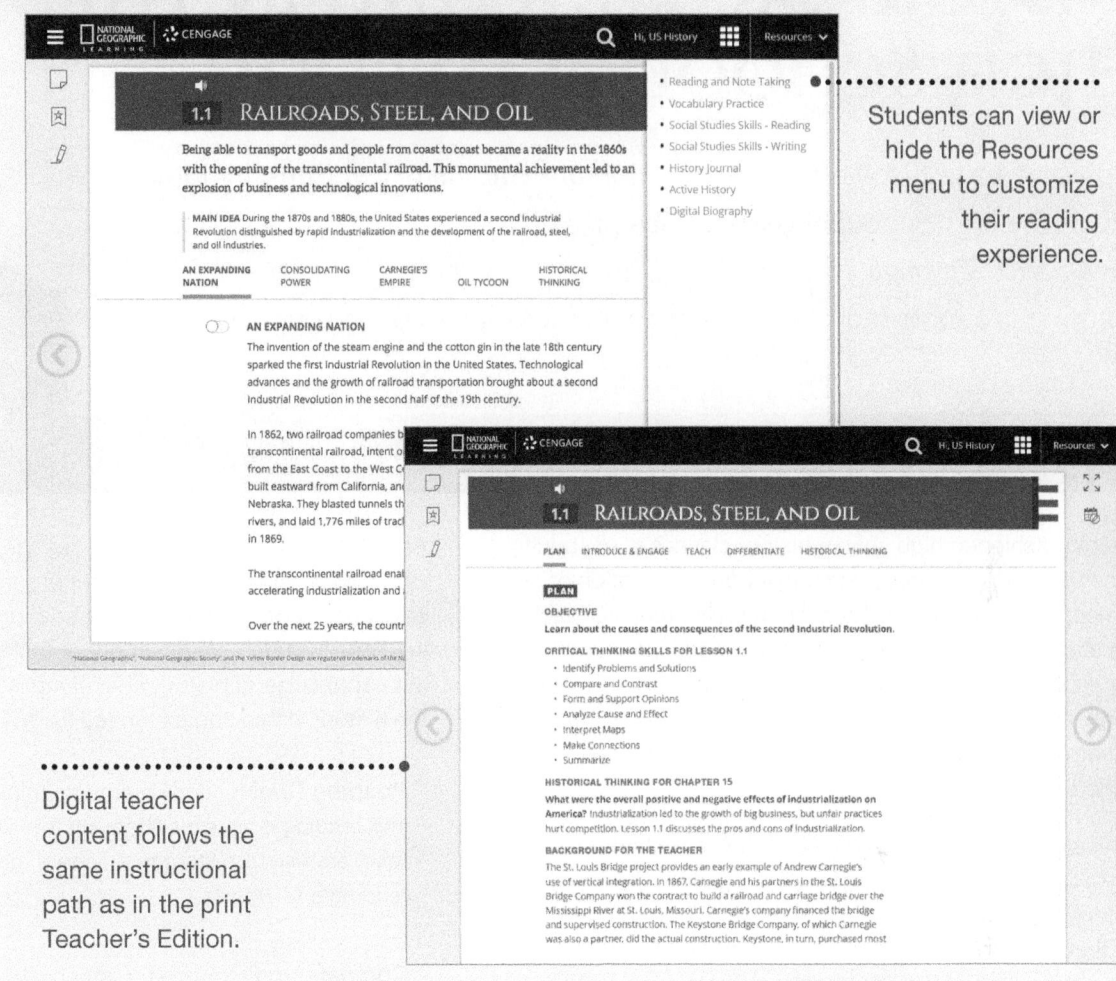

Students can view or hide the Resources menu to customize their reading experience.

Digital teacher content follows the same instructional path as in the print Teacher's Edition.

Class Management and Metrics

A series of tools provides teachers with flexibility and support.

Teacher Dashboard

- Assignments can be customized to control student access to content.

- Student progress can be tracked in the Gradebook.

- A series of reports allow teachers to measure student progress.

- A correlations tool allows teachers to search content by content standard.

EXAMPLE TEACHER DASHBOARD

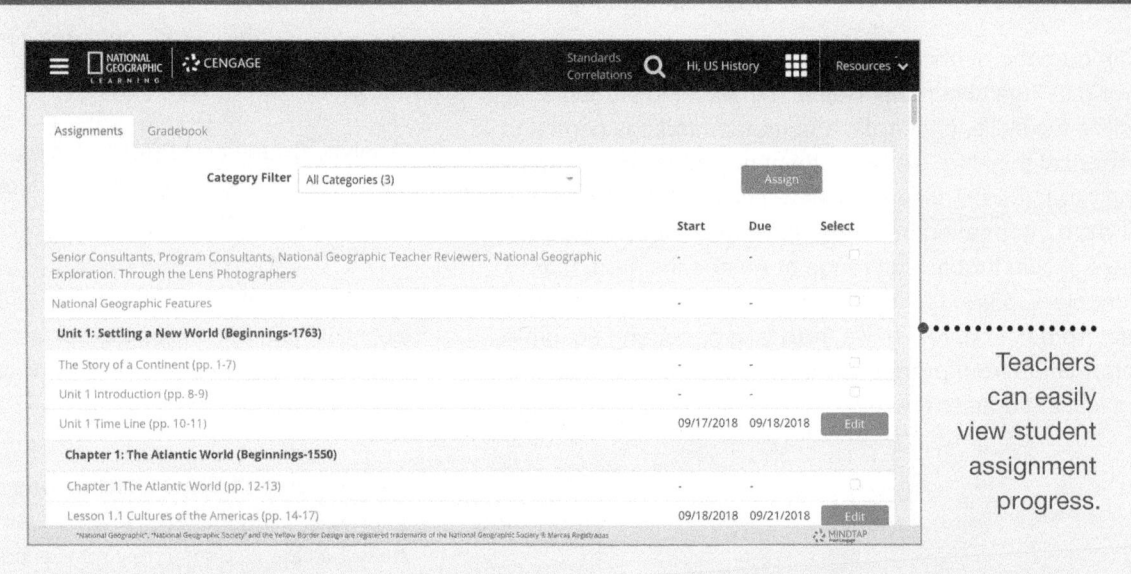

Teachers can easily view student assignment progress.

HISTORICAL THINKING IN THE HIGH SCHOOL CLASSROOM

Professor Fritz Fischer's understanding of what historical thinking looks like in the high school classroom has proved to be a powerful foundation for *America Through The Lens*. Here, he explains the ways historical thinking is supported in the chapters and lessons in this program.

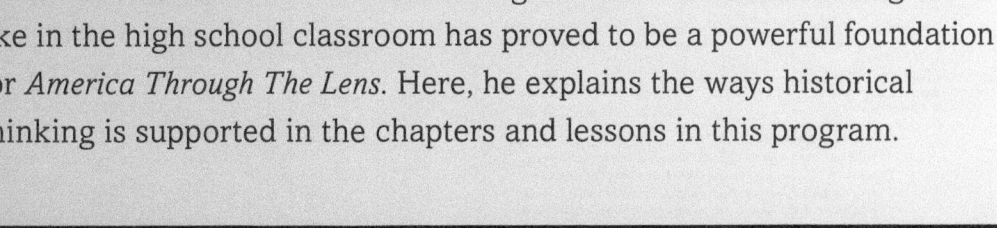

By Fritz Fischer, Professor of History and History Education, University of Northern Colorado

The old-fashioned high school history classes many adults remember too often devolved into a boring recitation of names, dates, and facts. Teachers merely presented facts in a stand-and-deliver lecture format, expecting students to regurgitate these facts on multiple-choice exams. Students were confronted with a blizzard of detail and often struggled to learn the content, only to forget what they learned in rushed bouts of memorization.

Ironically, historians themselves do not learn history in this way. History is about questions, not answers. To study history is to learn how to inquire. To understand the past, we first need to question the past. We learn how to gather and sift evidence from the past in order to answer these questions. Then we take this evidence and fashion it into an argument, or a logical story, about what happened. These are the basic processes in what historians and history educators now refer to as **historical thinking**.

The purpose of historical thinking is not to create a world of little historians. Rather, by teaching students to utilize the skills, concepts, and understandings central to historical thinking, we teach them how to better navigate their own lives. These abilities will help students gather and sift information in our current world. Recent studies have shown that a wide range of Americans, from high schoolers to adults, have tremendous difficulty separating fact from fiction, real news from fake news, and accurate information from propaganda. Historical thinking is a critical antidote to these problems.

America Through The Lens utilizes the skills, concepts, and understandings of historical thinking as a central organizational principle. Students will encounter a Historical Thinking section at the end of each lesson. These sections include a wide variety of tasks, all of which are important in building the capabilities of historical thinking in students. Here are some examples of the historical thinking exercises from *America Through The Lens*:

Reading Check Many historical thinking tasks overlap with literacy skills, and reading is no exception. History is a literary discipline, and history teachers must be literacy teachers, helping students become proficient at reading and writing.

Compare and Contrast Historical understanding requires students to be able to differentiate among various examples, ideas, and events.

Interpret Visuals Historical evidence comes in many forms, and often it is not written down. Paintings, photographs, and artifacts are important historical evidence. Yet their significance and connection to other historical evidence is not always clear, and students need practice in interpreting this evidence.

Analyze Cause and Effect This is one of the most basic requirements of historical thinking. As we all know, history is not a haphazard collection of unconnected events.

Make Inferences We need to look beyond the words in a document and try to connect them with the context of the times. Another way of stating this is that students need to learn to read between the lines to understand the subtext of a document.

Synthesize and Draw Conclusions Students need to be encouraged to put information together and develop their own interpretations of ideas and events based on the evidence they have encountered.

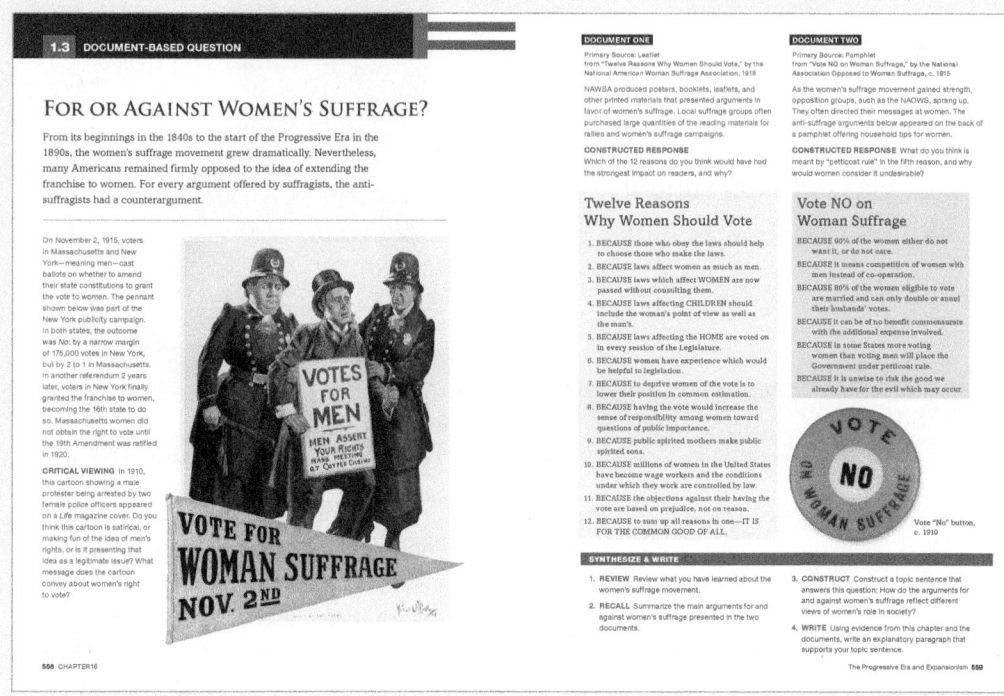

This is merely an introductory list and, as you will see in the program materials, not exhaustive.

Perhaps the most exciting historical thinking exercises in *America Through The Lens* are the Document-Based Questions, or DBQ, in each chapter. Fundamental to the concept of historical thinking is the understanding and use of *primary sources*, the building blocks of history. They are the documents and artifacts from the past, words spoken and artifacts fashioned by historical actors. Students need to be challenged to work to understand and then interpret these sources. Yet individual sources are insufficient to provide such an interpretation. Students need to learn how to examine a variety of sources with differing viewpoints if they are to have any chance of understanding the "truth" about the past. The DBQs in *America Through The Lens* include two or three important sources for students to examine and think about as they create their own interpretations of the past.

I often encounter teachers who want to learn more about historical thinking and how they can integrate these ideas into their method of telling the American story. One idea is to get connected to organizations where history teaching and historical thinking are discussed on a regular basis.

For much of my career, I have been intimately connected with the National Council for History Education (NCHE), an organization designed to bring together K–12 history teachers, university historians, and public historians on an equal playing field. These groups have much to teach each other about how to think historically and how students learn this method of thinking. NCHE annual conferences, the NCHE newsletter *History Matters!* and NCHE professional development workshops provide just such platforms.

There are also plenty of free resources online that provide more information and ideas for teachers about historical thinking. NCHE has a website (*nche.net*) that provides a "Blueprint for Student Learning in History" as well as an outline of "History's Habits of Mind," among other important resources.

The Stanford History Education Group has a brilliant website (*sheg.stanford.edu*) including lesson ideas and assessments all centered on historical thinking.

In the first decade of the 21st century, the federal government funded the Teaching American History Grant Program, which created an extraordinary free website at *teachinghistory.org*. This site includes valuable videos explaining historical thinking at all levels and also has links to hundreds of different lessons connected to historical thinking.

Basing classroom activities on historical thinking means creating an active, inquiry-based classroom. Students should be consistently questioning the past, questioning the teacher, and questioning each other. They should constantly be engaging and manipulating historical sources and creating interpretations about how these sources fit together. Finally, students should learn how to argue about their interpretations in a thoughtful and civil way. There is no better way to engage and excite a group of 11th graders than by creating such a historical thinking–based classroom.

For more on historical thinking in the classroom:

nche.net

sheg.stanford.edu

teachinghistory.org

ACTIVE LEARNING IN THE HISTORY CLASSROOM

Easily influenced by peers and distracted by text messaging and social media, high school learners can be challenging. A class of high school students is a highly diverse group of learners with myriad personalities and learning styles—what's the best way to reach them?

By Peggy Altoff, Senior Consultant, former teacher and past president of NCSS

As you know from experience, a high school teacher must be fully prepared to engage students each day and flexible enough to change plans at a moment's notice with the shifting classroom dynamic. National Geographic's U.S. History program, *America Through The Lens*, contains a wealth of teaching options that are perfect for the active teacher—and active students.

Variety and Flexibility

An expansive repertoire of proven strategies and appropriate activities provides the best preparation for each day's teaching. The structure of the Student Edition in this program is specifically designed to provide options that engage students in meaningful learning activities. The two- and four-page formats of the lessons in a chapter allow for several approaches, including

- selecting lessons and sections that are most appropriate for any given class of learners;

- focusing on one lesson each day to provide a depth of content knowledge;

- using cooperative learning activities that allow students to teach and learn from each other.

In a cooperative learning activity, for example, students can participate in a Jigsaw strategy, in which groups of students become "experts" on one lesson in a chapter. Next, all expert groups switch into new groups with each new group having one expert on each lesson. Each expert is then responsible for teaching the others in the group about the lesson. (See **Cooperative Learning Strategies** in this Teacher's Edition for a complete explanation of the Jigsaw strategy.)

Another cooperative learning possibility involves breaking a lesson into segments by subheading. Most of the lessons in the Student Edition have two to four subheadings. This makes it easy for students to work in pairs or small groups, with each student reading and learning about information in one segment and then sharing and discussing with the others.

You may also consider having students work in pairs or small groups to discuss a **Historical Thinking** question, a **Critical Viewing** question, or other text-based features. Experience suggests that each grouping strategy requires practice with students so that they can meet teacher expectations for appropriate conduct while acquiring knowledge of the content presented.

Student Edition activities are intended to address a variety of learning styles. The **Historical Thinking** questions at the end of each lesson provide skill practice with interpreting maps, analyzing visuals, sequencing events, and so on that can be completed individually, in small groups, or as a class. **Chapter Reviews** include an activity that requires students to demonstrate what they have learned through writing. A **Unit Wrap-Up** at the end of each unit offers students insight into the work of archaeologists, scientists, writers, and other experts. It also includes a **Unit Inquiry** project that asks students to present what they've learned using many different formats, including writing, video, and multimedia.

Components for the Teacher

The Teacher's Edition of *America Through The Lens* presents many possibilities for active learning and student engagement. The **Cooperative Learning Strategies** section offers a preview of the types of strategies located throughout the Teacher's Edition with a clear explanation of how to implement each one. For the highly experienced teacher, this may offer a review of practical procedures. Those new to the profession will probably want to return to these pages frequently to plan new experiences for students.

The **Chapter Planner** in the Teacher's Edition provides an overview of the lesson support in, each chapter and lists such tools as **Reading and Note-Taking**, **Vocabulary**

Practice, Social Studies Skills Lessons, Section Quizzes, and Formal Assessment Tests. The Strategies for Differentiation section that opens each Teacher's Edition chapter offers ideas that engage different groups of students under the headings Striving Readers, Inclusion, English Language Learners, Gifted & Talented, and Pre-AP. You can decide how to apply each of these strategies to individual learners.

For daily planning, refer to each lesson's Plan, Teach, and Differentiate sections. The Teach section includes discussion questions and activities that help students summarize and analyze the lesson. It also contains an Active Options component that especially engages students with Critical Viewing, National Geographic Learning Framework, and (my personal favorite) On Your Feet activities. We know that high school students are constantly moving and doing, and this feature provides ways to channel that bounding energy meaningfully.

Think carefully about how to select the options that are appropriate for your students. For me, Rule No. 1 in working with high school students has always been to start simple and move toward the complex.

It may not be a good idea, for example, to try to implement all of the available strategies and activities in one lesson. Start with those that make the most sense to you and gradually experiment with others. Inform students when you attempt a new strategy or activity and get their feedback on ways to improve it the next time. The activities and strategies in this program are not meant to provide a recipe for success. Instead, they form a menu of options that support daily decision-making based on your own abilities and preferences and those of your students.

EXAMPLE TEACHER'S EDITION LESSON ALIGNED WITH STUDENT EDITION LESSON 2.2 IN CHAPTER 15

Striking images, graphics, and detailed maps engage and inform students.

Each lesson offers two Differentiate options for instruction.

The Plan section helps teachers prepare to teach lessons.

The Introduce & Engage and Teach sections provide multiple access points for teaching content.

Project-Based Learning

Project-based learning is integral to successful history–social studies instruction. Well-designed projects allow students to

- explore a topic in depth;

- hone their skills in research, analysis, and critical thinking;

- work collaboratively with others toward a shared goal—an ability that is highly valued in both academic circles and the professional marketplace;

- become engaged and enthusiastic about a social studies topic;

- exercise creative control over their final product.

In addition, teachers may use projects to assess both students' grasp of content and their progress in developing collaboration and critical thinking skills.

The best projects not only allow students to express themselves creatively but also guide them through a rigorous, structured process of inquiry and research.

The best projects also ask students to create an end product that can be shared with their classmates. This project read-out can become part of each student's creative portfolio.

The Nature of Inquiry

The National Council for the Social Studies (NCSS) details the process of inquiry in the College, Career, and Civic Life Framework for Social Studies State Standards, or C3 Framework. The document proposes an Inquiry Arc that enumerates four dimensions of the process:

1. **Developing Questions and Planning Inquiries** Teachers or students generate a compelling question to guide research and supporting questions to help in seeking out specific evidence. The Historical Thinking Question at the beginning of each chapter in *America Through The Lens* is designed to spark inquiry-style thinking in students as they move through the text.

EXAMPLES

HISTORICAL THINKING QUESTION
How did World War I affect the United States politically, economically, and socially?

HISTORICAL THINKING QUESTION
How did the civil rights movement redefine American identity?

2. **Applying Disciplinary Concepts and Tools** Students determine which disciplines—economics, civics, geography, or history—relate to their guiding and follow-up questions. The tools and concepts from these disciplines will enable them to seek out and analyze evidence.

3. **Evaluating Sources and Using Evidence** Students conduct their research, determine which sources are both useful and reliable, and locate relevant evidence they can use for claims and counterclaims.

4. **Communicating Conclusions and Taking Informed Action** Students shape and present their final projects, which may take a wide variety of forms, such as traditional essays, multimedia presentations, performance pieces, or virtual museum galleries. When a project relates to a present-day issue, students may also follow up on their conclusions by taking constructive action within the school or in the wider community.

Of necessity, some projects during the school year will be smaller in scope and may not emphasize all four dimensions of the Inquiry Arc. For example, the inquiry question may be determined in advance by the teacher, or students may be directed to use the textbook or other preselected sources for their research. Similarly, students' choices of methods for communicating their conclusions may be limited to a few options that take less time to produce.

America Through The Lens offers a variety of options for inquiry and project-based learning:

- The History Notebook contains four long-term **Projects for Inquiry-Based Learning** that can be completed over a semester or a school year. Over the course of the projects, students conduct research and synthesize information from multiple sources to answer questions on broader themes.

- At the end of each unit, a **Unit Inquiry** challenges students with open-ended questions and guides them to gather evidence from the text, synthesize a response, and present their conclusion to the class in a creative, engaging format.

  For example, the Unit Inquiry for Unit 6 in *America Through The Lens* asks students to create a strategy they think could have been successful in resolving a conflict that took place in the United States between 1914 and 1940.

  Students use a chart to record the context in which their chosen conflict unfolded and shape a strategy that they present through a classroom debate, election campaign, or speech to the class.

  You may choose to expand the scope of the Unit Inquiry by having students conduct independent research using other sources or explicitly apply concepts from more than one discipline in their presentations. Alternatively, you might choose to limit the scope of the project by limiting students' options for presenting their projects.

- The National Geographic Learning Framework activities at the end of each unit also offer multiple opportunities for inquiry and creative thought. Depending on students' needs, you might select an activity and explicitly guide the class through the four dimensions of the Inquiry Arc to complete it, or you might have students complete the activities independently or in small groups.

EXAMPLE UNIT INQUIRY

Research Skills

Developing good research skills benefits students both inside and outside the classroom. Learning how to locate and evaluate information helps them improve the critical thinking skills they need not only to make and support an argument within a social studies project but also to make well-considered decisions in their everyday lives. Students can hone their research skills through instruction, guidance, and a great deal of practice.

Before launching the first inquiry project, make sure students understand the differences between quantitative and qualitative research:

quantitative research: "hard evidence"—numbers, facts, and figures that can support an assertion

qualitative research: opinions from scholars, scientists, and other experts; firsthand accounts of events; information that provides insights into reasons or motivations

You might also explain that quantitative research answers *who, what, where,* and *when* questions. Qualitative research helps answer *why* and *how* questions.

Social studies inquiry projects should incorporate both types of research. Often, it is qualitative research that enables students to form hypotheses or outline their arguments. Both qualitative and quantitative research can be used to support claims and counterclaims.

Teachers should provide examples of sources students can use to conduct both types of research. For example, government websites, scientific articles, newspaper articles, and encyclopedia entries can be mined for quantitative information.

Qualitative information can be found in firsthand accounts of historical events and analyses of those events written by scholars. Of course, many sources contain both types of information, and students might benefit from an activity in which they review an article to distinguish the qualitative and quantitative information it contains.

Similarly, at the beginning of the year, teachers should provide numerous examples of both reliable and unreliable sources and clearly explain the characteristics of each. You might also provide a list of approved sources for students to use or have students submit their sources before they proceed to gather evidence. As students gain confidence and skill, you can gradually release to them the responsibility for finding and evaluating sources.

USING KEY INSTRUCTIONAL STRATEGIES

It is important to use a variety of instructional strategies to support students' development of reading and thinking skills for content mastery. This Teacher's Edition provides numerous activities to scaffold and advance learning. Many of these are cooperative learning strategies for partners, small groups, or the whole class. Below are some additional strategies you might implement across all units or in selected chapters to support and engage students.

Before Reading a Chapter

Vocabulary The first page of each chapter includes a list of the Key Vocabulary terms students will find as they read. Review the vocabulary terms with the class. Point out that some terms are important names, places, and events (e.g., League of Nations, Great Migration), while others are general vocabulary words students will need to understand the chapters (e.g., alliance, sedition). The latter are Tier Two and Tier Three words for the most part.

Read all the Key Vocabulary terms aloud so that students can hear the pronunciation of those unfamiliar to them. Read each general vocabulary word and have students raise their hands if they understand it. Ask students to define the words or use them in sentences. Then encourage students to make as many connections as they can between the words and their own lives (e.g., "Dad says it's my *duty* to babysit my siblings sometimes.").

Tell students that all the vocabulary words for the entire text are gathered in a glossary in the reference section of the book. They can refer to the glossary as they read through the chapters. You can also assign the digital Vocabulary Practice page for each section of a chapter as homework.

Critical Viewing Have pairs or small groups briefly discuss the Critical Viewing question on the introductory image for each chapter. One student should record the group's answers. When the class has finished reading the chapter, tell the pairs or groups to reconvene and examine the photo again. Ask them to discuss whether they would change or expand their answers based on what they have learned. Encourage students to share their responses with the class.

American Stories Some students are most comfortable working on their own and find collaborative learning activities stressful. Use the American Story in each chapter as an opportunity to allow students to work independently from time to time. Ask students to perform a task appropriate to the American Story in question, such as

- finding connections between the topic and their own lives;

- choosing a photo or feature and explaining why they find it interesting;

- summarizing the key points.

You may have students present their answers to the class or write a short paragraph to turn in.

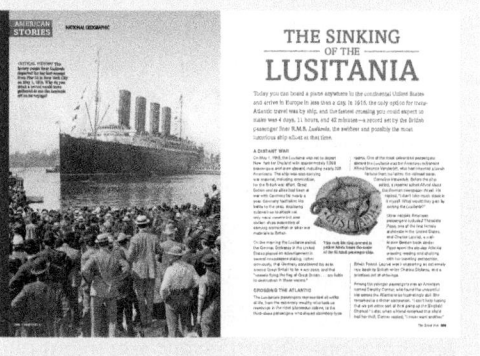

EXAMPLE AMERICAN STORY

THE SINKING OF THE LUSITANIA

When students work in small groups to read an American Story, you might choose one of the following strategies, depending on the format of the story:

- Give the groups a thematic question to guide their reading and to discuss after completing their reading. Group members might take turns reading aloud, or they might read independently and get together for discussion.

- Some American Stories lend themselves to a Jigsaw approach. Assign individual students to read separate sections or features and then share their understanding with the group. This strategy is especially effective for ELs or struggling readers because each student can take the time to focus on understanding a shorter portion of the text.

While Reading a Chapter

Reading Strategy Assign partners to make a copy of the graphic organizer mentioned in the chapter reading strategy (visible in the review at the end of each chapter). At the end of each lesson, allow partners time to briefly discuss their reading and update the graphic organizer. You may wish to have partners compare their graphic organizers with those of other pairs before they complete the review activities at the end of the chapter. Consider varying your pairing strategy, sometimes placing more advanced learners with students who are struggling or with ELs at the Emerging or Expanding level and sometimes pairing advanced learners and challenging them to find as many entries for their graphic organizers as possible.

EXAMPLE READING STRATEGY

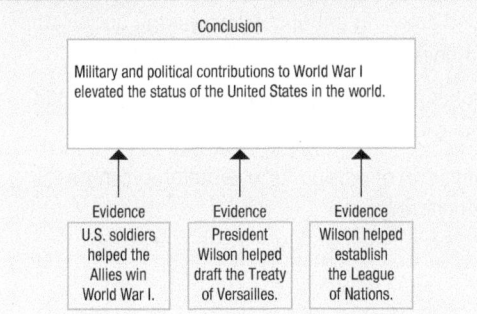

Conclusion

Military and political contributions to World War I elevated the status of the United States in the world.

Evidence
U.S. soldiers helped the Allies win World War I.

Evidence
President Wilson helped draft the Treaty of Versailles.

Evidence
Wilson helped establish the League of Nations.

Collaborative Conversations The Teach section that accompanies each lesson in this Teacher's Edition offers a variety of cooperative learning opportunities in the Guided Discussions and Active Options. Use these activities to introduce and practice the skills and concepts of collaborative conversations. The California History–Social Science Framework outlines some behaviors students should practice in order to have productive conversations. At the beginning of the year, explain these behaviors to students:

- Listen actively—Make eye contact and use body language to convey attentiveness.
- Use meaningful transitions—Make it clear to your classmates that you are reacting to their ideas by using transitions that indicate agreement or disagreement, clarification, building on an idea, and so forth.

- Be inclusive—Ensure that all members of the group participate.
- Take risks—Explore ideas that may be challenging and questions that have no easy answers.
- Focus on the prompt—Group members should help each other stay on topic.
- Use textual evidence—Cite specific evidence from the text to support your points.
- Keep an open mind—Consider all viewpoints presented in the conversation and be ready to change your opinion if someone presents solid evidence to support a claim.

Monitor conversations and provide feedback on students' use of these behaviors. As the year progresses, transfer responsibility for monitoring and rating their conversational skills to the students.

You may wish to provide sentence frames at the start of the year to help students use meaningful transitions and to support the participation of ELs and students who feel insecure about speaking up in a group. Some states' Departments of Education provide an extensive list of sentence frames that you may customize for your class.

Analyze Author's Choices Engage students in discussions analyzing the choices of visuals to illustrate the regular lessons and the special features such as Curating History (below) and American Voices. Ask questions such as: What do these objects tell about people's attitudes during the time period? What other objects could have been included in this feature? Why did the author choose to use a political cartoon in this lesson? Questions like these help students reach for a deeper understanding of the material and give them practice for interrogating other texts, such as primary sources.

After Reading a Chapter

Chapter Review Use the Chapter Review to assess students' mastery of the content, and review lessons as necessary. You may wish to have students work in pairs. In particular, consider pairing ELs at the Emerging or Expanding level with more proficient readers for the Analyze Sources item. Encourage ELs to ask questions about words or structures they find difficult, and tell the partners to answer to the best of their ability. This process will enable both partners to gain a deeper understanding of the primary source passage.

EXAMPLE CURATING HISTORY

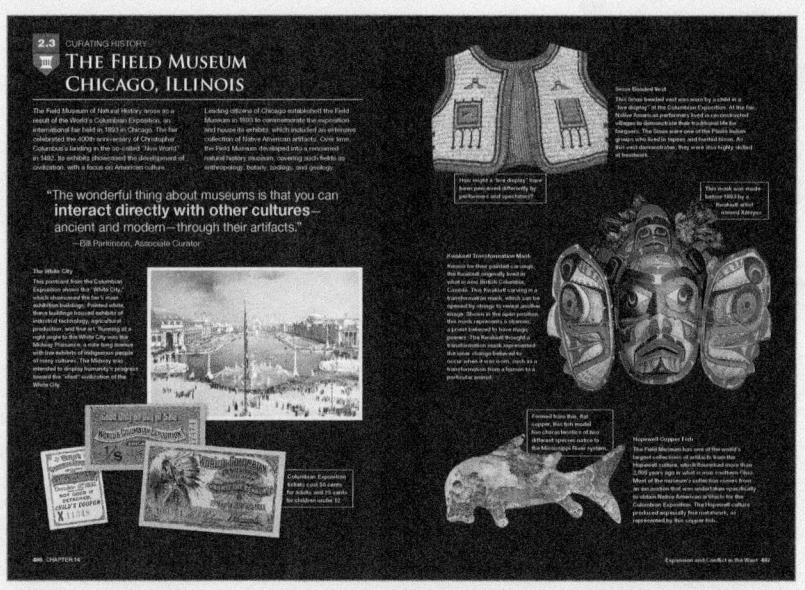

COOPERATIVE LEARNING STRATEGIES

Cooperative learning strategies transform today's classroom diversity into a vital resource for promoting students' acquisition of both challenging academic content and language. These strategies promote active engagement and social motivation for all students.

STRUCTURE & GRAPHIC	DESCRIPTION	BENEFITS & PURPOSES
CORNERS 1's 2's 1 Topic A 2 Topic B 3 Topic C 3's 4's 4 Topic D	• Corners of the classroom are designated for focused discussion of four aspects of a topic. • Students individually think and write about the topic for a short time. • Students group into the corner of their choice and discuss the topic. • At least one student from each corner shares about the corner discussion.	• By "voting" with their feet, students literally take a position about a topic. • Focused discussion develops deeper thought about a topic. • Students experience many valid points of view about a topic.
FISHBOWL	• Part of the class sits in a close circle facing inward; the other part of the class sits in a larger circle around them. • Students on the inside discuss a topic while those outside listen for new information and/or evaluate the discussion according to pre-established criteria. • Groups reverse positions.	• Focused listening enhances knowledge acquisition and listening skills. • Peer evaluation supports development of specific discussion skills. • Identification of criteria for evaluation promotes self-monitoring.
INSIDE-OUTSIDE CIRCLE	• Students stand in concentric circles facing each other. • Students in the outside circle ask questions; those inside answer. • On a signal, students rotate to create new partnerships. • On another signal, students trade inside/outside roles.	• Talking one-on-one with a variety of partners gives risk-free practice in speaking skills. • Interactions can be structured to focus on specific speaking skills. • Students practice both speaking and active listening.
JIGSAW Expert Group 1 A's Expert Group 2 B's Expert Group 3 C's Expert Group 4 D's	• Group students evenly into "expert" groups. • Expert groups study one topic or aspect of a topic in depth. • Regroup students so that each new group has at least one member from each expert group. • Experts report on their study. Other students learn from the experts.	• Becoming an expert provides in-depth understanding in one aspect of study. • Learning from peers provides breadth of understanding of overarching concepts.

STRUCTURE & GRAPHIC	DESCRIPTION	BENEFITS & PURPOSES
NUMBERED HEADS	• Students number off within each group. • Teacher prompts or gives a directive. • Students think individually about the topic. • Groups discuss the topic so that any member of the group can report for the group. • Teacher calls a number and the student with that number reports for the group.	• Group discussion of topics provides each student with language and concept understanding. • Random recitation provides an opportunity for evaluation of both individual and group progress.
ROUNDTABLE	• Seat students around a table in groups of four. • Teacher asks a question with many possible answers. • Each student around the table answers the question a different way.	• Encouraging elaboration creates appreciation for diversity of opinion and thought. • Eliciting multiple answers enhances language fluency.
TEAM WORD WEBBING	• Provide each team with a single large piece of paper. Give each student a different colored marker. • Teacher assigns a topic for a word web. • Each student adds to the part of the web nearest to him or her. • On a signal, students rotate the paper and each student adds to the nearest part again.	• Individual input to a group product ensures participation by all students. • Shifting points of view support both broad and in-depth understanding of concepts.
THINK, PAIR, SHARE	• Students think about a topic suggested by the teacher. • Pairs discuss the topic. • Students individually share information with the class.	• The opportunity for self-talk during the individual think time allows the student to formulate thoughts before speaking. • Discussion with a partner reduces performance anxiety and enhances understanding.
THREE-STEP INTERVIEW	• Students form pairs. • Student A interviews Student B about a topic. • Partners reverse roles. • Student A shares with the class information from Student B; then Student B shares information from Student A.	• Interviewing supports language acquisition by providing scripts for expression. • Responding provides opportunities for structured self-expression.

CROSS-DISCIPLINARY TEACHING

America Through The Lens includes numerous features to support students' reading development, including explicit vocabulary instruction, text within the grade-appropriate Lexile band, and differentiation notes in the Teacher's Edition to help teachers scaffold comprehension for striving readers.

Vocabulary support begins in the Student Edition. Striving readers will benefit from the highlighting that calls out key vocabulary, signaling each word's critical role in enhancing comprehension of content area text. In addition, a list of vocabulary and an intoductory activity are included on the first page of the chapter in the Teacher's Edition.

At the beginning of the year, you can identify striving readers in the class and provide ongoing support, such as additional vocabulary help and small-group time during which students can ask questions. Advanced readers can be offered activities from the Teacher's Edition differentiation notes for gifted and talented and pre-AP students.

The digital Vocabulary Practice page for each section of the Student Edition (example below) reinforces students' understanding of social studies terms.

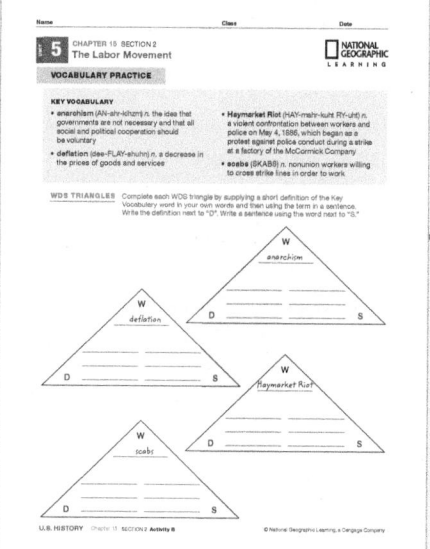

EXAMPLE VOCABULARY TREATMENT IN CHAPTER 19, LESSON 1.2

1.2 MAIN IDEA The phenomenal rise in stock prices came to a catastrophic end when the stock market crashed on October 29, 1929.

PANIC ON WALL STREET

We all know that what goes up must eventually come down. Investors in the 1920s didn't realize that old saying also applied to the stock market. On October 29, 1929, they learned just how wrong they were.

INVESTMENT FEVER

In the 1920s, Americans pointed to the growth of the stock market as an indication of the nation's growing prosperity. The market grew so quickly that many Americans saw it as the ideal place to make a fast buck. The U.S. Treasury's sale of Liberty Bonds during World War I had shown citizens that investments could lead to wealth.

More and more, corporations offered their stocks for sale to obtain cash to finance business growth. During the prosperous Harding and Coolidge years, generous government tax policies allowed the very wealthy to pay little or no income taxes, giving them extra money to invest in the stock market.

Smaller investors often bought stocks on **margin**. That is, they purchased stocks on credit, paying only 10 or 15 percent of the actual price up front. Buying on margin is a risky strategy because the investor is betting on being able to sell the stock at a higher price, pay off the stockbroker—the person who buys and sells stocks for his or her clients—and pocket a substantial profit. The lure of making easy money in the market was so great that people borrowed money to buy on margin. Banks happily loaned American investors that money, in spite of the Federal Reserve's warnings against the practice, which consequently gave rise to the establishment of weaknesses in the economy.

When this New York investor lost everything in the 1929 stock market crash, he put his car up for sale for less than 10 percent of its value.

Buying stocks on margin is a form of **speculation**. The buyer assumes, or speculates, that stock prices will always go up, even though there is no guarantee that they will. But in the 1920s, this looked like a sure bet. On September 3, 1929, the **Dow Jones Industrial Average (DJIA)**—a leading measure of general stock market trends—hit 381.17, a high for the decade, driven up in part by speculation and margin buying. Few suspected that the weakening market was headed for collapse.

OCTOBER 29, 1929

The problem began in September 1929. At the beginning of that month, the market hit its record high, but then stock prices declined. They regained some strength but began drifting downward again. Since there had been no abrupt collapse, many on Wall Street, their confidence unshaken, saw these events as one of the normal and temporary "corrections" that typically preceded another big increase in the stock market. A few people warned that problems lay ahead, but they were dismissed as chronic naysayers who had been wrong before.

But prices did not rise. On October 24, 1929, the day that became known as **Black Thursday**, stock trading began as usual, but few investors were willing to buy. Prices collapsed as investors, many of whom had bought on margin, tried to sell their stocks before prices fell even more. Nearly 13 million stocks were traded that day, which was then an all-time record. Stockholders absorbed, by some estimates, a $9 billion loss in the value of their stocks. During the afternoon, a large banking group led by bank executive J.P. Morgan, Jr., urged investors to be calm. Morgan even purchased some

Dow Jones Industrial Average Daily Index

Source: The Dow Jones Averages (1885–1995)

and the DJIA plummeted to 260.64. Then the hammer fell on October 29, a day that is still known as **Black Tuesday**. When trading began, the sell-off continued, with more than 16 million shares changing hands in a single day. The DJIA fell to 230.07 and continued to drop for nearly three years.

The consequences of the crash were immediate and striking. The prices of individual stocks continued on their downward slide. The DJIA reached a low of 41.22 on July 8, 1932. Within a few months of the

Buying stocks on margin is a form of **speculation**. The buyer assumes, or speculates, that stock prices will always go up, even though there is no guarantee that they will. But in the 1920s, this looked like a ⋯⋯⋯ Highlighted key terms are defined in context in the narrative.

Crash, I persuaded my mother in Rochester to let me talk to our family adviser. I wanted to sell stock which had been left me by my father. He got very sentimental. "Oh you father wouldn't have liked you to do that." He was so persuasive, I said OK, I could have sold it for $160,000. Four years later, I sold it for $4,000.

—from *Hard Times: An Oral History of the Great Depression*, by Studs Terkel, 1970

1. **READING CHECK** What effect did speculation and buying on margin have on stock prices?

2. **DRAW CONCLUSIONS** If trading reached record highs on October 24 and 29, why are these days called Black Thursday and Black Tuesday?

3. **INTERPRET GRAPHS** According to the graph, what were the highest and lowest averages in the DJIA in 1929, and how does the graph illustrate the cost and benefit of investing in the stock market?

686 CHAPTER 19

The Great Depression 687

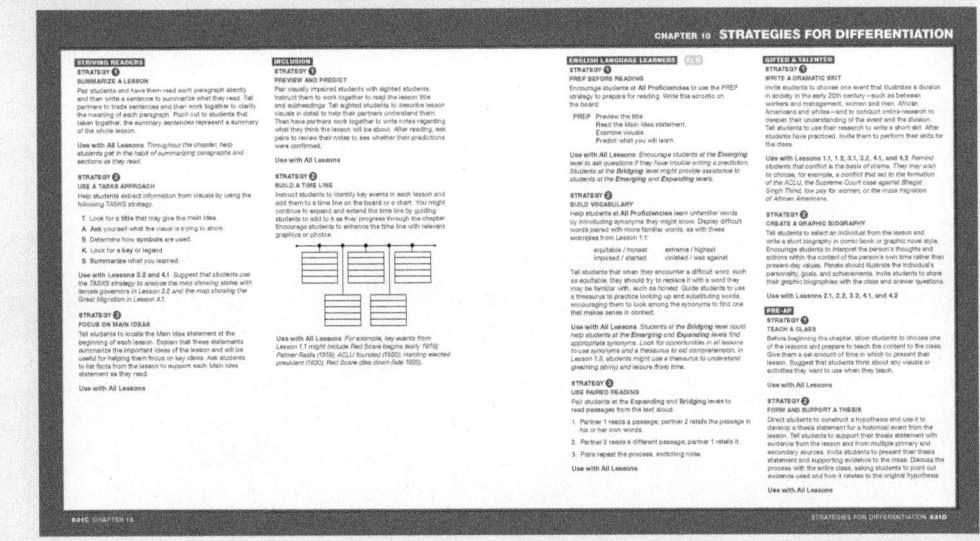

Pages 631C–631D in this Teacher's Edition

This Teacher's Edition also provides differentiation activities to customize instruction for ELs at the Emerging, Expanding, and Bridging levels. To support ELD, teachers should establish ongoing routines, such as previewing the lessons to identify language that may be challenging to ELs and providing specific help with these passages, working with small groups of ELs, and occasionally pairing ELs with more proficient readers.

You might also collaborate with the ELD teacher to incorporate content or language from the current *America Through The Lens* lesson. Where possible, it is valuable to encourage ELs to share the connections they can make between social studies content and their own experiences or home culture. This practice creates speaking opportunities for ELs and allows them to experience the rewards of making a unique and useful contribution to the classroom conversation.

In the Content Areas

STEM History–social studies topics often lend themselves to cross-disciplinary lessons with STEM concepts. Annotations throughout this Teacher's Edition highlight opportunities to connect to STEM instruction. You can also encourage students to look for such connections on their own and point them out to the class.

Geology and Geography An obvious cross-disciplinary connection for history students is geology. *America Through The Lens* leverages National Geographic assets to include Geology in History lessons in selected chapters. The approach is always on how geology can enhance our understanding of historical decisions and events.

The National Geographic maps in this program are created using real-time data as appropriate and are geared toward a student audience. An online National Geographic Atlas furnishes ample support for both history and geography.

In addition, a Geography Handbook in the reference section of the text provides support and practice for analyzing maps and covers common geographic concepts.

EXAMPLE ELL STRATEGIES

ENGLISH LANGUAGE LEARNERS

STRATEGY 1
PAIR PARTNERS FOR DICTATION

After reading a lesson, direct students of **All Proficiencies** levels to write a sentence in their own words that tells an important idea from the lesson. Then pair students and let them take turns dictating their sentences to each other. Encourage them to help each other with spelling and content accuracy.

Use with All Lessons *You may wish to pair students at the* **Emerging** *level with those at the* **Bridging** *level.*

Page 673D in this Teacher's Edition

ENGLISH LANGUAGE LEARNERS

STRATEGY 1
CREATE SENTENCE STRIPS

Choose a paragraph from a lesson and make sentence strips from it. Read the paragraph aloud while students at **All Proficiencies** follow along in their books. Then have students close their books, and give them the set of sentence strips. Students should put the strips in order and then read the paragraph aloud.

Use with All Lessons *Before reading, you may want to ask students at the* **Emerging** *level to read the sentence strips aloud. Then ask them to point out meaningful words in each sentence. Repeat the exercise with another paragraph.*

Page 773D in this Teacher's Edition

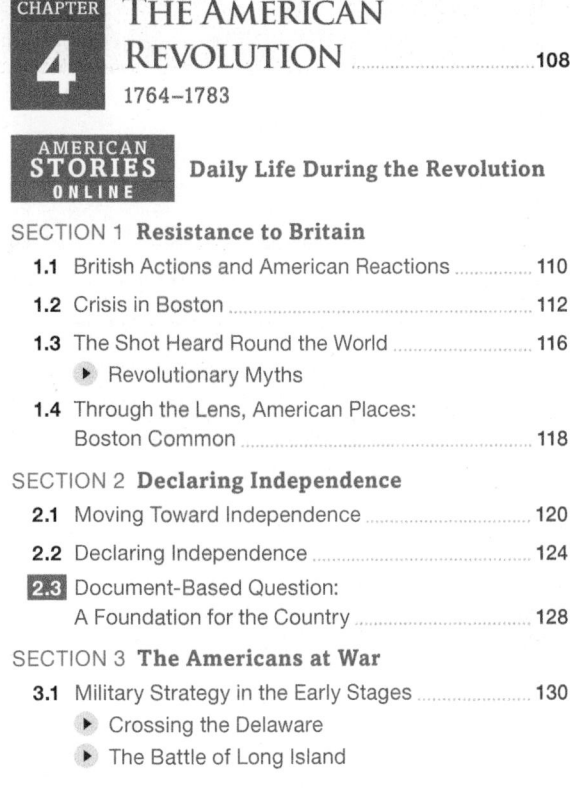

UNIT 3 1814–1854

EXPANDING THE NEW NATION

ARCHAEOLOGY AND U.S. HISTORY

Dr. Fredrik Hiebert
Archaeologist-In-Residence,
National Geographic Society **342**

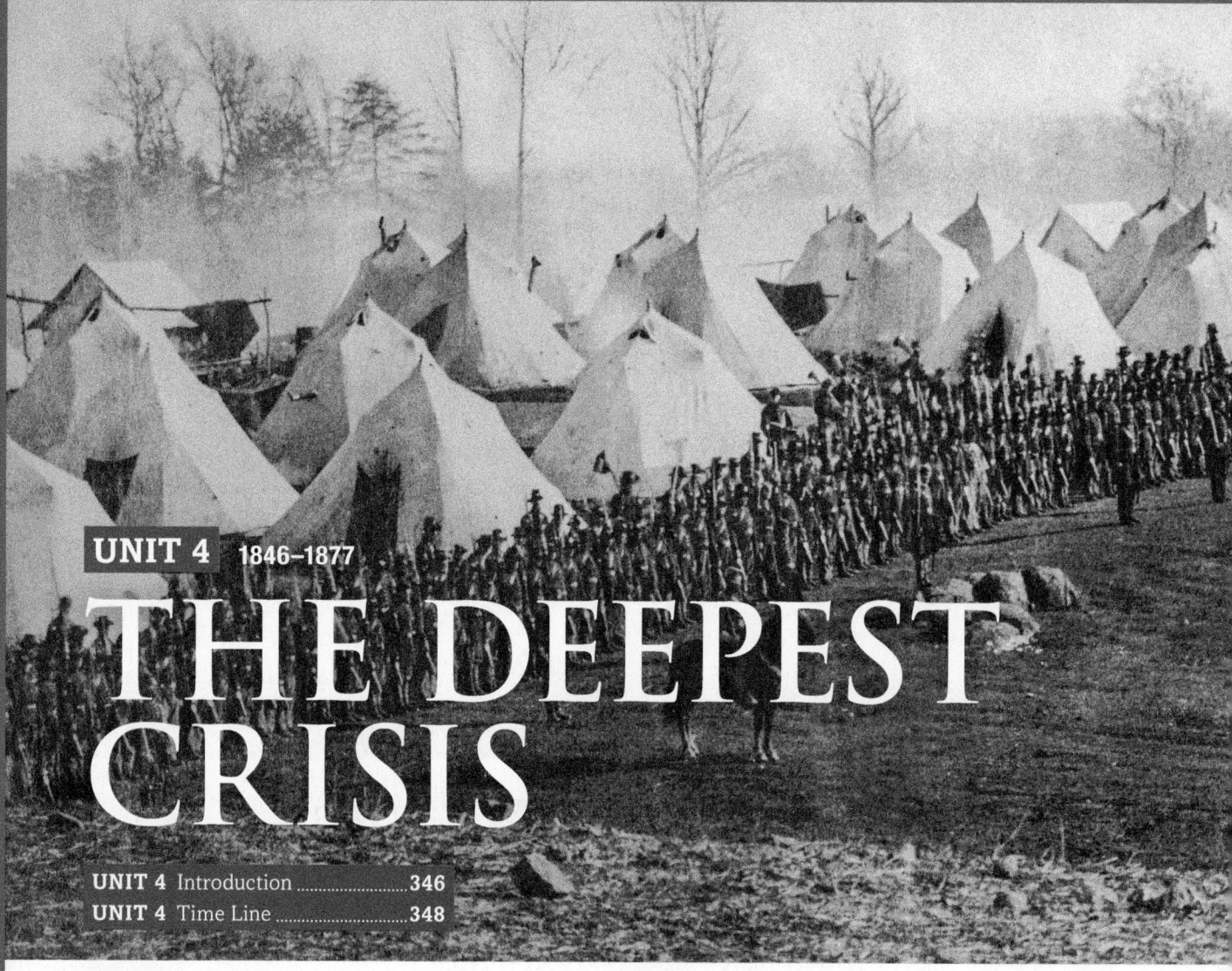

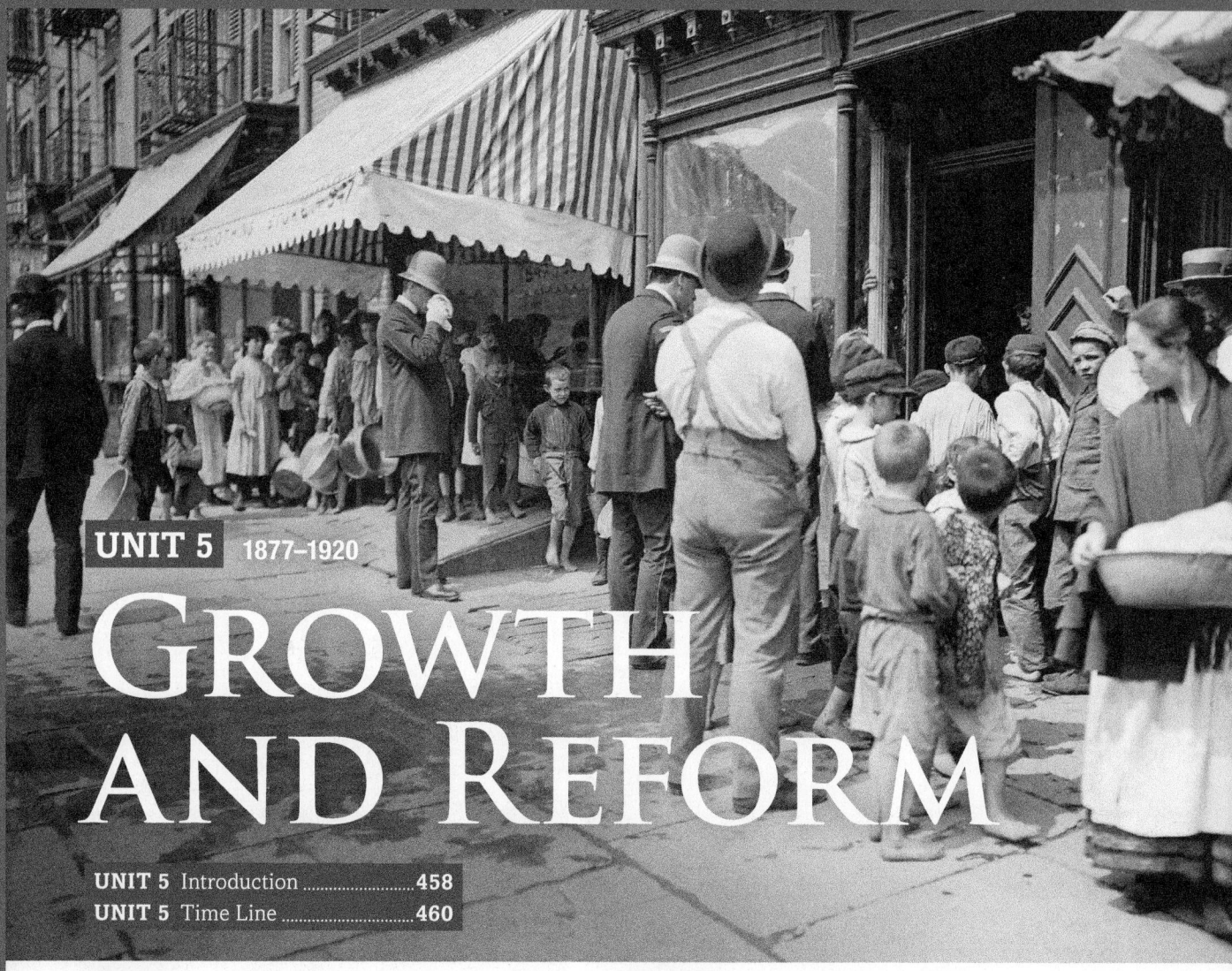

Franz Kline, *Lower East Side Market Scene* (detail), c. 1938

T38

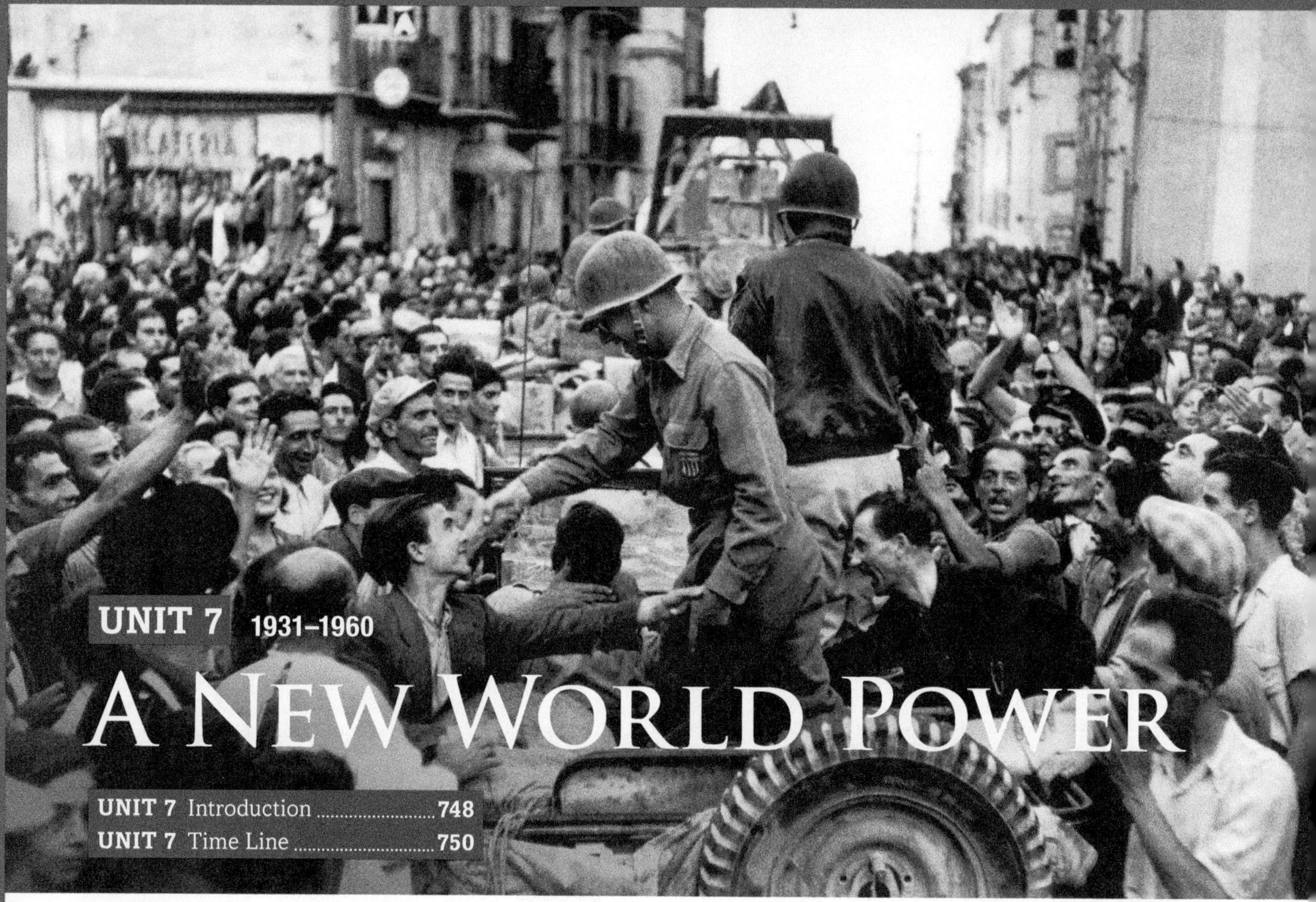

UNIT 7 1931–1960

A New World Power

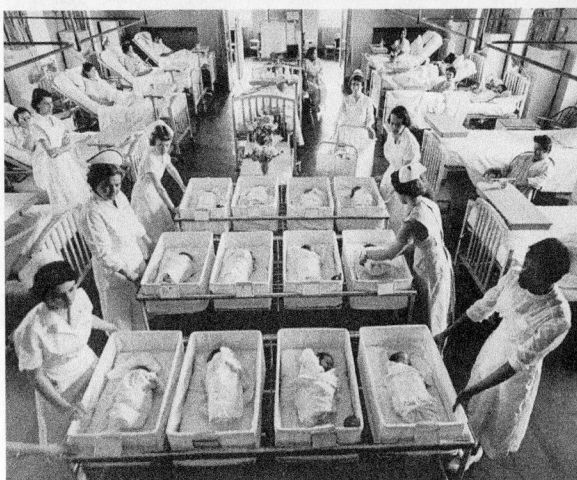

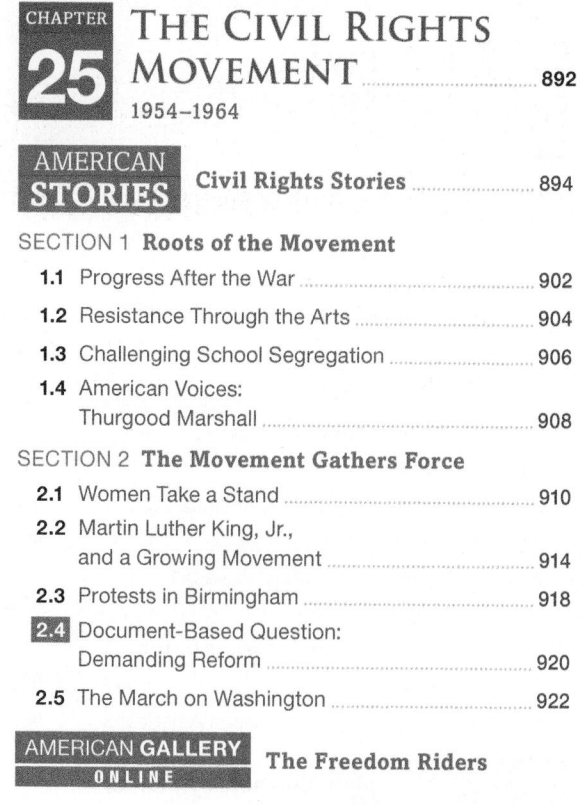

UNIT 8 1954–1975

YEARS OF TURBULENCE

NATIONAL GEOGRAPHIC FEATURES

Maps

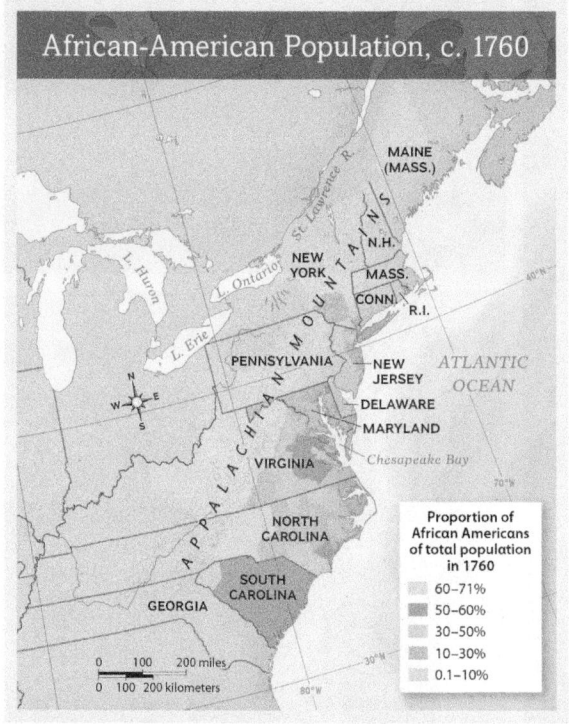

African-American Population, c. 1760

National Geographic Contributors

NATIONAL GEOGRAPHIC
EXPLORER SARAH PARCAK

Curating History

Document-Based Questions

GREENSBORO SIT-IN, 1960

SAILORS ON THE DECK OF THE USS MONITOR, 1864

Student Handbooks

Geology in History

American Voices Biographies

HARRIET TUBMAN

SEQUOIA NATIONAL PARK

Through The Lens Features

Featured Themes

Featured Photographers

Featured American Places

OBJECTIVES

- Explore the climate and landscapes of the North American continent and ways in which they have changed over time.
- Examine how plant and animal life throughout the continent have changed over time.
- Identify characteristics of the Pleistocene epoch.
- Understand how the earliest human populations came to North America, who they were, and where they settled.
- Analyze the causes and effects of the Agricultural Revolution on human populations and on the North American continent.
- Analyze artifacts that illustrate North American cultures in the era before European exploration.

CRITICAL THINKING SKILLS FOR "THE STORY OF A CONTINENT"

- Draw Conclusions
- Analyze Data
- Make Generalizations
- Compare and Contrast
- Analyze Cause and Effect
- Form and Support Opinions

CONNECT TO CHAPTER CONTENT

The Story of a Continent feature provides students with a brief history of the North American continent's climate, geography, and inhabitants from the Pleistocene epoch through the era just prior to European exploration. Using maps, time lines, illustrations, and artifacts, students will analyze how changes in climate and technology affected human migration to North America and the development of human cultures on the continent.

Use this feature to help students build their knowledge of North America as it existed before the arrival of European explorers. This knowledge will help students make connections as they read about the ways in which exploration and colonization, the founding of the United States, and the nation's expansion and growth affected North America's geography and cultures.

HISTORY NOTEBOOK

Encourage students to complete The Story of a Continent pages in their History Notebooks as they read.

THE STORY OF A CONTINENT

BY DR. WILLIAM PARKINSON
National Geographic Explorer
Associate Curator of Anthropology
Field Museum of Natural History

CRITICAL VIEWING This artist's rendering shows the Laurentide Ice Sheet, which, at times, covered large parts of North America during the Pleistocene epoch. Present-day glaciers, particularly in Canada, are remnants of this ice sheet. What does the image reveal about this glacial period?

EARTH'S TIME LINE ⊢—⊣ 100 Million Years

| Earth Forms 4.5 Billion Years Ago | First Life Appears on Earth 3.8 Billion Years Ago |

Close your eyes for a minute and try to imagine the United States without any of the familiar trappings of 21st-century life—no smartphones, hoverboards, or tablets. No iTunes, YouTube, or video games.

Imagine traveling from place to place without paved roads to follow—in fact, with no roads at all, and no wheeled vehicles or even horses to carry you. Instead of strip malls, fast-food chains, and electric streetlights, there are lush, dark forests, pristine rivers and streams, and abundant plant and animal life as far as your eye can see.

Take a deep breath while we travel back to the earliest history of North America, from the beginnings of civilization and even further back to a time when mammoths and mastodons, saber-toothed cats, and giant ground sloths roamed the lands of North America. It was a time when your own species, *Homo sapiens*, evolved and spread throughout the world.

This is the moment in a play just before the main curtain rises on North America—a continent with a story much longer than you may think.

GEOLOGY AND LANDSCAPE

North America is geologically dramatic, featuring towering mountains, vast deserts, sandy beaches, and rolling hills. But the landscape that Europeans like Christopher Columbus encountered when they arrived in the "New World" just a few hundred years ago was profoundly different from the world that the earliest humans experienced when they first came to North America.

Let's go way back in time to when the first modern humans arrived in North America. It was at the end of a more than 2-million-year period that geologists refer to as the **Pleistocene epoch** (PLEIS-to-seen EH-puhk). During this period, the climate and ecology of North America was completely different from the climate and ecology of today and included supersized animals and plants that no longer exist. During the Pleistocene epoch, modern humans across the world honed their skills in hunting, created early artwork, developed fire, and began to use language.

Many people think the climate during the Pleistocene was always cold when, in fact, there were dramatic fluctuations in temperature over relatively short periods of time. At some points, the climate during the Pleistocene was about the same as it is today. During **glacial periods**, or **ice ages**, when glaciers expanded across Earth's surface, the global average annual temperature was significantly colder.

During the Pleistocene epoch, there were more than 20 cycles of glacial periods in which the movement of ice and water changed the landscape and shorelines of the continents drastically, especially around the edges of the Arctic Circle and in present-day North America, Europe, and Asia.

In North America, ice sheets extended as far south as the Missouri and Ohio rivers and covered nearly all of Canada and much of the northern Great Plains, the Midwest, and the northeastern United States. Some recognizable bodies of water and landforms created by glacial movement include the Great Lakes, Cape Cod in Massachusetts, Long Island in New York, and Glacier National Park in Montana. When the glaciers retreated about 10,000 years ago, the North American landscape looked much like it does today.

INTRODUCE & ENGAGE

QUICKWRITE ABOUT MIGRATION

Give students a few minutes to write about human migration. Questions for students to consider might include the following: What causes people to migrate? How do migrations change populations? How do they affect natural resources? Have any migrations affected my life or my family's life—if so, how? Invite volunteers to share their writing with the class. Explain that in this lesson, students will learn about factors that prompted early human migration to North America and the kind of continent these migrants found when they arrived.

INTERPRET TIME LINES

Direct students' attention to Earth's Time Line. **ASK:** How much of this time line represents modern human existence? *(Human existence occupies only the tiny red sliver near the end of the time line.)* What does this fact suggest about the range of time we are dealing with when we study "human history" in North America? *(Possible response: When we study human history and events, we are focusing on a small fraction of not only Earth's history but also human history.)* Explain that in this lesson, students will learn about some of the major changes that took place within a very brief time in our planet's history.

CRITICAL VIEWING Possible response: The illustration reveals that major landmasses currently separated by oceans were once connected by an ice sheet. The illustration also suggests that for such a massive ice sheet to have existed, the climate for that half of the globe must have been much colder than it is now.

◂2.6 MILLION YEARS AGO — TODAY ▸

PLEISTOCENE EPOCH 2.6 Million to 11,700 Years Ago — 100 Thousand Years

People Arrive in North America 18–12,000 Years Ago
Modern Humans Evolve 75,000 Years Ago

HOLOCENE EPOCH 11,700 Years Ago to Today

North America Splits from Pangea 200 Million Years Ago

TODAY ▸

EARLY HUMANS

Modern humans followed a long line of hominid ancestors and even lived alongside one of them: the Neanderthal, or *Homo neanderthalensis*. Students may be familiar with Neanderthals via the pop culture image of the "caveman," with its somewhat derogatory associations. Explain that many scientists believe that Neanderthals would have been much like modern humans, although somewhat shorter and stronger, with differently shaped skulls but similarly sized brains.

Archaeological evidence shows that, like the earliest modern humans, Neanderthals hunted and gathered, made and used tools, and produced some forms of art. Modern genetic research shows that Neanderthals and modern humans did interbreed, although other evidence suggests this was probably a rare occurrence. In either case, the traits of modern humans won out, and Neanderthals eventually became extinct.

ENORMOUS ANIMALS

Around 11,000 years ago, larger mammals, such as woolly mammoths, bison, and bears, that had characterized the Pleistocene epoch in North America and elsewhere began to go extinct fairly quickly. Some scientists connect this extinction event to the arrival and spread of early modern humans in North America. They speculate that human hunters developed sufficent skills to hunt the larger mammals, whose reproductive rates were far lower than those of smaller mammals. In time, the larger mammals were hunted to extinction.

Other scientists think that climate fluctuations at the end of the Pleistocene, which led to warmer temperatures, higher sea levels, and changes in plant life, may have had a more devastating effect on these large mammal species. Most scientists agree, however, that both human activity and climate change played significant roles in this extinction event.

Some species of large mammals also seem to have had an influence on the cultural life of early humans. Woolly mammoths, bison, and bears appear more frequently in early cave paintings and carvings than do other types of animals, including human beings.

CLOVIS POINT DISCOVERIES MAP

The Clovis Point Discoveries map is a proportional symbol map. The map symbols vary in size to indicate differences in the amount of something in different locations. As a class, examine the map showing the locations of Clovis point discoveries in North America. **ASK:** What might have caused the largest clusters of points? *(Possible responses: These were areas where large populations lived. These were areas where large mammal hunting was most successful.)* Discuss how a cluster map of legal animal hunting in the United States today might compare with this map and why it might show a similar pattern of points.

BRIDGING THE CONTINENTS

In Europe, Asia, and Africa, modern humans evolved between 75,000 and 35,000 years ago—long before they arrived in North America. By the end of the Pleistocene, about 12,000 years ago, the only surviving hominid species was modern humans.

Scientists love debates, and one of the biggest debates in archaeology centers around the arrival of the earliest modern humans in North America. We know that when the Pleistocene ended, there were modern human societies living throughout the continent. The debate revolves around pinpointing when during the Pleistocene the first people migrated to the Americas and whether they came by boat or walked. Yes, it was possible for people to have *walked* from Europe and Asia to the Americas! Yes! But the continents are separated by oceans!

Today, the continents are separated by oceans, but during the Pleistocene, there were glacial periods when ice sheets covered the continents. In addition, the oceans contained less water, and the coastlines of the continents were much larger. After the last major glacial period, about 20,000 years ago, the two ice sheets that covered northern North America began to melt, leaving North America temporarily connected to Asia by a large stretch of land between modern-day Alaska and Siberia that scientists call the **Bering Land Bridge**. About 11,000 to 12,000 years ago, the land bridge disappeared as the ice melted, the oceans filled with the water, and the coastlines receded.

A team of paleontologists from the University of Michigan recovered this mastodon skull and more than 60 percent of the animal's skeleton in October 2016. Mastodons are extinct relatives of the elephant.

MAN   ELEPHANT   MAMMOTH MASTODON

ENORMOUS ANIMALS

About 12,000 years ago, we entered the Holocene (HO-luh-seen) epoch, which we are still in today. Many animals that lived during the Pleistocene went extinct around the beginning of the Holocene, including many species of large animals, or **megafauna**, such as mammoths, mastodons, and saber-toothed cats. Along with other oversize animals, like giant sloths, giant beavers, and American lions, horses also lived in North America until the end of the Pleistocene but were reintroduced by Europeans a few hundred years ago. They became a critical aspect of Native American culture, especially on the Great Plains. This was the incredible environment the earliest humans encountered when they first arrived in North America at the end of the Pleistocene.

THE GREAT DEBATE

Until recently, scientists believed that the earliest people to arrive in the Americas just before the land bridge disappeared were **hunter-gatherers** who specialized in hunting large herd animals that migrated back and forth across the continent. Archaeologists call them the Clovis Culture, based on a kind of stone tool—a Clovis point—that people made at that time.

But there is growing evidence that other groups may have reached the Americas before the Clovis Culture. Sites in Chile and Pennsylvania suggest that there was a pre-Clovis occupation of North America, and some scientists even speculate that people may have arrived by boats earlier in the Pleistocene, perhaps from Europe rather than Asia.

By the end of the Pleistocene, the climate began to stabilize, and modern humans spread throughout the Americas. They were specialized, mobile hunters and gatherers like their contemporaries elsewhere in the world, and they used the same technology— Clovis points—to hunt. These points have been found throughout North America, and similar ones have appeared as far south as Venezuela. People began to settle in different regions of the North American continent that can be distinguished according to the specialized stone tools that were made and used in the Holocene.

CLOVIS POINT DISCOVERIES

Coastline at 75 m below current sea level	Glacial ice 12,000 years before present
	Glacial ice 13,000 years before present

CLOVIS POINT DISTRIBUTION

·	•	●	●	●
1–4	5–12	13–24	25–54	88–142

No sites reported finding 55–87 Clovis points.

Clovis Point

Carbon dating of points like the one above indicates the Clovis Culture dates to around 11,500 years ago—a time archaeologists call the Paleoindian period. Examine the proportional symbol map to see where points have been found.

The Story of a Continent **3**

GUIDED DISCUSSION

1. **Draw Conclusions** What factors might have contributed to the migration of early hunter-gatherers across the Bering Land Bridge? *(Possible response: Because of the cold climate, hunter-gatherers may have been traveling in search of warmer temperatures, animals for hunting, or edible plants. They may also have been following herds of animals that migrated across the land bridge to North America.)*

2. **Analyze Data** What does the prevailing science tell us about the Clovis Culture? *(Evidence of the Clovis Culture suggests they were hunter-gatherers who migrated back and forth across the continent, but they may not have been the first people in the Americas. Sites have been found in Chile and Pennsylvania that show evidence of people who arrived before the Clovis Culture and may have traveled there from Europe or Asia.)*

MORE INFORMATION

The Folsom Culture Another early human culture that developed shortly after the Clovis Culture was the Folsom Culture. Archaeologists have identified this group by the artifacts left behind: knives and stone points (typically shorter and wider than Clovis points). Folsom artifacts, however, are not as widespread as their Clovis counterparts. They appear concentrated mostly in the Great Plains region. Folsom people seem to have hunted mainly bison, whereas the earlier Clovis people hunted mammoths. **ASK:** Why do you think the Folsom Culture differed in hunting tools and region from the Clovis? *(Possible response: The Folsom Culture came after the Clovis, and large mammals were beginning to go extinct at this time. Thus, the Folsom may have hunted bison because mammoths were scarce. They may have changed their weapon points to be more effective for hunting smaller animals. Changes in climate may have made it less necessary for the Folsom to spread out in search of food and enabled them to stay in one region.)*

ACTIVE OPTIONS

On Your Feet: Turn and Talk on Topic

Arrange students in three or four groups. Give the groups the following topic question: How did the domestication of corn forever change hunter-gatherer culture? Tell the groups to write a paragraph on this topic with each student contributing at least one unique sentence. Suggest that each group first discuss the wide-ranging implications of corn domestication on hunter-gatherer cultures. Then instruct them to write their sentences and organize them logically for presentation. Ask the groups to read their paragraphs to the class.

NG Learning Framework: Explore Cahokia Culture

SKILLS   Observation, Communication

KNOWLEDGE   Our Living Planet

Have pairs or small groups of students use digital and print resources to research the Cahokia community. Ask each group to focus on one element of Cahokia culture that is most interesting to them—agriculture, tools, social organization, Cahokia mounds, and so on. Groups should research their chosen topic and gather relevant graphics, photographs, maps, dates, and time lines for their presentation to the class. After all pairs or groups have presented their findings, discuss as a class any new patterns in human behavior or society that the Cahokia might have exhibited.

THE AGRICULTURAL REVOLUTION

For several thousand years during the Holocene, people continued to live in small groups and move frequently throughout the year, but everything changed when some groups of mobile hunters and gatherers started to experiment with planting their own crops. This transition from relying on gathering wild plants and hunting animals to planting crops and raising animals is called the **Agricultural Revolution**.

The practice of bringing plants and animals under human control is called **domestication**. Almost all the foods we eat today are domesticated instead of wild, which means they have been modified from their wild forms and are to some extent reliant upon humans for their existence. Corn, for example, is the domesticated form of a plant called *teosinte* (TAY-oh-SIN-tay), and cows are the domestic form of a wild herd animal called an *aurochs* (OR-auks). Domestication had a dramatic impact on society and actually transformed human life as people settled down and became reliant upon domestic plants and animals.

Out of all the plants domesticated in North America thousands of years ago, the real game changer was corn. The hunters and gatherers who began experimenting with the domestication of corn had no idea of the impact their little experiment would have on the world in the years to come. Corn is now grown almost everywhere in the world and tied to almost everything Americans eat and many things Americans produce, such as toothpaste and gasoline. But the biggest impact corn had in North America was its unparalleled ability to feed large populations.

This copper plate, discovered in 1906 near Malden, Missouri, provides evidence of Mississippian cultures outside of Cahokia.

SETTLING DOWN

It took a while for corn to be adopted and widely used in North America. In eastern North America, for example, it wasn't a major part of the human diet until about 1,000 years ago. Growing crops like corn and remaining in one location allowed social groups to grow larger and develop more complex political systems. In some places, these groups built massive cities and had extensive trade networks that moved goods across the continent.

One of these cities was located in present-day Illinois along the Mississippi River near the city of St. Louis, Missouri. Founded around A.D. 800, Cahokia would come to be the capital of a large community called a **chiefdom**. By A.D. 1250, Cahokia was a thriving community that controlled a massive geographic area at the confluence of three rivers (the Missouri, Illinois, and Mississippi), and at its height may have had a population of about 15,000 people. It is considered the most sophisticated prehistoric native civilization north of Mexico.

Since the fertile soil of Cahokia was easy to farm and was well suited to growing corn, people farmed more and hunted less. And archaeological evidence unearthed from the site indicates the people of Cahokia ate well.

Although Cahokia and other similar sites in the southeastern United States were heavily dependent upon domestic crops like corn, communities in other parts of North America were not. They continued to hunt and gather wild resources as a major part of their diet.

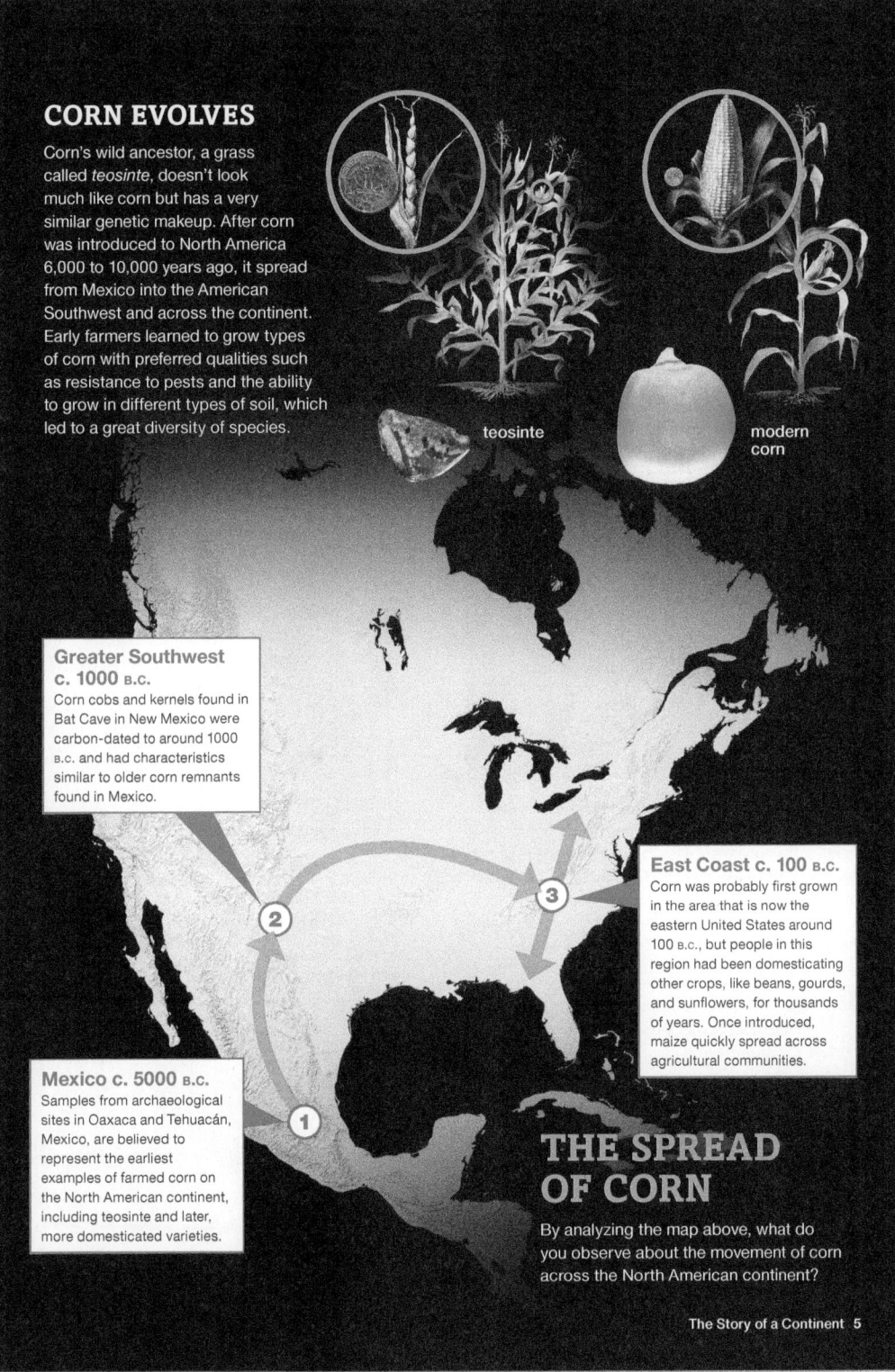

CORN EVOLVES

Corn's wild ancestor, a grass called *teosinte*, doesn't look much like corn but has a very similar genetic makeup. After corn was introduced to North America 6,000 to 10,000 years ago, it spread from Mexico into the American Southwest and across the continent. Early farmers learned to grow types of corn with preferred qualities such as resistance to pests and the ability to grow in different types of soil, which led to a great diversity of species.

teosinte

modern corn

Greater Southwest c. 1000 B.C.
Corn cobs and kernels found in Bat Cave in New Mexico were carbon-dated to around 1000 B.C. and had characteristics similar to older corn remnants found in Mexico.

East Coast c. 100 B.C.
Corn was probably first grown in the area that is now the eastern United States around 100 B.C., but people in this region had been domesticating other crops, like beans, gourds, and sunflowers, for thousands of years. Once introduced, maize quickly spread across agricultural communities.

Mexico c. 5000 B.C.
Samples from archaeological sites in Oaxaca and Tehuacán, Mexico, are believed to represent the earliest examples of farmed corn on the North American continent, including teosinte and later, more domesticated varieties.

THE SPREAD OF CORN

By analyzing the map above, what do you observe about the movement of corn across the North American continent?

CORN EVOLVES

Evidence from caves in southern Mexico suggests that ancient forms of corn quickly began evolving in ways that brought them closer to our modern corn plants. Nonetheless, the kernels they produced probably had a much lower nutritional value. Archaeologists and paleobotanists—scientists who study fossil plants—have also looked for evidence indicating how people used these plants for food. Tool artifacts suggest that some corn was ground for cooking or may have been eaten as a kind of popcorn.

For many years, paleobotanists could not agree about the evolution of the corn plant. Molecular biologists have now confirmed that it evolved from a wild grass called teosinte. Have students examine the side-by-side depictions of modern-day corn and teosinte. **ASK:** What details in these diagrams suggest that the plants are related? *(Possible response: The diagrams show that both plants have similar stalks and types of leaves, and both produce ears of corn with kernels, though modern ears are much larger and contain more kernels.)*

THE SPREAD OF CORN

Possible response: Corn took thousands of years to travel from Mexico into the greater Southwest and almost a thousand years more to spread to the East Coast. That time frame makes sense, given that people would have largely traveled on foot and would not have had any means of communicating with distant groups. In addition, corn's rapid spread in the East might have been related to the fact that people there were already skilled farmers, and their communities could begin using the corn right away.

GUIDED DISCUSSION

3. **Make Generalizations** What do these works of art from early North American cultures suggest about the people who made them? *(Answers will vary. Possible response: The works suggest the importance of wildlife to early North American cultures, as well as the need for people to reflect and document elements of their culture.)*

4. **Compare and Contrast** In what general ways were the human, cultural, and political landscapes of the "New World" similar to and different from the landscape of North America today? Explain. *(Answers will vary. Possible responses: In both eras, diverse people populated the continent and developed unique traditions, languages, and cultures. "New World" people wouldn't necessarily be aware of the many peoples and cultures spread out across North America. Today, North Americans share a much more common cultural identity. Although regional differences remain, modern communications and highways allow us to know about all the groups that make up the nation.)*

MORE INFORMATION

The Ancestral Pueblo Direct students' attention to the photograph of ancient Pueblo cliff dwellings at Mesa Verde National Park. **ASK:** What inferences can you make about the culture that built these dwellings? *(Answers will vary. Possible response: The culture was advanced. People were skilled at using the landscape to their advantage, and they favored a centralized, or urban, design for their dwellings.)*

Explain that the cliff dwellings shown here were built during a later phase of ancestral Pueblo civilization called Pueblo III. Earlier Pueblo groups lived first as nomadic hunter-gatherers, then dwelled in caves and covered pits, and later settled in small villages or large communities. The cliff dwellings were remarkable achievements. Their construction was high quality and durable. Because they were accessible only by ladder, they were easily defended against attack. Archaeological evidence suggests that a prolonged drought forced the Pueblo to abandon these communities. Later Pueblo dwellings were less well constructed. **ASK:** What does a decline in building quality suggest about Pueblo communities that followed the cliff dwellers? *(Possible responses: They were less prosperous. They had to construct their settlements quickly. They did not have enough high-quality resources for building.)*

Possible response: The emergence of art across so many cultures suggests that early humans were similar in many ways despite being geographically separated. It also suggests that making art is a fundamental human quality that expressed itself at an early stage.

A CULTURAL MOSAIC

This two-chambered pigment bowl in the form of a bird was found in the Pacific Northwest region of North America.

Before the 1500s, the Americas, Europe, and Africa had been isolated from one another, but as Europeans began looking beyond their shores for riches and resources, Africa's mighty empires wanted to show their strength. Both continents were on a collision course with the Americas, but the Europeans got there first.

When the Europeans arrived in the "New World," they experienced a mosaic of diverse cultures and landscapes. From the hierarchical chiefdoms of Florida to the more mobile, less hierarchical groups of the Great Basin, the cultures of North America made up a patchwork quilt of societies with distinct languages, economic practices, political systems, and traditions as varied as the landscape.

These petroglyphs in California's Chidago Canyon are thought to be the visions of ancient Paiute shamans.

Everyone has a personal American story to tell, and those stories often reflect the diversity of our cultural mosaic. It's not always easy to build consensus or get everyone "on the same page," but that diversity is one of the best things about life in the United States. With so many options and perspectives and our persistent American drive, we have the potential to develop amazingly creative solutions to 21st-century issues.

So raise the curtain on this incredibly rich and varied landscape, well equipped to sustain and nurture the promise of a unique new country and a vibrant people. The action and the drama are just about to begin.

NORTHWEST

PLATEAU

BASIN

CALIFORNIA

SOUTHWEST

Believed to be 1,000 years old, the Pilling Figurines from the Fremont group in Utah were named for the rancher who discovered them in 1950.

Like other groups in the Southwest, the Hohokam of southern Arizona created pottery painted with elaborate designs.

What does the fact that these diverse cultures all expressed themselves through art suggest about early humans?

6

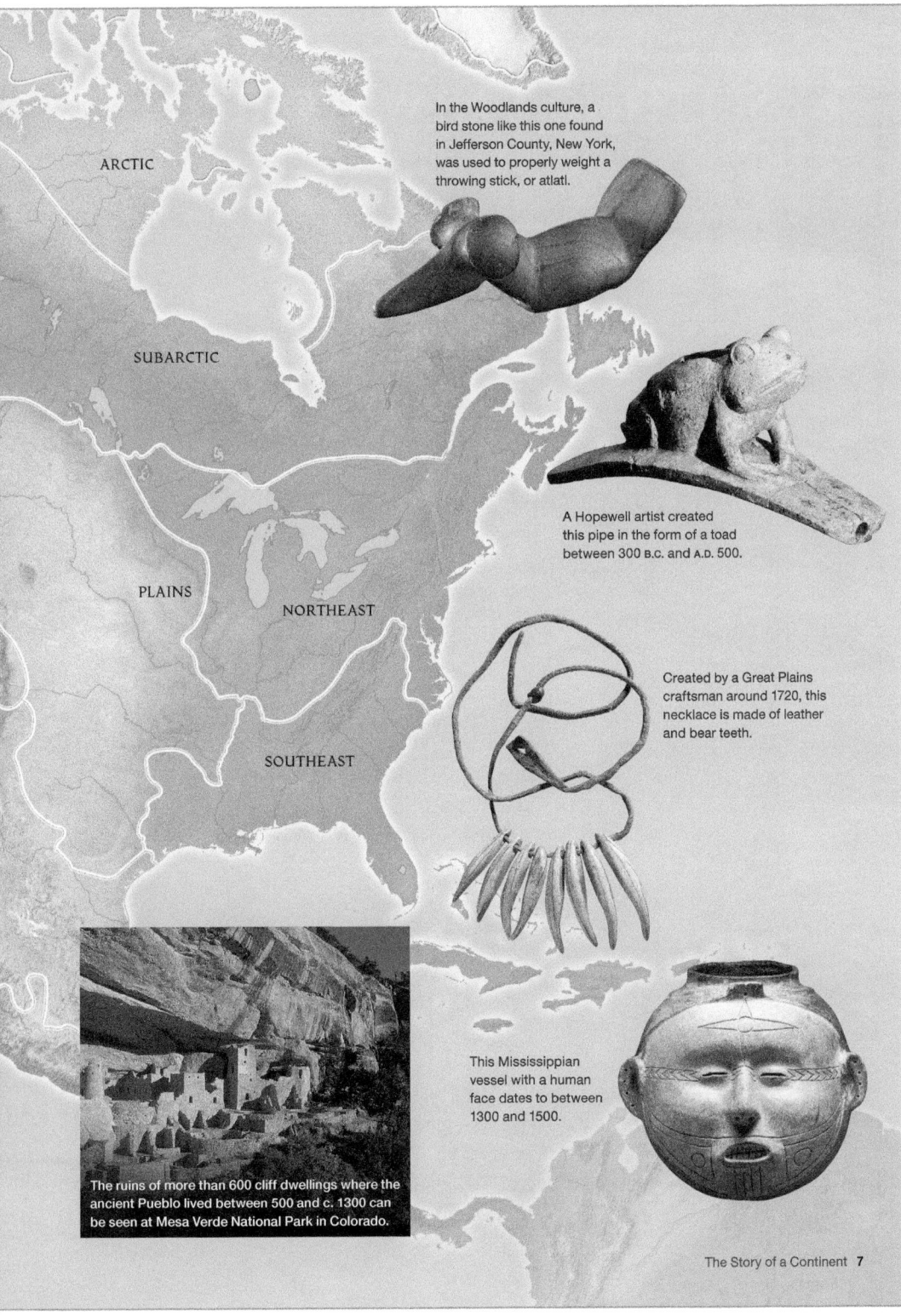

In the Woodlands culture, a bird stone like this one found in Jefferson County, New York, was used to properly weight a throwing stick, or atlatl.

ARCTIC

SUBARCTIC

PLAINS

NORTHEAST

SOUTHEAST

A Hopewell artist created this pipe in the form of a toad between 300 B.C. and A.D. 500.

Created by a Great Plains craftsman around 1720, this necklace is made of leather and bear teeth.

This Mississippian vessel with a human face dates to between 1300 and 1500.

The ruins of more than 600 cliff dwellings where the ancient Pueblo lived between 500 and c. 1300 can be seen at Mesa Verde National Park in Colorado.

The Story of a Continent 7

DIFFERENTIATE

STRIVING READERS

Understand Main Ideas Confirm students' understanding of the main ideas in The Story of a Continent by asking them to correctly complete statements such as the following:

- Glacial periods, or ice ages, created bodies of water and landforms such as _____ . *(the Great Lakes, Cape Cod, Glacier National Park)*
- The Bering Land Bridge refers to _____ . *(the ice sheets that connected modern-day Alaska and Siberia)*
- The biggest impact of corn domestication in North America was _____ . *(the ability to feed large populations of people)*

GIFTED & TALENTED

Compare and Contrast American Societies Instruct students to research both Cahokia and Inca cultures. Encourage them to use print and digital resources to research the social organizations, arts, architecture, religions, and economies of both societies. Students should look for maps, artifacts, photographs, and other visual evidence about both cultures. Have students create presentations that compare the cultures to share with the class.

See the Chapter Planner for more strategies for differentiation.

HISTORICAL THINKING

Ask and have students answer the following questions.

1. **READING CHECK** What was Earth's climate like during the Pleistocene epoch?

2. **ANALYZE CAUSE AND EFFECT** What effect did the development and spread of agriculture have on early human societies?

3. **FORM AND SUPPORT OPINIONS** What were some of the most important factors influencing human settlement of the North American continent?

ANSWERS

1. Earth's climate fluctuated between glacial periods (or ice ages) and periods of warmer climate, similar to what we know today. The Pleistocene epoch ended in a period of warmer temperatures.

2. Agriculture allowed humans to stay in one place and feed larger populations than did hunting and gathering. As a result, permanent villages developed, which led to larger communities and cities.

3. Possible responses: The ice age, which allowed humans to travel by foot into North America; the warming climate, which provided a longer growing season; the development of agriculture, which gave humans a relatively stable food supply throughout much of the year

NATIVE AMERICAN PETROGLYPHS

Native American petroglyphs can be found in many places in the Southwest, including Utah, Colorado, Arizona, Texas, and New Mexico. The petroglyphs in the photograph are known as the Butler Wash Petroglyph Panel and are located along the San Juan River in Utah. Researchers have tried to determine the meanings behind petroglyphs by studying the repetition of particular figures and shapes that appear in carvings in disparate locations. According to the National Park Service, petroglyphs are not examples of graffiti nor are they hieroglyphics since they do not represent specific words. Instead, petroglyphs are powerful symbols that reflect complex ideas and elements of cultures and religions.

While the meaning behind many petroglyphs remains a mystery, some likely served as tribal or clan markers, while others may have provided a record of those who came to and left a particular area. It is unlikely that Native Americans created petroglyphs simply as an artistic or leisure pursuit. They were intentionally created to record important aspects of a particular group's culture and society. **ASK:** What do you notice about the larger humanlike figures? *(Possible response: The largest figures are very broad through the shoulders and appear to be dressed in some kind of ceremonial clothing and headdresses.)* What do you think might have been ancient people's specific purpose in carving these petroglyphs? *(Answers will vary. Possible response: The carvings might serve as a notice or warning to outsiders who enter the area that powerful people occupy the territory.)*

UNIT
1

Beginnings–1763

SETTLING A NEW WORLD

CRITICAL VIEWING Petroglyphs, or rock carvings, created by ancient Native American artists can be found throughout the Southwest. The petroglyphs in this photo by National Geographic photographer Paul Chesley include many different figures. Describe some of the figures you see. What types of activities or events might they represent?

NATIONAL GEOGRAPHIC PHOTOGRAPHER
PAUL CHESLEY

Over a span of more than 40 years, National Geographic photographer Paul Chesley has photographed dozens of assignments for the National Geographic Society around the world. In addition to the ancient petroglyphs shown, Chesley has photographed Native American art depicted on a rock wall in Arizona's Canyon de Chelly National Monument. Chesley says that his international work, however, has brought him the greatest satisfaction and pleasure. His photographs demonstrate his particular fondness for capturing the colors, cultures, people, and natural beauty of Asia and the South Pacific. In 1988, the National Geographic Society acknowledged his valuable contributions by including Chesley's work in its prestigious 100-year retrospective of *National Geographic* photographs at the Corcoran Gallery in Washington, D.C. Chesley's photographic essays also have appeared regularly in publications such as *Newsweek, Time,* and *Life.*

In 2013, Chesley published a retrospective of his own work, *Paul Chesley: A Photographic Voyage.* The book is a memoir of Chesley's life as an artist, and it covers subjects around the globe from locations as diverse as Bali, Ukraine, and Cuba. The retrospective features Chelsey's ability to capture fleeting details of cultures in transition.

CRITICAL VIEWING Possible response: Some carvings look like spurts of water, as from a fountain, perhaps a symbol for water or a tribal symbol indicating generations of ancestors. The abstract figures could represent people or gods, with the larger, broad-shouldered figures depicting community leaders or deities of some type. Their size and the objects above their heads distinguish them from other figures, perhaps indicating power or dominance. The smaller figures might represent warriors and less powerful members of the group. Ancient people may have made the carvings to commemorate social and religious ceremonies, battles, and hunts, or other significant events in their history or culture.

1588 EUROPE:
THE DEFEAT OF THE SPANISH ARMADA

King Philip II of Spain had tried for years to find a way to restore the Roman Catholic faith in England. It was England's alliance with Dutch rebels against Spanish rule and repeated episodes of English piracy against Spanish trade ships that eventually provoked Philip to take action. After agreeing to join with a Spanish force stationed in Flanders under the command of the feared and respected Duke of Parma, the Spanish Armada set sail in May 1588 with 130 ships, 8,000 sailors, nearly 19,000 soldiers, and a plan to invade England. However, what the English fleet lacked in troops it made up for with smaller, faster, well-armed ships. On reaching the Strait of Dover, the Armada awaited backup from the Duke of Parma. But the Armada's unprotected position allowed the English to launch fire ships—boats loaded with explosives—that effectively broke the Armada's formation and sent it back out to sea. **ASK:** Why might the English have launched fire ships instead of engaging the unprotected ships in battle? *(Possible responses: The commander of the smaller English force may have wanted to drive the Armada back in order to decide whether a full battle would be necessary. Or the English may have been buying time to come up with a plan for conquering the larger Spanish fleet.)*

Meanwhile, Parma's forces found it impossible to get by the English fleet to join the Spanish with supplies and troops. The English used their artillary to hammer away at the Armada, sinking three ships. Eventually English forces—combined with troublesome winds—made the Armada break off the fight, and the planned invasion of England never happened. **ASK:** Given that Spain was known as Europe's greatest power in 1588, what might have been a consequence of the Armada's defeat? *(Possible response: Because the English fleet was much smaller than the Spanish Armada, the defeat would have been a significant blow to Spain's pride and its reputation for military superiority.)*

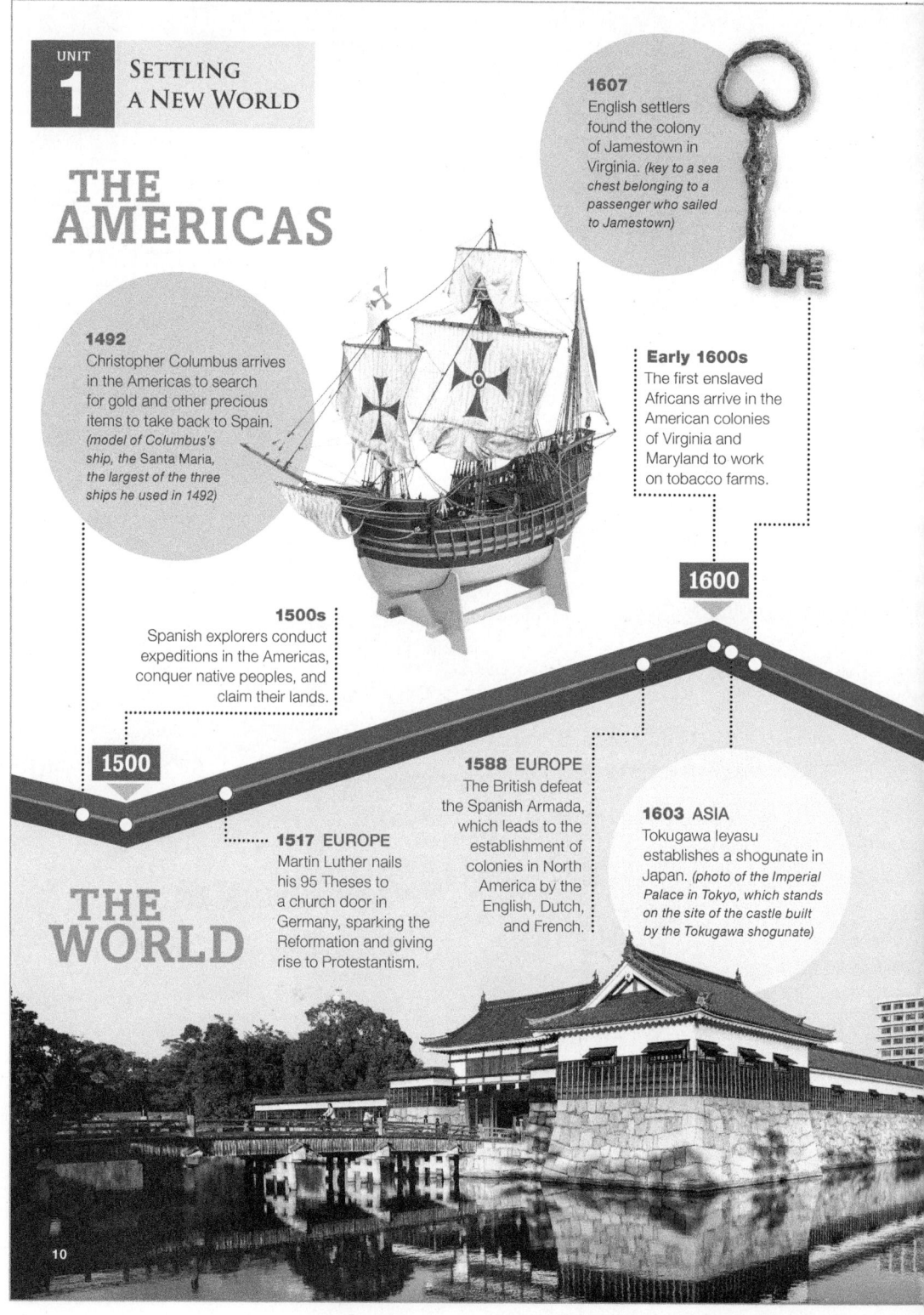

UNIT 1 SETTLING A NEW WORLD

THE AMERICAS

1607
English settlers found the colony of Jamestown in Virginia. *(key to a sea chest belonging to a passenger who sailed to Jamestown)*

1492
Christopher Columbus arrives in the Americas to search for gold and other precious items to take back to Spain. *(model of Columbus's ship, the Santa Maria, the largest of the three ships he used in 1492)*

Early 1600s
The first enslaved Africans arrive in the American colonies of Virginia and Maryland to work on tobacco farms.

1600

1500s
Spanish explorers conduct expeditions in the Americas, conquer native peoples, and claim their lands.

1500

1588 EUROPE
The British defeat the Spanish Armada, which leads to the establishment of colonies in North America by the English, Dutch, and French.

THE WORLD

1517 EUROPE
Martin Luther nails his 95 Theses to a church door in Germany, sparking the Reformation and giving rise to Protestantism.

1603 ASIA
Tokugawa Ieyasu establishes a shogunate in Japan. *(photo of the Imperial Palace in Tokyo, which stands on the site of the castle built by the Tokugawa shogunate)*

10

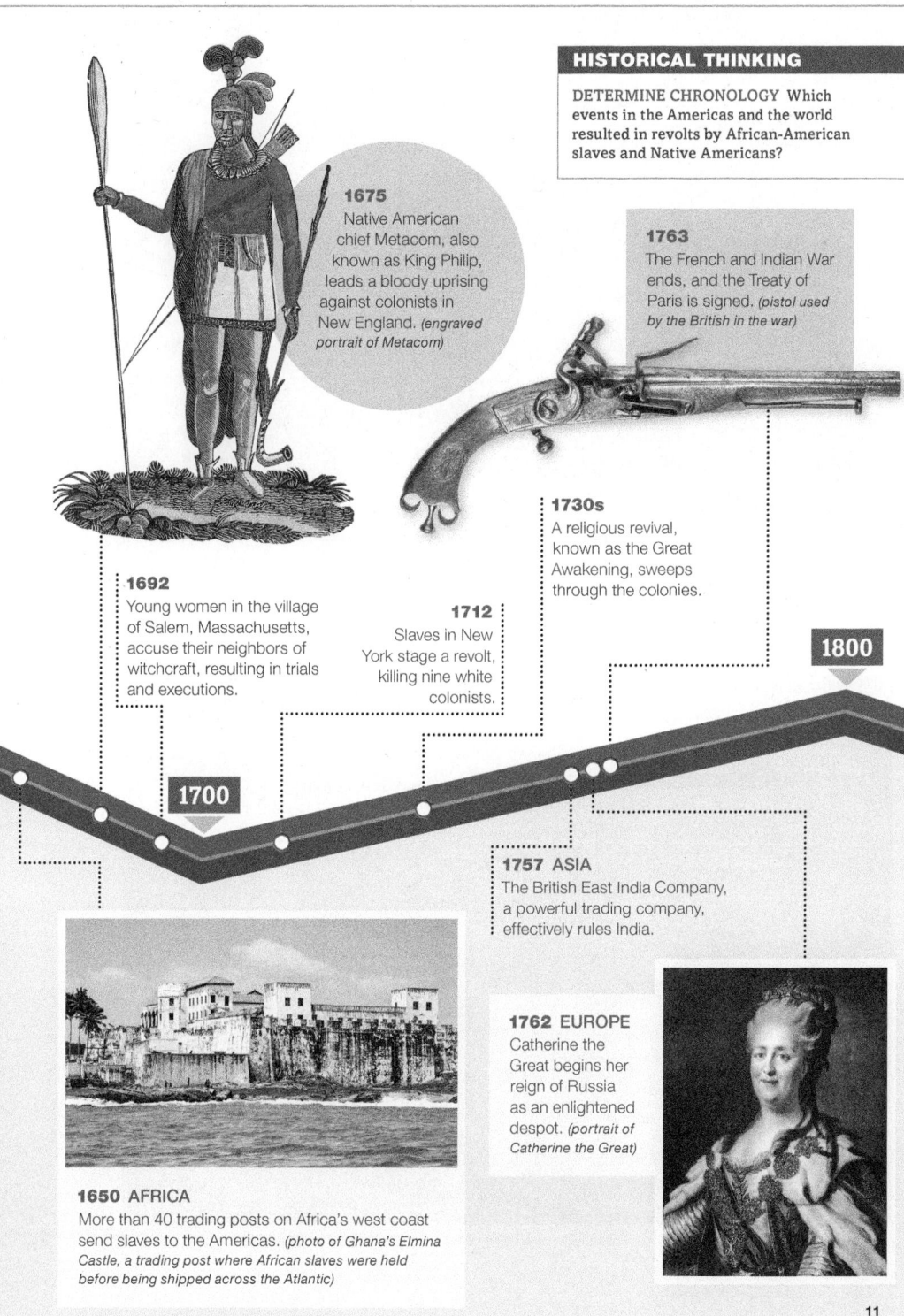

HISTORICAL THINKING

DETERMINE CHRONOLOGY Which events in the Americas and the world resulted in revolts by African-American slaves and Native Americans?

1675
Native American chief Metacom, also known as King Philip, leads a bloody uprising against colonists in New England. *(engraved portrait of Metacom)*

1763
The French and Indian War ends, and the Treaty of Paris is signed. *(pistol used by the British in the war)*

1730s
A religious revival, known as the Great Awakening, sweeps through the colonies.

1692
Young women in the village of Salem, Massachusetts, accuse their neighbors of witchcraft, resulting in trials and executions.

1712
Slaves in New York stage a revolt, killing nine white colonists.

1800

1700

1757 ASIA
The British East India Company, a powerful trading company, effectively rules India.

1762 EUROPE
Catherine the Great begins her reign of Russia as an enlightened despot. *(portrait of Catherine the Great)*

1650 AFRICA
More than 40 trading posts on Africa's west coast send slaves to the Americas. *(photo of Ghana's Elmina Castle, a trading post where African slaves were held before being shipped across the Atlantic)*

11

INTRODUCE TIME LINE EVENT

1762 EUROPE:
THE REIGN OF CATHERINE THE GREAT

German-born Catherine II, known as Catherine the Great, reigned from 1762 until her death in 1796. She married Grand Duke Peter, heir to the Russian throne, in 1745, but it was an unhappy marriage. Peter became czar in 1762 but was quickly overthrown, and Catherine was declared empress. She surrounded herself with a group of experienced ministers and reorganized the power structure and laws of her empire. Catherine expanded Russian territory, adding Crimea, Belarus, and Lithuania, as well as large areas of Poland. Passionate about social and political reform, education, and the arts, she convened a commission in 1767 to modernize Russian life.

Later in her reign, however, the Russian army put down a major rebellion in Russia's western territories. This event convinced Catherine of her reliance on and debt to Russian nobles. To reward them for their protection of her sovereignty, she created legislation giving them greater control over their lands, which enriched the nobility at the expense of the already downtrodden serfs. **ASK:** What general statement can you make regarding the change over time in Catherine's leadership? *(Possible response: Catherine's early leadership seemed to be liberal and broad-minded; but over time, she became more conservative and traditional, rewarding the nobles for their loyalty rather than seeing to the needs of all her people, as she appeared to do in her earlier reforms.)*

HISTORICAL THINKING

DETERMINE CHRONOLOGY

The enslaving of Africans by colonists and colonists' expansion into the lands of Native Americans inevitably resulted in revolts by both groups. In the early 1600s, enslaved Africans were put to work on tobacco farms in Virginia and Maryland. In 1650, trading posts on Africa's west coast began to send enslaved Africans to the Americas. A slave revolt took place 62 years later in New York in 1712. In 1675, Native American chief Metacom led an uprising in New England against colonists.

UNIT 1 RESOURCES

UNIT INTRODUCTION

UNIT TIME LINE

UNIT WRAP-UP

NATIONAL GEOGRAPHIC | CONNECTION

National Geographic Magazine Adapted Articles
- "Colonial New York"
- "The First Americans" ONLINE

Unit 1 Inquiry: Conceive a Utopia

NG Learning Framework Activities
- Map Migrations
- Establish a Trade Network

Unit 1 Formal Assessment

UNIT 1 | Beginnings–1763
SETTLING A NEW WORLD

CRITICAL VIEWING Petroglyphs, or rock carvings, created by ancient Native American artists can be found throughout the Southwest. The petroglyphs in this photo by National Geographic photographer Paul Chesley include many different figures. Describe some of the figures you see. What types of activities or events might they represent?

CHAPTER 1 RESOURCES

Available at NGLSync.Cengage.com

TEACHER RESOURCES & ASSESSMENT

Reading and Note-Taking

Vocabulary Practice

Document-Based Question Template

Social Studies Skills Lessons
- Reading: Analyze Cause and Effect
- Writing: Argument

Formal Assessment
- Chapter 1 Pretest
- Chapter 1 Tests A & B
- Section Quizzes

Chapter 1 Answer Key

ExamView®
  One-time Download

CHAPTER 1 | THE
ATLANTIC WORLD
Beginnings–1550

"This land is very populous, and full of inhabitants, and of numberless rivers, and animals."
—Amerigo Vespucci, Italian explorer

HISTORICAL THINKING What impact did European exploration have on the cultures of North America and Africa?

AMERICAN STORIES ONLINE | Cahokia
SECTION 1 | The Story of Two Hemispheres
SECTION 2 | Exploring the Americas
AMERICAN GALLERY ONLINE | Early American Civilizations

During its 100th anniversary in 2006, Mesa Verde National Park lit up Cliff Palace, Colorado's largest ancient cliff dwelling. From this image, it is possible to imagine a firelit evening among the ancient Pueblo people, who lived in the region more than 700 years ago. Cliff Palace has about 150 rooms and more than 20 kivas, or rooms for religious rituals.

12 CHAPTER 1

The Atlantic World 13

STUDENT DIGITAL RESOURCES

- eEdition
- Handbooks
- Online Atlas
- American Gallery Online
- History Notebook
- Active History
- Reid on the Road video series
- Literature Analysis
- Projects for Inquiry-Based Learning

Chapter 1 Spanish Resources are available at NGLSync.Cengage.com.

AMERICAN STORIES ONLINE | **Cahokia**

- Study Primary Sources: Images from the Birdman Tablet
- On Your Feet: Numbered Heads

| **NG Learning Framework:**
Make a Time Line

SECTION 1 RESOURCES

THE STORY OF TWO HEMISPHERES

LESSON 1.1
Cultures of the Americas

AMERICAN GALLERY ONLINE | Early American Civilizations

| **NG Learning Framework:**
Investigate a Legacy

LESSON 1.2
NATIONAL GEOGRAPHIC EXPLORER
SARAH PARCAK
Space, Satellites, and Archaeology

- Active History: Think Like an Archaeologist

| **NG Learning Framework:**
Explore High-Tech Archaeology

LESSON 1.3
15th-Century Europe

- On Your Feet: Create a Concept Web

| **NG Learning Framework:**
Celebrate Innovations

LESSON 1.4
West African Kingdoms

- On Your Feet: Kingdom Questions

| **NG Learning Framework:**
Compare West African Kingdoms

SECTION 2 RESOURCES

EXPLORING THE AMERICAS

LESSON 2.1
Opening Up the Ocean World

- ▶ Map of a Pizza
- On Your Feet: Four Questions About European Exploration

| **NG Learning Framework:**
Create a Technology Chart

LESSON 2.2
DOCUMENT-BASED QUESTION
Two Worlds Meet

- On Your Feet: Use a Jigsaw Strategy

CHAPTER 1 REVIEW

STRATEGY 1
TURN HEADINGS INTO OUTLINES

To help students organize and understand lesson content, explain that headings can provide a high-level outline of the lesson. Model for students how to use the lesson title and subheadings to create a basic outline. Encourage students to add information to their outlines as they read.

Use with All Lessons

STRATEGY 2
READ AND RECALL

Invite students to work in groups of two to four. First, have each student read the lesson independently. After reading, students should meet without the book and share ideas they recall. One student takes notes. As a group, students then review the lesson and decide what to add or change in the notes.

Use with All Lessons

STRATEGY 3
CLARIFY DIFFERENCES

Bondage	Chattel Slavery

Students may have difficulty understanding the differences between the practice of slavery (bondage) that existed in Africa and elsewhere for many centuries and chattel slavery, which occurred in Europe and the United States. To help students clarify the differences, instruct them to create a T-Chart and label the first column Bondage and the second column Chattel Slavery. Tell them to jot down key facts about each as they read about them in the lessons. Encourage students to compare their completed charts, noting any differences.

Use with Lessons 1.4 and 2.1 *To help students find information for their charts, bring their attention to the final paragraph of Lesson 1.4 and to the Growth of the Slave Trade subsection in Lesson 2.1.*

STRATEGY 1
PREVIEW AND PREDICT

Pair visually impaired students with students who are not visually challenged. Instruct them to read the lesson title and subheadings together. Tell sighted students to describe lesson visuals in detail to help their partners understand them. Then have pairs work together to write notes predicting what the lesson will be about. After they have finished reading the lesson, ask pairs to review their notes to see whether their predictions were confirmed.

Use with All Lessons *For example, in Lesson 1.1, ask sighted students to read the title and subheadings and describe the two artifacts, the map showing early American civilizations, and the photograph of Teotihuacan. Pairs will then write predictions, such as: This lesson will be about different Native American cultures, their artistic accomplishments, and the cities and civilizations they built.*

STRATEGY 2
USE SUPPORTED READING

Prompt pairs to read the chapter aloud lesson by lesson. Instruct them to stop at the end of each lesson and use these sentence frames to monitor their comprehension of the text:

- This lesson is mostly about _____.
- Other topics in this lesson are _____, _____, and _____.
- One question I have is _____.
- One of the vocabulary words is _____, and it means _____.
- One word I don't recognize is _____.

Use with All Lessons

ENGLISH LANGUAGE LEARNERS ELD

STRATEGY ❶
CREATE MEANING MAPS

Pair students at the **Emerging** level with those at the **Expanding** or **Bridging** level. Demonstrate how to use a Meaning Map for any of the Key Vocabulary or other important words and terms in the lesson. As students work, encourage them to discuss the words together and clear up any misunderstandings.

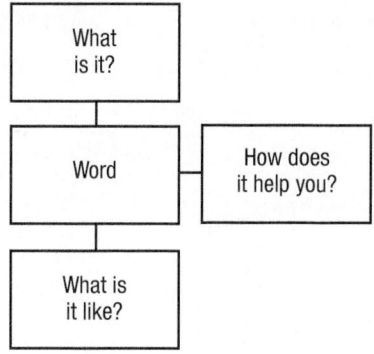

Use with All Lessons

STRATEGY ❷
USE PAIRED READING

Pair students at the **Expanding** and **Bridging** levels, and have them read passages from the text aloud.

1. Partner 1 reads a passage; Partner 2 retells the passage in his or her own words.

2. Partner 2 reads a different passage; Partner 1 retells it.

3. Pairs repeat the process, switching roles.

Use with All Lessons

STRATEGY ❸
ORDER SENTENCE STRIPS

Choose a key paragraph from the lesson to read aloud while students at **All Proficiencies** follow along in their books. After reading, tell students to close their books. Provide sentence strips of the paragraph and direct students to place the strips in order. Ask students to read their paragraphs aloud.

Use with All Lessons *You may wish to ask students at the* ***Emerging*** *level to read the sentence strips aloud and identify meaningful words before they start placing the strips in order.*

GIFTED & TALENTED

STRATEGY ❶
DESIGN AN INFOGRAPHIC

Instruct students to learn more about trading and the economy in the kingdom of Ghana, Mali, Songhai, Benin, or Kongo. Tell them to use the most compelling data and images from their research to create an infographic. Invite students to post their infographics on a class website or on the class bulletin board.

Use with Lesson 1.4

STRATEGY ❷
CREATE A MULTIMEDIA PRESENTATION

Direct students to create a multimedia presentation about the bubonic plague. Encourage them to use a cause-and-effect chart to keep track of the causes—those thought to be true during the Middle Ages and those recognized today—as well as the effects of the plague, including social, economic, and religious upheavals. Invite students to share their multimedia presentations with the class.

Use with Lesson 1.3

PRE-AP

STRATEGY ❶
WRITE A GRANT LETTER

Direct students to consider how an archaeological project could help add to our knowledge about one of the topics discussed in this chapter. Tell them to conduct research as necessary to help them write a letter from the perspective of a researcher requesting funding for a project. For example, students might research what techniques have been used to investigate plague burial sites, ancient mining sites, or trade routes; where such sites have been located; and what kinds of information can be gleaned from investigating these sites. Then prompt them to write a letter explaining why their project should receive funding, including information about where the project would take place, what means they would use to investigate, and what they hope to learn. Invite students to share their letters with the class.

Use with All Lessons

STRATEGY ❷
FORM AND SUPPORT A THESIS

Instruct students to develop a thesis statement for a specific topic related to one of the lessons in the chapter. Then have them conduct research to support their thesis with evidence. Tell students to use their research to write an essay, citing their sources. Encourage them to share their essays on a class or school blog.

Use with All Lessons

HISTORICAL THINKING What impact did European exploration have on the cultures of North America and Africa?

AMERICAN
STORIES | Cahokia
ONLINE

SECTION 1 **The Story of Two Hemispheres**
SECTION 2 **Exploring the Americas**

AMERICAN GALLERY | **Early American Civilizations**
ONLINE

"**This land is very populous,** and full of inhabitants, and of numberless rivers, and animals."
—Amerigo Vespucci, Italian explorer

During its 100th anniversary in 2006, Mesa Verde National Park lit up Cliff Palace, Colorado's largest ancient cliff dwelling. From this image, it is possible to imagine a firelit evening among the ancient Pueblo people, who lived in the region more than 700 years ago. Cliff Palace has about 150 rooms and more than 20 kivas, or rooms for religious rituals.

INTRODUCE THE PHOTOGRAPH

CLIFF PALACE

Have students study the photograph of Cliff Palace, the ancient Pueblo dwelling, that opens this chapter. Instruct them to read the quotation and look closely at the construction and layout of the historical site. **ASK:** What inferences can you make about the people who built this cliff dwelling? *(Answers will vary. Possible response: Given the engineering needed to construct the dwelling, the people must have attained a high level of technological skill to build these long-lasting structures in this particular setting and to use the landscape and its resources to their advantage. They also seem to have favored a centralized, or urban, design for the dwelling to support a large and dense population.)*

For Chapter 1 Spanish Resources, visit the Resources Menu. Chapter 1 Resources are available at NGLSync.Cengage.com.

SHARE BACKGROUND

The ancient Pueblo employed sandstone, mortar, and wooden beams as their main building materials when constructing Cliff Palace. They used hard river rock to shape the sandstone blocks and mixed local soil with ash and water to make the mortar to hold the blocks together. Tiny stones added to the mortar helped fill in any gaps. The ancient Pueblo decorated many of the walls with colored earthen plaster. But over the centuries, weather, wind, animals, and the natural breakdown of rock took their toll on Cliff Palace: The plaster deteriorated first, and walls and roofs eventually crumbled. Then in the late 1800s, visitors "discovered" the dwelling and hastened the damage through their curiosity and search for artifacts. The destruction slowed when the government established the Mesa Verde National Park in 1906 and launched a program of preservation to stabilize the ruins and keep them from further decline.

HISTORICAL THINKING QUESTION

> What impact did European exploration have on the cultures of North America and Africa?

Roundtable Activity: Impact of Exploration Arrange students into an even number of small groups and number each group. Assign odd-numbered groups these two questions: What are some ways that communities might react to the arrival of strangers? What factors affect how a community chooses to react to new people? Assign even-numbered groups these two questions: How might the arrival of explorers change a local economy? How might exploration affect the economy of the explorers' home country? Have the first student in each group write an answer to each question on a sheet of paper and pass the paper clockwise to the next student, who adds an answer, continuing until students are out of ideas. As a class, compile a master list of answers for each question. Then tell students that in Chapter 1 they will learn how European exploration affected cultures in Africa and the Americas.

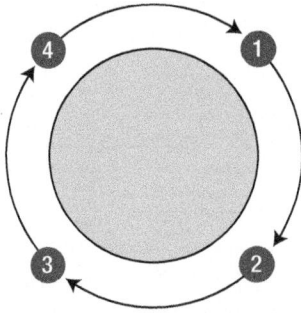

INTRODUCE THE READING STRATEGY

ANALYZE CAUSE AND EFFECT

Explain that identifying causes and effects helps students understand how one event brings about or influences later developments. Point out that one cause can have many effects. Turn to the Chapter Review and preview the graphic organizer with students. As they read the chapter, prompt students to analyze how the expansion of global trade impacted people living on different continents.

KEY DATES FOR CHAPTER 1

1324	Mansa Musa makes pilgrimage to Mecca
1347	Bubonic plague reaches Europe
c. 1452	Johann Gutenberg invents printing press
1483	Portuguese traders arrive in Kongo
1488	Bartholomeu Dias rounds Cape of Good Hope
1492	Christopher Columbus crosses the Atlantic
1494	Treaty of Tordesillas establishes Line of Demarcation
1498	Vasco da Gama reaches India by sea
1517	Martin Luther writes his 95 Theses

INTRODUCE CHAPTER VOCABULARY

KEY VOCABULARY

SECTION 1

caravan	manor system	Renaissance
Crusades	mercantilism	savanna
domesticate	nation-state	slash-and-burn agriculture
feudalism	nomadic	
humanism	potlatch	steppe
indulgence	Protestant Reformation	trans-Saharan
infrastructure		tundra

SECTION 2

caravel	chattel slavery	Columbian Exchange
cartographer	circumnavigate	quinine

DEFINITION CHART

As they read the chapter, encourage students to complete a Definition Chart. Ask them to list the Key Vocabulary terms in the left column of their charts. As students encounter each Key Vocabulary term in the chapter, they should write its definition in the center column and explain what it means, using their own words, in the right column. Model an example on the board, using the graphic organizer below.

Word	Definition	In My Own Words
caravan	a group of people and animals traveling together, usually for trade	traders and animals traveling together

 For instructional support for the online American Story "Cahokia," go to NGLSync.Cengage.com.

CULTURES OF THE AMERICAS

Imagine if you could travel back in time to the year 1492 and fly over the Western Hemisphere. You would see thousands of villages, cities, and even a sprawling empire or two. These vibrant cultures were unaware of the change that was coming, but their traditions and ways of life would soon alter the world.

Early American Civilizations and Environments, 1200 B.C.–A.D. 1535

- Arctic
- California
- Great Basin
- Great Plains
- Northeast
- Northwest Coast
- Plateau
- Southeast
- Southwest
- Subarctic
- **Mesoamerica**
- Aztec empire
- Mayan empire
- Olmec

A LARGE AND DIVERSE POPULATION

Archaeologists, scientists who study human history through the excavation and analysis of artifacts and other remains, generally believe the first humans to populate the Americas began arriving some 15,000 to 20,000 years ago. Many came in waves into the northern part of North America from Asia. Others came from Europe, traveling from island to island in the North Atlantic until they reached the continent. As small bands spread across the Americas, they found an abundant and challenging land. They faced frozen regions, grasslands, mountain ranges, deserts, and rain forests. In time, the migrants' languages, customs, and cultures became as different as their locations.

Historians don't know for sure how many people lived throughout North and South America in 1492, but their estimates range from 54 to 100 million. Trading networks crisscrossed North and South America, bringing items such as maize, or corn, from what is now Central America as far north and east as present-day Georgia. Ancient arrow and spear points made of obsidian, a hard, sharp stone quarried in northwestern Wyoming, have been unearthed in the Ohio River Valley, more than 1,600 miles to the east. Various cultures, traditions, and ways of life also traveled along these routes. Unfortunately, so did disease, which devastated the populations of both continents soon after their first contact with Europeans.

Native American groups of the Northwest Coast often wore masks during healing rituals, feasts, performances, or secret society meetings. This mask, most likely created by a Tsimshian (SHIHM-shee-uhn) artist, was made with wood, copper, paint, and shells.

THE FAR NORTH AND PACIFIC COAST

To the far north of North America, other Native American cultures thrived in the harsh climate of what is now Alaska and northwestern Canada. The Inuit (IH-noo-wit) were one of the largest Native American groups in this region. They lived in small communities along the northernmost coast of North America and inland on the flat, frozen **tundra**. The tundra's frozen ground made farming impossible, so the Inuit depended on fishing and hunting. They took to the sea in light boats called kayaks, made of wood and the hides of seal or walruses. Their hunting economy expanded when East Asian traders arrived. The Inuit traded furs and walrus ivory for Asian steel knives, hooks, and spear points. They could now hunt larger whales. As a result, they began using whale bones to build their houses. By the 1300s, the Inuit had spread across Canada and onto the island of Greenland, where they traded with the Vikings—European seafarers and warriors from Scandinavia—for iron tools and weapons.

The moderate climate farther south along the Pacific Coast made some farming possible and ensured that a greater variety of fish and game was available to those who settled the forests and coastal areas from present-day British Columbia to Baja California. The Kwakiutl (kwah-kee-YOO-tuhl) are one tribe that flourished along the Northwest Coast. To show their status and wealth, Kwakiutl families periodically held **potlatches**, or lavish feasts. Over several days they fasted, prayed, danced, and bestowed generous gifts on guests.

THE DESERTS AND THE PLAINS

Farming in the deserts that characterize the American southwest might seem an unlikely prospect. But the **ancient Pueblo** (PWAY-bloh) and the **Hohokam** (ho-ho-KOM) people made the most of their sparse water sources, which included only a few major rivers. They developed a series of canals to irrigate, or supply the fields with water, and produce abundant crops. Through trade, the people acquired maize from Mesoamerica. By adding maize to the number of plants they **domesticated**, or grew themselves, such as squash, beans, and cotton, they developed a diverse agricultural economy.

To house their growing populations, both groups built large adobe houses of sun-dried clay and straw in complexes that resembled modern-day apartment buildings. Many of these were tucked into cliffs on the edges of desert mesas, possibly as a defense against enemy attacks. It appears that these once-thriving communities were abandoned around A.D. 1200, perhaps due to warfare or **drought**, a prolonged period of little or no rainfall.

Northeast of the deserts were vast grasslands extending from the Mississippi River to the foot of the Rocky Mountains and north into Canada. Today

---

INTRODUCE & ENGAGE

EXPLORE REGIONAL DIFFERENCES

Draw a T-Chart on the board, labeling the first column Desert and the second column Woodland. **ASK:** What do you think of when you picture a desert or a woodland environment? *(Answers will vary. Possible responses: Desert: hot, dry, cacti, snakes, scorpions; Woodland: dense forests, running streams, bears, deer, small game)* Write students' responses in the chart. Ask them to identify ways life might be similar or different for humans living in these environments. Then tell students that in this lesson they will learn how Native Americans adapted to living in different environments in North America, Mesoamerica, and South America.

Desert	Woodland

TEACH

GUIDED DISCUSSION

1. **Identify Main Ideas and Details** How do historians know that Native Americans traded with one another? *(Possible response: Archaeologists have found objects and evidence of knowledge in one region that were native to a different region. For example, arrow and spear points made from obsidian mined in Wyoming have been found at sites in the Ohio River Valley, and Mesoamerican maize has been found in the Southwest and as far east as Georgia. There is also evidence that disease quickly spread across great distances, suggesting contact among tribes.)*

2. **Make Connections** What does the existence of potlatches among the Kwakiutl suggest about the natural environment of the Northwest Coast? *(Possible response: The region must have offered an abundance of fish, game, and other resources. If resources had been scarce, the Kwakiutl would not have been able to throw such lavish feasts and give generous gifts.)*

3. **Analyze Cause and Effect** How did trade result in benefits for the Inuit and the ancient Pueblo and Hohokam people? *(Trade with East Asians and Europeans provided the Inuit with steel knives, hooks, spear points, and iron tools and weapons, which enabled them to expand their hunting economy by hunting larger whales. The ancient Pueblo and the Hohokam acquired maize from Mesoamerica, which helped them develop a diverse agricultural economy.)*

MORE INFORMATION

Pueblo Bonito Pueblo Bonito, located in Chaco Canyon in present-day New Mexico, is an example of the large adobe houses built by the ancient Pueblo people. The ancient Pueblo built Pueblo Bonito in stages, somewhere between A.D. 850 and 1150. In addition to providing living quarters, the pueblo served as a ceremonial, political, and trading center. The structure was laid out in a D, or semicircular, shape and was positioned in relation to the cardinal directions—north, south, east, and west. Astronomical markers, earthen mounds, and devices to control water surrounded the pueblo. Although only the foundation remains today, archaeologists believe that the structure ranged from one to five stories high with two plazas in the center and was home to around 1,000 people at its height.

DIFFERENTIATE

ENGLISH LANGUAGE LEARNERS

Pronunciation Before reading, preview with students of **All Proficiencies** the words *archaeologists* and *infrastructure*. Point out the unusual group of vowels in the middle of the first word and the potentially difficult *str* consonant cluster in the second word. Then say each word slowly, and have students repeat it. You may also want to preview other words from the lesson that may be challenging to pronounce, such as *drought, Scandinavia, Mississippian, potlatches,* and *domesticated.* Suggest students make word cards for each word, writing definitions and pronunciation hints for themselves.

PRE-AP

Ask and Answer Questions About Native American Groups After they read the lesson, prompt students to choose a precontact Native American culture to learn more about, selecting one shown on the Early American Civilizations and Environments map or another they know of. Tell students to write three questions they have about that Native American group prior to its contact with Europeans. The questions should seek a deeper understanding of traditions and culture—addressing issues such as food, clothing, and housing; art and music; and language and systems of belief. Prompt students to conduct research to answer their questions and then share their findings with classmates, answering any questions their classmates may have.

See the Chapter Planner for more strategies for differentiation.

this region is called the Great Plains. Many Native American nations flourished here. In the western Great Plains, **nomadic** tribes such as the Blackfoot traveled the land following herds of game, particularly bison. The bison, or buffalo, was the center of their way of life, providing food, sinew for making thread, bones for making tools, and hides for clothing and shelter. Portable tents covered in hide, or tepees, could easily be packed up and moved over distances of hundreds of miles. On the eastern plains, Native Americans such as the Mandan and Pawnee lived more settled lives and farmed the land. They lived in villages of earthen lodges, some of which provided shelter for thousands of inhabitants.

THE MOUND BUILDERS

Around 1000 B.C., two hunter-gatherer cultures, the Adena and Hopewell, began building mounds across the upper and lower Midwest into present-day southern Ohio and Pennsylvania. Archaeologists refer to these cultures, which constructed the mounds along with the cities surrounding them, as **Mound Builders**. Built in a variety of shapes and sizes, the earthen mounds had different purposes, including as burial sites, temples, or ceremonial centers. The Serpent Mound in Ohio is one of the largest, winding more than 1,300 feet across the land. Seen from above, it appears to be a serpent holding an egg or jewel in its mouth. The mound may have been used as a burial site.

Beginning about A.D. 700, a new mound-building culture known as the Mississippians spread from present-day Georgia to Minnesota. Unlike the Adena and Hopewell, the Mississippians lived as settled farmers and could support large populations. Their capital, Cahokia (kuh-HO-kee-yuh), was built around a group of mounds in what is now southern Illinois. Between A.D. 1000 and 1100, Cahokia's population exceeded 15,000 people. At its center was Monks Mound, the largest human-made structure north of modern Mexico. About 100 feet high, its base is larger than Egypt's Great Pyramid of Giza. Some historians think Cahokia's population collapsed from the effects of a huge flood in about 1200. When Europeans first passed through the area, the city was gone.

THE EASTERN WOODLANDS

The land east from the Mississippi to the Atlantic Ocean and south to the Gulf of Mexico was covered with dense forests. Native Americans cleared portions of the woodlands to farm crops similar to those cultivated in the southwest: corn, beans, squash, and pumpkins. **Slash-and-burn agriculture**, the practice of cutting brush and burning trees to clear land for planting crops, forced the people to move their farms periodically to allow the soil to renew.

Plentiful crops meant large populations. In the south, these included the Cherokee, Chickasaw, and Choctaw, among others, who farmed the land surrounding their permanent villages. In the north and throughout much of the region, most tribes belonged to either the Algonquian (al-GAHN-kwee-uhn) or Iroquois (IHR-uh-kwoy) language group. The Algonquian speakers lived mainly along the Atlantic coast and to the foot of the Appalachian Mountains. The Iroquois-speaking nations lived mainly in the central part of present-day New York State and throughout the eastern Great Lakes region. They lived in longhouses, dwellings built of wood and bark that were large enough to house extended families. Although their ways of life were similar, Algonquians and Iroquois were usually enemies.

MESOAMERICAN EMPIRES

Mesoamerica once covered what is now southern Mexico and parts of Central America. Its fertile lands supported several civilizations, or complex societies. Among the best known are the **Olmec, Maya,** and **Aztecs**, civilizations that flourished in the region at different times from around 1200 B.C. to A.D. 1520. The oldest of these three, the Olmec settled along the coast of the Gulf of Mexico. They had an extensive trade network throughout Mesoamerica and greatly influenced the Maya, who thrived to their south. Visitors to Guatemala and the Yucatán (yoo-kuh-TAN) can still see the Maya's huge temple complexes and step pyramids, images of their solar and lunar calendars, and examples of their hieroglyphic, or picture-based, writing form.

The last Mesoamerican empire, the Aztec Empire, arose about A.D. 1200 in what is now central Mexico. At its height, nearly 6 million people lived under Aztec rule. The empire consisted of city-states controlled by the emperor, his council, and a strong military. Conquered city-states were allowed to govern themselves, but they were required to pay tribute, or bring rare and expensive gifts, to the emperor.

By the 1500s, the Aztecs' capital city of Tenochtitlán (tay-nohch-teet-LAHN) was one of the largest in the world. Built on small islands in a lake, the city grew rapidly. To increase its land, the Aztecs constructed artificial islands over the lake and nearby marshes to house lavish temples and palaces. The empire had plenty of food and developed a robust economy. But it also had a darker side: To appease their gods, the Aztecs sacrificed thousands of people each year. The army periodically raided nearby communities to keep the capital supplied with human victims.

This gold bee is one of many artifacts crafted by the Nasca people in ancient Peru.

Museo Larco, Lima – Perú

A SOUTH AMERICAN EMPIRE

Further to the south and west, the Inca developed an impressive civilization high in the Andes Mountains. The Inca rose to power in the 12th century, around the same period as the Aztecs, and built the largest empire on Earth at that time. Its boundaries ran 2,500 miles, from what is now Ecuador to central Chile, and boasted a population of around 10 million.

Inca engineers and architects created an **infrastructure**, or a series of connecting systems necessary for a society, that serves as an example of human planning even today. They developed terraced fields for agriculture and built miles of roadways and bridges to link all parts of their kingdom. Their stonework in the cities of Cusco (KOOS-koh) and Machu Picchu (MAH-choo PEE-choo) is so precise that not even a knife blade will fit between any two adjoining stones. The Inca adorned their cities with gold mined from the Andes. They amassed gold, silver, and gems for use in clothing, decorations, and jewelry, and their empire became the wealthiest and most powerful in the Americas.

HISTORICAL THINKING

1. **READING CHECK** How did present-day North and South America first become populated?

2. **ANALYZE CAUSE AND EFFECT** What made it possible for ancient Pueblo and Hohokam communities to grow crops?

3. **MAKE INFERENCES** What does the presence of a large trading network throughout North America imply about the different groups of people who lived on the continent?

4. **INTERPRET MAPS** What benefits did the Inuit and Aleut derive from their geographic locations?

Historians aren't certain who built the ancient city of Teotihuacan (tay-oh-tee-wah-KAHN) before the Maya and Aztec lived there. Located in present-day central Mexico, the city's Pyramid of the Sun rises high above ceremonial stone platforms along the Avenue of the Dead.

BUILD BACKGROUND

NORTHWEST COAST POTLATCHES

The potlatch played an important role in determining the social status of families. Since guests were expected to reciprocate by holding their own potlatch, a host could punish a rival by setting the bar so high that the other person's family is forced to give away all of their possessions to meet the obligation. Conversely, the potlatch could help a dishonored family regain status. The feasting and gifting associated with potlatches also served to redistribute resources within and among tribes, ensured that tribal members would contribute their labor for the common good, and helped prevent competition and conflict for resources. However, the idea that individuals would give away possessions—or even destroy them to prove they were wealthy enough to do so—ran counter to European views of property and wealth. The Canadian and U.S. governments outlawed potlatches in the late 1800s, but the ban was repealed in 1951, and potlatches are held today.

THE GREAT SERPENT MOUND

In the 1880s, Frederick W. Putnam excavated part of the Great Serpent Mound, but the artifacts he found could not establish who built the mound. Later archaeologists credited its creation to the Adena, based on the existence of nearby burial sites. This was the accepted interpretation until the 1990s, when samples from undisturbed areas of the mound yielded radiocarbon dates of around A.D. 1070—long after the Adena culture had ended. Some archaeologists used this new information to suggest that a Mississippian people created the mound. The discovery of Mississippian ruins nearby added support for this theory, as did the widespread use of rattlesnake imagery in Mississippian culture. But the issue is far from settled. In 2014, new radiocarbon testing dated the mound to around 300 B.C., once again suggesting that the Adena were responsible for its creation. A Mississippian group may have renovated the mound much later, leading to the very different radiocarbon dates.

TEACH

GUIDED DISCUSSION

4. **Analyze Environmental Concepts** How did Native American groups east of the Rocky Mountains both depend on and change their natural environments? *(Possible response: The nomadic tribes of the western plains built their cultures around following and hunting bison and other herd animals. Because they did not farm or create permanent settlements, they had little impact on the environment. Native Americans living in the eastern plains, the Mound Builders, and the eastern woodlands tribes hunted and fished, but most also farmed and created settlements. Farming enabled their populations to grow. These groups had an impact on the environment because of their size, the land they cleared, and the resources they used for settlements.)*

5. **Evaluate** What traits qualify the Olmec, Maya, Aztecs, and Inca as civilizations? *(Possible response: These groups created complex societies that engaged in activities such as extensive trade and agriculture; building roads, bridges, and large architectural structures, including temples and pyramids; creating complex governments that controlled city-states; developing forms of writing, calendars, elaborate art, and religious rituals; commanding large armies; and amassing great wealth.)*

MAKE CONNECTIONS

Point out the term *infrastructure* in the text. Invite a volunteer to use his or her own words to define the term. **ASK:** How does the term *infrastructure* describe the planning practices of both the ancient Inca and the United States today? *(Answers will vary. Possible response: The Inca created a system of terraced fields and extensive roadways and bridges that helped them feed and trade with all parts of their kingdom. In the United States today, governments at the local, state, and federal levels develop transportation, communication, sewage, water, and electrical systems that make economic and social development possible.)*

ACTIVE OPTIONS

AMERICAN GALLERY
ONLINE
Early American Civilizations Invite students to explore the American Gallery. Have them select one of the images and do additional research to learn more about it. Ask questions that will inspire additional inquiry about the chosen gallery image, such as: What is this? What is it designed to do? Why was it created? What is it made of? Why does it belong in this chapter? What else would you like to know about it?

NG Learning Framework: Investigate a Legacy   STEM

ATTITUDE Curiosity

SKILL Collaboration

Assign students to work with a partner to create a web page about the archaeological or cultural legacy of one of the Native American cultures discussed in the lesson. For example, students might investigate a Native American site that has been designated a national or state park or a World Heritage site. Alternatively, they might examine traditions that interest them, such as potlatches, that play a ceremonial role in modern Native American communities. Encourage students to include visuals, textual explanations, and hyperlinks in their web page.

For students who develop an interest in Native American archaeological sites, suggest that they read the online American Story "Cahokia."

HISTORICAL THINKING

ANSWERS

1. The first humans most likely came to North America in waves from Asia and Europe between 15,000 and 20,000 years ago. Small bands then spread throughout the Americas.

2. The Pueblo and Hohokam were able to farm in a desert environment because they dug irrigation canals that carried water from the few rivers in the region.

3. Possible response: Trading networks imply that different groups were aware of one another's cultures and traditions and that they were able to communicate well enough to conduct trade.

4. Possible response: The isolated locations of the Inuit and Aleut provided safety from other peoples. In addition, these two groups benefited from resources from the sea and from land animals that lived on the tundra.

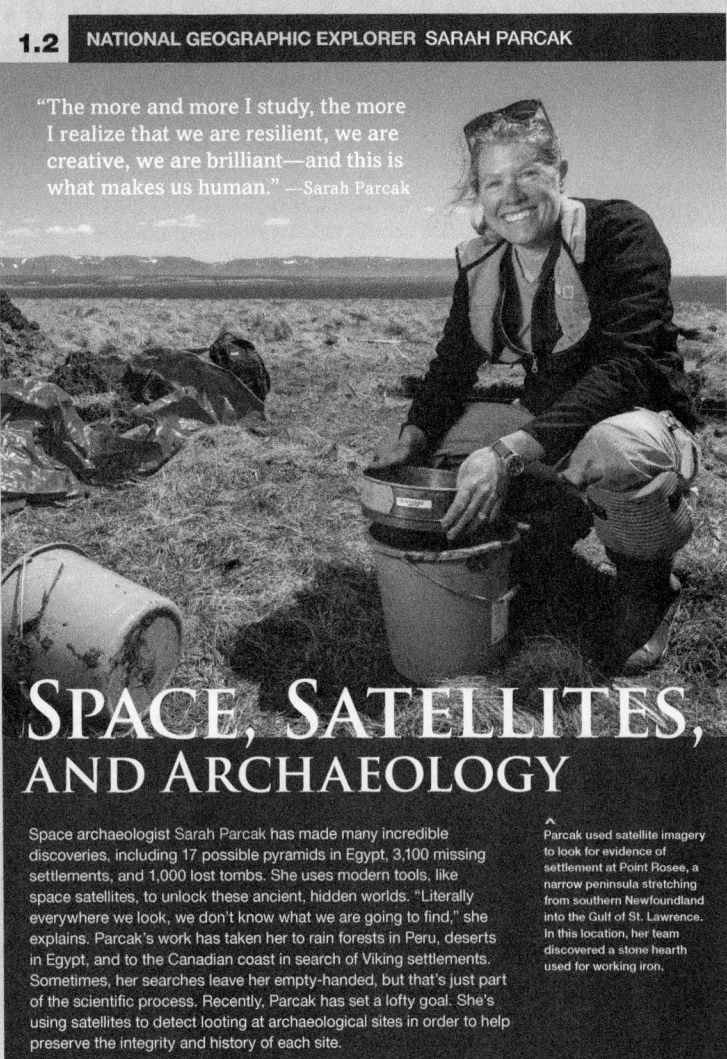

"The more and more I study, the more I realize that we are resilient, we are creative, we are brilliant—and this is what makes us human." —Sarah Parcak

SPACE, SATELLITES, AND ARCHAEOLOGY

Space archaeologist Sarah Parcak has made many incredible discoveries, including 17 possible pyramids in Egypt, 3,100 missing settlements, and 1,000 lost tombs. She uses modern tools, like space satellites, to unlock these ancient, hidden worlds. "Literally everywhere we look, we don't know what we are going to find," she explains. Parcak's work has taken her to rain forests in Peru, deserts in Egypt, and to the Canadian coast in search of Viking settlements. Sometimes, her searches leave her empty-handed, but that's just part of the scientific process. Recently, Parcak has set a lofty goal. She's using satellites to detect looting at archaeological sites in order to help preserve the integrity and history of each site.

^ Parcak used satellite imagery to look for evidence of settlement at Point Rosee, a narrow peninsula stretching from southern Newfoundland into the Gulf of St. Lawrence. In this location, her team discovered a stone hearth used for working iron.

MAIN IDEA Sarah Parcak, space archaeologist, uses satellite technology to discover civilizations that have been lost for thousands of years and look for signs of looting.

THE SPACE ARCHAEOLOGIST

When you picture an archaeologist, what comes to mind? Maybe someone wearing khaki-colored clothing and a large-brimmed hat, painstakingly brushing away the dirt that surrounds an artifact? That may be the typical image of an archaeologist, but Sarah Parcak doesn't fit this description. Instead of using brushes and shovels, this space archaeologist is more likely to use satellites and other remote sensing tools to locate and study ancient settlements.

One tool in Parcak's high-tech toolbox is a form of remote sensing called LIDAR, which stands for Light Detection and Ranging. LIDAR is used to collect data from an airplane, helicopter, or drone. It sends laser pulses down to ground level and records the rate at which the pulses return to build a map of the landscape below. But Parcak primarily uses satellite imagery to search areas of Peruvian rain forest or portions of the Egyptian desert for lost civilizations. As a result, more often than not, you'll find her in the lab. "We don't just grab an image, flip it into the computer, and press a button," she says. "I've spent more than 10,000 hours of my life staring at satellite imagery to understand what I'm seeing."

With satellite technology, Parcak has discovered ancient ruins—and sometimes entire civilizations—that have been hidden underground for tens to hundreds of thousands of years. "Satellite imagery is a powerful new tool that gives us eyes in the sky," explains Parcak. "We can process images captured from space in a way that lets us see patterns in the vegetation and the soil that might signal a man-made feature, hidden from view."

VIKINGS IN NORTH AMERICA?

One of Parcak's satellite imagery projects has taken place in North America. After studying the Canadian coastlines from above, one site—Point Rosee—stood out to Parcak as a place where humans might have lived long ago. During a June 2015 excavation of this site, which is hundreds of

To find evidence of looting in Egypt, Parcak compares current satellite images like this one to older satellite images. The winner of the 2016 TED Prize, she is funding a project in the Middle East that includes identifying and protecting archaeological sites through the use of satellite imagery.

miles south of the only known Viking settlement in North America, Parcak's team discovered an ancient iron hearth and bits of iron ore. The presence of the iron as well as other structures on the site pointed to a possible second Viking settlement in North America—a discovery that, if proven true, would shake the archaeological world to its core and potentially rewrite some of the history of the Americas.

Parcak was skeptical, and the discovery raised many questions—where the Norse people sailed, how they lived, and how long they settled in one region. Parcak and her team returned to Point Rosee in March 2016 to get some answers, but the dig did not turn up artifacts that reinforced the possibility of a second Viking settlement. For now, those questions remain unanswered, but Point Rosee will continue to be explored. "It's just the nature of science," says Parcak. "I think ultimately we just have to let the science speak for itself."

HISTORICAL THINKING

1. **READING CHECK** How does Sarah Parcak use satellite technology in the field of archaeology?
2. **SUMMARIZE** How could Parcak's research reshape the history of North America?
3. **FORM AND SUPPORT OPINIONS** If you were an archaeologist, would you embrace tools like LIDAR or stick with more traditional methods? Explain.

PLAN: 2-PAGE LESSON

OBJECTIVE
Examine how Sarah Parcak uses high-tech tools to find and preserve archaeological sites around the globe.

CRITICAL THINKING SKILLS FOR LESSON 1.2
• Summarize
• Form and Support Opinions
• Make Inferences
• Evaluate

HISTORICAL THINKING FOR CHAPTER 1
What impact did European exploration have on the cultures of North America and Africa?
Archaeologists have found that Vikings were one of the first European groups to explore and settle in North America. Lesson 1.2 describes some of the high-tech equipment used to identify and explore archaeological sites around the globe, including what may have been a previously unknown Viking settlement in North America.

NATIONAL GEOGRAPHIC EXPLORER
SARAH PARCAK

In addition to using space-age technology, Sarah Parcak also harnesses the power of crowd sourcing. Parcak wants to revolutionize the way archaeology is done by enlisting the aid of citizen explorers to help analyze the countless number of satellite images available to archaeologists. In January 2017, Parcak launched GlobalXplorer°, an online platform that brings archaeological exploration to anyone with an internet connection. Amateur archaeologists can log on to GlobalXplorer° and help find the next hidden site or help protect sites from potential looting. The platform may also deter thieves if they believe the world is watching them.

HISTORY NOTEBOOK
Encourage students to complete the Explorer page for Chapter 1 in their History Notebooks as they read.

INTRODUCE & ENGAGE

DESCRIBE HOW ARCHAEOLOGISTS WORK

Write the word *archaeologist* on the board. Ask students to define the term and volunteer words, phrases, or names they associate with it. Write their responses on the board. Then invite students to discuss their perceptions about what archaeologists do and the tools they use. Explain that in this lesson they will learn about National Geographic Explorer Sarah Parcak, who works with high-tech tools to locate and uncover hidden ancient settlements.

TEACH

GUIDED DISCUSSION

1. **Make Inferences** What skills might modern archaeologists need in order to use high-tech tools like LIDAR to search for sites? *(Possible response: To use high-tech tools, archaeologists might need technical skills to operate the equipment, computer skills to link data to other programs such as GPS to form maps, and an understanding of soil changes or other physical signs that will help them find hidden sites on the maps.)*

2. **Evaluate** Why are high-tech images often not enough to confirm an archaeological find, such as a settlement? *(Possible response: Archaeologists still need physical evidence, such as artifacts or bones, to determine whether a site was used as a settlement. High-tech images may or may not be able to detect such evidence, which must be dug out of the ground by hand.)*

MORE INFORMATION

High-Tech Tools of Archaeology Explain to students that LIDAR is only one of six major tools that have revolutionized archaeology. The other five involve satellite imagery, such as Google Earth, drones, shallow geophysics, soil geochemistry, and ground-penetrating radar. Drones are particularly useful for taking detailed aerial photographs in areas hard to reach on foot. Shallow geophysical and soil geochemistry techniques help gather data related to human settlement, such as soil disturbances, patterns of heavy metals, and magnetic traces left by fires and soil bacteria. Modern ground-penetrating radar enables archaeologists to make three-dimensional models of underground targets through hard surfaces. These tools can help locate, document, and protect ancient sites of human settlement on a global scale.

ACTIVE OPTIONS

Active History: Think Like an Archaeologist Extend the lesson by using either the PDF or Whiteboard version of the activity. These activities take a deeper look at a topic from, or related to, the lesson. Explore the activities as a class, turn them into group assignments, or assign them individually.

NG Learning Framework: Explore High-Tech Archaeology STEM

SKILL Observation

KNOWLEDGE New Frontiers

Share the National Geographic Explorer information about Parcak's GlobalXplorer° website and More Information text about high-tech tools used in archaeology. Then direct students to the GlobalXplorer° website's training video and information on how to spot looting. Have students train together in small groups, view images on the GlobalXplorer° platform, and record their observations. Ask groups to create a class presentation describing how the imaging equipment works, regions of the world on which it has been focused, important results achieved, and any contributions from the public.

DIFFERENTIATE

INCLUSION

Use Clarifying Questions Pair students with disabilities with students who can read the lesson aloud to them. Encourage students to ask and answer clarifying questions. You may also have the partner without disabilities describe the photograph of Parcak working at Point Rosee and the satellite image of Egyptian archaeological sites and read the captions. Direct students to work together to answer the Historical Thinking questions.

GIFTED & TALENTED

Tweet Space Archaeology Ask students to imagine they are working with Parcak on a project in the Peruvian rain forest, Egyptian desert, or Canadian coastline. Tell them to compose a series of tweets—including hashtags—about the project they choose, noting the purpose of the work, equipment and technology used, and discoveries made. Invite students to read their tweets to the class. After each one, ask the class to comment on the tweets using hashtags of their own.

See the Chapter Planner for more strategies for differentiation.

HISTORICAL THINKING

ANSWERS

1. Parcak uses satellite technology to access images taken from space. She studies the images to look for vegetation and soil patterns on Earth's surface that might indicate the presence of buildings and other features made by humans.

2. Parcak's research could prove that Vikings settled in more than one location in North America, contrary to accepted ideas. This research could suggest that Vikings had a bigger presence in North America than has previously been recognized.

3. Students should state their opinion and provide reasons to support it. Possible responses: If I were an archaeologist, I would use LIDAR in my research because it would allow me to cover a wide area quickly and detect places that people on the ground could easily miss. If I were an archaeologist, I would depend more on traditional excavation methods because artifacts need to be investigated on-site to confirm theories.

15TH-CENTURY EUROPE

Have you ever felt as if everything in your life was changing? During the 1400s, people in medieval Europe experienced such an upheaval. New ideas overturned centuries of traditional beliefs, sparking the creative rebirth of Europe.

THE MIDDLE AGES

The **Middle Ages** began with the fall of the Roman Empire in about A.D. 500 and lasted until the end of the 15th century. The western part of the empire split into several Germanic kingdoms, all warring against one another. To keep their lands and to protect their people, the Germanic kings developed a system known as **feudalism**. Under this system, the king granted land to the nobles, known as lords, who in turn gave land to lesser noblemen, called **vassals**. In exchange for a lord's protection, vassals paid taxes and pledged their military service.

Feudalism created a stable social structure organized like a pyramid. The king ruled at the top, lords were directly beneath him, and vassals beneath the lords. However, most people, including peasants and serfs, formed the broad base of the pyramid. Many were bound to a noble's land under the **manor system**. This system was a way of life in which peasants paid a landowner for his military protection through labor and with the agricultural goods they produced. They could buy their freedom, but few could earn the funds to do so. The majority of people, and their children after them, remained in bondage to the landowner.

PLAGUE SWEEPS EUROPE

From 1347 to 1351, the bubonic plague killed about 25 million people in Europe. Known as the Black Death because of the black spots that appeared on its victims' skin, the infection struck with frightening speed. People who went to bed healthy could be dead by morning. Symptoms began with swellings in the groin or armpits. Within hours, victims were racked by fever, chills, vomiting, and terrible pain until, finally, death came.

Today, antibiotics make the rare case of plague treatable, but in the Middle Ages, no one knew how the disease spread or how to fight it. One doctor speculated, "instantaneous death occurs when the aerial [air-borne] spirit escaping from the eyes of the sick man strikes the healthy person standing near." Other physicians, such as the French doctor who developed the "protective" uniform (shown here)in the 1600s, believed the plague was spread by bad air or odors. Doctors relied on their usual practices, such as bloodletting, burning aromatic herbs, and giving rosewater or vinegar baths. Nothing worked.

Christianity became another stabilizing force during the Middle Ages. The Roman Catholic Church unified medieval Europe under its spiritual and political authority. In the 11th century, the Church called on monarchs to launch the **Crusades**, a series of religious wars meant to battle the rise of **Islam** and regain the Holy Land—Jerusalem and the surrounding area. The followers of Islam, called **Muslims**, had captured the Holy Land and attacked the Christian Byzantine Empire, which had been the eastern half of the Roman Empire.

Although the Crusades ultimately failed, they enabled European monarchs to claim some lands in the east and establish trade routes between Europe and the Middle East. As trade increased, Europe began to prosper, encouraging the growth of towns and cities where merchants could sell their trade goods.

Trade routes also opened the continent to a terrifying threat. In October 1347, the bubonic plague, or Black Death, arrived in Italy on ships from the East. Spread by rats and the bite of infected fleas, the plague swept across Europe. Within two years, it had killed nearly a third of the population and left many towns and cities in need of workers. People lucky enough to survive left the manors for these jobs. The steady exodus, or departure, of people from the manors weakened the feudal system and helped end the Middle Ages. By the 1400s, Europe was ripe for change.

THE RENAISSANCE

In the years of conquest before the Crusades, Muslim scholars had acquired and preserved many ancient Greek and Roman texts and works of art. Returning crusaders and other travelers brought translations of classical thinkers such as Aristotle, Euclid, and Ptolemy back to their homes. In time, this knowledge inspired a cultural revolution in the royal courts, towns, and universities of Europe.

🏛 **National Gallery of Art, Washington, D.C.**

Woman Holding a Balance was painted by Renaissance Dutch artist Johannes Vermeer around 1664. Light, shadow, and photo-realistic details dominate Vermeer's scenes of everyday life. Some of his paintings are allegories—stories in which objects or people stand for abstract or spiritual ideas. As the woman in this painting contemplates the perfectly balanced pearls and gold on the scales, she may also be reflecting on the balance between enjoying earthly riches and leading a moral life.

By the 1400s, Europeans were making new advances in the arts, sciences, and technology. Historians call this era the **Renaissance**, or "rebirth." The Renaissance began in Italy and spread to many parts of Europe. The movement was founded on Greek and Roman ideas and on the philosophy of **humanism**. Humanists focused on individuality and encouraged critical thinking and the development of new ideas.

The Renaissance influenced all aspects of European culture. The revival of the arch and column, for instance, allowed architects to build in ways that seemed new, but that hadn't been used in nearly 1,500 years. New ideas regarding democracy and representative government made their way into

---

PLAN: 4-PAGE LESSON

OBJECTIVE

Learn how the Crusades, Renaissance, and Reformation changed life in medieval Europe.

CRITICAL THINKING SKILLS FOR LESSON 1.3

- Analyze Word Meaning
- Compare and Contrast
- Analyze Cause and Effect
- Make Inferences
- Summarize
- Analyze Primary Sources

HISTORICAL THINKING FOR CHAPTER 1

What impact did European exploration have on the cultures of North America and Africa?
Competition for trade spurred Europeans to search for sea routes to East Asia, ultimately leading to the exploration of the Americas. Lesson 1.3 examines the societal changes that took place in Europe, paving the way for this expansion.

BACKGROUND FOR THE TEACHER

Modern genome sequencing has shed light on how the Black Death relates to the modern bubonic plague—and helped settle a historical debate. The first breakthrough came in 2011 when a team of scientists extracted DNA from teeth found in the skeletal remains of people buried in a London "plague pit" during the height of the Black Death. From the DNA, the researchers were able to confirm that the victims were infected with *Yersinia pestis,* the same bacteria responsible for the modern bubonic plague. This finding put to rest claims by some that the Black Death might have been caused by a virus similar to modern Ebola that could spread directly from person to person. Furthermore, when the team compared the sequenced Black Death DNA with that of modern bubonic plague, they discovered that the two are remarkably similar. However, the medieval version may have been especially deadly due to the cold, wet climate of the time and the lack of developed immunities in the European population that could have helped protect people against the pathogen.

INTRODUCE & ENGAGE

K-W-L CHART

Provide each student with a K-W-L Chart. Lead students in a discussion to brainstorm what they already know about the Middle Ages, the Renaissance, and the Reformation. Ask them to record major points in the first column of their charts. Then ask students to write questions in the center column that they would like to have answered as they study Lesson 1.3, which discusses the factors that brought an end to the Middle Ages and transformed Europe in the 1400s. Allow time at the end of the lesson for students to complete the K-W-L Chart with what they have learned.

K What Do I Know?	W What Do I Want To Learn?	L What Did I Learn?

TEACH

GUIDED DISCUSSION

1. **Analyze Cause and Effect** What positive and negative consequences did the Crusades have on Europe? *(Answers will vary. Possible response: On the positive side, the Crusades opened Europe to trade with the Middle East, and the crusaders brought back translations of ancient Greek and Roman texts, helping spur the Renaissance. On the negative side, the trade routes brought the Black Death, which quickly wiped out nearly a third of Europe's population.)*

2. **Make Inferences** Why do you think peasants and serfs left manors for cities—despite the Black Death—during the Middle Ages? *(Possible response: Although cities were hit hard by the Black Death, peasants believed they had more opportunities there than on the manor of a feudal lord.)*

VIRTUAL MUSEUM VISIT

The National Gallery of Art was created through the generosity and efforts of financier Andrew W. Mellon, an avid art collector. Mellon got the idea for a world-class national art museum while serving as secretary of state from 1921 to 1932. He proposed his idea to President Franklin D. Roosevelt in 1936, offering to pay for construction of a building and to donate art. Congress approved the plan in 1937, and the National Gallery of Art opened in 1941. Encourage students to visit the museum's website and locate the essay that accompanies Vermeer's *Woman Holding a Balance*. Prompt students to work in groups to read the essay and discuss the following question: How does Vermeer's painting illustrate the tensions present in Renaissance Europe? Ask groups to share their thoughts with the class.

DIFFERENTIATE

STRIVING READERS

Create an Annotated Time Line To help students understand the order and significance of events presented in the lesson, provide pairs with a time line. Instruct them to note important dates, people, and events on the time line as they read the lesson. (You may wish to provide them with the dates 1347, 1400s, 1452, 1453, 1517, and 1530s, if needed.) Then have them reread the text, adding at least two details about each important person or event identified on their time line. Invite pairs to compare and discuss their completed time lines, making changes or additions if necessary.

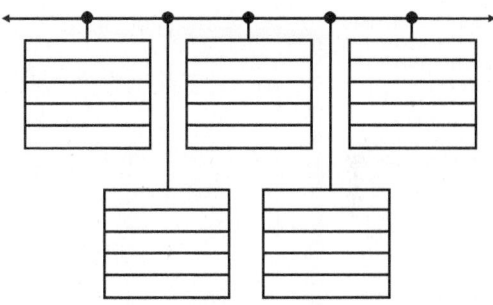

GIFTED & TALENTED

Explain and Illustrate Perspective Challenge students to explain and illustrate the use of perspective in Renaissance and contemporary art. First, have students conduct research to learn more about the math and history of perspective. Then prompt them to create a presentation that defines, explains, and provides examples of perspective. Students may use their own drawings or examples from Renaissance artists or contemporary pavement artists who use perspective to create 3-D optical illusions. Allow them to choose conventional art materials or presentation software to present their work to the class.

See the Chapter Planner for more strategies for differentiation.

intellectual circles. In the arts, the detailed study of human anatomy and perspective, a technique used to give the illusion of depth and distance, inspired the great artists of the Renaissance. Michelangelo, Raphael, and Leonardo da Vinci portrayed the human body realistically in their paintings and sculptures, even in their portraits of God. Today the term "Renaissance man" or "Renaissance woman" defines anyone who has many exceptional talents. **Leonardo da Vinci** may be the best example, excelling as an artist, inventor, scientist, engineer, and architect.

The Renaissance period also saw a steady rise in literacy, or the ability to read and write. Around 1452, **Johann Gutenberg** invented a printing press that used moveable type to set up pages of text. This invention allowed people to mass-produce and distribute commentary and literature, including classical and humanistic literary works. With more printed materials available, more people learned to read. Gutenberg's printed Bible allowed many Europeans to read Christianity's holy book for themselves, rather than having its contents interpreted for them by a priest. The combination of printing and increased literacy helped spread Renaissance ideas rapidly throughout Europe.

In the Middle Ages, scholars generally studied nature by reading what others had written about a topic. During the Renaissance, however, scholars preferred to find out for themselves through direct observation and experiments. One of the greatest Renaissance scientists, the Polish astronomer Nicolaus Copernicus, used mathematical calculations to show that Earth was not the center of the universe. Instead, it was only one of several planets revolving around the Sun. His work sent shock waves through Europe and opened the door to further discoveries.

Among the social changes taking place during the Renaissance was the rise of a wealthy merchant and financial class. The Medici (MEH-dee-chee) and Borgia (BOR-juh) families of Italy became more powerful than many European kings.

Members of the Medici family were bankers for the Roman Catholic pope and held government jobs. Some of the men became popes and some of the women became queens of France. As famous patrons of the arts, the Medici commissioned paintings, sculptures, buildings, and even their own mausoleums, or burial sites.

THE REFORMATION

By the time of the Renaissance, the Roman Catholic Church was beginning to lose some of its political power. The pope had once been the true ruler of Europe, commanding the loyalty of monarchs and clan leaders. But corruption often grows out of such widespread power, and as the Church's influence diminished, some Europeans began to speak out against several of its practices. The Renaissance humanist movement encouraged people to be more critical of the Church.

In 1517, German clergyman and university professor **Martin Luther** called for the Church to reject its corrupt practices. He singled out the selling of **indulgences**, or official forgiveness of sins. Luther believed that salvation for Christians was a gift from God in return for their faith, and it could not be bought. He wrote his ideas in a list of **95 Theses**, or statements of belief, and according to legend, nailed it to a church door.

Printed with movable type in 1455, this copy of Gutenberg's Bible features traditional hand-painted illustrations characteristic of earlier illustrated, or "illuminated," manuscripts. Fewer than 50 years after Gutenberg printed his Bible, print shops opened in more than 200 cities across Europe.

Luther didn't stop there. He challenged the Church's tight control over the Bible, which had been translated into Latin. Luther argued that Christians should be able to read the word of God themselves. He translated the Bible into German and used the printing press to distribute his translation widely.

In response to Luther's actions, the Church excommunicated, or ejected, him. But it was too late to stop the spread of Luther's ideas. Many rulers and their subjects sided with Luther and broke from the Church in a movement known as the **Protestant Reformation**. The word *protestant* referred to "protests" against the Catholic Church. However, reasons for leaving the Church were as much political as religious. A number of monarchs and nobles resented the power of the pope. By creating their own local churches, they could further weaken the Church's authority.

In Germany, some princes welcomed Luther's teachings and formed the new Lutheran Church. The spread of Lutheranism in northern Europe inspired other critics of the Catholic Church to offer their own Protestant doctrines. The most influential was **John Calvin**, a native of France. In the early 1530s, he attempted to create a model Christian society in Geneva, Switzerland. Calvin believed in predestination, or the idea that God had already decided who would go to heaven. People could not save themselves through faith or good works. Calvin's followers established churches in what became known as the Reformed tradition.

The pope and his allies, however, were equally determined to maintain control in Europe. Not surprisingly, the split between Catholics and Protestants led to a series of religious wars fought during the 1500s and 1600s.

NATIONS AND TRADE

By the 15th century, the political map of Europe was rapidly changing. Smaller kingdoms merged into larger **nation-states**, which united people who shared a common culture or language. The nation-states eventually organized into established nations, similar to modern-day countries. England, France, and Spain emerged as Europe's most powerful nations.

Their rise inspired a fierce competition for trade. As nations developed their own national economies, trade became crucial to their wealth. A growing merchant class expanded Europe's overland routes into the Middle East, Africa, and East Asia, where they traded European goods for salt, gold, silk, and exotic spices. Most countries adopted the practice

Thanks to the printing press, Luther's 95 Theses were quickly distributed throughout Germany after he posted them on the door of All Saints' Church in Wittenberg. The theses below express some of Luther's thoughts about the selling of indulgences. Purgatory is where souls go after death to repent and make amends for their sins in life.

32. Those who believe that they can be certain of their salvation because they have indulgence letters will be eternally damned, together with their teachers.

35. They who teach that contrition [repentance and regret] is not necessary on the part of those who intend to buy souls out of purgatory or to buy confessional privileges preach unchristian doctrine.

36. Any truly repentant Christian has a right to full remission [reduction] of penalty and guilt, even without indulgence letters.

of **mercantilism**, or government protection and encouragement of trade, based on the theory that such businesses create wealth. Under this system, nations tried to export more goods than they imported and fought to control the best trade routes.

But the best overland trade routes were becoming too costly to use. In 1453, the Turks of the Middle Eastern Ottoman Empire captured the city of Constantinople, which linked Europe and Asia, and gained absolute control of overland trade routes. They charged Europeans steep prices for Asian goods. European countries knew the only way to re-establish direct trade with Asia was by sea. This triggered a race to find the best sea route to East Asia and ultimately led to the exploration of the Americas. The winner of the race could become the wealthiest country in Europe.

HISTORICAL THINKING

1. **READING CHECK** What was the role of peasants in the manor system?

2. **ANALYZE WORD MEANING** Why do you think the word Renaissance was applied to artistic and intellectual changes of the 15th century?

3. **COMPARE AND CONTRAST** What were the main differences between the beliefs of Martin Luther and John Calvin?

4. **ANALYZE CAUSE AND EFFECT** How did the rise of powerful nations result in the development of mercantilism?

BUILD BACKGROUND

LEONARDO DA VINCI

Part of Leonardo da Vinci's genius rests in his blending of art and science. His notebooks show how he carefully dissected the human face to understand how the nerves and muscles worked to produce expression. He dissected the human eye to understand how the center of the retina sees detail and the edges discern shapes and shadows. His understanding of anatomy and physiology is expressed in the subtle smile of the woman in the painting *Mona Lisa*. While the corners of his subject's lips are turned slightly downward, Leonardo's use of light and shadows gives the impression of a slight smile when one looks directly at her face. However, the smile momentarily disappears and then reappears as the viewer's eyes scan across the painting. For Leonardo, art was a science, and he believed that artists—with their unique ability to accurately depict what they saw—were the purveyors of true empirical knowledge.

JOHANN GUTENBERG

Johann Gutenberg made his living at various times as a metallurgist, goldsmith, and gem cutter. Unsuccessful at business, he was deeply in debt, and his work on a printing press grew out of a need for money. At the time, most books were copied by hand or carved page by page into wooden blocks—processes both time-consuming and expensive. Gutenberg used his skills in metallurgy to create moveable type out of soft metals, such as lead and tin, that were easy to melt but strong enough to stand up to a printing press. He also created ink from soot and linseed oil that printed well on handmade paper. He modeled his printing press on a wine press, a design that allowed him to slide in paper, print a page, and squeeze out any extra water. Unfortunately, Gutenberg remained unlucky in business. He lost ownership of his printing press when his business partner sued him for repayment of debts.

TEACH

GUIDED DISCUSSION

3. **Make Inferences** In what ways did Johann Gutenberg's and Nicolaus Copernicus's accomplishments challenge the authority of the Roman Catholic Church? *(Answers will vary. Possible response: Gutenberg made the Bible available to more people, who could then read the text themselves and no longer had to rely on priests and other Church officials to interpret it. By challenging the view that Earth was the center of the universe, Copernicus's work challenged literal interpretations of the Bible.)*

4. **Summarize** What factors helped pave the way for the Reformation? *(Possible response: The humanist emphasis on analytical thinking and the power of the individual led Europeans to challenge the authority of the Roman Catholic Church and reject corrupt practices. The rise of nation-states and the merchant class weakened the Church's hold on government. The printing press helped spread humanist philosophy, scientific ideas, and religious critiques—including those of Martin Luther and John Calvin—to more people.)*

ANALYZE PRIMARY SOURCES

Direct students' attention to the Primary Source feature. **ASK:** What are the arguments against indulgences Luther makes? *(Possible response: Luther claims that those who think that salvation can be bought are eternally damned, that it is against Christian doctrine to teach that someone does not need to repent and can instead buy salvation, and that salvation comes through repentance—making indulgence letters unnecessary.)* Why do you think Luther was so opposed to this practice? *(Possible response: Indulgences favored the wealthy, they promoted the idea that people could act immorally and still buy themselves a place in heaven, and they made it seem that the Church was exchanging its principles in return for money.)*

ACTIVE OPTIONS

On Your Feet: Create a Concept Web Divide the class into five groups. Give each group a sheet of paper and have them draw a Concept Web. Assign each group one of the following topics: Crusades, Black Death, Renaissance, Reformation, Nations and Trade. Tell students to write their topic in the center oval. Then direct group members to take turns writing a detail about how their topic helped transform Europe, reading it aloud, and passing the paper clockwise to the next student. Instruct them to repeat the process until each group member has written at least two details. When students have finished, ask groups to share their completed Concept Web with the class.

NG Learning Framework: Celebrate Innovations

ATTITUDE Curiosity

KNOWLEDGE New Frontiers

Encourage students to learn more about the people mentioned in the lesson. Instruct them to work in pairs to research an individual who interests them, focusing on how that person helped transform society. Guide students to focus on the impact of one or more of the individual's innovations rather than writing a general overview. Students can publish their profiles electronically, on a class blog or website, or in a printed class magazine.

HISTORICAL THINKING

ANSWERS

1. Peasants were at the bottom of the social order. They provided labor and produced agricultural goods for landowners in return for military protection.

2. Answers will vary. Possible response: *Renaissance* means "rebirth." The period was marked by the reintroduction of ideas from ancient Greece and Rome, which sparked a new interest in science, art, architecture, and philosophy. It was as if Europeans' pursuit of ideas and knowledge was reawakened or reborn.

3. Possible response: Luther believed that salvation was God's gift to the faithful. Thus, salvation had to be earned by repenting one's sins. Calvin, on the other hand, believed in predestination, which meant that God had already decided who would and would not go to heaven.

4. Possible response: The rise of nations produced competition for trade, as trade created the wealth needed to grow national economies. This growth led governments to establish mercantilist policies designed to protect and promote trade.

As they have for centuries, camel caravans carry salt slabs cut from Lake Assale's dry seabeds in Ethiopia to distant market towns. A valuable commodity, salt provides the salt miners and camel keepers with a livelihood. But technology and big companies pose a threat to traditional salt harvesting and transportation methods.

WEST AFRICAN KINGDOMS

In the 800s, Arab traders were telling Europeans about a "land of gold" in West Africa. In this great kingdom, they said, even the dogs wore collars of gold. Those tales turned out to be true.

GEOGRAPHY AND TRADE

On the map, West Africa seems an unlikely place for great kingdoms to arise. To the north lie the semi-arid Atlas Mountains, forming a geographic barrier to the Mediterranean Sea and Europe beyond. The world's largest desert, the **Sahara**, stretches from the Atlantic Ocean to the Red Sea, covering most of northern Africa. South of the Sahara lies the Sahel, a region of **steppes**, or grasslands with few trees and moderate rainfall. The Guinean Forests lie south of the Sahel. These lush rain forests support more than a quarter of all African mammals.

You might think the vast Sahara would be an insurmountable barrier to trade, but by the early Middle Ages, West Africa had become a major hub of commerce, trading primarily with North Africa and the Middle East. What were they trading? The big-ticket items were gold and salt. Beneath the southern forests lay huge deposits of gold, while the Sahara had an abundant supply of salt. Vital for preserving foods, salt had been a form of currency in parts of the ancient world and was extremely valuable.

To transport these goods across the desert, traders established **trans-Saharan** trade routes. They crisscrossed the Sahara, extending from the Sahel and West Africa north to the shores of the Mediterranean Sea and as far east as Alexandria in Egypt. Camels made crossing the desert possible and profitable. These animals can walk nearly 100 miles without stopping for water, carrying heavy loads across the sands in scorching heat. Traders organized **caravans**, or groups of merchants traveling together, to carry their goods across the desert. Trans-Saharan trading fostered the development of market towns and, eventually, the rise of three West African empires—Ghana, Mali, and Songhai.

THE KINGDOM OF GHANA

The kingdom of **Ghana** began as a group of farming villages south of the Sahara that gradually banded together to form one state. By A.D. 500, Ghana had become the first great trading empire in West Africa. Its capital city, Koumbi-Saleh (KUHM-bee SAHL-uh), stood midway between the gold trade flowing north from Ghana's mines and the salt trade flowing south from the Sahara.

Ghana's kings grew rich by levying taxes on goods moving into and out of their empire. They also controlled the price of gold, decreeing that all nuggets belonged to the king and only gold dust could be traded. This made the supply of gold scarce and kept its price high. By the ninth century, Ghana had become wealthy and powerful. The kingdom was structured according to a feudal system. Although Ghana appeared stable, outside forces gradually began to weaken it.

One such force was Islam. As early as the 700s, Arab traders began to introduce the religion's scriptures and laws to the region. Literacy rose as people learned to speak, read, and write Arabic. Before that time, no West African culture had had a written language. Then, around 1050, an Islamic group known as the Almoravids attacked Ghana and tried to force its royal families and other leaders to convert, or change their religion. The Ghanians resisted, but were overpowered. The Almoravids captured Koumbi-Saleh in 1076.

Environmental changes also contributed to the demise of Ghana. Centuries of farming had exhausted the soil, and it could no longer support the population. By the early 1200s, Ghana's traders and farmers were leaving for better opportunities and more fertile lands to the south and west. The kingdom of Ghana gradually came to an end. Yet this "land of gold" had played a major role in developing West Africa's trade and culture.

THE KINGDOM OF MALI

After Ghana, the kingdom of **Mali** emerged as the new ruling power in West Africa, seizing control of the gold and salt commerce. The kingdom was fortunate in its geography and in its early leaders. Mali's land consisted largely of **savanna**, fertile grasslands where abundant rains fell. The soil was ideal for growing rice, millet, and other grains. Surplus crops allowed Mali to expand trade, support the development of art, and

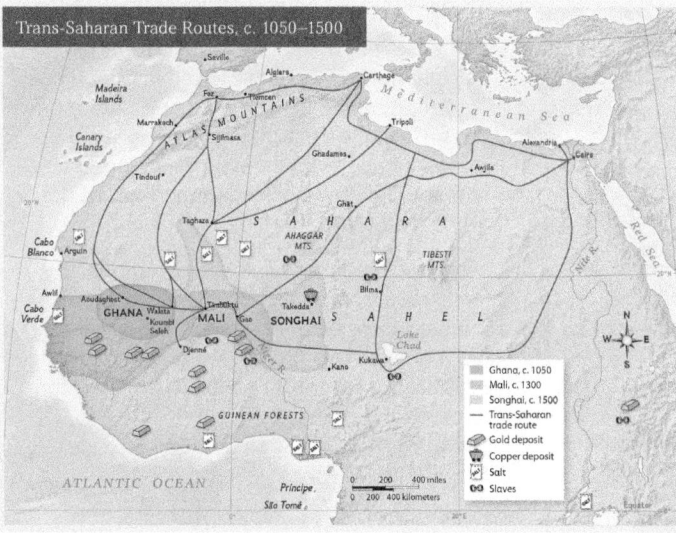

Trans-Saharan Trade Routes, c. 1050–1500

PLAN: 4-PAGE LESSON

OBJECTIVE

Discuss the reasons behind the rise and fall of wealthy kingdoms in West Africa.

CRITICAL THINKING SKILLS FOR LESSON 1.4

- Interpret Maps
- Determine Chronology
- Analyze Cause and Effect
- Analyze Environmental Concepts
- Evaluate
- Make Connections
- Summarize
- Analyze Primary Sources

HISTORICAL THINKING FOR CHAPTER 1

What impact did European exploration have on the cultures of North America and Africa? The arrival of the Portuguese changed the nature of the slave trade in West Africa. Lesson 1.4 examines how trade led to the rise and expansion of kingdoms in West Africa and the impact of European exploration on the region.

BACKGROUND FOR THE TEACHER

Caravans led by Berber traders started crossing the Sahara around the fifth century. By the eighth century, trade routes were well established, and caravans were an annual event. Transactions often took the form of the silent barter, an impersonal form of trade in which the two sides never met. North African salt traders would lay their salt in piles at a designated place, signal the beginning of trading with a drumbeat, and then leave. West African gold traders would arrive, inspect the salt, place bags of gold dust next to each pile, and retreat. The salt traders would return and, if they approved of the amount of gold, would take it, ending the transaction. If not, trading would continue until both sides were satisfied with the exchange.

FINANCIAL LITERACY

To extend their knowledge and understanding about the concepts in this lesson, refer students to the Financial Literacy handbook.

INTRODUCE & ENGAGE

PREVIEW USING VISUALS

Direct students' attention to the visuals in this lesson—the map, the photograph of the camel caravan, and the photograph of the Great Mosque of Djenné. Draw a two-column chart on the board, labeling the first column Questions and the second column Answers. Ask students what questions these visuals bring to mind. Record their questions in the chart. Later, after students have read and discussed the lesson, prompt them to answer as many of the listed questions as they can.

Questions	Answers

TEACH

GUIDED DISCUSSION

1. **Analyze Environmental Concepts** How did trans-Saharan traders overcome environmental challenges? *(Possible response: Traders needed to cross the vast expanse of the harsh Sahara. They traveled together in camel caravans because camels were well suited to the brutal heat, could carry heavy loads, and could walk great distances without stopping for water.)*

2. **Analyze Cause and Effect** How did the kings of Ghana utilize the economic idea of supply and demand? *(Possible response: The kings lowered the supply of gold by keeping all of the gold nuggets for themselves, allowing only gold dust to be traded. Because there was a strong demand for gold, limiting the supply increased its value, and people were willing to pay more for it.)*

3. **Evaluate** How did the introduction of Islam impact Ghana culturally and politically? *(Possible response: The introduction of Islam led to many people in Ghana learning to read, write, and speak Arabic. Prior to this, Ghana had not had a written language. Politically, the desire to spread Islam led the Almoravids to invade Ghana and try to force its rulers and other leaders to convert, weakening the power of the kings.)*

MAKE CONNECTIONS

Tell students to study the caption and photo of the modern camel caravan. **ASK:** Based on what you see in the photo and your knowledge of modern technology, why do you think the livelihoods of traditional salt miners and transporters are being threatened? *(Answers will vary. Possible response: Mining salt and transporting it in the traditional way is labor and time intensive. Salt producers could mine and transport greater quantities of salt if they used modern technology, such as trucks, drills, and computers. One truck alone could carry as much salt as many camels, could cover greater distances more quickly, and would not require the kind of care live animals need.)*

DIFFERENTIATE

INCLUSION

Understand Information in a Map Pair students who are strong readers with those who have reading or perception difficulties. Instruct pairs to study the information presented in the Trans-Saharan Trade Routes map. Direct them to read the legend together and use a finger to trace the perimeter of the territory of each African kingdom. Then have them point to slave markets and to the locations of gold, copper, and salt deposits. Finally, have them trace with a finger the main trade routes. To check students' understanding of the information presented in the map, prompt pairs to work together to answer the relevant Historical Thinking question.

PRE-AP

Analyze a Primary Source Direct students to use online or print sources to access additional portions or the full text of Ibn Battuta's *Travels in Asia and Africa*. Ask students to read a section and choose an excerpt to analyze. The analysis could include the reason Battuta began and continued his travels or the significance of specific cultural, historical, and religious details from the excerpt. Invite students to present their analysis to the class in a written or oral report.

See the Chapter Planner for more strategies for differentiation.

Built of mud, the Great Mosque of Djenné is an architectural wonder located in the ancient city of Djenné, Mali. National Geographic photographer Jimmy Chin captured this image of a colorfully dressed Malian approaching the mosque, a place of worship for Muslims.

construct impressive buildings. With its population of nearly 40 million people, Mali became one of the largest empires in West African history.

Unlike Ghana's original rulers, Mali's kings were Muslim. The kingdom's founder, Sundiata Keita (sun-JAHT-ah KAY-tah) brought peace, tolerance, and the rule of law to his diverse empire. In 1324, Sundiata's most famous descendent, **Mansa Musa**, expanded the empire and made a legendary pilgrimage to Islam's holy city of Mecca, in what is today Saudi Arabia, to fulfill his religious duty. His caravan is said to have included more than 60,000 servants and 80 camels loaded with gold. He distributed gold and lavish gifts to people along the way, and his generosity is credited with expanding Mali's trade network farther into the Middle East.

When Mansa Musa returned from Mecca, he laid the groundwork for making the trading city of Timbuktu a major center of Islamic learning and the arts. His finest achievements included the construction of the Great Mosque and the Sankara Madrassa, the largest library in Africa at the time. Weaker leaders followed Mansa Musa, however, and eventually their poor management allowed the empire to fragment into smaller kingdoms. One of these new kingdoms grew to surpass Mali in size and splendor.

THE KINGDOM OF SONGHAI

That kingdom was **Songhai**, the largest of the West African empires, extending some 2,500 miles from the Atlantic Ocean to the central Sahara. In the early 1300s, Mali, fearful of Songhai's growing power,

attacked the kingdom and captured its capital city, Gao. About 50 years later, Songhai rebelled, retaking Gao, attacking the weakened Mali kingdom, and capturing Timbuktu. Now that it controlled the region's gold and salt trades, Songhai accumulated enough wealth to build its own empire. The walled city of Gao became a multicultural marketplace that attracted traders from northern Africa, the Middle East, and Europe.

One of Songhai's greatest rulers, Askia Muhammad (ahs-KEE-ah moh-HA-muhd), built alliances, or agreements, with other Muslim states and reformed the government, banking, and education systems for the entire empire. But later Songhai rulers fought over control of the empire, leaving it vulnerable to envious neighbors. In 1591, Morocco seized Timbuktu and Gao, ending the Songhai empire.

BENIN AND KONGO

Two other African kingdoms, **Benin** (buh-NEEN) and **Kongo** (KAHNG-goh), established important trading networks in the 1400s. The kingdom of Benin dominated the forested region that covered the Niger River delta. Benin was known for its skilled artisans, or craftspeople, who created impressive ivory and wood carvings as well as bronze and brass objects.

The densely populated kingdom of Kongo arose in west-central Africa, south of the Congo River. It began as a loose partnership of smaller kingdoms that gradually banded together. By the mid-1500s, Kongo was a unified kingdom that had established a wide and well-organized trading network with other parts of the African continent.

Both Benin and Kongo were located along the coast, and as Portuguese mariners began exploring the sea routes surrounding Africa, they made contact with the people and kingdoms of the western part of the continent. For example, the Portuguese arrived in Kongo in 1483 and began a robust trade. They sent their missionaries and teachers to Kongo in exchange for goods such as ivory, salt, copper, and textiles. They also established a slave trade with both Kongo and Benin.

Slavery is a social system in which human beings are owned and completely controlled by other humans, usually as a source of forced labor. The practice had existed in West Africa and throughout most of the Eastern Hemisphere for centuries before the Portuguese began trading for slaves with the West African kingdoms. In fact, slavery existed in most civilizations throughout the world, including in the Americas. Up until the late 15th century, enslaved

PRIMARY SOURCE

Famous medieval traveler Ibn Battuta visited Mali on one of his many journeys through the Middle East, Europe, and Africa in the 14th century. While in Mali, he witnessed the sultan, Mansa Suleyman, enter his palace garden to hold court.

On certain days the sultan holds audiences in the palace yard, where there is a platform under a tree. The sultan comes out of a door in a corner of the palace, carrying a bow in his hand and quiver on his back. His usual dress is a velvety red tunic, made of the European fabrics called "mutanfas." The sultan is preceded by his musicians, who carry gold and silver guimbris [two-stringed guitars] and behind him come three hundred armed slaves. He walks in a leisurely fashion. As he takes his seat the drums, trumpets, and bugles are sounded.

—from *Travels in Asia and Africa*, by Ibn Battuta, 1325–1354

What detail in Battuta's description leads you to understand the extent of Mali's world trade?

people were usually prisoners who had been captured in war or people punished for committing a crime. Some had bonded themselves into slavery to pay off debts or to have food to eat and a roof over their heads. They were often able to buy or work off their bondage, and they sometimes had certain rights as slaves, even though they were not free. Their enslavement was not attached to their race, and their children were not automatically born into bondage. The Portuguese entry into the West African slave trade changed the very definition of slavery and expanded this new practice of slavery across the Atlantic Ocean and throughout the Western Hemisphere, triggering the greatest transfer of enslaved people in the history of the world.

HISTORICAL THINKING

1. **READING CHECK** What two valuable trade goods helped build the wealth and size of the West African kingdoms?

2. **INTERPRET MAPS** How did Ghana's location help it rise to power?

3. **DETERMINE CHRONOLOGY** Identify in order the rise and fall of the major West African empires.

4. **ANALYZE CAUSE AND EFFECT** How was West Africa important to the African continent and the known world in the late 15th century?

BUILD BACKGROUND

SAVING ANCIENT MANUSCRIPTS

The scholars who flocked to Timbuktu in the ancient kingdom of Mali possessed an array of manuscripts on religion, medicine, astronomy, history, geography, poetry, law, and mathematics. Over the centuries, families in Mali collected many of these works, passing them from generation to generation. In the late 1960s, UNESCO passed a resolution calling for Mali to create a center to collect and restore the manuscripts. As part of that effort, the Ahmed Baba Institute of Higher Learning and Islamic Research was established in Timbuktu in the early 1970s. Today, it is home to some 30,000 manuscripts. In addition, several hundred thousand more manuscripts are held in and around Timbuktu in private homes and libraries based on family collections. When Islamic extremists attacked Mali in 2012, the family-run Mamma Haidara Library rescued more than 300,000 rare manuscripts and transported them to safety.

NATIONAL GEOGRAPHIC PHOTOGRAPHER
JIMMY CHIN

If it weren't for Jimmy Chin's Chinese American heritage and love of rock climbing, he may have never become an award-winning photographer. When he was in his early 20s, Chin was climbing with a friend in Yosemite National Park. After scaling the face of El Capitan, the two camped for the night on the summit. Awaking to a spectacular sunrise, Chin grabbed his friend's camera and took a picture of him sleeping amid his climbing gear. The friend sold the photograph, and Chin used his share to buy his first camera. He is known for the expert composition of his photos, which he credits to the years he spent mastering Chinese calligraphy as a child. Chin says that the discipline and attention to detail required to draw each character helped him develop a sense for visual balance. As a result, composition came naturally to him when he began taking photos.

TEACH

GUIDED DISCUSSION

4. **Evaluate** What factors enabled Songhai to eclipse the power and size of Mali? *(Possible response: Songhai first came into existence when Mali fragmented into smaller kingdoms because of poor leadership, weakening Mali as a chief adversary. In addition, under the leadership of Askia Muhammad, Songhai formed alliances with other Muslim states, which eliminated possible rivals.)*

5. **Summarize** How did slavery change in West Africa after 1483? *(Prior to the arrival of the Portuguese, slavery in West Africa was not based on race, and most enslaved people were war prisoners, criminals, or people who had entered bondage as a way to survive. In addition, enslaved people had some rights, they could work or buy their way out of slavery, and their children were not automatically born into slavery. This all changed when the Portuguese entered the slave trade.)*

ANALYZE PRIMARY SOURCES

Direct students to read the Primary Source feature. Tell them that both Ibn Battuta and Mansa Musa began the journeys discussed in the text as a pilgrimage to Mecca, called the hajj. Point out that the hajj is a one-time holy duty required of all Muslims who are able to make the journey. Explain that the trip from his home in Morocco to Mecca should have taken Ibn Battuta about 16 months—but he ended up traveling some 75,000 miles over 24 years, visiting many courts, such as the one described in the Primary Source feature. He stopped in nearly every Muslim country, as well as China and India. **ASK:** Considering the description provided by Ibn Battuta and the information in the text about Mansa Musa's journey, how might the hajj serve a dual purpose? *(Possible response: Ibn Battuta and Mansa Musa both started out to fulfill a religious obligation but ended up achieving additional goals. The hajj sparked Ibn Battuta's curiosity to see the world. Mansa Musa used his pilgrimage in part to help expand Mali's trade by advertising the kingdom's wealth.)*

ACTIVE OPTIONS

On Your Feet: Kingdom Questions Use the Inside-Outside Circle strategy to check students' understanding of the factors that shaped the West African kingdoms of Benin and Kongo. Direct students in the outer circle to pose questions such as the following: Where did Benin arise? What was Benin known for? Where did Kongo arise? In what ways did contact with Portuguese mariners impact both kingdoms? Tell students in the inner circle to answer the questions. Then ask students to trade inside/outside roles.

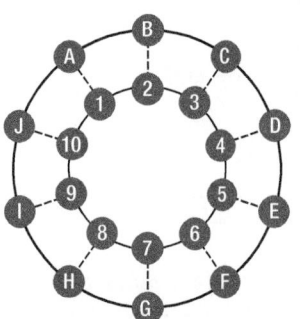

NG Learning Framework: Compare West African Kingdoms

ATTITUDE Curiosity

SKILL Communication

Instruct students to work in teams to brainstorm a list of conclusions about how Islam and trade impacted Ghana, Mali, and Songhai. Teams develop categories for their conclusions, such as positive, negative, economic, and cultural. Once they have completed their lists, prompt each team to exchange lists with another team. Ask teams to note similarities and differences between the lists in regard to both conclusions and categories. Reconvene as a class and review the lists, discussing any differences.

HISTORICAL THINKING

ANSWERS

1. Gold and salt were the most important trade goods that contributed to the wealth and size of the West African kingdoms.

2. Possible response: Ghana was located roughly midway between West African sources of gold and Saharan salt, which put it at the center of this important trade.

3. Ghana was the first great West African empire to rise to power, emerging by A.D. 500 as a major center of trade. It began to decline between the late 1000s and early 1200s due to conquest and environmental changes. Next, the kingdom of Mali arose as it seized control of the salt and gold trade. The kingdom reached its height under Mansa Musa, but the weak leaders that followed allowed Mali to fragment into smaller kingdoms. One of these kingdoms was Songhai. By the late 1300s, Songhai had defeated Mali. It became the largest West African kingdom, lasting until 1591, when Morocco seized Timbuktu and Gao.

4. Possible response: West Africa was a rich center of trade, where valuable goods such as gold and salt, along with enslaved people, were moved across the Sahara. Many of these goods and enslaved people ended up in Europe and the Middle East and eventually crossed the Atlantic after Portuguese seafarers arrived in West Africa.

PRIMARY SOURCE

Possible response: The fact that Mansa Suleyman is dressed in a robe made from European cloth suggests that the kingdom had access to European trade goods, either through long-distance trade or through Middle Eastern or European traders who came to Mali.

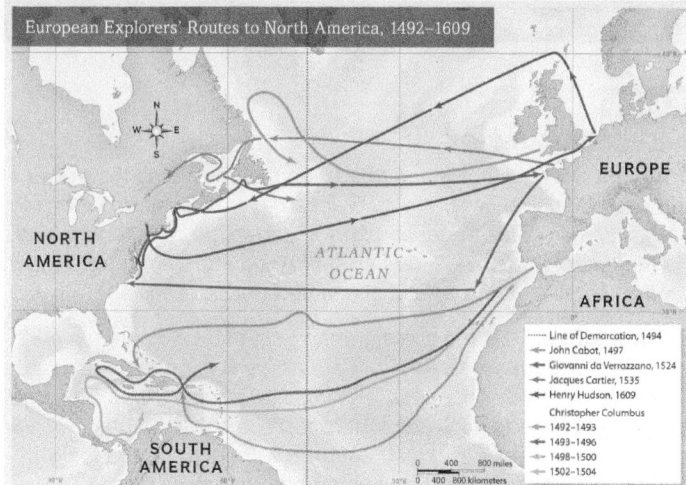

European Explorers' Routes to North America, 1492–1609

Line of Demarcation, 1494
John Cabot, 1497
Giovanni da Verrazzano, 1524
Jacques Cartier, 1535
Henry Hudson, 1609
Christopher Columbus
1492–1493
1493–1496
1498–1500
1502–1504

OPENING UP THE OCEAN WORLD

"Gold, Glory, and God!" Desire for wealth, national power, and the spread of Christianity drove the European explorers and their patrons. Success would bring power and wealth to many of them. To Europe and the Americas, it would bring catastrophic change.

EARLY EXPLORATION

As you have read, the Turks controlled overland trade routes to Asia, and they charged high tolls for European merchants to use them. In the 1400s, science, technology, and trade converged to help Europe establish ocean routes to the regions with which its countries traded. **Prince Henry of Portugal**, called "the Navigator," promoted and funded these efforts. He hoped to increase Portugal's political and mercantile power by claiming territory in different parts of the world where Portugal traded, promoting trade along the coast of Africa, and gaining converts to Christianity. But by around 1420, **cartographers**, or mapmakers, had charted only about 1,900 miles—or nearly one-fifth—of West Africa's coast. The true length and breadth of Africa were unknown.

Improvements in navigation and ship design during the 15th century made long sea voyages possible. The Portuguese had developed a small but sturdy ship called a **caravel**, whose triangular sails allowed it to maneuver more accurately at sea. As the Portuguese sailed southward along the western coast of Africa, they discovered just how large the continent was, and as far as they were concerned, most of it was theirs. In 1455, the pope had resolved a

dispute between Portugal and Spain over trade in West Africa by giving the Portuguese sole rights to coastal West Africa. In 1488, the Portuguese explorer **Bartholomeu Dias** sailed around the Cape of Good Hope at the southern tip of Africa. This voyage proved that a sea route around Africa to India was possible. Finally, in 1498, another Portuguese explorer, **Vasco da Gama**, and his crew became the first Europeans to reach India by sea.

This statue of Prince Henry the Navigator stands in Tomar, Portugal, where he was thought to have developed his plans for expanding the Portuguese empire.

COLUMBUS SETS SAIL

In the meantime, Ferdinand and Isabella, king and queen of Spain, had decided to sponsor **Christopher Columbus** in his search for a sea route to Asia. The devoutly Catholic monarchs wanted to find trading partners and establish colonies to increase their power, exploit colonial wealth, and spread Christianity. Columbus, a native of Genoa, Italy, was an experienced sailor and navigator. He believed that a European fleet could reach Asia by sailing west across the Atlantic Ocean. Like most Europeans, however, he supposed the Atlantic was far smaller and Asia far closer than either turned out to be.

In August 1492, Columbus and his men set sail from the Canary Islands, Spanish-ruled islands located in the Atlantic off the coast of northern Africa, with two caravels—the *Niña* and the *Pinta*—and the larger *Santa Maria*. Upon reaching land two months later—probably at present-day San Salvador Island in the Bahamas—Columbus thought they had arrived off the coast of China. Hoping to establish trade networks, they sailed southward to Cuba and then to Hispaniola, the island consisting of present-day Haiti and the Dominican Republic. There Columbus encountered the Taino (TIE-noh) people, who traded their gold trinkets for goods Columbus had brought.

The Spanish crew took timbers from one of their ships, which had wrecked nearby, and built the first Spanish fort in the Americas. Columbus left a portion of his crew at the fort and set sail for Spain.

On Columbus's return trip, a storm forced him to seek shelter in Portugal, and his reports of his voyage immediately set off another dispute between Spain and Portugal. Portuguese leaders refused to believe that Columbus had reached Asia. They insisted that those lands lay within Portugal's domain. Isabella and Ferdinand objected. In 1494, the pope negotiated the **Treaty of Tordesillas**, which established a north-south boundary—called the **Line of Demarcation**—that passed vertically through the Atlantic and present-day Brazil. The treaty gave Spain permission to colonize all land west of the line and gave Portugal a portion of land to the east of the line. It affirmed Portugal's right to the African sea route to India and its control of the Atlantic slave trade. This agreement would shape the political, economic, and cultural future of the Western Hemisphere.

Columbus returned to the Americas in 1493 with an even larger fleet, only to discover that the Taino had killed his men and destroyed the fort. He made two more voyages to the Americas, continuing to explore Caribbean islands and the South and Central

PLAN: 4-PAGE LESSON

OBJECTIVE

Identify important people, events, and consequences related to European exploration.

CRITICAL THINKING SKILLS FOR LESSON 2.1

• Analyze Cause and Effect
• Interpret Maps
• Interpret Visuals
• Make Inferences
• Make Connections
• Evaluate
• Summarize

HISTORICAL THINKING FOR CHAPTER 1

What impact did European exploration have on the cultures of North America and Africa?
Beginning in the late 15th century, European explorers fanned out across the globe. Lesson 2.1 examines how these voyages impacted the peoples of North America and Africa.

BACKGROUND FOR THE TEACHER

Mariners recognized that caravels could sail much faster than other ships. Consequently, caravels became popular choices for long-distance travel and exploration. The caravel's width and rounded bottom made it maneuverable in the water and suitable for hauling goods. Its shallow draft made it safer for sailing close to shore, a critical factor for voyages along the African coast. Caravels could be rigged with triangular sails or square sails. These modifications made any sort of trip possible, as triangular sails enabled ships to sail into the wind without capsizing, and square sails allowed the wind to push ships from behind. Christopher Columbus rigged his caravels with square sails because he assumed that he would be sailing in the same direction as the wind during his Atlantic crossing.

HISTORY NOTEBOOK

Encourage students to complete the Reid on the Road video series page for Chapter 1 in their History Notebooks after they view the video.

INTRODUCE & ENGAGE

SHARE TRAVEL EXPERIENCES

Encourage students to share personal experiences about trips they have taken or information about places they would like to visit. After sharing, invite students to discuss their motivations for travel. **ASK:** How do the reasons people travel today compare and contrast with those of people in the past? *(Answers will vary. Possible response: Modern people travel mostly for leisure, though some travel for business or to aid others. People in previous eras traveled mostly for economic reasons or to spread culture.)* Tell students that in this lesson they will learn about the reasons Europeans explored the world in the 1400s and the impact those explorations had on local populations.

TEACH

GUIDED DISCUSSION

1. **Analyze Cause and Effect** How did technological breakthroughs and economic motivations lead to increased European exploration? *(Better ship navigation and new ship designs, such as the caravel, made longer sea voyages possible. Consequently, Bartholomeu Dias was able to sail around the southern tip of Africa, Vasco da Gama was able to sail to India, and Columbus was able to sail across the Atlantic. In addition, wealthy benefactors, such as Prince Henry of Portugal, funded these expensive journeys with the hope of claiming resources and opening new trade routes.)*

2. **Make Inferences** Why do you think Ferdinand and Isabella were willing to finance Columbus's westward sea voyage? *(Possible response: The Spanish were interested in a western route to Asia so that they could gain a foothold there before the Portuguese, who had reached the region by sailing around Africa.)*

3. **Make Connections** How did Columbus's voyages reignite conflict between Portugal and Spain that required the pope's intervention? *(In 1455, the pope ended a dispute between Portugal and Spain by giving Portugal sole rights to coastal West Africa. When Portugal refused to accept Columbus's claim that he had reached Asia, Spain objected. In response, the pope negotiated the Treaty of Tordesillas, which established the Line of Demarcation running through the Atlantic Ocean and part of Brazil. The treaty gave Spain the right to colonize west of the line and Portugal rights to some land east of the line.)*

MORE INFORMATION

Columbus's Miscalculations Explain that Columbus made several mistakes that caused him to greatly underestimate the distance of his initial voyage. First, he rejected the common calculations of the width of the world in favor of the theories of Pierre d'Ailly, an early 15th-century French cosmographer who posited a much wider expanse of land, which meant less water to cross. Next, Columbus chose to value a degree of latitude at 56.67 miles, as suggested by medieval Persian astronomer al-Farghani, rather than at 59.5 miles, as more accurately described by Greek geographer Eratosthenes. Finally, he incorrectly assumed that al-Farghani used the 4,856-foot Roman mile; al-Farghani used the 7,091-foot Arabic mile. This series of errors caused Columbus to believe that the distance between the Canary Islands and Asia was approximately 3,000 miles—when in reality the distance was more than 7,000 miles. **ASK:** Why might Columbus have chosen calculations that made the voyage appear shorter? *(Possible response: He probably wanted to make the voyage seem likely to succeed so that he could find sponsors, and he may have wanted to convince himself that the trip was feasible.)*

DIFFERENTIATE

ENGLISH LANGUAGE LEARNERS

Create a Word Web Pair students at the **Emerging** and **Expanding** levels with students at the **Bridging** level, and direct them to create a Word Web on the topic of ocean travel. Tell partners to take turns reading paragraphs of the lesson, noting any terms related to ocean travel. Instruct students to write those terms on the spokes of the Word Web after each paragraph. Have pairs trade and compare their work, looking up unfamiliar words in a dictionary. Final Word Webs may include *coast, navigation, caravel, sails, sailed, sea route, sailor, navigator, set sail, fleet, circumnavigated,* and *mariner.*

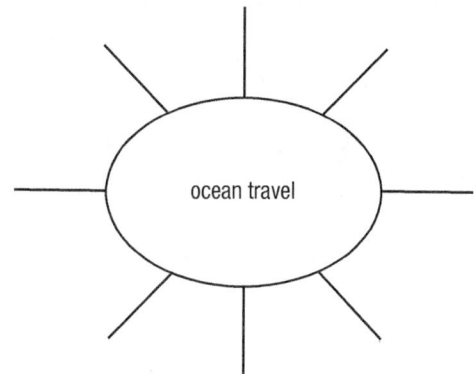

ocean travel

PRE-AP

Write a Book Review Challenge students to read and then write a book review of Stephen R. Bown's *1494: How a Family Feud in Medieval Spain Divided the World in Half.* Point out that a book review generally consists of a concise summary of the book and its overall argument, followed by a critical assessment of the book's strengths, weaknesses, effectiveness, and importance. Suggest that students look at newspaper or online book reviews for ideas about style and format. Encourage them to include details about the assumptions that underpinned the Treaty of Tordesillas, such as views of indigenous peoples and religious ideologies. Students may also mention details that they found particularly surprising or thought provoking. They might want to conclude their review by giving reasons for their classmates to read Bown's book. Ask students to share their reviews with the class by posting them to a class blog or reading them aloud.

See the Chapter Planner for more strategies for differentiation.

American coasts. Although he did not find the riches he hoped for, his voyages produced more accurate maps of the region than had ever before been available. While other explorers began to realize that two continents lay between Europe and Asia, Columbus himself refused to accept that idea. He died in 1506, poor and disgraced, still believing he had discovered a western route to Asia.

EXPLORATION CONTINUES

Between 1493 and 1529, Portugal and Spain sent many expeditions to the Western Hemisphere in search of gold. The Spanish found little on Hispaniola but assumed the Taino had obtained their supply of the precious metal from nearby islands or even from the mainland. European explorers obsessed with finding the source of the Taino gold began charting new lands in the Americas.

Other nations also searched for a western trade route to Asia. Italian sea captain **Amerigo Vespucci** made two separate voyages, one for Spain in 1499 and one for Portugal in 1501. His maps and charts revealed that South America was a huge landmass that had to be **circumnavigated**, or sailed around, to reach Asia. In recognition of his insight, a German mapmaker applied Vespucci's first name to the newly discovered continents, which became known as North America and South America.

England and France also entered the race. Ignoring the Treaty of Tordesillas, they searched for a northwest passage to Asia through North America. In 1497, Italian explorer **John Cabot**, sailing for England, arrived at Newfoundland and Nova Scotia. Like Columbus, he believed he had reached China. One of the most famous English explorers, **Henry Hudson**, made four voyages across the North Atlantic to what is now the northeastern United States. Hudson never found a passage to Asia, but some of the places he visited bear his name, including the Hudson River and Hudson Bay. Later, England used these voyages to reinforce its claims to land in North America.

In 1524, France sent another Italian mariner, **Giovanni da Verrazzano**, to look for the elusive northwest passage. Verrazzano sailed along the Atlantic coast to Newfoundland but found no waterway through the continent. French explorer **Jacques Cartier** tried in vain to locate the passage in 1534 and 1535, sailing into and down the St. Lawrence River. Although neither explorer found a passage to Asia, their voyages established France's claim to that region of the continent.

No one really knows what Christopher Columbus looked like, so his portraits vary considerably. This one was painted by the Italian artist Ridolfo Ghirlandaio around 1525.

GROWTH OF THE SLAVE TRADE

As Europeans began to establish colonies in the Americas, they needed laborers to work on their farms, plantations, and settlements. Spanish settlers initially enslaved Native Americans, mostly to work as forced labor in the sugarcane fields Spain had cultivated on Caribbean islands. But many Native Americans died, either from disease or from the brutal treatment they received. Although slavery and forced servitude had existed for centuries among civilizations in the Western Hemisphere, the practice grew under the Spanish and pitted tribe against tribe. The Spanish paid Native Americans for bringing them slaves, and this encouraged warfare as some tribes raided others to take prisoners to sell into slavery. Then Queen Isabella forbade the enslavement of Native Americans. Isabella's decision partly had a religious basis, but that did not stop Spain from turning to the African slave market.

The Atlantic slave trade began in the 1440s, with numbers of enslaved Africans being sent to Spain. Over the next four centuries, Africa lost more than 10 million people to bondage. Portugal, as you have read, was one of the first European nations to engage in the slave trade, and it dominated this harsh enterprise for almost 200 years. Once other European nations and the Americas became heavily involved, the enslavement of Africans only grew crueler. Unlike slavery in Africa, which was regarded as a temporary condition, the institution of **chattel slavery** that developed in Europe and the Americas required permanent bondage.

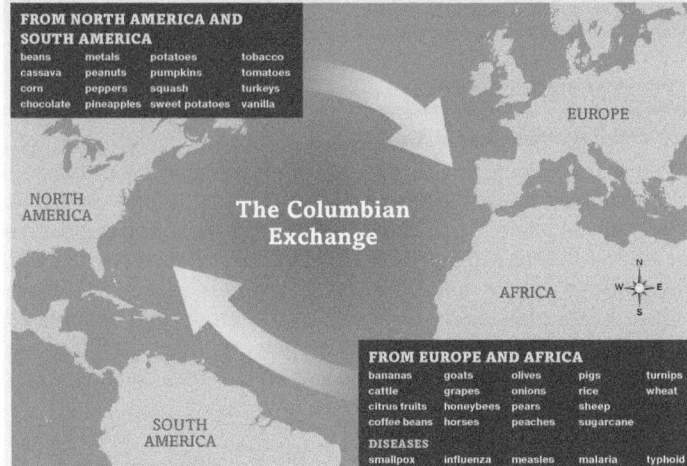

FROM NORTH AMERICA AND SOUTH AMERICA

beans	metals	potatoes	tobacco
cassava	peanuts	pumpkins	tomatoes
corn	peppers	squash	turkeys
chocolate	pineapples	sweet potatoes	vanilla

The Columbian Exchange

EUROPE

NORTH AMERICA

AFRICA

SOUTH AMERICA

FROM EUROPE AND AFRICA

bananas	goats	olives	pigs	turnips
cattle	grapes	onions	rice	wheat
citrus fruits	honeybees	pears	sheep	
coffee beans	horses	peaches	sugarcane	

DISEASES

smallpox	influenza	measles	malaria	typhoid

Chattel means "personal property." Under this system, the people enslaved lost all human rights and, as property, they and their children could be bought and sold at the enslaver's whim. At the time, Europeans believed their civilization was superior to others—enough to justify depriving other human beings of liberty and often of life itself. Nearly 600 years later, the legacy of slavery still influences the social, economic, and political life of the Americas, particularly in the United States.

THE COLUMBIAN EXCHANGE

From the first voyage of Columbus, the transfer of goods and culture between Europe and the Americas began to fundamentally transform world society. This process, known as the **Columbian Exchange**, led to an exchange of crops, animals, technology, and medicines across the Atlantic. Food crops such as corn, potatoes, tomatoes, chocolate, and peppers were shipped to Europe while wheat, rice, olives, bananas, and onions arrived in the Americas. Horses, brought to the Western Hemisphere by the Spanish, radically changed the lives of Native Americans.

Not all parts of the exchange were beneficial. Native Americans had no immunity to European diseases such as smallpox, typhoid, measles, chickenpox, and influenza. It is estimated that within three centuries after Columbus arrived, epidemic diseases had

killed up to 90 percent of the native population. As disease devastated Native Americans, **quinine**, a new medicine made from the bark of a South American tree, was developed in the 1600s. For three centuries, it was the only effective treatment for malaria, a disease carried by mosquitoes.

In part, the Columbian Exchange had a positive effect on all societies. For example, the availability of a greater variety of foods led to improved nutrition. But Native Americans experienced the worst negative effects, particularly through the decimation of their communities from European-introduced diseases and the resulting loss of Native American knowledge in areas such as agriculture and medicine.

HISTORICAL THINKING

1. **READING CHECK** What prompted Columbus to take his first voyage west?

2. **ANALYZE CAUSE AND EFFECT** What caused the practice of slavery to change in the late 1400s?

3. **INTERPRET MAPS** According to the sea routes on the explorers' map, which European nations sent explorers to North America?

4. **INTERPRET VISUALS** What lasting effects has the Columbian Exchange had on the Americas and the rest of the world?

BUILD BACKGROUND

THE PORTUGUESE SLAVE TRADE

In 1441, Prince Henry the Navigator sent two of his captains—Antão Gonçalves and Nuno Tristão—on separate ships to West Africa in search of goods to trade. After collecting seal skins and oil, Gonçalves called together his men and suggested that enslaved people would be a more lucrative cargo. He organized a raiding party and captured two native people, a man and a woman. After Tristão and members of his crew joined Gonçalves, the Portuguese took more captives, bringing them back to Europe in hopes of pleasing Prince Henry. Upon reaching Portugal, one of the captives suggested that he and several others would pay a ransom for their release in the form of enslaved sub-Saharan Africans. The next year, Gonçalves returned the captives to Africa and collected a payment of 10 enslaved people, some gold dust, and assorted goods.

SMALLPOX

While researchers are not certain where and when people were first infected with smallpox, some believe it may go back many thousands of years—to ancient Mesopotamia and the Nile River Valley. Several Egyptian mummies have been found with smallpox-like markings, and descriptions of diseases with symptoms matching smallpox appear in ancient Greek and Roman accounts of terrible plagues. Smallpox is thought to have traveled to Africa with Arab expansion and to Europe via soldiers returning from the Crusades. However, recent DNA research on a mummified child from the 1600s suggests that smallpox's origin may not be as old as once thought. But whatever its origin, in the 1980s, smallpox became the first infectious disease to be eradicated through vaccinations. Today, the virus exists in only two places—laboratories in the United States and Russia.

TEACH

GUIDED DISCUSSION

4. **Evaluate** How and why did England and France ignore the Treaty of Tordesillas? *(Possible response: England and France ignored the Treaty of Tordesillas by sending explorers across North America—a region already claimed, according to the treaty. England and France likely did this because they did not accept the decision of the pope and were eager to claim territory and discover the elusive northwest passage.)*

5. **Summarize** How did colonization lead to the expansion of chattel slavery in the Americas? *(European colonists needed laborers for their plantations, settlements, and farms. When disease and warfare decimated the Native American population and Queen Isabella outlawed enslaving Native Americans, the Spanish turned to Africa. The African slave trade quickly grew as colonization expanded, and enslaved people in the Americas were regarded as property rather than as being in temporary bondage.)*

INTERPRET VISUALS

Direct students' attention to the visual of the Columbian Exchange, and discuss the foods native to the Americas and to Africa and Europe. Then prompt students to consider if the Columbian Exchange has ended. Invite students to share their thoughts and reasons for their opinions with the class.

ACTIVE OPTIONS

On Your Feet: Four Questions About European Exploration Use a Four Corners activity to engage students in discussing four questions: What factors spurred European exploration? Why is it fair to say that Christopher Columbus's first voyage had unintended consequences? What were the causes and consequences of chattel slavery? What were the positive and negative effects of the Columbian Exchange? Assign each question to a corner of the room, and ask students to go to the corner of their choice to discuss the question. Then hold a class discussion to share each group's ideas.

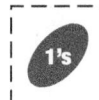 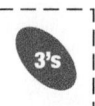

NG Learning Framework: Create a Technology Chart

SKILL Collaboration

KNOWLEDGE New Frontiers

Guide students to conduct research about the technologies that allowed European explorers during the 15th and 16th centuries to go farther and faster than their predecessors did. Divide the class into three groups, and assign each group a topic related to technology in the age of exploration: ship design, navigation, or mapmaking. Instruct group members to define and divide responsibilities among the group members. When groups have completed their research, ask them to present their findings to the class. Record each group's key ideas in a chart about the technology used in the age of exploration. Then hold a class discussion about the effects of these advances in transportation technology on those made in modern times, such as the space shuttle, high-speed train, or electric car.

HISTORICAL THINKING

ANSWERS

1. Columbus believed he could reach Asia by sailing west from Europe, and he hoped to open a new and faster trade route that Spain could claim.

2. Possible response: Before the late 1400s, slavery was not based on race. Most enslaved people were prisoners of war, criminals being punished, or those who had bonded themselves into slavery, and enslaved people could buy their way out of slavery. In the late 1400s, the chattel slavery system developed. Under this system, enslaved people were seen as property that could be bought and sold, bondage was permanent and passed on to children, and Africa became the main source for enslaved workers in the Americas. The primary factor that changed how slavery was practiced was the involvement of Europeans in the Atlantic slave trade.

3. According to the map, England sent John Cabot, the Netherlands sent Henry Hudson, and France sent Giovanni da Verrazano and Jacques Cartier. Some countries initially intended to find routes to Asia rather than claim lands in North America.

4. Answers will vary. Possible response: The Columbian Exchange resulted in cultures around the world adopting foods and other products not native to their home region. It also exposed the native population of the Americas to diseases for which they had no immunity, causing widespread illness and death. In the Americas, European culture dominated, while Native American populations never recovered in number.

TWO WORLDS MEET

When Europeans and Native Americans first encountered each other, they experienced people and cultures completely unknown to them. Their languages, clothing, tools, and customs were all extremely different. In some ways, it was like meeting someone from another planet.

Over the years, European and American artists and illustrators have depicted these encounters as meetings between civilized Europeans and primitive Native Americans. We now know that this interpretation is not accurate. In reality, Native Americans often thought the Europeans lacked a basic understanding of what many Native Americans believed to be the best, most productive ways to live.

Long after the age of exploration, these misconceptions often grew even more pronounced. In 1846, the famous printing company of Currier and Ives produced this hand-colored lithograph, *The Landing of Columbus Oct. 11th 1492*.

CRITICAL VIEWING How do you think the artist wanted Columbus to be portrayed, and what details in the painting might help represent him that way?

DOCUMENT ONE

Primary Source: Diary
from *The Diary of Christopher Columbus's First Voyage to America, 1492–1493*

Christopher Columbus and his crew had been at sea for two months when they first spotted the islands of the Caribbean. Convinced they were near mainland China, the men waded ashore, eager to make contact with the people of "Asia."

CONSTRUCTED RESPONSE How is Columbus's view of the Taino formed by his own beliefs and assumptions?

October 12, 1492: To some of them I gave red caps, and glass beads which they put on their chests, and many other things of small value in which they took so much pleasure and became so much our friends that it was a marvel. But it seemed to me that they were a people very poor in everything. They should be good and intelligent servants, for I see that they say very quickly everything that is said to them; and I believe that they would become Christians very easily, for it seemed to me that they had no religion.

DOCUMENT TWO

Primary Source: Speech
from a Native American leader after meeting Columbus, c. 1500

The Native Americans first encountered by Europeans did not have written languages. The only records of their words come from reports written by Europeans. The following speech by a Native American to Columbus was reported by Peter Martyr D'Anghera (MAR-tur dahn-GEHR-uh), an Italian historian in the service of Spain. Martyr did not witness the speech himself. He published the first volume of his account, *De Orbe Novo (On the New World)*, in 1516.

CONSTRUCTED RESPONSE What was one reaction Native Americans had to Europeans?

It is reported to us that you have visited all these countries . . . formerly unknown to you, and have inspired the inhabitants with great fear. Now I tell and warn you, . . . that the soul, when it quits the body, follows one of two courses; the first is dark and dreadful, and is reserved for the enemies and the tyrants of the human race; joyous and delectable is the second, which is reserved for those who . . . have promoted the peace and tranquility of others. If, therefore, you are a mortal, and believe that each one will meet the fate he deserves, you will harm no one.

DOCUMENT THREE

Primary Source: Retold Story
from a Wampanoag legend about the European arrival, c. 1700

Native Americans often passed down their history and culture through an oral tradition. Many of the stories told were fables or myths not meant to be taken literally. Instead, they were used to teach a lesson or to reflect a tribe's point of view. British settlers heard Wampanoag (wahm-puh-NOH-ag) legends about a giant named Maushop and recorded them in journals and letters as early as 1643.

CONSTRUCTED RESPONSE What does the change in Maushop's behavior convey about the Wampanoag's reaction to the arrival of Europeans?

On the west end of [present-day Martha's Vineyard] is a hill with a large cavity. A local Indian tradition says the deity Maushop lived there before the Europeans came to America. Maushop often invited Indians to share his meals. Once, to show their gratitude, they offered Maushop all the tobacco that grew on the island in one season. It barely filled his great pipe, but he . . . turned out the ashes into the sea, which formed Nantucket Island. Upon the Europeans' arrival in America, Maushop retired in disgust, and has never since been seen.

SYNTHESIZE & WRITE

1. **REVIEW** Review what you have learned about the impressions and reactions of Native Americans and Europeans toward one another.

2. **RECALL** List the main ideas expressed in each document.

3. **CONSTRUCT** Construct a topic sentence that answers this question: How did Native Americans and Europeans view one another during the time of exploration?

4. **WRITE** Using evidence from the chapter and documents, write an informative paragraph that supports your topic sentence in Step 3.

PLAN: 2-PAGE LESSON

OBJECTIVE

Synthesize information about early encounters between Native Americans and Europeans from primary source documents.

CRITICAL THINKING SKILLS FOR LESSON 2.2

- Synthesize
- Compare and Contrast
- Make Inferences
- Evaluate

HISTORICAL THINKING FOR CHAPTER 1

What impact did European exploration have on the cultures of North America and Africa?
Native Americans and Europeans represented vastly different cultures. Lesson 2.2 provides excerpts from documents that illustrate how these cultural differences colored perceptions on both sides when European explorers and Native Americans met.

BACKGROUND FOR THE TEACHER

When Christopher Columbus encountered the Taino, they were the largest Native American group in the Caribbean, possibly numbering 2 million people. While Columbus may have viewed them as poor and uncivilized, the Taino grew enough crops, such as yams, cassavas, corn, beans, and squashes, to support settlements of as many as 3,000 people. In addition, they hunted small animals, fished, gathered shellfish, and used large canoes to trade with people on other Caribbean islands. Contrary to Columbus's perception, the Taino had an elaborate religious system, with rituals, ceremonial centers, and carved representations. They also had a well-developed social structure with regional hereditary chiefs, nobles, commoners, and enslaved people. Nevertheless, the Spanish were able to conquer the Taino with little difficulty. By the 1550s, disease, starvation, and enslavement had all but rendered the Taino extinct.

INTRODUCE & ENGAGE

PREPARE FOR THE DOCUMENT-BASED QUESTION

Before students start on the activity, briefly preview the three documents. Remind students that a constructed response requires full explanations in complete sentences. Emphasize that students should use what they have learned about encounters between Europeans and Native Americans in addition to the information in the documents.

TEACH

GUIDED DISCUSSION

1. **Compare and Contrast** How would you characterize the difference in tone between the excerpt from Columbus and those from the Native Americans? *(Possible response: The excerpt from Columbus sounds patronizing. He depicts the Native Americans as childlike and awestruck over mere trinkets and suggests that they could be easily exploited. The tone of the Native American excerpts reflects anxiety over how the Europeans will behave toward the Native Americans and resentment over the changes the Europeans brought to traditional Native American ways of life.)*

2. **Make Inferences** How might the fact that Peter Martyr D'Anghera did not witness the Native American leader's speech have affected his retelling? *(Possible response: While Martyr may be accurate in indicating that the Native American leader warned Columbus not to harm or make war against Native Americans, his transcription seems to describe heaven and hell, so he might have added ideas from Christianity.)*

EVALUATE

After students have completed the Synthesize & Write activity, allow time for them to exchange paragraphs and read and comment on the work of their peers. Establish guidelines for comments prior to the activity so that feedback is constructive and encouraging in nature. Comments should focus on the most significant parts that address the purpose of the activity and the audience.

ACTIVE OPTION

On Your Feet: Use a Jigsaw Strategy Organize students into "expert" groups and assign each group one of the documents to analyze and summarize its main ideas in their own words. Then regroup students into new groups so that each new group has at least one member from each expert group. Students in the new groups take turns sharing the summaries from their expert groups.

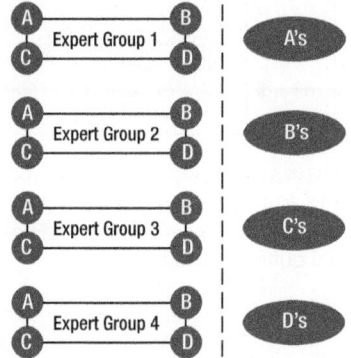

DIFFERENTIATE

STRIVING READERS

Provide Sentence Frames Instruct students to complete these sentence frames after reading the documents.

- **Document 1** Columbus believed the Taino would be good _____ because they repeated everything said to them. *(servants)*

- **Document 2** The writer is a(n) _____ historian recording the words of a(n) _____ leader, who believes that the Europeans should not _____ anyone. *(Italian; Native American; harm)*

- **Document 3** This document records part of a Wampanoag _____ about a giant who disappeared after the _____ arrived. *(legend; Europeans)*

GIFTED & TALENTED

Create a Visual Prompt students to conduct research to find and read a larger portion of one of the source documents or learn more about the context in which the work was created. Then invite them to create a drawing, photograph, cartoon, graphic, video, or other visual to represent the document. Encourage students to present their finished visuals to the class and explain how the cultural biases in the document are represented in their work.

See the Chapter Planner for more strategies for differentiation.

SYNTHESIZE & WRITE

ANSWERS

1. Answers will vary.

2. Answers will vary. Possible response: Columbus suggests that the Taino would make good servants and Christians; the Native American leader warns that Europeans will face punishment after death if they harm Native Americans; the Wampanoag legend depicts the arrival of the Europeans as bad for Native Americans.

3. Answers will vary. Possible response: Europeans viewed Native Americans as uncivilized and easily exploited, while Native Americans were fearful of European contact.

4. Answers will vary. Students' paragraphs should include their topic sentence from Step 3 and provide several details from the documents to support the sentence.

CONSTRUCTED RESPONSE

Document 1: Possible response: Columbus measures the Taino by European standards of wealth and class: Since the Taino are pleased with the cheap baubles, they must be poor, and because they're not Catholic, they lack religion.

Document 2: Possible response: Native Americans feared that Europeans were more likely to harm them than to promote peace.

Document 3: Possible response: Maushop's change indicates that the Wampanoag believed the arrival of the Europeans was a bad thing.

CRITICAL VIEWING The artist wanted to portray Columbus as a brave and heroic leader. He holds his sword aloft, claiming the land for Spain, and his men appear to bow down to him as a sign of respect.

VOCABULARY

Use each of the following vocabulary terms in a sentence that shows an understanding of the term's meaning.

1. infrastructure
   The Inca built an infrastructure of terraced fields and mountain roads and bridges.
2. domesticate
3. feudalism
4. humanism
5. mercantilism
6. nation-state
7. trans-Saharan
8. cartographer
9. chattel slavery
10. Columbian Exchange

READING STRATEGY
ANALYZE CAUSE AND EFFECT

Complete the following graphic organizer to show the major effects of European nations seeking to expand and claim global trade routes. Then answer the question.

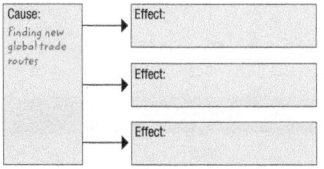

11. How did the expansion of global trade lead to a new view of the world for people on four continents?

MAIN IDEAS

Answer the following questions. Support your answers with evidence from the chapter.

12. How did geography influence early Native American cultures? LESSON 1.1
13. How was life in Europe changing by the 1400s and early 1500s? LESSON 1.3
14. Why did Martin Luther call for reform in the Roman Catholic Church? LESSON 1.3
15. What were the sources of wealth for three major kingdoms in West Africa? LESSON 1.4
16. How did European voyages of discovery change life for Native Americans and Africans? LESSON 2.1

HISTORICAL THINKING

Answer the following questions. Support your answers with evidence from the chapter.

17. MAKE INFERENCES What do structures such as the Great Serpent Mound reveal about ancient Native American cultures?
18. IDENTIFY PROBLEMS AND SOLUTIONS How did adopting the policy of mercantilism help strengthen some nations' economies?
19. ANALYZE LANGUAGE USE Why was the word *humanism* chosen to describe the philosophy that promotes individuality, critical thinking, and new ideas?
20. DRAW CONCLUSIONS Did Christopher Columbus's voyages confirm his ideas about world geography? Cite evidence from the text to support your conclusion.
21. FORM AND SUPPORT OPINIONS Should Native Americans have feared European explorers? Explain your answer.
22. COMPARE AND CONTRAST In what ways did Native American farming methods differ across North America?

INTERPRET MAPS

This detail of West Africa from a medieval map illustrates aspects of the region's culture, as well as the famous ruler of Mali, Mansa Musa. Study the map details and answer the questions.

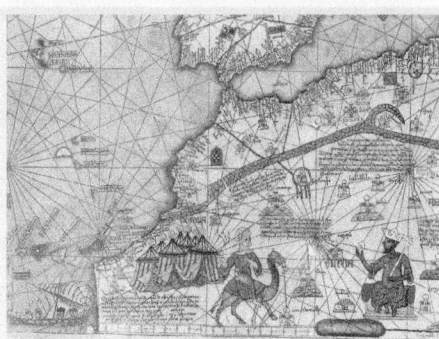

23. What details on the map reveal which figure is Mansa Musa?
24. What do the other illustrations on the map tell you about medieval trading in West Africa?

ANALYZE SOURCES

Jacques Cartier was unsuccessful in finding a northwestern water route to Asia, but he did learn much about the geography of the region he explored. He also frequently interacted with many Native American people during his voyages. This excerpt from the log of his first voyage in 1534 describes one such meeting. Read the passage and answer the question.

> Next day, having good weather, we sailed till noon. But, as we perceived there was no passage, we coasted along, and as we sailed saw some savages on the shores of a lake. The savages approached us and brought us pieces of cooked seal, which they placed on pieces of wood and then retired, giving us to understand that they gave them to us. We sent men ashore with hatchets, knives, chaplets [beads], and other articles, in which the savages took great delight, and they came all at once in their canoes to the shore where we were, bringing skins and other things they had to exchange for our articles, and there were more than three hundred of them—men, women, and children.

25. What words in Cartier's description help you understand how he regards this group of Native Americans?

CONNECT TO YOUR LIFE

26. ARGUMENT Columbus Day was established to honor Christopher Columbus's landing in America. Some people want the United States to stop celebrating this holiday because of what we know about Columbus's treatment of Native Americans. Do you agree? If so, whom might you honor instead? Write a letter to the editor of a newspaper explaining your views. Support your argument with evidence.

TIPS
- State your position about whether your city or state should celebrate Columbus Day.
- Use information from the chapter and your own ideas to support your argument.
- Research to learn more about both sides of the controversy.
- Address any counterarguments.
- Use two or three key vocabulary terms from the chapter in your letter.
- Conclude your letter with a sentence summarizing your position.

VOCABULARY ANSWERS

1. The Inca built an infrastructure of terraced fields and mountain roads and bridges.
2. The ability to domesticate maize and other plants helped Mesoamericans develop a diverse agricultural economy.
3. European society under feudalism was stratified, with the king and nobles at the top and peasants and serfs at the bottom.
4. By focusing on individuality, humanism helped foster critical thinking and new ideas.
5. European nations practiced mercantilism, which is why they competed for trade routes.
6. Small Renaissance kingdoms merged, forming nation-states.
7. Desert caravans carried salt along trans-Saharan trade routes.
8. A cartographer is someone who draws maps.
9. Under chattel slavery, enslaved people are considered property.
10. The Columbian Exchange introduced people around the world to new foods that came from faraway places.

READING STRATEGY ANSWER

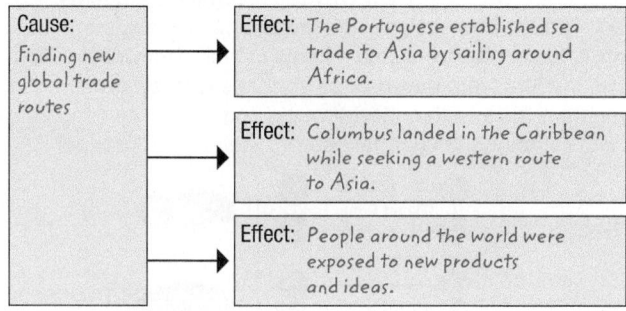

11. Possible response: The expansion of trade routes led people to new lands and encounters with cultures they never imagined existed, forever changing their understanding of the world and leading to global cultural diffusion.

MAIN IDEAS ANSWERS

12. Geography influenced the dwellings Native American groups built, what Native Americans ate and how they obtained their food, their traditions and beliefs, and the goods they traded.

13. Feudalism gave way to nation-states and global trade during this time period. This change was spurred by the effects of the Crusades, the Renaissance, the Reformation, and new technologies that improved literacy and ocean navigation.

14. Luther believed that the Catholic Church had become corrupt by controlling access to scripture and by selling indulgences that promised forgiveness for sins.

15. The primary sources of wealth for the three major West African kingdoms were gold and salt.

16. For Africans, European voyages of discovery led to the establishment of trade with Portugal. This commerce quickly focused on the slave trade, which decimated West African populations. For Native Americans, the arrival of the Europeans led to disease and warfare that quickly reduced Native American numbers and the amount of land to which they had access.

HISTORICAL THINKING ANSWERS

17. The existence of structures like the Great Serpent Mound suggests that ancient Native American cultures had complex societies with established religions, engineering skills, and populations large enough to build and use such structures.

18. The adoption of mercantilism helped strengthen the economies of some nations by focusing economic efforts on generating wealth through trade and the accumulation of valuable resources. Nations that succeeded in this effort dominated the era.

19. The word *humanism* underscores the philosophy's focus on the power of individuals to think for themselves in contrast to accepting without question traditional medieval views and the authority of the Church.

20. No, Columbus's voyages did not confirm his ideas. He believed that one could reach Asia by traveling west. Instead, he reached new continents—a fact he never fully understood or believed.

21. Answers will vary, but students might suggest that Native Americans should have feared European explorers because Europeans spread lethal diseases and came to claim Native American land for their home countries.

22. Native Americans adapted agricultural practices to local geography. For example, Native Americans in the desert southwest used canals to irrigate the arid land, and Native Americans in the eastern woodlands practiced slash-and-burn agriculture, clearing forests to grow crops.

INTERPRET MAPS ANSWERS

23. Mansa Musa can be identified as the figure who is sitting on a throne, holding a golden scepter and nugget, and has an Arab trader approaching him. In addition, his throne is located in the general area of Mali.

24. The map shows the diverse groups involved in West African trade, such as Arab traders and their tents, Portuguese traders in their caravel, and smaller towns that might be local trading centers.

ANALYZE SOURCES ANSWER

25. Possible response: Using the term *savages* to describe the Native Americans and reporting that they "took great delight" in inexpensive beads and other common articles suggest that Cartier regarded them as less sophisticated than Europeans.

CONNECT TO YOUR LIFE ANSWER

26. Letters will vary. Some students might argue in favor of keeping Columbus Day because of the societies that emerged from Columbus's discoveries. Others might oppose the holiday because of the devastation that the arrival of Europeans brought to Native Americans. Students should support their argument with information from the lesson and their own ideas and include Key Vocabulary terms in their letter.

UNIT 1 RESOURCES

UNIT INTRODUCTION

UNIT TIME LINE

UNIT WRAP-UP

NATIONAL GEOGRAPHIC | CONNECTION

National Geographic Magazine Adapted Articles
- "Colonial New York"
- "The First Americans" ONLINE

Unit 1 Inquiry: Conceive a Utopia

NG Learning Framework Activities
- Map Migrations
- Establish a Trade Network

Unit 1 Formal Assessment

CHAPTER 2 RESOURCES

Available at NGLSync.Cengage.com

TEACHER RESOURCES & ASSESSMENT

Reading and Note-Taking

Vocabulary Practice

Social Studies Skills Lessons
- Reading: Draw Conclusions
- Writing: Explanatory

Formal Assessment
- Chapter 2 Pretest
- Chapter 2 Tests A & B
- Section Quizzes

Chapter 2 Answer Key

ExamView®
   One-time Download

STUDENT DIGITAL RESOURCES

- eEdition
- Handbooks
- Online Atlas
- American Gallery Online
- History Notebook
- Active History
- American Voices (Biographies)
- Reid on the Road video series
- Literature Analysis
- Projects for Inquiry-Based Learning

Chapter 2 Spanish Resources are available at NGLSync.Cengage.com.

AMERICAN STORIES | The Colony of Jamestown

- Study Primary Sources: Excerpt from a pamphlet promoting the Virginia Colony, 1609
- On Your Feet: Jamestown Roundtable

NG Learning Framework:
Promote the Colony

SECTION 1 RESOURCES

SPAIN IN NORTH AMERICA

LESSON 1.1
Creating the Spanish Empire

- On Your Feet: Debate the Decline of the Aztec and Inca

NG Learning Framework:
Develop Guidelines for First Contact

LESSON 1.2
Spanish Rule of North America

- On Your Feet: Share Information About Spanish Colonization

NG Learning Framework:
Write a Report to the King

LESSON 1.3
Triangular Trade

- Active History: Analyze Primary Sources

NG Learning Framework:
Document the Economics of Slavery

SECTION 2 RESOURCES

COLONIZATION ON THE ATLANTIC COAST

LESSON 2.1
The English in Virginia

- ▶ Plimoth Plantation
- On Your Feet: English Colonists Roundtable

NG Learning Framework:
Create an Infographic

LESSON 2.2
NATIONAL GEOGRAPHIC EXPLORER
WILLIAM KELSO
Uncovering America's Birthplace

- On Your Feet: Question and Answer

NG Learning Framework:
Hold a Job Fair for Forensic Archaeology

LESSON 2.3
French and Dutch Colonies

- On Your Feet: Discuss the French and Dutch Colonies

NG Learning Framework:
Compare and Contrast North American Colonies

LESSON 2.4
New England

- On Your Feet: Debate Types of Colonial Government

NG Learning Framework:
Create an Annotated Time Line

American Voices Biographies
Anne Hutchinson and John Winthrop
Squanto

SECTION 3 RESOURCES

MIDDLE COLONIES AND SOUTHERN COLONIES

LESSON 3.1
Middle Colonies

- On Your Feet: Discuss William Penn's Vision

NG Learning Framework:
Compare Quakers Then and Now

LESSON 3.2
Southern Colonies

 Southern Plantations

NG Learning Framework:
Interview a Founder

LESSON 3.3
The Expansion of Slavery in the Americas

- On Your Feet: Word Webbing to Review Slave Codes

NG Learning Framework:
Investigate the Contributions of Enslaved Workers

CHAPTER 2 REVIEW

STRIVING READERS

STRATEGY ①
MAKE A TOP FIVE FACTS LIST

Tell students to reread the lesson and to review the visuals that it contains. Then ask students to close the book and write down five facts that they remember from the text. Have students meet with a partner to compare lists and consolidate the two lists into one final list. Encourage partners to state facts to each other from their lists.

Use with All Lessons *Throughout the chapter, help students develop the habit of making lists of facts as they read.*

STRATEGY ②
USE RECIPROCAL TEACHING

Tell partners to take turns reading each paragraph of the lesson aloud. At the end of the paragraph, the reading student asks the listening student questions about the paragraph. Students may ask their partners to state the main idea, identify important details that support the main idea, or summarize the paragraph in their own words. Then have students work together to answer the Historical Thinking questions.

Use with All Lessons

STRATEGY ③
CREATE A MAIN-IDEA AND DETAILS LIST

Direct students to read the Main Idea statements for each lesson aloud. Explain that these statements identify and summarize the lessons' key ideas. As students read the lessons, encourage them to find details in the text that connect to the Main Idea statements and write them in a Main-Idea and Details List, such as the one shown. Explain that this process helps students identify and remember the most important information.

```
Main Idea:
    Detail:
    Detail:
    Detail:
    Detail:
    Detail:
```

Use with All Lessons

INCLUSION

STRATEGY ①
PREVIEW USING MAPS

Preview maps to orient students to the lesson topic and to help them comprehend lesson text. Tell students to read the map title and legend and then place a finger on relevant information and trace arrows if present. For example, for the Conquistador Routes illustrated in Lesson 1.2, point out the color in the legend that represents each conquistador, and tell students to use a finger to trace each explorer's journey. For the Triangular Trade map in Lesson 1.3, encourage students to use a finger to trace the arrows showing the movement of raw materials, manufactured goods, and enslaved people.

Use with Lessons 1.2, 1.3, 2.3, 3.1, and 3.2

STRATEGY ②
PROVIDE A SUMMARY CHART

To help students better understand the reasons for Bacon's Rebellion, its outcomes, and impacts, provide them with a summary chart of the important dates, events, people, and outcomes, similar to the completed one below. You might alternatively provide a partially completed chart and guide students to identify and enter key information.

Date/Event	People Involved	Outcomes
1646/treaty giving the Powhatan land north of York River	Virginia officials, leaders of the Powhatan	Peaceful co-existence
Early 1670s/ cycle of raids and reprisals	the Powhatan, landless freemen who wanted land to grow tobacco	Landless colonists farmed land across York River; the Powhatan pushed back
1676/Bacon's Rebellion begins	Virginia governor William Berkeley, freeman Nathaniel Bacon, the Powhatan	Bacon wanted to remove the Powhatan and defied Berkeley, who wanted to protect the Powhatan and the profitable fur trade
September 1676/Bacon's Rebellion continues	Berkeley, Bacon and supporters, the Powhatan	Bacon and armed supporters attacked the Powhatan villages and burned much of Jamestown; Berkeley fled
1676/End of Bacon's Rebellion	Bacon and supporters, the Powhatan	Bacon died; many Powhatan killed; 1646 treaty broken; landowners replaced freeman laborers with enslaved Africans

Use with Lesson 3.2

ENGLISH LANGUAGE LEARNERS ELD

STRATEGY 1
USE TERMS IN A SENTENCE

Pair students at the **Emerging** level with those at the **Bridging** or **Expanding** level. Instruct pairs to work together to compose a sentence using selected Key Vocabulary words and terms. Ask the more proficient students to assist their partners in checking the accuracy of the sentences. Invite pairs to share their sentences and discuss different ways to use each word or term.

Use with All Lessons

STRATEGY 2
REVIEW TRANSITIONAL WORDS

To help students summarize what they read and put events relating to the colonization of North America in chronological order, display the following transitional words: *first, next, then, also, while, immediately, later, earlier, meanwhile, whenever, simultaneously, subsequently, during, following, before, afterwards*, and *finally*. Direct mixed pairs of students at the **Emerging** and **Expanding** levels to write a series of sentences that tell the major events in each lesson. Encourage them to use a variety of transitional words and to vary their sentence structure.

Use with All Lessons *You may expand the exercise by having students note transitional words as they read each lesson. For example, in Lesson 3.1, students may identify* at first, in spite of this, even so, first, *and* next.

STRATEGY 3
CREATE WORD SQUARES

Place students at **All Proficiencies** in mixed pairs and tell them to work together to identify at least three Key Vocabulary words or terms from the lesson that they have difficulty understanding. Instruct students to complete a Word Square for each word or term that they identify. Then have pairs exchange their Word Squares and ask and answer questions about the information they included.

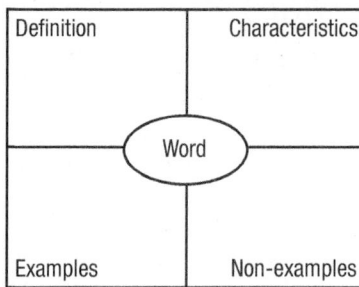

Use with All Lessons

GIFTED & TALENTED

STRATEGY 1
TEACH A CLASS

Allow students to choose one of the lessons in this chapter and prepare to teach the content to the class. Suggest that students think about visuals or activities they want to use as they teach. Give them a set amount of time in which to present their lesson.

Use with All Lessons

STRATEGY 2
WRITE A LETTER HOME

Tell students to conduct online research about Roger Williams or Anne Hutchinson to better understand their thoughts, beliefs, and experiences. Then ask them to write a letter from the point of view of one of the dissenters to a family member or friend about their experiences and their hopes for the future in Rhode Island. Invite volunteers to read their letters to the class or post them on a class website or blog.

Use with Lesson 2.4

PRE-AP

STRATEGY 1
REPORT ON CONCEPTS OF LAND OWNERSHIP

Direct students to conduct online and library research about the different concepts of land ownership held by Native Americans and Europeans. Tell them to use their findings to write a report about the basis for the misunderstandings between one of the following: the Lenape and the Dutch over the ownership of Manhattan (Lesson 2.3), the conflicts that led to the Pequot War (Lesson 2.4), the conflicts that led to Bacon's Rebellion (Lesson 3.2). Encourage students to assess the credibility and accuracy of their sources and to include properly formatted citations. Ask students to share their reports with the class.

Use with Lesson 2.3, 2.4, and 3.2

STRATEGY 2
CREATE AN ORAL PRESENTATION

Invite students to choose one term below to investigate. Students will then design and deliver an oral presentation that explains the significance of the term to the history of the colonization of North America.

conquistadors	dissenters
encomienda	pacifism
triangular trade	freedom of conscience
indentured servants	cash crop
heretics	slave code

Use with Lessons 1.1–1.3, 2.1, 2.3, 2.4, and 3.1–3.3

COLONIZING NORTH AMERICA

1513–1752

HISTORICAL THINKING How were the North American colonies shaped by their geography and by the people who settled them?

AMERICAN STORIES The Colony of Jamestown

SECTION 1 **Spain in North America**
SECTION 2 **Colonization on the Atlantic Coast**
SECTION 3 **Middle Colonies and Southern Colonies**

AMERICAN GALLERY ONLINE Southern Plantations

"We entered into the Bay of [Chesapeake] . . . I was almost ravished **at the first sight thereof.**"

—George Percy, early Virginia colonist

CRITICAL VIEWING The land around Chesapeake Bay attracted colonists with fresh water and fertile soil. They settled and formed communities in coastal locations such as Smith Island, Maryland, shown here. What features of the land do you think inspired Percy's quotation?

36 CHAPTER 2

Colonizing North America 37

INTRODUCE THE PHOTOGRAPH

SMITH ISLAND IN CHESAPEAKE BAY

Inform students that Smith Island was first spotted by English settlers as they sailed into Chesapeake Bay in 1607. Direct students to the quote by George Percy, one of those settlers who provided primary accounts of their experiences, and discuss the Critical Viewing question. Explain that Percy was aboard the *Susan Constant*, one of the three vessels that anchored at Chesapeake Bay on April 26. That night, Percy and a party of colonists had an altercation with local Native Americans, leaving two men injured. Three days later, the English staked a cross at the mouth of the bay and named it Cape Henry after the son of King James I, before moving on to explore the James River.
ASK: How have 400 years of settlement appeared to have changed the lands of Chesapeake Bay? *(Some of the islands are now inhabited or developed, and buildings and docks line the waterfront.)* Tell students that in this chapter they will learn how European settlement changed the geography and population of the Americas.

SHARE BACKGROUND

George Percy, the youngest son of the eighth earl of Northumberland, was a founding member of the Jamestown settlement. His father, charged with fomenting pro-Catholic conspiracies, died imprisoned in the Tower of London when Percy was a child. In 1602, after attending the University of Oxford, he sailed to the West Indies on a voyage that may have predisposed him for the Jamestown venture. Incentive to leave England may have come when his brother, Henry, was imprisoned for complicity in the Gunpowder Plot of 1605, in which English Catholics planned to blow up Parliament and kill King James I. Henry's association with Sir Walter Raleigh, a financier of the Roanoke voyages between 1584 and 1590, may have aided in the Virginia Company of London's royal charter and contributed to Percy's standing in the colony.

CRITICAL VIEWING Percy likely saw islands, meadows, and woods, with creeks or rivers running through them.

For Chapter 2 Spanish Resources, visit the Resources Menu. Chapter 2 Resources are available at NGLSync.Cengage.com.

HISTORICAL THINKING QUESTION

How were the North American colonies shaped by their geography and by the people who settled them?

Activate Prior Knowledge This activity helps students access prior knowledge of North American colonies and their geography. Arrange students into three groups, one for each chapter section. Prompt students to discuss what they already know about the topic and what they might learn. Ask them to consider the following questions and create summaries of the group's knowledge.

Spain in North America Section 1 is about the establishment of Spain's empire in the Americas and the beginning of the triangular slave trade. In what ways did the Spanish shape and influence North America? What role did the slave trade play in America's development?

Colonization on the Atlantic Coast Section 2 is about the settlement of what became the northeastern part of the United States and Canada. What types of settlers founded colonies along the Atlantic Coast? What were the goals of the settlers?

Middle Colonies and Southern Colonies Section 3 is about the colonization of the middle and southern areas of the future United States. Why were colonies founded there? How did the geography differ among the Northern, Middle, and Southern Colonies?

Regroup students so that new groups have representatives from each section who can share their knowledge of the assigned topics. Then tell them that they will review their summaries as they read the chapter to correct misconceptions or inaccuracies.

INTRODUCE THE READING STRATEGY

DRAW CONCLUSIONS

Explain that drawing conclusions about events and individuals' actions and the effects of those events and actions can help students better understand the relationships among historical events. Turn to the Chapter Review and preview the chart with students. As they read the chapter, encourage them to draw conclusions about the different settlements, events, religions, and policies that existed during the colonization of North America.

KEY DATES FOR CHAPTER 2

1519	Cortés meets the Aztec
1588	British defeat the Spanish Armada
1607	English establish Jamestown settlement
1619	Captive Africans are enslaved in North America
1620	Plymouth settlers sign Mayflower Compact
1627	Company of New France is established in Quebec
1632	King Charles I grants Maryland charter
1681	William Penn founds Pennsylvania
1691	North and South Carolina develop into distinct colonies
1733	Settlers establish Savannah, Georgia

INTRODUCE CHAPTER VOCABULARY

KEY VOCABULARY

SECTION 1

African diaspora	cultural diffusion	smallpox
beseige	encomienda	triangular trade
commodity	hacienda	viceroyalty
conquistador	Middle Passage	

SECTION 2

charter	heretic	joint-stock company
dissenter	indentured servant	separatist

SECTION 3

pacifism	slave code
proprietor	trustee

WORD MAPS

As students read the chapter, ask them to complete a Word Map for each Key Vocabulary word. Tell them to write the word in the oval and, as they encounter the word in the chapter, complete the Word Map. Model an example using the graphic organizer below.

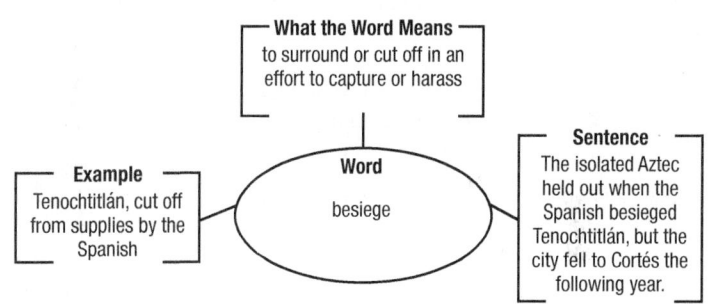

What the Word Means to surround or cut off in an effort to capture or harass

Example Tenochtitlán, cut off from supplies by the Spanish

Word besiege

Sentence The isolated Aztec held out when the Spanish besieged Tenochtitlán, but the city fell to Cortés the following year.

OBJECTIVES

- **Examine photographs of James Fort and artifacts from the Jamestown settlement.**
- **Explain how and why English settlers changed the environment of Virginia.**
- **Describe the ways in which Native Americans were affected by the colonists.**
- **Study a primary source: excerpt from a pamphlet promoting the Virginia colony, 1609.**

CRITICAL THINKING SKILLS FOR "THE COLONY OF JAMESTOWN"

- Make Connections
- Draw Conclusions
- Make Generalizations
- Compare and Contrast
- Analyze Cause and Effect

CONNECT TO THE CHAPTER

This American Story takes a deeper look at the settlement of Jamestown, Virginia, in 1607 by English colonists. Photographs of archaeological research provide details about where and how the colonists lived. Information about historical figures and an excerpt from a 1609 pamphlet promoting Virginia will deepen students' understanding of the interaction between colonists and Native Americans and the promises that first drew colonists to the area.

Chapter 2, Colonizing North America, introduces students to the reasons for and the experiences of Europeans colonizing the Americas. "The Colony of Jamestown" focuses specifically on English settlement of the Virginia colony and builds on information presented in Lesson 2.1 and Lesson 2.2.

HISTORY NOTEBOOK

Encourage students to complete the American Story page for Chapter 2 in their History Notebooks as they read.

CRITICAL VIEWING The photograph of the archaeological site shows that the fort was built very close to the water, making it more difficult for enemies to invade the fort. The excavation also reveals the location of the fort's walls and the size of some of its rooms.

AMERICAN STORIES

NATIONAL GEOGRAPHIC

CRITICAL VIEWING This aerial photograph of the Jamestown excavation site shows one corner of the triangular fort. Archaeologists have identified bulwarks, which were used to store artillery, at each of the fort's corners. What other details does this photo reveal about the site?

38 CHAPTER 2

THE COLONY OF
JAMESTOWN

For many Americans, the names John Smith, John Rolfe, and Pocahontas have been familiar since childhood. And so the basic outlines of early Jamestown are generally well known: In 1607, a group of English colonists established a settlement in a land they called Virginia—the rest was history.

Colonizing North America **39**

MAP THE JAMESTOWN SETTLEMENT

Point out the location of the Jamestown settlement on a physical map of contemporary Virginia. Ask students to consider why the settlement's location might have been attractive to colonists. As part of the discussion, guide students to consider the following topics:

- resources in the area
- proximity to the Atlantic Ocean
- benefits of living near a bay
- weather in the region

THE RESCUE OF JAMESTOWN

The 60 colonists who survived the "starving time" of November 1609 through early May 1610 had no idea that help had been stranded for almost a year in the islands of Bermuda and was soon to arrive. Sir Thomas Gates and his party of colonists arrived in Jamestown a few weeks after the Powhatan lifted the siege of the colony. Gates, likely shocked and disheartened by what he found, decided to abandon Jamestown and set sail for Newfoundland on June 8. As the colonists sailed up the James River, they met an arriving ship holding a year's supply of provisions. The ship also carried a new governor, Thomas West. It was likely on West's order that Gates and the Jamestown survivors returned to the colony.

Within two months, hostilities between the colonists and the Powhatan were no better than before the siege that began the previous November. In early August, colonists raided a Native American town, took corn, and killed 15 or 16 people. They also captured the chief's wife and two children, all three of whom they later executed.

GUIDED DISCUSSION

1. **Make Generalizations** What does the unsuitability of some of the colonists to settle Jamestown tell you about their previous lives in England? *(Possible responses: The colonists who were not farming the land, building shelters, or practicing survival skills may have been landowners with servants who worked for them or merchants who bought food and hired people to fulfill their needs. They may not have had the necessary skills to make Jamestown successful. Those who refused to work might have felt that laboring was beneath their social station, regardless of their skills.)*

2. **Make Connections** In what way do you think the location of Jamestown might have contributed to Native Americans contracting malaria? *(Possible response: The area around Jamestown was marshy, and mosquitoes—which can transmit malaria—thrive in stagnant water. The insects could have bitten colonists who carried the parasite that causes malaria in their blood, and then bitten the Native Americans, thus transmitting the disease from one group to the other.)*

MORE INFORMATION

Captain Bartholomew Gosnold, Jamestown Founder Draw students' attention to the replica of the ship *Godspeed* in the photograph of the re-created James Fort. Explain that Englishman Bartholomew Gosnold was the commander of *Godspeed* when it and two other ships set sail from England on December 20, 1606. Gosnold, an accomplished mariner, had spent three years promoting and planning the venture and was eventually granted a royal charter by James I that created the Virginia Company of London.

Upon arrival at Chesapeake Bay on April 26, 1607, Gosnold and six others formed the ruling council that would govern the new colony. That first summer, with temperatures in the upper 90s and high humidity, men began to die, falling to swamp fever, dysentery, and malaria. In August, Gosnold died. In 2002, the Jamestown Rediscovery Project uncovered remains buried just outside of the fort. The presence of a "gable-lidded" coffin (indicating status) and pieces of a captain's staff suggested that these were the remains of Gosnold. The results of a forensic analysis determined the age, height, and European ancestry to be consistent with known facts about him. The combined forensic and historical evidence pointed to the probable discovery of the burial site of one of the founders of Jamestown.

AMERICAN STORIES

This American Story is a deeper look at aspects of the well-known tale of Jamestown. It's an opportunity to explore the colonists' motivations and struggles and learn about their encounters—sometimes friendly, often hostile—with Native Americans. It also explores the ways the colonists irrevocably changed the land and its inhabitants by ultimately driving out most of the native groups.

GENTLEMAN COLONISTS

If you were planning an expedition to uncharted territory, knowing that you were months away from any possibility of resupply, whom would you choose to bring with you? Farmers, hunters, or others who could enable the expedition to live off the land? You might not bring many people who present themselves with the job description of "gentleman."

The first Jamestown expedition had a slightly different notion about necessary personnel. The list of names of the first 104 colonists includes 29 "gentlemen," a ruling council of 6 men, and 13 "labourers." There were also 6 carpenters and a handful of other craftsmen to round out the number of settlers with practical skills.

This ratio of useful workers to men who would hesitate to get their hands dirty seems frighteningly impractical to the modern-day mind. The Virginia Company, however, was certain the settlers could obtain most or all of their food from the local Indians, who were described as "generally very loving and gentle" by one writer in 1609. In the meantime, the settlers could occupy themselves searching for the gold and silver that they were certain existed in abundance in North America.

A historical interpreter leaves the gate of the re-created James Fort in 2007, the 400th anniversary of the founding of Jamestown. The festivities for the anniversary included the launch of a replica of the *Godspeed*, one of the three ships that carried the original settlers from England.

This breezy confidence proved to be a dangerous miscalculation. While they did trade with Jamestown to some extent, the Native Americans were either unable or unwilling to entirely support the colony. Starvation loomed, but the colony survived its first year, partly thanks to the leadership of John Smith, who decreed, "He that will not work shall not eat."

The overabundance of gentlemen was not the sole reason that only 38 colonists survived the first 9 months of Jamestown's existence. The colony had been established on a marshy plot of land with a tainted drinking water source. Archaeologists have also recently discovered evidence that many of the colonists worked very hard at fishing, woodworking, and other enterprises. Still, some testimony indicates that the work ethic of at least a few was an ongoing concern. One governor of Jamestown, arriving in 1611, was dismayed to find the inhabitants "bowling in the streets" rather than working in the few gardens they had planted.

PIGS, GERMS, AND TOBACCO

In Jamestown's earliest years, the region experienced a drought. While Native American groups seemed to manage, the colony teetered on the edge of disaster, saved only by the regular influx of additional settlers. Why, then, did the English prevail over the Native Americans in a relatively short time? Author Charles C. Mann, in a 2007 article for *National Geographic*, proposed an ecological explanation, noting that the colonists brought with them several organisms that were new to North America and destructive to the Native Americans' way of life.

Before 1607, there were few domestic animals in North America. Pigs, goats, cows, and horses all arrived with the Europeans, and when these animals wandered away from their enclosures,

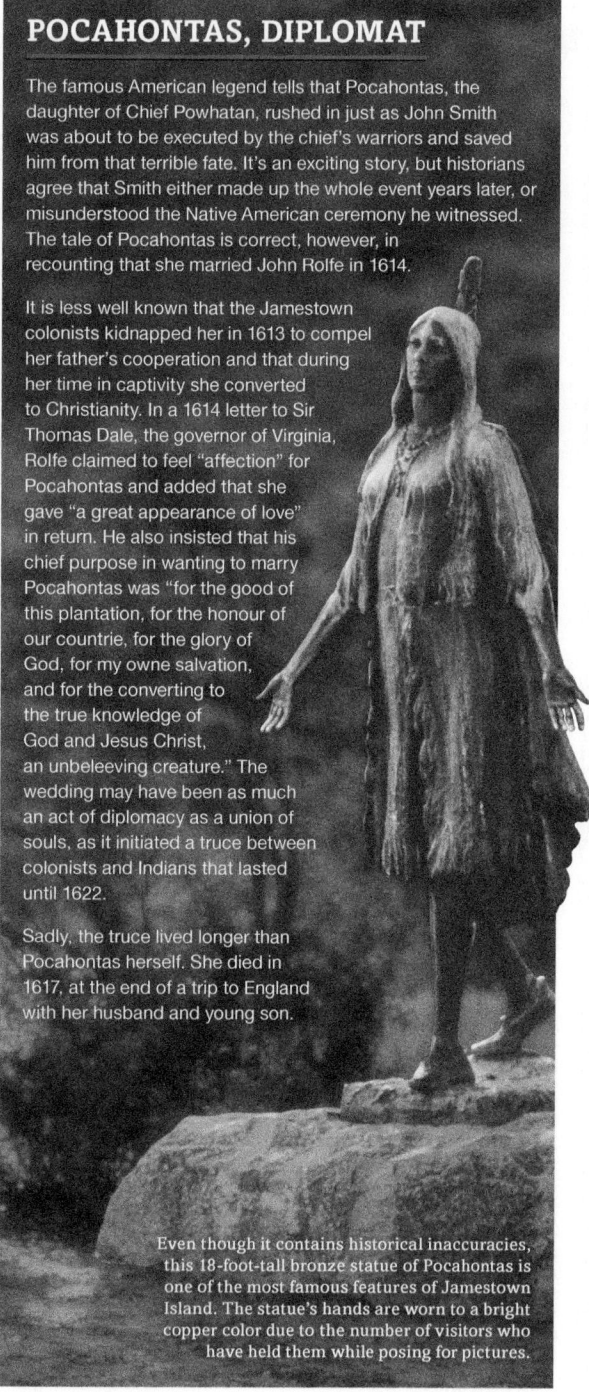

POCAHONTAS, DIPLOMAT

The famous American legend tells that Pocahontas, the daughter of Chief Powhatan, rushed in just as John Smith was about to be executed by the chief's warriors and saved him from that terrible fate. It's an exciting story, but historians agree that Smith either made up the whole event years later, or misunderstood the Native American ceremony he witnessed. The tale of Pocahontas is correct, however, in recounting that she married John Rolfe in 1614.

It is less well known that the Jamestown colonists kidnapped her in 1613 to compel her father's cooperation and that during her time in captivity she converted to Christianity. In a 1614 letter to Sir Thomas Dale, the governor of Virginia, Rolfe claimed to feel "affection" for Pocahontas and added that she gave "a great appearance of love" in return. He also insisted that his chief purpose in wanting to marry Pocahontas was "for the good of this plantation, for the honour of our countrie, for the glory of God, for my owne salvation, and for the converting to the true knowledge of God and Jesus Christ, an unbeleeving creature." The wedding may have been as much an act of diplomacy as a union of souls, as it initiated a truce between colonists and Indians that lasted until 1622.

Sadly, the truce lived longer than Pocahontas herself. She died in 1617, at the end of a trip to England with her husband and young son.

Even though it contains historical inaccuracies, this 18-foot-tall bronze statue of Pocahontas is one of the most famous features of Jamestown Island. The statue's hands are worn to a bright copper color due to the number of visitors who have held them while posing for pictures.

Colonizing North America **41**

On Your Feet: Jamestown Roundtable Arrange students in groups of four to take part in a Roundtable discussion about the various challenges the colonists faced after arriving in Jamestown. Ask each member of the group to name one difficulty the colonists needed to overcome. Then instruct each group to discuss and decide which of the challenges had the most devastating effect on the community and why.

NG Learning Framework: Promote the Colony

SKILL Communication

KNOWLEDGE Our Human Story

Ask pairs of students to create an advertisement for the Virginia Company to recruit potential colonists. Encourage students to consider what they have learned about the Jamestown colonists and to list specific skills and characteristics they are seeking in the people they recruit. Direct students to use available art supplies or software to create and illustrate era-appropriate advertisements. Invite pairs to present each advertisement for a class discussion about its accuracy and effectiveness in promoting the Virginia colony.

POCAHONTAS, DIPLOMAT

The woman known as "Pocahontas" (a nickname meaning "little playful one") was given the name "Matoaka" ("flower between two streams") at her birth in 1596 as the last daughter of Chief Powhatan. At 15, the customary age, she married a Powhatan named Kocoum and later gave birth to a son. Two years later, Captain Samuel Argall carried out a plot to kidnap Pocahontas and hold her hostage for the return of captured English prisoners. Argall pressed Chief Japazaw and his wife, under threat of attack, to aid in the plot to lure Pocahontas aboard his ship. He assured them that Pocahontas would be released unharmed. Argall broke his promise to release Pocahontas and, according to the sacred oral history of the Mattaponi tribe, had Kocoum killed before sailing to Jamestown. Historical accounts relate Pocahontas's conversion to Christianity, her marriage to John Rolfe, and voyage to England.
ASK: In what ways does Pocahontas's given name reflect her place in history? *(Possible response: "Flower between two streams" describes her role as the ambassador between the Powhatan and English cultures.)*

THE LIVELY TALE OF JOHN SMITH

As well as a famed explorer, John Smith was a skilled cartographer. He created invaluable maps of the colonies and published books detailing his observations about the New World. After returning to England in 1609, Smith sailed back to North America in 1614 to explore what he would call New England, and mapped the coastline that today runs from Maine to Massachusetts. In 1620, when the Mayflower arrived in Massachusetts, the English colonists used Smith's publications and maps to guide them. **ASK:** Why do you think John Smith's life is described as a "lively tale"? *(Possible response: The facts of Smith's life read like an exciting and adventurous tale crafted by a skilled storyteller, full of fighting in foreign lands, daring escapes, and great accomplishments.)*

THE NOT SO DISTANT PAST

In 2013, Jamestown Rediscovery archaeologists unearthed the remains of four men buried in the church within Historic Jamestowne Park. The remains were determined to be of a reverend, a knight, and two captains. **ASK:** What do these remains and the artifacts pictured reveal about the Jamestown inhabitants' lives? *(Answers will vary. Possible response: The four men indicate religious worship, connection to king, and the need for protection, things important to the colonists. The caltrops indicates preparedness against attacks. The wine bottles are evidence of storage of wine, perhaps made from native plants or brought from England. The tooth and ear picker suggest a concern for personal hygiene.)*

WRITE ABOUT HISTORY

Write a Diary or Journal Entry This American Story discusses the struggles of Jamestown settlers and discoveries archaeologists have made about them. Ask students to write a diary entry detailing a day in the life of a colony gentleman, council member, or craftsman, or write a journal entry of a member of an archaeological team that discovered a colonial artifact. Provide guidance about the writing process as necessary.

THINK ABOUT IT

Answers will vary. Possible response: The English created a new world in Virginia by bringing non-native domesticated cows, horses, and pigs and modifying the land through farming. They created a society based on English laws and culture and warred with, rather than joined, native cultures.

---

they wreaked havoc on the Native Americans' fields. Pigs were especially destructive, with their huge appetites, willingness to eat most anything, and ability to dig up roots and tubers.

The English settlers also carried a tiny, but no less powerful, import in their blood: the parasite that causes malaria, a disease that can sicken and weaken an individual for years. Some researchers theorize that malaria reached Virginia and infected the Native Americans in the early 1600s. It's even possible that malaria was responsible for the seeming laziness—or actual illness-related fatigue—of early colonists who failed to farm for food.

Tobacco was not an import to North America, but the Native Americans had never grown it in large quantities. As noted by scientist Leanne DuBois, "Tobacco has an almost unique ability to suck the life out of soil." To feed England's growing appetite for the crop, the colonists cleared acres of forest and left behind mostly depleted open lands. Mann sums up the results of the changes introduced by the English with a blunt conclusion: "Four centuries ago, the English didn't discover a New World—they created one."

A strain of sweet South American tobacco seed, brought to Jamestown by settler John Rolfe in 1610, quickly became Virginia's major cash crop and number one export.

THINK ABOUT IT

In what ways did the English create their own world in Virginia, rather than fitting into the existing environment and societies?

THE LIVELY TALE OF JOHN SMITH

Americans remember John Smith principally for his leadership of the Jamestown colony and his part in the Pocahontas legend. In fact, settling Jamestown was not Smith's first—or even his most exciting—adventure.

John Smith was born in 1580 and left home at 16 to become a soldier, joining a group in France that was fighting to free Holland from Spain's control. Later, he served as a sailor on a merchant ship and fought with Austrian troops against Turkey. In 1602, he was wounded and captured during a battle in present-day Romania and then sold into slavery. The Turk who bought Smith sent him as a gift to a woman he admired. Smith later claimed that the woman fell in love with him and arranged for him to train as a soldier in the Turkish army. He escaped and spent time in Europe and North Africa before returning to England in 1604 or 1605. Considering Smith's retelling of his encounter with Powhatan and Pocahontas, we might conclude that his greatness as an adventurer was matched by his brilliance as a storyteller.

A bronze statue of John Smith stands within the outlines of the original James Fort. The inscription on the base reads "John Smith, Governor of Virginia, 1608" and features Smith's coat of arms and motto, *vincere est vivere* ("to live is to conquer").

THE NOT SO DISTANT PAST

Smith and Rolfe, Pocahontas and Powhatan—these names often seem to belong to a remote, untouchable past. Modern-day research and archaeology, however, have helped to reveal the Jamestown colonists and Native Americans of the region as living, relatable people. Over several years of patient digging, researchers have unearthed the walls of the original fort and other buildings at Jamestown, as well as artifacts that allow valuable glimpses into the inhabitants' everyday lives.

The site is preserved within Historic Jamestowne Park, which is operated by the National Park Service and an organization called Preservation Virginia. At Historic Jamestowne, exhibits, tours, and costumed interpreters help visitors experience Jamestown as a real community that is not lost in distant history.

Glass wine bottles

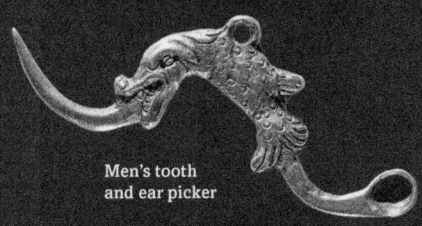

Men's tooth and ear picker

Iron caltrops were laid on the ground to injure enemies and prevent attacks.

PRIMARY SOURCE

In 1609, a pamphlet called "Nova Britannia" ("New Britain") appeared in England to promote the colony in Virginia to investors and potential colonists. At this point, Jamestown was still engaged in a desperate struggle against starvation and disease.

The country itself is large and great assuredly, though as yet, no exact discovery can be made of all. It is also commendable and hopeful in every way, the air and climate most sweet and wholesome, much warmer than England, and very agreeable to our natures. . . . the land naturally yields . . . [an] abundance of fish, both scale and shell; an infinite store of both land and water fowl.

There are valleys and plains streaming with sweet springs, like veins in a natural body; there are hills and mountains making an offer of hidden treasure, never yet searched; the land is full of minerals, plenty of woods (the wants of England).

—from "Nova Britannia," 1609

NOVA BRITANNIA.
OFFRING MOST
Excellent fruites by Planting in
VIRGINIA.

Exciting all such as be well affected
to further the same.

LONDON
Printed for SAMVEL MACHAM, and are to be sold at
his Shop in Pauls Church-yard, at the
Signe of the Bul-head.
1 6 0 9.

Colonizing North America **43**

DIFFERENTIATE

INCLUSION

Facilitate Comprehension Pair special-needs students with proficient readers who can help them understand the main text and features of this American Story. Coach special-needs students to jot down difficult words and concepts that confuse them. Coach their partners to use information from the story to help define words and answer questions.

GIFTED & TALENTED

Annotate a Graphic of James Fort Ask students to review information and photographs featured in this American Story and to conduct additional research to learn more about James Fort and its structures. Direct students to create a graphic of the fort and annotate its major structures, describing the function and use of each. Invite them to display their graphics and answer questions from the class.

See the Chapter Planner for more strategies for differentiation.

HISTORICAL THINKING

Ask and have students answer the following questions.

1. **READING CHECK** How have archaeology and science led to a greater understanding of the Jamestown settlers?

2. **COMPARE AND CONTRAST** How does the description of Virginia Colony in the Primary Source pamphlet compare with descriptions of the Jamestown colony in the rest of the text?

3. **ANALYZE CAUSE AND EFFECT** What reasons might Native Americans have had for not cultivating tobacco on a large scale?

ANSWERS

1. Possible response: Archaeological excavations revealed that colonists fished and worked with wood. Science helped to reveal that accounts of "lazy colonists" could have been describing symptoms of malaria.

2. The pamphlet boasts of an abundance of land and waterfowl and fish, but the Jamestown settlers actually faced starvation. "Sweet springs" does not describe the marshy land and tainted water supply that the colonists experienced. There is also no mention that the colony was located on land inhabited by native peoples with whom conflicts arose.

3. Possible responses: Native Americans thrived during the drought that killed many colonists, so they likely grew food crops rather than tobacco. Native Americans likely had no trade partners interested in tobacco, so without a market they probably grew only enough for their tribe's consumption.

CREATING THE SPANISH EMPIRE

Legend has it that Hernán Cortés told the Aztec, "We Spanish have a disease of the heart that can only be cured by gold." Native Americans might have thought Cortés was speaking literally, judging by Spanish conduct toward them.

CORTÉS AND THE AZTEC

For several decades after they settled in the Americas, the Spanish faced little competition from other European powers. This allowed them to explore large parts of North and South America. Between 1513 and 1598, **conquistadors**, or Spanish soldiers and adventurers, set out from their settlements in the Caribbean bound for the mainland to claim more land and riches for Spain.

One of the most famous of the conquistadors was **Hernán Cortés**. Cortés journeyed to the Caribbean in 1504 and took part in the Spanish conquest of the island of Cuba in 1511. In 1519, he sailed to the mainland of North America, leading an army of fewer than 600 soldiers deep into the Aztec Empire. The army carried firearms and rode horses, neither of which the Native Americans had seen before. Along the way, the Spanish recruited allies from smaller Native American

Cortés displays his military strength to impress Moctezuma's ambassadors in this painting, *The Arrival of Cortés in Vera Cruz*. It was created in the late 17th century by an unknown artist and is one in a series of scenes of the conquistador's visit.

tribes that had been conquered and enslaved by the Aztec. These new soldiers spoke local languages and helped Cortés communicate with his now-diverse army.

Cortés and his men arrived in Tenochtitlán (tay-nohch-teet-LAHN), the Aztec capital, without opposition. The Aztec ruler, Moctezuma (mahk-tuh-ZOO-muh), received them warily but peacefully. This proved to be a mistake. The Spaniards quickly seized Moctezuma and took control of the city and empire through him. Cortés's men demanded gold and attacked the Aztec during a religious ceremony. The Aztec rebelled and, during the battle, many people lost their lives, including Moctezuma and a third of the Spanish troops. The Spanish retreated from the city and attempted to **besiege** it, cutting off its access to supplies and reinforcements.

The Aztec victory was short-lived, however. About a year later, the siege, coupled with an epidemic of European diseases, had weakened the Aztecs' ability to defend Tenochtitlán, and Cortés and his troops attacked and conquered the city. After that, Spain quickly took charge of Mexico and began its large-scale colonization, claiming new territories for itself outside of its national borders. The Spanish also began enslaving native populations. They called their lands in the Americas "New Spain."

PIZARRO AND THE INCA

Spanish conquistador Francisco Pizarro arrived in the Americas in 1502. By 1520, he was living prosperously in Central America, in what is now Panama, but he had greater ambitions. Over the years, Pizarro had heard stories of cities to the south that were constructed of gold and silver. Pizarro led exploratory voyages down the Pacific coast of South America, where he and his companions found convincing evidence of a wealthy civilization in the Andes Mountains, the **Inca Empire**. Pizarro set out in January 1531 with about 180 men and a small number of horses to conquer the land we know as Peru on behalf of Spain.

Fortunately for Pizarro, the Inca's powerful emperor had died around 1527. Historians believe he died of **smallpox**, a deadly, infectious disease introduced by Europeans that was spreading throughout the empire. Without their emperor, the Inca fell into a civil war. The epidemic and the war had greatly weakened the Inca before Pizarro arrived.

When Pizarro visited the city of Cajamarca (kah-hah-MAHR-kah) in 1532, an Inca leader named **Atahualpa** (ah-tah-WAHL-pah) agreed to a peaceful meeting. Atahualpa arrived at the meeting

accompanied by 3,000 unarmed soldiers. He hoped his show of force would discourage the Spaniard from attacking. Much like Moctezuma before him, Atahualpa was wrong to trust the Spanish.

After a brief discussion in the city square, Pizarro's men opened fire, killing many of Atahualpa's soldiers. The Spanish took Atahualpa prisoner and held him for ransom, demanding a massive amount of gold and silver. The Inca complied, but the Spanish killed Atahualpa anyway. Then they installed a puppet leader at the Inca capital of **Cusco** (KOOZ-koh), which sparked a rebellion that continued for decades. The Spanish did not achieve full control of Peru until 1572.

How was it possible for so few Spanish soldiers to bring down such huge empires as the Inca and the Aztec? The Spanish had a number of advantages over Native Americans. They had firearms, cannons, armor, and horses, which made their armies more effective in battle. Aztec and Inca weapons were no match for them. The Spanish were masterful at forming alliances with Native American groups. They recognized that both empires consisted of conquered peoples who were not loyal to the Inca or the Aztec. They also realized that the organization of the Inca government allowed for one leader to replace another quite easily. Much like the leadership of the U.S. government today, Inca leadership could change and not directly affect commerce or the lives of its citizens.

The biggest factor contributing to Spain's success, however, was disease. Smallpox and other European illnesses killed or weakened many thousands of Native Americans throughout the Americas, and these epidemics aided the Spanish in their conquests. Smallpox eventually killed about half of all the Inca. Throw in a little luck, military skill, and utter ruthlessness, and the conquistadors' achievements begin to make a little more sense.

HISTORICAL THINKING

1. **READING CHECK** What error did both Moctezuma and Atahualpa make upon first encountering the Spanish?

2. **IDENTIFY MAIN IDEAS AND DETAILS** What factors led to the Spanish conquests in the Americas?

3. **MAKE GENERALIZATIONS** How did the Spanish desire for gold affect the people of Central and South America?

PLAN: 2-PAGE LESSON

OBJECTIVE

Explore how the Spanish conquered the Aztec and Inca empires in their pursuit of land and resources.

CRITICAL THINKING SKILLS FOR LESSON 1.1

- Identify Main Ideas and Details
- Make Generalizations
- Analyze Visuals
- Make Inferences

HISTORICAL THINKING FOR CHAPTER 2

How were the North American colonies shaped by their geography and by the people who settled them? Before the founding of the British colonies, the Americas were colonized by the Spanish. Lesson 1.1 describes how the Spanish gained a foothold in the region—setting the stage for massive cultural change.

BACKGROUND FOR THE TEACHER

The number of people killed by the Spanish during their conquest of the Americas was documented in all its brutality by an eyewitness—Friar Bartolomé de las Casas. In his work *A Short Account of the Destruction of the Indies*, de las Casas reports that the killing began on the island of Hispaniola and was repeated throughout the region. The Spanish would plunder the populations' resources—such as food and gold—and then begin to enslave and slaughter the people—killing, maiming, and burning them without regard to age, gender, or condition. In one particularly vivid passage, de las Casas describes a "gibbets," a gallows used to hang native people while they were burned alive in honor of God. De las Casas estimated that of the hundreds of thousands of inhabitants on Puerto Rico and Jamaica, fewer than 400 remained after Spanish contact, a chilling preview to the fate of indigenous people in the Aztec and Inca empires.

INTRODUCE & ENGAGE

IMAGINE A CHANGED WORLD

Ask students to recall works of fiction—such as novels, films, or television programs—in which a force from another planet invades Earth. Discuss how and why an invading force might conquer a people, prompting students with questions such as: Why does the invading force come to Earth? How do the invaders control and conquer the population? Where do they concentrate their efforts? How do the lives and culture of Earth's people change under the control of the invaders? How do Earth's people resist? After a few minutes of discussion, tell students that Lesson 1.1 describes a very real and devastating invasion by the Spanish that forever changed the lives of Native Americans, who had little means to resist the armed invaders on horseback.

TEACH

GUIDED DISCUSSION

1. **Analyze Visuals** In the painting *The Arrival of Cortés in Vera Cruz*, how does the artist portray the differences in strength between the Spanish and Native Americans? *(Possible response: The painter shows the Spanish are more powerful by allotting them more space in the painting, emphasizing their numbers and weapons, and highlighting their ships and royal flags. In contrast, the painter portrays the Native Americans as a small group, barely visible off to one side, without impressive symbols of their culture.)*

2. **Make Inferences** What does the ability of the Spanish to make alliances with surrounding tribes tell us about the Inca and Aztec empires? *(Possible response: The Aztec and Inca were harsh conquerors themselves and were so hated by other tribes that these conquered people were willing to fight with the Spanish, another conquering people, to overthrow them.)*

MORE INFORMATION

Modern-Day First Contact First contact between native peoples and outsiders is still occurring today. Some indigenous tribes, such as the Mashco in Peru's Amazon jungle, were unaffected by the Spanish conquistadors and only now are making contact with outsiders. The Mashco are vulnerable to the same threats experienced by Native Americans in the 1500s, having little immunity to diseases such as measles, flu, or even the common cold. Illegal drug trafficking, logging, and other invasive activities are forcing them out of their native region. José Carlos Meirelles, who has managed first contact with tribes in Brazil, cautions that it often takes years to gain a tribe's trust. It is difficult to establish contact without destroying their culture or physical well-being, but the goal is to ensure "their entry in our world is less painful," than with other native peoples in past centuries.

ACTIVE OPTIONS

On Your Feet: Debate the Decline of the Aztec and Inca Organize the class into groups of four and instruct members to number off from one to four. Ask each group to think about and discuss a response to the following question: Was the decimation of the Aztec and Inca inevitable? After a time, call out a number, and ask the students with that number to report for the group.

NG Learning Framework: Develop Guidelines for First Contact

ATTITUDE Empowerment

SKILL Communication

Share the More Information feature with students. Then ask them to work in small groups to develop first-contact guidelines to prepare members of a technologically developed culture to meet for the first time with an isolated indigenous culture. Encourage students to conduct online research about first-contact work and to use their findings to create a training brochure or guidelines for those who initiate first contact. Ask students to consider the following issues: respecting groups' cultures, preventing disease, language barriers, avoiding misunderstandings, and creating trust. Invite groups to share their work with the class.

DIFFERENTIATE

ENGLISH LANGUAGE LEARNERS `ELD`

Use Word Parts Pair students at the **Emerging** or **Expanding** level with students at the **Bridging** level. Direct pairs to identify the parts of the vocabulary word *besiege* and use a dictionary to investigate the meanings. Instruct students to write one sentence using the word, and another using the root *(siege)*. You may have students make similar sentence pairs with the following words: *bedevil, belittle, befriend, begrudge, bemoan, bejeweled.* Suggest that as students encounter unfamiliar words, they use word parts, along with context clues, to determine word meaning.

PRE-AP

Form and Support a Thesis Have students review what they learned about the factors behind the Spaniards' swift conquest of indigenous Aztec and Inca peoples. Then instruct them to develop a thesis regarding why Europeans became more technologically advanced than Native American peoples. Tell students to conduct research using a variety of print and online sources and then write an essay supporting their thesis with primary and secondary sources. Encourage students to share their essays on a class or school blog.

See the Chapter Planner for more strategies for differentiation.

HISTORICAL THINKING

ANSWERS

1. Both leaders initially met peacefully with the Spaniards instead of driving them away.

2. The main factors were a combination of superior weapons and the use of horses, alliances between the Spanish and tribes hostile to the Aztec and Inca people, weaknesses within the Aztec and Inca governments, and the spread of European diseases that decreased native populations.

3. The Spanish desire for gold had a devastating effect on the people of Central and South America, many of whom were killed or enslaved during the Spanish quest for gold.

MAIN IDEA Spanish explorers in Central America pushed deeper into North America in search of new territories and riches, bringing their rigid political and class systems with them.

SPANISH RULE OF NORTH AMERICA

You've probably heard the old saying that fortune favors the bold. Spain's expeditions into North America were both bold and very dangerous, but if the explorers survived, fortune might be theirs. The same was not true of the people they encountered on their journeys.

SPANISH EXPEDITIONS MOVE NORTH

As Cortés and Pizarro were conquering Mexico and Peru, Spanish explorers undertook several expeditions farther to the north, entering parts of what would become the United States. **Juan Ponce de León** (PAWN-say day lay-OHN) was the first European to set foot in Florida. In 1513, he landed near modern-day St. Augustine before sailing south through the Florida Keys.

More than two decades later, in 1539, **Hernando de Soto**, the Spanish governor of Cuba, landed in Florida and led a three-year expedition through what is now the southeastern region of the United States to claim land and search for treasure. The explorers trekked as far north as the Tennessee River Valley. On their way back, they destroyed Native American villages and killed or enslaved the inhabitants. De Soto died of a fever on the trail in 1542.

Álvar Núñez (NOO-nyehz) **Cabeza de Vaca** became the first European to cross the American West. In 1528, his expedition shipwrecked on the Gulf Coast of what is now Texas. He and a few survivors lived among Native Americans for four years before they traveled across present-day Texas, New Mexico, and Arizona to reach other Spaniards in northern Mexico. Cabeza de Vaca published an account of his remarkable journey and worked to change Spain's policies toward Native Americans.

From 1540 to 1542, **Francisco Vásquez de Coronado** led a large military expedition from Mexico to explore what is now California and parts of the Southwest. Spanish authorities sent Coronado in search of the Seven Cities of Cíbola (SEE-boh-lah), a wealthy kingdom rumored to be located north of Mexico. Expecting to discover silver, gold, and other riches, Coronado only found Native Americans hostile to Spanish rule.

As Coronado's expedition wound down, **Juan Rodríguez Cabrillo** (kuh-BREE-yoh) sailed up the Pacific coastline in search of a northern water route connecting the Pacific and Atlantic oceans. His ships may have traveled as far as the Pacific Northwest before turning back, but Cabrillo never returned to Mexico. He was injured during a battle with Native Americans in 1543 and died of his wound.

In early 1598, **Juan de Oñate** (oh-NYAH-tay) headed north from Mexico on a mission of colonization. His party of soldiers, settlers, and Franciscan friars (Catholic missionaries) established a colony in what is now Santa Fe, New Mexico. From there, Oñate journeyed as far as present-day Kansas and the Gulf of California seeking riches, but, like Coronado, he came back empty-handed.

Franciscan friars, such as those who accompanied Oñate, played a big part in colonizing New Spain. They established missions where they provided Native Americans with food and shelter in exchange for labor and attempted to convert them to Christianity. By 1629, more than 25 churches existed in New Mexico. Friars also built missions from Florida west to the Gulf Coast and north into present-day southeast Georgia.

THE SPANISH SYSTEM

By 1650, the Spanish colonies in the Americas stretched from New Mexico and Florida in the north to Chile in the south. How was it possible for the Spanish crown to control this huge overseas empire?

The king of Spain was the ultimate authority. He was aided by the Council of the Indies, a group of advisors who regulated trade, appointed officials, and made laws in the colonies. Beginning in the 16th century, Spain's colonies in the Americas were divided into two **viceroyalties**: New Spain and Peru. New Spain included portions of Central and North America. Peru covered portions of South America. Each viceroyalty was ruled by a viceroy, who reported to the king.

This hierarchical system existed to expand the power and wealth of the Spanish crown, in part by enriching Spanish settlers. To exploit the labor of the Native Americans and to profit from the natural wealth of the Americas, the Spanish king granted conquistadors large tracts of farmland called **haciendas** (hah-see-EHN-dahz). A hacienda included a second grant, or **encomienda** (ehn-koh-mee-EHN-duh), that allowed owners to enslave a certain number of Native Americans to work the land. However, so many Native Americans died under the harsh conditions of the encomienda system that the Spanish began to import enslaved African people to replace them, though the Portuguese dominated the slave trade.

Spain dominated colonization in the Americas until 1588, when the British defeated the **Spanish Armada**, a fleet of warships sent by Spain to attack Britain. As a result, Spain's reputation as a major political power in the world diminished. Britain and other European countries took advantage of this change to start their own colonies in the Americas.

CRITICAL VIEWING Founded in 1720, Mission San José is the largest of five missions in San Antonio, Texas. What details do you observe about the architecture of this mission, and what does it suggest about the people who built it?

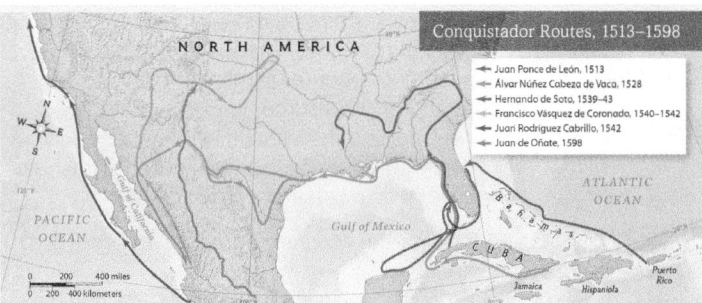

Conquistador Routes, 1513–1598

- Juan Ponce de León, 1513
- Álvar Núñez Cabeza de Vaca, 1528
- Hernando de Soto, 1539–43
- Francisco Vásquez de Coronado, 1540–1542
- Juan Rodríguez Cabrillo, 1542
- Juan de Oñate, 1598

HISTORICAL THINKING

1. **READING CHECK** What was Spain's ultimate goal in devising the viceroyalty and encomienda systems?

2. **DRAW CONCLUSIONS** Why do you think the Spanish were constantly exploring and attempting to colonize new areas?

3. **ANALYZE CAUSE AND EFFECT** How did the defeat of the Spanish Armada affect the colonization of the Western Hemisphere?

OBJECTIVE

Trace Spanish expeditions into North America and describe the Spanish colonial system.

CRITICAL THINKING SKILLS FOR LESSON 1.2

- Draw Conclusions
- Analyze Cause and Effect
- Evaluate
- Interpret Maps

HISTORICAL THINKING FOR CHAPTER 2

How were the North American colonies shaped by their geography and by the people who settled them? In the 16th century, the Spanish pushed northward, expanding their empire into what would become the United States. Lesson 1.2 describes the colonial system that the Spanish developed—a system that would eventually shape the region.

BACKGROUND FOR THE TEACHER

In 1493, Pope Alexander VI issued a document that became known as the Doctrine of Discovery, which included a key provision that set the foundation for European expansion in the Americas. The pope declared that any land not inhabited by Christians could be claimed by Christian rulers, providing justification for European conquest of the Americas. Over 300 years later, the doctrine was cited in a U.S. Supreme Court decision in which the federal government's exclusive right to claim land from Native Americans was upheld, arguing that the Native Americans were entitled to only a "right of occupancy," not land ownership. In modern times, indigenous groups and others have petitioned the Vatican to revoke the Doctrine of Discovery, yet it still remains in effect and has been cited in legal rulings made against Native Americans.

INTRODUCE & ENGAGE

BRAINSTORM NEXT STEPS

Write the following prompt on the board: After the Spanish initially conquered lands in the Americas, what next steps would you expect them to take? Work with students to brainstorm a list of steps, discussing the probability of each and how the Spanish might accomplish them. At the end of the discussion, inform students that this lesson describes two steps that the Spanish took next—acquiring wealth and land and increasing control over the peoples they conquered.

TEACH

GUIDED DISCUSSION

1. **Draw Conclusions** How did Spain profit from its northern expeditions? *(Possible response: Although Spain gained little in terms of wealth, it acquired more territory, learned about the interior of North America, encountered many Native American groups, and established missions in the Southeast and Southwest, extending Spain's power and influence into North America.)*

2. **Evaluate** What role did slavery play in the Spanish empire in North America? *(Slavery played a central role, with enslaved people providing the labor force in the colonies under the law of encomienda. The Spanish relied so heavily on enslaved labor that they imported enslaved people from Africa to replace enslaved native populations who died under their harsh rule.)*

INTERPRET MAPS

Direct students' attention to the map, Conquistador Routes, 1513–1598. **ASK:** Based on map details, which explorer likely encountered the most diverse terrain, climates, and Native American groups? Explain your answer. *(Álvar Núñez Cabeza de Vaca traveled the south coast of Cuba and along the western coast of Florida and the coast of the Gulf of Mexico, west through flat terrain and mountain ranges, and then south along the Gulf of California. His expedition would have endured high heat and humidity, wetlands and swamps, mosquitoes, desert conditions, mountainous trails, and lack of water. They likely encountered coastal, inland, and desert peoples with diverse economies and cultures.)*

ACTIVE OPTIONS

On Your Feet: Share Information About Spanish Colonization Use a Jigsaw configuration to organize students into "expert" groups and assign each a different aspect of the Spanish colonial system to research, such as the role of the viceroy, the lives of conquistadors, the lives of the Native Americans on the haciendas, or the work of missionaries. Then regroup students into new groups so that each new group has at least one member from each expert group. Students in the new groups take turns sharing information from their expert groups.

NG Learning Framework: Write a Report to the King

SKILLS Communication, Collaboration

KNOWLEDGE Our Human Story

Direct students' attention to the list of expeditions in the map. Point out that although Hernando de Soto died in 1542, his expedition ended when his men reached Mexico in 1543. Then divide the class into six groups, one for each expedition. Tell students to imagine that they must write a summary report to the king of Spain about the expedition. Ask them to conduct online research about the members of the expedition, the terrain they traveled, difficulties they faced, Native American groups they encountered, and the overall success of the mission. Instruct groups to divide and share research responsibilities and work together to assemble their report, which can include maps, illustrations, or quotes from primary sources. Invite groups to present their reports to the class.

DIFFERENTIATE

STRIVING READERS

Summarize Arrange students in pairs and tell them to read and summarize the text by writing at least three notes for each of the lesson's two subsections. After they have completed taking notes, guide students to review their notes and create a summary statement for each subsection. Then have students write a summary statement for the whole lesson.

PRE-AP

Create a Cause-and-Effect Chart Direct students to conduct online research on the encomienda system to better understand its causes and effects. Provide a Cause-and-Effect Chart for students to keep track of the reasons the system was instituted, its intended effects, and its actual impact. Encourage students to consider both economic and social causes and effects, such as intermarriage among Europeans and indigenous peoples. Invite students to share their charts with the class.

See the Chapter Planner for more strategies for differentiation.

HISTORICAL THINKING

ANSWERS

1. These hierarchical systems were meant to increase the Spanish crown's power and wealth in the Americas.

2. To the Spanish, more territory meant more natural resources, more labor to be exploited, and ultimately more subjects to serve the Spanish crown.

3. The defeat diminished the power and reputation of Spain, which gave other nations the opportunity to establish colonies in the Americas.

CRITICAL VIEWING Possible response: The variety of architectural features indicates a keen understanding of supporting structure and an appreciation for balance in design. The height of the bell tower, precision of the arches, height and extension of the walls, and symmetry of the dome suggest that the builders were skilled engineers and craftsmen.

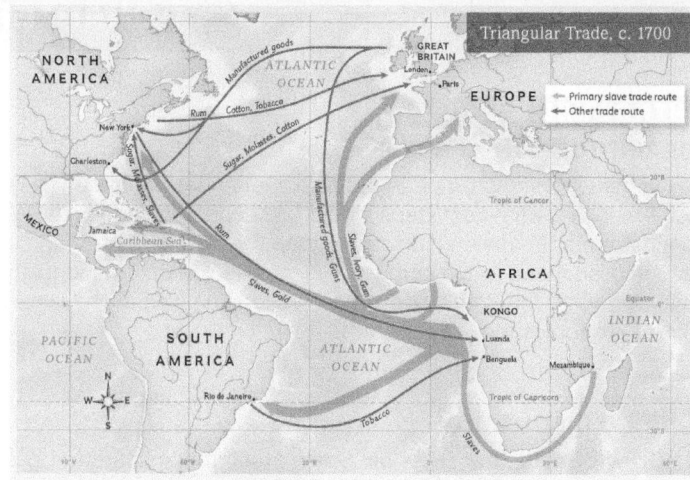
Triangular Trade, c. 1700

TRIANGULAR TRADE

Frederick Douglass, a former slave, once said, "No man can put a chain about the ankle of his fellow man without at last finding the other end fastened about his own neck." Those who benefited from the booming American slave trade, however, saw only wealth, not consequences.

THE PORTUGUESE SLAVE TRADE

To capitalize on the farms in the West Indies, hacienda owners forced enslaved Native Americans to work long hours under grueling conditions. Many of these Native Americans died. As a result, owners turned to slave traders from Portugal, who had been transporting kidnapped Africans since the 1440s.

For the Portuguese, the slave trade had been profitable since the 1480s. So many Africans were captured, traders had to build large forts along the West African coast to house them until they could be transported by ship. Slavery began on the islands of the Caribbean Sea around 1518. By the time the first documented enslaved African set foot on the mainland of North America, more than a million people were already in bondage throughout the European colonies of the Western Hemisphere.

This diagram of the lower deck of the British slave ship *Brookes* illustrates how 292 enslaved people were stowed, some under shelves, during their journey on the Middle Passage.

Meanwhile, in some areas of West Africa, the income generated from slavery rivaled that of other **commodities**, or products, of the region, including salt and gold. The demand for slaves required more traders to enter the business. Their raiders attacked villages in the African interior, marching their captives in chains to the slave forts. The trek was brutal, and only about half of those captured survived. From there, the enslaved were loaded onto ships bound for the Americas.

TRIANGULAR TRADE

As European colonies in the Americas began exporting resources and commodities across the Atlantic, a three-part trading route developed. Under this **triangular trade** system, ships exchanged goods from different continents and used the profits to fund the next leg of the journey. On the first leg, European ships carried textiles, firearms, gunpowder, iron, and brass to West Africa, where the items were sold to fund the purchase of enslaved Africans.

The second leg of the route, the infamous **Middle Passage**, transported captive Africans to the Americas. As the North American slave trade increased, slave ships shifted their primary ports from Central and South America to the West Indies. From there, enslaved people were transported to the English colonies on the mainland. Profits from North American slave markets were used to purchase goods to export to Europe—items that often depended on slave labor to produce. Once these goods reached Europe, the process began again.

As you can see from the map, trade across the oceans was not limited to this system. But for centuries, the main trade followed the triangular route that fueled it.

THE MIDDLE PASSAGE

The Middle Passage is referred to as "infamous" for good reason. The ships on that leg of the triangular trade route carried captives more than 5,000 miles from their homes and families. They had to survive brutal living conditions and starvation. The captives were chained to each other and to a floor of the hold below deck during the voyage. With 300 to 400 people crowded into a hold with only about three feet of headroom, there was little space to move. Ventilation was limited, and few ships were equipped to deal with human waste. Illnesses broke out often.

Approximately 10 percent of the captives who began the Middle Passage died of disease or despair before reaching the Americas.

During the four centuries of active Atlantic slave trading, ships carried more than 10 million people to the Western Hemisphere. Today, the removal of so many Africans from their homeland to the Americas is known as the **African diaspora**. The displaced Africans brought with them many traditions, which became the basis of a resilient culture that defied enslavement. Such spreading of traditions from one place to another is called **cultural diffusion**. Folktales such as the stories of Brer Rabbit and musical styles such as merengue are two examples of African traditions brought to the Americas and adapted by the descendants of the enslaved.

HISTORICAL THINKING

1. **READING CHECK** Why was the leg of the triangular trade route that transported slaves to the Americas called the Middle Passage?

2. **INTERPRET MAPS** What goods were exported from North America to Europe as part of the triangular trade system?

3. **DETERMINE CHRONOLOGY** How did the slave trade expand from Portugal, Spain, and their territories to the rest of the world?

PLAN: 2-PAGE LESSON

OBJECTIVE

Explore the development and impact of the triangular trade.

CRITICAL THINKING SKILLS FOR LESSON 1.3

• Interpret Maps

• Determine Chronology

• Summarize

• Make Inferences

• Analyze Language Use

HISTORICAL THINKING FOR CHAPTER 2

How were the North American colonies shaped by their geography and by the people who settled them? As the North American colonies grew, their economy increasingly relied on the importation of enslaved Africans. Lesson 1.3 examines the development of the triangular trade and the impact it had on both sides of the Atlantic.

BACKGROUND FOR THE TEACHER

Some Europeans opposed the slave trade even in the 1600s. One of them was Aphra Behn, a poet, novelist, and playwright who wrote a novel realistically portraying the brutality of slavery. Born in England, Behn traveled with her family to Surinam where she encountered African slaves for the first time. The experience is thought to be the basis for her work *Oroonoko: or, The Royal Slave*. The protagonist is the cultivated and intelligent West African prince Oroonoko, who is kidnapped by the English and brought to Surinam. His story gives Behn a chance to describe the inhumane treatment enslaved people endured and the heroic responses of those courageous enough to fight back. The novel, published in 1688, provided Europeans with one of the first positive characterizations of African people and helped to fuel the early movement to abolish the Atlantic slave trade.

INTRODUCE & ENGAGE

ACTIVATE PRIOR KNOWLEDGE

Draw a Word Web on the board and write the word *slavery* in the center. Ask students to associate words and phrases with the term, drawing on their knowledge of world history and the use of slavery in past civilizations. Discuss with them the different types of slavery they may have read or learned about. Then explain that this lesson describes how the Atlantic slave trade became one of the largest and most inhumane ventures in human history.

TEACH

GUIDED DISCUSSION

1. **Summarize** How did the Atlantic slave trade impact people on both sides of the Atlantic? *(Possible response: The slave trade created the African diaspora, breaking up families and causing a massive population loss. In the Americas, enslaved people influenced the culture of the colonies by bringing many traditions from Africa, including folktales and musical styles.)*

2. **Make Inferences** Based on the description of the Middle Passage, what can you infer about the people who survived it? *(Possible response: They likely had tremendous physical, mental, and emotional strength. Additionally, they may have formed bonds with one another, offering physical and psychological support to help each other survive.)*

ANALYZE LANGUAGE USE

Direct students' attention to the quote by Frederick Douglass in the lesson's introduction. **ASK:** How does Frederick Douglass use the word *chain* both literally and figuratively? *(Possible response: The literal meaning is a reference to the metal chains used to restrain enslaved people. The figurative meaning refers to the moral or ethical consequences for people engaged in the slave trade. Just as the slave cannot escape the physical chains, neither can the slave owner or trader escape having committed crimes in an immoral system.)*

ACTIVE OPTIONS

Active History: Analyze Primary Sources Extend the lesson by using either the PDF or Whiteboard version of the activity. These activities take a deeper look at a topic from, or related to, the lesson. Explore the activities as a class, turn them into group assignments, or even assign them individually.

NG Learning Framework: Document the Economics of Slavery

ATTITUDE Responsibility

KNOWLEDGE Our Human Story

Arrange the class in small groups and have students explore the economics of the triangle trade in the 1600s. Encourage students to conduct online and library research to find statistics for the number of slaves imported, expenditures for enslaved people, quantities of goods produced and traded, and types of companies involved (including manufacturers, insurance firms, banks, and investment firms) during this period. Suggest that students develop graphs and charts to display the data. Ask students to draw conclusions, based on their findings, about why it was difficult to outlaw the Atlantic slave trade. Invite representatives from each group to share their findings with the class.

DIFFERENTIATE

INCLUSION

Identify Diagram and Map Details Pair students with disabilities with students who can read the lesson aloud to them. Encourage the partner without disabilities to describe the slave ship diagram and the map in detail. When pairs have finished reading the lesson, you may want to have them work together to answer the Historical Thinking questions.

GIFTED & TALENTED

Prepare and Present an Oral History Tell students that of the millions of enslaved people who endured the Middle Passage, only a few left narratives of their experiences. Instruct students to conduct research using a variety of sources to discover details about the experiences of people such as Olaudah Equino and Venture Smith. Then have students select, prepare, and present a partial oral history or narrative to read to the class, prefacing their reading with information about the subject of the oral history.

See the Chapter Planner for more strategies for differentiation.

HISTORICAL THINKING

ANSWERS

1. It was called the Middle Passage because it was the second part of a three-part trading system that ran from Europe to Africa, from Africa to the Americas, and from the Americas to Europe.

2. Rum, cotton, tobacco, molasses, and sugar were transported from North America to Europe.

3. When too many enslaved Native Americans died, the demand for enslaved Africans in the Americas began to soar. Enslaved people became a commodity in the triangular trade, and the number of raiders capturing African people increased to meet the increasing demand. The system became so lucrative that it expanded to the rest of the world.

THE ENGLISH IN VIRGINIA

England soon followed Spain to the Americas. Hungry for gold, the first English colonists were blind to the true wealth of North America. In the end, it was the sale of tobacco, not precious metals, that filled the pockets of investors.

THE FOUNDING OF JAMESTOWN

During the late 15th and 16th centuries, England could not compete with Spain and Portugal in overseas exploration and colony building. The nation's attention was devoted to wars abroad and internal struggles. By the end of the 16th century, England had expanding agricultural and mining industries, land shortages, and an increasingly mobile population. These factors set the stage for England to challenge its rivals in the Americas.

England's first colonial venture in North America, a settlement on Roanoke Island in what would become North Carolina, took place in 1585. With the blessing of Queen Elizabeth I, English adventurer **Sir Walter Raleigh** sent about 100 settlers to Roanoke, but the settlers quickly realized that they lacked farming and fishing knowledge and returned to England. Raleigh organized a second attempt in 1587, but that colony was also abandoned.

In 1606, King James I awarded a **charter**, or a written grant of rights and privileges, to the Virginia Company to start a colony in North America. The Virginia Company was a **joint-stock company**, a business in which wealthy individuals pooled their money together and shared ownership. The company's investors hoped to find silver and gold and a viable trade route to Asia.

On April 26, 1607, three ships carrying about 105 colonists arrived at

Chesapeake Bay on the mid-Atlantic coast of North America. The group's leaders established a fort on an unoccupied peninsula at the mouth of what is now the James River. The swampy site had no spring to provide fresh water, and the surrounding river water was brackish, or salty. But here the colonists built Jamestown, England's first permanent settlement in the Americas. They named the surrounding land Virginia.

From the beginning, the colony was unstable. Relations with the local Native Americans, the Powhatan, were tense. The Powhatan resented the English intrusion on their territory, so they were not always interested in trading food with the settlers. Some of the early colonists did not have experience hunting, fishing, or farming, so they were often in need of supplies. Poor leadership, disease, and famine also kept the colony on the brink of failure.

On the grounds of Jamestown colony, a statue of John Smith faces the James River.

THE COLONY GAINS A FOOTING

In late 1608, Captain **John Smith** became leader of the colony, and circumstances began to improve. Smith had struck up a friendship with **Pocahontas**, the daughter of the Powhatan chief. This alliance helped Smith broker peace between the settlers and the Powhatan, who supplied food to Jamestown for the winter. Smith also required regular work, military training, and discipline for all the colonists. A year later, Smith was injured and, unfortunately for the colony, returned to England for good.

After Smith's departure, the Powhatan refused to supply food to Jamestown and attacked colonists who dared to leave the fort to hunt or forage. During the "starving time" in the winter of 1609–1610, the settlement's food ran out. When help from England finally came the following spring, only 60 of 500 colonists remained.

In the wake of Jamestown's almost total failure, a new leader, Thomas West, Lord Delaware, helped put the colony back on track. Just as important, the marriage of colonist **John Rolfe** and Pocahontas signaled a period of peace between the English and the Powhatan. Rolfe was a planter who had brought a new strain of tobacco to Virginia from the West Indies. The new tobacco sold well because of its sweet taste. In 1617, the colony shipped nearly 20,000 pounds of tobacco to England, stoking a demand in Europe. Rolfe's enterprise helped to raise the profits that Jamestown's English investors so desperately sought.

With a popular cash crop to back it up, the Virginia Company began to offer land in the colony to landless English farmers. The need for labor skyrocketed. The Virginia Company and then the planters themselves began to bring **indentured servants**, people who pledged to work for a period of four to seven years in exchange for ocean passage and necessities, to the colony.

The year 1619 brought two major institutions to Jamestown: slavery and a formal government. The colony's first slaves were African captives taken from a Portuguese ship by English raiders. That same year, the Virginia Company established the **House of Burgesses**, an assembly of elected delegates, or representatives, to help govern the colony. It was not a democracy. Only landowners could vote for delegates, a governor appointed by the English monarch could veto delegates' ordinances, and the Virginia Company chose more than a fifth of the delegates. The House of Burgesses was, however, the first form of representative government in English North America.

Ætatis suæ 21. A. 1616.

🏛 The National Portrait Gallery Washington, D.C.

In her portrait, Pocahontas wears the high lace collar and ornate clothing that was the fashion in England during the early 17th century. The painting was made while she and her husband visited England in 1616. Her clothing choice and the English name she took, Lady Rebecca Rolfe, indicate a desire to conform to European culture.

In March 1622, a surprise attack by Native Americans killed nearly one-third of the 1,240 Jamestown settlers in one day. In response, King James put the colony under direct British rule. Although its success as a business venture was decidedly mixed and it bears the stain of early slavery, the Jamestown colony is important as the first, lasting foothold of England in North America.

HISTORICAL THINKING

1. **READING CHECK** What disadvantages did the Jamestown colony have to overcome?

2. **IDENTIFY PROBLEMS AND SOLUTIONS** What difficulties plagued Jamestown settlers in the early years, and how could they have been avoided?

3. **COMPARE AND CONTRAST** How were English and Spanish colonies in the Americas similar and different?

PLAN: 2-PAGE LESSON

OBJECTIVE

Examine how England established a permanent settlement in North America and developed its first cash crop.

CRITICAL THINKING SKILLS FOR LESSON 2.1

- Identify Problems and Solutions
- Compare and Contrast
- Evaluate
- Analyze Cause and Effect

HISTORICAL THINKING FOR CHAPTER 2

How were the North American colonies shaped by their geography and by the people who settled them? The English chose a challenging site for their first settlement. Lesson 2.1 discusses the geographic obstacles Jamestown faced, its turbulent relations with Native Americans, and its economic salvation through the cultivation of tobacco.

BACKGROUND FOR THE TEACHER

The English were not the first European power to establish a colony in Virginia. Some eighty years earlier, the Spanish briefly settled the region, an undertaking which foreshadowed the problems the Jamestown settlement later faced. In 1526, a Spanish explorer founded a settlement which marked the first use of African slaves in what would become the mainland United States. The colony failed, but a second explorer, Pedro Menéndez de Avilés, arrived in the Chesapeake Bay area in 1565 and attempted to convert the Native Americans. In time, relations between the Spanish and the Powhatan devolved into direct violent conflict. Spain ultimately abandoned attempts to colonize Virginia, but the troubled relations between Native Americans and the ugly reliance on slavery would continue with the arrival of the English.

📄 HISTORY NOTEBOOK

Encourage students to complete the Reid on the Road video series page for Chapter 2 in their History Notebooks after they view the video.

INTRODUCE & ENGAGE

DISCUSS WHAT INVESTORS WANT

Ask students to suggest what investors might have expected for supporting a colonization effort, and write their ideas on the board. Students' responses might include the following: a quick return, huge profits, raw materials for export. Explain that since the English viewed colonization largely as a money-making enterprise, settlers were expected to establish relations and trade with locals and locate resources for export. Explain that in Lesson 2.1, the first English settlers quickly discovered how difficult it was to survive in an inhabited and unfamiliar location, let alone turn a profit for investors.

TEACH

GUIDED DISCUSSION

1. **Evaluate** What did investors fail to take into account when they financed voyages to settle North America? *(Possible response: They did not take into account colonists' potential troubles with establishing and sustaining the colony, dealings with Native Americans, and creating a revenue stream from found resources. Investors likely expected a quick return from gold and other resources for export.)*

2. **Analyze Cause and Effect** How did the West Indies colonies affect English colonization efforts in Virginia? *(Possible response: Tobacco from the West Indies gave Jamestown its first cash crop. This caused the Virginia Company to offer English farmers land in North America to increase the supply of tobacco.)*

VIRTUAL MUSEUM VISIT

The Smithsonian's National Portrait Gallery in Washington, D.C., authorized by Congress in 1962, contains the portraits of "men and women who have made significant contributions to the history, development, and culture of the people of the United States." Visitors to the website can search a large collection of items, including the portrait of Pocahontas, which was based on an engraving by Simon van de Passe. The artist made one error in copying the inscription beneath Pocahontas, identifying her husband not as John, but Thomas—which was the name of their son.

ACTIVE OPTIONS

On Your Feet: English Colonists Roundtable Arrange students in groups of four to discuss the following question: What advice would you give to English settlers as they prepared for their voyage to North America? Provide each group with a sheet of paper. The first student in each group writes an answer, reads it aloud, and passes the paper clockwise to the next student. Each student in the group adds at least one answer. Students circulate the paper around the table until they run out of ideas. Call on volunteers from each group to share their ideas.

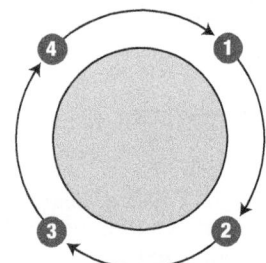

NG Learning Framework: Create an Infographic

SKILL Observation

KNOWLEDGE Critical Species

Organize students into four groups and assign each group one of the following topics about tobacco in the early years in Virginia: introduction and popularity, cultivation and processing, expansion and regulation as an industry, and impact on the economy and growth of Virginia. Tell students to conduct online research about their topic and create an infographic based on their findings. Encourage groups to include graphs or other visuals to represent data when appropriate and to display their infographic in the classroom. Use the completed infographics to discuss how the tobacco industry helped to shape areas surrounding Jamestown in the early years of English colonization.

DIFFERENTIATE

ENGLISH LANGUAGE LEARNERS ELD

Make Word Cards Tell students to use sticky notes to make word cards defining *joint-stock company*, *indentured servant*, and *delegate*, writing the term on one side and the definition on the other. Then pair students at **All Proficiencies** and have them take turns placing one of the sticky notes on the back of their partner, who then asks, "Who am I?" The first student provides clues, such as "You don't have much money," and the partner guesses whether the clue identifies a member of a joint-stock company, an indentured servant, or a delegate to the House of Burgesses.

PRE-AP

Analyze a Primary Source Invite students to access primary sources describing the "starving time" at Jamestown during the winter of 1609–1610, which can be found in online archives. Ask students to choose a short excerpt to analyze in terms of what it explains about the attitudes and experiences of early Jamestown settlers. Invite students to share their analysis with the class.

See the Chapter Planner for more strategies for differentiation.

HISTORICAL THINKING

ANSWERS

1. A location without fresh water and colonists who were inadequately prepared to hunt and fish were the colony's main disadvantages.

2. The colony was plagued by poor relations with the Powhatan and instability. Focused recruiting of leaders with proven skills at creating good relations with native peoples might have helped to establish a lasting friendship with the Powhatan. Colonists' ability to grow their own food or peacefully trade for food with the Powhatan could have prevented the high loss of life during the first winter at the settlement.

3. Possible response: Both English and Spanish colonies were established by nations seeking riches, both seized Native American lands and went to war with the tribes around them, and both used slave labor as their colonies grew. However, English colonies developed representative governments instead of the Spanish system of rigid hierarchies under the king.

UNCOVERING AMERICA'S BIRTHPLACE

"The American dream was born on the banks of the James River." — William Kelso

For years, most experts believed James Fort, the original fort built by the Jamestown colonists in 1607, had been washed away by the James River. But archaeologist William Kelso had his doubts. In 1994, he set out alone with his shovel to find signs of the triangular fort. After digging for just a few hours, he discovered an old trash pit containing glass beads, brass buttons, pottery shards, and copper scraps. His quest for Jamestown's buried truths was just beginning.

^ Kelso stands on the spot in the Jamestown church where Pocahontas, the daughter of Algonquian chief Powhatan, wed John Rolfe. According to Kelso, the church was the first major English church in the United States.

The 1607 map above depicts the Jamestown fort and settlement, with Chief Powhatan in the upper right. The lower left shows ships bringing settlers to the colony. On the right, an aerial photo shows a crooked row of grave sites uncovered by Kelso.

MAIN IDEA National Geographic Explorer William Kelso discovered evidence that has changed people's ideas about the Jamestown settlers.

EUREKA MOMENTS

Following his discovery, Kelso formed a team to excavate the Jamestown site. Within two years, they found evidence of a fort wall—earth stained dark by wooden posts that had decayed long ago. Kelso called that discovery "eureka moment number one."

Many more eureka moments followed. For more than 20 years, Kelso and his team have been excavating the site. They have identified evidence of all but one corner of the fort's structure. They also have discovered interior buildings, the settlement's first church, a well, several dump sites, and graves with human skeletons. The uncovered artifacts number more than a million.

REWRITING HISTORY

Kelso's discoveries have changed historical views of the Jamestown settlers. Some historians had portrayed the settlers as English noblemen who were unaccustomed to hard work. However, while reconstructing the fort using the kinds of materials and tools available to the settlers, Kelso discovered just how hard they had worked. He uncovered plenty of fishhooks and weapons as well as woodworking and glassmaking equipment. According to Kelso, "All of this flies in the face of conventional wisdom, which says that the colonists were underfunded and ill-equipped, that they didn't have the means to survive, let alone prosper. What we have found here suggests that just isn't the case."

During the winter of 1609–1610, called the "starving time," all but 60 of the 500 settlers died from starvation and disease. They resorted to eating rats, snakes, dogs, and shoe leather. But Kelso points out that a major drought occurred at that time, which would have dried up water supplies and killed crops.

Kelso hopes to uncover more about Jamestown. However, the sea level around Jamestown Island is rising. The river didn't wash away James Fort, but it's possible ocean water might. And Kelso believes the site is worth saving. He credits the settlers for developing a new form of government there when they organized a representative assembly about 1619. As Kelso says, "That's when liberty got out of the bag, and nobody could stuff it back in." Jamestown, Kelso insists, "is where America began."

HISTORICAL THINKING

1. **READING CHECK** What evidence has William Kelso uncovered on Jamestown Island?

2. **IDENTIFY MAIN IDEAS AND DETAILS** How has Kelso's work changed historians' views of the Jamestown settlers?

3. **DRAW CONCLUSIONS** How did the Jamestown settlers contribute to the development of American constitutional democracy?

PLAN: 2-PAGE LESSON

OBJECTIVE

Analyze archaeologist William Kelso's discoveries at Jamestown to uncover the true story of America's early settlers.

CRITICAL THINKING SKILLS FOR LESSON 2.2

- Identify Main Ideas and Details
- Draw Conclusions
- Ask and Answer Questions
- Interpret Visuals

HISTORICAL THINKING FOR CHAPTER 2

How were the North American colonies shaped by their geography and by the people who settled them? For years, experts believed that James Fort had been lost over time through erosion. Lesson 2.2 explains how archaeologist William Kelso's discoveries of a trash pit, a fort wall, and human graves began to reveal the true story of the early Jamestown inhabitants.

NATIONAL GEOGRAPHIC EXPLORER WILLIAM KELSO

In 2013, archaeologist William Kelso, along with historian James Horn and their team, discovered four bodies buried in Jamestown. To help identify the recovered remains and determine their connection to Jamestown, Kelso turned to high-tech forensic archaeology, including DNA analyses, CT scans, isotopic testing, and 3-D digital technology. After two years of research and analysis, the team identified the four men as Captain Gabriel Archer, an explorer; Reverend Robert Hunt, Jamestown's first minister; and two relatives of governor Thomas West: Sir Ferdinando Wainman, master of ordinance and horse troops, and Captain William West. Kelso was excited by the results. "We are talking about four of the first founders of English America from a crucial time in the history of the settlement."

HISTORY NOTEBOOK

Encourage students to complete the Explorer page for Chapter 2 in their History Notebooks as they read.

INTRODUCE & ENGAGE

DISCUSS HISTORIC SITES

Ask students to recall historic sites they know about or have visited. Prompt them to share stories or facts they remember about the sites, and then discuss why it might be important to verify the history of a site rather than simply to accept commonly held beliefs about it. Then explain that Lesson 2.2 describes how William Kelso's archaeological work is rewriting the story of the Jamestown settlement and its members.

For students who develop an interest in the Jamestown settlement, suggest that they read the American Story located at the beginning of this chapter.

TEACH

GUIDED DISCUSSION

1. **Draw Conclusions** Why are trash pits like the one at the Jamestown site an important find for archaeologists? *(Possible response: Trash pits usually contain many artifacts, food remains, and other debris that can tell archaeologists a great deal about the members of a community, including what they ate and how they lived.)*

2. **Ask and Answer Questions** What questions might you want to ask about the Jamestown site, and how would you find answers to them? *(Answers will vary. Possible responses: Who else is buried at the site? Are they male or female, young or old? Are Native Americans buried there? Is there evidence of battles between the settlers and Native Americans? Online research into current developments at the site might answer some of these questions.)*

INTERPRET VISUALS

Direct students' attention to the map in the lesson and have them study its details. **ASK:** How might the map have helped Kelso in his archaeological work at the site? *(Possible response: It likely gave him an idea of the shape and size of the fort, where buildings were located, and how close to the river the fort might be.)* **ASK:** What important features did Kelso and his team find that are not depicted on the map? *(the trash pits or dump sites and the burial sites)* **ASK:** Why might settlers have built the fort's gate where they did? *(The gate faces the river, so supplies from ships could easily be brought into the fort.)*

ACTIVE OPTIONS

On Your Feet: Question and Answer Tell half the class to write True-False questions based on the information about Jamestown and Kelso's discoveries. Tell the other half to create answer cards, with "True" written on one side and "False" written on the other. Then ask students who wrote questions to read them aloud. Direct students in the second group to respond by holding up either "True" or "False." When discrepancies occur, review the question and the text and discuss which answer is correct. After all questions are answered, if time permits, have groups reverse roles.

NG Learning Framework: Hold a Job Fair for Forensic Archaeology   **STEM**

SKILL Communication

KNOWLEDGE New Frontiers

Share the National Geographic Explorer information with students. Tell students to work in small groups to research the forensic archaeology field by conducting library and online research and, if possible, by interviewing people who work in the field. Then ask students to choose a technology to focus on, such as 3-D digital technology, DNA analysis, or CT scans, and investigate how that technology is used and its required training. Tell groups to use their findings to create a poster presentation of the technology they have chosen. Encourage students to include photographs of the equipment used and examples of test or analysis results. Invite groups to display their posters in the setting of a job fair of forensic technology careers.

DIFFERENTIATE

STRIVING READERS

Connect Details to a Main Idea Instruct students to work in pairs to complete a Main-Idea Diagram. Elicit the kinds of details (facts, dates, events, descriptions) that often support a main idea. Tell students to take turns reading the lesson, pausing after each paragraph to record relevant details, adding more boxes if necessary. Then have pairs work together to write a main-idea statement supported by the details.

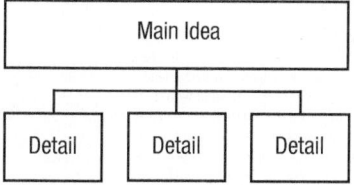

GIFTED & TALENTED

Illustrate a Quotation Direct students' attention to the implied metaphor in Kelso's statement, "That's when liberty got out of the bag, and nobody could stuff it back in." Challenge students to interpret Kelso's words visually. For example, they may draw a cartoon, or use a computer graphics program to create a meme that incorporates words or phrases from the quotation. Ask students to present their visual interpretations to the class and explain why they chose the style and images they did.

See the Chapter Planner for more strategies for differentiation.

HISTORICAL THINKING

ANSWERS

1. Kelso found remains of the fort's structures, uncovered interior buildings, the first church, a well, dump sites, over a million artifacts, and a burial site.

2. Historians previously thought the settlers were noblemen unused to hard labor, but Kelso uncovered evidence that the colony had skilled laborers and possessed the tools, equipment, and weapons needed to survive and prosper.

3. The settlers developed a new form of representative government, which allowed some members of the colony to govern its affairs.

FRENCH AND DUTCH COLONIES

Nobody likes to feel left out. At the turn of the 16th century, Spain and Portugal were far ahead of most other nations in exploration and colonization. When England got into the game, France and the Netherlands wanted in, too.

THE FRENCH FUR TRADE

While the English were turning their first North American colony into a large-scale agricultural settlement, French activity in the Americas focused on trading with Native Americans—especially in furs. This angle was virtually assured in 1582 when a French ship returned from North America with a cargo of furs that earned a 1,500 percent profit. More ships quickly followed.

In 1608, **Samuel de Champlain** established a base at Quebec, which means "the place where the river narrows" in Algonquian. As it turned out, Quebec was an ideal location for controlling what would become the Canadian interior. For almost 20 years, Champlain went about his business, acquiring furs and establishing good relationships with his Native American trading partners. He even went so far as to fight personally alongside France's Algonquian and Huron allies in conflicts with their enemies. His actions helped cement alliances between **New France** and various Native American nations. These alliances, in turn, earned the French access to valuable fur sources much farther to the west.

Quebec was still essentially a trading post with only a few hundred French inhabitants in 1627. In that year, the Company of New France, a joint-stock company, was established with Champlain as a member. The company's royal charter included total control of trade in the Americas, a requirement that 200 to 300 settlers be brought over each year, and the exclusion of Huguenots, a sect of French Protestants. As the ruler of a Roman Catholic nation, the French king frowned on Protestants, whom he considered to be heretics. **Heretics** are people who disagree with the established teachings or beliefs of a particular religion.

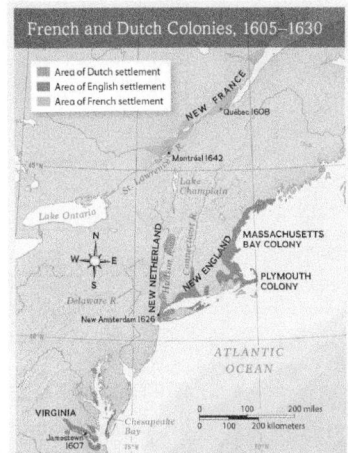

French and Dutch Colonies, 1605–1630

The city of Montreal, about 140 miles inland from Quebec along the St. Lawrence River, was founded in 1642, but the population of this settlement was also very slow to increase. The French king only allowed Catholics to settle there, and land distribution policies required most colonists to work for landowners instead of becoming landowners themselves. Consequently, peasants living in France saw little chance of improving their lives by moving to North America. France also sent missionaries to Native American villages in New France to learn their languages and traditions in hopes of converting them to Catholicism.

In 1663, when the crown dissolved the company, New France had only 2,500 inhabitants. However, it boasted a well-organized administration, along with schools and hospitals. The fur trade brought French colonists west into the Great Lakes region of New France, where their interactions with Native Americans were mostly friendly. The French set up trading posts and missions on the Upper Peninsula of Michigan. From there in 1673, Frenchmen Louis Jolliet and Jacques Marquette explored parts of Wisconsin and Illinois and navigated the Mississippi River as far south as present-day Arkansas.

NEW NETHERLAND

During the 16th century, the Netherlands had become an economic powerhouse. The Dutch—the people of the Netherlands—based their economy on the fishing and shipping industries. In 1609, the Dutch East India Company hired English seafarer Henry Hudson to search for the elusive northwestern route to Asia. Upon reaching the shore of North America, Hudson sailed 150 miles up what is now the Hudson River to present-day Albany, New York. Along the way, he traded for furs with local Native Americans. Trading was so lucrative that the Dutch established a post in the area, called Fort Nassau, in 1614.

In 1621, the Dutch government chartered the Dutch West India Company to trade and set up colonies in North America. In 1624, the company established **New Netherland** on Governors Island, just off the tip of what the Lenape—the Native American inhabitants of the region—called Manna-hata Island. The Dutch originally thought the tiny island would be easier for settlers to manage than the much larger Manna-hata. Soon, however, they were ready to expand.

A legend claims New Netherland leader Peter Minuit purchased Manna-hata, which we now know as Manhattan, in 1626 for $24 (60 Dutch guilders). The purchase, however, is not well documented. True or not, the result was plagued with misunderstanding. While the Dutch may have believed they owned the island outright, the Lenape believed they had only sold the Dutch the rights to share the land. Several years later the misunderstanding erupted into war.

Nevertheless, the colony's capital, **New Amsterdam** (present-day New York City), was built on this island. In the following years, food and lumber production and the fur trade aided in expanding the economy, and Dutch colonists began to move north and settle in the Hudson River Valley.

CRITICAL VIEWING A Native American man offers a pelt to a trapper in this print made by Jean-Adolphe Boquin in the 1870s. What does this print suggest about the relationship between these individuals?

HISTORICAL THINKING

1. **READING CHECK** How did Samuel de Champlain prove himself to France's Native American allies?

2. **FORM AND SUPPORT OPINIONS** Why do you think the French were successful in their commercial ventures in North America?

3. **INTERPRET MAPS** How many years separated the founding of Quebec, Jamestown, and New Amsterdam?

PLAN: 2-PAGE LESSON

OBJECTIVE

Discuss the motivations behind and impacts of the North American colonies of France and the Netherlands.

CRITICAL THINKING SKILLS FOR LESSON 2.3

• Form and Support Opinions

• Interpret Maps

• Summarize

• Draw Conclusions

HISTORICAL THINKING FOR CHAPTER 2

How were the North American colonies shaped by their geography and by the people who settled them? In the 1600s, France and the Netherlands launched their own colonial efforts in North America. Lesson 2.3 explores the motivations of the settlers and the characteristics of these colonies.

BACKGROUND FOR THE TEACHER

Slavery existed among Native American tribes in what is now the United States and Canada long before the arrival of European colonists. Indigenous peoples often enslaved men, women, and children captured in war as a way to boost tribal numbers and deal with vanquished enemies. However, with the arrival of Europeans, the indigenous slave trade accelerated. Tribes traded enslaved people to European settlers, and as a way to acquire greater numbers of slaves, Europeans were not above inciting wars among tribes as well as capturing and enslaving native North Americans on their own. Enslaving indigenous people became central to the early economy of England's southern colonies, and indigenous people constituted two-thirds of those enslaved in Canada for 150 years.

FINANCIAL LITERACY

To extend their knowledge and understanding about the concepts in this lesson, refer students to the Financial Literacy handbook.

INTRODUCE & ENGAGE

K-W-L CHART

Lead students in a discussion to brainstorm what they already know about French and Dutch exploration and their settlements in North America. Ask them to record their knowledge in the first row of a K-W-L chart. Then ask students to write questions they would like to have answered as they study Lesson 2.3. Allow time at the end of the lesson for students to complete the K-W-L Chart with what they have learned.

TEACH

GUIDED DISCUSSION

1. **Summarize** What role did the monarchy play in shaping the development of French colonies? *(The king had a direct influence on the number and types of settlers who came to North America. He allowed only Catholics, not Protestants, and required peasants to work for landowners rather than own land themselves. These policies discouraged emigration from France, slowed the growth of settlements, and made the French colonies less religiously diverse than those of England.)*

2. **Draw Conclusions** Why do you think relationships between Europeans and native North Americans were often violent? *(Possible response: Because the two cultures had fundamentally different ideas about things such as private property, misunderstandings were inevitable. In addition, European settlers were driven by profit and religious conversion, and they viewed native North American tribes as expendable and culturally inferior.)*

MORE INFORMATION

Inaccurate Depiction of Native Americans Tell students that the print by Jean-Adolphe Boquin depicting a trapper trading with Iroquois tribesmen (identifiable by their distinctive headdresses) contains a major inaccuracy. Ask volunteers to offer suggestions about what the inaccuracy might be. Then point out and discuss Boquin's inclusion of tepees in the background, which were not used by the Iroquois but by Plains Indians. Explain that the Iroquois lived in permanent longhouses built of wood, and that the name they called themselves, Haudenosaunee, means "People of the Long House." Discuss with students other inaccuracies and stereotypes connected with ideas about Native Americans, such as depictions found in movies, artwork, and commercial or sports logos.

ACTIVE OPTIONS

On Your Feet: Discuss the French and Dutch Colonies Arrange students in an Inside-Outside Circle configuration. Allow students time to write questions about the French and Dutch colonies. Ask them to focus their questions on the motivations, challenges, and successes of the two groups in establishing colonies in North America. Then tell students in the inside circle to pose questions to students in the outside circle. Have students switch roles. Students may ask for help from other students in their circle if they are unable to answer a question.

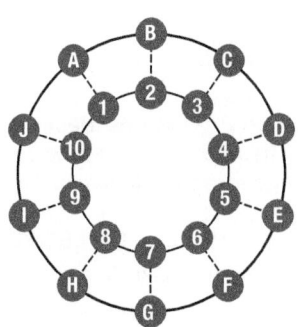

NG Learning Framework: Compare and Contrast North American Colonies

SKILL Communication

KNOWLEDGE Our Human Story

Arrange students in small groups and ask them to create a chart summarizing the similarities and differences among the Spanish, English, French, and Dutch colonies in the following categories: settlement patterns, demographics, economy, government, and relations with Native Americans. Encourage students to conduct online research as needed to supplement information in the text. Invite students to display their charts on a class website or around the classroom.

DIFFERENTIATE

INCLUSION

Describe a Historical Drawing Pair students who are visually impaired with students who are not. Ask the latter to describe in detail the print by Jean-Adolphe Boquin, focusing on the men's clothing, stances, and facial expressions. Then have the students read the caption and answer any questions their partners may have. You may also have pairs discuss the point of view conveyed by the drawing as well as inaccuracies in the background images outlined in the More Information section.

PRE-AP

Analyze Cross-Cultural Trade Relationships Ask students to reflect on the relationship between Native Americans and the French in the early years of the North American fur trade. Then direct them to conduct online research about present-day trade activities among diverse cultures. Assign a moderator and have students hold a panel discussion in which they discuss the similarities between present-day and early 17th-century trade relationships and analyze their impact on cross-cultural interactions.

See the Chapter Planner for more strategies for differentiation.

HISTORICAL THINKING

ANSWERS

1. Champlain proved to be a good trading partner with Native Americans and fought alongside the Huron and Algonquin against their enemies.

2. Answers will vary. Possible responses: Cultivating relationships with Native Americans was key to the success of the French. This allowed them to partner with a group familiar with the geography, which likely helped them learn where to hunt to acquire valuable furs.

3. Only one year separated the founding of Jamestown (1607) and Quebec (1608), but New Amsterdam (1626) was founded 19 years after Jamestown.

CRITICAL VIEWING Possible response: One Native American sits on the ground, and the European trader's gun rests along his side, suggesting that the individuals are at ease with one another. The men appear to be engaged in a transaction, which suggests a mutually beneficial trade relationship.

NEW ENGLAND

Have you ever felt so fed up with a situation that you just wanted to walk away and leave it all behind? Throughout their persecution by the English authorities and the Church of England, the Puritans held fast to their beliefs—even to the point of leaving their homes forever.

THE PLYMOUTH COLONY

While Jamestown was an almost purely commercial endeavor, the founding of New England had an added motivation: religious freedom. After King Henry VIII broke from the Roman Catholic Church and established the Church of England in 1534, different types of Christian worship became an increasingly troubling issue in England. The Church of England retained many elements of Catholicism. Puritanism, a Protestant movement in England in the late 16th and

17th centuries, sought to "purify" Christian worship by deleting these practices. Because of their beliefs and active opposition to the Church of England, Puritans were considered religious **dissenters**, or rebels. As such, they faced government persecution, including fines and imprisonment.

One group of Puritan dissenters, whom we now refer to as the Pilgrims, were **separatists** who believed that leaving England and its official church behind

was their only option. In September 1620, about 100 men, women, and children set sail for Virginia on the *Mayflower*. The voyage went astray, however, and the ship landed near what today is **Plymouth**, Massachusetts, more than 200 miles north of the original destination. Once they decided to found their colony there, the Pilgrims drafted the **Mayflower Compact**, a pledge signed by all of the adult males to establish a government and obey the laws and regulations that were subsequently enacted.

The colonists chose as a settlement site a Native American village abandoned by the Pawtuxet after a recent epidemic had killed most of the inhabitants. There, the Pilgrims endured their first winter, which only about half of them survived. **Squanto**, an English-speaking Pawtuxet, translated for the Pilgrims and helped them plant crops the following year. Historians believe Squanto had been kidnapped as a youth by English seafarers and taken to England, where he learned the language. He returned to North America years later. The colonists commemorated the 1621 harvest with three days of celebration shared with the area's Pokanoket people, with whom Squanto lived.

Governor **William Bradford** and military leader Myles Standish helped establish the Plymouth colony, maintaining order and keeping peace with the Pokanoket. Bradford served as governor for 30 years. He championed democratic institutions and acted as a stabilizing influence for the community. This stability, coupled with the colonists' hard work and thrift, helped the colony become self-sustaining by 1624. Although the Plymouth colony's success continued and its population reached about 2,000 by the mid-1640s, it remained separate from the other English dissenter colonies that soon began to spring up in New England.

THE MASSACHUSETTS BAY COLONY

Another group of dissenting Puritans arrived in 1630 and established the **Massachusetts Bay Colony**. Unlike the separatist Pilgrims, this colony's leaders sought to reform the church through their pious example, which they hoped would one day be taken up back in England. In the words of leader

Pilgrim Hall Museum
Plymouth, Massachusetts

Exhibits in Pilgrim Hall, the nation's oldest continuously operating public museum, tell the founding story of the United States. This wooden sculpture of Squanto from the 19th century forms part of the museum's collection. It shows what one artist imagined the Native American guide might have looked like.

John Winthrop, the colony would be "as a Citty upon a Hill, the Eyes of all people are uppon us . . . wee shall be made a story and a byword through the world."

The Massachusetts Bay Company obtained a charter from King Charles I that specified the colony's government and boundaries. The charter called for a governor, a deputy governor, and an executive board of 18 delegates to be elected by freemen, or company stockholders. Together, they would meet in a legislative body called the General Court to make laws and regulations, appoint lower officials, grant lands, and punish lawbreakers. The colony's leaders changed the rules, however, to allow all male church members, not just stockholders, to become freemen. In theory, every freeman would be a member of the General Court. But as the population grew and towns formed quickly, freemen voted in town meetings for representatives to the assembly.

According to their religious beliefs, the colony's founders thought if they maintained a moral society, God would help the colony prosper. To promote this end, church leaders dominated the government and took steps to guarantee their power. Laws required residents to attend Puritan church services, and, even though the Puritans were themselves dissenters from the Church of England, dissenters from Puritan beliefs were punished, often quite harshly.

Following English tradition, Puritan society in New England was strictly hierarchical. In the family, a husband was superior to his wife, and the children obeyed their parents. In general, Puritan women saw themselves not as individuals with rights equal

AMERICAN PLACES
Plimoth Plantation

Founded in 1947, Plimoth Plantation is a living museum in Plymouth, Massachusetts, that provides an experience of life in colonial America in 1620. Interpreters in period clothing answer visitors' questions and demonstrate how the colonists lived.

PLAN: 4-PAGE LESSON

OBJECTIVE

Examine how English Protestants' desire for religious freedom helped to create new colonies and new forms of government in North America.

CRITICAL THINKING SKILLS FOR LESSON 2.4

- Compare and Contrast
- Draw Conclusions
- Identify Main Ideas and Details
- Make Inferences
- Make Connections
- Evaluate
- Analyze Primary Sources

HISTORICAL THINKING FOR CHAPTER 2

How were the North American colonies shaped by their geography and by the people who settled them? Some people came to New England seeking religious freedom. Lesson 2.4 examines how Puritan settlers influenced the cultures and governments in Massachusetts, Connecticut, and Rhode Island.

BACKGROUND FOR THE TEACHER

The Plymouth Pilgrims and the Puritans of Massachusetts Bay were marked by key social, economic, and religious divergences. The small group of Pilgrims were largely working people without an ordained minister to lead them. Puritans were generally of a higher social status, more educated and wealthy, and brought ordained clergy to lead them. Plymouth's Mayflower Compact stated that elected officials and members of the colony were all bound by the same rules, giving the colony a degree of democracy. In Puritan society, leaders were accountable to God, not the people—an order with a tinge of theocracy. Indeed, while Puritan clergy held no official political authority, they exerted great influence on the state. In Pilgrim society, however, there was a more complete separation of church and state functions. Interestingly, the ideas of the poorer, working-class Pilgrims would turn out to have more influence on the emerging country.

INTRODUCE & ENGAGE

DISCUSS GROUPS THAT HAVE SPLIT

Invite students to share an example of a group with common beliefs or interests that eventually split into different factions. It could be a group in school, in the neighborhood or city, or with national connections. Have students describe what differences arose and how the group changed as a result. Chart students' responses on the board in an organizer such as the one shown. Then tell students that Lesson 2.4 explains how groups with religious differences profoundly influenced the founding and development of the New England colonies.

Common Beliefs/Interests	Differences That Arose	Resulting Change

TEACH

GUIDED DISCUSSION

1. **Identify Main Ideas and Details** What factors helped the Plymouth Colony succeed more quickly than other colonies? *(Possible response: Members had a shared system of beliefs and a common purpose, were made up of intact families, were helped by Native Americans, and benefited from strong leadership and rules of government that they agreed upon.)*

2. **Make Inferences** Why do you think the Massachusetts Bay colonists changed the rules in their charter about who could vote? *(Possible response: The settlers were no longer subject to constant scrutiny under British law and may have wanted more people to have a say in their government. They could have accomplished this either through their own vote or through electing representatives.)*

3. **Make Connections** In what ways did the colonists maintain English traditions in North America? *(Possible response: The English maintained a strictly hierarchical society and family structure. They viewed women as unequal to men, and they punished dissenters harshly.)*

VIRTUAL MUSEUM VISIT

The mission of Pilgrim Hall Museum, founded in 1820, is to "achieve worldwide awareness of the Pilgrims' significance as an enduring narrative of America's founding." It contains artifacts of both Pilgrim settlers and Native American groups. A tour of the museum provides guests with examples of the Pilgrims' letters, wills, and journals; their biographies; details of the Thanksgiving story; and pictures of items carried on the original *Mayflower*. Encourage students to work in groups to visit the museum's online collection and exhibits, select an area of interest about which to gather information, and then share their findings with the class.

DIFFERENTIATE

ENGLISH LANGUAGE LEARNERS

Create Words with Suffixes Bring students' attention to the word *separatist*. Explain that adding the suffix *-ist* creates a new word that refers to a person who practices or is associated with the action or principle of the root word. Elicit that, in this case, *separatists* were people who separated themselves from the Church of England. Have students at **All Proficiencies** work in pairs to add the suffix *-ist* to *real, survival, ideal, terror, novel, reform, and archaeology*. Discuss with students dropping the final *y* in *archaeology* before adding the suffix. Then tell them to discuss the meaning of each new word, using a dictionary as necessary, and write a sentence using it.

GIFTED & TALENTED

Write a Blog Post Challenge students to conduct online research to find information about the lives of specific Puritan women. Have students use what they learn to write a blog post in the voice of one woman whose story particularly interests them. Tell them to include the woman's age, daily activities, goals, obstacles, and vision for the future. Encourage students to include relevant letters, artifacts, or visuals that exemplify women's roles in Puritan society. Invite volunteers to post their work or present it to the class.

See the Chapter Planner for more strategies for differentiation.

The Fundamental Orders of Connecticut in 1639 was based on a sermon given by Thomas Hooker. The order joined together three settlements along the Connecticut River under one government. This document is essentially the first written constitution in North America. This excerpt includes 5 of the 11 orders presented in the document.

1. It is Ordered . . . that there shall be yearly two General Assemblies or Courts.

4. It is Ordered . . . that no person be chosen governor above once in two years.

5. It is Ordered . . . that to the aforesaid Court of Election the several Towns shall send their deputies.

7. It is Ordered . . . that . . . the Constable or Constables of each Town shall . . . give notice distinctly to the inhabitants of the same.

10. It is Ordered . . . that every General Court . . . shall consist of the Governor . . . and four other Magistrates.

to those of men, but as part of a community and a family, with duties determined by their gender and age. Aside from raising children, women's duties were many and important: keeping the house and garden; preserving fruits and vegetables; making cider, cheese, and butter; tending livestock; making cloth and sewing clothes; and more. The role of Puritan women in the church, where they were expected simply to listen and keep quiet, was indicative of their place in society. But they also were expected to administer a religious education to their children, and in that way, they were the spiritual equals of men.

CONNECTICUT AND RHODE ISLAND

By the mid-1640s, the Massachusetts Bay Colony had grown to more than 20,000 inhabitants, but not all of these residents were content with the colony's strict religious principles. In 1633, Puritan preacher **Thomas Hooker** arrived in Massachusetts Bay Colony and became a minister in the town of Newtown (later Cambridge). Hooker and his congregation weren't comfortable under the established Puritan leadership and migrated to the Connecticut River Valley to establish the town of Hartford. In 1639, prominent Hartford residents drafted a government framework called the **Fundamental Orders of Connecticut.** This influential document did not require church membership for voting and empowered voters

to elect both the legislature and the governor. Most important to the residents, it helped cement Connecticut's status as its own colony, independent of the authorities in the Massachusetts Bay Colony.

The founding of Rhode Island, too, resulted from unhappiness with the way the Massachusetts Bay Colony was governed. Minister **Roger Williams** arrived in Massachusetts in 1631. Williams's beliefs led him to openly criticize the Puritan establishment. First, he claimed that the colony rested on stolen property because the English king had no right to give away land that already belonged to Native Americans. Next, he attacked laws requiring church attendance as well as those that granted tax support for Puritan churches.

For his subversive, or rebellious, views, Williams was banished from Massachusetts Bay. In 1636, he established the settlement of Providence on land purchased from the Narragansett people. His settlement's policies of separation of church and government and religious tolerance, or allowing all people to freely practice their religion or beliefs, made Providence a destination for a variety of Christian dissenters.

One of these dissenters, **Anne Hutchinson,** accused Massachusetts Bay ministers of straying from accepted Puritan theology. She challenged the idea that understanding the Bible required the interpretation of ministers. This dispute was all the more serious to colony leadership because it came from a woman. Like Williams, Hutchinson was banished from Massachusetts Bay. With Williams's help, she and a group of supporters established a settlement they named Portsmouth on Narragansett Bay. Eventually, these settlements secured a charter, and Portsmouth and Providence united with nearby communities at Newport and Warwick to form the colony of Rhode Island.

CONFLICTS WITH NATIVE AMERICANS

During the 1600s, the colonial population grew, and settler communities spread across New England. As colonists sought to control and exploit an expanding share of territory and resources, Native Americans resented being pushed off their lands. The **Pequot War** of 1636–1637 was fought between the Pequot nation and an allied force of English colonists and other Native Americans. Throughout the war, colonists sold captured Pequot as slaves to other Native American tribes or to plantation owners in the West Indies. The largest battle involved a massacre of the Pequot, including women, children, and old men. The treaty to end the conflict led to the downfall of the Pequot nation.

CRITICAL VIEWING This woodcut of a Native American fort served as an attack plan in the final battle of the Pequot War in May 1637. What does this artwork reveal about this historical event?

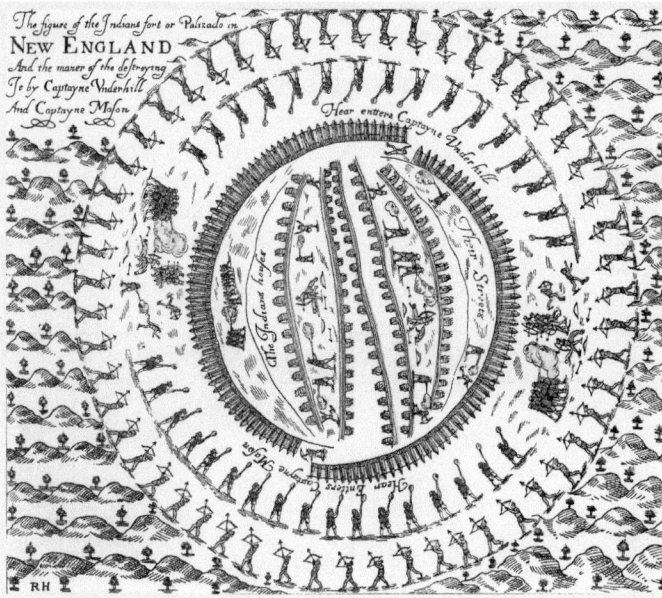

In the decades that followed the Pequot War, an uneasy peace prevailed between Native Americans and European colonists in New England. More than 50,000 Europeans settled in the region, occupying hunting, fishing, and agricultural lands of Native Americans. Resentments soon resurfaced. In 1671, colonists forced the Wampanoag nation to surrender its guns. Killings and retaliations followed. Wampanoag leader **Metacom** (known as King Philip in English) assembled raiding parties of Wampanoag and their Algonquian allies and attacked towns throughout New England. Colonial troops responded in kind. They also took this opportunity to attack their longtime allies, the Narragansett, whose land they sought to acquire. These battles came to be called **King Philip's War.**

In the end, about 600 colonial soldiers died in the conflict. Seventeen colonial towns were destroyed (including Providence, Rhode Island, which burned

in 1676), and roughly 50 more communities were seriously damaged. For the Native Americans of southern New England, the war was a calamity. Thousands died, and many others were captured and enslaved. Even groups that supported the English lost out. When the war was over, all Native Americans in the area either fled or stayed and lost their independence under English rule.

HISTORICAL THINKING

1. **READING CHECK** How did the Pilgrims and the founders of Massachusetts Bay differ in their views on the Church of England?

2. **COMPARE AND CONTRAST** How was the role of religion different in New England than in New France?

3. **DRAW CONCLUSIONS** In what ways did Native American tribes aligned with the colonists suffer as a result of King Philip's War?

BUILD BACKGROUND

ANNE HUTCHINSON'S BANISHMENT

The religious controversy surrounding Anne Hutchinson involved whether people needed to do good works to prove that they had received God's grace. Puritans in the colony believed that people entered a covenant with God by professing their belief in Christ, and in return, God bestowed salvation upon them. People then did "good works" as evidence of this covenant. Hutchinson argued that this put too much emphasis on "works." Hutchinson maintained that once a person accepted Christ and received grace, good works had no value as a sign of salvation. The clergy believed that this conclusion would lead to disastrous consequences for social order, and that without religious principles controlling behavior, social morality would quickly degenerate. Hutchinson's ideas threatened to split the colony into factions. In 1637, Hutchinson was tried, convicted, and banished from the colony. In 1638, a church trial resulted in her excommunication.

THE PEQUOT NATION

Before King Philip's War, the Pequot were the most powerful southern New England tribe and the primary makers of wampum—decorative beads crafted from shells that were used as an early currency. However, after the war, they lost their economic role and were confined to a small reservation. By the 1970s, only one tribal member, Elizabeth George Plouffe, remained on the land. After her death, her grandson, Richard A. Hayward, began calling other tribal members back home. Enough people returned by 1983 that the Pequot obtained federal recognition as a sovereign nation. The Pequot showed their business acumen again by opening Foxwoods Casino in 1992. Earnings from this highly successful venture have enabled them to buy back some of their traditional lands, give money to the state of Connecticut, and erect the Mashantucket Pequot Museum, which tells the story of the Pequot's rise, fall, and return as a nation.

TEACH

GUIDED DISCUSSION

4. Evaluate Why did the Massachusetts Bay colonists find the views of Roger Williams and Anne Hutchinson so threatening? *(Possible response: Williams's views struck at the foundation of the colony's land rights and tax laws, while both his and Hutchinson's views attacked the authority of the Puritan Church.)*

5. Compare and Contrast How do the Jamestown map in lesson 2.2 and the Pequot War woodcut in Lesson 2.4 reflect the change in power between colonists and Native Americans? *(Possible response: In the Jamestown map, the colonists are in the fort and threatened by the powerful Powhatan. In the woodcut, the members of the Pequot nation are in the fort, surrounded by the colonists and their allies. The power has shifted to the colonists, as evidenced by the defeat of the Pequot and, eventually, all the tribes.)*

ANALYZE PRIMARY SOURCES

Direct students' attention to the Primary Source feature. **ASK:** In what ways does the Fundamental Orders of Connecticut imply that the colonists are developing a representative form of government? *(Order 4 refers to choosing a governor; order 5 states that several towns will send deputies to the Court of Election, implying the deputies are chosen by the townspeople; and order 10 mentions a General Court that consists of the Governor and four other Magistrates, who may be chosen by the people.)* **ASK:** Why do you think colonists placed limits on the top government official? *(They were likely trying to prevent an absolute ruler such as the king of England.)*

ACTIVE OPTIONS

On Your Feet: Debate Types of Colonial Government Arrange the class into two teams and provide the following question: Which government is best during a colony's first years, authoritarian or representative? Assign teams the type of government they will argue for and then have students prepare for the debate, reflecting on what they have read about the colonies, the dangers and opportunities faced, and the mistakes made. Instruct students to prepare notes to support their arguments. When teams are ready, have them debate the topic. After a set amount of time, let the class vote on which team presented the strongest argument.

NG Learning Framework: Create an Annotated Time Line

SKILL Collaboration

KNOWLEDGE Our Human Story

Arrange students into four groups and assign each group one of the following topics: Plymouth Colony, Massachusetts Bay Colony, Connecticut and Rhode Island, and conflicts with Native Americans. Ask each group to create a time line from 1600 to 1680 showing significant events relative to their topic with annotations that include important details and visuals. Instruct students to assign specific time spans to each group member or divide the tasks equitably in another manner agreed upon by the group. Post each group's time line in the classroom or on a class website. Prompt students to discuss observations or insights they gained from viewing information laid out on the specific time lines.

HISTORICAL THINKING

ANSWERS

1. The Pilgrims wanted to eliminate many practices of the Church of England to purify its worship. The Massachusetts Bay Colony founders sought to reform the church through example, hoping they could influence the church's leaders back home.

2. In the New England colonies, Protestant separatists and dissenters, wanting religious freedom, established separate colonies where they formed new governments based on the rules of their religion. Colonists in New France, who were already Catholic and not fleeing religious persecution, did not need to establish a new form of government. Because non-Catholic settlers in New France were discouraged, slow population growth became a main concern.

3. At the end of King Philip's War, even Native Americans who had fought with the colonists suffered losses and were either forced off their land or remained and were subject to English rule.

CRITICAL VIEWING Possible response: The artwork provides an idea of how the British and their allies trapped many Pequot, including women and children, inside the fort and fired upon them.

William Penn (center) stands with Delaware Indians after signing a treaty that finalized the sale of Pennsylvania. This carving is housed in the U.S. Capitol building.

MIDDLE COLONIES

What's important to you when you think about places you'd like to live one day? A mild climate? Job opportunities? Tolerance and diversity? The Middle Colonies fit all those requirements. In fact, one of them was even founded on the principle of tolerance.

FROM NEW AMSTERDAM TO NEW YORK

The English **Middle Colonies** along the mid-Atlantic coast of North America were comprised of Delaware, New Jersey, Pennsylvania, and New York. In addition to the Dutch communities that were established there as part of New Netherland, the area attracted settlers from many other European countries who were searching for economic opportunities and religious freedom.

At first, to continue its lucrative fur trade, New Netherland maintained good relations with local Native Americans. But as you have read, in the Lower Hudson River Valley in the late 1630s and early 1640s, land disputes led to local wars between the Dutch colonists and Native Americans. In spite of this, by the 1650s, New Netherland was thriving.

Even so, New Netherland did not remain for long on the colonial map. The growing rivalry for sea power and trade dominance between England and the Netherlands ended up being the colony's undoing. King Charles II of England granted his brother, James, Duke of York, vast tracts of land in North America—including New Netherland. In 1664, a large English fleet arrived that vastly outnumbered the Dutch. The English took the colony without so much as a struggle. New Netherland was renamed New York, New Amsterdam became New York City, and the official Dutch presence on the mainland of North America came to an end.

PENNSYLVANIA

In 1681, King Charles II granted a charter for a colony to **William Penn**, in part on lands seized from the Dutch. Penn was a **Quaker,** a member of a religious group also called the Society of Friends. Quakers believe in a direct experience of God without need

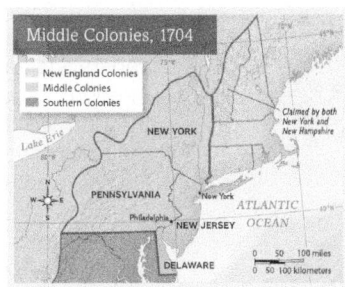
Middle Colonies, 1704
- New England Colonies
- Middle Colonies
- Southern Colonies

for traditional church hierarchies. In addition, they practice equality, simplicity, and pacifism. **Pacifism** is the belief that war is morally wrong.

William Penn had an ambitious plan for the colony. First, he wanted to make Pennsylvania a refuge for Quakers, who had been persecuted for years in England and in other colonies. Several unrepentant Quakers were even hanged for their beliefs in the Massachusetts Bay Colony.

Next, Penn wanted to guarantee freedom of conscience, or the right to hold different religious convictions than others, in the colony. But he believed in freedom *of* religion, not freedom *from* religion. Quakers tolerated diversity in beliefs, but still required Pennsylvanians to "acknowledge one almighty God to be the creator, upholder, and ruler of the world." Penn also supported fair treatment for Native Americans, and his policies translated into a long period of peaceful relations between Pennsylvania's settlers and Native Americans.

Penn's plans for government, too, were forward-thinking. His Frame of Government of 1682, a written plan for the government of Pennsylvania, included an elected General Assembly, and succeeding amendments increased the power of the voters in instituting public policy.

When Penn's policies were enacted, the colony became an attractive destination for people of many faiths and nationalities. Pennsylvania's diversity included large numbers of Amish and Mennonite believers from Germany and Switzerland. There were also Irish Catholics, French Huguenots, Spanish Jews, English Methodists—groups who felt a fresh start in a new land that, more or less, tolerated their religion was worth the risk of leaving their homeland.

Pennsylvania's harmonious society attracted hardworking people who were ready and able to cultivate its fertile lands. The agricultural output of the region surpassed local consumption, meaning there were surpluses of corn, wheat, rye, hemp, and flax to export. The port of Philadelphia became the trading hub through which agricultural and other exports flowed. Lumber, iron production, papermaking, and printing businesses flourished.

The colony's early economic success was in part due to enslaved labor. Though they would be known eventually for their antislavery views, Quakers owned slaves and were involved in the Philadelphia slave trade early in Pennsylvania's history.

NEW JERSEY AND DELAWARE

The colonies that existed on the land now known as New Jersey were a part of New Netherland. When the British took over, the land was divided between two British royal subjects, Lord Carteret and Lord Berkeley, and renamed New Jersey. In 1681, Penn and other Quakers bought the section owned by the Carteret family and incorporated it into Pennsylvania. The rest remained New Jersey.

In 1682, the king gave Penn three "lower" counties south of Philadelphia. Despite Penn's efforts to create an ideal colony, the non-English European settlers who lived in these counties were not happy being a part of Pennsylvania and at times clashed with colonial authority. Penn tried unsuccessfully to unite the English and the other Europeans. In 1704, after two decades of difficulties, he allowed the counties to split off. They joined together under the common name of Delaware and formed a government assembly.

HISTORICAL THINKING

1. **READING CHECK** Identify two reasons why William Penn was able to acquire the land that would eventually become Pennsylvania.

2. **DRAW CONCLUSIONS** In what ways were some Quaker beliefs reflected in the founding ideas of Pennsylvania?

3. **INTERPRET MAPS** Why might it have been easy for settlers in the lower counties of Pennsylvania to break away and form Delaware?

OBJECTIVE

Explore the establishment and characteristics of the Middle Colonies.

CRITICAL THINKING SKILLS FOR LESSON 3.1

- Draw Conclusions
- Interpret Maps
- Compare and Contrast
- Evaluate
- Analyze Visuals

HISTORICAL THINKING FOR CHAPTER 2

How were the North American colonies shaped by their geography and by the people who settled them? The Middle Colonies attracted people from multiple European countries and diverse religions. Lesson 3.1 reveals how these factors shaped colonial New York, Pennsylvania, New Jersey, and Delaware.

BACKGROUND FOR THE TEACHER

For William Penn, paying Native Americans for their land was part of his conception of a peaceful and pacifist Pennsylvania. He learned from earlier colonists that the Delaware, not the more powerful Iroquois, had the power to sell the territory he wanted. Acquiring legal title was important because without it investors might balk at financing the new colony. Once negotiations began, Penn had to navigate the Delaware's complex terms, such as tribal members having overlapping rights to use different areas. This meant that Penn might have to pay the same holder several times to satisfy all claims. From the 1680s to the early 1700s, Penn purchased several plots, creating what the Delaware called a "chain of friendship" with the tribe. This friendship proved vital when tribes went to war with colonists to reclaim their lands. The Quakers were spared as a result of Penn's fair and just treatment of the Delaware.

INTRODUCE & ENGAGE

PREVIEW NAMES AND VOCABULARY

Have students look up the meaning of Pennsylvania (Penn's woods) and Philadelphia (city of brotherly love). Then display the terms *pacifism* and *freedom of conscience*. Encourage students to identify the root words and speculate on each term's meaning. Discuss with them what a colony founded on these ideas might be like. Tell students that Lesson 3.1 describes a colony based on William Penn's vision.

TEACH

GUIDED DISCUSSION

1. **Compare and Contrast** What were some of the ways that colonial Pennsylvania differed from the Plymouth and Massachusetts Bay colonies? *(Possible response: Unlike Massachusetts, Pennsylvania accepted people with a diversity of religious beliefs and backgrounds, enjoyed rapid economic prosperity, and maintained peaceful relations with Native Americans. Both regions included a democratic form of government and were hostile to colonists with no religious beliefs.)*

2. **Evaluate** What role did the Dutch play in strengthening British dominance in North America? *(Possible response: The Dutch land holdings, well-developed settlements, and sea ports were taken over by the English, thus making England the dominant European power in the region. The former Dutch lands were used to create the colonies of New York, Pennsylvania, and New Jersey.)*

ANALYZE VISUALS

In the carving of William Penn and the Delaware, what does the artist depict about the reactions of the subjects to the signing of the treaty? *(Possible response: The artist depicts a range of reactions. The Quakers and Delaware on the left smile and watch the signing with interest, suggesting that they are pleased with the treaty. However, the groups behind and to the right of Penn appear conflicted or displeased. The Quakers wear frowns, and two men face away from the signing, with one watching the Delaware tribesmen farthest from the signing. In the latter group, the Delaware in the middle, holding a bow and a quiver of arrows, appears to stride purposefully toward the signing. One of his tribesman holds him back while another cowers fearfully in the rear.)*

ACTIVE OPTIONS

On Your Feet: Discuss William Penn's Vision Direct students to use the Think, Pair, Share strategy as they consider the following question: Did Pennsylvania live up to William Penn's ideals? Allow a few minutes for students to think, and then tell students to choose partners and discuss their ideas for five minutes. After discussion time, invite students to share their ideas with the class.

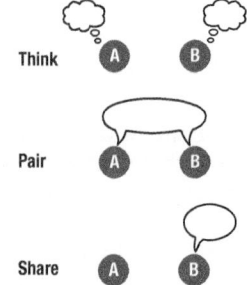

NG Learning Framework: Compare Quakers Then and Now

SKILLS Observation, Communication

KNOWLEDGE Our Human Story

Tell students to work in small groups to compare the beliefs and actions of colonial era Quakers with those of the present-day group. Encourage students to conduct online research, interview Quakers in their community if possible, and read information provided on Quaker websites. Ask students to consider the Quakers' main religious beliefs, major social concerns, public actions, and visions for the future. Invite students to summarize their findings in a written report, chart, or infographic. Have groups share their work with the class.

DIFFERENTIATE

STRIVING READERS

Chart Lesson Information Instruct students to draw a four-column chart and label the columns with the colonies named in the lesson's subsection headings. As they read, tell students to complete the chart with important details from each paragraph. After reading, encourage students to compare and revise their completed charts as necessary.

New York	Pennsylvania	New Jersey	Delaware
Summary			

GIFTED & TALENTED

Write a Dialogue Have students write a dialogue that could have taken place among the men involved in the signing of the treaty that transferred ownership of Pennsylvania from the Delaware to the colonists. Before they begin writing, tell students to conduct research to learn more about the negotiations and eventual purchase. You might suggest that they research excerpts of the sale agreement itself, including what the Delaware received in exchange for their land. Invite students to rehearse and perform their dialogue to the class if time allows.

See the Chapter Planner for more strategies for differentiation.

HISTORICAL THINKING

ANSWERS

1. Penn was able to acquire land for his colony because the English seized the land from the Dutch and because he was granted a royal charter by King Charles II.

2. Quakers believed in a direct experience of God, equality, simplicity, and pacifism. These beliefs were reflected in the tolerance of different religious beliefs, acceptance of many different groups of people, and establishment of peaceful relations with Native American tribes.

3. The lower counties were already isolated geographically from the rest of Pennsylvania and had probably developed close economic, social, and political ties among themselves.

The Rackliffe House near Berlin, Maryland, has stood on a ridge overlooking Sinepuxent Bay and Assateague Island since Captain Charles Rackliffe built it in the 1740s. Today it serves as a museum dedicated to preserving the culture of 18th-century Maryland colonists.

SOUTHERN COLONIES

The Southern Colonies were a bit of a mixed bag—new and old, poor and rich, Protestant and Catholic. The one thing that eventually unified them was a plantation economy and a heavy reliance on enslaved Africans for labor.

CHESAPEAKE BAY COLONY

George Calvert, the first **Lord Baltimore**, wanted to find a haven for English Catholics in North America. King Charles I granted a charter for a new colony called Maryland in June 1632. It was to be located north of Virginia. However, the charter did not arrive in time for Calvert, who had died in April, to take control. Instead, his son Cecilius, the second Lord Baltimore, became the **proprietor**, or owner of the colony. The first ships sailed through Chesapeake Bay in March 1634 with 17 landowning families and about 200 others who had come to work. Most were indentured servants.

The leaders of the settlement were determined not to repeat the mistakes of Virginia. They made sure to purchase land from the local Yaocomico (YAH-oh-com-ih-koh) people and establish friendly relations with them. They also set up farms and trading posts. Initially, most of the labor fell to indentured servants. Later, the owners of plantations began to purchase enslaved Africans to work their lands.

Maryland's charter was based on outdated feudal principles. The proprietor had sweeping civil and military powers and, like a medieval lord, could even confer titles. Maryland's first governor was Cecilius's younger brother Leonard, but it was not long before pressure from small landholders and local Protestants forced a colonial assembly to convene. Then, in 1638, the assembly established its right to initiate colonial legislation. This change brought the colony in line with legislative practices in England, where Parliament had the ability to propose laws. One of Maryland's better-known laws is the Religious Toleration Act, passed in 1649, which guaranteed freedom of worship, but only for Christians.

Maryland's status as a Catholic colony was a source of persistent problems. A Protestant rebellion, started by a Virginia trader named William Claiborne, forced the governor to briefly flee the colony in 1644. In 1650, spurred by the triumph of Puritans back home in the English Civil War, a successful Puritan revolt in Maryland led to more political upheaval. The new government revoked the Religious Toleration Act and essentially outlawed both Catholicism and Anglicanism—or membership in the Church of England. But in November 1657, England's Puritan leader, Oliver Cromwell, restored Lord Baltimore's proprietorship of Maryland along with the Religious Toleration Act. In the years that followed, the population of Maryland grew steadily, from about 8,000 in 1660 to about 16,000 by 1676.

BACON'S REBELLION

Twenty years after Maryland's religious tensions began, civil rebellion erupted in the Virginia Colony. This conflict, which began in 1676 and came to be known as **Bacon's Rebellion**, did not involve religion. Instead, it arose out of disputes with Native Americans, echoing battles farther north, such as the Pequot War and King Philip's War.

The tension was caused in part by a treaty signed in 1646 between the Virginia government and the Powhatan, which set aside territory north of the York River for the Powhatan. In the years following the treaty, Virginia's population continued to grow, and land available to farm tobacco became scarcer. Landless freemen grew resentful of the Powhatan and other local Native Americans and began to covet their land. As planters pushed into the frontier, the Native Americans pushed back.

Throughout the early 1670s, a cycle of raids and reprisals took place. When the frontier planters, led by Nathaniel Bacon, demanded permission to remove the Native American threat by any means they deemed necessary, Virginia's governor, William Berkeley, opted instead for a peaceful policy that would protect both the Native Americans and the colony's profitable fur trade with them.

Bacon, an ambitious 29-year-old councilman, saw an opportunity to challenge Berkeley's leadership. He stoked the hostility that many landless men

Map label: Southern Colonies, 1733

Map legend:
New England Colonies
Middle Colonies
Southern Colonies

PLAN: 4-PAGE LESSON

OBJECTIVE

Examine the establishment of the southern colonies and the role that cash crops and enslaved labor played in their success.

CRITICAL THINKING SKILLS FOR LESSON 3.2

- Compare and Contrast
- Make Predictions
- Evaluate
- Summarize
- Draw Conclusions
- Identify Problems and Solutions
- Form and Support Opinions

HISTORICAL THINKING FOR CHAPTER 2

How were the North American colonies shaped by their geography and by the people who settled them? The southern colonies attracted a wide variety of people. Lesson 3.2 explains how each colony was founded and developed in its early years.

BACKGROUND FOR THE TEACHER

The English Civil War set the Catholic royalists, who supported Charles I, against Protestant Parliamentary forces. The Catholic-Protestant wars eventually engulfed Scotland and Ireland and also provoked bitter debates between royalists and Protestants in the colonies. The Protestant-Puritan leader, Oliver Cromwell, defeated royalist forces and, in 1649, deposed and executed Charles I. The events overseas exacerbated long-held tensions in Maryland, exemplified during the Battle of the Severn, a skirmish outside Annapolis, Maryland, in which 400 Maryland Catholics and Puritans clashed. Despite the fact that religious tolerance was restored in 1657, the colony continued to experience religious, regional, and political conflicts between Catholics and Protestants for years.

HISTORY NOTEBOOK

Encourage students to complete the American Gallery page for Chapter 2 in their History Notebooks as they read.

INTRODUCE & ENGAGE
CHART COLONY DEVELOPMENT

Discuss with students what they recall about the way many New England and Middle colonies drifted from their founders' ideals as the settlements developed. Work with students to complete a Sequence Chain, such as the one shown, to record a progression of steps from idealism to conflict to eventual separation or transformation. Ask students whether they think such departure from an ideal is inevitable and, if so, why. Explain that in Lesson 3.2 they will read about southern colonies that were also founded on idealistic principles.

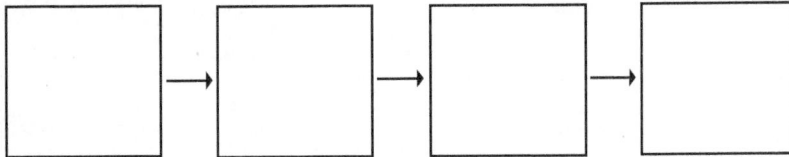

TEACH
GUIDED DISCUSSION

1. **Compare and Contrast** How did religious policies in Maryland compare to those in Massachusetts Bay Colony and Pennsylvania? *(Maryland allowed for religious tolerance, which was similar to policies in Pennsylvania and Rhode Island. Massachusetts Bay, however, did not support religious freedom, forcing residents to adhere to strict religious codes.)*

2. **Draw Conclusions** Why did the colonists in Maryland object to the original charter of the colony? *(Possible response: It concentrated too much power in the hands of the proprietor, and the colonists—especially smaller landowners and non-Catholics—had little say in their own affairs.)*

3. **Form and Support Opinions** Do you think landless members of Bacon's Rebellion felt they had achieved their goals? *(Possible responses: Yes. The protections for Native Americans were no longer enforced, and land previously held by the Powhatan was open for settlement. No. The revolt did not offer more opportunities for the landless whites. Instead, plantation owners imported enslaved Africans to take the place of white laborers.)*

MAKE PREDICTIONS

Direct students' attention to the map, Southern Colonies, 1733, and have them study its details, particularly the relative sizes of the New England, Middle, and Southern Colonies. **ASK:** Do you think the relatively larger size of the Southern Colonies would give them more political power during the colonial and revolutionary periods? Explain your response. *(Possible responses: Yes. Because of the size of the territory, these colonies were important economic and strategic assets. No. Even though the territory was large, except for Virginia, their populations were less dense than colonies such as Pennsylvania and New York.)*

DIFFERENTIATE
ENGLISH LANGUAGE LEARNERS `ELD`

Create a Word Web Pair students at the **Emerging** and **Expanding** levels with students at the **Bridging** level. Display a Word Web with the topic Southern Colonies in the center. Tell students to reread the text, noting and adding important words and phrases to the organizer. Then ask pairs to share and discuss their Word Webs, stating their ideas in complete sentences.

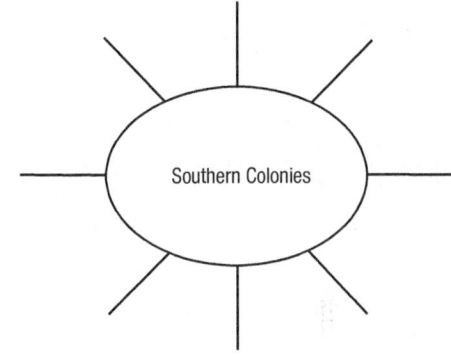

PRE-AP

Engage in a Debate Encourage students to conduct research about the founding principles of the Georgia colony and why they were eventually abandoned. Direct students to explore the Enlightenment principles underpinning James Oglethorpe's and John Viscount Percival's vision for Georgia and the social and economic forces that clashed with that vision. After students gather information and take notes, have them assume the role of a Georgia colonist who either supports or opposes the founding values. Then have the two sides participate in a debate over the best course to take for the future of the colony. After the debate, ask students to discuss how the opposing philosophies are relevant to today's discussions about social, economic, and racial injustice.

See the Chapter Planner for more strategies for differentiation.

and small farmers felt toward Berkeley and other substantial landowners. Bacon and a large group of armed supporters attacked Native American villages and then quickly turned their aggression on the authorities in Jamestown itself.

Berkeley submitted to the rebels' demands, permitting their war against the Native Americans, but that was not enough for Bacon. He went a step further, attempting to overthrow Berkeley and take control of the colony. A full-scale rebellion followed. Berkeley fled Jamestown. Bacon and his followers continued killing Native Americans, and, in September 1676, they set much of Jamestown on fire. A month later, however, Bacon was dead, possibly the victim of dysentery, and the energy that fueled his rebellion died with him.

Bacon's Rebellion marked a serious defeat for the area's Native Americans. Many were killed, and the protections of the 1646 treaty were no longer enforced. The landless freemen, for their part, found the rebellion to be a largely empty victory. Rather than opening up Virginia society to better opportunities, the freemen's revolt spurred landowners to replace them and their labor with enslaved Africans.

SETTLING THE CAROLINAS

After the English Civil War, the monarchy was re-established, and Charles II ascended the throne in 1660. However, the king had a serious problem. The upheavals of the previous 12 years had left the royal treasury empty, and there were large debts outstanding. By granting colonial lands to some creditors, he was able to both repay debts and bolster England's commerce and power.

The indigo plant is grown all over the world and was used to make the rich, blue dye that colored the woolen quilt shown at right.

In 1663, King Charles granted land south of the Virginia colony to prominent supporters, including Virginia governor William Berkeley and royalist politician Anthony Ashley Cooper. Cooper organized the colony of **Carolina** with the port of **Charles Town** as its major city that same year. The original Carolina charter was similar to Maryland's, and from it, the wealthy proprietors drew up the Fundamental Constitutions of Carolina to run the colony. But this document was complicated and feudal in nature—it even included a hierarchy of nobles and lords—and was soundly rejected by the colony's ordinary settlers.

By 1691, two colonies had developed out of the Carolina land grant. Small planters from Virginia moved into the first, which later became North Carolina. As early as 1653, people had settled on the shores of Albemarle Sound, where they raised tobacco, corn, and livestock. The Albemarle settlement, which remained poor, had been a haven for pirates and difficult to govern. Nevertheless, the population grew so large that eventually the proprietors appointed a governor.

The second colony attracted planters from the West Indian island of Barbados. Land on the island had become scarce, so a number of planters sailed to the mainland with enslaved Africans and bought large tracts of land on which they developed plantations. The region where they settled became South Carolina. At first, they shipped the goods they produced, such as food, livestock, firewood, and wooden planks for making barrels, back to Barbados. But the colony's plantation economy soon came to be dominated by such valuable cash crops as rice

and indigo (a natural source of deep blue fabric dye). A cash crop is produce grown to be sold for profit rather than for use by an individual farmer.

THE FOUNDING OF GEORGIA

The last British mainland colony, Georgia, received its charter from its namesake, King George II, in 1732. Enlightenment principles of human progress and freedom drove the colony's founders, **James Oglethorpe** and John Viscount Percival, to secure the charter. They envisioned Georgia as a place where the poor of England could get a fresh start in life. The idea attracted German, Scottish, and Scots-Irish settlers, too. Georgia would also serve as a shield between South Carolina and Spanish colonial Florida.

George II placed the colony in the hands of **trustees**, or managers who could neither receive financial benefits from the colony nor own land within its boundaries. The trustees, led by Oglethorpe, intended to create a peaceful, moral society of small farmers in which all except indentured servants worked for themselves. To this end, the trustees prohibited both rum and slaveholding and limited each landholder to 500 or fewer acres. Each free male immigrant was granted land at no charge, but no one could buy or sell land, and only men could inherit it. The prohibition on slavery and the limitations on landholding existed to prevent South Carolina's plantation culture and its use of slave labor from taking hold in Georgia.

In February 1733, the first settlers arrived and built the colony's first town, **Savannah**, on a high bluff overlooking the river of the same name. Oglethorpe purchased land from the Native Americans and went on to establish alliances with the Lower Creek, Cherokee, and Chickasaw nations against Spanish Florida. As more settlers arrived, the prohibitions on liquor, slavery, and land sales grew increasingly unpopular. Without hard liquor, Georgians could not engage in the rum trade with the West Indies, which would have been a ready market for Georgia's lumber. And the prohibition on creating plantations rankled some who aspired to the opulent lifestyle of the wealthiest plantation owners in South Carolina.

The settlers were powerless to make changes, however, because the colony lacked a representative assembly. As a result, many settlers chose to leave

The statue of James Oglethorpe in Savannah, Georgia, faces south in memory of the threat the Spanish settlers in Florida posed during Georgia's early years.

almost as soon as they arrived, which slowed the population growth of Georgia. Facing rising discontent and a fleeing population, the trustees eventually reversed course, allowing the importation of rum in 1742 and land sales and slavery in 1750. As they had feared, plantation agriculture, focused on rice, indigo, and sugar and powered by enslaved Africans, became common. Georgia's population swelled, but ownership of the colony transferred back to England in 1752. Oglethorpe's experiment had failed.

HISTORICAL THINKING

1. **READING CHECK** What issues in Virginia society helped lead to Bacon's Rebellion?

2. **COMPARE AND CONTRAST** In what way were the settlers of Maryland similar to the settlers of Massachusetts Bay?

3. **EVALUATE** How did differences in settlement patterns lead to distinct economic developments in North and South Carolina?

BUILD BACKGROUND

SOUTH CAROLINA AND THE COWBOYS

South Carolina included early examples of an iconic American figure—the cowboy. The colony, which included a large population of enslaved Africans, was ideal for raising cattle and hogs on its open grasslands. Many Africans had experience with herding and were able to utilize this skill with cattle. When the cattle were ready for sale, the cowboys rounded them up, branded them, and drove them to market—practices that predated the American West by nearly 150 years. These African cowboys experienced more freedom than most enslaved Africans in the Carolina colony until the rice plantation system began to take root. The colonists then adopted the Barbados slave codes, the harshest codes in all the colonies, which curtailed the freer life of the early cowboys.

THE BATTLE OF BLOODY MARSH

July 1742 marked the last time the Spanish attempted to invade Georgia, resulting in a decisive victory for Governor Oglethorpe and his troops. The Spanish governor of St. Augustine planned to stage the invasion from St. Simons, an island off Georgia's coast, but harsh weather delayed his ships. Oglethorpe, warned of the plan, raised an army of British regulars, local citizens, and Native Americans. Although his troops were outnumbered nearly five to one, Oglethorpe was able to defeat the Spanish first with a bold charge into their lines and then with an ambush in the surrounding marshes. The name Battle of Bloody Marsh came from its location, not its casualties, as about only 50 men were killed. The victory boosted the confidence of the Georgians and discouraged the Spanish from invading British North America in the future.

TEACH

GUIDED DISCUSSION

4. Summarize Why did a plantation economy develop so quickly in South Carolina? *(Possible response: South Carolina had a perfect climate for cash crops. Many settlers there came from the West Indies, where plantation economies were entrenched. Also, the colony welcomed slavery, which provided the labor force for the system.)*

5. Identify Problems and Solutions What problems did the Georgia trustees face, and at what cost did they resolve them? *(Possible response: Because of their restrictions on rum, land size, and slavery, the trustees faced slow growth in their colony and an increasingly discontented population. They solved these problems by lifting the restrictions. The colony thrived, but at the cost of the trustees' original ideals to keep hard liquor, plantations, and slavery out of Georgia.)*

MORE INFORMATION

Carolina Indigo Turning indigo plants into a rich blue dye required specialized equipment and skilled slave labor. The plants were first soaked in a vat of water, then transferred to a second vat where they were pounded until thick grains formed. The water in the vat was drained, and the remaining indigo paste was dried, cut into squares, and shipped to market in barrels. The English Parliament subsidized Carolina indigo growers for a time, making it a highly profitable crop for plantation owners. Indigo production peaked in 1775 but declined afterwards as England turned to India for the dye. In response, South Carolina started experimenting with cotton, another crop that would end up strengthening the plantation system and increasing slavery in the colonies.

ACTIVE OPTIONS

 **Southern Plantations** Invite students to explore the American Gallery. Have them select one of the images and do additional research to learn more about it. Ask questions that will inspire additional inquiry about the chosen gallery image, such as: Why is this building or location significant? What is the object, who made or used it, and what was its purpose? What does this art represent? What else would you like to know about the image you selected?

NG Learning Framework: Interview a Founder

SKILL Communication

KNOWLEDGE Our Human Story

Have students work in small groups to conduct research in order to engage in a panel interview of the founder or governor of a southern colony. Tell groups to investigate the founder's life and develop questions such as the following: What is the goal for the colony? What are the biggest challenges? What has been your greatest achievement? What is your overall assessment of the colony's success or failure? Group members can assume the roles of historical figures or panel interviewers and conduct the interviews in class or record them as a podcast.

HISTORICAL THINKING

ANSWERS

1. The landless residents of Virginia found it difficult to gain land—and therefore move up in society—because of the treaty that reserved land north of the York River for the Powhatan. This made colonists resent Governor Berkeley, large landowners, and especially the Powhatan.

2. The settlers of both colonies were initially composed of a religious group that needed a place to practice their religion freely.

3. North Carolina was settled largely by small planters from Virginia who remained poor despite raising some cash crops. South Carolina was settled by more prosperous planters from Barbados, who brought their agricultural knowledge and slaves with them and bought large tracts of land to establish plantations for cash crops.

THE EXPANSION OF SLAVERY IN THE AMERICAS

To be enslaved was to be treated as less than human. Enslaved African Americans could be bought and sold as property, worked beyond endurance, and thoughtlessly ripped away from their families. Yet it was their labor that produced much of the wealth of the American colonies.

CASH CROPS ARE KING

In many ways, cotton, tobacco, indigo, and rice were responsible for the success of colonial North America. As you have read, the economy of the Southern Colonies shifted from selling goods strictly to buyers in the West Indies to producing large amounts of cash crops to sell in the other colonies and across the Atlantic Ocean. The humid climate and fertile land of Maryland and Virginia were ideal for growing tobacco. The swampy coasts of South Carolina and Georgia were well suited for growing rice.

The trouble with growing rice in the Southern Colonies, however, was that colonists were not familiar with the delicate process of successful rice cultivation. To grow rice, farmers must flood the fields where it is grown in a controlled way. Proper harvesting of the grain requires a lot of backbreaking labor. The plants must be cut down and beaten to release the grains. Then the grains must be tossed to separate their parts and pounded to remove their hard covering. The colonists had to rely on enslaved laborers, many of whom came from rice-producing areas of Africa, to teach them how to grow enough rice to make their plantations profitable. The demand for labor caused by the expansion of rice and other cash crops initiated a boom in the slave trade.

Because of knowledgeable enslaved people, landowners in the Southern Colonies became wealthy, and even more landowners moved to the area to cash in. Rice plantations popped up along the region's rivers, which provided both the water necessary for growing the rice and a convenient way to transport the harvested and processed crops. Because rice cultivation took up so much land, plantations were enormous and the owners' homes were separated by large distances. Thus, many wealthy landowners moved to the bustling port city of Charles Town (known today as Charleston) for part of the year to escape the isolation. And as the demand for enslaved labor increased in the colonies, Charles Town and its slave markets became an important center of the North American slave trade.

SLAVE CODES

As slavery took hold, especially in the Southern Colonies, it became written into law in ways that deprived a whole group of people of their basic human rights. Before 1660, the status of black laborers in Virginia varied. Some were locked in their lives of enslavement, some were working in bondage until they paid off a debt, and a few were free. After 1660, however, Virginia enacted laws that defined enslavement in the South for African Americans and instituted the practice of chattel slavery. By law, an enslaved person's bondage lasted for his or her entire lifetime and passed from mother to child. This became the normal status of the majority of Africans from Africa and African Americans who were born in the colonies.

Slave codes, or racist laws passed by the governments of Virginia and Maryland during this period, codified severe discrimination based solely on skin color. The Virginia assembly, for example, ruled that an owner who killed a slave during punishment could not be charged with a felony. Further, slave codes banned interracial marriage and criminalized the freeing of slaves, except under certain conditions. As the codes evolved, enslaved people could no longer travel without permission, own property, testify against white people in court, or even gather in groups. Eventually, the other English colonies adopted aspects of these codes, with differing degrees of severity based on geography and slave population. For example, colonies in New England had relatively moderate codes, but South Carolina's were extremely harsh.

Enslaved women in Georgia use a tool called a pestle to grind rice in a vessel called a mortar.

Mortars and pestles can be made from many materials, including stone, metal, or ceramic. This set is carved from wood.

The slave codes of Virginia and Maryland significantly changed the social relationship between people of European and African descent by codifying legal discrimination. This Virginia law provided justification for holding people in slavery, even if they were fellow Christians.

Virginia, 1667

Act III. Whereas some doubts have arisen whether children that are slaves by birth . . . should by virtue of their baptism be made free, it is enacted that baptism does not alter the condition to the person as to his bondage or freedom; masters freed from this doubt may more carefully propagate [spread] Christianity by permitting slaves to be admitted to that sacrament.

The labor extracted from enslaved people varied by region. In the Chesapeake Bay and Carolina regions, most toiled in the plantation fields, tending to the cash crops. Some men and women were assigned domestic, or household, duties, and others became artisans, learning skilled trades. In the middle and northern colonies, farms that raised corn and wheat required fewer field hands, but many colonists still purchased enslaved people to work as servants in their households. Regardless of duties or region, one fact never changed: To be enslaved meant that someone else controlled your destiny.

Enslaved Africans who had lost their homelands and families found comfort by establishing new families and friendships in the colonies. They all knew, however, that their owners could destroy these relationships by selling them or their loved ones. This cruel and dehumanizing situation led to resistance during the 1700s, which you will read about in the next chapter.

HISTORICAL THINKING

1. **READING CHECK** How did enslaved people help establish the cultivation of rice in South Carolina?

2. **DRAW CONCLUSIONS** Why do you think slave codes contained differing levels of severity in different parts of the American colonies?

3. **MAKE PREDICTIONS** Predict the ways in which you think enslaved Africans and African Americans will resist control and servitude.

4. **MAKE INFERENCES** In the end, why could it be considered nearly irrelevant that some slave codes were not as harsh as others?

OBJECTIVE

Examine how and why slavery expanded in the North American colonies during the 17th century.

CRITICAL THINKING SKILLS FOR LESSON 3.3

- Draw Conclusions
- Make Predictions
- Make Inferences
- Describe
- Analyze Primary Sources

HISTORICAL THINKING FOR CHAPTER 2

How were the North American colonies shaped by their geography and by the people who settled them? As their economy developed, the Southern Colonies became increasingly reliant on slavery. Lesson 3.3 describes the geographic, economic, and political factors driving this trend.

BACKGROUND FOR THE TEACHER

The process of stripping enslaved people of their rights through discriminatory codes in North America was not uniquely aimed at enslaved Africans. Prior to 1700, enslaved Native Americans provided the main source of free labor throughout the colonies, and a legal justification for the system slowly developed. Underpinning slavery was a process known as "judicial enslavement." Practiced throughout New England, Native Americans were sentenced to long terms of involuntary servitude for debt or failure to pay fines incurred for minor crimes, such as trespassing. This, coupled with racially based tax codes and legal theory, worked to subjugate Native Americans and provide a free source of labor. The slave codes for Africans, however, went a step further, sentencing slaves and their descendants to a life in bondage. Even after slavery was abolished, the use of arbitrary arrests and court sentences to legally subjugate African Americans continued in many states until the 1950s.

INTRODUCE & ENGAGE

TAKE A POSITION

Have students imagine that they are 17th-century opponents of slavery who have been asked by a local plantation owner why they believe that the practice is wrong. Encourage them to think about the ethical, religious, and economic issues they might consider in their response and then explain and justify their position. Then tell students that Lesson 3.3 presents the expansion of slavery in the North American colonies and the legal controls used to keep African Americans enslaved.

TEACH

GUIDED DISCUSSION

1. **Describe** What geographic and economic factors allowed the plantation system to become entrenched in the Southern Colonies? *(Geography provided ideal growing conditions for cash crops. Economically, the slave trade provided unpaid labor, and abundant markets made cash crops lucrative.)*

2. **Make Inferences** Why do you think slave codes banned interracial marriage? *(Possible response: Slavery was built upon the premise that blacks were inferior to whites. Intermarriage undermined this premise by providing African Americans with legal status and allowing for the legitimized birth of mixed race children whose existence further questioned the racist ideology of slavery.)*

ANALYZE PRIMARY SOURCES

Direct students' attention to the Primary Source feature, an excerpt from the Virginia slave codes. **ASK:** What does this law allow holders of enslaved people to do? *(Holders of enslaved people could allow the enslaved to convert to Christianity without fear of having to set them free.)* **ASK:** Why might it be important to justify enslaving fellow Christians? *(Possible response: It would relieve the conscience of Christian holders of enslaved people and allow them to continue participating in the slave trade.)*

ACTIVE OPTIONS

On Your Feet: Word Webbing to Review Slave Codes Arrange the class into teams of four and provide each with a large sheet of paper. Give each team member a different colored marker and ask them to record details from the text about slave codes. Encourage students to build on their teammates' entries as they rotate the paper from one member to the next. Then call on volunteers from each group to make statements about how the passage of slave codes impacted society in the Southern Colonies.

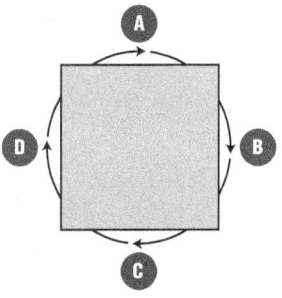

NG Learning Framework: Investigate the Contributions of Enslaved Workers

ATTITUDE Responsibility

KNOWLEDGE Our Human Story

Direct students to work in groups of four to create a chart to demonstrate the contribution enslaved workers made to the self-sufficiency and profitability of 18th-century plantations. Instruct students to conduct online and library research about the following two topics.

• Skilled enslaved workers: Categorize the various skills by craft, and note how, where, or why each craft was used. Then arrange the crafts in a hierarchy to demonstrate the importance of the skilled workers to the plantation.

• Labor systems using enslaved workers: List the characteristics of the gang system and the task system, emphasizing purposes and differences. Note the crop for which each system was typically used.

Encourage groups to display, compare, and discuss differences in their completed charts. Ask volunteers to share facts that they learned, especially those that challenged any previously held incorrect understandings about enslaved workers.

DIFFERENTIATE

STRIVING READERS

Rewrite a Passage Instruct pairs to read the introduction to the Primary Source feature and the excerpt from the Virginia slave codes. Based on context or research, have students define the following words and phrases: *codifying* (putting into legal code; making laws), *whereas* (since it is true that), *by virtue of* (because of), *it is enacted* (the law is), and *alter* (change). Tell pairs to work together to write the excerpt in conversational, or informal, English. Then have them share and compare their work with other pairs.

PRE-AP

Create a Flow Chart Direct students to conduct research and create a flow chart illustrating the long-term impact of the slave codes. Tell them to access multiple sources to explore connections to later injustices toward African Americans, such as Jim Crow laws, institutionalized racism, and mass incarceration of African Americans. Invite students to share their flow chart with the class.

See the Chapter Planner for more strategies for differentiation.

HISTORICAL THINKING

ANSWERS

1. Many enslaved people came from rice-growing regions, so they knew how to plant, cultivate, harvest, and process rice. Their knowledge and labor ensured the crop's success in South Carolina.

2. The Northeast was not dominated by plantations, which required a massive labor force, so enslaved individuals were fewer in number, and the jobs they did tended to be domestic or skilled labor. In areas where more slaves existed, there was a need for rigid control of those enslaved to maintain separation and dominance.

3. Answers will vary. Possible response: They will try to escape, revolt against their enslavers, or deliberately slow down the work.

4. Answers will vary. Possible response: No matter how slave codes varied, they justified total control over the lives of enslaved people, their families, descendants, and communities.

VOCABULARY

Use each of the terms below in a sentence that expresses an understanding about an event or topic from the chapter.

1. conquistador

   Conquistadors, such as Cortés, were the first Europeans to encounter many Native American groups.

2. indentured servant

3. commodity

4. viceroyalty

5. slave code

6. dissenter

7. joint-stock company

8. charter

9. heretic

READING STRATEGY
DRAW CONCLUSIONS

Drawing conclusions can help you make connections and better understand the text. Complete the following chart to draw conclusions about religion in the early American colonies. Then answer the question.

Text Clues	What I Know	My Conclusions

10. How great a role did religion play in the settlement of England's American colonies?

MAIN IDEAS

Answer the following questions. Support your answers with evidence from the chapter.

11. Why did the Aztecs' past military success actually make them more vulnerable to attack from an outside group such as the Spanish? **LESSON 1.1**

12. How did Catholic friars play a part in helping to broaden the Spanish empire in the Americas? **LESSON 1.2**

13. Why was the Middle Passage a dangerous journey for enslaved Africans? **LESSON 1.3**

14. What important role did John Rolfe play in the economy of Jamestown? **LESSON 2.1**

15. What religious issue hampered the development of the New France settlements along the St. Lawrence River? **LESSON 2.3**

16. What are two serious criticisms that Roger Williams leveled at the leaders of the Massachusetts Bay Colony? **LESSON 2.4**

17. What common disagreement between settlers and Native Americans was a contributing cause of both the Pequot War and King Philip's War? **LESSON 2.4**

18. What conflict helped England acquire New Netherland from the Dutch? **LESSON 3.1**

19. In what ways were Maryland's first settlers better equipped to start a colony than Virginia's first settlers? **LESSON 3.2**

20. How did Georgia's founder, James Oglethorpe, bolster the colony's standing as a barrier against Spanish Florida? **LESSON 3.2**

21. How did the slave codes fundamentally alter the status of Africans and African Americans in the colonies? **LESSON 3.3**

HISTORICAL THINKING

Answer the following questions. Support your answers with evidence from the chapter.

22. **COMPARE AND CONTRAST** How were the initial settlements of Massachusetts Bay and Georgia similar and different?

23. **ANALYZE CAUSE AND EFFECT** How did the large-scale adoption of slave labor in England's North American colonies affect global trade?

24. **IDENTIFY** Which two issues sparked Bacon's Rebellion?

25. **DRAW CONCLUSIONS** How and why were Native Americans' relations with New France and New England different?

INTERPRET MAPS

Look closely at the map below. Use information from the chapter and the map to answer the questions that follow.

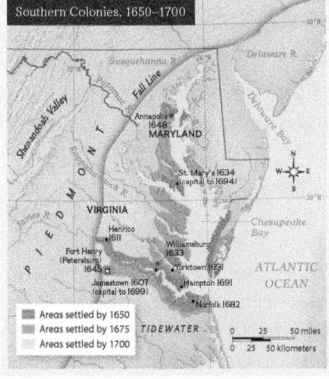

Southern Colonies, 1650–1700

26. What possible effects of Bacon's Rebellion can be seen on the map?

27. Using what you have learned in the chapter, what reasonable relationship can be drawn between the information on the map and levels of slave ownership in the Chesapeake region?

ANALYZE SOURCES

In September 1620, after their ship sailed off course, the Pilgrims arrived on the shore of Massachusetts. Before they disembarked from the ship, they wrote an agreement called the Mayflower Compact. Read the excerpt below and answer the question.

> [We] doe . . . covenant [agree] and combine ourselves together into a civill body politick, for our better ordering and preservation, and furtherance of the ends aforesaid; and by virtue hereof to enact, constitute, and frame such just and equall laws, ordinances, acts, constitutions and offices, from time to time, as shall be thought most meete [correct] and convenient for the generall good of the Colonie.

28. Why did the Pilgrims write the Mayflower Compact?

CONNECT TO YOUR LIFE

29. **EXPLANATORY** The discovery that there were two large continents—North and South America—that previously had been unknown to them changed the way Europeans viewed the world. In the past 30 years, advances in digital communications and computing have changed the way people perceive the world, as well. Review what you learned about the growth of the American colonies and find parallels between that development and the digital revolution. How do these modern parallels affect people's daily lives?

TIPS

- Use textual evidence from the chapter to support your explanation.

- Look for parallels between positive and negative aspects of the American colonies and the digital revolution.

- Focus on how people's lives changed in each instance and if people have truly benefited from the changes.

VOCABULARY ANSWERS

1. Conquistadors, such as Cortés, were the first Europeans to encounter many Native American groups.

2. After a specified term of labor, indentured servants could gain their freedom.

3. Sugar was an important commodity because of the revenue it generated along the triangular trade route.

4. To run the empire, the Spanish set up one viceroyalty in Mexico City and one in Lima, Peru.

5. The enforcement of slave codes allowed colonists to maintain control over the lives of enslaved people.

6. Pilgrim dissenters broke from the original Church of England.

7. Investors formed the Virginia Company of London, a joint-stock company, to finance colonization and share profits from exports.

8. A charter granted by the king gave colonists legal rights to land in North America.

9. Anne Hutchinson was labeled a heretic for her refusal to adhere to church doctrine.

READING STRATEGY ANSWER

Text Clues	What I Know	My Conclusions
Puritans founded Plymouth and Massachusetts Bay colonies; Puritan dissenters founded Connecticut and Rhode Island; Quakers founded Pennsylvania; Catholics founded New France	Puritan values were written into government and became social norms; dissenters had greater tolerance and separated church and state; freedom of conscience and religious tolerance applied only to Christians	Religion played a major role in the founding of North American colonies. It played a role in the development of their governments and cultures.

10. Possible response: Religion was a major motivating factor for founding many of the colonies and influenced the government and societies that developed in North American settlements. For example, Puritan values written into law in the Plymouth and Massachusetts Bay colonies became accepted social behaviors. Intolerance drove dissenters out, so they founded Connecticut and Rhode Island, where they separated the laws of religion and government.

MAIN IDEAS ANSWERS

11. People conquered by the Aztecs resented them, and some aided the Spanish to overthrow their Aztec rulers.

12. The friars established missions where they attempted to convert Native Americans to Christianity.

13. The ships were horribly overcrowded, lacked ventilation and sanitation, had inadequate food supplies, and fostered disease and illness. Many enslaved Africans did not survive the journey.

14. John Rolfe brought a new strain of tobacco from the West Indies that helped the colony become profitable.

15. The French King stipulated that only Catholics could settle the area, greatly reducing the number of settlers.

16. Roger Williams stated that the leaders had stolen land from Native Americans and disagreed with laws requiring church attendance.

17. Native Americans and settlers disagreed over land occupation and ownership. Native Americans were being forced off lands they had occupied for hundreds of years by Europeans who believed they owned the land by right of charters and land grants.

18. Although New Netherland was firmly under Dutch control, James, Duke of York, held land granted under the authority of King Charles II that included the Dutch colony. A large English fleet easily took New Netherland from the Dutch.

19. Maryland's settlers avoided mistakes that earlier settlers had made in Virginia. They established better relations with Native Americans, and rather than enslave native people for labor, they relied on indentured servants.

20. Oglethorpe forged alliances with the Lower Creek, Cherokee, and Chickasaw against the Spanish.

21. The slave codes wrote racial discrimination into law, fundamentally restricting the rights of Africans and African Americans based on their skin color.

HISTORICAL THINKING ANSWERS

22. Both colonies were founded on idealistic principles rather than profit, and neither initially had large plantations. They differed in that Massachusetts Bay was a refuge for Puritans, while Georgia was meant to be a place where England's poor could have a better life. Puritans governed Massachusetts, while a group of trustees governed Georgia.

23. The large-scale adoption of slave labor in North American colonies was a huge boost to the Atlantic triangular trade. As slaves increased production in the colonies, more goods were shipped to England. England then shipped goods to Africa and purchased more slaves.

24. Small farmers and landless men resented the treaties with Native Americans that prevented the colony from expanding. These men also resented wealthy leaders, particularly when Governor William Berkeley refused to support a war against Native Americans.

25. New France settlers generally coexisted with Native Americans while New Englanders frequently clashed with them. New France was sparsely settled, and as traders, the French settlers needed to maintain good relations with Native Americans. The English, however, wanted increasingly larger tracts of land and viewed Native Americans as enemies of progress, not economic partners.

INTERPRET MAPS ANSWERS

26. Settlement in Virginia greatly expanded in the 24 years following Bacon's Rebellion (1676), as a vast number of Native Americans had been killed and protections granted to them under treaty were ignored.

27. As the settlement expanded, tobacco became the number one cash crop, requiring a large labor force to plant, harvest, and process. As a result, the slave population sharply increased.

ANALYZE SOURCES ANSWER

28. The Pilgrims wrote the Mayflower Compact to affirm the need to establish "just and equall laws." They likely felt that having such an agreement would provide a guiding purpose—the "general good of the Colonie"—and help them preserve order and increase their chances of success.

CONNECT TO YOUR LIFE ANSWER

29. Answers will vary. Students find parallels between the growth of the American colonies and the development of the digital revolution and write an essay to explain how each development affected people's daily lives. Students use textual evidence and examples of aspects of the digital revolution, including positive and negative effects of both. Essays should focus on how people's lives changed and whether they benefited from the changes. Students use their evidence and examples to support their ideas.

UNIT 1 RESOURCES

UNIT INTRODUCTION

UNIT TIME LINE

UNIT WRAP-UP

NATIONAL GEOGRAPHIC | CONNECTION

National Geographic Magazine Adapted Articles
- "Colonial New York"
- "The First Americans" ONLINE

Unit 1 Inquiry: Conceive a Utopia

NG Learning Framework Activities
- Map Migrations
- Establish a Trade Network

Unit 1 Formal Assessment

CHAPTER 3 RESOURCES

Available at NGLSync.Cengage.com

TEACHER RESOURCES & ASSESSMENT

Reading and Note-Taking

Vocabulary Practice

Social Studies Skills Lessons
- Reading: Summarize
- Writing: Explanatory

Formal Assessment
- Chapter 3 Pretest
- Chapter 3 Tests A & B
- Section Quizzes

Chapter 3 Answer Key

ExamView®
One-time Download

STUDENT DIGITAL RESOURCES

- eEdition
- Handbooks
- Online Atlas
- American Gallery Online
- History Notebook
- Active History
- American Voices (Biographies)
- Literature Analysis
- Projects for Inquiry-Based Learning

Chapter 3 Spanish Resources are available at NGLSync.Cengage.com.

CHAPTER 3 PLANNER

AMERICAN STORIES ONLINE | **Colliding Cultures**

- Study Primary Sources: Letter from a Jesuit missionary
- On Your Feet: Identifying Issues
- **NG Learning Framework:** Make a Historical Connection

SECTION 1 RESOURCES
NEW ENGLAND AND THE MIDDLE COLONIES

LESSON 1.1
New England's Economy and Society

- On Your Feet: Navigation Acts Roundtable
- **NG Learning Framework:** Prepare for a Panel Discussion

LESSON 1.2
The Prosperous Middle Colonies

- On Your Feet: Interview William Penn
- **NG Learning Framework:** Create a Book of Proverbs

LESSON 1.3
Immigration and Growth in the Middle Colonies

- On Your Feet: Compare Social Classes
- **NG Learning Framework:** Compose a Journal Entry

SECTION 2 RESOURCES
THE SOUTHERN COLONIES

LESSON 2.1
An Agricultural Society

- On Your Feet: Colonial Agriculture Word Web
- **NG Learning Framework:** Craft an Informative Report

LESSON 2.2
Life Under Slavery

- On Your Feet: Fact-Finding Bee
- **NG Learning Framework:** Interpret Through Drawing

LESSON 2.3
AMERICAN VOICES
Olaudah Equiano

- On Your Feet: Fishbowl
- **NG Learning Framework:** Fact-Check a Historical Movie

LESSON 2.4
CURATING HISTORY
The Whitney Plantation Wallace, Louisiana

- On Your Feet: Sort the Artifacts

SECTION 3 RESOURCES
NEW DEVELOPMENTS IN THE COLONIES

LESSON 3.1
The Enlightenment
AMERICAN GALLERY ONLINE Colonial Landmarks
- **NG Learning Framework:** Create a Time Line

LESSON 3.2
The Great Awakening

- On Your Feet: Team Quiz
- **NG Learning Framework:** Write a Dialogue
- **American Voices Biography** Jonathan Edwards ONLINE

LESSON 3.3
English and Colonial Rights

- On Your Feet: Compare Bills of Rights
- **NG Learning Framework:** Host a Talk Show

SECTION 4 RESOURCES
THE FRENCH AND INDIAN WAR

LESSON 4.1
Conflict in the Colonies

- Active History: Compare North American Settlements
- **NG Learning Framework:** Craft an Editorial

LESSON 4.2
British Victory

- On Your Feet: Victory Q & A
- **NG Learning Framework:** Stage a Debate

CHAPTER 3 REVIEW

STRATEGY ❶
CREATE OUTLINES

Help students summarize the chapter by creating four outlines, one for each section. Tell them to write the titles of the sections at the top of each outline: *New England and the Middle Colonies*, *The Southern Colonies*, *New Developments in the Colonies*, and *The French and Indian War*. Instruct students to complete each outline with relevant information as they read the corresponding set of lessons.

I._____

    A._____

    B._____

II._____

    A._____

    B._____

III._____

    A._____

    B._____

Use with All Lessons

STRATEGY ❷
ASK EITHER/OR QUESTIONS

Monitor students' comprehension of the lesson by asking them to answer either/or questions. After students have answered the questions, ask partners to check one another's answers. Then have pairs work together to answer the Historical Thinking questions.

Use with All Lessons *For example, you may ask questions such as these for Lesson 3.1:*

- Was the Enlightenment a movement that encouraged people to obey or to challenge authority figures in politics and religion? *(challenge)*

- Did Benjamin Franklin reject or embrace Enlightenment ideas? *(embrace)*

STRATEGY ❸
MAKE A LIST

Post this heading on the board: Five Things I Know About the French and Indian War. Ask students to copy the heading onto a sheet of paper. As they read the lesson, prompt them to write at least five sentences under the heading, including reasons for various alliances and battles. Invite volunteers to share their sentences with the class.

Use with Lesson 4.1

STRATEGY ❶
PREDICT USING VISUALS AND CAPTIONS

Pair special needs students with students at higher proficiency levels. Ask more proficient students to assist special needs students in previewing the lesson by describing the photographs, artwork, maps, and other visuals and by reading the captions. Then have pairs work together to write predictions about what they will learn in the lesson. After students read the lesson, direct them to revise their predictions if necessary to match what they learned.

Use with All Lessons

STRATEGY ❷
MARK UP MAPS

Provide students with colored markers and a printout of the map African-American Population, c. 1760. Direct students to read the legend and to use a yellow marker to circle the areas where African Americans made up more than half the population. Then have them use a green marker to circle areas in which African Americans made up 30–50 percent of the population and a blue marker to circle areas in which African Americans represented 0.1–30 percent of the population. Provide sentence frames for students to complete based on their marked-up maps.

- In parts of _____, _____, and _____, African Americans made up more than half of the population. *(Virginia, North Carolina, South Carolina)*

- In the New England Colonies, African Americans made up a _____ part of the population. *(small)*

- In the Southern Colonies, higher concentrations of African Americans lived along the _____ rather than inland. *(coasts)*

- There were more African Americans than white Americans in nearly the entire colony of _____. *(South Carolina)*

Use with Lesson 2.2 *You can adapt this activity to help students understand the maps in Lessons 4.1 and 4.2.*

ENGLISH LANGUAGE LEARNERS

STRATEGY 1
USE CONTEXT CLUES

Pair students at the **Emerging** level with those at the **Expanding** or **Bridging** level. Model how to use context clues to learn the meaning of unfamiliar words. Instruct students to find the context clues or textual definitions that provide the meaning of the terms *maritime* (seafaring) and *subsistence farming* (producing only enough food for one's family, with little left over to sell). Then have students look for context clues to help them understand other unfamiliar words and write an original sentence using each word. Prompt more proficient students to assist others in checking the accuracy of the sentences. Invite pairs to share their sentences and discuss different ways to use each word. Encourage students to look for context clues whenever they encounter an unfamiliar word.

Use with All Lessons *For example, in Lesson 1.1, have students find context clues that help them determine the meaning of* smuggling *(trading goods illegally) and* apprentices *(young people living with craftsmen to learn a trade).*

STRATEGY 2
PRONOUNCE WORDS

Before reading, preview with students at **All Proficiencies** the terms *Parliament, salutary neglect,* and *libel.* Say each word slowly, and have students repeat after you. Suggest students make word cards for the terms, writing definitions and pronunciation hints for themselves. You may wish to preview additional terms from the lesson, such as *baron, levied, Glorious Revolution, Dominion, legislature, objectionable,* and *echoing.*

Use with Lesson 3.3 *You may wish to use this strategy with other lessons that contain words students find difficult to pronounce.*

STRATEGY 3
LOOK FOR COGNATES

Suggest that as students read they look for words that are similar in spelling and meaning to words in their home language. For each word they identify, have students of **All Proficiencies** make a vocabulary card with the English word and definition on one side and the word and definition in their home language on the other side. Encourage them to note any differences in the meanings of the two words.

Use with All Lessons *For example, in Lesson 1.1, the words* occupation, economic, colonies, *and* port *have cognates in Spanish:* ocupación, económico, colonias, puerto.

GIFTED & TALENTED

STRATEGY 1
CREATE A PODCAST

Allow students to choose one lesson as the basis for a history podcast. Tell them to establish a point of view that is both informative and entertaining, maybe even provocative. Suggest that students write a script and indicate sound effects if relevant. Then prompt them to present their episode live to the class or record it on a phone or other device to post on a class or school website.

Use with All Lessons

STRATEGY 2
CREATE A VISUAL BIOGRAPHY

Prompt students to create and annotate a visual biography of the most important events in the life of Olaudah Equiano as presented in his autobiography, using the text and additional research. Tell them to include dates, locations, and important people associated with Equiano's life events, as well as photographs, drawings, portraits, editorial cartoons, and other relevant images. Students could use presentation software or art supplies. Encourage them to share their biographies with the class.

Use with Lesson 2.3

PRE-AP

STRATEGY 1
EXPLORE IMPACTS

Instruct students to choose one of the people mentioned in the chapter and conduct research to write an essay that examines that person's impact on the history and maturation of the American colonies. Encourage students to incorporate photographs, art, and other visuals in their essays. Invite volunteers to share their finished essays with the class and answer any questions.

Use with All Lessons *Students could research one of the following: an accused Salem "witch," Benjamin Franklin, Francis Daniel Pastorius, the rebel slave leader Jemmy, Isaac Newton, John Locke, John Peter Zenger, or Chief Pontiac.*

STRATEGY 2
ANALYZE A SPEECH

Tell students that Chief Pontiac's speech in May 1763 was not recorded at the time. However, some of those who heard it wrote it down that same year, and that version is accessible in print and online. Instruct students to read and analyze the entire speech, including Pontiac's criticisms of his own people, his characterization of the French and British, his reasoning, and his call to action. Invite students to present their analysis to the class in a written or oral report.

Use with Lesson 4.2

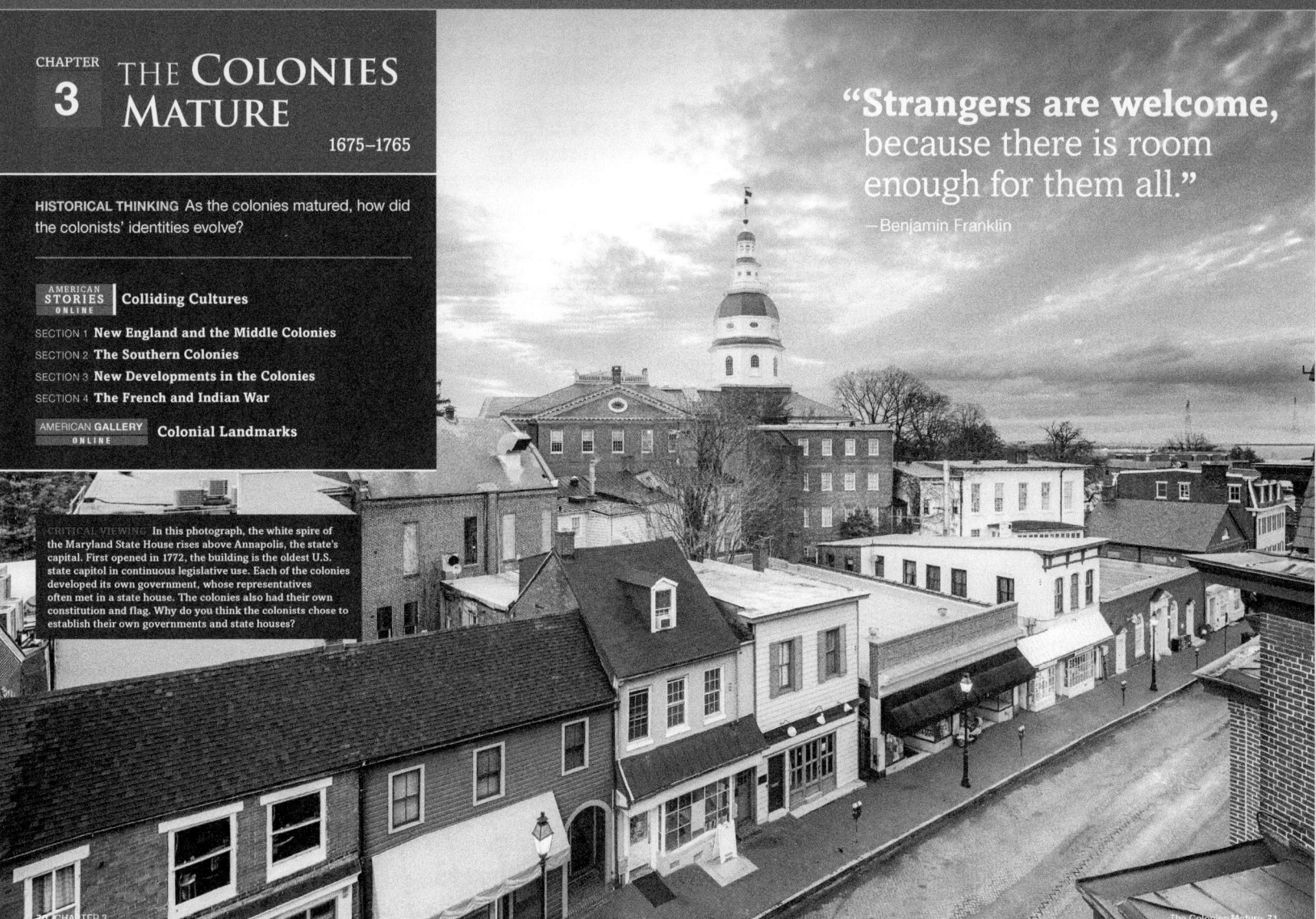

HISTORICAL THINKING As the colonies matured, how did the colonists' identities evolve?

AMERICAN **STORIES** ONLINE | **Colliding Cultures**

SECTION 1 **New England and the Middle Colonies**
SECTION 2 **The Southern Colonies**
SECTION 3 **New Developments in the Colonies**
SECTION 4 **The French and Indian War**

AMERICAN **GALLERY** ONLINE | **Colonial Landmarks**

CRITICAL VIEWING In this photograph, the white spire of the Maryland State House rises above Annapolis, the state's capital. First opened in 1772, the building is the oldest U.S. state capitol in continuous legislative use. Each of the colonies developed its own government, whose representatives often met in a state house. The colonies also had their own constitution and flag. Why do you think the colonists chose to establish their own governments and state houses?

"**Strangers are welcome,** because there is room enough for them all."

—Benjamin Franklin

INTRODUCE THE PHOTOGRAPH

COLONIAL ANNAPOLIS

Invite students to view the photograph, and guide them to discover details. **ASK:** What is implied by the architecture of the state house? *(The capitol building was clearly important, as it is the largest and grandest building in the photo and includes a spire that would have been visible from far away.)* Based on the photograph, what industries might have been located in colonial Annapolis? *(Possible response: Being located on a waterfront, Annapolis likely developed a shipping and transport industry and possibly a strong fishing industry.)* Read the Benjamin Franklin quote aloud. **ASK:** How does the photograph connect to Franklin's words? *(The photograph shows a peaceful, well-kept city with stores and housing to meet people's needs.)* Tell students that this chapter will explore more about life in the New England and Middle Colonies.

For Chapter 3 Spanish Resources, visit the Resources Menu. Chapter 3 Resources are available at NGLSync.Cengage.com.

SHARE BACKGROUND

Annapolis, Maryland, sits on the bank of the Severn River, which feeds into the Chesapeake Bay. It has long been home to thriving fishing, shipping, and recreational industries. Founded in 1649, Anne Arundel Town became Maryland's capital in 1695 and was later renamed Annapolis. The city offers a blend of architectural styles but is best known for its Georgian architecture. The Georgian period began with the crowning of England's King George I in 1714 and ended with the death of George IV in 1830. The Maryland State House in the city's historic district is one example of Georgian architecture. Most of this district's stately two- and three-story brick Georgians were built in the 1760s and 1770s.

CRITICAL VIEWING Each colony likely wanted to control its own government to ensure that its population would be able to access the land and resources and to guard against a situation in which one colony might dominate the others.

HISTORICAL THINKING QUESTION

As the colonies matured, how did the colonists' identities evolve?

Numbered Heads Activity: Shaping a Colonial Identity Divide the class into groups of four and have them count off within each group. Pose the following question: In what ways might life in the colonies help shape the identity of the people who live in them? Suggest students consider the following topics: society, economy, expansion and immigration, and government. Instruct group members to think about the question and discuss their answers. Encourage groups to identify the biggest factor in shaping a group identity and to explain why they think so. Call a number and invite students with that number to summarize their group's discussion for the class. As students read Chapter 3, periodically ask them if they still agree with their previous assessment of the factors shaping colonial identity based on what they've learned.

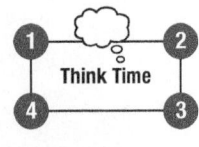

INTRODUCE THE READING STRATEGY

SUMMARIZE

Explain that summarizing texts can help readers identify which ideas are the most important. Turn to the Chapter Review and preview with students the diagram on summarizing. As they read the chapter, have students summarize information about why and how cities expanded in the New England and Middle Colonies.

KEY DATES FOR CHAPTER 3

1689	English Bill of Rights takes effect
1692	Salem witch trials begin
1701	Great Peace of Montreal is signed
1722	Iroquois Confederacy becomes Six Nations
1735	John Peter Zenger trial takes place
1739	Stono Rebellion erupts
1754	French and Indian War begins
1763	Treaty of Paris ends French and Indian War
1763	Pontiac's Rebellion begins

INTRODUCE CHAPTER VOCABULARY

KEY VOCABULARY

SECTION 1

backcountry	Conestoga wagon	Piedmont
common school	maritime	subsistence farming

SECTION 2

overseer	Stono Rebellion

SECTION 3

Enlightenment	libel	salutary neglect
Great Awakening	Parliament	salvation

SECTION 4

Proclamation of 1763

WORD MAPS

As students read the chapter, ask them to complete a Word Map for each Key Vocabulary word. Tell them to write the word in the oval and, as they encounter the word in the chapter, complete the Word Map. Model an example using the graphic organizer below.

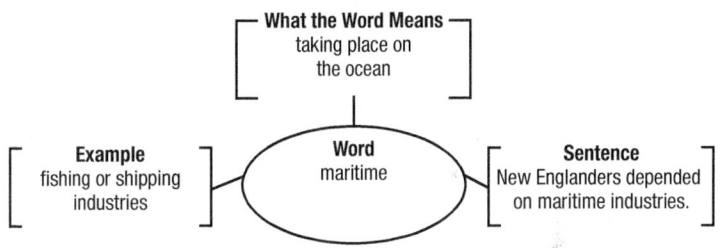

 For instructional support for the online American Story "Colliding Cultures," go to NGLSync.Cengage.com.

As settlers came to Boston, they filled low-lying areas along the water with land so they could build wharves to dock ships at their growing port. Today, the Port of Boston is one of the principal ports on the East Coast.

NEW ENGLAND'S ECONOMY AND SOCIETY

When people settle in a new place, they learn to take advantage of what it offers. In the 17th century, New Englanders learned to harvest both the land and the sea.

ECONOMIC ACTIVITIES

Most New England colonists were farmers, but farming in the region was a challenging occupation. New England's long, cold winters made for a short growing season. In addition, farms were often located on rocky soil amid thick forests, which made clearing the land difficult. Farming involved an entire family, with all members helping to plant and harvest crops and take care of the farm animals. These families practiced **subsistence farming**. This means that farmers produced only enough food to provide for their family with little, if any, left over to sell or trade. Many New England farm families raised livestock and grew wheat, rye, corn, and fruit.

The Atlantic Ocean provided more profitable economic opportunities for New Englanders, and fishing and whaling became important industries during the 17th century. Fishers sold their catches to London merchants in return for manufactured goods such as shoes, textiles, glass, and metal products. Colonial whalers hunted their prey along the coasts as well as in deeper waters. They sold and exported most parts of the huge creatures, including the whale meat, oil, bones, and blubber. Blubber is whale fat, and it was used to light oil lamps and make candles. These **maritime**, or seafaring, activities led to the development of a thriving shipbuilding industry. Forests in the region supplied plentiful lumber for the ships. In addition to the shipyards where the vessels were built, iron foundries and sawmills sprang up to meet the demand for ships, employing many workers.

CENTER OF TRADE

As a result of all this economic activity, New England found itself at the center of colonial trade. Merchants in the region traded with other colonies and exchanged goods directly with Europe. In the early 1700s, merchants in Boston and other port cities in Massachusetts and Rhode Island dominated colonial trade. In time, however, trade expanded across the Atlantic through the triangular trade routes. As you have read, these routes connected merchants in North America, Europe, and Africa. New England merchants sold such colonial goods as cotton and rum to Europe. In return, they received fruit and salt from Africa and sugar and dyes from the Caribbean. After 1750, the increased trade led to the growth of new port cities, including New York and Philadelphia in the Middle Colonies, and Charleston in the Southern Colonies.

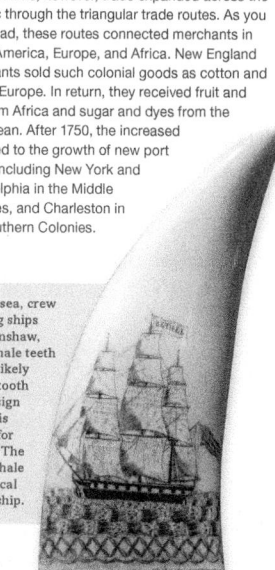

To pass free time at sea, crew members on whaling ships often practiced scrimshaw, the art of carving whale teeth and bones. A sailor likely carved this whale's tooth with an intricate design of a ship either for his own amusement or for loved ones at home. The whalers also used whale parts to make practical tools for use on the ship.

As trade in New England grew, British leaders decided they were entitled to their share of the profits. Beginning in 1651, Britain passed a series of laws called the **Navigation Acts**. The acts required that all goods brought to Britain or its colonies be transported on British or colonial-made ships. And colonial products, including tobacco, sugar, cotton, and dyes, could only be sold to Britain and its colonies.

The acts also allowed Britain to control and tax all trade to and from the American colonies. For example, all European products destined for the colonies had to go to a British port first. These products were then loaded onto British or colonial-made ships that carried the goods to colonial ports where additional taxes were levied on the imports. British authorities also taxed any colonial goods that were not shipped to Britain. The colonists, of course, resented the additional charges on both imports and exports. This led some to turn to smuggling, or trading goods illegally, a practice the British found hard to control.

PURITANISM DECLINES

When industry and trade developed in New England, Puritan leaders objected to the emergence of a merchant class in the region. They feared that making money would become more important to New Englanders than their religion. And, in fact, membership in the Puritan church began to decline around 1650. The Puritans also perceived other Protestant groups, including Quakers and Baptists, as threats to their authority. To maintain control, the Puritans only gave Puritan men the right to vote and hold office. Meanwhile, they punished those who voiced conflicting religious views. They even hanged some Quaker missionaries. However, after British king Charles II sent a letter forbidding the execution of Quakers, both Quaker and Baptist communities began to flourish in New England.

Still, Puritan leaders continued to overstep royal authority in religious and economic matters. As punishment, Charles II revoked the Massachusetts Bay Colony's charter in 1684. His successor, James II, further strengthened British control over Massachusetts. As of 1686, the king had combined Massachusetts, New Hampshire, Connecticut, the disputed Narragansett territory of Rhode Island, and the present-day state of Maine to form the **Dominion of New England**. Eventually, the Dominion was extended to include New York and New Jersey. The creation of the Dominion angered colonists, who felt

---

PLAN: 4-PAGE LESSON

OBJECTIVE

Summarize the influence of trade on colonial economic and religious culture.

CRITICAL THINKING SKILLS FOR LESSON 1.1

- Evaluate
- Make Inferences
- Summarize
- Identify Main Ideas and Details
- Analyze Cause and Effect
- Draw Conclusions
- Analyze Language Use

HISTORICAL THINKING FOR CHAPTER 3

As the colonies matured, how did the colonists' identities evolve? As the colonists adjusted to life in New England, they encountered new opportunities and new challenges. Lesson 1.1 explores how geography, trade, education, and religion reshaped the colonial identity.

BACKGROUND FOR THE TEACHER

Though Britain passed its first navigation law in 1381, it proved ineffective due to a shortage of ships. The laws Britain passed in the colonial era were more successful. The 1651 Navigation Act originally targeted the Dutch, then Britain's principal trade rival. But the Dutch were able to subvert the law, in large part due to American colonists' preference for Dutch goods and the deals the Dutch offered the colonists on commodities such as sugar. These factors led to a thriving Dutch smuggling trade, which threatened to upend Britain's shipping industry and led to the 1652 Anglo-Dutch War. The 1660 Navigation Act included a practice known as "enumerating," which meant the British could select product categories, such as sugar and tobacco, that the colonies could ship only to Britain, Ireland, or another British colony.

FINANCIAL LITERACY

To extend their knowledge and understanding about the concepts in this lesson, refer students to the Financial Literacy handbook.

INTRODUCE & ENGAGE

CONSIDER NATURAL RESOURCES

Work with students to brainstorm a list of natural resources common to their state or region. Guide them to create categories, such as soil, forests, minerals, and water, and to consider how these resources might boost the area's economy. Write the categories on the board. Then ask students to list businesses and commercial trade that might evolve from such resources. *(Possible responses: tourism, farming, energy production, lumber)* Tell students that Lesson 1.1 discusses colonial New England's economy and its effect on the region's culture and society.

TEACH

GUIDED DISCUSSION

1. **Identify Main Ideas and Details** Why did whales make a valuable target for whaling ships? *(Many parts of whales could be sold commercially, such as meat, oil, bones, and blubber for making candles. In addition, sailors used different parts of the whale to make practical tools they used on the ship, and they passed the time by making delicate carvings in whale teeth.)*

2. **Summarize** How did the Navigation Acts change the way European goods made it to market in the American colonies? *(Because of the Navigation Acts, European goods had to go to a British port. Once there, the goods were transferred onto British-owned ships. When the products were delivered to the colonies, the colonists had to pay new import taxes on them.)*

3. **Analyze Cause and Effect** How did the Puritans' political tactics help them maintain their power? *(Possible response: By allowing only Puritan men to vote or hold office, Puritan leaders controlled community laws, standards, and punishments. By executing Quaker missionaries, they probably slowed or stemmed the influx of new religious ideas and likely frightened those who might question their authority or religious views into silence.)*

MORE INFORMATION

17th-Century Plastic In the colonial whaling industry, baleen whales were particularly prized. Instead of teeth, these whales' mouths have baleen, long strips that hang down in two rows. Baleen is composed of keratin, a substance also found in human hair and fingernails. Each row of baleen contains hundreds of triangular plates. The longer sides are smooth, and the shorter sides are bristly. When removed from the whale's mouth, baleen retains its shape and flexibility, even if exposed to high heat. Because of these characteristics, baleen was used in many 17th-century products, including buggy whips, corset stays, and umbrella ribs. In fact, baleen was so versatile that it could be used for many purposes that today would require plastic or steel. The downside of baleen was that if it was not immediately dried and cleaned when removed from the whale's mouth, it retained a strong, rank smell that significantly lowered its value.

DIFFERENTIATE

STRIVING READERS

Sequence Events To help them better understand the Navigation Acts, direct pairs of students to make notes in two Sequence Chains—one about goods imported into the colonies and the other about exported goods. Notes should include information about what was loaded onto which nation's ship, where the ship went, when and where goods were unloaded or reloaded, and when the goods were taxed. When they have finished, instruct pairs to take turns reading the notes in their Sequence Chains aloud, using transition words to introduce the contents of each square.

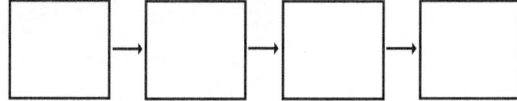

GIFTED & TALENTED

Write a Letter Tell students to conduct online research to learn about the experiences of specific categories of New England colonists. Students may choose to research the life of a blacksmith, fisherman, whaler, shipbuilder, farmer, wife and mother, or enslaved person. Then prompt them to write a letter from that person's perspective to loved ones far away, telling about their daily life in New England. If students choose a person who was likely unable to read or write, they can imagine they are dictating the letter to someone who could write it down. Invite volunteers to post their letters on a class blog or read them aloud to the class.

See the Chapter Planner for more strategies for differentiation.

they'd lost the rights and freedoms they'd enjoyed under their own colonial charters. Their resentment grew when James II appointed **Sir Edmund Andros** to be the Dominion's governor in 1686.

In April 1689, after news reached Boston that James II had been deposed, colonists overthrew the Dominion government and imprisoned Andros. With the Dominion gone, many of the colonies reactivated their charters. But Massachusetts, whose charter had been canceled under Charles II, was issued a new one by Britain's reigning king and queen, William and Mary. The 1691 Massachusetts charter guaranteed religious freedom for all Protestants and forbade religious restrictions on voting. The new charter greatly increased the number of voters in New England and caused Puritanism to decline even further.

NEW ENGLAND SOCIETY

Even as the Puritans lost some of their authority, they continued to influence colonial life—particularly in the realm of education. Puritans wanted children to learn to read so they could learn about God. In the 1640s, Massachusetts set up **common schools**, or elementary schools, which focused on instruction in the Bible and moral behavior. The colony also established secondary schools called Latin grammar schools. Neighboring colonies followed suit, and soon more people could read in New England than in any other region. Many children learned skills they would use later in life. Colonial boys often served as apprentices, living with a master craftsman to learn a trade, such as carpentry. Colonial girls typically stayed at home to learn cooking, sewing, and other skills necessary to run a household from their mothers.

The Puritans also founded colleges, including Harvard in Massachusetts in 1636 and Yale in Connecticut in 1701. Both colleges instructed only

male students, most of whom planned to become members of the clergy. Today, Harvard and Yale are modern institutions that offer classes to both men and women in a broad range of subjects and the opportunity to earn a variety of different degrees.

Some of the people in New England society were not free to attend school or learn the trade of their choosing. Enslaved African Americans made up about 2 or 3 percent of the region's population. The percentage was small because most New England farmers either didn't need or couldn't afford to buy enslaved workers. The slaves who did come

THE SALEM WITCH TRIALS

In 1689, British rulers William and Mary started a war with France that spilled into the American colonies, particularly the northern part of New York. Some of the colonists who fled the war ended up in Salem Village in the Massachusetts Bay Colony. These colonists put a strain on the village's resources and further heightened the existing tensions between its leading families. The quarrels that erupted were believed by many to be the work of the devil. This atmosphere of fear led Salem authorities to accuse three women of being witches in February 1692. All three were jailed, and soon villagers started accusing many others of witchcraft.

In all, nearly 200 women and men were accused and brought to trial for witchcraft. "Evidence" consisted largely of gossip. Twenty of the accused were put to death, most by hanging. Eventually the hysteria ran its course. In May 1693, Governor William Phips pardoned those still imprisoned and returned not-guilty verdicts in the remaining cases. About 200 years later, artist Joseph E. Baker created the engraving above called *The Witch No. 1*. In this fanciful take on the Salem witch trials, lightning breaks the chains that had bound the hands of the accused and strikes one of her questioners, knocking him to the floor.

Yale University, New Haven, Connecticut

The college was officially named Yale in 1718 in honor of Welsh merchant Elihu Yale. He had given 417 books, money from the sale of goods, and a portrait of Britain's king George I to the college. The first planned college campus in the United States, Yale became a university after it added multiple schools with instruction in many subjects. The aerial photo below shows the extent of the university today, which has produced five presidents among its graduates.

to New England usually worked as household servants, artisans, and laborers. In port cities, enslaved persons sometimes labored alongside their masters in the shipyards and as fishers, whalers, and shipbuilders. Free African Americans, many of whom had spent part of their lives as slaves, also lived in the New England colonies. Although they had some legal rights, they did not always receive equal treatment. A Massachusetts law, for instance, required all African Americans to remain indoors after 9 p.m. unless their owners had sent them out on business.

HISTORICAL THINKING

1. **READING CHECK** What were the major economic activities in 17th-century New England?

2. **EVALUATE** What role did geography play in the number of enslaved workers in New England?

3. **MAKE INFERENCES** How do you think some colonists viewed British authority after the passage of the Navigation Acts and the formation of the Dominion of New England?

4. **SUMMARIZE** Why did Puritanism decline?

BUILD BACKGROUND

SIR EDMUND ANDROS

Colonial resentment toward Edmund Andros often focused on his enthusiastic support for and enforcement of the Navigation Acts and on the harsh restrictions he placed on public gatherings. He also decreed that worship at Boston's Old South Meeting House would follow the Episcopalian tradition. After colonists imprisoned Andros, they sent him back to England, where he was tried and soon released. His time in the colonies did not end there, however. Although he was disliked in the colonies, British authorities considered him a competent administrator. Against that backdrop, he later returned to serve as governor of Virginia in 1692 and of Maryland from 1693 to 1694.

EXECUTION OF SALEM WITCHES

Because of popular lore and misconceptions, many people think that those who were convicted of witchcraft in Salem were burned at the stake. However, historical research reveals that was not the case. Researchers assert that while burning witches was common in French culture, the English punishment of choice was hanging, so it follows that hanging would also be the method employed in the American colonies. The one known exception was an accused farmer named Giles Corley, who was crushed to death under heavy stones for failing to plead either guilty or innocent.

TEACH

GUIDED DISCUSSION

4. **Draw Conclusions** How did the Puritans lay the groundwork for an eventual system of universal public education? *(New England Puritans were worried about people leaving the church, so they started common schools to teach children to read the Bible, a practice that quickly spread to other areas.)*

5. **Analyze Language Use** Using the context of the Salem witch trials, create a definition for the contemporary term *witch hunt*. *(A witch hunt is a baseless or unfounded accusation or campaign against a person or group that holds unpopular views and is usually based on little or questionable evidence.)*

AMERICAN PLACES

Though it began as an all-white, all-male institution, over the years Yale University has gradually diversified its student body. The first African American to receive a degree of any kind from Yale, Cortlandt Van Rensselaer Creed, earned a medical degree from the Yale School of Medicine in 1857. For women applicants, change came more slowly. Some alumni flatly opposed the idea of opening Yale to coeducational programming for undergraduate students. Although some women had been admitted for graduate studies as early as 1892, Yale did not become fully coeducational until 1969. In 1971, a group of women—all transfer students—became the first women ever to graduate from Yale.

ACTIVE OPTIONS

On Your Feet: Navigation Acts Roundtable Arrange students in groups of four or five. Provide a sheet of paper with this question for each group: In what ways did the Navigation Acts reshape New England's culture and economy? The first student in each group writes an answer and reads it aloud before passing the paper clockwise to the next student. Make sure that every student in the group adds at least one answer. When the groups have run out of answers, invite a volunteer from each to share their ideas.

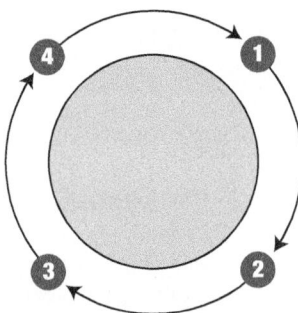

NG Learning Framework: Prepare for a Panel Discussion

SKILLS Communication, Collaboration

KNOWLEDGE Our Human Story

Divide the class into small groups. Direct each group to focus on a different aspect of the witch trials, such as who was on trial, who made the accusations, who served as judges, what happened at the trials, and how the trials affected the community. Encourage all students to combine what they learned about the witch trials in Lesson 1.1 with online and library research to develop further historical background about the events in Salem. Then bring the groups together to communicate their findings and hone their ideas. Ask each group to appoint a panelist to present the group's findings to the rest of the class in a brief panel discussion. Invite the class to ask questions of the panelists at the end of the presentation.

HISTORICAL THINKING

ANSWERS

1. Agriculture, lumber, and shipping and its related industries were all key economic activities. Fishing and whaling, as well as developing trade opportunities, were also important.

2. Due to long, cold winters and less than ideal soil, agriculture typically centered on families and subsistence farming. These farmers didn't need a large labor force and couldn't afford enslaved workers, so the percentage of enslaved workers in the population of New England was small.

3. Possible response: Many colonists increasingly resented British authority because they felt as though they'd lost some of the rights and freedoms to which they had become accustomed under colonial charters.

4. Puritanism began to decline about 1650 as a merchant class developed and as other Protestant groups moved into the area. Also, the Massachusetts charter, revised by the British, guaranteed religious freedom for all Protestants and did not allow voting restrictions on the basis of religion, which weakened Puritan control in the region.

THE PROSPEROUS MIDDLE COLONIES

A strong economy is a desirable characteristic in any location. But people also want to share the same rights and privileges. In the Middle Colonies, some people enjoyed equal treatment, but others did not.

BOOMING ECONOMY

The Middle Colonies were similar to New England colonies in some respects. Like New England, the Middle Colonies had access to wide, navigable rivers and to the Atlantic Coast, which provided lucrative, or moneymaking, trade and seafaring opportunities. Bustling port cities such as New York City and Philadelphia became centers of maritime trade in the Middle Colonies. This trade boosted shipbuilding and rope- and sail-manufacturing industries and created large numbers of jobs for dock workers and sailors.

Unlike New England, the Middle Colonies had a milder climate and fertile soil, which allowed the region to develop a profitable agricultural industry. Farmers in the Middle Colonies raised livestock and crops such as rye, barley, potatoes, oats, and wheat, the region's most important cash crop. In fact, wheat was the most popular grain in colonial America. By the early 1700s, more than 350,000 bushels of wheat and 18,000 tons of wheat flour flowed out of Middle Colony ports, bound for other colonies, Europe, and the Caribbean. Because of their production of wheat and other grains, the Middle Colonies became known as the "breadbasket of the colonies."

Through the wealth generated by the region's thriving economy, Middle Colony port cities attracted a variety of talented people. As a result, New York and Philadelphia also became leading cultural centers. A young man who would become one of Philadelphia's most famous residents, **Benjamin Franklin**, arrived in the city in 1723 at the age of 17. Franklin had left his hometown of Boston to seek a fresh start in a new city. Within five years, he owned a printing shop and published newspapers and *Poor Richard's Almanack*. An almanac is a publication that contains many types of information. Franklin's almanac included calendars, information on the weather and planting, and witty proverbs, such as "Three may keep a secret, if two of them are dead." The yearly volume was always a best seller. As you have read,

GRISTMILL

Middle Colony farmers often took their grain to a gristmill, a building that housed machinery for grinding grain. Colonial gristmills were usually built near a river so that its water could be used to power a waterwheel set outside the mill. The moving waterwheel turned gears inside the building that then rotated the top stone and bedstone. These worked together to crack the hard outer layers of the grain as it flowed through the hopper, grinding it into soft flour. Grinding flour at gristmills was an important industry in many communities in the Middle Colonies.

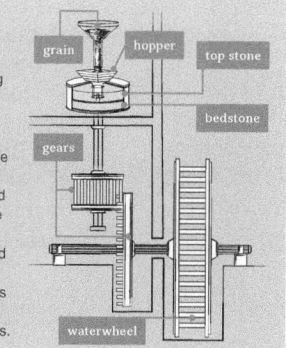

grain | hopper | top stone | bedstone | gears | waterwheel

Benjamin Franklin had only a couple of years of formal schooling. At the age of 12, he began to learn the printing trade under his older brother. This portrait of Franklin was painted from an original drawing by French artist Jean-Baptiste Greuze in 1777.

the literacy rate in the colonies was rising around this time, creating a big demand for newspapers and books—and almanacs.

TOLERANCE AND TENSION

You have read that William Penn encouraged tolerance of other religions when he founded Pennsylvania. This acceptance of others extended through much of the Middle Colonies and was due, in part, to the legacy of the original Dutch settlers. In the Netherlands, the Dutch had welcomed Jews and many Protestant groups. They carried their practice of religious tolerance with them when they founded New Netherland. In addition to different religions, the Dutch settlers embraced people from Sweden, Finland, and Norway. This diversity, or wide variety of people, in the Middle Colonies set them apart from the other American colonies.

The Quakers not only accepted people of different faiths, but they also believed that all people were equal before God. They were the first group in America to speak out against slaveholding.

Unfortunately, not everyone in the Middle Colonies extended a tolerance for diversity to African Americans. Most African Americans in the region lived in New York City, where about 40 percent of white families owned at least one slave by 1711. Many enslaved people were skilled artisans who worked for colonial craftsmen and manufacturers.

Enslaved African Americans in New York City often searched for paid work on their own when slaveholders had none available. But seeing many unaccompanied African Americans on the city streets frightened some white people. As a result, a law was passed that required all hiring of slaves to take place at a designated slave market. Of course, African Americans resented this further restriction on their lives.

Their resentment finally erupted on the night of April 6, 1712, when about 20 African Americans set fire to a building and attacked those who tried to extinguish it. In this first major slave rebellion in colonial America, nine whites were killed. The incident raised the fear that others would soon follow. To discourage new uprisings and punish those involved in the New York revolt, locals took revenge on the African-American community. Thirteen slaves were hanged, three were burned at the stake, and two others were tortured or starved to death. Although some whites questioned the morality of slavery and others opposed it out of fear of more revolts, the institution would be part of American life for more than 150 years. And even today, long after slavery's abolition, its legacy continues to have an impact on African Americans.

HISTORICAL THINKING

1. **READING CHECK** What factors accounted for the economic growth of the Middle Colonies?

2. **COMPARE AND CONTRAST** How were New England and the Middle Colonies similar economically and culturally, and how did they differ?

3. **SUMMARIZE** What was life like for African Americans in the Middle Colonies in general and in New York City in particular?

PLAN: 2-PAGE LESSON

OBJECTIVE

Analyze the economy and social structure of the Middle Colonies.

CRITICAL THINKING SKILLS FOR LESSON 1.2

- Compare and Contrast
- Summarize
- Analyze Cause and Effect
- Evaluate

HISTORICAL THINKING FOR CHAPTER 3

As the colonies matured, how did the colonists' identities evolve? Land suited to agriculture and the influence of the Quakers helped the Middle Colonies develop an identity based on prosperity and tolerance. Lesson 1.2 describes how the Middle Colonies, while thriving economically and intellectually, at times experienced tensions, violence, and fear built around the controversial issue of slavery.

BACKGROUND FOR THE TEACHER

Benjamin Franklin's writings were first published while he was a 16-year-old printer's assistant at his brother's newspaper, the *New England Courant*. During that time, he sent more than a dozen letters to the newspaper under the pen name of Silence Dogood. James Franklin published the letters, not realizing the identity of their author. When Franklin created *Poor Richard's Almanack*, he gave himself another pseudonym: Richard Saunders. The voice of "Poor Richard," though often laced with humor, was that of a slightly dull country bumpkin, a man of simple tastes who believed in hard work and good habits. Over the course of his life, Franklin wrote numerous articles for his own newspaper, the *Pennsylvania Gazette*, as well as letters on a wide range of subjects. Later, he gathered his letters together and published them as an autobiography. But *Poor Richard's Almanack* remained his most popular work. He published the almanac for 26 years, selling nearly 10,000 copies annually. The final volume that Franklin put together, entitled *Poor Richard Improved*, was printed in 1758.

INTRODUCE & ENGAGE

CONNECT TO TODAY

Write and display the term *economic prosperity* in the center of a Word Web. Ask students what factors help make a nation or region prosperous. Prompt them to consider these questions to generate ideas: What does it take for a nation or a community to achieve economic prosperity? *(Students might suggest factors such as natural resources, an educated workforce, and money from investors.)* Who is typically prosperous in a prosperous economy? *(entrepreneurs, investors, business owners)* Record students' responses on the Word Web. Tell students that Lesson 1.2 will explore the sources of wealth and prosperity in the Middle Colonies.

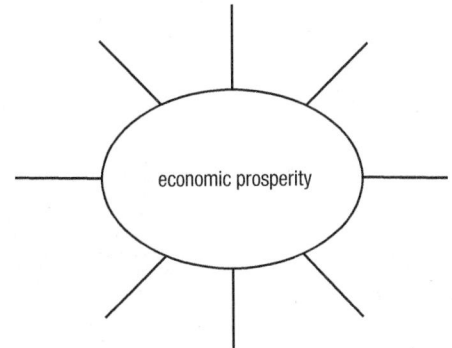

economic prosperity

TEACH

GUIDED DISCUSSION

1. **Analyze Cause and Effect** What effect did rising literacy rates have on colonial publications? *(Rising literacy rates helped create a demand for newspapers and almanacs.)*

2. **Compare and Contrast** How were the Quakers similar to and different from other religious groups that settled in the Middle Colonies? *(Possible response: The Quakers were like other religious groups in that they came to the colonies seeking religious freedom and tolerance. They differed from some groups in that they believed that all people were equal, and they consequently spoke out against slavery.)*

EVALUATE

Direct students to reread the second paragraph of the lesson and to review the diagram of the gristmill. **ASK:** How important was the invention of the gristmill in building the Middle Colonies' reputation as breadbasket of the colonies? *(Possible response: The gristmill was vitally important to the grain industry because it allowed farmers to sell not only bushels of wheat but also tons of processed wheat flour.)*

ACTIVE OPTIONS

On Your Feet: Interview William Penn Organize the class into groups of four for a Numbered Heads activity, instructing group members to number off from one to four. Ask groups to discuss questions they might pose if given the opportunity to interview William Penn and how Penn might answer the questions. Call a number and invite students with that number to present the questions and answers for their groups.

NG Learning Framework: Create a Book of Proverbs

SKILL Collaboration

KNOWLEDGE Our Human Story

Encourage students to work in pairs to explore online or library resources and familiarize themselves with some of the witty proverbs from *Poor Richard's Almanack*. Invite pairs to create proverbs focused on features of 21st-century life, such as digital technology, fast food, or air travel. Each partner could create a different section of the almanac, or partners could take turns contributing to each category. Remind students to title their work. Prompt them to create pen names for themselves as Benjamin Franklin did. Display completed almanacs around the classroom.

DIFFERENTIATE

STRIVING READERS

Dictate Sentence Summaries After students read the lesson, direct them to identify three sentences in the text that contain an important idea. Tell students to write that idea in a summary sentence using their own words. Then place students in pairs, and have partners take turns dictating their sentences to each other. Encourage them to check each other's work for accuracy and spelling.

PRE-AP

Research Religious Tolerance Ask students to generate a research question based on information presented in the text about the religious tolerance of the Dutch and the Quakers. Instruct them to research their question and take notes about their findings. Students might draw parallels or note contrasts with communities in regard to religious tolerance today. Invite them to share their findings with the class in an oral or written report.

See the Chapter Planner for more strategies for differentiation.

HISTORICAL THINKING

ANSWERS

1. Middle Colony farmers benefited from the mild climate and fertile soil, which helped them build thriving farms around livestock and crops. Access to ports and waterways supported maritime activities.

2. New England and the Middle Colonies were similar in that they had access to navigable rivers and to the Atlantic Coast, leading to maritime opportunities. However, the climate and soil of the Middle Colonies were better suited to agriculture than those of New England.

3. The Quakers and some other groups in the Middle Colonies were tolerant of diversity and vocally opposed slavery. In New York City, however, some white people fought for restrictions on the activities of African Americans. When African Americans revolted, white people retaliated, even going so far as to kill some African Americans.

IMMIGRATION AND GROWTH IN THE MIDDLE COLONIES

Think about what you might look for in a new home. If you wanted to live in a place with a strong economy, developing cities, and a history of tolerance, you might have chosen the Middle Colonies.

IMMIGRANTS

After the English took over the Middle Colonies, most of the region's new immigrants came from England and Germany. Between 1683 and 1783, more than 100,000 Germans immigrated to the region. Many of these immigrants fled religious persecution and other forms of oppression for the promise of religious freedom in the Middle Colonies. German immigrants were particularly diverse in their religious beliefs and brought Lutheran, Amish, and Mennonite traditions to the region. Other German immigrants looked to the Middle Colonies as a place of economic opportunity. They had heard about the region's arable, or fertile, and inexpensive land.

The majority of German immigrants settled in the backcountry of Pennsylvania to farm. The **backcountry** stretched along the Appalachian Mountains from Pennsylvania south through the Shenandoah Valley to the Carolinas. This region included the rich soil, rolling hills, and deep forests of the **Piedmont**, a relatively flat area between the mountains and the coastal plain.

The German farmers introduced new techniques to the region. For example, they built shelters for their animals in the winter. Germans also developed the Pennsylvania long rifle for hunting and designed the **Conestoga wagon**, a heavy covered wagon usually pulled by horses or oxen. The wagon could carry up to four tons of cargo. Few German farmers used slaves to work in their fields. As their land became more productive, many farmers were able to sell more of their harvest as cash crops and sell and export their livestock. German immigrants also settled in New York and other Middle Colony cities. There, some German artisans became ironworkers while others made glass, furniture, and kitchenware. By the 1740s, German artists were also creating distinctive house ornaments and elaborately illustrated documents.

In 1654, the first Jewish settlers arrived in Dutch New Amsterdam. Like many German immigrants, the Jews were fleeing religious persecution. Most of these early Jewish immigrants came from Spanish or Portuguese territories in South America and the Caribbean. But by the mid-1660s, the majority of them had left New Amsterdam. Other Jews returned to the site, which was then New York, in the early 1680s, and this time the settlers stayed. By 1685, about 100 Jews lived in New York City. By the late 1720s, that number had doubled. These immigrants built a synagogue—a Jewish place of worship—and established schools where religious subjects were taught as well as reading, writing, and arithmetic.

GROWING CITIES

Immigration from foreign countries and from other American colonies resulted in tremendous population growth in the cities of the Middle Colonies. Philadelphia was founded in 1681 as a village along the Delaware River and became the fastest-growing city in the colonies. Its population numbered more than 2,000 in 1700 and jumped to about 23,000 by 1760. At that time, more people lived in Philadelphia than in either New York City or Boston. Crops and trade made Philadelphia thrive. The city was also an attractive place to live. William Penn had envisioned Philadelphia as a large "green country town." As the city grew, planners built wide streets set in a grid pattern, public parks, and houses made of brick.

New York City also expanded. After it was acquired by the English in 1664, New York merchants maintained ties with the Netherlands and its colony, the Dutch West Indies. Trade goods continued to be shipped between New York and Amsterdam. As a result of these ties, the population of New York more than doubled between 1720 and 1760. The Dutch influence on New York could be seen in its architecture. The brick houses with low-sloping roofs that lined the city's streets strongly resembled those found in many Dutch towns. The English, however, soon put their stamp on New York by building houses made of brick and wood in their own style.

Although the economy in Middle Colony cities was booming, not everyone shared in the wealth. While rich merchants lived in mansions, many other city dwellers shared crowded quarters and scraped by, working for low wages. And the burgeoning, or expanding, cities lacked sanitation, putting those who lived in close quarters at particular risk from the spread of disease. These poorer inhabitants had little legal opportunity to improve their lives. Throughout the colonies, only white men who owned property had the right to vote. There were exceptions to that rule, however. Landowning men who were Catholic or Jewish were often denied voting rights.

Life was hard for women as well as men in the cities. Married women cared for their children and the household. Wealthier wives employed servants or used enslaved persons to perform domestic chores. In less wealthy urban families, some women worked alongside their husbands in shops and businesses. Women could also serve as midwives, helping to deliver babies and provide other medical care. The legal rights of women in the Middle Colonies were the same as those in other regions. They did not have the right to vote or manage their property once they married.

National Museum of American History, Washington, D.C.

Four to six horses were needed to pull a fully loaded Conestoga wagon. As the wagon bumped along the trails, its curved shape prevented the cargo from shifting. Its white canvas cover protected the goods against bad weather. From about 1750 to 1850, Conestoga wagons, like the one shown here, hauled farm products and manufactured goods on three- to four-week trips between rural areas and cities.

Francis Daniel Pastorius was a German immigrant to the colony of Pennsylvania. In 1683, he founded the city of Germantown, north of Philadelphia. In the 1690s, Pastorius wrote a description of this city and surrounding land, hoping to attract more Germans to immigrate and settle there.

On October 24, 1683, I, Francis Daniel Pastorius, with the good will of the governor, laid out another new city of the name of German-ton, or Germanopolis, at a distance of two hours' walk from Philadelphia, where there are a good black fertile soil, and many fresh wholesome springs of water, many oak, walnut, and chestnut trees, and also good pasturage for cattle. The first settlement consisted of only twelve families of forty-one persons, the greater part High German mechanics and wavers [weavers], because I had ascertained [learned] that linen cloth would be indispensable.

—from Francis Daniel Pastorius, 1690s

HISTORICAL THINKING

1. **READING CHECK** What attracted immigrants to the Middle Colonies?

2. **MAKE INFERENCES** How did the Middle Colonies probably benefit from the influx of immigrants?

3. **SUMMARIZE** Describe life for the rich and the poor in Middle Colony cities.

PLAN: 2-PAGE LESSON

OBJECTIVE

Analyze immigration trends, social class, and the rise of cities in the Middle Colonies.

CRITICAL THINKING SKILLS FOR LESSON 1.3

- Make Inferences
- Summarize
- Analyze Cause and Effect
- Analyze Primary Sources

HISTORICAL THINKING FOR CHAPTER 3

As the colonies matured, how did the colonists' identities evolve? As the colonies expanded, the Middle Colonies gained in popularity, and a steady flow of immigrants headed there to seek a better life. Lesson 1.3 explores the expansion of urban centers of the Middle Colonies in the 17th and 18th centuries.

BACKGROUND FOR THE TEACHER

The Conestoga wagon came out of the Pennsylvania Dutch craft tradition. Built tough enough to haul heavy loads over very rough terrain, it was the colonial version of an 18-wheeler. It was also huge, measuring 18 feet long and 21 feet high, and pulled by horses. In decent weather, it could cover as much as 15 miles a day. The frame was wood, and the wheels were rimmed with iron. An eye-catching vehicle, it was typically painted a rich blue with red trim. Once national roads existed, Conestoga wagons to some extent replaced steamboat travel. The Conestoga drivers were called wagoners, and they were a colorful crew. Wagoners drove the vehicle by riding the horse that was nearest the wagon on the left side or by walking alongside the wagon. Wagoners mostly lived outside, traveling specific routes and stopping at favorite inns and taverns along the way.

INTRODUCE & ENGAGE

DISCUSS CONTRIBUTIONS OF IMMIGRANTS

Prompt students to brainstorm a list of contributions made by immigrants to the United States over time. *(Students may suggest general contributions, such as foods, customs, music, and building techniques, as well as contributions of individual immigrants, such as Albert Einstein.)* Write their suggestions on the board. Remind students that since the colonial period, German immigrants to the United States have contributed greatly to American culture. Provide examples, such as Albert Einstein's theory of relativity and Levi Strauss's founding of the first company to manufacture blue jeans. Tell students that in this lesson they will learn about the impact of Germans and other immigrants on the culture and economy of the Middle Colonies.

TEACH

GUIDED DISCUSSION

1. **Analyze Cause and Effect** What were some of the causes and effects of the influx of German immigrants to the Middle Colonies in the 17th and 18th centuries? *(Possible response: Causes: Germans came seeking religious freedom and economic opportunity. Effects: They brought new farming and construction methods to the colonies; new technologies, such as the long rifle and Conestoga wagon; and the arts and crafts traditions of their homeland.)*

2. **Analyze Primary Sources** On what basis did Francis Daniel Pastorius choose specific German families to be part of the first settlement of Germantown? *(Pastorius chose families based on their potential contributions. He selected weavers and mechanics because he needed their expertise to satisfy colonial demand for fabric.)*

VIRTUAL MUSEUM VISIT

Part of the Smithsonian Institution, the National Museum of American History is home to more than 3 million historical artifacts, including a manuscript of the lyrics of "The Star-Spangled Banner." It also holds a vast archive of documents and photographs that spans the earliest colonial days through contemporary times. The museum hosts a full schedule of public education programs offering tours, lectures, and music and theater presentations. Many programs are available online, including a virtual tour of the museum's collections, and the museum hosts a blog, *O Say Can You See*, that keeps visitors updated on new developments.

ACTIVE OPTIONS

On Your Feet: Compare Social Classes Assign students to small groups, and tell them to locate information from the lesson and online to compare the upper and lower classes in the Middle Colonies. Ask them to complete a Venn diagram with their findings. Among other topics, students might compare housing and property rights, career and job potential, health and safety, and voting rights. When groups complete their diagrams, invite them to share their ideas with the class.

NG Learning Framework: Compose a Journal Entry

SKILLS Communication, Problem-Solving

KNOWLEDGE Our Human Story

Tell students to use online and library resources to explore the lives of 18th-century women in the Middle Colonies. Encourage students to take notes and analyze what women's day-to-day experiences might have been like. Then instruct them to compose a journal entry from the perspective of one such woman, discussing work, leisure, household tasks, or civil rights. Point out that journals are a forum for self-expression—where writers seek to clarify their own thoughts or work out problems. When students have completed their journal entries, invite volunteers to share their work with the class.

DIFFERENTIATE

ENGLISH LANGUAGE LEARNERS

Understand Related Words Direct students' attention to the words *immigrant*, *immigrate*, and *immigration*. Pair students at the **Emerging** or **Expanding** level with more proficient English speakers and have them make word cards with each word's definition, pronunciation, and a sentence using the word.

GIFTED & TALENTED

Present Information Graphically Challenge students to find population data online that supplements the information in the lesson. They might focus on the population growth of Philadelphia, New York, or another city in the Middle Colonies. Encourage students to display the information graphically, such as in a simple chart or bar graph or in a more creative infographic. Invite them to display their work on a class bulletin board, website, or blog.

See the Chapter Planner for more strategies for differentiation.

HISTORICAL THINKING

ANSWERS

1. Many immigrants moved to the Middle Colonies because of the promise of religious freedom and economic opportunity. Many came to farm the region's arable and inexpensive land.

2. The Middle Colonies benefited from the skilled work of immigrant artisans and from the innovations they created, such as the Conestoga wagon.

3. Rich merchants could afford to live in mansions, but many other city dwellers worked for low pay and had to live in cramped quarters. Poorer colonists living crowded together without effective sanitation systems faced disease and had few opportunities to improve their lives. As in the other colonies, the right to vote was limited to white Protestant men.

AN AGRICULTURAL SOCIETY

Unlike the economies of New England and the Middle Colonies, the economy of the Southern Colonies relied almost entirely on agriculture. The economy also rested on the unfortunate shoulders of an enslaved labor force.

SOUTHERN CROPS

As you have read, the fertile soil and mild climate of the Southern Colonies allowed farmers to grow such cash crops as cotton, tobacco, indigo, and rice. Tobacco flourished in the humid climates of Virginia and coastal Maryland. Rice grew well in the lowland swamps and tidewater areas of the Carolinas' coastal rivers. However, southern farmers had little experience with growing rice. Enslaved people who were brought from rice-growing regions in West Africa to the Southern Colonies shared their knowledge of rice cultivation with southern farmers, and rice yields increased dramatically. As the crop took hold, exports of rice from the Carolinas reached 1.5 million pounds per year by 1710 and nearly 20 million pounds by 1730. The chief markets for rice were Europe and the West Indies.

Among the Southern Colonies, North Carolina ranked third in tobacco production after Virginia and Maryland. Most of North Carolina's tobacco plantations were located along the coastal plain or near Virginia's border. In this photo taken in 2009, migrant workers from Mexico harvest tobacco leaves by hand in North Carolina.

Rice plantations sprang up along rivers in the Carolinas. Ships could sail up tributaries of the Chesapeake Bay to dock at the plantations and pick up the goods. The vessels then transported the exports to various markets. As a result, port cities did not emerge in the Southern Colonies as they had in the colonies to the north. The one exception was the busy port that developed in Charles Town (now known as Charleston, South Carolina). Wealthy plantation owners and merchants lived in Charles Town part of the year, and the city prospered through the export of rice and other crops. Charles Town became the fourth-largest city in the colonies, after Philadelphia, Boston, and New York.

SOUTHERN SOCIETY

As the plantation system in Maryland, Virginia, and the Carolinas became more entrenched, a distinct hierarchy of social classes developed in southern society. Wealthy plantation owners, also known as the southern gentry, were at the top of the social ladder. They lived like European nobles in their lavish mansions. With their armies of enslaved Africans, they enjoyed a leisurely lifestyle. Although relatively few in number, these rich landowners wielded tremendous political and economic power.

Below the southern gentry came farmers who owned much smaller portions of land. These farmers lived in modest houses and generally owned few, if any, slaves. They also struggled to compete with the large plantations. In fact, wealthy plantation owners often expanded their holdings by buying more land from small farmers. Colonists who rented rather than owned the land they farmed came next in the hierarchy. These farmers rarely owned enslaved workers. Some families could afford livestock, such as cows, pigs, and horses, as well as basic farming tools and equipment. Often, however, they secured these items on credit from wealthy merchant-planters to whom they could become indebted for a lifetime.

Enslaved men and women were at the bottom of the social hierarchy. They worked long hours in the fields planting, weeding, and harvesting crops. They usually labored until their **overseer**, or supervisor, allowed them to stop—often long after nightfall. Overseers and plantation owners sometimes used whips and other violent measures to make slaves work harder or to punish them for failing to obey orders. The development of rice cultivation significantly increased the slaves' workload. Work in a plantation owner's home was sometimes less brutal. Household slaves cooked, cleaned, and worked in the garden. Women often took care of the owners' children, and some served as nurses and weavers. Enslaved men were sometimes allowed to become artisans.

The immigrants who settled in the Piedmont area of the backcountry were also part of the society of the Southern Colonies. In the early 1700s, many of those who moved to the backcountry were Scots-Irish immigrants from the north of Ireland. They carved their farmland out of the forests and used the timber to build small log cabins. Land in the backcountry was not suited for large plantations. Instead, backcountry farmers hunted and raised only enough crops and livestock to feed their families. Women took part in every aspect of farm life. They worked in the home, in the fields, and in the forests, where they often hunted along with the men. Self-sufficient and determined, the farmers living in the backcountry did not rely on enslaved labor.

This ornately engraved silver mug, which was made in London around 1740, belonged to a wealthy plantation owner. Members of the southern gentry filled their homes with fine furniture, paintings, and silver. They also adopted the sports of English aristocrats, including horse racing and fox hunting.

HISTORICAL THINKING

1. **READING CHECK** How did the Southern Colonies' geography and climate support their main crops?

2. **IDENTIFY MAIN IDEAS AND DETAILS** What social classes developed in the Southern Colonies?

3. **EVALUATE** How did the southern gentry perpetuate the social hierarchy of the Southern Colonies?

PLAN: 2-PAGE LESSON

OBJECTIVE

Describe the agricultural economy and social structure of the Southern Colonies.

CRITICAL THINKING SKILLS FOR LESSON 2.1

- Identify Main Ideas and Details
- Evaluate
- Make Connections
- Compare and Contrast
- Summarize

HISTORICAL THINKING FOR CHAPTER 3

As the colonies matured, how did the colonists' identities evolve? The temperate climate in the Southern Colonies allowed farming to flourish and a booming agricultural economy to develop. Lesson 2.1 explains how economic prosperity led wealthy plantation owners to increase their reliance on enslaved workers.

BACKGROUND FOR THE TEACHER

Around 1612, a planter and colonial official named John Rolfe began cultivating a kind of tobacco from the West Indies, which was milder than the local tobacco and more suited to English tastes. Like rice, tobacco became a major crop and export for the Southern Colonies in the 17th century, and most farmers wanted to get in on the economic boom. In fact, so many farmers turned their fields over to tobacco that the colonial government eventually required farmers to cultivate food crops. Still, farmers continued to plant tobacco, which resulted in overproduction and plummeting tobacco prices. The government then limited the number of tobacco plants each farmer could grow to 1,500 seedlings. Prices did not rise substantially until the middle of the 18th century. Tobacco production waned again when the American Revolution began and the colonies opted to stop exporting tobacco to Europe.

INTRODUCE & ENGAGE

BRAINSTORM WORD ASSOCIATIONS

Write the word *plantation* on the board. Invite students to brainstorm words and phrases they associate with it. *(Possible responses:* cotton, slavery, wealth, large farm*)* Write their ideas on the board. Then ask students to sort the words into two categories: positive and negative. Ask volunteers to discuss which category is more often associated with the word *plantation*, and why. Tell students that in this lesson they will learn about how plantations fit into the economy and social structure of the Southern Colonies.

TEACH

GUIDED DISCUSSION

1. **Make Connections** What assumption can you make about West Africa given the fact that West African enslaved workers taught farmers in the Southern Colonies how to cultivate rice? *(Like the Southern Colonies, West Africa likely had lowland swamps and a humid climate favorable to cultivating rice, because the workers from West Africa had experience growing the crop.)*

2. **Compare and Contrast** How were the work conditions of enslaved field workers and enslaved household workers similar and different? *(Field workers did backbreaking outdoor labor, while house workers typically had less physically demanding tasks in and around the house. Both groups worked long hours.)*

SUMMARIZE

Direct students to reread the Southern Society subsection. **ASK:** How did the farms in the Piedmont backcountry differ from colonial rice plantations in terms of land and the people who worked it? *(Rice plantations were located near major waterways for crop cultivation and transport, while Piedmont farms were carved out of forests. Plantation owners built mansions, while Piedmont farmers built log cabins. Plantation owners relied on enslaved workers, while Piedmont farmers relied on family members to get work done.)*

ACTIVE OPTIONS

On Your Feet: Colonial Agriculture Word Web Arrange students into teams of four for a Team Word Webbing activity. Provide each team with a large sheet of paper, and give each student a different colored marker. Invite students to create a Word Web for the topic Agriculture in the Southern Colonies. Ask each team member to contribute a word to the part of the web nearest to him or her. Then have students rotate the paper and add words to the nearest part of the web again. Encourage teams to share, discuss, and display their completed Word Webs around the classroom.

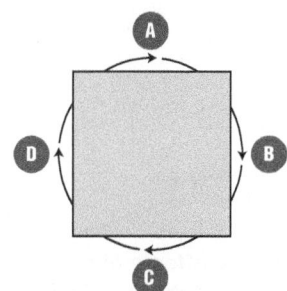

NG Learning Framework: Craft an Informative Report

SKILLS Communication, Collaboration

KNOWLEDGE Our Living Planet

Invite students to work in pairs to find out how U.S. rice cultivation and processing have changed since the colonial period. Tell partners to collaborate on an oral report that discusses statistics on the states that produce the most rice, the number of tons of rice currently exported to other nations, and the development of different rice varieties. If partners discover conflicting information, prompt them to work together to resolve the issue if they can. When they have completed their reports, have pairs communicate their findings to the class.

DIFFERENTIATE

ENGLISH LANGUAGE LEARNERS ELD

Identify Word Parts to Clarify Meaning Explain to students that when they encounter a new word, they can look for familiar word parts to help understand its meaning. Pair students at the **Emerging** level with students at the **Expanding** or **Bridging** level. Have pairs identify the three parts of the word *overseer* (*over*, *see*, and *-er*) and discuss the meaning of each word part. Partners then review the definition of *overseer*, a person who "sees over," or supervises, others.

GIFTED & TALENTED

Write and Deliver a Monologue Instruct students to research the life of someone who lived in the Southern Colonies, such as a plantation owner, an enslaved woman, a Native American, or a Scots-Irish settler from the backcountry. Then prompt them to write a dramatic monologue that focuses on one captivating event or a single day. Ask volunteers to perform their monologues and respond to questions from their classmates.

See the Chapter Planner for more strategies for differentiation.

HISTORICAL THINKING

ANSWERS

1. Farmers in the Southern Colonies were able to grow an abundance of cotton, tobacco, indigo, and rice due to the mild climate and fertile soil in the region.

2. At the top of society in the Southern Colonies were members of the southern gentry, wealthy owners of large plantations. Below them were farmers that owned smaller tracts of land, then farmers who rented farmland they could not afford to own, and finally, enslaved people.

3. The wealthy gentry continually expanded their holdings, whether in money, land, or enslaved workers. They maintained an economic advantage over smaller landowners by keeping them in debt.

MAIN IDEA As increasing numbers of enslaved Africans were brought to the Southern Colonies, they tried to hold onto their traditions and cope with their living and working conditions.

LIFE UNDER SLAVERY

People do what they can to cope in dire circumstances. It is almost impossible for us to imagine the conditions under which enslaved people lived. That makes their efforts to survive and preserve their identity all the more remarkable.

LIVING CONDITIONS

You may remember that planters in the Southern Colonies originally hired white indentured servants to farm their land. That changed in 1698 when English merchants were allowed to engage in the slave trade. Many of the enslaved people were sold in the American colonies. Southern plantation owners took full advantage of this new labor force.

These owners included planters who lived in the **Chesapeake**, the settled land around the Chesapeake Bay. The slave trade greatly increased the African population of the Chesapeake. In 1660, only 900 Africans lived there, some of whom were free of bondage. By 1720, Africans and African Americans made up one-fifth of the Chesapeake's population. Their population in Virginia and the Carolinas also soared. By 1750, African Americans were 40 percent of Virginia's population and more than half of South Carolina's. Nearly all of the African Americans in the Southern Colonies were enslaved.

Enslaved people were powerfully impacted by their slavery, but they were not entirely defined by their circumstances. Enslaved men and women often lived in the one-room cabins they had to build for themselves. They supplemented the meager amount of food the slave owners provided by planting vegetable gardens, raising hogs and chickens, and hunting and fishing. They also created a resilient and life-affirming culture through religion, music, food, and oral folktales.

Many of these cultural traditions found their way into colonial America. For example, enslaved Africans contributed words to the English language. Because slaves from different parts of West Africa frequently lived together on plantations, they sometimes used a mixture of African languages and English to communicate. As a result, words such as *yam*, *goober* (peanut), and *tote* were introduced to the colonists. Also, the rhythms of African music influenced colonists' music and dances and would later form the roots of jazz and the blues. African designs decorated the musical instruments, pottery, and baskets made by slaves. Enslaved Africans also contributed to the food culture of the colonies by popularizing okra, melons, and bananas.

SLAVE RESISTANCE

Enslaved people resisted the efforts of their enslavers to reduce them to commodities in both revolutionary and everyday ways. Some resisted by disrupting farm production. They slowed down their work, faked illness, and secretly destroyed crops and tools. Theft was another common form of resistance. Slaves stole food, livestock, tobacco, and money from their owners. In addition, slaves sometimes ran away. A few enslaved people turned to violence, killing plantation owners or setting fire to their fields and homes.

You've read about the slave uprising in the American colonies that occurred in New York in 1712. As you may recall, white colonists at that time feared more slaves would stage a revolt. That's just what happened in 1739, near the Stono River in South Carolina. A group of more than 50 enslaved people raided a firearms store and then killed 20 whites as they marched south. Their leader was a literate slave named Jemmy (also known as Cato) whose owner had taught him to read and write. By morning, armed white planters had killed nearly half the participants of the **Stono Rebellion**. The others managed to escape. Their goal was to reach St. Augustine, Florida, where Spanish authorities offered freedom and land to fugitive slaves from the British colonies, but few reached that destination. Most of the rebels were eventually captured and executed.

To prevent future revolts in South Carolina, the colony's legislature passed a new slave code in 1740. The code decreed that all slaves, their children, and later generations would remain permanently enslaved. In addition, it prohibited anyone from teaching an enslaved person to read or write. The code remained in force until 1865. In spite of such laws, some African-American slaves did learn to read and write. They employed their literacy to tell their stories and inform the world about the horrors of slavery.

This West African drum traveled with enslaved people to Virginia in the 1700s.

HISTORICAL THINKING

1. **READING CHECK** How did the slave trade affect the populations of the Southern Colonies?

2. **MAKE INFERENCES** Why do you think enslaved people tried to keep their African culture alive?

3. **SUMMARIZE** In what ways did enslaved African Americans rebel against their bondage?

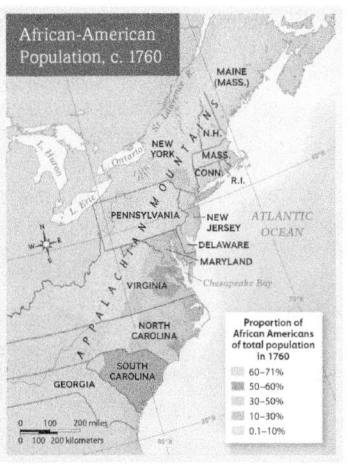

African-American Population, c. 1760

Proportion of African Americans of total population in 1760
- 60–71%
- 50–60%
- 30–50%
- 10–30%
- 0.1–10%

An enslaved person performs a traditional African stick dance, accompanied by a banjo player and drummer, in this late-1700s watercolor painting titled *The Old Plantation*.

PLAN: 2-PAGE LESSON

OBJECTIVE

Explore the causes and effects of rising rates of enslavement in the Southern Colonies.

CRITICAL THINKING SKILLS FOR LESSON 2.2

- Make Inferences
- Summarize
- Interpret Maps
- Analyze Cause and Effect

HISTORICAL THINKING FOR CHAPTER 3

As the colonies matured, how did the colonists' identities evolve? The growing number of enslaved workers led to many cultural changes in the Southern Colonies. Lesson 2.2 explores how cultures borrowed from one another and the various ways enslaved people rebelled against their bondage.

BACKGROUND FOR THE TEACHER

Historians aren't sure what led to the Stono Rebellion, but many believe the cause might have been the impending passage of the Security Act. Fueled by fear of slave uprisings, this legislation mandated that all white men carry guns on Sundays, the only day that enslaved people were allowed free time to work for themselves. There had also been a recent precedent for the uprising. In the 1720s and 1730s, many enslaved workers had escaped captivity and had journeyed to Spanish Florida. By 1739, about 100 enslaved workers were living in freedom at Fort Mose, a fort they had built with the Spanish at St. Augustine. Those who took part in the Stono Rebellion also hoped to find freedom in Spanish Florida. Things did not go as the rebels planned, however, and as a result, the Stono Rebellion became the bloodiest slave revolt in North American history, surpassed only by Nat Turner's slave uprising nearly 100 years later in 1831.

INTRODUCE & ENGAGE

PREVIEW USING VISUALS

Direct students' attention to the painting *The Old Plantation* and the caption that accompanies it. Tell students that although the painting is unsigned, it is believed to be the work of a white artist and slaveholder named John Rose. Elicit responses about the painting's subject matter, and invite students to point out specific details. **ASK:** What does this painting tell you about the lives of enslaved people on colonial plantations? *(Possible response: They retained many aspects of African cultures and spent some free time together away from their enslavers.)*

TEACH

GUIDED DISCUSSION

1. **Interpret Maps** According to the map, what geographic feature might account for the relatively low populations of African Americans in the western parts of North Carolina and Virginia, and why? *(The rough terrain of the Appalachian Mountains cut through western North Carolina and Virginia, making farming and other industries more problematic, thus lowering the need for enslaved workers.)*

2. **Analyze Cause and Effect** What effect did the new slave code of 1740 have on enslaved people in the Southern Colonies? *(The new code mandated that all enslaved people and all future generations of their families remain enslaved and illiterate in perpetuity.)*

MORE INFORMATION

Akan Drum Tell students that the drum pictured in this lesson is among the oldest surviving African-American artifacts. Constructed by members of the West African Akan ethnic group, from what is now Ghana, the drum is made of wood and vegetable fiber covered with stretched deerskin. It was most likely taken out of Africa by slave traders, as enslaved Africans couldn't bring any items from their homeland to the colonies. When the drum was collected in Virginia in 1730, it was mistakenly categorized as a Native American artifact. In the 1970s, researchers at the British Museum, where the drum is on display, used scientific evidence to show that the base of the drum came from a tree that grows in West Africa, and the fibers that secure the drum's skin were fashioned from plant material native to the same area.

ACTIVE OPTIONS

On Your Feet: Fact-Finding Bee Invite students to consider the facts they have learned in this lesson about life under slavery in the Southern Colonies. Arrange students into two teams, and give each a few minutes to create lists of facts. Have teams form two rows, face each other, and take turns providing a fact. Any student who makes an untrue statement sits down. The team with the most facts and fewest number of students sitting wins.

NG Learning Framework: Interpret Through Drawing

ATTITUDE Curiosity

KNOWLEDGE Our Human Story

Direct students' attention to the painting *The Old Plantation*. Remind them that the artist was most likely a white slave owner. Ask them to think about how the painting might be different if the artist had been an enslaved worker. Then invite students to draw or create a visual representation of a plantation scene, focusing on an aspect of everyday life that interests them. Invite students to share their visuals with the class and discuss the ways in which they interpreted plantation life.

DIFFERENTIATE

STRIVING READERS

Understand Main Ideas Confirm students' understanding of the main ideas in the lesson by asking them to complete sentence frames such as:

- Words that enslaved Africans contributed to American English include _____. *(yam, goober, tote)*

- The 1740 slave laws banned anyone from teaching an enslaved person _____. *(to read or write)*

- Some enslaved Africans learned to read and write and used the power of words to _____. *(tell about the horrors of slavery)*

PRE-AP

Investigate Contributions Ask students to choose an area of American culture to which enslaved Africans contributed, such as agricultural knowledge, food and cuisine, music, art, or language. Instruct them to gather information from a variety of sources to create an oral report detailing the contributions that enslaved Africans made. Then invite volunteers to share their findings with the class.

See the Chapter Planner for more strategies for differentiation.

HISTORICAL THINKING

ANSWERS

1. The slave trade greatly increased the African population in the Southern Colonies. In some areas African Americans made up more than half the population.

2. Possible response: By keeping alive cultural aspects of their former lives, African Americans created a sense of home, which may have helped them cope with living in bondage.

3. Some enslaved people disrupted work on plantations by faking illness or by destroying crops and tools. Others organized violent uprisings.

OLAUDAH EQUIANO 1745–1797

"I believe there are a few events in my life which have not happened to many."—Olaudah Equiano

The quotation above is quite an understatement, coming as it does from Olaudah Equiano (oh-LOW-duh ehk-wee-AHN-oh), a man who was repeatedly bought and sold as a slave, took part in an expedition to the Arctic, and wrote a best-selling autobiography—among many other episodes in an eventful life. The quote introduces his autobiographical work, *The Interesting Narrative of the Life of Olaudah Equiano, or Gustavus Vassa, the African*. Most of what is known about Equiano comes from this book.

CONTROVERSIAL BEGINNINGS

Equiano begins his autobiography with descriptions of life in the West African province of Eboe, an area in present-day southern Nigeria, where he says he was born. The enslavement of Africans by other Africans was part of the culture of the region and, indeed, of much of the continent. In fact, according to Equiano, his own family had slaves. His parents tried to protect their children from abduction, but one day Equiano was kidnapped and taken from his home. Before long, the 11-year-old boy was sold to European slave traders.

The traders took Equiano to the coast and the slave ship that would carry him to the Americas. Equiano says it was the first time he had ever seen white people, and his astonishment changed to terror as the slavers dragged him on board. As Equiano writes in his autobiography, "I was now persuaded that I had got into a world of bad spirits, and that they were going to kill me."

CRITICAL VIEWING This engraving of Equiano appears opposite the title page in his narrative. In the portrait, Equiano looks directly at his readers and is dressed in the elegant clothes of an English gentleman. He holds a Bible open to a passage whose subject is central to his narrative: salvation. Why do you think Equiano chose to be portrayed in this manner?

When he was brought below decks where the captured Africans were quartered, the awful stench of the place made him sick. The suffocating heat, the numbers of people crammed into the space, and the chains used to bind them "rendered the whole a scene of horror almost inconceivable." Many of the captives died on the Middle Passage to the Caribbean island of Barbados—some by suicide—but Equiano survived the journey.

His moving account of the conditions and suffering on the slave ship creates a vivid, unforgettable picture, but Equiano may not have actually experienced what he describes. In Vincent Carretta's 2005 biography of Equiano, the American writer revealed that he had found two documents that indicated his subject had been born in South Carolina, not Africa. The findings resulted in a fierce debate over Equiano's birthplace, which continues today. However, Equiano wrote his autobiography to inform readers about the brutal reality of slavery. Some historians believe he felt his narrative had to include a description of his abduction and the Middle Passage, whether it was based on his own experiences or those of others he'd heard or read about.

ABOLITIONIST AND WRITER

While Equiano's discussion of his early life has raised questions, Carretta and others have found evidence that backs up most of his story. In 1756, British naval officer Michael Pascal purchased Equiano in Virginia and gave him the name Gustavus Vassa. For about seven years, Equiano served and traveled with Pascal and became a seasoned sailor. When Britain was drawn into war, Equiano fought in battles alongside his owner. During this time, Pascal also sent Equiano to England, where he learned to read and write and converted to Christianity. After 1763, he was sold to other slaveholders who set him to work on trading ships. By engaging in some trading of his own, Equiano was able to buy his freedom in 1766.

But Equiano soon discovered that, as a free man, he lived "in constant alarm for [his] liberty." Several times, he was pursued by men who tried to capture him and return him to slavery. In part to escape from being seized, Equiano took to the seas again and worked in trade. He also joined an expedition in 1773 to find the Northwest Passage, a westward sea route that would connect the northern Atlantic and Pacific oceans by way of the Arctic Ocean. Explorers had been searching for such a route since the 15th century.

In 1777, Equiano returned to England where he became involved in the abolitionist, or antislavery, movement. He toured Britain and spoke out against

The title page of Equiano's narrative, like his portrait page, makes a reference to the Bible by quoting a passage from it. Once again, the Bible passage focuses on salvation and contains the words, "I will trust, and will not be afraid." Equiano devotes an entire chapter in his narrative to his conversion to Christianity, and religion is a constant theme throughout his book.

the cruelty of slaveholders, which he had witnessed firsthand. Urged to write about what he had seen, Equiano published his autobiography in 1789. The book was translated into several languages and became a best-seller. Sales of the book made Equiano a wealthy man.

He continued his work as an abolitionist, helping poor blacks in London and campaigning for an end to slavery. In his autobiography, Equiano writes, "I hope to have the satisfaction of seeing the renovation [renewal] of liberty and justice, resting on the British government, to vindicate [redeem] the honor of our common nature." Slavery was finally abolished in Britain in 1807, but Equiano did not live to see it. He had died 10 years earlier.

HISTORICAL THINKING

1. **READING CHECK** How does Equiano help his readers envision the horrors of the Middle Passage?

2. **MAKE INFERENCES** What characteristics helped Equiano survive life as a slave?

3. **FORM AND SUPPORT OPINIONS** If historians determined conclusively that Equiano was born in America, do you think that fact would discredit his entire story? Explain why or why not.

PLAN: 2-PAGE LESSON

OBJECTIVE

Examine how Olaudah Equiano's early life and experiences as an enslaved person led to his identity as an abolitionist and writer.

CRITICAL THINKING SKILLS FOR LESSON 2.3

• Make Inferences
• Form and Support Opinions
• Draw Conclusions
• Analyze Language Use

HISTORICAL THINKING FOR CHAPTER 3

As the colonies matured, how did the colonists' identities evolve? When Africans were brought to the colonies, they faced a new, forced identity— that of a slave. Lesson 2.3 describes how Olaudah Equiano overcame his enslaved condition and formed his own identity.

BACKGROUND FOR THE TEACHER

In London's African community in the late 1770s, another ex-slave, Quobna Ottobah Cugoano, worked alongside Olaudah Equiano to make the public aware of the brutal facts of slavery. Cugoano had been kidnapped from Ghana and taken to the West Indies in 1770. In 1772, he was brought to England, where he met Equiano. Cugoano's book *Thoughts and Sentiments on the Evil and Wicked Traffic of the Human Species*, thought to be written with Equiano's help, was the first published criticism of the slave trade. The two men's powerful oratory, letters, and books helped turn public opinion against slavery.

HISTORY NOTEBOOK

Encourage students to complete the American Voices page for Chapter 3 in their History Notebooks as they read.

INTRODUCE & ENGAGE

EXPLORE IDENTITY

Discuss with students factors that make up a person's identity. *(Possible responses: national origin, race, interests, personality, major life events, age, name, gender)* Ask them how names might influence people's identities, and how name changes might affect how people view themselves or how others view them. Tell students that in this lesson they will learn about the life of Olaudah Equiano and how his experiences as an enslaved person helped form his identity as an abolitionist and writer.

TEACH

GUIDED DISCUSSION

1. **Draw Conclusions** Direct students' attention to the engraving of Equiano and the title page of his autobiography. **ASK:** Why would Equiano include both his names on his autobiography? *(Possible response: He may have wanted to make readers aware of his African identity by using his African name as well as his identity as a slave in white society.)*

2. **Analyze Language Use** What did Equiano mean when he said he hoped Great Britain would end slavery and "vindicate the honor of our common nature"? *(Possible response: When Equiano says "common nature" he means that all people, regardless of race, share the same human characteristics. By "vindicate the honor," he refers to restoring the honor of slaves by freeing them and restoring the honor of whites by ending the trade of human beings.)*

AMERICAN VOICES

Explain to students that historians try to find primary sources whenever possible to verify the stories told by others, but they may find more than they expected. For example, Vincent Carretta, author of *Equiano the African: Biography of a Self-Made Man*, used ship and merchant logbooks, church baptismal records, and naval muster rolls to confirm nearly every detail of Equiano's record. He did not intend to start a controversy related to Equiano's place of birth. **ASK:** What steps might you take to verify family oral histories or stories in journals, letters, or memoirs? *(Possible responses: interview different family members or friends who were present during the events mentioned; check newspapers, historical documents, and public records)* Discuss with students what impact their research might have if the facts contradicted or disproved an important family story.

ACTIVE OPTIONS

On Your Feet: Fishbowl Arrange students in two concentric circles. Ask students in the inner circle to discuss this question: What different identities did Equiano need to adopt or develop during his life? Ask students in the outer circle to listen carefully to the discussion. After a time, direct the two circles to exchange places. Ask the new inner circle to discuss this question: How did whites in the colonies and in Europe view Equiano's identities? Then encourage both groups to draw conclusions about how Equiano might have seen himself.

NG Learning Framework: Fact-Check a Historical Movie

SKILLS Observation, Communication

KNOWLEDGE Our Human Story

Ask students to work in small groups to select and watch a movie related to the abolitionist movement and check the movie's historical facts. Students first record their reactions to and opinions about the movie and then conduct fact-checking using online research, print media, and/or interviews with experts on the subject. Ask them to write a report rating the movie's accuracy, describing changes made for dramatic effect, and summarizing how what they learned from fact-checking affected their reactions to or opinions about the movie and its subject. Invite groups to share their findings with the class.

DIFFERENTIATE

INCLUSION

Analyze a Portrait and Title Page At the beginning of the lesson, pair visually impaired students with sighted students. Ask the latter to describe the details shown in each photograph and read the captions. Tell visually impaired students to ask clarifying questions as necessary. Then have pairs work together to read the lesson and respond to the Critical Viewing and Historical Thinking questions.

GIFTED & TALENTED

Host a Talk Show Prompt pairs of students to assume the roles of a talk show host and Olaudah Equiano. Instruct them to plan, write, and perform a simulated television talk show in which Equiano is the guest. Tell students to focus on major events in Equiano's life and his commitment to abolition. Both Equiano and the host may also discuss the nature of truth in Equiano's narrative and the possible "higher truth" of conveying the experiences of millions of enslaved Africans unable to read, write, or tell their own truths.

See the Chapter Planner for more strategies for differentiation.

HISTORICAL THINKING

ANSWERS

1. Equiano uses first-person narration and vivid sensory details to show readers the true horror of how the slave ships felt, smelled, looked, and sounded.

2. Possible response: Based on what he accomplished, Equiano seems to have been resilient, adaptable, intelligent, enterprising, empathetic, and motivated to change society.

3. Possible responses: Yes. It would undermine his credibility with readers, who might believe that if he lied about one thing he might have lied about many other things. No. Readers might forgive such dramatic license if he described events truthfully. They might feel he was speaking for those who had died or who were silenced by what they had experienced.

CRITICAL VIEWING Possible response: Equiano was writing mainly for a white audience, so he probably wished to appear as an educated, Christian man—someone whites would take seriously. The topic of salvation might refer to his salvation as a Christian, to the salvation of freed slaves, and to the salvation that whites could obtain by abolishing slavery.

THE WHITNEY PLANTATION
WALLACE, LOUISIANA

Set on land where enslaved people labored for more than 100 years, the Whitney Plantation is the first museum dedicated exclusively to telling the story of slavery in the United States. More than 350 enslaved people worked on the plantation between 1752 and 1867, bringing great prosperity to its owners, a German immigrant family named the Haydels.

The Whitney Plantation employed one of the largest slave forces in Louisiana. Today, the names of those enslaved workers are etched in granite on the Wall of Honor at the plantation. Their stories and those of other slaves are told through the museum's restored buildings, artwork, exhibits, and hundreds of first-person narratives.

Slave Quarters
The Whitney Plantation has seven slave cabins that were acquired and moved there from nearby plantations. Before the Civil War, the Haydel plantation had 22 slave cabins, but most were torn down in the 1970s.

The number of enslaved workers on the plantation varied, but in 1819, there were 61 enslaved men and women. A sizeable labor force was required for the production and processing of sugarcane. Enslaved workers boiled sugarcane juice in large iron kettles like those shown in front of the cabins.

Plantation Kitchen
Enslaved cooks prepared meals for the master's family in this kitchen, which was located in a building separate from the large plantation house. Because they were hot, smoky, and smelly, kitchens were often detached from the main house. The loft above this kitchen served as a *pigeonnier*, a nesting place for pigeons that were a source of food and fertilizer.

Based on what you observe of these kitchen tools, how might plantation kitchens have been a challenging place to work?

Inside a Slave Cabin
This photograph shows the sparse, simple furnishings of a slave cabin. A two-room wooden shack on the Whitney Plantation might have housed two families, with as many as six people sharing a single room. People slept on simple beds like the one shown here or on pallets on the floor. In the hot summers, they might move their pallets to the porch and sleep outside.

Cabins contained a fireplace to provide heat and a place to cook, though cooking was also done on outside fires. Weekly food rations typically included cornmeal and bacon.

Slave Jail
At slave markets in New Orleans, enslaved people were locked up in jails similar to this one to await sale at auctions. The interior walls of the jail have small cutouts for attaching a slave's chains.

Posted near the jail at Whitney Plantation is a list of slaves and the prices for which they were bought and sold. Runaway slaves were also punished by being kept in these kinds of jails. The steel jails became like hot ovens in the summer. This jail was brought to Whitney Plantation to demonstrate the kind of brutal treatment slaves typically endured.

PLAN: 2-PAGE LESSON

OBJECTIVE
Study artifacts and exhibits about the lives of enslaved workers on a southern plantation.

CRITICAL THINKING SKILLS FOR LESSON 2.4
- Analyze Visuals
- Make Connections
- Draw Conclusions
- Make Inferences

HISTORICAL THINKING FOR CHAPTER 3
As the colonies matured, how did the colonists' identities evolve? Not all those coming to the colonies arrived voluntarily to seek a better life. People brought over as enslaved workers lost their homes, families, and identities. Lesson 2.4 guides students through exhibits and structures at the Whitney Plantation museum that tell the story of slavery on a southern plantation.

BACKGROUND FOR THE TEACHER
In 1998, John Cummings, a white New Orleans real estate magnate and retired lawyer, bought the Whitney Plantation to help preserve a historic Louisiana site. When he researched the plantation's history, however, he discovered household inventories that listed "the second most valuable property [t]here next to the real estate" as the enslaved workers—the labor force that produced indigo and sugarcane. Cummings, compelled to learn more about slavery, was appalled by what he discovered. His original plan evolved, and he decided to use the plantation as a museum dedicated to exhibiting the uncomfortable details about slavery and the realities of enslaved workers' lives. Cummings believes that educating people about slavery can change its legacy and help to improve race relations in the United States.

HISTORY NOTEBOOK
Encourage students to complete the Curating History page for Chapter 3 in their History Notebooks as they read.

INTRODUCE & ENGAGE

FACING DIFFICULT HISTORY

Direct students to read the introduction to the Curating History feature. Then ask them to think about what they have already learned about slavery and discuss what they think the public should know about slavery, such as how enslaved people actually lived or the toll slavery took on families. **ASK:** How might visiting a museum dedicated to educating people about the institution of slavery differ from visiting other kinds of museums, and why is such a museum important? *(Possible response: Museums often include items that relate to what people are proud of, such as works of art, examples of great architecture, or the history of technology. Slavery is not an institution to be proud of, so a visit to a preserved plantation is likely to be somber and evoke emotions of sorrow, anger, or shame. Even so, it's important to be educated about the failings in our history along with the achievements.)*

TEACH

GUIDED DISCUSSION

1. **Draw Conclusions** In what ways do the photographs collectively convey the purpose of the museum? *(Possible response: The photographs reveal details of the harsh lives of enslaved workers, including where they lived and worked, the rough tools given to them, and the inhumane use of steel jails to hold them for auction or punishment.)*

2. **Make Inferences** What can you infer about the plantation owners' attitude toward the enslaved workers from the caption and details in the photograph of the slave cabin? *(Possible response: The plantation owners treated the enslaved workers as they would treat livestock. They crowded too many into a small cabin, disregarding basic human needs for privacy, comfort, and living space. They obviously spent as little as possible to keep the enslaved workers sheltered and fed.)*

CURATING HISTORY

The Whitney Plantation museum includes the Big House and slave cabins, a Baptist church, a slave jail, and memorial statues and life-sized sculptures of enslaved children, giving visitors a vivid sense of the people who lived, worked, and died there. To further this end, John Cummings hopes to make available 4,000 oral histories of former enslaved workers and provide an international ancestry database. Ask students to access the museum's website, select a photograph, and then locate and read a related article from either the Slave Population or Historic Buildings/Memorials sections to find out more about the topic. Prompt students to identify, based on what they found, reasons why slavery is a difficult subject for Americans to discuss and in what ways the Whitney Plantation museum might help encourage the discussion.

ACTIVE OPTION

On Your Feet: Sort the Artifacts Arrange students into teams of four to examine the photographs and artifacts in the lesson and on the Whitney Plantation website and to skim through the articles. Then ask teams to complete two Concept Clusters, such as the ones shown. In one cluster, students should identify photographs and artifacts that reveal information about the work and daily lives of enslaved people. In the other, have them identify a different class of photographs and artifacts to be determined by the teams. When teams finish, have them compare their Concept Clusters. Guide the class in summarizing the new facts they learned.

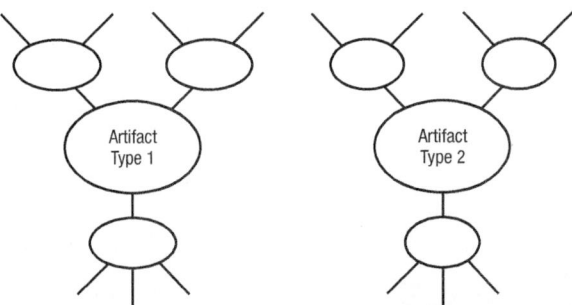

DIFFERENTIATE

STRIVING READERS

Use a K-W-L Chart Instruct students to create a K-W-L Chart titled Lives of Enslaved Workers at the Whitney Plantation. Tell them to look at the lesson's photographs and complete the first two columns of the chart. Then guide students to read the captions and complete the third column. If students have trouble understanding words or sentences, ask them to form clarifying questions and pose them to other students.

K What Do I Know?	W What Do I Want To Learn?	L What Did I Learn?

PRE-AP

Report on Sugarcane Plantation Labor Challenge pairs to research and report on the difficult and dangerous labor of enslaved workers in sugarcane fields. Tell students to conduct library and online research to locate information in the form of written descriptions, oral histories, engravings, prints, and other depictions. Ask pairs to assemble their findings and deliver an oral report to the class that includes specifics about the length of the workday, the physical labor involved, water and food breaks, and methods of punishment. Encourage them to prepare visuals to enhance their report.

See the Chapter Planner for more strategies for differentiation.

PLANTATION KITCHEN

Answers will vary. Possible response: Workers in such kitchens were likely expected to use only these basic tools to make food. If bowls and containers, like the ones shown, were hot, handling them could cause burns. Heavy metal or ceramic containers and sharp objects, like the hooks, could lead to accidental cuts that could become infected.

THE ENLIGHTENMENT

Ideas can be liberating, but they can be dangerous, too. They may be especially threatening when they question traditionally held beliefs and those in authority. Once such ideas take hold, they can be very hard to stop.

THE LIGHT OF HUMAN REASON

Around the mid-1600s, many European thinkers began to challenge the traditional religious ideas taught by the Catholic Church. The thinkers believed people should use reason and ask questions to help them understand the physical world and their place in it. The intellectual movement these thinkers sparked is called the **Enlightenment.** Rather than simply accept what religious and political figures had to say, Enlightenment thinkers encouraged others to employ logic and experience to gain knowledge and shatter the "darkness" of ignorance.

This movement was influenced, in part, by the Scientific Revolution, which began in Europe around 1550. Scientists applied the scientific method to conduct research and answer their questions. This step-by-step method involves identifying a problem; constructing a hypothesis, or a proposed solution to a problem; and collecting data through observation and experiments to test the hypothesis. English scientist **Isaac Newton** used the scientific method to investigate the natural world. By 1700, he had discovered the universal laws that predictably govern gravity, the natural bodies visible in the sky, and the ebb and flow of tides. Newton's work demonstrated that the universe operates according to fixed principles humans are capable of detecting and understanding. His findings and those of other scientists of the time challenged the idea that God was responsible for the placement and workings of the universe.

The 17th-century English philosopher **John Locke** developed Enlightenment thought by applying a logical approach to questions about society and government. In 1689, Locke published *An Essay Concerning Human Understanding,* in which he argued that people were not born with ideas implanted by God, but rather were "clean slates." He claimed humans had the ability to learn for themselves and to use their acquired knowledge to benefit society. That same year, in *Two Treatises of Government,* Locke declared that humans were born free and equal with natural rights, including life and liberty. He asserted that people should join together in what

John Locke published the radical ideas expressed in his *Two Treatises* anonymously. The excerpt below is from his second treatise, which contends that government should only exist by the consent of the people.

For no government can have a right to obedience from a people who have not freely consented to it; which they can never be supposed to do, till either they are put in a full state of liberty to chuse [choose] their government and governors, or at least till they have such standing laws, to which they have by themselves or their representatives given their free consent.

—from *Two Treatises of Government,* by John Locke, 1689

he called a "social contract" to form governments that would guarantee those rights. If a state failed in its obligation, the people had the duty to rebel and establish a new government. French Enlightenment philosopher **Jean-Jacques Rousseau** (roo-SOH) agreed with Locke and expressed his contempt for economic and political oppression and inequality. In *The Social Contract,* written in 1762, Rousseau maintained that the good of a community or society as a whole should have priority over the interests of individual citizens. He believed that only a government freely elected by the people had the authority to enact laws or constraints.

INFLUENCE ON THE COLONIES

The Enlightenment ideas of Locke, Rousseau, and others spread to the colonies in the 1700s. These ideas helped shape colonial thought. Benjamin Franklin became an important American Enlightenment leader. You've learned that Franklin was a printer, but he was also a writer, inventor, and scientist. As a scientist, he was influenced by the Scientific Revolution. For example, he used the scientific method to study the nature of electricity, and his findings brought him international fame.

In 1743, Franklin founded the American Philosophical Society in Philadelphia to promote "useful knowledge." He got the idea for the society from his friend, **John Bartram**, a naturalist and explorer. Bartram, who is considered the "father of American botany" for his exhaustive study of plants, had proposed forming a group of men to discuss nature, arts, and sciences. With the goal of using intellectual inquiry to further the common good, Franklin drew members from across the colonies to join his association and share new ideas and technologies. He also encouraged communication with members of similar associations in Europe. Soon philosophical societies began to spring up in other colonies. The books and newspaper articles on the Enlightenment penned by the members

When John Bartram purchased a 102-acre farm in Philadelphia in 1728 and dedicated it to the cultivation of native North American plants, he founded America's first garden. For more than 50 years, Bartram and his sons collected and studied the plants. He also built the stone house shown in this photo of the garden. In 1963, Bartram's Garden was designated a National Historic Landmark.

of some of these societies helped introduce the movement to colonial America. In addition, literacy rates increased as interest in the ideas grew.

Franklin would soon dedicate himself to public service. In fact, it is as a statesman that he is best known and honored. Enlightenment ideas influenced Franklin and other leaders who represented the colonists against British authority. Inspired by Locke's ideas on the role of rulers, Franklin and many other American Founders would eventually start to demand rights and freedoms for the colonies.

HISTORICAL THINKING

1. **READING CHECK** What were some of the ideas advanced by Enlightenment thinkers?

2. **MAKE CONNECTIONS** What type of government best reflects Locke's and Rousseau's ideas on the role of rulers?

3. **MAKE INFERENCES** Why do you think Franklin and others inspired by the Enlightenment began to be more critical of British authority?

PLAN: 2-PAGE LESSON

OBJECTIVE

Explore how the contributions of Enlightenment scientists and philosophers influenced thought in the American colonies.

CRITICAL THINKING SKILLS FOR LESSON 3.1

- Make Connections
- Make Inferences
- Analyze Primary Sources
- Summarize

HISTORICAL THINKING FOR CHAPTER 3

As the colonies matured, how did the colonists' identities evolve? During the Enlightenment, philosophers and scientists introduced the world to revolutionary new ideas and methods. Lesson 3.1 explores the impact of the Enlightenment on the colonial attitudes toward science, government, and freedom.

BACKGROUND FOR THE TEACHER

In 1743, Benjamin Franklin founded the American Philosophical Society, which is still in operation today. Its membership comprised doctors, clergy, lawyers, artists, and tradesmen, along with political luminaries of the day, such as George Washington, John Adams, and Thomas Jefferson. Today, the organization still adheres to Franklin's core mission to promote useful knowledge by honoring scientists and civic leaders, administering a number of scholarly fellowships and internships, and supporting research through publications, grants, exhibits, and educational programs.

HISTORY NOTEBOOK

Encourage students to complete the American Gallery page for Chapter 3 in their History Notebooks as they read.

INTRODUCE & ENGAGE

DISCUSS THE IMPACT OF NEW IDEAS

Ask students to recall examples from history when a person or group presented a new idea that changed the way people think. Examples might include the idea that the world is round or that the planets revolve around the sun. **ASK:** What emotions might people feel in response to new ideas that change their understanding of the world? *(Possible responses: excitement, confusion, anger, fear)* Guide students to discuss other ideas and movements, such as the civil rights movement, that led to major changes in U.S. society. Tell them that Lesson 3.1 explores a time when revolutionary ideas about science, society, and politics were commonplace.

TEACH

GUIDED DISCUSSION

1. **Analyze Primary Sources** Why might John Locke have published *Two Treatises of Government* anonymously? *(Answers will vary. Possible responses: The ideas he presented were considered radical at the time, and he may not have wanted to face political consequences or responses from friends and colleagues. Locke might have wanted his ideas to speak for themselves without engendering bias from others who supported or opposed him personally.)*

2. **Summarize** How did the ideas of the Enlightenment pave the way for the American Revolution? *(Possible response: The Enlightenment philosophers John Locke and Jean-Jacques Rousseau promoted the idea that people are born with a natural right to freedom, calling for people to create governments that would ensure that right, and this philosophy took hold in the colonies.)*

MORE INFORMATION

Sir Isaac Newton Explain to students that Newton believed the way to deep knowledge was through observation, not research in books. He once stuck a blunt needle into his eye socket between the eye and the bone to find out what the result would be. When he was inducted into the Royal Society, a group of prestigious thinkers and scientists that met regularly to discuss and critique each other's work, Newton agreed to share his theories about light. The other scientists tried to replicate his experiments and get the same results. When they failed, they accused him of not sharing his ideas accurately. Newton was a proud man, and he did not appreciate the criticism. He isolated himself from his peers and began a long period of self-imposed intellectual exile. **ASK:** Why did Enlightenment scientists try to replicate one another's work? *(Possible response: If they repeated an experiment but got different results, they would not trust the conclusions of the first experimenter.)*

ACTIVE OPTIONS

AMERICAN GALLERY ONLINE

Colonial Landmarks Invite students to explore the American Gallery. Guide them to select one of the images and do additional research to learn more about it. Ask *who, what, when, where* or *why* questions to prompt them to think more deeply about what the landmark represented in colonial America.

NG Learning Framework: Create a Time Line

ATTITUDE Curiosity

KNOWLEDGE Our Human Story

Encourage students to use online and library resources to find out about major highlights of the Enlightenment that they find intriguing, including information and important dates related to Enlightenment philosophers and scientists. Ask them to chart their findings in a time line that includes at least 10 items. When students have completed their time lines, invite them to present their work to the class and explain the importance of the events and dates they chose.

DIFFERENTIATE

ENGLISH LANGUAGE LEARNERS

Ask and Answer Questions Pair students at the **Bridging** level with students at the **Expanding** level. Tell them to write several short-answer questions, such as the ones below, about people and ideas in the lesson. Then each pair takes turns asking and answering questions with another pair.

1. What movement focused on human reason? *(the Enlightenment)*

2. Which English scientist used the scientific method to explore the natural world? *(Sir Isaac Newton)*

3. Who wrote that people are born free and equal, with natural rights? *(John Locke)*

4. Who was an important leader of the American Enlightenment? *(Benjamin Franklin)*

PRE-AP

Write an Editorial Encourage students to learn more about the ideas behind Rousseau's "social contract." Challenge them to find examples of present-day problems that they feel violate the social contract. For example, students might identify topics such as underfunded schools, polluted air or water, income inequality, or other issues. Then have them choose one problem and write an editorial that uses Rousseau's ideas to bring the problem to light. Invite students to share their editorials with the class.

See the Chapter Planner for more strategies for differentiation.

HISTORICAL THINKING

ANSWERS

1. Enlightenment thinkers encouraged people to base their ideas on logic and experience and to ask questions to understand the world and their place in it.

2. A government that reflects the ideas of Locke and Rousseau would be one freely elected by the people, one that stands for the rights and freedoms of the governed, and one that can be changed if it does not uphold those rights and freedoms.

3. British authority did not respect the rights and freedoms of the colonists. Following Enlightenment ideas, Franklin and others believed they had a right to demand that British laws be changed and to break free of British rule if their rights and freedoms were not respected.

THE GREAT AWAKENING

Are you persuaded by a message that appeals to your emotions, or are you more convinced by logic and reason? In the 18th century, emotional appeals persuaded colonists to adjust their ideas about religion, themselves, and the world.

CRITICAL VIEWING English artist John Collet illustrates George Whitefield delivering a sermon during one of his seven visits to the colonies in this mid-1700s painting. What does Whitefield's audience suggest about his appeal?

RELIGIOUS REVIVAL

Enlightenment ideas gained popularity among some Protestant colonial ministers who believed God had created humans as rational beings so they could use reason to determine right from wrong. However, other religious leaders pushed back against the Enlightenment. They feared that colonists were abandoning Christianity and losing sight of the importance of God in their lives.

As you know, many of the first colonists who settled in North America came seeking religious freedom. After they had gained that freedom, however, some of their earlier religious fervor died down. By the early 1700s, colonists had shifted their focus from religion to work and the attainment of material goods. Some even stopped attending church regularly. To revive religious life, many Protestant ministers began delivering stirring and emotional sermons during a series of religious revivals known as the **Great Awakening**. From about 1720 to the 1750s, these ministers sought to reconnect people with God and persuade them to recommit to their spiritual beliefs.

The revival began in western Europe in the late 17th and early 18th centuries and then spread to the colonies. In colonial America, the revival took hold primarily among members of the Dutch Reformed Church, which was established by the Dutch settlers in New Netherland; Congregationalists; Presbyterians; Baptists; and some Anglicans. They challenged the rationalism and emphasis on ritual and doctrine practiced by other Protestant denominations. The revivalists favored a more emotional and personal religious experience and preached that all people were equal before God. This spiritual equality appealed to African Americans in the Southern Colonies. Many of them began to move

away from traditional African religions and embrace Christianity. Some southern whites began allowing African Americans into their churches.

One of the most effective preachers of the Great Awakening was the minister **Jonathan Edwards** of Massachusetts. In 1734, he began preaching fiery sermons on **salvation**, or the deliverance from sin through the acceptance of Jesus Christ. Edwards drew large crowds for his sermons. He spoke calmly and made few movements, but his words had a dramatic effect on his listeners, who often wept and moaned aloud.

George Whitefield, an Anglican minister from England, was another important figure in the movement. Whitefield visited North America several times between 1739 and 1770 and preached

PRIMARY SOURCE

Jonathan Edwards delivered his most famous sermon, "Sinners in the Hands of an Angry God," in 1741 to a congregation in Connecticut. In the sermon, he described the fiery fate he believed was in store for those who failed to seek salvation.

The God that holds you over the pit of hell, much as one holds a spider, or some loathsome insect over the fire, abhors [hates] you, and is dreadfully provoked: his wrath [anger] towards you burns like fire; he looks upon you as worthy of nothing else, but to be cast into the fire; he is of purer eyes than to bear to have you in his sight. You have offended him infinitely more than ever a stubborn rebel did his prince; and yet it is nothing but his hand that holds you from falling into the fire every moment.

—from "Sinners in the Hands of an Angry God," by Jonathan Edwards, 1741

throughout the colonies. Because so many people wanted to hear him, his meetings were held in open fields. Unlike Edwards, Whitefield used dramatic gestures and varied the pitch of his voice for increased effect. It worked. Some listeners sobbed and even fainted during his sermons. Like Edwards, Whitefield called on his congregations to accept Jesus Christ. He claimed that by doing so, they would experience a "new birth."

IMPACT ON THE COLONIES

The Great Awakening profoundly affected the social and religious lives of the colonists. Congregations, communities, and some Protestant denominations split between the emotional "New Lights" revivalists and the rational "Old Lights" of established religion. Old Light clergymen resented the challenge to their authority and the new style of worship promoted by the New Light preachers. These revivalists encouraged the colonists to form their own church if they weren't satisfied with their established one. Some did just that. The new Protestant denominations that arose led to a greater tolerance of religious diversity throughout the colonies.

The Great Awakening also affected education. Some New Light preachers established colleges to train ministers for the new congregations. These colleges included Princeton University and Rutgers University in New Jersey, Brown University in Rhode Island, and Dartmouth College in New Hampshire.

The Great Awakening lessened the influence of the Enlightenment among many colonists and changed their view of religion and morality. In certain ways, however, the two movements had a similar impact on the colonies. Like the Enlightenment, the Great Awakening encouraged people to challenge authority and think themselves equal to those in power. In addition, both movements would eventually lead the colonists to question their British rulers and pave the way for revolutionary fervor.

HISTORICAL THINKING

1. **READING CHECK** What led to the Great Awakening?

2. **MAKE INFERENCES** Why do you think Edwards compared members of his audience to a spider?

3. **SUMMARIZE** How did the Great Awakening affect the colonists' ideas about authority and equality?

PLAN: 2-PAGE LESSON

OBJECTIVE

Analyze changes in religious thought and practice engendered by the Great Awakening.

CRITICAL THINKING SKILLS FOR LESSON 3.2

• Make Inferences

• Summarize

• Analyze Primary Sources

• Compare and Contrast

HISTORICAL THINKING FOR CHAPTER 3

As the colonies matured, how did the colonists' identities evolve? The Enlightenment gave many colonists a sense of control over their own destiny, which created a crisis for some religious leaders. Lesson 3.2 discusses the subsequent changes in religious expression and its impact on the colonies.

BACKGROUND FOR THE TEACHER

When his grandfather died in 1729, Jonathan Edwards, then in his mid-20s, took over as the minister of the Puritan Congregational Church in Northampton, Massachusetts. Soon after, he began to cause controversy. First, he spoke out against the ideas of his grandfather, who had allowed the unconverted to take part in religious sacraments. Edwards challenged this practice and insisted that such people were only trying to avoid the fires of hell. He used funeral sermons as opportunities to stress that death could happen at any time and that those who had not accepted Jesus before dying would be eternally damned. As a result, hundreds converted. But Edwards's hard-line approach began to fall out of favor by 1748, when some of the congregation rebelled against him. In 1750, the members voted to fire Edwards. The vote was 230 to 23 against him, and he was dismissed.

INTRODUCE & ENGAGE

PREVIEW VOCABULARY

Write the word *awakening* on the board. **ASK:** What does the word *awakening* mean in a literal sense? *(rousing from sleep)* Invite students to think about how the word *awakening* might be used as a metaphor. **ASK:** How might you use the word *awakening* to describe a personal, political, social, or religious event? *(Answers will vary. Possible response: Awakening might be used to describe a situation in which people have a new awareness of something, such as a societal wrong or a religious truth, almost as if they had previously been asleep and are newly conscious.)* Tell students that in this lesson they will learn about a major religious movement called the Great Awakening, which came on the heels of the Enlightenment.

TEACH

GUIDED DISCUSSION

1. **Analyze Primary Sources** What emotions might Jonathan Edwards have intended his sermons to instill in his listeners, and why? *(Possible response: Edwards may have wanted to terrify his listeners into either converting to or remaining true to the Christian faith by threatening them with images of spiritual and physical disaster if they failed to do so.)*

2. **Compare and Contrast** How were the colonial New Light revivalists similar to and different from the Old Lights? *(Both were factions of Protestantism, but New Light revivalists preached emotionally, encouraged individuals to pursue their personal faith, and had greater tolerance for diversity. In contrast, Old Light clergy adhered to long-established religious practices and resented the intrusion of new forms of worship.)*

MAKE INFERENCES

Remind students that in the early 1700s, some colonists had all but abandoned religion. **ASK:** Why do you think changing social conditions led to changing religious attitudes? *(Possible response: Many colonists had created businesses, and with financial and career success, the ability to use their free time as they saw fit may have been an option for the first time. In addition, as they acquired more control over their own lives, they may have felt less need to recognize a higher power and/or less willingness to accept the authority of church elders.)*

ACTIVE OPTIONS

On Your Feet: Team Quiz Arrange students into four teams and assign each team to a corner of the room for a Four Corners activity. Instruct each team to create a list of four or five questions about the effects of the Great Awakening in the colonies. Start the quiz by inviting Team One to ask Team Two one of the listed questions. When Team Two gives the correct answer, invite Team Two to ask Team Three a question. Continue until all teams have exhausted their questions.

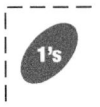 

NG Learning Framework: Write a Dialogue

SKILL Collaboration

KNOWLEDGE Our Human Story

Encourage pairs of students to work together to craft a script for an informal discussion between Great Awakening religious leaders Jonathan Edwards and George Whitefield. Tell them to use information from the lesson and from online and library sources to create their dialogue. Ask students to identify what ideas the two men might talk about and any details that might illustrate their personalities. When pairs have completed their script, invite them to perform the dialogue for the class as time permits, or post the script to a class blog.

DIFFERENTIATE

INCLUSION

Describe and Chart Details Pair students who are visually impaired with students who are not. Ask the latter to read the caption accompanying John Collet's painting and the paragraph about George Whitefield. Sighted partners describe the painting in detail, including clothing, gestures, and facial expressions. Tell visually impaired students to ask clarifying questions as necessary. Encourage partners to work together to answer the Critical Viewing question.

GIFTED & TALENTED

Perform a Dramatic Reading Direct students to look up the full text of "Sinners in the Hands of an Angry God." Challenge them to prepare a dramatic reading of an excerpt of their choosing. Suggest they practice reading it with Edwards's calm delivery and the more expressive voice and gestures of Whitefield. After they have practiced, encourage students to perform their reading for the class and to discuss how the dramatic reading affected their interpretation and understanding of the sermon.

See the Chapter Planner for more strategies for differentiation.

HISTORICAL THINKING

ANSWERS

1. Dissatisfaction with established church practices, leaders, and priorities led to the Great Awakening. Some religious leaders objected to Enlightenment ideals, which they saw as pulling the colonists away from religion.

2. He wanted his audience to understand the loathing God had for them by comparing them to a creature that they would loathe.

3. The Great Awakening helped colonists believe that they should challenge church leaders if they disagreed with those leaders. Challenging traditional church authority expanded to include challenging political authority.

CRITICAL VIEWING Details such as the size of the crowd and the people's emotional expressions and postures—bowing their heads, toasting, kneeling, weeping—reveal Whitefield's wide appeal.

ENGLISH AND COLONIAL RIGHTS

For hundreds of years, English monarchs ruled with absolute power. But, bit by bit, those under their thumb began to chip away at the monarchs' control. In time, the colonists would do the same.

THE RISE OF PARLIAMENT

The English began their quest for legal rights in 1215, when the **Magna Carta**, or "Great Charter," was created. The document served as a peace treaty between King John of England and his barons, or noblemen, who had objected to the heavy taxes the king had levied against them. Most of the 63 clauses in the Magna Carta dealt with the rights of the barons and other wealthy nobles. But two of the clauses protected all free English citizens from being stripped of their rights or possessions without "the lawful judgment of [their] peers or by the law of the land."

Britain's Parliament meets in London's Palace of Westminster, often called the Houses of Parliament. This 2017 photo shows a meeting of the House of Lords. Today, the legislative powers of this house are limited to ensure the government represents all its people. For example, an act passed in 1911 prevents the House of Lords from opposing laws strongly supported by the House of Commons.

The Magna Carta laid the groundwork for a more democratic government in England and became the first written constitution in European history.

The Magna Carta also fostered the rise of **Parliament**, England's legislative body. When it was first created, Parliament consisted of two houses: the House of Lords, made up of nobles and high church officials; and the House of Commons, whose members were elected by male landowners. In the late 1600s, Parliament's power significantly increased following the Glorious Revolution, the bloodless overthrow of King James II. As you may remember, this was the king who formed the Dominion of New England and took away some colonial rights in the region. Parliamentary leaders also thought James had overstepped his authority in England. When William and Mary ascended the throne in his place, Parliament permanently limited the monarch's control and balanced powers more equally between the ruler and the legislature. For example, Parliament would control taxation, pass laws, and be called on to give its consent for raising an army in peacetime and for sending an army to fight against foreign invasions. The **English Bill of Rights of 1689** formally protected the rights of English citizens and Parliament.

The American colonists modeled their governments on Parliament. Property owners in every colony elected representatives to serve in assemblies that were similar to the House of Commons. But unlike those in England's legislature, assembly officials lived in the area they represented so they would better understand local interests and needs. The colonists enjoyed making their own decisions and managing some of their affairs and resented the fact that they had no representation in Parliament, especially when it passed laws they didn't like. For the most part, though, the English government adopted a policy of **salutary neglect** toward the colonies, which means the government usually left them alone. The government generally avoided enforcing colonial policies—unless it suited them to do so.

THE ZENGER TRIAL

In 1733, the English government chose to enforce its laws in the colonies after a series of objectionable articles had appeared in the *New-York Weekly Journal*, a newspaper published by **John Peter Zenger**. The articles reported the corrupt activity of William Cosby, the British colonial governor of New York. Cosby had removed a judge who had ruled against him and had also tampered with the outcome of an election. The accusations were true, but at that time, it was illegal to criticize the government. Since the newspaper didn't print the name of the articles' author, Cosby turned on Zenger and accused him of **libel**, or the publishing of lies. Zenger was arrested in November 1734 and remained in jail until his trial began in August 1735.

Even though Governor Cosby felt confident about the trial's outcome, he packed the jury with his supporters just to make sure. But Zenger's wife Anna, who continued to publish the *New-York Weekly Journal* after her husband's arrest, found out what Cosby had done and reported the fact in the paper. The judge in the trial dismissed Cosby's jury and replaced it with a jury of colonists. However, the judge also dismissed Zenger's team of lawyers for questioning his authority. Andrew Hamilton, a well-known lawyer from Philadelphia, took over the case.

Hamilton knew that Zenger would be found guilty if he simply tried to defend his client against the libel charge. There was no question the paper had criticized the governor, and any such criticism, true or not, was considered libelous. So Hamilton decided to admit Zenger had printed the articles, but he also pointed out that the criticism was true. Why, he argued, should Zenger be punished for printing the truth? A free press, Hamilton insisted, needed to be protected. And wasn't it especially important that the colonists challenge colonial governors when the latter abused their authority? Echoing Enlightenment ideals, Hamilton reminded the jury to allow "that, to which Nature and the Laws of our country have given us a Right, . . . both of exposing and opposing arbitrary Power . . . by speaking and writing Truth."

After a brief deliberation, the jury returned a verdict of not guilty, stunning Cosby and the judge and delighting most of the colonists who thronged the courtroom. The verdict was a major victory for freedom of the press, and it helped ignite the colonists' determination to protect their rights. But the colonists still considered themselves British citizens. When British forces went to war, they would fight alongside them.

HISTORICAL THINKING

1. **READING CHECK** Why was the Magna Carta an important document?

2. **COMPARE AND CONTRAST** In what ways were Parliament and colonial assemblies alike and different?

3. **DRAW CONCLUSIONS** How might the Zenger trial have altered the colonists' attitude toward British authority?

OBJECTIVE

Examine how the structures of Parliament both inspired colonial governments and kept them in check.

CRITICAL THINKING SKILLS FOR LESSON 3.3

- Compare and Contrast
- Draw Conclusions
- Make Generalizations
- Make Connections

HISTORICAL THINKING FOR CHAPTER 3

As the colonies matured, how did the colonists' identities evolve? The colonists began to fashion their own governments, modeled on England's Parliament. Lesson 3.3 discusses the Magna Carta and the English Bill of Rights of 1689, the principles of which paved the way for colonial democracy.

BACKGROUND FOR THE TEACHER

In the years before the creation of the Magna Carta, King John raised a mercenary army, which suffered a major defeat at the Battle of Bouvines in northern France. To ensure that money would be on hand to pay the soldiers, King John ordered a scutage, a tax the barons could pay to the crown in lieu of sending their knights to perform military service. Scutage was not new at the time, and England, Germany, and France all engaged in it, but in King John's England, scutage had become commonplace. To make the burden worse, the king could still demand military service from his barons, and English laws mandated that if he did so, the barons had no choice but to obey. One of the stipulations of the Magna Carta forbade the levy of scutage unless approved by a council. Consequently, the practice dwindled, and by the 14th century it had become completely obsolete.

INTRODUCE & ENGAGE

ACTIVATE PRIOR KNOWLEDGE

Discuss with students what they already know about democratic systems of government. Remind them that although the United States and Great Britain are both democracies, their systems are somewhat different. Then write the term *parliament* on the board and discuss what students know about Britain's Parliament. Explain that in this lesson they will learn about how the British system of government gave rise to democracy in the colonies.

TEACH

GUIDED DISCUSSION

1. **Make Generalizations** How was England's system of salutary neglect regarding the colonies both positive and negative for the colonists? *(Positive: Under salutary neglect, the colonists enjoyed and got used to making decisions on their own. Negative: Because they were used to making their own decisions, they consequently resented intrusions of colonial laws, such as mandating certain taxes.)*

2. **Make Connections** In what way did the court's decision in the Zenger libel trial predict the future of the freedom of the press in the United States? *(Zenger's lawyer argued for the right to freedom of the press, which would one day become a guiding principle of U.S. government, insisting that if Zenger's criticisms of Cosby were true, the press must be allowed to print them.)*

MORE INFORMATION

English Bill of Rights of 1689 Though the English Bill of Rights would become one of the principal underpinnings of England's constitution, its initial purpose was mostly to point out and stop certain illegal practices of the monarch. King James II had fallen into the habit of suspending laws, interfering in the execution of justice, and raising taxes without first gaining consent from Parliament. The Bill of Rights of 1689 pushed for free elections, freedom of speech, and a separation of powers of Parliament and the Crown.

ACTIVE OPTIONS

On Your Feet: Compare Bills of Rights Direct students to locate and read the English Bill of Rights of 1689 and the U.S. Bill of Rights. Both are widely available online. Ask students to complete a Venn diagram that compares and contrasts the content of the documents. Then encourage them to share with the class their thoughts about the importance of the bills to the development of representative and parliamentary democracies.

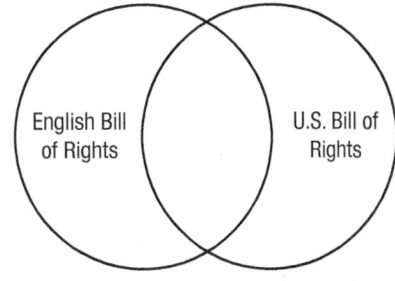

English Bill of Rights | U.S. Bill of Rights

NG Learning Framework: Host a Talk Show

SKILLS Communication, Collaboration

KNOWLEDGE Our Human Story

Divide the class into groups of three. Tell groups to imagine they are participants in a talk show after the libel trial of John Peter Zenger. Assign each group member the role of host, Zenger, or William Cosby. Encourage groups to learn more about the case by researching online resources to help them create their dialogue for the show. Details should include specifics about the case and the perspectives of plaintiff and defendant. Invite groups to share a recording of their talk show or present it to the class.

DIFFERENTIATE

STRIVING READERS

Write a Tweet As students read the lesson, direct them to write a tweet that summarizes each paragraph's main idea in their own words. Encourage students to read their tweets aloud to a partner, alternating paragraphs. Pairs continue the activity until they reach the end of the lesson.

PRE-AP

Report on Public Reaction Instruct students to conduct research and present an oral report about public reaction to the Zenger trial. Tell them to conclude their report by discussing the impact the trial had on freedom of the press and parallels to any other trials involving freedom of the press. Invite students to present their oral report to the class and to answer questions their classmates might have.

See the Chapter Planner for more strategies for differentiation.

HISTORICAL THINKING

ANSWERS

1. Much of the Magna Carta protected the rights of barons, but it also protected all free English citizens from losing their rights or possessions without a legal judgment, becoming the first written constitution in Europe.

2. The governing bodies were alike in that property owners in every colony elected representatives to serve in assemblies that were similar to the House of Commons. They were different because, unlike England's legislators, colonial assembly officials lived in the area they represented, so they had a better grasp of local issues.

3. At the time of the trial, criticism of the government was illegal, but Zenger's lawyer argued for freedom of the press—especially regarding cases in which colonial authorities abused their power. The court victory must have emboldened the colonists to stand up against British authority.

War would erupt between Britain and France in 1754. American artist Junius Brutus Stearns depicts the war's Battle of the Monongahela in his circa 1851 painting, *Washington as a Captain in the French and Indian War.* In this scene from the battle, the general leading the British and American troops falls wounded before George Washington, who sits astride his horse.

CONFLICT IN THE COLONIES

Can't we all get along? Many of the Native Americans who lived in North America didn't. But in the 1600s, some tribes united and agreed to defend each other against their common enemies. These agreements would influence where they would stand in the war that was brewing on the continent.

THE IROQUOIS CONFEDERACY

Before Europeans came to North America and claimed land there, Native Americans began forming alliances with one another. One of these alliances was formed by a group of tribes who called themselves the Haudenosaunee (hah-duh-NAH-suh-nee), or "People of the Longhouse," for the style of the houses they built. The French, however, called the group the Iroquois. As you have read, the Iroquois spoke the Iroquoian language and lived in the area around lakes Ontario, Huron, and Erie in present-day New York State and Pennsylvania and in the southern regions of Ontario and Quebec in present-day Canada. Five Iroquoian tribes living primarily in New York—the Mohawk, Oneida, Onondaga, Cayuga, and Seneca—forged the alliance

between 1570 and 1600. They wanted to put an end to the fierce wars they had been fighting against each other for years. The alliance was called the **Iroquois Confederacy**. With the addition of the Tuscarora tribe in 1722, the confederacy's name would change to the Six Nations.

The Iroquois also joined together to create a united force against their common enemies, the Algonquian and Huron. The Algonquian consisted of a band of tribes, including the Pequot and the Lenape, who spoke similar languages and lived along the Atlantic coast. The Huron lived along the St. Lawrence River.

As Europeans began to arrive in the region, Native Americans also began to form alliances with the British and French. The Iroquois—in particular, the

The Seneca Bark Longhouse at Ganondagan State Historic Site in Victor, New York, is a full-scale replica of a traditional longhouse.

Mohawk—formed an alliance with the British and Dutch, with whom they often traded furs for firearms. After the English took control of New York, the alliance came to be known as the Covenant Chain. Iroquois leaders maintained that their covenant, or binding promise, with the English was linked by a "chain of silver" that would never rust or break. The Iroquois believed the chain was linked by peace and friendship. Meanwhile, the Lenape and Huron allied with the French.

In the 1600s, the French and Iroquois battled for control of the fur trade. The Iroquois dominated the headwaters of the major waterways in the East, which were the key trade arteries to the interior of the continent. However, the Iroquois moved west after the demand for beaver fur led to a scarcity of the animals. The Native Americans warred with competing tribes along the way.

They also fought in New France, hoping to put an end to French trading in the Ohio Valley and beyond. In 1689, the Iroquois attacked the French settlement of Lachine (luh-SHEEN), a small fur-trading settlement

near Montreal. The attack was in retaliation for a raid on Iroquois corn two years before. The Iroquois killed about 250 settlers at Lachine and destroyed the trading settlement.

Clashes between the French and Iroquois continued until both sides grew weary of fighting. In 1701, at the request of the governor of New France, roughly 1,300 representatives from as many as 40 Native American tribes arrived in Montreal. The participants signed a treaty, known as the **Great Peace of Montreal**, that ended hostilities between the Iroquois and the French. In accordance with the treaty, the battle-weakened Iroquois agreed to remain neutral, or not take sides, in future wars.

CONFLICT BETWEEN BRITAIN AND FRANCE

As you have read, when French fur traders first came to North America in the 1600s, they set up a few forts and trading posts in the St. Lawrence River Valley. After they had trapped and killed many of the animals in the area, they resettled in the Ohio Valley. The British also claimed this land, and, in the 1740s,

---

OBJECTIVE

Analyze territorial disputes among the British, French, and Native Americans in the colonies.

CRITICAL THINKING SKILLS FOR LESSON 4.1

- Make Inferences
- Evaluate
- Interpret Maps
- Draw Conclusions
- Analyze Cause and Effect
- Analyze Visuals
- Make Generalizations
- Identify

HISTORICAL THINKING FOR CHAPTER 3

As the colonies matured, how did the colonists' identities evolve? As more settlers arrived in the colonies, conflicts between the British, the French, the colonists, and Native American groups escalated as each sought to control territory. Lesson 4.1 explores disputes among these groups and the various alliances that formed.

BACKGROUND FOR THE TEACHER

As other Native American groups did, the Iroquois, or Haudenosaunee, built homes that used available resources and suited their lifestyle. Trees were plentiful in the region, so longhouses featured frames made of saplings sunk into postholes, and bark panels formed the walls. Long and narrow, these permanent structures ranged in length from about 40 to 400 feet long, and most were not more than 23 feet wide. Inside, longhouses contained several small compartments along a central hall, each compartment intended for use by one family. Fires could be built along the hall, and four families shared a common fire that vented through a hole in the roof. In some instances, men and women entered through doors at opposite ends of the structure. Some Iroquois longhouses held 20 or more families.

INTRODUCE & ENGAGE

DISCUSS ALLIANCES

Ask students to recall a time when they formed an alliance with another person or group. Invite them to discuss the issues that created the need for the alliance as well as any benefits that might have come from it. Post a Cause-and-Effect Map like the one shown, and fill in the boxes with information from students' examples to show the process graphically. Then explain that in this lesson students will learn about North American territorial disputes among French, English, and Native American populations and the alliances that were formed to resolve them.

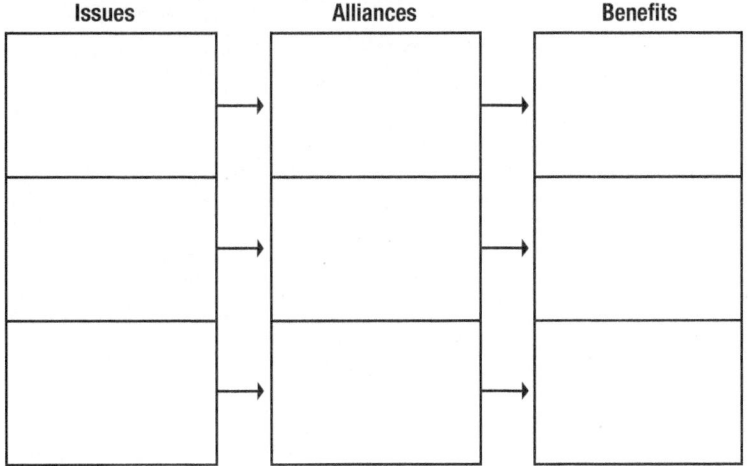

TEACH

GUIDED DISCUSSION

1. **Draw Conclusions** Why did some Native American groups form alliances with the British, while others formed alliances with the French? *(Possible response: Different tribes or groups of tribes had different interests. For example, some benefited from trade with the British, some competed with the French over fur trapping, and some probably had longstanding histories of peace or conflict with either the British or French. Each group would have formed alliances to further its own interests.)*

2. **Analyze Cause and Effect** What caused the French to move their trapping and trading operations to the Ohio River Valley? *(They had thinned out the animal population in the St. Lawrence Valley and sought new territory with more plentiful wildlife.)*

For students who develop an interest in clashes between Native Americans and Europeans, suggest that they read the online American Story "Colliding Cultures."

ANALYZE VISUALS

Draw students' attention to the painting *Washington as a Captain in the French and Indian War*. Invite students to call out compelling details they notice. **ASK:** What mood does this painting express? *(Possible response: The mood is chaotic. There is a smoky haze over the entire area, and several men have been wounded or killed.)* What details help you distinguish the British troops from the colonial forces they fought alongside? *(The British soldiers and officers wear bright blue uniform coats that stand out against the forest backdrop; the colonial troops wear more neutral colors that help them blend in.)*

DIFFERENTIATE

ENGLISH LANGUAGE LEARNERS   ELD

Identify Causes and Effects This lesson contains many examples of cause and effect. Provide the following sentence frames to help students discuss and write about important events that occurred leading up to and in the early years of the French and Indian War.

- **Emerging:** I read that _____ caused _____. _____ happened. The result was _____.

- **Expanding:** I read about how _____ caused_____. As a result of _____, _____ happened.

- **Bridging:** First the text tells about _____. Then the text explains how _____ resulted in _____. _____ happened. It may have been caused by _____ or _____. I think it was caused by _____ because _____.

PRE-AP

Explore Roots of Conflict Challenge students to learn how the European demand for fashionable felt hats drove the lucrative fur trade, which led to overhunting of beavers and the need to push into new territories, causing conflicts over land and ultimately leading to the French and Indian War. Tell students to use their findings to create a report that makes the connection between economic factors and conflicts. Encourage them to present their report to the class orally or post it on a class blog.

See the Chapter Planner for more strategies for differentiation.

began pushing the French traders out of the valley. Colonial settlers bought land shares in the fertile Ohio Valley from the Ohio Company of Virginia in 1749. Nevertheless, the French still tried to maintain their claim on the land.

To block the British, the French began building a chain of forts from Lake Ontario to the Ohio River. Then in 1752, the French destroyed Pickawillany, a colonial trading post. In an effort to settle the dispute over the Ohio Valley, the British governor of Virginia sent a young colonial army officer, **George Washington,** to Fort LeBoeuf (luh-BUHF) in October 1753. The French fort was located in northwest Pennsylvania near Lake Erie. Washington was charged with delivering a message from the governor, informing the French they were on British land and requesting that they leave the fort. However, the French politely refused.

In May 1754, the British sent the newly promoted Colonel Washington and a few troops under his command to capture Fort Duquesne (doo-KAYN) in present-day Pittsburgh. The French fort was strategically located on land where the Allegheny and Monongahela rivers meet to form the Ohio River. When he reached the fort, Washington realized he was outnumbered. He retreated about 40 miles from Fort Duquesne, where he and his troops hastily built a wooden stockade they fittingly called Fort Necessity.

But their situation was hopeless. French troops and their Native American allies soon surrounded the encampment and attacked. Washington's troops suffered heavy losses. After only a few hours of fighting, about 30 of Washington's men had been killed and about 70 were wounded. Accepting defeat, Washington surrendered to the French and abandoned Fort Necessity. Many historians consider this battle the start of the **French and Indian War.**

For Britain and France, this war would become part of a larger conflict, called the Seven Years' War, which officially began in 1756. The larger war involved all the great powers of Europe in a struggle over land on the continent. The French and Indian War was fought between Britain and France in their struggle to control North America.

Meanwhile, the colonists were also concerned about holding on to land in North America. In 1754, seven colonies sent delegates to a congress in Albany, New York, to negotiate an alliance with the Iroquois against the French. The Iroquois refused, however, because they were bound by the peace treaty they had signed with the French in 1701.

The delegates then discussed the defense measures the colonies might take against the French. They voted to adopt the **Albany Plan of Union** suggested by Benjamin Franklin. The plan proposed empowering a central government to tax, pass laws, and oversee military defense for the colonies. When the delegates returned home with the proposal, none of the colonies approved it. Nevertheless, the colonists were united in their determination to fight for the land they believed was theirs.

EARLY YEARS OF THE WAR

British general Edward Braddock landed in the colonies with two British regiments in 1755. In July of that year, he led his troops and about 700 colonial soldiers—including Washington, serving as an aide—through the Virginia backcountry on a mission to capture Fort Duquesne. Braddock's army was also accompanied by a group of Native Americans who served as scouts along the way.

The army's progress was slow, however. Braddock's wagons were too big for the narrow paths they encountered, and many of the scouts deserted, offended by the treatment they received at the hands of the British soldiers. The French and their Native American allies had plenty of time to track Braddock's progress and prepare for his arrival.

After Braddock and his troops crossed the Monongahela River about 10 miles east of Pittsburgh, the French forces ambushed them, shooting from behind trees. The **Battle of the Monongahela** lasted for several hours, as the French and their Native American allies continued to use the same tactic. Washington tried to convince Braddock to fight from behind trees as well, but the general refused. He and his troops were used to fighting on European battlefields, where the opposing armies formed neat rows.

The battle was a devastating defeat for Britain. About 1,000 of the 1,459 British soldiers who took part in the battle were killed or wounded, including Braddock himself. With his uniform pockmarked by bullet holes, Washington struggled to save what was left of Braddock's army and helped organize the retreat. British losses continued to pile up in the early years of the war. In New York, French forces seized Fort William Henry and Fort Oswego. Despite being outnumbered four to one, they captured 2,000 British soldiers at Lake George. In addition, between 1755 and 1757, France's Native American allies burned backcountry settlements in Virginia, Maryland, and Pennsylvania and killed or captured thousands of colonists. So far, the war was not going well for Britain and the colonies.

COLONIAL UNITY
Benjamin Franklin created this famous political cartoon in 1754 to urge the colonies to unite with Britain against the French. The segments of the snake represent the colonies: N.E. for New England; N.Y. for New York; N.J. for New Jersey; P. for Pennsylvania; M. for Maryland; V. for Virginia; N.C. for North Carolina; and S.C. for South Carolina. In time, the cartoon would come to symbolize colonial unity against Britain.

HISTORICAL THINKING

1. **READING CHECK** Why did some Iroquoian tribes form an alliance?

2. **MAKE INFERENCES** Why do you think none of the colonies approved the Albany Plan of Union?

3. **EVALUATE** What qualities did George Washington demonstrate during the Battle of the Monongahela?

4. **INTERPRET MAPS** Where were most of the battles of the French and Indian War fought?

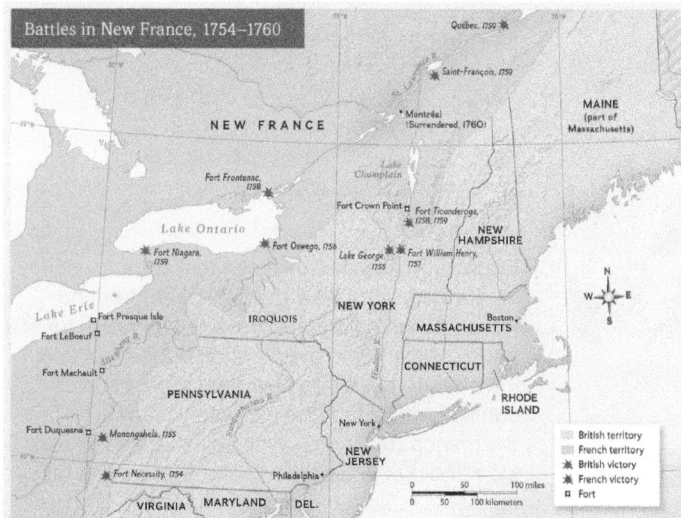

Battles in New France, 1754–1760

BUILD BACKGROUND

THE BATTLE OF THE MONONGAHELA

Surprise and confusion played a big role in the Battle of the Monongahela. As they surged toward Fort Duquesne, General Braddock's troops encountered little French resistance and considered that the fort might actually be abandoned. They didn't realize that the French had left the fort and planned to ambush them. When an advance guard, headed by British lieutenant colonel Thomas Gage, encountered the French, the clash forced Gage to retreat. His soldiers ran straight into General Braddock's, and chaos ensued. As British troops panicked, the French kept shooting, and Braddock suffered a bullet wound. He died a few days later, on July 13. Braddock's men buried him in the middle of a road and marched over the makeshift grave to stamp out all trace of it because they feared that Native Americans might dig up and vandalize his body.

JOIN, OR DIE

"Join, or Die" was the first political cartoon ever printed in an American newspaper. On May 9, 1754, it appeared in the pages of the *Pennsylvania Gazette* in an editorial written by Benjamin Franklin. The image caught wide attention and was soon reprinted in other newspapers. For years, mystified historians mistook the *P* (for Pennsylvania) above the snake for an *R* due to the small diagonal line on the right side of the letter, which turned out to be a flaw embedded in the paper.

TEACH

GUIDED DISCUSSION

3. **Make Generalizations** What general statement can you make about the British Army's intelligence information, given its attack on Fort Duquesne? *(Possible response: The fact that Washington's forces were greatly outnumbered and forced to retreat shows that the British Army did not always have accurate or up-to-date information about the movement of enemy forces.)*

4. **Identify** What roles did Native Americans fill in the early years of the French and Indian War? *(Answers will vary. Possible response: Native Americans served as scouts for the British. They also increased the fighting ranks, especially for the French, and may have done things that the French soldiers would not ordinarily do, such as burning villages and capturing or killing civilians, while French troops seized forts and captured British soldiers.)*

INTERPRET MAPS

Direct students' attention to the map Battles in New France, 1754–1760. Guide students to identify lakes, rivers, forts, and victory sites. **ASK:** What role did rivers and lakes play in the battles that took place in New France? *(Possible response: Many forts and settlements were located on or near lakes or rivers, which would have allowed the British and French armies to transport troops and supplies for battle.)* Why did many battles take place at or near forts? *(Possible response: Forts were valuable targets, as they provided shelter and protection and held ammunition and other supplies.)*

ACTIVE OPTIONS

Active History: Compare North American Settlements Extend the lesson by using either the PDF or Whiteboard version of the activity. These activities take a deeper look at a topic from, or related to, the lesson. Explore the activities as a class, turn them into group assignments, or even assign them individually.

NG Learning Framework: Craft an Editorial

SKILL Communication

KNOWLEDGE Our Human Story

Tell students to imagine they are newspaper editors in the year 1754 covering the delegation from seven colonies that deliberated on how best to defend against the French. Encourage students to use information from the lesson and online resources to create an editorial that argues for or against the Albany Plan of Union. Remind them to support their opinion with sound reasoning and explanations. When they have finished, invite students to present their editorials as speeches or in a panel discussion format.

HISTORICAL THINKING

ANSWERS

1. They had been fighting against each other for a long time and wanted to end the wars between them. They also wanted to join forces against a common enemy.

2. Possible response: The colonists might have rejected the Albany Plan of Union because it required a central government to tax, pass laws, and oversee military defense for the colonies. At the time, most colonists believed the colonies were too independent of each other for such a plan to work.

3. Possible response: Washington showed tactical sense and good judgment when he determined that the British should abandon fighting out in the open and instead fight from behind the trees, as the French were doing. He proved himself a strong leader when, after General Braddock's death, he organized the retreat of the remainder of Braddock's army.

4. Most of the battles of the French and Indian War were fought in New France.

BRITISH VICTORY

The colonists had fought valiantly alongside the British soldiers and rejoiced in Britain's victory. But soon after the war, the British government took steps that made the colonists wonder what they had fought for.

THE TIDE TURNS

The course of the conflict reversed after British statesman **Sir William Pitt** heavily financed the war and raised more troops to fight in it. In July 1758, the British captured Louisbourg in Nova Scotia, forcing the French in the Ohio Valley to pull out and rush to the defense of Quebec and Montreal. Soon after the removal of the French, supplies ran out for their Native American allies, and they, too, withdrew from the backcountry. As a result, the British took control of the western region.

Not even the French reinforcements from the Ohio Valley could save Quebec. In 1759, General James Wolfe laid siege to the city. Although both Wolfe and the commander of the French troops would die during the **Battle of Quebec**, the British captured the city. These victories persuaded many Iroquois to abandon their neutrality and join Britain and the colonies in the war effort. Then in 1760, General Jeffrey Amherst led his troops to Montreal. Only about 2,000 French soldiers remained to defend the city. Within three days, they surrendered to the British. The capture of Montreal ended French control of—and power in—Canada. It also marked the end of the French and Indian War.

In 1763, British diplomats traveled to Paris to negotiate a treaty with the French. Although many Native American tribes had been heavily involved in the conflict, no representatives from these groups were invited to take part in the negotiations. The **Treaty of Paris of 1763** officially ended the French and Indian War. According to its terms, Britain gained Canada from France. As Britain's ally, Spain acquired New Orleans and the Louisiana Territory west of the Mississippi River. Spain agreed to cede Florida to the British in exchange for Cuba and the Philippines, a group of islands in Southeast Asia. Britain now controlled all of the land in North America east of the Mississippi.

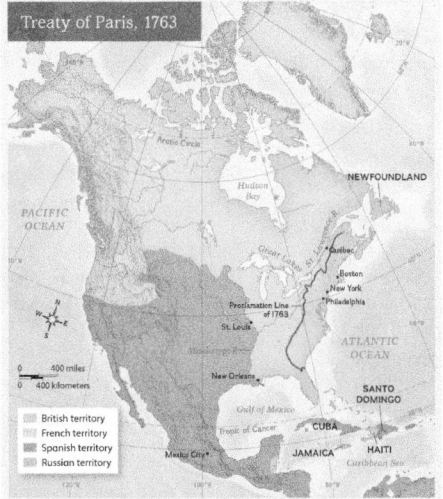

Treaty of Paris, 1763

NEWFOUNDLAND

PACIFIC OCEAN

Hudson Bay

Quebec
Boston
New York
Philadelphia
Proclamation Line of 1763
St. Louis

ATLANTIC OCEAN

New Orleans

Gulf of Mexico

SANTO DOMINGO

CUBA

Mexico City

JAMAICA   HAITI

0   400 miles
0   400 kilometers

☐ British territory
☐ French territory
☐ Spanish territory
☐ Russian territory

IMPACT OF THE WAR

With the end of the war, the colonists gained some advantages. The treaty gave them the right to fish the waters of the North Atlantic off the coast of Canada. And the colonists assumed they were now free to settle the Ohio Valley. For Native Americans, however, the war was a disaster. With the French removed from North America, they lost a powerful ally and trading partner. And trade with the British was much less favorable. The British didn't present the Native Americans with annual gifts as the French had. They also raised prices on trade goods and placed limits on what and how much Native Americans could trade. Perhaps worst of all, colonial settlers began streaming into Native American lands in the Ohio Valley, violating treaties that were still in effect.

The changes in trade policies and the land-grabbing by colonists drove large numbers of Delaware, Shawnee, Iroquois, and other Native Americans to rebel. Ottawa leader **Pontiac**, who had allied with the French during the war, urged Native Americans in the region to band together and fight against the British. In 1763, Pontiac began a series of coordinated attacks on British forts in what is known as **Pontiac's Rebellion**. His forces defeated 13 forts but were unable to seize the most important ones, including Fort Pitt (named in honor of William Pitt) in Pennsylvania. In addition, Pontiac had hoped to receive aid from the French, but that never came. During the siege at Fort Pitt, representatives from the Delaware tribe met with officers at the fort to ask them to give up. The British officers refused. Instead, some historians maintain that the officers gave the Native Americans smallpox-infested blankets to intentionally spread disease among them.

Fighting would continue for two more years. In the meantime, **King George III** of England grew frustrated with the ongoing war between the colonists and Native Americans. In an effort to keep the peace, King George issued the **Proclamation of 1763**, which required colonists to remain east of a line that, on a map, ran along the crest of the Appalachian Mountains from Maine to Georgia. The proclamation angered the colonists. The right to settle the lands west of the line had been the reason most of them had fought in the French and Indian War. Many colonists ignored the proclamation and continued to move westward. But the French and Indian War had been costly for the British government. It couldn't afford to send soldiers to enforce the proclamation. Soon Britain would demand that the colonists help pay down these expenses.

It is important for us, my brothers, that we exterminate from our lands this nation which seeks only to destroy us. You see as well as I do that we can no longer supply our needs, as we have done from our brothers, the French. The English sell us goods twice as dear [expensive] as the French do, and their goods do not last. Scarcely have we bought a blanket or something else to cover ourselves with before we must think of getting another; and when we wish to set out for our winter camps they do not want to give us any credit as our brothers the French do.

—from a speech to a council of Native Americans given by Chief Pontiac, near Detroit, May 1763

HISTORICAL THINKING

1. **READING CHECK** Why did the tide turn toward the British in the French and Indian War?

2. **SUMMARIZE** How did Britain's victory in the war affect Native Americans?

3. **ANALYZE CAUSE AND EFFECT** What led King George III to issue the Proclamation of 1763?

4. **INTERPRET MAPS** Why do you think Britain wanted to exchange Cuba and the Philippines for Florida?

PLAN: 2-PAGE LESSON

OBJECTIVE

Explore Britain's victory in the French and Indian War and its new role in North America.

CRITICAL THINKING SKILLS FOR LESSON 4.2

• Summarize
• Analyze Cause and Effect
• Interpret Maps
• Draw Conclusions
• Analyze Primary Sources

HISTORICAL THINKING FOR CHAPTER 3

As the colonies matured, how did the colonists' identities evolve? Victory over France brought Britain new land and massive debt. Lesson 4.2 explores the aftermath of the war and the ensuing tensions among Britain, Native American nations, and the colonies.

BACKGROUND FOR THE TEACHER

The fifth in a string of attacks on British-held forts during Pontiac's Rebellion took place at Fort Michilimackinac, perched on the northernmost tip of Michigan's Lower Peninsula. Once a French stronghold, the fort was abandoned after the war, and British soldiers moved in. The fort's commander ignored fur traders' warnings of an impending attack. On June 2, 1763, a group of Ojibwe invited British soldiers to watch them play a lacrosse-like game against an opposing team of Sauks. When the Ojibwe "accidentally" lobbed a ball into the fort, the soldiers allowed them inside to retrieve it. Once inside the fort, the Ojibwe attacked. The outnumbered soldiers were soon overrun, and the attack was a major victory for the Ojibwe. One year later, the British would reclaim the fort.

INTRODUCE & ENGAGE

DISCUSS INTERNATIONAL TREATIES

Write *international treaty* on the board and ask students to call out words they associate with this term. Invite the class to collaborate on a formal definition of the phrase. *(a written agreement among nations that legally binds two or more nations to its terms)* **ASK:** What are some different types of international treaties? *(trade agreements, peace agreements, environmental agreements)* Tell students that in this lesson they will learn about the Treaty of Paris, a peace treaty between Britain and France.

TEACH

GUIDED DISCUSSION

1. **Draw Conclusions** Why was the Battle of Quebec the conflict that ended the French and Indian War? *(The French had already lost a lot of territory to the British, their Iroquois allies were gone, and the loss of their Montreal stronghold was devastating.)*

2. **Analyze Primary Sources** Why might Native Americans setting out for their winter camp need credit from the French or British? *(Possible response: They likely needed extra supplies, such as blankets or tools, in preparation for the cold months of winter, especially if they were isolated from trading opportunities. They could then pay for those supplies in warmer weather, when they could more easily hunt and fish.)*

MORE INFORMATION

The Siege of Fort Detroit Share with students that in May 1763, Pontiac embarked on a daring plan for a surprise attack to capture Fort Detroit. The commanding officer at the fort was tipped off in time, however, so Pontiac went with his alternative plan and laid siege to the fort. The British shipped supplies and other aid to Fort Detroit. The British then sent troops, but Pontiac's allies intercepted at least one troop convoy. The siege dragged on through the summer. By the beginning of the harvest season, many of Pontiac's allies began to decamp for their villages. With fewer allies on hand to help him maintain pressure on the fort, Pontiac's siege began to erode. Eventually, he gave up the fight and returned to his village.

ACTIVE OPTIONS

On Your Feet: Victory Q & A Point out that several factors helped the British overcome their early losses to win the French and Indian War. Arrange students in a Fishbowl configuration. Assign the inner circle the discussion topic Components of British Victory in North America. Prompt them to identify the factors that helped the British win the French and Indian War, while the outside circle listens and takes notes. After a few minutes, have the circles change positions and restart the discussion.

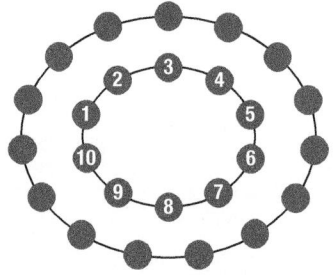

NG Learning Framework: Stage a Debate

SKILLS Collaboration, Communication

KNOWLEDGE Our Human Story

Tell students to imagine they are a group of colonists discussing the Proclamation of 1763. Divide the class into two teams and assign each team to argue either for or against the proclamation. Then encourage team members to work together to locate information about the proclamation in the lesson and online in preparation for their debate. Remind students to explore the pros and cons of the proclamation, searching for details that support their argument as well as any counterarguments they could make during the debate.

DIFFERENTIATE

STRIVING READERS

Read and Recall Invite students to work in pairs. First have each student read the lesson independently. After reading, partners meet without the book and take notes as they share ideas they recall. Pairs then review the lesson together and decide what to add or change in their notes.

GIFTED & TALENTED

Create a Multimedia Presentation Prompt students to learn more about the purpose, tactics, and battles of Pontiac's Rebellion, including events leading up to the rebellion and major battles. Tell students to create a multimedia presentation about Pontiac and the other Native Americans who fought to maintain control of their lands and way of life. The presentation might include maps, drawings, paintings, artifacts, and other visuals. Encourage students to conclude the presentation with the main positive and negative legacies of Pontiac's Rebellion.

See the Chapter Planner for more strategies for differentiation.

HISTORICAL THINKING

ANSWERS

1. Sir William Pitt increased the money spent on the war and raised more troops, giving the advantage to the British.

2. The British victory had a strong negative impact on Native Americans. Trade with the British was much less fair than it had been with the French. The British raised prices on goods and limited Native American trading opportunities and may have even knowingly infected goods with smallpox. Also, colonial settlers violated treaties by settling on Native American lands in the Ohio Valley.

3. Possible response: George III issued the proclamation primarily to end conflicts with Native Americans in the Ohio Valley by keeping colonists from settling there. It was also a way to keep control of valuable lands and restrict colonial expansion.

4. Possible response: Florida was on the mainland and shared a border with the colonies. Cuba was fairly close to the mainland, but it was an island, and the Philippines were on the other side of the world, so Florida was better strategically for the British.

VOCABULARY

Use each of the following vocabulary words in a sentence that shows an understanding of the term's meaning.

1. overseer
   The overseer didn't allow the enslaved laborers to stop working until well after sunset.

2. subsistence farming

3. backcountry

4. maritime

5. Parliament

6. salutary neglect

7. libel

8. salvation

READING STRATEGY
SUMMARIZE

When you summarize, you restate text in your own words and shorten it. A summary includes only the most important information and details. Use a diagram like this one to summarize the factors that led to the expansion of cities in the colonies.

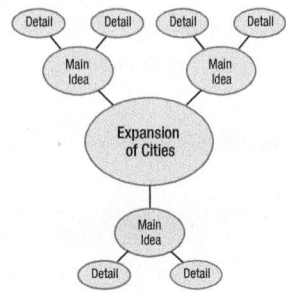

9. Why did most of the colonial cities arise in New England and the Middle Colonies?

MAIN IDEAS

Answer the following questions. Support your answers with evidence from the chapter.

10. Why did New England become the center of colonial trade in the early 1700s? LESSON 1.1

11. Why did the Middle Colonies come to be called the "breadbasket of the colonies"? LESSON 1.2

12. Where did most of the Germans who immigrated to the Middle Colonies settle? LESSON 1.3

13. Why did little industry develop in the Southern Colonies? LESSON 2.1

14. How did enslaved Africans in the Southern Colonies create resilient and rich cultures? LESSON 2.2

15. What was the Enlightenment? LESSON 3.1

16. In what way was the Great Awakening a reaction against the Enlightenment? LESSON 3.2

17. Why was John Peter Zenger arrested and jailed? LESSON 3.3

18. What sparked the French and Indian War? LESSON 4.1

19. How did the Proclamation of 1763 impact the colonists? LESSON 4.2

HISTORICAL THINKING

Answer the following questions. Support your answers with evidence from the chapter.

20. MAKE INFERENCES What was life probably like for subsistence farmers in the New England colonies?

21. DRAW CONCLUSIONS How did the Quakers live by the Bible's golden rule, which says to act toward others as you would want them to behave toward you?

22. ANALYZE CAUSE AND EFFECT What happened because enslaved people from West Africa taught southern plantation owners how to cultivate rice?

23. FORM AND SUPPORT OPINIONS Which movement do you think had the greater impact on the colonies—the Enlightenment or the Great Awakening? Remember to support your answer with evidence from the chapter.

24. COMPARE AND CONTRAST How did the relationship between the Native Americans and the British differ from that between the Native Americans and the French?

25. MAKE PREDICTIONS How do you think the colonists will react when Britain tries to make them help pay for the war?

INTERPRET GRAPHS

Study the graph below, which shows colonial population growth between 1670 and 1770. Then answer the questions.

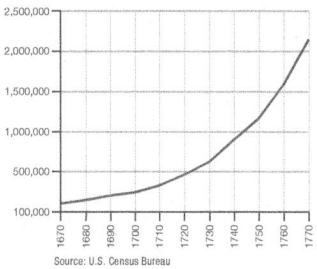

Population Growth in the Colonies, 1670–1770

Source: U.S. Census Bureau

26. In which decade did the American colonies experience the largest population growth?

27. What do you think accounts for the growth in population in that decade?

28. By how much did the population increase between 1670 and 1770?

ANALYZE SOURCES

In 1735, an essay supporting the education of women was reprinted in John Peter Zenger's *New-York Weekly Journal* after it had appeared in another newspaper. Read the excerpt from the essay and answer the question.

> I Have often wondered that Learning is not thought a proper Ingredient in the Education of a Woman . . . they have the same improvable Minds as the male Part of the Species, why should they not be cultivated by the same Method?
>
> Learning and Knowledge are Perfections in us, not as we are Men, but as we are reasonable Creatures, in which Order, of Beings the Female World is upon the same Level with the Male. We ought to consider in this Particular, not what is the Sex, but what is the Species to which they belong.

29. What Enlightenment ideals might have influenced the author of this essay?

CONNECT TO YOUR LIFE

30. EXPLANATORY Think about the challenges faced by those who moved to the American colonies. Then consider the difficulties immigrants to the United States encounter today. How are their challenges similar, and how do they differ? Write a paragraph in which you compare the two sets of experiences.

TIPS

- List the challenges the colonists faced in the cities, rural areas, and backcountry. Then list the challenges immigrants endure when they come to the United States today.

- Describe the factors that may have compelled the colonists and the modern immigrants to move.

- Use two or three vocabulary terms from the chapter in your paragraph.

- Conclude the paragraph with a sentence that ties the colonists' experiences to those of modern immigrants.

VOCABULARY ANSWERS

1. The overseer didn't allow the enslaved laborers to stop working until well after sunset.

2. Most colonists in New England practiced subsistence farming, growing food mainly for their families.

3. Many Scots-Irish immigrants settled in the backcountry of the Appalachian Mountains.

4. Transatlantic trade, shipbuilding, fishing, whaling, and other seafaring industries created a maritime economy in the Middle Colonies.

5. The power of Parliament, England's legislative body, increased in the 1600s.

6. Because of England's policy of salutary neglect, the government usually left the American colonists alone.

7. He sued the newspaper for libel because he thought the reporter lied about him.

8. During the Great Awakening, many preachers gave fiery sermons about salvation from sin.

READING STRATEGY ANSWER

9. Possible response: New England and the Middle Colonies had more ports along the coast than the Southern Colonies did. An increase in trade in the colonies after 1750 turned these ports into busy population centers.

MAIN IDEAS ANSWERS

10. Merchants in New England traded with other colonies and exchanged goods directly with Europe.

11. The Middle Colonies were called the "breadbasket" because they produced so much wheat and other grains.

12. German immigrants settled in the backcountry of Pennsylvania to farm.

13. The Southern Colonies were more heavily agricultural than the Middle Colonies or New England. In addition, unlike the Middle Colonies or New England, the Southern Colonies had few port cities. Industry developed fastest in urban population centers because of the abundance of labor.

14. Enslaved Africans contributed a number of words to the English language. The rhythms of African music also influenced the music and dances of colonial America. Enslaved people made musical instruments, pottery, and baskets decorated with African designs. They contributed to the food culture of the colonies by introducing okra, melons, and bananas.

15. The Enlightenment was a movement in which many European thinkers believed that people should use reason and ask questions to help them understand the physical world and their place in it.

16. Religious leaders feared that because of Enlightenment ideas, colonists were abandoning Christianity and losing the importance of God in their lives. Through revivals, religious leaders urged people to recommit to their spiritual beliefs.

17. Zenger was editor of the *New-York Weekly Journal*. Articles in his paper reported the corrupt activity of William Cosby, the British colonial governor of New York. The articles accused Cosby of removing a judge who had ruled against him and tampering with the outcome of an election. At the time, it was illegal to criticize the government.

18. The French and Indian War was sparked by territorial disputes between France and Britain over land in North America.

19. The proclamation stated that colonists had to remain east of a designated line marked by the Appalachian Mountains from Maine to Georgia. This angered the colonists because they had fought alongside the British in part so that they would be able to settle the lands beyond that line.

HISTORICAL THINKING ANSWERS

20. Life was challenging, as New England farm families produced only enough food to provide for themselves, with little, if any, left over to sell or trade. New England's long, cold winters made for a short growing season, and the soil was often rocky, so farmers were limited in what they could grow.

21. The Quakers accepted people of different faiths and believed that all people were equal before God. They were the first colonists to speak out against slavery.

22. Rice yields increased dramatically, and rice plantations sprang up along rivers in the Carolinas.

23. Answers will vary. Possible responses: The Enlightenment was more influential because applying the scientific method to problem solving transformed society in many ways, such as promoting the idea that universal laws governed the natural world rather than God. The Great Awakening was more influential because it lessened the influence of the Enlightenment among many colonists and changed their view of religion and morality.

24. The French abided by their treaties with Native Americans and also offered them gifts. The British did not honor their own treaties with Native Americans and did not offer gifts.

25. Answers will vary. Possible response: The colonists will balk at having to help pay for the war. They thought they were doing the British government a favor by helping in the conflict, and they went into the war believing that they would later settle on the lands they were fighting for against the French.

INTERPRET GRAPHS ANSWERS STEM

26. 1760–1770

27. Possible response: As trade increased, the colonial economy boomed, and the colonies drew more immigrants.

28. The population increased by about 2,000,000.

ANALYZE SOURCES ANSWER

29. Answers will vary. Possible response: The Enlightenment stressed the importance of science and reason. The writer draws on these ideas to argue that men and women—despite their differences—belong to the same species and are both reasonable and therefore can both be enriched by learning.

CONNECT TO YOUR LIFE ANSWER

30. Paragraphs will vary but should reflect both similarities and differences in immigrant experiences in areas such as language, education, employment, religion, and immigration law. Paragraphs should include two or three chapter vocabulary words and conclude with a sentence that ties colonists' experiences to those of modern immigrants.

Colonial New York

by Andrea Stone

Adapted from "New Online Archive Shows Colonial New York Was Rowdy, Filthy, Smelly," by Andrea Stone, news.nationalgeographic.com, December 21, 2014

Decrees limiting the sale of alcohol and outlining penalties for fighting were some of the first ordinances issued in the Dutch colony, New Netherland. Peter Stuyvesant, the colony's director-general, issued these decrees in the mid-1600s.

Most of the inhabitants of the colony's capital, New Amsterdam, likely never read the official decrees. But today, anyone with an internet connection can read them—some of the earliest laws declared in North America. New York City's Municipal Archives has posted a digitized collection of ordinances from 1647 to 1661, when the island of Manhattan in New York City was run by the Dutch and known as New Amsterdam.

The nation's origin story is dominated by the prim, religious monocultures of the Pilgrim and Puritan colonies of New England. The mixture of religions, races, and ethnic groups found in unruly New Amsterdam are often overlooked. However, we know New Amsterdam was an exuberant center of commerce, open to settlers of diverse backgrounds. Pauline Toole, commissioner of New York City's Department of Records and Information Services, remarks, "These ordinances show how New Amsterdam officials tried to maintain order in a fractious and rowdy city, and shed a light on our city's early development."

SUNDAY DRINKING AND FIGHTING

When Stuyvesant replaced an inept and tyrannical director-general, he found a city where alcohol was made or sold in one of every four buildings. Alcoholism was rampant. Despite his immediate crackdown on Sunday drinking and fighting, less than a year later, a frustrated Stuyvesant acknowledged that few had paid attention to his new regulations.

Stuyvesant, however, never tried to enact total prohibition. When he and his council weren't trying to moderate drinking, they were trying to tax it, often unsuccessfully. Several decrees dealt with the government's inability to collect excise taxes on illegal homemade beer and wine.

HOGS RUNNING FREE IN THE STREET

To tamp down frequent fires, Stuyvesant appointed chimney inspectors; required buckets, ladders, and hooks on street corners; and banned roofs made of hay and reeds. He also issued standards for bakers to follow and tried mightily to clean up the streets. The city's health and building departments can trace their beginnings back to Stuyvesant's New Amsterdam decrees.

In 1650, just 25 years after the Dutch built Fort Amsterdam to protect New Amsterdam and the rest of the colony, an ordinance was passed forbidding animals to run free. It noted the "decayed fortress, formerly in fair condition, has mostly been trodden down by hogs, goats and sheep." The loose animals also created an awful smell. To curb the stink lingering in the city, the council also banned the common practice of throwing "any rubbish, filth, ashes, oyster-shells, dead animals or anything like it" in the street.

The online portrait of New Amsterdam "sounds like kindergarten gone wild and the leaders trying to impose order desperately," says Russell Shorto, author of *The Island at the Center of the World*. But he added that the ordinances alone skew the picture of life in the colonial city. As thousands of court documents and other pieces of correspondence are posted to the archive, a more well-rounded portrait should emerge of New Amsterdam and North America's first Dutch colony.

"There's something about the actual written documents and something beyond the words—the paper, the texture, the change in handwriting, the stains on the document," Shorto says. "It's a physical document, and to get some sense [of it] in digital form is a wonder."

For more from National Geographic, check out "The First Americans" online.

UNIT INQUIRY: Conceive a Utopia

In this unit, you learned about the various groups of Europeans who came to North America seeking better lives for themselves and their families. Some groups, such as the Pilgrims and the Puritans, came to form communities based on shared religious beliefs and values. Others focused on building wealth by utiliizing the continent's abundant natural resources. What did these groups consider to be an ideal community? How did they conceive and form their new communities? What conflicts arose as they established their communities?

ASSIGNMENT

The colonies in North America were begun by people who imagined and sought a better way of life in a new place. Envision an ideal community, or a utopia, that you would like to live in. Think about such factors as the goals and values of your community and how it would function. Be prepared to present your utopia to the class.

Plan As you conceive your utopia, review the unit to gather evidence about the ways in which newcomers to North America devised or structured particular components of their communities and how they handled conflicts that arose. Use a graphic organizer like this one to take notes on the variety of ways you find.

Goals	Values
Religion	
Economy	
Government	
Education	
Gender roles	
Conflict	

Produce Review your notes and think about what you consider to be features of an ideal community. Produce a detailed conception of your utopia by writing a short paragraph on each feature.

Present Choose a creative way to present your community and its goals and values to the class. Consider one of these options:

- Create a commercial to persuade people to move to your new community. Include details telling where it is, what it's like, and what kind of people would prosper there.

- Lead a class discussion on the features of an ideal community. To begin the discussion, describe the features of your community.

- Develop a survey asking questions about what makes an ideal community. Encourage classmates to complete the survey, and then use their feedback to present ways your utopia matches their needs.

NATIONAL GEOGRAPHIC | LEARNING FRAMEWORK ACTIVITIES

Map Migrations

SKILLS Observation, Collaboration

KNOWLEDGE Our Human Story

Working with a partner, create a world map showing the migration routes of groups of people who settled in North America up to the mid-1700s. Skim the unit and make a list of immigrant groups and the dates of their migrations. Then create an outline map of the world. You might draw arrows of different colors to represent migration routes of various groups. Include a key that identifies the groups and provides dates of key movements. After you have finished your map, share it with your classmates and compare it with the maps of other partners. What patterns of migration do you notice? Why do you think these patterns occurred?

Establish a Trade Network

ATTITUDE Empowerment

SKILL Collaboration

Trade expanded the colonial economies and created important industries during the 17th century. Working with a small group, establish a trade network among your classmates. Decide what products or resources your group will trade with other groups and what products or resources you want to acquire. Negotiate prices and set quantities of products and resources to be traded. Then determine how the network will exchange goods. List the trading partners and details on the board. Discuss how the trade network might establish new industries or the need for additional infrastructure to support the exchange of goods.

NATIONAL GEOGRAPHIC CONNECTION

GUIDED DISCUSSION FOR "COLONIAL NEW YORK"

1. **Draw Conclusions** Why didn't Peter Stuyvesant declare prohibition to try to stop the rampant alcohol abuse in New Netherland? *(Possible response: The sale of alcohol generated taxes for the colony, so while Stuyvesant wanted to moderate its use, he and the council didn't want to prohibit its use completely.)*

2. **Make Inferences** Why might studying the city ordinances of only a particular time period present an inaccurate idea of the overall history of a community? *(Possible response: Ordinances are likely to point out only behavior to be avoided, which may relate to a particular portion of the population. Daily life is generally more varied and complex, so it's better understood by examining broader historical archives.)*

GUIDED DISCUSSION FOR "THE FIRST AMERICANS"

1. **Identify** What differences did researchers note between male and female skeletal remains of the earliest Americans? *(Male skeletons were larger and showed evidence of injuries from fighting. The female skeletons, on the other hand, showed fewer injuries but were much smaller and displayed signs of malnutrition.)*

2. **Summarize** Why do researchers believe the first long-term human inhabitation in North America might have occurred at the Friedkin site? *(Possible response: The area was ideal for hunter-gatherers, with plenty of game and edible plants, a source of water, and a temperate climate. The people also had access to chert, a type of rock useful for making tools.)*

HISTORY NOTEBOOK
Encourage students to complete the Unit Wrap-Up page for Unit 1 in their History Notebooks.

UNIT INQUIRY PROJECT RUBRIC

ASSESS

Use the rubric to assess each student's participation and performance.

SCORE	ASSIGNMENT	PRODUCT	PRESENTATION
3 GREAT	• Student thoroughly understands the assignment. • Student participates fully in the project process.	• Conception of the utopia is well thought out. • Conception includes a detailed paragraph on each feature of the utopia. • Conception contains all of the key elements listed in the assignment.	• Presentation is clear, concise, and logical. • Presentation does a good job of creatively representing a utopia. • Presentation engages the audience.
2 GOOD	• Student mostly understands the assignment. • Student participates fairly well in the project process.	• Conception is fairly well thought out. • Conception includes at least one paragraph describing one or two features of the utopia. • Conception contains most of the key elements listed in the assignment.	• Presentation is fairly clear, concise, and logical. • Presentation does an adequate job of creatively representing a utopia. • Presentation somewhat engages the audience.
1 NEEDS WORK	• Student does not understand the assignment. • Student minimally participates or does not participate in the project process.	• Conception is not well thought out. • Conception does not include a paragraph describing features of the utopia. • Conception contains few or none of the key elements listed in the assignment.	• Presentation is not clear, concise, or logical. • Presentation does an inadequate job of representing a utopia. • Presentation does not engage the audience.

NATIONAL GEOGRAPHIC LEARNING FRAMEWORK RUBRIC

ASSESS

Use the rubric to assess how each student applies the National Geographic Learning Framework.

SCORE	ASSIGNMENT	ASSIGNMENT	FINAL PRODUCTS
3 GREAT	• Map demonstrates **Observation** and **Collaboration** well. • Map explores **Our Human Story** well.	• Trade network simulation reflects **Empowerment** well. • Trade network simulation demonstrates **Collaboration** well.	• Final products are engaging, creative, and well presented.
2 GOOD	• Map demonstrates **Observation** and **Collaboration**. • Map explores **Our Human Story**.	• Trade network simulation reflects **Empowerment**. • Trade network simulation demonstrates **Collaboration**.	• Final products are interesting, logical, and complete.
1 NEEDS WORK	• Map does not demonstrate **Observation** or **Collaboration**. • Map does not explore **Our Human Story**.	• Trade network simulation does not reflect **Empowerment**. • Trade network simulation does not demonstrate **Collaboration**.	• Final products are not creative, complete, or interesting.

WEAPONS OF THE REVOLUTION

The earliest muzzle-loading firearm, or musket, was developed in Spain during the 16th century. It measured about 5 feet 6 inches long and weighed approximately 20 pounds. The musket was so unwieldy that it generally took two people just to get it into position. To gain more accuracy and control, soldiers generally set it onto a portable rest before firing. By the time of the American Revolution, the flintlock musket had become the most important weapon in battle. Although it was a single-shot weapon, the reloading process was easy and quick, with skilled soldiers able to fire up to three shots per minute. On the other hand, the long-barreled rifle, although more accurate, was difficult to load. This was a definite liability during battle when enemy forces were advancing at close range.

Guns were not the only weapons available to soldiers during the American Revolution. Many battles came down to weapons used for hand-to-hand combat, including bayonets. A socket bayonet could be fitted onto the end of a musket, transforming it from a gun to a spear. In addition, soldiers carried swords, knives, or axes. Sabers were also common—shorter ones for infantrymen and longer ones for cavalry. **ASK:** Based on this information, why do you think the soldiers stand in such close formation as they fire their weapons? *(Possible response: By concentrating firepower in a group, whether using muskets or rifles, the soldiers would be more likely to hit their targets. Also, groups of soldiers could alternate firing and reloading to maintain a steady barrage against oncoming troops.)*

UNIT 2

1764–1814

REVOLUTION AND A NEW NATION

104

CONTINENTAL ARMY UNIFORMS

At the start of the American Revolution, few colonial militias had access to uniforms of any kind, so soldiers typically wore their own clothing. Many donned long hunting shirts made of linen, with fringed capes that covered the shoulders. When the Continental Army was formed, the shortage of uniforms had yet to be resolved. To establish a sense of consistency, George Washington agreed for a time with the idea of using hunting shirts for all troops. By 1779, however, the official uniform had become a tight-sleeved blue woolen coat, a color that may have been chosen to contrast with the red uniforms of the British soldiers.

The sleeves, facings, linings, and buttons of the coats were one of three colors—red, white, or blue, depending on the region where the soldier was fighting. Soldiers in New York and New Jersey, for example, wore coats with off-white facings and white linings and buttons, while soldiers in North and South Carolina and Georgia wore uniforms with blue facings and white linings and buttons. All soldiers had white or beige waistcoats, breeches, and stockings. They topped off their uniforms with black three-cornered hats and brown or black shoes or boots. By 1782, blue coats with red facings had become the standard regimental uniform.

CRITICAL VIEWING The smoke from the weapons probably made it difficult to see the enemy at times. In addition, soldiers had to fire over the heads of the line in front of them, so there was the danger of being accidentally shot by one's own troops. Finally, the constricting uniforms and tight formations must have made fighting crowded, noisy, and difficult.

1779 AFRICA:
RISE OF LUANDA, SLAVE PORT

In 1576, slave traders from Portugal founded a colony at the West African port of Luanda to gain access to the area's ready supply of people who had been enslaved through war, trade, or tribute. Luanda was not densely populated, and the land along the coastline was extremely dry, so most food was imported from Europe or the Americas. Although it lacked many amenities, Luanda was home to an excellent natural harbor that the Portuguese knew would allow for easy export of enslaved people. Portuguese colonists began to acquire slaves by any means possible. By the turn of the 18th century, the city's population had greatly expanded, and most of its African residents were enslaved. Many enslaved people were shipped to Portuguese plantations and mines in Brazil. Others were sent to the Spanish Americas.

As demand for enslaved workers increased, the slave market became Luanda's primary economic industry. Luanda remained the principal center of the Atlantic slave trade to Brazil until 1836. By 1844, the port had opened to foreign trade shipping, welcoming diverse populations and ushering in new cultural developments. By 1850, Luanda had won a reputation as one of the most sophisticated cities of the Portuguese empire, and many referred to it as the "Paris of Africa." **ASK:** What might have created the change in public perception about the port of Luanda over time? *(Possible response: As the slave trade expanded, the city grew economically, and different business opportunities evolved. New people arriving from other lands introduced diverse cultures, trades, languages, and arts to the area; and the natural harbor provided easy access to travelers and merchants.)*

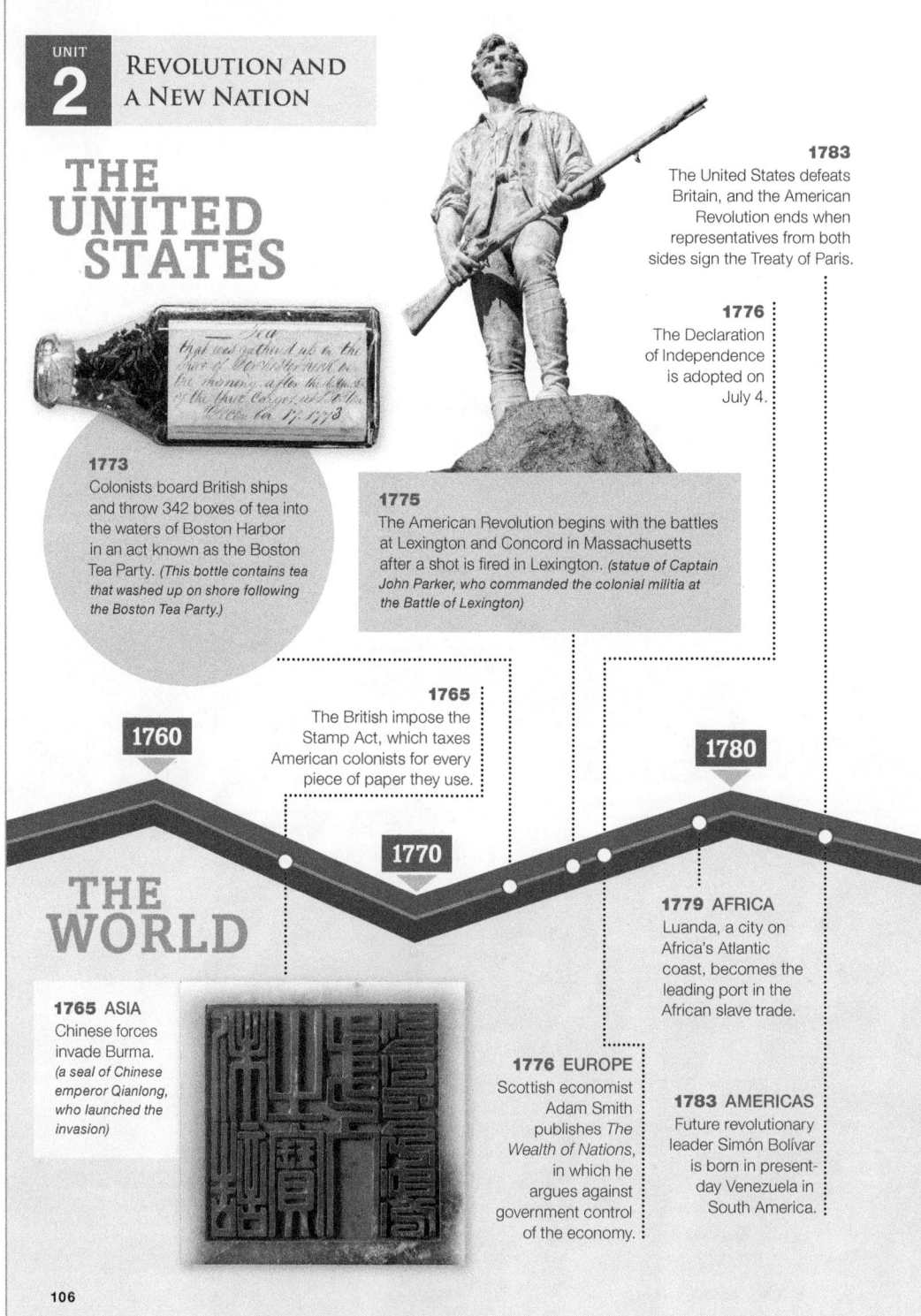

UNIT
2
REVOLUTION AND
A NEW NATION

THE UNITED STATES

1783
The United States defeats Britain, and the American Revolution ends when representatives from both sides sign the Treaty of Paris.

1776
The Declaration of Independence is adopted on July 4.

1773
Colonists board British ships and throw 342 boxes of tea into the waters of Boston Harbor in an act known as the Boston Tea Party. *(This bottle contains tea that washed up on shore following the Boston Tea Party.)*

1775
The American Revolution begins with the battles at Lexington and Concord in Massachusetts after a shot is fired in Lexington. *(statue of Captain John Parker, who commanded the colonial militia at the Battle of Lexington)*

1765
The British impose the Stamp Act, which taxes American colonists for every piece of paper they use.

1760

1780

THE WORLD

1770

1765 ASIA
Chinese forces invade Burma. *(a seal of Chinese emperor Qianlong, who launched the invasion)*

1776 EUROPE
Scottish economist Adam Smith publishes *The Wealth of Nations*, in which he argues against government control of the economy.

1779 AFRICA
Luanda, a city on Africa's Atlantic coast, becomes the leading port in the African slave trade.

1783 AMERICAS
Future revolutionary leader Simón Bolívar is born in present-day Venezuela in South America.

106

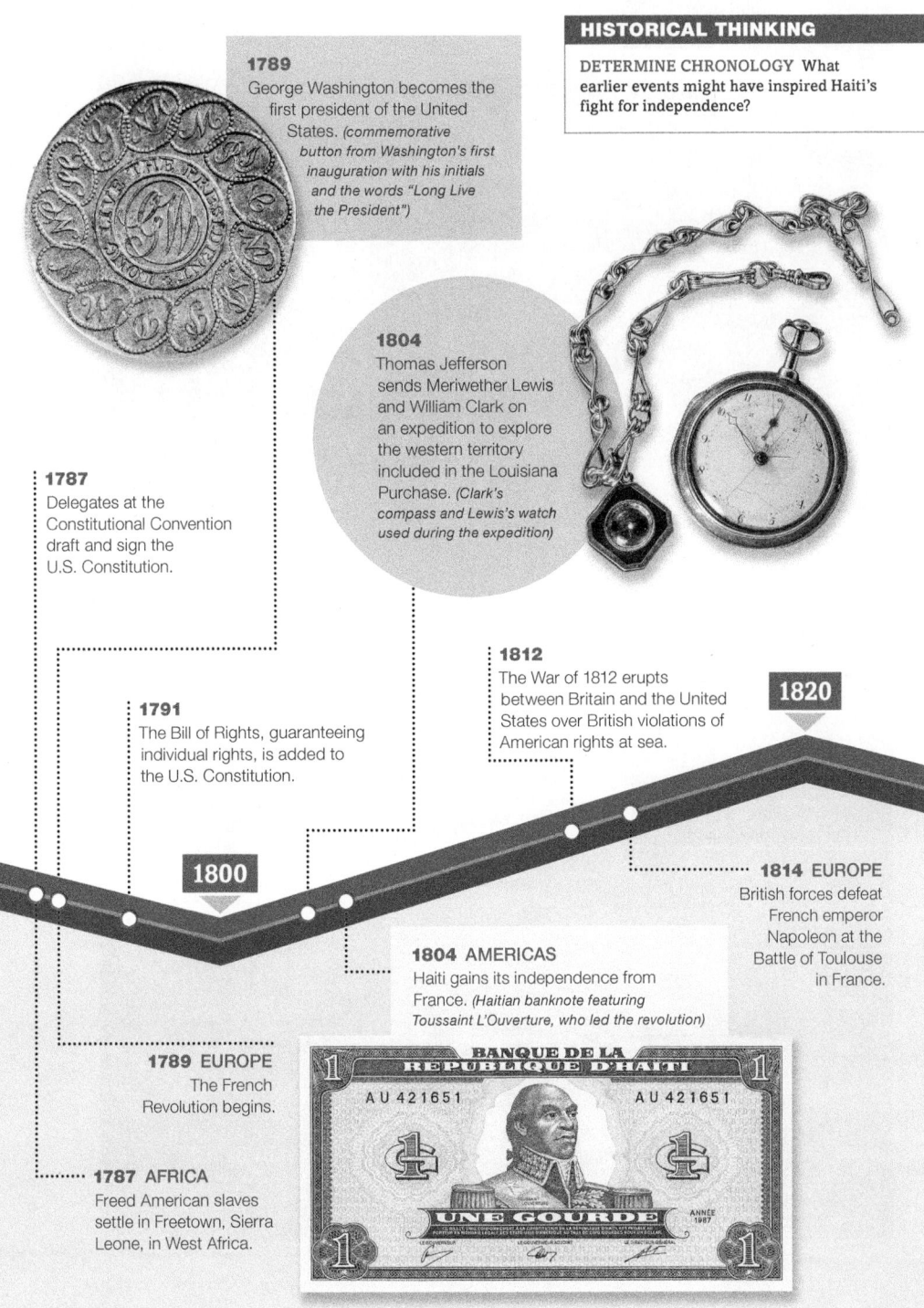

1789
George Washington becomes the first president of the United States. *(commemorative button from Washington's first inauguration with his initials and the words "Long Live the President")*

HISTORICAL THINKING

DETERMINE CHRONOLOGY What earlier events might have inspired Haiti's fight for independence?

1804
Thomas Jefferson sends Meriwether Lewis and William Clark on an expedition to explore the western territory included in the Louisiana Purchase. *(Clark's compass and Lewis's watch used during the expedition)*

1787
Delegates at the Constitutional Convention draft and sign the U.S. Constitution.

1812
The War of 1812 erupts between Britain and the United States over British violations of American rights at sea.

1820

1791
The Bill of Rights, guaranteeing individual rights, is added to the U.S. Constitution.

1800

1814 EUROPE
British forces defeat French emperor Napoleon at the Battle of Toulouse in France.

1804 AMERICAS
Haiti gains its independence from France. *(Haitian banknote featuring Toussaint L'Ouverture, who led the revolution)*

1789 EUROPE
The French Revolution begins.

1787 AFRICA
Freed American slaves settle in Freetown, Sierra Leone, in West Africa.

BANQUE DE LA
REPUBLIQUE D'HAITI
A U 421651   A U 421651
UNE GOURDE

107

INTRODUCE TIME LINE EVENT

1804 AMERICAS: REVOLUTION IN HAITI

Years before Haiti became an independent republic, it was a French colony called St. Domingue. With a slave-based economy, St. Domingue had large, highly successful coffee and sugar industries. By the mid-1700s, it had become the single most profitable colony in the Americas. Enslaved workers provided the labor to make that newfound wealth possible.

In 1789, the French Revolution drew much of the world into war. At the same time, in St. Domingue, people of mixed race began to push for French citizenship and other civil rights. In August 1791, a large group of enslaved workers began a rebellion at a French sugar plantation, setting in motion a chain of events that prompted the Haitian Revolution, led by a man named Toussaint L'Ouverture. The United States became concerned with events in Haiti because of its own use of slave labor and the colony's nearby location. Upon hearing of the slave revolt, American leaders rushed to defend St. Domingue's white population.

More than 10 years of war followed, involving French, Spanish, and British forces. At first, L'Ouverture fought alongside the Spanish. Later, hearing that the French planned to end slavery in the colonies, he switched sides to fight alongside them. France did outlaw slavery in its colonies in 1794, but then reinstated it in 1804 and wouldn't fully abolish it until 1848. Ironically, 1804 was the year in which Haiti gained its independence. **ASK:** Why might the United States have wanted to help put down a revolution in a French colony? *(Possible response: The United States allowed slavery, so slave holders there might have been worried that unrest among slaves in St. Domingue would spread to the mainland. The United States also may have had investments in St. Domingue's sugar or coffee industries and wanted to protect its interests.)*

HISTORICAL THINKING

DETERMINE CHRONOLOGY

The U.S. Declaration of Independence (1776), the U.S. victory over Britain (1783), and France's own revolution (1789) paved the way for Haiti to declare and win its independence from France in 1804.

AMERICAN STORIES ONLINE | **Daily Life During the Revolution**

- Study Primary Sources: Excerpts from George Washington's Rules of Civility & Decent Behaviour In Company and Conversation
- On Your Feet: Who Am I?

NG Learning Framework:
Create a Journal Entry

SECTION 1 RESOURCES

RESISTANCE TO BRITAIN

LESSON 1.1
British Actions and American Reactions

- Active History: Analyze Different Points of View

NG Learning Framework:
Investigate the Repeal of the Stamp Act

LESSON 1.2
Crisis in Boston

- On Your Feet: Four Corners

NG Learning Framework:
Write a Letter For or Against Standing Troops

LESSON 1.3
The Shot Heard Round the World

- ▶ Revolutionary Myths
- On Your Feet: Roundtable Discussion

NG Learning Framework:
Create a First Continental Congress Infographic

LESSON 1.4
THROUGH THE LENS—AMERICAN PLACES
Boston Common
Boston, Massachusetts

- On Your Feet: Advantages and Challenges Roundtable

NG Learning Framework:
Design a Unique Green Space

SECTION 2 RESOURCES

DECLARING INDEPENDENCE

LESSON 2.1
Moving Toward Independence

- On Your Feet: Consider Points of View

NG Learning Framework:
Convince the King to Reconcile

LESSON 2.2
Declaring Independence

- On Your Feet: Team Word Webbing

NG Learning Framework:
Publish a Common-Sense Pamphlet

American Voices Biography
Thomas Jefferson ONLINE

LESSON 2.3
DOCUMENT-BASED QUESTION
A Foundation for the Country

- On Your Feet: Think, Pair, Share

SECTION 3 RESOURCES

THE AMERICANS AT WAR

LESSON 3.1
Military Strategy in the Early Stages

- ▶ Crossing the Delaware
- ▶ The Battle of Long Island
- On Your Feet: Write a Feature Article

NG Learning Framework:
Conduct a Military Preview Panel

LESSON 3.2
Saratoga and Valley Forge

AMERICAN GALLERY ONLINE Valley Forge

NG Learning Framework:
Craft a Motivational Speech from George Washington

LESSON 3.3
Women's Roles in the Revolution

- On Your Feet: Numbered Heads

NG Learning Framework:
Create a Web Page

SECTION 4 RESOURCES

VICTORY FOR THE AMERICANS

LESSON 4.1
The War Moves South

- On Your Feet: Solve a Military Problem

NG Learning Framework:
Create a Chronological Exhibit

LESSON 4.2
Yorktown and the Legacy of the Revolution

- On Your Feet: Fishbowl

NG Learning Framework:
Create a Diversity Honor Roll

LESSON 4.3
CURATING HISTORY
Mount Vernon Museum and Education Center
Mount Vernon, Virginia

- On Your Feet: Sort the Artifacts

CHAPTER 4 REVIEW

STRIVING READERS

STRATEGY ①

USE A TASKS APPROACH

Help students analyze visuals to obtain information by using the following TASKS strategy.

T Look for a **title** that may give the main idea.

A **Ask** yourself what the visual is trying to show.

S Determine how any **symbols** are used.

K Look for a **key** or legend.

S **Summarize** what you learned.

Use with All Lessons *Students may find the TASKS strategy especially useful in analyzing and extracting information from the maps in Lessons 2.1, 3.1, and 4.1.*

STRATEGY ②

OUTLINE AND TAKE NOTES

To help students develop their reading and comprehension skills, ask them to work in pairs to write an outline for each lesson. Instruct them in using an outline format such as the one shown. Tell them to identify main ideas and then look for two details that support each main idea.

I. _____
  A. _____
  B. _____
II. _____
  A. _____
  B. _____
III. _____
  A. _____
  B. _____

Use with All Lessons *You might choose to pair students of mixed proficiency. Remind students that subsection headings in the lesson sometimes serve as the highest level (Roman numerals) of an outline.*

STRATEGY ③

SEQUENCE EVENTS

To build understanding of a lesson, direct students to note critical events in a Sequence Chain, such as the one shown, including the date and a brief summary of each event. Encourage students to add circles and arrows as necessary to show the number and complexity of the causes and effects of historical events and their relationship to each other.

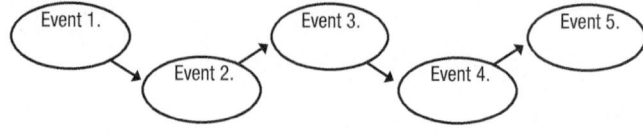

Use with Lessons 1.1–1.3, 2.1, 2.2, 3.1, 3.2, 4.1, and 4.2

INCLUSION

STRATEGY ①

PROVIDE TERMS AND NAMES ON AUDIO

Decide which of the terms and names are important for mastery and ask a volunteer to record the pronunciations and a short sentence defining each. Encourage students to listen to the recording as often as necessary.

Use with All Lessons *You might also use the recordings to quiz students on their mastery of the terms. Play one definition at a time from the recording and ask students to identify the term or name described.*

STRATEGY ②

DESCRIBE HISTORICAL PAINTINGS

Pair students who are visually impaired with students who are not. Ask the latter to read the captions and describe the historical paintings, providing specific details about setting, facial expressions, gestures, and clothing, as well as giving an overall impression of the style of the painting and the feelings it evokes. Instruct visually impaired students to ask clarifying questions as necessary. Sighted students might use an Attribute Web, such as the one shown, to organize details and what the students discuss.

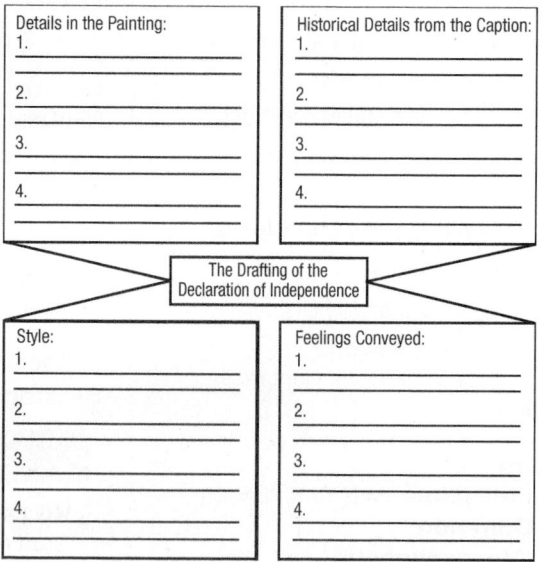

Use with Lessons 2.2, 3.1, 3.2, and 4.2 *Have students describe in detail* The Drafting of the Declaration of Independence *(Lesson 2.2),* Washington Crossing the Delaware *(Lesson 3.1),* Surrender of General Burgoyne *(Lesson 3.2), and* Surrender of Lord Cornwallis *(Lessons 4.2). Students may describe additional lesson visuals or graphics as time permits.*

ENGLISH LANGUAGE LEARNERS ELD

STRATEGY 1
CREATE A WORD WEB

Pair students at the **Emerging** and **Expanding** levels with those at the **Bridging** level. To activate prior knowledge and build vocabulary, have students create a Word Web for the word *resistance* before beginning Section 1 of the chapter, and the word *independence* before beginning Section 2. Tell students to take turns reading paragraphs of the lesson aloud, noting terms related to each word and adding them to the web.

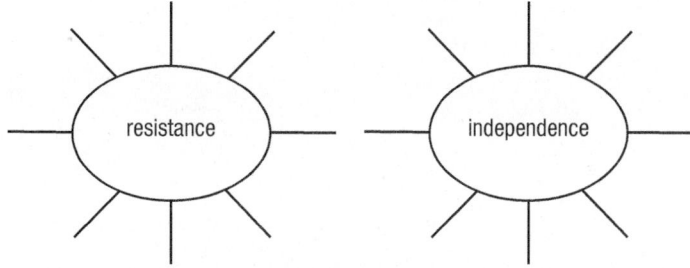

Use with Lessons 1.1–1.3, 2.1, and 2.2 *You might choose to tell pairs to trade and compare their completed Word Webs.*

STRATEGY 2
PAIR PARTNERS FOR DICTATION

After reading a lesson, ask students at **All Proficiencies** to write a sentence summarizing its main idea. Arrange students in pairs and ask them to dictate their sentences to each other. Then tell pairs to work together to check their sentences for spelling and accuracy.

Use with All Lessons *You might pair students at the Emerging level with those at the Bridging level and students at the Expanding level with each other.*

STRATEGY 3
CREATE WORD CHARTS

Help students understand unfamiliar words by completing charts such as the one shown. Pair students at the **Emerging** level with students at either the **Expanding** or **Bridging** level. Display and ask pairs to copy the chart and then work together to complete it as they encounter unfamiliar words.

Definition of _____.	Draw a visual.
Tell how it relates to the American Revolution.	Use it in a sentence.

Use with All Lessons

GIFTED & TALENTED

STRATEGY 1
WRITE AND PERFORM A SKIT

Tell students to choose one event illustrating the frictions between Patriots and the British that contributed to the War for Independence, and use it as the basis of a short skit. Allow time for students to prepare and practice before they perform their skits for the class.

Use with Lessons 1.1–1.3

STRATEGY 2
REPORT ON THOMAS JEFFERSON AND JOHN ADAMS

Inform students that Thomas Jefferson and John Adams died on July 4, 1826, only a few hours apart. Then tell pairs to conduct research to investigate and report on the friendship between them over their lifetimes, explaining when, how, and why the nature of the relationship changed. Ask students to use primary and secondary sources, including quotations from the men's letters to each another. Invite students to present their findings to the class in an engaging way, such as in character, as a news flash, or as an obituary that includes insightful comments on the men dying on the same day.

Use with Lesson 2.2

PRE-AP

STRATEGY 1
CREATE AN ANNOTATED TIME LINE

Direct students to choose events they consider most crucial to American independence and display them in an annotated time line. Instruct them to include dates, locations, key individuals, and impacts of events on larger social, economic, and political developments. Encourage students to present their time line to the class, stating how each event helped shape American independence.

Use with Lessons 1.1–1.3, 2.1, 2.2, 3.1–3.3, 4.1, and 4.2
You may wish to provide students with a list of events to choose from, including all major battles, major publications, the two Treaties of Paris, acts passed by Parliament, protests, and organizations.

STRATEGY 2
WRITE A PROFILE

Tell students to write a profile of any figure from the American Revolution that interests them. Ask them to conduct online research and draw on primary and secondary sources to supplement information from the text. Invite students to post their completed profile on a class blog or school website or read them to the class.

Use with Lessons 1.2, 1.3, 2.1, 3.2, 3.3, and 4.1 *Students may profile one of the individuals named in the chapter or one they discover while conducting research.*

HISTORICAL THINKING How did the colonists' emerging American identity lead to revolution?

The Old North Bridge, located in Concord, Massachusetts, is the site of a skirmish between the Continental and British armies in 1775.

"Here once the embattled farmers stood and fired **the shot heard round the world.**"

—Ralph Waldo Emerson

The American Revolution 109

INTRODUCE THE PHOTOGRAPH
THE OLD NORTH BRIDGE

Have students study the photograph and quotation that open the chapter. Ask students whether they have heard the phrase "the shot heard round the world." **ASK:** What do those words signify? *(They refer to the beginning of the American Revolution, an event closely followed by other nations.)* Then have students analyze Emerson's quote and relate it to the photograph that accompanies the lesson. **ASK:** How do Emerson's words connect to the photograph? *(Possible response: Emerson refers to the "embattled farmers" who skirmished at the site of the Old North Bridge, shown in the photograph.)* Tell students that in this chapter they will learn about the people, events, and involvement of foreign nations that shaped the course of the American Revolution.

SHARE BACKGROUND

On the night of April 18, 1775, the British sent about 700 men to Concord, Massachusetts, to seize military equipment that rebels had stored there. To prevent the rebels from stopping them, the British had to control two bridges—one of which was the famous Old North Bridge. Unknown to the British, a colonial militia of 400 men had already occupied the high ground above the bridge, so when the 96 British soldiers arrived to guard it, they were badly outnumbered. Around nine o'clock in the morning, the militia advanced toward the soldiers, forcing them to retreat to the east side of the bridge. Moments later, the famous shots were fired. The bridge shown in the photograph is not the original structure, which was torn down in 1788. This is the fifth reconstruction of the famous bridge and was built in 1956.

For Chapter 4 Spanish Resources, visit the Resources Menu. Chapter 4 Resources are available at NGLSync.Cengage.com.

HISTORICAL THINKING QUESTION

How did the colonists' emerging American identity lead to revolution?

Roundtable Activity: Explore National Identity Seat students around tables in groups of four. Ask groups questions about the concept of a national identity and discuss how forming such an identity might lead to revolution. Allow time for each student around the table to answer each question.

Question 1 What does it mean to have a national identity?

Question 2 What might motivate colonists to develop a national identity different from their British identity?

Question 3 In what ways might Britain's leaders react when colonists begin to establish an American identity?

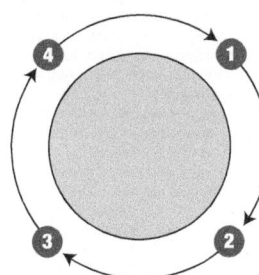

After students have finished the activity, tell them that in this chapter they will explore how the emergence of an American identity helped push the colonies into war.

INTRODUCE THE READING STRATEGY

FORM AND SUPPORT OPINIONS

Explain that if students want their opinions to be considered valid, they need to support them with reasons based on supporting evidence and established facts. Turn to the Chapter Review and preview with students the graphic organizer. Tell students to use a graphic organizer such as the one shown to collect supporting evidence and facts as they form opinions about events and the actions of individuals during the American Revolution.

KEY DATES FOR CHAPTER 4

1765	Parliament passes Stamp Act and Quartering Act
1770	Boston Massacre
1773	Parliament passes Tea Act; Boston Tea Party
1774	Parliament passes Intolerable Acts
1775	American Revolution begins
1776	Declaration of Independence approved and signed
1777	British forces capture Philadelphia
1778	France formally allies with America
1781	Cornwallis surrenders at Yorktown
1783	Treaty of Paris formally ends the war

INTRODUCE CHAPTER VOCABULARY

KEY VOCABULARY

SECTION 1

arsenal	committee of correspondence	martial law
Boston Massacre		minuteman
Boston Tea Party	duty	Patriot
boycott	guerrilla tactic	writ of assistance
	Loyalist	

SECTION 2

Articles of Confederation	Hessian	preamble
	mercenary	ratify
Declaration of Independence	mobilize	rule of law
earthworks		

SECTION 3

broadside	financier	privateer
deploy	garrison	profiteering
espionage	inflation	

SECTION 4

| adversary | nationalism | stalemate |
| irregular | provision | |

WORD WEBS

Tell students to complete a Word Web for Key Vocabulary words as they read the chapter. Direct them to write each word in the center of an oval and then look through the chapter to find examples, characteristics, and descriptive words that may be associated with the vocabulary word. After reading the chapter, ask students to share what they learned about each word. Model an example using the graphic organizer below.

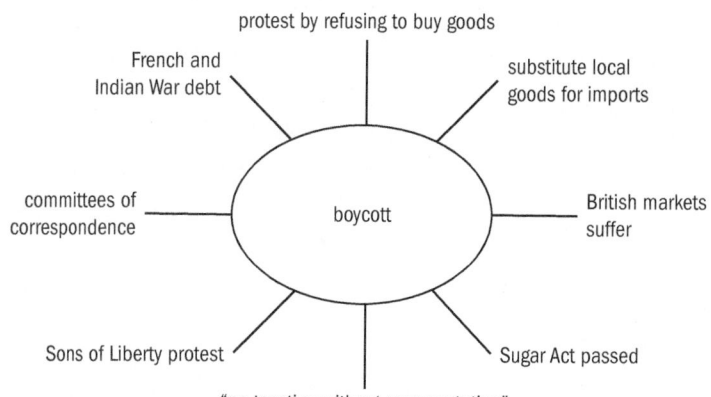

AMERICAN STORIES ONLINE

For instructional support for the online American Story "Daily Life During the Revolution," go to NGLSync.Cengage.com.

BRITISH ACTIONS AND AMERICAN REACTIONS

If you have an after-school job, you know about taxes. Even today, Americans complain about paying taxes. But we pay taxes that have been set by our elected representatives. The colonists had no such representatives in Parliament to promote their ideas about taxation.

TAXATION WITHOUT REPRESENTATION

American colonists were British subjects, but they had grown used to self-government and the concept of individual rights. When the British Parliament imposed new taxes on the colonists, it threatened more than just their pocketbooks. By the mid-1700s, the colonists had begun to shake off British influence and develop an American identity. Parliament's attempt to enforce new taxes drove another wedge between Britain and the North American colonies.

After the French and Indian War, the British government faced massive debt. British authorities argued that the colonists should pay a large share of that debt. **George Grenville**, the prime minister appointed by King George, agreed and issued laws to tax the colonies directly, rather than allowing colonial assemblies to impose taxes. Grenville, who believed that Britain should strictly control the colonies, saw these taxes as a way of raising revenue and reinforcing British power over the colonies.

Among the first of the new taxes was the **Sugar Act** of 1764, which established **duties**, or taxes, on imports of refined sugar, molasses, and other goods. Parliament also passed the **Currency Act**, which prohibited colonies from issuing their own paper money. This created a shortage of currency and further curbed colonial merchants and trade.

Many British subjects justified the Sugar Act by claiming that American colonists should start pulling their economic weight because they paid only a fraction of the annual taxes that people in Britain paid. Grenville believed that colonists should pay because the British army had reduced the threat of French colonial expansion by winning the French and Indian War. But some colonists openly accused the British of tyranny, coining the slogan "no taxation without representation." The colonists believed that because they had no representation in Parliament, Parliament had no right to impose direct taxes on them. As one Philadelphia merchant said, "The point in dispute is a very Important one, if the Americans are to be taxed by a Parliament where they are not nor can be Represented, they are no longer Englishmen but Slaves."

Colonial potters began making teapots with slogans to celebrate the repeal of the Stamp Act in 1766.

The original Sons of Liberty were a group of small merchants and craftsmen in Boston who called themselves the Loyal Nine and organized in protest of the Stamp Act. One of their first acts was hanging an effigy, or dummy, of a local man, Andrew Oliver, from a tree on Washington Street. The same night, an angry mob destroyed his home and carriage house. Ironically, the Act had appointed Oliver as distributor of the stamps without his knowledge and he had yet to accept the position. The Loyal Nine soon changed their name to the Sons of Liberty as the organization and its protest movement began to spread. By the end of 1765, there were Sons of Liberty operating in every colony.

In response to Britain's direct taxation, colonists began to organize protests, which included a series of **boycotts** against British goods. By refusing to import or purchase these goods, the colonists hoped to avoid taxes and send a clear message to Britain.

THE STAMP ACT

In 1765, Parliament passed the **Quartering Act**, which required colonists to provide housing for British soldiers in stables, inns, ale houses, and abandoned buildings. That same year, Parliament also passed the **Stamp Act**, a law that sent an even greater storm of protest sweeping through the colonies. Only documents marked with an official stamp were considered legal, and the only way to acquire the stamp was by paying a tax. Printed materials subject to this law included deeds, business licenses, court documents, newspapers, and even playing cards. The law also demanded the tax be paid with gold or silver coins, which colonists had difficulty doing because they generally used paper money and credit. British courts in the colonies enforced the act by confiscating any land, property, or goods involved in transactions conducted without the special government stamps.

Colonial assemblies formally protested the Stamp Act. **Patrick Henry**, newly elected to Virginia's House of Burgesses, led the protest. Henry was a strong supporter of colonial rights and would later become a leader in the fight for independence. He persuaded the House of Burgesses to pass a series of resolutions defending the colonists' right to tax themselves rather than to be taxed by Parliament. Massachusetts, Connecticut, New York, New Jersey, Pennsylvania, Maryland, and South Carolina passed resolutions similar to Virginia's. Rhode Island simply instructed its officials to ignore the stamp tax.

In October 1765, representatives from nine colonies traveled to New York City to attend the **Stamp Act Congress**. The congress upheld the power of representative colonial assemblies, not Parliament, to tax the colonists. It also defended the right to trial by jury, which the colonists believed was threatened by the expanded authority of the British colonial courts.

Protests broke out across the colonies, and by the end of 1765, they had forced official stamp distributors in every colony except Georgia to resign. The protest leaders called themselves **Sons of Liberty** and established networks throughout the colonies to organize boycotts and other protest actions. Merchants in New York City, Philadelphia, and Boston signed pacts to stop accepting British imports until Parliament repealed the act. Colonial resistance aimed to cancel the stamp tax, not end British authority. The efforts succeeded in 1766, when Parliament repealed the Stamp Act.

The controversies surrounding British actions led to a sharp division among colonists, and the erosion of individual rights and tax legislation created further animosity. **Loyalists** supported the authority of Parliament and wanted to continue living as British subjects. **Patriots** supported colonial self-government and increasingly began to call for independence from Britain.

HISTORICAL THINKING

1. **READING CHECK** How did British actions lead to resistance in the colonies?

2. **MAKE CONNECTIONS** Why did many colonists claim Parliament's decision to tax them was unfair?

3. **ANALYZE CAUSE AND EFFECT** How did the Sons of Liberty help bring about the repeal of the Stamp Act?

PLAN: 2-PAGE LESSON

OBJECTIVE

Examine how American colonists reacted to new taxes from Britain.

CRITICAL THINKING SKILLS FOR LESSON 1.1

- Make Connections
- Analyze Cause and Effect
- Form and Support Opinions
- Identify Main Ideas and Details
- Evaluate

HISTORICAL THINKING FOR CHAPTER 4

How did the colonists' emerging American identity lead to revolution? As their sense of American identity grew, many colonists began to resent British interference in colonial affairs. Lesson 1.1 discusses specific taxes that the British imposed on the colonies and how colonists responded.

BACKGROUND FOR THE TEACHER

Long before the Sugar Act of 1764, the British government had tried to use taxes to force the colonies to buy British goods. The Molasses Act of 1733 imposed a tax on sugar, molasses, and rum imported from the French and Dutch West Indies to make those products more expensive than imports from the British West Indies. The burdensome six-pence tax on a gallon of molasses could have crippled the rum manufacturing industry in the colonies if buyers had actually paid it. Instead, colonists used a thriving smuggling industry to buy cheaper products from non-British markets and to sell lumber, fish, and other products to those same markets. Although the Sugar Act reduced the tax levied on molasses, it also made the tax much harder to avoid and, therefore, far more onerous. In addition, the British West Indies would not buy the colonists' lumber and other products, which made the act's economic impact even more devastating.

INTRODUCE & ENGAGE

BRAINSTORM A MONEY PLAN

Prompt students to imagine that their city has built emergency levees for a smaller, neighboring town to help prevent a flood. Now their city asks the neighboring town to help with the cost. **ASK:** What would be a fair way to determine how much of the debt the town should pay? *(Possible responses: The expenses should be shared based on population and resources. The amount should be divided equally. The town should pay most of the debt because they benefited the most.)* **ASK:** Whatever percentage or amount is determined, what might be the best way to collect the money? *(Possible responses: Levy a tax on the town. Allow both sides to determine the method of payment. Allow the town to determine how they will pay.)* Explain that this lesson explores how the British government tried to collect money to pay for the French and Indian War and how the American colonists reacted.

TEACH

GUIDED DISCUSSION

1. **Form and Support Opinions** Do you think the American colonists had an obligation to help pay for the French and Indian War? Explain your answer. *(Possible responses: Yes. The British contained French colonial expansion and helped to protect American colonists and their interests, so colonists should share the cost. No. The British were protecting their own economic interests by repelling the French, and, with no representation in Parliament, the colonists had no voice in the kind and number of taxes levied.)*

2. **Identify Main Ideas and Details** Why was the Stamp Act so hated in the colonies? *(Possible responses: The necessity for the stamp complicated and threatened colonists' livelihoods and financial stability because it was required on a wide range of documents. The tax had to be paid in gold or silver coins. Without stamped documents, people could lose their property or goods.)*

EVALUATE

Direct students' attention to The Sons of Liberty feature. **ASK:** What positive and negative effects might result when individuals band together for a common cause? *(Possible response: Positive: Belonging to a group can give individuals the courage and inspiration they might not possess on their own. Negative: People can easily be influenced by others in a group and act emotionally and rashly, such as when the Sons of Liberty destroyed the house of the man appointed as stamp distributor before knowing the facts about him.)*

ACTIVE OPTIONS

Active History: Analyze Different Points of View Extend the lesson by using either the PDF or Whiteboard version of the activity. These activities take a deeper look at a topic from, or related to, the lesson. Explore the activities as a class, turn them into group assignments, or even assign them individually.

NG Learning Framework: Investigate the Repeal of the Stamp Act

SKILL Communicate

KNOWLEDGE Our Human Story

Arrange students in groups and instruct them to conduct online research about the actions taken by protesters and by Benjamin Franklin that led to the repeal of the Stamp Act. Tell groups to discuss the events and decide which were most effective. Then discuss each group's ideas as a class.

DIFFERENTIATE

ENGLISH LANGUAGE LEARNERS (ELD)

Use Monetary Terms To help students become familiar with financial terms, write the following words on the board: *taxes, debt, revenue, duties, coins, paper money, credit.* Say each word and have students repeat it after you. Pair students at the **Emerging** or **Expanding** levels with those at the **Bridging** level, and have partners create a Word Map for each word. Model an example for students on the board, using the graphic organizer shown. Monitor students and clarify as needed. Invite pairs to exchange and compare their Word Maps.

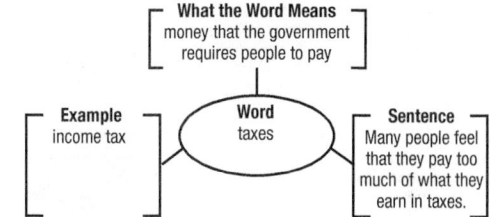

PRE-AP

Evaluate a Quotation Bring students' attention to the quotation from the Philadelphia merchant who concluded that if Americans were to be taxed without representation, then "they are no longer Englishmen but Slaves." Ask students to write a short essay stating whether they think the comparison of Americans taxed by parliament to slaves is strong or weak, and why. Ask students to state what purpose the writer might have had for making the comparison. Invite students to read their essay to the class.

See the Chapter Planner for more strategies for differentiation.

HISTORICAL THINKING

ANSWERS

1. Parliament passed several acts that directly interfered with colonial life and businesses. Colonists had grown accustomed to self-government, and Britain's attempts to exert control provoked them to resist.

2. Colonists regarded Britain's taxation policies as unfair because they had no representation in Parliament that could influence such decisions.

3. The Sons of Liberty coordinated efforts among the colonies to boycott British products, persuade merchants to refuse British imports, and force stamp distributors to resign. These and other actions eventually led Britain to repeal the Stamp Act.

Paul Revere's engraved print of the Boston Massacre, *The Bloody Massacre in King Street*, is not quite accurate. The print does not show the colonists fighting back, and it does not include Crispus Attucks, the African-American man killed in the clash.

CRISIS IN BOSTON

Everyone has a boiling point. The colonists had successfully forced the repeal of the Stamp Act, only to find Parliament saddling them with more taxes and regulations. Protests and boycotts led to a partial repeal, but rising tensions would eventually inspire revolt.

THE TOWNSHEND ACTS

Although Parliament repealed the Stamp Act, the threat of new taxes did not disappear. After all, Parliament had the authority to tax citizens living in Great Britain "in all cases whatsoever." It claimed that its authority also extended to subjects living in Britain's North American colonies.

Charles Townshend became Britain's finance minister shortly after the Stamp Act was repealed. He had strongly supported the Sugar Act. In fact, he was partially responsible for coming up with the legislation. He agreed with the British government that the colonists reaped economic and political benefits from their connection to Britain, and they should pay their fair share to that nation.

In 1767, Parliament passed four acts designed to generate colonial revenue for the British treasury as well as to force the colonists to comply with Parliament's authority. These acts were collectively called the **Townshend Acts**. Britain planned to use some of the revenue collected to pay colonial governors and judges, who previously had been paid by colonial legislatures. British leaders believed Parliament would have greater control over colonial officials if it held its own purse strings.

The acts established a Board of Customs Commissioners to collect customs duties, or taxes on imported goods, from colonial traders. These duties included taxes on lead, glass, paper, paint, and tea, all goods that the colonies were required to purchase from Britain. To stop smugglers, the British Parliament gave the board extensive powers to overtake ships and seize cargoes it believed to be contraband, or smuggled goods. The acts also expanded the authority of courts

to issue **writs of assistance**, or search warrants, which permitted customs officials to enter any building to search for and seize property from any trader who had not paid customs duties.

At first, there was little colonial reaction to the Townshend Acts. However, beginning in December 1767, John Dickinson, a Philadelphia lawyer who owned a Delaware plantation, published a series of 12 letters signed "A Farmer." Newspapers throughout the colonies reprinted these protest letters, and opposition to the acts soon grew. Colonists resisted paying the duties, and cries of "Tyranny!" rang through the streets.

John Singleton Copley painted this portrait of Mercy Otis Warren in 1763.

Contributing to rising tensions was the response from Great Britain to a letter sent by the Massachusetts assembly to the 12 other colonial assemblies. The letter was written by **Samuel Adams**, a prominent member of the Sons of Liberty, and lawyer James Otis. In the letter, they called once again for a boycott of British goods. The British monarchy saw this as a direct threat to its authority in the colonies. Parliament demanded that the Massachusetts assembly rescind, or withdraw, its call to action. It ordered colonial governors to dissolve their assemblies if they refused to ignore the call. Furthermore, Parliament sent British regiments into Boston to guard against further unrest. When the Massachusetts assembly refused to take back the letter, Parliament disbanded it, prompting a boycott in Boston that spread throughout the colonies.

Mercy Otis Warren, a writer and historian from Massachusetts, was close to many leading Patriots. After British troops were called to occupy Boston, she concluded that Britain was an enemy that could not be reasoned with. In her book *A History of the Rise, Progress, and Termination of the American Revolution*, she wrote, "the standing army is the most ready engine in the hand of despotism." For her, the stationing of troops in Boston represented the

point of no return in relations between the colonists and Britain. While the Townshend Acts were being passed, she opened her home to other Patriots, such as John Adams and Samuel Adams, and it became a center of political resistance to Britain.

THE BOSTON MASSACRE

The movement of British troops into Boston kept tensions charged for the next two years. Some troops set up camps on Boston Common, a wide field in the middle of the city meant for all citizens to use. The soldiers were not paid well, so many of them sought local work when they were not on duty. The people of Boston resented this, claiming the soldiers were taking jobs from colonists. Children taunted the soldiers in the streets, mocking their red uniforms by calling them "redcoats" and "lobsterbacks." All of this prompted plenty of fistfights between colonists and British soldiers. Within a few years, that violence turned deadly.

Early in the morning of March 5, 1770, authorities posted a handbill stating British troops would defend themselves against any colonial harassment. Later that night, an angry band of colonists roamed the streets of Boston, itching for a fight. They came upon a lone British sentry guarding the Customs House,

OBJECTIVE
Analyze how the Townshend Acts and the Tea Act led colonists to engage in acts of resistance and rebellion.

CRITICAL THINKING SKILLS FOR LESSON 1.2
- Identify Main Ideas and Details
- Analyze Visuals
- Form and Support Opinions
- Evaluate
- Make Inferences
- Identify
- Make Connections
- Analyze Primary Sources

HISTORICAL THINKING FOR CHAPTER 4
How did the colonists' emerging American identity lead to revolution? In response to more taxes from Britain, Patriots organized protests across the colonies. Lesson 1.2 discusses the escalating tensions between the American colonists and the British that led to the Boston Massacre and the Boston Tea Party.

BACKGROUND FOR THE TEACHER
John Dickinson had served in both the Delaware and Pennsylvania assemblies, but it was his pseudonymous "Letters from a Farmer in Pennsylvania" that caught public attention across the colonies and in Europe. In this series of published letters, Dickinson objected to British taxation in the colonies and advocated for peaceful acts of civil disobedience rather than armed revolution. Dickinson's "The Liberty Song," an early patriotic song, speaks to this sentiment: "Our purses are ready, / Steady, Friends, steady, / Not as SLAVES, but as FREEMEN our Money we'll give." He felt so strongly against armed revolution that, as a delegate from Pennsylvania, he refused to sign the Declaration of Independence. Sometimes called the "Penman of the Revolution," Dickinson had represented Pennsylvania at the Stamp Act Congress and wrote its resolution opposing the act. He published works about the First and Second Constitutional Conventions and proved instrumental in writing the Articles of Confederation and the U.S. Constitution.

INTRODUCE & ENGAGE

DISCUSS *BOILING POINT*

Read aloud the first sentence of the introductory paragraph. **ASK:** What does it mean to reach a boiling point, and in what context do you usually hear this expression used? *(Possible response: It signifies that something has reached a critical temperature or a crisis point. It is often used to describe the point at which a person's anger and frustration erupts into an outburst.)* **ASK:** In what ways could a community reach a boiling point, and what might happen if it does? *(Possible response: A community might be forced to endure increasingly oppressive measures, and some type of violence could result.)* Tell students that in this lesson they will learn how British actions in the colonies led to increased tensions in Boston that finally erupted in violence.

TEACH

GUIDED DISCUSSION

1. **Evaluate** If you had been a colonist, which aspect of the Townshend Acts might you have found most oppressive, and why? *(Answers will vary. Students might identify taxes because they affected the colonies' economies, the expanded powers of colonial customs authorities because search and seizure of goods on ships and buildings was made legal, or the targeting of smugglers because it eliminated ways to avoid paying customs duties.)*

2. **Make Inferences** Why might have Mercy Otis Warren considered the placement of standing troops in Boston to be "the point of no return"? *(Possible response: Warren might have felt that while British authority and ever-increasing taxes were oppressive, the threat posed by a standing army was a mark of tyranny.)*

3. **Identify** What factors led to rising tensions between citizens and soldiers stationed in Boston? *(Possible response: Encamping soldiers on Boston Common not only provided a constant reminder of British presence but prevented citizens from using the area. Soldiers probably resented their low pay, while residents resented the jobs soldiers took from Americans. Also, colonists and their children mocked and harassed the soldiers, who could not retaliate.)*

ANALYZE VISUALS

Direct students' attention to the engraving of the Boston Massacre. **ASK:** Why do you think this engraving does not show the colonists fighting back? *(Possible response: Paul Revere wanted to show the colonists in the most sympathetic light and the British as the aggressors, so the engraving depicts the colonists as victims rather than as combatants.)* **ASK:** How might a print of the event been different if a British sympathizer had engraved it? *(Possible response: It might have shown the British soldiers defending themselves against a mob of armed colonists.)*

DIFFERENTIATE

STRIVING READERS

Organize Lesson Information Arrange students in pairs. Break the lesson into manageable chunks to help students focus on and organize information section by section. Provide or instruct pairs to create a K-W-L Chart for each section heading. Tell students to complete the first two columns of each chart and then reread the section. Then have students complete the third column of each chart. If students demonstrate difficulty understanding what they have read, help them develop clarifying questions, and instruct them to pose them to their partner or another pair.

K What Do I Know?	W What Do I Want To Learn?	L What Did I Learn?

GIFTED & TALENTED

Write a Dialogue Tell students to write a dialogue that could have taken place among the Sons of Liberty as they planned the Boston Tea Party. Ask students to include reasons why the men decided to use Native American disguises and what they will do or will not do during the rebellion. Invite volunteers to read their dialogue to the class.

See the Chapter Planner for more strategies for differentiation.

and they began hurling insults at him. According to some accounts, the sentry responded by hitting a boy in the crowd with his gun. This attracted a larger crowd, and a British officer, Captain Thomas Preston, led seven more armed soldiers to the scene to try to calm things down. Instead, the situation got worse.

The crowd threw snowballs, ice, rocks, and other objects at the soldiers and attacked them with sticks and clubs. Then one of the soldiers fired his weapon, and the rest followed suit. Three colonists were killed immediately, including **Crispus Attucks**, an African-American sailor. Two other victims were wounded and died later, bringing the death toll to five, and six colonists were injured in what would go down in history as the **Boston Massacre**.

Governor Thomas Hutchinson promised that justice would be served. He arrested the soldiers involved and accused them of murder. To many colonists' dismay, John Adams, Patriot and lawyer, agreed to defend the soldiers in court, stating that everyone deserved the right to a fair trial, even the loathed British soldiers. Adams mounted an eloquent case, arguing that the soldiers had fired in self-defense, fearing their lives were in danger. His argument convinced the jury, which acquitted Captain Preston and all but two of the soldiers. Adams feared this trial would end his legal career, but over time he earned the respect of his fellow Patriots and played a vital role in the founding of the nation.

On the same day as the Boston Massacre, Lord North, Townshend's successor, asked Parliament to repeal the Townshend Acts, except for the tax on tea. He maintained Britain's right to tax the colonists and wanted to avoid the perception that he was giving in to colonial protesters. However, he also realized the American boycotts resulting from the Townshend Acts were harming Britain's economy. Parliament agreed to his request on April 12, 1770.

For the next two years, the conflict between Great Britain and the colonists eased, but the calm did not last. In 1772, after Patriots in Rhode Island burned a British ship that had been hunting for smugglers, Parliament once again started passing laws intended to control unrest in the colonies. Samuel Adams organized a **committee of correspondence** in Massachusetts to collect a list of British offenses against the colonies, publish them in public spaces, and communicate them as much as possible. Virginia soon had its own committee, and within a year most colonies had coordinated such opposition to Britain's actions.

THE BOSTON TEA PARTY

It wasn't long before the committees of correspondence had a new target for protest. In 1773, Parliament passed the **Tea Act**, which was enacted to bail out the failing British **East India Company** and gave the company the sole right to import and sell tea in North America. Without competition from colonial tea merchants, the company was able to lower the price of its tea. While the act was not intended to raise revenue, it stirred up old debates about the Townshend duties on tea, which were still in effect. Soon more protests were underway.

At first, the protesters simply made it difficult for the East India Company to deliver its tea to the colonies. Dockworkers in New York and Philadelphia refused to unload the company's ships and sent them back to England with their original cargoes. Then, in Boston, the Sons of Liberty staged a grand act of rebellion.

On December 16, 1773, the band of Patriots disguised themselves as members of the Mohawk nation and, under cover of night, headed to Boston Harbor. The choice of disguise was not simply to keep their identities secret. The act of dressing as Native Americans signaled that they no longer considered themselves to be subjects of the British crown, but true Americans. They boarded three ships and dumped 342 chests of East India Company tea overboard in what came to be known as the **Boston Tea Party**.

Reenactors dump crates of tea into Boston Harbor on December 16, 2017, the 244th anniversary of the famous protest. The men stand on a replica of one of the three ships the Sons of Liberty boarded that night.

The Sons of Liberty took great care in planning and executing the Boston Tea Party. No one was hurt that night, and only one person, Francis Akeley, was imprisoned for the crime. Crates of tea leaves reportedly washed ashore in Boston and nearby towns during the weeks following the protest.

The incident sparked more bold protests, including a second Boston Tea Party in March 1774 and a similar event that took place in New York in April. But these acts of defiance only hardened Britain's resolve against the protests. New and more punishing laws would soon be inflicted on the colonies.

HISTORICAL THINKING

1. **READING CHECK** Why was Boston considered a center of resistance against the British?

2. **IDENTIFY MAIN IDEAS AND DETAILS** What were Parliament's two main purposes in passing the Townshend Acts?

3. **ANALYZE VISUALS** What kinds of different information can an engraving and a photograph convey to a reader?

4. **FORM AND SUPPORT OPINIONS** Were the Sons of Liberty justified in destroying the British cargo? Support your opinion with evidence from the text.

BUILD BACKGROUND

CRISPUS ATTUCKS

Crispus Attucks is recognized as the first person to die in the American Revolution. Due to this distinction, he would later become an icon of the antislavery movement. As a young man, Attucks escaped from his enslavers and found freedom as a seaman sailing on whaling vessels and in Boston as a rope maker. Sources place Attucks at the center of two confrontations with British soldiers prior to the Boston Massacre—on March 2 between a group of rope makers and three soldiers in a bar, and on March 5, some hours before the massacre, with Attucks among a group of sailors and rope makers in a clash with British soldiers looking for work. At the soldiers' trial, witnesses' depositions about the massacre placed Attucks at the front of the mob, wielding a cordwood stick. Attucks and four others killed in the massacre, James Caldwell, Patrick Carr, Samuel Gray, and Samuel Maverick, were buried at the historic Granary Burying Ground. In 1888, a monument was erected at Boston Common to the men who died.

BOSTON TEA PARTY

The group of men, numbering between 60 and 70 by some accounts, who smashed the boxes and threw the tea into the harbor during the Boston Tea Party represented a cross section of colonial society, from laborers to artisans to doctors. Though they ranged in age, most were under 20 years old. They destroyed some 90,000 pounds of tea—worth about $1.7 million today—but were careful not to damage the ships or personal property aboard or harm the crew. Although the protesters wanted to send a forceful message to Parliament, the ships and their owners were American, not British. At least one of the owners, John Rowe, known as a smuggler with anti-British leanings, was said to have backed the plan to throw the tea overboard. While the Boston Tea Party was a major event leading up to the American Revolution, the actual destruction of the tea took only about three hours.

TEACH

GUIDED DISCUSSION

4. **Make Conections** How did the Townshend Acts ultimately affect money flowing to Britain? *(Possible response: Instead of raising revenues through taxation as intended, the Townshend Acts resulted in widespread boycotts of British goods in the colonies, which negatively impacted the British economy.)*

5. **Evaluate** Was the Boston Tea Party an effective means of protest? Explain your answer. *(Possible responses: Yes. It got the attention of the British and showed the strength of the colonists' resistance without injuring or killing anyone. No. It may have been a bold statement, but it ultimately resulted in harsher laws being forced on the colonies.)*

ANALYZE PRIMARY SOURCES

Direct students' attention to the Primary Source feature. **ASK:** What did John Adams think the trial against the soldiers proved and didn't prove? *(Possible response: Adams thought the trial proved that the soldiers did not deserve to be executed and that standing armies were dangerous. He also thought the verdict, while sparing the soldiers' lives, did not prove that the event was any less of a massacre nor did it prove that the authorities were right in sending the soldiers to Boston in the first place.)*

ACTIVE OPTIONS

On Your Feet: Four Corners
Post the following signs in four corners of the classroom: Townshend Acts, Tea Act, Boston Massacre, Boston Tea Party. Organize students into groups around each sign and prompt them to discuss how the event was a cause or effect of the growing unrest among colonists. Then have at least one student from each corner summarize the group's discussion for the other three groups.

NG Learning Framework: Write a Letter For or Against Standing Troops

ATTITUDE Empowerment

SKILL Communication

Direct students to work in small groups to write a letter to King George III in the aftermath of the Boston Massacre. Assign each group to write either in defense of standing troops, written from the British prime minister's point of view, or against standing troops, written from a Patriot's point of view. Prompt group members to discuss different approaches they might use in their letter, such as the tone and diction to employ and what reasons they might use to support their arguments. When groups have finished writing, invite them to share their letters with the class.

HISTORICAL THINKING

ANSWERS

1. Major activists in the resistance were from Boston, including John Adams, Samuel Adams, Mercy Otis Warren, and Paul Revere. When British troops moved into Boston, tensions increased, which led to the Boston Massacre and the Boston Tea Party. These major events likely inspired other colonies' resistance against British efforts to impose controls.

2. Parliament passed the Townshend Acts to generate revenue from the colonies for the British treasury and to force the colonies to recognize and submit to Britain's authority.

3. A photograph conveys realistic information more objectively and quantifiably than an engraving. However, as in the photo of the Boston Tea Party reenactment, a photo can also make a staged event seem factual. An engraving reflects the viewpoint of the artist, who manipulates a medium to depict a subject or event, choosing which details to include or exclude.

4. Opinions will vary, but students' answers should include evidence from the text to support their ideas. Some students might justify the actions by pointing out that the British overstepped their authority in passing the Townshend Acts and that the colonists sent a strong message to Parliament without inflicting harm on any individuals. Others might argue that the East India Tea Company was not responsible for Parliament's actions, so the destruction of its property was not justified.

THE SHOT HEARD ROUND THE WORLD

No one likes to be insulted. For King George III, the colonists' organized protests, such as dumping tea into Boston Harbor, were too great an insult to bear. Britain struck back at the colonists with all its might.

THE INTOLERABLE ACTS

In 1774, after the Boston Tea Party, Parliament and King George III decided to punish the colonies in the form of the Coercive Acts. Colonists quickly renamed these four acts the **Intolerable Acts**, because they were intended to prevent Massachusetts from governing itself. The acts closed the port of Boston until the colony repaid the East India Company for the tea it lost. They replaced the colonial assembly with a ruling council of the king's appointees. The acts increased British control on Massachusetts's courts, protecting British officials, who, if charged with a crime, could go to England or another colony to be tried. Finally,

CRITICAL VIEWING American artist Grant Wood depicted Paul Revere's journey in his 1931 work *The Midnight Ride of Paul Revere*. Why do you think the artist painted long shadows on the buildings?

Britain expanded the Quartering Act, which gave the colonial governors more authority to house British troops in buildings or in private citizens' homes, if necessary. Basically, the Intolerable Acts put Boston under **martial law**, or military control.

Colonists were furious. Protests and organized resistance increased in Massachusetts and the other colonies. When Boston suffered severe unemployment and food shortages due to the port closure, neighboring towns sent supplies.

On September 5, 1774, representatives from every colony but Georgia—56 delegates in all—met in Philadelphia at the **First Continental Congress** to determine how to respond to Britain's actions and to air their grievances. The meeting lasted more than a month. Although most of the delegates wanted to remain loyal to Britain, they agreed to petition the Parliament and the crown to repeal the Intolerable Acts and other restrictions. They passed resolutions to end all trade with Britain and suspend exports to the West Indies. They also established local committees, elected by citizens, to enforce the ban on trade. These committees eventually took on other functions of local government, including collecting taxes and raising militias.

Parliament refused the Congress's request, and King George concluded that the New England colonists were openly rebelling. He predicted that "blows must decide whether [colonists] are to be subject to this country or independent." Less than a month before the Congress was set to meet for a second time, King George's words came true.

LEXINGTON AND CONCORD

Believing that armed conflict with the British was inevitable, Patriots formed militias made up of **minutemen**, citizen-soldiers who would respond to a call to action at a moment's notice. In the spring of 1775, **General Thomas Gage**, commander of British troops in Boston, ordered his army to seize and secure all weapons and gunpowder and keep them out of the militias' hands. The order also required Gage to arrest Patriots Samuel Adams and **John Hancock** in nearby **Lexington**, in hopes of subduing protests. On April 18, British troops began marching toward **Concord**, about 20 miles west of Boston, to seize the **arsenals**, or stores of weapons and ammunition, believed to be held there. Things did not go according to plan.

A spy inside the British high command had informed the Patriots of Gage's plan, allowing **Paul Revere**, a local silversmith active in the Sons of Liberty, to make plans of his own. He arranged for the caretaker of the Old North Church to convey information to Patriots in Charlestown about British troop movements by signaling: one lantern in the steeple meant the British were advancing by land; two meant they were coming by sea. Legend has it that the caretaker hung two lanterns that night.

Upon learning the British were on the move, Paul Revere rowed from Boston to Charlestown. From there, he raced on horseback toward Lexington. Another Patriot, **William Dawes**, rode from Boston. Together, they sounded the alarm for the militia to gather at Lexington. A third Patriot, **Samuel Prescott**, rode on to Concord. The British troops, 700 men strong, reached Lexington at dawn on April 19. About 70 minutemen were waiting for them on Lexington Green. British major John Pitcairn planned to disarm the small militia and move on, but an unexpected shot rang out, and the fight was on. When the firing ended, eight minutemen lay dead, and ten were wounded. Only one British soldier was wounded, and none were killed.

After the confrontation at Lexington, the British set out for Concord. They knew the Patriots had already hidden most of their weapons and gunpowder. When the British arrived, they burned what few arms they found. Nearby minutemen thought the British were going to burn the entire town. They rushed to the North Bridge, exchanging gunfire with a group of British soldiers who were defending it. Meanwhile, hundreds of minutemen from the surrounding countryside arrived. The British troops began marching back to Boston, but the minutemen pursued them, using **guerrilla tactics**. They ambushed the British, launching small surprise attacks from behind trees and buildings. By day's end, British casualties included over 60 dead and 200 wounded or missing. At least 39 minutemen were missing or wounded, and 49 had died in what most historians recognize as the first battle of the American Revolution.

HISTORICAL THINKING

1. **READING CHECK** How did the Intolerable Acts lead to a more organized colonial resistance?

2. **DRAW CONCLUSIONS** Why did the Battle of Lexington increase the likelihood of full-scale war breaking out between Britain and the American colonies?

3. **MAKE PREDICTIONS** How might the Continental Congress respond to the Battles of Lexington and Concord?

PLAN: 2-PAGE LESSON

OBJECTIVE

Analyze how Britain's tightening grip on the colonies pushed their growing rebellion toward war.

CRITICAL THINKING SKILLS FOR LESSON 1.3

- Draw Conclusions
- Make Predictions
- Make Inferences
- Form and Support Opinions
- Compare and Contrast

HISTORICAL THINKING FOR CHAPTER 4

How did the colonists' emerging American identity lead to revolution? As Britain exerted greater political and military control over Massachusetts, Patriots united in their resistance. Lesson 1.3 discusses how the Intolerable Acts unified the colonies and prepared them to take up arms against Britain.

BACKGROUND FOR THE TEACHER

All the delegates to the First Continental Congress were against the Intolerable Acts, but they disagreed on how to respond. Delegate Joseph Galloway, a Loyalist from Pennsylvania, argued that the colonies owed their existence to Britain and should acknowledge the authority of Parliament to tax them. He offered a Plan of Union, in which the colonists would remain loyal British subjects in return for greater independence and a voice in Parliament. It was by a slim margin that his plan did not pass. Later Galloway helped the British, as he was convinced that aggressive British leadership would spur Loyalists in the southern colonies to rise up in support of British troops, but that support never materialized. He would eventually be charged with high treason, which forced him to flee to England.

HISTORY NOTEBOOK

Encourage students to complete the Reid on the Road video series page for Chapter 4 in their History Notebooks after they view the video.

INTRODUCE & ENGAGE

DISCUSS WHAT MAKES SOMETHING INTOLERABLE

Ask students to suggest definitions for the word *intolerable*. *(unable to be endured or put up with)* Ask students to recall actions by Britain that caused the colonists to protest, such as the Sugar Act, the Stamp Act, the Townshend Acts, issuing writs of assistance, and the Boston Massacre. Elicit from students what the colonists might find intolerable after enduring these oppressive measures from Britain. Then tell students that in this lesson they will learn how tensions in New England resulted in armed conflict.

TEACH

GUIDED DISCUSSION

1. **Make Inferences** Why would Britain have chosen to impose the harsh conditions of the Intolerable Acts on Massachusetts? *(Possible responses: The actions of the Patriots in Boston Harbor likely shook Parliament, so they reacted with laws aimed at suppressing further organization and uprising in other colonies. Britain wanted to protect its economic interests in the colonies at all costs.)*

2. **Form and Support Opinions** Would you consider the battle on Lexington Green a success or a failure for the Patriots? Explain your answer. *(Possible responses: It was a failure because the Patriots lost more men than the British. It was a success because, although the Patriots suffered more casualties, they stood their ground against a much larger British force, which could inspire others to fight the British as well.)*

COMPARE AND CONTRAST

Direct students' attention to the descriptions of the battles on Lexington Green and at Concord. **ASK:** How are the two conflicts similar and different? *(Possible response: In both battles, Patriot militias were expecting to confront trained British forces. At Lexington, the Patriots waited on the green and suffered more casualties than the British, while at Concord, the Patriots adopted guerrilla tactics and inflicted greater casualties on the British than they themselves sustained.)*

ACTIVE OPTIONS

On Your Feet: Roundtable Discussion Arrange students in groups of four, and give each group a large sheet of paper. **ASK:** Do you think war was inevitable after Parliament refused to address the grievances of the First Continental Congress? Why or why not? Tell one student in each group to write an opinion that they can support with evidence from the text. At your signal, a second group member adds another opinion with supporting text evidence, followed by the third and fourth members. After all students have written their opinions, allow time for each group to discuss the opinions and supporting text evidence. Then call on volunteers to share their group's ideas.

NG Learning Framework: Create a First Continental Congress Infographic

SKILLS Communication, Collaboration

KNOWLEDGE Our Human Story

Share the information under Background for the Teacher. Then tell students that they will work in small groups to research a delegate or action from the First Continental Congress and use their findings to create an infographic. Organize students into six groups and assign them one of the following topics: The Declaration of Rights and Grievances, the Suffolk Resolves, the Continental Association, Richard Henry Lee, Edward Rutledge, Samuel Adams. Ask students to include viewpoints, objectives, purpose, and goals, as appropriate. Encourage a representative of each group to present their infographic to the class.

DIFFERENTIATE

ENGLISH LANGUAGE LEARNERS

Practice Pronunciation Write the following words on the board: *martial*, *militia*, *information*, *ammunition*. Point out that in these words, *ti* is pronounced /sh/. Then pronounce each word and have students repeat. Pair students at the **Bridging** level with those at the **Emerging** or **Expanding** level, and instruct them to take turns finding passages in the lesson that contain any of the four words and read the passages aloud. Additionally, you might supply students with a list of commonly used words that include this pronunciation of *ti*, such as *cautious*, *partial*, *patient*, and *substantial*. Tell them to define the words, using a dictionary as necessary, and practice pronouncing them along with the words supplied from the lesson.

GIFTED & TALENTED

Interview a Minuteman Have pairs plan, write, and perform an in-depth news interview with a minuteman that could have taken place after the battle of Concord. Tell pairs to conduct online research to gather details about the battle and then formulate questions that will elicit in-depth answers about what the minuteman saw, heard, felt, and thought before, during, and after the battle. Allow pairs time to practice their interview and then record it for playback or perform it live for the class.

See the Chapter Planner for more strategies for differentiation.

HISTORICAL THINKING

ANSWERS

1. Anger stemming from the passage of the Intolerable Acts led to increased organization of resistance and the formation of the First Continental Congress, a unified, political body through which the colonies would address Britain's actions.

2. The Battle of Lexington was the first mutually armed confrontation between the British and colonists. Since no side claimed a clear victory, confrontations were likely to recur and escalate.

3. Possible response: The Continental Congress is likely to start organizing militias from all the colonies into a larger army for their common defense.

118 CHAPTER 4

1.4 THROUGH THE LENS AMERICAN PLACES

BOSTON COMMON
BOSTON, MASSACHUSETTS

Once used as an encampment for British soldiers during the American Revolution, Boston Common was the place where Americans, including George Washington and John Adams, gathered to celebrate their new independence from England. It was a place for antislavery speeches, Vietnam War protests, and rallies for civil rights—its grounds dedicated to free speech and public assembly.

Established in 1634, Boston Common is America's oldest public park. In the 1800s, residents leveled 50 acres of land where cows once grazed and added trees, fountains, and statues to transform the park into the popular public space we know today. Like Central Park in New York City, Boston Common embodies the trend in American cities to preserve nature within crowded areas of urban development.

CRITICAL VIEWING The sprawling Boston Common features landscaped paths, ballfields, a children's play area, and a pond for skating in the winter and splashing in the summer. Based on details in this photograph, how would you describe the urban setting that surrounds the park and the role the park likely plays in the city of Boston?

PLAN: 2-PAGE LESSON

OBJECTIVE

Examine the role Boston Common played in the history of Boston and the function of it and other parks in urban areas.

CRITICAL THINKING SKILLS FOR LESSON 1.4

- Analyze Visuals
- Make Connections
- Draw Conclusions
- Analyze Environmental Concepts

HISTORICAL THINKING FOR CHAPTER 4

How did the colonists' emerging American identity lead to revolution? Boston Common was one of the earliest locations where Americans came together to celebrate their freedom from England. Lesson 1.4 describes the history of the park and its place in urban development.

BACKGROUND FOR THE TEACHER

Coordinated green infrastructures help cleanse urban air, increase biodiversity, and manage rainwater runoff. Placing nature closer to where more people live has been found to reduce stress, elevate immune functions, improve concentration and creativity, relieve depression, and increase social interactions among residents. Some crowded cities have created a "green infrastructure" through a well-planned system of small parks, gardens, walkways, and other nature-based places. Two such green spaces were formerly abandoned, elevated freight lines—New York City's High Line in Manhattan and Chicago's 606, the Bloomingdale Trail. Both encourage pedestrians and cyclists to enjoy art and landscape installations, native and non-native plants and grasses, and events in an urban setting.

HISTORY NOTEBOOK

Encourage students to complete the American Places page for Chapter 4 in their History Notebooks as they read.

INTRODUCE & ENGAGE

PREVIEW USING VISUALS

Direct students' attention to the photograph of Boston Common and discuss it in terms of photographic technique, such as the angle or vantage point. **ASK:** Why do you think the photographer took the picture from this angle, and where might the photographer have been positioned? *(Possible response: This aerial view emphasizes the size of the park relative to the surrounding area and underscores its openness and greenness compared to the density and gray tones of the buildings. The photographer could have been in a helicopter or a plane or in a tall building not visible in the foreground.)* Tell students that this lesson explores Boston Common and the function of urban green spaces.

TEACH

GUIDED DISCUSSION

1. **Draw Conclusions** Based on the details in the photo, how might the park increase social ties among people? *(Possible response: People can play baseball in the diamond or bring their dogs and children to the park, connect with people on the lawn or walkways, enjoy the pond together, and meet others at park events.)*

2. **Analyze Environmental Concepts** How might a large park affect the ecosystem of the area in which it is located? *(Possible response: The trees might help reduce pollution and keep the area cooler in summer. The open land can absorb rainwater and reduce flooding, and the park can increase biodiversity by attracting birds and other animals.)*

AMERICAN PLACES

Boston Common was once land owned by one of the first settlers of the Boston area, minister William Blackstone. Later, a group of Puritan colonists purchased the area for use as pastureland for local livestock. Known as the Common Land, the site also operated as the public area for punishment of transgressions committed by Puritans and a few Quakers, and of crimes committed by alleged pirates, murderers, and witches. When the Stamp Act was repealed in 1765, Governor John Hancock and his wife supplied fireworks and a cask of wine for the Common Land celebration. In 1778, the couple entertained 300 French naval officers and used milk from the community cows to help feed them.

ACTIVE OPTIONS

On Your Feet: Advantages and Challenges Roundtable
Arrange students in groups of four to discuss the following question: What advantages and challenges do large parks offer to cities? Encourage students to consider such factors as the effect on nearby real estate, cost of maintaining the park, safety issues, access to the park, health benefits, social benefits, tourist value, and ecological benefits. Tell each student to provide a different advantage or challenge. Afterward, work with the class to compile the positive and negative aspects and form a general conclusion about large parks in urban areas.

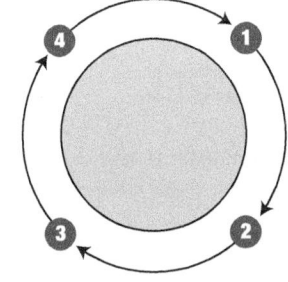

NG Learning Framework: Design a Unique Green Space

SKILLS Problem-Solving, Collaboration

KNOWLEDGE New Frontiers

STEM

Share the Background for the Teacher information with students. Then arrange them in small groups and tell them to design and write plans for a unique green space, including a drawing or model. Tell students to identify each feature in the green space and explain its intended function. Encourage students to conduct online research about green spaces, including small gardens and parks, walkways, and elevated gardens. Ask them to solve the problem of where and how to construct the space and how to incorporate "smart" technology into their design. Have students present their green space in class or on a class website or blog.

DIFFERENTIATE

INCLUSION

Describe Details in a Photograph Pair visually impaired students with sighted students. Ask the latter to describe in detail both the buildings and open areas shown in the photograph and record the details in a graphic organizer such as the one shown. You might also pair other inclusion students with a proficient student who could assist by prompting them to identify details and encouraging them to record details in the graphic organizer themselves. Encourage inclusion students to ask clarification questions as necessary. After pairs record as many details as possible, encourage them to continue working together to respond to the Critical Viewing question.

Photograph		
Detail	Detail	Detail

PRE-AP

Create an Annotated Time Line Tell students to research the uses of Boston Common and create an annotated time line of major events held there up to the present day. Encourage the use of an online time line creation tool, if available. Ask students to include the date and specific details for each event and visuals if relevant. Invite students to share their competed time lines with the class.

See the Chapter Planner for more strategies for differentiation.

CRITICAL VIEWING The urban area around the park is dense with buildings and surrounded by streets, and it offers little free space for people to use. The park provides people with an open, green space where they can enjoy nature and resident wildlife. In addition to recreational sports, the area could also serve as a gathering place for cultural activities such as concerts, rallies, festivals, and protests.

MOVING TOWARD INDEPENDENCE

The element of surprise is a powerful tool in war. An unexpected advance can send entire armies into disarray. One morning in 1775, British troops awoke to find the Continental Army right on top of them. They had to act quickly if they were going to survive.

THE SECOND CONTINENTAL CONGRESS

As many delegates at the First Continental Congress had expected, Parliament and King George ignored their list of grievances, so a **Second Continental Congress** convened on May 10, 1775. Many of those present had attended the First Continental Congress. The Second Continental Congress elected John Hancock from Massachusetts as its first president. A New York delegate named **John Jay** replaced Hancock as president in 1778. Other prominent delegates included Charles Carroll from Maryland, who was a radical member of the Board of War. John Witherspoon from New Jersey was an educator who had taught several other members of the Congress. A delegate from Pennsylvania, Benjamin Rush, published revolutionary newspaper articles promoting independence from Britain.

Early on, the Congress established the Continental Army. They named George Washington, the colonial army leader from Virginia, as its commander. Washington's job was to train recruits and maintain control over the armed forces in case war broke out. Washington proved to be an excellent choice.

Not all 65 delegates to the Second Continental Congress agreed on declaring independence or raising an army. A delegate from Pennsylvania proposed that the Congress refuse to discuss the possibility of independence during the meetings. In fact, the divide between Patriots and Loyalists within the Congress was wide. Patriots spoke of defending colonists' natural rights and liberties as a just cause. In contrast, Loyalists believed Patriot committees sometimes acted as mobs that gave individuals too much power and threatened the **rule of law**, or the idea that people and institutions are required to follow the regulations set forth by the government. Loyalists also argued that talk of a revolution threatened the stability they enjoyed as part of the British empire.

Soon after the Second Continental Congress convened, word came that a Patriot militia had won an important victory against the British at **Fort Ticonderoga**, a stronghold in northeastern New York. This significant event shifted the debate between Patriots and Loyalists to how effective military action would be in forcing Great Britain to accept their demands for change.

VICTORY AT FORT TICONDEROGA

In the early morning hours of May 10, 1775—the very day the Second Continental Congress first convened—**Ethan Allen**, a Patriot and military leader from Vermont, and **Benedict Arnold**, a captain from Connecticut, stood on the shore of Lake Champlain in northeastern New York. With them were about 300 members of a militia known as the Green Mountain Boys. They planned to use boats to cross the lake to Fort Ticonderoga and overtake the 40 people there.

Transporting the soldiers to the fort took longer than Allen and Arnold expected. Dawn quickly approached. Afraid they might lose the element of surprise, the commanders gave the order for the soldiers who had made the crossing to attack the southern gate of the fort. Without firing a shot, the men took the fort, gaining the first victory for the Patriot cause.

The colonial forces gained many advantages from their victory at Fort Ticonderoga. First, the fort's location was a key access point to towns in nearby British-held Canada and the Hudson River Valley.

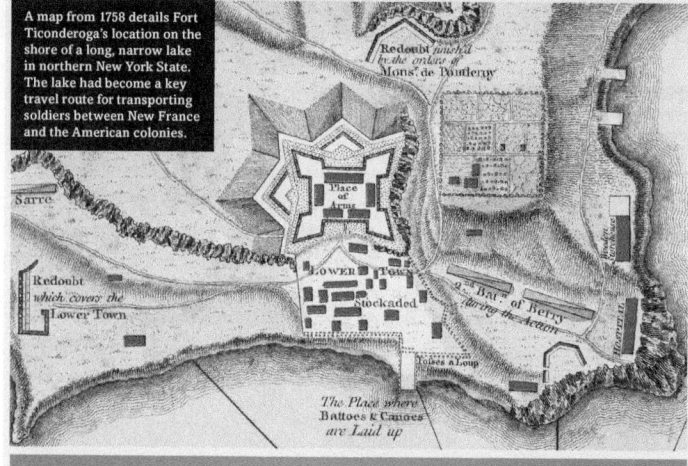

A map from 1758 details Fort Ticonderoga's location on the shore of a long, narrow lake in northern New York State. The lake had become a key travel route for transporting soldiers between New France and the American colonies.

CRITICAL VIEWING Built in 1755 by the French, the fort has a star shape that allowed cannons to be positioned along the perimeter to reach every part of the battlefield. This architectural style is called a bastion fort. What other features do you observe in the photograph and on the map that might aid soldiers in battle?

OBJECTIVE

Analyze how armed conflicts between Britain and the colonies drove them closer to war.

CRITICAL THINKING SKILLS FOR LESSON 2.1

- Analyze Cause and Effect
- Distinguish Fact from Opinion
- Evaluate
- Identify Main Ideas and Details
- Integrate Visuals
- Form and Support Opinions
- Make Inferences
- Interpret Maps

HISTORICAL THINKING FOR CHAPTER 4

How did the colonists' emerging American identity lead to revolution? Following the "shot heard round the world," clashes continued between British and American forces. Lesson 2.1 examines how two key battles, as well as the ill-fated Olive Branch Petition, helped solidify American resolve for independence.

BACKGROUND FOR THE TEACHER

The decision to appoint George Washington as commander of the Continental Army was advantageous from a political, tactical, and symbolic standpoint. As a slaveholder from Virginia, Washington brought the largest colony into the fight and dispelled the idea that American independence was primarily the concern of rabble-rousing New Englanders. In addition, as a veteran of the French and Indian War, Washington was perhaps the colonies' most experienced and decorated warrior—a vital asset, considering he would be leading ill-trained bands of state militias and citizen-soldiers against the greatest military force in the world. Finally, Washington looked and acted the part. At over six feet tall, he towered above his contemporaries; and his quiet, confident manner evoked loyalty and respect from nearly everyone, whether soldier or civilian.

DISCUSS RECONCILIATION

Write the term *reconciliation* on the board. Ask students what words or events they associate with the term. Tell students that though the colonists continued to protest Parliament's tyrannical actions, they hoped for reconciliation with the British. However, Britain was unwilling to give up control of the colonies. **ASK:** What do you think the terms of reconciliation with Britain would look like for the colonists? *(Possible response: The colonists would have representation in Parliament.)* Tell students that Lesson 2.1 discusses the events that finally pushed the colonies, after a final failed attempt to reconcile, to the brink of declaring independence.

TEACH
GUIDED DISCUSSION

1. **Evaluate** In what way did Loyalists have a valid point when they argued that Patriots were threatening the rule of law? *(Possible response: While actions such as boycotts were legitimate forms of protest, events such as destroying property during the Boston Tea Party were clear violations of the rule of law and could not be justified.)*

2. **Identify Main Ideas and Details** How did the Patriot victory at Fort Ticonderoga affect the discussions taking place at the Second Continental Congress? *(Possible response: The discussions among Congress shifted from the debate over some Patriot's, "mob-like" actions as Loyalists believed, versus the need to follow the rule of law to the effectiveness of military action against Britain to accept colonists' demands.)*

INTEGRATE VISUALS

Have students reread the subsection Victory at Fort Ticonderoga and examine the map from 1758. **ASK:** How do the details in the map illustrate the strategic importance of Fort Ticonderoga? *(The map shows the fort situated on a point jutting into Lake Champlain, a key trading route. The location of the fort allowed for the observation of approaching ships and men at multiple points.)* Then display a map of North America that indicates the location of Fort Ticonderoga and other locations significant to the American Revolution. Point out the locations to students. **ASK:** In addition to accessibility and defensibility, why might the location of Fort Ticonderoga have been advantageous for the British? *(Possible response: The fort is located close enough to Canada that British troops could have sailed north through the lake to defend Montreal if necessary, while still having access to New England, the center of colonial unrest and increasing numbers of armed confrontations.)*

DIFFERENTIATE
STRIVING READERS

Complete a T-Chart Instruct students to complete a T-Chart, labeling one column Loyalists and the other Patriots. Have students reread the lesson subsection by subsection and add details about each group in the correct column. After reading, encourage students to compare their completed charts, noting similarities and differences.

Loyalists	Patriots

PRE-AP

Profile an African-American Soldier Direct students to conduct online research to learn about enslaved and formerly enslaved people who fought for the Patriots or the Loyalists. Have students choose one such person to profile—for example, Harry Washington, Seymour Burr, Peter Salem, or Salem Poor. Encourage students to use multiple print and digital sources and to cite both primary and secondary sources in their profile. Ask students to include the person's background, motivations, and goals; experiences during specific battles; and ultimate fate. Invite volunteers to share their profiles with the class in an oral or written report, along with relevant visuals.

See the Chapter Planner for more strategies for differentiation.

CRITICAL VIEWING The fort has high stone walls and slots for cannons, which protected it from invasion from within, while redoubts and other earthworks and rock walls stalled advancements around the perimeter. The large interior areas designated for arms and supplies suggest that the fort was well stocked, and a separate hospital building indicates preparedness for treating wounded during confrontations or a siege.

With the capture of the fort, the Patriots blocked an important British military transit route between Canada and New York City. Without a direct way to transport troops, the British Army splintered. Also, capturing the artillery at Fort Ticonderoga provided the Continental Army with cannons and other pieces of heavy artillery at a time when munitions were in short supply. Less than a year later, the Patriots used these weapons to mount a successful attack on British forces in Boston, Massachusetts.

BATTLE OF BUNKER HILL

By April 1775, the British Army in Boston numbered about 5,000 troops, who positioned themselves throughout the city and the surrounding villages and towns. The British knew that by seizing control of Charlestown, they could prevent the Patriots from mounting an attempt to capture Boston. The British also saw an advantage in Charlestown's harbor. They sent long-distance communications by boat, so the harbor offered the British a base from which to stay in touch with their other forces. They planned to capture Charlestown's two hills, Bunker Hill and Breed's Hill, which provided clear views for observing Boston. But the Patriots had no intention of allowing the British to succeed.

George Washington ordered General Israel Putnam to lead a force of about 1,000 soldiers to block the British. On the night of June 16, 1775, Putnam's men marched to the hills above Charlestown and built **earthworks**, or human-made land modifications, to fortify their position on Breed's Hill. They also built small fortifications on Bunker Hill that would serve as a fallback point in case they needed to retreat.

The British awoke the next morning to find the Patriots overlooking their positions in Charlestown. General Thomas Gage instructed his soldiers to fire cannons at the Patriots. He ordered more than 2,000 troops to cross the Charles River and capture Breed's Hill. The British formed a line at the bottom of the hill and began their first charge. Through a stroke of luck, they had received the wrong size cannonballs from their armory, which meant their cannons were useless. Patriot General Putnam, keenly aware that his troops were also running out of ammunition, ordered his men to wait to open fire.

Well protected behind their earthworks, the Patriots forced the British to retreat, but the British soon regrouped and mounted a second charge. This charge was also unsuccessful, and soon hundreds

of British soldiers and officers lay dead or wounded. Forced to retreat for a second time, the British generals recognized that traditional fighting tactics would be unsuccessful. They ordered their troops to take off their knapsacks and coats so they would be more mobile. Colonel William Prescott, the commander, is said to have told his men, "Don't fire until you can see the whites of their eyes."

By the time the British advanced on Breed's Hill for the third time, the Patriots were resorting to throwing stones at them. General Putnam commanded his troops to retreat to Bunker Hill, but after a few unsuccessful attempts to defend it, he ordered a full retreat. In the end, more than 200 British soldiers and 100 Patriots lost their lives, and more than 750 British and 300 Patriots were wounded at the **Battle of Bunker Hill**. The British won the battle, but they suffered a great number of casualties, and fighting for control of the city of Boston continued. They realized that defeating the American colonists would be neither quick nor easy.

This Hessian brass drum was recovered from the Battle of Bennington in 1777. The sling in front was worn over the shoulder, leaving the drummer's hands free to hold drumsticks.

PEACE REJECTED

After the Battle of Bunker Hill, delegates from every colony except Georgia drafted a letter to King George, known as the **Olive Branch Petition**. The letter expressed hope for reconciliation while repeating the colonists' grievances against the Intolerable Acts. The colonists claimed that British "hostilities . . . have compelled us to arm in our own defense," but they made it clear that they were protesting Parliament's actions and were still loyal to Great Britain. King George did not believe them, though, and in August 1775, he declared without reading the petition that the colonists were in "open and avowed rebellion." In October, he stated that the colonists' actions were "carried on for the purpose of establishing an independent empire."

The king's statement dashed many Loyalists' hopes for reconciliation. They believed that the king had not realized how the Parliament's crippling

legislation would affect the colonists. The king's dismissal of the petition proved that he knew the consequences of the laws. Additionally, Parliament passed the Prohibitory Act on December 22, 1775, which authorized a blockade of all American ports to prevent any trade. Then the king made a deal with Germany allowing Britain to hire fierce German soldiers called **Hessians** and send them to North America. The Hessians were **mercenaries**, or soldiers for hire, who fought for whomever paid them. These acts increased tension between the Patriots and the British. John Adams noted that the blockade "throws the thirteen colonies out of the royal protections . . . and makes us independent in spite of our supplications and entreaties." However, many Loyalists continued to support efforts for reconciliation.

Attempting to divide the colonists even further, British authorities encouraged enslaved people in North America to revolt, claiming that their freedom rested on British military success. But the British only promised such freedom to those who fought on their side. Meanwhile, the colonists told enslaved people that the British were attempting to lure them away only to resell them in the West Indies, a much harsher place to be enslaved than the American colonies. With these conflicting narratives, enslaved people faced a tough decision. Predictably, some chose to join the British while others pledged their loyalty to the Patriot cause.

HISTORICAL THINKING

1. **READING CHECK** What was the significance of the Olive Branch Petition?

2. **ANALYZE CAUSE AND EFFECT** How did the capture of Fort Ticonderoga impact the Patriots' ability to wage war against Britain?

3. **DISTINGUISH FACT FROM OPINION** Was King George's claim that the colonies were taking actions "for the purpose of establishing an independent empire" fact or opinion? Explain your answer.

Battle of Bunker Hill, 1775

Mystic River

BUNKER HILL

Mill Pond

Warren's Earthworks

BREED'S HILL

First Landing

Glasgow

School Hill

Landing of the Reinforcements

CHARLESTOWN

Charles River

Falcon

BOSTON

Lively

- American forces
- British forces
- Fence
- Earthworks
- Cannon position
- British ship

0 500 1000 feet
0 100 200 meters

BUILD BACKGROUND

OLIVE BRANCH PETITION

The Olive Branch Petition was the brainchild of John Dickinson, the Pennsylvania Loyalist who continually tried to chart a moderate course between complete acceptance of Britain's authority and outright rebellion. From the start, however, Loyalist attempts at reconciliation proved to be a futile effort. The petition tried to appease both sides by framing the ongoing struggle as a temporary spat between friends, rather than as an inevitable separation. Dickinson spoke of the "tender regard" the colonists felt for their mother country, of which they remained "faithful subjects," and simply proposed a "humble petition" to end the bloodshed, which could be attributed to the actions of a few overly zealous participants.

DUNMORE'S PROCLAMATION

Britain's policy toward enslaved people was codified in Dunmore's Proclamation, named after Virginia's royal governor, John Dunmore. Written while Virginia was in a state of rebellion, the document offered freedom to slaves owned by Patriot sympathizers, if the slaves would fight for the British. However, the proclamation did not work as designed. First, it actually radicalized many moderate whites against the British, as they feared an open slave rebellion. Second, Dunmore misunderstood the essential motivation of enslaved people, whom he believed desired vengeance and would jump at the opportunity to rise against their oppressors. The promise of freedom, however, was the key to gaining their allegiance. Many enslaved people joined the British or the Patriots based on which group they believed offered the best possibility of casting off the shackles of slavery.

TEACH

GUIDED DISCUSSION

3. **Form and Support Opinions** Which event, the victory at Fort Ticonderoga or the Battle of Bunker Hill, was more important in shaping the course of the war, and why? *(Possible responses: The victory at Fort Ticonderoga was more important because it supported the Patriots' argument that independence was possible. The Battle of Bunker Hill was more important because, while technically a defeat, it proved that colonial soldiers could stand up against the British Army and that defeating American forces would be difficult.)*

4. **Make Inferences** Why do you think King George hired Hessian mercenaries from Germany to fight in North America? *(Possible response: He might have thought that foreign soldiers wouldn't be tempted to sympathize with the British colonists. Also, mercenary casualties likely reduced British casualties because they fought in place of British troops.)*

INTERPRET MAPS

Direct students' attention to the Battle of Bunker Hill, 1775 map. **ASK:** What strategic advantages did each side have at the onset of the battle? *(The British had more troops and controlled the main ports, which ensured their supply lines. The colonists controlled the important high ground, were well fortified with earthworks, and knew the terrain and people of Charlestown.)*

ACTIVE OPTIONS

On Your Feet: Consider Points of View Create five signs with the following labels: Colonial Soldier, British Soldier, Colonial Loyalist, Colonial Patriot, King George III. Place the signs around the classroom. Then arrange the students into five groups and assign each group one of the topics. Direct students to research the motivations causing each group to act as they did at the outset of the war. For example, Why did colonists join a militia? What motivated British soldiers to fight the colonists? Why did Loyalists continue to support reconciliation? How did the Patriots use the element of surprise in their attacks against the British? Why did the king dismiss the Olive Branch Petition? Then have groups discuss their topics. Finally, ask volunteers to summarize their group's discussion for the class.

NG Learning Framework: Convince the King to Reconcile

SKILLS Communication, Problem-Solving

KNOWLEDGE Our Human Story

Provide students with a copy of the Olive Branch Petition. As a class, read the document and note the various arguments made by the colonists. Then remind the class that King George refused to read the petition. Next have students form small groups and draft their own petition in one last attempt to achieve reconciliation between Britain and the colonies. Ask a small group of students to play the role of the king and his council. Direct petitioning groups to expand on the arguments in the original petition, form wholly new arguments, or brainstorm ways to present their petition so the king either reads or hears it. Finally, have groups share their petitions and allow the king and his council to respond.

HISTORICAL THINKING

ANSWERS

1. The Olive Branch Petition's failure indicated that reconciliation between Britain and the colonies would likely be impossible. King George called out the colonies as being in open rebellion without reading the petition and therefore did not grasp that the colonies' grievances were directed at Parliament, not Great Britain.

2. The capture of Fort Ticonderoga boosted the morale of Patriots, cut off British supply lines to the area, and gave the colonists much-needed arms and artillery.

3. Answers will vary. Possible response: The Patriots' acts of rebellion could have convinced King George that the colonists were defying Britain "for the purpose of establishing an independent empire." However, the king's claim was an opinion, not a fact, because the Olive Branch Petition was an attempt at reconciliation and clearly stated that the colonists were still loyal to Great Britain.

DECLARING INDEPENDENCE

Sometimes working as a team means putting differences aside for the greater good. In the years leading up to the American Revolution, people who held wildly differing views worked together to establish a government for all citizens. It was a tremendous undertaking.

HOSTILITIES AND *COMMON SENSE*

Two weeks after the Battle of Bunker Hill, George Washington arrived in Cambridge, Massachusetts, near Boston, to take charge of the Continental Army. Upset by the disorder he discovered there, Washington set out to instill strict discipline among the existing troops. He also began training new recruits whom he hoped would defeat the organized British troops.

In September 1775, the Second Continental Congress sent General Richard Montgomery and 1,200 members of the militia on a mission to attack Quebec City, a British military stronghold in Canada. Along the way, Montgomery's men battled British troops in Canada. But when they joined General Benedict Arnold's troops at their destination on December 31, the attack ended in a disastrous defeat. Montgomery died in the Battle of Quebec, and 400 Patriots were killed, captured, or wounded. Despite this loss, Benedict Arnold continued fighting against the British forces there.

Meanwhile, the fight for control of Boston raged on. In late January 1776, cannons, other artillery, and gunpowder from Fort Ticonderoga arrived. On the night of March 4, Washington had the cannons hauled to the top of a hill south of the city, which had clear views of the British troops below. Yet again, British soldiers awoke in the morning to find enemy guns aimed at them. General **William Howe** recognized he had been outmaneuvered. "These fellows have done more work in one night than I could make my army do in three months," he remarked. Washington agreed to allow the 10,000 British soldiers to evacuate safely in exchange for Britain's pledge not to burn the city as they went. The last of the British troops exited Boston on March 17, 1776. Howe sent his men to Nova Scotia, Canada, to regroup and resupply.

PRIMARY SOURCE

The cause of America is in a great measure the cause of all mankind. Many circumstances hath, and will arise, which are not local, but universal, and through which the principles of all Lovers of Mankind are affected, and in the Event of which, their Affections are interested. The laying a Country desolate with Fire and Sword, declaring War against the natural rights of all Mankind, and extirpating [destroying] the Defenders thereof from the Face of the Earth, is the Concern of every Man.

—from *Common Sense*, by Thomas Paine, February 14, 1776

Some members of the Second Continental Congress still wanted to reconcile with Britain even though battles had already taken place. The protection and stable economy that the British empire offered to colonists remained powerful reasons for their loyalty. But on January 9, 1776, as Arnold's campaign in Canada was failing and Patriots **mobilized** to protect the South from the British, **Thomas Paine** published a small pamphlet titled *Common Sense*.

Common Sense explained the struggle between the colonists and Britain from a new perspective. Rather than attacking King George directly, Paine defined the colonists' struggles as a question of how they wanted to be governed. Did they wish to have a representative democracy, or did they wish to continue to be ruled by a king or queen? Paine clearly chose the former. He called on colonists to declare independence, and he urged colonial merchants to break their ties to London businesses and expand their trade with other European countries for the sake of the colonial economy. "We have it in our power to begin the world over again," he wrote.

DRAFTING THE DECLARATION

The popularity of *Common Sense* spread rapidly among the growing number of Patriots both in the Congress and in the general public. In April 1776, the North Carolina delegates to the Congress pledged to vote in favor of independence. In May, New Jersey Patriots removed the last royal governor in the colonies from office. *Common Sense* won the endorsement of George Washington and many other leading Patriots, including Jonathan Trumbull, Sr., of Connecticut—the only colonial governor to favor independence. Loyalists, on the other hand, believed Paine's ideas were unrealistic and dangerous.

By the summer of 1776, 150,000 copies of *Common Sense* were in circulation. Colonists began destroying royal images and removing royal symbols from public buildings in their communities. A statue of King George in New York City was melted down for bullets by female volunteers

and used against British troops. The setting was now ripe for the Congress to draft a statement declaring the colonies' independence.

On June 11, 1776, the Congress chose five delegates—**Thomas Jefferson**, John Adams, Benjamin Franklin, Roger Sherman, and Robert Livingston—to draft a declaration of independence. The delegates became known as the **Committee of Five**. Among them, they selected Jefferson, a young politician and lawyer from Virginia, to write the official draft of the document. Jefferson had become famous for his writing skills through his publication of "A Summary View of the Rights of British America" in 1774, in which he argued that Parliament did not have authority over the colonies.

Jefferson incorporated many Enlightenment ideas into the **Declaration of Independence**, particularly John Locke's notions of natural rights and the existence of the social contract formed between people and their governments. Each section of the Declaration had a unique purpose. It began with a **preamble**, or introductory statement, which laid out the reasons colonists were declaring independence. A list of violations committed by King George followed, including the king's failure to approve certain laws created by colonial governments, his interruption of colonial trade,

The Committee of Five discuss the future of the country in this painting by Alonzo Chappel. He finished this piece in the 1850s as part of a series titled *The Drafting of the Declaration of Independence*.

PLAN: 4-PAGE LESSON

OBJECTIVE

Assess how the colonists worked together to form a new nation and government.

CRITICAL THINKING SKILLS FOR LESSON 2.2

- Form and Support Opinions
- Identify Main Ideas and Details
- Summarize
- Evaluate
- Draw Conclusions
- Make Connections
- Analyze Primary Sources
- Make Predictions

HISTORICAL THINKING FOR CHAPTER 4

How did the colonists' emerging American identity lead to revolution? As clashes with Britain continued, the colonists began to develop a stronger identity as Americans. Lesson 2.2 examines what led the colonists to declare independence and their first steps in forming a new nation.

BACKGROUND FOR THE TEACHER

The philosophical foundation of the American Revolution can be traced directly to the Enlightenment, an 18th-century European intellectual movement. Enlightenment thinkers stressed liberty and the notion that authority was illegitimate unless granted by the people. Indeed, the most famous portions of the Declaration, including the immortal phrases "all men are created equal" and "life, liberty, and the pursuit of happiness," were borrowed directly from Enlightenment thinker John Locke. Locke believed that all individuals were born equal with certain "unalienable" rights—namely "life, liberty, and property." Jefferson changed "property" to "the pursuit of happiness," whose broad meaning allowed for wider interpretation. However, asserting equality of all raised the thorny issue of slavery in colonial life. This fundamental contradiction would be an ongoing problem for the country.

INTRODUCE & ENGAGE

DISCUSS INDEPENDENCE AS A CONCEPT

Prompt students to discuss independence as a concept. Begin by writing the word in the center of a Concept Cluster, and add student responses to the map during classroom discussion. Prompt students to consider reasons why a person or group would want to be independent and what they would gain or lose as a consequence. At the end of the lesson, revisit the activity and discuss what gains and losses the colonies incurred, or might incur in the future, with the declaring of independence.

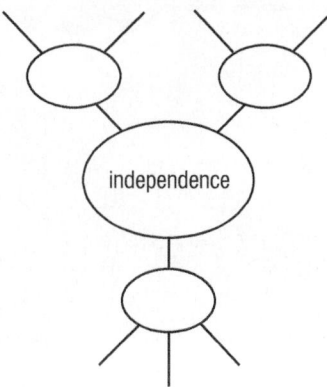

TEACH

GUIDED DISCUSSION

1. **Evaluate** What key qualities did the Continental Army demonstrate in confrontations with the British at Bunker Hill and during the defense of Boston? *(Possible response: At Bunker Hill, the Continental Army had become a disciplined fighting force with the ability to challenge British forces and inflict major losses. General Washington showed ingenuity in his command at Boston by having troops position cannons on a hill above the British. His troops showed strength and determination in accomplishing the feat overnight. Washington demonstrated tact and restraint by negotiating a British retreat without the British burning the city.)*

2. **Draw Conclusions** Why was it important in the Declaration to list the violations by King George and the colonists' appeals for justice? *(Possible response: These sections showed the king had broken the social contract between himself and the colonists and therefore justified the colonists' right to declare independence.)*

3. **Make Connections** How might collaborating on the Declaration of Independence have helped the delegates work together on the Articles of Confederation? *(Possible response: Collaborating on the Declaration gave them a philosophical framework for a new government structure and gave them experience in debating various issues and working out compromises with one another.)*

ANALYZE PRIMARY SOURCES

Direct students' attention to the Primary Source feature. Have them read the excerpt and note the words used by Thomas Paine to indicate that America's cause is of global concern. **ASK:** Why does Paine argue that the American cause is "universal"? *(He argues that natural rights apply to all mankind. Thus, if they are violated anywhere, it is the concern of all people.)* **ASK:** What do you think is his ultimate vision for the world? *(Possible response: Ultimately, Paine sees a world in which tyranny is recognized and destroyed because it wages war against people's natural rights.)*

DIFFERENTIATE

ENGLISH LANGUAGE LEARNERS

Read in Pairs Pair students at the **Emerging** or **Expanding** level with an English-proficient partner, and have them read the lesson together. Instruct students to ask their partners to pause whenever they hear a word or sentence construction that is confusing. Provide the following sentence frames to help students at different levels clarify information.

- **Emerging:** Please help me understand this (word, sentence).

- **Expanding:** I need some help understanding this (word, sentence, paragraph).

Suggest that students' partners point out context clues to help students understand the meanings of unfamiliar terms or constructions. Encourage them to restate sentences in their own words.

GIFTED & TALENTED

Sway a Group of Loyalists Challenge students to write and perform a speech in character as Thomas Paine trying to convince a group of Loyalists to become Patriots. Tell students to use the text and conduct additional research to determine three arguments that Loyalists made to justify their loyalty to Great Britain, and state them in their speech. Then have students access online excerpts or a full-text version of Paine's *Common Sense* and find ideas and quotations to use as counterarguments to sway the Loyalists in favor of independence. Encourage students to practice their speeches before delivering their speeches to the class.

See the Chapter Planner for more strategies for differentiation.

The painting is the first of four Revolutionary-era scenes that the U.S. Congress commissioned from painter John Trumbull. The artist had created a smaller version of this painting to document the events of the American Revolution, and he enlarged it for the Rotunda between August 1817 and September 1818. It was installed in 1826, along with three other Trumbull paintings.

and his levying of taxes without permission. The next section suggested that British citizens had ignored several appeals for justice from the colonists. The document concluded by declaring the newly independent nation as the United States of America, casting off all ties to Britain and pledging an oath that all states (all former colonies) supported the declaration.

The Committee presented the first draft of the Declaration to the Congress on June 28, 1776. However, delegates withdrew the draft because it included statements that morally objected to the institution of slavery and the slave trade. Those sentences were later deleted to gain the support from southern, as well as some northern, colonies.

APPROVING THE DECLARATION

By July 2, 1776, all of the colonial delegations except that of New York had a majority vote to approve the Declaration of Independence. The New York delegation approved it on July 9. However, there were individual holdouts. Some members of the Congress refused to sign it unless Jefferson withdrew statements that condemned the British people since many colonists wanted to avoid a direct attack on a culture to which they still felt connected. Jefferson made these revisions.

On July 19, the Congress titled the document "The Unanimous Declaration of the Thirteen United States of America," officially recognizing the new nation by this name. By August 2, most delegates had signed it. Newspapers printed copies, and colonists posted it on the doors of public buildings throughout the country. General George Washington instructed his officers to read it to the troops. Celebrations erupted throughout the nation, encouraging many Loyalists to support the Patriot cause. Suddenly, the Declaration had shifted the colonists' cause to a fight

for a united American republic instead of a struggle against Parliament in the king's name. You can read the Declaration of Independence in its entirety in the Citizenship Handbook.

CREATING A GOVERNMENT

On July 12, 1776, members of the Congress submitted their first draft of the **Articles of Confederation**, a list of resolutions loosely uniting the 13 states under a central government. The authors had worked hard to write resolutions that balanced the power of a central government with the power of state governments. The Articles created a central government with limited authority. For example, the government did not have the power to tax the states. The Articles also gave each state delegation one vote. This equalized the power of

states with large and small populations. For the Congress to approve any act, nine states had to vote in favor of the proposal. And to avoid the creation of an elite political class, delegates to the Congress could only serve for three years.

While delegates agreed on the structure of government created by the Articles, the Congress did not **ratify**, or formally approve, the document until 1781. This delay was due to some states' unresolved disputes over claims of lands outside the 13 colonies. States that held claims, such as Virginia, resisted giving up the land. States without claims wanted the central government to take control. In the end, the states without claims won, and the Congress ratified the Articles soon after. The Articles served as the foundation for the national government until 1789.

HISTORICAL THINKING

1. **READING CHECK** How did the publication of *Common Sense* encourage colonists to declare independence?

2. **FORM AND SUPPORT OPINIONS** Do you agree or disagree with the delegates' reasons for withdrawing the draft questioning the morality of slavery from the original draft of the Declaration of Independence? Support your opinion with evidence from the text.

3. **IDENTIFY MAIN IDEAS AND DETAILS** What were the weaknesses of the Articles of Confederation?

4. **SUMMARIZE** How did the colonies overcome their differences and unite in justifying a declaration of independence from Britain?

BUILD BACKGROUND

BRITISH REACTION TO THE DECLARATION

The Declaration was received by the British with both indifference and scorn. It wasn't until mid-August that a copy reached British shores, after which it was printed in a variety of newspapers, receiving mostly unfavorable coverage. While some periodicals were sympathetic to the colonists' cause, most argued that the document was nothing more than a declaration of treason and that Jefferson's ideas concerning equality were absurd. Others painted the colonists as ungrateful, petulant children whose complaints were outweighed by the protection afforded by the empire. In fact, many members of Parliament didn't even bother to comment, as the document was considered nothing more than the last words of a soon-to-be-suppressed rebellion. It wasn't until October that the king finally offered his opinion, calling the signers "daring and desperate . . . they have now openly renounced all allegiance to the crown."

THE ARTICLES OF CONFEDERATION

Rather than a proper constitution, the Articles of Confederation can be understood as a treaty among 13 separate but equal states. The power and authority of the states was placed firmly above that of the central government, whose restrained and clearly defined duties were confined to areas of foreign policy and defense, including the ability to declare war, select military officers, negotiate treaties and alliances, appoint ambassadors, and manage relationships with Native Americans. Many of the basic roles and characteristics of the modern federal government either did not exist or were purposely omitted from the Articles. For instance, there was no empowered president, and states could not be forced to provide federal funding through taxes. Instead, they could give the federal government money, if they wished. There was also no federal court, and the government could not draft soldiers to form an army.

TEACH

GUIDED DISCUSSION

4. **Make Predictions** How might disagreements over the content of the Declaration of Independence foreshadow problems in America's future? *(Possible responses: The demand to delete all language objecting to the institution of slavery foreshadows an issue that will haunt the nation throughout its history. The affinity for British culture hints at ethnic and cultural tensions that will arise as the country becomes more diverse.)*

5. **Draw Conclusions** How did Americans' experiences with Great Britain influence the provisions of the Articles of Confederation? *(Possible response: Americans did not want another strong central power such as a monarchy nor a political elite such as Parliament. As a result, they created a weaker central government and set term limits on delegates.)*

VIRTUAL MUSEUM VISIT

The U.S. Capitol Rotunda contains many depictions of events in American history, including sculptures of early explorers, carvings and frescos of colonial history, statues of presidents, and eight historical paintings—four completed by John Trumbull. Guide students to visit the Rotunda's website where they can view and read about Trumbull's paintings. Instruct them to take notes on the content of the paintings, including how the chosen events are depicted and the types of people included or excluded in all the works. Then discuss with students what these works tell us about how Americans in the 1800s viewed their history. Ask them which additional events or individuals they might add to provide a more complete history of early America.

ACTIVE OPTIONS

On Your Feet: Team Word Webbing Arrange students in groups of four or five. Hand each group a sheet of paper containing the following question: Which people or events helped forge a unifying American identity? Have the first students in each group write the name of a person or event with a short explanation and pass the paper clockwise to the next student. Each student in the group then adds at least one answer. Students circulate the paper until they run out of answers. Then direct each group to rank the people or events in order of importance. Call on volunteers from each group to share their list with the class.

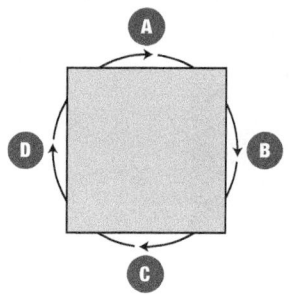

NG Learning Framework: Publish a Common-Sense Pamphlet

ATTITUDE Empowerment

SKILLS Communication, Problem-Solving

Remind students of the title of Thomas Paine's influential work and inform them that Paine believed declaring independence was nothing but "common sense." Then have students work in pairs to identify a current problem or issue and its common-sense solution. Tell pairs to create a pamphlet that explains the issue and solution, including why the solution is common sense. Encourage students to first research and read Paine's famous work, noting the arguments and rhetorical devices he uses. Invite students to print and distribute their pamphlets to the class. Then invite the class to discuss the topics and proposed solutions.

HISTORICAL THINKING

ANSWERS

1. *Common Sense* reframed the struggle between colonists and the British government as a choice between two systems of government. It essentially asked the citizens to decide how they wanted to be governed.

2. Possible responses: Disagree. Including the statements about a moral objection to slavery would give the document moral clarity and put the nation on a speedier path toward liberty for all people. Agree. The Declaration had to be unanimously ratified. Including the statements about the morality of slavery would have prevented the southern colonies from signing it, effectively blocking a unified vote for independence.

3. The Articles limited the ability of the central government to conduct basic functions such as raising taxes, and created 13 separate but equal governments which might have difficultly working together. In addition, it made it hard to pass laws because 9 of the 13 colonies, rather than a simple majority, had to agree on each law.

4. The colonies were able to overcome their differences and unite because they had all endured the violations inflicted by Great Britain, they developed a common language to frame their struggle, and they were willing to compromise to achieve independence.

A FOUNDATION FOR THE COUNTRY

Although the Declaration of Independence is not a legally binding document in the same way the U.S. Constitution and the Bill of Rights are, it is the basis on which the United States was founded. As such, it holds pride of place with the other two founding documents in the Rotunda for the Charters of Freedom in the National Archives Museum in Washington, D.C.

In addition to the founding documents, the archives house the population censuses taken every ten years since 1790, significant treaties, and military and naturalization records for all soldiers and immigrants in the United States. But the archives do not keep every government document. Only those files that are deemed valuable are kept, which works out to be between 2 and 5 percent of the federal records generated annually.

CRITICAL VIEWING Why is it important for a country to showcase historical documents, such as the Declaration of Independence?

DOCUMENT ONE

Primary Source: Legal Document
from the Declaration of Independence, 1776

The goal of the Declaration was to unite the colonies as one nation. To accomplish this goal, the colonists informed King George that he no longer held power over them, and why.

CONSTRUCTED RESPONSE What does this excerpt suggest about the colonists' reasons for declaring independence?

When in the Course of human events, it becomes necessary for one people to dissolve the political bands which have connected them with another, and to assume among the powers of the earth, the separate and equal station to which the Laws of Nature and of Nature's God entitle them, a decent respect to the opinions of mankind requires that they should declare the causes which impel them to the separation.

DOCUMENT TWO

Primary Source: Legal Document
from the Declaration of Independence, 1776

The colonists listed a set of principles for how they believed a government should treat its citizens. The Declaration was written in accordance with these principles.

CONSTRUCTED RESPONSE What beliefs about the origin and purpose of government did the colonists hold?

We hold these truths to be self-evident, that all men are created equal; that they are endowed by their Creator with certain unalienable rights; that among these are Life, Liberty, and the pursuit of Happiness; that, to secure these rights, governments are instituted among Men, deriving their just powers from the consent of the governed; that whenever any form of government becomes destructive of these ends, it is the right of the people to alter or to abolish it, and to institute new government, laying its foundation on such principles, and organizing its powers in such form, as to them shall seem most likely to effect their safety and happiness.

DOCUMENT THREE

Primary Source: Legal Document
from the Declaration of Independence, 1776

The Declaration ends with a list of human rights violations the colonists felt Great Britain had committed against them. They state that these violations justify their act of separating from the British empire.

CONSTRUCTED RESPONSE Why did the colonists feel it was their duty to establish independence?

When a long train of abuses and usurpations [illegal seizures of power], pursuing invariably the same object, evinces a design to reduce them under absolute despotism, it is their right, it is their duty, to throw off such government, and to provide new guards for their future security. Such has been the patient sufferance of these colonies; and such is now the necessity which constrains them to alter their former systems of government. The history of the present King of Great Britain is a history of repeated injuries and usurpations, all having in direct object the establishment of an absolute tyranny over these states.

Read the full Declaration of Independence
in the Citizenship Handbook.

SYNTHESIZE AND WRITE

1. **REVIEW** Review what you have learned about the writing and adoption of the Declaration of Independence.

2. **RECALL** On your own paper, write the main idea expressed in each excerpt of the document. Remember that main ideas should be supported by details from the excerpt.

3. **CONSTRUCT** Construct a topic sentence that answers this question: In what ways did the colonists feel Great Britain had violated their civil rights?

4. **WRITE** Write a paragraph that supports the statement in Step 3 using evidence from the excerpts.

PLAN: 2-PAGE LESSON

OBJECTIVE

Synthesize information about the Declaration of Independence by analyzing excerpts of this primary source document.

CRITICAL THINKING SKILLS FOR LESSON 2.3

- Synthesize
- Analyze Language Use
- Draw Conclusions
- Evaluate

HISTORICAL THINKING FOR CHAPTER 4

How did the colonists' emerging American identity lead to revolution? The Declaration of Independence formally separated the colonies from Britain and contains many of the ideas that are now deeply imbedded in the American identity. Lesson 2.3 examines excerpts from this seminal American document.

BACKGROUND FOR THE TEACHER

A signed document of the Declaration of Independence is housed at the National Archives, but hundreds of other versions of the document exist. Several rough drafts are known—some handwritten by Thomas Jefferson, others by John Adams. After Jefferson completed his work, the Declaration was reproduced as handwritten copies to preserve the original text. Many of these early copies are now archived in libraries and museums. Soon after the signing, colonial newspapers printed versions of the document, some of which included differences in punctuation and capitalization from Jefferson's version. John Dunlap, printer for the Continental Congress, produced 200 copies to be distributed throughout the colonies. In 1989, one of the 26 remaining Dunlap copies was discovered tucked behind a painting in an old picture frame that had been purchased for $4. The copy, valued at about $1 million, was eventually sold for $2.42 million.

INTRODUCE & ENGAGE

PREPARE FOR THE DOCUMENT-BASED QUESTION

Before students start on the activity, briefly preview the three documents. Remind students that a constructed response requires full explanations in complete sentences. Emphasize that students should use what they have learned about the Declaration of Independence in addition to the information in the excerpts.

TEACH

GUIDED DISCUSSION

1. **Analyze Language Use** In the second excerpt, what language did the colonists use that might reinforce King George's idea that they wanted to establish "an independent empire"? *(Possible response: The words "right of the people to alter or to abolish [the government], and to institute new government" probably sounded to King George as if colonists wanted to set up their own king and rule their own independent empire.)*

2. **Draw Conclusions** Why do you think the colonists were concerned about the "opinions of mankind" regarding their decision to separate from Great Britain? *(Possible response: The colonists were taking a historic step to "dissolve the political bands" between them and Great Britain, plus charting a new path based on Enlightenment principles. Therefore, they felt they needed to tell other people the reasons for their actions, which might also inspire others to throw off tyranny.)*

EVALUATE

After students have completed the Synthesize & Write activity, allow time for them to exchange paragraphs and read and comment on the work of their peers. Establish guidelines for comments prior to the activity so that feedback is constructive and encouraging in nature. Comments should focus on the most significant parts that address the purpose of the activity and the audience.

ACTIVE OPTION

On Your Feet: Think, Pair, Share Ask the following question and then allow a few minutes for students to think about it: On what grounds did the colonists think they were entitled to independence? Then tell students to choose partners and talk about the question for five minutes. After discussion time, invite students to share their ideas with the class.

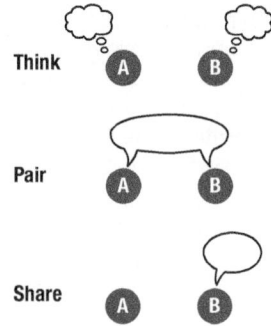

DIFFERENTIATE

INCLUSION

Paraphrase Using Sentence Frames Provide students with sentence frames to help them paraphrase and understand the text.

- **Document 1** When groups have to separate, they should spell out the _____ that make this step necessary. *(causes/reasons)*
- **Document 2** All people have certain rights which can't be taken away by a _____. *(government)*
- **Document 3** The colonies suffered under King George's rule, so they decided to _____ their system of government. *(change)*

GIFTED & TALENTED

Perform a Dramatic Reading Challenge students to prepare a dramatic reading of one of the excerpts. Encourage them to practice reading with appropriate expression, phrasing, and gestures and to consider how pace and volume might be used to convey meaning. Invite students to perform their dramatic reading for the class. Prompt comments about how the reading affected students' understanding of the excerpt.

See the Chapter Planner for more strategies for differentiation.

SYNTHESIZE & WRITE

ANSWERS

1. Answers will vary.

2. Answers will vary. Possible response: The colonies acknowledge the need to name reasons for declaring independence. When a government destroys the rights, given by their Creator, of a people, the people should form a new government. People have a duty to throw off tyranny and make their own safety and happiness.

3. Possible response: The colonists felt the king demonstrated "absolute despotism" and violated their "unalienable rights," noting "repeated injuries and usurpations," likely referring to taxing without representation, quartering troops, and conducting unwarranted searches and seizures.

4. Students' paragraphs should include their topic sentence from Step 3 and several details from the documents for support.

CONSTRUCTED RESPONSE

Document 1: Possible response: The colonists felt compelled by "the Laws of Nature and of Nature's God" to separate from, and have equal stature recognized by, Great Britain.

Document 2: Possible response: They believed that a government rules only at the consent of the people and that it should protect peoples' rights, keep them safe, and allow for their happiness.

Document 3: Possible response: They felt they had the right to throw off British rule because the king had repeatedly violated their rights and imposed tyrannical rule over them.

CRITICAL VIEWING Possible response: By showcasing historical documents, a nation makes its original founding principles and philosophy available for everyone to read. Thus, it is easier to preserve these original ideals and to recognize when they are ignored or challenged.

MAIN IDEA From late 1776 to late 1777, the Continental Army suffered major defeats that threatened to end the colonists' efforts to achieve independence.

MILITARY STRATEGY IN THE EARLY STAGES

Success in a competition often comes from knowing your own and your opponent's weaknesses and strengths. For a year, the well-trained and well-armed British Army dealt devastating losses to the Continental Army. But a weakness in the British plan let the Continental Army win an important victory that kept the colonists' hope for independence alive.

TWO ARMIES

As you might expect, the British military had distinct advantages over the Continental Army—it had the world's most powerful army and navy and had defeated its fiercest rivals, France and Spain, in several conflicts over the previous century. It was also well equipped and well supplied by Great Britain's strong central government. The British had the support of Loyalists throughout the colonies, including the Mohawk and a number of other Native American tribes and nations. Nearly 25,000 colonists would directly support British military actions during the war.

On the other hand, the Continental Army had its own strengths, which the British underestimated. First, most Americans had a strong belief in the cause of independence and self-government. Furthermore, Americans had a much more detailed knowledge of the local terrain, which gave them an advantage in battles. These factors contributed to the rise of resourceful American military leaders who were determined to use every strategy and resource necessary to win the nation's freedom.

Both forces had weaknesses, too. For the British, keeping troops supplied was a logistic and financial challenge. Ships carrying men, weapons, and food from Britain took months to reach North America. Distribution of those resources took time because the British Army was stationed up and down the eastern coast of the continent. British citizens quickly voiced concern about the cost of the war. In addition, the British soldiers found themselves far from home in a vast, unfamiliar country as they tried to control the widespread, rebellious colonists, move supplies over rough land and dangerous waters, and engage in combat. And some British generals hastily misjudged their enemy, which kept them from coordinating their own strategies effectively.

For its part, the Continental Army suffered from a woeful lack of training and discipline. It was constantly confronted by a shortage of supplies and ammunition and was so poorly funded that troops often received no payment for their service. Called to action by the Congress, soldiers followed their leaders into battles while worrying about the families and livelihoods they left behind. Meanwhile, the Articles of Confederation had stripped the Congress of the authority to collect taxes to pay the military or even to provide blankets and food.

General Washington quickly devised a plan to unite citizen-soldiers and state militias into a disciplined Continental Army. His first step was to create a structure similar to that used by the British Army, which was divided into smaller and smaller groups. Washington structured the Continental Army with even more levels of command, from brigades of thousands of soldiers to companies of about 40 privates. By organizing the troops into manageable groups, Washington's generals and officers could train and instill discipline more easily. In addition, troops could be more readily **deployed**, or put to use, in battle as large brigades or small companies, depending on what strategy was needed.

To increase the odds of winning the war, Washington tried to unite the army in two ways. First, he brought together state militias and regular forces under commanders from their own regions, so they could remain connected to the homes they were fighting for. But Washington also knew that his army had to represent the diversity of the new nation. To that end, he persuaded the Congress to recruit soldiers for long terms of service and organized them into regiments with soldiers from different regions.

AMERICAN LOSSES IN NEW YORK

Knowing the weaknesses of the Continental Army, British generals expected a rapid, victorious end to the conflict. They launched a plan to crush the rebellion by taking control of the Hudson River Valley and New York City, dividing the northern colonies from the middle and southern colonies. Because the British believed New England to be the stronghold of the Revolution, they hoped to cut off that region's supply lines. Colonists would certainly reconsider supporting the war if shipments of food and supplies stopped. The British also believed that large numbers of Loyalists in the middle and southern colonies would then welcome back British rule.

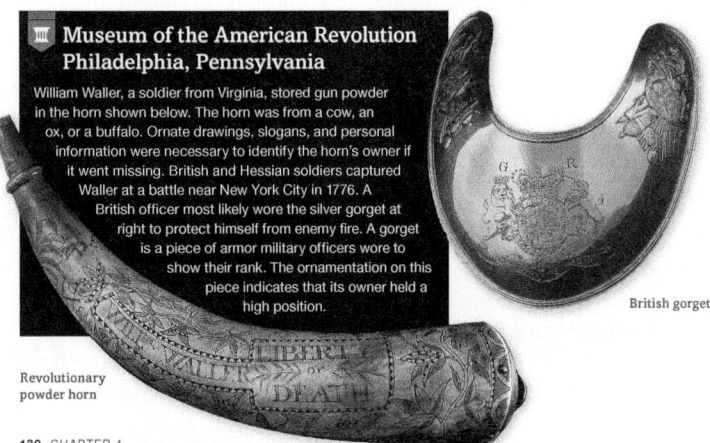

🏛 Museum of the American Revolution
Philadelphia, Pennsylvania

William Waller, a soldier from Virginia, stored gun powder in the horn shown below. The horn was from a cow, an ox, or a buffalo. Ornate drawings, slogans, and personal information were necessary to identify the horn's owner if it went missing. British and Hessian soldiers captured Waller at a battle near New York City in 1776. A British officer most likely wore the silver gorget at right to protect himself from enemy fire. A gorget is a piece of armor military officers wore to show their rank. The ornamentation on this piece indicates that its owner held a high position.

British gorget

Revolutionary powder horn

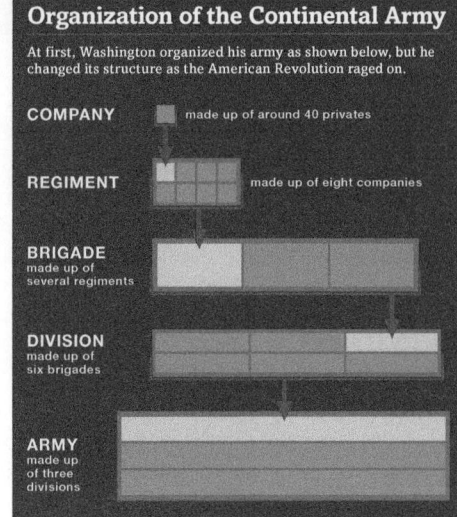

Organization of the Continental Army

At first, Washington organized his army as shown below, but he changed its structure as the American Revolution raged on.

COMPANY made up of around 40 privates

REGIMENT made up of eight companies

BRIGADE made up of several regiments

DIVISION made up of six brigades

ARMY made up of three divisions

PLAN: 4-PAGE LESSON

OBJECTIVE

Evaluate how the strengths and weaknesses of the Continental and British armies influenced early military strategies and battles.

CRITICAL THINKING SKILLS FOR LESSON 3.1

- Interpret Visuals
- Compare and Contrast
- Interpret Maps
- Make Inferences
- Draw Conclusions
- Summarize
- Analyze Cause and Effect
- Integrate Visuals

HISTORICAL THINKING FOR CHAPTER 4

How did the colonists' emerging American identity lead to revolution? Early military skirmishes proved costly to Americans, but their determination to win independence was spurred by the emergence of their identity as Americans rather than subjects of the crown. Lesson 3.1 describes repeated military setbacks faced by the Continental Army and a key victory that provided new hope.

BACKGROUND FOR THE TEACHER

The American Revolution drove a wedge between once-allied Native American tribes, such as those in the Iroquois Confederacy, which dominated the frontier northeast and northwest. The Confederacy consisted of six tribes who had been allies for 500 years. As the British-American conflict loomed, member nations attempted to remain neutral but soon found both sides pressuring them to join their cause. Unable to agree on whom to support, the Confederacy split, with four nations fighting for the British. These nations felt bound by old British alliances and believed they stood a better chance of keeping their lands if Great Britain won. A colonial victory would mean American expansion into tribal territory. The decision caused serious conflict within the Confederacy, as members of the same tribe ended up warring against one other.

📄 HISTORY NOTEBOOK

Encourage students to complete the Reid on the Road video series pages for Chapter 4 in their History Notebooks after they view the videos.

INTRODUCE & ENGAGE

CONSIDER KEYS TO VICTORY

Write the phrase "keys to victory" in the center of an Idea Web on the board. **ASK:** When two armies clash, what factors do you think are important in determining who will win? *(Possible response: size of the army, knowledge of terrain, quality of military leaders, availability of supplies and training)* Write students' responses in the surrounding circles. Then ask students to predict which factor will play the largest role in the first two years of the American Revolution. Allow volunteers to share their ideas. Finally, tell students that in this lesson, they will learn the strengths and weaknesses of British and Continental forces in the early battles of the war.

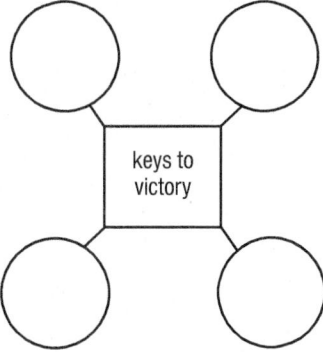

keys to victory

TEACH

GUIDED DISCUSSION

1. **Make Inferences** Why might the colonists' knowledge of the terrain be such an important advantage during battles? *(Possible response: Such knowledge would enable them to control strategic ground and waterways, know where to retreat when necessary, spy on the enemy, set up ambushes, and find food and water.)*

2. **Draw Conclusions** How did the forming of companies of soldiers into regiments affect the emergence of a common identity among Americans? *(Possible responses: Forming regiments of soldiers with men from the same area allowed the men to stay connected with soldiers from their home state while also serving the nation as a whole. Soldiers who served longer terms fought along with soldiers from different regions, but all had a stake in winning independence for the nation, which likely helped soldiers and those supporting them to think of themselves as Americans rather than colonists.)*

3. **Summarize** How did the weaknesses of the Articles of Confederation affect the Continental Army in the war? *(Possible response: Because Congress could not levy taxes on the states, raising money to pay soldiers, acquire supplies, and buy weapons was difficult.)*

🏛 VIRTUAL MUSEUM VISIT

The Museum of the American Revolution in Philadelphia, Pennsylvania, is home to a collection that highlights the ideas, events, and legacies from early resistance in Boston through the final victory at Yorktown. Visitors can see a life-size reproduction of the Boston Liberty Tree, George Washington's headquarters tent, design their own uniforms, experience a British infantry charge, or board a replica of a privateer ship. Instruct groups of students to explore the online collection found on the museum's website. Ask them to select one item and write a brief paragraph about how it helped them better understand this period of history. Encourage groups to present their artifacts and paragraphs to the class.

DIFFERENTIATE

ENGLISH LANGUAGE LEARNERS

Use *Good* and *Well* Remind students that used as an adjective, *good* describes a noun (a good singer), and used as an adverb, *well* describes a verb (sings well). Pair students at the **Emerging** and **Expanding** levels with students at the **Bridging** level. Provide them with Tree Diagrams similar to those shown. Model the activity using the second sentence in the lesson to complete a diagram using both *good* and *well*. Then instruct pairs to reread the fourth paragraph and add characteristics of the Continental Army to the diagram. *(The Continental Army was not well trained/disciplined/supplied/funded; They did not have good training/discipline/supplies/funding.)*

The British Army was well	equipped
	supplied

They had good	equipment
	supplies

The Continental Army was not well	trained

They did not have good	training

GIFTED & TALENTED

Design a Powder Horn Carving Encourage students to conduct online research about the meanings of the decorations and inscriptions found on powder horns used during the American Revolution. Then direct students to make detailed sketches of the designs and inscriptions for a powder horn that colonists might have used. Art students might make a model out of clay and carve their design directly on it. Ask students to share their illustrations or models and to explain the reasons for their designs.

See the Chapter Planner for more strategies for differentiation.

They decided to capture the city first. On August 22, 1776, Howe landed 20,000 troops on Long Island and overpowered General Washington and the 10,000 Continental soldiers stationed there, forcing them to retreat. On September 15, Howe's forces landed at Kip's Bay on the eastern side of Manhattan, where, once again, they soundly defeated the Continental Army. The Americans retreated a second time to the northern tip of Manhattan. They defended the stronghold at Harlem Heights for another month.

The defeat in New York City was a disaster for Washington and the Continental Army. About 2,000 men were killed, wounded, or captured, and about half of the remaining enlisted soldiers' terms of service were scheduled to expire by the end of the year. Reinforcements came from other regiments, swelling the army to about 5,000 soldiers, but Washington knew that he needed a win to gain the numbers required to defeat the British.

Through October and November 1776, Howe's forces continued to advance west, capturing 3,000 Continental soldiers at Fort Washington north of Harlem and forcing the rest into full retreat across the Hudson River and into New Jersey. Howe dispatched General **Charles Cornwallis** and his soldiers to pursue them. By December, Washington's force—which now consisted of 2,400 men—retreated to Pennsylvania.

VICTORY AT TRENTON

Meanwhile, Howe called off Cornwallis's pursuit of General Washington and ordered Cornwallis's troops to set up winter quarters at various locations across New Jersey, including Princeton and Trenton. Among those fighting for Britain were Hessian mercenaries, about 30,000 of whom served the British Army throughout the course of the American Revolution.

On the night of December 25, Washington and his men stealthily crossed the icy Delaware River and launched an attack on Hessian **garrisons**, or station posts, at Trenton. Early the following morning, they converged on the town. In only an hour and a half, the Continental Army took the city, killing 22 Hessians and capturing another 918 at the **Battle of**

Revolutionary Battles, 1775–1777

Trenton. The Americans only suffered two dead and five wounded. Encouraged by this victory, more men stayed on and continued fighting the British.

A few days after their defeat at Trenton, Cornwallis and his troops returned to the city, hoping to win it back. On the night of January 2, 1777, Washington instructed his men to light campfires before telling them to evacuate their camps. His deception fooled the British into believing that the Continental Army had not moved during the night. The next morning, Washington launched a surprise attack, inflicting heavy losses on three British regiments at Princeton, a town about 13 miles from Trenton. Howe called most of his remaining troops to New Brunswick, Canada, and British hopes for a speedy end to the war disappeared.

DEFEAT AT PHILADELPHIA

In the spring of 1777, British generals William Howe and **John Burgoyne**, in addition to Lieutenant Colonel **Barry St. Leger**, coordinated a new plan involving three armies. Burgoyne would march from Canada, St. Leger from western New York, and Howe from New York City to take control of the Hudson River Valley. They would join forces at Albany.

Burgoyne and St. Leger and their armies made their way from Canada and waited for Howe's arrival to attack Saratoga. However, Howe had changed his plan. He had decided it would be a good time to attack Philadelphia, the capital city of the new, rebellious nation. He thought the attack would send a strong message to the Americans about the futility of continuing the war. Capturing Philadelphia would also give Britain the advantage of controlling both major shipping and overland supply routes in North America. Because the three men were communicating by letter through their superiors in Britain, the men did not know each other's whereabouts.

In August, General Howe and his brother, Admiral Richard Howe, sailed with 13,000 troops from New York to the Chesapeake Bay. From there, they marched toward Philadelphia. As Washington

tried and failed to block the British advance, the Continental Congress fled the capital. Although Washington's soldiers mounted an attack on British-held Germantown on October 4, the British defeated them. Howe's army soon took control of Philadelphia and Germantown. Over the next month and a half, British forces captured key forts along the Delaware River, allowing Howe to establish supply lines and enabling him to control the entire region. Washington retreated, settling his troops into winter quarters, 20 miles northwest of Germantown.

HISTORICAL THINKING

1. **READING CHECK** What steps did Washington take to form and strengthen the Continental Army?

2. **INTERPRET VISUALS** About how many brigades were in the Continental Army?

3. **COMPARE AND CONTRAST** How were the advantages and disadvantages of the Continental Army different from those of the British military?

4. **INTERPRET MAPS** How many battles did the Americans win between 1775 and 1777?

General Washington (center left, standing) surveys the opposite shore in Emanuel Leutze's 1851 oil painting *Washington Crossing the Delaware*. On December 25, 1776, Washington and his army crossed the river on their way to attack Hessian troops in Trenton, New Jersey.

BUILD BACKGROUND

CANADIAN LOYALTY TO BRITAIN

As the 13 colonies asserted their independence, 7 North American territories in the province of Canada remained loyal to Britain. Throughout the war, American revolutionaries attempted to entice—and even force—their northern neighbors to join their cause. Both the First and Second Continental Congress made overtures to the Canadians, and the Continental Army planned and attempted multiple invasions of Quebec. In 1775, American forces led by Benedict Arnold marched toward the city, but a blizzard helped defeat them. In 1779, another expedition to St. Johns was recalled. The Articles of Confederation, ratified in 1781, included an invitation for Canada to join the Americans. However, both geography and culture ultimately prevented Canada from taking part in the American Revolution, as the mostly French-speaking Catholic population had little incentive to join their English-speaking, mostly Protestant neighbors.

WASHINGTON CROSSING THE DELAWARE

The iconic painting *Washington Crossing the Delaware* was completed by Emanuel Leutze 75 years after the event. Given the gap between the event and the painting, it's not surprising that the work contains several historical inaccuracies. For example, the flag depicted did not actually exist in 1775, the style of boat is incorrect, and Washington appears older than 44 years, his age at the time. Additionally, Washington certainly would not have been standing during the journey since such an action might have capsized the shallow craft. Leutze did not intend the work to be a literal documentation of the event. Instead, he hoped the painting would inspire similar calls for freedom in other nations across mid-19th century Europe.

TEACH

GUIDED DISCUSSION

4. Analyze Cause and Effect What was the significance of the American victory at Trenton and its aftermath? *(Possible response: Victory at Trenton provided a much-needed morale boost for Americans, causing many soldiers to remain in the army. Washington's surprise attack on General Cornwallis's returning troops a week later demonstrated to the British that they were up against brilliant leadership and a committed army that was resolved to win independence.)*

5. Summarize What symbolic and strategic goals did General Howe achieve when he captured Philadelphia? *(Possible response: By capturing the capital, he sent a strong signal about British military power to the Americans. With Philadelphia as a base, he was also able to capture Germantown and surrounding forts and gain control of major overland and shipping supply lines, which put the Continental Army at a serious disadvantage.)*

INTEGRATE VISUALS

Direct students' attention to the Revolutionary Battles map. Then ask them to recall the characteristics of the British military as discussed in the lesson. **ASK:** How does this map illustrate both the advantages and disadvantages of the British military? *(Advantages: The British Navy controlled sea routes and riverways from New Jersey to Chesapeake Bay, and therefore coastal shipping. British forces occupied areas to the north and south of American forces, largely located in New York and Massachusetts. Disadvantages: It was costly to bring supplies across the Atlantic and difficult to maintain supply lines to British units as far apart as Quebec and Chesapeake Bay.)*

ACTIVE OPTIONS

On Your Feet: Write a Feature Article Organize students into small groups and tell them to imagine they are wartime journalists working on a feature article. Their assignment is to report on one or more of the decisions made by George Washington as presented in the lesson. Assign half of the groups to write from a Loyalist point of view and the other half from a Patriot point of view. Encourage groups to begin their article with an attention-grabbing headline. Suggest that group members work together to outline their article before they begin writing. Invite groups to compile their completed articles into a magazine and print copies for the class or post it on a class website.

NG Learning Framework: Conduct a Military Preview Panel

SKILLS Communication, Collaboration

KNOWLEDGE Our Human Story

Arrange students in small groups to research, write, and present a panel analyzing the British and Americans as combatants before their major engagements. They can base their presentation on a "pregame show" format as they preview the upcoming conflicts. Tell students to include analysis of the strengths and weaknesses of each side, debates among panel members about the main issues of the conflict, evaluations of major leaders, and predictions for who will be victorious. If possible, direct groups to record and post their panel presentation for the class to view.

HISTORICAL THINKING

ANSWERS

1. Washington created a structure that included divisions, brigades, regiments, and companies; he had officers provide training and establish discipline among the troops; he united the troops both by bringing together state militias and regular forces under commanders from their own regions and by working with Congress to institute long terms of service for troops, organizing them into regiments of men from different regions to represent the diverse nation.

2. There were 18 brigades: 6 brigades to a division × 3 divisions = 18 brigades.

3. The American advantages stemmed from their knowledge of the terrain, their use of unconventional tactics, and their strong commitment to creating an independent nation. Their disadvantages involved the varying size, ability, and condition of their army. The British had a large, well-trained, and well-funded army but did not know the territory. They were fighting far from home against an enemy that often used guerrilla tactics, and they did not have a strong ideological commitment to the war.

4. The map shows six American victories.

MAIN IDEA As the war spread, the Continental Army and Navy celebrated decisive victories and faced terrible hardships. Meanwhile, the Second Continental Congress had to figure out how to pay for it all.

SARATOGA AND VALLEY FORGE

Keeping an opponent guessing about your next move can be a winning strategy. Both the British and the Americans used this tactic, but the Americans had to learn quickly how best to employ the element of surprise as they fought a much larger and better-equipped enemy.

CRITICAL THINKING General John Burgoyne (center left, in red) surrenders to General Horatio Gates (center, in blue) after the Battle of Saratoga. Painter John Trumbull used elements of composition in his 1821 painting *Surrender of General Burgoyne* to portray the transaction as peaceful. What details do you notice in the painting that indicate this?

AMERICAN VICTORY AT SARATOGA

As you have read, while the Howe brothers were on their way to attack Philadelphia, British general John Burgoyne was in Canada, preparing his march southward to gain control of the Hudson River Valley and overtake Albany, New York. He began his march with about 8,500 British, Hessian, and Canadian soldiers and almost 1,000 Native American warriors. Burgoyne might not have known that when General William Howe set sail to capture Philadelphia, he took most of his men with him, leaving a much smaller unit behind in New York City. Howe had no intention of leaving Philadelphia for Albany, so his decision left Burgoyne without the reinforcements he expected. And Burgoyne made some mistakes of his own.

At first, the plan to converge on Albany seemed to be working. Sailing southward on Lake Champlain, Burgoyne's forces easily recaptured Fort Ticonderoga in early July 1777. Greatly outnumbered by the British, the Continental soldiers abandoned the fort under cover of darkness and retreated south to the Hudson River.

After that victory, however, Burgoyne's progress slowed considerably. First, he had overloaded his troops with a mix of necessities and luxuries—along with heavy supplies and artillery. Soldiers also dragged cartloads of Burgoyne's personal possessions. Second, the rough terrain stalled the British as they marched on wilderness trails through marshes, ravines, and creeks swollen from rain. And finally, the Continental forces used guerrilla tactics to impede Burgoyne. They destroyed bridges, cut down trees and used them to block the path, and dug trenches to flood trails. British progress was reduced to one mile a day.

As Burgoyne was struggling to move south, St. Leger and his troops were advancing on Albany from the west. But St. Leger and a large group of Mohawk became involved in a 21-day siege at Fort Stanwix in the Mohawk Valley on their way to meet Burgoyne. When St. Leger learned that a substantial number of Continental reinforcements were marching toward the fort, he pulled his men out and headed north to Canada. Now, both St. Leger and Howe had abandoned the plan to capture the Hudson River Valley. Unaware that he was the only one still headed there, Burgoyne marched to Albany.

Meanwhile, forces of the Continental Army under the command of General **Horatio Gates** gathered along the Hudson River near Saratoga. With the help of Polish military engineer Tadeusz Kościuszko (tah-DAY-oosh kos-CHOOS-koh), the Continental troops had built fortified walls along Bemis Heights, overlooking the Hudson River and the nearby road, so they could see the British coming and fire on them. On September 19, 1777, the Americans and the British clashed at what is now called the First Battle of Saratoga, or the Battle of Freeman's Farm. Burgoyne's soldiers failed to cross Gates's lines. On October 7, Burgoyne attempted another attack, but General Benedict Arnold's unit drove the British back to their camp. This was the Second Battle of Saratoga.

By October 17, with the arrival of yet more Continental soldiers, Gates's forces numbered 20,000 or more. That was almost four times the strength of Burgoyne's army. Burgoyne sent out a desperate but futile call for reinforcements. The Americans surrounded him and cut his supply lines, forcing him to surrender. Upon learning about Burgoyne's defeat at Saratoga, both General Howe and Admiral Howe resigned. In 1778, General Henry Clinton took command of the British forces in North America.

The victory at Saratoga was a vital turning point in the American Revolution. In showing that they could defeat a large, professional army, the Americans impressed the French government. Despite having secretly sent money and military supplies to the Americans since 1776, France had yet to declare an official alliance. Finally convinced that the Americans could win the war, the French government negotiated in Paris with Benjamin Franklin. They signed a treaty in 1778 making the alliance official. Now the Americans had the backing of a wealthy nation with a large navy.

VALLEY FORGE

Meanwhile, after his defeat in Philadelphia, George Washington set up winter camp at **Valley Forge**. Valley Forge sat on a plateau above a series of hills in a forested area, which formed a natural protective barrier around the camp. About 11,000 men and 500 women and children lived there in wooden huts built by the men, but the winter of 1777–1778 was brutally harsh. Everyone suffered without enough clothing, blankets, or food. Washington remained at Valley Forge to share his troops' hardships, although he lived in a stone house and enjoyed somewhat better living conditions.

Despite the weather, the soldiers spent the winter training. In February 1778, **Friedrich von Steuben** (FREE-drihk von STOO-buhn), a former Prussian Army officer and expert in military tactics, arrived at Valley Forge. He instructed the Continental Army on how to care for their weapons, use the bayonet, march in drill formations, and plan their movements in the field, emphasizing the importance of taking care of their fellow soldiers. Von Steuben's training prepared the Continental Army to fight the British on equal terms. Unfortunately, the bitterly cold winter cost the lives of approximately 2,500 men in Washington's troop.

PLAN: 4-PAGE LESSON

OBJECTIVE

Analyze military successes and setbacks and financial problems of the new nation.

CRITICAL THINKING SKILLS FOR LESSON 3.2

- Analyze Language Use
- Determine Chronology
- Make Predictions
- Evaluate
- Analyze Environmental Concepts
- Ask and Answer Questions
- Make Inferences
- Identify Problems and Solutions
- Analyze Cause and Effect

HISTORICAL THINKING FOR CHAPTER 4

How did the colonists' emerging American identity lead to revolution? Following setbacks in New York and Philadelphia, the Continental Army won a major victory, but the outcome of the war remained in doubt. Lesson 3.2 describes the Americans' progress and problems as the war continued.

BACKGROUND FOR THE TEACHER

Ragtag Americans using guerrilla tactics against the powerful British is a popular image, but in reality, most of the fighting was done the traditional way. The two opponents—arranged in two straight lines, three rows deep—fired at one another while slowly marching forward. The reason for this seemingly absurd tactic was twofold. First, American tacticians had learned it from the British, and, second, the firearms were usually inaccurate. A tight formation allowed troops to fire volleys and launch hails of bullets, some of which would strike their targets.

FINANCIAL LITERACY

To extend their knowledge and understanding about the concepts in this lesson, refer students to the Financial Literacy handbook.

HISTORY NOTEBOOK

Encourage students to complete the American Gallery page for Chapter 4 in their History Notebooks as they read.

INTRODUCE & ENGAGE

PREDICT TURNING POINTS

Ask students to recall the fortunes of the Continental Army at the end of the previous lesson. Then review the advantages the British held over the Americans. Prompt a discussion using the following question: Considering that the Americans will ultimately achieve independence, what do you think will have to change for them to become victorious? Then inform students that Lesson 3.2 will look at two factors that helped turn the tide for the colonies: a resounding military victory and an important foreign alliance.

TEACH

GUIDED DISCUSSION

1. **Evaluate** What was the primary cause of John Burgoyne's defeat at Saratoga? *(Possible response: Burgoyne's defeat was caused by a lack of communication. He didn't know that Barry St. Leger and William Howe had decided not to march on Albany. Because of this, the Continentals had time to gather near Saratoga and gained the advantage in numbers and position. If Burgoyne had known he was advancing alone, he might have altered his plans.)*

2. **Analyze Environmental Concepts** How did geographic factors influence General Washington's decision to camp at Valley Forge? *(Washington chose the site because its higher ground and surrounding forest provided natural protection.)*

3. **Ask and Answer Questions** Imagine that you are able to interview one of the soldiers camped at Valley Forge. What questions would you ask, and how do you think they might respond? *(Answers will vary. Students might demonstrate their understanding of the conditions soldiers faced by asking why some of them stayed with Washington and the army throughout the winter, how they managed to survive the harsh winter, where supplies came from, and what they learned from their training.)*

MORE INFORMATION

The French Alliance Inform students that France's decision to formally back the colonies was made after years of negotiations involving American ambassador Benjamin Franklin and that the decision was a difficult one for France. The king and his court had to weigh the domestic and international consequences that would follow, whether the new nation won or lost. As an extension activity, allow students to work in pairs to research the diplomacy involved between Franklin and the French during the war. Encourage them to use a Decision Matrix to analyze the situation from France's point of view and decide whether it would be good for France to support the Americans' war for independence.

Should the French form an alliance with the Americans?	
Pros	Cons
Decision	

DIFFERENTIATE

STRIVING READERS

Recall and Record Facts After students have read the lesson, set a short time limit and tell them to write a list of facts they recall. Encourage them to group facts under the four subsection headings. Then direct them to work in pairs to compare and combine their lists. After pairs combine their lists, ask them to take turns reading facts aloud until all pairs run out of facts. Have students discuss facts they missed and add them to their lists.

PRE-AP

Analyze the Success of the Continental Army Tell students to conduct preliminary research to learn more about Polish military engineer Tadeusz Kościuszko, Prussian officer Friedrich von Steuben, or one of the French foreign officials with whom Benjamin Franklin negotiated an alliance. Instruct students to choose one person to investigate in detail and write an essay that analyzes that person's impact on the Continental Army's successes. Encourage them to use a graphic organizer, such as the one below, to keep track of their research. Invite students to post their essays on a class website or blog.

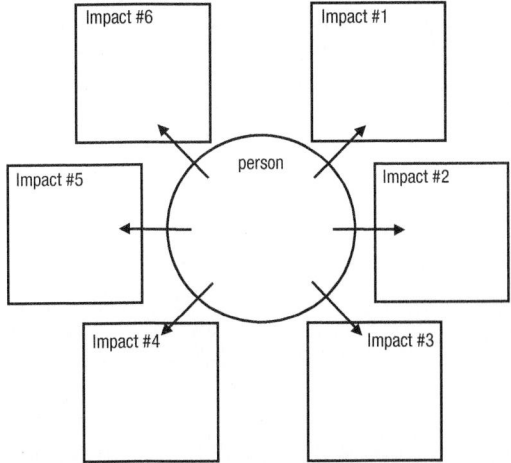

See the Chapter Planner for more strategies for differentiation.

CRITICAL VIEWING General Gates, in the center, holds both arms wide with his hands open, as if offering friendship to the surrendering British. The scene is peaceful, as few rifles are shown, and the other men are likely officers, depicted as relaxed and informally gathered, wearing no helmets or hats and leaning on the cannon or their swords. Light breaks through the dark clouds in the background, suggesting that the way to victory is clearing for the Americans.

During the hard winter of 1777, soldiers lived in log cabins similar to this reconstructed cabin at Valley Forge National Historic Park.

This lightweight cot was probably where Washington slept during his stay at Valley Forge. It is 6.5 feet in length, long enough for Washington's 6-foot frame.

WAR AT SEA

The soldiers in the Continental Army were discovering that they could defend themselves and defeat their enemy by using the terrain and the element of surprise to their advantage. But the new Continental Navy, officially established by the Congress in 1775, had fewer advantages. It lacked both funding and time to build more ships. The lack of money made hiring and adequately training sailors to fight Britain's vastly superior Royal Navy difficult. From the earliest days of the war, the need for American sailors to defend themselves against the British Navy had been great. The British seized or harassed American merchant ships and routinely blockaded harbors up and down the coast.

By 1777, the Continental Navy had about 18 ships. The Royal Navy boasted almost 260. Looking for a strategy to overcome their naval disadvantage, the Americans relied on a common maritime practice known as *guerre de course*, or "war of the chase," which allowed private ships to attack the merchant ships of an enemy power. The American government hired these **privateers**, or privately owned ships authorized to participate in war. The Continental Navy deployed privateers, often in pairs or with naval ships, to capture British equipment and supplies if possible, and to disrupt and delay British shipping in the Atlantic and around the Caribbean.

When Benjamin Franklin secured the help of France and Spain, two powerful navies joined the Continental Navy in battles. The United States' formal alliance with France also gave the Americans access to French ports. Now American ships could sail farther from home waters, even into the North Sea near Great Britain.

American captain **John Paul Jones**, commander of the merchant ship *Bonhomme Richard*, pursued British merchant vessels being escorted by the Royal Navy. In 1779, Jones intercepted the larger British ship H.M.S. *Serapis*. Early in the fighting, two of the *Bonhomme Richard's* cannons exploded. The ship caught fire, but the battle continued with the ships literally locked side by side in combat. According to legend, when the British captain demanded the Americans surrender, Jones replied, "I have not yet begun to fight." The British finally surrendered. By this time, the *Bonhomme Richard* was almost destroyed and sinking, so Jones and his crew boarded the *Serapis*. This was one of the most notable naval victories of the American Revolution. It boosted the morale of soldiers and civilians as the conflict moved into its final stage.

PAYING FOR WAR

You might be wondering why the Second Continental Congress didn't fund the Continental Navy. The short answer is because it couldn't. The Congress had very little money and no authority to raise it. Remember, the Articles of Confederation prohibited the Congress from taxing individual states. The country was too new to have a treasury or to borrow money on credit. So, to help pay for the navy, the army, and the war in general, the Congress began printing a new paper currency called "Continental" dollars, even though the government had no real wealth, such as stores of gold or silver, to back it up. At the beginning of June 1775, about $2 million Continental dollars were printed, but as the war dragged on, the Congress printed more money to cover its expenses. This led to rapid **inflation**, a rise in the price of goods and services that causes a decrease in the value of money.

By 1781, it took $146 to buy an item that had cost a dollar before the war. Washington even commented that "a wagon load of money will scarcely purchase a wagon load of provision." Merchants began to reject the currency. People came to view Continental currency as worthless.

Making matters worse, goods were hard to come by. For most of the war, the British controlled major ports, such as New York City and Philadelphia, negatively affecting American trade. Some merchants who supplied goods to the Continental Army participated in **profiteering**, or charging high prices for items in high demand and short supply to make a quick fortune.

Although the French, Dutch, and Spanish had granted the Americans several large loans, these funds were not enough to cover all the costs of war. To help stabilize the financial situation, the Congress turned to **Robert Morris** of Pennsylvania. As a former finance superintendent, Morris had helped the state reform its currency. The Congress hoped he could do the same for the nation. Morris chartered the First Bank of North America, which had the sole right to issue paper currency. Together with **Haym Salomon**, an American Jewish **financier**, or money broker, Morris funded the new bank with his own money, Salomon's, and some of the funds borrowed from the French. Among many Americans who loaned money to help pay the costs of the Revolution, Salomon was noted for extending large interest-free loans to the government. Never repaid for his generosity, Salomon died penniless in 1785. His and Morris's efforts helped to slow the rate of inflation and allowed Washington to continue the fight.

HISTORICAL THINKING

1. **READING CHECK** How did both an informal and formal alliance with France affect the Congress's ability to pay for the war?

2. **ANALYZE LANGUAGE USE** What did Washington mean when he stated that "a wagon load of money will scarcely purchase a wagon load of provision"?

3. **DETERMINE CHRONOLOGY** While Burgoyne's troops marched south toward the Hudson River Valley, what were the other participants in the plan to capture Albany doing?

4. **MAKE PREDICTIONS** As France enters the Revolutionary War, how might the strategies of the Continental Army and British forces change?

BUILD BACKGROUND

AMERICAN PRIVATEERS

During the American Revolution, over 2,000 privateers fought on the American side—an alliance critical to the Americans' ultimate success. Privateers seized and plundered hundreds of British ships in American waters, the North Atlantic, and the West Indies, causing the price of goods to skyrocket in England. The job was risky since captured privateers were treated harshly by the British, denied the typical rights of prisoners, and often held without trial. But the job could also be richly rewarding. After one raid, a 14-year-old New Hampshire privateer came away with a ton of sugar, 40 gallons of rum, and $100 in gold. Many other privateers became wealthy men. However, many on both sides in the conflict regarded privateers with contempt. George Washington said of these men, "I do believe there is not on earth a more disorderly set," while British newspapers denounced them as nothing more than "pyrates."

WARTIME ECONOMY

The American economy during the war years was weakened by too much paper money and inflation. Even before the war, individual colonies were printing their own currencies to hire soldiers and purchase supplies. With so many currencies floating around, determining their comparative values was difficult, if not impossible. The fledgling Continental currency was also in circulation but subject to rampant inflation because of overprinting and outright sabotage from the British, who conducted massive counterfeiting operations to undermine its value. As a result, merchants avoided paper currency at all costs and instead demanded hard currency in the form of domestic and foreign coins, usually from Spain or Portugal. If no coins were available, people used a barter system in which they paid for transactions by exchanging goods and services in the form of agricultural products, crafts, or labor.

TEACH

GUIDED DISCUSSION

4. Make Inferences Why might the Dutch, French, and Spanish have been willing to lend money to the Americans and give them military support in the war? *(Possible response: All three nations were competing with Great Britain for land, wealth, and influence around the world, so they were probably eager to help weaken the British empire in any way they could.)*

5. Identify Problems and Solutions What problem was Robert Morris given to solve, and how did he attempt to solve it? *(There was too much financial instability in the nation, which made it difficult to fund the war. Morris tackled this instability by chartering a single national bank, and only this bank could issue paper currency. As a result, Morris helped to stabilize the economy and fund the war.)*

ANALYZE CAUSE AND EFFECT

Share with students the Wartime Economy information under Build Background. Then tell them to reread the subsection Paying for War. Ask students to use the information in these sources to analyze the effects of the war effort so far on the American economy. To record the causes and effects they find, provide them with a Cause-Effect Organizer, such as the one shown below. Remind students that one cause might have more than one effect.

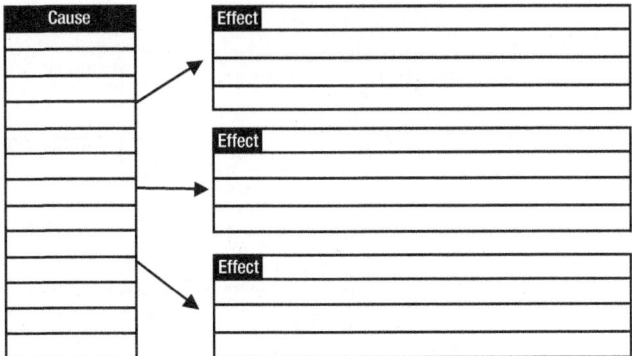

ACTIVE OPTIONS

 **Valley Forge** Invite students to explore the American Gallery. Have them select one of the items and do additional research to learn more about it. Ask questions that will inspire additional inquiry about the chosen gallery item, such as: Who created this and why? What does it tell about the people or event portrayed? What is the historic importance of this item?

NG Learning Framework: Craft a Motivational Speech from George Washington

ATTITUDE Empowerment

SKILLS Communication, Collaboration

Divide the class into small groups. Tell students to imagine they are aides to General Washington during the winter of 1777–1778 and are tasked with drafting a speech that the general will deliver to the soldiers to motivate them to stay with the revolutionary cause. Encourage groups to briefly research techniques used by motivational speakers and use a few to help them with their writing. Direct students to consider factors such as the importance of the soldiers' role in winning independence, Washington's personal qualities, the conditions of both armies, and the role of soldiers in the new nation. Tell students to work together to draft, revise, and refine their speeches and to select one group member to deliver the speech to the class. Invite students to provide constructive feedback about how well the speech might have motivated Washington's men.

HISTORICAL THINKING

ANSWERS

1. Before an alliance became official, France helped the new nation with secret economic and military assistance. Later, after signing an alliance with France in 1778, French loans were used to help fund the First Bank of North America.

2. Washington was commenting on the impact of rampant wartime inflation in which more and more printed currency bought fewer and fewer goods.

3. As Burgoyne's troops were making their way toward the Hudson River Valley, William Howe decided to focus on Philadelphia instead of heading north from New York City. Meanwhile, St. Leger and his forces, marching in from the west, became involved in the siege of a fort along the way and decided to retreat when faced with a larger force.

4. Possible response: With the French Navy entering the war, Washington might go on the offensive to take back key British strongholds along the coast. The British, on the other hand, might call back troops and ships from other areas to reinforce their coastal strongholds in preparation for naval attacks.

WOMEN'S ROLES IN THE REVOLUTION

Colonial women did not have the same rights as men, but they shared the responsibilities, hopes, and dangers of Revolutionary times. And most of the women resolved to make a difference in the fight for the nation's independence.

BEFORE THE REVOLUTION

As the possibility of war grew and debates raged, many women worked to build support for independence. You have read how the Sons of Liberty organized boycotts against the British, but it was the **Daughters of Liberty** who assured the success of the boycotts. They knew that women generally purchased the household goods, and they urged their friends and neighbors to participate. One of these women was **Sarah Morris Mifflin**. Born in Philadelphia to a prominent Quaker family, she was moved to action after the violent clashes at Lexington and Concord. Although she was wealthy, she joined others in refusing to purchase luxury items and textiles from Britain. To avoid buying British thread, Mifflin and many other women began spinning their own sewing thread and weaving their own cloth.

Other Daughters of Liberty, such as Mercy Otis Warren and **Abigail Adams**, wrote letters and articles supporting the cause of independence. Warren also wrote a series of satirical political plays that emphasized how the colonists' liberties were under attack not only by Parliament but also by corrupt royal officials within the colonies. She criticized Massachusetts governor Hutchinson for carrying out British policies and praised those who participated in the Boston Tea Party. Warren also published political pamphlets and articles in local newspapers in support of boycotts and other protests. She even urged women to be ready to take up arms. Her efforts prompted John Adams to call her the "most accomplished woman in America."

John Adams's wife, Abigail Adams, was a brilliant thinker in her own right. She influenced many Revolutionary leaders with her skillful writing about liberty, independence, and fair government. In letters to her husband, she also advocated for women's rights.

DURING THE REVOLUTION

Once the war began, women's roles increased in intensity and in range of activity. To provide for themselves, their children, and other relatives while the men were at war, women stepped in to run their husbands' businesses, which ranged from blacksmithing to publishing. On the farm, women took over the entire agricultural operation.

To aid the Continental Army, women formed public fundraising organizations. In Philadelphia, **Esther Reed**, the wife of Joseph Reed, a member of Philadelphia's Committee of Correspondence, published a **broadside**, or a single sheet of printed information, called "The Sentiments of an American Woman." It called on other women to show their patriotism by supporting activities that assisted the troops. As the wife of a high-ranking member of the Continental Army, she was well aware of equipment and clothing shortages, as well as the fact that many soldiers had not received the pay promised them. Canvassing the city, Reed's group gathered donations totaling more than $300,000 in paper currency. Similar women's organizations arose throughout the middle states.

The care of sick and wounded soldiers fell to women, both on and off the battlefield. In the summer of 1775, the Congress authorized the Continental Army to hire one nurse, at a monthly salary of $2, for every 10 soldiers needing care in a military hospital. Other women, such as Catherine Greene of Rhode Island, freely opened their homes as makeshift hospitals. In army camps and near battlefields, women often cooked meals and washed clothes.

Some women engaged in **espionage**, or spying, while others fought on the battlefield. As a member of a spy ring, **Anna Smith Strong** collected intelligence on British troop and ship movements along the coast of New York. Strong notified other spies of the information she had gathered through a code based on how she hung out her laundry. For example, a black petticoat on her clothesline meant a messenger was coming. Some female camp aides, known as Molly Pitchers because they brought water to the battlefield for the soldiers and to cool the cannons, are the subjects of Revolutionary legends. Famous Molly Pitchers **Margaret Corbin** and **Mary Ludwig Hays McCauly** are both said to have taken over firing artillery in the place of their wounded husbands.

Portrait of Abigail Adams, 1785

Sixteen-year-old **Sybil Ludington** rode 40 miles on horseback to warn her father's militia and villagers along her route that British troops were approaching. **Deborah Sampson** disguised herself as a man and joined the Fourth Massachusetts Regiment. She participated in multiple battles before she became ill and was relieved of service. She managed to keep her gender a secret until her illness required medical care. Even so, Sampson received an honorable discharge and became the only woman to receive a service pension from the Continental Army.

On a daily basis, colonial women helped the fight for independence and were a major influence in building the new nation. And, while their contributions to the war effort did not bring equal rights to women immediately, they expanded women's roles in society, laying the groundwork for women's rights campaigns a century later.

HISTORICAL THINKING

1. **READING CHECK** How did women build support for war efforts before the Revolution?

2. **DRAW CONCLUSIONS** How does Abigail Adams's letter to her husband signify that the war had sparked a movement among women?

3. **FORM AND SUPPORT OPINIONS** Which women's role discussed in this lesson do you think was most significant to the war effort? Cite evidence from the text to support your opinion.

PRIMARY SOURCES

I have retrenched every superfluous expense in my table and family. Tea I have not drank since last Christmas, nor bought a new cap or gown . . . and what I never did before, have learned to knit, and am now making stockings of wool for my servants; and this way do I throw in my might for the public good. I know this, that as free I can die but once; but as a slave I shall not be worthy of life. I have the pleasure to assure you that these are the sentiments of my sister Americans. They have sacrificed assemblies, parties of pleasure, tea-drinkings and finery, to that great spirit of patriotism which actuates all degrees of people throughout this extensive country.

—from a letter written by Sarah Morris Mifflin to a friend, 1776

I long to hear that you have declared an independency—and by the way in the new Code of Laws which I suppose it will be necessary for you to make I desire you would Remember the Ladies, and be more generous and [favorable] to them than your ancestors. Do not put such unlimited power into the hands of the Husbands. Remember all Men would be tyrants if they could. If [particular] care and attention is not paid to the Ladies we are determined to foment a [Rebellion], and will not hold ourselves bound by any Laws in which we have no voice, or Representation.

—from a letter written by Abigail Adams to her husband, 1776

PLAN: 2-PAGE LESSON

OBJECTIVE

Examine the roles and contributions of women during the American Revolution.

CRITICAL THINKING SKILLS FOR LESSON 3.3

• Draw Conclusions

• Form and Support Opinions

• Compare and Contrast

• Make Predictions

• Analyze Primary Sources

HISTORICAL THINKING FOR CHAPTER 4

How did the colonists' emerging American identity lead to revolution? The American Revolution was aided by and helped to create the emerging identity of American women. Lesson 3.3 explains how women engaged in civil disobedience, persuasion, medical work, and military operations in various roles as Patriots aiming to win independence from Britain.

BACKGROUND FOR THE TEACHER

Ironically, one of the colonists' grievances against the British—quartering their troops in colonial residences—proved to be a boon to American espionage efforts. When the British occupied Philadelphia, several high-ranking British officers lodged in the home of Lydia Barrington Darragh, a Quaker woman from Pennsylvania. When the officers held meetings—at times with General William Howe in attendance—Darragh secretly gathered intelligence as she brought refreshments or wood for the fire. She then wrote down the information, using a special shorthand, and hid it under the buttons of her son John's coat. The messages were then brought to another son, Charles, who served under George Washington. During one meeting in December 1777, Darragh hid in a closet and heard the officers planning a sneak attack against Patriot troops. That night, she personally brought the information to Continental soldiers, allowing them to prepare and stave off the British.

INTRODUCE & ENGAGE

BRAINSTORM WOMEN'S ROLES

Direct students to recount what they have read about the tactics used by exclusively male groups like the Sons of Liberty and men such as Thomas Paine to push for independence. Discuss with students what they recall about the status of women in the colonies. Then ask students to brainstorm a list of roles they think women might have played before and during the American Revolution. Tell them that this lesson describes some of the surprising roles women assumed as Patriots fighting for independence.

For students who develop an interest in what life was like for many during the late 18th century, suggest they read the online American Story "Daily Life During the Revolution."

TEACH

GUIDED DISCUSSION

1. **Compare and Contrast** How did the actions of the Daughters of Liberty differ from those of the Sons of Liberty? *(The Sons of Liberty focused on political organizing, drawing up foundation documents for the new country, and open acts of rebellion. The Daughters of Liberty engaged in actions such as boycotts, giving up imported British luxuries and making their own items. Barred from participating in government, women shared ideas in letters and broadsides rather than official documents.)*

2. **Make Predictions** Do you think women's participation in the American Revolution will improve their social standing after the war? *(Answers will vary. Possible responses: No. Women will likely remain in the subordinate roles they held prior to the war because legal and cultural standards will not change. Yes. Women will likely demand and achieve greater civic participation and education as a result of helping to win independence.)*

ANALYZE PRIMARY SOURCES

Direct student's attention to the Primary Source feature. Ask students to work in pairs to determine the main ideas and supporting details in the excerpts of the letters. Encourage students to use a graphic organizer, such as the Main-Idea and Details Chart shown, to organize their findings. Take time to clarify potentially confusing expressions or words—such as Mifflin's use of the term *slave*—so students clearly understand the main ideas. Then guide a discussion in which students compare and contrast the main ideas that they identified in both letters.

Main Ideas	Details

ACTIVE OPTIONS

On Your Feet: Numbered Heads Share the Background for the Teacher information with the class, and then arrange students in small groups. Ask students to think about the following question: How were women's roles, domestic skills, and lower social status an advantage and a disadvantage in their work as Patriots? Then tell groups to discuss the topic for several minutes. Finally, call out a number, and the student with that number in each group summarizes the group's discussion.

NG Learning Framework: Create a Web Page   `STEM`

`ATTITUDES` Empowerment, Responsibility

`SKILLS` Communication, Collaboration

Arrange students in small groups to create a web page about the Daughters of Liberty or Esther Reed's group, Ladies' Association of Philadelphia. Instruct them to choose one of the organizations, conduct research, and use their findings to promote the organization's work, using features such as graphics, news reports, political blogs, or fund-raising appeals. Have groups upload their web page to the class or school website.

DIFFERENTIATE

STRIVING READERS

Use Context Clues Tell students to copy the sentences containing the vocabulary words *broadside* and *espionage* on a piece of paper. Then ask them to underline the context clue that provides the meaning of each word. Encourage students to identify context clues whenever they encounter an unfamiliar word.

GIFTED & TALENTED

Write a Dramatic Monologue Provide students with a copy of "The Sentiments of an American Woman." After they have read it, challenge them to write a dramatic monologue in Esther Reed's voice in which she explains why she felt compelled to write her broadside and why she feels women have a strong role to play in the American Revolution. Alternatively, ask students to craft a brief biography of Reed and explain how her broadside was received by the public in general and women in particular. Encourage students to perform their dramatic monologues or read their biographies to the class.

See the Chapter Planner for more strategies for differentiation.

HISTORICAL THINKING

ANSWERS

1. Some women organized boycotts of British goods and formed groups to manufacture replacement goods. Others wrote letters and other materials criticizing colonial leadership and Parliament and promoting the cause of independence.

2. Abigail Adams draws a parallel between the grievances of the colonists toward Britain—namely lack of power and representation—and the position of women, who are subordinate to men. She mentions the ladies' readiness to rebel if their rights are not recognized.

3. Responses will vary. Students' responses should support their opinion with specific examples and evidence from the text.

THE WAR MOVES SOUTH

As a commander in the Continental Army, news of the French entering the war might give you high hopes of a quick victory. But subsequent defeats and a shift in British strategy put the end of the war temporarily out of sight.

ASSISTANCE ARRIVES

As you've read, France had been helping the Continental Army informally by sending supplies, but the French monarchy decided to adopt a wait-and-see strategy before it formally committed to aid the new nation. However, this earlier lack of a formal alliance didn't stop individual French volunteers from joining the fight. One such volunteer was the **Marquis de Lafayette**, a young aristocrat who had served in the French royal court. He arrived in Philadelphia in July 1777. Lafayette initially served on Washington's staff before taking command of his own division. But he soon found himself back in France, assisting Benjamin Franklin and John Adams on a diplomatic mission to secure French supplies and troops for the Patriot cause. He would eventually return to lead troops in Virginia as the war moved south.

Since the French and Spanish were already allied against the British, both nations pitched in to help the American war effort, drawing Britain's military and naval attention in different directions. The French navy pulled British resources away from the mainland by luring the Royal Navy into sea battles in the West Indies. On the mainland itself, Spaniard **Bernardo de Gálvez** led Spanish troops to the Mississippi Valley to re-occupy forts formerly held by Spain. This forced Britain to divert soldiers to the region, pulling them away from the Continental Army. Then Gálvez turned his attention to Florida, where he helped defeat the British, claiming the territory for Spain.

The Marquis de Lafayette (below) was also known as the "Hero of Two Worlds" because of his leadership in both the Continental and French armies. Born into a distinguished military family, Lafayette joined the French army when he was only 14 years old.

AFRICAN-AMERICAN RECRUITS

Meanwhile, many northern states recruited free African Americans to fight in the war. Even though African Americans had fought on the Patriot side during the battles of Lexington, Concord, and Bunker Hill, George Washington initially denied men of color the right to enlist in the Continental Army. The British, on the other hand, welcomed African Americans and lured enslaved African Americans into their ranks by promising them freedom. But when the need for fresh Patriot troops became dire, Washington lifted the ban, allowing all free men to enlist.

The British strategy of offering freedom to enslaved African Americans in exchange for their military service sometimes backfired on them. **James Armistead**, an enslaved man living in Virginia, sought and received his owner's permission to enlist in the Continental Army. He came to serve under Lafayette as a spy. Posing as a runaway slave, he joined a nearby British regiment and gained its leaders' trust. The information he gathered and shared with Lafayette and Washington helped the Americans win individual battles as well as the war itself.

By 1778, a significant number of free African Americans were recruited for service, with slaves and servants occasionally being accepted as substitutes for white landowners. That year, the First Rhode Island Regiment reformed, allowing recently freed African Americans to join because the state was unable to fill its quota of troops. Eventually, recruiters accepted any African American who chose to serve, whether free or enslaved. In all, an estimated 5,000 African Americans served in the Continental Army, in state militias, or at sea.

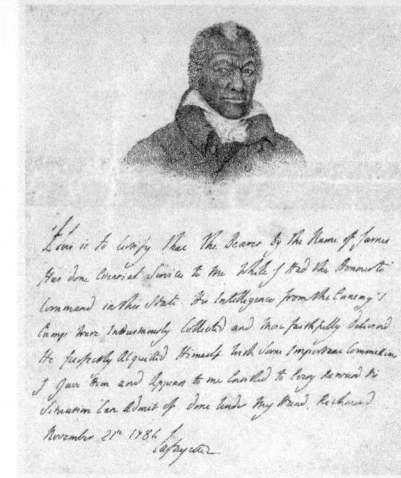

In this commendation letter dated November 1784, the Marquis de Lafayette writes of James Armistead, "His intelligences from the enemy's camp were industriously collected and faithfully delivered. He . . . appears to me entitled to every reward his situation can admit of." The illustration of Armistead at the top is by John Blennerhasset Martin.

THE FRONTIER WAR

From the beginning of the war, many Native American tribes formed alliances with the British because they had more weapons and supplies than the Patriots. The British also held more outposts in the frontier, so Native Americans often depended on them for trade. In addition, as many Americans began to settle west of the Appalachians, Native Americans saw them as a threat to their way of life. Soon, Native Americans launched devastating attacks on frontier settlements from the Great Lakes south to Georgia.

In early 1779, Virginia dispatched troops led by Lieutenant Colonel **George Rogers Clark** to deal with Native American attacks in the western backcountry. Clark's goal was to gain control of Fort Vincennes (also known as Fort Sackville), in present-day Indiana, from the British. By capturing the fort, he hoped to reduce British support for Native American raids on American settlements. Clark's surprise attack succeeded, and with the American victory at Vincennes, British domination in the frontier began to crumble. Once Native American tribes realized the British could no longer protect their interests, they began declaring neutrality. But although their frontier raids became less frequent, they did not end entirely.

Not all Native Americans on the frontier supported the British. The Catawba of South Carolina were a great help to the Patriots. They searched for Loyalists and escaped slaves who might aid the British and supplied food to the Patriots. After the war, the South Carolina assembly compensated them for their loyalty, refusing to support the governor's plan to claim and lease out their lands.

THE SOUTHERN CAMPAIGN

Despite the entry of the French forces into the Patriot cause, neither the Americans nor the British could claim a clear advantage in the war in the North. The two armies had reached a **stalemate**, or a tie, as they fought in New York in late 1778, so the British decided to take the war south. They knew that larger Loyalist populations existed in the South than in the North, and their strategy was to build strongholds of

---

PLAN: 4-PAGE LESSON

OBJECTIVE

Examine how American and British allies and the Southern Campaign affected the course of the American Revolution.

CRITICAL THINKING SKILLS FOR LESSON 4.1

- Draw Conclusions
- Interpret Maps
- Summarize
- Make Inferences
- Form and Support Opinions
- Analyze Language Use
- Evaluate
- Determine Word Meaning

HISTORICAL THINKING FOR CHAPTER 4

How did the colonists' emerging American identity lead to revolution? Key American allies and victories in the South were turning points in the war for independence. Lesson 4.1 discusses the contributions of the French, Native Americans, and African Americans and decisive successes in the southern states.

BACKGROUND FOR THE TEACHER

African-American participation in the American Revolution was not confined to the First Rhode Island Regiment. While that regiment was segregated, other African Americans served in integrated units, sometimes on the front lines but more often as cooks, wagon drivers, artisans, or manual laborers, such as ditch diggers. At sea, privateers serving the American cause often had African-American crewmembers. Even the southern states—who opposed arming African Americans—accepted them as seamen. Indeed, unlike the army, the navy didn't hesitate to recruit people of color. Although most African-American sailors performed menial tasks, some worked as skilled carpenters or ship pilots. Despite these contributions, after the war Congress passed laws making it illegal for African Americans to serve in the military. By the time pensions were offered to American Revolution veterans, most African Americans who served were no longer living.

INTRODUCE & ENGAGE

PREVIEW USING TEXT FEATURES

Guide students in using the lesson's introduction, subsection headings, and visuals to preview the lesson. **ASK:** Based on these features, what questions do you expect this lesson to answer? *(Answers will vary. Possible responses: What was the Frontier War? Who was the Swamp Fox? How did the movement of British forces affect the Continental Army? How and when did the French provide assistance? How did Southern patriots turn the tide of the war?)* Create and display a 5Ws Chart to categorize students' questions. Return to the chart at the end of the lesson and prompt students to provide explanations and answers. Urge students to research unanswered questions and report their findings to the class.

What?
Who?
Where?
When?
Why?

TEACH

GUIDED DISCUSSION

1. **Summarize** How did France and Spain help the Americans? *(Possible response: The Marquis de Lafayette helped the war effort by leading troops in Virginia as well as working in France with John Adams and Benjamin Franklin to gain aid for the war. The French Navy kept part of the Royal Navy occupied in the West Indies, and Bernardo de Gálvez and his Spanish troops diverted British forces to the Mississippi Valley and Florida, keeping the American forces from being overwhelmed by the British.)*

2. **Make Inferences** Why do you think George Washington initially opposed allowing African Americans to enlist in the Continental Army? *(Possible response: He may have considered the possibility that giving African Americans military training and providing them with weapons would encourage them to carry out armed revolts against slave owners.)*

3. **Form and Support Opinions** Do you think that all Native American tribes should have supported the Americans against Great Britain? *(Possible responses: Yes. They might have had their lands protected for a time after the war, like the Catawba did in South Carolina. No. Americans already threatened tribal lands west of the Appalachians and would eventually take even their allies' lands, so it made sense for Native Americans to fight against the side that posed the most immediate threat.)*

ANALYZE LANGUAGE USE

Direct students' attention to the commendation letter written by the Marquis de Lafayette and the accompanying text. **ASK:** How do the words used in the commendation hint that James Armistead was enslaved? *(The Marquis de Lafayette used the phrase "every reward his situation can admit of." This suggests that there are some rewards Armistead is not entitled to because he did not have the rights of a free man.)*

DIFFERENTIATE

STRIVING READERS

Use a Main-Idea Cluster Direct pairs of students to complete a Main-Idea Cluster for each subsection of the lesson. Tell partners to take turns reading paragraphs aloud and then work together to record the main idea and four details before moving on to the next subsection. Tell students to trade and compare their completed clusters, making revisions as necessary.

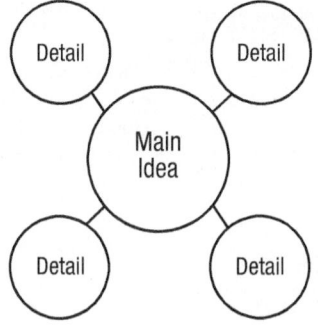

GIFTED & TALENTED

Write Journal Entries Instruct students to conduct research, using online and print sources, about James Armistead's activities as a double agent during the American Revolution. Tell them to use what they learn to write a series of journal entries from Armistead's point of view. Encourage students to include details about why Armistead agreed to serve the army of the country that enslaved him, how he gained the trust of British officers and was able to spy on them, how he conveyed intelligence to the Continental Army, and how that intelligence proved critical to American victories or successes. Encourage students to share their journal entries with the class or post them on a class website.

See the Chapter Planner for more strategies for differentiation.

This mural depicts General Francis Marion, the "Swamp Fox," and his men escaping British capture in a swamp in South Carolina in 1780. After seven hours of pursuit, the British gave up hope of finding them.

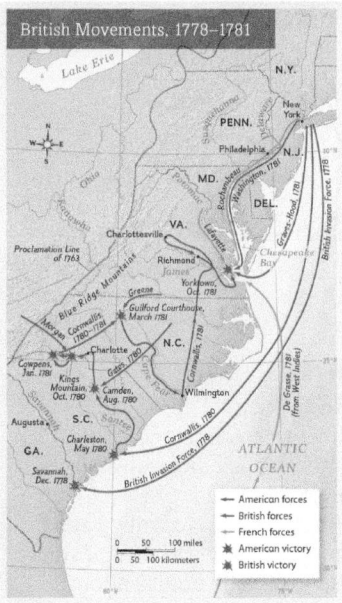

British Movements, 1778–1781

American forces
British forces
French forces
★ American victory
★ British victory

0   50   100 miles
0   50   100 kilometers

support throughout the region. In December 1778, British general Henry Clinton sent troops to Georgia and captured Savannah and Augusta.

In response, the Congress sent General Benjamin Lincoln, commander of the Southern Continental Army, to Charleston, South Carolina, to defend the city and organize a counteroffensive. The attempt, which took nearly a year to plan, resulted in a disastrous defeat for the Americans. By May 1780, the British had captured Charleston as well.

By July, desperate for a change in command, the Continental Army sent General Horatio Gates to build a new southern army. Less than a month later, the British soundly defeated Gates and his poorly prepared troops at Camden, South Carolina. By the end of August, Britain had gained control over much of South Carolina, and Clinton took part of his force back to New York. He left General Cornwallis in charge of about 8,000 soldiers. It seemed as if this strategy might just win the war for Britain, but once again, the British miscalculated. This time, they made the mistake of counting on a significant number of Loyalists to flock to their aid.

SOUTHERN PATRIOTS TURN THE TIDE

George Washington sent **Nathanael Greene**, one of his best generals, to take charge of American troops in the South. During 1780 and 1781, Greene rebuilt the army using both traditional soldiers and guerrilla forces called **irregulars**, or soldiers who joined the regular army for various periods of time. These smaller brigades of irregulars were led by Brigadier General **Thomas Sumter**, Colonel **Andrew Pickens**, and General **Francis Marion**. Marion had become famous as the "Swamp Fox" because of his ability to evade capture as he chased down the British through the swamps of Georgia and the Carolinas.

Together these officers and their troops cut British lines of communication and sabotaged local bands of Loyalists. A backcountry "civil war" erupted between Loyalists and Patriots that helped the Patriots regain control over parts of the Carolinas. This conflict also involved many African Americans who fought on both sides. On October 7, 1780, a Patriot militia defeated a large group of Loyalists at King's Mountain. This rare American victory sent the British retreating south and bolstered morale, but Britain still had the upper hand.

Two months later, General Greene arrived in North Carolina with a small force of only 1,500 men who lacked sufficient equipment and clothing. He decided their best chance was to force the British to split up and chase them through the Carolinas instead of engaging them in direct warfare. Greene split his small army into two groups. He led one, and General **Daniel Morgan** led the other. Cornwallis sent part of his force after Morgan's unit, confronting them at the **Battle of Cowpens**, in South Carolina, in January 1781. Morgan and his Continental troops decisively defeated Cornwallis. Meanwhile, in March 1781, a small force of British regulars caught up with Greene's unit at the **Guilford Courthouse** in North Carolina. Although historians give the victory to the British, it was hard-won. Cornwallis's troops suffered heavy casualties and retreated to the North Carolina coast seeking naval support.

Greene, now reunited with Daniel Morgan's troops, moved the Continental forces south to re-establish control of South Carolina and Georgia. Starting in April 1781, Greene's troops and the guerrilla brigades of Sumter, Pickens, and Marion fought two major battles in South Carolina. Although, like Guilford Courthouse, these were not American victories, they continued forcing the British to abandon their posts. One by one, Greene's soldiers picked off the remaining British garrisons, so that by September 1781, the British had retreated to a narrow strip of land near Charleston. Putting their hope in the southern Loyalists had failed. Now the British had to reconsider their strategy in the South.

HISTORICAL THINKING

1. **READING CHECK** Why did the British change their strategy at the end of 1778?

2. **DRAW CONCLUSIONS** Why was the battle at Guilford Courthouse a significant turning point in the war in the South?

3. **INTERPRET MAPS** How does the map demonstrate the strategy that General Greene and General Morgan used against British forces?

BUILD BACKGROUND

SOUTHERN LOYALISTS

Southerners' loyalty to the Crown was based on a variety of factors. Many southerners had close cultural and historical ties to England, such as the Highland Scots in North Carolina and the Anglicans along the coast who shared a common religion with the Crown. Merchants had economic reasons for remaining loyal, fearing that American independence would hurt the lucrative triangular trade. Those who traded with native tribes feared that with an American victory, Native Americans would lose the British protections that kept trade networks open. Others had simple self-preservation in mind—those running from the law feared that a change in local or state government might result in their arrest and imprisonment.

THE SOUTHERN CAMPAIGN

The Southern Campaign was bloody and destructive and in many ways a preview of the Civil War that would grip the nation less than a century later. Like the Civil War, the Southern Campaign split regions and forced individuals and families to choose sides. As Loyalists sided with the British, Patriot hostility rose sharply. The clash between Loyalists and Patriots led to mutual raids, murders, retribution for long-standing feuds, burning and plundering of plantations and crops, and the near total collapse of local governments. Also, like the Civil War, the Southern Campaign was plagued by brutality and heavy casualties. At the Battle of Cowpens, the British suffered a then-staggering 110 deaths, 200 men wounded, and 500 captured. Later, at Guilford Courthouse, the British lost one-third of their force, including many officers. It was these severe losses that forced the British to withdraw to the coast.

TEACH

GUIDED DISCUSSION

4. **Interpret Maps** What advantages did British forces have during the battles in Savannah and Charleston? *(Possible response: Both of these cities were on the coast, so the British could use their navy to bring in troops and keep them well supplied. In contrast, the Continentals had to march long distances overland and had to maintain long supply lines.)*

5. **Evaluate** Did the British make a mistake in waging the Southern Campaign? Support your answer with details form the text. *(Possible responses: No. The war in the North was at a stalemate, and French assistance likely would have turned the tide toward the colonists. Thus, an attempt to win in the South was a sound strategy. Yes. The British overestimated how many Loyalists and African Americans would help them. This support did not materialize, and the British strategy failed.)*

DETERMINE WORD MEANING

Tell students to reread the paragraph that describes the backcountry "civil war." Then ask a volunteer to state the definition of *civil war. (a war between citizens of the same country)* **ASK:** Overall, can the American Revolution be interpreted as a civil war? *(Possible responses: Yes. Both colonists and British troops were still subjects of the king and living in the same colonies, so the entire conflict could be regarded as a type of civil war. No. The British troops were viewed as an occupying army, not as fellow citizens; therefore, the conflict was between two different groups, not between citizens of the same country. Also, the fights between Loyalists and Patriots were limited skirmishes, not the main conflict.)*

ACTIVE OPTIONS

On Your Feet: Solve a Military Problem Arrange students in small groups and provide a Problem-and-Solution Organizer like the one shown. Instruct group members to choose a problem faced by either the British or Continental Army and complete the Problem-and-Solution Organizer to analyze how the problem was addressed. Encourage groups to discuss whether the solution was effective. Allow time for groups to share their work with the class.

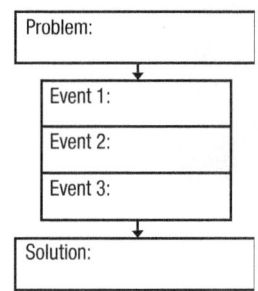

NG Learning Framework: Create a Chronological Exhibit

SKILLS Communication, Collaboration

KNOWLEDGE Our Human Story

Invite students to learn more about the events covered in the subsections The Southern Campaign and Southern Patriots Turn the Tide and then create an exhibit. Divide the class into small groups and assign each group one of the battles or events described. Tell groups to conduct online or library research to learn more about who was involved and the details of what happened. Ask each group to create a poster, infographic, or other display, that includes visuals and a description of the battle or event. Then have groups collaborate to create a chronological exhibit of the Southern Campaign. Invite each group to present its part of the exhibit to the class.

HISTORICAL THINKING

ANSWERS

1. The British had reached a stalemate with the Americans in the North. By shifting their strategy to the South, the British believed a large Loyalist population would help them defeat the Continental Army.

2. General Greene's unit inflicted heavy casualties on General Cornwallis's troops, forcing Cornwallis to retreat to the coast of North Carolina. This retreat was key in that it allowed Green's unit to continue south where it joined other Continental units. The combined forces battled together in South Carolina and forced the British to abandon their strongholds and retreat even further to a strip of land near Charleston.

3. The tactic to split the British forces and have them chase the Americans was used by Greene and Morgan. The map shows Morgan coming from the west to King's Mountain and then going to Cowpens. The British chase after him but are defeated at the Battle of Cowpens. Two months later, Greene comes from the east and the British rush to meet him at Guilford Courthouse.

MAIN IDEA As Cornwallis withdrew to Virginia, a combined French-American force surrounded him at Yorktown, causing his surrender and prompting the signing of a peace treaty to end the American Revolution.

YORKTOWN AND THE LEGACY OF THE REVOLUTION

Have you noticed how some people achieve success by knowing when to act? Sometimes in war, an opportunity presents itself while your opponent hesitates. As the British commanders disagreed on strategy, George Washington and the French seized the chance to defeat the British and end the war.

BRITISH SURRENDER AT YORKTOWN

As Greene and Morgan were winning the Carolinas and Georgia back for the Americans, Cornwallis returned to Virginia to take over the command of British general Benedict Arnold—the same Benedict Arnold who had been a Patriot hero at Fort Ticonderoga at the beginning of the war. Cornwallis decided to establish a stronghold in the area and requested additional troops from New York. But his superior, General Clinton, disapproved of this plan and refused the request. Cornwallis withdrew to the peninsula at Yorktown, Virginia, where he set up camp with an army of about 8,000 men. He fortified his position with the goal of keeping the harbor open for the British.

However, Cornwallis and Clinton continued squabbling, and the delay gave the Americans and the French a golden opportunity to organize an attack. Washington had been planning to combine forces with the French to launch a land-and-sea assault on New York City, but when he learned that a large French fleet under Admiral Comte de Grasse would arrive in the Chesapeake Bay in August, he changed his mind. Washington realized that a combined French-American force could attack from both land and sea to destroy Cornwallis's army before British reinforcements arrived. Washington marched south with his troops and the French soldiers commanded by Comte de Rochambeau (ROH-sham-BOH).

By the time Washington arrived in late September, the French fleet had already blockaded Chesapeake Bay, cutting off Cornwallis's escape route. The combined French and American forces now numbered around 16,000. Within weeks, the bombardments of artillery from Washington's troops forced Cornwallis to admit that he was trapped, and Yorktown was lost. General Clinton dispatched reinforcements from New York, but it was too late. Cornwallis surrendered on October 19, 1781.

Claiming illness, Cornwallis did not formally surrender by presenting his sword to Washington that day, however. His second-in-command performed the symbolic act. The British military band played a song called "The World Turned Upside Down," a fitting comment on the victory. The **Battle of Yorktown** was the last major battle of the Revolution. The British Parliament voted to end the war in 1782.

THE TREATY OF PARIS OF 1783

In negotiating peace terms, the United States had to reckon with its **adversary**, or enemy, Great Britain, as well as its allies, France and Spain. American peace commissioners Benjamin Franklin, John Jay, and John Adams shrewdly worked with each party to obtain a desirable settlement. The result was the **Treaty of Paris of 1783**. Signed on September 3, 1783, the treaty included two **provisions**, or legal conditions, that gave immediate authority to the new country. First, Great Britain recognized the United States of America as a sovereign nation. Second, the treaty established the United States' official boundaries: the Mississippi River on the west, the southern border of Canada on the north, and the border of Florida on the south. In separate agreements, Florida, which Britain had divided into **East Florida** and **West Florida**, was returned to Spain, and parts of the West Indies and Canada were ceded to France.

Besides forcing the British to remove troops from North America immediately, the treaty also secured American fishing rights off the Atlantic coasts of Newfoundland and the St. Lawrence River. In return, the Congress would prompt state governments to

BENEDICT ARNOLD, AMERICAN TRAITOR

Why did Benedict Arnold, who fought so valiantly for American independence at the beginning of the war, end up fighting for the British? According to most historians, his loyalties shifted after Saratoga, where he was wounded. Angered that General Gates did not give him the credit he thought he deserved when reporting the victory, Arnold switched his allegiance to Britain. In 1779, he plotted to surrender the American fort at West Point, New York, to the British. Before the plan could unfold, Washington's forces uncovered the plot and exposed Arnold as a traitor. Arnold escaped, and the British welcomed him as a commander of their forces in Virginia.

return property seized from Loyalists during the war and honor all prewar debts owed by citizens of each country to citizens of the other.

Not everyone was happy with the treaty. Native Americans felt that the British, ignoring the many treaties they had made over the years, had signed away their lands without the authority to do so. And despite the promises of freedom given by the British, thousands of African Americans were re-enslaved in the British West Indies in the years following the treaty. Some free African Americans, Loyalists, and Native Americans moved to Canada, where they felt welcome and less threatened. And in spite of the treaty, the British continued to contest territory between the Appalachian Mountains and the Mississippi River for decades.

The coming years would present a series of challenges to the new nation. Besides the creation of an independent United States, the Revolution had also established a new American identity. Based on the ideals of self-government, this identity embraced equality before the law, freedom of religion, and the values of education and **nationalism**, or a sense of loyalty and devotion toward one's nation. Citizens of the United States would have to decide exactly how to apply these ideals and values moving forward. They would also have to decide how to establish a stable government.

HISTORICAL THINKING

1. **READING CHECK** What was the significance of the Battle of Yorktown?

2. **FORM AND SUPPORT OPINIONS** Why was it important for Great Britain to recognize and accept the United States of America in the Treaty of Paris of 1783? Use text evidence to support your answer.

3. **INTERPRET VISUALS** Why do you think the artist chose to paint a dramatic background behind Cornwallis and his men?

CRITICAL VIEWING In John Trumbull's painting *Surrender of Lord Cornwallis*, British soldiers walk between French (left) and American (right) troops on horseback. What details suggest the historical significance of the scene?

OBJECTIVE

Understand the events that ended the American Revolution and the terms of the British-American peace treaty.

CRITICAL THINKING SKILLS FOR LESSON 4.2

• Form and Support Opinions
• Interpret Visuals
• Identify
• Draw Conclusions
• Evaluate

HISTORICAL THINKING FOR CHAPTER 4

How did the colonists' emerging American identity lead to revolution? The Battle of Yorktown and the Treaty of Paris signaled the end of the American Revolution. Lesson 4.2 describes these events and the sense of American nationalism that arose.

BACKGROUND FOR THE TEACHER

The years between General Cornwallis's surrender at Yorktown and the signing of the Treaty of Paris were filled with intense negotiations. The Yorktown victory in 1781 finally convinced Great Britain to consider American independence. In 1782, they offered the colonies autonomy within the British Empire—a proposal that Benjamin Franklin rejected. When formal peace treaty negotiations began later that year, the Americans asked for Canada, a request the British rejected. After months of hard work, during which the British eventually agreed to recognize full American independence, a preliminary version of the final treaty was drafted. However, the treaty would not take effect until France made a separate peace with England, which happened months later. In the end, the Americans and British left several issues unaddressed, including border disputes between the United States and the North American territories of Great Britain and Spain.

INTRODUCE & ENGAGE

DISCUSS THE LEGACY OF THE REVOLUTION

Ask students to read the title of the lesson and think about and offer suggestions about the meaning of and associations with the term *legacy*. Encourage them to suggest ways that the American Revolution has helped define what the nation is today. Prompt students to consider national attitudes toward religion, laws, politics, and culture that make up the American identity. Then inform students that this lesson will examine the end of the American Revolution and its immediate legacy.

TEACH

GUIDED DISCUSSION

1. **Identify** What circumstances and decisions led to the British defeat at Yorktown? *(Possible response: British General Clinton denied General Cornwallis's request for reinforcements in Virginia, so Cornwallis concentrated his troops at Yorktown, essentially isolating them on the peninsula. General Washington, learning that a French fleet was heading to Chesapeake Bay, abandoned his plans to take New York City and decided to wait for the fleet's arrival to combine forces and attack Cornwallis's position from land and sea.)*

2. **Draw Conclusions** Based on the information in the lesson, what can you conclude about Benedict Arnold's commitment to American independence? *(Possible response: Though he was a valiant fighter at the beginning, the basis for his commitment appears to be personal ambition and a desire for glory. When he felt he was denied proper recognition, he reversed his loyalties, apparently to obtain his own command.)*

EVALUATE

Have students read the subsection about the Treaty of Paris of 1783 and use online resources to find additional information about the pact. Then have the class complete a chart like the one shown, identifying the treaty's provisions and consequences and evaluating how they impacted different countries and groups. When students have finished, engage in a class discussion on the following topic: Who benefited the most and the least from the Treaty of Paris?

Provisions and Consequences	Who Gained	Who Lost

ACTIVE OPTIONS

On Your Feet: Fishbowl Arrange the class in two concentric circles, and then pose the following question: What could Great Britain have done differently to defeat the Americans? Have students in the inner circle discuss the question while those in the outer circle listen to the discussion and evaluate the points made. Instruct the groups to reverse roles and continue the discussion.

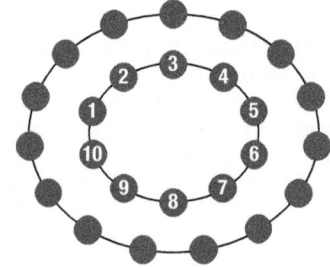

NG Learning Framework: Create a Diversity Honor Roll

ATTITUDE Responsibility

KNOWLEDGE Our Human Story

Discuss with students the diversity of people and groups mentioned in the chapter who contributed to the American war effort. Then organize students into small groups and have each group create a Diversity Honor Roll of the war, listing outstanding people or groups from different backgrounds and their main contributions. Groups can focus on people mentioned in the chapter or research other people or groups to add to their honor roll. Encourage groups to share their work with the class.

DIFFERENTIATE

ENGLISH LANGUAGE LEARNERS ELD

Use Synonyms Help students at **All Proficiencies** expand their English vocabulary by introducing familiar synonyms for unfamiliar words they encounter. Write the following word pairs on the board: *fortified/strengthened, squabbling/arguing, assault/attack, dispatched/sent, shrewdly/wisely.* Tell students to replace the first word with the second when they encounter it in a sentence. Guide students in using a thesaurus when they come across unfamiliar words to find a synonym that makes sense in context.

PRE-AP

Form and Support a Thesis Tell students to review what they learned about the territories acquired by the new United States under the Treaty of Paris. Ask them to develop a thesis regarding why the treaty makes no mention of the territorial rights and boundaries of Native American tribes. Tell students to conduct online research, including a variety of primary and secondary source materials, and use their findings to write an essay that supports their thesis. Invite volunteers to read their essays to the class.

See the Chapter Planner for more strategies for differentiation.

HISTORICAL THINKING

ANSWERS

1. The Battle of Yorktown, the last major battle of the war, demonstrated the combined strength of the Continental Army and its allies in the defeat of Cornwallis and effectively ended fighting in the South.

2. By recognizing the United States of America, Great Britain was acknowledging defeat and accepting the authority of America as a sovereign nation. Having done so, Great Britain would have to develop foreign relations with America, as they had with other nations.

3. Possible response: The dramatic background may have been a reminder of the artillery bombardments that had forced Cornwallis to surrender.

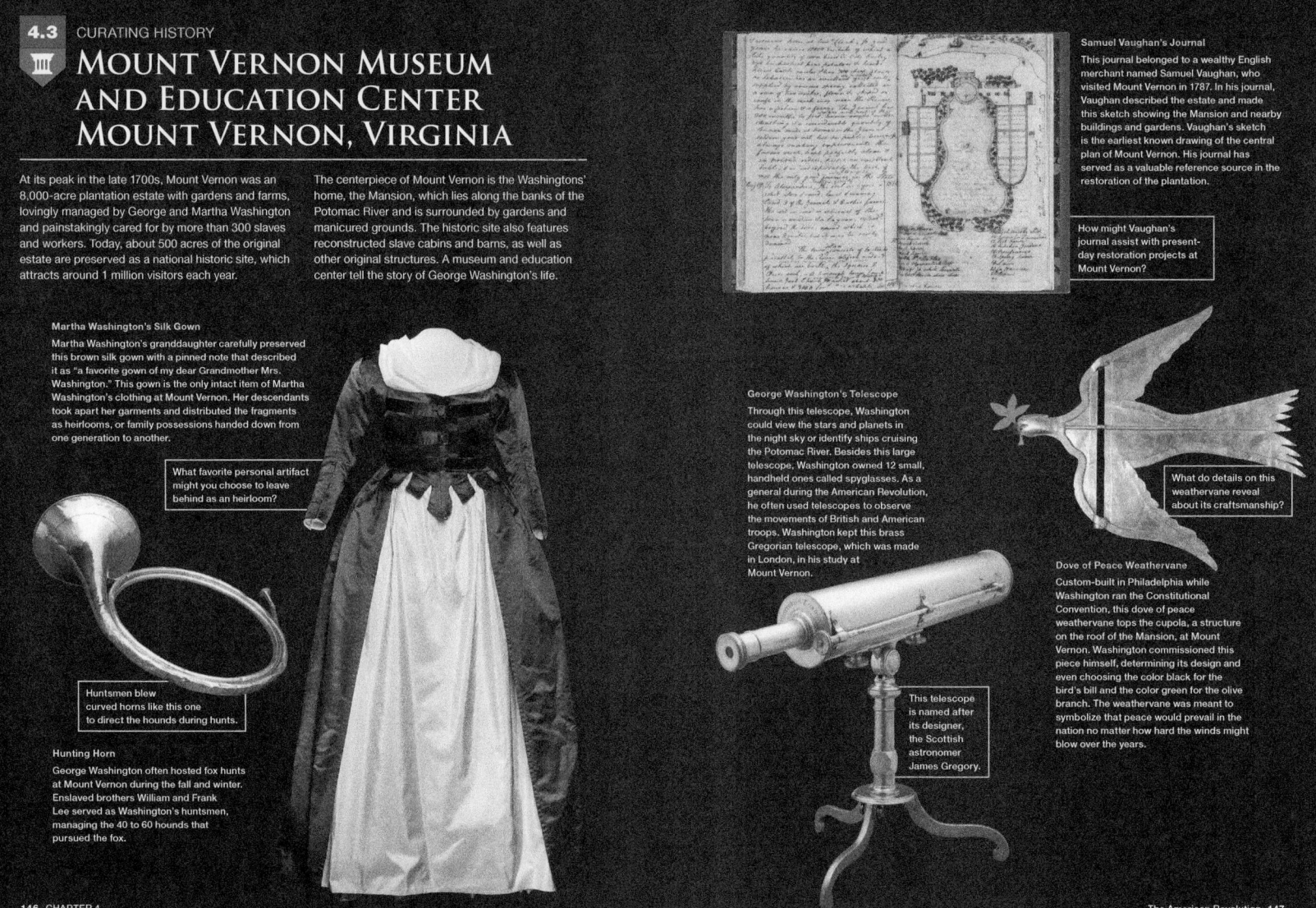

MOUNT VERNON MUSEUM AND EDUCATION CENTER MOUNT VERNON, VIRGINIA

At its peak in the late 1700s, Mount Vernon was an 8,000-acre plantation estate with gardens and farms, lovingly managed by George and Martha Washington and painstakingly cared for by more than 300 slaves and workers. Today, about 500 acres of the original estate are preserved as a national historic site, which attracts around 1 million visitors each year.

The centerpiece of Mount Vernon is the Washingtons' home, the Mansion, which lies along the banks of the Potomac River and is surrounded by gardens and manicured grounds. The historic site also features reconstructed slave cabins and barns, as well as other original structures. A museum and education center tell the story of George Washington's life.

Samuel Vaughan's Journal
This journal belonged to a wealthy English merchant named Samuel Vaughan, who visited Mount Vernon in 1787. In his journal, Vaughan described the estate and made this sketch showing the Mansion and nearby buildings and gardens. Vaughan's sketch is the earliest known drawing of the central plan of Mount Vernon. His journal has served as a valuable reference source in the restoration of the plantation.

How might Vaughan's journal assist with present-day restoration projects at Mount Vernon?

Martha Washington's Silk Gown
Martha Washington's granddaughter carefully preserved this brown silk gown with a pinned note that described it as "a favorite gown of my dear Grandmother Mrs. Washington." This gown is the only intact item of Martha Washington's clothing at Mount Vernon. Her descendants took apart her garments and distributed the fragments as heirlooms, or family possessions handed down from one generation to another.

What favorite personal artifact might you choose to leave behind as an heirloom?

George Washington's Telescope
Through this telescope, Washington could view the stars and planets in the night sky or identify ships cruising the Potomac River. Besides this large telescope, Washington owned 12 small, handheld ones called spyglasses. As a general during the American Revolution, he often used telescopes to observe the movements of British and American troops. Washington kept this brass Gregorian telescope, which was made in London, in his study at Mount Vernon.

This telescope is named after its designer, the Scottish astronomer James Gregory.

What do details on this weathervane reveal about its craftsmanship?

Dove of Peace Weathervane
Custom-built in Philadelphia while Washington ran the Constitutional Convention, this dove of peace weathervane tops the cupola, a structure on the roof of the Mansion, at Mount Vernon. Washington commissioned this piece himself, determining its design and even choosing the color black for the bird's bill and the color green for the olive branch. The weathervane was meant to symbolize that peace would prevail in the nation no matter how hard the winds might blow over the years.

Huntsmen blew curved horns like this one to direct the hounds during hunts.

Hunting Horn
George Washington often hosted fox hunts at Mount Vernon during the fall and winter. Enslaved brothers William and Frank Lee served as Washington's huntsmen, managing the 40 to 60 hounds that pursued the fox.

PLAN: 2-PAGE LESSON

OBJECTIVE
Study artifacts related to George Washington's life and his home at Mount Vernon.

CRITICAL THINKING SKILLS FOR LESSON 4.3
- Analyze Visuals
- Make Connections
- Evaluate
- Make Inferences

HISTORICAL THINKING FOR CHAPTER 4
How did the colonists' emerging American identify lead to revolution? Few people exerted more influence on the emerging nation than George Washington. Lesson 4.3 presents items preserved from his life at his home, Mount Vernon.

BACKGROUND FOR THE TEACHER
William and Frank Lee, mentioned in the hunting horn caption, were 2 of 317 enslaved people at the Mount Vernon plantation. These workers built Mount Vernon and labored in the fields to generate the wealth of the Washington family. As one descendant of these people said, ". . . We helped build this place and make it what it is. We helped make him who he was." In his lifetime, George Washington came to believe that slavery was wrong and was the only Founding Father to free his slaves upon his death in 1799. The museum, through its permanent and special exhibits, pays tribute to the shared journey of enslaved workers and the Washington family. The museum's online database allows visitors to search for individual stories and records of many slaves by name, skill, or date.

HISTORY NOTEBOOK
Encourage students to complete the Curating History page for Chapter 4 in their History Notebooks as they read.

INTRODUCE & ENGAGE

CURATE SCHOOL MEMORABILIA

Tell students to imagine their school is creating a museum and education center and they are curating items for the museum to commemorate their school's history. Discuss with students what categories they would use to sort memorabilia, such as sports, art, and science, as well as categories reflecting specific events or time periods. Ask students to tell what items they would include in each category and why. Talk about what students would want future students to know and remember about their school. Explain that in this lesson they will learn about the Mount Vernon Museum and Education Center, whose goal is to help visitors understand the lives and times of George and Martha Washington.

TEACH

GUIDED DISCUSSION

1. **Evaluate** What do items like the hunting horn and the telescope reveal about George Washington's interests and lifestyle? *(Possible response: The items confirm that Washington enjoyed sports like fox hunting and used advanced scientific equipment, such as the telescope, for his personal interest in astronomy as well as for practical reasons. The items also confirm the wealth and status of the family, since only the rich owned land for fox hunts or could afford expensive instruments.)*

2. **Make Inferences** Why might it be important to include primary sources from people outside the Washington family circle? *(Possible response: People outside the family might provide different perspectives about who the Washingtons were, what they did, and how they lived. Such sources could also give scholars and others more data to help them understand this historic family, place, and period.)*

CURATING HISTORY

The Mount Vernon Museum and Education Center is a rich resource for learning about the Washingtons, their families, and enslaved workers. The museum offers a virtual tour of the buildings and grounds; documentary movies and videos; extensive collections of artifacts, maps, and primary sources; and a range of digital educational resources. Access the website and guide students to the Clothing and Textiles collection to view the photograph of Martha Washington's silk gown. **ASK:** Why do you think the museum's curators felt that including a dress was important? What insights might such clothing give about the character of the wearer and the mood of the times?

ACTIVE OPTION

On Your Feet: Sort the Artifacts Arrange students into groups of three or four to examine the artifacts in the lesson and in the collections of the Mount Vernon Museum's website. Then have students complete two Concept Clusters such as the ones shown. In one cluster, have students sort the collection of furniture. In the other cluster, direct students to select a different collection to sort, considering the characteristics or uses that they identify. When groups are finished, ask them to share their Concept Clusters with the class.

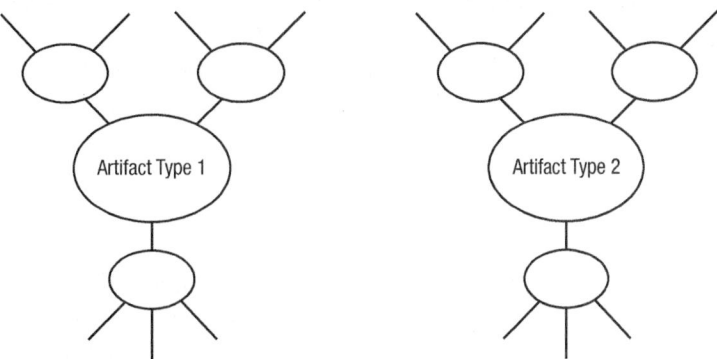

Artifact Type 1

Artifact Type 2

DIFFERENTIATE

STRIVING READERS

Preview and Review the Text Have students preview the lesson by reading the title and introductory text and examining the photographs. Instruct them to write questions about the photos that might be answered in the captions. After they read the lesson, have them discuss what they learned, review the text, and find answers to their preview questions.

PRE-AP

Research Mount Vernon Direct students to use online sources to learn how and why George Washington's private residence became the nation's first historical tourist attraction. Ask students to identify the people and main purpose behind the purchase, restoration, and opening of Mount Vernon to the public. Tell students to use their research to write a report or prepare an oral presentation. Invite students to share their completed work with the class.

See the Chapter Planner for more strategies for differentiation.

MARTHA WASHINGTON'S SILK GOWN

Answers will vary. Students' choices should represent an important or significant aspect of their lives that they would like to pass on to others.

SAMUEL VAUGHN'S JOURNAL

Vaughn's journal contains diagrams and drawings of Mount Vernon as it was in 1787, providing modern restorers with a rough model of the layout and details of original buildings and grounds.

DOVE OF PEACE WEATHERVANE

Possible response: The polished metal of the dove's body, wings, and tail feathers, along with detailed olive leaf in the dove's bill, show a high level of artistic skill of the craftsman and hint that Washington prized symmetry in design. The craftsman was knowledgeable about creating a vane that would resist damage, as evidenced by the raised edging around the perimeter and the metal bar down the length of the dove.

VOCABULARY

Use each of the following pairs of key vocabulary terms in a sentence that shows an understanding of their meanings.

1. boycott, committee of correspondence
   Samuel Adams set up a committee of correspondence to organize a widespread boycott of British goods.

2. guerrilla tactic, privateer

3. mercenary, deploy

4. rule of law, ratify

5. financier, profiteering

READING STRATEGY
FORM AND SUPPORT OPINIONS

Forming opinions as you read history is important to help clarify your understanding and sharpen your perceptions of the words and actions of the people involved. Use the graphic organizer to state and support your opinion about an important event of the American Revolution. Then answer the question.

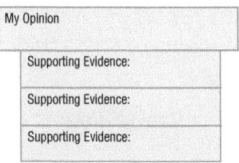

My Opinion

Supporting Evidence:

Supporting Evidence:

Supporting Evidence:

6. In your opinion, what was the most significant event of the American Revolution, and why?

MAIN IDEAS

Answer the following questions. Support your answers with evidence from the chapter.

7. How were the Sons of Liberty effective in leading resistance against British policies? **LESSON 1.1**

8. How was the Boston Massacre a result of both the Quartering Act of 1765 and the Townshend Acts? **LESSON 1.2**

9. Why did the colonies unite after the passage of the Intolerable Acts? **LESSON 1.3**

10. Why did King George III reject the Olive Branch Petition? **LESSON 2.1**

11. How were the ideas expressed in *Common Sense* put to use in the structure of the new national government established by the Articles of Confederation? **LESSON 2.2**

12. Why did the Continental Army's victories at Trenton and Princeton help keep the American effort for independence alive? **LESSON 3.1**

13. How did the Congress eventually find a way to help pay for the war? **LESSON 3.2**

14. How did women provide vital assistance to the Continental Army? **LESSON 3.3**

15. How did General Nathanael Greene help prevent the British from achieving success in their southern strategy? **LESSON 4.1**

16. What gave the Continental Army an advantage over the British at the Battle of Yorktown? **LESSON 4.2**

HISTORICAL THINKING

Answer the following questions. Support your answers with evidence from the chapter.

17. **ANALYZE CAUSE AND EFFECT** How did the Daughters of Liberty set the groundwork for changes in the social status of women during and after the war?

18. **MAKE CONNECTIONS** How did the United States' alliance with France contribute to the British defeat in the southern states?

19. **DRAW CONCLUSIONS** Why do you think that widespread public support for declaring independence was slow to form even after the events at Lexington and Concord?

20. **IDENTIFY PROBLEMS AND SOLUTIONS** What problem did the entry of the French into the war present for the British, and how did they attempt to solve it?

21. **DESCRIBE** How did women writers help to push colonial attitudes in favor of independence?

22. **IDENTIFY MAIN IDEAS AND DETAILS** How did disagreements among the British play a pivotal role in allowing George Washington to force the surrender at Yorktown?

23. **FORM AND SUPPORT OPINIONS** How would you rate Washington's handling of the Continental Army from late 1775 through late 1776? Support your opinion with evidence from the text.

INTERPRET MAPS

Look closely at the map that shows the boundaries of the original United States of America, established by the Treaty of Paris of 1783. Then answer the questions that follow.

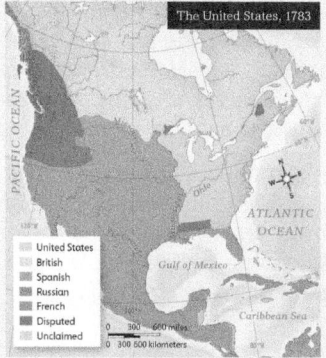

The United States, 1783

- United States
- British
- Spanish
- Russian
- French
- Disputed
- Unclaimed

24. What nations claim land bordering on the United States, and where, geographically, do those borders lie?

25. Assuming that North America includes the Caribbean Islands, which European nations hold the most and the least land in North America, according to this map?

ANALYZE SOURCES

During the run-up to the American Revolution, Native Americans faced the difficult question of whether to remain neutral or to side with the Americans or the British. Read the excerpt below, which explains the concerns of the Oneida about choosing sides. Then answer the question that follows.

> We cannot intermeddle in this dispute between two brothers. The quarrel seems to be unnatural. You are two brothers of one blood. We are unwilling to join on either side in such a contest, for we bear an equal affection to both you Old and New England. . . . We Indians cannot find, nor recollect in the traditions of our ancestors . . . a similar instance.

26. Based on the excerpt, why did the Oneida wish to remain neutral in the conflict between the Americans and the British?

CONNECT TO YOUR LIFE

27. **EXPOSITORY** The American Revolution was fueled by a desire to protect people's rights to life, liberty, and the pursuit of happiness. Yet this desire was not applied equally to African Americans, women, and Native Americans during and after the war. Think of a social conflict the United States is experiencing today. Using the war as one example, write a short essay explaining the importance of having fair solutions to social conflicts.

TIPS

- Use textual evidence and two or three key vocabulary terms from the chapter in your explanation.

- Describe the problems of equality during and after the American Revolution and the problem you are addressing today.

- Connect the two ideas, and explain how better understanding can help prevent social conflicts.

- Explain how Americans can improve their understanding of modern social conflicts.

VOCABULARY ANSWERS

1. Samuel Adams set up a committee of correspondence to organize a widespread boycott of British goods.

2. Privateers employed guerrilla tactics against the British by ambushing and attacking merchant ships.

3. The British hired Hessian mercenaries to fight against the American colonists, deploying them alongside British troops to bolster their numbers.

4. The rule of law required Congress to ratify the Articles of Confederation to put them into effect, but approval wasn't achieved until 1781.

5. Generous financiers provided funds for the war effort instead of engaging in profiteering and charging the Continental Army high prices for needed goods.

READING STRATEGY ANSWER

My Opinion:
The writing and signing of the Declaration of Independence was the most significant event of the American Revolution.

Supporting Evidence:
The Declaration announced the formation of the United States of America and severed ties between the new nation and Great Britain.

Supporting Evidence:
It clearly defined the colonists' reasons for independence.

Supporting Evidence:
It established democratic ideals and created a unified sense of American identity.

6. Answers will vary. Possible response: The Declaration of Independence unified the colonies and created a path to independence. Without it, conflicts between Great Britain and the colonies had no long-term goal. It gave Americans a separate identity, democratic ideals, and a reason to fight.

MAIN IDEAS ANSWERS

7. The Sons of Liberty organized networks among the colonies that provided leadership to initiate and maintain protests, such as boycotts of British goods.

8. Colonists already resented housing British soldiers, as required by the Quartering Act, and the repressive Townshend Acts that collected duties and allowed searches pushed that resentment to the point that it erupted into violence.

9. Although the Intolerable Acts were aimed at Massachusetts, they were viewed by colonists as an assault on all colonists' basic rights by Britain's growing tyranny.

10. King George made assumptions about what the petition said without reading it. He believed that the colonies were in open rebellion regardless of their attempt at reconciliation.

11. The Articles of Confederation reflected the *Common Sense* ideas of creating a representative democracy by giving one vote to each state's delegation and limiting representatives' terms to three years.

12. Devastating defeats in New York and Canada had reduced support for the patriot cause and the Continental Army. But the victories at Trenton and Princeton rekindled that support and helped draw more recruits into the army to continue the fight.

13. Congress acquired loans from foreign governments and financiers, such as Haym Salomon, to help stabilize the financial system. Robert Morris chartered a central bank, and he, Salomon, and others used their own money to fund it.

14. During the war, women worked as camp aides, nurses, cooks, spies, and even as soldiers in direct support of Continental troops. They also proved successful at gathering donations to contribute to soldiers who had not been paid.

15. General Greene split his forces, and he and General Daniel Morgan forced the British to split their troops and chase the Patriots through the Carolinas. The Patriots inflicted so many casualties on the British that they withdrew to the coast, abandoning their southern strategy.

16. The French gave the Continental Army a significant advantage during the battle by supplying troops on land and a fleet of ships that blockaded Chesapeake Bay, preventing British warships from aiding Cornwallis or allowing his escape.

HISTORICAL THINKING ANSWERS

17. The Daughters of Liberty effectively demonstrated women's abilities to organize for and have an impact during the fight for independence. By running businesses and farms in the absence of their husbands and fathers, they proved women to be capable and intelligent. Examples of their successes likely empowered women to keep fighting for equal treatment in society.

18. French assistance was critical to Britain's defeat in the South. The French not only provided troops, but their navy attacked British ships in the Atlantic and West Indies, forcing the British to divert troops and ships away from their Southern Campaign.

19. Although many British actions affected all the colonies, New England was the center of violent conflict between radical Patriots and Britain. People in the middle and southern colonies may have believed they could still achieve reconciliation with Britain.

20. The entry of the French into the war brought the northern war to a stalemate. As a result, the British attempted to establish control of the southern states, where they expected a large Loyalist force to assist them.

21. Women writers, such as Esther Reed and Abigail Adams, rallied public sentiment in favor of independence through publication of broadsides, letters, and articles, and instructed other women how to participate in the war effort.

22. Cornwallis and Clinton argued about where and when to commit their joint troops, leaving Yorktown undermanned and vulnerable to the American-French forces.

23. Washington's performance as commander was relatively poor from late 1775 through late 1776, despite the victory at Trenton. He was outmaneuvered and soundly defeated by British forces at New York, suffering many casualties and forced to retreat through New Jersey. However, he was also handicapped by colonial disunity, poorly trained soldiers, inadequate finances, and insufficient supplies.

INTERPRET MAPS ANSWERS

24. Spain claims land to the west of the Mississippi River extending from Canada to the Gulf of Mexico. Great Britain holds land north of the Great Lakes and extending east to the Atlantic Ocean.

25. Spain holds the most land, and France holds the least in North America.

ANALYZE SOURCES ANSWER

26. The Oneida felt it was unusual for people of the same heritage to be fighting, having no recollection in their history of such a conflict. They said they held both sides in equal esteem and probably saw no advantage—politically, economically, militarily, or socially—in allying with one group against the other.

CONNECT TO YOUR LIFE ANSWER

27. Essays will vary, but students should connect an example of a current social conflict in the United States to the American Revolution and use it as the basis for explaining the importance of having fair solutions to social conflicts. Essays should include textual evidence, two or three vocabulary terms, describe the problems of equality during and after the war and the current problem, connect the two ideas, and explain how better understanding can help prevent and improve modern social conflicts.

UNIT 2 RESOURCES

UNIT INTRODUCTION

UNIT TIME LINE

UNIT WRAP-UP

NATIONAL GEOGRAPHIC | CONNECTION

National Geographic Magazine Adapted Articles
- "Map Drawing"
- "Searching for Sacagawea" ONLINE

Unit 2 Inquiry: Explore a Contradiction

NG Learning Framework Activities
- Stage a Debate
- Create a Storyboard

Unit 2 Formal Assessment

Reenactors fire muskets as they portray an American Revolution battle scene in Mount Vernon, Virginia. What details in the photograph convey what it may have been like to fight in the American Revolution?

CHAPTER 5 RESOURCES

Available at NGLSync.Cengage.com

TEACHER RESOURCES & ASSESSMENT

Reading and Note-Taking

Vocabulary Practice

Document-Based Question Template

Social Studies Skills Lessons
- Reading: Compare and Contrast
- Writing: Argument

Formal Assessment
- Chapter 5 Pretest
- Chapter 5 Tests A & B
- Section Quizzes

Chapter 5 Answer Key

ExamView®
   One-time Download

STUDENT DIGITAL RESOURCES

- eEdition
- Handbooks
- Online Atlas
- American Gallery Online
- History Notebook
- Active History
- Literature Analysis
- Projects for Inquiry-Based Learning

Chapter 5 Spanish Resources are available at NGLSync.Cengage.com.

CHAPTER 5 FORGING A NEW GOVERNMENT 1780–1790

HISTORICAL THINKING How did American ideals and culture shape the new government?

AMERICAN STORIES ONLINE | The Northwest Ordinances
SECTION 1 Experiments with Liberty
SECTION 2 Writing a Constitution
SECTION 3 Ratifying the Constitution
AMERICAN GALLERY ONLINE | Crafting the Constitution

"The way to secure liberty is to **place it in the people's hands.**"
—John Adams

Independence Hall in Philadelphia, Pennsylvania, is the birthplace of the United States. The public can now tour this Georgian-style, red brick building where the Declaration of Independence and the Constitution were debated and signed.

 **The Northwest Ordinances**

- Study Primary Sources: Excerpt from the Northwest Ordinance of 1787
- On Your Feet: Good Ideas/Bad Ideas

NG Learning Framework:
Propose New States

SECTION 1 RESOURCES
EXPERIMENTS WITH LIBERTY

LESSON 1.1
Problems in the New Republic

- On Your Feet: Conduct a Three-Step Interview

NG Learning Framework:
Research Frontier Conflicts

LESSON 1.2
The Northwest Ordinances

- On Your Feet: Numbered Heads

NG Learning Framework:
Write Persuasive Materials

SECTION 2 RESOURCES
WRITING A CONSTITUTION

LESSON 2.1
The Constitutional Convention

- On Your Feet: Roundtable Discussion

NG Learning Framework:
Secrecy Versus Transparency

LESSON 2.2
A Constitutional Republic

- Active History: Categorize Government Responsibilities

AMERICAN GALLERY ONLINE Crafting the Constitution

NG Learning Framework:
Write an Op-Ed Piece

SECTION 3 RESOURCES
RATIFYING THE CONSTITUTION

LESSON 3.1
Federalists and Antifederalists

- On Your Feet: Fishbowl

NG Learning Framework:
Present an Essay

LESSON 3.2
Ratification and the Bill of Rights

- On Your Feet: Roundtable Discussion

NG Learning Framework:
Apply the Bill of Rights in the 21st Century

LESSON 3.3
DOCUMENT-BASED QUESTION
Setting a Balance

- On Your Feet: Use a Jigsaw Strategy

CHAPTER 5 REVIEW

STRATEGY ❶
PREVIEW THE TEXT

Work with students to preview each lesson in the chapter. Guide them to read each lesson's title, captions, and subsection headings. Then tell them to list the information they expect to find in the text. Instruct students to read a lesson and discuss with a partner what they learned and whether or not it matched their expectations.

Use with All Lessons

STRATEGY ❷
CONNECT MAIN IDEAS AND DETAILS

As they read each lesson, encourage students to work in pairs to complete a Main-Idea and Details Chart. Point out the kinds of details (facts, dates, events, reasons) that support main ideas. Then ask each pair to alternate reading paragraphs

Main Ideas	Details

aloud and write down main ideas and details. Tell them this process will help them identify and remember the most important information in the lesson. Ask volunteers to share their completed chart with other student pairs and discuss the similarities and differences in their responses.

Use with All Lessons

STRATEGY ❸
POSE AND ANSWER QUESTIONS

Arrange students in pairs and ask them to reread the lesson together. Instruct them to pause after each paragraph and ask each other *who, what, where, when,* or *why* questions about what they have just read. Suggest students use a 5Ws Chart to help organize their questions and answers. Encourage partners to assist each other as needed.

Use with All Lessons

STRATEGY ❶
DESCRIBE LESSON VISUALS

Pair students who have vision or perception issues with students who do not. Ask the latter to describe the details of each visual in a lesson and to respond to any questions their partner might have. Students should also read aloud and discuss the text accompanying each visual. Encourage pairs to continue working together to respond to any Historical Thinking or Critical Viewing questions related to the visuals.

Use with Lessons 1.1, 1.2, 2.1, and 3.2 *Students may describe the portrait of Mohawk leader Joseph Brant, the map of the Northwest Territory, the painting of Daniel Boone, the lithograph of Shays's Rebellion, and Howard Chandler Christy's painting of the signing of the U.S. Constitution.*

STRATEGY ❷
MODIFY VOCABULARY LISTS

You can modify the number of Key Vocabulary words that students will be required to master. As they read, instruct students to create a vocabulary card, such as the one shown, for each word in the modified list. Encourage them to write definitions, synonyms, antonyms, or examples on each word card. Direct students to refer to their vocabulary cards often as they read.

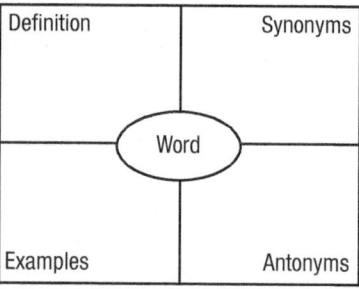

Use with All Lessons

ENGLISH LANGUAGE LEARNERS

STRATEGY ❶
ACTIVATE PRIOR KNOWLEDGE

Display the words below in a random "splash" arrangement. Tell students that all the words relate to the chapter topic of forging a new government. Ask students to discuss any ideas the words bring to mind. Then instruct them to work in pairs to write a sentence that uses each word. You may wish to pair students at the **Emerging** level with students at the **Expanding** or **Bridging** level, and ask more advanced students to assist less advanced students.

sovereignty   federalism   **legislative**
judicial   *electoral*   college   Framers
impeachment
checks and balances   executive
constitutional republic   Bill of Rights

Use with All Lessons

STRATEGY ❷
TEACH AND LEARN

Pair students at the **Emerging or Expanding** level with those at the **Bridging** level. Have the more English-proficient students teach words from the lesson that appear in various forms, such as an adjective related to a noun. Direct pairs to compose a sentence for each word, and invite them to share their sentences with other pairs. Suggest the following words:

constitution	constitutional
legislature	legislative
elector	electoral

Use with Lesson 2.2 *You may use a similar strategy for other lessons. For example, in Lesson 1.1, you could instruct students to write sentences for word pairs such as* republic/republicanism *and* equal/egalitarianism.

STRATEGY ❸
COMPOSE CAPTIONS

Pair students at the **Emerging** and **Expanding** levels with English-proficient students, and instruct them to work together to write original captions for the artwork or photographs in each lesson of the chapter. After they have finished, ask volunteers to share their captions.

Use with All Lessons *Suggest that students first read the printed caption aloud, then cover it with a piece of paper and write their original caption on the paper. Their caption may paraphrase and expand upon the one in the text. You may then lead a discussion comparing different students' captions.*

GIFTED & TALENTED

STRATEGY ❶
DESIGN AN INFOGRAPHIC

Instruct students to create an infographic that uses data from the text and their own research to show how the Three-fifths Compromise worked and why it was important in the crafting of the Constitution. Invite students to compare infographics and make predictions about what potential conflicts the Three-fifths Compromise might raise for the nation in the future.

Use with Lesson 2.2

STRATEGY ❷
RESEARCH AND ROLE-PLAY

Invite students to choose one advocate or opponent of federalism and prepare to role-play the part of that person. The person might be an important politician or writer or an average merchant, housewife, farmer, or servant. Instruct students to conduct research to learn why the person they choose would have supported or opposed federalism. Pair students who hold opposing views and invite them to role-play their parts with each other.

Use with Lessons 3.1 and 3.2 *If students role-play for the class, discuss how the performances enhanced students' understanding of federalist/antifederalist positions.*

PRE-AP

STRATEGY ❶
WRITE A PROBLEM-SOLUTION ESSAY

Remind students that the new republic faced many problems, including issues with internal governance, friction with other nations, and serious financial issues. Have them choose one specific problem introduced in the chapter and conduct additional research about the problem and the effectiveness of the solution. As students gather information, suggest they take notes using a Problem-and-Solution Diagram.

Use with Lessons 1.1, 2.2, and 3.2

STRATEGY ❷
EXTEND KNOWLEDGE

Invite students to show the relevance of a topic, person, idea, or event introduced in Chapter 5 to current events or issues being discussed today. For example, students might research republicanism, federalism, Joseph Brant, Shays's Rebellion, Alexander Hamilton, Abigail Adams, Mercy Otis Warren, or the ratification of the Constitution or the Bill of Rights. Invite students to report their findings to the class.

Use with All Lessons

HISTORICAL THINKING How did American ideals and culture shape
the new government?

"The way to secure
liberty is to **place
it in the people's
hands.**"

—John Adams

Independence Hall in Philadelphia, Pennsylvania,
is the birthplace of the United States. The public
can now tour this Georgian-style, red brick
building where the Declaration of Independence
and the Constitution were debated and signed.

INTRODUCE THE PHOTOGRAPH

INDEPENDENCE HALL

Direct students' attention to the photograph of
Philadelphia's Independence Hall and tell them to
look closely at the details. **ASK:** What inference can
you make about the historical importance of this
building from details in the photograph? *(Answers
will vary. Possible response: The building's old-style
architecture stands out from the modern buildings
around it; it has been kept in good condition; there
appears to be a sign with historical information
in the lower left-hand corner of the photograph.
These details indicate that the building has been
preserved because of its historical significance.)*
Tell students that in this chapter they will learn
that when the Articles of Confederation proved
inadequate, delegates of the young republic forged
a new government in this building.

SHARE BACKGROUND

Independence Hall originally served as the
Pennsylvania statehouse. Built between 1732
and 1753, it was home to all three branches of
Pennsylvania's colonial government. The state's
legislature allowed the delegates of the Second
Continental Congress and the Constitutional
Convention to meet in the statehouse's Assembly
Room, where both the Declaration of Independence
and U.S. Constitution had been signed.

After both the Pennsylvania and U.S. government
assemblies left Philadelphia, Pennsylvania wanted
to sell the statehouse property for redevelopment.
The city of Philadelphia protested and, in 1818,
bought the building for $70,000. Philadelphians
began referring to the Assembly Room, and
eventually the entire building, as Independence
Hall. In 1979, Independence Hall was designated
a UNESCO World Heritage Site and is under the
stewardship of the National Park Service.

*For Chapter 5 Spanish Resources, visit the
Resources Menu. Chapter 5 Resources
are available at NGLSync.Cengage.com.*

HISTORICAL THINKING QUESTION

How did American ideals and culture shape the new government?

Fishbowl Activity: The Impact of Ideals and Culture This activity helps students explore how ideals and culture shape the way people choose to govern themselves. Encourage students to use prior knowledge about why and how the American colonies broke away from Great Britain in the following discussions.

Have students form an inner circle and an outer circle, both facing the center. Tell the inner circle to discuss the following question while the outer circle listens and takes notes: What ideals and goals of American culture are reflected in the Declaration of Independence? Then have the circles switch places. Direct the new inner circle to discuss the following question while the outer circle listens and takes notes: What ideals and goals of American culture are reflected in the Articles of Confederation?

Reconvene as a class and discuss the common themes each circle touched upon in their discussions. Tell students that in this chapter they will learn about how American ideals and culture shaped the type of government the Framers created to replace the Articles of Confederation.

INTRODUCE THE READING STRATEGY

COMPARE AND CONTRAST

Explain to students that comparing and contrasting information can help them understand how a government evolves to meet specific challenges. Turn to the Chapter Review and preview the Venn diagram with students. As they read the chapter, have students compare and contrast the main features of the Articles of Confederation and the U.S. Constitution.

KEY DATES FOR CHAPTER 5

1785	Land Ordinance of 1785 is passed
1786	Shays's Rebellion begins
1787	Northwest Ordinance of 1787 is passed
1787	Constitutional Convention drafts the Constitution
1787	Three states ratify the Constitution
1788	Eight more states ratify the Constitution
1789	Washington is elected president, Adams vice president
1789	North Carolina ratifies the Constitution
1790	Rhode Island ratifies the Constitution
1791	Bill of Rights is ratified and added to the Constitution

INTRODUCE CHAPTER VOCABULARY

KEY VOCABULARY

SECTION 1

depression	precedent	speculator
egalitarianism	republicanism	suffrage
ordinance	sovereignty	war bond

SECTION 2

bicameral legislature	electoral college	impeachment
checks and balances	executive branch	interstate commerce
	federalism	judicial branch
constitutional republic	foreclosure	legislative branch
	Framer	separation of powers
credit	fugitive slave clause	specie
currency		
dual sovereignty		

SECTION 3

antifederalist	Bill of Rights	federalist

DEFINITION CHART

As students read the chapter, tell them to complete a Definition Chart for Key Vocabulary words. Instruct them to list Key Vocabulary words in the left column of the chart. Then, as they encounter each word, they write the word's definition in the center column and what the word means, in their own words, in the last column. Model an example using the graphic organizer below.

Word	Definition	In My Own Words
depression	a severe and long-term economic decline characterized by a number of business failures, reduced industrial output, and high unemployment	a severe economic downturn

For instructional support for the online American Story "The Northwest Ordinances," go to NGLSync.Cengage.com.

PROBLEMS IN THE NEW REPUBLIC

Have you ever tried to organize a new club or team? Imagine trying to create an entirely new kind of government. The nation's leaders grappled with this challenge and, like all of us, had to learn from their mistakes.

GOVERNING PROBLEMS

When the Patriots declared independence from Great Britain, they said that the American people had the power to create their own government. This new and radical idea was sparked in part by Enlightenment ideals of **egalitarianism**, the belief that all people should be treated equally, and **republicanism**, the belief that a government's power comes from its citizens and the representatives they choose to make their laws. According to John Jay, one of the American negotiators of the Treaty of Paris of 1783, Americans were "the first people whom heaven has favored with an opportunity of deliberating upon, and choosing the forms of government under which they should live."

In practice, however, the ideals of egalitarianism and republicanism did not apply to all people in the new republic. Women, Native Americans, most free men of color, and, of course, none of the enslaved had much of a political voice, if any. The individual states determined who qualified for **suffrage**, or the right to vote. In most states, only white males who owned property were allowed to vote.

As you have read, the United States' first plan of government—the Articles of Confederation—featured a weak central government. **Sovereignty**, or the power to govern, remained with each of the 13 new states. The Articles loosely bound these self-governing states together under a national legislature called the Confederation Congress, which acted as their agent. Each state had an equal vote in Congress. The national government did not include executive and judicial branches, which meant there was no president or federal court system. Congress itself had few powers. It could conduct foreign affairs, negotiate treaties, declare war, create a postal service, and issue money. But it could not impose taxes; that right belonged to the states. If Congress needed money, it had to request funds from the states.

This 1777 copy of the Articles of Confederation includes its full title. The reference to "Perpetual Union" reflects the representatives' hope that the union would continue forever.

FINANCIAL PROBLEMS

The emphasis on state sovereignty failed to promote a sense of national identity. This lack of unity made it difficult for the new nation to take effective action on important issues, such as paying off the huge debt amassed during the Revolution. Individual states refused to contribute enough money to help pay the debt. In 1785, Congress stopped making interest payments to France. By 1787, it was defaulting on loan payments to France, Spain, and private Dutch investors who had helped finance the war.

Meanwhile, the states faced their own financial difficulties. A postwar **depression**, or severe economic downturn, created hardship for farmers throughout the United States. State governments made the situation worse by imposing heavy taxes in order to repay **war bonds** issued to fund the Revolution. During the war, people had bought the bonds for less than their face value with the assurance they could sell them back for their full value when the bonds matured. As the war debt rose, many bond holders believed they would never be paid back, and they sold their bonds to wealthy lenders for cash, but at discounted prices.

When states levied high taxes, farmers had an especially hard time paying. Most farmers were used to paying debts with crops or livestock and rarely did business in cash. In many states, all or a portion of taxes had to be paid in gold and silver coins. If farmers failed to pay taxes, local courts seized their land and livestock and sold them, often at a fraction of their value. The courts imprisoned anyone whose assets failed to cover debts and back taxes until someone paid the sum owed.

CONFLICTS WITH OTHER NATIONS

Under the Articles of Confederation, conflicts with other countries also proved difficult to resolve. Without the ability to raise money and assemble a strong army, the American government could not enforce its policies. In the Treaty of 1783, for example, the British pledged to remove their troops from forts in the Great Lakes region. Through the 1780s, however, they refused to withdraw, hoping to regain the territory. They barred American ships from the Great Lakes and allied with Native Americans who wanted to halt white settlement. British diplomats claimed the actions were justified because Americans had failed to pay prewar debts to British creditors and to return property they had confiscated from Loyalists during the Revolution.

Native Americans allied with both Britain and Spain to slow the influx of American settlers. In return for an alliance and weapons, the Creek offered to block the Americans from settling in Spanish territory. The Cherokee and Shawnee also battled Americans through the 1780s, mostly in Tennessee, Kentucky, and Alabama, thus slowing settlement in what was then the southwestern frontier. In the Ohio Territory and surrounding northwest areas, Mohawk leader Thayendanegea (thahy-ehn-DAHY-naw-gah), also known as **Joseph Brant**, rallied Native Americans against white settlement.

During the 1780s, as settlers rapidly filled the region between the Appalachian Mountains and the Mississippi River, Spain feared it might lose control of Louisiana and Florida. In 1784, to protect its interests, the Spanish government closed the port of New Orleans to American ships and trade. The lower Mississippi River remained closed to U.S. navigation until 1788, when the Spanish permitted Americans to bring goods through New Orleans as long as they paid duties, or taxes, to Spain.

In 1786, Mohawk leader **Joseph Brant** sat for American portrait painter Gilbert Stuart in London. A renowned diplomat and warrior, Brant was in England to negotiate Iroquois land claims.

HISTORICAL THINKING

1. **READING CHECK** What problems did the nation experience under the Articles of Confederation?

2. **DRAW CONCLUSIONS** Why was the Confederation Congress unable to pay off the large national debt?

3. **COMPARE AND CONTRAST** How was the government of the new republic similar to and different from British rule of the colonies?

PLAN: 2-PAGE LESSON

OBJECTIVE

Explore how the emphasis on state sovereignty under the Articles of Confederation created serious problems for the new republic.

CRITICAL THINKING SKILLS FOR LESSON 1.1

- Draw Conclusions
- Compare and Contrast
- Make Predictions
- Analyze Cause and Effect
- Summarize

HISTORICAL THINKING FOR CHAPTER 5

How did American ideals and culture shape the new government? Americans had a deep distrust of a strong central government. Lesson 1.1 describes how the Articles of Confederation made it difficult to govern the country, pay off war debts, and deal with foreign nations.

BACKGROUND FOR THE TEACHER

Thayendanegea, or Joseph Brant, was a Mohawk leader, a Christian missionary, and a captain in the British Army. Born to Mohawk parents, he was educated at a Christian school and learned English, Greek, Latin, and European history. In the American Revolution, Brant fought so well against the Americans that George Washington offered a reward for his capture. After the war, Washington recognized the value of working with this powerful leader and invited Brant and other Iroquois Confederation elders to Philadelphia to improve U.S. relations with the tribes. During his life, Brant posed for several portraits, including the one by Gilbert Stuart. He often wore what came to be called "Indian dress," which was a blend of Native American clothing and ornamentation with items manufactured in Britain to look Native American.

FINANCIAL LITERACY

To extend their knowledge and understanding about the concepts in this lesson, refer students to the Financial Literacy handbook.

INTRODUCE & ENGAGE

CONSIDER GOVERNMENT POWER

Invite volunteers to share what they know about the division of power between the states and the federal government today. **ASK:** What powers are unique to the federal government? *(ability to sign treaties, declare war, coin money, control interstate trade, and settle disputes among states)* What would happen if the federal government had to ask states for money to carry out these powers? *(Possible response: States might be reluctant to comply, and the government would have trouble operating.)* Explain that in the 1780s the Articles of Confederation created financial troubles for the central government.

TEACH

GUIDED DISCUSSION

1. **Make Predictions** All states, regardless of size or population, had equal votes in Congress. What problems might this create in governing the new republic? *(Possible response: It might make it harder to pass national legislation and might increase friction among the states, since larger and smaller states would have an equal voice but very different needs and goals.)*

2. **Analyze Cause and Effect** After the war, why was there such an increase in the number of farmers who lost their land? *(Possible response: The states required farmers to pay taxes in coins, which many of them didn't have, instead of with livestock or crops. When farmers couldn't pay their debts or taxes, state courts seized and sold their property for nonpayment and imprisoned those who still owed money.)*

SUMMARIZE

Guide students to think about the conflicts with foreign nations confronting the United States in the postwar years. **ASK:** How did these conflicts impact the United States as a nation? *(Possible response: The republic faced interference with its trade and its territorial expansion. The British barred U.S. shipping in the Great Lakes region; Native Americans sided with Britain and Spain to slow western settlement and attacked white settlers; Spain limited access to the port of New Orleans.)*

ACTIVE OPTIONS

On Your Feet: Conduct a Three-Step Interview Have students work in pairs to interview each other regarding the financial problems the new nation faced. Direct one student to interview the other by asking this question: What economic challenges did the states face in the new republic? Urge the interviewer to ask follow-up questions based on the answers provided. Then tell students to reverse roles, with the second student asking this question: What economic challenges did the federal government face in the new republic? Finally, ask students to share information from the interviews with the class.

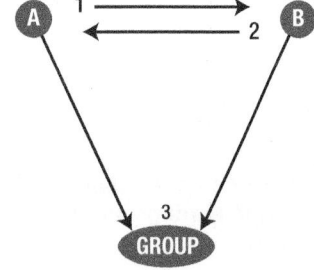

NG Learning Framework: Research Frontier Conflicts

SKILLS Communication, Collaboration

KNOWLEDGE Our Human Story

Have groups of students work together to develop a presentation about the frontier conflicts mentioned in the lesson. Assign each group a conflict to research: the British in the Great Lakes region, Native American actions against white settlers on the frontier, or Spain's actions involving the port of New Orleans. Students should lelarn details about the conflict and how both sides responded. When finished, ask groups to collaborate to construct a frontier map showing the locations of the conflicts. Then invite each group to share their findings with the class.

DIFFERENTIATE

STRIVING READERS

Summarize Using a Concept Cluster Tell students to write the lesson title in the center circle of a Concept Cluster and subsection headings in the other circles. As students read the lesson, instruct them to enter key information on the spokes, adding spokes as needed. Invite volunteers to summarize the lesson using their completed Concept Cluster and give examples of various problems and events that showed the serious weaknesses of the Articles of Confederation.

PRE-AP

Support a Position Ask students if they believe that the Americans' distrust of a strong federal government, as embodied in the Articles of Confederation, was justified. Instruct them to conduct online research to gather evidence and expert opinions and to take notes to construct an argument that supports their position and addresses the opposing viewpoint. Invite students to present their argument as a written or oral report.

See the Chapter Planner for more strategies for differentiation.

HISTORICAL THINKING

ANSWERS

1. Strong state sovereignty and a weak federal government led to a lack of national unity, serious financial problems at the state and federal levels, and conflicts with other nations.

2. Since the Confederation Congress had no ability to impose taxes or compel states to contribute money to the central government, it had no financial resources to pay off the national debt.

3. Possible response: Citizens now had a representative local and federal government, not one controlled by a distant, centralized monarchy, and they had a greater voice in running their own affairs. However, as under British rule, states could levy taxes on their citizens; and white males who owned property had more rights than women, white males without property, Native Americans, and people of color.

CRITICAL VIEWING The painting *Daniel Boone—The Home Seeker: Cumberland Valley* (c. 1940) by American artist N.C. Wyeth depicts the legendary frontiersman and his family moving westward. Boone's trailblazing helped later settlers reach the Northwest Territory. What do details in the painting imply about journeys through the wilderness?

THE NORTHWEST ORDINANCES

How do 13 separate governments resolve a shared problem? The 13 states all had overlapping claims to western frontier lands, and the new Congress faced one of its first challenges in crafting a fair solution.

LAND ORDINANCE OF 1785

As you have read, the Treaty of Paris of 1783 granted the United States most of the land between the Atlantic Ocean and the Mississippi River. Besides the original 13 states, this area consisted of the lands west of Pennsylvania, north of the Ohio River, and east of the Mississippi River. These "western lands" collectively became known as the Northwest Territory and included present-day Ohio, Indiana, Illinois, Michigan, Wisconsin, and part of Minnesota.

By ceding this territory to the United States, the Treaty of Paris also invalidated the many treaties between the British and the Native American nations who lived there. The question of who really controlled the area became a pressing issue. Some states claimed parts of the territory. Virginia, for example, claimed all the land between its western border and the Mississippi River. Other states argued that the

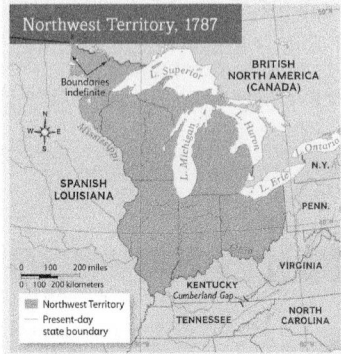

Confederation Congress should control the area. Clearly, the nation needed a system to guide the settlement of the Northwest Territory.

Operating under the Articles of Confederation, Congress passed three **ordinances**, or laws, designed to provide order and regulate settlement in the Northwest Territory. These ordinances established a system for transferring federally owned land into private holdings and forming townships and states.

The first ordinance, passed in 1784, divided the Northwest Territory into seven districts. The law allowed the settlers of each district to govern themselves by choosing a constitution and laws from any of the existing states. When a district's population reached that of Rhode Island, the smallest of the original 13 states, the district would become a state. Congress retained responsibility for selling public lands in the seven districts.

The second law, the **Land Ordinance of 1785**, set the procedures for surveying, dividing, and distributing land in the Northwest Territory. The ordinance called for dividing districts into townships 6 miles square, which could be further subdivided into 640-acre lots. Each lot would be sold at a minimum of $1 per acre, or $640 per lot.

The ordinance of 1785 reserved land in each township for a public school. By setting aside land for schools, Congress established a **precedent**, or example, of supporting public education, forwarding the ideals of egalitarianism, democracy, and republicanism. Thomas Jefferson pointed out that a republic could only work if voters were educated enough to make informed choices. About the importance of public education, Jefferson wrote, "Above all things I hope the education of the common

people will be attended to; convinced that on their good sense we may rely with the most security for the preservation of a due degree of liberty."

Because of the relatively high cost of the township lots, Congress had difficulty selling them to individuals. In fact, many settlers set up farms on lots without government approval. Frustrated by the lack of sales and in need of funds to pay off war debts, Congress agreed to sell 1.5 million acres for less than 10 cents an acre to the Ohio Company. The Ohio Company was a group of New England **speculators**. A speculator is a person who invests in property or stocks, hoping to sell at a profit.

NORTHWEST ORDINANCE OF 1787

The third ordinance, the **Northwest Ordinance of 1787**, created a process for organizing territorial governments and states. The ordinance called for Congress to appoint a governor, secretary, and three judges to administer a newly established territory. Once 5,000 adult males resided in a territory, they could elect an assembly. The right to vote was limited to free men who owned at least 50 acres of land. A territory qualified to enter the Union as a state when its population reached 60,000. Congress anticipated that three to five states would be created from the Northwest Territory.

The 1787 ordinance included provisions for such individual rights as religious liberty and trial by jury. It also banned slavery. After the Revolution, the issue of slavery grew in importance as some citizens noted that it conflicted with the principles of the Revolution. By the mid-1780s, several state governments had passed legislation against slavery. Vermont banned slavery in its constitution in 1777. In 1780, Pennsylvania passed a law providing for a gradual end to slavery in the state. In 1783, the Massachusetts Supreme Court declared that slavery violated the state constitution, which effectively ended slavery in the state. New Hampshire began abolishing slavery in the same year. In 1784, legislatures in Connecticut and Rhode Island followed Pennsylvania's example by passing laws gradually ending slavery.

HISTORICAL THINKING

1. **READING CHECK** What was the purpose of the three ordinances governing the Northwest Territory?

2. **INTERPRET MAPS** Besides land, what natural resources visible on the map of the Northwest Territory would benefit settlers?

3. **MAKE INFERENCES** How did the Northwest Ordinance of 1787 reflect democratic values?

PLAN: 2-PAGE LESSON

OBJECTIVE

Understand the ordinances passed by Congress in the 1780s to manage settlement of the Northwest Territory.

CRITICAL THINKING SKILLS FOR LESSON 1.2

- Interpret Maps
- Make Inferences
- Make Connections
- Identify

HISTORICAL THINKING FOR CHAPTER 5

How did American ideals and culture shape the new government? The Confederation Congress incorporated democratic ideals in dealing with the Northwest Territory. Lesson 1.2 discusses three ordinances passed by Congress to organize and regulate the territory.

BACKGROUND FOR THE TEACHER

For the Land Ordinance of 1785, surveyors used a rectangular survey system to create uniform parcels of land. Prior to this, the metes-and-bounds system had been used in much of colonial America, which caused numerous problems and boundary disputes. In the metes-and-bounds system, surveyors used natural features, such as creeks or ridges, and human-made structures, such as roads, to mark property boundaries. However, this system often created oddly shaped and sized lots. Also, the lot boundaries changed whenever features changed, such as a creek altering its course. People could gain or lose land arbitrarily, which led to many lawsuits. The rectangular survey system offered several advantages over the metes-and-bounds system. The surveys were less costly, boundaries did not shift, lot sizes were uniform, and good land was mixed with poor land, resulting in fewer hard-to-sell lots.

For students who develop an interest in these ordinances, suggest that they read the online American Story "The Northwest Ordinances."

INTRODUCE & ENGAGE

DISTRIBUTE LAND

Tell students to imagine they are in charge of a large piece of land that must be divided fairly among people who all claim a share of it. **ASK:** What method would you use to divide the land? What steps would you take to resolve people's competing claims? After discussing their ideas, tell students that in this lesson they will learn how Congress addressed these and other difficult challenges when deciding how the Northwest Territory should be settled and regulated.

TEACH

GUIDED DISCUSSION

1. **Make Connections** How did the ordinances of 1784 and 1785 extend the principles of republicanism in the Northwest Territory? *(Possible response: Congress allowed settlers to choose their own form of government from one of the existing states and required them to set aside land for public schools, believing a republic depended on educated voters making informed choices.)*

2. **Identify** What were the main flaws in the way Congress carried out the Land Ordinance of 1785? *(Possible response: Few people could afford the price of lots, people established their farms without permission, and the government was forced to sell the land at a steep discount to raise money for war debt payments.)*

MORE INFORMATION

The Ohio Company Also known as the Ohio Company of Associates, the company benefited in several ways in its dealings with Congress. It was allowed to make the first payment of its 1.5-million-acre purchase in military script, which meant investors put up less cash to buy the land. The company also got help from Congress when clashes with Native Americans threatened to slow settlement. Congress donated an additional 100,000 acres to the Ohio Company to act as a buffer between white settlements and Native Americans. The company allowed people to buy land in this buffer area if they were willing to defend their homesteads from the tribes. Finally, in 1795, the federal Treaty of Greenville forced many Native American tribes out of the region, which encouraged more settlers to purchase land from the Ohio Company.

ACTIVE OPTIONS

On Your Feet: Numbered Heads Arrange students in groups and have students number off within each group. Provide the following prompts for them to think about and discuss: What problems were the Land Ordinances of 1784 and 1787 trying to address? What future problems do you think either ordinance might create? After sufficient time, call a number and have each student with that number report on the group's discussion.

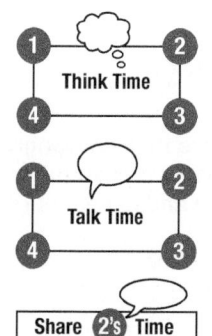

NG Learning Framework: Write Persuasive Materials

SKILLS Problem-Solving, Communication

KNOWLEDGE Our Human Story

Share the More Information paragraph with students. Tell them to imagine they are members of the Ohio Company faced with the problem of persuading settlers to purchase land and move to the Northwest Territory. Invite students to work in groups to solve this problem by developing materials such as a recruitment flier or poster. Suggest they use the text, map, and painting in the lesson as a starting point for their work and conduct online research on the topic as needed. Encourage students to think about what images and language would appeal to potential settlers, what skills and qualities settlers would need, what risks they might face, and what benefits Congress could promise them. Invite groups to share their persuasive materials with the class.

DIFFERENTIATE

INCLUSION

Ask Clarifying Questions Direct students who have perception issues to work with students who can read the lesson with them. Encourage students with perception issues to ask clarifying questions whenever they are confused about a word or topic. Have both students work together to answer the Critical Viewing and Historical Thinking questions.

GIFTED & TALENTED

Create a Multimedia Presentation Instruct students to use online and print sources to gather information about the effects of the Treaty of Paris and the Northwest Ordinances on the property rights, individual rights, and religious liberty of Native Americans living in the Great Lakes and Ohio Valley regions. Have students incorporate paintings, drawings, maps, artifacts, and quotations from primary sources into their multimedia presentations. Invite them to present their work to the class and answer questions about the topic.

See the Chapter Planner for more strategies for differentiation.

HISTORICAL THINKING

ANSWERS

1. The three ordinances established procedures to transfer federal land to personal ownership; to survey, divide, and distribute the land; and to set up territorial governments and create states.

2. Possible response: Other natural resources include major river systems and four of the Great Lakes.

3. The Northwest Ordinance of 1787 protected the rights of religious liberty and trial by jury, outlawed slavery, and created a process for organizing territorial governments and admitting new states to the Union.

CRITICAL VIEWING Mountains and hills in the painting imply that settlers had to cross challenging terrain with their families; the guns they carry suggest they had to be alert for danger; and the pack animals show that settlers had to carry most of their supplies with them.

THE CONSTITUTIONAL CONVENTION

If you had lived through more than six years of war, what would you most want? A peaceful life? That's probably what Americans wanted after the end of the Revolution. So what pushed a group of American farmers to take up rifles and fight again?

SHAYS'S REBELLION

As you have read, an economic depression after the Revolution caused great hardship for farmers. Before the war, British companies had encouraged Americans to buy goods on **credit**, which meant they could obtain the goods immediately and pay for them over time. Many farmers had paid their debts with such goods as crops or livestock or with **currency**, or paper money, issued by the states. Now that the war was over, the British manufacturers demanded Americans pay their debts in **specie**, or money in the form of gold and silver coins. Both specie and currency backed by specie were in short supply. At the same time, state governments imposed high taxes on their citizens, in part to repay war debts, and many demanded that a portion of these taxes be paid in specie.

The requirement to pay most debts and taxes in specie forced many Americans, particularly farmers, to run up enormous personal debts. As you have read, if people couldn't pay their debts or their taxes, they could be imprisoned. In addition, their property would be seized for nonpayment of taxes.

In this lithograph of Shays's Rebellion (1786–1787), a mob of rebels watch as one protester fights with a government official. The rebels gathered in September 1786 to prevent the court in Springfield, Massachusetts, from meeting.

Debtors around the country protested, but none more forcefully than the farmers of western Massachusetts. Beginning in August 1786, a farmer and veteran of the American Revolution named Daniel Shays staged an uprising that became known as **Shays's Rebellion**. Shays led armed farmers into Massachusetts courthouses to stop debt hearings and **foreclosures**, or the taking possession of property to cover outstanding debts.

In response to the attacks, Massachusetts called up 1,200 members of the state militia and implored Congress to help the state put down the armed rebellion. Congress, proving to be ineffectual in a crisis, responded by asking the states to send money and recruits to form a federal army. The Massachusetts government—and every state except Virginia—refused to raise the money. In late January 1787, Shays and the rebels attacked the federal armory at Springfield, intent on seizing its large store of weapons. Outnumbered but well-armed, the militia defeated them, and the rebellion was over by February. But the debt problem and the mounting discontent did not go away. The rebellion highlighted those issues, and voters turned to the ballot box to elect candidates who were sympathetic to debtors. Shays and many of his followers later received pardons.

The angry militancy of indebted farmers drew attention to the disastrous state of the nation's finances. The revolt highlighted the inability of Congress under the Articles of Confederation to resolve the nation's financial problems and maintain law and order. The rebellion concerned George Washington enough that he returned to public life.

A CONSTITUTIONAL CONVENTION

For years, Patriot leaders such as **Alexander Hamilton** of New York and Robert Morris of Pennsylvania had argued in favor of a more powerful central government. Shays's Rebellion brought more people around to their way of thinking.

In September 1786, as Shays's Rebellion grew stronger, state delegates assembled in Annapolis, Maryland, to discuss amending the Articles of Confederation in order to give Congress the power to regulate trade. But only five state delegations arrived on time, so the convention was canceled. Several delegates called for another convention to meet in May 1787 in Philadelphia to work on a broader revision of the Articles.

The Philadelphia meeting, called the **Constitutional Convention,** started on May 25, 1787. Every state except Rhode Island sent delegates. The delegates who gathered to create the Constitution—all wealthy and well educated—would become known as the **Framers**. Many of them, such as Benjamin Franklin of Pennsylvania, had been leaders during the Revolution and the first years of the republic. The Framers elected George Washington of Virginia as the leader of the convention.

To preserve the papers he acquired during the Constitutional Convention, George Washington stored them in this leather and brass-tack document box.

At the time of the convention, the weather in Philadelphia was punishingly hot and humid. Even so, the delegates insisted on keeping all the windows and doors shut in order to keep their discussions private. Men's fashions of the period added to the delegates' discomfort. Men wore coats and vests at all times, and the New England delegates were even wearing wool. Today, some historians believe that the delegates' desire to escape the stifling heat of Philadelphia made them more efficient and willing to compromise.

One of the most influential and prominent delegates was **James Madison** of Virginia, a 36-year-old planter, slaveholder, and intellectual who had served in the Virginia assembly and in Congress. In response to what he saw as major problems in Congress and in state governments, Madison felt compelled to push for a stronger central government. Ordinarily a shy man who avoided public speaking, he took such a dominant role in the proceedings that he was later called the "Father of the Constitution." Even though the purpose of the convention was to amend the Articles of Confederation, Madison arrived with a prepared document in which he proposed a powerful federal government to link all the states together. This document shifted the debate from how to revise the Articles to how to create an entirely new plan of government.

HISTORICAL THINKING

1. **READING CHECK** What was the historical significance of Shays's Rebellion?

2. **DRAW CONCLUSIONS** Why do you think the states wanted farmers to pay their debts in specie?

3. **IDENTIFY PROBLEMS AND SOLUTIONS** What financial problems did farmers and the states face after the Revolution, and why were they difficult to solve?

PLAN: 2-PAGE LESSON

OBJECTIVE

Identify the issues that led Congress to recognize problems presented by the Articles of Confederation and to call for revision.

CRITICAL THINKING SKILLS FOR LESSON 2.1

- Draw Conclusions
- Identify Problems and Solutions
- Analyze Primary Sources
- Make Inferences

HISTORICAL THINKING FOR CHAPTER 5

How did American ideals and culture shape the new government? The Articles of Confederation contained serious weaknesses that hampered the new republic. Lesson 2.1 describes how the government's inability to handle crises and unify the states led to the Constitutional Convention.

BACKGROUND FOR THE TEACHER

George Washington expressed his concerns over Shays's Rebellion in several letters to his friends. He wrote to David Humphreys that "commotions of this sort, like snow-balls, gather strength as they roll, if there is no opposition in the way to divide and crumble them." To Henry Knox, he noted, "If government shrinks, or is unable to enforce its laws; fresh manoeuvers will be displayed by the insurgents—anarchy & confusion must prevail—and every thing will be turned topsy turvey in that State; where it is not probable the mischiefs will terminate."

Following the rebellion, Washington again wrote to Knox, saying "that good may result from the cloud of evils which threatened, not only the hemisphere of Massachusetts but by spreading its baneful influence, the tranquility of the Union." Yet he remained concerned. "Our Affairs, generally, seem really, to be approaching to some awful crisis. God only knows what the result will be." He had little idea the result would be a new form of government.

INTRODUCE & ENGAGE

CONNECT TO THE PRESENT

Direct students' attention to the illustration of Shays's Rebellion and read the caption aloud. Ask students to recall news footage or photographs they have seen that show Americans protesting government actions or lack of action. Guide a short discussion about the influence of social protests on the actions of local or federal governments. Tell students that in this lesson they will learn how Shays's Rebellion helped pave the way for the Constitutional Convention.

TEACH

GUIDED DISCUSSION

1. **Analyze Primary Sources** Share the Background for the Teacher quotations with the class. Prompt students to think about George Washington's comments. **ASK:** Why was Washington so concerned about Shays's Rebellion? *(Possible response: Washington was concerned that Shays's Rebellion would spread if not put down. Because the federal government could not maintain law and order nor could the states act together, a spreading rebellion could threaten the very survival of the Union.)*

2. **Draw Conclusions** Why might Daniel Shays and his followers have felt justified in launching a rebellion? *(Possible response: Shays and his followers probably felt the government had become tyrannical. Their appeals and protests to state legislators had been in vain, so an armed rebellion was the only recourse they thought they had left to save their farms and stay out of prison. The fact that many rebels were later pardoned shows their cause had merit.)*

MAKE INFERENCES

At the start of the Constitutional Convention, the Framers agreed to follow a set of rules, including one that stated "nothing spoken in the House [would] be printed, or otherwise published, or communicated, without leave." **ASK:** Why do you think the Framers adopted the rule of secrecy even though it seems to contradict the democratic ideals that formed the basis of the Constitutional Convention? *(Possible response: The Framers probably wanted to debate their ideas, change their minds, make compromises, and establish the infrastructure for a new government free from outside pressure or the need to justify their positions to the public.)*

ACTIVE OPTIONS

On Your Feet: Roundtable Discussion Ask students to reread the information about Shays's Rebellion. Then arrange the class into groups of four and ask them to discuss the following question: How does Shays's rebellion compare and contrast to the American Revolution? Have each group consider the causes and demands of both rebellions, which class of people fought the ruling authority, and the goals of each rebellion. At the end, ask a volunteer from each group to summarize the main points of their discussion.

NG Learning Framework: Secrecy Versus Transparency

`ATTITUDE` Responsibility

`SKILL` Communication

Point out to students that lawmakers have long debated the question of secrecy versus transparency in government. Ask students to conduct research about both sides of this issue. Then divide the class into two groups to stage a debate about the merits of government secrecy versus transparency. Each group should develop their claim and their arguments based on information and examples from this lesson, their research, and their own knowledge. Then have each group pick their debate team members and hold the debate for the class. At the end, ask the class to vote on which side presented the better argument.

DIFFERENTIATE

ENGLISH LANGUAGE LEARNERS

Understand Related Words Write the words *debts*, *debtors*, and *indebted* on the board, reminding students that the *b* is silent: \det\ . Pair students at the **Emerging** or **Expanding** level with those at the **Bridging** level. Ask pairs to complete a diagram such as the one shown, writing a definition and an original sentence under each word. After they have completed the diagram, encourage students to discuss the different meanings of each word.

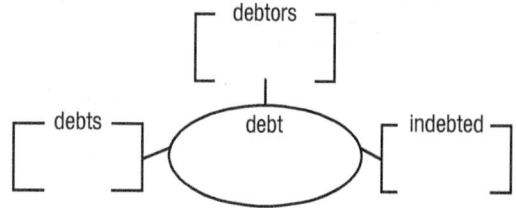

GIFTED & TALENTED

Analyze a Work of Art Instruct students to prepare a formal analysis of the lithograph of Shays's Rebellion. Suggest that they begin by taking notes on the setting and action, the expressions on bystanders' faces, and the artist's point of view. Then have students write an analysis that includes their informed thoughts about how the lithograph illustrates the reasons for Shays's Rebellion and how those reasons are related to the Articles of Confederation. Invite students to present their analysis to the class.

See the Chapter Planner for more strategies for differentiation.

HISTORICAL THINKING

ANSWERS

1. Shays's Rebellion showed Congress's inability to maintain order or address the nation's financial problems. This, in turn, increased support for a stronger central government, which led to the Constitutional Convention.

2. Possible response: Gold and silver coins were easier to use and had a stable value, unlike paper money, which was usually not backed by specie. Crops and livestock, whose value also fluctuated, would have to be sold to obtain specie.

3. Both had enormous debts and needed specie or currency backed by specie to pay them off. Farmers also needed specie to pay the taxes that states levied. Since specie and specie-backed currency were in short supply, states and farmers found it impossible to get out of debt.

A CONSTITUTIONAL REPUBLIC

Meet each other halfway. Make a deal. Find a happy medium. These expressions all mean the same thing: compromise. That's what the delegates to the Constitutional Convention did to create our American form of government.

THE GREAT COMPROMISE

In 1787, when the delegates in Philadelphia began to debate what form the new government of the United States should take, they had a variety of competing interests to consider and issues to resolve. But they could agree on a few things. For example, they wanted the federal and state governments to share power, a system called **federalism**. They also wanted the state governments to have certain powers that the federal government could not overrule, an idea called **dual sovereignty**. But how should power be divided? How would the rights of small states and large states be balanced? Should the federal government include a head of state, and how much power should that office hold? Should there be federal courts, and how much power should they have?

Convention delegates created a **constitutional republic**, a government in which the representatives gain their authority from the consent of the governed—that is, from the voters who elect them. The delegates agreed that the new government needed the same three branches as the British government: a **legislative branch** to make the laws, an **executive branch** to enforce the laws and lead the nation, and a **judicial branch** to interpret the laws. But the delegates expanded on the concept. Influenced by the writings of French political philosopher **Montesquieu** (MON-tuh-SKYOO), the Framers decided the three branches should have separate responsibilities and powers, so that no branch could become too powerful. This principle of **separation of powers** proved to be essential in the creation of the U.S. Constitution. As John Adams explained, "It is by balancing each of these Powers against the other two, that the Effort in human Nature towards Tyranny can alone be checked and restrained, and any degree of Freedom preserved in the Constitution."

During the first seven weeks of the Constitutional Convention, one issue overshadowed all others—the power of large states versus small states. James Madison's **Virginia Plan**, presented by fellow Virginian Edmund Randolph, proposed a powerful central government anchored by a **bicameral legislature**—one made up of two houses. Qualified voters would elect members to the lower house. For the upper house, members of each state's legislature would nominate candidates, and members of the lower house would choose from among them. The federal legislature would appoint members of the executive and judicial branches of the central government and could veto state laws. This plan gave more power to the larger states, because the number of representatives from each state depended on the state's population.

Several smaller states opposed the Virginia Plan. Delaware, Maryland, New Jersey, and Connecticut feared the power of Virginia, Pennsylvania, and Massachusetts, which together were home to almost half of the American population. If the Virginia Plan were adopted, just four states could dominate the legislature. In mid-June, William Paterson of New Jersey introduced the **New Jersey Plan**, which proposed a one-house, or unicameral, Congress in which all states had equal representation. In this plan, Congress would appoint an executive council, which would choose a supreme court. As in the Virginia Plan, Congress had greater authority than under the Articles of Confederation, with powers to tax, regulate commerce, and compel states to obey its laws. But the large states objected to the New Jersey Plan, arguing that Delaware, with a population of just 59,000, should not have as much power as Virginia, which had a population of 748,000.

TOTAL POPULATION OF THE UNITED STATES, 1790: 3,929,214

Population of Virginia 19%, 747,610

Population of New Jersey 4.7%, 184,139

= one representative from Virginia

= one representative from New Jersey

Edmund Randolph's **Virginia Plan**
TWO HOUSES
UPPER HOUSE
LOWER HOUSE
The number of representatives from each state is proportionate to the state's population.

William Paterson's **New Jersey Plan**
ONE HOUSE
Each state has an equal number of representatives, regardless of population.

ROGER SHERMAN'S
GREAT COMPROMISE

HOUSE OF REPRESENTATIVES
The number of representatives from each state is proportionate to the state's population.

SENATE
Each state has an equal number of representatives, regardless of population.

Source: United States Census Bureau

Roger Sherman of Connecticut finally broke the stalemate by proposing a plan known as the **Great Compromise**. This plan included a bicameral Congress. Representation in the lower house, the House of Representatives, would be based on population. The members of this house would be elected directly by the voters every two years. Only this house would have the power to initiate revenue bills, which meant that voters would elect the representatives who taxed them.

In the upper house, called the Senate, each state legislature would choose two senators to serve six-year terms. The idea of a bicameral Congress resolved the debate between small and large states. It also satisfied leaders who wanted to limit the influence of ordinary voters. These leaders expected that senators would come from the wealthier, upper classes of society. The senators' long terms and the fact that they were appointed by state legislators rather than elected by citizens would shield them from public opinion and provide a stabilizing influence. The plan required both houses of Congress to approve legislation.

Under the Great Compromise, the United States would become a single nation rather than a confederacy of states. At the same time, the states retained some rights, including equal representation in the Senate.

Forging a New Government **159**

PLAN: 4-PAGE LESSON

OBJECTIVE

Evaluate the reasons for and consequences of the compromises delegates made when drafting the Constitution.

CRITICAL THINKING SKILLS FOR LESSON 2.2

- Compare and Contrast
- Summarize
- Interpret Charts
- Make Connections
- Analyze Visuals
- Make Inferences
- Draw Conclusions
- Analyze Primary Sources

HISTORICAL THINKING FOR CHAPTER 5

How did American ideals and culture shape the new government? Compromise was necessary to create a constitutional republic. Lesson 2.2 examines the many arguments and compromises among delegates as they crafted a new government.

BACKGROUND FOR THE TEACHER

The Constitution created a Senate to give all states equal representation, but delegates then had to decide on the number of senators per state and their term limits. Some argued that one senator per state was too few; if the senator became ill or was called away, the state would be unrepresented. Also, more senators might make it easier to curb any unruly democratic tendencies of the House, something that concerned many delegates. Because the delegates deemed three senators per state too costly, they instead settled on two. As for term limits, James Madison and Edmund Randolph pushed for seven or nine years. Alexander Hamilton argued strongly for a life term as the only way to stem the "amazing violence & turbulence of the democratic spirit." In the end, the delegates settled on a six-year term for senators.

HISTORY NOTEBOOK

Encourage students to complete the American Gallery page for Chapter 5 in their History Notebooks as they read.

INTRODUCE & ENGAGE
BRAINSTORM CRITERIA

Write the word *compromise* on the board and ask volunteers for a definition of the word. Then ask the class to brainstorm criteria for what makes a good versus a poor compromise. Use a T-Chart to record the two lists of criteria. For example, under Good Compromise, students might list *solves the original problem; all sides gain something of value.* Under Poor Compromise, they might list *solves only part of the problem; one side feels short changed.* As students read the lesson, encourage them to use their criteria to evaluate the compromises the delegates made.

Good Compromise	Poor Compromise

TEACH
GUIDED DISCUSSION

1. **Make Connections** What impact did the Constitutional Convention have on the issue of sovereignty? *(Under the Articles of Confederation, sovereignty rested with the states. The convention delegates created a system based on federalism, which meant the federal and state governments shared power, and dual sovereignty, which meant the state governments retained certain powers that the federal government couldn't overrule.)*

2. **Compare and Contrast** How were the Virginia Plan and New Jersey Plan similar and different? *(Both plans gave Congress the authority to tax, regulate trade, and compel the states to obey federal laws. However, the two plans differed in the number of houses and in how representation was determined.)*

3. **Summarize** What concerns other than representation did the Great Compromise address? *(The House of Representatives solved the issue of raising federal revenue, since the House had the power to initiate revenue bills. Members of the Senate were appointed by state legislatures and served for longer terms, which addressed concerns about representatives having too much influence.)*

ANALYZE VISUALS

Direct students' attention to the infographic of the Great Compromise. Make sure students understand that the whole pie chart represents the size of the population of the United States in 1790, while the slices represent each state's proportion of that population. **ASK:** Which three states were the most populous? *(Virginia, South Carolina, Pennsylvania)* Based on the pie chart, about what percentage of the population lived in the eight smallest states? *(about 20 percent)* How does the infographic help you understand why large states favored the Virginia Plan, while small states favored the New Jersey Plan? *(Answers will vary. Possible response: Under the Virginia Plan, Virginia's representation in both houses of Congress would be four times greater than New Jersey's. This system benefited large states. Under the New Jersey Plan, representation would be equal in a single house of Congress. This benefited small states.)*

DIFFERENTIATE
STRIVING READERS

Understand Main Ideas Check students' understanding of the main ideas in the lesson by asking them to correctly complete either/or statements such as the following:

- The principle of separation of powers prevents any one branch of government from becoming too [powerful or weak]. *(powerful)*
- The bicameral Congress resolved the debate between [slave and free states or large and small states]. *(large and small states)*
- Delegates to the Constitutional Convention created an electoral college because they [trusted or distrusted] voters' ability to choose the president. *(distrusted)*
- The judiciary is the branch of government [most or least] clearly defined in the Constitution. *(least)*
- [Veto power or Interstate commerce] is one of the checks and balances written into the Constitution. *(veto power)*
- The Framers of the Constitution [supported or opposed] slaveholders. *(opposed)*
- It is relatively [easy or difficult] to make amendments to the Constitution. *(difficult)*

After students have finished, direct them to work with a partner to check their answers. Then ask pairs to work together to answer the Historical Thinking questions.

PRE-AP

Write a Biographical Profile Encourage students to locate a historical biography, either online or in a library, about one of the Framers of the Constitution. Tell them to read their chosen biography independently and then write a profile that includes the person's background, motivations, goals, actions, and impact on the Constitution. Encourage students to share their profile with the class.

See the Chapter Planner for more strategies for differentiation.

THE EXECUTIVE AND JUDICIAL BRANCHES

Remembering the colonies' problems with the British monarchy, delegates to the Constitutional Convention did not want to assign too much power to one person. But they also wanted the executive branch to serve as a check on the legislature. Ultimately, they decided that the executive branch would feature a single president who would serve a four-year term.

But how should the president be chosen? Some delegates thought the president should be directly elected by the voters. Others wanted Congress or the state legislatures to make the choice. The delegates finally arrived at a solution: an **electoral college** made up of electors from each state would cast official votes for the president and vice president. The number of electors from each state would be the same as the state's number of representatives in Congress, and each state could decide how to choose its electors.

Of the three branches of government, the judicial branch is least clearly defined in the Constitution. While the Framers created a judiciary with a Supreme Court to interpret the laws, they left many of the details to Congress. However, Section 2 of Article 3 prescribes one of the basic rights enjoyed by American citizens: the right to a trial by jury. The Framers felt this right was essential to protect citizens from tyranny.

To reinforce the separation of powers, the Framers included **checks and balances** in the Constitution. This system allows each branch of government to amend or veto acts of another branch so that the power of the three branches remains balanced. The president was given the power to veto laws passed by Congress, but legislators could override the veto if two-thirds of both houses approved. Congress had the authority to remove the president by **impeachment** and trial for treason, bribery, and "other high Crimes and Misdemeanors." Impeachment is the process of bringing formal charges against

a public official. Congress also had the power to declare war and raise an army and navy, but the president served as commander-in-chief of the military. Only with the "advice and consent" of the Senate could the president negotiate treaties and appoint ambassadors, Supreme Court justices, and other officials. The courts had the power to strike down laws judged to be unconstitutional.

SLAVERY AND COMMERCE

In addition to determining the structure of the government itself, the Framers had to address two other major issues: slavery and commerce. The words *slave*, *slavery*, and *slave trade* do not appear anywhere in the 1787 Constitution, and yet the issue influenced debates on representation in Congress, the election of the president, and the regulation of commerce. The southern states wanted to count slaves in a state's population when calculating the

TO BE SOLD, on board the Ship *Bance-Island*, on tuesday the 6th of *May* next, at *Afhley-Ferry*; a choice cargo of about 250 fine healthy **NEGROES**, just arrived from the Windward & Rice Coast. —The utmost care has already been taken, and shall be continued, to keep them free from the least danger of being infected with the SMALL-POX, no boat having been on board, and all other communication with people from *Charles-Town* prevented.

Auftin, Laurens, & Appleby.

N. B. Full one Half of the above Negroes have had the SMALL-POX in their own Country.

The 1787 Constitution allowed for the importation of slaves for at least 20 years. This advertisement from a Charleston, South Carolina, newspaper in the late 1700s announces the importation and sale of Africans on the ship *Bance Island*. To appeal to plantation owners seeking rice-farming expertise, the ad mentions that the captives are from the Windward and Rice Coast, the rice-growing area of Sierra Leone. The ad also notes that the Africans are likely free from or immune to smallpox.

number of delegates to the House of Representatives and votes in the electoral college. Because enslaved persons made up a significant portion of the population in southern states, northerners protested that white southerners would gain an unfair advantage by such a plan. They argued that slaves should not be counted because they could not vote. The convention settled on the **Three-fifths Compromise**, which stated that five enslaved African Americans would count as three free persons for determining representation and direct taxes, which were to be levied on income or profits rather than on goods or services.

The Framers approved other measures that upheld slavery, which was not surprising since George Washington himself owned more than 300 slaves. While few northern delegates supported slavery, they did almost nothing to promote its end. Instead, the Framers supported southern interests by approving a **fugitive slave clause**, which prevented people who had escaped slavery in the South from living as free people in the North. The delegates also included a slave importation clause, which stated that Congress could not prohibit the importation of slaves for 20 years. North and South Carolina and Georgia demanded this option because they expected settlement to expand into western Georgia and what are now the states of Alabama, Mississippi, and Tennessee.

Besides the issue of slavery, the Framers had to address the issue of **interstate commerce**, or trade between the states. Under the Articles of Confederation, Congress had no power to regulate trade, except with Native American nations, or to make trade agreements with foreign governments. Each state made its own trade regulations and agreements, which often conflicted with those of nearby states. In the commerce clause of the Constitution, the Framers gave the federal government the right to "regulate commerce with foreign nations, and among the several states, and with the Indian tribes."

Finally, the Framers understood that they needed to devise a method for adding amendments, or changes, to the Constitution when necessary. They

The Three-fifths Compromise

In some regions, the Three-fifths Compromise could make a big difference in the number of allotted representatives. As you can see from the table, enslaved people made up a small proportion of the population of New England in 1790. In contrast, enslaved people made up more than one-third of the South's population.

Under the Three-fifths Compromise, about 2,300 people would be added to the population of New England for the purpose of determining representation, which was not enough to add one representative. But more than 387,000 people would be added to the population of the South, thus giving a major boost to the power of southern white voters by increasing the number of their representatives in Congress by more than 12.

Percentage of Enslaved Population by Region, 1790

Region	Total Population	Enslaved Population	Percentage Enslaved
New England	1,009,522	3,886	0.38%
Middle Atlantic	1,017,726	45,371	4.46%
South	1,866,387	645,023	34.56%
TOTAL	**3,893,635**	**694,280**	**17.83%**

Source: United States Census Bureau

decided, however, that the process should not be too easy because frequent changes would make the Constitution less stable and enduring. To make changes possible—but not easy—they decided that two-thirds of both houses of Congress or two-thirds of the state legislatures must propose an amendment. Then three-fourths of the state legislatures must ratify the amendment for it to be added to the Constitution. In more than 225 years, only 27 amendments have been added.

HISTORICAL THINKING

1. **READING CHECK** How did the Framers create a strong central government with checks on its power?

2. **COMPARE AND CONTRAST** How is the form of government outlined in the Constitution different from that prescribed in the Articles of Confederation?

3. **SUMMARIZE** How did the Great Compromise address the concerns of both large and small states?

4. **INTERPRET CHARTS** How did the southern states benefit from the Three-fifths Compromise? Support your answer with evidence from the population chart and the text.

BUILD BACKGROUND

THE ELECTORAL COLLEGE

The electoral college addressed the concerns of delegates who opposed direct elections for president. Delegates who mistrusted the ability of state voters to understand national concerns believed that states would choose electors who were intelligent and well informed. Delegates from southern states believed that the electoral college would work to their advantage because votes would be based on population, not on the number of eligible voters. The Framers let the states decide how to choose their electors. In the Constitution, each elector could cast two votes, but one of these votes had to be for a person outside the elector's state. Later, the 12th Amendment allowed states to decide how their electors should vote. However, even when state law requires all electors to vote for the candidate who wins the state, individual electors, nicknamed "faithless electors," can still vote for a different candidate if they wish.

THE ISSUE OF SLAVERY

The delegates to the Constitutional Convention were well aware that slavery directly contradicted the lofty ideals of freedom and equality that underpinned the American Revolution. This ideological problem caused rancor among delegates whenever the moral and religious implications of slavery were raised. Even some slaveholders spoke out against the practice, calling it evil and repugnant and declaring that it turned slaveholders into tyrants. As James Madison noted, "The real difference of interests lay not between the large & small but between the N. & Southn [sic] States. The institution of slavery & its consequences formed the line of discrimination." Yet many delegates feared that taking a stand against slavery would result in the convention's failure to form a new government. As a result, the delegates made concessions toward slavery that would have long-lasting political and social implications.

TEACH

GUIDED DISCUSSION

4. Make Inferences Why do you think the southern states would likely favor the electoral college over a direct vote for president? *(Possible response: The number of electors in each state equaled the number of the state's representatives, so southern states would benefit from the Three-fifths Compromise, which gave them more representatives. In a direct election, they would lose this advantage because only eligible voters would be allowed to vote.)*

5. Draw Conclusions How did the debate surrounding the Three-fifths Compromise contradict the Founding Fathers' philosophy of natural rights? *(Possible response: The Three-fifths Compromise was based on the premise that a certain portion of African Americans could be counted as free people, but none of them would be granted the rights of free people. This contradicted the notion that all men are created equal and endowed with certain unalienable rights.)*

ANALYZE PRIMARY SOURCES

Share with students the following quote by James Madison: "The real difference of interests lies not between the large and small but between the northern and southern states. The institution of slavery and its consequences form the line of discrimination."
ASK: What evidence from the lesson supports Madison's point of view? *(Possible response: The Great Compromise settled the issue of small versus large states, yet objections to slavery presented real threats to the success of the convention. As the price of their support, the southern states insisted on the Three-fifths Compromise and on including both the fugitive slave clause and the slave importation clause.)*

ACTIVE OPTIONS

Active History: Categorize Government Responsibilities Extend the lesson by using either the PDF or Whiteboard version of the activity. These activities take a deeper look at a topic from, or related to, the lesson. Explore the activities as a class, turn them into group assignments, or even assign them individually.

AMERICAN GALLERY ONLINE

Crafting the Constitution Invite students to explore the American Gallery. Have them select one of the images and do additional research to learn more about it. Ask questions that will inspire additional inquiry about the chosen gallery image, such as: Why did you choose this particular image? What does it show? How does it aid your understanding of the Constitutional Convention? What else would you like to know about the person, items, or events depicted?

NG Learning Framework: Write an Op-Ed Piece

ATTITUDE Empowerment

SKILL Communication

Encourage pairs of students to write an op-ed piece from a Framer's perspective about one of the compromises suggested during the Constitutional Convention. Instruct pairs to research one Framer and any works written by him in order to familiarize themselves with his views, beliefs, and style of expression. Tell partners that the op-ed article should express the Framer's argument for or against a compromise. Encourage students to keep in mind the criteria for a good compromise that they developed in the Introduce & Engage activity. Invite pairs to share their op-ed article with the class.

HISTORICAL THINKING

ANSWERS

1. The Framers gave more power to the central government but split it into three branches, with each branch able to check the power of the other branches. The president can veto legislation passed by Congress, but Congress can override that veto with two-thirds approval. The president can take executive actions, but Congress can impeach the president with cause. The Supreme Court has the power to strike down laws it considers unconstitutional, but the president and Congress appoint the justices.

2. The government established under the Articles of Confederation had no executive or judicial branches and consisted of only a single house of Congress that had no power to tax or regulate interstate trade. Under the Constitution, the federal government consists of a bicameral legislative branch, an executive branch, and a judicial branch. The government has the power to levy taxes, make laws, and regulate interstate trade.

3. The Great Compromise addressed the concerns of large states by creating a House of Representatives, whose numbers are based on each state's population size. The Compromise addressed the concerns of small states by creating the Senate, which gives every state equal representation.

4. Possible response: The southern states benefited from the Three-fifths Compromise because it increased their numbers in the House of Representatives by allowing them to count every five enslaved African Americans as three free people. This added more than 387,000 people to the southern population, which translated into more than 12 additional representatives in Congress.

FEDERALISTS AND ANTIFEDERALISTS

Imagine a conversation among a group of small farmers in rural Pennsylvania in late 1787. They say the proposed Constitution will create a central government that is too large and powerful—and out of touch with the needs of everyday people. Sound familiar? Some of the original criticisms of the form of government outlined in the Constitution still surface in political arguments today.

THE BATTLE OVER RATIFICATION

In Philadelphia on September 17, 1787, the Framers signed the Constitution. They quickly sent it to the Confederation Congress, which forwarded it to the states without much debate. According to Article 7 of the Constitution, at least nine state conventions had to ratify, or approve, it for the Constitution to become the basis for a new government. Leaders who supported ratification knew the process had to move quickly, before an effective opposition could arise.

Disagreements flared over the key issue of power—specifically, who held most of it. How much power should the central government have, and how strong should the executive branch be? How much power should the states have? A significant argument against the Constitution was that it did not guarantee certain basic rights, which had factored so prominently in the Declaration of Independence.

The pro-ratification group included such powerful leaders as James Madison, Alexander Hamilton, and John Jay. This group came to be called **federalists** because they argued in favor of the Constitution's federalist provisions—those that kept certain powers for the states—in addition to supporting the elements calling for a strong central government. The anti-ratification group acquired the name **antifederalists** because they disagreed with the federalist position. Concerned about the potential abuse of power by the federal government, they opposed a strong central government and favored giving more power to state governments. The antifederalists also included a number of prominent political leaders, such as George Mason and Patrick Henry, both of Virginia.

THE TWO SIDES

Citizens in both cities and rural areas joined the ratification debate. People with federalist and antifederalist viewpoints could be found in every state and among every economic group, debating the Constitution's pros and cons intensely.

Merchants, professionals, artisans, and commercial farmers tended to be federalists. They favored ratifying the Constitution because it gave the federal government, not state governments, the authority to issue money. The Constitution would put an end to state-issued currencies and result in one national currency, which would facilitate trade. They believed a strong central government would encourage the growth of a market economy, make it easier to trade with other states and countries, provide greater stability and strength, and raise the stature of the United States in the eyes of European nations.

The federalists thought the purpose of government was to help balance the opposing interests of different groups. They believed that society benefited when people pursued their own individual goals. Madison claimed that the Constitution would establish a large republic with so many different factions that no single interest group could monopolize power.

Antifederalists disagreed with this viewpoint. They favored small, homogeneous republics or states in which people shared similar needs. Many antifederalists were small family farmers who were in debt to wealthy merchants. They believed that a central government would be too large and too remote and that the interests of the citizens of the 13 states were too diverse for one body to govern them all effectively. They argued that a member of Congress could not possibly know the will of 30,000 voters. With so few people elected to Congress and such large electoral districts, wealthy, well-known candidates would have a strong advantage over ordinary people who ran for office. To the antifederalists, the Constitution lacked important safeguards against corruption and abuse of power. They argued for term limits and more frequent elections. Antifederalists also objected to the lack of a list of citizens' rights in the Constitution.

PRESENTING THEIR CASES

The federalists had some advantages over the antifederalists. The federalists were organized nationally, and many lived in the coastal cities and towns, where it was easier to influence public opinion than it was in rural areas. To promote their position, three of the most prominent federalists—Hamilton, Jay, and Madison—began publishing anonymous essays in New York newspapers explaining in detail why the Constitution should be ratified. In 1788, these 85 essays were gathered together into a book called *The Federalist*, which gained attention beyond New York. It is still considered a major work in American political theory.

The antifederalists also wrote anonymous newspaper columns that explained their position on the Constitution. Two of the most prominent antifederalist essayists called themselves Brutus and Cato, after famous ancient Roman politicians, and wrote in response to an anonymous pro-ratification essayist called Caesar. However, the antifederalist columns were never published in a single volume.

WHY WERE THEY ANONYMOUS?

The war of words between the federalists and the antifederalists in American newspapers was waged anonymously. Why? Historians cannot be certain, but many have speculated that it was the name recognition of the writers themselves that forced them to adopt pseudonyms. They believed their arguments needed to be judged on their own merits, not on the notoriety or political power of the author. The antifederalists in particular adopted a number of pseudonyms, such as Cato, Brutus, a Columbian Patriot, and so on. It's been speculated that "Cato" was George Clinton, governor of New York; that "Brutus" was Judge Robert Yates; and "a Columbian Patriot" was Revolutionary playwright and essayist Mercy Otis Warren.

American artist Joseph Wright painted this portrait of federalist John Jay in 1786.

American artist Thomas Sully painted this portrait of antifederalist Patrick Henry in 1815.

HISTORICAL THINKING

1. **READING CHECK** What was the process for adopting the Constitution?

2. **COMPARE AND CONTRAST** What were the positions of the federalists and the antifederalists?

3. **MAKE GENERALIZATIONS** What groups tended to support the federalist view and why?

4. **MAKE INFERENCES** Why might small farmers in a largely rural state prefer that most power remain with their state government?

PLAN: 2-PAGE LESSON

OBJECTIVE

Examine the opposing arguments of two groups who debated the ratification of the new Constitution.

CRITICAL THINKING SKILLS FOR LESSON 3.1

- Compare and Contrast
- Make Generalizations
- Make Inferences
- Draw Conclusions
- Analyze Cause and Effect

HISTORICAL THINKING FOR CHAPTER 5

How did American ideals and culture shape the new government? Americans disagreed about how power should be shared in the new government. Lesson 3.1 discusses the main points argued by the federalists and antifederalists in the battle to ratify the Constitution.

BACKGROUND FOR THE TEACHER

When George Washington returned from the convention, he sent copies of the Constitution to Benjamin Harrison, Thomas Jefferson, and others who did not attend the convention. He admitted that while the Constitution was not perfect, it was the best that could be expected given the diverse interests among the states that had to be satisfied. Washington realized that the new government structure was likely to be attacked by many and warned that the Constitution's survival would depend "on literary abilities, & the recommendation of it by good pens."

James Madison turned out to be one of those "good pens." He wrote Washington in mid-November that enthusiasm for the Constitution in Virginia was turning into opposition, and he had decided to take action. Madison enclosed the first seven federalist essays in support of the document, hinting he was the author, and asked Washington to ensure that the essays were reprinted and distributed throughout Virginia.

THINK ABOUT POLITICAL PARTIES

Ask students to discuss the similarities and differences of the present-day Democratic and Republican parties in their attitudes toward the powers of federal and state governments. Draw a Venn diagram on the board and record students' responses, writing details about the Democratic Party in the left circle and about the Republican Party in the right circle. In the area of overlap, include details about how the parties are alike. Tell students this lesson addresses the opposing viewpoints of the federalists and antifederalists and their debates about federal and state powers.

TEACH

GUIDED DISCUSSION

1. **Draw Conclusions** Why might the antifederalists have opposed strong executive and legislative branches and supported term limits and more frequent elections? *(Possible response: The antifederalists worried that the central government would be too big and too removed to understand the concerns of voters. Term limits and frequent elections would ensure these officials were more attentive to their constituents.)*

2. **Analyze Cause and Effect** How did geography affect the federalist and antifederalist efforts to communicate their messages to the public? *(Possible response: Many federalists lived in coastal cities and towns, so it was easier for them to organize, reach larger populations, and spread their message through print media. Antifederalists were more broadly scattered in rural areas, so they had a harder time reaching the public.)*

MORE INFORMATION

Mercy Otis Warren In her guise as "a Columbian Patriot," Mercy Otis Warren was so concerned about protecting citizens' rights she even called for a second constitutional convention. Nevertheless, she argued that if the Constitution were to be ratified, antifederalists should accept the outcome to avoid civil unrest. Warren, who wrote a major history of the American Revolution, eventually changed her mind about the Constitution, saying, "Perhaps genius has never devised a system more congenial to their wishes, or better adapted to the condition of man than the American Constitution."

ACTIVE OPTIONS

On Your Feet: Fishbowl Arrange the class in concentric circles. Direct the inner circle to discuss the federalist and antifederalist viewpoints about whether the proposed Constitution distributes power in the most democratic way. The outer circle listens to this discussion and then the groups are signaled to reverse positions. Ask the new inner circle to continue the discussion, including what the consequences might be for equality and personal liberties should the proposed Constitution be adopted.

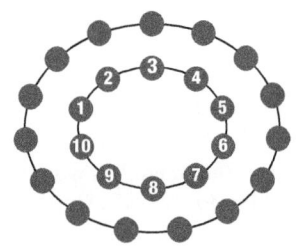

NG Learning Framework: Present an Essay

`ATTITUDES` Curiosity, Empowerment

`SKILLS` Communication, Collaboration

Arrange students in pairs or small groups and assign them either one federalist or one antifederalist paper to "translate" for a present-day audience. Encourage students to ask questions if they have trouble understanding the vocabulary, logical flow, or syntax of the original paper. Suggest ways that students might make the paper resonate with a modern audience, such as creating a social media post to express the ideas, designing a meme, or recording a PSA. Allow groups time to present their work to the class.

DIFFERENTIATE

STRIVING READERS

Dictate Subsection Summaries After students read each subsection of the lesson, ask them to write a sentence or two summarizing the main idea. Encourage pairs to dictate their sentences to each other. Then ask them to work together to check their sentences for accuracy and spelling. Provide these sentence frames:

The subsection is about _____.

The main idea in this subsection is _____.
I know this because _____.

The main idea is _____, supported in the subsection by these details: _____.

GIFTED & TALENTED

Create a Podcast Direct students to review the lesson and choose one of the federalists or antifederalists to feature in a podcast. Tell students to conduct research to learn more about the person's life and writings. Then have them write a script for their podcast and insert quotations from the writings to illustrate the person's views about the Constitution. Invite students to present their podcast to the class.

See the Chapter Planner for more strategies for differentiation.

HISTORICAL THINKING

ANSWERS

1. According to Article 7, at least nine state conventions had to ratify the Constitution.

2. The federalists supported a strong central government and specific powers for the states. The antifederalists, concerned about potential abuses of power, opposed a strong central government and wanted to give more power to state governments.

3. Many federalists were commercial farmers or merchants, artisans, and tradespeople who favored a strong central government. They believed it would stabilize the economy and allow it to prosper, encourage trade, and increase the international standing of the United States.

4. Possible response: Largely rural states had different concerns and needs than states with more industry and larger cities. Therefore, small farmers felt that local representatives would better understand the issues of a rural community.

CRITICAL VIEWING Artist Howard Chandler Christy's oil painting *Scene at the Signing of the Constitution of the United States* (1940) includes authentic period details and the likenesses of 40 men who attended the signing at Independence Hall in 1787, including George Washington, standing on the dais, and Benjamin Franklin, seated in the center. How would you characterize Chandler's portrayal of this historic event?

RATIFICATION AND THE BILL OF RIGHTS

Most Americans think of the Bill of Rights as an essential part of the U.S. Constitution. Probably few remember that it wasn't part of the original Constitution. A new Congress added it as a group of amendments, which persuaded two holdout states to agree to ratification.

THE ROAD TO RATIFICATION

As you have read, the Constitution required approval by the conventions of nine states to become law. Ratification proceeded smoothly at first. Delaware approved the Constitution unanimously on December 7, 1787, becoming the first state to ratify. In Pennsylvania, where supporters worried about resistance developing in the backcountry, federalists moved quickly and secured approval by a two-to-one margin. New Jersey and Georgia followed by ratifying unanimously. Connecticut ratified in January 1788. Except for Pennsylvania, these states were relatively small and recognized the advantages of joining a union in which they had equal representation in the Senate.

Soon the smooth road to ratification became bumpy. Maryland and South Carolina ratified easily, but the vote in Massachusetts was very close: 187 for and 168 against. The lack of a list of citizens' rights was a major obstacle to agreement, and Massachusetts recommended a series of amendments to protect individual rights and limit the powers of Congress. In June 1788, New Hampshire became the ninth state to ratify, satisfying the number of states required. Nevertheless, two crucial states had yet to accept the Constitution: Virginia and New York. While their ratification was technically not needed, their size and economic importance made their approval necessary to the success of the Constitution and the new government.

Virginia was home to some of the most vocal and respected antifederalists. Among their chief concerns was the Constitution's lack of a bill of rights that named and protected such fundamental liberties as freedom of speech and freedom of religion. The federalists argued that a bill of rights was superfluous, or unnecessary, because state constitutions already offered those protections. In reality, the protected rights varied from state to state. Federalists also argued that, while a bill of rights was necessary to protect citizens from a powerful king, the people themselves were sovereign under the Constitution and so there was no need to protect their rights.

Virginia won the battle over the bill of rights. It ratified the Constitution in late June after recommending a series of amendments that included a bill of rights, which Congress agreed to add. New York finally approved the Constitution in late July 1788. With ratification by 11 states, the United States began a new experiment in republican government. North Carolina and Rhode Island were the last two states to ratify.

THE BILL OF RIGHTS

In February 1789, members of the electoral college met in their state capitals to cast votes and elect the nation's first president. The unanimous election of George Washington came as no surprise. Washington's leadership during the war, his dignity and character, and his support for republican government made him the obvious choice. John Adams was elected vice president. On April 23, 1789, Washington arrived in New York City, which had been named the temporary federal capital, on a decorated barge. Thousands of cheering New Yorkers turned out to welcome him. He took the oath of office a week later.

Meeting for the first time on March 4, 1789, the newly elected Congress addressed the question of amending the Constitution. Several states had criticized the document for failing to protect the rights of citizens, and those objections still kept North Carolina and Rhode Island from joining the Union. James Madison became the chief advocate in Congress of the group of amendments that became known as the **Bill of Rights**, in spite of his earlier opinion that such amendments were not necessary. But some antifederalist leaders still wanted to scrap the Constitution entirely. They refused to support the Bill of Rights because they knew it would add to the Constitution's popular support.

After much negotiation between the Senate and the House, on September 25, 1789, Congress sent a total of 12 amendments to the states for ratification. The addition of the Bill of Rights was enough to secure the ratification of the two remaining states. North Carolina ratified the Constitution in November 1789, and Rhode Island followed suit in May 1790. By December 15, 1791, three-quarters of the states had approved 10 of the amendments, which formed the final and official Bill of Rights.

Of the 10 amendments that became the Bill of Rights, the First through Eighth Amendments enumerate basic individual rights. The Ninth Amendment protects any personal freedoms that are not specified in previous amendments. The Tenth Amendment states that "powers not delegated to the United States by the Constitution, nor prohibited by it to the States, are reserved to the States respectively, or to the people." It addressed concerns that the federal government might assume powers that were not mentioned in the Constitution.

HISTORICAL THINKING

1. **READING CHECK** Before voting for ratification, what did Virginia insist that Congress add to the Constitution?

2. **DRAW CONCLUSIONS** Why was it important for Virginia and New York to ratify the Constitution?

3. **SUMMARIZE** What were the federalists' arguments against adding a bill of rights to the Constitution?

4. **FORM AND SUPPORT OPINIONS** Do you think it was important to include the Bill of Rights in the Constitution? Support your opinion with evidence from the text.

PLAN: 2-PAGE LESSON

OBJECTIVE

Understand why the Bill of Rights was needed and how it was added to the U.S. Constitution.

CRITICAL THINKING SKILLS FOR LESSON 3.2

• Draw Conclusions

• Summarize

• Form and Support Opinions

• Determine Chronology

• Evaluate

HISTORICAL THINKING FOR CHAPTER 5

How did American ideals and culture shape the new government? Many states were concerned that the Constitution did not specifically protect individual rights. Lesson 3.2 discusses the process of ratifying the Constitution and creating the Bill of Rights, which was added later.

BACKGROUND FOR THE TEACHER

Artist Howard Chandler Christy strove above all for authenticity in his depiction of the signing of the U.S. Constitution. He researched period portraits of the signers to re-create the likenesses of those present. When he was unable to find portraits of Thomas FitzSimons and Jacob Broom, Christy obscured their faces rather than imagine how they looked. He also took care to depict clothing and artifacts accurately, even borrowing a pair of George Washington's breeches from the Smithsonian and some of Thomas Jefferson's books from the Library of Congress. To get the lighting right, Christy sketched the painting in Independence Hall in September at the same time of day the Constitution had been signed.

The artist did, however, exercise some creative license. He included John Dickinson, though Dickinson had signed by proxy; and he left out George Mason, Edmund Randolph, and Elbridge Gerry. All were present but had refused to approve or sign the document.

INTRODUCE & ENGAGE

COMPLETE A WORD WEB

Write the words *citizens' rights* in the center of a Word Web. Ask students to name citizens' rights they think the federal government should protect, and write them on the spokes. Pick one or two rights and discuss with students how their lives might be different if those rights were not protected. Then tell students that in this lesson they will explore why some states insisted that a Bill of Rights be included in the U.S. Constitution.

TEACH

GUIDED DISCUSSION

1. **Determine Chronology** In what basic order and time frame did the states ratify the U.S. Constitution? *(Delaware ratified on December 7, 1787; Pennsylvania, New Jersey, Georgia, and Connecticut by January 1788; Massachusetts, Maryland, South Carolina, and New Hampshire by June 1788—achieving the nine states needed. Virginia and New York followed by July 1788, North Carolina by November 1789, and Rhode Island by May 1790.)*

2. **Evaluate** What provisions of the Ninth and Tenth Amendments would reassure antifederalists who were reluctant to ratify the Constitution? *(Possible response: Both amendments prevent the federal government from taking on powers beyond those granted in the Constitution.)*

MORE INFORMATION

History of the Bill of Rights James Madison, serving as a U.S. representative, was the author of the Bill of Rights, but he did not start out to create a list of amendments. He first tried to address the antifederalists' concerns by going through the Constitution and making changes to the wording that he deemed appropriate. However, other representatives objected, stating Congress did not have the authority to change the Constitution as it was written. As a result, Madison's changes became a list of 17 amendments, of which 10 were ratified by the states. After Virginia finally ratified the Bill of Rights in 1791, these amendments were added after Article 7 in the Constitution. The Bill of Rights is regarded as part of the foundation of American democracy.

ACTIVE OPTIONS

On Your Feet: Discuss Individual Rights Arrange students in groups of four for a Roundtable discussion of the following question: Why were the antifederalists so insistent that the Constitution include a bill of rights, and why were the federalists equally certain it wasn't needed? Encourage students to recall events in the nation's past that might have influenced the antifederalists' position on this issue. After sufficient time, ask a volunteer from each group to summarize the group's discussion.

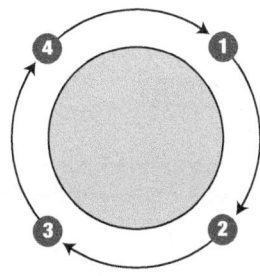

NG Learning Framework: Apply the Bill of Rights in the 21st Century

ATTITUDE Empowerment

KNOWLEDGE Our Human Story

Encourage students to use the Introduce & Engage activity as a springboard for exploring the current implications of the Bill of Rights. Assign pairs of students to research one of the amendments in the Bill of Rights as it applies to American life and politics in the 21st century. Students should research what rights the amendment protects, determine whether the amendment is a point of contention, and consider how American society today might be different if the right were not protected. Encourage pairs to find stories in the news that demonstrate ways in which their amendment is still relevant. Invite pairs to discuss their findings with the class.

DIFFERENTIATE

ENGLISH LANGUAGE LEARNERS ELD

Use a Term in a Sentence Pair students at the **Emerging** level with those at the **Expanding** or **Bridging** level. Direct students' attention to the terms *unanimously* and *two-to-one margin* in the first paragraph of The Road to Ratification subsection. Have pairs read the terms in context and discuss their meanings. Then challenge students to compose their own sentences using each term. Invite pairs to share their sentences.

GIFTED & TALENTED

Compare Documents Ask students to examine the Articles and Amendments in the Constitution and identify ways that they support the goals listed in the Preamble. You might provide a link to the Constitution online so that students can easily search for and locate connections among the three parts of the document. Ask students to assemble their findings in an outline, an infographic, or a chart. Invite them to share their work with the class.

See the Chapter Planner for more strategies for differentiation.

HISTORICAL THINKING

ANSWERS

1. Virginia insisted that a bill of rights be added.

2. The Constitution and new government were not likely to be successful without the support of New York and Virginia because both were major economic and population centers.

3. The federalists argued that a bill of rights was unnecessary because state constitutions already protected individual rights and because the people, not a powerful king, were sovereign under the Constitution.

4. Possible responses: Yes. Individual rights protected by state constitutions varied from state to state. No. Citizens were sovereign under the Constitution and could therefore protect their rights by voting.

CRITICAL VIEWING Possible response: The artist not only worked to make the details historically accurate but tried to convey what might have been a still-vigorous debate among delegates even at the signing. The artist shows George Washington as the imposing leader and Benjamin Franklin as the calm diplomat, both important figures who seem to be still points in the dramatic scene.

SETTING A BALANCE

The Framers of the Constitution wanted to establish an effective government, protect citizens' liberty, and guard against corruption and power-grabbing. To accomplish these goals, they crafted a government with three branches, assigned the branches different responsibilities, and provided ways for each branch to check the power of the others.

Gilbert Stuart painted portraits of five U.S. presidents, including James Madison. Dolley Madison wrote of Stuart, "He is a man of genius, and therefore does everything differently from other people." Her words could describe her husband's work to form a new nation.

CRITICAL VIEWING In this portrait of James Madison (c. 1805–1807), Gilbert Stuart placed drapery and other items typical in portraits of royalty in the background. In contrast, how do Madison's pose and the foreground reflect democratic ideals?

DOCUMENT ONE

Primary Source: Book
from *The Spirit of the Laws*, Book XI, Chapters 4 and 6, by Montesquieu, 1748

The Spirit of the Laws by French philosopher Montesquieu was one of the most influential books of 18th-century political thought. The book was widely read in the colonies and even excerpted in many newspapers. In the book, Montesquieu introduced and described the concept of separation of political powers. His ideas influenced the Framers as they debated the details of the Constitution.

CONSTRUCTED RESPONSE What kind of check on power does Montesquieu describe in this excerpt?

To prevent this abuse [of power], it is necessary from the very nature of things that power should be a check to power. A government may be so constituted, as no man shall be compelled to do things to which the law does not oblige him, nor forced to abstain from things which the law permits. . . . When the legislative and executive powers are united in the same person, or in the same body of magistrates, there can be no liberty. . . . Again there is no liberty if the judiciary power be not separated.

DOCUMENT TWO

Primary Source: Essay
from *Federalist* No. 51 by James Madison, 1788

In 1788, a group of American federalists published a collection of 85 essays entitled *The Federalist,* in which they argued in favor of the ratification of the U.S. Constitution. Essay No. 51, which James Madison originally published anonymously, dealt with the importance of autonomy, or independence, for the various departments of government.

CONSTRUCTED RESPONSE What does Madison prescribe as a way for each department of government to maintain its autonomy?

In order to lay a due foundation for that separate and distinct exercise of the different powers of government, which to a certain extent is admitted on all hands to be essential to the preservation of liberty, it is evident that each department should have a will of its own; and consequently should be so constituted that the members of each should have as little agency as possible in the appointment of the members of the others.

DOCUMENT THREE

Primary Source: Document
from The Constitution, Article 1, Section 7, Clause 3

The Framers took the ideas of Montesquieu and those of the federalists into account as they crafted their own version of a government. Each branch of this government would have the means to limit the power of the others. By extension, this form of government would help establish balance among the interests, classes, and factions of a diverse nation.

CONSTRUCTED RESPONSE How does Clause 3 set up a relationship of checks and balances?

Every Order, Resolution, or Vote to which the Concurrence [agreement] of the Senate and House of Representatives may be necessary (except on a question of Adjournment) shall be presented to the President of the United States; and before the Same shall take Effect, shall be approved by him, or being disapproved by him, shall be re-passed by two thirds of the Senate and House of Representatives, according to the Rules and Limitations prescribed in the Case of a Bill.

Read the full United States Constitution in the Citizenship Handbook.

SYNTHESIZE AND WRITE

1. **REVIEW** Review what you have learned about the idea of separation of powers and how it came to be part of the U.S. Constitution.

2. **RECALL** On your own paper, write notes about the responsibilities of each branch of government and the ways each branch checks the power of the others.

3. **CONSTRUCT** Construct a topic sentence that describes why the separation of powers is an important concept in a constitutional republic.

4. **WRITE** Using evidence from this chapter and the documents, write a paragraph explaining how the principle of separation of powers is applied in the United States government.

PLAN: 2-PAGE LESSON

OBJECTIVE

Synthesize statements and opinions from primary source documents about the balance of power in government.

CRITICAL THINKING SKILLS FOR LESSON 3.3

• Synthesize

• Compare and Contrast

• Make Connections

• Evaluate

HISTORICAL THINKING FOR CHAPTER 5

How did American ideals and culture shape the new government? The Framers created a three-branch government to balance its powers. Lesson 3.3 examines three documents that discuss the structure and nature of power in government.

BACKGROUND FOR THE TEACHER

In *Federalist* No. 51, James Madison observed: "If men were angels, no government would be necessary. If angels were to govern men, neither external nor internal controls on government would be necessary. In framing a government which is to be administered by men over men, the great difficulty lies in this: you must first enable the government to control the governed; and in the next place oblige it to control itself." For Madison, like Montesquieu, having three branches of government with independent powers was the best safeguard against tyranny. The most obvious way the Constitution accomplished this was by giving each branch of government its own powers and the tools to curb the powers of the other two branches. But Madison also believed that human nature provided a check in the form of ambition—each branch of government would check the other branches' power in order to protect its own power.

INTRODUCE & ENGAGE

PREPARE FOR THE DOCUMENT-BASED QUESTION

Before students start on the activity, briefly preview the three documents. Remind students that a constructed response requires full explanations in complete sentences. Emphasize that students should use what they have learned about the framing of the Constitution in addition to the information in the documents.

TEACH

GUIDED DISCUSSION

1. **Compare and Contrast** How are Montesquieu and Madison similar in their views concerning government power? *(Both believe that liberty cannot exist without a government in which power is divided among branches.)*

2. **Make Connections** How does Clause 3 in Article 1, Section 7 of the U.S. Constitution address the concerns of Montesquieu and Madison? *(The clause addresses their concern over one branch having too much power by describing the president's power of veto along with Congress's power to override that veto.)*

EVALUATE

After students have completed the Synthesize & Write activity, allow time for them to exchange paragraphs and read and comment on the work of their peers. Establish guidelines for comments prior to the activity so that feedback is constructive and encouraging in nature. Comments should focus on the most significant parts that address the purpose of the activity and the audience.

ACTIVE OPTION

On Your Feet: Use a Jigsaw Strategy Organize students into "expert" groups and assign each group one of the documents to analyze and summarize its main ideas in their own words. Then regroup students into new groups so that each new group has at least one member from each expert group. Students in the new groups take turns sharing the summaries from their expert groups.

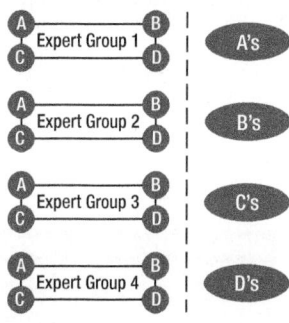

DIFFERENTIATE

INCLUSION

Highlight and Paraphrase Help minimize distractions for students with learning or perception issues by giving each student a handout that includes only the document excerpts. Pair these students with strong readers, and instruct partners to work together to highlight important words and ideas. Then ask pairs to write a sentence in their own words that summarizes each document's main idea.

PRE-AP

Form and Support a Thesis Challenge students to find and read a longer excerpt of Montesquieu's or Madison's document. Then have them conduct online research to develop a thesis regarding how the ideas in that document might have influenced the framing of the U.S. Constitution. Tell them to write an essay supporting their thesis with a variety of primary and secondary source material, plus their own analysis. Encourage students to share their essay on a class or school blog.

See the Chapter Planner for more strategies for differentiation.

SYNTHESIZE & WRITE

ANSWERS

1. Answers will vary.

2. Answers will vary. Possible response: The legislative branch initiates and passes laws, the executive branch approves and enforces laws, and the judicial branch determines whether laws are constitutional. This structure provides checks and balances since the executive branch has veto power, Congress can override a veto and has approval over cabinet members, and the judiciary serves for life.

3. Answers will vary. Possible response: The separation of powers in a constitutional republic helps prevent abuses of power by and within the government.

4. Answers will vary. Students' paragraphs should include their topic sentence from Step 3 and provide several details from the documents to support the sentence.

CONSTRUCTED RESPONSE

Document 1: Power is checked by power so that no one person functions as executive, legislative, and judiciary in one.

Document 2: To maintain autonomy, government departments need to have as little to do with the selection of members of the other departments as possible.

Document 3: Everything agreed to by Congress (except adjournment) can be vetoed by the president. However, Congress can override that veto by a two-thirds vote.

CRITICAL VIEWING Possible response: The furniture and clothing used for the portrait are modest and simple, without any sign of wealth or upper-class life. Even the books are modestly painted. Madison's pose is informal, with one arm over the back of the chair, as if inviting viewers to join him at the table.

VOCABULARY

Use each of the following vocabulary words in a sentence that shows an understanding of the word's meaning.

1. sovereignty
   Each state was guaranteed sovereignty and so had the authority to rule itself.

2. egalitarianism

3. ordinance

4. suffrage

5. federalism

6. bicameral legislature

7. constitutional republic

8. antifederalist

READING STRATEGY
COMPARE AND CONTRAST

To understand how a government evolves, it helps to compare and contrast its plans for governance. Use a Venn diagram to compare and contrast the main features of the Articles of Confederation and the U.S. Constitution, placing each feature in the proper circle. If the plans share any features, list them in the space where the circles intersect. Then answer the question.

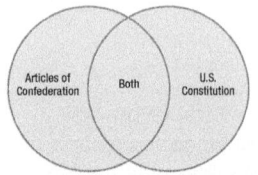

9. How did the U.S. government evolve from its founding to the ratification of the U.S. Constitution?

MAIN IDEAS

Answer the following questions. Support your answers with evidence from the chapter.

10. What was the main problem with the government formed under the Articles of Confederation? **LESSON 1.1**

11. What was the political status of the states under the Articles of Confederation? **LESSON 1.1**

12. What was a major problem with the Land Ordinance of 1785, and how was it solved? **LESSON 1.2**

13. Why did taxation lead to a revolt among farmers in 1786? **LESSON 2.1**

14. In what way did James Madison influence the direction of the 1787 convention in Philadelphia? **LESSON 2.1**

15. How did the Great Compromise combine elements of the Virginia Plan and the New Jersey Plan? **LESSON 2.2**

16. What are the main responsibilities of the three branches of the U.S. government? **LESSON 2.2**

17. How did the group that favored ratification of the Constitution get its name? **LESSON 3.1**

18. Why were some Americans opposed to ratification of the Constitution? **LESSON 3.1**

19. What issue slowed down the ratification of the Constitution? **LESSON 3.2**

HISTORICAL THINKING

Answer the following questions. Support your answers with evidence from the chapter.

20. **IDENTIFY PROBLEMS AND SOLUTIONS** How did the Articles of Confederation make it difficult for Congress to resolve conflicts with other countries?

21. **ANALYZE CAUSE AND EFFECT** What effect did the high price of lots have on land distribution in the Northwest Territory?

22. **MAKE CONNECTIONS** What political groups today oppose a strong central government, and what are their reasons?

23. **DRAW CONCLUSIONS** How might the Three-fifths Compromise have influenced the continuation of slavery in the United States?

INTERPRET VISUALS

American artist Ralph Earl and the subject of his portrait, Elijah Boardman (1760–1823), chose an unusual setting for this painting: Boardman's dry goods store. Boardman was a Revolutionary War veteran and a successful merchant in Connecticut. He eventually entered politics and became a U.S. senator. In this painting, he stands in front of his counting desk, where he managed bills and inventory. The open door reveals shelves of costly fabrics, including imports from Europe and Asia.

24. What do Boardman's clothing and manner imply about his status in the new republic?

25. How does Boardman typify the kind of leaders many Framers envisioned for the new republic?

ANALYZE SOURCES

As state legislators debated ratification of the U.S. Constitution, other citizens had fiery debates on its merits in the public press, most often signing their essays and letters to the editor with pseudonyms. In this excerpt from the October 18, 1787, edition of the *New York Journal*, antifederalist "Brutus" warns against establishing one large republic. Read the excerpt and answer the question.

> History furnishes no example of a free republic, any thing like the extent of the United States. The Grecian republics were of small extent; so also was that of the Romans. Both of these, it is true, in process of time, extended their conquests over large territories of country; and the consequence was, that their governments were changed from that of free governments to those of the most tyrannical that ever existed in the world.

26. What danger is "Brutus" warning readers about in this quotation?

CONNECT TO YOUR LIFE

27. **ARGUMENT** The U.S. Constitution is one of the oldest constitutions in use in the world. Its longevity is largely due to the amendment process, which allows the document to adapt to changing conditions. If you could propose a constitutional amendment, what would it be? Why is it important, and how might it affect Americans? Write a proposal describing your amendment and the problems it would alleviate. Include supporting reasons, details, and evidence.

TIPS

• Read the amendments to the Constitution to become familiar with the kinds of changes that have been made.

• Address opposition to your amendment.

• If appropriate, include two or three key terms from the chapter in your proposal.

• Conclude your argument by summarizing the benefits of your amendment.

VOCABULARY ANSWERS

1. Each state was guaranteed sovereignty and so had the authority to rule itself.

2. The Patriots believed in egalitarianism, the Enlightenment ideal that all people should be treated equally.

3. The Confederation Congress passed three ordinances that regulated how the Northwest Territory districts would be settled and eventually how they would enter the union as states.

4. Most state constitutions granted suffrage only to white male property owners; no other groups had the right to vote.

5. Under the system of federalism, a central government shares power with the states.

6. The Great Compromise called for a bicameral legislature consisting of the House of Representatives and the Senate.

7. In a constitutional republic, representatives and other officials derive their authority from the people who elect them.

8. The antifederalists opposed ratifying the Constitution because it lacked a bill of rights to protect individual liberties.

READING STRATEGY ANSWER

Articles of Confederation: weak central government, state sovereignty, Congress cannot tax or regulate trade, confederacy of states

Both: republican, issue money

U.S. Constitution: strong central government; dual sovereignty; Congress can tax and regulate trade, single nation

9. Possible response: The U.S. government began as a confederacy of self-governing states with a weak central government and a single-house Congress with almost no power. This arrangement caused so many problems that delegates got together to revise the confederacy. Instead, they created a new form of government composed of dual sovereignty and three equal branches with checks and balances that prevented any branch from gaining too much power. The states argued about a strong central government versus more power to the states but eventually ratified the Constitution and added the Bill of Rights.

MAIN IDEAS ANSWERS

10. The central government was so weak it didn't have the power to tax or regulate trade.

11. The states were sovereign powers, meaning they were self-governing.

12. The land prices were so high that Congress had difficulty selling township lots to individuals. Congress solved the problem by selling land to speculators.

13. Already in debt, farmers were required to pay heavy state taxes in specie or paper backed by specie, which they did not have. If they could not pay, the state could seize their property and have them arrested and put in jail.

14. Madison came to the Constitutional Convention with a plan for a new government, changing the discussion from fixing the Articles of Confederation to forging a new structure to govern the country.

15. The Great Compromise provided the small states with equal representation in the Senate, as in the New Jersey Plan. It provided for proportional representation in the House of Representatives, as in the Virginia Plan.

16. The legislative branch is charged with creating laws, the executive branch is charged with carrying out or enforcing the laws, and the judicial branch is charged with interpreting the laws.

17. The pro-ratification group, the federalists, took that name because they supported a federal system that shared power between the central government and the states.

18. The antifederalists opposed the Constitution because it took power away from the states, lacked a bill of rights, and featured a strong central government, which they feared would become tyrannical.

19. The lack of a bill of rights slowed ratification.

HISTORICAL THINKING ANSWERS

20. Under the Articles, Congress did not have the power to raise money for an army to confront Great Britain, Spain, or the Native American nations when they challenged the United States. The new country appeared weak to foreign nations.

21. High land prices meant that many individuals couldn't afford to buy lots directly from Congress. Congress decided to sell large amounts of land to speculators for resale. In some cases, people simply started farming the land without permission.

22. Possible response: Many Republicans, Libertarians, and conservative groups oppose a strong central government because of their concerns about protecting states' rights and individual liberties and about controlling government spending.

23. Possible response: In addition to giving tacit approval to slavery, the Three-fifths Compromise increased the southern states' representation in Congress, making it easier for them to pass laws favorable to maintaining slavery.

INTERPRET VISUALS ANSWERS

24. Boardman is dressed in fine clothes and stands with his hand on his counting desk, which contains what are probably accounting books. These details indicate he was a wealthy man with a high social standing.

25. The Framers envisioned wealthy, educated men like Boardman leading the country. Many of the Framers feared the influence of undereducated and less wealthy voters.

ANALYZE SOURCES ANSWER

26. Possible response: History shows that as a nation grows larger, its central government inevitably changes from a democratic to a tyrannical one.

CONNECT TO YOUR LIFE ANSWER

27. Essays will vary, but students' amendments should address a legitimate issue. Students should consider how their amendment will affect others; address arguments for and against their amendment; build a convincing case for adoption by using reasons, details, and evidence; and end by summarizing how people will benefit from their proposed amendment.

UNIT 2 RESOURCES

UNIT INTRODUCTION

UNIT TIME LINE

UNIT WRAP-UP

NATIONAL GEOGRAPHIC | CONNECTION

National Geographic Magazine
Adapted Articles
- "Map Drawing"
- "Searching for Sacagawea" ONLINE

Unit 2 Inquiry: Explore a Contradiction

NG Learning Framework Activities
- Stage a Debate
- Create a Storyboard

Unit 2 Formal Assessment

CHAPTER 6 RESOURCES

Available at NGLSync.Cengage.com

TEACHER RESOURCES & ASSESSMENT

Reading and Note-Taking

Vocabulary Practice

Social Studies Skills Lessons
- Reading: Summarize
- Writing: Explanatory

Formal Assessment
- Chapter 6 Pretest
- Chapter 6 Tests A & B
- Section Quizzes

Chapter 6 Answer Key

ExamView®
   One-time Download

STUDENT DIGITAL RESOURCES

- eEdition
- Handbooks
- Online Atlas
- American Gallery Online
- History Notebook
- Active History
- American Voices (Biographies)
- Reid on the Road video series
- Literature Analysis
- Projects for Inquiry-Based Learning

Chapter 6 Spanish Resources are available at NGLSync.Cengage.com.

AMERICAN STORIES — The Founding Fathers

▶ Monticello

- Study Primary Sources: Quotations from George Washington, Thomas Jefferson, and Benjamin Franklin
- On Your Feet: Perform a Reading

NG Learning Framework:
Evaluate and Improve an Invention

SECTION 1 RESOURCES

SHAPING THE NEW GOVERNMENT

LESSON 1.1
Washington's Leadership

- On Your Feet: Create a Plan for Government

NG Learning Framework:
Presidential Cabinets Then and Now

LESSON 1.2
Women's Roles in the New Republic

- On Your Feet: Three-Step Interview

NG Learning Framework:
Portray Present-Day Expectations for Women

American Voices Biography
Judith Sargent Murray ONLINE

LESSON 1.3
Opposing Visions of America

- On Your Feet: Think, Pair, Share

NG Learning Framework:
Design an Infographic

LESSON 1.4
Political Entanglements

- On Your Feet: Fishbowl

NG Learning Framework:
Understand the Free Press

SECTION 2 RESOURCES

JEFFERSON AND WESTWARD EXPANSION

LESSON 2.1
Jefferson's "Revolution"

- On Your Feet: Three-Step Interview

NG Learning Framework:
Write a Supreme Court Decision

American Voices Biographies
Alexander Hamilton and Aaron Burr ONLINE

LESSON 2.2
The Louisiana Purchase

▶ The River as Highway

- On Your Feet: Roundtable Discussion

NG Learning Framework:
Debate the Louisiana Purchase

LESSON 2.3
The Lewis and Clark Expedition

AMERICAN **GALLERY** ONLINE — On the Trail with Lewis and Clark

- Active History: Research Native Cultures

LESSON 2.4
AMERICAN VOICES
Sacagawea

- On Your Feet: Numbered Heads

NG Learning Framework:
Write Journal Entries

SECTION 3 RESOURCES

THE WAR OF 1812

LESSON 3.1
More Conflict with Britain

- On Your Feet: Create a Quiz

NG Learning Framework:
Analyze a Political Cartoon

LESSON 3.2
The War of 1812

- On Your Feet: Inside-Outside Circle

NG Learning Framework:
Analyze the Treaty of Ghent

CHAPTER 6 REVIEW

STRIVING READERS

STRATEGY 1
USE K-W-L CHARTS

Arrange students in pairs and provide each with a K-W-L Chart. Have partners brainstorm what they know about the early days of the republic and add their ideas to the chart. In the second column, tell students to write at least three questions they have, such as: How did the new government develop? Who were the first presidents and what did they accomplish? Why was the War of 1812 fought? Remind students to complete their charts as they read each lesson.

K What Do I Know?	W What Do I Want To Learn?	L What Did I Learn?

Use with All Lessons

STRATEGY 2
CLARIFY INFORMATION

Students may have trouble understanding aspects of the War of 1812, such as why the United States declared war, how different alliances were formed, and why particular battles were won or lost. To help students organize their reading and clarify information, instruct them to use a 5Ws Chart such as the one shown to take notes on the information under each subsection heading in the lessons.

What?
Who?
Where?
When?
Why?

Use with Lessons 3.1 and 3.2

STRATEGY 3
READ AND RECALL

Ask students to work in pairs. First have partners read the lesson independently. Then tell partners to meet without the book and share ideas they recall, with one student taking notes. Finally, direct partners to review the lesson and revise their notes.

Use with All Lessons

INCLUSION

STRATEGY 1
PREVIEW AND PREDICT

Pair students with reading or perception issues with proficient readers and direct them to read the lesson title and subsection headings together. Then ask proficient students to guide their partners in describing details in lesson visuals and reading the captions, working together to write notes predicting what the lesson will be about. After reading, ask pairs to review their notes to confirm their predictions and correct inaccuracies.

Use with All Lessons *For example, in Lesson 1.2, tell proficient students to read the title and subsection headings, and describe the painting. Then have students write predictions, such as the following: This lesson will be about the roles, rights, and responsibilities of women in the early days of the republic.*

STRATEGY 2
USE ECHO READING

Point out that the Main Idea statements all relate to important ideas and events that impacted the early days of the republic. Pair students with reading or perception issues with proficient readers who can read aloud the Main Idea statement at the beginning of each lesson. Direct students to "echo" by reading the same statement or by restating it using their own words.

Use with All Lessons *Pairs might continue to echo read selected paragraphs or entire subsections of each lesson.*

ENGLISH LANGUAGE LEARNERS

STRATEGY 1
CLARIFY VOCABULARY

Use the following strategies to help students at different proficiency levels clarify vocabulary.

- **Emerging:** Tell students to choose an unfamiliar word from the lesson. Provide these frames:

  I don't know the word _____.

  I think it means _____.

  Clues I found are _____ and _____.

  Point out any context clues and word parts and guide students to discover the word's meaning.

- **Expanding:** Provide students with these frames to help them clarify vocabulary:

  I don't know the word _____, but I think it means _____.

  The context and word parts suggest _____. The most likely meaning is _____.

- **Bridging:** Have students draw a three-column chart with the following headings: Word/Know/Learned. Tell students to write an unfamiliar word under Word, write what they already know about the word, noting context clues and word parts, under Know, and explain what they learned about the word under Learned.

Use with All Lessons

STRATEGY 2
USE PAIRED READING

Pair students at the **Expanding** and **Bridging** levels and have them read passages from the text aloud.

1. Partner 1 reads a passage; Partner 2 retells the passage in his or her own words.

2. Partner 2 reads a different passage; Partner 1 retells it.

3. Pairs repeat the process.

Use with All Lessons

STRATEGY 3
CREATE MEANING MAPS

Pair students at the **Emerging** level with those at the **Expanding** or **Bridging** level. Demonstrate completing a graphic organizer, such as a Meaning Map, for Key Vocabulary or other important words and terms in the lesson. Encourage students to discuss the words to clarify meanings.

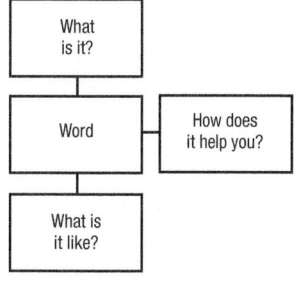

Use with All Lessons

GIFTED & TALENTED

STRATEGY 1
WRITE A DIALOGUE

Ask students to write imagined dialogues that might have taken place between people mentioned in the lessons. For example, you might suggest the following people in Section 1:

- Judith Sargent Murray and one of the Founding Fathers (Lesson 1.2)
- Alexander Hamilton and Lin-Manuel Miranda (Lesson 1.3)
- John Adams and Thomas Jefferson (Lesson 1.4)
- Benjamin Franklin (American Story) and Thomas Pinckney (Lesson 1.4)

Use with All Lessons

STRATEGY 2
CREATE DISPLAYS

Instruct students to conduct online research to learn more about how westward expansion affected the lives and the public perception of Native Americans. Tell students to locate paintings, headlines, and editorial cartoons from the late 1700s and early 1800s, as well as more recent images related to the impact of white settlement on native peoples during that time period. Ask students to work together to set up displays around the classroom. Use the displays to generate a discussion about public perception of Native Americans from the 1700s to the present.

Use with Lessons 1.4, 2.3, 2.4, 3.1, and 3.2

PRE-AP

STRATEGY 1
TEACH A CLASS

Before beginning the chapter, allow students to choose one of the lessons and prepare to teach the content to the class. Give them a set amount of time in which to present their lesson. Suggest that students think about any visuals or activities they want to use when they teach.

Use with All Lessons

STRATEGY 2
WRITE A NEWS REPORT

Assign students the role of journalists reporting on an aspect of the election of 1800. Remind them that news articles begin with the most important information and usually answer the questions *who*, *what*, *where*, *when*, *why*, and *how* by the end of the article. Invite students to post their articles on a class blog or on a school website.

Use with Lesson 2.1

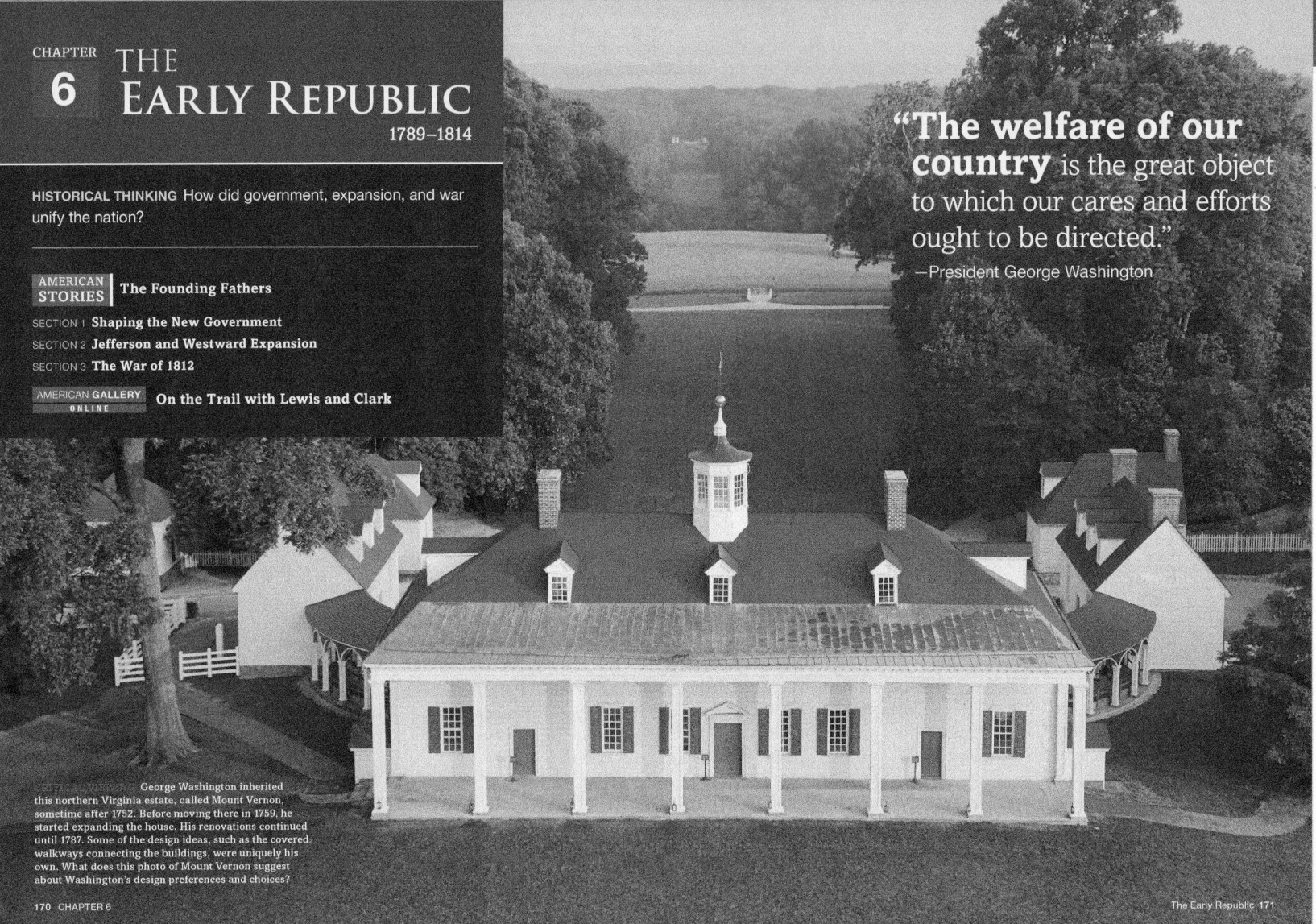

THE EARLY REPUBLIC

1789–1814

HISTORICAL THINKING How did government, expansion, and war unify the nation?

AMERICAN **STORIES** | The Founding Fathers

SECTION 1 **Shaping the New Government**

SECTION 2 **Jefferson and Westward Expansion**

SECTION 3 **The War of 1812**

AMERICAN **GALLERY** ONLINE **On the Trail with Lewis and Clark**

"**The welfare of our country** is the great object to which our cares and efforts ought to be directed."

—President George Washington

CRITICAL VIEWING George Washington inherited this northern Virginia estate, called Mount Vernon, sometime after 1752. Before moving there in 1759, he started expanding the house. His renovations continued until 1787. Some of the design ideas, such as the covered walkways connecting the buildings, were uniquely his own. What does this photo of Mount Vernon suggest about Washington's design preferences and choices?

INTRODUCE THE PHOTOGRAPH

GEORGE WASHINGTON AND MOUNT VERNON

Direct students to study the photograph, Critical Viewing caption, and quotation. **ASK:** Based on the photograph of Mount Vernon and what you read, what kind of background did George Washington bring to the presidency? *(Possible response: He brought a background of wealth and privilege that included original thinking, as evidenced by his original design ideas for Mount Vernon.)* Then discuss the quotation. **ASK:** Why might Washington have been especially concerned about the welfare of the country? *(Possible response: As the first president of a new nation, Washington understood that unifying the states was an immediate goal. He likely wanted a stable government and prosperity for Americans after the war.)* Tell students that in this chapter they will learn about how Washington and his successors proceeded to unify the new nation and establish the republic.

For Chapter 6 Spanish Resources, visit the Resources Menu. Chapter 6 Resources are available at NGLSync.Cengage.com.

SHARE BACKGROUND

George Washington's involvement in crucial events drew him away from the ongoing renovations at Mount Vernon. During the first expansion, which added a second story to the main building, Washington was fighting in the French and Indian War. He was attending the Second Continental Congress and leading the Continental Army during the second expansion, which added a two-story structure. The cupola on the roof was built in 1778, and years later, while attending the Constitutional Convention in 1787, Washington commissioned a dove-shaped weathervane, perhaps symbolizing the peace that he desired for the new nation.

CRITICAL VIEWING Washington preferred perfect symmetry in overall design, with embellishments such as gables, square columns, paned windows, and arches—all prominently featured in the house's three sections. An appreciation for functionality and unity is evidenced in his addition of the covered walkways that connect the three structures.

===

HISTORICAL THINKING QUESTION

How did government, expansion, and war unify the nation?

Team Word Webbing Activity: Consider What Brings About Unification of a Nation This activity will help students begin to consider how the establishment of the republic, westward expansion, and entering into war helped unify the diverse regions of the country into a single nation. Organize students into small teams and provide each with a large sheet of paper. Assign each team one of the following questions:

- How might becoming a republic unify a nation?
- How might expansion of its borders unify a nation?
- How might involvements in conflicts and engaging in war unify a nation?

Tell teams to write the question in the center of the paper and then brainstorm possible answers. Each student adds to the part of the web nearest him or her. On a signal, students rotate the paper, and each student adds to the nearest part again. Then call on volunteers from each team to make statements based on the ideas they expressed on their webs.

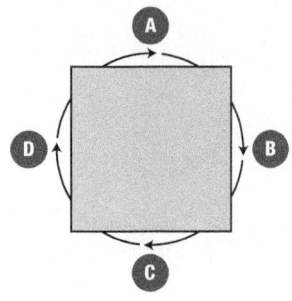

INTRODUCE THE READING STRATEGY

SUMMARIZE

Explain to students that when they summarize text, they restate main ideas and important details in their own words. Turn to the Chapter Review and preview the graphic organizer with students. After students have read Lesson 1.1, guide them in using the graphic organizer to take notes and write a summary of the lesson. Suggest that they use a similar graphic organizer to summarize the remaining lessons in the chapter.

KEY DATES FOR CHAPTER 6

1789	Washington becomes first U.S. president
1793	Washington issues Proclamation of Neutrality
1794	Whiskey Rebellion
1797	XYZ Affair worsens U.S. relations with France
1798	Alien and Sedition Acts pass
1801	Jefferson becomes third U.S. president
1803	*Marbury* v. *Madison* establishes judicial review
1803	Louisiana Purchase expands the United States
1805	Corps of Discovery heads west
1812	War erupts with Britain

INTRODUCE CHAPTER VOCABULARY

KEY VOCABULARY

SECTION 1

agrarian	dividend	loose constructionist
attorney general	envoy	nullification
Cabinet	excise tax	radical
census	impressment	republican motherhood
civic republicanism	inauguration	sedition
civil case	intermediary	strict constructionist
criminal case		

SECTION 2

estuary	Louisiana Purchase	portage
judicial review	midnight judge	secession

SECTION 3

embargo	War Hawk

WORD WEBS

Tell students to complete a Word Web for Key Vocabulary words as they read the chapter. Direct them to write each word in the center of an oval and then look through the chapter to find examples, characteristics, and descriptive words that may be associated with the vocabulary word. After reading the chapter, ask students to share what they learned about each word. Model an example using the graphic organizer below.

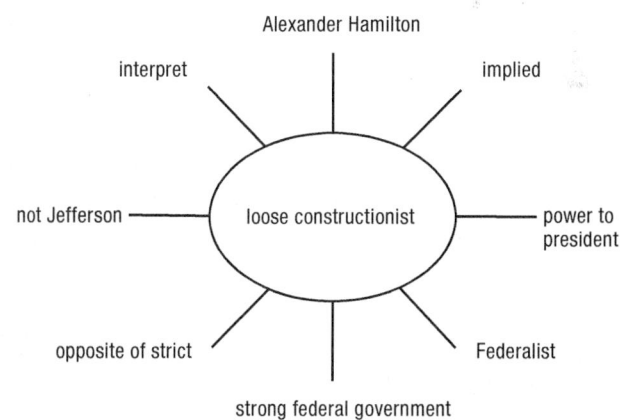

OBJECTIVES

- **Identify the Founding Fathers' roles in establishing the United States.**

- **Examine the contributions of Martha Washington.**

- **Learn about the accomplishments of the Founding Fathers in such areas as architecture, science, and music.**

- **Study primary sources: quotations from George Washington, Thomas Jefferson, and Benjamin Franklin.**

CRITICAL THINKING SKILLS FOR "THE FOUNDING FATHERS"

- Make Connections
- Draw Conclusions
- Make Inferences
- Analyze Primary Sources
- Synthesize
- Form and Support Opinions

CONNECT TO THE CHAPTER

This American Story focuses on the country's Founding Fathers and the diverse contributions they made to the newly created nation. Students will learn about George Washington, Thomas Jefferson, and Benjamin Franklin by examining their backgrounds, exploring quotations, and studying photographs and paintings of places and items associated with them.

Chapter 6, The Early Republic, discusses the formation of the country's government and the many challenges the republic faced in its early years. Students can use this American Story to examine the roles these three men played in the country's growth and development. Introduce "The Founding Fathers" before students begin the chapter so that they can familiarize themselves with the men's philosophies and then, later in the chapter, observe how the men's ideas influenced the republic.

HISTORY NOTEBOOK

Encourage students to complete the American Story and Reid on the Road video pages for Chapter 6 in their History Notebooks.

AMERICAN STORIES | NATIONAL GEOGRAPHIC

CRITICAL VIEWING American artist Gilbert Stuart painted this portrait of George Washington around 1800. How do you think the artist wanted to portray Washington, and what details in the painting might help represent him that way?

172 CHAPTER 6

THE **FOUNDING** FATHERS

Why do we use the term "Founding Fathers" to describe George Washington, Thomas Jefferson, Benjamin Franklin, and their contemporaries at the Constitutional Convention of 1787? The obvious answer is that these individuals helped establish the United States as an independent country and created its stable, lasting government structures. In a deeper sense, the Founding Fathers earned that title not just through their actions but by the qualities of character they embody. Each man personified traits such as patriotism, forward-thinking, and innovation that Americans admire and strive to incorporate into our national identity.

GEORGE WASHINGTON: THE PATRIOT

To most people, being elected president of the United States would most likely be cause for jubilation. George Washington, however, wrote to a friend that he was sacrificing "all expectations of private happiness in this world" by accepting the office. His personal aspirations lay elsewhere, on a plantation in Virginia called Mount Vernon.

When Washington inherited Mount Vernon sometime after 1752, he was already managing the plantation. He was dedicated to it, and his chief ambition was to remain there running the plantation in the company of his wife and stepchildren. Between 1775 and 1781, as Washington campaigned with the Continental Army, Mount Vernon remained on his mind. He gratefully returned there when the American Revolution ended.

Within a few years, however, Washington went back to public life and eventually became a key figure in the Constitutional Convention of 1787. Shortly afterward, the electoral college unanimously elected him president, and he felt obligated to serve his country.

> *"Every post is honorable in which a man can serve his country."*
> —George Washington, 1775

Washington knew his actions would set the tone for all future presidencies. In a letter to fellow Founding Father James Madison, he wrote "As the first of everything in our situation will serve to establish a precedent, it is devoutly wished on my part that these precedents may be fixed on true principles." He strove to fulfill his office with integrity and respect for the principles of democracy, and he retired after two terms.

Washington would have less than three years to enjoy his well-deserved and long-delayed retirement at Mount Vernon. On December 14, 1799, he died of a throat infection surrounded by his family members, trusted friends, and close members of his staff.

The Early Republic **173**

FOUNDING MOTHERS?

Each year in which George Washington commanded the Continental Army, Martha Washington would stay with him in the army camps when fighting ceased during the winter. There she tended to injured soldiers, assisted George in his correspondence, and hosted social gatherings. She also helped maintain George's morale and that of others at the camp. Though Martha likely enjoyed assisting her husband, these camp visits often required long, difficult journeys, forcing Martha to leave her son and grandchildren behind for months at a time. **ASK:** How do Martha's extended camp visits reflect Richard Norton Smith's characterization of her? *(Possible response: The visits are another example of how she supported George. Though she certainly had to make personal sacrifices, she performed this duty to assist her husband and to serve her country.)*

AT HOME IN MONTICELLO

For a place to be declared a UNESCO World Heritage Site, it must represent "outstanding universal value." It must also meet at least one of ten other criteria. Monticello's designation cites three criteria, the first of which is that the estate represents "a masterpiece of human creative genius." **ASK:** In what ways is Monticello a masterpiece of human creative genius? *(Possible response: The ingenuity of the dome and the clever mechanism connecting the two doors are examples of the creativity evidenced at Monticello.)*

CRITICAL VIEWING Possible response: Instead of a formal jacket and ruffled shirt, Jefferson is dressed in a garment with a fur collar, possibly a dressing gown.

CRITICAL VIEWING Possible response: The whiteness of Mrs. Washington's dress makes her appear angelic and pure, and the fabric has a sheen like silk, which gives her an air of refinement. The gentle look on Mrs. Washington's face conveys a calm temperament.

THOMAS JEFFERSON: THE FORWARD THINKER

On April 29, 1962, President John F. Kennedy hosted a banquet at the White House for 49 Nobel Prize winners. In his speech to some of the most brilliant people in the world, Kennedy said, "I think this is the most extraordinary collection of talent and of human knowledge that has ever been gathered together at the White House—with the possible exception of when Thomas Jefferson dined alone."

Kennedy had a point: Jefferson's intelligence, coupled with his curiosity and his relentless quest for knowledge, made him one of the

> *"The tree of liberty must be refreshed from time to time with the blood of patriots and tyrants."*
>
> —Thomas Jefferson, 1787

CRITICAL VIEWING American artist Rembrandt Peale painted this portrait in 1805 after Jefferson won re-election in a landslide victory. How might Jefferson's clothing reflect his preference for informality?

FOUNDING MOTHERS?

In 2016, when *The Atlantic* magazine asked, "Who is the greatest supporting player of all time?" historian Richard Norton Smith nominated Martha Washington, George's wife. According to Smith, "She ran Mount Vernon during his long absences; acted as his wartime secretary, sounding board, and surrogate; and charmed members of Congress who agreed on little else." Many historians acknowledge that Martha Washington was a patriot in her own right and played a pivotal role in supporting George in both the private and public spheres.

CRITICAL VIEWING This 1878 oil painting of Martha Washington is part of the White House art collection. What does artist Eliphalet Frazer Andrews convey about Mrs. Washington through the portrait's details?

leading intellectuals of his time. These qualities also allowed him to form a vision for the future of the North American colonies as an independent country, which he boldly articulated as the principal writer of the Declaration of Independence. Later, as president, he purchased the Louisiana Territory to ensure an expansive future for the United States.

Jefferson's restless intellect drove him to study topics as diverse as architecture, wine making, natural history, and many others. Wherever he found himself, he would take time each day to make notes about the weather, what plants were blooming, and the patterns of migratory birds. When he dispatched Lewis and Clark to explore the land west of the Mississippi, he was eager not just to stake the United States' claim to the territory, but to learn of the new animals, plants, people, and geographic features they would discover.

After his second term in office as president, Jefferson was succeeded in 1809 by his friend James Madison and retired to Monticello, his home in Virginia. At the age of 76, once again looking to the future, he founded the University of Virginia. Jefferson died on July 4, 1826.

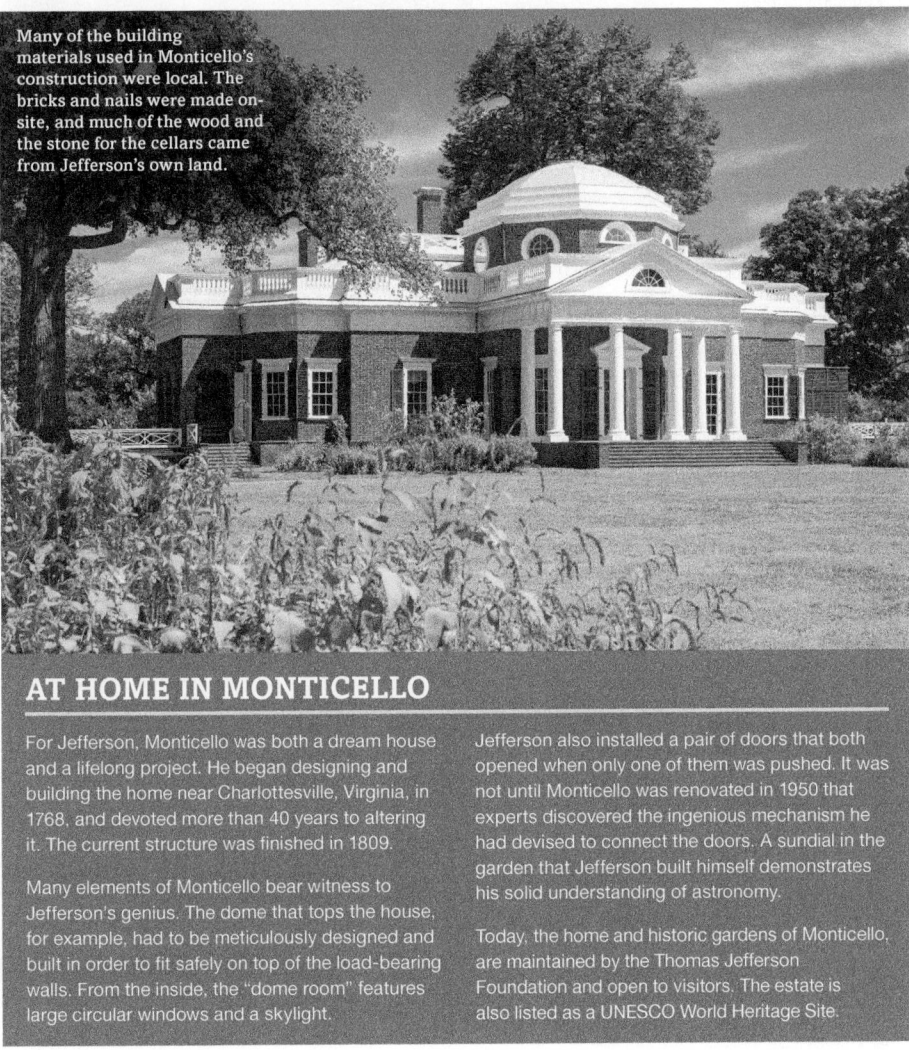

Many of the building materials used in Monticello's construction were local. The bricks and nails were made on-site, and much of the wood and the stone for the cellars came from Jefferson's own land.

AT HOME IN MONTICELLO

For Jefferson, Monticello was both a dream house and a lifelong project. He began designing and building the home near Charlottesville, Virginia, in 1768, and devoted more than 40 years to altering it. The current structure was finished in 1809.

Many elements of Monticello bear witness to Jefferson's genius. The dome that tops the house, for example, had to be meticulously designed and built in order to fit safely on top of the load-bearing walls. From the inside, the "dome room" features large circular windows and a skylight.

Jefferson also installed a pair of doors that both opened when only one of them was pushed. It was not until Monticello was renovated in 1950 that experts discovered the ingenious mechanism he had devised to connect the doors. A sundial in the garden that Jefferson built himself demonstrates his solid understanding of astronomy.

Today, the home and historic gardens of Monticello are maintained by the Thomas Jefferson Foundation and open to visitors. The estate is also listed as a UNESCO World Heritage Site.

TEACH

GUIDED DISCUSSION

1. **Make Inferences** Why do you think both Washington and Jefferson remain such widely respected presidents? Use details from the text to support your ideas. *(Possible response: Washington fought the American Revolution firsthand as a general and then led the country as its first president. He demonstrated honor, character, and "true principles" in both roles. As the principal writer of the Declaration, Jefferson defined the new nation. His intelligence and vision during his presidency helped to expand the country through the Louisiana Purchase and draw settlers westward after Lewis and Clark's discoveries.)*

2. **Analyze Primary Sources** What point was Thomas Jefferson making when he said, "The tree of liberty must be refreshed from time to time with the blood of patriots and tyrants"? *(Possible response: He was suggesting that liberty isn't won just once. For people to remain free, they must be ready to fight, and maybe die, to defend their freedom.)*

ACTIVE OPTIONS

On Your Feet: Perform a Reading Direct students to conduct online research on the writings of either George Washington, Thomas Jefferson, or Benjamin Franklin, such as those available on the Internet Archive or the Library of Congress websites. Instruct students to select essays, letters, autobiographical excerpts, or other types of writing that give insight into the personality, characteristics, or concerns of the Founding Father they choose. Tell students to select one or two excerpts from their research to read to the class and to provide an introduction that states the writer and the context. After the readings, discuss as a class what insight the pieces convey about the three Founding Fathers.

NG Learning Framework: Evaluate and Improve an Invention

ATTITUDE Curiosity

KNOWLEDGE New Frontiers

Tell students to research one of Franklin's inventions that is of particular interest to them. Instruct them to describe the original invention, how the invention has been improved over the years, and what further improvements they might provide today. Encourage students to provide a photograph, illustration, or diagram of Franklin's original invention and a drawing of their improved version to enhance their presentation.

WE ARE INDEBTED TO YOU, BEN FRANKLIN

Benjamin Franklin belonged to the Junto Club, a group of avid readers who discussed a wide range of subjects, philosophical ideas, and political issues. To have access to books they couldn't individually afford, they pooled their money to purchase books to share. In 1731, Franklin established the Library Company in Philadelphia, American's first subscription library. He solicited others to join and attracted 50 subscribers, mostly tradesmen. According to Franklin, libraries like this "made the common Tradesman and Farmers as intelligent as most Gentlemen." **ASK:** How did Franklin's library reflect the founding democratic ideals of the nation? *(Possible response: The library was open to all who could pay the subscription fee, and it encouraged education and free thinking.)*

THE GLASS ARMONICA

Share with students that Benjamin Franklin was inspired to create the glass armonica after witnessing musicians using water-filled wine glasses to produce notes. Then tell students that Franklin once noted: "That as we enjoy great Advantages from the Inventions of others, we should be glad of an Opportunity to serve others by any Invention of ours, and this we should do freely and generously." **ASK:** How were Franklin's ideas about inventing realized in his inspiration for and invention of the glass armonica? *(Possible response: Musicians had already created music using wine glasses, and Franklin expanded the idea and invented a glass instrument for the purpose of making music. He acknowledged that inventions were based on what others did earlier, and because of that, he suggested that they should be given for free for all to use.)*

WRITE ABOUT HISTORY

Analyze the Expression of American Ideals To help students think about how traits of the Founding Fathers are part of the American identity, ask them to write an essay in which they consider how patriotism, forward thinking, and self-reliance are expressed today in the United States and who takes on those roles. Provide guidance about the writing process as necessary.

THINK ABOUT IT

Answers will vary. Possible response: They represent independence, innovation, self-reliance, and patriotism.

BENJAMIN FRANKLIN: THE SELF-MADE MAN

By the time Benjamin Franklin died in 1790, he had been a printer, author, newspaper publisher, scientist, inventor, diplomat, and statesman. He is the only Founding Father to have signed the Declaration of Independence, the Treaty of Alliance with France, the Treaty of Paris, and the Constitution. He is also arguably the best-known entrepreneur among the Founding Fathers.

Such greatness probably seemed unimaginable when Franklin was born in 1706, the tenth son of a Boston soap maker. Franklin's family could not afford to educate him, and at 12 years old, he was apprenticed to his older brother, a printer. At 17, he ran away to Philadelphia, where he continued in the printing business. There he wrote and published the wildly popular annual *Poor Richard's Almanack* from 1732 to 1757. In addition to weather predictions and household advice, the almanac contained pearls of wisdom and wit, such as "Early to bed and early to rise, makes a man healthy, wealthy and wise" and "Three may keep a secret, if two of them are dead."

Like Jefferson, Franklin had a broad range of scientific interests and pursued them whenever the opportunity presented itself. When crossing the Atlantic Ocean to Europe, for example, he took accurate measurements of ocean temperatures that enabled him to make the first chart of the Gulf Stream, a powerful ocean current that flows from North America to Europe. This information helped reduce the sailing time from Europe to North America by two weeks. He also greatly advanced the understanding of electricity by conducting a variety of experiments, including the famous incident in which he flew a kite tied to a key during a lightning storm.

But it is as a statesman that Franklin is best known—and revered. When the Stamp Act was passed in 1765, he was in England, serving as a colonial representative of Pennsylvania. The colonists' negative response to the passage of the act took him completely by surprise. Stirred to action, he spoke eloquently to Parliament, condemning the act and explaining the colonists'

"*To succeed, jump as quickly at opportunities as you do at conclusions.*"
—Benjamin Franklin

Ben Franklin, shown above in a portrait by Joseph Siffred Duplessis, shared many important ideas with the world. But his proposal to eliminate the letters C, J, Q, W, X, and Y from the alphabet was not well received.

position. His speech was instrumental in its repeal. The experience made Franklin feel what he called his "Americanness" as never before. He also began to question his loyalty to Britain and its treatment of the colonies. As colonial protests mounted against Britain and the king, Franklin became a strong voice for independence and democracy. He would help draft the Declaration of Independence and was among the first to sign it.

Through his accomplishments, wit, energy, and personal charm, Franklin lived his final days wealthy and admired on both sides of the Atlantic.

THINK ABOUT IT

What American ideals do the Founding Fathers represent for you?

WE ARE INDEBTED TO YOU, BEN FRANKLIN

Some of Franklin's inventions, incorporating later improvements, are still in use, while others have been overtaken by more modern technologies. Here is a partial list of his creations, discoveries, and new ideas:

- bifocal glasses
- the lightning rod
- *Poor Richard's Almanack*
- the Franklin stove, which allowed for more efficient home heating
- swim fins (for the hands)
- the glass armonica (a musical instrument)
- extension arm (a device for reaching books on high shelves)
- the first successful lending library in the United States
- a map of the course of the Gulf Stream
- the terms "charge," "condenser," and "conductor" to describe concepts in electricity

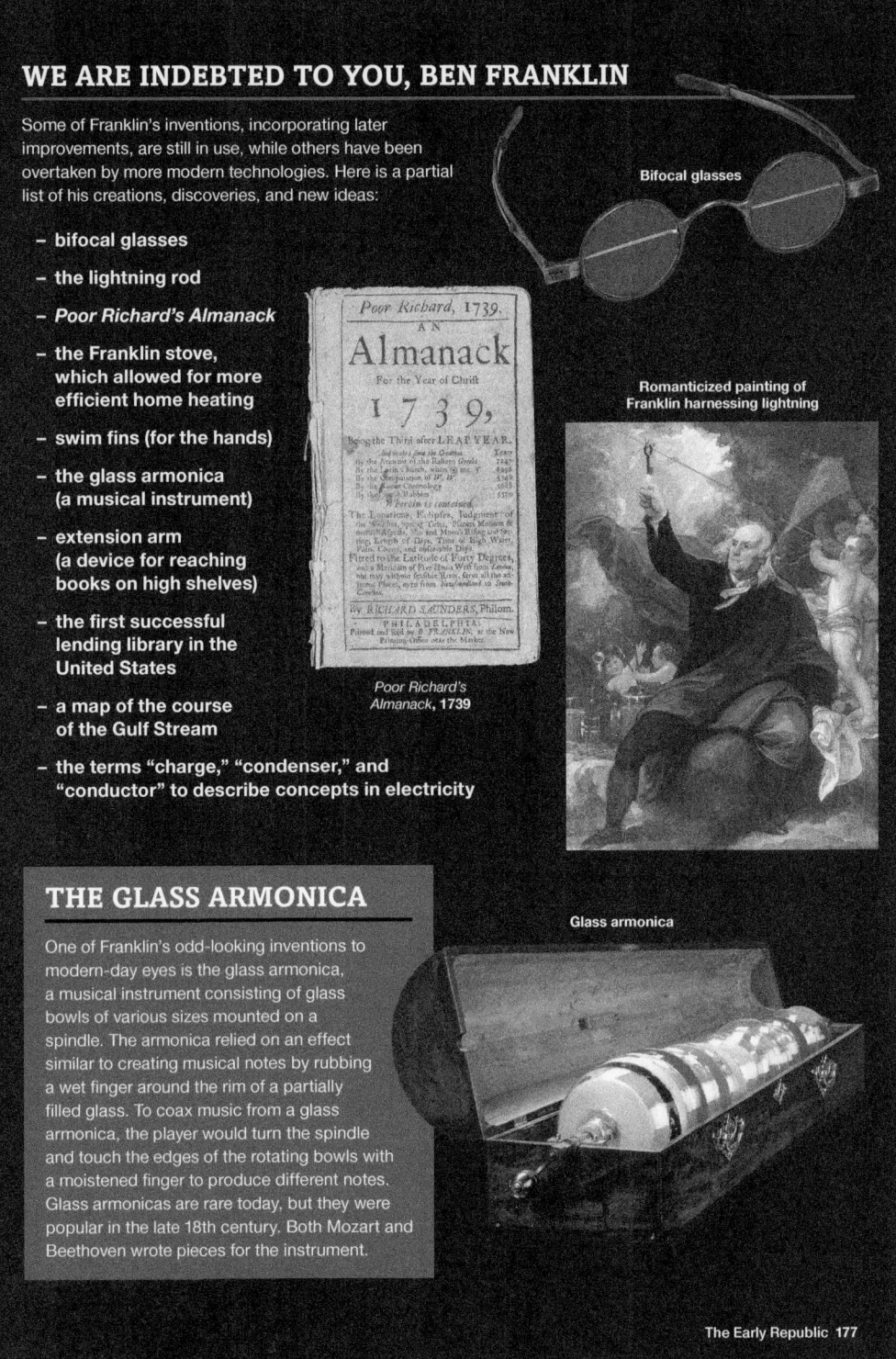

Bifocal glasses

Poor Richard's Almanack, 1739

Romanticized painting of Franklin harnessing lightning

Glass armonica

THE GLASS ARMONICA

One of Franklin's odd-looking inventions to modern-day eyes is the glass armonica, a musical instrument consisting of glass bowls of various sizes mounted on a spindle. The armonica relied on an effect similar to creating musical notes by rubbing a wet finger around the rim of a partially filled glass. To coax music from a glass armonica, the player would turn the spindle and touch the edges of the rotating bowls with a moistened finger to produce different notes. Glass armonicas are rare today, but they were popular in the late 18th century. Both Mozart and Beethoven wrote pieces for the instrument.

The Early Republic 177

STRIVING READERS

Chart Details About the Founding Fathers Pair students at **All Proficiencies** and instruct them to create a three-column chart with the columns labeled Washington, Jefferson, Franklin. Then direct pairs to take turns reading paragraphs of the American Story aloud to each other. Tell students to pause after each subsection, and record important details about the subject of the paragraph. Encourage students to write at least four details for each person, including notes about the person's character and contributions to the nation. Invite pairs to exchange and compare their completed charts.

GIFTED & TALENTED

Create a Founding Father Meme Challenge students to create a meme using a quotation from Washington, Jefferson, or Franklin that contains wit or wisdom that is still relevant today. Students may find Franklin's *Poor Richard's Almanack* as a source for inspiration. Tell students to add a photograph or artwork to enhance the social commentary or philosophical content of the quotation. Invite students to share their memes with the class.

See the Chapter Planner for more strategies for differentiation.

Ask and have students answer the following questions.

1. **READING CHECK** Why did George Washington have mixed feelings about serving as president?

2. **SYNTHESIZE** How did the nation change over the course of all three men's lifetimes?

3. **FORM AND SUPPORT OPINIONS** Which shared character traits among the Founding Fathers were crucial to America's success as a young nation? Explain your thoughts.

ANSWERS

1. Washington had been fighting in the American Revolution for several years, and he missed spending time at home. As a dutiful and dedicated Patriot, he also felt he needed to serve the country when asked.

2. Possible response: It went from being a collection of colonies to an independent nation with a Constitution, largely as a result of the work of these three men. The country also grew geographically, and institutions such as universities and libraries were established.

3. Possible response: Their sense of loyalty, dedication, intelligence, and fierce patriotism were crucial to America's success. Had they been less devoted to the cause, America might not have gained independence or become a republic.

WASHINGTON'S LEADERSHIP

Voted unanimously into office, George Washington reluctantly took on the role of president. As he himself described it, the nation faced "an ocean of difficulties." So what did he do? He gathered an A-list of team members to help him.

FORMING A GOVERNMENT

As you have read, the founders faced the unique challenge of forming a republican government from the ground up. The Articles of Confederation, which had given almost all the power to the states and practically none to the central government, hadn't worked well. Now the nation had a new Constitution that split power between a strong central government and the individual states. The challenge was to make that balancing act work.

As the newly written Constitution directed, the electoral college—not the people—determined who would be president in this first election. When the members of the electoral college met in their state capitals in February 1789 to cast their votes for president, they were instructed to vote for two candidates each. Every one of the 69 electors who participated cast one vote for Washington. Washington won the presidency hands down. John Adams, who was runner-up with 34 votes, became the vice president.

Washington's leadership during the revolution, his dignity and character, his support for republican government, and his commitment to the success of the new Constitution made him the obvious choice to unite the nation. He took great pains to make it clear that he would be the nation's president, not its king, and that he answered to the American citizens. At

his first presidential **inauguration**, or swearing-in ceremony, he did as he had when asked to lead the Continental Army: he renounced any formal salary for his position. Instead, in his inaugural address, he declared that any money paid to him as executive "be limited to such actual expenditures as the public good may be thought to require."

One of the first tasks the new president and Congress faced was to organize the government. In the summer of 1789, Congress created the Departments of State, Treasury, and War as part of the executive branch. Washington appointed the heads of these departments, called secretaries, and they formed his **Cabinet**.

CRITICAL VIEWING On April 30, 1789, Washington was sworn in as president on the balcony of a hall in New York City, the newly declared U.S. capital. What details in Ramon de Elorriaga's painting *The Inauguration of George Washington* show the importance of the event?

Washington chose a group of highly talented men from a variety of geographical areas and with a mix of political views to make up his Cabinet. He strongly advocated political moderation and tried to keep himself, as president, above the bickering that went on between political factions. He encouraged his Cabinet to do the same.

To oversee relations with foreign nations, Washington chose Thomas Jefferson as Secretary of State. Alexander Hamilton, well known as a good money manager, was chosen to be Secretary of the Treasury. And former general Henry Knox was selected to supervise the nation's military as Secretary of War. Congress created another Cabinet position, the office of **attorney general**, charged with the primary role of representing the United States before the Supreme Court. Unlike the other Cabinet members, the attorney general would not lead an executive department. Washington named lawyer and politician Edmund Randolph as the nation's first attorney general.

THE JUDICIARY AND THE CENSUS

President Washington and Congress also needed to establish a system of courts. With the **Judiciary Act of 1789**, Congress fleshed out the line of text in Article III of the Constitution, which states: "The judicial power of the United States shall be vested in one Supreme Court, and in such inferior courts as the Congress may from time to time ordain and establish." The act established a Supreme Court of six justices—one Chief Justice and five associate justices. (Today, eight associate justices sit on the court.) The Chief Justice was to preside over the judicial branch of the U.S. government as well as over the Supreme Court itself. John Jay, who had helped negotiate the Treaty of Paris in 1783, became the nation's first Chief Justice.

The act also created a dual-court system, with responsibilities split between state and federal courts. A few "inferior" federal courts, that is federal courts other than the Supreme Court, existed to deal with federal crimes. State courts presided over most civil and criminal cases. A **civil case** is a legal dispute between two or more individuals or organizations, often involving contract issues or other business problems. In a **criminal case** the defendant is

accused of breaking the law and endangering society, and the government initiates the case in coordination with law enforcement. The U.S. Supreme Court might agree to hear appeals for civil and criminal cases decided by the highest state courts.

Representing each state's population fairly with the right number of delegates in the House of Representatives and electoral college was a vital concern for the country. It meant the nation had to keep track of how many people were living in each state. The Constitution had stipulated that within three years of Congress's first meeting, a **census**, or population count, would be taken. It was to be repeated every ten years after that. Congress set August 1790 as the date of the first census, which took 18 months to complete.

Although sketchy and incomplete, the **U.S. Census of 1790** helped measure the dynamic population growth of an expanding nation. The first census results showed that the United States had nearly 3.9 million people, not including Native Americans. "Free white males" numbered about 1.6 million. "Free white females" numbered around 1.54 million. The category "All other free persons," mainly free African Americans, numbered nearly 60,000. Almost 700,000 of those counted in the census were enslaved.

THE CENSUS, THEN AND NOW

In 1790, the U.S. Census was little more than a head count. It measured race, age, gender, and whether someone was free or enslaved. Today, the census involves more than 200 different surveys that track information about people living in the United States, whether they are citizens or not. Why does the government need so much data? Information such as income, home ownership, and relationships among people sharing a residence help the government anticipate what its population will need. The number of people that live in a state continues to serve as the basis for determining how many representatives a state should have in the House. More specific information about each person helps government agencies decide how to allot government funds meant for maintaining education, healthcare, and other social systems nationwide.

HISTORICAL THINKING

1. **READING CHECK** What steps did Washington and Congress take to establish the new government?

2. **SUMMARIZE** Choose one political decision described in this lesson. How did it help organize the new nation's government?

3. **COMPARE AND CONTRAST** How were the nation's new federal and state courts different from one another?

PLAN: 2-PAGE LESSON

OBJECTIVE

Summarize how President Washington and the Congress organized the new government.

CRITICAL THINKING SKILLS FOR LESSON 1.1

- Summarize
- Compare and Contrast
- Evaluate
- Draw Conclusions
- Make Predictions

HISTORICAL THINKING FOR CHAPTER 6

How did government, expansion, and war unify the nation? As the first president, George Washington was charged with organizing a new government. Lesson 1.1 summarizes steps taken that were dictated by the Constitution and subsequent steps taken by Washington and Congress to serve the newly formed nation.

BACKGROUND FOR THE TEACHER

Because of the vague nature of Article III of the Constitution, it was left to Congress to decide how the courts would best function. The Judiciary Act established three tiers of courts: the Supreme Court, district courts which heard minor disputes, and circuit courts with jurisdiction over more important cases. The act also divided the country into thirteen districts and three circuits. However, one crucial component was omitted—permanent circuit court judges. In a practice known as circuit riding, district court and Supreme Court judges were tasked with traveling within a judicial district to preside over circuit court cases. In an era of cumbersome travel, this was an enormous burden. Early Supreme Court justices traveled during even the harshest weather in order to hold 27 circuit court sessions a year, from New Hampshire to Georgia, as well as two Supreme Court sessions in Philadelphia.

INTRODUCE & ENGAGE

K-W-L CHART

Provide students with a K-W-L Chart and ask them to record in the left column what they already know about the formation of the new government. Then ask them to record information they would like to learn in the middle column. Allow time at the end of the lesson for students to complete the chart with information they learned.

K What Do I Know?	W What Do I Want To Learn?	L What Did I Learn?

TEACH

GUIDED DISCUSSION

1. **Evaluate** Did Washington's decision to appoint people from different geographical areas with differing views contradict or support his desire to avoid bickering among political factions? Explain your answer. *(Possible responses: It contradicted his desire because factions were destined to arise due to regional issues, such as the importance of industry versus agriculture. It supported his desire because more people in the country probably felt their concerns were being represented and therefore were willing to compromise.)*

2. **Draw Conclusions** Why might the inclusion of a census question about citizenship be controversial? *(Possible response: Some people may fear that a citizenship question is a way for the government to locate residents who entered the country illegally, with the goal of deporting them. If this fear causes people not to respond to the census, the population count will be flawed.)*

MAKE PREDICTIONS

Inform students that the process for electing the president and vice president was changed by the 12th Amendment in 1804. **ASK:** What problems do you think were caused by the original system by which George Washington and John Adams were elected? *(Possible response: The two candidates with the most votes were likely political rivals, which could lead to serious or irreconcilable disagreements and damaging divisions in Congress.)*

ACTIVE OPTIONS

On Your Feet: Create a Plan for Government Direct small groups of students to separate areas of the room. Tell students to think about the role of George Washington, tasked with setting up a federal government. Ask them to review his initial actions and evaluate whether they were necessary first steps. Then ask groups to make a list of the first three actions they would take if they had been in Washington's place and provide a rationale for each. Allow groups to share their lists, and then, as a class, discuss and agree on a list of three first actions.

NG Learning Framework: Presidential Cabinets Then and Now

SKILL Communication

KNOWLEDGE Our Human Story

Divide the class into five groups and assign four groups one of Washington's first Cabinet positions (secretaries of state, treasury, and war, and attorney general). Direct groups to research the duties of the original position and summarize their findings for the class. Ask the fifth group to provide the class with a list of current Cabinet positions and when each was created. As a class, compare the list to Washington's first Cabinet and discuss possible reasons why departments that exist today were not formed by Washington.

For students who develop an interest in George Washington, suggest that they read the American Story at the beginning of this chapter.

DIFFERENTIATE

ENGLISH LANGUAGE LEARNERS   ELD

Create Word Squares Pair students at the **Emerging** level with those at the **Expanding** or **Bridging** level. Instruct students to create two Word Squares, writing *civil case* in the center oval of one and *criminal case* in the other. Have pairs use context clues in the lesson to write the definition and characteristics in the upper boxes, and examples and non-examples in the lower boxes.

GIFTED & TALENTED

Deliver a Speech of Introduction Tell students to choose and conduct research about one person from Washington's first Cabinet in order to deliver a formal speech of introduction about him. Encourage students to take notes in a three-column chart with the following headings: Cabinet Member, Personal Qualities, Professional Qualifications. Suggest that students use their notes to practice giving their speech to a partner. Invite volunteers to deliver their speech to the class.

See the Chapter Planner for more strategies for differentiation.

HISTORICAL THINKING

ANSWERS

1. Washington and the Congress established the Cabinet, created the judiciary, and oversaw the implementation of a national census.

2. Answers will vary. Possible response: By taking a national census, the government was able to determine the correct proportional representation for each state in the House of Representatives and the electoral college.

3. The federal courts tried only federal crimes, while state courts oversaw civil and nonfederal criminal cases. The Supreme Court could agree to hear cases when the judgments of lower courts were appealed.

CRITICAL VIEWING The importance of the event is conveyed by the men's formal dress, which included powdered wigs. A cheering crowd is depicted below the balcony and people wave banners from windows in the background. Washington stands with his right hand on the Bible and his left over his heart as a secretary transcribes the swearing in.

WOMEN'S ROLES IN THE NEW REPUBLIC

Two steps forward, one step back. During the war, women ventured outside of the home to battle, farm, and do business. Afterward, a new spotlight shone on the importance of women's household roles. Was this progress?

REPUBLICAN MOTHERHOOD

When George Washington traveled to his inauguration in New York, Americans along the route showed their patriotic spirit with celebrations, banners, and speeches. Americans also felt bound together by a new spirit of nationalism. They had a sense they were participating in **civic republicanism**—or the tradition of political thought that stresses individual freedom, active citizenship, and support for the common good.

Civic republicanism dates back to the ancient Greeks and Romans. In the United States, it represented a government and constitution that promised justice for all. In order to guarantee freedom and justice, a nation needed to promote principles such as civic virtue, patriotism, and individual freedom, and it needed to oppose excessive government power. In connection with these ideals, many Americans believed that raising children and educating them was important to the republic, as these activities passed the qualities of effective republican citizenship on to the next generation.

Women were crucial to civic republicanism in the role that historians now refer to as republican motherhood. The concept of **republican motherhood** was a powerful force in the late 18th and early 19th centuries. The goal was to raise children—especially sons—to participate actively and wisely in civic life by voting, becoming property owners, taking part in local government, and behaving morally. Though voting

Best known for his art depicting colonial America, John Singleton Copley painted this portrait of himself (top left) with his family in 1776–1777. Historians believe that through lighting, gesture, gaze, and color, Copley's work expresses some popular ideals of his time—including the concept of republican motherhood.

rights at the time varied from state to state, they were generally limited to property-owning white males. So the notion of republican motherhood mostly applied to upper- and middle-class white women.

The ideal was for a republican mother to pass on her wisdom in a tranquil home, a refuge protected from conflicts in the outside world of politics and business. By avoiding such outside influences, the republican mother was expected to live out her once-revolutionary principles by raising and teaching children. While this ideal elevated the traditional status of mother and wife, it also solidified gender roles in which men ruled the public sphere.

WOMEN, RESPONSIBILITIES, AND RIGHTS

During the war, women stepped in to manage farms and businesses while men served as soldiers. Some women even served on the battlefield. Many American women hoped that their lives would change after the Revolution, and they would be able to continue taking on more active roles as citizens.

After the war, women's rights did not improve. Women still could not vote or hold office. They still had very limited access to educational opportunities and had virtually no right to purchase property. Though they were allowed to inherit more property after the American Revolution, women usually came into their inheritance after marriage, so their husbands ended up being the legal owners of property they inherited. Ironically, as limited as the role of republican motherhood was, it was one of the only paths many women could follow to gain control over parts of their own lives.

A woman's stature as a republican mother opened up possibilities to serve the new nation in ways beyond just raising good citizens. Often seen as more "moral" than men who battled in politics, courtrooms, and businesses, the republican mother—tasked with shaping the moral and intellectual character of future generations—found opportunities to become active in church and community groups.

Women provided much of the support for establishing public schools and mental asylums. They opposed activities that they deemed immoral, such as alcohol abuse, and many worked to abolish slavery. They also formed "Maternal Associations" to teach new ideas about raising children and to provide childcare for working mothers who often took on domestic work for other families to support their own. And, since women were expected to teach their children to become responsible citizens, they argued for more educational opportunities for themselves.

SUPPORT FOR EDUCATION

Female essayist and playwright **Judith Sargent Murray** was a strong supporter of education for women. She argued against the common belief of the day that women were intellectually inferior to men, claiming that the nation's daughters could not reach their full capabilities if the only roles they were trained for in society were those of wife, mother, and housekeeper. She pointed out that if mothers were expected to teach their children the basics in all subjects, they should be educated in the sciences and higher mathematics, which were traditionally reserved for male students.

Through the first decades of the new republic, women would take an ever-increasing role in the education of children, both within the home and in public schools. They also became involved in establishing schools for other women. The more active women became in this enterprise and in promoting the public good, the more they began to work toward securing rights for themselves and their daughters. They formed organizations to help orphans, the physically handicapped, and war widows. These organizations would lead to larger social movements in the future.

PRIMARY SOURCE

I expect to see our young women forming a new era in female history. . . . The partial distribution of advantages, which has too long obtained, is, in this enlightened age, rapidly giving place to a more uniform system of [education] . . . and the revolution of events is advancing in that half of the human species, which [has until now] been involved in the night of darkness, toward the irradiating sun of science.

—from Judith Sargent Murray, 1798, as quoted in *No Small Courage: A History of Women in the United States*

HISTORICAL THINKING

1. **READING CHECK** What was "civic republicanism," and why did Americans feel they were participating in it?

2. **FORM AND SUPPORT OPINIONS** Did the concept of republican motherhood give women greater or less independence and autonomy? Support your opinion with details from the lesson.

3. **MAKE CONNECTIONS** What ideas that rose from the concept of republican motherhood might have led to later events in history, such as the fight for women's right to vote?

PLAN: 2-PAGE LESSON

OBJECTIVE

Identify how women's roles in society changed in the early years of the republic.

CRITICAL THINKING SKILLS FOR LESSON 1.2

• Form and Support Opinions

• Make Connections

• Draw Conclusions

• Analyze Primary Sources

HISTORICAL THINKING FOR CHAPTER 6

How did government, expansion, and war unify the nation? During the American Revolution, women had some opportunities to adopt nontraditional roles. Lesson 1.2 examines how the importance of passing the unifying principles of the new nation on to the next generation led to defining women's roles almost exclusively as wives and mothers.

BACKGROUND FOR THE TEACHER

Between 1760 and 1774, Loyalist John Singleton Copley established himself as the premier portrait artist in colonial America. His paintings served an upper-class colonial clientele—mainly well-off clergymen, merchants, and their wives—who desired English-style portraits, which were characterized by carefully posed subjects and objects in settings that conveyed social status. Ironically, Copley's most famous painting is his portrait of Paul Revere holding his chin in one hand and a silver teapot in the other. It stands as Copley's only finished portrait showcasing an artisan at work and wearing informal clothes. Unfortunately for Copley, the onset of the Revolution spelled the end of his colonial business, as many of his clients found themselves on the opposite side of history. Copley's deep Loyalist ties included his father-in-law, a merchant who consigned the tea which motivated the Boston Tea Party. In 1774 Copley left for Europe, never again to return to America.

INTRODUCE & ENGAGE

ACTIVATE PRIOR KNOWLEDGE

Ask students to recall what they learned previously about women's roles in society during the American Revolution. *(Students may recall that women maintained homes and ran businesses while men went to fight. They organized boycotts, wrote patriotic broadsides, and occasionally fought in battles.)* As a class, discuss how their experiences during the war might have changed women's expectations about their roles in the new republic. Then explain that in this lesson, students will examine how women's roles and opportunities became centered on family and home in a new era of societal barriers.

TEACH

GUIDED DISCUSSION

1. **Make Connections** Why was education and civic republicanism important for citizens of a democratic republic rather than for citizens of a monarchy? *(In a democratic republic, the citizens choose representatives who determine laws, so citizens must be educated to make informed decisions and think about the common good. In a monarchy, a citizen's knowledge and participation is not relevant to government because decisions are made by leaders who rule by birthright or succession.)*

2. **Draw Conclusions** Despite the lofty words of the Declaration of Independence, why did women still inhabit a limited role in the new republic? *(Answers will vary. Possible response: The Founders had a narrow definition of "men" in the phrase, "all men are created equal." They meant white, male property owners. African Americans and Native Americans were not considered "equal," and all women were also overlooked.)*

ANALYZE PRIMARY SOURCES

Direct students' attention to the Primary Source feature. **ASK:** What are Judith Sargent Murray's expectations for women in the new republic? *(Murray expects women to have better access to education.)* **ASK:** How does Murray use the theme of light and darkness to convey her message? *(Murray refers to the current inequitable system of education as "the night of darkness" and "the irradiating sun of science" as the education and advantages she believes will come with "this enlightened age.")*

ACTIVE OPTIONS

On Your Feet: Three-Step Interview Direct pairs to interview each other about women's education. First one student interviews the other using the following questions: What reasons did women in the early republic give for needing better education? What were the results of their increased participation in education? Based on the reasons and results you stated, how do you think women felt about their roles in the republic? Then have students reverse roles. Invite each student to share with the class the results of his or her interview.

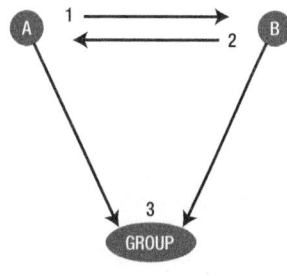

NG Learning Framework: Portray Present-Day Expectations for Women

SKILL Communication

KNOWLEDGE Our Human Story

Guide a discussion about the details that reinforce republican motherhood in the painting that accompanies the lesson, such as the attentive and loving mother, well-fed and happy children, and tranquil family setting. Then direct pairs to create a piece of art or literary work, such as a painting, song, mural, or short story, that depicts a role, expectation, or ideal for women in present-day society. Create a space for students to display their art and provide the opportunity for students to perform or read their written work. Ask students to comment on how the pieces demonstrate the ways women's lives have changed or stayed the same since the era of republican motherhood.

DIFFERENTIATE

STRIVING READERS

Summarize Using a Concept Cluster Help pairs summarize the lesson by guiding them to create a Concept Cluster with the lesson title in the center oval and the subsection headings in the smaller ones. As students read each subsection, tell them to record key facts and ideas on the spokes. After students complete the Concept Cluster, invite volunteers to summarize the lesson and explain how women's roles changed in the early years of the new republic.

PRE-AP

Explore Origins Instruct students to write an essay that examines the impact of ancient Greek and Roman ideas of civic republicanism on the forming of the new republic. Tell students to conduct online and print research to gather primary and secondary sources, and to cite them appropriately. Invite volunteers to share their essays with the class and answer questions their classmates may have.

See the Chapter Planner for more strategies for differentiation.

HISTORICAL THINKING

ANSWERS

1. Civic republicanism was an ideology that stressed freedom, the common good, and active citizenship. People felt they were participating in it because they had worked to gain America's independence, had a direct say in the new government, and were passing these values down to their children.

2. Answers will vary. Possible responses: Republican motherhood gave women greater independence, elevated the status of mothers in the home, opened possibilities for more education, and eventually led them into public works through community activism. Republican motherhood blocked women's independence and autonomy by idealizing women's roles as wives, mothers, and housekeepers confined to the home. As a result, women were mostly restricted to these roles.

3. By emphasizing the superior "moral" position of women and increasing their access to education, republican motherhood gave women the skills needed to work to improve their status in society and secure equal rights.

OPPOSING VISIONS OF AMERICA

Which came first, the United States or its national debt? If you said "its debt," you're right. Patriots had borrowed $54 million to fund the American Revolution. And now the already struggling nation was in conflict about how to pay it back.

Based on the life of the Founding Father, Tony Award-winning *Hamilton* mixes hip-hop music with traditional elements of Broadway musicals. The result is a unique biography that has propelled writer and actor Lin-Manuel Miranda (right) and his main character, Alexander Hamilton, into the national spotlight.

In addition to commemorating Hamilton's contributions to establishing the Federalist Party and advocating for the National Bank, the musical considers how Hamilton's childhood shaped his life and explores his roles as a soldier, a lawyer, and an economist throughout his political career.

OPPOSING VISIONS OF AMERICA

The arguments that had plagued the constitutional debates continued into the new government. During Washington's first term, these political divisions widened, and two political parties developed. Alexander Hamilton, Washington's secretary of the treasury, saw the nation's future greatness in commerce and manufacturing. His followers, who joined to form the **Federalist Party**, favored commercial development, a strong central government, and a **loose constructionist** interpretation of the Constitution, which gave expansive powers to Congress and the president.

On the other side of the political coin, the **Democratic-Republican Party** favored a **strict constructionist** interpretation of the Constitution, one that followed the document to the letter, honoring the rights of states over federal power. Thomas Jefferson and James Madison founded the party, and Jefferson became the Democratic-Republicans' chief spokesman. He believed that the United States should be an **agrarian**, or agricultural, society made up of small farmers. The role of commerce should be to allow these farmers to sell their surplus crops in Europe and purchase manufactured goods in return.

DISPUTES OVER DEBTS

The nation owed more than $10 million in war debts to foreigners, mostly the French, and more than $40 million to Americans in payment of bonds. The bonds were issued to civilians in exchange for wartime supplies and to soldiers in exchange for wages. After the war, many ordinary Americans, unable to wait for repayment, sold their bonds to wealthy speculators, often at only 10 or 15 percent of their value. In addition to the national debt, individual states owed about $25 million collectively.

In his *Report on the Public Credit* in January 1790, Alexander Hamilton presented a plan in which the national government took on the responsibility for all of these debts, including those owed by the states. He proposed repaying the foreign debt immediately but repaying the domestic debt more slowly, using import duties, income from the post office, and an **excise tax**, or a tax levied on one particular product, in this case on the purchase of whiskey.

The Democratic-Republicans opposed Hamilton's proposal. They argued the plan would allow speculators to profit from the hardships of citizens—many of them farmers—who had sold their bonds at a fraction of their value. And many of the southern states had already paid off their war debts. They did not want to be taxed again to pay debts of other states. Debate continued for months. The matter was finally settled after Hamilton, Jefferson, and Madison struck a bargain.

Jefferson and Madison wanted to move the nation's capital from New York to a place farther south, specifically, on the banks of the Potomac River, which separated Virginia from Maryland. If Hamilton agreed, Jefferson and Madison would persuade southern delegates to approve his financial proposal. He did, and Congress passed Hamilton's plan and authorized a new capital, carved out of Virginia and Maryland, but belonging to neither. The capital city would be called Washington, and it would lie on land renamed the District of Columbia. **Pierre L'Enfant**, a French architect who had served with Washington at Valley Forge, was hired to plan the new capital.

Finally, to stabilize the nation's finances, Hamilton proposed a national bank and a common currency. The **Bank of the United States** and its branches would hold federal funds and regulate state banks.

Its chief purposes would be to expand the money supply and encourage commerce and economic growth. As it prospered, stockholders would receive **dividends**, or interest for depositing their money. The government would also receive dividends, which would help to lower the national debt.

Madison and Jefferson took a strict constructionist stance on the national bank, arguing that the federal government lacked constitutional authority to create such an institution. Hamilton countered with the loose constructionist interpretation that some federal powers are implied rather than stated outright. He argued that the Constitution gave Congress and the president the power to collect taxes, pay debts, coin and regulate money—and to "make all laws which shall be necessary and proper for carrying into execution the foregoing powers." Congress chartered the bank in 1791 for 20 years. After studying the matter carefully, President Washington approved Congress's charter.

THE WHISKEY REBELLION

The excise tax on whiskey led to unrest in the states, particularly in western Pennsylvania. Farmers there had resisted the tax from the start, because whiskey was their main source of cash. It was much cheaper to transport and sell whiskey than the heavy grain it was made from. The excise tax harmed farmers'

finances and made them furious. In what became known as the **Whiskey Rebellion**, they tarred and feathered tax collectors, burned barns, and even destroyed the whiskey stills of fellow farmers who paid the tax. They believed their battle was a struggle for "the virtuous principles of republican liberty." The farmers had other complaints, too, about the federal government's failure to open lands in the Ohio Territory for settlement and to end trade restrictions with the Spanish on the Mississippi River.

In July 1794, about 500 farmers surrounded and burned a tax inspector's home, exchanging gunfire that killed several people. The violence soon spread to neighboring states. Washington sent 13,000 militia, but the revolt had ended before the troops arrived. The threat of military force had stopped the rebellion.

HISTORICAL THINKING

1. **READING CHECK** How did a loose constructionist and a strict constructionist interpret the Constitution differently?

2. **ANALYZE CAUSE AND EFFECT** What was the primary cause of the Whiskey Rebellion?

3. **DISTINGUISH FACT FROM OPINION** What was one fact and one opinion used in the debate over Hamilton's plan to repay the nation's war debt?

OBJECTIVE

Examine the political and economic divisions that arose in the early republic.

CRITICAL THINKING SKILLS FOR LESSON 1.3

- Analyze Cause and Effect
- Distinguish Fact From Opinion
- Summarize
- Make Connections
- Analyze Language Use

HISTORICAL THINKING FOR CHAPTER 6

How did government, expansion, and war unify the nation? As a new federal government took shape, disputes broke out concerning its proper role in America's affairs. Lesson 1.3 analyzes the political and economic divisions that arose amidst Washington's dream of a unified nation.

BACKGROUND FOR THE TEACHER

Central to understanding the Whiskey Rebellion is the fact that in Washington's day, the government raised revenue in vastly different ways than it does now. Today, most federal money comes from personal income, payroll, and corporate taxes—none of which existed in the early republic. Considering the role taxes played in sparking the American Revolution, the Founders were wary of taxes and included language in the Constitution that all but prohibited an income tax. Instead, the government turned to other means to raise money: tariffs and duties on some imported goods and excise taxes on goods including sugar, tobacco, and liquor. It wasn't until 1913, with the passage of the 16th Amendment, that a federal income tax was adopted. At the time, it applied only to the wealthiest one percent of the population.

FINANCIAL LITERACY

To extend their knowledge and understanding about the concepts in this lesson, refer students to the Financial Literacy handbook.

INTRODUCE & ENGAGE

DISCUSS WHY POLITICAL PARTIES FORM

Invite students to share what they know about the present-day Democratic and Republican parties. Then ask them to think about and discuss why political parties form and the functions they provide. Invite volunteers to share their ideas. Inform students that in this lesson, they will learn about the new nation's first political parties.

TEACH

GUIDED DISCUSSION

1. **Summarize** What was Hamilton's economic vision for America, and how did he hope to achieve it? *(Hamilton envisioned an economy based on industry and commerce that would require investment and international trade. It could be achieved by having a stable money supply, good relations with foreign partners, and a strong central government.)*

2. **Make Connections** What connections can you see between the Whiskey Rebellion and the American Revolution? *(The federal government needed cash and taxed a sure source of revenue, even though it unfairly burdened Pennsylvania farmers. This is similar to how Great Britain taxed the colonies to help finance the French and Indian War. Both the Patriots and the farmers complained of the unfair taxes. Their protests included burning property and tarring and feathering those they opposed, and they faced a strong government response in the form of troops.)*

ANALYZE LANGUAGE USE

Explain that the debate between Jefferson and Hamilton stemmed from the fact that the Constitution was vague about how powers given to the government could be implemented. For this, the Founders used the phrase "necessary and proper." The debate centered on the definition of the word "necessary." Jefferson believed it was best understood as "required," while Hamilton interpreted it as "conducive," or helpful. Thus, Jefferson believed that a bank was not required in order to regulate commerce, and was therefore unconstitutional. In 1819, the Supreme Court sided with Hamilton, and to this day the clause is used to justify new government activities. **ASK:** What interpretation of the "necessary and proper" clause do you favor and why? *(Possible responses: Since the word* necessary *is a synonym for* required, *Jefferson's interpretation makes the most sense. Adding only those powers that are required limits the power of the central government, which is proper. Hamilton's interpretation makes the most sense because as the needs of the nation change, new powers will help the government meet those needs.)*

ACTIVE OPTIONS

On Your Feet: Think, Pair, Share Give students a few minutes to think about the following topic: the Whiskey Rebellion was a battle for the "virtuous principles of republican liberty." Then have students choose partners and talk about the topic for five minutes. Finally, allow individual students to share their ideas with the class.

Think   A   B

Pair   A   B

Share   A   B

NG Learning Framework: Design an Infographic

SKILL Communication

KNOWLEDGE Our Human Story

Guide groups of four to conduct research and create an infographic that displays the differences between Hamilton's and Jefferson's views on the role of government. Ask students to contrast their perspectives on debt, the use of taxes, a national bank, the role of the federal government versus state and local governments, constitutional interpretation, and their vision of commerce. Invite students to share their infographics on a class or school website or in a classroom gallery.

DIFFERENTIATE

ENGLISH LANGUAGE LEARNERS

Build Vocabulary Bring students' attention to the use of the antonyms *loose* and *strict*. Pair students at the **Emerging** or **Expanding** level with students at the **Bridging** level, and have them work together to define the two words and then add intermediate words to a Synonym-Antonym Scale, using a thesaurus if necessary. The final scale may include words such as *vague*, *indefinite*, *general*, *firm*, *tough*, and *rigorous*. Encourage partners to compose a sentence for each word to demonstrate understanding.

← loose   strict →

GIFTED & TALENTED

Research and Perform Lyrics Provide or have students access the lyrics of "The Room Where It Happens," a song from the musical *Hamilton*. Tell students to research and provide context for the lyrics (the compromise that involved moving the capital to the Potomac). If there is time, ask volunteers to perform a portion of the lyrics, including an introduction explaining the context of the segment they will perform. Then discuss how the lyrics helped students understand the historical event.

See the Chapter Planner for more strategies for differentiation.

HISTORICAL THINKING

ANSWERS

1. Strict constructionists believed that the federal government could only do what was explicitly written in the Constitution. Loose constructionists believed the government had the latitude to take actions—such as setting up a national bank—that were implied by the Constitution, as long as the government did not take actions specifically forbidden, such as establishing a religion.

2. The primary cause of the Whiskey Rebellion was the implementation of an excise tax on whiskey, the main source of income for those who rebelled.

3. Answers will vary. Possible response: Fact: The imposition of an excise tax would tax citizens in states which had already paid off their war debts. Opinion: Speculators would profit from the hardships of citizens.

POLITICAL ENTANGLEMENTS

Washington's presidency wasn't getting any easier. As the young nation grew, so did its internal conflicts between political parties and external conflicts with other nations. Agreeing on which conflict to resolve first was a problem, too.

EXPANSION TO THE WEST

During the 1780s, the lands west of the Appalachian Mountains and south of the Ohio River developed quickly, as American settlers moved to Kentucky and Tennessee in search of available farmland. State governments, speculators, and frontiersmen took the land from the Cherokee who had inhabited the territory for thousands of years.

In the 1780s and 1790s, the Cherokee joined the Creek and Shawnee, who also lived in the region, in attacking the American settlers. To stop the attacks, the U.S. government issued the 1791 Treaty of Holston, which promised that if the Cherokee ceded settled territory, they could keep their remaining lands. However, Governor William Blount of the Tennessee Territory, known by Native Americans as "dirt king" for his greed for land, ignored the promise to the Cherokee. The treaty collapsed and the battles continued until 1794, when U.S. forces fought and defeated the Native Americans.

Farther north, settlement in Ohio country was slower. This was partly because the federal government kept a tighter control in the territory than in the West—but more so because Native Americans strongly resisted giving up their land there. Throughout the 1780s, the United States obtained land in the area from some Native American groups, while the Delaware, Shawnee, Iroquois, Miami, and other Native American nations rejected the agreements. Native American tribes in Ohio formed a confederacy against U.S. settlement and attacked any settlers that trespassed on their land. The confederacy extended its influence, forming alliances with Native Americans to the south. The Spanish and the British, who still had their eyes on these lands, provided aid to the Native American confederacy.

In the early 1790s, Washington sent two military expeditions against the confederacy. Both were unsuccessful. Then in 1794, U.S. forces defeated the Shawnee and the Miami at the **Battle of Fallen Timbers** near present-day Toledo, Ohio. The British, who had helped the confederacy in the past, refused to enter this battle because they were already fighting a war with France. The Native American confederacy eventually signed the **Treaty of Greenville** in 1795, giving up their lands in present-day Ohio and parts of Indiana, Illinois, and Michigan.

THE SPANISH FRONTIER

By the 1790s the young nation faced difficult relations with European rivals, both in North America and abroad. A major challenge came from Spain. At that time, Spain's lands in what is now the United States extended from Florida to Louisiana, Texas, New Mexico, Arizona, and California. Even though Spanish officials were wary of U.S. population growth, they opened their lands to U.S. settlers to bolster their own population and economy. Spain offered free land in Florida and Louisiana to American planters and relaxed restrictions to promote more trade. Such policies eventually led to the U.S. acquisition of Florida and Louisiana. As Jefferson had predicted, Spain provided "the means of delivering to us peaceably, what may otherwise cost us a war."

Meanwhile, **Thomas Pinckney**, an American statesman, traveled to Spain and negotiated the Treaty of San Lorenzo in 1795 to maintain friendly relations between the United States and Spain. Also known as "Pinckney's Treaty," it opened the Mississippi River to free navigation, allowing Americans free use of the Spanish port of New Orleans. The treaty also settled a conflict regarding the Spanish colony of West Florida.

DIFFICULTIES WITH FRANCE AND GREAT BRITAIN

In 1789, Americans were intrigued by the events unfolding in another country across the Atlantic. The people of France sought to put an end to upper-class privilege and demanded equality for the lower classes. This caused the country to change from a strict monarchy to a constitutional monarchy and started the **French Revolution**. Many in the United States, particularly the Democratic-Republicans, supported this revolution. However, in 1792, as the French Revolution continued, **radicals**, or people who support complete social or political change, took control and established the First French Republic. Within a year, the radicals had executed King Louis XVI. The French Republic then declared war on Britain, Spain, and other neighboring nations. In this international conflict, the Federalists sided with Britain, thereby increasing the division between the two American parties. So even though France

had supported the American Revolution, Washington declared in 1793 that the United States would remain neutral, not taking sides with anyone.

The 1778 Franco-American Alliance, forged during the American Revolution, did not require the United States to enter France's conflicts in Europe, but France expected favorable trade policies and informal American military help. Though Secretary of State Jefferson favored France, he agreed that neutrality, or official impartiality, was essential. Jefferson knew American commerce was tied to Britain, which could also sweep U.S. ships from the seas with its powerful navy.

Washington issued a Proclamation of Neutrality in April 1793, warning citizens to avoid hostile acts, including selling weapons and privateering, or licensing of private ships by a warring nation to attack enemy vessels. Still, France enlisted American privateers against British vessels.

On July 14, 1789, an angry crowd in Paris attacked and captured the Bastille, the fortress prison that had become a symbol of the tyranny of King Louis XVI. The event, as represented in this painting by Jean Pierre Houel, signaled the beginning of the French Revolution, a decade when long-oppressed French commoners seized power from the upper classes.

PLAN: 4-PAGE LESSON

OBJECTIVE

Explain how foreign and domestic events offered challenges to presidents Washington and Adams.

CRITICAL THINKING SKILLS FOR LESSON 1.4

- Summarize
- Form and Support Opinions
- Draw Conclusions
- Make Connections
- Analyze Visuals
- Identify

HISTORICAL THINKING FOR CHAPTER 6

How did government, expansion, and war unify the nation? During the 1780s and 1790s, events in Europe threatened America's emerging unity. Lesson 1.4 analyzes how the French Revolution and subsequent European war, further widened political divisions in the United States.

BACKGROUND FOR THE TEACHER

The settling of the Great Lakes region was marked by violence, war, and atrocities. In the 20 years leading up to the Treaty of Greenville, Native Americans across the region were under almost constant attack from American armies and militias who burned villages and sometimes massacred civilians. In one notorious incident in 1782 along the Upper Sandusky River in Ohio, members of a militia killed more than 90 Delaware people—the majority of whom were women and children, and all converted Christians and pacifists. The Treaty of Greenville established Indian lands and brought a temporary peace and respite from the suffering. However, further expansion quickly overran the agreed-upon boundaries, restarting the violence. The situation culminated in the War of 1812, in which many Native American nations on the frontier sided with the British against the United States.

INTRODUCE & ENGAGE

RESPOND TO A CONFLICT

Lead students in brainstorming tools that a government might use to resolve conflicts with foreign nations, such as military force, diplomacy, economic sanctions, and other ideas. Record students' responses, and then prompt a discussion with the following questions:

• Under what circumstances might a government go to war?

• How and why might a government avoid going to war?

Tell students that they will learn about how George Washington's and John Adams's administrations dealt with foreign and domestic conflict.

War	Avoid War

TEACH

GUIDED DISCUSSION

1. **Make Connections** How did conflicts between Native Americans and the United States government in the 1780s and 1790s illustrate the government's continued policy concerning them? *(Possible response: As in previous decades, tensions arose when settlers attempted to expand onto Native American lands. As had happened in the past, government treaties were broken or violated by the actions of settlers. When Governor William Blount ignored the Treaty of Holston in the Tennessee Territory, the federal government didn't step in to reinforce the treaty. During this period, the federal government began to use more force against Native Americans, as at the Battle of Fallen Timbers, and took more of their lands under the Treaty of Greenville.)*

2. **Draw Conclusions** Why do you think many Americans sided with the French in their conflict with Britain? *(Many Americans saw parallels between the French Revolution and the American Revolution, and appreciated the help from France during the war. In addition, many still felt hostility towards the British.)*

ANALYZE VISUALS

Direct students' attention to the painting of an angry crowd attacking the Bastille. **ASK:** What details about the French Revolution are conveyed in Jean Pierre Houel's painting? *(Answers will vary. Possible response: In the center of the painting three comrades—a uniformed soldier carrying a musket and two citizens, one of whom also carries a musket—stride amid the chaos. This suggests that some soldiers in the employ of King Louis XVI disagreed with his tyranny and took an active part in liberating the Bastille. The smoke from the burning of the Bastille suggests the violence and destruction that citizens used to overthrow the king.)*

DIFFERENTIATE

INCLUSION

Use Supported Reading Pair proficient with less proficient readers, and have them read the lesson aloud paragraph by paragraph. Instruct pairs to stop at the end of each paragraph and use these sentence frames to monitor their comprehension of the text:

• This paragraph is mostly about _____.

• Its main idea is _____.

• Details that support the main idea are _____ and _____.

• One word I don't recognize is _____.

• One question I have is _____.

PRE-AP

Analyze Precedents Tell students to conduct research to learn more about the precedents Washington set for his successors, such as taking control of treaty negotiations, establishing a policy of neutrality in foreign conflicts, limiting presidents to two terms in office, and the peaceful transition of power. Instruct students to gather information from a variety of credible sources. Then have students write an essay analyzing the impact of Washington's precedents, using properly formatted citations for quotations they may include. Invite volunteers to share their reports with the class.

See the Chapter Planner for more strategies for differentiation.

Meanwhile Washington also faced increasing aggression from the British. In the early 1790s, the British began **impressment**, or recruitment by force, of U.S. merchant sailors. They captured American sailors and forced them to serve the British navy. Then, in 1793, the British blockaded the French West Indies, seizing more than 250 American ships.

Problems eased when the British weakened their French West Indies blockade, allowing Americans to trade food and consumer goods, but not weapons. Washington sent John Jay, chief justice of the Supreme Court, to persuade the British to leave their Western forts, pay for the slaves who had left with Britain's army, end impressment, open the British West Indies to American trade, and compensate

the United States for their Caribbean shipping losses. **Jay's Treaty** succeeded only in obtaining British withdrawal from Western forts, payment for confiscated ships in the Caribbean, and began to open trade in the British West Indies to most ships.

Washington kept the treaty secret from the Senate until it was debated in June 1795. With heavy Federalist support, the Senate approved Jay's Treaty and Washington signed it. Jay's failure to achieve all of the treaty's goals enraged many politicians. Democratic-Republicans gained support from former Federalists, especially Southerners, as Americans throughout the nation protested what they viewed as a failed treaty. But the treaty had eased tensions with the British enough to avoid open war.

A GLOBAL PERSPECTIVE Chinese artist Ai Weiwei created 176 portraits of "prisoners of conscience"—people imprisoned for holding views of his work. Due to his public criticisms of the their governments do not allow—out of colorful LEGO® blocks. In 2014, his exhibit of the portraits, called *Trace*, was installed on the floor of Alcatraz Prison in San Francisco. From a distance, the images look cheerful. But details in them, such as handcuffs, surveillance cameras and Twitter bird logos (symbolizing tweets challenging authority), allude to a story of repression.

Ironically, Weiwei could not view the installation of his work. Due to his public criticisms of the Chinese government, he was not allowed to leave his country. There are many prisoners of conscience across the world today. Similar to the Sedition Act of 1798, which targeted anyone who criticized the U.S. government, laws exist in other countries that enable governments to violate citizens' basic freedoms. Governments that protect their citizens' civil and human rights have policies in place to limit and balance government power.

THE ADAMS PRESIDENCY

Once conflicts had subsided, American settlement and trade in the West increased. The economy flourished, and the success of the American republic seemed ensured. As the 1796 election approached, President Washington announced his retirement. His health had started to decline, and the angry Senate debate over Jay's Treaty had left him exhausted. He also wanted to establish the precedent, or example, of limiting the presidency to two terms. Before leaving office, Washington delivered a farewell address, in which he warned against the dangers of rivaling parties.

In spite of this warning, the Federalists and Democratic-Republicans waged a bitter campaign in 1796. John Adams ran on the Federalist side, and Thomas Jefferson represented the Democratic-Republicans. Other candidates ran too. As you have read, every elector of the electoral college cast two votes, but no more than one for any candidate. The 1796 election results were close: Adams won the presidency with 71 votes, and Jefferson won the vice presidency with 68. It was not a happy arrangement.

Adams's background was certainly presidential. A Patriot leader from the earliest rumblings of the Revolution, Adams had strongly supported Jefferson's writing of the Declaration of Independence and had served as a delegate to the Continental Congress. He had helped negotiate the Treaty of Paris of 1783 and had been minister, or ambassador, to Great Britain. Adams possessed an excellent understanding of government and diplomacy and had a reputation for honesty and fairness; but he lacked Washington's charisma, military bearing, and flair for leadership.

TROUBLE WITH FRANCE

Relations with France had worsened by the time John Adams took office. France began seizing American ships in an effort to prevent the United States from trading with Great Britain. War with France appeared inevitable. In 1797, the United States responded to the ship seizures by fortifying its harbors with warships and militia. Adams sent three **envoys**, or ambassadors, to France to settle the problem. The envoys communicated with the French foreign minister through **intermediaries**, or go-betweens, later known to the American public simply as X, Y, and Z. When the French agents made unreasonable demands and even insisted on being paid a bribe to begin negotiations, the shocked envoys turned them down and returned home.

The **XYZ Affair**, as the negotiations came to be called, further soured American relations with France. It also hurt the reputation of the Democratic-Republicans, who had supported the French Revolution. When Adams made reports of the affair public, most Americans felt their honor had been attacked, and war fever swept the country. Congress expanded the army, established the navy, and authorized naval vessels to attack French ships that threatened American merchant ships. Without officially declaring war, the United States battled France in the Caribbean from 1798 to 1800. After consistent French defeats at sea, the United States was reassured that France was not a threat.

THE ALIEN AND SEDITION ACTS

In 1798, as feelings of American patriotism rose against the French, the Federalists passed the **Alien and Sedition Acts**. The Alien Act allowed the president to expel, for any reason, new immigrants, or aliens, living in the United States—most of whom were Democratic-Republicans. The Sedition Act targeted U.S. citizens, including journalists, who criticized the government. **Sedition** is the act of provoking rebellion.

Democratic-Republican Thomas Jefferson condemned the Alien and Sedition Acts, claiming they violated citizens' freedom of speech and freedom of the press. His writings spurred a theory called **nullification**—the idea that a state could veto a federal law it considered unconstitutional. The theory represented a strict interpretation of the Constitution, denying implied powers of the federal government. By 1802, most of the acts had expired or been repealed, but they had undermined Adams's popularity. In the presidential election of 1800, Jefferson defeated him. The election marked the first peaceful transfer of power from one party to another.

HISTORICAL THINKING

1. **READING CHECK** What conflict did the United States have with Great Britain in the 1790s, and how was it resolved?

2. **SUMMARIZE** How did the United States deal with Native American groups who opposed U.S. settlement of the West in the 1780s and 1790s?

3. **FORM AND SUPPORT OPINIONS** Was John Adams successful as president? Support your opinion with evidence from the text.

4. **DRAW CONCLUSIONS** In what ways did the Proclamation of Neutrality that Washington issued in 1793 protect the United States?

BUILD BACKGROUND

ADAMS UNDER PRESSURE

As John Adams worked to avert war with France, numerous factions, people, and a nation attempted to undermine his efforts. Members of his own Federalist Party, including Alexander Hamilton, feared the anarchy of the French Revolution, pushed for war, and wished to turn public sentiment against France. Members of the rival party were equally skeptical of Adams. The Democratic-Republicans believed that the Federalists' pro-British leanings made Adams unreliable on the issue and demanded the release of details about the failed peace negotiations. In the meantime, the British, overjoyed with the anti-French hysteria overtaking America, prodded Americans to declare war on Britain's rival. Adams, however, was determined to avoid conflict. In 1800, an agreement was reached with France that avoided war but effectively ended the Revolutionary-era alliance between the two nations.

THE POLITICAL COST OF AVOIDING WAR

John Adams's actions during the XYZ affair avoided a war he felt the country wasn't ready for, but sank his chances for a second term. The Alien and Sedition Acts were tremendously unpopular and caused many voters to support Jefferson and the Democratic-Republicans. In addition, the Federalists were severely divided about Adams's steadfast refusal to declare war on France. This controversy caused Adams to fire his secretaries of state and war because they did not support his antiwar efforts and led Alexander Hamilton to declare Adams unfit to be president. During the election, opponents depicted Adams as soft on Britain, a would-be monarch, and an enemy of republicanism. At one point, he was even accused of plotting to have his son wed a daughter of the King.

TEACH

GUIDED DISCUSSION

3. **Identify** What factors made Adams a less popular president than Washington? *(Answers will vary. Possible response: Washington had been a military hero with broad support across the country. Adams was more closely linked to New England and did not have the support of the South, as Washington did. Adams's Federalist Party also passed the Alien and Sedition Acts, which targeted U.S. citizens. Many condemned the act and Adams as well.)*

4. **Draw Conclusions** Considering his role in founding the country, what do you think motivated Adams to sign the Alien and Sedition Acts? *(Possible response: Adams may have feared that the French would commit illegal acts in the United States after U.S. victories over them in the Caribbean. He may also have been motivated to target aliens because most of them were Democratic-Republicans, the Federalists' political rivals.)*

A GLOBAL PERSPECTIVE

Explore with students the photograph and caption. Then discuss laws that could lead to people becoming prisoners of conscience, such as when a journalist is imprisoned for not revealing sources. **ASK:** What policies does the United States have that protect the citizens' civil and human rights? *(Answers will vary. Possible response: freedom of speech, freedom of religion, minimum wage laws, and child labor laws.)* Lead a discussion about whether laws such as the Sedition Act could or do exist in modern America.

ACTIVE OPTIONS

On Your Feet: Fishbowl Direct half the class to sit in a circle facing inward and the other half to sit in a larger circle around them. Ask the inner circle to discuss these questions: Should constitutional rights be absolute? Is it ever okay to suspend constitutional rights? Students in the outer circle listen to the discussion and evaluate the points made. Then have the groups reverse roles and continue the discussion.

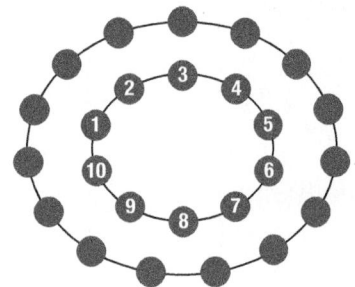

NG Learning Framework: Understand the Free Press

ATTITUDE Responsibility

SKILL Collaboration

To help students think more deeply about the issues surrounding the Sedition Act, ask them to work in pairs to explore the function and responsibilities of a free press. Tell one partner to research countries in which the press has a high degree of freedom, such as Finland, Costa Rica, and New Zealand, while the other partner researches countries without a free press, such as China, Cuba, and Libya. When students have finished their individual research, direct them to work together to analyze their findings and answer the following questions: What is the purpose of a free press? Can a free press be abused? Is it ever appropriate for a government to pass laws restricting the press? If so, when? In countries in which the free press is limited, are their ways to get around the restrictions? Was the Sedition Act justified? Invite pairs to share their analysis with the class.

HISTORICAL THINKING

ANSWERS

1. Britain was involved in a conflict with France which led the British to disrupt American maritime activities. In addition, there were multiple issues, such as Britain's occupancy of western forts, which dated back to the Revolution. Jay's Treaty resolved some issues but infuriated many people.

2. The United States used the army and militias to fight opposing Native American groups to drive them out of their lands. The federal government also used treaties to get Native American groups to sign over their land.

3. Answers will vary. Possible response: While John Adams achieved some successes as President, such as avoiding war with France, he overreached his powers when Federalists passed and implemented the Alien and Sedition Acts. Jefferson and others believed the acts violated the First Amendment, and the controversy about them contributed to Adams's failure to unite Americans and win a second term.

4. The Proclamation of Neutrality protected the United States by preventing an open alliance with France against Great Britain and by postponing a rift in the government that would likely result if the government chose a side.

JEFFERSON'S "REVOLUTION"

What happens when a presidential election is tied? Back in 1800, the House spent seven days casting votes to try to break it. The 36th time was the charm. Jefferson won.

THE ELECTION OF 1800

As the 1800 presidential election approached, the Federalists faced a growing backlash based on concerns over the Alien and Sedition Acts. At the same time, the United States was still hostile toward France. The Federalists hoped to take advantage of the continued conflict during the election. They planned to paint Jefferson and the Democratic-Republicans as pro-French and anti-American, since they had strongly supported the French Revolution when it began. However, President Adams did not halt negotiations with France for election strategies. The result was the Convention of 1800, an agreement with France that normalized relations and called for "a firm, inviolable, and universal peace."

Peace with France destroyed the Federalists' main campaign strategy and put the Democratic-Republicans in a good position going into

the election. The party chose Jefferson as its presidential nominee and supported **Aaron Burr**, an accomplished attorney and statesman, for vice president. President Adams once again received the Federalist nomination for president. Charles Pinckney was the Federalists' choice for vice president. When the electoral vote came in, the two Democratic-Republicans were tied at 73 votes, Adams had 65 votes, and Pinckney had 64.

No one had expected such a result. The Jefferson-Burr tie sent the election to the House of Representatives, with each state delegation receiving one vote. The House cast 36 ballots over seven days before awarding the presidency to Thomas Jefferson. Burr became vice president. To keep the arduous process from happening again, Congress approved the **12th Amendment** to the U.S. Constitution in 1803. The amendment requires each elector to cast

Jefferson Memorial
Washington, D.C.

The Jefferson Memorial, which faces the White House from across the Potomac River, was completed in 1943. It follows an architectural style, called neoclassical, that is prevalent on Capitol Hill. Like the earlier Greek and Roman styles that inspired it, the neoclassical style is characterized by symmetrical shapes, tall columns, and domes. Inside the memorial building, a bronze statue of Jefferson stands 19 feet tall.

a ballot for both a president and a vice president. The states ratified this amendment in 1804, just in time for the next general election.

Jefferson's inauguration took place in March 1801, the first to be held in the new capital city of Washington, D.C. The Democratic-Republicans dominated Congress. Many Federalists feared what they considered Jefferson's radical views. They saw what had happened in France, when revolutionaries took control and executed thousands of people. In his inaugural address, Jefferson tried to soothe such fears by saying, "We are all Republicans; we are all Federalists." His speech expressed his beliefs in power for state governments, freedom of religion and the press, majority rule with protection for political minorities, and the reduction of federal debt.

Jefferson aspired to create an agrarian republic in which the federal government minimized its role. In contrast to the Federalists' attempts at European grandeur, Jefferson adopted informality and frugality, or thriftiness, in his administration. He met Congressional delegates and foreign diplomats in small groups. He wrote Congress messages instead of making speeches. With Congressional support, he cut the defense budget and repealed all excise taxes, including the whiskey tax that had sparked a rebellion during Washington's administration. Almost two decades later, Jefferson described his election as "the revolution of 1800" because it was the first time that power passed from one party to another in the United States.

MARBURY v. MADISON

Although the Democratic-Republicans had won the presidency and Congress in 1800, the judiciary remained in Federalist control. Just before the Democratic-Republicans took over, Adams and his outgoing Federalist Congress passed the Judiciary Act of 1801, which amended the Judiciary Act of 1789. The act reduced the number of justices on the Supreme Court from six to five, thereby denying Jefferson the chance to appoint a new justice when the next justice died or resigned the lifetime position. The act also allowed Adams to appoint many new, Federalist lower-court judges before he stepped down. Adams worked late into the night of his last day signing commissions for these judges, who became known as the "**midnight judges**."

THE DUEL BETWEEN HAMILTON AND BURR

The rivalry between Aaron Burr and Alexander Hamilton had been building for a decade. In 1791, ill will began when Burr defeated Hamilton's father-in-law in an election. In 1800, Burr published a private essay Hamilton had written that criticized President John Adams. The essay publicly shamed Hamilton.

When Burr ran for governor of New York in 1804, Hamilton actively campaigned against him, and Burr lost the election. Irate, Burr challenged Hamilton to a duel with pistols, a common though illegal practice. Hamilton did not believe in dueling, but he accepted the challenge. The two men met at Weehawken, New Jersey, on July 11, 1804. Burr shot Hamilton in the stomach, and Hamilton died the next day. The murder ended Burr's political career. Despite being charged for Hamilton's death, Burr was never tried for it and received no punishment for the crime.

Adams also appointed a new Chief Justice of the United States, **John Marshall**—a Federalist. One of Marshall's earliest and most important cases was *Marbury v. Madison*. The case arose because the commission for one of the midnight judges, William Marbury, had not been delivered on time. Adams believed his signature alone made the commission valid. Jefferson disagreed and ordered his secretary of state, James Madison, to block the commission. Marbury sued to secure his commission.

The case seemed straightforward. Observers expected Chief Justice Marshall and his Federalist court to direct Secretary of State Madison to comply. Instead, Marshall explained that he could not remedy Marbury's problem because Congress had erred in giving the court such authority. In an unprecedented decision, Marshall declared that the existing 1789 Judiciary Act was unconstitutional.

With this ruling, Marshall established **judicial review**, the authority to invalidate any law the Court deems unconstitutional. By establishing judicial review, Marshall strengthened the balance among the three branches of government, promoting the principle of checks and balances.

HISTORICAL THINKING

1. **READING CHECK** How did judicial review strengthen the balance among the three branches of government?

2. **ANALYZE CAUSE AND EFFECT** Why did the election of 1800 lead to the adoption of the 12th Amendment?

3. **DRAW CONCLUSIONS** How did reduced tensions between the United States and France affect Jefferson's chances of winning the presidency?

PLAN: 2-PAGE LESSON

OBJECTIVE

Explain the historical significance of the election of 1800 and the establishment of judicial review.

CRITICAL THINKING SKILLS FOR LESSON 2.1

• Analyze Cause and Effect

• Draw Conclusions

• Evaluate

• Form and Support Opinions

HISTORICAL THINKING FOR CHAPTER 6

How did government, expansion, and war unify the nation? Following the election of 1800, fear spread that the nation would once again spiral into conflict. Lesson 2.1 describes the actions that Thomas Jefferson took to unify the nation after the country's first transfer of political power.

BACKGROUND FOR THE TEACHER

Marbury v. *Madison* granted the Supreme Court its best-known power: the ability to decide whether or not an action is constitutional. Because the Constitution itself does not specify its final arbiter, the question was hotly debated in early America. Just five years earlier, for example, after the passage of the Alien and Sedition Acts, Jefferson argued that it was the states, not the courts, who had the ability to decide the constitutionality of a federal law. In *Marbury*, however, the court disagreed, and in subsequent decisions the power of judicial review was expanded, allowing the court to rule on the constitutionality of any state, executive, judicial, or legislative action. Early 21st-century actions involving same-sex marriage, voter ID laws, gun restrictions, and abortion have all been challenged in court on the grounds that they violate the Constitution.

INTRODUCE & ENGAGE

DEFINE *REVOLUTION*

Guide students to discuss the meaning of the term *revolution*. Place the word in the oval of a Word Web. **ASK:** What are some concepts or events that you associate with the term? *(Answers will vary. Possible response: overthrow, civil war, violence, protest, radical change.)* Add student responses to the Word Web. Then have students consider whether a revolution must include violent conflict. Finally, inform students that in this lesson they will read about the election of 1800, a nonviolent affair some historians categorize as revolutionary.

TEACH

GUIDED DISCUSSION

1. **Evaluate** Was the election of 1800 truly a revolution? Explain your answer. *(Possible responses: The election was a nonviolent transfer of power, an event with almost no historical precedent, and thus revolutionary. The underlying fundamental principles of the government remained the same during this peaceful transition, so it was not a revolution in the sense of the American Revolution.)*

2. **Form and Support Opinions** Does judicial review give the Supreme Court too much power? Support your answer with evidence from the lesson. *(Answers will vary. Possible responses: Yes. The Court can declare both state and federal actions unconstitutional, and this is too much power for a Court whose members hold a lifetime appointment. No. Judicial review is necessary to check the powers of the legislative and executive branches and ensure that the constitutional rights of citizens of all states are protected.)*

⬡ AMERICAN PLACES

In building the Jefferson Memorial, the architects chose materials symbolizing the history and expansion of the United States. For example, the memorial represents the northernmost and southernmost of the original 13 colonies with marble from Vermont on the exterior and white Georgia marble on the interior. Stonework inside the memorial connects to westward expansion, featuring marble from Tennessee and limestone from Indiana. The statue of Jefferson is tied into his most lasting legacy, the Louisiana Purchase. It stands upon a large block of Minnesota granite with Missouri marble surrounding the base.

ACTIVE OPTIONS

On Your Feet: Three-Step Interview Have students work in pairs. One student interviews the other student using these questions: How did the election of 1800 lead to the approval of the 12th Amendment? Do you think electors deciding the outcome of an election is better than decision by popular vote? Why or why not? Then direct students to reverse roles. Ask students to share their responses and reasons in a class discussion.

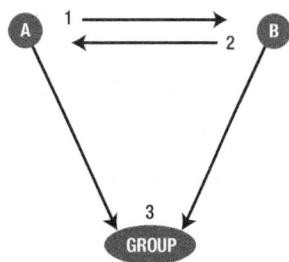

NG Learning Framework: Write a Supreme Court Decision

SKILL Communication

KNOWLEDGE Our Human Story

Assign students to work in groups to research the arguments Chief Justice Marshall used in *Marbury* v. *Madison* to declare part of the Judiciary Act of 1789 unconstitutional. Instruct students to investigate Article III Section 2 of the Constitution, which Marshall used to justify his position. Then have groups use their research to write a short Supreme Court opinion that mirrors Marshall's reasoning. Have groups share their opinions with the class.

DIFFERENTIATE

STRIVING READERS

List Details About a Topic After students read the lesson, have pairs create a table with the subsection headings of the lesson, Election of 1800 and *Marbury* v. *Madison*, and the sidebar heading, Duel Between Hamilton and Burr. Encourage pairs to take turns rereading paragraphs aloud, while their partner listens and identifies details to add to the table columns.

PRE-AP

Examine Jefferson's First Inaugural Address Assign each student a portion of the published text of Thomas Jefferson's 1801 Inaugural Address. Tell them to analyze and summarize its main ideas in their own words. Ask students to consider the following questions: Which passages specifically reflect Jefferson's political philosophy? What fears is Jefferson trying to calm? To which historical events does Jefferson refer, and where? Ask students to share their summaries with the class.

See the Chapter Planner for more strategies for differentiation.

HISTORICAL THINKING

ANSWERS

1. With judicial review, the Supreme Court established that it has the final say on the constitutionality of legislation, no matter how strongly Congress or the president might support that legislation.

2. Prior to the 12th Amendment, electors cast two votes and the top two candidates became president and vice president. In 1800, this practice led to a tie between two Democratic-Republicans. The 12th Amendment changed the procedure, requiring electors to vote separately for president and vice president.

3. Adams established normal relations with France before the election. This increased Jefferson's chances of winning because it prevented Federalists from attacking Jefferson and the Democratic-Republicans as anti-American supporters of a foreign enemy.

THE LOUISIANA PURCHASE

All purchases, even the greatest deals with the most benefits, have drawbacks. The Louisiana Territory was a great purchase for the United States that came with some big challenges.

NEGOTIATIONS FOR LOUISIANA

A chain of unlikely events led to the United States' purchase of the **Louisiana Territory.** It began in 1800, when France signed a treaty with Spain to recover the North American lands it had ceded to Spain in 1762. When Jefferson and Madison heard about the agreement, they instructed the U.S. minister to France, **Robert Livingston,** to prevent the territory from changing hands, or at least to obtain the important port of New Orleans.

Above all, the United States wanted to keep France from controlling the Mississippi River. As American settlers moved west, their economy increasingly depended on access to the Mississippi River and New Orleans. In October 1802, before the land transfer from Spain to France had gone through, Spain suspended the right of Americans to store goods in New Orleans, endangering the entire economy of what was then known as the American West. Americans believed that **Napoleon Bonaparte,** the leader of France, was behind the ban. Americans were anxious about what might happen when France took over the region. Many Americans—including frontiersmen and lawmakers—wanted to take New Orleans by force. Jefferson pushed for negotiations instead.

While U.S. minister Livingston negotiated in France, Napoleon made a surprising offer. Instead of selling only New Orleans to the United States, he suggested selling the entire Louisiana Territory—all 828,000 square miles of it. After years of rebellion, France's hold on its West Indian colony of Saint-Domingue on the island of Hispaniola (present-day Haiti) was

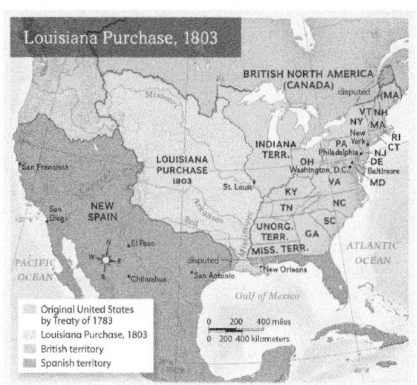
Louisiana Purchase, 1803

unstable. **Toussaint L'Ouverture** (TOO-sahnt LOH-ver-toor), a formerly enslaved man, led a successful rebellion to free slaves in the colony in 1791. He governed until 1802, when Napoleon staged an unsuccessful attempt to take it back. Without land in the Caribbean, Napoleon felt that Louisiana had little value. He had lost troops both to the revolt and to tropical diseases. The monetary costs of the conflict had also been high, and France was on the brink of war with Britain, another expensive enterprise.

In documents dated April 30, 1803, the United States agreed to pay France $15 million, or about three cents an acre, for the Louisiana Territory. The contract for the **Louisiana Purchase** did not specify the region's boundaries, however. The United States would have to negotiate those boundaries with Spain and Britain.

DOUBLING THE SIZE OF THE UNITED STATES

With the Louisiana Purchase, the United States nearly doubled in size, including land from the Gulf of Mexico north to Canada and from the Mississippi River west to the Rocky Mountains. Native Americans lived throughout the region. At the time of its purchase, the territory had a sparse white population of about 50,000 people, which included a mix of French, Spanish, Dutch, British, and Americans. Afterward, 3,000 free Africans moved into the region from Cuba. By 1810 approximately 7,600 free African Americans and 35,000 African-American slaves had entered the territory.

Some Federalists disapproved of the purchase, but most Americans celebrated it. The Mississippi River was once again open to commerce, while eastern merchants profited from the trade. As a strict constructionist, Jefferson worried that the federal government had no constitutional power to acquire territory. He put aside his concerns, however, confident that the Louisiana Purchase would provide spacious lands for generations of independent American farmers. Of those lands, Jefferson said, "The fertility of the country, its climate and extent, promise in due season important aids to our freedom, an ample provision for our posterity, and a widespread field for the blessings of freedom."

The United States took possession of Louisiana in December 1803, raising boundary issues and displeasing the Spanish, who had only recently transferred control to the French. Jefferson pushed for a generous interpretation for the United States, demanding that West Florida, Texas, and part of New Mexico be included. Spain, however, only agreed to give up a narrow strip along the west bank of the Mississippi River from northern Missouri to the Gulf of Mexico. More than a decade later, in 1819, the United States purchased Florida from Spain and came to an agreement on the Louisiana Territory's southwestern border.

THE TRIAL OF AARON BURR

As you have read, Aaron Burr killed Alexander Hamilton in a duel in 1804. Afterward, he fled arrest and alienated himself from Jefferson. He also hatched a plot or two, which included an invasion of New Spain and the **secession,** or political separation, of the American West. The plot fell through when an accomplice warned Jefferson of the plan. Burr was arrested and faced trial for treason in 1807. U.S. law defines treason as the act of anyone

In 1904, a centennial celebration of the Louisiana Purchase was held in St. Louis, Missouri. To honor the event, the march "A Deed of the Pen" was composed by Neil Morét. The title is a reference to the signing of the contract with France, and its sheet music had this specially designed cover.

"owing allegiance to the United States" who wages war against the United States or gives aid and comfort to its enemies.

Chief Justice John Marshall presided over Burr's trial. A jury acquitted Burr after Marshall argued that, according to the Constitution, treason required an overt act of war. Jefferson considered impeaching Marshall for favoring Burr during the trial, but found little support in Congress. Meanwhile, the president had other things to think about. He had been busy supervising an ambitious exploration of the new lands the nation had recently acquired.

HISTORICAL THINKING

1. **READING CHECK** What are some geographical borders that surround the area of land acquired in the Louisiana Purchase?

2. **INTERPRET MAPS** What rivers did the United States acquire the rights to in the Louisiana Purchase?

3. **FORM AND SUPPORT OPINIONS** Do you think Aaron Burr should have been found guilty of treason? Support your opinion with evidence from the text.

PLAN: 2-PAGE LESSON

OBJECTIVE

Describe the causes, effects, and controversies surrounding the Louisiana Purchase.

CRITICAL THINKING SKILLS FOR LESSON 2.2

• Interpret Maps

• Form and Support Opinions

• Make Connections

• Draw Conclusions

• Evaluate

HISTORICAL THINKING FOR CHAPTER 6

How did government, expansion, and war unify the nation? In 1803, Thomas Jefferson was offered the chance to nearly double the size of the United States. Lesson 2.2 describes the Louisiana Purchase, which accelerated westward expansion and was almost universally supported.

BACKGROUND FOR THE TEACHER

Federalists embraced loose constructionism and a strong executive branch, so granting the president the power to purchase the Louisiana Territory would seem to fit within their established ideology. The New England-based Federalists had long done poorly in the South and West, and they feared the Louisiana Territory would open new lands to small farmers and slaveholders, greatly expanding the base of Democratic-Republicans and giving them an unbreakable hold on the House, Senate, and presidency. Federalist opposition to the Louisiana Purchase, therefore, was motivated by political self-preservation. In the end, Federalist fears were warranted. Not long after the purchase, with their political power all but eroded, the Federalists faded into history and a new political party took their place.

HISTORY NOTEBOOK

Encourage students to complete the Reid on the Road video series page for Chapter 6 in their History Notebooks after they view the video.

INTRODUCE & ENGAGE

PREVIEW USING MAPS

Direct students' attention to the Louisiana Purchase map. Ask volunteers to point out the location of the original United States and its territories, the Mississippi River, New Spain, and finally, the Louisiana Purchase. **ASK:** Why might Thomas Jefferson have thought the Louisiana Purchase would benefit the United States? *(Answers will vary. Possible responses: It would enlarge the country, opening new land to settlement. It would limit the influence and reach of Spain.)*

TEACH

GUIDED DISCUSSION

1. **Make Connections** Why might Jefferson have been justified in his concerns about France controlling the Louisiana Territory rather than Spain? *(Answers will vary. Possible response: The United States had a history of peaceful relations with Spain, but relations with France were sometimes hostile despite its help during the American Revolution. In addition, Napoleon, France's new leader, was potentially hostile.)*

2. **Draw Conclusions** Why did Jefferson support the Louisiana Purchase despite his constitutional reservations? *(Possible response: Jefferson was motivated by the potential benefits of the purchase and by political shifts. He argued for a smaller, restrained government when the Federalists were in charge. He had fewer problems taking on a more powerful presidential role when the Democratic-Republicans were in charge.)*

EVALUATE

Provide students with the text of Article III Section 3 of the Constitution, which defines treason. **ASK:** Did Chief Justice John Marshall finding Aaron Burr innocent of treason rely on a strict or loose interpretation of the Constitution? *(He used a strict interpretation, as the Constitution states that treason is "levying war" and an "overt act of war," which Burr did not technically commit.)* **ASK:** How was this interpretation inconsistent with Marshall's other rulings? *(In* Marbury v. Madison *he adopted a loose interpretation, likely because he was a Federalist who disliked Jefferson, a Democratic-Republican, so he ruled against the wishes of a political opponent.)*

ACTIVE OPTIONS

On Your Feet: Roundtable Discussion Arrange students into five groups to discuss topics connected with the Louisiana Purchase. Assign each group one of the following topics: Robert Livingston, Mississippi River, Spain, Napoleon Bonaparte, Toussaint L'Ouverture. Tell students to research their topic as it connects to the Louisiana Purchase and to prepare a summary of their findings. Ask a volunteer from each group to share the group's summary with the class.

NG Learning Framework: Debate the Louisiana Purchase

ATTITUDE Empowerment

KNOWLEDGE Our Human Story

Invite students to engage in a class debate. Direct half the class to argue in favor of strictly adhering to the word of the Constitution, no matter the circumstances. Tell the other half of the class to argue in favor of the need to loosely interpret the document when the results are for the national good. Instruct groups to research their position in the context of the Louisiana Purchase and to use other historical examples to support their opinion. After the debate, encourage students to determine the strongest arguments presented by each side.

DIFFERENTIATE

ENGLISH LANGUAGE LEARNERS ELD

Practice Noun and Verb Forms Pair students at the **Emerging** and **Expanding** levels with students at the **Bridging** level. Elicit that the Key Vocabulary word *secession* is a noun, and that the verb form is *secede*. Provide students with other noun/verb pairs, such as: *concession/concede, recession/recede, procession/proceed,* and *confession/confess*. Instruct students to work together to write an original sentence for each word. Encourage pairs to exchange and read each other's sentences.

PRE-AP

Analyze the Negotiations of the Louisiana Purchase Tell students to research the negotiations of the Louisiana Purchase and then write an essay to share with the class. Tell them to include the principle participants, where and when negotiations took place, and the specific terms to which all parties agreed. Ask students to comment on the significance of the borders defined in the purchase. Invite students to share their essays with the class in an oral or written report.

See the Chapter Planner for more strategies for differentiation.

HISTORICAL THINKING

ANSWERS

1. The Louisiana Purchase is bordered by the Mississippi River to the east, the Gulf of Mexico along the coast of present-day Louisiana, and the Rocky Mountains to the northwest.

2. The United States acquired the rights to the Missouri River, Arkansas River, Red River, and Mississippi River.

3. Answers will vary. Possible responses: No. Although Burr held ill will against the United States, the text offers no evidence that he actually waged war against the country, which is central to the definition of treason. Yes. Burr promoted a secession plot, which involved giving aid to people who could be considered enemies of the United States.

In January 1806, Lieutenant William Clark and some Corps of Discovery members walked along the Oregon coast in search of a beached whale. On the way, they traveled past these sea stacks on what is now called Cannon Beach. The view inspired Clark to write, "from this point I beheld the grandest and most pleasing prospects which my eyes ever surveyed."

THE LEWIS AND CLARK EXPEDITION

Imagine the president asked you to explore unchartered territory. How would you prepare for your trip? When packing for the unexpected, Lewis and Clark made sure to bring their journals.

THE CORPS OF DISCOVERY

Even before the Louisiana Purchase was finalized, Thomas Jefferson had planned to explore the lands west of the Mississippi River. Several times since 1783, Jefferson had tried to organize expeditions for scientific knowledge and to promote American interests in the region. As president, he now had the authority and the country had the financial resources to support the enterprise. The Louisiana Purchase gave the plan a concrete purpose.

In 1803, Jefferson commissioned the exploration of those lands all the way to the Pacific Northwest. Jefferson named his private secretary, **Meriwether Lewis**, as captain of his **Corps of Discovery**, the group of men who undertook the expedition. Lewis chose as his co-leader his former military commander **William Clark**. In Lewis, Jefferson had the kind of leader he wanted: "a person who to courage, prudence, habits [and] health adapted to the woods, [and] some familiarity with the Indian character, joins a perfect knowledge of botany, natural history, mineralogy [and] astronomy." Lewis and Clark had battled Native Americans together in the Northwest Territory while serving in the army during the early 1790s. Both had experienced rugged frontier conditions. Clark also proved to be an expert mapmaker.

Jefferson had a list of goals for the Corps of Discovery. The explorers were to travel to the source of the Missouri River and from there try to find the elusive Northwest Passage, a transcontinental water route long sought by European mariners. However,

Born in 1774, Captain Meriwether Lewis (left) was four years younger than Second Lieutenant William Clark (right). Both men were born in Virginia and had successful military careers. Lewis helped quell the Whiskey Rebellion in 1794. That same year, Clark helped defeat the Shawnee and the Miami at the Battle of Fallen Timbers in the Ohio region.

repeated attempts to find the passage had all failed. The explorers would also be recording information about the plants and animals that lived throughout the new territory. The president hoped Lewis and Clark also would be able to make peaceful contact with Native Americans and expand the fur trade. Ultimately, the expedition would fill huge gaps in geographic, scientific, and cultural knowledge of the region.

Jefferson thought Lewis and Clark's expedition could solidify U.S. claims to the region. As you have read, the United States and Spain were still negotiating the boundaries of the Louisiana Territory. The United States could use exploration of the West and alliances with Native Americans to help support its claims to the broad boundaries of the territory.

Lewis and Clark were commissioned as U.S. army officers to lead the Corps of Discovery. In May 1804, the expedition departed St. Louis with about 40 men, traveling north along the Missouri River, sometimes navigating, sometimes pushing their 55-foot keelboat and towing two canoes. Clark charted their course and drew maps. Lewis frequently went ashore to investigate minerals, soil, plants, and animals.

Along the way, the expedition experienced threatening encounters with the Teton branch of the Lakota nation. In one tense meeting, Clark pulled his sword and Lewis brandished the boat's swivel gun. Thanks in part to the diplomacy of Teton Chief Black Buffalo, both sides calmed down before fighting broke out. At that point, the goal of friendly relations with Native Americans seemed distant.

The expedition navigated up the Missouri through autumn until, soon after the first snowfall, it arrived at the Mandan and Hidatsa villages in what is today North Dakota. The Corps of Discovery members constructed Fort Mandan nearby as a place to spend the winter, safe from the bitter, below-zero cold. Through the winter, they hunted buffalo, repaired

their gear, traded with the Mandan and Hidatsa, and learned about the surrounding lands from those Native Americans.

SEARCH FOR A WATER ROUTE WEST

In April 1805, some members of the Corps of Discovery returned to St. Louis with scientific notes, maps, artifacts, minerals, plants, and animals. The remaining 33 headed west in dugout canoes. By then the expedition had acquired two interpreters—French Canadian fur trapper Toussaint Charbonneau (TOO-sahnt shar-buh-NOH) and his Shoshone wife **Sacagawea** (SAK-uh-juh-WEE-uh), who had been captured by the Hidatsa at age 12. The interpreters brought along their baby, Jean-Baptiste, also known as Pomp.

Throughout the summer, the Corps made progress toward the Rocky Mountains, watching as the snow-capped peaks seemed to grow taller and taller. They had hoped to travel on the Missouri River all the way there. But then they reached the part of the river known as the Great Falls, where five waterfalls ranged over 21 miles of river, making navigation impossible. The expedition had to **portage**, or carry

---

PLAN: 4-PAGE LESSON

OBJECTIVE

Examine the purpose and significance of the Lewis and Clark Expedition.

CRITICAL THINKING SKILLS FOR LESSON 2.3

- Make Generalizations
- Interpret Visuals
- Determine Word Meanings
- Evaluate
- Analyze Language Use
- Make Inferences
- Analyze Primary Sources

HISTORICAL THINKING FOR CHAPTER 6

How did government, expansion, and war unify the nation? After the Louisiana Purchase, the United States was in possession of a vast unmapped territory. Lesson 2.3 describes Meriwether Lewis and William Clark's expedition to explore, map, and solidify U.S. land claims.

BACKGROUND FOR THE TEACHER

Before embarking on his historic journey, Meriwether Lewis had two important tasks: study and stock up. To gain the scientific skills he would need, Lewis invited some of the foremost scientists available to tutor him in mapmaking and surveying, mathematics, botany, zoology, fossils, anatomy, and medicine. Lewis also bought instruments to help with navigation, such as chronometers and sextants; weapons and ammunition; ink for journals; 193 pounds of soup concentrate; mosquito netting; and potential gifts for Native Americans, such as beads, knives, scissors, and tobacco. Perhaps most important was his purchase of Seaman, a Newfoundland dog, who, despite becoming lost and severely injured by a beaver, accompanied Lewis throughout the entire trip, serving as both hunter and watchdog.

HISTORY NOTEBOOK

Encourage students to complete the American Gallery page for Chapter 6 in their History Notebooks as they read.

INTRODUCE & ENGAGE

CONSIDER THE SCOPE OF A JOURNEY

Direct students' attention to a map of the present-day United States. Show them the general route Lewis and Clark took from the Mississippi River to the Pacific Ocean. If any students have traveled this expanse of the country, elicit how long the trip took and the sights they experienced. Ask students to imagine making the journey using unexplored waterways with the likelihood of encountering native people who may or may not be hostile. Then ask whether they would have taken such a trip, and why. Tell students that Lesson 2.3 discusses the motivations and results of the Corps of Discovery's famed expedition west of the Mississippi River.

TEACH

GUIDED DISCUSSION

1. **Evaluate** In what ways was Meriwether Lewis qualified to lead the Corps of Discovery? *(As a military captain who had some knowledge of Native Americans and experience with frontier living, Lewis was qualified to lead an expedition into unknown territory. In addition, he had knowledge of botany, natural history, mineralogy, and astronomy.)*

2. **Analyze Language Use** What do you think motivated William Clark to describe Cannon Beach as he did? *(Possible response: Clark may have been relieved and ecstatic that the Corps had finally reached the Pacific Coast. He had likely never seen sea stacks jutting from a beach before and may have been overwhelmed by the sight and the expanse of the ocean.)*

3. **Make Inferences** Why do you think some members of the expedition returned to St. Louis in 1805, rather than continue to the Pacific? *(Possible response: The Corps had likely amassed a great quantity of information about the territory, plants, and animals by that time, so those members may have returned to ensure that the discoveries already made would not be lost in case the journey failed.)*

MORE INFORMATION

The Northwest Passage Inform students that for centuries Europeans believed in the existence of an arctic route that would connect the Atlantic and Pacific Oceans—and offer easy access to Asian markets. Beginning shortly after Columbus's voyage, Europeans made several attempts to find the passage, but they all ended in failure, with ships cocooned in the ice and at the expense of many lives. It wasn't until 1906 that Roald Amundsen successfully completed the entire journey by boat. Explain that in recent years, journeys across the Northwest Passage have become easier and more frequent. Tell students to conduct research and use a Cause-and-Effect Chart to understand why this change has taken place, and the political, economic, and environmental effects this easier passage is having on the world.

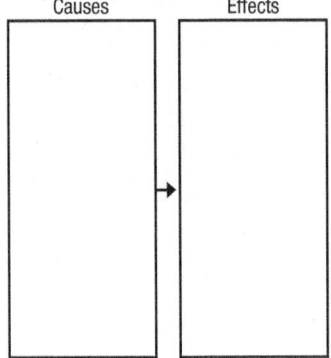

DIFFERENTIATE

STRIVING READERS

Use a Goal-and-Outcome Chart Pair students with proficient readers and instruct them to create a Goal-and-Outcome Chart. Tell pairs to reread the lesson and write specific obstacles and outcomes related to the scientific, economic, and political goals of the Lewis and Clark Expedition. Then direct students to write a few sentences summarizing the main goals and outcomes of the expedition. Ask pairs to compare their charts, noting similarities and differences.

Goals	Obstacles	Outcome
Scientific		
Economic		
Political		
Summary		

GIFTED & TALENTED

Create an Annotated Time Line Instruct students to create and annotate a time line of the most important events leading up to, during, and after the Lewis and Clark Expedition. Remind students to include dates and a brief description of the people, places, and actions associated with each event. Tell them to supplement text information with online research, and use photographs, graphics, and maps to enhance the information. Encourage them to use a graphics program if available. Invite students to present their finished time lines to the class and to answer classmates' questions.

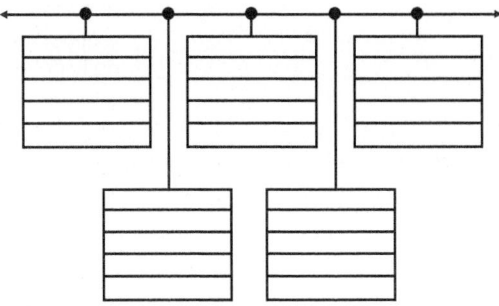

See the Chapter Planner for more strategies for differentiation.

their canoes and supplies overland for 18.5 miles in order to get around the falls. Extreme summer heat, dangerous storms, prickly pear cacti, and brush made the portage more challenging and time-consuming than anticipated, and the journey took about three weeks.

In August, the Corps reached a Shoshone village just east of the mountains, where they had hoped to buy horses to help them cross the mountains. To everyone's shock and delight, the villagers recognized Sacagawea. The chief of this group was her long-lost brother.

At the end of August, the party set out to cross the rugged mountains with 29 horses they had purchased. The expedition trekked the Lolo Trail through the Bitterroot Mountains for 11 days, passing over more than 200 miles of mountain crags and through dense forests. Clark wrote in his journal: "I have been wet and as cold... as I ever was in my life, indeed, I was at one time fearful my feet would freeze." After climbing over the Bitterroots, the explorers were overjoyed to finally see flat land. Lewis wrote, "The pleasure I now felt in having triumphed over the [Rocky] Mountains and descending to a level and fertile country where there was every rational hope of finding a comfortable subsistence [food supply] for myself and party can be more readily conceived than expressed, nor was the flattering prospect of the final success of the expedition less pleasing."

The explorers followed the Clearwater River to the Columbia River and then beyond to the Pacific Ocean. Paddling their canoes, they arrived at the Columbia in mid-October. They rested there before heading down the river to its estuary, 20 miles from the coast. An **estuary** is a wide body of mixed salty and fresh water where a river meets the ocean. There, torrential storms forced the explorers to remain for three weeks.

LEWIS AND CLARK'S RETURN

In mid-November 1805, the expedition finally reached the Pacific Ocean. There they built **Fort Clatsop**, which they named after the local Native Americans. They spent a rainy, uneventful winter there, making clothes and moccasins, drawing maps, writing in journals, and preserving food. The explorers hoped to meet one of the British or American ships that were reported to trade at the mouth of the Columbia River, but they never saw one. Finally, in late March 1806, the expedition began the long trip back home, first battling the strong current of the Columbia, then heading overland, including another difficult climb through the Bitterroots, sometimes through ten feet of snow.

Once across the Bitterroots, the expedition separated, taking two different routes to investigate more territory. Lewis led one group north along the Marias River, while Clark led the other south, heading

toward the Yellowstone River. The plan was to meet back up where the Yellowstone flowed into the Missouri. Along their route, Lewis's group had a violent encounter with eight Blackfeet. At first the Native Americans seemed friendly, and the two groups even camped together. But fighting broke out the next morning, and the explorers killed two of the Blackfeet. Fearful that the Blackfeet were pursuing them, Lewis and his group fled. On August 11, Lewis was shot below his left hip while hunting elk. Some of the expedition suspected Native Americans, but it's more likely Lewis was shot accidentally by one of his own men. Lewis's wound was painful but not life-threatening, and he continued the trek.

Meanwhile, Clark's party followed the Yellowstone River, taking notes and looking for good timber to construct carriages for their canoes. In his journal, Clark described finding the huge bones of a "fish" jutting out of a rock. Based on his account, scientists believe he discovered part of a dinosaur fossil. The day after Lewis was injured, the two groups reunited and began canoeing homeward along the swift current of the Missouri River.

After leaving Sacagawea and some other members of the expedition at the Mandan and Hidatsa villages, the Corps rode the river south. When they finally reached St. Louis at noon on September 23, 1806, they had traveled about 8,000 miles. Because the explorers had been gone for so long—two years, four months, and ten days—many Americans assumed that the Spanish or Native Americans had killed them. In fact, Spanish officials had tried unsuccessfully to intercept the expedition, which they correctly suspected would make Native American allies for the United States. When the Corps returned safely, they were met by a cheering crowd of about a thousand people.

A grateful president and Congress gave the explorers double the pay they had been promised as well as grants of land. Jefferson named Meriwether Lewis governor of Upper Louisiana Territory and promoted William Clark to brigadier general and made him an Indian agent. In 1809, Lewis was just 35 when he died of gunshot wounds at an inn in Tennessee while traveling to Washington, D.C. In 1813, Clark became the governor of the Missouri Territory.

National Museum of American History Washington, D.C.

The Corps of Discovery relied on compasses to navigate to the Pacific Ocean and back. Before the expedition, Lewis purchased 3 pocket compasses for $2.50 each, and this silver-plated compass in a mahogany box for $5.00. It was one of the few instruments to survive the journey.

A WEALTH OF NEW KNOWLEDGE

Although Lewis and Clark never found the Northwest Passage, the expedition was a great success. The explorers made contact with numerous Native American groups, including the Blackfeet, Lakota, and Nez Percé. They brought back information about Native American societies, noting that their interactions had been mostly friendly.

The expedition also gathered much scientific and geographical knowledge, such as identifying 178 new varieties of plants, including bitterroot, prairie sagebrush, Douglas fir, and ponderosa pine. They recorded 122 new species of animals, including the grizzly bear, the prairie dog, and the pronghorn antelope. The Corps collected valuable information about the geography and geology of the territory and brought back numerous mineral samples. Lewis, Clark, and at least five other Corps of Discovery members kept journals, providing notes on soil, climate, latitude, and longitude, as well as drawings of landforms and living things. Clark, a skilled cartographer, drew a series of detailed maps, published in 1810 and 1814, which became the most accurate maps of the West for decades. The expedition strengthened U.S. claims to the West, inspiring future exploration and waves of settlement.

HISTORICAL THINKING

1. **READING CHECK** What were Jefferson's political and scientific goals for authorizing the expedition?

2. **MAKE GENERALIZATIONS** How did the Corps of Discovery's interactions with Native American groups help the United States?

3. **INTERPRET VISUALS** What does the sketch on the journal page suggest about Lewis and Clark's priorities during the expedition?

4. **DETERMINE WORD MEANINGS** How would you explain the meaning of the word *expedition* as it is used in the context of this lesson?

BUILD BACKGROUND

THE JOURNALS OF LEWIS AND CLARK

Knowing that their journals would likely form the preeminent record of the expedition, Lewis and Clark took great care to fastidiously document their observations. They wrote in leather-bound journals and stored them in sealed tin boxes to protect against the elements. The men apparently made daily notes of their observations and experiences, and then periodically transcribed them into the journals. Today, numerous academic institutions have digitized the works and made them available for study online. The University of Nebraska, for example, offers nearly 5,000 pages of searchable text and digitized images of the original journal pages, including the explorers' hand-drawn maps and pictures.

THE MANDAN

The Mandan, with whom Lewis and Clark had famously peaceful relations, lived in complex permanent settlements and engaged in a sophisticated trade-based economy. They inhabited land along the banks of the Upper Missouri River in large collective villages of 40 or more lodges, each of which housed an average of 10 people. The more prominent families lived in the center of the village near a sacred central lodge. In fields outside their villages, the Mandan grew a variety of crops, including corn, beans, squash, and tobacco. The Mandan villages served as trade centers for the region, where other Native American tribes—including the Cheyenne, Cree, Crow, and Sioux—as well as Europeans, gathered in the fall to trade items such as musical instruments, horses, and meat products for Mandan corn.

TEACH

GUIDED DISCUSSION

4. Make Inferences Why do you think the Spanish were unsuccessful in their attempt to intercept the expedition? *(Possible response: The Corps did not have an exact route to follow as they searched for the legendary Northwest Passage. To cover as much of the new territory as possible, they returned via a different route. The Spanish probably searched for the expedition in likely places, and their determinations were incorrect. If they asked Native Americans for information, those who had been friendly with the Corps may not have been cooperative or purposefully given wrong directions.)*

5. Analyze Primary Sources What words or phrases in Lewis's description of the smelt indicate that he was describing the fish for scientific purposes? *(Lewis's description focuses on the anatomy of the fish rather than its general appearance. He precisely identifies "the first bone of the gills" and distinguishes among the parts of the eye. He notes the position of the "underjaw" and the lack of teeth.)*

VIRTUAL MUSEUM VISIT

The compass used by Meriwether Lewis is part of the National Museum of American History's online collection titled Treasures of American History. Selected from a trove of more than 3 million artifacts, the exhibition includes a mix of popular culture items—including Dorothy's red slippers from the *The Wizard of Oz* and Kermit the Frog—and items that resulted from scientific study and research, such as an original Edison light bulb from 1879. Direct small groups of students to explore the website and locate an artifact or essay that addresses or connects to the emerging national unity of the early 1800s. Invite a representative from each group to present and describe the item to the class.

ACTIVE OPTIONS

AMERICAN GALLERY ONLINE **On the Trail with Lewis and Clark** Invite students to explore the American Gallery. Have them select one of the images and do additional research to learn more about it. Ask questions that will inspire inquiry about the chosen gallery image, such as: Why is this of scientific importance? Who is shown here? What animal is this and where does it live? What might Jefferson have felt when told about or shown this?

Active History: Research Native Cultures Extend the lesson by using either the PDF or Whiteboard version of the activity. These activities take a deeper look at the topic from, or related to, the lesson. Explore the activities as a class, turn them into group assignments, or even assign them individually.

HISTORICAL THINKING

ANSWERS

1. Politically, Jefferson wanted to strengthen American claims to the Louisiana Territory, make contact with Native Americans, locate a Northwest Passage, and cement trading ties with existing networks. Scientifically, Jefferson wanted to learn about the landscape, geology, and animal and plant life of the unfamiliar territory.

2. Friendly relations with Native Americans allowed Lewis and Clark, and the United States, to gain valuable information about the land and knowledge of western tribes.

3. The level of detail in the sketch indicates that Lewis and Clark prioritized the acquisition of scientific knowledge during the expedition.

4. As used in this lesson, an expedition is a journey into unknown territory to learn, gather, and record information about the land and its geology and the people, plants, and animals found there.

SACAGAWEA C. 1788–1812

"[Sacagawea] deserved a greater reward for her attention and services on that route than we had in our power to give her." —William Clark

William Clark is referring to Sacagawea's contribution to the success of the expedition into the Louisiana Territory carried out by Clark, Meriwether Lewis, and other members of the Corps of Discovery between 1804 and 1806. The only woman on the expedition, she acted as a translator and shared her knowledge of the wilderness with the explorers as they moved westward—all while carrying her infant son. And, actually, for these services and others, Sacagawea received no reward at all.

VALUABLE TEAM MEMBER

Sacagawea is a legendary figure, but little is known about her life. Most historians agree that she was born in 1788 or 1789 and was a member of a Native American tribe called the Shoshone. However, they disagree about the spelling of her name and what it means. Spelled *Sacajawea*, the name may be a Shoshone word meaning "boat launcher." But spelled *Sacagawea* (or *Sakakawea*), the name is a word in the Native American language of Hidatsa and translates as "bird woman." Around 1800, when Sacagawea was 11 or 12 years old, the Hidatsa kidnapped her. She lived for a few years among the Hidatsa people until she was sold to French-Canadian fur trapper Toussaint Charbonneau and became one of his wives.

Lewis and Clark hired Charbonneau to be an interpreter on their expedition. Sacagawea set out with her husband and the explorers in 1805, even though she had given birth just two months before. During their travels, Lewis and Clark hoped to buy horses from the Native

Artists can only speculate about what Sacagawea looked like, but surviving records of her actions provide insight into her character. When a boat capsized during the expedition, she alone kept her head and fished out articles from the water that, according to Clark, were necessary to "insure the success of the enterprize."

Americans they encountered. Since Sacagawea could speak both Hidatsa and Shoshone, they thought she could serve as a translator during the transactions. By an amazing coincidence, when Lewis and Clark did cross paths with a group of Shoshone, its leader turned out to be Sacagawea's brother. After the siblings' emotional reunion, Sacagawea helped secure the horses the explorers needed.

She made herself useful in other ways as well. After Sacagawea joined the expedition, she sometimes recognized landmarks and provided important information on the terrain—even though she had not set foot on it since she was a little girl. She also knew the medicinal qualities of some of the roots and plants found along the way and used them to treat sick members of the expedition. On the return trip, she helped the explorers navigate a mountain pass—today known as the Bozeman Pass—to the Yellowstone River. The Corps probably benefited from her presence alone. A group of men traveling through the wilderness could appear threatening to others. As Clark wrote in his journal, "A woman with a party of men is a token of peace."

IN THE WORDS OF LEWIS AND CLARK

Most of what we know about Sacagawea comes from the journals of Lewis and Clark. In an early entry, Lewis seems to regard Sacagawea with contempt. He wrote, "If she has enough to eat and a few trinkets to wear, I believe she would be perfectly content anywhere." However, in at least one instance, she showed more spirit than Lewis initially gave her credit for. When the Corps reached the Pacific Ocean and saw a beached whale, Sacagawea asked the explorers to let her accompany them to witness these wonders. Eventually, they gave in. Lewis later commented in his journal, "She observed that she had traveled a long way with us to see the waters, and that now that monstrous fish was also to be seen, she thought it very hard she could not be permitted to see either."

Clark, on the other hand, was kind to Sacagawea, whom he nicknamed "Janey" and referred to as "pilot" in his journal. And he was quite fond of her child, Jean Baptiste. Clark called him "his little

CRITICAL VIEWING What details in this print by American illustrator N.C. Wyeth suggest that Sacagawea was a valuable member of the Corps of Discovery?

dancing boy, Pomp" and named a sandstone formation near the Yellowstone River "Pompey's Pillar" after the boy. When Jean Baptiste's neck was swollen, Clark himself applied an ointment, made of items such as beeswax and onions, to help reduce the swelling.

In August 1806, Sacagawea and her family returned to their village by the Missouri River. Then in 1812, Clark received word that she had died shortly after giving birth to a second child. However, just as debate surrounds Sacagawea's birth, controversy swirls around her death. Some historians maintain that another one of Charbonneau's wives died in childbirth, not Sacagawea. These researchers claim that Sacagawea rejoined the Shoshone and died on the Wind River Reservation in Wyoming Territory in 1884. Although much of her life remains a mystery, Sacagawea captured the American imagination. She has been honored with monuments, statues, a gold coin, and the title of honorary sergeant for her role on the Lewis and Clark expedition.

HISTORICAL THINKING

1. **READING CHECK** What are some of the mysteries that surround Sacagawea's life?

2. **EVALUATE** What do Sacagawea's actions and the journals of Lewis and Clark convey about her character?

3. **MAKE INFERENCES** Why do you think Sacagawea has captured the American imagination?

PLAN: 2-PAGE LESSON

OBJECTIVE

Explore the life of Sacagawea and her importance to the Corps of Discovery.

CRITICAL THINKING SKILLS FOR LESSON 2.4

- Evaluate
- Make Inferences
- Make Connections
- Analyze Language Use

HISTORICAL THINKING FOR CHAPTER 6

How did government, expansion, and war unify the nation? President Jefferson had ordered Lewis and Clark to explore and map newly acquired lands as they searched for the Northwest Passage. Lesson 2.4 discusses the life of Sacagawea and her pivotal role in this historic expedition.

BACKGROUND FOR THE TEACHER

After the expedition, Sacagawea and her husband, Toussaint Charbonneau, returned to their Hidatsa-Mandan village, and Clark gave Charbonneau more than $500 and 320 acres of farmland. Some accounts state that Clark adopted both of Sacagawea's children after her death, receiving custody of Jean Baptiste ("Pomp") and Lisette from Charbonneau and taking the children to live with him in St. Louis. While not much is known about Lisette, Pomp reportedly lived a life worthy of his mother. Well educated by age 18, he visited Europe and then returned to the American West to serve as a tracker, hunter, guide, and explorer with such famous men as Jim Bridger, Kit Carson, and John C. Frémont. He was praised as "the best man on foot on the plains or in the Rocky Mountains." In 1866, Sacagawea's son died at age 61.

HISTORY NOTEBOOK

Encourage students to complete the American Voices page for Chapter 6 in their History Notebooks as they read.

INTRODUCE & ENGAGE

SHARE AN EXPERIENCE

Ask volunteers to share a time when someone with experience helped them navigate a new situation, whether it was attending a new school, starting a new sport, or navigating a new culture. What feelings did they have before and after they received help? How did they feel about the person who helped them? Remind students that the Lewis and Clark Expedition continuously risked getting lost, and even attacked. However, as the lesson explains, they had an experienced and valuable member of the expedition in Sacagawea to help them succeed.

TEACH

GUIDED DISCUSSION

1. **Make Connections** How might have Sacagawea's past experiences prepared her for her role in the Corps of Discovery expedition? *(Possible response: Because of her kidnapping, she had become fluent in two Native American languages; she knew part of the terrain the Corps would cross; she had experience dealing with white men; and she had learned the medicinal qualities of some roots and plants.)*

2. **Analyze Language Use** How do the word choices of Lewis and Clark in their journal entries reflect their attitudes toward Sacagawea? *(Possible response: Lewis describes her as someone satisfied by "trinkets" and "something to eat," indicating she is unsophisticated and childlike. Clark calls her "Janey" and refers to her as "pilot," terms that show he regards her with kindness and also respects her abilities as a guide.)*

🛡 AMERICAN VOICES

Explain that for successful conversations to take place with the Shoshone, Sacagawea first translated what Shoshone tribesmen said into the Hidatsa language. Charbonneau then translated Hidatsa into French for the Corps' French-speaking member, Francois Labiche, who then translated the French into English for Lewis and Clark. To reply, the process was reversed. **ASK:** Considering this translation process, what added benefit—in addition to serving as interpreter—might have Sacagawea's presence provided to the Corps? *(Possible response: Sacagawea was the only one present who was a member of the Shoshone and therefore familiar with the culture as well as the language. In addition, her presence as a woman and mother might have had a calming effect during the laborious process and helped the men be patient with one another should misunderstandings arise.)*

ACTIVE OPTIONS

On Your Feet: Numbered Heads Arrange students in groups of four. Ask group members to number off. Instruct groups to think about and discuss the following question: Which characteristics or abilities of Sacagawea do you think were the most important in helping the Corps of Discovery succeed in its mission? Tell students to cite evidence from the text or other reliable sources to support their responses. Then call out a number and have students with that number summarize their group's discussion.

NG Learning Framework: Write Journal Entries

SKILL Communication

KNOWLEDGE Our Human Story

Invite students to work in small groups to deepen their understanding of Sacagawea by creating one or two journal pages from her point of view about the Corps of Discovery expedition. Students can use the text and visuals in this and the previous lesson as well as their own research as a basis for the journal entries. Groups might consider Sacagawea's thoughts, feelings, and impressions of events during the journey, including interactions with members of the Corps. Invite volunteers to present their journal entries to the class.

DIFFERENTIATE

INCLUSION

Describe Details in Artwork Pair students who are visually impaired with students who are not. Ask the latter to describe the two depictions of Sacagawea, providing specific details as well as giving an overall impression of the painting style and emotions conveyed. Tell visually impaired students to ask clarifying questions as necessary. Then instruct the partner to read each caption so partners can work together to answer the Critical Viewing question.

GIFTED & TALENTED

Design a Monument Tell students to research monuments and historical landmarks dedicated to Sacagawea and then design their own monument dedicated to her. Instruct them to write an essay describing the monument, including where they would put it and why. Encourage students to provide a sketch or other visual. Invite them to present their design ideas to the class and answer their classmates' questions.

See the Chapter Planner for more strategies for differentiation.

HISTORICAL THINKING

ANSWERS

1. Mysteries include the year and place of her birth, her early life with the Shoshone, the spelling and meaning of her name, and the circumstances and date of her death.

2. Possible response: She seems to have been determined, resourceful, courageous, and calm under pressure. Initially underappreciated by Lewis, she benefited the expedition as a healer, guide, and interpreter.

3. Possible response: Sacagawea provided an immense contribution to one of the most important expeditions in U.S. history. Americans are fascinated by her presence as a woman and resilience as a heroic figure in what would have been an unthinkable undertaking to many. Because many details of her early and later life are not documented, her story has become infused with fiction and possibility.

CRITICAL VIEWING Sacagawea stands at the front of the group and points to a landmark in the distance or in the direction that the Corps should travel. It appears that N.C. Wyeth placed her in this position of prominence to indicate the respect that the Corps had for her knowledge.

MORE CONFLICT WITH BRITAIN

Two sides are fighting. You say you don't want to get involved. Then you start trading supplies with both sides as they fight. Business is good for you. But there's a problem—now you *are* involved.

IMPRESSMENT AND INTERFERENCE

As you have read, Napoleon sold the Louisiana Territory to focus French efforts on a looming war with Britain. French expansion across Europe had sparked hostility between the two nations. Soon after France sold the Louisiana Territory to the United States in 1803, Great Britain declared war on France.

The United States took an official stance of neutrality in the war, and American merchants were more than willing to sell goods and weapons to both countries. But Britain and France were determined to keep their enemy from receiving supplies. By 1806, each country blockaded the other's harbor to keep American ships from delivering provisions. In addition, Britain authorized its navy to impress American sailors by capturing American ships and forcing the sailors to serve the British Navy.

Many Americans began calling for war. But Jefferson hoped to avoid hostilities and remain neutral during foreign disputes. He approved the Non-Importation Act of 1806, which banned specific British imports, and he attempted, unsuccessfully, to negotiate with Britain to end impressment and assure trading rights.

In June 1807, men on the British ship *Leopard* fired on and boarded the American ship *Chesapeake,* capturing four sailors. As more Americans clamored for war, Jefferson closed U.S. ports and waters to British vessels. But the British continued impressment and challenged Jefferson's port closures. They fired on coastal towns in Maine and sailed into Chesapeake Bay.

At Jefferson's urging, Congress passed the **Embargo Act of 1807**, which prohibited American exports to any country and most British imports. An **embargo** is a government order to ban trade with a particular nation or to halt the trading of a specified product. The embargo had devastating effects on American businesses, and merchants were soon staging protests. Congress replaced the Embargo Act with the Non-Intercourse Act in 1809. The new legislation banned trade only with Britain and France. Days later, Jefferson's second term as president ended without a resolution to the nation's problems with Britain.

HEADING FOR WAR

Despite the impact of the embargo, Jefferson remained popular. His endorsement of fellow Democratic-Republican James Madison in the 1808 presidential election resulted in a landslide victory against the Federalists. The election proved that Americans still supported the policies of Jefferson's Democratic-Republicans.

Madison moved into the still-unfinished president's mansion with his wife, **Dolley Madison**, who would play an important role in his presidency. According to one observer, "There was a frankness and ease in her deportment [behavior], that won golden opinions from all, and she possessed an influence so decided with [Madison]." The first lady transformed the presidential residence into a true executive mansion, frequently hosting gatherings and inviting Federalists and Democratic-Republicans to socialize together.

Meanwhile, the problems with Britain continued. In 1811, Madison appointed **James Monroe** of Virginia to be Secretary of State. Monroe hoped to ease tensions over British trade with diplomacy, but Britain continued to insist that American exports be licensed in England before shipping them to France. When Napoleon partially lifted France's blockade in 1811, the United States resumed trading with France. The British responded by attacking U.S. ships, and tensions between the two countries continued.

CRITICAL VIEWING Having started before dawn, much of the Battle of Tippecanoe took place in the dark. What details in this 1880s lithograph by Kurz and Allison reveal the difficulties that each side faced?

At the same time, conflict with Native Americans was brewing in the West—and Americans suspected the British were behind it. American settlement of the West was increasing, and many Native Americans feared they would be pushed out. Shawnee chief **Tecumseh** (tuh-KUM-suh) attempted to build an alliance among the Native Americans to protect their lands against the United States.

The last straw for the Native Americans had been the Treaty of Fort Wayne of 1809, in which several tribes were persuaded to sell the United States 2.5 million acres of their lands for about two cents an acre. Tecumseh met with **William Henry Harrison**, governor of the Indiana Territory, who refused to overturn the treaty. Next Tecumseh went south, seeking allies among the Creek and Seminole. But Tecumseh's plan for a broad Native American alliance failed. By 1811, American settlements in Tennessee, Kentucky, and Ohio had grown large enough to form a barrier between the Native Americans living to the north and south.

In November 1811, Harrison led about 1,000 troops toward Prophetstown, a village that Tecumseh and his brother, the Shawnee prophet Tenskwatawa (tens-qwah-TAH-wah), had founded on the Tippecanoe River in Indiana Territory. Tecumseh was still in the south. In the early morning on November 7, Tenskwatawa's forces attacked Harrison's camp.

The Native Americans were repelled and withdrew. At dawn, Harrison's forces struck back, destroying Prophetstown and claiming victory in what became known as the **Battle of Tippecanoe**.

When news of the battle reached Washington, D.C., many misinterpreted it as evidence of a threatening alliance between the British and Native Americans. **War Hawks** in Congress, led by Speaker of the House Henry Clay of Kentucky and John C. Calhoun of South Carolina, called for another war with Britain. In Calhoun's words, the United States had to show "the World, that we have not only inherited that liberty which our Fathers gave us, but also the will and power to maintain it." But many Americans wondered if the United States was prepared for such a conflict.

HISTORICAL THINKING

1. **READING CHECK** How did the United States become involved in the war between France and Great Britain?

2. **MAKE INFERENCES** What argument might Britain have made for its many acts against American commerce on the seas? Use evidence from the text to support your response.

3. **MAKE CONNECTIONS** Why do you think so many Americans thought that Britain was instigating the Native American unrest in the Northwest Territory?

PLAN: 2-PAGE LESSON

OBJECTIVE

Trace the events that pushed the United States toward war with Britain in 1812.

CRITICAL THINKING SKILLS FOR LESSON 3.1

• Make Inferences
• Make Connections
• Identify Problems and Solutions
• Analyze Language Use

HISTORICAL THINKING FOR CHAPTER 6

How did government, expansion, and war unify the nation? Despite the actions of Jefferson and Madison, events in the early 1800s again brought the United States into war with Britain. Lesson 3.1 analyzes the foreign events and domestic policies that threatened the emerging national unity.

BACKGROUND FOR THE TEACHER

The Embargo Act of 1807 had a devastating effect on the U.S. economy and took tremendous effort to enforce. Because of the law, U.S. exports dropped eighty percent, agricultural prices plummeted, farm foreclosures spiked, and customs revenue dried up. Backlash to the law was strong, particularly in the remaining Federalist stronghold of New England, whose economy depended on shipping. To combat the effects of the law, smuggling became rampant. Ships packed with goods left ports in New England under the pretense that they were sailing to other American ports. Instead they headed to banned foreign destinations, such as Canada, where illegal goods poured across the border. To enforce the law, Thomas Jefferson enacted policies that expanded federal power. He used militias, the army, and the navy to stop smugglers, and he declared the region of upstate New York along the Canadian border in insurrection.

INTRODUCE & ENGAGE

DISCUSS NEUTRALITY

Write the following lines from Thomas Jefferson's first inaugural address on the board: "It is proper you should understand what I deem the essential principles of our government . . . peace, commerce, and honest friendship with all nations, entangling alliances with none." Ask students to speculate on what Jefferson meant. If necessary, lead them to understand that Jefferson is referring to the United States remaining neutral in foreign wars. Then tell students that they will learn about the effects of Jefferson's views on neutrality in this lesson.

TEACH

GUIDED DISCUSSION

1. **Identify Problems and Solutions** What problem was the Embargo Act of 1807 trying to solve, and was it an effective solution? *(Jefferson wanted to remain neutral in the conflict between France and Britain. He believed that if the United States refused to trade with either, it could not be accused of taking sides, and thus avoid war. The tactic was successful for a few years, but eventually the country was drawn into war.)*

2. **Analyze Language Use** Direct students' attention to John Calhoun's quotation in the last paragraph of the lesson. **ASK:** What do John Calhoun's words convey about his views of his generation's role in U.S. history? *(Possible response: Calhoun's generation did not fight in the Revolution, but they benefited from it. He may have felt that his generation needed to act aggressively to preserve an inherited legacy and cement its own.)*

MORE INFORMATION

Kurz and Allison Explain that the lithograph featured in this lesson was produced by Kurz and Allison, a printing company located in Chicago. In the late 19th century, the printmakers were widely known for a series of 36 lithographs depicting Civil War battles. Their signature style, evident in their rendering of William Henry Harrison and the Battle of Tippecanoe, favored a panoramic point of view and heroic depictions of soldiers. **ASK:** How do you think a photograph of this event would differ from Kurz and Allison's interpretation? *(Possible response: The soldiers' uniforms would likely be dirty from fighting in the forest or have blood on them from their wounds. Some of the soldiers would likely be lying on the ground, as some Native Americans are shown. Harrison would probably have not been so close to the fighting.)*

ACTIVE OPTIONS

On Your Feet: Create a Quiz Organize students into two teams on opposite sides of the room. Instruct each team to write 10 True/False or multiple-choice questions focusing on Jefferson's efforts to remain neutral in the war between France and Great Britain and the domestic conflicts that interfered. Have teams alternate asking one of their questions, to which the other team responds. Keep track of the number of correct answers for each team. The team with the most correct answers is the winner.

NG Learning Framework: Analyze a Political Cartoon

SKILL Communication

KNOWLEDGE Our Human Story

Arrange students in small groups and tell them to conduct online research to locate and analyze a political cartoon from the early 1800s that comments on impressment or the Embargo Act. Ask students to determine the cartoonist's viewpoint and the literary and artistic elements used to convey the meaning. Invite groups to share the cartoon and their analysis with the class.

DIFFERENTIATE

ENGLISH LANGUAGE LEARNERS ELD

Clarify Multiple Meanings Remind students at **All Proficiencies** that some words have multiple meanings. Elicit that *impress* can mean to make someone feel admiration as well as to recruit by force. Pair students and ask them to use a dictionary to investigate the meanings of the following multiple-meaning words from the lesson: *found*, *interference*, *determined*, and *provision*. Challenge pairs to write sentences for two meanings of each word.

GIFTED & TALENTED

Host a Talk Show Instruct students to work in pairs to plan, write, and perform a simulated radio or television talk show in which Dolley Madison is the guest. Encourage them to conduct research to inform their questions and answers about Madison's life and her role in political affairs. Invite pairs to present their talk show to the class.

See the Chapter Planner for more strategies for differentiation.

HISTORICAL THINKING

ANSWERS

1. The United States attempted to remain neutral, but American merchants continued to trade with both sides. This led to blockades, embargoes, and an increase of impressment and ship confiscation by the British.

2. Possible response: The British likely justified blockading ports, detaining ships, and requiring licensing of American ships trading with France as necessary to stop the trade of supplies to an enemy nation. Britain may have wanted to increase its navy, but confiscating American ships and impressing American sailors were acts of aggression against the United States that could not be justified as essential to its war against France.

3. Possible response: Britain had allied with Native American nations and tribes against the Americans in the past, so many Americans believed they were still doing so.

CRITICAL VIEWING The Americans are fighting in what is likely unfamiliar territory, deep in a dark forest. The Native Americans are depicted using axes, spears, and a few rifles, largely technologically disadvantaged against soldiers who are all firing guns. For both sides, the dense forest and crowded combatants likely created confusion and chaos.

THE WAR OF 1812

Twenty-nine years after winning their war for independence, Americans were fighting the British again. The young United States was not the economic or military powerhouse it is today, and waging war against an empire was a risky prospect. But the war had consequences for Great Britain as well.

THE WAR BEGINS

Spurred on by Britain's interference with maritime commerce, cries from War Hawks, and rumors of a British-Native American alliance, Madison issued a war message on June 1, 1812. He signed Congress's declaration of war against Great Britain on June 18, and the **War of 1812** began.

The United States was ill-prepared for the war. The Democratic-Republicans in power supported a limited federal government that carried little debt and collected few taxes. They believed that financial responsibility, even for defense, lay with the states. The Bank of the United States charter had been allowed to expire in 1811, so state banks were the only source for war loans. The United States had declared war, but it did not have the financial resources to fight effectively. To make matters worse, the New England states refused to provide their share of funding for the war, and neither Massachusetts nor Connecticut sent militias.

Madison dispatched U.S. forces to Canada, hoping to win some victories while Britain focused on fighting France in Europe. U.S. General William Hull attacked Fort Malden, in Canada, which was commanded by British General Isaac Brock with support from Tecumseh's forces. Hull failed, though, and he even surrendered Detroit. The British went on to take control of much of the region. By this time, Britain really had joined forces with several Native American nations. Britain and its new allies captured Fort Dearborn, at the site of modern-day Chicago. American forces suffered another defeat in October near Fort Niagara.

Madison ran for reelection during the unsuccessful Canada campaign. His opponent, DeWitt Clinton of New York, criticized the war effort. However, the American navy won some surprising victories during the presidential campaign, including the U.S.S. *Constitution's* sinking of Britain's *Guerrière* near Nova Scotia. This boosted Madison's support, and he not only won the electoral vote 129 to 89, but his Democratic-Republican party secured a majority in Congress.

THE STAR-SPANGLED BANNER

This was the American flag that flew amid flaming rockets and exploding bombs at the battle of Fort McHenry. It inspired **Francis Scott Key** to memorialize the scene in his poem "Defense of Fort McHenry," which eventually became a song called "The Star-Spangled Banner." Congress made it the official U.S. national anthem in 1931.

Then 1813 began with another disaster. British and Native American forces staged a new offensive in the West, killing or capturing nearly 900 American troops near Detroit. The U.S. Army managed to hold Fort Meigs and Fort Stephenson in northern Ohio, but it needed naval support to end British control of Lake Erie. On September 10, U.S. ships commanded by **Oliver Hazard Perry** defeated the British at Put-in-Bay and seized control of Lake Erie.

Perry's victory allowed General William Henry Harrison to attack Fort Malden again, sending the British and Native Americans into retreat and reestablishing control of Detroit. Harrison's forces caught up with the British at Moraviantown in Upper Canada on October 5, winning the Battle of the Thames (tehmz) and killing Tecumseh. U.S. forces also burned York (Toronto), the capital of Upper Canada, but they met defeat in Montreal and lost Fort Niagara.

A WELCOME PEACE

After defeating Napoleon in April 1814, Britain turned greater attention to the American war. Britain sent forces into Chesapeake Bay and attacked Washington, D.C., in August. British troops burned the Capitol Building and the executive mansion. The president's family fled in the nick of time. Thanks to Dolley Madison's quick thinking, official documents and a famous portrait of George Washington were saved. In September, Americans won an important naval victory on Lake Champlain that saved New York City from invasion. That same month the British turned to Baltimore, but despite heavily bombarding Fort McHenry, they failed to take the city.

British forces sailed south to blockade the Mississippi River. However, as U.S. General **Andrew Jackson** prepared to defend New Orleans, Great Britain and the United States both realized a clear victory in the war was hopeless. As the British considered peace negotiations, they learned of American successes at Lake Champlain and Baltimore. Many in Britain now wanted to resume normal trade relations with the United States.

This painting by Tom Freeman, called *Burning of the White House, 1814*, shows the executive mansion in flames after British soldiers torched it during the War of 1812. Before their arrival, Madison's wife, Dolley, had a full-length portrait of George Washington carried from the building for safekeeping.

In August 1814, James Madison sent a delegation to Ghent, a city in what is now Belgium, and on Christmas Eve negotiators agreed to end the war. Due to the reliance on ships for communication, news of the **Treaty of Ghent** did not reach the United States until February 1815. Meanwhile, British forces continued to move against U.S. forces in New Orleans.

On January 8, 1815, the British unleashed a bold attack on the city, but they found Jackson ready and waiting. Jackson's troops, behind earthworks, fired into the charging British lines. In less than an hour, the British commander, two generals, and almost 300 British soldiers lay dead; more than 1,200 were wounded and 484 captured. Only 13 Americans were killed, with 39 wounded and 19 captured. News of the victory at the **Battle of New Orleans** reached Washington, D.C., just before notification of the Treaty of Ghent—signed two weeks before the Battle of New Orleans.

HISTORICAL THINKING

1. **READING CHECK** Why was the United States ill-prepared to fight the War of 1812?

2. **DESCRIBE** What major defeats and victories occurred for the United States at the beginning of the War of 1812?

3. **ANALYZE CAUSE AND EFFECT** What developments persuaded the British to agree to sign the Treaty of Ghent?

OBJECTIVE

Recount key events of the War of 1812, including the significance of the Treaty of Ghent.

CRITICAL THINKING SKILLS FOR LESSON 3.2

- Describe
- Analyze Cause and Effect
- Form and Support Opinions
- Make Predictions
- Analyze Language Use

HISTORICAL THINKING FOR CHAPTER 6

How did government, expansion, and war unify the nation? The War of 1812 tested Americans, who were again at war with Great Britain. Lesson 3.2 describes the course of the war and how a last-minute victory bolstered the spirits of the country after a series of devastating defeats.

BACKGROUND FOR THE TEACHER

The War of 1812 exposed growing regional divisions and hastened the death of the Federalist Party. The War Hawks were predominately Democratic-Republicans representing states in the South and West, and they believed that war with Britain would open new land for settlement, including possibly Canada and Spanish Florida. New England Federalists vehemently opposed the war, mainly because of its effects on shipping, and met in 1814 in what is known as the Hartford Convention. Some delegates raised the possibility of secession from the Union, but calmer heads quieted this idea, and the convention produced proposals to Congress calling for an end to the war and constitutional amendments to limit Democratic-Republican power. These proposals fell on deaf ears, however, when the news of the Treaty of Ghent arrived. A wave of patriotism that swept the country in the wake of the war helped to permanently erode the stature of the Federalist Party.

INTRODUCE & ENGAGE

PREVIEW USING VISUALS

Direct students' attention to the photograph of the tattered American flag and the painting of the White House burning. Inform them that these visuals signify events that occurred during the War of 1812. Call on volunteers to predict, based on these visuals, the impact that the war had on Americans. At the end of the lesson, have students review and discuss the accuracy of their predictions.

TEACH

GUIDED DISCUSSION

1. **Form and Support Opinions** Which political party do you think was to blame for the United States' poor preparation for the War of 1812? *(Answers will vary. Students might argue that Democratic-Republicans were to blame for failing to renew the charter of The Bank of the United States or to build a strong army and navy during the Jefferson years. Alternately, students might blame the Federalists, since the predominantly Federalist New England states refused to help fund the war, and in the case of Connecticut and Massachusetts, refused to provide militias.)*

2. **Make Predictions** How might have the timing of the news of the Treaty of Ghent influenced how Americans interpreted it? *(Possible response: Americans learned of the treaty in February, weeks after the defeat of the British at the Battle of New Orleans, so they might have assumed Britain had surrendered, when the war actually ended in a stalemate.)*

ANALYZE LANGUAGE USE

Ask students to consider the connections between the War of 1812 and issues that were left unresolved between the United States and Britain after the American Revolution. For example, point out lingering problems, such as Britain's refusal to withdraw troops from Western forts, its subsequent alliances with Native Americans, and its disrespect of America's maritime interests. Then tell students that some historians refer to the War of 1812 as "The Second War of American Independence." Lead a discussion about the accuracy of this phrase, eliciting details about the events surrounding the war that do or do not support it.

ACTIVE OPTIONS

On Your Feet: Inside-Outside Circle Arrange students in two concentric circles. Tell students in the outside circle to pose questions about the War of 1812, such as the following: Why was the United States ill-prepared for war? How did the Great Lakes region figure into events during the war? Was the War of 1812 worth fighting? Tell students in the inner circle to answer the questions. On a signal, students rotate to create new partnerships. On another signal, students trade inside/outside roles.

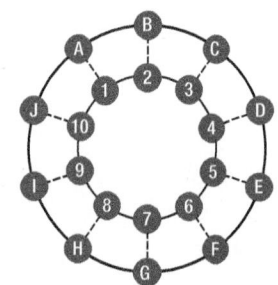

NG Learning Framework: Analyze the Treaty of Ghent

SKILL Communication

KNOWLEDGE Our Human Story

Arrange students in 11 small groups, numbered 1 through 11, and direct them to conduct online research about the Treaty of Ghent, with each group assigned to one of its 11 articles. Remind them that at the signing of the treaty the war was considered a draw, with the treaty offering neither side a distinct advantage. Then asks groups to determine which side, if either, benefited most from the provisions stated in the article they are examining. Ask groups to create a chart to display the provisions of the article and their determinations as bullet points. Bring students together to share their findings. Guide a discussion about whether, based on their collective study of the treaty, it truly offered neither side a distinct advantage.

DIFFERENTIATE

STRIVING READERS

Sequence Events Instruct students to work in pairs to complete a Sequence Chain detailing the major events of the War of 1812. Tell students to read the lesson, pausing after each paragraph to write notes in the chain about each event. Then tell students to take turns reading the notes aloud, using transition words to introduce the contents of each square. Provide students with a list of transition words to use, such as *first*, *then*, *also*, *and*, *but*, *next*, *although*, *second*, and *however*.

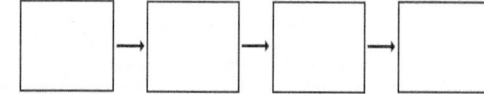

PRE-AP

Write a Biographical Essay Direct students to conduct research using a variety of online sources about how Tecumseh became a powerful warrior, orator, negotiator, and organizer. Tell students to use their research to form a thesis and then provide evidence and reasoning to support that thesis in a biographical essay about Tecumseh. Invite students to share their essays with the class.

See the Chapter Planner for more strategies for differentiation.

HISTORICAL THINKING

ANSWERS

1. The country had neither the financial and military resources required to wage war nor the support of all the states.

2. Early in the War of 1812, U.S. land advances on Canada as well as attempts to defend U.S. territories were unsuccessful, with losses at Fort Malden, Detroit, and Fort Dearborn. These losses were balanced by U.S. naval victories, such as the U.S.S. *Constitution* sinking the British ship *Guerrière*.

3. Having defeated France, Britain no longer needed to continue impressment of American sailors or a blockade of U.S. maritime trade—two causes of the war. News of U.S. successes such as those at Lake Champlain and Fort McHenry further convinced the British to pursue peace and resume trade relations with the United States.

VOCABULARY

Write a sentence using each of the following vocabulary terms.

1. civil case
   My family had a legal dispute with our insurance company, so we filed a civil case against them.

2. criminal case
6. sedition
3. civic republicanism
7. nullification
4. loose constructionist
8. judicial review
5. strict constructionist
9. secession
10. War Hawks

READING STRATEGY
SUMMARIZE

Summarizing can help a reader understand a text and see its important ideas. One way to summarize is to answer these questions: Who? What? Where? When? Why? and How? Use a graphic organizer like the one below to summarize a lesson in the chapter. Then answer the question.

Who?
What?
Where?
When?
Why?
How?
Summary

11. How did the events described in this lesson help unify the nation?

MAIN IDEAS

Answer the following questions. Support your answers with evidence from the chapter.

12. During the first presidential election, why did Americans see George Washington as the obvious choice to unite the nation? **LESSON 1.1**

13. In what ways did "republican motherhood" give women new freedom and autonomy, and in what ways did it maintain the status quo? **LESSON 1.2**

14. Describe the political divisions that arose in the early years of Washington's presidency. **LESSON 1.3**

15. What problems did the United States face in its relationships with foreign nations during the 1780s and 1790s? **LESSON 1.4**

16. What changes did Jefferson bring in his first term as president? **LESSON 2.1**

17. In what way did the Louisiana Purchase contradict Jefferson's political beliefs, and how did he rationalize the purchase? **LESSON 2.2**

18. In what ways was the Lewis and Clark Expedition successful in fulfilling Jefferson's goals for their exploration? **LESSON 2.3**

19. What pressures brought the United States closer to war with Britain in the years leading up to the War of 1812? **LESSON 3.1**

20. What developments helped bring an end to the War of 1812? **LESSON 3.2**

HISTORICAL THINKING

Answer the following questions. Support your answers with evidence from the chapter.

21. **COMPARE AND CONTRAST** In what ways was Jefferson's Democratic-Republican political philosophy different from that of the Federalists? Support your response with details from the text.

22. **MAKE INFERENCES** How did the Lewis and Clark Expedition help to secure U.S. claims to the Louisiana Territory and the Pacific Northwest, and open the entire West to American settlement?

23. **SYNTHESIZE** What effects do you think the Louisiana Purchase had on the American identity at that time?

24. **DRAW CONCLUSIONS** How do you think Britain's leaders viewed the outbreak of war with the United States in 1812?

25. **DISTINGUISH FACT FROM OPINION** As relations with France deteriorated, Federalists questioned the patriotism of Democratic-Republicans, journalists, immigrants, and all critics of the battles with France. Were their charges based on facts or opinions? Explain your response with evidence from the text.

INTERPRET VISUALS

In 1912, the Smithsonian Institution hired Amelia Fowler to repair the original Star-Spangled Banner. Fowler and her team of 10 workers replaced the deteriorating canvas backing that supported the flag, allowing it to be displayed for more than 80 years before its next, more extensive restoration, which began in 1998. The symbolic flag is now displayed in the National Museum of American History in Washington, D.C.

26. What tools were probably needed to restore the backing of the flag?

27. Why did Fowler require such a large team to finish the project?

ANALYZE SOURCES

George Washington announced his retirement as president in a letter published in Philadelphia's *American Daily Advertiser* on September 19, 1796. The letter, which came to be known as his "Farewell Address," advised building national unity by avoiding regionalism, factionalism (political parties), and foreign entanglements. Read the passage and answer the question.

> The common and continual mischiefs of the spirit of party are sufficient to make it the interest and duty of a wise people to discourage and restrain it.
>
> . . . It agitates the community with ill-founded jealousies and false alarms, kindles the animosity of one part against another, foments [provokes] occasionally riot and insurrection. It opens the door to foreign influence and corruption.

28. How does Washington believe the establishment of political parties can lead to corruption?

CONNECT TO YOUR LIFE

29. **EXPLANATORY** George Washington was adamantly opposed to political parties for the reasons he set forth in the excerpt quoted above. Today, there are wide divisions between the two major American political parties—the Republican Party and the Democratic Party. Choose one of Washington's arguments for avoiding the establishment of political parties, state whether or not you think it applies to American politics today, and write a paragraph explaining your thoughts on the matter.

TIPS

- List Washington's reasons for opposing political parties in your own words.
- Choose the one you think best applies to today's political situation.
- Support your response with evidence and examples from current events.
- Restate your main idea to help you write a strong conclusion to your paragraph.

VOCABULARY ANSWERS

1. My family had a legal dispute with our insurance company, so we filed a civil case against them.

2. Selling defective equipment could result in a criminal case.

3. Americans who practiced civic republicanism believed in individual freedoms and activities aimed at the common good.

4. Loose constructionists interpreted the Constitution broadly, allowing the government to have powers not explicitly prohibited.

5. Strict constructionists opposed the government using implied powers in the Constitution to establish a national bank.

6. A rebel act against the government may be an act of sedition.

7. A state could veto an unconstitutional law using nullification.

8. Through the process of judicial review, the Supreme Court upheld the new law as constitutional.

9. Aaron Burr's plan to start a new nation through the secession of the West proved to be a failure.

10. War Hawks might urge a president to prematurely declare war.

READING STRATEGY ANSWER

Who?	President Washington, Cabinet members, John Jay
What?	creating new governmental institutions
Where?	newly independent United States
When?	1789–1790
Why?	New institutions were necessary to a build a nation governed by the will of its people but with a federal government strong enough to fulfill its duties.
How?	form a Cabinet and federal judiciary, oversee first U.S. census
Summary	With its new Constitution and stronger central government, the nation selected George Washington as a president who could unite all Americans. To do so, Washington chose a nonpartisan Cabinet, worked with Congress to establish a judiciary system, and oversaw the first U.S. census to assure fair representation for Americans.

11. Possible response: By establishing a strong central government that still depended on the will of the people, Washington and his Cabinet built the foundation for a stable, unified government.

12. Washington displayed skilled military leadership during the Revolution and political leadership during the Constitutional Convention. Americans recognized and respected his strong commitment to the new government and Constitution.

13. The role of republican motherhood gave new freedom and status to some white middle- and upper-class mothers through their responsibility of passing on the values of civic republicanism to their children to make them productive citizens. However, it also solidified the status quo, keeping women in the home and largely out of the public sphere, thus limiting women's rights and liberties.

14. Political divisions arose early in Washington's presidency between the Federalists, who favored commerce, manufacturing, and a loose interpretation of the Constitution, and the Democratic-Republicans, who favored agriculture and believed in a strict interpretation of the Constitution.

15. During the 1780s and 1790s, the United States had to carefully handle France's expectation of favorable trade policies and informal help in its war with Britain, as well as Britain's impressment of sailors and confiscation of ships. National divisions existed over the Jay Treaty with Britain.

16. In his first term, Jefferson fulfilled his promises to decrease government expenditures, taxes, and the national debt. He cut the defense budget, repealed excise taxes, and adopted informality and frugality in the conduct of his administration.

17. As a strict constructionist, Jefferson promised limited rather than implied powers for the federal government. However, the Constitution did not explicitly allow the federal government to acquire territory. Jefferson set aside these concerns because he believed the Louisiana Purchase would provide spacious lands for an agrarian republic of self-supporting small farmers.

18. Jefferson wanted the expedition to fill gaps in geographic knowledge of the region, and it succeeded by providing a vast amount of new information. The expedition was somewhat successful in meeting Jefferson's goal of making peaceful contact with Native American groups, as many tribes traded with the expedition; shared food, shelter, and knowledge; and provided guides and interpreters. The expedition also fulfilled Jefferson's goal of strengthening U.S. claims on the region.

19. Pressures toward war mounted in the years leading up to 1812 due to British impressment of U.S. sailors, confiscation of ships, trade blockades, and an assumption among many Americans of a British-Native American alliance.

20. The war of 1812 approached an end as U.S. forces held off the British at Baltimore despite heavy bombardment of Fort McHenry. The British already had little hope of victory, and many wanted only to resume peaceful trade with the United States. News of American victories at Lake Champlain and Baltimore only strengthened Britain's desire for peace.

21. The Federalists favored a strong central government that would exercise powers implied in the Constitution. Centered in New England, they focused on commerce and manufacturing supported by high tariffs and a national bank. Democratic-Republicans believed in minimal government using powers stated in the Constitution. Centered in the South and West, Democratic-Republicans supported agriculture, with commerce seen as a way to sell farm surpluses and purchase manufactured goods. Federalists saw the nation's future in urban manufacturing and commerce. Democratic-Republicans followed Jefferson's vision of self-sufficient farmers only minimally restrained by government.

22. Lewis and Clark were the first Americans to explore the Louisiana Territory and Pacific Northwest so extensively. Their expedition recorded much new knowledge about the territory's geography, people, and wildlife. This information combined with alliances forged with Native Americans helped promote further American settlement in the West and solidify U.S. claims to the region.

23. Possible response: The Louisiana Purchase spurred national pride because it nearly doubled the size of the country and provided rich lands for future settlement. The promise of spacious lands to farm and news of Lewis and Clark's discoveries may have sparked Americans' sense of adventure.

24. Possible response: Britain's leaders probably considered the war a minor annoyance, distracting them from their war with France. They didn't make a major troop commitment to the American war until after defeating France in 1814.

25. Possible response: Federalists who questioned the patriotism of Democratic-Republicans, journalists, immigrants, and critics of the war effort based their accusations on opinions. Democratic-Republicans, such as Jefferson, had proven their patriotism throughout the Revolution and building of the government. They simply disagreed with Federalist policies, especially the Alien and Sedition Acts.

26. Restoring the backing probably required sewing needles and thread and perhaps a frame to hold the front to the canvas as it was being repaired and reattached.

27. A large restoration team was needed because the flag was large and the work was time consuming.

28. Washington believes that opposing parties make "mischief" to undermine each other, which fuels mutual hatred. Members of a party might resort to criminal or corrupt actions to advance their political agenda at the expense of rivals.

29. Paragraphs will vary. Students should first list Washington's reasons in their own words and then choose one reason and state whether it applies to American politics today. Paragraphs should include evidence and examples from current events and a strong conclusion that incorporates a restatement of the main idea.

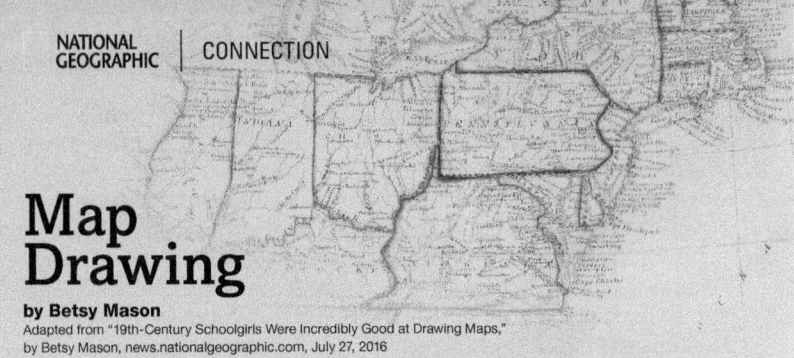

Map Drawing

by Betsy Mason
Adapted from "19th-Century Schoolgirls Were Incredibly Good at Drawing Maps,"
by Betsy Mason, news.nationalgeographic.com, July 27, 2016

The beautifully detailed early 19th-century map of the United States pictured above would be snapped up quickly by a collector if it were to hit the market today. It could go for several hundred or a couple thousand dollars. But not because it was made by a well-known cartographer or a prestigious map publisher. This map was hand-drawn by a 15-year-old girl as part of her schoolwork.

For a brief period at the beginning of the 19th century, many schoolgirls in the United States were expected to draw elaborate maps as a central part of their education. "It was hugely popular for about 30 years," says historian Susan Schulten of the University of Denver. "Chances are if you come across one [of these maps], it's from 1800 to 1835."

This practice likely originated in Europe and then spread to female academies, which were becoming popular in the states at the time. Though there are some nice examples of maps drawn by boys, boys were more often taught surveying and navigation instead of map drawing, Schulten says. For the girls, drawing maps wasn't to prepare them to be cartographers or even geographers. Instead, the activity was supposed to help them gain, retain, and demonstrate general knowledge, become good citizens, and show off their artistic skill.

"I think it very nicely fits in [with] what were the central goals of female education after the revolution," says Schulten, who first became interested in the schoolgirl maps while researching her book *Mapping the Nation*. Back then, geography was seen as an appropriate avenue for girls to become culturally literate, "to prepare them for a life of usefulness and social exchange," according to Schulten.

Another primary goal of drawing maps was mastery of the art of penmanship. The lettering on most of the schoolgirls' maps is very careful and neat, with multiple fonts, sizes, and weights for various kinds of features, like states, cities, and rivers, just like the professionally made maps these drawings were based on. "The lettering was sort of what drew me to them," Schulten says. "Sometimes I notice that [the girls] paid so much attention to penmanship and lettering that they chronically misspell words."

The maps were clearly labor-intensive assignments that would have taken weeks, if not months, to finish. So how did the schoolgirls create them? Information on how the maps were made is scarce, but a couple of techniques seem likely. Students who copied the maps by sight may have laid a grid over the original map as a guide. They would then put a similar grid on a blank sheet and copy the contents of each small box, one at a time—far easier than eyeballing an entire map at once.

Many of the maps were almost certainly traced, but some are on paper too thick to trace through. In this case, the girls could have used a common trick of the time to make a sort of carbon copy. They would use a pencil to cover an entire piece of paper with graphite, lay that facedown on a blank sheet of paper, and put the original map on top. Tracing the map with some sort of pointer would transfer the graphite outline to the blank sheet.

The various techniques, base maps, and personalities of the schoolgirls led to a wide range of map styles. Some girls just replicated versions of existing maps. Others displayed real artistry or added their own personal touches. Stephanie Cyr, co-curator of the "Women in Cartography" exhibit at Boston Public Library, comments, "[The girls] were able to express themselves artistically at a time when their whole world was dominated by men."

For more from National Geographic, check out "Searching for Sacagawea" online.

UNIT INQUIRY: Explore a Contradiction

In this unit, you learned about the American colonists' path to independence—from breaking ties with Great Britain and staging a revolution to establishing a new form of government for a new nation. The concept of liberty, or individual freedom, was a core ideal in the American Revolution and central to the emerging American identity. How did the Founding Fathers embrace liberty for all and yet allow the practice of slavery? Many of them owned slaves. Didn't they recognize the contradiction?

ASSIGNMENT

Research the Founding Fathers' positions on slavery and how they reconciled the practice of slavery with their ideal of liberty for all. Find out which of the Founding Fathers were slaveholders. Investigate the discussions of slavery that occurred during the drafting of the Articles of Confederation and the Constitution. Present your findings to the class.

Plan As you explore the contradiction between the Founders' ideal of liberty and the practice of slavery, gather evidence from this unit and the internet about the Founders' attitudes toward slavery. Research individuals such as John Adams, Samuel Adams, Samuel Chase, Benjamin Franklin, Alexander Hamilton, John Hancock, Patrick Henry, John Jay, Thomas Jefferson, James Madison, Thomas Paine, and George Washington. Think about motivations they may have had for accepting slavery. Use a graphic organizer like this to organize your notes.

Founding Father	State	Slaveholder, yes or no	Position on slavery
J. Adams			
S. Adams			
S. Chase			

Produce Review your notes and think about the reasons these prominent Founders failed to oppose slavery during the drafting of the Constitution. Write a summary that answers this question: How did the Founding Fathers reconcile their core value of liberty with their acceptance of the practice of slavery?

Present Choose a creative way to present your summary of the Founding Fathers' positions on liberty and slavery to the class. Consider one of these options:

- Taking on the role of one of the Founders, prepare and deliver a speech or monologue in which you present your views to the class.

- Write a journal entry or letter as one of the Founders in which you present your thoughts and feelings. Share your journal entry or letter with classmates.

- Design a poster or digital presentation that addresses the conflict between Americans' promotion of liberty for all and the practice of slavery.

NATIONAL GEOGRAPHIC | LEARNING FRAMEWORK ACTIVITIES

Stage a Debate

ATTITUDE Curiosity
SKILLS Communication, Collaboration

Review the unit and conduct further research to determine why some colonists did not support separating from Great Britain at the time of the American Revolution. Team up with a partner and prepare arguments for and against independence from Great Britain from the perspectives of both a Patriot and a Loyalist. Then create two props, such as different hats, to transform yourselves into a Patriot and a Loyalist. Begin by giving short speeches summarizing your positions and then debate the issue with your class.

Create a Storyboard

SKILLS Communication, Collaboration
KNOWLEDGE Our Human Story

Working in a small group, create a storyboard that tells the "story" of the formation of the United States. You might use a software program or simply pencil and paper to draft your storyboard. First review the chapters in this unit to determine which significant events to portray. Pick events that will show the story from the British taxation of the colonists to the election of President Washington. Make a list of the main events and their dates, and then work together to sketch the events and write a script. Display your storyboard in the classroom.

NATIONAL GEOGRAPHIC CONNECTION

GUIDED DISCUSSION FOR "MAP DRAWING"

1. **Make Inferences** How did expectations about the accomplishments of young men and young women differ in the early 19th century? *(Possible response: Young men were expected to have more physical, analytical, or math-related pursuits and skills. On the other hand, young women were expected to develop more general knowledge, display their artistic skills, and become good citizens.)*

2. **Draw Conclusions** What useful skills and habits do you think drawing maps might help a young person develop? *(Possible response: Map drawing might help develop a knowledge of geography, a steady hand and drafting skills, an artistic eye, powers of concentration or analysis, and strong planning and designing skills.)*

GUIDED DISCUSSION FOR "SEARCHING FOR SACAGAWEA"

1. **Summarize** What information in the article suggests that Sacagawea was a capable young woman? *(Possible response: Sacagawea was familiar enough with the terrain to know the Corps was heading in the right direction; she had knowledge of edible native plants; and she was part of the chain of translation among the Corps and Native Americans they encountered.)*

2. **Identify** Since the 19th century, how have various groups claimed Sacagawea as their own? *(Suffragists promoted Sacagawea as a smart, strong, capable woman and even as a heroic Native American patriot. Native Americans have included her story in their lore, and the Lemhi Shoshone hope to use ties to her to help establish their claim to ancestral lands.)*

HISTORY NOTEBOOK

Encourage students to complete the Unit Wrap-Up page for Unit 2 in their History Notebooks.

UNIT INQUIRY PROJECT RUBRIC

ASSESS

Use the rubric to assess each student's participation and performance.

SCORE	ASSIGNMENT	PRODUCT	PRESENTATION
3 GREAT	• Student thoroughly understands the assignment. • Student participates fully in the project process.	• Summary is well thought out. • Summary offers multiple reasons and evidence for the Founding Fathers' positions on liberty and slavery. • Summary contains all key elements listed in the assignment.	• Presentation is clear, concise, and logical. • Presentation does a good job of creatively summarizing the Founding Fathers' positions on liberty and slavery. • Presentation engages the audience.
2 GOOD	• Student mostly understands the assignment. • Student participates fairly well in the project process.	• Summary is fairly well thought out. • Summary offers one reason with evidence for the Founding Fathers' positions on liberty and slavery. • Summary contains most key elements listed in the assignment.	• Presentation is fairly clear, concise, and logical. • Presentation does an adequate job of summarizing the Founding Fathers' positions on liberty and slavery. • Presentation somewhat engages the audience.
1 NEEDS WORK	• Student does not understand the assignment. • Student minimally participates or does not participate in the project process.	• Summary is not well thought out. • Summary does not offer reasons or evidence for the Founding Fathers' positions on liberty and slavery. • Summary contains few or none of the key elements listed in the assignment.	• Presentation is not clear, concise, or logical. • Presentation does an inadequate job of summarizing the Founding Fathers' positions on liberty and slavery. • Presentation does not engage the audience.

NATIONAL GEOGRAPHIC LEARNING FRAMEWORK RUBRIC

ASSESS

Use the rubric to assess how each student applies the National Geographic Learning Framework.

SCORE	ASSIGNMENT	ASSIGNMENT	FINAL PRODUCTS
3 GREAT	• Debate reflects **Curiosity** well. • Debate demonstrates **Communication** and **Collaboration** well.	• Storyboard demonstrates **Communication** and **Collaboration** well. • Storyboard explores **Our Human Story** well.	• Final products are engaging, creative, and well presented.
2 GOOD	• Debate reflects **Curiosity**. • Debate demonstrates **Communication** and **Collaboration**.	• Storyboard demonstrates **Communication** and **Collaboration**. • Storyboard explores **Our Human Story**.	• Final products are interesting, logical, and complete.
1 NEEDS WORK	• Debate does not reflect **Curiosity**. • Debate does not demonstrate **Communication** or **Collaboration**.	• Storyboard does not demonstrate **Communication** or **Collaboration**. • Storyboard does not explore **Our Human Story**.	• Final products are not creative, complete, or interesting.

INTRODUCE THE PAINTING

ON THE OREGON TRAIL

Travelers in a wagon train bound for Oregon are captured in this painting, *Emigrants Crossing the Plains*, by American artist Albert Bierstadt. Though people tend to think of the Oregon Trail as a single track worn into the land, it was actually a series of tracks that changed shape and size with time and weather. In some places, ruts worn by wagon wheels and foot traffic converged into a single track, while in others, they split into two or more tracks half a mile apart. However, even where the tracks diverged the most, members of a wagon train would rarely be separated from one another by more than a few miles. Travelers often found shortcuts and easier routes across the plains, carving a new track in the land as they went. **ASK:** What detail in the painting helps the viewer understand where the migrants are headed? *(The wagon's cover has the words* For Oregon *painted on the side.)*

A number of mountain ranges stood between the eastern United States and the Oregon Territory, and explorers and settlers had to find safe passage around or through these peaks. One of the most commonly used routes led through the South Pass, which crossed over the Continental Divide. Also, to survive the 2,000-mile journey along the Oregon Trail, travelers needed steady supplies of water and food. Luckily, as they neared their destination, the trail to Oregon Territory followed the region's three largest rivers, the Platte, the Snake, and the Columbia. This section of the trail also offered plenty of grazing for herd and pack animals as well as good hunting and fishing. **ASK:** What impressions might Bierstadt have wanted to create through his use of light in this painting? *(Answers will vary. Possible response: Bierstadt painted a golden light suffusing the scene, with the sun glowing through the trees. He may have wanted to create impressions of peace and harmony with nature, and a sense of vast, open spaces, symbolizing a bright and hopeful future for the travelers.)*

UNIT **3**

1814–1854

EXPANDING THE NEW NATION

206

CRITICAL VIEWING New industries and inventions transformed the United States in the early 19th century. In this painting titled *Emigrants Crossing the Plains*, by American artist Albert Bierstadt, what details suggest how expanding transportation networks may have affected the growing country?

ALBERT BIERSTADT

The American painter Albert Bierstadt trained as an artist in Dusseldorf, Germany, where he took extended sketching tours through the Alps of Germany, Switzerland, and Italy. Bierstadt spent most of this time learning to draw the steep mountain peaks and craggy faces of alpine cliffs. This early landscape work, combined with his subtle use of color, mastery of composition, and ability to infuse his paintings with almost ethereal light, set him apart from many other artists of his day.

Bierstadt returned to the United States and in 1859 accompanied a group of surveyors on an expedition to the Rocky Mountains. He came home with stacks of sketches and photographs of the Rockies and set to work on a series of western landscapes. In a second trip to the West in 1863, Bierstadt chose to sketch more remote wilderness areas. He used these sketches as the basis for a series of paintings that won him wide acclaim.

Throughout the late 1800s, Bierstadt was regarded as the foremost painter of western landscapes in the country. But at the end of the century, tastes in art shifted, and his popularity began to wane. Today, art historians regard Bierstadt as one of the first painters to capture the panoramic vistas and sweeping grandeur of the American West.

CRITICAL VIEWING The worn path and number of people, wagons, and animals in the painting suggest that the Oregon Trail is becoming a well-known and well-traveled transportation network to the West. The emigrants seem undisturbed by the sight of abandoned goods and bleached bones along the way or by the Native American village in the distance. This implies that, despite the dangers, this growing transportation network will draw more people westward as the country's population increases.

1815 EUROPE: BATTLE OF WATERLOO

The Battle of Waterloo, which pitted British and allied forces against Napoleon Bonaparte and the French Army, was relatively brief by wartime standards, lasting only nine hours. Yet it significantly altered the course of history by marking the end of the Napoleonic Wars (1803–1815), a series of conflicts that claimed more than 5 million lives. The Battle of Waterloo was more than a military encounter; it was a fight for survival on the part of Europe's nation-states, which Napoleon wanted to conquer and rule as part of a new French empire.

The battle also signaled a change in how European wars were planned and fought. For the first time, Britain gathered a combined force that included Dutch, German, and Belgian soldiers to fight a single enemy. Working together, the allies decisively defeated the French Army. However, both sides sustained devastating losses. Allied forces suffered about 23,000 casualties, while Napoleon's losses totaled 25,000 killed or wounded and another 9,000 captured.

The victory at Waterloo and the end of the Napoleonic Wars had wider consequences as well. They not only strengthened the position of Great Britain, helping it to become a global power, but also affected the economy of the United States. From 1792 to 1807, the country had remained neutral in the wars and was able to greatly increase its trade with European nations that were blockaded or attacked by France. However, in 1807, President Thomas Jefferson placed an embargo on U.S. trade with all warring nations, and the foreign trade collapsed. It wasn't until after the defeat of Napoleon in 1815 that U.S. foreign trade began to pick up once again, gradually increasing the influence of the United States on the global stage. **ASK:** In what ways does trade help a nation become more influential in the world? *(Possible response: As a nation's trade increases, it has more economic and negotiating power to help or influence other countries. This would be particularly important for a new country like the United States.)*

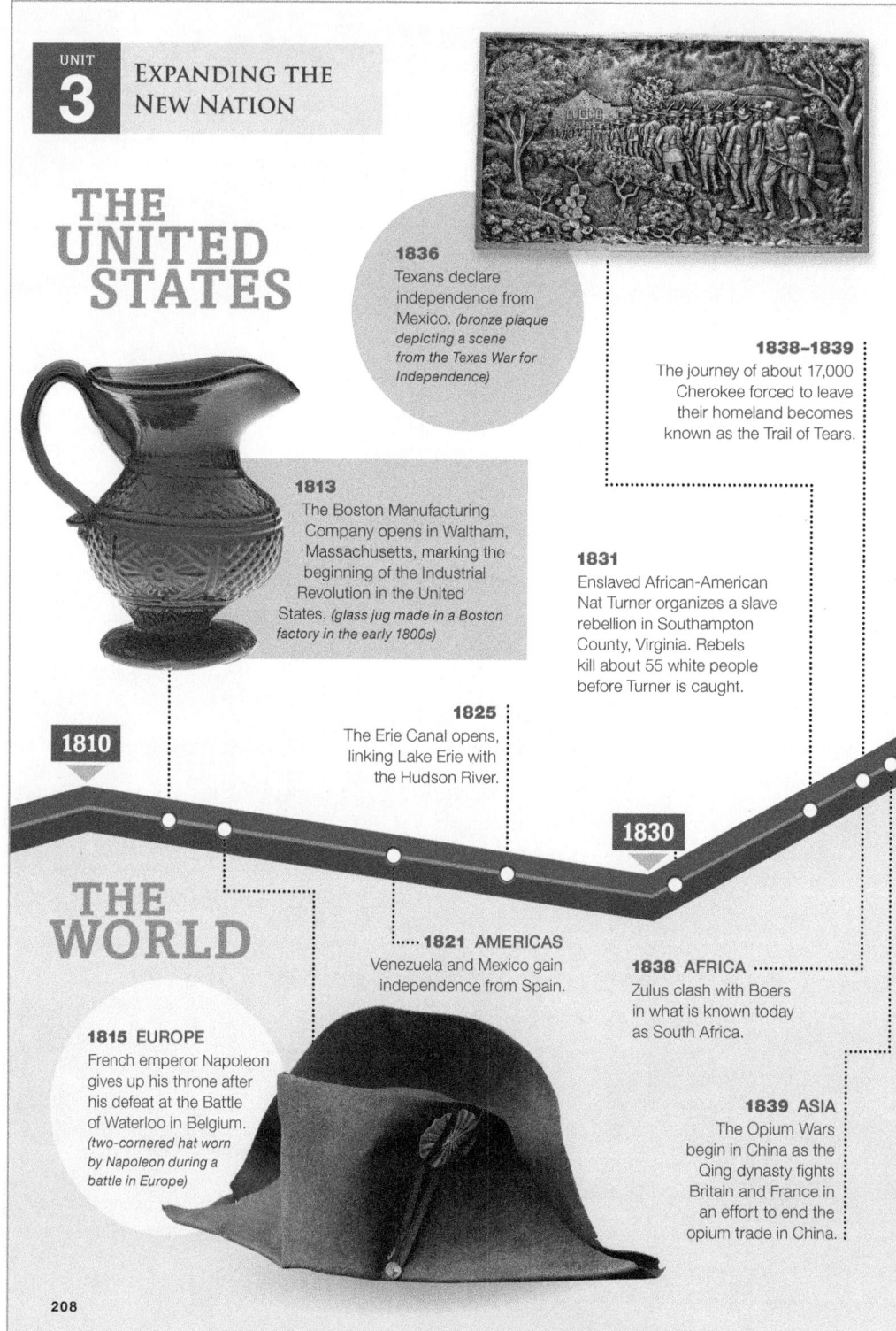

UNIT 3 EXPANDING THE NEW NATION

THE UNITED STATES

1836
Texans declare independence from Mexico. *(bronze plaque depicting a scene from the Texas War for Independence)*

1838–1839
The journey of about 17,000 Cherokee forced to leave their homeland becomes known as the Trail of Tears.

1813
The Boston Manufacturing Company opens in Waltham, Massachusetts, marking the beginning of the Industrial Revolution in the United States. *(glass jug made in a Boston factory in the early 1800s)*

1831
Enslaved African-American Nat Turner organizes a slave rebellion in Southampton County, Virginia. Rebels kill about 55 white people before Turner is caught.

1825
The Erie Canal opens, linking Lake Erie with the Hudson River.

1810

1830

THE WORLD

1821 AMERICAS
Venezuela and Mexico gain independence from Spain.

1838 AFRICA
Zulus clash with Boers in what is known today as South Africa.

1815 EUROPE
French emperor Napoleon gives up his throne after his defeat at the Battle of Waterloo in Belgium. *(two-cornered hat worn by Napoleon during a battle in Europe)*

1839 ASIA
The Opium Wars begin in China as the Qing dynasty fights Britain and France in an effort to end the opium trade in China.

208

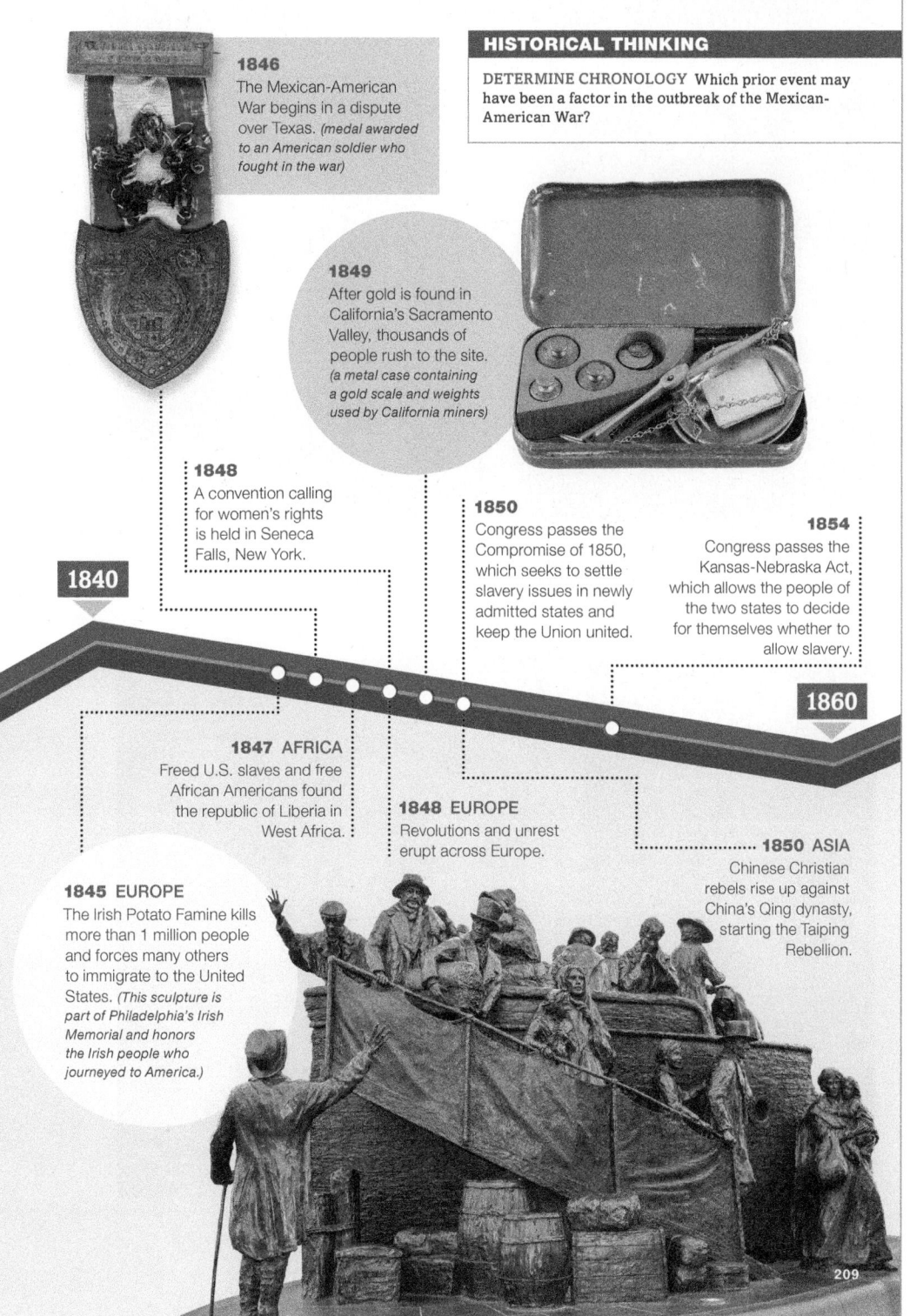

1846
The Mexican-American War begins in a dispute over Texas. *(medal awarded to an American soldier who fought in the war)*

HISTORICAL THINKING

DETERMINE CHRONOLOGY Which prior event may have been a factor in the outbreak of the Mexican-American War?

1849
After gold is found in California's Sacramento Valley, thousands of people rush to the site. *(a metal case containing a gold scale and weights used by California miners)*

1848
A convention calling for women's rights is held in Seneca Falls, New York.

1850
Congress passes the Compromise of 1850, which seeks to settle slavery issues in newly admitted states and keep the Union united.

1854
Congress passes the Kansas-Nebraska Act, which allows the people of the two states to decide for themselves whether to allow slavery.

1840

1860

1847 AFRICA
Freed U.S. slaves and free African Americans found the republic of Liberia in West Africa.

1848 EUROPE
Revolutions and unrest erupt across Europe.

1850 ASIA
Chinese Christian rebels rise up against China's Qing dynasty, starting the Taiping Rebellion.

1845 EUROPE
The Irish Potato Famine kills more than 1 million people and forces many others to immigrate to the United States. *(This sculpture is part of Philadelphia's Irish Memorial and honors the Irish people who journeyed to America.)*

INTRODUCE TIME LINE EVENT

1847 AFRICA: THE FOUNDING OF LIBERIA

In 1816, the American Colonization Society (ACS) proposed founding a colony in Africa where former slaves and free African Americans could live. Many ACS members were prominent leaders in American society, such as President James Madison, who helped raise public funding for migration to the colony. Despite resistance from most abolitionists, the ACS sent representatives to West Africa to locate an appropriate site. Several years and several failed attempts later, members finally chose a suitable piece of West African land and called it Liberia. Because another president, James Monroe, had secured further government funding for the colony, ACS members named its capital Monrovia in his honor.

In 1822, the first African-American colonists arrived. Over the next 40 years, more than 19,000 people relocated to Liberia. At first, ACS agents ran the colony, seeking to re-create a homogeneous American culture. However, intermarriage among colonists and indigenous people soon created a diverse population with a blend of cultural influences. By the time Liberia became an independent republic in 1847, the U.S. role in the colony had changed. Instead of governing Liberia, the United States provided financial and other types of aid. Also, white leaders were no longer at the helm, as Liberia was now governed by its black citizens. Even so, the country's power structure still favored those who had attended Liberian missionary schools or U.S. educational institutions. **ASK:** Why might abolitionists have argued against expatriation of African Americans to Liberia? *(Possible response: They might have believed that founding colonies in Africa was not the answer to the slavery question and that the United States should instead focus on ending slavery and integrating African Americans into American life and culture.)*

HISTORICAL THINKING

DETERMINE CHRONOLOGY

Answer: Texas declared its independence from Mexico in 1836; in 1846, the United States annexed Texas, which Mexico still considered as its territory.

UNIT 3 RESOURCES

UNIT INTRODUCTION

UNIT TIME LINE

UNIT WRAP-UP

NATIONAL GEOGRAPHIC | CONNECTION

National Geographic Magazine Adapted Articles
- "Nat Turner's Complex Legacy"
- "The Way West" ONLINE

Unit 3 Inquiry: Document a Migration

NG Learning Framework Activities
- Depict Nature
- Create Slogans to Promote Reforms

Unit 3 Formal Assessment

CHAPTER 7 RESOURCES

Available at NGLSync.Cengage.com

TEACHER RESOURCES & ASSESSMENT

Reading and Note-Taking

Vocabulary Practice

Social Studies Skills Lessons
- Reading: Draw Conclusions
- Writing: Argument

Formal Assessment
- Chapter 7 Pretest
- Chapter 7 Tests A & B
- Section Quizzes

Chapter 7 Answer Key

ExamView®
One-time Download

STUDENT DIGITAL RESOURCES

- eEdition
- Handbooks
- Online Atlas
- American Gallery Online
- History Notebook
- Active History
- Reid on the Road video series
- Literature Analysis
- Projects for Inquiry-Based Learning

Chapter 7 Spanish Resources are available at NGLSync.Cengage.com.

AMERICAN STORIES | American Inventions

- Study Primary Sources: Patent diagrams and an advertisement
- On Your Feet: Invention Impact

NG Learning Framework:
Describe a Useful Invention

SECTION 1 RESOURCES
REGIONAL GROWTH

LESSON 1.1
The Industrial Revolution

 AMERICAN **GALLERY** ONLINE Industrializing America

- Active History: Evaluate Industrial Revolution Inventions

LESSON 1.2
Cotton and Slavery in the South

- On Your Feet: King Cotton History Roundtable

NG Learning Framework:
Build or Draw a Scale Model

SECTION 2 RESOURCES
BUILDING A NATIONAL ECONOMY

LESSON 2.1
The Economy Expands

- On Your Feet: Use a Jigsaw Strategy

NG Learning Framework:
Profile a Canal Town

LESSON 2.2
NATIONAL GEOGRAPHIC EXPLORER
KEVIN CRISMAN
Wreck on the Red River

- On Your Feet: Impact of Steamships

NG Learning Framework:
Investigate a Shipwreck

LESSON 2.3
AMERICAN PLACES
The Great Lakes

- On Your Feet: Fishbowl

NG Learning Framework:
Investigate Great Lakes' Health

LESSON 2.4
Strengthening the National Government

- On Your Feet: Three Corners

NG Learning Framework:
Debate States' Rights Versus Federal Power

SECTION 3 RESOURCES
CHANGING POLITICS

LESSON 3.1
Nationalism and Foreign Policy

- On Your Feet: Team Word Webbing

NG Learning Framework:
Create a Community Service Plan

LESSON 3.2
Westward Expansion and Tensions Over Slavery

- ▶ State Shapes
- On Your Feet: 1824 Election Roundtable

NG Learning Framework:
Create a Political Cartoon

CHAPTER 7 REVIEW

STRIVING READERS

STRATEGY 1
SET A PURPOSE FOR READING

Before beginning a lesson, help students set a purpose for reading by prompting them to look at visuals and read the captions, titles, and headings. Tell students to write a question they expect the lesson to answer. After they have read the lesson, instruct students to answer the question in writing.

Use with All Lessons *For example, a question for Lesson 1.1 might be: How did the Industrial Revolution affect people's lives in Britain and New England?*

STRATEGY 2
FOCUS ON MAIN IDEAS

Tell students to locate the Main Idea statement at the beginning of each lesson. Explain that these statements summarize the important ideas of the lesson and help students focus on key facts and ideas. Ask students to copy the Main Idea statement into a Main Idea and Details List and then list details that support each Main Idea statement as they read the lesson.

Main Idea:
Detail:
Detail:
Detail:
Detail:
Detail:

Use with All Lessons *For example, key details from Lesson 2.4 may include ways the federal government gained greater power through the Supreme Court's landmark decisions in* Gibbons v. Ogden, Dartmouth College v. Woodward, *and* McCulloch v. Maryland, *as well as the economic outcomes of these rulings.*

STRATEGY 3
SUMMARIZE A LESSON

Instruct pairs of students to read each paragraph silently and write a sentence to summarize what they read. Tell partners to trade sentences and then work together to clarify the meaning of each paragraph. Point out to students that, taken together, the summary sentences represent a summary of the whole lesson.

Use with All Lessons *Throughout the chapter, help students get in the habit of summarizing paragraphs and sections as they read.*

INCLUSION

STRATEGY 1
USE SUPPORTED READING

Pair proficient readers with students who have reading or perception issues, and assign partners paragraphs to read aloud together. At the end of each paragraph, have students use the following sentence frames to monitor their comprehension:

• This paragraph is about _____.
• One fact that stood out to me was _____.
• I don't think I understand _____.

Be sure all students understand the content before moving on to the next paragraph.

Use with All Lessons

STRATEGY 2
WORK IN PAIRS TO UNDERSTAND MAPS

Allow students to work with others who can read the lesson aloud to them and describe the map in detail after reading the legend and other text related to the map. Instruct students to ask clarifying questions as necessary. When pairs have finished the lesson, have them work together to answer the lesson's Interpret Maps question.

Use with Lessons 2.1, 3.1, and 3.2 *Have students describe these maps in detail: U.S. Canals, 1821–1835 (Lesson 2.1), The United States, 1820 (Lesson 3.1), and Missouri Compromise, 1820 (Lesson 3.2).*

ENGLISH LANGUAGE LEARNERS

STRATEGY 1
CREATE A WORD WALL

Work with students at the **Emerging** and **Expanding** levels to select five terms from each lesson to display on a Word Wall. Choose terms students are likely to encounter in other lessons in the unit, such as *industrial revolution*, *invention*, *mass production*, *capital*, and *natural resources*. Keep the words displayed throughout the chapter, adding terms for each new lesson. Discuss each term as it comes up during reading.

Use with All Lessons

STRATEGY 2
DICTATE SENTENCE SUMMARIES

Pair students at the **Emerging** level with those at the **Bridging** level. After students read the lesson, direct them to identify three sentences that contain an important idea. Tell students to write that idea in a summary sentence using their own words. Partners then take turns dictating their sentences to each other. Encourage them to check each other's work for accuracy and spelling.

Use with All Lessons

STRATEGY 3
IDENTIFY WORD PARTS

Remind students of **All Proficiencies** that two words are often combined to make a new word. Write *waterways*, *downstream*, *upstream*, *keelboats*, *flatboats*, *backbreaking*, *steamboat*, *roadbuilding*, and *rainwater* on the board. Instruct students to copy the words and circle the two smaller words that make up each compound word. Then place students in mixed-proficiency pairs, and have them work together to define each of the two smaller words and the resulting compound word.

Use with Lesson 2.1

GIFTED & TALENTED

STRATEGY 1
CONDUCT AN INTERVIEW

Tell students to work in pairs to research the life of Denmark Vesey or Nat Turner. Prompt students to write questions a journalist might use to interview that person, focusing on the person's experiences, motivations, challenges, and achievements. Then tell them to use their research to write answers Vesey or Turner might give to those questions. Ask pairs to read their questions and answers for the class as if they are conducting an interview.

Use with Lesson 3.2

STRATEGY 2
PRESENT AN INVENTION

Direct students to choose one of the inventions or technological advances of the early 19th century. Then have them find out more about how it worked and how it impacted people's lives. Encourage students to incorporate diagrams, photographs, and other visuals to convey the mechanics and the importance of the item. Invite students to present their findings to the class and answer questions.

Use with Lessons 1.1, 1.2, and 2.1

PRE-AP

STRATEGY 1
WRITE A CAUSE-AND-EFFECT ESSAY

Remind students that most historical events have many causal factors and bring about many consequences. Challenge students to find out more about what caused the Panic of 1819 and to write an essay about both its causes and effects. Encourage them to use a graphic organizer to map out cause-and-effect relationships.

Use with Lesson 3.1

STRATEGY 2
EXPLORE IMPACTS OF GEOLOGIC HISTORY STEM

Tell students to choose a geographic feature of the Northwest Territory (lake, river, fertile valley, or plain) and to conduct research into its geologic history. Prompt them to use what they learn to write an essay examining how geologic processes created the feature and how that feature influenced westward expansion. Ask students to conclude the essay with their thoughts on the relationship of geography to history. Invite them to share their essays with the class.

Use with Lesson 3.2

REGIONAL AND NATIONAL GROWTH

1814–1831

In the mountains of West Virginia, this steam locomotive takes passengers on a scenic ride to the heights of Bald Knob, at the summit of Back Allegheny Mountain. The train, now part of Cass Scenic Railroad State Park, once hauled lumber from mountain logging camps to the sawmill in the town of Cass.

HISTORICAL THINKING How did rapid change create new opportunities and new tensions for the growing nation?

AMERICAN STORIES | American Inventions

SECTION 1 **Regional Growth**
SECTION 2 **Building a National Economy**
SECTION 3 **Changing Politics**

AMERICAN GALLERY
ONLINE | **Industrializing America**

"If we look to the history of other nations, ancient or modern, **we find no example of a growth so rapid, so gigantic, of a people so prosperous and happy.**"

—James Madison

210 CHAPTER 7

Regional and National Growth 211

INTRODUCE THE PHOTOGRAPH

A LAND OF OPPORTUNITY

Direct students' attention to the photograph and quotation that introduce this chapter. Invite them to discuss details they notice. **ASK:** What does James Madison's quotation indicate about his view of the history of the world and the place of the United States within it? *(Possible response: The quotation indicates that Madison believes the United States is superior to every other nation in world history and that it is a nation that is bigger, richer, happier, and more rapidly changing.)* **ASK:** How does the photograph connect to Madison's words? *(Possible response: The steam locomotive in the photograph is a symbol of progress and growth that made some people prosperous.)* Tell students that in this chapter they will learn how the nation grew and changed along with technological innovation and westward expansion.

SHARE BACKGROUND

In the mid-1700s, when pioneers first came to the mountains of the area that is now West Virginia, they found miles of pristine woodlands. It did not take the newcomers long to realize the area's economic potential. The earliest loggers used crosscut saws to slice up felled trees, but this method proved difficult and labor intensive and soon gave way to new technology. The development of the steam engine and the circular saw set the stage for production mills. From there, the lumber industry moved very quickly. In 1835, there were 15 steam-powered sawmills in West Virginia. By 1880, 472 lumber facilities existed. Eventually, easy access to rail lines would make logging and lumber production even more lucrative. In fact, by the late 1800s, 82 sawmills were operating just along the Chesapeake and Ohio Railroad.

For Chapter 7 Spanish Resources, visit the Resources Menu. Chapter 7 Resources are available at NGLSync.Cengage.com.

HISTORICAL THINKING QUESTION

How did rapid change create new opportunities and new tensions for the growing nation?

Numbered Heads: Challenges, Opportunities, and Growth Invite students to think about what they already know about the effects of geographic, economic, and political factors on nations. Divide the class into groups of four and direct group members to number off. Assign each group one of the following questions:

Question 1 How might geographic factors help create or shape regional economies?

Question 2 What factors might cause major changes to a nation's employment opportunities over time?

Question 3 What effects could the institution of slavery have on U.S. politics?

Question 4 What happens when a region's primary concerns are not the same as the nation's primary concerns, and how could the issue be resolved?

Allow groups sufficient time to think about their topic before coming together for a class discussion. Remind groups to give each member a chance to contribute. Then call a number and invite students with that number to report for the group.

INTRODUCE THE READING STRATEGY

DRAW CONCLUSIONS

Explain that when readers draw conclusions they connect pieces of evidence to help them formulate a larger idea. Direct students to turn to the Chapter Review and preview the graphic organizer. As students read the chapter, encourage them to draw conclusions about events, policies, movements, and people during the early decades of the 19th century.

KEY DATES FOR CHAPTER 7

1816	Second Bank of the United States is chartered
1818	National Road opens
1819	Panic of 1819 begins
1820	Missouri Compromise takes effect
1823	Monroe Doctrine is formalized
1824	John Quincy Adams is elected president
1825	Erie Canal is completed
1831	Nat Turner leads revolt

INTRODUCE CHAPTER VOCABULARY

KEY VOCABULARY

SECTION 1

abolitionist	exploitative	long-staple cotton
capital	Industrial Revolution	mass production
cotton gin	interchangeable part	short-staple cotton

SECTION 2

American System	landmark decision	patent
aqueduct	lock	subsidy
bankruptcy	market revolution	tariff
corporation	monopoly	turnpike

SECTION 3

coalition	Missouri Compromise	spoils system
49th parallel	sectionalism	unorganized territory
glacial till		

DEFINITION CHART

As students read the chapter, tell them to complete a Definition Chart for Key Vocabulary words. Instruct them to list the Key Vocabulary words in the left column of the chart. Then, as they encounter each word, they write its definition in the center column and what the word means, in their own words, in the last column. Model an example using the graphic organizer below.

Word	Definition	In My Own Words
capital	money and other assets needed to start and fund a business	start-up money

OBJECTIVES

- **Evaluate the economic effects of major inventions and innovations of the 19th century.**
- **Analyze the evolving status of women during the 19th century.**
- **Investigate the functions of the U.S. Patent Office.**
- **Study primary sources: patent diagrams and an advertisement.**

CRITICAL THINKING SKILLS FOR "AMERICAN INVENTIONS"

- Make Connections
- Draw Conclusions
- Analyze Cause and Effect
- Make Inferences

CONNECT TO THE CHAPTER

This American Story examines pivotal inventions that profoundly changed the U.S. economy in the 19th and 20th centuries. Through a narrative that focuses on the effects of innovation on agriculture and other sectors—accompanied by photographs and patent diagrams—students will recognize how technological advances are important to U.S. history.

The chapter, Regional and National Growth, examines the expansion of the United States, both as a nation and as an economic force in the world. This American Story will help students better understand how specific innovations developed during the American Industrial Revolution raised U.S. economic potential. Introduce "American Inventions" after students have completed Lesson 1.1 to illustrate ways in which the Industrial Revolution impacted American society.

HISTORY NOTEBOOK

Encourage students to complete the American Story page for Chapter 7 in their History Notebooks as they read.

CRITICAL VIEWING Possible responses: Inventions like the steel plow made work easier and faster. Technological improvements meant that more crops or other goods could be produced with less labor, making them cheaper for consumers. With less labor needed, however, some people might have lost their jobs.

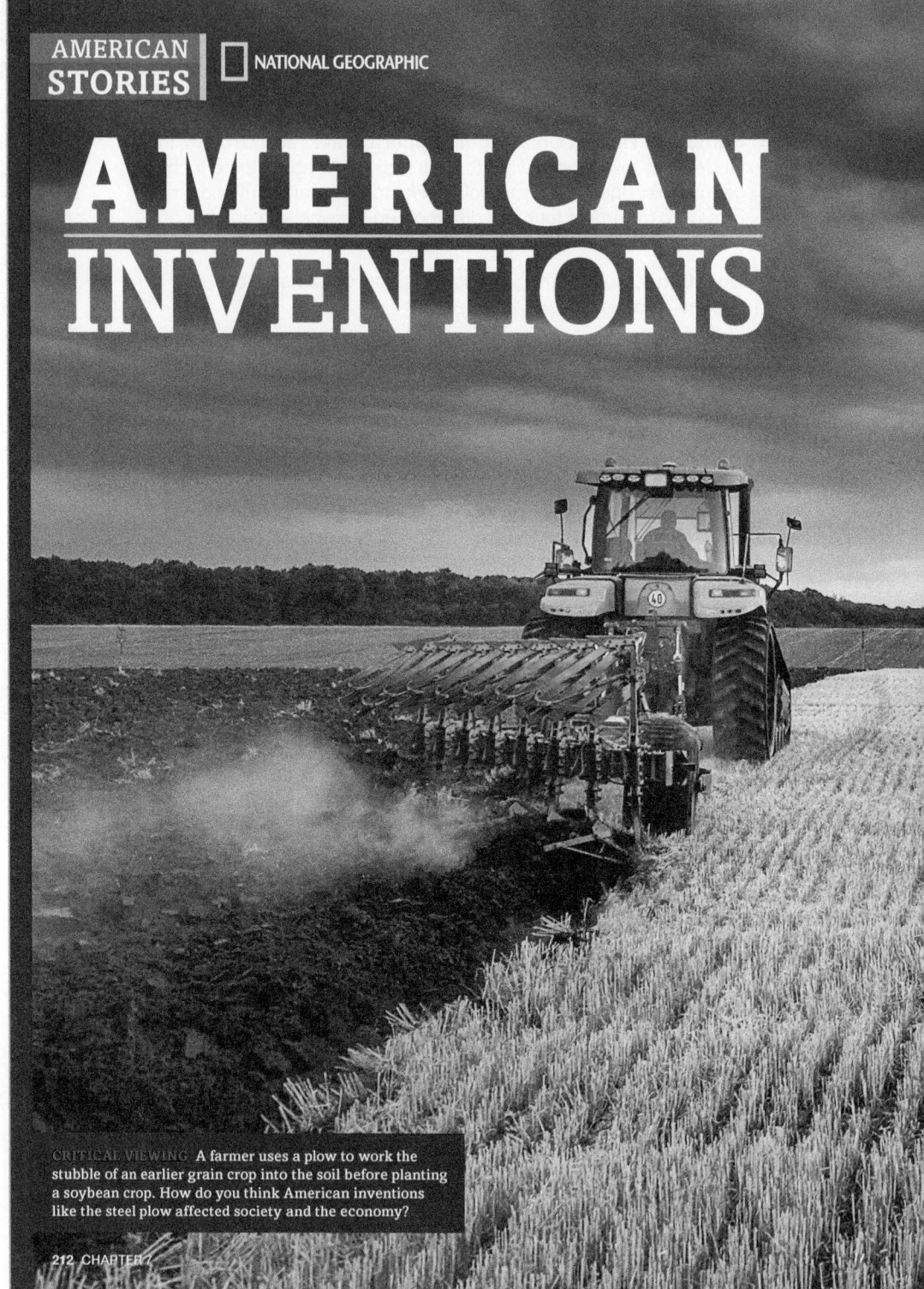

AMERICAN STORIES | NATIONAL GEOGRAPHIC

AMERICAN INVENTIONS

CRITICAL VIEWING A farmer uses a plow to work the stubble of an earlier grain crop into the soil before planting a soybean crop. How do you think American inventions like the steel plow affected society and the economy?

The first half of the 19th century was a time of vigorous economic growth in the United States, fired in part by industrial innovations imported from Britain, but also by American inventions that revolutionized the fields of manufacturing, communication, and agriculture. This American Story highlights a few of the American inventions that helped spur the country's growth in the 19th century and laid the groundwork for the economy and technologies of the 21st century.

AGRICULTURE: THE COTTON GIN AND THE STEEL PLOW

The agriculture and economy of two American regions, the Midwest and the South, were each largely shaped by a single invention. In the South, that invention was the cotton gin, patented by Eli Whitney in 1794. The cotton gin consisted mainly of a rotating drum with protruding hooks that could separate the seeds from cotton plants 50 times more quickly than a person doing the job by hand. Whitney's invention had an enormous effect on the economy of the southern states, vastly improving the productivity of cotton plantations. By the middle of the 19th century, cotton was the United States' leading export. Cotton's increased profitability due to the cotton gin had unintended social consequences. Both the plantation system and slavery became more deeply entrenched in the South as the demand for labor to harvest the ever larger cotton crops increased.

In the region we now call the Midwest, the crucial invention was the steel plow. The fields of grain that stretch from horizon to horizon in Iowa, Nebraska, Kansas, and other states may be said to have originated from this innovation. In the first decades of the 19th century, settlers were pouring into the western territories seeking to establish farms. The cast iron plows they brought with them from the East, however, did a poor job of breaking through the rich but sticky prairie soil. Farmers were forced to stop frequently and remove the clumps of soil that accumulated on their plow blades.

In 1837, a young blacksmith from Illinois named John Deere forged a plow using steel instead of cast iron while also giving the plow a slightly different shape. Combined, these two innovations allowed Deere's plow to cut cleanly through the dense soil. Farmers eagerly adopted the invention, which they nicknamed the "singing plow" because they claimed it made a musical sound as it dug furrows in the prairie soil. John Deere continued innovating and improving his designs, and by 1846, he was producing 1,000 plows a year. In the 21st century, the John Deere Company is one of the world's largest manufacturers of agricultural equipment.

DISCUSS THE IMPORTANCE OF CREATIVITY

Ask students to discuss their thoughts about human creativity, focusing on contemporary examples of American creativity in the following areas:

- science and medicine
- technology
- manufacturing
- literature
- visual and performing arts

Encourage students to elaborate on how the United States benefits from the creativity of its citizens. Then tell them that the 19th century was a time of enormous creative output, leading to a wealth of important American inventions and innovations.

BACKGROUND FOR THE TEACHER

JOHN DEERE, INNOVATOR

Soon after John Deere moved from Vermont to Grand Detour, Illinois, in 1837, he discovered that the soil in this rural area was thicker and tougher than the soil in the East. Inspired by the desire to make it easier to plow this soil, Deere and his partner, Major Leonard Andrus, fashioned a new plowshare by repurposing an old steel blade from a sawmill. A plowshare is the part of a plow that cuts a path through the soil. They polished the new blade until it was so smooth that not even the dampest soil would stick to it. The end product was the steel plow, patent number 46,454, and it would make Deere a rich man. Determined to stay far ahead of his competitors, Deere continued refining his designs and pioneered the idea of mass-producing plows. By the mid-1800s, he was selling more than 13,000 plows a year. The company Deere founded in 1868 still survives, with international manufacturing contract revenues of more than $34 billion.

INVENTIONS BY AMERICAN WOMEN

Sybilla Masters, the wife of a Philadelphia merchant, is among the earliest known female colonial inventors. In 1712, she invented a corn mill that used mechanical hammers instead of the typical grinding wheels to process maize into meal. Unable to successfully file a patent in the colonies, she took her design to England. In 1715, her husband filed the patent, but the design plans and description on the filing clearly show that it was Sybilla Masters's invention. With this filing, she became the first colonist, male or female, to receive an English patent. After the formation of the United States, the Patent Act of 1790 was passed, allowing citizens the right to patent their inventions, and women, such as those noted on the time line, could apply for patents in their own names. **ASK:** In your opinion, what does the time line reveal about the place of women in the 19th and 20th centuries? *(Possible response: While women in the 19th and 20th centuries struggled for equal rights, they also developed complex and ingenious inventions.)*

TYPING IT UP

Tell students that QWERTY keyboards are named for the order of the first letters in the top letter row, but debates continue over why QWERTY became the standard letter arrangement. One theory says that a typewriter's mechanical levers jammed less often when commonly used pairs of letters were spatially separated. Another suggests that placing the letters out of alphabetical order slowed typists down, again leading to fewer lever jams. A third suggests that the QWERTY arrangement allowed telegraph operators to type more quickly by placing certain letter combinations close together. **ASK:** Why do you think the QWERTY arrangement is used on computer keyboards today, even though jamming levers and telegraph-operator speed are no longer issues? *(Possible response: Once QWERTY became the standard and people learned to type in that system, they would buy only QWERTY typewriters. New generations learned on available machines, so the cycle continued.)*

CRITICAL VIEWING Possible response: The advertisement suggests that buyers will feel happy to have the best machine and confident that they can sew stylish clothing for people of all ages, suggested by the variety of clothing shown on the people in the ad.

MANUFACTURING: THE SEWING MACHINE

Elias Howe, an American machinist, was not the first person to imagine or even to build a sewing machine. However, he was the first to create and patent a device that incorporated key features of modern home and industrial sewing machines. One of these was a new form of needle that allowed for a type of stitching called a lockstitch. To see an example of lockstitch sewing, you can examine the hem of almost any machine-sewn garment in your wardrobe.

With Howe's sewing machine, garments could be made much more quickly and cheaply. The New York clothing maker Brooks Brothers, for example, was able to make its overcoats in six days, rather than three weeks, and sell the coats at a lower price. As companies adopted sewing machines, garment factories expanded, and employment opportunities opened up for workers, especially women. A *New York Times* article from January 7, 1860, paints an optimistic picture of "sewing girls," claiming that "it is no uncommon thing for those who, toiling night and day, could earn only one or two dollars per week, to now receive from three to ten dollars per week for operating a sewing machine." By the early 20th century, the Chicago clothing maker Hart, Schaffner & Marx alone employed 8,000 workers. Today, garment factories using sewing machines based on Howe's novel ideas employ millions of people worldwide.

CRITICAL VIEWING The French phrase *la meilleure* in this 1900 advertisement for an Elias Howe sewing machine means "the best." How do you think the ad is supposed to make people feel about purchasing a Howe sewing machine? What details in the image support your response?

INVENTIONS BY AMERICAN WOMEN

There is no way of knowing how many American inventions were created, at least in part, by women because women were not allowed to apply for patents in the country's early years. Some historians believe, for example, that plantation owner Catherine Greene was the principal designer of the cotton gin, but she could not patent the invention under her name. This time line traces notable inventions by American women between 1813 and 1975.

1871 machine for making paper bags (Margaret Knight)

1813 circular saw (Tabitha Babbitt)

1825

TYPING IT UP

The first commercially successful writing machine—or typewriter—was the result of intensive research by inventors Christopher Latham Sholes, Carlos Glidden, and Samuel Soulé in Milwaukee, Wisconsin. Others had tried to invent similar machines, but most of them were difficult to use and very large—as big as a piano in some cases.

In June 1868, Sholes filed a patent for a small, more efficient typewriter that could put words onto paper far faster than a pen. The machine featured the QWERTY keyboard still used on computer keyboards today, a cylinder that placed equal spaces between each typed line, and key levers that struck an ink ribbon to print each letter on the inserted sheet of paper.

In 1873, Sholes contracted with the New York gun manufacturer E. Remington and Sons, to mass-produce the typewriters. The machines were soon renamed "Remingtons." Author Mark Twain owned a Remington and was the first writer to submit a typed book manuscript to a publisher.

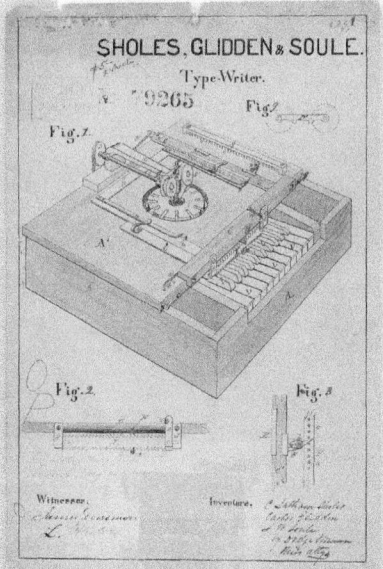

Sholes's 1868 typewriter patent (above) featured a machine that could type only in capital letters. A shift key introduced in 1878 allowed capitals and lowercase letters.

CRITICAL VIEWING The design of this typewriter prevented the typist from seeing the words while he or she typed. What differences do you observe between early typewriters and computer keyboards?

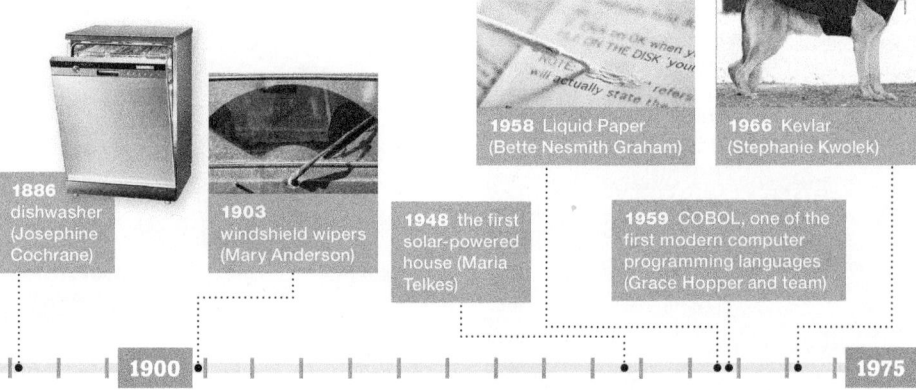

1886 dishwasher (Josephine Cochrane)

1903 windshield wipers (Mary Anderson)

1948 the first solar-powered house (Maria Telkes)

1958 Liquid Paper (Bette Nesmith Graham)

1959 COBOL, one of the first modern computer programming languages (Grace Hopper and team)

1966 Kevlar (Stephanie Kwolek)

1900   1975

TEACH

GUIDED DISCUSSION

1. **Analyze Cause and Effect** How did the cotton gin, used mostly in the South, likely impact the economy of the industrial Northeast? *(Possible response: The cotton gin likely caused the economy of the Northeast to grow immensely, because it allowed greater quantities of cotton to be produced in the South and shipped to textile mills in the Northeast. The influx of raw product probably led to an increase in hiring at the textile mills.)*

2. **Make Inferences** Why do you think a sewing girl's basic pay rose from $1 or $2 per week to between $3 and $10 per week following the invention of the sewing machine? *(Possible response: Sewing girls gained a valuable skill in learning how to use a sewing machine. Some of the increased revenue from faster and more profitable manufacturing was likely passed along to the workers.)*

ACTIVE OPTIONS

On Your Feet: Invention Impact Post the following signs in different corners of the classroom for a Three Corners activity: Steel Plow, Sewing Machine, Telegraph. Organize students into groups around these signs, and prompt them to discuss the role their assigned invention played in building the 19th-century U.S. economy. Encourage students to consider changes to society, business, and politics that took place as a result of the invention. Ask a representative from each group to share a summary with the class.

NG Learning Framework: Describe a Useful Invention STEM

SKILL Problem-Solving

KNOWLEDGE Our Human Story

Ask students to reflect on the daily activities of people in their community and then think of an invention that would make a household or community task easier to accomplish. Tell them to write a description of the invention and to include sketches or diagrams to illustrate how it would work. Invite students to share their finished designs with the class.

CRITICAL VIEWING Possible responses: The keys on a computer keyboard are flatter than on a typewriter. There are more keys on computer keyboards, such as function keys, arrow keys, and a numeral pad.

EVERYDAY TREASURES

Until the beginning of the 19th century, rotten teeth, gum infections, and tooth extractions were commonplace, largely because of limited dental hygiene practices. Then a dentist named Levi Spear Parmly encouraged his patients to use silk thread to clean the spaces between their teeth. Dental floss didn't catch on at first, but improvements to both the dispenser and the thread helped it gain in popularity. Today dental floss is sold everywhere. **ASK:** Which inventions on the time line are less important today than they once were? *(Possible responses: Mail-order catalogs are outdated because of television shopping channels and online retailers. Pencil erasers and paper clips have declined in use as a result of paperless technologies.)*

THE U.S. PATENT OFFICE

The U.S. Patent and Trademark Office grants different types of patents. Utility patents protect functional inventions or improvements to existing inventions, such as machines or processes. Design patents protect the design or appearance of an invention, not how it works. When applying for a patent, inventors must submit detailed specifications. **ASK:** Why must patent applications and specifications be as accurate as possible? *(Possible response: The specifications need to be accurate because other people might want to design improvements and because the Patent Office needs to determine whether the submitted invention or improvement is unique.)*

WRITE ABOUT HISTORY

Write an Obituary Invite students to write an obituary for Catherine Greene, Christopher Latham Sholes, or another of the inventors mentioned. Tell them to include biographical information from the American Story and from online resources. Provide guidance about the structure of and elements in most obituaries. After students have completed their first drafts, encourage them to exchange their work with a partner and suggest corrections and revisions. Invite students to read the completed obituaries aloud to the class or post them on the class or school website.

THINK ABOUT IT

Answers will vary. Possible response: The telegraph was the most influential invention because it opened up communications across the United States and led the way for the telephone, cable television, and the Internet.

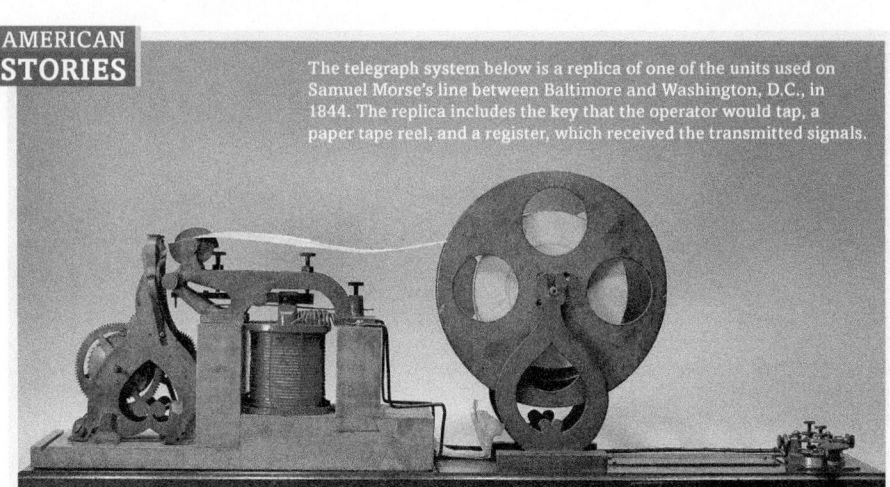

AMERICAN STORIES

The telegraph system below is a replica of one of the units used on Samuel Morse's line between Baltimore and Washington, D.C., in 1844. The replica includes the key that the operator would tap, a paper tape reel, and a register, which received the transmitted signals.

COMMUNICATION: THE TELEGRAPH

At the start of the 19th century, long-distance communication was carried out via trains, horseback riders, mail carriages, and ships. As a consequence, it was both slow and unreliable. In the 1830s and 1840s, the American inventor and painter Samuel Morse built on the work of other thinkers to solve this problem by designing an easy-to-operate telegraph.

Morse's telegraph was a simple device. An operator tapped a key that completed an electrical circuit, sending a signal along a wire to another telegraph. The operator could transmit patterns of long and short signals (called "dots" and "dashes") that would be recorded on a piece of paper moving through the receiving telegraph. Each pattern represented a letter of the alphabet in a code developed by Morse, which is still known as Morse Code.

The telegraph quickly found a multitude of civilian and military uses. Journalists on assignment could rapidly transmit stories to newspapers back home. During the Civil War, army units would string telegraph wires as they advanced so that they could receive orders and relay intelligence without delays.

An article in *Harper's Weekly* magazine from 1862 reported on the Union Army's use of the telegraph: "The army signal-telegraph has been so far perfected that in a few hours quite a large force can be in constant connection with head-quarters. This, while a battle is progressing, is a great convenience."

Perhaps as important as the telegraph device itself was the network of wires that were strung across the continent, and then the world, to connect all the individual telegraphs. This network would evolve into the system that carries 21st-century instant communication through telephones and the Internet.

THINK ABOUT IT

Which invention do you think had the greatest influence on the American economy or society in the 21st century?

EVERYDAY TREASURES

Not every invention must be large or momentous to have a noteworthy effect on our everyday lives. Each of these American innovations dating from the 19th century or earlier has made its particular contribution to our comfort, convenience, or pleasure.

1774 mail order catalog

1796 cupcake

1806 coffee percolator

1775   1800

THE U.S. PATENT OFFICE

The framers of the U.S. Constitution were anxious to encourage new ideas by ensuring that inventors could reap the benefits of their work. Article 1, Section 8, Clause 8 of the Constitution states that the legislative branch should "promote the progress of science and useful arts, by securing for limited times to authors and inventors the exclusive right to their respective writings and discoveries."

The United States Patent and Trademark Office is the agency that oversees the fulfillment of this constitutional mandate. An inventor can file an application with the patent office, describing the invention in detail. If the agency recognizes that the invention is original and does not duplicate an existing invention, it issues a document called a patent. Receiving a patent provides certain rights and protections to an inventor, including the right to exclude all others from exploiting the invention to make money for up to 20 years. At the same time, the patent document is available to the public, so that others may study the invention and improve on it.

The United States is not the only country with a government patent office. An international treaty exists to allow inventors to seek patents internationally.

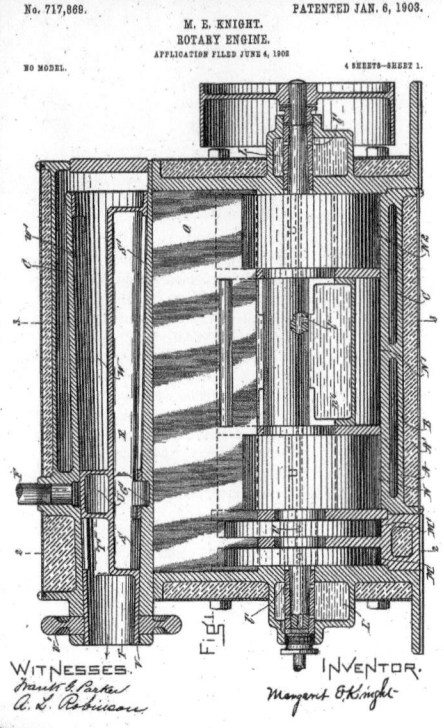

This specification for improvements to the rotary engine was filed by Margaret Knight with the U.S. Patent Office in 1902.

1815 dental floss
1829 Graham cracker
1843 ice cream maker for home use
1847 doughnut
1849 safety pin
1859 pencil eraser
1867 paper clip
1874 spork

1825 — 1850 — 1875

Regional and National Growth **217**

DIFFERENTIATE

ENGLISH LANGUAGE LEARNERS

Expand Vocabulary Direct students at the **Emerging** level to reread the lesson and list any words they would like to better understand. Then ask them to work with a partner at the **Bridging** or **Expanding** level who can help them add two or three synonyms or examples after each word. Model using the word *garment*.

> *garment*: clothes, dress, shirt

After pairs have completed their lists, prompt them to create an original sentence for each word.

PRE-AP

Report on an Invention Direct students to choose a product used today that has its roots in a 19th-century invention. Prompt them to conduct research about the invention's origins, its patent history (including patents for improvements), and its evolution into the product available today. Invite students to present their findings to the class as an oral report, and encourage them to display photographs or illustrations of the invention at different points in its development.

HISTORICAL THINKING

Ask and have students answer the following questions.

1. **READING CHECK** What new technologies were responsible for the massive growth of the U.S. economy in the first half of the 19th century?

2. **ANALYZE CAUSE AND EFFECT** What effects might the sewing machine have had on middle-class families following its availability to the public?

3. **MAKE INFERENCES** Why do you think it took so long for female inventors in the United States to receive patents for their work?

ANSWERS

1. The cotton gin and the steel plow drove production in the agricultural sector, the sewing machine drove growth in the manufacturing sector, and the telegraph revolutionized communication and laid the groundwork for future innovations.

2. Possible response: Having a sewing machine would have made making clothes for the family quicker and easier and freed time for other pursuits. Some people might have started a home sewing business.

3. Possible response: American society was more patriarchal in the 18th and 19th centuries than it is today. Women lacked many rights, and their ideas were not valued as highly as men's.

THE INDUSTRIAL REVOLUTION

By definition, a revolution involves dramatic change. The American Revolution gave birth to the United States. Just a few decades later, a different type of revolution transformed the way most Americans lived.

THE EFFECTS OF THE WAR OF 1812

Even though the War of 1812 ended in a stalemate, many Americans felt a sense of triumph. The United States had held its own against Great Britain, the most powerful military force in the world. The war inspired nationalism among Americans as it reinforced the nation's independence and sovereignty. Soon after peace returned, the newly confident United States entered a period of economic growth driven by industry.

Riding the wave of optimism that swept across the country, James Monroe, Madison's secretary of state, easily won the 1816 presidential election, becoming the third straight Democratic-Republican

from Virginia to hold that office. During his distinguished career, Monroe had served as a delegate to the Continental Congress, senator from Virginia, and governor of Virginia before Jefferson sent him to France to help negotiate the terms of the Louisiana Purchase. He had earned a reputation for honesty and dependability.

Monroe and his wife Elizabeth set a new tone for the presidency, with greater emphasis on style, entertaining, and celebrating the new national stature of the United States. The Monroes had the executive mansion painted a brilliant white to cover the smoke stains that remained from the fire set by the British forces during the war. The mansion has ever since been known as the "White House."

Between 1831 and 1866, this steam locomotive powered New Jersey's first railroad train. The British-built engine was called the "John Bull," after a fictional figure that represents Great Britain in the same way Uncle Sam personifies the United States for some people.

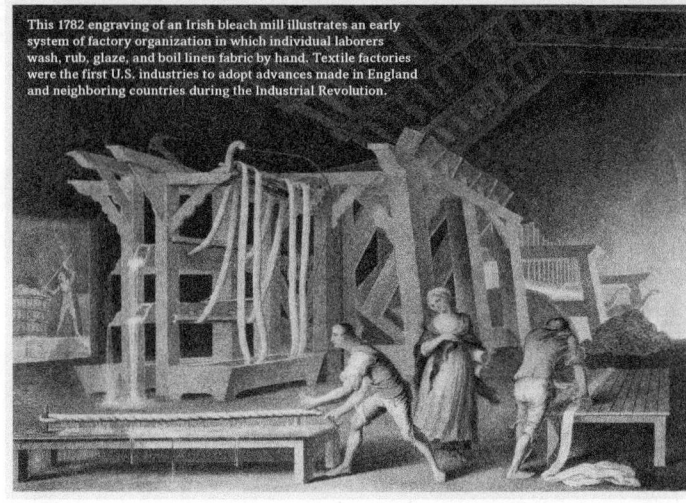

This 1782 engraving of an Irish bleach mill illustrates an early system of factory organization in which individual laborers wash, rub, glaze, and boil linen fabric by hand. Textile factories were the first U.S. industries to adopt advances made in England and neighboring countries during the Industrial Revolution.

The country that Monroe presided over was united in name, but its various regions had developed different economic strengths and distinct cultures. Sometimes the states had sharply conflicting policies, and their economies did not connect with one another very effectively. Certain similarities persisted across all regions, however. For example, most Americans in the early 1800s supported themselves through farming. They had few possessions and little money, and they made many of the things they needed by hand, including clothing and basic tools. For other items, they relied on skilled artisans, or craftspeople, in their communities. But a change was coming.

THE INDUSTRIAL REVOLUTION IN BRITAIN

Roughly a half-century earlier, in the mid-1700s, a sweeping transformation had begun in Great Britain that historians would later call the **Industrial Revolution**. The name implies rapid change, but this revolution unfolded over the course of many decades. It was characterized by a number of technological developments, each influencing the next advancement. One of the most significant of these developments was the invention of the steam engine to power factories and, when used in a vehicle such as a train locomotive, to transport goods. New machines greatly increased production

while decreasing the amount of human effort needed to perform specific tasks. These machines included the spinning jenny, which spun thread, and the power loom, which wove thread into cloth. The two inventions played a major role in completely transforming the way textiles were produced.

Another key development was the introduction of **interchangeable parts**, or precisely manufactured parts that are identical to one another. Using such parts, unskilled workers could quickly assemble products such as firearms. Interchangeable parts made possible **mass production**, or the production of manufactured goods in great quantities. Previously, such goods were made in small workshops by skilled artisans who crafted each part individually.

The Industrial Revolution began in Britain for many reasons. Britain enjoyed an abundance of flowing rivers and coal, natural resources that could provide energy to power the newly invented machines. Further, Britain's expanding network of roads, canals, and, eventually, railroads made it relatively easy and inexpensive to transport raw materials and finished goods over long distances. British investors were willing to provide large amounts of **capital**, or money needed to fund a business. They invested

---

OBJECTIVE

Explore the rise of American manufacturing during the U.S. Industrial Revolution.

CRITICAL THINKING SKILLS FOR LESSON 1.1

- Draw Conclusions
- Analyze Cause and Effect
- Form and Support Opinions
- Summarize
- Identify Main Ideas and Details
- Analyze Visuals
- Evaluate
- Analyze Primary Sources

HISTORICAL THINKING FOR CHAPTER 7

How did rapid change create new opportunities and new tensions for the growing nation? The transition from an agrarian to a manufacturing economy dramatically altered the lives of many working Americans. Lesson 1.1 describes some of the changes put in motion by the Industrial Revolution.

BACKGROUND FOR THE TEACHER

In the early 1830s, a young steamboat mechanic named Isaac Dripps built a locomotive engine from parts sent from England to New Jersey's Camden and Amboy Railroad. The "John Bull" was considered one of the highest quality locomotives of the day, but it tended to derail. To improve on the design, Dripps added a frame with an extra set of wheels out in front of the train. These wheels made the train more stable by guiding it over uneven rails and around tight curves. The new American design worked so well that the Camden and Amboy Railroad bought 15 more. Within a decade, American manufacturers had created a thriving business exporting locomotives to other countries. The Smithsonian Institution eventually acquired the original John Bull locomotive, which is still on display for the public.

HISTORY NOTEBOOK

Encourage students to complete the American Gallery page for Chapter 7 in their History Notebooks as they read.

INTRODUCE & ENGAGE

EXPLORE MASS PRODUCTION

Write the term *mass production* on the board. Ask students to discuss what they already know about mass production and provide a class definition for the term. Write their collective definition on the board. **ASK:** What types of products do you think are mass produced, and what types do you think are not? Explain your answer. *(Answers will vary. Possible response: Automobiles, computers, and other standard products are mass produced because building many at one time makes each one cheaper to build and to buy. Original artwork is not mass produced because each piece is meant to be unique.)* Tell students that in this lesson they will learn how the Industrial Revolution in the United States moved the country from an agrarian to a manufacturing economy.

TEACH

GUIDED DISCUSSION

1. **Draw Conclusions** Why do you think different U.S. regions developed widely varying economic and cultural trends? *(Possible response: Geography and settlement patterns influence both the economy and the culture that develops in a place. The economies and cultures of two regions could be as different as the natural resources available in each area and the heritage of the settlers who live there.)*

2. **Summarize** How did the textile industry change during the Industrial Revolution? *(The Industrial Revolution introduced such inventions as the spinning jenny, which spun thread by machine rather than by hand, and the power loom, which could automatically weave cloth from thread. These devices saved time, increased textile output, and lowered production costs.)*

3. **Identify Main Ideas and Details** How did the natural resources available in Britain and the United States help bring about each nation's Industrial Revolution? *(In both countries, rivers and waterways provided energy to power mills, and an abundance of mineral resources, such as coal and iron ore, was mined and used to fuel industrial furnaces.)*

ANALYZE VISUALS

Guide students to view the color engraving of the workers at the bleach mill, and prompt them to discuss details they notice. **ASK:** How does the engraving of the millworkers illustrate workplace and production changes leading up to the Industrial Revolution? *(The workers are in a large building instead of in their homes and there are different stations, each for a different purpose. However, there are no machines, and each worker is carrying out a task by hand.)* Invite students to write a brief paragraph about the mood the engraving evokes.

DIFFERENTIATE

STRIVING READERS

Complete a Venn Diagram Tell students to use a Venn diagram to take notes while they read about the similarities and differences between the British Industrial Revolution and the American Industrial Revolution. Invite them to compare their completed diagrams with a partner's and discuss any differences. Encourage students to think about the roles that natural resources, people, and inventions played in each revolution and about how the American Industrial Revolution built upon the British one.

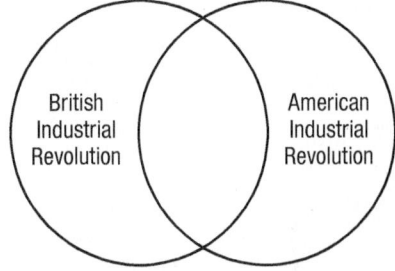

PRE-AP

Connect Past and Present Instruct students to conduct research into Francis Cabot Lowell's business and financial practices. In particular, they might investigate how Lowell "researched" the technology of textile mills in Britain, then raised money from wealthy individuals and used it to build a mill that covered the entire production process from raw fiber to finished cloth. Students might also explore how the mill generated large profits for the mill's shareholders. Tell them to use what they learn to write an essay about Lowell's practices and how they relate to corporations, stock shareholders, venture capital, vertical integration, intellectual property, and industrial espionage today.

See the Chapter Planner for more strategies for differentiation.

heavily in machines and factories, hoping to make a healthy profit when the enterprises succeeded. They eventually extended their investments throughout the United Kingdom, which, by 1801, included the countries of England, Scotland, Wales, and Ireland.

The Industrial Revolution brought profound changes to Britain. The old economy based on agriculture and handicrafts gave way to a new economy focused on manufacturing and industry. Society shifted from an agrarian economy and became far more urbanized as large numbers of people left farms to work in factories, which were usually located in cities.

THE AMERICAN INDUSTRIAL REVOLUTION

The advances of the early Industrial Revolution gave Great Britain's textile industry a tremendous advantage over its rivals in other countries. To keep this advantage, the government prohibited skilled workers from emigrating and forbade the export of textile machinery and drawings of that machinery.

In late 1789, a young cotton-mill worker named Samuel Slater left Britain illegally and sailed to the United States. In 1793, with the support of a wealthy American businessman, he built the first water-powered textile mill in Pawtucket, Rhode Island. Amazingly, he built it from memory. Slater constructed a spinning frame, a machine that produced stronger threads than regular spinning wheels. Since no satisfactory power loom yet existed, Slater's mill performed only the first two steps of cloth production: carding, or preparing the cotton fibers for spinning, and spinning the thread. Slater distributed the thread to local farm families, who wove cloth on looms in their homes. The textile industry became the first American industry to use methods of mass production. Slater has been called the "father of the American factory system" for the way he divided factory work into simple steps.

Even so, the United States continued to rely heavily on Great Britain for imports of textiles and other manufactured goods into the early 1800s. But then Britain imposed trade restrictions on the United States for continuing to do business with France while the two European powers were at war with each other. As you have read, Congress responded by passing the Embargo Act of 1807, which prohibited all foreign trade. This act and the subsequent War of 1812 nearly cut off all British imports. The U.S. economy suffered, leading to hardship among farmers, who could no longer sell their produce for export, and New England merchants, who had relied on international trade. The American textile industry, however, eventually benefited from the trade disruption. U.S. manufacturers developed their own power looms and other technologies to increase production and sell to people who had formerly bought imported textiles.

As in Great Britain, a wealth of natural resources played an important role in the early stages of the American Industrial Revolution. The United States had an abundance of waterpower, the energy derived from flowing rivers and waterfalls, that could be harnessed to drive machinery. It also had plenty of iron ore and coal. The coal could be burned to power steam engines and to fuel the furnaces used in the production of iron and steel.

NEW ENGLAND'S TEXTILE MILLS

In 1810, almost 20 years after Samuel Slater's textile mill began operating, a Boston businessman named Francis Cabot Lowell traveled to Great Britain for a two-year visit. Through his business connections, he toured textile mills in Scotland and in the English county of Lancashire and became fascinated by the water-powered looms that wove thread into cloth at great speed, generating wealth for the mill owners. He carefully studied the looms, memorizing details of their construction and workings.

Upon returning home, Lowell worked with an engineer to recreate a power loom from memory. He and two business partners raised $400,000 in capital—a spectacular sum at the time—from a group of investors called the Boston Associates. In 1813, ten miles west of Boston, they opened the Boston Manufacturing Company, the first factory that combined all the steps of making cloth under a single roof. The company started as a four-story textile mill built along the Charles River in Waltham, Massachusetts, where a waterfall with a ten-foot drop offered free waterpower. Bales of cotton entered the mill, and bolts of cloth left it. This represented the real beginning of the Industrial Revolution in the United States.

Unlike earlier textile mills, Lowell's Waltham factory used unskilled labor and machines for weaving, which had been the most expensive part of the cloth-making process. Lowell and his partners were concerned that the introduction of factories into the United States might create the same problems with child labor and poverty-stricken workers they had seen during their visits to England. With this in mind, they recruited young New England farm women and girls as "operatives," or factory workers. The operatives, unlike British laborers, considered millwork a three- or four-year commitment before they left the factory, often to marry and raise a family. They worked 14 hours a day, 6 days a week, and earned $2.00 a week or more, depending on the type of job they performed.

By today's standards, the long hours and the often unpleasant and dangerous working conditions that the "mill girls" endured seem **exploitative**, or unfair and abusive. At the time, however, their employment

PRIMARY SOURCE

Harriet Hanson Robinson worked in a textile mill in Lowell, Massachusetts, from 1834, when she was only 10 years old, until 1848. In a report for the state of Massachusetts and later in her autobiography, she describes how work in the mills transformed the lives of local women.

We can hardly realize what a change the cotton factory made in the status of the working women. Hitherto woman had always been a money saving rather than a money earning, member of the community. Her labor could command but small return. If she worked out as servant, or "help," her wages were from 50 cents to $1.00 a week; or, if she went from house to house by the day to spin and weave, or do tailoress [seamstress] work, she could get but 75 cents a week and her meals. As teacher, her services were not in demand, and the arts, the professions, and even the trades and industries, were nearly all closed to her.

—from *Early Factory Labor in New England* by Harriet H. Robinson, 1889

represented a significant step forward for society. It was rare in the early 1800s for women to have the freedom to leave their homes, live on their own, and earn their own money. The Boston Manufacturing Company provided housing and offered greater educational and cultural opportunities than the girls and women would have encountered at home.

The Waltham mill was tremendously profitable, and in 1822 its investors broke ground for a larger mill located 30 miles northwest of Boston. The mill was the centerpiece of the country's first planned industrial town, which was given the name "Lowell" in honor of the man who had transformed the U.S. textile industry. In the following decades, the Boston Associates continued to expand their textile empire into Lawrence, Massachusetts, and other parts of New England.

HISTORICAL THINKING

1. **READING CHECK** How were most goods produced in the United States before the Industrial Revolution?

2. **DRAW CONCLUSIONS** What role did capital play in the Industrial Revolution?

3. **ANALYZE CAUSE AND EFFECT** How did trade with Britain affect the American Industrial Revolution?

4. **FORM AND SUPPORT OPINIONS** Do you think the "operatives" who worked at the Lowell mill were exploited as workers? Support your opinion with evidence from the text.

This illustration, copied from an oil painting by an unknown artist, shows Samuel Slater's first U.S. mechanical cotton mill rising up above nearby buildings and Rhode Island's Pawtucket Falls.

BUILD BACKGROUND

THE RHODE ISLAND SYSTEM

When Samuel Slater left Britain, he had memorized the designs of the textile machines he had worked with, but he had no capital or business organization. Once in the United States, however, Slater found a backer for his ultimate plan—an American textile mill based on the latest British innovations. His benefactor was a wealthy Quaker businessman named Moses Brown. By 1803, Slater and his brother were employing entire families to live and work at the mill. This model proved highly successful, and the Slaters had no problem attracting plenty of workers. They later expanded the mill into a village, Slatersville, adding a company store and tenement housing for their workers. Slater's idea of a village dedicated to the needs of millworkers caught on. Known as the Rhode Island System, it served as a model for other mill owners throughout New England, including Francis Cabot Lowell.

THE BOSTON ASSOCIATES

In creating the Boston Manufacturing Company, Francis Cabot Lowell and his associates realized that a small partnership would not fit the needs of their large-scale operation. Instead, Lowell proposed a system of joint-stock shareholders who could hold or sell their stock in the company and gain dividends from company profits, which they could then reinvest. In normal partnership undertakings of the day, the owners gained the company's rewards, but they also suffered its setbacks. With Lowell's model, stockholders had only very limited liability for the company's losses. The state of Massachusetts also granted Lowell and his associates a great deal of flexibility to create the company's internal systems and by-laws, as long as they complied with certain rules, such as maintaining a corporate treasurer. In creating this system, Lowell revolutionized how corporations were financed.

GUIDED DISCUSSION

4. Evaluate How did British trade restrictions against the United States during the War of 1812 both damage and improve the U.S. economy? *(British import-export restrictions damaged the agricultural economy through Britain's refusal to import U.S. crops and other products. However, by stopping exports of goods to the United States, Britain led U.S. manufacturers to increased levels of self-reliance and technological innovation, which fueled the rise of the U.S. textile industry.)*

5. Analyze Primary Sources What evidence does Harriet H. Robinson use to assert that working in textile mills benefited female workers? *(Instead of telling about specific benefits from working in a mill, Robinson tells about the disadvantages women had previously faced—charged with saving money for the household rather than making it themselves, making little money from the few opportunities that were open to women, and being excluded from those jobs that offered better pay.)*

6. Analyze Visuals Direct students' attention to the painting of Pawtucket Falls. **ASK:** What details in the painting convey the idea that the river would be a good resource for Samuel Slater's mill? *(Possible response: The river is large and seems to be moving quickly over the falls, both making it a reliable source of power for the mill.)*

MORE INFORMATION

Harriet Hanson Robinson Harriet Hanson Robinson's talents went far beyond her childhood work as a bobbin doffer at a Lowell textile mill. In fact, over the years, she became a well-known writer and activist. While still employed at the mill she supplied the millworkers' newspaper, the *Lowell Offering*, with prose and poems that went on to be republished and achieve national recognition. In 1881, Robinson organized the National Woman Suffrage Association of Massachusetts, and, in the early 1890s, she founded the General Federation of Women's Clubs, an organization that promoted the arts, the environment, and public education.

ACTIVE OPTIONS

Active History: Evaluate Industrial Revolution Inventions Extend the lesson by using either the PDF or Whiteboard version of the activity. These activities take a deeper look at a topic from, or related to, the lesson. Explore the activities as a class, turn them into group assignments, or even assign them individually.

AMERICAN **GALLERY**
ONLINE
Industrializing America Invite students to explore the American Gallery. Have them select one of the images and do additional research to learn more about it. Ask questions about the chosen gallery image, such as: What is this? Where is this? What is its purpose? Why does it belong in this chapter? What else would you like to know about it?

For students who develop an interest in Industrial Revolution inventions, suggest that they read the American Story at the beginning of this chapter.

ANSWERS

1. Before the Industrial Revolution, skilled craftspeople made goods by hand.

2. The new machines and large factories that characterized the Industrial Revolution were costly to build and maintain but could lead to big profits. Investors offered capital to pay for these things expecting to make money on their investments.

3. Before the Embargo of 1807 and the War of 1812 disrupted trade, most textiles were imported from Britain. When British textiles became unavailable, American manufacturers developed new technology and built more factories to meet the demand and reap the profits.

4. Answers will vary. Possible responses: No. The operatives were not exploited but instead given an opportunity to earn money and live away from home not afforded to many women at the time. Yes. The operatives were exploited because they were required to work long hours under dangerous conditions, and it was ultimately the mill owners who profited most from the operatives' hard work.

COTTON AND SLAVERY IN THE SOUTH

Comfortable, versatile, and attractive, cotton cloth was the high-performance fabric of the 1800s, and everyone wanted it. As factories spun and wove, planters in the South picked up speed to meet the demand for cotton fiber.

KING COTTON

As Britain's textile mills continued to produce cotton cloth more cheaply and in larger quantities, the market for affordable cotton garments expanded. After the War of 1812, demand soared for raw cotton that British factories could spin and weave into the popular fabric. And no region of the world was as well prepared to meet this demand as the American South.

Cotton is categorized by staple length—that is, the length of the fibers. **Long-staple cotton** is prized because its long, silky fibers can be used to produce fine cloth and lace. But it is difficult to grow. In the United States, it flourished only in the coastal lowlands of Georgia and the Carolinas. **Short-staple cotton**, on the other hand, could be grown successfully across nearly the entire South. Cotton fibers are found in the plant's bolls, or pods, which contain small, sticky seeds. Separating the seeds from the raw fiber was an extremely slow and laborious process.

In 1793, while visiting a cotton plantation in Georgia, a New Englander named **Eli Whitney** came up with the idea for a machine that could quickly separate the cotton fibers from the seeds. His invention was called the cotton engine, or **cotton gin**, and it greatly increased the efficiency of cotton production. A single gin could produce as many as 50 pounds of cleaned cotton fiber each day. In contrast, a person removing the seeds by hand could produce only about one pound of fiber in a day. Since seeds accounted for more than half the weight of harvested cotton, removing the seeds before the cotton was shipped dramatically lowered transportation costs from plantation to cotton mill. Textile factories in the North began to purchase more cotton from

the South. As profits increased, cotton growers expanded their production, causing the demand for enslaved workers to grow.

Seeking fertile land to meet the demand for cotton, small farmers and planters moved westward to the new states of Alabama, Mississippi, and Louisiana. Cotton soon surpassed tobacco as the most important southern crop, accounting for more than half of all U.S. exports. **King Cotton**, as the industry came to be called, would have a long reign and would profoundly affect the South and the country.

EXPANDING SLAVERY

By the late 1700s, more and more voices were being raised against slavery, mostly in the northern states. In 1807, at the urging of **abolitionists**, or activists who work to end (or abolish) slavery, Congress passed an act that prohibited "the importation of slaves into any port or place within the jurisdiction of the United States . . . from any foreign kingdom, place, or country." The United States would no longer be part of the trans-Atlantic slave trade, which had begun 300 years earlier. The 1807 act did not, however, prohibit owning slaves or selling them within the borders of the United States.

The enslaved population continued to grow even after it became illegal to import slaves. As you have read, under chattel slavery, children born to enslaved parents were themselves enslaved. Also, traders persisted in smuggling slaves into the United States. In 1810, nearly 1.2 million enslaved people lived in the United States. By 1820, that number increased by roughly 29 percent to nearly 1.54 million. Although the enslaved population was much higher in the South than in the North, both sections of the country participated in and benefited from slavery and the slave trade.

The quick expansion of cotton plantations from southeastern coastal states into Alabama, Mississippi, and Louisiana created a tremendous demand for labor. Large numbers of field workers were needed to do the backbreaking work of clearing and cultivating the land and harvesting the cotton. Enslavers in the states along the Atlantic seaboard, faced with a surplus of labor, eagerly sold enslaved people to planters moving west. As a result, around

The Henry Ford Museum Dearborn, Michigan

The cotton gin designed by Eli Whitney pulled the cotton through a set of narrow wire teeth mounted on a spinning cylinder, leaving behind the larger seeds. Capable of being operated by people, animals, or water power, the machine was both simple and efficient. In the 1790s, the first saw-tooth gin was developed by several inventors, including Eli Whitney and Hodgen Holmes. The saw-tooth cotton machine in the photograph below was made around 1830.

HAULING THE WHOLE WEEKS PICKING

CRITICAL VIEWING Artist William Henry Brown used pen, watercolor, and cut-out figures to create *Hauling the Whole Weeks Picking* (c. 1842), a four-panel artwork depicting life on a South Carolina plantation. What does the title of this illustration mean, and what are the enslaved people doing?

PLAN: 4-PAGE LESSON

OBJECTIVE

Analyze political and social implications of the rise of cotton in the 19th century.

CRITICAL THINKING SKILLS FOR LESSON 1.2

• Analyze Cause and Effect

• Draw Conclusions

• Determine Word Meanings

• Compare and Contrast

HISTORICAL THINKING FOR CHAPTER 7

How did rapid change create new opportunities and new tensions for the growing nation? The South was well suited to growing cotton, which soon became a product in high demand. Lesson 1.2 explores how the institution of slavery expanded to meet the growing demand.

BACKGROUND FOR THE TEACHER

The trans-Atlantic slave trade emerged as a controversial issue during the Constitutional Convention of 1787. But those in attendance hammered out a compromise that allowed the southern states to continue importing enslaved workers for another 20 years beyond the passage of the Constitution. By the time the law prohibiting the importation of slaves to the United States took effect, all states except South Carolina had banned the practice. Four million enslaved people were already living in slaveholder states, so, figuring the law would have little practical impact, some southern congressmen voted to pass the legislation, which went into effect on January 1, 1808. Great Britain had banned slave importation in 1807. However, Brazil did not outlaw the slave trade until 1850, and Cuba continued to import enslaved workers from Africa until the 1860s.

INTRODUCE & ENGAGE

DISCUSS THE IMPORTANCE OF COTTON

Take an informal survey to find out how many students are wearing clothing, purses, backpacks, or shoes made from cotton. Tell them that cotton has been one of the most important fabrics in history. Ask what qualities they think contribute to cotton's usefulness and what kinds of products could be manufactured from it. Record their responses in a Word Web. Tell students that in this lesson they will learn about the rise of cotton production in the United States and its effects on U.S. society and politics.

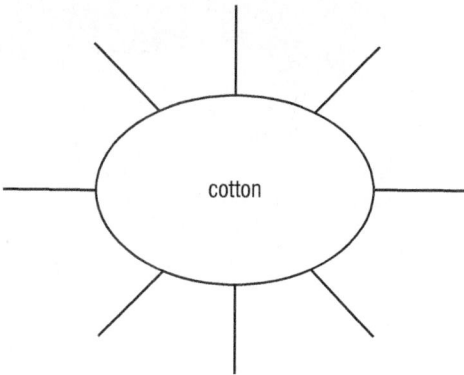

TEACH

GUIDED DISCUSSION

1. **Compare and Contrast** What were the differences and similarities between short- and long-staple cotton? *(Both were valuable crops. The fibers of long-staple cotton were very long and soft, which made it more desirable, but it could only be grown in certain coastal areas. Short-staple cotton had shorter fibers, making it less prized, but it was easy to grow in most areas of the South.)*

2. **Analyze Cause and Effect** What effect did the 1807 act prohibiting the importation of enslaved workers have on slavery in the United States? *(The act ended legal U.S. participation in the trans-Atlantic slave trade, but because it did not make enslavement illegal, the institution of slavery continued to grow, and traders began smuggling slaves into the United States.)*

🏛 VIRTUAL MUSEUM VISIT

The Henry Ford Museum houses many unusual and iconic historical artifacts and provides educational experiences for visitors. The museum's eponymous founder, Henry Ford, began collecting artifacts of the American experience in 1914. His collection grew to 26 million items that tell not only the story of America's technological achievements but also the story of everyday American life. Ford collected everything from clocks to major symbols of U.S. history and culture. Today, the museum's collection includes the bus on which Rosa Parks refused to give up her seat and the limousine John F. Kennedy was riding in when he was assassinated.

DIFFERENTIATE

ENGLISH LANGUAGE LEARNERS

Use Terms in Sentences Pair students at the **Emerging** level with those at the **Expanding** or **Bridging** level. Ask the more proficient students to model the exercise by using the first Key Vocabulary term in a sentence. Then have students take turns composing sentences for the other vocabulary terms. They can expand the exercise to write sentences for terms related to cotton *(cloth, garments, spin, weave, fabric, fibers, bolls, seeds, textile)* and slavery *(abolish, import, smuggle, highest bidder).* Invite pairs to share their sentences and discuss different ways to use each term.

GIFTED & TALENTED

Create a Historical Silhouette Prompt students to examine the mixed-media artwork by William Henry Brown in this lesson. Guide them to learn more about the art of the silhouette and about Brown, one of the last silhouettists, or artists who created portraits and tableaux with paper cutouts. Instruct students to choose a person, event, or scene from the lesson and render it visually in a style similar to that of Brown. Invite them to present their work to the class, explain why they chose the subject they did, and describe how they created their artwork.

See the Chapter Planner for more strategies for differentiation.

CRITICAL VIEWING The title refers to the heavy physical labor that plantation life required of enslaved people. The men, the woman, and the children are moving all the cotton they have picked during the week—on an oxcart, in small pails, and in huge baskets carried on their heads or backs.

1815, the price of enslaved people began to rise, and the practice of separating families in order to sell individuals to the highest bidders also increased.

Hundreds of thousands of enslaved people were forced to migrate to the new states in the 1810s and 1820s. Some moved along with their enslavers to the new plantations, but many individuals were sold to slave traders in the East and North. The traders, then brought them to slave markets in New Orleans, Mobile, and other cities in the new states. This domestic slave trade, a complex network of traders, suppliers, and insurers, contributed to the northern economy and made up as much as 13.5 percent of the total southern economy. The combined population of Alabama, Mississippi, and Louisiana more than tripled between 1810 and 1820, and by 1860, nearly half of those people were enslaved.

But not all African Americans were enslaved, even in the South. In 1810, the South was home to around 97,000 free African Americans, and roughly 77,000 lived in the North. Some had purchased their freedom, some had been freed by their former enslavers, and some had managed to escape slavery, take new identities, and start new lives.

Free African Americans were a small minority, however. Slavery was expanding, partly in response to developments in the North, particularly in the growing textile industry. In northern mills, demand increased for the South's cheap cotton, which was made possible by enslaved labor. But even as slavery became more deeply ingrained in the South and in the country's economy, opposition to it was growing in the North. Slavery was becoming a fault line that would threaten to split the nation.

EFFECTS OF KING COTTON

The Industrial Revolution began making itself felt in the United States by the 1810s, but its immediate effects were largely confined to northern states. While an industrial society began to develop in the North, the South remained primarily agricultural, in large part because of the cotton boom.

The expansion of King Cotton's realm did not occur in a direct east-to-west sweep across the South. Instead it followed the geographic and political outlines of lands once controlled by Native Americans. As you have read, during the War of 1812 many Native Americans had fought on the side of the British. They did so in a desperate effort to stop the United States

CRITICAL VIEWING Enslaved African Americans place baskets of cotton into a cotton-press machine, which flattens it to be packed into square bales, or bundles. From the details in this illustration, what role do you think the young man on the horse plays in the process?

Now a museum of African-American history, arts, and crafts, the Old Slave Mart in Charleston, South Carolina, is the former site of many slave auctions. In locations such as this one, slaves were displayed and inspected by buyers prior to purchase.

from intruding farther into their territories. The end of the war dealt a strong blow to this hope as the United States took quick steps to establish firm control over the entire eastern half of the continent.

Andrew Jackson, the general who had won the Battle of New Orleans, negotiated with the Creek, Cherokee, Chickasaw, and Choctaw nations of Alabama, Florida, and Mississippi. Using heavy-handed tactics, he forced Native Americans to sign treaties giving away their lands. Many resisted the enforcement of these treaties, objecting that the leaders who signed them had no authority to do so. Their resistance and arguments were in vain, and they were driven off the land.

After Jackson secured the lands from the Native Americans, white settlers rushed into the newly acquired territories, eager for the fertile land and the fortunes they planned to earn from it. Meanwhile, the Native Americans of the region, all of whom lived in agrarian societies, were pushed into hilly and mountainous areas poorly suited to farming.

Another effect of the cotton boom was to tie the South more closely to the economy of Britain. To meet the demand of its booming textile industry,

Britain imported raw cotton from the West Indies, the East Indies, Brazil, and the Mediterranean region as well as from the southern United States. In 1790, cotton from the South represented less than one percent of total British cotton imports. By 1800, the figure had risen to 24 percent, and by the late 1820s, Britain imported nearly 75 percent of its cotton from the southern United States.

HISTORICAL THINKING

1. **READING CHECK** Why was cotton referred to as "King Cotton"?

2. **ANALYZE CAUSE AND EFFECT** Why did the auction prices of enslaved people rise, even after the international slave trade was outlawed on American soil?

3. **DRAW CONCLUSIONS** How did the Industrial Revolution affect the lives of the people who were enslaved in the South?

4. **DETERMINE WORD MEANINGS** What context clues help you understand what "heavy-handed" means in describing Andrew Jackson's tactics in negotiating with Native Americans in the South?

BUILD BACKGROUND

OLD SLAVE MART

Charleston, South Carolina, was the vibrant commercial hub of the South's cotton plantation economy. For years, sales of enslaved people took place at auctions held outside the Custom House in full public view. But in 1856, the city passed an ordinance that outlawed the practice of public slave auctions. Instead, a number of small sales rooms were established along Charleston's streets. One of these buildings, Ryan's Mart, belonged to a city alderman and former sheriff named Thomas Ryan. He sold the property in 1859 to auctioneer Z.B. Oakes, but a few years later the outcome of the Civil War ended the practice of slavery and slave auctions. Beginning in about 1878, the building was used as a tenement. Finally, in 1938, Miriam B. Wilson bought the property and converted it to a museum of African-American culture, history, and arts.

FREED AFRICAN AMERICANS

Though hampered by a long list of discriminatory laws, many free African Americans in northern states were able to purchase land, homes, and businesses. They paid taxes and sometimes, though typically for only brief periods, were allowed to vote. Many spoke out—in churches, in meetings, and in print—against racial inequality and the injustice of slavery. The first African-American-owned newspaper, *Freedom's Journal*, began in 1827. Such publications, written exclusively by African Americans, led the way in the ongoing fight against slavery. Another option existed for freed African Americans as well. With the help of the American Colonization Society, thousands left the United States to colonize what would later be the West African nation of Liberia. Still, most freed African Americans saw themselves as Americans and opted to stay in the United States.

TEACH

GUIDED DISCUSSION

3. **Analyze Cause and Effect** What effect did signing treaties with Andrew Jackson have on the Creek, Cherokee, Chickasaw, and Choctaw nations? *(White settlers moved onto the lands that Native Americans ceded and forced Native Americans to move to mountainous areas not suitable for farming.)*

4. **Draw Conclusions** In what ways did the cotton boom tie the South more closely to the economy in Britain? *(Britain needed to import raw cotton to meet the demand of its textile industry, and once the cotton boom occurred in the South, imports from the South grew from less than 1 percent in 1790 to more than 75 percent by the 1820s.)*

MORE INFORMATION

Eli Whitney's Patent Woes In the fall of 1793, Thomas Jefferson received a drawing of a new invention, the cotton gin, from Eli Whitney. Jefferson told Whitney that he would have to send along a working model of the invention if he wanted to obtain a patent. Whitney struggled to build a full-size working model, but he finally achieved it in February 1794 and received his patent. Making a profit on the machine, however, turned out to be harder than Whitney expected. His plan was to set up cotton gins all over the South and charge farmers a fee for ginning the cotton. The farmers rebelled against this system, which they found inconvenient and expensive. Instead, they made their own copies of Whitney's machine. To make matters worse, a wording issue in the 1793 patent law prevented Whitney and his partner from winning any lawsuits over the patent until the law was revised in 1800.

ACTIVE OPTIONS

On Your Feet: King Cotton History Roundtable Arrange students around tables in groups of four. Pose the following question for discussion: What social and economic effects in the southern and the northern states followed the rise of cotton? Prompt each student to answer in a different way. Allow time for groups to share the different answers with the class.

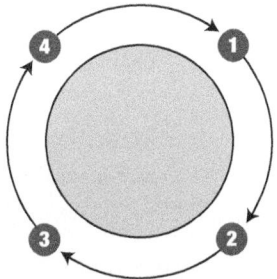

NG Learning Framework: Build or Draw a Scale Model   STEM

ATTITUDE Curiosity

SKILL Collaboration

Invite pairs of students to use information from the lesson and from online resources about the workings of the cotton gin to create a scale model or drawing of the machine. If students build the model, prompt them to use cardboard, glue, cotton balls, and any other materials that help demonstrate how the cotton gin works. Students should make sure their models or drawings are well labeled to show how the machine operates to process cotton, remove seeds, and move the seeded bolls to a holding area. Encourage pairs to share their completed projects with the class.

HISTORICAL THINKING

ANSWERS

1. King Cotton was so named because it became the most important crop to the South's economy.

2. The demand for enslaved workers increased as cotton planters moved west and set up new plantations in Alabama, Mississippi, and Louisiana, and the rise in demand for enslaved workers caused prices to rise at slave auctions.

3. Possible response: The Industrial Revolution in Britain indirectly caused additional distress to enslaved people in the South because Britain's increased demand for cotton prompted American planters to seek new fertile lands farther west. Large numbers of enslaved people were forced to move to the new plantations, and many of them were torn from their families to be sold separately.

4. The referenced paragraph states that Jackson forced Native Americans to sign treaties. Therefore, "heavy-handed" indicates that the treaties were harsh and unfair to the Native Americans.

CRITICAL VIEWING Answers will vary. Possible response: The horse is hitched to a movable beam that attaches to a spindle that probably presses a heavy plate or surface down on the cotton, so it is likely that the young man's task is to keep the horse moving in a circle to turn the spindle and power the cotton press.

CRITICAL VIEWING This 1803 wooden scale-model reveals the technology of Robert Fulton's first steamboat. The black metal engine, a steam boiler, powered the two paddle wheels placed on either side of the hull. Why do you think inventors build scale-models like this one?

THE ECONOMY EXPANDS

Today, goods travel all over the world on container ships, airplanes, trucks, and high-speed trains. Two hundred years ago, the pace of life was slower, but merchants were beginning to call for speedier modes of transportation.

FULTON'S STEAMBOAT

From the earliest days of European settlement, the fastest and cheapest way to travel and transport goods long distances in North America was by boat on natural waterways. However, rivers could be dangerously fast in some seasons and so slow and shallow as to be impassable in others. They often froze for months in the winter. Floating downstream was easy, but traveling upstream against the current could be almost impossible. Flatboats that carried goods down the Ohio and Mississippi rivers to New Orleans did not make the return trip. Instead, they were broken up and their crews journeyed home on foot. Keelboats, longer and slimmer than flatboats, could be poled, paddled, sailed, or pulled upstream, but the work was backbreaking and the progress slow. Not surprisingly, soon after the power of steam was harnessed in the mid-1700s, people began to dream of riverboats propelled by steam engines.

The first practical steamboat in the United States was built by an inventor named John Fitch. He successfully tested the boat on the Delaware River in 1787, and four years later he received a U.S. **patent**, or a license that gave him the sole right to manufacture and sell his steamboats. He built several more steamboats, but because they were very costly to make and operate, he failed to start a profitable business. Another person excited by the possibility of steam propulsion was Robert Livingston, the statesman who, as the American minister to France, had negotiated the Louisiana Purchase. Livingston secured a 20-year monopoly on all steam navigation in the state of New York. A **monopoly** is the complete control of an industry or business venture by one person or company. Once Livingston had his monopoly, he partnered with an inventor named **Robert Fulton** to build a steamboat.

By the fall of 1807, a Fulton-designed steamboat was making regular trips on the Hudson River between New York City and Albany, the state capital. By 1811, Fulton managed to build a steamboat that was powerful and sturdy enough to take on the powerful currents of the Mississippi River. Soon, dozens of steamboats designed by other engineers were traveling up and down the river in competition with Fulton's model. Within a decade, the upstream journey on the Mississippi and Ohio rivers from New Orleans to Louisville, Kentucky, had been reduced from several months to just 14 days. "If anyone had said this was possible thirty years ago," a journalist marveled, "we should have been ready to send him to a mad-house."

Steamboats, along with the invention of the cotton gin and demand from textile mills, contributed to the rapid growth of the cotton industry in the South by providing efficient transportation between the plantations of the lower Mississippi Valley and the port of New Orleans. The increasing speed and frequency of the steamboats also encouraged the growth of villages and towns along the rivers. Louisville, Kentucky; Pittsburgh, Pennsylvania; Cincinnati, Ohio; and St. Louis, Missouri, were among many cities that grew into major business centers thanks to the arrival of the steamboat.

CLAY'S AMERICAN SYSTEM

The United States was experiencing a transition from a pre-industrial economy to a market-oriented, capitalist economy—the **market revolution**. While each region in the United States developed differently, the country's leaders saw the need to improve transportation between the regions in order to build the national economy. The Democratic-Republicans had long been known for

their opposition to federal power, but the surge of nationalism after the War of 1812 inspired leading members of the party to view the central government more favorably. Younger party members, such as **Henry Clay** of Kentucky and **John C. Calhoun** of South Carolina, urged Congress and the president to take strong steps to promote economic stability and encourage the growth of businesses.

Clay and Calhoun believed the future of the country lay in commerce and industry, and this led them to propose a three-part economic plan that Clay dubbed the **American System**. First, the plan called for internal improvements, such as clearing rivers and constructing roads and canals, which would make it easier to transport agricultural produce and manufactured goods from one part of the country to another. To provide the funds for these improvements, Clay and Calhoun supported the use of government subsidies. A **subsidy** is an amount of money or land granted to an individual or business by the government to promote commerce or fund improvements.

Second, the plan called for the re-establishment of a national bank to stabilize currency and encourage trade. Finally, the American System advocated a tariff to protect the United States' growing industries. A **tariff** is a tax on goods imported from other countries. By making imported goods more expensive, tariffs encourage people to buy goods produced in their own countries. Tariffs are also a way for governments to collect money.

THE NATIONAL ROAD

Relying on the support of the American System, the United States experienced a frenzy of roadbuilding after 1815. Investors, states, and even the federal government built thousands of miles of private roads, called **turnpikes**, that charged tolls to cover the roads' notoriously high maintenance costs. In 1818,

the U.S. government opened the **National Road**, also called the Cumberland Road, which wound through the rugged Allegheny Mountains and connected Cumberland, Maryland, on the Potomac River, with Wheeling, Virginia (now West Virginia), on the Ohio River. Both George Washington and Thomas Jefferson had pushed for the construction of such a road as a means of unifying the country and opening western lands for expansion.

The National Road was the best that technology could provide at the time, and it proved to be wildly popular. It featured excellent bridges and a relatively smooth stone surface. To ensure that rainwater drained quickly, the center of the roadway was raised higher than the sides. The road was soon crowded with travelers—on foot, on horseback, in carriages, in stagecoaches—and livestock. Traffic jams often slowed movement to a crawl. As a result of heavy usage, the road's condition quickly deteriorated due to wear and tear.

THE ERIE CANAL

In addition to building roads, state governments and private **corporations**, businesses that have most of the legal rights of an individual, began planning the construction of dependable canals. These canals would have **locks**, or gated enclosures used to raise or lower boats as they pass from one level to another. Locks solved the problem of building canals through hilly or uneven terrain.

In New York, ground was broken in 1817 on an extremely ambitious project: a canal that would connect the Hudson River with Lake Erie. It would allow water transportation between the Atlantic Ocean and the entire Great Lakes system, which extends deep into North America's interior. When completed, the **Erie Canal** would be roughly 365 miles long—more than 10 times longer than any existing canal at the time.

PLAN: 4-PAGE LESSON

OBJECTIVE

Explore economic, technological, and infrastructure advances that took place in the 19th century.

CRITICAL THINKING SKILLS FOR LESSON 2.1

- Draw Conclusions
- Analyze Cause and Effect
- Interpret Maps
- Identify Main Ideas and Details
- Make Connections
- Evaluate
- Compare and Contrast
- Analyze Visuals

HISTORICAL THINKING FOR CHAPTER 7

How did rapid change create new opportunities and new tensions for the growing nation? Technological advances made travel and shipping faster and safer. Lesson 2.1 examines the impact of major road and canal projects on the U.S. economy.

BACKGROUND FOR THE TEACHER

Pioneering steamboat designer John Fitch created several functional steamboats—some of which used steam-powered oars—but none was financially practical. Robert Fulton's model, the *Clermont*, was the first truly successful steamboat because it made travel and shipping not only useful but also lucrative. Traveling from New York City to New York State's capital city of Albany every four days, the *Clermont* carried up to 100 passengers at a time. Most steamboats of the 19th and early 20th centuries featured a paddle-wheel design. Side-wheelers, like the Clermont, had a paddle wheel on either side; stern-wheelers had a single wheel in the back. In 1814, during the War of 1812, Fulton built a steam-powered warship, the *Fulton*. It was heavy and slow, and though it went through a series of successful trials, it never saw battle.

FINANCIAL LITERACY

To extend their knowledge and understanding about the concepts in this lesson, refer students to the Financial Literacy handbook.

CONSIDER TRAVEL AND TRANSIT

Encourage students to discuss the means by which goods flow across the United States today. Remind them that infrastructure did not always look the way it does today and that long distances, bad weather, and rough terrain between economic hubs often made travel and shipping difficult. **ASK:** What methods did people in the 18th and 19th centuries use to ship goods across wide expanses of the country? *(trains, wagons, boats, and barges)* Prompt them to consider the cost of improving infrastructure. **ASK:** How are improvements to roads and waterways funded today? *(Possible response: States and the federal government can levy taxes, charge tolls, or provide grants and other subsidies.)* Tell students that in this lesson they will learn about some of the transportation technologies, projects, and systems that helped American businesses move goods to market.

TEACH

GUIDED DISCUSSION

1. **Identify Main Ideas and Details** How did the invention of the steamboat change travel in the United States? *(Possible responses: The steamboat had enough power to travel against strong river currents, which had not been possible for boats powered by hand or by sail. Steamboats required smaller crews, and their powerful engines greatly reduced travel time.)*

2. **Make Connections** Why did Henry Clay and some other Democratic-Republicans think the time was right to promote the federal government's role in massive infrastructure projects? *(Possible response: The United States was moving from a pre-industrial economy to a market-oriented economy, and Clay and his allies thought that it was crucial to the nation's future to move goods easily from one region to another. Although Democratic-Republicans usually opposed giving power to the federal government, they must have recognized that the federal government would be key in developing a transportation system that spanned the country.)*

3. **Draw Conclusions** How did the building of the Erie Canal affect trade throughout the United States? *(Answers will vary. Possible response: The Erie Canal connected the Atlantic Ocean and the Hudson River to the Great Lakes system and also connected to roads, expanding trade throughout the United States.)*

EVALUATE

Prompt students to consider the objectives of the National Road. **ASK:** Did the road serve its purpose and accomplish all that its developers hoped it would? Explain your answer. *(Possible responses: Yes. The National Road was extremely successful and resulted in a huge increase in westward travel, which helped fulfill the government's desire for national expansion. No. Though the road was built with the finest technology available and offered travelers a better travel option, it turned out to be very difficult and expensive to maintain, especially given the constant flow of traffic that often slowed travel times to a crawl and led to worsening road conditions.)*

ENGLISH LANGUAGE LEARNERS ELD

Clarify Word Meaning Explain that readers can often use context clues to figure out the meaning of unfamiliar words. Pair students at the **Emerging** level with students at the **Expanding** or **Bridging** level. Prompt partners to find the Key Vocabulary word *bankruptcies* and the context clue *business failures*. Then have students look for additional Key Vocabulary words or other words that are unfamiliar. Prompt them to read the sentences before and after the target word to look for clues to the word's meaning. Encourage them to look up the word in a dictionary to verify its meaning.

PRE-AP

Analyze the Impact of Tariffs Instruct students to research the Tariff of 1816 and analyze its consequences, both positive and negative. Tell them to briefly research some other tariffs and compare the outcomes. Then prompt students to use their findings to write an essay on the overall effectiveness of tariffs, citing details from the tariffs they investigated. Invite them to share their essays with the class.

See the Chapter Planner for more strategies for differentiation.

CRITICAL VIEWING Inventors build scale-models to show in greater detail what the drawing and plans for the invention represent. A scale-model could show moving parts and structural innovations that could then be replicated at full size. It could also be useful in helping potential investors visualize how the invention will work—and at a much lower cost than it would take to build a full-size model.

Mockingly called "Clinton's Big Ditch" after the governor of New York State who promoted its construction, the Erie Canal soon won over its critics. Several engineers who helped build the canal traveled to Britain to study canal construction, and local U.S. workers often invented tools to solve specific problems. Over the life of the canal, laborers, like those in this photograph taken around 1907, have maintained and rerouted the canal and locks.

Year by year, the canal advanced steadily toward Lake Erie, transforming the countryside along the way. As soon as workers completed a segment, canal boats crowded its waters, paying tolls that financed the portions yet unfinished. The Erie Canal was completed in October 1825, seven years after work had begun and two years ahead of schedule. It was considered one of the engineering marvels of its time. It boasted 83 stone locks and 18 stone **aqueducts**, or water bridges, that carried it over streams and ravines. Cutting through swamps, forests, and solid rock, it climbed more than 500 feet in elevation from east to west. Near its western end, a staircase-like series of locks transported it up a steep 75-foot-high slope called the Niagara Escarpment.

From the start, the canal was a spectacular success. The cost of transporting goods between Lake Erie and New York City, at the mouth of the Hudson River, plummeted. Canal traffic became so heavy that boats sometimes had to wait a day or two to pass through the locks. Buffalo, Rochester, Syracuse, and other canal-side cities flourished, and New York City became more firmly established as the country's most important seaport and commercial center. Like the National Road, the Erie Canal played a large role in westward expansion. By providing a safe and reliable route as well as easier, cheaper access to more markets, it drew large numbers of settlers to western New York and, from there, to the country's western territories.

Early 20th century postcards highlighted engineering feats of the Erie Canal such as this series of step-like locks in Lockport, New York. Eventually, the Erie Canal connected to the National Road and feeder canals, such as those in Ohio, Indiana, and Illinois.

U.S. Canals, 1821–1835

- National Road
- Other road
- Canal

TARIFFS

As you have read, the War of 1812 disrupted trade between the United States and Britain. By the end of the war in 1815, the British had large stockpiles of iron products, glassware, and textiles. At the same time, production of these goods had been growing in the United States. In an effort to reduce their inventories and to restrain American manufacturing, the British began sending their goods to the American market at very low prices. Most Americans bought the cheaper British goods, leaving American goods unsold. **Bankruptcies**, or business failures, among American manufacturers grew sharply.

In their proposed American System, Henry Clay and John C. Calhoun promoted a tariff as the best way to protect and promote U.S. industry. Congress agreed and passed the **Tariff Act of 1816**, which imposed a tax on British imports, leveling the playing field between Britain's strong manufacturing sector and the United States' emerging one. Revenue from the tariff was intended to help fund the internal improvements that were also part of Clay and Calhoun's grand plan.

Tariffs became one of the country's most divisive issues. Manufacturers in the Northeast welcomed them because they protected the region's growing industries. On the other hand, farmers in the South, West, and Midwest opposed tariffs because they raised the price of imported goods. Southerners also worried that the British would retaliate and impose a tariff on cotton and other agricultural imports, which would hurt the South's cotton-centered economy. The issue of tariffs would continue to raise problems throughout the first half of the 19th century.

HISTORICAL THINKING

1. **READING CHECK** What was the American System?

2. **DRAW CONCLUSIONS** How would a British tariff on cotton imports from the United States hurt the South's economy?

3. **ANALYZE CAUSE AND EFFECT** How did the American System drive the building of roads and canals in the United States in the early 1800s?

4. **INTERPRET MAPS** How could someone send goods from coastal Maryland to Detroit in 1835?

Regional and National Growth **229**

BUILD BACKGROUND

THE NIAGARA ESCARPMENT

An escarpment is the steep face of a cuesta, or a landform made up of layers of tilted rocks. These cliffs are created when erosion wears away soft rock, such as shale, from underneath harder rock, such as limestone, causing the unsupported harder rock to break off. The Niagara Escarpment began to form out of a seabed more than 450 million years ago. Over time, the sea's sediment compressed to form rock. Then glaciers and other natural elements weathered the shale more rapidly than the sturdier stone, creating the spectacular landforms still visible today, which include deep valleys, waterfalls, hills, cliffs, and caves. Extending more than 650 miles, the Niagara Escarpment spans southeastern Wisconsin up through the Manitoulin Islands of Ontario, Canada, back across the U.S.-Canada border, and ends just east of Rochester, New York.

THE ERIE CANAL

The Erie Canal has had a lot of nicknames over the course of its long history—from "Clinton's Big Ditch" and "Clinton's Folly" in the early days of its construction to "the Eighth Wonder of the World" once it was up and running. In 1808, the New York State Assembly ordered feasibility studies on the project. Because legislators knew the United States had a deep interest in opening up new territory in the West, they thought the time might be right to push for the massive canal project, and they approached Congress for funding. Though President Thomas Jefferson believed firmly in westward expansion, as evidenced by the Louisiana Purchase, he thought the building of the canal was a good idea proposed far too soon. He was certain that the canal could not be completed using only the technology available at the time. As a result, Congress denied federal funding for the project.

TEACH

GUIDED DISCUSSION

4. **Compare and Contrast** How did people from different regions of the United States respond to the Tariff Act of 1816, and why? *(Manufacturers in the Northeast approved of the tariffs because they benefited economically from them—the tariffs raised the prices of British goods and therefore cut down on competition for sales. Farmers in the South, West, and Midwest were economically hurt by the tariffs, which meant higher prices for goods they bought from Britain, and southern farmers in particular worried about the potential of retaliatory tariffs by the British on American cotton.)*

5. **Analyze Visuals** Direct students' attention to the black-and-white photograph of workers at the Erie Canal and ask them to read the caption. **ASK:** What details in the photograph provide clues about the possible challenges workers encountered while building the Erie Canal? *(Answers will vary. Possible responses: The steep walls and the ladders could lead to worker falls and injuries. Water collecting in the bottom could slow or stop work and would make it challenging to move materials by wheelbarrow—as evidenced by the boards laid across the puddles.)*

MAKE CONNECTIONS

Review with students the major public works projects of the early 19th century: the National Road and the Erie Canal. **ASK:** In what ways did these massive projects provide a model for infrastructure and technological improvements of today? *(Possible responses: The National Road led the way for the networked state and federal highway system that links the United States from coast to coast. The success of the Erie Canal, especially since it was finished two years ahead of schedule, probably increased confidence in the future of large-scale infrastructure projects.)*

ACTIVE OPTIONS

On Your Feet: Use a Jigsaw Strategy Organize students into "expert" groups. Assign each group one of the following goals of the American System: strengthening infrastructure, stabilizing the economy to increase trade, and strengthening American industry. Instruct groups to consider the assigned goal and determine whether the American System was successful in meeting that goal, based on information from the lesson and from additional research. After groups have discussed their topic in depth, regroup students so that each new group has at least one member from each expert group. Then ask experts to share the results of their study.

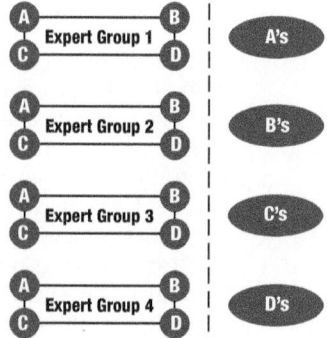

NG Learning Framework: Profile a Canal Town

SKILL Communication

KNOWLEDGE Our Human Story

Invite students to choose a major city located along the Erie Canal—such as Albany, Rochester, or Buffalo, New York—as the subject of a historical profile. Direct them to conduct online and library research to learn how the selected city changed due to construction of the canal. Prompt them to consider areas such as population, trade, quality of life, and other social, political, and economic factors.

HISTORICAL THINKING

ANSWERS

1. The American System, an economic plan proposed by Henry Clay and John C. Calhoun, sought to create economic stability and strengthen the federal government by making improvements to the nation's transportation system, establishing a national bank, and imposing tariffs on foreign goods.

2. Britain was an important market for cotton. If the British imposed a tariff on cotton from the United States, it would likely make American cotton more expensive in Britain than cotton from other countries, and that would hurt U.S. sales.

3. To make it faster and easier to get goods to market, the American System provided funding to build better roads and canals by establishing government subsidies and by imposing tariffs on imports from other nations.

4. Possible response: Goods could be sent overland on the National Road, then shipped up a canal to the shores of Lake Erie at Cleveland, and finally moved by boat across Lake Erie and onto a river or waterway into Detroit.

Reproduced Textbook Page

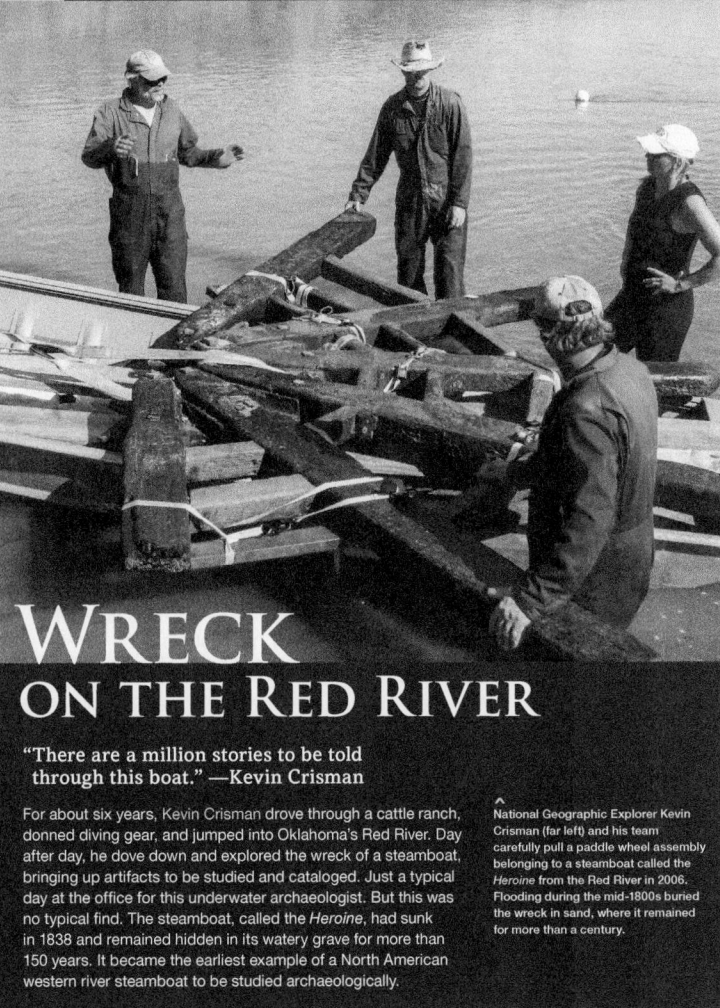

WRECK ON THE RED RIVER

"There are a million stories to be told through this boat." —Kevin Crisman

For about six years, Kevin Crisman drove through a cattle ranch, donned diving gear, and jumped into Oklahoma's Red River. Day after day, he dove down and explored the wreck of a steamboat, bringing up artifacts to be studied and cataloged. Just a typical day at the office for this underwater archaeologist. But this was no typical find. The steamboat, called the *Heroine*, had sunk in 1838 and remained hidden in its watery grave for more than 150 years. It became the earliest example of a North American western river steamboat to be studied archaeologically.

National Geographic Explorer Kevin Crisman (far left) and his team carefully pull a paddle wheel assembly belonging to a steamboat called the *Heroine* from the Red River in 2006. Flooding during the mid-1800s buried the wreck in sand, where it remained for more than a century.

MAIN IDEA Underwater archaeologist Kevin Crisman's study of the *Heroine* has provided new information about early steamboats and river culture.

LOST AND FOUND

The 140-foot-long *Heroine* was bringing supplies to soldiers at Oklahoma's Fort Towson when a snag, or submerged log, in the river tore through its hull and brought the boat down. Stories about the *Heroine* circulated for years, but no one really tried to find it. After all, many steamboats from the 1800s had sunk, but very few had been found. Some sank when the steam boilers that powered their engines exploded—a common occurrence. Other hazards lurked beneath the river's surface, with sandbars, shifting logs, and snags lying in wait for unwary ship captains. It's no wonder the average lifespan of a steamboat in the early to mid-1800s was less than six years. The *Heroine* itself was about that age when it sank into the sands of the Red River. It remained there until the 1990s, when flooding led to its discovery on the riverbank.

In 2002, enter National Geographic Explorer Kevin Crisman. Working with the Oklahoma Historical Society and Texas A&M University's Institute of Nautical Archaeology, Crisman led the exploration of the steamboat—while it remained in the water. Crisman and his team couldn't remove the *Heroine* from the river because doing so would have caused its wooden frame to shrink, crack, and fall apart. Besides, the boat was well preserved in the sand.

So Crisman extracted everything he could from the wreck, but the process was challenging. After the team carefully dug a hole in the sediment, rain sometimes washed sand back in, filling up the hole. And much of the work was carried out in dark, murky water. As Crisman says, he and his team often "saw with our fingertips." Still, they managed to bring many artifacts to the surface: tools, machinery, cargo, and personal items. Based on data and pieces of the steamboat gathered at the site, researchers have also been able to create models of the *Heroine*.

TRANSPORTATION REVOLUTION

Among the cargo found on the *Heroine* were two intact pork barrels, the first ever recovered. The finding gave researchers insight into the meatpacking practices of the early 1800s. "That's the thing about shipwrecks," claims Crisman. "You find all of these

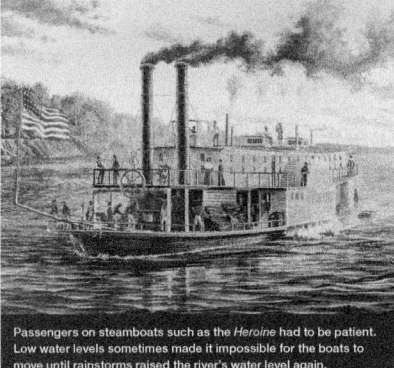

Passengers on steamboats such as the *Heroine* had to be patient. Low water levels sometimes made it impossible for the boats to move until rainstorms raised the river's water level again.

things that you would have never thought to ask questions about." In their haste to abandon ship, passengers left some items behind. The spoons, buttons, and shoes help archaeologists imagine the lives of the passengers.

The items also help identify the social standing of the passengers. According to Crisman, the boats were "cultural blenders." For a couple of weeks, people from all walks of life were thrown together as they sailed on a steamboat: the wealthy and the poor, businessmen and laborers, mountain men and settlers. The boats sometimes even carried African Americans to slave auctions.

People sailed on steamboats in the early 1800s because they provided a quick—an astounding five to eight miles per hour!—and inexpensive form of transportation. Also, unlike earlier craft, steamboats could run upstream; they didn't have to be hauled manually. The boats brought about a transportation revolution that transformed the West. Steamboats carried immigrants and their cultures all over the region, and goods such as oranges made their way west for the first time as well. As Crisman says, "The floodgates opened, and the world rushed in."

HISTORICAL THINKING

1. **READING CHECK** Why didn't Crisman haul the *Heroine* out of the river to explore it?
2. **MAKE INFERENCES** What does Crisman mean when he says, "The floodgates opened, and the world rushed in"?

PLAN: 2-PAGE LESSON

OBJECTIVE

Examine how underwater archaeologists explore shipwrecks, and discuss Kevin Crisman's work on the wreck of the *Heroine*.

CRITICAL THINKING SKILLS FOR LESSON 2.2

- Make Inferences
- Describe
- Identify Main Ideas and Details

HISTORICAL THINKING FOR CHAPTER 7

How did rapid change create new opportunities and new tensions for the growing nation?
Steamships greatly aided expansion and settlement of the country's interior but often didn't have a long lifespan. Lesson 2.2 describes what the shipwreck of the *Heroine* is teaching Kevin Crisman and his team about life in America 150 years ago.

NATIONAL GEOGRAPHIC EXPLORER KEVIN CRISMAN

Dr. Kevin Crisman specializes in maritime history from 1450 to 1950; in North American river, canal, and lake navigation; and in shipboard life and seafaring communities. During his career, he's been involved in investigating numerous wrecks in the Gulf of Mexico and the Great Lakes, including naval ships sunk in Lake Champlain during the War of 1812, as described in his book *Coffins of the Brave*. Crisman holds a faculty fellowship at the Institute of Nautical Archaeology at Texas A&M University. Crisman is very passionate about what he does, particularly about the different perspective his work offers on the past. He says, "The great thing about archaeology is that it lets you tell the stories about people that didn't get written down."

HISTORY NOTEBOOK

Encourage students to complete the Explorer page for Chapter 7 in their History Notebooks as they read.

INTRODUCE & ENGAGE

BRAINSTORM A LIST OF QUESTIONS

Discuss with students famous shipwrecks, such as the *Titanic*, they may have heard of or learned about in the media. **ASK:** If you could interview the archaeological teams who explored these wrecks, what questions would you ask? *(Possible responses: What equipment did the team use? How did the ship sink? What condition was the wreck in when they located it? What artifacts survived? What did the artifacts tell them?)* Write students' questions on the board. Tell them that in this lesson they will discover how an underwater archaeology team explores old shipwrecks and what the team learns from the artifacts.

TEACH

GUIDED DISCUSSION

1. **Describe** What factors caused so many steamboats sink? *(A combination of river conditions and 1800s technology caused many steamboats to sink. Some steamboats sank when their boilers exploded, and others sank when they hit submerged hazards, such as sandbars and logs.)*

2. **Identify Main Ideas and Details** What does Crisman believe artifacts recovered from shipwrecks reveal? *(Possible response: Artifacts can tell us a great deal about the people, culture, and technology of the past, such as what people wore, the social classes represented by those that traveled on a ship, methods of preserving food, what tools and machinery were used on board, and what cargo the ship carried.)*

MORE INFORMATION

Nautical Archaeology George F. Bass and his fellow students at the University of Pennsylvania Museum of Archaeology and Anthropology first developed the discipline of underwater, or nautical, archaeology in the early 1960s. The group devised technologies for locating wrecks underwater, communicating between underwater and surface teams, and using deep-water submersibles. They were involved in exploring ancient shipwrecks off the coast of Turkey. By 1973, Bass had formed the American Institute of Nautical Archaeology, which eventually found a home at Texas A&M University as the Institute of Nautical Archaeology.

ACTIVE OPTIONS

On Your Feet: Impact of Steamships Arrange students in groups and ask them to fill out a Cause-and-Effect Web to show the effects of steamboats on American life. Instruct students to use information from the lesson and from their own knowledge to complete their web. Then direct groups to discuss what these effects might reveal about how the country was changing and developing in the 19th century.

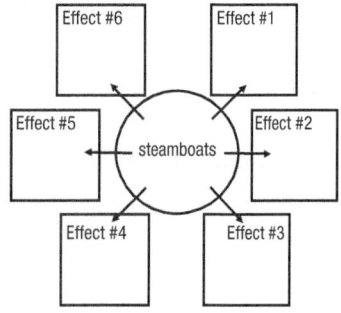

NG Learning Framework: Investigate a Shipwreck `STEM`

ATTITUDE Curiosity

SKILLS Observation, Communication

Ask students to work in groups to investigate either a famous shipwreck (such as the *Titanic*, the *Indianapolis*, or Spanish treasure ships) or one of the shipwrecks that Kevin Crisman has explored. Direct groups to conduct online and library research and put together a report or display that includes a map showing the wreck's location and an explanation of the scientific tools and equipment used to find, explore, and retrieve artifacts from the wreck. Students can use their list of questions from the Introduce & Engage activity to help guide their research. Invite groups to share their reports or displays with the class.

DIFFERENTIATE

ENGLISH LANGUAGE LEARNERS `ELD`

Make Word Cards As they read the lesson, prompt students at the **Expanding** level to keep a list of unfamiliar words, such as *donned*, *gear*, *submerged*, *hazards*, *unwary*, *sediment*, *intact*, and *manually*. Direct students to look up each word in a dictionary and make a word card to help them understand and pronounce the word. Tell them to write the word on one side of a card and define the word and spell it phonetically on the other side.

PRE-AP

Write a Letter Home Instruct students to use library or online sources, both primary and secondary, to learn more about the journey of the *Heroine* and about what artifacts from the *Heroine* reveal about people's diet, clothing, and daily life in the 1830s. Tell students to use what they discover to imagine themselves as passengers on the *Heroine*. Prompt them to write a letter home telling a friend or family member about their experiences on the boat.

See the Chapter Planner for more strategies for differentiation.

HISTORICAL THINKING

ANSWERS

1. The *Heroine* was well preserved in the water and sand but would have broken apart had it been pulled from the water and allowed to dry out.

2. Crisman probably means that with steamboat travel along rivers, more people and products from all over the world could access the territory inland far more easily and quickly than they could using land routes.

The largest surface freshwater system on Earth, the Great Lakes have played a major role in the colonization and development of North America. The movement of massive glaciers gave the Great Lakes basin its shape through a geological process that began about one million years ago.

In the early days of European exploration and expansion, the lakes served as a convenient transportation route into the middle of the continent. Explorers soon realized the value of the fertile land, thick forests, and mineral-rich vast shorelines. These resources, plus the endless supply of fresh water, drew people and industries to the region, where cities grew and flourished. Today, over 30 million people live in the Great Lakes basin. Lakes Michigan, Ontario, Superior, Erie, and Huron continue to attract people and businesses. But the lakes themselves have not benefited from this development. They have been seriously affected by such issues as pollution, overfishing, and invasive species—issues environmentalists are scrambling to address today.

CRITICAL VIEWING Snow is a way of life for the people who settle in the Great Lakes region. This image of Montrose Harbor in Chicago shows the icy waters of Lake Michigan and the lake's snowy shoreline. What impact, both positive and negative, might human modifications have on the natural landscape along Lake Michigan?

232 CHAPTER 7

Regional and National Growth 233

PLAN: 2-PAGE LESSON

OBJECTIVE

Examine the effects of human modifications on the Great Lakes.

CRITICAL THINKING SKILLS FOR LESSON 2.3

• Analyze Visuals

• Make Connections

• Analyze Environmental Concepts

HISTORICAL THINKING FOR CHAPTER 7

How did rapid change create new opportunities and new tensions for the growing nation? The Great Lakes have been integral to expansion and development since the early days of European exploration. Lesson 2.3 shows how human activities have affected the shoreline and health of the lakes.

BACKGROUND FOR THE TEACHER

The health of the Great Lakes has never been of greater concern. These lakes supply 90 percent of the fresh water in the United States and provide 56 billion gallons of water a day for industrial, urban, and agricultural use. Even though the water is essential, the future of the lakes is uncertain. Organizations such as the Great Lakes Environmental Research Laboratory and Ecosystem Dynamics use scientific research to battle pollutants, invasive species, and habitat destruction. Native American groups near the Great Lakes are also raising awareness about the lakes' problems. Members of a group called Mother Earth Water Walkers trek 2,000 miles around the Great Lakes every year to focus public attention on the declining water quality. As one walker said, "I walk for my grandchildren, and those that are coming."

HISTORY NOTEBOOK

Encourage students to complete the American Places page for Chapter 7 in their History Notebooks as they read.

INTRODUCE & ENGAGE

PREVIEW USING VISUALS

Direct students' attention to the photograph of Montrose Harbor on Lake Michigan.
ASK: What details in the photo indicate how people use the harbor? *(Possible response: The empty boat slips in the protected part of the harbor at the left show that people dock boats there during warmer seasons. The trees laid out in rows suggest that the area is used for recreation—there might be picnic areas or parking spots beneath the snow. The two piers seem as if they would make good fishing spots.)* Explain to students that this lesson explores some of the ways that humans have used and altered the Great Lakes.

TEACH   STEM

GUIDED DISCUSSION

1. **Make Connections** Why are areas near lakes usually developed? *(Possible response: Lakes provide a means for transportation as well as valuable resources, such as water and fish. Some people develop lakeside areas to take advantage of recreational opportunities.)*

2. **Analyze Environmental Concepts** Based on the text and the photograph, how might the ecology of this area have changed since Europeans arrived? *(Possible response: There were probably thick forests, wetlands, and many plants and animals there. The photograph shows significant development, so there has likely been a significant reduction in biodiversity in the area, with trees being the current main plant species.)*

🛡 AMERICAN PLACES

With the Montrose Harbor and beach area, constructed in the 1930s, city planners tried to strike a balance between recreation and conservation. Although nearly deserted in winter, the harbor and park are popular recreational sites in the summer months. In addition to the boat slips and launches in the photograph, the beach area also has a dog park, kayak and volleyball sections, a complex of food concessions, and a swimming beach. At the south end, the city has preserved both a dune habitat that shelters endangered plant life and a natural area where migratory birds stop during the fall and spring.

ACTIVE OPTIONS

On Your Feet: Fishbowl Arrange students in two concentric circles. Ask the inner circle to discuss the following questions and arrive at conclusions: What things does a body of water such as Lake Michigan provide to the people who live around it? What responsibilities do people have toward such a body of water? Students on the inside discuss the questions while those outside listen for new information. Then direct the two circles to switch places. Encourage volunteers to summarize the conclusions discussed in their circle.

NG Learning Framework: Investigate Great Lakes' Health   STEM

ATTITUDE Responsibility

SKILLS Observation, Collaboration

Share the Background for the Teacher information with students. Arrange the class into five groups and explain that they will create a collaborative snapshot of the Great Lakes' health today. Assign each group one of the Great Lakes and direct them to conduct online research about the health of their lake, considering such factors as erosion, pollution levels, and biodiversity. Prompt groups to work together to create a Great Lakes map or infographic that displays their findings. Ask a volunteer from each group to present the information their group contributed. As a class, assess the current physical condition of the Great Lakes.

DIFFERENTIATE

STRIVING READERS

Complete a T-Chart Instruct pairs to create a T-Chart to summarize how people have benefited from and harmed the Great Lakes. Tell them to label one column Benefited and the other one Harmed. Ask students to closely examine the photograph and then read the text aloud to each other, pausing to add details under each column. Encourage pairs to compare their completed charts, noting similarities and differences.

GIFTED & TALENTED   STEM

Investigate Invasive Species Direct students to conduct online research about zebra mussels, round gobies, or another invasive species in the Great Lakes. Tell them to analyze the causes and effects of the species' introduction to the lakes and to share their findings in a multimedia presentation. Encourage students to use a chart to track causes and effects, including environmental, economic, social, and political impacts. Invite students to share their presentations with the class.

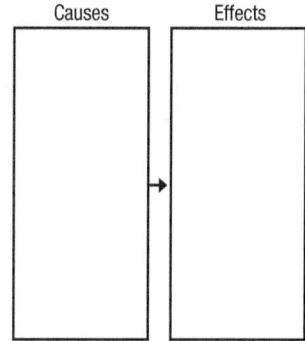

See the Chapter Planner for more strategies for differentiation.

CRITICAL VIEWING Positive impacts include the creation of recreational areas and preservation of open spaces and natural habitats that might attract birders and others who enjoy nature. Negative impacts include pollution from boats and people, introduction of invasive species, and destruction of native species.

STRENGTHENING THE NATIONAL GOVERNMENT

Since the nation's founding, Americans have argued over how much power they should grant the federal government. That question drove decisions of voters, lawmakers, and the Supreme Court in the first half of the 19th century.

AMERICAN PLACES
The Supreme Court, Washington, D.C.

Surprisingly, the Supreme Court was not provided with its own building until 1935. Chief Justice William Howard Taft, who had also served as president, persuaded Congress to construct a permanent home for the Court. The architect built it in the style of an ancient Roman temple. The result was as Taft wished: "a building of dignity and importance suitable for its use as the permanent home of the Supreme Court of the United States."

THE SUPREME COURT AND NATIONAL POWER

Between 1814 and 1828, a series of Supreme Court decisions further expanded federal power and encouraged economic development. One case, **Gibbons v. Ogden**, focused on the steamboat monopoly New York State had granted to Robert Livingston. The case required the court to interpret the Constitution's vaguely worded commerce clause, which grants Congress the power "to regulate Commerce with foreign Nations, and among the several States, and with the Indian Tribes."

Aaron Ogden, who owned a fleet of steamboats, had an agreement with monopoly holder Robert Livingston to operate his boats in waters between New Jersey and New York. Thomas Gibbons joined him in this enterprise, but the partnership fell apart when Gibbons ran his own steamboat from Elizabethtown, New Jersey, to New York City. Ogden sued him. Gibbons argued that Congress alone had the power to regulate interstate commerce, or business affairs between states, and that New York had been wrong to grant the monopoly in the first place. The Court decided in favor of Gibbons, ruling that federal laws regulating interstate commerce take precedence over state laws.

This ruling greatly expanded Congress's power to regulate commerce between states. By making it illegal for states to grant monopolies and enact laws restricting interstate commerce, the decision also encouraged competition. It triggered a boom in steamboat traffic on the Mississippi and other major rivers, accelerating the country's westward expansion and economic development.

New Hampshire's Dartmouth College was at the center of another key Supreme Court ruling. In 1769, King George III of England had granted the college a charter, giving authority for managing the school to a board of trustees. In 1815, after a religious controversy led the board to remove the college's president, the New Hampshire legislature passed laws that amended the charter. Its actions made the once-private school a public college, changed the duties of the trustees, and altered the trustee selection process.

The trustees sued, and the case, called **Dartmouth College v. Woodward**, eventually reached the Supreme Court. The court ruled in favor of the trustees, holding that the charter was a contract, and the Constitution prohibits states from passing laws that alter the obligations of a contract. The ruling had a powerful effect on the U.S. economy. Shielded from one form of state interference, businesses were more secure and likelier to attract investors and expand.

THE SECOND BANK OF THE UNITED STATES

The Bank of the United States played an invaluable role in helping the young country handle its huge Revolutionary War debt and establish an effective financial system. But, as you have read, the bank faced strong political opposition based on questions of its constitutionality. After a bill to renew its charter failed in Congress, the Bank of the United States was forced to close its doors in 1811. It didn't take long for economic problems to arise again.

The United States at this time relied heavily on credit, or the ability to borrow money or obtain goods or services before paying for them. Credit is given based on trust that payment will be made in the future. Because far too little cash was available in the country's growing territory, business dealings were often based solely on trust. But when a chain of transactions is based on credit, the failure of one borrower can bring down many lenders. By 1815, states had chartered more than 200 private banks in an effort to solve their cash-shortage problems. These banks issued notes that served as currency in cash-starved areas.

Many influential leaders, including Henry Clay, John Calhoun, and President Monroe, wanted to create a new national bank to stabilize the economy and distribute scarce cash more uniformly. They argued that the state bank notes varied too much in value. Some were at risk of losing value entirely, destabilizing the whole economic system. The expanding nation needed a central financial institution to coordinate the flow of money.

In 1816, Congress chartered the **Second Bank of the United States**. Based in Philadelphia, the bank was a blend of public institution and private enterprise. The federal government deposited funds in the bank, controlled a fifth of its shares of stock, and appointed a fifth of the directors, but otherwise the bank operated as a private business. It pumped large amounts of paper currency into the system in an attempt to fuel the postwar economy and make it easier to pay debts. This was especially helpful in the new states of the West, where buyers were making numerous land purchases on credit.

The Second Bank provoked as much hostility as the first had. Its opponents still argued that the Constitution did not grant Congress the power to establish corporations of any type, including a national bank. In the case of **McCulloch v. Maryland**, 1819, the Supreme Court ruled the bank was constitutional and protected it from state taxation. In his decision, Chief Justice John Marshall declared that the laws of the federal government "form the supreme law of the land." Business flourished in the new legal environment created by the Supreme Court's **landmark decisions**, or legal cases that settle important questions about new or existing laws.

HISTORICAL THINKING

1. **READING CHECK** How did a Supreme Court ruling affect traffic on the Mississippi River?

2. **DRAW CONCLUSIONS** How did the Supreme Court decision in *Dartmouth College* v. *Woodward* affect the relationship between state governments and businesses?

3. **IDENTIFY PROBLEMS AND SOLUTIONS** What problems led to the call for a second national bank?

PLAN: 2-PAGE LESSON

OBJECTIVE

Explore connections among Congress, the Supreme Court, and the banking industry after the War of 1812.

CRITICAL THINKING SKILLS FOR LESSON 2.4

• Draw Conclusions

• Identify Problems and Solutions

• Summarize

• Describe

HISTORICAL THINKING FOR CHAPTER 7

How did rapid expansion create new opportunities and new tensions for the growing nation? As the nation grew, tensions flared regarding how much power should be wielded by the states and by the federal government. Lesson 2.4 discusses several landmark decisions by the Supreme Court that helped define the powers states did and did not have.

BACKGROUND FOR THE TEACHER

The Constitution did not specifically define the powers and rights of the Supreme Court, so Congress, along with a set of appointed justices, took on the task of developing a system for creating federal law. The Judiciary Act of 1789 set the protocols for organizing and maintaining the U.S. Supreme Court as well as the federal lower court system. George Washington appointed the first six justices, appointing new ones as openings occurred. The Court was originally structured with one Chief Justice and five associate justices. The number of justices on the court changed several times before 1869, at which time it was set at nine and has remained so ever since. The job of a Supreme Court justice is a lifetime appointment. With an average tenure of 16 years, only 17 Chief Justices and 101 associate justices have served since the Court's 1790 founding.

INTRODUCE & ENGAGE

ACCESS PRIOR KNOWLEDGE

Write the term *Supreme Court* on the board. Have students brainstorm words or phrases they associate with this term. Record their ideas on the board. Invite them to identify any historic Supreme Court cases they know of and discuss why they believe those cases were important. Tell students that in this lesson they will learn about three Supreme Court cases in the 19th century that engendered or clarified important changes to U.S. laws regarding banking regulation, tax structure, and corporate transactions.

TEACH

GUIDED DISCUSSION

1. **Summarize** What was the outcome of the case of *Dartmouth College* v. *Woodward*? *(The court ruled that the New Hampshire legislature couldn't force a private college to become a public one because the school had a preexisting charter, which is a contract, and the Constitution prohibits states from passing laws that change contractual obligations.)*

2. **Describe** How did the federal government help stabilize the economy of some states in the West? *(The government placed large sums of cash in the Second Bank of the United States, controlled a percentage of the bank's assets, and infused western states with paper currency. This greatly enhanced the postwar economy by helping people pay off debts on land they had bought on credit.)*

◎ AMERICAN PLACES

At first, the Supreme Court met in the New York City Merchants Exchange Building. But when Philadelphia became the U.S. capital in 1790, the government and the Court moved there—first sharing space in the State House, also known as Independence Hall, then in City Hall. The federal government relocated again in 1800, this time to Washington, D.C., where it has remained, and the Supreme Court took up residence in the newly constructed Capitol Building. More than a century later, in 1932, Congress finally approved construction of a building specifically for the Supreme Court.

ACTIVE OPTIONS

On Your Feet: Three Corners Label three corners of the room with one of the landmark cases discussed in the lesson: *Gibbons* v. *Ogden*, *Dartmouth College* v. *Woodward*, and *McCulloch* v. *Maryland*. Instruct students to move to the corner of their choice for a focused discussion that addresses the question: How did the Supreme Court's ruling affect the lives of U.S. citizens? Reconvene as a class and allow members of each group to summarize their discussions. Invite students to draw conclusions about how the landmark cases might have influenced subsequent U.S. laws.

NG Learning Framework: Debate States' Rights Versus Federal Power

| ATTITUDE | Empowerment |

| KNOWLEDGE | Our Human Story |

Pose the following question: Should individual states be able to create laws that take precedence over federal laws? Divide the class into two groups and assign one to argue for states' rights and the other to argue for federal power. Instruct groups to use information from the lesson and from outside research to craft their arguments. Guide each group to anticipate the arguments of the opposing side and explore ideas to rebut them. Ask students from each side to take turns presenting their arguments.

DIFFERENTIATE

STRIVING READERS

Determine Chronology Assign students to work in pairs. Explain that they are to determine the chronology of events relating to the Second Bank of the United States. Suggest that they first scan the lesson and write the dates mentioned in chronological order in a Sequence Chain. Then ask students to read carefully and add notes. Invite pairs to trade Sequence Chains and note any differences.

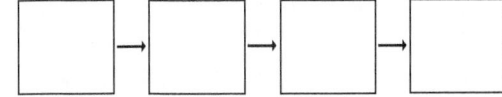

PRE-AP

Extend Knowledge Prompt students to gather information from a variety of sources to learn more about one of the Supreme Court decisions during the 1800s that gave more power to the federal government. Encourage students to quote or paraphrase and cite primary and secondary sources as appropriate. Invite volunteers to share their findings in an oral or written report.

See the Chapter Planner for more strategies for differentiation.

HISTORICAL THINKING

ANSWERS

1. *Gibbons* v. *Ogden* prohibited states from granting monopolies to steamboat companies and from passing laws restricting interstate transportation, which opened the doors to competition among steamboat companies on the Mississippi River.

2. The *Dartmouth College* v. *Woodward* decision prohibited states from passing laws that changed contractual obligations, which protected businesses from some kinds of state interference.

3. A shortage of cash hindered commerce, forcing people to rely on credit, and the notes issued by banks varied greatly in value and were often unsound.

NATIONALISM AND FOREIGN POLICY

Picture a jigsaw-puzzle map of the United States with its present-day borders. After the War of 1812, the puzzle was far from complete, but the fast-growing nation would soon add several key pieces.

SETTLING THE COUNTRY'S BOUNDARIES

When the War of 1812 ended, a wave of nationalism swept over the United States. As you have read, nationalism is a strong feeling of loyalty and devotion to one's country, often emphasizing the idea that the nation is superior to all others. The optimistic national mood influenced—and was influenced by—developments in foreign affairs as the United States began to increase its interactions with other countries.

After taking office in early 1817, President James Monroe worked to establish clearer borders for the United States. **John Quincy Adams**—a skilled diplomat, a member of the U.S. delegation that had negotiated the Treaty of Ghent that ended the War of 1812, and the son of second president John Adams—helped negotiate the Rush-Bagot Agreement of 1817 with Britain. The goal of this treaty was to calm diplomatic tensions on the Great Lakes and Lake Champlain, near the Canadian border, by limiting naval fleets that patrolled the waters. Under its terms, each side was allowed one military vessel each on Lake Champlain and Lake Ontario and two on each of the other Great Lakes. As Monroe's Secretary of State, Adams also helped negotiate the Convention of 1818, an agreement with Britain that fixed the border between the United States and Canada at the **49th parallel**—that is, the line of latitude established at 49 degrees north latitude.

Monroe and Adams also negotiated with the Spanish minister to settle the U.S. borders with Spain's territories. In the resulting **Adams-Onís Treaty** of 1819, Spain ceded both East and West Florida to the United States and dropped its claim to the Oregon Territory. The United States, in return, recognized Spanish sovereignty over the vast territory stretching

The United States, 1820

from Texas to present-day California. Adams referred to the accord as the Transcontinental Treaty because it extended the borders of the United States from the Atlantic to the Pacific.

THE PANIC OF 1819

As world demand for cotton cloth increased each year, prices skyrocketed for land on which to grow cotton in the southern United States. This led to a dramatic spike in Southern cotton prices. British manufacturers turned to other cotton suppliers, such as India. This sent American cotton prices tumbling, and the value of land that produced cotton fell with them. Meanwhile, something similar was happening in the country's new western lands, where easy credit and high European demand for American agricultural products helped to create a speculative "bubble" in land prices. The cost of land kept increasing, and many people thought it would continue to rise indefinitely. But the bubble burst, in part for the same

reasons as the drop in Southern cotton values. Prices for American crops had risen along with the cost of the land on which they grew, which in turn caused European demand to decrease.

As land prices fell, many who had borrowed money based on future profits were unable to repay their loans. Banks and businesses began to fail, and they fell like dominoes. The **Panic of 1819** had begun, an economic crisis that sent the nation into the worst financial downturn it had yet experienced. The economy took three years to recover.

Farmers were hit hard, but many managed to get by through subsistence farming. In the cities, business ground to a halt due to bank failures and a lack of sources of credit. About half a million workers lost their jobs. Americans shuddered to see "children freezing in the winter's storm—and the fathers without coats and shoes." Charitable groups opened soup kitchens, while many families who had moved to towns and cities for work returned to the countryside to live with relatives.

THE MONROE DOCTRINE

Despite the economic downturn, President Monroe remained popular, and he easily won re-election in 1820. The years of his presidency became known as the **Era of Good Feelings** because of the near absence of party politics and conflict, both within the United States and in its direct dealings with European nations. Elsewhere in the Western Hemisphere, however, conflict abounded.

Throughout the first two decades of the 19th century, South and Central America faced one struggle after another. Once-powerful Spain had been weakened by war and domestic upheaval, and colonial leaders such as Simón Bolívar in Venezuela and José de San Martín in Argentina pushed ahead with their long-simmering plans for independence. By 1822, the former Spanish colonies of Chile, Mexico, and Venezuela had won their independence, as had the former Portuguese colony of Brazil.

Fearing that France or Russia might attempt to fill the vacuum left by Spain in the Americas, President

As the fifth president of the United States, James Monroe was the last of the Founding Fathers to remain active in national politics. Like Thomas Jefferson and John Adams, two presidents who preceded him, Monroe died on the Fourth of July.

Monroe urged Congress to recognize the new Latin American republics. In December 1823, the president formalized a new foreign policy that eventually became known as the **Monroe Doctrine**: "The American continents, by the free and independent conditions which they have assumed and maintained, are henceforth not to be considered as subjects for future colonization by any European power." Monroe made it clear that, while the United States would not involve itself in any European wars, it would defend the Americas against any interference from Europe. Through this bold statement, the United States claimed the role of protector and leader of the Western Hemisphere.

HISTORICAL THINKING

1. **READING CHECK** What was the Monroe Doctrine?

2. **DRAW CONCLUSIONS** Why do you think Americans did not blame President Monroe for the Panic of 1819?

3. **INTERPRET MAPS** What areas of North America did the United States gain under the Adams-Onís Treaty?

4. **MAKE CONNECTIONS** What connections existed between Spain's domestic situation and the terms of the Adams-Onís Treaty?

PLAN: 2-PAGE LESSON

OBJECTIVE

Explore agreements the United States made with other nations to expand its territorial borders and assert its independence.

CRITICAL THINKING SKILLS FOR LESSON 3.1

- Draw Conclusions
- Interpret Maps
- Make Connections
- Analyze Cause and Effect
- Make Generalizations

HISTORICAL THINKING FOR CHAPTER 7

How did rapid change create new opportunities and new tensions for the growing nation? As western expansion continued, the United States pushed for clearer international borders, and the economy flourished for a time. Lesson 3.1 discusses the economic collapse that occurred in 1819.

BACKGROUND FOR THE TEACHER

The Panic of 1819 spread rapidly and left devastation in its wake. In New York State, property values plummeted from $315 million to $256 million in just two years, and land prices in Pennsylvania dropped in a single year from $150 to $35 per acre. More than 1,800 people were sent to prison for their debts in Philadelphia; in Boston, the number was nearly twice as high. Protests broke out as financially strapped Americans demanded laws to protect them from rising debt and to bring an end to debtors' prisons. Though the panic subsided by 1823, it continued to influence U.S. politics. One result was the population's widespread mistrust, resentment, and hostility toward banking institutions, large corporations, and politicians. Americans began to demand state constitutions that were more democratic and placed fewer restrictions on who could vote or hold office.

INTRODUCE & ENGAGE

CONNECT TO TODAY

Write the term *Era of Good Feelings* on the board. Ask students what qualities they would expect to encounter in their daily lives during a time known by this description. Record their responses on the board. Tell students that in this lesson they will learn why this nickname was applied to James Monroe's two terms as president.

TEACH

GUIDED DISCUSSION

1. **Analyze Cause and Effect** What events led to the economic downturn and bank failures of 1819? *(Global demand for cotton cloth caused the price of U.S. cotton to rise dramatically, which led Britain to start buying cotton from other countries. That caused a sharp drop in the price of U.S. cotton. Meanwhile, land speculation and easy credit in the new western territories drove land prices up. As prices got higher, demand fell. Land was not worth as much, and banks began to fail when people couldn't pay back loans.)*

2. **Make Generalizations** What effect do you think the Era of Good Feelings might have had on the day-to-day lives and attitudes of Americans? *(Possible response: Because of fewer conflicts outside and within the United States and between the nation's political parties, average Americans might have been more upbeat, less angry, and less fearful about the future—even through difficult economic times.)*

MORE INFORMATION

Treaty of 1818 Share with students that the treaty establishing the 49th parallel as the boundary between U.S. and Canadian territories was also known as the "Convention respecting fisheries, boundary and the restoration of slaves" between the United States and Great Britain. Among other things, the treaty cleared the way for U.S. fishing rights in the waters off Newfoundland and Labrador. The United States and Britain also agreed to a joint control of the Oregon Territory, which would later lead to conflict. Though the treaty establishing the 49th-parallel boundary improved U.S. relations with Britain and Canada, it had a devastating effect on the area's native population. Overnight, native peoples on both sides of the boundary line became subject to different laws and ownership rights than they had followed before. Settlers often homesteaded on lands that had long been home to native communities, sometimes tearing down dwellings and whole villages and leaving the former residents homeless.

ACTIVE OPTIONS

On Your Feet: Team Word Webbing Organize students into groups of four. Have them record on a sheet of paper how they think countries in Europe and South and Central America likely reacted to the Monroe Doctrine. Encourage students to build on their teammates' entries as they rotate the paper from one member to the next. Then call on volunteers to make statements about international reactions to the Monroe Doctrine based on their Team Word Webs.

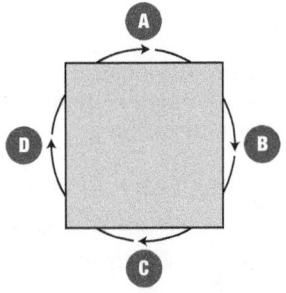

NG Learning Framework: Create a Community Service Plan

ATTITUDE Responsibility

SKILL Problem-Solving

Divide students into small groups and ask them to imagine it is the winter of 1820; the Panic of 1819 has damaged the U.S. economy, and many people are suffering. Prompt students to take on the role of community members working together to devise a plan to supply food, shelter, and clothing to the hardest hit residents of their community. Invite group members to discuss ideas to prepare their plan. When they have finished, ask groups to share their plans with the class.

DIFFERENTIATE

STRIVING READERS

Summarize with Tweets As students read the lesson, direct them to pause after each paragraph and write a tweet summarizing the paragraph's main idea in their own words. Then place students in pairs, and have partners take turns reading their tweets aloud to each other, discussing differences in their summaries.

GIFTED & TALENTED

Create a Graphic Instruct students to create a graphic comparing the economic downturns of 1819 and 2008, conducting additional research as necessary. Prompt them to consider in what ways the downturns were alike and in what ways they were different. Invite students to present their finished graphic to the class and make a statement summarizing their findings.

See the Chapter Planner for more strategies for differentiation.

HISTORICAL THINKING

ANSWERS

1. The Monroe Doctrine was a foreign policy asserting that the American continents were free and independent and that the United States would no longer allow European powers to colonize or interfere in the Americas and would not get involved in wars in Europe.

2. Possible response: Americans didn't blame Monroe because he had done so much to expand the nation, had helped to ease diplomatic tensions with Britain, and had already served one full term as president.

3. Spain gave control of both sides of Florida to the United States and relinquished all claims on the Oregon Territory, which the United States co-administered with Great Britain.

4. Because Spain had been weakened by war and domestic chaos, it might have been more willing to rid itself of some of its overseas colonies and claims, such as Florida and the Oregon Territory, which drained its shrinking resources.

WESTWARD EXPANSION AND TENSIONS OVER SLAVERY

Think about a time you had to make a compromise. What did you give up in order to get what you originally wanted? Were you satisfied? Compromises are important ways to manage conflict, but they don't always solve the underlying problem.

SETTLING THE NORTHWEST TERRITORY

The growing nationalism in the United States was mirrored by a dramatic expansion to new territories in the West. In the first two decades of the 19th century, the number of Americans living west of the Appalachian Mountains grew from about 300,000 to more than 2 million. "Old America seems to be breaking up, and moving westward," one man wrote in 1817, as he watched people move their possessions down the Ohio River on flatboats.

The region called the Old Southwest—the area that included Alabama and Mississippi—was growing fast due to the cotton boom, but the Northwest Territory, or Old Northwest, was growing even faster. Bounded by the Appalachian Mountains in the east, the Ohio River in the south, and the Mississippi River in the west, much of the region's land was ideally suited for farming, thanks in large part to its glacial past. For millions of years, ending about twenty thousand years ago, vast sheets of ice had plowed across this part of North America, smoothing and flattening the land and leaving behind thick deposits of silt, sand, clay, and rock called **glacial till**. Over the centuries, it became exceptionally fertile soil.

As you have read, when the Northwest Territory was formally opened for settlement, the Northwest Ordinances of 1784, 1785, and 1787 established laws calling for the territory to be divided into a number of self-governing districts. The plan was for these to become states once they met certain requirements. The laws also specified such things as lot sizes and prices. Importantly, the Northwest Ordinance of 1787 prohibited slavery from the region forever.

Most white settlers were dissatisfied with the first land they claimed; about two-thirds of them moved again within a few years. There was always talk of

In this illustration from a series called "Life of Lincoln," the very young future president Abraham Lincoln maneuvers a flatboat full of cargo down a river in the early 1800s. The flatboat was a practical mode of transportation at the time.

richer land a bit farther west, or a new town that was certain to mushroom into a major city, or greater opportunity just over the horizon. Settlers who remained in a community often became its leading citizens, consolidating land into larger farms, setting up gristmills and sawmills, holding political offices, and establishing the small towns that served as county seats and trading centers. In many cases, the storekeepers who were among the first to arrive often made small fortunes through trade.

THE MISSOURI COMPROMISE

As the United States expanded, each region began to establish a separate identity. People came to feel strong loyalty toward the part of the country in which they lived, a concept known as **sectionalism**. Several factors drove the development of sectionalism in the United States, including economic differences among regions—dependence on industry in the northeast, for example, as opposed to the agriculture that drove the southeast and west—and a variety of cultural differences. But slavery was one of the major causes of sectionalism, and westward expansion was making that more evident.

In 1815, the United States was evenly divided between slave states and free states; there were nine of each. The balance held over the next four years as Mississippi and Alabama were admitted to the Union as slave states and Indiana and Illinois were admitted as free states. Politically, this balance was extremely important. Although the free states held a large and growing numerical advantage in the House of Representatives, the two sides were equally represented in the Senate. That meant neither could force through legislation opposed by the other. Southerners feared that if the free states gained control of the Senate, they would outlaw the practice of slavery nationwide.

The upcoming statehood of the Missouri Territory threatened to upset that balance in 1819. About 10,000 enslaved people lived in the territory. If Missouri were admitted as a slave state, as its territorial legislature had decreed, then the slave states would have a majority in the Senate. Slavery in Missouri, an area at roughly the same latitudes as much of Illinois, Indiana, and Ohio, seemed to violate the assumption, long held by many in the free states, that if slavery expanded at all, it would do so only in the South. The Constitution's Three-fifths Compromise, which allowed states to count enslaved people as a fraction of free persons in the census, had already given the slave states 20 more members of Congress and 20 more electors for the presidency. The South seemed to be getting extra and unfair representation.

Missouri Compromise, 1820

OREGON COUNTRY
Disputed territory occupied jointly by Great Britain and United States

BRITISH NORTH AMERICA (CANADA)

Admitted as free state, 1820.

UNORGANIZED TERRITORY

MICHIGAN TERRITORY

Admitted as slave state, 1821

Missouri Compromise Line, 36°30'

NEW SPAIN

ARKANSAS TERRITORY

FLORIDA TERRITORY

Ceded by Spain, 1819

PACIFIC OCEAN

ATLANTIC OCEAN

Gulf of Mexico

- Closed to slavery by Missouri Compromise
- Open to slavery by Missouri Compromise
- Free states and territories
- Slave states and territories

0 100 200 miles
0 100 200 kilometers

PLAN: 4-PAGE LESSON

OBJECTIVE

Analyze how westward expansion and changing populations influenced political developments in the 19th century.

CRITICAL THINKING SKILLS FOR LESSON 3.2

- Form and Support Opinions
- Interpret Maps
- Draw Conclusions
- Analyze Cause and Effect
- Make Inferences
- Compare and Contrast
- Analyze Primary Sources

HISTORICAL THINKING FOR CHAPTER 7

How did rapid change create new opportunities and new tensions for the growing nation?
Westward expansion threatened the delicate balance between slave states and free states. Lesson 3.2 explores how the Missouri Compromise was created to keep the balance and sidestep this divisive issue.

BACKGROUND FOR THE TEACHER

In the 19th century, before steamboats were viable, the flatboat was the most common form of river transport into the Old Southwest. This craft had many nicknames: johnboat, keelboat, scow, and joe boat. Flat on the bottom and typically oblong or rectangular, the largest flatboats were about 28 feet long. They were made of cheap, durable materials. Some were used by fishermen to collect clams. When going downriver, speed was completely dependent on the river's current. The upriver return journey, however, required crew members to use long poles they sank into the river bottom to push and pull the boat against the current. Some flatboat round trips took up to nine months.

HISTORY NOTEBOOK

Encourage students to complete the Reid on the Road video series page for Chapter 7 in their History Notebooks after they view the video.

INTRODUCE & ENGAGE

PREVIEW USING VISUALS

Direct students' attention to the illustration from the "Life of Lincoln" series. Ask them to point out any details they notice, such as the construction of the flatboat, how the crew steers it, the amount and placement of its cargo, and the other boats in the background. **ASK:** Why do you think people might have used a vessel like this one despite access to steamboats? *(Possible responses: It was probably much cheaper to travel by flatboat, especially if hauling freight. It looks self-propelled and simply built, so perhaps people built and operated flatboats themselves rather than paying a steamboat company, but trips probably took longer.)* Tell students that in this lesson they will learn about people packing up and moving to newly opened land in the west.

TEACH

GUIDED DISCUSSION

1. **Analyze Cause and Effect** Why did westward expansion serve to entrench public opinion on the issue of slavery? *(The United States was evenly divided between slave and free states, so when the country began to expand there was much concern about whether states would be admitted as free or slave states in order to maintain a political balance. Americans expressed their support for or against slavery based on the region in which they lived and if that region relied on enslaved labor or not.)*

2. **Draw Conclusions** Why did the Three-fifths Compromise benefit the South? *(Possible response: The Three-fifths Compromise added enslaved people to a state's census, counting an enslaved person as three-fifths of a free person. By increasing the population count of slave states, it entitled those states to increased representation in Congress and a greater number of electors.)*

3. **Make Inferences** Why were many white settlers in the Northwest Territory dissatisfied with the first land they claimed? *(Possible responses: Their expectations might have been too high, based on rumors or their own desires. They might have experienced rough weather, drought, or flooding that ruined crops. They might have felt isolated by living too far from towns or cities.)*

MORE INFORMATION

The Hostilities of Sectionalism Remind students that to a great extent, sectionalist hostilities were based on anxiety over the economy. New Englanders had watched as their best workers left for new opportunities in the West. Later, when the rail network was fully up and functioning, they saw proof that the West could produce commodities such as wool and grain at lower prices than much of New England. The West had sectionalist tendencies of its own, partly based on westerners' gnawing belief that eastern business interests were exploiting them. On a more personal level, many westerners felt that other parts of the country disparaged them as uncultured or uneducated.

In the South, meanwhile, though plantation owners did not make up the majority of the population, they were the richest and most powerful members of society, and their way of life was dependent on enslaved workers. Rather than opposing slavery, small farmers with no slaves typically supported slavery, hoping to become prosperous enough to buy slaves of their own. The South's near universal acceptance of slavery was what allowed plantations to flourish. Anything that threatened that way of life was met with resistance. Slavery was the South's economic backbone and the foundation of its sectionalism.

DIFFERENTIATE

INCLUSION

Describe and Predict Using a Cartoon Pair students to work together to describe the Nast cartoon in detail. Instruct them to read the caption, discuss what they think is meant by "the spoils system," and predict what they will learn about Jackson and the spoils system in the lesson. Then ask pairs this question: Does the cartoonist have a positive or negative point of view about Jackson and the spoils system? *(The details convey the cartoonist's negative view of Jackson and the spoils system.)*

GIFTED & TALENTED

Create a Podcast Prompt students to prepare an episode of a history podcast about a topic discussed in this lesson, such as opportunities and tensions as settlers moved west, details of the Missouri Compromise, slave leaders and rebellions, the end of the Era of Good Feelings, the rise of the spoils system, or the formation of the Democratic Party. Suggest that students write a script for their podcast, including sound effects. Invite them to present their episode to the class live or record it on a device and play it for the class.

See the Chapter Planner for more strategies for differentiation.

Debate in the Senate raged for weeks in early 1820. Finally, a group led by Henry Clay succeeded in negotiating the **Missouri Compromise**. Under its terms, Missouri would be admitted to the Union as a slave state and Maine would be admitted as a free state, preserving the balance between slave and free states. Going forward, slavery would be prohibited in all the lands acquired in the Louisiana Purchase north of the southern border of Missouri, which was 36° 30' north latitude. Under this provision, slavery would be allowed to continue in the Arkansas territory, but it would be prohibited in **unorganized territory**, the vast expanses of the Louisiana Territory that lay farther north. This included the future states of Iowa, Minnesota, Wisconsin, the Dakotas, Nebraska, and Kansas. Another provision stipulated that any slaves who escaped to the free states would be returned to their owners upon capture.

DISAGREEMENTS OVER SLAVERY

The dispute over Missouri made it clear that slavery was becoming an increasingly divisive issue, but no one seemed to have a solid plan for what might happen should slavery end. Slavery had entrenched in Americans' minds the idea that whites and African Americans were somehow fundamentally different. Many white citizens, both in the North and the South, believed it would be impossible for the two races to live together in the United States. That was the message of the **American Colonization Society**, founded in 1816 and based in Washington, D.C. The society bought land in western Africa where it established a colony called **Liberia**, which means "land of freedom." Over the next 50 years, the society sent about 12,000 free African Americans to the colony, many of whom died of tropical diseases. As time went by, fewer African Americans migrated—and most were never interested in emigrating in the first place.

Meanwhile, unrest brewed among African Americans, both free and enslaved. In Charleston, South Carolina, a free and literate African American named **Denmark Vesey** had followed the Missouri controversy in the newspapers, which reinforced his belief that slavery was immoral. Taking inspiration from a successful slave revolt in Haiti decades earlier, Vesey organized a large-scale rebellion scheduled for June 16, 1822.

The rebels planned to seize Charleston's arsenals, guardhouses, and roads, and then to kill slaveholders before fleeing to Haiti, where slavery had been abolished. Before the rebellion could take place, insiders leaked the plans, and Vesey called

off the attack. Over the next two months, authorities captured and hanged 35 alleged conspirators, including Vesey. White southerners blamed Vesey's rebellion on the agitation against slavery in the Missouri debate.

Nine years later, **Nat Turner**, an enslaved but literate field hand and traveling preacher, led a deadly revolt in Virginia. Turner claimed God sent him visions urging him to lead a slave rebellion. During the night of August 22, 1831, Turner and his followers moved from farm to farm, slaughtering white families, including children and infants. By dawn, Turner's band of about 75 men had killed more than 50 people. A militia of 3,000 soon arrived to put down the rebellion, and Turner and his men were either killed or captured, later to be hanged.

Fearing more uprisings, the Virginia legislature met to discuss the issue. Some argued for a crackdown on the free black community's activities. Others

Denmark Vesey statue by sculptor Ed Dwight in Charleston, South Carolina

PRIMARY SOURCE

At his trial, Denmark Vesey kept his head held high, facing his prosecutors with the heroism of someone who believed he was doing the right thing even though he was resigned to bear the most severe punishment for it. His behavior rattled the sentencing judge, who addressed him directly at trial.

It is difficult to imagine, what infatuation could have prompted you to attempt an enterprise so wild and visionary. You were a free man, comely, wealthy, and enjoyed every comfort compatible with your situation. You had, therefore, much to risk and little to gain.

—from Judge to Denmark Vesey at his trial, 1822

called for an end to slavery, either immediately or gradually. Finally, Virginia and other southern states passed laws further limiting the freedom of both enslaved and free African Americans.

THE REINVENTION OF POLITICS

Slavery and the power of the federal government were central issues in the presidential election of 1824. James Monroe had run unopposed in 1820, but the 1824 election featured five strong candidates, including Secretary of State John Quincy Adams, Secretary of War John C. Calhoun, Secretary of the Treasury William Crawford, House speaker Henry Clay, and war hero Andrew Jackson. The election ended with Adams, Crawford, Clay, and Jackson vying for the presidency. Jackson won the popular vote and more electoral votes than the other candidates, but he needed more than half of the electoral votes to win the election.

Per the Constitution, it fell to the House of Representatives to decide the election. Adams narrowly prevailed with Clay's help. Although he had been a brilliant secretary of state, Adams struggled as president and could not rally public or political support for a stronger national government, internal improvements, or a tariff to protect American industry. This was due in part to fierce opposition from Jackson's supporters who remembered what they called Adams's "corrupt bargain" with Clay to win the election.

As the Era of Good Feelings faded, a very different era was coming into view. In New York, politicians developed a political strategy based on party organization and the **spoils system**, also known as the patronage system. Candidates who won an election were expected to remove people who had been appointed to city and state jobs by their predecessors and replace them with their own campaign workers and supporters. They were also expected to distribute political favors to loyal supporters. **Martin Van Buren**, a young lawyer and politician from New York, took advantage of the spoils system to create a powerful statewide organization. His goal was to combine party unity with personal advancement for party members, creating a self-reinforcing network of political power.

In the 1824 election, Van Buren had thrown his support behind Andrew Jackson, who shared his political ideas. Traveling throughout the United States, Van Buren forged a **coalition**, or group united to achieve a common goal, of ambitious state politicians willing to back Jackson. The coalition eventually split from the Democratic-Republicans to

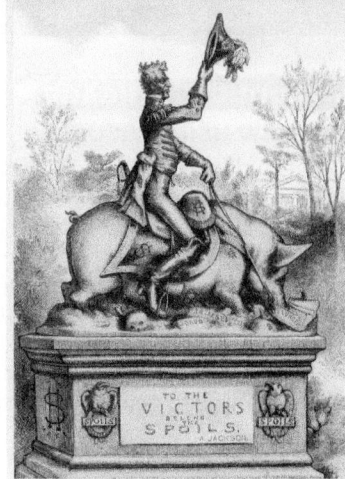

CRITICAL VIEWING Cartoonist Thomas Nast illustrates the spoils system as a statue of Andrew Jackson surrounded by money bags while riding a pig. On the pedestal is the motto "To the Victors Belong the Spoils." How does the image of the pig add to the cartoon's ironic message?

form a new party called the Democratic Party, or the Democrats. Their candidates did extremely well in the congressional elections of 1827, exploiting public disapproval of Adams and his party, the National Republicans. After the election, the Democrats controlled both the House and the Senate. The stage was set for a showdown in the 1828 elections.

HISTORICAL THINKING

1. **READING CHECK** Why was the balance between slave states and free states politically important?

2. **FORM AND SUPPORT OPINIONS** Were white southerners correct in believing Denmark Vesey's rebellion was caused by debates about the Missouri Compromise? Support your opinion with evidence from the text.

3. **INTERPRET MAPS** Which areas did the Missouri Compromise close to slavery, and which did it open?

4. **DRAW CONCLUSIONS** Why did politicians establish the spoils system?

BUILD BACKGROUND

DENMARK VESEY

After living as an enslaved worker for more than 25 years, Denmark Vesey bought his own freedom in 1799, but he could not free his wife and children. Some historians believe that the loss of his family persuaded Vesey to pursue his assault on the institution of slavery. In 1817, he joined the African Methodist Episcopal (AME) Church, where he often preached to small gatherings at his home. Through the church, Vesey met people who would help him plot a rebellion, and by 1821, they had begun making plans. But long before Vesey and his followers ever even discussed an uprising, Charleston city officials had targeted the church as a potential threat. Within months of the AME's founding, the city accused the congregation of worshipping in violation of Charleston ordinances and arrested 140 free men and slaves.

THE 1824 ELECTION

During the Era of Good Feelings, political partisanship had nearly disappeared, and a single party, the Democratic-Republicans, controlled U.S. politics. But the election of 1824 revealed a nation divided over issues of protectionism and trade, not to mention differing views on the role of the federal government. Unlike today, a presidential candidate in 1824 did not openly campaign for the job of president. Instead, candidates used well-connected friends to pass newspapers positive stories about them as well as smears against the opposition. Andrew Jackson's 1824 bid for the presidency received particularly energetic endorsement from Tennessee's elite. His campaign team was made up of speculators, creditors, and political leaders. Jackson, himself a land speculator and cotton planter with 100 enslaved workers, was well positioned to win their support.

TEACH

GUIDED DISCUSSION

4. **Draw Conclusions** Why did the American Colonization Society fail to attract African Americans to colonize Liberia? *(Answers will vary. Possible responses: Most African Americans likely had little interest in moving to an unfamiliar place with no way to make a living or feed their families. Though life was difficult for African Americans in the United States, many preferred to try to create a better life where they were rather than set out for a new home thousands of miles away.)*

5. **Compare and Contrast** How were Denmark Vesey's planned slave rebellion and Nat Turner's revolt similar and different? *(Similarities: Participants in both hoped to kill many people; both were statements against slavery; both had dozens of participants; both had leaders who were put to death for their crimes. Differences: Vesey was not able to carry out his plan, but Turner and his group killed more than 50 people; Vesey planned to seize Charleston's arsenals, take over its roads, and kill all the slaveholders, but Turner rampaged through Virginia farming country killing whole families; Vesey planned to escape to Haiti, but it is not clear what Turner planned.)*

ANALYZE PRIMARY SOURCES

Tell students to read the Primary Source and consider the quote from Denmark Vesey's sentencing judge. Invite them to discuss reasons why Vesey may have chosen to comport himself the way he did at trial. **ASK:** What does the judge's choice of words indicate about his attitude toward Vesey? *(Possible response: The judge's words indicate that he respects and even admires Vesey to a certain extent, but at the same time, he believes Vesey is guilty of a serious crime and cannot imagine why he would throw away all the advantages he had to commit such a crime.)*

ACTIVE OPTIONS

On Your Feet: 1824 Election Roundtable Divide students into groups of four and seat each group in a circle. Pose the following question for discussion: How did the U.S. political system change between 1824 and 1828? Encourage each student to answer the question in a different way. When groups are finished discussing the question, invite them to share their ideas with the class.

NG Learning Framework: Create a Political Cartoon

SKILL Communication

KNOWLEDGE Our Human Story

Instruct students to conduct online research about a recent local, state, or national election. Guide them to look for specifics about the campaign, the election outcome, or one or more of the candidates to use as the basis for a political cartoon. Before they begin, encourage them to review Thomas Nast's "To the Victors Belong the Spoils" as a point of reference. When students have completed their work, gather their cartoons to post in a classroom gallery.

HISTORICAL THINKING

ANSWERS

1. Maintaining a balance between slave and free states meant that neither side had a majority in the Senate, and therefore neither side could pass legislation that the other side opposed.

2. Answers will vary. Possible responses: Yes. Vesey kept a close eye on the debate, and he staged his rebellion after it was decided. No. There were enough reasons to object to slavery without the Missouri Compromise, and he was particularly inspired by an earlier slave revolt in Haiti.

3. The Missouri Compromise closed the unorganized territory to slavery. It opened the Arkansas Territory, which closed up a gap and created an unbroken proslavery block in the South.

4. Politicians established the system to obtain and consolidate power. They could buy votes by promising people public jobs. Once in office, the patronage jobholders would continue to vote for them and also support their policies.

CRITICAL VIEWING The cartoon shows the pig, itself a symbol of gluttony and overindulgence, rooting around in documents emblazoned with words that connote greed, such as *fraud*, *plunder*, and *bribery*. The image of Jackson removing his hat like a gentleman soldier while riding a pig gives the cartoon extra irony.

VOCABULARY

Use each of the terms below in a sentence that demonstrates an understanding of a concept or development discussed in the chapter.

1. capital
   The Industrial Revolution was dependent on investors willing to provide capital to fund the purchase of factories and machinery.

2. cotton gin

3. mass production

4. short-staple cotton

5. abolitionist

6. tariff

7. landmark decision

8. 49th parallel

9. sectionalism

10. spoils system

READING STRATEGY
DRAW CONCLUSIONS

Drawing conclusions about how events and ideas connect is important to building understanding. Complete a graphic organizer like the one below to draw a conclusion about the importance of technology during the early 19th century. Then answer the question.

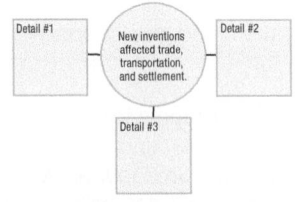

11. How did technology help transform the United States' economy?

MAIN IDEAS

Answer the following questions. Support your answers with evidence from the chapter.

12. Why were waterfalls important in the early decades of the Industrial Revolution? LESSON 1.1

13. How did the Embargo Act of 1807 and the War of 1812 affect industry in the United States? LESSON 1.1

14. How did Eli Whitney contribute to the expansion of cotton production? LESSON 1.2

15. What effect did the cotton boom have on slavery? LESSON 1.2

16. What three things did Henry Clay propose in the economic plan he called the American System? LESSON 2.1

17. How did the Tariff Act of 1816 help American industry? LESSON 2.1

18. In what area did the Supreme Court's decision in *Gibbons* v. *Ogden* expand the federal government's power? LESSON 2.4

19. What was the purpose of the Convention of 1818? LESSON 3.1

20. Why was Maine important to the Missouri Compromise? LESSON 3.2

HISTORICAL THINKING

Answer the following questions. Support your answers with evidence from the chapter.

21. IDENTIFY Identify five major changes or developments that took place in the United States in the period after the War of 1812.

22. DRAW CONCLUSIONS What economic reasons might the British have had for wanting to repair diplomatic relations with the United States after the War of 1812?

23. COMPARE AND CONTRAST In the early decades of the 1800s, were the North and the South becoming more or less alike? Explain.

24. SUMMARIZE What were the overall negative and positive effects of the Tariff Act of 1816 on the American people?

25. FORM AND SUPPORT OPINIONS Do you think Denmark Vesey should be viewed as a hero? Support your opinion with evidence from the chapter.

26. ANALYZE CAUSE AND EFFECT Why did President Monroe initiate the foreign policy that became known as the Monroe Doctrine?

INTERPRET GRAPHS

Between 1810 and 1830 the percentage of people enslaved in the North went from about 0.7 to 0.3 percent; in the South, it went from about 33 percent to 34 percent. Study the graph below, which shows the sizes of the enslaved populations of southern states in 1810 and 1820. Then answer the questions that follow.

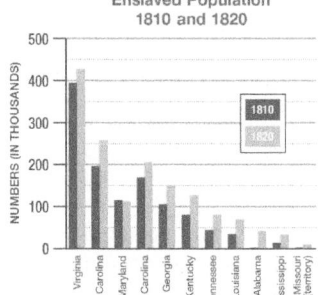

Enslaved Population
1810 and 1820

Source: U.S. Census Bureau

27. Identify which state on the graph had the greatest growth in slave population between 1810 and 1820. How many more people were enslaved in that state in 1820 than in 1810?

28. What conclusion can you draw about where slavery increased the most during the decade between 1810 and 1820?

ANALYZE SOURCES

In August 1807, Robert Fulton conducted the first trial of his newly built steamboat, traveling from New York City up the Hudson River to Albany and back. Afterward, he described the successful trip in a letter to his friend, Mr. Barlow.

My steamboat voyage to Albany and back has turned out rather more favorable than I had calculated. The distance from New York to Albany is one hundred and fifty miles; I ran it up in thirty-two hours, and down in thirty. I had a light breeze against me the whole way, both going and coming, and the voyage has been performed wholly by the power of the steam engine. I overtook many sloops and schooners [sailboats] . . . and parted with them as if they had been at anchor. The power of propelling boats by steam is now fully proved.

29. Why do you think Fulton included the sentence about sloops and schooners?

CONNECT TO YOUR LIFE

30. ARGUMENT In this chapter you learned about the rise in nationalism after the War of 1812. Now think about the role nationalism plays in American life today. Do you think nationalism is a good thing or a bad thing? Write a short argumentative essay in which you explain why you feel this way.

TIPS

• Find evidence in the text that shows how nationalism affected the United States after the War of 1812.

• List examples of nationalism you see in the United States today.

• Weigh positive and negative aspects of nationalism against each other.

• Begin your essay by stating your claim.

• Include details and evidence that support your argument.

• End your essay with a concluding statement.

VOCABULARY ANSWERS

1. The Industrial Revolution was dependent on investors willing to provide capital to fund the purchase of factories and machinery.

2. The invention of the cotton gin made growing cotton more profitable for plantation owners in the South.

3. One hallmark of the Industrial Revolution was mass production.

4. Short-staple cotton gets its name from its short fibers.

5. Abolitionists wanted to end the institution of slavery.

6. Henry Clay advocated for a tariff to protect U.S. industry from foreign competition.

7. The Supreme Court gave Congress more power to regulate business in its landmark decision in *Gibbons* v. *Ogden*.

8. The Convention of 1818 established the 49th parallel as the dividing line between the United States and Canada.

9. People favored the politics and customs of their own regions, a development known as sectionalism.

10. The spoils system was based on the awarding of political favors.

READING STRATEGY ANSWER

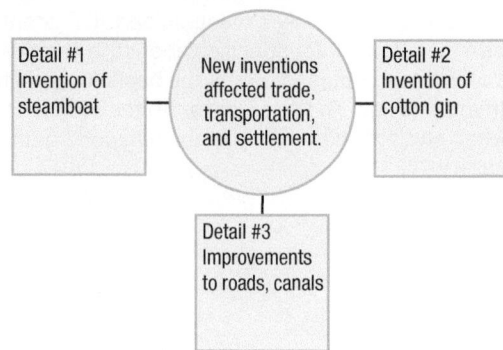

11. Possible response: Technology boosted the U.S. economy in several ways: Steamboats made river travel faster, increasing trade and transport of goods to ports; the cotton gin made the processing of cotton fibers more efficient and profitable; and the construction of better roads and canals increased trade and westward movement.

MAIN IDEAS ANSWERS

12. Waterfalls provided free waterpower to run the machinery in factories.

13. By temporarily cutting off the flow of British manufactured goods to the United States, the embargo and the war encouraged technological development in the U.S. textile industry.

14. He invented the cotton gin, which could quickly separate cotton fibers from the seeds. The invention made growing cotton more profitable and led to a boom in cotton production across the southern states.

15. As cotton cultivation expanded across the southern states and became more important to the southern economy, plantation owners expanded slavery to secure a bigger labor force.

16. He proposed internal improvements, such as the construction of roads and canals, the reestablishment of a national bank, and a tariff on imported goods.

17. The establishment of a tax on British goods made them more expensive and therefore encouraged Americans to buy more goods manufactured in the United States.

18. *Gibbons* v. *Ogden* expanded the federal government's power regarding the regulation of interstate commerce.

19. The purpose of the Convention of 1818 was to clarify the location of the border between the United States and Canada.

20. Admitting Maine to the Union as a free state at the same time that Missouri was admitted as a slave state preserved the balance between free and slave states.

HISTORICAL THINKING ANSWERS

21. Accept any five of the following as well as other reasonable answers: The Industrial Revolution took root in the Northeast; nationalism increased; Supreme Court rulings greatly expanded the powers of the federal government; through treaties with Britain and Spain, the United States settled its borders and gained new territories; transportation improved as new roads and canals were built and steamboats began to ply major rivers; westward expansion accelerated; both cotton production and slavery expanded dramatically in the southern states; tensions over slavery led to the Missouri Compromise; the United States became more assertive in its foreign policy.

22. The British had become dependent on American cotton for their flourishing textile industry, and the United States was an important market for textiles and other British manufactured goods.

23. They were becoming less alike. The northern states were beginning to industrialize, urbanize, and show signs of growing discomfort with slavery. Meanwhile, the cotton boom was keeping the South agrarian and rural and more dependent on slavery.

24. By raising the price of foreign goods, the tariff helped to protect and promote U.S. manufacturers located in the Northeast, while the South and West received little benefit but had to pay more for goods. It also raised the threat that the British might retaliate with a tariff on American cotton, which would hurt the South's economy.

25. Answers will vary. Possible responses: Vesey should be viewed as a hero because slavery was immoral, and he planned the rebellion with the noble goal of freeing thousands of enslaved people. Vesey was not a hero because even though slavery was immoral, it was also immoral of him to kill many people.

26. Monroe initiated the Monroe Doctrine as insurance against the possibility of France or Russia seizing control of formerly Spanish-controlled lands in the Americas.

INTERPRET GRAPHS ANSWERS

27. According to the graph, Alabama's enslaved population grew the most, by about 50,000 people.

28. Slavery increased much more in the southern states to the west of the original 13 states as well as Missouri Territory—the states that achieved statehood (or in the case of Missouri, that nearly did) during the decade. These areas were likely opening up to cotton production.

ANALYZE SOURCES ANSWER

29. He wanted to make sure his friend understood that the steamboat was traveling much faster than the boats under sail.

CONNECT TO YOUR LIFE ANSWER

30. Responses will vary, but students should state their argument clearly and provide solid examples and evidence of the role of nationalism after the War of 1812 and today, including both positive and negative aspects. They should end with a concluding statement supporting their claim.

UNIT 3 RESOURCES

UNIT INTRODUCTION

UNIT TIME LINE

UNIT WRAP-UP

NATIONAL GEOGRAPHIC | CONNECTION

National Geographic Magazine Adapted Articles
- "Nat Turner's Complex Legacy"
- "The Way West" ONLINE

Unit 3 Inquiry: Document a Migration

NG Learning Framework Activities
- Depict Nature
- Create Slogans to Promote Reforms

Unit 3 Formal Assessment

CHAPTER 8 RESOURCES

Available at NGLSync.Cengage.com

TEACHER RESOURCES & ASSESSMENT

Reading and Note-Taking

Vocabulary Practice

Social Studies Skills Lessons
- Reading: Distinguish Fact from Opinion
- Writing: Argument

Formal Assessment
- Chapter 8 Pretest
- Chapter 8 Tests A & B
- Section Quizzes

Chapter 8 Answer Key

ExamView®
   One-time Download

STUDENT DIGITAL RESOURCES

- eEdition
- Handbooks
- Online Atlas
- American Gallery Online
- History Notebook
- Active History
- American Voices (Biographies)
- Literature Analysis
- Projects for Inquiry-Based Learning

Chapter 8 Spanish Resources are available at NGLSync.Cengage.com.

AMERICAN STORIES | The Cherokee

- Study Primary Sources: Excerpt from an interview with a descendant of the Cherokee freedmen
- On Your Feet: Team Word Webbing

NG Learning Framework:
Analyze Cherokee Myths, Legends, Folktales

SECTION 1 RESOURCES
JACKSONIAN DEMOCRACY

LESSON 1.1
Champion of the Common Man

- On Your Feet: Roundtable

NG Learning Framework:
Create a Storyboard

LESSON 1.2
The People's President?

- On Your Feet: Think, Pair, Share

NG Learning Framework:
Debate the Spoils System

SECTION 2 RESOURCES
TAXES AND STATES' RIGHTS

LESSON 2.1
Tension over Taxes

- On Your Feet: Stage a Quiz Show

NG Learning Framework:
Research Tariffs

LESSON 2.2
The Nullification Crisis

- On Your Feet: Team Word Webbing

NG Learning Framework:
Create a Presentation

SECTION 3 RESOURCES
NATIVE AMERICAN POLICIES

LESSON 3.1
Seizing Native American Land

- On Your Feet: Numbered Heads

NG Learning Framework:
Form an Opinion

LESSON 3.2
Putting Up Resistance

- Active History: Analyze a Different Perspective

AMERICAN GALLERY ONLINE   The Trail of Tears

American Voices Biography
Black Hawk ONLINE

LESSON 3.3
CURATING HISTORY
Gilcrease Museum
Tulsa, Oklahoma

- On Your Feet: Sort the Artifacts

SECTION 4 RESOURCES
ECONOMIC POLICIES

LESSON 4.1
The End of the Second Bank

- On Your Feet: Four Corners

NG Learning Framework:
Create a Political Cartoon

LESSON 4.2
An Economic Crisis

- On Your Feet: Arguments For and Against Intervention

NG Learning Framework:
Write a Campaign Speech

CHAPTER 8 REVIEW

STRIVING READERS

STRATEGY 1
OUTLINE AND TAKE NOTES

To help students develop their reading and comprehension skills, ask them to work in pairs to write an outline for each lesson. Instruct them in using an outline format such as the one shown. Tell them to identify main ideas and then look for two details that support each main idea.

I. _____

    A. _____

    B. _____

II. _____

    A. _____

    B. _____

III. _____

    A. _____

    B. _____

Use with All Lessons *You may wish to pair students of mixed proficiencies. Remind students that subsection headings in the lesson sometimes serve as the highest level (Roman numerals) of an outline.*

STRATEGY 2
USE A TASKS APPROACH

Help students analyze visuals to obtain information by using the following TASKS strategy.

T Look for a **title** that may give the main idea.

A **Ask** yourself what the visual is trying to show.

S Determine how any **symbols** are used.

K Look for a **key** or legend.

S **Summarize** what you learned.

Use with Lessons 3.2 and 4.2

STRATEGY 3
USE RECIPROCAL TEACHING

Tell partners to take turns reading each paragraph of the lesson aloud. At the end of the paragraph, the reading student asks the listening student questions about the paragraph. Students may ask their partners to state the main idea, identify important details that support the main idea, or summarize the paragraph in their own words. Then have students work together to answer the Historical Thinking questions.

Use with All Lessons

INCLUSION

STRATEGY 1
USE CLARIFYING QUESTIONS

Allow students with disabilities to work with students who can read the lesson aloud to them and describe the photographs if necessary. Instruct pairs to ask and answer clarifying questions about the text, visuals, and text features.

Use with All Lessons

STRATEGY 2
USE MODIFIED MAIN IDEA STATEMENTS

To help students anticipate and organize content, provide modified Main Idea statements before reading. Several examples are provided below.

1.1 White men who did not own property were given the right to vote, and that helped Andrew Jackson win the presidency in 1828.

1.2 Jackson brought changes to American democracy, but not everyone liked those changes.

2.1 President Adams supported a tariff law hated by the people in the South, and he lost the 1828 election.

2.2 When South Carolina ignored federal laws, Jackson sided with the federal government.

3.1 President Jackson passed laws that forced Native Americans off their homelands so white settlers could use the land.

3.2 Many Native Americans did not want to leave their land, but they were forced to move and suffered greatly.

Use with All Lessons

ENGLISH LANGUAGE LEARNERS ELD

STRATEGY ❶
CREATE WORD CHARTS

Help students understand unfamiliar words by completing word charts such as the one below. Pair students at the **Emerging** level with those at the **Expanding** or **Bridging** level. Ask students to copy the chart and then work together to complete the four parts for unfamiliar words they encounter.

Definition of _____.	Draw a visual.
Tell how it relates to the Jackson Era.	Use it in a sentence.

Use with All Lessons

STRATEGY ❷
USE SENTENCE STRIPS

Choose a key paragraph from the lesson to read aloud while students at **All Proficiencies** follow along in their books. Tell students to close their books. Provide sentence strips of the paragraph and direct students to place the strips in order. Ask students to read their paragraphs aloud.

Use with All Lessons *You may wish to ask students at the Emerging level to read the sentence strips aloud and identify meaningful words before they start placing the strips in order.*

STRATEGY ❸
PAIR PARTNERS FOR DICTATION

After reading a lesson, ask students at **All Proficiencies** to write a sentence summarizing its main idea. Arrange students in pairs and ask them to dictate their sentences to each other. Then tell partners to work together to check the sentences for spelling and accuracy.

Use with All Lessons *You may wish to pair students at the Emerging level with those at the Bridging level and students at the Expanding level with one another.*

GIFTED & TALENTED

STRATEGY ❶
WRITE AND PERFORM JOURNAL ENTRIES

Tell students to imagine they attended Jackson's inaugural reception. Encourage them to access primary and secondary source materials to learn more about the event. Then have students write journal entries providing specific details of their expectations and experiences. Instruct students to practice and then perform a reading of their journal entries.

Use with Lesson 1.2

STRATEGY ❷
CREATE A GRAPHIC BIOGRAPHY

Tell students to learn more about one of the figures of the Jackson Era. Prompt them to use what they learn to create a graphic biography in the style of a comic book or graphic novel. Students may include quotations from or about the individual and visuals illustrating that person's ideas and actions. Invite students to share their completed graphic biographies with the class.

Use with Lessons 1.1, 1.2, 2.1, 2.2, 3.1, 3.2, 4.1, and 4.2 *You might suggest students research Andrew Jackson, Martin Van Buren, John Calhoun, Daniel Webster, Robert Hayne, Henry Clay, or Osceola.*

PRE-AP

STRATEGY ❶
EXPLORE LONG-TERM CONSEQUENCES

Direct students to write a research essay about the long-term impacts of the Indian Removal Act. Suggest that students use print and online sources to learn more about the act's immediate effects as well as its present-day repercussions. Invite students to share their essays with the class.

Use with Lessons 3.1 and 3.2 *You may wish to provide students with a list of Native American groups that lived in the students' region and suggest they focus their essay on one of those groups.*

STRATEGY ❷
FORM AND SUPPORT A THESIS

Challenge students to research the economic, political, and psychological factors that led to the Panic of 1837. Instruct them to develop a thesis regarding what they consider the predominant factor. Tell them to write an essay supporting their thesis with a variety of primary and secondary source material, plus their own analysis. Encourage students to share their essays on a school website or class blog.

Use with Lesson 4.2

THE JACKSON ERA
1828–1840

HISTORICAL THINKING How did Andrew Jackson change politics and the presidency?

CRITICAL VIEWING This statue of Andrew Jackson, erected in 1856, stands at the center of Jackson Square in New Orleans, Louisiana. It is one of four identical statues by sculptor Clark Mills. The equestrian monuments celebrate Major General Jackson's 1815 victory against the British at the Battle of New Orleans during the War of 1812. At the dedication of this statue, Mills said that he tried to capture Jackson reviewing his troops just before leading them into battle. How would you describe Jackson's attitude as portrayed here by Mills?

"I have great confidence in **the virtue of the great majority of the people.**"

Andrew Jackson

MAJOR GENERAL ANDREW JACKSON

244 CHAPTER 8

The Jackson Era 245

INTRODUCE THE PHOTOGRAPH

JACKSON'S EQUESTRIAN STATUE

Direct students to study the photograph and the Critical Viewing text. Then read the quotation from Andrew Jackson aloud. **ASK:** What do Andrew Jackson's words convey about his outlook and vision for the United States? *(Possible response: Andrew Jackson believes most of the people of the United States are moral, and they will use their goodness and intelligence to make the republic strong and preserve the country's democratic ideals.)* Tell students that in Chapter 8, they will learn about the influence Jackson had on national politics and on the nation's economy. The chapter also explains how Jackson's policies dramatically affected Native Americans and forever changed their way of life.

SHARE BACKGROUND

The statue that stands in Jackson Square is a replica of the one Clark Mills cast for Lafayette Park across from the White House in Washington, D.C. When prominent citizens in New Orleans learned that Mills was creating a statue of Jackson for Washington, D.C., they lobbied for one for their own city. The original statue boasts two distinctions: it is the first bronze statue cast in the United States and the first equestrian statue in the world that balances on only the horse's hind legs. Mills, who had never created an equestrian statue before, used his own horse as a model, training it to stand on its hind legs in his studio. He also studied horse anatomy, even dissecting a few horses. To add to the statue's authenticity, he borrowed Jackson's saddle, bridle, and military uniform.

CRITICAL VIEWING Answers will vary. Possible response: Jackson appears to be a strong, confident leader who is looking forward to engaging in battle.

For Chapter 8 Spanish Resources, visit the Resources Menu. Chapter 8 Resources are available at NGLSync.Cengage.com.

HISTORICAL THINKING QUESTION

> How did Andrew Jackson change politics and the presidency?

Four Corners Activity: Presidential Policies Guide students to consider some of the issues that have challenged presidents in general and Andrew Jackson in particular. Label each corner of the room with one of the following: Democracy, Economy, States' Rights, Native Americans. Divide the class into four groups and tell each group to move to a corner to discuss one of these questions.

Group 1: Democracy: Who should be allowed to vote? How might changing who can vote change the kind of candidates who are elected?

Group 2: States' Rights: Should states have the right to override or ignore a law made by federal lawmakers, and if so, under what circumstances? What is a president's role in the discussion?

Group 3: Native Americans: What responsibilities does a president have regarding Native Americans? Should policies help Native Americans maintain their cultural identity or assimilate?

Group 4: Economy: What is the foundation for a strong economy? How might a president's policies help or hurt an economy?

Instruct students in each group to discuss their questions. Ask a volunteer from each group to summarize the group's ideas for the class. Record students' ideas and revisit them at the end of the chapter.

INTRODUCE THE READING STRATEGY

DISTINGUISH FACT FROM OPINION

Explain that as students read, they should decide which statements are facts that can be proved to be true and which are opinions that tell what someone thinks or believes but cannot be proved. Turn to the Chapter Review and preview with students the chart about distinguishing fact from opinion. As they read the chapter, encourage them to distinguish fact from opinion when encountering statements about people, events, policies, or ideas.

KEY DATES FOR CHAPTER 8

1828	Andrew Jackson is elected president
1828	Tariff of 1828 passes
1830	Indian Removal Act passes
1832	Jackson is re-elected; Black Hawk War takes place
1834	Whig Party is founded
1836	Martin Van Buren is elected president
1837	Panic of 1837 occurs
1837	Federal forces capture Osceola
1838	Trail of Tears begins
1840	William Henry Harrison is elected president

INTRODUCE CHAPTER VOCABULARY

KEY VOCABULARY

SECTION 1

Jacksonian democracy   kitchen cabinet

SECTION 2

doctrine of nullification   Tariff of Abominations

SECTION 3

assimilate   Indian Territory   Trail of Tears

Indian Removal Act   syllabary

SECTION 4

mandate   Panic of 1837   Whig Party

WORD WEBS

Tell students to complete a Word Web for Key Vocabulary words as they read the chapter. Direct them to write each word or term in the center of an oval and then look through the chapter to find examples, characteristics, and descriptive words that may be associated with the vocabulary word. After reading the chapter, ask students to share what they learned about each word or term. Model an example using the graphic organizer below.

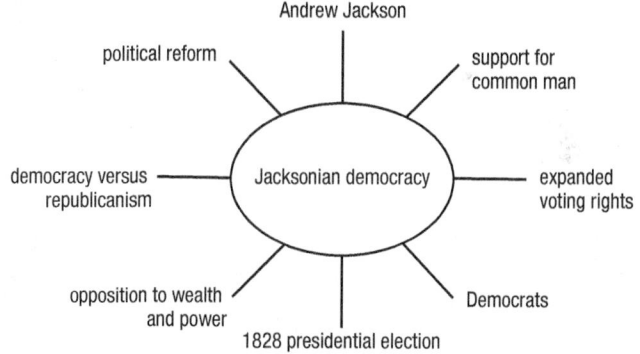

OBJECTIVES

- **Trace the causes and effects of conflicts between the Cherokee and white settlers.**

- **Learn about the forced removal of the Cherokee from their lands and how they established themselves in present-day Oklahoma.**

- **Analyze the developments and changes in the language, culture, and economy of the Cherokee people.**

- **Compare past and present-day experiences of the Cherokee.**

- **Study a primary source: excerpt from an interview with a descendant of the Cherokee freedmen.**

CRITICAL THINKING SKILLS FOR "THE CHEROKEE"

- Make Connections
- Draw Conclusions
- Form and Support Opinions
- Make Generalizations
- Identify

CONNECT TO THE CHAPTER

This American Story explores the history of the Cherokee people and how interactions with European settlers and the United States government affected their culture and history. Features inform about the Cherokee writing system and the controversy regarding the tribal status of Cherokee freedmen, the descendants of African-Americans who had been enslaved by the Cherokee and then freed after the Civil War.

Chapter 8, The Jackson Era, examines how Andrew Jackson shaped economic and social policies, including those that greatly affected Native Americans. This American Story details how policies before, during, and after Jackson's presidency impacted the Cherokee. Introduce "The Cherokee" after Lesson 3.2, which discusses the Trail of Tears.

HISTORY NOTEBOOK

Encourage students to complete the American Story page for Chapter 8 in their History Notebooks as they read.

CRITICAL VIEWING Cherokee people might choose to wear traditional clothing at today's festivals to show their pride in their Cherokee identity and respect for their heritage. Stereotypes have sometimes led outsiders to group all Native Americans together, so some Cherokee might also want to emphasize differences between themselves and other Native American groups.

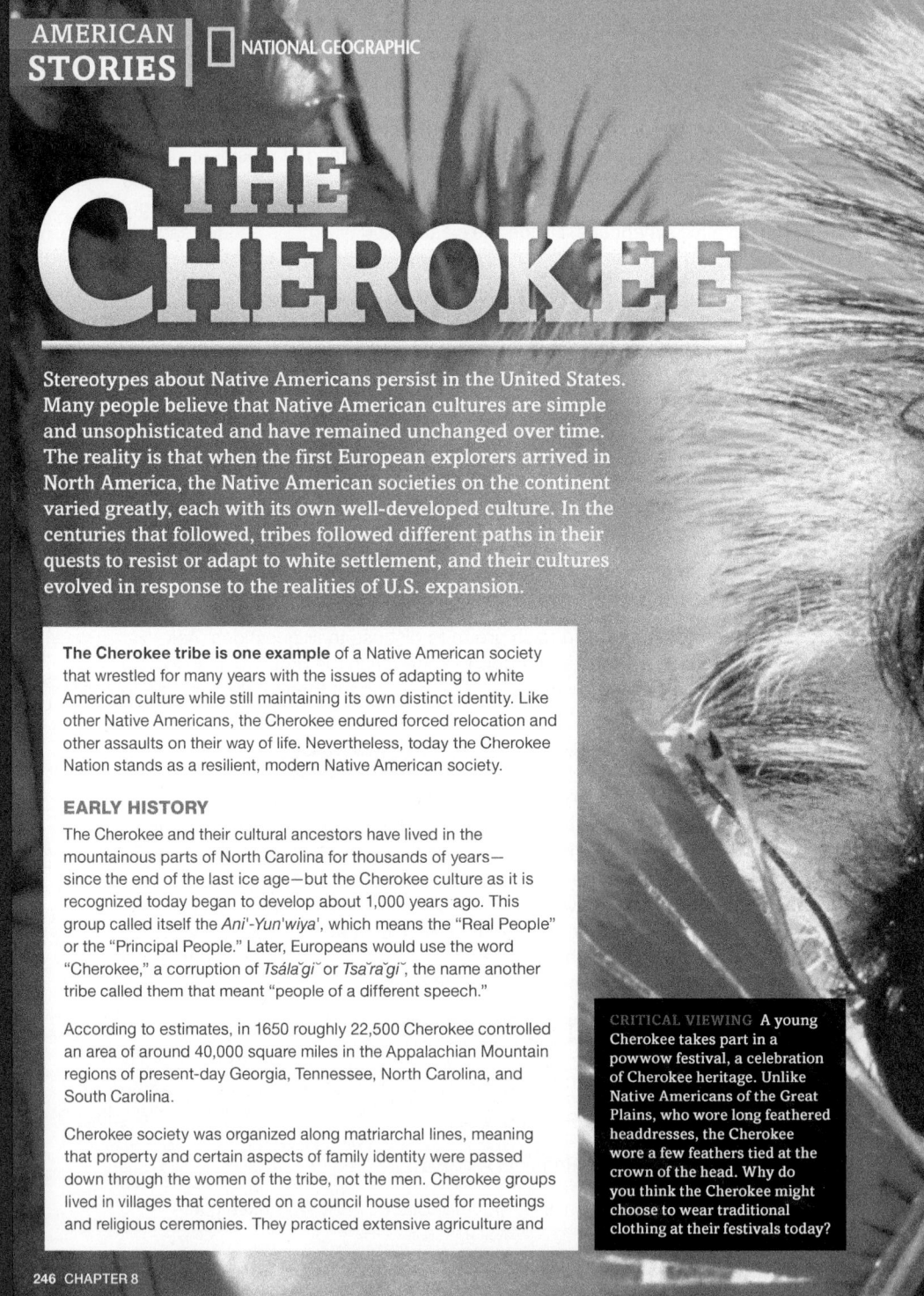

THE CHEROKEE

Stereotypes about Native Americans persist in the United States. Many people believe that Native American cultures are simple and unsophisticated and have remained unchanged over time. The reality is that when the first European explorers arrived in North America, the Native American societies on the continent varied greatly, each with its own well-developed culture. In the centuries that followed, tribes followed different paths in their quests to resist or adapt to white settlement, and their cultures evolved in response to the realities of U.S. expansion.

The Cherokee tribe is one example of a Native American society that wrestled for many years with the issues of adapting to white American culture while still maintaining its own distinct identity. Like other Native Americans, the Cherokee endured forced relocation and other assaults on their way of life. Nevertheless, today the Cherokee Nation stands as a resilient, modern Native American society.

EARLY HISTORY

The Cherokee and their cultural ancestors have lived in the mountainous parts of North Carolina for thousands of years— since the end of the last ice age—but the Cherokee culture as it is recognized today began to develop about 1,000 years ago. This group called itself the *Ani'-Yun'wiya'*, which means the "Real People" or the "Principal People." Later, Europeans would use the word "Cherokee," a corruption of *Tsála̱gi̱* or *Tsa̱ra̱gi̱*, the name another tribe called them that meant "people of a different speech."

According to estimates, in 1650 roughly 22,500 Cherokee controlled an area of around 40,000 square miles in the Appalachian Mountain regions of present-day Georgia, Tennessee, North Carolina, and South Carolina.

Cherokee society was organized along matriarchal lines, meaning that property and certain aspects of family identity were passed down through the women of the tribe, not the men. Cherokee groups lived in villages that centered on a council house used for meetings and religious ceremonies. They practiced extensive agriculture and

CRITICAL VIEWING A young Cherokee takes part in a powwow festival, a celebration of Cherokee heritage. Unlike Native Americans of the Great Plains, who wore long feathered headdresses, the Cherokee wore a few feathers tied at the crown of the head. Why do you think the Cherokee might choose to wear traditional clothing at their festivals today?

The Jackson Era **247**

PREVIEW USING VISUALS

Read the title of the American Story and guide students to preview the visuals that appear throughout. **ASK:** Which, if any, of these visuals introduces information about the Cherokee that is new to you or surprising? *(Answers will vary. Possible responses: The photograph of the Cherokee Female Seminary is surprising because it is a massive brick or stone building in a European architectural style, and the Native American students are wearing the formal clothing and hairstyles of white Americans. The photograph of the protesting African Americans identifying as Cherokee citizens is surprising because I would expect Cherokee citizens to be Native American. The image of an asi is interesting because this winter dwelling of the Cherokee is very different from other Native American structures that are more often depicted, such as tepees made of animal skins, wooden longhouses, or adobe dwellings.)*

BACKGROUND FOR THE TEACHER

CHEROKEE TEAR DRESSES

The Cherokee tear dress is another example of how Cherokee culture has adapted and changed over time. In precolonial times, Cherokee traditionally wore buckskin clothing. When European settlers introduced them to woven cloth, they quickly recognized the utility and convenience of using fabric to fashion garments. Tear dresses, usually made from calico, feature a full skirt and a ruffle at the bottom. But what makes these dresses distinctive is the way they are constructed—the fabric is not cut into precise pattern pieces as most commercial garments are. Instead, the fabric is torn into basic squares and rectangles, then stitched to fit the woman who will wear the dress. Researchers differ on the origins of the dress. Some believe it evolved out of necessity as the Cherokee journeyed on the Trail of Tears. Having few possessions with them—and no scissors—the tear dress solved a practical problem. Others suggest that the Cherokee learned this technique from missionaries who wanted a quick solution for getting the Cherokee to conform to European ideas of modesty. Whichever the origin, Cherokee women have embraced the tear dress, and it is now designated as the official tribal dress of women in the Cherokee Nation of Oklahoma, where it is often worn at powwows and other special occasions.

GUIDED DISCUSSION

1. **Form and Support Opinions** In the context of the 1780s, do you think it was a sound strategy for the Cherokee to assimilate to the white settlers' culture? Explain your response. *(Answers will vary. Possible responses: Yes. By the 1780s, the Cherokee had already lost much of their land to the settlers, so assimilation might have been the best way for them to keep some of their remaining land and to maintain peace with the settlers. No. Assimilation did not guarantee that white settlers and the federal government would leave them alone.)*

2. **Make Generalizations** Which aspects of a culture are most important for a group to maintain its cultural identity? *(Possible responses: It is important to maintain cultural aspects that bring people together, such as foods, faith, and celebrations. Retaining a central philosophy or worldview is more important than retaining material details, such as traditional clothing styles. It's important to keep a group's language alive since language both reflects and influences how speakers of it view others and the world around them. A group must be able to evolve to preserve its culture. For example, creating a written version of a traditionally oral language helped the Cherokee culture to endure, even though some of the symbols are derived from a different culture, and the Cherokee's adoption of a constitution proved to be practical and helped its culture survive.)*

AMERICAN STORIES

farmed large plots of land. Crops included corn, beans, and squash, which were known as the "three sisters" because they benefited from being planted close together. Spirituality was an important part of Cherokee life, with beliefs and ceremonies focused on maintaining a sense of balance among humans, nature, and the spiritual world.

The Cherokee first encountered Europeans in 1540, when the Spanish explorer Hernando de Soto led his expedition across the tribe's land in search of gold and other riches. This first meeting was devastating for the Native Americans. De Soto and his followers demanded food and tribute from the Cherokee, and they enslaved people from the villages. Worst of all were the diseases the Europeans introduced, such as smallpox and measles. The Cherokee, like other Native American groups, lacked immunity to these illnesses, and their population suffered great losses. According to some estimates, European diseases wiped out up to 95 percent of the Native American population within 150 years of Columbus's arrival.

FRIENDS AND FOES

By 1650, the Cherokee had established regular trade relationships with English settlers. Contact with the new immigrants brought about some changes in farming patterns as the Cherokee began to cultivate species brought from Europe, such as

An asi, a traditional Cherokee winter house, is a small, dome-shaped structure that is partially underground to help keep in the heat.

peaches and watermelons. Alliances between the Cherokee and settlers were marked by outbreaks of hostility. For example, in 1693, the tribe sent a delegation to the British authorities in Charleston, South Carolina, to formally protest after colonists purchased some Cherokee people taken as slaves by enemy groups.

Trade and conflict continued in the 18th century as white settlers encroached on Cherokee land in rapidly increasing numbers. When the American Revolution erupted, most Cherokee allied with

This illustration depicts a 1566 meeting between the Spanish conquistador Juan Pardo and members of the Creek and Cherokee nations.

the British and fought for the return of their land. Receiving little support from Britain, however, the Cherokee were defeated in 1777 by the Continental Army and forced to sign away even more territory in western North Carolina, South Carolina, and portions of present-day Tennessee and Kentucky.

During the 1780s, a steady stream of settlers flowed from Virginia and North Carolina into the region west of the Appalachians and south of the Ohio River in search of fertile land. State governments, speculators, and frontiersmen quickly proceeded to push out the Cherokee. Colonial governments did sometimes declare in favor of Cherokee land rights, but the progress of white settlement was unstoppable.

The Cherokee began to explore the strategy of assimilation and adopted elements of white culture. They established a new government and constitution that they modeled on that of the United States. They also abandoned their traditional log dwellings to build homes in the American style and used American agricultural methods. Many Cherokee children even attended schools run by Christian missionaries, who persuaded a considerable number of tribe members to convert to Christianity. White authorities praised the Cherokee for adapting so well to European culture and adopting what the authorities considered to be "civilized" behavior.

Despite their many adaptations, the Cherokee and other tribes of the Southeast had no desire to leave their home regions. In their view, they had already given up more land than they should have and were determined to hold on to what they had left. The pressure to force the Indians out, however, was intense. Most whites, especially those who coveted the rich lands under the Native Americans' control, bristled at the continuing presence of the native inhabitants. The discovery of gold in Georgia only served to intensify their hunger for land.

In 1830, President Andrew Jackson required tribes in the Southeast to move west of the Mississippi to a dry prairie region called the Great American Desert. The Cherokee contested their removal in the Supreme Court and through other peaceful means, but to no avail. After years of negotiations and resistance, the Cherokee were among the last of the southeastern tribes to go. Their journey was brutal and became known as the "Trail of Tears." Thousands of Cherokee died of hunger, disease, exposure, or sheer exhaustion during the journey.

THE CHEROKEE TODAY

As tragic as it was, the Trail of Tears did not put an end to the Cherokee. Resilient in the face of hardship, they promptly began rebuilding their institutions and businesses after their removal. The new Cherokee capital was the town of Tahlequah, in present-day Oklahoma. There, the Cherokee reinstated their democratic form of government, and in 1839, they adopted a new constitution. In 1828, the Cherokee began printing periodicals in their own language. The tribe also established an extensive school system with 144 elementary schools and 2 institutes of higher learning—the Cherokee Male and Female Seminaries. These schools were so well regarded that white settlers living nearby paid to have their children attend. Some historians have termed this time of relative calm and prosperity the "Cherokee Golden Age."

THE CHEROKEE WRITING SYSTEM

Around 1809, a Cherokee named Sequoya began creating a system to write words in the tribe's language using symbols to represent syllables. After the Cherokee people adopted the writing system—known as a syllabary—literacy rates within the tribe soared. In 1824, the General Council of the Cherokee Nation awarded Sequoya a silver medal to honor his achievement. In 1828, the U.S. Congress granted him an honorary award of $500, although he only received $300. Texas leader Sam Houston once told Sequoya, "Your invention of the alphabet is worth more to your people than two bags full of gold in the hands of every Cherokee."

The symbols in the Cherokee syllabary, shown here, are similar to English letters and usually written from left to right.

THE CHEROKEE WRITING SYSTEM

A stint as a soldier in the U.S. Army stoked Sequoya's interest in developing a writing system for the Cherokee people. Neither he nor his fellow Cherokee soldiers were able to perform tasks such as reading military orders or describing in writing events that had taken place. After returning from service, Sequoya devoted much of his time to completing the Cherokee syllabary, and thousands of Cherokee people became literate in a short period of time. **ASK:** Why do you think the Cherokee people adapted so quickly to Sequoya's writing system after living without one for so long? *(Answers will vary. Possible response: The fact that a fellow Cherokee developed the writing system would have made it seem less of an intrusion from white culture and more of an expansion of their own. The Cherokee probably also realized the value of reading and writing in maintaining status in a society of literate whites.)*

ACTIVE OPTIONS

On Your Feet: Team Word Webbing Arrange students in groups of four, and provide each group with a large sheet of paper for a Word Web. Assign the following topic: the Cherokee. Tell one member of each group to add a detail to the web, then on a signal, rotate the paper to the next group member. Call on a volunteer from each group to share the group's web.

NG Learning Framework: Analyze Cherokee Myths, Legends, Folktales

SKILL Communication

KNOWLEDGE Our Human Story

Prompt students to research Cherokee myths, legends, or folktales using library or online sources. Then instruct them to meet in small groups to discuss how the myths, legends, or folktales they found explain natural phenomena, teach how people should behave in certain situations or as part of a community, or illustrate another message. Then ask groups to summarize their findings for the class.

THE CHEROKEE FREEDMEN CONTROVERSY

Inaccurate historical records have often served to deny freedmen Cherokee citizenship. The federal government's Dawes Rolls (1898–1914) were census documents that identified whether individuals were Native Americans, freedmen, or mixed Native American and white, but did not specify whether, through intermarriage, some freedmen were also part Cherokee. The omission is significant because these rolls are used for proving "Indian blood." **ASK:** Why might it be important to freedmen's descendants to be granted Cherokee citizenship? *(Possible response: The descendants may want to acknowledge their shared ancestry and history with the Cherokee. Also, a citizen of the Cherokee Nation might be entitled to resources or programs that others are not.)*

RIGHTS RESTORED

Marilyn Vann is a descendant of enslaved African Americans—and of the wealthiest Cherokee slaveholder, James Vann. Vann, who was the son of a Cherokee mother and a Scots father, enslaved around 100 workers. **ASK:** How might Marilyn Vann describe the experience and outcome of the lawsuit against the Cherokee? *(Possible response: She might say she was angry when the Cherokee amended their constitution and frustrated that the court battle dragged on, but felt relieved that freedmen's tribal citizenship rights were upheld.)*

WRITE ABOUT HISTORY

Compose a Newspaper Editorial Tell students to imagine that they are descendants of a family that was forced to relocate under President Jackson's policies during the 1830s. Prompt them to write an editorial formatted as a posthumous open letter to Jackson, that captures the experience of the migration itself and its lasting effects. Assist students in the writing process and formatting their editorials as necessary.

CRITICAL VIEWING The Cherokee might have considered education key to governing themselves and protecting their rights against settlers and the federal government.

CRITICAL VIEWING The Cherokee Female Seminary opened in Park Hill, Oklahoma, in 1851. It was the first school of higher learning for women west of the Mississippi. After the school burned down in 1887, a new one—shown in this photo—opened in 1890 in Tahlequah. Why might education have been important to the Cherokee people?

In the 1860s, the Civil War put an end to the golden age. Tribal members, some of whom were slave owners, were divided over which side to take in the bloody conflict. Over the course of the war, Cherokee territory was overrun by both the Union and Confederate armies at different times, leaving the tribe's economy in tatters.

Still, the Cherokee maintained a partly independent state until 1906. At that point, in the lead-up to Oklahoma's statehood, the land was divided into lots, some of which were given to individual Cherokee who had been listed in a special census. Other lots were given to freed slaves or homesteaders or retained by the federal government. Many of the Cherokee who held the lots became U.S. citizens, and the tribal government was essentially dissolved.

In the later 20th century, the Cherokee government saw a revival as the tribe regained a large measure of independence. In 1990, the Cherokee Nation negotiated and signed an agreement with the U.S. Congress on self-governance. The Cherokee Nation today numbers around 300,000 members throughout the United States and governs a jurisdictional service area—not a reservation—in northeastern Oklahoma, where around 126,000 members live. The tribal government is founded on democratic principles and is composed of executive, judicial, and legislative branches. It also owns several successful businesses, including Cherokee Nation Entertainment, which operates entertainment venues, and Cherokee Nation Industries, which supplies defense contractors. According to the Cherokee Nation's website, its businesses have "a positive financial impact of over one billion dollars annually" for the state of Oklahoma.

In North Carolina, the descendants of those few who succeeded in avoiding the enforced removal formed the Eastern Band of the Cherokee. Like the Cherokee Nation, they operate under a tribal government with three branches. The Eastern Band has more than 14,000 enrolled members, the majority of whom live in the 57,000-acre area the group purchased, called the Qualla Boundary.

Like all groups of people, the Cherokee are diverse in their thoughts, opinions, and ways of navigating the modern world. Some adhere closely to tribal traditions, while others have largely abandoned them. The Cherokee Nation hosts numerous celebrations and ceremonies, and members are free to choose whether or not to attend. What all Cherokee have in common is belonging to a living, evolving culture that defies flat stereotypes of Native American life and occupies a unique place in today's United States.

THINK ABOUT IT

What aspects of Cherokee society do you think helped the tribe survive and move toward success in the 21st century?

In 2007, a group of Cherokee freedmen in Oklahoma City demonstrated for their right to tribal citizenship.

THE CHEROKEE FREEDMEN CONTROVERSY

When the Cherokee assimilated into white American society in the early 1800s, some established plantations and acquired African-American slaves to work on them. The enslaved people were forcibly moved along with their masters to the Great American Desert, where they continued in servitude.

After the Civil War, the Cherokee signed a treaty with their former slaves, or freedmen, granting them "all the rights of Native Cherokees." However, in 2007, the Cherokee amended their constitution and made having "Indian blood" a requirement for being considered a citizen of the tribe. As a result, about 2,800 descendants of the freedmen lost their Cherokee citizenship. The freedmen responded with protests, demonstrations, and, eventually, lawsuits.

Finally, in 2017, 10 years after the amendment's passage, U.S. District Court judge Thomas Hogan ruled that Cherokee freedmen had tribal citizenship rights. In his decision, Judge Hogan wrote, "The Cherokee Nation can continue to define itself as it sees fit but must do so equally and evenhandedly with respect to native Cherokees and the descendants of Cherokee Freedmen." The attorney general for the Cherokee Nation stated that the decision would not be appealed.

RIGHTS RESTORED

Marilyn Vann was a leader of the descendants and a plaintiff in the lawsuit against the Cherokee.

PRIMARY SOURCE

Following the ruling, Vann told a reporter what it meant to her.

There can be racial justice—but it doesn't always come easy. What this means for me is the freedmen people will be able to continue our citizenship . . . and also that we're able to preserve our history. All we ever wanted was the rights promised us to continue to be enforced.

—from an interview with National Public Radio, 2017

STRIVING READERS

Compare Past and Present Tell students to complete a T-Chart relating to past (before 1990) and present (1990 to present) experiences of the Cherokee Nation. Tell students to label the columns Past and Present and then list four or five relevant details from the American Story under each heading.

GIFTED & TALENTED

Explore Cherokee Culture Direct students to conduct research on one aspect of Cherokee culture. Ask students to assemble material from a variety of resources, such as photographs, illustrations, and video and audio clips, that relate to their chosen topic. Have students use the material to prepare a brief oral summary of the topic and present it to the class.

See the Chapter Planner for more strategies for differentiation.

HISTORICAL THINKING

Ask and have students answer the following questions.

1. **READING CHECK** In what ways have encounters with outsiders threatened the Cherokee?

2. **IDENTIFY** How did the Cherokee benefit from establishing a constitution and a government that was independent of the federal government?

3. **DRAW CONCLUSIONS** Why do you think Sam Houston told Sequoya that his invention of the Cherokee writing system was "worth more to your people than two bags full of gold in the hands of every Cherokee"?

ANSWERS

1. Diseases brought by the Spanish in the mid-1500s killed the Cherokee in large numbers. Both the Spanish and the British enslaved Cherokee people. Settlers and the federal government forced the Cherokee to move from their lands.

2. Possible response: Having a constitution and a government gave the Cherokee the authority and structure to legally protect themselves, negotiate with the federal government, and maintain their Cherokee identity and autonomy.

3. Possible response: Houston knew that a writing system would offer improved communication. Its value lay in its lasting effect, which, unlike gold, would help to keep the Cherokee united.

THINK ABOUT IT

Possible response: The Cherokee are resilient. After the tribe's forced relocation, they re-established their government and newspaper and instituted a school system while maintaining their cultural identity.

CHAMPION OF THE COMMON MAN

A loss in any contest can be hard to take, but it is especially so when you believe your opponent used underhanded methods to win. That's exactly how Andrew Jackson felt about his loss in the 1824 election. By 1828, he was ready for a rematch.

THE COMMON MAN

When the House of Representatives chose John Quincy Adams as president in 1824, Andrew Jackson viewed the win as another triumph for the rich. Jackson claimed to represent the rights of hardworking people, whom he called the "common man," and he considered himself one of them. Born into poverty in 1767, Jackson grew up on the border between North and South Carolina. His father died before his birth, so his mother struggled to raise him and his brothers on her own. During the American Revolution, young Jackson risked his life carrying messages to the Continental Army. British soldiers captured him during a mission and took him prisoner. While held captive, the boy was ordered to shine a soldier's shoes. When Jackson refused, the soldier slashed him with his sword. By the age of 14, Jackson had lost his mother and brothers to various illnesses. Jackson himself contracted smallpox but survived the disease.

Jackson was determined to overcome his hard childhood and make a success of his life. As a young man, he studied law and became a lawyer. Then he moved to Tennessee, where he met the woman he would marry, Rachel Donelson Robards. Jackson also served in the House of Representatives and Senate. In 1804, he purchased a 425-acre farm, later called the Hermitage, near Nashville. As you've read, Jackson rose to national prominence when he defeated the British at the Battle of New Orleans in the War of 1812.

After he lost the presidential election in 1824, Jackson and the Democratic Party that eventually formed sought to limit Adams to a single term and lay the groundwork for the next election. Jackson's allies in Congress weakened Adams's presidency by blocking many of his programs. The Democrats also benefited from the expansion of voting rights in many states, which granted suffrage to white men who did not own property, including farmers, craftsmen, laborers, and middle-class businessmen. (Women, African Americans, and Native Americans still could not vote, however.) To appeal to these new voters, the Democrats tried to make political participation attractive. They organized barbecues and picnics at political rallies and wrote entertaining campaign songs. Political gatherings became events that united people with common interests.

The movement that supported the rights of the common man became known as **Jacksonian democracy**. Due in part to broadened voting rights, over 800,000 more men voted in the 1828 presidential election than in the 1824 election. As the 1828 election approached, there was a general restlessness and desire for change. Many voters were ready for a president who had risen from a humble background through hard work rather than one who had inherited his wealth and power. Andrew Jackson would be their man.

THE ELECTION OF 1828

The election once again pitted Jackson against Adams. During the campaign, both sides did everything in their power to get their candidate elected. They organized speeches, held parades, and came up with slogans and songs to build enthusiasm for their man. These tactics changed the way all future American politicians would run their campaigns.

Soldiers cheer for Jackson astride his white horse as he surveys the battle scene in this 1856 painting by Dennis Malone Carter, *The Battle of New Orleans*. In the background, British soldiers fall before the Americans' fire.

PRIMARY SOURCE

You are supported by the great body of the people . . . because they have entire confidence in your wisdom, and integrity; and it is believed that the men now in power have obtained, and are endeavoring to retain their places by "bargain management and intrigue," and in direct violation of the will of the people.

—from a letter written by Robert Y. Hayne to Andrew Jackson, 1828

The 1828 campaign was also marked by mudslinging, or nasty personal attacks. Previous campaigns had used insults to criticize an opponent, but communication had been more limited then. In 1828, newspapers across the country carried the candidates' attacks. Jackson's supporters portrayed Adams as a man who only represented the interests of the wealthy and who had gained the presidency through a "corrupt bargain" with key members of the House. The Adams campaign, in turn, charged that Jackson was a slave trader and murderer. In fact, Jackson used slaves at the Hermitage and had engaged in many duels, one of which resulted in the death of his challenger. But the most vicious attacks directed against Jackson involved his wife, who had divorced her first husband. Rachel's divorce had not been properly finalized when she and Andrew married in September 1793. Once the divorce went through, however, the couple legally remarried in January 1794. Still, the Adams campaign characterized Rachel as a bigamist, or someone who is married to two people at the same time.

In spite of the mudslinging, Jackson won in a landslide, with 178 electoral votes to Adams's 83. Sadly, Jackson would enter the White House without Rachel by his side. She died of a heart attack a few weeks after the election. Jackson believed his political enemies and their personal attacks had caused his wife's death. In December, he buried Rachel on the grounds of the Hermitage in the dress she had planned to wear to her husband's inauguration.

HISTORICAL THINKING

1. **READING CHECK** How did the expansion of suffrage benefit Jackson in the election of 1828?

2. **DISTINGUISH FACT FROM OPINION** How did both Adams and Jackson use facts and opinions to try to sway voters?

3. **DRAW CONCLUSIONS** Why were so many people excited over the prospect of Jacksonian democracy?

PLAN: 2-PAGE LESSON

OBJECTIVE

Examine how the expansion of suffrage and new campaign tactics influenced the 1828 presidential election.

CRITICAL THINKING SKILLS FOR LESSON 1.1

• Distinguish Fact from Opinion
• Draw Conclusions
• Compare and Contrast
• Analyze Primary Sources

HISTORICAL THINKING FOR CHAPTER 8

How did Andrew Jackson change politics and the presidency? Andrew Jackson benefited from the expansion of suffrage among white men. Lesson 1.1 examines how Jackson and what would become the Democratic Party won the presidential election of 1828 through new campaign tactics that appealed to the common man.

BACKGROUND FOR THE TEACHER

The duel in which Andrew Jackson killed his opponent resulted from a conflict over two of his great passions—horse racing and defending his and his wife Rachel's honor. In late 1805, fellow Tennessean Joseph Erwin proposed a horse race between his horse Ploughboy and Jackson's prized horse Truxton. When Erwin began to doubt his horse would win, he forfeited the race to minimize the amount of money he would lose, which led to an argument about the value of the notes offered to cover his debt. Although Truxton won a rescheduled race against Ploughboy, Erwin's son-in-law Charles Dickinson and Jackson continued to exchange barbs about each other's character, leading to a duel. Jackson, who was just an average shot, wore an oversized coat to conceal the shape of his body and let crack-shot Dickinson fire first, hoping to survive the bullet. His plan worked. Dickinson shot, but stood perplexed, thinking he had missed. The wounded Jackson took careful aim. On his first try, his gun locked up, but he fired again, fatally wounding Dickinson.

INTRODUCE & ENGAGE

TALK ABOUT POLITICAL CAMPAIGNS

Prompt students to consider the candidates and major issues of some local or national political campaigns. Guide them to discuss the campaigns, including the tone and content of advertisements, any debates between the candidates, and how the candidates communicate their messages to their audience. Encourage students to identify character traits or defining issues for a candidate they would support. **ASK:** Do you think it's important for voters to vote for a national candidate based on regional issues? Why or why not? *(Possible response: Yes. People in one region might face completely different problems from people in another region, and they need to know a candidate will work to address their problems. No. Important traits, such as honesty, experience, and temperament, are important to everyone.)* Tell students that in Lesson 1.1 they will learn about the campaign tactics used in the 1828 presidential election.

TEACH

GUIDED DISCUSSION

1. **Compare and Contrast** In what ways did the differences between Jackson and John Quincy Adams reflect the different regions and people who supported them? *(Possible response: Adams was a successful, well-educated member of Massachusetts society who inherited his wealth and power. He appealed to the merchants, businessmen, professionals, and wealthy landowners in the Northeast, where commerce and industry fueled the economy. Jackson was a self-made man from the western region of the South. As a prominent slaveholder, he appealed to southern slaveholders. He came from humble beginnings, so he appealed to the farmers who settled the western frontier, who probably viewed him as a fellow laborer.)*

2. **Distinguish Fact from Opinion** What facts and opinions about Rachel Jackson are reflected in the last paragraph of the lesson? *(Facts: Rachel died of a heart attack before Jackson became president; she was buried in the dress she had planned to wear to the inauguration. Opinion: Attacks against Rachel by Jackson's opponents caused her death.)*

ANALYZE PRIMARY SOURCES

Direct students' attention to the Primary Source feature. **ASK:** Who are "the men now in power" that Hayne references? *(Adams and his administration)* **ASK:** According to Hayne, why do "the great body of the people" distrust them? *(The people believe that Adams won the presidency unfairly by making a bargain with Clay and other members of Congress.)*

ACTIVE OPTIONS

On Your Feet: Roundtable Organize students into teams of four. Pose the following question: How did the 1828 election change presidential politics? Have each student answer the question within the group and explain his or her answer based on what they learned in the lesson. Allow time for groups to share the different answers with the class.

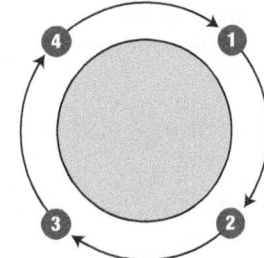

NG Learning Framework: Create a Storyboard

SKILLS Collaboration, Communication

KNOWLEDGE Our Human Story

Invite students to work in groups to create storyboards about events in Jackson's life that shaped his character and political appeal, including the 1824 election. Encourage groups to conduct additional research to enrich their storyboards. When the storyboards are completed, encourage groups to share them with the class.

DIFFERENTIATE

ENGLISH LANGUAGE LEARNERS

Identify Word Parts Write these words on the board and have students copy them on a sheet of paper.

*hardworking   groundwork   craftsmen
mudslinging   landslide*

Pair students at the **Emerging** and **Expanding** levels with students at the **Bridging** level. Instruct them to work together to circle and define the two smaller words within each word. Then have them define the smaller words and the resulting compound word. Ask them to write an original sentence for each compound word.

PRE-AP

Analyze Campaign Songs Challenge students to locate and listen to Adams's campaign song "Little Know Ye Who's Coming" and Jackson's song "Hunters of Kentucky." Then prompt them to write an essay that analyzes the lyrics and musical style of each. Instruct students to consider the target audience of each song; what it reveals about that candidate's background, character, and political party; and how the song fits into the candidate's overall campaign strategy. Invite students to share their essays with the class.

See the Chapter Planner for more strategies for differentiation.

HISTORICAL THINKING

ANSWERS

1. When white males who did not own property were given the right to vote, more than 800,000 "common men" joined the voting population. Jackson fashioned himself as a candidate for the common man and so attracted many of these new voters.

2. Jackson used the facts that Adams was wealthy and had won the 1824 election with Clay's help to promote the opinion that he represented only the wealthy elite and had won as the result of a "corrupt bargain." The Adams campaign, meanwhile, used the facts that Jackson was a slaveholder, had fought in duels, and had to remarry his wife after her divorce was finalized to portray Jackson as a murderous slave trader married to a bigamist.

3. Possible response: Jacksonian democracy held out the prospect that men of humble origin, not just wealthy men, would have a say in government.

THE PEOPLE'S PRESIDENT?

Seeing a new president installed in the White House is always a cause for celebration—at least among his or her supporters. But Andrew Jackson's backers may have been a bit too enthusiastic.

CRITICAL VIEWING President Jackson—in the black jacket—is pinned against a wall by his supporters during the White House reception following his inauguration in this 1970 painting by Louis S. Glanzman, *The Rowdy Party*. What details in the painting convey a negative impression of the people at the reception?

A NEW POLITICAL CLASS

About 20,000 people arrived in Washington, D.C., to witness Andrew Jackson's inauguration on March 4, 1829. Some traveled 500 miles to attend the event. In a tradition established by Thomas Jefferson, Jackson opened the White House to the public so that he could greet the people. However, the White House staff was not prepared for the thousands who showed up. As the crowd grew and became more unmanageable, the new president fled the White House and was taken to a hotel.

Rumors circulated that the guests had destroyed items in the White House and stood on the furniture in their muddy shoes. But Jackson supporters claimed these accounts were exaggerated. And actually, most newspapers reported little or no damage. At least one writer, Margaret Bayard Smith, was dismayed by the simply dressed men and women who came to the White House. Nevertheless, she recognized that their presence—and Jackson's—represented a fundamental change in American democracy. Smith wrote, "What a pity what a pity! No arrangements had been made, no police officers placed on duty and the whole house had been inundated [invaded] by the rabble mob." However, as she also pointed out, "Ladies and gentlemen only had been expected at this Levee [reception], not the people en masse [as a whole]. But it was the People's day, and the People's President and the People would rule."

To the established political class, the scene at the White House represented the dangers of Jacksonian democracy. Members of the establishment thought they were better able to govern the country than the common man. But Jackson's election had broadened democracy, and he symbolized the age. He was the first president who did not come from a wealthy family in Virginia or Massachusetts. To many supporters, he also represented the shift of power to the West. Many people believed they finally had a president who represented them and their interests.

A ROCKY START

When Jackson took office, he began to carry out the reforms he'd promised during his campaign. He started by replacing a number of government officials from the previous administration with people who had supported him during the campaign, including newspaper editors. Jackson replaced only about 10 percent of the officials he had authority over, but this was far more than other presidents had replaced. The new president referred to his actions as "the principle of rotation in office." He claimed this rotation prevented government officials from permanently holding on to their jobs and becoming too powerful. Jackson's opponents, however, claimed he was simply rewarding his friends.

Critics charged Jackson with instituting the spoils system, which comes from the saying "to the victors belong the spoils of the enemy." They claimed that what he had done was corrupt and that he was using his appointments to gain greater control of the federal government. You may remember that Martin Van Buren had used the spoils system to create a powerful statewide network when he served as a New York senator. Jackson was the first to use the spoils system in the federal government.

Like the presidents before him, Jackson also selected his Cabinet members. He made Van Buren, who had directed the 1828 campaign, his Secretary of State. His close friend, John Eaton, became Secretary of War. Jackson's vice president, John C. Calhoun, recommended men for some of the other Cabinet positions.

Meanwhile, gossip was swirling about Eaton's new wife, Peggy, who was said to have a scandalous past. As a result, many of the Cabinet members' wives and Calhoun's wife refused to socialize with Peggy. Calhoun supported his wife, which angered Jackson. The rumors recalled those that had upset Jackson's wife during the 1828 campaign. The Eaton affair, as it came to be called, caused a rift between Jackson and Calhoun. Van Buren, on the other hand, behaved courteously to Peggy Eaton and would become Jackson's most trusted advisor. Policy issues would also divide the Cabinet. To ease the tension, Van Buren and Eaton withdrew from their positions. Jackson fired most of the other members in 1831.

Instead, he turned to a group of unofficial advisors—all trusted friends. Jackson's opponents dubbed this group the **kitchen cabinet**, suggesting that the members had "back door" access to the president.

For a time, Van Buren was a member of the kitchen cabinet. Calhoun, who wanted to succeed Jackson as president, became increasingly resentful of Van Buren. His resentment turned out to be well founded. When Jackson ran for re-election in 1832, Van Buren replaced Calhoun as his running mate.

HISTORICAL THINKING

1. **READING CHECK** What did Jackson symbolize to his supporters?

2. **MAKE INFERENCES** Why might some people have wanted to characterize those who came to the White House after Jackson's inauguration as a "rabble mob"?

3. **FORM AND SUPPORT OPINIONS** Do you think a president should only appoint friends and supporters to positions of power? Why or why not?

PLAN: 2-PAGE LESSON

OBJECTIVE

Discuss Andrew Jackson's 1829 inauguration and the consequences of his political appointments.

CRITICAL THINKING SKILLS FOR LESSON 1.2

- Make Inferences
- Form and Support Opinions
- Analyze Primary Sources

HISTORICAL THINKING FOR CHAPTER 8

How did Andrew Jackson change politics and the presidency? After the election of 1828, Andrew Jackson rewarded his supporters and friends with political appointments. Lesson 1.2 discusses Jackson's 1829 inauguration and the controversies that arose after he became president.

BACKGROUND FOR THE TEACHER

The informality of Andrew Jackson's inauguration and the passions it raised in its spectators fanned the fears of Washington insiders that the mob rule of democracy was overtaking the republican order. Rather than ride in a fancy procession to the Capitol to be sworn in and deliver his address, Jackson traveled without pretension—hatless and on foot. In the wake of the bitter campaign, John Quincy Adams chose not to attend the inauguration and ordered the military not to provide an escort for the president-elect. Therefore, a group of Revolutionary War veterans volunteered to accompany Jackson. The huge crowd that gathered to witness the event roared with approval and encouragement at the end of Jackson's speech. When the excited crowd snapped the cable that blocked the stairs to the Capitol's East Portico where Jackson stood, Jackson's men whisked him inside and out the west end of the Capitol, where he mounted his horse and rode to the White House.

INTRODUCE & ENGAGE

CREATE A KITCHEN CABINET

Guide students to consider the political meaning and connotation of the term *kitchen cabinet*. If necessary, explain that the kitchen cabinet is a group of informal advisors to the president. Ask students to identify people they might like to include in their own kitchen cabinet, people to whom they could turn for information, advice, and decision-making help in different areas of their lives. Invite volunteers to share who they would include and why they chose those people. Tell students that in this lesson they will learn about Jackson's inauguration as president and his early administration.

TEACH

GUIDED DISCUSSION

1. **Analyze Primary Sources** How would you characterize Margaret Bayard Smith's reaction to inaugural-day events at the White House? *(Possible response: Smith seems both awed and disturbed by the events. She sees the crowd as unruly and crude, but she also understands that "everyday people" are excited about being included and about finally having a president that they feel represents them.)*

2. **Form and Support Opinions** Do you think Jackson's swift replacement of government officials helped to fulfill his campaign promise to reform government? Why or why not? *(Possible responses: Yes. He offered a new vision, but he could not have begun any reforms if he had kept all the officials that had served under the previous administration. No. "Rotation in office" sounded like a reform, but Jackson just replaced some of Adams's appointments with his own friends and supporters.)*

MORE INFORMATION

Political Appointees Explain to students that Jackson's practice of rewarding his political supporters with government jobs led to some unfortunate choices. One of his most notorious appointments involved Samuel Swartwout, an early and enthusiastic Jackson supporter. Jackson appointed Swartwout as a customs collector at the port of New York during both of his terms in office. Duties at the port accounted for anywhere from one-half to two-thirds of U.S. Treasury funds each year. While in this position, Swartwout embezzled more than $1.2 million from the port before escaping to London in 1838. In today's dollars, that would be around $30 million. **ASK:** How does this story illustrate the negative connotation of the term *spoils system*? *(Possible response: Swartwout received his appointment because he was a friend of the candidate, not based on merit, and he used the opportunity for his gain only.)*

ACTIVE OPTIONS

On Your Feet: Think, Pair, Share Give students a few minutes to think about this question: How did Andrew Jackson's own history and friendships contribute to problems in his Cabinet? Then have students choose partners and talk about the question for five minutes. Finally, allow individual students to share their ideas with the class.

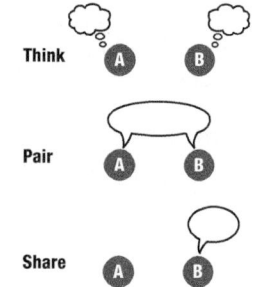

Think A B

Pair A B

Share A B

NG Learning Framework: Debate the Spoils System

ATTITUDE Responsibility

SKILL Communication

Divide the class into two groups. Direct one side to argue the pros of the spoils system and the other side to argue the cons. To organize their arguments, instruct the pro group to discuss reasons why the spoils system does benefit the workings of government and the policy decisions of the president, and direct the con group to identify reasons that support why the spoils system does not. Prompt each group to anticipate arguments the other side might make and generate some ideas to rebut those concerns. Invite the groups to debate the topic by taking turns presenting their arguments to the class.

DIFFERENTIATE

INCLUSION

Describe Details in a Painting Pair visually impaired students with sighted students. Ask the latter to describe in detail the participants in and setting of Jackson's inaugural party. Encourage students to ask clarifying questions as necessary. Then have pairs work together to read the caption and respond to the Critical Viewing question and the second Historical Thinking question.

GIFTED & TALENTED

Write a Letter Instruct students to find out more about the Eaton affair. Ask them to choose a figure who played a prominent role in the situation and its consequences, such as Peggy or John Eaton, John C. or Floride Calhoun, Jackson, or others. Then prompt them to write a letter to a friend describing the Washington, D.C., social scene from that person's point of view, describing the attitudes, feelings, and justifications of the chosen figure. Invite students to read their letter to the class.

See the Chapter Planner for more strategies for differentiation.

HISTORICAL THINKING

ANSWERS

1. To Jackson's supporters, his election represented a broadening of democracy and a shift in political power to the West, and they saw Jackson as a president who would represent their interests.

2. Possible response: The established political class would have wanted to show Jackson's supporters in the worst possible light because Jacksonian democracy was a threat to their power and status.

3. Possible response: Being a friend or supporter should not disqualify someone from being considered for appointment as long as the person is qualified. However, friendship or the obligation to reward supporters could cloud a president's judgment and result in the appointment of unqualified people.

CRITICAL VIEWING Possible response: The painting shows drunken individuals, broken dishes and glasses, people standing on the furniture, and a barefoot child carrying the flag in a disrespectful manner.

TENSION OVER TAXES

Sometimes you take a stand, and it doesn't work out. In 1828, Adams supported a bill he hoped would help him get re-elected, but the move backfired. Andrew Jackson won the election but had to deal with southern opposition to the bill.

DIFFERENCES BETWEEN THE NORTH AND THE SOUTH

The Eaton affair and Cabinet infighting weren't the only problems Andrew Jackson faced early in his presidency. Tensions between the North and the South were rising over tariffs, the taxes a government charges on imported goods. By the 1820s, the two regions had developed strong, but very different, economies. You've learned that the economy of the North had become increasingly industrialized by the 1820s. The trend had brought great population growth and wealth to the region. Some of this population growth was due to the influx of immigrants drawn by the hope of obtaining work in northern factories. By contrast, the agrarian South depended largely on agricultural production, particularly cotton. And, as you know, large plantation owners used enslaved labor to work their fields.

Industries in the North benefited from tariffs because the taxes increased the price of foreign manufactured goods. The tariffs made the lower-priced goods produced in the North more attractive, which boosted local sales. On the other hand, tariffs hurt the South. Southern farmers bought manufactured goods from Europe. Tariffs on these goods made them more expensive. In 1828, Congress would pass a bill that underscored the economic differences between the North and the South.

THE TARIFF OF 1828

The bill, which would be called the Tariff of 1828, was passed in the final months of John Quincy Adams's presidency. It greatly raised tariffs and, therefore, the prices of foreign goods sold in the United States. The bill was intended to protect northern industries from foreign competition. As you know, Adams represented the interests of the Northeast, where many factories were located. With the next presidential election approaching, Adams promoted the bill, in part to appeal to northeastern voters. The bill, he believed, would also benefit the federal government. At that time, tariffs represented the government's main source of revenue. Defenders of the tariff pointed out that its passage would be in the interest of the entire country. Southerners didn't buy it. They hated the tariff so much they called it the **Tariff of Abominations**.

The Tariff of 1828 made the foreign goods the South needed more expensive. However, it also contained a clause that raised taxes on some of the imported raw materials that were necessary to both the North and the South, including wool. Democrats in Congress had proposed the clause because they believed its inclusion would persuade northeastern representatives to vote against the tariff. After all, many textile manufacturers in the Northeast depended on imports of wool, and the clause made the fiber more expensive. Nevertheless, the bill passed with the support of representatives from the middle and western states as well as a few key congressmen from New England.

Adams signed the bill into law even though he knew it would probably hurt him in his bid for re-election. People in many regions of the country disliked the bill, but southerners especially loathed it. The South voted against Adams partly in reaction to the tariff. One of its greatest opponents was John C. Calhoun, who was John Quincy Adams's vice president. As you know, Calhoun was also elected vice president under Andrew Jackson. Once in office, Jackson supported the tariff, but Calhoun continued to voice his opposition to it. As a result, the split between the two would deepen even further.

TARIFFS TODAY
Americans continue to disagree over tariffs. In 2017, the U.S. government threatened to impose tariffs on steel imported from China and other countries. Ships carrying containers of imported steel continually arrived in American ports, including this one in South Carolina.

The president at that time, Donald Trump, claimed the countries were using the United States as a "dumping ground" for their cheap steel. He also insisted that the imported steel was harming national security by preventing the United States from manufacturing steel for its own defense purposes. Critics said the tariffs would raise the price of domestic steel and, as a result, the price of U.S. goods made of steel. Opponents also pointed out that European countries might retaliate by levying tariffs on some U.S. imports. In spite of these objections, President Trump ordered tariffs on most imported steel and aluminum in 2018.

HISTORICAL THINKING

1. **READING CHECK** How did the economies of the North and the South differ in the 1820s?

2. **IDENTIFY MAIN IDEAS AND DETAILS** Why did southerners call the Tariff of 1828 the Tariff of Abominations?

3. **MAKE INFERENCES** Why might those in the middle and western states have supported the tariff?

4. **DRAW CONCLUSIONS** In what ways was the passage of the Tariff of 1828 a no-win situation for Adams?

PLAN: 2-PAGE LESSON

OBJECTIVE

Describe how tariffs led to tension between the North and South and within the Jackson administration.

CRITICAL THINKING SKILLS FOR LESSON 2.1

- Identify Main Ideas and Details
- Make Inferences
- Draw Conclusions
- Make Connections
- Distinguish Fact from Opinion

HISTORICAL THINKING FOR CHAPTER 8

How did Andrew Jackson change politics and the presidency? Andrew Jackson came to support the Tariff of 1828, which was signed into law by John Quincy Adams. Lesson 2.1 discusses the regional tensions caused by the tariff and how Jackson's acceptance of the tariff widened the divide between himself and his vice president.

BACKGROUND FOR THE TEACHER

In the wake of the War of 1812, John C. Calhoun encouraged passage of the Tariff of 1816. He did this in part because he believed that the United States needed to establish economic self-sufficiency as a matter of national security in the event of another war with Britain. In the 1820s, his views on tariffs changed. Nevertheless, he convinced the South Carolina delegation to temper its response to the Tariff of 1828 out of fear that a strong protest would cause a backlash that would hurt Andrew Jackson's chance for victory in the presidential election. Calhoun hoped that Jackson would ease the burden on the South by reassessing the tariff schedules if he won the election. That hope proved to be false. The South saw its costs rise and its revenues drop while the North experienced an economic boom.

FINANCIAL LITERACY

To extend their knowledge and understanding about the concepts in this lesson, refer students to the Financial Literacy handbook.

INTRODUCE & ENGAGE

ACTIVATE PRIOR KNOWLEDGE

Invite students to share what they have already learned about the purpose of tariffs and the differing views of the North and South concerning their implementation. Record and display students' responses in a Concept Cluster. Ask students to use ideas from the Concept Cluster to discuss why the North favored tariffs while many in the South opposed them. Tell students that in Lesson 2.1 they will learn about the Tariff of 1828.

TEACH

GUIDED DISCUSSION

1. **Make Connections** Why was immigration a bigger factor in population growth in the North than it was in the South, given that both regions had strong economies? *(Possible response: Both economies were strong, but the economy in the North centered on manufacturing, which needed workers in factories, while the economy in the South was agricultural. Because much of the labor needed on plantations and farms was supplied by enslaved workers or family members, immigrants seeking jobs could not expect to find many opportunities in the South.)*

2. **Identify Main Ideas and Details** What unsuccessful tactic did Democrats use to try to block passage of the Tariff of 1828? *(Congressional Democrats inserted a clause in the bill that raised taxes on imported wool and other raw materials used in both the North and South in hopes of defeating its passage. It didn't work, though, because the bill had enough support to pass, even with the clause.)*

DISTINGUISH FACT FROM OPINION

Direct students' attention to the Tariffs Today feature. **ASK:** Which points in the feature are facts and which are opinions? *(Possible response: It's a fact that President Trump threatened and then ordered tariffs. The dumping of cheap steel might be a fact, if it is verified. The point that imported steel is a security risk is an opinion. The objections made by the opponents of the tariffs are also opinions, since they are possible outcomes, not events that have actually happened.)*

ACTIVE OPTIONS

On Your Feet: Stage a Quiz Show Instruct students to write one question about the Tariff of 1828. Encourage students to consider regional differences and political and economic consequences. Collect the questions. Then have groups of five students take turns coming to the front of the class to take part in a quiz. Pose a few of the questions to each group and allow students to confer about the answers. Tell them to signal their readiness to respond by raising their hands.

NG Learning Framework: Research Tariffs

ATTITUDE Curiosity

KNOWLEDGE Our Human Story

Arrange students in groups to learn more about Trump's push for tariffs on imported steel and other goods. Instruct groups to investigate which goods were singled out for tariffs, how the affected nations responded to the tariffs, and what consequences the tariffs had on American businesses and the U.S. economy. Invite groups to share their findings with the class and discuss the pros and cons of tariffs in a modern global economy.

DIFFERENTIATE

ENGLISH LANGUAGE LEARNERS ELD

Understand Shades of Meaning Pair students at the **Emerging** level with those at the **Bridging** or **Expanding** level, and provide them with a Synonym-Antonym Scale based on the words *love* and *hate*, such as the one shown below. Instruct students to reread the sentence in the last paragraph of the subsection The Tariff of 1828 that contains the words *disliked* and *loathed*. Tell students to use context clues to determine the meanings of the words *dislike* and *loathe* and then write these meanings at the appropriate places on the scale. Encourage students to think of two or three more words with meanings between *love* and *hate* and add them to the scale.

◄─────────────────────────►
hate   love

GIFTED & TALENTED

Write a Dialogue Direct student pairs to write a brief dialogue based on the views that Calhoun and Jackson held about tariffs. Share with students the information provided in Background for the Teacher and suggest that they do further research to learn more about the reasons for the men's positions. Encourage pairs to perform their finished scripts with appropriate vocal and facial expressions.

See the Chapter Planner for more strategies for differentiation.

HISTORICAL THINKING

ANSWERS

1. The North's economy was based on industry, while the South's economy remained dependent on agricultural production, particularly cotton.

2. The tariff benefited northerners at the expense of southerners, making foreign goods and raw materials more expensive.

3. Possible response: The middle and western states would likely benefit from the growth of the home market for manufactured goods and agricultural products that resulted from the tariff.

4. Possible response: Adams needed to sign the tariff to please his industrial base in the Northeast, but in doing so, he alienated voters in the South and elsewhere who relied on foreign trade or raw materials from Britain.

THE NULLIFICATION CRISIS

Where do you stand on states' rights? Do you believe a state should be able to decide which federal laws it will obey? The people in many southern states thought they should have that right after Congress passed the Tariff of 1828.

THE DOCTRINE OF NULLIFICATION

Vice President John C. Calhoun represented South Carolina, his home state, in the fight against the Tariff of 1828. He invoked the **doctrine of nullification**, also known as the states' rights doctrine, to make his case. As you may recall, nullification refers to an idea first proposed around 1798 by Thomas Jefferson and James Madison. According to this idea, states have the right to determine when the federal government has exceeded its power. In these instances, states can reject federal laws and declare them "void [invalid] and of no force." The doctrine of nullification became a key issue in the debate over states' rights versus federal power.

Calhoun further developed this doctrine in a document called the *South Carolina Exposition and Protest*, which was published in 1829 without his name on it. In the document, Calhoun insisted that a state should only be compelled to obey a federal

Daniel Webster debates the doctrine of nullification in the Senate while his opponent, Robert Y. Hayne, sitting cross-legged in the foreground, listens. This bronze relief is set in the pedestal of a statue of Webster in Washington, D.C.

The Webster-Hayne debate took place over several days in January 1830 and established Webster's reputation as a gifted orator. In the following excerpts from their speeches, first Hayne and then Webster state their views on nullification.

If the Federal Government, in all or any of its departments, is to prescribe [impose] the limits of its own authority, and the States are bound to submit to the decision, and are not to be allowed to examine and decide for themselves when the barriers of the Constitution shall be overleaped, this is practically "a Government without limitation of powers." The states are at once reduced to mere petty corporations [insignificant organizations] and the people are entirely at your mercy.

—Robert Y. Hayne, 1830

I . . . have kept steadily in view the prosperity and honor of the whole country, and the preservation of our federal Union. It is to that Union we owe our safety at home, and our consideration and dignity abroad. It is to that Union that we are chiefly indebted for whatever makes us most proud of our country. . . . And although our territory has stretched out wider and wider, and our population spread farther and farther, they have not outrun its protection or its benefits.

—Daniel Webster, 1830

law with which it disagreed if the law were amended to the Constitution. This process would protect states' rights—especially those of the less populated South—from being violated by a northern majority. Otherwise, Calhoun believed, federal enforcement of the law should be considered unconstitutional.

Andrew Jackson was angered by the position his vice president had taken on nullification. Jackson didn't like the tariffs, but he didn't repeal the Tariff of 1828. His inaction disappointed many of the southerners who had voted for him. They'd expected he would at least modify the law once he became president. Jackson supported states' rights, but he opposed Calhoun's notion that states should have the power to prevent the federal government from enacting national laws. Only the Supreme Court, Jackson asserted, had the power to declare a law unconstitutional. He also feared the doctrine of nullification threatened the preservation of the Union.

THE WEBSTER-HAYNE DEBATE

Daniel Webster, a senator from Massachusetts, disagreed with Jackson on many issues, but he also perceived nullification as a threat to the Union. Other politicians joined in the debate over nullification, but the **Webster-Hayne debate** held in 1830 became the most famous. Over the course of the debate, Webster argued against nullification, calling for "Liberty and Union, now and forever, one and inseparable." Senator Robert Y. Hayne of South Carolina presented Calhoun's ideas and made the case in favor of nullification. Hayne criticized those whom he said "are constantly stealing power from the States and adding strength to the Federal Government."

The nullification crisis escalated in 1832. In an effort to make some concessions to the South, Congress passed the Tariff of 1832, which reduced tariffs. However, most southerners viewed the new law as little better than the old one, and South Carolina decided to put Calhoun's nullification theory to a test. The South Carolina legislature declared the tariffs of 1828 and 1832 "null and void." Furthermore, if the federal government used force to collect the tariffs, the representatives claimed South Carolina would secede, or withdraw, from the Union. South Carolina tried to persuade other states to join their protest, but none did.

Jackson responded by issuing a statement reaffirming the authority of the federal government and warning that any attempt to leave the Union would be considered treason. In addition, Congress authorized the president to use force against any state that refused to pay the tariffs. Finally, Senator Henry Clay of Kentucky proposed the Compromise Tariff of 1833, which would gradually reduce tariffs over the next 10 years. South Carolina agreed to the compromise, and the nullification crisis ended. Jackson had succeeded in preventing secession. However, tensions over states' rights would continue to grow and divide the country throughout much of the 1800s.

HISTORICAL THINKING

1. **READING CHECK** What is the doctrine of nullification?

2. **DISTINGUISH FACT FROM OPINION** How did Hayne and Webster use facts and opinions to make convincing arguments in their debate?

3. **DRAW CONCLUSIONS** Why did Jackson believe the nullification crisis could lead to secession?

PLAN: 2-PAGE LESSON

OBJECTIVE

Analyze how the Tariff of 1828 sparked the nullification crisis and how Andrew Jackson responded.

CRITICAL THINKING SKILLS FOR LESSON 2.2

- Distinguish Fact from Opinion
- Draw Conclusions
- Summarize
- Make Connections
- Analyze Primary Sources

HISTORICAL THINKING FOR CHAPTER 8

How did Andrew Jackson change politics and the presidency? Andrew Jackson was from the South, but he was also a strong Unionist. Lesson 2.2 discusses how Jackson responded to John C. Calhoun's doctrine of nullification and prevented South Carolina from seceding.

BACKGROUND FOR THE TEACHER

Each year republican-minded politicians gathered on April 13 to celebrate Thomas Jefferson's birthday with a dinner and toasts. Jackson and Calhoun both planned to attend the 1830 dinner and offer toasts. When Jackson received the dinner's program and examined the list of toasters, he found it full of supporters of nullification. Jackson prepared three short toasts, settling on one. Many at the dinner hoped that Jackson's toast would indicate whether he planned to compromise or fight nullification. Jackson made his opposition to nullification clear, toasting, "Our Federal Union— It must be preserved." Vice President Calhoun, in turn, responded with his own declaration, "The Union—next to our Liberty, the most dear; may we all remember that it can only be preserved by respecting the rights of the States, and distributing equally the benefit and burden of the Union."

INTRODUCE & ENGAGE

TAKE A STAND

Engage in a short class discussion about which body enacts which kinds of laws in the United States today: state governments or the federal government. Point out that laws regarding some issues, such as immigration, are decided at the federal level, while others, such as medical malpractice, are decided at the state level. Ask students what types of laws they believe should be developed at the state or federal level. Then tell students that they will read about the issue of states' rights and the debate that almost divided the nation.

TEACH

GUIDED DISCUSSION

1. **Summarize** What ideas underpinned Calhoun's *South Carolina Exposition and Protest*? *(Calhoun built on Jefferson and Madison's idea of nullification, which said that states had the right to declare a federal law void if they thought the federal government had overstepped its power in passing it. Calhoun extended the idea by arguing that states should only be forced to obey a law they disagreed with if the law became an amendment to the Constitution.)*

2. **Make Connections** Why did Jackson take the stands that he did during the nullification crisis even though he believed in states' rights and did not like the tariffs? *(Jackson believed that states didn't have the right to prevent the federal government from enacting federal laws, so he felt justified in using force against states that refused to pay the tariffs. Jackson believed that by taking this stand he was protecting the Union.)*

ANALYZE PRIMARY SOURCES

Direct students' attention to the Primary Sources feature. **ASK:** What is Robert Y. Hayne's main point? *(Possible response: Hayne argues that if the federal government alone can set the limits of its own power and states can't challenge it, then the federal government will grant itself virtually unlimited power at the expense of states and the American people.)* **ASK:** What is Daniel Webster's main point? *(Possible response: Webster argues that the Union has given Americans individual liberty, security at home, prestige in the world, and pride in their country, and everyone throughout the country benefits from its preservation.)*

ACTIVE OPTIONS

On Your Feet: Team Word Webbing Arrange teams of students around a large sheet of paper. Give half the teams this topic sentence: State governments should have the power to reject a federal law if they believe the federal government has exceeded its power. Give the other half this topic sentence: The U.S. Constitution created a government, not just an association of states, so leaving the union is treason. Instruct students to create a paragraph by having each student contribute one sentence to support the topic sentence. Ask volunteers to read their team's paragraph aloud.

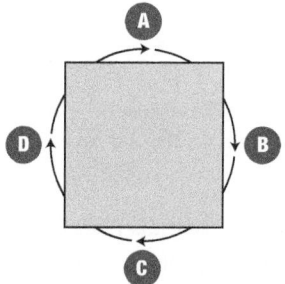

NG Learning Framework: Create a Presentation

ATTITUDE Curiosity

SKILLS Collaboration, Communication

Direct students to work in pairs to learn more about the Webster-Hayne debate. Then instruct pairs to take an in-depth look at one aspect of the debates that they find interesting. For example, they could evaluate one of the speeches, analyze why the Webster-Hayne debate is one of the most celebrated debates in American history, or assess public reaction to the debate. Prompt partners to collaborate on writing a short oral or multimedia presentation discussing their findings. Invite pairs to share their presentations with the class.

DIFFERENTIATE

STRIVING READERS

Write a Tweet As students read the lesson, direct them to write a short tweet to summarize each paragraph's main idea in their own words. Encourage students to read their tweets aloud to a partner, alternating so that the first student reads his or her tweet about the first paragraph and the second student reads a tweet about the second paragraph. Partners continue until they reach the end of the lesson.

PRE-AP

Explain the Compromise of 1833 Instruct students to conduct research and present an oral report about how the Compromise Tariff of 1833 was crafted and accepted by both sides. Suggest students use a graphic organizer to keep track of their research and to organize their report. Students may wish to conclude with their thoughts on whether the art of compromise is alive in Congress today. Invite students to present their oral reports to the class.

See the Chapter Planner for more strategies for differentiation.

HISTORICAL THINKING

ANSWERS

1. The doctrine of nullification asserts that states could nullify federal laws when the federal government exceeds its power.

2. Possible response: Hayne's use of fact: If the government determined the limits of its own power, it could choose almost limitless power for itself. Hayne's use of opinion: The states would be reduced to "petty corporations" and the people would be at the government's mercy. Webster's use of fact: The Union contributed to the safety and prosperity of the nation. Webster's use of opinion: Everything that citizens take the most pride in should be attributed to the Union.

3. Possible response: He probably believed that a state might choose to secede if the Supreme Court did not allow it to nullify a federal law that it objected to strongly.

SEIZING NATIVE AMERICAN LAND

Almost from the moment Europeans arrived in North America, Native Americans had struggled to hold on to their homes. They would encounter one of the greatest threats to their traditional lands in Andrew Jackson.

PROMISES MADE AND BROKEN

You may remember that Andrew Jackson had dealings with Native Americans before he became president. After the War of 1812, the federal government authorized then-General Jackson to negotiate treaties with Native Americans in the Southeast, including the Creek, Cherokee, Choctaw, and Chickasaw. The Creek signed their treaty after losing a war against U.S. Army troops led by Jackson, and the treaty's terms were highly unfavorable to the Native Americans. They were required to hand over about 22 million acres of land—an area roughly the size of South Carolina—to the federal government. After more battles and treaties with other Native Americans, white settlers moved into the fertile lands the tribes had occupied for generations. The Native Americans were edged onto lands less suitable for farming.

As president, Jackson wanted to get hold of more Native American territory for white settlers. He offered Native Americans two options. They could either **assimilate**, or adopt, European culture and submit to the laws of their state government, or they could move west of the Mississippi River. Some Native American tribes chose assimilation. The Cherokee, Chickasaw, Creek, Choctaw, and Seminole adapted so well to European culture that some people referred to them as the "Five Civilized Tribes." Among these tribes, none assimilated as fully as the Cherokee. They dressed in western-style clothing and owned businesses and farms. Some built plantations and ranches and even used enslaved people to work their land.

One Cherokee named **Sequoya** (sih-KWOY-uh), who had fought for the United States during the War of 1812, developed a **syllabary**, written symbols or characters used to represent a word's syllables,

for the Cherokee language. The syllabary was used to translate many books, including the Bible, and literacy spread rapidly among the Cherokee. The Cherokee also printed a newspaper called the *Cherokee Phoenix*, the first newspaper published by Native Americans as well as the first in a Native American language. They even wrote a constitution based on the U.S. Constitution and, having established a sovereign government, founded the **Cherokee Nation**.

However, assimilation did not protect the Cherokee or any of the southeastern tribes from being pressured to leave their homes. The pressure mounted when gold was discovered on Cherokee land in Georgia in 1828. As a result, southern states passed laws that ignored previous treaties and allowed farmers, miners, and other settlers to claim Native American lands for themselves.

THE INDIAN REMOVAL ACT

Jackson supported the laws enacted in the southern states and went even further. In 1830, he pushed Congress to pass a law called the **Indian Removal Act**, which reversed the federal government's policy of respecting Native American claims to their lands. The law granted the president power to negotiate removal treaties with Native American groups living east of the Mississippi. The treaties required Native Americans to give up any claim to their homes and move to an area of land that came to be known as **Indian Territory**, which included present-day Oklahoma and parts of Kansas and Nebraska. Native Americans who wished to remain in the eastern states would become citizens of their home state.

The Indian Removal Act called for peaceful negotiations and specified that Native Americans would not be forced off their land. But Jackson did

Native Americans continue to fight for their homes today. In 2016, Native Americans protested the installation of an oil pipeline that crossed the Missouri River near North Dakota's Standing Rock Sioux Reservation, claiming that it could contaminate the reservation's drinking water. In this photo, U.S. Army veteran Catcher Cuts the Rope leads a protest march. Despite protesters' efforts, the pipeline opened in June 2017.

not always abide by this ruling. He regarded Native Americans as children who needed to be guided. Jackson believed removal was in their best interests. Not all Americans agreed with the removal act, however. Some protested the cruelty of sending Native Americans to unknown lands. Others, like the Quakers, objected on moral grounds, claiming the Indian Removal Act was neither just nor right. But their protests had little impact. The removal of Native Americans soon got underway.

The act affected not only Native Americans in the Southeast but also tribes farther north. Many Native Americans left their homes peacefully. The Choctaw became the first southeastern tribe to sign a treaty. While some Choctaw chose to remain in Mississippi under the terms of the act, thousands elected to move westward beginning in 1831. On foot and carrying insufficient supplies, the first group to

relocate encountered the worst winter yet recorded. About 2,500 Choctaw died of exposure, starvation, and disease during the move. The Chickasaw faced similar hardships when they headed west in the winter of 1837. But not all Native Americans gave up their homes. Some would not go without a fight.

HISTORICAL THINKING

1. **READING CHECK** What options did Jackson offer Native Americans in his effort to acquire land for white settlers?

2. **DISTINGUISH FACT FROM OPINION** Was Jackson's attitude toward Native Americans based on fact or opinion or both? Explain your answer.

3. **MAKE INFERENCES** Why do you think many Native Americans chose to leave their homes peacefully and relocate to Indian Territory?

PLAN: 2-PAGE LESSON

OBJECTIVE

Identify how westward expansion into Native American lands affected Native Americans in the eastern states.

CRITICAL THINKING SKILLS FOR LESSON 3.1

• Distinguish Fact from Opinion
• Make Inferences
• Draw Conclusions
• Make Connections

HISTORICAL THINKING FOR CHAPTER 8

How did Andrew Jackson change politics and the presidency? Andrew Jackson pushed Congress to pass the Indian Removal Act, then circumvented its provisions. Lesson 3.1 describes how white settlers' demand for land led Native Americans to be pushed off eastern lands and relocated westward.

BACKGROUND FOR THE TEACHER

From its first issue—published on February 21, 1828, in New Echota, Georgia, the capital of the Cherokee Nation—the *Cherokee Phoenix* worked to inform and unite the Cherokee people and to garner support for Cherokee resistance to being forcibly removed. To communicate to Cherokee people from a range of backgrounds, the newspaper used a two-column format for articles, one column in English and one column in the Cherokee syllabary. Articles included coverage of congressional debates and Supreme Court cases relevant to the Cherokee Nation; issues concerning assimilation, removal, and Cherokee land rights; Cherokee news; and practical advice on agriculture and animal husbandry. Established and paid for by the Cherokee National Council, the paper ceased publication on May 31, 1834, when the government ran out of money for it. Ultimately, the Georgia militia seized and destroyed the press.

INTRODUCE & ENGAGE

EXPLORE MOTIVATIONS

Ask the class to identify reasons why the federal government would want to take land that Native Americans had occupied for generations. List students' responses on the board. Then tell students that in this lesson they will learn how the federal government sought to move Native Americans off their land so that white settlers could occupy it and how Native Americans responded.

TEACH

GUIDED DISCUSSION

1. **Draw Conclusions** What evidence shows that efforts to assimilate did little to protect Native American rights? *(Possible response: The Chickasaw, Creek, Choctaw, Seminole, and particularly the Cherokee adopted American dress and culture, opened businesses, and established farms and plantations. In spite of these signs of assimilation, the majority were forced to give up their lands and relocate to Indian Territory.)*

2. **Make Connections** How did events in the southern states foreshadow Congress's efforts to open Native American lands to white settlers? *(Possible response: When gold was discovered in Georgia, the southern states passed laws that allowed miners, farmers, and other settlers to claim Native American lands in spite of treaties. The Indian Removal Act authorized the president to negotiate new treaties that required Native Americans to give up their land claims.)*

MORE INFORMATION

Sequoya's Syllabary Tell students that Sequoya first used symbols to represent whole words in his writing system. When that became too cumbersome, Sequoya devised a new system where a unique symbol stood for each syllable in the Cherokee language. Eventually, Sequoya devised a total of 86 symbols. **ASK:** Why would a writing system like the one Sequoya developed be important for the Cherokee during the Age of Jackson? *(Possible response: Having a written language made it possible to use newspapers and other printed material to communicate with Cherokee people no matter where they lived to coordinate efforts or sway opinions. The Cherokee probably also felt a need to get information provided by and for the Cherokee, instead of depending on information—or misinformation—from people that didn't have their best interests at heart.)*

ACTIVE OPTIONS

On Your Feet: Numbered Heads Organize students into groups of four. Tell students to think about and discuss a response to this question: Considering the specific gains and losses sustained by different groups, did the Indian Removal Act reflect a time of progress? Then call a number and ask the student from each group with that number to report for the group.

NG Learning Framework: Form an Opinion

ATTITUDES Responsibility, Empowerment

SKILL Problem-Solving

Assign students to small groups. Ask them to imagine they are leaders of the Cherokee, Choctaw, or other southeastern group in the 1830s. Congress has passed the Indian Removal Act, and Jackson is pushing for Native Americans to relocate to Indian Territory. Ask students which choice they think their group should make—to move or to become citizens of the state in which they live. Tell each group to discuss the options and arrive at a decision and plan of action using information from the text and additional research, if necessary. Invite groups to share their decisions with the class and explain their reasoning.

DIFFERENTIATE

ENGLISH LANGUAGE LEARNERS `ELD`

Use a Word Map Pair students at the **Emerging** level with those at the **Expanding** or **Bridging** level, and provide them with a Word Map such as the one shown. Instruct students to write *assimilate* in the center oval and to use context clues from the text to complete the Word Map. As students work, encourage them to use a dictionary to confirm meanings and clear up any misunderstandings.

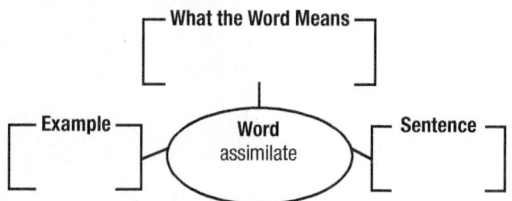

GIFTED & TALENTED

Create a Multimedia Presentation Invite students to examine the photograph of the 2016 protest near the Standing Rock Sioux Reservation and read the caption. Prompt students to learn more about the treaties relating to the Sioux and other tribes. Challenge them to connect some of the issues underlying the Standing Rock protest to the Indian Removal Act. Instruct students to assemble their findings into a multimedia presentation to share with the class.

See the Chapter Planner for more strategies for differentiation.

HISTORICAL THINKING

ANSWERS

1. Jackson offered Native Americans two options. They could remain in the eastern states if they were willing to assimilate and follow the laws of their state governments, or they could give up their claims to their homes and move west of the Mississippi River to Indian Territory.

2. Possible response: Jackson's attitude toward Native Americans was based on opinion—that they were childlike and needed to be guided to do what was in their own best interest.

3. Possible response: They may have wanted to avoid conflicts with white settlers and the federal government, or they may have thought that moving to Indian Territory was the best way to save their traditional way of life.

PUTTING UP RESISTANCE

Sometimes people stand up to injustice, even when they're outnumbered and overpowered. Despite the size and strength of the United States, some Native Americans tried to defy Andrew Jackson and the U.S. government.

THE SECOND SEMINOLE WAR

The Seminole, who had first settled in the northern area of Florida, were among the Native Americans who fought against relocation. Most of the Seminole refused to sign a removal treaty, and President Jackson and the U.S. government declared war on them in 1835.

This wasn't the first time Jackson had gone to war against the Seminole. The First Seminole War was waged between 1817 and 1818, when General Jackson led his troops on frequent raids into Florida, which belonged to Spain at that time. The Seminole had provided a refuge for slaves who had escaped from their owners. Jackson and his soldiers invaded the Spanish territory to combat the Native Americans, burn their villages, and recapture the slaves. The Americans also seized Spanish-held territory. As a result, Spain ceded Florida to the United States in 1819, and the Seminole were confined to an area of land in the central and southern parts of the territory.

The Second Seminole War posed a tougher challenge for the U.S. Army. Under their leader Osceola (ahs-ee-OH-luh), the Seminole used guerrilla tactics to fight the American soldiers. The warriors hid within the swamplands of the Everglades, a wetlands region in southern Florida,

CRITICAL VIEWING Little is known about Osceola's early life, but many historians believe he was born in Alabama in 1804 to a Creek mother and a Scottish father. He was known as Billy Powell until he went to live among the Seminole in the Everglades. There, he embraced his Native American heritage and became known as Osceola. What does this 1838 portrait of Osceola, painted by American artist George Catlin, convey about the leader?

and took the Americans by surprise during battles. Armed with tomahawks and muskets, the Seminole ambushed and attacked the soldiers. The Seminole also tried to drive out white settlers already living in the region by setting fire to their homes and farmland.

In 1837, the U.S. government and the Seminole called a truce, or an agreement to stop fighting, and the Americans arranged to meet Osceola at a peace conference. But the conference turned out to be a trap. Osceola was taken prisoner and died in captivity three months later.

Occasional skirmishes in Florida continued for five more years before the Seminole finally surrendered. Nearly 2,000 American soldiers died during the war, which cost the government more than $40 million. Some Seminole eventually migrated to Indian Territory and became one of the Five Civilized Tribes. However, many remained in the Everglades. The Seminole still live there today.

THE BLACK HAWK WAR

As you've learned, Native Americans in other parts of the country faced removal. Some of them resisted relocation as well. Tribes in Illinois, including the Shawnee, Ottawa, Potawatomi, Sauk, and Fox, signed a treaty and moved west of the Mississippi River. However, once they settled in their new home, they struggled to grow enough food on the land. Rather than starve, they rebelled. In April 1832, Sauk warrior **Black Hawk** led about 1,000 Sauk, Fox, and other Native American people to take back their lands in Illinois.

Their return angered and frightened the white settlers who had moved onto the lands the tribes had surrendered. A force of about 7,000 volunteers, consisting of settlers, U.S. soldiers, and even members of other Native American tribes, joined together to fight Black Hawk and his followers. The brief but bloody Black Hawk War ended in August and resulted in the deaths of as many as 600 Native Americans and 70 soldiers and settlers. A number of those who participated in the war on the American side would become prominent figures in U.S. history. For instance, a young **Abraham Lincoln** served as a captain in the Black Hawk War. Another future president, **Zachary Taylor**, also took part.

Black Hawk surrendered and was held prisoner by the U.S. Army for several months. While imprisoned, he told his captors that he was not sorry for trying to take back Native American land. Black Hawk believed he was defending the land and his people from those he said aimed to "cheat them." When the American public learned what Black Hawk had said, many people sympathized with him.

Following his imprisonment, Black Hawk was brought to Washington, D.C., to face Andrew Jackson. The president had Black Hawk take a tour of four major eastern cities to show the Sauk leader that he was no match for such a large, powerful nation. Many Americans turned out to see the famous Sauk warrior. While in Baltimore, Black Hawk was quoted as saying, "I ought not to have taken up the tomahawk, but my people have suffered a great deal." He died in 1838.

National Museum of the American Indian Washington, D.C.

Seminole men wore pouches called bandolier bags strapped over their shoulders. Made of wool and decorated with beads, the bags were used to carry flint, steel, and tobacco. The bag shown at right is believed to have been taken from a Seminole chief during the Second Seminole War.

OBJECTIVE

Assess how Andrew Jackson's stance on Native American relocation and his defiance of the Supreme Court affected Native Americans.

CRITICAL THINKING SKILLS FOR LESSON 3.2

- Draw Conclusions
- Evaluate
- Interpret Maps
- Compare and Contrast
- Identify
- Make Inferences
- Analyze Primary Sources

HISTORICAL THINKING FOR CHAPTER 8

How did Andrew Jackson change politics and the presidency? Andrew Jackson took a hard-line approach to implementing the Indian Removal Act. Lesson 3.2 examines the consequences for the Seminole, Cherokee, and other eastern Native Americans.

BACKGROUND FOR THE TEACHER

In 1832, a group of Seminole leaders signed the Treaty of Payne's Landing. The terms of the treaty required the Seminole to move to Creek lands in Mississippi within three years, provided the Seminole found the lands suitable. After a Seminole delegation visited and declared the lands acceptable, they were pressured into signing the Treaty of Fort Gibson in 1833, confirming the terms of removal. When the federal government learned that the Seminole had no intention of honoring the treaty, General Wiley Thompson warned that he had the authority to remove them by force. The Seminole responded with their own show of force. On December 28, 1835, in separate incidents, Osceola killed General Thompson, and Seminoles attacked and killed a large group of soldiers under the command of Major Francis Dade.

HISTORY NOTEBOOK

Encourage students to complete the American Gallery page for Chapter 8 in their History Notebooks as they read.

INTRODUCE & ENGAGE

K-W-L CHART

Provide each student with a K-W-L Chart. Tell students to brainstorm what they already know about the forced relocation of Native Americans. Then direct students' attention to the map. After reviewing the map, tell students to write questions inspired by the map, such as: Why were Native Americans moved so far from their native lands? What hardships did Native Americans face during removal? Allow time at the end of the lesson for students to complete their charts.

K What Do I Know?	W What Do I Want To Learn?	L What Did I Learn?

TEACH

GUIDED DISCUSSION

1. **Draw Conclusions** How might past experiences with the federal government have colored the Seminoles' decision to resist removal? *(Possible response: The Seminole had fought Jackson in the First Seminole War when Florida still belonged to Spain. They likely distrusted the president and the U.S. military, since troops under Jackson had burned Seminole villages and the government had confined the Seminole to central and south Florida following the war. In addition, during the Second Seminole War, U.S. forces had taken Osceola prisoner during a supposed peace conference.)*

2. **Compare and Contrast** How were the experiences of Osceola and Black Hawk similar and different? *(Possible responses: Both leaders fought U.S. forces over land, but Osceola fought to keep Seminole land and Black Hawk tried to regain land lost through a treaty. Both were taken into captivity, but Osceola was captured through trickery and Black Hawk surrendered. Osceola died in captivity, but Black Hawk was released after several months.)*

3. **Evaluate** Do you think Black Hawk's tour of four major eastern cities met Jackson's objective? Why or why not? *(Answers will vary. Possible responses: Yes. Black Hawk said that he shouldn't have waged war—probably because the tour made him realize he couldn't possibly have won. No. Black Hawk was unapologetic about trying to take back Native American land because he recognized the suffering of his people, and the tour likely did not change his mind about the justness of his cause even if he realized it was futile to fight.)*

VIRTUAL MUSEUM VISIT

The National Museum of the American Indian (NMAI) is located in Washington, D.C., on the National Mall, with additional facilities in New York City and in Suitland, Maryland. NMAI holds more than 800,000 items spanning over 12,000 years of history and representing more than 1,200 cultures throughout the Americas, including almost all tribal groups in the United States. Encourage students to visit the NMAI's "Infinity of Nations" exhibit online and investigate other Native American pouches and shoulder bags and cultural items under the Woodlands tab. Ask students to work in groups to gather information from the exhibit and share their findings with the class.

DIFFERENTIATE

STRIVING READERS

Determine Chronology Assign students to work in pairs to determine the chronology of events presented in the lesson. Suggest that they scan the lesson and write the dates mentioned in chronological order in a Sequence Chain, adding more ovals as needed. Then ask students to read the lesson, pausing to jot down notes in their Sequence Chain about significant events that happened on various dates. When they have finished, instruct students to take turns reading the notes in their Sequence Chain aloud, using transitional phrases such as *and then* or *after that* to indicate connections between events.

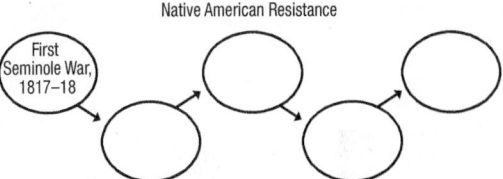

Native American Resistance

PRE-AP

Write a Book Review Challenge students to read and then write a review of Steve Inskeep's book *Jacksonland: President Andrew Jackson, Cherokee Chief John Ross, and a Great American Land Grab.* Tell students that a book review generally consists of a concise summary of the book and its overall purpose, followed by a critical assessment of the book's strengths, weaknesses, effectiveness, and importance. Suggest that students include details about Ross's ancestry, his use of diplomacy and legal argument, and his successes and failures in protecting the Cherokee, their land, and way of life. Encourage students to share their reviews with the class by posting them to a class blog or reading them aloud.

See the Chapter Planner for more strategies for differentiation.

CRITICAL VIEWING Possible response: The artist depicts Osceola as dignified, proud, and stately. He wears a concerned expression, as if he predicts trouble ahead for his people. He is dressed elaborately in Seminole clothing, reinforcing his Native American roots and his status among the Seminole.

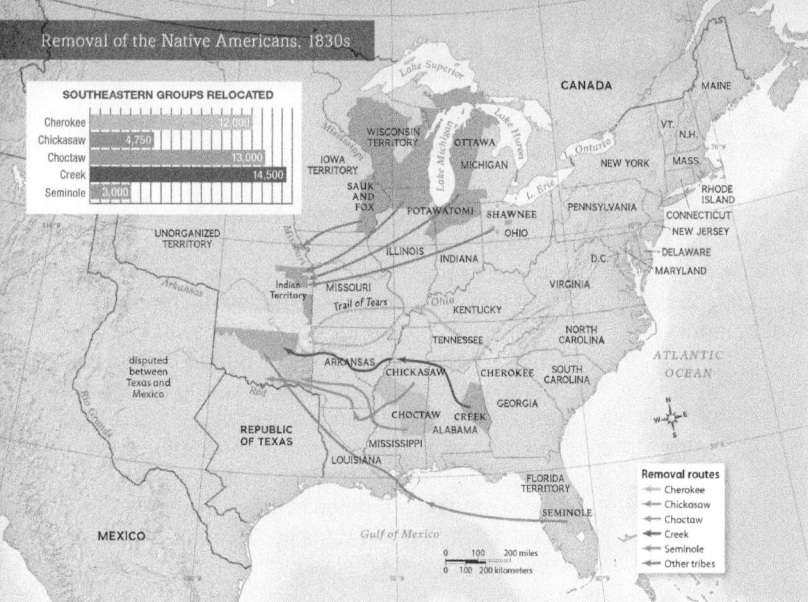

SOUTHEASTERN GROUPS RELOCATED

Cherokee	12,000
Chickasaw	4,750
Choctaw	13,000
Creek	14,500
Seminole	3,000

Removal routes
- Cherokee
- Chickasaw
- Choctaw
- Creek
- Seminole
- Other tribes

In 1988, thousands of reenactors embarked on the journey taken by the Cherokee to commemorate the 150th anniversary of the Trail of Tears.

THE TRAIL OF TEARS

As a sovereign nation, the Cherokee took legal action to resist their removal from Georgia. In the 1823 case *Johnson* v. *M'Intosh*, the Supreme Court declared that only the U.S. government could buy land from Native Americans, not private citizens. The Cherokee brought two cases before the Court in their fight: *Cherokee Nation* v. *Georgia* in 1831 and *Worcester* v. *Georgia* in 1832. In the second case, the Supreme Court ruled that the Cherokee Nation could not be regulated by the state and determined the Indian Removal Act violated previous treaties with the Cherokee. However, the decision did not help the Cherokee. Both the state of Georgia and Jackson ignored the Supreme Court ruling. The president reportedly declared, "[Supreme Court Chief Justice] John Marshall has made his decision, now let him enforce it!"

A few Cherokee leaders negotiated a removal treaty with the U.S. government and headed to Indian Territory in the mid-1830s. But most of the Cherokee—about 17,000—opposed the treaty and remained on their land. **John Ross**, the principal chief of the Cherokee, tried to work out a more favorable treaty with the United States, but Jackson refused to engage in further negotiations. In 1838, General **Winfield Scott** and 7,000 troops were sent into Cherokee lands in Georgia and Alabama. The soldiers took the Cherokee from their homes and placed them in camps. White settlers then destroyed the Cherokee villages and stole the people's belongings, leaving the Native Americans with only the few items they'd taken to the camps.

After months of confinement, the Cherokee were forced to begin the long march to Indian Territory. They were ill-equipped for the long journey, which took place over the fall and winter of 1838 and continued through the spring of 1839. And the soldiers didn't provide the Cherokee with adequate food, shelter, or clothing. Some soldiers even stole what few supplies the Native Americans possessed. As a result, about 4,000 Cherokee died.

One of the soldiers accompanying the Cherokee later described the march: "On the morning of November the 17th [1838] we encountered a terrific sleet and snow storm with freezing temperatures and from that day until we reached the end of the fateful journey on March the 26th 1839, the sufferings of the Cherokee were awful. The trail of the exiles was a trail of death. They had to sleep in the wagons and on the ground without fire. And I have known as many as twenty-two of them to die in one night of pneumonia." Survivors described the journey as "the place where they cried." Today it is known as the **Trail of Tears**.

PRIMARY SOURCE

Before the Cherokee were taken from their homes and forced on the march to Indian Territory, John Ross still hoped to appeal to the U.S. government for justice. In this excerpt from a letter Ross wrote to members of the House of Representatives, he describes what his people had already suffered.

We are stripped of every attribute of freedom and eligibility for legal self-defense. Our property may be plundered before our eyes; violence may be committed on our persons; even our lives may be taken away, and there is none to regard our complaints. We are denationalized; we are disfranchised [denied legal rights]. We are deprived of membership in the human family! We have neither land nor home, nor resting place that can be called our own.

—from Cherokee chief John Ross's letter to the U.S. House of Representatives, 1836

The Cherokee who survived the march faced more challenges when they reached Indian Territory. During the journey, the American soldiers had made the Cherokee pay settlers for the right to cross their land and boatmen for passage across rivers. By the time the Cherokee arrived in their new home, they had little money left. And the Native Americans who had already settled in the territory weren't pleased to see the newcomers. The Cherokee fought with the Osage over land. They also sought revenge against their people who had signed the removal treaty.

More than 47,000 people from the five southeastern tribes were moved to Indian Territory. As one historian has said, "All went through their own versions of the Trail of Tears."

HISTORICAL THINKING

1. **READING CHECK** How did the Seminole use the geography of the Everglades to fight the U.S. Army in the Second Seminole War?

2. **DRAW CONCLUSIONS** Why were the numbers of U.S. soldiers and Native Americans killed in the Black Hawk War so unequal?

3. **EVALUATE** What did Jackson reveal about his presidency when he challenged the Supreme Court to enforce its ruling in the Cherokee cases?

4. **INTERPRET MAPS** Why was Indian Territory probably established where it is shown on the map?

BUILD BACKGROUND

WORCESTER V. GEORGIA

Worcester v. *Georgia* stemmed from the arrest of Samuel Worcester, a missionary with the American Board of Commissioners for Foreign Missions. Worcester took an active interest in the Cherokee resistance movement, working closely with Elias Boudinot, the editor of the *Cherokee Phoenix*. Consequently, the state of Georgia feared the influence Worcester might have over the Cherokee. The state passed a law outlawing whites from living within the Cherokee Nation without the state's permission. This led to the arrest and conviction of Worcester and several other missionaries. The Cherokee Nation hired lawyers to represent Worcester and the other missionaries and appealed the convictions, leading to the Supreme Court case. The Cherokee hoped that the Court's ruling that the Cherokee Nation was sovereign and beyond Georgia's control would help stop removal, but that proved not to be the case.

REMEMBER THE REMOVAL

Since 2009, the Cherokee Nation has held an annual three-week Remember the Removal bike ride to commemorate the Trail of Tears. Riders from the Cherokee Nation join riders from the Eastern Band of Cherokee Indians to bike the northern route of the Trail of Tears. The ride begins near New Echota, Georgia, and ends in Tahlequah, Oklahoma, the capital of the Cherokee Nation. Most riders are between 16 and 24 years old. The ride is designed to educate young people about Cherokee history, culture, and language and to develop leadership and teamwork skills among participants. Along the 950-mile journey, which runs through seven states, riders stop at sites important to the history of removal. One such site is Blythe Ferry, located at the confluence of the Tennessee and Hiwassee rivers in Tennessee, where 9 of the 13 groups led by Chief John Ross departed their ancestral land on the Trail of Tears.

TEACH

GUIDED DISCUSSION

4. **Identify** Remind students that Andrew Jackson indicated that removal was in the best interest of Native Americans. **ASK:** What evidence suggests that Jackson's desire for Cherokee land outweighed any concern he might have had for the best interests of Native Americans? *(Possible responses: Jackson ignored the Supreme Court rulings stating that the Indian Removal Act violated previous treaties. When many Cherokee resisted removal, Jackson used military force to round them up and placed them in camps in preparation for removal to Indian Territory. The military did nothing to prevent white settlers from stealing Cherokee property and destroying villages.)*

5. **Make Inferences** In the *Worcester* v. *Georgia* case, why did the Supreme Court rule that states could not regulate the Cherokee Nation? *(Possible response: The Cherokee Nation, as other Native American nations, is designated as a sovereign nation, similar to France, for instance. Only the federal government negotiates with other nations—states do not have that authority.)*

ANALYZE PRIMARY SOURCES

Direct students' attention to the Primary Source feature. **ASK:** How does Ross describe the plight of the Cherokee? *(Ross says that the Cherokee are being deprived of freedom and their legal rights, including self-defense. In addition, they have lost property and been subjected to violence and death.)* **ASK:** Why do you think Ross uses the words *freedom, property,* and *denationalized*? *(Possible response: Ross uses the same terms that white citizens would use if they were protesting the federal government curtailing their rights. He is portraying the Cherokee as equal participants in American society that deserve equal treatment.)*

ACTIVE OPTIONS

Active History: Analyze a Different Perspective Extend the lesson by using either the PDF or Whiteboard version of the activity. These activities take a deeper look at a topic from, or related to, the lesson. Explore the activities as a class, turn them into group assignments, or even assign them individually.

AMERICAN **GALLERY**
ONLINE

The Trail of Tears Invite students to explore the American Gallery. Instruct them to select one of the photographs and do additional research to learn more about it. Ask questions that will inspire additional inquiry about the chosen gallery photo, such as: How does the photo capture the hardship of the Trail of Tears? What does the photo suggest about the importance of remembering Native American history? What else would you like to know about the subject of the photo?

For students who develop an interest in the Cherokee, suggest that they read the American Story at the beginning of this chapter.

HISTORICAL THINKING

ANSWERS

1. The Seminole used guerrilla tactics during battles by hiding in the swamplands of the Everglades in order to surprise the U.S. troops.

2. Possible response: Black Hawk's forces were outnumbered 7 to 1. The military probably also had far superior weaponry.

3. Jackson's actions show that he was willing to break the law openly by defying the Supreme Court in order to get his way. This indicates that he believed that the executive branch was the most powerful branch of government and did not have to answer to the other branches.

4. Possible response: The government wanted to establish Indian Territory in unorganized territory to separate Native Americans from state lands being settled by whites. It was probably also located on less desirable land.

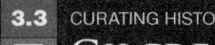

3.3 CURATING HISTORY

GILCREASE MUSEUM
TULSA, OKLAHOMA

A Scotch-Irish, French, and Native American heritage and a love for American history and artwork inspired Tulsa oilman Thomas Gilcrease to found Gilcrease Museum in 1949. He had admired artwork by the masters in Europe but chose to curate a collection that reflected Native American history and culture—a nod to his Creek ancestry.

With a focus on the preservation and study of American art and history, Gilcrease Museum and its research center house the world's largest collection of art, artifacts, and historical documents relating to the American West. Its collection includes more than 12,000 pieces of western fine art and more than 100,000 rare books and manuscripts.

Antelope Head with Pedernal by Georgia O'Keeffe
A modern artist who trained in New York City and Chicago, O'Keeffe (1887–1986) spent many summers in New Mexico developing a love for the Southwest. This 1954 oil painting embodies what O'Keeffe is best known for—abstract close-ups of animal bones, flowers, clouds, and landscapes. She is considered the mother of American modernism.

Wooden Kachina Doll
Within the traditional beliefs of the Hopi and Zuni groups, a kachina is considered one of many spirit-beings that interact with humans. These spirit-beings can be represented through masks and hand-carved wooden dolls, such as this one. The dolls teach children about ceremony, legends, and history. Many kachina are elaborately decorated and presented as gifts on special occasions.

Silver Thunderbird Necklace
In some Native American folklore, the thunderbird is a symbol of power, but it may also represent a trickster—the interpretations abound. Regardless, the thunderbird appears on Native American artifacts from many different groups and regions.

This 1900s necklace from the Zuni group in the American Southwest features seven thunderbird pendants adorned with turquoise, jet, coral, and mother-of-pearl.

To many Native American groups of the Southwest and Mexico, turquoise symbolized life: the blue of water and the green of growing plants.

What types of materials were used to decorate this kachina?

The Night Rider by Frederic Remington
Remington was one of the premier artists of the American West, and his oil paintings are an important part of the Gilcrease collection. This 1905 painting and others still serve as source material for modern filmmakers and historians of this region.

The Cheyenne
Frederic Remington wasn't just a painter. This 1913 bronze sculpture is part of a collection of riders and horses he sculpted after traveling through the Southwest in the 1880s with "a desire to record the vanishing wilderness." The details in the sculpture capture the strength and grace of both the horse and its Native American rider.

Remington was also a writer, authoring short stories and eight books about the West.

Ceramic Vessel by Annie Healing Nampeyo
While some modern southwestern potters now experiment with different colors and effects in their work, many adhere to techniques dating back to 300 B.C. A Hopi Tewa potter from Arizona, Annie Healing Nampeyo (1884–1968) followed in her mother's footsteps, using traditional Puebloan designs and patterns in her work. This piece dates to around 1900.

How would you describe the imagery on this Hopi pottery?

What can you infer about Native American warriors from this sculpture?

266 CHAPTER 8

The Jackson Era 267

PLAN: 2-PAGE LESSON

OBJECTIVE
Study artifacts and artwork related to Native American cultures and the American West.

CRITICAL THINKING SKILLS FOR LESSON 3.3
- Analyze Visuals
- Make Connections
- Draw Conclusions
- Make Inferences

HISTORICAL THINKING FOR CHAPTER 8
How did Andrew Jackson change politics and the presidency? During Andrew Jackson's administration, the United States expanded its territory by forcing Native Americans to move west of the Mississippi or assimilate into white culture. Lesson 3.3 presents art and artifacts of Native American cultures, some of which originated east of the Mississippi.

BACKGROUND FOR THE TEACHER

Gilcrease Museum has been called "a kind of Smithsonian Institution of the American West," and for good reason. Collector Thomas Gilcrease amassed thousands of artifacts, paintings, documents, rare books, and artworks representing both Native American and western U.S. history. He first exhibited his collection in San Antonio, Texas, but when the public failed to appreciate it, he moved his entire collection to Tulsa, Oklahoma, where it remains. To keep this impressive collection intact, the City of Tulsa purchased the museum in the 1950s and today manages it in partnership with the University of Tulsa. In addition to the more than 250,000 items related to the native people of the Americas, the museum houses the only certified handwritten copy of the Declaration of Independence known to exist.

HISTORY NOTEBOOK
Encourage students to complete the Curating History page for Chapter 8 in their History Notebooks as they read.

INTRODUCE & ENGAGE
PREVIEW USING VISUALS

Direct students to view the items in this lesson without reading the captions. Ask them to speculate on the purpose and meaning of the artifacts and why paintings might have been included in this collection. Explain to students that in this lesson they will learn about the Gilcrease Museum, which has preserved thousands of items related to the history of Native Americans and the American West.

TEACH
GUIDED DISCUSSION

1. **Draw Conclusions** What characteristics of Zuni and Hopi cultures do the artifacts reveal? *(Possible response: They show that these cultures have a high level of artistic knowledge and skill in working with metal, stone, clay, and paints to create decorative and practical objects. They also show that spiritual beliefs are woven into everyday life, as revealed by the kachina doll and the thunderbird design in the jewelry.)*

2. **Make Inferences** Why do you think that modern filmmakers and historians view Remington's paintings as source material? *(Possible response: Through his art, some of which was created around the turn of the 20th century, Remington documented details of Native American dress, their lives, and the land as it appeared when he painted it. Filmmakers and historians can view his art as a source of authentic information about that time and place.)*

CURATING HISTORY

The Gilcrease Museum maintains the Gilcrease Online Collections with a searchable database that allows visitors to access more than 25,000 items, including rare documents from the time of the Cherokee Removal. Encourage students to select and research one of the Native American artifacts shown in this lesson or browse the online collections to find an artifact or document that interests them. **ASK:** What did you learn about the people who made the artifact? What is the significance of the document, and how does it enhance your understanding of the effect of westward expansion on Native Americans? Why is it important to preserve this item?

ACTIVE OPTION

On Your Feet: Sort the Artifacts Arrange students into teams of four to examine the paintings, sculptures, and artifacts in the lesson and on the Gilcrease Museum website. Then ask students to complete two Concept Clusters like those shown below. In one cluster, students identify various artifacts that reveal information about the daily lives of Native Americans in the West. In the other, students identify a different class of materials and artifacts, to be determined by the teams. When teams finish, invite them to share and discuss their Concept Clusters. Guide the class in summarizing new information they learned about Native Americans and the American West, especially anything that challenged previously held misconceptions.

DIFFERENTIATE
ENGLISH LANGUAGE LEARNERS ELD

Pose and Answer Questions Arrange students at the **Emerging** and **Expanding** levels in mixed pairs and ask them to reread the captions together. Instruct them to pause after each caption and ask one another *who, what, where, when,* or *why* questions about each item pictured. Ask students at the **Bridging** level to assist others as needed.

PRE-AP

Create an Online Profile Instruct students to gather information and write a profile about Annie Healing Nampeyo or another Native American artist of note. Encourage students to use multiple print and digital resources and to cite both primary and secondary sources. The profile should include a brief biography and an overview of the person's art, including how and why the artist made it, and where, if applicable, the art has been curated. Invite volunteers to share their profiles with the class.

See the Chapter Planner for more strategies for differentiation.

CERAMIC VESSEL BY ANNIE HEALING NAMPEYO

Possible response: The shapes are geometric and seem to be abstract depictions of beings important to Hopi mythology. At the left is a bird drawn symmetrically with outstretched wings. Next to it is a coiled serpent, possibly a rattlesnake, based on its segmented tail.

WOODEN KACHINA DOLL

Possible response: The kachina doll appears to be decorated with feathers and paint. Yarn in the feathers and the necklace appear to be woven from animal hair and some kind of fiber.

THE CHEYENNE

Possible response: Details in the sculpture suggest that Native American warriors were skillful riders, since this warrior uses only a simple bit and rope to control the horse rather than the bridle, reins, saddle, and stirrups used by cowboys. Warriors must have also been courageous to ride into battle with only a spear and shield.

THE END OF THE SECOND BANK

What do you do when you perceive something as a threat? Do you run from it, or do you confront it head-on? Never one for running away from anything, President Andrew Jackson went on the attack against the Second Bank of the United States.

JACKSON'S BANK WAR

You've read that Congress approved the creation of the Second Bank of the United States in 1816. This bank was established after the charter, or permit to do business, of the First National Bank, proposed by Alexander Hamilton, expired. During Andrew Jackson's presidency, the Second Bank had helped regulate the economy and stimulate its growth. Because the huge federal bank controlled the country's money supply, inflation had been kept down. Inflation is a decrease in the value of money that causes an increase in the price of goods and services. The bank had also provided loans to finance the purchase of property and businesses.

Much of the success of the Second Bank was due to its president, **Nicholas Biddle**, who had assumed the post in 1823.

In spite of the prosperity fostered by the Second Bank, Jackson hated the bank. Under Biddle's leadership, the number of bank notes, or paper money, issued by the Second Bank had increased, and Jackson distrusted paper money. In 1795, he had sold some land, and the buyer had paid Jackson in bank notes. When the buyer went bankrupt, the bank notes were worthless. Jackson believed the nation's money supply should only consist of specie, or silver or gold coins. He also thought the Second Bank favored wealthy industrialists over working people

and limited its support of farmers and westward settlers. In addition, the president felt the bank and those who directed it were too powerful. Because the Second Bank could grant loans to members of Congress, Jackson feared that Biddle could use his power to influence these legislators.

The Second Bank became the central issue during Jackson's run for re-election in 1832. The charter for the bank was due to expire in 1836. But Jackson's opponent in the presidential race, National Republican Henry Clay, supported the bank and sponsored a bill to renew its charter early. Congress passed the bill, but Jackson vetoed it. In his veto message to Congress, Jackson wrote, "[It is my] belief that some of the powers and privileges possessed by the existing bank are unauthorized by the Constitution, subversive of the rights of the States, and dangerous to the liberties of the people."

When Jackson beat Clay in the 1832 election, he interpreted the win as support for his position on the Second Bank and as a **mandate**, or authorization, to destroy it. So during the four years that remained of its charter, Jackson directed funds from the Second Bank to be deposited in various state banks. Critics called these state banks Jackson's "pet banks." Biddle fought back by withholding bank loans from customers, but his actions backfired and turned more people against the Second Bank. By the time the bank's charter expired, Jackson had already stripped it of its power. Although Biddle tried to keep the Second Bank in operation with a state charter from Pennsylvania, the bank went out of business in 1841.

A NEW PARTY

In 1834, Henry Clay, who lost the presidential race but remained senator of Kentucky, persuaded Congress to censure Jackson over his handling of the Second Bank and refusal to hand over classified documents relative to the veto. Jackson was the first president to receive this "formal disapproval" from Congress. That same year, Clay and fellow senator Daniel Webster formed a new political party. They called it the **Whig Party** after a political party in Britain that had criticized the monarchy's abuse of power. The Whigs believed Jackson had exceeded his authority as president. In fact, members of the new party often referred to Jackson as "King Andrew." The Whigs promoted a national program to improve infrastructure, such as roads and buildings, much like the one Clay had laid out in his American System. They also supported business and industry interests.

CRITICAL VIEWING This political cartoon, "King Andrew the First," was issued around 1833. What details in it convey the idea that Jackson abused his power when he vetoed the Second Bank bill?

After the Second Bank lost its power, Jackson's pet banks made it easier to take out loans, and people flocked to them. At first, the federal government benefited from these loans because many citizens used them to purchase government land in the West. The revenue from these land sales was so great that, in 1835, Jackson paid off the national debt. However, the flow of easy credit led to inflation. To help curb this trend, Jackson required purchasers of government land to pay in gold or silver instead of paper money issued by banks. But this policy prompted banks to reduce available credit. An unstable currency and banking system would lead to a severe economic downturn shortly after Jackson's second term in office ended.

After Jackson's presidency ended, money began to lose its value. The 50-cent bank note below is actually a political cartoon showing Jackson, on the far right, grabbing for gold. The token, which features Jackson and the words "I take the responsibility," mocks his economic policies.

FIFTY CENTS

FIFTY CENTS

PLASTER

5

50

HISTORICAL THINKING

1. **READING CHECK** Why did Jackson hate the Second Bank of the United States?

2. **SYNTHESIZE** How did Jackson's attitude toward the Second Bank reflect his role as the representative of the common man?

3. **MAKE INFERENCES** Why did the Whigs call Jackson "King Andrew"?

PLAN: 2-PAGE LESSON

OBJECTIVE

Analyze how Andrew Jackson's war against the Second Bank of the United States ended in the bank's demise.

CRITICAL THINKING SKILLS FOR LESSON 4.1

• Synthesize

• Make Inferences

• Form and Support Opinions

• Analyze Cause and Effect

HISTORICAL THINKING FOR CHAPTER 8

How did Andrew Jackson change politics and the presidency? Andrew Jackson used his presidential power to destroy the Second Bank of the United States. Lesson 4.1 examines Jackson's efforts and how the bank became a campaign issue in 1832.

BACKGROUND FOR THE TEACHER

When Henry Clay first suggested renewing the charter for the Second Bank of the United States early, Nicholas Biddle cautioned against it. While Clay hoped to make the bank a campaign issue, Biddle wanted to keep the bank out of the political fray. But Clay, with the help of Daniel Webster, who was on the bank's payroll, kept pressing Biddle to reconsider. Finally, Biddle agreed, convincing himself that Andrew Jackson would not veto the bill purely for political gain and that it was the best option for the bank should Jackson win the election. In the Senate, Webster lobbied hard and successfully for renewal, arguing that the Second Bank of the United States was the best safeguard against the detrimental practices of the state banks, which often competed with one another to issue bank notes—a situation that led to inflation. This situation, Webster argued, harmed ordinary people the most.

INTRODUCE & ENGAGE
PRESIDENTS VERSUS KINGS

Prompt students to consider ways in which presidents are like and unlike kings. Draw a Venn diagram on the board and ask students to identify similarities and differences on issues such as how each usually attains the position and relinquishes it; to whom each one answers; and how much power each wields. Then direct students' attention to the political cartoon "King Andrew the First." Tell students that in Lesson 4.1 they will learn about why and how Jackson set out to destroy the Second Bank of the United States and why some people felt Jackson had overstepped his presidential authority.

TEACH
GUIDED DISCUSSION

1. **Form and Support Opinions** Do you think Jackson's hatred for the Second Bank of the United States was justified? Explain. (Answers will vary. Possible responses: No. The bank under Biddle had been good for the economy, keeping inflation down and providing business and property loans. Yes. Jackson had firsthand experience that banks and paper money could hurt regular people while benefiting wealthy people.)

2. **Analyze Cause and Effect** How did Jackson's use of pet banks have both positive and negative consequences? (Possible response: Positive: The pet banks made it easier to take out loans, which helped people, particularly after Biddle began denying loans. Many people used these state bank loans to buy federal land, which helped the government pay off the national debt. Negative: Jackson funneled money from the Second Bank of the United States to pet banks, weakening the Second Bank. The easy credit they offered led to inflation.)

MORE INFORMATION

Political Cartoon Direct students' attention to the political cartoon of the 50-cent bank note. Explain that the man on the donkey is Missouri senator Thomas Hart Benton, one of Jackson's defenders in Congress, and the man on the fox is Martin Van Buren. At the base of the cliff, Biddle watches from the roof of the Second National Bank. **ASK:** What does the political cartoon suggest about the consequences of Jackson's actions? (Possible response: The cartoon suggests that Jackson's war on the bank and insistence on the use of specie put the U.S. economy in danger and that Jackson is leading people over a cliff.)

ACTIVE OPTIONS

On Your Feet: Four Corners Divide students into four teams and assign each team a corner of the room. Ask each team to write down several questions based on the lesson's discussion of arguments for and against the Second Bank of the United States. When teams are ready, Team 1 asks a question. The first team to signal by raising a hand gets to answer the question. If the answer is correct, that team asks the next question. If the answer is not correct, another team gets the chance to respond. If no team has the correct answer, Team 1 provides the answer and asks another question. Correct any misconceptions revealed in the questions or answers and continue until teams have exhausted their questions.

NG Learning Framework: Create a Political Cartoon
ATTITUDE Responsibility
SKILLS Collaboration, Communication

Ask small groups to consult online or library resources to learn more about Congress's passage of the bill to renew the charter of the Second Bank of the United States and Jackson's veto of the bill. Tell groups to use their research to help them create a political cartoon that reflects the views of one side or the other in the conflict. Encourage groups to delve into the congressional debates and Jackson's and Biddle's actions and reactions to enrich their cartoons. Invite groups to share their cartoons with the class and discuss what they convey.

DIFFERENTIATE
STRIVING READERS

Use a Main-Idea Cluster Pair students at mixed levels of proficiency and direct partners to use a Main-Idea Cluster to check their understanding of each lesson subsection. Tell students to take turns reading a section and then work together to record the main idea and four details. Instruct pairs to trade and compare their Main-Idea Clusters.

PRE-AP

Write Diary Entries Instruct students to conduct online research to learn more about President Jackson's thoughts about the Second Bank. Based on their research, have students date and write a series of diary entries that Jackson might have written about the bank and its president, Nicholas Biddle. Students may also include Jackson's thoughts about the bank as a campaign issue and a political strength or liability. Have students present their diary entries to the class, including background information from their research.

See the Chapter Planner for more strategies for differentiation.

HISTORICAL THINKING
ANSWERS

1. Part of Jackson's dislike for the Second Bank of the United States stemmed from his distrust of paper money, resulting from a failed land deal that left him holding worthless bank notes. Under Biddle, the bank had increased the amount of paper money in circulation.

2. Jackson sided with the common man by criticizing the Second Bank for favoring wealthy industrialists over working people and for its limited support of farmers and westward settlers.

3. The Whigs believed Jackson had exceeded his authority as president, so they compared him to a British king who could abuse his power without answering to an electorate.

CRITICAL VIEWING Jackson stands before a throne, is dressed in royal garments, wears a crown, holds a scepter, and is standing on the tattered remains of the U.S. Constitution.

MAIN IDEA Andrew Jackson's economic policies helped trigger a depression that devastated the country and influenced the presidential election of 1840.

AN ECONOMIC CRISIS

In good economic times, people tend to be content with the government in office. But when the economy plunges, people often cast blame on those officials. Martin Van Buren was about to find that out.

THE PANIC OF 1837

As the 1836 presidential election approached, the U.S. economy still seemed to be in good shape. With his second term coming to an end, Andrew Jackson backed his vice president, Martin Van Buren, as the Democratic candidate, and Van Buren won easily. The young Whig Party had nominated three candidates to try to gain support from three different regions of the country. Senator Daniel Webster of Massachusetts was chosen to attract voters in the East. Senator Hugh White from Jackson's own state of Tennessee was the Whigs' hope for support in the South. And William Henry Harrison, a congressman from Ohio, represented the West. You may recall that Harrison became well known after he fought the Shawnee at the 1811 Battle of Tippecanoe in Indiana. He'd also been a hero during the War of 1812. Harrison was the most popular Whig candidate and secured more electoral votes than Webster or White. Nevertheless, Van Buren won more electoral votes than the three Whig candidates combined.

Van Buren had had his eyes on the presidency for years. As Jackson's trusted friend and advisor, Van Buren was the most likely candidate to succeed the president. Van Buren was a skilled politician, but he lacked Jackson's charisma, or charm. Still, his supporters were confident that he would continue Jackson's policies and defend the rights of working people. However, just weeks after Van Buren's inauguration, the state banks began to struggle. Americans soon realized an economic crisis was brewing. Jackson's impact on the banking system and insistence on the use of specie were among the factors that led to the crisis. The fear over the state of the economy that swept the country became known as the **Panic of 1837**.

Many people rushed to the banks to exchange their paper money for gold and silver. But the banks didn't have enough of the precious metals to meet the demand. As a result, about 800 banks closed in 1837. The closures led businesses to collapse, which in turn caused many thousands of Americans to lose their jobs and land. Some of the unemployed went hungry and were forced to live on the streets. Before long, the country had spiraled into a deep economic depression that would last for seven years. Van Buren, who believed the federal government should not interfere with the economy, did little to address the problem. Because the depression didn't improve throughout his presidency, many voters blamed him for the nation's economic woes.

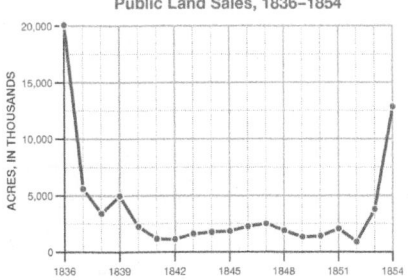

Public Land Sales, 1836–1854

ACRES, IN THOUSANDS

Data: United States Census Bureau

THE 1840 ELECTION

Van Buren's opponents were quick to criticize the new president's reaction to the crisis. Henry Clay and Daniel Webster insisted that the federal government should help dig the country out of the depression. They called for higher tariffs on imports to raise the price of imported goods and encourage Americans to buy products made in the United States. But Van Buren didn't take their advice. As the depression dragged on and more and more people turned against Van Buren, the Whigs believed they had a good chance of winning the presidential election in 1840.

This time, the Whigs nominated William Henry Harrison as their sole candidate. They chose **John Tyler** of Virginia to be Harrison's running mate. During the campaign, the Whig Party focused on Harrison's war experience, particularly at the Battle of Tippecanoe. Banners and flags carried the slogan "Tippecanoe and Tyler too." Harrison was also portrayed as a frontier man of the people and the "log cabin" candidate. The Whigs painted Van Buren as rich and out of touch with the common man. Actually, although Harrison lived on a farm, he was born into a wealthy family. It was Van Buren who came from a humble background. Whig Party organizers held parades for their candidate and came up with catchy songs. Harrison himself went out on the campaign trail to meet with people. He was the first presidential candidate to do so.

Harrison won the election with 234 electoral college votes to Van Buren's 60. It was a huge victory for Harrison and for the Whigs, who took control of both houses of Congress. At age 67, Harrison was the oldest man ever elected president up to that time, but his term was brief. On a chilly day in March 1841, Harrison delivered an inaugural address that lasted almost two hours. He caught a cold that developed into pneumonia and died 31 days later. Harrison became the first president to die in office.

Consequently, Tyler became the first vice president to assume the presidency after his predecessor's death. Even though he was a Whig working with a Whig Congress, Tyler received little support from his party. Many of his views aligned with those of the Democrats. The Whigs had only chosen him for vice president to appeal to southern voters. Dubbed "His Accidency" by his enemies, Tyler used the veto 10 times during his presidency and was kicked out of the Whig Party. Even though the country began to emerge from the depression in the early 1840s, Tyler would be limited to one term in office.

HISTORICAL THINKING

1. **READING CHECK** Why did voters blame Van Buren for the economic depression?

2. **ANALYZE CAUSE AND EFFECT** What happened as a result of the depression?

3. **DISTINGUISH FACT FROM OPINION** How did the Whig Party use facts and opinions to promote Harrison during the 1840 presidential campaign?

The Democrats gave the Whigs the idea for running a "log cabin campaign" after one of their newspapers ridiculed Harrison as a dull backwoodsman who, with a small pension, would be content "to sit the remainder of his days in his log cabin." This pin from the 1840 campaign shows Harrison standing in front of a log cabin shaking Uncle Sam's hand.

PLAN: 2-PAGE LESSON

OBJECTIVE

Analyze how Andrew Jackson's economic policies helped spark an economic depression that affected the 1840 presidential election.

CRITICAL THINKING SKILLS FOR LESSON 4.2

- Analyze Cause and Effect
- Distinguish Fact from Opinion
- Make Predictions
- Compare and Contrast
- Interpret Graphs

HISTORICAL THINKING FOR CHAPTER 8

How did Andrew Jackson change politics and the presidency? Andrew Jackson's policies as president led to economic problems. Lesson 4.2 examines the Panic of 1837 and the resulting depression—and its political impact.

BACKGROUND FOR THE TEACHER

Land sales were a major factor in the economic boom in the first half of the 1830s. Fueled by easy credit from state banks, land speculators bought up land with bank notes that varied widely in value, depending on the bank. Because the state banks were unregulated, many did not have sufficient amounts of gold and silver to back the notes. When Andrew Jackson issued his Specie Circular executive order in July 1836, which required payment in specie to purchase public lands, these banks were forced to tighten their credit, causing land sales to plummet. By the end of the year, sales were down 30 percent compared to the previous four quarters. Sales continued to plummet in 1837, even as land prices dropped. The price of land in Indiana and Illinois, for example, dropped from $10 an acre in 1836 to $3 or less in early 1837. Congress repealed the Specie Circular in mid-1838, but it would take years for the U.S. economy to start growing well again.

INTRODUCE & ENGAGE

CREATE A WORD WEB

Create a Word Web like the one shown with the term *economic crisis* in the center. Ask students to suggest words or phrases they associate with economic crises, such as *recession* or *depression*. Add the words and phrases to the Word Web. Tell students that this lesson discusses some of the causes and consequences of the Panic of 1837.

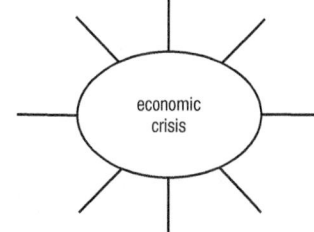

TEACH

GUIDED DISCUSSION

1. **Make Predictions** How might the economic events of 1837 have been different if Jackson had not destroyed the Second Bank of the United States? *(Possible response: The widespread state bank failures might have been avoided if the Second Bank of the United States had been open to control the distribution of specie to failing banks.)*

2. **Compare and Contrast** How did the Whigs change their campaign tactics between the elections of 1836 and 1840? *(Possible response: In the election of 1836, they tried to appeal to each section of the country by running several candidates. In the election of 1840, they ran only William Henry Harrison for president and John Tyler for vice president. In the 1840 election, Harrison also became the first presidential candidate ever to go out on the campaign trail.)*

INTERPRET GRAPHS

Share the information from the Background for the Teacher with students. Then direct students' attention to the graph of public land sales between 1836 and 1854. **ASK:** What happened to land sales between 1838 and 1839, and what might account for this change? *(Possible response: Land sales increased slightly because Congress repealed the Specie Circular requirement that public lands be purchased with gold or silver coin.)* **ASK:** What might have caused the uptick to reverse course and trend downward? *(Possible response: The worsening effects of the depression on the overall economy may have left few people with the funds to buy land or caused people to feel pessimistic about investing in land.)*

ACTIVE OPTIONS

On Your Feet: Arguments For and Against Intervention Divide the class into small groups. Provide each group with a large sheet of paper and instruct them to identify arguments for and against the following position: The federal government should intervene in the economy during times of economic crisis. Tell groups to use the paper to make a two-column chart, labeling the columns For and Against. Group members should brainstorm arguments and write them in the appropriate column. When groups have finished, encourage them to present their arguments to the class and identify which position they find most compelling.

NG Learning Framework: Write a Campaign Speech

SKILL Communication

KNOWLEDGE Our Human Story

Arrange students in small groups. Prompt the groups to choose one of the two presidential candidates who ran in the 1840 election: William Henry Harrison or Martin Van Buren. Instruct students to review information presented in the lesson and to conduct additional research about their candidate. Prompt them to work together to craft a campaign speech for their candidate, based on what they learned about the candidate's personality, his political beliefs, and events leading up to the election. Each group should then choose one person to deliver the speech to the class.

DIFFERENTIATE

INCLUSION

Work in Pairs Allow students with disabilities to work with students who can read the lesson aloud to them. Encourage the partner without disabilities to describe the graph and explain what it illustrates about the quantity of land sold in different years. When pairs have finished the lesson, direct them to work together to answer the Historical Thinking questions.

GIFTED & TALENTED

Design an Infographic Guide students to conduct additional research into how and why the Panic of 1837 happened. Suggest that students use a Cause-and-Effect Chain to keep track of what they learn. Then direct students to create an infographic that uses data and visual information to show the main causes and effects of the Panic. Encourage students to use the chain as a framework for their infographic. Invite students to compare infographics and generate a list of the causes and effects of the Panic.

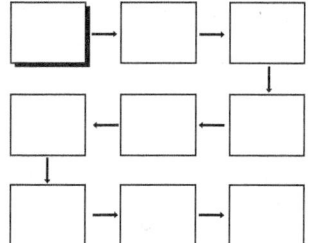

See the Chapter Planner for more strategies for differentiation.

HISTORICAL THINKING

ANSWERS

1. The crisis started shortly after Van Buren began his presidency, and he did nothing to solve the problem because he believed the government should not intervene.

2. The depression caused thousands of Americans to lose their jobs and land as businesses failed. Some of the unemployed lived on the streets and went hungry. People blamed Van Buren, so the depression also resulted in Harrison winning the 1840 presidential election in a landslide.

3. The Whigs noted Harrison's war experience, particularly in the Battle of Tippecanoe, which was a fact. They also used opinions, for example, saying that Van Buren was out of touch with the common man.

VOCABULARY

Use each of the following vocabulary words in a sentence that shows an understanding of the term's meaning.

1. **Tariff of Abominations**
Southerners called the Tariff of 1828 the Tariff of Abominations because it made the imported goods the South needed more expensive.

2. kitchen cabinet
3. Whig Party
4. syllabary
5. assimilate
6. Trail of Tears
7. Jacksonian democracy
8. Panic of 1837

READING STRATEGY
DISTINGUISH FACT FROM OPINION

When you separate someone's personal beliefs and feelings on a topic from information that can be proved to be true, you distinguish fact from opinion. Use a chart like this one to record statements from the chapter and identify them as fact or opinion. Then answer the question.

Facts	Opinions

9. What facts and opinions were voiced during Andrew Jackson's war on the Second Bank of the United States?

MAIN IDEAS

Answer the following questions. Support your answers with evidence from the chapter.

10. What groups of people did Andrew Jackson promise to represent as president? **LESSON 1.1**

11. Why did the Eaton affair cause a rift between Jackson and his vice president, John C. Calhoun? **LESSON 1.2**

12. Why did President John Quincy Adams promote the Tariff of 1828? **LESSON 2.1**

13. How did Jackson respond to the nullification crisis? **LESSON 2.2**

14. Why did Jackson strongly support passage of the Indian Removal Act? **LESSON 3.1**

15. What measures did the Cherokee take to resist relocation? **LESSON 3.2**

16. Why did Henry Clay and Daniel Webster call their new party the Whig Party? **LESSON 4.1**

17. How did the Panic of 1837 affect Martin Van Buren's presidency? **LESSON 4.2**

HISTORICAL THINKING

Answer the following questions. Support your answers with evidence from the chapter.

18. **EVALUATE** How would you describe Jackson's character?

19. **MAKE INFERENCES** Why do you think some Native Americans were willing to adopt European culture?

20. **DRAW CONCLUSIONS** How did Calhoun's call for states' rights during the debate over the Tariff of 1828 underscore the divide between the North and the South?

21. **COMPARE AND CONTRAST** In what ways were the presidencies of Van Buren and John Tyler similar and different?

22. **MAKE CONNECTIONS** How has Jacksonian democracy influenced politics today?

23. **FORM AND SUPPORT OPINIONS** In your opinion, is Jackson's legacy primarily good or bad? Explain your answer.

INTERPRET VISUALS

This 1831 political cartoon, "The Rats Leaving a Falling House," was published after members of Jackson's Cabinet resigned. Jackson is seated in the chair. The rats represent, from left to right, Secretary of War John Eaton, Secretary of the Navy John Branch, Secretary of State Martin Van Buren, and Secretary of the Treasury Samuel Ingham. Study the cartoon and then answer the questions that follow.

24. Why is Jackson's foot pressing down on the tail of the rat represented by Van Buren?

25. What details in the cartoon tell you that its creator was not a Jackson supporter?

26. Why do you think these department secretaries are shown trying to flee Jackson's Cabinet?

ANALYZE SOURCES

In his inaugural speech in 1829, President Jackson discussed his policies on the economy and Native Americans. Read the following excerpt from his speech and then answer the questions.

> Under every aspect in which it can be considered, it would appear that advantage must result from the observance of a strict and faithful economy. This I shall aim at the more anxiously both because it will facilitate the extinguishment [elimination] of the national debt . . . and because it will counteract that tendency to public and private profligacy [wastefulness] which a profuse expenditure [extravagant spending] of money by the Government is but too apt to engender [cause]. . . . It will [also] be my sincere and constant desire to observe toward the Indian tribes within our limits a just and liberal policy, and to give that humane and considerate attention to their rights and their wants which is consistent with the habits of our Government and the feelings of our people.

27. What were Jackson's goals with regard to the nation's economy?

28. How well did Jackson carry out the position he states here on Native Americans?

CONNECT TO YOUR LIFE

29. **ARGUMENT** In the 1828 presidential campaign, mudslinging on both sides was used to sway voters. Think about the campaign ads, speeches, remarks, and tweets made by recent candidates for government offices. Did they use mudslinging against their opponents? Do you think such personal attacks persuade voters or disgust them? Write a paragraph in which you make the case for or against mudslinging in political campaigns.

TIPS

- Review the mudslinging tactics used in the 1828 presidential campaign.
- Recall or research the campaign ads and speeches made by a recent candidate for government office and note the mudslinging used.
- Determine whether the mudslinging helped or hurt the candidate.
- State your position on mudslinging in political campaigns and support it with evidence from the text or your own experience and observations.
- Conclude your paragraph with a sentence summarizing your position.

VOCABULARY ANSWERS

1. Southerners called the Tariff of 1828 the Tariff of Abominations because it made the imported goods the South needed more expensive.

2. The unofficial advisors that made up Andrew Jackson's kitchen cabinet helped him deal with conflicts in his official cabinet.

3. Jackson's political opponents formed the Whig Party during the president's second term.

4. In the Cherokee syllabary, written symbols represent syllables, not individual letters.

5. Many Cherokee chose to assimilate, adopting European culture.

6. The Cherokee's forced removal to Indian Territory was so brutal it came to be called the Trail of Tears.

7. One of the goals of Jacksonian democracy was to defend the rights of hardworking people against abuses by the political establishment.

8. Jackson's bank policies caused the economic crisis called the Panic of 1837.

READING STRATEGY ANSWER

Facts	Opinions
The Second Bank stimulated economic growth.	Money supply should only consist of specie.
It increased the number of bank notes.	The bank favored wealthy industrialists.
It could make loans to Congress.	Nicholas Biddle might use his loan power to influence legislators.
	The Second Bank was unconstitutional.

9. Possible response: During his war against the Second Bank, Jackson cited the facts that the bank had increased the number of bank notes in circulation and that the bank had the ability to grant loans to members of Congress. He expressed the opinions that the money supply should only consist of specie, that the bank favored the wealthy over the common man, that Nicholas Biddle might use the bank's loaning power to influence Congress, and that the bank was unconstitutional.

MAIN IDEAS ANSWERS

10. Jackson promised he would represent the "common man"—hardworking people, such as farmers, craftsmen, laborers, and middle-class businessmen.

11. Vice President John C. Calhoun supported his wife when she refused to socialize with John Eaton's wife, Peggy, and led many other cabinet wives to do the same. This angered Jackson, since Eaton was his close friend, and the bad treatment of Peggy reminded him of the way his wife Rachel had been hurt by terrible rumors.

12. President Adams promoted the Tariff of 1828 because he represented the interests of the Northeast and needed to appeal to voters in that region and because he thought the tariff would help the federal government raise money.

13. Even though he supported states' rights, Jackson believed nullification was an act of treason against the authority of the federal government. As such, he promised to use force against any state that refused to pay the tariff.

14. Foremost, Jackson wanted to make Native American land available to white settlers. He also claimed that the removal would be in the best interest of Native Americans.

15. The Cherokee fought relocation through legal actions, resulting in two Supreme Court cases: *Cherokee Nation* v. *Georgia* in 1831 and *Worcester* v. *Georgia* in 1832. When the court cases didn't help the situation, John Ross attempted unsuccessfully to negotiate a better removal treaty.

16. Henry Clay and Daniel Webster called their party the Whig Party after the British Whigs who had criticized the monarchy's abuse of power.

17. The Panic of 1837 weakened Martin Van Buren's presidency and cost him re-election because he refused to let the federal government intervene in the economy, which many people believed should have been done to help end the depression.

HISTORICAL THINKING ANSWERS

18. Possible response: Jackson was stubborn, easy to anger, authoritarian, and convinced that he knew what was best for the country. His actions related to the Eaton affair, the nullification crisis, Indian Removal Act, and the bank war are evidence of this.

19. Some Native Americans probably believed that adopting European culture might help them retain their land, gain legal rights, or reduce white hostility.

20. When Calhoun called for states' rights, he believed that the federal government was exceeding its power by establishing a tariff that helped the industrial North but hurt the agricultural South.

21. The presidencies of Van Buren and Tyler were similar in that they both disappointed their base. Van Buren failed to intervene in the economy to lessen the depression, and Tyler held policies that were closer to the Democrats than the Whigs, vetoing many bills. They were also alike in being limited to one term. They were different in their party affiliation, where they were from, and in how they came to office.

22. Jacksonian democracy expanded voting rights to white men without property. This trend toward inclusiveness in civic life has continued over time and broadened to include other groups, such as women and minorities, who today are entitled to vote and participate in government.

23. Possible responses: Jackson's legacy is primarily good, because he gave the common man a voice in government and pursued policies that helped everyday people. Jackson's legacy is primarily bad because his economic policies resulted in a depression, and his Native American policies uprooted people from their homes and caused a great deal of human suffering.

INTERPRET VISUALS ANSWERS

24. Jackson wants Van Buren to leave his cabinet to help ease the internal conflict. However, he wants to retain him as part of his kitchen cabinet.

25. Jackson looks exhausted, his cabinet members are portrayed as rats, there is an imp or bat atop the altar of reforms, the furniture and building are collapsing, and the title indicates that the creator believes that Jackson's administration is falling apart.

26. The basis of the political cartoon is that the Jackson administration is falling apart. The secretaries are depicted as rats trying to flee a sinking ship.

ANALYZE SOURCES ANSWERS

27. Andrew Jackson wanted to pay down the national debt and control government spending.

28. Andrew Jackson adopted policies and took actions that directly opposed the view on Native Americans that he expressed in his inaugural speech, unjustly forcing them from their lands along the Trail of Tears, where many died.

CONNECT TO YOUR LIFE ANSWER

29. Arguments will vary, but paragraphs should support students' positions with references to specific mudslinger tactics and campaign ads and speeches. They should also determine whether the mudslinging helped or hurt the candidate, take a stand on the mudslinging, include supporting evidence, and conclude their paragraph with a summary of their position.

UNIT 3 RESOURCES

UNIT INTRODUCTION

UNIT TIME LINE

UNIT WRAP-UP

NATIONAL GEOGRAPHIC | CONNECTION

National Geographic Magazine Adapted Articles
- "Nat Turner's Complex Legacy"
- "The Way West" ONLINE

Unit 3 Inquiry: Document a Migration

NG Learning Framework Activities
- Depict Nature
- Create Slogans to Promote Reforms

Unit 3 Formal Assessment

CHAPTER 9 RESOURCES

Available at NGLSync.Cengage.com

TEACHER RESOURCES & ASSESSMENT

Reading and Note-Taking

Vocabulary Practice

Document-Based Question Template

Social Studies Skills Lessons
- Reading: Make Inferences
- Writing: Expository

Formal Assessment
- Chapter 9 Pretest
- Chapter 9 Tests A & B
- Section Quizzes

Chapter 9 Answer Key

ExamView®
  One-time Download

STUDENT DIGITAL RESOURCES

- eEdition
- Handbooks
- Online Atlas

- American Gallery Online
- History Notebook
- Active History

- American Voices (Biographies)
- Literature Analysis

- Projects for Inquiry-Based Learning

Chapter 9 Spanish Resources are available at NGLSync.Cengage.com.

AMERICAN STORIES ONLINE | **The Writers and Artists of Concord, Massachusetts**

- Study Primary Sources: Excerpts from Ralph Waldo Emerson, Henry David Thoreau, and Walt Whitman
- On Your Feet: Roundtable

NG Learning Framework:
Create a Transcendentalist Collage

SECTION 1 RESOURCES

RELIGIOUS AWAKENINGS AND SOCIAL REFORMS

LESSON 1.1
Religion and Reform

- On Your Feet: Fishbowl

NG Learning Framework:
Propose a Reform

LESSON 1.2
A Young Nation's Literature and Arts

 **AMERICAN GALLERY ONLINE** The Hudson River School

NG Learning Framework:
Create a Book Jacket

LESSON 1.3
THROUGH THE LENS—AMERICAN PLACES
Rocky Mountain National Park, Estes Park, Colorado

- On Your Feet: Think, Pair, Share

NG Learning Framework:
Compare Names of the Park Summits

SECTION 2 RESOURCES

THE ABOLITION MOVEMENT

LESSON 2.1
Life Under Slavery

- On Your Feet: Numbered Heads

NG Learning Framework:
Create a Class Collage

LESSON 2.2
Abolitionists Speak Out

- On Your Feet: Inside-Outside Circle

NG Learning Framework:
Debate How to End Slavery

American Voices Biography
Frederick Douglass ONLINE

SECTION 3 RESOURCES

WOMEN FIGHT FOR RIGHTS

LESSON 3.1
Seneca Falls and a Call for Rights

- Active History: Analyze Primary Sources

NG Learning Framework:
Analyze Depictions of 19th-Century Women

American Voices Biography
Lucretia Mott ONLINE

LESSON 3.2
AMERICAN VOICES
Elizabeth Cady Stanton, 1815–1902

- On Your Feet: Four Corners

NG Learning Framework:
Write a Speech

LESSON 3.3
DOCUMENT-BASED QUESTION
The Seneca Falls Convention

- On Your Feet: Host a DBQ Roundtable

CHAPTER 9 REVIEW

STRIVING READERS

STRATEGY 1
USE A K-W-L CHART

Provide each student with a K-W-L Chart. Ask students to brainstorm what they know about historical events of the early to mid-1800s, such as religious revivals, slavery, abolition, and women's rights. Direct students to add these ideas to the first column of the chart. Then have them write in the second column of the chart questions they have about each topic, such as: What progress did abolitionists make? or What rights did women receive? Remind students to complete their charts as they read each lesson in the chapter.

K What Do I Know?	W What Do I Want To Learn?	L What Did I Learn?

Use with All Lessons

STRATEGY 2
TURN HEADINGS INTO OUTLINES

To help students organize and understand lesson content, explain that headings can provide a high-level outline of the lesson. Model how to use the lesson title and subheadings to create a basic outline. Encourage students to add information to their outlines as they read.

Use with All Lessons *For example, in Lesson 1.1, help students begin an outline such as the one shown to complete as they read.*

Religion and Reform

I. The Second Great Awakening
   A. _____
   B. _____
   C. _____
II. Middle-Class Reforms
   A. _____
   B. _____
   C. _____
III. Workers Begin to Organize
   A. _____
   B. _____
   C. _____

STRATEGY 3
CLARIFY INFORMATION

To help students clarify information about the factions that arose within the antislavery movement, instruct them to create a T-Chart and label the first column Liberty Party and the second Friends of Universal Reform. Tell them to jot down key facts about each faction as they read. Encourage students to compare their completed charts, noting any differences.

Liberty Party	Friends of Universal Reform

Use with Lesson 2.2 *To help students find information for their charts, direct their attention to the paragraphs under the heading "Differences Among Abolitionists."*

INCLUSION

STRATEGY 1
USE ECHO READING

Point out that the Main Idea statements all relate to important ideas and events that impacted the Age of Reform. Pair students with a proficient reader who can read aloud the Main Idea statement at the beginning of each lesson. Students will "echo" by reading the same statement or by re-stating it in their own words.

Use with All Lessons *Pairs might also echo-read selected paragraphs or entire sections of each lesson.*

STRATEGY 2
PREVIEW AND PREDICT

Pair visually impaired students with sighted students. Instruct them to work together to read the lesson title and subheadings, as well as photo and art captions. Tell sighted students to describe lesson visuals in detail to help their partners understand them. Then have partners work together to write notes regarding what they think the lesson will be about. After reading, ask pairs to review their notes to confirm their predictions.

Use with All Lessons *For example, in Lesson 1.2, have sighted students read the title subheadings and captions, and then describe the three paintings and photograph. Pairs will then write predictions such as This lesson will be about the important artists and writers of the 19th century.*

ENGLISH LANGUAGE LEARNERS ELD

STRATEGY 1
CREATE MEANING MAPS

Pair students at the **Emerging** level with those at the **Expanding** or **Bridging** level. Demonstrate how to use the Meaning Map shown here for Key Vocabulary or other important words in the lesson. Encourage students to discuss the words and clear up any misunderstandings.

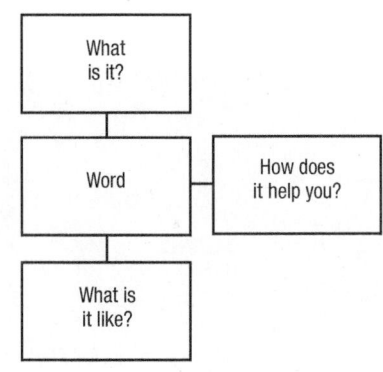

Use with All Lessons

STRATEGY 2
USE PAIRED READING

Pair students at the **Expanding** and **Bridging** levels and have them read passages from the text aloud.

1. Partner 1 reads a passage; Partner 2 retells the passage in his or her own words.

2. Partner 2 reads a different passage; Partner 1 retells it.

3. Pairs repeat the process, switching roles.

Use with All Lessons

STRATEGY 3
BUILD VOCABULARY

Help students at **All Proficiencies** learn unfamiliar words by introducing synonyms they might know. Display difficult words paired with more familiar words, as with these examples from Lesson 1.1:

> zealous/passionate
>
> masterful/skillful
>
> refrain from/avoid
>
> controversy/argument

Tell students that when they encounter a difficult word, such as *zealous*, they should try to replace it with a word they are familiar with, such as *passionate*. Guide students to use a thesaurus to practice looking up and substituting words to find a synonym that makes sense in context.

Use with All Lessons *Students at the **Bridging** level could help students at the **Emerging** and **Expanding** levels find appropriate synonyms. Look for opportunities in all lessons to use synonyms and a thesaurus to aid comprehension.*

GIFTED & TALENTED

STRATEGY 1
CREATE A GALLERY WALK

Instruct students to choose an artist or writer that helped define 19th-century American culture and to use online resources to find photographs, quotations, and excerpts related to that person. Ask students to work together to group their findings, chronologically or by medium, and to set up stations around the classroom. Each station should include gallery-style signage. Then conduct a Gallery Walk, inviting students to stop at each station and share reflections.

Use with Lesson 1.2

STRATEGY 2
PERFORM A DRAMATIC READING

Ask students to conduct online research to find the full text of an abolitionist's essay or speech. Challenge them to prepare a dramatic reading of the entire piece or part of it. After they have practiced, invite students to perform their reading in front of the class.

Use with Lesson 2.2

PRE-AP

STRATEGY 1
WRITE A BIOGRAPHICAL PROFILE

Instruct students to locate a historical biography on an individual they encountered in this chapter and explain his or her influence on American society. Tell students to read the biography independently and then develop a profile for that person. Encourage students to post their completed profile on a class blog or school website.

Use with Lessons 1.1, 1.2, 2.2, 3.1, and 3.2

STRATEGY 2
CREATE AN ANNOTATED TIME LINE

Direct students to choose events they consider the most important in the fight for women's rights and create an annotated time line for display. The time line should include dates, locations, people, and the impact of each event, as well as how the event might connect to larger social, economic, and political developments. Encourage students to present their time lines to the class and state how each event moved the fight for women's rights forward.

Use with Lessons 3.1 and 3.2 *Students may extend their time lines to events before and after the Age of Reform, from Abigail Adams to the ongoing attempts to ratify the Equal Rights Amendment to the Constitution.*

AN AGE OF REFORM

1820–1850

HISTORICAL THINKING How did cultural and social reform influence American society?

AMERICAN STORIES ONLINE | **The Writers and Artists of Concord, Massachusetts**

SECTION 1 **Religious Awakenings and Social Reforms**

SECTION 2 **The Abolition Movement**

SECTION 3 **Women Fight for Rights**

AMERICAN GALLERY ONLINE | **The Hudson River School**

"Nothing can bring you peace but **the triumph of principles.**"

—Ralph Waldo Emerson

CRITICAL VIEWING The Hudson River begins high in the Adirondack Mountains of New York and runs south to the Atlantic Ocean. North of New York City, the river winds through the Hudson River Valley, where this photograph captures the region's unspoiled fall beauty. In the early 19th century, writers and landscape painters flocked to the valley. Why do you think the terrain of the Hudson River Valley inspired 19th-century Americans?

274 CHAPTER 9

An Age of Reform 275

INTRODUCE THE PHOTOGRAPH

HUDSON RIVER VALLEY

Direct students' attention to the photograph of the Hudson River Valley. **ASK:** What feelings does the photo inspire? *(Possible responses: awe, tranquility, appreciation, reverence)* Then have students read the quotation by Ralph Waldo Emerson. **ASK:** What do you think Emerson meant by "the triumph of principles"? *(Possible response: living according to your own instincts)* How might taking inspiration from the natural setting shown in the photo and living according to your own principles lead to peace? *(Possible response: The natural beauty of the photo inspires connection and peaceful feelings and, as Emerson suggests in his quote, being true to oneself and acting on those principles can bring a feeling of connection and peace of mind.)* Tell students that in this chapter they will learn how cultural and social movements led Americans to discover and act upon their principles.

SHARE BACKGROUND

In the early 17th century, English explorer Henry Hudson was the first European to set foot in the Hudson River Valley. In the 19th century, the region became culturally significant when its natural beauty inspired local artists and writers whose works helped form a new American identity. Their paintings and literary works—which historians consider the beginning of a uniquely American culture—embody the major philosophies of the time and highlight the close relationship between people and nature. This 19th-century connection between art and nature has inspired current efforts in environmental and historical conservation. In 1996, Congress designated the Hudson River Valley as a National Heritage Area to preserve this region.

CRITICAL VIEWING Possible response: People may have felt a connection to the beauty of the Hudson River Valley's gently rolling hills, dense forests, and winding rivers—particularly when fall revealed the valley's colors.

For Chapter 9 Spanish Resources, visit the Resources Menu. Chapter 9 Resources are available at NGLSync.Cengage.com.

HISTORICAL THINKING QUESTION

How did cultural and social reform influence American society?

Jigsaw Activity: Preview Content This activity will generate student discussions about ways cultural and social reform movements influence American society. Divide the class into three groups and assign one of the sections of Chapter 9 to each group. Instruct group members to discuss what they know about the topic and what they think they will learn.

Group 1 Section 1 is about ways 19th-century American society and culture reflected religious values. How might religion influence people's actions?

Group 2 Section 2 is about slavery and the movement to end it. Why might people disagree about ending slavery?

Group 3 Section 3 is about the fight for women's rights. What social beliefs might restrict women's rights?

Regroup students so each new group includes at least one member from each original group. Invite students to share their prior knowledge and predictions about their assigned section so all students can anticipate what they might learn as they read Chapter 9.

INTRODUCE THE READING STRATEGY

MAKE INFERENCES

Remind students that inferences are not stated in the text. Direct students' attention to the chart in the Chapter Review and point out the relationship among what the text states, what the reader already knows, and the inference the reader makes. Encourage students to use the chart to record inferences as they read the chapter.

KEY DATES FOR CHAPTER 9

1800	Second Great Awakening begins
1830	Transcendentalism takes root
1831	William Lloyd Garrison publishes *The Liberator*
1833	American Anti-Slavery Society is founded
1836	Ralph Waldo Emerson publishes *Nature*
1841	*Amistad* trial takes place
1844	Lowell Female Labor Reform Association is established
1848	Seneca Falls Convention is held in New York

INTRODUCE CHAPTER VOCABULARY

KEY VOCABULARY

SECTION 1

civil disobedience	penitentiary	transcendentalism
common school movement	Romanticism	utopian community
evangelist	Second Great Awakening	
labor union	temperance movement	

SECTION 2

emancipation	gag rule	stewardship

SECTION 3

cult of domesticity	Seneca Falls Convention	suffragist

WORD MAPS

As students read the chapter, ask them to complete a Word Map for each Key Vocabulary word. Tell them to write the word in the oval and, as they encounter the word in the chapter, complete the Word Map. Model an example using the graphic organizer below.

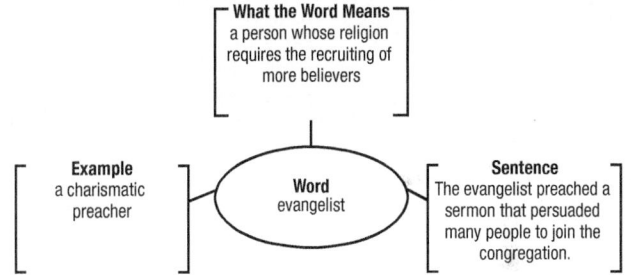

For instructional support for the online American Story "The Writers and Artists of Concord, Massachusetts," go to NGLSync.Cengage.com.

RELIGION AND REFORM

If you've been part of a large crowd at a sports event or concert, you know how exhilarating that experience can be. In the early 19th century, enthusiastic crowds flocked to religious events known as revivals.

CRITICAL VIEWING In *The Progress of Intemperance*, four panels of a 19th-century print concisely illustrate the path to alcoholism, which the temperance movement blamed for much family hardship. What does each step describe, and what is the overall purpose of this illustration?

TEMPTED.   PERSUADED.   HARDENED.   WRECKED.

THE SECOND GREAT AWAKENING

The 1820s and 1830s marked a period of reform in the United States motivated by new ideas about religion and a changing society. Many adults were leaving home at a younger age to take advantage of newly available land in the West. Emerging industrial work drew young men to growing cities, leaving their family farms or businesses. Young women and girls, too, left their communities to work in mills and factories. As people sought to cope with these changes, revival meetings brought many people together for a common purpose.

Revivalism was not a new idea. As you've read, Jonathan Edwards and George Whitefield hosted revival meetings in frontier towns during the First Great Awakening in the late 1700s. During the first few decades of the 19th century, similar gatherings attracted thousands of people who listened to stirring sermons, prayed, studied the Bible, and sang hymns. The movement became known as the **Second Great Awakening**, which emphasized a new idea: having a direct and emotional relationship with God encouraged personal responsibility and would lead to spiritual salvation.

This print, titled *Methodist Camp Meeting*, captures the typical activities of a 19th-century revivalist meeting held in the wilderness. After building the preachers' shelter, participants set up tents, listened, prayed, and socialized.

The influential ministers of this movement shifted the religious viewpoint of American society in an important way. Like the leaders of the First Great Awakening, these **evangelists**, or preachers of the Gospel—the part of the Bible that describes the life and teachings of Jesus—enthusiastically urged believers to experience a spiritual rebirth and accept Jesus as their personal savior. However, later revivalist preachers broke with their predecessors on the crucial point of salvation. Edwards and Whitefield believed that only the grace of God could save people, while preachers of the Second Great Awakening taught that people could achieve salvation for themselves through their own actions. They believed that by turning away from sin, helping others to do so, and improving the overall morality of society, individuals could work to establish the kingdom of God on Earth and, by doing so, save their own souls.

One minister in particular, **Charles Grandison Finney**, embodied the movement's zealous spirit. As a young attorney living in Adams, New York, Finney began attending church at his fiancée's request. There, he unexpectedly found himself struck by what he identified as the power of God's love, saying that "an overwhelming sense" of his wickedness brought him to his knees. Speaking in the plain, direct language of everyday life, Finney set himself apart from other ministers. His masterful sermons delivered his hopeful message to believers and nonbelievers alike: he believed that all people had it within themselves to embrace God and turn away from sin.

Those converted by Finney brought his optimistic message to their own churches and communities. Women's prayer groups met daily, traveling from home to home to spread their religious message. Employers encouraged their workers to attend revivals. All the Protestant denominations worked together, setting aside differences in their beliefs to recruit hundreds of new and former Christians, spread the message of salvation, and work to improve the moral character of their families and communities. These efforts led to reforms throughout 19th-century society.

MIDDLE-CLASS REFORMS

People looked to churches for moral direction, and church ministers responded by encouraging their congregations to build a solid, religious home life for their children. The church pointed specifically to middle-class women to serve as the moral center of the American family. As you may remember, the idea of Republican Motherhood was much admired in the years following the American Revolution. In the early 1800s, with more children attending school and husbands' incomes rising in a growing economy, housewives and mothers had more time and resources to teach their children and encourage their husbands to live devout, or faithful, lives. They could also spend their free time improving the lives of people in the community.

The **temperance movement** became a center of social reform for many of these women. The word *temperance* means "self-restraint" or "moderation."

OBJECTIVE

Discover the connection between Christian religious revivalism and the social reforms of the early 1800s.

CRITICAL THINKING SKILLS FOR LESSON 1.1

- Make Inferences
- Draw Conclusions
- Form and Support Opinions
- Compare and Contrast
- Analyze Cause and Effect
- Analyze Visuals
- Evaluate
- Analyze Primary Sources

HISTORICAL THINKING FOR CHAPTER 9

How did cultural and social reform influence American society? The growth of religious revivalism motivated people to improve American society. Lesson 1.1 discusses the problems that plagued early 19th-century America and how reformers sought to solve them.

BACKGROUND FOR THE TEACHER

Charles Finney's emotion-based preaching skills became hallmarks of revivalism. Building on successful styles of earlier preachers, and unlike the more staid Puritan ministers, Finney spoke directly to his audiences and entertained them with relevant stories. He instituted an "anxious bench" for people struggling with conversion and an "inquiry room" for those who had spiritual questions. Both innovations allowed him to preach directly to those in need of guidance. Finney's revivals lasted two to three weeks, during which he ignited religious fervor among his listeners with sermons and music. He inspired people to commit their lives to Christ and empowered them to believe that their actions could reform society. His well-advertised revivals drew large crowds and resulted in thousands of conversions.

FINANCIAL LITERACY

To extend their knowledge and understanding about the concepts in this lesson, refer students to the Financial Literacy handbook.

INTRODUCE & ENGAGE

CONNECT TO TODAY

Ask students to brainstorm a list of social problems they think are significant today. Record their responses on the left side of a class T-Chart like the one below. Then have students discuss the kinds of reform movements aimed at solving these problems, and record the responses on the right side of the chart. **ASK:** What motivates people to become involved in social reforms? *(Possible responses: a sense of responsibility, religion, pressure from family or peers, personal experience)* Tell students that in this lesson they will learn what motivated people to address the social problems of the early 19th century.

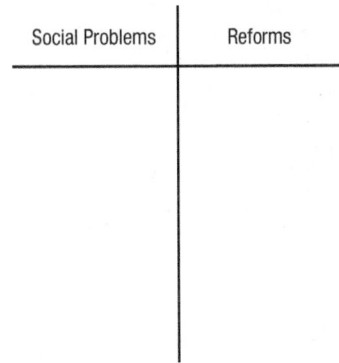

Social Problems	Reforms

TEACH

GUIDED DISCUSSION

1. **Compare and Contrast** What were some similarities and differences between the First and Second Great Awakenings? *(Both movements attracted gatherings of thousands of people, were based around Protestantism, and encouraged spiritual rebirth. However, the first movement taught that God's grace alone could save believers, while the second movement taught the idea of achieving salvation through actions. Thus, the Second Great Awakening is more closely tied to reform movements than the first.)*

2. **Make Inferences** Why was religion a major influence on reform movements of the early 1800s? *(Possible response: Influential evangelists and church groups taught personal responsibility for improving one's life. If it was possible to improve oneself, it naturally followed that people could improve society as a whole.)*

3. **Analyze Cause and Effect** What effect did a growing economy have on middle-class gender roles in the 19th century? *(An increase in incomes made it possible for women to have more time to devote to taking care of their families, rather than having to work. Religion offered a way for women to become active in society, and many middle-class women founded or joined groups devoted to social reform.)*

ANALYZE VISUALS

Direct students to analyze the print titled *Methodist Camp Meeting* and list as many details as they notice in one minute. When time is up, invite students to share their lists. **ASK:** Based on your observations, what generalizations can you make about revivalist meetings in the early 19th century? *(Possible responses: Meetings were held outside cities and outdoors, probably so people could get away from the distractions of daily life; some people are dressed nicely, so the meetings must have been regarded as special occasions. The wooden stage, benches, and tents indicate people stayed for a while or perhaps used the same setting for multiple meetings. Half the group is focused on the preacher, and half the group is focused on other people, so there must have been socializing as well as evangelizing taking place.)*

DIFFERENTIATE

ENGLISH LANGUAGE LEARNERS

Create a Word Web Pair students at the **Emerging** and **Expanding** levels with students at the **Bridging** level. Tell partners to take turns reading the paragraphs, noting religious terms they find. Instruct them to write those terms on the spokes of a Word Web, adding more spokes if needed. Direct pairs to compare webs, ask and answer questions about the terms, and look up the definitions of any unfamiliar terms. Webs may include *revivalism, sermons, Bible, hymns, God, ministers, preachers, evangelists, Gospel, Jesus, spiritual rebirth, personal savior, sin, morality, souls, churches, prayer groups, Protestant denominations,* and *congregations.*

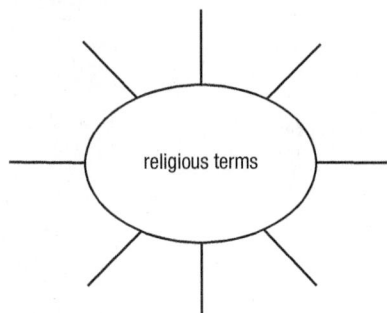

PRE-AP

Research and Write a Report Ask students to choose one of the social reforms sparked by the Second Great Awakening and write three questions about it. Challenge them to formulate questions that seek a deeper understanding of the roots of the problem and the proposed reforms and their effectiveness. Tell students to use a variety of sources to help them answer their questions and to write a report summarizing their findings. Invite volunteers to read their reports to the class.

See the Chapter Planner for more strategies for differentiation.

CRITICAL VIEWING Possible responses: The first step shows a well-dressed man declining a drink offered by another man. The second step shows the man has succumbed to the offer and is drinking in a social setting. In the third step, the man is pouring himself a drink at a bar, his clothes are rumpled, and he appears to be drunk. In the last step, the man, now in tattered clothing, reaches for what may be his last dollar to pay for the drink. The purpose of the illustration is to indicate that even social drinking can lead to dependence on alcohol, which will destroy one's life.

Most women in this movement saw drinking as a sin, and they believed that those who drank alcohol lacked self-control. And members of the temperance movement had evidence to back up their beliefs.

At that time, alcohol consumption was a real problem. By 1830, the average American drank about seven gallons of pure alcohol a year—triple the amount that Americans drink today. Drunkenness resulted in impoverished families, immoral behavior, damaged health, and poor job performance. By 1833, around 6,000 temperance societies had sprung up around the nation. These were generally religious groups, and the majority of their members were women. Temperance societies spread their anti-alcohol message through marches, meetings, and published literature, often urging people to make public pledges to refrain from drinking.

Reformers also took up the cause of universal public education. They campaigned for a public investment in education for every American child as the path to good citizenship and a more moral society. But when education depended on a family's ability to pay for private schools, many lower-income, working-class, and immigrant children, who had to work to help support their families, could not attend. Men, who were typically the main wage earners, were more likely to receive formal educations than women, whose main duties were to home and family. Enslaved African Americans were prohibited from obtaining any education at all, while free African Americans could only attend certain schools.

To address some of these issues, **Prudence Crandall** opened the Canterbury School for girls in 1831, and soon repurposed it as a school for African-American girls only, stirring controversy in her small Connecticut town. The local authorities arrested Crandall more than once for "unlicensed instruction," and the school was threatened and attacked. Meanwhile, reformers began to push for all American children to have free public education managed by local governments, an education reform known as the **common school movement**.

In Massachusetts, **Horace Mann** put the ideas of this movement into action. He championed the need to set basic standards for the training of professional teachers, especially women. He also wanted public schools to prepare students of all social classes, genders, races, ethnicities, and faiths for society and the workforce. Mann put another common school movement idea into action: funding free public schools through local property taxes. Soon other states began to follow Massachusetts's lead.

Reformers also looked to change institutions housing prisoners, the poor, and the mentally ill. Instead of concentrating only on punishment, reformers sought to establish a different kind of prison called a **penitentiary**, whose goal was to rehabilitate criminals. In a penitentiary, inmates were confined in individual jail cells, alone with their thoughts and the Bible. Reformers hoped that the inmates might become penitent, or remorseful, as a result and later return to society as better people. Reformers also sought to establish compassionate asylums, or hospitals, for the deaf and blind, the mentally ill, orphans, and the poor. At the time, many of these people were locked away in prisons or confined to poorhouses because there was no other place for them to go.

A social reformer named **Dorothea Dix** became famous throughout the country for her crusade on behalf of the mentally ill and people otherwise forgotten. Dix lobbied tirelessly for cleaner, healthier, and safer institutions for people in need. She persuaded at least nine state legislatures to establish publicly funded asylums to help care for those patients. Dix also worked on improving conditions in jails and poorhouses.

In addition to pursuing prison and asylum reforms, Dorothea Lynde Dix was an innovative educator. She wrote numerous books, including the popular *Conversations on Common Things*, a guidebook to help schools and parents answer a variety of children's questions.

PRIMARY SOURCE

The lead story in the December 1840 edition of the *Lowell Offering* was a spirited response to an editorial from the *Boston Quarterly Review* that painted an unflattering picture of the lives and morals of "factory girls."

"'She has worked in a factory' is sufficient to damn to infamy the most worthy and virtuous girl." So says Mr. Orestes A. Brownson [writer of the original editorial]; and either this horrible assertion is true, or Mr. Brownson is a slanderer. . . . And whom has Mr. Brownson slandered? A class of girls who in this city alone are numbered by thousands, . . . girls who generally come from quiet country homes, where their minds and manners have been formed under the eyes of the worthy sons of the Pilgrims, and their virtuous partners, and who return again to become the wives of the free intelligent yeomanry [farmers and small business owners] of New England, and the mothers of quite a portion of our future republicans.

—from *Lowell Offering*, December 1840

WORKERS BEGIN TO ORGANIZE

By the 1820s, widespread factory work was changing how people lived and worked. Industry provided many new jobs, but working conditions in most factories were far from ideal. The employees often worked 14 hours per day, 6 days a week, regardless of age. Children as young as 10 commonly worked in some factories, such as textile mills. Worker safety was a low priority, and serious on-the-job injuries and even deaths occurred too frequently. An injured employee was either fired for being unable to work or received no pay until he or she could return to work.

Naturally, workers wanted better treatment, including safer working conditions, shorter hours, and job protection following accidents. They also wanted better pay because the country's growing economy meant that the cost of living, reflected in prices for food, clothing, and rent, kept rising. Workers realized they stood little chance of changing conditions individually, so in the 1820s, they began to organize **labor unions**, or groups that advocate for workers' rights and protections. Because they bargain and act collectively, labor unions can promote reform and advancement efforts more effectively. Craftspeople and artisans who practiced a specialized skill, such as carpenters and shoemakers, also formed their own organizations known as craft unions. While most members of craft unions did not work in factories, their goals for better wages and working conditions were the same.

Despite heavy resistance from factory owners, unions made progress in improving workplace conditions until an economic depression hit the nation, prompting the Panic of 1837. Within a year, many factory workers and artisans were unemployed. As the economy struggled, the power of labor and craft unions decreased. Improved work conditions became less important than having work to begin with, as jobs became scarce. When the economy improved again in the early 1840s, unions began to regain some of their power.

Women in the Massachusetts textile mill town of Lowell joined together in 1844 to establish the Lowell Female Labor Reform Association (LFLRA), the first union of working women. Female millworkers built public support for their goals by writing and publishing the *Lowell Offering*, a monthly magazine of articles, poetry, and songs about their lives. By courting public opinion and pressuring the Massachusetts legislature to support their cause, the LFLRA was able to shorten millworkers' average workday from 14 to 10 hours.

HISTORICAL THINKING

1. **READING CHECK** Who was Charles Grandison Finney?

2. **MAKE INFERENCES** Why do you think universal public education was considered an important part of the 19th-century reform movement?

3. **DRAW CONCLUSIONS** Why did changes in society lead to religious revivalism in the early 19th century?

4. **FORM AND SUPPORT OPINIONS** Why do you think business owners fought against workers' demands during this era? Support your opinion.

BUILD BACKGROUND

DOROTHEA DIX

Although her experiences were varied—including serving as the Superintendent of United States Army Nurses during the Civil War—Dorothea Dix is best remembered for her campaign on behalf of the mentally ill. Her interest in this subject remains a bit of a mystery. Some biographers suggest there was a personal connection, as Dix suffered from a variety of ailments throughout her life, including tuberculosis, possible depression, and physical exhaustion. Dix had great compassion for the mentally ill people who endured horrific mistreatment in institutions, such as being chained to walls or kept in cages. She petitioned Congress and state legislatures to initiate changes by delivering her "memorials," in which she provided detailed descriptions of the terrible conditions found in hospitals and jails. Her efforts led to the creation of more than 100 mental health facilities, in which patients were treated more humanely.

LIFE IN LOWELL'S TEXTILE MILLS

Many young women came to the Lowell textile mills believing they could earn their own living and be independent from their paternalistic families. The reality they found was far different. Lowell women worked long hours in huge, dusty rooms, enduring the racket of hundreds of looms and the constant pressure to produce more cloth. After work, they lived in boardinghouses, where they slept six to a room, often having to share a bed with another without the privacy to read a book, write a letter, or enjoy a quiet moment to themselves. The Lowell Female Labor Reform Association (LFLRA) was formed in response to these conditions and to the lack of recourse available to the workers. In 1842, for example, a Lowell factory cut wages by 20 percent but increased the workload. When 70 workers staged a walkout in protest, all were promptly fired and were never allowed to work in a Lowell factory again. Owners hoped such tactics would discourage further protests.

TEACH

GUIDED DISCUSSION

4. **Evaluate** How did Horace Mann's ideas about public education impact women? *(Possible response: Mann recommended standards for teacher training, which would improve a profession that was dominated by women. He also worked to provide equal educational opportunities for students of both genders, which would improve schooling for girls.)*

5. **Compare and Contrast** How were mid-19th-century labor unions alike and different? *(Possible responses: All unions worked toward the same goals of improving wages and working conditions. Labor unions organized people, such as factory workers, who worked for large employers. Craft unions organized people who had special skills, such as shoemakers and carpenters. Unions also used different tactics, such as collective bargaining, publications, and pressuring legislatures, to gain support for their causes.)*

ANALYZE PRIMARY SOURCES

Direct students' attention to the Primary Source feature. **ASK:** What stereotypes and preconceptions concerning women do Mr. Brownson and the writer of the article in the *Lowell Offering* promote? *(Mr. Brownson promotes the stereotype that any woman working away from her family must be morally loose. Conversely, the article writer promotes the stereotype that all the factory girls come from virtuous Pilgrim descendants and will return to become virtuous wives of respectable New Englanders. Both writers have the preconception that the true proper role of a woman is that of a morally responsible wife and mother.)*

ACTIVE OPTIONS

On Your Feet: Fishbowl Arrange students in two concentric circles facing inward for a discussion about the role of religion in reform movements. Pose the following question: Is religion as influential today as it was in the 1820s and 1830s? Direct students in the inner circle to discuss their answers, while students in the outer circle listen and evaluate the ideas they hear. Then reverse roles and ask students in the new inner circle to continue the discussion of the posed question by supporting or refuting the ideas they just heard. Provide time for both groups to exchange ideas and summarize the results of the discussions.

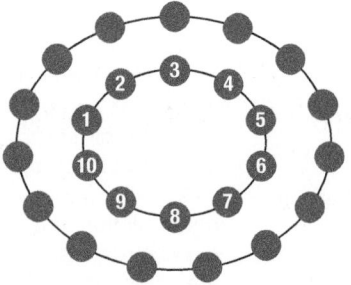

NG Learning Framework: Propose a Reform

ATTITUDES Responsibility, Empowerment

SKILL Problem-Solving

Follow up on the Introduce & Engage activity by organizing students into groups and asking them to choose one of the social problems they listed. Encourage group members to work together on a proposed reform to address the problem. Have each group present a proposal to the class. Then discuss as a class how the proposed reforms are similar to or different from the 19th-century reforms discussed in the lesson.

HISTORICAL THINKING

ANSWERS

1. Charles Grandison Finney was an evangelist who believed everyone could reject sin and embrace God. His sermons promoted optimism and activism among those who attended his revivals and led to a wave of reform movements throughout the country in the early 19th century.

2. Possible response: If they received a free, quality education, citizens might be better prepared to live their lives in a rational, prosperous way and avoid problems such as alcoholism, poverty, and criminality.

3. Society became unsettled when the lure of industrial work in cities caused many young men and women to break established family and community ties. Thus, people sought order and comfort in religious revivals, which brought them together for a common experience and purpose.

4. Possible response: Business owners focused on making as much money as possible. They resisted workers' demands for shorter workdays, higher wages, better working conditions, and job protection because such reforms would cut into their profits.

A YOUNG NATION'S LITERATURE AND ARTS

Writers and artists help create and define a nation's culture and identity. Which writers and artists do you think best capture the American spirit? In the 19th century, as the United States grew and changed, so did its art and literature.

AN AMERICAN LITERATURE

Culture in the United States during the 19th century had its roots in the colonial era. But in the country's early days, literature and art took a backseat to war, economic panic, and political conflict. As the American people grew more prosperous, they started to create a new identity separate from their European past. Artists and writers played a significant role in that effort.

In 1773, **Phillis Wheatley** became the first African-American woman to achieve fame as a poet. About seven years before she wrote or published her poems, Wheatley was a child kidnapped from Africa and taken to Boston on a slave ship. Purchased by a couple who recognized her talents, she soon learned to read and write in English, Greek, and Latin. Some of Wheatley's poetry addresses the colonial struggle for independence, as well as racial freedom. The couple freed her shortly after her book *Poems on Various Subjects, Religious and Moral* was published in London.

By the early 1800s, a uniquely American literature was taking hold and gaining recognition. **Washington Irving** became an internationally recognized writer, best known for his short stories "Rip Van Winkle" and "The Legend of Sleepy Hollow," both published between 1819 and 1820. In 1823, **James Fenimore Cooper** began publishing his five-book series of novels known as the "Leather-Stocking Tales" that include *The Last of the Mohicans*, an American classic. These popular books recount the life and exploits of the idealized frontiersman Natty Bumppo, or Hawkeye. Poet **Henry Wadsworth Longfellow**

In the legend of Rip Van Winkle, who sleeps through the Revolutionary War, author Washington Irving cleverly contrasts America's sleepy colonial society to that of the bustling United States. Artist N.C. Wyeth is one of many American artists who portrayed the aged Rip Van Winkle after his 20-year nap.

immortalized the earliest days of the American Revolution in his famous poem, "Paul Revere's Ride," bringing the event into the realm of national myth. His poems made many American legends famous, including the legend of Hiawatha, the Iroquois leader who helped establish the Iroquois Confederacy.

Some authors of the time wrote about both historic and contemporary conflicts and individualism. Although he wrote and published in the mid-1800s, **Nathaniel Hawthorne** set his major novels in Massachusetts during its early years when Puritanism ruled. *The House of the Seven Gables* was inspired by a home one of Hawthorne's relatives owned and a curse supposedly placed on his relatives by a woman accused of being a witch during the Salem witch trials. His best-known novel, *The Scarlet Letter*, focuses on love, guilt, revenge, and judgment in the Massachusetts Bay Colony of the 1640s. In his more contemporary novel, *Moby Dick*, **Herman Melville** describes life on a whaling ship as he recounts the tale of Captain Ahab, who relentlessly pursues the great white whale of the book's title. The novel is Melville's allegory for Americans' obsession with wealth and westward expansion.

In their writing, poets **Walt Whitman** and **Emily Dickinson** turned away from the flowery, sentimental poetry popular in the 1800s. Instead, they both wrote honestly and directly about their beliefs and experiences. In his most important work, *Leaves of Grass*, Whitman wrote in free verse, or poetry that does not rhyme or depend on a strict meter. The collection includes the poem "Song of Myself," in which he celebrates his life as a journey toward individual growth and a more democratic self. While Dickinson's poetry is leaner and more abstract, she also played with rhythm and theme in unexpected ways. During her life, she wrote over 1,700 poems.

THE TRANSCENDENTALISTS

Many American writers embraced a philosophical movement called **transcendentalism** in the 1830s and 1840s. Transcendentalism was based on the goal of transcending, or rising above, the

Walt Whitman was in his 30s and about to publish his first book of poetry, *Leaves of Grass*, when this photograph was taken. Many of his poems praise America as an experiment in democracy.

expectations society typically placed on people. The movement started in New England with a group of people who attended the Unitarian Church—a liberal, Christian church that urged members to embrace their feelings rather than texts and sermons. Like the revivalists of the Second Great Awakening, the Unitarians believed in the need to work toward social reform. Rather than a quick conversion experience at a revival meeting, however, Unitarians believed individual spiritual changes took time, as people relied on reason and their own consciences to lead them on the correct path.

Transcendentalists took this a step further. They believed that the path to spirituality lay in following one's heart and taking inspiration from nature, art, and literature. They emphasized the importance of practicing self-reliance as opposed to conformity. As a group, transcendentalists supported women's rights, abolition, and other social reforms, and they believed that organized religion, restrictive laws and social institutions, and industrialization kept individuals from fully expressing themselves and their spirituality.

Transcendentalist leader **Ralph Waldo Emerson** incorporated **Romanticism**, another philosophy that rejected the logic and rationality of the Enlightenment and emphasized imagination, emotion, and action, into his movement. Emerson's book *Nature* (1836) reflects his belief that experiencing nature leads one to grasp the divine, spiritual, or mystical aspects of life. In a speech at Harvard University, Emerson famously argued that action, risk, and endeavor should be the hallmarks of a true American scholar.

The New England writer, editor, and educator **Margaret Fuller** was closely associated with Emerson and his philosophy. She edited the transcendentalist magazine *The Dial* in the early 1840s and also wrote *Woman in the Nineteenth Century* (1845). The book states her feminist beliefs, which included her conviction that women deserved to have political equality and the right to seek emotional fulfillment.

PLAN: 4-PAGE LESSON

OBJECTIVE

Analyze how 19th-century literature and art reflected a uniquely American style.

CRITICAL THINKING SKILLS FOR LESSON 1.2

- Make Connections
- Make Inferences
- Analyze Visuals
- Analyze Language Use
- Compare and Contrast
- Form and Support Opinions
- Draw Conclusions
- Analyze Primary Sources

HISTORICAL THINKING FOR CHAPTER 9

How did cultural and social reform influence American society? In the early 1800s, a uniquely American artistic culture and philosophical movement emerged. Lesson 1.2 discusses how 19th-century art, literature, and transcendental philosophy reflected the maturing nation.

BACKGROUND FOR THE TEACHER

Phillis Wheatley's poems are both mournful and exuberant works about American history. More than one third of her poems are elegies for friends, famous people, and even strangers who died. She also employed religious imagery to show the contradiction of a supposedly Christian nation tolerating the evils of slavery. The rest of her works are celebrations of America, which attracted famous supporters like John Hancock. When local publishers refused her work on racial grounds, she published her book in London and earned international fame. Unable to obtain financial support for another book, she took a job as a maid. Wheatley died in obscure poverty in 1784. Her work is a testimony to the spirit that characterized the beginnings of American literature and a sad reminder of the history of racial discrimination.

HISTORY NOTEBOOK

Encourage students to complete the American Gallery page for Chapter 9 in their History Notebooks as they read.

INTRODUCE & ENGAGE

BUILD A WORD WEB

Invite students to preview the color illustrations of 19th-century paintings in Lesson 1.2. Challenge them to complete a class Word Web, like the one shown, by adding adjectives to describe the paintings or adding nouns to indicate what the paintings depict. Tell students that this lesson discusses how 19th-century art and literature reflect an emerging American spirit. At the end of the lesson, provide time for students to revisit the Word Web and add to it.

19th-century American art

TEACH

GUIDED DISCUSSION

1. **Analyze Language Use** What does the term *national myth* suggest about the influence of Longfellow's poem "Paul Revere's Ride"? *(Possible response: The work popularized the event so much that the poetic version, not the real story, became part of the collective American myth.)*

2. **Compare and Contrast** How were transcendentalists' beliefs similar to and different from those of revivalists? *(Both groups believed in the need for social reform and the ability of people to bring about change. However, revivalists were Christian, believing in conversion and the study of biblical texts, while transcendentalists relied on inspiration from nature as a path to spirituality.)*

3. **Make Inferences** As America matured, why do you think philosophies like transcendentalism and Romanticism became hostile to the logic of the Enlightenment? *(Possible response: The Enlightenment supplied a rationale for revolution and a framework for government, but it did not provide artistic inspiration nor spiritual answers. Thus, as the nation became more established and people began to prosper, they looked for inspiration and answers in other places.)*

FORM AND SUPPORT OPINIONS

Ask students to recall the artists and writers discussed in the lesson. Pose the following question: How and why do you think a new American identity emerged at this time in the country's history? Arrange students in small groups and ask them to discuss their opinions with other members of their group. Suggest they consider factors such as what was happening in the country and the types of subject matter, style, and audience that writers and artists chose to address. Invite each group to present and explain their opinions.

DIFFERENTIATE

STRIVING READERS

Summarize Using Sentence Frames Assign partners to read each subsection of the text together and then write a summary. When all pairs are finished, call on them to read their summaries aloud in the order in which the material appears in the text for an overview of the entire lesson.

Provide the following sentence frames to help students write effective summaries.

- This subsection is about _____ and _____.
- In summary, this subsection states _____.
- This subsection makes the following points: _____.

GIFTED & TALENTED

Create an Online Profile Have students conduct research about one of the writers or artists mentioned in the text to write a profile about that person and his or her work. Direct students to use multiple print and digital sources and to cite both primary and secondary sources in their profile. The profile should incorporate examples of the person's work and elucidate the person's background, philosophy, motivations, and influence on the development of American art or literature. Invite volunteers to post their profiles on a class or school website.

See the Chapter Planner for more strategies for differentiation.

In July 1846, Thoreau was briefly jailed for refusing to pay taxes he believed supported slavery and the Mexican-American War. He framed his refusal to pay as an act of protest and civil disobedience, which he outlined in his essay "Civil Disobedience."

I ask for, not at once no government, but at once a better government. . . . Must the citizen ever for a moment, or in the least degree, resign his conscience to the legislation? Why has every man a conscience then? I think that we should be men first, and subjects afterward. It is not desirable to cultivate a respect for the law, so much as for the right. The only obligation which I have a right to assume is to do at any time what I think right. . . . How does it become a man to behave toward the American government today? I answer, that he cannot without disgrace be associated with it. I cannot for an instant recognize that political organization as my government which is the slave's government also.

—from "Civil Disobedience," by Henry David Thoreau, 1849

CRITICAL VIEWING Inspired by his trips westward, Albert Bierstadt's painting *Sunset in the Rockies* is a romantic landscape with the luminism, or clear, radiant light, characteristic of the Hudson River School. How might this painting have influenced Americans to participate in the country's westward expansion?

One of Emerson's students, **Henry David Thoreau**, however, was probably America's best-known transcendentalist. In his book *Walden: Life in the Woods* (1854), Thoreau describes the two years he lived alone in harmony with nature in a simple cabin beside Walden Pond, a small lake in Concord, Massachusetts. He also wrote a famous essay, "Civil Disobedience," which explains why he supported **civil disobedience**, or the purposeful breaking of a law that contradicts one's conscience. Fuller and Emerson shared Thoreau's beliefs. All three believed the United States was waging a war in Mexico to expand slavery in the Southwest, and they denounced it. Emerson and Thoreau were ardent abolitionists who opposed the institution of slavery.

Louisa May Alcott, famous for her novels about family relationships and what it was like to grow up female in 19th-century society, was the daughter of transcendentalist leader Bronson Alcott. She grew up in the company of Thoreau, Fuller, and Emerson, and her father's dedication to transcendentalist philosophy and the importance of education informed her life and work. She is best known for her novel *Little Women*.

Some transcendentalists, including Bronson Alcott, organized **utopian communities**. The word *utopian* means "ideal or perfect," and the aim of these small towns was to gather believers together to live in a way that was as close to ideal as possible. These communities attempted to be self-sustaining, but few, if any, could thrive on their own. Most of them disbanded after only a few years.

PAINTERS OF NATURE

Romanticism and transcendentalism also influenced American visual artists as they sought inspiration in the natural world. **Thomas Cole**, a key figure in American fine arts in the 1830s and beyond, lived on the Ohio frontier. After visiting New York's Hudson River Valley in 1825, Cole began to paint its dramatic landscapes. Soon younger painters, such as **Asher B. Durand** and **Frederic Edwin Church**, joined Cole in their fascination with the stirring American landscape, both along the Hudson River and throughout the region. The style created by these painters and their followers became an American art movement known as the **Hudson River School**. **Albert Bierstadt**, a German immigrant and accomplished artist, traveled far to the West. He gained international fame for using the style of the Hudson River School in his panoramic paintings of the Rocky Mountains, the Grand Canyon, the high Sierra, and the hanging valleys of Yosemite. In their paintings, all of these artists celebrated the diverse beauty of the American landscape and often emphasized the human relationship with nature.

Several noted artists of the time began painting in the style of the Hudson River School, but went on to embrace other less precise and realistic styles of painting. For example, **George Inness** began his career painting finely rendered American landscapes, but over the years and under the influence of French painters of the era, his focus changed to vivid colors and depictions of shimmering light. Like the transcendentalists and their belief that the divine and spiritual could be found in nature, Inness's later paintings transcend realism and reveal a mystical world where light and color work in harmony to suggest, rather than strictly depict, a landscape.

Little Blue Heron exemplifies the scientifically precise images John James Audubon created in his paintings. But Audubon also reveals the bird's intangible qualities, explaining, "You may see this graceful Heron, quietly and in silence walking along the margins of the water, with an elegance and grace."

Other important artists followed their own paths through the American landscape. Beginning in the 1830s, **George Catlin** lived among the Native Americans of the Great Plains and made hundreds of drawings and paintings. As a young man, Catlin was moved by the sight of a Native American delegation visiting Philadelphia. He vowed that "nothing short of the loss of my life shall prevent me from visiting their country and becoming their historian." Art and nature enthusiasts could also view the country's wildlife in the remarkable watercolors of **John James Audubon**, who set out on daunting journeys to record the birds of the young nation in their natural environments. It took ten years for Audubon to produce four immense volumes. He completed the project in 1838.

1. **READING CHECK** How does James Fenimore Cooper's work mark him as a writer of truly American literature?

2. **MAKE CONNECTIONS** What philosophical belief do the transcendentalists and the members of the Hudson River School have in common?

3. **MAKE INFERENCES** Why might members of the Hudson River School of painting be considered followers of Romanticism?

4. **ANALYZE VISUALS** How does the Bierstadt painting reflect the views of transcendentalists?

BUILD BACKGROUND

UTOPIAN COMMUNITIES: BROOK FARM

Brook Farm, a utopian community founded in 1841, covered a site roughly 180 acres in West Roxbury, Massachusetts. To join the community, members paid an initial investment that entitled them to housing, food, and a percentage of the profits from enterprises, such as selling flowers or making doors. In return, members agreed to work 300 days a year at a job of their choice. Families lived simply, surrounded by nature and involved in cooperative activities. The community provided education for children from infancy through a six-year college preparatory course. Brook Farm School became a highly successful enterprise. The community, however, was short lived. Its amateur farmers found it difficult to till the rocky soil. Disappointed investors began demanding their money back, and in 1846, fire destroyed a central building. By 1847, the experiment had ended in failure.

JOHN JAMES AUDUBON

John James Audubon was born in Haiti, raised in France, lived in several places in the United States, and worked diverse jobs to support his family and his fascination with birds. With the help of an assistant who drew backgrounds, Audubon created life-size portraits of hundreds of American birds in their natural habitats. He developed a method of mounting recently killed birds on wires so he could arrange them in lifelike positions. A self-taught artist, Audubon used watercolors to accurately portray the delicate colors and textures of bird feathers. To find an engraver for his large prints, he traveled to Europe, where his good looks and charming personality soon made him famous. Exhibitions of Audubon's paintings helped finance the publication of the impressive four-volume work *The Birds of America*, which was accompanied by five volumes of "bird biographies" based on detailed notes that Audubon had taken in the field.

TEACH

GUIDED DISCUSSION

4. **Make Connections** How did Henry David Thoreau's life reflect the beliefs that Ralph Waldo Emerson expressed in his book *Nature*? *(Possible response: Emerson believed that experiencing nature leads a person to understand the spiritual aspects of life and to take risks. Thoreau reflected this by living alone in the woods in harmony with nature, which inspired him to take risks by doing acts of civil disobedience.)*

5. **Draw Conclusions** Share the Brook Farm information with students. **ASK:** Why do you think utopian communities failed after a short time? *(Possible response: These communities attempted to be self-sustaining cooperatives, but members did not always have the skills or patience to make a community successful. Also, outside influences and events may have tempted members away from the group.)*

ANALYZE PRIMARY SOURCES

Direct students' attention to the Primary Source feature. **ASK:** What is the purpose of Thoreau's essay? *(Its purpose is to argue that it's more important for people to follow their conscience than to be subservient to a government.)* Why does Thoreau feel it is right to disobey the law? *(Possible response: Thoreau feels strongly that the government is wrong to allow slavery. Because the government's laws violate his conscience, he can neither support the government nor obey its laws.)* Allow students to discuss their opinions of civil disobedience. **ASK:** When, if ever, is a person justified in disregarding the law? *(Answers will vary. Possible response: A person is justified in violating a law when it clearly infringes on peoples' human or civil rights.)*

ACTIVE OPTIONS

AMERICAN GALLERY
ONLINE
The Hudson River School Invite students to explore the American Gallery. Have them select one of the images and do additional research to learn more about it. Ask questions that will inspire additional inquiry about the chosen gallery image, such as: Who is this? What does the painting depict? Is the work a good example of early 19th-century art? Why does it belong in this chapter? What else would you like to know about it?

NG Learning Framework: Create a Book Jacket

SKILLS Observation, Communication

KNOWLEDGE Our Human Story

Display examples of book jackets to ensure students are familiar with the format: an attractive front cover with title and author, inside flap with a brief summary of the story that entices readers, back flap with a picture and biographical notes about the author, back cover with reviews from readers. Challenge students to choose a book by one of the authors discussed in the lesson and create a book jacket for it. If students have not read the book, encourage them to find accurate information about the work and author. Have students create a display to share their book jackets with the class. Use the display to synthesize ideas about 19th-century American literature.

For students who develop an interest in 19th-century American culture, suggest that they read the online American Story "The Writers and Artists of Concord, Massachusetts."

HISTORICAL THINKING

ANSWERS

1. Cooper's "Leather-Stocking Tales" were written about the American wilderness, featured an idealized frontiersman named Natty Bumppo, and portrayed Native Americans as disappearing. The setting, main character, and stories are uniquely American.

2. Both believed in the power of nature to help people attain spiritual insight.

3. Both philosophies rejected the logic and rationality of the Enlightenment. Romanticism emphasized imagination, emotion, and action. The Hudson River School paintings portrayed the beauty of the American landscape, which inspired viewers' imaginations and emotions. Some paintings might have motivated people to visit these places.

4. Possible response: Bierstadt's *Sunset in the Rockies* reflects a more spiritual view of nature through his choice of suffused light and color, suggesting that viewers can also receive inspiration from nature—a concept that transcendentalists regarded as the path to spirituality.

CRITICAL VIEWING Possible response: The painting presents an idealized view of the West that portrays the natural beauty and open spaces of western landscapes and suggests adventure and opportunity. Such a portrayal must have appealed to people who wanted to leave the crowded eastern cities and seek their fortune in the West.

ROCKY MOUNTAIN NATIONAL PARK, ESTES PARK, COLORADO

Artifacts prove humans began exploring the Rocky Mountain region 11,000 years ago. Recently, archaeologists have discovered evidence of migration patterns of these early native peoples within the area. We do know the Ute tribe dominated the area until the 1700s, reaping the benefits of the lush valleys, meadows, and clear, cold lakes. With the 1803 Louisiana Purchase, the United States acquired the land that includes what we now call Rocky Mountain National Park, and it was only a matter of time before the stunning landscape attracted more and more visitors.

Like the Grand Canyon, the valleys of Yosemite, and the Hudson River, the landscape of Rocky Mountain National Park inspired many Romantic artists—and continues to inspire artists today. The geography and diversity of life in this unique region allow artists to capture the human relationship with nature, something painters like Albert Bierstadt and Charles Partridge Adams aspired to do. And surely the elk, mule deer, and moose, along with hundreds of species of birds and plants, make it easy to feel inspired.

CRITICAL VIEWING Beginning millions of years ago, massive glaciers scraped across the earth, shaping the meadows and peaks of Rocky Mountain National Park. Compare this photograph to the Bierstadt painting, *Sunset in the Rockies*, you saw earlier in this chapter. What elements from this natural environment likely influenced and inspired Bierstadt and other Romantic artists?

284 CHAPTER 9

An Age of Reform 285

PLAN: 2-PAGE LESSON

OBJECTIVE

Learn about the historical relationship between humans and the natural landscapes of Rocky Mountain National Park.

CRITICAL THINKING SKILLS FOR LESSON 1.3

- Analyze Visuals
- Make Connections
- Make Inferences
- Evaluate

HISTORICAL THINKING FOR CHAPTER 9

How did cultural and social reform influence American society? Drawn to the acquired lands of the Louisiana Purchase, artists were inspired by the scope and beauty of newly discovered American landscapes. Lesson 1.3 discusses the influence of Rocky Mountain National Park's geography on the work of Romantic artists, what visitors might experience, and what geologists have learned there.

BACKGROUND FOR THE TEACHER

The Rocky Mountains comprise more than 100 separate ranges divided into five groups—the Canadian, Northern, Middle, and Southern Rockies and the Colorado Plateau. They all exhibit similar elevations (10,000 to 14,000 feet), steep vertical descents, spectacular scenery, and great mineral wealth. During the Great Depression, the Civilian Conservation Corps planted trees, built lodges, put out fires, and built roads inside the Rocky Mountain National Park. Present-day visitors can experience four ecological zones in the park: montane (large meadow valleys), subalpine (forests and lakes), alpine tundra (cold, high winds, no trees), and glaciers. Humans' relationship with the region has always been divided between exploiting its resources and preserving the park as public land.

HISTORY NOTEBOOK

Encourage students to complete the American Places page for Chapter 9 in their History Notebooks as they read.

DISCUSS ATTITUDES TOWARD NATURE

Remind students that the Romantics and transcendentalists believed that being in nature allowed people to experience life deeply. Discuss with students their personal experiences in wilderness areas, in city and national parks, or near lakes and oceans, and what and how their experiences made them feel. **ASK:** Why is a connection between humans and nature important? Then tell students that this lesson features Rocky Mountain National Park, whose beauty has inspired many artists and drawn millions of visitors over the years.

TEACH

GUIDED DISCUSSION

1. **Make Inferences** Why might the photographer have framed this photograph at this angle and not included any people? *(Possible response: This angle contrasts the expanse of the meadow against the inspiring height of the mountains that surround it. The photographer, like the Romantics, may have wanted viewers to feel they were present at the scene, experiencing its beauty and inspiration firsthand, without being distracted by the presence of other people.)*

2. **Evaluate** What is the public's responsibility toward such places as Rocky Mountain National Park? *(Possible responses: The public has a responsibility to protect and preserve the park and the diverse species that live there and keep it free of human development for current and future generations. If resources from the park will benefit the country, the public should support opening it to commercial development.)*

⬡ AMERICAN PLACES

President Woodrow Wilson dedicated Rocky Mountain National Park in January 1915. Enos Mills, an early naturalist and lodge owner in the park, had a vision for future generations: "In years to come . . . thousands of families will find rest and hope in this park." Only two hours from Denver along Trail Ridge Road, the park offers visitors towering summits, alpine meadows and lakes, and stunning vistas. Although Rocky Mountain is only about one-eighth the size of Yellowstone, its beauty and accessibility draw an equal number of visitors each year. Over time, however, the impact of 3 million visitors annually has created serious problems of overcrowding, pollution, and ecological damage. Current efforts aim to preserve the park for future generations, as Mills and other early conservationists envisioned.

ACTIVE OPTIONS

On Your Feet: Think, Pair, Share Tell students to think individually about the following topic: How does protecting wilderness areas reflect American culture and values? Then arrange students in pairs and ask them to discuss the topic. After a sufficient time, invite students to share individually the ideas they discussed and any conclusions they reached.

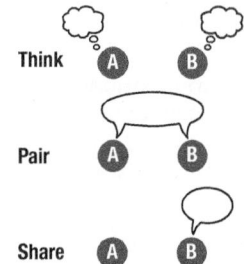

Think ⒶⒷ

Pair ⒶⒷ

Share ⒶⒷ

NG Learning Framework: Compare Names of the Park Summits

ATTITUDE Responsibility

KNOWLEDGE Our Human Story

Ask students to work in groups to conduct online and library research to identify the English names of various Rocky Mountain summits and compare them with the Ute and Arapaho names. Encourage them to describe how the names were chosen, what they mean, and what they imply about the differences between European and Native American relationships with nature. Ask groups to share their findings with the class.

INCLUSION

Describe Details in a Photograph Pair visually impaired students with sighted students. Ask the latter to describe in detail the foreground and background elements in the photograph and to give an overall impression of the scene and the feelings it conveys. Encourage vision-impaired students to ask clarifying questions. Then have pairs work together to answer the Critical Viewing question.

PRE-AP

Create an Infographic Challenge students to learn how the Ute viewed their relationship with nature and how they used specific items from their environment for food, clothing, and shelter, as well as for making soap, baskets, rope, and other items used in their daily lives. Direct students to use relevant information and visuals from several library or online sources to create an infographic to display their findings. Encourage them to share their infographics with the class.

See the Chapter Planner for more strategies for differentiation.

CRITICAL VIEWING The golden reflection of the setting sun, the sheer face of the mountains rising above the water, the height of the cascading waterfall, the undisturbed beauty of the shoreline, and the water flowing through the scene are all elements in this natural environment that likely influenced and inspired Bierstadt and other Romantic artists.

Slave owners placed these heavy iron shackles on young children's ankles to punish them or keep them from running away.

LIFE UNDER SLAVERY

The fact that fewer than 200 years ago, our country allowed people to hold others captive, buy and sell them, force them to work, and freely abuse them is unjustifiable to us today. It was unjustifiable to many people then, too.

AFRICAN AMERICANS AND THE SOUTH

As you have read, in the early 1800s the domestic slave trade expanded beyond the southern coast as planters in Alabama, Mississippi, and Louisiana cleared more land to plant cotton. Enslaved people also helped grow and harvest many other agricultural commodities, such as hemp, wheat, corn, rice, sugar, and tobacco. They worked with livestock, practiced trades such as carpentry and blacksmithing, and even labored in southern factories, in shipyards, and on docks. Wherever there was work to be done in the South, enslaved African Americans were likely being forced to do it.

Despite their bondage, African Americans created a strong, uplifting culture that influenced the larger American culture. Families were at the center of this culture, but they were often split apart by the slave trade. You may remember reading that slave owners could sell a child away from his or her mother, or a husband away from his wife. Enslaved African Americans had to rely on extended families for support, and grandparents, aunts, and uncles often played significant roles in child rearing. When even extended family was unavailable, enslaved people created "fictive kin," or friends and neighbors given honorary titles of "brother" or "aunt" and treated as relatives. These kinship bonds helped enslaved families stay resilient.

THE SLAVE DWELLING PROJECT
In 2010, Joseph McGill, Jr., was an office worker who had a unique hobby: Civil War reenactment. In "battle," he wore the uniform of the 54th Massachusetts Volunteer Infantry Regiment, the first Union military unit of African-American soldiers during the Civil War. For McGill, it was a thrilling way to experience history, so when an opportunity to sleep in a former slave cabin arose, he said yes. It led him to found the Slave Dwelling Project, a journey to locate and stay overnight in former slave dwellings.

The project's mission is to encourage people to preserve the places where enslaved people lived. McGill believes that when people—black and white—know the history, they are more able to have frank discussions about slavery's legacy. In this photograph, Johnnie Leach looks over a slave cabin slated for restoration in South Carolina. Leach once lived with his family in a slave cabin like this one while working nearby.

PLANTATIONS AND FARMS

Plantation owners commonly placed responsibility for day-to-day operations in the hands of professional overseers, or supervisors. These overseers were often young white men hoping to gain experience and money to buy their own land one day. Slave owners and overseers held the ultimate threat of force against slaves, but they much preferred to keep the work moving smoothly. Conflicts and discipline problems meant the loss of productive work. On larger plantations, enslaved people often worked in groups called gangs, which were managed by trusted male slaves who served as "drivers." These men tended to be especially intelligent, strong, and skilled. Some drivers were respectful to and, in turn, were respected by the people they managed. Others took advantage of their authority, and they were neither liked nor respected by the people who worked under them.

Slavery was an institution of power, designed to create profit for the slaveholder and break the will of the enslaved. In addition to working as many as 15 hours a day in the fields or as domestic servants, enslaved African Americans had very little privacy and were subject to severe discipline by their owners. Slaves who were accused of being disobedient or disrespectful were often whipped, branded, shackled, or even locked up in sweltering enclosures. Female slaves often suffered sexual abuse. Partly because most expectant mothers were forced to continue working in the fields until giving birth, about a third of all enslaved babies died before they reached their first birthday. Enslaved people generally ate poorly, were provided only meager shelter, and had little or no access to effective health care. Many constantly feared violence from the drivers and overseers.

Slave owners often justified their behavior by claiming they provided "their people" a better life than they would have had in Africa. Indeed, southern plantation owners tried to justify slavery to themselves and to the North by stressing their Christian **stewardship**, or careful and responsible management, of the slaves. As one clergyman wrote to his fellow slaveholders in the early 1840s, slaves "were placed under our control . . . not exclusively for our benefit but theirs also."

POLITICS OF THE SOUTH

In southern cities, white plantation owners and cotton merchants enjoyed among the highest per capita incomes in the nation. They had the finest homes and access to public entertainment that rivaled any city in the country. They owed their position to slavery. Without it, the southern economy would collapse. So it is not surprising that southern landowners were determined to protect the institution of slavery.

Both of the major U.S. political parties in the South—the Whigs and the Democrats—clamored for the southern landowners' votes. The Whigs, who portrayed themselves as the party of progress and prosperity, appealed to lawyers, editors, merchants, and wealthy planters. They believed the best way to protect slavery was for the South to develop its region's economy and build strong economic and political ties with the North and Europe.

The Democrats, on the other hand, found their strongest supporters among the small farm owners of the South who resented paying taxes on their property, including any slaves they owned. They saw the Democrats' platform of limiting the power of the federal government as the best way to protect slavery. They also liked the party's approach to western expansion and its policy of removing American Indians from locations that had fertile, rich soil or mineral resources.

HISTORICAL THINKING

1. **READING CHECK** Why did some enslaved people create a network of "fictive kin"?

2. **DRAW CONCLUSIONS** Why do you think both Whigs and Democrats in the South positioned themselves as friends of slavery?

3. **DISTINGUISH FACT FROM OPINION** What facts from the lesson prove false the claim of the southern preacher that African Americans were enslaved "not exclusively for our benefit but theirs also"?

PLAN: 2-PAGE LESSON

OBJECTIVE

Examine how African Americans devised ways to survive the institution of slavery in the South.

CRITICAL THINKING SKILLS FOR LESSON 2.1

• Draw Conclusions

• Distinguish Fact from Opinion

• Make Inferences

• Analyze Visuals

HISTORICAL THINKING FOR CHAPTER 9

How did cultural and social reform influence American society? As slavery expanded across the South, the institution affected all aspects of southern life. Lesson 2.1 discusses the lives of enslaved African Americans as well as the political and economic consequences of slavery for the South.

BACKGROUND FOR THE TEACHER

Many stories of enslaved people were preserved because of the Federal Writers' Project (FWP), established during the Great Depression. Between 1936 and 1938, the FWP sent writers to 17 states to interview people who had been enslaved. To document the stories, writers received instructions about the kinds of questions to ask and how to accurately record the answers—which were often spoken in local dialects. Some of the interviewees related memories from their childhood or stories their parents had told them. A few people, mostly in their 90s, even remembered what it was like to have been an enslaved adult. Today, their recollections are an important reminder of the realities of slavery. The interviews and photos are available on the Library of Congress's website in a 17-volume collection titled *Born in Slavery: Slave Narratives from the Federal Writers' Project.*

INTRODUCE & ENGAGE

EXAMINE THE POWER OF WORDS

Write the terms *slave* and *slave owner* on the left side of the board. Write the terms *enslaved person* and *slaveholder* on the right side. Point out that the terms refer to the same groups of people. **ASK:** How does a change in terminology affect the way we think about these groups? *(Answers will vary. The term* slave *describes a position in society, whereas* enslaved person *acknowledges humanity. The term* slave owner *perpetuates the idea that one person can own another, whereas the term* slaveholder *indicates a temporary relationship.)* Tell students Lesson 2.1 discusses life under slavery.

TEACH

GUIDED DISCUSSION

1. **Make Inferences** Why do you think plantation owners broke up enslaved families? *(Possible responses: The owners had no regard for enslaved families, so keeping them together was not a consideration. Splitting families was a way for the slaveholder to exhibit power by destroying an enslaved person's spirit and removing support.)*

2. **Analyze Visuals** Based on the photograph of the slave cabin, what can you infer about how enslaved people lived? *(Possible response: The building looks simple with only a door and window and what appears to be a metal roof, which would make the cabin hot in summer and cold in winter. These dwellings were far more primitive when compared to those of the landowner.)*

MORE INFORMATION

Re-creating Culinary Traditions Inform students that what we today call "southern cuisine" has direct ties to food dishes that enslaved people developed. This connection is being explored by Michael Twitty, an African-American chef and historian. He has studied the cooking traditions of enslaved people, and he re-creates their recipes, preparing meals using the ingredients and cooking techniques of the 18th century. For example, he prepares a typical meal of rabbit, hominy, and okra soup in iron pots over an open fire. Through his presentations, Twitty educates audiences about the culinary contributions of enslaved African Americans. Invite students to conduct further research about Michael Twitty's work and recipes and to share their findings with the class.

ACTIVE OPTIONS

On Your Feet: Numbered Heads Review the information about the Slave Dwelling Project. Pose the following questions for students to think about: Would you stay overnight in a slave dwelling? Do you think it is worthwhile to experience history in this way? Why or why not? Then divide students into groups of four and have them count off within each group. Direct group members to discuss the questions. After sufficient time, call out a number and have the student in each group with that number summarize the group's discussion for the class.

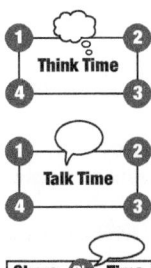

NG Learning Framework: Create a Class Collage

| ATTITUDE | Curiosity |

| KNOWLEDGE | Our Human Story |

Direct students to access the Library of Congress website and examine the *Born in Slavery* narratives, which are first-person accounts and photographs of formerly enslaved people. Ask students to work in groups and choose photographs or quotations they find particularly significant. Then tell them to use the photographs and words to create a class collage. Provide time for students to discuss their choices and explain how this activity deepened their understanding of life under slavery.

DIFFERENTIATE

ENGLISH LANGUAGE LEARNERS   ELD

Create Words with Suffixes Bring students' attention to the words *kinship* and *stewardship*. Explain that the suffix *-ship* means having the qualities or condition of the first part of the word. Elicit the meaning of *kinship* and *stewardship*. Tell students to add the suffix *-ship* to *friend, relation, owner, citizen, sportsman, craftsman,* and *reader*. Ask students of **All Proficiencies** to work in pairs to discuss the meaning of each new word and then write a sentence using it.

PRE-AP

Investigate Contributing Factors Challenge students to gather information from a variety of sources to learn more about the economic, political, social, religious, and geographic factors that encouraged slaveholding. Instruct them to write an essay that examines the relative contributions of at least three of these factors. Remind students to cite their sources and to quote or paraphrase them as appropriate. Invite students to post their essays on a class website or blog.

See the Chapter Planner for more strategies for differentiation.

HISTORICAL THINKING

ANSWERS

1. They created such kinship bonds with friends and neighbors because members of their own families had been separated from them by being sold to work on other plantations.

2. Because the institution of slavery was so deeply ingrained in the South, both parties had to support it in order to survive politically.

3. The facts include that enslaved African Americans were held against their will under threat of violence and forced to work extremely long hours in all types of weather without compensation. They could be bought or sold at an owner's whim, which often separated families permanently. They could also be physically abused or even killed.

Despite being respected for his speaking and writing, Frederick Douglass often faced racism, exclusion, and isolation. In a subtle response to bigotry, Douglass engaged in a 19th-century version of "photo ops." Photographed frequently, he purposefully chose to dress formally and to convey the image of a stern, dignified, and educated African American.

ABOLITIONISTS SPEAK OUT

If you speak up about a cause or injustice from personal experience, people usually listen with more interest and empathy. In the 19th century, when former slaves spoke out with powerful stories about their horrifying experiences, more people listened and joined the abolitionist cause.

THE ABOLITION MOVEMENT

The first efforts to end slavery in North America arose even before the United States was founded, but in the late 1820s, the push to abolish slavery began to gain momentum. The Second Great Awakening had sparked interest in social reform, and some northern church members argued that it was their Christian duty to work for immediate **emancipation**, or freedom, of the enslaved. These abolitionists called for slaveholders to free their slaves as soon as possible; hire them as free, paid workers; and reimburse them for their years of unpaid labor.

A crusading newspaper writer and editor, **William Lloyd Garrison** was also one of the leaders of the abolition movement. He became involved by working with the colonization movement, which, as you've read, aimed to relocate freed slaves to West Africa. After attending antislavery meetings organized by African Americans, he realized that the colonization movement was not good-hearted, but racist. In 1831, Garrison began to publish *The Liberator*, a newspaper that promoted the antislavery cause.

This cotton and silk banner was designed to spread the abolitionist message and honor journalist William Lloyd Garrison (above). It was displayed at antislavery gatherings.

In it he condemned the colonization plan and pushed the idea of emancipation. "*I will* be as harsh as truth," Garrison announced, "and as uncompromising as justice. On this subject, I do not wish to think, speak, or write, with moderation. . . . AND I WILL BE HEARD." And he was heard. Although his message was no different from those running in newspapers published by African Americans, through *The Liberator* these ideas reached a larger white audience.

In 1833, Garrison joined with other abolitionists to found the American Anti-Slavery Society. By the late 1830s, the organization had more than 2,000 chapters and as many as 250,000 members, primarily in the Northeast and Midwest. The organization held that slavery violated not only natural law but also the will of God and that the U.S. Constitution gave people the right to end slavery. It spread this message through its publication, the *National Anti-Slavery Standard* and through meetings, petitions, and lectures. Other abolition groups also published and distributed antislavery articles in their publications, which were powerful weapons for their cause.

Both whites and African Americans banded together to support the abolitionist cause. **Frederick Douglass** was among the most prominent African-American abolitionists. He wrote the *Narrative of the Life of Frederick Douglass, an American Slave* (1845) to detail his years of enslavement in Maryland. While there, he broke the law by learning to read. Sent to Baltimore by his owner, Douglass worked in the shipyards, read widely, and plotted his escape to freedom. After several attempts, he finally succeeded in 1838. He borrowed the papers of a free African-American sailor and rode a train to freedom in New York City. There, he met a man who introduced him to the New York Anti-Slavery Society.

Douglass was a compelling speaker who lectured throughout the North with William Lloyd Garrison. He also cofounded and edited an influential abolitionist newspaper called the *North Star*. The newspaper's name referred to the fact that escaping slaves used the North Star to guide them to freedom. Douglass eventually became a consultant to President Abraham Lincoln and, in later years, a U.S. official and diplomat.

SPREADING THE WORD

Between 1834 and 1835, abolitionists sent out a million pieces of mail, much of it to the South where they hoped to appeal directly to ministers and others open to the idea of emancipation. Angry white southerners protested, declaring that the literature would provoke more rebellions such as those led by Nat Turner and Denmark Vesey. In Charleston, South Carolina, mobs of southern slavery sympathizers burned sacks of mail that came from northern cities. A group of plantation owners from Georgia offered a $12,000 reward for the capture of a wealthy abolitionist merchant who funded much of the antislavery postal campaign.

Among the abolitionists who went on the lecture circuit, **Angelina** and **Sarah Grimké** were popular speakers for the cause because they were the daughters of a prominent South Carolina slave-owning planter. The Grimkés' personal experiences with slavery gave them a credibility that white northern abolitionists could not match. "All moral beings have essentially the same rights and the same duties, whether they be male or female," Angelina Grimké said. The women of the South, who "now wear the iron yoke of slavery in this land of boasted liberty and law . . . are our countrywomen—they are our sisters."

African Americans were more effective at spreading the word than any other abolitionists. They electrified audiences and readers with descriptions of their captivity and their daring escapes to the North.

PLAN: 4-PAGE LESSON

OBJECTIVE

Compare the methods that different abolitionist groups used in their struggle to outlaw slavery.

CRITICAL THINKING SKILLS FOR LESSON 2.2

- Make Inferences
- Analyze Cause and Effect
- Draw Conclusions
- Make Predictions
- Analyze Language Use
- Evaluate
- Analyze Primary Sources

HISTORICAL THINKING FOR CHAPTER 9

How did cultural and social reform influence American society? In the early 1800s, the abolitionist movement gained momentum throughout the United States. Lesson 2.2 discusses the different ways that white and African-American abolitionists spread their messages and fought for change.

BACKGROUND FOR THE TEACHER

Frederick Douglass became drawn to the abolition movement through reading the *Liberator* and hearing William Lloyd Garrison speak. Garrison, in turn, was impressed by Douglass and invited him to become a lecturer for the Anti-Slavery Society. Douglass considered Garrison his mentor, and the two men promoted similar ideologies for nearly a decade. Then their views began to diverge. Garrison—a pacifist who favored persuasion rather than violence—denounced the U.S. Constitution as a proslavery document and promoted dissolving the Union. Douglass, on the other hand, believed rebellion and politics were effective abolitionist tactics. He did not view the Constitution as inherently proslavery but thought it could be used to justify emancipation. Douglass also did not favor dissolution of the Union because it would leave enslaved people at the mercy of southerners.

INTRODUCE & ENGAGE

BRAINSTORM CHARACTERISTICS OF INFLUENTIAL SPEAKERS

Invite students to name influential speakers who persuaded them to accept a new or different point of view. List the responses on the board. Then ask them to brainstorm characteristics that make people influential speakers, and record their answers in an Idea Web. Suggest that students use these characteristics to evaluate the abolitionist speakers mentioned in Lesson 2.2. At the end of the lesson, invite students to revisit the Idea Web and discuss whether the characteristics that make people influential speakers today also apply to influential speakers of the 19th century.

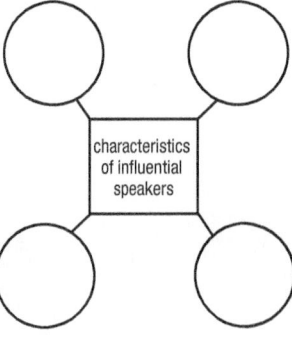

characteristics of influential speakers

TEACH

GUIDED DISCUSSION

1. **Make Predictions** In what ways do you think southern slaveholders would react to the abolitionist demands of northern church members? *(Possible response: To southern slaveholders, slavery was an economic and social issue. They would likely strongly reject the demands for immediate emancipation, hiring of formerly enslaved people, and compensation of formerly enslaved people for unpaid labor. Such actions would destroy their economy and imply that African Americans were equal to whites.)*

2. **Draw Conclusions** Why might a lecture featuring both William Lloyd Garrison and Frederick Douglass have provided audiences with a persuasive argument for abolition? *(Possible response: Douglass described his personal experiences of the horrors of slavery, and Garrison called upon white people to reject slavery and demand emancipation in the name of justice and freedom. The two approaches would have been a powerful combination.)*

3. **Analyze Language Use** In the quotation from the *Liberator* and the illustration of the banner, what effect does the use of italics and capitalization have on Garrison's message? *(Possible response: The italics and capital letters grab the reader's attention and communicate the strength and urgency of Garrison's beliefs and intentions.)*

MORE INFORMATION

Portraits of Frederick Douglass Frederick Douglass is recognized as the most photographed American of the 19th century. More photos were taken of him than of President Abraham Lincoln or the notoriously famous army officer George Custer. Douglass was a fan of the relatively new and expanding field of photography and even wrote speeches about it, declaring that the "picture-making faculty is . . . a mighty power." Part of photography's power, he believed, was its democratic appeal—both the working classes and the wealthy could afford to be photographed and to purchase the pictures. Yet Douglass saw an even greater potential in photography's ability to sway people's views about abolition: "The few think, the many feel. The few comprehend a principle, the many require illustration." Photographs of Douglass are available online at the websites of the Library of Congress and the Massachusetts Historical Society.

Tell students to study the photograph of Frederick Douglass in the lesson and to read the caption. **ASK:** Do you think Douglass's plan to represent himself as a dignified, respectable man in photographs may have succeeded in changing people's view of slavery? Why or why not? *(Answers will vary. Possible responses: Yes. Even today people use their photos to convince other people of their positive qualities. Douglass's lined face suggests his struggles, yet he looks directly into the camera as if to say, "I have made a good life." This might have made people realize that all enslaved people should be free. No. Douglass is so grim in the photo that it might have scared people and made them feel threatened. Photos don't always change people's minds. Even today, although there are many photographs of successful African Americans and other minorities for people to see, racism and prejudice are still part of our society.)*

DIFFERENTIATE

INCLUSION

Use Clarifying Questions Allow students to work with a partner who can read the lesson aloud to them. Encourage students to ask and answer clarifying questions about the photographs and the accompanying text. Then instruct pairs to work together to answer the Historical Thinking questions.

PRE-AP

Compare Strategies Then and Now Remind students that the abolitionists used a variety of strategies to raise awareness and prompt action. Ask them to choose a contemporary movement or cause and conduct research to learn how that movement spreads its message and rallies people to the cause. Then invite students to write an essay comparing contemporary strategies with those the abolitionists used. Encourage them to use a chart like the one shown to organize their research and thoughts. Students may conclude their essays with ideas about which strategies have best stood the test of time and why. Invite them to read their essays to the class or post them on a school website.

Strategy	Abolitionist Cause	Contemporary Cause
Moral appeals		
Logical appeals		
Emotional appeals		
First-person accounts		
Writing (newspapers, direct mail, other)		
Speaking (lectures, sermons, other)		
Political lobbying		
Direct actions		
Other		

See the Chapter Planner for more strategies for differentiation.

Sojourner Truth, born into slavery in New York around 1797, attracted a wide readership with her book, *The Narrative of Sojourner Truth*. So, too, did Solomon Northup, a free man of color from New York who was kidnapped and sold into slavery in the deep South, with his account *Twelve Years a Slave*. Harriet Tubman, who escaped bondage in 1849, helped hundreds of enslaved people escape

the South. She was a riveting speaker who pulled no punches in her description of slavery and the dangers of trying to escape it. Despite the respect they gained from telling their stories, African-American abolitionists continued to face restrictions from fellow reformers and enemies alike. They responded by demanding greater rights for African Americans in the North, as well as those in the South.

David Walker was another powerful, resourceful abolitionist voice. Born in the South to a free mother and an enslaved father, Walker moved to Boston, where he opened a secondhand clothing store in the 1820s. Walker printed antislavery pamphlets and sewed them into the clothes he sold to sailors. He hoped his pamphlets would travel to many ports, reaching as many people as possible, especially in the South. In 1829, Walker printed his pamphlet *Appeal to the Colored Citizens of the World*, which became one of the most radical antislavery documents of the abolitionist movement. In the pamphlet, he denied that slaves felt or owed any loyalty to their masters and called for African Americans to be full American citizens in both the government and the economy, even if that required violent revolt.

DIFFERENCES AMONG ABOLITIONISTS

Just as Americans could not agree on the subject of slavery, abolitionists themselves differed on how to react to the opposition they faced. William Lloyd Garrison told his followers not to respond to any acts of violence. He renounced all ties to either major political party because both were tolerant of slavery. But other abolitionists courted political parties and politicians, seeing them as the most effective way to achieve abolition.

The differences among the abolitionists became clear at the annual meeting of the American Anti-Slavery Society in 1839. The various factions differed in their attitudes toward the role of women in the movement. Women made up perhaps half of all antislavery organizations, but some male abolitionists believed it best to keep them in a subordinate role, preventing women members from voting, speaking publicly, and serving on committees with males. Unable to resolve their differences, the society split. The more conservative members, who advocated for the gradual emancipation of enslaved peoples, created the Liberty Party. They put their hope in politics, attempting to run a candidate for president in the 1840 election. Garrison founded the Friends of Universal Reform, which continued to work for the immediate emancipation of slaves and welcomed women as full and equal members.

Actor Chiwetel Ejiofor picks cotton in his role as Solomon Northup in the 2013 film *12 Years a Slave*, based on Northup's autobiography. The movie illuminates the terrible choices for survival all enslaved people faced.

Both sides overwhelmed Congress with more than 300 petitions signed by 40,000 people demanding the abolition of slavery in the District of Columbia. Once again, southerners argued that the petitions threatened to incite slaves to rebellion and called for Congress to reject them. Seeking to avoid conflict, Congress set the petitions aside without consideration. This congressional practice of disregarding petitions is called the gag rule. During the next decade, many northern abolitionists spoke out against the gag rule, which they believed violated a basic American freedom and supported slavery.

Former president John Quincy Adams, now a Massachusetts congressman, thought the gag rule unconstitutional and fought for Congress to recognize the antislavery petitions. Finally, the gag rule was overthrown in December 1844. Adams also successfully defended Africans who had taken control of the slave ship *Amistad* on its way to Cuba and sailed it to Long Island, New York. The Africans were arrested and charged with murdering the ship's captain. Supported by a large network of abolitionists, Adams tried the case before the U.S. Supreme Court. In 1841, he won the case, securing the acquittal and freedom of the defendants.

As the antislavery movement grew stronger, it met with more determined opposition in the North as well as in the South. In 1835, mobs in Boston destroyed the homes of African Americans, pelted antislavery speakers, and dragged William Lloyd Garrison through the streets of town at the end of a rope. After denouncing a local judge who prevented the trial of a crowd that had burned a black man alive in Missouri, abolitionist editor Elijah P. Lovejoy moved across the Mississippi River to the free state of Illinois to escape the wrath of offended readers. He didn't move far enough. In November 1837, a pro-slavery mob shot and killed him as he and his assistants tried to protect his printing equipment from them. Local law officers arrested Lovejoy's assistants for inciting the violence. Clearly, there was no agreement, in the North or South, on the question of abolishing slavery.

HISTORICAL THINKING

1. **READING CHECK** What methods did abolitionists use to spread their message?

2. **MAKE INFERENCES** Why do you think William Lloyd Garrison came to believe the colonization plan was racist?

3. **ANALYZE CAUSE AND EFFECT** What effect did publications such as *The Liberator* have on the public, and why was this effect important?

4. **DRAW CONCLUSIONS** How did learning to read affect Frederick Douglass's life?

BUILD BACKGROUND

THE GRIMKÉ SISTERS

The Grimké sisters witnessed firsthand the grim reality of slavery on their family's plantation. Sarah recalled being disciplined by having to pick cotton alongside enslaved workers, and Angelina described hearing the screams of enslaved people being punished. The sisters' hatred of the institution prompted them to move to Philadelphia, where their abolitionist writings quickly gained them notoriety. In a letter to William Lloyd Garrison, Angelina wrote that abolition was a "cause worth dying for," which angered local Quakers who balked at the radical message. When Angelina wrote an appeal urging southern women to become abolitionists, authorities in Charleston threatened to imprison the sisters if they came to the city. The sisters also offended northerners who felt that women should not speak in public about controversial issues.

THE *AMISTAD* CASE

The *Amistad* case, although a seminal moment in the abolition movement, did not deal directly with the legality of slavery but with the more mundane issue of property rights. The question put before the U.S. Supreme Court was who, if anyone, owned the Africans. Three parties claimed ownership: the captain of the ship that captured the *Amistad* after the revolt sought salvage rights to its cargo of enslaved people; two Spanish slavers claimed ownership of the Africans; and the Spanish government demanded extradition of the Africans to Cuba for trial. John Quincy Adams, however, argued that none of the parties had ownership rights to the Africans, as they were free citizens of Sierra Leone and had been illegally abducted, transported, and enslaved against their will. The Supreme Court agreed with Adams's argument and ordered the Africans returned to their homeland.

TEACH

GUIDED DISCUSSION

4. **Make Predictions** Considering the cultural barriers of the time, how do you think antislavery messages from women such as the Grimké sisters, Sojourner Truth, or Harriet Tubman were received? *(Possible response: Because, in general, men believed the place for women was the home, public arguments made by female abolitionists may have been viewed as examples of women overstepping their proper bounds and, therefore, could be disregarded.)*

5. **Evaluate** How would you evaluate the gag rule as a strategy for dealing with the slavery controversy in Congress? *(Possible response: It was not effective in the long run. The rule only postponed the need to deal with the issue of abolition. By ignoring abolitionists, congressmen avoided offending constituents who disagreed with antislavery views.)*

ANALYZE PRIMARY SOURCES

Direct students' attention to the Primary Source feature. **ASK:** What is Walker's basis for rejecting the colonization plan? *(He insists that African Americans have as much right to live in America as whites.)* What threat does Walker make? *(He indicates that white Americans will regret their failure to act if enslaved people resort to violence in order to win their freedom.)* How did Walker's message differ from that of other abolitionists? *(Walker was more radical than some other abolitionists, and he voiced the possibility of violence, if necessary, to obtain justice.)*

ACTIVE OPTIONS

On Your Feet: Inside-Outside Circle List names of the abolitionists discussed in Lesson 2.2 on the board. Arrange students in two concentric circles facing each other. Instruct students in the outside circle to ask questions about the abolitionists, and tell the students on the inside to answer them. On a signal, students rotate to create new partnerships. On another signal, students trade inside/outside roles.

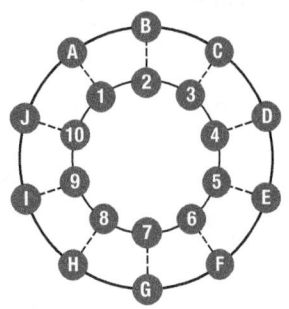

NG Learning Framework: Debate How to End Slavery

SKILL Communication

KNOWLEDGE Our Human Story

Ask students to work in groups to role-play one of the 19th-century abolitionists they read about in this lesson. Direct each group to research the life and views of this abolitionist, especially the person's ideas about how to best end slavery. Then have each group choose a member to assume the role of the abolitionist and engage in a debate with the other "abolitionists" in class. Prompt students with questions such as: Is violence ever acceptable? Is there a political solution to ending slavery? Allow time for students to present their abolitionist's views and respond to members of other groups.

HISTORICAL THINKING

ANSWERS

1. Abolitionists held meetings and gave speeches and lectures, the most effective of which were by African Americans with firsthand knowledge of slavery. They also published newspapers, mailed flyers, and circulated petitions.

2. The colonization plan seemed to suggest that while African Americans should not be enslaved, they were not good enough to live in the United States. The plan suggested that Africa was the appropriate place for black people—even those born in the United States who had no knowledge of Africa, its languages, or its cultures.

3. The publications made white people in the North confront an injustice that they otherwise would have avoided. This was important because once people actually took a side, they were more likely to try to spread the word and convince others to join the abolitionist cause.

4. Learning to read became a key to freedom for Douglass. It gave him the ability to write his narrative, which described his years of enslavement and educated others about slavery. As a literate, educated man, Douglass could voice his opposition to slavery by publishing the *North Star* and became an influential speaker.

SENECA FALLS AND A CALL FOR RIGHTS

Today women vote, protest, and are active in social and political causes. But before the 1830s, the idea of women demanding to vote was considered laughable, and the thought of a woman governor, member of Congress, or president was unimaginable. Then women began to find and use their collective voice.

THE CULT OF DOMESTICITY

As the rapid advances of the Industrial Revolution changed the U.S. economy in the first half of the 19th century, a substantial middle class began to form in the United States. In middle-class homes of that era, men left home each day to go to work, and women took care of the children and the household. Middle-class women were expected to be the moral center of the household and provide strong models of clean living for their children and husbands. This social ideal became known as a **cult of domesticity**.

Catharine Beecher, the sister of Harriet Beecher Stowe, renowned abolitionist and author of *Uncle Tom's Cabin*, was a teacher, author, and advocate for women's education. While Beecher felt that women's duties were as important as men's, she also believed that each partner had a distinct sphere to which he or she was suited. And for Beecher, a woman's sphere was the home and family. She opposed women's suffrage for this reason, claiming that politics were corrupting and far removed from women's place in the home. Her 1841 book, *A Treatise on Domestic Economy*, was a comprehensive guide for domestic duties. It contained practical lessons in how to keep a home, feed a family, raise children, and provide simple medical care. For the middle-class women who could afford luxuries such as domestic servants and store-bought foods, following such advice for efficient household management allowed them more free time.

The cult of domesticity empowered some women to consider restrictions they faced in society. Individual state laws, for instance, governed women's rights

Catharine Beecher, 1848

and freedoms according to their marital status. Often, unmarried women shared many legal rights with men, including the ability to own property and make contracts. In contrast, married women deferred these rights to their husbands the moment they married. A married woman could not give away or sell any property. She could not bring a lawsuit, nor could she be sued. She could not enter into a contract or make a will. And every American woman was barred from voting in national elections and serving on juries. Chafing under these restrictions, women began to demand reforms.

SENECA FALLS CONVENTION

Of course, some women had been speaking out about their lack of rights since before the American Revolution. You'll recall that Abigail Adams admonished her husband John, who was then serving as a delegate to the Continental Congress, to "remember the ladies" because they will not "hold [themselves] bound by any laws in which [they] have no voice or representation." But for more than 50 years, American women had allowed themselves to be bound by those very laws. That was about to change.

In 1840, abolitionist **Elizabeth Cady Stanton** attended the World's Anti-Slavery Convention in London, England. As a female delegate, she found herself seated in a separate, roped-off area away from the important discussions, and she felt "humiliated and chagrined" by the experience. While there, Stanton met another attendee, **Lucretia Mott**, a devout Quaker and feminist, who shared her feelings. In fact, the Quakers had recognized the spiritual equality of women from the faith's earliest days, allowing them the same rights to speak in meetings as men and expecting them to take on social causes with the same vigor. Just as Quakers were staunch abolitionists, they enthusiastically embraced the fight for equal rights for women.

Stanton and Mott vowed to begin a movement for women's rights in the United States. Their plan was temporarily set aside when both women returned to the United States. Mott, meanwhile, joined a group of Quaker women who traveled around the nation, spreading the word about both abolition and women's rights. They hoped to bring the idea of equality for women into the national consciousness. Then in 1847, Stanton moved from Boston to Seneca Falls, a small town in upstate New York.

Living in Seneca Falls, Stanton grew frustrated with the limitations the small town placed on her and other women. She reached out to Mott and, in 1848, the two women joined together with three of Mott's Quaker friends to plan a convention for women's rights activists in Seneca Falls. Their plan included the drafting of a list of rights all women should strive for. They called their plan the **Declaration of Sentiments and Resolutions**. Using the Declaration of Independence as a model, Stanton and Mott demanded women's suffrage, or the right to vote, and insisted on equal treatment concerning property rights, education, employment, divorce, and legal matters.

A historical roadside marker designates the Wesleyan Chapel in Seneca Falls, New York, as the site of the first national women's rights convention in 1848.

PLAN: 4-PAGE LESSON

OBJECTIVE

Explain how the abolition movement led to the struggle for women's rights and the Seneca Falls Convention.

CRITICAL THINKING SKILLS FOR LESSON 3.1

- Determine Chronology
- Make Inferences
- Make Connections
- Synthesize
- Form and Support Opinions
- Summarize
- Evaluate
- Analyze Primary Sources

HISTORICAL THINKING FOR CHAPTER 9

How did cultural and social reform influence American society? In the 19th century, many women were restricted to the domestic roles of wife and mother. Lesson 3.1 discusses how women worked to break free of these restrictions and gain equality in American life.

BACKGROUND FOR THE TEACHER

Quakers were at the forefront of the women's rights movement because their denomination allowed greater equality for women than did other religious groups. Quakerism taught that both genders were equal in the eyes of God. For example, Quaker women, if they felt the call, could embark on long journeys of ministry, leaving their husbands to care for the children and manage the house. Seneca Falls in upstate New York was a center of Quaker activism. In 1848, a group of Quakers formed an organization called the Progressive Friends that advocated for women's equality. Both the planning for the Seneca Falls Convention and the drafting of the Declaration of Sentiments took place in the homes of Quaker leaders. Twenty-three of the women who signed the declaration were Quakers—the largest representation from any religious group. For many years, Quaker women used their valuable organizing and public-speaking skills to campaign for women's rights.

INTRODUCE & ENGAGE

CREATE A CHARACTER MAP

Discuss the current roles of women in American society. Ask students to describe a "typical" American woman. Display an Idea Web, like the one shown, and write "American woman" in the center. Challenge students to fill in the circles with the characteristics they feel exemplify the image of today's American woman. Discuss the similarities and differences among the responses. Tell students that Lesson 3.1 describes characteristics of women in the 19th century and how some women attempted to break free from the restrictions of society.

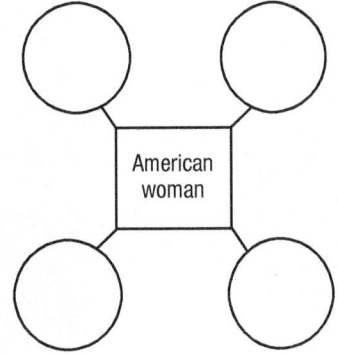

TEACH

GUIDED DISCUSSION

1. **Synthesize** How did Catharine Beecher's opposition to women's suffrage reflect the values of the cult of domesticity? *(Beecher opposed women's suffrage because becoming involved with politics would distract women from their primary responsibilities of caring for family and home.)*

2. **Form and Support Opinions** Do you think the fact that single women had more rights than married women was a deterrent to marriage in the 19th century? Why or why not? *(Answers will vary. Possible responses: Yes. A single woman could retain more independence by having rights such as owning property, making contracts, or keeping her own wages. No. A woman's value to society was defined by her role as wife and mother, so single women were likely ostracized. Also, there were likely few professions open to women that would allow them to support themselves financially.)*

3. **Make Connections** How did Quakerism influence the fight for women's rights? *(Possible response: Quakers believed in spiritual equality and had always given women and men equal rights. Quaker women probably wanted society to reflect this same equality and so spoke out for abolition and women's rights.)*

MAKE INFERENCES

Remind students that the cult of domesticity applied mainly to middle- and upper-class women and that many of the early women's rights activists were also from these social classes. **ASK:** Why do you think this ideal wasn't applied to all women in American society? *(Possible response: Women from the lower classes were often employed out of the home because the family needed their income. They were not around to care for the family or tend to the home and had little time to participate as rights' activists or protectors of moral values. Racial prejudices excluded African-American women from this social ideal, regardless of their economic status.)*

DIFFERENTIATE

STRIVING READERS

List Subsection Facts Ask students to read each subsection of the lesson and write a list of facts they learned from each subsection. Then have partners compare their lists and fill in any facts they may have missed. Direct students to explain what each subsection was about in their own words, using their list of facts as a memory prompt.

GIFTED & TALENTED

Interview a Seneca Falls Convention Attendee Have pairs plan and write an interview with a person who attended the Seneca Falls Convention. Tell partners to conduct online research to gather details about what happened during the convention and about specific men and women who attended. Tell pairs to turn their research notes into a scripted interview. Challenge them to formulate questions that will elicit in-depth answers about what the attendee saw, heard, thought, and felt during the convention. After pairs practice their interview, invite them to record it or perform it for the class.

See the Chapter Planner for more strategies for differentiation.

They held the **Seneca Falls Convention** in July 1848. Stanton read the 12 resolutions of the declaration. Afterwards, those attending voted to pass each resolution individually. The only resolution that failed to pass was the call for women's suffrage. Many attendants felt that resolution asked for too much and might hurt their efforts to achieve their other goals. The convention ended with 68 women and 32 men signing Stanton and Mott's document.

IMPACT OF THE CONVENTION

The Seneca Falls Convention—and the declaration, when it was published—was met with considerable hostility, even from those who believed in improved rights for women. But the organizers of the convention succeeded in their major goal: calling attention to the need for women's rights in the United States.

The Seneca Falls Convention is viewed as the beginning of the women's rights movement and the organized attempt to gain women's suffrage. News of the convention spread to women's rights and reform groups across the country. Beginning with the 1850 women's rights convention in Worcester, Massachusetts, national meetings convened regularly and their goals became national talking points for the growing women's rights movement.

The work of abolitionists and women's rights activists often overlapped in the 1800s. Frederick Douglass was one of the men who attended the Seneca Falls Convention and signed the Declaration of Sentiments. He returned to Rochester, New York, where he was living, and gave the convention a positive review in his newspaper, the *North Star*. At a women's rights meeting in Akron, Ohio, in 1851, African-American abolitionist and women's rights activist Sojourner Truth addressed the audience. She told her story of escaping slavery in New York in 1826, leaving all but one of her children behind. When New York freed all enslaved people in 1827, she was reunited with most of her children. She learned that her son Peter had been sold illegally to a plantation owner in Alabama. Truth sued both Peter's former owner and the Alabama planter and won. In 1844, she joined a reform group run by abolitionists that advocated for women's rights. She soon began speaking for both causes.

In her speech, later named "Ain't I a Woman?," Truth criticized the abolitionists who failed to seek the same freedoms for both African-American men and women. She worried that when slavery ended, African-American men would receive rights and become citizens, leaving behind the cause

CRITICAL VIEWING People gather at a Respect Rally in Park City, Utah, in 2018 on the anniversary of the first Women's March, which was held on January 20, 2017. Thousands of demonstrations took place around the world on the same day in 2018. Why do you think people choose to participate in public demonstrations? Support your answer with details from the photograph.

I think that 'twixt the negroes of the South and the women at the North, all talking about rights, the white men will be in a fix pretty soon. That man over there says that women need to be helped into carriages, and lifted over ditches, and to have the best place everywhere. Nobody ever helps me into carriages, or over mud-puddles, or gives me any best place! And ain't I a woman? Look at me! Look at my arm! I have ploughed and planted, and gathered into barns, and no man could head me! And ain't I a woman? I could work as much and eat as much as a man—when I could get it—and bear the lash as well! And ain't I a woman? I have borne thirteen children, and seen most all sold off to slavery, and when I cried out with my mother's grief, none but Jesus heard me! And ain't I a woman?

—from "Ain't I a Woman?," by Sojourner Truth, 1851

for women's rights, black or white. Her speech highlighted the complex relationship among white abolitionists, white **suffragists**, or people who supported granting voting rights to women, and African Americans. White women's rights advocates generally phrased their demands for equal rights in terms of education and a broad range of freedoms, and this appeared to neglect African-American women and their needs.

Several years after the 1848 Seneca Falls Convention, Elizabeth Cady Stanton and **Susan B. Anthony** met. Like Lucretia Mott, Anthony was a Quaker, and she also began her activism with the abolition movement, working with William Lloyd Garrison. Later, she crusaded for temperance and founded the Woman's New York State Temperance Society after she was barred from speaking at a New York state Sons of Temperance meeting in 1852.

Stanton and Anthony quickly became friends and joined forces. Stanton's and Anthony's backgrounds, personalities, and strengths were different, but these differences worked together to make them a formidable team. They complemented each other, with Stanton providing the intellectual and theoretical foundations of the movement, and Anthony acting as its chief organizer, activist, and agitator. For the next 50 years, the two drove and dominated the crusade for women's rights and suffrage.

HISTORICAL THINKING

1. **READING CHECK** What rights did married women lack in the mid-1800s?

2. **DETERMINE CHRONOLOGY** What events led to Elizabeth Cady Stanton becoming a leader in the women's rights movement?

3. **MAKE INFERENCES** Why might Sojourner Truth worry that some activists would stop supporting the women's suffrage movement once African-American men won the right to vote?

4. **MAKE CONNECTIONS** Describe the connection between the abolition and women's rights movements.

BUILD BACKGROUND

SENECA FALLS CONVENTION

A small notice that appeared in the *Seneca County Courier* on July 11, 1848, served as the major publicity for a convention that is widely regarded as the formal beginning of the ongoing women's rights movement. The newspaper announcement stated that a convention to discuss women's rights would be held on Wednesday and Thursday, July 19 and 20, in the Wesleyan Chapel in Seneca Falls, New York. Although the Wednesday meeting was for women only, the general public was invited on Thursday to hear addresses by both ladies and gentlemen. The convention drew approximately 300 attendees, mostly from the local area. The first day's meeting presented the all-female audience with a discussion of the rights of women. On the second day, participants discussed the Declaration of Sentiments and Resolutions of the convention, which were defended in speeches by Elizabeth Cady Stanton and Frederick Douglass.

THE BLOOMER COSTUME

Nineteenth-century reforms extended into many aspects of women's lives, including fashion. *The Lily*, the first newspaper for women, began as a temperance publication in 1849, but editor Amelia Bloomer soon became interested in women's rights. She began publishing articles about a new outfit that became known as the "Bloomer costume." Instead of long, heavy skirts, the Bloomer costume consisted of a knee-length dress worn over loose trousers fitted at the ankle. Women's rights activists, including Elizabeth Cady Stanton and Susan B. Anthony, quickly adopted the comfortable style for public appearances. Women who wore the Bloomer outfit were severely criticized for their "masculine" attire. As a result, the costume became a short-lived fad. Many activists abandoned the Bloomer style, choosing to focus instead on the more important goals of voting rights and equal status.

TEACH

GUIDED DISCUSSION

4. **Summarize** Why did some activists feel the Declaration of Sentiments and Resolutions might ultimately hurt the women's rights movement? *(Possible response: The declaration incorporated demands for suffrage, property rights, equal education and employment, and legal status. Some activists felt the declaration was trying to do too much at once and would hurt women's ability to achieve any single goal.)*

5. **Evaluate** Do you think Frederick Douglass's participation in the Seneca Falls Convention helped or hindered the fight for women's rights? *(Answers will vary. Douglass was a well-known and respected abolitionist. His newspaper provided positive media coverage for audiences that otherwise might not have learned about the convention and the declaration. However, his race and activism in the abolitionist movement made him unpopular in the South and may have negatively impacted possible southern support of the women's rights movement.)*

ANALYZE PRIMARY SOURCES

Direct students' attention to the Primary Source feature. **ASK:** What is the primary argument Sojourner Truth is making about gender and race? *(Truth argues that African-American women face dual prejudices because of their race and gender.)* How does the title of the excerpt connect to Truth's argument? *(The title "Ain't I a Woman?" connects to the argument that because Truth was black, she was never offered the courtesies that white women were, such as being helped over a puddle. When she says the phrase, she is pointing out that in American society black women were not viewed as "women." Therefore, solving this problem would require overcoming multiple cultural barriers.)*

ACTIVE OPTIONS

Active History: Analyze Primary Sources Extend the lesson by using either the PDF or Whiteboard version of the activity. These activities take a deeper look at a topic from, or related to, the lesson. Explore the activities as a class, turn them into group assignments, or even assign them individually.

NG Learning Framework: Analyze Depictions of 19th-Century Women

SKILLS Observation, Communication

KNOWLEDGE Our Human Story

Direct students to conduct online research to find illustrations portraying 19th-century women. Instruct them to choose one illustration that depicts either the cult of domesticity or the women's rights movement. Then ask students to work in small groups to create a collage of their illustrations. Invite each group to display their collage and explain how it portrays women in the 19th century. Challenge students to identify the illustrators' points of view by asking questions such as: Are they promoting a stereotype? Are they critical or supportive? What 19th-century cultural beliefs do they reflect? Provide time for display and discussion of the collages.

HISTORICAL THINKING

ANSWERS

1. Married women lacked the right to give away or sell property. When a woman married, she deferred any property she owned to her husband. Married women could not sue, make a will, or enter into any legal contract. Neither married nor single women could vote or serve on juries.

2. Stanton helped organize the 1848 Seneca Falls Convention. She presented the Declaration of Sentiments at the convention, gaining attention from newspapers, politicians, and other women's rights groups around the country. She later met Susan B. Anthony, and together they led women's rights and suffrage movements for the next 50 years.

3. Many people did not think women's rights were important. Truth might have believed that once activists achieved the goal of enfranchising African-American men, they would give up the fight for women's suffrage.

4. Both African Americans and women lacked basic rights in American society. Women had been a major part of the abolition movement for years, learning to publicize, organize, and agitate. They brought their abilities and sentiments from that movement to the campaign for women's rights. Leading abolitionists, including Frederick Douglass, actively supported women's rights.

CRITICAL VIEWING Possible response: Large demonstrations attract media attention and can win new supporters for a cause. Displaying signs and posing for cameras are examples of how demonstrators try to get their message across to the public and, hopefully, influence people's attitudes in favor of their cause.

ELIZABETH CADY STANTON 1815–1902

"The history of the past is but one long struggle upward to equality."
—Elizabeth Cady Stanton

Elizabeth Cady Stanton certainly joined the historical struggle for equality. She fought the uphill battle for women's rights and suffrage for most of her life. Many of Stanton's views, including those on marriage and divorce, were considered radical in her time. Brave and outspoken, she often alienated others—sometimes even those on her own side—but Stanton never backed down. As she said, "The best protector any woman can have . . . is courage."

A YOUNG REBEL

At an early age, Elizabeth Cady recognized the unequal treatment accorded women. She grew up in a wealthy home in Johnstown, New York, where her father, Daniel Cady, was a prominent lawyer and statesman. Tragedy repeatedly struck the family, however, and only 4 of the 11 Cady children survived into adulthood—all daughters. After his last remaining son died, Elizabeth's father said to her, "Oh, my daughter, I wish you were a boy!" Elizabeth tried to make his wish come true. She later wrote: "I thought that the chief thing to be done in order to equal boys was to be learned and courageous. So I decided to study Greek and learn to manage a horse."

Daniel Cady probably didn't believe that women were inferior, but he was realistic about their status in society. He knew his daughter would never have the rights and

Elizabeth Cady Stanton put her views on equal rights into practice in her own marriage. At her insistence, the promise to obey her husband, which was typically included in a woman's wedding vows at that time, was removed. Stanton fought for women's political rights and their social and cultural rights.

opportunities that men enjoyed. Still, he made sure Elizabeth received the best education available to girls at that time. She attended the Johnstown Academy and graduated from Emma Willard's Troy Female Seminary in 1832. Elizabeth also gained an education by helping out in her father's law office, where she learned firsthand about the legal restrictions imposed on women. Visits to the home of her abolitionist cousin, Gerrit Smith, also opened Elizabeth's eyes. Through Smith, Elizabeth met some of the leading social and political reformers of the day.

One of these reformers was Henry Stanton. An abolitionist and ten years older than Elizabeth, Henry had donated most of his money to the fight against slavery. In spite of her father's objections, Elizabeth and Henry married in 1840. The couple decided to spend their honeymoon in London where they attended the World's Anti-Slavery Convention. It was there, as you have read, that Elizabeth Stanton met Lucretia Mott. They would soon join forces and organize their own convention at Seneca Falls.

A CONTROVERSIAL LEADER

Stanton worked with Mott at Seneca Falls, but it was with Susan B. Anthony that she forged an enduring partnership beginning in 1851. The two were an impressive political team. Stanton was the better writer and orator. While she stayed at home to care for her seven young children, she wrote pamphlets, essays, letters, and speeches for herself and for her partner. Anthony, on the other hand, had greater organizational skills. She planned meetings, distributed Stanton's pamphlets, and pressured the New York legislature to pass laws that supported women's rights.

Many of their efforts focused on marriage and divorce. Stanton called for the government to grant married women property rights. At that time, all property in a marriage belonged to the husband by law. Stanton also wanted to relax divorce laws and allow women the right to leave an unhappy marriage, which scandalized other crusading women.

As you know, Stanton was an abolitionist, and she intensified her work in the abolition movement during the Civil War. After the war, however, she criticized the 14th and 15th amendments, which granted voting rights to African-American men. Stanton believed the government should pass

CRITICAL VIEWING This cartoon ridicules the women who chose to join Stanton and Anthony's National Woman Suffrage Association. How does the cartoonist portray women who demanded the right to vote?

legislation that granted universal suffrage and so refused to support the amendments. Her stand created a rift with other abolitionists. As a result, Stanton and Anthony established the exclusively female National Woman Suffrage Association in 1869. Less radical feminists formed the American Woman Suffrage Association.

Stanton cut back on her speaking tours as she got older and focused on her writing. Together with Anthony and suffragist Matilda Joselyn Gage, Stanton wrote the *History of Woman Suffrage*, which would become a six-volume publication on the struggle for women's rights. The work helped heal the split between the two rival suffrage organizations, and they merged to form the National American Woman Suffrage Association in 1890. However, Stanton stirred controversy once again by claiming that organized religion and the teachings in the Bible discriminated against women. She enraged many people in the suffrage movement in the mid-1890s when she published her critique of biblical texts in *The Woman's Bible*. Stanton anticipated her critics by stating in that work: "Come, come, my conservative friend, wipe the dew off your spectacles, and see that the world is moving."

HISTORICAL THINKING

1. **READING CHECK** What elements of Stanton's upbringing led her to support women's rights?

2. **FORM AND SUPPORT OPINIONS** Do you think Stanton was justified in her opposition to the 14th and 15th amendments? Why or why not?

3. **EVALUATE** What did Stanton mean when she urged her critics to "see that the world is moving"?

PLAN: 2-PAGE LESSON

OBJECTIVE

Examine Elizabeth Cady Stanton's impact on the women's rights and abolition movements in the 1800s.

CRITICAL THINKING SKILLS FOR LESSON 3.2

• Form and Support Opinions

• Evaluate

• Make Connections

• Summarize

HISTORICAL THINKING FOR CHAPTER 9

How did cultural and social reform influence American society? American women had worked to gain equal rights since the foundation of the nation. Lesson 3.2 describes how Elizabeth Cady Stanton fought against slavery and for women's political, social, and cultural rights.

BACKGROUND FOR THE TEACHER

Elizabeth Cady Stanton juggled being an activist, wife, and mother—something many modern activists would understand. Because her husband traveled a great deal for the cause of abolition, Stanton raised their seven children primarily on her own. While she enjoyed her role as a mother, she also wrote in her essay "The Solitude of Self": "Accompany your children through their lives . . . but always remain an independent woman." While her children were still young, Stanton decided to run for a seat in Congress and received 24 votes, the first ever cast for a female candidate. Once her children were grown, she began traveling to promote women's rights. After Stanton's death in 1902, her daughter Harriot worked toward the passage of the 19th Amendment, ratified in 1920.

HISTORY NOTEBOOK

Encourage students to complete the American Voices page for Chapter 9 in their History Notebooks as they read.

INTRODUCE & ENGAGE

DETERMINE LEADERSHIP QUALITIES

Direct students to study the photograph of Stanton without reading the caption. **ASK:** What qualities of Stanton does the photo convey? *(Possible response: Her direct gaze suggests determination, intelligence, fearlessness, and a strong sense of self. The cross on her necklace suggests strong Christian values.)* Then tell students to read the caption. **ASK:** Based on this information, what qualities might Stanton bring as a leader and organizer? *(Possible response: courage, willingness to break social norms, perhaps too radical for some people, honesty)* Elicit from students the qualities they think make a great leader. After reading the lesson, ask students to state the specific qualities that made Stanton so effective.

TEACH

GUIDED DISCUSSION

1. **Make Connections** Why do you think Stanton worked for the abolition of slavery as well as for women's rights? *(Possible response: She probably saw a link between the political and legal rights denied enslaved people and those denied women.)*

2. **Summarize** In what ways did Stanton's tendency to speak her mind both help and hurt her as a leader? *(Possible response: It helped her define what rights women should have, persuade others to support her causes, and even get legislation passed in New York. Speaking her mind about marriage, the 14th and 15th Amendments, and ideas expressed in the Bible undermined her leadership, alienating some women and men who might have joined her.)*

AMERICAN VOICES

Direct students' attention to Stanton's statements about courage: "The best protector any woman can have . . . is courage," and "I thought that the chief thing to be done in order to equal boys was to be learned and courageous." **ASK:** What do you think Stanton meant by *courage?* *(Possible response: Stanton probably meant the ability to challenge society on behalf of herself and other women and to stand firm in her own beliefs, regardless of the consequences.)*

ACTIVE OPTIONS

On Your Feet: Four Corners Post the following signs in different sections of the classroom: Work, Sports, Politics, Entertainment. Organize the class into groups around each sign. Tell students in each group to write about what women have achieved in this area in the 20th and 21st centuries, and what women of the 19th century might think about these achievements. Ask students to discuss their responses with the group. Then call on one or two students from each group to share ideas from the group's discussion.

NG Learning Framework: Write a Speech

ATTITUDE Responsibility

SKILLS Communication, Problem-Solving

Ask students to work in groups to write a speech about a present-day women's rights issue, such as equal pay or career advancement, in the style and tone of Elizabeth Cady Stanton. Direct groups to use online or library resources to locate Stanton's speeches or articles in order to familiarize themselves with her expression and phrasing. Encourage them to offer a solution for the issue and to conclude with a call to action. Invite groups to deliver their speeches to the class.

DIFFERENTIATE

ENGLISH LANGUAGE LEARNERS `ELD`

Use a Definition Chart Pair students at the **Emerging** level with students at the **Expanding** and **Bridging** levels. Ask pairs to work together to create a Definition Chart for words they struggle with in the lesson. Direct pairs to trade Definition Charts, review them, and then work together to write a sentence using each word. You may invite students to discuss how the words help them understand Stanton's ideas and accomplishments.

GIFTED & TALENTED

Create a Meme Challenge students to create a meme using a quotation by Stanton. Tell them to conduct online research to locate and read Stanton's quotations, select one that resonates with them, and then use conventional materials or a computer graphics program to create the meme. Have students present their memes to the class and explain the reasons for choosing their quotations and visuals.

See the Chapter Planner for more strategies for differentiation.

HISTORICAL THINKING

ANSWERS

1. She knew her father wished she were a son, so she learned skills beyond the limits of her gender. Her father made sure she received a good education, and while working at her father's law practice, she observed that many laws were biased against women.

2. Possible responses: Yes. Again women's rights had been ignored, and she could not in good conscience support the amendments. No. She should have supported the amendments as a triumph of the abolition movement and a step in the right direction for universal suffrage.

3. Possible response: Stanton meant that society was changing and religion needed to change with it in order to erase the bias against women in religion and society.

CRITICAL VIEWING All the women are depicted as unattractive or behaving in an unwomanly manner, including dominating men ("man-tamer" poster), being free of family obligations (woman glaring and gesturing at the man holding a baby), dressing in a provocative manner (woman showing her legs below the knee), and smoking.

THE SENECA FALLS CONVENTION

As the 19th century progressed, women played huge roles in reform movements that took hold in the United States. They held meetings, gave talks, protested, and generally helped raise awareness about abolition, temperance, the needs of the poor and mentally ill, and many other issues in society. But by mid-century, the women who played leading roles in attempting to help others faced another problem within U.S. society—the subordinate, or lesser, role of women. Their work in previous reform movements armed them with tools to take action.

On July 19, 1948, the United States issued a three-cent stamp commemorating the first women's rights convention at Seneca Falls, New York, and celebrating the 100 years of progress toward equality made by women following the convention. Featured on the stamp were three 19th-century activists and reformers, Elizabeth Stanton, Carrie Chapman Catt, and Lucretia Mott. Besides serving a practical purpose, postage stamps are sometimes valuable to historians for the cultural and historical insights they contain.

CRITICAL VIEWING If you were a historian, what would this stamp tell you about how people in 1948 thought about the Seneca Falls convention of 1848? Include information about the three women portrayed on the stamp in your answer.

UNITED STATES POSTAGE

ELIZABETH STANTON · CARRIE C. CATT · LUCRETIA MOTT

3¢ 100 YEARS OF PROGRESS 1848 OF WOMEN 1948 3¢

DOCUMENT ONE

Primary Source: Historic Document
from the Declaration of Sentiments,
by Lucretia Mott and Elizabeth Cady Stanton, July 20, 1848

Mott and Stanton issued the Declaration of Sentiments and Resolutions at the Seneca Falls Convention in New York. It begins by echoing the Declaration of Independence to establish that women should have the same rights as men. This excerpt is from the Declaration of Sentiments, a pointed list of women's grievances against men.

CONSTRUCTED RESPONSE Why do you think the right to vote is listed as the first grievance? Explain.

Declaration of Sentiments

He has never permitted her to exercise her inalienable right to the elective franchise [right to vote].

He has compelled her to submit to laws, in the formation of which she had no voice.

He has made her, if married, in the eye of the law, civilly dead.

He has taken from her all right in property, even to the wages she earns.

He has denied her the facilities for obtaining a thorough education— . . .

He has endeavored, in every way that he could to destroy her confidence in her own powers . . .

DOCUMENT TWO

Primary Source: Newspaper Article
from "Women Out of Their Latitude," the *Mechanic's Advocate*, August 12, 1848

The reaction to the Seneca Falls Convention and the Declaration of Sentiments and Resolutions was mostly negative and often dismissive or condescending. This newspaper article is a typical example of these reactions, making reference to both the concept of proper "womanliness" and the Bible.

CONSTRUCTED RESPONSE What part of this writer's critique of the convention might the organizers actually agree with? Explain.

The women who attend these meetings, no doubt at the expense of their more appropriate duties. . . . affirm, as among their rights, that of unrestricted franchise [right to vote], and assert that it is wrong to deprive them of the privilege to become legislators, lawyers, doctors, divines [members of the clergy].

Now, it requires no argument to prove that this is all wrong. Every true hearted female will instantly feel that this is unwomanly. Society would have to be radically remodeled . . . and the order of things established at the creation of mankind . . . would be completely broken up.

DOCUMENT THREE

Primary Source: Speech
from "Solitude of Self," by Elizabeth Cady Stanton, January 18, 1892

After the 1848 Women's Rights Convention at Seneca Falls, Elizabeth Cady Stanton continued her work for women's suffrage. For more than 20 years, she led suffrage organizations, including the National American Woman Suffrage Association. This excerpt is from her resignation speech from that group, 28 years before the 19th Amendment guaranteed women the right to vote in 1920.

CONSTRUCTED RESPONSE What overall effect does Stanton believe the contemporary state of women's rights in 1892 was having on American women?

To throw obstacle in the way of a complete education is like putting out the eyes; to deny the rights of property, like cutting off the hands. To deny political equality is to rob the ostracized of all self-respect; of credit in the market place; of recompense in the world of work; of a voice among those who make and administer the law; a choice in the jury before whom they are tried, and in the judge who decides their punishment.

SYNTHESIZE & WRITE

1. **REVIEW** Review what you have learned about the reasons and theories behind the movement for improved women's rights in the mid-1800s.

2. **RECALL** List the main ideas about the women's rights movement expressed in the three documents.

3. **CONSTRUCT** Construct a topic sentence that answers this question: Why did American women campaign for increased rights?

4. **WRITE** Using evidence from the chapter and the documents, write an informative paragraph that supports your topic sentence in Step 3.

PLAN: 2-PAGE LESSON

OBJECTIVE

Synthesize information about the Seneca Falls Convention and the women's rights movement from primary source documents.

CRITICAL THINKING SKILLS FOR LESSON 3.3

- Synthesize
- Make Inferences
- Analyze Language Use
- Evaluate

HISTORICAL THINKING FOR CHAPTER 9

How did cultural and social reform influence American society? Women's attempts to gain equal rights were well organized but met with fierce opposition. Lesson 3.3 examines primary sources that express women's grievances and a reaction to their reform movement.

BACKGROUND FOR THE TEACHER

The Seneca Falls Convention caused controversy not only in 1848 but in 1997 as well, as the convention's 150th anniversary was coming up the following year. Many people took offense when the U.S. Postal Service refused to issue a commemorative stamp in honor of the anniversary. Supporters of the stamp considered the convention second only to ratification of the 19th Amendment in importance to the women's movement, equated the Declaration of Sentiments with the Declaration of Independence, and insisted that the Seneca Falls Convention merited recognition of its historic significance. Despite their letters and appeals, the Postal Service maintained its position, citing many past examples of stamps that honored women's achievements. These included the 1948 stamp that commemorated 100 years of women's progress, a 1995 stamp honoring women's suffrage, and more than 80 stamps celebrating individuals who contributed to the women's rights movement.

INTRODUCE & ENGAGE

PREPARE FOR THE DOCUMENT-BASED QUESTION

Before students start on the activity, briefly preview the three documents. Remind students that a constructed response requires full explanations in complete sentences. Emphasize that students should use what they have learned about the Seneca Falls Convention and the women's rights movement during the 19th century in addition to the information in the documents.

TEACH

GUIDED DISCUSSION

1. **Make Inferences** Why do you think the Seneca Falls Convention and the Declaration of Sentiments provoked a mostly negative reaction? *(Possible response: The convention threatened the "natural order" of 19th-century society, which relegated women to the home and assigned political and economic power to men. In addition, the entire social order would have to be overhauled to accommodate the demands of women's rights advocates.)*

2. **Analyze Language Use** What is the effect of Elizabeth Cady Stanton's use of similes in the first sentence of her speech? *(The similes equate the effect of the loss of rights experienced by women with the loss of their sight and hands, which is a more dramatic way to make people think about the impact of inequality on women's lives.)*

EVALUATE

After students have completed the Synthesize & Write activity, allow time for them to exchange paragraphs and read and comment on the work of their peers. Establish guidelines for comments prior to the activity so that feedback is constructive and encouraging in nature. Comments should focus on the most significant parts that address the purpose of the activity and the audience.

ACTIVE OPTION

On Your Feet: Host a DBQ Roundtable Discuss with the class some of the current women's issues they know about. Then divide the class into groups of four. Hand each group a sheet of paper with the following question: How similar are current women's issues, and the reactions to them, to those of the 19th century? Instruct the first student in each group to write an answer, read it aloud, and pass the paper clockwise to the next student. The paper may circulate around the table several times. Then reconvene the class and discuss the groups' responses.

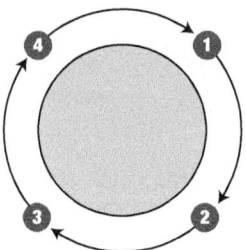

DIFFERENTIATE

INCLUSION

Highlight and Summarize Help students with attention issues minimize distractions by creating a handout that includes only the three document excerpts. Give a copy to each student along with a highlighter. Provide a brief introduction to each document, then read the excerpt aloud. Tell students to follow along and highlight important words and ideas as you read. Instruct them to write a summary sentence for each excerpt, using several of the words and phrases they highlighted. Invite students to share and discuss their summaries.

GIFTED & TALENTED

Research and Role-Play Tell students to conduct online research to find out more about Carrie Chapman Catt, who is featured on the postage stamp in the lesson. Encourage students to locate primary source documents as well as other information. Then have them use what they learn to role-play a talk show in which Carrie Chapman Catt, Elizabeth Cady Stanton, and Lucretia Mott are interviewed by the host to respond to the writer of the newspaper article "Women Out of Their Latitude." Invite students to perform their role-play for the class.

See the Chapter Planner for more strategies for differentiation.

SYNTHESIZE & WRITE

ANSWERS

1. Answers will vary.

2. Answers will vary. Possible responses: A male-dominated society has denied women their basic rights. Granting women the rights they demand would upset the natural order of society. Creating obstacles to equality is comparable to physically crippling women.

3. Possible response: American women realized that the lack of full political and social equality with men obstructed their development as individuals and responsible citizens.

4. Students' paragraphs should include details from the documents to support their topic sentence from Step 3.

CONSTRUCTED RESPONSE

Document 1: If women gained the right to vote, they could elect lawmakers who supported their causes, and they could influence local and national legislation.

Document 2: The organizers would likely agree with the assertion that the attendees wanted the right to vote, to participate in professional fields, and to radically remodel society.

Document 3: Stanton believes the limitations placed on American women are crippling their ability to educate themselves and depriving them of property, self-respect, and the ability to participate fully in society.

CRITICAL VIEWING The 1948 stamp would indicate that people in the 20th century honored the convention at Seneca Falls because it formally began the women's rights movement. Stanton, Catt, and Mott are being recognized for their leading roles in planning and organizing the convention and for their work on behalf of women's rights.

9 REVIEW

VOCABULARY

Use each of the following terms in a sentence that shows an understanding of the term's meaning.

1. **Romanticism**
   Followers of Romanticism rejected logic in favor of emotion.

2. penitentiary
3. suffragist
4. labor union
5. stewardship
6. temperance movement
7. gag rule
8. transcendentalism
9. emancipation

READING STRATEGY
MAKE INFERENCES

When you make inferences, you use what you already know to understand the meaning of a text. Use a chart like the one below to make inferences about how the era's social and cultural reforms influenced America. Then answer the question.

I Read	I Know	And So
"Americans seemed to fear that their society was becoming less unified."	People can react strongly to change and disunity.	An upsurge in religious zeal, the Second Great Awakening, took hold.

10. What changes did the era's social and cultural reforms make to American society?

MAIN IDEAS

Answer the following questions. Support your answers with evidence from the chapter.

11. Where did the Second Great Awakening have its geographical roots? **LESSON 1.1**

12. What overall outcome did Dorothea Dix hope for in her movement to help the mentally ill and those who were imprisoned? **LESSON 1.1**

13. What set John James Audubon apart from the painters of the Hudson River School? **LESSON 1.2**

14. Why might it be to a slave owner's advantage to use one of his slaves as a driver? **LESSON 2.1**

15. What role did violence play in the running of a plantation? **LESSON 2.1**

16. Why did the speeches of Frederick Douglass and the sisters Angelina and Sarah Grimké carry more significance for some northerners than those of other white abolitionists? **LESSON 2.2**

17. Explain the ways in which former president John Quincy Adams contributed to the abolitionist movement. **LESSON 2.2**

18. How was the legal status of men and women both similar and different in the mid-1800s? **LESSON 3.1**

19. How did the cult of domesticity influence the women's rights movement? **LESSON 3.1**

HISTORICAL THINKING

Answer the following questions. Support your answers with evidence from the chapter.

20. **FORM AND SUPPORT OPINIONS** In what ways do you think Charles Grandison Finney epitomized the spirit of not only the Second Great Awakening but also of the reform era?

21. **ANALYZE CAUSE AND EFFECT** What methods did members of the temperance movement use to try to persuade people to refuse or drink less alcohol?

22. **MAKE CONNECTIONS** Explain how Romanticism and transcendentalism are related to each other.

23. **DRAW CONCLUSIONS** Which of the middle-class reform movements do you think had the most concrete, long-lasting effect on U.S. society? Explain.

INTERPRET VISUALS

George Catlin is famous for his paintings of Native Americans and their lives and cultures in the early 1800s. Look closely at his painting *Buffalo Chase, a Single Death*. Use your observation of the painting and information from the chapter to answer the questions that follow.

24. How does this painting illustrate the contribution George Catlin made to the development of uniquely American art forms?

25. In what ways does Catlin's painting reflect the ideas of Romanticism and transcendentalism?

ANALYZE SOURCES

Elizabeth Cady Stanton was in many ways well ahead of her time. In this quotation from her book, *The Woman's Bible*, published in 1895 and 1898, she expresses a desire for equality between men and women that many would argue has still not been achieved to this day.

> We should give to our rulers, our sires and sons no rest until all our rights—social, civil and political—are fully accorded. How are men to know what we want unless we tell them? They have no idea that our wants, material and spiritual, are the same as theirs; that we love justice, liberty and equality as well as they do; that we believe in the principles of self-government, in individual rights, individual conscience and judgment, the fundamental ideas of the Protestant religion and republican government.

26. In what ways does this quotation from Elizabeth Cady Stanton echo the motives and tactics of the Second Great Awakening and the middle-class reforms that followed?

CONNECT TO YOUR LIFE

27. **EXPOSITORY** Think about the movement for women's rights that had its beginnings in the era of reform and the fact that this movement is ongoing today. Write a paragraph that discusses the progress of the movement over time and its status today.

TIPS
- Introduce the topic with a clear main idea statement concerning your assessment of the progress of women's rights over time.
- Use textual evidence from the chapter to highlight the ways in which U.S. society and government limited women's rights at the time the movement began.
- Summarize which of these limitations have been done away with.
- Include at least two areas in which U.S. society still falls short of giving equal rights to women.
- Provide a concluding statement that follows from and supports the ideas and information you have presented.

VOCABULARY ANSWERS

1. Followers of Romanticism rejected logic in favor of emotion.

2. Convicted criminals are often locked up in a penitentiary.

3. The suffragist movement continued to work for women's right to vote, despite heavy resistance.

4. A labor union gives workers more power to bargain with management for better wages and working conditions.

5. Slaveholders claimed their stewardship improved the lives of enslaved African Americans through the care they provided.

6. Supporters of the temperance movement pressured the government to outlaw the sale of alcohol.

7. The gag rule allowed Congress to avoid confronting the issue of slavery by refusing to read abolitionists' petitions.

8. Henry David Thoreau embraced transcendentalism when he found inspiration in nature from living at Walden Pond.

9. Some abolitionists wanted slaveholders to grant emancipation to their enslaved workers and hire them for pay as freed workers.

READING STRATEGY ANSWER

I Read	I Know	And So
"Just as Americans could not agree on the subject of slavery, abolitionists themselves differed on how to react to the opposition they faced."	Splits within a movement can interfere with its success.	Opposing opinions caused Congress to enact a gag rule by which they avoided taking action on slavery.
"The Seneca Falls Convention—and the declaration, when it was published—was met with considerable hostility, even from those who believed in improved rights for women."	People may be reluctant to accept too many changes at one time.	The campaign for women's rights continued for decades before it achieved success.

10. Social and cultural reforms, often organized by middle-class women, addressed alcohol addiction, established free public education, and improved conditions for prisoners, the mentally ill, and workers in industry.

MAIN IDEAS ANSWERS

11. As with the First Great Awakening, the roots of the Second Great Awakening were in the revival camps in the wilderness and in the women's prayer groups held in frontier homes and churches.

12. Dix hoped to help people whom society had forgotten. She sought cleaner, healthier, and safer places for the care of the mentally ill and improved living conditions for the poor and imprisoned.

13. Hudson River School painters focused on American landscapes that they often romanticized, whereas Audubon focused on creating precise and detailed records of American birds.

14. Enslaved people might be more willing to take directions from someone they liked or trusted, which would improve the efficiency of work on a plantation.

15. Many plantation owners and their overseers used violence, including whippings, beatings, and even sexual assaults, to force enslaved people to work.

16. They had firsthand knowledge of the dehumanizing nature of slavery: Douglass was a former enslaved person, and the Grimké sisters were the daughters of a plantation owner and had developed a hatred of the institution of slavery.

17. As a congressman from Massachusetts, John Quincy Adams helped to overthrow the gag rule that kept Congress from recognizing antislavery petitions. He served as legal counsel for Africans who had seized control of the slave ship *Amistad*, helping them win their freedom.

18. In the mid-1800s, single women could own property and make contracts like men. However, married women surrendered their property and wages to their husbands and could not enter into contracts, sue someone, or make wills.

19. Some women began to resent the restrictions the cult of domesticity imposed on their lives. In addition, middle-class women began to have free time, which led them to be more active in community affairs. These circumstances allowed women to become involved in reform movements, including women's rights.

HISTORICAL THINKING ANSWERS

20. Finney became a preacher to reform and change society. His sermons connected with everyday people and inspired them to make changes in their communities. His message that individuals could find salvation through their own actions mirrored the reform spirit of the era.

21. In addition to linking alcohol with immoral behavior, temperance reformists focused on exposing the effects of alcohol: damaged health, impoverished families, and weak job performance.

22. Ralph Waldo Emerson, a leading transcendentalist, took inspiration from Romanticism. Romanticism's emphasis on imagination, emotion, and action fit well with transcendentalism's emphasis on finding inspiration in nature.

23. Answers will vary. Possible response: The movement for universal public education probably had the longest-lasting effect on society. It led the way for all children in the United States to receive a free public education and for teaching to become a standardized profession.

INTERPRET VISUALS ANSWERS

24. Catlin depicted Native Americans of the Great Plains in their surroundings, which included native species, such as the American bison, and the grasslands.

25. Catlin's painting of Native Americans involved in a buffalo hunt reflects Romanticism by emphasizing action. It also reflects transcendentalism by highlighting nature and showcasing the American landscape and animal life.

ANALYZE SOURCES ANSWER

26. Stanton combines spiritual needs with social reform. She calls for action by prodding women to give men no rest until they understand that women's needs for social, civil, and political rights are equal to their own. Her sentiments echo the reform movement's zeal and belief that individuals have a responsibility to help people and change society for the better.

CONNECT TO YOUR LIFE ANSWER

27. Paragraphs will vary but should introduce the topic with a clear main idea statement concerning students' assessment of the progress of women's rights over time, use text evidence to highlight how U.S. society and government limited women's rights at the beginning of the movement, summarize which limitation has been eliminated, include at least two areas in which U.S. society still falls short of giving equal rights to women, and provide a concluding statement that follows from and supports the ideas and information presented.

UNIT 3 RESOURCES

UNIT INTRODUCTION

UNIT TIME LINE

UNIT WRAP-UP

NATIONAL GEOGRAPHIC | CONNECTION

National Geographic Magazine Adapted Articles
- "Nat Turner's Complex Legacy"
- "The Way West" ONLINE

Unit 3 Inquiry: Document a Migration

NG Learning Framework Activities
- Depict Nature
- Create Slogans to Promote Reforms

Unit 3 Formal Assessment

CHAPTER 10 RESOURCES

Available at NGLSync.Cengage.com

TEACHER RESOURCES & ASSESSMENT

Reading and Note-Taking

Vocabulary Practice

Social Studies Skills Lessons
- Reading: Analyze Cause and Effect
- Writing: Argument

Formal Assessment
- Chapter 10 Pretest
- Chapter 10 Tests A & B
- Section Quizzes

Chapter 10 Answer Key

ExamView®
One-time Download

STUDENT DIGITAL RESOURCES

- eEdition
- Handbooks
- Online Atlas
- American Gallery Online
- History Notebook
- Active History
- American Voices (Biographies)
- Reid on the Road video series
- Literature Analysis
- Projects for Inquiry-Based Learning

Chapter 10 Spanish Resources are available at NGLSync.Cengage.com.

AMERICAN STORIES | Chicano History and Culture

- Study Primary Sources: Excerpts from interviews with Sandra Cisneros
- On Your Feet: Compare Immigration Plans

  NG Learning Framework:
  Depict the Influence of Mexican Americans

SECTION 1 RESOURCES
MANIFEST DESTINY

LESSON 1.1
The Call of the West

- Active History: Illustrate the Rain Shadow Effect

  NG Learning Framework:
  Chart a Western Trail

  American Voices Biographies
  Brigham Young and Joseph Smith ONLINE

LESSON 1.2
THROUGH THE LENS
Michael Nichols

- On Your Feet: Fishbowl

  NG Learning Framework:
  Create a Composite Photograph

LESSON 1.3
Pioneers and Native Americans

- On Your Feet: Create a Quiz

  NG Learning Framework:
  Investigate How Tribes Adapted to Indian Territory

SECTION 2 RESOURCES
THE TEXAS REVOLUTION

LESSON 2.1
Settling the Southwest

- On Your Feet: Jigsaw

  NG Learning Framework:
  Create a Classroom Resource

LESSON 2.2
Texas Fights for Independence

- On Your Feet: Generate a Cause-and-Effect Chain

  NG Learning Framework:
  Research the Defenders of the Alamo

  American Voices Biography
  Sam Houston ONLINE

LESSON 2.3
CURATING HISTORY
Mexic-Arte Museum Austin, Texas

- On Your Feet: Sort the Artifacts

SECTION 3 RESOURCES
THE MEXICAN-AMERICAN WAR

LESSON 3.1
Tensions with Mexico

- On Your Feet: Analyze Character Traits

  NG Learning Framework:
  Take a Stand on the War

LESSON 3.2
Waging War in the Southwest

- On Your Feet: Examine the Benefits of Acquiring Territory

  NG Learning Framework:
  Compare Artistic Depictions

SECTION 4 RESOURCES
CALIFORNIA: THE GOLDEN STATE

LESSON 4.1
Settling California

- On Your Feet: Explore California's History

  NG Learning Framework:
  Investigate Mission Histories

LESSON 4.2
The Gold Rush

- ▶ The Gold Rush

  AMERICAN GALLERY ONLINE The Gold Rush

  NG Learning Framework:
  Evaluate Primary Sources

LESSON 4.3
GEOLOGY IN HISTORY
How Geology Built the Transcontinental Railroad

- On Your Feet: Team Word Webbing

  NG Learning Framework:
  Investigate Construction Problems and Solutions

CHAPTER 10 REVIEW

STRIVING READERS

STRATEGY 1
CREATE IDEA WEBS

Guide students to summarize the chapter by creating an Idea Web for each section. Tell them to write the section titles in each square: Manifest Destiny, The Texas Revolution, The Mexican-American War, California: The Golden State. Instruct students to complete each Idea Web with relevant information as they read each section's lessons.

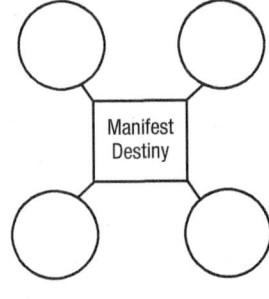

Use with All Lessons *For example, for Manifest Destiny, students may add the following information: Large numbers of people migrated west; people used the idea of manifest destiny to allow them to take Native American lands; the journey west was difficult and often dangerous; Native Americans were pushed off their lands by the federal government.*

STRATEGY 2
USE RECIPROCAL TEACHING

Tell partners to take turns reading each paragraph of the lesson aloud. Instruct the reading student to ask the listening student questions about the text at the end of the paragraph. Students may ask their partner to state the main idea, identify important details that support the main idea, or summarize the paragraph in their own words. Then have students work together to answer the Historical Thinking questions.

Use with All Lessons

STRATEGY 3
UNDERSTAND MAIN IDEAS

Direct students to read the Main Idea statements aloud. Explain that these statements identify and summarize the lesson's key idea. As students read, encourage them to find details in the text that connect to the Main Idea statements and to record them in a Main Idea and Details List. Explain that this process will help them identify and remember the most important information.

Main Idea:
Detail:
Detail:
Detail:
Detail:
Detail:

Use with All Lessons

INCLUSION

STRATEGY 1
PREDICT USING VISUALS AND CAPTIONS

Pair students with classmates who can assist in previewing the lesson. Tell the assisting student to describe the photographs, artwork, maps, and other visuals and read the captions. Then have pairs work together to write predictions about what they think they will learn in the lesson. After students read the lesson, encourage them to confirm or revise their predictions to reflect what they learned.

Use with All Lessons

STRATEGY 2
USE SUPPORTED READING

Assign pairs of students selected paragraphs to read aloud together. At the end of each paragraph, have students use the following sentence frames to identify what they do and do not understand:

- This paragraph is about _____.
- One fact that stood out to me was _____.
- I had trouble understanding _____, so I tried to figure it out by _____.

Confirm that all students understand the content before moving on to the next paragraph. When they have completed the lesson, tell them to use these sentence frames to demonstrate comprehension:

- This lesson is mostly about _____.
- It also contains information about _____ and _____.

Use with All Lessons

ENGLISH LANGUAGE LEARNERS

STRATEGY 1
USE A TERM IN A SENTENCE

Pair students at the **Emerging** level with those at the **Expanding** or **Bridging** level. Instruct pairs to work together to compose a sentence using selected Key Vocabulary terms, names, and places. Ask the more proficient students to assist their partner in checking the accuracy of the sentences. Invite pairs to share their sentences and discuss different ways to use each word or term.

Use with All Lessons

STRATEGY 2
IDENTIFY COGNATES

Suggest that as students read they look for words that are similar in spelling and meaning to words in their home language. For each word they identify, have students at **All Proficiencies** make a vocabulary card with the English word and definition on one side and the word and definition in their home language on the reverse. Encourage them to note differences in the meanings of the two words.

Use with All Lessons *For example, in Lesson 2.2, the words* immigration, dictator, revolution, *and* independence *have Spanish cognates:* inmigración, dictador, revolución, *and* independencia.

STRATEGY 3
CREATE WORD SQUARES

Arrange students at **All Proficiencies** in mixed pairs and direct them to work together to identify at least three Key Vocabulary words or terms from the lesson that they have difficulty understanding. Instruct partners to create Word Squares for each word or term and then trade them with another pair. Encourage pairs to ask and answer questions about the information they included.

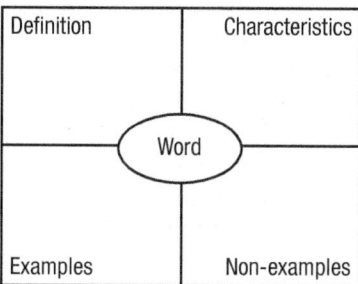

Use with All Lessons

GIFTED & TALENTED

STRATEGY 1
TEACH A CLASS

Allow students to choose one of the lessons in this chapter and prepare to teach the content to the class. Suggest that students think about any visuals or activities they want to use as they teach. Give them a set amount of time in which to present their lesson.

Use with All Lessons

STRATEGY 2
WRITE A LETTER HOME

Tell students to imagine that they participated in the gold rush. Instruct them to write a letter to a friend or family member about their journey to California, their challenges along the way, and whether their prospecting was successful. Before students write their letter, tell them to conduct online research to learn more about the overland and sea routes people took to California in the mid-1800s, the conditions and life in the boomtowns, and the various successes and failures of prospectors. Have students post their letters on a class blog or read them to the class.

Use with Lesson 4.2

PRE-AP

STRATEGY 1
EXPLAIN THE SIGNIFICANCE OF A TERM

Invite students to choose one term below as the focus of a class presentation. Direct them to design and deliver an oral presentation that explains the significance of the term in the history of westward expansion. Encourage students to provide a visual, such as an infographic, to enhance their presentation.

mountain men	prairie schooner	presidio
manifest destiny	*empresario*	rancho
Mormon Trail	Tejanos	forty-niner
Pueblo Revolt	annexation	transcontinental railroad

Use with Lessons 1.1, 1.3, 2.1, 2.2, 3.2, and 4.1–4.3

STRATEGY 2
REPORT ON RAILROAD WORKERS

Direct students to gather information from library or online sources to write a report about Chinese laborers on the transcontinental railroad. Suggest that they focus on specific details, such as the number of Chinese workers, their hours and pay compared with workers of European descent, and their lives after the railroad was completed. Invite students to share their reports with the class.

Use with Lesson 4.3

10 WESTWARD EXPANSION

1830–1854

HISTORICAL THINKING How did the idea of manifest destiny shape the future of the United States?

"The expansive future is our arena."

—John O'Sullivan, newspaper editor

As the United States expanded westward, it gained such natural treasures as these huge sandstone pillars in Utah's Valley of the Gods. Adjacent to Bears Ears National Monument, Valley of the Gods is protected public land managed by the Bureau of Land Management. In 2017, the U.S. government reduced the size of Bears Ears by 85 percent to allow natural resources to be extracted from the land.

For Chapter 10 Spanish Resources, visit the Resources Menu. Chapter 10 Resources are available at NGLSync.Cengage.com.

INTRODUCE THE PHOTOGRAPH

WESTWARD EXPANSION

Have students study the photograph and quotation. **ASK:** How do the photograph and quotation relate to one another? *(Possible response: The quotation suggests that the future of the United States will play out in the open land to the west. The photograph illustrates this point by presenting a huge stretch of western land.)* Point out that as a newspaper editor, John O'Sullivan would have had a wide audience for his views. Prompt students to discuss what O'Sullivan meant by *arena* and why people might have shared his view. *(Possible response: By* arena, *O'Sullivan may have meant that there was a competition to be won or something to display in the future as a result of expansion to the west. Some people might have considered moving to the undeveloped West as an opportunity to live as they chose and create their own futures in this new arena.)* Tell students that in this chapter they will learn why Americans in the 1840s increasingly pushed westward and the impact this expansion had on the nation.

SHARE BACKGROUND

The federal government's decision to vastly reduce the size of Bears Ears National Monument overturned more than 100 years of conservation work. Bears Ears is the ancestral home of several Native American tribes and features tens of thousands of archaeological sites, including petroglyphs, pictographs, cliff dwellings, and graves. In 1903, archaeologists began to push for protection. Preservation efforts gained momentum during Barack Obama's presidency, when representatives from Utah's five tribes, whose ancestors lived on the land, proposed designating the region a national monument to protect it from development. In December 2016, President Obama established the 1.35-million-acre Bears Ears National Monument. The decision immediately sparked controversy, with critics calling it a massive land grab and an overreach of executive authority. President Donald Trump's decision to reduce the size of the monument went into effect on February 2, 2017.

HISTORICAL THINKING QUESTION

How did the idea of manifest destiny shape the future of the United States?

Numbered Heads Activity: The Role of Expansion Divide the class into groups of four and have students count off within each group. Pose the following question: Based on what you've already learned, what role has expansion played in the history of the United States? Instruct group members to think about the question individually and then discuss their answers. Tell students that many people believed it was God's will for the United States to spread across all of North America. Ask group members to discuss and predict the impact this view might have on the United States in the 1840s. Call out a number and invite the person with that number in each group to summarize the group's discussion for the class.

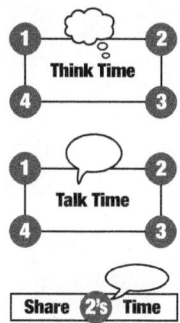

INTRODUCE THE READING STRATEGY

ANALYZE CAUSE AND EFFECT

Explain that analyzing cause and effect can help students understand the complexity of historical events and their multiple causes and effects. Turn to the Chapter Review and preview the graphic organizer with students. As they read the chapter, tell students to analyze and record the causes and effects of events during the era of westward expansion.

KEY DATES FOR CHAPTER 10

1830	Indian Removal Act relocates Native Americans
1836	Texas declares independence
1845	John O'Sullivan coins the term *manifest destiny*
1845	The United States annexes Texas as a slave state
1846	Mexican-American War begins
1848	Treaty of Guadalupe Hidalgo is signed
1848	Discovery of gold at John Sutter's mill
1850	California becomes a free state

INTRODUCE CHAPTER VOCABULARY

KEY VOCABULARY

SECTION 1

| manifest destiny | mountain men | prairie schooner |

SECTION 2

| annexation | empresario | *vaquero* |

SECTION 3

| amphibious force | dark horse | presidio |
| contiguous | insurrection | |

SECTION 4

boomtown	mountain pass	topography
entrepreneur	prospector	transcontinental railroad
forty-niner	rancho	

DEFINITION CHART

As students read the chapter, tell them to complete a Definition Chart for Key Vocabulary words. Instruct them to list the words in the left column of the chart. Then, as they encounter each word, they write the word's definition in the center column and what the word means, in their own words, in the last column. Model an example using the graphic organizer below.

Word	Definition	In My Own Words
entrepreneur	a person who starts, manages, and is responsible for a business	a person who begins and owns a business

OBJECTIVES

- **Assess how historical events have impacted Mexicans immigrating to the United States.**
- **Analyze how Mexicans have influenced American history and cultural traditions.**
- **Evaluate the issues surrounding current immigration policy.**
- **Study a primary source: excerpts from interviews with Sandra Cisneros.**

CRITICAL THINKING SKILLS FOR "CHICANO HISTORY AND CULTURE"

- Make Connections
- Draw Conclusions
- Compare and Contrast
- Form and Support Opinions
- Analyze Cause and Effect
- Interpret Maps
- Make Inferences

CONNECT TO THE CHAPTER

This American Story explores Chicano history and culture. Before the United States spanned North America to the Pacific Ocean, much of the Southwest was part of Spain, and then Mexico, and home to people with unique histories and cultures—now referred to as "Chicano." By studying an absorbing narrative that includes primary sources, maps, charts, and photographs, students will understand how an often overlooked and sometimes disrespected people have helped shape the United States.

This chapter, Westward Expansion, explores America's era of manifest destiny—a time when thousands pushed westward into territory inhabited by Native Americans and Mexicans. Some Mexicans eventually became American citizens when the border of the United States was extended farther south. Introduce this American Story after completing the chapter, as it provides insight into how expansionism altered the cultural makeup of the nation.

HISTORY NOTEBOOK

Encourage students to complete the American Story page for Chapter 10 in their History Notebooks as they read.

AMERICAN STORIES

NATIONAL GEOGRAPHIC

CHICANO
HISTORY AND CULTURE

CRITICAL VIEWING Vehicles draped in Mexican flags and banners are a familiar sight at the annual Cinco de Mayo parade in Modesto, California. What impressions of Chicano culture do you gain from the photo?

304 CHAPTER 10

In 1821, Mexico was the largest country in North America, reaching well into what is now the northern United States. Newly independent from Spain, Mexico was nearly twice the size it is today. It encompassed territories that include parts or all of the present-day states of California, Utah, Nevada, Colorado, Wyoming, New Mexico, Oklahoma, and Arizona.

Away from the Pacific Coast, the land north of the Rio Grande was sparsely inhabited. To spark economic development, the Mexican government enticed settlers from the United States and Europe by granting them colonies in Texas. Americans flocked into the region, but they soon rebelled against the laws imposed by the distant central government in Mexico City. In 1836, Texas gained its independence from Mexico, unleashing debates within the United States over whether to annex, or add, the new republic as a state—which would guarantee war with Mexico. In 1845, the annexation was approved, and war followed.

The Mexican-American War was hard-fought and bloody. In 1847, Mexico was defeated and forced to cede all of its land north of the Rio Grande to the United States. After the war, many Mexicans who had made their homes north of the Rio Grande found themselves living in the United States. Over time, these Mexican Americans and their descendants helped form the unique cultures of the states they lived in.

In the nearly 200 years since the end of the Mexican-American War, later waves of immigrants from Mexico have continued to enrich the cultures of the border states, creating unique art forms, music, and cuisines. Today, a number of states have large Mexican American populations, especially those that once formed part of Mexico, including New Mexico, Colorado, Nevada, Arizona, California, and Texas. This American Story highlights the Mexican American, or Chicano, history and culture of those states.

Westward Expansion **305**

CONNECT CULTURE TO HISTORY

Brainstorm with students examples of how Mexican American heritage has influenced American culture. Examples might include food, music, architecture, language, or religion. Then ask students to identify regions of the country most influenced by Chicano culture. **ASK:** Why have Mexican Americans left such a large imprint on the United States? *(Possible response: In the past, Mexico stretched farther north than it does now, and it shares a border with the United States. Cultural influences likely remained as the nation expanded.)* Then tell students they are going to read an American Story about the history and culture of Mexican Americans, also known as Chicanos.

CONSIDER THE IMPACT OF IMMIGRANTS

Tell students that during the westward expansion of the United States, people of Spanish and Mexican descent already inhabited the newly acquired territories. Ask students to consider how the influx of thousands of white settlers of European descent might impact the people already living there. Suggest that students consider topics that will aid in their discussion, such as clashing cultures, federal government policies, settlement patterns, and establishing local government. Ask students to volunteer a few topics, and write them on the board as headings. Then guide a discussion and write key points that students make under the relevant headings. After reading "Chicano History and Culture," direct students back to their key points to see how they connect to information in the text.

CRITICAL VIEWING Possible response: Chicano symbols and decorations favor primary colors—red, yellow, and blue are prominent in the photograph. Mexican and American flags are displayed, so Chicanos are proud of their combined heritage.

CALIFORNIA'S HISTORIC MISSIONS

Although the last of California's missions was built in 1823, all 21 of the structures still stand, stretching from San Diego to Sonoma, just north of San Francisco. Due to weather, neglect, and the occasional earthquake, many of them have been reconstructed, and most are still active Catholic parishes. Several of these missions are located in, or just outside, some of the largest cities and popular tourist destinations in the United States. About 10 miles from Los Angeles, San Gabriel Arcángel appears to visitors as a fortress, with its five-foot-thick walls and narrow windows. The walls protect its original winery, kitchen garden, and graveyard. Mission San Francisco de Asis (also known as Mission Dolores) lies in the heart of San Francisco and is the city's oldest structure. San Francisco Solano in Sonoma, the center of wine country, houses the widely known Sebastiani Vineyards, much of which includes the vineyards of the original mission.

CHICAGO'S CHICANOS

The growth of Chicago's Mexican American community was part of the 20th-century wave of Mexican Americans leaving the countryside for U.S. industrial centers. While most of the first Mexican Americans and other Latin Americans to come to Chicago were passing through as itinerants or entertainers, many stayed. Thousands more came during World War I to replace military personnel sent overseas, filling vacant positions in meatpacking, steel production, and light industries. The predominately male workers lived in the surrounding communities, where they eventually settled and had families. These communities developed strong political, religious, and cultural institutions, as well as lasting ties to Mexico. By as early as 1929, Chicago had become known for its strong Mexican American roots, and as a result became a magnet for Mexican Americans throughout the region.

EARLY CALIFORNIA

Before the Mexican-American War, the state we know as California was called Alta California, or Upper California, to distinguish it from Baja California, or Lower California. Baja California extends as a long peninsula south of the present-day border of California. The Spanish settlement of Alta California began in 1769 with the establishment of the first Catholic missions and the military forts called presidios.

Alongside the missions and presidios, a civilian society of Spanish-speaking landowners arose. The Californios, as they were known, received generous land grants from the Spanish government to encourage settlement in Alta California. The Californios established large farms and cattle ranches, relying on the labor of Native Americans and Mexicans from lower social classes. Some Californio families controlled enormous estates. Legally, a land grant could not exceed about 50,000 acres, but some families received multiple grants.

The Californios had comfortable lifestyles, supported through trade with U.S. merchants who arrived by sea to buy hides and tallow produced at the ranches. The elite families were known for their lavish entertainments and parties. A Californio wedding celebration could last a week or more.

After the Mexican-American War ended in 1847, all Mexicans living in the lands ceded to the United States became American citizens by default, unless they officially declared themselves to be Mexican citizens. On paper, the Californios retained title to their land. But the reality was that their vast holdings and control of society were quickly threatened. The California gold rush caused large numbers of people to pour into California from the United States. Additionally, westward-expanding railroads demanded land grants from the government. Soon the Californios were facing legal challenges to their land ownership. Many families were forced to sell their property piece by piece to pay legal fees. By the end of the 19th century, most elite Californios had lost much or all of their property.

A NEW CENTURY OF SETTLEMENT

The 20th century saw new waves of immigration from Mexico into California and other southwestern states. The Mexican migrants were not seeking land but better-paying jobs. At times, the new arrivals faced prejudice and open hostility, even when they were filling existing labor gaps.

In the early 1900s, the spread of irrigation, agriculture, railroads, and mining in California created a demand for inexpensive labor. Many migrants worked for a few months and then returned to Mexico, but between 35,000 and 75,000 stayed every year. Some cities in California developed lively centers of Mexican American culture, but prejudice against Chicanos remained strong.

In 1942, a new wave of Mexican workers arrived at the invitation of the U.S. government in response to a shortage of farm and transportation workers caused by World War II. Under the Bracero Program, Mexican laborers replaced American workers who were serving in the armed forces. Over a span of 22 years, the Bracero Program brought more than 4 million Latino workers into the country.

ENGLISH FROM SPANISH

Hundreds of English words have Spanish origins, and many of these words made their way into the United States via the former Mexican territories that now form the American Southwest. This chart features words that are related to the experiences of early Mexican cowboys working on ranches in the region.

ENGLISH	SPANISH	SPANISH MEANING
buckaroo	vaquero	cowboy
lasso	lazo	tie
lariat	la reata	rope
mustang	mustango or mesteño	wild horse
patio	patio	courtyard
ranch	rancho	ranch
rodeo	rodear	to encircle

The Bracero Program had a strong influence on California's economy and resulted in an increase in long-term Mexican American residents. Like earlier waves of immigration, this one caused flare-ups of prejudice and hostility. In 1943 in Los Angeles, for example, white soldiers, sailors, and civilians went on a weeklong spree of violence against Mexican American youths. The outbreak came to be called the Zoot Suit Riots because of a style of dress that was fashionable among young Mexican American men: extravagant-looking outfits called zoot suits and a distinctive duck-tail haircut. The aggressors forcefully removed the Mexican American young men's suits, cut their hair, and beat them brutally. At the time, rumors were spread that Mexican Americans were hindering the war effort by evading the draft. In fact, the reverse was true: Mexican Americans served in the armed forces in World War II in numbers far greater than their percentage of the general population. Seventeen were awarded the Congressional Medal of Honor.

In the 1950s and 1960s, Mexican Americans in California joined with other groups to counter the effects of prejudice and to empower communities. A union called the United Farm Workers, organized by labor activist Cesar Chávez, took up the cause of migrant farmworkers, demanding better pay and improved working conditions. In 1968, a group of Mexican American high school students and their supporters organized what became known as the Los Angeles Blowouts. About 15,000 students walked out of 5 East Los Angeles high schools to protest their substandard education. Both the union and the students were part of a larger civil rights movement called the Chicano Civil Rights Movement. The term *Chicano* had long existed as a negative nickname for Mexican Americans, but the movement adopted it as a symbol of cultural pride.

A Catholic religious order called the Franciscans founded Old Mission Santa Barbara in Santa Barbara, California, in 1786. Still home to a community of Franciscan friars, the mission is considered a cultural and historic landmark.

Today, California's Mexican roots are visible throughout the state. The names of cities such as Los Angeles, San Francisco, San Diego, and Sacramento all originated with the Spanish colonizers. California streets and towns bear the names of old Californio families, such as Yorba, Pico, Vallejo, and Peralta. Many cities proudly celebrate their Mexican heritage and the state's unique Mexican American cultures. Olvera Street in Los Angeles, for example, has been called the heart of that city's Chicano community and hosts an annual celebration of the Mexican Revolution and such religious festivals as *Día de los Muertos* (Day of the Dead) and the feast of the Virgin of Guadalupe.

Westward Expansion **307**

GUIDED DISCUSSION

3. **Make Connections** How have unemployment and labor shortages in the United States impacted Mexican immigration to Texas? *(When unemployment was high, as during the Great Depression, immigration slowed down, and people were even deported. When workers were needed during World War II, the opposite happened because policies such as the Bracero Program encouraged immigration to fill the labor shortage.)*

4. **Analyze Cause and Effect** What were the short-term and long-term effects of the Bracero Program on California? *(In the short term, the program brought needed workers into the United States to fill jobs left open by people who were serving in the military. Even as some Mexican Americans served during the war, others who filled job openings faced hatred and violence from whites, notably in the Zoot Suit Riots. Tensions between Americans and Mexicans still exist, as some Americans believe that immigrants take jobs that should go to U.S. citizens.)*

ACTIVE OPTIONS

On Your Feet: Compare Immigration Plans Have students compare current immigration laws with the latest proposals on immigration. Direct them to reliable and credible online sources that describe the immigration laws currently in place and proposals for changes or new laws under discussion in Congress. Ask students to gather details in note form about existing immigration laws versus laws under discussion, identify the pros and cons of each, and explain which laws they believe should be in place and why. As an alternative, students may choose to compare current immigration laws with past immigration laws. Then arrange students in small groups, and prompt them to use their notes to share and discuss their findings.

NG Learning Framework: Depict the Influence of Mexican Americans

ATTITUDE Responsibility

KNOWLEDGE Our Human Story

Organize students into small groups and ask them to choose a city with a large Mexican American population. Instruct groups to conduct research in order to create an infographic explaining the history of Mexican Americans in that city and the impact of their cultural traditions. Information could include a line graph depicting changes in the Mexican American population over time, a time line illustrating important historical events, and photographs or other visuals. Invite groups to display their infographics around the classroom.

ON BEING MEXICAN AMERICAN

Mexican American novelist and poet Sandra Cisneros (left) was born in Chicago, but in her youth, she frequently traveled with her family to Mexico to visit relatives. In interviews, she commented on the experience of growing up in multiple cultures.

PRIMARY SOURCE

If you know two cultures and two languages, that intermediate place, where the two don't perfectly meet, is really interesting.

I think that Mexican American kids live in a global world. It's not even bi-, it's multi-. You know, for those of us who grew up with different countries on our block, different nationalities, you know, we moved into multiple worlds.

San Francisco's Mission District, with its historic buildings and bright murals, is home to local Chicano organizations. A carnival is held every May in the district to celebrate the food, music, and dance of the Chicano culture. In 1999, the city of San Jose opened Mexican Heritage Plaza, a community and cultural arts center with a theater, art gallery, and classrooms. Visitors from all ethnic backgrounds come to California every year to enjoy the riches of the state's Mexican American heritage.

THE CHICANOS OF TEXAS

It's a popular question for trivia contests: How many flags have flown over Texas? In fact, beginning in the 1500s, Texas has been under six flags: those of France, Spain, Mexico, the Republic of Texas, the Confederacy, and the United States. Over the centuries, the governments have changed, but the Tejanos have remained.

The word *Tejano* refers to Texans of Mexican or Spanish descent. Unlike the Californios, the Tejanos did not form an upper-class landowning society, though the majority earned a living by farming or ranching. Throughout the 1700s, the Spanish government tried to persuade people to settle in Texas, but the isolation, poor living conditions, and danger from Native American attacks held most prospective settlers back. By the end of the 18th century, Texas had only about 5,000 residents of Mexican heritage.

In the 1800s, the trickle of Mexican settlers increased to a larger flow, and in 1850, a federal census counted 14,000 residents of Mexican descent. Like California, Texas also had an influx of Mexican immigrants at the start of the 20th century. By one estimate, the number of Tejanos had reached about 700,000.

The immigration tide turned during the Great Depression, which began in 1929. Faced with growing unemployment in the Southwest—and throughout the United States—President Herbert Hoover created a program to deport Mexicans and other Hispanics so that Americans could take their jobs. Mexican Americans remaining in the country struggled to find jobs or federal assistance.

All southwestern states were affected but Texas was impacted the most. In all, between 400,000 and 500,000 Mexicans and their American-born children returned to Mexico, more than half of them from Texas. Not all the returnees were officially deported. Some left on their own in fear that they would be forced out of the country.

Immigration to the United States from Mexico increased once again in the 1940s due to labor shortages in the United States, the Bracero Program, and a high rate of poverty in Mexico. In 1990, the census counted about 3.9 million people of Mexican descent in Texas, and more than 80 percent were born in the United States.

308 CHAPTER 10

As in California, Chicanos in Texas have encountered prejudice, segregation, and sometimes violent treatment. Before World War II, most Tejanos lived in rural areas, farming, working as ranch hands, or building railroads. In towns, some managed to start small businesses that catered to Tejano communities. During World War II and after, many Tejanos moved to larger cities for better-paying, more highly skilled jobs. In the 1960s, many organizations worked as part of the Chicano Movement to fight for equal rights and greater political involvement for Mexican Americans in Texas.

Tejanos have developed their own unique culture based on Mexican traditions but incorporating outside elements. One example is the music genre called *conjunto*. Combining musical elements from two continents, conjunto mixes themes from northern Mexican traditions with accordion sounds and polka music borrowed from 19th-century German settlers in the region. A typical conjunto band features an accordion, guitars, and drums. The Tejano Conjunto Festival draws appreciative audiences to San Antonio, Texas, every year, and the Conjunto Hall of Fame has inducted more than 70 musicians.

Another prominent aspect of Tejano culture is Tex-Mex food, which blends elements of Mexican and American cooking. Cheese, beans, beef, and the spices cumin and chili powder are common ingredients in Tex-Mex cooking. Fajitas and nachos are popular Tex-Mex creations.

CHICANOS TODAY

Southwestern states, especially California and Texas, continue to attract the majority of Mexican immigrants today. After California and Texas, the state that receives the largest number of Mexican immigrants is Illinois. Chicago, the city with the third highest population in the United States, has a large and vibrant Mexican American community that has attracted new immigrants for decades.

ON BEING MEXICAN AMERICAN

Sandra Cisneros, the sole daughter in a family of seven children, was born to a Mexican father and Mexican American mother. During her childhood, the family frequently moved, often to poor neighborhoods. This constant upheaval, characterized by new schools, friends, and neighbors, inspired Cisneros to write *The House on Mango Street*, a novel depicting a year in the life of a young Mexican American girl named Esperanza growing up in a diverse neighborhood in Chicago. Direct students' attention to the Primary Source feature. **ASK:** What are the multiple worlds Cisneros speaks about, and what impact might living in multiple worlds have on a young person? *(Possible response: Cisneros is saying that Mexican American kids have several distinct influences, such as their family, their neighbors, their home country, and American society. A person living within multiple cultures might develop a broader and richer understanding of the world or may feel torn between different cultural identities.)*

CRITICAL VIEWING The painting shows workers crowded behind barbed wire, appearing imprisoned or corralled like livestock rather than being housed. While the men were probably grateful for the work, their expressions range from blank stares to misery, suggesting despair, possibly due to being overworked or mistreated.

CRITICAL VIEWING Artist Domingo Ulloa was committed to promoting social justice through his artwork. He painted *Braceros* in 1960 after visiting a migrant workers' camp in Holtville, California. What does this painting suggest about the experiences of migrant workers under the Bracero Program?

NATIONAL GEOGRAPHIC EXPLORER
JASON DE LEÓN

The seed that brought about the Undocumented Migration Project (UMP) was a change in U.S. immigration policy implemented in the mid-1990s. The goal of the policy is to deter migrants from crossing the southern U.S. border near urban areas that have no official entry points and where migrants have found routes to illegally enter the United States. U.S. immigration officials have increased security around these areas, forcing migrants further south, as planned, to remote border areas, such as in the Sonoran Desert. As a result, migrants often take life-threatening routes on foot through the desert, traveling with as few possessions and as much water as possible. As traveling becomes increasingly difficult, migrants cast aside expendable possessions. The UMP was founded to collect these objects in order to expose the realities of migrant experiences. Jason De León and his team work in the brutal desert heat, collecting and documenting artifacts, including sneakers, personal photos, prayer cards, and even food wrappers. "This is not garbage," De León argues. "These objects are an important historical record of the shared migration story of Americans and Latinos, but I think it is important that these artifacts are returned to the communities of people who have been so directly impacted…These artifacts belong to the migrants that have faced the harsh Sonoran Desert."

WRITE ABOUT HISTORY

Examine Local Cultural Influences This American Story focuses on how Chicano history and culture helped shape the United States. To help students make connections between the American Story and their own lives, ask them to choose one local place or event to research—such as a restaurant, historic building, or annual festival—and write an essay explaining how it has been shaped by a specific culture. Provide guidance about the writing process as necessary.

THINK ABOUT IT

Answers will vary. Students' responses might include hearing Chicano classmates' references to their culture, visiting Chicano friends' homes and eating food or seeing decorations from their culture, listening to music by Chicano musicians or composers, or viewing murals or other works created by Chicano artists.

AMERICAN STORIES

Between 1965 and 2000, 4.3 million Mexicans moved to the United States. In 2014, more than 11.7 million Mexicans came to the United States, making up 28 percent of the foreign-born population. Since the end of the Great Recession of 2007–2009, however, more Mexican migrants have returned to Mexico than have arrived in the United States.

While the Mexican American community is well established in the United States, some people have concerns about illegal immigration from Mexico. The number of unauthorized immigrants coming into the country has dropped in recent years. But millions of illegal immigrants remain in the United States, some of whom were brought here as children. Under President Trump, who was elected in 2016, the U.S. government has increased its efforts to stop illegal immigration and to deport unauthorized immigrants.

Americans have differing opinions on the subject of deporting unauthorized immigrants. Some oppose deportation, arguing that unauthorized immigrants help the American economy by performing jobs that few citizens want. Others favor deportation, claiming that unauthorized immigrants take jobs that would otherwise go to American citizens. The treatment of illegal immigrants who came to the United States as children is a particularly divisive issue.

In the meantime, Mexican Americans continue to enrich the culture of the United States with their contributions in literature, art, architecture, government, agriculture, science, and other fields. Cities and small towns across the country boast restaurants serving Mexican and Tex-Mex food. Vibrant Chicano neighborhoods invite visitors to join in appreciating Mexican American art, music, and celebrations. Two major Spanish-language television networks, Univision and Telemundo, are headquartered in the United States, providing news and entertainment to a diverse audience. Mexican American culture will always be an integral part of the American scene.

THINK ABOUT IT

What elements of Chicano culture do you experience in your everyday life?

Mexican Americans in the United States, 2014

San Francisco 269,000
Los Angeles 1,753,000
Chicago 640,000
New York 340,000
Dallas 605,000
Houston 609,000
PACIFIC OCEAN
ATLANTIC OCEAN
Gulf of Mexico

Mexican-born population in metropolitan areas, 2014
- More than 1 million
- 500,000–1 million
- 200,000–499,999
- Less than 200,000

Percentage of total population, 2014
- 20–30
- 10–19.9
- 5–9.9
- Less than 5

In the period between 2010 and 2014, most immigrants from Mexico settled in California (37 percent), Texas (21 percent), and Illinois (6 percent). The U.S. cities with the largest number of Mexican immigrants were greater Los Angeles, Chicago, Houston, and Dallas. These four metropolitan areas were home to about 39 percent of the Mexican immigrants in the United States.

What conclusions can you draw about the distribution of the Mexican American population in the United States?

NATIONAL GEOGRAPHIC

JASON DE LEÓN

A spiky cactus bristles in the scorching Sonoran Desert sun. Caught on its thorns—a baby diaper. Miles away, a tattered backpack contains one roll of toilet paper, a love letter, and a prayer card. Beside it, a tiny child's shoe. Until Jason De León, a National Geographic Explorer and the founder of the Undocumented Migration Project, arrived on the scene, such items were all considered garbage, or never discovered at all.

People view undocumented migration into the United States from Mexico from a wide variety of perspectives, often focusing on the effects the immigrants have on the politics, culture, or economy of the United States. De León may be the first to study the topic from the perspective of an archaeologist. He applies scientific techniques to gain a deeper understanding of the migrants' experiences. In addition to collecting the objects they leave behind, he conducts interviews to help illuminate the meaning of the items. De León explains, "We use archaeological surveys, linguistics, forensics, and ethnography to document how people prepare to cross the border, who profits from helping them, how they deal with physical and emotional trauma during their journey, and what happens to those who don't make it." His goal is to learn more about the effects of immigration on all who are involved in it on both sides of the border, including migrants, law enforcement officers, smugglers, and everyday citizens. "It's an emotional subject, but my focus has to be science first," explains De León.

De León is a Mexican American who grew up in South Texas and Southern California. "Being raised on the border in a bicultural household with a long immigration history makes me very attuned to issues of cultural identity and discrimination," he explains.

What might the study of undocumented migrants reveal about U.S. history?

De León collaborated with American artist Amanda Krugliak and photographer Richard Barnes on a traveling exhibit called *State of Exception*, a wall of discarded backpacks left by migrants trying to cross into the United States through the Sonoran Desert.

Westward Expansion 311

STRIVING READERS

Read and Recall Arrange students in pairs and tell them to read the American Story first independently and then share information they recall, with one partner taking notes. Then direct pairs to review the text and decide what to add or change in the notes.

PRE-AP

Create and Annotate a Time Line Direct students to create an annotated time line showing important events in the history of Chicano people in what is now the United States. Tell students to supplement the lesson with information, photographs, cartoons, and other relevant visuals from online sources. Remind them to include dates, locations, events, and key figures in their annotations and to show connections with larger social and economic trends. Invite students to present their time lines to the class, stating how each entry represents a significant contribution to Chicano history and culture.

See the Chapter Planner for more strategies for differentiation.

HISTORICAL THINKING

Ask and have students answer the following questions.

1. **READING CHECK** What is the meaning of *Chicano*?

2. **ANALYZE CAUSE AND EFFECT** How did the Mexican-American War impact Californios?

3. **INTERPRET MAPS** How does the distribution of the Mexican American population in 2014 compare with what it was prior to the annexation of Texas and the Mexican-American War?

4. **MAKE INFERENCES** Why is the treatment of people who were brought here illegally as children a particularly divisive issue?

ANSWERS

1. A Chicano is a person of Mexican American heritage.

2. After the war, California became part of the United States. This resulted in the loss of property by Californios who owned large tracts of land.

3. While Mexican Americans continue to live across the Southwest and California, they have also migrated to places such as New York, Chicago, and Florida.

4. Possible response: Even though the children did not choose to immigrate to the United States, some people insist they should be deported because they are undocumented. People may fear that a path to citizenship for this group will diminish their own economic opportunities. Others maintain that returning the children to Mexico, with which they may have no connection, would punish them for an illegal act over which they had no control.

THE CALL OF THE WEST

What is "the West" to you? Americans' notions of "the West" have changed over time. Almost every section of the United States beyond the eastern coastal region has been considered "the West" at some time in American history. As Americans migrated, the designation of the West changed.

REASONS FOR MIGRATING

Europeans began pushing westward shortly after they established their first settlements along the eastern seaboard of North America. Many people migrated west along the same latitudes as they lived, moving to places with familiar weather and soil. For example, in the early 1800s, people from New York migrated to Michigan, while people from Virginia, Tennessee, and Kentucky headed to Missouri.

In the 1840s, the number of people moving west of the Mississippi River increased dramatically, forming one of the largest migrations in U.S. history. Between 1841 and 1866, up to a half million Americans migrated west of the Mississippi. Most of these migrants were young men in their teens and early adulthood. About 30 percent were women and children. While people from all over the United States moved west in the 1840s and 1850s, the largest number came from the South and the Midwest.

People packed up and headed west for a variety of reasons. One of the main reasons was population growth. The population of the United States grew from 5.3 million in 1800 to a whopping 23 million by 1850.

During this period, most people in the United States needed land because they made their living by farming. Younger children in farm families often inherited little or no property. In some places, overuse had made existing farmland less fertile and productive, so it took more acreage to produce the same yields. Tobacco and cotton, the cash crops of the South, were particularly tough on the soil, depleting it of nutrients and decreasing its fertility. Many southern farmers were looking for fertile land to grow these crops. Recent immigrants wanted land as well.

Changes in government policy in the 1830s made moving to the West much more attractive, contributing to the boom in migration and settlement. In 1801, a settler had to pay $2.00 per acre and buy a minimum of 320 acres to secure public land from the government. In the 1830s, the price was about $1.25 per acre and a settler only had to buy 80 acres.

CRITICAL VIEWING *Westward the Course of Empire Takes Its Way*, a painting by German-American artist Emanuel Leutze, completed in 1861, shows weary travelers catching their first glimpse of California. What does the title of the painting suggest about the westward migration of Americans?

Iron bands were added to wooden wagon wheels to withstand the long journeys of pioneers through the rugged terrain of the West.

PLAN: 4-PAGE LESSON

OBJECTIVE

Explain why people moved west in the 1840s and 1850s.

CRITICAL THINKING SKILLS FOR LESSON 1.1

- Analyze Cause and Effect
- Identify Main Ideas and Details
- Interpret Maps
- Draw Conclusions
- Analyze Visuals
- Make Connections
- Integrate Visuals

HISTORICAL THINKING FOR CHAPTER 10

How did the idea of manifest destiny shape the future of the United States? During the 1840s and 1850s, more Americans began moving west than ever before. Lesson 1.1 examines the motivations behind this migration, including the expansionist philosophy of manifest destiny.

BACKGROUND FOR THE TEACHER

Emanuel Leutze, painter of the famed *Washington Crossing the Delaware*, came to the United States as a child with his family, seeking political refuge from the autocracy of Germany. At around age 25, Leutze returned to Germany to study at the renowned Dusseldorf Academy, where he completed a series of paintings depicting major events in U.S. history. Noted for attention to color and detail, the paintings reflect the style popular at the academy. Leutze became a fierce advocate for democracy, supporting the Revolutions of 1848, a string of democratic protests across Europe against existing monarchies. When Leutze returned to the United States, he was greeted as an artistic master. The painting featured in this lesson was commissioned by the U.S. Congress to decorate the stairway of the U.S. Capitol Building.

FINANCIAL LITERACY

To extend their knowledge and understanding about the concepts in this lesson, refer students to the Financial Literacy handbook.

INTRODUCE & ENGAGE

CONSIDER PUSH AND PULL FACTORS

Ask students to recall people they know who have moved to another part of the United States or to another country. Use questions such as the following to prompt class discussion: Why did they move? What might motivate you to move to a different region or country? Where would you go and why? Write the questions on the board and record students' responses. Explain the differences between push factors—reasons pushing someone to leave home—and pull factors—reasons pulling, or motivating, the move to a specific place. Ask students to consider as they read how the push and pull factors of people today compare and contrast with the motivations of Americans who moved to the West in the 19th century.

TEACH

GUIDED DISCUSSION

1. **Draw Conclusions** Why do you think most of the western migrants were young men? *(Possible response: Young men looking for work weren't tied down by family obligations that a husband or father would have. They could move freely to the new territory, likely finding jobs along the way to support themselves.)*

2. **Analyze Cause and Effect** What prompted the federal government to change its policies about the pricing and availability of land in the 1830s? *(In the 1830s, a majority of the population farmed for a living, and some people needed land to farm. The government wanted to populate the West, so government land policy encouraged migration with offers of cheap land. In addition to reducing the price per acre, the government reduced the amount of acreage people were required to buy, likely opening the way for a range of settlers, from those wanting to buy as few as 80 acres for a farm to those buying thousands of acres to raise cattle.)*

ANALYZE VISUALS

Share the information from Background for the Teacher about artist Emanuel Leutze. Remind students that Leutze's paintings are generally considered celebrations of events in U.S. history that exemplify American ideals. **ASK:** How does *Westward the Course of Empire Takes Its Way* depict the hardships, character, and experiences of western migrants? *(Possible response: The western migrants, including women and children, are shown struggling over crowded and rough terrain. Their faces express fatigue and concern. Most are on foot, demonstrating both strength of character and determination. Others guide the mules and horses pulling the wagons through the narrow trail. Men using axes to break up a fallen tree blocking the way, a woman with an infant likely born on the trail, and a burial scene vividly represent the difficulties that western migrants experienced.)*

DIFFERENTIATE

STRIVING READERS

Use a Main-Idea Cluster Pair students and direct them to construct a Main-Idea Cluster for each subsection of the lesson. Tell partners to take turns reading each paragraph and then work together to record the main idea and four details before moving on to the next subsection. After partners complete a Main-Idea Cluster for each subsection, instruct them to trade and compare their work with another pair, making any changes necessary for accuracy.

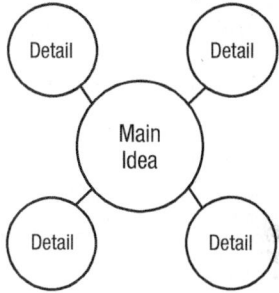

PRE-AP

Engage in a Debate Tell students they will debate the validity of the concept of manifest destiny. Assign or have students choose a position for or against the concept. Review the text and share information from Build Background on the next page. Then instruct students to conduct additional research to find strong historical, economic, and cultural support for their position, including examples of real-life impacts. After students have gathered information and prepared their notes, have them conduct a debate. After the debate, guide a discussion about new information the class identified and how the debate deepened their understanding of the concept and impact of manifest destiny.

See the Chapter Planner for more strategies for differentiation.

CRITICAL VIEWING The title suggests that the United States was expanding and becoming an empire as a natural course of its development as a nation.

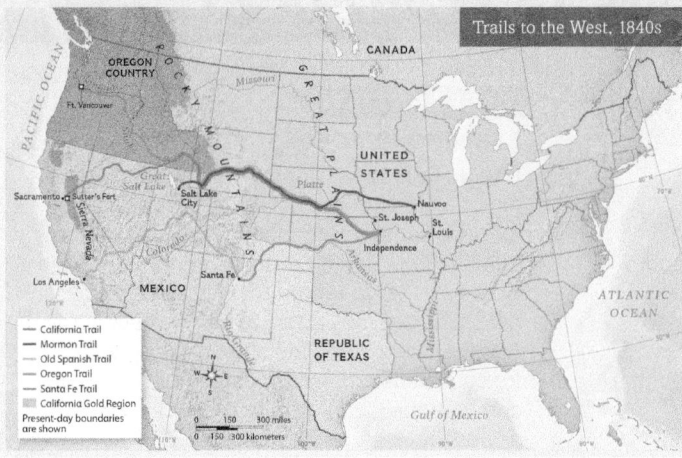

Trails to the West, 1840s

- California Trail
- Mormon Trail
- Old Spanish Trail
- Oregon Trail
- Santa Fe Trail
- California Gold Region

Present-day boundaries are shown

Jim Beckwourth, an American mountain man and explorer, established a trail through the Sierra Nevada for migrants traveling to California.

Besides needing farmland to make a living, Americans tended to link open land and land ownership with the ideals of liberty and independence. Many moved several times in their lives, looking for better land and more freedom.

As Americans pushed west, they gained access to natural resources that either had been depleted in the East or did not exist there. For example, while farmers gained fertile land, trappers and fur traders, called **mountain men**, made fortunes selling beaver pelts and other furs. The Great Plains provided ranchers with grazing land for livestock. The discovery of valuable deposits of coal, copper, silver, gold, and other minerals drew miners to the West. The area's forests prompted the development of the timber industry in the Pacific Northwest.

THE CONCEPT OF "MANIFEST DESTINY"

The West was not simply an area of vast, unoccupied land, however. Hundreds of Native American groups lived there, while Spain and later Mexico claimed much of the territory. Americans needed a justification for taking the land from the people who already lived there or considered it theirs. In 1845, newspaper editor John O'Sullivan provided that justification. He wrote that it was the **manifest destiny**, or inevitable fate, of the United States "to overspread the continent allotted by Providence for the free development of our yearly multiplying

millions." In other words, O'Sullivan proposed that God intended for the people of the United States to take over the North American continent.

Not surprisingly, the idea of manifest destiny and the westward expansion of the United States led to disputes with Native Americans who already lived in the West and with Mexicans who claimed much of the region. Not only was land at stake, but also the culture and way of life of many groups of people.

TRAILS WEST

While some migrants sailed to California and the Pacific Northwest, most traveled overland by wagon. The overland migrants followed trails marked by earlier trappers and fur traders who, to some degree, probably used even earlier trails made by Native Americans as well as by migrating herds of animals.

Some of the trappers and traders became legends to the people of the eastern United States. One of the most famous was **Jim Beckwourth**, a free African American who worked on western expeditions and lived with various Native American tribes. Beckwourth established a trail west through the Sierra Nevada, the high mountain range along part of the eastern border of California.

Other explorers also blazed trails and drew maps to guide westward migrants. **John C. Frémont** and **Kit Carson** were two of the most important

trailblazers. Frémont was a soldier with the U.S. Army, and Carson was a famous mountain man who served as his guide. They explored the Rocky Mountains region in 1842, making use of a gap through the mountains in what today is southern Wyoming. This crossing point, called the South Pass, became essential to overland travel to the West Coast. In the following years, the pair traveled through the Oregon Territory, California, and the Southwest. Their journeys led to Frémont's famed map of the West, the first map of the area that was scientifically based.

Migrants and traders typically followed two main trails west. The **Santa Fe Trail** started at Independence, Missouri, and led to Santa Fe in present-day New Mexico. From Santa Fe, the trail extended into Mexico. Access to the city of Santa Fe gave traders the chance to exchange U.S. products for Mexican silver, furs, and mules. The **Oregon Trail** stretched for about 2,000 miles from Independence, Missouri, to Oregon City, near present-day Portland, Oregon. A southern spur, the California Trail, led to Sacramento, California.

Hundreds of thousands of people traveled the Oregon Trail from the 1840s through the 1860s. Those who traveled the spur trail to California sent back reports of crowded campsites and dust-filled air from the large number of oxen and wagons.

Ruts made by the wheels of the many wagons that rolled over the land can still be seen in parts of the Great Plains today.

MIGRATION OF THE MORMONS

One of the groups migrating west was the **Mormons**, who believed in a religion founded by Joseph Smith in New York in 1830. Members of the religion, called the Church of Jesus Christ of Latter-day Saints, believe in the Christian Bible but consider it incomplete. They also follow additional scriptures found by Smith, who claimed they had been revealed to him by divine beings.

Smith and his followers moved from New York and established settlements in Ohio and Missouri. However, their non-Mormon neighbors viewed them with suspicion and hostility. Forced to leave Ohio and Missouri, they gathered in Illinois in 1839 and founded the town of Nauvoo.

By the mid-1840s, Nauvoo had become one of the largest cities in Illinois, with a population exceeding 15,000 people. However, the Mormons again faced harassment, which erupted into violence. After a mob killed Smith in 1844, the Mormons chose a new leader, **Brigham Young**. He decided to lead the Mormons west to find a remote and protected place where they could practice their religion.

Young and his followers chose the region around the southern shore of the Great Salt Lake in what is now the state of Utah. Surrounded by mountains in the east and deserts in the west and south, the site was effectively cut off from the rest of the country. Two years after the death of Joseph Smith, 15,000 Mormons followed what came to be called the **Mormon Trail** and began arriving at their new home. About 55,000 Mormons traveled the Mormon Trail to Salt Lake City over the next 20 years.

HISTORICAL THINKING

1. **READING CHECK** What was the concept of manifest destiny, and how was it connected to westward migration?

2. **ANALYZE CAUSE AND EFFECT** Why did so many Americans move west of the Mississippi River in the 1840s and 1850s?

3. **IDENTIFY MAIN IDEAS AND DETAILS** What role did geography play in the Mormons' choice of a site to settle in the West?

4. **INTERPRET MAPS** What physical features did all the trails shown on the map pass over or through?

Westward Expansion **315**

BUILD BACKGROUND

MANIFEST DESTINY

Although John O'Sullivan coined the famous phrase "manifest destiny," the idea was not a new one. The Puritans who first set foot on the continent believed that they arrived with both God's approval and the duty to spread Christianity. In the 1800s, settlers pushed Native Americans aside because they believed the territory was rightly theirs. Even in modern times, the philosophy persists. Some observers argue, for example, that U.S. policy in Southwest Asia has been motivated by the belief that the region is destined to become more like the United States—democratic and open—and that the U.S. military has the might and the duty to make this vision a reality.

OPPOSITION TO MORMONS

The hostility aimed at the Mormons was motivated by a number of factors. In a broad sense, the Mormons considered themselves Christian, but some of their beliefs contradicted those of Protestantism and caused suspicion. Perhaps the most controversial idea was polygamy. While Mormons believed that men had a sacred right to have multiple wives, the federal government disapproved, setting off a struggle over the relationship between church and state that culminated in the United States outlawing the practice. Mormons' economic and political power also bred resentment. Non-Mormons feared Mormon influence on the regions with established Mormon communities. Supporters of slavery were especially fearful that a large influx of Mormons, who opposed slavery, would disturb the status quo in slave states and in territories that allowed the practice.

GUIDED DISCUSSION

3. Make Connections What historical evidence might 19th-century Americans have used to justify manifest destiny? *(Possible response: Americans might have pointed to their defeat of the British, their conquest of Native Americans, and the gradual expansion of U.S. territory through treaties and war as evidence that they were destined to control the continent. Americans could have also referred to the importance of religion—from the Puritans to the First and Second Great Awakenings—in American history as evidence of a divine cause.)*

4. Analyze Cause and Effect Why do you think many of the western trails began in Independence, Missouri, and what effect might this have had on the city? *(Possible response: Situated on the Missouri River in one of the westernmost states, the city was probably already a center for transportation of goods and travelers. Independence likely grew in population and size as a result of providing supplies and services to migrants.)*

INTEGRATE VISUALS

Guide students to view additional paintings depicting westward expansion, such as the following, available online: *American Progress* (1872), *Across the Continent* (1868), and *Emigrants Crossing the Plains* (1869). Challenge students to closely examine Leutze's painting and the others. **ASK:** What details illustrate ideas related to manifest destiny? *(Possible response: Leutze's painting and the others present an expansive scene in which migrants are traveling westward, often toward a golden horizon. The light suggests the dawn or a new beginning for Americans going west. Across the Continent conveys the idea differently, with a railroad track that disappears into the distant western horizon. All reinforce the belief central to manifest destiny that Americans were destined to occupy all land to the West Coast. All but Leutze's painting depict scenes of an orderly progression west. His view includes hardships as well as hope for the travelers as they eagerly hurry over a steep rocky trail to get their first look at California.)*

ACTIVE OPTIONS

Active History: Illustrate the Rain Shadow Effect Extend the lesson by using the PDF or Whiteboard version of the activity. These activities take a deeper look at a topic from, or related to, the lesson. Explore the activities as a class, turn them into group assignments, or even assign them individually.

NG Learning Framework: Chart a Western Trail | STEM |

SKILL Problem-Solving

KNOWLEDGE Our Living Planet

Assist small groups of students in locating a map that depicts the physical features and climate zones of the United States. Challenge groups to take the role of trailblazers and chart a western trail from Independence, Missouri, to the California coast. Remind students to factor in river systems and landforms such as mountains, deserts, canyons, and plains, and consider climate when plotting their route. Direct groups to compose a short report explaining the decisions they made for their route and comparing their route with the trails mapped in the lesson. Invite groups to present their routes and discuss similarities and differences among their choices.

HISTORICAL THINKING

ANSWERS

1. Manifest destiny was the belief that God had destined the United States to stretch across the continent. It justified the acquisition of new land and conquest of native peoples in order for migrants to inhabit the land.

2. They moved because the East was overcrowded, they wanted the opportunity to own land, and government policies offered land at a low cost.

3. Because the religion was controversial and Mormons faced persecution, they settled in an isolated region cut off from the rest of the nation by mountains and desert.

4. The trails crossed the Great Plains and the Rocky Mountains. Northern trails crossed the Platte and Snake rivers, while southern trails crossed the Arkansas and Colorado rivers.

National Geographic photographer **Michael Nichols** worked more than two weeks with a crew of climbers and assistants to get this shot of a giant sequoia named "the President." Then he climbed the tree himself to "say goodbye." Born in Alabama, Nichols has devoted his career to capturing the wonders of the natural world, striving to inspire people to conserve Earth's amazing living things, from African elephants to giant sequoias.

CRITICAL VIEWING The giant sequoias of California inspired awe in the first pioneers who encountered them in the 1850s. This tree in Sequoia National Park is the second largest in the world, measured not by height but by volume. It contains at least 54,000 cubic feet of wood and bark and, at 3,200 years old, is still growing. How does the perspective from which Nichols captured this shot help convey the tree's size?

OBJECTIVE

Examine how nature photography captures the natural wonders of the world.

CRITICAL THINKING SKILLS FOR LESSON 1.2

• Analyze Visuals

• Make Connections

• Ask and Answer Questions

• Evaluate

HISTORICAL THINKING FOR CHAPTER 10

How did the idea of manifest destiny shape the future of the United States? People traveling west encountered many natural wonders. Lesson 1.2 shows how photography can be used as a means of helping to preserve wildlife and natural wonders, such as the giant sequoias on California's western coast.

NATIONAL GEOGRAPHIC PHOTOGRAPHER
MICHAEL NICHOLS

Michael "Nick" Nichols is a photographer, a storyteller, and someone who feels part of a world larger than himself. He has combined his two talents to create photographic stories of trees and animals, such as elephants, tigers, and gorillas, that have made people see his subjects as part of a complex world. Nichols often uses camera traps and remote-controlled robots to capture shots of animal behavior in the wild, unaffected by human presence. To photograph the full height of "the President," he worked with a team of scientists, three cameras, a robotic dolly, and a gyroscope. To capture the height of the giant sequoia, Nichols hoisted a camera on the dolly and snapped individual segments. Later he combined 126 photos into a composite to show the entire tree.

HISTORY NOTEBOOK

Encourage students to complete the Through the Lens page for Chapter 10 in their History Notebooks as they read.

INTRODUCE & ENGAGE

NATURE AND PEOPLE

Direct students' attention to the photograph and have them read the introduction. Discuss with them why a nature photographer might be interested in the conservation of all living things. Then ask students what impact the photograph could have on viewers regarding the relationship between nature and people. Tell them that in this lesson they will learn how Michael Nichols attempts to show this human connection to the natural world through photography.

TEACH

GUIDED DISCUSSION

1. **Ask and Answer Questions** What questions does the photograph of "the President" inspire, and how might you answer them? *(Possible responses: How tall is the tree? How did crew members attach the wires to the tree and then take them down? How did they use the wires to raise and lower themselves? Answers would likely be found online in articles about the photographing of the tree.)*

2. **Evaluate** How does the photograph relate to Michael Nichols' mission? *(Possible response: The photo shows the immenseness of the giant sequoia by revealing its size compared with the humans dangling from its branches. It illustrates Nichols' mission of "capturing the wonders of the natural world" in a manner that may inspire others to become involved in conservation efforts.)*

THROUGH THE LENS

Photojournalist Michael Nichols has spent his career trekking to some of the most dangerous and remote places of the world to bring back pictures that move people to action because he believes that, "Even with our deluge of images, people still are moved by imagery." One of his most iconic, poetic shots is of hippos swimming together in the Atlantic Ocean, a sight few have ever seen. The photo, "Surfing Hippos," together with Nichols' other work in central Africa, inspired the president of Gabon to create 13 national parks, an area that covers 11 percent of the country. It also helped conservationists to convince authorities to expand one of Central African Republic's national parks. According to Nichols, "Although we focus on…tigers or grizzly bears or elephants or spotted owls because they're the hook—all that matters in conservation really is land."

ACTIVE OPTIONS

On Your Feet: Fishbowl Share the Through the Lens information with students and ask them to view Nichols' photographs online and read more about his conservation work. Then arrange the class in two concentric circles, and pose the following question: How is nature a part of our history and our human story? Have students in the inner circle discuss the question while those in the outer circle listen to the discussion and evaluate the points made. Instruct the groups to reverse roles and continue the discussion.

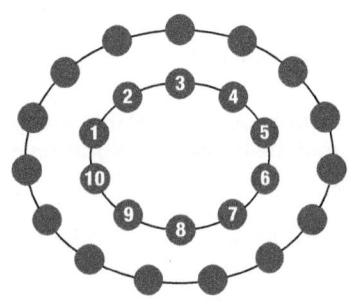

NG Learning Framework: Create a Composite Photograph

ATTITUDE Responsibility

SKILL Communication

Tell students to create a composite photograph that shows an important aspect of nature in their neighborhood or city. They may make a digital composite or make a collage using printed photos. If necessary, direct students to online instructions for photographing and creating a digital composite photo. Invite volunteers to present their completed work to the class, explaining the concept behind it, including why they chose the subject matter, and how they constructed it.

DIFFERENTIATE

INCLUSION

Analyze Photographic Content Some students may find the photograph difficult to decipher in terms of its perspective and scale. Pair students who are visually impaired with students who are not. Have them discuss where the photographer was when he took the photo and how its composition enhances the text. Then direct partners to work together to answer the Critical Viewing question.

GIFTED & TALENTED

Create a Web Page Prompt students to conduct online research to identify a Michael Nichols' photograph they find particularly compelling. Challenge them to design an informative web page about the photograph, including links to related information. Suggest that they include information about the subject of the photograph, the location, technical details about how Nichols took the photograph, and how the photo furthers his mission to inspire the preservation of the natural world. Encourage students to post their web page on a school or class website.

See the Chapter Planner for more strategies for differentiation.

CRITICAL VIEWING Nichols' perspective shows how small the people are compared with the width of the trunk, making the sequoia appear more like a tall building or a rock wall than a tree.

PIONEERS AND NATIVE AMERICANS

Can you imagine traveling in a covered wagon for six months across vast grasslands and over mountains to make a new life in an unknown land? Or watching your homeland being overtaken by people who do not respect your rights? Pioneers and Native Americans faced these separate challenges in the mid-1800s.

THE PIONEER EXPERIENCE

Traveling west on the Oregon Trail was nothing like the relatively safe and easy cross-country trips of today. An estimated 4 to 10 percent of travelers died on the trail, mostly from diseases or accidental shootings. People often contracted such diseases as cholera, dysentery, and typhoid fever from drinking unsanitary water or eating contaminated food. In the mountains, migrants faced the threat of early snowstorms. Some mountain passes were so dangerous and steep that wagons had to be dragged up one side and then carefully eased down the other using ropes, chains, and pulleys. Before reaching the end of the trail, some travelers ran out of food and suffered from malnutrition. But contrary to popular myth, conflicts with Native Americans were rare along the trails west.

Most pioneers traveled overland in a smaller version of a Conestoga wagon, which, as you have read, is a type of covered wagon. The vehicles' white canvas covers reminded people of the sails on ships called schooners, which led people to call the wagons **prairie schooners**. During the day, the pioneers rode in or walked next to their wagons, herding their livestock along the way. When they stopped, they had to set up camp, find fuel and make a fire, cook meals, and make any necessary repairs on wagons and other equipment.

On the journeys west, women typically did not follow strict gender roles. They still cared for the children, gathered fuel, and cooked meals, but they also took on such traditionally male roles as driving wagons, repairing equipment, herding cattle, putting up tents, and pulling oxen out of the mud.

CONFLICTS OVER LAND AND CULTURE

As you have read, millions of Native Americans lived in North America when Columbus first set foot in the Western Hemisphere. However, European diseases soon began to decimate their population. Despite these losses, hundreds of established tribes still lived west of the Mississippi when explorers and settlers began moving there. According to some historians, more than 325,000 Native Americans lived in the Southwest, the Great Plains, California, and the Pacific Northwest in 1840.

Westward migration from the United States threatened these Native Americans with the loss of their homeland, access to vital resources, and ways of life. The United States forced many tribes into treaties that took away their land and limited their freedom. When they resisted the changes pressed upon them, the U.S. government's reaction was usually swift and brutal.

These changes particularly threatened the nomadic way of life of the Plains tribes, who moved from place to place following the herds of bison, or buffalo. These tribes depended on the buffalo for most of their needs, including food, clothing, shelter, weapons, and tools. The wild buffalo herds migrated seasonally across enormous areas of open grazing land. The nomadic culture of the Plains tribes clashed with that of settlers who sought their own plots of land for farming, ranching, and mining.

The settlers even encroached upon land that had been specifically set aside for Native Americans. Under the Indian Removal Act of 1830, several southeastern tribes were forced to move to Indian Territory in present-day Oklahoma and parts of Kansas and Nebraska. Eventually, the pioneers began to claim that land as well.

As depicted in this 1858 painting titled *Fort Laramie* by American artist Alfred Jacob Miller, Fort Laramie was a busy trading post along the Oregon Trail, frequented by both Native Americans and pioneers. The fort was located near present-day Laramie, Wyoming.

While traveling west, pioneers used Dutch ovens like this one to cook food on hot coals.

PRIMARY SOURCE

Amelia Stewart Knight set out on the Oregon Trail in 1853 with her husband and seven children. She recorded their experiences in her diary.

Cold; breakfast the first thing; very disagreeable weather; wind east, cold and rainy, no fire. We are on a very large prairie, no timber can be seen as far as the eye can reach. Evening—Have crossed several bad streams today, and more than once have been stuck in the mud. We . . . have just crossed Grand river, and will camp in a little bottom, plenty of wood, and we will have a warm supper, I guess. Came 22 miles today. My head aches, but the fire is kindled and I must make some tea, that will help it, if not cure it.

—from the diary of Amelia Stewart Knight,
April 18, 1853

HISTORICAL THINKING

1. **READING CHECK** How did the westward migration of people from the United States affect Native Americans?

2. **MAKE INFERENCES** Why do you think pioneer women did not follow strict gender roles on their journeys west?

3. **EVALUATE** In your opinion, what were the greatest hardships that pioneers faced on their journeys west?

4. **ANALYZE LANGUAGE USE** What inspired the pioneers to call their covered wagons "prairie schooners"? Cite evidence from the lesson in your response.

PLAN: 2-PAGE LESSON

OBJECTIVE

Summarize the experiences of migrants along the Oregon Trail and the impact of migration on Native Americans.

CRITICAL THINKING SKILLS FOR LESSON 1.3

- Make Inferences
- Evaluate
- Analyze Language Use
- Make Connections
- Compare and Contrast
- Analyze Primary Sources

HISTORICAL THINKING FOR CHAPTER 10

How did the idea of manifest destiny shape the future of the United States? As settlers pushed farther west, many people's lives changed. Lesson 1.3 examines how the realities of manifest destiny affected women and Native Americans.

BACKGROUND FOR THE TEACHER

Migrants along the Oregon Trail traveled in parties often made up of relatives or neighbors. Parties usually had rules that specified procedures for camping and traveling, set limits on drinking and gambling, provided for assistance for the sick, and clarified what to do if a member died. A day's travel covered an average of 15 miles, starting before sunrise with a breakfast of coffee, bread, and bacon, stopping midday for a cold lunch, and ending around five o'clock with, if possible, a hot dinner. Children attended school in the evening while other members of the party performed tasks and chores or entertained themselves around campfires with songs, dancing, and telling stories. As the journey progressed, some travelers, realizing they had packed too many belongings, lightened their wagons by unloading large or heavy cargo. These abandoned items, known as "leeverites"—from the traveler's choice to "leave 'er right here"—were often seen along difficult stretches of trail.

INTRODUCE & ENGAGE

DISCUSS THE DIFFICULTIES OF A LONG JOURNEY

Invite students to discuss problems or inconveniences people might encounter today on a long trip through unfamiliar surroundings. *(Possible responses: A car might break down. An airplane flight might be delayed or canceled. Travelers might get lost or become sick. Baggage might be misplaced.)* As they read the lesson, ask students to recall these present-day travel problems and consider how they compare or contrast with the hardships pioneers would likely face on their journey west.

TEACH

GUIDED DISCUSSION

1. **Make Connections** Based on the text, how do you think migrants prepared for the long journey west? *(Possible responses: Migrants likely began by putting their affairs in order in their hometowns, closing businesses, selling property, and packing up what they would take with them. They might have arranged to join a large group to avoid traveling alone or planned their own route. Migrants would have needed tents, food, a wagon and equipment to repair it, and horses or mules. Because of the possibility of diseases or accidental injuries, migrants would have also carried medical supplies.)*

2. **Compare and Contrast** How does the scene depicted in Alfred Jacob Miller's painting *Fort Laramie* differ from what would eventually happen to Native Americans? *(Possible response: The painting shows Native Americans living peacefully near Fort Laramie and apparently engaging in trade with the soldiers and migrants passing through, with all three groups likely benefiting from the contact. In reality, the U.S. Army had built the fort on inhabited Native American land, and its occupation and the settlements of migrants would eventually force Native Americans to leave, either peacefully or as a result of hostilities from the federal government. This scenario would take place throughout the West as the United States expanded.)*

ANALYZE PRIMARY SOURCES

Direct students' attention to the Primary Source feature. **ASK:** What can you infer about Amelia Stewart Knight's experiences along the Oregon Trail from her diary entry? *(Possible response: In this excerpt, Knight focuses on the hardships of the journey, including the weather, lack of timber, and her discomfort. She doesn't write about her family or sights along the way. This might mean that Knight was so exhausted by the long trek that feelings of excitement and optimism had worn off.)*

ACTIVE OPTIONS

On Your Feet: Create a Quiz Arrange students in teams and direct them to create a quiz about information in the lesson. Allow time for teams to write a variety of true-false, short-answer, or complete-the-sentence questions. Then have teams alternate posing a question to which the other team responds. Clarify incorrect answers and keep track of the number of correct answers for each team.

NG Learning Framework: Investigate How Tribes Adapted to Indian Territory

ATTITUDE Responsibility

KNOWLEDGE Our Human Story

Remind students that under the Indian Removal Act, some tribes were moved to Indian Territory. Divide the class into groups and tell students to investigate how the southeastern tribes adapted to living in Indian Territory in the West. Instruct students to conduct research to identify the tribes' original locations and how they lived, hunted, and sheltered. Then ask groups to determine the climate of the tribes' new location in Indian Territory and how they adapted to living there. Invite a representative from each group to present the group's findings to the class.

DIFFERENTIATE

ENGLISH LANGUAGE LEARNERS `ELD`

Pronounce Words Remind students of the three pronunciations of *ch* in English: /tch/ as in *child*, /k/ as in *school*, and /sh/ as in *machine*. Display the following words from the chapter:

/tch/	ranching	encroached	challenges
/k/	cholera	schooner	aches
/sh/	Chicago		

Model pronunciations and have students repeat. Suggest that they make word cards, noting definitions and pronunciation hints.

PRE-AP

Investigate Conflict Have students gather information from a variety of sources to create an oral or written report about specific conflicts between Native Americans and the federal government during the mid-1800s. Suggest that students use a Sequence Chain to take detailed notes on the events in the order that they happened, including information from firsthand accounts, if available. Invite volunteers to share their findings with the class, including their sources.

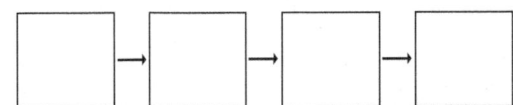

See the Chapter Planner for more strategies for differentiation.

HISTORICAL THINKING

ANSWERS

1. Native Americans lost access to the resources they depended on as they were pushed onto smaller and smaller areas of land. Settlements deprived nomadic Plains tribes of places where they traditionally traveled and hunted.

2. The journey west was long and difficult, so group members shared a variety of chores. This included women performing tasks traditionally assigned to men.

3. Possible response: The greatest hardships were disease and navigating unfamiliar terrain. Travelers sometimes drank contaminated water, causing cholera or dysentery. Crossing desert, rivers, and mountains was dangerous and resulted in injury and death.

4. The white canvases that covered settlers' wagons looked like sails on ships. Additionally, the journeys were very long, which may have made people feel like they were on a voyage across the ocean.

SETTLING THE SOUTHWEST

It's impossible to look at a map of the Southwest without recognizing the Spanish influence on the region's place names: San Antonio, Los Angeles, Rio Grande. Can you identify the Native American influence as well? Of course, the names you read reflect the region's history.

SPANISH COLONIES IN THE SOUTHWEST

As people from the United States moved westward, they encountered not only Native Americans but also Spanish citizens. As you have read, beginning in the 1500s, Spanish conquistadors explored and claimed the parts of western and southwestern North America that became Arizona, New Mexico, Nevada, Texas, Utah, and California.

Spain had a different colonial system than that of Great Britain. Spain was more interested in converting local Native Americans to Christianity and exploiting their labor than in replacing them with Spanish settlers. As a result, Roman Catholic clergy traveled with the conquistadors and set up missions throughout Spanish America. The goal was to gather the Native Americans into a community ruled by soldiers and priests, teach them European agricultural techniques, and make them Christians. Some Spanish treated the Native Americans well, but many punished and enslaved those who refused to convert or openly rebelled.

Some Native American tribes sought to build alliances with the Spanish against their enemies, but many resisted Spanish colonization. You have read about the Pueblo rebellion against the Spanish conquistador Juan de Oñate in New Mexico in the late 1500s. It was followed by more uprisings, including a revolt at Acoma Pueblo, during which the community was destroyed. The largest and most successful rebellion in New Mexico was the 1680 **Pueblo Revolt**, also called Popé's—or Po'pay's—Rebellion. During the rebellion, the Pueblo killed a number of priests, destroyed missions and Christian artifacts, and drove all 2,400 Spanish settlers out

Mexico, c. 1821

[map: Mexico, c. 1821 showing UNITED STATES, NEW CALIFORNIA, NEW MEXICO, PACIFIC OCEAN, ARIZPE, DURANGO, COAHUILA, TEJAS, NUEVO LEÓN, NUEVO SANTANDER, Gulf of Mexico, Mexico City. Scale: 300 miles / 300 kilometers]

United States
Mexico
—— Mexican state border

of New Mexico. After 4 attempts over 12 years, the Spanish recaptured the territory and subdued the Pueblo people once again.

The Spanish had a significant impact on North American culture, including agriculture, language, music, art, law, and food. The Spanish introduced goats, sheep, horses, and cattle to the Western Hemisphere. Many ranching techniques come from the Spanish, including the use of *vaqueros*, or cowboys, to manage large herds of cattle. The words *lariat* and *lasso* are Spanish in origin. So are many western and southwestern place names, including Colorado, California, Los Angeles, and Tucson. In Spanish America, new cultures emerged that combined elements of Spanish culture and a number of Native American cultures of the Southwest.

The Spanish government left North America in 1821 after Mexico won its 11-year revolution against Spain. The new nation of Mexico included lands that make up parts or all of present-day Texas, New Mexico, Arizona, California, Nevada, Utah, Colorado, and Wyoming.

The newly independent nation had difficulty establishing a stable government and a healthy economy. Its northernmost states and territories, which included Tejas (TAY-hahs), or present-day Texas, were distant from the center of government in Mexico City, and few Mexicans were interested in settling there.

GONE TO TEXAS

Hoping that a larger population would help stabilize Tejas and prevent the territory from becoming part of the quickly expanding United States, the Mexican government offered land grants to encourage American immigration. Agents called **empresarios** contracted with the Mexican government to settle a certain number of families in Tejas in exchange for large land grants. An empresario controlled how property on a land grant was allotted and even how the law was enforced. The Mexican government gave out 41 empresario grants over 14 years after the country gained its independence.

Many Americans found the idea of migrating to Tejas enticing. Tejas had fertile soil for farming, vast forests for providing lumber, and expansive grasslands for raising cattle. In 1827, the Mexican government agreed it would not ban slavery entirely in Tejas. As a result, a number of plantation owners immigrated there, bringing along enslaved people.

The first and most famous empresario was **Stephen F. Austin**, an American who agreed to settle 300 families on land between the Brazos and Colorado rivers in Tejas. These first settlers are still called the Old Three Hundred. Most of them were farm families from west of the Appalachian Mountains rather than the East Coast. The majority were from Louisiana, and others hailed mostly from Alabama, Arkansas, Missouri, and Tennessee. They had been part of an earlier westward migration and were now seeking to move even farther west.

American empresario Stephen F. Austin, known as the "Father of Texas," established settlements of English-speaking people in Tejas in the 1820s.

Mexico's immigration plan was a far bigger success than Mexico expected or ultimately wanted. By 1830, about 21,000 Americans were living in Tejas, significantly more than the number of **Tejanos**, or settlers of Hispanic descent. Only 5 years later, the number of American settlers in Tejas had grown to about 38,000, which included about 3,000 enslaved African Americans.

HISTORICAL THINKING

1. **READING CHECK** What parts of North America did Spain control in the early 1800s?

2. **COMPARE AND CONTRAST** How was the Spanish colonial system different from the British system?

3. **ANALYZE CAUSE AND EFFECT** Why did the Americans in Tejas outnumber the Tejanos by the 1830s?

4. **INTERPRET MAPS** Based on the map, why do you think Tejas was so attractive to settlers from the United States?

PLAN: 2-PAGE LESSON

OBJECTIVE

Describe the Spanish influence on the American Southwest and how Mexican independence affected the United States.

CRITICAL THINKING SKILLS FOR LESSON 2.1

• Compare and Contrast
• Analyze Cause and Effect
• Interpret Maps
• Synthesize

HISTORICAL THINKING FOR CHAPTER 10

How did the idea of manifest destiny shape the future of the United States? In 1821, Mexico won independence from Spain after an 11-year revolt. Lesson 2.1 analyzes how Mexico's victory opened the door for American immigration to the Southwest.

BACKGROUND FOR THE TEACHER

The history of the *vaquero* dates back to long before American settlement of the Southwest. Around 1600, Spanish migrants crossed the Rio Grande, bringing longhorn cattle with them. Eventually, large ranches were established, and ranch owners hired *vaqueros* as independent laborers who were not bound to the land and able to come and go as they pleased. The *vaqueros*—many of whom were of Native American and Spanish descent—were experts at herding cattle and taming wild horses. Seasoned *vaqueros* could control a horse with the slightest pull on the reins and knew cattle so well that they could locate strays with a seemingly uncanny ability. In addition to the expert handling of horses and cattle, *vaqueros*' reputations depended on how well they could wield a rope from the back of a running horse.

INTRODUCE & ENGAGE

PREVIEW USING THE MAP

Point out the map of Mexico in the lesson, and ask students to preview the information in the legend. Have volunteers share questions they have about the map and its content. List the questions on the board and guide students to frame them in a way that can be answered through study and research. At the end of the lesson, revisit the questions to see which ones have been answered and which require additional investigation.

TEACH

GUIDED DISCUSSION

1. **Synthesize** How did Mexican independence help reshape the United States? *(Possible response: With powerful Spain out of North America, the United States expanded into the Southwest and came closer to fulfilling its manifest destiny. As Mexico encouraged Americans to settle its land, Americans eventually outnumbered Tejanos. The United States would eventually take Tejas as part of the Union.)*

2. **Analyze Cause and Effect** How did empresarios affect settlement in Tejas? *(Possible response: Empresarios seemed to have absolute power within their land grants, including allotting the land and law enforcement. With such power, they determined who would settle in Tejas and where and chose who would be in charge of law and order. Empresarios, such as Stephen F. Austin, established settlements of English-speaking migrants from the United States, eventually outnumbering Spanish speakers.)*

MORE INFORMATION

The Old Three Hundred The families who settled under the terms of Stephen F. Austin's land grants were different from the typical U.S. families that migrated west. Hoping to ensure peace and a successful settlement, Austin recruited educated, wealthier settlers and awarded them enormous tracts of land. Farming families received 177 acres, and ranchers received an astounding 4,428 acres. Many of the families were slaveholders, and their large plantations became the center of power for the future state. **ASK:** What effect do you think allotting more land to ranchers than farmers might have on Texas's early history? *(Possible response: To get more land, more people may become cattle ranchers than farmers, causing ranching to become important to the state's economy.)*

ACTIVE OPTIONS

On Your Feet: Jigsaw Organize students into "expert" groups and assign each group one of the following topics: the Pueblo Revolt, Mexican War of Independence, American settlers in Texas, Tejano settlers in Texas. Tell groups to research and discuss the topic and summarize their findings. Then regroup students so that each new group has at least one member from each expert group. Students in the new groups take turns sharing the summaries from their expert groups.

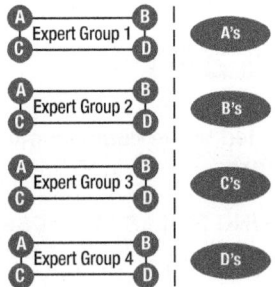

NG Learning Framework: Create a Classroom Resource

SKILLS Communication, Collaboration

KNOWLEDGE Our Human Story

Organize students into six groups and direct them to write lessons to be combined into a chapter about Spanish influence on North American culture. Assign each group one of the following topics: agriculture, language, music, art, law, or food. Tell groups to create a single lesson about their assigned topic that includes visuals, written explanations, and discussion questions. Invite groups to present their lessons to the class. Later, have students combine the lessons into a single volume that can serve as a classroom resource.

DIFFERENTIATE

ENGLISH LANGUAGE LEARNERS   ELD

Explore Spanish Word Origins Point out the Spanish origins of *lasso* and *lariat*, and add that *vaquero* comes from *vaca*, Spanish for *cow*. Ask students at **All Proficiencies** whose home language is Spanish to help their classmates learn these and other words related to *vaqueros*: boot (*bota*), stirrup (*estribo*), spur (*espuela*), stampede (*estampida*), and rodeo (*rodear*).

GIFTED & TALENTED

Write and Perform an Interview Tell pairs to research details about Stephen F. Austin in order to prepare and perform an interview about his work as an empresario, in which one student asks questions and the other answers as Austin. Encourage students to frame questions through their research, such as: What were your goals as an empresario? Why did you choose specific families and specific locations for settlement? How did you persuade the Mexican government to allow slavery in Tejas when it was illegal in Mexico? Invite pairs to perform their interviews for the class.

See the Chapter Planner for more strategies for differentiation.

HISTORICAL THINKING

ANSWERS

1. Spain controlled Mexico and all or part of present-day Arizona, New Mexico, Nevada, Wyoming, Texas, Colorado, Utah, and California.

2. The Spanish did not bring as many people to settle the land as the British did. Instead, they wanted to enslave and convert native people and use their labor to gain resources.

3. The Mexican government offered land grants to encourage American immigration, and many more settlers migrated than the Mexican government expected. Farmers and plantation owners who wanted to expand their holdings may have seen migrating to where slavery was allowed as a way to make their businesses more profitable.

4. Tejas shared an eastern border with Louisiana, making it easier to migrate there than to places farther west, such as New California.

TEXAS FIGHTS FOR INDEPENDENCE

Perhaps you've heard this saying by Mark Twain: "It's not the size of the dog in the fight, it's the size of the fight in the dog." Texans would likely apply this saying to those who fought to free their state from Mexico.

REBELLION IN TEXAS

As you have read, Americans in Tejas, or Texas as they called it, vastly outnumbered Mexicans by 1830. Concerned about the imbalance, the Mexican government outlawed further immigration from the United States and also prohibited Americans from bringing any more enslaved people into Texas. The ban did not actually stop immigration—of free or enslaved Americans—but it angered many Texans.

Both Americans and Tejanos, all proud residents of the Texas territory, began to call for greater representation in the central government and statehood within Mexico for Texas. Texans staged two revolts in 1832 and 1833. Then in 1834, General **Antonio López de Santa Anna** suspended the Mexican constitution and named himself dictator of Mexico. Both Americans and Tejanos were outraged at the disregard for their rights. Stephen Austin

and other Texans formally petitioned the Mexican government to allow Texas to become a separate Mexican state under its own administration. When their request was denied, they decided to fight.

As with the American Revolution, the **Texas War for Independence**, also called the Texas Revolution, started with a skirmish. In early October 1835, Mexican commander Francisco de Castañeda (kah-stah-NYAY-duh) led a small troop of soldiers to Gonzales, Texas, to retrieve a cannon that the Mexican government had provided the town. Castañeda had orders to avoid conflict, but the town's local militia attacked him and his men, forcing them to retreat. This incident became known as the Battle of Gonzales. More battles followed, and soon Santa Anna was on the march, leading an army north to put down the rebellion.

In February 1836, Santa Anna and his army attacked and occupied San Antonio, Texas, where about 180 Texan rebels refused to surrender an old mission called the **Alamo**. About 1,800 Mexican soldiers held the rebels under siege for 13 days, during which time no food, ammunition, or reinforcements could enter the mission. Among those who occupied the Alamo were **Davy Crockett**, a famous frontiersman and congressman from Tennessee, and **James Bowie**, a Texan slave trader. Bowie commanded the volunteer troops at the Alamo. He shared power with **William Barrett Travis**, who commanded the regular troops. On March 2, 1836, Texas declared its independence from Mexico and named itself the **Republic of Texas**.

The Alamo's defenders held out for nearly two weeks. On March 6, the Mexicans stormed the mission and killed almost everyone inside. On orders from Santa Anna, the Mexican Army stripped the bodies of the rebels and burned them. After the battle, "Remember the Alamo!" became a rallying cry, and all those who died were considered heroes of Texas independence.

Another major skirmish began on March 23, 1836. The Mexican Army captured about 400 men from the United States who had joined the Texan army at Goliad, Texas. Many of these men surrendered with the understanding that they would be allowed to return to the United States. They did not know that the agreement depended on Santa Anna's approval. Santa Anna instead ordered the execution of all the captives. "Remember Goliad!" now became a rallying cry alongside "Remember the Alamo!" Santa Anna's cruelty at the Alamo and Goliad not only roused people in Texas but also many in the United States and other countries who decided to support the Texan cause.

THE LONE STAR REPUBLIC

In the spring of 1836, Santa Anna was on the verge of ending the Texas Revolution. But on April 21, the Texan army, led by **Sam Houston**, surprised a larger Mexican force at the San Jacinto (yuh-SIHN-toh) River. A force of 910 Texans attacked Santa Anna's 1,200 soldiers during their afternoon nap, taking only 18 minutes to win the **Battle of San Jacinto**. Santa Anna was wounded but escaped, only to be captured a day later. Houston forced Santa Anna to sign treaties withdrawing Mexican troops from Texas, granting Texas its independence, and recognizing the Rio Grande as the boundary between Mexico and the Republic of Texas.

Mexico's Congress renounced the treaties on the grounds that Santa Anna had signed them under penalty of death. But the fight was over, and Texas became an independent nation. Its flag featured a single large star, which earned Texas the nickname **Lone Star Republic**. The new nation legalized slavery and banned free African Americans from entering or living in the country. Texans elected Sam Houston, the hero of San Jacinto, as president. The people of Texas also voted to seek immediate **annexation**, or takeover, by the United States. However, Texas remained independent longer than anyone expected.

HISTORICAL THINKING

1. **READING CHECK** What events led to the Texas War for Independence?

2. **DETERMINE CHRONOLOGY** When did the tide turn in favor of the Texans during their fight for independence?

3. **MAKE INFERENCES** Why did Tejanos fight for independence from Mexico?

TEXAS WAR FOR INDEPENDENCE
1835–1836

October 10, 1835 Texans win the Battle of Goliad.

December 9, 1835 Texan troops seize the Alamo. *(Alamo building located in San Antonio, Texas)*

February 23, 1836 Santa Anna and his troops begin the siege of the Alamo.

March 6, 1836 Santa Anna storms the Alamo.

March 23, 1836 Santa Anna orders the Goliad Massacre.

April 21, 1836 Texans win the Battle of San Jacinto and capture Santa Anna a day later. *(Surrender of Santa Anna by William Huddle)*

| OCT | NOV | DEC | JAN | FEB | MAR | APR | MAY | JUN |

October 2, 1835 Texans win the Battle of Gonzales.

December 1835 Antonio López de Santa Anna arrives in San Luis Potosí to raise troops against Texans. *(portrait of Santa Anna by Carlos París)*

March 2, 1836 Texas declares its independence from Mexico. *(flag of the Republic of Texas)*

May 14, 1836 Santa Anna signs the Treaties of Velasco.

322

323

BRAINSTORM RALLYING CRIES

Define the term *rallying cry* as a word or phrase used to encourage people to unite in support of a cause. Ask students to brainstorm rallying cries, and list the words or phrases on the board. Then lead a class discussion about why rallying cries garner support for an issue. Tell students that in this lesson they will learn why "Remember the Alamo!" became a rallying cry for Texas.

TEACH
GUIDED DISCUSSION

1. **Compare and Contrast** How were the reasons Texas declared independence from Mexico similar to and different from the reasons the American colonies declared independence from Great Britain? *(Both Texans and the colonists believed that they lacked adequate political representation and that governmental restrictions unfairly limited immigration. Specific grievances differed in that Texans were angry at the prohibition of slavery, and colonists resented excessive taxation.)*

2. **Make Predictions** What do you think caused Texas to remain independent "longer than anyone expected," as stated in the lesson? *(Possible response: Texas's legalization of slavery might have delayed its annexation by the United States because adding another slave state would have disrupted the balance achieved by the Missouri Compromise.)*

INTERPRET TIME LINES

Direct students' attention to the time line in the lesson. **ASK:** How did Santa Anna's involvement affect the course of the war? *(The Texans had achieved victories at Gonzales and Goliad and seized the Alamo before Santa Anna assembled troops and stormed the mission. Santa Anna's involvement prolonged the war and led to the brutal deaths of many Texans.)*

ACTIVE OPTIONS

On Your Feet: Generate a Cause-and-Effect Chain Draw and display a large Cause-and-Effect Chain on the board or on chart paper. In the first box write: Mexican government outlaws American immigration to Texas. For each subsequent box, ask a volunteer to write an effect and explain how it was caused by the event preceding it. Continue to have students write effects and explain causes until they exhaust information from the lesson.

NG Learning Framework: Research the Defenders of the Alamo

ATTITUDE Curiosity

KNOWLEDGE Our Human Story

Tell students to conduct preliminary research about the defenders of the Alamo, choose one to fully research, and then write a report to present to the class. Students may choose a well-known leader, such as William Barret Travis, Susannah Dickinson, James Bowie, Davy Crockett, or Gregorio Esparza, or a less famous defender they discover. Invite students to share their reports with the class. After the presentations, use the following questions to prompt a class discussion: What did these individuals have in common? Why were they willing to give their lives for Texas independence?

STRIVING READERS

Pose and Answer Questions Have students work in pairs to read the text and time line. Instruct them to pause after each paragraph and after each entry in the time line to ask each other *who, what, where, when,* and *why* questions about what they have just read. Suggest students use a 5Ws Chart to organize their questions and answers.

PRE-AP

Compare Impacts Then and Now Instruct students to conduct research to learn more about the massacres at Goliad and the Alamo and their impact on support for the Texas Revolution. Also tell them to research a recent instance of brutality or injustice that rallied people to respond. Have students use a Venn diagram to organize their information and then create a presentation comparing and contrasting both events. After the presentations, lead a discussion about how brutality or injustice can bring people together to demand change.

See the Chapter Planner for more strategies for differentiation.

ANSWERS

1. The following events led to the Texas War for Independence: Mexico banned immigration, representation in the government was denied, Santa Anna became dictator, and Texas was denied Mexican statehood.

2. The battles at the Alamo and at Goliad made Texans more determined to win their independence. Santa Anna's cruelty strengthened their resolve and brought them support from the United States and other countries. In battle, the tide turned with Sam Houston's victory in the Battle of San Jacinto.

3. Tejanos wanted greater representation in the Mexican government and felt their rights were disregarded.

2.3 CURATING HISTORY

MEXIC-ARTE MUSEUM
AUSTIN, TEXAS

The Mexic-Arte Museum presents traditional and contemporary Mexican, Latino, and Latin American art with the goal of reaching visitors of all ages. Its permanent collection and special exhibitions showcase the work of established and emerging artists in such media as prints, sculptures, photographs, masks, murals, and installations.

The museum's mission of youth outreach is evident in its educational programs. For example, artist educators teach courses for underserved students at local schools. The museum also provides formal gallery space for local teens to display their artwork and teams up with other museums to present teacher workshops during the summer.

Illustrated Encyclopedia

Among the Mexic-Arte Museum's collection of rare books is this encyclopedia volume titled *México a través de los siglos (Mexico Through the Centuries)*. When the encyclopedia was published in 1884, it was advertised as the complete social, political, religious, military, artistic, scientific, and literary history of Mexico from ancient times to the late 1800s. This rare book is among the more than 5,000 books and periodicals housed in the museum's library, which has a collection that dates from the 19th century to the present day.

Calaveras Print

This 19th-century print by Mexican artist Manuel Alfonso Manilla (1830–1895) features imagery of skeletons, or *calaveras*, which is common in indigenous Aztec art. Manilla often used calaveras to depict religious themes and create caricatures. A caricature is an illustration that exaggerates prominent characteristics of a subject, usually in order to ridicule the subject.

From 1882 to 1892, Manilla worked as an illustrator and engraver with a Mexico City publishing house. He created artwork to accompany songs, or *corridos*, and drew story characters and scenes of street life, bullfighting, and circuses.

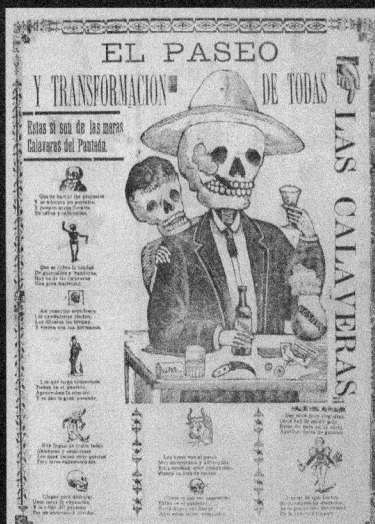

EL PASEO
Y TRANSFORMACION DE TODAS
LAS CALAVERAS

Tree of Life

A Tree of Life is a form of Mexican folk art inspired by the metal candelabras, or candleholders, and incense burners that Spanish friars brought to Mexico. Originally sculpted from clay, early Trees of Life depicted the biblical story of creation. Today's sculptures display a wide variety of themes. This ceramic Tree of Life by renowned Mexican potter Alfonso Castillo Orta (1944–2009) focuses on the theme of spring. The goddess of spring appears in the center of the tree near the bottom.

How does Alfonso Castillo Orta represent spring in this Tree of Life?

Queen of the Huipil

In this 1988 photograph, Mexican-born photographer Jesse Herrera (1945–) captures the coronation of the Queen of the Huipil during an annual festival held in the community of Cuetzalan in Mexico. Elders from the community select a festival queen based partly on the quality of her *huipil*, a traditional woven garment. The queen is crowned with a white cloth and paraded on an ornate chair, as shown here.

Tecuani Mask and Costume

Tecuani means "jaguar" or "tiger" in Nahuatl, a language spoken by indigenous people in central and southern Mexico. This mask and costume come from the state of Guerrero in southwestern Mexico. Dancers wear this kind of costume in performances of a traditional Mexican dance called *Danza de los Tecuanes*, or Dance of the Jaguars.

Originally, the dance represented an event in which two tribes joined together to fight a jaguar that had been attacking their livestock. Today, the dance is performed at religious celebrations and cultural events in Mexico and in the United States, including Day of the Dead celebrations. Day of the Dead is a Mexican holiday in November that focuses on remembering family members and friends who have died.

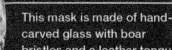

This mask is made of hand-carved glass with boar bristles and a leather tongue.

324 CHAPTER 10

Westward Expansion 325

PLAN: 2-PAGE LESSON

OBJECTIVE

Study artifacts and art related to traditions of ancient and modern Mexican, Latino, and Latin American cultures.

CRITICAL THINKING SKILLS FOR LESSON 2.3

• Analyze Visuals
• Make Connections
• Identify
• Make Inferences

HISTORICAL THINKING FOR CHAPTER 10

How did the idea of manifest destiny shape the future of the United States? Before Americans migrated westward, Spain and Mexico controlled the vast territory of the West, influencing the culture of North America. Lesson 2.3 explores artifacts and artwork from artists that reveal their Spanish and indigenous origins.

BACKGROUND FOR THE TEACHER

The Mexic-Arte Museum in Austin, Texas, is one of the country's few Mexican art museums. It began as the vision of three artists—Sylvia Orozco, Sam Coronado, and Pio Pulido—who wanted to share Mexico's pre-Columbian and modern art and culture with Texas. Founded in 1984, the museum showcased its first cultural program with a Day of the Dead festival in the fall of that year. In 2009, the museum launched one of several of its youth outreach programs. *Screen It!* provides printing skills and art education to more than 2,000 underserved African-American and Latino youth in the surrounding community. The museum's print collection has inspired many of these students to express through art their own stories and heritage.

HISTORY NOTEBOOK

Encourage students to complete the Curating History page for Chapter 10 in their History Notebooks as they read.

INTRODUCE & ENGAGE

SHARE EXAMPLES OF ART AS CULTURE

Guide a class discussion about the ways in which art can teach others about a specific culture. Then tell students that in this lesson, they will learn about the Mexic-Arte Museum, which showcases traditional and contemporary artwork relating to Mexican, Latino, and Latin American cultures.

TEACH

GUIDED DISCUSSION

1. **Identify** What themes do some of the artifacts represent? *(Possible response: The Tree of Life and the skeletons on the calaveras print suggest themes of life and death.)*

2. **Make Inferences** What might be the cultural value to Mexican people today of preserving the 1880s Spanish encyclopedia? *(Possible response: From the description given, the authors might have been able to preserve some of the stories and traditions of indigenous people before Columbus and give an account of how the Spanish invasion contributed to modern Mexican culture.)*

CURATING HISTORY

The Mexic-Arte Museum offers a rich collection of artifacts and artwork and a variety of educational programs. Access the museum website and guide students to explore the Random Images at the Online Collections Database. **ASK:** How do the items you see reflect the museum's mission to highlight established and new artists? What insights do the paintings, drawings, and other artwork give you into Mexican culture?

ACTIVE OPTION

On Your Feet: Sort the Artifacts Arrange students in groups of four or five to examine the museum's online collection of art and photographs. Instruct them to use the details they see on the website and in the lesson to complete a Concept Cluster, sorting the art into categories. When the groups are finished, they can share their Concept Clusters with the class and note the details that most of them identified.

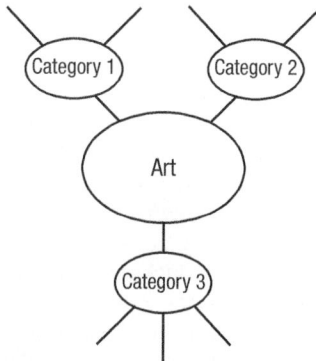

For students who develop an interest in Mexican art and culture, suggest they read the American Story at the beginning of this chapter.

DIFFERENTIATE

ENGLISH LANGUAGE LEARNERS

Create a Word Web Pair students at the **Emerging** and **Expanding** levels with students at the **Bridging** level. Tell partners to take turns reading sentences, identifying art terms, and writing the terms on the spokes of a Word Web. Instruct pairs to trade and compare their completed Word Webs and to use a dictionary to determine the meaning of unfamiliar words. Final webs may include the following: *prints, sculptures, photographs, masks, murals, installations, gallery, imagery, caricature, illustrator, engraver,* and *folk art.*

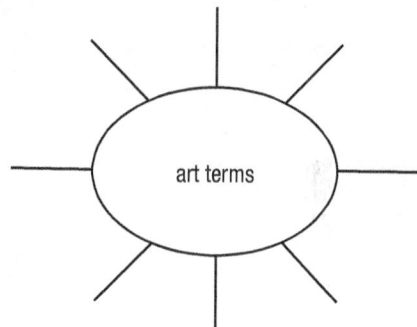

GIFTED & TALENTED

Propose an Exhibition Ask students to plan an exhibition that might be added to the Mexic-Arte Museum. Encourage them to jot down notes about the kinds of artifacts and artwork they would include as well as what they hope viewers would gain from the display. Instruct them to write a proposal, stating the purpose, goals, and contents of the exhibition. Invite students to present their proposal to the class.

See the Chapter Planner for more strategies for differentiation.

TREE OF LIFE

Answers will vary. Possible response: In his Tree of Life, Alfonso Castillo Orta represents spring through the use of bright colors; a variety of colorful birds, leaves, and flowers; and a goddess of spring. The goddess and most of the figures that represent people have raised arms or arms stretched out in a gesture welcoming the season of growth.

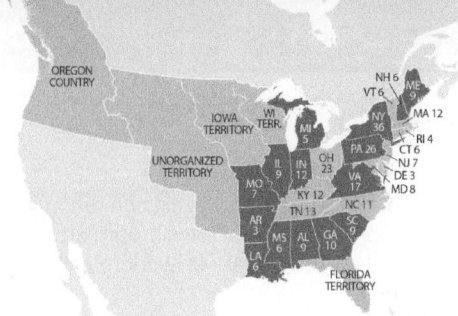

The 1844 Election

Henry Clay, Whig
Electoral Vote: 105 votes, 38.2%
Popular Vote: 1,300,004 votes, 48.1%

James K. Polk, Democrat
Electoral Vote: 170 votes, 61.8%
Popular Vote: 1,339,494 votes, 49.6%

James G. Birney, Liberty
Electoral Vote: 0 votes, 0%
Popular Vote: 62,000 votes, 2.3%

TENSIONS WITH MEXICO

What would you consider a legitimate reason to wage war? Like people around the world, Americans have different answers to this question. In the 1840s, many Americans—both prominent leaders and everyday citizens—doubted the reasons for waging war with Mexico.

THE ELECTION OF 1844

Debate about adding Texas as a state in the Union began almost as soon as the Republic of Texas won its independence in 1836 and continued for years. The presidential campaign of 1844 brought the issue to the forefront of American politics. The Democrats nominated **James K. Polk**, a former governor of Tennessee and a staunch supporter of manifest destiny, as their candidate. Polk had supported Martin Van Buren as the party's presidential nominee and had only wanted to be vice president. But Van Buren did not support the annexation of Texas, which cost him the support of southerners—and the nomination.

Polk was the first **dark horse** to run for the nation's highest office. A dark horse is a little-known candidate whose nomination is unexpected and usually the result of a compromise between factions. Polk and the Democrats appealed to both northerners and southerners with a platform promoting U.S. expansion. They addressed the issue of slavery by proposing to balance the admission of Texas as a slave state with the admission of Oregon as a free territory.

The Whigs nominated prominent Kentucky statesman Henry Clay for president on a platform opposing further U.S. expansion. However, Clay soon came to believe that such a stance would cost him the presidency. He changed his position and supported the annexation of Texas on the condition that it be achieved peacefully. But his strategy backfired, and he won only a few expansionist votes while losing those of abolitionists and other opponents of annexation. Clay's campaign was damaged even more by the presence of a third party, the abolitionist Liberty Party, in the election. Though the Liberty Party only won 62,000 votes, its strong showing in New York drew enough votes away from Clay to give the state's electoral votes to Polk, which made the difference in the national election. Although Polk won only 49.5 percent of the popular vote, he received 170 votes from the electoral college against Clay's 105 votes. That was enough to secure him the election. He entered office with the clear goal of annexing Texas and Oregon.

This presidential campaign ribbon from 1844 features portraits of Democratic candidate James Polk and his running mate, George Dallas.

POLK'S FOUR GOALS

Polk had promised to serve only one term as president, but he planned to accomplish a great deal in those four years. He had campaigned on four goals. One was to add two new states to the Union by annexing the Republic of Texas and acquiring full control of the Oregon Territory from Great Britain. His second goal was to reduce tariffs on imports, which he believed would lower the cost of products for American consumers. His third goal was to re-establish an independent U.S. Treasury, which would manage all government funds, thus limiting the influence of unregulated state banks. The lending practices of the state banks had contributed to a depression in the late 1830s. Polk's fourth goal was to acquire the territories of California and New Mexico. Polk eventually would achieve all four goals.

Even before Polk took office, Congress voted to annex Texas as a new slave state in 1845. But the admission of Texas to the Union meant that slave states outnumbered free states in the U.S. Senate. The admission of Oregon as a free state would be needed to restore the balance.

For years, expansionists had sounded the rallying cry "Fifty-Four Forty or Fight." They wanted the United States to gain control of all the Oregon Territory up to its boundary with Russian territory at the latitude of 54° 40'. During the presidential campaign, Polk had agreed. But after winning the election, he instructed his secretary of state, James Buchanan, to negotiate secretly with Great Britain to relinquish, or give up, its claims to the Oregon Territory below the 49th parallel, which formed the northern boundary of the United States to the east. This deal angered northern Democrats, who had supported Polk on Texas,

because it would decrease the size and eventual electoral power of Oregon. In 1846, the United States and Great Britain signed the Oregon Treaty, setting the border between Oregon and Canada at the 49th parallel.

POLK PROVOKES WAR

The Mexican government had never recognized the independence of Texas, so the United States' annexation of Texas increased tensions between the two countries. In addition, the two countries did not agree on the boundary between them. Polk insisted that the **Rio Grande** was the border between Texas and Mexico, but Mexico considered the **Nueces River**, which was much farther north, to be the border.

Polk wanted to fight Mexico but did not want to be blamed for starting a war. Instead, he provoked one. In July 1845, Polk ordered American troops under the command of General Zachary Taylor to cross the Nueces River into disputed territory. The Mexican government claimed that the United States had invaded Mexico, committing an act of war. Even though the Mexican Army lacked funds, effective weapons, and training, Mexican president José Joaquín de Herrera ordered troops to assemble at the Rio Grande.

There, on April 25, 1846, American and Mexican forces fought a battle that left 11 Americans dead and 5 wounded. The Mexicans captured the remainder of the American troops. More skirmishes followed, and on May 11, President Polk announced to Congress that Mexico had "invaded our territory and shed the blood of our fellow citizens on our own soil." In response, Congress declared war, and the **Mexican-American War** began on May 13, 1846.

OBJECTIVE

Analyze the reasons for and consequences of the U.S. annexation of Texas.

CRITICAL THINKING SKILLS FOR LESSON 3.1

- Analyze Cause and Effect
- Distinguish Fact and Opinion
- Compare and Contrast
- Draw Conclusions
- Interpret Maps
- Analyze Primary Sources
- Make Inferences

HISTORICAL THINKING FOR CHAPTER 10

How did the idea of manifest destiny shape the future of the United States? President James K. Polk's election was viewed as a mandate for manifest destiny. Lesson 3.1 analyzes how his election and the annexation of Texas led to the Mexican-American War.

BACKGROUND FOR THE TEACHER

Although James K. Polk may have seemed a dark horse to most Americans, he was well known to Andrew Jackson, a person with a great deal of influence. Polk had become one of Jackson's staunchest allies while serving in the House of Representatives, backing the president's policies and actions, including the war on the Second National Bank, his opposition to internal improvements, and his actions during the nullification crisis. Polk's support had earned him the nickname "Young Hickory," a play on Jackson's familiar moniker "Old Hickory." Ironically, Polk's loyalty cost him a second term as governor of Tennessee when the Whigs blamed the economic crash of the late 1830s on Jackson and, by implication, on Polk. Yet it was Jackson who resurrected Polk's career. At the 1844 Democratic Convention, Jackson accurately sensed the mood of the nation and argued the party needed a candidate committed to manifest destiny. On the ninth ballot, a person fitting that description was selected—James K. Polk.

INTRODUCE & ENGAGE

PREDICT CAMPAIGN ISSUES

Direct students' attention to the campaign ribbon shown in the lesson. Ask them to use details from the ribbon to anticipate the issues Polk would support as a presidential candidate. Inform students that Polk supported the annexation of Texas, which would have lasting consequences for the nation and the Southwest. Then use a Cause-and-Effect Web to help students predict the effects of Polk's position. *(Possible responses: war with Mexico, an increase in slave states, new cultural influences in the country)* After completing the lesson, revisit the Cause-and-Effect Web and discuss which effects were realized and why.

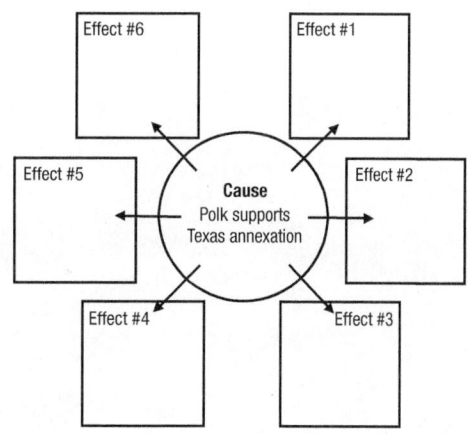

TEACH

GUIDED DISCUSSION

1. **Make Inferences** Why did Henry Clay believe he had to support expansionism to win the election? *(Possible response: Clay likely knew that only a small portion of the country, such as abolitionists, opposed U.S. expansion. Thus, he had to support the policy to have a chance at winning the election.)*

2. **Distinguish Fact and Opinion** How did Polk's claim that Mexico "invaded our territory and shed the blood of our fellow citizens on our own soil" reflect both fact and opinion? *(Possible response: Because American soldiers died, the claim that "blood was shed" was a fact. However, the assertion that Mexico "invaded" American "soil" is based on Polk's opinions that Texas was part of the United States and that the Rio Grande was the legitimate boundary, opinions Mexico disagreed with.)*

INTERPRET MAPS

Provide students with demographic maps from the presidential elections of 1836 and 1840, and guide them to compare these maps with the one in this lesson. **ASK:** Did either the Democrats or Whigs consistently win only in free states or only in slave states in these elections? *(No. Both political parties were able to garner support from both slave and free states.)* Have students explain why they think both parties were able to maintain this type of joint support. *(Possible response: Neither party took a hard position on slavery, which would have turned portions of the North or South against them.)* Then remind students that in 1844 the Liberty Party ran on an abolitionist platform. **ASK:** What do you think would happen if the major political parties no longer appealed to both slave and free states? *(Possible response: Negotiations and compromises would cease, leading the country closer to civil war.)*

DIFFERENTIATE

STRIVING READERS

Create a T-Chart Instruct students to use a T-Chart such as the one shown to compare candidates Polk and Clay in the election of 1844. Ask them to reread the lesson, adding details under each column, including the candidate's home state, political party affiliation, past political experience and degree of popularity, position on expansionism and slavery, and percentage of popular and electoral votes won in the election. Encourage students to compare their completed charts, noting similarities and differences.

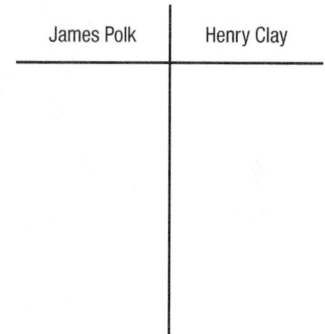

PRE-AP

Analyze Lincoln's "Spot Resolutions" Instruct students to read and analyze Abraham Lincoln's "Spot Resolutions," which are available in the Library of Congress and other online archives. Their analysis should include the reasoning behind Lincoln's demand that Polk provide specific facts to Congress and describe how the numbered resolutions build Lincoln's case regarding the U.S. pretext for the Mexican-American War. Encourage students to extend their analysis to other wars in which a U.S. president has involved the nation, perhaps invoking reasons similar to Polk's, such as a "just war" or to "support the troops." Invite students to present their analysis to the class in a written or oral report.

See the Chapter Planner for more strategies for differentiation.

While the United States was negotiating a peace treaty with Mexico, Senator John Calhoun of South Carolina delivered a speech to his peers in which he opposed a proposal to annex all of Mexico because he did not want Mexicans or Native Americans to become American citizens. In this excerpt from his speech, he explains why he argued against the Mexican-American War from the beginning.

I opposed the war then, not only because I considered it unnecessary, and that it might have been easily avoided; not only because I thought the President had no authority to order a portion of the territory in dispute and in possession of the Mexicans, to be occupied by our troops; not only because I believed the allegations upon which it was sanctioned by Congress, were unfounded in truth; but from high considerations of reason and policy, because I believed it would lead to great and serious evils to the country, and greatly endanger its free institutions.

—from a speech to the Senate by John C. Calhoun, January 4, 1848

DIFFERENT ATTITUDES TOWARD WAR

The Mexican-American War had widespread support in the South and West, where people hoped a victory would open new lands for American settlement and the expansion of slavery. Although many northerners denounced the war and American motives, Polk had no difficulty getting congressional approval because he linked the war to support for U.S. troops.

Debate over the war continued, however. Some Americans, particularly those who opposed slavery, viewed the conflict as an immoral land grab that violated the nation's democratic principles. Former president John Quincy Adams opposed the war, as did such northern abolitionists as William Lloyd Garrison and Charles Sumner, who believed that it was being fought so that southerners could expand slavery and increase cotton production. Author Henry David Thoreau spent a night in jail for refusing to pay taxes that would fund the war. In response to the opposition, Polk accused his critics of treason and insisted that the war was just and necessary.

As the war dragged on for more than a year, opposition grew. In December 1847, Illinois congressman Abraham Lincoln, then a young newcomer to the U.S. House of Representatives, introduced the "Spot Resolutions." This legislation called on President Polk

to identify the "spot" where American blood had first been spilled in order to determine if the bloodshed had actually occurred on U.S. soil. Congress never acted on the resolutions. But in January 1847, the House of Representatives passed a law censuring Polk for "unnecessarily and unconstitutionally" beginning the Mexican-American War.

AMERICAN PLACES
The Rio Grande, Texas

The Rio Grande forms the southern boundary of Big Bend National Park, a protected area of canyons and waterfalls at the southernmost bend of the river in southwest Texas. The huge bend in the river curves around the largest protected portion of the Chihuahuan Desert. The Rio Grande serves as the border between Mexico (top) and the United States for about 1,000 miles. Early in the Mexican-American War, this border, and therefore access to this important river, was disputed.

HISTORICAL THINKING

1. **READING CHECK** What were the four goals of James Polk's 1844 presidential campaign?

2. **ANALYZE CAUSE AND EFFECT** How did James Birney and the Liberty Party affect the election of 1844?

3. **COMPARE AND CONTRAST** How did attitudes about the Mexican-American War differ among Americans?

4. **INTERPRET MAPS** How would you describe the voting pattern in the 1844 election?

BUILD BACKGROUND

RIVER BOUNDARIES

Mexico's claim that the Nueces River constituted the southern border of Texas was supported by historical precedent. Spain established the Nueces as a border in 1816; the United States approved the boundary when purchasing Florida from Spain in 1819. Even after Mexico's independence, American mapmakers placed Texas's southern boundary at the Nueces River. After annexation, however, the United States abruptly switched its position and argued that an additional 150 miles claimed by Texas—the distance from the Nueces to the Rio Grande—was now part of U.S. territory. To ease tensions, President Polk sent negotiator John Slidell to Mexico to attempt to establish the Rio Grande as the formal boundary. When Mexican leaders refused to hear the offer and reaffirmed their claim to all of Texas, Polk quickly sent troops across the Nueces, beginning the war.

OPPOSITION TO THE WAR WITH MEXICO

Opposition to the Mexican-American War was largely an anti-slavery issue voiced by powerful abolitionist speakers. Former U.S. president John Q. Adams led the northern Whigs' opposition, declaring the war an act of aggression by the United States. Adams understood the implications of annexing Texas as early as 1838 when he filibustered in Congress for 22 days to block the annexation over the issue of slavery. By 1845, Adams and other political leaders voiced concerns about the war's constitutionality, including President Polk's ordering U.S. troops into disputed Mexican territory to provoke war. Charles Sumner, another fierce abolitionist, delivered speeches in northern cities, publicly berating politicians who supported the war. Sumner declared himself a Conscience Whig, stating, "A war of conquest is bad; but the present war has darker shadows. It is a war for the extension of slavery over a territory which has already been purged by Mexican authority from this stain and curse."

TEACH

GUIDED DISCUSSION

3. Draw Conclusions What evidence supported the claim of northern abolitionists that the Mexican-American War was being fought to expand slavery? *(Possible response: Southern slaveholders supported the war, Texas already had established slavery, and any new territory in addition to Texas would be southern and potentially open to slavery.)*

4. Analyze Primary Sources Direct students' attention to the Primary Source feature. **ASK:** What reasons does John C. Calhoun give for opposing the Mexican-American War? *(Possible response: It was unnecessary, unconstitutional, and founded on lies. It would lead to great evils and endanger the country's free institutions.)*

AMERICAN PLACES

The photograph clearly shows how the Rio Grande changes the landscape around it, allowing plants and animals to thrive in the arid Southwest. Because the river keeps changing its course, Mexico and the United States must adjust to the new international boundaries the river creates. The Rio Grande's water is vital to farms and ranches on both sides of the river, so a change in the "ownership" is a source of friction between the two countries. The Rio Grande has at times been the setting of immigration conflicts between the United States and Mexico.

ACTIVE OPTIONS

On Your Feet: Analyze Character Traits Divide the class into small groups. Have groups work in separate areas of the room to complete a graphic organizer like the one shown. Direct them to use information from the text and other sources to list Polk's actions and identify the character traits demonstrated by each action. Then have each group share its analysis. Use the activity as the basis for a class discussion about how Polk's character traits contributed to the Mexican-American War and divided the nation.

Person	Actions	Character Traits

NG Learning Framework: Take a Stand on the War

SKILL Communication

KNOWLEDGE Our Human Story

Divide the class into teams of four or five and provide each team with a primary source either supporting or opposing the Mexican-American War, such as Polk's "Declaration of War" and Josh Giddings's speech from May 11, 1846. Ask teams to analyze their assigned source and note the major arguments. Then invite teams with opposing sources to engage in a debate about whether the country should have declared war on Mexico. When the teams finish, lead a class discussion about which arguments were the most persuasive and why.

HISTORICAL THINKING

ANSWERS

1. Polk's four goals were acquiring Texas and Oregon, reducing tariffs, re-establishing an independent U.S. Treasury, and acquiring California and New Mexico.

2. The Liberty Party drew votes from the Whigs in the key state of New York, allowing Polk to become president.

3. Many southerners and westerners supported the war as a way to acquire more land and to expand slavery. Abolitionists opposed it because they feared the expansion of slavery into any new territory acquired. Other people opposed the war because they believed it was unconstitutional, unnecessary, and started under false pretenses.

4. The Whigs did well in New England and some western states, while the Democrats did well in the South, West, and the North outside New England.

WAGING WAR IN THE SOUTHWEST

The Southwest is known for its breathtaking landscape. The Grand Canyon, Bryce Canyon, and Yosemite Valley are just a few of the region's stunning features. Once belonging to Mexico, these natural treasures are part of the bounty the United States gained with its victory in the Mexican-American War.

An 1851 print by German artist Carl Nebel captures the moment General Winfield Scott discovered that the Mexican Army had retreated from Mexico City overnight, forcing local politicians to surrender the capital to the Americans.

WAR WITH MEXICO

The United States began the Mexican-American War on strong footing. In June 1846, General **Stephen Kearny** led about 1,700 American soldiers from Fort Leavenworth, Kansas, to Santa Fe, the capital of the New Mexico Territory. Kearny's troops traveled for two months before reaching their destination, but they took control of the city without firing a shot. With this one victory, the United States claimed all of the New Mexico Territory.

Kearny's next goal was to gain control of California. By the time Kearny arrived in San Diego in December 1846, U.S. Navy Commodore Robert Stockton had captured and blockaded the three major ports of California: San Francisco, Los Angeles, and San Diego. A power struggle emerged between the two men, each believing that President Polk had put him in charge. When Lieutenant Colonel John C. Frémont, also under orders from Polk, joined the two officers, he sided with Stockton. In return, Stockton named Frémont governor of California.

Frémont had been serving in California clandestinely, or secretly, with possible orders to encourage Americans living in California to rebel against the Mexican government. On June 14, 1846, about 30 American settlers in Sonoma, California, took control of the town and raised their own flag, which featured a grizzly bear. The design later became the inspiration for California's state flag. The flag also inspired the name of the **insurrection**, or rebellion, which became known as the **Bear Flag Revolt**. The rebels declared California an independent republic—the **Bear Flag Republic**. A few weeks later, Frémont

took command of the American rebels and seized the **presidio**, or Spanish military settlement, of San Francisco, which was empty at the time.

The independent Bear Flag Republic ended three weeks after it began, however. American forces soon claimed San Francisco and the surrounding region for the United States. By January 1847, all of California was under American control. Kearny took over and became territorial governor of California. He arrested Frémont and sent him east to Washington, D.C., where he was court-martialed for disobedience and other offenses. But President Polk stepped in and reversed Frémont's sentence. Frémont retained public support and eventually returned to California, where he became the first senator to represent the state in the U.S. Congress.

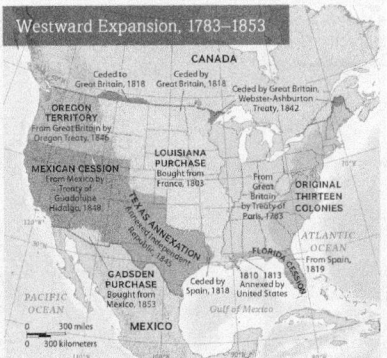

Westward Expansion, 1783–1853

AMERICANS INVADE MEXICO

Meanwhile, in Texas, General Zachary Taylor had been moving south. He crossed the Rio Grande on May 18, a few days after war was officially declared. In September 1846, he conquered the city of Monterrey after a five-day siege. In early 1847, at the Battle of Buena Vista (BWAY-nuh VEES-tuh), Taylor fought against Mexican troops led by General Santa Anna. While no clear winner emerged, the Mexican Army suffered far greater casualties than the Americans did, and Taylor became a hero in the United States.

Taylor's troops next joined those commanded by General Winfield Scott on the east coast of Mexico, near Veracruz. The Mexican fort at Veracruz was considered to be nearly impossible to capture. Scott employed the largest **amphibious force** ever used by the United States up to that time. An amphibious force consists of troops attacking from both land and sea. After a three-week siege, Scott succeeded in taking Veracruz without losing many of his soldiers. Then he headed inland toward Mexico City, where Americans fought for days before they finally captured the last fort protecting the city in September 1847. With its capital city under American control, Mexico surrendered.

Mexico and the United States signed the treaty that officially ended the war, the **Treaty of Guadalupe Hidalgo**, on February 2, 1848. Under the terms of the treaty, the Rio Grande became the boundary

between Texas and Mexico. In exchange for $15 million, Mexico relinquished all of its northernmost territories, including all or part of the present-day states of California, New Mexico, Arizona, Utah, Nevada, Colorado, and Wyoming. The U.S.-acquired territory constituted more than half of Mexico's total territory and increased the area of the United States by one-third. Polk had achieved his fourth goal of acquiring the territories of California and New Mexico.

In 1853, the United States completed its last land deal with Mexico. In the **Gadsden Purchase**, the United States paid $10 million for an area of land located along the southern borders of present-day Arizona and New Mexico. The United States wanted this land to complete a southern transcontinental railroad. The transaction completed the borders of the **contiguous**, or connected, United States.

HISTORICAL THINKING

1. **READING CHECK** How did the Mexican-American War end?

2. **SUMMARIZE** What were the consequences of the Mexican-American War for the United States and for Mexico?

3. **INTERPRET MAPS** Through what single land purchase or treaty did the United States gain the largest area of land between 1845 and 1855?

OBJECTIVE

Evaluate the end of the Mexican-American War and how the Treaty of Guadalupe Hidalgo expanded U.S. territory.

CRITICAL THINKING SKILLS FOR LESSON 3.2

- Summarize
- Interpret Maps
- Make Inferences

HISTORICAL THINKING FOR CHAPTER 10

How did the idea of manifest destiny shape the future of the United States? In 1847, the United States won the Mexican-American War. Lesson 3.2 discusses the U.S. victory and how subsequent treaties realized one of the goals of manifest destiny.

BACKGROUND FOR THE TEACHER

The decision to mount an amphibious assault at Veracruz stemmed from Mexico's geography. Although Zachary Taylor had won early victories in the north, Mexico was simply too large to conquer through individual battles. U.S. military leaders decided it was necessary to invade and capture central Mexico to force a surrender. They chose Veracruz as the landing site, and a massive amphibious effort was soon underway to prepare for the invasion. Because this type of assault was so novel, ships had to be custom-designed. For example, steamships used to bring troops to Veracruz required special landing boats to transfer the troops from ship to land. The boats had to be carefully constructed not only to fit aboard the steamships but also to maneuver in the rough surf. This large-scale effort foreshadowed the use of amphibious assaults in the Civil War and in two world wars.

INTRODUCE & ENGAGE

ACTIVATE PRIOR KNOWLEDGE

Ask students to recall what they learned about the beginning of the Mexican-American War. Create a 5Ws Chart on the board and call on volunteers to complete *who, what, where, when*, and *why* details describing the start of the war. Tell students that in this lesson they will learn about the end of the war and the terms of the treaties signed. At the end of the lesson, ask students to add information to the chart regarding the results of the war.

TEACH

GUIDED DISCUSSION

1. **Make Inferences** Why do you think American forces defeated Mexican forces in California and Mexico relatively easily? *(Possible response: Mexico had only recently achieved independence from Spain and had gone through changes in its government. As a result, its army was probably not well organized or supplied. For the Mexican forces in California, communicating with the government would have been a problem since the Mexican capital was several hundred miles to the south.)*

2. **Summarize** How did the Bear Flag Revolt lead to the United States gaining control of California? *(Possible response: Lieutenant Colonel John C. Frémont encouraged Americans in California to rebel against the Mexican government. In Sonoma, citizens took over the town and declared California to be independent, renaming it the Bear Flag Republic. With Frémont in command, the rebels took over the empty presidio in San Francisco, and three weeks later, U.S. forces claimed the city and the area around it for the United States.)*

MORE INFORMATION

Paintings of War The print featured in this lesson was included in a book by journalist George Kendall, *The War Between the United States and Mexico*, published in 1851. As a newspaper correspondent, Kendall traveled with the U.S. Army during the war and based the book on his experiences. He hired artist Carl Nebel to provide the illustrations. It proved a difficult task for Nebel, who had no firsthand knowledge or experience of the war. Instead, he had to rely on the sketches and accounts of others. Despite these obstacles, historians generally consider Nebel's paintings accurate depictions of events in the Mexican-American War.

ACTIVE OPTIONS

On Your Feet: Examine the Benefits of Acquiring Territory Organize students into four groups and assign one of the following topics to each: Texas Annexation, Oregon Territory, Mexican Cession, and Gadsden Purchase. Instruct each group to research why the United States acquired each territory. Groups should focus on the benefits the country hoped to gain from the expansion, such as resources or land for railroads. Once groups have finished, ask a representative from each group to explain their findings. Then lead the class in a discussion about which benefits would have the greatest impact on the United States.

NG Learning Framework: Compare Artistic Depictions

ATTITUDE Curiosity

KNOWLEDGE Our Human Story

Share with students the More Information feature about Carl Nebel's paintings. Then have them research Christian Friedrich Mayr and his painting of the same event. Suggest students work in pairs to discuss the following questions: How are Nebel's portrayal of the event and his historical point of view different from Mayr's? How does an artist's point of view affect our understanding of history? Call on volunteers to share their responses with the class.

DIFFERENTIATE

INCLUSION

Understand a Map Instruct pairs to examine the map Westward Expansion, 1783–1853 chronologically, from the original colonies to the Gadsden Purchase. Tell them to state the name of each acquisition and identify when and how the United States acquired it. Students can then use their knowledge to answer the Interpret Maps question.

GIFTED & TALENTED

Create a Multimedia Presentation Direct students to conduct online research to learn more about the Bear Flag Revolt, the Bear Flag Republic, and the Bear Flag itself, including its history, symbolism, and evolution over time. Have students assemble their findings into a compelling multimedia presentation. Invite students to share their presentation with the class and answer questions from their classmates.

See the Chapter Planner for more strategies for differentiation.

HISTORICAL THINKING

ANSWERS

1. Mexico and the United States signed the Treaty of Guadalupe Hidalgo, which set the Rio Grande as the boundary between Texas and Mexico. Mexico also relinquished all its northernmost territories for $15 million.

2. The United States acquired territory equal to more than half of Mexico's total area, increasing its own area by one-third.

3. In 1848, the Treaty of Guadalupe Hidalgo ended the Mexican-American War and brought the United States all or parts of California, New Mexico, Arizona, Utah, Nevada, Colorado, and Wyoming.

SETTLING CALIFORNIA

Today, California is the leading economic powerhouse of the United States. But both the Spanish and the Mexicans largely ignored the territory when they owned it. Even so, their influence on California is readily apparent.

CRITICAL VIEWING In his 1790 painting *Portrait of Fray Junipero Serra*, how does Spanish artist Francesc Caimari Rotger emphasize Father Serra's religious devotion?

MISSIONS AND RANCHOS

As you have read, Spain first explored and claimed California in the 1500s but was slow to establish settlements there. In the mid-1700s, Russian and British fur trappers in the Pacific Northwest began to expand their hunting and trading activities farther south. To reinforce their land claims, the Spanish then sent priests and soldiers to establish settlements.

In 1769, **Father Junípero Serra** (hoo-NEE-peh-roh SEH-rah), a Catholic priest from Spain, built the first mission in California at San Diego. The Spanish went on to establish 21 missions throughout California, each a day's ride apart. Protected by soldiers housed in nearby presidios, these church-centered missions grew into villages and agricultural centers. They formed the foundations for many California cities, including San Diego, Los Angeles, and San Francisco.

Like other mission priests, Father Serra sought to convert the local Native Americans to Christianity. As you have read, the mission system was devastating to many Native Americans, who were often mistreated and exploited for their labor. Father Serra's relationship with the Native Americans under his authority is the subject of controversy. While a number of historians believe he was a generous, caring, and courageous man who did his best to improve the lives of Native Americans, others claim he participated in the abuse and oppression of Native Americans at the Spanish missions.

Mexico won its independence from Spain in 1821 and ended the mission system in California in 1833. The Mexican government granted most of the mission land to **Californios**, or settlers of Spanish or Mexican descent. These land grants formed large estates called **ranchos**. Each rancho covered thousands of acres. The rancheros, or owners, raised large herds of cattle for their hides and tallow, or processed fat. They traded the hides and tallow for manufactured goods, which were shipped along the Pacific Coast. Most of the hides went to New England boot- and shoemakers, while the tallow was processed into candles and soap in South America. Many Native Americans ended up working on the ranchos, often receiving only basic housing and food for their labor.

California was too far away for the authorities in Mexico City to govern it effectively. Feeling neglected and yet also increasingly independent, Californios staged numerous revolts against the Mexican government. By 1845, residents had effectively achieved home rule and had a locally born governor, Pío Pico, a ranchero of mixed Mexican and African descent. But California remained sparsely populated, with a Native American population numbering less than 150,000 and about 7,000 non-native people living there. By the end of 1849, the non-native population would reach nearly 100,000.

A GROWING AMERICAN PRESENCE

In the 1830s, Americans began migrating to California as part of the overall westward movement. A majority of the American immigrants were male traders, who typically blended into the local culture, married local women, learned Spanish, and became Mexican citizens. Most of these traders lived in the coastal cities, such as Los Angeles, San Diego, and San Francisco.

Fur trappers and farming families also moved to California, following the California spur of the Oregon Trail. These groups settled more often in northern California and usually remained separate from the Californios, due to differences in culture and religious beliefs. While most Californios were Roman Catholics, the majority of immigrants were Protestants. The immigrants tended to form their own settlements. Some received land grants from the Mexican government to establish ranchos.

One of the largest of these immigrant settlements was Nueva Helvetia, or New Switzerland, which later became the city of Sacramento. Swiss immigrant **John Sutter**, who received several land grants from the Mexican government to start a colony, founded the settlement. By the late 1840s, Sutter's settlement had become a thriving farm community. Besides raising herds of cattle like other California rancheros, residents also grew grapes and wheat, thus helping to diversify the region's agriculture.

Despite the influx of immigrants from the United States and other countries, Californios still formed the majority of the population when the United States acquired California in 1848 through the Treaty of Guadalupe Hidalgo. But that situation would soon change.

HISTORICAL THINKING

1. **READING CHECK** What was a rancho?

2. **SUMMARIZE** How did Native Americans in California fare under Spanish rule?

3. **MAKE INFERENCES** Why was it difficult for the government in Mexico City to effectively govern California?

4. **COMPARE AND CONTRAST** How is the history of Mexican California similar to the history of Mexican Texas?

PLAN: 2-PAGE LESSON

OBJECTIVE

Examine how the mission system and immigration shaped California.

CRITICAL THINKING SKILLS FOR LESSON 4.1

- Summarize
- Make Inferences
- Compare and Contrast
- Draw Conclusions

HISTORICAL THINKING FOR CHAPTER 10

How did the idea of manifest destiny shape the future of the United States? Dating back to Spanish settlement, California's history was shaped by a variety of influences. Lesson 4.1 examines the impact of diverse peoples on California's development.

BACKGROUND FOR THE TEACHER

California's missions had lasting effects on the region. For Native Americans, Spanish colonization was disastrous, resulting in the deaths of thousands and the destruction of many cultures. Historians estimate that prior to contact there were approximately 300,000 native people in California. By 1860, around 30,000 remained. Ironically, many missions helped preserve native cultures by storing their art and artifacts, which are available for study today. Detailed records kept by priests allow modern scholars to track the change from a Native American hunter-gatherer society to an economy based on ranching and agriculture. Missions left their mark in other ways, such as building aqueducts, some of which are still used today in the city of Santa Barbara, and inspiring California's iconic mission-style architecture with its spacious courtyards, tall adobe walls, fountains, and patios.

INTRODUCE & ENGAGE
PREVIEW USING MAPS

Display a present-day map of California and challenge students to locate all the cities that begin with *San* or *Santa*. Explain that *San* or *Santa* means "saint" in Spanish and that many cities in California are named for saints, reflecting the Catholic heritage of the state. Tell students that several of these cities grew up around Spanish missions established in the 1700s. Explain that this lesson describes how the mission system shaped California's history.

TEACH
GUIDED DISCUSSION

1. **Draw Conclusions** Why did California remain sparsely populated by the Spanish and Americans until as late as 1845? *(Possible response: California was far from both the United States and central Mexico, was difficult for most people to travel to, and had no obvious wealth to attract settlers.)*

2. **Compare and Contrast** How did the ethnic and religious makeup of California compare with that of the rest of the United States? *(Possible response: California was home to more Roman Catholics and people of Spanish and Mexican ancestry than other parts of the United States, with the possible exception of Florida.)*

SUMMARIZE

Guide students to recall the different reasons Americans began to migrate to California. **ASK:** Why did the interaction between Americans and the Spanish change over time? *(Possible response: At first, most American immigrants were traders—single men who blended into the culture, intermarried, and became citizens of Mexico. In time, however, Protestant trappers and farmers arrived. Religious and cultural differences caused these Americans to form communities separate from Spanish communities.)*

ACTIVE OPTIONS

On Your Feet: Explore California's History Organize students into groups of three. Provide each group with a Concept Cluster and instruct students to label it as shown. Tell students to write words or phrases on the spokes for each topic, adding spokes as necessary. Encourage students to build on other group members' entries. After all groups have written on all three topics, call on volunteers to summarize the information from their clusters.

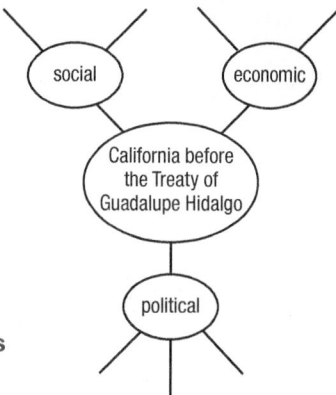

NG Learning Framework: Investigate Mission Histories

SKILLS Communication, Collaboration

KNOWLEDGE Our Human Story

Direct students to work in small groups to investigate the history of a particular California mission, focusing on the art, architecture, and layout; daily life for adults and children; the type of work done there; and significant contributions to the culture or history of the state. Encourage students to search for maps, time lines, and other documents with information about the mission. Invite groups to develop creative ways to share their findings, such as creating an infographic, video, or written first-person account.

DIFFERENTIATE
STRIVING READERS

Identify Facts Post the following heading: Five Facts About California's Early History. After students read the lesson, ask them to copy the heading and write five sentences under it. Invite students to share and compare their sentences with a partner.

GIFTED & TALENTED

Create a Visual Biography Direct students to create and annotate a visual biography of Pío Pico, the last governor of California under Mexican rule, whose long life spanned many events in the history of California, Mexico, and the United States. Students should include dates and locations. Some students might wish to explore Pico's cultural heritage and make connections to contemporary Latino and African-American communities of California. Invite students to present their biography to the class, explaining why they chose the events, annotations, and visuals they included.

See the Chapter Planner for more strategies for differentiation.

HISTORICAL THINKING
ANSWERS

1. A rancho was a large land grant given to certain residents or immigrants in California by the Mexican government. The lands were once the property of the Roman Catholic missions.

2. Native Americans were used as forced labor, many died from European diseases, and many of their cultures were destroyed.

3. California was far from Mexico City and sparsely populated, so residents regarded themselves as independent from the Mexican government.

4. Both territories were established by Spain as colonies, had diverse populations, were taken over by Americans, and became independent states before becoming part of the United States.

CRITICAL VIEWING Father Serra is depicted holding a cross and looking at it with reverence while a priest reads the Bible to him. The priest uses an aspergillum to bless Father Serra with a sprinkle of holy water.

THE GOLD RUSH

Eureka is an ancient Greek word meaning "I have found it." Supposedly, shouts of "Eureka!" rang through the Sierra Nevada foothills in the first few months of the California gold rush. But the supply of easy gold had dwindled by the time most of the gold seekers showed up.

GOLD DIGGERS

The Native Americans of California had always known about the gold in the rocks and creeks of their homeland, but they did not value it the way Europeans did. On January 24, 1848, when a worker building a sawmill for John Sutter spied glittering flecks of gold in the stream that powered the mill, everything changed. Sutter swore the worker to secrecy, but it didn't take long for word to spread. By the end of the year, **prospectors**, or people in search of valuable natural resources, swarmed the western foothills of the Sierra Nevada, collecting nuggets and gold dust worth about $6 million. Local Native Americans were among the first to participate in the mining. Territorial governor Richard Mason estimated that in 1848, more than half the gold miners were Native Americans. By the end of 1849, more than 700 ships carrying in excess of 45,000 prospective gold miners—most of them from the eastern United States—had sailed to California. About 55,000 new settlers followed, arriving from the overland trails that cut across the continent. The newcomers formed a **gold rush**, a large-scale, rapid movement of people to a place where gold has been discovered.

CRITICAL VIEWING American and Chinese miners work on a site outside Sacramento, California, in 1852. Based on what the men hold and wear, what equipment was essential to search for gold?

Whether they came by sea or land, the fortune-seekers were a mixed group. The majority of **forty-niners**—gold miners named for the year they began arriving in California—were Americans, but people came from all over the world. Stories of *Gam Saan*, or "Gold Mountain," sparked gold fever in China. In 1852 alone, over 20,000 Chinese gold seekers arrived in California. Prospectors from Peru, Chile, and especially from Sonora, Mexico, which had experienced a gold rush of its own in the early 1800s, also streamed into California. In fact, many Latino gold-seekers were skilled miners. Some African Americans came too. Most were from the cities of New England or were enslaved people bound to southern forty-niners. Women were less likely to be victims of gold fever. By 1850, only 8 percent of California's entire population was female. But a few women made a good living as **entrepreneurs**, or organizers of new businesses. And some women did try their luck at mining and struck gold.

Whatever their ethnicity or gender, few miners made a fortune, aside from the lucky handful present at the beginning of the gold rush. However, California flourished. Many who first came to find gold decided to stay and became farmers, teachers, builders, and traders. In fact, the largest fortunes in California were made not in the gold fields, but from supplying miners with clothing, food, and equipment. One of the most famous California gold rush entrepreneurs was Levi Strauss, a dry goods salesman who had emigrated from Germany. He moved to San Francisco, where he produced and sold the tough denim blue jeans still popular today.

THE MINING FRONTIER

Although movies and books romanticized it, mining was a dangerous, unpleasant business. Disease, violence, and miserable living conditions were part of daily life in mining camps. The death rate from illness, accident, murder, and suicide was extremely high. One out of every five forty-niners died within six months of arriving in the gold fields.

Mining life was especially hard for certain ethnic groups. Some Native Americans were worked to death, while others were driven away or murdered. The government sanctioned this violence. In 1851, California's first governor, Peter Hardeman Burnett, declared that "a war of extermination will continue to be waged between the two races until the Indian race becomes extinct." Latino and Chinese miners also were frequently exploited as laborers, sifting gold from the sand and gravel of streambeds. The Foreign Miners License Tax, passed in 1852, was imposed almost solely on the Chinese. Until it was declared unconstitutional in 1870, it provided nearly a quarter of California's yearly revenue.

Most miners did not intend to settle in California permanently; they planned to make their fortunes and go back home. Mining camps that had turned into **boomtowns**, or towns that grow suddenly, were abandoned on an almost daily basis. Maintaining law and order amid such chaos was extremely difficult. The territorial, and later the state, government passed mining codes and established mining districts. But many mining areas were too remote to govern effectively, and the stream of new prospectors was constant. Miners ended up forming their own self-governing districts. Each district elected an official who recorded all the claims and settled disputes. Miners administered justice themselves, often by banishing or hanging offenders.

The lawlessness in the mining camps created a demand for stronger government, which statehood would bring. California easily met the population requirements for statehood, but residents wanted it to be admitted as a free state. California's constitution explicitly stated: "neither slavery nor involuntary servitude . . . shall ever be tolerated in this state." Even though its admission would upset the balance between slave and free states, California became the nation's 31st state in September 1850.

HISTORICAL THINKING

1. **READING CHECK** How were the largest fortunes in California made during the gold rush?

2. **ANALYZE CAUSE AND EFFECT** How did the discovery of gold in 1848 affect California?

3. **IDENTIFY MAIN IDEAS AND DETAILS** What was life like in the mining camps of California during the gold rush?

PLAN: 2-PAGE LESSON

OBJECTIVE

Explain how the discovery of gold affected the history of California.

CRITICAL THINKING SKILLS FOR LESSON 4.2

- Analyze Cause and Effect
- Identify Main Ideas and Details
- Make Connections
- Analyze Primary Sources

HISTORICAL THINKING FOR CHAPTER 10

How did the idea of manifest destiny shape the future of the United States? When first acquired by the United States, California was a sparsely populated, remote territory. Lesson 4.2 explains how the gold rush ultimately changed California into the newest state in the Union.

BACKGROUND FOR THE TEACHER

In spite of California's fertile farmlands, many forty-niners faced starvation. The food supply could not keep up with the rapid influx of settlers, and the growing demand allowed merchants to charge outrageous prices. A slice of bread or a single chicken egg sold for a dollar or more, the equivalent of more than $30 today. Some entrepreneurs found a new source of eggs for the protein-hungry newcomers. They sailed to the Farallon Islands off the coast of San Francisco to gather murre eggs, which they sold to restaurants and grocery stores. Murres are penguin-like birds that lay their large eggs on steep cliffs. Egging, as the gathering work was called, was dangerous, and the enterprise touched off a competitive—and often violent—egg rush in California.

HISTORY NOTEBOOK

Encourage students to complete the American Gallery and Reid on the Road video series pages in their History Notebooks.

INTRODUCE & ENGAGE

DISCOVER WORD RELATIONSHIPS

Display a Word Web with *gold fever* in the center. Ask students to tell what they associate with the phrase. *(Possible responses: excitement or enthusiasm about gold; miners focused on getting as much gold as they can; people becoming preoccupied with finding gold)* Tell students that this lesson describes how an event in California in the 1840s caused people across the country to develop gold fever and drew them to the newly acquired territory.

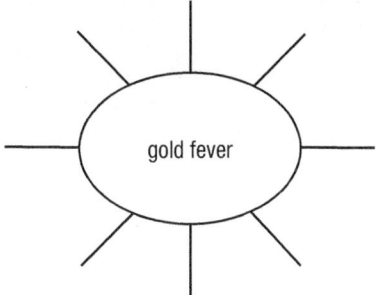

gold fever

TEACH

GUIDED DISCUSSION

1. **Make Connections** How might 19th-century views about gender roles have contributed to the predominantly male population of early California? *(Possible response: Women were considered fragile, and society dictated that their proper place was in the home or as caretakers and teachers. Thus, traveling cross-country to participate in a gold rush, enduring harsh conditions, and living in lawless camps was not an option for most women.)*

2. **Analyze Cause and Effect** What caused California to push so quickly for statehood? *(Possible response: Because the population rapidly increased and much of the state was disorganized and lawless, residents saw statehood as a way to bring stability and order to the region.)*

ANALYZE PRIMARY SOURCES

Direct students' attention to the Primary Source feature. **ASK:** What symptoms of gold fever does James H. Carson notice in himself? *(He envisions himself as suddenly wealthy, with a castle, slaves, and many adoring women seeking his attention.)* Discuss the obstacles that prevented Carson and others from achieving their dreams, including the fierce competition for gold and the lawless, dangerous gold fields and camps.

ACTIVE OPTIONS

AMERICAN GALLERY ONLINE **The Gold Rush** Invite students to explore the American Gallery. Have them select one of the images and do additional research to learn more about it. Ask questions that will inspire additional inquiry about the chosen gallery image, such as: Who or what is this? What action is taking place? What was this item used for? How is it related to the gold rush?

NG Learning Framework: Evaluate Primary Sources

ATTITUDE Curiosity

SKILL Communication

Instruct students to work in small groups to research primary source information about the California gold rush. Encourage them to examine newspaper articles, songs or poems from the era, and journals and diaries written by forty-niners. Then direct each group to choose one or two sources and evaluate their credibility, including the author's experience, language and tone, purpose for writing, and intended audience. Invite each group to share one or two sources with the class and explain what information the sources added to their understanding of the gold rush.

DIFFERENTIATE

ENGLISH LANGUAGE LEARNERS

Understand a Loan Word Bring students' attention to the word *entrepreneur* and model its pronunciation. Then pair students at the **Emerging** and **Expanding** levels with native English speakers and have them make a word card, writing the definition of the word *entrepreneur*, pronunciation hints, and an original sentence using the word.

PRE-AP

Investigate the Impact of the Gold Rush Tell students to investigate specific short- and long-term impacts of the gold rush. Assign them one of the following aspects on which to focus:

- economic impacts
- social impacts
- environmental impacts

Suggest that students use a Cause-Effect Organizer to record their thinking. Invite students to present their findings in a written or oral report.

See the Chapter Planner for more strategies for differentiation.

HISTORICAL THINKING

ANSWERS

1. The largest fortunes were made by merchants who supplied miners with food, clothing, and equipment. Miners who came at the beginning of the gold rush were also more likely to make fortunes than those who arrived later.

2. The discovery of gold attracted thousands of people from many countries into the territory. The need for stability and order eventually led residents to demand that California become a state.

3. The mining camps were characterized by disease, violence, and poor living conditions, resulting in the death of one out of every five miners.

CRITICAL VIEWING As shown in the photograph, mining gold required shovels, rakes, a trough with a source of water, pans for sifting, and rugged clothing, boots, and hats.

4.3 GEOLOGY IN HISTORY

MAIN IDEA In the 1850s and 1860s, geology largely determined the railroad route that would connect California with the rest of the country.

Donner Pass

Andesite Peak
8,215 ft (2,504 m)

Donner Pass
7,093 ft (2,162 m)

DONNER RIDGE

Donner Lake

Mount Judah
8,245 ft (2,513 m)

Mount Lincoln
8,369 ft (2,551 m)

Transcontinental Railroad

Elevation above sea level

7,550–9,200 ft	2,301–2,804 m
6,700–7,549 ft	2,042–2,301 m
6,200–6,699 ft	1,890–2,042 m
1,800–6,199 ft	549–1,889 m

scale varies with perspective

HOW GEOLOGY BUILT THE TRANSCONTINENTAL RAILROAD

By Andrés Ruzo, National Geographic Explorer

People often say that the shortest distance between two points is a straight line. But a railroad route between two places is rarely straight. The area's geology has to be dealt with.

CONNECTING THE EAST WITH THE WEST

After California achieved statehood, many people believed the United States needed a **transcontinental railroad**—a railroad that would cross the continent to the West. Trains already linked the East, South, and Midwest. But settlers heading to the Pacific Coast had to travel by wagon or stagecoach on a journey that took months. A railroad connecting the regions would not only provide more efficient transportation but also unite all parts of the growing country.

Many of those who supported the creation of a transcontinental railroad were nonetheless divided over what route it should take. In general, northerners called for a route passing through northern states and territories. Southerners, on the other hand, advocated for a route that would run through the territory acquired in the Gadsden Purchase: present-day southern Arizona and southern New Mexico. Both sides knew that a transcontinental railroad would bring new businesses and industries and increased trade to the stops along the route.

In the 1850s, Congress sponsored several groups of surveyors to explore possible routes for the railroad. The surveyors mapped the **topography** of the land west of the Mississippi, studying its physical features, including mountains, valleys, and bodies of water, as well as its human-made features. They also documented the Native American tribes living in the West and the region's plants and animals. The surveyors looked for areas with fertile soil, forests, and navigable rivers. Having these resources accessible along the chosen route would not only make construction cheaper and easier but also promote settlements along the way. Above all, the surveyors tried to plot routes that would run mostly along flat or gently sloping terrain.

OVERCOMING GEOLOGIC FEATURES

A man named Theodore Judah, however, had his own ideas about the route. Judah was a construction engineer who had helped build the first railroad in California. For the transcontinental railroad, he proposed a northern route through Nebraska, Wyoming, Utah, Nevada, and California. Those who objected to Judah's plan pointed out the many

Trains used the Summit Tunnel at Donner Pass, shown here, for 130 years. Today, this line of the railroad is bypassed, and the tunnel has been abandoned.

physical obstacles, including the Sierra Nevada, the mountain range running along the eastern edge of California. To build level tracks, engineers would use explosives to blast tunnels through the range's granite peaks.

Daniel Strong, a drugstore owner in California, liked Judah's proposed route and offered his help. Strong showed Judah a path through the Donner Pass, a mountain pass in the northern Sierra Nevada. A **mountain pass** is a passageway through a mountain range that is lower than the surrounding peaks. As geologic forces, such as glaciers and earthquakes, eroded and shaped mountain ranges over millions of years, they created these passes. The Donner Pass would require the railroad route to cross one of the Sierra Nevada's summits rather than two. Judah's route would also follow already established trails, including the Oregon and Mormon trails.

Together, Judah and Strong found investors to fund their plan, and Judah presented it to Congress in 1861. The legislators expressed doubts about the proposal, but President Abraham Lincoln, who was a great supporter of a transcontinental railroad, endorsed it. And by that time, the country was engaged in the Civil War between the North and the South. That meant that the southern route was no longer under consideration. Congress passed the **Pacific Railways Acts** in 1862 and 1864, which authorized two companies to build the railroad: the **Central Pacific Company** and the **Union Pacific Company**. It was decided that the Central Pacific Company would begin laying tracks in Sacramento, California, while the Union Pacific Company would start in Omaha, Nebraska. The two lines would meet in the middle.

After laborers worked 12 to 16 hours a day, 7 days a week for about 6 years building bridges, blasting tunnels, and laying tracks, locomotives from each company met nose to nose at Promontory Point, Utah, on May 10, 1869. The president of the Central Pacific Company drove a golden spike into the tracks to commemorate the route—an achievement dictated by geology.

THINK LIKE A GEOLOGIST

1. **READING CHECK** Why did many Americans want to build a transcontinental railroad in the 1850s?

2. **MAKE INFERENCES** What physical features besides mountains might have posed a challenge to those building the transcontinental railroad?

3. **DRAW CONCLUSIONS** In what ways did geology dictate the railroad's route?

PLAN: 2-PAGE LESSON

OBJECTIVE

Analyze how geology determined the route for a transcontinental railroad built between California and Nebraska.

CRITICAL THINKING SKILLS FOR LESSON 4.3

- Make Inferences
- Draw Conclusions
- Identify
- Evaluate
- Interpret Maps

HISTORICAL THINKING FOR CHAPTER 10

How did the idea of manifest destiny shape the future of the United States? After California became a state, people pushed the federal government to build a railroad that would connect the East with the West. Lesson 4.3 explains how planners used geologic features to determine the route for the railroad.

NATIONAL GEOGRAPHIC EXPLORER ANDRÉS RUZO

Andrés Ruzo is familiar with the challenges of working with extreme geology, whether it's his own Boiling River project in the jungles of Peru or writing about the transcontinental railroad in the 1860s. What Ruzo loves about the Boiling River project is that "it forces you to be extremely intentional with every step, because there can be really serious consequences." For instance, in the dry season the river's heated springs are hot enough to kill anything that falls into the water. In the 1860s, railroad workers used highly volatile explosives to blast through solid granite. One mistake in these situations could have had deadly consequences. A geoscientist, conservationist, author, and science communicator, Ruzo is dedicated to educating others about geologic science.

HISTORY NOTEBOOK

Encourage students to complete the Geology in History page for Chapter 10 in their History Notebooks as they read.

INTRODUCE & ENGAGE

ACTIVATE PRIOR KNOWLEDGE

Display a map of the United States. Ask volunteers to trace what might serve as a continuous overland route from Nebraska to the Pacific Ocean. Prompt them to share their observations about waterways and mountain ranges that must be navigated or crossed. Then explain that planning a railroad connecting the East to the West involved examining the proposed path at ground level, mile by mile. Tell students that in this lesson they will read about the geology and politics that determined the eventual route. After students read the lesson, ask them to compare their proposed route with a map of the actual route and suggest reasons for the differences.

TEACH

STEM

GUIDED DISCUSSION

1. **Identify** Although geology was a main factor, what other factors influenced where the railroad would eventually be constructed? *(Possible response: Regional competition between the North and South led to both proposing routes that favored their interests, one through northern areas and the other through Arizona and New Mexico. The onset of the Civil War eliminated the southern route.)*

2. **Evaluate** How did Theodore Judah's and Daniel Strong's ideas for the railroad's route take advantage of geologic and man-made features? *(Possible response: Judah's proposed northern route would use part of the existing Oregon and Mormon trails. Strong knew about a mountain pass through the Sierra Nevadas, which would require crossing only one summit.)*

GEOLOGY IN HISTORY

Interpret Maps Direct students' attention to the map of the Donner Pass and ask them to study the legend, the route of the railway, and the topography of the terrain. **ASK:** What details in the map illustrate why the railroad was constructed through the Donner Pass? *(Possible response: The Donner Pass is more than 1,000 feet lower than the surrounding summits. From the east, it increases elevation gradually as it passes through the Sierra Nevada range.)* Direct students' attention to the right side of the map where the route makes a long loop. **ASK:** Why might the railway have taken this course? *(Possible response: The waterway probably affected the route. The track may have been built to cross the water at narrow sections, where construction of bridges would have been possible.)*

ACTIVE OPTIONS

On Your Feet: Team Word Webbing Arrange students in groups of four or five. Hand each group a sheet of paper containing the following topic sentence: Geology both helped and hindered the building of the transcontinental railroad. Tell groups to build a paragraph based on the topic sentence. Have the first student in each group write a sentence and pass the paper clockwise to the next student. Students circulate the paper until each group member has added at least one sentence and the group runs out of sentences to add. Then direct each group to collaborate on a concluding sentence for their paragraph. Call on volunteers from each group to share the group's paragraph with the class.

NG Learning Framework: Investigate Construction Problems and Solutions

ATTITUDE Curiosity

SKILL Communication

Arrange students in small groups and have them research the actual construction of the transcontinental railroad. Ask them to find out how engineers and workers solved some of the geologic problems they faced building tunnels and bridges, protecting tracks from blizzards, and meeting quotas to keep construction on schedule. Direct students to summarize their findings in a written report, including illustrations or other visuals. Invite groups to share their work with the class.

DIFFERENTIATE

STRIVING READERS

Tweet a Summary As students read the lesson, direct them to write a tweet for each paragraph that summarizes the paragraph's main idea in their own words. Ask students to read their tweets aloud to a partner, comparing and correcting them for accuracy. Encourage pairs to develop hashtags for each tweet.

GIFTED & TALENTED

Perform a Dramatic Reading Challenge students to conduct research to find an eyewitness account or a newspaper report about the joining of the Union Pacific and Central Pacific railroads at Promontory Point. Instruct students to prepare a dramatic reading of the account or an excerpt from it. After they have practiced, invite students to perform their readings for the class.

See the Chapter Planner for more strategies for differentiation.

HISTORICAL THINKING

ANSWERS

1. The country was growing, particularly along the West Coast, and those traveling west wanted a faster, more efficient mode of transportation. A transcontinental railroad would also encourage new businesses and settlement along the route.

2. In addition to mountains, transcontinental railroad construction had to cross rivers and canyons, go around lakes or wetlands, and navigate through or around dense forests.

3. Route planners had to determine the flattest route with the most gradual slope, accessible mountain passes, and whether land with adequate supplies for workers was suitable for settlement. Adapting to geologic features made building the transcontinental railroad easier, faster, and cheaper.

VOCABULARY

Use each of the following vocabulary words in a sentence that shows an understanding of the term's meaning.

1. mountain man

   The mountain man lived alone and trapped beaver in the Rocky Mountains.

2. manifest destiny
3. vaquero
4. empresario
5. dark horse
6. presidio
7. rancho
8. gold rush
9. forty-niner
10. boomtown

READING STRATEGY
ANALYZE CAUSE AND EFFECT

Analyzing causes and effects can help a reader understand the reasons that an event occurred. Complete the following graphic organizer with reasons for the westward migration of the 1840s and 1850s and answer the question.

Causes → Effects

Large numbers of Americans moved west in the 1840s and 1850s.

11. What push and pull factors contributed to the westward migration of Americans in the 1840s and 1850s?

MAIN IDEAS

Answer the following questions. Support your answers with evidence from the chapter.

12. What role did the concept of manifest destiny play in the westward migration of Americans? **LESSON 1.1**

13. Why did the westward migration of the pioneers particularly threaten the way of life of the Plains tribes? **LESSON 1.3**

14. Why did the Mexican government encourage American immigration to Tejas? **LESSON 2.1**

15. Why did both Tejanos and Americans in Tejas want to separate from Mexico? **LESSON 2.2**

16. Why did the Mexican-American War have widespread support in the South? **LESSON 3.1**

17. How did the outcome of the Mexican-American War benefit the United States? **LESSON 3.2**

18. How did the change from Spanish to Mexican rule affect California? **LESSON 4.1**

19. How did the gold rush of 1848 affect the drive for statehood in California? **LESSON 4.2**

HISTORICAL THINKING

Answer the following questions. Support your answers with evidence from the chapter.

20. **IDENTIFY PROBLEMS AND SOLUTIONS** What problems did the annexation of Texas create for the United States?

21. **SEQUENCE EVENTS** In what order did the United States acquire the lands west of the Louisiana Purchase?

22. **ANALYZE CAUSE AND EFFECT** What effect did the gold rush of 1848 have on Native Americans in California?

23. **DRAW CONCLUSIONS** What was the ultimate goal of the Texan fight for independence from Mexico?

24. **FORM AND SUPPORT OPINIONS** What is your opinion of the concept of manifest destiny?

25. **DESCRIBE** Who were the forty-niners? Describe their characteristics and backgrounds.

INTERPRET IMAGES

The political cartoon by Nathaniel Currier at right is titled "The Independent Gold Hunter on His Way to California" and was first published in 1849. This cartoon contrasted with other popular depictions of the forty-niners. Newspapers sensationalized stories of miners getting rich after a short time in California. Many artists portrayed the forty-niners as brave and ambitious heroes. Study this illustration closely. Then answer the questions that follow.

26. What equipment is the man carrying?

27. What is unusual about the way the man is dressed?

28. Based on details in the cartoon, what is the artist's attitude toward the gold hunter?

ANALYZE SOURCES

The United States Constitution states that only Congress can declare war. On May 11, 1846, after American forces had clashed with Mexican troops in eastern Texas, President Polk addressed Congress and requested a declaration of war on Mexico. Read this excerpt from his address. Then answer the question.

> Mexico has passed the boundary of the United States, has invaded our territory and shed American blood upon American soil. She has proclaimed that hostilities have commenced and that the two nations are now at war.
>
> As war exists, and, notwithstanding all our efforts to avoid it, exists by the act of Mexico herself, we are called upon by every consideration of duty and patriotism to vindicate with decision the honor, the rights, and the interests of our country.

29. How does Polk characterize Mexico's actions and the position of the United States?

30. How does Polk justify declaring war on Mexico?

CONNECT TO YOUR LIFE

31. **ARGUMENT** Think about the migrants who headed west in the 1840s. Many were Americans who were moving to Mexican territories in search of land and better opportunities. Today, emigrants from Mexico and many other nations come to the United States in search of a better life. Should the United States welcome such immigration or severely limit it? Write a short essay stating your opinion and supporting it with reasons and evidence.

TIPS

- State your opinion on whether immigration to the United States should be encouraged or severely restricted.
- Provide at least two reasons that support your opinion.
- Use information from the chapter, if possible, as well as your own observations and facts obtained by research to provide evidence for your argument.
- Address any counterarguments.
- Conclude your essay by summarizing your position.

VOCABULARY ANSWERS

1. The mountain man lived alone and trapped beaver in the Rocky Mountains.

2. Manifest destiny describes what many believed to be God's plan for the United States to extend to the Pacific Ocean.

3. Spanish cowboys were known as *vaqueros*.

4. The empresario approved and settled 300 families in Texas.

5. The dark horse candidate surprised everyone by winning the nomination.

6. The soldiers stationed at the presidio were tasked with guarding the mission.

7. Gentlemen farmers of Spanish-Mexican descent came to California and established huge estates known as ranchos.

8. The gold rush resulted in a flood of people migrating to California.

9. Forty-niners headed to California's gold rush beginning in 1849.

10. Like many boomtowns, the settlement was abandoned when nearby gold mines stopped producing gold.

READING STRATEGY ANSWER

Causes | Effects

Causes:
- Population growth
- Existing farmland scarce and depleted
- Western land cheap and plentiful
- Land ownership believed to promote liberty
- Idea of manifest destiny justified expansion

→ Effects:
Large numbers of Americans moved west in the 1840s and 1850s.

11. Push factors included the lack of fertile farmland and overcrowding at home. Pull factors included the availability and affordability of western land. The United States had acquired all the territory west of the Mississippi River to the Pacific Ocean. With such an expanse of open land, offering it cheaply to people who wanted to be landowners encouraged many Americans to migrate west in the mid-1800s.

MAIN IDEAS ANSWERS

12. Manifest destiny provided an ideological justification for westward expansion. People believed they were fulfilling God's plan.

13. The nomadic way of life of the Plains tribes clashed with the desire of settlers to own private plots of land. As tribes followed their historical movements, they became trespassers on lands now occupied by settlers who claimed ownership.

14. The Mexican government hoped that a larger population would help stabilize Tejas, so it offered land grants to encourage immigration.

15. Many Tejanos and Americans in Tejas thought the central government in Mexico was too far away and didn't understand their needs. Anglo Texans were also upset that Mexico had banned further immigration from the United States of free or enslaved people.

16. Southerners hoped the war would lead to new states open to slavery.

17. The United States increased its size by one-third by acquiring Mexico's territories north of the Rio Grande.

18. The missions fell out of power, and Mexican citizens and immigrants received land grants to establish ranchos.

19. The gold rush brought a wave of people into California. This led to problems such as crime and instability. Statehood was seen as a way to bring order.

HISTORICAL THINKING ANSWERS

20. The annexation of Texas as a slave state upset the balance of slave versus free states, which increased tensions surrounding the issue of slavery. The problem was solved eventually by admitting Oregon as a free state.

21. Oregon (1846), California, New Mexico, Arizona, Utah, Nevada, and parts of Colorado and Wyoming (1848)

22. Some Native Americans working in the gold fields were worked to death, and others were intimidated, murdered, or driven away.

23. Texans wanted Texas to become part of the United States.

24. Answers will vary. Some students might argue that westward expansion was a natural progression, as the United States had already grown substantially westward since its original founding. Others might claim that the idea was wrong because it ignored the rights and claims of Native Americans and other groups already inhabiting western lands.

25. Forty-niners were a diverse group of mostly male miners who flocked to California during the gold rush in an attempt to make a fortune. Most were from the United States, but many came from all over the world, including Mexico, China, Chile, and Peru.

INTERPRET IMAGES ANSWERS

26. The man is carrying a shovel, scale, teapot, and a gold pan and is wearing what appears to be a kettle on his head.

27. The man is formally dressed in a long coat and shiny leather boots rather than wearing durable clothes that would be necessary for working in a mine.

28. The artist likely believed that many people traveled to California optimistically and were hopelessly unprepared to do the work required to successfully find gold.

ANALYZE SOURCES ANSWERS

29. Polk is arguing that Mexico invaded the United States when it crossed the U.S. border and Americans were killed. The U.S. position, he believes, is to defend the "honor, the rights, and the interests of our country."

30. Polk claims that the war already exists because Mexico "has claimed that hostilities have commenced." Thus, the United States must fight to defend its ideals and to protect itself and its interests.

CONNECT TO YOUR LIFE ANSWER

31. Essays will vary but should state an opinion about whether the United States should encourage or severely limit immigration and then include the following: at least two reasons for support, information from the chapter (if applicable), the student's own observations, facts obtained through research, response to possible counterarguments, and a conclusion that summarizes the student's position.

Nat Turner's Complex Legacy

by Justin Fornal
Adapted from "Nat Turner's Slave Uprising Left Complex Legacy"
by Justin Fornal, news.nationalgeographic.com, October 5, 2016

Nat Turner was an African-American slave preacher in Virginia who led the bloodiest slave rebellion in American history.

In the 185 years that followed, Turner's place in history has been reinterpreted and revised. His legacy is debated, and even more so today, with Turner's Bible now on display in the National Museum of African American History and Culture and the release of the 2016 film *The Birth of a Nation*, chronicling Turner's life and revolt.

After the revolt, Turner was captured, tried, and executed. Much of our knowledge of Turner comes from the town where he was jailed, which is today Courtland, Virginia. There, he was interviewed by lawyer Thomas Ruffin Gray. The interviews were compiled in a pamphlet titled "The Confessions of Nat Turner: The Leader of the Late Insurrection in Southampton, Virginia." This serves as the main historical record of who Nat Turner was. But it's an imperfect record. Some historians think Gray took personal liberties with how he presented Turner.

Nat Turner was born into slavery on October 2, 1800, on the Benjamin Turner family plantation in Virginia. Having learned to read at an early age, Turner was considered an intellectual at the time, as teaching slaves to read was highly frowned upon.

Throughout his life, Turner would look to the Bible to better understand the reasons behind slavery. His wisdom and natural oratorial skills led him to become a respected preacher among the surrounding slave community. Early on, he interpreted that the Bible said that slaves should remain subservient to their earthly masters, but a series of prophetic visions and a solar eclipse changed his views. These events convinced Turner that it was his destiny to unite black men and women, both enslaved and free, to fight against slavery.

On August 21, 1831, Turner met with a group of fellow conspirators and took a vow to kill all slave owners they encountered, including women and children. The group traveled from farm to farm, slaughtering whites and freeing blacks. Many of the enslaved chose not to join the revolt, and some even fought to protect their masters. At most stops the rebel force grew, at one point reaching around 40 recruits. Over the next two days the rebels killed at least 55 whites. Soon the local militia caught the group. However, Turner delayed capture by hiding in the woods for two months. Once found, Turner was sentenced to death for "conspiring to rebel and make insurrection." On November 11, he was hanged.

Desperate to regain control in the wake of the rebellion, white militias unleashed a wave of violence and intimidation against both enslaved and free blacks throughout the region. Many innocent people who had nothing to do with the incident were killed.

It is rumored that after Nat Turner was hanged, he was decapitated, quartered, and skinned. Allegedly, pieces of his skin were given out as souvenirs. This would have been done in an attempt to crush Turner's legacy and prevent him from being a martyr.

But Turner's story is now undergoing a resurgence. The 2016 film presents Turner as a patriot. And his descendants and the descendants of survivors of the revolt are in the news debating his legacy.

Today in Courtland, monuments stand in honor of the Confederate military. There's a plaque noting the rebellion, but those who see Nat Turner as a hero believe that just as the Confederate memorials stand to benefit descendants of southern soldiers, it is only fair that descendants of the enslaved should have a place to pay homage to figures such as Nat Turner, who gave his life to fight for their freedom.

For more from National Geographic, check out "The Way West" online.

UNIT INQUIRY: Document a Migration

In this unit, you learned about the physical expansion and growth in population of the United States during the first half of the 19th century. As the nation enlarged its boundaries, hundreds of thousands of Americans migrated westward, undertaking long and challenging journeys. What drove Americans to pull up roots and move their families west? What were their journeys like? What did they find when they arrived at their final destinations?

ASSIGNMENT

Assume the role of a 19th-century American who is moving west. Create a journal in which you describe:

- who you are and where you live now
- the reasons you want to move (push-pull factors)
- why you chose a particular destination
- the route you take
- what you pack
- challenges and encounters on the journey
- how many miles and days you travel
- what you find and do at your destination

Be prepared to share your journal with the class.

Plan As you plan your journal entries, review the unit to gather evidence about the experiences of those who journeyed west in the early 1800s. Conduct additional research as necessary. Use a graphic organizer like this one to take notes.

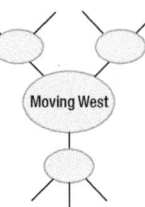

Moving West

Produce Begin your journal entries with actual dates. Include a map of your route and sketches or photographs of the landscapes you travel through. Focus on creating a realistic account of the experiences of migrants of the time. Be sure to cover these topics: *decision* (push-pull factors); *planning* (route and destination, what to pack); *journey* (landscapes, challenges, hardships, encounters); *destination* (miles covered, number of days, result).

Present Choose a creative way to present your journal to the class. Consider one of these options:

- Introduce yourself and select a few journal entries to read aloud to the class. Then allow class members to pose questions for you to answer.

- Post your journal online and invite the class to access it. Encourage readers to share their reactions and comments and to ask questions. Answer classmates' questions after they are posted.

- Hold a discussion in which classmates share what they learned from the journal writing assignment. Take a poll of the class, asking how many would actually be willing to risk such a trip.

NATIONAL GEOGRAPHIC | LEARNING FRAMEWORK ACTIVITIES

Depict Nature

SKILL Observation

KNOWLEDGE Our Living Planet

During the 19th century, many artists and writers celebrated the beauty and wonder of the American landscape in their work. Select and explore a natural site near you. It could be a park, beach, nature trail, or some other natural site. While you are there, take notes or photographs of what you observe, including physical features, animals, or plant life. Choose a way to depict your observations to share with your class. Either present the photos you took or use your notes to write a poem or create a drawing.

Create Slogans to Promote Reforms

ATTITUDE Responsibility

KNOWLEDGE Our Human Story

While many Americans moved west in the early 1800s, others worked to address social problems in settled parts of the country. Working in a small group, review the unit to make a list of the various problems and injustices that reformers focused on. Write a short summary of each problem or injustice, including who was affected and how they were affected, and then create a slogan that identifies the kind of change that reformers sought. Share your slogans with the class in a creative way.

NATIONAL GEOGRAPHIC CONNECTION

GUIDED DISCUSSION FOR "NAT TURNER'S COMPLEX LEGACY"

1. **Form and Support Opinions** Do you think Nat Turner deserves a monument? Support your opinion with evidence from the article. *(Possible responses: Yes. Turner deserves a monument because he fought for his own and others' freedom, as the American colonists had done. No. Turner does not deserve a monument because he started out wanting to unite black and white people to end slavery but ended up trying to kill all slave owners and their families.)*

2. **Analyze Cause and Effect** What were some of the short- and long-term effects of Turner's slave rebellion? *(Turner's forces killed many people; he and his followers were caught and hanged; white militias took vengeance by murdering African Americans in and around Virginia; descendants of people on both sides of the rebellion continue to argue about its meaning and about Turner's ultimate place in history.)*

GUIDED DISCUSSION FOR "THE WAY WEST"

1. **Make Connections** What were the dangers of westward migration, and why did migrants still undertake the journey? *(Dangers included disease, economic hardship, starvation, attacks by Native Americans, and loss of livestock. Migrants risked the journey for gold, more land, a more temperate climate, and dreams of a better life, and to fulfill the country's Manifest Destiny.)*

2. **Summarize** What general opinion did Horace Greeley have about overland migration? *(Possible response: Greeley thought migrants' journeys had an "aspect of insanity" about them since the trips were dangerous; also, he believed the majority of migrants would not improve their lives by moving west.)*

HISTORY NOTEBOOK

Encourage students to complete the Unit Wrap-Up page for Unit 3 in their History Notebooks.

UNIT INQUIRY PROJECT RUBRIC

ASSESS

Use the rubric to assess each student's participation and performance.

SCORE	ASSIGNMENT	PRODUCT	PRESENTATION
3 GREAT	• Student thoroughly understands the assignment. • Student participates fully in the project process.	• Journal entries are well thought out. • Journal entries offer a number of dates and descriptions of decision making, planning, and the journey itself. • Journal entries contain all of the key elements listed in the assignment.	• Presentation is clear, concise, and logical. • Presentation does a good job of creatively representing western migration. • Presentation engages the audience.
2 GOOD	• Student mostly understands the assignment. • Student participates fairly well in the project process.	• Journal entries are fairly well thought out. • Journal entries offer a few dates and a few descriptions of decision making, planning, and the journey itself. • Journal entries contain most of the key elements listed in the assignment.	• Presentation is fairly clear, concise, and logical. • Presentation does an adequate job of creatively representing western migration. • Presentation somewhat engages the audience.
1 NEEDS WORK	• Student does not understand the assignment. • Student minimally participates or does not participate in the project process.	• Journal entries are not well thought out. • Journal entries do not offer dates or descriptions of decision making, planning, or the journey itself. • Journal entries contain few or none of the key elements listed in the assignment.	• Presentation is not clear, concise, or logical. • Presentation does an inadequate job of representing western migration. • Presentation does not engage the audience.

NATIONAL GEOGRAPHIC LEARNING FRAMEWORK RUBRIC

ASSESS

Use the rubric to assess how each student applies the National Geographic Learning Framework.

SCORE	ASSIGNMENT	ASSIGNMENT	FINAL PRODUCTS
3 GREAT	• Depiction demonstrates **Observation** well. • Depiction explores **Our Living Planet** well.	• Slogans reflect **Responsibility** well. • Slogans explore **Our Human Story** well.	• Final products are engaging, creative, and well presented.
2 GOOD	• Depiction demonstrates **Observation**. • Depiction explores **Our Living Planet**.	• Slogans reflect **Responsibility**. • Slogans explore **Our Human Story**.	• Final products are interesting, logical, and complete.
1 NEEDS WORK	• Depiction does not demonstrate **Observation**. • Depiction does not explore **Our Living Planet**.	• Slogans do not reflect **Responsibility**. • Slogans do not explore **Our Human Story**.	• Final products are not creative, complete, or interesting.

OBJECTIVES

- Learn about different career paths in archaeology.
- Identify the importance of a material record of past history.
- Explore the use of context in the study of archaeology.
- Investigate tools and methods unique to archaeology.
- Compare and contrast archaeological sites across various regions.

CRITICAL THINKING SKILLS FOR "ARCHAEOLOGY AND U.S. HISTORY"

- Make Inferences
- Synthesize

NATIONAL GEOGRAPHIC ARCHAEOLOGIST-IN-RESIDENCE
FREDRIK HIEBERT

Fred Hiebert's passion for finding the interconnections among cultures, both ancient and modern, has led him into unusual places and projects throughout the world. He has excavated at the bottom of Lake Titicaca in the South American Andes Mountains, and he has explored deep below the Black Sea in Eurasia in search of the wreckage of submerged human settlements. In Turkmenistan, he and his team excavated a 4,000-year-old city located along the ancient trade route known as the Silk Road. In Afghanistan in 2003, Hiebert took part in work that led to the identification and cataloging of a legendary trove of treasure—the Bactrian gold. The treasure included 20,000 pieces of exquisite gold jewelry and artifacts that had been hidden by curators shortly after being excavated in the late 1970s to protect them from the ravages of war and occupation.

HISTORY NOTEBOOK

Encourage students to complete the Archaeology and U.S. History page in their History Notebooks as they read.

ARCHAEOLOGY AND U.S. HISTORY

Fredrik Hiebert

Archaeologist-in-Residence,
National Geographic Society

Dr. Hiebert directs archaeology projects around the world and recently curated an exhibition of more than 500 Greek artifacts in the National Geographic Museum.

Making sense of past events can be a complicated process. If history is the study of the past through written documents, such as firsthand accounts, letters, news reports, and inscriptions, then archaeology is the study of the human past through the **material record**—the buildings and objects that survive from a previous era. Archaeologists and historians are partners in preserving the human record.

Archaeology is the study of human-made objects, or **artifacts**, and the artifacts' context. An artifact tells a story by its style of manufacture, decoration, or inscription (words written on it). **Context** is the location of artifacts in the place of their last use or disposal. Context refers to where the artifacts were found, whether in the remains of buildings, in burial sites, on battlefields, or even in garbage pits.

This archaeological information sheds light on written histories that might tell only one side of the story. In fact, archaeology is one of the most important contributors to the interpretation of history here in the United States, from the original peopling of the continent right up to contemporary events.

For a look at American archaeology, start with the features on the opposite page. Then check out the map of U.S. archaeological sites that follows—archaeology may be just around the corner.

How does archaeology add to our understanding of U.S. history?

Pueblo Bonito (which means "beautiful town" in Spanish) was a great house in Chaco Canyon used by ancestral Puebloans between A.D. 850 and 1150. Built of sandstone blocks cemented with adobe mortar, this building once had hundreds of rooms—many of them round kivas, or ceremonial rooms—and in some areas was more than four stories high.

ARCHAEOLOGY AT A GLANCE

Archaeologists as First Responders

When disaster strikes, archaeologists are often among the first emergency personnel on the scene. Their expertise in proper excavation techniques is vital to the careful recovery of human remains and material evidence. The work of archaeologists, for example, sheds light on the real impact of the 9/11 devastation in New York City and the extent of the damage from Hurricane Katrina in New Orleans.

When the World Trade Center towers were destroyed, first responders included archaeologists. Instead of collecting artifacts such as ancient pottery, they collected wallets, briefcases, office supplies, and personal memorabilia of terrified workers forced to leave their belongings behind.

NatGeo Archaeology

National Geographic Society has a long history of archaeological exploration, including Hiram Bingham's work at the Inca site of Machu Picchu in the Andes in 1911. Today, Dr. Fredrik Hiebert is archaeologist-in-residence at National Geographic's headquarters in Washington, D.C. The Society has also been instrumental in conducting repatriations, the return of illegally excavated artifacts to their countries of origin.

National Geographic helps support ongoing excavation at Jamestown in Virginia, the site of the first permanent European settlement in North America.

State Archaeologist

Did you know that every state in the union has an official archaeologist? These experts help direct archaeological research and discovery on nonfederal land and bring that information to the public through stewardship and education.

Native American Graves Protection and Repatriation Act (NAGPRA)

This 1990 act provides protection for Native American burial sites and better control over the removal of Native American human remains and artifacts. The act requires federal agencies to return excavated cultural items, including human remains, funerary objects, sacred objects, and objects of cultural heritage, to descendants and culturally affiliated Indian tribes.

PREVIEW WITH VISUALS

Tell students to look closely at the photographs of Pueblo Bonito and the ruins of the World Trade Center towers as you read the captions aloud. **ASK:** Based on details you notice in the photographs, what do these two sites have in common? How are they different? *(They are both ruins of buildings formerly inhabited by human beings. They differ in their location, time period, building materials, and methods by which they were destroyed.)*

ARCHAEOLOGY WORD WEB

On the board, write the name of your state in the center circle of a Word Web. Direct students to think about the state in terms of its history and archaeological sites. Ask students to suggest words and terms to create a Word Web that identifies the state's early people, natural resources, and history.

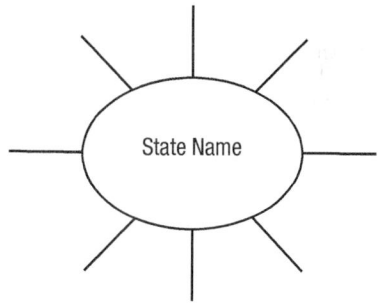

DISCOVER CLASSROOM ARTIFACTS

Instruct students to look around the room for one minute and to imagine that a team of archaeologists has discovered this classroom many years from now. Have students suggest some of the artifacts archaeologists might identify as important to a material record of classroom life. Write students' suggestions on the board.

GUIDED DISCUSSION

1. **Make Inferences** Why might archaeologists have needed to take sediment samples from Pearl Harbor's sunken battleship U.S.S. *Arizona*? *(Answers will vary. Possible responses: Archaeologists studied possible toxic effects from human waste and chemicals around the site and in the water. Archaeologists tried to gain some understanding of the areas hardest hit by the bombing and what the lives and final moments of the people in those areas might have been like.)*

2. **Synthesize** How can archaeological information about historical sites serve to change long-held beliefs or perceptions about events in U.S. history? Support your response with evidence from the text and provide one example to support your synthesis. *(Possible response: Using scientific processes, archaeologists can provide details showing discrepancies between long-held beliefs or legends and actual historical evidence, which in some cases results in reviewing history through the lens of science. One example would be the archaeological evidence that demonstrates that Native Americans and not the U.S. Army won the famous Battle of the Little Bighorn.)*

ACTIVE OPTION

STEM

NG Learning Framework:
Investigate Archaeological Research Methods

SKILLS Collaboration, Communication

KNOWLEDGE Our Human Story

Divide students into four teams and assign each team one of the following methods of scientific research that archaeologists use:

- remote sensing
- radiocarbon dating
- excavation
- satellite archaeology

Direct teams to conduct research for their assigned archaeological method using online or library sources. Teams should investigate the steps involved in each method, how archaeologists use the method in their work, and any recent advances in that technology. When teams have completed their work, invite representatives to extend their collaboration by sharing their findings with the class.

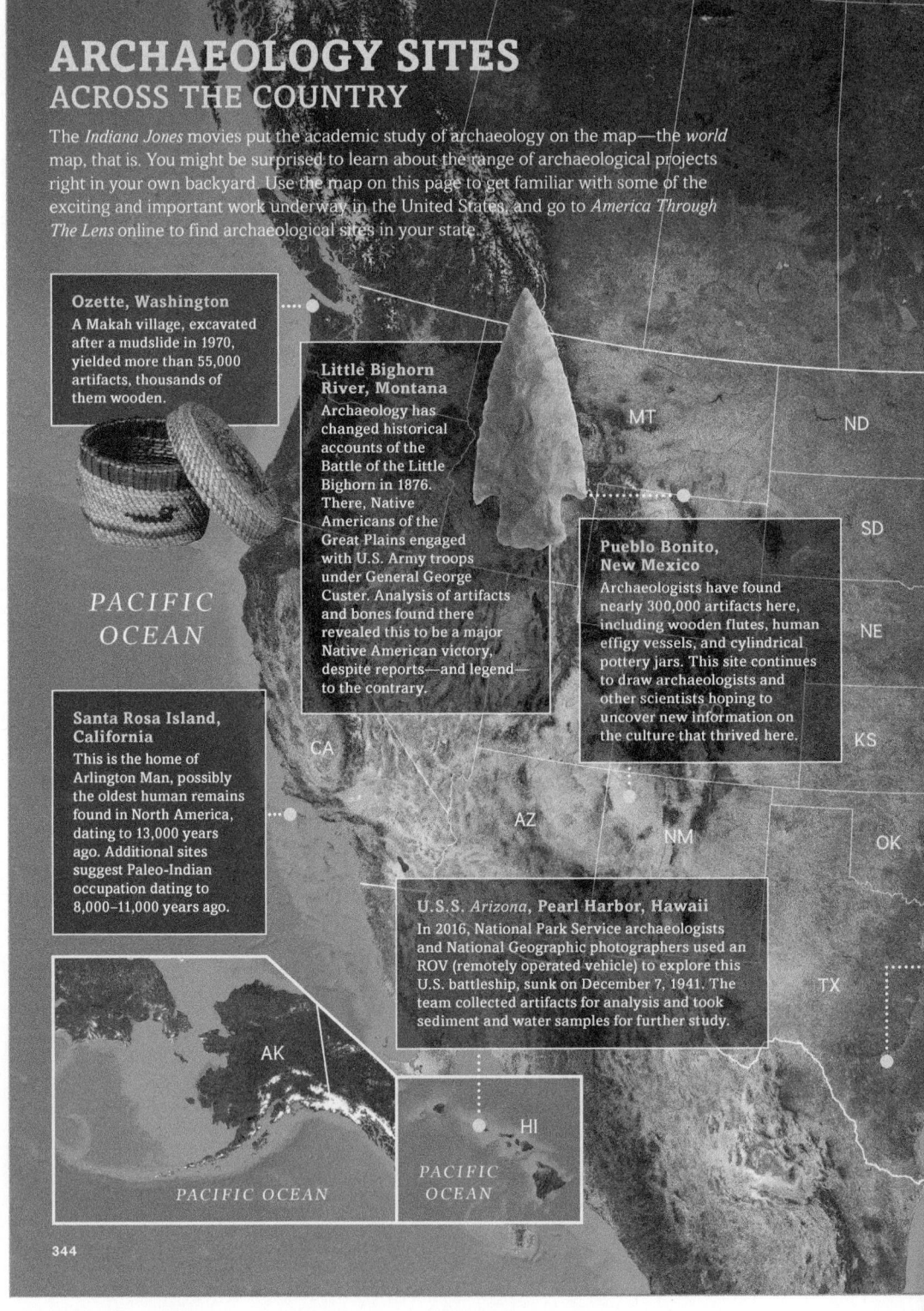

ARCHAEOLOGY SITES
ACROSS THE COUNTRY

The *Indiana Jones* movies put the academic study of archaeology on the map—the *world* map, that is. You might be surprised to learn about the range of archaeological projects right in your own backyard. Use the map on this page to get familiar with some of the exciting and important work underway in the United States, and go to *America Through The Lens* online to find archaeological sites in your state.

Ozette, Washington
A Makah village, excavated after a mudslide in 1970, yielded more than 55,000 artifacts, thousands of them wooden.

Little Bighorn River, Montana
Archaeology has changed historical accounts of the Battle of the Little Bighorn in 1876. There, Native Americans of the Great Plains engaged with U.S. Army troops under General George Custer. Analysis of artifacts and bones found there revealed this to be a major Native American victory, despite reports—and legend—to the contrary.

Pueblo Bonito, New Mexico
Archaeologists have found nearly 300,000 artifacts here, including wooden flutes, human effigy vessels, and cylindrical pottery jars. This site continues to draw archaeologists and other scientists hoping to uncover new information on the culture that thrived here.

Santa Rosa Island, California
This is the home of Arlington Man, possibly the oldest human remains found in North America, dating to 13,000 years ago. Additional sites suggest Paleo-Indian occupation dating to 8,000–11,000 years ago.

U.S.S. *Arizona*, **Pearl Harbor, Hawaii**
In 2016, National Park Service archaeologists and National Geographic photographers used an ROV (remotely operated vehicle) to explore this U.S. battleship, sunk on December 7, 1941. The team collected artifacts for analysis and took sediment and water samples for further study.

PACIFIC OCEAN

344

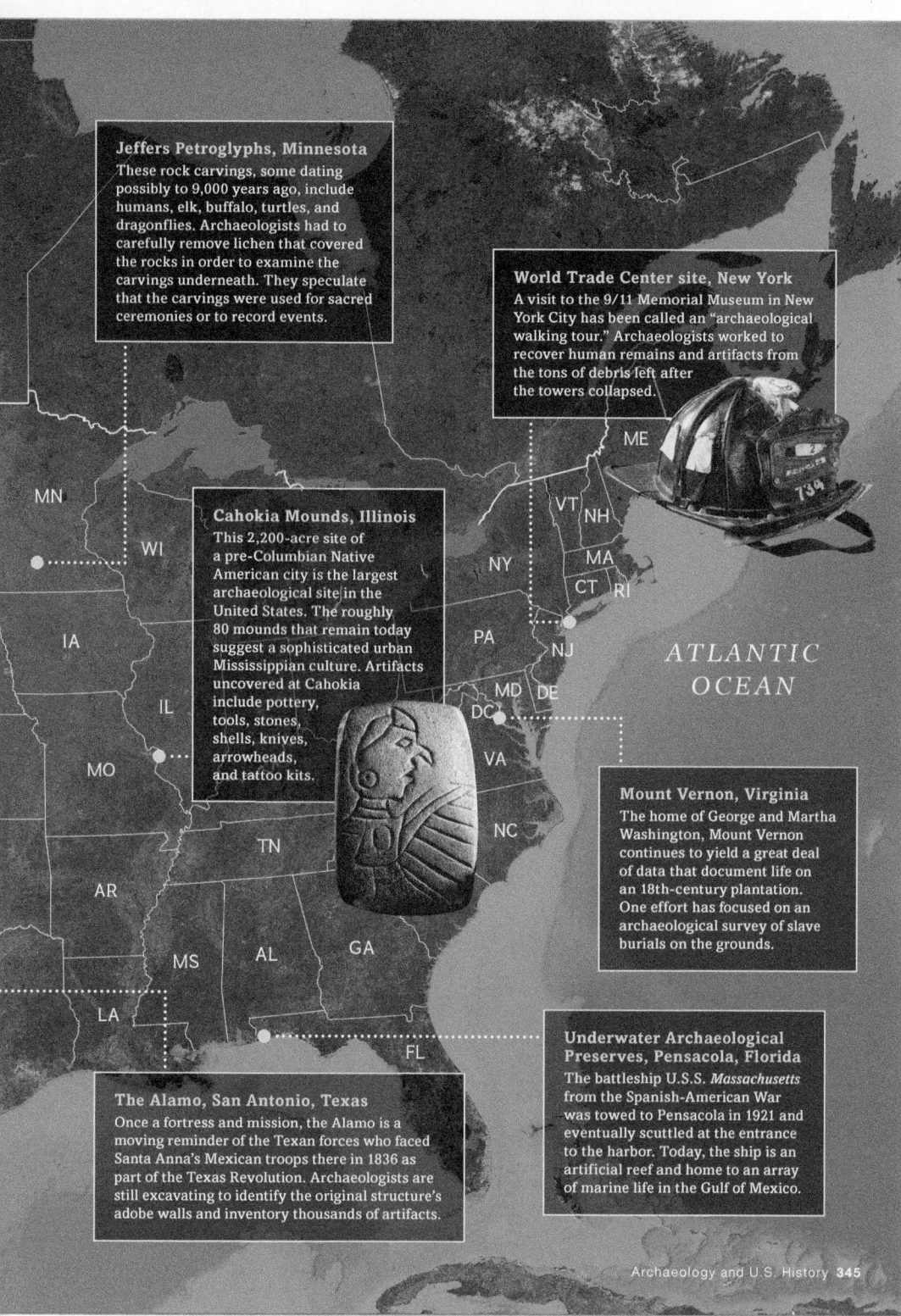

Jeffers Petroglyphs, Minnesota
These rock carvings, some dating possibly to 9,000 years ago, include humans, elk, buffalo, turtles, and dragonflies. Archaeologists had to carefully remove lichen that covered the rocks in order to examine the carvings underneath. They speculate that the carvings were used for sacred ceremonies or to record events.

World Trade Center site, New York
A visit to the 9/11 Memorial Museum in New York City has been called an "archaeological walking tour." Archaeologists worked to recover human remains and artifacts from the tons of debris left after the towers collapsed.

Cahokia Mounds, Illinois
This 2,200-acre site of a pre-Columbian Native American city is the largest archaeological site in the United States. The roughly 80 mounds that remain today suggest a sophisticated urban Mississippian culture. Artifacts uncovered at Cahokia include pottery, tools, stones, shells, knives, arrowheads, and tattoo kits.

Mount Vernon, Virginia
The home of George and Martha Washington, Mount Vernon continues to yield a great deal of data that document life on an 18th-century plantation. One effort has focused on an archaeological survey of slave burials on the grounds.

Underwater Archaeological Preserves, Pensacola, Florida
The battleship U.S.S. *Massachusetts* from the Spanish-American War was towed to Pensacola in 1921 and eventually scuttled at the entrance to the harbor. Today, the ship is an artificial reef and home to an array of marine life in the Gulf of Mexico.

The Alamo, San Antonio, Texas
Once a fortress and mission, the Alamo is a moving reminder of the Texan forces who faced Santa Anna's Mexican troops there in 1836 as part of the Texas Revolution. Archaeologists are still excavating to identify the original structure's adobe walls and inventory thousands of artifacts.

ATLANTIC OCEAN

Archaeology and U.S. History **345**

DIFFERENTIATE

STRIVING READERS

Write a Text Message As students read the lesson, instruct them to take a moment after they finish each paragraph to write a short text message paraphrasing the main idea. Pair students and direct them to compare their text messages about each paragraph. Then tell pairs to collaborate on a new text message that uses the best ideas from both texts. Call on pairs to select a paragraph, read it aloud, and then read their corresponding text message.

GIFTED & TALENTED

Create a Podcast Direct students to select one of the U.S. archaeological sites on the map as a subject for a podcast. Guide them to conduct online research to find more information from various sources about the history of their chosen site. Once students have the information, instruct them to write a script. They may choose to deliver the podcast on their own or work with a partner. Invite volunteers to present their podcasts to the class.

CIVIL WAR ENCAMPMENTS

Though many soldiers on both sides of the Civil War took part in combat, most spent only a fraction of their time on the front lines. Even during times of heavy fighting, most men spent only 1 out of every 30 days on the battlefield. The rest of the time they lived in military camps, where the days revolved around mundane tasks. To maintain a semblance of discipline, they took part in daily military drills, and then typically spent much of their free time listening to music or playing cards. The arrival of packages, letters, and newspapers provided some relief from boredom and homesickness. During the war, most soldiers had more to fear from disease and lack of adequate food and shelter than from enemy fire. In fact, between 400,000 and 600,000 Civil War soldiers lost their lives to illness and deprivation. **ASK:** What fact about soldiers' lives is the most surprising? *(Possible response: It's surprising that so little time was spent in combat and that so many deaths were from disease or reasons other than enemy fire.)*

The Union Army was known for having good rations— that is, when adequate supplies could be delivered. Daily camp rations typically included varying amounts of starch in the form of soft bread or hardtack (hard, unleavened bread), flour, or cornmeal; three-quarters of a pound of pork or bacon or one and a quarter pounds of fresh or salted beef; small amounts of rice, peas, beans, or dried vegetables; and coffee, sugar, and tiny allotments of salt and pepper. Fresh fruits and vegetables were rare, but one-half ounce of vinegar a day helped to prevent scurvy. Because the war was spread over a vast front, it was often difficult to get food to the troops. **ASK:** Besides distance, what other factors might have made it difficult to transport food to the troops? *(Possible response: Fighting might have taken place in mountainous or marshy areas that would have made transport difficult; enemy troops might have been between the food transports and the Union troops; severe weather conditions, such as heavy snow, rain, or flooding, might have made it hard to get supplies through.)*

UNIT
4
1846–1877
THE DEEPEST CRISIS

346

CRITICAL VIEWING The first major conflict to be extensively photographed was the American Civil War. This photo, taken by G.H. Houghton in the early 1860s, shows Union troops stationed at Camp Griffin in Langley, Virginia—a Confederate state. Based on the details in this photograph, what do you predict may have taken place shortly after it was taken?

WARTIME SHELTER

In the early years of the Civil War, many soldiers slept in large, cone-shaped shelters called Sibley tents, which could accommodate 10 or 12 men. However, at military encampments after 1862, the main form of shelter became the shelter tent, also known as the "dog tent." Invented for maximum portability, this type of tent was smaller than the Sibley and was intended to hold only two men. As part of a soldier's kit, each man received a six-foot section of heavy cloth with buttons on three sides. Pairs of soldiers buttoned their tent sides together, pulled them down over forked sticks at either end, and pinned the sides down tight to the ground. To form the floor, or sleeping area, they laid a rubberized blanket or a sheet of tarred cloth on the ground to keep out the cold and wet as best they could. Each soldier was also issued a heavy wool blanket.

The portability of the shelter was useful, but on long marches or in combat situations, exhausted soldiers often discarded their tents along the way to shed the extra weight and bulk in their packs. As a result, as the war dragged on, many soldiers slept on nothing more than a blanket spread over bare ground. Historians believe that in many cases the soldiers' prolonged exposure to cold, wet weather and heat resulted in many illnesses and deaths on both sides of the conflict.

CRITICAL VIEWING Possible response: Details such as the ranks of troops lined up in tight formation and holding their rifles, the officers on horseback in front of them, and the American flag overhead suggest that the men are about to engage Confederate forces in battle.

1857 ASIA:
INDIAN MILITARY REVOLT

By 1857, the British East India Company had effectively ruled most of India for nearly 100 years. During this period, the British governed by replacing India's Hindu aristocracy with British officials and missionaries, often using educational and military methods that deliberately challenged orthodox Hindu and Muslim beliefs. British officers also introduced the Enfield rifle to the sepoys, the Indian troops under their command, that required soldiers to bite off the ends of cartridges—rumored to be lubricated with pig and cow fat—before inserting the cartridges into the rifle. Hindu sepoys considered the cow sacred and did not eat beef, and Muslim sepoys did not eat pork as part of their religious observance. Consequently, all sepoys regarded putting the cartridges in their mouths as a direct violation of their religious beliefs. **ASK:** How would you generalize the sepoys' main concern? *(They believed the British were showing a grave disrespect for their traditional cultures and religions.)*

The British command ignored the sepoys' objections and rising anger over this issue. When a group of sepoys refused to use Enfield cartridges, British officers imprisoned them. Other enraged sepoys then marched into Delhi, where they temporarily restored an aging Mughal emperor to power. The revolt spread across northern India, as sepoys killed British officers and massacred men, women, and children at Delhi and Kanpur. The British, eager to end the revolt, took reprisals against many sepoys who were not part of the uprising. Their actions were particularly harsh and vengeful and included executing captured sepoys with bayonets or by tying them to the mouth of a cannon loaded with powder and firing. The British finally managed to put down the revolt in July 1858. **ASK:** Why do you think the British ignored the sepoys' rising anger? *(Answers will vary. Possible responses: The British might have ignored the sepoys' complaints because they regarded their concerns as unimportant or as defying orders; the British viewed themselves as the dominant culture, ruling a conquered people.)*

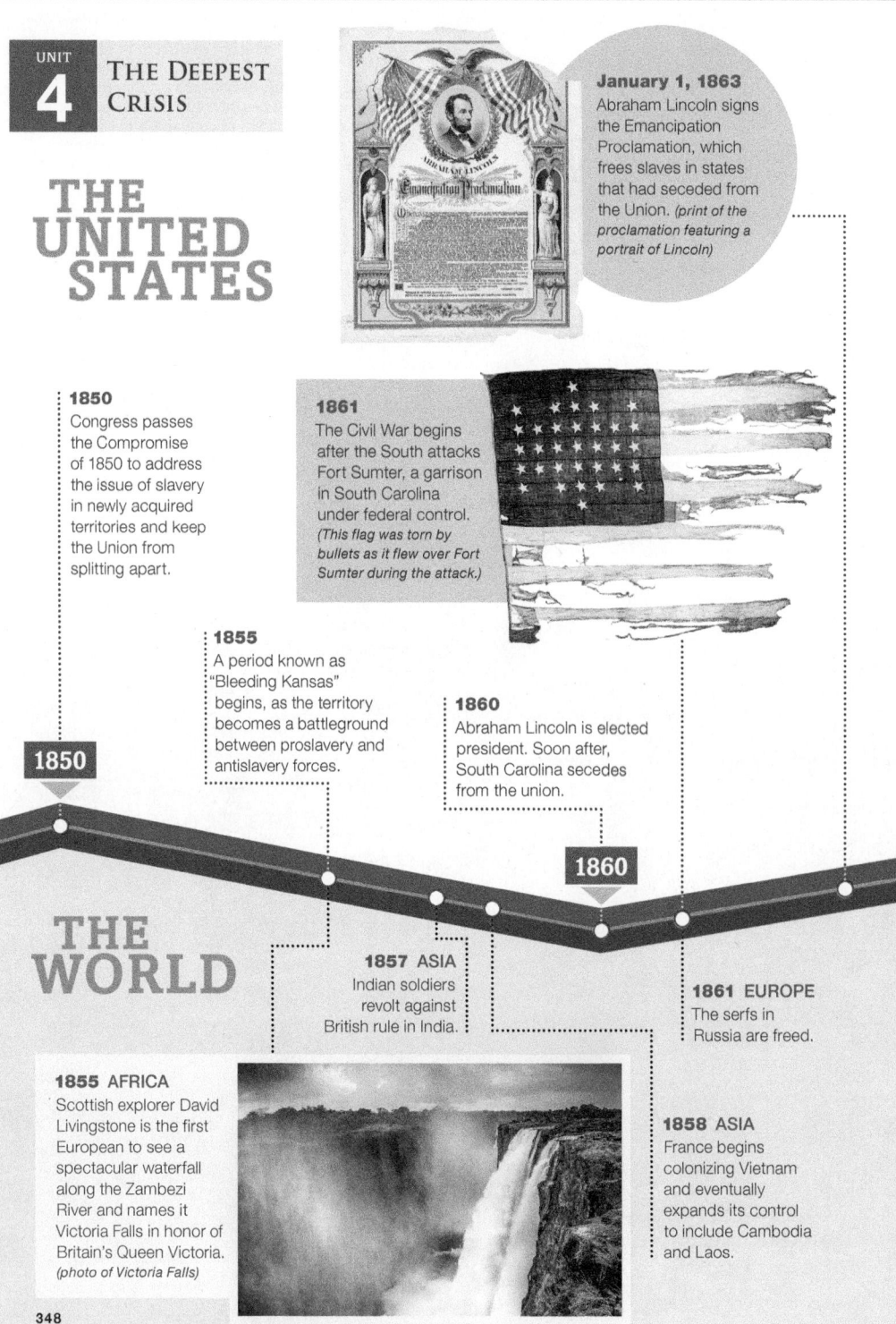

UNIT **4** THE DEEPEST CRISIS

THE UNITED STATES

January 1, 1863
Abraham Lincoln signs the Emancipation Proclamation, which frees slaves in states that had seceded from the Union. *(print of the proclamation featuring a portrait of Lincoln)*

1850
Congress passes the Compromise of 1850 to address the issue of slavery in newly acquired territories and keep the Union from splitting apart.

1861
The Civil War begins after the South attacks Fort Sumter, a garrison in South Carolina under federal control. *(This flag was torn by bullets as it flew over Fort Sumter during the attack.)*

1855
A period known as "Bleeding Kansas" begins, as the territory becomes a battleground between proslavery and antislavery forces.

1860
Abraham Lincoln is elected president. Soon after, South Carolina secedes from the union.

1850

1860

THE WORLD

1857 ASIA
Indian soldiers revolt against British rule in India.

1861 EUROPE
The serfs in Russia are freed.

1855 AFRICA
Scottish explorer David Livingstone is the first European to see a spectacular waterfall along the Zambezi River and names it Victoria Falls in honor of Britain's Queen Victoria. *(photo of Victoria Falls)*

1858 ASIA
France begins colonizing Vietnam and eventually expands its control to include Cambodia and Laos.

348

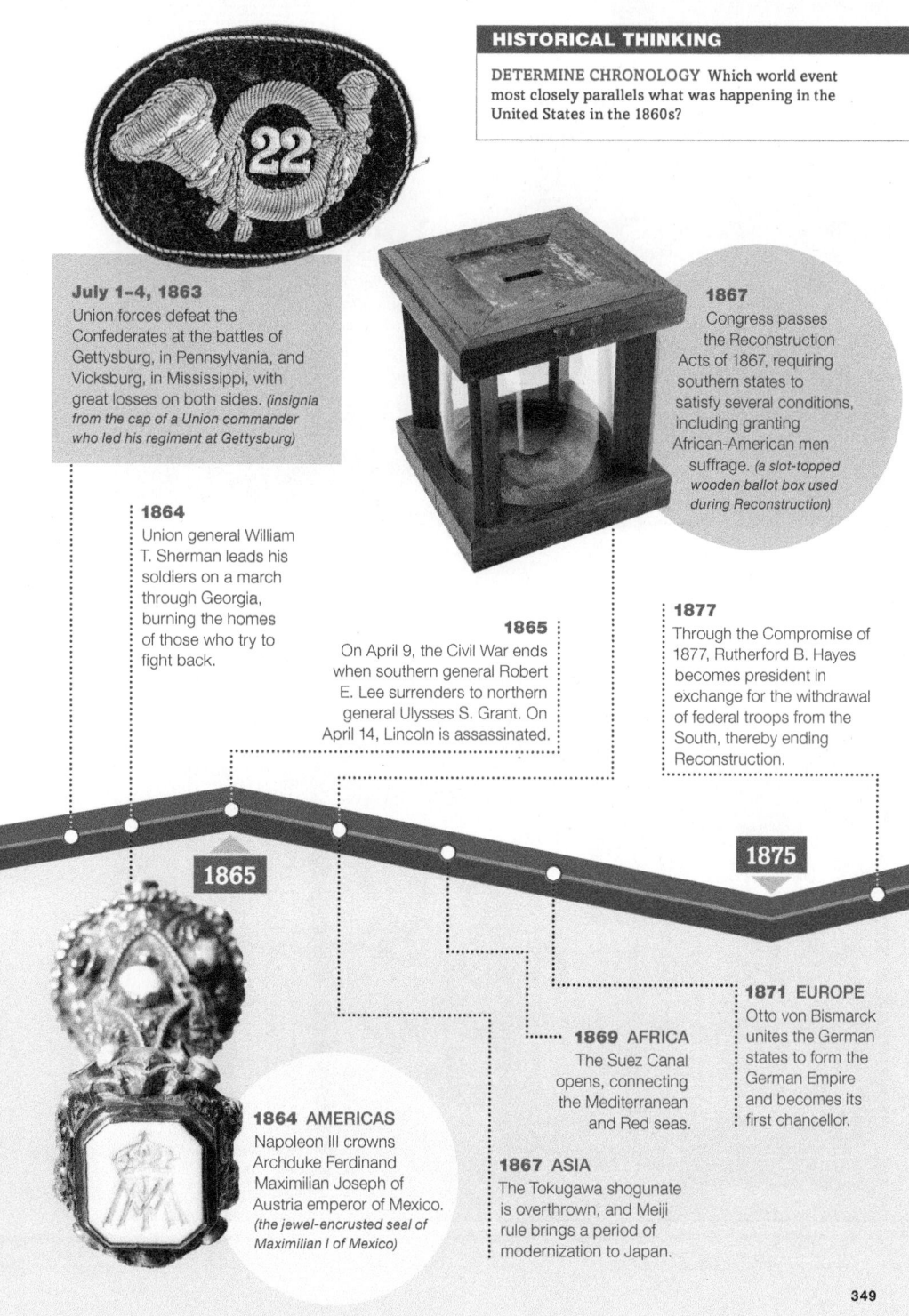

DETERMINE CHRONOLOGY Which world event most closely parallels what was happening in the United States in the 1860s?

July 1–4, 1863
Union forces defeat the Confederates at the battles of Gettysburg, in Pennsylvania, and Vicksburg, in Mississippi, with great losses on both sides. *(insignia from the cap of a Union commander who led his regiment at Gettysburg)*

1864
Union general William T. Sherman leads his soldiers on a march through Georgia, burning the homes of those who try to fight back.

1865
On April 9, the Civil War ends when southern general Robert E. Lee surrenders to northern general Ulysses S. Grant. On April 14, Lincoln is assassinated.

1867
Congress passes the Reconstruction Acts of 1867, requiring southern states to satisfy several conditions, including granting African-American men suffrage. *(a slot-topped wooden ballot box used during Reconstruction)*

1877
Through the Compromise of 1877, Rutherford B. Hayes becomes president in exchange for the withdrawal of federal troops from the South, thereby ending Reconstruction.

1865

1875

1864 AMERICAS
Napoleon III crowns Archduke Ferdinand Maximilian Joseph of Austria emperor of Mexico. *(the jewel-encrusted seal of Maximilian I of Mexico)*

1867 ASIA
The Tokugawa shogunate is overthrown, and Meiji rule brings a period of modernization to Japan.

1869 AFRICA
The Suez Canal opens, connecting the Mediterranean and Red seas.

1871 EUROPE
Otto von Bismarck unites the German states to form the German Empire and becomes its first chancellor.

349

INTRODUCE TIME LINE EVENT

1871 EUROPE: OTTO VON BISMARCK FORMS THE GERMAN EMPIRE

Otto von Bismarck began his political career as a legislator, but he quickly rose to power as a Prussian representative and later served as Prussia's ambassador to Russia and France. At the age of 47, he was named prime minister of Prussia by King Wilhelm I. Bismarck's goal was to unite the German states to form one powerful empire in which Prussia would be the dominant force. Although unsure that such an ambitious goal could be achieved during his lifetime, Bismarck began attempting to link northern and southern German states together. When the powerful state of Austria refused to go along with his plan, Bismarck orchestrated a war between Austria and Prussia. Prussia won the war but allowed Austria to retain its autonomy. In a relatively short time, Bismarck established the North German Confederation, with Prussia as its center and Austria now a secondary power.

However, the southern German states were still firmly opposed to unification. Bismarck then provoked a war with France, hoping to draw the southern states into a combined German action against a common enemy. He also spread anti-French propaganda to influence the four southern German states to join the North German Confederation. If the combined states could conquer France, they would form the German Empire. His tactics worked. In the end, only Austria, with its population of 7 million German speakers, still remained outside the unified German state. Bismarck was called a national hero and later named the first imperial chancellor of the newly formed German Empire. **ASK:** What reasons might Austria and other states have had for refusing to join the unified German Empire? *(Possible response: They might have feared a loss of autonomy, new laws they did not approve of, or a general lack of control over their own political futures.)*

HISTORICAL THINKING

DETERMINE CHRONOLOGY

Answer: Two years before Abraham Lincoln signed the Emancipation Proclamation and freed slaves in secessionist states, the serfs, or slave laboring class in Russia, were set free.

AMERICAN STORIES | Abraham Lincoln: The Great Emancipator

- Study Primary Sources: Quotations from Abraham Lincoln's speeches and letters
- On Your Feet: Research Liberia

NG Learning Framework:
Present a Speech

SECTION 1 RESOURCES
CONFLICT OVER SLAVERY

LESSON 1.1
Industrial North and Agricultural South

- On Your Feet: Numbered Heads

NG Learning Framework:
Write a News Article

LESSON 1.2
Tensions Over Expanding Slavery

- On Your Feet: Roundtable

NG Learning Framework:
Craft a Protest Speech

SECTION 2 RESOURCES
GROWING OPPOSITION TO SLAVERY

LESSON 2.1
The Underground Railroad

AMERICAN GALLERY ONLINE | The Underground Railroad

NG Learning Framework:
Create a Visual Itinerary

American Voices Biography
Harriet Beecher Stowe ONLINE

LESSON 2.2
AMERICAN VOICES
Harriet Tubman

- On Your Feet: Fishbowl

NG Learning Framework:
Develop Opposing News Stories

LESSON 2.3
Kansas and Nebraska

- On Your Feet: Jigsaw

NG Learning Framework:
Write an Editorial

American Voices Biography
John Brown ONLINE

LESSON 2.4
Dred Scott and the Debate Over Slavery

- Active History: Debate an Issue

NG Learning Framework:
Evaluate the Candidates

SECTION 3 RESOURCES
LINCOLN'S ELECTION AND SOUTHERN SECESSION

LESSON 3.1
The Election of 1860

- On Your Feet: Who's Who in the 1860 Election

NG Learning Framework:
Design a Social Media Campaign

LESSON 3.2
The Confederacy Forms

- On Your Feet: Compare Inaugural Addresses

NG Learning Framework:
Generate a Time Line

CHAPTER 11 REVIEW

STRATEGY ①
SET A PURPOSE FOR READING

Before students begin a lesson, help them set a purpose for reading by scanning the title and headings, studying visuals, and reading the captions. Tell students to write a question they expect the lesson to answer. After they have read the lesson, instruct students to answer the question in writing.

Use with All Lessons *The purpose students set for reading Lesson 1.1 may be: How did the economies of the North and the South differ, and how did people in each region feel about the federal government?*

STRATEGY ②
ASK EITHER/OR QUESTIONS

Monitor students' comprehension of the lesson by asking them to answer questions containing two choices. After students have answered the questions, have partners check each other's answers. Then have pairs work together to answer the Historical Thinking questions.

Use with All Lessons *For example, you may ask questions such as these for Lesson 3.1:*

- *Was William Seward or Abraham Lincoln more strongly vocal about opposition to slavery? (Seward)*

- *Did the delegates to the Democratic National Convention find common ground or split over their differences? (split)*

- *Did members of the southern Democratic Party or the northern Democratic Party vote for Stephen Douglas in the 1860 election? (northern Democratic Party)*

STRATEGY ③
LIST FACTS

Post this heading on the board: Five Things I Know About Tensions Between the North and South. Ask students to copy this heading on a sheet of paper. As they read each lesson, have them write at least five sentences under the heading. Invite volunteers to share their sentences with the class.

Use with All Lessons *Throughout the chapter, help students acquire the habit of listing facts they learn as they read.*

STRATEGY ①
PREVIEW USING MAPS

Preview the maps in the lesson to orient students to the lesson topic and to help them understand the text. Tell students first to read the map title and legend and then identify relevant information.

Use with Lessons 1.2, 2.3, and 3.1 *For example, on the Compromise of 1850 map in Lesson 1.2, students should note the colors in the legend that represent free, slave, or potentially slaveholding territory and then point out the borders of each area. In the Kansas-Nebraska Act, 1854 map in Lesson 2.3, students can review the legend and identify the areas that allowed, banned, or were open to slavery.*

STRATEGY ②
BUILD A TIME LINE

To increase understanding of factors that heightened or lessened tensions between the North and the South, instruct students to identify and list key events on a time line, such as the one shown below. Each entry should include the date and a brief summary of the event and its significance. Encourage students to add graphics or photographs to the time line.

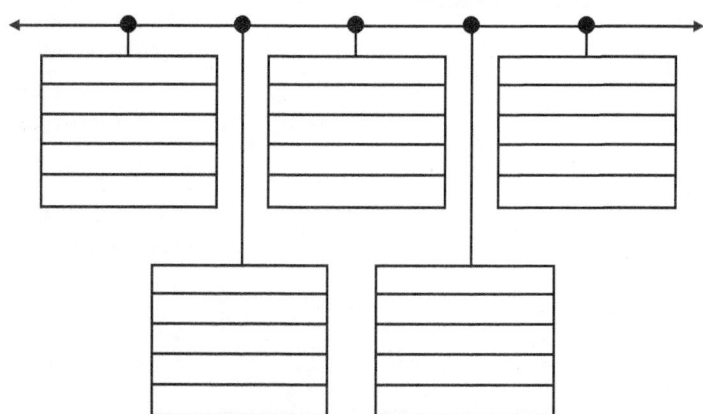

Use with All Lessons *For example, key events from Lesson 1.2 might include: Missouri Compromise kept balance of free and slave states (1820); Wilmot Proviso proposed to prohibit slavery in any territory acquired from Mexico (1846); Wilmot Proviso defeated (1847); Free-Soil Party formed to fight slavery (1848); California constitution bans slavery (1849); Compromise of 1850 balances interests of North and South (1850); Fugitive Slave Act of 1850 punishes anyone who aids slaves and raises tensions between North and South (1850).*

ENGLISH LANGUAGE LEARNERS ELD

STRATEGY 1
CREATE A WORD WALL

Work with students at the **Emerging** and **Expanding** levels to select five words from each lesson to display in a grouping on a Word Wall. Choose words and terms students are likely to encounter throughout the chapter, such as *slave state*, *free state*, and *abolition*. Keep the words displayed and discuss each one as it comes up during reading.

Use with All Lessons *You might suggest that students at the Bridging level write example sentences using each word.*

STRATEGY 2
USE CONTEXT CLUES

Pair students at the **Emerging** level with those at the **Expanding** or **Bridging** level. Instruct pairs to underline the context clues or textual definitions that provide the meaning of Key Vocabulary words. Then have students write original sentences using the words. Have the more proficient students assist others in checking the accuracy of the sentences. Invite pairs to share their sentences and discuss different ways to use each word or term.

Use with All Lessons *For example, in Lesson 1.2, have pairs underline context clues that help them determine the meaning of the following words:* proviso *(condition),* popular sovereignty *(right of local citizens to determine their own laws), and* omnibus bill *(comprehensive legislation).*

STRATEGY 3
REVIEW TRANSITIONAL WORDS

To help students summarize what they read and put events relating to North-South tensions in chronological order, write these transitional words on the board: *first, next, then, while, immediately, later, earlier, meanwhile, whenever, subsequently, during, following, before, after,* and *finally.* Direct students at the **Emerging** and **Expanding** levels to work together to write a series of sentences that explain what happens in each lesson. Encourage them to use a variety of transitional words and to vary their sentence structure.

Use with All Lessons *You might expand the exercise by having students identify transitional words as they read each lesson. For example, in Lesson 3.1, students may identify* after, meanwhile, as, *and* then.

GIFTED & TALENTED

STRATEGY 1
CREATE A PODCAST

Direct students to choose one of the lessons as the basis for an episode of a history podcast. Tell students that their podcast should express a point of view so that it is both informative and entertaining. Suggest they write a script for their podcast and include sound effects and music. Then have students either present their episode to the class or record it on a phone or other device.

Use with All Lessons

STRATEGY 2
WRITE AN ONLINE PROFILE

Tell students that Harriet Tubman, John Brown, and William Seward used very different means to fight for abolition of slavery. Instruct students to choose one of the three abolitionists and use multiple print and digital sources to investigate the person's tactics. Then encourage students to create an online profile with both text and visuals to describe these tactics and evaluate their effectiveness. Invite volunteers to share their online profiles with the class.

Use with Lessons 2.1–2.4 and 3.1

PRE-AP

STRATEGY 1
REVIEW A BOOK

Challenge students to read and review a book on events leading up to the Civil War, such as David Reynolds's book *Mightier Than the Sword: Uncle Tom's Cabin and the Battle for America.* Remind them that a review briefly summarizes the main topic and then provides a critical assessment of the book's strengths and weaknesses. Students may conclude their review by suggesting reasons that their classmates should or should not read the book. Encourage them to post their reviews on a class blog or read them aloud in class.

Use with Lesson 2.1

STRATEGY 2
EXTEND KNOWLEDGE

Invite students to conduct online research to learn more about a topic, person, or event introduced in this chapter. For example, students might choose to research the Fugitive Slave Act, Compromise of 1850, Underground Railroad, Harriet Beecher Stowe, Jacob Lawrence, Kansas-Nebraska Act, Republican Party, John Brown, "Bleeding Kansas," Harpers Ferry, Dred Scott decision, or Fort Sumter. Invite students to present their findings in an oral report to the class or in a digital report posted on a class website or blog.

Use with All Lessons

HISTORICAL THINKING How did tensions over slavery divide the North and the South?

AMERICAN STORIES | Abraham Lincoln: The Great Emancipator

"I believe
this government
cannot endure,
**permanently
half** *slave*
and half *free.*"

—Abraham Lincoln, 1858

CRITICAL VIEWING This monumental statue of Abraham Lincoln overlooks the National Mall from within the Lincoln Memorial in Washington, D.C. The memorial was dedicated in 1922. A team of sculptors had spent 4 years carving the 19-foot-tall and 19-foot-wide marble statue. Its designer, Daniel Chester French, wanted to depict Lincoln at the height of the Civil War. What do Lincoln's posture, clothing, and expression say about him as a leader?

INTRODUCE THE PHOTOGRAPH

ABRAHAM LINCOLN

Direct students' attention to the statue of Abraham Lincoln and the quotation. Encourage them to think about the emotions the designer and sculptor wanted to evoke with this work. **ASK:** What effect does the lighting have on your perception of the sculpture? *(Possible response: The golden light on the statue, in contrast to the darkness behind it, evokes feelings of awe and admiration of Lincoln as an inspired leader in the country's darkest time.)* What does the quotation from Lincoln reveal about him? *(He believes the nation cannot survive trying to accommodate slavery.)* What does the quotation reveal about Lincoln's sense of purpose? *(He will do what he can to remove slavery and preserve the Union.)* Tell students that in this chapter they will learn about issues and events that divided northern and southern states and eventually split the nation into two warring factions.

For Chapter 11 Spanish Resources, visit the Resources Menu. Chapter 11 Resources are available at NGLSync.Cengage.com.

SHARE BACKGROUND

Before designing the statue of Lincoln, Daniel Chester French spent a great deal of time researching Lincoln's life and studying photographs of him. French wanted his statue to provide a clear sense of the many hardships Lincoln had endured while at the same time depicting him as a man of spirit, strength, and character. The statue's hands illustrate French's intent. Lincoln's left hand is clenched into a fist, symbolizing his determination to end both slavery and the Civil War during his presidency. The right hand, not shown in this photograph, is relaxed and slightly open, providing a glimpse into Lincoln's compassionate side.

CRITICAL VIEWING Lincoln is dressed in formal attire and sits with both arms resting on the posts of the chair, as if he had just sat down or was about to rise. The look on his face is serious, but he also seems reflective, as if pondering the difficult tasks ahead. These elements convey that Lincoln takes his responsibilities seriously and is likely to be a strong, compassionate, and thoughtful leader.

HISTORICAL THINKING QUESTION

How did tensions over slavery divide the North and the South?

Activate Prior Knowledge This activity will allow students to access prior knowledge about the years before the Civil War to help them understand how the issue of slavery led to increasingly serious conflicts between the North and the South. Arrange the class into three groups, one for each chapter section. Prompt students to discuss what they already know about their group's topic and ask them to consider the following questions:

Conflict Over Slavery: Section 1 describes issues and events that led to the early regional conflicts over slavery. What were the main differences in the economies of the North and South? How might these differences fuel the conflicts?

Growing Opposition to Slavery: Section 2 discusses increasing opposition to the institution of slavery. How strong were the abolitionists becoming in the North? What tactics might they use to influence public opinion?

Lincoln's Election and Southern Secession: Section 3 examines events leading up to Abraham Lincoln's election in 1860 and the response of the South. Had southerners talked about leaving the Union before the 1850s? How do you think southern states will view Lincoln's election?

Invite each group to choose a representative to summarize the group's responses.

INTRODUCE THE READING STRATEGY

IDENTIFY MAIN IDEAS AND DETAILS

Explain that identifying main ideas and details helps readers link ideas and expand on concepts to better understand history. Turn to the Chapter Review and preview with students the graphic organizer used for identifying main ideas and details. As students read the chapter, encourage them to locate the main ideas and details of each lesson to understand how tensions over slavery eventually split the nation in two and led to the Civil War.

KEY DATES FOR CHAPTER 11

1845	Irish potato famine begins
1850	Fugitive Slave Act is passed
1852	*Uncle Tom's Cabin* is published in book form
1854	Kansas-Nebraska Act is passed
1856	Proslavery activists attack Lawrence, Kansas
1857	*Dred Scott* v. *Sandford* case is decided
1858	Abraham Lincoln and Stephen A. Douglas debate
1859	John Brown raids Harpers Ferry
1860	Lincoln is elected president
1860	South Carolina secedes from the Union

INTRODUCE CHAPTER VOCABULARY

KEY VOCABULARY

SECTION 1

omnibus bill	proviso	recession
popular sovereignty		

SECTION 2

Bleeding Kansas	nativist	Underground Railroad
Dred Scott decision	sack of Lawrence	

SECTION 3

Confederacy	Crittenden Plan

WORD WEBS

Tell students to complete a Word Web for Key Vocabulary words as they read the chapter. Direct them to write each word in the center of an oval and then look through the chapter to find examples, characteristics, and descriptive words that may be associated with the vocabulary word. After reading the chapter, ask students to share what they learned about each word. Model an example using the graphic organizer below.

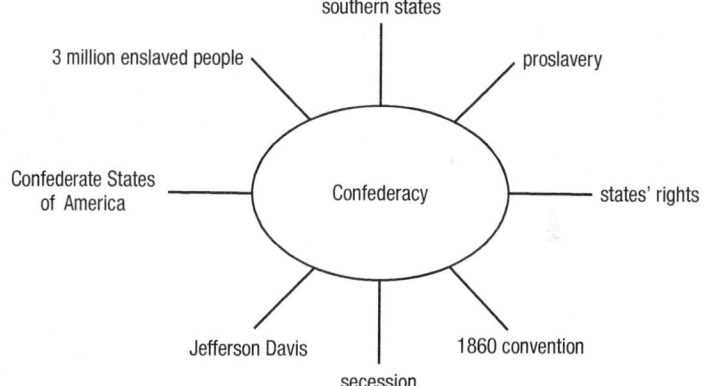

OBJECTIVES

- **Examine key events in Abraham Lincoln's life.**
- **Analyze Lincoln's response to the practice of slavery.**
- **Understand the role African Americans played during the Civil War.**
- **Study primary sources: quotations from Abraham Lincoln's speeches and letters.**

CRITICAL THINKING SKILLS FOR "ABRAHAM LINCOLN: THE GREAT EMANCIPATOR"

- Analyze Language Use
- Form and Support Opinions
- Draw Conclusions
- Evaluate

CONNECT TO THE CHAPTER

This American Story traces Abraham Lincoln's entry into politics and the challenges he faced running for elected office. A time line presents the major events and achievements of Lincoln's life, while photographs of Lincoln, his wife, Mary Todd Lincoln, and some of the items he used lend a personal touch to the narrative.

Chapter 11, Tensions Between North and South, examines the conflicts between the northern and southern states leading up to the Civil War. In particular, the chapter discusses the role slavery played in dividing the nation and how the dispute over slavery affected the presidential election of 1860. Introduce "Abraham Lincoln: The Great Emancipator" after students have completed the chapter to give them greater insight into Lincoln—the victor of the 1860 election—and his evolving position on how to end the institution of slavery.

HISTORY NOTEBOOK

Encourage students to complete the American Story page for Chapter 11 in their History Notebooks as they read.

AMERICAN STORIES | NATIONAL GEOGRAPHIC

CRITICAL VIEWING
Alexander Hesler's 1860 photograph of Abraham Lincoln captures the man before his presidency. How does this photo compare to others you have seen of Lincoln later in his life? Explain.

352 CHAPTER 11

ABRAHAM LINCOLN
THE GREAT EMANCIPATOR

Over the course of his life, Lincoln was called many names. Barbarian. Unshapely man. Even the original gorilla. But those who admired him called him Honest Abe, the Ancient One, and with the highest level of respect—the Great Emancipator.

In 1864, Lincoln wrote, "I am naturally anti-slavery. If slavery is not wrong, nothing is wrong." His actions and writings indicate not just lifelong opposition but also personal disgust with slavery. In an undated note, he reflected sarcastically that "although volume upon volume is written to prove slavery a very good thing, we never hear of the man who wishes to take the good of it, by being a slave himself." Lincoln abhorred the institution of slavery, but his attitudes toward African Americans could not be described as "modern." Although he never publicly embraced the idea of full equality, his ideas about the capabilities of African Americans and their roles in society did evolve with time and experience.

Lincoln's negative view of slavery may date back to his early childhood and to his parents' position on the matter. When he was born in Kentucky in 1809, slavery was legal in the state, and some of his family members were slaveholders. Lincoln's parents, however, appear to have been against it. In fact, when their church divided over the question of whether slavery was justified, they joined the antislavery group. In 1816, Lincoln's father moved the family across the Ohio River into Indiana, a free state. In his autobiography, Lincoln wrote that his father made this change "partly on account of slavery."

Lincoln witnessed slavery on many occasions during his youth in Kentucky and while traveling on the Mississippi and Ohio rivers. The experiences disturbed him, as is indicated in a letter he wrote to his friend Joshua Speed. "In 1841 you and I had together a tedious low-water trip, on a Steam Boat

TIME LINE OF LINCOLN'S LIFE

February 12, 1809
Abraham Lincoln is born in a one-room log cabin in Kentucky to parents Thomas Lincoln and Nancy Hanks Lincoln.

1824
At 15, Lincoln is an avid reader and hard worker. He attends school in the fall and winter and plows, plants, and does odd jobs for neighbors.

1827
Lincoln gets a job ferrying passengers to steamboats on the Ohio River.

1830
The Lincolns move to Illinois. Lincoln makes his first political speech.

| 1800 | 1810 | 1820 | 1830 |

Tensions Between North and South 353

GUIDED DISCUSSION

1. **Analyze Language Use** After passage of the Kansas-Nebraska Act, which allowed for the expansion of slavery in part of the Midwest, Lincoln responded that slavery "deprives our republican example of its just influence in the world—enables the enemies of free institutions, with plausibility, to taunt us as hypocrites." **ASK:** What did Lincoln mean by this statement? *(Possible response: He meant that the United States should be recognized as an example of freedom to the rest of the world but the practice of slavery shows a hypocritical denial of freedom for many that reflects badly on the nation.)*

2. **Form and Support Opinions** If Lincoln had lived longer, how do you think his policies regarding African Americans might have continued to change? Use details from the text to support your opinion. *(Possible response: Lincoln was already in support of partial suffrage just before his death, so he likely would have eventually supported full suffrage for all African Americans.)*

ACTIVE OPTIONS

On Your Feet: Research Liberia Ask groups of four or five to conduct online research on the early history of Liberia. Tell students to investigate the country's beginning as a home for freed slaves and to analyze the motivations of those who promoted the transport of freed slaves to the country. After groups have conducted their research, lead a class discussion about why Lincoln's proposal to send freed slaves to Liberia was unacceptable to many abolitionists.

NG Learning Framework: Present a Speech

SKILL Communication

KNOWLEDGE Our Human Story

Ask students to conduct online research to choose one of Lincoln's speeches to present to the class, either in its entirety or in excerpts. For example, students may choose the Gettysburg Address, the House Divided speech, or an inaugural address from Lincoln's first or second term. Before reading the speech, students should first introduce it by stating the date of its delivery and the context in which Lincoln presented it. After students present the speech, guide the class to identify and discuss a few of the rhetorical devices (allusion, alliteration, metaphor, parallelism) that Lincoln often used to communicate his meaning.

AMERICAN STORIES

from Louisville to St. Louis. You may remember, as I well do, that from Louisville to the mouth of the Ohio there were, on board, ten or a dozen slaves, shackled together with irons. That sight was a continual torment to me; and I see something like it every time I touch the Ohio, or any other slave-border."

Lincoln supporters wore pins like this one during his second presidential campaign.

Lincoln began his career as a public servant in 1834, when he was elected to the Illinois General Assembly for the first of four terms. Despite his personal beliefs, he did not advocate for the immediate abolition of slavery. He believed it was permitted under the Constitution in the states where it existed and that the federal government did not have the power to abolish it in those states. In 1837, at the age of 28, Lincoln made one of his first public statements about slavery before the Illinois General Assembly, and it neatly summarized his views:

> [We] believe that the institution of slavery is founded on both injustice and bad policy; but that the promulgation of abolition doctrines tends rather to increase than to abate its evils.

> [We] believe that the Congress of the United States has no power, under the constitution, to interfere with the institution of slavery in the different States.

In 1846, Lincoln was elected to the U.S. House of Representatives. During his single term in office, he became known for his antislavery views, and he proposed legislation to begin abolishing slavery in the District of Columbia. Because this zone was directly under federal government control, Lincoln believed Congress did have the authority to make

rules regarding slavery there. After completing his term in 1849, Lincoln returned to Illinois and retired from politics to practice law, but he was unable to embrace life as a private citizen for long. In 1854, the topic of slavery drew Lincoln back to the public stage after Senator Stephen A. Douglas persuaded Congress to pass the Kansas-Nebraska Act, which opened up the possibility of slavery's expansion into a large part of the Midwest. Incensed, Lincoln delivered three speeches from Illinois in which he eloquently outlined the case against slavery. "I hate it because of the monstrous injustice of slavery itself," he said. "I hate it because it deprives our republican example of its just influence in the world—enables the enemies of free institutions, with plausibility, to taunt us as hypocrites."

At the same time, however, he didn't insist on the abolition of slavery in the South, and he admitted he didn't know what steps should be taken if all the slaves were to be liberated at once. "My first impulse would be to free all the slaves, and send them to Liberia—to their own native land," he remarked.

Mary Todd had a life of privilege before she married Lincoln.

TIME LINE CONTINUED

April 1832
The Black Hawk War breaks out. Lincoln joins the Illinois militia but sees no action.

August 4, 1834
Lincoln is elected to the Illinois General Assembly as a member of the Whig Party. He begins to study law, using books borrowed from a friend.

November 4, 1842
Lincoln and Mary Todd marry and live in Springfield.

August 3, 1846
Lincoln is elected to the U.S. Congress as a member of the Whig party.

1830

1840

Liberia, on Africa's Atlantic coast, had been settled by freed American and Caribbean slaves since 1822 and had become a republic in 1847. Lincoln went on to admit he viewed African Americans as somewhat less than equal. If it were not practical to send all the former slaves to Liberia, he asked, "What next? Free them, and make them politically and socially, our equals? My own feelings will not admit of this; and if mine would, we well know that those of the great mass of white people will not."

During a debate against Senator Douglas in 1858, Lincoln made himself even clearer. "I will say then that I am not, nor ever have been, in favor of bringing about in any way the social and political equality of the white and black races," he declared, going on to assert his opposition to African Americans serving on juries, voting, or holding office. He did insist, however, that African Americans had the right to be free, receive pay for their labor, and improve their conditions through their own hard work.

In the years that followed, Lincoln continued to support the concepts of gradually ending slavery and sending former slaves out of the country—an idea called colonization that was popular among some leaders. In 1862, while drafting the Emancipation Proclamation, which would outlaw slavery in the South, President Lincoln met with a group of formerly enslaved people at the White House and presented a plan to send emancipated slaves to colonize a region of Central America. Abolitionists and African-American leaders alike angrily disagreed with this plan, insisting African Americans had the same right to live in the United States as whites.

As the tensions over slavery mounted and the country moved inexorably into the Civil War, Lincoln continued to speak out, although his message seemed contradictory at times. In a famous speech in Springfield, Illinois, in 1858,

Frederick Douglass Appeals to President Lincoln by William Edouard Scott, 1943

LINCOLN AND DOUGLASS

When Lincoln happily spotted his friend Frederick Douglass at the reception following the president's second inauguration, he immediately asked what Douglass thought of the inaugural speech. "There is no man in these United States whose opinion I value more than yours," Lincoln explained.

The friendship between Lincoln and Douglass seems both unlikely and perfectly logical. They were self-made men who were born into poverty and educated themselves before rising to positions of prominence. But Douglass had experienced the cruelties of being enslaved. He was also an abolitionist who demanded immediately ending slavery, while Lincoln favored gradually phasing it out. With the brutal honesty of a friend, Douglass criticized Lincoln's colonization plans, writing that the president "seems to have an ever increasing passion for making himself appear silly and ridiculous."

LINCOLN AND DOUGLASS

As an enslaved worker, Frederick Douglass was the victim of terrible abuse, which included starvation, daily whippings, and witnessing the whippings of other slaves. He eventually made a plan to escape to the North, but when his plan came to light, Douglass was sent to jail as punishment. **ASK:** How might Douglass's personal experience with enslavement account for differences between him and Lincoln on the issue of slavery? *(Possible response: Lincoln felt slavery was wrong, but he had not suffered personally from it, so it probably seemed reasonable to him to consider social and political aspects and support the gradual decline of slavery. Douglass had suffered abusive treatment as an enslaved worker and witnessed the abuse of others, so he had more reason to want slavery ended quickly.)*

TIME LINE OF LINCOLN'S LIFE

Explain that Abraham Lincoln was admitted to the Illinois bar in 1836, and in 1844, he established a new partnership with another lawyer. During this time, Lincoln spent several months of the year traveling hundreds of miles throughout central Illinois, which allowed him to meet many voters in the region. Just two years later, in 1846, Lincoln took a leave from his law practice to serve in the U.S. Congress. **ASK:** How do you think Abraham Lincoln's work as a lawyer might have helped him develop his career in politics? *(Possible response: As a traveling lawyer, Lincoln would have met people with a wide variety of backgrounds, viewpoints, and concerns. The people, in turn, would have learned about Lincoln's character, abilities, and political ambitions. As a result, his travels helped build his name and reputation with potential voters.)*

March 31, 1849 Lincoln returns to Springfield, leaving politics to practice law.

1854 Lincoln re-enters politics to oppose the Kansas-Nebraska Act. He chooses to run for the U.S. Senate, but loses the Senate election in 1855.

June 16, 1858 Lincoln gives his "House Divided" speech in Springfield and engages in seven debates with Stephen Douglas, his Democratic opponent in the Senate race. In 1859, Lincoln loses the Senate election to Douglas.

November 6, 1860 Lincoln is elected as the first Republican president of the United States.

1850   1860

VIRTUAL MUSEUM VISIT

The Abraham Lincoln Presidential Library and Museum offers numerous activities to help visitors gain a deeper understanding of President Lincoln, his home state of Illinois, and the time period during which he lived. The museum features educational workshops and discussions on topics related to Lincoln's life and offers walking tours of Springfield, where Lincoln spent many years developing his career and family life. In addition, a museum gallery guides visitors through re-creations of significant events during his presidential terms. Access the library's website and direct students to a collection of items related to Abraham Lincoln's life or presidency. Have groups of students explore the material, choose one item to research further, and present their findings to the class.

WRITE ABOUT HISTORY

Compose a Eulogy Ask students to compose a eulogy for Abraham Lincoln to be spoken at his funeral or at another event just after his death. Students' eulogies should emphasize the main accomplishments of Lincoln's presidency, along with any personal characteristics that made him an admirable person. Since eulogies are intended for reading aloud, ask students to consider how they would sound when presented orally. Pair students to edit each other's eulogies and make suggestions for revision. Provide guidance about the writing process as necessary. Encourage students to read their completed eulogies to the class.

CRITICAL VIEWING Possible response: This photograph seems to reveal a strained relationship between Lincoln and McClellan. Neither man is looking at the other, and Lincoln is even turned slightly away from McClellan. They may have been discussing the battle of Antietam or perhaps Lincoln's frustration with his commanding general.

AMERICAN STORIES

CRITICAL VIEWING In this 1862 photograph, Lincoln confers with General George McClellan in Antietam, two weeks after that bloody battle. What does this photograph reveal about Lincoln's relationship with McClellan?

he declared, "A house divided against itself cannot stand. I believe this government cannot endure permanently half slave and half free. I do not expect the Union to be dissolved . . . but I do expect it will cease to be divided. It will become all one thing or all the other." Lincoln gave his first inaugural address as president in 1861 a little more than a month before fighting broke out between the Union and the Confederacy. However, he insisted, "I have no purpose, directly or indirectly, to interfere with the institution of slavery in the States where it exists. I believe I have no lawful right to do so, and I have no inclination to do so."

On December 20, 1860, South Carolina became the first state to secede from the Union. On April 12, 1861, the Civil War began with the Confederate Army attack on Fort Sumter, South Carolina. By August 1862, the Confederacy had won several important victories, and Lincoln had written a preliminary draft of the Emancipation Proclamation. Lincoln's change in attitude toward abolition was more a matter of strategy than a serious change of heart.

By the summer of 1862, thousands of African Americans had fled their places of enslavement and sought shelter behind Union lines. Neither the federal government nor the Union Army had a policy for dealing with these individuals. Lincoln realized that proclaiming freedom for those enslaved in the South could serve two purposes: First, giving the former slaves an official status in the Union would allow them to support Union army units. Second, more slaves might be encouraged to free themselves, deserting the plantations in the South and thus helping to starve the Confederacy.

In an August 22, 1862, letter to Horace Greeley, Lincoln explained his priorities: "My paramount object in this struggle is to save the Union, and is not either to save or to destroy slavery. If I could save the Union without freeing any slave I would do it; and if I could save it by freeing all the slaves I would do it; and if I could save it by freeing some and leaving others alone I would also do that."

TIME LINE CONTINUED

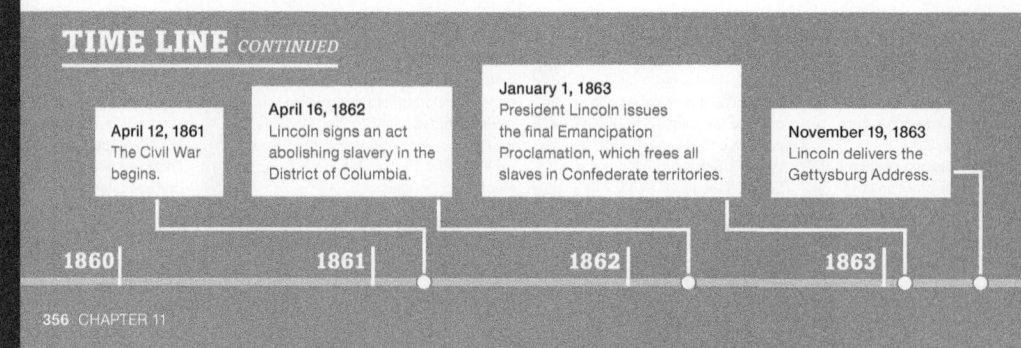

April 12, 1861
The Civil War begins.

April 16, 1862
Lincoln signs an act abolishing slavery in the District of Columbia.

January 1, 1863
President Lincoln issues the final Emancipation Proclamation, which frees all slaves in Confederate territories.

November 19, 1863
Lincoln delivers the Gettysburg Address.

1860   1861   1862   1863

The Abraham Lincoln Presidential Library and Museum
Springfield, Illinois

From 1837 until he moved into the White House in 1861, Lincoln made his home in Springfield, Illinois. Today, Springfield's Abraham Lincoln Presidential Library and Museum shares his legacy with thousands of visitors every year. The library houses a unique collection of Lincoln-related papers and artifacts, and the museum immerses visitors in Lincoln's life and career through interactive exhibits.

Lincoln's letter sealer

In reality, when the final version of the Emancipation Proclamation was issued on January 1, 1863, it did not actually free any slaves, because it applied only to the Confederate states that were fighting against the Union—states that did not recognize Union laws. Border slave states and parts of the Confederacy that had been taken by the Union were exempted. Still, it was a powerful statement and a meaningful step toward the true abolition of slavery that would come with the 13th Amendment in 1865. The proclamation also marked an evolution in Lincoln's own thinking, as it did not mention colonization at all, and Lincoln never alluded to it again.

In the turbulent years following the Emancipation Proclamation, Lincoln's attitude toward African Americans continued to evolve and was likely influenced by the actions of the formerly enslaved. As historian T.J. Stiles observed, "The enslaved moved *themselves* off farms and plantations and into federal lines, asserting their autonomy in a positive act of resistance. Many carried it further by enlisting as soldiers, with profound implications for the status of African Americans." The escaping slaves were the Great Emancipators in their own lives, and their service in the Union Army cast them in an entirely new light. By the end of the war, 200,000 African Americans had served in the U.S. Army and Navy,

many of them with great bravery and distinction. Some historians connect the former slaves' self-assertion and courage in defense of the Union with Lincoln's willingness to envision a greater role for them in society.

In his last speech, Lincoln took one step farther away from his earlier prejudices, promoting partial suffrage for African Americans, an idea that seems timid by today's standards but was radical for its time. He declared, "It is also unsatisfactory to some that the elective franchise [voting] is not given to the colored man. I would myself prefer that it were now conferred on the very intelligent, and on those who serve our cause as soldiers." Three days later, Abraham Lincoln was assassinated. It's impossible to know whether and how his views on African Americans would have continued to evolve had he been given the chance to live to a ripe old age.

THINK ABOUT IT

How did Lincoln's views toward slavery and racial equality evolve throughout his lifetime?

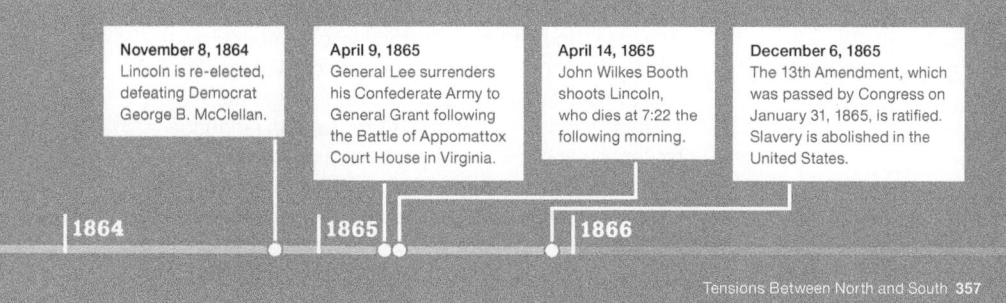

November 8, 1864
Lincoln is re-elected, defeating Democrat George B. McClellan.

April 9, 1865
General Lee surrenders his Confederate Army to General Grant following the Battle of Appomattox Court House in Virginia.

April 14, 1865
John Wilkes Booth shoots Lincoln, who dies at 7:22 the following morning.

December 6, 1865
The 13th Amendment, which was passed by Congress on January 31, 1865, is ratified. Slavery is abolished in the United States.

1864   1865   1866

Tensions Between North and South 357

DIFFERENTIATE

INCLUSION

Predict Using Photos and Captions Pair students to examine the photographs in the lesson and take turns reading the captions. Then have pairs write notes predicting what they will learn in this American Story. After they read the lesson, ask students to review their notes to confirm or revise their predictions.

PRE-AP

Describe an Event or Era Direct students to conduct research about a particular incident or time period in Lincoln's life. Tell them to use their research to compose an article focused on that event or time, including quotations by and about Lincoln. Invite students to share their findings with the class in an oral or written report.

See the Chapter Planner for more strategies for differentiation.

HISTORICAL THINKING

Ask and have students answer the following questions.

1. **READING CHECK** What struggles did President Lincoln face in his attempts to limit slavery?

2. **DRAW CONCLUSIONS** Why do you think President Lincoln saw colonization as a possible solution to the problem of slavery?

3. **EVALUATE** What part did military service play in Lincoln's evolving vision for African Americans in society?

ANSWERS

1. Lincoln struggled with his own attitude about the inferiority of African Americans and his belief that the federal government did not have the power to abolish slavery in the South.

2. Possible response: Moving enslaved people to Central America would end slavery in the United States and prevent greater conflict between the North and South.

3. Possible response: Lincoln pointed out that partial suffrage should be granted to those who served, which showed he valued their military service.

THINK ABOUT IT

Lincoln opposed slavery his entire life but did not support racial equality. He believed African Americans should be free and earn wages for their work but should not be on juries or in elected office. His experience with Frederick Douglass and as president opened his mind to the possibility of full racial equality.

MAIN IDEA As a sharp distinction developed between the economies of the North and the South, the two regions also formed different ideas about what they expected from the federal government.

INDUSTRIAL NORTH AND AGRICULTURAL SOUTH

If you've spent your entire life living on a farm, it might be difficult to envision life in a huge city. Likewise, if you've lived in towns or cities your whole life, you may have trouble understanding life in the country. How might rural and urban communities have different expectations of their federal government?

NORTHERN INDUSTRY AND COMMERCE

During the 1830s and 1840s, economic differences between the North and the South started to form. The northern economy, though still primarily agricultural like the South, began to be driven more and more by industry.

As you have read, textile mills represented one of the earliest major industries in the North. Samuel Slater brought the British secrets of textile machinery to New England in the 1790s, where he established a number of plants. In the early 1800s, Francis Cabot Lowell helped develop the first power loom and revolutionized the conversion of raw cotton into finished cloth so the entire process could be done under one roof. He created company towns around his factories, providing housing, stores, and other businesses to support the needs of his wage workers. Lowell's factories also changed the makeup of the worker population by recruiting young, female immigrants, who would work for lower wages than other laborers.

The geography of New England, with its many swift rivers, provided the water power to run the mills' mechanical looms. Other industries soon emerged throughout the North, using that same water power to manufacture machinery, guns, paint, paper, and other products. Manufacturing, in turn, boosted secondary industries that supported the factory-based economy. Banking expanded to provide loans and capital, or money for investment, to businesses. And business owners needed better transportation systems, such as canals and railroads, to transport supplies and goods. Many wealthy northern

industrial families, such as the Lowells, invested in railroads, financial institutions, and other businesses that helped their manufacturing endeavors.

Factory workers toiled long hours in often unsafe conditions for wages that barely covered their basic needs. Still, for many, such work offered greater security and a better life than they might have had otherwise. The growth of American factories and the need for more workers in the North coincided with natural and political crises in Europe. Millions of Europeans fled their homelands for a better life in the United States, providing a ready and willing workforce for northern industries.

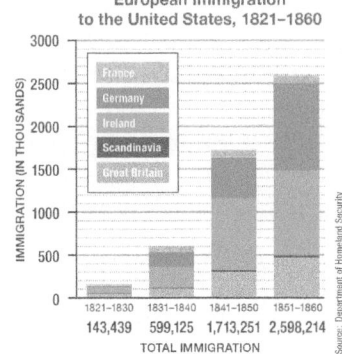

European Immigration to the United States, 1821–1860

	1821–1830	1831–1840	1841–1850	1851–1860
TOTAL IMMIGRATION	143,439	599,125	1,713,251	2,598,214

(Legend: France, Germany, Ireland, Scandinavia, Great Britain)

IMMIGRATION (IN THOUSANDS) — vertical axis 0 to 3000

Source: Department of Homeland Security

From 1845 to 1849, a blight, or disease, struck potato crops in Ireland. Potatoes had become a staple Irish food following their introduction to Ireland in the late 1500s, and the extended crop failure caused a devastating famine, or time of mass starvation. More than 2 million people fled the **Irish potato famine**, hoping to find work in the northern United States. Once they landed, Irish immigrants faced hard times and discrimination because of their Roman Catholic faith and their willingness to take almost any job for any pay. Some workers born in the United States complained that Irish immigrants drove down wages for everyone.

As the Irish potato famine came to an end, a political upheaval in Germany caused another wave of immigrants to move to the North. Many German immigrants came with money to invest in businesses and land. Most of them settled in cities or headed to the Midwest and beyond. Some German immigrants maintained their culture and language by settling in large groups. As industries and transportation expanded and Americans continued to move west, German immigrants settled and established businesses in growing midwestern cities, such as Chicago and Detroit.

SOUTHERN AGRICULTURAL ECONOMY

As the North became more industrial and urban, the southern economy and culture continued to focus on agriculture, especially growing cotton. Large-scale plantations were so profitable that few wealthy southerners saw value in investing in factories, although the availability of cotton drove the development of textile mills in the South. Still, few other types of manufacturing took hold. Great Britain purchased so much southern cotton for its textile factories that a healthy trade system grew between Great Britain and the South. Rather than make goods themselves, southerners relied on British manufactured goods. And some southern states traded more cotton with Britain and other foreign countries than they did with the northern states.

Most wealthy southerners invested in property, especially land and enslaved people. Some historians have argued that the region's reliance on plantation agriculture delayed economic diversity. Southern leaders defended their agricultural system against criticisms about its dependence on slavery by declaring it was more stable than northern industries and less prone to the ups and downs of economic **recessions**, periods of decline in economic activity. They argued that northern factory owners used and abused their workers, discarding

Irish immigrants brought this brooch, or pin, to America during the potato famine. Carved from an ancient oak tree, it features Ireland's national emblem, a harp. The gold shamrocks, or clover, refer to Saint Patrick, the country's patron saint.

them if they got hurt or became ill and could not work. In contrast, they reasoned, enslavers had an interest in looking out for the welfare of their enslaved workers, even in illness and old age.

Some newer southerners, however, questioned this system and its reliance on slavery. Few mid-century German immigrants who settled in Texas supported slavery. Some spoke out loudly against it. But since most immigrants did not want to cause disputes with their new neighbors, the majority of German immigrants opposed to slavery kept their thoughts to themselves.

HISTORICAL THINKING

1. **READING CHECK** Other than geography, what circumstances helped the textile industry to flourish in the North?

2. **ANALYZE CAUSE AND EFFECT** How did northern industries benefit from overseas crises like the Irish potato famine?

3. **COMPARE AND CONTRAST** How did the southern economy develop differently from that of the North?

4. **INTERPRET GRAPHS** According to the graph, what happened to Irish and German immigration in the period between 1851–1860?

PLAN: 2-PAGE LESSON

OBJECTIVE

Explore the increasing economic, political, and social distinctions between the industrial North and the agrarian South.

CRITICAL THINKING SKILLS FOR LESSON 1.1

• Analyze Cause and Effect

• Compare and Contrast

• Interpret Graphs

• Make Inferences

• Summarize

HISTORICAL THINKING FOR CHAPTER 11

How did tensions over slavery divide the North and the South? As the North's economy and population diversified, its regional differences with the South increased. Lesson 1.1 explores the growing separation between the North and the South in the 1830s and 1840s.

BACKGROUND FOR THE TEACHER

During the 19th century, the Erie Canal made it easier to travel from the East to the Midwest. As a result, Michigan became a popular destination for immigrants. By 1830, German immigrants began moving to the city of Detroit in large numbers; by 1866, they represented 20 percent of Michigan's population. The arrival of so many immigrants created a ready-made market for foreign language materials, and it wasn't long before ambitious German printers stepped in to supply them. The first Detroit German-language newspaper, *Allgemeine Zeitung von Michigan*, was published in 1844. More German newspapers appeared, many of them highly vocal on issues such as Congress's efforts to curb immigration. By the late 1800s, people in 15 different Michigan communities could choose from among 40 German-language newspapers to read.

FINANCIAL LITERACY

To extend their knowledge and understanding about the concepts in this lesson, refer students to the Financial Literacy handbook.

INTRODUCE & ENGAGE

EXPLORE REASONS BEHIND IMMIGRATION

Write the word *immigration* on the board. Invite students to discuss what they already know about why people leave their home countries to immigrate to the United States. *(poverty, a poor economy, search for religious freedom, war, political persecution, famine)* Write their responses on the board and discuss how people's reasons for immigrating might change over time. Tell students this lesson describes factors that prompted many people to immigrate to the United States during the 19th century.

TEACH

GUIDED DISCUSSION

1. **Make Inferences** Why might a worker in the North choose factory work as a better, more secure way of life, despite low wages and unsafe working conditions? *(Possible response: Many workers were women seeking to escape their family life or farm life or were immigrants fleeing harsh conditions in their own countries. Both groups would be willing to take available work even at a low rate of pay.)*

2. **Summarize** Why did southerners claim that agriculture was a better economic system than industry? *(Southerners claimed that agriculture was more stable and less prone to recession and that workers were treated better, even though they were enslaved.)*

MORE INFORMATION

Irish Potato Famine By the time of the great Irish potato famine, most of Ireland's tenant farmers were already poor because the land was difficult to farm and crop yields were low. The potato, on the other hand, had become a staple, especially for poor rural populations, because it was relatively easy to grow, highly nutritious, and dense in calories. Irish farmers had begun to depend almost exclusively on only two of the hardiest varieties of potato and failed to plant other strains. This reliance diminished the potatoes' genetic diversity and made the plants more vulnerable to disease. In 1845, the potato blight was accidentally brought to Ireland from North America. Unfortunately, the growing season that year had been unusually cold and rainy, which provided perfect conditions for the blight to spread. It killed entire fields of potatoes, which in most cases rotted while still in the ground.

ACTIVE OPTIONS

On Your Feet: Numbered Heads Organize students in groups of four and have the members in each group number off. Direct groups to discuss the economic information in the lesson and then conduct research to find out more about the economic differences between the North and the South in the 19th century. For example, groups might explore the number of farms, factories, and immigrants in each region or the main types of products made. Then call out a number and have students with that number report on their group's findings.

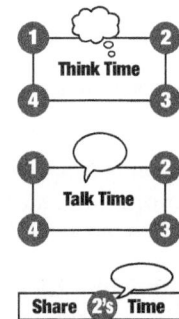

NG Learning Framework: Write a News Article

ATTITUDES Curiosity, Responsibility

SKILL Communication

Instruct students to imagine they are working for a newspaper in the 1840s and have been assigned to write an article about the daily lives of workers at one of Francis Cabot Lowell's textile factories. Ask them to combine information from the text with primary and secondary sources they find online to provide further background for their stories. Encourage students to focus on working conditions, wages, and worker demographics. Invite students to read their completed articles to the class.

DIFFERENTIATE

ENGLISH LANGUAGE LEARNERS

Dictate Sentence Summaries Pair students at the **Emerging** level with those at the **Bridging** level. After students read the lesson, direct them to identify three sentences that contain an important idea. Then tell each student to write that idea in a summary sentence using his or her own words. Partners then take turns dictating their sentences to each other. Encourage pairs to work together to check each other's work for accuracy and spelling.

PRE-AP

Evaluate a Claim Have students evaluate the claim by some slaveholders that enslaved workers in the South were treated better than factory workers in the North. Tell students to conduct research to learn more about the treatment of each group of people and then to write an essay evaluating the claim. Instruct them to use primary and secondary sources to support their evaluation. Invite them to post their essays on a class or school blog.

See the Chapter Planner for more strategies for differentiation.

HISTORICAL THINKING

ANSWERS

1. Industrial inventions, capital investment, and new transportation systems such as railroads and canals helped the textile industry to flourish in the North.

2. Northern industries benefited from crises overseas because they gained an immigrant work force that would accept low wages. For example, between 1845 and 1849, the Irish potato famine prompted about 2 million people to flee to the United States.

3. The southern economy remained tied to plantation agriculture and slavery while the northern economy became more industrial and urban.

4. From 1851 to 1860, German immigration nearly doubled compared with the previous decade. Irish immigration, on the other hand, remained fairly constant, with an increase of only about 100,000 immigrants between 1851 and 1860.

TENSIONS OVER EXPANDING SLAVERY

The call of the West continued to inspire Americans. There was no stopping the rush of settlers toward new land. But what about the spread of slavery across the country? Was that inevitable, too?

THE WILMOT PROVISO

Before the Mexican-American War ended in 1848, debates about the expansion of slavery were heating up. Would slavery be allowed in any of the new territory acquired by the United States? Should it be? Not surprisingly, northerners and southerners had opposing views.

At issue was the balance of political power between slave and free states. So far, Congress had kept a balance under the Missouri Compromise of 1820, which simultaneously admitted Missouri as a slave state and Maine as a free state—keeping the total number of free and slave states equal. At this point, the more densely populated free states held a majority of seats in the House of Representatives. In the Senate, each state received equal representation, preserving a balance. But this balance was challenged as the United States acquired more land.

In 1846, a bill before Congress addressed the acquisition of more land. It proposed that the United States spend $2 million to end the Mexican-American War and purchase California and Mexican territory north of the Rio Grande. Representative **David Wilmot**, a Pennsylvania Democrat, seized the opportunity to address slavery. Like most northerners, Wilmot was concerned that the expansion of slavery to new territory would strengthen the institution and increase southern political power. He proposed adding a **proviso**, or condition, to the bill that would prohibit the establishment of slavery in any territory the United States might acquire from Mexico. His plan is known as the **Wilmot Proviso**.

The House passed the proviso, with most votes in favor of it coming from the North. But the proviso was defeated in the Senate in 1847, with 15 slave states and 14 free states in the Union at that time. This spurred a desire among the representatives of free states to weaken the influence of the slave states in Congress. From 1846 onward, divisions between the North and the South would threaten party unity.

THE PONY EXPRESS
After California's statehood in 1850, better communication was needed between the East and the West. In 1860, a service to deliver mail by horseback riders—called the Pony Express—was introduced as a solution. Riders traveled in relays at full speed on a nearly 2,000-mile route between Missouri and California. Along the way, fresh riders and horses were exchanged at stations, such as the one shown in this painting by Frederic Remington titled *The Coming and Going of the Pony Express*.

The Compromise of 1850

(map showing states and territories of the United States, with legend:)
- Free state or territory
- Slave state
- Territory open to slavery
- County with more than 50% slave population

To further complicate matters, part of the agreement that had been established by the Missouri Compromise was now in question. It had to do with its allowance of slavery into new territories south of Missouri's southern border. Many residents in the Southwest opposed the idea of slave states in their region. Though some settlers in isolated areas of the Southwest had slaves, most communities in the newly acquired territories did not accept slavery. This was especially true in California, where the discovery of gold, among other factors, contributed to its status as one of the fastest-growing areas of the far West.

A good portion of California fell below the Missouri Compromise line, so it did not clearly fit the geographic boundaries established for being a free state or slave state. But as a former territory of Mexico, California had been "free" since 1829. And many Americans who had migrated there did so to establish small farms or to work on large ones. Introducing slave labor into California's agricultural economy would cost them their livelihoods. In 1849, a year before California became a state, the California constitution banned slavery. Californians petitioned for California to enter the Union as a single free state in violation of the Missouri Compromise.

Southerners drew a hard line at allowing California to break the Missouri Compromise and join the Union as a free state. If they gave in to California, they feared a balance of representation and power in government could not be maintained. Outraged southern politicians even argued that to deny slave states equal representation in the Senate was to risk war between the North and the South.

COMPROMISE OF 1850

As debates heated up over California's petition to join the Union as a free state, tensions rose between the North and the South over yet another slavery issue: runaways. Under the Fugitive Slave Act of 1793, authorities of one state could order the return of runaway slaves to their owners in another state. Northern states increasingly ignored this law, however, often turning a blind eye to abolitionists who helped many enslaved people flee to freedom. Southern enslavers argued that by refusing to enforce the Fugitive Slave Act, authorities in the North encouraged enslaved people to flee and unfairly deprived enslavers of their property. They wanted a tougher federal law to ensure that runaways would be returned to bondage or owners would be compensated for their loss of slave labor.

PLAN: 4-PAGE LESSON

OBJECTIVE

Analyze the increasingly serious debate over whether new territories and states would become free states or slave states.

CRITICAL THINKING SKILLS FOR LESSON 1.2

- Identify Main Ideas and Details
- Summarize
- Interpret Maps
- Make Connections
- Compare and Contrast
- Analyze Cause and Effect
- Analyze Primary Sources

HISTORICAL THINKING FOR CHAPTER 11

How did tensions over slavery divide the North and the South? The U.S. expansion westward threatened the balance of slave and free states. Lesson 1.2 discusses various political and legislative attempts to satisfy proslavery and antislavery factions.

BACKGROUND FOR THE TEACHER

After the migrations of Mormons to Utah, the steady flow of pioneers along the Oregon Trail, and the frantic 1849 gold rush, the need for faster cross-country mail service became obvious. Postal companies existed, such as the Butterfield Overland Mail Service, but they were too slow. In addition, by 1858, the U.S. postmaster general had begun to cut back on mail service to California.

Then the Leavenworth & Pike's Peak Express Company stepped in and offered a faster mail service that became popularly known as the Pony Express. The company paid riders about $100 per month plus food and lodging. The mail route stretched nearly 2,000 miles, but tag teams of horses and riders could cover that distance in just 10 days. Crowds lined up along sections of the route to cheer the riders who swept past them. The Pony Express lasted only 18 months but became deeply ingrained in the American imagination.

INTRODUCE & ENGAGE

DISCUSS THE SIGNIFICANCE OF LAWS

Draw a Word Web on the board and write the term *effective law* in the center. Invite students to offer words or phrases that describe an effective law. Then ask volunteers to give examples of important local, state, or federal laws that are up for debate or that have been passed in recent years. Choose one example with which most students are familiar and ask whether they think the law is effective, based on the characteristics listed in the Word Web. Tell students this lesson discusses 19th-century laws that attempted to maintain the balance between slave and free states as tensions between the North and the South increased.

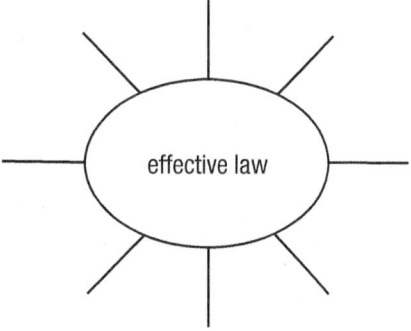

effective law

TEACH

GUIDED DISCUSSION

1. **Identify Main Ideas and Details** How did the Pony Express accomplish its purpose? *(To speed up mail service between the eastern and western United States, the Pony Express set up a series of stations along a 2,000-mile route and had teams of riders and horses carry the mail at top speed across the country.)*

2. **Interpret Maps** According to the map, which state had the most counties where slaves were more than 50 percent of the population? *(South Carolina)*

3. **Make Connections** Why was the issue of slave or free states so important at the federal level? *(Possible response: If the balance of slave and free states tipped in one direction or the other, the makeup of Congress would change. Whichever side gained more seats could introduce laws that would promote or restrict slavery.)*

COMPARE AND CONTRAST

Tell students to think about the Compromise of 1820 and the Compromise of 1850, and then discuss with them the changes that occurred in the United States in the 30 years between the two resolutions. **ASK:** What were both compromises meant to accomplish, and how did they differ in their results? *(Possible response: Both compromises attempted to balance the number of slave and free states. However, while the Compromise of 1820 achieved a balance that lasted 30 years, the Compromise of 1850 pushed the two sides even further apart because of the stronger Fugitive Slave Act, which outraged the North.)*

DIFFERENTIATE

STRIVING READERS

Understand Main Ideas Monitor students' understanding of the main ideas in the lesson by asking them to complete either/or sentences such as the following:

- The Missouri Compromise [balanced or unbalanced] the number of slave and free states. *(balanced)*

- Many people in the Southwest [supported or opposed] slavery. *(opposed)*

- Admitting California to the Union as a free state would have [upheld or violated] the Missouri Compromise. *(violated)*

- Many northern states [ignored or enforced] the Fugitive Slave Act of 1793. *(ignored)*

- President Fillmore [supported or opposed] the Compromise of 1850. *(supported)*

- The Fugitive Slave Act of 1850 gave slaveholders [more or less] power. *(more)*

GIFTED & TALENTED

Evaluate the Wilmot Proviso Direct students to conduct further research on the background and terms of the Wilmot Proviso. Then ask them to set up a panel discussion for a news show to evaluate whether the proviso would have united or divided the country further if it had been passed into law. Challenge students to use graphics, primary and secondary sources, and cite evidence from their research to support their views. Invite them to present the panel discussion for the class.

See the Chapter Planner for more strategies for differentiation.

In Charleston, South Carolina, enslaved laborers hired out by their owners were required by law to be licensed and to wear copper identification badges like these while they were leased out. Stamped on each badge is the city name, the job, such as porter or carpenter, an identification number, and the year. Although badge laws existed in several cities, Charleston was the only city known to have followed a formal regulatory system for the leasing of enslaved people, and only metal badges from that city have been found. Leased slaves were sometimes allowed to keep a percentage of what they earned.

Slave tax badges

In the meantime, these various debates were reshaping political alliances. In August 1848, supporters of the Wilmot Proviso, upset by the actions of northern Democrats and Whigs whom they felt were too moderate on slavery, held a convention to launch a new political party. The **Free-Soil Party** brought together antislavery forces from the Whig, Democratic, and Liberty parties to oppose any further spread of slavery. Adopting the motto "free soil, free speech, free labor, and free men," the Free-Soil Party attracted a wide coalition of voters. Small farmers and wage laborers who opposed the spread of slavery on the basis of economic competition rather than moral grounds supported the new party. Former president Martin Van Buren ran as the Free-Soil Party's presidential candidate in 1848. Although he did not win, the party picked up numerous seats in state and local legislatures, proving that its stance was growing in appeal.

The rise of the new party contributed to split loyalties among voters. As a result, war hero and Whig Party candidate **Zachary Taylor** was elected U.S. president in 1848. Taylor angered those on both sides of the slavery issue by supporting California statehood without any reference to its slave or free status. He proposed that the courts should decide the fate of slavery in the region. When California applied for statehood as a free state in December 1849, some southern states threatened to secede, or separate politically, from the Union. Kentucky Representative Henry Clay hoped to broker a compromise but received little support from Taylor.

Clay proposed what would become known as the **Compromise of 1850**. It attempted to balance the political interests of free states and slave states, while also taking into consideration **popular sovereignty**, or the right of local citizens to determine their own laws. Clay's proposal was an **omnibus bill**, or comprehensive legislation, which addressed almost all divisive slavery concerns. He hoped to balance the territory issue with other matters that drove debates about slavery. He suggested keeping slavery legal in the District of Columbia, but abolishing the domestic trading of slaves there. On the one hand, the bill called for a stronger fugitive slave law in the North. On the other hand, it announced that Congress had no power to regulate the interstate slave trade. The legislation sought to admit California

---

PRIMARY SOURCES

When the Compromise of 1850 was proposed, it set off a great debate in the Senate between northerners and southerners. The arguments below illustrate how the slavery issue was starting to threaten the Union.

Unless something decisive is done, I again ask, What is to stop this agitation before the great and final object at which it aims—the abolition of slavery in the States—is consummated? Is it, then, not certain that if something is not done to arrest it, the South will be forced to choose between abolition and secession? If the agitation goes on, . . . nothing will be left to hold the States together except force.

—from speech by John C. Calhoun, March 4, 1850

I wish to speak to-day, not as a Massachusetts man, nor as a Northern man, but as an American, . . . I speak to-day for the preservation of the Union. . . . I speak to-day, out of a[n] . . . anxious heart for the restoration to the country of that quiet and that harmony which make the blessings of this Union so rich, and so dear to us all.

—from speech by Daniel Webster, March 7, 1850

---

as a free state, but broke from the Wilmot Proviso by leaving the status of other territories won from Mexico undetermined. Hard-liners on both sides of the issues opposed the compromise. Fierce debate raged among members of Congress.

DEBATING THE COMPROMISE

In January 1850, John C. Calhoun, Henry Clay, and Daniel Webster—among the most influential American legislators of the time—took the lead in the national debate over California. Calhoun, from South Carolina, was the most vocal and extreme spokesman for the South. He warned that if slave states did not unite, they would be overtaken by free states in the North and West. Clay of Kentucky reassumed the role of the Great Compromiser that he had played during the Missouri Compromise 30 years earlier. Massachusetts's Webster tried to convince angry northerners that accepting the South's demand for respect was in the best interests of the Union because it would keep the nation together. Arguments went on for months. Meanwhile, President Taylor offered no support for the legislation. The Compromise of 1850 seemed doomed.

Then a series of unexpected events brought new interest to the legislation. In the summer of 1850, Zachary Taylor died from a sudden illness. The new U.S. president, **Millard Fillmore**, openly supported the compromise. John Calhoun, who had been ill throughout most of the debates, passed away. Daniel Webster left the Senate to become Secretary of State. And the elderly and exhausted Henry Clay left Washington, D.C., to recover. Younger, less prominent members of Congress began to build coalitions in support of the compromise. **Stephen A. Douglas**, a promising young Democrat from Illinois, steered the various components of the compromise through committees and votes.

By September, the five major components of the Compromise of 1850 had become law. California was admitted as a free state, and the boundary of Texas was established. Congress formed the territories of Utah and New Mexico, where popular sovereignty would decide the slavery issue. And to balance ending the slave trade in Washington, D.C., Congress passed a much more restrictive and controversial fugitive slave law.

The **Fugitive Slave Act of 1850** raised much dissent in free states because it allowed for the punishment of anyone who aided runaway slaves in their escape. Marshals and sheriffs had the authority to force any bystanders, including abolitionists, to help capture fugitives. Once arrested, an alleged runaway could

CAUTION!!
COLORED PEOPLE
OF BOSTON, ONE & ALL,
You are hereby respectfully CAUTIONED and advised, to avoid conversing with the
Watchmen and Police Officers of Boston,
For since the recent ORDER OF THE MAYOR & ALDERMEN, they are empowered to act as
KIDNAPPERS
AND
Slave Catchers,
And they have already been actually employed in KIDNAPPING, CATCHING, AND KEEPING SLAVES. Therefore, if you value your LIBERTY, and the *Welfare of the Fugitives* among you, *Shun* them in every possible manner, as so many *HOUNDS* on the track of the most unfortunate of your race.
Keep a Sharp Look Out for KIDNAPPERS, and have TOP EYE open.
APRIL 24, 1851.

Printed by abolitionists as a warning to runaway slaves, this poster reflects the impact of the Fugitive Slave Act of 1850 in Boston.

not testify in his or her own defense or call witnesses. And no matter how long it had been since a person had escaped, no matter how settled or accepted the runaway had become in a new place, an enslaver could capture and return the fugitive to bondage. Abolitionists adamantly opposed the Fugitive Slave Act. While parts of the Compromise of 1850 quieted conflict between the North and the South, the law provoked it.

HISTORICAL THINKING

1. **READING CHECK** What connection did the Wilmot Proviso have to California statehood?

2. **IDENTIFY MAIN IDEAS AND DETAILS** What political factions made up the Free-Soil Party?

3. **SUMMARIZE** How did the Fugitive Slave Act of 1850 acknowledge and enforce slave states' practice of slavery?

4. **INTERPRET MAPS** Based on the map, how did the Compromise of 1850 balance the issue of free versus slave states?

BUILD BACKGROUND

LEASING ENSLAVED WORKERS

The majority of southern white families did not have enslaved workers but could hire them when needed through lease arrangements with slaveholders. This allowed slaveholders, in turn, to make more money from their enslaved workers. The workers performed different types of jobs, including domestic and agricultural work, industry and factory labor, and road, canal, or railroad work. Unskilled enslaved people usually labored in mines or processed tobacco, while those with more training and skills might be leased to do carpentry or blacksmithing. The practice of leasing could lead to friction between employers who wanted to get the most out of leased workers and slaveholders who wanted to protect their long-term investment. Slaveholders who discovered their leased slaves were being injured or weakened could immediately cancel the lease and take their slaves back.

FUGITIVE SLAVE ACT OF 1850

In 1850, the annual number of escaped slaves was around 1,000 out of an estimated 3.2 million enslaved workers. For those opposed to slavery, the numbers demonstrated that southerners who demanded stricter fugitive slave laws were being unreasonable. Southern slaveholders, on the other hand, saw that some escaped slaves—notably Frederick Douglass—were speaking out about the cruelties of slavery and attracting greater sympathy for the abolitionist movement. Ironically, the Fugitive Slave Act, created to support the institution of slavery, had the opposite effect. Because of its harshness and penalties against northern whites as well as escaped slaves, the act inspired more resistance, increased the use of the Underground Railroad, and helped new legislation pass in the North that protected personal liberty.

TEACH

GUIDED DISCUSSION

4. Analyze Cause and Effect What happened as a result of the launch of the Free-Soil Party? *(Forces from three different parties that opposed the expansion of slavery pulled together, chose former president Martin Van Buren as their presidential candidate, and gained a number of seats in legislative races, increasing the party's visibility and credibility with voters.)*

5. Analyze Primary Sources Direct students' attention to the excerpts from John Calhoun's and Daniel Webster's speeches. How are their two points of view similar and different? *(Possible response: Calhoun and Webster both seemed to want the Union preserved. However, Webster believed that preservation could be achieved by appealing to the patriotism of all, while Calhoun believed that unless the forces of abolition were curbed, they would provoke the South into leaving. If that happened, then only the use of force would keep the Union together.)*

🏛 VIRTUAL MUSEUM VISIT

Incorporated as a not-for-profit enterprise in 1857 and originally called the Chicago Historical Society, the Chicago History Museum is the oldest cultural institution in Chicago. Its collections hold millions of historical objects, documents, and pictures of life in the United States over the past century and a half. Its mission is to create a place of scholarship, education, and civic engagement for people and, through its collections, exhibits, and publications, to "touch the lives of all Chicagoans and help them make meaningful and personal connections to history." The museum offers temporary exhibits on a rotating basis as well as a number of permanent exhibits, with items such as the slave tax badges. Invite students to visit the online exhibit "Facing Freedom in America" and explore how the concept of freedom has influenced political and social developments in the United States.

ACTIVE OPTIONS

On Your Feet: Roundtable Remind students that some aspects of the Compromise of 1850 served to calm conflicts between the free and slave states even as other aspects inflamed the controversy. Arrange students in groups of four and ask them the following question: If you were a representative from a free or a slave state, would you be for or against the Compromise? Direct each student to respond to the question, providing reasons to support their answers. Afterward, invite groups to share their answers with the class.

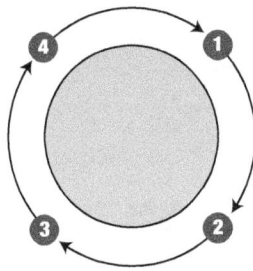

NG Learning Framework: Craft a Protest Speech

ATTITUDES Responsibility, Empowerment

KNOWLEDGE Our Human Story

Divide the class into small groups to craft a protest speech. Tell groups to imagine they are writing a protest speech for an abolitionist who is part of a planned protest against the Fugitive Slave Act of 1850. Ask them to develop a speech that gives all the reasons the act should not be allowed to pass. Direct them to use information from the lesson and conduct research to gather primary and secondary sources. When students have completed their work, invite each group to elect one member to deliver the speech to the class.

HISTORICAL THINKING

ANSWERS

1. The Wilmot Proviso focused on prohibiting slavery in any new lands acquired from Mexico. This applied to California, which wanted to enter the Union as a free state.

2. The Free-Soil Party was made up of antislavery Democrats, Whigs, and Liberty Party members.

3. The Fugitive Slave Act of 1850 acknowledged the right of slaveholders to pursue escaped slaves no matter where the slaves lived or how long ago they had escaped. It also added provisions to punish anyone who either aided runaway slaves or refused to help authorities recapture them.

4. The Compromise of 1850 tried to keep the balance of free and slave states by allowing California to enter the Union as a free state; by declaring a large part of the territory in the Great Plains, Northwest, and West as free; and by giving the Southwest territories of New Mexico and Utah the right to choose whether they would be free or slave states.

CRITICAL VIEWING African-American artist Jacob Lawrence depicts an escape from slavery in his 1997 silkscreen *Forward Together (Harriet Tubman and the Underground Railroad)*. What shapes, colors, and other details in the work help convey what it was like for runaways on the Underground Railroad?

THE UNDERGROUND RAILROAD

It's the mid-1800s and your family is part of a secret operation to help slaves escape through the North to Canada. From all outward appearances, it's just a regular day of chores. But family members are on edge. Then a soft, coded knock signals that your guests have arrived.

GROWTH OF THE ABOLITION MOVEMENT

As you have read, the abolition movement grew out of religious groups who opposed slavery on moral grounds. White abolitionists, free African Americans, and enslaved people who had successfully escaped bondage in the South pooled their efforts to work to end American slavery.

As the movement grew, the role of African Americans, especially former slaves, also expanded within the movement. Sharing their personal experiences helped put human faces to the political issue. Abolitionist publishing houses and newspapers produced numerous narratives recounting life under slavery, horrifying incidents of abuse, and harrowing experiences of escape. As you have read, abolitionist groups sponsored inspiring speakers such as Frederick Douglass and Sojourner Truth. But the most dangerous and daring abolitionist effort, especially in the face of the Fugitive Slave Act, was the **Underground Railroad**, a network of secret routes and safe houses run mainly by free African Americans and devoted white abolitionists in the North.

A ROAD TO FREEDOM

Escaping from slavery was very difficult. Runaways were hunted like animals, and if they were captured, they were returned to bondage where they faced whippings and other terrible, sometimes deadly, punishments. With the passage of the Fugitive Slave

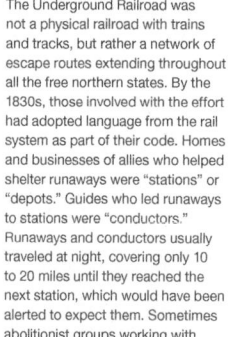

Today people read *Uncle Tom's Cabin* very differently than they did in 1852. They often discuss how Stowe's use of literary elements moved the nation.

Act of 1850, the best way for escaping slaves to avoid being caught was to make it all the way into Canada, where U.S. authorities and slave hunters had no jurisdiction, or legal power. This effort required months of slow, careful travel to avoid detection.

The Underground Railroad was not a physical railroad with trains and tracks, but rather a network of escape routes extending throughout all the free northern states. By the 1830s, those involved with the effort had adopted language from the rail system as part of their code. Homes and businesses of allies who helped shelter runaways were "stations" or "depots." Guides who led runaways to stations were "conductors." Runaways and conductors usually traveled at night, covering only 10 to 20 miles until they reached the next station, which would have been alerted to expect them. Sometimes abolitionist groups working with the Underground Railroad provided new clothes to help disguise the runaways' appearance or paid their passage on boats for quicker movement north. Wealthy abolitionists who secretly donated money to keep the Underground Railroad running were code-named "stockholders."

One of the most famous conductors on the Underground Railroad was Harriet Tubman, who, as you have read, escaped slavery and then helped hundreds of runaway slaves reach freedom in the North. After her escape in 1849, she worked and

saved her money so she could return to the South to smuggle more slaves to freedom. Over the next 10 years she made approximately 13 trips back and forth, leading about 70 people to freedom. Tubman perfected a variety of techniques to avoid capture. Her bravery and skill earned her the admiration of other abolitionists and the hatred of southern slaveholders. In 1849, southern authorities had offered a reward for her arrest. Tubman once bragged to Frederick Douglass that as a conductor on the Underground Railroad she "never lost a single passenger."

UNCLE TOM'S CABIN

While some abolitionists actively helped enslaved people escape, others used the power of the pen to spread their message. In 1852, author **Harriet Beecher Stowe** published a popular antislavery novel that some historians believe persuaded many readers to oppose slavery. Stowe was one of minister and reform activist Lyman Beecher's 13 children. Raised to believe that they had a duty to address injustices in the world, almost all of the Beecher children grew up to be involved in reform causes, including abolition and women's rights.

Objecting to the Fugitive Slave Act and its effects, Stowe wrote *Uncle Tom's Cabin* in the style of popular melodramas, appealing to readers who might otherwise not read abolitionist literature. The main character, Uncle Tom, is a kindly older slave who lives under a wicked, abusive master named Simon Legree.

The plot involves tragedy, redemption, and heart-pounding escapes north for some of the characters. Although a work of fiction, the book reflects real-life experiences of African Americans who told their stories of escape to northern audiences.

Uncle Tom's Cabin sold an unheard-of 300,000 copies within a year of publication. It was the bestselling novel of the 19th century, as readers throughout the world empathized, or felt a connection, with the enslaved people in the story and were mortified by their treatment. Abolitionist groups held theatrical performances of the story to further spread its message. Southerners, however, harshly criticized the book, arguing that the reprehensible Simon Legree did not reflect the actions of most slaveholders. Some historians who claim the book was partly responsible for the Civil War cite the story of Abraham Lincoln meeting Stowe and declaring, "So this is the little lady who made this big war."

HISTORICAL THINKING

1. **READING CHECK** How did the Underground Railroad get its name?

2. **DRAW CONCLUSIONS** How did the Fugitive Slave Act of 1850 affect abolitionists who wanted to help people who had escaped slavery?

3. **IDENTIFY MAIN IDEAS AND DETAILS** What major contributions did African Americans make to the abolitionist movement?

PLAN: 2-PAGE LESSON

OBJECTIVE

Understand how the Underground Railroad developed and what led white abolitionists to help enslaved people escape.

CRITICAL THINKING SKILLS FOR LESSON 2.1

- Draw Conclusions
- Identify Main Ideas and Details
- Summarize
- Make Connections

HISTORICAL THINKING FOR CHAPTER 11

How did tensions over slavery divide the North and the South? In the North, public opposition to slavery escalated following the Fugitive Slave Act of 1850. Lesson 2.1 examines the abolitionist movement and the expanding operations of the Underground Railroad.

BACKGROUND FOR THE TEACHER

Harriet Beecher Stowe's *Uncle Tom's Cabin* appeared during a period of intense social and political turmoil in the country. The novel struck a chord with the public and became such a literary success that it led to some of the first mass-marketing products. Companies created dolls and children's books based on the novel's characters.

After the 1800s, however, the book produced mixed reactions in readers. Some regarded it as a nostalgic view of history rather than as a scathing attack on slavery. Others claimed the novel was a sanitized version of slavery, stressing slaves' docile behavior and willingness to suffer without complaint. As a result, "Uncle Tom" was used as a negative term by some African Americans to refer to those who wouldn't fight segregation.

HISTORY NOTEBOOK

Encourage students to complete the American Gallery page for Chapter 11 in their History Notebooks as they read.

INTRODUCE & ENGAGE

ACTIVATE PRIOR KNOWLEDGE

Discuss with students what they already know about the Underground Railroad. Remind them about the various mandates of the Fugitive Slave Act of 1850. Then ask them to make predictions about how those mandates might affect enslaved people and their abolitionist allies. Explain that this lesson describes some of the people and organizations that helped enslaved people escape to the North, many using the Underground Railroad.

TEACH

GUIDED DISCUSSION

1. **Summarize** How did abolitionists publicize facts about slavery to the American public in the North? *(They published escaped slaves' stories in newspapers, sponsored escaped slaves as speakers, and wrote articles detailing the horrors of slavery.)*

2. **Make Connections** In what ways do you think Harriet Beecher Stowe's family and background helped her write and publish *Uncle Tom's Cabin*? *(Possible response: She was from an activist family who taught her and her siblings that it was their duty to fight against injustice and work for causes such as women's rights and abolition. Meeting former enslaved people would have helped Stowe write her novel, and being part of a large network of abolitionists and women's rights advocates would have given her a ready-made audience for her novel.)*

MORE INFORMATION

Jacob Lawrence Although Jacob Lawrence was born more than 50 years after the Civil War, slavery was one of the subjects he focused on in his paintings about African-American life in the United States. Lawrence was an avid researcher and spent long hours in the library, studying historical texts and newspapers. At times, he added lengthy explanatory captions to his work. He liked to create series of paintings with multiple panels that tell a particular story. Some of his subjects included stories of African Americans coping with war, mass migration, and mental illness. In 1941, Lawrence rose to national fame when his 60-panel *The Migration Series* was unveiled in New York City. This work illustrated the mass movement of African Americans from the agrarian South to the industrial North between World War I and World War II. Eventually, New York City's Museum of Modern Art and the Phillips Collections jointly purchased the entire *Migration* series.

ACTIVE OPTIONS

AMERICAN GALLERY ONLINE

The Underground Railroad Invite students to explore the American Gallery. Have them select one of the images and do additional research to learn more about it. Ask questions that will inspire additional inquiry about the gallery image, such as: What or who is this? What is the intended purpose of this image? Why do you think it is included in this chapter? What more would you like to know about it?

NG Learning Framework: Create a Visual Itinerary

ATTITUDE Curiosity

KNOWLEDGE Our Human Story

Instruct students to work in small groups to conduct research to locate maps and other information about Underground Railroad routes from the South to northern cities, such as Detroit, Chicago, or New York City. Challenge groups to lay out different routes in a visual itinerary that includes maps, captions, icons for cities, and photographs or illustrations of prominent Underground Railroad conductors or other supporters. When groups finish, invite them to share their work with the class.

DIFFERENTIATE

INCLUSION

Support Critical Viewing Pair students to work with a partner who can describe Jacob Lawrence's *Forward Together* silkscreen and read the caption to them. Ask the partner to describe the elements in detail, including postures, colors, and mood. Instruct pairs to ask and answer questions about the silkscreen and to work together to answer the Critical Viewing question.

GIFTED & TALENTED

Present a Personal Narrative Remind students that abolitionists used the power of personal stories to effect change. Ask students to think about a contemporary social issue, such as bullying, racial profiling, or income inequality. Then instruct them to use online resources to research a personal narrative related to that issue which draws upon a person's life experiences and shares meaningful facts to build empathy and spark action. Invite students to present the personal narrative to the class.

See the Chapter Planner for more strategies for differentiation.

HISTORICAL THINKING

ANSWERS

1. The secret, or underground, network adopted a name and the vocabulary similar to actual rail systems, with stations, depots, and conductors.

2. Abolitionists became more organized, working to expand the Underground Railroad to ensure safe passage for more enslaved people willing to risk escape. The risks for abolitionists also became greater.

3. African Americans made many contributions to the abolitionist movement, including telling stories of their former enslavement and escape and working to help others to freedom on the Underground Railroad.

CRITICAL VIEWING The image of the North Star in the upper right corner points to the escaping slaves' destination and purpose. The brown and black figures have their arms outstretched, their legs racing to climb hills and cross rivers, and their babies and belongings clutched tightly to their bodies. The dark background and jagged, snakelike shapes rising from the ground convey the peril of a night journey over dangerous terrain.

HARRIET TUBMAN c. 1820–1913

"There are two things I've got a right to, and these are, Death or Liberty—one or the other I mean to have."—Harriet Tubman

Born into slavery, Harriet Tubman fought for her right to liberty—and, as she says, would have chosen death if she couldn't be free. When she was a teenager, she even defended the rights of another enslaved person by refusing to help capture him. The man's overseer threw a two-pound weight at Tubman and hit her in the head. As a result of the blow, she suffered headaches and seizures for the rest of her life. But none of the abuse she endured as a slave kept her from seeking freedom.

UNDERGROUND CONDUCTOR

Tubman seized her chance to escape in 1849 when her master died. She fled the Maryland plantation and the fields she'd worked for years and set off on foot for Pennsylvania. With the help of a sympathetic white woman along the way and guided by the North Star, Tubman made her way to Philadelphia. Recalling her feelings upon her arrival, she said, "I looked at my hands to see if I was the same person. . . . I felt like I was in Heaven."

She found work in the city and used the money she earned to return to Maryland and bring members of her family to freedom along the Underground Railroad. In time, as you know, Tubman rescued many other enslaved people and claimed, "I never ran my train off the track."

Much of her success on the Underground Railroad was due to the strategies she perfected. Tubman carried drugs to keep fretful babies quiet, and she typically set

Unlike many photographs that captured Harriet Tubman later in her life, this one shows her as a young woman in her 40s. It was taken by Benjamin Powelson after the Civil War for use as Tubman's calling card. As was the custom of the time, Tubman would have left this card when she paid someone a visit.

off with her passengers on a Saturday night, knowing that the escape wouldn't be reported in the newspapers until Monday. Tubman could also improvise. Once, after a bounty had been placed on her head, she overheard some men reading her wanted poster. When they read aloud the part that stated she was illiterate—she was—she picked up a book and pretended to read it.

SPY AND MILITARY LEADER

In recognition of her achievements on the Underground Railroad, Tubman earned the nickname "Moses." The name referred to the Jewish prophet who, according to the Hebrew Bible, led his people out of Egyptian slavery. She was also known to some as "General Tubman." This would prove prophetic.

During the Civil War, Tubman decided she could free more slaves by working with the Union Army. She served as a spy and even led a military expedition—the first woman to do so. On one occasion, she and other former enslaved people gathered information about Confederate positions and maneuvers along a river in South Carolina. Tubman helped plan a raid on the southern troops that resulted in the destruction of buildings, bridges, and plantations and freed about 750 slaves. In this and all the challenges she faced, Tubman's religious faith sustained her. As she once said, "I prayed to God to make me strong and able to fight."

After the war, Tubman retired to New York, where she lived until her death in 1913. Tubman will always be remembered as the most famous conductor on the Underground Railroad, but a more tangible memorial of her legacy may be in the works. In 2016, President Barack Obama's treasury secretary announced his plan to replace Andrew Jackson with Harriet Tubman on the $20 bill in 2020. However, after a new administration entered the White House in 2017, President Donald Trump's treasury secretary suggested he might block that plan or place Tubman on a $2 bill. Still, the honor of being on the $20 bill would be fitting. After all, Tubman, once enslaved herself, would take the place of a man who had been a slave owner.

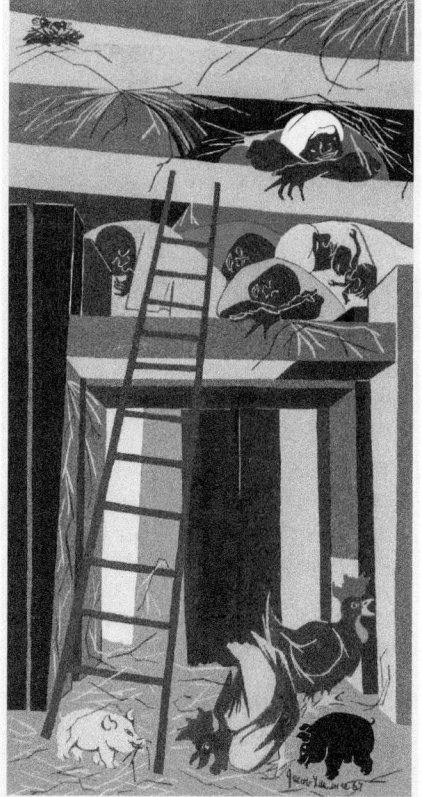

Tubman keeps watch over a group of fugitive slaves as they sleep in a barn in this illustration from *Harriet and the Promised Land*, a book about the Underground Railroad by Jacob Lawrence.

HISTORICAL THINKING

1. **READING CHECK** What did Tubman decide to do after she gained her freedom?

2. **MAKE INFERENCES** Based on Tubman's accomplishments, what inferences can you make about her character?

3. **FORM AND SUPPORT OPINIONS** Do you think Tubman should appear on U.S. currency? Explain.

PLAN: 2-PAGE LESSON

OBJECTIVE

Learn more about the life of Harriet Tubman, one of the most active and influential leaders in the struggle to end slavery.

CRITICAL THINKING SKILLS FOR LESSON 2.2

- Make Inferences
- Form and Support Opinions
- Analyze Language Use
- Make Connections

HISTORICAL THINKING FOR CHAPTER 11

How did tensions over slavery divide the North and the South? The North became a haven for enslaved people who had escaped from bondage in the South. Lesson 2.2 describes Harriet Tubman's life as an enslaved person, her role as an Underground Railroad conductor, and her military service during the Civil War.

BACKGROUND FOR THE TEACHER

Harriet Tubman employed cunning and personal courage in her fight to free enslaved people. In one remarkable incident, she helped prevent an escaped slave, Charles Nalle, from being taken back to the South. Tubman sent out a call for a crowd to gather around the building where Nalle was being held, disguised herself as an old woman, and entered the building. When the federal marshals tried to leave with Nalle, Tubman signaled the crowd to attack and joined in the fight, pulling Nalle away from his captors. She and others got him safely across a nearby river, but he was captured again. Tubman once more led the fight to free him, physically carrying the injured man down the stairs and out of the house where he was being held. This time, Nalle escaped to freedom.

HISTORY NOTEBOOK

Encourage students to complete the American Voices page for Chapter 11 in their History Notebooks as they read.

INTRODUCE & ENGAGE

WEIGH THE RISKS

Discuss with students the dangers enslaved people faced if they tried to escape and the grave consequences if they were caught. Ask students to consider people in the news today who might be taking similar risks to escape oppression or danger and to find safety. What consequences might they face if they fail to reach their goal? Tell students this lesson discusses how Harriet Tubman constantly took great risks not only to free herself and others but also to help the Union win the war.

TEACH

GUIDED DISCUSSION

1. **Analyze Language Use** What did Tubman mean when she claimed, "I never ran my train off the track"? *(Possible response: She probably meant that as a conductor on the Underground Railroad, she never failed to complete a journey and never lost any of the people she led out of slavery.)*

2. **Make Connections** What skills and qualities did Tubman develop as a conductor that may have helped her become a successful spy and leader for the Union Army? *(Possible response: As a conductor, she developed strategies to outsmart her pursuers and improvised to avoid capture, skills a spy would need. She also had to be courageous and dedicated, qualities that probably gave her the confidence to lead military operations.)*

🎖 AMERICAN VOICES

Harriet Tubman's wartime service included working as a volunteer at Fort Monroe and as an assistant to Dr. Durant at the freedman's hospital in Port Royal, South Carolina. Her knowledge of medicinal roots made her a legendary healer among the soldiers. In 1863, Tubman was made commander of a team of scouts and reported directly to Generals Hunter and Saxon. It was during this time that she led a troop of 150 black soldiers in a raid that freed more than 700 trapped slaves. **ASK:** Why do you think white Union officers trusted Tubman with so much responsibility? *(Possible responses: They may have trusted her based on her success with the Underground Railroad. Her past experiences demonstrated her ability to complete difficult missions. She must have given an impression of authority that led the officers to trust her judgment and abilities.)*

ACTIVE OPTIONS

On Your Feet: Fishbowl Arrange students in two concentric circles and tell the inner circle to discuss the following question: Given Harriet Tubman's dedication to fighting for the freedom of others, what groups of people might she fight for today? The outer circle listens to the discussion, and then, at a signal, the inner and outer circles reverse positions. The new inner circle continues the discussion by focusing on this question: In what ways might Tubman lead these groups or inspire them to act? At the end of the activity, have students summarize their discussions.

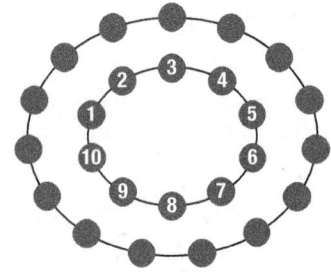

NG Learning Framework: Develop Opposing News Stories

SKILL Communication

KNOWLEDGE Our Human Story

Tell students that northerners and southerners viewed Harriet Tubman in very different ways. Organize students into small groups to write a news story about Harriet Tubman. Assign half the groups to write their articles for a southern newspaper and the other half for a northern newspaper. Direct groups to research Harriet Tubman's prewar activities and to find examples of proslavery and antislavery news stories of the 1850s. Direct students to consider the language and tone that each side would use to describe Tubman and her actions. Invite groups to share their work with the class.

DIFFERENTIATE

STRIVING READERS

List Biographical Facts Post this heading: Five Facts About Harriet Tubman. After students read the lesson, ask them to copy the heading onto a piece of paper and write five sentences that each contain one fact about Tubman's life. Invite volunteers to share their sentences with the class.

PRE-AP

Investigate Primary Sources Tell students that late in her life, Tubman petitioned the federal government for a pension based on her Civil War service. Challenge them to discover relevant primary source documents about this event, including those regarding the basis, support, and resolution of her petition. Tell students to analyze the evidence in the documents and assess the strength of Tubman's claim that she was eligible for a pension and the strength of the reasons behind the House and Senate decisions. Ask students to present their findings in an oral or written report.

See the Chapter Planner for more strategies for differentiation.

HISTORICAL THINKING

ANSWERS

1. After Tubman achieved her freedom, she decided to do all she could to lead other enslaved people to freedom as well.

2. Possible response: Her accomplishments show that she was fearless, determined, resourceful, physically strong with great stamina, intelligent, and deeply spiritual.

3. Answers will vary. Possible responses: Yes. She is a remarkable American patriot who deserves to have her picture on the $20 bill. No. Pictures on U.S. currency should be limited to presidents, Founders, or Treasury secretaries, and no one else, no matter how deserving they might be.

KANSAS AND NEBRASKA

Just four years after the Compromise of 1850 was finally passed, the balance between free and slave states was upset again. And this time the controversy erupted into violence. What was it going to take to resolve this recurring, seemingly unending problem?

THE KANSAS-NEBRASKA ACT

As you have read, the Missouri Compromise of 1820 prohibited slavery in any territory north of the 36° 30' line of latitude. When California, located partly below this boundary, petitioned to join the Union as a free state, Congress eventually passed more extensive legislation known as the Compromise of 1850, which appeased both sides of the issue yet again.

Illinois Senator Stephen A. Douglas, who worked to pass the Compromise of 1850, soon turned his attention to the future of the unorganized territory west of Iowa and Missouri. Douglas supported the vision of a railroad system that would cross the entire continent, passing through his home state of Illinois. However, the railroad could not be built through unorganized territory. Douglas believed the next step toward realizing the railroad system was to organize the lands into two new territories named Kansas and Nebraska, which could later become states. These new territories lay north of the 36° 30' latitude line. Once again, the balance of power between free and slave states was a hotly debated issue.

Douglas was not a supporter of slavery, but he was an advocate of popular sovereignty. He submitted a bill to the Senate that would repeal the Missouri Compromise and let the residents of each new territory and state decide on the matter of slavery for themselves—regardless of whether they resided on land north of the 36° 30' latitudinal line. Douglas hoped his legislation, which became the Kansas-Nebraska bill, would help him gain southern support for organizing the two territories. He also believed

The Kansas-Nebraska Act, 1854

NEBRASKA TERRITORY

KANSAS TERRITORY   MISSOURI

Free states
Territories closed to slavery
Slave states
Territories open to slavery

that, even if the territories opted to allow slavery, the practice would not survive in any northern territories or states. The proposal unleashed a wide range of objections that had supposedly been resolved by earlier compromises. Free-Soil Party members and abolitionists protested loudly and angrily against a bill that might allow slavery to spread beyond its current borders.

The opposing factions could not coordinate their efforts to fight the bill, though, and the **Kansas-Nebraska Act** passed in 1854. It repealed the Missouri Compromise and created two new territories—Kansas and Nebraska—that would decide the legality of slavery through popular sovereignty. Both sides on the slavery issue knew there was still a chance to influence the voting. Plans for how to do so were already underway.

FORMATION OF THE REPUBLICAN PARTY

The issue of slavery was having an impact on political parties. As you have read, slavery was a major reason for the formation of the Free-Soil Party. As old alliances began to fracture, new ones formed. The fight over slavery in the new territories sped up these changes. But slavery wasn't the only matter driving the political shifts that were taking place.

For many political leaders in the early 1850s, halting the flood of immigrants to the United States was a higher priority than stopping the spread of slavery. **Nativists**, or those who opposed foreign immigration, organized the American Party around this issue. People began to call this political faction the **Know-Nothing Party** because it was initially organized much like a secret society, and when asked about party platforms or business, members were instructed to respond, "I know nothing." At first, the Know-Nothings shook up conventional party politics by winning a number of elections, many by write-in vote, in 1854. Eventually, however, the party

was unable to keep its promise to citizens to stem the tide of immigrants. The American Party's members split along proslavery and antislavery lines. By 1856, it had lost almost all its influence.

New parties such as the Know-Nothings had benefited from the declining power and unity of the Whigs, who were also being torn apart over slavery. The Kansas-Nebraska Act brought about the end of the Whig Party. By 1854, most northern antislavery Whigs had split from the party, while most of the proslavery members had joined the Democrats.

Some former Whigs, Free-Soilers, Know-Nothings, and Democrats were fed up with their party's support for southern causes and met at Ripon, Wisconsin, in May 1854 to form a new party more firmly devoted to stopping the spread of slavery. Its platform stated it would not permit slavery in the territories or in new states. This new political faction, called the **Republican Party**, was relatively successful as a new party. Its members quickly won election to

CRITICAL VIEWING A Know-Nothing political cartoon published in 1854 portrays an Irish and a German immigrant running from a voting site with the ballot box, which they have stolen in the midst of a brawl. What details in the cartoon reflect nativist attitudes toward immigrants?

PLAN: 4-PAGE LESSON

OBJECTIVE

Examine how conflicts over slavery gave rise to regional violence and the formation of new political parties.

CRITICAL THINKING SKILLS FOR LESSON 2.3

- Identify Main Ideas and Details
- Summarize
- Interpret Maps
- Identify
- Compare and Contrast
- Interpret Visuals
- Make Inferences

HISTORICAL THINKING FOR CHAPTER 11

How did tensions over slavery divide the North and the South? Unorganized territories became a new battleground in the fight over slavery. Lesson 2.3 discusses these regional conflicts and their political consequences in the mid-1800s.

BACKGROUND FOR THE TEACHER

A colleague of Stephen A. Douglas once dubbed him "a steam engine in breeches"—a fitting description of his considerable energy. Douglas channeled that energy into his political career, rising quickly through the ranks of the Illinois Democratic Party. He had ambitious plans for his home state and believed that a railroad system linking Illinois to the western territories would make the state economically competitive. First, however, he would need to obtain land to build the Illinois Central Railroad. As a member of the powerful U.S. Senate Committee on Territories, he petitioned the federal government for a land grant to Illinois to help get the project underway. In return, the Central Railroad would pay interest to the state and allow federal officials to ride for free. The success of this transaction encouraged Douglas to aim even higher. Eventually, he introduced the Kansas-Nebraska Act with the goal of expanding the country's railroad network and settling the dispute over slavery in the territories.

INTRODUCE & ENGAGE

CONNECT TO TODAY

Draw a Concept Map on the board and write *political parties* in the center. Ask students to name some contemporary U.S. political parties, such as the Democratic, Republican, Libertarian, Socialist, and Green parties. Write students' answers in the smaller circles. Invite volunteers to describe what each party claims to stand for. Tell students that this lesson discusses some of the political parties that arose in the mid-19th century and how they attempted to deal with the issue of slavery.

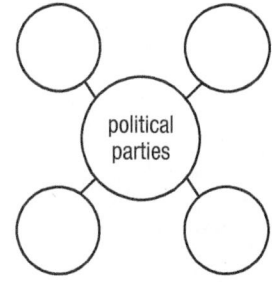

TEACH

GUIDED DISCUSSION

1. **Identify** In what way did the question of transportation influence the development of the Kansas-Nebraska Act? *(Railroads could not be built in the unorganized western territory; therefore, dividing it into two new territories, Kansas and Nebraska, would allow a transcontinental railroad system to be built and connect the entire country east to west.)*

2. **Identify Main Ideas and Details** How did the highly unpopular Kansas-Nebraska Act become law? *(Free-Soil Party members and abolitionists could not organize their efforts well enough to defeat the bill, and Douglas had sufficient support to get the law passed in Congress.)*

3. **Summarize** What influences led to the formation of two new political parties in the early 1850s? *(For some, stopping the flood of immigrants was a more pressing issue than slavery and gave rise to the nativist American Party. For others, the strong desire to stop slavery led them to found the new Republican Party.)*

MORE INFORMATION

The Know-Nothings The American Party, formed in 1849 in New York City, was originally known as the Order of the Star Spangled Banner. Its secrecy soon earned it the nickname Know-Nothing Party. The party's membership, which grew from a small brotherhood to more than 50,000 members, came mostly from the working class. Members were not only anti-elitist but also strongly anti-Catholic, which led them to demand limits on immigration from Ireland and Germany. Their platform also included provisions that would have made it nearly impossible for immigrants to become U.S. citizens. They argued that anyone not born in the United States should not be given the right to vote or hold public office. By 1855, the Know-Nothing Party had gained control of the Massachusetts legislature, where members were able to pass a number of anti-immigration bills. **ASK:** Why would working-class people be more likely to view immigration and not slavery as the main political issue? *(Possible response: Immigrants competed more directly with native-born workers for jobs in urban areas, while slavery was an issue mainly in the agricultural South and in unorganized territories.)*

DIFFERENTIATE

ENGLISH LANGUAGE LEARNERS

Explore New Terms Students at the **Emerging** or **Expanding** level might be unfamiliar with the adjective *full-fledged*. Tell students to locate the phrase "full-fledged abolitionists" in the lesson and to use context clues to ascertain its meaning. Ask them to write a definition of *full-fledged* and then use a dictionary to confirm or revise the definition. If time permits, encourage students to look up the term's etymology. (It originally referred to having feathers; the word *fledgling* refers to a young bird whose first feathers enable it to fly.) Instruct students to write original sentences using *full-fledged* to modify nouns such as *member*, *abolitionist*, and *war*. Invite them to share their sentences with other students.

PRE-AP

Write an Essay Some historians contend that the Kansas-Nebraska Act made the Civil War inevitable. Direct students to gather evidence from a variety of sources and develop a thesis that agrees or disagrees with this claim. Tell them to write an essay that supports their position with evidence from both primary and secondary sources. Remind students to assess the credibility of their sources, to include properly formatted citations, and to paraphrase their data and conclusions to avoid plagiarism. Invite them to share their essays with the class.

See the Chapter Planner for more strategies for differentiation.

CRITICAL VIEWING The two immigrants, depicted as unshaven and rough looking, are stealing the ballot box while others fight behind them. The implication is that politicians use immigrants to steal elections. The two wear barrels labeled with the alcoholic drinks associated with Ireland (whiskey) and Germany (beer). The cartoon reflects nativist views that such immigrants were heavy drinkers, violent, and unworthy of citizenship.

local offices throughout the country. In 1856, the Republican presidential candidate, John C. Frémont, won 11 northern states and two-fifths of the electoral vote overall. The presidential winner, Democrat **James Buchanan**, held no strong position on the slavery issue and was considered by most to be noncontroversial. Buchanan seemed happy to let the courts decide the future of slavery.

"BLEEDING KANSAS"

In spite of the disputes surrounding the Kansas-Nebraska Act, the future of slavery in the Nebraska Territory was not controversial. The territory's climate was not conducive to plantation agriculture, and only a few slaves resided in the area. The 1860 census identified a total of 15 enslaved African Americans in the entire territory.

Kansas was a different story. Activists on both sides of the slavery issue believed they had the opportunity to turn the Kansas Territory in their favor. Antislavery

In this 1872 painting, artist Ole Peter Hansen Balling portrays the severity of the militant abolitionist John Brown, who engaged in extreme tactics in his fight against slavery.

forces quickly organized emigrant aid societies to provide assistance to those who would move to Kansas and vote against allowing slavery in the territory. Expecting trouble from proslavery forces, some of these societies encouraged the settlers to arrive well armed. Abolitionist minister Henry Ward Beecher, of the famous Beecher family, personally outfitted some migrants with new rifles. These gifts came to be known as "Beecher's Bibles."

In response to these efforts, proslavery forces from neighboring Missouri organized to cross the border and influence the territorial vote. In November 1854, when Kansas residents went to the polls to choose between a proslavery or antislavery congressional representative, proslavery Missourians flowed into Kansas Territory to stuff the ballot boxes with illegal votes. The proslavery delegate won the election.

Election tampering was even worse in March 1855, when Kansas voters had to choose between a proslavery and antislavery territorial government. Illegal voting increased as so-called "border ruffians" crossed over from Missouri to threaten anyone opposed to slavery. Their efforts were unnecessary, however, because many Kansas residents had migrated from the South and were proslavery in the first place. Once again, the proslavery delegates won. They took over the territorial legislature and passed laws prohibiting "free-soilers" and other antislavery men from serving on juries and holding public office. The proslavery delegates made assisting a fugitive slave a capital offense, punishable by death.

But this time antislavery forces in Kansas refused to recognize the proslavery legislature's authority. As the newly elected Kansas government passed laws protecting slavery in the territory, antislavery forces established their own government with its own elected legislature and governor, and a separate constitution. Most antislavery supporters in Kansas were not

A number of antislavery emigrant parties came to Kansas Territory armed with cannons to fight any proslavery forces that tried to keep them out. A photographer captured this group of northerners and their cannon in Topeka, Kansas Territory, in 1856.

full-fledged abolitionists. They were simply opposed to competing with plantation agriculture and its institution of slavery. While federal authorities tried to find a way to fix the election mess in Kansas, the territory was split between the two opposing state governments. In 1856, the proslavery government moved its capital to Lecompton, not far from Lawrence, which was a center of antislavery activism in the territory. The conflict in Kansas dragged on and became increasingly violent.

Violence escalated in May 1856 when a group of proslavery advocates ransacked Lawrence, set a hotel on fire and destroyed a newspaper office. They burned down the newspaper office and the Free State Hotel. The "**sack of Lawrence**," as this attack came to be known, shocked people throughout the country. Even more shocking, three days later the zealous abolitionist **John Brown** led his sons and several other followers in a violent revenge attack on a group of proslavery supporters. Brown's men dragged five men from their homes and hacked them to death on the banks of Pottawatomie Creek. Each of the victims had been connected in some way with the territorial court, but Brown's motives for choosing whom to attack have never been clearly established. Neither Brown nor his sons were ever punished for the murders.

Newspapers began to refer to the region as "**Bleeding Kansas**." The brutality even extended to the halls of Congress. During the height of the Kansas violence, Massachusetts senator and

abolitionist Charles Sumner gave a speech calling out fellow senators, whom he blamed for causing the chaos in Kansas. He targeted Stephen Douglas, the popular sovereignty advocate from Illinois and author of the Kansas-Nebraska Act, and Andrew Butler, a proslavery leader from South Carolina. Sumner's verbal attacks on the elderly Butler were particularly harsh and personal. Congressman Preston Brooks, Butler's nephew, decided to avenge his family's honor by taking action against Sumner. On May 22, 1856, Brooks attacked Sumner as he was sitting at his desk in the Senate chamber, beating him over the head with a metal-tipped cane. The attack left Sumner severely injured and permanently scarred. Though the storm of violence in Kansas finally subsided after a new territorial governor took charge in September 1856, its rippling effect in Congress indicated a greater disturbance in the nation was to follow.

HISTORICAL THINKING

1. **READING CHECK** Why were abolitionists opposed to the Kansas-Nebraska bill?

2. **IDENTIFY MAIN IDEAS AND DETAILS** What was the main platform of the newly formed Republican Party?

3. **SUMMARIZE** What incidents led to the use of the term "Bleeding Kansas"?

4. **INTERPRET MAPS** How did the Kansas-Nebraska Act affect the balance of power between slave states and free states?

BUILD BACKGROUND

SACK OF LAWRENCE

On April 23, 1856, in Lawrence, Kansas, Sheriff Samuel Jones was shot while arresting a free-state advocate. Although he survived, supporters of the free-state movement forced him out of town. News about the troubles in Lawrence soon spread and alarmed proslavery forces from southern states. On May 2, 400 proslavery troops from Alabama and Georgia arrived at the Kansas border and, three days later, killed an abolitionist named John Stewart. On May 21, some of the troops entered the Lawrence city limits, carrying an American flag and a "Southern Rights" flag. This set off a round of violence that included cannon fire and explosions that rocked the Free State Hotel. One resident was killed, and a proslavery advocate died of injuries from falling debris. Although the fighting subsided, emotions remained high, setting the stage for John Brown's attack.

SUMNER'S SPEECH AND THE AFTERMATH

Charles Sumner, a freshman Republican senator, stood out from his colleagues not only for his six-foot-two-inch frame but also for his fiercely vocal opposition to slavery. He was particularly angry about the Kansas-Nebraska Act and wrote a 112-page speech against it titled "The Crime Against Kansas." Before he addressed the U.S. Senate on May 19, 1856, he handed out printed copies of his speech for Senate members to read.

He then proceeded to deliver the speech over two days, May 19 and 20, having memorized all 112 pages. Unfortunately, his bombastic style, in which he appeared to regard his opponents as somewhat dull witted, added more fuel to his insults about Stephen Douglas and Andrew Butler, both supporters of the act. After the assault by Butler's nephew, described in the text, Sumner never fully recovered. He eventually returned to the Senate but continued to have nightmares about the attack and severe headaches for most of his life.

TEACH

GUIDED DISCUSSION

4. **Compare and Contrast** Describe the difference in attitudes toward slavery in the Nebraska and Kansas territories. *(Possible response: Since Nebraska did not have good land or the climate for growing cotton or tobacco, proslavery forces had little interest in it. Kansas, on the other hand, did have the right conditions, and both proslavery and antislavery factions fought bitterly for control of the territory.)*

5. **Identify Main Ideas and Details** How did Kansas end up with two governments? *(Election tampering, illegal voting, and proslavery advocates from Missouri gave the election victory to proslavery forces. Antislavery forces refused to accept the outcome and formed their own government, giving Kansas two governors and two legislatures.)*

6. **Interpret Visuals** What does the photograph of the men with their cannon suggest about the division of the country over slavery? *(Possible response: The photo shows the extremes that people were willing to go to in the battle over slavery and suggests that a time is coming when only violence can settle the issue.)*

MAKE INFERENCES

Discuss with students the violent behavior of John Brown and his sons following the sack of Lawrence. **ASK:** Why do you think John Brown and his sons were never prosecuted for the crime of killing five proslavery supporters? *(Answers will vary. Possible response: Officials might have been reluctant to inflame the situation further by arresting Brown. Also, since Brown carried out his attack as revenge for the proslavery sack of Lawrence, many antislavery people may have felt his violent actions were justified.)*

ACTIVE OPTIONS

On Your Feet: Jigsaw Organize students into "expert" groups and assign each group one of the following topics: the fight over the Kansas-Nebraska Act, John Brown's attack, the conflicts in Kansas, the fight over slavery on the Senate and House floors. Ask groups to discuss the following question: What effect did each event have on the divisions in the country? After groups have had time for discussion, rearrange students into new groups so that each new group has at least one member from each expert group. Students in the new group take turns sharing what they learned in their former groups.

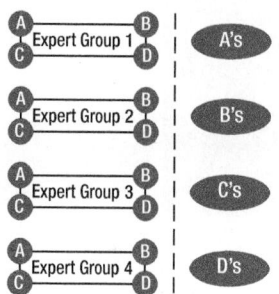

NG Learning Framework: Write an Editorial

| SKILL | Communication |

| KNOWLEDGE | Our Human Story |

Direct students to work in small groups to write an editorial about one of the events or people discussed in the lesson. Tell them to conduct additional research about the topic they select, including how the person or event influenced the nation. Inform students that their editorials should express an opinion about their topic and include evidence from their research to support their viewpoints. Ask students to read their editorials to the class or post them on a class blog or website.

HISTORICAL THINKING

ANSWERS

1. Abolitionists feared the Kansas-Nebraska Act would encourage the spread of slavery by repealing the Missouri Compromise and by allowing popular sovereignty to decide whether a state or territory should be slave or free.

2. The Republican Party announced it would not permit slavery in territories or new states, a platform that brought it early success in national elections.

3. Kansas was called "Bleeding Kansas" because of ongoing violent clashes that occurred between proslavery and antislavery advocates over elections and because of incidents like the "sack of Lawrence" and the Pottawatomie Massacre.

4. By allowing two large territories to decide for themselves whether to allow slavery, the Kansas-Nebraska Act potentially tipped the balance of power in favor of the slave states.

DRED SCOTT AND THE DEBATE OVER SLAVERY

Boundaries between slave states and free states were negotiated to maintain a balance of power in Congress. But what happens when a slave owner moves with his slave from a slave state to a free state? What do these boundaries mean *then*?

DRED SCOTT DECISION

In 1857, the U.S. Supreme Court made a ruling that would increase discord about slavery. The case involved an African American named **Dred Scott**. John Emerson, a doctor in the U.S. Army, had purchased Scott as a slave in 1833. Emerson then relocated to the Wisconsin Territory, where slavery was illegal under the provisions of the Missouri Compromise. Scott continued to work for Emerson without wages while in the territory. However, because Emerson's work required him to be away for long periods, Scott was hired out to others for pay. While living in Wisconsin Territory, Scott also met and married Harriet Robinson, who was enslaved by a federal Indian agent. Emerson purchased Harriet, and the Scotts eventually had two daughters, who were also Dr. Emerson's property.

Emerson married in 1838 and moved back South, bringing the Scotts with him. Three years later, Emerson died in Missouri. In his will, he instructed that the Scott family and his other slaves be left to his wife's family. Dred Scott wanted to use the money he had been saving to purchase freedom for himself, his wife, and their daughters, but the family's new owners refused. Dred Scott sued, arguing that his time living in the free Wisconsin Territory made him a free man. The case worked its way up through the court system, with various outcomes for and against Scott until it finally wound up before the Supreme Court in 1846.

At this time, southerners, led by Chief Justice **Roger B. Taney**, dominated the Supreme Court. Its 1857 decision in *Dred Scott v. Sandford*, written by Taney, not only went against Scott's request, but went further than anyone expected. In the **Dred Scott decision**, the Court declared that it could not rule on the merits of Scott's request because as property, enslaved African Americans "had no rights which the white man was bound to

respect." In other words, Scott had no standing to sue in federal court as African Americans could not be considered U.S. citizens, even those who had been born free. Furthermore, the decision declared that the ownership of slaves was a property right, and Congress had no authority to limit slavery in territories such as Wisconsin, so the Missouri Compromise had been illegal. This essentially meant that slavery could extend anywhere in the United States, regardless of local opinion or established law.

Reaction to the decision was swift. Many southerners were relieved, although even they were surprised by how far the Court went. Rather than resolving the issue, however, the decision only enraged abolitionists and Free-Soil supporters. If the Dred Scott decision were followed to its logical conclusion, they warned, the United States would reopen the slave trade with Africa and even extend slavery into northern states, where it had been banned. Most authorities quietly ignored the ruling rather than enforce it. The case unintentionally boosted support for the rising Republican Party.

You are probably wondering what happened to Dred Scott and his family. During the trial and its many appeals, Dred Scott received assistance from a surprising source: the original family who had sold him to John Emerson. The adult sons of Scott's first owner paid his legal fees as the case worked its way through the courts. After the Supreme Court decision, the family purchased Scott and his family and granted them their freedom. Dred Scott died just 16 months after finally becoming free.

LINCOLN-DOUGLAS DEBATES

The Dred Scott case played an important role in the 1858 race for U.S. senator from Illinois, which would set the stage for the next presidential election. Incumbent Democratic Senator Stephen A. Douglas was running for re-election against Republican lawyer Abraham Lincoln. Although state legislatures, rather than individual voters, elected U.S. senators at this time, the candidates held seven public debates that newspapers covered nationally.

The Lincoln-Douglas debates highlighted the candidates' differing views on expanding slavery into new territories. Douglas reaffirmed his commitment to popular sovereignty. Lincoln expressed his personal belief that slavery was immoral and should be placed on a path toward "ultimate extinction." In terms of policy for the meantime, however, Lincoln reaffirmed the Free-Soil position that slavery needed to be confined rather than rashly abolished. Douglas

🏛 **Missouri History Museum St. Louis, Missouri**

During the 1880s, the artist Louis Schultze painted this life-size portrait of Dred Scott for the Missouri Historical Society as part of a series depicting notable residents of St. Louis. Although painted after Scott's death, the image was based on the only known photograph taken of Scott, who wore a similar suit jacket, white shirt, and bow tie.

Lincoln and Douglas gained the attention of the nation during their race for the Illinois U.S. Senate seat. Because they mainly debated the issue of slavery, the outcome of their contest had repercussions for the entire country.

Judge Douglas declares that if any community want[s] slavery, they have a right to have it. He can say that, logically, if he says that there is no wrong in slavery; but if you admit that there is a wrong in it, he cannot logically say that anybody has a right to do wrong.

—from a speech by Abraham Lincoln during one of the Lincoln-Douglas debates, 1858

I hold that the people of the slaveholding States are civilized men as well as ourselves; . . . It is for them to decide, therefore, the moral and religious right of the slavery question for themselves within their own limits.

—from a speech by Stephen Douglas during one of the Lincoln-Douglas debates, 1858

seized on Lincoln's statements to portray him as a dangerous radical whose views could further tear the country apart.

During one of the debates held in Freeport, Illinois, Lincoln challenged Douglas to discuss how popular sovereignty could exist after the Dred Scott decision. Douglas argued that local communities could undermine the ruling by refusing to enact slave codes (similar to local police regulations), which were used to control enslaved people and prevent them from running away. And because few slaveholders would choose to live in communities without laws protecting their right to hold humans as property, slavery would be kept at a minimum in the areas where communities refused to enact slave codes. This concept became known as Douglas's **Freeport Doctrine**.

But Douglas's doctrine only widened a growing sectional division within the Democratic Party. Some northern Democrats were satisfied with Douglas's position. Many southern Democrats adamantly opposed it. To them, Douglas was not an ally they could count on to protect their interests. Although Douglas won the election and retained his seat in the U.S. Senate, he lost national standing within his own party. Lincoln, on the other hand, lost the election but won a national following within the Republican Party.

PLAN: 4-PAGE LESSON

OBJECTIVE

Learn how proslavery and antislavery factions fought for political dominance in the 1850s.

CRITICAL THINKING SKILLS FOR LESSON 2.4

- Identify Main Ideas and Details
- Summarize
- Form and Support Opinions
- Analyze Primary Sources
- Draw Conclusions
- Analyze Cause and Effect
- Compare and Contrast
- Analyze Visuals

HISTORICAL THINKING FOR CHAPTER 11

How did tensions over slavery divide the North and the South? Battles between proslavery and antislavery forces became more violent in the 1850s. Lesson 2.4 explores the Dred Scott decision and abolitionist John Brown's raid on Harpers Ferry.

BACKGROUND FOR THE TEACHER

Between August and October of 1858, U.S. Senate candidates Abraham Lincoln and Stephen A. Douglas debated each other in seven different congressional districts across Illinois. The format of the debates was simple: One candidate would present an hour-long address, and then the other candidate would speak for 90 minutes. The first speaker would get 30 minutes to present a rebuttal. There were no moderators and no breaks except for a pause to allow the first candidate to leave the podium as the other approached. Douglas, as the incumbent, presented first in four of the seven debates. Even though Douglas won the election, the debates proved beneficial for Lincoln. After his loss, Lincoln edited and published the debate transcripts. Their success brought Lincoln more attention from the press and a wider national audience, both of which helped him win the Republican presidential nomination in 1860.

INTRODUCE & ENGAGE

DISCUSS THE NATURE OF DEBATES

Find a video recording of excerpts from a recent or famous presidential debate to play for students. Before presenting the excerpts, discuss with students what they already know about typical debate formats, venues, and issues. Play the excerpts and guide students to identify issues important to the candidates. Then draw a Venn diagram on the board. Tell students that although debates are meant to differentiate candidates, they also reveal the candidates' common ground. Play the excerpts again, and invite students to complete the Venn diagram. Then tell them that Lesson 2.4 discusses a series of political debates between Abraham Lincoln and Stephen O. Douglas three years before the Civil War.

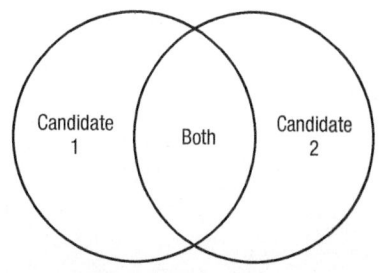

TEACH

GUIDED DISCUSSION

1. **Analyze Primary Sources** Read the excerpts from the Lincoln-Douglas debate in the Primary Sources feature. What point is Lincoln making in response to Douglas's statement about the right of people to decide the slavery issue for themselves? *(Possible response: Lincoln plays on the word* right *by turning Douglas's words against him. His point is that Douglas's argument falls apart if you admit slavery is wrong. As a result, no one has a "right to do wrong," that is, to allow slavery to exist.)*

2. **Draw Conclusions** Why did the Dred Scott decision attract new supporters to the Republican Party? *(Possible response: Many antislavery supporters were angered by the idea that no African Americans could ever be U.S. citizens and that Congress had no authority to limit slavery in territories. The Republican Party with its antislavery platform drew many of these angry supporters into its ranks.)*

3. **Analyze Cause and Effect** What was the intended purpose of the Freeport Doctrine, and what were its actual effects? *(Possible response: Stephen Douglas intended to help defuse the slavery conflict by arguing that communities could limit slavery by not enacting slave codes. However, the doctrine's actual effects were to further split the North-South factions in the Democratic Party and strengthen Lincoln's following within the Republican Party.)*

🏛 VIRTUAL MUSEUM VISIT

The Missouri History Museum is a wing of the Missouri Historical Society, which was founded in St. Louis in 1866. Its mission is to save "from oblivion the early history of the city and state." Each year, more than 36,500 students view the museum's artifacts and exhibits and attend its programs and educational events, all of which focus on the local and regional history of Missouri, including the Dred Scott decision. The museum's website is a rich resource of historical materials for scholars and history buffs alike. Encourage students to take a virtual tour of both the museum and the affiliated Missouri Historical Society and to explore the online materials from the Dred Scott Collection.

DIFFERENTIATE

STRIVING READERS

Summarize Using a Concept Cluster Instruct pairs to summarize the lesson by creating a Concept Cluster. Tell students to write the lesson title in the center oval and the subsection headings in the outer ovals. As pairs read each subsection, have them enter key events and ideas on the spokes, adding spokes as needed. After students complete their Concept Clusters, invite volunteers to summarize the lesson.

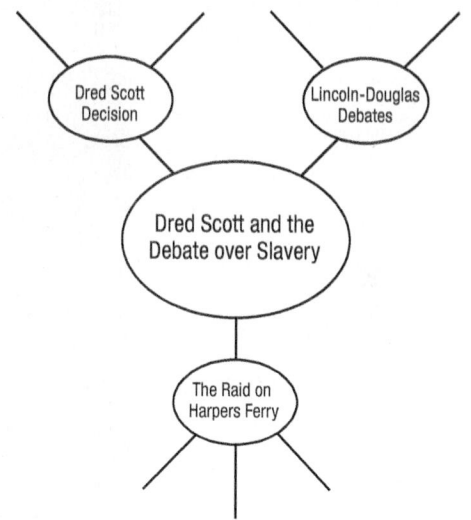

GIFTED & TALENTED

Perform a Readers' Theater Challenge students to prepare a readers' theater script using 1857 editorials written about the Dred Scott decision, many of which are available online at such websites as the Secession-Era Editorials Project of Furman University. Direct students to choose and arrange excerpts from northern and southern state newspapers to show the clash of opinions. They can create a script for one reader or recruit classmates to read different parts. Suggest readers use their voice, facial expressions, and gestures to convey the original writers' emotions and ideas. Invite students to perform their scripts, and then ask listeners to discuss how the readers' theater enhanced their understanding of why the Dred Scott decision had such an impact.

See the Chapter Planner for more strategies for differentiation.

THE RAID ON HARPERS FERRY

With tensions already rising over slavery in the territories, a familiar face reemerged to fan the flames of conflict. Radical abolitionist John Brown, who had worked with the Underground Railroad and led the murderous attack on slavery supporters at Pottawatomie Creek during the "Bleeding Kansas" crisis, launched his boldest effort yet. After his action in Kansas, Brown and his followers led a group of newly freed slaves to assured freedom in Canada.

Brown had fled capture in Kansas, and for the next few years he spent most of his time in the North, speaking about slavery and abolition to audiences. Hatching a plan to lead a larger-scale slave revolt in Maryland and Virginia, Brown solicited money from wealthy and willing contributors to fund this insurrection. With this money, he purchased weapons for his planned initial attack.

On October 16, 1859, Brown led 21 men—only 5 of them African American—in an attack on the federal arsenal at **Harpers Ferry, Virginia**. The group took several slave owners hostage, believing their slaves would take arms from the arsenal and join the revolt. They hoped an army of liberators would rise up across the South and overthrow slavery in a bloody rebellion.

Instead, U.S. Army forces overtook the arsenal, killing several of Brown's followers and wounding Brown himself, whom they captured alive. The federal government quickly tried Brown and sentenced him to hang for treason. A defiant Brown went to the gallows, still claiming that his actions were necessary and called for by God.

Once again, reactions to John Brown's deeds and execution varied by region. Some northern abolitionists hailed him as a righteous victim who had sacrificed himself to the antislavery cause. Southerners were horrified by the violence carried out by Brown and his followers. To them, he was an example of growing extremism within the abolition movement.

HISTORICAL THINKING

1. **READING CHECK** What legal argument did Dred Scott rely on when he sued for his freedom?

2. **IDENTIFY MAIN IDEAS AND DETAILS** What reasons did the Supreme Court give to support its decision in the Dred Scott case?

3. **SUMMARIZE** Why did national newspapers cover the debates in Illinois between Lincoln and Douglas?

4. **FORM AND SUPPORT OPINIONS** Was John Brown justified in attempting to raid the Harpers Ferry arsenal? Support your opinion.

AMERICAN PLACES
Harpers Ferry National Historic Park, West Virginia

Harpers Ferry lies where the Potomac and Shenandoah rivers converge, as shown in this aerial image taken by National Geographic photographer Ken Garrett. The scene of John Brown's 1859 raid on the armory, the town later became the site of one of the nation's first integrated schools—attended by both African Americans who had been enslaved and whites. Today it is part of Harpers Ferry National Historical Park at a point in the Blue Ridge Mountains where West Virginia, Virginia, and Maryland meet.

BUILD BACKGROUND

JOHN BROWN'S ARMY

John Brown's small army at Harpers Ferry included a mix of young farm boys, an African-American college student, a formerly enslaved man, two Quaker brothers, and battle-scarred veterans of Brown's Kansas campaign. All of them were committed to the fight against slavery and were determined to lead an uprising of white and African-American liberators. Once a large federal force arrived at Harpers Ferry, however, Brown's group had few options but to surrender or try to escape. Two young men, Albert Hazlett and Osborne Anderson, managed to slip over a back wall of the arsenal and escape in a boat up the Potomac River. Hazlett got as far as Pennsylvania before he was captured and extradited back to Virginia. Anderson, however, was one of just five men—and the only African American—to survive the fight. Later, he wrote an account of his experiences at Harpers Ferry before, during, and after the raid.

"BATTLE HYMN OF THE REPUBLIC"

When John Brown was executed for his role at Harpers Ferry, an unknown lyricist took an old religious camp meeting song and wrote new words to reflect the antislavery movement's determination to continue the fight. The new version proclaimed that though Brown's body was decaying in the grave, his soul—symbolizing the abolitionist cause—was still marching forward. Once the Civil War began, this new version of the old song became popular with the Union Army. The Confederate Army, meanwhile, created its own version, which mockingly described John Brown's body hanging from a tree, implying he had been lynched. Later, Julia Ward Howe, an abolitionist writer, wrote yet another version in which the lyrics stressed the justice of the Union cause. Howe's version, known as "The Battle Hymn of the Republic," caught the imaginations of northern soldiers and civilians alike and became a rallying song for the Union.

TEACH

GUIDED DISCUSSION

4. **Compare and Contrast** How were northern and southern reactions to the execution of John Brown similar and different? *(Possible response: Both had strong reactions to the execution, but northerners believed John Brown was a martyr to the abolitionist cause, while southerners believed the execution was justified due to Brown's violence and antislavery stance.)*

5. **Identify Main Ideas and Details** How did Brown and his followers misjudge the situation at Harpers Ferry? *(Possible response: Brown took only 21 men, probably because he expected that enslaved workers around Harpers Ferry would rise up and join him during the attack. Instead, Brown and his men fought alone, and U.S. Army forces quickly put an end to the raid.)*

6. **Analyze Visuals** What details in the aerial photograph of Harpers Ferry and the photograph's caption reveal the site as a good location for the U.S. Army's arsenal? *(Possible response: It offered proximity to three different states and was built where two rivers converge, which made it easy to move supplies and troops in and out of the area.)*

AMERICAN PLACES

Visitors to Harpers Ferry National Historic Park can step back in time and watch reenactors dramatize historical events throughout the year. Among the most popular is "Reacting to the Raid: Local Militia and the U.S. Marines," which depicts John Brown's attack on Harpers Ferry and his subsequent capture two days later, performed by volunteers from the U.S. Marine Corps Historical Company. The park also features 20 miles of public hiking trails that take visitors to Civil War battlefields or to lookout points where they can view West Virginia's landscape from atop a mountain. In affiliation with the Harpers Ferry Historical Association, the park offers workshops that teach visitors about 19th-century blacksmithing, tin-making, cooking, and gardening.

ACTIVE OPTIONS

Active History: Debate an Issue Extend the lesson by using either the PDF or Whiteboard version of the activity. These activities take a deeper look at a topic from, or related to, the lesson. Explore the activities as a class, turn them into group assignments, or even assign them individually.

NG Learning Framework: Evaluate the Candidates

| SKILL | Communication |

| KNOWLEDGE | Our Human Story |

Invite students to work in small groups to gather information from the lesson and from their own research about the Lincoln-Douglas debates. Tell them to use the information to write an article for a 19th-century newspaper evaluating each candidate for the voting public. Instruct groups to identify details about both candidates' backgrounds, reputations, appearance, oratorial skills, and arguments as representatives of their political parties. Encourage students to include direct quotations from candidates' speeches in their evaluation. When groups are finished, invite them to share their articles with the class.

HISTORICAL THINKING

ANSWERS

1. Scott was born a slave in Virginia but had been taken by his master to a free territory in the upper Midwest where they lived for several years. He petitioned for his freedom, using the legal argument that residence in the free territory entitled him to free status.

2. The Supreme Court reasoned that enslaved African Americans were property and, as such, had no rights as U.S. citizens, including the right to sue. They also reasoned that Congress didn't have the authority to limit slavery in territories.

3. Douglas already had a national reputation as a states' rights advocate, which meant he had sympathies toward the South, while Lincoln was known for his strong antislavery stance. Because their debates had national implications for the makeup of the Senate, the national media would be on hand to cover the story, allowing the public in both the North and the South to follow the debates closely.

4. Answers will vary. Possible responses: Yes. Brown could see that current political solutions would never eradicate slavery, so he took action to force people to choose sides. He truly believed that enslaved people would revolt and join him to eliminate slavery from the country. No. Brown badly misjudged his ability to end slavery in a single assault against an arsenal of the federal government. His violent approach probably alienated many people who otherwise sympathized with his antislavery stance.

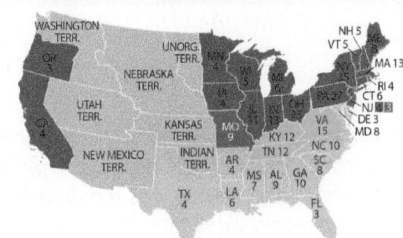

The 1860 Election

Abraham Lincoln, Republican

Electoral Vote: 180 votes, 59.4%

Popular Vote: 1,866,452 votes, 39.8%

Stephen A. Douglas, Northern Democrat

Electoral Vote: 12 votes, 3.9%

Popular Vote: 1,380,202 votes, 29.5%

John C. Breckinridge, Southern Democrat

Electoral Vote: 72 votes, 23.8%

Popular Vote: 847,953 votes, 18.1%

John Bell, Constitutional Unionist

Electoral Vote: 39 votes, 12.9%

Popular Vote: 590,901 votes, 12.6%

THE ELECTION OF 1860

It was clear that "a house divided" couldn't stand, and a presidential election wasn't going to fix the problem. It was becoming obvious that whoever won the election of 1860 would have the unlucky task of keeping the nation from falling.

NOMINATING LINCOLN

Going into the national Republican convention of 1860, the front-runner, or leading candidate, for the presidential nomination was U.S. Senator **William Seward**, a former governor of New York. Seward was a fierce abolitionist who had left the Whigs to join the Republican fight against the expansion of slavery into new territories. However, a relative newcomer to the national spotlight overshadowed Seward. As you have read, just two years before the convention, Abraham Lincoln had lost his bid for the U.S. Senate seat from Illinois to Stephen A. Douglas. But Lincoln's riveting performances during the much-publicized Lincoln-Douglas debates had won him nationwide attention.

Lincoln was firm in his stance on slavery: he did not expect it to be abolished anytime soon, but it should not be allowed to spread. Seward was much more outspoken in his opposition to slavery. Slavery was such a divisive issue in the country that many Republican party members viewed Lincoln as the more moderate, practical choice. And it didn't hurt Lincoln's chances for nomination that the 1860 Republican National Convention was being held in Lincoln's home state of Illinois. Thousands of Lincoln's supporters descended upon the convention site in Chicago—a makeshift structure called the

Wigwam—to promote "Honest Abe." The majority of Republicans at the convention soon saw Lincoln as the future of the party. After three ballots, Lincoln had secured the party's nomination.

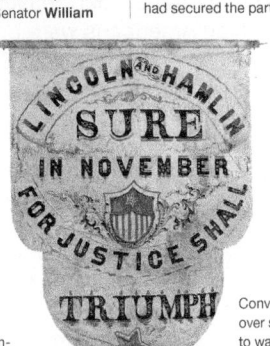

A political banner from 1860 advertises presidential candidate Lincoln and his running mate Hannibal Hamlin.

A BROKEN PARTY

Meanwhile, as the Republican Party rallied behind Lincoln, sectional differences were splitting the Democratic Party in two. The Democrats had long depended on attracting voters and support from both the South and the North, but that ability was nowhere to be found in Charleston, South Carolina, at the first Democratic National Convention of 1860. Disagreements over slavery led southern Democrats to walk out of the convention.

As Stephen A. Douglas, Lincoln's former senatorial opponent, was securing his candidacy at the convention, the southern delegates who had walked out were holding their own separate convention. They nominated **John C. Breckinridge** of Kentucky as their candidate.

Northern democrats staged yet another convention in Baltimore, Maryland, to try to bring the southern delegates back into the fold, but it became clear the split could not be mended. The race now had a northern Democrat, Douglas, and a southern Democrat, Breckinridge, running against one another—as well as against Republican candidate Lincoln—for the presidency.

Then a fourth candidate entered the race. Hoping to unite the country beyond sectional differences, some former members of the Whig Party and what few remnants were left of the Know-Nothings joined forces to create the **Constitutional Union Party**. The party appealed to people who believed that preserving the Union and protecting the Constitution outweighed concerns about slavery. It nominated **John Bell**, a highly regarded former U.S. senator from Tennessee and a slaveholder. With so many candidates for the presidency, the Unionists—as members of the Constitutional Union Party were called—counted on there being a deadlock that the House of Representatives would have to settle. Unionists hoped that legislators in the House would end up voting for Bell.

A FIERCE ELECTION

With four candidates running in an increasingly divided nation, the individual campaigns operated as if there were two separate elections taking place: one in the North and one in the South. Northern voters focused on choosing between Lincoln and Douglas, while southern voters considered Bell and Breckinridge as options. Some southern states did not even include Lincoln or Douglas on their ballots.

Lincoln did not campaign in the South, or in the North for that matter. Following the practice of the time, he remained at home in Springfield, Illinois, where he received Republican delegations and discussed important issues of the day. Constitutional Union Party candidate Bell did not go out on the campaign trail either, and southern Democrat Breckenridge gave only one speech, in Lexington, Kentucky. Stephen A. Douglas, on the other hand, traveled

all over the North and as far South as Alabama warning voters not to let sectionalism drive their votes. However, Douglas's efforts went unrewarded, especially in the South, where he endured insults and had rotten fruit thrown at him.

On election day, Lincoln won 40 percent of the overall popular vote and a commanding 60 percent majority of electoral votes. He swept the North—with the exception of New Jersey, which he split with Douglas—and the western states of Oregon and California. Lincoln did not win electoral votes in a single southern state. Douglas won almost 30 percent of the popular vote but received a mere 12 electoral votes: 9 from Missouri and 3 from New Jersey. Breckinridge won the entire South except for the three states that straddled the North and the South—Tennessee, Kentucky, and Virginia—which voted for Bell. Southerners were shocked that Lincoln had won the presidential election without a single electoral vote from the South.

HISTORICAL THINKING

1. **READING CHECK** What factors helped Lincoln defeat Seward in the Republican Party nomination of 1860?

2. **IDENTIFY MAIN IDEAS AND DETAILS** What did the Constitutional Union Party hope to achieve?

3. **DRAW CONCLUSIONS** Why were there two Democratic candidates in the 1860 presidential election?

4. **INTERPRET MAPS** Would the winner of the 1860 presidential election have been different if the states that voted for Bell had voted for another candidate? Explain your answer.

PLAN: 2-PAGE LESSON

OBJECTIVE

Analyze the divided nation's response to the 1860 presidential election.

CRITICAL THINKING SKILLS FOR LESSON 3.1

• Identify Main Ideas and Details

• Draw Conclusions

• Interpret Maps

• Make Generalizations

• Compare and Contrast

HISTORICAL THINKING FOR CHAPTER 11

How did tensions over slavery divide the North and the South? Disputes over slavery had pushed the nation to the breaking point by 1860. Lesson 3.1 examines the parties' campaign strategies during the 1860 presidential election and the election's outcome.

BACKGROUND FOR THE TEACHER

John C. Breckinridge came in second in the 1860 presidential election and was headed for a bright political future but circumstances intervened. After the election, he finished presiding over the Senate as vice president and then, in 1861, won a seat as a senator from Kentucky. Because many southern states had seceded, Breckinridge was almost alone in the Senate in his support of slavery. However, he truly wished to avoid war at all costs. He pleaded with Lincoln to compromise with the Confederacy and to withdraw federal troops from Confederate states as an act of good faith. Lincoln refused his request. Breckinridge tried to keep Kentucky neutral, but when his home state sided with the Union, he sent a letter resigning his seat. The Senate quickly voted him out. Breckinridge fled to Virginia and joined the Confederate Army, becoming a major general. He served as the last secretary of war to the Confederacy.

INTRODUCE & ENGAGE

DISCUSS CAMPAIGN MATERIALS

Discuss with students how modern candidates use banners, slogans, and other materials as part of their strategies to win an election. Then direct students' attention to the banner and caption in this lesson. **ASK:** What message is the banner conveying to voters? *(The banner claims that Lincoln and Hamlin are "sure" to get elected in November and that a vote for them will let justice triumph, that is, strike a blow against slavery.)* How might this banner help attract voters to Lincoln and his party? *(Possible response: It connects Lincoln and the Republicans to the American ideal of justice for all.)* Explain that Lesson 3.1 discusses the strategies that each party adopted in an effort to win the 1860 election.

GUIDED DISCUSSION

1. **Make Generalizations** In what way did the election of 1860 foreshadow the onset of the Civil War in 1861? *(Possible response: The 1860 election was handled as if it were two elections—one in the North and one in the South, foreshadowing the South's secession from the Union the following year and the creation of two governments.)*

2. **Compare and Contrast** How did Abraham Lincoln and Stephen Douglas differ in their 1860 presidential campaign strategies? *(Lincoln remained in Illinois and dealt strictly through delegates. Douglas, on the other hand, campaigned in the North and the South, trying to convince voters to choose him and not let separatist tendencies determine their vote.)*

MORE INFORMATION

Seward's "Higher Law" Speech William H. Seward came to prominence in part because of his first speech as a new member of the Senate. Known as the "Higher Law" speech, it was the highlight of what would be Seward's long Senate career. At the time, Henry Clay and others had suggested a number of compromises to deal with the issue of "slave or free" in the western territories. On March 11, 1850, Seward stood up and began to read his speech. Although he was not an impressive speaker, his words captured the public's attention. Among other points, he insisted that California be admitted as a free state and warned southerners that slavery was doomed. Their threats of secession would not save it. The speech immediately established Seward as a major force in the fight against slavery.

ACTIVE OPTIONS

On Your Feet: Who's Who in the 1860 Election Divide students into groups of four and assign each group member one of the four candidates in the 1860 election. Direct group members to stand one at a time and describe everything they have learned about their assigned candidate, and, without mentioning the person's name, ask, "Who am I?" The other members write down their answer. When all the group members have taken a turn, ask students to compare their answers.

NG Learning Framework: Design a Social Media Campaign

`SKILL` Communication

`KNOWLEDGE` Our Human Story

Invite students to work in small groups and conduct research to create a social media campaign for one of the candidates in the 1860 election. Tell them to showcase the candidate's biography, political goals, campaign slogans, and fund-raising activities. Have them consider what strategy the candidate might use to convince people to volunteer for the campaign and vote for the person on election day. Invite students to share their finished social media campaigns with the class.

DIFFERENTIATE

ENGLISH LANGUAGE LEARNERS `ELD`

Clarify Multiple Usages Pair students at the **Emerging** and **Expanding** levels with students at the **Bridging** level. Ask them to take turns reading aloud sentences from the subsection A Fierce Election, stopping at each use of *campaign* to determine whether the word is used as a noun, verb, or adjective. Tell students to compose a sentence using the word *campaign* in that same way. Encourage partners to read their original sentences to each other.

PRE-AP

Analyze Political Cartoons Direct students to find political cartoons from the year 1860. Tell them to write an essay analyzing one cartoon or comparing two related cartoons. Students should explain what historical event or idea is described or alluded to, what symbols the cartoonists used and what their viewpoints are, and whether the cartoons effectively convey their messages. Invite students to share their finished analyses with the class.

See the Chapter Planner for more strategies for differentiation.

HISTORICAL THINKING

ANSWERS

1. Lincoln won the nomination for several reasons: The Lincoln-Douglas debates had elevated him to national prominence, he was considered more moderate than Seward, and the Republican convention was held in his home state, giving him more support.

2. The Constitutional Union Party hoped to turn people's attention from regional conflicts and concerns about slavery and focus on preserving the Union and protecting the Constitution.

3. Southern and northern Democrats could not agree on a single candidate and instead nominated Douglas in the North and Breckinridge in the South.

4. No. Even if all the popular votes for Bell had gone to Douglas, giving him a majority, Bell did not have enough electoral votes to overcome Lincoln's lead. Douglas would have had only 51 electoral votes to Lincoln's 180.

THE CONFEDERACY FORMS

In hindsight, it's hard to believe that some people wanted to leave their country after finding out that Abraham Lincoln was their president. Yet Lincoln's election was the straw that broke the camel's back—or broke the nation in two, in this case.

AMERICAN PLACES
Fort Sumter, South Carolina

Fort Sumter is one of a series of forts built after the War of 1812 revealed the need for added defense along U.S. coasts. Located on a human-made island, the five-sided brick structure was designed to protect Charleston Harbor. On April 12, 1861, the first fighting of the Civil War took place at Fort Sumter. Today it is preserved as part of the Fort Sumter National Monument.

SECESSION

"THE DEED'S DONE" shouted a Mississippi headline announcing that Abraham Lincoln had won the presidential election. Lincoln's victory outraged many southerners. To them, it signaled the eventual destruction of slavery, and sooner rather than later. Despite Lincoln's assurances that he did not intend to threaten slavery where it already existed, many southern leaders believed it was only a matter of time before abolitionists achieved their goal. Few southerners believed that popular sovereignty or appeals to states' rights would protect the institution of slavery within the United States. Instead, they began seriously discussing the matter of secession.

Different perspectives of secession existed in both the South and the North. Some white southerners argued that secession was treason, while others felt it was the best way to present a united front against the North. Northerners were also split, with some northern Democrats calling for conciliation with the South. In December 1860, Kentucky Senator John J. Crittenden tried to play the role of peacemaker, proposing a compromise plan in Congress that he hoped would stop talk of secession. His **Crittenden Plan**, which was also called the Crittenden Compromise, would remove any federal power to abolish slavery in states where it already existed. It would also restore the north-south division of the Missouri Compromise and extend it to the Pacific Ocean. This would nullify the Compromise of 1850 and disregard popular sovereignty, except in states south of the Missouri Compromise line.

The plan found support in both the North and the South, and President James Buchanan pushed for its speedy approval in Congress. However, many Republicans—including President-elect Abraham Lincoln—strongly objected to extending slavery into any new territories. By the middle of January 1861, the Senate had killed the plan.

Many southerners saw their options dwindling, with secession as the only remaining solution. Although southern leaders had repeatedly threatened to secede from the Union over the first half of the 19th century, no state had formally attempted it. Lincoln did not even believe secession was legal under the U.S. Constitution. Others argued that since the United States was originally formed as an agreement between states, any state had the right to leave the Union if it so desired.

Lincoln was due to take office in March 1861, and some southern states wanted to secede before his inauguration. In South Carolina, delegates held a convention in December 1860 to declare they were leaving the Union. Among their reasons were that northern states had "denounced as sinful the institution of slavery" and elected a president "whose opinions and purposes [were] hostile to slavery." Southerners serving in President Buchanan's outgoing cabinet began to resign. In January and February 1861, six states from the Deep South followed South Carolina's lead and seceded: Mississippi, Florida, Alabama, Georgia, Louisiana, and Texas. Delegates from these states met in Alabama to create a provisional constitution, which was similar to that of the United States except in its explicit guarantee of slavery and states' rights.

Although he publicly declared that states did not have the right to secede, President James Buchanan did little else in response. In fact, he refused to take any action to stop the secession.

THE CONFEDERATE STATES OF AMERICA

At their February 1861 meeting, delegates from the seceding states formally established a new country, called the **Confederate States of America**, also referred to as the **Confederacy**. They launched a temporary government headquartered in Montgomery, Alabama, where they inaugurated **Jefferson Davis** as provisional president with Alexander H. Stephens as vice president. The Confederacy eventually adopted a constitution that limited its president to one six-year term.

In the meantime, with President Buchanan refusing to use force against the seceding states, local militias in the Confederacy began seizing U.S. government property. In most cases, U.S. officials and military forces gave up the property peacefully and retreated from the seceded state back into Union territory. However, in some places stalemates occurred. That's what happened at **Fort Sumter**, a U.S. fort located on an island in Charleston Harbor, South Carolina.

Two days after South Carolina seceded, U.S. Army Major Robert Anderson and his troops secured control of the fort, which was still under construction, and they refused to surrender. Rather than attack Fort Sumter and drive out the troops, the South Carolinians held siege, preventing supply ships from reaching the island. Anderson alerted authorities in Washington, D.C., that his troops had about four months' worth of supplies. By that time, Abraham Lincoln would be president. James Buchanan decided to let Lincoln deal with the crisis.

As Lincoln prepared for his inauguration, he faced challenges on numerous fronts. Seven slave states had seceded from the Union, and eight slave states remained. The use of force or threats would likely cause the remaining slave states to secede. People throughout the country waited to see what would happen next.

HISTORICAL THINKING

1. **READING CHECK** Why did Lincoln's election prompt the secession of some states?

2. **SUMMARIZE** What process did the first seven states to secede follow to separate themselves from the United States?

3. **DRAW CONCLUSIONS** Why do you think most U.S. officials in the South gave up federal property without a fight?

4. **MAKE CONNECTIONS** How did the Crittenden Plan build on past legislation in its effort to resolve the secession crisis?

PLAN: 2-PAGE LESSON

OBJECTIVE

Explore the repercussions of Abraham Lincoln's election in the North and in the South.

CRITICAL THINKING SKILLS FOR LESSON 3.2

- Summarize
- Draw Conclusions
- Make Connections
- Compare and Contrast
- Make Inferences

HISTORICAL THINKING FOR CHAPTER 11

How did tensions over slavery divide the North and the South? Even before Lincoln took office, southern states were debating whether to remain in the Union. Lesson 3.2 examines the South's journey toward secession and the initial confrontation that started the Civil War.

BACKGROUND FOR THE TEACHER

John J. Crittenden began his Senate career in 1817 and, over a 40-year span, gained a reputation as a highly respected negotiator and one of the nation's top lawyers. When someone was needed who might craft a peaceful solution to secession, Crittenden's colleagues immediately turned to him. The compromise Crittenden developed met with broad support not only from powerful senators such as William Seward but also from the public, which petitioned Congress to adopt it. However, the mood in Congress was too divisive by that point. Two months before the plan was finally defeated in the Senate, Crittenden tried to introduce a resolution to demand a national referendum on the issue, but again Congress failed to act. Though the Crittenden Plan did not pass, it serves as a reminder that even after the South had begun to secede, legislative leaders did not give up searching for a peaceful solution that would satisfy both sides and avoid war.

INTRODUCE & ENGAGE

ANALYZE DIVISIVE ISSUES

Tell students to read the lesson title and introduction. Then invite students to name issues that divide citizens today and issues that increasingly divided the United States in the 1850s. List students' responses and then lead a class discussion about the factors behind the divisive issues. **ASK:** What factor do you think was most important in the South's decision to secede from the Union? Give reasons for your answer. *(Possible response: The preservation of slavery was the most important factor. If slavery were abolished, the economic and social consequences would be devastating for the South.)*

TEACH

GUIDED DISCUSSION

1. **Compare and Contrast** How did Abraham Lincoln's belief about the Constitution and secession differ from the beliefs of many southerners? *(Possible response: Lincoln believed that secession was illegal under the Constitution, while southerners argued that the Constitution was an agreement among states to form a nation. Any state that decided to leave that agreement was within its legal rights.)*

2. **Make Inferences** Why do you think that President James Buchanan left the crisis at Fort Sumter for Lincoln to resolve? *(Possible response: Buchanan had no particularly strong antislavery views, took no action to stop secession, and was about to leave office. He probably had little desire to persuade or force the Confederates to abandon their siege of Fort Sumter.)*

AMERICAN PLACES

Fort Sumter was one of only two forts in the South that were still under federal control at the time of the Confederate siege. The fort held no particular value for the North, but it quickly became a symbol in the fight to preserve national unity. Today, the national monument at Fort Sumter preserves the ruins of the fort, which has been only partially rebuilt. The monument park is also part of the National Park Service's Open Parks Network, a long-term education and research project funded by the Institute of Museum and Library Services. The Open Parks Network provides downloadable archives related to the fort's history.

ACTIVE OPTIONS

On Your Feet: Compare Inaugural Addresses Provide students with printouts of the 1861 inaugural addresses of President Abraham Lincoln and Confederate president Jefferson Davis. Divide the class into two groups and assign one of the speeches to each group. Invite students to analyze the speech's main points and to collaborate on an adaptation that presents the essential ideas in more contemporary language. Encourage group members to take turns reading portions of their assigned inaugural address aloud and to make notes on points they wish to highlight. When both groups have completed their drafts, have each group select one member to deliver the adapted speech to the class. Lead the class in a discussion comparing the main points of the two addresses.

NG Learning Framework: Generate a Time Line

SKILL Communication

KNOWLEDGE Our Human Story

Instruct students to work in groups and use facts from the lesson and from additional research to generate an annotated and illustrated time line of events in U.S. history from Abraham Lincoln's election on November 6, 1860, to the Confederate siege at Fort Sumter on April 12, 1861. Encourage students to include a variety of items in their time lines, such as quotes from speeches and other documents, and visuals of relevant artifacts, people, and artwork. Ask groups to share their time lines with the class.

DIFFERENTIATE

STRIVING READERS

Pose and Answer Questions Have pairs take turns reading paragraphs of the lesson aloud. Instruct partners to pause after each paragraph and ask one another *who, what, where, when,* or *why* questions about what they have just read. Suggest students use a 5Ws Chart to help organize their questions and answers.

Who? _____

What? _____

Where? _____

When? _____

Why? _____
_____
_____

GIFTED & TALENTED

Write and Perform Diary Entries Tell students to conduct research to learn more about the events between Lincoln's election and his inauguration. Then ask them to write a series of diary entries that Lincoln might have written in reaction to events such as the secession of southern states, the Confederacy seizing U.S. property, and President Buchanan's lack of response. Invite students to perform a dramatic reading of their diary entries for the class.

See the Chapter Planner for more strategies for differentiation.

HISTORICAL THINKING

ANSWERS

1. Many southern states viewed Lincoln's election as signaling the end of slavery, an institution essential to the South's economy.

2. They seceded, formed the Confederate States of America, named Jefferson Davis as president, and adopted a constitution.

3. Possible response: President Buchanan took no action to halt secession, so there were probably no orders to resist the takeovers.

4. It sought to re-establish the Missouri Compromise and nullify the Compromise of 1850. Under the Plan, new states south of the compromise line could decide for themselves whether to be slave states or free states.

VOCABULARY

Use each of the following vocabulary terms in a sentence that shows an understanding of the term's meaning.

1. recession

   During the recession, many factories closed because people could no longer afford to buy their products.

2. proviso

3. popular sovereignty

4. omnibus bill

5. nativist

6. Dred Scott decision

7. Underground Railroad

8. Confederacy

READING STRATEGY
IDENTIFY MAIN IDEAS AND DETAILS

Identifying the main ideas and details of a text helps a reader understand the content and follow all the parts of a narrative. Use a graphic organizer like the one shown here to identify the details contributing to the growing problem of sectionalism in the United States. Then answer the question.

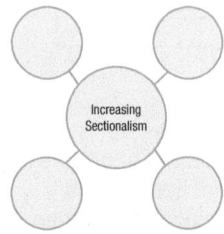

Increasing Sectionalism

9. In what ways did slavery divide the North and the South in the mid-19th-century United States?

MAIN IDEAS

Answer the following questions. Support your answers with evidence from the chapter.

10. During the 1840s and 1850s, why did large groups of Irish and Germans immigrate to the United States? **LESSON 1.1**

11. What were the main provisions of the Compromise of 1850? **LESSON 1.2**

12. Why was Harriet Beecher Stowe famous? **LESSON 2.1**

13. Why was the Kansas-Nebraska Act so controversial? **LESSON 2.3**

14. Explain the Freeport Doctrine. **LESSON 2.4**

15. When and why was the Constitutional Union Party formed? **LESSON 3.1**

16. How were Abraham Lincoln's and Stephen Douglas's ideas about the issue of slavery alike and how were they different? **LESSON 3.1**

17. What was the Crittenden Plan? **LESSON 3.2**

HISTORICAL THINKING

Answer the following questions. Support your answers with evidence from the chapter.

18. **SUMMARIZE** What role did cotton play in both the northern textile industry and southern plantation agriculture?

19. **IDENTIFY MAIN IDEAS AND DETAILS** What was the most controversial part of the Compromise of 1850 for northerners, and why?

20. **ANALYZE CAUSE AND EFFECT** What political developments led to the creation of the Republican Party?

21. **EVALUATE** How did the Dred Scott decision by the U.S. Supreme Court worsen the conflict over slavery?

22. **MAKE INFERENCES** What trends and events in the United States gave rise to the American Party, also called the Know-Nothing Party?

23. **FORM AND SUPPORT OPINIONS** Based on the evidence provided in this chapter, do you think it was inevitable that the South would split from the North? Explain your response.

INTERPRET VISUALS

This lithograph by T. H. Maguire titled *Outward Bound, The Quay of Dublin*, depicts a man in Dublin, Ireland, studying a poster advertisement about ocean voyages to New York City. It was engraved sometime before 1860. Examine the cartoon and answer the questions that follow.

24. Why do you think the artist chose to show this particular view from within the city of Dublin?

25. What details in the lithograph help you understand why the man might be interested in leaving Ireland?

ANALYZE SOURCES

On July 5, 1852, Frederick Douglass delivered a scathing speech against slavery in Rochester, New York. The city's leaders had asked him to speak at the local Independence Day festivities, and speak he did. Read the excerpt from the speech and answer the question that follows.

> It is not light that is needed, but fire; it is not the gentle shower, but thunder. We need the storm, the whirlwind, and the earthquake. The feeling of the nation must be quickened [made to live]; the conscience of the nation must be roused; the propriety of the nation must be startled; the hypocrisy of the nation must be exposed; and its crimes against God and man must be proclaimed and denounced.

26. How does this excerpt explain Douglass's reasons for giving a fiery speech against slavery rather than delivering a standard flag-waving Fourth of July address?

CONNECT TO YOUR LIFE

27. **EXPLANATORY** Think about how the issue of states' rights surrounding slavery divided the nation to the point of its breaking apart. Now consider the issues that divide American citizens today. Choose one of these issues and write an essay summarizing its impact on the United States.

TIPS

• Brainstorm a list of divisive issues the people of the United States are facing today and choose the one you find most compelling.

• Research to learn more about both sides of the issue.

• Form a topic sentence naming the issue and explaining why you believe it to be important.

• Develop the topic with relevant facts and concrete details. Be sure to address both sides of the issue.

• Conclude your essay by restating and briefly supporting your topic sentence.

VOCABULARY ANSWERS

1. During the recession, many factories closed because people could no longer afford to buy their products.

2. David Wilmot added a proviso to the bill stating the condition that slavery could not be instituted in any territory that the United States had acquired from Mexico.

3. Stephen Douglas believed that the territories should use popular sovereignty, letting citizens decide whether to allow slavery.

4. Henry Clay proposed an omnibus bill to address all the issues pertaining to slavery.

5. Many members of the Know-Nothing Party were nativists who wanted to stop all immigration to the United States.

6. Abolitionists were outraged by Judge Taney's ruling in the Dred Scott decision that no African American could be a U.S. citizen.

7. Conductors on the Underground Railroad took great risks to help their passengers escape to freedom.

8. Southern states that seceded from the Union formed the Confederate States of America, also called the Confederacy.

READING STRATEGY ANSWER

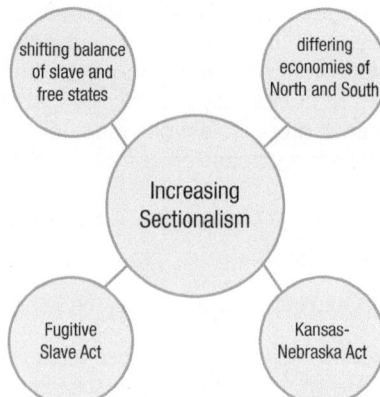

shifting balance of slave and free states

differing economies of North and South

Increasing Sectionalism

Fugitive Slave Act

Kansas-Nebraska Act

9. Answers will vary, but responses should state that slavery divided the North and the South along economic, social, and political lines. This included the shifts in political power between free and slave states, the industrial economy of the North and the agricultural economy of the South, the Fugitive Slave Act, the Kansas-Nebraska Act, and the publication of *Uncle Tom's Cabin*.

MAIN IDEAS ANSWERS

10. Many Irish fled from the potato famine, and the Germans escaped from political upheaval and persecution.

11. It allowed California to enter the Union as a free state but added more powers to the Fugitive Slave Act.

12. Her bestselling novel, *Uncle Tom's Cabin*, encouraged readers throughout the world to oppose slavery, and it inflamed regional divisions within the United States.

13. It repealed the Missouri Compromise of 1850 and asserted that two new territories, Kansas and Nebraska, were to decide through popular sovereignty whether to allow slavery or remain free.

14. It was Stephen Douglas's plan whereby local communities could keep slavery out by not enacting slave codes, despite the Dred Scott decision.

15. It was formed before 1860 to attract people who wanted to preserve the Union and the Constitution in spite of their regional differences over slavery.

16. Douglas believed that communities and states should be able to decide for themselves the question of slavery, while Lincoln believed that if slavery was wrong it was wrong in all cases.

17. It was a plan to preserve the Union by removing the federal government's power to end slavery in states where it existed, by restoring and extending the provisions of the Missouri Compromise to the Pacific Ocean, and by nullifying the Compromise of 1850.

HISTORICAL THINKING ANSWERS

18. It was the most important cash crop on southern plantations and vital to the operation of northern textile mills.

19. The Fugitive Slave Act was the most controversial part because it provided for the punishment of whites who aided runaway slaves or refused to help capture them. Also, runaway slaves could not appeal to the courts and could be sent back to bondage years after they had escaped.

20. Passage of the Kansas-Nebraska Act and the weakening of the Whig and Know-Nothing parties led to the creation of the Republican Party, which was devoted to stopping the spread of slavery and eventually abolishing it.

21. The decision implied that slavery could be extended anywhere in the country, which enraged abolitionists and Free-Soilers.

22. Increasing numbers of immigrants were arriving in the United States, making anti-immigrant sentiments the driving force behind the Know-Nothing Party.

23. Answers will vary. Students who answer yes might cite the failed compromises and proposed solutions as evidence that the split was inevitable. Students who say no might point out that with more effort and patience on both sides, a solution might have been found to prevent secession and war.

INTERPRET VISUALS ANSWERS

24. Possible response: The artist probably wanted to show how hopeless economic conditions seemed to be in Ireland at that time.

25. Possible response: The city looks run down with its cracked sidewalks and dim light. The man is dressed in a ragged coat and battered hat, and he carries what may be all of his belongings on a stick. The details convey there is no future for him in Ireland, so it's understandable why he would consider leaving for New York.

ANALYZE SOURCES ANSWER

26. Answers may vary, but students should note that Douglass is pointing out the hypocrisy of celebrating a day of independence while there are still millions of people enslaved in the country. He probably wanted to arouse the nation to confront this injustice rather than simply give another patriotic speech.

CONNECT TO YOUR LIFE ANSWER

27. Essays will vary. Students should clearly state their chosen issue and why it is important, include a topic sentence and develop it with facts and details, discuss both sides of the issue, and end by restating and supporting their topic sentence to show the issue's impact on the country.

CRITICAL VIEWING The first major conflict to be extensively photographed was the American Civil War. This photo, taken by O.H. Houghton in the early 1860s, shows Union troops stationed at Camp Griffin in Langley, Virginia—a Confederate state. Based on the details in this photograph, what do you predict may have taken place shortly after it was taken?

UNIT 1846–1877
4 THE DEEPEST CRISIS

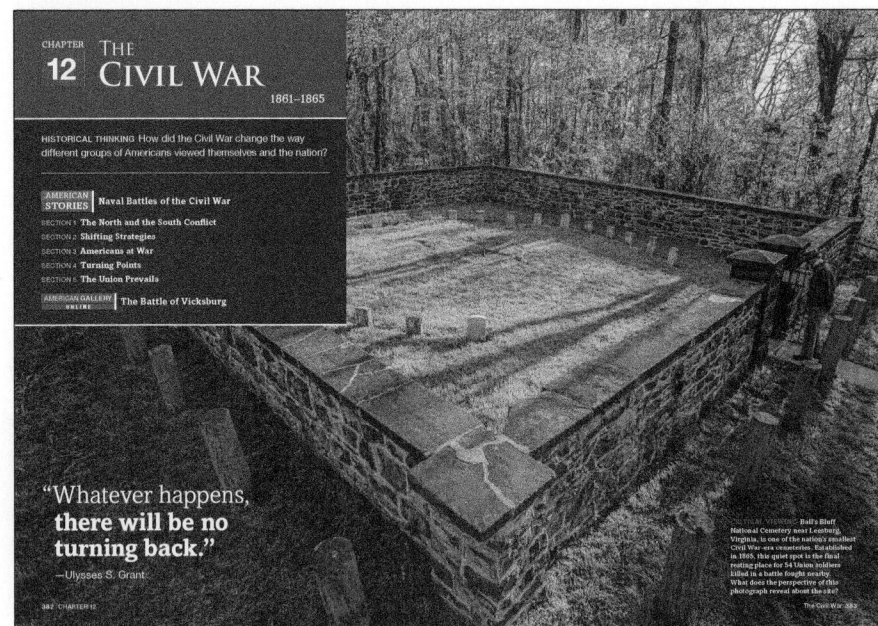

CHAPTER
12 THE CIVIL WAR
1861–1865

HISTORICAL THINKING How did the Civil War change the way different groups of Americans viewed themselves and the nation?

AMERICAN STORIES | Naval Battles of the Civil War
SECTION 1 The North and the South Conflict
SECTION 2 Shifting Strategies
SECTION 3 Americans at War
SECTION 4 Turning Points
SECTION 5 The Union Prevails
AMERICAN GALLERY ONLINE | The Battle of Vicksburg

"Whatever happens, there will be no turning back."
—Ulysses S. Grant

Ball's Bluff National Cemetery near Leesburg, Virginia, is one of the nation's smallest Civil War-era cemeteries. Established in 1865, this quiet spot is the final resting place for 54 Union soldiers killed in a battle fought nearby. What does the perspective of this photograph reveal about the site?

382 CHAPTER 12   The Civil War 383

AMERICAN STORIES | Naval Battles of the Civil War

- Study Primary Sources: Excerpt from a letter describing the Battle of Hampton Roads
- On Your Feet: Roundtable

NG Learning Framework:
Compare Naval Ships, Past and Present

SECTION 1 RESOURCES

THE NORTH AND THE SOUTH CONFLICT

LESSON 1.1
Beginnings of War

- Active History: Compare Resources

NG Learning Framework:
Represent Data

LESSON 1.2
Early Course of the War

- On Your Feet: Roundtable

NG Learning Framework:
Write a News Story

American Voices Biography
Clara Barton ONLINE

LESSON 1.3
THROUGH THE LENS—AMERICAN PLACES
Manassas, Virginia

- On Your Feet: Fishbowl

NG Learning Framework:
Create a Photo Collage

SECTION 2 RESOURCES

SHIFTING STRATEGIES

LESSON 2.1
Early Battles on Land and Sea

- On Your Feet: Three-Step Interview

NG Learning Framework:
Report on Frémont's Martial Law

LESSON 2.2
The Battles of 1862

- On Your Feet: Use a Jigsaw Strategy

NG Learning Framework:
Commemorate a Battle

American Voices Biography
William T. Sherman ONLINE

SECTION 3 RESOURCES

AMERICANS AT WAR

LESSON 3.1
Shifting the Focus to Slavery

- On Your Feet: Inside-Outside Circle

NG Learning Framework:
Analyze a Speech

LESSON 3.2
Discontent in the North and the South

- ▶ Civil War Medicine
- On Your Feet: Analyze the Effect of Civil War Weapons

NG Learning Framework:
Debate Draft Exemptions

SECTION 4 RESOURCES

TURNING POINTS

LESSON 4.1
Vicksburg and Chancellorsville

AMERICAN GALLERY ONLINE | The Battle of Vicksburg

NG Learning Framework:
Publish a Civil War Newspaper

LESSON 4.2
NATIONAL GEOGRAPHIC PHOTOGRAPHER SAM ABELL
Compose and Wait

- On Your Feet: Team Word Webbing

NG Learning Framework:
Tell a Story Using Photographs

LESSON 4.3
The Battle of Gettysburg

- ▶ Gettysburg Reenactors
- On Your Feet: Numbered Heads

NG Learning Framework:
Explore the Geography of Gettysburg

LESSON 4.4
CURATING HISTORY
National Civil War Museum Harrisburg, Pennsylvania

- On Your Feet: Sort the Artifacts

SECTION 5 RESOURCES

THE UNION PREVAILS

LESSON 5.1
Total War

- On Your Feet: Roundtable

NG Learning Framework:
Journal from Two Perspectives

LESSON 5.2
DOCUMENT-BASED QUESTION
Lincoln's Vision

- On Your Feet: Think, Pair, Share

LESSON 5.3
Surrender and Tragedy

- On Your Feet: Numbered Heads

NG Learning Framework:
Write a Eulogy

CHAPTER 12 REVIEW

STRATEGY 1
OUTLINE AND TAKE NOTES

To help students develop their reading and comprehension skills, ask them to work in pairs to write an outline for each lesson. Instruct them in using an outline format, such as the one shown. Tell them to identify main ideas and then look for two details that support each one.

I. _____

   A. _____

   B. _____

II. _____

   A. _____

   B. _____

III. _____

   A. _____

   B. _____

Use with All Lessons *You might wish to pair students of different proficiencies.*

STRATEGY 2
SEQUENCE EVENTS

To build understanding of critical events in a lesson, direct students to take notes in a Sequence Chain, such as the one shown, including the date and a brief summary of each event. Encourage them to add circles and arrows as necessary to show the complexity of the causes and effects of historical events and their relationship to each other.

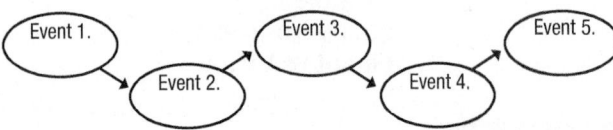

Use with Lessons 1.1, 1.2, 2.1, 2.2, 3.1, 3.2, 4.1, 4.3, 5.1, and 5.3

STRATEGY 3
USE A TASKS APPROACH

Help students analyze maps to obtain information by using the following TASKS strategy.

T Look for a **title** that may give the main idea.

A **Ask** yourself what the map is trying to show.

S Determine how any **symbols** are used.

K Look for a **key** or legend.

S **Summarize** what you learned.

Use with Lessons 1.1, 2.2, and 5.1

STRATEGY 1
USE CLARIFYING QUESTIONS

Pair students with disabilities to work with students who can read the text elements and describe visual details of the illustration of the Anaconda Plan: Scott's Great Snake, including the resource icons on the map. Instruct students to ask and answer clarifying questions. Encourage them to discuss any patterns they notice on the map regarding where different resources were abundant.

Use with Lesson 1.1

STRATEGY 2
MODIFY MAIN IDEA STATEMENTS

To help students anticipate and organize content, provide modified Main Idea statements before reading. Several examples are given below.

1.1 The Civil War began with Confederate and Union forces fighting over control of Fort Sumter.

1.2 The first battles showed that the Civil War would not be easy to win.

2.1 Fighting spread to the West, but neither side was clearly winning.

2.2 In the second year of the Civil War, many more soldiers died on both sides.

3.1 As war continued, Lincoln declared that the Union's main goal for fighting was to end slavery.

Use with All Lessons

ENGLISH LANGUAGE LEARNERS

STRATEGY ①
PRONOUNCE WORDS

Before reading, preview with students at **All Proficiencies** the vocabulary terms *writ of* habeas corpus, *offensive war, defensive war, Anaconda Plan*, and *promissory note*. You may also wish to preview other terms from the lesson, such as *loyal, Fort Sumter, emphasized, extensive, resigned,* and *negotiate*. Say each word slowly, and have students repeat, noting the pronunciation, syllable stress, and stress patterns in phrases. Suggest that students make word cards for each word, writing definitions and pronunciation hints for themselves.

Use with Lesson 1.1 *You may wish to adapt this strategy to use with other lessons and with other words students find difficult to pronounce. Encourage students to practice using online dictionary recordings to hear correct pronunciations.*

STRATEGY ②
CREATE WORD CHARTS

Help students understand unfamiliar words by completing Word Charts, such as the one below. Pair students at the **Emerging** level with students at the **Expanding** or **Bridging** level. Ask partners to copy the chart and then work together to complete the four parts for any unfamiliar word they encounter.

Definition of _____.	Draw a visual.
Tell how it relates to the Civil War.	Use it in a sentence.

Use with All Lessons

STRATEGY ③
PAIR PARTNERS FOR DICTATION

After students at **All Proficiencies** read a lesson, ask them to write a sentence summarizing its main idea. Arrange students in pairs, and ask them to dictate their sentences to each other. Then tell partners to work together to check the sentences for spelling and accuracy.

Use with All Lessons *You may wish to pair students at the **Emerging** level with those at the **Bridging** level and pair students at the **Expanding** level with one another.*

GIFTED & TALENTED

STRATEGY ①
RESEARCH AND ROLE-PLAY

Instruct students to prepare for role-playing by learning more about why Radical Republicans and Copperheads held the views they did on slavery. Assign pairs of students opposing roles, and direct them to take notes in a chart, such as the one shown, to support their assigned position and argue against their partner's position. Prompt students to use their notes to role-play for the class a meeting between a Copperhead and a Radical Republican.

Viewpoint	Support	Opposing Viewpoint

Use with Lesson 3.1

STRATEGY ②
DESIGN AN INFOGRAPHIC

Direct students to create an infographic that presents information about a specific Civil War battle. Guide them to conduct research to learn more about the battle and collect compelling data and other visual information before designing their infographic. Invite students to share their infographics with the class.

Use with Lessons 1.1, 1.2, 2.1, 2.2, 4.1, 4.3, and 5.1

PRE-AP

STRATEGY ①
WRITE A PROFILE

Assign students to write a profile of a Civil War nurse who broke the gender barrier, such as Clara Barton, Dorothea Dix, Kate Cumming, Phoebe Pember, or Louisa May Alcott. Direct them to conduct online research to supplement information from the text. Invite students to post their completed profiles on a class blog or school website or read them to the class.

Use with Lesson 1.2

STRATEGY ②
SUPPORT A POSITION

Tell students to conduct research to decide if General William Tecumseh Sherman's "total war" was justified. Instruct them to gather expert opinions and evidence and present their argument in a report. Suggest that students state whether they think Sherman's tactics were aberrant or were consistent with past and present U.S. military actions.

Use with Lesson 5.1

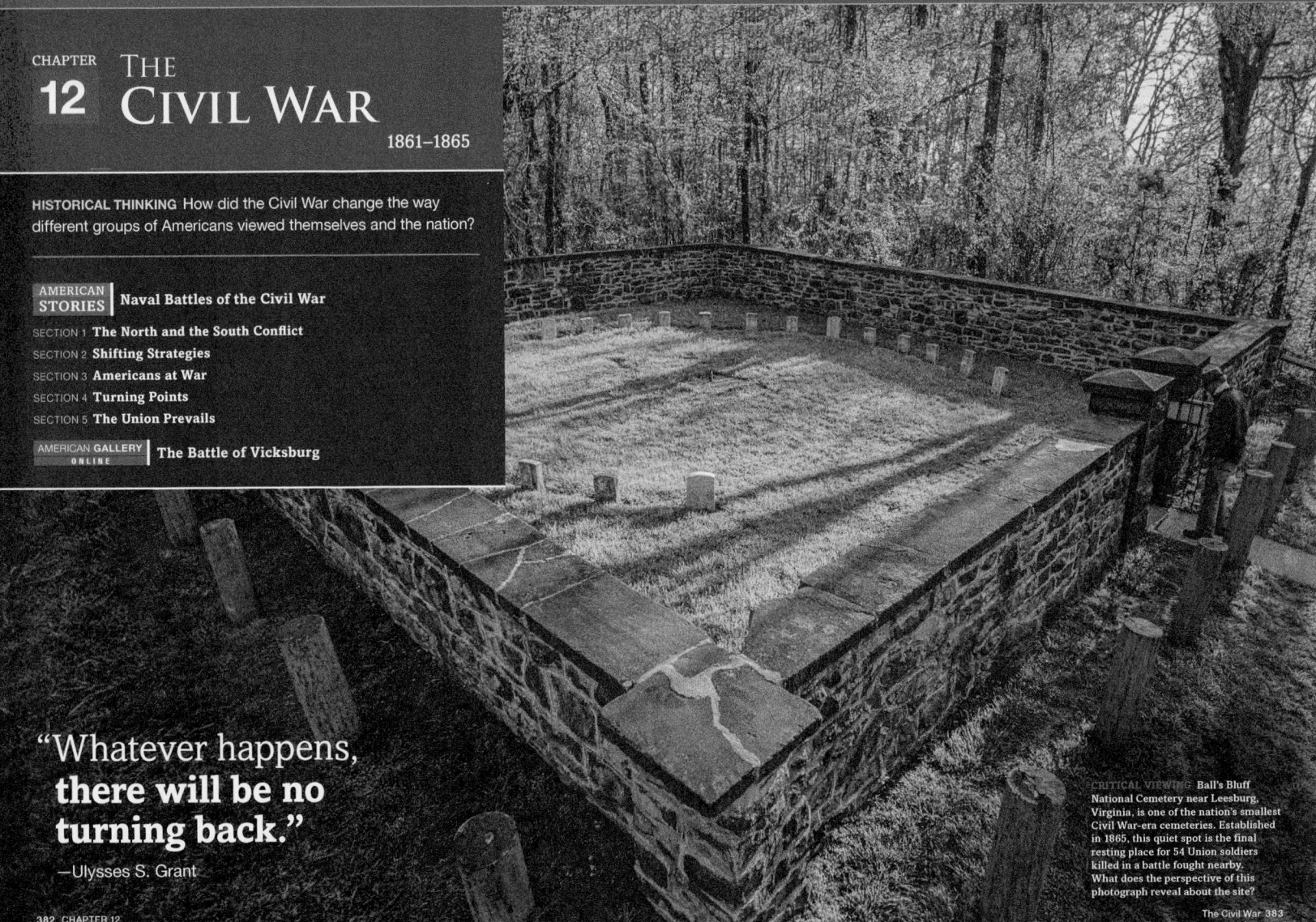

HISTORICAL THINKING How did the Civil War change the way different groups of Americans viewed themselves and the nation?

"Whatever happens, there will be no turning back."

—Ulysses S. Grant

CRITICAL VIEWING Ball's Bluff National Cemetery near Leesburg, Virginia, is one of the nation's smallest Civil War-era cemeteries. Established in 1865, this quiet spot is the final resting place for 54 Union soldiers killed in a battle fought nearby. What does the perspective of this photograph reveal about the site?

The Civil War 383

INTRODUCE THE PHOTOGRAPH

BALL'S BLUFF NATIONAL CEMETERY

Direct students' attention to the photograph. Point out that the cemetery honors Union losses in one of the early battles of the Civil War. In 1861, Union troops crossed the Potomac River at Ball's Bluff, hoping to capture Leesburg, Virginia. Instead, they tangled with Confederate soldiers on patrol. The struggle that followed pushed the Union soldiers down the steep slope of the bluff and into the river. Laden with heavy gear, many of them drowned. Others died from Confederate gunfire. Only one of the 54 soldiers buried here has ever been identified. ASK: Why do we honor soldiers fallen in battle even if we don't know who they are? (Possible responses: It helps us remember the tragedy of war. It reminds us of everyday people who made a great sacrifice for what they believed in.) Tell students that in this chapter they will learn about the impact of the Civil War on soldiers, civilians, and the nation.

For Chapter 12 Spanish Resources, visit the Resources Menu. Chapter 12 Resources are available at NGLSync.Cengage.com.

SHARE BACKGROUND

Two monuments stand outside the walls of the half-acre Ball's Bluff National Cemetery. One commemorates Clinton Hatcher, a fallen Confederate soldier. The other honors Union colonel Edward D. Baker, a senator from Oregon and a close personal friend of President Lincoln. Hatcher and Baker are both buried elsewhere. Baker led the Union charge at Ball's Bluff. His death triggered the hasty retreat that resulted in 900 fallen and injured Union soldiers. In addition, 700 Union troops were captured in the battle.

CRITICAL VIEWING Answers will vary. Possible response: The perspective reveals a small, square plot with a semicircular layout of headstones, which is surrounded by woods and enclosed by a thick stone wall with a single entrance and exit. Some of these details would have been lost if the photographer had not chosen a diagonal shot from a higher vantage point.

HISTORICAL THINKING QUESTION

How did the Civil War change the way different groups of Americans viewed themselves and the nation?

Jigsaw Activity: Make Predictions This activity will help students make predictions about how the Civil War changed the perspective of many Americans. Arrange the class into five groups and assign each group a section title. Tell students to discuss what they think they will learn in the section to help them answer the Historical Thinking question. Provide the following clues.

Group 1 Section 1 examines the beginning of the Civil War and the resources and strategies of each side.

Group 2 Section 2 examines early battles on the land and sea and the stalemate in 1862.

Group 3 Section 3 examines the North's shift to ending slavery as the goal of the war and discontent on the home front on both sides.

Group 4 Section 4 examines the battles that broke the stalemate and began to turn the tide in the Union's favor.

Group 5 Section 5 examines the North's final assault on the South, the South's surrender, and President Lincoln's assassination.

Regroup students so that each new group has at least one member from each original group. Invite students to share their predictions about their assigned section so that other students can anticipate what might be covered in Chapter 12.

INTRODUCE THE READING STRATEGY

MAKE INFERENCES

Explain to students that by pairing information they read with what they already know and have experienced, they can make inferences—"educated guesses"—about events. Turn to the Chapter Review and preview the graphic organizer with students. As they read the chapter, guide them to make and record inferences about the major challenges the nation faced because of the Civil War.

KEY DATES FOR CHAPTER 12

April 1861	Confederates fire on Fort Sumter
July 1861	First Battle of Bull Run is fought
September 1862	Battle of Antietam is fought
December 1862	Battle of Fredericksburg is fought
January 1863	Lincoln issues Emancipation Proclamation
July 1863	Battle of Gettysburg is fought
November 1863	Lincoln delivers Gettysburg Address
September 1864	Sherman captures Atlanta
April 1865	Lee surrenders at Appomattox Court House
April 1865	Lincoln is assassinated

INTRODUCE CHAPTER VOCABULARY

KEY VOCABULARY

SECTION 1

Anaconda Plan	defensive war	offensive war
border state	greenback	promissory note
cavalry	infantry	writ of *habeas corpus*

SECTION 2

front	ironclad	pontoon

SECTION 3

confiscate	Emancipation Proclamation	lynch
conscription		Radical Republican
contraband	exemption	scapegoat
Copperhead	freedman	trench warfare
draft		

SECTION 4

barrage	contingent	flanking maneuver
battery		

SECTION 5

assassination	Reconstruction	veteran
morphine	total war	

WORD MAPS

As students read the chapter, ask them to complete a Word Map for each Key Vocabulary word. Tell them to write the word in the oval and, as they encounter the word in the chapter, complete the Word Map. Model an example using the graphic organizer below.

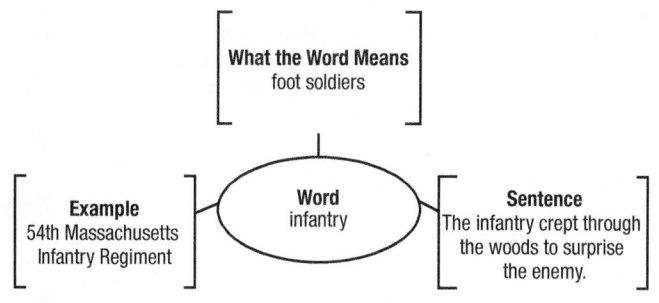

What the Word Means
foot soldiers

Example
54th Massachusetts
Infantry Regiment

Word
infantry

Sentence
The infantry crept through the woods to surprise the enemy.

OBJECTIVES

- Compare and contrast the naval actions of three Civil War battles.
- Draw conclusions about Union and Confederate military strategies.
- Discuss how the navy helped the Union win the Civil War.
- Study a primary source: excerpt from a letter describing the Battle of Hampton Roads.

CRITICAL THINKING SKILLS FOR "NAVAL BATTLES OF THE CIVIL WAR"

- Make Connections
- Draw Conclusions
- Identify Main Ideas and Details
- Compare and Contrast
- Summarize
- Evaluate

CONNECT TO THE CHAPTER

This American Story paints three vivid portraits of Civil War battles in which naval forces played a pivotal strategic role. The narrative first examines the Battle of Hampton Roads and the fighting between two ironclads, the U.S.S. *Monitor* for the North and the C.S.S. *Virginia* for the South. It describes the fairly bloodless Battle of Mobile Bay and the fierce combat at the Battle of Vicksburg for control of the Mississippi River. Special features provide details about the structure of a warship, describe efforts to preserve a shipwrecked ironclad, and include an excerpt from a first-person account of the clash between the *Monitor* and the *Virginia* during the Battle of Hampton Roads.

Chapter 12, The Civil War, examines the causes of the Civil War and its aftermath. While land battles and war strategies make up the bulk of the events described in the chapter, narratives of the three naval battles highlight the contributions of the Union and Confederate navies to the war efforts. Introduce "Naval Battles of the Civil War" as a supplement to Lesson 2.1.

HISTORY NOTEBOOK

Encourage students to complete the American Story page for Chapter 12 in their History Notebooks as they read.

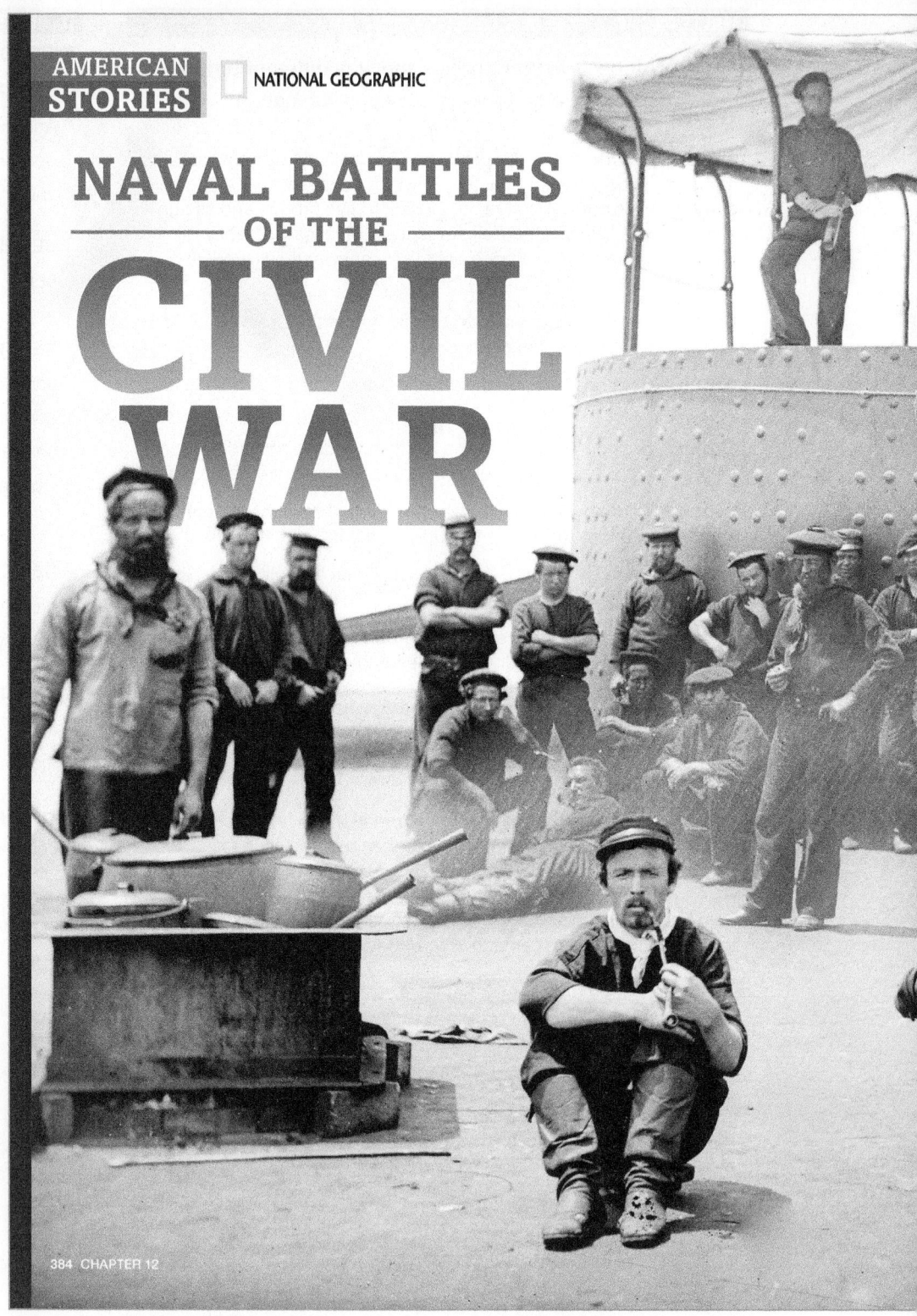

AMERICAN STORIES   NATIONAL GEOGRAPHIC

NAVAL BATTLES OF THE CIVIL WAR

384 CHAPTER 12

CRITICAL VIEWING The crew of the U.S.S. *Monitor* pose for a photo on deck while the cook (left) tends the stove. The ship's revolving gun turret rises in the background. What do you think life was like for the sailors aboard the ironclad?

The Battle of Hampton Roads in 1862 pitted a Confederate ship once described as "a floating barn roof" against a Union ship called a "tin can on a shingle." The vessels may have not have been graceful, but they heralded the beginning of modern naval warfare.

The confrontation between these two ships, the Confederacy's C.S.S. *Virginia* and the Union's U.S.S. *Monitor* is the most famous naval battle of the Civil War. It marked a turning point in military technology and secured the Union's dominance when it came to sea power. Hampton Roads was, however, just one of several key naval battles of the Civil War. This American Story spotlights three of these engagements.

HAMPTON ROADS

Both the *Virginia* and the *Monitor* were ironclads, a new breed of steam-powered warship. As the name implies, an ironclad was sheathed in iron plates. The Confederates salvaged a Union ship called the U.S.S. *Merrimack* and renamed it the *Virginia*. They then replaced its upper hull with a structure made of iron. In all, the ship was 263 feet long. The *Monitor*, the Union ship, was an entirely new design. Its 172-foot hull rose just above the waterline, making it hard to hit. It also had a revolving gun turret so that its cannons could fire in any direction.

Hampton Roads is a harbor at the mouth of the James River in Virginia. On March 8, 1862, it was under blockade by powerful wooden Union warships, including the *Congress* and the *Cumberland*, when the *Virginia* steamed into the harbor. The *Congress* unleashed its 20 cannons in a thunderous bombardment, but the *Virginia* shrugged off the assault. It pushed forward, one sailor recalled, "like the horrid creature of a nightmare," and pounded the *Congress* with multiple rounds of cannon shot. The *Virginia* next attacked the *Cumberland*. As the Union ship fired volley after volley, the *Virginia* rammed the *Cumberland* and sank it. Finally, the *Virginia* turned back to the *Congress* and finished it off, too.

Three other Union warships had hurried into the harbor to pursue the *Virginia*, but all three had run aground. Two had managed to escape, leaving the *Minnesota*,

DISCUSS BRANCHES OF THE MILITARY

Explain to students that the U.S. military has distinct branches, each of which fulfills specific functions and areas of specialization. List these main U.S. military branches on the board:

    Army
    Marine Corps
    Navy
    Air Force
    Coast Guard

Invite students to discuss what they already know about each branch, how the branches differ from one another, and instances in which a particular branch would be most effective. Share with students that in this American Story they will focus on how advancements in technology changed strategic naval warfare during the Civil War.

BACKGROUND FOR THE TEACHER

THE BEGINNING AND THE END OF THE U.S.S. *MONITOR*

In 1861, upon receiving the news that the Confederate Navy was building a powerful new battleship, President Lincoln called for a Union naval board to build an ironclad of its own. Swedish American inventor John Ericsson came up with the design. Construction began in New York City, and approximately three months later, on January 30, 1862, the 987-ton *Monitor* was launched into the East River. After less than a year in operation, the *Monitor* hit rough weather and towering waves. As the ship pitched, leaking water doused its engines, cutting off the steam pressure that powered the vessel. The ship took on water, its pumps failed, and the sailors had to bail the excess water. The crew sent up a distress signal, and a nearby ship, the *Rhode Island*, rushed to answer, quickly deploying its lifeboats. But as the *Monitor*'s crew tried to escape, many drowned.

CRITICAL VIEWING Possible response: When not engaged in battle, sailors were likely exposed to weather on the deck or crowded in their quarters below. Conditions were probably dirty and noisy—even during meals—with few opportunities for rest or privacy.

THE SIEGE OF VICKSBURG

The siege of Vicksburg lasted 47 days, leading to widespread illness and hunger. As supplies dwindled, the publisher of the local newspaper, *The Daily Citizen*, had to print on wallpaper. The publisher escaped as Union forces marched into the city. When the soldiers located the newspaper office, they added their own note to the final edition:

JULY 4, 1863
Two days bring about great changes. The banner of the Union floats over Vicksburg. Gen. Grant has "caught the rabbit;" he has dined in Vicksburg, and he did bring his dinner with him. The "Citizen" lives to see it. For the last time it appears on "Wall Paper." No more will it eulogize the luxury of mule meat and Fricasseed kitten—urge Southern warriors to such diet nevermore. This is the last wall-paper edition, and is, excepting this note, from types as we found them. It will be valuable hereafter as a curiosity.

INSIDE THE *MONITOR*

The *Monitor*'s design differed starkly from other naval vessels of the Civil War era. On the typical ship of that time, the commanding officer occupied the most luxurious quarters, always located at the very back of the vessel. Next came the cabins of high-ranking officers. Lower-ranking officers lived amidships, or in the middle of the vessel, while the lowest-ranking sailors slept on the decks and elsewhere. When John Ericsson designed the *Monitor*, he threw out these conventions entirely. He placed all the ship's systems below the waterline, and the engine, not the commander's quarters, was located at the back of the vessel. Ericsson moved the commander's and officers' quarters to the front, just behind the pilothouse. To help facilitate this change in protocol, Ericsson used his own funds to make the officers' quarters as luxurious as possible. **ASK:** Do you think a Civil War sailor would have preferred to serve on the *Monitor* or on a conventional wooden ship? Explain your thinking. *(Possible responses: Sailors would have preferred the* Monitor *because it was probably safer in battle and had modern features, such as flush toilets. Serving on the new ironclad may have also brought status to sailors. Sailors would have preferred the older wooden ships because they were less cramped, less noisy, and had more natural light.)*

still stuck, to exchange fire with the *Virginia*. When evening fell and it became too dark to shoot, the *Virginia* returned to its moorings. Later that night, the *Monitor* quietly slid into Hampton Roads and tied up to the *Minnesota*. The next day would see a change in fortunes for both the Union and Confederacy.

When the *Virginia* approached the *Minnesota* on the morning of March 9, it was confronted by the Union ironclad. However, neither the *Virginia* nor the *Monitor* could gain the advantage. Eventually, the *Virginia* scored a hit on the *Monitor*'s pilothouse that partially blinded the ship's commander, Lieutenant John Worden. Worden immediately turned over command to his executive officer, and the *Monitor* retreated to shallow water where the *Virginia* could not follow. The *Virginia* prepared to renew its attack on the *Minnesota*, but it had a leak in its bow and was running short of ammunition. The Confederate ship was forced to withdraw for repairs.

Today, historians still debate who won the Battle of Hampton Roads. The fight between the *Monitor* and the *Virginia* was inconclusive. Craig Symonds, professor emeritus of history at the U.S. Naval Academy, believes the results of the fight favored the Union. "The battle was certainly a draw in the tactical sense," he says, "but in the strategic sense it was a clear Union victory. The *Monitor* neutralized the offensive potential of the *Virginia*, which allowed the Union Navy to remain in Hampton Roads." In terms of naval history, the battle was a landmark. March 8, 1862, came to be seen as the day the wooden warship died.

VICKSBURG

It is almost impossible to overestimate the importance of the Mississippi River to both sides in the Civil War. The Father of Waters, as the river was often called, was a major route for transporting goods to markets. When Mississippi and Louisiana seceded from the Union, free passage down the great river was blocked. Once the war began, the blockade threatened the northern economy and prevented the Union from transporting troops to southern battlefields.

The Union had gained control over much of the Mississippi by 1862, but the Confederacy still held a 200-mile stretch along Vicksburg, Mississippi. Sitting on a high bluff above a bend in the river,

INSIDE THE *MONITOR*

The *Monitor* was a radical departure from previous warship designs. Among the most revolutionary features was the gun turret that could pivot in any direction using steam power. Other innovations included a steam engine specially designed to fit into a tight space, a forced-air ventilation system, and flush toilets. Modern warships may not look much like the "tin can on a shingle," but the *Monitor* is the ancestor of today's battleships. The cutaway diagram below of the *Monitor* reveals its interior and compartments and provides information on the ship's size, speed, and engine.

Engineer and inventor John Ericsson designed the Union's first ironclad and even gave it its name: the *Monitor*.

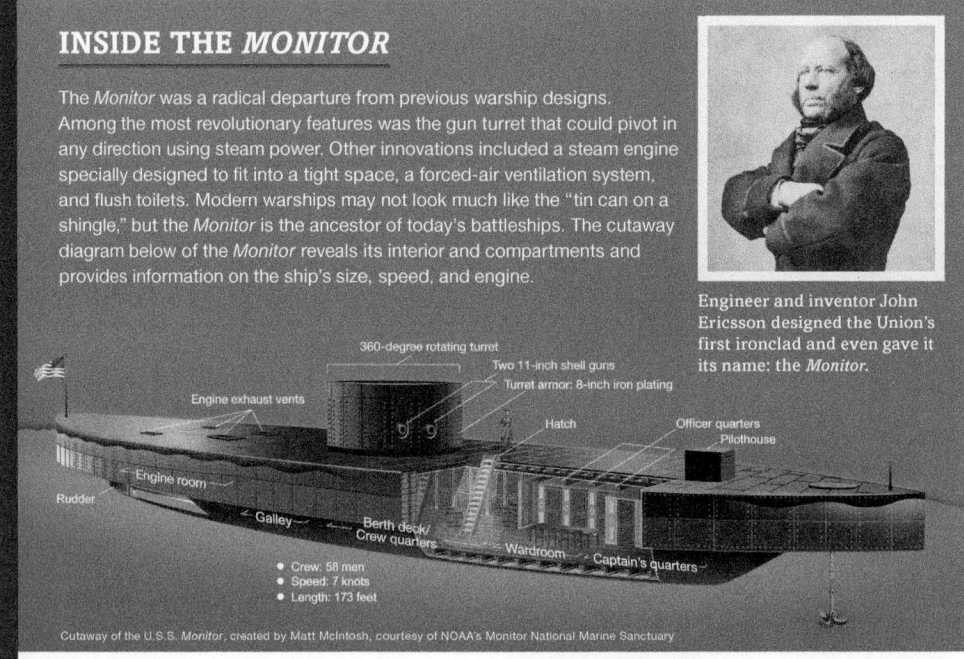

360-degree rotating turret
Two 11-inch shell guns
Turret armor: 8-inch iron plating
Engine exhaust vents
Hatch
Officer quarters
Pilothouse
Engine room
Rudder
Galley
Berth deck/ Crew quarters
Wardroom
Captain's quarters

- Crew: 58 men
- Speed: 7 knots
- Length: 173 feet

Cutaway of the U.S.S. *Monitor*, created by Matt McIntosh, courtesy of NOAA's Monitor National Marine Sanctuary

CRITICAL VIEWING
Vicksburg's Battery Sherman, shown here in a photograph taken between 1863 and 1865, was built by the Union after it won the Battle of Vicksburg in 1863. The battery was named for Union general William Tecumseh Sherman, who played an important role in the battle. What geographic advantages did the battery give the Union over the Confederate Army?

Vicksburg commanded the perfect position to block passage on the Mississippi. Heavily fortified batteries, or artillery units, in and around the city could target any ship that attempted the stretch with a punishing barrage. To Abraham Lincoln, Vicksburg was the key to all the productive land in the southern states. As long as Vicksburg commanded the river, southern troops could be supplied with food by ships plying the Mississippi.

The difficult job of taking Vicksburg fell to General Ulysses S. Grant. Grant's troops were on the east side of the river, across from the city. His plan of attack required him to find a way to land the soldiers on the west side of the river south of Vicksburg. To make it happen, Grant called on Union admiral David Porter. Grant later recalled in his memoirs, "The cooperation of the navy was absolutely essential to the success (even to the contemplation) of such an enterprise."

At first, Grant requested only that Porter supply a few gunboats, but Porter proposed a bolder scheme. He would take nearly half of his squadron down the Mississippi, including ironclad gunboats and transports, in two separate sorties, or defensive attacks. At 10 p.m. on April 16, 1863, the first fleet, consisting of 7 ironclads, 1 warship equipped with rams, and 3 army transports, set out to make its way past the Vicksburg batteries under cover of night. Each ship had barges tied to it carrying baggage and supplies. Porter had also ordered bales of cotton and hay and sacks of grain to be stacked around the ships' boilers to protect them from Confederate shots and to conceal the boiler fires. The Union Army could use these supplies, too, once they were unloaded downstream.

In the end, the effort at secrecy was in vain. As Grant recalled, "The enemy were evidently expecting our fleet, for they were ready to light up the river by means of bonfires on the east side and by firing houses on the point of land opposite the city on the Louisiana side. The sight was magnificent, but terrible."

The night was turned to thunderous daylight by the bonfires and the nonstop firing of the Vicksburg batteries. Grant observed that the fleet was under attack for more than two hours, while other accounts claimed that the barrage lasted for four. Witnesses claimed the sound of the guns could be heard from 30 miles away.

Despite the furious shelling, Porter's small first fleet suffered very little damage. One transport was destroyed, but its crew abandoned ship and was rescued. Other ships suffered some damage but remained largely intact. Even better, no men were killed during the passage, although a dozen were wounded. The second fleet also emerged relatively unharmed. Grant's men, meanwhile, marched south to meet the boats and gain transport across the river to the Vicksburg side. Once the troops landed, the Union Navy continued to provide support by bombarding key sites from the river.

The Battle of Vicksburg was far from over with the landing of the troops. The city finally surrendered to Grant on July 4, 1863, after hard fighting and high casualties on both sides. However, without the participation of Porter and his fleets, the battle to completely open the Mississippi might have been even more costly in lives lost.

The Civil War **387**

TEACH

GUIDED DISCUSSION

1. **Identify Main Ideas and Details** Why is the Battle of Hampton Roads considered a landmark Civil War battle despite the fact that it had no clear winner? *(Hampton Roads was the first major battle fought between ironclads, and it signaled the beginning of the end for wooden ships. The ironclads were much bigger, stronger, and capable of more massive firepower.)*

2. **Compare and Contrast** How did the Battle of Vicksburg differ from the two other battles in this American Story? *(Possible responses: Unlike the Battle of Hampton Roads and the Battle of Mobile Bay, the purpose of the Battle of Vicksburg was to seize control of the Mississippi River for the Union. The battle was fought from the river and on the ground, with the Union Navy bombarding the city and later transporting General Grant's troops. Although a clear Union victory, the battle resulted in many casualties on both sides.)*

ACTIVE OPTIONS

On Your Feet: Roundtable Divide the class into groups of four. Tell each group to answer the following question: What important long- and short-term consequences arose from strategies and technologies used in Civil War naval battles? Direct groups to have each member answer the question with a different response. Then reconvene the class and discuss the groups' responses.

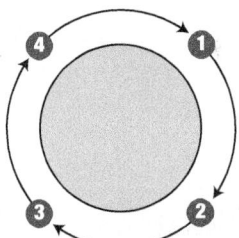

NG Learning Framework: Compare Naval Ships, Past and Present

SKILL Collaboration

KNOWLEDGE Our Human Story

Organize students in small groups to do further research on Civil War naval ships and to gather information about modern-day naval ships, such as frigates, aircraft carriers, destroyers, cruisers, patrol ships, littoral combat ships, corvettes, and amphibious assault ships. When groups have completed their research, conduct a whole-class discussion in which students compare naval ships of the past with those of the present.

CRITICAL VIEWING Battery Sherman was located on high, flat ground. With a lookout of 360 degrees and cannons mounted on rotating disks, it could defend Vicksburg in all directions.

SAVING THE *MONITOR*

At the beginning of summer 2016, preservation professionals removed the fragile metal nut guards that lined the interior of the *Monitor*'s turret. Hoping to find a trove of artifacts, they could locate only one: a bone-handled knife of the type commonly used by *Monitor* crew members. **ASK:** Why might finding personal items be helpful in understanding the *Monitor*'s history? *(Possible response: Personal items provide clues about the daily lives of the sailors aboard the* Monitor *who may have taken part in its battles. These clues add to our understanding of the human story behind the ship and its battles.)*

DURING THE BATTLE OF HAMPTON ROADS

Tell students that William F. Keeler was also aboard the U.S.S. *Monitor* on December 30, 1862, when it sank during a storm off Cape Hatteras. After a wave carried him from the deck into the sea, he grasped a line thrown to him and was hauled to safety. His legacy is his letters, which were collected and published 100 years after the events he recounted. **ASK:** How does Keeler paint a picture of what it was like on the *Monitor* in the midst of battle? *(Possible response: Keeler uses concrete details and descriptions, such as the "howling" of the shells and the "crash of solid shot" to help the reader imagine the battle.)*

WRITE ABOUT HISTORY

Compose a Letter Home Ask students to imagine they are sailors on the *Monitor* just a few hours after the Battle of Hampton Roads, and direct them to write a letter to a relative back home. Encourage students to reflect on information from the lesson and to think about daily life aboard the ship as well as the battle itself. After they complete a first draft, invite students to exchange letters with a partner and provide feedback. When students have created polished drafts, invite volunteers to read their letters aloud to the class.

THINK ABOUT IT

Battle narratives can provide insight into the human aspect of the conflict in addition to providing key information about the events.

CRITICAL VIEWING The two ironclads must have been evenly matched or one would have sunk the other. The rotating turret on the *Monitor* didn't provide an advantage in a head-on battle with the *Virginia*, whose guns appear to be too high to damage the *Monitor*'s hull.

AMERICAN STORIES

CRITICAL VIEWING The *Monitor* (in the foreground) and the *Virginia* exchange fire in this 19th-century print. Note that shots from the *Monitor* issue from its round, rotating turret. Why do you think the battle between the two ironclads ended in a stalemate?

MOBILE BAY

Have you ever heard the expression "Damn the torpedoes, full steam ahead!"? People use the phrase to express a determination to go forward with an action, no matter the obstacles. Few know that it originated with Union admiral David Farragut, the victor at the Battle of Mobile Bay.

In August 1864, Mobile Bay, Alabama, was a heavily fortified Confederate naval base. The bay's entrance was defended by two forts and by a field of floating mines, which were called torpedoes at that time. The Confederates had left a narrow channel free of torpedoes so that their blockade runners could slip into the harbor. Inside Mobile Bay lurked the *Tennessee*, a powerful ironclad under the direction of Confederate admiral Franklin Buchanan, who had also commanded the *Virginia*. His fleet included two lesser ironclads.

Admiral Farragut was in command of a fleet of four ironclads and several wooden steamships. He formed a plan to enter Mobile Bay through the narrow torpedo-free channel with his ironclads arranged in one column and the wooden vessels in another. The plan quickly went wrong, however, when some of the ships veered from their columns, and the ironclad *Tecumseh* hit a torpedo that sank it within 25 seconds. In an attempt to avoid total defeat, Farragut directed his own ship, the wooden-hulled *Hartford*, into the field of floating mines, shouting, "Damn the torpedoes!"

Incredibly, the *Hartford* proceeded through the minefield without setting off any torpedoes, possibly because many of them had faulty trigger mechanisms. The rest of the Union ships followed carefully in the *Hartford*'s path. As the ships entered the bay, Buchanan tried to ram them with the *Tennessee*, but the ironclad couldn't keep up with the faster wooden warships.

Then, Buchanan and Farragut engaged in a duel between the *Tennessee* and the *Hartford*. The ships slowly sailed toward each other—it took 15 minutes to cover the 4 miles that separated them. When they finally faced off, a sailor on the *Hartford* threw a spittoon at the other ship, and a sailor on the *Tennessee* succeeded in stabbing a *Hartford* crewman with his bayonet. Neither ship, however, scored a fatal hit against the other.

After the odd confrontation concluded, the *Tennessee* found itself surrounded by Union ships, all firing as rapidly as possible. The *Tennessee*, meanwhile, was experiencing problems with its ammunition. The fight was all but over when Buchanan was struck by flying debris and fell with a broken leg. He passed command to his captain, who surrendered shortly thereafter.

THINK ABOUT IT

What do battle narratives like these help you understand about events in history?

The two cannons shown in this photograph were removed from the *Monitor*'s revolving gun turret in 2004.

SAVING THE *MONITOR*

Both the *Monitor* and the *Virginia* ended their careers as wrecks on the sea bottom. Because the *Virginia* was scuttled intentionally in 1862, its location was known, and several salvage operations after the war brought up parts of the ship. Finding the *Monitor*, which sank in a storm off North Carolina in 1862, was more of a challenge.

In 1973, an expedition partially funded by the National Geographic Society located the shipwreck at last, using sonar, photography, and remotely operated vehicles. In 1975, the site of the *Monitor* shipwreck became the nation's first national marine sanctuary. In more recent years, the Mariners' Museum and Park in Virginia, the National Oceanic and Atmospheric Administration, the U.S. Navy, and other agencies have joined forces to raise and conserve parts of the *Monitor*. The ship's propeller was raised in 1998, and its innovative steam engine was returned to daylight in 2001. The *Monitor*'s most famous feature, its unique turret, was brought to the surface in 2002, after lying under the warship's overturned hull on the sandy sea bottom for 140 years.

The next step in the conservation process was to plunge the massive artifacts back into water, this time in special tanks at the Mariners' Museum and Park. These tanks contained a solution designed to remove the salt that had accumulated on all the artifacts' surfaces after sitting on the ocean floor for more than a century. Today, the propeller has been fully preserved and is on display in the museum's extensive *Monitor* exhibit. Other artifacts are still undergoing the preservation process in the museum's lab complex, where visitors can watch conservators at work revealing the secrets of the gun turret and other items.

In addition to many artifacts large and small, researchers made a gruesome discovery when they found the remains of two crewmen among the wreckage. These unknown sailors were among the 16 who perished when the *Monitor* went down.

DURING THE BATTLE OF HAMPTON ROADS

William F. Keeler, paymaster on board the *Monitor* during the Battle of Hampton Roads, described the harrowing experience in a letter to his wife.

> **PRIMARY SOURCE**
>
> In this excerpt from his letter, Keeler describes a moment during the battle when the *Monitor* and *Virginia* are firing at each other, and the grounded Union ship, the *Minnesota*, also joins the fight against the *Virginia*.
>
> *The sounds of the conflict at this time were terrible. The rapid firing of our own guns amid the clouds of smoke, the howling of the* Minnesota's *shells, which was firing whole broadsides [a barrage of fire from one side of a ship] . . . just over our heads (two of her shots struck us), mingled with the crash of solid shot against our sides & the bursting of shells all around us. Two men had been sent down from the turret, who were knocked senseless by balls striking the outside of the turret while they happened to be in contact with the inside.*
>
> —from William F. Keeler's letter, 1862

The Civil War **389**

DIFFERENTIATE

ENGLISH LANGUAGE LEARNERS `ELD`

Use New Words in Sentences Pair students at the **Emerging** or **Expanding** level with students at the **Bridging** level. Direct the latter to pronounce the following words from the American Story and clarify meanings as necessary: *bayonet, blockade, ironclad, squadron,* and *torpedoes.* Then instruct partners to work together to compose an original sentence for each word. Suggest that students compile their own word lists as the basis for additional sentences.

PRE-AP

Create a Time Line Ask students to choose one of the three Civil War naval battles they learned about in this American Story, conduct online and print research to learn more about the battle, and use their findings to construct an annotated time line. Direct them to access reliable sources as they locate maps, primary sources, and in-depth descriptions of the battle they selected. Invite them to post their completed time lines around the classroom.

See the Chapter Planner for more strategies for differentiation.

HISTORICAL THINKING

Ask and have students answer the following questions.

1. **READING CHECK** How was Union admiral David Farragut able to defeat Confederate admiral Franklin Buchanan at the Battle of Mobile Bay?

2. **SUMMARIZE** What was the eventual fate of the Union ship the *Monitor*?

3. **EVALUATE** What were some larger implications of the Union victory in the Battle of Vicksburg?

ANSWERS

1. When the ships in Farragut's fleet were unable to navigate safely through a narrow channel free of mines, Farragut led his own ship through the floating minefield, and the rest of the fleet followed in its path to enter Mobile Bay. Once there, Union ships surrounded and fired on Buchanan's ship, injuring Buchanan and leading the new commander to surrender.

2. The *Monitor* went down in a storm, but technological advances led to its discovery in 1973. The site of the *Monitor* shipwreck later became the first marine sanctuary in the United States, and efforts to conserve the ship continue.

3. Possible response: When Mississippi and Louisiana seceded, they blocked Union passage down the Mississippi River, greatly endangering the Union economy. The Union's victory at Vicksburg reopened the river for the North and blocked the delivery of supplies to southern Confederate troops.

BEGINNINGS OF WAR

It was January 9, 1861. The *Star of the West* was headed to secessionist South Carolina to resupply army forces holed up at Fort Sumter. Suddenly the ship was overtaken by rebel gunfire and retreated. What would become of the soldiers at Fort Sumter now?

DECISION AT FORT SUMTER

In February 1861, president-elect Abraham Lincoln began a long railway trip from Illinois to Washington, D.C., pausing to speak to the people who came out to meet him along the way. At first, he downplayed the talk of secession coming from the South. But as the train rolled on, threats of war and even threats against the president himself increased. For his own safety, Lincoln sneaked into the nation's capital in the dark of night.

Abraham Lincoln took the oath of office on March 4, 1861. In his inaugural speech, he addressed concerns from the southern states, assuring that he had no intention of interfering with slavery where it already existed, that he would not use force against the South, and that he would not attempt to fill offices with men not supported by local communities. But he also warned that secession was illegal and that it was his duty to maintain the integrity of the federal government. Lincoln pleaded with his countrymen to move slowly and let heated feelings cool.

Lincoln believed the country was best served by having the most talented people in the Cabinet, even if they disagreed with him, so he appointed several Cabinet members who had previously been his political rivals. Three in particular—Secretary of State William H. Seward, Treasury Secretary Salmon P. Chase, and Attorney General Edward Bates—had run against him for the

Republican presidential nomination. This "team of rivals" grew to respect and become extremely loyal to Lincoln. He hoped that bringing together these men, some of whom held opposing ideas, would help him find ways to avoid war. However, events soon took over, elevating the simmering conflict into violence.

As you have read, by the time Lincoln took his oath of office, Fort Sumter, a Union fort on an island in Charleston Harbor, was surrounded by Confederate

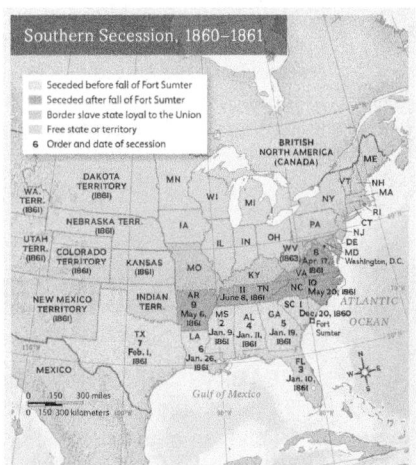

Southern Secession, 1860–1861

forces in South Carolina. Union soldiers held the fort, refusing to surrender. After Lincoln's inauguration, the commander at Fort Sumter reported that his troops would soon be out of food. Lincoln decided to send noncombat supplies to the fort.

Meanwhile, Jefferson Davis and his Confederate government had already decided that they would consider any attempt to supply the fort to be an act of war, and they determined that the Confederate commander in Charleston, P. G. T. Beauregard, should attack Fort Sumter before the Union relief ships had a chance to arrive. In the early hours of the morning on April 12, 1861, Beauregard's troops opened fire on Fort Sumter. The shelling continued for more than 30 hours before the Union forces finally surrendered. Luckily, no lives were lost in the attack, and the southern forces allowed the northern troops to evacuate the fort peacefully.

To Lincoln and other leaders of the federal government, the shelling of Fort Sumter was an act of war. As the president prepared to defend the Union by force, it became clear that the time for a peaceful resolution to political disagreements between the North and the South had run out.

ADVANTAGES AND DISADVANTAGES

The day after the Confederates raised their flag over Fort Sumter, President Lincoln called out 75,000 soldiers to help put the rebellion down. As a result, Virginia seceded. Confederate leaders then voted to move their capital to Richmond, Virginia, the largest and most industrialized city in the South.

Arkansas, Tennessee, and North Carolina soon followed Virginia's example and joined the Confederacy. Lincoln knew that if Maryland seceded, the District of Columbia would be completely surrounded by Confederate territory. Accordingly, he acted quickly to keep Maryland in the Union, jailing secessionist advocates and suspending the **writ of *habeas corpus***, a law that allowed prisoners to petition to a judge if they believed they had been arrested unlawfully. The suspension only applied to areas near rail lines between Philadelphia and Washington, and its goal was to protect the movement of troops, supplies, and weapons to the capital. With *habeas corpus* suspended, any secessionist arrested as a threat to the Union was effectively blocked from being released. Despite being a slave state, Maryland chose to remain in the Union. The other slave states on the border of the South—Kentucky, Missouri, and Delaware—also remained in the Union under pressure from the federal government.

PRIMARY SOURCE

In your hand, my dissatisfied fellow countrymen, and not in mine, is the momentous issue of civil war. The government will not assail you. You can have no conflict without being yourselves the aggressors. You have no oath in Heaven to destroy the government, while I shall have the most solemn one to preserve, protect, and defend it. . . . We are not enemies, but friends. We must not be enemies. Though passion may have strained, it must not break our bonds of affection. The mystic chords of memory, stretching from every battlefield and patriot grave, to every living heart and hearthstone, all over this broad land, will yet swell the chorus of the Union, when again touched, as surely they will be, by the better angels of our nature.

—from Abraham Lincoln's First Inaugural Address, March 4, 1861

Even in strongly pro-Confederate states, some people remained loyal to the federal government. In the mountains of western Virginia, delegates met to declare their allegiance to the Union. These 50 counties formed the new state of **West Virginia**, which joined the Union in 1863 as a slave state. The strategic need to keep the slave-holding **border states** from seceding was one of the reasons Lincoln did not focus on the future of slavery in the initial days of the war, but instead emphasized the illegality of secession and the need to preserve the Union. Many people in the North and the South found his tactics, such as suspension of the writ of *habeas corpus*, to be an abuse of federal power.

At the outset of the war, the North held an advantage in terms of overall resources. The Union states had greater industrial capacity; a more extensive system of railroads and canals; more food, draft animals, and ships; and four times as many free citizens eligible for military service as the South. However, the North faced fighting an **offensive war**, meaning that victory depended on invading the Confederates' home territory. Lincoln's government also had to convince skeptical northerners that it would be worth the cost in lives and resources to keep the southern states in the Union by force.

The Confederacy possessed considerable military advantages. It could wage a **defensive war**, protecting its homeland and fighting on ground that was familiar to local forces. The Confederates also had an initial advantage in military leadership. Some of the most experienced U.S. military generals resigned to fight for the South. For example,

---

PLAN: 4-PAGE LESSON

OBJECTIVE

Explore the factors that influenced the strategies of both sides during the Civil War.

CRITICAL THINKING SKILLS FOR LESSON 1.1

- Compare and Contrast
- Form and Support Opinions
- Interpret Maps
- Make Inferences
- Summarize
- Make Connections
- Analyze Primary Sources
- Analyze Visuals

HISTORICAL THINKING FOR CHAPTER 12

How did the Civil War change the way different groups of Americans viewed themselves and the nation? War broke out soon after Abraham Lincoln's inauguration, and the states had to choose sides. Lesson 1.1 discusses how events at Fort Sumter helped spark the war and explores the advantages, disadvantages, and strategies of each side.

BACKGROUND FOR THE TEACHER

Abraham Lincoln based his power to suspend the writ of *habeas corpus* on Article I, Section 9 of the U.S. Constitution, which declares that "the privilege of the writ of *habeas corpus* shall not be suspended, unless when in cases of rebellion or invasion the public safety may require it." Although the section applies to the powers of Congress, Congress was not in session, and Lincoln believed he had the right to take action. Not everyone agreed. When Union soldiers arrested Maryland state militiaman John Merryman for burning rail bridges and held him without legal counsel at Fort McHenry, Chief Justice Roger B. Taney issued a writ, which the fort's commander would not accept. Taney responded with a written opinion that only Congress could suspend the writ of *habeas corpus*, but Lincoln refused to honor that opinion.

FINANCIAL LITERACY

To extend their knowledge and understanding about the concepts in this lesson, refer students to the Financial Literacy handbook.

INTRODUCE & ENGAGE

ACTIVATE PRIOR KNOWLEDGE

Ask students to consider and discuss this question: How did Lincoln's election and the failure of the North and the South to reach a compromise contribute to the outbreak of the Civil War? Complete a K-W-L Chart with student responses that show what they already know about factors that led to the war. If necessary, guide the discussion by asking about southern reactions to Lincoln's electoral victory and the congressional debate over the Crittenden Plan. Then elicit and record in the K-W-L Chart questions that students would like answered as they study the lesson. At the end of the lesson, provide time for a discussion to complete the last column of the K-W-L Chart with what students have learned.

K What Do I Know?	W What Do I Want To Learn?	L What Did I Learn?

TEACH

GUIDED DISCUSSION

1. **Make Inferences** What did Lincoln's choice of Cabinet members suggest about his method of decision making? *(Possible response: Lincoln chose Cabinet members who didn't necessarily agree with him or with each other. However, each was qualified in his own way. This suggests that Lincoln liked to hear a range of opinions, even conflicting ones, so he could make informed decisions.)*

2. **Summarize** Why and how did Lincoln use his presidential power to protect Washington, D.C.? *(Knowing that Washington, D.C., would be surrounded by Confederate states if Maryland seceded, Lincoln suspended the writ of habeas corpus in areas near rail lines between Philadelphia and Washington, D.C. This enabled him to have Maryland's secessionists arrested and kept in jail. The main goal was to keep troop and supply lines to the capital open.)*

3. **Make Connections** Why do you think the Union admitted West Virginia as a slave state and Lincoln focused on secession rather than slavery as the reason to go to war? *(Possible response: The Lincoln administration didn't want to anger or alarm the border states because it wanted them to remain in the Union. Therefore, the Union didn't make slavery an obstacle to granting West Virginia statehood. Lincoln focused on secession rather than slavery in his response to the Confederacy because the border states had not illegally seceded—but those states did allow slavery—so he focused on an issue they agreed with in order to keep the border states happy.)*

ANALYZE PRIMARY SOURCES

Direct students' attention to the Primary Source feature. **ASK:** How are Lincoln's words both an attempt at reconciliation and a warning? *(Possible response: Lincoln is telling secessionists in the South that he will not make the first move toward war and that Americans on both sides can still find common ground and affection for one another. However, if states move against the federal government, Lincoln will not hesitate to preserve, protect, and defend it.)*

DIFFERENTIATE

ENGLISH LANGUAGE LEARNERS

Understand Antonyms Pair students at the **Emerging** level with those at the **Expanding** or **Bridging** level. Instruct pairs to reread the paragraphs in the lesson that contain the terms *offensive war* and *defensive war*. Help them understand that *offensive* and *defensive* are antonyms and that these adjectives can be used to describe things other than war, such as styles of driving, aspects of sports games, and actions in personal relationships. Ask pairs to make word cards for *offensive* and *defensive*, writing the word on one side and the definition on the other. Tell them to use context clues from the lesson to help them write each definition and then to check their work against a dictionary definition. Challenge students to compose original sentences for each word and then read the sentences to their partner.

GIFTED & TALENTED

Perform a Historic Speech Guide students to access the full text of Lincoln's first Inaugural Address. Prompt them to prepare and present a dramatic reading of a portion of the speech. Suggest that they practice using gestures and dramatic pauses and emphasize Lincoln's strong verbs, vivid imagery, alliteration, and other poetic devices. After they have practiced, have students perform the speech for the class. Invite listeners to discuss how the reading enhanced their understanding of Lincoln's use of both logic and emotion in his attempt to avoid civil war.

See the Chapter Planner for more strategies for differentiation.

SCOTT'S GREAT SNAKE.

The Anaconda Plan was meant to strangle the South by cutting off trade between slave states in the East and the West and between the Confederacy and Europe. General Winfield Scott believed his plan would put an early end to the war and limit the number of casualties.

Scott proposed sending a large naval force down the Mississippi River that would capture forts and towns along its banks.

Union ships patrolled the coastal border to prevent deliveries of weapons and supplies to southern states.

Scott's plan was never fully implemented, but a naval blockade was maintained throughout the war, largely cutting off the South's access to money, food, and war supplies from abroad. Scott himself believed the war would last for two years.

coal
corn
cotton
peaches
oranges
cattle
hay
banking
tobacco
sheep
apples
sugar cane
horses

A Confederate hundred-dollar bill (left) features enslaved African Americans working fields, the Greek goddess Minerva, and former Vice President John C. Calhoun. An eagle, Liberty, and Abraham Lincoln are featured on the U.S. ten-dollar bill (below).

Robert E. Lee, who had served the United States as an officer in the Mexican-American War and as superintendent of the United States Military Academy at West Point, refused to fight against his home state of Virginia. Although he did not strongly support secession, Lee eventually became commander of the Army of Northern Virginia. Meanwhile, Lincoln struggled to find a leader for the Union Army who could win decisive victories on the battlefield.

STRATEGIES ON BOTH SIDES

When fighting first broke out, neither side expected the conflict to last long. Lincoln's initial call for troops was supposed to be for only 90 days of service. The Confederates believed northerners lacked the desire to fight an offensive war and would quickly negotiate a settlement. But by summer, both North and South began to recognize that the war might last beyond a few months. The Confederate Congress authorized 400,000 volunteers in May 1861, and in July 1861, the U.S. Congress authorized 500,000 troops. New soldiers enlisted for three years.

In terms of military strategy, the South saw itself as purely on the defensive, but if the opportunity arose, it hoped to carry out a decisive strike against Washington, D.C. The North, for its part, counted on General Winfield Scott's **Anaconda Plan,** named after the large snake that squeezes its prey to death. That plan depended on sending an overpowering force down the Mississippi, dividing the South in two. At the same time, the Union Navy would blockade southern seaports on the Atlantic coast and Gulf of Mexico to seal the South off from its global trading partners.

On the civilian side, Confederate leaders decided to print paper money to help fund the expensive war effort. Since the Confederacy had little gold or silver to back the value of this money, Confederate currency was really more like a **promissory note**, or an agreement to pay, that could be redeemed once the South won the war. As the war dragged on, the Confederates printed millions of dollars of currency even as the value of their money tumbled, leading to massive inflation and dire economic circumstances for the South. The Union relied more on taxes and bonds—loans to be repaid later—to fund the costs of the war. Eventually, however, it also had to issue paper money. More than $450 million in U.S. paper currency, called **greenbacks** because the backs of the bills were printed in green ink, circulated during the war.

HISTORICAL THINKING

1. **READING CHECK** Why did the Confederates fire on Fort Sumter?

2. **COMPARE AND CONTRAST** What advantages and disadvantages did each side have in the conflict?

3. **FORM AND SUPPORT OPINIONS** How do you think the Anaconda Plan could have shortened the war?

4. **INTERPRET MAPS** Of the four states that seceded after the attack on Fort Sumter, which one shared a border with only Confederate states?

BUILD BACKGROUND

WINFIELD SCOTT

A hero from the War of 1812 and the Mexican-American War, General Winfield Scott was a talented military tactician. By the time Abraham Lincoln took office in 1861, however, Scott was 74 years old and so heavy and wracked with ailments that he could not even mount his horse. Known as "Old Fuss and Feathers" because of his love of military discipline and pomp, he was an easy target for critics. A series of disappointments marked his command of the Union Army. First, Scott offered Robert E. Lee, a trusted member of his staff during the Mexican-American War, the chance to lead the Union troops in the field, but Lee resigned and soon commanded Virginia's troops for the Confederacy. Then Lincoln, fearing Scott's Anaconda Plan would produce slow results and involve too many troops, cut its implementation to just the blockade and sent the army instead to fight what would become the disastrous First Battle of Bull Run (First Manassas). Scott resigned in November 1861.

CONFEDERATE CURRENCY

The assortment of paper money circulating in the Confederacy baffled citizens and led to fraud. The Confederate treasury issued some 70 different types of notes, while state and county governments, banks, and even businesses issued their own. A shortage of paper fueled the confusion. Many bills were printed on the back of canceled bonds, misprinted currency, or even wallpaper. The wide array of notes and different papers made it difficult for ordinary people to detect counterfeits. Samuel C. Upham was one northerner who took advantage of this situation. An enterprising shopkeeper, Upham began printing Confederate notes as souvenirs, or what he called "Mementos of the Rebellion." He soon realized that he could be patriotic and also turn a profit by counterfeiting a large quantity of different Confederate notes for distribution in the South, thereby devaluing the legitimate currency.

TEACH

GUIDED DISCUSSION

4. **Interpret Maps** How does the map of Scott's Anaconda Plan help you understand why dividing the Confederacy in two would impact the South's war effort? *(Possible response: The cattle industry was centered in the western region. If Union forces controlled the Mississippi River, they could cut off meat supplies coming from Confederate states west of the Mississippi, contributing to food shortages in the Confederate states east of the river.)*

5. **Form and Support Opinions** Do you think the South's method of funding the war was a sound strategy? Why or why not? *(Answers will vary. Possible responses: No. The decision to rely on printing money was not sound because the notes could only be redeemed after the war, assuming that the South won, and printing more money as needed led to inflation and other economic problems. Yes. Given the fact that the Confederacy had little gold and silver, issuing promissory notes was the best strategy because Confederate leaders had no other options.)*

ANALYZE VISUALS

Direct students' attention to the photograph of the Confederate hundred-dollar bill. Point out the visuals on the bill and read the caption. Explain that the goddess Minerva is associated with wisdom, the arts, and war. **ASK:** What do the images on the Confederate bill suggest about how the South viewed the Civil War? *(Possible response: The prominent placement of enslaved workers on the bill shows that the South viewed slavery as central to the Confederate identity and that the war was mostly about slavery. The presence of Minerva seems to be a claim that the Confederacy had wisdom and divine favor on its side as it went to war. The engraving of John C. Calhoun might point to the importance of states' rights, the institution of slavery, and the right to secede.)*

ACTIVE OPTIONS

Active History: Compare Resources Extend the lesson by using either the PDF or Whiteboard version of the activity. These activities take a deeper look at a topic from, or related to, the lesson. Explore the activities as a class, turn them into group assignments, or even assign them individually.

NG Learning Framework: Represent Data `STEM`

`ATTITUDE` Curiosity

`SKILLS` Collaboration, Communication

Remind students that data can be presented in a variety of ways. For example, the lesson presents information about Confederate and Union resources in a text format, and the Active History activity uses a table to compare numbers and percentages. Challenge students to conduct online research to learn more about the economic, transportation, or military advantages and disadvantages on both sides and present the data in graph form. Allow them to work in pairs or small groups to create an appropriate means of representing the data. Display the completed graphs. Then discuss as a class which ways of presenting the data are most helpful and why.

HISTORICAL THINKING

ANSWERS

1. Lincoln sent ships to deliver food and supplies, and the Confederates considered any attempt by the Union to resupply Fort Sumter an act of war.

2. The North had the advantage of more resources, which included greater industrial capacity, canals and railroads, food, draft animals, ships, and citizens eligible for military service. The North faced the disadvantage of fighting an offensive war. The South had the advantages of fighting a defensive war on familiar territory and having stronger military leadership, but it lacked industrial resources, a transportation network, and a large pool of available soldiers.

3. The Anaconda Plan could have shortened the war by disrupting trade and supplies and by dividing the Confederacy, making it more difficult for the South to wage war.

4. North Carolina shared a border with only Confederate states.

EARLY COURSE OF THE WAR

Can you imagine packing a lunch and spending the afternoon watching a battle? In July 1861, civilians from Washington, D.C., heard that Confederate and Union troops were about to clash just outside town. Expecting a quick and exciting Union victory, many lined the battlefield carrying picnic baskets and champagne. The realities of war soon dimmed their spirits.

BATTLE OF BULL RUN

In the summer of 1861, both the North and the South were strategizing for a quick victory. With the opposing capitals of Richmond, Virginia, and Washington, D.C., so close to one another, a decisive attack by either side on the other's capital could mean a swift end to hostilities, which is why many of the early battles occurred in Virginia. Some Union leaders thought they should attack before the Confederates had time to mobilize, or organize and train, their forces. But both Union and Confederate armies already had troops in position in northern Virginia.

Lincoln made the first move, sending out Union troops under the command of General Irvin McDowell with the goal of capturing Richmond. The soldiers marched south from Washington to Manassas, Virginia, where, on July 21, 1861, they faced off against Confederates commanded by General P.G.T. Beauregard in the first major battle of the war. Because it took place near a stream called Bull Run, the action is known in the North as the **First Battle of Bull Run**. In the South, it's called the First Battle of Manassas. Civilian spectators came out from Washington to watch, expecting a quick Union victory.

The fighting was harder than anyone expected, but Confederate troops took heart when one of their leaders pointed out General Thomas J. Jackson and his men holding their line and shouted, "There is Jackson standing like a stone wall!" From that time on, the general was known as **Stonewall Jackson**. The Confederates rallied and took the advantage when **J.E.B. Stuart**, the leader of the Confederate **cavalry**, or soldiers on horseback, sent his men to charge through the Union lines of **infantry**, or foot soldiers, forcing the Union troops to retreat. The Confederates won their first victory, but at a cost. The casualties were high on both sides.

Lincoln soon replaced McDowell with **George B. McClellan**, a hero of the Mexican-American War who had studied military tactics in Europe. McClellan had already frustrated Confederate forces under Robert E. Lee in western Virginia. Lincoln had high hopes for McClellan, but soon grew impatient as his general hesitated to launch a major offensive. Meanwhile, weakened by heavy casualties, Confederate forces failed to pursue further attacks against the North to follow their Bull Run victory.

WOMEN AND WAR

As both sides recruited men to fight in the war, women were also called upon to serve in a variety of ways. Within two weeks of the war's beginning, Union and Confederate women organized thousands of local aid societies to help supply uniforms and other necessities to their respective armies.

Many of these supplies were destined for hospitals. The sheer number of troops involved, along with the new and ever more destructive weapons used in the war, led to high numbers of casualties that overwhelmed understaffed hospitals. Women began filling nursing positions, even though only men had served as military nurses prior to the Civil War. Secretary of War Simon Cameron appointed Dorothea Dix, long known as a champion of the poor and mentally ill in the years before the war, to be superintendent of nurses for the Union Army. In spite of her title and responsibilities, neither she nor any of the female nurses who served in the Civil War received official military appointments.

Female nurses worked long hours and tended to gruesome injuries previously believed to be too horrific for women to handle. Many distinguished themselves, earning the respect of career military men. **Kate Cumming**, from Alabama, was among the most honored Confederate nurses in the Mississippi region. She later wrote one of the most accurate memoirs about life in Confederate field hospitals. **Phoebe Pember**, the daughter of a prominent Jewish family in the South, wrote another famous southern hospital memoir. Pember served as a nurse and administrator at what was at the time the world's largest military hospital, in Virginia.

For some women, serving as Civil War nurses inspired future careers. Union nurse **Clara Barton**, nicknamed the "Angel of the Battlefield" for her service, went on to found the American Red Cross. Another Union nurse, Louisa May Alcott, became a famous author. Her wartime experiences shaped her fiction books, including *Little Women*.

On the home front, women took on the work of men serving in the war. In the North, women ran farms and worked in factories in addition to raising families all by themselves. In the South, women managed plantations, farmed, and fed their families in the face of high inflation and increasing food shortages. The burden of war was heavy for women on both sides.

HISTORICAL THINKING

1. **READING CHECK** How did the Battle of Bull Run end?

2. **IDENTIFY MAIN IDEAS AND DETAILS** Why did many early battles take place in Virginia?

3. **MAKE INFERENCES** In what ways did the Civil War affect the northern workforce?

4. **MAKE CONNECTIONS** How has the role of women in the medical profession changed since the Civil War?

National Geographic photographer Ken Garrett captured a smoke-filled reenactment of the Battle of Bull Run in Manassas, Virginia.

PLAN: 2-PAGE LESSON

OBJECTIVE

Describe the First Battle of Bull Run and how the roles of women changed during the Civil War.

CRITICAL THINKING SKILLS FOR LESSON 1.2

• Identify Main Ideas and Details

• Make Inferences

• Make Connections

• Form and Support Opinions

• Analyze Cause and Effect

• Analyze Primary Sources

HISTORICAL THINKING FOR CHAPTER 12

How did the Civil War change the way different groups of Americans viewed themselves and the nation? Both sides expected a swift end to the conflict. Lesson 1.2 looks at how the First Battle of Bull Run altered perceptions about the war and led to changing roles for women.

NATIONAL GEOGRAPHIC PHOTOGRAPHER KEN GARRETT

National Geographic photographer Ken Garrett is carrying on a family tradition. His father, Wilbur "Bill" Garrett, was a longtime National Geographic photographer and also served as the editor of *National Geographic* magazine in the 1980s. Bill Garrett believed that photographers should be photojournalists and visual storytellers. Ken Garrett agrees but admits that he grew into that view. As a child, he thought of photography as a way to explore. He now focuses on telling the story of the past, as is shown in his work documenting the Journey Through Hallowed Ground National Heritage Area. This route, which extends 180 miles from Gettysburg, Pennsylvania, to Thomas Jefferson's home at Monticello in Charlottesville, Virginia, contains the nation's largest concentration of Civil War sites, including Manassas, Virginia, the site of the First Battle of Bull Run.

INTRODUCE & ENGAGE

DISCUSS GENDER ROLES

Prompt students to recall how women participated in the American Revolution and that the positions they filled had been previously unavailable to them. Discuss how women's lives changed again after the war, when they returned to traditional roles as wives, mothers, and keepers of the home. Tell them that in this lesson they will learn how the Civil War also affected gender roles for some women.

TEACH

GUIDED DISCUSSION

1. **Form and Support Opinions** What was the Confederacy's greatest advantage in the Battle of Bull Run? Why do you think so? *(Possible response: Confederate forces were under the command of strong military leaders like Stonewall Jackson and J.E.B. Stuart, and they had a cavalry unit, which proved decisive in the battle.)*

2. **Analyze Cause and Effect** Why do you think both the Union and the Confederate military began using female nurses during the Civil War? *(Possible response: More nurses were needed during the Civil War because the weapons were deadlier than in previous wars, resulting in increased casualties. In addition, male nurses could serve as soldiers, so shifting nursing duties to women resulted in more fighting forces.)*

ANALYZE PRIMARY SOURCES

Direct students' attention to the Primary Source feature. **ASK:** What point is Clara Barton trying to convey about war? *(Possible response: Barton is lamenting that history focuses on the political outcomes of war—the victories—and portrays the glory of war rather than focusing on the pain and human destruction, something that nurses face after every battle.)*

ACTIVE OPTIONS

On Your Feet: Roundtable Arrange students in groups of four for a Roundtable discussion. Ask them the following question: What changes did women experience during the Civil War? Instruct groups to have each member contribute to the answer and then come to a consensus about the changes that had the most significance to society. Invite groups to share their ideas with the class.

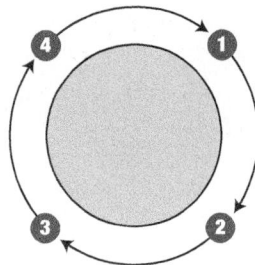

NG Learning Framework: Write a News Story

`SKILLS` Collaboration, Communication

`KNOWLEDGE` Our Human Story

Ask students to work in groups to write a news story about the First Battle of Bull Run. Instruct half of the groups to write a story for a Union newspaper and half for a Confederate newspaper. Tell students to conduct research, making sure to use credible primary and secondary sources, to learn more about the public's changing perceptions of the war. Invite groups to present their news stories to the class.

DIFFERENTIATE

STRIVING READERS

Use a Main-Idea Cluster Direct pairs of students to use a Main-Idea Cluster to check their understanding of the lesson. First, tell partners to take turns reading the paragraphs within a subsection. Then ask them to work together to record the main idea and four details. Instruct pairs to trade and compare clusters.

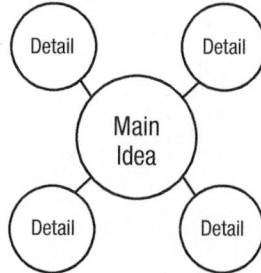

PRE-AP

Analyze a Battle Instruct students to conduct research to analyze what happened at the First Battle of Bull Run and why. Suggest that students use a graphic organizer to keep track of their research. Then prompt them to use their notes to craft an oral report about the goals, tactics, events, and outcome of the battle. Invite students to present their oral reports to the class.

See the Chapter Planner for more strategies for differentiation.

HISTORICAL THINKING

ANSWERS

1. A Confederate cavalry charge forced the Union troops to retreat.

2. The Confederate capital was located in Virginia, and the U.S. capital was just outside Virginia, in Washington, D.C. Each side wanted to capture the other side's capital to end the war quickly, so the fighting centered on that area.

3. When the men went off to war, the number of women in the workforce increased because women took over running farms and working in factories.

4. Answers will vary. Possible response: Women now fill roles in all areas of the medical profession, including working as doctors, technicians, nurses, surgeons, and researchers.

MANASSAS, VIRGINIA

Near the town of Manassas, Virginia, flows a small stream called Bull Run. This was the site of the two major Civil War battles named after both the town and the stream. The First Battle of Bull Run, also known as the First Battle of Manassas, was fought on July 21, 1861, near the residence in the photograph, called the Stone House. During the battle, wounded Union soldiers sought refuge in the home's basement. Soon they could hear the cries of other wounded soldiers seeking shelter on the floor above.

The Second Battle of Bull Run, or the Second Battle of Manassas, took place more than a year later. Once again, the Stone House served as a Union aid station where medical officers treated wounded soldiers. Both battles resulted in Confederate victories and a staggering number of casualties. Today, the Stone House is part of Manassas National Battlefield Park, which covers about eight square miles and preserves the sites of the two historic battles.

CRITICAL VIEWING The landscape of Manassas National Battlefield Park features gently rolling hills covered by a patchwork of open meadows and mostly deciduous forests. The park spans nearly 5,100 acres with more than 40 miles of hiking trails, including paths that loop through the sites of the two battles. How would you characterize the mood of this photograph by National Geographic photographer Ken Garrett?

The Civil War 397

PLAN: 2-PAGE LESSON

OBJECTIVE

Describe the significance of Manassas National Battlefield Park in Virginia and how photographer Ken Garrett conveys its history.

CRITICAL THINKING SKILLS FOR LESSON 1.3

- Analyze Visuals
- Make Connections
- Draw Conclusions
- Ask and Answer Questions

HISTORICAL THINKING FOR CHAPTER 12

How did the Civil War change the way different groups of Americans viewed themselves and the nation? A crucial part of American history, the Civil War continues to have a strong influence on American identity. Lesson 1.3 describes the importance of the site of two major Civil War battles and how that history lives on through Ken Garrett's photography.

NATIONAL GEOGRAPHIC PHOTOGRAPHER
KEN GARRETT

Ken Garrett had covered a wide range of subjects before he received an assignment to photograph some of the most historic and sacred sites in the United States. He traveled from Gettysburg, Pennsylvania, to Thomas Jefferson's home in Charlottesville, Virginia, producing a book called *Journey Through Hallowed Ground*. As Garrett explains, "We think these places are so important that they have a spiritual meaning." His approach is to study a site, such as the Manassas National Battlefield Park, from every angle until something speaks to him. He then converts that feeling into photographs that touch the viewer. In the words of Jon James, superintendent of the park, Garrett's body of work unifies the historic sites into "a chain of the history and heritage of the area."

HISTORY NOTEBOOK

Encourage students to complete the American Places page for Chapter 12 in their History Notebooks as they read.

INTRODUCE & ENGAGE

SHARE EXPERIENCES VISITING A MONUMENT

Discuss with students national battlefields or wartime monuments they have visited, read about, or seen in the media. Ask them to consider whether they think the site or monument adequately conveys the story of the people or the meaning of the event it commemorates. Then invite students to discuss what impression the site might have on visitors. Tell them that in this lesson they will learn about the historic site of two major battles of the Civil War.

TEACH

GUIDED DISCUSSION

1. **Draw Conclusions** Why do you think Garrett photographed the site with the Stone House in the foreground rather than in the background? *(Possible response: He might have wanted to emphasize the importance of the Stone House as a place of refuge for the soldiers and not just as a building on the battlefield.)*

2. **Ask and Answer Questions** What else might you want to know about this battlefield park, and how would you find the answers? *(Answers will vary. Possible responses: How close to the Stone House did fighting take place? Who tended to the soldiers there? Is there a cemetery near the park where Civil War soldiers are buried? Online and library research about the two battles and the park would likely provide answers to these questions. Staff at the park might be able to answer them as well.)*

AMERICAN PLACES

The 600,000 visitors a year to Manassas, Virginia, can still see the Stone House and Stone Bridge, but few other traces of the battles remain, as nature has covered most of the evidence. Even in 1865, a visiting reporter remarked, "Delicate flowers growing out of the empty ammunition boxes . . . Wasn't that peace growing out of war?" Yet visitors can still find reminders of the battles in the Stone House. In an upstairs room, two wounded soldiers carved their names, "E.P. Ge" and "Brehm Aug 30," in the floorboards. When the government restored the house to its pre–Civil War appearance, the original floorboards were left in place. Records show that only Brehm survived the war.

ACTIVE OPTIONS

On Your Feet: Fishbowl Configure half of the class to sit in a small circle facing inward. Have the other half of the class sit in a larger circle around them. Pose the following question: Why is it important to keep Civil War sites such as Manassas National Battlefield Park open to the public? Students in the inner circle should discuss the question while those in the outer circle listen and evaluate the points made. Then the groups reverse roles and continue the discussion, expanding the topic to include the importance of preserving such sites for future generations.

NG Learning Framework: Create a Photo Collage

ATTITUDES Curiosity, Responsibility

KNOWLEDGE Our Human Story

Share with students the National Geographic Photographer information about Garrett. Then have them work in groups to conduct online research to find other photographs of historic battlefields. Direct groups to select two or three photographs and write a caption explaining the location and significance of each site. Then tell groups to assemble their photos into a collage. Invite them to share their collages with the class, describing what the photographers may have wanted viewers to understand or feel about the subject of each photo.

DIFFERENTIATE

INCLUSION

Describe the Photograph At the beginning of the lesson, pair visually impaired students with students who can describe details in the photograph and clarify the text as necessary. Have pairs work together to respond to the Guided Discussion and Critical Viewing questions.

GIFTED & TALENTED

Create a Multimedia Presentation Instruct students to conduct research using print and online sources to learn more about Manassas as a historic battle site and as a modern town. Prompt them to find written, audio, video, and photographic materials and assemble their findings into a compelling multimedia presentation that provides insight into the past, present, and possible future of Manassas. Invite them to share their presentation with the class.

See the Chapter Planner for more strategies for differentiation.

CRITICAL VIEWING Possible response: At first glance, the mood seems tranquil, with the serene meadow and woods in the background. However, the stark presence of the deserted Stone House, along with what look like cannons in the background, are reminders of the suffering that soldiers experienced here when battles raged over the surrounding hills.

Artist J. G. Wells illustrated the close-range battle between the *Monitor* (front left) and the *Virginia* (front right) in this 1891 oil painting.

EARLY BATTLES ON LAND AND SEA

Maryland brothers Andrew and William Shriver not only grew up together, but lived next to one another as adults. When war broke out, however, Andrew sided with the Union while William aided the Confederacy. Their situation was a real-life example of the divisions that pitted brother against brother and neighbor against neighbor.

THE WAR IN THE WEST BEGINS

While Union and Confederate leaders eyed each other's capitals in the East, fighting expanded in the western border states, especially Missouri. Southern forces hoped to rally slaveholders in divided communities to their side, believing that victories over Union troops might lead those states to secede and join the Confederacy.

A few days after the Battle of Bull Run, Lincoln installed former Republican presidential candidate John C. Frémont as commander of the forces in Missouri. On August 10, 1861, two regiments of Confederate troops attempted to surround Union forces near Springfield, Missouri. Although the Union soldiers were outnumbered, they attacked the poorly equipped Confederates. Both sides suffered heavy casualties during the fighting, and both sides retreated, but the Union troops withdrew the farthest. For the time being, southwestern Missouri remained under Confederate control.

Confederate forces also staged guerrilla attacks throughout the state. With Missourians divided over the war, Frémont placed the entire state under martial law, or military authority. He ordered the death penalty for captured guerrillas and seized the slaves and other property of Confederate sympathizers. Slaveholders in the border states of Kentucky and Maryland threatened to join the Confederacy if Lincoln did not make Frémont back off. When Frémont resisted, Lincoln removed him from his post. Missouri remained in a state of turmoil throughout the war.

A descendant of Massachusetts Bay colonists, Ulysses S. Grant was born in Ohio in 1822. After graduating from West Point, he served with Winfield Scott in the Mexican-American War, participating in the sieges of Veracruz and Mexico City.

By 1862, Union generals in the West began to advance aggressively. Troops under the command of General **Ulysses S. Grant** pushed Confederates from southern Kentucky down the Tennessee and Cumberland rivers and across the Kentucky border into Tennessee. Important Confederate forts guarded both rivers, but Grant hoped to overwhelm them with combined attacks from water and land. He successfully assaulted Fort Henry on the Tennessee River in early February. He then marched his men overland to Fort Donelson on the Cumberland River. There, the Confederates fought desperately, destroying several Union gunboats, but Grant ultimately won control of the fort and the region it served. When the Confederate general in command of Fort Donelson attempted to negotiate with Grant for its surrender, Grant responded: "No terms except an unconditional and immediate surrender can be accepted." Within days, Union troops took nearby Nashville, the capital of Tennessee, the first capture of a southern state's capital during the war.

BATTLE OF THE IRONCLADS

From the beginning of the war, the Confederacy had hoped to win support from European trade partners that relied on southern cotton, especially France and England, both of which had already abolished slavery. But citizens of other nations were also divided by the Civil War in the United States. Many Europeans sympathized with the Confederates' desire for self-determination. European abolitionists, however, opposed any efforts to protect slavery. The South also overestimated its importance to European markets. British factories had stockpiled cotton in anticipation of the war, and Britain and other nations also began investing heavily in Egyptian cotton. European countries planned to remain neutral until they were more certain of which side would win the conflict. Meanwhile, the Union Navy continued to tighten its blockade under the North's Anaconda Plan, limiting the ability of southern smugglers to sneak cotton overseas.

As the naval war heated up, both sides began to experiment with new and improved maritime weapon technologies. The Confederacy was the first to build an **ironclad**, or ship covered in iron plates. After southern shipbuilders redesigned and cladded a captured Union ship, the U.S.S. *Merrimack*, the Confederacy changed the ship's name to the C.S.S. *Virginia*. The Union countered by designing its own ironclad, the U.S.S. *Monitor*. On March 8, 1862, the *Virginia* attacked several Union ships in the harbor at Hampton Roads, Virginia. Luckily for the Union Navy, the *Monitor* was nearby. The next day, the two ironclads engaged in a battle that lasted for hours

and technically ended in a draw. Many consider the battle a victory for the Union, which remained in possession of Hampton Roads.

Naval experiments eventually led to the first combat submarines—and the first combat submarine attack. The Confederates built a vessel they hoped could strike the enemy while remaining entirely underwater. The work was very dangerous. Several men lost their lives in test runs of the tiny, hand-cranked submarine called the *H. L. Hunley*. Despite this poor track record, by the latter part of the war Confederate leaders were so desperate to break the Union blockade that they called the experimental submarine into action. On February 17, 1864, the *Hunley* torpedoed the U.S.S. *Housatonic* in Charleston Harbor. Although most of the *Housatonic* crew escaped, the ship became the first ever sunk by a submarine. But the *Hunley* crew never lived to celebrate the victory. The submarine failed to resurface.

HISTORICAL THINKING

1. **READING CHECK** Why did Lincoln remove John C. Frémont as commander of the Union forces in Missouri?

2. **ANALYZE CAUSE AND EFFECT** What effect did the Battle of Hampton Roads have on the Union blockade of the South?

3. **MAKE CONNECTIONS** How did the war influence later naval technology?

OBJECTIVE

Discuss why and how fighting expanded in the West and the role of maritime innovations in naval warfare.

CRITICAL THINKING SKILLS FOR LESSON 2.1

• Analyze Cause and Effect

• Make Connections

• Make Inferences

• Analyze Visuals

HISTORICAL THINKING FOR CHAPTER 12

How did the Civil War change the way different groups of Americans viewed themselves and the nation? The Civil War not only divided the nation but also caused rifts within families and between friends. Lesson 2.1 describes the early fighting in the West and the naval war in the East.

BACKGROUND FOR THE TEACHER

After capturing Nashville, the Union Army stationed enough troops and support personnel to outnumber the city's population. They set up supply depots and opened military hospitals to treat wounded soldiers. Although the occupiers kept the city's markets, schools, and churches open, some residents complained about Union soldiers attending church services. In an attempt to maintain order, army officials pressured prominent leaders and business owners to sign loyalty oaths to the Union. When many people refused, officials responded by ordering every white citizen older than 18 to sign a loyalty oath or be evicted from Nashville, a threat that induced many citizens to sign. As difficult as the occupation was, it did offer some benefits. The Union Army provided important city services to Nashville residents, such as health care, policing, fire protection, and aid to needy families.

INTRODUCE & ENGAGE

BRAINSTORM A LIST

Write the term *martial law* on the board and explain that when a government imposes martial law, it turns the normal civilian functions of the government over to the control of the military. Ask students to brainstorm reasons why a government might take this action. Write volunteers' answers on the board and then prompt students to discuss the pros and cons of a government's use of this measure. Tell students that in this lesson they will learn about the imposition of martial law in the border state of Missouri and its consequences for the Union.

TEACH

GUIDED DISCUSSION

1. **Make Inferences** Why would capturing Nashville be an advantage for the Union Army? *(Possible response: Nashville's capture would be an important psychological victory, since it would be the first southern state capital in Union hands. Also, the city and the area around it might be strategically important as a source of food and supplies for Union troops as they moved deeper into the South.)*

2. **Make Connections** What factors kept European nations from offering the support and aid the Confederacy had hoped for? *(Abolitionists in Europe did not want to protect slavery, Britain and other European nations had stockpiled cotton or invested in Egyptian cotton and did not need to help the South protect their cotton supply, and European governments wanted to remain neutral until the outcome of the war became clearer and they could side with the winner.)*

ANALYZE VISUALS

Direct students' attention to the painting by J. G. Wells. **ASK:** How does this painting help you understand why the North quickly built its own ironclad after the South designed the *Virginia*? *(Possible response: The painting shows the vulnerability of wooden ships to the Confederate ironclad—one Union ship is on fire and the other is nearly capsized. With no ironclad, the Union would have been at a clear disadvantage in sea battles.)*

For students who develop an interest in Civil War naval battles, suggest that they read the American Story at the beginning of this chapter.

ACTIVE OPTIONS

On Your Feet: Three-Step Interview Ask students to work in pairs. Direct one partner to interview the other by asking questions about naval warfare, such as: What were the ironclad ships? Direct the interviewer to ask follow-up questions. Then have partners reverse roles, with the second interviewer asking questions about the topic. Partners continue to interview each other until they run out of questions. Encourage students to draw on information from the lesson and their own knowledge of the subject. Invite pairs to share information from their interviews with the class.

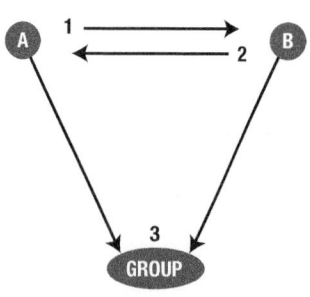

NG Learning Framework: Report on John C. Frémont's Martial Law

ATTITUDE Responsibility

SKILLS Communication, Collaboration

Organize students into three groups to present a collaborative report on John C. Frémont's imposition of martial law in Missouri. Group 1 researches the rules and regulations of martial law that Frémont put in place. Group 2 researches how these rules and regulations affected people's lives. Group 3 researches public responses to Frémont's martial law. Have each group choose a member for a three-person panel to report their findings to the class. Then guide a discussion in which students state whether they agree or disagree with Frémont's decision to impose martial law and with Lincoln's decision to remove Frémont from command.

DIFFERENTIATE

ENGLISH LANGUAGE LEARNERS ELD

Understand Battle Terms As they read the lesson, prompt students at the **Expanding** level to keep a list of military terms they may not know, such as *regiments*, *casualties*, *engaged*, *retreated*, *withdrew*, *assaulted*, *surrender*, *neutral*, *blockade*, and a *draw*. Direct students to make word cards to help them understand and remember the words for future use. Ask them to write the word on one side of the card. On the other side, have them define the word, spell it phonetically, and use it in an original sentence.

GIFTED & TALENTED

Write and Present a Skit Challenge students to write and present a skit that dramatizes the surrender of Fort Donelson. Prompt them to conduct research to learn more about the battle and the messages exchanged between General Grant and General Buckner of the Confederate Army. In addition to portraying the two generals, students may recruit classmates to play other characters, such as subordinate officers or soldiers on either side. Invite students to present their skits to the class.

See the Chapter Planner for more strategies for differentiation.

HISTORICAL THINKING

ANSWERS

1. Lincoln removed Frémont after Maryland and Kentucky threatened to join the Confederacy because of Frémont's harsh policies in Missouri, which included imposing martial law, ordering the death penalty for captured guerrillas, and seizing the slaves and property of Confederate sympathizers.

2. The battle helped the Union maintain its naval blockade of the South by keeping the harbor at Hampton Roads under Union control.

3. Both sides developed new naval technologies, such as ironclads and the first combat submarines. Both ironclads and submarines paved the way for the more sophisticated vessels used in modern navies.

THE BATTLES OF 1862

The pictures were startling. Using recently developed technology, Civil War photographers started capturing graphic images of bodies that lay strewn about battlefields after the fighting. The gruesome photos undermined any remaining optimism about a quick end to the war.

Civil War Battles, 1861–1865

400

BATTLES IN THE EAST AND WEST

Combat on all **fronts**, or battle lines between armies, heated up by the spring of 1862. It seemed as if Union general George McClellan was finally ready to launch his long-delayed offensive in the East. McClellan planned to attack Richmond from the south to shift fighting farther away from Washington, D.C. But even after getting the go-ahead from President Lincoln, McClellan took several more weeks to prepare his men for what he expected to be the war's conclusive, or final, battle.

Meanwhile, in the West, generals Ulysses S. Grant and **William Tecumseh Sherman** pushed their troops deeper into Tennessee after their victories at Fort Henry and Fort Donelson. Their objective was Corinth, Mississippi, a major southern rail center, where 45,000 Confederate soldiers waited for them. If the Union could capture the railroads at Corinth, it would control most of the western Confederacy. However, Confederate general Albert Sidney Johnston learned about the plan and ambushed Grant's troops near a church in Shiloh, Tennessee, on April 6, 1862. The **Battle of Shiloh** began as a series of brutal fights among scattered groups of desperate men with little coordinated leadership. When General Johnston was killed leading an attack, he was replaced by P.G.T. Beauregard, who then succeeded in pushing the Union troops back two miles.

The Confederate advantage proved short lived, however, as 20,000 Union reinforcements arrived overnight. The next day Grant and his army regained the ground they had lost, and the Confederates retreated to Corinth. Although the southern forces had been badly beaten, Grant's troops were too exhausted to pursue them. The loss of life at what the press called "Bloody Shiloh" exceeded anything anyone had ever seen. With more than 23,000 casualties overall, Shiloh was the deadliest battle of the war so far. Horrified at the loss of life, some people urged Lincoln to remove Grant from his command, but the president refused. He is said to have responded, "I can't spare this man [Grant]; he fights!"

As Grant's forces were working to secure the upper Mississippi, Union naval forces under Commander **David Farragut** were trying to seize control of New Orleans. The city was protected by two well-armed

Confederate Memorial Hall New Orleans, Louisiana

Confederate and Union soldiers launched these three- to five-pound hand grenades like darts into enemy territory during the battles at Vicksburg and Petersburg, among others. New Yorker William Ketchum designed and patented this particular grenade. On impact, metal parts inside the grenade would grind against each other, causing a spark that would ignite gunpowder.

forts as well as a river blocked with thick cables. On April 24, Farragut and his fleet of 43 ships attacked the city, breaching the cables and sailing right up to the New Orleans docks. On April 25, Confederate leaders ordered more than 3,000 southern soldiers to evacuate New Orleans. Union ground troops soon arrived to occupy the city while Farragut's fleet continued up the Mississippi River, capturing Baton Rouge, Natchez, and Memphis. However, they were unable to dislodge the Confederate forces holding Vicksburg, Mississippi.

FIGHTING TO A STALEMATE

Throughout the war so far, Washington, D.C., remained a target for the Confederates. Lincoln and McClellan feared the capital faced a direct threat from Confederate troops stationed in the Shenandoah Valley under the command of Stonewall Jackson. For three months in the spring of 1862, Jackson led his men up and down the valley, creating the impression that his forces were larger than they were. As a result, the Union divided its troops, and McClellan cancelled his plans for an overland assault on Richmond, which would have required his army to march through the Shenandoah Valley. Instead, McClellan set sail from Washington, D.C., with around 100,000 soldiers, landing on the Virginia Peninsula and battling to within a few miles of Richmond. There, rather than pushing forward, McClellan decided to pull his men back because he feared they might be outnumbered when they reached the Confederate capital.

Meanwhile, in early June, Robert E. Lee replaced the wounded Joseph Johnston as commander of the Army of Northern Virginia, the largest field army of the Confederacy. Lee then ordered an attack against McClellan's larger force. He sent out cavalry leader

The Civil War **401**

PLAN: 4-PAGE LESSON

OBJECTIVE

Analyze how the battles of Shiloh, Antietam, and Fredericksburg affected the course of the war.

CRITICAL THINKING SKILLS FOR LESSON 2.2

- Form and Support Opinions
- Make Inferences
- Identify Main Ideas and Details
- Compare and Contrast
- Draw Conclusions
- Interpret Maps
- Identify
- Analyze Language Use

HISTORICAL THINKING FOR CHAPTER 12

How did the Civil War change the way different groups of Americans viewed themselves and the nation? In 1862, the two armies engaged in some of the heaviest fighting of the war. Lesson 2.2 examines how three of these battles affected the nation.

BACKGROUND FOR THE TEACHER

The effort to preserve Civil War battlefields, where so many lives were lost, has been an ongoing struggle. In 1993, the Civil War Sites Advisory Commission studied more than 380 major battlefields—including Shiloh, Antietam, and Fredericksburg—to determine their condition and to suggest steps for preservation. The resulting report led to some restoration projects. In 2012, the commission issued an updated report that evaluated the level of progress and noted new areas of concern. Among the 3.7 million acres of land and water included in the original study, only 54 percent of the sites retained enough battlefield features in 2012 to warrant preservation. For individual battlefields, 31 had more than half of their land permanently preserved, 227 had less than half of their land preserved, 65 did not have any protection, and the remaining sites had either been destroyed by development or could no longer be located.

INTRODUCE & ENGAGE

CONSIDER THE POWER OF AN IMAGE

Ask students to consider how modern news coverage and the wide distribution of phones with camera and video capabilities have influenced our views about how war impacts civilians and soldiers. List students' ideas on the board and briefly discuss the implications of these technologies. Explain to students that the gruesome images of the dead produced by Civil War photographers after the Battle of Antietam had a profound effect on citizens who were far from the battlefields. Tell students that Lesson 2.2 describes some of the bloodiest battles of the war.

TEACH

GUIDED DISCUSSION

1. **Compare and Contrast** How did General George McClellan and General Ulysses S. Grant differ in their battle strategies? *(Possible response: McClellan was cautious and reluctant to engage the enemy, such as choosing not to march through the Shenandoah Valley for fear that Confederate forces outnumbered his troops. Grant, on the other hand, actively sought out and fought the enemy, such as pushing his soldiers through to Corinth, Mississippi, battling Confederate troops along the way.)*

2. **Draw Conclusions** Why might the Battle of Shiloh be considered only a partial victory for the Union, even though General Grant won? *(Possible response: Grant's forces were so exhausted by the fighting that they could not pursue the retreating Confederates, allowing them to escape. Also, the loss of life was so great that people urged Lincoln to replace Grant, which showed they didn't have faith in Grant's abilities.)*

3. **Interpret Maps** How does the map help you understand why the failure to capture Vicksburg in 1862 was a problem for the Union? *(Possible response: Commander Farragut and his forces were able to capture New Orleans, Baton Rouge, Natchez, and Memphis, but without Vicksburg, the Union couldn't take complete control of the Mississippi River.)*

VIRTUAL MUSEUM VISIT

Confederate Memorial Hall Museum, the oldest museum in Louisiana, opened on January 8, 1891, with the goal of commemorating southern heritage. The museum was built through the efforts of the Louisiana Historical Association and philanthropist Frank Howard, the first president of the association. The museum contains one of the largest collections of Confederate artifacts in the United States. The online collection displays flags, personal items, weapons, uniforms, and special exhibits. Prompt students to visit the museum's website, select artifacts that interest them, and conduct additional research on one or two of the artifacts they have chosen. Then invite volunteers to share their findings with the class and explain how the artifacts helped them better understand the war.

DIFFERENTIATE

INCLUSION

Understand a Map Pair students with a partner who can assist them in understanding the information presented in the map Civil War Battles, 1861–1865. First, instruct pairs to read each line in the legend and trace the corresponding colored areas of the map and sites of Union and Confederate victories. Make sure students understand that the inset is an enlarged map showing battles near Washington, D.C., and the Confederate capital of Richmond, Virginia. As they read the lesson, encourage students to use the map to trace troop movements and battles—for example, McClellan's route from Washington, D.C., to the Virginia peninsula and Farragut's fleet movements from New Orleans northward up the Mississippi.

PRE-AP

Report on the Impacts of Shiloh Direct students to conduct research about the various impacts of the Battle of Shiloh. Tell them to consider such effects as the number of Union and Confederate dead and wounded, the amount of artillery used, and how long the battle lasted, as well as its impact on civilians and politicians who witnessed or learned of the horrific cost. Encourage students to keep track of their research in a graphic organizer such as the one below. Invite them to share their findings in an oral or written report.

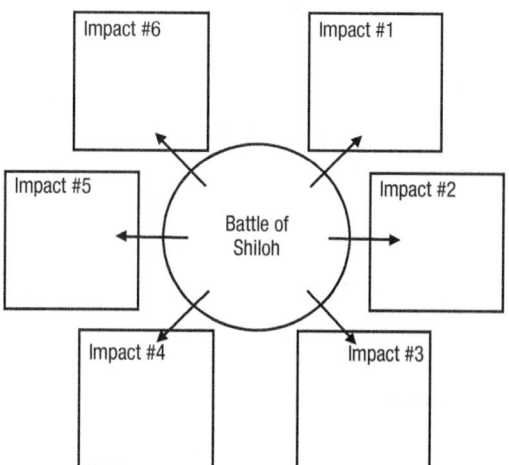

See the Chapter Planner for more strategies for differentiation.

J.E.B. Stuart, whose soldiers rode all the way around McClellan's troops, scoping out their position and stealing their supplies. Lee soon brought in Jackson and his men to join the effort. The series of clashes that followed are called the **Seven Days' Battles** because they took place over seven days, between June 25 and July 1. The Confederates managed to protect Richmond and drive the Union troops back down the Virginia Peninsula, but they sustained heavy losses.

By July 1862, the war seemed to have reached a stalemate, with neither side gaining the upper hand. McClellan's hesitant performance in the Seven Days' Battles weakened Lincoln's already waning confidence in his leadership. Lincoln placed Major General Henry Halleck, who advocated a more aggressive stance, in charge of all the Union forces. McClellan remained a commander working under Halleck's command.

ANTIETAM

To better protect Washington, Lincoln and Halleck decided to remove McClellan from the Virginia Peninsula and consolidate his troops with others from the Shenandoah Valley. This unit would be under the joint command of McClellan and General John Pope. As McClellan's forces began to retreat from the peninsula in August, the Confederates saw a window of opportunity for an offensive attack. Lee decided to strike Pope's troops near Bull Run, before McClellan's group could join them. After defeating the Union at the Second Battle of Bull Run, Lee decided to continue his offensive and push into Maryland. But as McClellan's men were on the move, one soldier made a fortuitous discovery. He

stumbled upon a packet of cigars in a field, dropped by a careless Confederate officer. Wrapped around the cigars were Lee's detailed plans for his attack on Maryland. The plans revealed that Lee had split his forces into two groups marching several miles apart. If McClellan moved quickly, he could ambush Lee's army before the two groups could meet up again. But once again, McClellan took action too late.

On September 17, Lee and McClellan met in battle once more, this time at Antietam (an-TEE-tuhm) Creek, near Sharpsburg, Maryland. The Confederates had only 35,000 men to McClellan's 72,000, but Lee's forces held their ground. The terrible **Battle of Antietam** ended in confusion and stalemate. More men were killed, wounded, or declared missing on this day than on any other single day during the war. Lee lost nearly a quarter of his army. Despite the massive Confederate casualties and the weakened state of Lee's troops, McClellan held back, allowing them to retreat.

Charles Carleton Coffin, a journalist who was present at Antietam, reported a chilling description of the battle in the magazine *The Century Illustrated*: "It was no longer alone the boom of the batteries, but a rattle of musketry—at first like pattering drops upon a roof; then a roll, crash, roar, and rush, like a mighty ocean billow upon the shore, chafing the pebbles, wave on wave, with deep and heavy explosions of the batteries, like the crashing of the thunderbolts."

Neither side was satisfied with the battle's outcome. The Confederate offensive had failed, but McClellan, despite his numerical advantage, had been unable to win a decisive victory. Many historians have argued that if McClellan had continued to attack Lee's

After the Battle of Antietam in 1862, photographer Alexander Gardner documented a few of the thousands of soldiers who lost their lives.

forces, the war might have been over at this point. Lincoln complained, "If General McClellan does not want to use the army, I would like to borrow it for a time." The president named Ambrose E. Burnside as the new commander of Union forces working under Major General Halleck.

Despite Lincoln's dissatisfaction with the outcome at Antietam, the Union won an important political and economic advantage. Seeing the South thwarted in such an important battle, the European powers decided to withhold their support from the Confederacy for the time being.

FREDERICKSBURG

In November, Burnside planned another assault on Richmond. Hoping to fool Lee by taking an unusual route, he decided to cross the Rappahannock River at Falmouth, near Fredericksburg, Virginia, then follow the railroad lines to Richmond. Burnside's engineers needed hollow metal cylinders called **pontoons**, to build floating bridges over the river, but these did not arrive until two weeks after Burnside reached the Rappahannock. Two Confederate units arrived at Fredericksburg and took potshots at Burnside's men as they worked on the bridges.

Meanwhile, Lee positioned his troops and artillery high in the hills above Fredericksburg. When the Union soldiers finally crossed the Rappahannock, they had to march through a valley where the Confederate troops perched above could easily

pick them off. "A chicken could not live on that field when we open on it," declared one Confederate at Fredericksburg. With southerners able to fire down on them at will from protected positions, more than 12,000 Union soldiers were killed, wounded, or declared missing during the three-day **Battle of Fredericksburg**. Burnside was eventually forced to retreat across the river. Watching the attack, Lee noted, "It is well that war is so terrible. We should grow too fond of it."

At battle's end, both armies found themselves where they had been at the battle's beginning. The North fell into mourning, humiliation, and anger at this sacrifice. By the winter of 1862–1863, many men had died for little apparent purpose and with no end in sight to the increasingly bloody war.

HISTORICAL THINKING

1. **READING CHECK** Why was Corinth, Mississippi, an important objective for the Union Army?

2. **FORM AND SUPPORT OPINIONS** Was the battle of Antietam a greater loss for the Union or the Confederacy? Explain your answer.

3. **MAKE INFERENCES** Why were the Confederates successful in fighting the Union Army to a stalemate in the East?

4. **IDENTIFY MAIN IDEAS AND DETAILS** Why did McClellan attack Richmond from the Virginia Peninsula?

CRITICAL VIEWING In December 1862, army engineers built floating bridges for Union troops to cross a river near Fredericksburg, Virginia. What materials were needed to construct them?

BUILD BACKGROUND

THE BATTLE OF ANTIETAM

The Battle of Antietam began at dawn as thousands of Union soldiers crept through a cornfield to attack Confederate lines. The battle raged throughout the morning, with the cornfield changing hands at least six times as one side or the other drove the enemy back. By the time this part of the battle ended, there were nearly 8,000 casualties. To the southwest, both sides fought along Sunken Road, worn some five feet below ground level by wagon traffic. The road provided cover for more than 2,000 Confederate troops. Union forces attacked around 9:30 A.M. By midday, they had captured the road but were soon driven back, leaving more than 5,000 Confederate and Union soldiers dead or wounded. Farther south, the Union's effort to take a bridge over Antietam Creek and scale a Confederate-held bluff added to the day's carnage, which climbed to some 23,000 casualties from both sides.

PONTOON BRIDGES

The engineers who built pontoon bridges during the Civil War worked in crews, each assigned specific tasks. The abutment crew built the land approach to the bridge by using stakes to anchor a pontoon close to shore and securing long beams from the shore to the pontoon. The next crew leveled the approach by adding or taking away dirt or, in marshy areas, by using logs. At the same time, the boat crews began moving the pontoons into place in the water and anchoring them. As the pontoons were anchored into place, the balk crew laid long, heavy beams called balks from the abutment to the center of the first pontoon and then from pontoon center to pontoon center until the bridge reached the other shore. Lashers used rope to lash the pontoons together. The chess crew followed, laying wide planks called chesses across the bridge, which the side-rail crew secured in place by adding heavy side rails.

TEACH

GUIDED DISCUSSION

4. **Identify** What factors allowed the Civil War stalemate to continue in 1862? *(Possible response: Neither side was able to gain a decisive victory. Also, General McClellan's slowness to commit troops and his reluctance to pursue the enemy made it difficult to break the stalemate. He failed to attack General Robert E. Lee when Lee was weakened and allowed Lee and his soldiers to escape.)*

5. **Analyze Language Use** What did General Lee mean when he said, "It is well that war is so terrible. We should grow too fond of it"? *(Possible response: Lee probably meant that war can be seen as glorious or heroic, as when Confederate troops forced General Ambrose E. Burnside to retreat. This could lead to a fascination with war, but the horror of dead and wounded soldiers balances those views with harsh reality.)*

MORE INFORMATION

Photographer Alexander Gardner Direct students' attention to the photograph of the dead soldiers taken by Alexander Gardner. Explain that photography equipment used during the Civil War could not capture motion or scenes in low light. To depict the horror of war, Gardner decided to photograph dead soldiers where they fell on the battlefield in full daylight. He was the first photographer to do so. **ASK:** What impact do you think photos like this one had on people's perception of the war? *(Answers will vary. Possible response: Such photos likely brought home the realities and horrors of the war in ways that even vivid news stories could not.)*

ACTIVE OPTIONS

On Your Feet: Use a Jigsaw Strategy Organize students into "expert" groups and assign each group one or two of the generals discussed in the lesson, focusing on their leadership style and battle tactics. Regroup students so that each new group has at least one member from each expert group. Ask the new groups to compare and contrast the generals they studied. At the end, invite one student from each group to summarize the main differences and similarities among the generals.

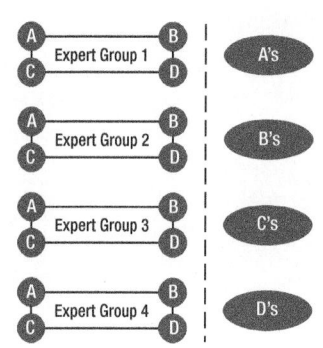

NG Learning Framework: Commemorate a Battle

SKILL Communication

KNOWLEDGE Our Human Story

Arrange students in groups and ask each group to choose a battle from the map of Civil War battles and then research it to create a commemorative exhibit. Instruct groups to use maps, photographs, time lines, or other visuals to create an appropriate display. Then direct students to write a brief summary describing the battle and honoring those who participated. When groups have finished, invite them to share their exhibit with the class.

HISTORICAL THINKING

ANSWERS

1. Corinth was a major railroad center, so capturing it would enable the Union to control the rail lines and, therefore, most of the western Confederacy.

2. Answers will vary. Possible responses: Antietam was a greater loss for the Confederacy. The Confederates couldn't afford the casualties they suffered there, and the battle convinced European powers to hold off supporting the South. Antietam was a greater loss for the Union. Even though Union troops stopped the Confederate advance, McClellan allowed Lee to escape, which prolonged the war.

3. Although the Confederates had a smaller army, they had better military leaders and used better strategies, such as when Stonewall Jackson fooled Union general McClellan into thinking he had a larger force, when J.E.B. Stuart scouted the Union's position and stole supplies, and when Lee placed his troops in the hills above Fredericksburg. In contrast, Union generals in the East often over- or underestimated their opponents, did not act quickly enough, or failed to pursue the Confederates when they were retreating.

4. McClellan thought Jackson's army was much larger than it actually was. As a result, McClellan decided to move his troops by water to the peninsula to avoid encounters with Jackson's forces.

CRITICAL VIEWING The text says that the pontoons supporting the bridges were hollow metal cylinders. It looks like the crews also needed ropes and wooden planks, posts, and rails to construct the bridges.

SHIFTING THE FOCUS TO SLAVERY

It was dusk on the evening of July 18, 1862. The men of an African-American regiment in the Union Army readied themselves to lead a dangerous charge against a heavily protected fort in South Carolina. Many in the North and the South doubted the fighting ability of African-American soldiers. Their commander told the men, "The eyes of thousands will look upon what you do tonight."

The 54th Massachusetts Infantry Regiment, led by Colonel Shaw, stormed the walls of Fort Wagner on July 18, 1863. For their bravery, soldiers wounded in the battle were each given a badge like the one above. The 1890 print shown here was made by Kurz and Allison, a printing company based in Chicago.

SLAVERY UNDER ATTACK

Although neither side was satisfied with the bloody outcome at Antietam, President Lincoln decided that it represented enough of a Union victory to justify tying the outcome of the war to the end of slavery. This would stir greater support for the war among northern abolitionists, and it might also discourage European powers that had banned slavery on their own soil from supporting the Confederacy. Even northerners who did not support abolition could see that slavery offered the South an economic advantage. Slaves provided a huge labor force at home while white males went off to fight for the Confederacy. Anything that undermined that system was good for the Union.

Up to this point, slavery in captured territories had presented a dilemma for advancing Union forces. Military leaders had to decide whether enslaved people should be treated as **contraband**—captured enemy property—or as free. When Union soldiers overran South Carolina's Sea Islands during the Battle of Port Royal in November 1861, most of the white residents fled, leaving behind 10,000 slaves and a wealth of cotton fields. Rather than treat the enslaved people as contraband, Union leaders put the **Port Royal Experiment** in place, treating the former slaves as free. Most of these **freedmen** continued to work in the islands' cotton fields, but now they received wages. In January 1862, a Union general put in a request for teachers to help educate the freedmen. Soon after, the federal government expanded this call into a formal effort to not only educate the freedmen, but also to build hospitals for them and help them gain ownership of lands from the plantations they had once worked as slaves.

Some northerners saw the Port Royal Experiment as a model for what could be done throughout the South. In the spring of 1862, abolitionist and Union general David Hunter declared slavery abolished in South Carolina, Georgia, and Florida. President Lincoln immediately revoked Hunter's proclamation. In the months before Antietam, he was not yet prepared to end slavery where it existed.

Some legislators sided with General Hunter. **Radical Republicans**, or abolitionist members of Congress who supported African-American rights, wanted to make abolition a condition for ending the war. Many northern Democrats who were sympathetic to the South, called **Copperheads**, opposed this position, believing it would spur the Confederates to fight harder. They wanted slavery to remain in place so that the South would return to the Union, and they were hostile to ideas of racial equality. In the first year of the war, Lincoln tried to steer a course between the Radical Republicans and the Copperheads.

PRIMARY SOURCE

That on the first day of January . . . all persons held as slaves within any State or designated part of a State, the people whereof shall then be in rebellion against the United States, shall be then, thenceforward, and forever free; and the Executive Government of the United States, including the military and naval authority thereof, will recognize and maintain the freedom of such persons, and will do no act or acts to repress such persons, or any of them, in any efforts they may make for their actual freedom.

—from Abraham Lincoln's Emancipation Proclamation, 1863

THE EMANCIPATION PROCLAMATION

By the end of 1862, Lincoln was shifting course. The loss of life had made many northerners question whether keeping the Union together was worth the cost. Lincoln needed a moral cause to rally the Union.

In the wake of Antietam, Lincoln issued the **Emancipation Proclamation**, which decreed all slaves in states that were still in rebellion against the United States were "thenceforward, and forever free." The official document took effect on January 1, 1863, and was denounced throughout the South and in much of the North as well. The proclamation did not free any of the enslaved people in the border states, for fear that those states would shift their loyalty to the Confederacy. And, of course, slaveholders in the Confederacy did not consider themselves bound by U.S. law, so the proclamation did not affect them. However, the decree ruled out any compromise that would bring the Confederate states back into the Union with slavery intact. Slavery had been the central cause of the war, and now Lincoln proclaimed that a Union victory would end it.

AFRICAN-AMERICAN SOLDIERS

Although northern civilian and military leaders remained deeply divided over abolition, many began to realize that African Americans could be of great value to the Union. Very quickly after Lincoln announced the Emancipation Proclamation, Union leaders began to enlist African-American troops. In May 1863, two African-American regiments stormed a fortified Confederate installation at Port Hudson, Louisiana. That same month, the War Department founded the **Bureau of Colored Troops** and began a wide-scale effort to recruit African-American soldiers.

In February 1863, the governor of Massachusetts issued the first formal call for African Americans to enlist in the **54th Massachusetts Infantry Regiment**, led by white colonel **Robert Gould Shaw**. In two weeks, more than 1,000 African Americans had enlisted, including Charles and Lewis Douglass, two of Frederick Douglass's sons. In July 1863, the unit lost Shaw and nearly half of its 600-man attack force when the regiment stormed **Fort Wagner**, which guarded the port of Charleston, South Carolina. Greatly outnumbered and forced into hand-to-hand combat, the regiment lost the battle, but the valor of the 54th inspired many more African Americans to enlist and fight for the Union.

HISTORICAL THINKING

1. **READING CHECK** Who were the Radical Republicans?

2. **DISTINGUISH FACT FROM OPINION** Does the statement "The Emancipation Proclamation ended slavery in the United States" represent a fact or an opinion? Explain your response, based on evidence from the text.

3. **MAKE INFERENCES** Why do you think so many African Americans enlisted to fight for the Union after the Emancipation Proclamation was issued?

OBJECTIVE

Explain why Abraham Lincoln issued the Emancipation Proclamation and describe its effect.

CRITICAL THINKING SKILLS FOR LESSON 3.1

- Distinguish Fact from Opinion
- Make Inferences
- Identify Problems and Solutions
- Analyze Language Use

HISTORICAL THINKING FOR CHAPTER 12

How did the Civil War change the way different groups of Americans viewed themselves and the nation? The Emancipation Proclamation encouraged Americans to view the Civil War as a moral fight to end slavery. Lesson 3.1 focuses on why President Lincoln issued the Emancipation Proclamation and how the proclamation influenced the war effort.

BACKGROUND FOR THE TEACHER

Abraham Lincoln first informed the Cabinet of his intention to issue the Emancipation Proclamation on July 22, 1862. Secretary of State William Seward argued that Lincoln should wait until after a Union victory so that the proclamation would not look like the act of a desperate administration. Lincoln heeded Seward's advice, waiting until after Antietam to issue a preliminary Emancipation Proclamation on September 22. The preliminary proclamation served as a warning to the Confederacy to stop its rebellion or face the end of slavery. When no Confederate states responded, Lincoln made some edits to the document and signed the final proclamation on January 1, 1863. The differences between the two versions reflected Lincoln's changing views. In order to frame the Emancipation Proclamation as a war measure, Lincoln applied emancipation only to those southern states still in rebellion. Nevertheless, the proclamation helped pave the way for full emancipation by making slavery the focus of the war.

INTRODUCE & ENGAGE

DISCUSS THE VALUE OF PURPOSE

Remind students that Thomas Jefferson used the Declaration of Independence to outline colonial grievances against Great Britain and to justify declaring independence. Discuss the value of Jefferson's purpose with the class. **ASK:** What are the benefits for a leader to publicly state the purpose of a military or political action? *(Answers will vary. Possible responses: If people understand the purpose of a painful action, they are more likely to support it. Having a common purpose unifies people. Appealing to people's emotions and passions encourages them to fight harder or contribute more.)* Tell students that in Lesson 3.1 they will learn about how President Lincoln used the Emancipation Proclamation to define a greater moral purpose for the Civil War in an effort to defeat the Confederacy.

TEACH

GUIDED DISCUSSION

1. **Identify Problems and Solutions** What political problems did the Port Royal Experiment present for Lincoln? *(Possible response: At this point in the war, Lincoln tried to hold a neutral position between Radical Republicans, who favored General Hunter's proclamation abolishing slavery in South Carolina, and Copperheads, who opposed it. If Lincoln accepted Hunter's proclamation, it would clearly indicate his support for abolition.)*

2. **Make Inferences** Why might northerners opposed to abolition still support enlisting African-American troops? *(Possible response: African-American troops provided additional manpower dedicated to the Union cause. As northerners realized that the war would not end quickly, the additional troops were an advantage.)*

ANALYZE LANGUAGE USE

Direct students' attention to the Primary Source feature. **ASK:** What point do you think Lincoln was trying to make when he stated that all slaves in rebel states "shall be then, thenceforward, and forever free"? *(Answers will vary. Possible response: Lincoln was making the point that the weight of the federal government was firmly behind enslaved workers in the Confederate states and would not allow them to escape slavery in one state only to be captured and enslaved again in another.)*

ACTIVE OPTIONS

On Your Feet: Inside-Outside Circle Arrange students in concentric circles facing each other. Tell students in the outside circle to pose questions about the goals and consequences of the Emancipation Proclamation, such as: Why didn't the Emancipation Proclamation free all slaves? Ask students in the inner circle to answer their partner's question. On a signal, tell students to trade roles so that those in the inside circle ask questions and those in the outside circle answer the questions.

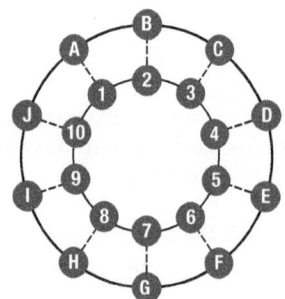

NG Learning Framework: Analyze a Speech

| ATTITUDE | Empowerment |
| KNOWLEDGE | Our Human Story |

Prompt students to explore the enduring significance of the Emancipation Proclamation by working in groups to analyze the speech Dr. Martin Luther King, Jr., gave on September 12, 1962, commemorating the centennial of the proclamation. Direct students to research the speech and summarize King's major points. Then lead a class discussion about which of King's points they found most compelling.

DIFFERENTIATE

INCLUSION

Use Supported Reading Assign pairs of students selected paragraphs to read aloud together. At the end of each paragraph, ask them to use the following sentence frames to identify what they do and do not understand:

• This paragraph is about _____.

• One fact that stood out to me was _____.

• I had trouble understanding _____, so I tried to figure it out by _____.

Be sure all students understand the content before moving on to the next paragraph.

GIFTED & TALENTED

Create a Museum Exhibit Direct students to use information from the text and their own research to design and prepare a museum exhibit about the experiences of African-American soldiers in the Civil War. Suggest that students look for letters, photographs, reports, artifacts, and other primary and secondary source materials. Prompt them to address bias and prejudice in reports and historical interpretations of African-American soldiers. Invite students to display their exhibit in the classroom.

See the Chapter Planner for more strategies for differentiation.

HISTORICAL THINKING

ANSWERS

1. The Radical Republicans were the abolitionist members of Congress who wanted to link ending the war to ending slavery.

2. Since the Emancipation Proclamation did not address slavery in the border states, which had not seceded from the Union, it is not factual to say that it ended slavery in the United States. The Emancipation Proclamation only applied to Confederate states still in rebellion. In addition, the proclamation could only end slavery in the Confederate states if the Union won the war. The statement is an opinion based on what Lincoln said would happen if the Union won.

3. Possible response: The Emancipation Proclamation opened the way for African-American men to serve in the Union military. Many African Americans seized that opportunity so that they could take part in ending slavery.

CRITICAL VIEWING A soldier stands in the trenches of fortifications at Yorktown, Virginia, in May 1862. Based on the photograph, what do you believe were the advantages of living and fighting in the trenches?

DISCONTENT IN THE NORTH AND THE SOUTH

Few places reflected the human cost of war more than military hospitals. As one witness recalled, "The surgeon snatched his knife . . . wiped it rapidly once or twice across his bloodstained apron, and the cutting began. The operation accomplished, the surgeon would look around with a deep sigh, and then—'Next!'"

SOLDIERS AND THE MEANING OF WAR

As the war dragged on, both sides used new technologies to gain an edge over the enemy. In addition to advances in maritime technology, such as the ironclad, each side made improvements in land transportation and communication. The Union, which already held an advantage in terms of the railroad and telegraph lines it controlled at the beginning of the conflict, greatly expanded these networks. Telegraph lines could be rapidly extended in the wake of troops on the march, permitting nearly instant communication even from the battlefield. Both the North and the South also experimented with using hot-air balloons to spy on enemy lines from above.

Some of the most significant technological advances involved the weapons and equipment carried by everyday soldiers. The development of the Minié ball, a cone-shaped bullet, made rifles more accurate and easier to load. By 1863, Union soldiers were using repeating rifles, which allowed them to shoot more than one bullet without reloading. The fastest of these could fire off 7 rounds in less than 30 seconds. Due to its industrial advantage, the Union was better able to equip its troops with

these newer rifles, while the South lagged behind. Both sides were using rifles with grooved barrels, an invention that became commonplace in the 1850s. The grooves caused bullets to spin, making them much more accurate at longer ranges than the bullets fired from the smooth-barreled muskets used in the American Revolution.

To counter the increasingly efficient rifles and larger cannons, Civil War soldiers resorted to **trench warfare**. Opposing armies dug ditches, or trenches, roughly parallel to each other. The trenches provided each army with both a vantage point from which to fire at the enemy and a place to shelter from incoming fire.

Improved weaponry added to higher casualty rates on the battlefield. In addition, poor hygiene in military camps and hospitals led to high rates of infection and disease. Doctors did not understand the role germs play in spreading infections, so they did not employ practices that are considered basic today, such as hand-washing. A Civil War soldier was actually more likely to die from illness than from battle wounds. In some ways, those killed quickly in battle faced an easier end than the majority of those who died slowly from infected wounds. Often the only way to treat infection in an arm, leg, or foot was to amputate. Thousands of wounded who survived the war returned home missing parts of their bodies.

Despite the miserable conditions in the camps, which also included poor food and long, lonely hours, soldiers found ways to keep their spirits up. They sang songs, played games, and gambled. Many spent long hours writing letters home and savored any letters from loved ones that reached them at the front.

CHALLENGES IN THE CONFEDERACY

Although many of the battles of the spring of 1862 had been close, with high casualties on both sides, the outcomes generally favored northern goals. As the war dragged on and the body count grew, Confederate leaders had a hard time keeping experienced troops in the field. Many of those who had enthusiastically volunteered for service had expected the fighting would be over quickly. They were not prepared to spend years in fear and misery far away from their homes and families. When the first year-long enlistments in the Confederate Army ran out in April 1862, many soldiers opted to return home rather than re-enlist.

The Confederate Congress, fearful that its army would be short of men as the Union stepped up its attacks, decided that it had no choice but to enact **conscription**, issuing an order that forced men into military service. Conscription is also known as the **draft**. All white men between the ages of 18 and 35 were required to serve in the Confederate military for three years. However, the order exempted

PRIMARY SOURCE

Surgeons and nurses who staffed the hospitals of the Civil War wrote letters describing the horror of combat and the hardships their patients suffered.

The days after the battle are a thousand times worse than the day of the battle—and the physical pain is not the greatest pain suffered. How awful it is. . . . The dead appear sickening but they suffer no pain. But the poor wounded mutilated soldiers that yet have life and sensation make a most horrid picture. I pray God may stop such infernal work—though perhaps he has sent it upon us for our sins. Great indeed must have been our sins if such is our punishment.

—from a letter written by Dr. William Child, Union Army surgeon, 1862

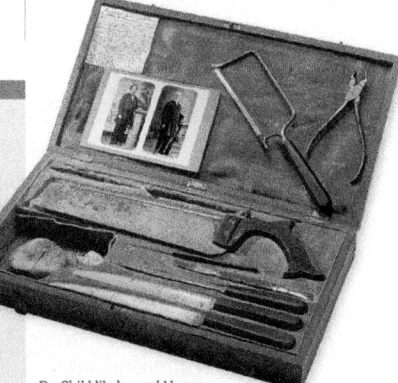

Dr. Child likely would have used a medical kit such as this one. Saws, knives, and scalpels were a military doctor's most useful tools during the Civil War.

OBJECTIVE

Analyze the effects of improved weapons on Civil War soldiers and reactions to the military draft in the North and South.

CRITICAL THINKING SKILLS FOR LESSON 3.2

- Analyze Cause and Effect
- Compare and Contrast
- Make Predictions
- Identify
- Make Inferences
- Analyze Primary Sources
- Evaluate
- Form and Support Opinions
- Summarize

HISTORICAL THINKING FOR CHAPTER 12

How did the Civil War change the way different groups of Americans viewed themselves and the nation? Poorer citizens in the North and the South resented mandatory service and draft exemptions. Lesson 3.2 examines improved weapons and reactions to the draft.

BACKGROUND FOR THE TEACHER

Both sides in the Civil War used trenches throughout the war. Early on, troops dug a trench in preparation for battle or after a battle to provide cover for shocked and weary soldiers. However, trenches became more elaborate in later years. Digging in was particularly important when troops faced off against each other over extended periods of time, such as at Petersburg, Virginia, in 1864. Over the months, the trenches at Petersburg stretched across some 35 miles, crossing railroad lines, roads, and rivers. In addition to deep trenches, both sides positioned obstructions to delay attacks and planted mines to guard against enemy approaches from underground. The trenches helped repel attacks and placed the two sides within striking distance of each other while still providing cover from artillery fire.

HISTORY NOTEBOOK

Encourage students to complete the Reid on the Road video series page for Chapter 12 in their History Notebooks after they view the video.

INTRODUCE & ENGAGE

CONSIDER DRAFT OPTIONS

Pose this situation to students: There is a war, and every able-bodied man and woman between 20 and 35 years of age must serve in the military. However, people are able to pay a fee equal to half the average worker's annual income to avoid service. Ask students to consider the advantages and disadvantages of this arrangement, and use a T-Chart like the one shown to record their ideas. Revisit the chart after reading the lesson and guide students to compare their ideas with the consequences they read about in the lesson.

Advantages	Disadvantages

TEACH

GUIDED DISCUSSION

1. **Identify** What communication advantage did the North have over the South, and why was it important? *(Possible response: The North had control of more telegraph lines and could extend them as soldiers took control of new areas. This made it easier to communicate from the battlefield.)*

2. **Make Inferences** Why do you think medical technology might not have advanced as fast as military technology did during the Civil War? *(Possible response: Government resources were focused on the war instead of on medical research. The advances in weapon technologies were new, and medical professionals had not previously encountered the types of injuries those technologies caused.)*

3. **Analyze Primary Sources** How does information in the lesson support the view of the war that Dr. William Child presents in the Primary Source feature? *(Possible response: Child believes that the aftermath of the battle is much worse than the battle itself because, unlike those who died during the fighting, the injured soldiers suffer great pain and mutilation. The lesson points out that wounded soldiers often died slowly from infected wounds, and many survivors returned home missing body parts.)*

MORE INFORMATION

Minié Balls Explain to students that the Minié ball bullet was named for its inventor, French army officer Claude-Étienne Minié. Unlike earlier balls, which were the same size as the rifle barrel and thus had to be jammed into the barrel, the Minié ball was small enough to be dropped in. When the powder ignited, the ball expanded so that it engaged the firing mechanism. Minié balls caused the vast majority of injuries treated by Civil War surgeons. The bullet's conical shape flattened out when it struck a person, greatly damaging tissue and bone and carrying cloth, skin, and dirt into the wound, which led to infections. Minié balls often resulted in amputations. **ASK:** Why did surgeons perform so many amputations rather than try to save limbs? *(Possible responses: The tissue damage was too severe to repair with Civil War medical technology, and doctors did not have an effective way to treat infections. It was faster and safer to amputate than to attempt complicated surgery under field conditions.)*

DIFFERENTIATE

STRIVING READERS

Use a Sorting Activity Write the following terms and phrases on the board:

> trench warfare
> conscription
> exemption
> repeating rifles
> lynched
> casualty rates
> maritime technology
> working class
> ironclad
> re-enlist
> "a rich man's war and a poor man's fight"
> New York City draft riots
> scapegoats
> Irish immigrants
> draft

Instruct pairs to work together to sort the terms and phrases into groups. Then challenge students to write a paragraph that shows how each set of terms is related.

PRE-AP

Analyze a Primary Source Direct students to access letters and diary entries written by soldiers during the Civil War, which can be found in many online archives. Instruct them to choose one diary entry or letter, ideally from someone who lived in their state or region, to analyze in detail. Tell students to focus their written analysis on the soldier's motivation for writing, the main idea and purpose, and the most compelling or revealing details. Invite students to share their analyses with the class.

See the Chapter Planner for more strategies for differentiation.

CRITICAL VIEWING The trenches would have provided cover from enemy fire, and supplies could be stored there to be ready when needed.

one white man on plantations with 20 or more slaves, a provision known as the "twenty negro law." This loophole divided southerners by class, since those with few or no slaves could not escape the draft. Many resented this **exemption**, or release from the obligation to serve. They claimed the Confederacy was simply using poor white southerners to benefit the interests of wealthy planters. Some derided it as "a rich's man's war and a poor man's fight."

Class conflict also broke out in the streets of the Confederate capital in the spring of 1863. Convinced that greedy merchants were holding supplies of flour until shortages and inflation drove prices even higher, a crowd of poor women in Richmond broke open merchants' stores and took what they needed. The **Richmond Bread Riot** subsided after authorities threatened violence and arrests, in addition to promising free supplies, but similar events occurred in several other southern cities.

The rioters were not the only ones who took what they needed. That same spring, the Confederate government passed several laws, including the Impressment Act, that allowed it to **confiscate**, or seize and hold, crops and other supplies from citizens. Volunteer efforts were not producing enough food, clothing, and other necessities to supply the Confederate Army. Some desperate soldiers had

already taken to stealing crops. Under the new laws, farmers were supposed to receive a fair price in exchange for their goods. Instead, many felt used, further fueling tensions within the South.

THE NORTHERN HOME FRONT

The war also made life difficult in the North. Prior to the Emancipation Proclamation, many northerners objected to the war and Lincoln's approach to it. Wealthy business owners were eager to re-establish trade with their former southern partners. Northerners whose families had come from the South wanted to renew connections that the war had broken. As a result of these feelings, Copperheads won significant victories in congressional elections in 1862.

Opponents of the war feared, for good reason, that the Union would establish a draft that would force men to fight for a cause they did not support. The Union was facing the same problem as the South—volunteer recruitment efforts could not keep up with the needs of the battlefield. Congress passed the Conscription Act in March 1863, instituting its first draft. Like the Confederate draft, the law allowed wealthy men to avoid service. If drafted, a man with enough money could hire a substitute to fight in his place, or he could pay a fee of $300 directly to the government.

After a battle at Savage Station, Virginia, in 1862, wounded Union soldiers wait for medical care. Confederates captured the hospital the day after this photograph was taken.

In the 2016 film *Free State of Jones*, Newton Knight, center, and fellow soldiers defend themselves against Confederate troops trying to put down their rebellion.

THE FREE STATE OF JONES

Southern class conflict manifested itself in unusual places and ways. Angered by what he believed to be unfair conscription laws, a white farmer in Mississippi named Newton Knight initiated a local guerrilla war against the Confederacy in October 1863. His "Jones County Scouts" eventually declared Jones County, Mississippi, to be the Free State of Jones, aligned with the Union. They even raised the American flag over the county courthouse. Knight and his supporters managed to elude Confederate capture for the remainder of the Civil War.

Poor and working-class northerners, especially those who lived in cities, opposed the draft. Emotions were particularly strong in areas with large communities of Irish immigrants. They had fled famine in Ireland only to face discrimination and difficulty finding jobs upon arriving in the United States. Few wanted to risk their lives to free slaves who might compete with them for jobs after the war ended.

Protest demonstrations broke out in several northern cities. The worst occurred in New York City. On July 13, 1863, a group of protesters destroyed a draft office, sparking the **New York City draft riots**. Violence escalated into four days of attacks on newspaper offices, businesses that supported the war effort, and African Americans. In fact, African Americans became **scapegoats**, or innocent people blamed for the mistakes or faults of others. In this case, some of the rioters blamed African Americans for the war and taking jobs away from white workers. During the uprising in New York, rioters destroyed homes owned by African Americans and **lynched**, or hanged, 11 African Americans. Many African-American families abandoned the city.

Local police were unable to calm the rioting. By July 16, some 4,000 Union troops, fresh off the battlefield of Gettysburg, were called to assist. When the smoke cleared, more than 100 people were dead and millions of dollars in property had been destroyed. Nearly 20 percent of the African-American

population left the city. Those that stayed either moved to neighborhoods with police stations close by or to the outskirts of the city where the danger of race rioting was lower.

The draft continued to be enforced, but with one important difference: Some New York men with families who had no other means of financial support were now eligible to receive exemptions.

HISTORICAL THINKING

1. **READING CHECK** How did both the Union and Confederacy respond to the lack of military volunteers?

2. **ANALYZE CAUSE AND EFFECT** How did new battlefield technology contribute to higher casualties?

3. **COMPARE AND CONTRAST** How were the uprisings in Richmond and New York City similar and different?

4. **MAKE PREDICTIONS** What simple advancement in medical science do you think was needed before army surgeons and nurses would be able to save a greater number of wounded soldiers?

BUILD BACKGROUND

THE RICHMOND BREAD RIOT

The Richmond Bread Riot was a desperate reaction to the severe conditions in Richmond, a city with a population that had tripled to more than 100,000 during the war. Inflation had driven up prices, and the effectiveness of the Union blockade, coupled with fewer crops being planted and the need to feed the Confederate troops, made food scarce. Adding to the problem, a spring snowstorm had melted, turning the roads to mud and making it difficult to get crops to the city. Frustrated and hungry, a group of women met at Belvidere Hill Baptist Church on April 1, 1863, to plan a strategy. They decided to protest at the governor's office to demand a remedy. The next day, a large crowd of women marched to Capitol Square, wielding axes and knives and shouting "Bread or Blood!" and gathering more people along the way. Refused by the governor, they broke into government warehouses, stores, and businesses, seizing food, clothing, and other necessities, as well as some jewelry and other luxury items.

THE NEW YORK CITY DRAFT RIOTS

Many among New York City's working class opposed the Emancipation Proclamation and the draft. Democratic Party newspapers and politicians, including New York governor Horatio Seymour, fanned this opposition by railing against the draft and warning the city's Irish and German immigrants that the Emancipation Proclamation would result in waves of African Americans coming to New York City to take their jobs. Opposition was particularly high among Irish immigrants, who already competed with African Americans for jobs. Like other laborers, the Irish had been hit hard by the economic downturn in the first year of the war and by rising prices as the war progressed. The mounting casualties among Irish units in the Union Army also discouraged and alarmed them. Word that 23,000 Union soldiers had been killed or injured or were missing at Gettysburg only heightened opposition to the draft.

TEACH

GUIDED DISCUSSION

4. **Evaluate** Why did some people argue that the Civil War was "a rich man's war and a poor man's fight"? *(Possible response: In the South, white men with more than 20 slaves were exempt from the draft, while those with few or no slaves were required to fight in a war to protect the interests of wealthy people on large plantations.)*

5. **Form and Support Opinions** Was the Confederate government justified in passing the Impressment Act? Use evidence from the text to support your opinion. *(Answers will vary. Possible responses: No. Civilians already suffered from food shortages, so confiscating crops and other supplies just made their lives more difficult. Yes. The crops and supplies were needed to feed and clothe soldiers fighting for the Confederacy. According to the new law, farmers were supposed to be paid for their goods, which is better than having them stolen.)*

SUMMARIZE

Focus students' attention on the subsection about the northern home front. **ASK:** How did issues of race, class, and economics contribute to the scapegoating of African Americans during the New York City draft riots? *(Possible response: Many poor and working-class northerners opposed the draft in part because they resented being forced to fight to end slavery. They worried that once slavery ended, freed African Americans would take their jobs. They unjustly blamed African Americans for the war and for threatening their economic future. In New York City, these fears boiled over into violence against African Americans.)*

ACTIVE OPTIONS

On Your Feet: Analyze the Effect of Civil War Weapons Organize students into groups. Ask each group to create a Cause-and-Effect Web about Civil War weapons, such as the one shown. Instruct group members to take turns writing the effects of different weapons in the outer boxes. Guide students to consider both the military advantages as well as negative repercussions. If a student cannot think of an effect, allow group members to help. Invite groups to share and compare their completed webs.

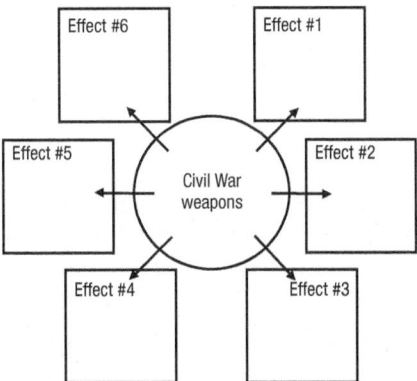

NG Learning Framework: Debate Draft Exemptions

ATTITUDE Responsibility

SKILL Communication

Organize the class into two groups to conduct additional research on the draft in the North and the South. Direct groups to use their research to debate this topic: Were the military service exemptions on both sides warranted, based on wartime conditions? Instruct one group to argue the affirmative and the other group the negative. Prompt groups to compile their arguments in written form in preparation for the debate and to support their claims with evidence from their research. When both sides have argued their cases, conduct a class discussion on which arguments were most compelling.

HISTORICAL THINKING

ANSWERS

1. As the number of volunteers dwindled and initial enlistments came to an end, both the Union and Confederacy instituted drafts.

2. Inventions like the Minié ball, which made rifles easier to load and more accurate, and repeating rifles, which allowed soldiers to shoot more rounds without reloading, resulted in greater numbers of dead and wounded on both sides.

3. Both riots were products of class conflict that resulted when poor citizens believed they were exploited by wealthier citizens. Poor women in Richmond rioted because they believed that greedy merchants withheld flour to drive up prices. Poor men who rioted in New York City were angry over being drafted to fight against slavery, especially when the rich could afford to take advantage of exemptions.

4. Answers will vary. Possible response: Medical science needed to understand the role of germs in spreading infection. If surgeons had understood germ theory, they would have cleaned their hands and surgical equipment and paid more attention to camp hygiene.

VICKSBURG AND CHANCELLORSVILLE

A good leader knows just what actions are necessary to get the desired results. General Grant knew that if his troops could capture Vicksburg, it would work in the Union's favor. In Virginia, Union forces were thinking the same thoughts about Richmond. But first they had to fight their way through Chancellorsville.

THE SIEGE OF VICKSBURG

As you have read, the Union gained control over much of the Mississippi River in the spring of 1862 when its forces captured New Orleans, Baton Rouge, Natchez, and Memphis. The Confederacy, however, still held a nearly 200-mile-long stretch of the river between **Vicksburg**, Mississippi, and Port Hudson, Louisiana. Vicksburg was the only remaining location in Mississippi where the Confederacy controlled railroad heads on both sides of the river.

Vicksburg's geography made it a formidable stronghold. The city sat atop high bluffs overlooking a hairpin bend in the river. Union ships attempting to sail around the bend had to make it past a multitude of Confederate cannons positioned along the cliffs' edges. From the start of the war, President Lincoln had considered Vicksburg one of the keys to a Union victory.

In May and June 1862, Union gunships shelled the city's defenses, but with little effect. Meanwhile, Union troops started digging a three-mile-long canal across the DeSoto Peninsula, a long finger of land surrounded by the river bend, hoping to change the course of the river to bypass Vicksburg entirely, rendering the city irrelevant. However, disease, heat exhaustion, and sunstroke claimed the lives of many of these soldiers, and the Union gave up working on the canal in July.

In December, General Ulysses S. Grant moved on Vicksburg once again. He ordered General William Tecumseh Sherman to lead an attack on the city in late December. Sherman's troops advanced on Vicksburg from the northeast, struggling across muddy bayous. At Chickasaw Bayou, Sherman's men

encountered Confederate forces waiting for them in strong defensive positions. Sherman was soon sounding the retreat.

Following this defeat, Grant decided to try again to build the canal and reroute the river. Day after day from January through March, soldiers as well as slaves from nearby plantations dug in the cold mud. Disease once again plagued the project, and so did clouds of mosquitoes, continuous rain, floodwater from the rising river, and shelling from Confederate **batteries**, or groups of artillery pieces.

In spring 1863, Grant finally gave up on the canal in favor of a bold new plan. He marched his 40,000 soldiers down the west side of the Mississippi to a point roughly 30 miles south of Vicksburg. From there, they crossed the river on barges and gunboats that Union admiral **David Porter** had managed to run south past Vicksburg under cover of night. The army marched northeast, capturing Jackson, Mississippi, the state's capital, and several other towns along the way. Then Grant's troops turned and battled their way westward to the eastern edge of Vicksburg. After two unsuccessful assaults on the well-entrenched Confederates, Grant blocked every road leading into the city, beginning the Siege of Vicksburg.

Over time, the situation became increasingly grim for the city's residents and its 31,000 defenders. To escape Union shelling, many people began living in caves dug into the hills. Supplies of ammunition, food, and water began to run perilously low. After 47 days, Confederate general John C. Pemberton surrendered the city to Grant on July 4, 1863. The Union soon controlled the entire Mississippi River, and the Confederacy was split in two. "The Father of the Waters again goes unvexed to the sea," said President Lincoln.

CRITICAL VIEWING During the siege of Vicksburg, the Shirley family, who owned the house shown in this 1863 photograph, was forced to live in an artificial cave, like the ones dug into the hillside. What sacrifices might be required of the people living in these caves?

THE BATTLE OF CHANCELLORSVILLE

Meanwhile, back in Virginia, Lincoln replaced General Burnside after the Union's disastrous defeat at Fredericksburg. General **Joseph Hooker** took command of the Army of the Potomac, the official name of the Union forces battling in Virginia. But no one was certain how "Fighting Joe" Hooker would fare against Robert E. Lee, who had yet to be decisively defeated despite the men, resources, and determination the Union had thrown against him.

As Grant's soldiers were landing south of Vicksburg, Hooker staged an attack on Lee's Army of Northern Virginia, which remained entrenched in the hills south of Fredericksburg. Hooker commanded 130,000 troops, but rather than trying to overwhelm Lee with numbers, Hooker intended to outsmart him. He planned to send a large Union force to sweep around Lee in a **flanking maneuver**, or a troop movement around the side of an enemy line in the hope of gaining an advantage. Some of the soldiers would attack the Confederates from behind as others attacked from the front, forcing Lee out of his strong defensive position. But Lee wasn't so easily fooled. He divided his troops and sent General Stonewall Jackson to circle around Hooker's men and attack, outflanking Hooker's own flanking maneuver.

On May 2, Jackson surprised and defeated Hooker's troops near a crossroad called **Chancellorsville**. Southern jubilation over the victory ended that very night, though, when nervous Confederate soldiers accidentally shot Stonewall Jackson as he returned from surveying the front lines.

The next day, Lee managed to contain another Union assault on Fredericksburg, forcing Hooker's troops to retreat. Lee had overcome Hooker's superior numbers, but his losses were staggering: 13,000 casualties, or roughly 22 percent of his men. The most significant loss was General Jackson, who died of his wound after the fighting ended.

HISTORICAL THINKING

1. **READING CHECK** Why was the Battle of Chancellorsville both a victory and a loss for General Lee?

2. **ANALYZE CAUSE AND EFFECT** What was the effect of Hooker's flanking maneuver around Lee's troops?

3. **MAKE INFERENCES** Why do you think Grant decided to put Vicksburg under siege?

4. **ANALYZE LANGUAGE USE** What do you think President Lincoln meant when he said "The Father of the Waters again goes unvexed to the sea"?

PLAN: 2-PAGE LESSON

OBJECTIVE

Explain how the capture of Vicksburg divided the Confederacy and changed the course of the Civil War.

CRITICAL THINKING SKILLS FOR LESSON 4.1

• Analyze Cause and Effect

• Make Inferences

• Analyze Language Use

• Evaluate

• Draw Conclusions

HISTORICAL THINKING FOR CHAPTER 12

How did the Civil War change the way different groups of Americans viewed themselves and the nation? Defeating the Confederacy proved more difficult than the Union had expected. Lesson 4.1 discusses how the battles of Vicksburg and Chancellorsville influenced the Union's expectations.

BACKGROUND FOR THE TEACHER

Many Vicksburg residents had opposed secession, but they rallied in support of the Confederacy. Their first experience with the reality of war occurred when Union ships began shelling the city in May 1862. Newspaper accounts describe civilians running through the streets seeking safe shelter. The resourceful Mississippians furnished hillside caves with tables, chairs, and mattresses. However, eyewitness reports indicate the 47 days of siege were anything but comfortable. Shelters were tight, housing African-American slaves and their enslavers, both suffering the same terrors and deprivations of war. Meager supplies of food and water were sold at exorbitant prices to those who could afford them. Citizens of Vicksburg who survived the siege found their city devastated and the Union flag flying above their courthouse.

HISTORY NOTEBOOK

Encourage students to complete the American Gallery page for Chapter 12 in their History Notebooks as they read.

INTRODUCE & ENGAGE

CHOOSE BATTLES

Ask students what criteria they might use to determine which battles to include in a book or website about the Civil War. Create a graphic organizer, such as the one shown, to record their responses. Suggest that students include battles they have already studied. For example, one criterion might be the first battle of the war (Fort Sumter) because it marked the beginning of fighting. Tell students that in this lesson they will learn about two significant battles—Vicksburg and Chancellorsville. As they read, ask them to consider why these battles are included in the text. At the end of the lesson, revisit the chart and allow students to share their ideas.

Criterion	Battle(s)	Reason

TEACH

GUIDED DISCUSSION

1. **Evaluate** Was the plan to bypass Vicksburg by rerouting the Mississippi River a feasible strategy? Why or why not? *(Answers will vary. Possible responses: Yes. Rerouting the river would have made Vicksburg irrelevant to the war, and it would have enabled the Union to gain control of the Mississippi without risking the lives of soldiers in battle. No. The strategy was poorly planned, impossible to execute, and bound to result in many deaths from disease and exposure.)*

2. **Draw Conclusions** How might a flanking maneuver help one side gain an advantage? *(Possible response: Previous battles had involved direct attacks, but a flanking maneuver offers the element of surprise and gives one side the advantage of catching the other side off guard.)*

MORE INFORMATION

Jackson and Lee Thomas "Stonewall" Jackson was a West Point graduate who had fought in the Mexican-American War and taught at Virginia Military Institute. He served under Robert E. Lee's command in several significant Civil War battles, including the Second Battle of Bull Run (Second Manassas), Antietam, and Fredericksburg, and he became one of Lee's most trusted officers. At Chancellorsville, Lee's confidence was justified when Jackson successfully carried out the maneuver that assured victory. As a result of the wounds Jackson suffered from friendly fire, his left arm had to be amputated. Upon hearing the news, Lee stated, "He has lost his left arm, but I have lost my right."

ACTIVE OPTIONS

AMERICAN GALLERY ONLINE **The Battle of Vicksburg** Invite students to explore the American Gallery. Have them select one of the images and do additional research to learn more about it. Ask questions that will inspire additional inquiry about the chosen gallery image, such as: Why does it belong in this chapter? How does it relate to the battle? What else would you like to know about it?

NG Learning Framework: Publish a Civil War Newspaper

SKILLS Communication, Collaboration

KNOWLEDGE Our Human Story

Discuss how the public learned about Civil War battles during the war. Suggest that students conduct research to find examples of northern and southern newspapers issued during the Civil War. Then have students work in groups to create their own newspaper articles about the battles of Vicksburg and Chancellorsville, either from the northern or southern perspective. Some may write from the viewpoint of a war correspondent who witnessed the battles. Others might write sidebars about the generals involved or provide human interest stories about the impact on local civilians. Instruct group members to collaborate on publishing their related articles in newspaper format to share with the class.

DIFFERENTIATE

STRIVING READERS

Read and Recall Direct students to work in pairs. First, each student reads the lesson independently. Then pairs meet without the book and take notes as they share ideas they recall. Finally, partners review the lesson together and decide what to add or change in their notes.

GIFTED & TALENTED

Create a Military Campaign Map Have students conduct research and create a map showing General Grant's troop movements and battles along the way to the capture of Vicksburg. Prompt them to label and date the troops' starting point, the route south of Vicksburg, and the battles of Port Gibson, Raymond, and Jackson, as well as the siege of Vicksburg. Students may also show the DeSoto Peninsula and the railroad heads at Vicksburg. Encourage them to add relevant photographs, paintings, artifacts, and other visuals. Invite students to present their maps to the class and answer any questions.

See the Chapter Planner for more strategies for differentiation.

HISTORICAL THINKING

ANSWERS

1. Lee defeated General Joseph Hooker and repulsed the Union assault, but he lost one of his top generals, Stonewall Jackson.

2. The maneuver failed because Lee divided his forces and sent General Jackson to circle around Hooker's men, thereby using Hooker's own tactic against him. In the end, Jackson was able to surprise and defeat Hooker's troops.

3. After Union assaults on Vicksburg failed, Grant concluded that the city could not be taken by a direct attack, so he decided a siege was the Union's best chance to capture the city.

4. The Confederate control of Vicksburg had prevented the Union from passing freely down the Mississippi River. Lincoln meant that by regaining control of Vicksburg, the Union had unblocked the full course of the river.

CRITICAL VIEWING People gave up the use of their possessions, the comforts of living in a house, and food prepared in a kitchen. The makeshift shelters provided little protection against military action and left people vulnerable to the weather.

COMPOSE AND WAIT

"Photography is an act of appreciation. If it can become an act of affection, you are at one with your subject."
—Sam Abell

When a young Sam Abell became a photography intern at *National Geographic* magazine in 1967, he thought to himself, "This is the right place for me; this is my life." He was also convinced he was the least qualified person ever hired for the role, having graduated from a college that did not have an actual photography program. Fifty years and thousands of memorable photos later, Abell has amply proved himself wrong about his qualifications—but he was correct in his realization that National Geographic was the perfect place for him.

∧ In 2001, Abell captured this photograph of the swollen Mississippi River overtaking its banks and spilling floodwater onto Water Street near Muscatine, Iowa.

Perched on the limestone bluffs overlooking the Mississippi River near Savannah, Illinois, Abell was able to frame a broad vista of river, wooded green islands, and the curving train tracks. Then he waited for a train.

MAIN IDEA National Geographic photographer Sam Abell captures American culture and geography with his camera.

NOT THE TYPICAL PHOTOGRAPHER

Born in Sylvania, Ohio, in 1945, Sam Abell had a camera in his hand at an early age. His first photography teacher was his father, an enthusiastic amateur photographer. In a darkroom they built in their home, Abell and his father spent hours learning to develop photos and forging a loving bond over their shared fascination with the photographic image.

The University of Kentucky, where Abell went to college, didn't have an official photography program, but he received an abundance of real-world practice taking pictures for the university's School of Journalism. After graduating in 1967, he was hired by National Geographic as a photography intern and became a staff photographer for *National Geographic* magazine in 1970. In a decades-long career, he photographed subjects as diverse as maritime culture in Newfoundland, the tiny town of Hagi, Japan, and the expansive American West.

Abell is not the typical journalistic photographer, and his images have often been described as "quiet," not a quality generally associated with the lively, action-oriented scenes that magazines often seek. He considers himself a charter member of the "compose and wait" school of photographic thought. He will choose a location and frame his shot, then wait—for weeks, if necessary—for the perfect moment, gesture, or even shadow that brings what he calls a "breath of life" to the image. A photo editor once noted that Abell "records everyday physical existence but simultaneously suggests other possibilities. It is this steady looking for another life behind things that characterizes his work." Abell elaborates, "I have been drawn to that which in life is enduring."

CONNECTING TO THE MISSISSIPPI

One subject that Abell has returned to more than once is the Mississippi River, which he has explored extensively, recording both its pristine wildernesses and its bustling industrial areas—geographic America and economic America.

Reflecting on why the river is such an iconic symbol of the American story, Abell observes that if you spread out a map of North America, it looks like the entire continent drains into the Mississippi. That's not quite true, of course, but for Abell, visualizing the continent in this way illustrates "the power of the Mississippi's physical location." He also acknowledges the sophisticated Native American civilizations that grew along its banks, the role of its tributaries in carrying Lewis and Clark westward, and the river's importance during the Civil War as the North and South fought for control of its waters. "It's the great confluence of water and exploration and the history of North America," he says.

HISTORICAL THINKING

1. **READING CHECK** What does Sam Abell mean by the expression "compose and wait"?

2. **ANALYZE VISUALS** Look at the photos on these pages. How do they reflect Abell's ideas about photography?

PLAN: 2-PAGE LESSON

OBJECTIVE

Describe Sam Abell's approach to photographing the American landscape.

CRITICAL THINKING SKILLS FOR LESSON 4.2

- Analyze Visuals
- Make Inferences
- Summarize

HISTORICAL THINKING FOR CHAPTER 12

How did the Civil War change the way different groups of Americans viewed themselves and the nation? Photographs capture moments of history and change in a country and around the world. Lesson 4.2 describes the philosophy and work of Sam Abell, who has documented American life and landscapes for more than 30 years.

NATIONAL GEOGRAPHIC PHOTOGRAPHER SAM ABELL

In April 2001, the Mississippi River flooded the Quad Cities, an area in Iowa and Illinois, and crested at more than 22 feet, the third-highest level in the Quad Cities' history. In photographing scenes like the one shown, Abell said, "I looked for those aspects of the Mississippi that were timeless . . . I thought the water covering up a fair portion of the contemporary landscape made it old-seeming and historic—that is, the history of flooding." Abell visited nearby towns and rural locations to find the scenes that he thought best captured the effects of the historic floodwaters on the people and landscapes. His distinctive photographs were included in the book *The Mississippi and the Making of a Nation*.

HISTORY NOTEBOOK

Encourage students to complete the National Geographic Photographer page for Chapter 12 in their History Notebooks as they read.

INTRODUCE & ENGAGE

CONNECT PAST AND PRESENT

Ask students to recall a photograph of a place, person, or event that stands out for them. Prompt them to discuss what story the photo tells and what elements make it memorable, such as lighting, composition, the subject, or other factors. Tell students that in this lesson they will learn about Sam Abell's approach to taking memorable photographs and his fascination with the historic Mississippi River.

TEACH

GUIDED DISCUSSION

1. **Make Inferences** What in Abell's youth and early training might have contributed to his method of approaching subjects and creating memorable photographs? *(Possible response: He and his father pursued photography as a hobby. This informal training and experience probably allowed him to follow his own natural interests and style instead of learning a specific method or developing a journalistic style.)*

2. **Summarize** What makes the Mississippi River such a compelling subject for Abell? *(Possible response: He is interested in the river's historic role in the exploration and development of the nation, its size and location, its importance to Native American cultures, and the contrast of wilderness and industrial areas that still exists today.)*

MORE INFORMATION

Photographer of His Time Abell is drawn to photography's expressive power. "I think of myself as a writer who photographs. Images, for me, can be considered poems, short stories or essays." His most memorable assignments have included hiking the 2,600-mile Pacific Crest Trail and flying inside a cyclone in Australia to photograph sheet lightning. He stays passionate about his art by teaching classes and workshops. "Nominally the classes are about photography but the real thing I'm teaching is life, and about how photography is a positive way of 'being in life.'" Abell is currently busy photographing the United States. "I now want to be a photographer of my time, and our common culture."

ACTIVE OPTIONS

On Your Feet: Team Word Webbing Share the More Information section with the class. Then arrange students into groups of four. Hand each group a sheet of paper and ask students to complete the following sentence: A photograph has the power to _____. Tell one member in each group to add a word or phrase and pass the paper clockwise to the next member. Each group member adds at least one response. Students circulate the paper until they run out of responses. Call on a volunteer from each group to share the group's responses with the class.

NG Learning Framework: Tell a Story Using Photographs

SKILLS Observation, Communication

KNOWLEDGE Our Human Story

Instruct students to work in small groups or pairs to tell a story of their own with photographs they create. Suggest that they look for settings or subjects around them, such as their rooms or homes, families and friends, or neighborhoods. Invite groups or pairs to form a collage of their photographs to display in the classroom. Allow time for students to talk about why they chose their subjects and why they set up and framed their shots as they did.

DIFFERENTIATE

ENGLISH LANGUAGE LEARNERS ELD

Make Word Cards Pair students at the **Emerging** level with students at the **Expanding** or **Bridging** level. Instruct partners to read the sentences in the lesson containing the adjectives *pristine*, *bustling*, and *iconic* and make a word card for each word, including the definition, pronunciation, and an original sentence using the word. Ask pairs to discuss how the words help them understand Abell's connection to the Mississippi River.

PRE-AP

Analyze a Photograph Direct students to browse some of Abell's photographs online and choose one to analyze. Tell them to first analyze the photograph's subject, its composition (the position and framing of people and/or objects relative to one another), and Abell's perspective. Then prompt them to consider what Abell may have waited for before taking the photograph and why. Invite students to share their analysis with the class in an oral report.

See the Chapter Planner for more strategies for differentiation.

HISTORICAL THINKING

ANSWERS

1. Abell chooses a location and composes a scene and then waits for the right moment when something happens that brings the scene to life.

2. Possible response: Both photographs show Abell's idea of "compose and wait." He frames a scene that contains key elements, such as the vista of the bend in the river seen from above or the row of mailboxes surrounded by water with the street sign marking the submerged roadway. Then he waits to capture a moment when something happens—the train rounds the curve of the river, an elderly man wades through the knee-high water and steadies himself against a protruding branch. These elements add a human dimension to each scene that tells a story—the quality that Abell says he values most.

THE BATTLE OF GETTYSBURG

As you walk among statues and monuments, a group of children exit the Gettysburg Museum and Visitor Center, running and laughing across the grass. It's a peaceful place now, but you can't help but be reminded of how many fought and died on this very spot, and how it changed the course of the war.

LEE INVADES THE NORTH

General Lee's stunning victory at Chancellorsville was one bright spot in an otherwise gloomy picture for the Confederacy in early May 1863. In Mississippi, Union forces under General Grant were winning battle after battle as they marched toward the key city of Vicksburg. The Union's Army of the Cumberland, commanded by General William Rosecrans, was threatening to break through Tennessee into Georgia. And the Union's blockade was drawing an ever-tighter net around the southern coast.

Some of Lee's generals urged him to pull Grant away from Vicksburg by rushing his troops to Tennessee to defend the center of the Confederacy. But Lee decided that his most effective move would be to invade the North again, taking the pressure off Virginia, where much of the fighting had taken place up to that point. A successful invasion of the North would dishearten the Union, and it might persuade Britain and France to recognize the Confederacy. It might also strengthen the position of Peace Democrats, northerners who wanted to abandon the war effort and negotiate a settlement with the South. These were the same people the Union called "Copperheads."

In early June 1863, Lee began to move his army of 75,000 men north through the Shenandoah and Cumberland valleys into southern Pennsylvania. There, they occupied several towns and advanced within striking distance of Harrisburg, the state capital. Meanwhile, General Hooker had also been moving northward, keeping the 95,000-strong Army of the Potomac between Lee's forces and Washington, D.C.

Hooker's relationship with his superiors and President Lincoln had grown increasingly strained, and in late June, Hooker threatened to resign his command. Lincoln abruptly replaced him, putting General **George Meade** in charge. Now it was up to Meade to figure out how best to stop the greatest threat the

Born into a celebrated Virginia family, Robert E. Lee enrolled in the U.S. Military Academy at West Point in New York and was one of only six soldiers in his class who graduated with a clean record of behavior.

Union had yet faced from Confederate forces. Washington and Baltimore were vulnerable, along with the cities, towns, and farms of Pennsylvania. Confederate troops not only helped themselves to the abundant food and livestock the rich land offered as they marched through, but they also seized free African Americans and fugitive slaves and forced them to the South and into slavery.

Still, Lee and his men found themselves in a dangerous situation. Lee had sent a cavalry corps commanded by his "eyes and ears," J.E.B. Stuart, to gather information about Meade's forces, but Stuart ranged too widely from the main army. As a result, Lee had little idea of the Union Army's plans. For their part, Meade and his fellow officers decided to pursue Lee, but not too aggressively; they wanted to choose the right time and place for a decisive battle.

On June 30, fate intervened. That day, a Confederate brigade in search of supplies happened upon a large Union cavalry force in a place that neither side knew or cared much about: Gettysburg, Pennsylvania. Gettysburg was a crossroad town of about 2,400 people located some 35 miles south of Harrisburg.

Lee's army was scattered across a large area of south-central Pennsylvania, and Meade's army was strung out along a 25-mile-long front moving northward from Maryland into Pennsylvania. Messengers quickly spread the news of the Gettysburg encounter, and reinforcements from both armies hurried to the town.

FIGHTING FOR THE HIGH GROUND

The **Battle of Gettysburg** began the morning of the following day, July 1, when a large **contingent**, or group, of Confederates advancing from the west clashed with Union cavalry that had taken up positions on a set of ridges along the town's western border. Union infantry soon arrived to support the cavalry, but the Union forces were still outnumbered. The fighting intensified and spread as the two sides battled for the high ground. By afternoon, the Union forces were in retreat through Gettysburg.

At first, the Confederates thought they had gotten the better of the first day's fighting, but as the smoke cleared late in the day, they discovered that the Union forces had consolidated themselves on the most advantageous ground. Meade's men occupied

AMERICAN PLACES
Gettysburg Battlefield, Pennsylvania

In 1863, most roads in south-central Pennsylvania led to Gettysburg, so it was not surprising that enemy armies would encounter one another here. This statue of Union general Gouverneur K. Warren stands on Little Round Top, a hill overlooking the battlefield that he and his troops defended from a Confederate assault. Warren, who was nicknamed the "Hero of Little Round Top," survived the furious fighting. The statue of Warren shown in this photograph was raised after his death in 1882.

The Civil War 415

OBJECTIVE

Describe the outcome of General Lee's second invasion of the North.

CRITICAL THINKING SKILLS FOR LESSON 4.3

- Identify Main Ideas and Details
- Make Connections
- Draw Conclusions
- Identify Problems and Solutions
- Make Inferences
- Summarize
- Analyze Language Use
- Compare and Contrast
- Analyze Primary Sources

HISTORICAL THINKING FOR CHAPTER 12

How did the Civil War change the way different groups of Americans viewed themselves and the nation? As the Civil War dragged on, General Lee faced a decision that would determine the fate of the Confederacy. Lesson 4.3 describes how the Battle of Gettysburg marked a turning point in the war.

BACKGROUND FOR THE TEACHER

Robert E. Lee's legacy is still hotly debated: Is Lee an American icon, worthy of respect for his honorable service and gentlemanly conduct, or does his reputation rest on a myth that overlooks his racial prejudices? In the 150 years since Lee's death, his biographers and other historians have cast him in different lights as Americans' views of racial equality have changed. In the early 20th century, writers portrayed Lee as a noble defender of the southern cause. As the civil rights movement focused public attention on the African-American experience, however, Lee's white-supremacist views received greater scrutiny. Writers began to portray Lee as a defender of the racial inequality upon which the Confederacy rested. The controversy continues as Americans struggle to separate the man from the cause.

HISTORY NOTEBOOK

Encourage students to complete the Reid on the Road video series page for Chapter 12 in their History Notebooks after they view the video.

INTRODUCE & ENGAGE

CREATE A WORD WEB

Direct students' attention to the lesson's photograph of Robert E. Lee in military uniform. Invite a volunteer to read the caption aloud. Ask students to characterize General Lee based on the photo and caption and add the characteristics to a Word Web, like the one shown. You may wish to share information about Lee from Background for the Teacher and allow students to add or change information on the web. Tell them that in this lesson they will learn about some of Lee's military decisions, accomplishments, and failures. At the end of the lesson, revisit the web, add any new traits students identify, and discuss how the text influenced their opinions of Lee.

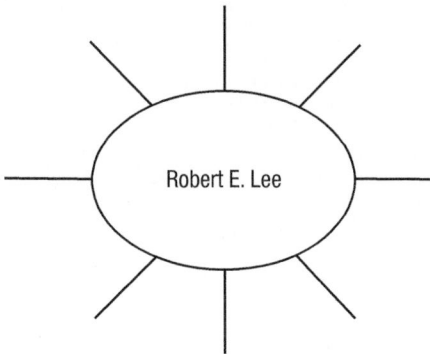

Robert E. Lee

TEACH

GUIDED DISCUSSION

1. **Identify Problems and Solutions** What problem did Lee's generals hope to solve by recommending that troops be sent to Tennessee in May 1863? *(Victorious Union forces targeted Vicksburg and posed a threat to Georgia, while the Union blockade cut off supplies to the southern coast. Confederate generals believed that sending troops to Tennessee would pull Grant's forces away from Vicksburg.)*

2. **Make Inferences** Why do you think President Lincoln swiftly replaced General Hooker after he threatened to resign? *(Possible response: Lincoln probably saw Hooker as unreliable because he already had a strained relationship with superiors, and Lincoln probably did not want to live with the threat that Hooker might resign at any time. By replacing him, Lincoln might have lost a good general, but he gained stability in military leadership.)*

3. **Summarize** What advantages and disadvantages did the Union have when the Battle of Gettysburg began? *(The Union cavalry had an advantageous position on ridges above the town, and the infantry soon joined them. However, Confederate troops did outnumber the Union forces.)*

AMERICAN PLACES

In 1895, the federal government designated Gettysburg Battlefield as a National Military Park to honor veterans of both armies who fought there. The National Park Service took over administration in 1933. Today, the site provides opportunities for visitors to experience this historic battle through tours led by park rangers or living history demonstrations in which reenactors bring the events to life. The park's museum includes collections of Civil War artifacts that provide insights into the lives of soldiers who fought at Gettysburg.

DIFFERENTIATE

ENGLISH LANGUAGE LEARNERS

Use Terms in Sentences Pair students at the **Emerging** level with those at the **Expanding** or **Bridging** level. Direct their attention to the Key Vocabulary words *contingent* and *barrage*. Ask them to read the words in context and discuss their meanings. Then challenge pairs to compose original sentences using each word. Tell more proficient students to assist their partners in checking the accuracy of the sentences. Invite pairs to share their sentences with other pairs and discuss different ways to use each word.

PRE-AP

Form and Support a Thesis Direct students to conduct preliminary research about Pickett's Charge and to develop a thesis regarding why General Lee ordered Pickett and his men to cross open space and attack Union troops occupying higher ground. Then ask students to write an analysis based on their thesis using a variety of primary and secondary source material for support. They might conclude that Lee was strategic or overconfident or that Pickett's Charge was brave or foolhardy. Invite students to read their analysis to the class and answer classmates' questions.

See the Chapter Planner for more strategies for differentiation.

CRITICAL VIEWING Artist Paul Philippoteaux painted this scene of Pickett's Charge in the early 1880s. It is part of a larger mural that measures 42 feet high and 377 feet long. How would you describe the nature of the fighting at the Battle of Gettysburg?

a four-mile-long, fishhook-shaped line of hills and ridges—including Cemetery Hill, Cemetery Ridge, Culp's Hill, Little Round Top, and Big Round Top—that permitted them to protect their flanks. When Meade arrived during the night, he strengthened the Union positions with artillery and additional troops.

During the second day of the battle, the Confederates slowly mobilized their forces to attack the Union positions late in the afternoon. Fierce attacks and counterattacks raged on the slopes of Little Round Top and the boulder-strewn hill known as the Devil's Den, as well as in a nearby wheat field and peach orchard. The fighting produced horrific casualties—35,000 men were killed or wounded—but the Union managed to keep control of the high ground.

PICKETT'S CHARGE

Despite the Union's superior position, and against the advice of General James Longstreet, one of his top officers, Lee decided to mount a frontal attack the next day. Early in the afternoon, his artillery forces began a massive, deafening bombardment of Union positions. For nearly 2 hours, some 150 Confederate cannons blazed, focusing much of their shelling on the middle of the Union lines along Cemetery Ridge. Union artillery forces shot back, but because of limited space they had fewer than half as many big guns. To fool the Confederates and to save ammunition for later battles, the Union commander ordered his men to slow their fire.

Mistakenly believing that the artillery **barrage**, or bombardment, had substantially weakened the Union forces, Lee ordered General **George E. Pickett** and two other generals to lead roughly 13,000 men in an assault on the middle of the Union line. As Confederate attackers marched and then raced in waves toward Cemetery Hill across nearly a mile of open ground, many were mowed down by deadly artillery crossfire or by rifle fire from the Union soldiers. Nevertheless, in what would later be called "the high-water mark of the Confederacy," several hundred of the attackers managed to pierce Union lines. Within an hour, however, they were repulsed and forced to retreat. **Pickett's Charge** had been a catastrophic failure.

Lee's troops spent the next day, July 4, on Seminary Ridge, a short distance west of Cemetery Ridge, waiting in a drenching rain for a Union counterattack that never came. That night, as the rain continued to fall, the Confederates began their long retreat back to Virginia. Meanwhile, a thousand miles away, General Pemberton had just surrendered Vicksburg to General Grant.

AFTER THE BATTLE

The three days of fighting at Gettysburg had been a disaster for the Army of Northern Virginia. About one-third of the entire force—around 28,000 of Lee's men—had been killed or wounded. The Confederates, short of supplies and soldiers, had gambled on an aggressive assault and lost. Although the North's casualty count was similar, its total number of troops was still far greater than the South's. Elation swept the North. The Union's victories at Gettysburg and Vicksburg would prove to be major turning points in the Civil War.

Hoping to end the war as soon as possible, President Lincoln used persuasion as well as fighting to try to entice the Confederacy back into the Union. In early December 1863, five months after Gettysburg, he issued a proclamation of amnesty and reconstruction. To southerners who would take an oath of loyalty to the Union, Lincoln promised a full pardon and the return of all property with the exception of slaves. Although he excluded Confederate leaders and high officers from this offer, Lincoln tried to include as many white southern men as possible. He decreed that once 10 percent of the number of voters in a state had sworn their loyalty to the Union, they could begin forming a new state government. He also promised education and apprenticeship programs that would aid formerly enslaved people in the transition to full freedom. He made no allowances for African-American participation in the new state governments of the South, however.

Implementing this plan turned out to be problematic. Lincoln, northern Republicans, and much of the public had underestimated the intensity of southern bitterness over years of war and occupation. Even in Tennessee and Kentucky—areas that were under Union control—guerrilla bands and raiders terrorized the local population and disrupted elections. Civilians in border states often found themselves in an impossible situation. Washington Elliott, a brigadier general in the Union Army, called citizens of the border states who failed to aid Union forces "enemies of mankind" with "the rights due to pirates and robbers." Those who actively aided the Union, on the other hand, were liable to find their crops trampled, their barns burned, and other acts of vandalism carried out by secessionist neighbors.

Abolitionists and their allies attacked Lincoln's plan as far too lenient to Confederates and not helpful enough for former slaves. In February 1864, Republican members of Congress introduced the **Wade-Davis Bill**, which attempted to enforce a standard set of laws to be enacted and administered across the South after the war ended. These laws would require 50 percent, rather than 10 percent, of a state's population to swear an oath of past as well as future loyalty before the state could form a new government. Lincoln hoped to entice Arkansas and Louisiana to rejoin the Union, and he was looking ahead to the upcoming election. He decided he had no choice but to refuse to sign the bill.

HISTORICAL THINKING

1. **READING CHECK** What are two things that General Lee believed might be accomplished by a Confederate invasion of the North?

2. **IDENTIFY MAIN IDEAS AND DETAILS** Why were the casualties at Gettysburg a greater blow to the Confederacy than to the Union?

3. **MAKE CONNECTIONS** What connection can you make between Lee's victory at Chancellorsville and his strategy at Gettysburg?

4. **DRAW CONCLUSIONS** Why do you think General Meade did not order a Union counterattack the day after Pickett's Charge?

BUILD BACKGROUND

THE MEDAL OF HONOR

The nation's highest military award—the Congressional Medal of Honor—originated during the Civil War. The government presented more than 1,500 Medals of Honor to Union soldiers, sailors, and marines who served during the war. As requirements underwent review and revision, some of those awards were rescinded because the recipients were civilians or members of an honor guard rather than combatants. By 1918, the honoree had to have been an officer or enlisted person who participated in combat and performed gallantly at the risk of life "above and beyond the call of duty." Although the Medal of Honor is supposed to be presented within three years of an act of heroism, President Obama made an exception in 2014, posthumously awarding one to 1st Lt. Alonzo Cushing, an artillery commander who died at Gettysburg on July 3, 1863, while defending Cemetery Ridge during Pickett's Charge.

RESTORING A BATTLEFIELD

The topography of Gettysburg served a crucial role in battle strategies. Generals put their West Point training into practice as they studied sight lines for artillery and available cover and concealment for infantry. As years passed, however, Civil War–era farm fields transformed into forests, and fences and walls deteriorated. In 2000, Gettysburg National Military Park undertook the project of restoring the battlefield to its 1863 condition. The task involved studying historical maps and photographs, soldiers' diaries, and officers' reports and then plotting information on digitized maps to obtain an accurate picture. The work of restoring the landscape included removing some trees and planting others, rebuilding wooden fences and stone walls, and restoring roads. Today, visitors can stand where soldiers stood and see what they saw more than 150 years ago. The restoration has provided new insights into the historic Battle of Gettysburg.

TEACH

GUIDED DISCUSSION

4. **Analyze Language Use** What is meant by calling Pickett's Charge "the high-water mark of the Confederacy"? *(Possible response: A high-water mark is the highest peak of something. During Pickett's Charge, the Confederate attackers reached their highest level of achievement, managing to break through Union lines.)*

5. **Compare and Contrast** What were the similarities and differences between the Wade-Davis Bill and President Lincoln's proclamation of amnesty and reconstruction? *(Possible response: Both plans aimed at restoring Confederate states to the Union once southerners took an oath of loyalty. Lincoln's plan stated that a secessionist state could form a new state government if just 10 percent of that state's voters pledged loyalty to the Union, but the Wade-Davis Bill required 50 percent of a state's voters to take the oath.)*

ANALYZE PRIMARY SOURCES

Direct students' attention to the Primary Source feature. **ASK:** What emotions does the battlefield description evoke? *(Possible responses: sadness, horror, compassion, confusion)* **ASK:** How do you think the eyewitness's age influenced her reaction? *(Answers will vary. Possible response: Although Tillie lived nearby, she had likely not witnessed anything like the devastation she saw after the battle, and it would be shocking to such a young person. The fact that she could describe it in such great detail 25 years later indicates the lasting effect the experience had on her.)*

ACTIVE OPTIONS

On Your Feet: Numbered Heads Pose the following questions for discussion: Do you agree with historians who consider Gettysburg the most significant battle of the Civil War? Why or why not? What do you think was the most important outcome of the battle? Divide the class into groups of four and ask students to count off within each group. Provide time for groups to discuss the questions. Then call a number and have the student with that number from each group summarize the group's discussion for the class.

NG Learning Framework: Explore the Geography of Gettysburg

`ATTITUDE` Curiosity

`SKILLS` Collaboration, Communication

Divide the class into three groups and assign one day of the Battle of Gettysburg to each group. Instruct group members to explore how the geography of the region impacted troop movements and military tactics on the assigned day. Direct them to prepare a map, with a key or legend, showing the movements of both armies. Prompt students to prepare a narration of the battle, which may incorporate images and primary source quotations, to accompany the map. Provide time for groups to share their work with the class.

HISTORICAL THINKING

ANSWERS

1. Lee believed that, in addition to taking pressure off Virginia, invading the North could demoralize northerners, persuade Britain and France to recognize the Confederacy, and bolster the arguments of Peace Democrats, who opposed the war.

2. The Confederates lost one-third of their total troop strength at Gettysburg, with about 28,000 dead and wounded. The Union suffered a similar number of losses, but the amount was a smaller percentage of its fighting force.

3. Lee's bold strategy at Chancellorsville had led to victory, which might have influenced his decision at Gettysburg to order the daring attack known as Pickett's Charge.

4. Possible responses: Meade might have been unwilling to move his forces off the high ground they held. He might have felt that the rain made conditions unfavorable for a major battle. He might have suspected that after their heavy losses on July 3, the Confederates would soon retreat to Virginia.

CRITICAL VIEWING The painting depicts furious hand-to-hand combat in the midst of smoke and fire from cannons and the confusion of disorganized units fighting within a small area.

NATIONAL CIVIL WAR MUSEUM
HARRISBURG, PENNSYLVANIA

The National Civil War Museum in Harrisburg, Pennsylvania, describes itself as the only museum in the United States to tell the entire story of the Civil War "without bias to Union or Confederate causes." The museum immerses visitors in the Civil War period through living history demonstrations, videos, dioramas, and interactive exhibits that represent the experiences of common soldiers, civilians on the home front, enslaved African Americans, and prominent leaders. Artifacts on display include drums and bugles carried by young boys in the armies, a wide variety of weapons, and a brass slave collar. The great suffering caused by the war becomes evident through the museum's collection of war photography.

Union Navy Flare Gun
Guns that launch flares—bursts of bright, colored light—were used by the Union Navy for signaling during the Civil War. The guns shot cartridges high up into the night sky, where they exploded as flares. Ships could send coded messages by launching flares of different colors in various combinations. The flares might convey orders, distress, the location of troops, or other messages.

How does this flare gun appear to differ from a pistol?

Lincoln's Note to McClellan
On August 27, 1862, President Abraham Lincoln sent this brief note to Major General George McClellan in Alexandria, Virginia, inquiring: "What news from the front?"

At the time, McClellan had been ordered to move Union troops toward Manassas to aid General Pope's soldiers in an upcoming battle with Confederate forces. McClellan failed to follow orders and never sent troops to Manassas, which led to a disastrous defeat for the Union at the Second Battle of Bull Run.

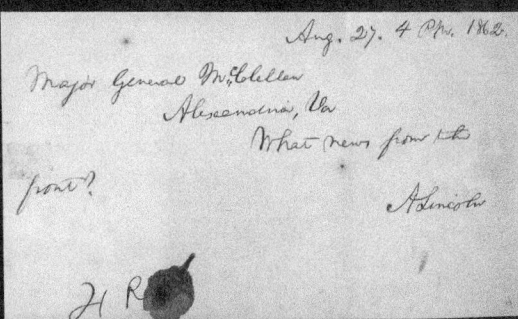

Union Signal Corps Decoding Device
Both the Union and the Confederate armies had signal corps—squads of soldiers who were responsible for communicating information across a battlefield.

A signal corps member typically waved flags or torches to send messages from one commander to another. These flag or torch movements represented different numbers, which were then translated into letters using a decoding device like this one. The codes themselves could be changed by rotating the disk to alter the alignment of numbers and letters.

A lead musket ball like the one lodged in this Bible would create a large wound.

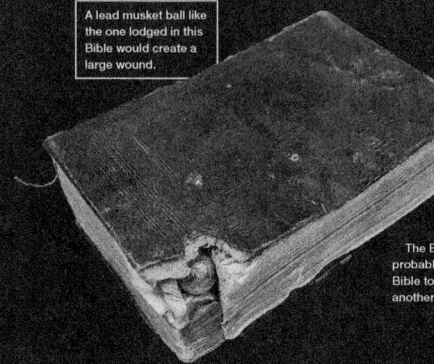

Bible with Musket Ball
Private Adam Troutman of the Confederate Army of Northern Virginia carried this Bible in his pocket during the Battle of Antietam in 1862. The Bible stopped a musket ball and probably saved his life. Troutman gave the Bible to his brother and was later killed in another battle.

Do research to identify modern veterans' groups similar to the G.A.R.

Grave Marker
The Grand Army of the Republic (G.A.R.) was an organization made up of veterans who had fought for the Union in the Civil War. The Ladies of the G.A.R. is a still-active organization of female descendants of those veterans. The members place markers like this one on the graves of their deceased family members.

PLAN: 2-PAGE LESSON

OBJECTIVE
Examine both sides of the Civil War through artifacts at the National Civil War Museum.

CRITICAL THINKING SKILLS FOR LESSON 4.4
- Analyze Visuals
- Make Connections
- Evaluate
- Make Inferences

HISTORICAL THINKING FOR CHAPTER 12
How did the Civil War change the way different groups of Americans viewed themselves and the nation? The dispute over slavery divided the nation into the Union and the Confederacy. Lesson 4.4 displays items from the Civil War that reveal how both sides fought the war and were affected by the conflict.

BACKGROUND FOR THE TEACHER
The inclusive theme of the National Civil War Museum is symbolized by a sculpture in front of the entrance that depicts a Confederate soldier giving water to a wounded Union fighter. Inside, exhibits tell the war's story in chronological order. The museum offers basic information about most battles but focuses primarily on the lives and experiences of the soldiers. Visitors can listen to Civil War–era music and look up individual military records provided by the Civil War Preservation Trust, which is working to put the records online. The museum also chronicles the nation's efforts to come to terms with the war through Reconstruction. The military records clearly show, however, that the conflict over slavery profoundly changed the United States and its people.

HISTORY NOTEBOOK
Encourage students to complete the Curating History page for Chapter 12 in their History Notebooks as they read.

INTRODUCE & ENGAGE

PRESENT BOTH SIDES

Before beginning the lesson, prompt students to share their opinions about the best way for a museum to teach the public about the Civil War. **ASK:** How might a museum present the causes and goals of both sides? What kinds of displays or artifacts might express what the conflict was like for people? Explain that in this lesson students will learn about the National Civil War Museum, whose goal is to inspire lifelong learning about the Civil War and present a balanced view of "the American people's struggles for survival and healing."

TEACH

GUIDED DISCUSSION

1. **Evaluate** In what ways did both sides try to keep their communications secret? *(Both sides sent coded messages via flags or torches and deciphered them with decoders, communicating information only one side could interpret. If the other side learned the code, however, it had to be changed.)*

2. **Make Inferences** Why do you think the Troutman family and the museum left the musket ball embedded in the Bible? *(Possible response: They probably wanted to show the unusual way the Bible had prevented Troutman from being killed. Leaving the musket ball in place makes the point more dramatically, bringing home the dangers the men faced, rather than simply telling the story or showing the damage left by the ball.)*

CURATING HISTORY

In addition to its on-site exhibits, sculptures, and displays, the National Civil War Museum also partners with Dickinson College to offer the online House Divided Project, accessed through the Manuscripts section under Our Collection. The project provides primary and secondary resources for learning about the common soldiers, such as William Elisha Stoker, and their families during the Civil War. Access the website and guide students to find the William Elisha Stoker and House Divided Project archives as well as the photographs and battle maps. **ASK:** How do personal stories help people understand the larger issues of the Civil War? What experiences or feelings might be common to soldiers and families on both sides?

ACTIVE OPTION

On Your Feet: Sort the Artifacts Arrange students into groups of three or four to examine the artifacts shown in the lesson, choose two, and determine what the focus of a museum exhibit might be that includes each artifact. Have groups complete Concept Clusters such as those shown and then share their ideas with the class.

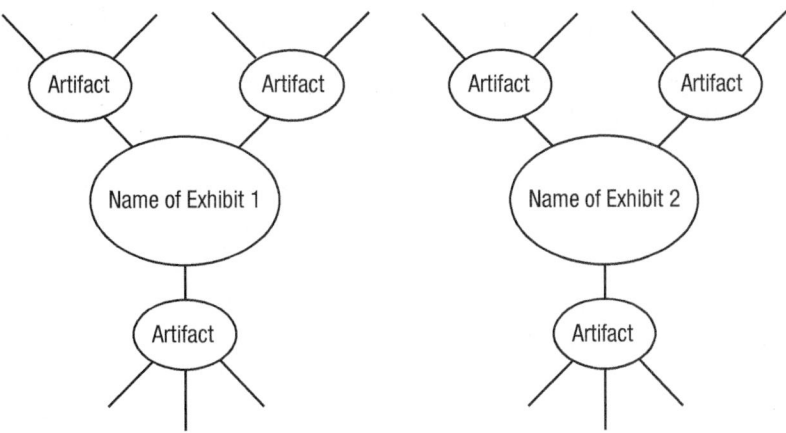

DIFFERENTIATE

STRIVING READERS

Organize Information Instruct students to draw a K-W-L Chart on a sheet of paper. Tell them to look at the artifacts shown in the lesson and complete the first two columns of the chart. Then direct students to read the captions, examine the photographs, and complete the third column.

K What Do I Know?	W What Do I Want To Learn?	L What Did I Learn?

PRE-AP

Write an Unbiased Summary Prompt students to consider the National Civil War Museum's claim that it tells the story of the Civil War "without bias" toward either side. Ask them to reflect on what they have learned in this chapter about the Civil War and what taking an unbiased approach to its history would involve. Then challenge students to write a brief summary describing the Civil War that both sides would agree is a fair and unbiased account. Invite volunteers to read their summaries to the class. Encourage students to comment on evidence of bias in the summaries, such as highly connotative words or statements of opinion.

See the Chapter Planner for more strategies for differentiation.

UNION NAVY FLARE GUN

The flare gun has no chamber to hold bullets and consequently has a much shorter barrel or muzzle. The flare gun's trigger sits on top of the barrel, while the trigger on a pistol is located immediately in front of the grip.

GRAVE MARKER

Students may find veterans' groups for World War I, World War II, the Vietnam War, and the Iraq and Afghanistan wars.

TOTAL WAR

Sometimes duty calls us to do things we'd rather not. According to some historians, William Tecumseh Sherman wept when he learned that South Carolina had voted to secede and civil war had become inevitable. Four years later, Sherman led a brutal campaign through the South that all but assured a Union victory.

BATTLES IN SPRING 1864

In late November 1863, four and a half months after his successful siege of Vicksburg, General Ulysses S. Grant helped lead Union forces to victory in two battles near another key city, Chattanooga, Tennessee. The victories ended a Confederate siege of the city and opened a path for the Union to enter Georgia, as Chattanooga lay just north of the Georgia-Tennessee state line. This development ultimately spelled disaster for the Confederacy.

Grant had earned President Lincoln's confidence with his battlefield successes and the strategic initiative he displayed. In March 1864, Lincoln awarded him command of the Union Army. Grant and Lincoln agreed that the Union should use its superior numbers, naval strength, military equipment, and supplies to attack the Confederacy on every front at once and force it to sacrifice at least some of its territory. Grant would head to Virginia to meet General Robert E. Lee head on and fight toward the goal of capturing Richmond. Lincoln left General Sherman in charge of Union forces in Chattanooga. From there, Sherman would launch an invasion of Georgia and attack Atlanta, a vital industrial and railroad center. A Union capture

REMOVING CONFEDERATE STATUES

In the first half of the 20th century, organizations dedicated to remembering Confederate Civil War heroes erected statues of Confederate military officers in parks and other public spaces in more than 30 states. In the 2010s, many Americans began to question why Confederate officers should be so honored, viewing the statues as symbols of the white supremacist ideals that are the legacy of slavery.

A controversial movement began, urging city governments to remove these monuments. Two descendants of Stonewall Jackson even joined in, writing an open letter asking for his statue on Monument Avenue in Richmond, Virginia, to be taken down. Several cities responded. The statue of Jefferson Davis at left, for example, was removed from a New Orleans, Louisiana, monument in May 2017. The worker is wearing a bulletproof vest to protect him from the possibility of a violent protest.

of Atlanta would disrupt rail transportation throughout the South and cut the Confederacy into pieces too small to resist the Union forces.

More than 180,000 African Americans enlisted just when the Union needed them most. By spring 1864, the Union Army had established the means of recruitment, training, and pay for these soldiers. The Confederates, however, refused to recognize the same rules of warfare for African-American soldiers that they acknowledged for whites. In April 1864, at Fort Pillow in western Tennessee, Confederate cavalry under the command of **Nathan Bedford Forrest** shot down African-American Union soldiers who attempted to surrender. The **Fort Pillow Massacre** and other racist atrocities committed by the Confederates provoked outrage in the North and strengthened the determination of African-American soldiers, for whom "Remember Fort Pillow!" became a battle cry.

In May 1864, two months after assuming command of the entire Union Army, Grant marched into Virginia with his largest unit, the Army of the Potomac, to destroy Lee's forces and capture the Confederate capital of Richmond. The first engagement between Grant and Lee was the **Battle of the Wilderness**, which took place in thick woods near Chancellorsville. Two days of savage fighting ended in horrible losses on both sides. Shells exploding in dry brush caused fires that trapped wounded men, burning them alive. Grant lost more men than Hooker had at the Battle of Chancellorsville. Hooker had treated such losses as a decisive defeat and retreated, but Grant pushed forward.

Hoping to position a large Union force between Lee's army and Richmond, Grant hurried his soldiers southward to the crossroad of **Spotsylvania Court House**. Lee's troops got there first, however. For two weeks, both sides fought fiercely around Spotsylvania until the Confederates managed to halt the Union advance. After withdrawing, Grant tried repeatedly to swing his troops around Lee's right flank, but each time Lee anticipated his move and blocked him. Finally, in mid-June, Grant tried another strategy.

Grant aimed to capture Petersburg, a vital rail center located 25 miles south of Richmond, but the Confederates were able to repulse the North's

The National Museum of American History, Washington, D.C.

Abraham Lincoln used the latest technology to his full advantage during the 1860 and 1864 elections. His campaign team made pins featuring a portrait of the candidate that supporters could wear on their jackets. Though Lincoln's pins didn't become popular again until the 1890s, they are a precursor to the campaign buttons we are familiar with today.

initial attack. Grant then began a siege, pinning down Lee's main force around Richmond and Petersburg and forcing the Confederates to construct longer lines of earthworks to protect the capital. In an attempt to break through Lee's defenses, Union soldiers from Pennsylvania who had been coal miners before the war volunteered to tunnel under the South's fortifications and plant explosives. Throughout July, they dug; finally, at the end of the month, they detonated 320 kegs of gunpowder, blowing an enormous crater in the Confederate lines and killing several hundred Confederate soldiers. The attack that followed the explosion, however, failed. Union troops piled into the crater, where the rallying Confederates trapped them.

LINCOLN'S RE-ELECTION

In early May 1864, as Grant set off on his Virginia campaign, Sherman began his invasion of Georgia, moving southward from Chattanooga with an army of about 110,000 men. Throughout June and July, he pushed relentlessly through northern Georgia. By the end of July, the Confederates had fallen back to Atlanta, preparing to defend it from siege. It seemed only a matter of time before the Union triumphed, but how much time? This question loomed large for the Confederacy because 1864 was a presidential election year for the Union. If Lincoln were to lose the election, southern leaders might be able to negotiate an end to the war and recognition of Confederate independence.

Forced to fight off strong political challenges even within his own party, Lincoln himself believed that his chances of winning a second term were low. The Republicans tried to broaden their appeal by nominating Andrew Johnson, a former Democrat from Tennessee, for the vice presidency.

PLAN: 4-PAGE LESSON

OBJECTIVE

Analyze the tactics President Lincoln and Union generals used to try to end the Civil War.

CRITICAL THINKING SKILLS FOR LESSON 5.1

- Make Inferences
- Compare and Contrast
- Interpret Maps
- Make Connections
- Form and Support Opinions
- Summarize
- Draw Conclusions

HISTORICAL THINKING FOR CHAPTER 12

How did the Civil War change the way different groups of Americans viewed themselves and the nation? African Americans joined the Union Army to help the North win the war. Lesson 5.1 discusses the consequences of the enlistment of some of these men and the pivotal battles and events of 1864.

BACKGROUND FOR THE TEACHER

According to a memoir by Union soldier Mack J. Leaming, no single event led to more universal condemnation from the North than the massacre at Fort Pillow. At the time of General Forrest's attack, Fort Pillow was defended by 500–600 Union troops, about half of them African Americans. When those troops surrendered, the Confederates shot nearly all the African-American soldiers. A few days after the battle, President Lincoln delivered an emotional address condemning the massacre. Because the Confederates refused to treat African-American soldiers as prisoners of war, the Union stopped participating in prisoner exchanges. Lincoln later called on his Cabinet to decide how to punish the Confederacy, but members could not agree on a course of action. According to Leaming, the only punishment delivered to the Confederacy came from Union soldiers when they later defeated General Forrest's men at Tupelo, Mississippi.

INTRODUCE & ENGAGE

BRAINSTORM THE MEANING OF "TOTAL WAR"

Draw a Word Web on the board and write the term *total war* in the center. Ask students to consider how total war might differ from the usual idea of war and what kinds of weapons and tactics might be used. Prompt students to brainstorm words and phrases they associate with *total war*. Record all responses on the Word Web. Then ask students to go through the responses together and decide which words to keep and which to discard to create a possible definition of *total war*. Tell students the term will be explained in this lesson, and invite them to write a definition in their own words once they have completed their reading.

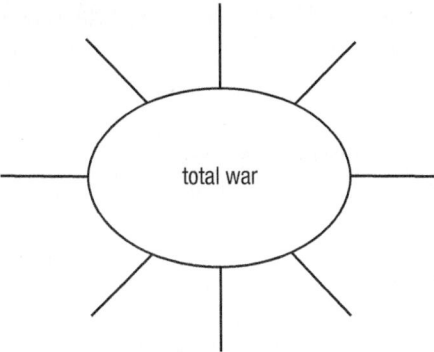

TEACH

GUIDED DISCUSSION

1. **Make Connections** Why did President Lincoln and Ulysses S. Grant decide to attack the Confederacy on all fronts at once? *(Their strategy was to force the Confederacy to give up some territory, disrupt its communication and transportation networks, and divide the South into sections too small to defend against Union troops. They hoped this strategy would help end the war more quickly.)*

2. **Form and Support Opinions** Why do you think the question of removing statues of Confederate war heroes remains so controversial today? *(Answers will vary. Possible response: Some believe that the statues symbolize white supremacist ideals and that celebrating Confederate leaders ignores the fact they fought to split the Union and preserve slavery. Others believe that the statues simply reflect important figures in history and should be preserved.)*

VIRTUAL MUSEUM VISIT

The National Museum of American History in Washington, D.C., brings the Civil War to life with its online exhibit "Civil War 150," which commemorates the 150th anniversary of the war's end. The exhibit offers a rich resource of items that gives viewers a detailed look at the Civil War era, including flags, documents, photographs, and posters, along with collections of military and civilian objects. Each digital photo of an item can be enlarged and expanded to provide more description and background information. Exhibit features include "Funding a War," focusing on the currency used by both sides; "Soldier's Way of Life," showing soldiers' uniforms and objects used daily; "Tools of War," displaying weapons; and "Leaders," presenting items owned and used by Civil War officers.

DIFFERENTIATE

ENGLISH LANGUAGE LEARNERS

Read in Pairs Pair students at the **Emerging** or **Expanding** level with English-proficient students and ask them to read the lesson together. Instruct English-proficient students to pause whenever their partners encounter a word or sentence construction they find confusing and point out subjects, predicates, and context clues to help them understand syntax, idioms, or unfamiliar terms. For example, "a rich agricultural resource, providing crops to feed the Confederate Army," helps students understand that *agricultural resource* refers to land used to grow food. And "successes lifted spirits" means that the successes made people feel hopeful and cheerful. Encourage students to restate sentences containing unfamiliar terms in their own words.

GIFTED & TALENTED

Create a Flowchart Tell students to create a flowchart that documents the main events during the total war phase of the Civil War. Instruct them to supplement the information in the lesson with primary or secondary sources from online research. Suggest that students use a graphic organizer such as the one below to keep track of dates, events, impacts, and other information. Encourage them to find newspaper headlines, photographs, editorials, and cartoons to illustrate each event in the flowchart. Invite students to present their completed flowcharts to the class.

See the Chapter Planner for more strategies for differentiation.

The Democrats, meanwhile, felt they were in a good position to win back the presidency. They knew that in the eyes of his critics, Lincoln had caused the war, trampled on constitutional rights, consolidated too much power, and refused to end the war when he had a chance. To take full advantage of such criticisms, they chose as their candidate General George McClellan, one of many generals Lincoln had removed from command. McClellan and the Democrats portrayed themselves as the party committed to restoring the United States to its prewar unity and grandeur. McClellan campaigned on a promise to end the war by re-admitting the southern states to the Union and allowing them to continue to practice slavery. It was a bargain that appealed to many in the North.

Just when it appeared certain that the Democrats would win the election, news from the battlefield began to alter the political landscape dramatically. Sherman had swung around Atlanta and begun destroying the railroads that made the small city an important transportation hub. Unable to defend Atlanta, the Confederates set much of it on fire and abandoned it. Sherman and his army marched into the city on September 2. About two weeks later, Union general **Philip Sheridan** soundly defeated Confederate forces in the Shenandoah Valley and then set about systematically destroying the valley's ability to support the South's war effort again.

Throughout most of the war, the Shenandoah Valley had been a rich agricultural resource, providing crops to feed the Confederate Army. The railroads that ran through the valley supplied southern soldiers with food, clothing, and ammunition, much of which was stored at Staunton, Virginia. Sheridan burned the valley's fields, farms, and mills; ripped up its railroad tracks; and destroyed the storehouses in Staunton. Then he took a regiment across the Blue Ridge Mountains to Charlottesville and destroyed the railroad hub there.

These successes lifted spirits in the North and gave a tremendous boost to Lincoln's campaign. On Election Day in November, Lincoln won with relative ease, capturing 55 percent of the popular vote and 212 of the available 233 electoral votes. Unexpectedly strong support from Union soldiers contributed significantly to his victory.

SHERMAN'S MARCH TO THE SEA

In the first few years of the war, the Union had generally refrained from targeting civilians and their property. By 1864, however, generals Grant and Sherman had come to believe, as had President Lincoln, that in order to bring the South to its knees, the Union must wage **total war**. In this harsh method of warfare, illustrated by Sheridan's destruction of the Shenandoah Valley, traditional rules and laws of war are ignored and all resources are poured into defeating the enemy no matter what. Little distinction

Union soldiers dismantle railroad tracks in Atlanta, Georgia, in 1864.

is made between combatants and noncombatants, private property is considered fair game, and every effort is made to destroy the enemy's economic and emotional capacity to continue fighting. "We are not only fighting hostile armies," explained Sherman, "but a hostile people, and must make old and young, rich and poor, feel the hard hand of war."

A week after Lincoln's re-election, Sherman and his troops set out from Atlanta toward Georgia's Atlantic coast, taking the war to the southern people themselves. The march was as much a demonstration of northern power as a military maneuver. "If we can march a well-appointed army right through [Confederate] territory," Sherman argued, "it is a demonstration to the world, foreign and domestic, that we have a power which [Confederate president] Davis cannot resist."

As Sherman's army of 62,000 men swept triumphantly across the state, living off food confiscated from farms along its route, it left a wide path of devastation. The troops tore up railroads, blew up bridges, cut telegraph lines, destroyed fences, and burned crops and supplies. Large numbers of deserters from both sides, fugitive slaves, and outlaws took advantage of the situation to prey on the towns and plantations in Sherman's wake, inflicting additional destruction and panic.

On December 10, Sherman's force reached the important coastal city of Savannah and took up positions around it. Sherman demanded that the city surrender, and on December 21 it did so. Savannah was spared the destruction Atlanta had endured. "I beg to present to you, as a Christmas gift, the city of Savannah," Sherman buoyantly telegraphed Lincoln. Contrasting sharply with the devastation of the South, the president's annual message to Congress presented a portrait of a North gaining strength with "more men now than we had when the war began."

HISTORICAL THINKING

1. **READING CHECK** What developments brought new life to Lincoln's 1864 presidential campaign?

2. **MAKE INFERENCES** Why do you think Lincoln assigned Grant to lead the Army of the Potomac rather than allowing him to continue waging war in the West?

3. **COMPARE AND CONTRAST** How did Lincoln and McClellan differ in their positions on the slavery issue? Support your answer with text evidence.

4. **INTERPRET MAPS** Where did Sherman and his troops go after they captured Savannah?

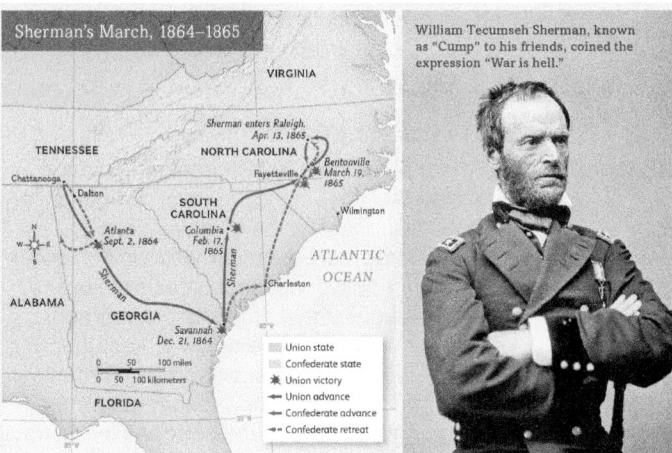

Sherman's March, 1864–1865

VIRGINIA

TENNESSEE

NORTH CAROLINA

Sherman enters Raleigh. Apr. 13, 1865

Chattanooga

Dalton

Bentonville March 19, 1865

Fayetteville

SOUTH CAROLINA

Wilmington

Atlanta Sept. 2, 1864

Columbia Feb. 17, 1865

ATLANTIC OCEAN

ALABAMA

Charleston

GEORGIA

Savannah Dec. 21, 1864

0 50 100 miles
0 50 100 kilometers

FLORIDA

Union state
Confederate state
Union victory
Union advance
Confederate advance
Confederate retreat

William Tecumseh Sherman, known as "Cump" to his friends, coined the expression "War is hell."

BUILD BACKGROUND

GEORGE B. McCLELLAN

General McClellan had a difficult time finding other employment after President Lincoln removed him as commander of the Union Army. In the 1864 presidential election, he agreed to run against Lincoln even though he disagreed with the Democratic Party's claim that the entire war effort had been a failure. McClellan's overwhelming defeat in the election left him so disillusioned that he could not imagine being drawn into public life again. He resigned his military commission and took his family on a trip to Europe. After the Civil War, misfortune continued to follow him when he tried to reclaim his prewar job as a railroad consultant. Company officials no longer wanted his services since they feared his past conflicts with Lincoln might keep them from winning large government contracts. McClellan's only return to political life came in 1877 when he was elected for one term as governor of New Jersey.

SHERMAN IN SAVANNAH

General Sherman's description of Savannah, Georgia, as a "gift" to President Lincoln and the Union was an apt one. Not only did the city surrender without bloodshed, but Sherman was able to confiscate a great deal of equipment and supplies, including 150 guns and cannons plus a large cache of ammunition, 190 train cars and 13 locomotives, 3 steamboats, and 25,000 bales of cotton. Sherman's forces took only 800 prisoners of war, as the roughly 20,000 citizens of Savannah accepted the capture of their city quietly and peacefully. However, Sherman's gift was missing one key part. Confederate general William J. Hardee and most of his infantry, who had been stationed in Savannah, had already escaped the city and crossed the river. There they were able to destroy Confederate battleships and burn down the navy yard, presumably to keep them from falling into Union hands.

TEACH

GUIDED DISCUSSION

3. **Summarize** What made the Democrats believe they had a good chance to win the 1864 presidential election? *(Possible response: People were tired of the war, they felt Lincoln had abused his power and disregarded constitutional protections, and the Democrats offered a plan to negotiate an end to the war and reunite the United States.)*

4. **Draw Conclusions** Why was it vital to the Union war effort to capture the Confederate city of Savannah, Georgia? *(Possible response: Savannah was an important business and trade center on the Atlantic coast, and it was deep in Confederate territory. Capturing the city would be both a military and a psychological victory.)*

MORE INFORMATION

Union Deserters and Reenlistment Despite the fact that desertion was punishable by death, many soldiers on both sides assumed the risk and left their armies. For instance, after the disastrous Union defeat at the Battle of Fredericksburg, Union troop morale plummeted, and more than 100 soldiers deserted each day. In addition, in late 1863, many Union soldiers were reaching the end of their first three-year tour of duty, and the army feared they would decide not to reenlist. Union leadership devised a clever solution by offering regiments special benefits and favors if they were able to retain a certain percentage of their original forces for a second tour of duty. Also, those who planned to stay in the army pressured those who planned to leave. For many soldiers, peer pressure proved too great, and they ended up staying with their units.

ACTIVE OPTIONS

On Your Feet: Roundtable Arrange students in groups of four or five. Tell each group to answer the following question: What factors contributed to the Union's decision to wage total war on the Confederacy? Direct groups to have each member answer the question with a different response. Then reconvene the class and discuss the groups' responses.

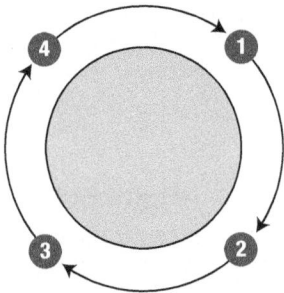

NG Learning Framework: Journal from Two Perspectives

SKILL Communication

KNOWLEDGE Our Human Story

Ask students to work in small groups to conduct online research to find more information about Sherman's march across Georgia and how it affected civilians in both the North and the South. Suggest that students consider such factors as where the civilians lived, their family life, their attitudes toward the war, and how they coped with wartime conditions. Prompt students to use the information to write journal entries from both a northern and southern perspective. Invite students to share their journal entries with the class.

HISTORICAL THINKING

ANSWERS

1. General Sherman's capture of Atlanta and General Sheridan's routing of Confederate forces in the Shenandoah Valley and his destruction of crops and supplies both helped Lincoln's campaign.

2. Possible response: Grant had scored numerous successes in the West by attacking persistently, while commanders in the East repeatedly hesitated to attack or failed to follow up on victories. Lincoln may have moved Grant to the East because he thought the general would take more initiative and give the North a better chance of defeating the South.

3. Lincoln was firmly opposed to slavery and had abolished it symbolically through the Emancipation Proclamation, whereas McClellan was willing to accept the continued practice of slavery as a condition for reunification with the Confederate states.

4. According to the map, Sherman and his troops went north to Columbia, South Carolina, and then marched into North Carolina, capturing Fayetteville and Bentonville before advancing to Raleigh.

LINCOLN'S VISION

Abraham Lincoln's speeches are remembered today as among the finest in the history of the United States. Lincoln was not known as a speaker gifted with a captivating voice or dramatic delivery. The force of his speeches—and of his most significant written documents—came from the words themselves.

The beginning of 1862 was not a happy time for Abraham Lincoln. His son Willie died of typhoid fever, the Union Army was in a deadlock with the Confederates, and the American people were restless. In the summer, Lincoln moved his family to a cottage north of Washington, D.C. There, he wrote one of the most important laws in U.S. history.

On July 22, 1862, Abraham Lincoln read a first draft of the Emancipation Proclamation to his Cabinet. Although he was not delivering a formal speech, he knew his words must win over his chief advisors if his plan to change the focus of the war was to succeed.

The painting below shows Lincoln alone in a messy study. His left hand is resting on a Bible and the U.S. Constitution. A bust of former president James Buchanan, who was seen as a weak leader against secession, hangs from a noose in the corner. Pro-Union Andrew Jackson stares at Lincoln from the mantle of the fireplace. With these details, the artist is hinting at the great weight of history Lincoln must have felt as he wrote the Emancipation Proclamation.

CONSTRUCTED RESPONSE Study the painting carefully. What other examples of symbolism do you notice in the painting?

President Lincoln, Writing the Proclamation of Freedom by David Gilmour Blythe, 1863

DOCUMENT ONE

Primary Source: Speech
The Gettysburg Address, by Abraham Lincoln, November 19, 1863

In November 1863, Abraham Lincoln was invited to speak at the dedication of a cemetery at Gettysburg for the Union soldiers who had perished in the battle. Despite its extreme brevity, or shortness, Lincoln's address to the gathered crowd soon came to be seen as one of the greatest speeches in American history. In it, Lincoln attempted to frame the war as not simply a struggle to keep the Union together but as a fight for the principles of freedom and democracy upon which the country was founded.

CONSTRUCTED RESPONSE To what is Lincoln referring when he speaks of "unfinished work" and "the great task"?

Four score and seven years ago our fathers brought forth on this continent a new nation, conceived in Liberty, and dedicated to the proposition that all men are created equal. Now we are engaged in a great civil war, testing whether that nation or any nation so conceived and so dedicated, can long endure. We are met on a great battlefield of that war. We have come to dedicate a portion of that field, as a final resting place for those who here gave their lives that that nation might live. It is altogether fitting and proper that we should do this. But, in a larger sense, we cannot dedicate—we cannot consecrate—we cannot hallow—this ground. The brave men, living and dead, who struggled here, have consecrated it, far above our poor power to add or detract. The world will little note, nor long remember what we say here, but it can never forget what they did here. It is for us the living, rather, to be dedicated here to the unfinished work which they who fought here have thus far so nobly advanced. It is rather for us to be here dedicated to the great task remaining before us—that from these honored dead we take increased devotion to that cause for which they gave the last full measure of devotion—that we here highly resolve that these dead shall not have died in vain—that this nation, under God, shall have a new birth of freedom—and that government of the people, by the people, for the people, shall not perish from the earth.

DOCUMENT TWO

Primary Source: Speech
from Abraham Lincoln's Second Inaugural Address, March 4, 1865

The war that had begun a month after Lincoln first took office as president was still dragging on when he began his second term in 1865. In his brief second inaugural address, Lincoln suggested that the war was God's punishment for slavery—a sin for which the South and the North shared guilt. And although the end of the war was in sight, he spoke not of triumph but of reconciliation and healing.

CONSTRUCTED RESPONSE What do you think a *bondsman* is, and to what is Lincoln referring with the phrase "two hundred and fifty years of unrequited toil"?

Fondly do we hope, fervently do we pray, that this mighty scourge of war may speedily pass away. Yet, if God wills that it continue until all the wealth piled by the bondsman's two hundred and fifty years of unrequited toil shall be sunk, and until every drop of blood drawn with the lash shall be paid by another drawn with the sword, as was said three thousand years ago, so still it must be said "the judgments of the Lord are true and righteous altogether." With malice toward none, with charity for all, with firmness in the right as God gives us to see the right, let us strive on to finish the work we are in, to bind up the nation's wounds, to care for him who shall have borne the battle and for his widow and his orphan, to do all which may achieve and cherish a just and lasting peace among ourselves and with all nations.

SYNTHESIZE AND WRITE

1. **REVIEW** Review what you have learned about Lincoln's Gettysburg Address and Second Inaugural Address.

2. **RECALL** On your own paper, write the main ideas expressed in each document.

3. **CONSTRUCT** Select one to three key words from either the Gettysburg Address or the Second Inaugural Address and then construct a topic sentence to answer this question: What is the significance of these words to the speech?

4. **WRITE** Using evidence from this chapter and the documents, write a one-paragraph argument that supports your topic sentence in Step 3.

PLAN: 2-PAGE LESSON

OBJECTIVE

Synthesize information about the contexts of Abraham Lincoln's Gettysburg Address and Second Inaugural Address.

CRITICAL THINKING SKILLS FOR LESSON 5.2

- Synthesize
- Draw Conclusions
- Summarize
- Evaluate

HISTORICAL THINKING FOR CHAPTER 12

How did the Civil War change the way different groups of Americans viewed themselves and the nation? As the Civil War dragged on, it produced a sense of weariness and sorrow in the nation. Lesson 5.2 explores two speeches that reflect Lincoln's attempts to rededicate people to the war's cause and to future peace and healing.

BACKGROUND FOR THE TEACHER

President Abraham Lincoln delivered his now famous Gettysburg Address just four months after the Battle of Gettysburg. Though a victory for the Union, the battle resulted in massive casualties on both the Union and Confederate sides. The main speaker scheduled for the cemetery dedication that day was Edward Everett, a former U.S. senator and Massachusetts governor and one of the most popular speakers of his era. Lincoln had been invited to make a few remarks as well. In all, a crowd of about 15,000 attended the dedication ceremony. Everett spoke for about two hours, but it was Lincoln's brief speech that stirred the audience and, ultimately, became enshrined in history. Everett later wrote that he wished he could have come as close to hitting the central point and message of the dedication in two hours as Lincoln had done in only two minutes.

INTRODUCE & ENGAGE

PREPARE FOR THE DOCUMENT-BASED QUESTION

Before students start on the activity, briefly preview the two documents. Remind students that a constructed response requires full explanations in complete sentences. Emphasize that students should use what they have learned about the Civil War in addition to the information in the documents.

TEACH

GUIDED DISCUSSION

1. **Draw Conclusions** How does Lincoln describe what the men who fought at Gettysburg did? *(Possible response: Lincoln describes the soldiers who died at Gettysburg as making a great sacrifice to advance the noble ideals on which the United States was built. He also says that by spilling their blood for such a worthy cause, they made the battlefield a sacred place.)*

2. **Summarize** What future responsibilities did Lincoln assign his listeners in these two speeches? *(He asked the people to rededicate themselves to supporting the war to its conclusion and then to come together as one nation to honor the dead, move forward, and harbor no hatred or ill will toward either side.)*

EVALUATE

After students have completed the Synthesize & Write activity, allow time for them to exchange paragraphs and read and comment on the work of their peers. Establish guidelines for comments prior to the activity so that feedback is constructive and encouraging in nature. Comments should focus on the most significant parts that address the purpose of the activity and the audience.

ACTIVE OPTION

On Your Feet: Think, Pair, Share Ask the following question and allow a few minutes for students to think about it: What influence do you think Civil War events of 1864 might have had on the tone and content of Lincoln's Second Inaugural Address? Then tell students to choose partners and talk about the question. Finally, invite students to share their ideas with the class.

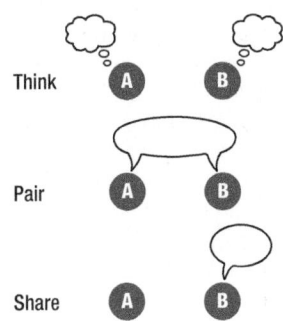

Think   A   B

Pair   A   B

Share   A   B

DIFFERENTIATE

INCLUSION

Highlight and Summarize Help students minimize distractions by creating a handout that includes only the two document excerpts. Give a copy to each student, along with a highlighter. Tell students to highlight important words, phrases, and ideas—first after reading silently and again after reading aloud. Then ask them to write a summary sentence for each document, using several of the words and phrases they highlighted.

PRE-AP

Identify Patterns Instruct students to locate and read the complete text of Lincoln's second inaugural address. Then direct students to compare that speech with the Gettysburg Address, identifying patterns or similarities in theme, language use, or tone or noting other connections between the two speeches. Prompt students to write a brief essay discussing their findings. Invite volunteers to share their essay with the class.

See the Chapter Planner for more strategies for differentiation.

SYNTHESIZE & WRITE

ANSWERS

1. Answers will vary.

2. Answers will vary. Possible responses: The Founding Fathers created a nation that declared equality for all. The terrible war is worth fighting to protect those values and to maintain the United States as a united democratic nation. When the war is over, the two sides must not show malice to one another but instead must work together to care for those affected and to unite the nation in a just, lasting peace.

3. Possible response: Lincoln builds the Gettysburg Address around the different meanings of the word *dedicate*, referring to the nation's commitment to principle, to the burial ground at Gettysburg, and to the people's resolve to continue the fight.

4. Students' arguments should be well reasoned and should include and build upon their topic sentence from Step 3 to reflect clear understanding of the chapter and the documents, backed by relevant textual evidence.

CONSTRUCTED RESPONSE

Document 1: Possible response: He is referring to winning the war not only to save the Union but also to preserve a democratic form of government that is free of slavery.

Document 2: Possible response: A bondsman is a slave. The phrase "two hundred and fifty years of unrequited toil" refers to the fact that in 1865 slavery had existed in North America for two and a half centuries.

CRITICAL VIEWING Possible response: The U.S. flag pulled back to let in light symbolizes America's enlightened ideals, the tipped scales symbolize justice, the globe symbolizes America's place in the world, and the sword on the map symbolizes war.

SURRENDER AND TRAGEDY

Have you ever wondered how two opposing forces can work together after waging war on one another? When it became clear that the Union was the victor in the Civil War, the next challenge for the North and the South was to reunite as one nation. Would both sides win that victory?

CRITICAL VIEWING The National Geographic Society commissioned Tom Lovell to paint *Surrender at Appomattox* in 1965. Why do you think the artist chose to show the Union officers gazing toward Lee, who is dressed in gray and seated apart from them?

SURRENDER AT APPOMATTOX

In mid-January 1865, several weeks after achieving his triumphant March to the Sea, General Sherman issued Special Field Order No. 15. This order reserved confiscated land along the coasts of South Carolina, Georgia, and Florida for former slaves, granting 40-acre plots to those who settled there. Two weeks later, the Republicans in Congress passed the **13th Amendment**, which abolished slavery in the United States forever. One congressman wrote to his wife that "we can now look other nations in the face without shame."

Sherman's 60,000-man army had begun moving northward from Georgia into the Carolinas. As they had during the March to the Sea, the troops lived off the countryside and destroyed much of the local infrastructure. Meanwhile, growing numbers of Confederate soldiers were deserting their armies.

President Lincoln met with Confederate officials in early February at Hampton Roads, Virginia, to try to negotiate an end to the war. He offered slave owners compensation for their freed slaves if the Confederacy would immediately cease fighting, but Confederate president Jefferson Davis refused to submit to the "disgrace of surrender." A month later, Lincoln was sworn in for his second term as president. In his inaugural address, he offered a message of forgiveness and reconciliation, calling for his fellow citizens to "bind up the nation's wounds."

Meanwhile, Grant was finally poised to capture Richmond, which the Union had besieged for months. As Grant's troops worked to surround Petersburg and cut Confederate supply lines, Lee's force was stretched thinner and thinner. Finally, on the night of April 2, Lee evacuated both Richmond and Petersburg, hurrying the Army of Northern Virginia westward along the Appomattox River. Union forces entered Richmond, only to find the Confederates had burned it to the ground rather than allow it to fall intact into enemy hands.

Grant's army set off in hot pursuit of Lee. Seven days later, they confronted each other near the village of **Appomattox Court House** in central Virginia. Lee was moving his troops south to reinforce Confederate forces battling Sherman in North Carolina, but now he was surrounded. With all avenues of escape blocked, Lee had no choice but to surrender.

On April 9, 1865, Lee and Grant met in the living room of a civilian's home in Appomattox Court House, Lee in his full dress uniform and Grant in his muddy field outfit. Lee accepted Grant's terms and surrendered. All Confederate soldiers were pardoned and allowed to keep their private property—including their horses, which they would need for farm work when they returned home. Confederate officers were allowed to keep their sidearms. "The war is over," Grant said. "The Rebels are our countrymen again." But the Confederate soldiers were in bad shape. Many were starving. Grant made sure that all of Lee's men received Union rations.

Though a number of Confederate troops had yet to surrender, and Jefferson Davis remained at large, it was clear that the war had ended. All of the passion and courage the Confederates displayed throughout the war was not enough to defeat the resources and manpower of the industrial North. Celebrations erupted among relieved citizens in cities and towns throughout the North.

In the South, Confederate soldiers and displaced persons began to straggle home. On April 11, 1865, Lincoln addressed a crowd outside the White House on **Reconstruction**, or the process of reorganizing and rebuilding the former Confederate states. He admitted that northerners differed "as to the mode, manner, and means of Reconstruction" and that the white South was "disorganized and discordant."

LINCOLN'S ASSASSINATION

Among the crowd that had gathered to hear Lincoln's address on Reconstruction was a failed actor and southern sympathizer named **John Wilkes Booth**. The previous summer, Booth and several co-conspirators had begun plotting to kidnap the president, but their plans eventually changed from kidnapping to **assassination**, or murder committed for political reasons.

On the evening of April 14, Lincoln and his wife went to Ford's Theater in Washington to see a play. There, Booth approached Lincoln from behind and shot him in the back of the head before leaping to the stage and fleeing. Lincoln died early the next morning. The news stunned Americans and sparked an explosion of anti-southern sentiment in the North. One newspaper mourned that Booth and his conspirators "have stricken down the MAN who stood forth their best intercessor [negotiator] before the nation . . . their truest, most forgiving friend, he who pleaded with his people to temper justice with mercy." In death, Lincoln was transformed from a careworn president into a hero who had given his life to hold the nation together.

Lincoln's funeral train left Washington, D.C., on April 21. Its final destination was Springfield, Illinois, where Lincoln had lived before becoming president. Along the train route, thousands of Americans lined up to mourn and pay respects to the president, who was finally buried on May 4.

THE EFFECTS OF THE WAR

The costs and consequences of the Civil War were profound. The Union expended about $3 billion on for the conflict, while the cost to the Confederacy was about $1 billion. But the monetary cost was dwarfed by the price paid in suffering and loss of life. Total casualties on both sides—including soldiers who were wounded, killed in action, died in prisoner

---

PLAN: 4-PAGE LESSON

OBJECTIVE

Examine the end and the immediate aftermath of the Civil War.

CRITICAL THINKING SKILLS FOR LESSON 5.3

- Determine Word Meaning
- Identify Problems and Solutions
- Form and Support Opinions
- Determine Chronology
- Draw Conclusions
- Analyze Cause and Effect
- Make Inferences
- Compare and Contrast

HISTORICAL THINKING FOR CHAPTER 12

How did the Civil War change the way different groups of Americans viewed themselves and the nation? The Civil War caused economic divisions to deepen between the South and the North. Lesson 5.3 explores postwar laws that helped the nation rebuild.

BACKGROUND FOR THE TEACHER

For about a month after Robert E. Lee's surrender, Jefferson Davis remained at large, pursued by Union forces. On May 3, 1865, Davis and some of his cabinet crossed into Georgia heading west, hoping to gather Confederate forces and continue the fight. In the early morning of May 10, however, Davis and his followers were hemmed in by two different groups of Union cavalry, neither of which recognized the other as belonging to the Union. The Union forces fired on one another, and two cavalrymen were killed before the soldiers realized they were on the same side. Subsequently, they captured Davis and escorted him to a military prison. Accused of treason, he spent two years in prison but never faced a trial and was finally released. Davis never requested a pardon. Until his death in 1889, he remained convinced of the South's right to secede from the Union.

INTRODUCE & ENGAGE
ACTIVATE PRIOR KNOWLEDGE

Discuss with students what they already know about the period just after the end of the Civil War. Remind them that once the war ended, people had to do a lot of work to reunify the nation. Ask students to speculate about what life might have been like in the North and in the South during the post–Civil War period. Explain that in this lesson they will learn important details about the first steps the government took to improve the lives of people in all areas of the nation.

TEACH
GUIDED DISCUSSION

1. **Determine Chronology** Describe in order the actions that led to Lee's surrender to General Grant at Appomattox Court House. *(The Union laid siege to Richmond, Virginia, exhausting Lee's Army of Northern Virginia to the point where Lee had to evacuate his troops. Grant's forces tracked and surrounded them near Appomattox Court House, Virginia, and forced them to surrender.)*

2. **Draw Conclusions** What forms of aid did the South need during Reconstruction? *(Possible response: Much of the South's infrastructure, such as railroads, bridges, and shipyards, had to be rebuilt. Farmers had lost fields and homes to fire or other damage, and many people had lost businesses or land and needed a way to support themselves. Towns heavily damaged by shelling and fires had to be rebuilt. Southerners had to adjust to new laws and a new way of life.)*

3. **Analyze Cause and Effect** What were the immediate results of the assassination of President Lincoln? *(The assassination set off a wave of northern anger against the southern states and turned Abraham Lincoln into a national hero overnight.)*

MORE INFORMATION

Lincoln's Assassination Several people close to Lincoln mentioned that on April 14, 1865, the president seemed happier than he had been in a long time. He and his wife ate an early supper with friends and headed to Ford's Theatre, where Lincoln had seen many performances during the war—including one that featured John Wilkes Booth. When Booth heard by chance of the Lincolns' plans to attend the theater on the evening of April 14, he devised his plan. The actor knew the building well. Still, he prepared by visiting the theater to watch a dress rehearsal on April 13. Immediately after Booth shot Lincoln, however, his plan went awry. The stage was 15 feet below the presidential box, and one of Booth's spurs caught in the flag draped over the side of the box. This caused Booth to tumble onto the stage rather than landing on his feet. He broke one of his legs in the fall, but he managed to stagger offstage, shouting, "*Sic semper tyrannis!*" ("Thus always to tyrants!") before disappearing into the alley that ran alongside the theater. Booth believed that in the end, history would come to show his assassination of Lincoln as the killing of a tyrant.

DIFFERENTIATE
STRIVING READERS

Create Idea Webs Ask students to summarize the lesson by creating four Idea Webs, one for each subsection. Instruct them to complete each web with at least four important ideas from the subsection. Guide students to use their Idea Webs to write a summary statement for each subsection and then a summary statement for the entire lesson. Invite them to compare their summary statements and note similarities and differences.

GIFTED & TALENTED

Create a Podcast Direct students to conduct online research to learn more about the Homestead Act, focusing on who benefited and who did not. Tell them to find primary source documents, such as newspaper articles and posters, as well as secondary sources. Challenge students to discover the impact on Native Americans, African Americans, white families, single women, and the urban poor. Then prompt them to write a script in the form of a podcast, incorporating what they have learned and analyzing the Homestead Act from the perspective of the present day. Invite students to share their podcasts with the class.

See the Chapter Planner for more strategies for differentiation.

CRITICAL VIEWING Possible responses: The Union officers may face Lee because the surrender is a momentous occasion deserving somber respect; every Union officer is likely considering how he would feel if the situation were reversed and the Union forced to surrender; the artist shows that although the Confederates are surrendering, the two sides do not fully trust one another and so are keeping their distance.

of war camps, and succumbed to disease—topped 1 million: about 640,000 from the Union and more than 480,000 from the Confederacy.

Two out of three deaths occurred not on the battlefields, but in the field hospitals, as diseases and infections took their toll. Army surgeons prescribed millions of doses of **morphine**, a highly addictive medication, to ease their patients' pain, and many Civil War **veterans**, or people who served in the military, became addicted to it.

The war affected the financial situations of families in both the North and the South. Many wounded veterans were permanently disabled and could no longer work, and thousands of fathers, sons, and brothers never returned home at all, resulting in the loss of the family breadwinner. Some families fell into poverty, and many homes, farms, and businesses had to be rebuilt. This was especially true in the former Confederacy.

Major southern cities had been reduced to ruins and ash. Much of the South's infrastructure had been destroyed; weeds and brush had taken over fields, and farm values fell by half. However, abolition of slavery and the resulting loss of "free" slave labor was the largest blow to the southern economy. Paying wages for the masses of workers needed to keep a large plantation going hit the owners hard.

Things were not as dire in the North. While the war did not fundamentally change the North's economy, it did speed up processes already well underway. Northern manufacturers saw their businesses and profits expand during the war due to the demand for their products. Northern farmers began using machinery to plant, harvest, and process their crops, reducing the amount of farm labor required.

The war also resulted in a major change in the United States government. The balance of power shifted from individual states and regions to Washington, D.C., and the Union victory boosted Republican power in both the legislative and executive branches. The success of the Republican party—which would continue for decades—and the creation of a national currency and banking system aided the flow of money, spurred the growth of business, and triggered an expansion of the federal government.

NEW LAWS LOOK FORWARD

Before the war even ended, the federal government began asserting its new power. In 1862, the Republicans succeeded in passing three important pieces of legislation. The **Morrill College Land Grant Act** provided each state with 30,000 acres of federal land grants for each member of its congressional delegation. The states then sold the land and used the proceeds to fund 69 public colleges, most of which focused on agriculture and the mechanical arts. These "land grant colleges" include Cornell University, the Massachusetts Institute of Technology, and the University of Wisconsin at Madison.

The **Homestead Act** also involved land grants, but the recipients were individuals. Any adult citizen who headed a family could qualify for a grant of 160 acres of public land by paying a registration fee and living on the land continuously for 5 years. The act also permitted a farmer to purchase the land from the government at a reduced rate after only six months of residency. By the end of the 19th century, the U.S. government had distributed more than 80 million acres to Americans through the provisions of the Homestead Act.

Finally, the Pacific Railway Acts provided funds and land grants for the creation of a nationwide railroad network, specifically one that would connect the Atlantic and the Pacific coasts by train—a transcontinental railroad. The acts authorized both the Union Pacific and the Central Pacific companies to construct rail lines from the Missouri River to the continent's west coast. The war slowed this effort, but interest in a transcontinental railroad picked back up once the conflict was over.

The United States emerged from the Civil War a changed nation. The demands of wartime had led to the draft and government involvement in transportation and business. The war had also profoundly shifted the balance of power among the regions of the country: After Lee's surrender at Appomattox, the South's political dominance over the national agenda was broken. Now it was time to bring the South back into the Union.

HISTORICAL THINKING

1. **READING CHECK** What happened at Appomattox Court House?

2. **DETERMINE WORD MEANING** Reread the last sentence of "Surrender at Appomattox." What do you think *discordant* means in this context?

3. **IDENTIFY PROBLEMS AND SOLUTIONS** What problem was Sherman addressing when he issued Special Field Order No. 15?

4. **FORM AND SUPPORT OPINIONS** What do you think was the biggest problem facing the United States after the Civil War? Explain your answer.

War Department, Washington, April 20, 1865.
$100,000 REWARD!
THE MURDERER
Of our late beloved President, Abraham Lincoln,
IS STILL AT LARGE.
$50,000 REWARD
Will be paid by this Department for his apprehension, in addition to any reward offered by Municipal Authorities or State Executives.
$25,000 REWARD
Will be paid for the apprehension of JOHN H. SURRATT, one of Booth's Accomplices.
$25,000 REWARD
Will be paid for the apprehension of David C. Harold, another of Booth's accomplices.
GENERAL ORDER – All persons harboring or secreting the said persons, or either of them, or aiding or assisting their concealment or escape, will be treated as accomplices in the murder of the President and the attempted assassination of the Secretary of State, and shall be subject to trial before a Military Commission and the punishment of DEATH.

A PRESIDENTIAL FUNERAL

Lincoln's assassination caused a frenzy in Washington, D.C., and his family scrambled to plan the president's funeral. Soldiers carried Lincoln's body from the boardinghouse where he died to the White House. A hearse, shown above, transported the body to a ceremony near the Capitol and then to a train headed for Springfield, Illinois, where Lincoln was to be buried. Meanwhile, law enforcement set to work on capturing Booth and his accomplices. Wanted signs (left) for Booth's arrest were posted all over Washington, D.C., and the surrounding areas.

BUILD BACKGROUND

THE RAILROAD PRESIDENT

When the train carrying Abraham Lincoln's coffin pulled out of the depot in Washington, D.C., on April 19, 1865, it embarked on a journey that in many ways reflected the fallen president's legacy. Lincoln had first come to public life just as new locomotive technologies were evolving into major American rail systems. As a young Illinois legislator, he argued for construction of more train lines and later worked directly for a railroad company. These factors fueled his reputation as a champion of America's railroads. On his journey to Washington when first elected president, Lincoln took a circuitous route over railways through the northern and midwestern states, giving speeches to assure crowds of his intention to unify the nation. On his sad return journey four years later, every railroad crossing was lined with people of all ages who came to pay their final respects as his funeral train passed by.

19TH-CENTURY OPIATE USE

To 19th-century physicians and patients, morphine and other opiates must have seemed like medical magic. They could relieve pain quickly and completely and treat the symptoms of many conditions—from asthma to gastrointestinal disease to gunshot wounds. During the Civil War, the Union Army alone doled out nearly 10 million opium pills and 2.8 million ounces of opium powder and tinctures to its wounded soldiers, many of whom became addicted. These medications were so commonplace among both military and civilian doctors that soldiers who were not addicted when they came home from the war often found themselves treated by family physicians more than willing to inject them with opiates for all manner of complaints. Fifteen percent of all medical prescriptions in Boston in the late 1880s were for opiates, and by 1890 pharmacists were openly selling the drugs in an unregulated marketplace to doctors and self-medicating patients alike.

TEACH

GUIDED DISCUSSION

4. Make Inferences Why do you think the death toll from disease and infections was higher than that for wounds from battle during the Civil War? *(Answers will vary. Possible response: Soldiers' health on both sides was likely affected by limited access to medicine or nutritious food. In addition, troops had to travel long hours through bad weather, camp in makeshift shelters, and live in very close proximity to one another. All of these factors would have contributed to a high possibility of death from disease and infections.)*

5. Compare and Contrast What was the most crucial difference between postwar life in the northern and the southern states? *(Possible response: The war devastated the South's economy through neglected and destroyed farmland and the loss of slave labor, but the North still had a thriving manufacturing economy, which had benefited from wartime production.)*

DRAW CONCLUSIONS

Review with students the post–Civil War legislation described in the lesson, including the Morrill College Land Grant Act, the Homestead Act, and the Pacific Railway Acts. **ASK:** In what ways did these acts affect the spirit and mission of Lincoln's vow to bring the nation together? *(Possible response: All these acts provided Americans with opportunities to help pull themselves out of poverty or hardship and gain an economic foothold, whether through education, land and housing, or expanded business opportunities through improved transportation and shipping.)*

ACTIVE OPTIONS

On Your Feet: Numbered Heads Organize students into groups of four and ask each group member to number off. Instruct groups to analyze and discuss how the United States might be different today—economically, socially, and politically—if the Confederacy had won the Civil War. Then call a number and have the student with that number in each group report for the group.

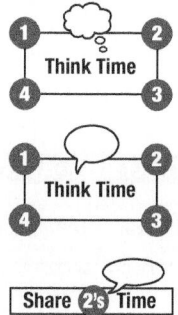

NG Learning Framework: Write a Eulogy

SKILLS Communication, Collaboration

KNOWLEDGE Our Human Story

Instruct students to work in pairs to conduct online research to look at examples of eulogies, or speeches crafted to honor someone who has died. Tell them to imagine that their task is to write a eulogy for Lincoln, highlighting what they consider to be his greatest accomplishments. Prompt pairs to collect details for their eulogies from the text and additional online research. Invite them to present their completed eulogies to the class.

HISTORICAL THINKING

ANSWERS

1. General Lee surrendered the Confederate Army of Northern Virginia to General Grant, ending the Civil War.

2. It means "not in agreement with one another."

3. The South's enslaved workers had been freed, but they had no land of their own.

4. Answers will vary. Possible responses: The biggest problem was incorporating freed slaves into society because they had no land and faced open hostility and discrimination. The biggest problem was overcoming bitterness and anger between northerners and southerners because the war had a clear winner and a clear loser and many casualties on both sides. The biggest problem was rebuilding the South's economy and infrastructure, both of which had been badly damaged by the war and had to be addressed without the use of enslaved labor.

VOCABULARY

Write a sentence using each of the following key terms.

1. writ of *habeas corpus*
   Thanks to the writ of habeas corpus, he was able to appear before a judge and claim that his arrest was illegal.

2. border state
3. defensive war
4. cavalry
5. ironclad
6. contraband
7. Copperhead
8. draft
9. total war

READING STRATEGY
MAKE INFERENCES

When you make inferences, you use what you already know to understand the meaning of a text. Complete the following chart to make inferences about the major challenges the nation faced immediately following the Civil War. Then answer the question.

Before the War	During the War	After the War

10. What major challenges did the nation face as it began to reunite after the war?

MAIN IDEAS

Answer the following questions. Support your answers with evidence from the chapter.

11. Why was fighting a defensive war an advantage for the South? LESSON 1.1

12. Why did civilian spectators come out from Washington to watch the First Battle of Bull Run? LESSON 1.2

13. What was the outcome of the battle between the *Monitor* and the *Virginia*, the first two ironclads that faced each other in the war? LESSON 2.1

14. Why was the Battle of Antietam considered a stalemate? LESSON 2.2

15. What did the Emancipation Proclamation declare about slaves in rebelling states? LESSON 3.1

16. Why was General Grant's capture of Vicksburg a turning point in the war? LESSON 4.1

17. What was the outcome of the Battle of Gettysburg? LESSON 4.3

18. Why was the Union's presidential election of 1864 important to the Confederacy? LESSON 5.1

19. What was the outcome of the siege of Richmond and Petersburg? LESSON 5.3

HISTORICAL THINKING

Answer the following questions. Support your answers with evidence from the chapter.

20. IDENTIFY How did views about the "proper" role of women in the medical field change during the war?

21. DRAW CONCLUSIONS Why did Missouri become the site of heated conflict during the war?

22. MAKE INFERENCES Why might some people have thought General McClellan was an indecisive leader?

23. DISTINGUISH FACT AND OPINION Some Copperheads said the Radical Republicans' insistence on making the end of slavery a condition of peace would only lead to more bloodshed. Is this statement a fact or an opinion? Explain.

24. COMPARE AND CONTRAST How were the siege of Vicksburg and the siege of Richmond and Petersburg alike and different?

25. FORM AND SUPPORT OPINIONS Should Robert E. Lee and other Confederate officials be remembered as heroes or as villains? Explain your answer.

INTERPRET GRAPHS

Examine the graph at right, which illustrates how inflation affected the North and the South by showing how much buying power Americans had in each region throughout the war. Then answer the questions.

26. If a northerner paid $1.46 for three pounds of tea in 1865, how much would a southerner pay for the same item?

27. How many times higher was the cost of that tea in the South in 1865 compared with 1862?

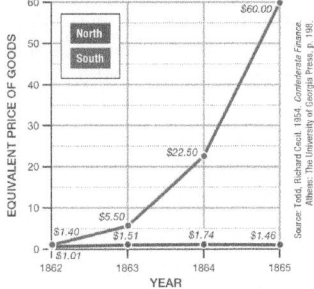

Inflation: North and South

ANALYZE SOURCES

In the early years of the Civil War, Confederate forces often took advantage of the rich agricultural resources of Virginia's Shenandoah Valley. In September 1864, Union general Philip Sheridan embarked on a strategic campaign of destruction throughout the valley. In November, a Confederate soldier named Richard Habersham described the devastation he saw as his army marched through the area.

> It is a sad sight to see this beautiful valley desolated as it is. All along the route from Staunton to this place houses are leveled to the ground and tack wantonly destroyed and horses by the hundreds lying scattered over the fields or stretched off on the roadside either killed in [Confederate general Jubal] Early's last fight or died and left unburied. . . . Our infantry is now in line of battle[,] the bugle is sounding for the horses to be taken up and we are—I think about to have a little excitement of some kind, probably a battle, as the sharpshooters are all in the front ready for action.

28. What emotions does Habersham express in this excerpt?

CONNECT TO YOUR LIFE

29. ARGUMENT Think about the principles that people were willing to fight for during the Civil War. Consider how people battled to abolish slavery or uphold it, to preserve the Union or secede from it. Now think about the principles you believe are worth fighting to protect. Would you be willing to go to war to uphold them? Write a paragraph defending your principles and explaining why it is important to stand up for them.

TIPS

- Make a list of what you consider to be the most important principles a person should follow. Note where you see a potential conflict between two of your listed principles.

- Note events in your life when you needed to stand up for your beliefs and how you dealt with these challenges.

- Connect one of the events in your personal life with the struggle over principles that took place during the Civil War.

VOCABULARY ANSWERS

1. Thanks to the writ of *habeas corpus*, he was able to appear before a judge and claim that his arrest was illegal.

2. Lincoln believed that it was important to keep the border states in the Union, even if it meant allowing slavery there.

3. Southerners fought a defensive war, protecting their homes, families, and communities.

4. General Lee ordered his cavalry to ride out and scout the Union troops' positions.

5. The metal covering on the ironclads changed the way sea battles were fought.

6. General Lee welcomed the contraband that J.E.B. Stuart's men seized from Union troops.

7. The Copperheads would have tolerated slavery in return for the South rejoining the Union.

8. The draft required men to serve in the military during the war.

9. The Union Army under Grant and Sherman waged total war, devastating towns and countrysides.

READING STRATEGY ANSWER

Before the War	During the War	After the War
Southern economy is based on enslaved labor.	Lincoln issues Emancipation Proclamation and Congress passes the 13th Amendment.	South must rebuild its economy using wage labor.
Southern states secede.	Nation is divided into the Confederacy and the Union.	Southern states must be readmitted to the Union.
Political power rests with the states.	Federal power grows.	States must adjust to the new balance of power.

10. Answers will vary. Possible response: Prior to the war the southern economy was based on enslaved labor, but when slavery ended, the South had to rebuild its economy using wage labor. In addition, political power had rested with the states prior to the war, but federal power grew during the war, and states faced the challenge of adjusting to the new balance of power after the war—especially states that had seceded.

MAIN IDEAS ANSWERS

11. Southerners often fought in familiar territory and among civilians who supported their cause.

12. The spectators viewed the battle as entertainment because they expected to witness a quick victory.

13. The two ships fired on each other for hours, but the battle ended in a draw. Overall, however, the result favored the Union because that side retained control of Hampton Roads.

14. Antietam was considered a stalemate because neither side gained a meaningful objective. Lee's army held its ground but took major casualties, and McClellan did not succeed in destroying Lee's army.

15. The Emancipation Proclamation declared that slaves in rebelling states would be considered free as of January 1, 1863.

16. The capture of Vicksburg gave the Union control of the entire Mississippi River, splitting the Confederacy in two.

17. Union forces defeated Lee's Confederate forces at Gettysburg, ending Lee's invasion of the North.

18. The presidential election of 1864 was important to the Confederacy because its outcome could determine the fate of the South. George McClellan, Lincoln's challenger, had indicated that he was willing to allow slavery to continue if the Confederate states rejoined the Union.

19. After months of enduring the siege, Lee hastily pulled his troops out of both cities and led them westward, letting the cities fall to the Union.

HISTORICAL THINKING ANSWERS

20. Before the war, nursing was not considered a "proper" pursuit for women. During the war, a shortage of male nurses and high demand led to women serving as nurses. As a result of their efforts, it became acceptable and more common for women to become nurses.

21. Missouri was a Union state that permitted slavery, and the population was divided over the issue. Lincoln had placed John C. Frémont in command of Union forces in the state. When Frémont imposed martial law in an attempt to put down Confederate guerrilla attacks, border states threatened to secede and the imposition of martial law angered Missouri citizens.

22. People might have considered McClellan an indecisive leader because he was slow to implement his war plans and repeatedly let Confederate troops retreat without pursuing them.

23. The Copperheads' claim that making the end of slavery a condition of peace would only lead to more bloodshed is an opinion because it is based on a future outcome and cannot be verified. It tells what the Copperheads believe will happen.

24. Possible response: The sieges were alike in that they were carried out by Union forces commanded by General Grant, involved cities of great importance to the Confederacy, and ultimately resulted in Union capture of the besieged cities. The sieges differed in duration and outcome. The siege of Vicksburg lasted 47 days, while the siege of Richmond and Petersburg went on for months. Confederate forces surrendered in Vicksburg but fled Richmond and Petersburg.

25. Answers will vary. Possible responses: Lee and other Confederate officials should be remembered as villains because they were fighting to defend slavery, an immoral institution. In addition, secession was an act of treason against the United States. Lee and other Confederate officials should be remembered as heroes because they were fighting to save the southern economy and way of life.

INTERPRET GRAPHS ANSWERS   STEM

26. $60.00

27. almost 43 times higher

ANALYZE SOURCES ANSWER

28. Habersham expresses sadness over the destruction he sees, but he seems excited about the prospect of an impending battle.

CONNECT TO YOUR LIFE ANSWER

29. Arguments will vary, but students' paragraphs should identify principles they believe are worth fighting for and explain why. They should support their positions with references to specific principles and potential conflicts between those principles. They should also make references to times in their lives when they had to defend their beliefs and then relate one of those events to the ways people struggled over principles during the Civil War.

UNIT 4 RESOURCES

UNIT INTRODUCTION

UNIT TIME LINE

UNIT WRAP-UP

NATIONAL GEOGRAPHIC | CONNECTION

National Geographic Magazine Adapted Articles
- "A Sketch in Time"
- "Lincoln" ONLINE

Unit 4 Inquiry: Analyze the Legacy of Slavery

NG Learning Framework Activities
- Create a Compromise Guide
- Investigate Medical Care

Unit 4 Formal Assessment

UNIT 4 1846–1877
THE DEEPEST CRISIS

CRITICAL VIEWING The first major conflict to be extensively photographed was the American Civil War. This photo, taken by G.N. Houghton in the early 1860s, shows Union troops stationed at Camp Griffin in Langley, Virginia—a Confederate state. Based on the details in this photograph, what do you predict may have taken place shortly after it was taken?

CHAPTER 13 RESOURCES

Available at NGLSync.Cengage.com

TEACHER RESOURCES & ASSESSMENT

Reading and Note-Taking

Vocabulary Practice

Social Studies Skills Lessons
- Reading: Compare and Contrast
- Writing: Explanatory

Formal Assessment
- Chapter 13 Pretest
- Chapter 13 Tests A & B
- Section Quizzes

Chapter 13 Answer Key

ExamView®
One-time Download

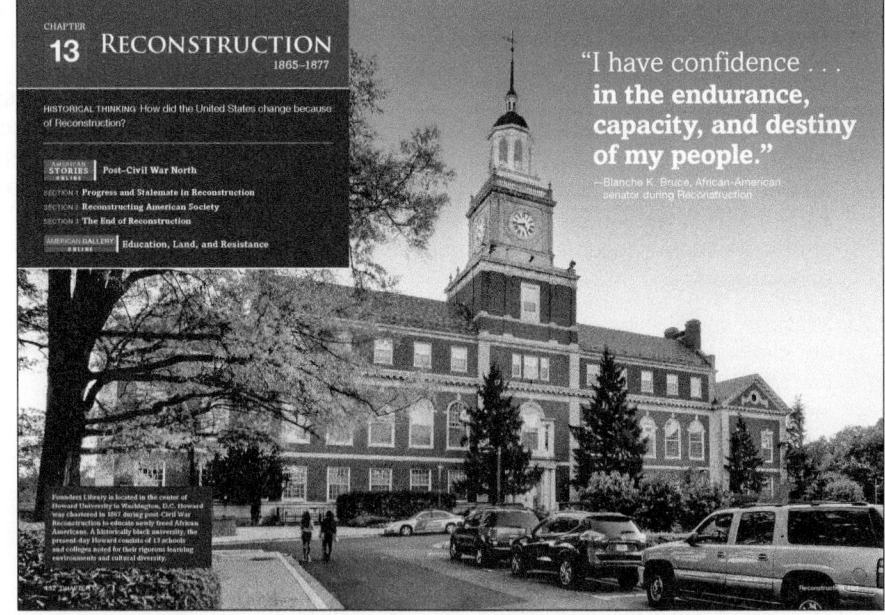

CHAPTER 13 RECONSTRUCTION 1865–1877

HISTORICAL THINKING: How did the United States change because of Reconstruction?

AMERICAN STORIES ONLINE | Post-Civil War North

SECTION 1 Progress and Stalemate in Reconstruction
SECTION 2 Reconstructing American Society
SECTION 3 The End of Reconstruction

AMERICAN GALLERY ONLINE | Education, Land, and Resistance

"I have confidence . . . **in the endurance, capacity, and destiny of my people.**"
—Blanche K. Bruce, African-American senator during Reconstruction

Founders Library is located in the center of Howard University in Washington, D.C. Howard was chartered in 1867 during post-Civil War Reconstruction to educate newly freed African Americans. A historically black university, the present-day Howard consists of 13 schools and colleges noted for their rigorous learning environments and cultural diversity.

STUDENT DIGITAL RESOURCES

- eEdition
- Handbooks
- Online Atlas
- American Gallery Online
- History Notebook
- Active History
- American Voices (Biographies)
- Literature Analysis
- Projects for Inquiry-Based Learning

Chapter 13 Spanish Resources are available at NGLSync.Cengage.com.

AMERICAN
STORIES
ONLINE **The Post–Civil War North**

- Study Primary Sources: Viewpoints on civil rights from the post–Civil War period

- On Your Feet: Write a Eulogy

NG Learning Framework:
Compile a Centennial Display

SECTION 1 RESOURCES

PROGRESS AND STALEMATE IN RECONSTRUCTION

LESSON 1.1
Reconstruction Under Andrew Johnson

- On Your Feet: Fishbowl

NG Learning Framework:
Create a Unified Cause-and-Effect Chain

LESSON 1.2
Radical Reconstruction

- On Your Feet: Analyze Goals and Outcomes

NG Learning Framework:
Prepare Trial Arguments

SECTION 2 RESOURCES

RECONSTRUCTING AMERICAN SOCIETY

LESSON 2.1
The South After the War

- On Your Feet: Numbered Heads

NG Learning Framework:
Write an Opinion Piece

LESSON 2.2
Promises and Reforms

AMERICAN **GALLERY** ONLINE   Education, Land, and Resistance

NG Learning Framework:
Create a Display of Progress

American Voices Biography

Hiram Revels ONLINE

SECTION 3 RESOURCES

THE END OF RECONSTRUCTION

LESSON 3.1
Grant's Presidency

- Active History: Amend the Constitution

NG Learning Framework:
Write a Letter to the President

LESSON 3.2
The End of an Era

- On Your Feet: Compete in a True-False Quiz

NG Learning Framework:
Create an Editorial Cartoon Gallery

CHAPTER 13 REVIEW

STRIVING READERS

STRATEGY ①
READ AND RECALL

Tell students to read the lesson independently. After they read, pair students and have them take notes as they share content that they recall. Then direct pairs to review the lesson and decide what to add or change in their notes.

Use with All Lessons

STRATEGY ②
CLARIFY INFORMATION

Help students clarify information about Ku Klux Klan activities following the Civil War and congressional efforts to counteract them. As they read the lesson, instruct students to create and label a T-Chart as shown. Tell them to note key facts about Klan activities and efforts to suppress them.

Klan Activities	Anti-Klan Efforts

Encourage students to compare their completed charts, note differences, and make corrections as necessary.

Use with Lesson 2.1

STRATEGY ③
MAKE A CHART

Instruct students to create a chart to help them understand the main purpose and details of the constitutional amendments discussed in the chapter. Tell them to note each amendment's number and main purpose as they read. After students read independently, place them in pairs and tell them to take turns, with one partner rereading paragraphs related to each amendment aloud while the other listens and identifies details to add to the third column.

Amendment	Main Purpose	Details
13th		
14th		
15th		

Use with Lessons 1.1, 1.2, and 3.1

INCLUSION

STRATEGY ①
PROVIDE TERMS AND NAMES ON AUDIO

Decide which of the terms and names are important for mastery and ask a volunteer to record the pronunciations and a short sentence defining each term and name. Encourage students to listen to the recording as often as necessary.

Use with All Lessons *You might also use the recording to quiz students on their mastery of the terms and names. Play one definition at a time and ask students to identify the term or name described.*

STRATEGY ②
USE ECHO READING

Point out that the Main Idea statements all relate to important ideas and events that impacted post–Civil War Reconstruction. Pair students with proficient readers who can read the Main Idea statement at the beginning of each lesson aloud. Have the partner "echo" the statement and then restate it in his or her own words.

Use with All Lessons *Pairs might continue to echo read selected paragraphs or entire subsections of each lesson.*

ENGLISH LANGUAGE LEARNERS ELD

STRATEGY 1
ACTIVATE PRIOR KNOWLEDGE

Display the words and terms below in a random "splash" arrangement. Tell students that all the terms relate to the period of Reconstruction following the Civil War. Ask them to discuss ideas the terms bring to mind. Then instruct them to work in pairs to write sentences using one or two of the terms in each one. You may wish to pair students at the **Emerging** level with students at the **Expanding** or **Bridging** level.

military rule

integrate

carpetbaggers

equal rights sharecropping tenant farmers

freedmen

debt social justice poll taxes

black codes literacy tests

scandal

citizen corruption economic panic

Use with All Lessons

STRATEGY 2
USE SENTENCE STRIPS

Choose a paragraph from the lesson and make sentence strips from it. Read the paragraph aloud while students follow along in their books. Pair students at the **Emerging** and **Expanding** levels and ask them to close their books. Then give pairs the set of sentence strips and instruct them to put the strips in order. Invite students to take turns reading the resulting paragraph aloud.

Use with All Lessons *You may ask students at the Emerging level to read the sentences aloud and ask their partners to explain unfamiliar words before working together to arrange the sentences in the correct order.*

STRATEGY 3
CREATE MEANING MAPS

Pair students at the **Emerging** level with those at the **Expanding** or **Bridging** level. Demonstrate using a Meaning Map for Key Vocabulary or other important words and terms in the lesson. Encourage students to discuss the words to clarify meanings.

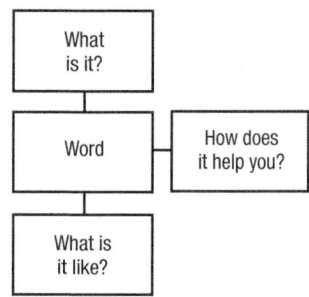

Use with All Lessons

GIFTED & TALENTED

STRATEGY 1
WRITE AND PERFORM JOURNAL ENTRIES

Tell students to access primary and secondary source materials to learn more about the experiences of freedmen during Reconstruction. Then ask them to imagine themselves to be recently freed African Americans living in one of the former Confederate states. Instruct students to write journal entries from this perspective and based on their research about what freedmen experienced, thought, felt, and hoped. Invite students to practice and then perform a reading of their journal entries for the class.

Use after Lesson 2.2

STRATEGY 2
CONDUCT AN INTERVIEW

With students in pairs, have them plan and write an interview with one student playing the role of interviewer and the other responding as Oliver Otis Howard. The interview should focus on Howard's actions, motivations, failings, and achievements. Direct pairs to conduct research and then formulate questions and in-depth responses about Howard's Christian beliefs, his experiences as a teacher and Union general, and his work at the Freedmen's Bureau. Ask students to clarify Howard's moral and philosophical stances, especially regarding voting rights, land, and education for African Americans. Students may perform the interview live or record it.

Use with Lesson 2.2

PRE-AP

STRATEGY 1
EXPLORE INTEGRATION DURING RECONSTRUCTION

Direct students to write a research essay about the short- and long-term consequences of the efforts to integrate African Americans as equal citizens during Reconstruction. Suggest that they use print and online sources to explore both the immediate effects and their present-day repercussions. Invite students to share their essays with the class.

Use with Lessons 1.1 and 2.2

STRATEGY 2
EVALUATE GRANT'S LEGACY

Inform students that historians and biographers have had sharply divergent interpretations of President Grant's presidency. Challenge students to conduct research on the topic, taking notes on the evidence for different viewpoints. Then have them evaluate Grant's presidency based on their findings. Invite them to present their evaluation to the class in an oral or written report.

Use with Lessons 3.1 and 3.2

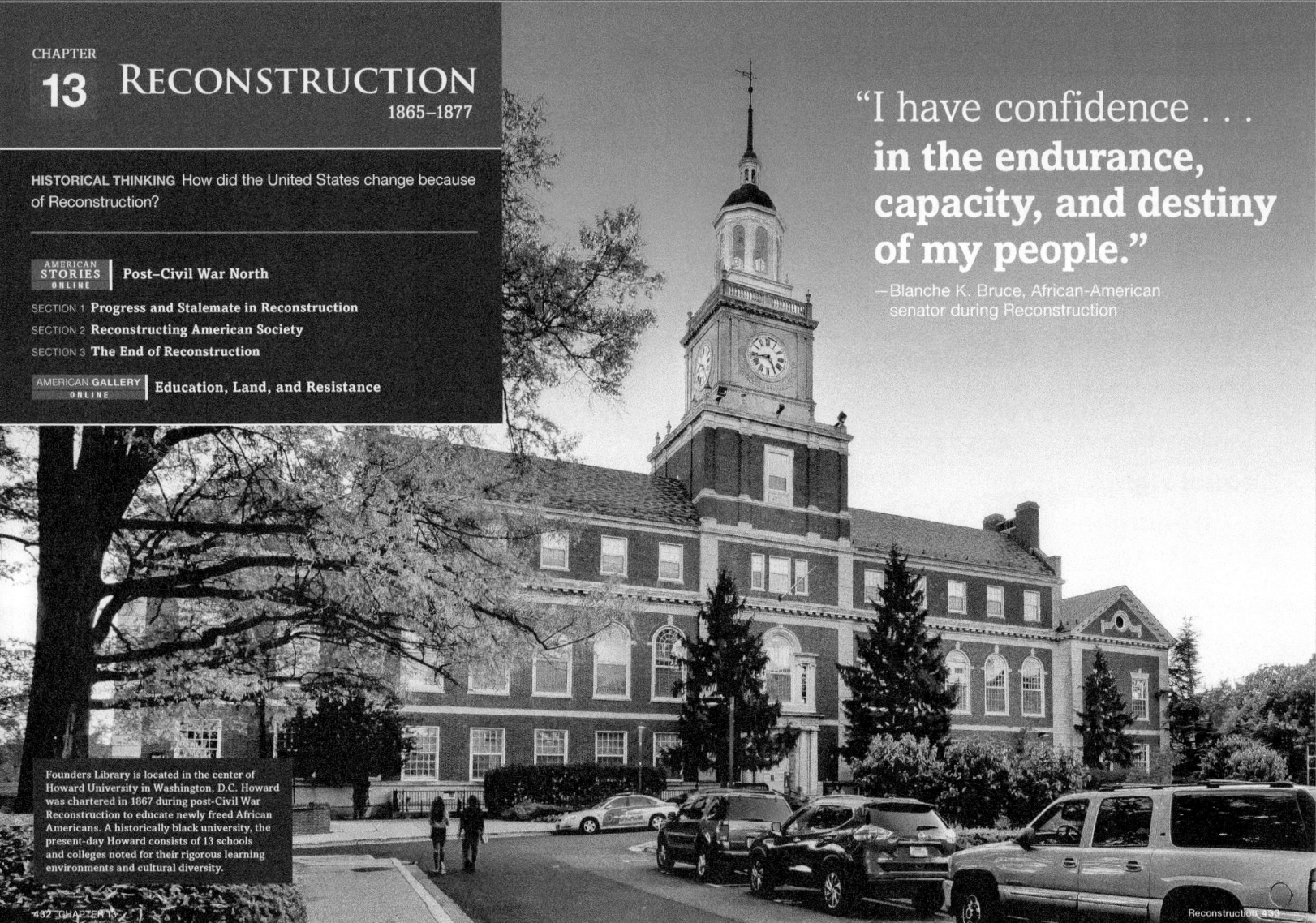

13 RECONSTRUCTION
1865–1877

HISTORICAL THINKING How did the United States change because of Reconstruction?

AMERICAN STORIES ONLINE Post–Civil War North

SECTION 1 **Progress and Stalemate in Reconstruction**

SECTION 2 **Reconstructing American Society**

SECTION 3 **The End of Reconstruction**

AMERICAN GALLERY ONLINE Education, Land, and Resistance

"I have confidence . . . **in the endurance, capacity, and destiny of my people.**"

—Blanche K. Bruce, African-American senator during Reconstruction

Founders Library is located in the center of Howard University in Washington, D.C. Howard was chartered in 1867 during post-Civil War Reconstruction to educate newly freed African Americans. A historically black university, the present-day Howard consists of 13 schools and colleges noted for their rigorous learning environments and cultural diversity.

Reconstruction 433

INTRODUCE THE PHOTOGRAPH

HOWARD UNIVERSITY FOUNDERS LIBRARY

Direct students' attention to the photograph, caption, and quotation, and ask them to study the details of Founders Library. Then provide a photograph of Independence Hall, and explain that the style of architecture of Founders Library is called colonial revival. **ASK:** Why do you think the architect chose to base his design on colonial architecture? *(Possible response: Since the design is similar to Independence Hall, the architect must have wanted Founders Library to represent a place of freedom, learning, expression, and new beginnings.)* **ASK:** How does Blanche K. Bruce's quotation relate to the photograph? *(Possible response: Howard University represented new educational opportunities for African Americans. Bruce's quotation underscores the belief that, given equal rights and opportunities, African Americans could succeed, as evidenced by Bruce's position as senator during Reconstruction.)*

SHARE BACKGROUND

The four-story Founders Library was designed by African-American architect Albert I. Cassell, who used Philadelphia's Independence Hall as his inspiration. The library, which opened in 1939, also housed the university's law school from 1944 to 1955, a time when key civil rights cases were being decided in the courts. Today, the library system houses 1.8 million volumes and contains the Moorland-Spingarn Research Center, one of the largest collections of records documenting black experience worldwide. In 2016, the National Trust for Historic Preservation designated the Founders Library building as a national treasure. National Trust president Stephanie Meeks said of the preservation, ". . . we're going to make Founders a creative learning space for the 21st century, while maintaining its distinctive character and central place in the life of the university."

For Chapter 13 Spanish Resources, visit the Resources Menu. Chapter 13 Resources are available at NGLSync.Cengage.com.

How did the United States change because of Reconstruction?

Jigsaw Activity: Preview Content In this activity, students draw on what they have learned to suggest ways to reunify the divided country in the aftermath of the Civil War. Arrange the class into three groups and assign each group a chapter section title. Guide students to discuss what they think they will learn. Ask them to consider the following clues and questions:

Group 1 Section 1 describes two competing plans designed to bring southern states back into the Union. What requirements should be placed on the former Confederate states? What might be the most important needs of freed African Americans?

Group 2 Section 2 presents efforts to rebuild the economic and social structures of the South. After the destruction of war, what are some of the best ways to restore a state or region? At what pace should changes be made?

Group 3 Section 3 examines the nation's new crises and shifting priorities in the 1870s. How can a government ensure that hard-won rights and freedoms are protected in the face of new challenges?

Regroup students so that each new group has at least one member from each original group. Have students share their predictions about their assigned section so that other students can anticipate what might be covered in Chapter 13.

INTRODUCE THE READING STRATEGY

COMPARE AND CONTRAST

Explain to students that comparing and contrasting can help them more deeply understand historical concepts and events. Turn to the Chapter Review and preview using the Venn diagram. As students read the chapter, guide them to compare and contrast topics related to Reconstruction, such as the similarities and differences between Presidential Reconstruction and Radical Reconstruction.

KEY DATES FOR CHAPTER 13

1865	Andrew Johnson assumes the presidency
1865	Presidential Reconstruction begins
1865	Freedmen's Bureau is created
1866	Civil Rights Act becomes law
1867	Radical Reconstruction begins
1868	14th Amendment ratified
1870	15th Amendment ratified
1871	Ku Klux Klan Acts become law
1873	Financial panic triggers depression
1876	Supreme Court weakens 14th and 15th amendments
1877	Compromise of 1877 ends Reconstruction

INTRODUCE CHAPTER VOCABULARY

KEY VOCABULARY

SECTION 1

amnesty	integrate	Radical Reconstruction
carpetbagger	Presidential Reconstruction	scalawag
collateral		

SECTION 2

debt peonage	sharecropping	voter intimidation
Freedmen's Bureau	social justice	wage economy
lien	tenant farmer	

SECTION 3

Compromise of 1877	Panic of 1873	poll tax
literacy test		

DEFINITION CHART

As students read the chapter, tell them to complete a Definition Chart for Key Vocabulary words. Instruct them to list Key Vocabulary words in the left column of the chart. Then, as they encounter each word, they write the word's definition in the center column and what the word means, in their own words, in the last column. Model an example using the graphic organizer below.

Word	Definition	In My Own Words
amnesty	the pardon of a large group of individuals by a government or other authority	forgiving people for the offenses they committed

AMERICAN
STORIES
ONLINE

For instructional support for the online American Story "The Post–Civil War North," go to NGLSync.Cengage.com.

RECONSTRUCTION UNDER ANDREW JOHNSON

Even the best of friends can break up after a bitter argument. But how do you become friends again? The Civil War had divided the United States between the North and the South. After the war, would it be possible to repair this division and reunite the nation?

THE NATION'S CHALLENGES

The nation was still deeply divided after the surrender of the Confederacy. Plans for a postwar Reconstruction had first been discussed in December 1863, when President Lincoln proposed an **amnesty**, or pardon, plan. This plan would allow Confederate states to organize new governments once 10 percent of the male population took an oath of loyalty to the United States. Lincoln's approach echoed his call from the Second Inaugural Address to act "with malice toward none, with charity for all."

But Lincoln was dead, assassinated in April 1865, and the nation was left to steer the course of rebuilding without his thoughtful guidance and strong leadership. Vice President **Andrew Johnson**, a former Democrat from Tennessee who was chosen for the 1864 Republican ticket to attract more voters, assumed the presidency. Johnson was a southerner and a former slaveholder who had remained loyal to the Union. He had served in Congress and retained his seat in the Senate even after his home state of Tennessee seceded. Before being elected vice president, Johnson had also served as the military governor of Tennessee. Now he faced the difficult challenge of rebuilding the United States politically, socially, and economically.

Although loyal to the Union, Johnson did not support equal rights for African Americans. This position, along with his southern background, did little to win him the trust of northern Republicans. But southerners did not trust him either, due to his support of the Union. As Lincoln had, Johnson believed that moderate measures would be most effective in reuniting southern states with the Union.

Andrew Johnson, the 17th president of the United States, was born in 1808. After the death of his father, his family struggled financially. Johnson never went to school and was apprenticed to a tailor at age 14, but he taught himself to read and write. His eloquent speaking style helped propel his advance in politics.

Incorporating the South back into the political life of the United States in a fair and just manner was one of the largest challenges looming for Johnson. While the new president supported more lenient treatment of former Confederates, northern Republicans in Congress argued for harsher punishment for the South. They thought the South should pay a heavy political price for the war, which would include banning Confederate leaders from participating in the nation's politics in the future. Northern politicians also realized that if African Americans were granted the right to vote, southern representation in the House of Representatives would increase—a possible threat to northern Republicans' control in the House.

The nation also had to grapple with the South's continued resistance to granting any rights to African Americans or taking steps to **integrate**, or bring them into society as equals. Many African Americans worried that their former owners and other white southerners would keep them from owning property

and taking advantage of employment opportunities. President Johnson had made no secret of the fact that he did not support equal rights for the newly freed African Americans. This, along with his support of states' rights, led many Republicans and other northerners to fear that the president's actions would only encourage white southerners to resist African-American equality.

Perhaps the most overwhelming and immediate problem facing the nation was rebuilding the South and its economic system. By the war's end, large portions of the South lay in ruins, and its economy had crumbled. Land values had decreased dramatically, crop fields had been destroyed, and herds of livestock had been reduced significantly. Confederate money and bonds were worthless. Before emancipation, planters had used their slaves as collateral for loans, since the enslaved were, legally, property. **Collateral** is property or money a borrower puts up as security when he or she takes

---

OBJECTIVE

Assess the effectiveness of President Johnson's Reconstruction plans for the South.

CRITICAL THINKING SKILLS FOR LESSON 1.1

- Summarize
- Identify
- Make Inferences
- Analyze Cause and Effect
- Compare and Contrast
- Make Connections
- Identify Main Ideas and Details
- Make Generalizations
- Analyze Primary Sources

HISTORICAL THINKING FOR CHAPTER 13

How did the United States change because of Reconstruction? Following the Civil War, action was needed to rebuild the South and unite the nation. Lesson 1.1 discusses President Andrew Johnson's plan to address the issues of reunification and African-American rights.

BACKGROUND FOR THE TEACHER

Conflicts over Reconstruction were shaped as much by religious belief as by military and political concerns. Both the North and South believed that God was on their side, even though their sides had decidedly contradictory goals. As the war dragged on, the northern Protestant churches began to argue that slavery had to be extinguished in order for the North to win and God's kingdom to be realized. This line of thought caused many northerners to support emancipation and contributed to the North's determination to pass the 13th Amendment. The South's defeat gave rise to the fervor of a "Lost Cause," an ideology based on the belief that God still favored the South and that the horrors of the Civil War were a test for a yet unknown higher purpose. These competing religious ideologies set the stage of an ongoing clash over the goals of Reconstruction.

INTRODUCE & ENGAGE

PARTICIPATE IN A POLL

Discuss the definition of *reconstruction* with students and explain that in the context of the Civil War it involved policies meant to restore the Union and rebuild the South. Remind students that the Civil War had been difficult and prolonged and that many in the North still felt grief and anger over the assassination of Abraham Lincoln. Then take a poll, asking students this question: If you were a northerner, would you want the government to be harsh or lenient with the South? Write the results of the poll on the board. Tell students that in this lesson they will learn how President Andrew Johnson and Congress disagreed over this very question and what the consequences were for all Americans, including African Americans, in the South.

TEACH

GUIDED DISCUSSION

1. **Analyze Cause and Effect** What decisions undermined Johnson's ability to be an effective president? *(Possible response: Johnson's decision to remain loyal to the Union alienated southern politicians, and his decision to pardon Confederates and his stance on African-American rights lost him northern Republicans' support.)*

2. **Compare and Contrast** How did the North and the South differ in their reasons for denying African Americans full civil rights, such as the right to vote? *(Possible response: Northerners feared southern states would gain too many seats in the House of Representatives if African Americans in the South received full citizenship and were allowed to vote. Southerners resisted any steps toward equal rights for African Americans, including allowing them to change jobs and own land, to maintain economic and social control in the southern tradition of white dominance.)*

3. **Make Connections** How did the South's reliance on slavery contribute to its devastating economic problems after the war? *(Possible response: Because enslaved people were viewed as property, they had been used as collateral for loans. When African Americans were freed, the loans couldn't be paid back, and the wealth of many slaveholders vanished. As a result, southerners couldn't rebuild. In addition, the South had relied on slavery and agriculture and never diversified its economy, which made its economic collapse worse and recovery much more difficult.)*

🏛 AMERICAN PLACES

Arlington National Cemetery contains several unique Civil War features. It holds the graves of 3,800 formerly enslaved African Americans who lived in the Freedman's Village on land that became part of the cemetery. Confederate soldiers whose graves were originally scattered in several sections and marked with civilian-style headstones are also buried in Arlington. Confederate veterans led an effort to rectify this situation, so 482 Confederates, including soldiers, wives, and 15 civilians, were reburied together in one section. To distinguish their graves from those of Union soldiers, the markers feature pointed tops rather than the rounded headstones typical of Union graves. Near Arlington House, formerly the home of Robert E. Lee, is the Civil War Unknown Monument, America's first tomb to an unknown soldier. Its burial vault contains the remains of 2,111 Union and Confederate soldiers.

DIFFERENTIATE

ENGLISH LANGUAGE LEARNERS `ELD`

Create Word Squares Arrange students at **All Proficiencies** in mixed pairs, and tell them to write the word *collateral* in the center oval of a Word Square. Have them consult a dictionary and write the word's definition and characteristics in the appropriate boxes. Then instruct students to write examples or non-examples of collateral using information from the text, current events, or their own knowledge. Direct pairs to exchange their Word Squares with another pair and ask and answer questions about the information.

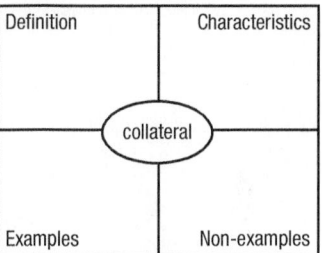

PRE-AP

Investigate the Memphis Riots Inform students that the three days of violent riots in Memphis in 1866 are well documented but until recently were rarely discussed by historians or the public. Prompt them to conduct research using multiple print and online sources about the riots, including the immediate and underlying causes as well as the short- and long-term effects. Challenge students to discover the extent of the violence and destruction, including the number of homes, schools, and churches that were burned and the number of people killed and wounded. Tell them to present their findings in a written or oral report, concluding with their thoughts on why this well-documented event in U.S. history is not well known to the public.

See the Chapter Planner for more strategies for differentiation.

out a loan. If the borrower does not repay the loan, the lender can take the collateral as payment. With the destruction of that "collateral," the fortunes of many formerly wealthy southerners collapsed, and few banks outside the South were willing to loan money to them to rebuild or revive the economy. The emancipation of African Americans destroyed the South's slave-based agricultural system and left nothing in its place.

PRESIDENTIAL RECONSTRUCTION

Congress was in recess when Lincoln was assassinated, and it was not scheduled to reconvene until December 1865. Johnson used the opportunity to implement his plan to reunite the North and the South. Through his **Presidential Reconstruction** plan, Johnson offered amnesty to former Confederates who agreed to take an oath of loyalty to the Union, restoring their political and civil rights and assuring that the government would not seize their property or prosecute them for treason. High-ranking Confederate leaders and wealthy planters were not offered amnesty at this time, although Johnson eventually pardoned many of them

individually. In fact, by 1866, Johnson had granted more than 7,000 pardons to wealthy southerners and Confederate senior officers.

In addition to loyalty oaths, Johnson also mandated that states convene constitutional conventions to reject secession and ratify the 13th Amendment, which abolished slavery nationwide. Johnson's Reconstruction plans, however, left out any provision for allowing African Americans the right to vote or participate in politics.

For the most part, the southern states met Johnson's conditions and began electing new members to Congress. Little had changed politically, however. Many of the thousands of former Confederates whom Johnson had pardoned were elected to seats in Congress, including Alexander H. Stevens, the former vice president of the Confederacy, who represented Georgia. With the entire African-American population now counted as single individuals when apportioning representatives—not merely as three-fifths of a person as before the war—the South stood to gain even greater legislative power than it had held before the war.

This wood engraving by Alfred R. Waud depicts the May 1866 riot in which white men shot at unarmed African-American citizens in Memphis, Tennessee. Although the violence began after a minor disturbance between former Civil War African-American soldiers and local police, it quickly escalated.

RESISTANCE IN THE SOUTH

The South welcomed the lenient terms established by Johnson's Presidential Reconstruction. Many southerners and their state legislatures, including members of the state conventions elected in 1865, proudly displayed their contempt for the North. Some refused to fly the American flag, some refused to ratify the 13th Amendment, and some even refused to admit that secession had been illegal. Even Johnson recognized that "there seems, in many of the elections something like defiance."

Beginning with Mississippi in 1865, southern states began passing post–Civil War black codes, which were special laws to control and limit the rights of African Americans. These laws were not all that different from those enacted in the colonial era when slavery first took hold. By keeping African Americans poor and dependent on white society for work, these black codes, although varying from state to state, were all intended to maintain the constant supply of available cheap labor that the 13th Amendment had removed. Although the southern state legislatures granted African Americans some rights, such as the right to marry, to own personal possessions, and to sue and be sued, most black codes defined what African Americans could not do: move from one job to another, own or rent land, testify in court, or practice certain occupations.

As African Americans adjusted to the new black codes in southern states, they also faced a wave of violence in many areas of the postwar South. In Texas alone, roughly 1,000 African Americans were murdered by whites between 1865 and 1868, some for merely refusing to remove a hat or for not obeying a command issued by a white person.

Sometimes the violence turned into rioting. For three days in May 1866, white mobs in Memphis, Tennessee, angered when a group of African Americans attempted to stop a white policeman from arresting an African-American man, attacked the camps and neighborhoods of African Americans. Even white police officers and firefighters joined in the violence. A Congressional investigation concluded that competition over jobs fueled the rioting and reported that 46 African Americans and 2 whites were murdered in the uprising. Many more of both races were injured, and homes, churches, and schools were robbed, burned, or destroyed. The violence and jailing of hundreds of blacks forced most of Memphis's African-American community to flee the city until order was restored.

Riots also broke out in July 1866 in New Orleans, when white citizens murdered 35 black citizens and wounded more than 100. As with the Memphis riots, the New Orleans attacks were carried out with the tacit, or unspoken, approval of local government officials and the city's police force. This violence showed the failings of Reconstruction: No one group seemed to have the political will necessary to punish the perpetrators and protect African Americans.

Northerners and congressional Republicans were enraged by the enacting of black codes and the recurring violence against African Americans in the South. In response, they took action against Johnson's Reconstruction efforts.

HISTORICAL THINKING

1. **READING CHECK** Why did most congressional Republicans resist President Johnson's Reconstruction plans?

2. **SUMMARIZE** What challenges did President Johnson face in trying to rebuild the nation?

3. **IDENTIFY** What requirements did the former Confederate states have to meet before being readmitted to the Union under Presidential Reconstruction initiated by Johnson?

4. **MAKE INFERENCES** Why might Lincoln, a northerner, have advocated for a plan that was lenient in its treatment of the former Confederate states and its leaders?

BUILD BACKGROUND

SLAVE CODES AND BLACK CODES

Andrew Johnson firmly believed that the federal government should not dictate how states run their affairs. This attitude continued a long tradition of allowing southern colonies and states to devise rules restricting African Americans' civil rights. While colonial slave codes had defined African Americans and their children as property rather than people, the black codes declared that freed African Americans were not truly free. For instance, some state codes allowed orphaned African-American minors to be apprenticed to white planters as unpaid labor. Other codes required African Americans to show written evidence each January that they had employment contracts for the coming year. Just as slave codes had been the precursors to black codes, so would black codes become precursors to the even more restrictive Jim Crow laws that emerged in the late 19th century.

THE NEW ORLEANS RIOT

The riot in New Orleans was one of the few early examples of white officials held accountable for the killing of African Americans. Upon capturing the city early in the Civil War, the Union imposed martial law. After the war, martial law was lifted, and the original mayor was reinstated. A short time later, 130 African-American delegates tried to attend the Louisiana Constitutional Convention, which was to address voting rights and the black codes recently passed by the Louisiana state legislature. A mob of white police, ex–Confederate soldiers, and white supremacists attacked the unarmed delegates, and many were beaten, shot, or killed. The riot spread over several blocks, claiming the lives of bystanders as well. Federal martial law was immediately reimposed, and city officials—including the mayor—were removed from office for their part in allowing the massacre.

TEACH

GUIDED DISCUSSION

4. **Identify Main Ideas and Details** How did the Presidential Reconstruction plan affect the political standing of the South? *(Possible response: The makeup of Congress didn't change, but Johnson's plan gave the South more political influence than before the Civil War. Former southern politicians were elected to office, and now that African Americans counted as single individuals, increasing the southern states' number of representatives, the South had more legislative power.)*

5. **Make Generalizations** Why did white southerners pass black codes after the war? *(Possible responses: By limiting African Americans' civil rights, they wanted to show their contempt for northern policies. They feared that giving African Americans civil rights would remove a supply of cheap labor and allow African Americans in political offices. They believed that African Americans were inferior and did not deserve full civil rights.)*

ANALYZE PRIMARY SOURCES

Direct students' attention to the Primary Source feature. Ask students to reread it carefully, paying attention to what constituted being deemed a vagrant. **ASK:** Why do you think white people are included in the amended vagrant law, and what seems to be the purpose for the different punishments prescribed? *(Possible response: Authors of the codes probably wanted to prevent white people who sympathized with African Americans from meeting or working with them. Making the cost of violating the code much higher for whites was meant to deter them from getting involved. It also reinforced the economic disparity and segregation of whites from African Americans.)*

For students who develop an interest in the economic conditions and social issues in the North after the Civil War, suggest that they read the online American Story "The Post–Civil War North."

ACTIVE OPTIONS

On Your Feet: Fishbowl Arrange students in two concentric circles. Tell students in the inner circle to discuss the following topic: How well did the Presidential Reconstruction plan address the issues facing the country at the end of the Civil War? Tell students in the outer circle to listen and takes notes on the discussion. Then have the groups reverse position, and ask the new inner circle to discuss this question: What do you predict will happen next in Reconstruction? At the end of each discussion, have students from the outer circle summarize their conclusions.

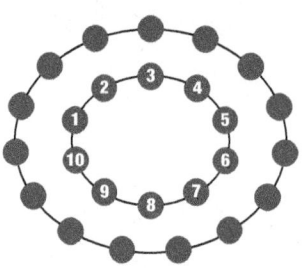

NG Learning Framework: Create a Unified Cause-and-Effect Chain

`SKILLS` Communicate, Collaborate

`KNOWLEDGE` Our Human Story

Arrange the class into three teams, and assign each a subsection from the lesson for which to create a Cause-and-Effect Chain. Since the first subsection is long, you may want to assign more students to this team. Ask each team to read through the assigned subsection and use a graphic organizer such as the one shown to identify the various causes and effects. When teams have completed their individual chains, have them collaborate to create a unified Cause-and-Effect Chain for the lesson to display in the classroom.

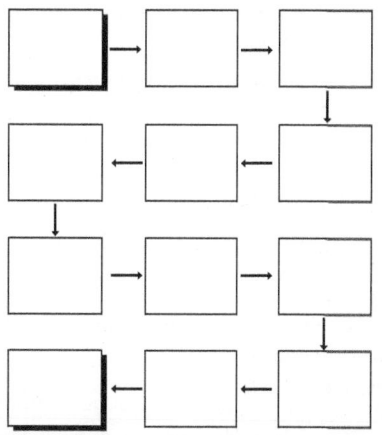

HISTORICAL THINKING

ANSWERS

1. Northern Republicans felt that Johnson's policies were too lenient on the defeated South and did not provide enough support for rights of African Americans.

2. Johnson had to devise a way to bring southern states back into the Union, deal with southern resistance to civil rights for African Americans, and rebuild the South's infrastructure and economy.

3. States had to pass the 13th Amendment abolishing slavery and repudiate secession. Individuals had to take an oath of loyalty to the United States.

4. Lincoln was probably appalled by the destruction and death caused by the Civil War. Since preserving the Union had been his main goal, he may have realized that if the North punished the South too severely, it would be much more difficult to reunite and rebuild the nation.

RADICAL RECONSTRUCTION

You may have heard the saying, "To the victor belong the spoils." And, after the Civil War, that's why many northern congressional Republicans believed they should win control of the South's reconstruction. But many southerners and the president himself had different plans, inciting a power struggle for the South.

CONGRESS TAKES CONTROL

The South might have been generally pleased with Johnson's Presidential Reconstruction plan, but northerners—and especially Republicans in Congress—were not. In the North, public opinion called for severe punishment of the South. As you have read, the Radical Republicans, who had supported abolition during the war, agreed with this plan. They were led by Representative **Thaddeus Stevens** of Pennsylvania and Senator Charles Sumner of Massachusetts. You may recall that Sumner was the senator who was beaten with a cane on the Senate floor during debates surrounding the Kansas-Nebraska Act in 1856. Stevens was a

fierce abolitionist who fought for the rights of African Americans before, during, and after the Civil War. He had practiced law in Pennsylvania and served in Congress from 1859 to 1868, where he became an early leader of the Republican Party.

The Radical Republicans were furious over the South's institution of black codes and Johnson's lenient Reconstruction plans. They argued for harsher treatment of former Confederate leaders and wealthy plantation owners, such as seizing their land and giving it to those who had been enslaved on it. They supported immediate and universal voting rights for African Americans. As violence against African Americans increased in the

South, many moderate Republicans allied with the Radical Republicans. In December 1865, House and Senate Republicans created a Joint Committee on Reconstruction, tasked with investigating the political and social conditions in the former Confederate states before considering their readmission to the Union.

Attempting to eliminate the black codes through federal legislation, the House passed the **Civil Rights Act of 1866**. The act granted full equality and citizenship to "every race and color," with the exception of Native Americans. Johnson vetoed the bill, but Congress overrode the veto.

As you know, upon the ratification of the 13th Amendment in December 1865, all enslaved people were released from bondage. To prevent any future erosion of African-American rights, Radical Republicans proposed the **14th Amendment**, which guaranteed citizenship and equal protection under the law to all American-born people. The amendment decreed that any state that abridged, or reduced, the voting rights of any male citizen who was older than 21 would suffer a proportionate reduction in its congressional representation. On Johnson's advice, the southern states refused to ratify the amendment.

For much of the summer and fall of 1866, northerners watched in disbelief as southerners ignored the reforms Congress had crafted. Delegates at southern state conventions refused to ratify the 14th Amendment and resisted further attempts to rebuild the South. Then Republicans won control of Congress in the 1866 elections, and they decided it was time to take Reconstruction out of the president's hands.

RECONSTRUCTION ACTS OF 1867

The results of the 1866 elections overwhelmingly reflected northern disapproval of Johnson's plans for Reconstruction. Even though Johnson undertook a speaking tour to regain support for his policies, his Republican opponents won control of two-thirds of the seats in both the House and Senate as well as the governorships and legislative majorities of every northern state.

The Republicans felt they had a mandate, or command from the people, to institute a harsher Reconstruction plan, but they couldn't agree among themselves about the vote, land distribution, the courts, and education. Some wanted to put the South under military control and keep it there for an undetermined time, while others thought it was better to return southern states to civilian control as

PRIMARY SOURCE

Only months after Andrew Johnson took office, Thaddeus Stevens—the leader of the Radical Republicans in Congress—wrote him a letter arguing against his plan for Presidential Reconstruction.

His Excellency Andrew Johnson,

Sir
I am sure you will pardon me for speaking to you with a candor [frankness] to which men in high places are seldom accustomed. Among all the leading Union men of the North with whom I have had [communication] I do not find one who approves of your policy. They believe that "restoration" as announced by you will destroy our party (which is of but little consequence) and will greatly injure the country. Can you not hold your hand and wait the action of Congress and in the meantime govern them by military rulers? Profuse pardoning also will greatly embarrass Congress if they should wish to make the enemy pay the expenses of the war or a part of it.

With great respect Your obt Servt [obedient Servant]
Thaddeus Stevens

—from Representative Thaddeus Stevens's letter to President Andrew Johnson, July 6, 1865

soon as possible. Finally, in March 1867, they passed the **Reconstruction Acts of 1867**, which undid all of Johnson's policies and began the period of **Congressional Reconstruction**, which lasted until the end of 1877.

The Reconstruction Acts, which collectively came to be called **Radical Reconstruction**, placed the South under military rule. All southern states except Tennessee, which had been readmitted to the Union in July 1866 after ratifying the 14th Amendment, were divided into five military districts. A Union general was placed in charge of each district. Southern states were required to convene conventions to write new constitutions, which had to grant the right to vote to all adult male citizens, regardless of race. After ratifying its new constitution, each state had to ratify the 14th Amendment before it was allowed to elect members to Congress. Once these conditions were met and both the U.S. Senate and House of Representatives had approved its new constitution, the state could be readmitted to the Union.

With Radical Reconstruction underway, some northerners began to move to the South looking for business opportunities created by the rebuilding efforts. Southern Democrats and others called these northern immigrants **"carpetbaggers"** because

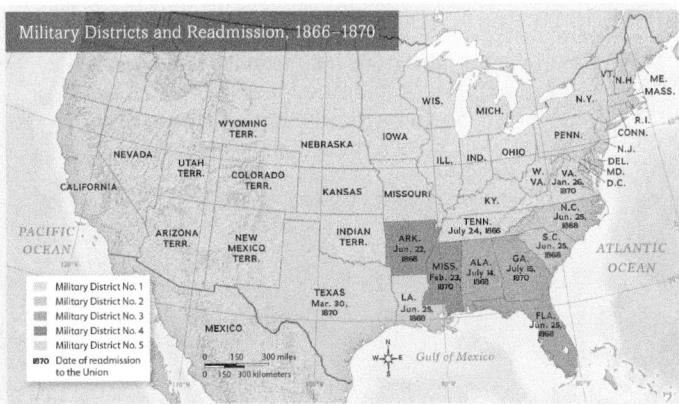

Military Districts and Readmission, 1866–1870

Military District No. 1
Military District No. 2
Military District No. 3
Military District No. 4
Military District No. 5
1870 Date of readmission to the Union

PLAN: 4-PAGE LESSON

OBJECTIVE

Examine why Radical Republicans took over Reconstruction and passed their own civil rights legislation.

CRITICAL THINKING SKILLS FOR LESSON 1.2

- Make Inferences
- Determine Word Meanings
- Interpret Maps
- Identify Main Ideas and Details
- Summarize
- Analyze Primary Sources
- Analyze Language Use
- Draw Conclusions

HISTORICAL THINKING FOR CHAPTER 13

How did the United States change because of Reconstruction? Angered by events in the South, members of Congress decided to take action. Lesson 1.2 describes how Republicans enacted a plan of Radical Reconstruction and sought to remove Andrew Johnson from office.

BACKGROUND FOR THE TEACHER

The Civil Rights Act of 1866 was originally offered by Illinois senator Lyman Trumbull as a compromise bill. Although the bill guaranteed all citizens equal protection under the law, it did not guarantee political rights, including the right to vote, or social rights, such as equal access to public accommodations. Congress proposed the 14th and 15th amendments and passed civil rights acts in 1870 and 1875 to remedy these oversights. In the late 1800s, however, the U.S. Supreme Court ruled that the laws and amendments had no authority over private individuals, businesses, or organizations, which were left free to discriminate. As a result, for decades African Americans and other minorities were segregated from mainstream political, economic, and social life. Yet the 1866 act did not disappear. In the 1960s, many of its provisions were incorporated into landmark civil rights legislation and are still cited in court cases today.

INTRODUCE & ENGAGE

REVIEW AND PREDICT

Review with students what they've learned about the power struggle between President Johnson and Congress over Reconstruction. With students, complete a T-Chart that lists the executive powers that Johnson had and the legislative powers that the Republicans had to enact their respective visions for Reconstruction. *(Executive powers included veto, executive orders, hiring and firing. Legislative powers included passing laws, overriding a veto, impeachment.)* Then discuss how each side might use its powers to tip the balance in its favor. Tell students that this lesson discusses how far each side was willing to go in the battle over Reconstruction.

Executive Powers	Legislative Powers

TEACH

GUIDED DISCUSSION

1. **Identify Main Ideas and Details** How did Congress try to protect African Americans during Presidential Reconstruction? *(Congress passed federal legislation and proposed a constitutional amendment. The Civil Rights Act of 1866 was passed, and the 14th Amendment protected those rights against any future assault by southern legislators.)*

2. **Make Inferences** Why do you think Johnson urged the southern states to reject the 14th Amendment? *(Possible response: Johnson was a former slaveholder and probably believed, like many southern leaders, that African Americans were inferior and should not have the right to vote. He may also have felt the amendment overreached federal power into states' affairs.)*

3. **Summarize** What conditions did Radical Reconstruction place on southern states before they could rejoin the Union? *(The states had to convene new constitutional conventions, write and ratify new constitutions granting voting rights to all adult males, and ratify the 14th Amendment. Once Congress approved the new constitutions, the states would be readmitted to the Union.)*

ANALYZE PRIMARY SOURCES

Direct students' attention to the Primary Source feature. **ASK:** What image of himself does Thaddeus Stevens present to the president? *(Possible response: Stevens acknowledges the higher status of the president and signs the letter "Your obt Servt," but he speaks to the president as an equal, likely because he has the support of other Republicans, and one who is thinking in terms of the best interests of the country rather than his party.)* **ASK:** What is Stevens asking the president to do, and how does he try to influence Johnson? *(Stevens is asking that Johnson establish military rule in the South, wait for Congress to act, and stop pardoning so many southerners. Stevens points out that not one leading Union man of the North approves of the president's policy. He also tries to appeal to Johnson's desire to do what is best for the United States by stating that the harm caused by this policy will extend beyond the Radical Republicans, hurting the entire country.)*

DIFFERENTIATE

INCLUSION

Describe a Political Cartoon Pair students who are visually or perceptually challenged with students who are not. Ask the latter to describe the caricature of Carl Schurz, including details about his expression, hand gesture, and the bags he carries. Encourage partners to ask clarifying questions about the details, including the writing on the bags. Then have pairs work together to answer the Critical Viewing question.

GIFTED & TALENTED

Research and Role-Play Direct students to work in pairs to role-play a dramatization of a possible encounter between President Johnson and Representative Stevens after Johnson received Stevens's letter. Instruct students to conduct research to discover more about each man's background, personality, and political beliefs. Then tell them to use what they learn to create a list of talking points to guide them in the role they will play. Encourage students to use language from the letter in the Primary Source excerpt as well as language gleaned from their research. Allow time for pairs to rehearse their dramatization, and then invite them to perform it for the class. Ask students to comment on how the dramatization enhanced their understanding of the conflicts between the president and the Radical Republicans.

See the Chapter Planner for more strategies for differentiation.

they often arrived carrying cheap suitcases made of carpet fabric. Most southerners viewed these people as intruders, looking to take advantage of others and exploit the South. Some of them were buying up the property of southerners who, due to the region's dire economic situation, could not afford to pay taxes. If a property owner failed to pay taxes, his or her land could be sold for pennies on the dollar. The northerners who came South included Republicans who wanted to engage in politics, and many of them became delegates to the constitutional conventions in the former Confederate states. But most of the northerners who traveled South were former Union soldiers, preachers, teachers, and social workers who hoped to help African Americans adjust to society as free individuals.

White southerners who supported Radical Reconstruction also earned the disdain of many in the South, who considered them traitors and called them "scalawags." The term *scalawag* is an insult used to describe a worthless, dishonorable person. Southern supporters of Radical Reconstruction came from a variety of backgrounds. Many were small plantation owners or backcountry farmers who wanted to prevent the wealthy planters from regaining power. Others were southern business owners who supported the North's efforts to rebuild the South's economy. Enough "scalawags" were scattered throughout the South to help build the Republican Party into a political force in the mountains of eastern Tennessee, western North Carolina, eastern Kentucky, northern Alabama, and northern Georgia.

THE IMPEACHMENT OF JOHNSON

As Republicans in southern state governments carried on with their rebuilding efforts, congressional Republicans sought to curb Andrew Johnson's presidential power. In a special session of Congress, Republicans voted to limit Johnson's authority as commander in chief of the army and passed the Tenure of Office Act, which prevented the president from removing officials who had been confirmed by the Senate. The passage of this act clearly violated the U.S. Constitution, which granted the president the right to hire or fire Cabinet members.

In August 1867, Johnson defied the new law by replacing his Secretary of War, Edwin Stanton, with war hero Ulysses S. Grant. Stanton, a strong supporter of the Republicans in Congress, had been the only member of Johnson's Cabinet to support Radical Reconstruction. Stanton, with the support of his Radical Republican allies, locked himself in his office and refused to leave.

On February 24, 1868, the House of Representatives voted to impeach Johnson, charging him with 11 articles of impeachment, most centered on the violation of the Tenure of Office Act. The Senate trial began in March 1868 and lasted for 11 weeks. Finally, in May, Johnson was acquitted in the Senate by one vote. Even his political foes realized that using impeachment to address anything less than criminal offenses was unwise. However, the constitutional and political significance of Johnson's impeachment endured.

CRITICAL VIEWING Republican Carl Schurz moved from Wisconsin to Missouri, where he was elected U.S. senator in 1868. In this 1872 political cartoon by Thomas Nast, Schurz appears as a carpetbagger. What qualities does Nast link to Schurz, and whose opinion would that caricature most likely represent?

A GLOBAL PERSPECTIVE Andrew Johnson was neither the first nor the last head of state to be tried for impeachable offenses. As early as the 14th century in England, a member of Parliament faced impeachment, and the process eventually became a law in many nations. In the 21st century, several world leaders have been impeached, including President Park Geun-hye of the Republic of Korea. Removed from office in 2016, Park was arrested and put on trial for bribery, abuse of power, and coercion. She was accused of receiving around $70 million in bribes from South Korean corporations in exchange for "favorable treatment." The bribes were revealed when files kept by Park's friend, Choi Soon-sil, were leaked to the press. In 2018, Choi and Park were convicted in separate trials. Choi was sentenced to 20 years in jail, and Park to 24 years. In this photograph, South Koreans protest the corruption by displaying an effigy of Park tied to the logos of companies accused of the bribery.

HISTORICAL THINKING

1. **READING CHECK** What issues concerning Reconstruction plans divided President Johnson and the congressional Republicans?

2. **MAKE INFERENCES** What political purpose did the Radical Republicans have for supporting equal rights for African Americans?

3. **DETERMINE WORD MEANINGS** Why might some people call the Reconstruction Act of 1867 "radical"?

4. **INTERPRET MAPS** Based on the map, which Military District was first to return to the Union in its entirety, and which states were part of this district?

BUILD BACKGROUND

NATIVE AMERICANS AND CIVIL RIGHTS

Both the 14th Amendment and the Civil Rights Act of 1866 excluded Native Americans from citizenship and the benefits of equal protection and due process under the law. In fact, when the Civil Rights Act was first introduced, both parties feared that the bill's language covering "every race and color" would confer citizenship on Native Americans. If tribes were granted this status, state and federal governments would have a much harder time seizing native lands. The bill's sponsor, Senator Lyman Trumbull, assured colleagues that only individuals who left their tribes and who "pay taxes and live in civilized society" would be covered. This wasn't enough, and language was added that specifically prohibited Native American birthright citizenship. Native Americans were not granted full citizenship until 1924 and not guaranteed the right to vote in all states until the Voting Rights Act of 1965.

EDMUND ROSS AND ANDREW JOHNSON

Senator Edmund Ross cast the deciding vote during the trial of President Johnson. Ross was a partisan Republican who had long supported the party's agenda, and nearly everyone expected him to vote against Johnson. The reasons for Ross's sudden turnabout remain a mystery. Some claim that while Ross had no sympathy for the president and his policies, he was concerned that Johnson was not being given a fair trial. Thus, he reasoned that if the impeachment succeeded, any president could be forced from office by partisan politics. Others point out that Ross received a large campaign donation from Johnson's supporters—a factor that may have determined his decision. Regardless of motivation, Ross was defamed in the press and lost his re-election bid. Later, the U.S. Supreme Court declared the Tenure of Office Act unconstitutional, validating Ross's decision.

TEACH

GUIDED DISCUSSION

4. **Analyze Language Use** What were southerners trying to accomplish by labeling people "carpetbaggers" and "scalawags"? *(Possible response: They used the terms to disparage northerners and southerners who worked to change the social and economic conditions of the South. The ultimate goal was to keep the old system in order.)*

5. **Draw Conclusions** Why did some people feel that impeaching the president for anything less than criminal offenses was unwise? *(Possible response: The impeachment of Johnson was based primarily on his violations of the Tenure of Office Act, which, even though passed by Congress, was unconstitutional. This made the impeachment charges appear politically motivated rather than based on criminal offenses. With the vote to acquit, Congress acknowledged that impeaching a president for political reasons could lead to parties trying to impeach the president over differences in political views.)*

A GLOBAL PERSPECTIVE

Explore with students the photograph of the protest in South Korea and its caption.
ASK: What are the makers of the effigy suggesting about Park Geun-hye and her actions? *(Possible response: The makers of the effigy depict Park tied by rope, impeached and convicted for taking bribes from corporations in return for favors. The effigy is sneering, so the makers are suggesting that Park is not remorseful and feels contempt for the people who elected and impeached her.)* Guide a discussion about the differences between Park's impeachment trial and Andrew Johnson's. *(Park was charged with bribery, a crime that directly impacted her ability to govern fairly. Johnson was charged with breaking the Tenure of Office Act, which concerned the protocol of firing Cabinet members and was not a crime.)*

ACTIVE OPTIONS

On Your Feet: Analyze Goals and Outcomes Arrange students in groups of four to analyze Radical Reconstruction. Provide each group with a Goals-and-Outcomes Chart like the one shown. Tell groups to complete the chart by identifying the goals of Radical Reconstruction, the obstacles impeding those goals, and the final outcome. In the summary section of the chart, ask each group to assess the overall success of Radical Reconstruction. Have groups share their summaries with the class.

Goals of Radical Reconstruction	Obstacles	Outcome
Summary		

NG Learning Framework: Prepare Trial Arguments

ATTITUDE Responsibility

KNOWLEDGE Our Human Story

Divide the class into two teams to act as the prosecution and defense at Johnson's Senate trial following his impeachment. Direct each team to conduct online and library research to discover and prepare the major arguments for their side. Suggest that the prosecution team print out the Tenure of Office Act as part of their source material. Have teams present their arguments to the class. Lead a class discussion about whether the 1868 impeachment trial was justified, based on the arguments presented.

HISTORICAL THINKING

ANSWERS

1. Congressional Republicans wanted to treat former Confederate leaders and plantation owners harshly, were angry about black codes, and advocated universal voting rights for people, regardless of color or former status. Johnson advocated leniency for the South, did not support equal rights for African Americans, and advised southern states not to ratify the 14th Amendment.

2. By championing equal rights, the Republicans attracted the support of African Americans throughout the South, strengthening the party.

3. The act placed the southern states under federal military control and divided the South into five districts, each controlled by a Union general. Some Americans might regard the act as an extreme departure from democratic government.

4. Military District Number 2 was the first to return to the Union on June 25, 1868. It consisted of North Carolina and South Carolina.

CRITICAL VIEWING Thomas Nast presents Schurz with a stern expression and a tight fist, suggesting that he is harsh and greedy. The bulging carpetbag on his back suggests that he is in the South to enrich himself. Nast was likely representing the opinion of most southerners.

THE SOUTH AFTER THE WAR

Imagine what it would be like if the foundation of your local economy were destroyed, seemingly overnight. That's what the South faced after the war. Along with the end of slavery came a massive shift in the labor force, especially on the huge plantations that had supported the region's once-thriving agricultural economy. Change would not be easy.

ECONOMIC DEVASTATION

As profound social and political problems plagued the South after the Civil War, Republican leaders in the early years of Reconstruction keenly focused on economic development. These politicians believed that with appropriate aid, the South could be transformed. It could become a modern society dominated by large, prosperous cities, productive factories, and an agricultural industry not based on the plantation system and enslaved labor.

The Civil War left large parts of the South in ruins and devastated its economy. Most of the fighting had taken place in the South, and its major cities, such as Atlanta, Charleston, and Richmond, were severely damaged. Little infrastructure remained standing. Energy supplies were depleted, and nearly two-thirds of the South's railroad system was in a shambles. Steamboats no longer traveled the rivers, and roads had been mangled by wartime use. Protective levees near rivers had been demolished, ruining large strips of Mississippi delta cotton lands. Cotton that had not been destroyed in the war had been seized by Union troops.

Throughout the South, land values had decreased dramatically, wiping out hundreds of millions of dollars in insurance investments and bank assets based on the value of now nearly worthless property. Confederate money and bonds were also worthless. Consequently, little capital was available to pay for rebuilding. Perhaps the greatest impact on the South's economy was the emancipation of African Americans. Enslaved workers accounted for the largest share of capital investment in the South, roughly $4 billion, which was more than the land itself was worth. Emancipation completely upended the South's agricultural system, which relied on enslaved labor. Consequently, the disappearance of both enslaved labor and capital meant that the South's agricultural economy required a complete overhaul.

Naturally, these factors had a negative effect on southern crop production. The cotton crop would not rise to prewar levels until 1879. Likewise, tobacco and sugar production didn't rebound until the 1880s and 1890s. Other traditional southern crops fared worse. Some, such as the rice industry along the East Coast and the hemp industry of Kentucky, never returned to their prewar levels.

A CHANGED SOCIETY

The southern economy clung to life as both whites and African Americans struggled to find an alternative to slavery and the plantation system. People responded in a variety of ways. Some former slaveholders simply gave up and left the country to settle in Latin America, while others continued to treat the freed African Americans as though they were still enslaved to keep them from leaving. Other planters provided living accommodations to former slaves and paid them wages for the work they performed on the plantations.

Immediately after the war, in the spring of 1865, many planters insisted that their formerly enslaved workers continue to work in "gangs," as they had before emancipation. In exchange for their labor, they received a portion of the crop, shared among all the workers. Few African Americans agreed to this method. They preferred to work as individuals or in family groups. Landowners soon found they had little choice but to permit African Americans and their families to take primary responsibility for farming a portion of land under an agricultural system called **sharecropping**.

Under this system, sharecroppers—who were also known as **tenant farmers** because they did not own the land they worked—provided all the labor on a portion of land and turned over the majority of the crop to the landowner. The profit on the crop served as payment of rent on land and shelter, and the sharecroppers also were allowed to keep a very small portion of the profit for themselves. Some poor white families, devastated by the war, also became sharecroppers.

But sharecropping could also leave sharecroppers in debt to landowners. Most sharecroppers lacked necessary supplies, including seeds and tools for farming their allotted land. Landowners and local supply shops would often step in to rent or sell the supplies to the sharecroppers on credit at a high rate of interest. To assure that they would be paid back, the landowners and merchants would place **liens**, or legal claims on a borrower's crops and any property owned. By the time the crops were harvested, the sharecropper had usually run up a considerable amount of debt, and as a result, would receive only a tiny part of the profits, or none at all. If sharecroppers could not pay back their loans, the planter and anyone else they owed could claim even more of the profits on the crops they grew.

CRITICAL VIEWING A man stands above a deep crater near burned-out buildings in the ruins of postwar Richmond, Virginia. What does this photograph reveal about the challenges southern cities faced after the Civil War?

During the 1890s, African-American men, women, and children sharecroppers pick cotton in a Savannah, Georgia, cotton field.

PLAN: 4-PAGE LESSON

OBJECTIVE

Explore how conditions in the "New South" both diverged from and closely resembled those under slavery.

CRITICAL THINKING SKILLS FOR LESSON 2.1

- Analyze Cause and Effect
- Draw Conclusions
- Identify
- Summarize
- Form and Support Opinions
- Compare and Contrast
- Identify Problems and Solutions
- Integrate Visuals

HISTORICAL THINKING FOR CHAPTER 13

How did the United States change because of Reconstruction? The Civil War devastated the South's economy and altered its social structure. Lesson 2.1 examines the conditions in the postwar South and the different ways that southerners and northerners attempted to remake or restore southern society.

BACKGROUND FOR THE TEACHER

After the Civil War, increasing cotton production was important to the South and to the North as well. The federal government and many northern businessmen realized that money from cotton exports would be critical to help reduce the enormous federal war debt, stabilize the nation's monetary system, and help fund economic recovery and development. These same businessmen opposed confiscating large plantations and instead supported resuming the plantation economy. Because of racial attitudes, many northerners opposed freed slaves migrating to the North and viewed keeping African Americans contracted to the plantations as part of the solution. Thus, conditions were ripe for binding freedmen and poor whites to the land. By 1880 King Cotton was seemingly reborn—the South was exporting more cotton than it had in 1860, continuing America's reign as the world's leading cotton exporter.

INTRODUCE & ENGAGE

CONSIDER POSTWAR HOPES AND FEARS

Guide students to recall conditions in the postwar South. Then ask them to think about the hopes and fears that both African Americans and whites might be feeling. Elicit and display volunteers' responses in a Venn diagram, like the one shown, and discuss their similarities and differences. Tell students that Lesson 2.1 explains how steps toward economic recovery in the South affected people of both races. After students have read the lesson, revisit the Venn diagram and revise it if necessary.

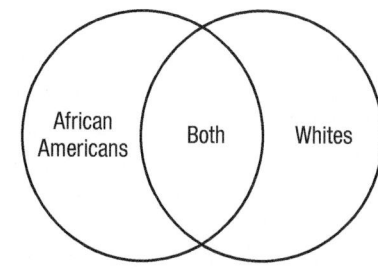

TEACH

GUIDED DISCUSSION

1. **Summarize** What factors made a quick recovery of the southern economy difficult? *(Possible response: Most of the fighting had occurred in the South and had destroyed infrastructure and cities. The South also endured the loss of farmland and plummeting land values, and emancipation eliminated a workforce worth billions of dollars.)*

2. **Form and Support Opinions** Do you think the Republican vision for a transformed South was realistic? Explain your thinking. *(Possible responses: Yes. The old agricultural system based on slavery was gone. It would take years, but the South would have to build a new system more like the one in the North. No. The South had based its economy almost entirely on agriculture. Changing to a new economy would require tremendous investments and social changes that the South would resist and the federal government would be unlikely to carry out.)*

3. **Compare and Contrast** How were the problems of African Americans and poor white southerners similar and different? *(Possible response: African Americans and poor whites who became sharecroppers were at the mercy of landowners and others in power and became trapped by debt. However, poor white southerners did not face the discrimination, threats, and fears for their safety that African Americans did.)*

MORE INFORMATION

White Farmers in the South After the Civil War, two-thirds of all sharecroppers in the South were white, but this had not always been the case. Before the war, many whites were yeoman farmers who owned their own land and grew crops other than cotton. After the war, however, many of these farmers converted their fields to cotton, hoping the crop would yield enough profit to pay off debts incurred during the war and taxes levied during Reconstruction. Unfortunately, prices stayed depressed long enough for many farmers to lose their land, so they had no recourse but to become sharecroppers. The loss of status was economic and social. Sharecroppers were considered near the bottom of the "agricultural ladder" of the South, just slightly above wage laborers.

DIFFERENTIATE

ENGLISH LANGUAGE LEARNERS

Explore an Unfamiliar Phrase Arrange students at **All Proficiencies** in mixed pairs. Bring their attention to the phrase "in a shambles" in the second paragraph. Instruct students to use context clues to determine its meaning and then use a dictionary to confirm the meaning. *(in a state of great destruction, disorder, or confusion)* Ask pairs to work together to write two original sentences using the phrase. Encourage students to share their sentences with the class.

PRE-AP

Research and Write an Essay Tell students to use print and online materials to research the Enforcement Acts. To help them organize the information they gather, suggest that they take notes in a Goal-and-Outcome Diagram, such as the one shown. Direct students to use their notes to write an essay about why the acts were needed, what happened after their passage, and how effective they were. Encourage students to conclude their essays with their thoughts about whether similar legislation is needed today to combat hate crimes. Ask volunteers to read their essays to the class.

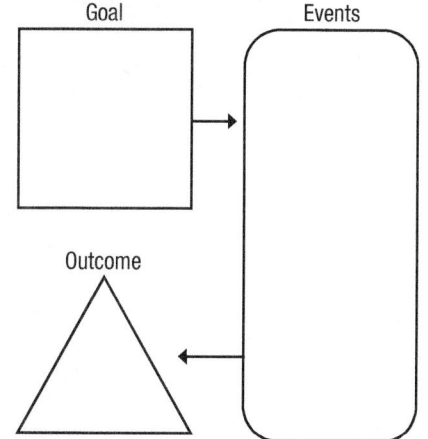

See the Chapter Planner for more strategies for differentiation.

CRITICAL VIEWING The photograph shows the scale of the destruction and the amount of construction needed to restore buildings and infrastructure in southern cities. Also, people left in the cities would require immediate aid in the form of food, clothing, and shelter.

The cycle would continue for many sharecroppers, leading to a financial condition called **debt peonage**. In this situation, sharecroppers were financially bound to continue under the unfair sharecropping system because they could not make enough money to pay off their debts or move off the land. Sharecroppers who failed to pay off debts could be sent to prison or placed into forced labor. So many African Americans fell into debt peonage that some people called the condition "black peonage."

Despite the challenges facing the South, the region was making economic progress. Wealthy, powerful northern and southern politicians and business owners provided money to rebuild infrastructure and to develop new industries. These efforts to transform the South from a mostly agrarian society into an industrial one reflected the desire for a "New South." For example, the land around Birmingham, Alabama, contained large deposits of coal, iron ore, and limestone necessary for producing steel. By the late 1880s, Birmingham had become one of the largest producers of iron and steel in the nation. But despite the industrial progress, most southerners remained closely linked to traditional agriculture, which remained the driving economic force in the South.

THE KU KLUX KLAN

As Radical Reconstruction gained traction in the South, southern whites looked for ways to fight racial integration that they believed the North was forcing on them. Because they were politically powerless to battle the Republicans running their state governments, many organized secret societies to undermine efforts to promote African-American equality. The largest and most powerful of these societies was the **Ku Klux Klan**, founded in 1866 by Confederate veterans in Pulaski, Tennessee. The Ku Klux Klan, also known as the KKK or simply, the Klan, dedicated itself to maintaining white supremacy. It saw itself as a military wing of the Democratic Party, intimidating and killing both whites and African Americans who dared to associate with Republicans or support African-American rights. Under the leadership of its "grand wizard" Nathan Bedford Forrest, the KKK rallied resistance against Radical Reconstruction. Forrest was a former Confederate general who had won a handful of victories over Union forces in the war. His reputation attracted many members to the organization.

Klan violence spread across the South and continued into the 1870s. Local Klan members, along with other white supremacist groups such as the Knights of the White Camelia, White Leagues, and the White Brotherhood, terrorized communities in many parts of the South. Hooded and robed to disguise their identities, the KKK attacked at night, breaking up Republican meetings; burning African-American homes, churches, and schools; and running their political opponents out of their communities. They even lynched, or tortured and hanged, their victims.

The Klan threatened both African Americans and white Republicans, pledging to harm or kill them and their families if they tried to cast a ballot, and these **voter intimidation** tactics proved very effective. By keeping opponents away from the polls, the Democratic Party began to regain its political foothold in the South. Driven by white racism, the KKK framed each election as a battle between African Americans and whites. With these tactics, the Klan helped the Democratic Party eventually win back the support of many southern whites who had been voting for Republicans. By the mid-1870s, the Democrats regained power in all but three southern states.

ANTI-KLAN EFFORTS

Republicans realized that racist violence and brutality were undermining the party's ability to survive and grow in southern states, but they were split on how to address the issue. Many came to the conclusion that using military forces to influence politics was not working in the South. Others, influenced by the persistent violence, questioned if staying in the South was worth the party's cost and effort.

Unable to ignore the Klan's violent activities, Congress passed three Enforcement Acts between 1870 and 1871 to address the problems in the South. The first, in 1870, made it illegal for groups of people to "go in disguise upon the public highways, or upon the premises of another" in order to violate any citizen's rights. The two Enforcement Acts passed in 1871, also known as the **Ku Klux Klan Acts of 1871**, gave the federal government control of national elections (including the supervision of polling places), outlawed organized attempts to deprive voters of their civil rights, and banned efforts to bar any citizen from holding public office.

The Enforcement Acts also gave the federal government broader powers to fight the Klan, including the right to override state laws. The acts gave the president the authority to use military force to detain and aid the prosecution of Klan members, resulting in the arrests of more than 5,000 Klan leaders and the eventual conviction of 1,250 of them. Although the Enforcement Acts were used to force southern states to comply with the rule of law, sentiment in the North for such stern measures was fading, and the United States Supreme Court declared the Ku Klux Klan Acts unconstitutional in 1882.

HISTORICAL THINKING

1. **READING CHECK** What is sharecropping?

2. **ANALYZE CAUSE AND EFFECT** Why were many African Americans trapped by the sharecropping system in the postwar South?

3. **DRAW CONCLUSIONS** What impact did the actions of the Ku Klux Klan have on Republican Reconstruction?

4. **IDENTIFY** What were the chief aims of the Ku Klux Klan Acts of 1871?

Following the Civil War, James Sloss founded the Sloss Furnace Company in Birmingham, Alabama, to take advantage of the region's coal and iron ore deposits. Paying better than farm work, the furnace jobs attracted rural African Americans and whites to Birmingham. This photograph shows Sloss Furnace in 1906, when it was one of the largest producers of pig-iron, used in making cast-iron pipe and steel. Closed in 1970, Sloss is now a National Historic Landmark and an industrial museum.

BUILD BACKGROUND

THE SLOSS FURNACE COMPANY

The Sloss Furnace Company was one of the most successful businesses in the New South, but it had demonstrably racist employment policies. White and African-American employees were strictly segregated, having separate bathhouses, time clocks, and even picnics. The top of the company hierarchy included all-white groups of managers and white-collar professionals, such as chemists, accountants, and engineers. In the middle was a racially mixed group of skilled laborers whose white workers were paid more and had higher positions than their African-American counterparts. At the bottom were the exclusively African-American wage-labor gangs. Beginning in 1928, many African Americans were replaced with cheaper convict labor. These conditions persisted to the 1960s.

KU KLUX KLAN SYMBOLS

Some of the most infamous symbols of the Ku Klux Klan have unusual histories. Night riders, for instance, can be traced back to pre–Civil War America when groups of deputized white men patrolled the roads looking for runaway slaves, enforcing curfews, and fighting slave revolts. The white sheet and hood originated when Klansmen played "pranks" on African-American families by riding in disguise through their neighborhoods and farms, claiming to be Confederate "ghost" soldiers. As Reconstruction wore on, the pranks turned violent as Klansmen began attacking African Americans and northerners. The burning cross, surprisingly, was not part of early Klan symbolism. It first appeared in the 1915 movie *Birth of a Nation*, which showed Klansmen setting fire to crosses. The Klan copied this act from the movie and has used it ever since.

TEACH

GUIDED DISCUSSION

4. Draw Conclusions Why did some white southerners support organizations like the Ku Klux Klan? *(Possible response: They felt that integration was being forced on them, had little power to counter Republican Reconstruction efforts, and feared the rise of African-American political and social power.)*

5. Identify Problems and Solutions How did Republicans attempt to solve the problem of the Ku Klux Klan? *(Possible response: They decided to solve the problem through legal means by passing the Enforcement Acts and prosecuting Klan leaders and members in the courts. The attempts were cut short when the Supreme Court ruled the acts unconstitutional.)*

INTEGRATE VISUALS

Direct students' attention to the photographs of workers picking cotton and the Sloss Factory. **ASK:** How do these two photos reflect the reality of the New South? *(Possible response: The factory reflects the new direction the economy of the New South was forced to take. The cotton workers reflect how the New South's economy largely still resembled that of the old South and was based primarily on agriculture and African-American labor.)*

ACTIVE OPTIONS

On Your Feet: Numbered Heads Organize students into groups of four and have them number off. Ask the following question: How did changes in the South's economy affect the lives of African Americans and southern whites? Give the group members time to think about the question individually. Then tell groups to discuss the topic so that any member can report for the group. After sufficient time, call a number and ask students with that number to report for their group.

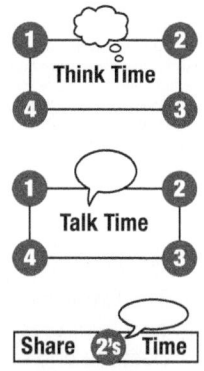

NG Learning Framework: Write an Opinion Piece

SKILLS Problem-Solving, Communication

KNOWLEDGE Our Human Story

Arrange students in small groups, and instruct each group to choose a problem or issue facing the postwar South and write a letter to the editor identifying the causes of their selected problem. Groups can conduct further online or library research if they need more information. Urge students to respond to potential arguments and historical realities that would challenge the causes they identify or render them invalid. Invite groups to share their letters with the class.

HISTORICAL THINKING

ANSWERS

1. In sharecropping, farmers raise crops and give most of the harvest to the landowner. When the crops are sold, rent for the farmers' land and homes comes out of the profits. The farmers are allowed to keep a small part of the profits.

2. For most African Americans, farming was the only way they could support themselves. To operate as sharecroppers, however, they had to buy supplies on credit. Most accumulated such high levels of debt that they could neither pay off their loans nor leave the land without risking imprisonment, effectively becoming trapped in the system.

3. The Klan intimidated voters, disrupted Republican meetings, and frightened political opponents into leaving. These actions made it more difficult for Republican Reconstruction to achieve its goals and helped Democrats regain power in the South.

4. The Ku Klux Klan Acts aimed to put the federal government in charge of national elections, prosecute Klan members and any others who tried to deprive people of their civil rights, and make it illegal to prevent any citizen from holding public office.

CRITICAL VIEWING Thomas Nast's overall message is that things have gotten worse for African Americans in the years following the Civil War, as shown by the motto "Worse Than Slavery" under the skull at the top of the shield. Depictions of members of the White League and the Klan, cowering African Americans, and the phrase "this is a white man's government" convey this point.

PROMISES AND REFORMS

Like many Americans, you probably take your education and political rights for granted. But to African Americans during Reconstruction, opportunities to learn and participate in politics were significant signs of their new freedoms.

In this 1877 oil painting, *Sunday Morning in Virginia*, Winslow Homer captures young African Americans as they practice a new freedom—learning to read.

SOUTHERN LAND REFORM

Reconstruction aimed not just to rebuild the South but also to reunite the nation without slavery. Those efforts began even before the war was over. As Union forces took over Confederate territories near the end of the Civil War, they freed enslaved people they encountered. Some African Americans seized their freedom at the first opportunity; others moved to Union camps or even joined the army. For most, simple survival remained the highest priority. This meant being able to find shelter and food.

Most newly freed African Americans stayed in the South, and many based this decision on rumors that the government would award them land. As you have read, after General Sherman completed his "March to the Sea" and confiscated roughly 400,000 acres of coastline stretching from South Carolina to

Florida, he issued Special Field Order No. 15. The order set the land aside exclusively for the settlement of freedmen, with each family receiving no more than 40 acres. By June 1865, more than 40,000 African Americans had established a self-governing community on the confiscated "Sherman Land." Sherman also instructed his army to lend mules to the community to help in development. This was the source of the promise of "40 acres and a mule." But after the war, in the fall of 1865, President Johnson overturned Sherman's order and returned most of "Sherman Land" to its former owners.

In early 1865, in anticipation of the war's end, Congress created the Bureau of Refugees, Freedmen, and Abandoned Lands, more commonly called the **Freedmen's Bureau**. The bureau's main purpose was to oversee the South's transition from a

African-American women and children practice reading in this photograph, taken at the Freedman's Village in Virginia. The federal government established the village to aid enslaved people who were escaping from the South during the Civil War.

slave economy to a **wage economy**, or an economy in which people are paid for their work. Army officers, who acted as bureau agents, dispensed medicine, food, and clothing to formerly enslaved African Americans and poor white southerners. The Freedmen's Bureau created courts to draw up labor contracts between landowners and laborers and resolve conflicts. It also established schools and coordinated female volunteers who came from the North to teach in them. In fact, the bureau's commissioner, former Union general Oliver Otis Howard, believed education was the key to improving the lives and opportunities of former slaves. By 1869, the Freedmen's Bureau had built thousands of schools for African Americans.

THE IMPORTANCE OF EDUCATION

Having been denied educational opportunities during slavery, many southern African Americans were eager to attend school. They viewed education as a path to better jobs as they adjusted to a wage economy. Learning to read and write and gaining a basic understanding of mathematics would help them deal with contracts, budgets, and other labor issues. A solid education would also allow them to become active, informed citizens, aware of their civil rights and knowledgeable about the political process.

The Freedmen's Bureau worked with African-American churches, individuals, and aid groups to help fund, build, and staff hundreds of schools for African-American children and adults. The schools were often built on land owned by African Americans. Although the schools were free, sending children to school often cut into total household income. As you have read, many recently freed African Americans, including children, continued to work at the same jobs they had performed when they were enslaved, whether on farms or in towns, only now they were being paid for their labor. Most families relied on their children's wages to help cover living costs.

African-American schools grappled with many challenges, including shortages of teachers and classroom space. Students often had to rotate in and out of a classroom in shifts. Typically, teachers taught children all day and then held classes for adults at night. Teachers included soldiers who had a basic education and were stationed in the area to oversee Reconstruction. In some schools, children and adults learned side by side in the same classroom.

Along with establishing schools to teach basic skills, the Freedmen's Bureau also created institutions of higher learning for African-American students

---

PLAN: 4-PAGE LESSON

OBJECTIVE

Analyze the causes and effects of education and political representation for African Americans during Reconstruction.

CRITICAL THINKING SKILLS FOR LESSON 2.2

- Summarize
- Analyze Cause and Effect
- Describe
- Make Inferences
- Identify Problems and Solutions
- Draw Conclusions
- Integrate Visuals

HISTORICAL THINKING FOR CHAPTER 13

How did the United States change because of Reconstruction? Radical Reconstruction allowed for a period of social and political reform. Lesson 2.2 describes how government and private organizations helped bring educational opportunities and congressional representation to African Americans.

BACKGROUND FOR THE TEACHER

The Freedmen's Bureau was originally intended as a temporary agency that was to last a year past the end of the Civil War. However, reality soon proved this estimate overly optimistic, as the agency, placed under the War Department, faced a daunting task. The goals of Reconstruction were ambitious, but there was no precedent for the federal government to undertake such a project. Indeed, 4 million freed slaves needed immediate aid, and the large welfare and land reform program envisioned by many would require the creation of an enormous federal bureaucracy that did not exist and never had. With the odds stacked against it, the bureau had mixed success. However, it marked the government's first involvement in social welfare and justice issues, a trend that would resurface in the 20th century.

HISTORY NOTEBOOK

Encourage students to complete the American Gallery page for Chapter 13 in their History Notebooks as they read.

INTRODUCE & ENGAGE

DISCUSS LACK OF EDUCATION

Tell students to imagine they haven't learned to read, write, or do basic math. Ask questions such as the following: What would be the effects on your life in a world where others had these skills? In what ways would you be vulnerable? Record and display students' answers in a Cause-Effect Organizer, like the one shown. Then ask students which skill they would want to learn first, and why. Tell them that Lesson 2.2 explains how social reforms and educational opportunities impacted the lives of several million formerly enslaved people.

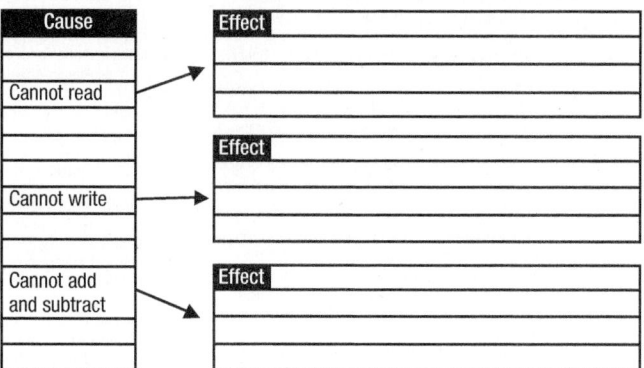

TEACH

GUIDED DISCUSSION

1. **Make Inferences** Why do you think President Johnson overturned Field Order No. 15? *(Possible response: General Sherman's order promised to radically reorganize the region, something President Johnson did not want to do. Johnson wanted to keep the economic and social structure of the South as it was, and giving large swaths of land to African Americans would do the opposite.)*

2. **Identify Problems and Solutions** What problems did the Freedmen's Bureau face in setting up schools for African Americans, and how did the bureau try to solve them? *(The bureau needed to build thousands of schools, staff the schools, and find ways to accommodate the number of children and adults who wanted to attend classes. The bureau solved the problems by working with African-American landowners and groups to fund and build schools, using locally stationed military and volunteers as teachers, and rotating students in shifts and holding night classes.)*

3. **Draw Conclusions** Why were skills like reading contracts important to formerly enslaved workers now working in a wage economy? *(Possible response: In a wage economy, unlike in a slave economy, people were paid for their work. They needed to understand the specifics of their pay and employment arrangements. If workers didn't understand a contract or other employment document, they could be exploited.)*

INTEGRATE VISUALS

Tell students that the Freedman's Village was established by the federal government in 1863 on land that became part of Arlington National Cemetery. Managed by the federal government and American Missionary Association, the village was intended to house, train, and educate freed African Americans and their children. Direct students' attention to the photograph and oil painting. **ASK:** How do the photograph and painting illustrate the challenges faced by African Americans who wanted an education? *(Possible response: The photo shows children and adults practicing reading outside with no apparent oversight or direct instruction, which would likely make progress slow and difficult. The painting shows the lack of school materials, with one book serving an entire family trying to read in a dimly lit room. The older woman facing away from the young students may symbolize a generation who missed the opportunity of receiving an education and can only hope for a better life for the young.)*

DIFFERENTIATE

STRIVING READERS

Create a Lesson Outline To help students understand the promises and reforms of Reconstruction while developing their reading and comprehension skills, ask them to work in pairs and use a simple format, such as the one shown, to write an outline for the lesson. Tell them to identify a main idea for each subsection and two details that support it. Encourage pairs to exchange outlines and suggest possible corrections or revisions.

I. _____

    A. _____

    B. _____

II. _____

    A. _____

    B. _____

III. _____

    A. _____

    B. _____

GIFTED & TALENTED

Write a Profile Assign individuals or pairs of students 1 of the 16 African Americans elected to Congress during Reconstruction and have them conduct research using multiple print and digital sources to write a profile. Tell students to incorporate photographs and other relevant images to provide background about the motivations, challenges, successes, and overall impact of the assigned representative. Invite volunteers to share their profiles with the class.

See the Chapter Planner for more strategies for differentiation.

during Reconstruction. As you have read, General Oliver Otis Howard, the commissioner of the Freedmen's Bureau, supported education within African-American communities. Howard University in Washington, D.C., founded in 1867 and named in Howard's honor, established the first law school for African Americans. Howard served as the university's third president. Other African-American colleges and universities were founded throughout the South, creating a vital education network for formerly enslaved people and their families. Many of these colleges and universities are still thriving today.

THE FIGHT FOR SOCIAL JUSTICE

Following the Civil War, African Americans quickly established their own churches. Many African Americans were drawn to the Baptist denomination because of its flexible organization, which allowed congregations the freedom to determine how they wanted to worship. More than a million southern African Americans were members of a Baptist church by 1890, significantly more than those who joined any other denomination.

Churches were central to the lives of African-American families and helped to strengthen their growing communities. Importantly, churches led the battle for **social justice**, or the fair distribution of opportunities and privileges, including racial

African-American men, dressed according to their profession, cast their ballots during Virginia's 1867 election in *The First Vote*, an illustration by Alfred Waud. That year, African Americans in Virginia were given the right to vote.

equality and rights, for all. In addition to conducting religious services, churches hosted political, social, and educational events. In places where African Americans did not have strong political representation, African-American ministers stepped in to become community leaders and advocates for social justice. African Americans also formed a range of fraternal and benevolent societies, clubs, and lodges, and even trade associations to provide aid and support within their communities.

Like religion, family was a foundation of African-American life. Slavery had torn apart unimaginable numbers of families, and during Reconstruction, many African Americans tried to reunite with lost family members. Many turned to the Freedmen's Bureau to locate missing relatives. The Freedmen's Bureau also helped strengthen African-American families by legitimizing marriages that had usually been prohibited during slavery.

GAINING A VOICE

Radical Reconstruction gave southern African Americans the right to vote, allowing them to gain a political voice and become active participants in the nation's electoral process. Ambitious African-American southerners, many of whom had been free and relatively prosperous before the Civil War, put themselves forward as natural leaders. African Americans from the North came to the South, also hoping to secure appointed and elective offices. During their service in the Union military, African-American veterans had gained useful leadership skills. Such men became the backbone of the Republican Party in districts that had a predominantly African-American population.

Many African Americans looked to the **National Equal Rights League** for political support. This organization advocated the expansion of civil rights and established state leagues throughout the nation. With the help of the Equal Rights leagues, many local African-American leaders mobilized enormous numbers of African-American voters in the fall of 1867. African Americans were the majority of delegates in South Carolina's and Louisiana's conventions, although they accounted for smaller proportions of convention delegates in the other southern states. Even so, African-American delegates throughout the South played an instrumental role in drafting democratic constitutions for their states.

Republican support and voter turnout among African Americans propelled many formerly enslaved men into community and political leadership positions. More than 1,400 African Americans were elected to

This 1872 print depicts the first seven African Americans to serve in the U.S. Congress. Representing five southern states, the men are (from left to right), Senator Hiram Rhodes Revels of Mississippi (who filled the Senate seat that Jefferson Davis had once held) and Representatives Benjamin S. Turner of Alabama, Robert C. De Large of South Carolina, Josiah T. Walls of Florida, Jefferson F. Long of Georgia, Joseph Rainey of South Carolina, and Robert B. Elliot of South Carolina.

political office in the South during Reconstruction, including a total of 16 African Americans elected to Congress. Of those, **Blanche K. Bruce** and **Hiram Revels** represented Mississippi in the U.S. Senate.

Although Bruce had been born into slavery, the son of an enslaved woman and a white planter, he was a well-educated man. The Republican-led Mississippi legislature elected Bruce to a seat in the U.S. Senate in 1874, where he served until 1881, fighting for equal rights for African Americans and Native Americans, as well as for Chinese immigrants.

Born to free African Americans in the South, Hiram Revels was a minister who was educated in the North. After winning a seat in the Mississippi State Senate in 1869, Revels was elected to assume a vacant Mississippi U.S. Senate seat in 1870, where he worked to integrate public schools and passenger rail service. He left the Senate to become president of Alcorn Agricultural and Mechanical College, which today is Alcorn State University, in Claiborne County, Mississippi.

African-American politicians, including Revels and Bruce, worked with other Republicans to repeal black codes, increase the number of elective political offices open to African Americans, and establish state hospitals and other institutions for people with disabilities. They passed legislation to rebuild roads, railways, and other infrastructure, and they achieved a major goal when Reconstruction governments established public school systems in the South.

Despite their many political achievements during Reconstruction, no African American was elected governor of a state in that era. However, after a

corruption scandal toppled the elected governor of Louisiana, **Pinckney Pinchback** stepped in to serve as acting governor from late 1872 to early 1873. Pinchback had been born free in Macon, Georgia, the son of an African-American mother and a white planter who raised him together. After his father's death, Pinchback and his mother fled the South for Ohio in fear of being enslaved. During the war, Pinchback returned South to recruit soldiers for the Union in New Orleans and remained in the region.

Oscar Dunn was the nation's first elected African-American lieutenant governor, serving in Louisiana from 1868 to 1871. Born into slavery in New Orleans, Dunn was self-educated and learned public speaking from actors who rented rooms in his mother's boarding house. After escaping slavery, he purchased his freedom. During Reconstruction, he served in the Louisiana State Senate and helped organize the 1870 Republican convention. Before his death in 1871, Dunn was a vocal supporter of African-American suffrage, equal rights, and land ownership. He was a fierce opponent of leniency for former Confederate officials.

HISTORICAL THINKING

1. **READING CHECK** What does the term "social justice" mean?

2. **SUMMARIZE** How did the Freedmen's Bureau help African Americans in the South?

3. **ANALYZE CAUSE AND EFFECT** How did education empower African Americans?

4. **DESCRIBE** How did the social and political lives of African Americans change during Reconstruction?

BUILD BACKGROUND

HOWARD UNIVERSITY

Howard University, originally founded to train African-American students to become preachers, soon expanded its offerings to include liberal arts courses and medical training. General Oliver Otis Howard served as Howard's third president (1869–1874), by which time the school had educated approximately 150,000 formerly enslaved persons. Unlike other colleges and universities at the time, Howard opened its doors to women as well. But it wasn't until 1926 that the university had its first African-American president, Dr. Mordecai Wyatt Johnson. Today, Howard University is part of a network of educational institutions known collectively as HBCUs, or historically black colleges and universities, and many leaders, including Supreme Court justice and civil rights icon Thurgood Marshall, are among its graduates.

FIRST AFRICAN AMERICANS IN CONGRESS

The first African Americans in Congress were among the best-educated and relatively prosperous African Americans in the nation, and they arrived in Washington eager to work on advancing civil rights. Although welcomed by Republican colleagues, they faced public skepticism about their abilities and discrimination from many other congressmen, who refused to yield to them in debates, grant them good committee assignments, or pass their legislation. They also faced open racism, such as when Democrat John Harris asked, "Is there not one gentleman on the floor who can honestly say he really believes that the colored man is created his equal?" African-American representative Alonzo Ransier replied simply, "I can."

TEACH

GUIDED DISCUSSION

4. **Summarize** What factors enabled the Baptist church to become such an important part of the fight for social justice? *(Possible response: The Baptist church, with its flexible organization, attracted many African Americans, and its ministers became community leaders and advocates for equal rights. In this way, the church could provide both leadership and a large number of members in the fight for social justice.)*

5. **Make Inferences** Why do you think African Americans were unable to elect an African-American state governor during Reconstruction? *(Possible response: While African Americans could elect congressmen from their districts, and African-American senators were elected by legislatures, a candidate for governor would need significant white voter support to win in a statewide election, which would have been difficult or impossible to attain.)*

MORE INFORMATION

Alfred Waud Inform students that British-born American illustrator Alfred Waud, creator of *The First Vote*, worked as a battlefield artist during the Civil War and that his drawings are among the finest representations of Civil War battles. After the war, Waud sketched scenes of life during Reconstruction in the South. Direct students to study Waud's illustration. **ASK:** Why do you think Waud emphasized the different professions of African Americans in this drawing? *(Possible response: He probably wanted to counter stereotypes that whites had about African Americans' capabilities and to show how important the vote was to a diverse group of working men that included laborers, a well-dressed businessman, and a soldier.)*

ACTIVE OPTIONS

 **Education, Land, and Resistance** Invite students to explore the American Gallery. Have them select one of the images and do additional research to learn more about it. Ask questions that will inspire additional inquiry about the chosen gallery image, such as: Who or what is this? Why is the person or place important in Reconstruction history? Why does the image belong in this chapter? What else would you like to know about it?

NG Learning Framework: Create a Display of Progress

ATTITUDE Responsibility

SKILL Communication

Have students work in groups to create an infographic to display the kinds and degrees of progress made during the early years of Reconstruction. Suggest that groups select topics such as politics, education, social justice, or land reform and then conduct research to analyze how successful African Americans were in achieving equality in each category. Invite groups to display and explain their infographic. Then use the infographics as a basis for a class discussion about the relative success of this era of Reconstruction.

HISTORICAL THINKING

ANSWERS

1. Social justice means that opportunities and privileges are distributed fairly to all in society.

2. The Freedmen's Bureau's main purpose was to see that the South transitioned from a slave economy to a wage economy. To do so, it provided legal help with labor contracts and conflicts; distributed clothing, food, and medicine; and established schools.

3. Education empowered African Americans to have the knowledge to handle labor and wage issues, become aware of their rights as citizens, and participate in the political process.

4. During the early years of Reconstruction, African Americans made significant social and political gains, moving from a state of slavery to becoming full citizens. Many were able to acquire a basic education and gain a political voice, and some even attained state and federal political offices. They also founded equal rights organizations, helped draft state constitutions and pass laws to rebuild infrastructure, repealed black codes, and helped establish public school systems in the South.

GRANT'S PRESIDENCY

Elections have consequences. The Republicans knew that they needed to win the presidential election to keep their Reconstruction policies going. Few, if any, realized that electing a popular but inexperienced executive might cause a host of other problems.

THE ELECTION OF 1868

Politically wounded and weak, Andrew Johnson finished his term in office but decided against running in the 1868 election. Republicans nominated Union war hero Ulysses S. Grant, whom they trusted to support their Reconstruction policies. Although Grant had no political experience, Republicans thought his independence and reputation would lead to less partisanship throughout the country. Accepting the nomination, Grant said, "Let us have peace," a phrase that became the theme of the Republican campaign.

The Democrats nominated the former governor of New York, **Horatio Seymour.** Seymour was a Copperhead, a former Confederate sympathizer, who relied on racial bigotry and white supremacy to attract voters. Seymour's message resonated with midwestern farmers and urban whites who felt misunderstood by Eastern politicians or threatened by freedmen, whom they thought would take their jobs.

Grant prevailed over Seymour, thanks in part to African-American support in the South. Even in the face of violence and voter intimidation, enough federal troops were stationed in southern states to protect and enable the large numbers of African-American voters—nearly 500,000 of them—who turned out to cast their ballots. Grant carried six states in the South and most states in the North to win the election with 53 percent of the vote, and the Republicans retained their large majorities in both houses of Congress.

This 1868 campaign badge promotes Ulysses S. Grant's presidential candidacy with patriotic symbols.

In his inaugural address, Grant declared, "I shall on all subjects have a policy to recommend, but none to enforce against the will of the people." He promised to uphold the laws Congress passed, and he was true to his word. With Andrew Johnson and his veto pen a memory, Congress was finally able to put one final Reconstruction amendment into place.

THE 15th AMENDMENT

You have read about the 13th Amendment, which abolished slavery in the United States. The 14th Amendment, which guaranteed citizenship to all American-born people and equal protection under the law for all citizens, was finally ratified in July 1868. In the years that followed, the 14th Amendment opened the door to other landmark legislation, including laws that expanded rights for women, mandated school integration, and guaranteed voting rights and equal employment opportunities for women and minorities.

After Grant's election, Congress passed the **15th Amendment,** which prohibited federal and state governments from restricting the right to vote because of race, color, or previous condition of servitude, or slavery. The amendment was intended to limit the legal right of the southern states to exclude African Americans from the political process, and it completed the political reforms sought by Reconstruction.

Congress approved the amendment quickly in February 1869. Democrats viewed it as a step toward equality for African Americans and heavily opposed it. In fact, the amendment did not ensure African

Americans the right to hold office, and it left in place certain restrictions that both southern and northern states imposed on voting rights. These restrictions included **poll taxes**, or fees charged when people register to vote, and **literacy tests**, which require voters to prove they can read and write before registering. Such measures were enacted mainly to keep African Americans from voting. Even so, state legislatures ratified the 15th Amendment promptly, and it became part of the Constitution in 1870.

WEAK LEADERSHIP

By 1870, many Americans were thinking less of the war and more of the future. Northern voters were losing interest in the South's issues and becoming more concerned about those closer to home. But Grant's inexperience impeded his ability to help the nation face challenges. Because of his "hands-off" approach to governing and attempts to avoid partisan battles, he seemed weak. Congress stepped in to make decisions about controversial issues.

The Republicans were losing support in the South to the Democratic Party as Reconstruction-era policies faded. And within the party itself, rifts arose over protective tariffs, currency issues, and competing Reconstruction plans. Among the most powerful party factions were a group of disgruntled, unhappy members who called themselves the **Liberal Republicans.** In the 1870s, the word *liberal* described someone who favored smaller government, lower tariffs, civil-service reform, and, most important, an end to Reconstruction. But Grant's administration had other problems, too. Rumors of scandal were beginning to surface.

HISTORICAL THINKING

1. **READING CHECK** What effect did the 15th Amendment have on voting rights for African Americans in the North?

2. **ANALYZE CAUSE AND EFFECT** How did African Americans help pass the 15th Amendment?

3. **COMPARE AND CONTRAST** How closely did Grant's inaugural promises align with his actions as president? Support your response with evidence.

PLAN: 2-PAGE LESSON

OBJECTIVE

Explain why voters elected Ulysses S. Grant as president and the impact of the 15th Amendment.

CRITICAL THINKING SKILLS FOR LESSON 3.1

- Analyze Cause and Effect
- Compare and Contrast
- Make Inferences
- Identify
- Analyze Primary Sources

HISTORICAL THINKING FOR CHAPTER 13

How did the United States change because of Reconstruction? By 1868, the final reforms of Reconstruction were being put in place even as support for the plan was fading. Lesson 3.1 explores how the passage of the 15th Amendment proved to be both the culmination and last gasp of Reconstruction-era policies.

BACKGROUND FOR THE TEACHER

The historical legacy of Ulysses S. Grant is almost as interesting as his life. Following the Civil War, many historians adopted the "Lost Cause" interpretation of the conflict, which argued that noble southerners waged a courageous war against the industrialized and more populous North. Under this framework, Robert E. Lee was the hero of history, and Grant was the villain. However, in more recent decades, the perspective has begun to shift. Modern historians point to Grant's strengths and accomplishments, such as an unshakable calm under fire and a strong sense of fairness and justice, which led him to support the 15th Amendment and anti-Klan legislation, to send troops to end Klan violence in the South, and to reform the government's policies toward Native Americans. In a 2018 survey of American historians conducted by the *New York Times*, Grant ranked as the 21st best president, up seven slots from his previous ranking.

INTRODUCE & ENGAGE

CHOOSE A PRESIDENTIAL CANDIDATE

Review with students the reasons for Republican frustration with Andrew Johnson. Then ask them to imagine they are a committee of Republicans in 1868 charged with choosing a Republican candidate for president. **ASK:** What qualities should the candidate have? *(Possible responses: commitment to Reconstruction, support for African Americans, respect for the will of Congress)* Record and display their responses on a Word Web. Tell students that Lesson 3.1 examines the presidency of Ulysses S. Grant, the Republican successor to Johnson. When students finish reading the lesson, revisit the Word Web and ask them to compare and contrast their responses with the qualities that Grant exhibited as president.

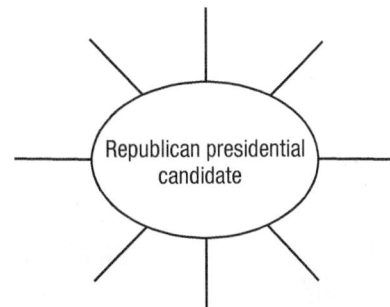

Republican presidential candidate

TEACH

GUIDED DISCUSSION

1. **Make Inferences** Why might voters have felt that Grant would make a good president? *(Possible response: As a general, Grant had demonstrated his ability as a strong leader and the ability to pursue a long-term course of action, qualities that would aid in directing Reconstruction. Voters might have considered that George Washington had served as a general and then had been an exemplary president, so they assumed that Grant would be exemplary as well.)*

2. **Identify** What factors caused Reconstruction to lose support in the North? *(Northern voters began to tire of the issue and became more concerned about local problems. Also, the Republican Party was divided about Reconstruction, and Liberal Republicans turned to other issues that they felt were more important.)*

ANALYZE PRIMARY SOURCES

Remind students that in his inaugural address, Grant said, "I shall on all subjects have a policy to recommend, but none to enforce against the will of the people." **ASK:** In what way does this quotation reinforce his campaign theme of "let us have peace"? *(Possible response: Grant was suggesting that unlike President Johnson, who acted against the will of Congress, he would be a unifying figure by promoting peaceful relationships in government and, hopefully, in the country.)*

ACTIVE OPTIONS

Active History: Amend the Constitution Extend the lesson by using either the PDF or Whiteboard version of the activity. These activities take a deeper look at a topic from, or related to, the lesson. Explore the activities as a class, turn them into group assignments, or even assign them individually.

NG Learning Framework: Write a Letter to the President

SKILL Communication

KNOWLEDGE Our Human Story

Ask students to work in groups to write a letter to President Grant from the perspective of either a midwestern farmer or urban worker, an African-American or white sharecropper, or a Radical or Liberal Republican. The letter should express the person's concerns and what the person hopes Grant will do to address them. Direct students to conduct research about the perspective they are assuming. When groups finish writing their letters, invite a representative from each to read their letter to the class.

DIFFERENTIATE

INCLUSION

Describe and Analyze Pair students to examine the print celebrating the 15th Amendment and its caption. Have partners take turns describing each scene in detail. Encourage analysis of the printmaker's point of view about the 15th Amendment. Then have pairs work together to answer the Critical Viewing question.

GIFTED & TALENTED

Create a Poster Challenge students to create a poster illustrating the shortcomings of the 15th Amendment. Suggest that they use scenes and images showing the voter restrictions and other forms of discrimination faced by African Americans. Invite students to share their posters with the class. Guide a class discussion about how, taken together, the student posters and the 1870 print in the lesson enhance their understanding of what the 15th Amendment did and did not do for African Americans.

See the Chapter Planner for more strategies for differentiation.

HISTORICAL THINKING

ANSWERS

1. Since the 15th Amendment did not lift voting restrictions for African Americans living in the North, it had little effect on their voting rights.

2. African Americans in the South, protected by federal troops, turned out in large numbers to vote for Grant and Republican candidates, which eventually helped Congress pass the 15th Amendment.

3. Grant promised to put the concerns of the people first and to uphold the laws passed by Congress. He kept his word about the laws, but by leaving decisions about controversial issues to Congress, he appeared weak and ineffective.

CRITICAL VIEWING The 15th Amendment specifically tried to protect African Americans' participation in the political process. The scenes of African Americans fighting in the Civil War, becoming educated, and getting married provide justification for the political process that the amendment would help protect.

THE END OF AN ERA

Think about how complicated and difficult it is to keep track of U.S. economic and political issues today. In the 1870s, Americans were also faced with a host of political scandals and a financial panic that nearly took their minds off the problems of Reconstruction. Nearly.

SCANDAL AND PANIC

The first accusations of scandal arose in the summer of 1869. Two speculators, Jay Gould and Jim Fisk, were caught manipulating the gold market to make huge profits for themselves. The scheme involved members of Grant's own family, leading many Americans to question the ethical standards of Grant and his administration.

But despite Grant's weak leadership and connection to scandal, Republicans chose him again as their 1872 presidential candidate. The Liberal Republicans allied with Democrats to throw their support behind newspaper publisher Horace Greeley, whose platform was based on ending Reconstruction. Grant, who supported Reconstruction, remained popular enough with the public to win re-election easily, even though more government scandals were already brewing.

Corruption in the railroad industry surfaced in September 1872. The **Crédit Mobilier** (KREH-diht moh-BEEL-yay) was a construction company created by directors and stockholders of the Union Pacific Railroad. The stockholders signed contracts with the company to work on the railroad, and then they overcharged for work completed,

American illustrator Howard Pyle captures the fear and chaos sparked by the Panic of 1873 in this painting, *The Rush from the New York Stock Exchange on September 18, 1873.*

passing the huge profits on to themselves. To avoid a congressional investigation, Crédit Mobilier's managers bribed some congressional Republicans and, allegedly, Vice President Schuyler Colfax, allowing them to buy company shares at prices well below market value. When the lawmakers sold their shares, they pocketed the difference. A newspaper, the *New York Sun*, broke the story in late 1872, sparking an investigation that further damaged the Grant administration's credibility. Another scandal arose when Congress forced Secretary of War William Belknap to resign after accusing him of accepting cash gifts from army suppliers.

Then, in September 1873, the influential banking firm of Jay Cooke and Company declared bankruptcy due to a European stock market crash and bad investments made in the Northern Pacific Railroad. More bank and railroad business failures followed, sending a wave of fear known as the **Panic of 1873** through the financial industry and the country. Thousands of businesses closed, many people lost their savings, and unemployment increased. To make matters worse, there was no system of unemployment insurance or social security to cushion workers against the economic shocks. The nation slid into a depression that lasted until 1879.

Scandals and economic panic harmed Grant and the Republicans politically, and in the 1874 midterm elections, Democrats won control of the House of Representatives and secured more seats in the Senate. Grant's administration retreated from southern politics, and southern Democrats gained more power. Racial intimidation and racist propaganda increased, and in 1876, two important Supreme Court cases diminished African Americans' hopes of securing equal rights.

RECONSTRUCTION ENDS

In *U.S.* v. *Cruikshank*, the Court ruled that, while the 14th Amendment allowed the federal government to prohibit states from abusing African Americans' civil rights, only the states could prosecute and punish violations of the amendment. In *U.S.* v. *Reese*, decided the same day, the Court ruled that the 15th Amendment only made it illegal to deny a citizen's voting rights based on race. States were free to use other criteria to determine a voter's fitness, such as poll taxes and literacy tests. These decisions paved the way for nearly a century of racial discrimination.

Democrats felt optimistic as the 1876 presidential election approached. They nominated the governor of New York, Sam Tilden, a vocal opponent of

corruption. Republicans nominated Rutherford B. Hayes, a respected Union officer, former member of the House of Representatives, and governor of Ohio. Both candidates were known for their honesty.

Tilden captured 184 electoral votes against Hayes's 165, but Tilden needed one more electoral vote to secure a victory. Of the 20 votes still in doubt, 19 were from the southern states of Louisiana, South Carolina, and Florida, and one was from Oregon. Both sides declared victory. The Constitution did not provide guidance on contested presidential elections, but the two houses of Congress had specific roles. The House of Representatives was responsible for electing the president if no one won an electoral majority, and the Senate was responsible for verifying the electoral vote. Neither the Republican Senate nor the Democratic House could proceed without the support of the other.

Congress created a 15-member electoral commission with five members each from the House, Senate, and Supreme Court. The commission's eight Republicans and seven Democrats voted along party lines, recommending the disputed electoral votes go to Hayes, but the Democratic House would still have to accept Hayes as the winner. To prevent a crisis, Republicans and Democrats struck a deal that became known as the **Compromise of 1877**: Democrats agreed to award Hayes the presidency in exchange for ending Reconstruction. Within a month of taking office, Hayes pulled federal troops out of the South.

Reconstruction had begun the long struggle to overcome the racism borne of centuries of chattel slavery, but to complete the effort would have required an expansion of federal power few Americans, even those in the North, were willing to accept. Instead, racial discrimination became entrenched throughout the nation. Reconstruction may have fallen short of its goals, but the 13th, 14th, and 15th amendments eventually paved the way for the civil rights movement of the 1960s.

HISTORICAL THINKING

1. **READING CHECK** What was the outcome of the Compromise of 1877?

2. **DRAW CONCLUSIONS** Why was the Crédit Mobilier scandal particularly disturbing to many Americans?

3. **ANALYZE CAUSE AND EFFECT** What set off the Panic of 1873 and how did it affect the nation?

4. **COMPARE AND CONTRAST** How were the two Supreme Court cases involving the 14th and 15th amendments similar and different?

PLAN: 2-PAGE LESSON

OBJECTIVE

Examine how scandal, economic panic, Supreme Court decisions, and a contested election brought an end to Reconstruction.

CRITICAL THINKING SKILLS FOR LESSON 3.2

• Draw Conclusions

• Analyze Cause and Effect

• Compare and Contrast

• Summarize

• Identify Problems and Solutions

HISTORICAL THINKING FOR CHAPTER 13

How did the United States change because of Reconstruction? Following the Grant administration, the nation turned away from Reconstruction-era reforms. Lesson 3.2 describes how economic panic and a contested election led to the end of Reconstruction.

BACKGROUND FOR THE TEACHER

The legacy of Reconstruction is mixed. Although it gave African Americans full citizenship, overturning centuries of racist policy, W.E.B. Du Bois judged the era "a splendid failure." The decades following the Civil War proved that racial animosity was not confined to the South. For Reconstruction to be successful, the United States needed to develop a national strategy for African Americans to progress economically. Many white northerners who opposed this type of aid felt trapped in urban poverty—competing with new immigrants for menial jobs. While it was acknowledged that the development of apprenticeship programs and government enforcement of civil rights laws was necessary, attitudes in the North made this politically unsupportable, leaving many formerly enslaved people no road to prosperity.

FINANCIAL LITERACY

To extend their knowledge and understanding about the concepts in this lesson, refer students to the Financial Literacy handbook.

INTRODUCE & ENGAGE

COMPLETE A SEQUENCE CHAIN

Direct students' attention to the painting and caption in this lesson and discuss details in the men's body language and facial expressions that tell what is happening. Then work with students to complete a Sequence Chain of political events that a financial panic might trigger. Suggest that they consider how people might feel toward political officials and the party in power. Tell them that Lesson 3.2 describes how a serious financial panic contributed to the end of Reconstruction.

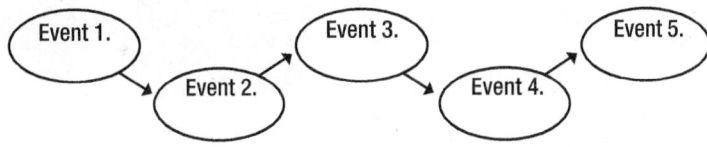

TEACH

GUIDED DISCUSSION

1. **Summarize** How did the economic panic and scandals during Grant's administration affect the balance of power in Congress, and what were the consequences? *(Democrats gained control of the House of Representatives and obtained more Senate seats. This weakened Grant's support, and he withdrew from political action in the South, which led to an increase in white racial hostility toward African Americans.)*

2. **Identify Problems and Solutions** What problems arose in the 1876 presidential election, and how were they resolved? *(Neither candidate received a majority of electoral votes, and the Constitution had little to say on the matter. Congress tried to solve this problem by creating a committee that eventually chose Republican Rutherford B. Hayes as president. With the Compromise of 1877, the Democratic House gave Hayes the victory in return for agreeing to the Republicans' demand to end Reconstruction.)*

MORE INFORMATION

Democratic Convention of 1876 Even before its historic finish, the 1876 election reflected how the nation was changing. The Democrats held their convention in St. Louis, Missouri, the first major political party convention west of the Mississippi River, marking the growing importance of the region. Both presidential candidates, though disagreeing on civil rights, were sympathetic to the South—something that hadn't happened since before the Civil War. In their platform, Democrats called for federal government and civil service reforms and restrictions on Chinese immigration, reflecting a growing unease with the rise in the country's Asian population.

ACTIVE OPTIONS

On Your Feet: Compete in a True-False Quiz Divide the class into two teams and have each write a series of True-False questions about the lesson for a quiz competition. Tell teams to provide the correct answers for false questions. Choose one team to begin the competition and then have teams take turns reading questions until both teams run out of questions. The team with the most correct answers is the winner.

NG Learning Framework: Create an Editorial Cartoon Gallery

ATTITUDES Empowerment, Responsibility

SKILL Communication

Arrange students in small groups. Ask each group to choose an event from the lesson as the basis for an editorial cartoon. Direct groups to conduct research to learn more about the event and to find examples of editorial cartoons printed in the late 1800s. Tell them to make sure that the group agrees on an opinion about the event and that it is clearly expressed in their cartoon. Invite groups to arrange their cartoons in a gallery so that they may comment on and ask questions about each other's work.

DIFFERENTIATE

STRIVING READERS

Summarize in a Tweet Arrange students in pairs and instruct them to write a tweet for each paragraph in the lesson to summarize its main idea in their own words. Encourage partners to read their tweets aloud, alternating paragraphs. Then have pairs compare their tweets with another pair to help check their comprehension.

PRE-AP

Write an Analytic Essay Instruct students to conduct preliminary research to learn more about the Supreme Court rulings in *U.S.* v. *Cruikshank* and *U.S.* v. *Reese*. Then tell them to choose one of the cases to research in detail and write an analytic essay. Suggest that they analyze the arguments presented in the case, the logic of the Court's ruling, and the impact the decision had on African Americans' voting and civil rights. Invite students to post their essays on a class blog or website.

See the Chapter Planner for more strategies for differentiation.

HISTORICAL THINKING

ANSWERS

1. The Compromise of 1877 gave the presidential election to Rutherford B. Hayes in exchange for an end to Reconstruction in the South.

2. The scandal involved members of Congress and the vice president, who had been bribed by Crédit Mobilier to prevent a congressional investigation of the company.

3. A European stock market crash led to the bankruptcy of a large banking corporation. As more banks and businesses failed, workers lost their jobs and people lost their savings, plunging the nation into a deep depression.

4. The Supreme Court decisions were similar in that they narrowed federal protections for African Americans, giving more power to the states and ushering in an era of discrimination. They were different in that the 14th Amendment decision dealt with civil rights in general, while the 15th Amendment decision centered on voting rights.

VOCABULARY

Use each of the terms below in a sentence that expresses an understanding about an event or topic from the chapter.

1. amnesty
   President Johnson's support of amnesty for former Confederates suggested he would willingly grant them official pardons.

2. carpetbagger

3. scalawag

4. sharecropping

5. voter intimidation

6. social justice

7. integrate

8. collateral

9. poll tax

READING STRATEGY
COMPARE AND CONTRAST

Use a Venn diagram like the one shown below to compare and contrast the principles of Presidential and Congressional (Radical) Reconstruction. Then answer the question.

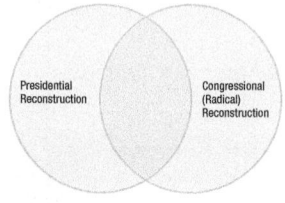

Presidential Reconstruction / Congressional (Radical) Reconstruction

10. On which issues were Presidential Reconstruction and Congressional Reconstruction alike and on which issues were they different?

MAIN IDEAS

Answer the following questions. Support your answers with evidence from the chapter.

11. Why were many congressional Republicans not surprised that Andrew Johnson supported leniency toward former Confederate states? **LESSON 1.1**

12. Why did the Radical Republicans think it necessary to implement their own Reconstruction plans? **LESSON 1.1**

13. What pushed congressional Republicans to consider impeaching Johnson? **LESSON 1.2**

14. What proposals were made to help rebuild the South and reform its economy? **LESSON 2.1**

15. In what area of African-American life did the Freedmen's Bureau have the most impact? **LESSON 2.2**

16. Why was education considered crucial as well as a symbol of freedom to African Americans in the South? **LESSON 2.2**

17. Why did Congress wait until Grant was elected to pass the 15th Amendment? **LESSON 3.1**

18. How was the 1876 election dispute settled? **LESSON 3.2**

HISTORICAL THINKING

Answer the following questions. Support your answers with evidence from the chapter.

19. **SEQUENCE** How did ratification of the 13th, 14th, and 15th amendments advance the rights of African Americans?

20. **DRAW CONCLUSIONS** What impact did the emergence of sharecropping in the South have on the region after the Civil War?

21. **SUMMARIZE** What were the political ramifications of the Panic of 1873?

22. **MAKE INFERENCES** Why were the elections and political successes of Hiram Revels and Blanche K. Bruce important to African Americans in the South?

23. **FORM AND SUPPORT OPINIONS** Given what you have read about Presidential and Congressional (Radical) Reconstruction, which plan do you think offered the best way to reunite the nation? Explain your opinion.

INTERPRET VISUALS

Look closely at the two-panel political cartoon, which compares the South during Reconstruction with the South after Reconstruction. Use information from the chapter and the cartoon to answer the questions that follow.

24. What does the woman in the first panel symbolize, and why?

25. How does the artist depict the South in the second panel?

ANALYZE SOURCES

In this excerpt from President Grant's Second Inaugural Address delivered on March 4, 1873, Grant discussed his approach to civil rights in the South as Reconstruction continued. Read the excerpt and answer the question.

> The effects of the late civil strife have been to free the slave and make him a citizen. Yet he is not possessed of the civil rights which citizenship should carry with it. This is wrong, and should be corrected. To this correction I stand committed, so far as Executive influence can avail.
>
> Social equality is not a subject to be legislated upon, nor shall I ask that anything be done to advance the social status of the colored man, except to give him a fair chance to develop what there is good in him, give him access to the schools, and when he travels let him feel assured that his conduct will regulate the treatment and fare he will receive.

26. What distinction does Grant make between the meaning of "civil rights" and "social equality"?

CONNECT TO YOUR LIFE

27. **EXPLANATORY** Ratification of the 15th Amendment in 1870 prohibited the government from denying a person's right to vote on the basis of race. Recall what you learned about the issues during Reconstruction that drove many African-American men to feel empowered and to take an active role in the political process by voting. Think about the first time you were or will be eligible to vote as an active citizen in your local, state, and national elections. Write a paragraph identifying an issue about which you have strong opinions and why you think your vote and your voice should be heard.

TIPS

- Use textual evidence from the chapter in your explanation.

- Address the issues that arose when some southern states tried to limit the legal rights of African Americans to vote.

- Explain under what circumstances voters can have their voices suppressed either legally or illegally.

VOCABULARY ANSWERS

1. President Johnson's support of amnesty for former Confederates suggested he would willingly grant them official pardons.

2. After the Civil War, northerners who went to the South looking for easy economic opportunities were known as carpetbaggers.

3. Southerners used the derogatory term *scalawag* to refer to white southerners who supported Reconstruction.

4. Many former slaves made their living sharecropping, working someone else's land for a small portion of profits from the crops.

5. Voter intimidation by the Klan kept both African-American and white Republican voters away from the polls.

6. Social justice requires equal rights and opportunities for all.

7. Radical Republicans sought to integrate freedmen into society.

8. After emancipation, plantation owners could not use their former slaves as collateral for loans.

9. Requiring African Americans to pay a poll tax before voting excluded poorer voters from the political process.

READING STRATEGY ANSWER

Presidential Reconstruction: amnesty, civil rights/political rights for Confederates

Both: 13th Amendment, new or amended constitutions for southern states

Congressional (Radical) Reconstruction: 14th Amendment, 15th Amendment, military presence in South

10. The two sides agreed on abolition of slavery and that southern states needed to have constitutional conventions. The main differences were that Presidential Reconstruction granted amnesty for former Confederates and protected their rights, while Congressional Reconstruction sought to remake the South through two constitutional amendments and military occupation of the region.

MAIN IDEAS ANSWERS

11. Johnson was a former Democrat and a former slaveholder from Tennessee who did not support equal rights for African Americans.

12. Radical Republicans believed Johnson was too lenient, and they wanted to eliminate black codes and keep former Confederate states from returning to the Union until they met strict requirements.

13. Initially, they were angered by Johnson's Reconstruction plans but decided to impeach him when he violated the Tenure in Office Act.

14. Many Americans thought the South's economy had to be transformed from agrarian to industrial. Financial support from wealthy southerners and northerners aided in rebuilding and helped to spur industrial growth.

15. The Freedmen's Bureau had the most impact on education in the lives of African Americans by building, funding, and staffing thousands of schools that would provide a free education.

16. African Americans viewed education as a path to help them live free and independent lives and to gain entry into the political process.

17. Grant's election, ensured by the overwhelming support of African Americans, was accompanied by large Republican majorities and signaled that the country supported the 15th Amendment.

18. Congress created an electoral commission to decide the election. Meanwhile, Democrats and Republicans negotiated the Compromise of 1877, in which Democrats agreed to give Hayes the presidency if Republicans agreed to end Reconstruction.

HISTORICAL THINKING ANSWERS

19. The 13th Amendment freed all enslaved African Americans. The 14th Amendment granted citizenship to all African Americans and gave them equal protection under the law. The 15th Amendment granted all African-American men the right to vote.

20. The sharecropping system severely limited the economic freedom of both African Americans and poor whites by preventing them from earning enough money to pursue other opportunities.

21. After the panic of 1873, the Republicans lost control of the House of Representatives and several Senate seats. This shifted the balance of power and led indirectly to the end of Reconstruction.

22. Revels and Bruce were among the first group of African-American politicians to assume office and leadership positions. African Americans in the South saw them as role models and hoped they could introduce and pass civil rights laws.

23. Answers will vary. Possible responses: Presidential Reconstruction exhibited leniency toward the already devastated South and would have ensured a smooth transition into the postwar era. Instead of seeking retribution, President Johnson offered amnesty and pardons to former Confederates in return for an oath of loyalty. Congressional Reconstruction was the best plan to reunite the nation because it established order with military rule and created clear requirements for Confederate states to reenter the Union, such as ratifying the 14th Amendment, writing new state constitutions, and allowing all adult males to vote.

INTERPRET VISUALS ANSWERS

24. With Grant as president, the woman symbolizes a South that is weak, chained, heavily burdened by Union troops, and exploited by carpetbaggers.

25. With Hayes as president, depicted plowing under a carpetbag, the South is portrayed as prospering, having returned to an agricultural economy. Factories in the background represent developing industry.

ANALYZE SOURCES ANSWER

26. Grant believes civil rights are something the government can and should guarantee but that social equality cannot be legislated and is dependent on fair opportunities, education, and people's own behavior.

CONNECT TO YOUR LIFE ANSWER

27. Paragraphs will vary. Students should identify an issue about which they have a strong opinion and explain why their vote and voice should be heard. Paragraphs should include textual evidence from the chapter, address issues that arose as a result of limiting the legal rights of African Americans to vote, and explain the circumstances under which votes can be legally or illegally suppressed.

A Sketch in Time

by Harry Katz

Adapted from "A Sketch in Time: Bringing the Civil War to Life," by Harry Katz, *National Geographic*, May 2012

At the time of the Civil War, camera shutters were too slow to record movement sharply. Photographers, burdened by large glass negatives and bulky horse-drawn processing wagons, could neither maneuver the rough terrain nor record images in the midst of battle. So newspaper publishers hired illustrators to sketch the action for readers at home and abroad. Embedded with troops on both sides of the conflict, these "special artists," or "specials," were America's first pictorial war correspondents or reporters. They were young men—none were women—from diverse backgrounds, including soldiers, engineers, fine artists, and a few veteran illustrators, all seeking income, experience, and adventure.

The English-born Alfred Waud and Theodore Davis were the only specials who covered the war from the opening gun battle in April 1861 through the fall of the Confederacy four years later. Davis later described what it took to be a war artist: "Total disregard for personal safety and comfort; an owl-like propensity [ability] to sit up all night and a hawky style of vigilance during the day; capacity for going on short food; willingness to ride any number of miles horseback for just one sketch, which might have to be finished at night by no better light than that of a fire."

In spite of the remarkable courage these men displayed and the events they witnessed, their harrowing stories have gone unnoticed. W.T. Crane heroically covered the events taking place in Charleston, South Carolina, from within the rebel city. D.H. Strother, a Union supporter, was arrested as a spy for sketching the Confederate Army encampments outside Washington, D.C. Frank Vizetelly witnessed Jefferson Davis's final flight into exile.

Special artists worked fast, identifying a war scene's focal point, blocking out the composition in minutes, and fleshing it out later in camp. They took great pride in making their renderings as faithful as possible. The artists dispatched their sketches from the battlefield by horse, train, or ship to the publisher's office, where the image was copied onto blocks of wood and engraved for printing. Usually it took two to three weeks for the drawing to be published, although important events or battles could be rushed into print in a matter of days.

Two journals led the national scene in 1861, *Harper's Weekly* and *Frank Leslie's Illustrated Newspaper*. *Leslie's* claimed to be strictly neutral in its coverage of the growing divide in the country and then of the war. In contrast, *Harper's* stood firmly with the Republican Party, President Lincoln, the abolitionists, and the Union. Both publishers, however, censored images considered too negative or graphic and altered drawings to make them more stirring or upbeat. *Harper's* editors, for instance, made Alfred Waud's drawing of a leg amputation at an Antietam field hospital look less gory to accommodate squeamish readers. Engravers freshened another Waud sketch of exhausted horses dragging artillery carts, giving them lifted heads and spirited tails and making them kick up clods of mud. The enhanced sketch provided an animated portrait of the drivers of the team of horses racing ammunition to the front.

Nonetheless, by depicting scenes as realistically as they could, specials undermined the popular myth of the war as a romantic adventure. As citizens grew accustomed to the violent imagery, censorship eased.

Within a generation, photographers using Kodak cameras surpassed sketch artists. But artists are still going to battlefronts. For instance, both the military and the media send artists to Afghanistan to interpret warfare in ways cameras cannot, capturing for the record the inner lives of the soldiers caught up in a larger drama.

For more from National Geographic, check out "Lincoln" online.

UNIT INQUIRY: Analyze the Legacy of Slavery

In this unit, you learned about one of the most divisive periods in American history—the years before, during, and after the Civil War—when the issue of slavery ripped the country apart. Did the practice of slavery, and the racism that accompanied it, cause problems that continue to affect the lives of Americans today? Do the effects of slavery and racism still cast a shadow over the country, more than 150 years after the end of the Civil War?

ASSIGNMENT

Compare the social, political, and economic status of African Americans during the Civil War era and today. Identify areas of progress as well as lingering problems that are part of the legacy of slavery and racism. Be prepared to present your analysis to the class.

Plan As you consider the legacy of slavery and racism, review the unit to gather evidence about the treatment of both free and enslaved African Americans during the Civil War era. Make a list of the areas in which African Americans experienced discrimination and describe the treatment. Then consider the situation today. Do additional research if necessary. Use a graphic organizer like this one to help organize your findings and observations.

	Civil War Era	Today
Segregation		
Employment		
Education		
Property ownership		
Voting rights		
Family units		
Hate group activity		

Produce Use your notes to write an essay in which you analyze the legacy of slavery and racism in the United States. Describe what life was like for free and enslaved African Americans during the Civil War era. Then identify the strides that have been made as well as the connection between slavery and problems of racism, prejudice, and privilege that remain.

Present Choose an engaging way to present your analysis to the class. Consider one of these options:

- Team up with a partner to present an imaginary dialogue between two people, one from the Civil War era and one from the present time, discussing educational and employment opportunities for African Americans in the United States.

- Create your own graphic that clearly compares the situation in the two time periods.

- Prepare talking points for both sides of a debate on this question: Have the issues of race, prejudice, and privilege improved in the United States since the Civil War era? Work with a partner to stage the debate for the rest of the class.

NATIONAL GEOGRAPHIC | LEARNING FRAMEWORK ACTIVITIES

Create a Compromise Guide

SKILLS Collaboration, Problem-Solving

ATTITUDE Responsibility

The Missouri Compromise, the Compromise of 1850, and the Kansas-Nebraska Act helped keep the United States together, postponing the Civil War. Review information about the three acts. Then think about a time you, or a group you are part of, compromised. Consider this question: What makes compromise successful? Then work with a partner to create a guide for successful compromise. Include conditions necessary for agreement. Present your guide to the class and discuss the conditions that existed during the creation of the acts in the 1800s.

Investigate Medical Care

ATTITUDE Curiosity

KNOWLEDGE Our Human Story

About 620,000 soldiers died in the Civil War, and about two-thirds of those deaths were caused by disease rather than injury. Research the medical care that soldiers received in camps and field hospitals. Find out the factors that contributed to the high rate of disease and the large number of deaths. Investigate treatments for diseases and surgical techniques used. Then give an oral report to the class in which you identify medical advances that would have reduced the disease and death rate.

NATIONAL GEOGRAPHIC CONNECTION

GUIDED DISCUSSION FOR "A SKETCH IN TIME"

1. **Compare and Contrast** How were *Harper's Weekly* and *Leslie's Illustrated Newspaper* similar and different? *(Similarities: Both were top-rated journals; both edited special artists' sketches to alter images they feared would strike readers as overly gruesome or negative; both sometimes changed sketches to make them more exciting. Differences: Politically, Harper's Weekly stood firmly with the Republicans and Lincoln, while Leslie's Illustrated Newspaper claimed to be neutral on wartime issues.)*

2. **Make Inferences** What aspects of modern soldiers' inner lives might artists capture that cameras cannot? *(Possible response: Artists could portray the unseen in modern soldiers' lives, such as dreams, memories, or nightmares. They can also create abstract or impressionistic portraits that emphasize a mood or tone. These are aspects that cameras can't record.)*

GUIDED DISCUSSION FOR "LINCOLN"

1. **Identify Main Ideas and Details** What did the events surrounding Lincoln's procession in Manhattan reveal about post-Civil War America? *(Despite the outcome of the Civil War, many white Americans in the United States were still conflicted over the issue of equality and freedom for African Americans.)*

2. **Make Connections** Why did many Americans mourn the loss of President Lincoln so acutely? *(Many people in both the North and the South had lost family and other loved ones in the Civil War but often never recovered the bodies, which made it more difficult to mourn them. Also, the war's end was not a victory against a foreign power but against their fellow citizens. Lincoln's assassination was probably an outlet for people to grieve these losses.)*

HISTORY NOTEBOOK

Encourage students to complete the Unit Wrap-Up page for Unit 4 in their History Notebooks.

UNIT INQUIRY PROJECT RUBRIC

ASSESS

Use the rubric to assess each student's participation and performance.

SCORE	ASSIGNMENT	PRODUCT	PRESENTATION
3 GREAT	• Student thoroughly understands the assignment. • Student participates fully in the project process. • Student works well with partner.	• Analysis is well thought out. • Analysis of the effects of slavery and racism is detailed. • Analysis contains all the key elements listed in the assignment.	• Presentation is clear, concise, and logical. • Presentation provides strong analysis. • Presentation engages the audience.
2 GOOD	• Student mostly understands the assignment. • Student participates fairly well in the project process. • Student works fairly well with partner.	• Analysis is fairly well thought out. • Analysis includes the effects of slavery and racism. • Analysis contains most of the key elements listed in the assignment.	• Presentation is fairly clear, concise, and logical. • Presentation provides analysis. • Presentation somewhat engages the audience.
1 NEEDS WORK	• Student does not understand the assignment. • Student minimally participates or does not participate in the project process. • Student does not work well with partner.	• Analysis is not well thought out. • Analysis of the effects of slavery and racism is not offered. • Analysis contains few or none of the key elements listed in the assignment.	• Presentation is not clear, concise, or logical. • Presentation does not provide analysis. • Presentation does not engage the audience.

NATIONAL GEOGRAPHIC LEARNING FRAMEWORK RUBRIC

ASSESS

Use the rubric to assess how each student applies the National Geographic Learning Framework.

SCORE	ASSIGNMENT	ASSIGNMENT	FINAL PRODUCTS
3 GREAT	• Guide demonstrates **Collaboration** and **Problem-Solving** well. • Guide reflects **Responsibility** well.	• Oral report reflects **Curiosity** well. • Oral report explores **Our Human Story** well.	• Final products are engaging, creative, and well presented.
2 GOOD	• Guide demonstrates **Collaboration** and **Problem-Solving**. • Guide reflects **Responsibility**.	• Oral report reflects **Curiosity**. • Oral report explores **Our Human Story**.	• Final products are interesting, logical, and complete.
1 NEEDS WORK	• Guide does not demonstrate **Collaboration** and **Problem-Solving**. • Guide does not reflect **Responsibility**.	• Oral report does not reflect **Curiosity**. • Oral report does not explore **Our Human Story**.	• Final products are not creative, complete, or interesting.

NEW YORK CITY HEAT WAVE, 1896

On August 4, 1896, a powerful heat wave settled over New York. For the next 10 days, New Yorkers sweated their way through searing temperatures and humidity that effectively shut the city down. The poorest residents experienced the worst conditions. Inside the apartments in brick tenement buildings, recorded temperatures climbed as high as 120°F in the sweltering afternoons, cooling off only slightly once the sun went down. People took whatever refuge they could find, but many died of heat exhaustion or dehydration. Some died accidentally by tumbling off tenement rooftops or fire escapes while attempting to sleep outside. Others risked personal safety by sleeping in the open alongside the East River. **ASK:** What household problems might result from the extreme heat in a crowded city without access to cooling or refrigeration? *(Answers will vary. Possible response: Food storage would be very difficult. The elderly, the disabled, and the debilitated would be especially vulnerable to heat exhaustion and dehydration.)*

Finally, Theodore Roosevelt, who was at the time president of New York's Board of Police Commissioners, persuaded the city to buy several hundred tons of ice to distribute to poorer neighborhoods. On August 13, the city delivered ice to police precincts throughout New York, and throngs of women and children showed up carrying large pots and pans to haul the ice home to their suffering families. The heat finally broke on August 14. By that time, approximately 1,500 people had died of causes related to the heat wave. The disastrous consequences of the heat wave in August 1896 led to increased scrutiny of and public debate about the living conditions of lower-income families, especially those living in the city's many tenements.

GROWTH AND REFORM

Similar to today, New York City around 1900 was a bustling, congested place where cultures and social classes intermingled, influenced one another, and sometimes clashed. Rapid urban growth and the influx of immigrants contributed to some of the social challenges cities like Chicago, San Francisco, and New York faced. In this photo, children eagerly wait in line with empty tubs to collect free ice that could be used to keep food from spoiling.

458

459

POST–HEAT WAVE REFORM

The 1896 heat wave caught New York City by surprise, and city residents and officials were woefully unprepared for its magnitude. Consequently, during the crisis, the city lacked the infrastructure to assist residents, who were for the most part left to fend for themselves. Even when help was available, as in the case of the city's ice delivery to lower-income neighborhoods, things did not always go as planned. In a note to his sister, Theodore Roosevelt lamented that in some precincts, members of the police force took bribes from wealthier residents, providing ice to some and denying it to others.

Once the crisis was over, reforms followed slowly. The epic scale of the heat wave led to at least one strong piece of reform legislation, however. In 1901, the state of New York passed the Tenement House Act, which instituted new standards of hygiene, ventilation, and fireproofing for the city's large public apartment houses.

1884 AFRICA:
THE BERLIN CONFERENCE

The continent of Africa has a long history as a source of latex from rubber trees, diamonds, ivory, and other resources. In the mid-1800s, European competition for African commodities began to build. To gain a stronger foothold in Africa, a number of European nations expanded their existing colonies, which led to conflicts with Africans. Beyond that, colonial expansion increased political polarization and squabbling among the colonizing European powers. At a conference held in Berlin, Germany, beginning in 1884, the major European powers and the United States gathered to divide up the entire African continent. With no African leaders in attendance, the attending nations decided that any one of them could lay claim to specific lands in Africa as long as the claiming nation was able to occupy and govern the territory in question. **ASK:** Why were no African nations invited to the Berlin Conference? *(Answers will vary. Possible response: European nations intended to take Africa by force if they had to, so they didn't invite leaders to discuss the situation.)*

It did not take European nations long to overpower African countries. In addition to taking the land, Europeans imposed Western laws, languages, and religious practices on Africans. This imposition was based on the racist assumption that European nations were more advanced and civilized. The effects of European racism and exploitation would reach far into Africa's future. **ASK:** Why might Europeans have felt it necessary to replace African religious practices, languages, and values with Western ones? *(Possible response: The Berlin Conference stipulated that territory colonized by European forces had to be occupied and administered by those forces, so to gain full cooperation from Africans, European colonists tried to make Africa over in their own image. In addition, Europeans wanted to grab land and subjugate people, so disrupting the native peoples' culture was in the Europeans' interest.)*

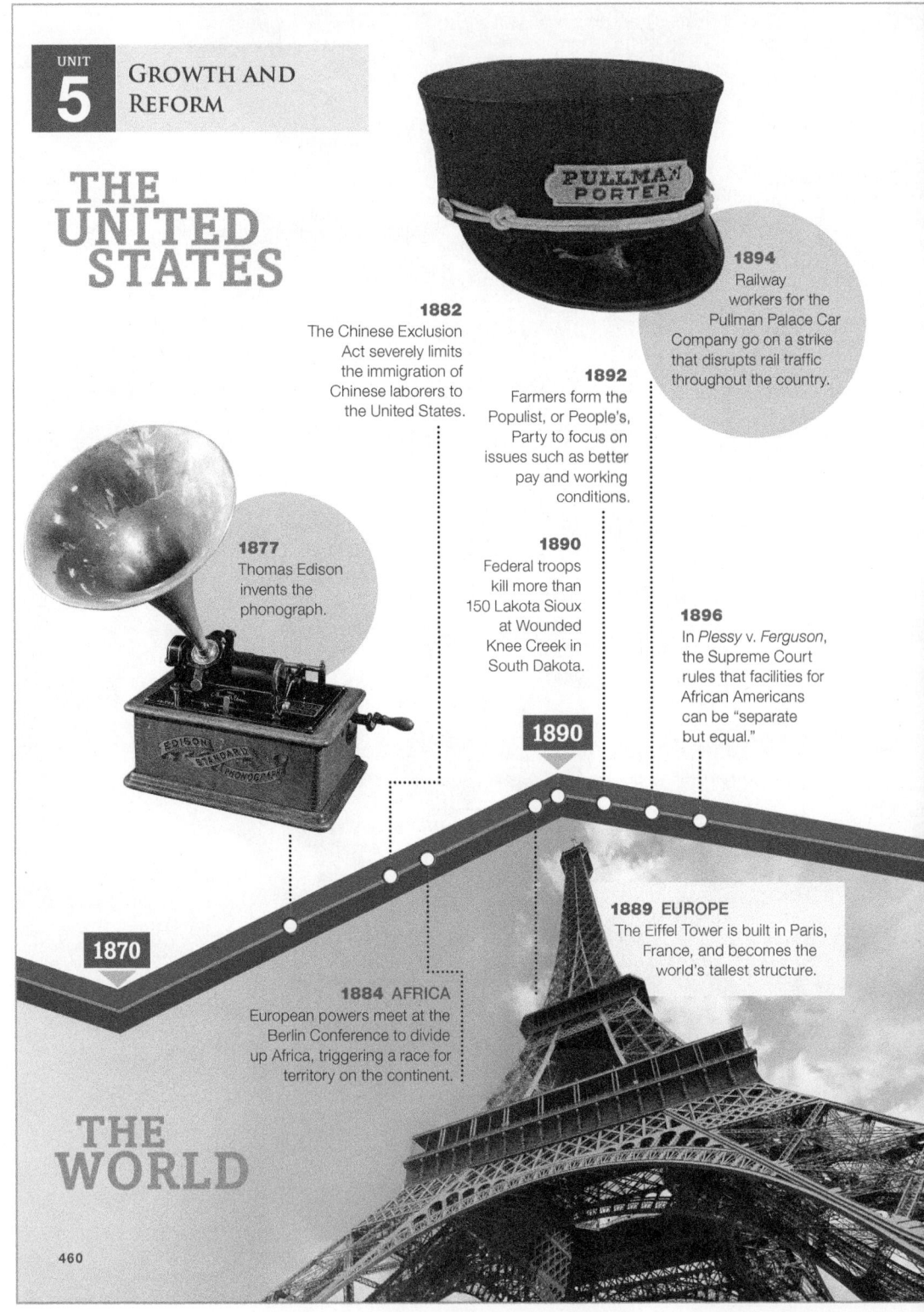

UNIT **5** GROWTH AND REFORM

THE UNITED STATES

1882
The Chinese Exclusion Act severely limits the immigration of Chinese laborers to the United States.

1894
Railway workers for the Pullman Palace Car Company go on a strike that disrupts rail traffic throughout the country.

1892
Farmers form the Populist, or People's, Party to focus on issues such as better pay and working conditions.

1877
Thomas Edison invents the phonograph.

1890
Federal troops kill more than 150 Lakota Sioux at Wounded Knee Creek in South Dakota.

1896
In *Plessy* v. *Ferguson*, the Supreme Court rules that facilities for African Americans can be "separate but equal."

1890

1870

1889 EUROPE
The Eiffel Tower is built in Paris, France, and becomes the world's tallest structure.

1884 AFRICA
European powers meet at the Berlin Conference to divide up Africa, triggering a race for territory on the continent.

THE WORLD

460

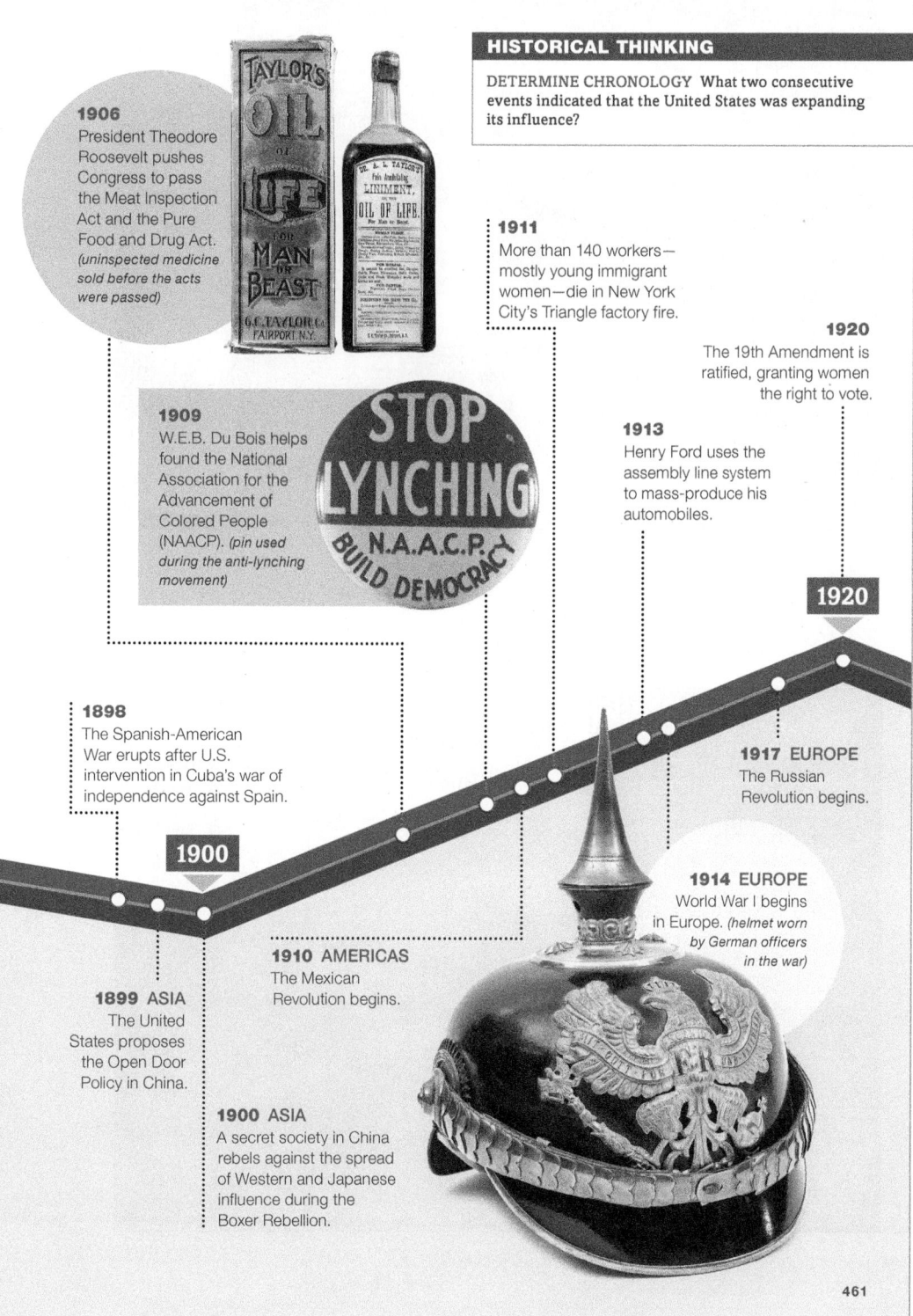

HISTORICAL THINKING

DETERMINE CHRONOLOGY What two consecutive events indicated that the United States was expanding its influence?

1906
President Theodore Roosevelt pushes Congress to pass the Meat Inspection Act and the Pure Food and Drug Act. *(uninspected medicine sold before the acts were passed)*

1909
W.E.B. Du Bois helps found the National Association for the Advancement of Colored People (NAACP). *(pin used during the anti-lynching movement)*

1911
More than 140 workers—mostly young immigrant women—die in New York City's Triangle factory fire.

1920
The 19th Amendment is ratified, granting women the right to vote.

1913
Henry Ford uses the assembly line system to mass-produce his automobiles.

1898
The Spanish-American War erupts after U.S. intervention in Cuba's war of independence against Spain.

1899 ASIA
The United States proposes the Open Door Policy in China.

1900 ASIA
A secret society in China rebels against the spread of Western and Japanese influence during the Boxer Rebellion.

1910 AMERICAS
The Mexican Revolution begins.

1914 EUROPE
World War I begins in Europe. *(helmet worn by German officers in the war)*

1917 EUROPE
The Russian Revolution begins.

1900

1920

461

1917 EUROPE: THE RUSSIAN REVOLUTION

World War I devastated Russia. It lost millions of soldiers, and its army broke down completely in 1916. Meanwhile, the nation suffered massive food shortages due to the collapse of Russian factories and farms. A number of political factions rose up calling for revolution. One, led by Vladimir Lenin, argued for violent overthrow of the government to replace the failed structure with communism, a system that in theory provides for the distribution of lands and wealth to promote the common good. **ASK:** Why might food shortages lead a nation to revolution? *(Possible response: People need food for survival, and the lack of it would mobilize them to support a person who convinced them of how they could get it. In addition, the Russian people, exhausted by the ongoing hardships of war and widespread hunger, blamed the government and became desperate for change and reform.)*

In 1917, food-shortage protests in the Russian capital of Petrograd escalated into revolution. Czar Nicholas II abdicated the throne in March 1917, and a temporary government known as the Petrograd Soviet of Workers' and Soldiers' Deputies took power. The most powerful wing of the Soviets, the Bolsheviks, soon took over under the leadership of Vladimir Lenin. After three years of bloodshed and civil war, the Bolsheviks seized control of the Russian Empire. **ASK:** How did the Russian government change between 1916 and 1917? *(Possible response: The czar resigned and ceded power to the Petrograd Soviet of Workers' and Soldiers' Deputies. One of the internal factions of the Petrograd Soviet, the Bolsheviks, rose up and took power.)*

HISTORICAL THINKING

DETERMINE CHRONOLOGY

In 1898, victory over Spain in the Spanish-American War gave the United States valuable overseas assets that greatly increased its international profile. As part of a postwar treaty, Spain transferred sovereign control over the Philippines to the United States and ceded both Puerto Rico and Guam to U.S. interests. With these new holdings, the United States was ready to take on a new role in world politics. In 1899, armed with its new international clout, the United States proposed the Open Door Policy, which gave all nations equal trading privileges with China. The policy remained the mainstay of U.S. policy in East Asia for the next 50 years.

UNIT 5 RESOURCES

UNIT INTRODUCTION

UNIT TIME LINE

UNIT WRAP-UP

NATIONAL GEOGRAPHIC | CONNECTION

National Geographic Magazine Adapted Articles
- "Nature for Everyone"
- "21st Century Cowboys" ONLINE

Unit 5 Inquiry: Produce a Documentary

NG Learning Framework Activities
- Write a Position Statement
- Plan a Protest

Unit 5 Formal Assessment

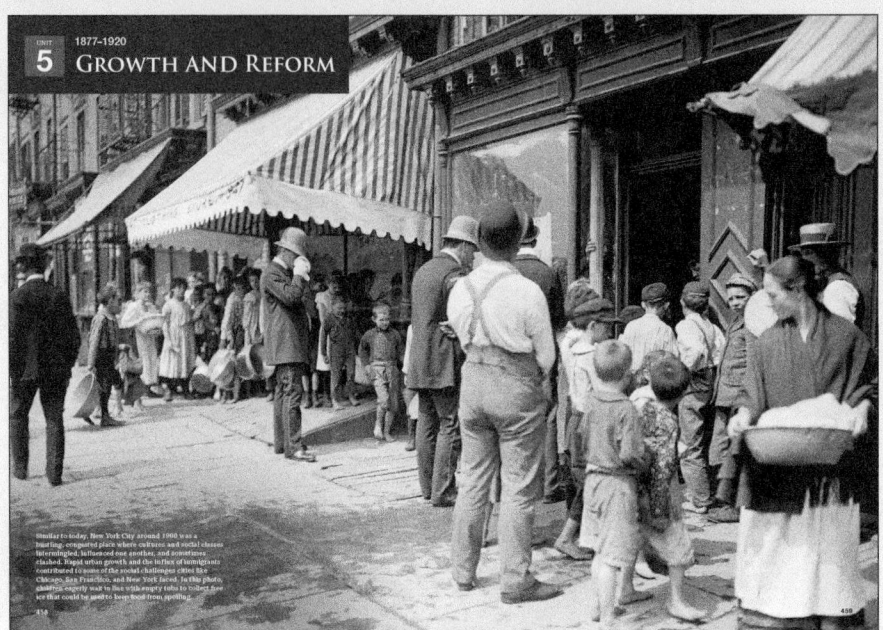

CHAPTER 14 RESOURCES

Available at NGLSync.Cengage.com

TEACHER RESOURCES & ASSESSMENT

Reading and Note-Taking

Vocabulary Practice

Social Studies Skills Lessons
- Reading: Draw Conclusions
- Writing: Argument

Formal Assessment
- Chapter 14 Pretest
- Chapter 14 Tests A & B
- Section Quizzes

Chapter 14 Answer Key

ExamView®
One-time Download

STUDENT DIGITAL RESOURCES

- eEdition
- Handbooks
- Online Atlas
- American Gallery Online
- History Notebook
- Active History
- American Voices (Biographies)
- Literature Analysis
- Projects for Inquiry-Based Learning

Chapter 14 Spanish Resources are available at NGLSync.Cengage.com.

- Study Primary Sources: Introduction from *The Lone Ranger* radio show
- On Your Feet: Take a Virtual Tour of the Wild West

NG Learning Framework:
Analyze the Western Film

SECTION 1 RESOURCES
THE CHANGING FRONTIER

LESSON 1.1
Farming, Ranching, and Mining

- On Your Feet: Three Corners

NG Learning Framework:
Publish a Flyer

American Voices Biography
Aaron Montgomery Ward ONLINE

LESSON 1.2
GEOLOGY IN HISTORY
How Geology Waters the Great Plains

- Active History: Analyze Causes of the Dust Bowl

NG Learning Framework:
Make a Plan

LESSON 1.3
Farmers and the Populist Movement

- On Your Feet: Think, Pair, Share

NG Learning Framework:
Investigate Crop Diversity

American Voices Biography
William Jennings Bryan ONLINE

LESSON 1.4
THROUGH THE LENS—AMERICAN PLACES
America's Breadbasket: The Great Plains

- On Your Feet: Roundtable

NG Learning Framework:
Research the Breadbasket

SECTION 2 RESOURCES
BROKEN TREATIES AND WAR

LESSON 2.1
Growing Pressures on Native Americans

AMERICAN **GALLERY** ONLINE | The Battle of the Little Bighorn

NG Learning Framework:
Research Massacres and Wars

American Voices Biography
Geronimo ONLINE

LESSON 2.2
Broken Promises

- On Your Feet: Inside-Outside Circle

NG Learning Framework:
Design a Policy

American Voices Biography
Helen Hunt Jackson ONLINE

LESSON 2.3
CURATING HISTORY
The Field Museum Chicago, Illinois

- On Your Feet: Sort the Artifacts

LESSON 2.4
Closing the Frontier

- On Your Feet: Stage a Quiz Show

NG Learning Framework:
Research Buffalo Bill's Show

LESSON 2.5
Literature of the West

- On Your Feet: Compare and Contrast Primary Sources

NG Learning Framework:
Investigate Native American Boarding Schools

CHAPTER 14 REVIEW

STRIVING READERS

STRATEGY 1
FOCUS ON MAIN IDEAS

Tell students to locate the Main Idea statement at the beginning of each lesson. Explain that these statements summarize the important ideas of the lessons and will be useful for helping them focus on what matters most in the text.

Use with All Lessons *Throughout the chapter, help students get in the habit of using the Main Idea statements to set a purpose for reading.*

STRATEGY 2
SEQUENCE EVENTS

To build understanding of the critical events in a section and their relationship to one another in time, encourage students to note them in a Sequence Chain like the one shown.

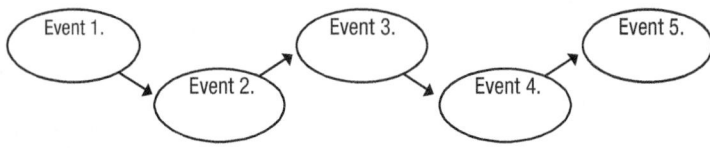

Use with Lessons 1.2 and 2.1 *Suggest that students use the Sequence Chain to trace the sequence of events related to various aspects of westward migration, including water access (Lesson 1.2) and conflicts with Native Americans (Lesson 2.1).*

STRATEGY 3
TURN HEADINGS INTO OUTLINES

To help Striving Readers organize and understand lesson content, explain that headings can provide a high-level outline of the lesson. Model for students how to use the lesson title and subheadings to create a basic outline structure. Encourage students to flesh out their outlines as they read.

Use with All Lessons

INCLUSION

STRATEGY 1
MODIFY VOCABULARY LISTS

Using your standards as a guide, limit the number of Key Vocabulary words that students will be required to master. As they read, instruct students to create a vocabulary card for each word in the modified list. Students may write definitions, synonyms, or examples on the back of each word card. Encourage students to refer to their vocabulary cards often as they read.

Use with All Lessons

STRATEGY 2
DESCRIBE LESSON VISUALS

Pair visually challenged students with students who are not visually challenged. Ask the latter to describe the visuals and answer any questions the visually impaired students might have.

Use with Lessons 1.2, 2.1, and 2.3 *Specifically, students may describe the Ogallala Aquifer diagram in Lesson 1.2, the map showing Indian reservations and battles in Lesson 2.1, and the photographs of Native American artifacts in Lesson 2.3. Students could also read aloud the text accompanying each visual.*

ENGLISH LANGUAGE LEARNERS

STRATEGY ❶
PREP BEFORE READING

Encourage students at **All Proficiencies** to use the PREP strategy to prepare for reading. Write this acrostic on the board:

PREP **P**review the title.
Read Main Idea statement.
Examine visuals.
Predict what you will learn.

Use with All Lessons *Encourage students at the **Emerging** level to ask questions if they have trouble writing a prediction. Students at the **Bridging** level could help students at the **Emerging** and **Expanding** levels write their predictions.*

STRATEGY ❷
REVIEW TRANSITIONAL WORDS

To help students put events in chronological order and summarize what they read, write these transitional words on the board: *first, next, then, also, while, immediately, later, earlier, meanwhile, whenever, simultaneously, subsequently, during, following, before, afterward,* and *finally.* Direct students at the **Emerging** and **Expanding** levels to work together to write a series of sentences that tell what happens in each lesson. Encourage them to use transitional words to tell about the time order of events. Prompt students at the **Bridging** level to construct a paragraph that summarizes the material. Encourage them to use a variety of transitional words and to vary their sentence structure.

Use with All Lessons

STRATEGY ❸
USE PAIRED READING

Pair students at the **Expanding** and **Bridging** levels to read passages aloud from the text.

1. Partner 1 reads a passage; partner 2 retells the passage in his or her own words.

2. Partner 2 reads a different passage; partner 1 retells it.

3. Pairs repeat the process, switching roles.

Use with All Lessons

GIFTED & TALENTED

STRATEGY ❶
WRITE A DRAMATIC SKIT

Invite students to use a variety of documents to deepen their understanding of the frictions that developed between population groups during westward expansion between 1877 and 1900. Instruct them to choose one event illustrating such frictions and use it as the basis of a short skit. Allow time for students to prepare and practice their skits. After they have practiced, invite them to perform their skits for the class.

Use with Lessons 1.1, 1.2, 1.3, 2.1, 2.2, and 2.5 *Remind students that conflict—with others or with oneself—is the basis of drama.*

STRATEGY ❷
CREATE A GRAPHIC BIOGRAPHY

Tell students to select an individual mentioned in this chapter and create a short biography in the style of a comic book or graphic novel. Encourage students to interpret the person's thoughts and actions within the context of that person's own time rather than in terms of present-day norms and values. In the biography, students may include quotations from the individual and descriptions and visuals illustrating that individual's personality, goals, actions, and ideas. Students should share their completed biographies with the class and answer questions.

Use with Lessons 1.3, 2.1, 2.2, and 2.4 *You may suggest William Jennings Bryan, Sitting Bull, George Custer, Chief Joseph, William Cody, and Annie Oakley.*

PRE-AP

STRATEGY ❶
WRITE AN ESSAY

Instruct students to write an essay connecting the concept of manifest destiny with the trend toward westward migration. Their essays should explain the idea of manifest destiny, summarize how the idea arose, and describe the short- and long-term consequences for Native Americans, African Americans, and settlers of European ancestry. Students may read their essays to the class or publish them on a school blog.

Use with Lessons 1.1, 2.1, and 2.2

STRATEGY ❷
FORM A THESIS

Ask students to develop a thesis statement for a specific topic related to one of the lessons in the chapter. The statement must make a claim that is supportable with evidence either from the chapter or through further research. Ask students to present their thesis statements to the class.

Use with All Lessons

HISTORICAL THINKING How did expansion alter the West and its native populations?

AMERICAN STORIES | The Wild West

SECTION 1 **The Changing Frontier**

SECTION 2 **Broken Treaties and War**

AMERICAN GALLERY ONLINE | The Battle of the Little Bighorn

"These soldiers cut down my timber; they kill my buffalo; and when I see that, **my heart feels like bursting.**"

—Chief Satanta of the Kiowa

National Geographic photographer Jim Brandenburg captured these wild American bison crossing the prairie near the Missouri River in South Dakota. In the first half of the 19th century, millions of bison roamed freely over North America. During the second half of the century, however, their numbers fell sharply, in part because settlers pushed westward, and farmers and ranchers killed off many of the animals. By the early 20th century, only a few hundred wild bison remained in North America.

Expansion and Conflict in the West 463

INTRODUCE THE PHOTOGRAPH
WILD BISON

Ask students to examine the photograph, caption, and quotation that open this chapter. Invite connections between the photograph and the Satanta quotation. **ASK:** How did Satanta feel about the bison (called buffalo in this quotation), and how might the soldiers' feelings have differed? *(Possible response: Satanta felt a possessive kind of connection to the bison and grieved their loss. The soldiers might have viewed the bison merely as a resource or even a nuisance.)* You may wish to point out that both *bison* and *buffalo* are used to refer to these animals. The terms often are used interchangeably, but *bison* is technically the correct term. Tell students that in this chapter they will learn how the movement of settlers westward (and the presence of the military there) changed the land and affected the people, plants, and animals living there.

NATIONAL GEOGRAPHIC PHOTOGRAPHER
JIM BRANDENBURG

Throughout his career, Jim Brandenburg has used his camera to draw people's attention to the environment. Both his photographs and the proceeds from them further his mission of promoting, preserving, and expanding the native prairie in his home state of Minnesota. Since establishing the Brandenburg Prairie Foundation in 1999, Brandenburg has helped purchase more than 1,000 acres of land in Minnesota, partnering with the U.S. Fish and Wildlife Service to restore the land to its natural state. During a dedication ceremony for the Touch the Sky Prairie, a Lakota tribal elder acknowledged that it is rare for a white man to turn land back over to nature.

For Chapter 14 Spanish Resources, visit the Resources Menu. Chapter 14 Resources are available at NGLSync.Cengage.com.

HISTORICAL THINKING QUESTION

How did expansion alter the West and its native populations?

Four Corners Activity: Moving Westward This activity encourages students to consider how settlers might interact with the environment and with Native Americans in the West as demographics shifted after the Civil War. Post the following topics, one in each corner of the classroom:

1. Ways to make a living from the land

2. Effects of technology on settlers

3. Division of land among settlers

4. Cultural differences between Native Americans and settlers

Instruct students to choose a topic and think about how it might have affected settlers as they moved west. Then have students go to the corner of their chosen topic and discuss their ideas. Ask one member of each group to summarize the group's ideas for the class.

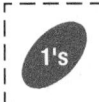 

INTRODUCE THE READING STRATEGY

DRAW CONCLUSIONS

Explain that drawing conclusions about people's actions and the effects of those actions can help students better understand the relationship between historical events. Turn to the Chapter Review and preview the Draw Conclusions Diagram with students. As they read the chapter, encourage students to analyze facts, make inferences, and use their own judgment to draw conclusions about the impact of expansion upon the West.

KEY DATES FOR CHAPTER 14

1876	Colorado becomes a state
1876	Battle of the Little Bighorn
1877	Chief Joseph of the Nez Perce surrenders
1887	Dawes Severalty Act
1889	Dakotas, Montana, and Washington become states
1890	Massacre at Wounded Knee
1892	Boll weevil begins to attack southern crops
1892	Populist Party forms

INTRODUCE CHAPTER VOCABULARY

KEY VOCABULARY

SECTION 1

aquifer	gold standard	reservoir
cooperative	hydraulic mining	shaft mining
dry farming	lode	sluice
Exoduster	placer mining	subtreasury system
free silver movement	populism	

SECTION 2

allotment	genocide	posse
dime novel	Ghost Dance	reservation
forage		

WORD MAPS

As they read the chapter, encourage students to complete Word Maps for Key Vocabulary words. Tell students to begin by making a Word Map for each word, writing the word in the center oval. Then, as they encounter the word in the chapter, they should complete the Word Map for that word. Model an example for students on the board, using the graphic organizer below.

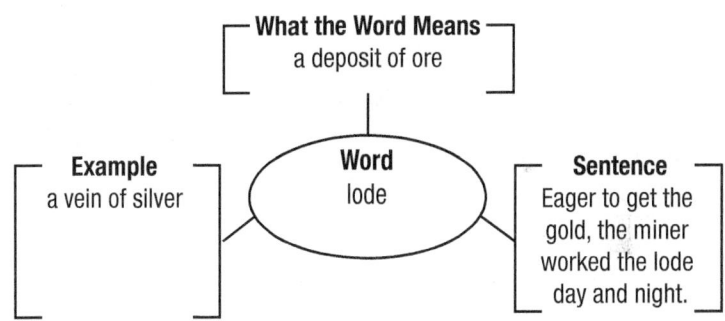

OBJECTIVES

- **Compare and contrast the legend of the Wild West to the historical reality.**

- **Understand the role of popular culture in forming the mythology of the West.**

- **Identify bias and prejudice in historical interpretations.**

- **Study a primary source: the introduction from *The Lone Ranger* radio show.**

CRITICAL THINKING SKILLS FOR "THE WILD WEST"

- Make Connections
- Draw Conclusions
- Distinguish Fact and Opinion
- Form and Support Opinions
- Compare and Contrast
- Summarize

CONNECT TO THE CHAPTER

This American Story introduces students to the concept of the Wild West. Through the study of a compelling narrative touching on history, myth, and popular culture, students will understand the importance of the legend of the Wild West in forming the American identity and how legend differs from historical reality.

This chapter, Expansion and Conflict in the West, tells the story of westward migration in the decades following the Civil War. While the chapter analyzes the political and economic consequences of this event, of equal importance is how the settlement of the West—and the mythology created by popular culture—shaped the American identity for decades. This American Story introduces students to the myth of the Wild West and can be used after completing the chapter to illustrate how popular culture can influence people's perception of historical reality.

HISTORY NOTEBOOK

Encourage students to complete the American Story page for Chapter 14 in their History Notebooks as they read.

CRITICAL VIEWING The cast is diverse, with men of varying ethnicities and ages. The men are packing guns and scowling, so they look like a tough group.

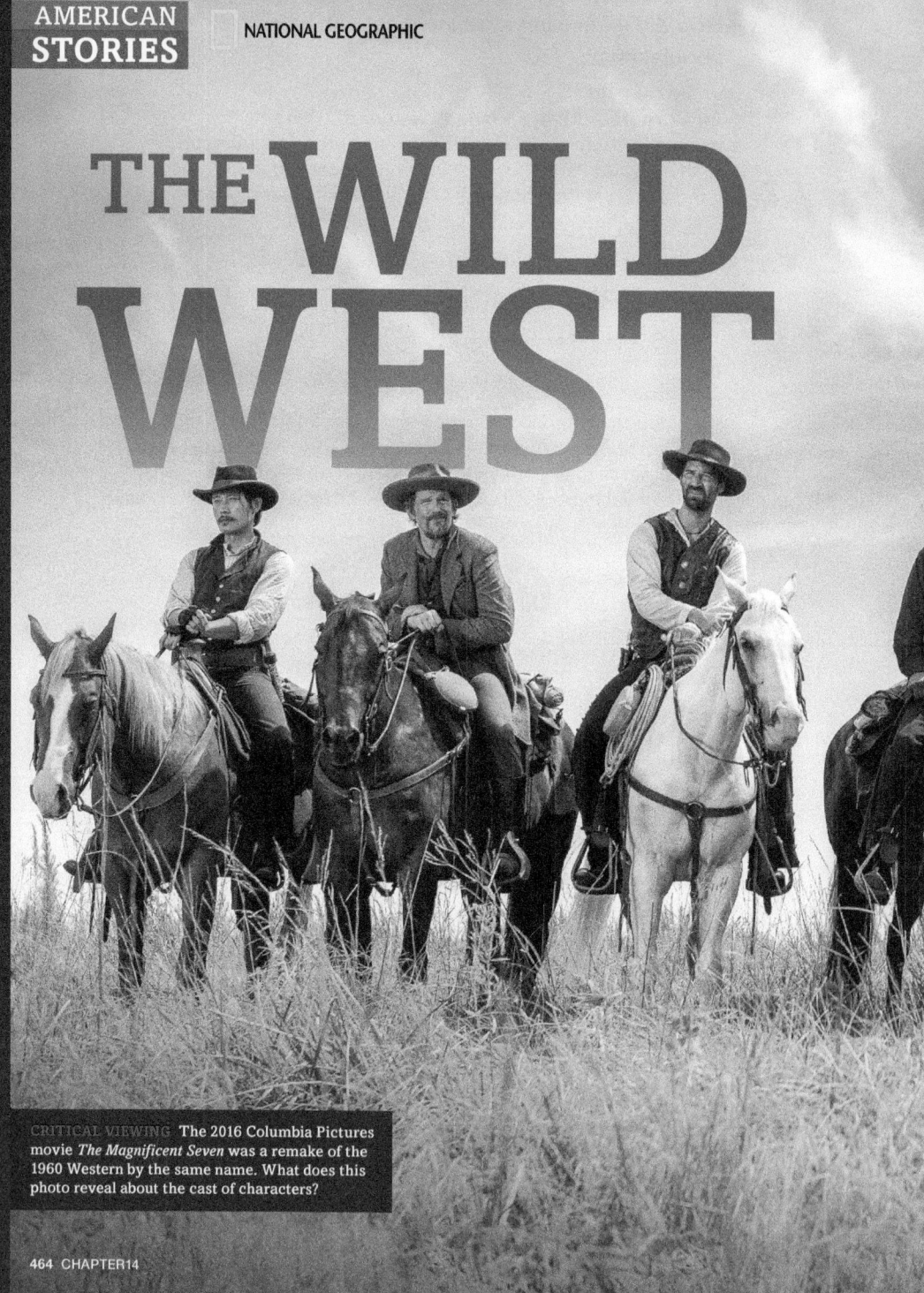

AMERICAN STORIES   NATIONAL GEOGRAPHIC

THE WILD WEST

CRITICAL VIEWING The 2016 Columbia Pictures movie *The Magnificent Seven* was a remake of the 1960 Western by the same name. What does this photo reveal about the cast of characters?

464 CHAPTER 14

In the 1950s and 1960s, you couldn't flip through the television channels during prime time without seeing at least one Western—a fictional series about the American West set in the late 1800s. Movie screens were also filled with images of scheming outlaws pursued by handsome, heroic lawmen, and cool, confident cowboys protecting herds from cattle thieves. In other words, the Wild West lived and breathed through the entertainment industry, and the American public loved it.

Expansion and Conflict in the West 465

PREVIEW USING VISUALS

Tell students to examine the photograph. **ASK:** What evidence in the photograph suggests that the West was actually wild? *(Possible response: The men look unshaven and rough. They have guns and other weapons, suggesting that they needed protection against lawlessness.)* **ASK:** What occupations might the men have? *(Possible responses: They might be cowboys since they have horses and ropes, or they could be gunslingers. One appears to be a Native American, and he might also be a scout or an interpreter.)* Tell students that they will learn how stories about the Wild West became an important part of American popular culture and how these stories largely conflicted with the reality of the West in the late 1800s.

REALITY VERSUS THE STORY

On the board, list a series of professions often depicted in film and television, such as police officer, doctor, or lawyer. Have students brainstorm what people in these professions do on a daily basis according to popular culture. Then ask students to discuss what the daily activities of these jobs realistically include. Tell students that the realities of jobs, events, and historical eras are often exaggerated when depicted for the purpose of entertainment. Explain that this American Story will examine how legends developed around the life of cowboys and historical figures during the settling of the West.

EXPLORE IDEAS ABOUT THE WILD WEST

Explain that popular culture often romanticizes or idealizes historical events to make people and events from the past more appealing to readers and viewers. Work with students to demonstrate this concept. Write *Wild West* on the board and the headings Preconceptions and Source below. Then ask students to name what comes to mind when they hear the phrase Wild West. List their responses in the Preconceptions column. Then ask students where their preconceptions of the Wild West come from and list their responses in the Source column. Have students distinguish pop culture sources (television, films, comic books) from nonfiction sources (academic texts). Guide students to compare and discuss their preconceived notions about the Wild West and to recognize how dramatic historical events and activities of the Wild West led to the development of exaggerated and romanticized accounts of the West in popular culture.

AFRICAN-AMERICAN COWBOYS

One quarter of the cowboys in the Old West were African Americans, but popular culture often ignored them. Leading up to the Civil War, more than 30 percent of Texas' population was enslaved people. At the outbreak of the war, many ranchers joined the fight and relied on their slaves to maintain the land and cattle. When the ranchers returned after the war, they could no longer rely on slave labor because of the emancipation of slaves. So they turned to free African Americans, many of whom were now skilled cattle handlers and in great demand in a booming cattle industry. African-American cowboys found work from Texas to shipping points in Kansas, Colorado, and Missouri, and, although they faced discrimination in many towns, other members of their profession treated them with respect and a degree of equality.

DIME NOVELS

From the middle to late 1900s, dime novels proved to be tremendously successful. At their height, the most popular titles had a circulation of more than 400,000. Historians point to three changes that led to their massive popularity: the increased efficiency of printing, the ease of shipping goods due to rails and canals, and rising literacy rates. Vivid illustrations, exciting plots, and flowery prose contributed to their success as well. **ASK:** What examples of flowery prose are found in the titles of the dime store novels? *(Phrases such as "deeds of daring," "scenes of thrilling peril," and "romantic incidents" are examples of flowery prose.)*

CALAMITY JANE

In 1953, Warner Bros. released the musical comedy/Western *Calamity Jane*, loosely based on Martha Jane Cannary's life in Deadwood. Two attractive singing film stars of the day—Doris Day and Howard Keel—portrayed Calamity Jane and Wild Bill Hickok as feuding, and later romantically linked, characters. Part of the plot involves Calamity Jane's unrequited love for a young soldier and her cleaning herself up and learning to be more feminine. **ASK:** What details in the movie plot are likely romanticized aspects of Calamity Jane's life? *(The text doesn't mention Calamity Jane wanting to be cleaned up and more feminine, so these plot points, along with the songs and love interest, were likely added to romanticize her life and tell a story that audiences would find appealing.)*

AMERICAN STORIES

THE REAL WEST

The legend of the Wild West did not start with TV or the movies. First came the dime novels (pictured below): short, inexpensive paperback books that told thrilling tales of adventure, hardship, and daring rescues. Even as the real cowboys, outlaws, lawmen, and pioneers went about their business in the real West, dime novel writers were spinning the stories of these individuals into tall tales and wild adventures. At the same time, Buffalo Bill's Wild West show was touring the eastern states. This outdoor extravaganza featured mock shootouts, cowboys demonstrating their skills, buffalo, and other Wild West icons.

And so was born the larger-than-life image of the West as a place of theatrical violence, with masked bandits stalking every bank and frequent shootouts between the good guys and the bad guys. Life in the real West was by no means boring, and the West did have its colorful characters. But the day-to-day reality was not nearly as exciting as the stories on the pages and screens.

Two of the most popular "set" pieces from Westerns—the shootout between the sheriff and the villain in the town streets and the daring bank robbery—were extremely uncommon in real life. Historians have studied crime statistics for several western towns in the late 1800s. Using the information, these researchers estimated that the Wild West was no more violent than cities and towns today. Historian Larry Schweikart concluded

> *There are more bank robberies in modern-day Dayton, Ohio, in a year than there were in the entire Old West in a decade, perhaps in the entire frontier period!*
>
> — Historian Larry Schweikart

that fewer than a dozen bank robberies likely took place in the final decades of the 19th century. He remarked, "There are more bank robberies in modern-day Dayton, Ohio, in a year than there were in the entire Old West in a decade, perhaps in the entire frontier period!"

As for dramatic shootouts on Main Street, most of the life-altering disagreements in the West were over land, and people fought them out in court. In a book about the frontier, historian Patricia Nelson Limerick commented, "The showdowns would occur in the land office or the courtroom; weapons would be deeds and lawsuits, not six-guns."

DIME NOVELS

"Purple prose" is an expression used to describe writing that is elaborate, flowery, and over the top. It's also a good description of the style in which many dime novels were written. This 1910 novel features a dramatic image of Buffalo Bill in action. But the novel's title is relatively tame compared to more "purple" ones like *Adventures of Buffalo Bill from Boyhood to Manhood: Deeds of Daring, Scenes of Thrilling Peril*; and *Romantic Incidents in the Early Life of W. F. Cody, the Monarch of Bordermen*.

GREAT WESTERN LIBRARY No. 145

BUFFALO BILL'S RECORD JUMP

by COL. PRENTISS INGRAHAM

CALAMITY JANE

Men weren't the only real-life characters who found their way into the myth of the Wild West. Martha Jane Cannary was orphaned in 1867, soon after her family moved to Salt Lake City, Utah. The 12-year-old girl was uneducated and desperately poor, but she was tall, strong, and able to do the jobs that were mainly available to men. Dressing and working like a man, taking whatever jobs she could, the teenager acquired the nickname Calamity Jane.

We know for certain that Calamity Jane moved to Deadwood, South Dakota, in 1876 and met American frontiersman, army scout, and officer of the law, Wild Bill Hickok. At that point, the stories take over. Jane, an enthusiastic participant in the creation of her own tall tale, claimed that she had single-handedly caught the man who killed Hickok—a fact disproved by newspaper accounts of the time. She also claimed to have rescued a runaway stagecoach with its six passengers and driver.

In 1895, Jane joined Buffalo Bill Cody's Wild West show as a horseback rider and sharpshooter, further expanding both her legend and her fan base. Dime novels about Calamity Jane spun ever more fanciful tales of her adventures, including a marriage to Hickok. Though reports of a relationship between Calamity Jane and Hickok are highly suspect, she was buried next to him at Mount Moriah Cemetery in South Dakota.

An accomplished rider, Jane was often photographed on horseback. Here she poses in front of tepees and tents at the Pan-American Exposition in Buffalo, New York.

The life of the cowboy, too, was not exactly as portrayed in the Westerns. On-screen cowboys were almost exclusively white, and they seemed to spend their days with pistols drawn. In reality, of the approximately 40,000 cowboys on the Great Plains, 30 percent or more were African-American or Mexican. Several hundred were Native Americans. And the actual work of a cowboy? It was unromantic, poorly paid, and often revolved around the boredom of 14-hour days in the saddle herding cattle.

WILD BILL HICKOK: A CASE STUDY

The story of Wild Bill Hickok is a useful case study for examining how a real-life event was turned almost instantly into a Wild West legend. The tale begins with one of the few true instances of a quick-draw gun duel in the street. In 1865, James Butler Hickok,

known as "Wild Bill," was a gambler and a drifter who made his temporary home in Springfield, Missouri. He got into a disagreement over a gambling debt with a man named Davis Tutt. It culminated on the evening of July 20, when both men drew their pistols and fired at each other in the town square. Tutt fell dead, with a bullet through the heart; Hickok was unharmed.

Within a few months, Hickok was on his way to Wild West stardom. Colonel George Ward Nichols started the process with an article about the showdown for *Harper's New Monthly Magazine*. Nichols's account of the shootout was mostly factual, but he went on to tell his readers that Hickok had once fought off 10 attackers on his own and that he had killed 100 men, among other fictions. The article was hugely popular and was soon followed by dime novels with titles such as *Wild Bill, the Indian Slayer*.

TEACH

GUIDED DISCUSSION

1. **Distinguish Fact and Opinion** What evidence has been used by historians to evaluate and dispel some of the myths in the debate about the level of violence in the Wild West? *(Historians compared crime statistics from the late 1800s with present-day statistics. They found that the Wild West was not more violent than present-day cities. This fact dispels the myth of rampant violence in the Wild West as depicted in popular culture.)*

2. **Form and Support Opinions** How did the circumstances of Wild Bill Hickok's death conflict with the legend of his life? Support your response with details from the text. *(Possible response: Hickok was known as an expert gunfighter, able to fight off nearly a dozen attackers. However, one man was able to shoot and kill him while he played poker.)*

ACTIVE OPTIONS

On Your Feet: Take a Virtual Tour of the Wild West Direct students to form small groups and search online for historical photos of people and places in the West in the late 1800s. First ask students to brainstorm search terms and make a list. Terms might include "historical Deadwood," "historical west," or African-American cowboys." Then tell students to use the terms they listed to search online for historical photos. Ask students to note details in the pictures that differ from popular notions of the Wild West. Have groups reconvene and discuss their findings.

NG Learning Framework: Analyze the Western Film

SKILL Observation

KNOWLEDGE Our Human Story

Divide students into small groups and assign each a Western film from a different decade. Examples include *Stagecoach* (1939), *The Ox-Bow Incident* (1943), *High Noon* (1952), *The Man Who Shot Liberty Valance* (1962), *True Grit* (1969), *The Outlaw Josey Wales* (1976), *Silverado* (1985), *Dances with Wolves* (1990), *Wyatt Earp* (1994), and *3:10 to Yuma* (2007). Instruct students to research and watch portions of the assigned film outside of class, taking notes on plot and character that answer the following questions: What is being mythologized in this film? What characters are presented as heroes? Villains? What are their goals? In what way, if any, do the films represent bias or prejudice in historical interpretation? Choose a completion date for students to present their films and their findings in order by decade. After the presentations, discuss the role of the genre in popular culture and how Westerns have evolved based on the films students sampled.

THE LONE RANGER

As originally conceived, the Lone Ranger was a solitary figure who traveled the West by himself. However, this caused a problem dramatically, as the character had no one to interact with, and this did not make for the most exciting dialogue for radio listeners. The problem was solved in episode 11 with the introduction of a sidekick, Tonto, who was originally designed simply to give the Lone Ranger someone to talk to. **ASK:** Based on the primary source, what attributes did people of the 1930s view as heroic? *(People valued attributes such as bravery, integrity, resourcefulness, and the championing of justice.)*

WRITE ABOUT HISTORY

Create Your Own Myth Remind students that much of the myth of the Wild West was created by popular culture. Have students create their own myth about themselves, a friend, or a family member. Ask them to think about the attributes their selected person has— such as heroism, honesty, or trustworthiness—and how these attributes could be exaggerated or mythologized. Then prompt students to write a brief myth—in the style of *The Lone Ranger* introduction, a dime novel, a Western film script, or other creative avenue—for the selected person.

CRITICAL VIEWING Possible response: This scene from *Red River* was set outdoors but filmed indoors on a production stage. Production staff used sand, fake steers, boulders, and desert plants to create a realistic outdoor setting. An artist painted a background painting, and lighting, such as the light visible at the top of the photo, simulated the time of day and created mood.

THINK ABOUT IT

Answers will vary. Possible response: Depictions of the Old West often glorify and feature events, such as shootouts, that were rare and ignore some groups of people, such as African Americans or Mexicans, who were present during the time.

CRITICAL VIEWING American film stars Montgomery Clift (left), John Wayne (center), and Noah Beery, Jr., (right) endured long days of filming on the set of the 1948 Western *Red River*. What do you observe about the sets and process used to produce this film?

Hickok himself contributed to his legend by appearing in Buffalo Bill's Wild West show. It was as a gambler, however, that Hickok would meet an abrupt and unglamorous end, when a man named Jack McCall crept up and shot him while he was playing poker in a saloon in Deadwood, South Dakota, in 1876. Even after his death, the dime novels continued to embellish the Wild Bill Hickok lore with titles such as *Wild Bill, the Pistol Prince; Buffalo Bill, the King of the Border Men;* and *Wild Bill's Last Trail.*

WHY THE LEGEND?

Why have the tall tales of the Wild West persisted for more than a century after the real American frontier began to fade from memory? Perhaps it is because the Old West embodies a spirit of toughness and independence that Americans admire. Perhaps, too, the legends recall a time when much of the country was untamed and new—to American settlers, at least. For the Native Americans of the West, many of the events of the frontier period are distinctly lacking in romance or nostalgia. For those who still enjoy the legends of the Wild West, and those who seek out the truth behind them, perhaps the greatest draw is the universal human love of a good story.

THINK ABOUT IT

How do films or TV shows you have seen that feature the Old West or the American frontier compare to the legends and realities you have learned about? What evidence of bias or historical inaccuracies have you observed?

THE LONE RANGER

"Hi-Yo Silver! Away!" was a call recognized by millions of Americans in the 1930s through the 1950s and beyond. It was the signature call of the Lone Ranger to his valiant horse, Silver, as he set off on another weekly adventure to bring order to the lawless West. Accompanied by his Native American sidekick, Tonto, the Lone Ranger protected the innocent and brought evildoers to justice. Unlike some heroes of Wild West tales, the Lone Ranger was entirely fictional and not based on a real-life individual.

The Lone Ranger began as a radio show in 1933, featuring the adventures of a mysterious masked man who fought for justice in the Wild West. In 1949, it debuted as a TV show and became wildly popular in its own right, running in syndication well after the series was canceled in 1957. The appeal of *The Lone Ranger* has continued into the 21st century. A TV movie with that title was made in 2003, and a new version was released in 2013.

PRIMARY SOURCE

Across the country in the 1930s, families would tune in their radios to hear the thrilling introduction to *The Lone Ranger* radio show, which many could recite by heart:

A fiery horse with the speed of light, a cloud of dust and a hearty Hi-Yo Silver! The Lone Ranger! With his faithful Indian companion Tonto, the daring and resourceful masked rider of the plains led the fight for law and order in the early western United States! Nowhere in the pages of history can one find a greater champion of justice! Return with us now to those thrilling days of yesteryear! From out of the past come the thundering hoofbeats of the great horse Silver! The Lone Ranger rides again!

—from *The Lone Ranger*, by Fran Striker, 1933

Actor Clayton Moore took his job as a role model very seriously and made frequent public appearances as the Lone Ranger when he wasn't filming episodes.

Collectors love television memorabilia, and items from *The Lone Ranger* television series are no exception. This 1954 metal lunch box is a prized piece of pop culture.

DIFFERENTIATE

ENGLISH LANGUAGE LEARNERS

Understand Main Ideas and Details Pair students at the **Emerging** and **Expanding** levels together and students at the **Expanding** and **Bridging** levels together. Partners should take turns reading sections of the American Story aloud and work together to complete a Main Idea Cluster. Encourage students to include at least four details per cluster and to compare their results with those of other pairs.

PRE-AP

Investigate Depictions of Native Americans Direct students to conduct online research to learn more about biased or racially prejudiced depictions of Native Americans in television and film. Ask students to write a short report that references specific movie or television clips. Invite students to conduct a panel discussion with the class to share and discuss their findings.

See the Chapter Planner for more strategies for differentiation.

HISTORICAL THINKING

Ask and have students answer the following questions.

1. **READING CHECK** What was the Wild West?

2. **COMPARE AND CONTRAST** How were notions about the Wild West and the historical West of the late 1800s different?

3. **SUMMARIZE** How did the legend of the Wild West spread in popular culture?

ANSWERS

1. The Wild West was a term used to describe the mythology of the West centered on heroes, villains, and theatrical violence.

2. Notions about the Wild West included much more violence, lawbreaking, shootouts, and crime than actually took place. Historically, disputes during the late 1800s in the West were usually about land and were settled in courts rather than through violence.

3. Ideas about the Wild West started with dime novels and then moved on to theatrical, film, radio, and television productions.

FARMING, RANCHING, AND MINING

When there's a lot of open space, people tend to spread out. After the Civil War ended, Americans once again hitched their wagons and headed west of the Mississippi River, eager to settle the untamed land and begin their new lives.

MANIFEST DESTINY

As you have read, many of those who migrated west were inspired by the concept of manifest destiny, the belief that Americans were intended to settle all the land between the Atlantic and Pacific coasts. While American communities were thriving in the East, many eastern farmers, hungry for greater stretches of land, moved westward. In 1860, the unsettled West included the grassland prairie region in the middle of North America, called the Great Plains, an area that was wide open for new settlement.

During the Civil War, the U.S. government had tried to make it easier for farmers to migrate to the Great Plains by passing the Homestead Act in 1862. As you know, the act offered plots of land in the region to American citizens or to those intending to become citizens. For a small filing fee, each person was eligible for 160 free acres as long as he or she lived on the land and cultivated it for five years. That may sound like a lot of land, but a settler had to purchase two or three times that acreage to grow enough crops for a reasonable profit. And the Homestead Act did not provide the money to go west, file a claim on the land, or purchase farming equipment.

Still, many pioneers left their homes and settled on the Great Plains. They were rewarded for their efforts when the transcontinental railroad opened in 1869. The railroad provided transportation for the settlers and brought new immigrants across the frontier. The lines also carried household goods, tools, and other merchandise to the homesteaders—items sometimes purchased through catalog companies such as Montgomery Ward.

After the Civil War, many African Americans also migrated west with the goal of seeking a life free from discrimination and establishing communities of their own. The settlers were called **Exodusters** because they made their exodus, or exit, from the South after Reconstruction had failed to end the racial oppression of African Americans. On the Great Plains, many became farmers, and some even established towns of their own. Many African-American men also worked as miners and cowboys. By 1890, about 520,000 African Americans lived west of the Mississippi River.

LIFE ON THE GREAT PLAINS

The settlers' lives weren't easy. The first order of business upon arrival on the Great Plains was building a house. Because there were no forests on the plains, and therefore no lumber, homesteaders cut thick blocks of earth, called "sod bricks," out of the prairie soil. It took about 3,000 sod bricks to construct a single sod house. The thick sod walls kept out the cold in the winter and the heat in the summer. Some homes were built right into a hill or ridge with only a single opening for a door and grass growing on the "roof." Lacking firewood, farmers burned buffalo chips—dry dung—or sunflower plants for fuel to cook their meals and provide warmth.

The arid climate and tough prairie soil proved challenging for farmers, but new technology in farming machines helped increase productivity. In 1837, an Illinois blacksmith named John Deere invented a plow tough enough to break through the prairie's dense soil. Cyrus McCormick's reaper, a machine that helped harvest grain, was widely used by 1850. During the 1880s, inventors created steam-powered threshers to process wheat and machines that husked corn, or removed the ears' outer leaves. In 1873, Joseph Glidden devised a practical form of barbed wire for fencing. Soon a machine could produce this wire on a large scale, and it was used widely to keep livestock in and predators out.

Technology alone could not help the farmers cultivate crops. The region received little rain, and few rivers crossed the plains. Farmers who lived near the Rocky Mountains could build irrigation systems to bring water from mountain streams, but farther east, farmers came to rely on **dry farming** techniques to make the most use of what little rain did fall. They plowed widely spaced rows and planted their seeds between deep furrows so that rainwater would drain into the trench formed between the rows. They kept fields free of weeds to ensure that only food-producing plants received moisture.

One of the challenges of living on the Great Plains was dealing with its sheer size. On the vast prairie, tall grass stretched as far as the eye could see, and farms were far apart. The nearest neighbor was often miles away. Although families set up networks to meet socially and support each other during difficult times, homesteads were isolated. Loneliness was a fact of life.

THE LIFE OF A COWBOY

While lonely, the grasslands of the western plains were perfect for grazing cattle, and a number of wealthier settlers established ranches from Texas to Montana. At the same time, the once numerous herds of bison that had roamed the region were dwindling, victims

PRIMARY SOURCE

In 1880, former slave Benjamin "Pap" Singleton testified at congressional hearings regarding the migration of African Americans to the Great Plains. In this excerpt from the hearings, he states his reasons for promoting the exodus.

Well, my people, for the want of land—we needed land for our children—and their disadvantages—that caused my heart to grieve and sorrow; pity for my race, sir, that was coming down, instead of going up—that caused me to go to work for them. I sent out there perhaps in '66—perhaps so; or in '65, any way—my memory don't recollect which; and they brought back tolerable favorable reports; then I . . . went into Southern Kansas, and found it was a good country, and I thought Southern Kansas was congenial [agreeable] to our nature, sir; and I formed a colony there, and bought about a thousand acres of ground.

—from Benjamin "Pap" Singleton at congressional hearings, 1880

CRITICAL VIEWING In 1888, Solomon Butcher took this photograph of an African-American family posed in front of their sod house. What details in the photo suggest what their lives might have been like on the plains?

PLAN: 4-PAGE LESSON

OBJECTIVE

Understand the economic opportunities taken and the challenges faced by settlers traveling west to farm, ranch, and mine.

CRITICAL THINKING SKILLS FOR LESSON 1.1

- Analyze Environmental Concepts
- Draw Conclusions
- Make Inferences
- Compare and Contrast
- Analyze Primary Sources
- Analyze Cause and Effect
- Identify

HISTORICAL THINKING FOR CHAPTER 14

How did expansion alter the West and its native populations? New economic opportunities and technologies encouraged settlers to establish communities on the Great Plains. Lesson 1.1 examines this settlement and its effect on the land.

BACKGROUND FOR THE TEACHER

Benjamin "Pap" Singleton, the "Father of the Exodus," led his people to Kansas because of its antislavery history and inexpensive land. He tried to ensure the success of his colonies by welcoming only migrants who had money to contribute and the will to work hard. The trickle of settlers led by Singleton was followed by a much larger migration of thousands of people in 1879, a surge so immense that it became a national issue. Since free African Americans tended to vote for Republicans, Democrats in Congress accused Republicans of encouraging the migration to Kansas to increase Republican power there and to decrease the congressional representation of the southern states the migrants had left. Southern whites began to call for the government to stop the exodus, and the Senate formed a committee in 1880 to investigate the forces behind the migration.

GET SET TO SETTLE

Guide students to recall what they already know about western lands and to consider what possessions and traits a farmer, rancher, or miner in the late 1800s might need in order to settle successfully in the West. Ask students to record their ideas in a three-column table, including reasons why each item or trait would be useful in the context in which the events unfolded. Then prompt students to identify items or traits in the table that would still be important to people seeking employment in the West, such as in Silicon Valley, and any that would not be as helpful as they were in the context of people settling in the late 1800s.

Type of Settler	Item or Trait Needed	Reason(s)

TEACH

GUIDED DISCUSSION

1. **Draw Conclusions** How would life have been different for pioneers had the transcontinental railroad not been built, and how might the settlement of the West have taken a different turn? *(Possible responses: Life would have been more difficult because the railroad made it possible to get supplies easily; communities would have grown more slowly without all the new immigrants that the railroad transported.)*

2. **Compare and Contrast** How was the experience of farmers near the Rocky Mountains different from that of farmers farther east? *(Farmers farther east could not get rain from mountain streams. Instead, they had to weed their fields to save moisture for crops and plow their fields to channel rainwater to their plants.)*

ANALYZE PRIMARY SOURCES

Direct students' attention to the Primary Source feature. **ASK:** How does Benjamin "Pap" Singleton explain why he worked for the exodus? *(Possible response: He says that his people needed land for their children and that they were faced with disadvantages that hurt their chances for success in life.)* **ASK:** What parts of Singleton's speech indicate that he truly believed the migration was good for his people? *(Possible response: He says that he heard favorable reports from people sent to Kansas to study the land, so he made his decision based on evidence. He also backed his belief with action and money by buying land for a colony in Kansas himself.)*

DIFFERENTIATE
STRIVING READERS

Make a Chart Before they read the lesson, instruct pairs of students to make a chart titled Life on the Great Plains, and tell them to label three columns: Farmers, Ranchers, and Miners. When students have finished reading, prompt them to work together to list as many details as they can about life on the Great Plains for each group. One student can reread paragraphs aloud while the other student listens and adds details to the lists. Invite volunteers to share their lists with the class.

GIFTED & TALENTED

Write a Skit Prompt students to briefly research the life of Benjamin Singleton and the context of the Primary Source excerpt. Encourage students to frame questions to answer through research, such as: Why was Singleton called to testify before Congress? What were some of his goals? What was his probable tone as he delivered his testimony? Direct students to prepare and then present a short skit that incorporates their research and the primary source material.

See the Chapter Planner for more strategies for differentiation.

CRITICAL VIEWING Possible response: The family made good use of the available natural resources because the house looks as if it was constructed from sod. The people may have been lonely because aside from their home and a small shed in the background, no signs of other settlements are visible. On the other hand, they must have had some way to acquire supplies because they own manufactured goods and equipment, such as the glass windows in their home and the windmill in the background.

of overhunting and conflicts between the U.S. government and Native Americans. Their loss left even more land for cattle to roam.

Ranchers employed cowboys to round up their cattle and drive them to "cow towns" in Kansas, Nebraska, and Wyoming. From there the animals were loaded into boxcars and shipped by rail to the stockyards and meatpacking plants of Chicago. Improved slaughtering and packaging techniques as well as ice-cooled boxcars made beef more widely available throughout the nation. Americans developed a taste for beef, and its consumption soared.

Cattle drives took three to five months, depending on how far the ranch was from a cow town. More than 2,000 head of cattle were rounded up for a big cattle drive. Before the drive could begin, cowboys had to check each animal's brand—an identifying mark burned into its hide—to make sure that all the cattle belonged to the ranch they were working for. Cowboys also tamed horses, branded calves, herded the cattle safely across rivers, and prevented stampedes, or animals racing out of control.

Men of many different ethnicities worked as cowboys, but they all used the techniques and traditions developed by Mexican vaqueros, or cattle drivers. These cowboys also adopted Mexican tools and apparel, such as spurs, chaps, and lariats. One of every seven cowboys was an African American. Although they were paid the same wages, African-American cowboys were not as likely to manage herds or hold other positions of authority on the cattle trail. Even so, some African-American cowboys became successful ranchers themselves when they retired from driving cattle.

When the use of barbed wire spread across the plains, and fences enclosed the once open range, the role of the cowboy faded. Today, as you know, many Western movies and novels portray cowboys as rugged heroes who led exciting lives, but wrangling cattle was hard work. Cowboys could easily work 14 hours or more every day. During cattle drives, cowboys worked in shifts to watch the herds through the night, rode throughout the day, and pocketed only about $30 or $40 per month for their labors.

IN SEARCH OF TREASURE

Farmers, ranchers, and cowboys worked hard for their money, but some people hoped to gain instant wealth. After the California gold rush of 1849, prospectors found gold and silver deposits in Colorado, Montana, and the Dakotas, as well as rich deposits of copper in New Mexico and Arizona.

The story was almost always the same. With the discovery of a **lode**, or vein of ore, a horde of hopeful miners rushed to the area, staked claims, and set up camp. Then the merchants arrived, bringing goods to sell to the miners at exorbitant, or very steep, prices. As in California during the gold rush, if the mineral lode was substantial, a wild and lawless mining camp might grow quickly into a boomtown. Some boomtowns, such as Denver, Colorado, grew into large, prosperous cities. But most of the boomtowns went bust once the lode had been mined out. Abandoned as quickly as they sprang up, these boomtowns became ghost towns.

Initially, miners used **placer mining** techniques to search for gold, panning for gold nuggets and dust in riverbeds and streams with lightweight tools. They set up wooden runs called **sluices** to strain the water. But these techniques were not enough to eke, or obtain, every bit of precious metal from a rich lode. Soon mining companies stepped in and funded a much more intensive, aggressive process.

The companies used dynamite for **shaft mining**, blasting vertical channels into mountains. Once these dark passageways were carved out, men were lowered down shafts to mine for 10 to 12 hours a day using picks and shovels. Lack of oxygen, pockets of toxic gases, and cave-ins made these mines dangerous places to work. Other companies shot pressurized water onto the mountainsides to remove topsoil and gravel and expose the precious minerals beneath, a process known as **hydraulic mining**, or hydropower mining. Debris and the toxic chemicals used in the process—including mercury—flowed downstream, contaminating farmers' water sources. Farmers sued the mining companies and put an end to hydraulic mining, but it took decades for the land and water to recover.

Mining spawned many stories of fortune and failure. It also helped to spread the Union from coast to coast. People demanded law enforcement and government in the hastily organized, unruly mining camps. This eventually led to the creation of new territories and several new states, including Colorado in 1876. The Dakotas, Montana, and Washington were admitted to the Union in 1889.

Western expansion and advances in technology enriched the nation and made work more efficient, but this progress often came at a price—especially for farmers. Even as their farms became productive, many farmers found themselves falling into a cycle of debt. In time, they decided to get together and do something about it.

🏛 **Art Institute of Chicago**

On a trip to Mexico in 1889, American artist Frederic Remington made sketches of the horsemen he saw there. He used this material to create many illustrations and paintings, including this one in 1890 called *A Mexican Vaquero*. The portrait of the *vaquero*, shown here sitting on his horse and looking directly at the viewer, was also made into a wood engraving for *Harper's New Monthly Magazine* in 1891.

HISTORICAL THINKING

1. **READING CHECK** What attracted settlers to the Great Plains after the Civil War?

2. **ANALYZE ENVIRONMENTAL CONCEPTS** In what ways were the byproducts of shaft mining and hydraulic mining detrimental to several natural systems?

3. **DRAW CONCLUSIONS** How was the establishment of new states and territories in the West connected to unruly behavior in mining camps?

4. **MAKE INFERENCES** What qualities did settlers need to survive on the Great Plains?

BUILD BACKGROUND

FROM BOOMTOWN TO GHOST TOWN

The boomtowns that sprang up near mining camps featured fancy hotels, busy saloons and restaurants, boardinghouses, doctors' and dentists' offices, and even opera houses, stock exchanges, and bowling alleys. One such boomtown—Bodie, California—grew to include 2,000 buildings and a population of perhaps as many as 10,000 people by 1879, buoyed by the excavation of almost 10,000 tons of gold ore from its nearby mine. Once the gold ran out and the mining companies folded, however, the town shrank. By the 1940s, after two devastating fires, people basically abandoned Bodie. Calico, California, another boomtown, thrived for 12 years while its 500 mines produced more than $20 million of silver ore but then shriveled up as the worth of silver plunged just before the turn of the century.

While many ghost towns disappeared, others found a second life as tourist attractions. For example, after being named a State Historic Park and a National Historic Landmark in 1962, Bodie has been preserved by the California Department of Parks and Recreation in a state of "arrested decay." As much as possible, the department has kept the interiors of the buildings the same, leaving all items exactly as they were when the town was abandoned. It has repaired the exteriors only enough to keep them from falling down. Many buildings show damage from fires and the passage of time. The buildings in Calico, on the other hand, have been not just rebuilt but repurposed. Visitors to Calico Ghost Town can dine in themed restaurants, shop in old-fashioned stores, and enjoy experiences such as panning for gold.

TEACH

GUIDED DISCUSSION

3. **Analyze Cause and Effect** How did the development of new technologies affect cowboys? *(Possible response: Developments such as better slaughtering and packaging techniques and ice-cooled boxcars helped cowboys by making it easier to transport beef to consumers, increasing the appetite for this product. The development of barbed wire hurt cowboys because fences took over the job of corralling cows.)*

4. **Identify** What factor prompted mining companies to turn to shaft mining and hydraulic mining instead of using placer mining techniques, despite the impact of the new methods on the environment? *(Efficiency was the factor that changed which mining techniques were used: Shaft mining and hydraulic mining were more efficient ways to collect large amounts of ore.)*

🏛 VIRTUAL MUSEUM VISIT

Explain that the Art Institute of Chicago displays many other works by Frederic Remington on its website. Note that Remington was a sculptor as well as a painter. Access the museum's website and search for the Frederic Remington collection. Arrange students in groups and ask each group to locate and study a work by Remington that depicts the life of an American cowboy, such as *The Bronco Buster, Coming Through the Rye (Over the Range), The Branding Chute*, or *The Rattlesnake*. Ask groups to consider how the depiction of a cowboy's life in their chosen artwork compares with that in *A Mexican Vaquero*. Invite them to present their comparisons to the class.

ACTIVE OPTIONS

On Your Feet: Three Corners Post these signs in three corners of the classroom: Mining, Dry Farming, Ranching. Organize students into groups around each sign and prompt them to discuss how the practices of that industry influenced the geographic extent, composition, biological diversity, and viability of natural systems in the West after the Civil War. Then have students of each group travel to summarize their discussion for each of the other two groups.

NG Learning Framework: Publish a Flyer

ATTITUDE Curiosity

SKILLS Communication, Collaboration

Tell students that they have been hired to design flyers meant to persuade new settlers to move to the West to work as farmers, cowboys, or miners. Direct groups of students to use library and online resources to find contemporary examples of such flyers. Encourage groups to include specific facts and persuasive language as well as a visually appealing layout. Once groups have printed and distributed their flyers, lead a discussion about the techniques and language that they used.

HISTORICAL THINKING

ANSWERS

1. Eastern farmers wanted to farm larger plots in an area open for settlement. African Americans wanted to start communities of their own that would be free of discrimination.

2. Shaft mining broke apart mountains and exposed workers to toxic gases. The pressurized water used in hydraulic mining carried away debris and toxic chemicals, such as mercury, contaminating the water supply.

3. Unchecked lawlessness in western mining camps caused people to seek protection from law enforcement and governmental institutions, prompting the establishment of states and territories for safety and a reliable judicial system.

4. Settlers had to be strong and healthy to survive harsh conditions and build homes, farms, and communities from scratch and to cope with social isolation. They had to be creative, as when they turned sod into houses and used dry dung and sunflowers for fuel.

1.2 **GEOLOGY IN HISTORY**

MAIN IDEA A huge underground reservoir of water allows the farmers of the Great Plains to water their crops.

HOW GEOLOGY WATERS THE GREAT PLAINS
By Andrés Ruzo, National Geographic Explorer

Fresh water is one of our most rare and precious resources. We can't survive without it. Thanks to modern plumbing and water purification techniques, about 99 percent of Americans can get water right from the tap, but this ease of access is misleading. Only about 3 percent of Earth's water is fresh, and most of this water is locked away in ice caps and glaciers. Of all the water on Earth, less than 1 percent is available to humans as usable fresh water.

FROM THE GREAT AMERICAN DESERT

Most Americans get their fresh water from either surface or groundwater **reservoirs**, contained bodies of water that can be tapped. As rain flows over the land's surface, some of it collects in rivers and lakes, and some seeps into the earth. The water that soaks into the surface fills the space between soil particles and fractures in rock to become groundwater. Certain geologic formations have the right conditions below the surface to hold large groundwater reservoirs. These formations are called **aquifers**.

The water in some aquifers flows to the surface naturally. To get water from other aquifers, however, engineers must drill down and raise the water to the surface. Depending on the type of rock, an aquifer will produce different amounts and types of water. Fault zones, areas of easily dissolved rock, and expanses of gravel often result in productive aquifers. The groundwater can effectively flow through the fractures and spaces in the rock. Areas of rock that are solid and not porous or fractured usually do not form aquifers because water cannot penetrate.

In 1820, U.S. Army major Stephen H. Long dubbed the Great Plains, "the Great American Desert." He considered this dry, flat land, "almost wholly unfit for cultivation, and of course uninhabitable by a people depending upon agriculture for their subsistence." Despite this warning, settlers moved to the Great Plains in droves beginning in the 1860s and 1870s. While many did manage to make a living,

it was tough. The thick sod of the plains had to be broken up before crops could be planted. And though farmers were able to use pumps powered by windmills to bring some underground water to the surface, this technique had its drawbacks. Farmers were not usually able to dig deep enough wells, and the pumping mechanisms did not work when the wind was not blowing. By the 1930s, drought and poor farming practices had so eroded parts of the Great Plains, they became known as the Dust Bowl because of the terrible dust storms that blew through the region.

Before pump technology improved in the 1950s, farmers struggled to create irrigation systems to water their fields, as shown in this photo of an Oklahoma farmer in the 1930s.

TO AMERICA'S BREADBASKET

Those settlers would never have believed that this same region would become part of America's breadbasket by the 1950s—all thanks to the **Ogallala Aquifer** (also called the High Plains Aquifer). For the past 15,000 years, water has been slowly collecting in the space between underground sand and gravel grains to form the Ogallala Aquifer. Spanning eight states, it's one of the world's largest aquifers.

Unfortunately, farmers didn't have access to this aquifer during westward expansion. In fact, full access to this reservoir wasn't available until the 1950s, when new technology made it economically viable to drill deep into the aquifer and access its water using powerful pumps. Today, Ogallala waters help grow nearly one-fifth of the wheat, corn, and beef cattle produced in the United States.

However, overuse has been drying up the Ogallala Aquifer. By the 1960s, geologists realized its water was limited, and natural processes refill it very slowly. Without rules for responsible groundwater extraction, some estimates indicate the aquifer will run dry as early as 2028. Once drained, it will take more than 6,000 years for it to naturally replenish.

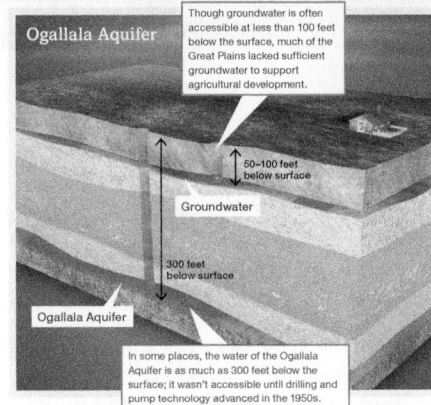

Ogallala Aquifer

Though groundwater is often accessible at less than 100 feet below the surface, much of the Great Plains lacked sufficient groundwater to support agricultural development.

50–100 feet below surface

Groundwater

300 feet below surface

Ogallala Aquifer

In some places, the water of the Ogallala Aquifer is as much as 300 feet below the surface; it wasn't accessible until drilling and pump technology advanced in the 1950s.

THINK LIKE A GEOLOGIST

1. **IDENTIFY MAIN IDEAS AND DETAILS** Why are aquifers important to humans?

2. **DRAW CONCLUSIONS** Why is the fact that early settlers were unable to fully tap into the Ogallala Aquifer beneficial to farmers today?

3. **ANALYZE ENVIRONMENTAL CONCEPTS** What human practices in the 1950s altered the natural processes within the Ogallala Aquifer?

CRITICAL VIEWING Center-pivot irrigation systems, widely used to distribute water from the Ogallala Aquifer, operate equipment and sprinklers that rotate around a central point, or pivot, giving farm fields this circular pattern. How might this current form of irrigation be more efficient than others in this region?

PLAN: 2-PAGE LESSON

OBJECTIVE

Discuss how farmers on the Great Plains struggled to water their crops and how farming practices resulted in environmental problems.

CRITICAL THINKING SKILLS FOR LESSON 1.2

- Identify Main Ideas and Details
- Draw Conclusions
- Analyze Environmental Concepts
- Describe

HISTORICAL THINKING FOR CHAPTER 14

How did expansion alter the West and its native populations? For decades, farmers on the Great Plains struggled to find a way to bring adequate water to their crops. Lesson 1.2 explains what aquifers are and how use of the Ogallala Aquifer has changed the land and the way people farm on the Great Plains.

NATIONAL GEOGRAPHIC EXPLORER ANDRÉS RUZO

Geoscientist Andrés Ruzo has an interest in developing local resources in responsible ways that will not harm the environment while allowing businesses to function and prosper. He believes that environmentalists and companies can and should find ways to work together to solve the world's energy problems. He notes, "Energy can turn deserts into fertile cropland, alleviate the struggle for resources, and permit 7 billion people to live longer, healthier, more comfortable lives. Simultaneously, a nation's economic and environmental prosperity, as well as its international power, are also tied with how that nation uses and creates energy." His main area of study is green energy, especially geothermal energy.

HISTORY NOTEBOOK

Encourage students to complete the Geology in History page for Chapter 14 in their History Notebooks as they read.

INTRODUCE & ENGAGE

ACTIVATE PRIOR KNOWLEDGE

Display a glass or bottle of water. Ask students to consider how they use fresh water and how their lives would be different without access to clean, fresh water. Review how the water cycle moves water around Earth. *(Water evaporates from surface bodies of water or is released by plants into the atmosphere through transpiration; it condenses into clouds; and it falls back to Earth as precipitation, sometimes soaking into the ground to form groundwater.)* Invite students to describe ways to collect fresh water. *(Possible responses: digging wells, collecting rainwater in barrels, using nets to extract water from the air)* Tell students that in this lesson they will learn about how farmers on the Great Plains have worked to grow crops in a dry environment and about the unintended consequences of some of their actions.

TEACH

STEM

GUIDED DISCUSSION

1. **Describe** What set of conditions forms the best aquifer? Why? *(A place with fault zones, easily dissolved rock, and lots of gravel will form the best aquifer because there will be many small spaces where water can flow and collect.)*

2. **Analyze Environmental Concepts** How did farming on the Great Plains change after people could access water from the Ogallala Aquifer, and how does that relate to the idea of the Dust Bowl versus the breadbasket? *(At first, farmers struggled to pump underground water to the surface. Bad farming practices eroded the land, turning parts into the Dust Bowl. With access to water from the Ogallala Aquifer, farmers grew crops more easily and turned this area into America's breadbasket.)*

GEOLOGY IN HISTORY

Analyze Visuals Direct students' attention to the diagram of the Ogallala Aquifer. Explain that the water cycle is a natural system in which water evaporates from Earth's surface, forms clouds in Earth's atmosphere, and falls back to Earth as precipitation in a continuous cycle. Some water seeps into the ground, adding to groundwater held in aquifers. Point out that when human activities take water out of aquifers faster than it is replaced, the water table is lowered. **ASK:** If overuse of the Ogallala Aquifer causes the water table to drop, what could that mean for people who depend on it for water? *(They will likely have to drill deeper.)* Explain that water from aquifers also feeds into rivers, streams, and wetlands. **ASK:** How might overuse of aquifers like the Ogallala Aquifer affect habitats for plants and animals? *(Removing too much water from aquifers could affect the ability of a habitat, such as a wetland area, to support native plant and animal life.)*

ACTIVE OPTIONS

Active History: Analyze Causes of the Dust Bowl Extend the lesson by using either the PDF or Whiteboard version of the activity. These activities take a deeper look at a topic from, or related to, the lesson. Explore the activities as a class, turn them into group assignments, or even assign them individually.

NG Learning Framework: Make a Plan

ATTITUDE Responsibility

SKILL Problem-Solving

Assign students to small groups. Ask them to imagine that they have been chosen to make a plan for how people living on the Great Plains will use the Ogallala Aquifer in the future. Direct groups to conduct online research to learn more about current environmental policy regarding the use of the water from the aquifer, particularly by examining the Ogallala Aquifer Initiative launched by the National Resources Conservation Service. Prompt them to consider how to balance economic needs with environmental ones. Invite groups to share their finished plans with the class.

DIFFERENTIATE

INCLUSION

Analyze Visuals Provide concrete questions to help students describe and understand the graphic representation of the Ogallala Aquifer. For example: What layer would you see if you were standing on the ground? *(sod/grass)* How far would someone have to dig to get to the groundwater? *(50–100 feet)* How much deeper would someone have to dig to reach the water in the aquifer? *(about another 200–400 feet)* Encourage students to identify details they don't understand, and help them frame questions about these details that other students may answer.

GIFTED & TALENTED

Write a Ballad Instruct students to briefly search library or online sources for first-person accounts of life during the Dust Bowl. Then prompt them to write a ballad from the perspective of someone who lived through the experience. Some students may wish to set their ballad to music.

See the Chapter Planner for more strategies for differentiation.

THINK LIKE A GEOLOGIST

ANSWERS

1. Aquifers contain rich supplies of fresh water that humans can access to meet their needs for agricultural and other uses.

2. Because early settlers were not able to drill deep enough to access the Ogallala Aquifer, farmers today have had a vast store of water to draw upon for irrigation.

3. No limits were placed on how much water people could pump out, so people began to drain the aquifer more quickly than natural processes could refill it. Now there is a danger that the aquifer could run dry.

CRITICAL VIEWING Possible response: This sprinkler system allows farmers to cover a wide area of land with an even spray of water without having to dig and maintain extra channels in the ground to direct water to the crops or to move sprinkler systems from one area to another.

FARMERS AND THE POPULIST MOVEMENT

Staying afloat in any business is tough. You've probably seen restaurants and stores close after they failed to thrive. In the late 19th century, small farmers struggled against the odds to make a profit. Some just didn't make it.

FARMERS ORGANIZE

Around 1870, farmers in the South, Midwest, and West all faced economic hardship. Technology had increased farm productivity, but the surplus of agricultural products resulted in falling prices. For example, a bushel of wheat cost $1.50 in 1865. By 1894, the price had fallen to $0.49. The loss of income and the rising costs of farm equipment and shipping charges put farmers in a cycle of debt.

To make matters even worse, a boll weevil infestation struck the South in 1892. The boll weevil is a beetle that eats the buds and flowers of the cotton plant, preventing the boll, or the rounded, fluffy seed capsule of the cotton, from forming. The boll is what is harvested, processed, and spun into thread. Without the boll, there is no crop. The failed crops

affected the livelihoods of southern landowners, sharecroppers, and merchants. Many people were ruined financially and fled the South. Those who remained diversified their crops and eventually brought new agricultural industry to the region.

Dependent on merchants, railroads, and banks, which also charged high interest rates, farmers started to organize and unite in protest. In the 1870s, a group of farmers in Texas formed the first **Farmers' Alliance**. By the 1880s, other alliances arose with millions of members in the South and the Midwest. These alliances served not only a social, cultural, and political purpose but also an economic one.

To help resolve their economic grievances, farmers in local Granges, or lodges within an alliance, formed

cooperatives. **Cooperatives** are organizations run and funded by their members, who contribute funds into a pool of money. The farm cooperatives used the money to buy seeds and equipment. The larger the order for goods or services, the easier it was to negotiate good prices, lower shipping and storage rates, and lower-interest bank loans.

One of the most significant problems farmers faced was overproduction, which kept farm prices low. To address this problem, Charles Macune proposed the **subtreasury system**. The government would set up storage silos, or subtreasuries, in urban centers. When a farmer deposited a crop in the silo, the government would give the farmer a low-interest loan for a percentage of the crop's value to buy seeds for the next season. In 1889, Macune presented his system at a conference in St. Louis, but politicians refused to support it. The plan was never tried.

African-American farmers, who were banned from joining the mostly white Farmers' Alliances, formed the **Colored Farmers' National Alliance** in 1886. At its peak, about 250,000 African-American farmers belonged to the alliance. In 1891, the Colored Alliance went on strike, refusing to pick cotton unless landowners raised their wages. The strike, organized by Ben Patterson of Arkansas, ended when 15 strikers were lynched, including Patterson himself. The Colored Alliance soon dissolved.

THE POPULIST PARTY

In 1892, Farmers' Alliance leaders formed a third political party, known as the **People's Party** or the **Populist Party**, declaring that the Republican and Democratic parties did not support their interests. **Populism** is the belief that ordinary people should control government rather than elite politicians. The populists' political platform promoted subtreasuries and called for regulations to control rates for storage and shipping. It also supported workers' rights, specifically an eight-hour workday.

The Populist Party's most well-known concern was the issue of silver coinage. At the time, American currency was backed by gold. The **gold standard** required the U.S. government to print only an amount of money equal to the total value of its gold reserves. Strictly following the gold standard kept a limited amount of currency in circulation, which, in turn, kept the economy from growing, even though the nation's population was rapidly expanding. The only way the United States could distribute more money was to obtain more gold. The limited number of dollars in circulation affected the value of each one. Farmers found they had to work harder to maintain the same

At the Democratic Convention in 1896, William Jennings Bryan gave a fiery speech in support of free silver. He compared the gold standard to the crown of thorns Christians believe was placed on Jesus' head before he was crucified.

If they dare to come out in the open field and defend the gold standard as a good thing, we shall fight them to the uttermost, having behind us the producing masses of the nation and the world. Having behind us the commercial interests and the laboring interests and all the toiling masses, we shall answer their demands for a gold standard by saying to them, you shall not press down upon the brow of labor this crown of thorns. You shall not crucify mankind upon a cross of gold.

—from William Jennings Bryan's "Cross of Gold" speech, 1896

level of income. As a result, they looked for ways to inflate the currency—that is, put more dollars into circulation—and help lift themselves out of debt.

With western mines providing an abundant supply of silver, the Populist Party supported the **free silver movement**. According to the plan proposed, anyone holding silver could have it minted into U.S. coins for a small fee, and the coins could then be placed into circulation. Introducing free silver would increase the money supply and inflate prices substantially. In 1896, the Democratic nominee for president, **William Jennings Bryan**, supported free silver. The Republican nominee, **William McKinley**, was for the gold standard. As a result, farmers threw their support behind the Democrats. When the Populist Party as a whole supported Bryan, its members joined the Democratic Party. The Populist Party came to an end. However, Bryan's support of free silver lost him the 1896 election. The Republicans fanned voters' fears that free silver would lead to inflation, and McKinley won the presidential election. The gold standard remained in place until 1933.

HISTORICAL THINKING

1. **READING CHECK** How were farmers affected by industrialization?

2. **DRAW CONCLUSIONS** Why do you think Bryan used a biblical metaphor to argue his case in favor of free silver?

3. **ANALYZE CAUSE AND EFFECT** How did the free silver movement affect the Populist Party and the 1896 presidential election?

A GLOBAL PERSPECTIVE

Today, farmers' cooperatives, like those that arose in the late 1800s in the United States, have been established in countries all over the world. In this photo, African farmers belonging to the Orinde Farmers' Cooperative Society in Kenya sort coffee beans on a drying bed. About 700,000 small-scale farmers belong to more than 500 cooperatives in Kenya. These agricultural cooperatives help create jobs and provide training and financial help for members.

PLAN: 2-PAGE LESSON

OBJECTIVE

Analyze the struggles of farmers in the late 1800s and learn how farmers strengthened their economic status and their political voice.

CRITICAL THINKING SKILLS FOR LESSON 1.3

- Draw Conclusions
- Analyze Cause and Effect
- Determine Chronology
- Summarize

HISTORICAL THINKING FOR CHAPTER 14

How did expansion alter the West and its native populations? In the late 1800s, new technologies and economic policies made it hard for farmers to make a living. Lesson 1.3 examines those difficulties and some of the strategies farmers tried to resolve them.

BACKGROUND FOR THE TEACHER

Reformers called for agricultural diversification in the South even before the boll weevil struck. They thought that if farmers produced more of the products needed for their families, they would owe less money to merchants. Reformers did encourage farmers to raise some cotton as a cash crop, but they hoped that a smaller supply of cotton would lead to higher prices. In addition, crop diversification could help restore worn-out soil—growing only cotton season after season had caused some fields to erode and run low on nutrients. To this end, reformers suggested growing grass and legumes—both of which could be used as feed for livestock. Doing so would save farmers the cost of buying hay, and livestock manure could serve as a free, natural fertilizer for cotton fields.

FINANCIAL LITERACY

To extend their knowledge and understanding about the concepts in this lesson, refer students to the Financial Literacy handbook.

INTRODUCE & ENGAGE

DISCUSS THE COST OF DOING BUSINESS

Write the phrase "a successful farm" in the center of an Idea Web on the board. **ASK:** What do people need to make a farm successful? *(Answers will vary. Possible responses: workers; seeds and other supplies; a place to store crops; a way to transport crops to market; a demand for the farm's goods; profit from one year to purchase supplies for the next year; money to replace or update equipment)* Tell students that they will learn how small farmers struggled to keep their farms afloat when many of these necessities were threatened.

TEACH

GUIDED DISCUSSION

1. **Determine Chronology** Describe how one event led to another once the boll weevil disaster began. *(First, the boll weevils ate cotton plants, and cotton crops failed. Many people—not just farmers—suffered financially. As a result, many of those people left the South. Next, the people who stayed diversified their crops. Finally, the region enjoyed profits from new agricultural industries.)*

2. **Summarize** What were the issues that created economic hardships for farmers in the South, Midwest, and the West in the late 1800s? *(The farmers faced a surplus of crops, which caused lower prices for their products; a boll weevil infestation in the South destroyed cotton crops; railroads, banks, and merchants charged high interest rates on loans and services that increased farmers' debt; and low profits.)*

A GLOBAL PERSPECTIVE

Explore the photograph and caption of the Kenyan cooperative with students. **ASK:** What connection do you see between the cooperatives in Kenya and those in the United States during the late 1800s? *(Possible response: Both cooperatives formed when many farmers joined together to help one another.)* **ASK:** How are the benefits offered by the cooperatives alike and different? *(Possible response: They are alike because both offer financial help. They are different because the United States cooperatives focused on pooling resources to buy supplies and banding together to negotiate better shipping deals, while the Kenyan cooperatives focus on creating jobs and helping their members obtain training.)* Conduct a class discussion about why farmers in the United States and in Kenya might choose to join a cooperative.

ACTIVE OPTIONS

On Your Feet: Think, Pair, Share Direct students to use the Think, Pair, Share strategy to consider which economic policy to support—the gold standard or the free silver platform. Tell them to form pairs to discuss the benefits and drawbacks of each system for people in different economic situations, deciding finally which system they believe would have been better overall for the nation. Then invite one student from each pair to present and explain the pair's conclusion to the class.

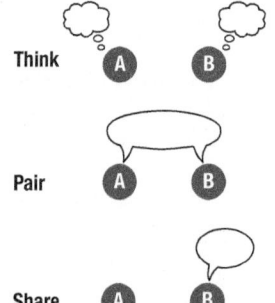

Think A B

Pair A B

Share A B

NG Learning Framework: Investigate Crop Diversity

ATTITUDE Curiosity

KNOWLEDGE Our Living Planet

Encourage small groups of students to consult online or library sources to research the way a southern community diversified its crops and to evaluate how much success the community found with its new products. Potential topics include peanuts in Alabama and sweet potatoes in Georgia. Remind students to assess the relevancy of each source for their task and audience. Work with groups to create a format for sharing their findings.

DIFFERENTIATE

STRIVING READERS

Use Reciprocal Teaching Tell partners to take turns reading each paragraph of the lesson aloud. At the end of the paragraph, the reading student asks the listening student questions about the paragraph. Students may ask their partners to state the main idea of the paragraph, identify important details that support the main idea, or summarize the paragraph.

PRE-AP

Conduct a Debate Explain to students that even today some people want to return to the gold standard. Proponents believe it would help stabilize the economy. Opponents think it would slow down the economy and introduce more instability. Instruct students to research expert opinions about re-instituting the gold standard today and to compare current ideas about it with those held by people in 1896. Then have two students debate the pros and cons of returning to the gold standard today.

See the Chapter Planner for more strategies for differentiation.

HISTORICAL THINKING

ANSWERS

1. Developments in technology made it easier for farmers to produce more crops, but the result was a crop surplus that caused the prices for these agricultural products to fall. Farmers made less money, but at the same time, they needed more money to buy new equipment to stay competitive with other farms and to pay the railroad shipping rates.

2. Possible response: Bryan probably realized the importance of faith to a large number of his supporters. He knew that through his metaphor, many of his listeners would identify advocates of the gold standard with the people who crucified Jesus, and they would therefore begin to back the free silver movement instead.

3. Wealthy business owners worried that free silver would hurt their business interests, and other voters worried it would cause inflation. These voters switched their support to the Democratic Party, ending the Populist Party and resulting in the election of the Republican candidate, William McKinley.

AMERICA'S BREADBASKET: THE GREAT PLAINS

For a long time, the term "breadbasket" referred literally to the basket that held your family's bread or rolls during meals. Today, it's a common name for a country's food-producing region, and in the United States, that's the Great Plains. Parts or all of 10 different states fall within the Great Plains, and most of them—Nebraska, Kansas, Iowa, Illinois, Indiana, and North Dakota, to name a few—are considered the breadbasket of North America because of the abundance of grains they produce.

The notion that an agricultural region could provide grain to cities that can't produce their own food isn't a new one. It dates back to the classical Greeks and Romans. In the United States, the farmers, fertile soils, and inexpensive available land of the Midwest have been growing reliable staple crops since the 1700s, and feeding not only Americans, but people across the world. Chances are great that the wheat, barley, corn, rice, or soybeans you eat each day are the product of your country's breadbasket.

Like other breadbasket states, Iowa is known for its cornfields. In 2015, the state's farmers grew 2.5 billion bushels of corn on 13 million sprawling acres of farmland. To preserve soil quality, corn is rotated with soybeans, growing here in front of the corn in the distance.

PLAN: 2-PAGE LESSON

OBJECTIVE

Learn about the role the Great Plains region continues to play in providing grain to American cities and to other countries.

CRITICAL THINKING SKILLS FOR LESSON 1.4

• Analyze Visuals

• Make Connections

• Analyze Environmental Concepts

HISTORICAL THINKING FOR CHAPTER 14

How did expansion alter the West and its native populations? Taking advantage of the fertile soil of the Great Plains, settlers transformed grassland prairies into fields of grain. Lesson 1.4 discusses the importance of "America's Breadbasket" to life in the past as well as today.

BACKGROUND FOR THE TEACHER

The Great Plains region owes the fertility of its soil to the decaying of the roots of its prairie grasslands, the natural process through which humus is formed. Wheat, corn, soybeans, canola, and other staples grown on farms across the Great Plains feed people throughout the United States and are exported to markets around the world. Iowa, for example, devotes about 90 percent of its land to agriculture. The state's economy thrives by transforming corn into products such as corn oil, corn syrup, cornmeal, cornstarch, popcorn, and animal feed. Grain processing plants that manufacture cereal also boost the state's economy. Additionally, Iowa is the United States' primary producer of ethanol—a biofuel used to supplement or replace gasoline—turning about 1.5 billion bushels of corn into more than 4.1 billion gallons of ethanol each year.

HISTORY NOTEBOOK

Encourage students to complete the American Places page for Chapter 14 in their History Notebooks as they read.

INTRODUCE & ENGAGE

PREVIEW WITH VISUALS

Direct students' attention to the photograph of an Iowa farm. **ASK:** What do you notice about the land that appears to be cultivated? *(Answers will vary. Possible responses: The fields are arranged in neat rows. Two different crops are being grown.)* **ASK:** What do you notice about the land farther back? *(Answers will vary. Possible response: That land is covered with trees and other greenery. Buildings are visible on the horizon in the far distance.)* Discuss the varied use of this land, with its cultivated crops, natural plants, and human settlements.

TEACH

GUIDED DISCUSSION

1. **Make Connections** What is the relationship between agricultural regions and cities? *(Cities, which usually cannot produce enough food to meet the needs of their many residents, rely on fertile farming regions to supply them with the food they need.)*

2. **Analyze Environmental Concepts** Share the information presented in Background for the Teacher. **ASK:** How might the health of natural systems on the Great Plains impact the quality, quantity, or reliability of the agricultural products the region produces to feed people in the United States and other nations? *(Possible responses: Disruptions to the natural systems on which agriculture depends—caused, for example, by destructive insects, flood or drought, disease, or natural disasters—would disrupt the growing cycle and lead to smaller yields and lower-quality products.)*

AMERICAN PLACES

Over time, Iowa planters have studied farming closely to discover the planting methods that will yield the best results. Along with deciding what to plant and when to do so, farmers must determine how deeply to plant the seeds, how far apart to set the rows, and how many plants to cultivate per acre. Farmers may be tempted to space rows closely together to cram more plants into a field and grow a larger crop to make a larger profit; however, research at Iowa State University has found that after a certain point, placing plants too close together does not yield additional corn.

ACTIVE OPTIONS

On Your Feet: Roundtable Divide the class into groups of four or five. Hand each group a sheet of paper containing the following question: How does the existence of America's Breadbasket affect our country and the rest of the world? The first student in each group should write an answer, read it aloud, and pass the paper clockwise to the next student. Have students circulate the paper until they run out of answers or the time is up.

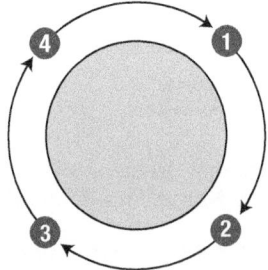

NG Learning Framework: Research the Breadbasket

SKILL Collaboration

KNOWLEDGE Our Living Planet

Explain that the ever-increasing global population puts pressure on natural systems on the Great Plains as more wheat, corn, and other farm products are needed to supply the growing demand for food. Point out that farmers could expand productivity by cultivating more land or by increasing the crop yield on current farmland. Organize students into groups to research how farmers on the Great Plains boost their output. Groups could focus on ideas such as the use of pesticides, improved farm equipment, or the adoption of hybrid or genetically modified species, including those designed to be resistant to insects, drought, or disease. Ask them to consider any potential drawbacks to the strategies they research. Allow time for groups to present their findings to the class.

DIFFERENTIATE

ENGLISH LANGUAGE LEARNERS `ELD`

Pose and Answer Questions Arrange students at the **Emerging** and **Expanding** levels in mixed pairs and ask them to reread the American Places text together. Instruct them to pause after each sentence to ask one another *who, what, when, where,* or *why* questions about what they have just read. Suggest students use a 5Ws Chart to help organize their questions and answers. Ask students at the **Expanding** level to assist students at the **Emerging** level as needed.

What?
Who?
Where?
When?
Why?

GIFTED & TALENTED

Illustrate the Breadbasket Challenge students to artistically interpret the phrase "America's Breadbasket." For example, students may create a drawing, painting, collage, or edited photographic image that incorporates both the literal and metaphorical meanings of *breadbasket*. Invite students to present their artistic renderings to the class and to answer questions about the materials they used and their artistic processes.

See the Chapter Planner for more strategies for differentiation.

GROWING PRESSURES ON NATIVE AMERICANS

When settlers pushed westward, the Native Americans in the region were forced to leave their homelands. Some went quietly, but many Native Americans chose to resist and fight back.

Indian Reservations and Battles in the West, 1864–1890

Native American land, 1861–1890
★ Major battle
Present-day boundaries are shown

BATTLES AND RESERVATIONS

Approximately 325,000 Native Americans inhabited the lands west of the Mississippi River prior to white settlement. Each tribe or nation had its own culture and customs, and sometimes groups fought one another for land and access to resources. As migrants began to head west along the Oregon and Santa Fe trails and miners pursued gold in California in 1848, Native Americans in the region sometimes launched attacks on the settlers and miners who were pushing westward.

In an attempt to stop the violence, U.S. officials and Native Americans met in Wyoming in 1851 and signed the **Treaty of Fort Laramie**. The treaty guaranteed the Native Americans in the territory an annual cash payment. In exchange, the Native Americans agreed to remain within specified boundaries, end their attacks on settlers, and allow the U.S. military to build forts in the area. The treaty worked. Wagon trains filled with settlers passed safely through tribal lands, and the U.S. Army encountered no resistance as it built its forts.

However, conflicts arose once again when even greater numbers of American pioneers and homesteaders began to migrate to the West in the 1860s. The constant flow of white settlers and the expansion of the transcontinental railroad threatened to push the Native Americans off the lands they'd been guaranteed. In addition, the settlers' cattle, sheep, and horses competed for grazing land with the vast herds of bison that roamed the region, and commercial hunters slaughtered many of the huge animals. Native Americans living in the West relied on bison for food and supplies, using every part

of the animal. Throughout the 1860s and 1870s, growing tensions over land and the bison erupted into frequent battles between Native Americans and U.S. forces.

The U.S. government tried to put an end to the conflicts by establishing reservations to confine Native Americans. A **reservation** is an area of land designated for and managed by a particular Native American tribe. However, most Native Americans found it hard to survive on reservations, which were typically located on undesirable land that was not good for farming. Most Native American cultures were based on a lifestyle of hunting and **foraging**, or searching for plants. The animals and plants Native Americans traditionally sought for food, medicines, and rituals were often scarce on reservations.

Native Americans were supposed to be safe on their reservations, but that was not always the case. In 1864, the governor of the Colorado Territory told the Cheyenne living there to gather near Fort Lyon on Sand Creek. He promised them protection from the battles raging in the region. Chief Black Kettle, leader of the Cheyenne, had his people set up camp along the creek. To show that the Cheyenne were friendly, he flew an American flag. Others in the village raised white flags, indicating their desire to communicate.

Ignoring these signs of peace, Colonel John Chivington, commander of a group of volunteer militiamen, swept into the camp after the able-bodied men had left to hunt. The militiamen slaughtered at least 150 unarmed women, children, and elderly men in the **Sand Creek Massacre**. In retaliation, the Cheyenne, Lakota, and Arapaho living in the territory conducted raids on unsuspecting settlers.

THE LITTLE BIGHORN

Few Native Americans liked being confined to a specific territory. But after the U.S. government promised the Lakota that miners and settlers would not encroach on their territory, they reluctantly agreed to settle on a reservation in the Black Hills in present-day South Dakota. When gold was discovered in the Black Hills, however, Colonel **George A. Custer** allowed miners to cross into Lakota hunting territory, in violation of a new Fort Laramie Treaty drawn up in 1868.

In 1874, the treaty was officially voided, and the commissioner of Indian affairs demanded that all Lakota leave the Black Hills by the end of January 1876. Sitting Bull, leader of the Lakota, refused to move, and troops arrived to force the relocation. Eventually Sitting Bull moved his band to a camp in the valley of the Little Bighorn River in Montana.

There the Cheyenne, Lakota, and other Native Americans who had abandoned their reservations joined Sitting Bull in his fight.

On June 25, 1876, Colonel Custer and his 7th Cavalry entered Sitting Bull's encampment on the Little Bighorn River. The roughly 2,000 Native American warriors were in an advantageous position. Custer had only about 200 men, but the U.S. troops attacked anyway. The warriors killed nearly all of them, including Colonel Custer, in the **Battle of the Little Bighorn**. It marked the worst defeat for the U.S. Army in the Native American wars.

After their victory, the Lakota did not go on the offensive, but the U.S. government did. Fighting continued for another five years, and the U.S. Army ultimately forced the Lakota to relinquish their hunting grounds and relocate to reservations. The United States seized the Black Hills.

PLAN: 4-PAGE LESSON

OBJECTIVE

Analyze the conflicts that arose as settlers moved west and onto Native American lands.

CRITICAL THINKING SKILLS FOR LESSON 2.1

- Interpret Maps
- Make Predictions
- Draw Conclusions
- Analyze Cause and Effect
- Form and Support Opinions
- Identify
- Analyze Primary Sources

HISTORICAL THINKING FOR CHAPTER 14

How did expansion alter the West and its native populations? The federal government tried to end conflicts between settlers and Native Americans in the West through treaties and the establishment of reservations. Lesson 2.1 describes how and why Native Americans resisted these changes.

BACKGROUND FOR THE TEACHER

At the council for the first Treaty of Fort Laramie, federal officials asked each Native American tribe to pick a representative. The officials did not understand that tribes would not feel bound to follow an agreement made without the approval of all tribe members. Though this treaty tried to make peace by designating land for each tribe, the representatives who agreed to the treaty could not force other tribal members to respect its terms. Conflicts escalated, especially when settlers discovered gold in Montana and built the Bozeman Trail through Lakota lands to connect the East to the new mines. Another council led to a new Treaty of Fort Laramie in 1868; there, the Lakota agreed to live in the Black Hills, and the government agreed to close the Bozeman Trail.

HISTORY NOTEBOOK

Encourage students to complete the American Gallery and Growing Pressures on Native Americans pages for Chapter 14 in their History Notebooks as they read.

INTRODUCE & ENGAGE

SETTLE A CONFLICT

Ask students to suppose that two different groups of people want control of the same land for different reasons. Lead students in discussing the merits of different ways to resolve the conflict, such as cooperative use of the land, negotiation, or warfare. Prompt them to consider such ideas as whether it should matter what each group wants the land for or who was there first. **ASK:** How could you judge whether the resolution was a good one or not? *(Answers will vary. Possible responses: Both sides get something out of the deal; there is no longer conflict over the land; the stronger side achieved its goal.)*

TEACH

GUIDED DISCUSSION

1. **Analyze Cause and Effect** What are some of the complex causes that led to the clash between settlers and Native Americans in the West? *(Possible responses: White settlers and new railroad lines moved onto lands that had been guaranteed to Native Americans. The settlers' livestock competed for grazing land with bison, on which Native Americans depended. Miners wanted access to land that might contain ore, and Native Americans wanted the same land for different reasons.)*

2. **Form and Support Opinions** Should the Lakota have agreed to leave the Black Hills when the commissioner of Indian affairs demanded that they relocate? Support your opinion with evidence from the text. *(Answers will vary. Possible responses: No; the government had no right to void a treaty that the Lakota were willing to follow. Yes; the Lakota had been reluctant to settle in the Black Hills anyway, and they might have been happier in another location.)*

INTERPRET MAPS

Instruct students to read the names of the various tribes represented on the Indian Reservations and Battles in the West map. Explain that Native Americans did not all belong to one single culture. Instead, each tribe had its own traditions, beliefs, and ways of using the land to make a living. **ASK:** How does this map help you better understand why it might have been difficult for the federal government to come up with a solution for how settlers and Native Americans could live together in peace? *(Possible response: The map shows how spread out the tribes were. If each tribe had its own way of doing things, the government probably found that no single solution met the needs of all the tribes.)*

As an extension to this activity, have students work in groups or individually to research one of the tribes listed on the map. Instruct them to learn more about the traditions, beliefs, and ways of using the land of the tribe of their choice. Create a table like the one below and host it on a document-sharing site so students can complete it with the results of their research. Use the completed chart to further discuss the difficulty of coming up with a single solution for how settlers and Native Americans could peacefully coexist.

Tribe	Traditions	Beliefs	Land Use

DIFFERENTIATE

ENGLISH LANGUAGE LEARNERS

Use Sentence Strips Choose a paragraph from the lesson, such as the paragraph about the Sand Creek Massacre or about the Battle of the Little Bighorn. Instruct students of **All Proficiencies** to make sentence strips out of it by writing each sentence on a separate strip of paper. Read the paragraph aloud, having students follow along in their books. Then tell students to close their books and arrange their sentence strips in order. Call on students to read the paragraph aloud and summarize it in their own words.

PRE-AP

Create a Time Line and Essay Instruct students to review the lesson and decide which events most affected Native Americans, such as massacres, treaties, and broken treaties. Then instruct students to create an annotated time line. Each event should include the date and at least two details, and students should conduct research to supplement their time line with additional details, images, or maps. Prompt students to use their time lines as the basis for an essay arguing why the events they chose were important.

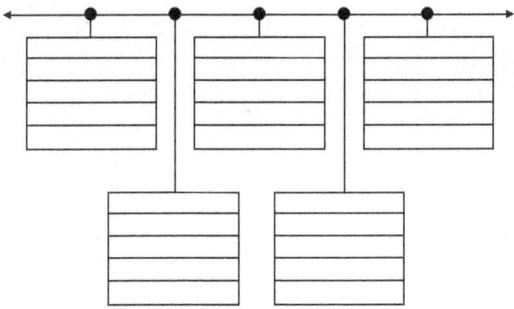

See the Chapter Planner for more strategies for differentiation.

Black Hills of South Dakota

National Geographic photographer Anand Varma captured this scene overlooking a canyon in the Black Hills, a small mountain range that rises in South Dakota and extends into Wyoming. The Lakota—often called the Sioux—have refused offers of payment as compensation for the land from the U.S. government. The Lakota only want the Black Hills, which they consider their spiritual home.

CHIEF JOSEPH AND GERONIMO

A similar pattern of resistance played out in other regions as well. The Nez Perce (NEHZ PURSE), who had traditionally lived in the Pacific Northwest, refused to give up their territory and relocate to a small reservation in Idaho. Despite being outgunned and outnumbered, **Chief Joseph** fought U.S. troops while leading his band of about 700 Nez Perce in a retreat toward the Canadian border. The Nez Perce journeyed about 1,600 miles, climbing steep mountains and trudging across hot plains, but the U.S. Army apprehended them just 30 miles from the border.

PRIMARY SOURCE

Chief Joseph made his surrender speech at Bear Paw, Montana, in 1877. In this excerpt from the speech, Chief Joseph reflects the despair of all Native Americans whose efforts to resist the U.S. government had failed.

It is cold, and we have no blankets; the little children are freezing to death. My people, some of them, have run away to the hills, and have no blankets, no food. No one knows where they are— perhaps freezing to death. I want to have time to look for my children, to see how many I can find. Maybe I shall find them among the dead. Hear me, my chiefs! I am tired; my heart is sick and sad. From where the sun now stands, I will fight no more forever.

—from Chief Joseph's surrender speech, 1877

When Chief Joseph's band finally surrendered at Bear Paw Mountain in Montana, they were guaranteed settlement in Idaho, but the government broke that promise. Instead, the Nez Perce were sent to the Oklahoma Territory, where disease caused mass casualties. In 1884, after the public became aware of the tribe's plight, advocates pressured the government to allow the Nez Perce to return to their native lands. Today, they belong to a confederation of tribes in eastern Washington State.

In the Southwest, Apache chief **Geronimo** also resisted forced government confinement. In the 1870s, the Apache had been confined to a reservation in Arizona. Geronimo frequently left the reservation with a small band of followers to raid towns and settlements. In September 1886, Geronimo and 400 other Apaches were captured, exiled to Florida, and imprisoned there. Many of the prisoners died in Florida because the unfamiliar tropical environment made them susceptible to diseases. The U.S. government denied Geronimo's request to return his people to Arizona. Instead, in 1894, his band was transferred to Fort Sill in Oklahoma, where Geronimo died at the age of 80 in 1909.

Some people call the treatment of Native Americans **genocide**, or the deliberate killing of a large group of people and its culture. Many historians consider the Native American wars to have ended with Geronimo's capture. While in captivity, the Apache chief became a celebrity and sometimes appeared in public. When his autobiography was published in 1906, he dedicated the book to President Theodore Roosevelt. Geronimo believed Roosevelt was "fair-minded" and would treat the Apache people with justice in the future. However, on his deathbed, the chief told his nephew, "I should never have surrendered; I should have fought until I was the last man alive."

HISTORICAL THINKING

1. **READING CHECK** Why did the U.S. government break the Treaty of Fort Laramie?

2. **INTERPRET MAPS** Locate areas on the map with several reservations clustered together. What inferences can you make about the type of land in these areas and why tribes were placed there?

3. **MAKE PREDICTIONS** How might history have unfolded differently if the United States had not forced Native Americans to relocate to reservations?

4. **DRAW CONCLUSIONS** What did Chief Joseph mean when he said, "From where the sun now stands, I will fight no more forever"?

BUILD BACKGROUND

BLACK HILLS MONUMENTS

In October 1927, workers blasted the first bits of rock away from the side of a Black Hills mountain to start carving what would become a popular South Dakota attraction: Mount Rushmore, featuring the faces of four presidents. Each year, almost 3 million people visit this monument, which many Lakota see as an embodiment of the wrongs done to them by the federal government. What to sculptor Gutzon Borglum was a ledge firm enough to support his huge work was to the Lakota a sacred rock named "Six Grandfathers" (representing the earth, the sky, and the four directions). In response to this monument honoring white U.S. presidents, a Lakota chief decided to build a memorial to Lakota warrior Crazy Horse on a neighboring Black Hills mountain.

NATIONAL GEOGRAPHIC PHOTOGRAPHER ANAND VARMA

Photographer Anand Varma grew up wanting to study exotic fish. Once he began college, however, his interests expanded. He started conducting field research on topics such as how primates take care of their young and how the ecology of a mangrove forest works. That inquisitive spirit led Varma into a career of photographing and sharing the wonders of the natural world. He has dedicated his life to drawing people's attention to creatures, environments, and people that they might not otherwise notice or know about. His assignments take him around the world to photograph amazing places, such as the Black Hills.

TEACH

GUIDED DISCUSSION

3. **Identify** What danger did some Native Americans face when forced to relocate to lands far from their home territory? *(Many of the Nez Perce and the Apache succumbed to diseases when they were forced to travel through and live in unfamiliar climates and environments.)*

4. **Analyze Primary Sources** How is Chief Joseph's view on surrender similar to and different from Geronimo's deathbed view on surrender? *(Possible response: Both leaders hoped that surrender would help their people: Chief Joseph hoped to have time to find and take care of his missing people, while Geronimo hoped the president would secure justice for his people. However, Chief Joseph seems resigned to his choice and indicates that he will never be willing to fight again, while Geronimo on his deathbed regrets his surrender.)*

AMERICAN PLACES

Archaeologists believe that people began visiting the region now known as the Black Hills around 10,000 years ago. Native Americans used the area for spiritual rites and as a neutral place where warring groups could meet safely to make peace. The Lakota gave the area a name that means "hills that are black" because its dense pine forests look black from a distance. Stretching 125 miles in length and 65 miles in width, this area includes forested hills and mountains, canyons, lakes, grasslands, and caves. Today, the government protects part of the region as the Black Hills National Forest, where visitors can enjoy recreational activities, such as camping, hiking, and fishing.

ACTIVE OPTIONS

AMERICAN GALLERY ONLINE **The Battle of the Little Bighorn** Invite students to explore the American Gallery. Have them select one of the images and do additional research to learn more about it. Ask questions that will inspire inquiry about the chosen gallery image, such as the following: What is this? Where and when was this created? By whom? Why was it created? Why does it belong in this chapter? What else would you like to know about it?

NG Learning Framework: Research Massacres and Wars

SKILL Collaboration

KNOWLEDGE Our Human Story

Ask small groups of students to work together to develop a presentation about one of the Native American massacres or wars mentioned in the lesson's text and map. Once each group has picked a massacre or war, instruct group members to divide tasks among themselves, researching who was involved in the conflict, what spurred the clash, where it occurred, how long it lasted, what was at stake for each side, and what effects it had. Encourage students to integrate information from their sources into a coherent understanding of the massacre or war. Invite each group to share its findings with the class.

HISTORICAL THINKING

ANSWERS

1. The U.S. government broke the Treaty of Fort Laramie and sent miners into Native American territory because gold was discovered in the Black Hills, which previously had been given to the Lakota.

2. The land in these areas was probably less desirable than the land in the surrounding areas, and it was most likely poor for growing crops. Native American tribes were probably placed there because white settlers did not want that land anyway.

3. Answers will vary. Possible response: Native Americans might have had land of their own—land that they chose for themselves, spacious enough to allow them to spread out and hunt, forage, and enjoy their traditional way of life.

4. Answers will vary. Possible response: Chief Joseph meant that from that moment until the end of time, he vowed never to fight again.

BROKEN PROMISES

Relations between the U.S. government and Native Americans were characterized by a trail of broken promises. No matter how many treaties Native Americans signed, their situation grew ever more desperate.

DAMAGE TO NATIVE CULTURES

The American public began to recognize the wrongs committed against Native Americans. In 1877, President Rutherford Hayes spoke out about how the nation had repeatedly broken its promises to them. Writer **Helen Hunt Jackson** also drew attention to the Native American plight in her 1881 book *A Century of Dishonor*. She submitted her work to Congress, hoping to stir its members to pass legislation that would improve Native American lives.

To that end, Congress passed the **Dawes Severalty Act** in 1887, which divided reservations into land **allotments**, or sections, of 160 acres. Native Americans who received an allotment were expected to establish farms. After 25 years, those who had successfully established a farm could become U.S. citizens. Sponsors intended the law as a positive alternative to the reservation system. However, the law also allowed the public to purchase any unoccupied allotments. Since most Native Americans of the Great Plains had lived as nomadic hunters and gatherers, few wanted to settle on the farms. So white settlers rushed to purchase the best reservation land. In the end, the allotments only weakened Native American communities.

THE TRAGEDY AT WOUNDED KNEE

By the 1880s, many Native Americans lived in poverty on reservations. They also suffered from illness, malnutrition, and despair. This was the case at the Pine Ridge Reservation on Wounded Knee Creek, to which Lakota leader Sitting Bull and his band had been sent. The United States considered Sitting Bull an agitator, or someone who seeks to rouse anger and stir rebellion as a means of forcing change. Sitting Bull refused to sign government treaties and boldly voiced his doubts over government promises.

U.S. officials also believed Sitting Bull was the driving force behind the **Ghost Dance** movement.

Actually, the movement got underway in 1889 after a Northern Paiute named Wovoka had a vision of a rescuer destroying white men and restoring the world to Native Americans. Wovoka taught followers the ceremonial Ghost Dance, which would usher in this deliverer. Once every six weeks, the participants danced for five nights; on the final night, they danced until morning. The practice spread to many reservations in the West—including the Pine Ridge Reservation—giving demoralized Native Americans hope. Fearing the Ghost Dance would result in uprisings, the U.S. government tried unsuccessfully to ban it.

In autumn 1890, when government officials came to the Pine Ridge Reservation to distribute land allotments to the Lakota, Sitting Bull declared he and his followers would refuse them. This rebuff, as well as the fact that the officials believed Sitting Bull had instigated the Ghost Dance, led the government to issue a warrant for his arrest. On December 15, 1890, authorities tried to seize Sitting Bull. He resisted arrest and was fatally shot during the scuffle.

But his death did not end the Ghost Dance. Two weeks later, the U.S. Army confronted Lakota Ghost Dancers gathered at Wounded Knee Creek and demanded they hand over their weapons. During the tense transaction, a shot was fired—no one knows by whom—but U.S. troops immediately opened fire in return, killing about 300 Lakota. The **Massacre at Wounded Knee** failed to put an end to the Ghost Dance, but from then on, the ceremony was conducted in secret. However, the massacre did halt any further Native American resistance.

CRITICAL VIEWING In 1890, the U.S. government attempted to assimilate Native American children, or change their language, habits, and dress, by sending them to boarding schools to learn white values and culture. The Apache children shown in these two photos taken by John Choate were among those captured with Geronimo in Arizona in 1886. The children were sent to the Carlisle Indian Industrial School, a boarding school in Pennsylvania.

Choate took the top photo shortly after the children's arrival at the school. The bottom photo, showing the same children, was taken after four months at the school. What does the children's physical appearance reveal about the ways they were changed by the school?

HISTORICAL THINKING

1. **READING CHECK** What were the aim and results of the Dawes Severalty Act?

2. **MAKE INFERENCES** Why might U.S. officials have believed that Sitting Bull started the Ghost Dance movement?

3. **SYNTHESIZE** What series of misunderstandings led to the Massacre at Wounded Knee?

4. **DRAW CONCLUSIONS** What effect did assimilation have on the Native American community?

PLAN: 2-PAGE LESSON

OBJECTIVE

Analyze how the federal government's actions caused its relationship with Native Americans to deteriorate in the late 19th century.

CRITICAL THINKING SKILLS FOR LESSON 2.2

- Make Inferences
- Synthesize
- Draw Conclusions
- Evaluate
- Compare and Contrast

HISTORICAL THINKING FOR CHAPTER 14

How did expansion alter the West and its native populations? Federal policies designed to help Native Americans alienated them by not taking into account entrenched Native American ways of life. Lesson 2.2 discusses the flaws of the Dawes Severalty Act and the escalating conflicts that led to the Massacre at Wounded Knee.

BACKGROUND FOR THE TEACHER

The term *severalty* in the name of the Dawes Severalty Act means that the law treated people as separate individuals. By encouraging Native Americans to think of themselves as independent farmers instead of as members of a tribe, reformers hoped to persuade them to exchange their customs for more "civilized" ways and assimilate into American society. However, reformers did not understand the Native American mind-set. For example, because the Lakota believed that all living things are spiritually related, they did not think that one person could own land, and farming horrified them because it required a farmer to change the ground by plowing it. Because they valued interpersonal relationships highly, they governed by consensus, making decisions only with input from all tribal members. Therefore, even when the Lakota did accept allotments, extended family groups cultivated each plot together.

INTRODUCE & ENGAGE

ACTIVATE PRIOR KNOWLEDGE

Invite students to recall what they learned in the previous lesson about promises the federal government made to Native Americans but then broke. Tell students to identify some specific promises, explain how the promises were broken, and discuss whether they believe that any of those promises were made in good faith, citing facts and details to support their opinions. Ask students to look for new broken promises described in this lesson.

TEACH

GUIDED DISCUSSION

1. **Make Inferences** Why do you think Helen Hunt Jackson titled her book *A Century of Dishonor*? (*Possible response: Jackson believed that Native Americans had been mistreated for a long time—more than 100 years—and that treating people so unfairly did not bring honor to the federal government.*)

2. **Evaluate** How effective were the methods of resistance that Sitting Bull used within the context of 19th-century conflicts? Explain. (*Answers will vary. Possible response: Sitting Bull tried to resist peacefully by objecting to government policies and refusing to sign treaties, but his approach ultimately failed—he was shot, and many of his people ultimately were massacred—because the military held all the power in that time and place.*)

COMPARE AND CONTRAST

Prompt students to compare the motivations of the reformers behind the Dawes Severalty Act with those of the reformers who wanted to send Native American children to boarding schools. **ASK:** What approach did both groups take to the problem of making Native Americans' lives better? (*Possible response: Both groups attempted to guide Native Americans to adopt new, "white" ways of life.*) **ASK:** Why do you think Native Americans resisted both reforms? (*Answers will vary. Possible response: Rather than giving up their own culture and accepting a foreign culture, Native Americans may have wanted to preserve their own traditions or create a blended culture.*)

ACTIVE OPTIONS

On Your Feet: Inside-Outside Circle Arrange students in concentric circles facing each other. Instruct each student in the outside circle to ask a question about interactions between the federal government and Native Americans. Each student in the inside circle answers his or her partner's question. On a signal, have students in the inside circle rotate counterclockwise to meet new partners and begin again. On a different signal, students trade roles so that those in the inside circle ask questions and those in the outside circle answer questions.

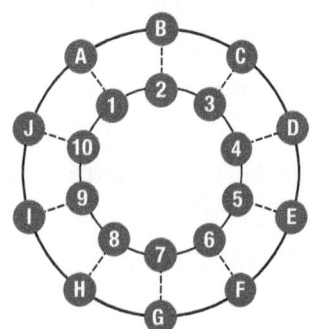

NG Learning Framework: Design a Policy

| ATTITUDE | Responsibility |
| SKILL | Problem-Solving |

Guide students to think more deeply about the relationship between the federal government and Native Americans and to consider how their joint history might have unfolded differently. Instruct them to use information from the chapter and additional print or online sources to evaluate the Dawes Severalty Act and either revise it to better meet the needs of Native Americans or come up with a new approach or law to help Native Americans live peacefully and prosperously in the United States. Invite students to share their finished solution with the class, explaining why it is a better approach toward truly helping Native Americans.

DIFFERENTIATE

INCLUSION

Compare and Contrast Photographs Pair students who are visually impaired with students who are not. Ask the latter to compare and contrast John Choate's photographs of the Apache children before and after they were sent to boarding school. Students should consider details such as the children's clothing, hair, postures, and facial expressions. Then have the pairs of students work together to answer the Critical Viewing question.

GIFTED & TALENTED

Create a Podcast Tell students to prepare an episode of a history podcast relating to Sitting Bull, the Ghost Dance, or the assimilation of Native American children. Suggest that students write a script for their podcast and include sound effects if possible. Tell them to take a point of view on the subject so that the podcast is informative, entertaining, and maybe even provocative. Then have students present their podcast to the class or record it on a phone or other device and play it back to the class.

See the Chapter Planner for more strategies for differentiation.

HISTORICAL THINKING

ANSWERS

1. The Dawes Severalty Act was designed to encourage Native Americans to farm and become U.S. citizens. Few opted to farm, though, and settlers bought much of the land.

2. The dancers sought to take back control of their lives and land, and Sitting Bull was a leader in resisting the government.

3. Mistakenly blaming Sitting Bull for the Ghost Dance, federal authorities arrested him and he was accidentally shot. Then, when the U.S. Army demanded that the Ghost Dancers turn over their weapons, someone's gun went off and the army opened fire on the Lakota.

4. Because of assimilation policies, many children lost their Native American identity; tribal members struggled with lifestyles, such as farming, that were neither familiar nor desirable to them; and many lived in poverty.

CRITICAL VIEWING Possible response: In the first picture, the children's appearance is traditional. In the second, their hair has been cut and they are wearing uniforms. The pictures show that the school was trying to teach the children to adopt white culture.

THE FIELD MUSEUM
CHICAGO, ILLINOIS

The Field Museum of Natural History arose as a result of the World's Columbian Exposition, an international fair held in 1893 in Chicago. The fair celebrated the 400th anniversary of Christopher Columbus's landing in the so-called "New World" in 1492. Its exhibits showcased the development of civilization, with a focus on American culture.

Leading citizens of Chicago established the Field Museum in 1893 to commemorate the exposition and house its exhibits, which included an extensive collection of Native American artifacts. Over time, the Field Museum developed into a renowned natural history museum, covering such fields as anthropology, botany, zoology, and geology.

> "The wonderful thing about museums is that you can **interact directly with other cultures**— ancient and modern—through their artifacts."
>
> —Bill Parkinson, Associate Curator

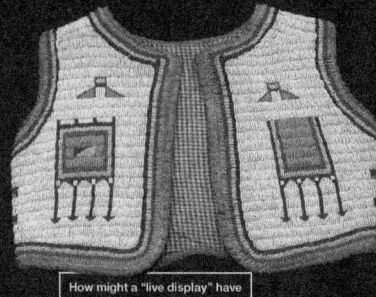

Sioux Beaded Vest
This Sioux beaded vest was worn by a child in a "live display" at the Columbian Exposition. At the fair, Native American performers lived in reconstructed villages to demonstrate their traditional life for fairgoers. The Sioux were one of the Plains Indian groups who lived in tepees and hunted bison. As this vest demonstrates, they were also highly skilled at beadwork.

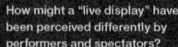
How might a "live display" have been perceived differently by performers and spectators?

This mask was made before 1893 by a Kwakiutl artist named Xániyus.

The White City
This postcard from the Columbian Exposition shows the "White City," which showcased the fair's main exhibition buildings. Painted white, these buildings housed exhibits of industrial technology, agricultural production, and fine art. Running at a right angle to the White City was the Midway Plaisance, a mile-long avenue with live exhibits of indigenous people of many cultures. The Midway was intended to display humanity's progress toward the "ideal" civilization of the White City.

Kwakiutl Transformation Mask
Known for their painted carvings, the Kwakiutl originally lived in what is now British Columbia, Canada. This Kwakiutl carving is a transformation mask, which can be opened by strings to reveal another image. Shown in the open position, this mask represents a shaman, a priest believed to have magic powers. The Kwakiutl thought a transformation mask represented the inner change believed to occur when it was worn, such as a transformation from a human to a particular animal.

Columbian Exposition tickets cost 50 cents for adults and 25 cents for children under 12.

Formed from thin, flat copper, this fish model has characteristics of two different species native to the Mississippi River system.

Hopewell Copper Fish
The Field Museum has one of the world's largest collections of artifacts from the Hopewell culture, which flourished more than 2,000 years ago in what is now southern Ohio. Most of the museum's collection comes from an excavation that was undertaken specifically to obtain Native American artifacts for the Columbian Exposition. The Hopewell culture produced especially fine metalwork, as represented by this copper fish.

PLAN: 2-PAGE LESSON

OBJECTIVE
Identify artifacts relating to the World's Columbian Exposition (1893).

CRITICAL THINKING SKILLS FOR LESSON 2.3
• Make Connections
• Analyze Visuals
• Describe
• Analyze Cause and Effect

HISTORICAL THINKING FOR CHAPTER 14
How did expansion alter the West and its native populations? Interacting with settlers changed Native American cultures, but it also brought those cultures to the attention of more Americans. Lesson 2.3 discusses the Columbian Exposition, which included exhibits of Native American artifacts—as well as live people—and the Field Museum, which has preserved artifacts from the exposition.

BACKGROUND FOR THE TEACHER
In 1890, Chicago competed for and won the honor of hosting the World's Columbian Exposition—a world's fair marking the 400th anniversary of Columbus's landing in the New World and celebrating American civilization. Fair designers juxtaposed dazzling arrays of electrical lights and the latest home-improvement gadgets with displays of artifacts that presented people from native cultures as exotic but primitive stereotypes. The fair fostered a unifying sense of pride in American civilization at the cost of treating other cultures as inferior. Today, the Field Museum partners with members of these cultures so they can influence the ways in which their history is presented.

HISTORY NOTEBOOK
Encourage students to complete the Curating History page for Chapter 14 in their History Notebooks as they read.

INTRODUCE & ENGAGE
BRAINSTORM A LIST

Ask students to brainstorm a list of types of artifacts that would help museum visitors learn about a past culture. Compile and display a master list. Invite students to discuss what each artifact might convey about its origin and the people who made it. Tell students that they will learn about artifacts that were first displayed at the World's Columbian Exposition in 1893 and then used to start Chicago's Field Museum of Natural History.

TEACH
GUIDED DISCUSSION

1. **Describe** Explain the purpose and design of the Midway Plaisance. *(This long avenue featured exhibits on both sides showcasing various cultures, carrying visitors toward the "White City" of main exhibition buildings. It was intended to show how humans had developed more sophisticated societies over time, finally reaching the highest level of civilization.)*

2. **Analyze Cause and Effect** How might a successful exhibition, such as the World's Columbian Exposition, support a trend toward funding new expeditions and discoveries? *(Possible response: As noted in the Hopewell Copper Fish caption, most of the Field Museum's Hopewell collection comes from one excavation made specifically to collect such objects for the Columbian Exposition. A popular exhibition that attracts a lot of people might prompt institutions to fund additional expeditions.)*

CURATING HISTORY

The Field Museum opened with approximately 500,000 objects from the Columbian Exposition. As its collection expanded to include millions of other natural history artifacts, the number of fair objects on display shrank to 2,000. From 2013 to 2014, the museum hosted an exhibit called *Opening the Vaults: Wonders of the 1893 World's Fair* that presented fair treasures once again. The museum's website showcases many of these artifacts. Ask groups of students to access the website, select an artifact, and read about it. Then invite students to explain to the class why this artifact was worth displaying at the Columbian Exposition and what people today can still learn from it.

ACTIVE OPTION

On Your Feet: Sort the Artifacts Direct students to work in teams of four to examine both the artifacts in the lesson and images related to the Columbian Exposition that are available at the Field Museum's website. Then have students complete two Concept Clusters like those shown below. In one cluster, students should identify artifacts and photographs that reveal information about past American cultures. In the other, they should identify a different class or genre of artifacts and/or photographs to be determined by them. When teams are finished, they can share their Concept Clusters with the class and note details that most of the teams identified.

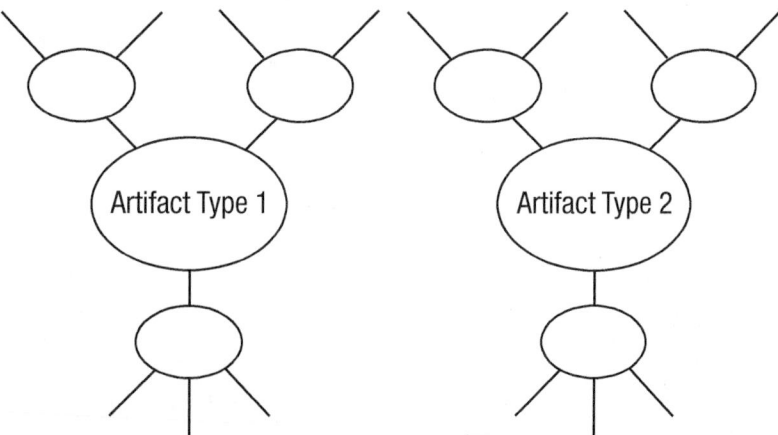

DIFFERENTIATE
STRIVING READERS

Organize Information Instruct students to draw four small K-W-L Charts on a blank piece of paper and label each chart with the heading of one of the pictured artifacts or group of artifacts. Tell students to examine the artifacts and complete the first two columns of each chart. Then direct students to read the captions and complete the third column of each chart. If students have trouble understanding some of the proper nouns or other information, ask them to formulate clarifying questions to ask other students.

K What Do I Know?	W What Do I Want To Learn?	L What Did I Learn?

PRE-AP

Give a Speech Challenge students to research, prepare, and present an informative speech about a Native American artifact. They may access online collections of the National Museum of the American Indian or other online sources of images and information about Native American artifacts. Students should choose one item and learn as much as they can about it, including where it is from, what it is made of, and how it was used. Encourage students to use a computer slide presentation as part of their informative speech to the class.

See the Chapter Planner for more strategies for differentiation.

SIOUX BEADED VEST

Answers will vary. Possible response: Spectators might be fascinated at the sight of people wearing traditional clothing and representing different ways of life. However, people on display might feel embarrassed or exploited, or they might resent being treated as objects or like zoo animals rather than as human beings with dignity and feelings.

CLOSING THE FRONTIER

Westerns, with their strong, quiet heroes and dastardly bad guys, have been a staple of films for more than 100 years. That tradition was born after the frontier vanished and stories of the rugged people who settled it took hold in people's imaginations.

TRANSFORMED BY THE FRONTIER

As the U.S. government forced Native Americans onto reservations, white settlers flooded deeper into western states and territories. By 1890, census data showed there was no longer a western region in which the population numbered fewer than two people per square mile. The frontier, once marked by open, unpopulated land, had ceased to exist.

In response to the census data, historian **Frederick Jackson Turner** developed a theory about the importance of the frontier. He presented his frontier theory in the paper "The Significance of the Frontier in American History," which he delivered to the American Historical Association in 1893. His views influenced generations of historians. Turner maintained that

western settlement had shaped America's national identity. He portrayed the frontier as a place that encouraged individualism and the belief that a person's independence and self-reliance were more important than the rules and concerns of society as a whole. As each generation pushed farther west, it became more democratic and egalitarian, or equal. The people relied on themselves and their neighbors instead of institutions or government officials. For example, if a horse was stolen, the sheriff often gathered together a **posse**, or group of armed men formed to capture an outlaw.

Turner's characterization of the frontier and the people who conquered it became widely accepted. Like most Americans of the late 19th century, he ignored the stories of many groups of people who were an important part of western history: Native Americans, Latinos, African Americans, Asians, and women of all ethnicities. Turner's frontier was solely one of white settlement and expansion.

THE WILD, WILD WEST

Incomplete though it may have been, Turner's characterization of the West began to be reflected in popular culture. Easterners and those living in urban areas developed a particular fascination with stories of the West, no matter how embellished, or exaggerated, they were. Novels, songs, plays—and, in time, films—portrayed bold characters and their adventures on the now vanished frontier.

One figure in particular captured the imagination of Americans from all walks of life: **Buffalo Bill Cody**. William Cody was born on the prairie in 1846, and he worked as a messenger, livestock wrangler, gold prospector, and Pony Express rider delivering mail

throughout the West. In 1867, he began hunting bison—which many people at the time referred to as *buffalo*—to feed railroad construction crews. He hunted and killed more than 4,000 buffalo in 17 months, but he actually earned his nickname by taking part in an 8-hour buffalo shooting match with another hunter named William. Cody also fought in numerous battles during the Native American wars.

Cody became the larger-than-life protagonist, or main character, of a series of novels penned by E.Z.C. Judson. Judson wrote **dime novels**, popular fiction that sold for 10 cents a book, that were made widely available through improved printing methods and shipping. Dime novels were the forerunners of modern paperback books. Judson, who published his books under the pen name Ned Buntline, created a Buffalo Bill character that became as iconic as American folk hero and frontiersman Davy Crockett had been to earlier generations.

In 1872, Judson encouraged Cody to portray his fictional character on stage. Cody discovered he was a natural showman, and his first performances were so well received that he launched Buffalo Bill's Wild West show, a traveling act that was part circus and part theater. In his Wild West show, Cody featured Native Americans and bison in different scenes, telling mostly true—but often sensationalized—stories. Besides Buffalo Bill himself, the indisputable star of the show was **Annie Oakley**, an excellent markswoman. She performed for crowds at the Wild West show for 16 years and is widely considered America's first female superstar. Lakota leader Sitting Bull also joined the show for a short time. The show toured for three decades throughout the United States and Europe.

Dime novels laid the foundation for Western films, which appeared at the dawn of the movie industry. The first Western, *The Great Train Robbery*, was a black-and-white film released in 1903. It was so successful that producers quickly made more films in the same genre. Initially, Westerns were filmed in eastern cities, but as plots grew more complicated, they required more authentic-looking scenery. Thus, producers moved to California-based studios, where Westerns became a significant percentage of the movies produced—and Hollywood was born. The public viewed cowboy characters as heroes. In the 1950s and early 1960s, Westerns were the most popular genre of television programming. Though tastes in entertainment have changed somewhat since then, Western stories continue to find eager audiences in movies, television, and novels.

Annie Oakley was born Phoebe Ann Moses in 1860. Her family had a small farm, and as a child, Annie helped support it by shooting small wild game to sell to grocery stores. At age 15, she won a shooting contest against a traveling marksman named Frank Butler, who was charmed by Annie. The two married and soon began performing together, with Annie using the name "Oakley." Sitting Bull saw their show and gave Annie the Lakota name *Watanya Cicilla*—"Little Sure Shot." In 1885, she joined the Wild West show. Oakley continued performing into her sixties.

HISTORICAL THINKING

1. **READING CHECK** According to Frederick Jackson Turner, how did western settlement shape America's national identity?

2. **MAKE INFERENCES** Why do you think city dwellers became especially entranced with tales of the West?

3. **FORM AND SUPPORT OPINIONS** Do you agree with Turner's theory about the impact of western settlement on American identity? Explain why or why not.

PLAN: 2-PAGE LESSON

OBJECTIVE

Learn how the settling of the frontier helped shape an American identity and inspired tale-telling about the Wild West.

CRITICAL THINKING SKILLS FOR LESSON 2.4

- Make Inferences
- Form and Support Opinions
- Evaluate
- Integrate Visuals
- Analyze Primary Sources

HISTORICAL THINKING FOR CHAPTER 14

How did expansion alter the West and its native populations? As settlers filled the West and the last of the actual frontier vanished, tales of the Wild West grew in popularity. Lesson 2.4 describes how the frontier's settlement affected Americans' view of themselves and their nation.

BACKGROUND FOR THE TEACHER

At first, Buffalo Bill Cody's Wild West show presented only an entertaining mix of restaged scenes and showcases of skills such as roping and shooting. Over time, however, Cody developed a clearer dramatic narrative that emphasized how the westward movement of settlers had civilized the frontier. Despite his championing of white settlers, for the most part Cody treated Native Americans fairly. Although his Native American performers still had to dress and act in stereotypical ways and reenact historical scenes that cast them as violent aggressors or losers—scenes in which some of the performers had participated in real life—Cody provided them with equal pay and housing and urged them to preserve their culture and traditions.

INTRODUCE & ENGAGE

CONSIDER THE FRONTIER

Point out the title of this lesson. **ASK:** What is a frontier? *(Possible response: The boundary between something that is known and an area that has yet to be explored.)* **ASK:** What are some modern frontiers? *(Answers will vary. Possible responses: space; places with harsh environments, such as Antarctica; deep-sea trenches)* Guide students to think about frontiers in relation to what they learned about the idea of manifest destiny earlier in the chapter. Tell students that in this lesson they will find out one aspect of what happened once people actually settled the land between the Atlantic and Pacific coasts and the frontier officially "closed."

TEACH

GUIDED DISCUSSION

1. **Evaluate** What value was there in having posses, and what potential dangers might posses have presented? *(Answers will vary. Possible response: Posses helped sheriffs bring lawbreakers to justice. However, since they worked beyond the reach of most government officials, posses had the potential to act as vigilantes, answering to no one but the sheriff who led them.)*

2. **Integrate Visuals** What information does the photograph convey about Annie Oakley, and how does it add to the text? *(Answers will vary. Possible response: Her gun and medals show that she is an accomplished markswoman. Details such as the dress she is wearing and how she has styled her hair in long curls show that she is presenting herself not just as an expert shot but specifically as a woman who can shoot well, probably because it was much rarer for women to exhibit their marksmanship skills.)*

ANALYZE PRIMARY SOURCES

Prompt students to read the excerpt from William Cody's autobiography. **ASK:** What motivation does Cody mention for staging his Wild West show? *(He believed that getting people in the East interested in the West would help the West's development.)* **ASK:** Why do you think Cody says that he felt "a little sorry that my Western adventures would thereafter have to be lived in spectacles"? *(Answers will vary. Possible response: The West that his show depicted was changing and disappearing, so he may have felt bad that the only way to have Western adventures was to simulate them on stage. He also may have felt sad because instead of having fun adventuring in the real West, he felt obligated to manage his show.)*

For students who develop an interest in the Wild West, suggest that they read the American Story located at the beginning of this chapter.

ACTIVE OPTIONS

On Your Feet: Stage a Quiz Show Instruct students to write one question about the frontier or about popular depictions of the Wild West. Collect the questions. Then have groups of five students take turns coming to the front of the class to take part in a quiz. Pose a few of the questions to each group and allow students to confer about the answers. Tell them to signal their readiness to respond by raising their hands.

NG Learning Framework: Research Buffalo Bill's Show

ATTITUDE Curiosity

KNOWLEDGE Our Human Story

Arrange students in small collaborative teams to research one of the acts featured in Buffalo Bill's Wild West show. Direct students to collect biographical information about the person or people in the act before, during, and after participating in the show. Urge teams to include contemporary descriptions, photographs of the act, and recordings of the music played by the show's band. Invite teams to compile their efforts into a multimedia presentation to share with the class.

DIFFERENTIATE

ENGLISH LANGUAGE LEARNERS

Dictate Sentence Summaries Pair students at the **Emerging** level with those at the **Bridging** level. After students read the lesson, direct them to identify three sentences that contain an important idea. Then tell each student to write that idea in a summary sentence using his or her own words. Partners then take turns dictating their sentences to each other. Encourage them to work together to check each other's work for accuracy and spelling.

GIFTED & TALENTED

Create a Poster Direct students to conduct online research to find posters from the Wild West show era. Although the shows claimed authenticity, the posters generally included elements that revealed stereotypical views of cowboys, Indians, and the frontier life. Ask students to identify stereotypical images and then create their own poster that includes more authentic images. Encourage students to display their own poster alongside an image of a poster from the 19th century and discuss similarities and differences.

HISTORICAL THINKING

ANSWERS

1. Because settlers depended on themselves instead of on institutions, they valued independence and self-reliance—two traits that became strongly linked with America's national identity.

2. Answers will vary. Possible response: City people had to follow rules to live closely together and keep society working. Therefore, the freedom portrayed in tales of the West appealed to them.

3. Answers will vary. Possible responses: Yes; many Americans value individual self-expression and think that rules should change if they clash with how someone chooses to live life. No; instead of relying on themselves or local help, many people think that the government should be in charge of providing essential services.

LITERATURE OF THE WEST

As a writer, how would you describe a place that is unfamiliar to most people so that they could imagine being there? In the late 1800s, authors captivated readers with strange and elaborate depictions of the West and new American experiences.

SETTLERS' VOICES

The dime novels that mythologized the Wild West grew out of a much larger literary movement of the late 1800s, marked by a writing style known as regional realism, or **local color**. Through this writing style, the unique and sometimes very peculiar traits of a region came to life through vivid descriptions of its people, customs, dialects, folklore, and landscape. Local color grew in popularity after the Civil War, as Americans became intrigued with areas of the country they had once found too distant or strange to consider settling in.

Humorist **Mark Twain**, whose real name was Samuel Langhorne Clemens, was one of the most notable local colorists of the era. Before he began writing travel narratives and fiction, Twain piloted steamboats up and down the Mississippi River, mined for silver, and worked as a newspaper reporter in Nevada and California. His accounts of traveling down the Mississippi and throughout the West paint

a detailed picture of life in those regions, and his most famous novels, *The Adventures of Tom Sawyer* and *Adventures of Huckleberry Finn*, rely on his rich memories of growing up in Missouri.

The mining camps and boomtowns of the American West also inspired local colorists. **Bret Harte**, famous for his exaggerated characters in short stories, such as "The Luck of Roaring Camp" and "The Outcasts of Poker Flat," spent time in the gold camps of California before becoming a journalist,

Mark Twain's first famous story was "The Celebrated Jumping Frog of Calaveras County," the source of this fanciful illustration of the author.

PRIMARY SOURCE

Roughing It is an account of author Mark Twain's experiences in the West.

And now, at last, we . . . were perched upon the extreme summit of the great range of the Rocky Mountains. . . . We were in such an airy elevation above the creeping populations of the earth, that now and then when the obstructing crags stood out of the way it seemed that we could look around and abroad and contemplate the whole great globe, with its dissolving views of mountains, seas and continents stretching away through the mystery of the summer haze.

—from *Roughing It* by Mark Twain, 1872

fiction writer, and poet. Author **Mary Hunter Austin** wrote about life on the eastern slopes of the Sierra Nevada and in the Great Basin. Her most famous work, *The Land of Little Rain*, describes the animals, plants, and people of that region in the late 1800s.

NATIVE AMERICAN VOICES

Native Americans were among the emerging Western literary voices after the Civil War. The nations and tribes of the Great Plains had long passed down oral histories of their lives and beliefs. But as more Native Americans were sent to boarding schools in the late 1800s, a number of them began to write extensively about their experiences. Activist **Sarah Winnemucca Hopkins**, the daughter of a Paiute chief, was one of the first Native Americans of the plains to have such accounts published. Her autobiography and only book, *Life among the Piutes [Paiutes]: Their Wrongs and Claims*, describes the lives of the Northern Paiute and how they were affected by U.S. settlement.

Two Lakota writers of the late 1800s struggled to reconcile the cultures in which they were raised with their assimilation into white society. **Zitkala-Sa** (ziht-KAH-lah SAH), or "Red Bird," was born and raised on the Pine Ridge Reservation in South Dakota. After attending a Quaker missionary school in Wabash, Indiana, where Lakota ways were discouraged, Zitkala-Sa found herself caught between two cultures. She drew on her personal experience to write essays and short stories, a number of which were published in literary magazines of the time.

Charles Alexander Eastman was raised in the Lakota tradition until his father, who had converted to Christianity, encouraged him to convert as well. Eastman became a doctor and eventually returned to the Lakota as a government physician on the Pine Ridge Reservation, where he witnessed the aftermath of the massacre at Wounded Knee. He

later described the event in *From the Deep Woods to Civilization*, but his most notable work is an account of his Lakota upbringing, called *Indian Boyhood*.

BORDER BALLADS

American settlement of the Southwest changed the lives of the Spanish-speaking people in this region. Newly introduced cultural and language differences sparked conflicts, especially near the Mexican border. Mexican ballads called *corridos* (koh-REE-dohs), told dramatic stories of heroes' defiant encounters with the new U.S. authorities, based on real events.

The earliest known corrido is about Mexican folk hero Juan Nepomuceno Cortina, who shot a U.S. marshal for mistreating his mother's servant in the late 1850s. The incident escalated into a series of border conflicts that inspired a ballad and established the typical plot for most corridos that followed: an outnumbered Mexican hero north of the border outwits and outruns American forces. The most famous corrido, "El Corrido de Gregorio Cortez," tells the story of a ranch hand who was falsely accused of stealing a horse in 1901. He led his pursuers for hundreds of miles before he was captured.

The exciting literature that came out of the American West helped define the region and the nation as a whole. Some critics even credit the literary trend with helping the nation mend after the Civil War and establish a new American identity for the future.

HISTORICAL THINKING

1. **READING CHECK** What topic was common among the Native American writers discussed in this lesson?

2. **DETERMINE WORD MEANING** Why do you think the terms "local color" and "regional realism" are used to describe the literature of the West?

3. **MAKE INFERENCES** Why do you think the border corridos became so popular in the Southwest?

PRIMARY SOURCE

In Zitkala-Sa's "The Soft-Hearted Sioux," a young man returns to his Lakota village after attending a Christian mission school.

I did not grow up the warrior, huntsman, and husband I was to have been. At the mission school I learned it was wrong to kill. . . . In the autumn of the tenth year I was sent back to my tribe to preach Christianity to them. With the white man's Bible in my hand, and the white man's tender heart in my breast, I returned to my own people.

Wearing a foreigner's dress, I walked, a stranger, into my father's village.

—from "The Soft-Hearted Sioux" by Zitkala-Sa, 1901

PLAN: 2-PAGE LESSON

OBJECTIVE

Explore how writers' experiences in the West inspired literature that captured the imaginations of Americans in the late 1800s.

CRITICAL THINKING SKILLS FOR LESSON 2.5

- Determine Word Meaning
- Make Inferences
- Identify
- Make Connections
- Evaluate

HISTORICAL THINKING FOR CHAPTER 14

How did expansion alter the West and its native populations? As settlers arrived in the West during the late 1800s, they gradually displaced native populations. Lesson 2.5 focuses on the role writers played in depicting the geographic wonders that enticed settlers to the West and the harsh realities for many Native Americans and Spanish-speaking people in the region as a result of westward expansion.

BACKGROUND FOR THE TEACHER

As students read earlier in the chapter, in the late 1800s, the federal government was sending Native American children to government-run boarding schools, many of which were located hundreds of miles from their homes. The goal of this removal was to take control of children's lives and suppress their Native American beliefs, behaviors, and culture. Isolated from their families, children were prohibited from using their given names, dressing in native clothing, and speaking their native language. Reports of students' recollections of their experiences include receiving no instruction in basic math or English, being forced to perform hard labor, and being beaten. The founder of the first such school was an army officer who had previous experience educating inmates at a prison for Native Americans. Some Christian missionary schools sought to "civilize" Native Americans by neutralizing their culture. Authors, such as Zitkala-Sa, would later provide details in their writing that documented this contemptible practice.

INTRODUCE & ENGAGE

ACCESS PRIOR KNOWLEDGE

Ask volunteers to share what they know about Mark Twain and his writing. *(Possible responses: Twain is famous for writing novels about Tom Sawyer and Huckleberry Finn. There are film adaptations of those and other Twain novels, including* A Connecticut Yankee in King Arthur's Court *and* The Prince and the Pauper.*)* Tell students that in this lesson they will read an excerpt from one of Twain's famous experiences as a traveler and read about other writers whose experiences and descriptions attracted interest in and provided insight to the West during the late 1800s.

TEACH

GUIDED DISCUSSION

1. **Identify** How did Mark Twain's and Bret Harte's early careers and experiences influence their writing? *(Twain's work as a steamboat pilot on the Mississippi River influenced his use of the river as a setting. Harte's early experiences in mining camps likely brought him into contact with interesting people and situations that provided the basis for some of his stories.)*

2. **Make Connections** How did the literature of the West contribute to the American identity? *(Possible response: Authors' descriptions of the western landscapes and the experiences of the people who lived there, including conflicts between settlers and Native Americans and Mexicans, defined the West as a strange, captivating place made up of different cultures. Some critics credit the literature for establishing a new American identity.)*

EVALUATE

What benefit is gained from Native American authors writing their stories versus providing strictly oral accounts? *(Possible response: Oral accounts stay entirely within the Native American community, but published accounts can reach a larger audience. As a result, white culture has the opportunity to better understand the effects that western expansion had—and continues to have—on Native American populations.)*

ACTIVE OPTIONS

On Your Feet: Compare and Contrast Primary Sources Draw students' attention to the Primary Source features. Divide the class into groups of three or four, and tell students to review the two excerpts to compare and contrast how the authors depict their experiences. Encourage them to use a Compare Texts graphic organizer to record similarities and differences in elements such as purpose, point of view, theme, tone, style, and mood. Tell students to discuss and determine each excerpt's main idea as it relates to the West. Guide a class discussion in which groups refer to their graphic organizers as they share how and why the two depictions of the West differ.

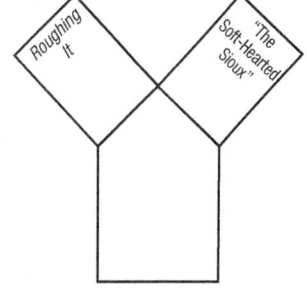

NG Learning Framework: Investigate Native American Boarding Schools

ATTITUDE Responsibility

KNOWLEDGE Our Human Story

Instruct students to work in small groups to investigate the experiences of Native American children relocated to boarding schools during the late 1800s. Tell them to use reliable primary and secondary source materials to gather information about the organizations that established the schools and their goals, facilities for housing and education, and the treatment and overall experiences of the children. Ask students to share their findings during a class discussion.

DIFFERENTIATE

STRIVING READERS

Summarize Using a Concept Cluster Direct pairs to summarize the lesson by creating a Concept Cluster. Guide students to write the lesson title in the center oval and the subsection headings in the outer ovals. As they read each subsection, tell them to write key names and information on the spokes, adding more spokes as needed. Invite volunteers to use their Concept Cluster to summarize the lesson, explaining the contributions by authors to the literature of the American West.

GIFTED & TALENTED

Write a Corrido Instruct students to compose a short corrido about an outnumbered "hero" who outwits someone of authority. Students may base their lyrics on one of the events described in the text or devise their own scenario. Suggest that they listen to or read examples of corridos online and examine them for content and structure before composing their own. When students have finished writing, invite them to read or sing their corrido to the class.

See the Chapter Planner for more strategies for differentiation.

HISTORICAL THINKING

ANSWERS

1. The Native American writers focused on their forced assimilation into white culture and the negative effects it had on them and their communities.

2. The stories are unique to the western region. The style of writing captures a realistic sense of the setting while focusing on the historical events and local people who shaped the West.

3. Possible response: By making heroes out of those who defied U.S. authorities, writers of corridos gave Mexicans an outlet for expressing their feelings about conflicts near the border.

VOCABULARY

Use each of the following vocabulary terms in a sentence that shows an understanding of the term's meaning.

1. **shaft mining**
   Some companies used shaft mining to blast the passageways needed to reach the veins of gold deep within the mountain.

2. **Exoduster**

3. **lode**

4. **populism**

5. **forage**

6. **allotment**

7. **cooperative**

8. **dime novel**

9. **local color**

READING STRATEGY
DRAW CONCLUSIONS

When you draw conclusions, you make a judgment based on what you have read. You analyze the facts, make inferences, and use your own experiences to form your judgment. Use a diagram like this one to draw conclusions about the impact of expansion and conflict in the West.

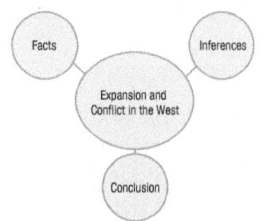

10. What impact did westward expansion and conflict with Native Americans have on American identity in the late 1800s?

MAIN IDEAS

Answer the following questions. Support your answers with evidence from the chapter.

11. Why did Exodusters migrate west? **LESSON 1.1**

12. How did farmers respond to industrialization? **LESSON 1.1**

13. Why did farmers in the South and the Midwest form alliances? **LESSON 1.3**

14. What happened when William Jennings Bryan basically co-opted much of the Populist Party platform and ideology? **LESSON 1.3**

15. What contributed to the decline of the great bison herds? **LESSON 2.1**

16. What was the result of the Lakota victory at the Battle of the Little Bighorn? **LESSON 2.1**

17. Why did the U.S. government try to ban the Ghost Dance? **LESSON 2.2**

18. What piece of data clearly indicated that there was no longer a western frontier? **LESSON 2.4**

19. How did local colorists bring the West to life for Americans in other regions? **LESSON 2.5**

HISTORICAL THINKING

Answer the following questions. Support your answers with evidence from the chapter.

20. **SYNTHESIZE** How did the federal government affect the country's growth in the years following the Civil War?

21. **ANALYZE CAUSE AND EFFECT** How did the boll weevil infestation affect cotton production in the South?

22. **EVALUATE** What impact—both good and bad—did settlement have on the Great Plains?

23. **MAKE INFERENCES** How did Buffalo Bill Cody's life serve as inspiration for a character in a dime novel?

24. **DRAW CONCLUSIONS** In the context of westward expansion, why did the U.S. government believe Native Americans would benefit from being assimilated into white culture?

25. **COMPARE AND CONTRAST** In what ways were the lives of Chief Joseph and Geronimo both similar and different?

INTERPRET VISUALS

This poster advertises land a railroad company sold on the Great Plains in 1872. Look at the poster and then answer the questions that follow.

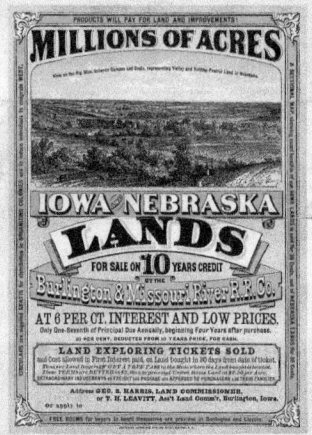

26. Based on what you've learned about the Great Plains, do you think the image in this poster of land in Iowa and Nebraska is an accurate depiction? Why or why not?

27. Why might those trying to sell this land use both valid and fallacious, or flawed, arguments in a poster like this one?

ANALYZE SOURCES

Helen Hunt Jackson was best known as a poet, but in 1881, she published *A Century of Dishonor*, a nonfiction book that exposed the injustice of U.S. government policies toward Native Americans. Read the excerpt from the book below and answer the question.

> There is not among these three hundred bands of Indians one which has not suffered cruelly at the hands either of the Government or of white settlers. The story of one tribe is the story of all, varied only by differences of time and place. Colorado is as greedy and unjust in 1880 as was Georgia in 1830, and Ohio in 1795, and the United States government breaks promises now as deftly [effortlessly] as then, and with the added ingenuity [inventiveness] from long practice.

28. What does the passage tell us about Jackson's historical interpretation of the U.S. government?

CONNECT TO YOUR LIFE

29. **ARGUMENT** You've read that westward expansion helped shape a new American identity. What do you think our identity is today, and what factors have shaped it? Write a paragraph in which you defend your ideas about what American identity means today.

TIPS

- Think about how westward expansion shaped American identity in the late 1800s.

- Consider present-day events that have had a similar impact on our identity, including immigration and technology.

- Determine how these events have affected and changed our national identity.

- Write an opinion statement in which you state what you believe our American identity is today.

- Support your opinion with facts and reasons.

VOCABULARY ANSWERS

1. Some companies used shaft mining to blast the passageways needed to reach the veins of gold deep within the mountain.

2. Exodusters were the African Americans who made an exodus from the South to western territories after Reconstruction failed.

3. A lode, also called a vein, is a deposit of ore.

4. Populism appealed to the ordinary people in the country, but not the political elite.

5. Some tribes preferred to forage to get food, gathering edible plants and berries instead of growing crops.

6. An allotment is a specific parcel of land that the government designates for an individual.

7. The farmers formed a cooperative and ran it as a group to buy supplies for the members at good prices.

8. Dime novels about fictional adventures in the West became popular at the end of the 19th century.

9. Local color in Mark Twain's stories came from regional dialect.

READING STRATEGY ANSWER

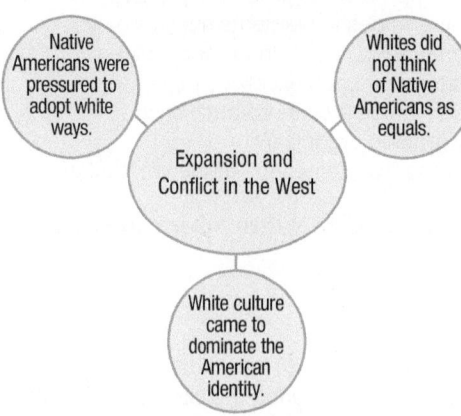

10. Answers will vary. Possible response: As white settlers moved west seeking land to mine and farm, Native Americans and their cultures were pushed aside, and white culture came to dominate the American identity.

MAIN IDEAS ANSWERS

11. Exodusters migrated west to take advantage of chances for an improved life with less discrimination and better job opportunities.

12. Farmers responded to industrialization by taking advantage of new technologies that helped them increase productivity, such as Deere's plow, McCormick's reaper, and machines to help process wheat and husk corn.

13. They formed alliances to help fix the financial problems they faced as the prices of their produce decreased and their shipping, storage, and new equipment costs rose.

14. Because Bryan was a Democrat, many members of the Populist Party joined the Democratic Party to support him, and the Populist Party ended.

15. Commercial hunters shot huge numbers of bison in order to sell their hides. In addition, the bison could not find enough food once they had competition for grazing lands from domesticated livestock, and a long drought was also a factor.

16. Federal forces retaliated and forced the Lakota to give up their land.

17. The U.S. government tried to ban the Ghost Dance because it gave Native Americans hope that they could reclaim their lands, and the government feared that the activity would encourage uprisings.

18. The population counts gathered by the 1890 census indicated that the western frontier was gone.

19. Writers who were local colorists brought to life unique aspects of the West in their dime novels and literature. They used language to vividly describe landscapes, people, and their customs in both dramatic and humorous tales.

HISTORICAL THINKING ANSWERS

20. Possible responses: The government used treaties and the establishment of reservations to try to move Native American people to certain areas of land so that white settlers could develop other areas. The government passed the Dawes Severalty Act to encourage Native Americans to farm plots of land, with the result that white settlers also purchased and settled many of these allotments.

21. The cotton industry survived the boll weevil infestation, but individual farmers, laborers, and communities suffered. Eventually, the infestation caused many farmers and communities to diversify their crops, thus helping to renew their economies.

22. It added greatly to the amount of land that was cultivated for crops—which resulted in massive erosion during the Dust Bowl but also in the creation of the nation's "breadbasket." It opened more areas for people from the East to build homes and start farms but also resulted in the displacement of Native Americans who had lived on the Great Plains for generations.

23. The events in Buffalo Bill's life provided good material for dime novels because Buffalo Bill participated in many exciting events in western history, from the jobs he held and his buffalo hunting to his career as a soldier during the Native American wars.

24. Answers will vary. Possible response: The U.S. government believed that "civilized" white values were the best and would improve the lives of Native Americans while reducing friction between whites and Native Americans and opening up more land for permanent settlement.

25. Possible responses: Both Chief Joseph and Geronimo resisted the relocation of their people. Chief Joseph fought U.S. troops defensively while trying to lead his people to Canada, while Geronimo actively sought battles by leaving his reservation to raid nearby settlements.

INTERPRET VISUALS ANSWERS

26. Answers will vary. Possible response: The picture on the poster shows a landscape of rolling hills with meadows and stands of trees. It is not an accurate depiction: The Great Plains of the 1870s was a region of mostly flat grasslands, without many trees.

27. Answers will vary. Possible response: Sellers might use valid arguments to convince buyers that the sellers can be trusted but also mix in fallacious arguments, such as the claim that essentially the land will pay for itself, to make a potential land purchase hard to resist.

ANALYZE SOURCES ANSWER

28. Jackson characterizes the U.S. government as untrustworthy, unfair, and cruel. By citing specific examples of broken promises that span a century, her historical interpretation seems to be that the government has not and will not change its treatment of Native Americans.

CONNECT TO YOUR LIFE ANSWER

29. Answers will vary, but students should include an opinion statement about what American identity means today. They should support their opinion using concrete examples of events they believe have shaped this identity and details that present and explain the relationships between the events and our modern identity as Americans.

UNIT 5 RESOURCES

UNIT INTRODUCTION

UNIT TIME LINE

UNIT WRAP-UP

NATIONAL GEOGRAPHIC | CONNECTION

National Geographic Magazine Adapted Articles
- "Nature for Everyone"
- "21st Century Cowboys" ONLINE

Unit 5 Inquiry: Produce a Documentary

NG Learning Framework Activities
- Write a Position Statement
- Plan a Protest

Unit 5 Formal Assessment

CHAPTER 15 RESOURCES

Available at NGLSync.Cengage.com

TEACHER RESOURCES & ASSESSMENT

Reading and Note-Taking

Vocabulary Practice

Document-Based Question Template

Social Studies Skills Lessons
- Reading: Identify Problems and Solutions
- Writing: Argument

Formal Assessment
- Chapter 15 Pretest
- Chapter 15 Tests A & B
- Section Quizzes

Chapter 15 Answer Key

ExamView®
  One-time Download

STUDENT DIGITAL RESOURCES

- eEdition
- Handbooks
- Online Atlas
- American Gallery Online
- History Notebook
- Active History
- American Voices (Biographies)
- Reid on the Road video series
- Literature Analysis
- Projects for Inquiry-Based Learning

Chapter 15 Spanish Resources are available at NGLSync.Cengage.com.

AMERICAN STORIES | Working in America

- Study Primary Sources: Quotations from noted labor activists
- On Your Feet: Roundtable

NG Learning Framework:
Create a Union Poster

SECTION 1 RESOURCES

THE GROWTH OF CORPORATIONS

LESSON 1.1
Railroads, Steel, and Oil

- On Your Feet: Question and Answer

NG Learning Framework:
Research Philanthropy

American Voices Biography
John D. Rockefeller and Ida Tarbell ONLINE

LESSON 1.2
CURATING HISTORY
California State Railroad Museum, Sacramento

- On Your Feet: Sort Artifacts

LESSON 1.3
Inventions and New Technologies

AMERICAN **GALLERY** ONLINE The Age of Invention

NG Learning Framework:
Create a Virtual Museum Exhibit

American Voices Biography
George Washington Carver ONLINE

SECTION 2 RESOURCES

THE LABOR MOVEMENT

LESSON 2.1
The State of Workers

- On Your Feet: Tell Me More

NG Learning Framework:
Create a Photo Exhibit

LESSON 2.2
Organizing into Unions

- On Your Feet: Roundtable

NG Learning Framework:
Conduct a Legislative Hearing

LESSON 2.3
Labor Conflicts

- On Your Feet: Fishbowl

NG Learning Framework:
Write Press Releases

SECTION 3 RESOURCES

A WAVE OF IMMIGRATION

LESSON 3.1
Ellis Island and Angel Island

- ▶ Angel Island
- Active History: Map Countries of Origin

NG Learning Framework:
Trace the Americanization Movement

LESSON 3.2
THROUGH THE LENS
Immigration

- On Your Feet: Delve into a Photograph

NG Learning Framework:
Create Immigration Presentations

LESSON 3.3
Difficult Lives in a New Land

- On Your Feet: Think, Pair, Share

NG Learning Framework:
Write an Immigrant Story

LESSON 3.4
AMERICAN VOICES
Jane Addams, 1860–1935

- On Your Feet: Rotating Discussion

NG Learning Framework:
Profile Jane Addams

SECTION 4 RESOURCES

THE GILDED AGE

LESSON 4.1
Growing Urbanization

- On Your Feet: Inside-Outside Circle

NG Learning Framework:
Understand Urban Innovations

LESSON 4.2
Tackling Urban Problems

- On Your Feet: Three-Step Interview

NG Learning Framework:
Be a Reformer

LESSON 4.3
Jim Crow and Segregation

- On Your Feet: Use a Jigsaw Strategy

NG Learning Framework:
Create a Social Media Page

LESSON 4.4
DOCUMENT-BASED QUESTION
Confronting Racial Violence

- On Your Feet: Host a DBQ Roundtable

CHAPTER 15 REVIEW

STRATEGY ❶
TURN TITLES INTO QUESTIONS

To help students set a purpose for reading, have them read the title of each lesson in a section and then turn that title into a question they believe will be answered in the lesson. Students can record their questions and write their own answers, or they can ask each other their questions.

Use with All Lessons *For example, in Section 2, questions from the titles of Lessons 2.1, 2.2, and 2.3 could be "What was life like for factory workers?", "Why did workers join unions?", and "What caused labor conflicts and how were disputes resolved?" respectively.*

STRATEGY ❷
MAKE A TOP FIVE FACTS LIST

Tell students to reread the lesson and review any visuals it contains. Then ask students to write down five facts that they remember from the text. Arrange for students to meet with a partner to compare and consolidate their lists into one final list. Encourage pairs to share their facts lists.

Use with All Lessons *Throughout the chapter, help students get in the habit of making lists of facts as they read.*

STRATEGY ❸
USE A TASKS APPROACH

Help students get information from visuals by using the following TASKS strategy:

T Look for a **title** that may give the main idea.

A **Ask** yourself what the visual is trying to show.

S Determine how **symbols** are used.

K Look for a **key** or legend.

S **Summarize** what you learned.

Use with Lessons 1.1 and 3.1 *Suggest that students use the TASKS strategy to analyze the Railroad Network map in Lesson 1.1 and the Immigrants Arriving in the United States in 1900 graph in Lesson 3.1.*

STRATEGY ❶
USE SUPPORTED READING

To monitor students' comprehension, ask student pairs to read the chapter aloud, lesson by lesson. Instruct them to stop at the end of each lesson and use these sentence frames:

This lesson is mostly about _____.

Other topics in this lesson are _____.

One question I have about the lesson is _____.

One of the vocabulary words is _____.

It means _____.

One word I do not recognize is _____.

I don't think I understand _____.

Use with All Lessons

STRATEGY ❷
PROVIDE TERMS AND NAMES ON AUDIO

Decide which of the terms and names are important for mastery and ask a volunteer to record the pronunciations and a short sentence defining each. Encourage students to listen to the recording as often as necessary.

Use with All Lessons *You might also use the recordings to quiz students on their mastery of the terms. Play one definition at a time from the recording and ask students to identify the term or name described.*

ENGLISH LANGUAGE LEARNERS ELD

STRATEGY 1
USE VISUALS TO PREDICT CONTENT

Direct students at the **Emerging** and **Expanding** levels to read each lesson title and examine the visuals. Then ask them to write a sentence predicting how the visual is related to the lesson. After reading, you may wish to have students verify their predictions and reword their sentences if necessary.

Use with All Lessons *Encourage students at the **Emerging** level to ask questions if they have trouble writing a prediction, for example, about the photos of inventors and their inventions (Lesson 1.3) or the photos of immigrants (Lesson 3.1). Students at the **Bridging** level could help students at the **Emerging** and **Expanding** levels write their predictions.*

STRATEGY 2
SET UP A WORD WALL

To help broaden vocabulary, work with students to choose three words from each section to display in a grouping on a classroom Word Wall. Keep the words displayed throughout the chapter and discuss each one as it comes up during reading. Invite volunteers to add unfamiliar words and phrases as they encounter them in their reading.

Use with All Lessons

STRATEGY 3
BUILD A CONCEPT CLUSTER

To activate prior knowledge and build vocabulary, write a Key Vocabulary word in the center of a Concept Cluster drawn on the board. Invite volunteers to add words, phrases, and pictures to the cluster. Clarify any misunderstandings about the Key Vocabulary word's meaning. Then challenge students to say sentences that make use of the word.

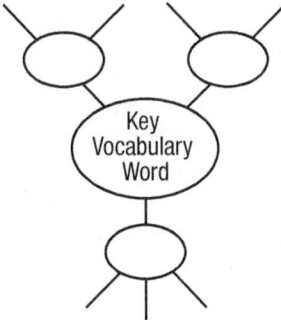

Use with All Lessons

GIFTED & TALENTED

STRATEGY 1
TEACH A CLASS

Before beginning the chapter, allow students to choose one of the lessons listed below and prepare to teach the content to the class. Give them a set amount of time in which to present the lesson. Suggest that they plan ahead for any additional visuals or activities they may want to use as they teach.

Use with Lessons 2.1–2.3 and 3.4

STRATEGY 2
WRITE NEWS REPORTS

Assign students the role of journalists reporting on the violation of African Americans' constitutional rights as granted by the 13th, 14th, and 15th Amendments. Point out that they are reporting within the context of the time and should not overlay their report with present-day values. Remind students that news reports begin with the most important information and answer the questions *Who?, What?, Where?, When?, Why?,* and *How?* Students may post their articles on a class blog or publish them on a class or school website.

Use with Lesson 4.3

Pre-AP

STRATEGY 1
EXTEND KNOWLEDGE

Invite students to do research to find out more about a topic, person, event, or movement introduced in Chapter 6. For example, students might choose to research Social Darwinism, Jane Addams, or the founding of the National Association for the Advancement of Colored People (NAACP). Students may present their findings in an oral report to the class.

Use with All Lessons

STRATEGY 2
ANALYZE EFFECTS

Tell students to work individually or in pairs to research and examine the long-term effects of slavery, which resulted in racism and slavery-like conditions for African Americans in the late 19th and early 20th centuries. Alternatively, assign teams and have each choose one of the following aspects of racism on which to focus:

- social inequality
- economic inequality
- educational inequality

Use with Lessons 4.3 and 4.4

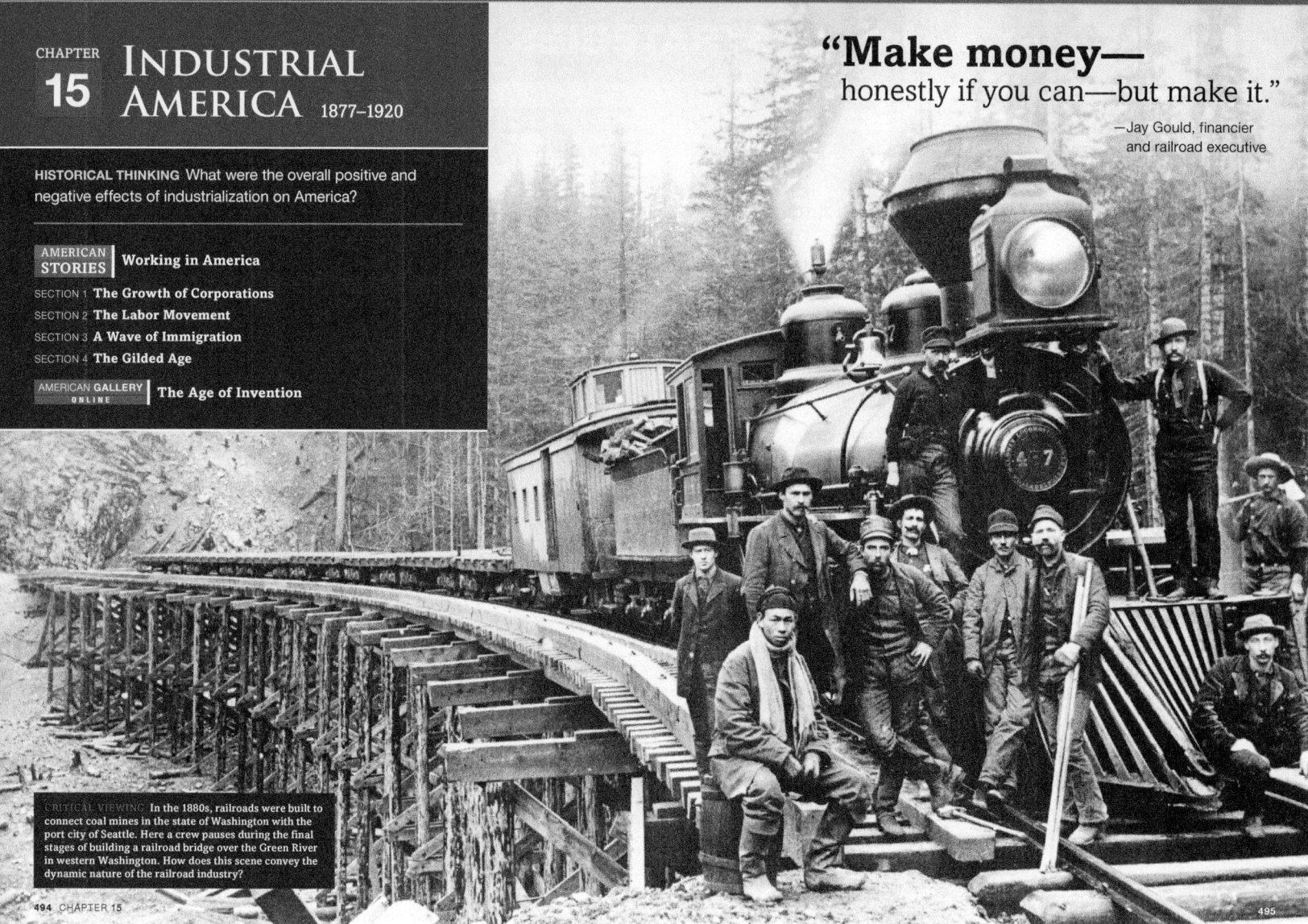

CHAPTER 15
INDUSTRIAL AMERICA 1877–1920

HISTORICAL THINKING What were the overall positive and negative effects of industrialization on America?

AMERICAN STORIES | **Working in America**

SECTION 1 **The Growth of Corporations**

SECTION 2 **The Labor Movement**

SECTION 3 **A Wave of Immigration**

SECTION 4 **The Gilded Age**

AMERICAN GALLERY ONLINE | **The Age of Invention**

"Make money—
honestly if you can—but make it."
—Jay Gould, financier and railroad executive

CRITICAL VIEWING In the 1880s, railroads were built to connect coal mines in the state of Washington with the port city of Seattle. Here a crew pauses during the final stages of building a railroad bridge over the Green River in western Washington. How does this scene convey the dynamic nature of the railroad industry?

495

INTRODUCE THE PHOTOGRAPH

THE RAILROAD

Have students study the photograph and quotation that open this chapter. Direct students to focus on the terrain in the photograph. **ASK:** Based on this photo, how would you describe the work of building the railroads in the western part of the United States? *(Answers will vary. Possible response: Building railroads through mountainous terrain and across rivers was treacherous and dangerous work. The work was physically exhausting and difficult.)* Tell students that in this chapter they will learn about the importance of railroads and the growth of large corporations in the United States in the late 1800s.

SHARE BACKGROUND

This 1885 photograph is of a construction crew standing next to a woodburning balloon-stack locomotive at a crossing of the Green River on the western slope of the Cascade Mountains. Wood-fired locomotives put out a large amount of sparks that often set fire to the surroundings. As a result, a variety of smokestacks were designed to help control the spark emission.

Financier Jay Gould acquired and took control of several railroad lines in the late 1800s. At one point Gould controlled nearly 16,000 miles of track, about 15 percent of the total rail mileage in the United States. However, Gould's acquisitions often came about through manipulative and illegal practices.

CRITICAL VIEWING Answers will vary. Possible response: The photograph shows how railroad workers had to push through physical features such as mountains and rivers to build tracks.

For Chapter 15 Spanish Resources, visit the Resources Menu. Chapter 15 Resources are available at NGLSync.Cengage.com.

HISTORICAL THINKING QUESTION

What were the overall positive and negative effects of industrialization on America?

Jigsaw Activity: Preview Content This activity will help students preview and make predictions about the topics covered in Chapter 15. Divide the class into four groups. Assign one of the section titles to each group and have them discuss what they think they'll learn. Ask students to consider the following clues and questions:

Group 1 Section 1 is about the growth of corporations. **ASK:** What kinds of industries developed in the United States in the late 1800s? What helped the corporations grow during this time?

Group 2 Section 2 is about the labor movement in the United States. **ASK:** What kinds of issues might workers in the new industries face? How might workers deal with the issues?

Group 3 Section 3 is about an increase in immigration to the United States in the late 1800s and early 1900s. **ASK:** What reasons might people have for immigrating to the United States? What issues did immigrants face?

Group 4 Section 4 is about the Gilded Age. **ASK:** Why did more people move from rural to urban areas in the late 1800s? Why might the time between 1870 and 1900 be known as the Gilded Age?

Regroup students so each new grouping has at least one member from each original group. Have students share what they predicted about their assigned section so that other students can learn what to expect from their reading in Chapter 15.

INTRODUCE THE READING STRATEGY

IDENTIFY PROBLEMS AND SOLUTIONS

Explain that identifying problems faced by individuals and nations and tracking their solutions can help students understand the way history unfolds. Turn to the Chapter Review and preview the Problem-and-Solution Chart with students. As they read the chapter, have students analyze several problems and solutions that faced the United States as it continued to industrialize.

KEY DATES FOR CHAPTER 15

1877	Bell Telephone Company founded
1882	Chinese Exclusion Act
1886	Statue of Liberty unveiled
1886	American Federation of Labor founded
1892	Immigration station opens at Ellis Island
1894	Pullman strike
1896	*Plessy* v. *Ferguson*
1905	NAACP founded
1906	Upton Sinclair publishes *The Jungle*
1910	Immigration station opens at Angel Island

INTRODUCE CHAPTER VOCABULARY

KEY VOCABULARY

SECTION 1

Bessemer process	parent company	subsidiary
horizontal integration	phonograph	telegraph
	robber baron	trust
monoculture	Social Darwinism	vertical integration
muckrakers		

SECTION 2

anarchism	laissez-faire economics	socialism
deflation		workers' compensation
Haymarket Riot	scab	

SECTION 3

Americanization	propaganda	tenement
anti-Semitism	push-pull factors	

SECTION 4

department store	referendum	streetcar
grandfather clause	sanitation	suburb
Jim Crow laws	segregation	vaudeville
political machine	"separate but equal"	
progressivism		

DEFINITION CHART

As they read the chapter, encourage students to complete a Definition Chart for Key Vocabulary words. Ask students to list the Key Vocabulary words in the far left column of their charts. Then, as they encounter the words in the chapter, tell them to write the Key Vocabulary word's definition in the center column and then what the word means using their own words in the far right column. Model an example for students on the board using the graphic organizer below.

Word	Definition	In My Own Words
referendum	public vote on an individual issue	a vote by people on a particular issue

OBJECTIVES

- **Discuss the labor movement and growing prosperity during the late 19th and early 20th centuries.**
- **Learn about the labor activists who championed for workers' rights.**
- **Analyze why workers form and support unions.**
- **Identify causes for the decrease in union membership rates over time.**
- **Study primary sources: quotations from noted labor activists.**

CRITICAL THINKING SKILLS FOR "WORKING IN AMERICA"

- Make Connections
- Draw Conclusions
- Identify Problems and Solutions
- Describe
- Synthesize

CONNECT TO THE CHAPTER

This American Story familiarizes students with the development of the labor movement during the late 19th century. As mass production and manufacturing increased in the United States, the labor force—and earnings—increased. Through the study of key activists of the labor movement, quotations, personal testimony, and photographs, students will learn how growing prosperity shaped the American landscape, from the growth of the working class to the birth of workers' unions.

The upcoming chapter, Industrial America, discusses the rapid growth of various industries during the second Industrial Revolution. This American Story will help students better understand how the growth directly affected workers in both positive and negative ways. Introduce the American Story after the class has learned about union organizing in Lesson 2.2.

HISTORY NOTEBOOK

Encourage students to complete the American Story page for Chapter 15 in their History Notebooks as they read.

AMERICAN STORIES | NATIONAL GEOGRAPHIC

WORKING IN AMERICA

496 CHAPTER 15

CRITICAL VIEWING Workers build a truck engine on a General Motors assembly line in Flint, Michigan. What does this photograph reveal about the physical demands of a job like this and the skills a worker might need to have?

During the late 19th century, the nature of labor in the United States changed profoundly. In 1877, the country had 15 million non-domestic workers, with more than half in agriculture and another 4 million in manufacturing. In the decades that followed, the balance would shift as increasing numbers of Americans and new immigrants were attracted to factory work because it paid well. Manufacturing earnings went up about 50 percent between 1860 and 1890, prices of everyday goods fell, and wages increased. Earnings jumped again by 37 percent between 1890 and 1914.

Despite these improvements, working conditions weren't even close to what would be considered safe or even reasonable today. In 1890, the average pay rate for factory work was less than 16 cents per hour. The average workweek was 53 hours, and 2-day weekends were unheard of. In many industries, workers put in 12-hour workdays. At the same time, factory conditions were unsafe and largely unregulated by state or federal governments. At even greater risk than the adult workers—and earning lower wages—were the 1.75 million child laborers who were at work then.

The frustrations of the growing working class provided fertile soil for the seeds of the modern labor movement. Several large unions took up the cause of workers in industries such as steel, the railroads, and mining. Some of those unions no longer exist, but others, such as the American Federation of Labor, are still major forces today. In many ways, labor unions molded the 21st-century workplace. It is to their efforts that we owe reforms such as a 40-hour workweek and the end of child labor in factories and mines.

The story of American labor was shaped by a diverse group of charismatic activists, and it has influenced the lives of millions. This American Story focuses on a few of the many individuals who exemplify the diversity of labor in the United States.

Industrial America **497**

ACTIVE OPTIONS

On Your Feet: Roundtable Divide students into groups of four and allow them time to research one or more union strikes that have been in the news. Ask them to consider the makeup of the union membership and its grievances and how the two relate to the physical characteristics and/or human characteristics of the area. When students' research is done, direct the class to move their desks into a circle and guide a discussion based on the following question: In the strike you researched, how does what the union wants connect to who the members are and where they work and live?

NG Learning Framework: Create a Union Poster

ATTITUDE Empowerment

SKILL Communication

Instruct students to work together in groups of four to create a poster promoting membership in a particular union or organization mentioned in this American Story. Tell students that each poster should include a list of benefits that came with membership and graphic elements they create by hand or using a computer. Ask groups to present their posters to the class when they are finished. Invite constructive criticism from the class about the effectiveness of the posters.

MOTHER JONES

Examine the photo of Mother Jones and the striking textile workers. Emphasize that strikes end quickly if the two sides come to an immediate agreement but that strikes can continue for months if the two sides reach an impasse.
ASK: Why do you think Mother Jones's actions provoked some people to consider her "the most dangerous woman in America"? *(Possible response: The company owners probably saw Mother Jones as a threat because she organized workers. If workers formed unions, then company owners would have to negotiate with union representatives and likely pay higher wages and meet other union demands to avoid a labor strike and lost revenue.)*

MOTHER JONES

Round-faced, with a kindly expression and white hair in a messy bun atop her head, Mary Harris Jones looked like somebody's sweet elderly grandmother, and not the firebrand that she was in reality.

Born in Ireland around 1837, Harris and her family crossed the Atlantic to flee the devastation of the Great Irish Famine. In 1861, she married an American ironworker who was also a union supporter, but he and their children died in a yellow fever outbreak. Jones moved to Chicago and worked as a seamstress until she lost her home in the Great Chicago Fire of 1871. She then became a labor activist, campaigning for unions and workers' rights. In the 1870s, she traveled extensively, giving speeches to striking coal miners, railroad workers, and other laborers. The workers nicknamed her "Mother," a nod to her care for them. In 1905, Mother Jones helped found the Industrial Workers of the World union.

Mother Jones's efforts continued well into retirement age. While in her eighties, she actively supported a mine strike in West Virginia and traveled through Pennsylvania to encourage steel workers to vote in favor of a nationwide strike. She was arrested more than once for her activities but

The first thing is to raise hell. That's always the first thing to do when you're faced with an injustice and you feel powerless. That's what I do in my fight for the working class. —Mother Jones

Mother Jones (center-right) and her army of striking textile workers are shown here descending upon New York City to protest unfair working conditions.

was never deterred. When one judge asked her who had given her a permit to speak on public property, she answered tartly, "Patrick Henry; Thomas Jefferson; John Adams!"

Unsurprisingly, Mother Jones elicited strong and varying reactions from workers, union organizers, factory owners, and government officials. Labor leader Eugene Debs called her the "heroine of a thousand battles." On the other side, one U.S. congressman condemned Mother Jones as a "notorious and troublesome woman" in a speech to the House of Representatives. One attorney for the government is said to have called her "the most dangerous woman in America," a label that is frequently used in biographies and other writings about the colorful activist.

THE JAPANESE-MEXICAN LABOR ASSOCIATION

Some early labor unions were exclusive, refusing to admit African Americans, women, or workers from certain ethnic groups. But others created bonds across ethnic groups as workers united to improve their conditions.

One such mixed union was the Japanese-Mexican Labor Association (JMLA), which was the first labor union formed by members of different racial backgrounds. The JMLA represented workers who had been hired by the Western Agricultural

Contracting Company (WACC), a labor contractor, to work for a beet farming company in Oxnard, California. In February 1903, the JMLA presented a list of grievances to the WACC claiming workers were being paid less than they had been promised, and demanding that workers be allowed to shop in places other than the overpriced company store. When the JMLA went on strike, 90 percent of the laborers in the American beet industry stopped work to support them. Eventually, the WACC agreed to most of the JMLA's demands.

Justice is never given; it is exacted and the struggle must be continuous for freedom is never a final fact, but a continuing evolving process to higher and higher levels of human, social, economic, political, and religious relationship.
—A. Philip Randolph

A. Philip Randolph is considered one of the most important civil rights leaders to emerge from the labor movement.

A. PHILIP RANDOLPH

Asa Philip Randolph was born in Florida in 1889. In 1911, he moved to New York City, where he attended college at night and ran an employment agency. He attempted to organize black workers through his employment agency and later, during World War I, he advocated for more jobs for African Americans in the armed forces.

In 1925, Randolph became the founding president of the Brotherhood of Sleeping Car Porters, the first successful black trade union. At the time, long-distance travel within the United States often meant riding on a passenger train and, perhaps, spending the night in a sleeping car—a specialized railroad car with small bedroom compartments. Nearly all the porters who assisted sleeping-car passengers were African-American men. In 1937, the Brotherhood contracted with the Pullman Company, which manufactured and operated sleeping cars. Randolph's vision, however, extended well beyond any single union—he was determined to improve African Americans' job prospects overall.

In 1941, the American defense industry was rapidly expanding to provide arms and supplies to the country's European allies in World War II. Randolph observed that few African Americans were being hired to fill the new job openings, and the federal government was not taking action. Randolph began to plan a massive protest march on Washington, D.C., warning President Franklin D. Roosevelt that thousands of African-American workers would converge on the city. In response, Roosevelt issued an executive order forbidding defense contractors and the federal government from discriminating against African Americans. After the war, Randolph was instrumental in prompting President Harry S. Truman to eliminate segregation in the armed forces.

In 1955, Randolph became vice president of the American Federation of Labor and Congress of Industrial Organizations (AFL-CIO), where he continued to fight discrimination within the member unions. In 1963, he revived his plan for a giant protest in the country's capital, helping to organize the March on Washington for Jobs and Freedom. On August 28 of that year, around 200,000 people joined to support equal opportunities for African Americans—a goal that motivated A. Philip Randolph for decades.

Industrial America **499**

THE JAPANESE-MEXICAN LABOR ASSOCIATION

Explain to students that Samuel Gompers, the national head of the American Federation of Labor (AFL), had refused to admit the JMLA as an affiliate of the federation unless it omitted Asians from its ranks. The JMLA refused to comply. **ASK:** Why would Japanese and Mexican workers band together instead of aligning themselves in separate unions? *(Possible responses: Since they were both working in the agriculture industry, they likely had the same grievances; a large, unified group gave them more power than two smaller, separate unions.)*

A. PHILIP RANDOLPH

Discuss with students the common use of protests and marches to air grievances and bring about change in society. Mention some examples of causes or movements known for using these methods, such as the woman suffrage movement of the early 19th century or the civil rights movement of the 1960s. Call students' attention to the response A. Philip Randolph received from President Roosevelt when Randolph threatened to organize a protest in Washington, D.C., about the hiring of few African Americans in the rapidly growing defense industry. **ASK:** Why do you think the threat of a protest had such an effective outcome for Randolph? *(Possible responses: President Roosevelt may have wanted to avoid a major protest that could have caused chaos in the capital; Roosevelt may have recognized the inequality in government defense hiring that Randolph had brought to light and decided to act upon it.)* **ASK:** How does the quotation from Randolph relate to the use of protests? *(Possible response: He is making the point that people have to struggle for justice, and protesting is one way of demanding fair treatment on a large scale rather than just waiting for it to happen.)*

Ask students to consider the meaning, implication, and impact of Randolph's threatened protest and to discuss how events could have taken another direction had Roosevelt not issued his executive order.

STUDS TERKEL

Emphasize that Studs Terkel used interviews and firsthand accounts of American workers in his book *Working* rather than merely describing in his own words what motivated them. **ASK:** Why do you think Terkel used this approach? *(Possible response: Terkel might have wanted to hear what many people had to say about their jobs to see whether there were common ideas. Also, stories told by workers themselves can have a more powerful impact than second-hand accounts.)*

MEET LENNY RYBCZYK

Discuss with students different professions that commonly offer union representation. Point out that the text mentions that Lenny and other members of his family belonged to unions representing upholsterers and carpenters. **ASK:** Why do you think Lenny decided to follow his mother and brother's lead and join a union? *(Possible response: He probably saw that they had benefited from their membership in the unions, and he thought it would benefit him as well.)*

WRITE ABOUT HISTORY

Express an Opinion This American Story describes how American workers organized to secure better pay and working conditions for themselves. To help students make connections between the text and their own lives, ask them to write an opinion piece about what guarantees a job should provide to a worker and why. Remind students of the circumstances that initially led to workers forming unions and ask students to consider what Studs Terkel's interviews revealed about workers. Pair students to edit each other's opinion pieces and make suggestions for revision. Provide guidance about the writing process as necessary.

CRITICAL VIEWING Unions protect and look out for the best interests of their members. This makes workers feel like part of a community, and in return they feel loyalty and pride in their membership.

THINK ABOUT IT

Possible responses: Companies might discourage or intimidate employees from forming unions. If few jobs are available, workers might not have the option of taking a union job and take what work they can find. Companies might move union jobs offshore and hire nonunion labor for less. Legislation could affect union membership by making it difficult for unions to operate effectively on behalf of members.

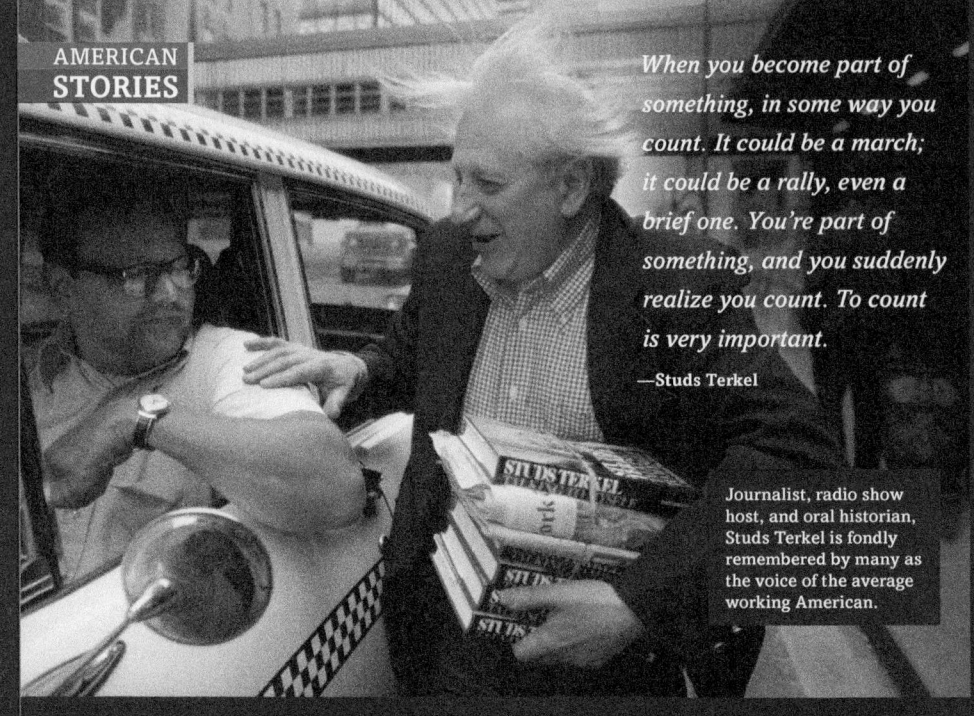

AMERICAN STORIES

When you become part of something, in some way you count. It could be a march; it could be a rally, even a brief one. You're part of something, and you suddenly realize you count. To count is very important.

—Studs Terkel

Journalist, radio show host, and oral historian, Studs Terkel is fondly remembered by many as the voice of the average working American.

STUDS TERKEL

Louis Terkel was born in 1912, but later adopted the name "Studs" after the title character in a trio of books about a fictional youth growing into troubled manhood during the Great Depression.

Unlike the character in the book, Terkel was well educated, earning a law degree from the University of Chicago in 1934. After a varied career that included stints as a radio actor and writer and a period in the Air Force, he began hosting his own radio show in 1944. He found his voice in radio with a program that mixed music and interviews with Americans from all walks of life, both celebrities and everyday workers. Terkel's guests regularly opened up to him, revealing fascinating insights into their experiences, thoughts, and feelings. Of his gentle questioning style, he remarked, "The thing I'm able to do, I guess, is break down walls. If they think you're listening, they'll talk."

Terkel wrote books on many topics, including firsthand accounts of life during the Great Depression and World War II. In 1974, he published *Working*, a collection of interviews with dozens of people about their working lives. In the book, Terkel allowed individuals to tell their own stories. He took a broad view of the definition of labor, speaking with factory workers, farmers, office workers, stay-at-home mothers, business executives, musicians, and athletes, among many others.

One theme that runs through the book is workers' desire to find meaning in their work by taking pride in their jobs and asserting some control over their working conditions. According to Terkel, when that sense of purpose eludes them, they despair. Some of the people Terkel interviewed found meaning and satisfaction even in jobs that were poorly paid and sometimes perceived as menial. For example, waitress Dolores Dante described the highs and lows of her work to Terkel, explaining how she provided a special level of service. "I don't want to change the job," she told him during her interview.

Terkel once interviewed a union organizer who found his purpose in helping auto factory workers. These laborers often struggle to find meaning in their own jobs when they feel they have little or no say in their working conditions. The union organizer explained that workers "don't want to tell the company what to do, but simply have something to say about what *they're* going to do. They just want to be treated with dignity."

500 CHAPTER 15

THE STATE OF THE UNIONS

The nature and power of labor unions have changed somewhat since the days of Mother Jones and A. Philip Randolph. Union density—the proportion of union members in the workforce—peaked in 1955, when it reached nearly 35 percent. Since then, union membership has declined steadily, especially in the private, or nongovernment, sector. Between 1970 and 1984, the number of private-sector union members dropped from 17 million to 11.6 million. By 2016, it dropped to 7.4 million. Public-sector unions representing teachers, police officers, and firefighters have had more success in keeping up their numbers, maintaining a density of around 35 percent between 1980 and 2016.

Various reasons may account for the decline in union membership. Many companies vigorously resisted attempts to unionize their workforces. Some moved the manufacturing of their products to factories in countries with lower labor costs. In the 1980s, the federal government enacted legislation that weakened unions' power. More recently, several state governments have also passed laws that make it harder for unions to organize workers and to bargain collectively for pay and benefits.

With the decline in private-sector unions, the face of union membership has changed. While the term "labor movement" often brings to mind gritty black-and-white images of 1930s factory strikes, a large proportion of 21st-century union members are white-collar workers. In fact, today, there are millions more unionized teachers than unionized truckers.

Nobody can predict with any certainty the future of labor unions in the United States. Some commentators believe the unions' influence will continue to be eroded by powerful corporations, government policies, and market forces such as globalization and the automation of workplaces. Others see hope in new ways of organizing and the increasing diversity of union membership. While the future is uncertain, unions will continue to search for ways to evolve as American workers confront the challenges of the 21st-century workplace.

THINK ABOUT IT

How do forces beyond workers' control affect union membership?

MEET LENNY RYBCZYK

In the present day, millions of workers still belong to unions. Lenny Rybczyk, who retired in 2016 after a 43-year career as a carpet installer, credits his union with his successful and satisfying work life.

Rybczyk has a family history of union membership. His mother belonged to the upholsterer's union in the 1950s and 1960s. His older brother apprenticed with the Chicago Carpenters Local Union 1185 in 1962, working four days a week and attending trade school (with pay) one day a week. When Rybczyk graduated from high school in 1973, he followed in his brother's footsteps,

signing up as an apprentice to learn his trade. Recalling his early years, he says, "The work gave me structure as a young man, confidence, loyalty, equality, camaraderie, and also the ability to work independently with no supervisor."

Looking back on his career, Rybczyk takes pride in his work, which took him to such locations as Chicago's Sears Tower, the tallest building in the world at the time, and Argon National Laboratories, a high-level scientific research facility—in addition to banks, hospitals, and everyday office buildings. Without Local 1185, he believes, the story of his life would have been very different. "I have what I have only because of the union," he explains.

CRITICAL VIEWING Rybczyk takes tremendous pride in his union button collection. Based on what you have read about American laborers, what do you think fuels the intense pride many take in their unions?

Industrial America 501

DIFFERENTIATE

INCLUSION

Predict Using Photos, Captions, and Quotations
Pair special needs students with students at higher proficiency levels. Have them look at each photograph together, taking turns reading captions and quotations. Instruct students to predict what they will learn based on these features.

GIFTED & TALENTED

Interview a Labor Activist Ask pairs to plan and write a brief television interview with Mother Jones, A. Philip Randolph, or Studs Terkel that elicits in-depth answers from the interviewee about labor issues he or she was concerned with. Allow pairs time to research issues important to the chosen interviewee. You may also suggest the interviewer plan to ask the interviewee to what degree their efforts were successful. Students may perform the interview live and/or record it.

See the Chapter Planner for more strategies for differentiation.

HISTORICAL THINKING

Ask and have students answer the following questions.

1. **READING CHECK** How has union membership changed over the years?

2. **DESCRIBE** What characteristics made Mother Jones and A. Philip Randolph effective leaders?

3. **SYNTHESIZE** How do Lenny Rybczyk's statements reflect Studs Terkel's findings about what workers consider important?

ANSWERS

1. Union membership used to be much higher but has declined, especially in the private sector where it lost almost 10 million members between 1970 and 2016. Unionized white-collar workers now outnumber physical laborers, such as factory workers and truckers.

2. Both had perseverance and a keen sense of justice, continuing to fight despite criticism or resistance. They also had the courage to stand up to leaders in government and industry.

3. Studs Terkel found that workers need to take pride in their work and feel like they have some control over their jobs. Lenny Rybczyk affirmed this finding, stating that his job allowed him to work independently and made him feel confident.

MAIN IDEA During the 1870s and 1880s, the United States experienced a second Industrial Revolution distinguished by rapid industrialization and the development of the railroad, steel, and oil industries.

RAILROADS, STEEL, AND OIL

Being able to transport goods and people from coast to coast became a reality in the 1860s with the opening of the transcontinental railroad. This monumental achievement led to an explosion of business and technological innovations.

AN EXPANDING NATION

The invention of the steam engine and the cotton gin in the late 18th century sparked the first Industrial Revolution in the United States. Technological advances and the growth of railroad transportation brought about a second Industrial Revolution in the second half of the 19th century.

With the passage of the Pacific Railway Acts in 1862, two railroad companies began work on the nation's first transcontinental railroad, intent on making it

easier to travel and move goods from the East Coast to the West Coast. The work crews of the Central Pacific, including thousands of Chinese immigrants, built eastward from California, and Union Pacific crews built westward from Nebraska. They blasted tunnels through mountains, constructed bridges over rivers, and laid 1,776 miles of track before connecting the railroad lines in Utah in 1869. The transcontinental railroad enabled overland commerce from coast to coast, accelerating industrialization and affecting every aspect of American society.

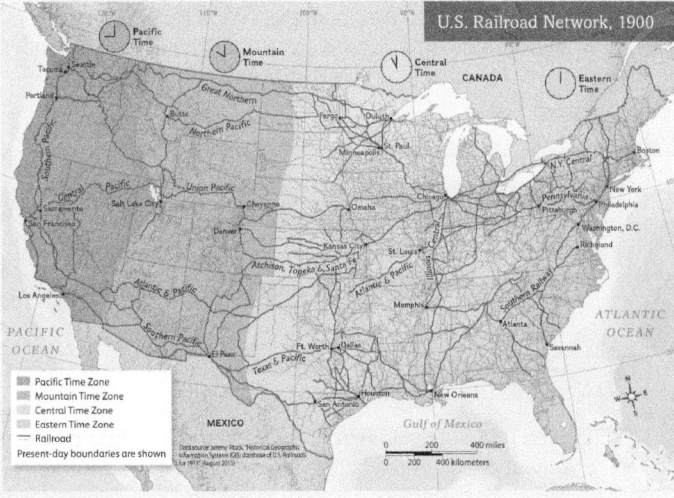

U.S. Railroad Network, 1900

Over the next 25 years, the country added four more transcontinental rail lines, and railroad companies employed tens of thousands of employees. Goods such as coal and industrial machinery moved from one part of the country to another on a nationwide network of railroads. Special railroad cars transported food and livestock. Railroads became the nation's first big business.

CONSOLIDATING POWER

Entrepreneurs, or people who accept risk in starting a business, found that they could pool capital with partners to create security. As workers built the railroads, businessmen built corporations, companies or groups of people that invest in a business and then share its profits. The many investors that make up a corporation provide access to large amounts of capital. Such access is useful, and even necessary, for large industries. Large corporations were able to accumulate cash reserves, enabling them to weather a depression that began in the 1870s, as well as several recessions in the 1880s. As you have read, a depression is a severe and long-term economic decline in which many businesses fail, industrial output is reduced, and unemployment is high. A recession, often part of a normal business cycle, is a shorter-lasting downturn.

While some business owners were largely immune to economic fluctuations, downturns affected workers substantially. As corporations hired more and more people, when the economy faltered, more workers lost their jobs. The perceived economic progress of the late 19th century was repeatedly disrupted by prolonged periods of decline as the country suffered a number of economic recessions during the intense boom-and-bust cycles.

Entrepreneurs generated levels of wealth not imagined before, even in spite of economic ups and downs. People began to question the practices of industry executives and owners. For example, railroad owners **Cornelius Vanderbilt** and **Jay Gould** had reputations for treating competitors ruthlessly. Their behavior earned them the negative description of "**robber barons**," or businessmen who sought to buy out their competitors and who conspired to set prices, enriching themselves, but often violating state laws. Such practices eventually enabled larger railroad companies to consolidate and control even more of the railroad business, forming the nation's first industrial giant.

In response, states set up commissions, or agencies composed of experts, to investigate the railroads' practices and settle issues of rates, finance, and

service. Railroads rejected such oversight, and in the mid-1870s, the Illinois commission was challenged in the Supreme Court case *Munn v. Illinois* by a grain warehouse. The firm argued that it could set its own storage and railroad rates. Regulations that varied from state to state violated its 14th Amendment right to equal protection. But the court upheld the right of a state to regulate private industries that affect public interest and all railroads. In 1887, Congress passed the **Interstate Commerce Act**, establishing a commission to investigate complaints and sue companies that violated its regulations.

CARNEGIE'S EMPIRE

As the railroad industry grew, it created a demand for more steel for railroad tracks and train parts. As a result, the steel industry vastly increased its production between 1877 and 1880 alone. The main technology for steel production was the **Bessemer process**. In this process, workers forced air through molten pig iron to remove impurities. Doing this first made the process of adding carbon to transform the iron into steel cheaper and more efficient.

Andrew Carnegie became the dominant figure in the steel industry. To build his empire, Carnegie adopted the strategy used by Gustavus Swift in the meatpacking industry: **vertical integration**, or the control of all phases of production from start to finish. Carnegie purchased the mines to gather raw materials, bought boats and railroads to transport materials, built and controlled the steel mills, and developed a sales force to sell his products. By employing vertical integration, Carnegie maximized profits by not having to pay outside companies.

In dealing with his competition, Carnegie employed **horizontal integration**, which means he purchased other companies to reduce the number of competitors. Carnegie's use of horizontal integration allowed him to come close to achieving a monopoly on, or exclusive control over, the steel industry.

Carnegie believed the ability to create wealth came naturally for some people because the natural order of society determined that some people would be wealthy while others would be resigned to poverty. His assumption derived from a misapplication of Charles Darwin's theory of evolution, which states, in part, that the fittest animals and plants survive to reproduce and pass on their genes, while the less fit die off. British writer Herbert Spencer applied Darwin's theory to human society in a new philosophy. According to the ideas of **Social Darwinism**, wealthy individuals, who represented the fittest of humans, were destined to survive and succeed.

OBJECTIVE

Learn about the causes and consequences of the second Industrial Revolution.

CRITICAL THINKING SKILLS FOR LESSON 1.1

- Identify Problems and Solutions
- Compare and Contrast
- Form and Support Opinions
- Analyze Cause and Effect
- Interpret Maps
- Make Connections
- Summarize

HISTORICAL THINKING FOR CHAPTER 15

What were the overall positive and negative effects of industrialization on America?

Industrialization led to the growth of big business, but unfair practices hurt competition. Lesson 1.1 discusses the pros and cons of industrialization.

BACKGROUND FOR THE TEACHER

The St. Louis Bridge project provides an early example of Andrew Carnegie's use of vertical integration. In 1867, Carnegie and his partners in the St. Louis Bridge Company won the contract to build a railroad and carriage bridge over the Mississippi River at St. Louis, Missouri. Carnegie's company financed the bridge and supervised construction. The Keystone Bridge Company, of which Carnegie was also a partner, did the actual construction. Keystone, in turn, purchased most of its structural iron and iron supplies from the Union Iron Mills, of which Carnegie was the main owner. In addition, Carnegie earned a commission from selling the bonds he used to finance the bridge. This arrangement meant that Carnegie earned money at every level of construction.

INTRODUCE & ENGAGE

ACTIVATE PRIOR KNOWLEDGE

Point out the title of the lesson. **ASK:** What connections might there be between railroads, steel, and oil? *(Possible response: Railroads are built with steel and need oil to run. In addition, railroads are an important way to transport natural resources and finished products related to steel and oil.)* Tell students that in this lesson they will learn about business practices that gave exclusive control of these resources to a few wealthy individuals.

TEACH

GUIDED DISCUSSION

1. **Analyze Cause and Effect** How did the rise of corporations assist business expansion in spite of economic turbulence in the late 19th century? *(The fact that corporations had multiple investors provided businesses with access to large pools of money for industrial expansion and helped them weather downturns in the economy that hurt workers and smaller businesses.)*

2. **Compare and Contrast** What impacts might horizontal and vertical integration have on consumers? *(Possible response: Horizontal integration lessens competition. This means there would be fewer businesses supplying competing goods or services, thereby limiting consumer choices and driving up prices. Vertical integration maximizes profits for producers, but it could be either positive or negative for consumers, depending on the quality, availability, and pricing of products.)*

3. **Interpret Maps** What evidence on the map supports the idea that railroads linked cities in a network of industry and trade? *(Possible responses: Railroads link the East and West coasts; railroads link cities; port cities are hubs; major industrial and agricultural cities are hubs.)* How would this network affect the spread of goods and ideas? *(Possible response: Goods and ideas could more quickly and easily be exchanged between hubs and cities connected by the railroad network.)*

MORE INFORMATION

Social Darwinism in Popular Culture Once British writer Herbert Spencer applied Charles Darwin's doctrine of "survival of the fittest" to human society, this new philosophy made its way into popular culture. Horatio Alger, a well-known writer of the day, created a series of novels featuring teenage boys who underwent a rags-to-riches transformation based on their ability to work hard and triumph in a competitive world through determination, courage, and honesty. Alger wrote 106 books with titles such as *Paddle Your Own Canoe* and *Brave and Bold*. Although Alger's plots were trite and predictable, his novels were highly popular and had a lasting impact on readers well into the 20th century.

DIFFERENTIATE

ENGLISH LANGUAGE LEARNERS

Determine Point of View Pair students and have them analyze the primary source feature from Ida Tarbell's "History of the Standard Oil Company" that appears in the lesson. Ask partners to consider the following questions as they discuss: How does Tarbell feel about Rockefeller's actions? How can you tell? Provide the following sentence frames to help students at different proficiency levels formulate their responses:

- **Emerging:** Tarbell thinks _____. This is what she writes about it: "_____."

- **Expanding:** Tarbell's viewpoint is _____. She shows this by _____.

- **Bridging:** The words _____ show that Tarbell thinks _____.

PRE-AP

Analyze a Primary Source Invite students to access one of the articles in Ida Tarbell's "History of the Standard Oil Company," which can be found in many online archives. Ask students to read a portion of it and choose an excerpt to analyze in terms of its main idea and purpose. Invite students to share their analyses with the class.

See the Chapter Planner for more strategies for differentiation.

In an 1889 article "The Gospel of Wealth," Carnegie refined his ideas about wealth and Social Darwinism. He acknowledged his belief in a natural division between the wealthy and the poor, but Carnegie also believed that the wealthy were duty-bound to share that wealth with society. His philanthropy, or desire to promote the welfare of others through financial support, set an example for business leaders. Throughout his life, Carnegie donated millions of dollars to many causes, including educational institutions, libraries, and theaters. Between 1883 and 1929 he funded 2,509 libraries worldwide, 1,689 of them in the United States.

OIL TYCOON

In 1859, oil prospectors struck the first American oil near Titusville, Pennsylvania. The rise of the railroad and steel industries made oil more readily available nationwide. Railroads transported oil long distances, and the steel industry provided a strong material for constructing pipelines, drilling equipment, and tanks. Initially, oil's main purpose was to fuel lamps, but soon oil became necessary to lubricate the machinery that ran American industries. In the early 1900s, oil was an essential part of the new automobile industry and would later provide heat and electric power to the country as well.

Another successful and powerful business leader who shaped American industry was the oil tycoon, **John D. Rockefeller**. Rockefeller built his first oil refinery in Ohio in 1863 to convert crude, or raw, unprocessed oil into specialized oil products. Just a few years later, in 1870, he founded the **Standard Oil Company**. Rockefeller used tactics such as price-cutting to lure customers to his company. Like Carnegie, he also employed horizontal integration, taking over most of his competitors to ensure his company's dominance in the market.

Within a decade, Rockefeller controlled about 90 percent of the country's oil-refining capacity. But he had done so by engaging in secret deals to get railroad companies to charge him less than other producers for transportation costs. Regulators put a stop to that, so in 1881, he reestablished his corporation as a **trust**, or a company managed by members of a board rather than by owners or stockholders. These board members are called trustees. Unlike those who oversee the management of a company, trustees are not investors with a stake in profits. The switch allowed Rockefeller, through his trustees, to buy controlling amounts of stock in other oil companies, and to do so across various states.

Rockefeller's questionable business tactics did not go unnoticed by state and federal government or by the general public. Beginning in 1902, journalist **Ida Tarbell** wrote a series of articles called "The History of the Standard Oil Company" for *McClure's Magazine*. Tarbell's father had worked in the oil industry in Pennsylvania, and she learned firsthand the effects of Rockefeller's strategies. For example, the secret rebates Rockefeller had arranged with the railroad companies made the costs of transporting oil prohibitively high for independent producers like Tarbell's father, but generously low for Standard Oil. As a result, Tarbell's well-to-do family was soon living in poverty. Tarbell spent nearly two years researching Standard Oil before writing her articles exposing Rockefeller's unethical practices. Her reporting had a profound influence on the public's opinion of corporations and trusts in general. In fact, Tarbell and other investigative reporters became known as **muckrakers**, or journalists who expose misconduct by an organization or a person.

Still, despite Rockefeller's suspicious business strategies, he, like Carnegie, contributed enormous sums of money to philanthropic organizations, such as educational institutions and medical facilities. Additionally, in 1913 he established the Rockefeller Foundation, which for more than 100 years has

PRIMARY SOURCE

In the excerpt below, journalist Ida Tarbell evaluates John D. Rockefeller's takeover of oil producers in and around Cleveland, Ohio, by fixing transportation costs.

Mr. Rockefeller's capture of the Cleveland refineries in 1872 was as dazzling an achievement as it was a hateful one. The campaign . . . viewed simply as a piece of brigandage [piracy], was admirable. The man saw what was necessary to his purpose and he never hesitated before it. His courage was steady—and his faith in his ideas unwavering. He simply knew what was the thing to do, and he went ahead with the serenity of the man who knows.

—from "The History of the Standard Oil Company," by Ida Tarbell, in *McClure's Magazine*, 1903

supported research and initiatives to improve the well-being of people and the planet.

The second Industrial Revolution profoundly changed Americans' relationships with work, transportation, and communication. As in the first Industrial Revolution, the development of new materials and new processes upended the roles of labor and attracted more people to jobs in cities. However, the second Industrial Revolution was characterized by government's increased role in social and business affairs. Ownership in company stocks became more common, unlike during the first Industrial Revolution. The trend toward groundbreaking inventions and the growth of big business continued throughout the late 19th century, ushering in the modern United States and a new American identity.

HISTORICAL THINKING

1. **READING CHECK** What strategies did leaders of different industries use to maximize profits and reduce competition?

2. **IDENTIFY PROBLEMS AND SOLUTIONS** What solution did the states and Congress create to investigate concerns about the railroad industry's practices?

3. **COMPARE AND CONTRAST** In what ways are vertical integration and horizontal integration similar and different?

4. **FORM AND SUPPORT OPINIONS** Do you think Ida Tarbell is biased in her assessment of John D. Rockefeller's practices in her articles? Use evidence from the text to support your opinion.

AMERICAN PLACES
Carnegie Hall, New York City

Andrew Carnegie donated 90 percent of his wealth to worthy organizations and causes. He also supported educational institutions and promoted American arts and culture. One of his most long-lasting contributions is Carnegie Hall, which opened in New York City in 1891 as the "Music Hall." The first performances in the hall featured Peter Tchaikovsky, the Russian composer, conducting his own works.

BUILD BACKGROUND

STANDARD OIL

The Standard Oil Trust was the brainchild of Standard Oil attorney Samuel C. T. Dodd. The structure was designed as a way to get around regulations in several states that prohibited one corporation from owning stock in another corporation. Individual companies turned over their stock to the trust in exchange for trust certificates, which entitled the certificate holders to shares in the profits of the entire group of companies. The trust's nine trustees, one of whom was John D. Rockefeller, held control over the actions of the companies in the trust, which eventually numbered nearly 40. For a while, the trust enabled Rockefeller to hide the size of Standard Oil's business holdings and the fact that the different companies were working together to control nearly all oil refining, pricing, and distribution in the United States. However, in 1892, the Ohio Supreme Court ruled that Standard Oil Trust was an illegal monopoly. In response, Rockefeller disbanded the trust but kept control of the individual companies by establishing overlapping boards of directors. He then converted Standard Oil of New Jersey into a holding company that owned majority shares in the former trust companies. This action was made possible by the New Jersey Holding Company Act, which allowed corporations to hold stock in other corporations in other states.

GUIDED DISCUSSION

4. **Make Connections** How did Andrew Carnegie's belief in Social Darwinism color his views toward business and philanthropy? *(Possible response: Carnegie accepted the Social Darwinist view that some people were destined by the natural order to be wealthy and succeed while others were destined to be poor. Carnegie's acceptance of this perspective possibly led him to feel justified in using monopolistic business practices. But Carnegie also came to believe that the wealthy were duty-bound to help the poor by sharing their wealth.)*

5. **Summarize** Why was oil an essential part of industrial expansion during the late 19th and early 20th centuries? *(Possible response: In addition to providing kerosene for lamps, oil was needed to lubricate machinery. Oil was also essential in the automobile industry and later in heating and generating electric power.)*

AMERICAN PLACES

The plan for Carnegie Hall was hatched while Andrew Carnegie and his new bride, Louise Whitfield Carnegie, were sailing to Scotland for their honeymoon in 1887. The couple struck up a friendship with shipmate Walter Damrosch, who was the musical director of the Symphony Society of New York and the Oratorio Society of New York. The young conductor was anxious to develop a new concert hall where his orchestra would have enough room to play. Carnegie agreed to fund the project and chose a site near Central Park. Louise Carnegie laid the cornerstone for the building on May 13, 1890. Carnegie Hall escaped demolition in the 20th century when New York City purchased the building and established it as a public trust.

ACTIVE OPTIONS

On Your Feet: Question and Answer Tell half the class to write True-False questions about the lesson's information on big business in the late 19th century. Tell the other half to create answer cards, with "True" written on one side and "False" on the other. Ask each question-writing student to read his or her question aloud. Instruct students in the second group to display their answer to the question. When discrepancies occur, the answering students should review the question and discuss which answer is correct, supporting their answers with evidence from the lesson, until they reach consensus. After all questions are answered, if time permits, have groups reverse roles.

NG Learning Framework: Research Philanthropy

ATTITUDE Curiosity

SKILLS Collaboration; Communication

Assign groups of students to learn more about the philanthropic efforts of Andrew Carnegie and John D. Rockefeller. Instruct groups to select a specific area of philanthropic interest, such as Carnegie's focus on public educational institutions and libraries or Rockefeller's interest in research and initiatives to improve the well-being of people and the planet. Then have each group use its research to create a profile of Carnegie or Rockefeller that juxtaposes his business and philanthropic practices. Encourage students to evaluate the men's actions from the context of their historical era rather than in terms of present-day norms and values. Invite groups to share their profiles with the class.

ANSWERS

1. Industrial leaders used vertical integration, the pooling of capital, and price setting to maximize profits, and they used horizontal integration and underhanded tactics to reduce competition.

2. States set up commissions to investigate and regulate the railroads' practices. Congress passed the Interstate Commerce Act, which established a commission to investigate and regulate business practices and sue violators.

3. Vertical and horizontal integration are similar in that both strategies attempt to maximize profits. They are different in their tactics. Vertical integration maximizes profits by controlling all phases of production. Horizontal integration maximizes profits by limiting competition.

4. Possible response: Tarbell's assessment is probably fair, even though she might have been influenced by her father's experiences in the oil industry. She spent almost two years researching the company before writing her articles. In addition, for a long time before Tarbell wrote her articles, Rockefeller had been engaged in questionable business tactics, such as price-cutting, making secret deals with railroads, and using horizontal integration and trusts to crush his competition.

CALIFORNIA STATE RAILROAD MUSEUM, SACRAMENTO

Home to 225,000 square feet of exhibits, restored railroad cars, and iconic engines, this museum brings railroad history in California and the West to life. One exhibit features early communication methods—the bells, whistles, flags, lanterns, and lights used by railroads before modern electronic communication methods existed. Another tells the story of Abraham Lincoln and his steadfast support of the railroad, highlighting the construction of the world's first transcontinental railroad, the Union Pacific Railroad, which has carried America through natural disasters, wars, and a changing transportation industry. There's even a train simulator for museum visitors who want to "pilot" a high-speed train.

Southern Pacific Motor Car

Completed in 1908 and retired in 1920, the Southern Pacific Railroad's McKeen Motor Car Number 9 operated along the railway's Sacramento Valley Lines. McKeen Motor Cars were the first steel self-propelled train cars in the world, and the first example of aerodynamic design in North America. This postcard, dated 1915, demonstrates the comfort of traveling via motor car.

Steam Locomotive

Built in New Jersey in 1863, this small steam-powered locomotive traveled on a ship called the *Mary Robinson*, which departed from New York, sailed around Cape Horn, and arrived in San Francisco in March 1864. The Central Pacific Railroad would have preferred to purchase a larger engine, but because of the Civil War, only smaller engines were available.

Why would the Civil War have impacted the availability of train engines? Do research to find the answer.

Railroad Time Schedule

Railroad companies proposed dividing North America into four time zones as a way to make rail transportation more efficient. Before the implementation of time zones in 1883, most towns in the United States kept their own local time based on the movement of the sun. As railroads made it easier and faster to move between cities, the fact that each city had its own local time made it impossible to track and set arrival and departure times. Major railroad companies collaborated on a plan to divide the country into four time zones, which greatly helped regulate their train schedules.

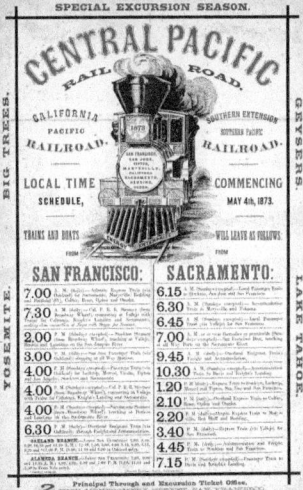

How might this 1873 schedule for the Central Pacific Railroad, which was based on local times, have contributed to confusion?

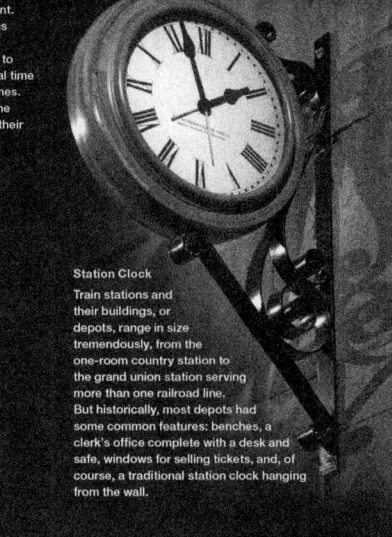

Station Clock

Train stations and their buildings, or depots, range in size tremendously, from the one-room country station to the grand union station serving more than one railroad line. But historically, most depots had some common features: benches, a clerk's office complete with a desk and safe, windows for selling tickets, and, of course, a traditional station clock hanging from the wall.

A Car Load of California Peaches.

Moving Fresh Foods

By combining images, photographers and artists around the turn of the century created humorous scenes boasting of a region's agricultural capabilities. In this exaggeration or tall-tale postcard, a Southern Pacific flat car is loaded with six enormous California peaches. Since the late 1890s, real peaches have been shipped worldwide in refrigerated railcars and containers.

506 CHAPTER 15

Industrial America 507

PLAN: 2-PAGE LESSON

OBJECTIVE

Identify artifacts related to railroad transportation in the late 1800s and early 1900s.

CRITICAL THINKING SKILLS FOR LESSON 1.2

- Analyze Visuals
- Make Connections
- Make Inferences

HISTORICAL THINKING FOR CHAPTER 15

What were the overall positive and negative effects of industrialization on America? Industrialization increased the need to move people, goods, and resources coast to coast. Railroads provided solutions as well as new challenges. Lesson 1.2 looks at the early days of railroad transportation through exhibited items at a California railroad museum.

BACKGROUND FOR THE TEACHER

The California State Railroad Museum complex, which opened to the public in 1976, is located in the Old Sacramento Historic District of the state's capital. The museum is home to 19 steam locomotives built between 1862 and 1944, ranging in size from the small Southern Pacific Number 1 pictured in the lesson to the giant Southern Pacific Number 4294, built in 1901 and weighing in at a million pounds. The museum's rolling stock includes a variety of cabooses, freight cars, and passenger cars built between 1874 and 1950. The museum is also home to a library and archive that supports its railroad conservation and education efforts. Included in the library are documentary materials that describe the locomotives, rolling stock, and other artifacts included in the museum's collections.

HISTORY NOTEBOOK

Encourage students to complete the Curating History page for Chapter 15 in their History Notebooks as they read.

INTRODUCE & ENGAGE

PREVIEW WITH VISUALS

Instruct students to begin by examining the artifacts in the lesson without reading the captions. **ASK:** What do these objects suggest about railroad transportation in the late 1800s and early 1900s? *(Answers will vary. Possible responses: Train companies cared about design as well as function; trains ran on regular schedules; equipment varied by use.)* List students' ideas on the board, highlighting any ideas that suggest a link between railroads and industrialization or new technologies. Tell students that in this lesson they will explore railroad transportation by examining railroad artifacts.

TEACH

GUIDED DISCUSSION

1. **Make Inferences** Why was the Southern Pacific Railroad's McKeen motor car a significant step in railroad transportation history? *(Possible response: It was the first steel self-propelled train car in the world and the first aerodynamic design in the United States.)*

2. **Make Connections** Why might turn-of-the-century postcards that promoted California have often highlighted trains? *(Answers will vary. Possible response: Trains were becoming a vital part of American life at the turn of the century. They were important for transporting people to, from, and within California and for carrying California's goods and natural resources to other parts of the country.)*

CURATING HISTORY

The California State Railroad Museum website is a useful resource for learning about the history of railroads in California and the West. Access the website and guide students to the Exhibits section. Under Locomotives in that section, direct them to the description of the locomotive shown in the lesson: the Southern Pacific Railroad Number 1, also called the C.P Huntington. As a class, find the answers to the following questions: Who built the locomotive? *(Danforth, Cooke & Company)* How was the locomotive used when it was in service? *(It was used for construction of the transcontinental railroad, pulling passenger trains, pulling maintenance and construction trains, and clearing tracks.)* Encourage students to explore on their own other locomotives, rolling stock, and exhibits on the website and to share their observations with the class.

ACTIVE OPTIONS

On Your Feet: Sort Artifacts Ask students to work in teams of four to complete two Concept Clusters using the museum's online collection. In one cluster, students should sort the collection of locomotives by a defining characteristic, such as gauge, size, or design. In the other cluster, students should sort the collection of rolling stock by function. When teams are finished, have them share and discuss their Concept Clusters with the class.

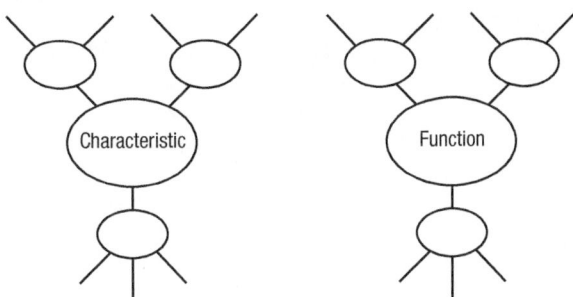

DIFFERENTIATE

ENGLISH LANGUAGE LEARNERS ELD

Explore the 5 Ws Remind students of the questions reporters use to guide their reporting: *Who? What? Where? When?* and *Why?* Pair students at the **Emerging** level with English-proficient students. Tell them to take turns asking and answering questions about each of the photos and captions using these question words. Suggest that English-proficient students help their partners understand the meaning of any new vocabulary words as they pose and answer questions.

PRE-AP

Compare Historical and Current Rail Uses Explain that railroads and the freight they move remain important to Americans today. After students read the lesson, ask them to research what goods were moved by rail through their town or state in the late 19th century and what goods are moved through their area by rail today. Students may also compare passenger rail use then and now. Encourage students to share what they learn with the rest of the class.

See the Chapter Planner for more strategies for differentiation.

STEAM LOCOMOTIVE

Many locomotives were needed to pull supply and troop trains during the Civil War. The need to supply the war effort would have meant that fewer construction materials and finished locomotives were available for nonmilitary use.

RAILROAD TIME SCHEDULE

Because Sacramento and San Francisco set their own local times, travelers from one or the other city would likely have their watches set to the city in which they originated, making it difficult to use the schedule effectively.

MAIN IDEA In the late 1800s, Americans invented new devices and technologies that changed everyday life in dramatic ways and stimulated even more economic and industrial growth.

INVENTIONS AND NEW TECHNOLOGIES

Without even realizing it, you have been experimenting with and inventing things since you were young. During the late 19th century, men and women of varied backgrounds also experimented—and they created transformative technologies.

BELL'S TELEPHONE

The growth of the railroad, steel, and oil industries changed American life, but their rise was not the only economic development to transform the United States. At the same time, inventors were developing technologies and creating devices that would have profound impacts on daily life.

During the 19th century, people relied on the **telegraph**, a machine that transmitted messages along connected wires, to communicate over long distances. An operator tapped out the electric signals for a word with the telegraph key. The key completed an electric circuit and sent the message to a receiver at the other end, where the message could be transcribed or printed. In the 1870s, **Alexander Graham Bell**, a Scottish scientist, began to experiment with sending multiple messages at the same time. While trying out ways to subdivide a telegraph wire into many channels, Bell began transmitting musical tones over the telegraph. Ultimately, he hoped to transmit people's voices.

Bell devised a simple machine from which sounds were carried over wires—the first telephone. In February 1876, Bell filed a request for a patent, or a license that would give him the sole right to make and sell his new invention. He was just in time. Bell had submitted his patent request just two hours before another inventor

Surrounded by curious onlookers, Alexander Graham Bell speaks into his new invention. By the time the first telephone connection opened between Chicago and New York City in 1892, 950 miles of copper wire had been strung between the two cities to make telephone communication possible. Bell became president of the National Geographic Society in 1898. Under his leadership, photography became a central feature of the Society's magazine, *National Geographic*.

presented his own plans for a similar device. A few weeks later, the U.S. Patent and Trademark Office awarded Bell his patent. Within a week, Bell spoke the first words ever heard on a telephone, saying to his assistant: "Mr. Watson—come here—I want to see you."

Later that year, Bell demonstrated his invention at the Centennial Exposition in Philadelphia, and in 1877, he and two partners formed the Bell Telephone Company. In 1885, Bell created the American Telephone and Telegraph Company as a wholly owned **subsidiary**, or secondary business, of American Bell. The original purpose of American Telephone and Telegraph was to build and operate long-distance telephone lines, but its role expanded, and it eventually became the **parent company**, or controlling company, of the Bell System. The company, also known as AT&T, still exists today.

THE WIZARD OF ELECTRICITY

Not long after the debut of the telephone, another inventor unveiled one of the most important advancements of the 19th century. In 1880, **Thomas Edison** patented his most famous work: a practical electric light bulb. Just three years later, Edison put this invention to work by establishing the first electrical system in New York City. Within a year, 500 customers in the city had electric lights.

Although Edison's first career was as a telegraph operator, by the time he was in his 20s, he was an active inventor who had already patented some of his almost 1,100 inventions. His range of patents included both entirely new devices and improvements to existing ones, such as an efficient electrical generator, a motion picture projector, and an electric pen.

In 1876, Edison established an industrial research laboratory—the first of its kind—to work on his inventions. The lab, located in Menlo Park, New Jersey, became the site of many future discoveries. While there, Edison invented the **phonograph**, or record player, in 1877. The Menlo Park lab was also the site of Edison's experiments with electric lighting.

Edison's light bulbs relied on a direct electric current, which initially caused some problems. When the current traveled long distances, the amount of usable electric power decreased. A former colleague of Edison's, an immigrant named **Nikola Tesla**, developed a system for delivering electric power using an alternating current. Alternating current, or AC, electric power could travel longer distances

than the direct current, or DC, power Edison and his team developed. Tesla sold his patent to industrialist **George Westinghouse**, who quickly embraced and marketed Tesla's new and improved method.

In 1886, Edison built a second research lab in West Orange, New Jersey, known as the Edison Laboratory. At this lab, Edison and his workers invented a motion picture camera and built the first motion-picture stage, launching the silent-film industry. They also improved his phonograph and developed an alkaline storage battery. For the wealth of contributions he made to technology, Edison became known as the "Wizard of Menlo Park."

A WAVE OF INVENTIONS

Although Bell and Edison undoubtedly produced some of the most important inventions of the late 19th century, many other inventors also introduced life-changing technologies. Products such as the cash register, the typewriter, and the linotype, which the newspaper industry used to set type, helped improve efficiency in the workplace. The Kodak Company's portable camera allowed anyone to become a photographer.

George Washington Carver was among the many African-American innovators who emerged during the late 19th century. Carver served as the head of the agriculture department at the Tuskegee Institute in Alabama, where he encouraged crop diversification in the South to address a major problem: soil quality. Because of decades of **monoculture**, or the practice of growing only one crop, the quality of soil in the South had diminished. Carver experimented with solutions by asking southern farmers to grow a variety of crops, such as peanuts and sweet potatoes. The problem was, however, that these crops didn't generate enough market demand. So Carver began developing new products derived from these crops, such as oils, flour, soap, and cosmetics. Peanuts eventually became one of the South's biggest cash crops.

Another African-American innovator was **Lewis Latimer**, who drew the blueprints for Alexander Graham Bell's telephone patent and also worked in the field of electric lighting. Latimer was a mechanical draftsman for the U.S. Electric Lighting Company, and in 1882, he invented an improved process for manufacturing the carbon filaments inside lamps. Latimer then went to work for Edison, first as an engineer and then as an inventor—the only African-American member of Edison's team.

PLAN: 4-PAGE LESSON

OBJECTIVE

Analyze how inventions and new technologies improved life and work for Americans and led to economic growth in the late 1800s.

CRITICAL THINKING SKILLS FOR LESSON 1.3

- Make Inferences
- Identify Problems and Solutions
- Analyze Cause and Effect
- Summarize
- Draw Conclusions
- Analyze Primary Sources

HISTORICAL THINKING FOR CHAPTER 15

What were the overall positive and negative effects of industrialization on America?
Inventions such as the telephone and electric lights changed the way many Americans lived and worked. Lesson 1.3 explores some of the major inventors, inventions, and technological innovations of the late 1800s.

BACKGROUND FOR THE TEACHER

Thomas Edison waged a very public battle against George Westinghouse for control of the electric power market. Heavily invested in direct current (DC) and convinced that alternating current (AC) was dangerous, Edison and his associates launched lawsuits, publicity stunts, and newspaper attacks against Westinghouse. Edison had much to lose; Westinghouse's use of AC meant that he could bring electricity to rural areas, something that DC systems could not do efficiently or cost effectively. Cost and efficiency were highlighted when the DC-powered General Electric Company, which had taken over Edison's company, competed against the Westinghouse Corporation to supply electricity to the 1893 World's Columbian Exposition. Westinghouse undercut GE's bid by about half and won the contract, primarily because the GE system required so much copper wire. GE soon converted to AC.

HISTORY NOTEBOOK

Encourage students to complete the American Gallery and Inventions and New Technologies pages for Chapter 15 in their History Notebooks as they read.

INTRODUCE & ENGAGE

CREATE A TOP 10 TECH LIST

Direct students to make a Top 10 list of their favorite recent technological inventions. Ask them to describe how each invention meets their needs and how their lives might be different without the invention. Invite volunteers to share inventions from their lists and discuss their reasons for including them. Explain that this lesson explores how inventions and new technologies transformed people's lives and accelerated economic and industrial growth in the late 1800s.

TEACH

GUIDED DISCUSSION

1. **Make Inferences** Why was Nikola Tesla's use of alternating current significant to the spread of electric lighting? *(Edison relied on direct current, which could only travel short distances without losing power. This meant that a DC-powered electrical system could only serve a small geographic area. Tesla's alternating current allowed electricity to travel greater distances without losing power, thereby expanding the service area and allowing people beyond the geographically concentrated cities to use electric lights.)*

2. **Identify Problems and Solutions** What obstacle did George Washington Carver face in trying to solve the South's soil problem, and how did he get around that obstacle? *(Peanuts, potatoes, and other crops that Carver asked southern farmers to grow to improve soil quality did not generate enough market demand to make the farmers turn a profit. To increase market demand, Carver developed new products made from the crops.)*

MORE INFORMATION

Inventing the Telephone Alexander Graham Bell was not the only inventor experimenting with transmitting musical tones over the telegraph. Elisha Gray was also working on a "harmonic telegraph," which led him—like Bell—to the idea of the telephone. Because Gray submitted his papers later than Bell, and because Gray's papers were merely a statement of his intent to file for a patent later, Bell seemed the clear winner. Controversy arose, however, when it turned out that the device outlined in Bell's patent would not actually work as described. On the other hand, Gray's design would have worked. Bell's final design included features similar to Gray's design, which led the two inventors to years of court battles. Bell eventually won the legal disputes, but debates continued among historians over who should actually get credit for inventing the telephone. **ASK:** What evidence might historians use to inform their debate over this issue? *(Possible responses: the timing of the filings; the content of the papers that were filed; the discrepancy between the filed papers and the finished design; court rulings)*

DIFFERENTIATE

STRIVING READERS

Chart Inventors Assign students to create a multiple-column inventors' chart. Each time they encounter a new inventor in the lesson, they should write the name at the top of one of the columns and add a brief description of the invention below the name. At the end of the lesson, ask students to compare their charts.

Alexander Graham Bell		
invented the telephone		

GIFTED & TALENTED

Write a Script Direct student pairs to write a brief script based on the battle between Thomas Edison and George Westinghouse over control of the electric power market. Share with them the information provided in Background for the Teacher and suggest that they do further research as necessary to locate additional details about the dispute. Encourage pairs to perform their finished scripts with appropriate vocal and facial expressions.

See the Chapter Planner for more strategies for differentiation.

African-American inventor and electrical engineer **Granville T. Woods** left elementary school at the age of 10, yet went on to develop many important patents related to the field of transportation. One of his inventions was a telegraph system that enabled the transmission of messages between moving trains and train depots. Another was a safety feature that helped people avoid injury from accidental contact with electrical wires by running them above streetcars. Woods and his brother Lyates also received patents for emergency braking systems. In total, Woods patented more than 45 inventions during his lifetime, and he sold the rights to many of them to large companies.

Elijah McCoy was born in Canada to a family who had escaped slavery in Kentucky on the Underground Railroad. After studying mechanical engineering in Scotland, he returned to the United States and worked for the Michigan Central Railroad. Like Woods, McCoy also invented an important product related to transportation. Over the course of two years, McCoy experimented with a device to lubricate railroad engines automatically. In 1872, he patented the "lubricating cup," which continuously oiled a steam engine's gears.

During the late 1800s, enterprising women were also carving out a place as inventors, developing new labor-saving devices and safety-inspired products. **Margaret Knight** received patents for a variety of machines and products relating to both industry and the home. Some of Knight's patents were for shoe-manufacturing devices and rotary engines, while others related to sewing machines and clothing. By the time she died in 1914, Knight held a total of at least 27 patents for her inventions.

In 1886, **Josephine Garis Cochrane** patented the first commercially successful dishwasher. The daughter of a civil engineer and granddaughter of an inventor, Cochrane was also someone who entertained often. She set out to find a way to wash dishes quickly and safely. In 1886, Cochrane patented her dishwasher design and began building them for friends. She displayed her invention at the 1893 World's Columbian Exposition and later formed a company to sell the product, although the dishwasher did not become popular in American homes until the 1950s.

The number and variety of inventions developed during the late 19th century helped create factory and office jobs, and the country's workforce grew as a result. These innovations also enabled greater efficiency and constructive improvements in work, which led to greater economic gains and better working conditions for some, although not for all. The country's desire for inventions may have been motivated by practical considerations, but it also provided opportunities for resourceful and creative women and African Americans.

HISTORICAL THINKING

1. **READING CHECK** What contributions did Alexander Graham Bell and Thomas Edison make to American innovation in the late 19th century?

2. **MAKE INFERENCES** Why do you think the inventions of the women mentioned were oriented toward safety and efficiency?

3. **IDENTIFY PROBLEMS AND SOLUTIONS** What problem was George Washington Carver hoping to solve by diversifying crops in the South?

4. **ANALYZE CAUSE AND EFFECT** What factors contributed to the invention and innovation that occurred during the 19th century?

TWO PATHBREAKING INNOVATORS

Innovators and inventors throughout history share a common skill: problem-solving. George Washington Carver lived in the South and witnessed the effects of monoculture on southern farmers, so he innovated ways to improve soil nutrition. Margaret Knight was frustrated by slow and inefficient production in the factory where she worked, so she improved the process by inventing a machine.

GEORGE WASHINGTON CARVER

As an agricultural chemist, George Washington Carver spent a lot of time experimenting in his lab, as he is doing in the photo above. Carver's ideas about replenishing soil nutrients and growing more varied crops helped southern farmers, both in their harvests and their nutrition. His reputation earned him many invitations to work in other labs, but he declined, preferring to stay at Tuskegee.

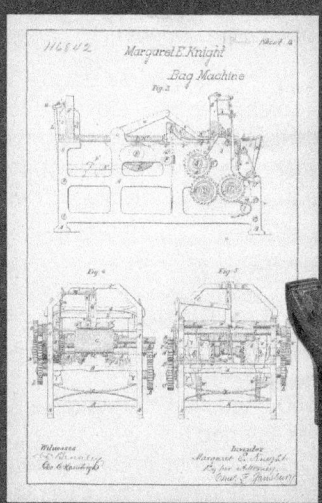

MARGARET KNIGHT

In 1870, Margaret Knight invented a machine that produced flat-bottomed paper bags by cutting, folding, and gluing paper together. In 1871, she submitted the drawing at the left with her patent application. Knight built her first paper-bag machine from wood and brass, and it produced more than 1,000 bags. It also served as the prototype, or example, for a stronger machine made with iron, which was used in mass production.

BUILD BACKGROUND

MARGARET KNIGHT

Like many young girls in New England, Margaret Knight went to work in a textile factory to help support her family. While working at the factory, she witnessed the injury of a fellow worker when a shuttle flew off a mechanical loom. Knight, only 12 years old at the time, invented a device to prevent similar accidents. The invention became popular, but neither Knight nor her family had the insight or means to patent the device. By the time Knight went to work for the Columbia Bag Company, where she invented her flat-bottom paper bag machine, she had learned more. Still, she almost did not get her patent. When she took her wooden prototype to a machinist to have it cast in iron, another customer who saw the prototype copied and patented Knight's idea. Knight hired a lawyer to defend her claim, providing as evidence her detailed journals. Luckily, the patent commission sided with her. Knight's flat-bottom bags had a huge impact on retail stores. Department stores such as Macy's and Lord & Taylor saw the efficiency of using the bags rather than requiring clerks to wrap and tie each purchase.

TEACH

GUIDED DISCUSSION

3. **Summarize** How did the inventions of Granville T. Woods and Elijah McCoy help improve transportation in the United States? *(Woods improved transportation safety with his telegraph system that allowed messages to be transmitted between moving trains and train depots and his and his brother's emergency braking system. He improved streetcar safety by running electrical wires above the streetcars to avoid contact with people. McCoy's automatic lubricating cup made trains operate more efficiently by not forcing trains to stop often to manually oil the gears.)*

4. **Draw Conclusions** Why might it be said that the labor-saving device Josephine Garis Cochrane invented was ahead of its time? *(Cochrane invented a dishwasher in 1886, but dishwashers did not become popular until much later.)*

ANALYZE PRIMARY SOURCES

Direct students' attention to the Primary Sources feature. Ask them to work with partners to determine the main idea and supporting details in Lewis Latimer's letter. Encourage students to use a graphic organizer like the Main Idea and Details List shown to organize their thoughts. Then hold a class discussion in which pairs share their analyses. Take time to clarify any discrepancies so students clearly understand Latimer's main idea.

Main Idea:
Detail:
Detail:
Detail:
Detail:
Detail:

ACTIVE OPTIONS

AMERICAN GALLERY ONLINE **The Age of Invention** Invite students to explore the American Gallery. Have them select one of the inventions and do additional research to learn more about it. Ask questions that will inspire additional inquiry, such as: What is the invention? Who invented it? What is its purpose or function? How has it improved people's lives or work?

NG Learning Framework: Create a Virtual Museum Exhibit

SKILLS Collaboration, Communication

KNOWLEDGE New Frontiers

Arrange students in groups and explain that each group will create a multimedia presentation about one of the inventors in this lesson. Guide each group to include information about their assigned inventor's life and inventions, accompanied by an explanation of the inventor's impact on American life. Encourage them to include photographs and other visuals to enhance their presentation. Allow time for groups to share their presentations and answer questions.

HISTORICAL THINKING

ANSWERS

1. Possible response: Alexander Graham Bell invented the telephone, and Thomas Edison invented electric lights. These were both significant inventions that still have an impact on people's lives throughout the world. In addition to electric lights, Edison's inventions include the phonograph and motion picture devices.

2. Possible response: In the late 1800s, women's main sphere was the home, where efficiency and safety in completing domestic tasks would be a benefit. Women who were employed outside the home often worked in factories, where safety and efficiency also would be major concerns.

3. Carver was trying to improve the soil's quality. Because farmers had been planting only cotton, the soil was poor. Carver thought introducing different crops would improve the soil's quality.

4. Possible response: Railway and westward expansion, improvements in steel production, and the discovery of new resources such as oil spurred invention and innovation as people sought to improve long-distance communication, serve new markets, and improve production, safety, and efficiency. New innovations and inventions, in turn, spurred additional innovations and inventions. For example, Lewis Latimer invented a device used to manufacture the carbon filaments inside of lamps. This would not have occurred had not electric lights already been invented.

THE STATE OF WORKERS

Rapid societal changes can have both positive and negative consequences. During the late 19th and early 20th centuries, many changes took place in the workforce—some for the better and some for the worse.

NEW INVENTIONS, NEW JOBS

Amid the explosion of technology in the late 1800s, the labor force expanded rapidly. In the 1870s alone, it increased by a whopping 29 percent. As new machines and office equipment made their way onto the market, factories and offices became common places of employment. This new work environment signaled a switch from work involving independent, skilled craftspeople to machine-driven jobs in large organizations—jobs that required little or no skill. Suddenly, many workers found themselves at the mercy of managers whose only concerns were maintaining order in the workplace and meeting profit expectations. Many workers had little chance of improving their circumstances.

When photographer Lewis Hine asked this cotton mill worker her age, she replied that she didn't remember, but that she knew she was too young to work. Hine took this 1908 photo in his role as an investigative photographer for the National Child Labor Committee.

People moving to urban areas as part of this workforce expansion included immigrants as well as native-born Americans. Workers experienced some benefits from the growth of factory and office work. Increased productivity made possible by technology created a surplus of goods, resulting in **deflation**, or a decrease in the prices of goods and services. Workers' buying power increased, and in many cases, employees could work fewer hours. Women's participation in the workforce also expanded, as they took positions as teachers, office workers, sales assistants, domestic workers, and factory workers. However, women earned less than men, and fewer opportunities were available to them.

DANGEROUS WORK

Though wages and work hours improved during the late 19th and early 20th centuries, safety conditions did not. Workers in the railroad, coal mining, steel, and meatpacking industries faced constant danger of mishaps and even death on the job. A 1906 novel by **Upton Sinclair**, *The Jungle,* described the deplorable working conditions in the meatpacking industry. In his novel Sinclair wrote that men "fell into the vats . . . sometimes they would be overlooked for days, till all but the bones of them had gone out to the world." In the coal mining industry, an estimated 3,242 miners died in job-related accidents in 1907. More than 350 of those deaths resulted from just one mine explosion in West Virginia. That same year, a journalist investigating a U.S. Steel plant in Chicago found that as many as 12 percent of its employees died or suffered injuries every year.

Factory managers often blamed the workers themselves for the accidents that caused their injuries. But many observers realized that the hazards workers faced in many industrial jobs were real. In response, states began providing **workers' compensation**, which meant that a worker who had been injured could receive assistance for medical care and loss of income. Wisconsin passed the first comprehensive workers' compensation law in 1911. By 1920, 43 states had passed some type of workers' compensation.

As the workforce expanded in the late 19th and early 20th centuries, child labor also peaked. Factory managers hired children because they were easier to control than adults, and they could be paid lower wages. Often, children worked to help support their families. In 1880, nearly 182,000 children younger than age 16 worked in such places as textile mills, glass factories, and even coal mines. Like adults, children endured long hours under dangerous

PRIMARY SOURCE

In 1907, the Russell Sage Foundation brought investigators together to study industry in Pittsburgh, Pennsylvania, particularly the city's steel mills. One of these investigators was lawyer Crystal Eastman, whose survey of work accidents helped inspire workplace reforms.

The principal classes of fatalities which result, strictly speaking, from the process of making steel . . . are only 19 percent of the fatalities that occur in the mills where steel is made. It can be asserted that nearly twice as many men are killed in the process of transporting materials and finished product from place to place in mill and yard, as are killed in the actual process of making steel.

—from *Work-Accidents and the Law: The Pittsburgh Survey,* by Crystal Eastman, 1916

conditions with few safety or health protections. Many children could not attend school because they had to spend their entire day at work.

The nonregulatory approach to business that allowed practices such as child labor is called **laissez-faire economics**, in which the government rarely interferes in the free market and businesses choose how they will operate, with little or no oversight. An American sociologist named **William Graham Sumner** offered the ideas of Social Darwinism as justification for this approach, arguing that social reforms imposed a financial burden on the "forgotten men" of the middle class. However, despite the popularity of Social Darwinism—or indeed perhaps because of it—workers of the late 19th and early 20th centuries began to assert their rights and demand improvements and protections in their workplaces.

HISTORICAL THINKING

1. **READING CHECK** What changes took place in the workforce during the late 19th and early 20th centuries?

2. **ANALYZE CAUSE AND EFFECT** What larger social and economic issues did the large-scale use of child labor in 1880 impact?

3. **DRAW CONCLUSIONS** How common were injuries in the coal and steel industries in 1907?

4. **IDENTIFY MAIN IDEAS AND DETAILS** What protections did workers have during the late 19th and early 20th centuries? Support your answer with details from the text.

PLAN: 2-PAGE LESSON

OBJECTIVE

Examine the causes and consequences of working conditions that many Americans faced in the late 1800s and early 1900s.

CRITICAL THINKING SKILLS FOR LESSON 2.1

- Analyze Cause and Effect
- Draw Conclusions
- Identify Main Ideas and Details
- Make Inferences
- Make Connections
- Analyze Primary Sources

HISTORICAL THINKING FOR CHAPTER 15

What were the overall positive and negative effects of industrialization on America?
Industrial progress fueled a growing workforce but led to dangerous working conditions for many workers. Lesson 2.1 describes the hazardous working conditions many men, women, and children faced.

BACKGROUND FOR THE TEACHER

The 1870 U.S. Census reported that 750,000 children under the age of 15 worked in jobs not connected to family businesses or farming. By 1890, that number had grown to 1.5 million and by 1910, to 2 million. Textile mills, glass factories, and coal mines were not the only industries employing large numbers of children. Canneries, for example, employed children as young as six or seven, many of them hired along with their parents. In the late 1880s, nearly one in five workers at fruit and vegetable canneries was under the age of 16. Workdays for child laborers often began at 5 a.m. or earlier. In seafood canneries, children shucked oysters or processed shrimp for longer than 12 hours a day. In vegetable and fruit canneries, the workdays could stretch to 18 hours, with children hauling heavy crates of fruits and vegetables, husking corn, peeling fruit, and cutting the ends off green beans.

FINANCIAL LITERACY

To extend their knowledge and understanding about the concepts in this lesson, refer students to the Financial Literacy handbook.

INTRODUCE & ENGAGE

CREATE A CONCEPT CLUSTER

Display a Concept Cluster like the one shown. Write the term *working-class jobs* in the center. Ask students what characteristics they associate with working-class jobs today. Encourage students to consider both positive and negative aspects of those jobs. Tell students that in this lesson they will explore the conditions faced by the working class in the late 1800s and early 1900s.

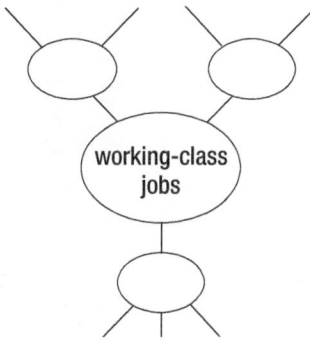

TEACH

GUIDED DISCUSSION

1. **Make Inferences** What was Upton Sinclair suggesting about the consequences of safety conditions in the meatpacking industry when he wrote "all but the bones of them had gone out to the world"? (*Sinclair was suggesting that if workers who fell into the vats were not discovered soon enough, their soft tissue became part of the meat product being manufactured in the vats.*)

2. **Make Connections** How did William Graham Sumner use Social Darwinism to justify the principles of laissez-faire economics? (*In line with the Social Darwinian belief that the structure of society represented a natural order, Sumner argued that social reforms, such as regulating child labor, would violate this natural order and place a financial burden on the "forgotten men" of the middle class by taking money out of their pockets and giving it to the poor and unproductive.*)

ANALYZE PRIMARY SOURCES

Call on a volunteer to read aloud the quotation from Crystal Eastman. Discuss the point that Eastman makes about workplace safety. **ASK:** According to Eastman, what percentage of steel-mill fatalities result from making steel? (*19 percent*) **ASK:** What killed more workers than making steel? (*Twice as many were killed while transporting materials and finished products as were killed in making steel.*)

ACTIVE OPTIONS

On Your Feet: Tell Me More Instruct students to form four teams and assign each team one of the following topics: changes in the workforce; dangerous working conditions; child labor; and laissez-faire economics. Each group should write down as many facts about their topic as they can. Reconvene the class and have one group stand up. Invite the rest of the class to call out, "Tell me more about [the topic]!" The standing group reads aloud one of their facts. The class again calls out, "Tell me more!" until the group runs out of facts to share. Then the other groups stand, one at a time, to present their facts as classmates ask for more information. Monitor which group shares the most facts.

NG Learning Framework: Create a Photo Exhibit

ATTITUDE Curiosity

KNOWLEDGE Our Human Story

Ask students to work in groups to locate and select photographs by Lewis Hine that show children laboring in coal mines, textile mills, glass factories, canneries, and other workplaces. Instruct the groups to write research-based captions to accompany the photos. Then have groups organize their photos and captions into a single electronic or print gallery exhibit to be viewed by other classes.

DIFFERENTIATE

ENGLISH LANGUAGE LEARNERS

Summarize Place students of **All Proficiencies** in pairs, and assign each pair one or more paragraphs from the lesson. Ask them to read their assigned paragraphs and then work together to summarize each paragraph in one or two sentences. When all pairs have finished, invite them to read their summaries aloud in the order in which the material appears in the lesson.

PRE-AP

Write a Profile Ask students to access multiple print and online sources to gather information about the National Child Labor Committee, for which photographer Lewis Hine worked. Encourage them to locate information about the committee's origins, purpose, and early challenges. Students should then use their research to write a profile about the committee. Remind them to cite the sources they use. Invite volunteers to share their profiles with the class.

See the Chapter Planner for more strategies for differentiation.

HISTORICAL THINKING

ANSWERS

1. The workforce expanded as immigrants, urban dwellers, women, and children worked at the many new jobs created by growing businesses.

2. Children often needed to work to support their families, and factories liked to hire children because they worked for less pay.

3. Injuries were extremely common, as evidenced by 3,242 miners dying from job-related accidents in 1907 and 12 percent of the employees being injured or killed each year in one Chicago steel plant.

4. Under laissez-faire economics, workers had very little protection until Wisconsin passed the first workers' compensation law in 1911.

ORGANIZING INTO UNIONS

Fighting for your rights takes a lot of perseverance, courage, and conviction. You could be putting your job or maybe even your life on the line. In the late 1800s, dangerous and unfair working conditions led many workers to fight for their rights—but not without a cost.

ORGANIZING FOR CHANGE

You have read that American workers began to organize labor unions, or groups of workers who band together to achieve better pay, safer working conditions, and other benefits, in the 1820s. After the Civil War, this effort gathered new energy. Unions formed in the cigar manufacturing, shoe-making, and coal mining industries, but their popularity grew in other industries as well—most notably, the railroads. Strikes, or work stoppages, became a strategic tactic employed by unions when companies or bosses refused to negotiate with them. In industries with highly trained employees who performed specific jobs, such as a railroad brakeman, management struggled to replace workers when all of them walked off the job at once. Unionized workers knew they had a lot of leverage in this situation, and they used it.

PRIMARY SOURCE

The demand for an 8-hour workday dates from the early 1800s, but nearly 100 years later, it was not yet a reality. In this excerpt, Terence Powderly provides arguments in its favor.

Men who work short hours are better educated than those who do not; they have more time in which to study. A thinking, studious man will learn that overexertion shortens life, and he will guard against it. Thousands go to early graves through overwork every year, and until the struggle for existence is shortened by cutting down the hours of toil, this condition of affairs will continue.

—from "The Plea for Eight Hours," by Terence V. Powderly, 1890

What does Powderly imply will happen if workers' hours aren't reduced?

In July 1877, railroad workers launched a strike in Martinsburg, West Virginia, when the Baltimore and Ohio (B&O) Railroad Company announced it would immediately cut pay by 10 percent. Workers had already experienced one pay cut that year, and they balked at the company's decision. Soon the strike had spread to larger cities such as Baltimore, Pittsburgh, and Chicago. In total, about 100,000 workers across the country participated in what came to be known as the Great Railroad Strike. When management's attempt to break the strike resulted in rioting, federal troops arrived. Though the riots led to the deaths of about 100 people, the strike succeeded in sharpening the focus on workers' rights.

One of the first major unions was the **Knights of Labor**, founded in 1869. Like other unions at the time, the Knights of Labor sought an 8-hour workday to replace the more typical 10- to 12-hour workday. But the union also pressed for social reforms and equality. It offered membership to women and African Americans. Its inclusivity set the Knights of Labor apart from other 19th-century labor and trade unions.

In 1879, **Terence V. Powderly** assumed control of the Knights of Labor. After the Great Railroad Strike of 1877, the union's membership climbed from approximately 9,000 members in 1879 to more than 100,000 in 1885. Though Powderly himself did not generally support the practice of striking, the Knights of Labor mobilized a strike in 1885 against Jay Gould, an executive for the Union Pacific railroad known for his ruthless dealings with both employees and competitors. In 1886, the Knights of Labor called another strike against Gould's company—this one much more widespread than the first. Prompted by

THE CHICAGO RIOT

A RECORD OF THE

Terrible Scenes of May 4, 1886.

Chicago and New York:
BELFORD, CLARKE & CO.
1886.

the firing of a union member in Texas, the Great Southwest Strike spread to several states and halted railroads in the region, but Gould held fast, and the strike ended after a month and a half.

DESCENT INTO CHAOS

Meanwhile, Chicago experienced its own labor uprising in 1886. On May 3, striking union members at McCormick Works, a McCormick harvesting machine factory, were harassing **scabs**, or nonunion workers willing to cross strike lines in order to work, who were going into and out of the factory. The situation turned violent, and police killed one person and injured several others. In response, labor leaders called for a public protest rally in Haymarket Square the following day.

The May 4 rally began peacefully. In fact, Chicago's mayor, who lived only a mile away, even visited the event. Unconcerned that trouble might start, he returned home. However, the situation became chaotic when someone threw a bomb and police responded with gunfire. The blast was so powerful, the mayor heard it from his home. In the end, several police officers and protesters died, and dozens of people suffered injuries. Police blamed labor leaders for the bombing, giving rise to the argument that the labor movement supported terrorism and **anarchism**, or anti-government beliefs.

The event, later known as the **Haymarket Riot**, resulted in the arrests of eight people. Despite the fact that their guilt was questionable and the evidence flimsy, seven of those arrested were sentenced to death, and the eighth defendant was sentenced to life in prison. Though the Knights of Labor had no direct association with the events in Haymarket Square, many people nonetheless

blamed the organization for what took place, and the union's membership declined.

In contrast, the **American Federation of Labor (AFL)**, which formed the same year that the Haymarket Riot occurred, suddenly drew many members to its ranks. Leader **Samuel Gompers**, a critic of the Knights of Labor, wanted to focus on labor's economic gains and less on social reform. He emphasized issues such as better wages, benefits, and working conditions rather than changing the structure of society. As labor unions gained strength in numbers, the steel and railroad industries faced increasing numbers of labor strikes.

HISTORICAL THINKING

1. **READING CHECK** In what way was the Knights of Labor a unique labor union in the late 1800s?

2. **IDENTIFY PROBLEMS AND SOLUTIONS** What problem did workers hope to solve by calling a strike? Explain by using information from the text.

3. **DETERMINE CHRONOLOGY** What was the order of the main events around the Haymarket Riot? Explain what happened before, during, and after the riot.

PLAN: 2-PAGE LESSON

OBJECTIVE

Explore the rise of unions in the late 1800s and the causes and outcomes of major strikes.

CRITICAL THINKING SKILLS FOR LESSON 2.2

• Identify Problems and Solutions

• Determine Chronology

• Analyze Cause and Effect

• Compare and Contrast

HISTORICAL THINKING FOR CHAPTER 15

What were the overall positive and negative effects of industrialization on America? Labor unions grew and new ones formed during the late 1800s to work for shorter hours, better pay, and safer conditions. Lesson 2.2 discusses the growth of unions.

BACKGROUND FOR THE TEACHER

The Haymarket Riot followed a May 1, 1886 nationwide strike against employers not offering eight-hour-workdays. As the strike began, the *Chicago Mail* singled out two of the city's union leaders, Albert Parsons and August Spies, as likely instigators of trouble and suggested holding them responsible for any violence during the strike. In the wake of the riot, Parsons and Spies were arrested and convicted along with six other men. Although neither Parsons nor Spies were present when the bomb exploded, they were hanged in 1888 along with two of the other Haymarket prisoners. A fifth prisoner committed suicide in jail. The remaining three were pardoned in 1893, approximately seven years after the riot, when a petition signed by 60,000 people led to an investigation that revealed bias and falsified evidence in their trials.

INTRODUCE & ENGAGE

CONSIDER CONSEQUENCES

Point out to students that industrial workers in the late 1800s, including children and adolescents, worked 10- to 12-hour days. **ASK:** How would your life be different if you had to work 10 to 12 hours a day for low wages in a factory or mine? *(Answers will vary. Possible responses: no time for school, socializing, sports, or leisure-time activities.)* Explain that in this lesson students will learn what labor unions did in the late 1800s to achieve the 8-hour workday and other reforms that we now take for granted.

TEACH

GUIDED DISCUSSION

1. **Analyze Cause and Effect** What were the causes and consequences of the Great Railroad Strike? *(Causes: The B&O Railroad Company said it would cut workers' pay by 10 percent after an earlier pay cut the same year. Consequences: The strike spread to large cities across the country, and federal troops were eventually called in to stop rioting; 100 lives were lost; the strike focused attention on workers' rights.)*

2. **Compare and Contrast** How did Samuel Gompers differ from Terence V. Powderly in his view of the role of unions? *(Possible response: Gompers opposed Powderly's and the Knights of Labor's focus on social reform. He was more interested in focusing on economic gains for labor, such as better wages, benefits, and working conditions.)*

🏛 VIRTUAL MUSEUM VISIT

The Chicago History Museum was founded in 1856. Though the Great Chicago Fire of 1871 destroyed the museum's original building and much of its contents, a new structure was completed in 1896. The museum's current home, built in 1932, allowed for the expansion of the collection. Paul Hull's *The Chicago Riot* is part of the museum's online exhibit "The Dramas of Haymarket." Encourage students to visit the exhibit, where they can view the book cover and other artifacts and read in depth about the Haymarket affair. The exhibit provides background information about Chicago and the labor movement in the late 1800s and describes the strike, riot, trial, and aftermath. Ask students to work in groups to gather information from the exhibit and share their findings with the class.

ACTIVE OPTIONS

On Your Feet: Roundtable Have students gather in groups of four and give each group a large sheet of paper. **ASK:** Do you think the goals of strikes in the late 1800s justified the tactics and outcomes? Tell one student in each group to write his or her opinion. Remind students to support their ideas with evidence from the text. At your signal, a second group member adds an opinion, followed by the third and fourth. After all students have written their answers, allow time for groups to discuss members' responses. Then call on volunteers to share their group's ideas.

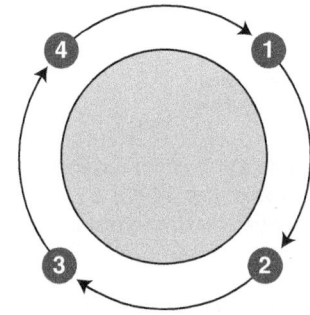

For students who develop an interest in the labor movement, suggest that they read the American Story at the beginning of this chapter.

NG Learning Framework: Conduct a Legislative Hearing

ATTITUDE Responsibility

KNOWLEDGE Our Human Story

Ask students to conduct a mock legislative hearing to investigate the causes and consequences of the Haymarket Riot, noting the complexity of determining the causes. Assign students the roles of state or federal legislators and testifying individuals, including union leaders, McCormick managers, and the police superintendent. Encourage students to do additional research to help formulate the legislators' questions and testifiers' responses.

DIFFERENTIATE

STRIVING READERS

Create a Word Square Ask students to write the term *labor unions* in the center oval of a Word Square and then add the appropriate information noted in each quadrant.

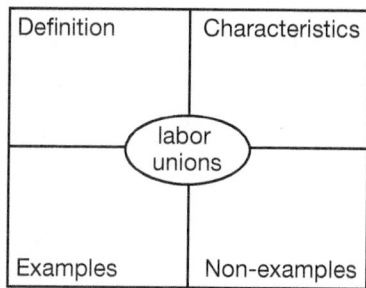

GIFTED & TALENTED

Tweet the Riot Invite students to imagine they were present at the Haymarket Riot. They may be one of the people mentioned in the lesson (mayor, police, reporter, or protestor) or a bystander of any gender, race, age, or profession. Challenge each student to compose a series of 140-character updates before, during, and after the riot, complete with hashtags. Invite students to read their tweets aloud as the class guesses who the tweets are from.

See the Chapter Planner for more strategies for differentiation.

HISTORICAL THINKING

ANSWERS

1. The union accepted women and African Americans.

2. Workers thought strikes could give them bargaining leverage. Trained workers who performed specific duties assumed that they would be hard to replace and that employers would have little choice but to bargain with them.

3. Police killed one person and injured others on May 3 during violence between strikers and scabs at the McCormick Works. On May 4, a bomb went off at a protest rally in Haymarket Square, and police responded with gunfire, causing more deaths and injuries. Eight people were arrested, tried, and convicted.

PRIMARY SOURCES

Powderly implies that workers will have shortened lifespans if their hours are not reduced.

LABOR CONFLICTS

Worker protests and union strikes might not seem newsworthy today, but in the late 1800s, they made headlines. When labor unions took on the giants of industry, they encountered the combined forces of police, the National Guard, and the U.S. government.

STRIKING AGAINST STEEL

Though union membership grew in the late 1800s, the public reactions to two major strikes—the **Homestead Strike** and the **Pullman Strike**—set the labor movement back in the 1890s. As you have read, Andrew Carnegie controlled much of the steel industry. Workers at his steel plant in Homestead, Pennsylvania, belonged to the Amalgamated Association of Iron and Steel Workers union, and their contract with Carnegie Steel was scheduled to expire on July 1, 1892. Carnegie, away in Scotland, gave permission to his operations manager, **Henry Clay Frick,** to break the union, or destroy its power, in advance of this date.

Frick strongly opposed the union—more so than Carnegie—and wasted no time. First, he tried cutting the workers' wages, a move the union rejected. Next, Frick locked the workers out of the mill, literally, by surrounding the mill with barbed wire so that workers could not get in. Then on July 2, he fired all of the union workers at the mill—a total of 3,800 employees.

Union workers knew that Frick would try to replace them with scabs, so the strikers charged the mill. Meanwhile, Frick had hired 300 security guards from the **Pinkerton Detective Agency,** whom industrialists often enlisted to break strikes, to guard the mill. In the battle that ensued, at least seven workers and three Pinkerton guards died. The workers took control of the mill for several days, but the National Guard advanced on July 12 and removed them at the mill. A few days later, scabs replaced union workers at the mill.

Neither labor nor Carnegie Steel fared well in the wake of the Homestead Strike. Union workers lost their jobs, and some also faced criminal charges for their roles in the violence. Public opinion of Carnegie Steel suffered because of the way the company had treated its workers.

THE PULLMAN STRIKE

In 1894, another major strike made headlines, this time in the railroad industry. Workers struck against the Pullman Palace Car Company near Chicago, Illinois. The company, owned by George Pullman, manufactured railway sleeper cars known as Pullman cars.

In 1881, Pullman had established a company town—Pullman, Illinois—near his factory to accommodate its workers. The town featured housing, shops, a library, parks, and other amenities for the workers. It might sound ideal, but it allowed Pullman great control over his workers. He did not allow free discussion, independent newspapers, or the observance of any religion other than Protestant Christianity. Pullman also charged a higher rent than landlords in nearby areas, enabling him to profit from his ownership of the company town.

When an economic recession hit in 1893, Pullman cut his workers' wages and extended their work hours, but he still expected Pullman residents to pay the same amount in rent and other expenses. In response, angry workers joined the American Railway Union, a new union led by **Eugene V. Debs.**

The American Railway Union was the country's first union to consolidate workers across an entire industry. Before Debs succeeded in combining the many different railway unions, workers had organized themselves according to their individual crafts.

PULLMAN PORTERS
The Pullman company hired mostly southern African-American men to attend train passengers on their journeys. George Pullman supposed men who had previously been enslaved would be accustomed to a role of serving and would work for low wages.

For the Pullman porters, work shifts could be as long as 20 hours a day, and the pay was not enough to live on. On the plus side, however, porters received tips from passengers, they got to see the country, and the job didn't require heavy manual labor. In 1925, Pullman porters began fighting for better conditions by forming a union, called The Brotherhood of Sleeping Car Porters. The Brotherhood provided the first instance in which an African-American group negotiated terms with a powerful corporation.

The solidarity, or united purpose, of the American Railway Union turned a local strike into a national labor conflict.

When the Pullman union workers tried to discuss their grievances with their employer, he fired them. In response, the workers called for a strike. Debs coordinated a union boycott of Pullman cars on all rail lines. With members of the American Railway Union refusing to handle any Pullman cars, rail traffic in the Midwest screeched to a halt. Debs hoped the work stoppage would cause the railroads to discontinue their relationship with Pullman.

Instead, President Grover Cleveland sent federal troops to Illinois to facilitate train movement. Violence erupted, and members of the National Guard shot and killed several strikers. As a result of the bloodshed, Debs tried to end the strike, but his involvement with the boycott and strike led to his arrest. While in prison, Debs became interested in **socialism**, the political theory that advocates that the community as a whole should control the production, distribution, and exchange of goods and services. Debs later formed and became the leader of the Socialist Party of America.

Labor was not the only segment of society to experience change during the late 1800s. Greater transformations lay ahead for the United States as more immigrants began to arrive.

HISTORICAL THINKING

1. **READING CHECK** What actions led to the Homestead Strike and the Pullman Strike?

2. **IDENTIFY PROBLEMS AND SOLUTIONS** Describe solutions that indicate different directions events could have taken in the cases of the Homestead and the Pullman strikes.

3. **EVALUATE** What does the structure of the company town of Pullman say about George Pullman's attitude toward its residents? Use examples from the text to support your answer.

OBJECTIVE

Analyze the growth of labor unrest in the steel and railroad industries of the 1890s and the response from employers and the federal government.

CRITICAL THINKING SKILLS FOR LESSON 2.3

• Identify Problems and Solutions

• Evaluate

• Analyze Cause and Effect

• Draw Conclusions

HISTORICAL THINKING FOR CHAPTER 15

What were the overall positive and negative effects of industrialization on America? In the 1890s, unions staged strikes for better pay and shorter hours, and companies used force to break strikes. Lesson 2.3 focuses on the Homestead and Pullman strikes.

BACKGROUND FOR THE TEACHER

Management was not the only side that prepared for confrontation at Homestead. Before strikers occupied the mill, they set up sentries and communication signals. When Henry Clay Frick tried to sneak in the Pinkerton guards on river barges in the predawn hours of July 6, the strikers and their families were ready. From their position on higher ground, they fired on the barges. The Pinkerton guards, mostly unseasoned new recruits, fired back but were left stranded when the towboat cut the barges loose. Eventually, the guards surrendered and came ashore, only to be attacked by the strikers and their families lining the shore. Although the strikers could hold off the Pinkerton guards, they were no match for 8,500 National Guardsmen. Frick was able to break the strike, drive the Amalgamated Association of Iron and Steel Workers union out of Carnegie's only unionized plant, and cut wages.

INTRODUCE & ENGAGE

ANALYZE OUTCOMES

Direct students to recount what they read in Lesson 2.2 about labor strikes and the reactions of management and the government in the late 1800s. **ASK:** What impact might earlier labor strikes have had on how labor and management dealt with one another? *(Answers will vary. Possible response: Both sides would have been likely to mistrust each other. On the other hand, to avoid possible violent outcomes, both sides might have realized the importance of negotiation and compromise.)* Tell students that they will read about two major strikes in the 1890s in this lesson.

TEACH

GUIDED DISCUSSION

1. **Analyze Cause and Effect** In what ways did the Homestead Strike negatively affect both union workers and Carnegie Steel? *(Union workers lost their jobs, a few were killed, and some were charged with crimes because of the violence. Carnegie Steel's treatment of its workers damaged the company's public reputation.)*

2. **Draw Conclusions** How did the Pullman boycott and strike shift Eugene V. Debs's future in a new direction? *(Debs was arrested and convicted because of his involvement in the boycott and strike. While in prison, he became interested in socialism and later formed and led the Socialist Party of America.)*

EVALUATE

Read the Pullman Porters feature aloud. **ASK:** Based on the information, do you think the benefits of a porter's job outweighed the drawbacks in working conditions? Why or why not? *(Answers will vary. Possible responses: Yes. Although the porters worked long hours and for low wages, they were able to see the country, supplement their incomes with tips, and avoid heavy manual labor at a time when opportunities were limited for African Americans; No. The porters' low wages and long hours were a form of racial discrimination because white men probably would have been paid more for fewer hours.)*

ACTIVE OPTIONS

On Your Feet: Fishbowl Tell one half of the class to sit or stand in a close circle, facing inward, and the other half of the class to sit or stand in a larger circle around them. **ASK:** What evidence supports a conclusion that unions suffered setbacks in the 1890s? Students in the inner circle should discuss the question for five minutes while those in the outer circle listen to the discussion and evaluate the points made. Then have the groups reverse roles and continue the discussion.

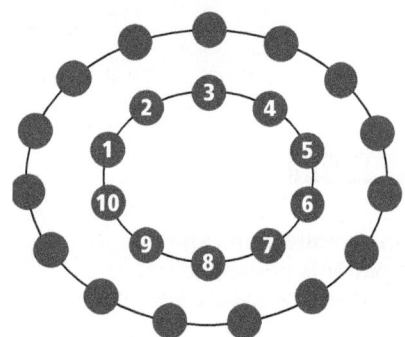

NG Learning Framework: Write Press Releases

SKILL Communication

KNOWLEDGE Our Human Story

Organize students into groups to write press releases about the Homestead and Pullman strikes. Assign each group to write a release about one of the strikes that gives the viewpoint or "spin" of a key party, such as the union, industry management, railroad owners, the Pinkerton Detective Agency, or the federal government. Encourage groups to conduct additional research to inform their press releases. Groups should then present their press releases and discuss as a class how bias and prejudice affect historical interpretations.

DIFFERENTIATE

INCLUSION

Use Supported Reading Assign pairs of students paragraphs to read aloud together. At the end of each paragraph, have students use the following sentence frames to identify what they do and do not understand:

• This paragraph is about _____.

• One fact that stood out to me was _____.

• I had trouble understanding _____, so I figured it out by _____.

Be sure all students understand the content before moving on to the next paragraph.

PRE-AP

Investigate the Government's Role Ask students to gather information from a variety of sources to create an oral report on why the government sided with management in the Homestead and Pullman strikes. Encourage students to use primary and secondary sources. Invite volunteers to share their findings with the class.

See the Chapter Planner for more strategies for differentiation.

HISTORICAL THINKING

ANSWERS

1. Before the Homestead Strike, managers cut pay, locked out workers, and fired union workers. Pullman cut pay and lengthened work hours but charged workers the same for rent and expenses and then fired union workers rather than discuss grievances.

2. Possible responses: In the Homestead strike, Andrew Carnegie could have extended the workers' contract; he could have appointed someone other than Henry Clay Frick to deal with the workers in his absence. In the Pullman strike, George Pullman could have lowered rent for his residents during the 1893 recession; he could have refrained from firing workers who wanted to discuss grievances. In the context of these possible solutions, both strikes might have been averted.

3. Possible response: Pullman wanted full control over his employees' lives and saw residents as a source of income. For example, he only allowed people to practice Protestantism, curbed discussion, and kept rents high.

ELLIS ISLAND AND ANGEL ISLAND

Athlete. Artist. Gamer. Musician. Environmentalist. Your identity is a combination of traits and experiences, and it is likely to change as you grow. Likewise, the American identity was reshaped by the arrival of millions of new immigrants in the late 1800s.

THE NEW IMMIGRANTS

Until the early 1870s, most immigrants to the United States were from northern and western Europe. But between 1890 and 1920, immigrants began to arrive from southern and eastern European countries such as Italy, Greece, Hungary, Poland, Russia, and Czechoslovakia. Unlike many of their predecessors, few of these new immigrants were Protestant Christians, but instead were largely Catholic, Jewish, and Orthodox. They also typically did not speak English. Although seeking a better life, just as those who arrived before them, they were often treated with prejudice.

Like earlier groups of immigrants to the United States, southern and eastern European and Asian immigrants were motivated by several **push-pull factors**, or pressures that forced them from their home countries and drew them to a new one. The factors that pushed immigrants away from their home countries included a lack of economic opportunities, a shortage of farmland, too few educational opportunities, religious discrimination, and the threat of being drafted to fight in wars. For the Irish, the massive emigration that began with the Great Potato Famine of 1845–1849 stretched into the latter half of the century, as hunger and poverty continued to plague Ireland.

The pull factors that drew immigrants to the United States included the hope for greater economic opportunity, plentiful farmland available for purchase at affordable prices, political and religious freedom, and the absence of war. Following the Civil War, rapid industrial growth created an unprecedented demand for labor. Industries across the country needed both skilled and unskilled workers. Communities established by previous groups of immigrants in cities such as Chicago and New York welcomed the newcomers.

As the influx of non-English-speaking immigrants continued into the early 20th century, an **Americanization** movement emerged. Proponents of Americanization wanted to immerse immigrants in what they defined as American culture and transform them into "true" Americans. During the 1910s, schools, community organizations, and businesses offered immigrants English classes and lessons in American history and government. Some immigrants embraced Americanization efforts, but others rejected them, preferring instead to maintain their own languages and cultures.

Support for Americanization peaked during World War I and waned in the 1920s. In its place came a new appreciation by some for the coexistence of different groups, known today as pluralism. This new appreciation also applied to religious beliefs, as growing numbers of Catholics and Jews continued arriving from Europe.

WELCOME TO ELLIS ISLAND

Beginning in 1892, most of the European immigrants who arrived on the East Coast were processed through the immigration station at **Ellis Island** in New York Harbor. Before it opened, immigrants had arrived at a facility called Castle Garden in Lower Manhattan. Between 1855 and 1890, officials processed 8 million immigrants at the Castle Garden location, but the facility was no longer large enough to manage the large numbers of new immigrants. Ellis Island became the site of a new and more comprehensive immigration processing facility.

THE FACES OF ELLIS ISLAND

Augustus Francis Sherman was the chief registry clerk at Ellis Island in the early 1900s. He took photographs of incoming immigrants, and in 1907, *National Geographic* magazine published some of them. In 2016, artist Jordan Lloyd digitally colorized many of these photos, including the four that appear below. The colorization specialists took care to reproduce historically accurate colors in order to bring to life the intricacies and beauty of the traditional clothing worn by immigrants who walked through the doors of Ellis Island.

Woman from Ruthenia, a region of present-day Ukraine and Belarus, wearing an embroidered linen blouse and sheepskin jacket

Bavarian man, wearing a trachtenjanker, or wool jacket, with horn buttons

East Indian boy, wearing a topi (cap), homespun cotton cloth called khadi, and prayer shawl

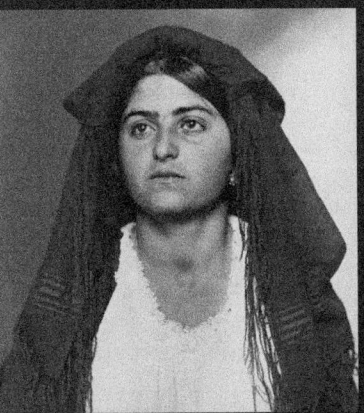
Italian woman, wearing a traditional dress with blue shawl and veil

---

OBJECTIVE

Analyze the push-pull motivations and experiences of immigrants coming to the United States in the late 1800s and early 1900s.

CRITICAL THINKING SKILLS FOR LESSON 3.1

- Interpret Graphs
- Identify Problems and Solutions
- Make Generalizations
- Describe
- Compare and Contrast
- Identify

HISTORICAL THINKING FOR CHAPTER 15

What were the overall positive and negative effects of industrialization on America?
Industrialization drew immigrants from southern and eastern Europe and Asia to the United States, raising concerns among people already in America. Lesson 3.1 explores this immigration.

BACKGROUND FOR THE TEACHER

Because of his job as Ellis Island's chief registry clerk, amateur photographer Augustus Francis Sherman (1865–1925) had unique access to the immigrants he photographed. It is believed that those he portrayed were detainees persuaded to have their photos taken while awaiting receipt of money, transport tickets, or the arrival of relatives to retrieve them from the island. The elaborate outfits worn by his subjects were most likely not the clothing these immigrants arrived wearing. Rather, historians think these costumes were special national or holiday garb that the people had brought with them from their countries of origin.

HISTORY NOTEBOOK

Encourage students to complete the Reid on the Road video series page for Chapter 15 in their History Notebooks after they view the video.

INTRODUCE & ENGAGE

THUMBS UP, THUMBS DOWN

Ask students to volunteer reasons that might cause a person to move from one country to another. List their reasons on the board. Then read the list aloud and have students give each reason a thumbs-up or a thumbs-down, depending on whether they would emigrate for that reason. Tell them that in this lesson they will learn about the reasons immigrants left their homelands to come to the United States in the late 1800s and early 1900s.

TEACH

GUIDED DISCUSSION

1. **Make Generalizations** How were European immigrants who arrived after 1870 different from those who arrived earlier? *(Prior to 1870, most European immigrants were Protestants from western and northern Europe. The immigrants who came between 1890 and 1920 were primarily from southern and eastern Europe, spoke little English, and most were mostly Catholic, Jewish, or Orthodox.)*

2. **Describe** How did views of cultural differences in the United States change after support for Americanization began to wane? *(The attempt to make America more homogenous gave way to a new appreciation for cultural and religious differences as Catholics and Jews continued to arrive from Europe.)*

MORE INFORMATION

Americanization in Context The Americanization movement arose within the context of a society transformed by industrialization, beset by labor strife and economic swings, and grappling with rapid urbanization and ballooning immigration. As the gap widened between middle-class and wealthy Americans of Anglo-Saxon descent and the masses of working-class and poor immigrants, support for laissez-faire approaches to economic and social problems began to waver. Protestant ministers of the Social Gospel movement rebelled against Social Darwinism's idea that the ills of society were the results of natural selection. They preached the Gospel to poor slum dwellers in the cities and helped immigrants assimilate. Social Darwinist beliefs did not disappear, however. Some proponents of Americanization pushed for forced assimilation, arguing that the failure of immigrants to assimilate was a threat to national identity. **ASK:** How do you think proponents of the Americanization movement might have reacted to the photographs of the four immigrants? *(Possible response: They would likely have been struck by the fact that each person was wearing traditional clothing from his or her country of origin and would have wanted them instead to wear American styles to better blend with American culture.)*

DIFFERENTIATE

ENGLISH LANGUAGE LEARNERS ELD

Build Vocabulary Remind students of **All Proficiencies** that analyzing word parts can help them build their vocabulary. Write *Americanization* on the board. Point out that the adjective *American* acts as the base word and that the two suffixes *–ize* and *–ation* combine with *American* to create a noun meaning "the process of making someone or something American." Ask students to look for other words in the lesson that can be broken down into word parts in order to decipher their meaning—for example, *pluralism, immigration,* and *exclusionary.* Provide the following sentence frames to help students at different proficiency levels analyze word parts:

- **Emerging:** This part means _____. So that word means _____.

- **Expanding** and **Bridging:** _____ is a suffix. It means _____. So the word _____ means _____.

GIFTED & TALENTED

Perform an Oral History Ask students to access the Ellis Island Oral History Collection, which is available online. Invite them to listen to several interviews of immigrants from different countries and then select a portion of one interview that can be read aloud in three or four minutes. Encourage them to rehearse their performances using the interview transcripts. After students perform their oral history excerpts, ask them to identify any specific information in the lesson that is reinforced by their oral histories.

See the Chapter Planner for more strategies for differentiation.

Once they arrived at Ellis Island, immigrants faced a series of examinations that generally took anywhere from three to seven hours. They answered questions about how they were going to support themselves in the United States and received medical exams to ensure they were free of contagious diseases. Aid workers and social workers also provided immigrants with other needs, such as clothing, counseling, or even money. Immigrants who were found to have a contagious disease or deemed unable to support themselves could be barred entry and sent back to their home countries. About 2 percent of immigrants met this fate. By the time Ellis Island stopped functioning as an immigration center in 1924, more than 12 million immigrants had passed through its doors.

One experience shared by immigrants entering the United States through Ellis Island was seeing the **Statue of Liberty** as they arrived in New York Harbor. Unveiled on a wet and foggy day on October 28, 1886, with President Grover Cleveland in attendance, the statue was greeted with great celebration. The copper figure was designed and constructed as a gift from France, and the pedestal was built by the United States. Holding the torch of freedom in her upraised hand, "Lady Liberty" came to symbolize the welcoming spirit of the United States. **Emma Lazarus**'s poem "The New Colossus" was etched into a plaque at the base of the statue in 1903, reinforcing a message of inclusion: "From her beacon-hand / Glows world-wide welcome."

CONTROLLING IMMIGRATION

On the West Coast, immigrants arrived at **Angel Island,** a facility in San Francisco Bay that processed immigrants during the early 20th century. Unlike the mainly European immigrants who arrived at Ellis Island, those who arrived at Angel Island came from Asia, primarily China and Japan. Other Asian immigrants included Filipinos, Hindus, and Sikhs.

The Angel Island facility opened in 1910 not only to process immigrants but also to control the number of Chinese immigrants allowed into the country. Many native-born Americans harbored prejudices toward Chinese immigrants and believed Chinese laborers, who often worked for low wages, took jobs away

Immigrants Arriving in the United States in 1900

NUMBERS (IN THOUSANDS)

- 300
- 200
- 100
- 0

Northern and Western Europe
Southern and Eastern Europe
Asia

Source: U.S. Census Bureau

from American workers. Anti-Chinese sentiment had intensified in the 1870s when unemployment ran especially high. In 1882, Congress passed the **Chinese Exclusion Act** to prevent Chinese immigrants from working in the United States. Although states had already passed their own versions of immigration laws, the Chinese Exclusion Act became the nation's first federal immigration law.

Immigration from Asia continued despite laws created to suppress it. Those who came for purposes other than work could still seek admission to the United States. However, they had to prove they were not laborers by providing certification from the Chinese government. Because the act included such a wide definition of who qualified as a laborer, proving their occupation was difficult for immigrants.

As a result, the act severely limited Chinese immigration for 10 years. Officials turned away more than 5 percent of Chinese immigrants who tried to enter the country—far more than the 2 percent of European immigrants turned away from Ellis Island. Even the Chinese people already living in the United States had to obtain certification to reenter the country if they traveled outside the United States and wanted to return. When the Chinese Exclusion Act expired in 1892, Congress enacted the **Geary Act,** which extended the restrictions on Chinese labor for an additional 10 years. When that act expired in 1902, Congress made the extension permanent. In fact, Congress did not finally repeal these exclusionary acts until the 1940s.

Chinese immigrants denied admission and detained at Angel Island could appeal, but they often had to endure difficult conditions while waiting to hear the results. The wait could last weeks, months, or

Japanese women aboard an incoming ship await processing at Angel Island in 1925. Between 1900 and 1925, more than 250,000 Japanese immigrated to the United States.

in some cases more than a year, and prospective immigrants had to submit to lengthy interrogations about their families and villages in China. To pass the time and express their feelings while waiting, some detainees carved poems in the walls. Facilities on Angel Island were often crowded, and some featured barbed wire and armed guards to prevent people from escaping. The island seemed more like a prison than an immigration center.

Also contributing to the diversity of the United States in the early 20th century was the openness of its southwestern borders. People crossed freely between the United States and Mexico. But the migration process could be difficult for new arrivals to the United States, and the struggle did not end there. Once admitted to the country, immigrants frequently faced prejudice and poverty as they settled into their new homes.

HISTORICAL THINKING

1. **READING CHECK** What were some of the push-pull factors that led immigrants to come to the United States during the late 19th and early 20th centuries?

2. **INTERPRET GRAPHS** From what region did the most immigrants to the United States come in 1900?

3. **IDENTIFY PROBLEMS AND SOLUTIONS** How could a Chinese person immigrate legally under the terms of the Chinese Exclusion Act?

4. **MAKE GENERALIZATIONS** Explain connections between the experiences of immigrants arriving in the late 19th and early 20th centuries with the larger issue of worldwide migration in the 21st century.

BUILD BACKGROUND

MEXICAN IMMIGRATION

Mexicans who chose to enter the United States during this period were motivated by economic and political problems in Mexico and by economic expansion in the southwestern United States. Falling wages and higher prices in Mexico and the possibility of work on railroad projects in northern Mexico pushed workers, mostly men, from the interior to the border. From there they discovered better wage opportunities in the United States. The upheavals of the Mexican Revolution sparked further immigration after 1910, and more families began to cross the border. The demand for Mexican labor in the southwestern United States was also spurred by new technologies, such as refrigerated train cars and large-scale irrigation, which boosted agriculture in the region. In addition to southwestern railroads and agriculture, Mexican immigrants also picked cotton in Texas, worked in the mines in New Mexico and Arizona, and provided seasonal farm labor in California and elsewhere.

Immigrants came both legally and illegally across the border from Mexico, often staying temporarily in the United States to work and then returning home. The demand for Mexican labor increased with the decline in immigration from China, Japan, and eventually, Europe. Depending on the level of demand for Mexican workers in the United States, border agents often looked the other way when immigrants entered illegally.

TEACH

GUIDED DISCUSSION

3. **Compare and Contrast** How was the immigrant experience similar and different at Ellis Island and Angel Island? *(Possible response: Immigrants faced a series of examinations and possible denial of admittance at both facilities. However, Chinese immigrants coming through Angel Island were much more likely to be denied entry or detained; also, the facility was more like a prison.)*

4. **Identify** How did the United States use legislation to control Asian immigration? *(Congress passed the Chinese Exclusion Act in 1882 and the Geary Act in 1892 to extend the effects of the Chinese Exclusion Act an additional 10 years; legislation in 1902 made the extension last until 1940.)*

MORE INFORMATION

Asian-American History Students may want to explore the history of Asian immigrants to the United States in books by historians Erika Lee and Ronald Takaki. Among Lee's books are *The Making of Asian America: A History; At America's Gates: Chinese Immigration during the Exclusion Era, 1882–1943;* and *Angel Island: Immigrant Gateway to America,* coauthored with Judy Yung. The late Ronald Takaki, the grandson of Japanese immigrants, taught and wrote about multiculturalism and race relations in the United States. Among his works are *Strangers from a Different Shore: A History of Asian Americans* and *Democracy and Race: Asian Americans and World War II.*

ACTIVE OPTIONS

Active History: Map Countries of Origin Extend the lesson by using either the PDF or Whiteboard version of the activity. These activities take a deeper look at a topic from, or related to, the lesson. Explore the activities as a class, turn them into group assignments, or even assign them individually.

NG Learning Framework: Trace the Americanization Movement

ATTITUDE Curiosity

SKILLS Collaboration, Communication

Have groups of students conduct online research regarding the effects of the Americanization movement on immigrants, on policies in the United States, and on other stakeholder groups. Alternatively, they may research the causes of the shift from Americanization toward pluralism. Suggest that they use a Cause-and-Effect Web to organize their findings. Ask groups to share their research in a class discussion.

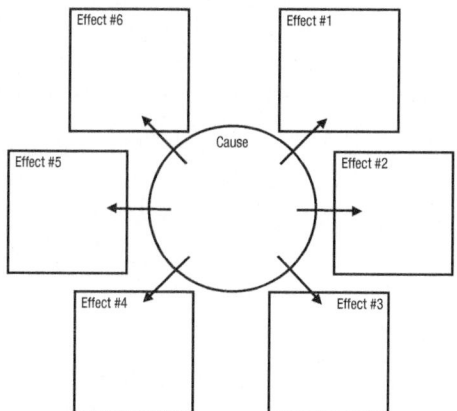

HISTORICAL THINKING

ANSWERS

1. Push factors included the lack of farmland and economic and educational opportunities in immigrants' homelands, as well as religious persecution, the military draft, and, in the case of the Irish, famine. Pull factors included economic opportunity, affordable farmland, political and religious freedom, and the absence of war.

2. In 1900, most immigrants came from southern and eastern Europe.

3. To immigrate legally, a Chinese person would have to provide certification from the Chinese government that he or she was not a laborer.

4. Many immigrants arriving in the late 19th and early 20th centuries left their homelands to escape war, discrimination, and persecution, which is also the case with many immigrants in the 21st century. Likewise, some immigrants in the late 19th and early 20th centuries were subject to quotas and exclusionary laws based on their countries of origin, an issue that also impacts worldwide migration today.

Sikh immigrants from India, Angel Island, c. 1925

Japanese immigrant, Angel Island, c. 1925

Mexican immigrants at an immigration station in El Paso, Texas, 1938

Between 1870 and 1915, New York City's population more than tripled, and about 75 percent of its residents were immigrants and their children. Many Italian immigrants settled on or near Mulberry Street, the so-called Main Street of the neighborhood known as Little Italy, shown here.

THROUGH THE LENS

IMMIGRATION

As President John F. Kennedy famously acknowledged in the title of a book he published as senator in 1959, the United States is "a nation of immigrants." Except for those of us with Native American ancestry, we all can trace our heritage back to somewhere else. From English colonists seeking religious freedom on the shores of a distant land, to Asian, Latin American, and European immigrants eager for work opportunities and a chance to make a better life, the rich tapestry of this country is interwoven with the stories of many immigrants. How is immigration a piece of your American story?

European immigrants arriving at Ellis Island, 1921

522 CHAPTER 15

Somalian immigrant outside the Mayo Clinic in Minnesota, where she works as a nurse

Salon Cuba BARBER SHOP

Little Havana, Miami, Florida

A Chinese shop owner uses an abacus in New York City's Chinatown.

Industrial America 523

PLAN: 2-PAGE LESSON

OBJECTIVE

Analyze how photographs tell the story of immigration.

CRITICAL THINKING SKILLS FOR LESSON 3.2

• Analyze Visuals

• Make Connections

• Identify

• Make Inferences

HISTORICAL THINKING FOR CHAPTER 15

What were the overall positive and negative effects of industrialization? Industrialization and its associated jobs motivated many immigrants to move to the United States. Lesson 3.2 examines photographs of immigrants over the past 100-plus years, proof of John F. Kennedy's statement that we are "a nation of immigrants."

BACKGROUND FOR THE TEACHER

Though newcomers have not always been welcomed with open arms, immigrants from Asia in particular experienced severe discrimination and open hostility in the West during the late 19th and early 20th centuries. In addition to the Chinese Exclusion Act of 1882, which barred Chinese immigrants (see the previous lesson), California's Alien Land Act of 1913 primarily prohibited Japanese immigrants from owning land in the state. Even though the Land Act was easily circumvented by methods such as purchasing land in the name of a child, it reflects the often intense anti-immigrant sentiment found in the western United States during this period.

HISTORY NOTEBOOK

Encourage students to complete the Through the Lens page for Chapter 15 in their History Notebooks as they read.

INTRODUCE & ENGAGE

EXPLORE THE PERSONAL CONNECTION TO IMMIGRATION

Call attention to the question presented at the beginning of this lesson: How is immigration a piece of your American story? Have volunteers discuss their responses. If possible, encourage students with varying stories to share with the class—for example, someone whose relatives recently immigrated and someone whose family arrived in the United States long ago. Explain to students that in this lesson they will examine photographs and analyze what they tell us about the immigrant experience in America.

TEACH

GUIDED DISCUSSION

1. **Identify** What distinction do you see between the photographs on the left page and the photographs on the right page? *(The photographs on the left show newly arrived immigrants who are entering the United States. The photographs on the right show immigrants who are already living in the United States.)*

2. **Make Inferences** Share with students the information provided in Background for the Teacher. **ASK:** Based on this information, in addition to the photographs and captions, which person depicted would have been directly impacted by California's Alien Land Act of 1913? *(the Japanese immigrant at Angel Island, c.1925)*

◉ THROUGH THE LENS

Examining the photographs of immigrants in this feature, as well as the captions, it is easy to see differences in the dates, places, and people depicted. However, similarities do exist. **ASK:** How would you describe the mood or attitude of the people depicted in the photographs on the left page? *(Possible response: The people seem serious, thoughtful, and perhaps a bit apprehensive about their relocation.)* What similarities do you observe in the photographs on the right page? *(Possible response: Even though each place shown is different, all the photographs depict immigrants making a living and thus participating in American society.)*

ACTIVE OPTIONS

On Your Feet: Delve into a Photograph Arrange students into eight small groups. Assign each group one of the photographs featured. Have groups identify the time period and country (or countries) of origin of the subjects of the photograph. Then ask them to research immigration from that country and time period. Groups should focus on questions such as the following: Why did the people come to America? Where did/do they live? What types of jobs did/do they do? Choose a volunteer from each group to share the group's findings.

NG Learning Framework: Create Immigration Presentations

ATTITUDE Responsibility

KNOWLEDGE Our Human Story

Build on the Introduce & Engage discussion by asking students to find out more about their own family's immigrant experience or the family immigrant experience of someone they know. Suggest that they conduct interviews with older relatives or friends and examine family trees and photographs. Invite each student to create a presentation based on what they discover, incorporating any pertinent artifacts, photographs, recipes, and so on, that help tell the story of the family's immigration. After students share their presentations, create a class time line with entries that show when each family immigrated to this country.

DIFFERENTIATE

INCLUSION

Describe Lesson Visuals At the beginning of the lesson, pair visually impaired students with sighted students. Ask the latter to describe the details shown in each photograph and to clarify any points of confusion as necessary. Encourage pairs to continue working together to respond to the Guided Discussion and Through the Lens questions.

GIFTED & TALENTED

A Nation of Immigrants Encourage students to create their own "Through the Lens" features by combining several immigrant photographs that they either research or take themselves, depending on their location. Ask them to include captions that tell what each photograph depicts. Display the features and have students discuss why they chose the photographs they did.

See the Chapter Planner for more strategies for differentiation.

DIFFICULT LIVES IN A NEW LAND

Adapting to a new country was especially difficult for newly arrived immigrants, whose languages, religions, food, and traditions often set them apart as they searched for shelter and work.

A PLACE TO LIVE AND WORK

Immigrants brought with them a hopeful optimism about a new future in a new country. At the same time, navigating daily life in an unfamiliar place sometimes brought a series of complex and frustrating encounters. For some, the language barrier was significant. In 1910, almost one-quarter of all immigrants spoke languages other than English. They were further isolated by their traditional dress, ethnic foods, and religious practices that were sometimes unfamiliar to the largely Protestant American population. Catholics and Jews, in particular, often faced religious prejudice, such as anti-Catholicism and **anti-Semitism**, or prejudice against Jewish people. For instance, throughout the late 19th century, American Jews were often barred from attending particular universities and conducting certain businesses.

Once settled, immigrants gained employment in a variety of jobs. Many immigrant men worked in construction. They dug tunnels and laid rails for the new subway system in New York, and they built steel mills in Pittsburgh. In Chicago, immigrants helped construct some of the world's first skyscrapers, or very tall buildings.

Some immigrant groups migrated toward specific types of work. For example, Italian women often sewed for the garment industry, Greek immigrants took jobs with the railroads, and Filipinos, Japanese, and Hindus and Sikhs from India, moved to California and other western states to work in the agriculture and service industries. Many immigrants started businesses.

The influx of new immigrants added to the population growth of cities across the country. In cities such as Chicago and New York, housing could not keep up

with increased demand. Wealthier residents lived in spacious apartment buildings and townhomes, but working-class residents—including newly arriving immigrants—often found housing in structures called **tenements**. Most tenements were six- or seven-story, multi-resident buildings, constructed on narrow lots. They were typically poorly ventilated, crowded, and ill-maintained.

In New York City, tenements were designed to house as many people as possible. Individual residences featured small, narrow rooms and few windows. The space between the tenement buildings was often so narrow that people could reach out a window and touch someone living in the next building. Only the top floors actually received much light. Because of poor ventilation and substandard or nonexistent sanitation, diseases spread quickly in the tenements. The structures were also prone to fires because of overcrowding and poor construction.

STRENGTH IN NUMBERS

Many immigrants settled in neighborhoods that reflected their own ethnic backgrounds so their native languages and customs surrounded them. They built churches and synagogues and formed mutual aid, or self-help, societies to provide services and support for residents and incoming immigrants.

One of these societies was the Polish National Alliance, formed in Philadelphia and Chicago in 1880. Its purpose was to bring Polish immigrants together in support of Poland's independence and to help one another assimilate, or blend in with and adopt American ways of life in the United States. One year after forming, the alliance established a Polish-language newspaper. Later, it set up an insurance program for members and provided loans and scholarships to those seeking an education.

CRITICAL VIEWING Children play in the streets of New York City, amid traffic and trash. Lewis Hine captured this photograph in 1910. Based on details you notice in the photo, how would you describe this street and its tenements?

The Hebrew Immigrant Aid Society, founded in 1881 on Manhattan's Lower East Side, originally formed to aid eastern European immigrants fleeing to the United States to escape religious persecution. The organization provided food, clothing, transportation, and employment to Jewish refugees. In 1904, it established a bureau on Ellis Island to assist newly arrived immigrants with translation and other services, such as loans for the $25 landing fee.

In addition to forming self-help societies, immigrants also contributed to their neighborhoods by constructing schools, theaters, and concert halls. These investments demonstrated the immigrants' commitment to their new country—an idea the Americanization movement promoted. The Polish National Alliance and the Hebrew Immigrant Aid Society still operate today, helping immigrants and others in need.

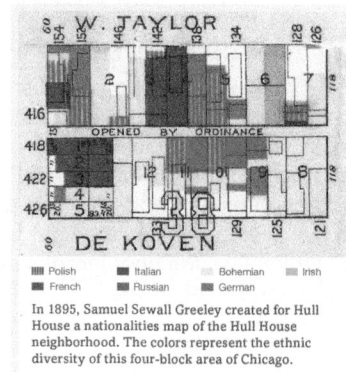

In 1895, Samuel Sewall Greeley created for Hull House a nationalities map of the Hull House neighborhood. The colors represent the ethnic diversity of this four-block area of Chicago.

OBJECTIVE

Learn about the immigrant experience in the United States in the late 1800s and early 1900s.

CRITICAL THINKING SKILLS FOR LESSON 3.3

- Describe
- Evaluate
- Identify Problems and Solutions
- Make Connections
- Analyze Cause and Effect
- Analyze Visuals

HISTORICAL THINKING FOR CHAPTER 15

What were the overall positive and negative effects of industrialization on America?
Immigrants faced hardships as well as opportunities as they adjusted to life in a new country that was not always welcoming. Lesson 3.3 explores the immigrant experience.

BACKGROUND FOR THE TEACHER

To date, the Hebrew Immigrant Aid Society (HIAS) has aided more than 4.5 million people fleeing persecution. In the 1930s, the organization helped Jews emigrate from Nazi Germany and assisted refugees fleeing eastern Europe. After World War II, it helped resettle some 150,000 people evacuated from displaced persons camps in Europe. From the 1950s onward, HIAS has helped Jews flee the Russian invasion of Hungary and the Cuban Revolution and has aided Jews caught in uprisings, pogroms, and other conflicts in Egypt, Algeria, Libya, Czechoslovakia, Poland, Ethiopia, Iran, and the former Soviet Union. HIAS has also helped non-Jewish refugees resettle, including Vietnamese, Cambodians, and Laotians following the fall of Saigon in 1975. Since 2000, HIAS has increased its efforts to assist non-Jewish refugees around the globe who are in immediate danger from conflict and persecution.

INTRODUCE & ENGAGE

PREVIEW USING VISUALS

Direct students' attention to the photos, diagram, and political cartoon in the lesson. **ASK:** What can you infer about the immigrant experience from these visuals? *(Possible responses: Living conditions were crowded and unhealthy; immigrants from the same country settled near one another; not everyone welcomed the new immigrants; immigrants started their own businesses.)* Tell students that in this lesson they will learn about difficulties immigrants faced as they adjusted to life in the United States and how some groups formed by earlier immigrants helped those who arrived after them. At the end of the lesson, have students review their inferences to see how accurate they were.

GUIDED DISCUSSION

1. **Make Connections** In what ways did new immigrants contribute to the growth of cities? *(Possible responses: Immigrant men dug tunnels and laid track for subways and built steel mills and skyscrapers; immigrants constructed neighborhood schools, theaters, and concert halls.)*

2. **Identify Problems and Solutions** What problems did tenements solve and what new problems did they create? *(Possible response: Tenements helped solve housing shortages caused by the influx of new immigrants. However, their poor ventilation and sanitation let diseases spread, and their poor construction and overcrowding contributed to fires.)*

3. **Evaluate** Why do you think the Polish National Alliance and the Hebrew Immigrant Aid Society are still in operation today? *(Answers will vary. Possible responses: Members of the organization still realize the importance of helping newly arrived immigrants; for reasons of empathy and compassion, members are motivated to help current refugees in the same way in which their ancestors were assisted years ago.)*

MORE INFORMATION

Lower East Side Tenement Museum New York City's Lower East Side Tenement Museum, founded by Ruth Abram and Anita Jacobson, offers glimpses into the lives of tenement residents in the late 1800s and early 1900s. The museum is housed in a former tenement at 97 Orchard Street. Abram and Jacobson conducted extensive research to accurately portray immigrant life in the restored apartments. Students can experience tenement life by going on virtual tours of the recreated apartments of the Levine, Confino, Rogarshevsky, and Baldizzi families. Guide them to use the museum's downloadable applications and to read online about the histories of these families.

DIFFERENTIATE

INCLUSION

Analyze a Political Cartoon Pair visually impaired students with students who are not. Ask the latter to describe the two men pictured in the cartoon (see next page) and to read all the words written on the immigrant's clothing and luggage. Tell visually impaired students to ask clarifying questions as necessary. Then have the pairs work together to answer the Critical Viewing question.

PRE-AP

Research and Role-Play Invite students to research both the mutual aid societies that helped immigrants and the nativist groups that opposed immigration. Then ask students to prepare to play the part of a pro- or anti-immigration person of the era. Instruct them to use their research as the basis for their role-play.

See the Chapter Planner for more strategies for differentiation.

CRITICAL VIEWING The street and tenements look crowded, dirty, unhealthy, and possibly dangerous.

ENCOUNTERING PREJUDICE

Despite many immigrants' attempts to assimilate into their new home, some Americans still harbored prejudices against them. These nativists felt threatened by what they saw as changing cultural values and competition for employment. They vehemently opposed immigration and wanted to restrict it by using literacy tests and quotas based on national origin. Many nativist groups worked actively against immigrants, taking particular aim at certain religious groups, such as Catholics and Jews.

For example, in 1887, the American Protective Association formed in Iowa. In essence, this organization was a secret society of white, native-born Protestants that exploited Americans' fears about an unstable economy and what they perceived as a negative influence of immigrants in the country. The organization specifically targeted Catholic immigrants, spreading rumors and **propaganda**, or purposely misleading and usually negative information, to try to bar Catholics both from entering the United States and from serving in public office. In fact, the oath that members took included a pledge that they would not "vote for, or counsel others to vote for, any Roman Catholic." The organization boasted more than 2 million members in the 1890s, though by 1900, its membership had dwindled significantly, and it had little or no influence.

Of course, prejudice extended beyond anti-Catholic and anti-Semitic boundaries. Just as the

CRITICAL VIEWING Anti-immigrant sentiment, though prevalent, was not unchallenged. This 1896 cartoon drawn by Frank Beard appeared in *The Ram's Horn*, a Social Gospel magazine. How does Beard portray both the United States and the immigrant trying to enter the country?

Jukichi Harada, standing fifth from the left behind two of his children, immigrated with his family to southern California from Japan in 1905. He started a restaurant, which he named the "Washington Restaurant" in honor of America, his new home.

Chinese Exclusion Act of 1882 had barred many Chinese immigrants from entering the country, the **Gentlemen's Agreement of 1907** between the United States and Japan had a similar effect, though not quite as severe.

This understanding between President Theodore Roosevelt and the Japanese government affirmed that the Japanese would grant passports for Japanese emigration to the United States only to educated businessmen and other professionals and their direct family members—not to peasants (farmers) or laborers. In exchange, Roosevelt agreed that the San Francisco School Board would stop separating Japanese schoolchildren from white students. Californian nativists had drummed up the need for the Gentlemen's Agreement out of a fear that Japanese immigrants would ultimately control all the best farmland in the state. At the time, 1,000 Japanese immigrants were arriving in the state every month, and most of them were farmers.

Like the Chinese, most Japanese arrived at Angel Island in San Francisco Bay. But thanks to the Gentlemen's Agreement, Japanese immigrants rarely had to stay on the island beyond a couple of days. In the end, both Roosevelt and the Japanese government stuck to their promises, but the agreement did nothing to end discrimination against the Japanese in the United States.

Urban centers continued to expand as native-born Americans and newly arrived immigrants moved to the growing, crowded cities. At the same time, the gap between the wealthy and the poor continued to increase.

HISTORICAL THINKING

1. **READING CHECK** Who immigrated to the United States between 1877 and 1911, and why?

2. **DESCRIBE** Why did immigrants form self-help societies?

3. **EVALUATE** In what ways did the treatment of immigrants to the United States show both the strengths and weaknesses of American democracy at the turn of the 20th century?

4. **IDENTIFY PROBLEMS AND SOLUTIONS** Explain the problem that the Gentlemen's Agreement set out to address.

BUILD BACKGROUND

AMERICAN PROTECTIVE ASSOCIATION

Although the American Protective Association achieved a national presence as chapters spread from state to state, its origins were very local. The organization formed after Arnold Walliker, the mayor of Clinton, Iowa, failed to win reelection in 1887. Walliker, his brother Jacob, and their friend Henry Francis Bowers blamed the town's Irish Catholics for the defeat, in part because the priest of the local Catholic church had urged the congregation to vote against the mayor. From its small handful of Iowa founders, membership exploded; in less than a decade the association claimed 2.5 million members.

In addition to vowing not to vote for or support Catholic candidates, members pledged to denounce the Pope and the Roman Catholic Church, not strike with Catholic workers, and not hire Catholics if Protestant workers were available. The association's propaganda included a forged document, purported to be from the Catholic Church, that instructed Catholics to take over the U.S. government in an uprising and kill all non-Catholics. The association, whose membership was primarily Republican, also expected Republican candidates to kowtow to its demands or face the consequences. When William McKinley failed to meet with members of the American Protective Association before running for president, members launched a campaign against him, charging that he was a Catholic who took advice from Church hierarchy. After McKinley won the presidency in 1896 in spite of the attacks, the association began to lose membership. It completely disappeared after Henry Bowers' death in 1911.

TEACH

GUIDED DISCUSSION

4. **Analyze Cause and Effect** What factors fueled nativists' opposition to immigration? *(Nativists felt threatened by changing cultural values; opposed Catholics, Jews, and other non-Protestants; and resented competition for employment.)*

5. **Describe** What tactics did nativists use to gain support for their positions? *(Nativists exploited Americans' fears about an unstable economy and stoked fear of immigrants, particularly Catholics, by spreading false rumors and propaganda and by requiring members to pledge not to vote for Catholics.)*

ANALYZE VISUALS

Have students revisit the photograph of Jukichi Harada's restaurant. **ASK:** Why is Harada's restaurant a good example of the effects of the Americanization movement? *(Possible response: Even though Harada was from Japan, he started a restaurant that was named after an American president and featured American food.)*

ACTIVE OPTIONS

On Your Feet: Think, Pair, Share Give students a few minutes to think about the following question: What evidence supports the idea that the late 1800s and early 1900s was a period of both religious intolerance and religious pluralism? Then have students choose partners and talk about the question for five minutes. Finally, allow individual students to share their ideas with the class.

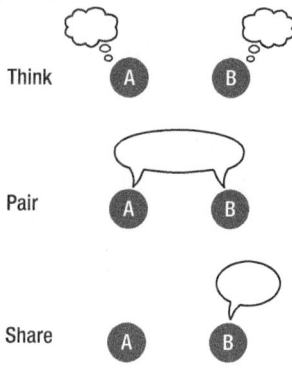

NG Learning Framework: Write an Immigrant Story

ATTITUDE Empowerment

SKILL Communication

Instruct students to write short stories set in the late 1800s or early 1900s about the experiences of newly arrived immigrants to the United States. Provide the option of using individuals, families, or groups as the characters. Explain that the stories should highlight specific experiences, such as tenement life, immigrant neighborhoods, self-help societies, and/or nativist responses. Revisit the use of narrative techniques with students, like dialogue, pacing, description, and reflection. Share stories on a class website or blog, or have volunteers read their stories in class.

HISTORICAL THINKING

ANSWERS

1. Immigrants came from countries such as the Phillipines, Japan, and India, as well as many European countries like Italy, Greece, Poland, and Russia. They came to escape religious persecution and for economic reasons.

2. Immigrants formed self-help societies to provide services and support—such as food, clothing, transportation, employment, insurance programs, loans, and help in assimilation—for residents of immigrant neighborhoods and for incoming immigrants.

3. Answers will vary. Possible response: Religious discrimination, such as barring American Jews from attending certain universities or conducting certain businesses or encouraging people to vote against Catholic candidates, showed weaknesses; the formation of communities where immigrants could continue traditional cultural and religious practices and seek aid showed strengths within our American democracy.

4. Japan agreed to grant emigration passports only to educated businessmen and other professionals. In exchange, Theodore Roosevelt ensured that the San Francisco Board of Education would stop segregating Japanese and white students.

CRITICAL VIEWING Frank Beard portrays the immigrant as poor, superstitious, disease-ridden, unfaithful, alcoholic, anarchistic, and non-Protestant. He portrays the United States as unwelcoming even though it professes to freely accept all immigrants.

JANE ADDAMS 1860–1935

"She is the truest American I have ever known, and there has been none
braver."—Harold Ickes, United States Secretary of the Interior

The well-used rocking chair (right) belonged to Addams and helped
relieve the chronic back pain she suffered from for much of her life.

In the late 1800s, Chicago was a tough
place to live for the thousands of
immigrants who came to work in the
city's booming factories and stockyards.
The journalist Lincoln Steffens described
Chicago as "first in violence, deepest in
dirt, loud, lawless, unlovely, ill-smelling.
Criminally, it was wide-open; socially it
was thoughtless and raw." Onto this grim
and seemingly hopeless stage stepped an
unlikely hero: Jane Addams.

THE FOUNDING OF HULL HOUSE

Jane Addams was born into a financially comfortable
family in the small town of Cedarville, Illinois—far
from the poverty and bustle of Chicago. A bright and
intellectually curious young woman, she attended
college and went on to study medicine, although
she did not complete her medical degree. Instead,
she spent several years traveling in Europe and
considering her choices for leading a meaningful
life. During a visit to London, Addams and her friend
Ellen Starr toured a settlement house—an urban
community center that provided needed services to
people in the neighborhood. There, Jane Addams
discovered her purpose.

In 1889, Addams and Starr leased a house, called
Hull House after the man who had built it, in a
poor, immigrant neighborhood of Chicago. Hull
House would be Addams's home for the rest of
her life. Addams and her partner, Starr, moved into
the house and immediately began renovating the
space, creating programs to help the people in
the neighborhood, and fundraising among wealthy
Chicagoans to support their work.

In this photo taken in 1930, Jane Addams holds a
little girl during the celebration of Hull House's 40th
anniversary. The settlement house was located in a
neighborhood that, at the time, had one of the city's
highest infant mortality rates. In response, Hull
House residents researched this problem as well as
others that affected people in their neighborhoods.
Their findings, often published in sociology journals,
provided evidence for activists lobbying for reforms.

Hull House provided a generous range of desperately
needed services, including a kindergarten, day
care, afternoon clubs for older children, classes
and activities for adults, a playground, a library, and
a boarding house for girls. Addams crusaded for
improvements throughout the city as well as in her
own neighborhood. She served on the city's board of
education and, at one point, worked as the garbage
inspector in the ward where Hull House was located.

BEYOND HULL HOUSE

Addams's work at Hull House gained her respect
and admiration from people throughout the country.
However, when she took her activism onto the
national scene, she was not afraid to take public
stances she knew would make her deeply unpopular.
She was opposed to war under any circumstance
and spoke out against fighting in World War I, even
after the United States had joined the war and
most Americans strongly supported it. After the
war, she continued to be critical of the military. She
also supported labor unions and openly criticized
elements of the American capitalist system. By the
1920s, J. Edgar Hoover, the director of the Federal
Bureau of Investigation (FBI), was calling Jane
Addams "the most dangerous woman in America"—
the same description that had been applied to
Mother Jones several years earlier by a U.S. attorney.

Then came the stock market crash of 1929 and the
beginning of the Great Depression, a time of poverty
and struggle for many Americans. Once again,
Addams's efforts on behalf of the poor came to the
forefront. She rose in the national esteem at the same
time she received international recognition. In 1931,
she was awarded the Nobel Peace Prize.

Jane Addams died only a few years later. Her
legacy of support for all people continues today in
the organizations she helped found, including the
National Association for the Advancement of Colored
People (NAACP), the American Civil Liberties Union
(ACLU), and the Women's International League for
Peace and Freedom. After 122 years of service, Hull
House closed in 2012. However, the site now houses
a museum dedicated to continuing Addams's vision
through research, education, and social engagement.

HISTORICAL THINKING

1. **READING CHECK** Why was Jane Addams
   unpopular during World War I?

2. **IDENTIFY PROBLEMS AND SOLUTIONS** What
   are some of the problems that Jane Addams worked
   to solve during her lifetime?

3. **MAKE CONNECTIONS** Think of an issue of local,
   national, or international concern today. What do
   you think Jane Addams would say about it?

PLAN: 2-PAGE LESSON

OBJECTIVE

**Examine how Jane Addams helped immigrants
and encouraged social reform.**

CRITICAL THINKING SKILLS FOR LESSON 3.4

• Identify Problems and Solutions

• Make Connections

• Identify

• Form and Support Opinions

HISTORICAL THINKING FOR CHAPTER 15

**What were the overall positive and negative
effects of industrialization on America?**
Industrialization fostered immigration to cities,
but many new immigrants dwelled in poverty.
Lesson 3.4 looks at how Jane Addams helped poor
immigrants and worked for social reform.

BACKGROUND FOR THE TEACHER

Jane Addams was a product of her upbringing in a
middle-class family that believed in individual rights
and a community's responsibility for its members.
Addams's time at college only reinforced her
belief in community service. But like others among
America's first generation of college-educated
women, she found few nonfamily roles available
to her other than teaching and missionary work.
Addams rejected both in favor of social work, civic
action, and social reform. Addams worked closely
with the social science faculty at the University
of Chicago and helped to found the university's
School of Social Work. She strongly believed
that social scientists should go beyond merely
investigating social problems and use the data they
gather to seek social reform through legislation
and advocacy.

HISTORY NOTEBOOK

Encourage students to complete the
American Voices page for Chapter 15 in their
History Notebooks as they read.

INTRODUCE & ENGAGE

BRAINSTORM A LIST

Ask students to imagine that they are planning an urban community center to help poor immigrants during the late 1800s and early 1900s. Have them brainstorm the services that the center should offer, using what they have learned about the time period to generate ideas. Then compile their ideas in a class list. Explain that this lesson describes the services and activities of Jane Addams at Hull House in Chicago.

TEACH

GUIDED DISCUSSION

1. **Identify** What services did Hull House provide? *(children's services, such as a playground, day care, kindergarten, and afternoon clubs for older children; adult classes and activities; a library; and a boarding house for girls)*

2. **Form and Support Opinions** Do you agree with Harold Ickes's description of Jane Addams as brave? Why or why not? *(Answers will vary. Possible response: Jane Addams was brave because she was willing to live and work in a poor neighborhood, challenge the Chicago city government to make improvements, and stand up for unpopular positions.)*

🛡 AMERICAN VOICES

Jane Addams did not limit Hull House's purpose to philanthropy and cultural uplift. She also viewed it as a place to gather information about immigrant needs, which she used to spur action from Chicago's government bureaucracy. Addams facilitated an exchange of knowledge that she believed was beneficial to all classes. Poor immigrants learned to navigate American culture and society, while politicians and other middle-class and wealthy native-born Americans came to appreciate what it meant to be poor. **ASK:** Why might Addams's approach yield longer-lasting results than would simple charity? *(Possible response: Addams's approach was designed to institute reforms at the societal level, not just to help individuals deal with immediate crises.)*

ACTIVE OPTIONS

On Your Feet: Rotating Discussion Divide students into four teams and assign each team a corner of the room. Ask each team to think of several questions based on the lesson's discussion of Jane Addams's life and reform efforts. Start the discussion by tossing a beanbag or other soft object to Team 1 and asking a question. After Team 1 answers the question, members should toss the beanbag to another team and ask one of their prepared questions. Correct any misconceptions revealed in the questions or answers and continue until teams have exhausted their questions.

NG Learning Framework: Profile Jane Addams

| ATTITUDE | Empowerment |
| KNOWLEDGE | Our Human Story |

Invite students to learn more about Jane Addams's ideas and reform efforts. Instruct them to write a short magazine article profiling Addams's work as a social reformer and activist. Encourage students to focus on a particular effort—such as sanitation, education, or peace—rather than write a general overview. Students can publish their profiles electronically, in a class blog or website, or in print in a class magazine.

DIFFERENTIATE

STRIVING READERS

Make a List Write this heading on the board: Five Things I know About Jane Addams and Her Work. After students read the lesson, ask them to copy the heading and list five statements under it. Invite volunteers to share their lists with the class.

GIFTED & TALENTED

Interpret Quotations Direct students' attention to the two quotes about Jane Addams in this lesson, one by Harold Ickes and the other by J. Edgar Hoover. Challenge students to interpret one or both comments artistically. For example, they might create a drawing, painting, or cartoon that incorporates a comment, or they might compose a song that includes the comment in its lyrics. Encourage students to collaborate on creating a format for presenting their creations to the class.

See the Chapter Planner for more strategies for differentiation.

HISTORICAL THINKING

ANSWERS

1. Addams was opposed to war and spoke out against U.S. participation in World War I, even though most Americans supported the war.

2. Addams focused on the plight of immigrants and the poor, education, sanitation, African-American civil rights, civil liberties, and peace.

3. Answers will vary. Students' responses should be consistent with information in the lesson.

MAIN IDEA In the late 19th and early 20th centuries, cities across the country grew in size and number as people seeking opportunity and excitement moved to them.

GROWING URBANIZATION

Some people prefer the wide-open spaces of a rural environment, but others crave the energy of city life. In the late 19th and early 20th centuries, Americans moved to cities for a host of reasons, and the cities grew to accommodate them.

FROM COUNTRY TO CITY

Between 1860 and 1920, American cities grew immensely, especially in the Northeast and Midwest. For example, Chicago's population swelled from about 109,000 in 1860 to about 1.1 million by 1890. However, rapid urbanization was not confined to the Northeast and Midwest. In the 1890s, a new railroad connected south Florida, including Miami, with northeastern cities. By the following decade, the swampy land of southern Florida was drained to attract new residents with its affordable property and warm climate. Miami's expansion was so rapid that it acquired the nickname "Magic City."

Many factors contributed to American urbanization. The ever growing number of immigrants—more than 8 million between 1870 and 1890 alone—generally settled in the cities where they arrived. Increased industrialization and trade played a role as well. As a result of extensive railroad systems, cities such as Chicago could receive large shipments of food and other goods, which brokers then sold and transported to markets throughout the nation. Declining crop prices also drove people from rural areas into the cities when farming no longer provided them with a livable income.

Cities offered exciting opportunities for people to meet others, enjoy cultural events, and live independent lives. Many single men and women took advantage of these opportunities. A great many of them rented rooms in boardinghouses, a living arrangement where a landlord or lady leased rooms in his or her home for a reasonable amount of money per week. The proprietor of the boardinghouse provided three meals a day, served in a common dining room, and kept the boarders' rooms clean. Boarders also had access to the parlor, where they could socialize with each other. It was an economical way for newcomers to make friends and learn about the city in a safe home environment.

Cities also offered a wide variety of entertainments. Young and old Americans alike enjoyed amusement parks, dance halls, and **vaudeville** theaters. Vaudeville, a type of show featuring a variety of specialty acts such as singing and instrumental music, dancing, comedy, drama, and acrobatics, was popular with urban audiences.

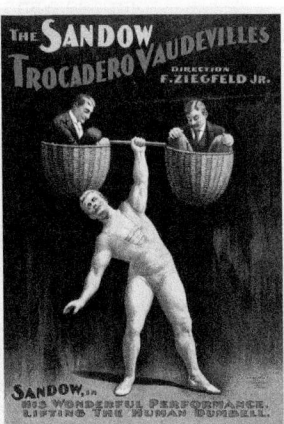

Colorful posters like this one from 1894 advertised vaudeville productions and promised thrilling and exotic entertainment—including strongmen lifting humans high overhead.

CITY STRUCTURES

Busy, crowded, and growing cities need efficient forms of public transportation. In the 1880s, **streetcars** became the main form of transportation in urban centers, and cities that had streetcar systems, such as Boston, San Francisco, Chicago, and New York, became known as "streetcar cities." Streetcars helped foster the development of a city's central district because they gave people a means for traveling to and from the city to shop and work. At the same time, streetcars allowed people to travel easily to the outskirts of the city, so those who wanted to escape city living could move to emerging communities on the city's edge, called **suburbs**.

A city's central district featured businesses such as banks, railroad terminals, and the growth of new places to shop: **department stores**. First introduced in the United States in the mid-1800s, department stores offered a unique shopping experience by providing a wide variety of merchandise all under one roof. They drew shoppers from the suburbs. Chicago's Marshall Field & Company and New York's R.H. Macy & Company brought many customers into the big city.

As city populations grew, finding enough space to house all the residents quickly became a problem.

When cities could not spread out, they found another solution: they built up. The revolutionary use of steel frameworks in construction allowed builders in Chicago to erect the first skyscraper—an incredible 10-story building—in the 1880s. Skyscrapers were soon standing 30 stories high or more in American cities, making efficient use of limited available urban space. Moreover, the development of the commercial electric passenger elevator just a few years after the first skyscraper's construction added to the practicality and usefulness of these tall buildings. But not everyone could afford to live in a roomy apartment in a skyscraper or move to the suburbs. Many city dwellers rented space in tightly packed, poorly ventilated tenements. The intense overcrowding in poor urban neighborhoods led to many public health problems that required solutions, and reformers ultimately took up the cause.

HISTORICAL THINKING

1. **READING CHECK** What factors contributed to urbanization between 1860 and 1920?

2. **ANALYZE CAUSE AND EFFECT** What effect did the use of steel have on building construction and the growth of cities?

3. **EXPLAIN** How and why did suburbs emerge in the late 19th century?

CRITICAL VIEWING Shoppers who patronized R.H. Macy & Company (center) in New York City in 1906 arrived by streetcar, horse-and-carriage, walking, or an elevated train line. How does the photo convey that commerce, transportation, and people are all interdependent?

PLAN: 2-PAGE LESSON

OBJECTIVE

Identify factors that contributed to urban growth in the late 1800s and early 1900s, including characteristics of city life, demographic shifts, and other developments.

CRITICAL THINKING SKILLS FOR LESSON 4.1

• Analyze Cause and Effect

• Explain

• Make Connections

HISTORICAL THINKING FOR CHAPTER 15

What were the overall positive and negative effects of industrialization on America?
Industrialization prompted a population shift from rural to urban areas, contributing to rapid city growth. Lesson 4.1 focuses on this growth.

BACKGROUND FOR THE TEACHER

Architects and engineers faced a geological challenge building skyscrapers in Chicago. Tall buildings need a solid base to carry their weight. New York had solid rock close to the surface, but bedrock in Chicago was buried as deep as 85 feet from the surface under a mixture of clay, sand, and gravel that journalists in the 1800s compared to jelly. Architects and engineers designed several solutions to address the problem, including sinking evenly spaced piers into the mushy clay to distribute a structure's weight. Eventually, construction workers built watertight chambers to work underground, allowing them to extend skyscraper foundations to the bedrock.

INTRODUCE & ENGAGE

THINK LIKE A CITY PLANNER

Have students think about life in large cities. **ASK:** Why might a crowded city prefer to build up rather than simply spread out? *(Answers will vary. Possible responses: Spreading out means providing city services over a wider geographic area, which complicates transportation in terms of roads, transit, and travel time and results in smaller customer bases for individual businesses; building up means more people can live and work in the city center.)* Tell students in this lesson they will read about the growth of cities in the late 1800s and early 1900s.

TEACH

GUIDED DISCUSSION

1. **Make Connections** What evidence supports the idea that cities provided men and women the opportunity to live independent lives? *(Possible response: Boardinghouses offered single men and women an inexpensive living arrangement in which they could rent just one room in a house. That gave people a chance to live independently from their families.)*

2. **Explain** How did department stores benefit shoppers and a city's central business district? *(Department stores provided shoppers with the convenience of accessing a variety of goods under one roof. They benefited central business districts by bringing customers to the city centers.)*

MORE INFORMATION

Electric Elevators Early elevators were used for freight. The possibility of the ropes breaking and plunging the elevator to the ground made them unfit for moving people. Elisha Graves Otis solved the problem and paved the way for passenger elevators by developing a safety clamp that locked the elevator to the side rails if a rope broke. The first passenger elevator, which was powered by steam, was installed at New York's Haughtwout & Company department store in 1857. It was almost 30 years before an electric motor replaced steam in passenger elevators. **ASK:** Why do you think installing the first passenger elevator would have appealed to owners of a department store? *(Answers will vary. Possible responses: They might have thought the novelty would attract customers; they might have seen the elevator as key to expanding their business's offerings.)*

ACTIVE OPTIONS

On Your Feet: Inside-Outside Circle Allow students time to write questions about the demographic shift from rural to urban, the growth and structure of cities, and city life in the late 1800s and early 1900s. Then have students form two concentric circles facing each other. Students in the inside circle pose questions to students in the outside circle; then the circles switch roles. Students may ask for help from other students in their circle if they are unable to answer a question.

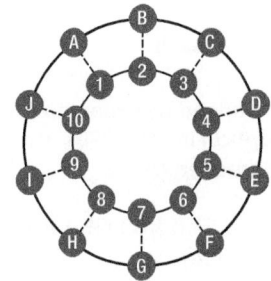

NG Learning Framework: Understand Urban Innovations

SKILL Communication

KNOWLEDGE New Frontiers

Ask students to conduct further research on one of the developments affecting the growth and structure of turn-of-the-century cities, such as streetcars, suburbs, or skyscrapers. Instruct them to write a short description of this development based on information in the lesson and their research. Then direct students to use their descriptions to discuss how the growth of cities might have been different if these developments had not occurred.

DIFFERENTIATE

ENGLISH LANGUAGE LEARNERS

Make Word Cards Invite students at the **Expanding** level to make word cards for the terms *streetcar, suburbs,* and *department store.* You may add other words from the lesson, such as *outskirts, skyscraper,* and *overcrowding.* Tell students to write each term on one side of a card and illustrate it on the opposite side. Students then pair with another student, present each illustration, and ask their partner to determine which term is being illustrated. Each pair continues until all cards are shared.

GIFTED & TALENTED

Create a Vaudeville Show Ask students to research vaudeville shows in late 19th- and early 20th-century America. Then have them create a program for a vaudeville show, including a variety of performances ranging from comedy to serious lectures, from classical to popular music, and from dance to drama. If time permits, encourage students to develop some of their acts and present a short vaudeville show to the class.

See the Chapter Planner for more strategies for differentiation.

HISTORICAL THINKING

ANSWERS

1. Increased immigration, industrialization and trade, declining crop prices that drove rural workers to cities in search of work, and people seeking new opportunities all contributed to urbanization.

2. Steel frameworks enabled the development of skyscrapers, which provided living and working space for more people.

3. Streetcars aided the emergence of suburbs by making it possible for people to live on the outskirts of the city but still work and shop in the city center.

CRITICAL VIEWING Transportation is carrying people and goods to and from the city. Some people are carrying packages, suggesting that they have been shopping in the stores.

MAIN IDEA In the 1890s, a new set of reformers addressed various problems stemming from urbanization and political corruption.

TACKLING URBAN PROBLEMS

When big problems are not solved by those in charge, sometimes ordinary citizens step up and become the agents of change. In the late 1800s, reformers took on social and political problems that had been brewing for several decades.

CITY PROBLEMS, CITY POLITICS

The growing density of urban populations during the late 19th century caused great concern among both public health officials and social reformers. Before 1895, effective departments of **sanitation**, or proper waste disposal and a system for providing clean water, did not exist in cities. Horse manure and garbage accumulated in the streets, while noxious factory smoke filled the air. Such unsanitary conditions made poor sections of cities particularly susceptible to outbreaks of illnesses such as

cholera, a deadly disease that people sometimes contract after drinking contaminated water. Crowded conditions increased the amount of damage caused by fires and the likelihood of violent and criminal acts.

Corruption in big city governments was an accepted practice, and political machines were in charge. **Political machines**, or agreed upon, exclusive power structures, involved city officials bribing politicians, contractors, and constituents with all manner of favors to keep the city running. Bribes, promises, and favors were the oil that greased the political machine. In cities such as Chicago and New York, political machines were efficient but corrupt methods of city management.

New York's William Magear Tweed, or "Boss Tweed," ran one of the most notorious political machines. In the 1860s, Tweed led a Democratic Party committee called **Tammany Hall**, and, similar to the spoils system that arose during the Jackson presidency, he used his position to award city contracts to associates and supporters. Newspapers accused Tweed of corruption, but the inner-city residents, whom the machine depended on for votes, saw value in the system. The contracts that Tweed awarded improved the residents' neighborhoods by paving roads, installing sewers and gas lines, and building parks and elevated train lines. Corruption charges eventually brought Tweed down in the early 1870s but did not disable political machines as a whole.

Because of the political corruption and gaudy excesses of the wealthy, the years between 1870 and 1900 became known as the **Gilded Age**. To gild something means to coat it with a thin layer of gold that can disguise what lies underneath. The phrase "Gilded Age" originated with the novel *The Gilded Age* by Mark Twain and Charles Dudley Warner. The authors used the term to highlight the way spectacular wealth masked the greed and corruption of industrialists and politicians.

REFORMING SOCIAL ILLS

Many Americans knew what was underneath the gilded layer, and they believed that governments did not do enough to solve the problems that stemmed from urbanization. In the 1890s, individuals organized a number of different reform movements to address social problems. These reformers were mostly native-born, middle class, white, and Protestant. They believed that society was responsible for the common good of all its citizens and that social ills resulting from industrial growth and political corruption had to be addressed.

Because one of the root values of these reformers was a belief in progress, the various reform movements became known as **progressivism**. Progressive reformers worked in many different capacities to achieve reforms. Some focused on improving urban living conditions. Some addressed the injustices of child labor, and others challenged big-city bosses and government corruption. While they may have focused on different issues, progressive reformers shared similar goals: addressing social problems such as poverty and exploitation, exposing corruption, reforming government, and expanding democracy.

Thanks to the writings of several novelists and journalists, even Americans who did not live in places like New York City or Chicago learned about the horrendous living conditions in these cities. As you have read, Upton Sinclair's 1906 novel *The Jungle* exposed the dangerous and filthy working conditions of Chicago's stockyards and the abusive treatment immigrant workers endured in the city. Like Ida Tarbell and other muckrakers, Sinclair shined a light on suffering and injustice and the need for reform.

The authors **Theodore Dreiser** and **Frank Norris** also highlighted social problems in their novels. Dreiser had grown up in poverty, and he used his experiences to inform his writing. He described urban poverty in *Sister Carrie* and targeted the legal system in *An American Tragedy*. Likewise, Frank Norris, in his novels *McTeague* and *The Octopus*, explored social issues such as the wheat industry's conflicts with railway monopolies.

Besides addressing social problems, progressive reformers aimed to clean up government by passing new laws that gave citizens the right to initiate **referendums**, or public votes on individual issues, and the right to recall, or remove, an elected official from office. These measures were one way to keep political figures and political machines from gaining too much power. Other progressive reforms included enforcing state regulation of industry and giving voters, instead of party officers, the chance to choose nominees for important political offices.

The late 1800s saw the beginning of many reforms in society and government. Even so, some deeply held prejudices still lurked in American society.

Butchers pause for a photo in Chicago's meatpacking district in 1904. Upton Sinclair exposed the ill treatment of workers and unsanitary and dangerous conditions in slaughterhouses. Through one of his characters in *The Jungle*, he asserts that "one of the consequences of civic administration by ignorant and vicious politicians, is that preventable diseases kill off half our population."

HISTORICAL THINKING

1. **READING CHECK** What steps did reformers take to try to improve citizens' lives and government practices?

2. **IDENTIFY PROBLEMS AND SOLUTIONS** In what ways did change in the late 19th and early 20th centuries affect politics, values, and beliefs?

3. **DESCRIBE** Why did poor city residents have positive feelings about political machines such as Tammany Hall?

PLAN: 2-PAGE LESSON

OBJECTIVE

Identify problems caused by urbanization and political corruption in the 1890s and the reformers who addressed them.

CRITICAL THINKING SKILLS FOR LESSON 4.2

• Identify Problems and Solutions

• Describe

• Form and Support Opinions

• Analyze Visuals

HISTORICAL THINKING FOR CHAPTER 15

What were the overall positive and negative effects of industrialization on America?
American industrialization led to several urban problems. Lesson 4.2 describes the poor living conditions and the political corruption in cities and the efforts made by reformers to combat these problems.

BACKGROUND FOR THE TEACHER

The amount of money plundered from New York City by Boss Tweed's ring is estimated at between $30 million and $200 million. Boss Tweed was toppled in large part through the efforts of the *New York Times* and the political cartoons of Thomas Nast in *Harper's Weekly*. In 1871, the *New York Times* obtained information that detailed how Tweed planned to pocket public money that was intended for furnishing a new courthouse. Tweed offered the newspaper $5 million to squash the story. However, the editor of the paper refused, and the articles were published in July 1871. Tweed was convicted of the theft two years later and sent to prison.

Tweed also at one point offered Nast $500,000 to stop creating and publishing the damaging cartoons, which Nast refused.

INTRODUCE & ENGAGE

CREATE A WORD WEB

Create a Word Web like the one shown with the term *urban problems* in the center. Ask students to suggest words they associate with present-day problems in cities. Then discuss solutions that have been attempted to solve the problems listed. Tell students that this lesson discusses the problems facing cities and the attempts at reform.

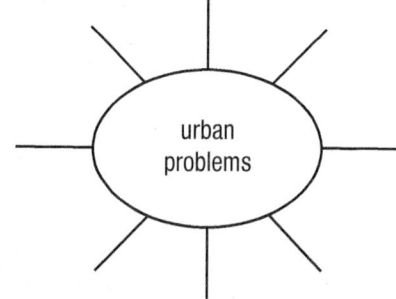

TEACH

GUIDED DISCUSSION

1. **Form and Support Opinions** Do you think that the phrase *Gilded Age* was a good description for the time between 1870 and 1900 in the United States? Explain. *(Answers will vary. Possible response: The Gilded Age described the time period well. It was a time that appeared to be one of wealth and prosperity, but this phrase disguised the greed and political corruption that was prevalent and the poor conditions under which many people lived and worked.)*

2. **Identify Problems and Solutions** How did progressive reformers attempt to clean up government and stem political corruption? *(Progressive reformers passed laws giving citizens the right to initiate referendums and recall elected officials in an attempt to keep political figures and political machines from gaining too much power. The reformers also pushed for enforcing state regulation of industry and giving voters the chance to choose nominees for important political offices.)*

ANALYZE VISUALS

Direct students' attention to the photo of butchers in Chicago's meatpacking district. **ASK:** What sanitation issues in the meatpacking industry does this photo illustrate? *(Answers will vary. Possible response: Workers carry meat while wearing no gloves to protect them from transmitting bacteria. They wear filthy coats over regular clothes. Non-workers appear to be allowed in the meatpacking plant.)* Discuss with students why Upton Sinclair might have written about the scene in this photo in *The Jungle*. Then ask students to write a caption for the photo that could be included in Sinclair's book. Have students share their captions with the class.

ACTIVE OPTIONS

On Your Feet: Three-Step Interview Have students work in pairs. One student should interview the other using these questions: Why were the years between 1870 and 1900 known as the Gilded Age? How did progressive reformers attempt to achieve political change in the late 1800s? Then students should reverse roles. Finally, each student should share the results of his or her interview with the class.

NG Learning Framework: Be a Reformer
ATTITUDE Responsibility
SKILL Problem-Solving

Organize students into small groups and have them discuss social problems today that they believe need to be addressed. Encourage them to consider problems on the school, community, or national level. Then ask them to take on the role of reformers and do research using different forms of media to write an article that describes the problems and also suggests possible ways in which the government or individuals could solve them. Ask group representatives to read the finished articles. Finally, hold a class discussion in which students compare the problems and solutions they identified.

DIFFERENTIATE

STRIVING READERS

Summarize With students working in pairs, assign each student to read a paragraph aloud while a partner listens and takes notes. Tell students that after the first student reads, the partner will summarize the paragraph in one or two spoken sentences. Encourage students to ask each other questions as they come across complex information.

PRE-AP

Present an Oral Report Ask students to prepare and present oral reports on one of the books featured in the lesson, such as *The Jungle, Sister Carrie,* or *An American Tragedy.* Students can choose one or more excerpts to highlight and present to the class. Instruct them to focus on excerpts that illustrate the social problems the author targeted. Encourage students to include visuals in their reports to enhance interest and understanding.

See the Chapter Planner for more strategies for differentiation.

HISTORICAL THINKING

ANSWERS

1. They formed a new movement called progressivism, which encouraged the government to take a more active role in fixing society's problems and called for an expansion of democracy. Some writers, like Upton Sinclair, also wrote books about these problems, increasing the public's awareness of them.

2. Possible response: Growing urbanization in the late 19th and early 20th centuries led to many instances of political corruption, with city officials deciding what services and improvements were to be made based on favors, bribes, and promises. Many Americans realized that social reform was necessary to rid the cities of their problems, which led to a shift toward progressive values and beliefs.

3. The contracts that Boss Tweed awarded to supporters and associates ended up helping improve the inner-city neighborhoods. The neighborhoods got roads, sewers, gas lines, parks, and elevated trains as a result of the contracts.

JIM CROW AND SEGREGATION

Sometimes the struggle against injustice runs into obstacles, as personal and institutional prejudices get in the way of making laws that are fair for everybody. Although progressive reformers had made headway with social and political reforms, many African Americans still faced massive challenges.

SUPPRESSING THE VOTE

As you have read, during Reconstruction, laws were enacted in the South to protect the rights of African Americans and bring them into the larger society as full-fledged citizens. The 13th, 14th, and 15th amendments, respectively, abolished slavery, granted equal protection under the law to all Americans, and extended the right to vote to African-American males. But after Reconstruction ended, southern states and communities passed laws meant to undermine these reforms. African Americans experienced what historians refer to as the "black nadir," or the lowest point since the end of the

Civil War. Racial violence and legalized discrimination inhibited African Americans' economic opportunities and political participation.

Southern state, county, and local legislatures set their sights on the 15th Amendment in particular. Tactics targeting African-American voting rights, such as the implementation of poll taxes and literacy tests, were complicated and difficult to get around. For example, poll taxes were typically between one and two dollars, but the equivalent of a dollar in 1877 equaled more than $22.00 by 2017 standards. That was unaffordable for many poor people of any

Poll taxes were common throughout the nation in the latter 19th century, and faded away in the 20th century, except in the South. This receipt from San Francisco, California, shows that James Leonard paid a poll tax of $2.00 in 1890. California abolished the tax in 1914. Fifty years later, the 24th Amendment abolished the poll tax nationwide.

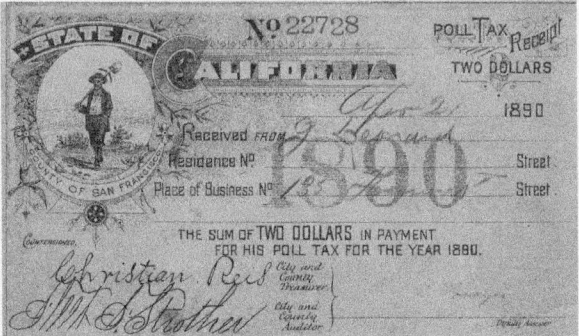

ethnicity. In addition, counties, cities, and towns sometimes each levied their own separate poll taxes, which put an even greater burden on those hoping to register.

Poll taxes were an impediment to poor white citizens as well as African Americans, but several southern states found a way around that problem through the use of a legal provision called a **grandfather clause**. The clause stated that those who had the right to vote prior to 1866 or 1867—or their direct descendants—were not subject to some or all voting requirements, such as poll taxes or literacy tests. This allowed poor and illiterate white men to register to vote, but denied that right to many African Americans.

The first literacy tests required for voter registration didn't arise in the South, but in New England. In 1855, Connecticut instituted a law requiring a year's residency in the state and successful completion of a literacy test before a citizen could register to vote. The state's intent was to discourage Irish immigrants from voting. After Reconstruction, southern states adopted this practice. Literacy tests took many forms, from requiring a citizen to read and answer questions to interpreting a portion of a state's constitution. But the registrar of voters had the final say over who passed. A white applicant might answer all questions incorrectly and pass, while an African-American applicant might provide accurate answers and fail.

Perhaps the worst hurdle for African Americans wishing to register to vote was intimidation. Most voter registration applications had to be made at the courthouse where, in some places, white police officers waited to arrest applicants on petty or made-up charges. In many southern locales, white business owners organized White Citizens Councils that retaliated against minorities who attempted to vote. Registrars released applicants' personal information to the councils, which then punished prospective voters by encouraging their employers to fire them or persuading their landlords to evict them.

Many council members were also part of the Ku Klux Klan. Due to the federal anti-Klan legislation of the early 1870s, Klan membership had dwindled by 1880, but the racism that fueled the organization never died out. Despite the low profile of the Klan during the 1890s, the practice of lynching continued, and its members murdered on average 187 African Americans every year throughout the decade. The Klan began to build its membership again in 1915.

People wear badges to identify as members of a group. In the 1920s, some Americans wore these badges to be identified as Klan members. The badge on the left is in the shape of a Klan hood.

SEPARATION BASED ON RACE

Discrimination against African Americans was common practice throughout the United States, but it occurred most rampantly in the South. After the end of Reconstruction, southern politicians remained intent on enforcing **segregation**, or the separation of different groups of people, usually based on race. They passed a series of laws to ensure that African-American and white citizens attended separate schools and used separate public facilities, such as restrooms, theaters, restaurants, and public transportation. In states such as Florida, Louisiana, and Mississippi, whites enforced these laws, known as **Jim Crow laws**, to establish and maintain power in society. Jim Crow was an African-American character in minstrel shows of the day—a dim-witted, comic fellow, portrayed by a white actor in blackface, who was the target of ridicule and the butt of jokes. That the name of this character became associated with segregation laws is just one more affront to those to whom the laws applied.

One Jim Crow law had a particularly significant effect. In 1890, Louisiana passed the Separate Car Act, which required "equal but separate accommodations" for white and African-American train passengers. In other words, the railroads had to offer the same accommodations to whites and African Americans, but in separate rail cars.

A New Orleans committee that supported African-American rights decided to test the act's constitutionality. Because the act did not define the meaning of *white* or *African-American*, the committee

---

INTRODUCE & ENGAGE

CONNECT TO TODAY

Write the term *equal rights* in the center of a Concept Cluster on the board. **ASK:** What do you think of when you hear that term? How does the term apply to issues of equal rights facing the nation today? *(Answers will vary. Possible responses include African Americans' fight against discrimination, women's rights for equal pay, equal rights for transgender people, and the fight against continued voter suppression.)* Tell students that they will learn about the struggles of African Americans in the late 1800s in facing prejudice and discrimination and about their response.

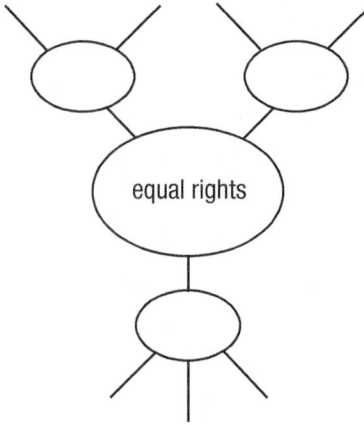

equal rights

TEACH

GUIDED DISCUSSION

1. **Evaluate** What is the connection between Reconstruction and poll taxes and literacy-test requirements? *(Reconstruction attempted to correct injustices against African Americans; however, Southern communities passed laws to prevent African Americans from voting and participating politically.)*

2. **Form and Support Opinions** After the Civil War, why do you think discrimination against African Americans was common practice throughout the United States, not just in the South? *(Answers will vary. Possible response: Though some people in the North maintained strong beliefs about the importance of equal rights for African Americans, discriminatory practices had already taken a serious hold on American society in general; therefore, though the North did not adopt severe discriminatory regulations such as the South's Jim Crow laws, discrimination remained a common practice.)*

ANALYZE VISUALS

Tell students to examine the photo of the KKK badges and read the caption. **ASK:** What was the purpose of the badges? *(The badges identified the person wearing them as a member of the KKK.)* Why do you think a person would want to be identified as a KKK member? *(Possible responses: People who would wear the badges would have been proud to be a member of the KKK and would have supported the organization's views about violent tactics toward African Americans; badge wearers could use the badges to intimidate any African Americans they encountered.)*

DIFFERENTIATE

STRIVING READERS

Create a Concept Cluster In the center oval of a Concept Cluster, write the word *segregation*. Add *voting rights*, *Jim Crow Laws*, and *African-American activism* to the other three ovals. Tell students to copy the graphic organizer. Have them reread the lesson to complete the cluster, citing specific examples of discrimination regarding voting rights, Jim Crow laws, and African Americans' activism in response to segregation. When students have completed their Concept Clusters, tell them to share them with a partner, noting similarities and differences.

PRE-AP

Research a Court Ruling Point out to students that after a legal decision is made by the U.S. Supreme Court, justices are chosen to prepare majority and dissenting opinions. A majority opinion states the decision of the court and provides reasons for the court's decision. A dissenting opinion expresses disagreements with the court's decision. Ask students to research the majority opinion and the dissenting opinion in *Plessy* v. *Ferguson*. Have them summarize the two opinions in their own words. Hold a class discussion about the reasons for and against the court ruling presented in the opinions.

See the Chapter Planner for more strategies for differentiation.

CRITICAL VIEWING Possible response: The words suggest that though slavery had been dismantled, African Americans after Reconstruction continued to face discrimination and violence. As a result, their lives were not much better than they were under slavery.

CRITICAL VIEWING White bi-plane passengers tow a group of African-American passengers behind them in this 1913 cartoon from the New York humor magazine, *Puck*. What details in the cartoon demonstrate a northern critique of the "separate but equal" policies legalized by *Plessy v. Ferguson*?

Our greatest danger is that in the great leap from slavery to freedom we may overlook the fact that the masses of us are to live by the productions of our hands, and fail to keep in mind that we shall prosper in proportion as we learn to dignify and glorify common labor and put brains and skill into the common occupations of life. No race can prosper till it learns that there is as much dignity in tilling a field as in writing a poem. It is at the bottom of life we must begin, and not at the top. Nor should we permit our grievances to overshadow our opportunities.

—from the "Atlanta Compromise" speech, by Booker T. Washington, 1895

How does Washington's speech reflect the Tuskegee Institute's goals?

The supplementary truths must never be lost sight of: first, slavery and race-prejudice are potent . . . causes of the Negro's position; second, industrial and common-school training were necessarily slow in planting because they had to await the black teachers trained by higher institutions . . . and, third, while it is a great truth to say that the Negro must strive and strive mightily to help himself, it is equally true that unless his striving be not simply seconded, but rather aroused and encouraged, by the initiative of the richer and wiser environing group, he cannot hope for great success.

—from *The Souls of Black Folk*, by W.E.B. Du Bois, 1903

What is Du Bois's main critique of Washington's theories?

claimed the railroads could not consistently apply the act. To prove its point, in 1892, the committee enlisted Homer Plessy to purchase a train ticket in Louisiana. Plessy was one-eighth African-American. When he purposely sat in the car reserved for whites, a conductor told Plessy to move to the African-American car. Plessy refused and was arrested.

Plessy challenged the railroad company in the 1896 Supreme Court case *Plessy v. Ferguson*. The court decided that the Separate Car Act did not violate the 14th Amendment's guarantee of "equal protection of the laws" because the railroad company offered equal accommodations, even if they were separate. In a strong dissent from the majority of the court, Justice John Marshall Harlan wrote, "I am of the opinion that the statute of Louisiana is inconsistent with the personal liberties of citizens, white and black, in that State, and hostile to both the spirit and the letter of the Constitution of the United States." By ruling against Plessy, the Supreme Court upheld the practice of segregation, thereby allowing other businesses and institutions to apply a "**separate but equal**" treatment to African Americans for decades.

Public schools enforced "separate but equal" segregation policies. African-American and white students attended different schools, but they were rarely equal. Whites had much better access to schools and the public funding needed to pay for them. African Americans, on the other hand, often had to pay to build schools themselves and resort to using second-hand supplies, such as outdated textbooks that white schools gave them.

SELF-RELIANCE VS. SOCIAL REFORM

African-American leaders responded to segregation laws, but in very different ways. Some supported the idea of working to make changes from within the system. Others championed open protest because they believed that was the only route to securing their denied rights.

Booker T. Washington was an educator who founded the Tuskegee Institute in Alabama in 1881 to train African Americans to be teachers. Eventually, though, Washington incorporated vocational classes at the institute, teaching manual trades and developing students' agricultural skills.

Washington also promoted self-reliance among African Americans, believing they should focus on hard work and personal development rather than on trying to reform entrenched, systemic racism. He thought the best way for African Americans to win the respect of whites was for them to prove themselves worthy of that respect. In 1895, Washington presented his ideas in a speech at the Cotton States and International Exposition in Atlanta, Georgia. In his speech, known as the "Atlanta Compromise" speech, Washington encouraged African Americans to refrain from openly and actively promoting social equality.

Washington's emphasis on self-reliance helped him raise money for the institute, especially from white donors. Although Washington did not publicly promote social reform, he did privately fund court challenges to segregation.

In contrast, historian, sociologist, and reformer **W.E.B. Du Bois** (doo-BOYS) believed that protest was the best path toward gaining equality and ending segregation. Du Bois charged that Washington's acceptance of discrimination helped promote bigotry rather than deter it. He critiqued the ideas of self-reliance in his book *The Souls of Black Folk*, and, in the process, motivated others to oppose Washington's approach.

By 1903, the year *The Souls of Black Folk* was published, eight years had passed since Washington's "Atlanta Compromise" speech. Little had improved in the daily lives of African Americans, however. Racial violence, discrimination, and segregation worked against African Americans' limited ability to participate in the political process, and the activism proposed by Du Bois gained favor.

In 1905, Du Bois founded a small organization called the Niagara Movement, which attacked Washington's ideas. The organization died out in 1909, but that same year Du Bois co-founded the **National Association for the Advancement of Colored People (NAACP)** with other African-American leaders and white supporters. DuBois served as the organization's director of research and edited its magazine, *The Crisis*. His hope was that the NAACP could be a force for change in ending segregation and discrimination against African Americans. In fact, reform did begin to attract greater attention as the nation entered a new period of rapid change.

HISTORICAL THINKING

1. **READING CHECK** What were Jim Crow laws, and why were they instituted?

2. **ANALYZE CAUSE AND EFFECT** How might poor white citizens in the South avoid voter suppression tactics such as poll taxes and literacy tests?

3. **EVALUATE** Regarding the events discussed in this lesson, evaluate what aspects of African Americans' lives changed and what aspects stayed the same.

4. **IDENTIFY PROBLEMS AND SOLUTIONS** What different solutions did Booker T. Washington and W.E.B. Du Bois propose as ways to fight discrimination against African Americans?

BUILD BACKGROUND

DIFFERENT BACKGROUNDS AND VIEWS

Booker T. Washington and W.E.B. Du Bois came from vastly different backgrounds. Washington was born into slavery in Virginia in 1856. After emancipation, his family moved to West Virginia. Poverty forced Washington to begin working at nine years of age. In 1872, he enrolled at the Hampton Normal and Agricultural Institute in Virginia, one of the first all-black schools in the United States. In 1881, he was selected to lead the Tuskegee Normal and Industrial Institute in Alabama. The school provided African Americans with practical work skills to be successful in the industrial world. Washington believed that becoming economically independent and productive members of society would eventually result in true equality for African Americans.

W.E.B. Du Bois was born in Massachusetts in 1868 to a free black family. His family lived in a basically integrated community. He attended local schools and graduated as valedictorian of his class. Du Bois first faced discrimination when he began attending Fisk University in Tennessee. That experience greatly influenced him. His goal upon returning to the North to further his education was to push for equal rights for African Americans. He earned a doctorate degree from Harvard University in 1895, the first African American to do so. His dissertation, "The Suppression of the African Slave Trade to the United States of America, 1638–1870," was one of the first papers on the subject.

TEACH

GUIDED DISCUSSION

4. **Draw Conclusions** How did the ruling in *Plessy* v. *Ferguson* promote segregation in the United States? *(The ruling legalized segregation in public places.)*

5. **Identify Problems and Solutions** What problem was W.E.B. Du Bois trying to solve and how did he attempt to solve it? *(Possible response: Du Bois wanted to solve the problem of segregation and discrimination that African Americans faced. He attempted to solve the problem by calling for activism to push for immediate equality for African Americans. He founded the Niagara Movement and co-founded the NAACP.)*

ANALYZE PRIMARY SOURCES

Direct students' attention to the Primary Sources feature. Have them work with partners to compare and contrast Washington's and Du Bois's views on how to gain equality for and end the segregation of African Americans. Encourage students to use a graphic organizer like the Venn diagram shown here to organize their thoughts. Then hold a class discussion in which pairs share their comparisons. Take time to clarify any descrepancies so students clearly understand each man's point of view. Ask students to use evidence to evaluate which person provided a better argument for how to fight discrimination.

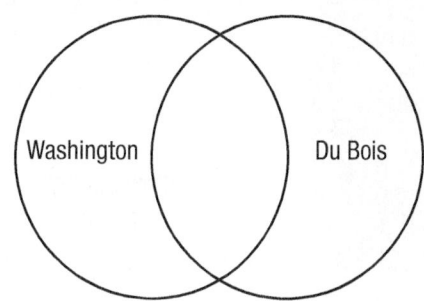

ACTIVE OPTIONS

On Your Feet: Use a Jigsaw Strategy

Organize students into "expert" groups and have students from each group analyze one of the following amendments: 13th Amendment, 14th Amendment, 15th Amendment. Ask students in each group to summarize their analysis in their own words. Then have the members of each group count off using the letters A, B, C, and so on. Regroup students so that each new group has at least one member from each expert group. Have students in the new groups take turns sharing the simplified summaries they came up with in their expert groups.

NG Learning Framework: Create a Social Media Page

SKILL Communication

KNOWLEDGE Our Human Story

Have students work in groups to research the founding of the NAACP and to create a social media page about the founding. Explain that their page should reenact the announcement of the formation of the organization, as if such technology had been available in 1909. Direct students to include the organization's mission statement, short biographies of the founding members, and the initiatives that the organization expects to launch. Encourage students to include photographs where appropriate.

HISTORICAL THINKING

ANSWERS

1. Jim Crow laws were laws that enforced the segregation of whites and African Americans in order to maintain the white power structure.

2. Poor white citizens in the South avoided poll taxes or literacy tests by qualifying for exceptions under a grandfather clause, or if the registrar of voters let them vote even if they failed any tests.

3. Possible response: African Americans' lives changed in the sense that they had attained equal protection under constitutional law and that males had been granted the right to vote. However, realistically, their lives hadn't really changed; voting was close to impossible, economic opportunities were denied, and "separate but equal" rulings limited access to education.

4. Booker T. Washington thought that African Americans should fight discrimination by focusing on hard work and personal development to improve themselves, rather than by focusing on social reform. W.E.B. Du Bois thought that protest was the only way to fight discrimination, and he thought Washington's approach actually encouraged, rather than discouraged, discrimination.

PRIMARY SOURCES

Answers will vary. Possible response: In his speech, Booker T. Washington stressed that having skills that can be applied to common occupations is the way for African Americans to succeed economically. He believed a vocational education would accomplish that. His belief reflected the goals of the Tuskegee Institute, which included vocational classes that taught manual trades and agricultural skills.

Answers will vary. Possible response: Du Bois's main critique of Washington's theories was that although Washington called for vocational education for African Americans, there were not enough trained African-American teachers who would be able to train them.

CRITICAL VIEWING Answers will vary. Possible response: The African Americans are separate from the white passengers and crowded together under an air balloon that is connected to the bi-plane. Their form of transportation is dependent on the bi-plane to work; therefore, it is not equal to the form of transportation used by the white people in the bi-plane.

CONFRONTING RACIAL VIOLENCE

Beginning in the 1870s, African Americans realized the freedoms they had gained following the Civil War were under attack. Many white people sought to manipulate laws to return African Americans to what, in effect, would be slavery. When laws failed to work, some white people turned to violence, wrecking the property of African Americans and resorting to lynching. In retaliation, some African Americans fought violence with violence. Others fled their homes. But many turned to nonviolent protest.

CRITICAL VIEWING One way white southerners terrorized African Americans during the years after the Civil War—and well into the 20th century—was by burning down their houses and farms and destroying their crops and belongings. *Burned Out*, painted by William H. Johnson around 1943, depicts an African-American couple standing in front of their burning house with the few possessions they managed to rescue. How does the painting convey the vulnerability of African Americans in a hostile society?

🏛 Smithsonian American Art Museum Washington, D.C.

William H. Johnson grew up in South Carolina, left for New York at age 17, and studied art in Paris. He traveled throughout Europe and North Africa with his Danish wife before returning to New York, where he spent most of the rest of his life. There, he developed his distinctive style, using a limited number of colors applied to a flat surface such as plywood. Like many artists, Johnson brought his own life experiences into his art. From his studio in New York, Johnson recalled life in the South from his childhood, which he depicted in paintings and in works on paper. After his death in 1970, more than 1,000 of Johnson's paintings and drawings were discovered by friends. His work is now housed in the Smithsonian American Art Museum.

DOCUMENT ONE

Primary Source: Newspaper Editorial
from "Mrs. Ida Wells-Barnett Calls on President McKinley," by Ida B. Wells-Barnett, 1898

Ida B. Wells-Barnett, an African-American journalist, wrote extensively about lynching. She traveled to England to speak about the topic and formed anti-lynching societies. Wells-Barnett devoted particular attention to the topic after mobs lynched three of her friends.

CONSTRUCTED RESPONSE How does Wells-Barnett characterize lynching in the United States?

For nearly twenty years lynching crimes . . . have been committed and permitted by this Christian nation. Nowhere in the civilized world save the United States of America do men . . . go out in bands of 50 and 5,000 to hunt down, shoot, hang or burn to death a single individual. Statistics show that nearly 10,000 American citizens have been lynched in the past twenty years. To our appeals for justice the stereotyped reply has been that the governor could not interfere in a state matter. We refuse to believe this country, so powerful to defend its citizens abroad, is unable to protect its citizens at home.

DOCUMENT TWO

Primary Source: Document
from "Platform Adopted by the National Negro Committee," 1909

In response to racial violence, William English Walling and others, mostly whites, formed the National Negro Committee, which eventually became the NAACP. Written by the committee, the platform's signers include Ida B. Wells-Barnett and Jane Addams. This document emphasized that violence benefits no one.

CONSTRUCTED RESPONSE According to the statement, who is affected by violence against African Americans?

The systematic persecution of law-abiding citizens . . . on account of their race alone is a crime that will ultimately drag down to an infamous end any nation that allows it . . . and it bears most heavily on those poor white farmers and laborers whose economic position is most similar to that of the persecuted race. Indeed persecution of organized workers, peonage, [and] enslavement of prisoners . . . already threaten large bodies of whites in many southern States.

DOCUMENT THREE

Secondary Source: Newspaper Article
from *Fort Worth Star-Telegram*, by Tim Madigan, 2011

In July 1910, a white mob, emboldened by rumors, randomly attacked African-American residents of Slocum, Texas. Anywhere from 20 to 200 people were killed. Newspaper accounts of the massacre were conflicting, and most articles falsely reported that it was begun by armed African Americans. Not until 2011 did the town officially acknowledge the massacre. This newspaper article relates what is known of the killings 100 years after they happened.

CONSTRUCTED RESPONSE What important information does this source provide about the 1910 events in Slocum?

Some initial newspaper accounts erroneously reported that whites had also been killed, describing the Slocum incident as a race riot. But Slocum was no riot. "Men were going about killing Negroes as fast as they could find them, and, so far as I was able to ascertain, without any real cause," Anderson County Sheriff W.H. Black, a white from nearby Palestine, was quoted as saying. Seven white men were indicted on murder charges and had their cases transferred to Houston on a change of venue. But none ever came to trial.

SYNTHESIZE & WRITE

1. **REVIEW** Review what you have learned about racial violence from the passages and the painting.

2. **RECALL** On your own paper, write down some of the different reactions American citizens had to racial violence in the late 19th and early 20th centuries, as demonstrated in the passages.

3. **CONSTRUCT** Construct a topic sentence to answer this question: In what ways did African-American journalists and activists reveal the extent of racial violence?

4. **WRITE** Write an informative paragraph supporting your topic sentence in Step 3 by using evidence from the passages, the art, and the chapter.

PLAN: 2-PAGE LESSON

OBJECTIVE

Synthesize information about responses to racial violence from primary and secondary source documents.

CRITICAL THINKING SKILLS FOR LESSON 4.4

• Synthesize

• Compare and Contrast

• Evaluate

HISTORICAL THINKING FOR CHAPTER 15

What were the overall positive and negative effects of industrialization on America?

Racial violence limited economic and political gains for African Americans. Lesson 4.4 provides excerpts from documents addressing this violence.

BACKGROUND FOR THE TEACHER

Tim Madigan's 2011 Fort Worth *Star-Telegram* article about the 1910 massacre of African Americans in Slocum, Texas, led the Texas state legislature to officially recognize the killings. In 2014, Constance Hollie-Jawaid, whose ancestor was killed in the massacre, and E.R. Bills, who wrote a book about the event, petitioned the Texas Historical Commission to erect a historical marker acknowledging what happened in 1910. Some residents of Anderson County argued against the marker, claiming that historical reports of the massacre were too conflicting to unravel or that a marker would bring unwarranted shame to the community. In the end, the Texas Historical Commission honored the pair's request. The marker was erected in January 2016. Hollie-Jawaid hopes that the recognition of the massacre will help spur a thorough investigation of events and possibly uncover the mass grave of the victims.

INTRODUCE & ENGAGE

PREPARE FOR THE DOCUMENT-BASED QUESTION

Before students start on the activity, briefly preview the three documents. Remind students that a constructed response requires full explanations in complete sentences. Emphasize that students should use what they have learned about the Civil War and Reconstruction in addition to the information in the documents.

TEACH

GUIDED DISCUSSION

1. **Compare and Contrast** How are the two primary source documents similar and different in the ways in which they confront racial injustice? *(Possible response: Both documents viewed the racial injustices as crimes. Wells-Barnett's editorial focused on how the national government had failed to take action, while the National Negro Committee's statement argued that the nation and poor whites would be harmed by allowing the crimes to happen.)*

2. **Evaluate** How does the 2011 newspaper article about the Slocum Massacre support the idea that historical interpretations can be biased and prejudiced? *(Possible response: The article notes that some papers at the time reported erroneously that the massacre was a race riot and that whites died in the violence.)*

EVALUATE

After students have completed the Synthesize & Write activity, allow time for them to exchange paragraphs and read and comment on the work of their peers. Establish guidelines for comments prior to this activity so that feedback is constructive and encouraging in nature. Comments should focus on the most significant parts that address the purpose of the activity and the audience.

ACTIVE OPTIONS

On Your Feet: Host a DBQ Roundtable Divide the class into groups of four and have groups discuss the following question: How do the authors of these excerpts use evidence to support their points of view? The first student in each group should write an answer, read it aloud, and pass the paper clockwise to the next student, who does the same. The paper should circulate around the table several times. Reconvene as a class and discuss the groups' responses.

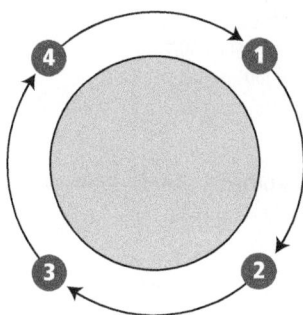

DIFFERENTIATE

STRIVING READERS

Summarize Assign pairs to reread each document and summarize it. Read each constructed response question aloud and make sure all students understand it. Encourage volunteers to share responses.

GIFTED & TALENTED

Perform a Dramatic Reading Challenge students to prepare a dramatic reading of one of the documents in the lesson. Encourage them to practice reading it with appropriate expression and gestures. Students can then perform their dramatic reading in front of the class. Discuss how each dramatic reading affected their interpretation and understanding of the document.

See the Chapter Planner for more strategies for differentiation.

SYNTHESIZE & WRITE

ANSWERS

1. Answers will vary.

2. Possible response: Some people, such as the journalist Ida Wells-Barnett and the National Negro Committee, condemned and tried to bring attention to the violence. Others, such as some in Slocum, Texas, seemed to ignore it.

3. Possible response: African-American journalists and activists used newspapers and committee platforms to reveal the extent of racial violence.

4. Answers will vary. Students' paragraphs should include their topic sentence from Step 3 and provide several details from the documents to support the sentence.

CONSTRUCTED RESPONSE

Document 1: She characterizes lynching as uncivilized and a failure of the United States to protect its citizens; she provides shocking statistics to back up her claims.

Document 2: The statement argues that racial violence hurts the nation and poor white farmers and laborers.

Document 3: The passage states that the incident was not a race riot, backing up the claim with a quote by Sheriff W.H. Black about men killing African Americans without cause.

CRITICAL VIEWING Possible response: The painting shows no public services, such as the fire department, assisting the couple, implying that African Americans were left on their own to deal with hardships.

15 REVIEW

VOCABULARY

Write a paragraph using each key vocabulary term from the chapter listed below in a way that conveys its importance. A sample beginning sentence is provided for the first term.

1. push-pull factors
   Lack of opportunity in their home countries and opportunities in the United States were push-pull factors for immigrants.
2. muckraker
3. tenement
4. sanitation
5. propaganda
6. progressivism

READING STRATEGY
IDENTIFY PROBLEMS AND SOLUTIONS

Identifying problems faced by individuals and nations and tracking their solutions can help readers understand the way history unfolds. Complete the Problem-and-Solution Chart to analyze several problems the United States faced as it continued to industrialize and solutions to those problems. Then answer the question.

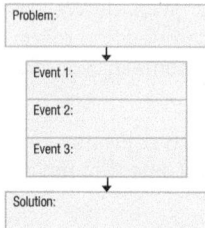

Problem:

↓

Event 1:

Event 2:

Event 3:

↓

Solution:

7. Describe one problem the United States faced as industrialization grew, beginning in the 1890s. Then list events that led to a solution.

MAIN IDEAS

Answer the following questions. Support your answers with evidence from the chapter.

8. How did expansion of the railroad industry help the steel industry grow? LESSON 1.1

9. Why are Alexander Graham Bell and Thomas Edison considered significant inventors of the late 19th century? LESSON 1.3

10. Why did states provide workers' compensation? LESSON 2.1

11. Why did workers resume forming labor unions in the late 1800s? LESSON 2.2

12. What was unique about the American Railway Union's structure? LESSON 2.3

13. What did the Americanization movement hope to accomplish? LESSON 3.1

14. Why did nativists oppose immigration? LESSON 3.3

15. Why were fires and diseases especially deadly in large cities such as Chicago and New York? LESSON 4.2

16. Why did many white southerners react the way they did to Reconstruction reforms after Reconstruction ended? LESSON 4.3

HISTORICAL THINKING

Answer the following questions. Support your answers with evidence from the chapter.

17. ANALYZE CAUSE AND EFFECT What part did greed play in the growth of industry?

18. EVALUATE In what ways did the late 19th and early 20th centuries represent both advancement and turmoil for African Americans?

19. SYNTHESIZE How did writers in the late 19th and early 20th centuries help expose injustices in society, and why was it important?

20. IDENTIFY PROBLEMS AND SOLUTIONS What problems did progressive reformers seek to solve?

21. DRAW CONCLUSIONS How did Jim Crow laws and "separate but equal" treatment impact economic mobility and opportunity for African Americans?

22. FORM AND SUPPORT OPINIONS What were positive effects of industrialization on living and working conditions? Support your opinion using evidence from the chapter.

INTERPRET GRAPHS

Look carefully at the graph showing causes of death on the job for workers at steel mills in one Pennsylvania county. Then answer the questions that follow.

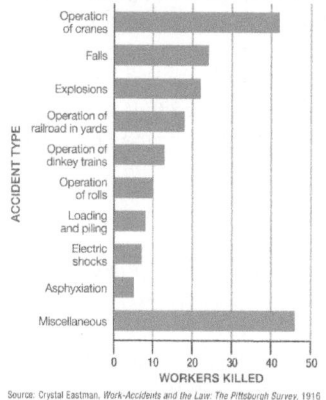

Steel Worker Deaths in Allegheny County, Pennsylvania, 1906–1907

ACCIDENT TYPE: Operation of cranes, Falls, Explosions, Operation of railroad in yards, Operation of dinkey trains, Operation of rolls, Loading and piling, Electric shocks, Asphyxiation, Miscellaneous

WORKERS KILLED: 0 10 20 30 40 50

Source: Crystal Eastman, *Work-Accidents and the Law: The Pittsburgh Survey*, 1916

23. How many workers were killed by various causes not specified in the graph?

24. How do the numbers of deaths from operating different types of equipment, such as cranes, the railroad in yards, dinkey trains, and rolls, compare?

25. What were the causes of the third and fourth highest numbers of deaths?

ANALYZE SOURCES

In 1900, writer and journalist Theodore Dreiser published *Sister Carrie*, a novel about a young woman who moves from rural Wisconsin to Chicago. In this scene, the narrator describes Carrie's visit to a department store, a new kind of consumer experience that arose in the late 1800s.

> Carrie passed along the busy aisles, much affected by the remarkable displays of trinkets, dress goods, stationery, and jewelry. Each separate counter was a show place of dazzling interest and attraction. She could not help feeling the claim of each trinket and valuable upon her personally, and yet she did not stop. There was nothing there which she could not have used—nothing which she did not long to own.

26. What was the effect of the department store on Carrie?

CONNECT TO YOUR LIFE

27. ARGUMENT This chapter discusses the rise of cities and some of the benefits and drawbacks of city life. Is solving the problems of cities worthwhile, or should people just move out of cities? Write an argument supporting your position.

TIPS

- Reread the chapter, listing the advantages and disadvantages of urban living.
- Look over your lists and add your own thoughts and experiences to them.
- Decide on a position to take. Then choose two or three of your strongest pros or cons to develop and support your argument.
- Include two or three vocabulary terms from the chapter in your argument.
- Address any opposing views you identify. Use your list to help in choosing an opposing view to challenge.
- Conclude with a summary that explains your arguments clearly and directly.

VOCABULARY ANSWERS

One sample paragraph is provided below, followed by topic sentences for the remaining paragraphs. Students' paragraphs should flesh out the idea stated in each topic sentence.

1. Lack of opportunity in their home countries and opportunities in the United States were push-pull factors for immigrants. Push factors included a lack of economic opportunities, a shortage of farmland, and discrimination. Pull factors included economic opportunities, affordable farmland, and religious freedom.

2. Muckrakers used journalism to uncover questionable business practices by leading industrialists.

3. Many newly arrived immigrants were forced to live in poorly ventilated and crowded tenements.

4. Crowded cities suffered from severe sanitation problems, particularly in poor neighborhoods.

5. Nativists often spread untrue and negative propaganda about immigrants.

6. Reformers who operated under the banner of progressivism felt that society's ills could be solved through social action.

READING STRATEGY ANSWER

Problem: New industries led to poor working conditions.

↓

Event 1: Workers were hurt or killed on the job.

Event 2: Child labor increased.

Event 3: Many began to see that the dangers were real.

↓

Solution: States began to provide workers' compensation; workers formed unions.

7. Responses will vary but should demonstrate the impact of industrialization on how Americans lived and worked.

MAIN IDEAS ANSWERS

8. The railroads needed a lot of steel for railroad tracks and train parts, so as the railroad industry grew, so did the steel industry.

9. Alexander Graham Bell invented the telephone, and Thomas Alva Edison invented electric lights. These were both significant inventions that still have an impact on people's lives throughout the world. Edison also invented other products, such as the phonograph and motion picture devices.

10. States provided workers' compensation because employers often blamed workers for the accidents that caused injuries.

11. More workers joined unions and established new ones in the late 1800s to get better pay, safer work conditions, and other benefits, such as shorter workdays. At the time, workers were facing pay cuts, long workdays, and very unsafe conditions at work.

12. The American Railway Union was the country's first union to bring together workers across an entire industry, no matter which geographical area or special trade they worked in.

13. The Americanization movement wanted to immerse immigrants in the American way of life so they would become "true" Americans.

14. Nativists felt they had to protect the interests of people born in the United States. They felt threatened by changing cultural values and competition for employment, and they harbored prejudices against certain religious groups, such as Catholics and Jews.

15. Crowded conditions made for poor sanitation and dirty water, which helped spread diseases; flimsy construction made buildings fire-prone, and crowding allowed fires to spread.

16. Reconstruction had facilitated improvements for African Americans, such as the abolition of slavery and the establishment of voting rights for African-American men. Many southerners wanted to go back to the time of slavery, after Reconstruction ended, they began making and enforcing laws that diminished the effects of these reforms.

HISTORICAL THINKING ANSWERS

17. Possible response: Company leaders employed underhanded tactics that enabled them to dominate their industries. For example, in the railroad industry, Cornelius Vanderbilt and Jay Gould bought out competitors so they had less competition. Likewise, in the oil industry, John D. Rockefeller used horizontal integration to take over competitors, which eventually enabled him to control about 90 percent of the country's oil-refining capacity.

18. Possible response: During the late 1800s, several constitutional amendments brought about important changes for African Americans, such as the abolition of slavery. Also, African-American inventors, such as George Washington Carver, had success during this time. However, the time period also featured Jim Crow laws and the formation of the Ku Klux Klan, which both restricted the rights of and instilled terror in African-American citizens.

19. Ida Tarbell wrote a series of articles that exposed the questionable tactics that John D. Rockefeller employed in the oil industry. Ida Wells-Barnett wrote newspaper editorials that raised awareness of lynching. Upton Sinclair made the general public more aware of issues surrounding work conditions and the treatment of immigrants in the workplace. The awareness these writers raised helped bring about social change.

20. Progressives sought to help the poor and African Americans, reform urban living conditions, end child labor, challenge big city bosses and government corruption, and curtail abuses by big business.

21. Jim Crow laws and "separate but equal" treatment hampered economic mobility and opportunity for African Americans by blocking access to comparable education and institutionalizing discrimination.

22. Answers will vary. Possible response: Industrialization resulted in new technologies and inventions that improved daily life and work, such as electric lights, the telephone, streetcars, better railroads and bridges, elevators, and workplace innovations. Industrialization also enabled cities to expand upward by building skyscrapers.

INTERPRET GRAPHS ANSWERS STEM

23. Around 45 workers were killed by causes not specified in the graph.

24. Workers were much more likely to be killed operating cranes than they were operating the railroad in the yard, dinkey trains, or rolls.

25. Excluding "Miscellaneous," explosions were the third highest cause of death; operation of railroad in yards was the fourth highest.

ANALYZE SOURCES ANSWER

26. Carrie wants to buy everything she sees, but she doesn't act on the impulse.

CONNECT TO YOUR LIFE ANSWER

27. Paragraphs will vary, but students should state a clear position, support their positions with sound reasons and evidence, acknowledge opposing views, and include two to three vocabulary terms from the chapter.

UNIT 5 RESOURCES

UNIT INTRODUCTION

UNIT TIME LINE

UNIT WRAP-UP

NATIONAL GEOGRAPHIC | CONNECTION

National Geographic Magazine Adapted Articles
- "Nature for Everyone"
- "21st Century Cowboys" ONLINE

Unit 5 Inquiry: Produce a Documentary

NG Learning Framework Activities
- Write a Position Statement
- Plan a Protest

Unit 5 Formal Assessment

CHAPTER 16 RESOURCES

Available at NGLSync.Cengage.com

TEACHER RESOURCES & ASSESSMENT

Reading and Note-Taking

Vocabulary Practice

Document-Based Question Template

Social Studies Skills Lessons
- Reading: Analyze Language Use
- Writing: Argument

Formal Assessment
- Chapter 16 Pretest
- Chapter 16 Tests A & B
- Section Quizzes

Chapter 16 Answer Key

ExamView®
  One-time Download

STUDENT DIGITAL RESOURCES

- eEdition
- Handbooks
- Online Atlas
- American Gallery Online
- History Notebook
- Active History
- American Voices (Biographies)
- Literature Analysis
- Projects for Inquiry-Based Learning

Chapter 16 Spanish Resources are available at NGLSync.Cengage.com.

AMERICAN STORIES | **The Triangle Waist Company Factory Fire**

- Study Primary Sources: Quotations from firsthand accounts and archival photographs of the factory fire

AMERICAN GALLERY ONLINE New York City at the Turn of the Century

NG Learning Framework: Establish a Commission

SECTION 1 RESOURCES
PROGRESSIVISM

LESSON 1.1
The Roots of Progressivism

- On Your Feet: Create a Team Word Web

NG Learning Framework: Explore Opposing Viewpoints

American Voices Biography Billy Sunday and William Graham Sumner ONLINE

LESSON 1.2
Women Fight for Rights

- On Your Feet: Conduct a Three-Step Interview

NG Learning Framework: Create a Documentary

American Voices Biography Margaret Culbertson ONLINE

LESSON 1.3
DOCUMENT-BASED QUESTION
For or Against Women's Suffrage?

- On Your Feet: Host a DBQ Roundtable

LESSON 1.4
Reforming Government

- On Your Feet: Become an Expert

NG Learning Framework: Research Local Government

SECTION 2 RESOURCES
PROGRESSIVE ADMINISTRATIONS

LESSON 2.1
Reform Under Roosevelt

- On Your Feet: Card Responses

NG Learning Framework: Analyze Impact of Humans on the Environment

American Voices Biography Theodore Roosevelt ONLINE

LESSON 2.2
THROUGH THE LENS—AMERICAN PLACES
The Grand Canyon Northwestern Arizona

- On Your Feet: Build a Model of the Geologic Record

NG Learning Framework: Explore Land-Use Controversies

LESSON 2.3
Progressivism Under Taft and Wilson

- On Your Feet: Inside-Outside Circle

NG Learning Framework: Trace a Philosophy Across Time

SECTION 3 RESOURCES
AMERICA IN THE AGE OF EMPIRE

LESSON 3.1
American Expansionism

- On Your Feet: Debate Isolationism

NG Learning Framework: Explore the Impact of Expansionism

American Voices Biography Queen Liliuoakalani ONLINE

LESSON 3.2
Extending Influence in Asia

- On Your Feet: Build a Paragraph

NG Learning Framework: Analyze American Attitudes Toward China

LESSON 3.3
The Spanish-American War

- On Your Feet: Spanish-American War Roundtable

NG Learning Framework: Draw Conclusions About Military Conflicts

LESSON 3.4
The Philippine-American War

- Active History: Analyze Achievements of Emilio Aguinaldo

NG Learning Framework: Take a Position

LESSON 3.5
Involvement in Latin America

- On Your Feet: Rotating Discussion

NG Learning Framework: Hold a Mock Trial

CHAPTER 16 REVIEW

STRIVING READERS

STRATEGY ❶
MAKE "TOP FIVE FACTS" LISTS

After students finish a lesson, direct them to write in their own words five important facts they have learned. Then ask them to compare lists with a partner and consolidate their two lists into one. If time permits, have each pair turn their facts into questions and then work with another pair, taking turns asking and answering their "Top Five" questions.

Use with All Lessons

STRATEGY ❷
CLARIFY MULTIPLE MEANING WORDS

To help improve striving readers' text comprehension, point out words that likely have more familiar meanings. List these words and definitions on the board:

cabinet: a piece of furniture for storing things; a council that gives advice
strike: to hit forcibly and deliberately; work stoppage by employees as a form of protest
sweeping: using a broom to clean; describes something far-reaching in range or effect

Tell students to identify which meaning fits the context of the sentence in which the word is used.

Use with Lesson 2.3 *Throughout the chapter, call out and clarify other multiple meaning words.*

STRATEGY ❸
SET A PURPOSE FOR READING

Before beginning a lesson, help students set a purpose for reading by turning the Main Idea statement into a question. Tell students to answer the question in writing after they read. Below are sample questions for Lessons 1.1 and 1.2.

1.1 What were some of the social, economic, and political problems that progressive reformers addressed in the United States in the early 1900s?

1.2 Who were the women who played leading roles in fighting for women's right to vote?

Use with All Lessons

INCLUSION

STRATEGY ❶
USE ECHO READING

Point out that the Main Idea statements all relate to important aspects of progressivism and expansionism. Pair students with a proficient reader. Ask the proficient reader to read the Main Idea statement at the beginning of a lesson aloud. Tell the less proficient partner to "echo" the statement and then restate it in his or her own words.

Use with All Lessons

STRATEGY ❷
DESCRIBE A POLITICAL CARTOON

Pair students who are visually impaired with well-sighted students. Ask the latter to describe the political cartoon "The Lion Tamer" in detail, including the setting, Roosevelt, and the labels on the lions and on the den they are emerging from. Tell the well-sighted students to answer questions their partner may have. Then ask pairs to discuss the point of view conveyed by the cartoon.

Use with Lesson 2.1 *You may repeat this strategy for the political cartoons in Lesson 1.3 (women's suffrage) and Lesson 3.5 (also featuring Roosevelt).*

ENGLISH LANGUAGE LEARNERS

STRATEGY ①
ACTIVATE PRIOR KNOWLEDGE

Display the words below in a splash arrangement. Tell students the words relate to U.S. expansionism in the age of empire. Ask students to talk about and research word meanings. Then have them write sentences, using two of the words in each one.

Use with Lessons 3.1–3.5 *You may wish to pair students at the Emerging level with students at the Expanding and Bridging levels, with the more proficient students providing assistance.*

STRATEGY ②
USE PRONUNCIATION KEYS

Preteach the meaning and pronunciation of Key Vocabulary terms for students at **All Proficiencies**. Model pronunciation and help students create a pronunciation key on note cards. Encourage students to use the words to write sentences about the lesson and read them aloud. Encourage students at the **Bridging** level to develop more complex sentences for each word and to share their sentences with the group.

Use with All Lessons

STRATEGY ③
CREATE A WORD WALL

Work with students at the **Emerging** and **Expanding** levels to select three words from each lesson to display in a grouping on a Word Wall. Choose words students are likely to encounter in other chapters, such as *reform, dispute,* and *settlement.* Keep the words displayed throughout the chapter and discuss each one as it comes up during reading. Suggest that students at the **Bridging** level contribute by adding phrases or examples to each word to develop understanding.

Use with All Lessons

GIFTED & TALENTED

STRATEGY ①
CREATE A PODCAST

Before beginning the chapter, allow students to choose one lesson and use the information to prepare an episode of a history podcast. Tell students to be creative and that their podcast should establish a point of view that is both informative and entertaining. Invite students to present their podcast live or record it and play it for the class.

Use with All Lessons

STRATEGY ②
CREATE AN ANNOTATED TIME LINE OF WOMEN'S SUFFRAGE

Have students create and annotate a time line of events leading up to the 19th Amendment. Students should supplement text information with online research. Tell students to graphically indicate connections among events and larger social and economic trends. Encourage the use of an online time line creation tool if available. Have students share their finished time lines with the class.

Use with Lessons 1.2 and 1.3

PRE-AP

STRATEGY ①
WRITE A HISTORICAL DIALOGUE

Instruct pairs to conduct online research, accessing multiple primary and secondary sources, to gather information about the interactions between Queen Liliuokalani and President Cleveland leading up to the annexation of Hawaii. Tell students to write a dialogue that might have taken place between the two leaders that addresses such issues as sovereignty, imperialism, self-determination, economic and strategic interests, and the Treaty of Annexation signed by President Benjamin Harrison.

Use with Lesson 3.1

STRATEGY ②
EXPLORE LONG-TERM CONSEQUENCES

Direct students to write a research essay about the long-term impacts of U.S. imperialist policies of the early 20th century. Suggest that students concentrate on one nation (Cuba, Colombia, Panama, or the Philippines) and use print and online sources to explore past imperialist policies and their present-day repercussions. Invite students to share their essays with the class.

Use with Lessons 3.1–3.5

THE **PROGRESSIVE ERA** AND **EXPANSIONISM**

1890–1920

HISTORICAL THINKING What reforms and expansion took place during the Progressive Era?

AMERICAN STORIES | The Triangle Waist Company Factory Fire

SECTION 1 **Progressivism**

SECTION 2 **Progressive Administrations**

SECTION 3 **America in the Age of Empire**

AMERICAN GALLERY ONLINE | New York City at the Turn of the Century

"A great democracy has got to be progressive, or it will soon **cease to be either great or a democracy.**"

—President Theodore Roosevelt

At the same time Americans were working to solve social, economic, and political problems at home, the United States was expanding its overseas territories. The island chain of Hawaii, where American companies operated pineapple plantations like the one pictured here, became a U.S. territory in 1900.

542 CHAPTER 16

The Progressive Era and Expansionism 543

INTRODUCE THE PHOTOGRAPH

PROGRESS AND EXPANSION

Tell students to study the photograph and quotation that open this chapter. Draw students' attention to the word *progressive* in the quote. Ask them to think about what the root word—*progress*—means. **ASK:** How does the photograph of a pineapple plantation relate to the idea of progress? *(Answers will vary. Possible response: A pineapple is a tropical fruit that is shipped to and sold in the continental United States. Acquiring land able to grow different crops is one way of making progress.)* Tell students that in this chapter they will learn about how the United States expanded its influence across the globe, as well as how progressive administrations attempted to better the lives of citizens.

SHARE BACKGROUND

The introduction of the pineapple to Hawaii predates American arrival to the islands, but the fruit's production accelerated shortly after U.S. missionaries arrived in 1820. U.S. pineapple canning began in the 1860s in Baltimore, Maryland, initially using fruit imported from the Caribbean. In the late 1800s, a group of entrepreneurs from California—including James D. Dole of the Dole Food Company—arrived in Hawaii and began to develop the pineapple industry. The industry was slow to take off, with high tariffs cutting into profitability. (Hawaii was not yet part of the United States.) This changed in 1898 when the islands were annexed, eliminating the tariffs and making trade easier. This development—along with plentiful land available for homesteading—eventually made Hawaii home to the largest pineapple industry in the world.

For Chapter 16 Spanish Resources, visit the Resources Menu. Chapter 16 Resources are available at NGLSync.Cengage.com.

What reforms and expansion took place during the Progressive Era?

Brainstorm Issues of the Progressive Era and Reasons for Expansion Invite students to begin thinking about the problems within the United States at the end of the 1800s and reasons the country might look to expand. Ask students to brainstorm ideas in response to the following questions.

1. What were some of the major problems facing the United States in the late 1800s?

2. In the conflict between business and labor, which side had previous presidents supported?

3. For what reasons might the United States want to expand overseas?

4. What conflicts could result from this expansion?

Write each question on chart paper and add students' ideas. Revisit the questions at the end of each lesson and ask students to suggest additional answers based on what they have learned.

INTRODUCE THE READING STRATEGY

ANALYZE LANGUAGE USE

Explain that analyzing the specific language used by authors is vital to understanding the meaning behind complex passages. Turn to the Chapter Review and preview the Word Map with students. As they read the chapter, have students analyze several primary source passages concerning the issues of the Progressive Era and U.S. expansionism.

KEY DATES FOR CHAPTER 16

1898	United States annexes Hawaii
1898	Treaty of Paris concludes Spanish-American War
1900	Boxer Rebellion ends
1902	Philippine-American War ends
1904	Construction begins on Panama Canal
1906	Roosevelt signs Pure Food and Drug Act
1911	Triangle Waist Company factory fire
1913	16th and 17th Amendments ratified
1914	Congress passes Clayton Antitrust Act
1920	19th Amendment ratified

INTRODUCE CHAPTER VOCABULARY

KEY VOCABULARY

SECTION 1

Children's Bureau	exposé	recall
commission government	franchise	
direct primary	initiative	
enfranchisement	Progressive Era	
	prohibition	

SECTION 2

conservation	scientific management	syndicate
income tax		trustbuster
merger	social security	

SECTION 3

American Anti-Imperialist League	imperialism	protectorate
archipelago	isolationism	reparations
Boxer Rebellion	isthmus	sphere of influence
expansionism	Open Door Policy	yellow journalism

VOCABULARY PYRAMIDS

As students read the chapter, have them complete a Vocabulary Pyramid for each Key Vocabulary word. Tell students to make a pyramid for each word, adding what they know about each word before reading and then adding to or correcting the pyramid after they encounter the word in the chapter. Model an example for students on the board using the graphic organizer shown.

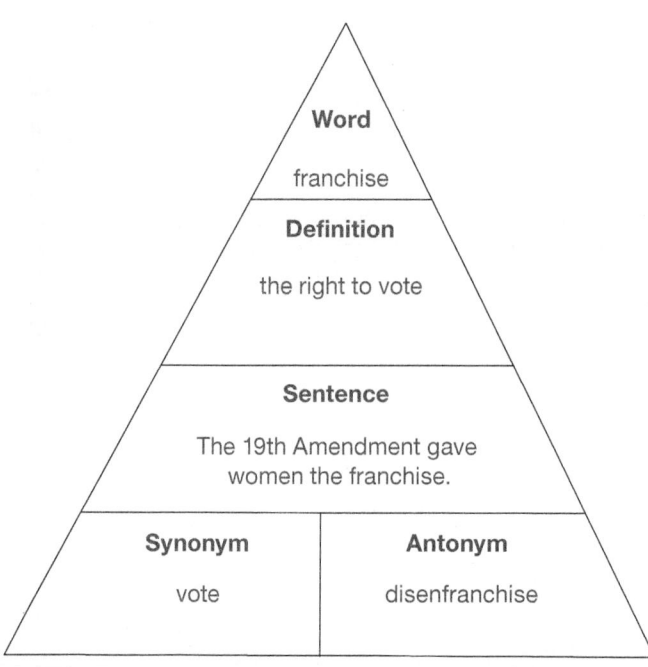

Word
franchise
Definition
the right to vote
Sentence
The 19th Amendment gave women the franchise.
| **Synonym** | **Antonym** |
| vote | disenfranchise |

OBJECTIVES

- **Understand the causes and consequences of the Triangle Waist Company factory fire.**
- **Compare conditions experienced by factory workers in the past and present.**
- **Describe the roles of women in the industrial economy.**
- **Trace the development of workers' protections across American history.**
- **Study primary sources: quotations from firsthand accounts and archival photographs of the factory fire.**

CRITICAL THINKING SKILLS FOR "THE TRIANGLE WAIST COMPANY FACTORY FIRE"

- Make Connections
- Draw Conclusions
- Form and Support Opinions
- Evaluate
- Describe
- Identify Problems and Solutions
- Analyze Language Use
- Analyze Cause and Effect

CONNECT TO THE CHAPTER

This American Story explores the Triangle factory fire, a seminal event in the development of workers' rights in the United States. Through the study of a harrowing narrative that weaves together individual accounts, archival photographs, diagrams, and connections to the present, students will understand the human toll of this terrible event as well as the political and economic repercussions.

This chapter, The Progressive Era and Expansionism, explores a time in American history when the federal government took on greater responsibility in protecting its citizens from unregulated institutions. One such institution was the workplace, which did not offer the protections extended to present-day workers. Use this American Story after reading Lesson 2.3, which places the Triangle factory fire in the context of the Taft administration.

HISTORY NOTEBOOK

Encourage students to complete the American Story page and the American Gallery page for Chapter 16 in their History Notebooks as they read.

THE TRIANGLE WAIST COMPANY

FACTORY FIRE

March 25, 1911, was a normal day for the 500 workers at the Triangle Waist Company, a factory located on the 8th, 9th, and 10th floors of the Asch Building in New York City. That is to say, the workers, most of them immigrant women between the ages of 16 and 23, had put in several grueling hours sewing shirtwaists—a type of women's blouse—for a pay rate that came to around $15 for a week of 12-hour days.

In 1909, the Ladies Garment Workers Union had led a strike against New York clothing manufacturers. Their demands had included higher pay, shorter hours, and safer working conditions. Most of the smaller factories quickly agreed to the union's demands, but Isaac Harris and Max Blanck, the owners of the Triangle factory, resisted. Instead, they joined a group of manufacturers who fought back with dirty tactics, including paying police officers to beat or intimidate the striking workers. Eventually, Harris and Blanck relented, offering their employees higher wages and shorter working hours but refusing to allow them to unionize. Despite these improvements, work at the Triangle Waist Company was still exhausting, unsafe, and poorly paid. The factory remained a sweatshop with working conditions just as harsh as that name implies.

Around 4:40 p.m. on March 25, 1911, Isidore Abramowitz was preparing to go home from his job cutting fabric on the eighth floor, when he spotted sparks in a bin used for discarded scraps of fabric. At once, he seized one of the buckets of water placed throughout the factory in case of fires and dumped it on the flames. Abramowitz's fellow cutters rushed to throw water from other buckets onto the fire, but the workers were in a gigantic room filled with long wooden tables and piles of fabric scraps. They were surrounded by extremely flammable materials.

Within moments, the fire was out of control, and panicked employees were struggling toward the exits. Sylvia Kimeldorf, an 18-year-old who was working on the eighth floor that day, recalled, "The place was filling up with heavy black smoke, and we were all choking."

Limited **firefighting technology,** including short ladders and poor water pressure, made battling the Triangle factory fire and rescuing factory workers a serious challenge for firefighters.

In 1909, a fire insurance inspector recommended that Triangle factory owners keep the building's doors unlocked during the day and conduct fire drills with factory workers. Harris and Blanck did not follow through on either request. As a result, when Ladder Company 20 arrived on the scene of the horrific fire there two years later, there was little they could do.

Fabric scraps provided fuel for what one fire captain called "a mass of traveling fire." Staircases were too few in number, and the fire escape didn't reach the ground. Short ladders and poor water pressure made putting out the fire and rescuing workers nearly impossible. All firefighters could do was mist the outside of the building.

The Progressive Era and Expansionism **545**

INTRODUCE & ENGAGE

PREVIEW USING VISUALS

Inform students that the fire at the Triangle Waist Company factory affected the entire garment industry. Have students view the photograph and read the caption. **ASK:** What factors, other than those stated in the caption, might have hindered firefighters? *(Possible responses: There might not have been enough hoses and firefighters on the scene. Heavy smoke probably made finding trapped workers almost impossible.)* **ASK:** Why are events like this less likely to happen today? *(modern firefighting technology, safety regulations)* Explain that many present-day safety regulations grew out of reforms that followed in the wake of disasters such as the Triangle factory fire.

CONNECT TO YOUR LIFE

Tell students that this American Story concerns the development of workplace safety regulations. Then ask students to raise their hands if they have a job, or if not, ask them to think about a friend's or family member's job. **ASK:** What safety regulations or requirements are present at workplaces that you know? *(Possible responses: mandatory breaks, minimum wage, safety equipment such as glasses or goggles, protective clothing and shoes)* Next discuss with students why these regulations exist. Explain that the events described in this American Story helped to usher in laws protecting the rights of workers.

DISCUSS WOMEN IN THE WORKFORCE

Discuss the topic of women in the workforce with students. Ask the following questions:

- What types of jobs were often associated with women in the workforce in the past? Today?
- Have the types of jobs for women changed over the years? How so?
- Why were some jobs heavily segregated by gender? Is this the case currently?

At the end of the discussion, tell students that in this American Story they will learn about garment workers, an occupation almost exclusively filled by women in the 19th and early 20th centuries.

FEDERAL WORK SAFETY REGULATIONS

Although the Triangle factory fire led to several reforms in New York City, federal work safety laws were slow to follow. The first breakthroughs came in the early 1930s with Franklin Roosevelt's New Deal, which set a minimum wage, banned child labor, and established Social Security. However, it wasn't until the 1960s that serious efforts to establish national work safety guidelines were undertaken. The debates were long and arduous as business and labor interests clashed over the details. These efforts culminated in 1970 with the passage of the Occupational Safety and Health Act (OSHA), which set safety standards for all 50 states, covered most private employees in the nation, and included regulations that required items such as safety harnesses for construction workers and needles with built-in protection for nurses.

THE TRIANGLE FACTORY FLOOR

Have students imagine they are factory workers situated at the table adjacent to Greene Street. **ASK:** What escape routes are available from your location, and what are the problems with these routes? *(Possible response: The closest exits are the stairs and elevator, but these are blocked by fire. Alternatively, the fire escape is available, but the stairs are narrow, making it difficult to descend.)* Tell students that because of modern building codes, much about the ninth floor of the Asch Building is now illegal. For example, according to California law, stairways must be 44 inches wide—not 33—and doors must be fire resistant. In addition, rules about the placement and structure of fire escapes are much stricter than in the past. **ASK:** Why do you think the factory floor was arranged in such a crowded and dangerous manner? *(Possible response: The floor was arranged to fit as many people as possible so that the maximum number of shirtwaists could be produced.)*

AMERICAN STORIES

The Asch Building had stairways and elevators located on the northeast and southwest corners, but the northeast corner was almost instantly consumed by flames. On the eighth and ninth floors, workers rushed for the stairway doors on the southwest side of the building but found them locked. It was company policy to lock the doors during working hours to prevent workers from stealing supplies or taking unauthorized breaks. On the eighth floor, one employee had a key, and most of the workers on that floor were able to escape.

Workers on the 10th floor managed to take the stairs up to the building's roof, from which they were rescued by a group of students at the neighboring New York University School of Law building, who placed ladders between the rooftops. Factory owners Isaac Harris and Max Blanck were able to escape the fire in this way. But for workers on the ninth floor, there was no escape via the staircases. They were unable to unlock or force the doors open, so their only hopes for survival were the southwest elevators or the fire escape.

Elevator operators Joseph Zito and Gaspar Mortillalo saved as many people as they could, making several trips to the burning floors before conditions became unbearable. Later, bodies of workers who had tried to escape down the elevator shaft but had fallen to their deaths were found piled on top of the elevators. A few people did survive the breakneck trip down the elevator shaft by gripping the cables. One of them, Sam Levine, recalled, "I can remember getting to the sixth floor. While on my way down, as slow as I could let myself drop, the bodies of six girls went falling past me."

The metal fire escape ladder on the outside of the building was not sufficiently strong to support the weight of the fleeing crowd, and it was further weakened by the fierce heat of the fire. Some workers were able to descend the fire escape to the sixth floor before the fragile ladder crashed to the ground. Nellie Ventura was one of those survivors. "At first I was too frightened to try to run through the fire," she recalled. "Then I heard the screams of the girls inside. I knew I had to go down the ladder or die where I was."

THE TRIANGLE FACTORY FLOOR

This diagram shows how the ninth floor of the Asch Building was laid out. The fire blocked access to the stairs and freight elevators on the Greene Street side of the building. Look at the spacing of the long tables and the location of the passenger elevators on the Washington Place side. One survivor described the space between the rows as "narrow and blocked by chairs and baskets." Other sources indicate that the stairs in the stairwells were 33 inches wide and the stairs of the fire escape were 17½ inches wide. In addition to the locked stairway door, what difficulties did the workers face in trying to escape the fire?

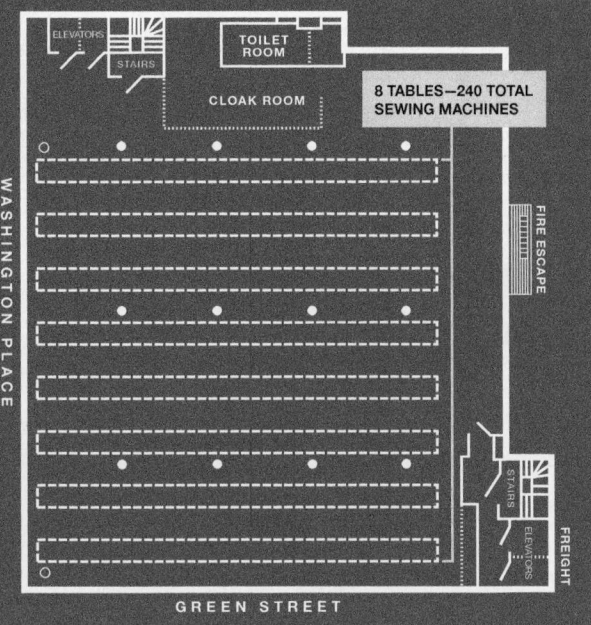

ELEVATORS · STAIRS · TOILET ROOM · CLOAK ROOM · 8 TABLES—240 TOTAL SEWING MACHINES · WASHINGTON PLACE · FIRE ESCAPE · STAIRS · ELEVATORS · FREIGHT · GREEN STREET

WHAT IS A SHIRTWAIST?

It is ironic that the shirtwaist, produced in sweatshops by an underpaid, mainly female workforce, was a symbol of social progress and women's growing empowerment. Popular in the late 19th and early 20th centuries, the shirtwaist was a style of blouse for women, featuring buttons down the front and modeled after men's shirts.

Practical and relatively comfortable, shirtwaists came to symbolize the modern working woman who earned her own wages and thus was not fully dependent on a man to support her. Women wearing shirtwaists as they demonstrated in the streets were the backbone of the women's movement around the turn of the 20th century.

As it gained in popularity, the shirtwaist also had a democratizing effect on fashion. Because the blouses were available in a range of prices, from 25 cents to 7 dollars, they were worn by women from every economic level, from salesclerks to wealthy socialites. According to the *Gimbel Brothers Illustrated 1915 Catalog*, "the women of other lands occasionally wear a shirtwaist—the American woman occasionally wears something else. Her daily apparel is a smart tailored skirt and neat blouse."

CRITICAL VIEWING What can you infer about women's fashions during the early part of the 1900s based on this 1905 shirtwaist and 1901 advertisement?

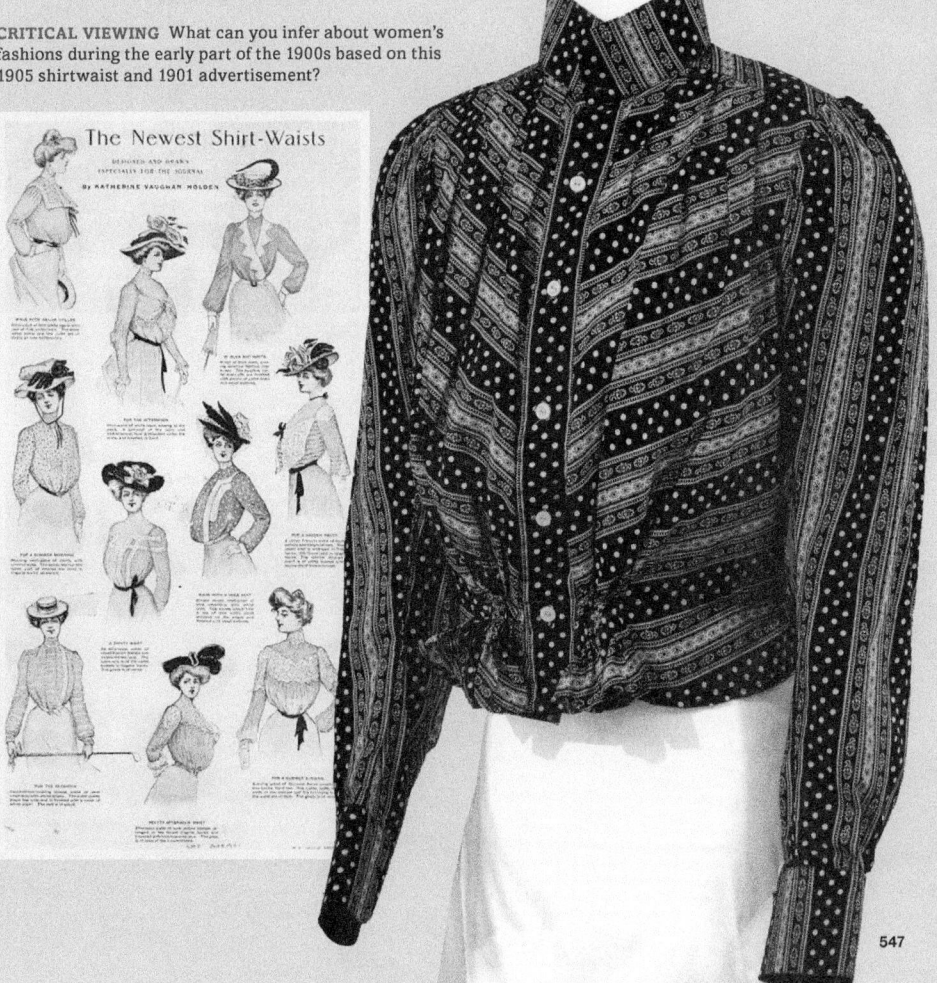

547

TEACH

GUIDED DISCUSSION

1. **Form and Support Opinions** In 1909, based on the negotiations between the factory workers and Harris and Blanck, who held more power in the workplace, management or labor, and why? *(Possible response: Management had more power because they determined workers' pay and whether or not workers could unionize. In addition, they were able to use unfair tactics to suppress strikes.)*

2. **Evaluate** In the context in which the events unfolded, which causes of the loss of life were due to ineffective building practices and which were due to decisions made by management? *(Locking the doors was a costly decision made by management. However, narrow and short fire escapes—as well as the narrowness of the building stairs—were structural issues most likely related to building practices at the turn of the 20th century.)*

WHAT IS A SHIRTWAIST?

The shirtwaist was an iconic symbol of women's social liberation, and it played an important role in the story of industrialization and immigration. As shirtwaists became more popular, factories sprang up to support the industry. More than 450 textile factories were located in Manhattan and employed some 40,000 workers, most of whom were immigrants. This influx of workers and industry helped the city become known as an industrial powerhouse. **ASK:** Why is it ironic that women in a sweatshop produced the shirtwaist? *(The shirtwaist was a symbol of social progress, so wearing one asserted the burgeoning equality between men and women. However, women working for low wages in terrible conditions undercut this supposed progress.)*

CRITICAL VIEWING Shirtwaists were popular items along with hats and skirts. Based on the dates mentioned in the caption, shirtwaists were popular for several years and produced in many different styles. The garment was obviously a key item in a modern woman's wardrobe.

GUIDED DISCUSSION

3. **Describe** What factors contributed to firefighters being unable to control the blaze and save factory workers? *(Possible response: Firefighting equipment was inadequate. For example, ladders were not long enough to reach the top floors, and weak water pressure from the hoses provided little relief. Nets were not strong enough to hold the weight of workers trying to jump off the building.)*

4. **Identify Problems and Solutions** What additional laws—besides those mentioned in the text—could have been passed to prevent such tragedies as the Triangle factory fire? *(Answers will vary. Possible response: Laws governing the number of people allowed on a factory floor, the material used to construct factories, and the length of ladders on fire engines could have prevented such tragedies.)*

CRITICAL VIEWING The fire was intense enough to reduce equipment, furniture, and other items in the building to rubble and ash or to an otherwise unrecognizable state.

CRITICAL VIEWING The devastating impact of the fire is evident in the solemn tone of the photograph and by the expressions of the men who are gazing downward and looking somber.

AMERICAN STORIES

CRITICAL VIEWING The Triangle factory fire caused extensive damage. What can you infer about the intensity of the fire from this photo?

CRITICAL VIEWING The bodies of the Triangle factory workers who did not survive the fire were taken to the New York City morgue to be identified by their loved ones. What does this photo reveal about the impact the fire had on New Yorkers?

548 CHAPTER 16

Meanwhile, on the ground, the New York City fire department was trying desperately to quell the blaze, but the department's ladders reached only as high as the sixth floor of the Asch Building. Firefighters and onlookers watched helplessly as young women, trapped and in danger of burning to death, leapt from the factory windows.

Some firefighters tried to deploy safety nets to catch the falling workers, but all those who jumped died on impact. Sylvia Kimeldorf, who had managed to escape by the stairs, remembered reaching the ground floor of the building and being held back by firefighters: "The bodies were falling all around us and they were afraid to let us go out because we would be killed by the falling bodies." Within 40 minutes, all three floors of the Triangle factory had been destroyed by the blaze, and 146 workers were dead. Even seasoned police officers were appalled by the grim scene. "It's the worst thing I ever saw," one older officer told the *New York Times* that night.

Could the Triangle factory fire have been prevented, or could it at least have resulted in fewer fatalities? In the aftermath, angry New Yorkers and factory workers believed so. Outraged crowds took to the streets to protest dangerous factory working conditions. On April 5, 1911, a mourning parade of more than 100,000 factory workers marched along one of New York City's main streets as 300,000 spectators turned out to witness the event.

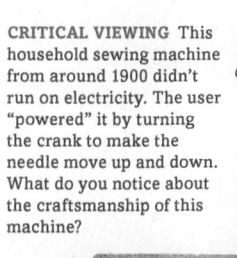

CRITICAL VIEWING This household sewing machine from around 1900 didn't run on electricity. The user "powered" it by turning the crank to make the needle move up and down. What do you notice about the craftsmanship of this machine?

SEWING MACHINES AT HOME AND AT WORK

The sewing machine is arguably one of the most influential American inventions in both the industrial and domestic domains. Before the sewing machine, garments were mostly stitched by women working at home. In New York City in 1850, around 5,000 women were employed hand-stitching shirts in their homes for very little pay. Beginning in the late 1800s, industrial sewing machines allowed entrepreneurs to hire women to work in factories, turning out clothing much more quickly and cheaply. Some sources touted the benefits of the new invention for "sewing girls," but as the Triangle story illustrates, the move from home to factory did not necessarily improve the situation for poor, immigrant working women.

In middle-class and wealthier homes, the sewing machine helped support the "cult of domesticity," the idea that a woman's home was her particular sphere of influence. In the words of an 1860 *New York Times* article, the sewing machine had "stitched its way onward as an agent of domestic economy." By acquiring a sewing machine—and perhaps a sewing room—a woman proved that she could master relatively complex machinery and produce and mend clothing for the family. Believers in the cult of domesticity conveniently overlooked the fact that the men in the home were usually in charge of the finances, and thus the decision to purchase a sewing machine.

The Progressive Era and Expansionism **549**

ACTIVE OPTIONS

AMERICAN **GALLERY** ONLINE

New York City at the Turn of the Century Invite students to explore the American Gallery. Have them select one of the images and do additional research to learn more about it. Ask questions that will inspire additional inquiry about the chosen gallery image, such as: What kind of construction is going on? What does this photo have in common with the rest of the gallery? How is present-day New York City different from what is shown in the photo?

NG Learning Framework: Establish a Commission

SKILL Problem-Solving

KNOWLEDGE Our Human Story

Following the fire, New York State established a commission to investigate ways to prevent future workplace accidents. Arrange students in small groups to serve as mock commissions investigating workplace issues. Their task is to identify a current workplace issue, such as the 2012 or 2013 factory disaster in Bangladesh, and investigate the problems that led to the disaster. Each group will create a report that includes the problems and their recommendations to remedy the issue. Tell students to support their findings with evidence from primary and secondary sources. Allot time for commissions to present their reports to the class.

SEWING MACHINES AT HOME AND AT WORK

The sewing machine was a symbol for the growing divide between the experiences of upper- and working-class white women in the 19th and early 20th centuries. While this period saw the creation of the middle class—complete with homeownership, a single wage earner, the ability to purchase consumer goods, and the creation of the homemaker wife—it was also an era of steep economic inequality. In working-class, agricultural, and immigrant households, women needed to earn wages or contribute to the farm and thus could not live up to the era's glorified domestic image of women. **ASK:** How did the sewing machine affect women and the economy of the American landscape? *(For working-class women, the sewing machine was a tool used to earn money. For wealthy women, it was a luxury item kept in the home for personal use.)*

CRITICAL VIEWING The intricate workings of the sewing machine were meticulously crafted and pleasingly designed. This suggests that it was meant to be both a machine for the necessary construction of clothing and a piece to display when not in use.

THE MINK BRIGADE

Explain that since the activism of the Mink Brigade, much has been done to advance American women. Women are now more likely to have a bachelor's degree than men, and the Civil Rights Act of 1964 barred institutions, businesses, and schools from discriminating based on gender. **ASK:** Why do you think Anne Morgan was interested in defending and advancing the rights of women workers? *(Answers will vary. Possible response: Morgan was probably educated and well-read in social issues. Helping working women get better pay and working conditions may have been her way of contributing to society.)*

MODERN-DAY TRIANGLES

Explain that in December 2016, garment workers who produce major Western-brand clothing in Bangladesh protested their low pay, and many protesters were arrested or fired. Guide students to discuss the disasters described in the text and to consider lessons that were learned during the evolution of the garment industry in the United States. **ASK:** What might American consumers do to pressure factories and brand companies to improve workers' pay and working conditions in China, India, and Bangladesh? *(Answers will vary. Possible response: American consumers could boycott products manufactured in countries where workers are underpaid, unprotected, and otherwise treated unfairly.)*

WRITE ABOUT HISTORY

Solve a Current Problem Tell students that events such as the Triangle fire can lead to adoption of laws or policies, such as the USA PATRIOT Act after terrorist attacks on September 11, 2001. Ask students to identify a recent event that they believe has a legislative remedy and to compose an essay in which they explain the law or policy that could prevent such an event in the future. Provide guidance about the writing process as needed.

CRITICAL VIEWING The machines are close together, but the room seems clean and well lit, and the workers appear to be comfortable. It's impossible to say whether the building has adequate exits, stairs, and safety features or whether workers are locked in, such as workers were at the Triangle factory.

THINK ABOUT IT

Possible response: Disasters like this are possible, but improvements in safety standards and fire prevention make them less likely.

Later that year, the New York state legislature formed a commission, which included union leader Samuel Gompers, to investigate ways to prevent disastrous workplace fires in the future. In 1912, the commission issued the first of a series of reports that resulted in numerous changes to health and safety laws in New York. Buildings were required to have fire alarms, fire extinguishers, well-built fire escapes, and sprinkler systems on higher floors. In addition, it became illegal to lock fire exits during working hours or to block stairways. Many of these laws were adopted in other states as well. Future Secretary of Labor Frances Perkins had been in New York on March 25, 1911, and had watched the tragedy unfold with gruesome swiftness. "Something must be done," she said, encapsulating the country's mood. "We've got to turn this into some kind of victory, some kind of constructive action."

THINK ABOUT IT

Do you think a workplace disaster like the Triangle factory fire could happen in the United States today? Why or why not?

An unlikely trio, a young garment worker, mink brigade member and social activist Flora Dodge LaFollette, and social reformer and missionary Rose Livingston (from left to right), march together during a 1913 strike of New York City garment workers.

THE MINK BRIGADE

When female garment workers went on strike in 1909, prior to the Triangle factory fire, they garnered unlikely allies in wealthy, prominent women. Anne Morgan, daughter of the powerful financier J.P. Morgan, had never needed to earn a living—much less toil at a sewing machine for 12 hours a day. Still, she and her friends were moved by the plight of the young immigrant sweatshop workers. Morgan recruited other upper-class women, including social activist Flora Dodge LaFollette, to come to the workers' defense. The "mink brigade," as the women were mockingly called because of their extravagant furs, walked the picket lines, feeling less likely to be attacked due to their social status. The mink brigade also defended striking workers who had been arrested and paid their fines.

Women like Anne Morgan and Flora Dodge LaFollette engaged in other philanthropic projects and worked to advance women's rights. In a statement in 1927, Morgan pictured a time when women "will take their places beside men as partners, unafraid, useful, successful, and free." To what extent do you think this vision has been realized in the 21st century?

MODERN-DAY TRIANGLES

In the 21st century, factory disasters in China, India, and Bangladesh have served as disturbing modern-day reminders of the Triangle factory fire. Bangladesh has become a world leader in garment manufacturing. The country's more than 5,000 factories, staffed with a largely female workforce, produce clothing for major international brands.

In November 2012, more than 100 people died in a fire at the Tazreen Fashions factory outside Dhaka, the capital of Bangladesh. The problems in the Tazreen factory—and other factories in Bangladesh—resembled those in the Triangle Waist Company factory: insufficient fire escapes, blocked exits, and poor safety measures. Then, in April 2013, the Rana Plaza building, in Savar, which is northwest of Dhaka, collapsed.

Rana Plaza had housed several garment factories. More than 1,100 workers were killed and 2,500 more injured in the catastrophe. The ensuing investigation revealed that the top four floors of the building had been built illegally, with no permits issued, and that the foundation was poorly constructed.

The disasters sparked a public outcry against the factory owners, the international brands that contracted the factories to make their garments, and the Bangladeshi government. Activists demanded improved safety measures and working conditions in the country's garment factories. The case of the Rana Plaza collapse resulted in criminal charges against the owners of the building and the factories housed inside. In addition to building code violations, charges in the case included murder.

CRITICAL VIEWING Workers in India stitch clothing in a garment factory in this 2012 photo. How would you describe working conditions in this factory?

ENGLISH LANGUAGE LEARNERS ELD

Create a Word Web Pair students at the **Emerging** and **Expanding** levels with students at the **Bridging** level. Display a Word Web with the topic Fire in the center. Tell students to reread the text, noting and adding words and phrases to the organizer that describe or relate to the factory fire. Then ask pairs to share and compare their organizers.

PRE-AP

Write a News Report Instruct students to conduct online research to learn more about the Triangle factory fire. Then have them write a detailed news story from the point of view of a New York City journalist in 1911, including quotes from eyewitnesses. Invite students to post their stories on a class blog or publish them on a school website.

See the Chapter Planner for more strategies for differentiation.

HISTORICAL THINKING

Ask and have students answer the following questions.

1. **READING CHECK** Who, if anyone, is to blame for the Triangle factory fire?

2. **ANALYZE LANGUAGE USE** What do the quotations from the firsthand accounts in this American Story reveal about the fire? Cite specific remarks to support your answer.

3. **ANALYZE CAUSE AND EFFECT** What reforms were made after the fire?

ANSWERS

1. Possible response: The owners of the factory are to blame because they made the decision to keep outside doors locked during work hours even though a fire insurance inspector recommended leaving them unlocked.

2. The quotations reveal the horror that individuals experienced as they struggled to escape. Nellie Ventura "heard the screams of the girls inside" as she descended a fire escape. Sam Levine lowered himself to safety by gripping the cables in an elevator shaft. On his way down, "the bodies of six girls went falling past" him.

3. The practice of locking doors was outlawed, and reforms mandated fire protections such as alarms and sprinkler systems.

THE ROOTS OF PROGRESSIVISM

At the dawn of the 20th century, children as young as eight years of age helped support their families by working in dusty mines sorting coal. This situation was one of many that reformers at the time wanted to change.

GOALS OF PROGRESSIVISM

As you have read, the United States had quickly become more industrialized and urbanized after the Civil War, and its immigrant population had grown dramatically. These changes brought new social and economic problems that reformers pressured the government to address. The push for reform reached a peak during the **Progressive Era**, a period from about 1890 to 1920 in which reformers sought to correct many social, economic, and political inequalities and injustices in the United States. The era brought sweeping changes that had a lasting impact on American society. In fact, many laws, policies, and ideas that shape life in the United States today trace back to this period.

The Progressive Era featured numerous reform campaigns led by progressive-minded people who were primarily white, middle class, Protestant, and college educated. The various campaigns often shared the same general aims of helping the disadvantaged and making the United States a more equitable and democratic country. One of the progressives' major goals was to end the widespread corruption of political bosses and government officials. Progressives wanted government at all levels to be honest and more open, efficient, democratic, and responsive. The people, they felt, should have a stronger and more direct role in electing officials and creating laws.

Many progressives also sought reforms in business and labor. Rejecting the laissez-faire, or hands-off, approach to economic affairs that had prevailed previously, they called for the government to regulate business practices and to break up monopolies and trusts. They hoped to end child labor and bring about improved working conditions, higher pay, and better benefits for all workers, including immigrants.

Theodore Roosevelt was an avid horseback rider throughout much of his life. In this photo from 1902, Roosevelt jumps a horse over a fence on a friend's farm near Washington, D.C.

Women played a major role during the Progressive Era and fought for an equal voice in government. At the time, only a few states allowed women to vote in elections. Progressives sought an amendment to the U.S. Constitution guaranteeing women's suffrage.

SPREADING PROGRESSIVISM

Progressivism arose in response to a multitude of problems. These included poverty, the spread of urban slums, poor working conditions in factories and mines, corruption in government, and the power of large corporations over the economy and government. These problems gained the attention of most Americans through **exposés**, writings that publicize a scandal or injustice. You have read about Upton Sinclair and his book *The Jungle,* which exposed the horrors of working in the meatpacking industry. You have also read about Ida Tarbell and her exposé of Rockefeller's Standard Oil Company. Sinclair and Tarbell were just two of the many muckrakers who helped bring the nation's social ills to wide public attention.

Helen Hunt Jackson, who had achieved fame as a poet and novelist, became a fierce advocate for the rights of Native Americans. In her nonfiction book *A Century of Dishonor,* published in 1881, Jackson condemned the federal government and white settlers for their shameful and often brutal treatment of Native Americans. Her popular 1884 novel *Ramona* called attention to the struggles of Native Americans living on missions in the Southwest.

Journalist and photographer **Jacob Riis** drew public attention to the crime, disease, and squalor in New York City's slums, which he had experienced firsthand as a struggling immigrant and a police beat reporter. His influential book *How the Other Half Lives,* published in 1890, jolted readers with stark photographs, unsparing descriptions, and shocking statistics. The book helped bring about laws regulating tenements, and it strongly influenced then president-to-be Theodore Roosevelt.

Joseph Mayer Rice, a physician by training, became a leader in a movement to reform education. From 1891 to 1897, he authored a series of articles that appeared in a journal called *The Forum.* Rice's articles shocked Americans by revealing poor teaching methods, low achievement, and unhealthy conditions in the nation's public schools.

In his 1902 magazine article "Tweed Days in St. Louis," muckraker **Lincoln Steffens** revealed the destructive effect of corruption on the government of St. Louis, Missouri, then one of the country's largest cities. The popularity of that article led Steffens to report on the troublesome relationship between business and government in five other major cities. His articles were collected and published in 1904 in a book called *The Shame of the Cities.* They made a powerful impression on the American public.

The Lithuanian-born political activist and anarchist **Emma Goldman** spoke out in her writings and lectures for the rights of workers and the empowerment of women. When World War I erupted, she fought strongly against U.S. involvement in the war and against military conscription, in which the government requires men to enlist and serve in the armed forces. As a result of her antiwar activism, she was arrested and convicted of conspiracy against the conscription law. She spent two years in prison. After her release, she was deported to her home country.

The progressive movement coincided with and was strongly influenced by a religious movement known as **Social Gospel**, which originated around 1870 among Protestant ministers who sought to apply Christian liberal theology to societal problems. This theology emphasized helping others by following the moral and ethical example of Jesus. Like Social Darwinism, Social Gospel addressed the poverty in urban, industrial society. However, followers of Social Gospel rejected the tenet of Social Darwinism that people are engaged in a struggle for existence in which only the strong survive. In contrast, they believed that by creating a kinder and more equitable society, they could help build the kingdom of God on Earth. They worked for such reforms as an end to child labor, a living wage for workers, a shorter workday, and safer working conditions.

SOCIAL GOSPEL AND FUNDAMENTALISM

Two distinct religious movements, Social Gospel and fundamentalism, took root during the Progressive Era. Social Gospel was based on Christian liberal theology, fundamentalism on a literal interpretation of the Bible. Two leading fundamentalists of the time were **Dwight L. Moody** and **Billy Sunday**. A former shoe salesman, Moody began preaching in the mid-1800s and devoted his life to winning souls and educating impoverished children in Chicago. Sunday left professional baseball to travel the country preaching against alcoholic beverages, declaring, "Whiskey and beer are all right in their place, but their place is in hell." Fundamentalists and followers of Social Gospel alike opposed the teachings of such Social Darwinists as William Graham Sumner, who portrayed the results of dire poverty as a natural mechanism to weed out the "unfit" in society.

HISTORICAL THINKING

1. **READING CHECK** What were the goals of progressivism?

2. **ANALYZE CAUSE AND EFFECT** How did journalists help spread progressivism?

3. **COMPARE AND CONTRAST** How do the teachings of Social Gospel conflict with the theory of Social Darwinism?

PLAN: 2-PAGE LESSON

OBJECTIVE

Identify how social, political, and economic inequalities informed the actions of the progressives in the early 20th century.

CRITICAL THINKING SKILLS FOR LESSON 1.1

• Analyze Cause and Effect

• Compare and Contrast

• Make Inferences

• Form and Support Opinions

HISTORICAL THINKING FOR CHAPTER 16

What reforms and expansion took place during the Progressive Era? Industrialization, urbanization, and immigration resulted in social and economic problems. Lesson 1.1 describes the conditions that caused progressive reformers to seek changes in business and government.

BACKGROUND FOR THE TEACHER

When Jacob Riis immigrated to the United States from Denmark in 1870, he became part of the "other half" that he later wrote about. Without a job, Riis experienced the poverty of New York City's lower class. Theodore Roosevelt had grown up with the privileges of wealth, yet this unlikely pair forged a long-term friendship based on mutual respect and a strong commitment to reform. As New York police commissioner, Roosevelt worked with Riis, who was then a police reporter and photojournalist, to investigate and improve the city's housing policies. Roosevelt called Riis "the best American I ever knew" and praised Riis's "great gift of making others see what he saw and feel what he felt."

INTRODUCE & ENGAGE

CONNECT THE PRESENT WITH THE PAST

Ask students to read the introductory paragraph to this lesson and identify the problems it describes. *(poverty, child labor, health)* Invite students to brainstorm a list of social and economic problems that exist in the present-day United States. *(Possible responses: poverty, discrimination, unemployment, violence, crime, drug addiction)* **ASK:** Who are the reformers who seek changes today? Discuss students' responses. After reading the lesson, direct students to draw parallels between past and present efforts to remedy social and economic problems.

TEACH

GUIDED DISCUSSION

1. **Make Inferences** Why did progressive reformers believe it was the government's role to address social and economic problems? *(Possible response: Reformers felt that changes in laws and policies were necessary to bring about widespread reforms.)*

2. **Form and Support Opinions** Which of the reformers' strategies was most effective? *(Possible responses: Exposés publicized and sensationalized problems to focus public attention on social issues. Books and articles provided in-depth coverage of injustices. Graphic photographs vividly illustrated the stark and unsafe living and working conditions experienced by marginalized groups.)*

MORE INFORMATION

Washington Gladden With sensibilities as a Protestant minister and an observant eye as a past editor of the *New York Independent* to bring into play, Washington Gladden became pastor of the Congregational Church in Springfield, Massachusetts, in 1875. Within a year, Gladden found himself on the brink of crossing a long-held Protestant tradition of noninterference in the forward march of capitalism. In reaching out to striking shoe factory workers, Gladden felt sympathetic to their situation. The next year he published *Working People and Their Employers*, advocating for workers' right to unionize during the industrializing late 19th century and helping to usher in the Social Gospel Movement. Gladden went on to advocate for African Americans and helped form the NAACP.

ACTIVE OPTIONS

On Your Feet: Create a Team Word Web Ask teams of four to gather around a large sheet of paper. Each student should write a word or phrase related to progressivism on the part of the web nearest him or her. At your signal, students should rotate the paper and continue to add words or phrases to the web. Tell teams to use their completed web to summarize a main idea about progressivism.

NG Learning Framework: Explore Opposing Viewpoints

`ATTITUDE` Responsibility

`KNOWLEDGE` Our Human Story

Instruct students to analyze the similarities and differences between the ideologies of Social Darwinism and Social Gospel. Guide students to use print and online resources, including the biographies of William Graham Sumner, Billy Sunday, and Dwight L. Moody, to investigate the positions, goals, and opponents. Then group students by movement and ask them to discuss their findings, including the views of the movement's opponents. Ask a member from each of the groups to present an overview of the movement, along with who opposed it and why, to the class.

DIFFERENTIATE

STRIVING READERS

Read and Recall Invite students to work in pairs. First have each student read the lesson independently. After reading, students should meet without the book and take notes as they share ideas they recall. Students then review the lesson together and decide what to add or change in their notes.

GIFTED & TALENTED

Create a Social Media Profile Have students choose one of the social reformers mentioned in this lesson. Instruct them to do online research to learn more about the person and his or her activism regarding social issues and solutions. Then ask students to create a social media profile for the reformer. Invite students to share their profiles with the class.

See the Chapter Planner for more strategies for differentiation.

HISTORICAL THINKING

ANSWERS

1. Progressives wanted to correct social and economic injustices by ending political corruption, regulating business practices, improving working conditions, and giving women the right to vote.

2. Through exposés, books, articles, and photographs, journalists and other writers created public awareness of the need for progressive reforms.

3. Social Gospel promoted helping poor people by following the example of Jesus and creating a better society. Social Darwinism taught that poverty was a natural means of separating the strong from the weak in society.

WOMEN FIGHT FOR RIGHTS

When the Progressive Era began, the campaign to allow women to vote was about a half century old. How much longer would women have to fight before they gained something as basic as the right to cast a ballot?

MIDWEST LEADERS

In the early 20th century, American society still strongly restricted the roles of women. Women could not vote or hold office in most states, and many companies barred women from working in certain professions. For decades, American women had been working in support of social reforms, even as they began to demand that their own rights be expanded to include all the rights and responsibilities of citizenship. Women were the foot soldiers of progressive reform.

One of the best known foot soldiers was Jane Addams. As you have read, she founded Hull House in Chicago, one of the most famous settlement houses in the nation. Hull House provided many resources and services to struggling immigrants. Addams also fought for such progressive causes as workers' rights, women's suffrage, or women's right to vote, and the regulation of tenements. She helped bring about the first juvenile law court, and she played a role in the founding of the **American Civil Liberties Union (ACLU)**, an organization that fights to this day for the constitutional rights of all citizens.

Hull House became a magnet for bright, ambitious women who were dedicated to social work and reform. One such women was **Florence Kelley**. While residing at the settlement house, she investigated sweatshops and tenement conditions and conducted a thorough survey of Chicago's 19th Ward, a political district in the city. Her reports on the appalling conditions she observed helped bring about an Illinois law that banned child labor, limited working hours for women, and established regulations for sweatshops. Kelley's reports earned her an appointment as the state's chief factory inspector.

In 1899, Kelley moved to New York City to become the general secretary of the newly created **National Consumers League**, an organization dedicated to defending the rights of consumers and workers. For the next 30 years, she led the league's fight for a minimum wage law for women, protection of in-home workers from exploitation, and restrictions on child labor.

Another social reformer drawn to Hull House was **Julia Lathrop**, who arrived in 1890. Lathrop worked to improve the lives of children, the disabled, and the mentally ill. In 1893, after becoming the first female member of the Illinois Board of Charities, Lathrop set out to inspect all of the state's poorhouses and "poor farms." These facilities housed, at state expense, people who could not support themselves, which included the mentally ill, physically ill, disabled, and aged—all mixed together. The inspections led her to push for separate facilities for the mentally ill. In 1912, President Taft appointed Lathrop as the first head of the **Children's Bureau**, the first federal agency dedicated to improving the lives of children and families. Lathrop worked to address the issues of child labor, infant and maternal mortality, juvenile delinquency, and the treatment of the mentally ill.

WEST COAST REFORMERS

On the West Coast, in San Francisco, women were working to solve other kinds of problems. The Chinese Exclusion Act of 1882 banned the immigration of Chinese laborers. As a result, Chinese men who had emigrated before the ban were cut off from their wives and families. Secret criminal societies called *tongs* arose in San Francisco's Chinatown, as well as in Chinese neighborhoods in other cities, to bring Chinese women to the United States. The tongs

🏛 **Jane Addams Hull-House Museum, Chicago**

Jane Addams appears with children at Hull House, the settlement house she established, in this photo from the collection of the Jane Addams Hull-House Museum. By 1907, Hull House consisted of 13 buildings occupying an entire block in Chicago. The museum is housed in one of the two original Hull House buildings.

kidnapped women and girls from China, smuggled them into California, and sold them as slaves to men or to brothels, or houses of prostitution. **Margaret Culbertson**, superintendent of the Occidental Mission Home for Girls, a Chinatown settlement house, was fearless in her efforts to rescue these women and girls. Once safe at the mission house, they received shelter, food, clothing, education, and security.

When Culbertson became too ill to continue her rescues, her assistant, **Donaldina Mackenzie Cameron**, took over. In the nearly 4 decades that she served as superintendent, Cameron rescued more than 3,000 women and girls from slavery, daring to run across rooftops and break down doors to carry out her work. The tongs hated and feared her, but those she rescued and sheltered called her *Lo Mo*, or "Beloved Mother."

COMBINING FORCES

In 1890, two competing women's rights organizations merged to form the **National American Woman Suffrage Association (NAWSA)**. Elizabeth Cady Stanton and Susan B. Anthony, pioneers in the women's suffrage movement, served as the new organization's first presidents. When Anthony retired in 1900, the presidency went to **Carrie Chapman Catt**, who stated that the enfranchisement of women would be the crowning glory of democracy. **Enfranchisement** is the act of granting full citizenship, including the right to vote. The right to vote is also referred to as the **franchise**.

For several decades, the strategy of suffragists, or people seeking the franchise for women, had been to push for a national constitutional amendment guaranteeing women the right to vote. By 1910, however, the movement had stalled. Southern Democrats in Congress opposed women's suffrage for fear it would include the enfranchisement of African-American women. In addition, companies that manufactured liquor worried that women's suffrage would strengthen the movement to prohibit the sale of alcohol. Faced with those roadblocks, suffragists began focusing their efforts at the state level. The result was a string of victories in western

---

OBJECTIVE

Describe contributions to social reform movements by Midwest and West Coast women.

CRITICAL THINKING SKILLS FOR LESSON 1.2

- Form and Support Opinions
- Compare and Contrast
- Identify Problems and Solutions
- Make Connections
- Analyze Cause and Effect
- Analyze Visuals
- Analyze Primary Sources

HISTORICAL THINKING FOR CHAPTER 16

What reforms and expansion took place during the Progressive Era? Women fought for expansion of voting rights while focusing on other social issues. Lesson 1.2 explains how women's efforts impacted the needs of marginalized groups.

BACKGROUND FOR THE TEACHER

Some Progressive Era women's reform movements have been called "municipal housekeeping," referring to an expansion of women's traditional roles into a broader sphere of influence. Although some women's efforts aimed at cleaning up streets and parks in local communities, the success of their reforms surpassed mere "housekeeping." Women's clubs in the early 1900s worked to improve public health concerns by promoting food inspections, clean water, and better sanitation through street cleaning and garbage removal. Women took responsibility for improving schools by opening free kindergartens and providing hot lunches for children. Female reformers often expanded their efforts from local issues to state and national concerns by playing an active role in lobbying for federal legislation to address social and environmental problems.

📝 HISTORY NOTEBOOK

Encourage students to complete the Women Fight for Rights page for Chapter 16 in their History Notebooks as they read.

INTRODUCE & ENGAGE

CONSIDER GOALS AND TRACK OUTCOMES

Ask students to make statements about the status of women in the United States in the early 20th century. Then ask students to make statements about the status of women in present-day American society. Encourage students with different viewpoints to support and explain their statements. Tell students that in this lesson they will learn how women fought for an expansion of their rights during the Progressive Era. As students read the lesson, suggest that they use a chart like the one below to record the goals and outcomes of the women's movement. At the end of the lesson, provide time for students to share their summaries.

Goals	Obstacles	Outcome
1.	1.	1.
2.	2.	2.
3.	3.	3.
SUMMARY		

TEACH

GUIDED DISCUSSION

1. **Make Connections** How did female reformers at the local level influence national reforms? *(Possible response: Several women who were successful at the local level, such as Jane Addams, Florence Kelley, and Julia Lathrop, went on to lead national reform organizations, such as the American Civil Liberties Union, the National Consumers League, and the Children's Bureau.)*

2. **Compare and Contrast** In what ways were the problems faced by West Coast reformers different from the problems faced by Midwest reformers? *(Possible response: In both cases, reformers tried to protect women and children from exploitation. However, West Coast reformers had to battle secret, organized criminal societies that exploited women and girls specifically by kidnapping and enslaving them.)*

3. **Analyze Cause and Effect** How did bias and prejudice interfere with passing a constitutional amendment giving women the right to vote? *(Possible responses: Southern Democrats opposed the enfranchisement of African-American women. Liquor manufacturers wanted to block the women's temperance movement.)*

🏛 VIRTUAL MUSEUM VISIT

The Jane Addams Hull-House Museum is located on the campus of the University of Illinois at Chicago in the former Hull Home and the Residents' Dining Hall, two of the buildings on the original site of the settlement house founded in 1889. Visitors may view more than 5,500 artifacts and displays relating to the residents and immigrant neighbors served by Hull House. The museum also offers workshops for teachers and special exhibits and tours for children and adults. The museum website provides valuable research aids as well as information about current initiatives. Students may be interested in learning about Cities of Peace, which carries out the ideals of Jane Addams's work by partnering with young people in Chicago and Phnom Penh, Cambodia, to promote shared healing for harm caused by violence.

DIFFERENTIATE

ENGLISH LANGUAGE LEARNERS `ELD`

Summarize Place students of **All Proficiencies** in pairs and assign them one or two paragraphs from the lesson. Instruct students to read their assigned paragraphs individually and then work together to summarize each paragraph in one or two sentences. When all pairs are finished, have them read their summaries in the order in which the material appears in the lesson. Provide the following sentence frames to help students at different proficiency levels create an effective summary.

- **Emerging:** This paragraph is about _____.
- **Expanding:** This paragraph is about _____ and _____.
- **Bridging:** To summarize, the paragraph provides information about _____.

PRE-AP

Write a Compare and Contrast Essay
Instruct students to conduct online research about the women who rescued Chinese girls sold into slavery or prostitution in San Francisco in the late 19th century, and how the women accomplished this. Then have students research the work of organizations fighting present-day slavery and human trafficking. Tell students to use their research to write an essay in which they compare and contrast the reasons for human trafficking and the tools used to fight it in both the late 19th century and today. Invite them to share their essays with the class.

See the Chapter Planner for more strategies for differentiation.

states as well as several eastern states. Some of the victories were only partial—that is, women were granted the right to vote only in certain elections—but others fully enfranchised women. In California, women gained full voting rights in 1911.

Another important figure in the suffrage movement was **Alice Paul**, who led its radical wing. She had fought for the vote in England and now wanted to apply aggressive tactics, such as marches and protests, in the United States. Other women joined her, including Harriot Stanton Blatch, who was the daughter of Elizabeth Cady Stanton.

For a few years, Paul and her allies worked on NAWSA's congressional committee. NAWSA stressed that female voting would result in purer and more honest politics. The organization also played down the argument that women should have equal political rights. Instead, it argued that suffrage would offset the votes of immigrants and racial minorities in large cities. Thus, suffragists would be protecting traditional values against "alien" assaults. Frustrated with NAWSA's cautious tactics, Paul left the organization in 1913. Along with **Lucy Burns**, the suffragist known for spending the most time in jail for the cause, she formed the Congressional Union for Woman Suffrage.

In 1916, the Congressional Union for Woman Suffrage reorganized itself as a single-issue political party and adopted a new name: the **National Woman's Party (NWP)**. Although the NAWSA and the NWP were fighting for the same cause, their strategies could not have been more different. While the NAWSA continued to rely on lobbying, petition gathering, and state-level campaigns, the NWP opted for direct action. Its members staged marches, picketed the White House, went on hunger strikes, and committed acts of civil disobedience. The effort to win the vote for women would take several more years and a war to bring about victory.

THE PROHIBITION MOVEMENT

Women also took the lead in reviving the temperance movement, which had first emerged in the early 1800s and encouraged people to temper, or moderate, their consumption of alcohol, or to abstain from alcohol altogether. Temperance reformers pointed out that although men did much of the drinking, alcohol-related problems often hit women and children hardest. Some men, they argued, spent money on alcohol that could be used to provide for the needs of their families. Excessive alcohol consumption, reformers believed, often caused men

PRIMARY SOURCE

Six feet tall and wielding a hatchet, temperance leader **Carry Nation** was famous for destroying bars and saloons to impede the selling and drinking of alcoholic beverages. Before she started using a hatchet, she collected bricks and stones—which she called "smashers"—to use as her weapons. Here, she describes her first experience "smashing" a saloon in Kiowa, Kansas, in 1899.

I threw as hard and as fast as I could, smashing mirrors and bottles and glasses and it was astonishing how quickly it was done. [The] men seemed terrified, threw up their hands and backed up in the corner. My strength was that of a giant. I felt invincible. God was certainly standing by me.

—from The Use and Need of the Life of Carry A. Nation, by Carry Nation, 1909

to become abusive, abandon or neglect their families, turn to crime, or fall into poverty and homelessness.

The Anti-Saloon League, founded in 1893, became one of the leading national organizations in the crusade against alcohol. Through propaganda and educational materials that often focused on women, children, and families, the league developed a strong base, especially among devout Protestant Christians. Promoting the idea of **prohibition**, the league pressured local and state governments to create laws restricting or prohibiting the production, sale, and consumption of alcohol. Oklahoma was the first state to adopt prohibition in 1907, and by 1914, eight other states had done the same. Militant prohibitionists, however, were discouraged by the state-by-state approach. The Anti-Saloon League set its sights on a bigger goal: a constitutional amendment to ban the sale of alcohol in the United States.

HISTORICAL THINKING

1. **READING CHECK** What reforms did Florence Kelley help bring about?

2. **FORM AND SUPPORT OPINIONS** What is your opinion of the NAWSA's claim that granting women the right to vote would offset the votes of immigrants and racial minorities? Give reasons for your opinion.

3. **COMPARE AND CONTRAST** How did the strategies of the NAWSA and the NWP differ?

4. **IDENTIFY PROBLEMS AND SOLUTIONS** What social problems did leaders in the temperance movement work to solve?

BUILD BACKGROUND

TACTICS OF NAWSA AND NWP

The NAWSA used elaborate tactics to spread the word and gain support for its cause. The 1913 national suffrage parade, for example, took place in Washington, D.C., one day before Woodrow Wilson took the oath of office as president. Timed to take advantage of the crowds on hand for the inauguration, the parade included between 5,000 and 10,000 suffragists (sources disagree), marching bands, and elaborate floats made its way along Pennsylvania Avenue. Well-organized participants wore sashes, hats, pins, or buttons advertising the cause and conducted themselves with dignity. A pageant on the steps of the Treasury Building included women and children dressed in classical costumes presenting a tableau portraying ideals, such as Freedom and Justice, and historical figures, such as Joan of Arc and Queen Elizabeth I of England.

The NWP, which was much smaller than the NAWSA, used tactics that were not as grand but just as effective. Picketing, for example, targeted President Wilson for several months during 1917, and suffragists marched to the White House carrying banners that demanded the right to vote. Each day, these "silent sentinels" walked a picket line outside the president's residence. The arrest of more than 200 of them for obstructing traffic fueled the protesters. Jailed NWP leaders used hunger strikes to attract public support for their cause, and in some cases, female inmates suffered physical violence and force-feeding. A "Jailed for Freedom" pin became a sign of honor among NWP members.

TEACH

GUIDED DISCUSSION

4. **Analyze Visuals** In the 1874 print, to what is the artist comparing the temperance movement? *(Answers will vary. Possible response: The artist compares the temperance movement to the Crusades. The women wear armor and carry weapons. The leader resembles Joan of Arc, and the banner invokes religious justification for the cause. The eagles and star-spangled shield appeal to patriotism.)*

5. **Make Connections** What characteristics and experiences likely prepared Alice Paul and Lucy Burns for their leadership roles in women's suffrage? *(Possible response: Both Alice Paul and Lucy Burns were aggressive in their tactics to win the vote for women. Paul had a deep history with the movement, having organized protests in England. Burns was a dedicated activist as well, having spent more time in jail than other activists of her time. Both women appear to have been fearless about speaking out and standing up for women's rights.)*

ANALYZE PRIMARY SOURCES

Explain that moral fiber is defined as the strength and ability to do what one believes is right. Invite students to offer aspects of Carry Nation's moral fiber that led to the actions she describes in the Primary Source feature and display their suggestions. **ASK:** Do you think Carry Nation was justified in smashing a saloon? Consider Nation's actions within the context of her times rather than solely in terms of present-day values. *(Possible responses: Nation believed she was justified because she felt God gave her the strength to hurl the bricks and stones. Given the obstacles to women at the time and the violence many women endured from men who abused alcohol, Nation was justified in smashing the saloon and bringing attention to the issue.)*

ACTIVE OPTIONS

On Your Feet: Conduct a Three-Step Interview Tell students to think about which female reformer made the greatest contribution to the civic principles and social reform movements of the Progressive Era. Students must be able to support their choice with evidence from the text or other sources. Ask students to work in pairs to interview each other about their choices. Finally, each student should share with the class the choice and reasons expressed by the classmate he or she interviewed.

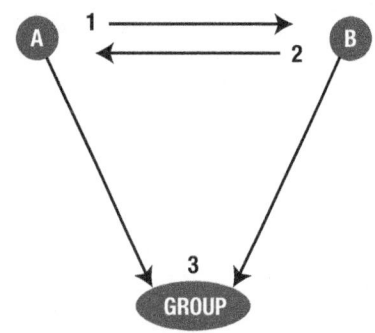

NG Learning Framework: Create a Documentary

ATTITUDE Responsibility

SKILLS Communication, Collaboration

ASK: Which of the social problems and issues discussed in this lesson have relevance in present-day American society? *(Possible responses: gender inequality, minimum wage, poverty, discrimination)* Tell students to work in groups to research a current social issue that has roots in the reform movements of the Progressive Era. Instruct students to write and present to the class a documentary that explores the differences between past and present-day reformers' approaches to the issue, focusing on consequences of past events and decisions and determining the lessons that were learned.

HISTORICAL THINKING

ANSWERS

1. At the state level, Florence Kelley helped bring about a law that banned child labor, limited working hours for women, and regulated sweatshops. With the National Consumers League, she fought for consumers and better working conditions and a minimum wage law for women.

2. Answers will vary. Students may note that the claim was an attempt to win support for women's suffrage by appealing to people who opposed rights for immigrants and racial minorities. Some students may view this as an effective tactic; others may feel it was biased and prejudiced to promote equal rights for one group while discriminating against others.

3. NAWSA members garnered support by lobbying, gathering petitions, and holding campaigns at the state level. NWP members took a more direct and high-profile approach by marching, picketing, going on hunger strikes, and promoting civil disobedience.

4. Temperance leaders worked to solve alcohol-related problems, such as poverty, homelessness, crime, and abuse or neglect of women and children.

CRITICAL VIEWING Possible responses: The reformers' actions were violent and destructive. At that time, there was no law against the sale and consumption of alcohol, so the reformers' tactics were illegal.

FOR OR AGAINST WOMEN'S SUFFRAGE?

From its beginnings in the 1840s to the start of the Progressive Era in the 1890s, the women's suffrage movement grew dramatically. Nevertheless, many Americans remained firmly opposed to the idea of extending the franchise to women. For every argument offered by suffragists, the anti-suffragists had a counterargument.

On November 2, 1915, voters in Massachusetts and New York—meaning men—cast ballots on whether to amend their state constitutions to grant the vote to women. The pennant shown below was part of the New York publicity campaign. In both states, the outcome was *No*: by a narrow margin of 175,000 votes in New York, but by 2 to 1 in Massachusetts. In another referendum 2 years later, voters in New York finally granted the franchise to women, becoming the 16th state to do so. Massachusetts women did not obtain the right to vote until the 19th Amendment was ratified in 1920.

CRITICAL VIEWING In 1910, this cartoon showing a male protester being arrested by two female police officers appeared on a *Life* magazine cover. Do you think this cartoon is satirical, or making fun of the idea of men's rights, or is it presenting that idea as a legitimate issue? What message does the cartoon convey about women's right to vote?

DOCUMENT ONE

Primary Source: Leaflet
from "Twelve Reasons Why Women Should Vote," by the National American Woman Suffrage Association, 1918

NAWSA produced posters, booklets, leaflets, and other printed materials that presented arguments in favor of women's suffrage. Local suffrage groups often purchased large quantities of the reading materials for rallies and women's suffrage campaigns.

CONSTRUCTED RESPONSE
Which of the 12 reasons do you think would have had the strongest impact on readers, and why?

Twelve Reasons Why Women Should Vote

1. BECAUSE those who obey the laws should help to choose those who make the laws.
2. BECAUSE laws affect women as much as men.
3. BECAUSE laws which affect WOMEN are now passed without consulting them.
4. BECAUSE laws affecting CHILDREN should include the woman's point of view as well as the man's.
5. BECAUSE laws affecting the HOME are voted on in every session of the Legislature.
6. BECAUSE women have experience which would be helpful to legislation.
7. BECAUSE to deprive women of the vote is to lower their position in common estimation.
8. BECAUSE having the vote would increase the sense of responsibility among women toward questions of public importance.
9. BECAUSE public spirited mothers make public spirited sons.
10. BECAUSE millions of women in the United States have become wage workers and the conditions under which they work are controlled by law.
11. BECAUSE the objections against their having the vote are based on prejudice, not on reason.
12. BECAUSE to sum up all reasons in one—IT IS FOR THE COMMON GOOD OF ALL.

DOCUMENT TWO

Primary Source: Pamphlet
from "Vote NO on Woman Suffrage," by the National Association Opposed to Woman Suffrage, c. 1915

As the women's suffrage movement gained strength, opposition groups, such as the NAOWS, sprang up. They often directed their messages at women. The anti-suffrage arguments below appeared on the back of a pamphlet offering household tips for women.

CONSTRUCTED RESPONSE What do you think is meant by "petticoat rule" in the fifth reason, and why would women consider it undesirable?

Vote NO on Woman Suffrage

BECAUSE 90% of the women either do not want it, or do not care.

BECAUSE it means competition of women with men instead of co-operation.

BECAUSE 80% of the women eligible to vote are married and can only double or annul their husbands' votes.

BECAUSE it can be of no benefit commensurate with the additional expense involved.

BECAUSE in some States more voting women than voting men will place the Government under petticoat rule.

BECAUSE it is unwise to risk the good we already have for the evil which may occur.

Vote "No" button, c. 1910

SYNTHESIZE & WRITE

1. **REVIEW** Review what you have learned about the women's suffrage movement.

2. **RECALL** Summarize the main arguments for and against women's suffrage presented in the two documents.

3. **CONSTRUCT** Construct a topic sentence that answers this question: How do the arguments for and against women's suffrage reflect different views of women's role in society?

4. **WRITE** Using evidence from this chapter and the documents, write an explanatory paragraph that supports your topic sentence.

PLAN: 2-PAGE LESSON

OBJECTIVE

Synthesize information about women's suffrage in the early 1900s from primary source documents.

CRITICAL THINKING SKILLS FOR LESSON 1.3

- Synthesize
- Draw Conclusions
- Make Inferences
- Evaluate

HISTORICAL THINKING FOR CHAPTER 16

What reforms and expansion took place during the Progressive Era? The struggle to expand voting rights to women was long and hard-fought during the Progressive Era. Lesson 1.3 examines arguments for and against women's suffrage.

BACKGROUND FOR THE TEACHER

Anti-suffragists worked at the local level for decades before the National Association Opposed to Woman Suffrage was founded (by a woman) in 1911. Some 20th-century women apparently opposed an expansion of their rights based on a need to preserve their way of life. Female anti-suffragists generally came from the wealthy upper class, where their social status provided privileges working-class women did not share. Consequently, they had the time and the means for involvement in charity work—tasks that reinforced traditional gender roles. The anti-suffragists viewed enfranchisement as a disruption of the status quo, which would result in a loss of femininity. Their motives were not solely self-serving, however. They believed involvement in politics would threaten women's ability to carry out charitable works that aided underprivileged groups.

INTRODUCE & ENGAGE

PREPARE FOR THE DOCUMENT-BASED QUESTION

Before students start on the activity, briefly preview the two documents. Remind students that a constructed response requires full explanations in complete sentences. Emphasize that students should use what they have learned about the struggle for women's suffrage in the United States during the Progressive Era in addition to the information in the documents.

TEACH

GUIDED DISCUSSION

1. **Draw Conclusions** What conclusion can you draw from the results of the 1915 referenda on women's suffrage in New York and Massachusetts? *(Possible responses: The majority of voters opposed women's suffrage. Since only men could vote, the results show that some men supported women's suffrage.)*

2. **Make Inferences** What bias did the National Association Opposed to Woman Suffrage convey by printing anti-suffragist arguments on the back of a pamphlet of household tips? *(Possible response: Women should concern themselves with domestic tasks rather than political matters.)*

EVALUATE

After students have completed the Synthesize & Write activity, allow time for them to exchange paragraphs and read and comment on the work of their peers. Establish guidelines for comments prior to this activity so that feedback is constructive and encouraging in nature. Comments should focus on the most significant parts that address the purpose of the activity and the audience.

ACTIVE OPTION

On Your Feet: Host a DBQ Roundtable Divide the class into groups of four. Have each group move desks to form a table where all four students can sit. Give each group a sheet of paper with the following question: Why did women want the right to vote, and what obstacles did they have to overcome to get it? The first student in each group should write an answer, read it aloud, and pass the paper clockwise to the next student. Students should circulate the paper around the table several times. Reconvene as a class and discuss groups' responses.

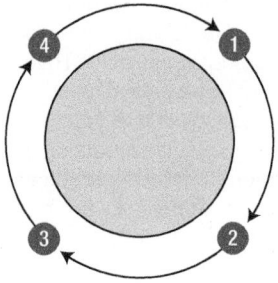

DIFFERENTIATE

INCLUSION

Support Critical Viewing Have visually impaired students work with sighted partners, who describe the cartoon in as much detail as possible, including facial expressions and postures. Then have the sighted partner read the caption aloud. Instruct students to work together to determine their answers to the Critical Viewing questions.

GIFTED & TALENTED

Debate Women's Suffrage Pose this scenario: Students are living in New York, and the 1915 referendum on women's suffrage is one week away. Pair students and tell them to flip a coin to decide who will debate for or against women's suffrage. Students must defend their position based on the primary source documents in this lesson and other primary and secondary source materials they research that date prior to the 1915 vote. Have partners work individually to prepare their arguments and then debate women's suffrage in small groups or in front of the class. Invite students to reflect on the reasoning of each side and to discuss the attitudes toward women that have and have not changed during the past century.

See the Chapter Planner for more strategies for differentiation.

SYNTHESIZE & WRITE

ANSWERS

1. Answers will vary.

2. Answers will vary.

3. Answers will vary. Possible response: Suffragists believed in the equality of women and men, whereas anti-suffragist arguments supported the superiority of men and specific feminine roles for women.

4. Answers will vary. Students' paragraphs should include the topic sentence from Step 3 and several details from the documents to support the sentence.

CONSTRUCTED RESPONSE

Document 1: Possible response. Students should support their choice with evidence from what they have learned about the women's suffrage movement.

Document 2: Possible response. The term "petticoat rule" means that women would have more influence than men. Women would consider the term undesirable because it implies a sexist view that women are inferior.

CRITICAL VIEWING The portrayal of powerful female police officers and the comparatively weak male protester indicates the cartoon is satirical. It conveys the message that men are not in danger of losing their rights if women are granted suffrage.

1.4

MAIN IDEA During the Progressive Era, reform-minded Americans worked to make city and state governments more democratic, more efficient, and less corrupt.

REFORMING GOVERNMENT

If you were running for political office, how would you convince people to vote for you? Offer them money? Promise them jobs? Across the United States, candidates were using such tactics to gain and keep political offices in the late 1800s and early 1900s.

REFORMING CITY GOVERNMENT

The earliest push for political reform during the Progressive Era occurred at the level of city government. The city mayors and councils struggled to deal with expanding populations divided by ethnicity, race, religion, and economic class. Council members often traded favors with one another and blocked legislation that hurt their districts, which made city government ineffective.

This situation gave rise to "boss politics." You have read about Boss Tweed and his political machine, Tammany Hall, but Tweed was not an isolated example. Throughout many big cities, powerful bosses commanded hierarchical political party organizations that operated at the district, the neighborhood, and even the block level. These corrupt political machines provided services, jobs, and favors in exchange for votes.

Reformers worked to take city government out of the hands of corrupt officials. After a hurricane devastated Galveston, Texas, in 1900, the Texas legislature suspended Galveston's city council and established a five-member commission to temporarily oversee the city. This new form of **commission government**, dubbed the "Galveston plan," worked so well that it was made permanent. It quickly spread to Dallas, Fort Worth, and other Texas cities.

CRITICAL VIEWING Two boys explore the wreckage of St. Patrick's Church in Galveston, Texas, after a devastating hurricane in 1900. The city council handled the disaster so poorly that a new form of government was instituted, and a commission of experts took charge of the various city departments. What details in the photograph indicate the scale of the hurricane damage?

In 1907, Des Moines, Iowa, became the first city outside Texas to adopt commission government, but it staged a vote so citizens could choose their own city commissioners. Des Moines became a model for cities around the United States that were seeking to overhaul their governments.

Staunton, Virginia, became another model. In 1908, Staunton's city council hired a professional manager to take charge of the city's struggling public services. The council-manager approach proved to be an effective way of taking politics out of city administration. Dayton, Ohio, adopted and popularized this form of government in 1913 following a devastating flood.

REFORMING STATE GOVERNMENT

The reform movement soon spread from the city level to the state level. Progressives, including future presidents Theodore Roosevelt and **Woodrow Wilson**, worked to make state government less corrupt, more efficient, and more democratic. Progressives instituted such structural changes as the **direct primary**, in which party candidates are nominated by a direct vote, and the direct election of U.S. senators.

At the time, party political bosses often controlled who was nominated to run for political offices. Direct primary elections gave this control to voters. In accordance with the U.S. Constitution, senators had always been elected by state legislatures, which often were strongly influenced by rich and powerful political supporters. In 1899, Nevada changed its law to allow voters to elect U.S. senators directly. Soon, other states did the same. Then, in 1913, progressive efforts helped pass and ratify the **17th Amendment**, which mandated that all U.S. senators be elected by popular vote.

Progressives also promoted such democratic reforms as the **initiative** and the referendum. An initiative enables citizens to bypass the legislature and propose new laws to be voted on. In a referendum, as you have learned, a proposal is submitted to voters directly for approval or rejection. During the Progressive Era, nearly 20 states adopted statewide processes for initiatives and referendums.

After he was elected New York's governor in 1898, Theodore Roosevelt worked with the state legislature to enact laws regulating tenements, corporations, and the civil service, and he fought against corruption and political machines. In 1906, New York gained another reform-minded governor with the election of Charles Evans Hughes. Hughes helped

regulate public utilities, such as gas and water, and expanded the state's involvement in policing. He also pushed through laws that made political campaigns more open, honest, and democratic.

During his two-year tenure as governor of New Jersey beginning in 1911, Woodrow Wilson established a commission to oversee the state's public utilities and helped pass a workers' compensation law to help employees who were injured on the job. On the other side of the country, California governor **Hiram Johnson** led the charge for constitutional state amendments on the initiative, referendum, and **recall**, or the right of citizens to remove an elected official by direct vote.

But the leading symbol of state reform was **Robert M. La Follette**, a Republican who was elected governor of Wisconsin in 1900. During his two terms, he established direct primary elections, regulated Wisconsin's railroads, and levied higher taxes on corporations. He forged a close relationship between the state government and the University of Wisconsin faculty, who advised him on policy. This reliance on academic experts as government advisors was called the "Wisconsin Idea."

HISTORICAL THINKING

1. **READING CHECK** How did progressives give voters a larger voice in state government?

2. **MAKE CONNECTIONS** How did reforms instituted in city governments help shape reforms adopted in state governments?

3. **DRAW CONCLUSIONS** Why do you think Governor La Follette sought the advice of the faculty at the University of Wisconsin?

INTRODUCE & ENGAGE

PROPOSE A SOLUTION

Remind students of conditions that existed in U.S. cities in the late 1800s and early 1900s. If time permits, read excerpts from the works of Lincoln Steffens, Jacob Riis, or Jane Addams aloud. Discuss how conditions in cities related to ineffective and corrupt city governments. Then challenge students to propose solutions to the problems as you record their responses on the board. Tell students that in this lesson they will learn how progressives reformed city and state governments. At the end of the lesson, have students revisit their suggested solutions and compare them with historical progressive reforms.

TEACH

GUIDED DISCUSSION

1. **Analyze Cause and Effect** What was the relationship between commission government and the power of political machines? *(Possible response: Commission government allowed voters to choose city officials, depriving corrupt political bosses of the power to buy the votes that kept them in office.)*

2. **Summarize** What corruption existed in state governments prior to progressive reforms? *(Possible response: Political bosses controlled the selection of nominees for office, and state legislatures crafted laws beneficial to rich supporters. Both of these practices undermined the democratic process.)*

ANALYZE PRIMARY SOURCES

Direct students' attention to the quotation from Governor Hiram Johnson's first inaugural address. Based on context or research, have students define the words *thug (a violent criminal)* and *broadcloth (woven fabric often made of wool)*. Ask them to restate the quote to express Johnson's ideas in modern terms. *(Possible response: I prefer the obvious criminal to criminal politicians who appear to be respectable but use thugs as a violent means to get what they want.)*

ACTIVE OPTIONS

On Your Feet: Become an Expert Group students into four "expert" groups. Assign each group one of the following examples of city government to study in depth: Tammany Hall model; Galveston model; Des Moines model; Staunton model. When groups have completed their research, regroup students so that each new group has at least one member from each expert group. Ask experts to report on their study. As a whole class, discuss reasons why political machines gained power in cities and how reform models of city government spread throughout the United States in the early 1900s.

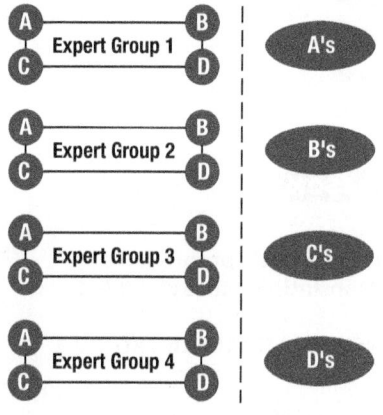

NG Learning Framework: Research Local Government

ATTITUDE Curiosity

SKILL Collaboration

Arrange students into small groups and instruct them to research the history of their local government to compare the present form with past forms it has taken. Use the following questions to guide students' research: What form or forms did the government take in the past? What is the present-day form? What specifically changed, and why? What stayed the same? Encourage students within groups to collaborate on a presentation, using appropriate media to share the results of their research.

DIFFERENTIATE

STRIVING READERS

Understand Main Ideas Check students' understanding of the main ideas in Lesson 1.4 by asking them to correctly complete either/or statements such as the following:

- The first political reforms of the Progressive Era happened at the [state or city] level of government. *(city)*
- The 17th Amendment mandated that all U.S. [senators or representatives] be elected by popular vote. *(senators)*
- An initiative is a way that [citizens or state legislatures] can propose new laws. *(citizens)*

PRE-AP

Explore the Etymology of *Thug* Point out Hiram Johnson's use of the word *thug* in the Primary Source feature. Tell students to research the circuitous route the word *thug* has taken from ancient Sanskrit to modern English. Invite students to present their research to the class orally or in writing.

See the Chapter Planner for more strategies for differentiation.

HISTORICAL THINKING

ANSWERS

1. Progressives promoted reforms, such as the direct primary, the initiative, and the referendum, that expanded the role of voters in choosing candidates by election and proposing or rejecting legislation.

2. The success of city government reforms that reduced corruption and increased voter power inspired similar changes at the state level.

3. Possible response: La Follette recognized the value of academic expertise in making political decisions.

PRIMARY SOURCE

Possible responses: Corrupt politicians appear respectable while engaging in criminal acts and corruption. Outright thugs are openly criminal, so people expect them to engage in violence and criminal activity.

CRITICAL VIEWING Much of the church is in rubble, with windows broken and walls caved in. Sunlight has created a shadow of the boy at the right on a fallen wall, so it appears that the roof has also collapsed.

REFORM UNDER ROOSEVELT

Theodore Roosevelt had a strong commitment to reform, which fit perfectly with the mood of Americans at the start of the 20th century. He led the way in expanding the power of the federal government in order to carry out the reforms he thought were necessary.

ROOSEVELT BECOMES PRESIDENT

In November 1900, voters elected President William McKinley to a second term. McKinley's presidency was cut short, however. On September 6, 1901, a young Michigan-born anarchist, a person who opposes all government, shot the president at a world's fair in Buffalo, New York. The president died eight days later. His vice president, Theodore Roosevelt, took over as president.

At 42, Roosevelt was the youngest person ever to hold the office of president. Roosevelt was brash and energetic. He loved the outdoors, and he led an active lifestyle that included horseback riding, swimming, boxing, and hunting.

Roosevelt came to office at a time when there was strong momentum for social, economic, and political change in the United States. He became the first progressive president and took the lead in bringing about many reforms.

Since entering politics around 1880, Roosevelt had been either elected or appointed to a variety of government positions, including member of the New York State Assembly, assistant secretary of the U.S. Navy, and governor of the state of New York. He had earned a reputation for political independence and for commitment to eradicating, or getting rid of, political corruption.

After the deaths of his wife and his mother on a single day in 1884, Roosevelt had retreated to a cattle ranch he owned in the Dakota Territory and spent much of the next two years there. He became increasingly dedicated to **conservation**, or the management and protection of natural resources, as he saw how human activities were damaging the land and reducing the populations of such wildlife as bison, bighorn sheep, and elk.

An original Teddy bear

🏛 The National Museum of American History, Washington, D.C.

Rose Michtom, the wife of a candy store owner, created the first Teddy bear in Brooklyn, New York, in 1902, after she and her husband saw a political cartoon involving President Theodore "Teddy" Roosevelt on a bear hunt. The couple put the bear on display in their store window, and many passers-by wanted to buy it. Rose and her husband, Morris, wrote to Roosevelt asking permission to use the name *Teddy* for the bear. On receiving the president's approval, Morris formed a toy company and began manufacturing Teddy bears.

THE SQUARE DEAL

Nine months after taking office, President Theodore Roosevelt faced one of the first major challenges of his presidency. On May 12, 1902, the 140,000 members of the United Mine Workers union, an organization formed to protect the interests of workers, walked off their jobs in the coal fields of eastern Pennsylvania after the mine operators refused to meet with union representatives. The miners were seeking higher pay, shorter hours, and recognition of their union. The mine operators, who had lost a strike two years earlier, wanted to break the strike—and the union.

The drop in production caused coal prices to soar. As the walkout stretched into autumn, the threat of winter coal shortages loomed. Republicans worried that if voters' homes were cold, people might vote against the Republican Party in the congressional elections in November. Roosevelt, in a letter to Massachusetts's governor Winthrop Murray Crane, expressed concern that the shortages could cause "untold misery . . . with the certainty of riots which might develop into social war."

After much agonizing, Roosevelt decided to act. But he did not call in troops to break up the strike, as President Grover Cleveland had done in the Pullman Strike eight years earlier. Instead, he brought the two sides together and worked with them to negotiate a reasonable settlement. Roosevelt called his approach the **Square Deal** because he wanted to ensure fairness and balance to both sides. This approach in disputes between big business and labor would be a hallmark of Roosevelt's presidency.

Roosevelt believed that as president, he should take action to promote the general welfare of the people and to protect the country's natural resources. He saw the presidential office as a "bully pulpit," or a position of high authority and prestige from which he could promote his ideas and push his social and economic agenda more aggressively than presidents who came before him. For this reason, many historians consider Theodore Roosevelt the first modern president.

BUSTING THE TRUSTS

Corporations were a major source of concern for Roosevelt. Some of them were growing large and extremely powerful through **mergers**, in which two or more companies combine as one. One example was the 1901 merger of the Carnegie Steel Company with steel companies owned by J.P. Morgan, which created the mammoth United States Steel Corporation. Valued at more than $1.4 billion, it was the largest corporation in U.S. history. It had 168,000 employees, and it controlled 60 percent of the steel industry's production. By eliminating other employment opportunities, United States Steel used its size to drive down workers' wages, and so other steel companies were able to do the same.

In a cartoon entitled "The Lion Tamer," which appeared on the cover of *Harper's Weekly* in 1904, President Roosevelt is portrayed as taming the power of trusts in various industries.

OBJECTIVE

Examine Theodore Roosevelt's progressive philosophy and its translation into legislation.

CRITICAL THINKING SKILLS FOR LESSON 2.1

- Make Inferences
- Analyze Environmental Concepts
- Analyze Primary Sources
- Make Connections
- Make Predictions
- Compare and Contrast
- Analyze Visuals

HISTORICAL THINKING FOR CHAPTER 16

What reforms and expansion took place during the Progressive Era? Labor unrest, unregulated trusts, conservation, and splintered race relations were hallmarks of the Progressive Era. Lesson 2.1 examines President Theodore Roosevelt's approach to these issues.

BACKGROUND FOR THE TEACHER

Roosevelt developed his progressivism in New York, a city infamous for its impoverished immigrants, inadequate public services, political bosses, and rampant corruption. As an assemblyman, he targeted corrupt judges and tried to address the conditions in tenements. Later, he supported civil service exams, a direct criticism of the "urban political machine" in which party bosses doled out jobs to their supporters rather than the most qualified candidates. In 1899, he was elected governor and pushed for reforms that included factory inspections and tenement housing laws. Roosevelt was so successful that corporations and financial institutions wanted to remove him from office. In 1900, Roosevelt left office after being nominated as vice president—a job he did not want, saw as a dead end, but eventually accepted.

FINANCIAL LITERACY

To extend their knowledge and understanding about the concepts in this lesson, refer students to the Financial Literacy handbook.

INTRODUCE & ENGAGE

THE FIRST MODERN PRESIDENT

Inform students that historians consider Theodore Roosevelt to be the first modern president because he had many of the personality traits, the leadership style, and the cultural visibility present in modern leaders. Ask students to think about what we expect from modern presidents. Do they take an active or passive role in running the country? Are they more or less visible than leaders in other branches of government? Are they outspoken or introverted? Draw a Concept Cluster on the board and ask students to volunteer specific characteristics of their idea of a modern president. Revisit the Concept Cluster at the end of the lesson and determine whether President Roosevelt embodied any of these characteristics.

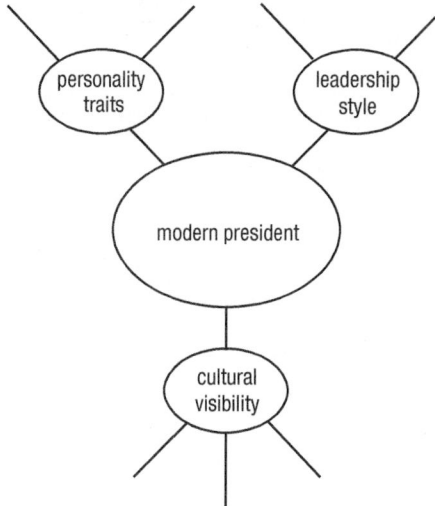

TEACH

GUIDED DISCUSSION

1. **Analyze Primary Sources** What do the details of the political cartoon tell you about the artist's viewpoint? *(Possible response: The artist views Roosevelt as a trustbusting hero taming the beasts of industry—the beef, oil, and steel trusts. The artist portrays the trusts as threatening lions to suggest the dangers they pose to the nation. Roosevelt is depicted heroically, cracking his whip and dominating the trusts to protect Americans from the evils of big business.)*

2. **Make Connections** Why did Roosevelt sign the Elkins Act into law? *(The Interstate Commerce Commission had not been enforcing the Interstate Commerce Act, which regulated federal railroad transportation. The Elkins Act established fines that discouraged corrupt policies of railroad leaders, such as providing reduced transportation rates to favored companies.)*

VIRTUAL MUSEUM VISIT

The National Museum of American History in Washington, D.C., has a collection of more than 3 million items, including Dorothy's ruby slippers from the film *The Wizard of Oz*, one of Abraham Lincoln's top hats, and sheet music from Duke Ellington. Using the museum's website, one can view online exhibitions and artifacts. Instruct groups of students to search the museum's collections for objects related to Theodore Roosevelt's life and presidency. Tell groups to select one object and give a short presentation explaining how it reflects Roosevelt's progressive governing philosophy or personality.

DIFFERENTIATE

ENGLISH LANGUAGE LEARNERS `ELD`

Write Key Vocabulary Sentences Pair students at the **Emerging** level with those at the **Bridging** or **Expanding** level. Direct the more proficient students to model the exercise by stating an original sentence using a Key Vocabulary word. Then tell students to take turns composing a sentence for each Key Vocabulary word (*conservation, mergers, trustbuster*) and also for *anarchist, corruption, monopolize*, and any other unfamiliar words in the lesson. Invite pairs to share their sentences and discuss different ways to use each word. Use the following sentence frames to help students at different proficiency levels engage in discussion.

- **Emerging:** This word means _____.
- **Expanding:** The word _____ means _____.
- **Bridging:** The author used the word _____; its connotative meaning is _____, and it shows _____.

GIFTED & TALENTED

Create a Multimedia Presentation Instruct students to use online and print sources to research the path and purpose of the camping trip that President Roosevelt and John Muir took into the Yosemite wilderness. Then have students create a multimedia presentation using any presentation tool that will help them show as much information about the trip as possible, including the beginning and the end, stopping points, and the topics the two men discussed. Encourage students to end their presentation with the legislation that was likely a result of this camping trip. Invite students to give their presentations to the class.

See the Chapter Planner for more strategies for differentiation.

In 1903, President Theodore Roosevelt (left) went on a three-night camping trip with conservationist John Muir in the Yosemite region in California. Here the two men stand together atop Glacier Point, with Yosemite Falls in the distance behind and below them.

Roosevelt saw industrial mergers as unavoidable, but he thought that the federal government should play an active role in regulating business instead of sitting back and allowing corporations to do as they pleased. He believed in encouraging corporations to behave in a socially responsible way and in monitoring and controlling those that did not. Roosevelt's idea of a good company was one that paid a living wage to its employees, provided safe working conditions, did not overcharge its customers, and did not contribute to political corruption to gain an advantage.

In 1890, Congress had passed the **Sherman Antitrust Act**, which gave the federal government the power to prosecute and break up corporations and trusts that monopolized, or threatened to monopolize, specific markets and industries. Unlike previous presidents, Roosevelt used the act aggressively. His first target was the powerful Northern Securities Company, which controlled three railroads. In 1904, the Supreme Court ruled that the company had violated the Sherman Antitrust Act and ordered it to be dismantled. Americans saw Roosevelt as a **trustbuster**, someone who would fight to curb the power of big business by vigorously enforcing antitrust legislation.

REGULATING BUSINESS

Progressives had a strong belief in the power of government to do good and to promote a better society. They rejected laissez-faire economics, feeling the government's hands-off approach had allowed corporations to abuse their power at the expense of workers, consumers, and smaller businesses. Instead, progressives pushed the government to regulate business more closely. This work fell to agencies such as the **Federal Trade Commission (FTC)** and the **Interstate Commerce Commission (ICC)**, which employed experts on the industries they supervised.

The ICC was created in 1887 through the Interstate Commerce Act, which was intended to control corruption in the railroad industry. It required the railroad companies to offer reasonable and fair rates for transporting goods, and it prohibited them from offering preferred rates to certain customers. The act had not been strongly enforced, however, and the railroads and corporations still engaged in unfair practices. In 1903, Roosevelt took action. He signed the Elkins Act, which levied heavy fines on railroads that offered rebates, or partial returns on money paid, and on the companies that received them. Three years later, he signed the Hepburn Act, which gave the ICC the power to establish maximum transportation rates and review the accounts and records of the railroads.

Other industries also came under the watchful eyes of the Roosevelt administration. In late 1905, Congress began writing a bill intended to ensure the purity and safety of foods and drugs. Roosevelt strongly supported the bill, but it faced steep business opposition.

Then, in the winter of 1906, Upton Sinclair's muckraking novel *The Jungle* was published. As you have read, the book described the unsanitary practices of the meatpacking industry. Roosevelt was among the thousands of Americans who read the book and were shocked and disgusted by its revelations. He launched an investigation of the industry and supported legislation that established a federal program for meat inspection. Meanwhile, Sinclair's novel produced a public outcry that spurred the House to pass what would become the **Pure Food and Drug Act**, which Roosevelt signed into law in June of 1906.

RACE RELATIONS

While breaking up corporations and establishing food safety laws, Roosevelt also wanted to be seen as a friend to African Americans. In October 1901, he invited Booker T. Washington, who had built a political machine among black Republicans in the South, to dine with his family at the White House.

Southerners were infuriated, and a Tennessee newspaper editor called the occasion "the most damnable outrage that has ever been perpetrated by any citizen of the United States." Roosevelt felt the backlash of his decision and never again invited another African American to dine at the White House. However, he appointed African Americans to positions in post offices and customs houses. The appointments could only help him win votes from black delegates in the upcoming election of 1904.

Beyond symbolic actions, however, Roosevelt did not challenge the racism that existed throughout the nation. Discrimination, segregation, poverty, and violence continued to be a scourge on the lives of African Americans.

THE CONSERVATION PRESIDENT

As a boy, Theodore Roosevelt had been frail and sickly, but he grew into a strong man who loved outdoor activities. As you have read, the two years he spent on a cattle ranch in the Dakota Territory helped transform him into a committed conservationist. He saw how human activities were ruining the land and destroying wildlife, and he felt an urgent need to protect the country's natural resources.

Conservation became one of the defining aspects of Roosevelt's presidency. He used his power as president to create 4 national game preserves, or areas set aside to protect wild animals, 51 refuges for wild birds, and 150 national forests. He also helped establish Crater Lake and Mesa Verde national parks. Through the Antiquities Act, he protected the Grand Canyon and many other areas of scenic or historical interest from destruction and development. He worked closely with Gifford Pinchot (PIN-show), head of the newly created National Forest Service, to create a policy that balanced the protection of natural resources with their industrial use. Because of his efforts, Roosevelt is remembered as the Conservation President.

HISTORICAL THINKING

1. **READING CHECK** Why did many Americans think of Theodore Roosevelt as a trustbuster?

2. **MAKE INFERENCES** What political reason might Roosevelt have had for inviting Booker T. Washington to the White House?

3. **ANALYZE ENVIRONMENTAL CONCEPTS** What actions did Roosevelt take to improve the viability of natural systems?

BUILD BACKGROUND

PRESENT-DAY PROGRESSIVISM

A hallmark of the Progressive Era was the passage of laws aimed at expanding the power of government through the establishment of regulatory agencies. Many progressive achievements, such as the Federal Trade Commission, still exist today. Signed into law by Woodrow Wilson in 1914, the FTC was given the mission to protect consumers and promote competition. Today, the commission aids consumers by allowing them to file complaints against businesses, report identity theft, receive a free credit report, avoid telemarketing calls by registering with the National Do Not Call Registry, and get alerts on illegal robocalls and scams such as fake prizes and real estate timeshares.

CONTROVERSY AT THE WHITE HOUSE

The controversy surrounding President Roosevelt's decision to dine with Booker T. Washington is difficult to understand. Other presidents had invited African Americans to meals at the White House but never to a formal dinner. Many—especially those in the South—saw an invitation to dine as a tacit acceptance of social equality, an idea that was anathema to racial segregationists of the time. After the dinner, the outrage lasted for years. Assassins were hired to go after Washington, and Roosevelt and his wife were harshly criticized and depicted in vulgar cartoons. Other Republicans, in an attempt to suppress the controversy, claimed that the meal was not in fact a "dinner," but a less objectionable "lunch." When pressed by a journalist years later as to the nature of the engagement, Mrs. Roosevelt checked her calendar and confirmed that the engagement had indeed been a dinner.

TEACH

GUIDED DISCUSSION

3. **Make Predictions** What are some possible drawbacks of the progressives' rejection of laissez-faire economics and the government taking a more active role in the economy? *(Possible response: By becoming more active in the economy, the government could play favorites by incentivizing some industries over others, thus harming competition.)*

4. **Compare and Contrast** How did Theodore Roosevelt change the government's philosophy toward the natural environment? *(Previous administrations had not viewed the protection of the environment as an important issue, exploiting the land rather than protecting it. Roosevelt's camping trip with John Muir probably drew attention to the beauty of places such as Yosemite and the necessity of preserving them.)*

ANALYZE VISUALS

Direct students' attention to the photograph of Theodore Roosevelt and John Muir. Ask them to examine the way the men are dressed, particularly Roosevelt. Ask students to think about how Roosevelt's appearance compares with how we typically imagine the appearance of the president. **ASK:** Why do you think Roosevelt chose to dress this way? *(Answers will vary. Possible response: By dressing "ruggedly," Roosevelt was reinforcing his image as a tough man of action who was also attuned to the natural world.)*

ACTIVE OPTIONS

On Your Feet: Card Responses Direct students to work in groups to create a quiz about what they learned in the lesson. Students can write true-false, complete-the-sentence, or short-answer questions. Have groups trade sets of questions and answer them. Encourage groups to check answers against the text and to keep track of group scores.

NG Learning Framework: Analyze Impact of Humans on the Environment

| ATTITUDE | Responsibility |

| SKILLS | Communication, Collaboration |

Instruct students to work in teams to investigate Theodore Roosevelt's observations about the effects humans had already had on the land and wildlife in the Dakota Territory by the time of his retreat there in 1884. Tell students to use both print and online sources to gather information about the state of the Dakota Territory when Europeans first arrived and the resulting impact of their activities on the land and wildlife by the time of Roosevelt's retreat. Ask teams to divide research tasks fairly and to combine their findings into a coherent understanding of the facts, noting discrepancies among sources. Teams should create a report that includes visuals such as maps and photos. Allow time for groups to share their reports with the class.

HISTORICAL THINKING

ANSWERS

1. Roosevelt aggressively used the Sherman Antitrust Act to fight monopolies.

2. Roosevelt might have been seeking to increase his support among African-American voters.

3. Roosevelt protected land, such as the Grand Canyon, from development through the Antiquities Act. He created national game preserves and refuges for wildlife and established national forests and the National Forest Service.

THE GRAND CANYON
NORTHWESTERN ARIZONA

One of the seven natural wonders of the world, the Grand Canyon is the most spectacular gorge on Earth. Over millions of years, the Colorado River carved the canyon, which displays through its layers of rock the most extensive record of geologic history on Earth. In fact, rocks at the bottom of the canyon date back 2.5 billion years. Still, the aesthetic and geologic value of the Grand Canyon have not been enough to ensure its protection. When mining and tourism interests posed a threat, President Theodore Roosevelt stepped in to safeguard the canyon by making it a national monument in 1908. Roosevelt expressed the hope that no human activity would "mar the wonderful grandeur, the sublimity, the great loneliness and beauty of the canyon." Congress established Grand Canyon National Park in 1919, but developers have not stopped devising plans to "mar" the canyon. Today, environmentalists affiliated with National Geographic and other organizations continue to battle against commercial groups who have proposed building a tram near the park's eastern edge to shuttle visitors to the canyon's bottom.

CRITICAL VIEWING Although mostly red, as revealed in this photo by National Geographic photographer Pete McBride, the Grand Canyon's rock layers also display hues of green, pink, gray, brown, and violet. What do you think motivates activists like McBride to protect the Grand Canyon from development?

PLAN: 2-PAGE LESSON

OBJECTIVE

Understand the tension between the preservation and development of America's vast natural heritage.

CRITICAL THINKING SKILLS FOR LESSON 2.2

• Analyze Visuals

• Make Connections

• Analyze Environmental Concepts

• Form and Support Opinions

HISTORICAL THINKING FOR CHAPTER 16

What reforms and expansion took place during the Progressive Era? The birth of the conservation movement is one of the lasting legacies of the Progressive Era. Lesson 2.2 discusses the Grand Canyon, which was protected by President Roosevelt and is America's most iconic example of environmental preservation.

NATIONAL GEOGRAPHIC PHOTOGRAPHER
PETE McBRIDE

In 2015, photographer Pete McBride, along with writer Kevin Fedarko, undertook an ambitious adventure accomplished by only 24 other people—a hike through all 800 miles of the Grand Canyon. The goal of the trip was to raise awareness about the threats facing this American icon. The arduous journey involved hiking the vertical face of the canyon, finding passable routes where none were established, and locating water in the searing heat. Because of the difficulty, it took the pair eight trips and nearly a year to complete the trek. Films, photographs, and information about the adventure are available at the National Geographic website.

HISTORY NOTEBOOK

Encourage students to complete the American Places page for Chapter 16 in their History Notebooks as they read.

INTRODUCE & ENGAGE

PREVIEW USING VISUALS

Direct students' attention to the photograph. **ASK:** How would you describe the landform in the photograph? *(Possible responses: It's immense, covering miles of land. The jagged rock formations are beautiful and awe inspiring.)* Ask students to share their experiences visiting the Grand Canyon, a local landform, or another historic geologic site. Encourage students to discuss what they think and feel when they visit such sites.

TEACH

GUIDED DISCUSSION

1. **Analyze Environmental Concepts** What threats to the Grand Canyon made Theodore Roosevelt want to preserve it, and what present-day threats exist? *(Roosevelt feared mining and tourism would mar the canyon's beauty. Present-day threats include an effort to build a tram to the bottom of the canyon, which would destroy some of the natural landscape that Roosevelt wanted to preserve.)*

2. **Form and Support Opinions** Do you think Roosevelt and environmental groups were justified in supporting the creation of Grand Canyon National Park? *(Answers will vary. Students should support their opinions with sound reasons that are supported by details and facts.)*

📍 AMERICAN PLACES

The Grand Canyon is located in Arizona close to the borders of Utah and Nevada. Visitors have the option of exploring the canyon along the North or South Rim. The canyon's total area includes more than a million acres of land and stretches 277 miles along the Colorado River, which snakes along the canyon's floor. The width of the national park is about 10 miles, although in some places it spans as many as 18 miles. Hikers who wish to travel rim-to-rim generally take three days. Those who attempt to raft the length of the river can travel for two weeks or even longer.

ACTIVE OPTIONS

STEM

On Your Feet: Build a Model of the Geologic Record Divide the class into five groups. Remind students that the geologic record is the history of Earth that is recorded in the rocks of Earth's crust. Direct students to use print or online sources to locate and examine a labeled diagram or photo of a segment of rock wall in the Grand Canyon that indicates when the layers of rock developed. Instruct students to use found materials to build a 3-D model of the segment they examined and label it. Ask a student from each group to present the group's model to the class and explain the segment of geologic record that it represents. As a class, discuss what the visible geologic record in the Grand Canyon walls has contributed to science.

NG Learning Framework: Explore Land-Use Controversies

ATTITUDE Responsibility

SKILL Problem-Solving

Land-use issues along the Grand Canyon have remained controversial. Divide the class into small groups. Have each group briefly research a land-use controversy along the Grand Canyon or other piece of protected land. Groups should prepare a short report and present the arguments for and against the proposed development to the class. Encourage students to weigh the pros and cons of the proposed development and identify any possible alternatives to the proposed use of land.

DIFFERENTIATE

STRIVING READERS

Create a Concept Cluster Write *Grand Canyon* in the center oval of a Concept Cluster and *aesthetic value (beauty)*, *geologic value (science)*, and *commercial value (money)* in each of the other three ovals. Instruct students to reread the American Places feature and then write specific examples of different ways of valuing the Grand Canyon on the spokes. Encourage students to add their own ideas. Then have students share and discuss their Concept Clusters with a partner.

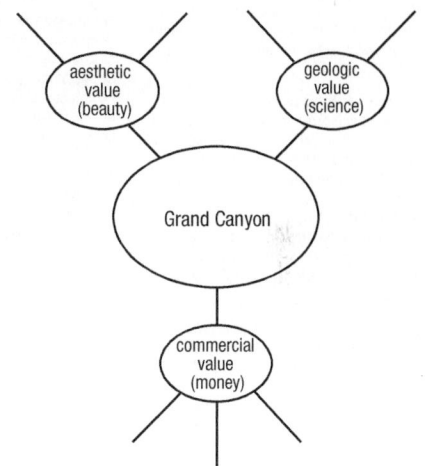

PRE-AP

Research Impacts of Tourism Have students conduct research on the economic and environmental impact of Grand Canyon tourism. Instruct students to gather information from a variety of unbiased sources. Then have students write an essay analyzing the impact of tourism on the Grand Canyon. Challenge students to conclude their essay with a recommendation to the National Park Service that would reduce the environmental impact of human activity and also be a source of revenue. Ask students to share their analyses and recommendations with the class.

See the Chapter Planner for more strategies for differentiation.

CRITICAL VIEWING The sheer massiveness of the Grand Canyon and the geologic record it provides, as well as its astounding beauty, are motivating factors for its preservation.

PROGRESSIVISM UNDER TAFT AND WILSON

The description "a tough act to follow" could certainly be applied to Theodore Roosevelt. His popularity helped the Republicans retain the presidency in 1908, but his successor looked weak in comparison.

A MIXED COURSE

Theodore Roosevelt had stepped into the presidency early in McKinley's second term, so by 1908, he felt he had already served two terms in office. Citing George Washington's decision to limit his presidency to two terms, Roosevelt declined to run again. Instead he supported his secretary of war, **William Howard Taft**, as the next Republican candidate. Taft handily won the presidency against William Jennings Bryan, a Democrat who had run and been defeated twice before.

Roosevelt chose Taft as his successor because he believed Taft would carry on his progressive agenda. He did not realize that Taft disagreed with his expansive view of presidential power. Taft believed that the president should act within the strict constitutional boundaries of his office. Although he aggressively enforced antitrust legislation, Taft lacked the will to urge progressive policies on the more conservative members of the Republican Party. Roosevelt's progressive agenda continued under Taft, but it faced setbacks.

Taft started off on the wrong foot after he failed to name any progressives to his cabinet. Then he offended progressives again when he sided against Gifford Pinchot, the Forestry Service chief and Roosevelt's good friend, in a dispute over the commercial use of public lands in Alaska. Pinchot had barred the lands from development, but Richard A. Ballinger, Taft's secretary of the interior, opened the lands to coal-mining companies. Pinchot accused Ballinger of acting as a member of a **syndicate**, or group of criminals, trying to sell valuable coal lands for profit. Taft investigated the charges and

publicly agreed with Ballinger. He fired Pinchot for insubordination, or defiance of authority. This incident led progressives to doubt Taft's commitment to conservation. Some even sent letters to Roosevelt, at the time on safari in Africa, saying as much.

As the president and the progressives argued, Americans struggled with major social issues. In 1910, some 200,000 youngsters below the age of 12 labored in mills and factories. Attempts to limit child labor in southern textile mills brought few results. In 1912, after a six-year struggle, progressive reformers succeeded in establishing the Children's Bureau. Its mission was to investigate and report on the conditions of children working in factories and living in orphanages. Unfortunately, Congress failed to pass any legislation that would have allowed reformers to take action against businesses that overworked child laborers. One such measure was a bill that would have prohibited interstate shipment of products made using child labor.

Another pressing social issue was immigration, which had nearly tripled from 1910 to 1914. Many of the immigrants were from southern and eastern Europe, and some Americans felt that their presence threatened traditional American values. The growing Americanization movement strongly encouraged immigrants to adopt American culture, including speaking and writing English instead of their native languages. While many immigrants quickly assimilated, others refused to give up their own languages and customs. By 1913, both houses of Congress had passed a bill to impose a literacy test on immigrants. President Taft, however, vetoed the bill as a largely anti-immigration measure.

LABOR AND THE WORKPLACE

The progressive movement had made huge strides during Roosevelt's presidency, but it fell short in brokering deals between labor unions and corporations. During Taft's presidency, unions made progress in organizing workers and improving working conditions for their members. That progress was partly driven by a public outcry over workplace tragedies.

On March 25, 1911, a fire broke out near closing time on the top floors of the Triangle Waist Company in New York City. The company employed about 500 people, mostly young immigrant women, to produce fashionable blouses. The workers ran to the stairway doors, but they were locked. Many trapped, terrified women chose to jump out of the 10-story building, hoping to survive the fall. Tragically, 146 people died in the **Triangle Waist Company factory fire**, and an outraged American public cried out for factory reform.

As the Triangle Waist Company factory went up in flames, a reporter, who happened to be walking nearby, called his pressroom and narrated events as they occurred. Here is part of his story.

Two windows away two girls were climbing onto the sill; they were fighting each other and crowding for air. Behind them I saw many screaming heads. They fell almost together, but I heard two distinct thuds.

Suddenly the flame broke out from the windows below them and curled up into their faces.

—from an account of the fire by William Shepherd, United Press reporter, 1911

The intense heat of the factory fire at the Triangle Waist Company weakened the metal of the fire escape ladder. Some workers were able to descend to a lower floor before the ladder collapsed.

PLAN: 4-PAGE LESSON

OBJECTIVE

Learn how William Howard Taft and Woodrow Wilson tried to promote progressive goals.

CRITICAL THINKING SKILLS FOR LESSON 2.3

- Interpret Maps
- Analyze Cause and Effect
- Make Inferences
- Compare and Contrast
- Evaluate
- Analyze Primary Sources
- Summarize
- Form and Support Opinions

HISTORICAL THINKING FOR CHAPTER 16

What reforms and expansion took place during the Progressive Era? Roosevelt, Taft, and Wilson compose the three "Progressive Presidents." Lesson 2.3 examines the philosophies and policies of Roosevelt's two progressive successors.

BACKGROUND FOR THE TEACHER

Remembered largely as an ineffective president, William Howard Taft achieved his life's ambitions *after* serving the country's highest office. The son of a distinguished judge, who became a judge himself at age 34, Taft always felt more at home in the court than in the political arena. In fact, he called his own political campaign "one of the most uncomfortable four months of my life." After losing to Woodrow Wilson in 1912, he became a law professor at Yale. Then, in 1921, President Harding appointed Taft as Chief Justice of the United States—the only former president ever to hold the position. After being appointed, Taft wrote: "I don't remember that I ever was President."

INTRODUCE & ENGAGE

PREDICT CHANGE

Inform students that after Theodore Roosevelt left office, he was followed by two more progressive presidents, William Howard Taft and Woodrow Wilson. Although progressives, each of these presidents differed from Roosevelt in both philosophy and action. Display a Main Idea and Details Chart. Ask students to recall Roosevelt's reforms and then brainstorm how his successors might change what he had accomplished in conservation, presidential power, and promoting antitrust legislation. Tell students that in this lesson, they will examine the progressive actions that Taft and Wilson advanced.

Roosevelt's Reforms	Possible Changes
Conservation	
Presidential Power	
Trusts	

TEACH

GUIDED DISCUSSION

1. **Compare and Contrast** How did Taft's activities and policies compare with Roosevelt's? (Possible response: Like Roosevelt, Taft believed in regulating business, but he lacked Roosevelt's forcefulness to advance progressive policies past conservative Republicans. Taft allowed land in Alaska to be used for coal mining.)

2. **Evaluate** Why were progressives unable to combat child labor even with the establishment of the Children's Bureau but able to succeed in improving working conditions for adults? (Possible response: Congress did not pass legislation aimed at businesses that exploited child laborers possibly due to catering to special interests. In the aftermath of the Triangle factory fire, the public and Congress may have been more concerned with adult workplaces and reform.)

ANALYZE PRIMARY SOURCES

Direct students' attention to the Primary Source feature and the photograph of the Triangle Waist Company fire escape. Remind students that when analyzing history, historians use multiple pieces of evidence to come to their conclusions. Tell students to read the account by William Shepherd, taking note of the specific details used in his eyewitness report. Then have students analyze the photograph of the incident and refer to Shepherd's account for similarities and differences. **ASK:** What parts of William Shepherd's account of the fire are verifiable using the photograph? What parts are not? (The photograph supports the idea that multiple floors were engulfed by fire, and the damage to the building confirms the ferociousness of the flames. However, the number of girls involved and the fact that they fell cannot be verified.)

For students who develop an interest in the Triangle Waist Company fire, suggest that they read the American Story at the beginning of this chapter.

DIFFERENTIATE

INCLUSION

Analyze a Photo and Primary Source Pair students who are visually impaired with students who are not. Ask the latter to describe the photograph of the Triangle Waist Company after the fire and to read the Primary Source feature aloud. Tell visually impaired students to ask clarifying questions as necessary. Then have the pairs work together to explain how the tragedy led to workplace reforms.

GIFTED & TALENTED

Investigate Union Art and Music Instruct students to gather information from a variety of sources to create an oral or written report about the IWW or about labor union poster art or music that emerged from the "bread and roses" strike. Encourage students to use primary and secondary sources and to quote or paraphrase as appropriate. Remind students to cite their sources. Invite volunteers to share their reports with the class.

See the Chapter Planner for more strategies for differentiation.

On March 4, 1913, Woodrow Wilson was inaugurated as the nation's 28th president. In this photograph taken at the White House just before the inauguration, Wilson appears on the left and his predecessor, President William H. Taft, is on the right.

The 1912 Election

Woodrow Wilson, Democrat
Electoral Vote: 435 votes, 81.9%
Popular Vote: 6,294,327 votes, 41.8%

Theodore Roosevelt, Progressive
Electoral Vote: 88 votes, 16.6%
Popular Vote: 4,120,207 votes, 27.4%

William H. Taft, Republican
Electoral Vote: 8 votes, 1.5%
Popular Vote: 3,486,343 votes, 23.2%

Eugene Debs, Socialist
Popular Vote: 900,370 votes, 6.0%

Another outcry arose after soldiers moved in to clear a tent city in Ludlow, Colorado. For about seven months, mine workers had been striking against the Colorado Fuel and Iron Company for higher pay and better treatment in company camps. The company owner, John D. Rockefeller, had the governor call in the National Guard to end the strike, which resulted in clashes between soldiers and miners. On April 20, 1914, troops shot into the workers' camps and set fire to tents. As many as 20 people, including women and children, were shot or died in the fire.

Labor unions such as the American Federation of Labor (AFL) and the International Workers of the World (IWW) had existed prior to the turn of the 20th century, but their membership swelled between 1900 and 1914. The IWW grew, in part, because it aimed to unite workers of every industry, including unskilled and African-American workers. The IWW played a major role in a strike against textile mills in Massachusetts. Workers walked out of the mills in January 1912 after company owners announced pay reductions. Strikers sang of "bread and roses,"

symbolizing both a living wage and hope for the future. With production at a standstill, company owners were eager to negotiate. By March 1, 1912, with the IWW's help, the workers won a raise in pay.

As labor unions made important gains for workers, company owners looked at ways to make their businesses more efficient. A mechanical engineer named **Frederick Winslow Taylor** developed **scientific management**, a method of running factories and other workplaces efficiently. Taylor studied individual tasks and determined the best way to complete them in the shortest amount of time. Taylor's findings resulted in sweeping changes in many industries. Factory managers expected workers to perform one specific activity for hours at a time, which made many workers feel like little more than machines. As workers in other countries attained benefits such as **social security**, a program in which the government provides money to the elderly, disabled, and unemployed, Americans continued their fight for improved working conditions and higher pay.

A PROGRESSIVE DEMOCRAT

As Taft neared the end of his first term in office, many Americans viewed him as a weak president. Political divisions in the country became apparent during the 1912 election. Theodore Roosevelt, apparently forgetting his pledge not to seek another presidential term, started his own party, the Progressive Party, to run against Republican Taft. The Democrats nominated Woodrow Wilson, then the governor of New Jersey.

Another candidate, Eugene Debs, ran as the Socialist candidate. With the Republican vote split, Woodrow Wilson won the election by a landslide. Taft won only 8 electoral votes to Wilson's 435.

President Wilson set to work immediately on his pet project: lowering tariffs, or taxes imposed on imported goods. This issue was important to progressives because tariffs added to the price of imported household items. Cutting tariffs would cut prices for consumers. Wilson fought hard to persuade Congress to pass the Revenue Act of 1913 to reduce tariffs. However, there was a glaring problem: how to make up for the income lost by reducing tariffs.

To remedy this shortfall, Congress added another provision to the bill: an **income tax**, or money paid to the government based on how much a person earns. Earlier in the year, the states had ratified, or approved, the **16th Amendment**, which granted Congress the power to collect income taxes nationwide. Wilson's success with the Revenue Act helped build his image as an effective leader.

The Wilson administration then turned its attention to banking and trustbusting, or breaking up monopolies. The country needed a central bank to control the money supply and make sure it was adequate to meet the demands of the growing economy. Wilson's

solution was to form the **Federal Reserve System**, a system of 12 banks located around the country and overseen by board members appointed by the president. The Federal Reserve System functioned as the nation's central bank.

Wilson also urged Congress to strengthen the nation's antitrust laws. As you have read, the Sherman Antitrust Act, passed in 1890, gave the government the right to break up monopolies and illegal trusts. However, it did not forbid businesses from engaging in some questionable practices, such as allowing one person to direct two or more "competing" companies. The **Clayton Antitrust Act**, passed in 1914, closed many of the loopholes, or ways around the law, not specifically prohibited by the Sherman Antitrust Act.

While Wilson made significant contributions to the progressive movement, he opposed African-American causes. In addition, like Taft, he did not support women's suffrage, at least initially. Of the three progressive presidents, only Roosevelt supported women's right to vote.

HISTORICAL THINKING

1. **READING CHECK** How did Taft and Wilson further the progressive agenda?

2. **INTERPRET MAPS** If Roosevelt and Taft had not split the Republican vote, is it likely that the Republican candidate would have won the election? Use electoral and popular vote data from the map to explain your answer.

3. **ANALYZE CAUSE AND EFFECT** How did the Revenue Act of 1913 affect American consumers?

4. **MAKE INFERENCES** Why did many Americans view Taft as a weak president?

The Progressive Era and Expansionism **571**

BUILD BACKGROUND

PROGRESSIVE INCOME TAX

While some progressive achievements, such as ending corruption, trustbusting, and improving working conditions, fit easily into progressives' overall goal of correcting social, economic, and political inequalities, the progressive roots of the income tax are less obvious. Prior to the 16th Amendment, the federal government collected money mainly through tariffs, duties, and excise taxes placed on goods. Because of their nature, these taxes impacted everybody equally—a tax on tobacco was the same for everyone, no matter their income. However, beginning during the Civil War, the idea of a progressive income tax—a percentage of one's earnings going directly to the government—began to surface.

When an income tax was passed in 1894, it was ruled unconstitutional because it applied to only the top 2 percent of earners—a small bloc of voters—rather than uniformly across the whole country. The concept of having the wealthy take a disproportionate role in funding the government continued to interest progressive reformers, and with the passage of the 16th Amendment in 1913, they achieved their goal of taxing higher earners more than lower earners.

TEACH

GUIDED DISCUSSION

3. **Summarize** How did the efficiencies promoted by scientific management impact workers and labor unions? *(Scientific management practices quantified the optimal productivity of a worker in a specific amount of time. This pressured workers into keeping up repetitive tasks for long hours, a condition that labor unions wanted to improve in addition to getting workers higher pay.)*

4. **Form and Support Opinions** Instruct students to review the philosophy of the Progressive Era—the belief that the government has a role in promoting social, economic, and political justice. **ASK:** Which president—Roosevelt, Taft, or Wilson—best achieved the goals of progressivism? *(Answers will vary. Students should relate the goals of progressivism to the actions of the chosen president.)*

INTERPRET MAPS

Tell students to examine the map of the election of 1912 and the tally of electoral votes. Explain that because of the unique nature of this election, Wilson won in an electoral landslide by winning traditionally Republican areas. Guide students to use the map to help them understand the meaning, implication, and impact of the 1912 election and to recognize that events could have taken another direction. Prompt students with questions such as: Why did a popular president such as Roosevelt lose his bid for another term? What reasons would voters have had for retaining Taft? What impact did Eugene Debs's candidacy have? What does the difference between the electoral vote and the popular vote tell you about the results of the election?

ACTIVE OPTIONS

On Your Feet: Inside-Outside Circle Use the Inside-Outside Circle strategy to check students' understanding of reforms and policies under the Taft and Wilson administrations. Have students in the outer circle pose questions (for example, What was the purpose of the immigration literacy test?), and have students in the inner circle answer them. Then tell students to trade inside/outside roles and rotate to create new partnerships.

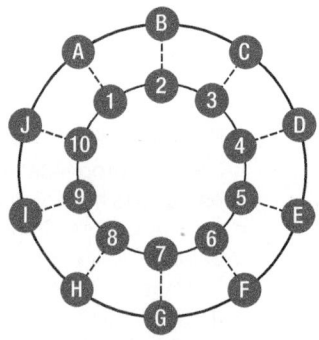

NG Learning Framework: Trace a Philosophy Across Time

ATTITUDE Curiosity

KNOWLEDGE Our Human Story

Explain that the term *progressive* is prevalent in present-day U.S. politics, and many politicians, particularly those from the Democratic Party, use the term to describe themselves. Break students into small groups and ask them to research the policies, philosophies, and important issues of modern progressives. Then have groups choose one modern politician who is known as a progressive and prepare a short presentation outlining his or her philosophy, policies, and issues. Encourage a discussion about the links between modern and historical progressivism.

HISTORICAL THINKING

ANSWERS

1. Taft promoted progressive issues such as antitrust reform, vetoed the anti-immigration literacy bill, and saw labor unions making strides in advancing the rights of workers. He fell short on conservation efforts, having opened land in Alaska to coal-mining companies. Wilson's administration saw actions against big business, such as the Clayton Antitrust Act and the Revenue Act. Under Wilson, Congress passed a bill authorizing the collection of a federal income tax. Wilson created the Federal Reserve System to centralize the nation's funds.

2. Answers will vary. Students could note that Wilson won only 41.8 percent of the popular vote, meaning nearly 60 percent of the country voted for his opponents. However, if Roosevelt had not run, all his supporters would not necessarily have voted for Taft.

3. The Revenue Act lowered prices on imported goods.

4. Answers will vary. Responses could include Taft's failure to lead the progressives by not including progressives in his Cabinet, not continuing Roosevelt's commitment to conservation, not getting legislation through Congress to protect children against labor abuses, and—when anti-immigration sentiments in the nation were high—not allowing the bill to pass that would have required literacy tests for immigrants.

Kennecott Mines National Historic Landmark, shown here, preserves the main buildings and land of Kennecott, Alaska, a historic mining town. In 1900, copper was discovered near this site. Its mining and processing gave rise to a multinational company, the Kennecott Copper Corporation. The Kennecott mines closed in 1938, and the site fell into disrepair.

AMERICAN EXPANSIONISM

For more than a hundred years, the United States grew in size until it stretched from coast to coast. Then, in the late 1800s, the nation sought to gain a foothold in distant lands.

THE ROOTS OF IMPERIALISM

As Americans struggled with social issues at home, the United States began to take an interest in expanding its influence overseas. For most of its short history, the nation had kept a low profile in world affairs. While European powers pursued **imperialism**, a policy of exerting economic, political, or military control over weaker nations, Americans had followed the course of **isolationism**, avoiding entanglements in foreign countries. By the 1880s, however, the United States had begun to look beyond its borders.

Trade played a big role in this new outlook. American business was booming, and one of the results was a surplus of American-made goods. Business leaders wanted to increase opportunities to sell these goods overseas. Their desire to do so led many of them to endorse **expansionism**, a policy similar to imperialism. Expansionism focuses on increasing a country's territory. Such a policy would open up new markets for American products and provide access to more raw materials.

American leaders had watched closely as European powers carved up territories in Africa and Asia, adding colonies and **protectorates**, or countries that are partly controlled by a stronger country. Americans worried about being left behind. One expansionist leader, Captain **Alfred T. Mahan** of the U.S. Navy, proposed an international network of naval bases, a powerful battleship fleet, and an aggressive foreign policy that would make the United States a competitive world power.

More than a hint of racism ran through the aims of the imperialists and expansionists. They believed in the superiority of white, English-speaking people and thought the rest of the world should bend to their will.

EYES ON ALASKA AND HAWAII

Americans had already taken the first steps toward expansion years earlier. In 1867, the United States paid $7.2 million to purchase Russia's territory in Alaska. Most Americans believed the land was useless, but the discovery of gold there in the 1880s and 1890s lured prospectors to the territory, and the population began to grow. At the same time, the Alaskan salmon fishing industry began to thrive. When Alaskans discovered copper in 1898, Americans started to recognize the great deal they had made with the Russians.

The Hawaiian Islands, an **archipelago**, or island chain, in the midst of the Pacific Ocean, attracted American interest even earlier than Alaska did. American missionaries began preaching in the islands in the early 1800s, and by the 1850s,

Americans were establishing businesses there, primarily growing and exporting sugarcane and pineapples. As early as the 1870s, the United States had recognized the strategic value of a naval base in Hawaii for protecting the Pacific Coast in wartime.

As more Americans came to the islands, their growing influence on the local economy and government soon sparked conflict with the Hawaiian monarchy. When **Queen Liliuokalani** came to power in 1891, she dismissed the legislature, which she felt was too sympathetic to Americans, and she presented a constitution that stripped white settlers of the powers they had secured for themselves. Most native Hawaiians agreed with the new constitution. But by this time, there were enough Americans and pro-American Hawaiians—including 150 U.S. Marines—living on the islands to stage a revolt against the queen. They overthrew the queen, established their own government, and requested that the United States annex, or take possession of, the islands.

President Benjamin Harrison agreed to sign a treaty with the pro-American, and mostly white, rebels to annex the islands, effective on February 14, 1893. But in the meantime, he lost the 1892 election to Grover Cleveland, who did not approve of the rebels' actions. Cleveland put the treaty on hold.

The fate of the islands remained unsettled until 1898, when the United States annexed Hawaii. By then, the islands were viewed as an essential naval asset in the Spanish-American War. In the "Organic Act" of 1900, Congress established a government for Hawaii, and the islands became an official U.S. territory. Meanwhile, the United States had set its sights on securing trading deals in Asia.

PRIMARY SOURCE

After losing her throne in 1893, Queen Liliuokalani of Hawaii continued to demand that the United States give her country back to her. Here she presents her case to the U.S. government.

Therefore, supplementing my protest of June 17, 1897, I call upon the President and the National Legislature and the People of the United States to do justice in this matter and to restore to me this property, the enjoyment of which is being withheld from me by your government under what must be a misapprehension [misunderstanding] of my right and title.

—from Queen Liliuokalani's letter of protest addressed to the House of Representatives, 1898

HISTORICAL THINKING

1. **READING CHECK** What were some reasons that the United States began an expansionist course in foreign policy in the late 1800s?

2. **EVALUATE** How did the acquisitions of Alaska and Hawaii benefit the United States?

3. **COMPARE AND CONTRAST** How are imperialism and expansionism alike and different?

PLAN 2: PAGE LESSON

OBJECTIVE

Understand the motivations and early impacts of United States expansionism.

CRITICAL THINKING SKILLS FOR LESSON 3.1

• Evaluate

• Compare and Contrast

• Analyze Primary Sources

HISTORICAL THINKING FOR CHAPTER 16

What reforms and expansion took place during the Progressive Era? In the mid to late 19th century, the United States began to expand its influence around the globe. Lesson 3.1 analyzes the motivations for this expansion and its impact on Hawaii and Alaska.

BACKGROUND FOR THE TEACHER

Prior to Europeans exploring Hawaii, the islands had a long history of self-governance and a strong internal culture. Originally, a series of individual chiefs or kings governed the islands—each overseeing a specific area. In 1778, when Captain James Cook arrived, Western culture began to exert its influences. As white planters filtered in, the islands were united under a single monarch and later ruled by a constitutional government chosen by a few selected voters. The system used to hold land was changed, and certain aspects of traditional culture were prohibited. Today, many native Hawaiians are trying to bring back and preserve their unique heritage by once again teaching the native language, learning traditional ways of sea travel, and celebrating previously banned practices, such as the hula dance.

INTRODUCE & ENGAGE

UTILIZE PRIOR KNOWLEDGE

Have students recall early American ideas about foreign policy. Remind them that George Washington favored avoiding entanglements with foreign countries. Then tell students that beginning in the mid to late 1800s, the United States began to deviate from this idea. **ASK:** What do you think might have led the United States to become more involved in world affairs? *(Answers will vary. Students could discuss economic issues such as trade or competition with other countries for resources.)* Inform students that in Lesson 3.1 they will learn why the United States began an era of expansion.

TEACH

GUIDED DISCUSSION

1. **Compare and Contrast** How was this period of U.S. expansion like and different from earlier periods of expansion in U.S. history? *(Earlier periods were confined to the North American continent. During this period, expansion extended overseas. The subjugation of native peoples by white people of European descent occurred in both periods.)*

2. **Evaluate** What was controversial about the acquisition of Hawaii? *(Unlike Alaska, which was peacefully purchased from Russia, Hawaii was a monarchy and not for sale. Thus, the United States used a different means to acquire it—the overthrow of the queen and annexation of the islands.)*

ANALYZE PRIMARY SOURCES

Direct students' attention to the Primary Source feature. **ASK:** What is Queen Liliuokalani's main argument? *(She argues that by her title Hawaii is rightfully hers and should be restored to her.)* **ASK:** What effect does using the word *misapprehension* have on the meaning of the queen's demand? *(Answers will vary. Possible response: The queen underscores the injustice done to her by suggesting that only through a misunderstanding would the U.S. government overthrow the rightful monarch of a sovereign country.)* Ask students to volunteer an oral response to the queen, stated from the perspective of an expansionist.

ACTIVE OPTIONS

On Your Feet: Debate Isolationism Divide the class into small groups. Provide each group with a large sheet of paper and inform students they are going to debate the following position: The United States should end its policy of isolationism. On the paper, have the groups make a two-column chart and list arguments for and against ending isolationism. Group members should brainstorm arguments and write them in the appropriate column. When all arguments are exhausted, groups should prepare and present their debate, making sure to follow established rules.

NG Learning Framework: Explore the Impact of Expansionism

SKILL Collaboration

KNOWLEDGE Our Human Story

Direct students to the Library of Congress website. Guide small groups in using the site, including searching for key terms and time periods. Present students with the following question: How did American expansionism impact the society, economy, and politics of Hawaii? Have each group locate multiple primary sources from the Library of Congress that help answer the question. Ask groups to write short explanations of their findings and share them with the class.

DIFFERENTIATE

ENGLISH LANGUAGE LEARNERS

Look for Cognates Suggest that as students read, they look for words that are similar in spelling and meaning to words in their home language. For example, the words *imperialism*, *isolationism*, and *expansionism* have cognates in Spanish: *imperialismo*, *aisacionismo*, *expansionismo*. For each word they identify, have students of **All Proficiencies** make a vocabulary card with the English word and definition on one side and the cognate on the other side.

PRE-AP

Form and Support a Thesis Challenge students to research the economic, political, military, and racist roots of American imperialism. Then instruct them to develop a thesis regarding what they consider the predominant factor. Have them write an essay supporting their thesis with a variety of primary and secondary source material, plus their own analysis. Encourage students to share their essays on a class or school blog.

See the Chapter Planner for more strategies for differentiation.

HISTORICAL THINKING

ANSWERS

1. The United States desired overseas markets for trading of excess goods. Colonization of Africa and Asia had proved profitable for European countries, and the United States wanted similar opportunities.

2. Alaska provided valuable natural resources, such as gold, copper, and salmon. Hawaii provided land with valuable resources and strategic value in the Spanish-American War.

3. Imperialism and expansionism both involve a country spreading its influence beyond its borders. With imperialism, a powerful country dominates a weaker one to exploit its resources. Expansionism involves acquiring territory and trade partners, but not necessarily dominating another nation.

EXTENDING INFLUENCE IN ASIA

Near the end of the 19th century, Japan and several of the most powerful European nations had secured exclusive trading deals in China. The United States wanted to trade in China as well. How did the Americans open the door to trade in China? They simply made a proposal.

OPENING THE DOOR TO CHINA

The United States successfully established a diplomatic and trading presence in Asia after Naval Commodore Matthew C. Perry negotiated the Treaty of Kanagawa with Japan in 1854. For centuries, Japan had a policy of isolation and limited trade with other countries. In 1853, Perry was sent to negotiate diplomatic relations and trade between Japan and the United States. As a result of the treaty the two countries signed, Japan opened its ports to American ships for the first time in more than 200 years. As the 19th century came to a close, the United States had begun to turn its attention to Japan's neighbor: China.

At that time, Great Britain had the strongest presence of any foreign power in China. But other countries, such as France, Germany, Italy, Russia, and Japan, had also carved out **spheres of influence**, or claims of exclusive economic and trading authority, in parts of the country. Within each sphere of influence, the controlling nation made deals with local banks and businesses that allowed it exclusive economic benefits within the community. The United States wanted a part of this economic action.

In 1900, U.S. Secretary of State **John Hay** proposed the **Open Door Policy** to all of the countries with spheres of influence in China. Hay suggested that all Chinese ports accept ships from every nation, not just those with which China had brokered deals. The plan honored the trading arrangements China had already made, but it extended those same provisions to other nations as well, giving the United States a foothold in China. The policy also calmed Chinese fears that the competition between the foreign powers would change the spheres of influence into colonies and tear China apart. While the nations affected by this policy may not have agreed with the American proposal, they did not openly oppose it either.

Meanwhile, many Chinese were fed up with foreign interference in their country. Their discontent was about to erupt into open rebellion.

THE BOXER REBELLION

A secret society in China called the Righteous and Harmonious Fists had long opposed the presence of so many Westerners and Japanese in the country. Members of the society particularly resented the influence of Christian missionaries, who questioned the teachings of traditional religions. Bands of rebels started wandering the countryside outside Beijing, attacking foreigners, mostly Christian missionaries. The rebels were dubbed "the Boxers" because they exercised by sparring in a boxing ring. The Boxers also attacked Chinese leaders whom they believed were responsible for the preferential treatment that foreigners received. The attacks were called the **Boxer Rebellion**.

In 1898, forces within the Chinese government also began calling for an end to foreign meddling. The Boxers then changed the group's name to the Righteous and Harmonious Militia, and the government enlisted the militia and encouraged its violent actions.

The Boxers began burning Christian churches and buildings that housed foreign businesses. By the spring of 1900, the Boxers were staging attacks in the capital city of Beijing. An international relief force arrived in the city in June to stop the violence. China's empress dowager Cixi—the emperor's adoptive

CIXI, EMPRESS DOWAGER OF CHINA

Yehenara, a middle-class Chinese girl, started her political career by giving birth to a son in 1856. A mistress of the Chinese emperor, she became known as Cixi, meaning "kind and virtuous." Her son was the emperor's only male heir. When the emperor died, the six-year-old boy took the throne. Cixi became one of the regents, or officials who govern in place of a child monarch.

Cixi gave up the regency when her son became 17 years old. But he died two years later, and her three-year-old nephew, whom Cixi had adopted, ascended to the throne. Cixi again became a regent.

She ruled China until 1889, when she retired to a palace she had built near Beijing. However, Chinese officials returned her to power in 1898 after the country suffered a major defeat in a war with Russia and Japan. She fled Beijing during the Boxer Rebellion but returned in 1902 and continued to rule until her death in 1908.

A bright and ambitious woman, Cixi ruled China for almost half a century. She ranks as one of the most powerful women in Chinese history.

mother and the person who actually ruled China—sent troops to fight the relief force and declared war on the United States, the United Kingdom, France, Germany, Italy, Russia, Japan, and Austria-Hungary.

Another international force of 20,000 soldiers captured Beijing in August 1900. The empress dowager and her court escaped the city, and she had little to do with the negotiations that followed. In September 1901, China signed the treaty that officially ended the Boxer Rebellion. The treaty forced China to pay **reparations**, or forced compensation, to the foreign powers for damages and lost lives. Payment of these reparations had a disastrous effect on the Chinese economy, fueling a resentment that resurfaced later in the 20th century.

HISTORICAL THINKING

1. **READING CHECK** How did the United States gain a foothold in China in the late 1800s?

2. **ANALYZE CAUSE AND EFFECT** What were the causes of the Boxer Rebellion?

3. **DRAW CONCLUSIONS** Why do you think John Hay proposed the Open Door Policy instead of negotiating directly with China?

4. **COMPARE AND CONTRAST** How did the political system in China differ from that in the United States in the 1800s? Support your answer with evidence from the text.

OBJECTIVE

Understand the impact of Western expansion into East Asia.

CRITICAL THINKING SKILLS FOR LESSON 3.2

- Analyze Cause and Effect
- Draw Conclusions
- Compare and Contrast
- Evaluate
- Make Inferences

HISTORICAL THINKING FOR CHAPTER 16

What reforms and expansion took place during the Progressive Era? The large market of goods for trade in China was a tempting prize for many Western nations. Lesson 3.2 discusses their attempts to exert influence in East Asia.

BACKGROUND FOR THE TEACHER

The Open Door Policy was not the first instance of American relations with China. Dating back to the colonial days, Chinese goods such as silks, pots, and dishes could be found across the continent. After American independence, commercial ties between the two countries continued, and some Americans built great fortunes in this endeavor. Throughout this period, China was the dominant nation in East Asia and was largely able to control its interactions with the West. However, this changed with the Opium War, a conflict with Britain that left China extremely weakened and exposed its technological disadvantages. This weakness led Japan, France, Britain, and Russia to carve up the declining empire—a development that worried the United States and led to the proposal of the Open Door Policy.

INTRODUCE & ENGAGE

PREVIEW VOCABULARY

Write *Open Door Policy* on the board. Tell students that this was the policy the United States attempted to apply to China during the period of American expansionism. **ASK:** According to what this phrase implies, how do you think the United States would want China to act toward other countries? Write and display students' suggestions and revisit them at the end of the lesson. Tell students that in this lesson they will examine the causes and effects of the Open Door Policy in China.

TEACH

GUIDED DISCUSSION

1. **Draw Conclusions** To what extent should the Open Door Policy be considered imperialistic? *(Possible response: The Open Door Policy had some commonalities with imperialism in that it allowed powerful nations to have influence over a foreign country without ruling it, as is done with imperialism.)*

2. **Evaluate** Did the Boxer Rebellion achieve its intended goals? Why or why not? *(Possible response: No. The goal of the Boxer Rebellion was to rid China of foreign influences, but the rebellion resulted in foreign countries sending troops to China and a disastrous treaty that crippled the country's economy.)*

MAKE INFERENCES

Have students read the feature on Cixi, the empress dowager of China. Tell students that the term *dowager* refers to a widow who inherits property or title from her husband. Review with students the details of the empress dowager's life, particularly the method by which she ruled. **ASK:** What does the empress dowager's life tell us about the status of women in this era of Chinese history? *(Possible response: The fact that the empress ruled China—without being a direct descendant of the late emperor—for nearly 50 years implies that women could, under certain circumstances, achieve high status and power. It's important to note that for most of her rule she was a regent, ruling on behalf of young male heirs. This tells us that men generally wielded more power than women.)*

ACTIVE OPTIONS

On Your Feet: Build a Paragraph Arrange students in four groups in different corners of the room. Provide each group with the same topic sentence: The Boxer Rebellion had many effects on China. Each group should build a paragraph about the topic, with each student contributing one sentence. Then have groups record and share their paragraphs with the class.

NG Learning Framework: Analyze American Attitudes Toward China

ATTITUDE Responsibility

KNOWLEDGE Our Human Story

Tell students to gather and record information that answers the following prompt: What attitudes did many Americans have toward China during the era of the Open Door Policy? How did these attitudes impact U.S. objectives and actions in Asia? Instruct student groups to conduct an online search to locate primary and secondary sources, including books, speeches, and political cartoons. Ask a volunteer from each group to share the group's findings with the class.

DIFFERENTIATE

STRIVING READERS

Write a Tweet As students read the lesson, direct them to pause after each paragraph and write a tweet summarizing the paragraph's main idea in their own words. Remind students to keep their tweets within the 140-character limit. Direct students to read their tweets aloud to the group, alternating paragraphs throughout the lesson.

GIFTED & TALENTED

Write and Deliver a Monologue Instruct students to briefly research the life of Cixi, the empress dowager of China, and then write a dramatic monologue focusing on Cixi's role in a particular event described in the lesson, such as the Boxer Rebellion. Alternately, students might write a monologue "from the grave" with Cixi relating high and low points of her life. Ask volunteers to perform their monologues for the entire class.

See the Chapter Planner for more strategies for differentiation.

HISTORICAL THINKING

ANSWERS

1. The United States gained a foothold through the Open Door Policy, which proposed that China open its ports to all nations, not just those nations with which it had trade deals.

2. The Boxer Rebellion started because the Boxers were opposed to the increasing presence and influence that foreigners had in China.

3. Possible response: John Hay may have wanted to negotiate with the powerful nations who were already dealing with China because he respected their political and military strength more than he respected the Chinese government.

4. Unlike the United States, a democracy with elected officials who represent the will of voters, China was a monarchy, whose rule is inherited. Cixi ruled as regent for her son, the child monarch, who inherited the crown from his father, the late emperor.

THE SPANISH-AMERICAN WAR

At the same time the United States was seeking to expand its territory, Spain was losing hold on its empire. In the late 1800s, the paths of the two nations collided.

SPANISH HOLDINGS

By the late 1800s, Spain had lost most of its once vast colonial empire stretching around the world. It still retained a few colonies, including Cuba and Puerto Rico in the Caribbean and the Philippines in the Pacific. Yet people in these lands had begun to demand their independence from Spanish rule.

In Cuba, a revolt against Spanish rule broke out in February 1895. The Cuban rebels waged a strong campaign, and Spain responded with brutal tactics. When the Spanish could not defeat the rebels in direct combat, they herded the civilian population into fortified camps so the people could not aid the rebels. In these disease-ridden and overcrowded camps, more than 100,000 Cubans died, many of them from starvation.

For a number of reasons, Americans took a keen interest in events in Cuba. One reason was the island's proximity—it lies only about 90 miles south of the tip of Florida. Another factor was economic interest. American companies had millions of dollars invested in sugarcane plantations on the island. In 1894, the United States accounted for 85 percent of Cuba's exports, while Spain was responsible for only 6 percent. Thus, Cuba was an economically valuable neighbor of the United States. In addition, Americans identified with the Cubans' desire for independence. Spain's brutal measures to end the Cuban rebellion, which American newspapers graphically portrayed, aroused the sympathy of the American public.

REMEMBER THE *MAINE*

By the time William McKinley was inaugurated as president in 1897, many Americans were calling for the United States to intervene in Cuba and aid the rebels. At first, McKinley attempted to negotiate a peace settlement between the Cuban rebels and the Spanish. The president succeeded in getting Spain to offer the Cubans limited self-government.

Then a dramatic event changed the course of American involvement. The United States had sent a battleship, the U.S.S. *Maine*, to Havana, Cuba, to protect American citizens and property there. On February 15, 1898, the ship exploded in the Havana harbor, killing more than 250 men, or about two-thirds of the crew. Modern research suggests that naturally occurring chemical reactions in one of the ship's coal bunkers caused the explosion. At the time, however, a naval board of inquiry, along with the American public, blamed Spain.

Though they lacked any evidence, American newspapers claimed that Spain had blown up the battleship. The *New York Journal and Advertiser*, owned by newspaper publisher William Randolph Hearst, printed such unfounded headlines as "Destruction of the War Ship *Maine* Was the Work of an Enemy!" and "Spanish Treachery!" This type of sensationalized newswriting, using exaggeration, melodrama, and outright lies to attract readers, became known as **yellow journalism**.

While a Navy investigation never pinned blame on Spain, many Americans readily believed that the Spanish had caused the explosion. Proponents of U.S. military intervention in Cuba used the slogan "Remember the *Maine!*" to rally public support. As public opinion in the United States increasingly favored war, Spain tried to avert it by conceding to many U.S. demands. But then the U.S. Congress authorized the president to use force to gain the withdrawal of Spain's armed forces from Cuba.

Spain responded by declaring war on the United States on April 24, and the United States in turn declared war on Spain the next day, on April 25.

WAR IN THE PACIFIC

Although events in Cuba led the United States into war, the first battle of the Spanish-American War actually took place in the Philippines. The U.S. Navy believed their superior forces could easily disable the Spanish fleet in the Philippines, where Spain was also battling rebels. Because they wanted freedom from Spain, the Filipino rebels joined forces with the Americans.

On May 1, 1898, a U.S. naval squadron under the command of Commodore **George Dewey** attacked the Spanish navy at Manila Bay. Within hours, the Spanish fleet was destroyed in an uneven fight.

CRITICAL VIEWING This print, published in 1898 by the printmakers Kurz and Allison, shows the explosion of the U.S.S. *Maine*. The men featured at the top of the print are American naval officers Admiral Montgomery Sicard (left) and Captain Charles Sigsbee (right). What kind of reaction might this print have aroused in Americans at the time it was published?

In an article entitled "Naval Officers Think the *Maine* Was Destroyed by a Spanish Mine," the *New York Journal and Advertiser* led Americans to believe that the U.S.S. *Maine* was deliberately blown up.

Assistant Secretary of the Navy Theodore Roosevelt says he is convinced that the destruction of the Maine in Havana Harbor was not an accident. The Journal offers a reward of $50,000 for exclusive evidence that will convict the person, persons or government criminally responsible for the [destruction] of the American battleship and the death of 258 of its crew. The suspicion that the Maine was deliberately blown up grows stronger every hour. Not a single fact to the contrary has been produced.

—from the *New York Journal and Advertiser*, February 17, 1898

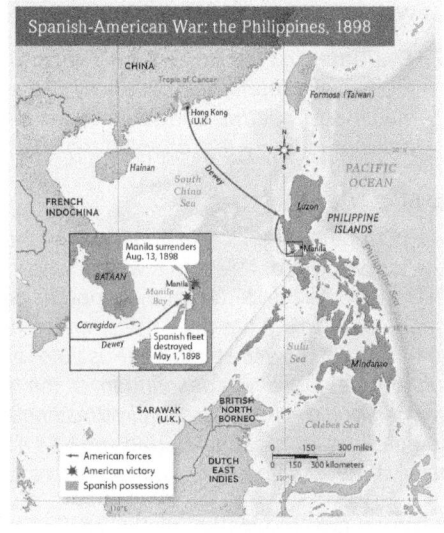

Spanish-American War: the Philippines, 1898

CHINA
Tropic of Cancer
Formosa (Taiwan)
Hong Kong (U.K.)
Hainan
South China Sea
FRENCH INDOCHINA
Luzon
PACIFIC OCEAN
PHILIPPINE ISLANDS
Manila surrenders Aug. 13, 1898
BATAAN
Manila
Manila Bay
Corregidor
Dewey
Spanish fleet destroyed May 1, 1898
Sulu Sea
Mindanao
SARAWAK (U.K.)
BRITISH NORTH BORNEO
Celebes Sea
DUTCH EAST INDIES

→ American forces
✶ American victory
■ Spanish possessions
0 150 300 miles
0 150 300 kilometers

PLAN: 4-PAGE LESSON

OBJECTIVE
Analyze the causes and consequences of American involvement in Cuba and the Pacific in the late 1800s.

CRITICAL THINKING SKILLS FOR LESSON 3.3
- Interpret Maps
- Analyze Cause and Effect
- Make Connections
- Form and Support Opinions
- Draw Conclusions
- Analyze Primary Sources
- Integrate Visuals

HISTORICAL THINKING FOR CHAPTER 16
What reforms and expansion took place during the Progressive Era? Cuba, close to the southern border of the United States, offered an obvious place to expand U.S. interests. Lesson 3.3 examines the results of the expansion that led to the Spanish-American War.

BACKGROUND FOR THE TEACHER
American interest in Cuba dated to before the Spanish-American War and was closely tied to slavery. During the territorial expansion of the early 19th century, many pro-slavery southerners viewed Cuba, the Caribbean, and South America as potential new territory into which slavery could expand. These views were supported by wealthy Cuban slave owners who feared Spain would abolish the institution. The situation came to a head in 1854, when the U.S. minister to Spain wrote a document known as the Ostend Manifesto, arguing that the United States should purchase Cuba. The manifesto was highly controversial and resulted in Cuba taking measures to free slaves and organize an antislavery militia. In addition, it angered the Spanish government and antislavery groups in the United States, forcing the United States to abandon its attempts to acquire the island.

INTRODUCE & ENGAGE

CONSIDER MOTIVATIONS FOR WAR

Have students recall wars or conflicts currently taking place around the world. Questions to prompt class discussion include: Why did the conflict start? What motivated different parties to become involved in the conflict? Was any deceit or misinformation used to gain support for the conflict? Call on volunteers to share their responses with the class. Ask students to consider as they read how present-day motivations of people and countries are similar to and different from motivations during the Spanish-American War. When the lesson is completed, complete a Venn Diagram such as the one shown.

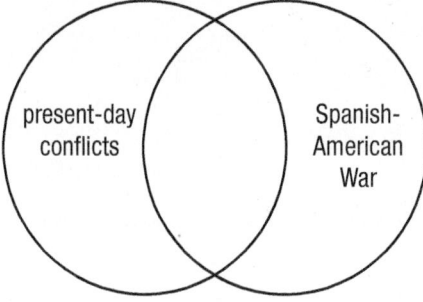

present-day conflicts   Spanish-American War

TEACH

GUIDED DISCUSSION

1. **Form and Support Opinions** Explain that present-day scientists have determined that Spain did not in fact cause the explosion that destroyed the U.S.S. *Maine*. **ASK:** If this information had been available in 1898, would the United States still have declared war? Collect and evaluate information about the explosion and then explain your answer. *(Answers will vary. Possible response: Yes. Pressure from business groups and those outraged by the brutal methods of the Spanish against Cuban citizens would have eventually pushed the country to war.)*

2. **Draw Conclusions** What does the fact that the first battle of the Spanish-American War took place in the Philippines—and not Cuba—tell us about the motivations of the United States for declaring the war? *(Answers will vary. Possible response: The war was not simply to liberate Cuba. The United States had a broader goal of acquiring territory from the weakened Spanish empire.)*

ANALYZE PRIMARY SOURCES

Have students review the definition of yellow journalism and then read the Primary Source feature. **ASK:** Why is this piece of writing considered yellow journalism? *(The writing sensationalizes the incident by playing up the melodramatic parts, such as the number dead and the possible involvement of Spain, rather than reporting hard facts.)* **ASK:** What biases are present in the writing? *(The article asserts that the explosion of the* Maine *was deliberate, stating there is no evidence that proves it was accidental. However, the article offers no evidence to prove the involvement of Spain.)*

DIFFERENTIATE

STRIVING READERS

Identify Facts Arrange students in pairs and ask them to generate a list of facts from the lesson for three to five minutes. Then guide students to conduct a round-robin activity to review what they learned. Invite one student from each pair to share their list. Write all the facts on the board.

GIFTED & TALENTED

Present a Skit Invite students to research analyses of the explosion aboard the U.S.S. *Maine* and use what they learn to write a short skit about the explosion and its aftermath. Encourage students to write two different endings, one that reflects historical events by assigning blame to Spain and one that imagines a different outcome. Encourage students to present their skits to the class and to perform both endings. Then guide the class in a discussion of what direction events might have taken had Spain been cleared of involvement in the explosion.

See the Chapter Planner for more strategies for differentiation.

CRITICAL VIEWING The print highlights the intensity of the blast that destroyed the ship with graphic depictions of smoke, fire, a bright flash, and bodies of U.S. crew members flung into the air. Americans at the time probably felt outrage about the explosion and animosity toward Spain.

Theodore Roosevelt appears near the center in this 1898 photograph of the Rough Riders, a volunteer cavalry unit. The photograph was taken at the top of Kettle Hill, which the Rough Riders captured as part of the Battle of San Juan Hill. The battle became legendary, due largely to Roosevelt's fame. Although the Rough Riders trained as cavalry, they never fought on horseback because their horses did not arrive in Cuba in time.

Dewey had brought six steel ships to the battle, while the Spanish fleet consisted of seven unarmored wooden ships. The Spanish lost more than 350 men in the battle, while no Americans lost their lives. After the battle, Dewey reported to his superior officer: "There were . . . only seven men in the squadron very slightly wounded."

Dewey's victory was widely celebrated in the United States, even though it was incomplete. Though his squadron had control of Manila Bay, Dewey lacked enough troops to take Manila itself. He estimated that he would need 5,000 additional troops to seize the city. He soon received twice that number, and by August, U.S. troops occupied Manila. However, the United States still had to battle the Spanish in Cuba.

WAR IN THE CARIBBEAN

While Dewey's victory demonstrated the superiority of U.S. naval forces, the U.S. Army consisted of only about 25,000 troops, too small a force for the scale of fighting that was anticipated. The United States had to turn to volunteers to fight the war. With enthusiasm for the war running high, about 1 million men volunteered, which was far more than the army could handle. About 280,000 men actually saw active duty in the war.

The war in the Caribbean began in late June 1898 with U.S. troops landing at Guantanamo Bay in Cuba and additional forces converging on the harbor city of Santiago. The most famous land battle in Cuba, the Battle of San Juan Hill, was fought near Santiago on July 1. A volunteer cavalry regiment called the Rough Riders and two African-American regiments, the Ninth and Tenth Cavalries, charged up Kettle Hill while other units attacked San Juan Hill. The Rough Riders were commanded by Leonard Wood and Theodore Roosevelt, who had resigned as assistant secretary of the Navy to lead the regiment. American newspapers portrayed Roosevelt as a hero in the battle, which contributed to his success in his future campaign for president.

At the time the war broke out, the U.S. Army included four regiments of African-American soldiers who had been headquartered in the West and on the northern plains. When they were ordered to Cuba and traveled through the southern United States, they encountered segregation and racial threats. Despite such unfair treatment, they fought fiercely in Cuba and earned numerous citations for bravery, including five Congressional Medals of Honor.

The war in the Caribbean came to an end after the U.S. Navy destroyed the Spanish fleet as it attempted to escape from the harbor at Santiago. The Spanish surrendered on July 16. American troops then invaded and took control of Puerto Rico on July 25, meeting with no opposition. On August 12, Spain and the United States signed a cease-fire agreement. From the first battle in the Pacific to the cease-fire agreement, the entire war had lasted just 16 weeks.

Representatives of the two countries met in Paris on December 10, 1898, to agree on a peace treaty. In the **Treaty of Paris**, Spain granted independence to Cuba, gave Puerto Rico and Guam to the United States, and allowed the United States to buy the Philippines for $20 million. The United States later convinced the new Cuban government to lease land for the Guantanamo Bay Naval Base. As the United States gained new territory, Spain's 400-year run as a colonial power in the Americas ended.

Spanish-American War: the Caribbean, 1898

UNITED STATES

Spanish fleet destroyed July 3, 1898

Tampa
FLORIDA
Gulf of Mexico

July 1: San El Caney
Kettle Hill
July 1: San Juan
Santiago

San Juan Hill
July 1, 1898

Caribbean Sea

USS *Maine* exploded Feb. 1898

Havana
Cuba
Santiago

Bahamas

ATLANTIC OCEAN

HAITI
DOMINICAN REPUBLIC

San Juan
Puerto Rico

Jamaica

Caribbean Sea

0   200   400 miles
0   200   400 kilometers

→ American forces
→ Spanish forces
✴ American victory
----- U.S. Naval blockade
▓ Spanish possessions

HISTORICAL THINKING

1. **READING CHECK** Why did the United States fight in the Spanish-American War, and what did the country gain from it?

2. **INTERPRET MAPS** Which American fleet had to travel farther, the one sailing from Hong Kong to Manila in the Philippines or the one departing from Tampa, Florida, to fight in Cuba? Use the scale of miles on the maps to determine your answer.

3. **ANALYZE CAUSE AND EFFECT** How did yellow journalism help drive the United States into war with Spain?

4. **MAKE CONNECTIONS** Describe a recent example of yellow journalism, and compare its effect with the effect of the reporting about the *Maine* explosion.

BUILD BACKGROUND

WAR AND DISEASE

The fighting during the Spanish-American War was relatively brief, lasting only a few months, but the experiences of many soldiers were harrowing. In total, close to 2,500 American soldiers died during the conflict, with the majority dying from disease. The primary culprit was typhoid fever, which swept through military camps in the United States before soldiers even left the mainland. Those who made it to Cuba were subject to tropical ailments such as malaria and yellow fever, as well as diarrhea, dysentery, and stomach disorders from eating chemically adulterated, poorly preserved beef. These deaths resulted in a major response. Dr. Walter Reed headed the Typhoid Board, which inspected the conditions of the military camps. In doing so, breakthroughs were made in the understanding of typhoid transmission, once considered a waterborne disease but now correctly understood as transmitted through contact. Ultimately, officials determined that the existing medical practices were woefully inadequate. Camps were not sanitized, too few nurses were employed and valued, and there were not enough medical officers. These findings led to a reorganization of the Army Medical Department.

TEACH

GUIDED DISCUSSION

3. **Integrate Visuals** How does the photograph of Theodore Roosevelt atop Kettle Hill compare with the text's version of the events? *(Like the text, the photograph portrays Roosevelt as the hero of the battle by placing him in the center. However, African-American soldiers, who played an important role in the event, are absent from the photograph.)*

4. **Draw Conclusions** What do the United States' actions in Cuba and the Philippines reveal about the nation's attitudes toward those two countries and their people? *(Answers will vary. Possible response: In both instances it is difficult to discern if the United States was engaged in the conflict to add territory or bring freedom to people. However, the text states that Americans celebrated Dewey's victory, so the belief existed that the citizens of the two countries needed to be delivered from the rule of Spain.)*

INTERPRET MAPS

Tell students to examine the two maps. **ASK:** Based on the maps, what strategic advantages over Spain did the United States have in the Philippines and the Caribbean? *(In both conflicts the United States had a geographic advantage, namely a place to resupply and anchor ships. In the Philippines, this was accomplished in Hong Kong. In Cuba, the close proximity of Florida gave U.S. forces an edge.)*

ACTIVE OPTIONS

On Your Feet: Spanish-American War Roundtable Arrange students in groups of four. Have students hold a roundtable discussion on the causes and effects of the Spanish-American War. Tell each student to offer a cause or effect based on information from the text. Ask a volunteer from each group to record students' statements. Afterward, have groups share their collected statements with the class. Allow time to hold a class discussion on the primary and secondary causes and effects of the war.

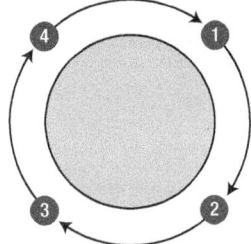

NG Learning Framework: Draw Conclusions About Military Conflicts

ATTITUDE Curiosity

KNOWLEDGE Our Human Story

With the alleged deliberate sinking of the U.S.S. *Maine*, the Spanish-American War became one of several conflicts in U.S. history that began under controversial circumstances. Break the class into small groups. Assign each group a different U.S. conflict or near conflict, such as the XYZ Affair with France or the controversial decision made by the United States and other allies in 2003 to invade Iraq based on information that Saddam Hussein had undisclosed weapons of mass destruction (WMDs). Based on preliminary research, invite students to create a hypothesis about the conflict. Then have groups prepare and give a short presentation in which they analyze what was factually known at the time, what the government or other parties asserted, and what was later found to be true. After all groups have finished, discuss the main themes and conclusions from the presentations as well as the lessons learned.

HISTORICAL THINKING

ANSWERS

1. The United States entered the war because of the sinking of the U.S.S. *Maine* and to aid Cuban rebels. After the war, Cuba gained independence, and the United States received Puerto Rico and Guam and the ability to purchase the Philippines.

2. According to the map scale and the routes indicated, the fleet that traveled farther sailed from Hong Kong to the Philippines, approximately 750 miles. The fleet that sailed from Tampa to Cuba traveled approximately 600 miles.

3. Through sensationalized, unsubstantiated stories claiming that Spain was responsible for the explosion of the U.S.S. *Maine*, yellow journalism swayed public opinion toward war.

4. Answers will vary. Students should describe a recent news article that made an unsubstantiated claim and provided no credible evidence to support it. Students should point to exaggerated statements and inflammatory language used to attract readers' attention and sway their opinions.

The Philippine-American War

After just 16 weeks of fighting, the United States defeated Spain in what the American secretary of state dubbed "a splendid little war." The United States gained Puerto Rico, Guam, and the Philippines, but not all of the countries involved felt "splendid" about it.

AN OPPORTUNITY TO EXPAND

Once Spain signed the Treaty of Paris in 1898, its empire dwindled to almost nothing. The United States, on the other hand, had become an imperialist nation at the stroke of a pen, claiming control over three island territories in two oceans. Americans were divided about McKinley's diplomatic success in acquiring those lands, however. The Americans who favored manifest destiny believed acquiring foreign territories was the next logical step for the nation. Many others, however, disapproved of such expansion, recalling how American colonists felt about British rule many years before.

As the Treaty of Paris was being negotiated, President McKinley headed to the Midwest in October 1898 to convince his fellow citizens that annexing the Philippines was in the nation's best interests. The president gave many speeches stating his case for a more expansive foreign policy. A territory in the South Pacific would bolster trade with China, he argued, and the Philippines could supply certain goods that Americans needed, such as sugar. McKinley explained that the Germans and the Japanese had positioned ships around the Philippines, waiting for a chance to occupy the archipelago. He reasoned that it was better for the Filipinos to be taken under the wing of the United States than to be governed by any other nation. In Iowa, McKinley told his audience, "We do not want to shirk a single responsibility that has been put upon us by the results of the war."

Many Filipinos, however, did not agree with McKinley's reasoning. **Emilio Aguinaldo**, one of the leaders of the rebellion against Spain before and during the Spanish-American War, believed the United States had promised the Filipinos their independence. Now he felt that Filipinos had battled one colonial power only to be handed over to another. Aguinaldo and his men readied themselves to fight yet again.

A BRUTAL WAR

Only two days after ratifying the treaty ending the Spanish-American War, the United States became embroiled in the Philippine-American War. Aguinaldo and his troops took control of the largest island in the Philippines and proclaimed it a republic, prompting a swift U.S. reaction. President McKinley sent a fleet of ships to put down the rebellion.

During 1899, the U.S. Army defeated the Filipinos in conventional battles. However, when faced with the highly organized and fully supplied American army, Aguinaldo and his men switched strategies. They started a guerrilla war, a war fought by unconventional means, such as sabotage, ambushes, and unexpected raids. Aguinaldo's troops were a grassroots group—untrained and assembled from local residents—but they had some advantages. They knew the geography of their island, and they looked like the civilian population. They could hit selected targets and then escape by blending in with the crowd. Individual soldiers slipped into the American troops' camps at night and sabotaged or stole equipment. Faced with this new threat, the American military responded by killing and torturing Filipino prisoners to gain information about the rebels' plans. American troops also looted and burned down villages, moving the inhabitants into camps that they then failed to supply with food.

The American press reported the soldiers' brutality, and enthusiasm waned in the United States for pursuing further expansion. People who opposed imperialism began to organize. The **American Anti-Imperialist League** became a voice against McKinley's foreign policy decisions. By 1900, many Americans believed the existing empire should be retained and protected—but not increased.

Even some of the soldiers fighting in the Philippines struggled with their purpose in the war. One soldier wrote, "I am not afraid, and am always ready to do my duty, but I would like someone to tell me what we are fighting for." A Minnesota general lamented, "It seems to me that we are doing something that is contrary to our principles in the past."

American troops captured Aguinaldo in 1901, effectively ending the rebellion. Some minor uprisings occurred through the next summer, but without Aguinaldo, who took an oath of allegiance to the United States, the rebel forces slowly disbanded. On July 4, 1902, President Theodore Roosevelt forgave the Filipino nationalists and proclaimed the end of the war. The fighting had claimed the lives of 4,200 American soldiers and more than 20,000 Filipino rebels. In addition, some 200,000 Filipino civilians perished in the warfare or from starvation and disease. The Philippines would not become an independent nation until more than four decades later, in 1946.

HISTORICAL THINKING

1. **READING CHECK** What were the reasons for the Philippine-American War, and what were the results?

2. **ANALYZE CAUSE AND EFFECT** How did the Philippine-American War affect some Americans' views on expansionist foreign policy?

3. **ANALYZE LANGUAGE USE** The word *guerrilla* means "little war" in Spanish. How does this meaning help you understand the difference between conventional and guerrilla warfare?

4. **MAKE CONNECTIONS** How did the Spanish-American War lead to the Philippine-American War?

A GLOBAL PERSPECTIVE In the Umbrella Revolution of 2014, tens of thousands of people took to the streets of Hong Kong to protest attempts by mainland China to control the island's elections. After police tried to break up the protests, the people used colorful umbrellas to protect themselves from pepper spray, as shown in this photo. Although Hong Kong became part of mainland China in 1997, the people were promised their autonomy for 50 years. How does the reaction of the people of Hong Kong compare to the reaction of many Filipinos when the United States claimed control of the Philippines?

580 CHAPTER 16

The Progressive Era and Expansionism **581**

PLAN: 2-PAGE LESSON

OBJECTIVE

Describe the outcome of the United States' possession of the Philippines.

CRITICAL THINKING SKILLS FOR LESSON 3.4

- Analyze Cause and Effect
- Analyze Language Use
- Make Connections
- Categorize
- Evaluate

HISTORICAL THINKING FOR CHAPTER 16

What reforms and expansion took place during the Progressive Era? Following the Spanish-American War, the United States took possession of the Philippines. Lesson 3.4 discusses this decision, its outcome, and the reaction at home.

BACKGROUND FOR THE TEACHER

Formed in 1898, the American Anti-Imperialist League was opposed to the United States' attempted acquisition of the Philippines. Among its members were many of the nation's most famous and influential citizens, including industrialist Andrew Carnegie, author Mark Twain, and labor leader Samuel Gompers. The league argued against annexation of the Philippines primarily on moral grounds, claiming the forcible governing of a people was antithetical to the ideas of the country and constitution. However, there was also a deep conservatism within the group. Many members feared that extension into Asia and inclusion of Asian people within U.S. society would endanger traditional American values.

PREVIEW ARGUMENTS

Inform students that following the Spanish-American War, an intense debate broke out across the nation concerning the status of the Philippines. Some supported annexing the island, while others strongly opposed it. Display a T-Chart labeled Arguments For and Arguments Against. Have students brainstorm possible arguments for and against the addition of a new territory. When finished, inform students that Lesson 3.4 concerns the consequences of the U.S. acquisition of the Philippines.

TEACH

GUIDED DISCUSSION

1. **Categorize** What were the economic, strategic, and moral arguments used by President McKinley to support the annexation of the Philippines? *(McKinley argued that economically, annexation would boost trade and supply needed goods; strategically, it would prevent a foe from gaining the island; and morally, he believed it was better for the United States to govern the Filipino people than another power.)*

2. **Evaluate** Remind students of the United States' complaints that Spain denied independence to Cuba and used brutal tactics against the Cuban people.
ASK: Considering the U.S. expansion into the South Pacific and its treatment of the Filipino people, is it fair to call the United States hypocritical? Why do you think so? *(Answers will vary. Possible response: Yes. The United States committed actions in the Philippines for which it criticized Spain. The United States did not grant the country independence, and American soldiers tortured prisoners and burned and looted villages.)*

A GLOBAL PERSPECTIVE

Explore the photograph of the Umbrella Revolution and its caption with students.
ASK: What were the people of Hong Kong protesting? *(mainland China's interference in their elections)* **ASK:** Why do you think people in protest movements often use colors, such as the Orange Revolution in Ukraine, or objects, like umbrellas, to identify themselves? *(These identifiers offer a way to show support or solidarity with others who believe in the same cause.)* Conduct a discussion of protests taking place in the United States and around the world. Ask students to think about and discuss why some protests are peaceful and some are violent.

ACTIVE OPTIONS

Active History: Analyze Achievements of Emilio Aguinaldo Extend the lesson by using either the PDF or Whiteboard version of the activity. These activities take a deeper look at a topic from, or related to, the lesson. Explore the activities as a class, turn them into group assignments, or even assign them individually.

NG Learning Framework: Take a Position

ATTITUDE Responsibility

KNOWLEDGE Our Human Story

Provide small groups of students with primary sources—such as the platform of the Anti-Imperialist League or a speech by President McKinley—that support and oppose involvement in the Philippines. Ask students to read the sources and summarize the types of arguments presented, such as economic, moral, or strategic. Then have students choose a present-day international controversy to study. Instruct students to write their own support or opposition to it in the style of one of the primary sources provided.

STRIVING READERS

Make a List Post this heading: Five Things I Know About the Philippine-American War. After students read the lesson, ask them to copy the posted heading and add five sentences under it. Invite volunteers to share their sentences with the group.

PRE-AP

Write a Synthesis Essay Direct students' attention to the Primary Source feature and the quotation in the text from the Minnesota general. Challenge students to write a synthesis essay, using these sources to substantiate a claim regarding an underlying similarity or difference. Tell students to develop an idea about the quotations and then express a claim in a clear thesis statement. Invite them to read their essays to the class. Allow a Q&A session if time permits.

See the Chapter Planner for more strategies for differentiation.

ANSWERS

1. The United States had bought the Philippines from Spain, but the Filipino people had other ideas. When Emilio Aguinaldo and his troops declared the Philippines a republic, President McKinley sent a fleet in response. The war ended with the rebellion quashed and many lives lost, including 200,000 civilians.

2. The brutality of the war led many Americans to believe that the nation should maintain its current territories but not pursue further expansion. Americans opposed to imperialism began to organize.

3. Possible response: Conventional warfare involves moving supplies and large numbers of armed and uniformed troops who act under a hierarchical command. The Filipino rebels used "little war" tactics, such as local, small-scale sabotage and secret raids, and effectively blended in with civilians.

4. The Philippine-American War was an effect of Spain ceding the Philippines, Guam, and Puerto Rico to the United States. The Filipino rebels fighting against Spanish imperialism banded together again to fight against the new imperialists.

A GLOBAL PERSPECTIVE Like the Filipinos, the people of Hong Kong were upset about being ruled by a foreign government. The events in Hong Kong appear to have been a peaceful protest, while Filipino rebels engaged in war.

INVOLVEMENT IN LATIN AMERICA

Have you ever felt overshadowed by a stronger opponent in an athletic contest? In the early 1900s, the United States cast such a shadow over Latin America.

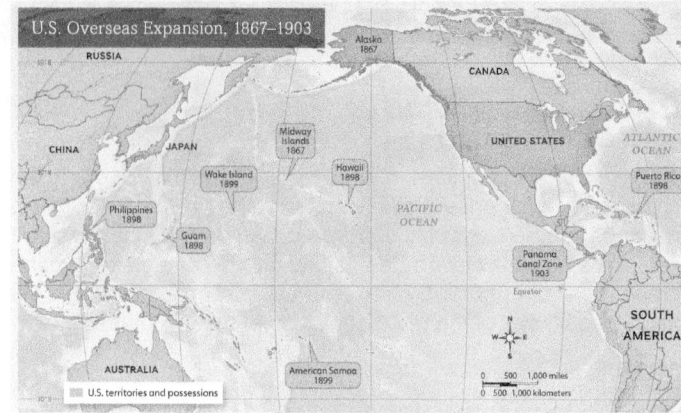

U.S. Overseas Expansion, 1867–1903

U.S. territories and possessions

ACQUIRING PUERTO RICO

As you have read, the United States gained control of Puerto Rico at the end of the Spanish-American War in 1898. Before the war, many Puerto Ricans had long sought independence from Spanish rule. **Luis Muñoz Rivera,** a leader of the Puerto Rican independence movement, had worked with the Spanish government to negotiate for the island's independence. By 1897, Puerto Rico had won the right to self-governance, though it remained a Spanish colony. When the United States acquired Puerto Rico, Muñoz Rivera continued to advocate for independence. But the U.S. government had its own ideas.

After gaining control of Puerto Rico, the United States initially appointed military officers to govern the island. But on April 12, 1900, Congress ratified the Foraker Act, which established the island's first House of Representatives and Supreme Court. The act reserved for the U.S. president the authority to appoint a governor and an executive council, but it gave some political power to Puerto Ricans as well.

Control of high government positions in Puerto Rico was important to U.S. interests for a number of reasons. The tropical island could supply goods, such as sugar, to the United States, and it served as a new market for American goods, such as coal, a natural resource Puerto Rico lacked. The United States could enjoy exclusive rights to trade. In addition, Puerto Rico would become the site of an important U.S. naval base.

BIG STICK DIPLOMACY

In 1901, Theodore Roosevelt became president. By then, in addition to the territories discussed, the United States possessed the previously uninhabited Wake Island as well as part of the island chain of Samoa, which became American Samoa. Earlier, in 1867, the United States had annexed Midway Islands. Roosevelt began making plans to extend American influence worldwide, especially in Latin America. He relied on recommendations made by Alfred T. Mahan years before: build a strong navy, adopt an aggressive foreign policy, and connect the Atlantic and Pacific oceans by digging a canal through Central America.

In terms of foreign policy, Roosevelt said the United States should "speak softly and carry a big stick," meaning the nation should negotiate peacefully while

This cartoon from 1904 shows President Roosevelt pulling the Great White Fleet, a fleet of battleships that he ordered to sail around the world to demonstrate American naval strength.

flexing its military strength. Roosevelt employed his **Big Stick Diplomacy** early in his presidency during an incident involving Venezuela. In 1902, German and British ships destroyed the Venezuelan economy by blockading its ports in order to collect debts owed to them. The event forced the president to act. Roosevelt "spoke softly" by negotiating a deal to end the crisis, and he "carried a big stick" by writing a declaration that, when necessary, the United States would intervene in the affairs of Latin American nations. The declaration, called the **Roosevelt Corollary,** amended the Monroe Doctrine, a much earlier U.S. declaration that opposed European interference in the Americas.

The Roosevelt Corollary came into play later as Roosevelt set out to build a canal in Central America. The canal would dramatically cut shipping times between the East and West coasts of the United States. Ships at the time had to sail around all of South America to complete this journey. In 1902, Congress pursued a treaty to lease a tract of land for the canal on an **isthmus**, or strip of land between two bodies of water, in Colombia. When the Colombian government refused, Roosevelt gently encouraged the people who lived on the isthmus to start an insurrection, or rebellion, against the Colombian government. The presence of American ships around the isthmus discouraged the Colombians from putting down the insurrection, which in turn allowed the newly formed nation of Panama to quickly claim its independence.

The Panamanians agreed to lease a 10-mile tract of land to the United States, giving it control over the area. On March 3, 1904, construction began on the **Panama Canal** and continued long after Roosevelt's presidency. The canal opened in 1914. With the Panama Canal Zone, the United States added another foreign territory to its collection. Technically, the acquisitions had all taken place by treaty and not by force, but that did not stop people around the world from calling the United States an empire.

Roosevelt passed the responsibilities of his administration to President Taft in 1909. Taft generally followed Roosevelt's diplomatic techniques, although when opportunities to invest in China arose, he replaced Roosevelt's "big stick" with money. For instance, when the Chinese asked for help to buy Japanese-owned railroads in their country in 1909, Taft and other world leaders loaned the money to them. In return, Taft requested that the Chinese be more accommodating to American trade. American journalists dubbed this approach "Dollar Diplomacy."

HISTORICAL THINKING

1. **READING CHECK** How did President Roosevelt apply Big Stick Diplomacy in gaining land for the Panama Canal?

2. **INTERPRET MAPS** Which territories did the United States acquire in 1898?

3. **FORM AND SUPPORT OPINIONS** What do you think were the pros and cons of Big Stick Diplomacy?

The Progressive Era and Expansionism **583**

PLAN: 2-PAGE LESSON

OBJECTIVE

Examine the impact of U.S. foreign policy on Latin America at the turn of the 20th century.

CRITICAL THINKING SKILLS FOR LESSON 3.5

• Interpret Maps

• Form and Support Opinions

• Compare and Contrast

• Analyze Visuals

HISTORICAL THINKING FOR CHAPTER 16

What reforms and expansion took place during the Progressive Era? Following the Spanish-American War and continuing with the presidency of Theodore Roosevelt, the United States expanded its influence in Latin America. Lesson 3.5 examines the policy and consequences of this expansion.

BACKGROUND FOR THE TEACHER

Construction of the Panama Canal was extremely difficult and considered to be one of the greatest engineering feats in history. The 50-mile-long waterway would cut through the continental divide and across land prone to landslides, flooding, and disease, and flow through a series of locks. Railways were used to truck out dirt, preventing mudslides and the formation of pooled water, a breeding ground for mosquitoes, known carriers of malaria and yellow fever. To build the locks, American corporations, such as U.S. Steel and Portland Cement, provided steel and concrete. The project cost in excess of $350 million, the most expensive U.S. construction project at the time. The cost in human lives is estimated at 5,600 of the 70,000 total workers who labored on the canal.

INTRODUCE & ENGAGE

ANALYZE NONLITERAL LANGUAGE

Write the phrase *speak softly and carry a big stick* on the board. Tell students that this phrase refers to one of Theodore Roosevelt's foreign policies. Discuss the literal meaning of the phrase and possible nonliteral meanings. Ask students to speculate how this phrase might describe Roosevelt's actions toward other countries. Inform students that Lesson 3.5 will examine Roosevelt's foreign policies in action in Latin America.

TEACH

GUIDED DISCUSSION

1. **Compare and Contrast** How did the foreign policy ideas of William Howard Taft differ from those of Roosevelt? *(While Roosevelt believed in using force to achieve his ends, Taft used economic persuasion.)*

2. **Form and Support Opinions** Remind students of previous U.S. foreign policies, including George Washington's isolationism and the Monroe Doctrine. **ASK:** Was the Roosevelt Corollary a significant departure from previous U.S. foreign policy? *(Possible response: Roosevelt's policy was in opposition to Washington's isolationism, which preached nonintervention. Roosevelt's policy was are closer to the Monroe Doctrine, which declared the Western Hemisphere as America's domain. Roosevelt's belief that the United States had the right to preemptively intervene in the affairs of its neighbors was a new idea.)*

ANALYZE VISUALS

Instruct students to examine the political cartoon. **ASK:** What point is the artist making, and what bias, if any, can you identify? *(The artist shows a giant Roosevelt dominating the Caribbean with military might. The ship is labeled "Debt Collector," suggesting that Roosevelt thinks countries in the Caribbean owe him something. The artist portrays Roosevelt negatively as a bully, tromping in foreign waters and dragging the threat of the U.S. fleet behind him.)*

ACTIVE OPTIONS

On Your Feet: Rotating Discussion Divide students into four teams and assign each a corner of the room. Tell teams to prepare several questions about the role of the United States in the independence of Panama and the building of the Panama Canal. Start the discussion by having Team 1 ask a question of Team 2, who answers and then asks a question of Team 3, and so on. Continue until the teams have exhausted all their questions.

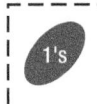 

NG Learning Framework: Hold a Mock Trial

ATTITUDE Responsibility

SKILL Collaboration

Arrange students in four groups and guide them in conducting a mock trial centered on the following question: Did the United States become an imperial power? Assign one group to build a "prosecution" to answer the question affirmatively. Assign another group to build a defense. A third group will be witnesses and play the parts of important people of the era, such as Theodore Roosevelt, William McKinley, and Emilio Aguinaldo. The fourth group will be the jury and weigh the arguments and arrive at a verdict. After the trial, encourage a discussion of the verdict and the effectiveness of the prosecution and defense.

DIFFERENTIATE

ENGLISH LANGUAGE LEARNERS ELD

Sound Out Words Before reading, preview the Key Vocabulary word *isthmus* with students of **All Proficiencies**. You may also want to preview other words from the lesson, such as *insurrection, negotiate, tropical, exclusive,* and *flexing*. Point out the unusual combination of consonants in the word *isthmus*. Model pronunciations and have students repeat. Suggest that students make word cards, noting definitions and pronunciation hints.

GIFTED & TALENTED

Create an Annotated Time Line Instruct students to research U.S. involvement in Colombia and Panama and create an annotated time line of key events leading to the construction of the Panama Canal. Remind students to include dates and brief descriptions of people, places, and actions associated with events. Students may use images and maps to add further information. Encourage students to compare their finished time lines and discuss items they chose to include or omit and why.

See the Chapter Planner for more strategies for differentiation.

HISTORICAL THINKING

ANSWERS

1. Roosevelt encouraged the rebellion of people on the isthmus and used naval power to prevent Colombia from stopping the insurrection. This allowed Panama to claim its independence and permit construction of the canal.

2. In 1898, the United States acquired the Philippines, Guam, Hawaii, and Puerto Rico.

3. Answers will vary. Possible response: Gaining land in the Americas was good for U.S. trade and military strategy, but this form of diplomacy turned the focus of the government outside of the U.S. mainland and changed the image of the nation around the world.

VOCABULARY

Use each of the following vocabulary words in a sentence that shows an understanding of the term's meaning.

1. **Progressive Era**
   As a result of Progressive Era initiatives, fewer children worked as laborers in factories.

2. enfranchisement

3. conservation

4. initiative

5. syndicate

6. isolationism

7. reparations

8. yellow journalism

9. trustbuster

10. protectorate

READING STRATEGY
ANALYZE LANGUAGE USE

Complete the Word Map to analyze the meaning of the quotation from Theodore Roosevelt that appears at the beginning of the chapter. Then answer the question.

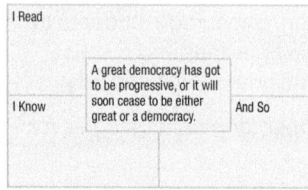

I Read

A great democracy has got to be progressive, or it will soon cease to be either great or a democracy.

I Know

And So

11. How did Roosevelt's progressivism impact the future of American democracy?

12. Where did women's suffrage fit within the progressive movement?

MAIN IDEAS

Answer the following questions. Support your answers with evidence from the chapter.

13. Why did the constitutional amendment guaranteeing women the right to vote become stalled? LESSON 1.2

14. Why were direct primaries considered a progressive idea? LESSON 1.4

15. Why is Theodore Roosevelt's presidency so strongly associated with the Progressive Era? LESSON 2.1

16. Why did progressives reject laissez-faire economics? LESSON 2.1

17. What problem did the Federal Reserve System solve? LESSON 2.3

18. What were some of the factors that changed Americans' minds about the purchase of Alaska from the Russians? LESSON 3.

19. Why did the United States seek to replace China's spheres of influence with the Open Door Policy? LESSON 3.2

20. What territories did the United States gain at the end of the Spanish-American War? LESSON 3.3

21. Why did some Americans oppose the United States' actions during the Philippine-American War? LESSON 3.4

22. How did President Roosevelt apply Big Stick Diplomacy in Latin America? LESSON 3.5

HISTORICAL THINKING

Answer the following questions. Support your answers with evidence from the chapter.

23. **MAKE GENERALIZATIONS** What methods did reformers use to achieve their goals during the Progressive Era?

24. **EVALUATE** In what way was President Roosevelt's Square Deal an innovative approach to labor disputes?

25. **MAKE INFERENCES** How did the United States' role in the world change after the Spanish-American War?

26. **SYNTHESIZE** What were the purpose and effects of the Open Door Policy?

27. **COMPARE AND CONTRAST** How did Roosevelt's Big Stick Diplomacy differ from Taft's Dollar Diplomacy?

28. **DRAW CONCLUSIONS** What was the impact of the Children's Bureau?

INTERPRET GRAPHS

Study the line graph below, which shows the results of censuses conducted on the Hawaiian Islands. Then answer the questions.

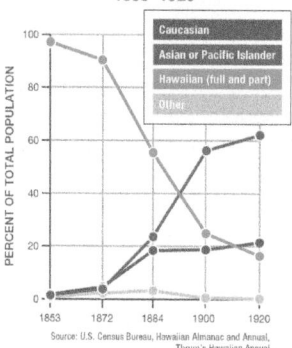

Hawaii's Changing Population, 1853–1920

Caucasian
Asian or Pacific Islander
Hawaiian (full and part)
Other

PERCENT OF TOTAL POPULATION

1853   1872   1884   1900   1920

Source: U.S. Census Bureau, Hawaiian Almanac and Annual, Thrum's Hawaiian Annual

29. Which population group declined the most and which increased the most during the time period covered on the graph?

30. What does the graph reveal about the non-native population of Hawaii during that time period?

ANALYZE SOURCES

In 1917, Carrie Chapman Catt delivered an address to Congress explaining why women's suffrage was inevitable and essential. Read the excerpt from the speech and answer the question that follows.

Behold our Uncle Sam floating the banner with one hand, "Taxation without representation is tyranny," and with the other seizing the billions of dollars paid in taxes by women to whom he refuses "representation." Behold him again, welcoming the boys of twenty-one . . . to "a voice in their own government" while he denies that fundamental right of democracy to thousands of women public school teachers from whom many of these men learn all they know of citizenship and patriotism.

31. What point is Catt making about the United States government?

CONNECT TO YOUR LIFE

32. **ARGUMENT** Once the West was settled in the late 1800s, the United States turned its sights to the world outside its borders. American involvement in world affairs has increased ever since. Write an essay arguing whether or not the United States should have so much global influence, citing examples from the chapter and your own research.

TIPS

• Review American actions in the Pacific and the Caribbean discussed in the chapter.

• Research two or three current U.S. foreign involvements.

• Develop your topic by comparing U.S. actions described in the chapter with the present-day situations you researched.

• Use two or three vocabulary words from the chapter in your argument.

• End your essay with a recommendation on the role you believe the United States should have in world affairs.

VOCABULARY ANSWERS

1. As a result of Progressive Era initiatives, fewer children worked as laborers in factories.

2. Women achieved enfranchisement in a few states before voting rights for women became a federal law.

3. Thanks to conservation, some of America's most beautiful natural places are protected and preserved.

4. To address abusive child labor, citizens put an initiative on the ballot to specify the minimum age of workers.

5. Police agencies develop strategies to break up syndicates in order to reduce organized crime.

6. The president's position on isolationism kept the United States out of the affairs of foreign nations.

7. As part of the peace agreement, the defeated state agreed to pay $3 billion in reparations to the victors.

8. Some publications rely on the sensationalized, exaggerated, and false statements common to yellow journalism in order to attract readers' attention.

9. Trustbusters fought to keep large corporations from having too much control over an industry, its workers, and the economy.

10. The powerful nation built naval bases on several of its island protectorates.

READING STRATEGY ANSWER

For a democracy to function it must be progressive.

A great democracy has got to be progressive, or it will soon cease to be either great or a democracy.

Roosevelt and other progressives believed the government should attempt to solve society's ills.

I know why Roosevelt advocated for progressivism.

11. Roosevelt's belief in a role for government in solving society's problems set a precedent for later administrations.

12. It was a reform sought during the Progressive Era.

MAIN IDEAS ANSWERS

13. Southern Democrats in Congress worried that giving women the right to vote would lead to African Americans voting. The liquor industry worried that if women got the right to vote, it would lead to the prohibition of alcohol.

14. Up until then, political bosses often controlled the nomination of candidates for political offices. Direct primary elections let voters decide who was nominated.

15. When Roosevelt became president, there was momentum in the United States for big changes. Roosevelt, who was young, energetic, and already a national hero, was an inspiring advocate of progressive causes.

16. Progressives believed that the hands-off approach had allowed corporations to treat their employees, consumers, and small businesses unfairly.

17. The Federal Reserve System organized the nation's money supply under one agency, thus making the government able to act quickly to address problems.

18. The discovery of gold and copper, plus a thriving salmon fishing industry, justified the purchase of Alaska.

19. The countries with spheres of influence did not include the United States, and those countries wanted exclusive control over a sector of the Chinese economy. The United States wanted to be able to trade directly with China without having to go through those other countries.

20. The United States gained Puerto Rico and Guam and the option to purchase the Philippines.

21. American troops responded to the Filipino guerrilla tactics by burning and looting villages, torturing and killing prisoners to get tactical information, and moving villagers into camps where they were starved. Americans were likely repulsed by news of these actions and lost their enthusiasm for expansionism.

22. Instead of attacking Colombia to take desirable land, Roosevelt used the threat of American military power to help Panama gain independence, thus allowing for the building of the Panama Canal.

HISTORICAL THINKING ANSWERS

23. Possible response: Progressives were trying to reform the country and ensure that all people, regardless of wealth or social status, would be treated fairly; women would be able to vote and be seen as equals to men; and workers wouldn't be exploited by their employers. Methods used to achieve these goals included the passage of laws and amendments, engaging in protests and marches, and the use of writing and journalism to expose problems.

24. Instead of using police action, as did Grover Cleveland, Roosevelt worked with both sides to negotiate a settlement. It was a superior approach because both sides would get some of what they wanted, and there would be no violence or death.

25. After the Spanish-American War, the United States became an expansionist—and arguably imperialist—power with newly acquired possessions Puerto Rico, Guam, the Philippines, and the annexed Hawaii.

26. The purpose was to open China to trade with the United States, but one of the effects was the Boxer Rebellion because China came to resent the influence of various foreign countries within its borders.

27. While Roosevelt relied on U.S. military prowess to intimidate other countries, Taft's foreign policy involved loaning money to foreign nations in return for trade accommodations.

28. Although the Children's Bureau was charged with issues such as improving the condition of children living in orphanages and working in factories, it did not succeed in pushing legislation through Congress to address child labor.

INTERPRET GRAPHS ANSWERS   STEM

29. The population of native Hawaiians declined the most. The population of other (mostly Asian) people increased the most.

30. The graph shows that the non-native population, composed of other Asians and Caucasians, grew as the Hawaiian population declined.

ANALYZE SOURCES ANSWER

31. Catt makes the point that the government itself is tyrannical and hypocritical in taxing women and denying them the vote while at the same time condemning taxation without representation. Catt also points out the irony in "boys of twenty-one" being taught "all they know of citizenship and patriotism" by women who were themselves denied the rights of citizenship.

CONNECT TO YOUR LIFE ANSWER

32. Answers will vary, but students should argue whether the United States should have so much global influence, cite examples from the chapter and their own research of present-day situations, use two or three vocabulary words, and conclude with a recommendation on the role of the United States in world affairs.

Nature for Everyone

by Gary Strauss

Adapted from "Biologist Wants Nature for Everyone—Including Prisoners"
by Gary Strauss, news.nationalgeographic.com, September 2016

National Geographic Explorer Nalini Nadkarni developed a reputation as "queen of the forest canopy," thanks to her extensive research among the towering branches of the forests of Costa Rica. On solid ground, she brings her knowledge of the natural world to unconventional settings. It's a long way from the Costa Rican rain forest to a U.S. prison, but Nadkarni navigates both environments with ease.

As a forest ecologist, Nadkarni spent her early career enmeshed in tree canopies. But after years of fieldwork and university life, she decided that her efforts needed a broader audience than scientists, academics, and natural history buffs. "I was preaching to the choir, so I began to ask myself how can I bring my message to others," says Nadkarni. "Rather than saying you need to read my articles or attend my lectures to understand my science, I took the approach of appealing to people in their own venues."

Nadkarni coordinated with rap artists to develop nature programs for at-risk youth, created a fieldwork outfit for a Barbie doll, and organized eco-fashion shows. She hoped that these entertaining yet educational initiatives would better connect people to trees and forests. Her work bringing science and nature programs to prisons could have that impact.

While teaching at Washington's Evergreen State College, she studied the movement of tree branches by attaching a paint brush to twigs. Measuring wind-aided changes and calculating them over 12 months, she found that a tree can sway back and forth up to 186,540 miles in a single year. "I began to think of other entities that are perceived to be static and stuck," she explains. "Prisoners are also stuck. But whether you're a CEO or an inmate stuck in solitary confinement, what we have in common is humanity and a connection to nature."

She put her observations into action by developing science and nature programs at Washington's Cedar Corrections Center. There, inmates working with biologists raised threatened Oregon spotted frogs. They also grew mosses in an effort to help replace what had been commercially harvested in old growth forests.

Those efforts evolved into the Sustainability in Prisons Project, funded in part by the National Science Foundation. The project spread to 10 Washington state prisons and facilities in Oregon, California, Ohio, and Maryland. The group's efforts include recycling programs, beekeeping, organic vegetable farms, tree planting, and flower nurseries. Inmates develop skills for future employment and gain a sense of purpose, responsibility, and teamwork. Nadkarni asserts that prisoners who participate are less likely to return to criminal activity after their release.

Now a biology professor and head of the University of Utah's Center for Science and Mathematics Education, Nadkarni has also brought nature to inmates housed in solitary confinement. She beamed images and videos of forests, oceans, mountains, and skies into their recreation rooms. While limited in scope, the impact has been dramatic. Some inmates housed for violent crimes or tendencies in the isolation unit at Oregon's Snake River Correctional Institution were shown nature videos. Those shown recordings of nature scenes committed 26 percent fewer violent infractions, according to a study presented in August 2016 to the American Psychological Association.

"We can't bring nature programs to maximum security," Nadkarni says. "But what we've found is that exposing violent offenders to images of nature for an hour a day brings down their stress and anxiety levels and reduces violent tendencies." She wants to bring her successes to other prisons as well to further demonstrate her simple but profound approach.

For more from National Geographic check out "21st Century Cowboys" online.

UNIT INQUIRY: Produce a Documentary

In this unit, you learned about the changes that occurred in the United States in the late 1800s and early 1900s. From the displacement of Native Americans on the western frontier to the influx of immigrants into the growing industrial cities of the Northeast and Midwest, these changes produced a wide range of social, political, and economic problems. Writers and photographers documented the problems to call public attention to them.

ASSIGNMENT

Assume the role of a reporter and produce a short documentary that examines an important problem in American life between 1877 and 1920. Topics include poverty, child labor, substandard housing, unsafe working conditions, and political corruption in city governments. Explain the causes and effects of the problem and outline attempted solutions. Be prepared to present your documentary to the class.

Plan Review the social, economic, and political problems covered in this unit and choose one to investigate. Reread the text's description of the problem and make a list of questions you have about its causes, effects, and solutions. Use library and online resources to research multiple points of view on the issue. Evaluate each source's explanation of the cause of the problem. Determine which explanation best agrees with the text evidence provided to include in your documentary. Take notes using a graphic organizer like this one.

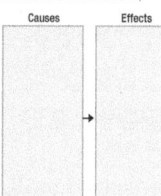

Produce Create an outline for your documentary. Then write a script in which you introduce the problem, identify its causes and effects, describe attempted solutions, and conclude by stating the outcome of the events. Revise the script as necessary. Consider your audience, and make sure to address the most significant points of the problem and solution. Choose photographs and other graphics from books and online sources to help convey your main points. Make a video of the narration and graphics.

Present Show your documentary to the class. You might consider one of these options:

- Post the documentary on a class website and invite your classmates and friends to view it. Invite viewers to share their feedback and questions with you. Respond to the feedback and questions you receive.

- Work with your teacher to schedule a class viewing of the documentary. After the viewing, ask classmates for their reactions and lead a class discussion of the issue.

LEARNING FRAMEWORK ACTIVITIES

Write a Position Statement

ATTITUDE Responsibility
SKILL Communication

In the late 1800s and early 1900s, disadvantaged groups of Americans struggled to gain rights and improve their situations. These groups included farmers, Native Americans, laborers, immigrants, African Americans, and women. Choose one of these groups and research the group's struggles. Write a position statement addressed to a government official or agency of the time in which you detail your concerns and demands. Present your position statement to the class and discuss possible reactions of the government official or agency, taking into account historical context.

Plan a Protest

ATTITUDE Empowerment
KNOWLEDGE Critical Species

The settlement of the West and the expansion of farming had a negative impact on the natural environment in the late 1800s and early 1900s. A prime example of this negative impact was the fate of the American bison, which were hunted to the point of near extinction. Working with a partner or small group, research the bison's decline and plan a protest to persuade the government to take action to protect current and future herds. Create a slogan and protest signs. Outline where you will stage the protest and how you will draw participants. Present your plan to the class and solicit their reactions.

NATIONAL GEOGRAPHIC CONNECTION

GUIDED DISCUSSION FOR "NATURE FOR EVERYONE"

1. **Identify Main Ideas and Details** What is the central idea that has driven Nalini Nadkarni's work throughout her career? *(Nadkarni has devoted her life to building a bridge between the natural world and human beings, even where there is little access, such as in prisons. She believes that access to nature induces calmness and peacefulness and reduces stress. Nadkarni brings people to nature using methods such as hands-on recycling programs, farming and tree planting, wildlife-care programs, and sometimes videos and still images of natural scenes.)*

2. **Make Connections** How does Nadkarni's work with professionals, such as rap artists and doll-clothing manufacturers, reflect her larger mission? *(Nadkarni works closely with effective communicators to develop nature programming geared to the particular needs of specific groups, such as at-risk youths or prison inmates.)*

GUIDED DISCUSSION FOR "21ST CENTURY COWBOYS"

1. **Describe** What overall personality traits does the author ascribe to typical, 21st-century American cowboys? *(They are typically comfortable with solitude, independent minded, and conscious of tradition. Since they are itinerant, they are somewhat vain about their appearance, taking special pride in their hats and saddles.)*

2. **Summarize** What role does technology play in the life of the contemporary cowboy? *(Cowboys use computer technology to tag and track cattle and record brands.)*

HISTORY NOTEBOOK

Encourage students to complete the Unit Wrap-Up page for Unit 5 in their History Notebooks.

UNIT INQUIRY PROJECT RUBRIC

ASSESS

Use the rubric to assess each student's participation and performance.

SCORE	ASSIGNMENT	PRODUCT	PRESENTATION
3 GREAT	• Student thoroughly understands the assignment. • Student participates fully in the project process.	• Documentary is well thought out. • Documentary offers a number of examples of causes, effects, and attempted solutions. • Documentary contains all of the key elements listed in the assignment.	• Presentation is clear, concise, and logical. • Presentation does a good job of creatively representing the problem in question. • Presentation engages the audience.
2 GOOD	• Student mostly understands the assignment. • Student participates fairly well in the project process.	• Documentary is fairly well thought out. • Documentary offers at least two examples of causes, effects, and attempted solutions. • Documentary contains most of the key elements listed in the assignment.	• Presentation is fairly clear, concise, and logical. • Presentation does an adequate job of representing the problem in question. • Presentation somewhat engages the audience.
1 NEEDS WORK	• Student does not understand the assignment. • Student minimally participates or does not participate in the project process.	• Documentary is not well thought out. • Documentary does not offer examples of causes, effects, and attempted solutions. • Documentary contains few or none of the key elements listed in the assignment.	• Presentation is not clear, concise, or logical. • Presentation does an inadequate job of representing the problem in question. • Presentation does not engage the audience.

NATIONAL GEOGRAPHIC LEARNING FRAMEWORK RUBRIC

ASSESS

Use the rubric to assess how each student applies the National Geographic Learning Framework.

SCORE	ASSIGNMENT	ASSIGNMENT	FINAL PRODUCTS
3 GREAT	• Position statement reflects **Responsibility** well. • Position statement demonstrates **Communication** well.	• Plan reflects **Empowerment** well. • Plan explores **Critical Species** well.	• Final products are engaging, creative, and well presented.
2 GOOD	• Position statement reflects **Responsibility**. • Position statement demonstrates **Communication**.	• Plan reflects **Empowerment**. • Plan explores **Critical Species**.	• Final products are interesting, logical, and complete.
1 NEEDS WORK	• Position statement does not reflect **Responsibility**. • Position statement does not demonstrate **Communication**.	• Plan does not reflect **Empowerment**. • Plan does not explore **Critical Species**.	• Final products are not creative, complete, or interesting.

LOWER EAST SIDE MARKET SCENE (DETAIL)

The neighborhood depicted in this painting was and still is a bustling area of New York City's Lower East Side. The artist is likely paying homage to Greenwich Village as well, which by the end of the 19th century was a natural choice for financially strapped artists who wanted to try their luck in New York City. For decades, Greenwich Village—centrally located with affordable rents—served as a vibrant international hub for creative artists and thinkers.

The zenith of Greenwich Village artistic activity occurred during the 1940s and 1950s, as new musical and visual art movements took hold. One such movement was abstract expressionism, a distinctly American form that veered sharply from European art traditions, spurning familiar landscapes, still lifes, and portraits in favor of purely emotional, or expressive, imagery. At some point, nearly every major abstract expressionist of the time lived and worked in Greenwich Village, including Mark Rothko, Jackson Pollock, and Franz Kline, the artist who created the work shown here.

Kline began his career as a figurative painter, fusing vibrant, colorful social scenes with the flat, two-dimensional qualities of cubism. He painted *Lower East Side Market Scene* between 1938 and 1940, just after his move to New York City after having studied in London. This work, currently part of Allentown Art Museum's permanent collection in Pennsylvania, depicts a contemporary and familiar view of an open-air neighborhood street market.

Direct students' attention to the painting. **ASK:** What emotion or mood does this painting evoke, and what might it tell you about New York's Lower East Side in the late 1930s and early 1940s? *(Answers will vary. Possible response: Although the people in the painting are busy with a variety of different tasks, the image projects a feeling of calm and patience, which establishes the sense of a close-knit community.)* **ASK:** Why might artists have wanted to move away from the classical traditions of Europe? *(Answers will vary. Possible response: Artists tend to be creative thinkers who are interested in staking out new creative territory and exploring new styles. Kline and his contemporaries may have felt that older traditions restricted their creativity.)*

UNIT

6

1914–1940

FROM THE GREAT WAR TO THE NEW DEAL

588

CRITICAL VIEWING Artist Franz Kline painted *Lower East Side Market Scene* (detail) around 1938, soon after moving to New York City. It shows an open-air market likely inspired by the artist's Greenwich Village neighborhood, with its older buildings and working-class residents. What does the painting reveal about American culture?

589

FRANZ KLINE

American painter Franz Kline was a leading force in the postwar abstract expressionism movement. He was born in Pennsylvania, and he trained at Boston University and the Heatherley Art School in London. After he completed his education in 1938, he moved to New York City, where he lived and worked until his death in 1962.

Kline's style and subject matter shifted radically over time. By 1949, he had begun to explore his own brand of abstract expressionism, which emphasized emotion and line over more familiar scenes and imagery. Using tools and materials more common to house painting than to fine art—large, crude brushes and inexpensive commercial paints—Kline worked almost exclusively in bold strokes of black and white throughout the 1950s.

CRITICAL VIEWING The scene seems vibrant and a bit ramshackle. The rich colors, tight spaces, and broad brushstrokes point to the bustle of a busy, culturally diverse neighborhood. Despite the work's soft focus, the details in the clothing and the activities indicate people from a broad mix of cultural backgrounds who live and work closely with one another. The people also exhibit a hands-on, no-nonsense approach to work and commerce. Open-air markets, such as the one featured here, have become a cultural mainstay and are common features of present-day urban areas.

1919 EUROPE:
TREATY OF VERSAILLES

On November 11, 1918, after four long years of fighting, the Central Powers surrendered to the Allies, ending World War I. The following year, the Allies met at the Paris Peace Conference and drafted the Treaty of Versailles, which officially assigned Germany sole blame for the war. The Allies did not consult Germany in advance about the terms of the treaty, and the Germans were deeply shocked and angered by the punitive nature of the agreement. Among other stipulations, the Treaty of Versailles demanded that Germany, still reeling from its human and capital losses from the war, be forced to pay out massive financial sums to the Allies. In addition, it forced Germany to give up territory to Great Britain, France, Poland, Japan, Belgium, and Denmark. Consequently, Germany lost 10 percent of its population, as people living in the reassigned areas were no longer subject to German jurisdiction.

Although the terms of the treaty were harsh, enforcement was ineffective. Germans resented having to shoulder all blame for the world conflict as well as all financial reparations, and this simmering resentment was partially responsible for Adolf Hitler's rise to power in the 1930s. **ASK:** Why might the Allies have believed it necessary to assign only one nation complete responsibility for the war? *(Possible responses: The world had only recently come through a long, bloody conflict that Germany started, so the Allies wanted to punish Germany and recoup their losses. Assigning Germany sole blame and therefore making it give up territory, population, and financial reparations was supposed to disempower Germany and be a warning against future acts of aggression by any nation.)*

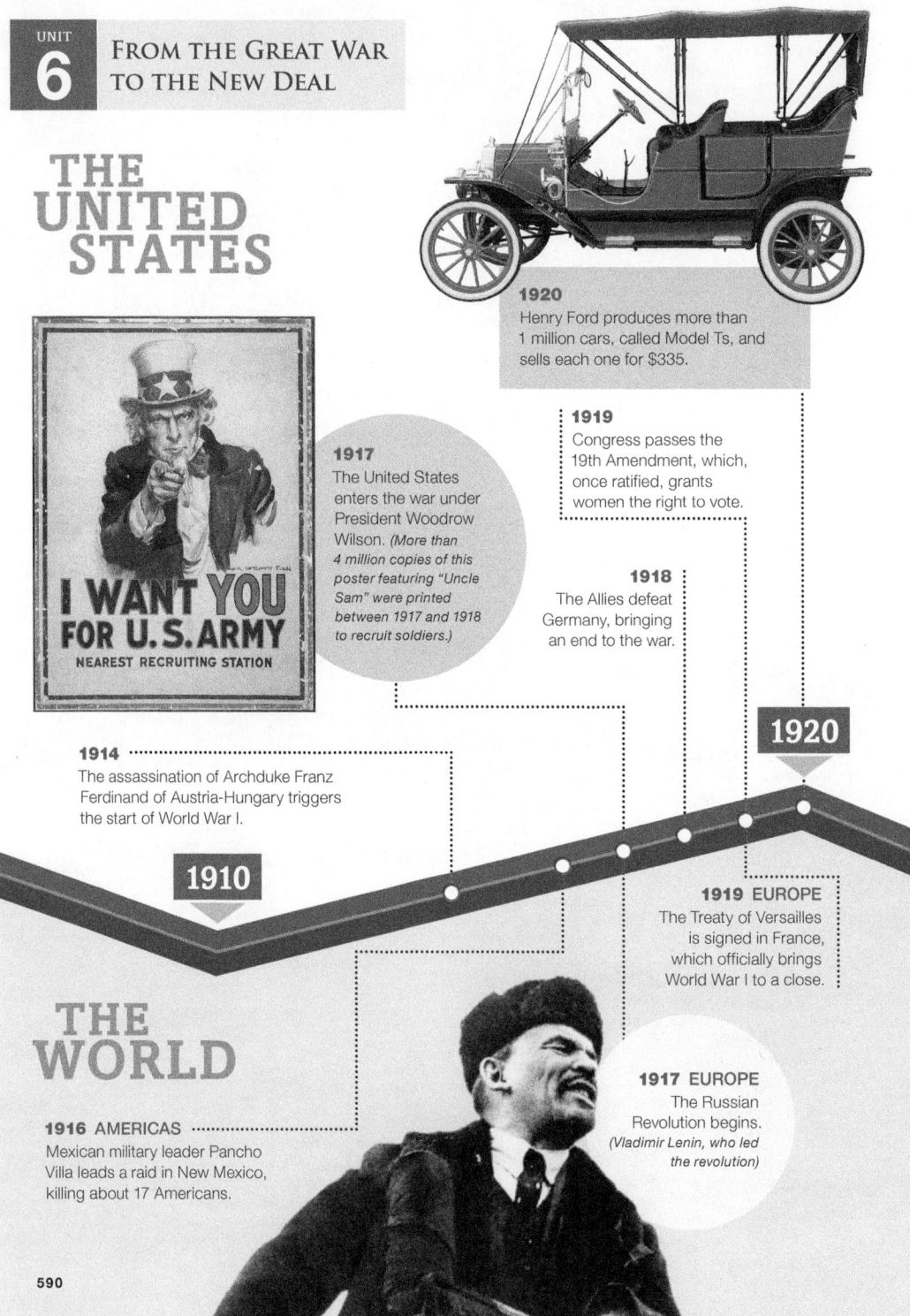

UNIT
6
FROM THE GREAT WAR
TO THE NEW DEAL

THE UNITED STATES

1920
Henry Ford produces more than 1 million cars, called Model Ts, and sells each one for $335.

1917
The United States enters the war under President Woodrow Wilson. *(More than 4 million copies of this poster featuring "Uncle Sam" were printed between 1917 and 1918 to recruit soldiers.)*

I WANT YOU FOR U.S. ARMY
NEAREST RECRUITING STATION

1919
Congress passes the 19th Amendment, which, once ratified, grants women the right to vote.

1918
The Allies defeat Germany, bringing an end to the war.

1920

1914
The assassination of Archduke Franz Ferdinand of Austria-Hungary triggers the start of World War I.

1910

1919 EUROPE
The Treaty of Versailles is signed in France, which officially brings World War I to a close.

THE WORLD

1917 EUROPE
The Russian Revolution begins. *(Vladimir Lenin, who led the revolution)*

1916 AMERICAS
Mexican military leader Pancho Villa leads a raid in New Mexico, killing about 17 Americans.

590

1929
The stock market crashes, marking the start of the Great Depression. *(men wearing signs in downtown Chicago advertising their qualifications, 1934)*

HISTORICAL THINKING

DETERMINE CHRONOLOGY What other conflict began the year the United States entered World War I?

1933
To address the Great Depression, Roosevelt enacts a series of domestic programs called the New Deal. *(mural created by Charles Wells under the New Deal's Works Progress Administration)*

1940
Roosevelt signs into law an act creating the first peacetime draft in U.S. history.

1931
As a result of drought and overplowed land, terrible dust storms sweep across the Great Plains states, a region some call the Dust Bowl.

1932
Franklin Delano Roosevelt is elected to his first term as president.

1937 ASIA
Japan goes to war with China and occupies Chinese cities including Shanghai, Beijing, and Nanjing.

1933 EUROPE
Adolf Hitler becomes dictator of Germany. *(postage stamp of Hitler made by the Nazi regime)*

1922 AFRICA
Egypt gains independence from Great Britain.

INTRODUCE TIME LINE EVENT

1937 ASIA: JAPANESE OCCUPATION OF CHINA

In 1931, after many years of economic decline, Japan began to expand its resources by invading and taking over the province of Manchuria in China. Japan's own government was not stable, and in 1936, the military gained control of the Japanese state. The new leadership continued the expansionist policies, and by 1937, Japan had taken complete control of northern China, including the region's wealthy major cities. In the process of gaining this territory, Japan massacred 300,000 Chinese citizens. In 1940, Japan joined the Axis Powers, continuing its takeover of parts of Asia, including European colonies there. Meanwhile, the United States monitored Japanese aggression in the region very closely. **ASK:** Why might the United States have had concerns about Japan's takeover of European holdings in Asia? *(Possible response: The United States had valuable Pacific assets to lose if Japan stepped up aggression, including holdings acquired after the Spanish-American War, such as Guam.)*

HISTORICAL THINKING

DETERMINE CHRONOLOGY

The Russian Revolution began in 1917, the same year the United States entered World War I. By late 1916, losses from World War I had devastated Russia's farm and factory production, leaving the country financially strapped and its people starving. In early 1917, chaos and protests over widespread food shortages erupted in Russia's capital city of Petrograd and escalated into a revolution. Feeling the pressure but lacking any power or resources to set Russia back on course, Czar Nicholas II abdicated. His brother refused the throne, which brought an end to 300 years of rule by the Romanov dynasty. A provisional government took over. Later that year, the Russian Revolution ended when Vladimir Lenin and his Bolshevik faction overthrew the provisional government and seized power.

591

UNIT 6 RESOURCES

UNIT INTRODUCTION

UNIT TIME LINE

UNIT WRAP-UP

NATIONAL GEOGRAPHIC | CONNECTION

National Geographic Magazine Adapted Articles
• "The Hidden World of the Great War"
• "1918 Flu Pandemic" ONLINE

Unit 6 Inquiry: Create a Conflict Resolution Strategy

NG Learning Framework Activities
• Write a Conflict Negotiator Profile
• Settle a Dispute

Unit 6 Formal Assessment

UNIT 6 | 1914–1940
FROM THE GREAT WAR TO THE NEW DEAL

CRITICAL VIEWING: Artist Franz Kline painted *Lower East Side Market Scene* (detail) around 1930, soon after moving to New York City. It shows an open-air market likely inspired by the artist's Greenwich Village neighborhood, with its older buildings and working-class residents. What does the painting reveal about American culture?

CHAPTER 17 RESOURCES

Available at NGLSync.Cengage.com

TEACHER RESOURCES & ASSESSMENT

Reading and Note-Taking

Vocabulary Practice

Social Studies Skills Lessons
• Reading: Draw Conclusions
• Writing: Expository

Formal Assessment
• Chapter 17 Pretest
• Chapter 17 Tests A & B
• Section Quizzes

Chapter 17 Answer Key

ExamView®
   One-time Download

CHAPTER 17 | THE **GREAT WAR** 1914–1920

HISTORICAL THINKING: How did World War I affect the United States politically, economically, and socially?

AMERICAN STORIES | The Sinking of the *Lusitania*
SECTION 1 | European Conflict and U.S. Neutrality
SECTION 2 | Joining the Fight
SECTION 3 | Waging War Across the Atlantic
SECTION 4 | The War Ends
AMERICAN GALLERY ONLINE | Selling World War I at Home

"It is a fearful thing to lead this great peaceful people into war . . . **civilization itself seeming to be in the balance.**"
—President Woodrow Wilson

CRITICAL VIEWING: Trench warfare meant endless hours in muddy, wet conditions for soldiers during the Great War. In this 1916 photograph taken by John Warwick Brooke, British troops prepare to fight the Battle of the Somme in France, one of the bloodiest battles of the war. On the first day alone, the British suffered more than 57,000 casualties. What details in this photo convey the hardships of trench warfare?

STUDENT DIGITAL RESOURCES

• eEdition
• Handbooks
• Online Atlas

• American Gallery Online
• History Notebook
• Active History

• American Voices (Biographies)
• Literature Analysis

• Projects for Inquiry-Based Learning

Chapter 17 Spanish Resources are available at NGLSync.Cengage.com.

AMERICAN STORIES | The Sinking of the *Lusitania*

- Study Primary Sources: Eyewitness accounts of the sinking of the *Lusitania*
- On Your Feet: Debate the *Lusitania's* Voyage

NG Learning Framework:
Present an Account

SECTION 1 RESOURCES

EUROPEAN CONFLICT AND U.S. NEUTRALITY

LESSON 1.1
War Breaks Out in Europe

- Active History: Analyze Causes and Effects of World War I

NG Learning Framework:
Present Dramatic Monologues

LESSON 1.2
Wilson's Neutrality

- On Your Feet: Card Response

NG Learning Framework:
Write a Letter to the Editor

American Voices Biography
Uncle Sam ONLINE

SECTION 2 RESOURCES

AMERICA ENTERS THE WAR

LESSON 2.1
Pressures to Enter the War

- On Your Feet: Inside-Outside Circle

NG Learning Framework:
Develop a Presentation

LESSON 2.2
America Enters the War

- On Your Feet: Team Word Webbing

AMERICAN GALLERY ONLINE | Selling World War I at Home

SECTION 3 RESOURCES

WAGING WAR ACROSS THE ATLANTIC

LESSON 3.1
A Brutal War

- On Your Feet: Roundtable Discussion

NG Learning Framework:
Explore Warfare Technology

LESSON 3.2
THROUGH THE LENS
Jeffrey Gusky

- On Your Feet: Descriptive Words

NG Learning Framework:
Write a Photo Caption

LESSON 3.3
The Home Front

- On Your Feet: Use a Jigsaw Strategy

NG Learning Framework:
Design an Infographic

SECTION 4 RESOURCES

VICTORY AND WILSON'S PEACE

LESSON 4.1
Road to Victory

- On Your Feet: Team Word Webbing

NG Learning Framework:
Create an Annotated Time Line

LESSON 4.2
Victory and Wilson's Peace

- On Your Feet: Numbered Heads

NG Learning Framework:
Discuss Widespread Change

CHAPTER 17 REVIEW

STRIVING READERS

STRATEGY ❶
ANALYZE MAIN IDEAS

Direct students to read the Main Idea statements aloud for each lesson. Explain that these statements identify and summarize the key idea for each lesson. As students read the lessons, encourage them to make notes about details they find in the text that connect to the Main Idea statements. Tell them this process will help them identify and remember the most important information.

Use with All Lessons

STRATEGY ❷
CREATE IDEA WEBS

Prompt students to summarize the chapter by creating four Idea Webs, one for each section, and label the center sections as follows: *War in Europe, America Enters War, On the Home Front,* and *The Road to Peace.* Instruct students to complete each web with relevant information as they read the corresponding set of lessons.

Use with All Lessons *For example, for* War in Europe, *students may add these topics to their Idea Web: Assassination starts the war; brutal trench warfare on two fronts; President Wilson remains neutral; strong economic ties between U.S. and Allies.*

STRATEGY ❸
CLARIFY INFORMATION

Students may have trouble understanding the complicated alliances that led to World War I (Lesson 1.1) and the multi-step peace process and redrawing of national boundaries at the end of the war (Lesson 4.2). To help students organize the information, instruct them to take notes on information under each subheading in the text using a 5Ws Chart.

Use with Lessons 1.1 and 4.2

INCLUSION

STRATEGY ❶
PREVIEW USING MAPS

To help students better understand the major changes in national boundaries that resulted from World War I, direct them to preview the maps in Lessons 4.1 and 4.2. First have students use a finger to trace the territory held by the Allied Powers and the Central Powers in the map of Major Battles of World War I, 1917–1918. Then have them trace the territories lost by the Russian, Austro-Hungarian, and German empires in the map of National Boundaries After World War I, 1920. Explain that the areas lost by the empires were returned to populations that had been taken over by the empires.

Use with Lessons 4.1 and 4.2

STRATEGY ❷
DESCRIBE LESSON VISUALS

Pair students who are visually impaired with students who are not. Ask the latter to describe the visuals in the lesson and read all captions. Encourage visually impaired students to ask questions to clarify anything they do not understand, and instruct partners to answer the questions. Prompt sighted partners to identify any important or dramatic details they notice.

Use with All Lessons *For example, in the Warbirds of World War I illustrations in Lesson 3.1, sighted students would describe the colors and markings on each fighter airplane and read the associated text.*

ENGLISH LANGUAGE LEARNERS

STRATEGY ❶
CREATE SENTENCE STRIPS

Choose a paragraph from the lesson and make sentence strips from it. Read the paragraph aloud while students follow along in their books. Pair students at the **Emerging** and **Expanding** levels and ask students to close their books. Then give pairs the set of sentence strips and instruct them to put the strips in order. Invite students to take turns reading the resulting paragraph aloud.

Use with All Lessons *You may ask students at the Emerging level to read the sentences aloud and ask their partners to explain any unfamiliar words before working together to arrange the sentences in the correct order.*

STRATEGY ❷
MODIFY VOCABULARY LISTS

Limit the number of vocabulary words, terms, and names students at the **Emerging** level will be required to master. Direct students to write each word from your modified list on a colored sticky note and put it on the page next to where it appears in context.

Use with All Lessons

STRATEGY ❸
CREATE A DEFINITION CHART

Place students in mixed pairs, such as students at the **Emerging** level with those at the **Bridging** level. Tell pairs to work together to identify at least three Key Vocabulary words from the lesson that they have had difficulty understanding. Instruct students to create a Definition Chart for those words. Then tell pairs to trade their chart with another pair and ask and answer questions about the information in the chart.

Word	Definition	In My Own Words

Use with All Lessons

GIFTED & TALENTED

STRATEGY ❶
CREATE A POSTER

Instruct students to research the images, slogans, and persuasive appeals used in World War I posters and in Prohibition posters. Then have them create a poster in a similar style. They could use conventional art materials or an online design program. Invite students to display their posters and explain the images, colors, and words they chose to use based on their research.

Use with Lessons 2.2 and 3.3

STRATEGY ❷
CREATE A MUSEUM EXHIBIT

Direct students to use the chapter text and online resources to design and prepare a museum exhibit about the experiences of African Americans during World War I, both on the home front and on the battlefields of Europe. Suggest students look for letters, newspaper articles, photographs, and other primary source materials. Encourage students to also use secondary source documents and address bias and prejudice in historical interpretations of the subject. Invite students to display their exhibits in the classroom.

Use with Lessons 3.1, 3.3, and 4.2

PRE-AP

STRATEGY ❶
WRITE A FEATURE ARTICLE

Instruct students to conduct online research about women's roles in World War I. Tell students to select one woman and write a feature article about her and what she did during the war. Prompt students to make connections between women's experiences during the war and broader social, economic, and political trends during and after the war.

Use with Lessons 2.2 and 3.3 *You may wish to provide examples of feature articles as a guide.*

STRATEGY ❷
ANALYZE LONG-TERM EFFECTS

Tell students to research and examine one of the following topics related to World War I:

- the long-term consequences of World War I
- race and/or gender inequities
- economic changes
- political changes

Suggest that students develop an infographic to display the results of their investigation. Encourage students to share their research projects with the class in a panel discussion.

Use with Lessons 3.1, 3.3, and 4.2

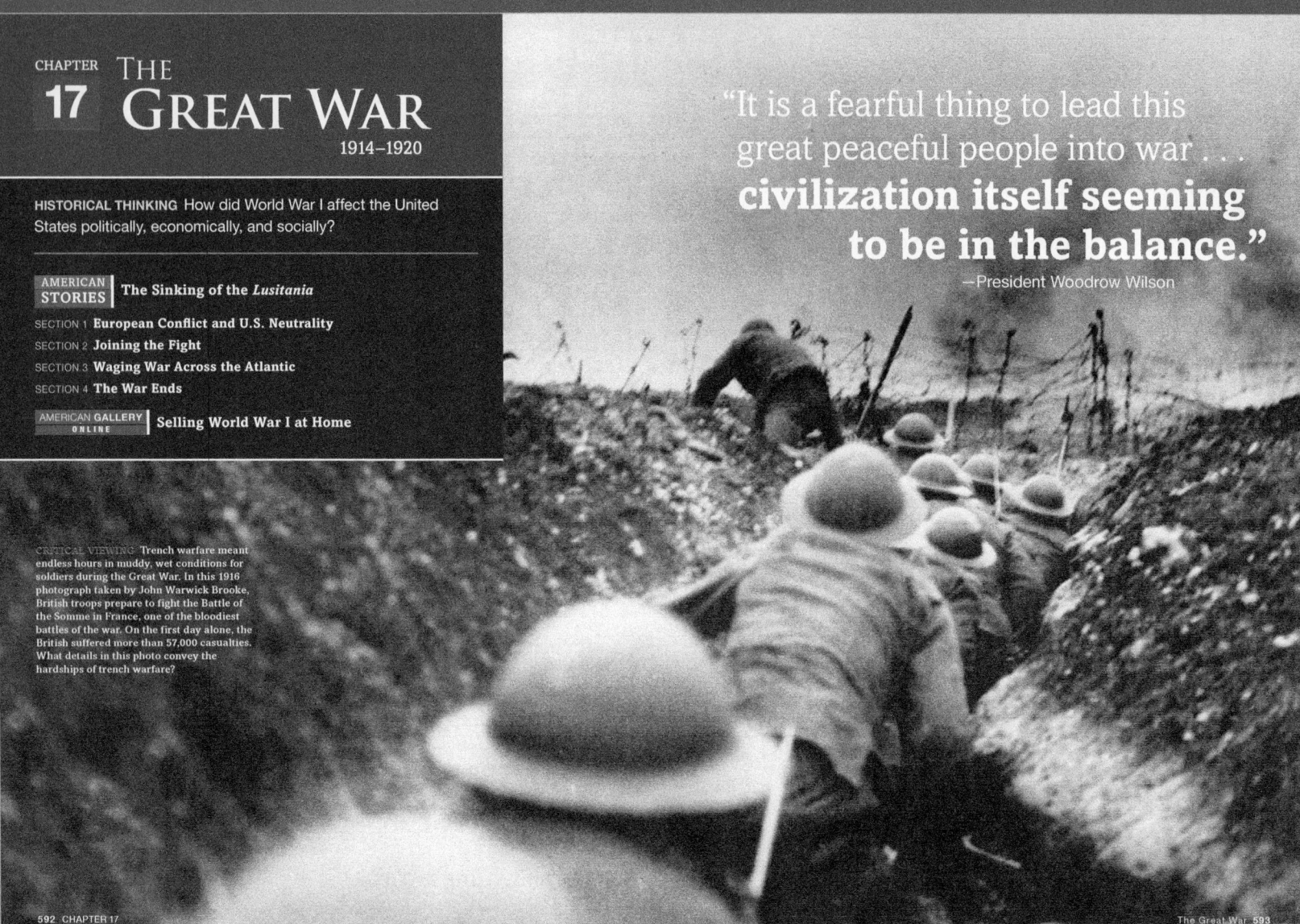

THE GREAT WAR

1914–1920

HISTORICAL THINKING How did World War I affect the United States politically, economically, and socially?

CRITICAL VIEWING Trench warfare meant endless hours in muddy, wet conditions for soldiers during the Great War. In this 1916 photograph taken by John Warwick Brooke, British troops prepare to fight the Battle of the Somme in France, one of the bloodiest battles of the war. On the first day alone, the British suffered more than 57,000 casualties. What details in this photo convey the hardships of trench warfare?

"It is a fearful thing to lead this great peaceful people into war . . . **civilization itself seeming to be in the balance.**"

—President Woodrow Wilson

INTRODUCE THE PHOTOGRAPH

TRENCH WARFARE

Draw students' attention to the photograph and quotation that open this chapter. Ask them to focus on the soldiers and the landscape. **ASK:** How does the photograph add meaning to the quotation? *(Answers will vary. Possible responses: The soldiers huddle in trenches in the midst of artillery fire—they must feel a lot is at stake to keep going under those circumstances. The landscape looks bleak and barren, as if civilization may already be crumbling.)* Tell students that in this chapter they will learn about the United States' entry into World War I and the effects of that war on the United States.

SHARE BACKGROUND

Assigned to document the movements of the British army, John Warwick Brooke joined Ernest Brooks in 1916 as the second official photographer assigned to the Western Front. Both photographers were expected to take as many photographs as they could, with variety also an important consideration. During two years at the Western Front, Brooke took an estimated 4,000 photographs. Prior to the war, Brooke had worked as a photographer for the Topical Press Agency, which photographed the daily routine of London Transport. Brooke's photographs thus serve to document both daily life in prewar London and the war itself.

CRITICAL VIEWING The soldiers had to crouch down and could move only in single file in the crowded, mud-walled trench. Eventually, they would have to crawl out, as the soldier in front is doing, and expose themselves to enemy fire.

For Chapter 17 Spanish Resources, visit the Resources Menu. Chapter 17 Resources are available at NGLSync.Cengage.com.

HISTORICAL THINKING QUESTION

How did World War I affect the United States politically, economically, and socially?

Four Corners: Preview Content This activity will help students preview and discuss the topics covered in Chapter 17. Provide a brief description and question for each section of the chapter, such as the ones shown below, and designate each of four corners as being "home" to one of the sections. Divide the class into four groups. Each group goes to one of the corners and discusses the topic of the section for a short time.

Group 1 Section 1 is about European conflict and U.S. neutrality. **ASK:** What reasons might European nations have for fighting one another, and why might the United States want to remain neutral?

Group 2 Section 2 is about America's entry into the war. **ASK:** How might a war in a foreign land have ramifications for people back home economically, socially, or politically?

Group 3 Section 3 is about waging war in Europe. **ASK:** What strategies or technologies might be important for a good offense and a good defense in war?

Group 4 Section 4 is about victory and Wilson's peace. **ASK:** What are some ways that a war could end?

Then ask each group to summarize their ideas for the class.

INTRODUCE THE READING STRATEGY

DRAW CONCLUSIONS

Explain that drawing conclusions based on evidence can help students understand the way history unfolds. Turn to the Chapter Review and preview the graphic organizer with students. As they read the chapter, encourage students to use both facts from the text and their own inferences to draw conclusions about aspects of World War I.

KEY DATES FOR CHAPTER 17

1914	World War I begins in Europe
1915	German submarine sinks the *Lusitania*
1917	United States enters the war
1917	Russian Revolution
1918	Flu epidemic begins
1918	Armistice ends fighting
1919	Paris Peace Conference
1919	The Great Steel Strike
1920	States ratify 19th Amendment

INTRODUCE CHAPTER VOCABULARY

KEY VOCABULARY

SECTION 1

| militarism | moral diplomacy | Schlieffen Plan, The |

SECTION 2

American Expeditionary Forces (AEF)	conscientious objector	War Industries Board (WIB)
civil liberties	Liberty Bond	Zimmermann Telegram
Committee on Public Information (CPI)	U-boat	

SECTION 3

antiaircraft gun	machine gun	Prohibition
Great Migration	pandemic	tank
influenza		

SECTION 4

| armistice | Fourteen Points | Treaty of Versailles |
| communism | League of Nations | |

WORD MAPS

As they read the chapter, have students complete Word Maps for Key Vocabulary terms. Tell students to make a Word Map for each term. Have them write the term in the center oval and then, as they encounter the term in the chapter, complete as much of the Word Map for that term as they can. Model an example for students on the board, using the graphic organizer below.

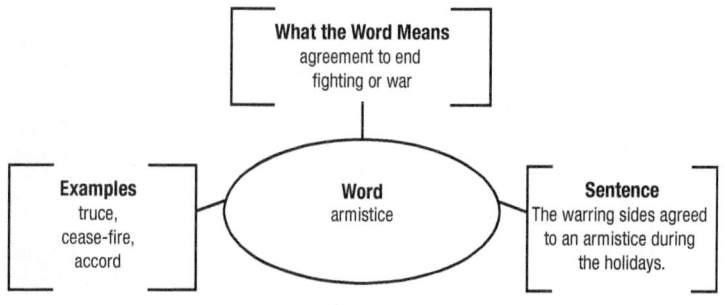

What the Word Means agreement to end fighting or war

Examples truce, cease-fire, accord

Word armistice

Sentence The warring sides agreed to an armistice during the holidays.

OBJECTIVES

- Learn about the sinking of the R.M.S. *Lusitania* and its ramifications.
- Recognize the complexity of the cause for the attack and the effects of the disaster.
- Understand the impact of the event and the role it played in U.S. involvement in World War I.
- Study primary sources: eyewitness accounts of the sinking of the *Lusitania*.

CRITICAL THINKING SKILLS FOR "THE SINKING OF THE *LUSITANIA*"

- Make Connections
- Draw Conclusions
- Identify
- Integrate Visuals
- Describe
- Summarize

CONNECT TO THE CHAPTER

This American Story provides students with details about one of the most notorious events of the early 20th century: the sinking of the R.M.S. *Lusitania*. Students will learn about the historical context of the ship's voyage and the reasons why it was in danger from the very outset. Primary sources help students to visualize the graphic events surrounding the ship's sinking from those who witnessed it firsthand.

The upcoming chapter, The Great War, discusses World War I and the United States' eventual entry into the war. This American Story will provide students with important background information about an event that helped sway public opinion in favor of the nation's involvement. Introduce the American Story before the class learns about the pressure the United States was under to enter World War I in Lesson 2.1.

HISTORY NOTEBOOK

Encourage students to complete the American Story page for Chapter 17 in their History Notebooks as they read.

CRITICAL VIEWING Possible response: People were probably interested in witnessing the impressive sight of the world's fastest passenger liner leaving New York.

AMERICAN STORIES · NATIONAL GEOGRAPHIC

CRITICAL VIEWING The luxury ocean liner *Lusitania* departed for her last voyage from Pier 54 in New York City on May 1, 1915. Why do you think a crowd would have gathered to see the *Lusitania* off on its voyage?

THE SINKING
OF THE
LUSITANIA

Today you can board a plane anywhere in the continental United States and arrive in Europe in less than a day. In 1915, the only option for trans-Atlantic travel was by ship, and the fastest crossing you could expect to make was 4 days, 11 hours, and 42 minutes—a record set by the British passenger liner R.M.S. *Lusitania*, the swiftest and possibly the most luxurious ship afloat at that time.

A DISTANT WAR

On May 1, 1915, the *Lusitania* was set to depart New York for England with approximately 2,000 passengers and crew aboard, including nearly 200 Americans. The ship was also carrying war material, including ammunition, for the British war effort. Great Britain and its allies had been at war with Germany for nearly a year. Germany had taken the battle to the seas, deploying submarines to attack not only naval vessels but also civilian ships suspected of carrying ammunition or other war materials to Britain.

On the morning the *Lusitania* sailed, the German Embassy in the United States placed an advertisement in several newspapers stating, rather ominously, that Germany considered the seas around Great Britain to be a war zone, and that "vessels flying the flag of Great Britain . . . are liable to destruction in these waters."

This cork life ring covered in yellow fabric bears the name of the ill-fated passenger ship.

CROSSING THE ATLANTIC

The *Lusitania*'s passengers represented all walks of life, from the extremely wealthy who took up residence in the most glamorous cabins, to the third-class passengers who shared dormitory-type rooms. One of the most celebrated passengers aboard the *Lusitania* was the American millionaire Alfred Gwynne Vanderbilt, who had inherited a lavish fortune from his father, the railroad baron Cornelius Vanderbilt. Before the ship sailed, a reporter asked Alfred about the German newspaper threat. He replied, "I don't take much stock in it myself. What would they gain by sinking the *Lusitania*?"

Other notable American passengers included Theodate Pope, one of the first female architects in the United States, and Charles Lauriat, a well-known Boston book dealer. Pope spent the six-day Atlantic crossing reading and chatting with her traveling companion, Edwin Friend. Lauriat was transporting an extremely rare book by British writer Charles Dickens, and a priceless set of drawings.

Among the younger passengers was an American named Dorothy Conner, who found the uneventful trip across the Atlantic to be frustratingly dull. She remarked to a dinner companion, "I can't help hoping that we get some sort of thrill going up the [English] Channel." Later, when a friend remarked that she'd had her thrill, Conner replied, "I never want another."

The Great War **595**

GUIDED DISCUSSION

1. **Identify** Why did the *Lusitania's* crew and passengers think the voyage would be safe, despite warnings? *(Possible response: They probably were not aware that the* Lusitania *would be carrying war materials and ammunition and didn't think it was likely that the Germans would actually target a passenger liner.)*

2. **Integrate Visuals** How does the May 18, 1915, headline of the *New York Times* connect the event of the *Lusitania's* sinking to larger political developments? *(Possible response: The "grave crisis" mentioned in the headline likely refers to whether Wilson was considering the death of American passengers to be an act of war against the United States. One potential political development could be the U.S. entry into the war in Europe.)*

A DISASTROUS COURSE

Explain to students that additional accounts of the sinking of the *Lusitania* include descriptions of the weather and detailed information about how Captain Turner was guiding the ship. There was patchy fog in the area as the ship approached Ireland, and in addition to not zigzagging, Captain Turner slowed and sailed close to the shore. **ASK:** How might the fog have influenced the captain's decisions about the course of the ship, and how might a different decision have caused events to take a different direction? *(Possible response: It probably made him more reluctant to zigzag the ship because it would have been more difficult for him to see where the ship was going in the fog. If he had made different sailing decisions, however, the* Lusitania *may have been spared.)*

A DISASTROUS COURSE

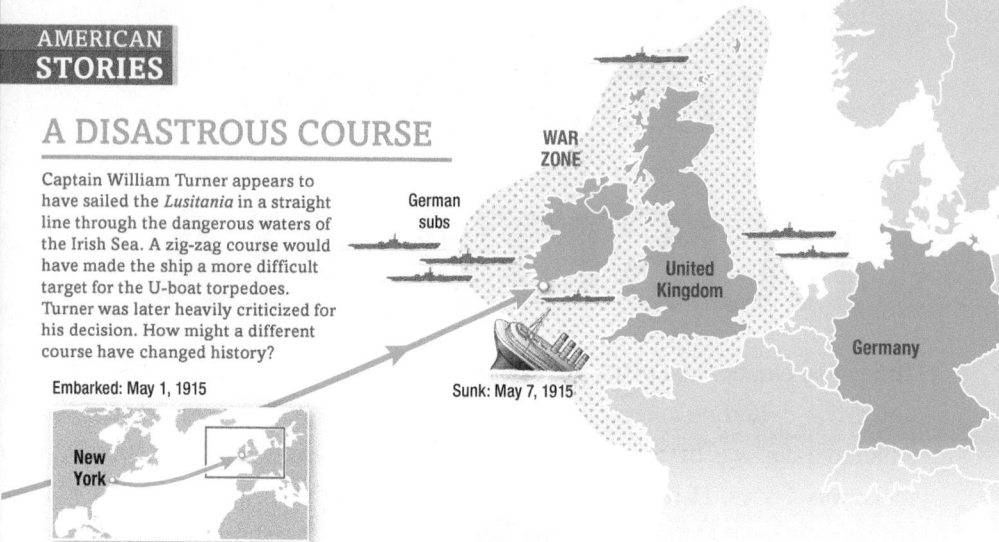

Captain William Turner appears to have sailed the *Lusitania* in a straight line through the dangerous waters of the Irish Sea. A zig-zag course would have made the ship a more difficult target for the U-boat torpedoes. Turner was later heavily criticized for his decision. How might a different course have changed history?

Embarked: May 1, 1915

WAR ZONE

German subs

United Kingdom

Germany

Sunk: May 7, 1915

New York

ATTACK NEAR IRELAND

At a little after 2 p.m. on May 7, the *Lusitania* was steaming into the Irish Sea, about 20 miles from the Irish Coast. Lurking in the same waters was the U-20, a German submarine with a mission to target British ships. The *Lusitania's* captain ordered a turn to starboard, unknowingly placing the liner directly within the submarine's sights.

Passengers and crew alike watched, transfixed, as a German torpedo streaked toward the helpless ship. One passenger described himself as "spellbound" by the sight, adding, "I felt absolutely sick."

This moment of fearful anticipation ended when the torpedo slammed into the *Lusitania's* side, blasting a hole in the hull. Immediately, seawater began to pour into the vessel at an estimated rate of 100 tons per second. The *Lusitania* began to list—or tilt—at an extreme angle, making it nearly impossible for passengers to

clamber into the lifeboats. Panicked passengers and crew members scrambled to find and put on their life vests, and parents desperately searched for their children in the crowds. Some people leaped into the sea while others clung to the sinking ship. Within 18 chaotic minutes, the *Lusitania* had disappeared beneath the surface of the sea.

Newspapers, including this May 8, 1915, edition of the *New York Times*, spread word of the event across the world.

ONE SHIPWRECK: TWO PERSPECTIVES

There are many survivor accounts of the sinking of the *Lusitania*, and it is valuable to compare these primary sources to better understand the event. The captain of the German U-boat that sank the ship offers a different perspective entirely from that of the survivors. Read and compare the two accounts below.

PRIMARY SOURCE

A SURVIVOR'S STORY

Dwight Harris, a young New Yorker, was carrying an engagement ring when he boarded the *Lusitania*, planning to propose to his beloved in England. He also brought with him a custom-made life preserver he had bought the day before. Pacing anxiously on deck on the day of the attack, he saw the torpedo: "a white and greenish streak in the water!" Harris hurried to his room to locate his life preserver, failed to get into a lifeboat, and jumped overboard.

Floating in the sea, he witnessed the *Lusitania's* plunge toward the bottom. He later described, "A terrible mass of iron, wood, steam, and water! And worst of all, human forms!—A great swirling greenish white bubble formed where the ship went down, which was a mass of struggling humanity and wreckage!" The ring Harris carried survived the catastrophe and he later offered it to Aileen Cavendish Foster, whom he married on July 2, 1915.

This illustration of survivors fleeing in lifeboats from the sinking of the *Lusitania* appeared in an Italian weekly newspaper.

PRIMARY SOURCE

THE SUBMARINE CAPTAIN'S STORY

The submarine that sank the *Lusitania* was the U-20, under the command of Captain Walther Schwieger. The U-20 left Germany on April 30 with a mission to destroy shipping vessels destined for Liverpool, England. It was a successful cruise: by May 7, the submarine had already sunk three vessels off the coast of Ireland. That morning, Captain Schwieger decided to turn for home, since the U-20 was running low on both fuel and torpedoes. Then, at 1:20 p.m., an officer at the periscope spotted the distinctive shape of the *Lusitania*.

In his ship's log, Schwieger provided one of the clearest eyewitness accounts of the torpedo's aftermath. He recorded, "There was a terrific panic on her deck. Overcrowded lifeboats, fairly torn from their positions, dropped into the water. Desperate people ran helplessly up and down the decks. Men and women jumped into the water and tried to swim to empty, overturned lifeboats. It was the most terrible sight I have ever seen."

The "terrible sight" did not dampen Schwieger's enthusiasm for his job. On a single cruise in September 1915, he sank 11 ships, including the passenger ship *Hesperian*, which was carrying home the body of a Canadian passenger who had been killed on the *Lusitania*. By the time the war in Europe was over, German submarines had sunk more than 4,000 ships, around one-fourth of the world's shipping vessels.

ONE SHIPWRECK: TWO PERSPECTIVES

Remind students that over 700 people ultimately survived the sinking of the *Lusitania*, and firsthand accounts of the survivors provide information about the disaster. Have students compare the two accounts. **ASK:** What does each account help you understand about the event? *(Possible response: Both accounts convey the emotion of the disaster and give a physical description of the sinking. Harris's account describes how he survived and provides a dramatic description of the actual sinking. Captain Schwieger describes the panic and actions of the passengers as they try to survive.)* **ASK:** How do you think the event affected Harris and Captain Schwieger? *(Answers will vary. Possible response: Harris was probably grateful to survive and go on to marry his girlfriend. Although Captain Schwieger noted the event as "the most terrible sight," as a captain in the German navy, he continued to wage war on enemy vessels, as evidenced by his sinking of many more ships after the* Lusitania.*)*

ACTIVE OPTIONS

On Your Feet: Debate the *Lusitania's* Voyage Ask students to think about the cruise line's decision to send war supplies and civilian passengers in the same ship during wartime. Then divide the class into two groups: one to argue in support of the decision and one to argue against it. Instruct each group to compile a list of reasons in support of its position. Then have the groups debate each other, allowing one member of each group to speak at a time. When finished, encourage the class to discuss the effectiveness of the arguments presented.

NG Learning Framework: Present an Account

SKILL Communication

KNOWLEDGE Our Human Story

Encourage students to briefly search online for an additional eyewitness account of the sinking of the *Lusitania* that interests them. Accounts could be from passengers or crew members from the ship, rescuers, or crew members of the U-20. Once students have chosen an account, instruct them to prepare and perform a reading of it for the class. Students should first introduce the account by telling the person's name and providing relevant background information. After each reading, invite the class to briefly discuss it before continuing with the next one.

LUSITANIA SURVIVAL OUTCOME

Nettie Moore was an Irish passenger on the *Lusitania*. Both Nettie's husband and baby son died when the *Lusitania* sank, but Nettie survived because her brother was there to save her. An estimated 82 Irish passengers did not survive when the ship went down. **ASK:** What approximate percentage of the number of passengers lost from the British Isles does the number of Irish passengers represent? *(About 11 percent of the total deaths among passengers from the British Isles were Irish.)*

NATIONAL GEOGRAPHIC EXPLORER
ROBERT BALLARD

Robert Ballard is a deep-sea explorer famous for discovering hydrothermal vents and the wreck of the *Titanic*, in addition to other shipwrecks. Ballard's ship, the E/V *Nautilus*, spends several months of the year exploring the oceans. The general public can view E/V *Nautilus* video footage by visiting the Nautilus Live website.

WRITE ABOUT HISTORY

Describe a Civilian's Perspective This American Story describes the sinking of the passenger liner *Lusitania* by a German U-boat during World War I. To help students make connections between the American Story and their own lives, ask them to write an essay about how a single wartime event can affect civilians. Remind students of the *Lusitania* survivor accounts they studied. Also ask students to think about current conflicts in the world and the impact of events on civilians in war zones or living far away from the fighting. Pair students to edit each other's essays and make suggestions for revision. Provide guidance about the writing process as necessary.

THINK ABOUT IT

1. Possible response: The *Lusitania* sailed through what was considered a war zone, and the fact that the ship continued on a straight course probably made it an easy target for the German torpedo. There also might have been a second explosion after the torpedo hit the ship, and this probably contributed to the ship sinking.

2. Possible response: The United States probably would have entered the war eventually. The text says that it was just "the first in a series of events" that led to American involvement and that by 1917 public opinion had definitely turned against Germany.

AFTERMATH

During the hours and days immediately following the disaster, the main concern for family and friends of the victims was the frantic search for survivors—or for the bodies of those who had perished. Alfred Vanderbilt had last been seen helping others escape the wreckage. His body was never found. Dorothy Conner survived the sinking and went on to serve in France, supporting the troops. Charles Lauriat also survived, but his irreplaceable book and drawings were lost in the icy Irish Sea. When rescuers pulled Theodate Pope aboard their boat, they believed she was dead and left her on deck with the other bodies. Fortunately, another rescued passenger realized she was alive and called for help to revive her. Her companion, Edwin Friend, was among those who disappeared.

It is believed that 1,191 people died in the sinking of the *Lusitania*. Of those, 129 were Americans. Exact totals have remained elusive because of the difficulty in identifying stowaways and last-minute changes to crew and passenger lists. Naturally, the news of the sinking sparked shock and horror in the United States. In private, President Wilson expressed his fury to his secretary. "In God's name, how could any nation calling itself civilized purpose [plan] so horrible a thing?" he asked. In public, however, he made speeches counseling a restrained response to the German aggression.

Despite their anger, most Americans agreed with Wilson; they opposed the idea of the United States entering the war in Europe. Still, the sinking of the *Lusitania* can be seen as the first in a series of events that did finally engage the United States in the conflict that would engulf the world. By the time Wilson declared war in 1917, American public opinion had turned firmly against Germany.

THINK ABOUT IT

1. What factors likely contributed to the sinking of the *Lusitania*?

2. If the ship hadn't been sunk, do you think the United States would have been drawn into the war? Why or why not?

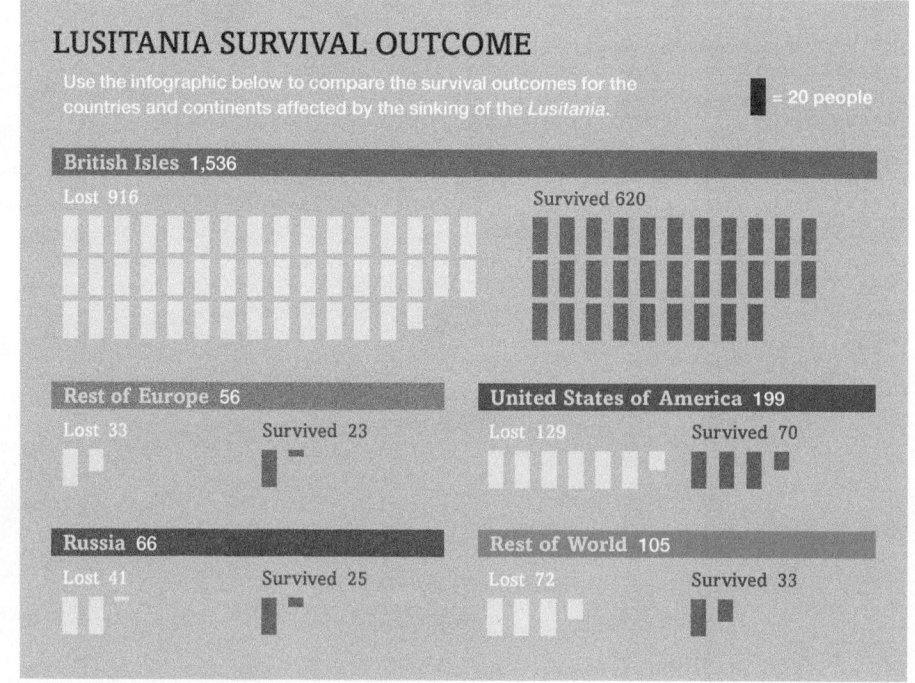

LUSITANIA SURVIVAL OUTCOME

Use the infographic below to compare the survival outcomes for the countries and continents affected by the sinking of the *Lusitania*.

■ = 20 people

British Isles 1,536

Lost 916   Survived 620

Rest of Europe 56
Lost 33   Survived 23

United States of America 199
Lost 129   Survived 70

Russia 66
Lost 41   Survived 25

Rest of World 105
Lost 72   Survived 33

SOURCE: Merseyside Maritime Museum

NATIONAL GEOGRAPHIC

A SECOND EXPLOSION?

The *Lusitania* was a well-constructed ship, designed to survive the flooding of one or two of its internal compartments. Why, then, did it sink almost instantly after just one torpedo strike? Many witnesses claimed that a second explosion followed the torpedo strike, and several theories have been used to explain this blast, but none have been proven.

Some have claimed that the *Lusitania* was secretly carrying explosives for Britain's military and that these were ignited by the torpedo strike. As you have read, the ship was in fact carrying rifle ammunition and other war supplies, but none of these materials would have caused a massive explosion.

National Geographic Explorer-in-Residence Robert Ballard explored the *Lusitania's* wreck in 1993 and proposed the theory that the ship's coal bunkers exploded. The coal bunkers were enormous compartments that stored the 5,690 tons of coal needed to fuel the engines. By the end of the long voyage, only highly combustible coal dust remained in those spaces, but the dust may have been too damp to explode.

During hearings after the sinking, the *Lusitania's* captain proposed that the torpedo could have ruptured the line that carried steam from the boiler rooms to power the propellers. Tests conducted by a National Geographic team in 2012 seem to support this explanation, but definitive proof remains elusive. The wreck of the *Lusitania* guards its secrets.

Says Robert Ballard of the *Lusitania* wreckage: "She is now a faint ghost of the ocean greyhound she once was, one of the saddest wrecks I've ever seen. But when I visualize her upturned bow, I can imagine the pride of those who once sailed on the swiftest ship in the world."

A small submersible called *Delta* took Ballard to the *Lusitania* for a firsthand look at the wreckage.

STRIVING READERS

Pose and Answer Questions Arrange students in pairs to read the American Story. Instruct them to pause after each paragraph and ask one another *who, what, where, when* or *why* questions about the content. Suggest students use a 5Ws Chart to help organize their questions and answers.

GIFTED & TALENTED

Create a Cause-and-Effect Presentation Direct students to conduct online research to learn more about the sinking of the *Lusitania* in order to create a multimedia presentation about its causes and effects. Encourage students to use a Cause-and-Effect Chart to keep track of the relationship among events. Invite students to share their cause-and-effect presentations with the class.

See the Chapter Planner for more strategies for differentiation.

HISTORICAL THINKING

Ask and have students answer the following questions.

1. **READING CHECK** How did passengers and the general public react to the attack?

2. **DESCRIBE** Why were some passengers unable to get into lifeboats?

3. **SUMMARIZE** Why is the exact cause of the second explosion on the ship still not known?

ANSWERS

1. People were generally surprised and angry because the *Lusitania* was not a military vessel. Accounts of those who survived described their horror and disbelief as the ship was hit and sank.

2. Water began filling the ship, which caused it to tilt. The tilting made it difficult for people to get into the lifeboats.

3. Because the ship sank so quickly, it was impossible at the time to examine the hull and therefore difficult to determine the exact damages so the cause could be traced.

WAR BREAKS OUT IN EUROPE

Have you ever built a house of cards? Each card must be placed perfectly in order to support the delicate structure. Nudge just one card, and the whole building collapses. In 1914, Europe was a house of cards, just waiting for the nudge that would lead to fighting and chaos.

EUROPE AT THE EDGE OF WAR

In 1914, Europe was divided into hostile nations and poised for war. At the heart of the tension was lingering animosity between France and Germany in the wake of the Franco-Prussian War. In 1870, Germany had conquered France and then demanded $1 billion. Germany also seized the eastern French provinces of Alsace and Lorraine. For Germany, the acquisition of the provinces was the final step in unification. German leaders brought together several regions under the control of the kingdom of Prussia and declared a German Empire in 1871.

Frustrated by the military loss and determined to reclaim the lost provinces, the French worked to rebuild their economy and military. To further strengthen its position against Germany, France also formed alliances, or agreements of mutual support, with Russia and Great Britain. The German government had similar understandings with Austria-Hungary and the Ottoman Empire. Italy had been part of an earlier alliance with Germany and Austria-Hungary, but those ties had become frayed by 1914.

Because of these complex and delicate networks of treaties and alliances, an attack on one country could—and did—trigger retaliation by others and plunge all of Europe into a state of war. The conflict would come to be called "the Great War" because of the enormous number of casualties that resulted from it and the large number of nations involved in it. As war once again loomed in Europe in the 1930s, many historians began to refer to the conflict that began in 1914 as "World War I."

THE THREE –ism's

Alongside the alliances, three cultural attitudes helped push Europe down the path to conflict. Nationalism is a strong belief in one's own country and its superiority to others. In Europe, nationalism often conflicted with individuals' ethnic ties to a certain region or group of people.

Imperialism is the drive to conquer or colonize other territories and form an empire. Great Britain, Germany, and France were imperial powers, competing for colonies in Africa and Asia and the raw materials and markets that the colonies provided.

Militarism is the belief that a government must create a strong military and be prepared to use it to achieve the country's goals. By 1914, Germany was a major military power, and France was working to catch up. Britain did not have a strong military presence on the ground, but it did have a large and powerful navy and felt threatened by Germany's push to expand its own seagoing forces.

AN ASSASSINATION SPARKS WAR

On June 28, 1914, **Archduke Franz Ferdinand** of Austria-Hungary and his wife were assassinated, or murdered for political reasons, during a parade in the capital city of Bosnia. Their killer was a Serbian nationalist. Serbia was allied with Russia and had a history of conflict with Austria-Hungary.

One after another, European alliances were activated. The Austrians, supported by the Germans, made harsh demands of the Serbs to punish them for the assassination. Russia came to Serbia's defense, and France declared its support for its ally Russia.

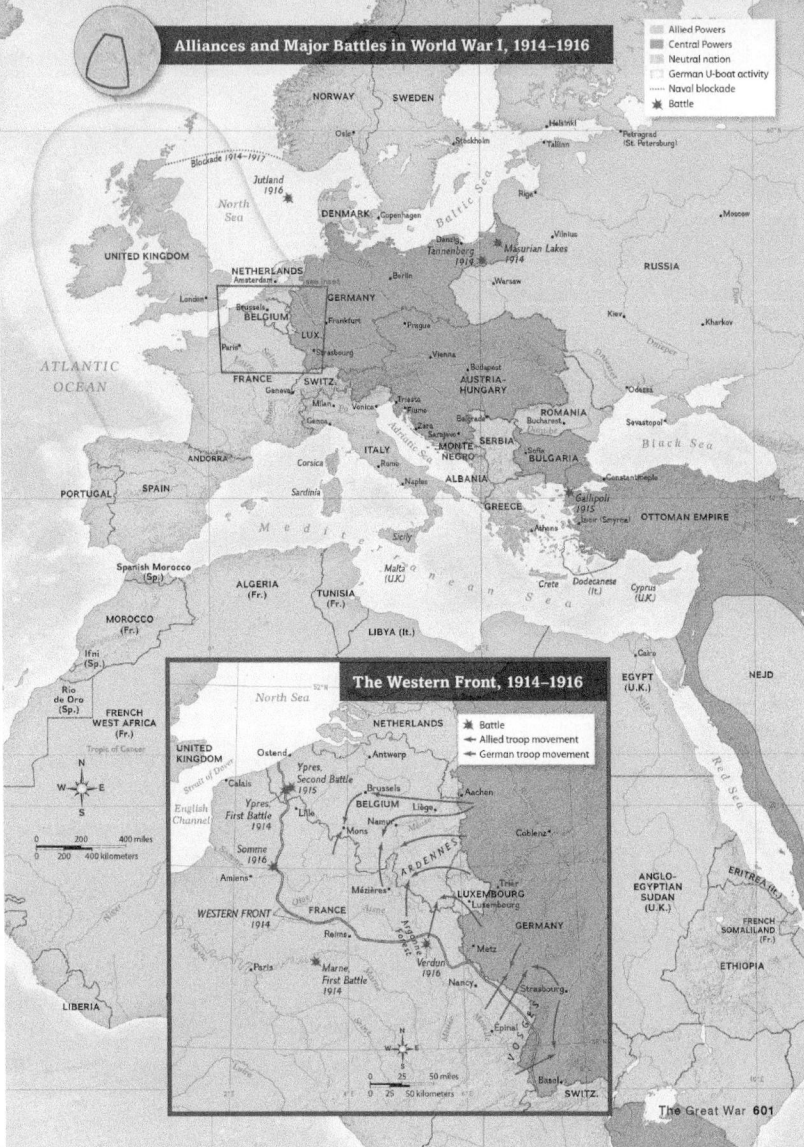

Alliances and Major Battles in World War I, 1914–1916

The Western Front, 1914–1916

The Great War **601**

PLAN: 4-PAGE LESSON

OBJECTIVE

Understand the complex relationships among nations that fought in the Great War.

CRITICAL THINKING SKILLS FOR LESSON 1.1

- Analyze Cause and Effect
- Make Generalizations
- Make Inferences
- Compare and Contrast
- Draw Conclusions
- Interpret Maps
- Evaluate
- Analyze Primary Sources

HISTORICAL THINKING FOR CHAPTER 17

How did World War I affect the United States politically, economically, and socially? The outbreak of World War I took the United States by surprise, but tensions had been simmering across Europe. Lesson 1.1 describes how European nations honored their alliances as fighting began.

BACKGROUND FOR THE TEACHER

Even before the Franco-Prussian War, control of Alsace and Lorraine had been a matter of dispute. In the 9th century, Alsace and Lorraine were ruled by Charlemagne, the emperor of what came to be known as the Holy Roman Empire. Centuries later, at the end of the Thirty Years' War, the 1648 Peace of Westphalia ceded Alsace and Lorraine to France. Alsace and Lorraine remained French until 1871, when Germany reclaimed them at the end of the Franco-Prussian War. However, control of these provinces arose as an issue at the end of both world wars.

INTRODUCE & ENGAGE

UNDERSTAND THE NUMBERS

Use comparisons to help students put the human toll of World War I in perspective. **ASK:** How many people do you think would fill a stadium at a professional football game? *(about 75,000)* **ASK:** About how many people live in the most populous U.S. city? *(about 8.5 million)* **ASK:** How many thousands of people are in a million? *(one thousand thousands)* Point out that some wars have lasted for hundreds of years and have resulted in hundreds of thousands of people killed. Explain that World War I lasted only four years, but 9 million soldiers were killed and an additional 21 million soldiers were wounded or listed as missing. Tell students that in this lesson they will learn how World War I started.

TEACH

GUIDED DISCUSSION

1. **Compare and Contrast** How was militarism in Germany and in France similar prior to World War I, and how was it different? *(Both countries built up their military, but they had a different focus. The purpose of Germany's militarism was to acquire and support a German Empire; the purpose of France's militarism was to win back Alsace and Lorraine from Germany.)*

2. **Make Inferences** How did imperialism add to tensions among European nations? *(European powers such as Great Britain, Germany, and France competed for colonies in Africa and Asia and so saw each other as rivals.)*

3. **Draw Conclusions** In the context of looming war in the early 1900s, what might be some advantages and disadvantages of maintaining alliances and the understood agreement that an attack against one is an attack against all? *(Possible responses: Advantages: With tensions rising and war on the horizon, a nation with allies can count on other nations to come to its defense in case of attack. Alliances might prevent an attack in the first place, since an aggressive nation might think twice about attacking a small or weak nation with powerful allies. Disadvantages: A nation might be drawn into a war it doesn't want to defend another nation. A nation might have to cut ties with nations with which it has no quarrel.)*

INTERPRET MAPS

Guide students to analyze the map of alliances and major battles and the inset map of the Western Front. **ASK:** In which countries did most of the fighting take place? *(France and Belgium)* **ASK:** What was the general direction of the Allied troop movements and the Central Powers troop movements? *(Allied troops moved north and northeast. Central Powers troops moved west and southwest.)* **ASK:** Which land battle was waged farthest from the front? *(Marne, First Battle)* **ASK:** Which battle was waged at sea? *(the Battle of Jutland)*

DIFFERENTIATE

STRIVING READERS

Turn Headings into Questions To help students set a purpose for reading, tell them to read each subsection heading and then turn it into a question they think will be answered in the lesson, such as Why was Europe at the edge of war? Direct students to record their questions. After reading the lesson, have students write the answer to each question.

PRE-AP

Research Trench Warfare Tell students to conduct a short research project to answer specific questions about trench warfare. Ask students to generate an initial research question based on information in the lesson. As they research, encourage them to use their question as a springboard for generating additional questions for which they'd like to find answers. Prompt students to share their findings with the class in an oral or written report.

See the Chapter Planner for more strategies for differentiation.

We entered the trenches about midnight, we found them very uncomfortable, as there was only one dug-out for our company. . . . I spent six hours making myself a shelter in a communication trench, a sort of sofa with a waterproof sheet above it, cut out of one side of a five-foot trench. I worked most of the night throwing earth up to shield my bed, as the Germans were sniping at our parapet all day long. Meals were wretched, as we had nowhere decent to eat them, and we also lost our principal ration bag, containing tinned fruits and other joys.

—from the personal account of British Lieutenant William Andrew Turnbull, regarding the trenches near Hooge, France, 1915

In early August, Germany declared war on both Russia and France, invading Belgium in a push to reach France's northern border.

Alarmed by the actions of belligerent, militaristic Germany, which lay just across the English Channel, Britain declared war on the country. Within months, Europe was consumed by a war between two alliances: the **Central Powers** (primarily Germany, Austria-Hungary, and Turkey) and the **Allies** (primarily Great Britain, France, and Russia). Italy remained neutral at first but eventually joined the Allies in 1915.

The sudden outbreak of fighting in Europe surprised Americans. Although the arms race among the great powers had seemed potentially dangerous, it had been a century since a war involving all of the major European countries had erupted. Additionally, American faith in progress and the betterment of humanity, a principal part of the Progressive Era's creed, made war unthinkable.

TRENCH WARFARE ON TWO FRONTS

For years before the events of 1914, Germany had been preparing to wage war on France and Russia. **The Schlieffen Plan**, devised by a German army officer and completed in 1906, called for a rapid conquest of France, so that German troops could then turn east and

CRITICAL VIEWING This colorful 1917 postcard features the flags of the Allies in the Great War. From left: Portugal, Serbia, Belgium, Italy, France, Great Britain, the United States, Romania, Russia, and Japan. What might have been the goal behind the creation of artwork like this during the Great War?

FOR FREEDOM

IN THE TRENCHES

The Great War is known for its trench warfare. Troops fighting for the Allies and Central Powers dug trenches fairly close to each other to attack and defend from below ground level. Trench warfare is typically used when the troops defending themselves from an attack have superior firepower, forcing the opposition to give up their mobility by digging trenches for protection.

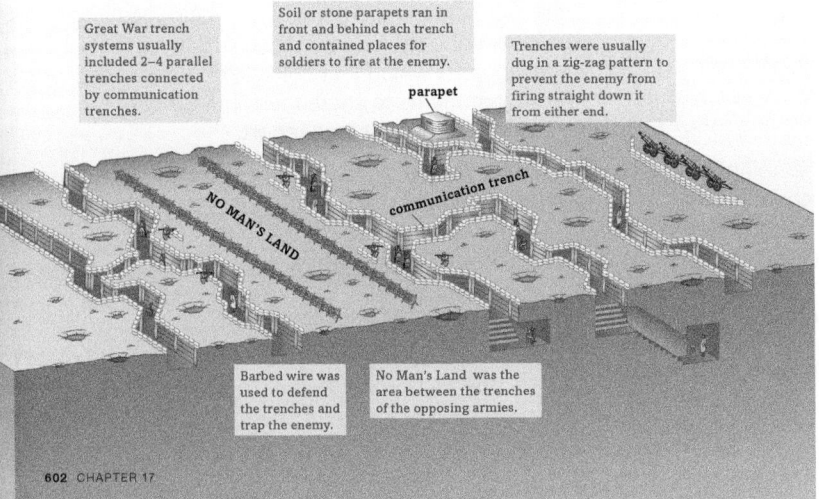

Great War trench systems usually included 2–4 parallel trenches connected by communication trenches.

Soil or stone parapets ran in front and behind each trench and contained places for soldiers to fire at the enemy.

Trenches were usually dug in a zig-zag pattern to prevent the enemy from firing straight down it from either end.

parapet

NO MAN'S LAND

communication trench

Barbed wire was used to defend the trenches and trap the enemy.

No Man's Land was the area between the trenches of the opposing armies.

march on Russia. This strategy failed, however, when the British Army joined France in stalling the advance of the German Army before it reached Paris. By the end of 1914, Germany found itself fighting enemies on two fronts, or battle lines. On the Western Front in northern France, German troops battled French and British forces; on the Eastern Front, Germany faced off with Russia.

On both fronts, a type of fighting called trench warfare prevailed. To shelter from enemy artillery fire, troops would dig complex networks of trenches into the ground, often starting with simple foxholes that could hold one or two soldiers. The holes were then deepened and connected by shallow crawling trenches. From there, the trenches were excavated further underground to strengthen them, and lined with boards to ease movement along the passageways. The boards also helped troops avoid potential diseases caused by mud and dirty water.

Fighting between the trenches took a brutal toll on all sides. One army might take an enemy trench at the cost of thousands of lives, only to lose it again within a matter of weeks. In one battle along the Somme River in France, more than a million soldiers were killed or wounded in order for the Allies to advance

a meager six miles. The space between enemy trenches, called "No Man's Land," had an average width of 150 to 250 yards, but the distance could vary from just a few yards to miles across. Once productive farm fields or lush open meadows, No Man's Land quickly turned into a nightmarish dead landscape filled with rubble, bomb craters, and the bodies of soldiers killed by artillery or machine-gun fire. Sometimes wounded soldiers suffered for days there before they died.

HISTORICAL THINKING

1. **READING CHECK** Why was trench warfare so costly in human lives?

2. **ANALYZE CAUSE AND EFFECT** How did the conclusion of the Franco-Prussian war lead to hostilities between Germany, France, and Britain?

3. **MAKE GENERALIZATIONS** How do militarism and nationalism affect a country's attitude toward going to war?

4. **MAKE INFERENCES** Based on the diagram of trench warfare and what you have read in the chapter, what can you infer about the effectiveness of this type of fighting?

BUILD BACKGROUND

A CONTROVERSIAL PLAN

Count Alfred von Schlieffen, a chief of the German general staff, devised a plan to consolidate the German Empire by defeating both France and Russia in a two-front war. Schlieffen was inspired by Hannibal, a Carthaginian general whose tactics resulted in the defeat of a Roman force in 216 B.C. Schlieffen's plan involved four army groups and a detailed timetable. It relied on continuous forward movement of the army—a departure from German military thinking. One strategist disapproved of the plan because it required the creation of new military units, potentially weakening the regular army. The German navy objected because the plan called for land engagements rather than the building of battleships. Schlieffen first proposed his plan in 1905, but it was not put into action until World War I. At the war's end, German military leaders blamed the plan for Germany's defeat. The Schlieffen Plan was then locked in an archive at Potsdam, where it was destroyed during a British bomber attack on April 14, 1945.

TRENCH WARFARE

Trenches had been used strategically in previous battles and wars, including the Civil War, but they took on a new prominence during World War I. Technological advances to weaponry, such as rapid-fire machine guns and improved artillery, made it necessary to make adjustments to defensive systems, too. Troops responded by building earthen shelters to protect soldiers from the increased firepower and to provide cover from which to fire on the enemy. In addition to soldiers and weapons, trenches housed stores of ammunition, food and areas to prepare it, first-aid supplies, and pits dug for latrines. Networks of trenches could be quite elaborate, including passages along which fresh soldiers, additional supplies, and even mail could be sent.

TEACH

GUIDED DISCUSSION

4. Make Inferences Why do you think one particular event, the assassination of two people, led to the development of a war that spread across and even beyond Europe? *(Answers will vary. Possible responses: Some nations were looking for an excuse to fight or invade other nations, and the assassination provided one. The incident directly affected only a few nations, Austria-Hungary and Serbia, but other nations felt the need to assist nations with whom they were allied.)*

5. Evaluate What circumstances might have helped strategists predict that Germany's Schlieffen Plan might fail? Explain your answer with evidence from the text. *(Answers will vary. Possible response: The plan was completed in 1906 but not carried out until 1914. By then, alliances and the political environment might have changed radically. The plan also relied on conquering the French quickly, which might not have happened for many reasons.)*

ANALYZE PRIMARY SOURCES

Direct students' attention to the Primary Source feature. **ASK:** Which details in Turnbull's account might describe the experience of any soldier who occupied the trenches? *(The trenches were crowded and uncomfortable. Turnbull and his comrades were subjected to sniper attacks. They had poor food and nowhere decent to eat.)* **ASK:** What part of the description applies only to the author? *(his description of making a shelter)* Encourage students to draw a conclusion about the writer's character and to cite evidence for their answer. *(Answers will vary. Possible response: He was resourceful, as evidenced by the way he made a shelter for himself in a communication trench.)*

ACTIVE OPTIONS

Active History: Analyze Causes and Effects of World War I Extend the lesson by using either the PDF or Whiteboard version of the activity. These activities take a deeper look at a topic from, or related to, the lesson. Explore the activities as a class, turn them into group assignments, or even assign them individually.

NG Learning Framework: Present Dramatic Monologues

ATTITUDE Curiosity

KNOWLEDGE Our Human Story

Prompt small groups of students to review the information about trench warfare in the lesson and Primary Source feature and to further research the topic. Groups should use their findings to write a set of dramatic monologues that represent the views of trench warfare from a variety of fighters—from both sides of the war, if possible. For example, monologues might portray a soldier who lived, a soldier who died, a commanding officer, and a medic. Instruct students to think about the context (World War I, early 1900s) as they consider the norms and values of the people they are portraying. Remind them to avoid present-day slang when expressing their characters' views. Allow groups to choose a format for presenting their dramatic monologues, possibly including period photographs and music.

HISTORICAL THINKING

ANSWERS

1. It took a great deal of fighting to capture an enemy trench. Furthermore, in order to advance and secure more territory, soldiers had to cross No Man's Land, where they were completely exposed to the enemy.

2. At the end of the Franco-Prussian War, Germany acquired the French territories of Alsace and Lorraine. Germany further demanded a million dollars from France. As a result, France began rebuilding its military in the hope of reacquiring its lost territories. France also formed an alliance with Britain to that end.

3. Nationalism, the belief that one's country is superior to others, coupled with militarism, the belief that a strong army is essential, can lead to a country's belief that it has both the right and the might to overcome a country that it considers inferior.

4. Trench warfare was not a very effective way to fight because an enormous number of lives could be lost in gaining even a small amount of territory.

CRITICAL VIEWING Answers will vary. Possible response: The artwork was probably intended to symbolize the Allies' unity and inspire confidence in their cause.

WILSON'S NEUTRALITY

In 1914, Americans were eagerly following the baseball pennant race between the New York Giants and the Boston Braves and flocking to the movies to escape into the world of silent films. The guns of war in Europe seemed like distant and muffled thunder.

WILSON'S MORAL DIPLOMACY

In 1914, when the war began in Europe, the United States began to supply the Allies with weapons and goods. However, President Woodrow Wilson firmly declared the country would follow a policy of neutrality, or refusal to support either side in the war. He asked his fellow citizens to "be neutral in fact as well as in name" and "impartial in thought as well as in action." Elected president in 1912, Wilson had wanted to concentrate on a domestic policy of economic reform. In 1913, he remarked to a friend,

"it would be the irony of fate if my administration had to deal chiefly with foreign affairs." When confronted with the question of whether to support one of the warring sides in Europe, Wilson left no doubt of his opinion. "Our whole duty for the present . . . is summed up in the motto America First," he said. "Let us think of America before we think of Europe."

In fact, however, Wilson did actively pursue matters of foreign policy even before being confronted with the war in Europe. Wilson believed in a concept called **moral diplomacy**, which required that the

Woodrow Wilson, shown here giving a speech after his 1912 nomination for president of the United States, had been elected New Jersey's governor in 1910 and was elected U.S. president just two years later.

United States drastically reduce its intervention in the affairs of other countries. Wilson felt that the role of the United States should be to act as an example of democracy and to support the efforts of other peoples to elect their own governments. Wilson contrasted his philosophy to the "dollar diplomacy" practiced by his predecessor. Dollar diplomacy was a theory used to justify U.S. interference with the governments of countries in which American companies stood to make a profit. Pursuing the ideal of moral diplomacy, Wilson tried to lessen U.S. involvement in the Philippines and Latin America.

AMERICAN PUBLIC OPINION

Most Americans were solidly in agreement with Wilson's stance on the war in Europe. Still, many expressed sympathy for one or more of the countries embroiled in the fighting. The United States was home to more than five million German Americans, who tended to favor the Central Powers. The three million-plus Irish Americans strongly resented England and cheered for its enemies. Russia, with its authoritarian government, was generally regarded with suspicion. On the other hand, many Americans felt a kinship with Britain and France, which were both democracies and had a great deal of shared history with the United States.

Germany initiated an extensive propaganda campaign to sway American public opinion in its favor. The campaign was conducted principally through pamphlets and newspaper advertisements. At the same time, the German government used espionage, or spying, and sabotage to harm the Allied war effort by preventing American goods from being shipped to Britain. German agents would find ways to destroy the goods in the United States before they could be loaded onto ships, costing American businesses a great deal of money and sometimes injuring or killing civilians. When instances of sabotage were eventually discovered, they helped turn American public opinion against Germany.

American public opinion of the Central Powers was further soured by stories appearing in the *New York Times* in December 1915, reporting the killing or forced deportation of millions of Armenian civilians by the Turkish government. This campaign by the Turks became known as the **Armenian genocide**.

ECONOMIC TIES

While Americans were divided in their emotional loyalties to the European powers, the U.S. government had close economic ties to the Allies. In 1914, exports to Britain and France totaled $754

million. In contrast, that same year Germany received $190 million worth of imported products from the United States. As the war continued, the economic difference widened. In 1916, exports from the United States to Britain and France stood at $2.75 billion, while trade with Germany had dwindled to practically nothing because the British Navy was blockading German ports.

The United States had other growing financial ties to the Allies. In order to pay for American goods used in their war efforts, the Allies borrowed billions of dollars from the U.S. government, as well as from American banks and investors. Thus, a victory for the Allies would benefit many American investors.

This political cartoon draws attention to the U.S. government's conflicting attitude toward the war. It portrays Uncle Sam advertising peace on the front of his two-sided "sandwich board" and promoting the sale of ammunition to warring countries on the back.

HISTORICAL THINKING

1. **READING CHECK** Why did some Americans favor the Central Powers while others favored the Allies?

2. **COMPARE AND CONTRAST** What are the differences in the principles behind moral diplomacy and dollar diplomacy?

3. **MAKE INFERENCES** Why might a military defeat for the Allies cause a loss to American investors?

INTRODUCE & ENGAGE

PREVIEW WITH VISUALS

Direct students' attention to the political cartoon. **ASK:** Who does the figure in the cartoon represent, and what conflicting policies does he advertise? *(Possible response: He represents the United States. At the same time that he promotes peace, he also offers ammunition for sale—using the war to make a profit.)* Tell students that in this lesson they will learn how the United States struggled with those opposing attitudes when war broke out in Europe.

TEACH

GUIDED DISCUSSION

1. **Compare and Contrast** How were Wilson's policy of neutrality and his belief in moral diplomacy similar, and how were they different? *(Moral diplomacy and neutrality both advocated a lack of intervention into the affairs of other nations. Unlike the policy of neutrality, however, moral diplomacy advocated that the United States should support democracy in other nations.)*

2. **Analyze Cause and Effect** How did acts of sabotage help to shape public opinion in the United States about the war in Europe? *(German agents sometimes sabotaged goods destined for Britain, costing U.S. businesses money and harming American civilians. These actions helped to turn public opinion against Germany.)*

MORE INFORMATION

Woodrow Wilson's Speech While following his policy of neutrality in regards to the war in Europe, President Wilson's interests beyond U.S. borders revolved around the idea that exporting American goods and democratic and capitalistic ideals would be good for the United States and other countries. Share with students the following passage from Woodrow Wilson's 1916 address to the Salesmanship Congress in Detroit, Michigan.

Lift your eyes to the horizons of business: do not look too close at the little processes with which you are concerned, but let your thoughts and your imaginations run abroad throughout the whole world, and with the inspiration of the thought that you are Americans and are meant to carry liberty and justice and the principles of humanity wherever you go, go out and sell goods that will make the world more comfortable and more happy, and convert them to the principles of America.

ASK: How does this passage reflect Wilson's belief in the concept of moral diplomacy? *(President Wilson believed that open markets were an effective way to support democracy in other nations.)*

ACTIVE OPTIONS

On Your Feet: Card Response Tell half the class to write 10 True-False questions based on the lesson. Instruct the other half to create answer cards, writing "True" on one side and "False" on the other side. Students from the first group take turns asking their questions. Students from the second group hold up their cards, showing either "True" or "False."

NG Learning Framework: Write a Letter to the Editor

SKILL Communication

KNOWLEDGE Our Human Story

Ask students to consider the point of view of a German American at the start of World War I. Suggest they think about these issues: attitudes toward the war, neutrality, or sabotage; worries about war in Europe or discrimination in the United States; divided loyalties; growing popular support for the Allies. Instruct students to write a letter for publication in a newspaper, expressing and supporting the point of view a German American may have held in the context of World War I. Students may want to compile the letters into a classroom display or post them on a classroom website.

DIFFERENTIATE

ENGLISH LANGUAGE LEARNERS ELD

Understanding Loan Words Call students' attention to the words *espionage* and *sabotage*. Model the pronunciation and explain that these loan words retain elements of French pronunciation in the final syllable. Pair students at the **Emerging** or **Expanding** levels with proficient English speakers, and ask them to make word cards that include the spelling of each word and its pronunciation. Encourage students to create several sentences using the words and take turns reading them aloud to one another.

PRE-AP

Research "America First" Direct students to research and write a paper about the meaning and use of the phrase "America First" from the time Wilson first used it until the present day. Suggest that students establish Wilson's original meaning, and then choose several examples of how the phrase has been used by others since then. You may wish to suggest students research its use by the America First Committee, which opposed U.S. involvement in WW II, and by nationalists in recent times. Invite students to share their findings with the class and explain why the phrase is controversial.

See the Chapter Planner for more strategies for differentiation.

HISTORICAL THINKING

ANSWERS

1. Many Americans with German backgrounds favored the Central Powers, as did Irish Americans, who generally disliked England. Some Americans favored the Allies because they had business interests with Allied countries or because Britain and France were democracies.

2. Moral diplomacy calls for reduced intervention in the affairs of other nations. Dollar diplomacy justifies interference in the governments of countries in which American companies stand to make a profit.

3. Many American businesses had dealings with Allied nations. An Allied defeat would likely mean a loss of business, the income that business would have produced, and the nonpayment of business loans.

MAIN IDEA Germany's aggressive actions posed an increasing threat to American lives and business, leading the United States to declare war with Germany in 1917.

PRESSURES TO ENTER THE WAR

In 1914, the war in Europe seemed remote. Its violence was taking place on the far side of the ocean and was hardly relevant to life in the United States. By 1917, the war was on America's doorstep, and American blood had been shed.

GERMAN ATTACKS AT SEA

Since colonial times, the U.S. government had generally followed a policy of isolationism by declining to become involved in politics or wars in Europe. Even though certain groups within the United States sympathized with either the Allies or the Central Powers, the American public as a whole saw no reason to depart from the centuries-old policy. Even so, two strong forces were slowly pushing the United States toward engagement in the war: the economic ties with Britain and France that have already been discussed and the risk posed to American lives by the fighting.

American civilians were mainly at risk when they were at sea. Germany was confronted with a British naval blockade that prevented imported goods such as food and ammunition from reaching German ports. In 1914, the German Navy turned to a new

This 1916 campaign button reflected Wilson's isolationist platform.

PREPAREDNESS PEACE WILSON PROSPERITY

weapon to combat the blockade: submarines, also called **U-boats** (short for *unterseeboot*, the German word for "submarine"). German submarines targeted not only enemy warships but also merchant ships that might be carrying war-related supplies from the United States to British or French ports. Even trans-Atlantic passenger ships, which often carried U.S. citizens, were not safe from the U-boats, since they were often suspected of also carrying cargo destined for the Allied war effort.

As you have read, on May 1, 1915, the passenger ship *Lusitania* left New York harbor for Liverpool, England. The *Lusitania* was huge, luxurious, and the fastest ship afloat. Its legendary speed offered no protection, however, when a German submarine encountered the ship in the Irish Sea on May 7 and sank it with a torpedo. Wilson and the nation were angered by the deaths of 129 Americans aboard the ship. The president demanded an apology from the German government, as well as a pledge to limit submarine warfare. Eventually, Germany agreed to **stop attacking civilian ships without warning.**

GERMANY BREAKS ITS PROMISE

Despite the sinking of the *Lusitania* and the deaths of American citizens in other submarine attacks, Wilson refused to join the war. In the 1916 election, he ran on a platform of prosperity, progressivism, and peace. He won re-election after a campaign that featured the slogan "He kept us out of the war." Wilson then proposed ending the war through negotiation, but both Britain and Germany rejected his offer to broker a peace treaty. In response, Wilson addressed the Senate in January 1917 with a speech that called for a "Peace Without Victory" in which he argued that "only a peace among equals can last." The warring powers remained unwilling to cooperate, convinced that the only place to find a solution was the battlefield.

By 1917, the British naval blockade was successfully starving Germany of much-needed war supplies. On land, the Central Powers' armies were bogged down in the trenches and making no progress in either the east or the west. Becoming desperate, Germany decided to resume unrestricted submarine attacks to choke off the stream of supplies arriving in Great Britain by sea. The German military commanders knew this move would enrage Wilson and the American public, but they gambled that all-out submarine warfare would bring down the Allies before the United States could declare war and send troops to Europe.

THE ZIMMERMANN TELEGRAM

At the same time, another incident helped propel the country toward war. British intelligence had intercepted and decoded a secret telegram from the German foreign minister, Arthur Zimmermann, to Germany's ambassador in Mexico. The **Zimmermann Telegram** laid out a plan to ally with Mexico and offer financial aid to the country if it attacked the United States. The telegram promised that Arizona, Texas, and New Mexico would be returned to Mexico as part of this deal. Wilson released this diplomatic bombshell to the public on March 1, 1917.

From that point, events moved quickly to bring the United States to war. On March 18, the Germans sank three American ships. On April 2, Wilson called Congress to a special session and asked for a declaration of war against Germany. He pledged to fight for "the ultimate peace of the world and for the liberation of its peoples, the German peoples included." In many ways, Wilson's war declaration was also an effort to continue promoting America's vision for the world. Congress agreed and declared war on Germany on April 6, 1917.

HISTORICAL THINKING

1. **READING CHECK** What events led President Wilson to ask Congress to formally declare war on Germany?

2. **IDENTIFY PROBLEMS AND SOLUTIONS** Why did Germany choose to launch unrestricted submarine warfare in 1917?

3. **EVALUATE** For Germany, what were the advantages and disadvantages of submarine warfare?

GERMAN U-BOAT

The German U-boat was less than 150 feet long and only 12 feet in diameter. The crew of 35 were packed into a tiny space no bigger than a double-decker bus.

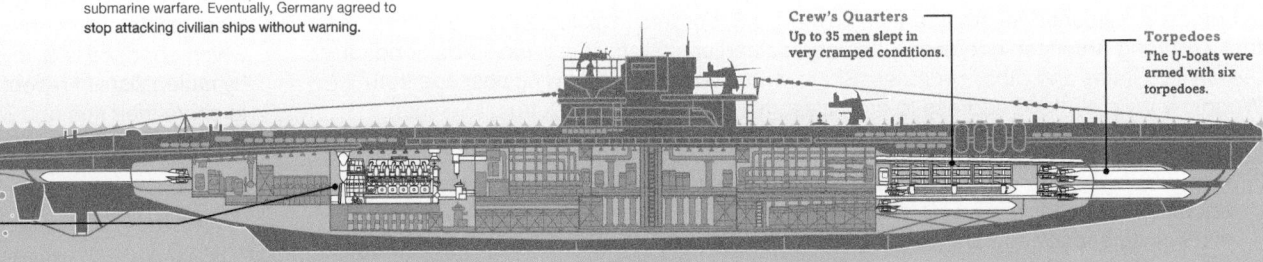

Crew's Quarters
Up to 35 men slept in very cramped conditions.

Torpedoes
The U-boats were armed with six torpedoes.

Ship's Engines
Ship's battery engines generated explosive hydrogen gas.

OBJECTIVE

Discuss how successful naval blockades caused Germany to escalate attacks, pushing the United States to join the war.

CRITICAL THINKING SKILLS FOR LESSON 2.1

• Identify Problems and Solutions
• Evaluate
• Make Inferences
• Form and Support Opinions
• Analyze Primary Sources

HISTORICAL THINKING FOR CHAPTER 17

How did World War I affect the United States politically, economically, and socially? Although business and other interests pulled the United States toward war, Wilson maintained U.S. neutrality for much of World War I. Lesson 2.1 discusses the events that finally pushed the United States to declare war.

BACKGROUND FOR THE TEACHER

Woodrow Wilson was an idealist as well as a pacifist. He envisioned a world in which nations agreed to avoid arms races and in which the United States would help to negotiate peace. As a boy, Wilson had witnessed the Civil War; as president, he was determined not to send American troops into similar conditions in Europe. Even after approving the idea of loans to Britain—prompted by the sinking of the *Lusitania*—Wilson clung to his neutrality stance. Various groups, including the Women's Christian Temperance Union and the United Mine Workers, participated in anti-war rallies that supported Wilson's policy of neutrality. But even Wilson's "Peace Without Victory" speech of January 22, 1917, in which he reiterated his policy of neutrality, could not forestall the United States' entry into war.

INTRODUCE & ENGAGE

TALK ABOUT WINNING

Prompt students to think about various instances in which one person or group faces off against another, such as a sporting event or an argument. **ASK:** What does it mean to be the victor? *(Answers will vary. Possible responses: One side wins, proving it is stronger or better than the other. One side gets what it wants.)* **ASK:** If there is a winner, does there also have to be a loser? *(Possible responses: Yes, both sides cannot be the best. No, there could be a tie, or both could win in different ways.)* **ASK:** What do you think the phrase "Peace Without Victory" means? *(Possible response: It means that both sides agree to end a conflict without declaring that one side won and the other lost.)* Tell students that in this lesson they will learn about President Wilson's ideas about a possible outcome for the war.

TEACH

GUIDED DISCUSSION

1. **Make Inferences** Considering the context of when World War I began, why would Germany expect their new weapon, the U-boat, to be more successful in combating the British blockade? *(U-boats could travel under water, which would have made them difficult for ships of that era to detect.)*

2. **Form and Support Opinions** Was Germany justified in attacking U.S. merchant and passenger ships? Support your answer with evidence from the chapter. *(Answers will vary. Possible responses: No, because Germany and the United States were not at war; yes, because the United States was exporting war supplies to aid the Allies, Germany's enemies.)*

ANALYZE PRIMARY SOURCES

Ask students to reread the Primary Source feature. **ASK:** What does Wilson see as the role of the United States in the world? *(to be one of many nations that seek to preserve people's rights)* **ASK:** To what "sacrifices" do you think he refers? *(Possible responses: the loss of life and injuries in battle; the financial cost of the war; the use of the nation's resources)*

ACTIVE OPTIONS

On Your Feet: Inside-Outside Circle Arrange students in concentric circles facing each other. Direct each student in the outside circle to ask a question about the events leading up to and including the declaration of war against Germany. Each student in the inside circle answers his or her partner's question. On a signal, students should rotate to create new partnerships. On another signal, students trade inside/outside roles.

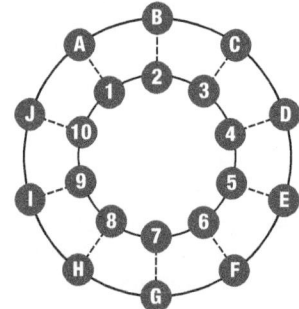

NG Learning Framework: Develop a Presentation

ATTITUDE Curiosity

KNOWLEDGE Our Human Story

Prompt students to work in groups to research the German U-boat campaign during World War I and to develop a presentation based on their research. Suggest that they incorporate a time line into their presentation. Instruct them to include an evaluation of how successful they judge the campaign to have been in the context of World War I. When students have finished, invite groups to make their presentations to the class.

For students who develop an interest in the sinking of the Lusitania *and the effects of U-boat warfare, suggest that they read the American Story at the beginning of this chapter.*

DIFFERENTIATE

STRIVING READERS

Use a Concept Cluster Guide pairs of students to summarize the lesson by creating a Concept Cluster. Tell them to write the lesson title in the center circle and the lesson subheadings in the outer circles: *German Attacks at Sea, Germany Breaks its Promise,* and *The Zimmermann Telegram.* As students read the information under each subheading, prompt them to enter key events on the spokes radiating from each subsection. After students complete their Concept Cluster, invite volunteers to summarize the lesson and explain how various events increased pressure on the United States to enter the war.

GIFTED & TALENTED

Create a Flowchart Instruct students to create a flowchart with dates, events, and visuals that demonstrate President Wilson's changing views from 1914 to 1917 about U.S. involvement in the war. Instruct students to conduct online research focusing on primary sources, including Wilson's speeches, campaign posters, buttons and slogans, as well as newspaper editorials and political cartoons from early 1917. As students present their completed flowcharts to the class, lead a class discussion on how and why President Wilson changed from an isolationist and pacifist to a wartime president.

See the Chapter Planner for more strategies for differentiation.

HISTORICAL THINKING

ANSWERS

1. Germany resumed its U-boat attacks on merchant and passenger ships and sent the Zimmermann Telegram, which urged Mexico to attack the United States.

2. Germany launched unrestricted submarine warfare to stop supplies from reaching Great Britain in the hopes of winning the war before the United States could enter it.

3. Advantage: Submarines were effective in sinking Allied cargo and warships. Disadvantage: Unrestricted submarine warfare increased the risk that the United States would declare war on Germany.

AMERICA ENTERS THE WAR

On every public surface, colorful posters encouraged young men to join the armed forces. Factories converted their assembly lines to make uniforms instead of children's clothes. Americans were asked to have a "meatless" and a "wheatless" day each week so that more food could be sent to Europe. The United States was going to war, and life was changing for everyone.

CRITICAL VIEWING During the war, women were recruited into jobs vacated by men who had gone off to fight. New factory jobs, especially in munitions factories like the ones shown above, were also created as part of the war effort and became the largest employers of women in 1918. How might the work women did during the war have related to their quest for suffrage?

BUILDING A MILITARY—AND FAST

By 1917, both Germany and the Allies were battle weary, and the number of casualties on both sides was staggering. On the Western Front, where the Allies and the Germans confronted each other in France, more than 1.4 million French soldiers had been killed or wounded in 1915 alone. In a single battle at the French town of Verdun in 1916, both sides lost more than 300,000 men. Gigantic battles also occurred on the Eastern Front between the Russians and the Germans and their Austrian allies.

Although American entry into the Great War came later than the Allies had hoped, they greatly welcomed the help. Unfortunately, in 1917, the United States was in a poor position to supply desperately needed soldiers to the Allies; together, the regular U.S. Army and National Guard numbered only 379,000 troops. The power of the federal government began to increase in response to the need to mobilize people for war. In fact, the war initiated a century-long growth of the federal government. Average citizens found they had to respond to government programs in strange and unfamiliar ways, including accepting new rules for their businesses and changing their eating habits.

The government grew first through the administration of the draft. In May 1917, Congress adopted the **Selective Service Act**, which required all men between the ages of 21 and 30 to register for the draft. By the end of World War I, 3.7 million American men would serve as soldiers or sailors. The corps of soldiers sent to fight in Europe was called the **American Expeditionary Forces (AEF)**. At the head of these troops was

General **John J. Pershing**, an experienced military leader who had commanded troops in Cuba, Mexico, and the American West.

THE WARTIME ECONOMY

As the United States entered into the most extensive conflict it had ever faced in terms of dollars, American businesses were also caught unprepared for war. The war effort would require the manufacturing of ships, airplanes, guns, and ammunition, but after a decades-long peacetime economy, American factories were accustomed to producing items like cars, bicycles, and kitchen stoves. They too would need to be readied for war.

To help solve this problem, the government undertook the organization of the war at home. Wilson began by establishing the **War Industries Board (WIB)**. The WIB oversaw manufacturing in the United States, finding ways to make factories more efficient as they converted to wartime production. Some labor unions threw their support behind the war effort and the WIB. In exchange for a voice in deciding economic policy, the American Federation of Labor promised that it would not strike or insist that factories hire only union members. Through the creation of the WIB and other agencies, the federal government increased its role in the U.S. economy.

Outside of the workplace, the government also promoted civilian support for the war. All Americans were asked to buy **Liberty Bonds**. As you have read, purchasing a war bond was, in essence, loaning money to the U.S. government. The government would repay the cost of the bond after 30 years, and in the meantime, the buyer received

annual interest at a rate of 3.5 percent. Those who failed to buy war bonds were deemed unpatriotic and said to be helping the Germans. Ultimately, the total cost of the war to the United States exceeded $35 billion. The United States had loaned over $11.2 billion to the Allies, most of which was never repaid. Yet President Wilson counted on the Allies' financial dependence on the United States to leverage achieving the goals he had for postwar diplomacy.

WARTIME FOOD

In addition to financial support, the Allies needed food. To mobilize the agricultural resources of the United States, Congress passed the Lever Act, which established the Food Administration. Wilson named **Herbert Hoover** to head the agency. A mining engineer from California, Hoover had gained international fame through his work to feed the starving people of Belgium. He asked Americans to observe days without meat and wheat because "wheatless days in America make sleepless nights in Germany." Additionally, families planted "victory gardens" to grow fruits and vegetables. With the price of wheat rising higher, farmers were induced to expand their production, increasing the wheat crop from 637 million bushels in 1917 to 921 million bushels a year later.

PRIMARY SOURCE

Internationally, the Great War led to many important advances for women, including increased support for women's suffrage in the United States.

If the women in the factories stopped work for twenty minutes, the Allies would lose the war.

—Joseph Joffre, French Field Marshall, 1916–1918

What does this quote reveal about the global perspective on the role women played in the Great War?

PLAN: 4-PAGE LESSON

OBJECTIVE

Explore how the federal government made military and economic changes and changes in civil liberties after entering the war.

CRITICAL THINKING SKILLS FOR LESSON 2.2

- Analyze Cause and Effect
- Draw Conclusions
- Interpret Visuals
- Identify Problems and Solutions
- Analyze Language Use
- Compare and Contrast
- Describe

HISTORICAL THINKING FOR CHAPTER 17

How did World War I affect the United States politically, economically, and socially? World War I affected Americans even before the United States joined the war. Lesson 2.2 describes how entering World War I led to the expansion of the U.S. federal government, which created a wartime economy and placed limitations civil liberties.

BACKGROUND FOR THE TEACHER

In the summer of 1917, General John J. Pershing, head of the American Expeditionary Forces, arrived in Paris with the first American troops and was greeted by cheering crowds. With the United States having entered the war in support of France, one of Pershing's aides made a visit to the tomb of a French aristocrat who had supported the American colonies in their war for independence. At the tomb of the Marquis de Lafayette, the aide is reported to have said on Pershing's behalf, "Lafayette, we are here." Lafayette had helped the colonies during the American Revolution, and now the United States was coming to the aid of France.

HISTORY NOTEBOOK

Encourage students to complete the American Gallery page for Chapter 17 in their History Notebooks as they read.

INTRODUCE & ENGAGE

CONNECT TO TODAY

Ask students to imagine that the United States has declared war today. Discuss the following questions:

• How might your daily life change?

• How would you feel if you were ordered to serve in the military?

• How could you or your family contribute to the war effort?

• How would you feel if you had to give up some of your rights, such as freedom of speech?

Tell students that Americans were faced with these kinds of issues when the United States entered the Great War.

TEACH

GUIDED DISCUSSION

1. **Identify Problems and Solutions** What problem kept the United States from immediately supplying troops to the Allies in 1917, and how did the government's solution impact American society? *(The United States had a small military force in 1917. The solution was the military draft created by the Selective Service Act, which required millions of men to register.)*

2. **Analyze Language Use** As World War I unfolded, Herbert Hoover said that "wheatless days in America make sleepless nights in Germany." What did he mean in the context of war? *(He meant that if Americans were willing to go without wheat on occasion, the unused grain could go to feed soldiers in Europe, making them stronger to fight—and, thus, a greater threat to Germany.)*

MORE INFORMATION

Funding the War Having declared war on Germany, the United States was faced with the problem of paying for its involvement. With factories already producing consumer goods at full capacity, retooling them to produce munitions and other necessities of war would be extremely expensive. The government had three options: Print more money, raise taxes, or borrow. The option to print more money was off the table almost immediately, as "greenbacks" printed during the Civil War had resulted in inflation. Instead, the government instituted the Liberty Bonds program and raised individual and corporate income taxes, estate taxes, and excise taxes.

DIFFERENTIATE

INCLUSION

Use Clarifying Questions Allow students with disabilities to work with students who are able to read the lesson aloud to them. Encourage partners to ask and answer clarifying questions. Ask the partner without disabilities to describe the photographs of the women working in munitions factories and the posters from the National World War I Museum. Then prompt partners to work together to answer the Historical Thinking questions.

PRE-AP

Write Diary Entries Instruct students to conduct research using online and print sources to find examples of Americans affected by the Sedition Act. Tell students to choose one person, perhaps from their state, and learn as much as they can about that person's life, work, and family. Then prompt students to use what they've discovered to write diary entries from that person's point of view, concentrating on how the Sedition Act affected his or her life. Suggest that students present their findings in an oral report that includes background information and a dramatic reading of their diary entries.

See the Chapter Planner for more strategies for differentiation.

PRIMARY SOURCE

Joffre's comment reveals a global recognition of the importance of the work that women were doing in the factories, replacing men who left to serve in the military and continuing to produce materials needed to support the Allies.

CRITICAL VIEWING The work women did, often in jobs traditionally done by men, showed that they were equal to men in the workplace, which lent support to their quest for the right to vote.

DISSENT AND CIVIL LIBERTIES

Americans on the home front had mixed reactions to the war. Some were vocal in expressing their dissent, or disagreement, with the government's official opinion. Many men proclaimed themselves **conscientious objectors**—people who refuse to fight in a war for religious reasons—while others simply failed to register for the draft. Opposition to the war was especially prevalent among German Americans and Irish Americans.

To counter possible dissent and raise the country's enthusiasm for the war, the government established the **Committee on Public Information (CPI)**, which launched a massive campaign of advertising and propaganda. George Creel, the head of the committee, declared that its task was to create a spirit of "[brotherhood], devotion, courage, and deathless determination." The CPI used pamphlets, posters, billboards, movies, and dynamic public speakers to spread its message. This was no easy task for Creel, who called it "the world's greatest adventure in advertising."

The campaign stirred up strong feelings of patriotism but also hostility toward everything German. Hamburgers, named after the German town of Hamburg, came to be called "Salisbury steak" or "liberty steak." Sauerkraut was renamed "liberty cabbage," and the people in some cities gave up pretzels. German literature vanished from library shelves, and schools stopped teaching the German language. More alarming, German Americans experienced prejudice and extreme nativism, or a policy that favors the interests of native inhabitants over those of immigrants, and became the targets of suspicion, threats, and even violence.

The government had legitimate reasons to be concerned about German espionage, but the measures taken to combat it during the war were excessive. The government began a campaign against radicals and progressives, a position that Wilson had opposed during his run for re-election in 1916. This reversal of policy undermined public support for the president in domestic politics. In his eagerness to win the war, Wilson alienated part of his own political base.

ENSURING PATRIOTIC BEHAVIOR

The Wilson administration and Congress enacted a number of laws designed to place limits on the rights of Americans to criticize the government or the war effort. National Security concerns led to the passage and enforcement of the Espionage Act of

ARE YOU A SLACKER?

Nobody likes to be called a slacker, but nowadays acting like one will only get you in trouble with a teacher, parent, or boss. In 1917 and 1918, the term "slacker" referred to a man who failed to register for the draft or declare a conscientious objection. At first, the government tried using publicity to shame slackers into registering. Then, in 1918, the Justice Department took more serious steps. Agents began raiding restaurants and ballparks or just approaching groups on street corners. Any man who could not show draft registration papers was promptly arrested and taken to jail.

1917. The act was designed to prevent sabotage and spying, but simply speaking out against the war could be considered illegal. The Trading with the Enemy Act authorized the postmaster general to suspend the delivery of foreign-language publications or any material he believed might be offensive to the government.

The Sedition Act of 1918 prohibited "uttering, printing, writing, or publishing any disloyal, profane, scurrilous [slanderous], or abusive language" about either the government or the armed forces. Thus, nearly any public criticism could be deemed punishable by law in an attempt to prevent sedition, the criminal act of trying to persuade individuals to undermine the government. These acts severely encroached on Americans' **civil liberties**—the right to engage in legal activities such as free expression without being hindered by the government. People were even jailed for making negative comments about Woodrow Wilson or calling the conflict a "rich man's war."

HISTORICAL THINKING

1. **READING CHECK** What steps did the U.S. government take to prepare for war?

2. **ANALYZE CAUSE AND EFFECT** How did entering the war affect the organization of the economy of the United States?

3. **DRAW CONCLUSIONS** How did the government's actions both unite and divide Americans?

4. **INTERPRET VISUALS** Select one of the propaganda posters (right) and consider its purpose. Who was its intended audience and what techniques were used to make the poster effective?

National World War I Museum and Memorial Kansas City, Missouri

The National World War I Museum in Kansas City, Missouri, is positioned beneath the Liberty Memorial, a 217-foot granite monument to the veterans of World War I. The museum opened in 2006 to national acclaim and was recognized by Congress in 2014 as the National World War I Museum and Memorial. More than one million people have visited the museum, including presidents and American veterans like Frank Buckles, the country's last surviving Great War veteran.

The museum houses a vast collection of World War I-era propaganda posters, including those pictured here. Their high-interest, colorful graphics and thought-provoking messages called Americans to action and attempted to inspire great patriotism.

Shortly after the start of the war, the poster was recognized as an effective way to distribute national propaganda to a wide audience cheaply, vividly, and quickly. In almost every country involved in the war, posters like these played a significant role in spreading patriotism.

This poster features Uncle Sam and Germany's ruler, Kaiser, or emperor, Wilhelm II.

Posters encouraged people to plant victory gardens at home to provide food for soldiers.

Prominent studios produced short propaganda films to foster pro-war public sentiments.

BUILD BACKGROUND

VICTORY GARDENS

As head of the U.S. Food Administration, Herbert Hoover had power over just about everything involving food, from purchasing to storage and distribution. Americans took to heart his comment that "food will win the war," planting vegetables and fruit not just in their backyards but in many other kinds of yards and parks. In fact, Americans were encouraged to consume fresh fruits and vegetables because those foods could not easily be sent overseas. Hoover's efforts to decrease consumption became known as "Hooverizing," and Hoover is credited with keeping the United States from having to impose wartime rationing. After the war, Hoover continued to send large quantities of food to Europe, where farms and food distribution chains had been disrupted by wartime activities.

TRADING WITH THE ENEMY

Shortly after the United States entered World War I, Congress enacted the Trading with the Enemy Act of 1917, its purpose being to oversee trade with enemies of the United States and its allies. According to the act and executive orders that followed, all property located within the United States but belonging to the enemy was placed under control of an "Alien Property Custodian." In addition, the Federal Trade Commission (FTC) received the power to control enemy-owned patents, which covered a wide range of products. Such measures had far-reaching consequences, as the FTC further gained the right to set conditions for how products were to be used and to fix prices for synthetic drugs used at that time.

TEACH

GUIDED DISCUSSION

3. **Compare and Contrast** How were the attitudes and related behavior of conscientious objectors and slackers alike, and how were they different? *(Both groups opposed serving in the war. Conscientious objectors declared their position to the government, but slackers did not. Unlike conscientious objectors, slackers did not register for the draft.)*

4. **Describe** How did the U.S. entry into World War I connect to the social and political developments regarding the civil liberties of ordinary Americans? *(Possible response: Congress passed the Espionage Act of 1917, the Trading with the Enemy Act, and the Sedition Act of 1918. Together, these acts limited and even punished some previously legal activities such as speaking or writing critically about the government or reading foreign-language publications.)*

VIRTUAL MUSEUM VISIT

Access the National World War I Museum's website and then find and read aloud the museum's mission statement. Ask students to identify the three goals of the museum. *(remembering, interpreting, and understanding the war and its impact)* Then ask small groups to explore the site on their own and choose an online exhibition to visit. Groups should summarize the exhibit for the class and explain how the exhibit fulfills one or more of the museum's goals.

ACTIVE OPTIONS

On Your Feet: Team Word Webbing Arrange students in groups of four and provide each group with a large sheet of paper. Tell group members to take turns contributing a detail to a word web with the topic *America Prepares for War* at the center. When time for the activity has elapsed, call on a volunteer from each group to share the group's web.

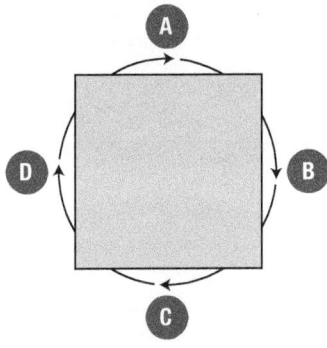

AMERICAN GALLERY ONLINE **Selling World War I at Home** Invite students to explore the American Gallery. Have them select one of the images and do additional research to learn more about it. Ask questions that will inspire additional inquiry about the chosen gallery image, such as: Who or what is the subject of the image? How does it relate to the war in Europe?

HISTORICAL THINKING

ANSWERS

1. Preparation for war included enacting the Selective Service Act, creating the War Industries Board, and issuing Liberty Bonds.

2. The war gave the federal government a larger role in the economy. Factories converted to production of wartime goods, such as ammunition and airplanes, and women entered the workforce in great numbers to replace men who served in the armed forces.

3. Government propaganda united many Americans by instilling a sense of patriotism, but a government campaign against radicals and progressives alienated others.

4. Answers will vary. Students should support their ideas using evidence from the poster's images, visual style, and wording.

MAIN IDEA Millions of American soldiers arrived in Europe and engaged in fighting made more deadly than ever before by advanced weapons technology and unsanitary conditions in the trenches.

A BRUTAL WAR

The trainee pilots were young and hopeful. They were eager to engage in daring aerial duels against the Germans, just like the glamorous Allied flying aces they idolized. Within weeks of their arrival in Europe, at least half of these young flyers died in action.

LETHAL TECHNOLOGY

When they arrived in France, American troops entered a war unlike any fought before. New technologies, as well as improvements to existing military machines, led to enormous numbers of casualties in every battle. **Machine guns**, for example, had existed since the late 1800s, but they were refined and improved over the course of World War I. Mounted atop trenches and able to fire hundreds of bullets per minute, machine guns could mow down attacking soldiers much more efficiently than single-shot rifles.

To counter the machine gun, the British invented the **tank**, an armored, heavily armed vehicle that used treads instead of wheels. Tanks could cross No Man's Land in the face of intense machine-gun fire and plow directly into enemy trenches. By the end of the war, both sides were using tanks to assault enemy lines.

This rotary engine came from the red Fokker Dr.1 Triplane of German ace pilot, the Red Baron.

For the first time ever, war also took to the skies. Only 11 years after the Wright brothers' first flight, airplanes were transformed into fighting machines and deployed over the battlefield. Pilots used cameras to take photos of enemy troop movements on the ground. German and Allied pilots engaged in one-on-one battles in the air, guiding their planes through acrobatic maneuvers high above the ground. At first, the pilots shot at each other with pistols, but eventually guns were installed on the planes themselves.

Being a pilot was extremely dangerous. On average, a new pilot survived three to six weeks in combat conditions. The most famous flyer on the Allied side was American ace fighter pilot, Eddie Rickenbacker, who was credited with shooting down 26 enemy planes. His impressive attack on 7 German aircraft in September 1918 earned him the U.S. Medal of Honor. On the opposing side, German Manfred von Richtofen, known as the Red Baron, was considered the ace of aces and credited with shooting down 80 Allied planes.

Nowhere near as nimble as airplanes, but also useful, were airships—also called dirigibles—whose cockpits were held aloft by gigantic rigid balloons filled with lighter-than-air gas. Airships could conduct aerial surveillance of enemy troop movements. Countering both planes and airships was the **antiaircraft gun**, a piece of heavy artillery modified so that it could be pointed skyward.

At sea, the Allies used a new strategy to end the threat of German submarines to Allied shipping. Convoys of destroyers and other warships—whose torpedoes, guns, and depth charges (bombs designed to explode under water) could easily sink a German submarine—surrounded and protected vulnerable merchant ships as they crossed the Atlantic. Escorted across the Atlantic by destroyers and other patrol vessels, these otherwise defenseless merchant vessels could move safely in groups.

612 CHAPTER 17

WARBIRDS OF WORLD WAR I

The first aircraft used in World War I were extremely basic. Vulnerable pilots sat in open cockpits using unsophisticated and sometimes nonfunctional instruments. Navigation devices didn't exist, so they relied on paper maps and glimpses of the railway signs down below them. Sometimes lost pilots even landed in fields and asked directions! But air technology advanced throughout the war, and increasingly effective aircraft replaced the simple machines that took to the skies in 1914, transforming the airplane into a war machine.

BRITISH SOPWITH CAMEL BIPLANE
This plane's unusual name came from the slight hump in front of the cockpit. It shot down more German aircraft than any other Allied plane using twin machine guns that easily destroyed its flimsy opponents.

NIEUPORT 28
War hero Eddie Rickenbacker and many other American pilots flew these biplanes, which had a distinctive pair of machine guns mounted on their left sides.

SPAD XIII
Known as one of the most successful fighter planes of the Great War, this plane was widely used by French, American, and other Allied squadrons. Nearly 8,500 of them were produced.

FOKKER D VII
This popular German biplane was one of the best World War I fighters and was considered easy to fly, highly maneuverable, and safe. The Red Baron endorsed it wholeheartedly.

NORTH SEA 6 AIRSHIP
Along with the NS7, this airship became one of the more famous North Sea Class airships of the Great War. It could fly for 30 hours or more, escorting convoys and hunting for submarines.

The Great War 613

INTRODUCE & ENGAGE

COMPARE TECHNOLOGIES

Ask students to name examples of technology used in current wars. Use a chart like the one shown here to list the examples. Invite students to suggest examples of technology that might have been invented and used during World War I. Add their suggestions to the chart. Finally, have students list examples of technology used in earlier wars around the world. Tell students to copy the chart and update it as they read about technology during World War I. If time permits, revisit the chart after students have read the lesson, and discuss how weapons technology has evolved over time.

Weapons in War Today	Weapons in World War I	Weapons in Earlier Wars

TEACH

GUIDED DISCUSSION

1. **Compare and Contrast** How was World War I weapons technology similar to and different from that used in previous wars? *(Possible response: Technology was similar in that guns continued to be used as weapons. Differences included the use of machine guns, tanks, airplanes and dirigibles, and antiaircraft guns.)* Students may add this information to the chart begun in the Introduce & Engage activity and expand their answer after reading the rest of the lesson.

2. **Identify Problems and Solutions** What problem did Allied forces encounter while shipping goods and supplies, and what solution did they devise? *(The problem was that German submarines hunted and destroyed Allied merchant ships. The Allies overcame the problem by using warships to escort and protect the merchant ships.)*

ANALYZE VISUALS

Direct students' attention to the illustration of the various "warbirds." Ask students to determine which planes were flown by the Allies and which were flown by the Central Powers. *(Allies: the Sopwith Camel, Nieuport 28, SPAD XIII, and NS6 and NS7 airships; Central Powers: the Fokker D VII)* **ASK:** How does the airship differ, in design and function, from the planes shown? *(The airship is larger than the planes, and it has a very different design. Its purpose was to hunt for submarines and escort convoys rather than to engage individual enemy pilots.)*

DIFFERENTIATE

ENGLISH LANGUAGE LEARNERS ELD

Read in Pairs Pair English language learners at the **Emerging** or **Expanding** level with English-proficient speakers, and have them read the lesson together. Instruct English language learners to ask their partners to pause whenever they hear a word or sentence construction that is confusing.

Provide the following sentence frames to help students at different proficiency levels clarify information.

- **Emerging:** Please help me understand this (word, sentence, paragraph).

- **Expanding:** I need some help understanding this (word, sentence, paragraph).

Suggest that English-proficient speakers point out context clues to help their partners understand the meanings of unfamiliar terms or constructions. Encourage English language learners to restate sentences in their own words.

GIFTED & TALENTED

Illustrate War Trauma Challenge students to interpret visually the phrase *shell shock*, conveying what happens when minds and bodies are pushed to the limit by battlefield stress and trauma. For example, students may create a drawing, painting, collage, or digitally altered photograph incorporating World War I scenes and metaphorical representations of psychological states. You may encourage students to expand their research and incorporate contemporary visuals related to veterans suffering from post-traumatic stress disorder (PTSD) that indicate what has been learned about diagnosing and treating this condition since World War I. Invite students to present their artistic renderings to the class and answer questions about their work.

See the Chapter Planner for more strategies for differentiation.

AMERICANS ON THE WESTERN FRONT

In 1917, the situation for Britain and France took a dangerous turn when a revolution overturned the monarchy in Russia. The country's new government pulled out of the war, which freed the German troops from the Eastern Front to go fight in the west. At the same time, few American troops had arrived to reinforce the Western Front.

But in 1918, millions of American soldiers poured into France to turn the tide against Germany and eventually helped bring an end to the war. In contrast to the Allied troops, who were exhausted after years of brutal fighting, the Americans were fresh and well fed. In May 1918, one million American troops helped stop the German advance at the town of Cantigny.

Many members of minority groups who experienced discrimination at home served with distinction on the battlefields of Europe. A number of Asian Americans chose to serve in the armed forces and received U.S. citizenship as a result. Many Hispanic Americans from Texas and New Mexico also fought, although some refused to register for the draft to protest the discrimination they faced in everyday life. African-American leaders debated the merits of serving in the armed forces of a country that did not grant them equal rights. Still, thousands of black men did serve in segregated army units in Europe. With the exception of three exclusive fighting divisions, most African Americans were assigned behind-the-scenes duties instead of combat roles with white soldiers. But their wartime experience broadened the soldiers' views. Young men serving abroad found European ideas about race and sexuality very liberating.

HAZARDS FOR SOLDIERS

Charging into a barrage of machine-gun fire wasn't the only danger to soldiers fighting in the trenches. The Germans first used poison gas in 1915, but eventually both sides employed this fearsome weapon. Tossed into enemy trenches, the gas caused agonizing pain and killed soldiers by suffocation. After the Great War, most countries banned the use of poison gas. In addition, exposure to intense bombardment while in the trenches sent some soldiers home with physical injuries and others with a new syndrome known as "shell shock," a disorder brought on by the stress of war. Now known as PTSD, or post-traumatic stress disorder, symptoms included extreme nervousness, inability to sleep, and other severe emotional problems.

The trenches themselves posed other dangers to soldiers. Heavy rains filled the trenches with water

and mud, leading to diseases such as trench foot, which was caused by standing for hours in cold water with no possibility of changing into dry socks or boots. A severe case of trench foot could require amputation. Even the mud that filled the trenches could pose a drowning hazard for wounded soldiers waiting for medical assistance.

Many of the lesser-known heroes of World War I were women. Women and men drove ambulances, ferrying the sick and wounded from the front to hospitals behind the lines. The majority of the corps of nurses who treated the injured and comforted the dying were women. **Julia C. Stimson**, an American nurse, arrived at an army hospital in France just weeks after the United States joined the war. She was later appointed chief nurse of the Red Cross in France and then head of the nursing services of the American Expeditionary Forces. After the war, Stimson was awarded medals by the United States, Britain, and France for her bravery and life-saving service.

🏛 The National Portrait Gallery, Washington, D.C.

W.E.B. Du Bois, an African-American historian and author, is pictured here in Winold Reiss's 1925 drawing. In 1909, Du Bois helped found the National Association for the Advancement of Colored People (NAACP), which fought for equal rights for African Americans. He supported the war effort but believed the patriotism and heroism of African-American soldiers was not appropriately acknowledged or rewarded.

CRITICAL VIEWING The African-American soldiers of the 369th Infantry from New York City, nicknamed the "Harlem Hellfighters," fought with the French and were the first Americans to receive the French Croix de Guerre (War Cross) for Gallantry. What questions does this image—and what you've learned in this lesson—raise for you about the experiences African Americans had in the Great War?

PRIMARY SOURCE

The day has been tremendous, and the first in which I have not lost a life. We soldiers are hard pressed these days. The wounded pour in day and night by trains, by American autos too, but I can't take a minute to run out to salute my countrymen [American ambulance drivers]. We discharge our patients as fast as we can, and bury dozens a week. It is all like a weird dream, laughter (for they laugh well, the soldiers) and blood and death and funny episodes, and sublime also, all under the autumn stars.

—from *Mademoiselle Miss*, letters from an American nurse in France, entry dated October 27, 1915

HISTORICAL THINKING

1. **READING CHECK** How did women and minorities contribute to the war effort in Europe?

2. **DRAW CONCLUSIONS** Why did the Great War have more casualties than previous wars?

3. **ANALYZE CAUSE AND EFFECT** What effect does war have on the development of technology?

4. **EVALUATE** In 1918, W.E.B. Du Bois wrote in the NAACP's monthly journal that "while the war lasts [we should] forget our special grievances and close our ranks shoulder to shoulder with our white fellow citizens and allied nations that are fighting for democracy." This was viewed by some as puzzling, given his views on racial equality. What do you think about Du Bois's statement, based on what you know about the civil rights movement?

BUILD BACKGROUND

RUSSIA'S EXIT FROM THE WAR

Although Russia fought on the side of the Allies, its participation went badly and made many existing problems worse. Russia could not support a war; its soldiers didn't have enough weapons, ammunition, or food to fight effectively. In addition, Russia's troops were poorly led, and Germany constantly outfought Russia. By October 1916, millions of Russian soldiers had been wounded, killed, or captured. At this same time, Russia's factory and farm production collapsed, creating terrible shortages of fuel and food. Most Russians blamed their suffering on Czar Nicholas II, head of the Russian Empire, paving the way for the revolution that would take Russia out of the war.

CHEMICAL WARFARE

World War I is sometimes known as "the chemist's war," due to the large-scale use of chemical weapons. The French first used gas as a weapon whose purpose was not to kill but to render soldiers unable to fight. The Germans used poison gas, initially chlorine, in 1915 against the French, but the British picked up the idea quickly. However, the gas sometimes blew back into the faces of the attackers, incapacitating them as well. Later, troops used phosgene and mustard gas, which were more lethal. Mustard gas damaged lungs and raised blisters on skin. These poison gases were the most feared weapons of the war, and both sides quickly developed gas masks. Over the course of the war, gas killed about 10 percent of its victims, but it left hundreds of thousands with long-lasting damage.

TEACH

GUIDED DISCUSSION

3. **Determine Word Meaning** How does the term *shell shock* describe a condition that some soldiers suffered as a result of the war? *(Answers will vary. Possible response: For some soldiers, the experience of being shelled by the enemy resulted not in lost limbs or other physical problems but in severe mental or emotional stress, or "shock.")*

4. **Form and Support Opinions** What do you think the main impact might have been if American troops had not arrived in Europe in 1918? Explain whether and how you think the war might have gone in a different direction. *(Answers will vary. Possible response: The Allies might have lost the war—they desperately needed America's military might, not just its supplies.)*

🏛 VIRTUAL MUSEUM VISIT

According to its website, the National Portrait Gallery's collections are designed to bring visitors, whether online or in person, "face to face with America." In addition to the portraits themselves, the collections include information about the subjects of the portraits. Exhibitions are arranged according to various themes, such as Presidential Portraits and Women's Suffrage. Direct pairs of students to access the gallery's website, find other portraits relating to World War I, and choose a work to present to the class. Encourage students to explain how the work they chose can help viewers come "face to face with America."

ACTIVE OPTIONS

On Your Feet: Roundtable Discussion Have students sit in groups of four around a table. Ask them to discuss the following question: How did World War I change the way war was fought? Provide each group with a large sheet of paper. Tell group members to take turns jotting down as many answers to the question as possible. Encourage them not only to include warfare technology but also to make other connections—numbers of nations, people killed, alliances, impact on medical personnel such as the nurse cited in the Primary Source feature, and any other response they can justify to show ways in which World War I was different from previous wars. When time for the activity has elapsed, call on a representative from each group to share the group's ideas. You may wish to compile a master list of responses.

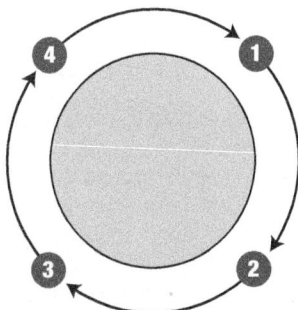

NG Learning Framework: Explore Warfare Technology STEM

SKILLS Observation, Collaboration

KNOWLEDGE Our Human Story

Ask students to revisit the lesson's information about the new warfare technology and its effect on the war. Students then should work in pairs to create a list of observations about one specific new weapon and how its use affected battlefield operations, the troops themselves, and perhaps civilian populations during or after the war. Once students have completed their list of observations, each pair should exchange lists with another pair and discuss the new list.

HISTORICAL THINKING

ANSWERS

1. Women drove ambulances and served as nurses. Members of several American minorities fought in the war or served behind the front lines in support roles.

2. Advanced technologies resulted in deadlier weapons; furthermore, conditions of trench warfare were hazardous and unsanitary.

3. War results in the development of more advanced technology as each side tries to gain an offensive advantage and then must improve its own defenses against the other side's improved weapons.

4. Answers will vary. Possible response: Du Bois may have felt that fighting alongside white soldiers would change negative attitudes toward African Americans and advance the civil rights movement.

CRITICAL VIEWING Answers will vary. Possible response: Why did the U.S. Army segregate African-American soldiers?

CRITICAL VIEWING Stairs lead from the relative safety of an underground quarry to the trenches. What sorts of challenges might soldiers have faced while living below ground?

Carving of "the disasters of the 20th century"

German military leader Field Marshal Paul von Hindenburg

THROUGH THE LENS

JEFFREY GUSKY

During World War I, some troops took refuge in centuries-old underground cities in northeastern France. They left their mark in the soft limestone in the form of signatures, sketches, carvings, and relief sculptures. National Geographic photographer Jeffrey Gusky captured the intimate stories of these soldiers, many of whom never made it out from the trenches.

French officer

German infantryman

U.S. troops of the 26th "Yankee Division did around 500 carvings during the 6 weeks they spent in an underground quarry in France in 1918.

616 CHAPTER 17

The Great War 617

PLAN: 2-PAGE LESSON

OBJECTIVE

Discover the carvings and drawings that soldiers in World War I inscribed on cave walls in France.

CRITICAL THINKING SKILLS FOR LESSON 3.2

- Analyze Visuals
- Make Connections
- Draw Conclusions
- Make Inferences

HISTORICAL THINKING FOR CHAPTER 17

How did World War I affect the United States politically, economically, and socially? The United States mobilized its military to help the Allies win the war. Trench warfare resulted in soldiers enduring devastating conditions in the trenches. Lesson 3.2 displays the carvings and sketches that soldiers created in the quarries beneath the trenches to pass the time and tell their stories.

NATIONAL GEOGRAPHIC PHOTOGRAPHER
JEFFREY GUSKY

National Geographic photographer and physician Jeffrey Gusky has documented a network of underground cities from World War I. These cities lay beneath World War I trenches in the French countryside. A French government official introduced Gusky to local officials residing along what was the Western Front. These officials then introduced Gusky to the local residents, who revealed their secrets about many hidden WWI remnants both above and below the ground. To photograph the underground cities, Gusky had to work in total darkness, often crawling through small holes in the ground or climbing over jagged rocks.

HISTORY NOTEBOOK

Encourage students to complete the Through the Lens page for Chapter 17 in their History Notebooks as they read.

INTRODUCE & ENGAGE

PREVIEW WITH VISUALS

Direct students to the photographs in the lesson. Ask students what they think the photographs show. Point out that, in addition to a passageway, the photos show carvings that soldiers during World War I created while living in the trenches in France. Discuss with students why they think soldiers would have wanted to create these carvings.

TEACH

GUIDED DISCUSSION

1. **Draw Conclusions** What do you think the carvings indicate about the soldiers and life in the trenches? *(Answers will vary. Possible response: The detail in the carvings and the number of carvings indicate that soldiers spent a great deal of time living in the trenches. The carvings also seem to indicate that the soldiers wanted to tell a story about their experiences in and feelings about the war.)*

2. **Make Inferences** Soldiers in the underground cities often left inscriptions on the walls, such as their names, hometowns, and addresses. Considering the context in which these events unfolded, why do you think they might have wanted to leave that kind of information behind? *(Answers will vary. Possible response: The soldiers faced the possibility of dying in the war at any moment. They wanted to leave behind evidence that they were there, and that their contributions to the war mattered. They wanted people to remember them.)*

THROUGH THE LENS

Although many people think that World War I was a trench war, in actuality it went even deeper. As the soldiers dug their trenches, they discovered quarries and caves below the forests of northeastern France. Soldiers would rotate from the front lines down to these underground spaces for rest and refuge. In these quarries and caves, soldiers created offices, kitchens, and artwork, which have remained unchanged for the last 100 years. Very few people were aware of their existence. But Jeffrey Gusky's photography has brought awareness to more people of these underground cities and the objects and wall artwork found there. Soldiers left behind their boots, beds, and equipment as well as carvings and inscriptions that revealed soldiers' personal information, such as their religion, poetry they liked, and favorite sports teams. The U.S. soldiers of the 26th "Yankee" Division appeared to be the most productive artists during their six-week stay underground in 1918.

ACTIVE OPTIONS

On Your Feet: Descriptive Words Distribute five sticky notes to each student. Then have students closely examine each photograph. Direct students to write one word or a short phrase describing each photograph on one sticky note. Tell students to place their notes on the board or a wall. As a class, discuss the posted descriptions.

NG Learning Framework: Write a Photo Caption

SKILL Observation

KNOWLEDGE Our Human Story

Have students learn more about the WWI carvings photographed by Jeffery Gusky. Direct students to Gusky's website to find additional carvings that Gusky recorded with his camera. Ask students to choose two photographs and write a caption for each photograph that describes what soldier's story each photograph captured. Hold a class discussion in which students discuss why they think the soldiers chose to carve those particular items.

DIFFERENTIATE

INCLUSION

Visual Partners Pair visually impaired students with sighted students to interpret the photographs in this lesson. Ask sighted students to describe each of the visuals in the lesson to the visually impaired students. Remind partners to identify details in the photographs and to discuss why they think the soldiers included what they did in the carvings.

GIFTED & TALENTED

Create a Carving Have students review the photographs and the information in this lesson. Discuss what soldiers during World War I carved in the quarries and why they might have chosen to inscribe those items. Then have students think about what kinds of things or feelings soldiers fighting in a war today might choose to illustrate and leave behind. Direct students to either describe what the soldiers might illustrate or actually draw what they might leave behind for others to see. Ask students to share their illustrations and to explain the reasons for their choices.

See the Chapter Planner for more strategies for differentiation.

CRITICAL VIEWING Answers will vary. Possible response: It must have felt cramped and airless, and it must have been strange not to see daylight for long periods of time. It might also have been a damp and unhealthy environment.

MAIN IDEA The war abroad and reform movements at home combined to bring about changes in social and economic conditions for many Americans. At the same time, the world confronted a massive, deadly outbreak of a familiar disease.

THE HOME FRONT

Life didn't come to a halt in the United States while the young men fought overseas. The war accelerated far-reaching social changes that had already begun in America's cities, workplaces, and among the voting public. When the soldiers returned, they would find that home was not exactly the way they had left it.

The Phillips Collection, Washington, D.C.

Jacob Lawrence is considered one of the most influential visual artists of the 20th century. The painting above is Panel 1 of his 1941 series, *The Migration of the Negro*. This 60-painting collection pays tribute to southern African Americans, including his parents, who fled to cities in the American North and West during the Great Migration. To escape racial inequality, many migrants landed in cities like New York, St. Louis, and Chicago, transforming the culture, music, and politics of these locations.

Jacob Lawrence, "Panel 1," from "The Migration Series," credit: © 2017 The Jacob and Gwendolyn Knight Lawrence Foundation, Seattle / Artists Rights Society (ARS), New York

THE WAR'S IMPACT AT HOME

Nearly every racial or ethnic group in the United States was affected by economic and cultural changes brought about by the war. As you've read, German Americans were viewed with suspicion by their fellow citizens. German Americans lost connections with their culture, as German-language newspapers were shut down, and speaking German in public was banned in half the states. Dissenters of any national background suffered a similar fate, being viewed with hostility by other Americans and persecuted by the government.

Some minority groups saw more positive changes. Jewish Americans had formerly been grouped according to their country of origin in Europe. Now they united to play a stronger international role by forming charities and donating millions to help victims of the war. Mexican American workers living in the southern and southwestern states moved north to follow job opportunities that opened up in factories when young men enlisted. Many women, too, left their traditional roles to take paying jobs in factories, offices, or loading docks.

For African Americans, the war years brought enormous changes. In the South, a variety of natural disasters crippled southern agriculture, which resulted in increasingly poor job prospects for black farm workers. African Americans had begun leaving the South for cities in the North around 1910, a mass movement known as the **Great Migration**. The outbreak of the war played a key role in this process. As immigration from Europe ended and white American factory workers enlisted, thousands of jobs opened up in industrial centers in northern cities. Between 1914 and 1920, more than 600,000 African Americans moved north.

African Americans who moved to these centers, however, were often met with hostility. And even after the war, the prospect of improved rights for African Americans remained bleak. The Wilson administration and the Democratic Party resisted efforts to reduce racism, and harsh policies toward black Americans persisted in many states.

PROHIBITION

At the start of the 20th century, saloons could be found in cities throughout the United States. They not only served beer and other alcoholic drinks, they offered places where working men could gather to socialize. Women were not permitted to enter a saloon—and many didn't want to. Reform organizations, such as the Anti-Saloon League and the Women's Christian Temperance Union, believed saloons encouraged drunkenness and overspending by men. Feeling that they were defending their families, many women supported **Prohibition**—making the sale of liquor illegal.

During the war, the Prohibition movement gained ground because the grain used to make beer was needed for food, and because most brewers (beer makers) were German. In December 1917, Congress approved the **18th Amendment** to the Constitution, prohibiting the sale of alcohol in the United States. The amendment was ratified after the war, in January 1919. Congress also passed the **Volstead Act**, which contained measures to enforce Prohibition.

In 1910, the National Woman's Christian Temperance Union (NWCTU) produced this "Vote No" Prohibition postcard. "Vote no" refers to localized "no license" campaigns that attempted to deny the license renewals of taverns in order to protect children and preserve family unity and values.

PLAN: 4-PAGE LESSON

OBJECTIVE

Analyze the social upheaval of the Great Migration, Prohibition, the woman suffrage movement, and the flu pandemic.

CRITICAL THINKING SKILLS FOR LESSON 3.3

- Make Generalizations
- Evaluate
- Form and Support Opinions
- Make Inferences
- Analyze Cause and Effect
- Identify
- Determine Chronology
- Analyze Primary Sources

HISTORICAL THINKING FOR CHAPTER 17

How did World War I affect the United States politically, economically, and socially? World War I brought about social and cultural changes in the United States. Lesson 3.3 discusses the Great Migration, as well as events leading up to the enactment of the 18th and 19th amendments.

BACKGROUND FOR THE TEACHER

African Americans who came to the North secured work in the coal mines of West Virginia, the stockyards of Chicago, and the steel mills of Pittsburgh. Sixty thousand African Americans moved to Chicago between 1916 and 1920, representing a 148 percent increase in the city's African-American population. Similar increases occurred in Pittsburgh, Cincinnati, and Detroit. As their population in the North grew, African Americans encountered discrimination in housing and public services, including from long-standing residents of African-American communities in northern cities who looked down on the new arrivals. Nevertheless, southern African Americans continued to move north in a historic population shift that reshaped the politics and culture of the nation's largest cities.

HISTORY NOTEBOOK

Encourage students to complete the Home Front page for Chapter 17 in their History Notebooks as they read.

INTRODUCE & ENGAGE

USE VISUALS AS A SPRINGBOARD

Direct students' attention to the visuals in this lesson—the painting, the postcard, the photograph, and the poster. Draw a T-Chart on the board, labeling the fist column Visuals and the second column Questions. Ask students what questions these visuals bring to mind. Record their questions in the T-Chart. Later, after students have read and discussed the lesson, prompt them to answer as many of the listed questions as they can.

Visuals	Questions

TEACH

GUIDED DISCUSSION

1. **Make Inferences** How were German Americans viewed by their fellow Americans during World War I, and why? *(German Americans were often viewed with suspicion by other Americans. The United States was at war with Germany, causing many people to think that German Americans might be in league with the enemy.)*

2. **Analyze Cause and Effect** What combined factors gave rise to the Great Migration before and during the war years? *(Possible response: At the same time that natural disasters in the South reduced opportunities for African-American agricultural workers, industrial jobs opened up in northern cities as workers enlisted to fight in World War I.)*

3. **Identify** What wartime circumstances strengthened the Prohibition movement? *(Grain normally used for making beer was being used for food. Furthermore, most brewers were of German heritage, and anti-German sentiment caused many Americans to oppose anything associated with Germany.)*

VIRTUAL MUSEUM VISIT

Founder Duncan Phillips opened the Phillips Collection in 1921, making it the nation's first museum devoted to modern art. The collection now contains more than 4,000 works, including many by French impressionists and American modernists. Invite pairs of students to visit the museum online and read the background about Jacob Lawrence's series *The Migration of the Negro*. Prompt pairs to select another panel from the series and present their selection to the class, explaining why they chose that particular panel and how it might fit into the context of the larger work.

DIFFERENTIATE

ENGLISH LANGUAGE LEARNERS

Use Terms in Sentences Pair students at the **Emerging** level with those at the **Bridging** or **Expanding** level. Ask the more English-proficient partner to model the exercise by using the first Key Vocabulary term in a sentence. Then direct students take turns composing sentences for each of the Key Vocabulary terms: *Great Migration, Prohibition, influenza,* and *pandemic*. You may expand the exercise to other lesson words such as *dissenters, pickets, contagious,* and *vulnerable*. Invite pairs to share their sentences with the class. Discuss different ways to use each word. Use the following sentence frames to help students at different proficiency levels engage in discussion.

• **Emerging:** This word means _____.

• **Expanding:** I can use this word to mean _____ or _____.

• **Bridging:** I can use the word _____ for _____ or _____ .

PRE-AP

Research the Pandemic Remind students that the 1918 pandemic was unusual in that it was more lethal to people in their prime (ages 20 to 40) than to infants or the elderly. Challenge students to conduct research utilizing online medical journals to shed light on why the 1918 influenza pandemic was so deadly and how recent scientific knowledge may improve vaccination strategies and prevent future pandemics. After students complete their research, invite them to present their findings to the class in an oral or written report.

See the Chapter Planner for more strategies for differentiation.

Suffragists align with Woodrow Wilson during his 1916 re-election campaign. While Wilson's political platform favored women's suffrage, the president didn't fully support it until 1918.

PRIMARY SOURCE

Do you realize that when you ask women to take their cause [suffrage] to state referendum . . . you drive women of education, refinement, achievement, to beg men who cannot read for their political freedom?

Do you realize that such anomalies as a college president asking her janitor to give her a vote are overstraining the patience and driving women to desperation? Do you realize that women in increasing numbers indignantly resent the long delay in their enfranchisement?

Your party platforms have pledged women suffrage. Then why not be honest, frank friends of our cause, adopt it in reality as your own, make it a party program, and "fight with us"? As a party measure —a measure of all parties—why not put the amendment through Congress and the legislatures? We shall all be better friends, we shall have a happier nation, we women will be free to support loyally the party of our choice, and we shall be far prouder of our history.

—from Carrie Chapman Catt's address to the U.S. Congress, November 4, 1917

WOMEN GAIN THE VOTE

Women had been demanding the right to vote since the 1840s, and by 1914, they could vote in several states. However, after Wilson's re-election, his support for a constitutional amendment giving women suffrage seemed lukewarm at best to those in the movement. In 1917, women picketed the White House, and many were imprisoned. Still, they continued to demonstrate, in spite of the threat of increasingly long jail terms.

World War I finally provided the context in which women's activism to secure the vote could finally succeed. Women saw the opportunity to strengthen their argument. Carrie Chapman Catt, a leader of the National American Woman Suffrage Association, claimed that women were patriotic voters. According to her argument, giving women the right to vote would counteract the potential influence of dissenters at the polls. At the same time, the pickets in front of the White House continued.

The combined impact of these tactics pushed the House of Representatives to pass the **19th Amendment**, granting suffrage to women in January 1918. The Senate took another year to approve the amendment, and the states ratified it in August 1920. Beyond the success of women's suffrage, however, the war did not produce lasting changes in the everyday lives of American women. As soon as the war ended, women were expected to relinquish their office and factory jobs to the returning soldiers and resume their traditional roles at home.

USE THE HANDKERCHIEF AND DO YOUR BIT TO PROTECT ME!

THE PUBLIC

TREASURY DEPARTMENT UNITED STATES PUBLIC HEALTH SERVICE

COLDS, INFLUENZA, PNEUMONIA, AND TUBERCULOSIS ARE SPREAD THIS WAY

Flu Epidemic 1918–1919

First cases reported at U.S. military bases
August 1918

September 1918 total U.S. deaths
12,000

October 1918 total U.S. deaths
195,000

Total U.S. deaths 1918–1919
600,000

Total deaths worldwide 1918–1919
50,000,000

Sources: PBS, U.S. National Library of Medicine

Despite attempts at public health education, like displaying this 1919 poster, the 1918 influenza pandemic was widespread and deadly. Scientists have since learned the virus was H1N1, which has resurfaced at various times throughout history.

THE FLU STRIKES

At the end of 1918, a particularly powerful strain of **influenza**, the contagious virus we now call "the flu," struck with dramatic suddenness and spread rapidly throughout the U.S. population. Scientists were not able to develop a vaccine quickly enough against the Spanish flu, as it was called. Antibiotics did not come into widespread use until around 1940, so they were not yet available to fight secondary infections, such as pneumonia, that could accompany the flu. More than 600,000 Americans died of the disease in 1918 and 1919, overwhelming the funeral facilities of many major cities. It was most deadly for people aged 20–40, which was unusual, since influenza is typically more likely to be fatal among the very young and the very old. As a result, soldiers and officers were in the most vulnerable age group.

The outbreak was a **pandemic**—a sudden spread of disease that covers a very large geographic area and affects a major portion of the population. By the time it receded in 1920, the flu had killed more than 50 million people worldwide. It is estimated that one-third of the world's population became infected. The pandemic sapped the strength of the Allied forces who had already lived through brutal trench warfare and had been tasked with enforcing the peace treaty at the end of the war. The outbreak also diverted attention from important social problems, and illustrated how vulnerable humanity was to infectious diseases.

PRIMARY SOURCE

1918 has gone: a year momentous as the termination of the most cruel war in the annals of the human race; a year which marked the end, at least for a time, of man's destruction of man; unfortunately a year in which developed a most fatal infectious disease causing the death of hundreds of thousands of human beings. Medical science for four and one-half years devoted itself to putting men on the firing line and keeping them there. Now it must turn with its whole might to combating the greatest enemy of all—infectious disease.

—from the *Journal of the American Medical Association,* 1918

HISTORICAL THINKING

1. **READING CHECK** What changes were reform movements able to bring about during and immediately after the war?

2. **MAKE GENERALIZATIONS** In what ways can a war help bring about social changes on the home front?

3. **EVALUATE** In Catt's appeal to Congress, what details suggest her frustration with having to beg for women's suffrage?

4. **FORM AND SUPPORT OPINIONS** Do you believe women and African Americans made large strides toward civil rights during the war years? Explain.

BUILD BACKGROUND

WILSON'S GROWING PROGRESSIVISM

After 1914, progressive reformers looked to the federal government for help with the agenda of social change. In the light of the results of the 1914 congressional elections, Woodrow Wilson understood that he must move left to win four more years in office. During the months before the election campaign began, Wilson came out in support of laws to restrict child labor, promote federal loans to farmers, provide federal aid for highway construction, and cover federal employees with workers' compensation laws. When a national railroad strike threatened in August 1916, Wilson compelled Congress to pass the Adamson Act, which mandated an eight-hour workday for railroad employees. Labor responded with strong support for Wilson's re-election bid. Meanwhile, the improving economy, driven by orders from the Allies for American products and foodstuffs, helped the Democrats.

One notable step that Wilson took was to nominate Louis D. Brandeis to the U.S. Supreme Court in January 1916. Brandeis had won renown as the "People's Lawyer" and as a foe of consolidated business enterprise. Since Brandeis was a longtime champion of reform causes and a prominent Jew, his appointment aroused intense, often anti-Semitic, feelings among conservatives. In the end he was confirmed, and Wilson's strong endorsement of him convinced progressives that the president was on their side.

TEACH

GUIDED DISCUSSION

4. **Determine Chronology** What individual events served as milestones in the women's suffrage movement? *(1840s—the movement begins; 1914—some states allow women to vote; 1918—the U.S. House of Representatives passes the 19th Amendment; 1919—the Senate passes the 19th Amendment; 1920—states ratify the 19th Amendment)*

5. **Analyze Cause and Effect** How and why did the flu outbreak in 1918 affect troop strength in particular? *(The flu was most deadly for people aged 20–40, the age group to which most members of the military belonged, so the outbreak decreased the fighting strength of troops.)*

ANALYZE PRIMARY SOURCES

Direct students' attention to the Primary Source feature from the *Journal of the American Medical Association.* **ASK:** How does the writer's comment support the use of the term "the Great War"? *(The writer refers to the conflict as "the most cruel war in the annals of the human race.")* **ASK:** How does the excerpt reflect the grim mood as the war ended and the influenza outbreak raged? *(Possible response: The writer refers to the cruelty and destructiveness of the war and then indicates, almost with a sense of exhaustion, that now medical science must go to war with "the greatest enemy of all—infectious disease.")*

ACTIVE OPTIONS

On Your Feet: Use a Jigsaw Strategy Arrange students into four "expert" groups and instruct students from each group to analyze the effect of one of the following events on American society: the Great Migration; Prohibition; woman suffrage; the influenza epidemic. Regroup students into four new groups such that each new group has at least one member from each original expert group. Instruct experts to report on their event to their new group.

NG Learning Framework: Design an Infographic

SKILL Communication

KNOWLEDGE Our Human Story

Invite students to research the difficulties and opposition that American women encountered as they worked over time to gain the right to vote, especially during the years of the Great War. Suggest students consider how change happens at different rates at different times and how that principle is reflected in the history of the women's suffrage movement. Challenge small groups of students to design an infographic based on their research. Encourage them to incorporate text and visuals that point to the norms and values of the time periods their infographic represents. Work with the groups to create a classroom display of the results.

HISTORICAL THINKING

ANSWERS

1. Reform movements brought about women's suffrage and Prohibition.

2. War can bring about social changes by offering more job opportunities to women and minorities and by relying on citizens to support the war effort in various ways.

3. Details that suggest Catt's frustration include her statements that women are dependent on men to gain suffrage; that the delay to enact the vote for women has been long; and that political parties have pledged women's suffrage but have failed to put the amendment through Congress.

4. Possible response: Women made large strides toward civil rights by receiving the right to vote. African Americans did not make large strides because they still suffered widespread discrimination.

ROAD TO VICTORY

As you know, many people referred to the fighting as the Great War because it consumed so many countries in its fires. By the end, they were calling it "the war to end all wars" because the bloodshed and ruin were unlike anything that had gone before. But the participation of American troops in the war helped establish the United States as a global power.

Major Battles of World War I, 1917–1918

ATTACK AND COUNTERATTACK

During the late winter of 1918, the Allies faced a dangerous military crisis. As you may recall, by November 1917, revolution had erupted in Russia, and the second of two revolutions had taken that nation out of the Allied coalition. The revolutionaries placed the Bolsheviks, a party of communist extremists, in power and overthrew the Russian imperial government. This turmoil enabled the Germans to move troops to the Western Front. Berlin hoped to achieve victory before the Americans could reinforce the Allies.

On March 21, 1918, the German Army launched a renewed offensive to conquer France and end the war before large numbers of American forces landed in Europe. Over the next two months, the Germans gained ground in Belgium and France, only to be stopped in May by the American counterattack at Cantigny, France. With millions of U.S. soldiers now in France, the German drive for a quick victory had failed. The following month, the American Expeditionary Forces (AEF) stopped Germany from advancing in battles near Belleau Wood and Château-Thierry. In addition to their strategic value, these victories provided a tremendous morale boost to the flagging Allied armies.

The Germans made one more offensive push in July, but the British, French, and American troops repelled it. After that, the Allies went on the offensive, driving the German forces back, trench by trench. In September, the Allies began an operation called the **Meuse-Argonne offensive**, in which American divisions cut off the railroads that were bringing supplies to the German Army. As part of the offensive, General Pershing led AEF troops in the bloody and decisive **Battle of Argonne Forest** in October 1918. Looking back on the offensive years later, German general Erich Ludendorff wrote, "America thus became the most decisive power in the war." Still, American casualties in the Battle of Argonne were staggering, reaching 117,000, including 26,000 killed. French casualties totaled 70,000, and German casualties came to 100,000 soldiers.

WILSON'S PEACE PROGRAM

As the war ground toward its end, Wilson proposed a program for peace that he called the **Fourteen Points**. Among the key provisions of this plan were freedom of the seas, free trade among countries, and no more secret treaties. Wilson also advocated national self-determination, the idea that countries should reflect the national origins of the people who lived within their boundaries.

PRIMARY SOURCE

President Wilson's **Fourteen Points** were presented in a speech to Congress on January 8, 1918.

Points 1–5 dealt with diplomatic issues that Wilson believed were essential for preventing further war:

1. Open covenants [binding agreements] of peace, openly arrived at, after which there shall be no private international understandings of any kind but diplomacy shall proceed always frankly and in the public view.

2. Absolute freedom of navigation upon the seas, outside territorial waters, alike in peace and in war, except as the seas may be closed in whole or in part by international action for the enforcement of international covenants.

3. The removal, so far as possible, of all economic barriers and the establishment of an equality of trade conditions among all the nations consenting to the peace and associating themselves for its maintenance.

4. Adequate guarantees given and taken that national armaments [weaponry] will be reduced to the lowest point consistent with domestic safety.

5. A free, open-minded, and absolutely impartial adjustment of all colonial claims, based upon a strict observance of the principle that in determining all such questions of sovereignty, the interests of the populations concerned must have equal weight with the equitable [fair] claims of the government whose title is to be determined.

[Points 6–13 are not included here. These points dealt with boundary changes and called for ensuring the sovereignty of several nations. They also included a request for the break-up of the Ottoman Empire and the development of an independent Polish state.]

Point 14 called for the creation of an assembly of nations that would help safeguard the sovereignty of all countries:

14. A general association of nations must be formed under specific covenants for the purpose of affording mutual guarantees of political independence and territorial integrity to great and small states alike.

Which of the Fourteen Points do you think might have been controversial in the context of the war? Explain your answer.

PLAN: 4-PAGE LESSON

OBJECTIVE

Understand how American forces helped achieve an Allied victory and how Woodrow Wilson attempted to forge a peace plan.

CRITICAL THINKING SKILLS FOR LESSON 4.1

- Make Inferences
- Evaluate
- Make Predictions
- Analyze Cause and Effect
- Identify Main Ideas and Details
- Analyze Primary Sources
- Determine Word Meaning
- Compare and Contrast
- Draw Conclusions

HISTORICAL THINKING FOR CHAPTER 17

How did World War I affect the United States politically, economically, and socially?
The United States became a decisive force in ending the war and subsequently took its place as a world leader. Lesson 4.1 describes the last major battles of the war and the Paris Peace Conference.

BACKGROUND FOR THE TEACHER

American forces at Cantigny, Belleau Wood, and Château-Thierry were instrumental in bringing the war to an end. At Belleau Wood, it was the U.S. Marines who carried the day. In the annals of Marine Corps history, Belleau Wood stands out, for prior to World War I the Corps had been small and undistinguished. However, in response to the U.S. entry into the war, Marines were deployed to France in 1917. Marines at Belleau fought so heroically that the French officially renamed the Belleau Wood "Wood of the Marine Brigade." It also was at Belleau Wood that the Marines earned the nickname of "Devil Dogs." When commanded to take a steep hill, some Marines climbed on all fours. Gas masks in place, eyes bloodshot, and foaming at the mouth from the heat, they gave the appearance of an attack by "dogs from hell."

INTRODUCE & ENGAGE

DISCUSS DESPERATE ACTIONS

Write this sentence on the board: *Their backs were to the wall.* Discuss its meaning with the class. Ask students when a sports team might have its "back to the wall." *(Possible response: when a team is tied or is down a point just seconds before the end of a game)* **ASK:** What could be done to turn the situation around? *(Possible response: The team could try harder, adopt a new strategy, or bring in a star player.)* Tell students that in this lesson they will connect that expression to the war effort and learn how American forces helped to turn a potential loss into a victory when the Allies had "their backs to the wall."

TEACH

GUIDED DISCUSSION

1. **Evaluate** Why were the Allied victories at Cantigny, Belleau Wood, and Château-Thierry of critical importance? *(They stopped Germany from advancing and provided a morale boost to the Allied armies.)*

2. **Analyze Cause and Effect** How did cutting off the railroads affect the German Army, and how might events have taken a different turn if this strategy had not been successful? *(Possible responses: As a result of this action, the German Army was unable to receive supplies; if the supply lines had not been disrupted, the Germans might well have fended off the historically important Meuse-Argonne offensive and won the war. There would likely have been even higher casualties among the Allied forces if supplies had gotten through; the war might have dragged on, and the role of the United States might not have been considered as significant in the war's outcome.)*

3. **Identify Main Ideas and Details** What was the main objective of the first five of Wilson's Fourteen Points? *(The main objective was to establish diplomatic understandings that could prevent further war.)*

ANALYZE PRIMARY SOURCES

Direct students' attention to the Primary Source feature and have them read the text. **ASK:** How could each of the different points help to prevent further war? *(Answers will vary. Possible response: Point 1 addresses transparency, discouraging nations from making secret pacts and alliances against other nations. Point 2 emphasizes free passage on the seas, prohibiting the kind of naval actions that helped cause the United States to enter World War I. Point 3 promotes trade between nations, and strong, fair trade connections would be a strong incentive for peace. Point 4 calls for reduced weapons, which would promote peace. Point 5 deals with fair treatment of colonies, potentially easing the kind of situation that led to the American Revolution. Points 6–13 settle specific boundary and sovereignty issues, which could remove reasons some nations had for fighting. Point 14 provides for an international organization to help assure compliance with international standards.)* Use a Main-Idea and Details List like the one shown here to record students' ideas.

Main Idea: Wilson's Fourteen Points could help prevent further war.
Detail:
Detail:
Detail:
Detail:
Detail:

DIFFERENTIATE

STRIVING READERS

Sequence Events Direct students to work in pairs to determine the sequence of events leading to the end of World War I. Have students use a Sequence Chain graphic organizer like the one shown. Tell students to decide on four major events leading up to the Paris Peace Conference, which will serve as the final event in their chain. Instruct them to include the date and a summary of each event. Invite students to share their Sequence Chains with other pairs and discuss any differences.

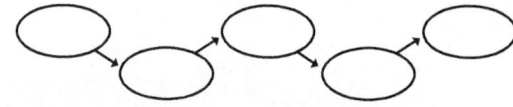

PRE-AP

Connect to Policies Instruct students to conduct library or online research to answer the question: How were Wilson's Fourteen Points an extension of earlier Progressive policies and his doctrine of moral diplomacy? When students have completed their research, prompt them to hold a panel discussion for the class, addressing such issues as setting a positive example for other nations regarding democracy and freedom, promoting good relations between nations, and being prepared to use force when necessary.

See the Chapter Planner for more strategies for differentiation.

PRIMARY SOURCE

Answers will vary. Possible response: The fourth point might have been the most controversial in the context of war, because it called for reducing weapons. Other points, such as the third point that dealt with trade, might have been more controversial during times of peace, but during and immediately after World War I, nations were probably most concerned about their ability to defend themselves.

The Fourteen Points would not be easy to achieve. Britain and France objected to the proposal because it did not include heavy sanctions on Germany. After four years of slaughter, these European nations wanted to punish Germany and cripple its ability to wage war in the future. They also disliked Wilson's interference with European policies. For the desperate Germans, however, the Fourteen Points seemed much more appealing than direct negotiations with Britain and France.

In early October, the German government asked Wilson to arrange an **armistice**, an end to the fighting, based on the provisions of the Fourteen Points. Britain and France objected to this proposal. However, by threatening to make a separate peace between the United States and Germany, Wilson convinced the two European nations to accept the Fourteen Points in general terms and attend a peace conference with Germany.

The fighting officially ended on November 11, 1918, at 11:00 a.m.—the 11th hour on the 11th day of the 11th month, or Armistice Day, as it would be called. Earlier that morning, Germany, lacking supplies and manpower and facing invasion at any moment, had signed an armistice, or peace agreement, with the Allies in a railroad car outside Compiégne, France. The details of the peace treaties among the formerly warring nations would be decided over the next year, but the relief that day was evident. British prime minister David Lloyd George stated, "This is no time for words. Our hearts are too full of gratitude to which no tongue can give adequate expression."

Nine million soldiers died in the Great War, and 21 million were wounded. France, Germany, Russia, Austria-Hungary, and Great Britain each lost nearly a million or more soldiers, and at least five million more civilians died from factors such as exposure, starvation, and disease. The Great War killed more people, involved more countries, and cost more money than any previous war in history. Its technology transformed the nature of modern warfare, introducing newer, deadlier, more effective weapons onto the battlefield.

The impact of the war was staggering, and many major global events that took place later in the 20th century can be tied to this first World War. The Russian Revolution, World War II, the Holocaust, and the creation of the atomic bomb, which you will read about later in this book, are all directly linked to the Great War. Even the Great Depression and the Cold War are connected to it in significant ways.

THE PARIS PEACE CONFERENCE

Breaking with the tradition that presidents did not travel outside the country, Wilson decided to attend the Paris Peace Conference. By the time he left for the conference, which began in January 1919, Wilson's political position at home had weakened considerably. He had alienated Republicans by keeping them out of the highest levels of his government and angered progressives with his harsh repression of dissent. In the October 1918 congressional elections, Americans voted Republican majorities into both the Senate and House of Representatives. This situation promised to make it difficult for a peace treaty negotiated by Wilson to be ratified.

In Europe, however, Wilson was heralded as a hero when he traveled to the Paris Peace Conference. The people greeted him with lavish applause and the nickname "Wilson the Just." Wilson, David Lloyd George, Georges Clemenceau, the president of France, and Italy's prime minister, Vittorio Orlando, made up the "Big Four" who directed the conference. The European leaders were hard-headed realists who did not share Wilson's idealism, and they were skeptical of the Fourteen Points. "God gave us the Ten Commandments and we broke them," said Clemenceau. "Wilson gives us the Fourteen Points. We shall see."

Notably absent from the Paris Peace Conference was one of the original Allies—Russia. As a result of the Russian Revolution, Russia's monarchy had given way to **communism**, a form of government in which all the means of production and transportation are owned by the state. The revolutionaries changed Russia's name to the Union of Soviet Socialist Republics (U.S.S.R.), or the **Soviet Union** for short. Its leader was Vladimir Ilyich Lenin. In March 1918, the Russian revolutionary party had made its own peace treaty with Germany.

HISTORICAL THINKING

1. **READING CHECK** What effect did the arrival of American troops have on the outcome of the war?

2. **MAKE INFERENCES** Why did Germany prefer to negotiate the terms of peace with Wilson rather than with France and Britain?

3. **EVALUATE** How did Wilson's Fourteen Points serve as a justification for America's entry into the war?

4. **MAKE PREDICTIONS** How might a later event in history, such as World War II or the Great Depression, be connected to the Great War?

The Great War **625**

BUILD BACKGROUND

THE MEUSE-ARGONNE OFFENSIVE

When American soldiers arrived in Europe, the British and French hoped to absorb them into their own armies, thereby shoring up their depleted ranks. General John J. Pershing, commander of the American Expeditionary Forces, refused to comply. He supported the view of the U.S. government: If American soldiers were going to fight, they would do so as an independent army. Therefore, it was as the U.S. First Army that 1.2 million Americans participated in the 47-day Meuse-Argonne offensive, which contributed significantly to ending the war.

THE LOST BATTALION

On October 2, 1918, 550 U.S. soldiers moved forward in the Argonne Forest as part of the Argonne-Meuse offensive. Survivors of four battalions of the U.S. Army's 77th Infantry Division entered a ravine where German soldiers cut them off from their higher command. The Germans pounded the trapped Americans mercilessly for five days. In addition, an American plane unwittingly shelled the Americans. During that time, the U.S. soldiers endured with little food and with no overcoats or blankets. They relied on carrier pigeons to communicate with higher command. When reinforcements finally reached them, only 194 Americans emerged alive.

TEACH

GUIDED DISCUSSION

4. **Determine Word Meaning** What is the difference between an armistice and a peace treaty? *(An armistice is an agreement to end fighting. A peace treaty hammers out the details that will ensure peace.)*

5. **Compare and Contrast** At the war's end, how did most Americans' view of Woodrow Wilson differ from that of the nation's European allies, and why? *(Most Americans were disillusioned with Wilson because of his policies at home, but most Europeans from Allied nations admired and praised him because he had helped end the war.)*

DRAW CONCLUSIONS

Discuss with students Clemenceau's reaction to Wilson's proposed Fourteen Points. **ASK:** What does Clemenceau mean when he compares the Fourteen Points to the Ten Commandments? *(Clemenceau is implying that if people broke the Ten Commandments, which came from God, governments and individuals would be even less likely to keep the Fourteen Points, which came from a human being.)*

ACTIVE OPTIONS

On Your Feet: Team Word Webbing Arrange students into teams. Provide each team with a large piece of paper. Give each student a different colored marker. Assign the topic "The Great War." Each student then adds to the part of the web nearest to him or her. On a signal, students rotate the paper, and each student adds to the nearest part again. Encourage teams to compare their completed webs.

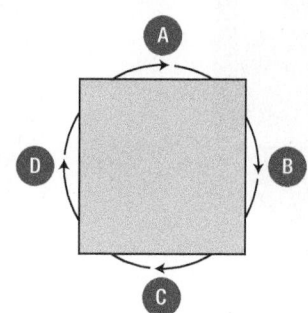

NG Learning Framework: Create an Annotated Time Line

SKILL Collaboration

KNOWLEDGE Our Human Story

Tell students to work in small groups to research important World War I battles that involved U.S. troops in Europe. Then tell each group to create a time line showing the chronology of the battles. Instruct students to annotate their time lines with details about the different battles and how the Americans fared in each. Invite groups to share their time lines.

HISTORICAL THINKING

ANSWERS

1. The arrival of American troops ultimately resulted in the Allies winning the war.

2. Germany felt that the United States would not impose heavy sanctions, as the British and French were likely to do.

3. Answers will vary. Possible response: The Fourteen Points stated that nations should have absolute freedom to navigate the seas during wars as well as during times of peace—a policy that Germany had not honored when it sank the *Lusitania* and other ships.

4. Answers will vary. Possible response: World War II may have been the result of dissatisfaction with the terms of the World War I peace treaty.

CRITICAL VIEWING The exhibition's name reflects the bloody battles and horrendous loss of life in World War I.

National Boundaries after World War I, 1920

VICTORY AND WILSON'S PEACE

Woodrow Wilson had a lofty dream of a world at peace and a great gathering of nations. It was a vision that blinded him to the necessities of everyday politics. In the end, the nations gathered, but the United States was not among them.

THE TREATY OF VERSAILLES

The **Treaty of Versailles**, which officially brought the war to a close, was signed in the Hall of Mirrors at the Palace of Versailles outside of Paris, France, on June 28, 1919. Although Wilson had a significant role in designing the Versailles Treaty, the negotiations over peace terms with Germany had produced both victories and defeats for the American president. Against his wishes, the final wording of the treaty included a clause assigning Germany the "guilt" for starting the war in 1914. The treaty also exacted severe financial penalties from Germany in the form of reparations, payments to make up for damages and casualties caused by the war, that eventually amounted to $33 billion. Both of these provisions fueled bitter resentment in Germany that would only deepen in the decades that followed.

With regard to self-determination for nations, Wilson was somewhat more successful. In the aftermath of the war, the Austro-Hungarian Empire was dissolved, and new boundaries were drawn. It was not possible to fully align national borders with the ethnic origins of the groups within each country. Still, borders in postwar Europe did more closely follow ethnic divisions than the prewar boundaries.

THE LEAGUE OF NATIONS

Wilson's main goal in the negotiations was to establish a **League of Nations**, a general assembly of countries that would stabilize relations among countries and help preserve peace. The final Treaty of Versailles included the league's charter. Each member country would have an equal voice in the general assembly, and the league would have an international court of justice. For Wilson, the "heart of the covenant" of the League of Nations was Article X,

which required member nations to take unified action when any member country was attacked.

Because Democrats were in the minority in the Senate, Wilson would need some Republican votes to ratify the Treaty of Versailles. Many Republicans, however, objected to establishing the League of Nations, believing it infringed on U.S. sovereignty,

Three global powerhouses, British prime minister David Lloyd George (left), French prime minister Georges Clemenceau (center), and American president Woodrow Wilson (right), take a stroll during the Versailles Peace Conference in June 1919.

or freedom from external control. Senator **Henry Cabot Lodge**, a Republican and chair of the Senate Foreign Relations Committee, was especially vocal in his opposition. Lodge and Wilson had been political enemies for a long time and disliked each other personally. Wilson did not help matters when he indicated that since the treaty's critics had offered no alternate plan, "it is a case of 'put up or shut up'".

In the political battle over the treaty, Lodge focused on Article X and the issue of whether Congress should be able to approve American participation in any actions taken by the league to defend its members from aggression. By September 1919, with the treaty in trouble, Wilson decided to take his case to the American people in a series of speeches in the Midwest and on the West Coast. The grueling schedule—32 major speeches in 22 days—exhausted him, and the heart and blood disorders that had

bothered him for years became aggravated. He was rushed back to Washington where he suffered a massive stroke that left his left side paralyzed.

The president's wife and his doctors did not reveal how sick Wilson was. As the first lady screened his few visitors and decided what documents he would see, Wilson became a shell of a president, and the government drifted. The Treaty of Versailles came up for a vote in the Senate in November 1919 and March 1920, and both times it was defeated. Wilson ultimately could not convince Congress to join the League of Nations. He died in 1924.

THE DECLINE OF PROGRESSIVISM

As you have read in this chapter, many goals of progressivism, including women's suffrage, a stronger labor movement, and Prohibition, had been attained by 1919. Enough states had ratified the 18th

---

PLAN: 4-PAGE LESSON

OBJECTIVE

Understand the peace process at the end of World War I and the postwar political, social, and economic unrest in the United States.

CRITICAL THINKING SKILLS FOR LESSON 4.2

- Compare and Contrast
- Form and Support Opinions
- Make Inferences
- Identify Problems and Solutions
- Evaluate
- Interpret Maps
- Analyze Cause and Effect
- Analyze Language Use
- Make Predictions

HISTORICAL THINKING FOR CHAPTER 17

How did World War I affect the United States politically, economically, and socially? The United States transitioned from a wartime to a peacetime economy, resulting in social unrest. Lesson 4.2 discusses the war's end and its effects on the United States.

BACKGROUND FOR THE TEACHER

The League of Nations was established in 1920, with headquarters in Geneva, Switzerland. Its two main bodies were an Assembly of Member States and a Council made up of five permanent members—the United Kingdom, France, Italy, Japan, and Germany (from 1926 to 1933)—and up to ten rotating members. The Secretariat aided in administrative matters, and a Court of International Justice met in The Hague, in the Netherlands, to rule on international disputes. Although the United States never joined, the Harding, Coolidge, and Hoover administrations were sympathetic to much of the League's work.

INTRODUCE & ENGAGE

DEVELOP A WORD MAP

Prompt students to discuss the meaning of the word *cooperation*. Begin by adding the word to the center of a Word Map, and complete the map during classroom discussion. Guide students to consider the root of the word, allowing them to use a dictionary if necessary. Revisit this activity at the end of the lesson, and discuss how a spirit of cooperation failed in the following situations: discussions about the League of Nations in Congress; relations between workers as well as between workers and management; and relations between blacks and whites in both the North and the South.

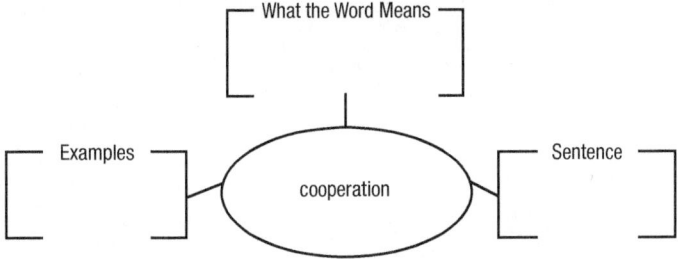

TEACH

GUIDED DISCUSSION

1. **Identify Problems and Solutions** What problem did Wilson confront regarding Congress and the League of Nations, and how did he try to solve it? *(Possible response: Problem: Many members of Congress objected to the League of Nations as part of the Treaty of Versailles because they worried it would weaken U.S. sovereignty. Solution: Wilson undertook a speaking tour to convince the American public—rather than politicians—of the League's value.)*

2. **Evaluate** How successful was Wilson in negotiating the Treaty of Versailles? Cite evidence to support your answer. *(Possible response: He was moderately successful because he experienced both victories—peace was established—and defeats— Congress refused to have the United States join the League of Nations.)*

3. **Interpret Maps** Which countries lost territory as a result of the war? *(the German, Russian, and Austro-Hungarian empires and Bulgaria)* Which countries had been part of the Russian Empire before the war? *(Finland, Estonia, Latvia, Lithuania, Poland, and Bessarabia)*

MORE INFORMATION

Edith Bolling Galt Wilson Historians disagree on exactly how much governmental power Edith Wilson, President Wilson's second wife, wielded after her husband's debilitating stroke. While some historians suggest she was more or less the acting president at the end of his second term, others argue that she functioned more as a gatekeeper to the president and did not make weighty decisions. She herself denied making any decisions on matters facing the nation—only on those regarding her husband's health. It is clear, however, that she served as an intermediary between almost everyone and President Wilson—including the members of his cabinet. Just by choosing which communications he could receive and which issues might be brought to his attention, she exerted an extraordinary influence on the Wilson administration.

DIFFERENTIATE

INCLUSION

Trace Maps Direct students to read the legend for the National Boundaries after World War I map and then to use a finger to circle the territories lost by the three major empires. Provide sentence frames for students to complete based on the map.

- After the war, the Baltic Republics of Latvia, Lithuania, and Estonia were created from what had been the _____ Empire. *(Russian)*
- West Prussia had previously been part of the _____ Empire. *(German)*
- Yugoslavia and Czechoslovakia became new nations, carved out of what had been the _____ Empire. *(Austro-Hungarian)*
- The _____ Empire and the _____ Empire lost the largest territories after World War I. *(Russian; Austro-Hungarian)*

PRE-AP

Write a Report Direct students to gather relevant information from several library or online sources to write a report on post-war economic and social problems in the United States. Suggest that students limit their report to one problem, such as labor unrest or racial tensions. Encourage students to assess the credibility and accuracy of their sources, include properly formatted citations, and paraphrase their data and conclusions to avoid plagiarism. Invite volunteers to share their reports with the class.

See the Chapter Planner for more strategies for differentiation.

Mounted Chicago police officers escort African Americans to a safety zone during the Chicago Race Riots of 1919. Thirty-eight people, most of them black, were killed, and another 500 were injured over the course of five violent days.

The photograph on the left shows a large crowd gathering at the entrance of the Skinner and Eddy Shipbuilding Corporation on Seattle's central waterfront during the nation's first citywide general strike. It began in the shipyards in January 1919, paralyzing the city for several days. On the right is the front page of the *Seattle Union Record* announcing the strike.

Amendment (the Prohibition amendment) by January 1919 to make it part of the Constitution. Additionally, thanks to the 19th Amendment, women could "take their appropriate place in political work," according to Carrie Chapman Catt. Americans began to turn their attention away from progressive ideas as they faced the switch from a wartime to a peacetime economy.

The end of the war created an uncertain situation for American businesses. Orders for guns, ammunition, and other wartime goods were canceled, leaving factories with a pressing need to retool themselves once again, this time to produce peacetime consumer items. When the war had broken out, the WIB had stepped in to help American industry remake itself, but now the government retreated from its earlier organizational role. At the same time, inflation raised prices considerably. By 1920, the government's cost of living index had gone up 105 percent over prewar levels, making goods more expensive. As returning soldiers began to seek jobs, unemployment soared, reaching nearly 12 percent by 1921.

In the midst of economic hardship, social unrest also flared. In early 1919, labor unions staged major strikes demanding higher wages at shipyards in Seattle and steel mills across the country. The Industrial Workers of the World called for a general strike to support the shipyard and steel strikers. When 60,000 laborers took part in the strike, the mayor of Seattle, Ole Hanson, mobilized police and soldiers, earning himself the nickname "the Savior of Seattle." Inflammatory newspaper articles depicted the strike as a precursor to a communist revolution.

The largest industrial strike of the year was the Great Steel Strike of 1919. The American Federation of Labor tried to rally all steelworkers to end the grueling 7-day workweek and the 12-hour workday. In September 1919, 350,000 midwestern steelworkers left the mills. Steel manufacturers refused to recognize the union and replaced striking workers with unemployed minority workers and immigrants to keep their factories running during the strike. They waited for the strike to break due to police harassment and internal divisions within the unions themselves. Striking workers held their position for months, but could not withstand the financial and political pressure being exerted on them by management. The strike failed in early 1920.

Racial tensions also flared up in the turbulent postwar atmosphere. There were frequent lynchings in the American South. In the North, the flow of African-American migrants produced confrontations with angry whites. This tension erupted into race riots in Washington, D.C., Elaine, Arkansas, and Chicago, Illinois, during the summer of 1919, which one black leader came to call "the red summer." Racism and antilabor sentiments fueled each other during these tense months.

With Wilson ill and the government leaderless, the Republicans expected Theodore Roosevelt to be their nominee in 1920, but he died in 1919. The party then turned to Senator **Warren G. Harding**, who promised frustrated voters a "return to normalcy." By *normalcy* he meant reducing government's role in business and stepping back into a more isolationist stance. Harding was elected by a large majority over the Democratic candidate, James M. Cox of Ohio. Voters wanted to turn the Democrats out of office because of their anger over big government, high taxes, and labor unrest. Americans were also prepared to let Europe grapple on its own with its new postwar realities. Although World War I transformed America into a world leader, the aftermath of the war ushered in a decade of isolationism. By the end of the 1920s, this policy would have serious consequences for the world economies.

HISTORICAL THINKING

1. **READING CHECK** How did the end of the war affect the U.S. economy?

2. **COMPARE AND CONTRAST** Compare the social climate of the United States at the beginning of the Great War to the social climate at the end of the war. How did they differ?

3. **FORM AND SUPPORT OPINIONS** Should the Senate have ratified the Treaty of Versailles? Support your opinion.

4. **MAKE INFERENCES** Why did some newspapers compare the steelworkers' strike to the beginning of a communist revolution?

BUILD BACKGROUND

WORLD LEADERSHIP VS. ISOLATIONISM

The end of World War I raised the international stature of the United States. U.S. military forces helped win the war for the Allies, and President Wilson was instrumental in crafting the Treaty of Versailles—circumstances that transformed the nation into a world leader. Shortly after returning from Paris, Woodrow Wilson addressed Congress. Campaigning for support of American membership in the League of Nations, he declared, "There can be no question of our ceasing to be a world power. The only question is whether we can refuse the moral leadership that is offered us, whether we shall accept or reject the confidence of the world . . . a new role and a new responsibility have come to this great nation that we honor and which we would all wish to lift to yet higher levels of service and accomplishment."

But instead of following Wilson's vision, the United States veered toward isolationism. Americans were still reeling from the tremendous toll the war took on U.S. soldiers and did not want to be drawn into new conflicts. In addition, U.S. workers resented competing with immigrants for jobs and wanted to stop new immigrants from coming into the country. Americans also blamed Europe for rising ideas of anarchism, socialism, and communism. The United States, therefore, focused on protecting itself and its own interests.

TEACH

GUIDED DISCUSSION

4. Analyze Cause and Effect In what ways did economic problems lead to social problems in the context of the United States at the end of World War I? *(Answers will vary. Possible responses: The return of millions of soldiers caused high unemployment and thus competition for jobs, creating tensions—particularly with minority and immigrant workers; inflation caused prices to rise; and workers, hurt by rising prices, held strikes. Many Americans were upset over high taxes, labor unrest, and big government—all factors that they blamed on Democratic policies.)*

5. Analyze Language Use What did Harding mean by promising voters a "return to normalcy," and why might voters have found that idea appealing as the 1920 presidential campaign unfolded? *(Possible response: Harding was promising them a reduction in the government's role in business and less involvement in the affairs of other nations; voters were probably tired of the expanded government role in their lives that had been necessary during the war years, when the government exerted influence on everything from food to manufacturing to civil liberties, and they were tired of being involved in the problems between other nations.)*

MAKE PREDICTIONS

Share the Build Background information with students. Then explain that the U.S. move toward isolationism resulted in new policies, such as the Emergency Quota Act of 1921. This law limited immigration, especially from southern and eastern Europe. Congress also set high tariffs on imported products to keep out foreign goods. **ASK:** What consequences do you think isolationist policies such as these might have for the world economies? *(Answers will vary. Possible responses: Europe, devastated by the war, would have too many people and not enough jobs—and perhaps not enough food. Other nations might retaliate against U.S. tariffs by setting their own tariffs, and that could result in a tariff war that would not benefit anyone.)*

ACTIVE OPTIONS

On Your Feet: Numbered Heads Arrange students in four groups and assign each group one of the following topics: the Treaty of Versailles; the League of Nations; the effect of the war's end on American businesses; or racial tensions following World War I. Students should number off within each group; then group members should review information in the lesson about their topic. Groups should discuss the topic so that any member can report for the group. Finally, call a number and have the students with that number report for their group.

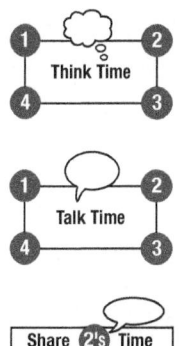

NG Learning Framework: Discuss Widespread Change

ATTITUDE Curiosity

KNOWLEDGE Our Human Story

Ask small groups to discuss this question: How did America change because of World War I? Instruct groups to generate as many responses as they can, referring to as many aspects of American life that they can address with confidence. In a follow-up discussion with the entire class, compile a master list of responses and invite comments.

HISTORICAL THINKING

ANSWERS

1. The end of the war affected the U.S. economy by contributing to inflation and unemployment.

2. At the beginning of the Great War, Americans actively supported progressive ideas, such as women's suffrage and the labor movement. At the war's end, interest in progressive ideas declined.

3. Answers will vary. Possible responses: Yes; even if the treaty contained some problematic elements, it would have solidified the leadership role of the United States. No; the Senate was right to uphold U.S. sovereignty.

4. The steelworkers' strike and the communist revolution both resulted from widespread organized dissatisfaction and promoted the power of the worker over the power of management.

VOCABULARY

For each pair of vocabulary words, write one sentence that explains the connection between the words.

1. conscientious objector; civil liberties
   A conscientious objector might have had to hide his negative feelings about the Great War to keep his civil liberties.

2. militarism; moral diplomacy

3. influenza; pandemic

4. machine gun; tank

5. armistice; Fourteen Points

6. Treaty of Versailles; League of Nations

READING STRATEGY
DRAW CONCLUSIONS

When you draw conclusions, you make a judgment based on what you have read. You analyze evidence, make inferences, and use your own experiences to form your judgment. Use a chart like this one to draw a conclusion about how the war changed the perception of the United States in the world. Then answer the question.

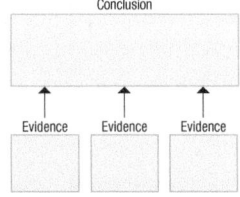

Conclusion

Evidence   Evidence   Evidence

7. In what ways did World War I mark the beginning of a new role for the United States on the world stage?

MAIN IDEAS

Answer the following questions. Support your answers with evidence from the chapter.

8. How did the networks of alliances in Europe lead to the beginning of World War I? LESSON 1.1

9. Why did President Wilson declare a policy of neutrality toward the war in Europe? LESSON 1.2

10. What German actions eventually led the United States to declare war? LESSON 2.1

11. In what ways did the U.S. government support the war effort? LESSON 2.2

12. How were members of minority groups treated during the war? LESSON 3.1

13. What effect did the flu pandemic of 1918–1919 have on the Allied forces? LESSON 3.3

14. In what ways did Wilson and the Allies disagree about a peace treaty for Europe? LESSON 4.1

15. Why did the United States refuse to ratify the Treaty of Versailles? LESSON 4.2

HISTORICAL THINKING

Answer the following questions. Support your answers with evidence from the chapter.

16. MAKE GENERALIZATIONS What general statement could you make about the power and usefulness of propaganda?

17. DRAW CONCLUSIONS How did Wilson's view of the United States' role in the world change during the war?

18. IDENTIFY MAIN IDEAS AND DETAILS What advantages made the United States instrumental in helping the Allied side win the war?

19. SYNTHESIZE How did the United States change its policies, both at home and abroad, because of World War I?

20. MAKE CONNECTIONS In what ways is the flu pandemic of 1918–1919 similar to modern disease outbreaks you have heard of? In what ways is it different?

21. FORM AND SUPPORT OPINIONS What do you think is the most important lasting effect of World War I on life in the United States? Explain your answer.

INTERPRET VISUALS

Study this propaganda poster created by the U.S. Food Administration during the war. Then answer the questions that follow.

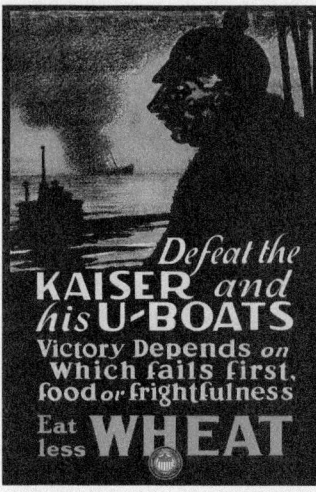

22. How do the poster's visuals and artistic details inspire fear?

23. What does the poster's slogan, "Victory depends on which fails first, food or frightfulness," mean?

ANALYZE SOURCES

Supporters of women's suffrage stood outside the White House day after day carrying signs and hoping to influence President Wilson. Often, the signs would elicit angry, or even violent, responses. Read the text of one such sign below. Then answer the question that follows.

> Kaiser Wilson
> Have you forgotten your sympathy with the poor Germans because they were not self-governed? 20,000,000 American women are not self-governed.
>
> —banner of the National Woman's Party, 1917

24. Why does the writer of this sign use the term "Kaiser Wilson"?

CONNECT TO YOUR LIFE

25. EXPOSITORY Imagine the year is 1919, and you spent the war working on the home front. The war has ended, and you are writing a letter to a friend explaining how events during and just after the war have changed your feelings about what it means to be an American.

TIPS

- Consider how the war affected all Americans, including the government's efforts to influence citizens' thoughts.

- Determine your identity as the letter writer. Are you male or female? Are you white, African American, a recent immigrant, or a member of a different group?

- Develop your topic by discussing ways in which your circumstances and your attitudes changed—and did not change.

- Use two or three vocabulary terms from the chapter in your letter.

- End the letter with a brief summary statement about how you feel at the current point in time.

VOCABULARY ANSWERS

1. A conscientious objector might have had to hide his negative feelings about the Great War to keep his civil liberties.

2. The candidates debated whether a country could practice moral diplomacy at the same time it pursued defensive militarism.

3. Not all strains of influenza will lead to a pandemic like the one that occurred in 1918.

4. The tank was invented in part to counter the deadly effect of more efficient machine guns.

5. To end World War I, President Wilson called for an armistice based on the principles put forth in his Fourteen Points.

6. The Treaty of Versailles marked the official end of World War I and included the League of Nations charter, which would establish an assembly of countries to help maintain peace.

READING STRATEGY ANSWER

Conclusion

Military and political contributions to World War I elevated the status of the United States in the world.

Evidence
U.S. soldiers helped the Allies win World War I.

Evidence
President Wilson helped draft the Treaty of Versailles.

Evidence
Wilson helped establish the League of Nations.

7. World War I marked the beginning of the role of the United States as a world power because the U.S. military helped the Allies win the war, and the U.S. government helped establish a structure for world peace.

MAIN IDEAS ANSWERS

8. When Archduke Franz Ferdinand of Austria-Hungary was assassinated by a Serb, Austria-Hungary's ally, Germany, became involved. Serbia was allied with Russia, which also had alliances with France and Britain. When fighting arose, all the allies were drawn in.

9. Wilson wanted to focus on affairs within the United States. In addition, he believed that the United States should serve as a role model to other countries but not try to interfere in their governments.

10. German submarines sank civilian ships, including the *Lusitania*, that carried American passengers. Then, in 1917, the German foreign minister sent a telegram proposing that Mexico attack the United States as a distraction.

11. The government created the War Industries Board to coordinate businesses and factories as they converted to war production, sold Liberty Bonds to raise money, and conducted an extensive publicity campaign to persuade Americans to support the war.

12. Although many Americans from minority groups served with distinction, African Americans served in segregated units, often working behind the scenes instead of serving in combat roles.

13. The flu pandemic reduced numbers among the Allied forces, which were populated largely by the age group most vulnerable to the disease.

14. The Allies wanted to punish Germany with heavy sanctions, but Wilson did not want to include such sanctions in the treaty. In addition, the Allied leaders were skeptical of the Fourteen Points, Wilson's vision for how Europe should be structured after the war.

15. The Republican Party, which opposed Wilson and his policies, had won a majority in both houses of Congress. Wilson's adversaries raised concerns about whether Congress would be able to approve U.S. participation in certain League of Nations actions. After Wilson had a serious stroke, he was no longer able to vigorously advocate for the treaty.

HISTORICAL THINKING ANSWERS

16. Answers will vary. Students should mention details that describe the way propaganda swayed U.S. public opinion against Germans and dissenters and in favor of the war.

17. Before the war, Wilson believed that the U.S. should lead by example and should avoid direct intervention in other countries' affairs whenever possible. As the war ended, he took a much more interventionist stance by trying to dictate postwar European policies.

18. The United States had millions of fresh troops to send. It also had a large industrial base, which was quickly converted to manufacturing war goods. Even before it entered the war, the United States sold various types of supplies to Britain and France.

19. Answers will vary. Students might point out that the United States adopted foreign policies that tied it to Europe in unprecedented ways and supported domestic policies that curtailed freedom of speech and allowed for discrimination.

20. Answers will vary. Students might connect the flu pandemic with the Ebola outbreak of 2014–2015. Students might compare the greater availability of drugs and treatments in modern times with the availability of drugs and treatments in 1918.

21. Answers will vary. Students should clearly state an opinion on the most important lasting effect of the war, and they should use details from the chapter in addition to other sources or prior knowledge to support it.

INTERPRET VISUALS ANSWERS

22. The poster depicts a ship sinking in the distance, presumably having been torpedoed by the submarine in the foreground, and a dark, sinister-looking German soldier. The lurid colors and crude artistic style convey a feeling of threat. These elements combine to cast the Germans as malevolent and fearsome.

23. The slogan means that Americans should eat less wheat to send more food to the Allies, so that the soldiers can continue fighting and outlast their "frightful" enemies.

ANALYZE SOURCES ANSWER

24. The writer is accusing Wilson of hypocrisy by equating him with the ruler of Germany and pointing out that Wilson expressed sympathy with Germans who had no say in their government while denying women at home the chance to have a say in their government through voting.

CONNECT TO YOUR LIFE ANSWER

25. Answers will vary, but students should present the information in the form of a well-organized letter. Students should clearly state their own identity as the letter writer and use details from the chapter to support an explanation of how their circumstances and attitudes about being an American changed over the course of the war and its immediate aftermath.

UNIT 6 RESOURCES

UNIT INTRODUCTION

UNIT TIME LINE

UNIT WRAP-UP

NATIONAL GEOGRAPHIC | CONNECTION

National Geographic Magazine Adapted Articles
- "The Hidden World of the Great War"
- "1918 Flu Pandemic" ONLINE

Unit 6 Inquiry: Create a Conflict Resolution Strategy

NG Learning Framework Activities
- Write a Conflict Negotiator Profile
- Settle a Dispute

Unit 6 Formal Assessment

CHAPTER 18 RESOURCES

Available at NGLSync.Cengage.com.

TEACHER RESOURCES & ASSESSMENT

Reading and Note-Taking

Vocabulary Practice

Social Studies Skills Lessons
- Reading: Compare and Contrast
- Writing: Argument

Formal Assessment
- Chapter 18 Pretest
- Chapter 18 Tests A & B
- Section Quizzes

Chapter 18 Answer Key

ExamView®
One-time Download

STUDENT DIGITAL RESOURCES

- eEdition
- Handbooks
- Online Atlas
- American Gallery Online
- History Notebook
- Active History
- American Voices (Biographies)
- Reid on the Road video series
- Literature Analysis
- Projects for Inquiry-Based Learning

Chapter 18 Spanish Resources are available at NGLSync.Cengage.com.

AMERICAN STORIES | All That Jazz

- Study Primary Sources: Excerpt from an interview and period media
- On Your Feet: Write Blues Lyrics
- **NG Learning Framework:** Compare Present-Day Music with the Past

SECTION 1 RESOURCES

RETURN TO NORMALCY

LESSON 1.1
The Red Scare

- On Your Feet: Discuss Supreme Court Opinions
- **NG Learning Framework:** Debate Civil Liberties Versus National Security

LESSON 1.2
Divisions in Society

- On Your Feet: Fishbowl
- **NG Learning Framework:** Research Prohibition

LESSON 1.3
GEOLOGY IN HISTORY
How Geology Kept the '20s Roaring

- On Your Feet: Turn and Talk
- **NG Learning Framework:** Create a Presentation About Caves and Prohibition

LESSON 1.4
A New Consumer Society

- ▶ The Model-T
- On Your Feet: Three Corners
- **NG Learning Framework:** Explore 1920s Radio Advertising

SECTION 2 RESOURCES

A VIBRANT CULTURE

LESSON 2.1
The Birth of Jazz

- ▶ This Is Jazz
- On Your Feet: Inside-Outside Circle
- **NG Learning Framework:** Write a Magazine Article

LESSON 2.2
Popular Culture and Artistic Achievement

- Active History: Analyze Primary Sources
- AMERICAN **GALLERY** ONLINE   Going to the Movies
- **NG Learning Framework:** Analyze a Selection by a "Lost Generation" Writer

SECTION 3 RESOURCES

NEW ROLES FOR WOMEN

LESSON 3.1
Changing Roles for Women

- On Your Feet: Think, Pair, Share
- **NG Learning Framework:** Compare Women's Roles Over Time

LESSON 3.2
Women in Politics

- On Your Feet: Team Word Webbing
- **NG Learning Framework:** Create a Radio Ad

SECTION 4 RESOURCES

THE HARLEM RENAISSANCE

LESSON 4.1
The Great Migration

- On Your Feet: Roundtable
- **NG Learning Framework:** Collaborate on a Biography

LESSON 4.2
The Harlem Renaissance

- On Your Feet: Jigsaw
- **NG Learning Framework:** Create a Biographical Infographic
- **American Voices Biography** Zora Neale Hurston ONLINE

LESSON 4.3
AMERICAN VOICES
Langston Hughes

- On Your Feet: Numbered Heads
- **NG Learning Framework:** Analyze Points of View

CHAPTER 18 REVIEW

STRATEGY ❶
SUMMARIZE A LESSON

Pair students and have them read each paragraph silently and then write a sentence to summarize what they read. Tell partners to trade sentences and then work together to clarify the meaning of each paragraph. Point out to students that taken together, the summary sentences represent a summary of the whole lesson.

Use with All Lessons *Throughout the chapter, help students get in the habit of summarizing paragraphs and sections as they read.*

STRATEGY ❷
USE A TASKS APPROACH

Help students extract information from visuals by using the following TASKS strategy.

T Look for a **title** that may give the main idea.

A **Ask** yourself what the visual is trying to show.

S Determine how **symbols** are used.

K Look for a **key** or legend

S **Summarize** what you learned.

Use with Lessons 3.2 and 4.1 *Suggest that students use the TASKS strategy to analyze the map showing states with female governors in Lesson 3.2 and the map showing the Great Migration in Lesson 4.1.*

STRATEGY ❸
FOCUS ON MAIN IDEAS

Tell students to locate the Main Idea statement at the beginning of each lesson. Explain that these statements summarize the important ideas of the lesson and will be useful for helping them focus on key ideas. Ask students to list facts from the lesson to support each Main Idea statement as they read.

Use with All Lessons

STRATEGY ❶
PREVIEW AND PREDICT

Pair visually impaired students with sighted students. Instruct them to work together to read the lesson title and subheadings. Tell sighted students to describe lesson visuals in detail to help their partners understand them. Then have partners work together to write notes regarding what they think the lesson will be about. After reading, ask pairs to review their notes to see whether their predictions were confirmed.

Use with All Lessons

STRATEGY ❷
BUILD A TIME LINE

Instruct students to identify key events in each lesson and add them to a time line on the board or a chart. You might continue to expand and extend the time line by guiding students to add to it as they progress through the chapter. Encourage students to enhance the time line with relevant graphics or photos.

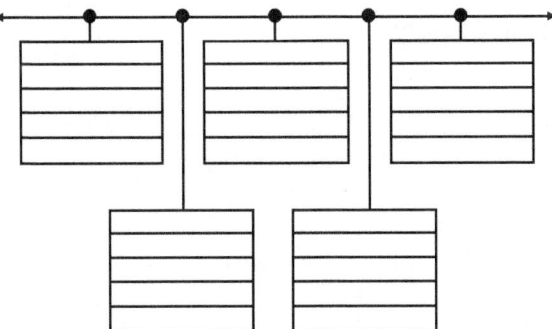

Use with All Lessons *For example, key events from Lesson 1.1 might include Red Scare begins (early 1919); Palmer Raids (1919); ACLU founded (1920); Harding elected president (1920); Red Scare dies down (late 1920).*

ENGLISH LANGUAGE LEARNERS

STRATEGY ❶
PREP BEFORE READING

Encourage students at **All Proficiencies** to use the PREP strategy to prepare for reading. Write this acrostic on the board:

> **PREP** **P**review the title.
> **R**ead the Main Idea statement.
> **E**xamine visuals.
> **P**redict what you will learn.

Use with All Lessons *Encourage students at the **Emerging** level to ask questions if they have trouble writing a prediction. Students at the **Bridging** level might provide assistance to students at the **Emerging** and **Expanding** levels.*

STRATEGY ❷
BUILD VOCABULARY

Help students at **All Proficiencies** learn unfamiliar words by introducing synonyms they might know. Display difficult words paired with more familiar words, as with these examples from Lesson 1.1:

equitable / honest	extreme / highest
imposed / started	violated / was against

Tell students that when they encounter a difficult word, such as *equitable*, they should try to replace it with a word they may be familiar with, such as *honest*. Guide students to use a thesaurus to practice looking up and substituting words, encouraging them to look among the synonyms to find one that makes sense in context.

Use with All Lessons *Students at the **Bridging** level could help students at the **Emerging** and **Expanding** levels find appropriate synonyms. Look for opportunities in all lessons to use synonyms and a thesaurus to aid comprehension. In Lesson 1.3, students might use a thesaurus to understand* gleaming (shiny) *and* leisure (free) *time.*

STRATEGY ❸
USE PAIRED READING

Pair students at the **Expanding** and **Bridging** levels to read passages from the text aloud.

1. Partner 1 reads a passage; partner 2 retells the passage in his or her own words.

2. Partner 2 reads a different passage; partner 1 retells it.

3. Pairs repeat the process, switching roles.

Use with All Lessons

GIFTED & TALENTED

STRATEGY ❶
WRITE A DRAMATIC SKIT

Invite students to choose one event that illustrates a division in society in the early 20th century—such as between workers and management, women and men, African Americans and whites—and to conduct online research to deepen their understanding of the event and the division. Tell students to use their research to write a short skit. After students have practiced, invite them to perform their skits for the class.

Use with Lessons 1.1, 1.2, 3.1, 3.2, 4.1, and 4.2 *Remind students that conflict is the basis of drama. They may wish to choose, for example, a conflict that led to the formation of the ACLU, the Supreme Court case against Bhagat Singh Thind, low pay for women, or the mass migration of African Americans.*

STRATEGY ❷
CREATE A GRAPHIC BIOGRAPHY

Tell students to select an individual from the lesson and write a short biography in comic book or graphic novel style. Encourage students to interpret the person's thoughts and actions within the context of the person's own time rather than present-day values. Panels should illustrate the individual's personality, goals, and achievements. Invite students to share their graphic biographies with the class and answer questions.

Use with Lessons 2.1, 2.2, 3.2, 4.1, and 4.2

PRE-AP

STRATEGY ❶
TEACH A CLASS

Before beginning the chapter, allow students to choose one of the lessons and prepare to teach the content to the class. Give them a set amount of time in which to present their lesson. Suggest that students think about any visuals or activities they want to use when they teach.

Use with All Lessons

STRATEGY ❷
FORM AND SUPPORT A THESIS

Direct students to construct a hypothesis and use it to develop a thesis statement for a historical event from the lesson. Tell students to support their thesis statement with evidence from the lesson and from multiple primary and secondary sources. Invite students to present their thesis statement and supporting evidence to the class. Discuss the process with the entire class, asking students to point out evidence used and how it relates to the original hypothesis.

Use with All Lessons

THE JAZZ AGE AND MASS CULTURE

1921–1929

HISTORICAL THINKING How did the Roaring Twenties both divide and unite Americans?

AMERICAN STORIES | **All That Jazz**

AMERICAN GALLERY ONLINE | **Going to the Movies**

"Everybody's **youth is a dream.**"
—F. Scott Fitzgerald, author

The 2013 film version of F. Scott Fitzgerald's novel *The Great Gatsby* portrayed the Jazz Age as a swirl of activity. Director Baz Luhrmann interpreted the extravagant, self-indulgent world of the wealthy Jay Gatsby with vibrant party scenes like this one.

The Jazz Age and Mass Culture 633

INTRODUCE THE PHOTOGRAPH

THE ROARING TWENTIES

Tell students to study the photograph, caption, and quotation. Have students compare what they see in the photograph with what they know of dress and behavior in the 1920s. **ASK:** What does the photograph suggest about how society changed during the Jazz Age? *(Answers will vary. Possible responses: People look more free and fun loving. The women are dressed in revealing, flashy dresses and are wearing makeup, unlike during the late 1800s and prewar 1900s, when dresses covered more of women's bodies.)* Tell students that in this chapter they will learn more about the Roaring Twenties, a time when Americans rushed headlong into a modern world of increased wealth, consumer goods, wailing jazz, roaring city life, and the excitement of youth.

SHARE BACKGROUND

An autobiographical writer, F. Scott Fitzgerald wrote about the excesses of the Jazz Age that he experienced. Stationed at an army base in Montgomery, Alabama, in 1918, Fitzgerald met and fell in love with the free-spirited and creative Zelda Sayre, a pampered southern belle. Sayre was unwilling to wait for Fitzgerald to make his fortune, so she broke off their engagement in 1919. Spurred by the rejection, Fitzgerald completed his first novel, *This Side of Paradise*, which found immediate success. With their future now bright, Sayre and Fitzgerald married in New York City in 1920. Their time together in New York and later in Paris during the 1920s epitomized the excesses of the Jazz Age. Wealthy and famous, they partied and traveled constantly. By the 1930s, Fitzgerald had begun a descent into alcoholism, and Zelda had suffered the first of a series of mental breakdowns.

For Chapter 18 Spanish Resources, visit the Resources Menu. Chapter 18 Resources are available at NGLSync.Cengage.com.

HISTORICAL THINKING QUESTION

How did the Roaring Twenties both divide and unite Americans?

Roundtable: Uniting and Dividing Prompt students to recall prior knowledge about present and past issues or events that have united and divided Americans. Arrange groups of four or five students and number each group. Assign odd-numbered groups this question: How can cultural or social change unite people? Assign even-numbered groups this question: How can cultural or social change divide people? Have the first student in each group write an answer on a sheet of paper and pass the paper clockwise to the next student, who adds an answer, and so on, until students are out of ideas. Discuss the groups' answers. Revisit the questions after studying the chapter to see how students' understanding of causes of unity and division may have changed.

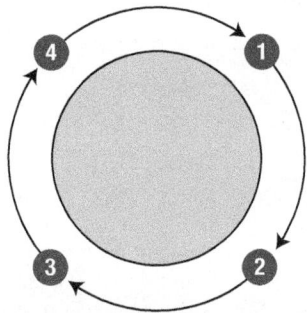

INTRODUCE THE READING STRATEGY

COMPARE AND CONTRAST

Preview the Comparison Chart in the Chapter Review. Explain that comparing and contrasting in such a chart can help readers better understand similarities and differences among people, events, or movements in history. As they read the chapter, have students compare traditional ways with modern ones that emerged in the 1920s.

KEY DATES FOR CHAPTER 18

1923	Warren G. Harding dies
1923	Calvin Coolidge inaugurated
1924	National Origins Act of 1924 passes
1925	Nellie Tayloe Ross of Wyoming is first female governor
1925	Scopes trial pits evolution against fundamentalism
1925	Alain Locke publishes *The New Negro*
1927	Charles A. Lindbergh makes historic transatlantic flight
1927	Nicola Sacco and Bartolomeo Vanzetti executed
1927	*The Jazz Singer* is first major sound film
1928	Amelia Earhart makes historic transatlantic flight

INTRODUCE CHAPTER VOCABULARY

KEY VOCABULARY

SECTION 1

American Civil Liberties Union (ACLU)	bootlegger	Red Scare
	capitalism	speakeasy
Anti-Defamation League (ADL)	eugenics	stalactite
	fundamentalism	stalagmite
assembly line	mass market	welfare capitalism

SECTION 2

jazz	modernism

SECTION 3

constituency	flapper

SECTION 4

back-to-Africa movement	Harlem Renaissance	Pan-Africanism

DEFINITION CHART

As they read the chapter, have students complete a Definition Chart for Key Vocabulary terms. Tell students to list Key Vocabulary in the left column and, as they encounter each term in the chapter, write the definition in the center column. In the right column they can write an explanation of the definition in their own words. Use the graphic organizer below to model an example for students.

Word	Definition	In My Own Words
assembly line	a method of manufacturing in which the work passes from one worker to another, each of whom has a specific, specialized task	a way of mass producing in which workers stay in place and the product being manufactured moves along a conveyor belt

OBJECTIVES

- **Discuss the origins and geographic diffusion of jazz and the blues.**
- **Study the connections between jazz music, social trends, and other forms of popular music.**
- **Understand the effects of radio on the diffusion of jazz music.**
- **Study primary sources: excerpt from an interview and period media**

CRITICAL THINKING SKILLS FOR "ALL THAT JAZZ"

- Make Connections
- Draw Conclusions
- Summarize
- Analyze Language Use
- Compare and Contrast
- Analyze Cause and Effect

CONNECT TO THE CHAPTER

This American Story focuses on uniquely American music genres—jazz and the blues—from their inception to their influences on later genres. Through photos of innovators, a painting of a jazz club scene, an interview, and a chart tracing American music influences over time, students learn about the origins and evolution of jazz and blues music in America.

This chapter, The Jazz Age and Mass Culture, discusses the social, political, and cultural changes that took place in the United States during the 1920s. This American Story will help students better understand the connections among jazz and the blues and early 20th-century culture and individual expression. Use this American Story after the class's initial introduction to jazz in Lesson 2.1.

HISTORY NOTEBOOK

Encourage students to complete the American Story page for Chapter 18 in their History Notebooks as they read.

AMERICAN STORIES | NATIONAL GEOGRAPHIC

ALL THAT JAZZ

634 CHAPTER 18

CRITICAL VIEWING The Preservation Hall Jazz Band is a contemporary jazz ensemble formed in 1963 with the aim of preserving the original spirit of New Orleans jazz. The band takes its name from Preservation Hall, a music venue located in New Orleans' French Quarter. Based on this photograph, what musical instruments appear in a typical jazz band?

It seems that every generation chooses to rebel against previous ones, partly through the rhythms and melodies of new styles of music. In the 1950s and 1960s, the rebellious music of choice was rock and roll, described as "savage music" in an advertisement by the Citizens' Council of Greater New Orleans. In the 1980s and 1990s, rap and hip-hop came on the scene, once again rattling the sensibilities of older generations.

Though they are each unique, rock, rap, and hip-hop are cousins, bearing family resemblances because they are all descended from an earlier musical and social revolution—the birth of jazz and the blues.

THE ORIGINS OF JAZZ

New Orleans is generally considered to be the birthplace of jazz. A city like no other in the late 1800s, New Orleans was home to an extremely diverse population of whites, African Americans, and people of mixed races.

In this cultural whirlwind could be heard the sounds of music that had originated with enslaved people who worked in the cotton fields. The music was based on traditional African work songs and "field hollers." Work songs often had a call-and-response structure, with one person singing a line and other people singing a response. Field hollers were high-pitched calls used by individuals working alone to communicate with workers in other fields.

Late in the 19th century, New Orleans also hosted a lively European classical music scene, with several well-attended opera houses. At this time, new kinds of sounds emerged that blended various African and European influences. By the turn of the 20th century, the strains of jazz could be heard in the

The Jazz Age and Mass Culture **635**

INTRODUCE & ENGAGE

BRAINSTORM IDEAS ABOUT JAZZ MUSIC

Display a Word Web with the term *jazz music* in the center circle. Ask students what they think of when someone mentions jazz music. Guide students to discuss their ideas about jazz and the decades or eras they associate with the genre. Then, as a class, identify as many famous jazz musicians and vocalists as possible and add the details to the Word Web. If there is time, repeat the same activity for blues music. Then tell students they are going to read an American Story that explains how jazz and the blues developed into uniquely American forms of music.

MAKE A LIST OF MUSIC GENRES

Write the following headings on the board: Jazz, Blues, Rock, Pop, Hip-Hop, Rap. Ask students to write each heading on a piece of paper and list examples of songs or musicians in each category. Then have the class share and discuss the lists. Tell students to keep notes on their lists about origins and influences as they read to see what connections they can make among contemporary genres, jazz, and the blues.

MAP LOCATIONS

Display a map of the United States and explain that jazz started in New Orleans and then spread to other cities. Point out on the map the cities where jazz music originally thrived, such as New Orleans, Chicago, New York, and Los Angeles. **ASK:** Why might these cities have been places where jazz first became popular? *(Possible response: These were growing cities with a large and diverse population that included music enthusiasts and musicians who enjoyed various types of music. Also, Chicago is directly north of New Orleans, so it would have made sense for musicians to travel between the two cities.)*

CRITICAL VIEWING A typical jazz band might include drums, a trumpet or some kind of horn, an upright bass, a clarinet, a piano, and a banjo.

CRITICAL VIEWING This 1943 oil painting by Chicago artist Archibald J. Motley, Jr., called *Nightlife*, depicts a crowded nightclub in a Chicago South Side neighborhood. What kind of mood does the painting convey?

streets of New Orleans. Two key features stood out as hallmarks of the jazz style: syncopation and improvisation. Syncopation is the temporary placement of stress on normally weak beats in a piece of music to create a complex rhythm. Improvisation is the act of composing and performing music on the spot. Modern-day jazz styles still feature catchy syncopated rhythms and dizzying original riffs improvised by performers.

NEXT STOP: CHICAGO

If New Orleans was the birthplace of jazz, Chicago was its nursery. In the 1910s and 1920s, many African Americans migrated north in search of better economic opportunities. Jazz musicians were part of this trend, and some of the most notable musicians landed in Chicago. Joe "King" Oliver was one of the best-known New Orleans transplants, playing with King Oliver's Creole Jazz Band on Chicago's South Side.

Today, Oliver is remembered not only for his own musical accomplishments but also for hiring one of jazz's legendary greats for his band. Trumpet player Louis Armstrong, also originally from New Orleans, brought the art of improvisation to new heights. Ron David, the author of *Jazz for Beginners*, describes Armstrong this way: "He built his improvisations like songs within a song, and his trumpet sound glowed." Also a singer, Armstrong had a distinctive vocal style and specialized in scatting, or singing improvised melodies in meaningless syllables.

The jazz craze spread like wildfire among diverse audiences in the 1920s, a decade now known as the Jazz Age. Young people flocked to nightclubs in Chicago, New York, Los Angeles, and other cities to hear jazz and to dance in ways their elders considered immodest. One of the most popular dances of the Jazz Age was the fast-paced, energetic Charleston, which featured quick kicking steps.

Jazz singer Ella Fitzgerald performs with Duke Ellington's band in this 1964 photograph.

THE WOMEN OF JAZZ

The female jazz musicians who have received the most acclaim are the great vocalists of the swing era and later, such as Ella Fitzgerald, Billie Holiday, and Lena Horne. Fitzgerald was a master of scatting, using her voice to weave complex improvised melodies around the beat of the band. Holiday, nicknamed "Lady Day," was known for her soulful and moving ballads. Horne, a dancer, singer, and actress, became one of the top African-American performers of her time, appearing in theater and movies and on television. She refused to accept any acting roles that stereotyped African-American women, and she became an activist in the civil rights movement.

A 1922 photograph shows Lil Hardin (center) performing with King Oliver's Creole Jazz Band in California.

Other lesser known but equally talented female jazz musicians include Lil Hardin and Mary Lou Williams. Born in 1898, Hardin was a pianist and composer. She started her career in New Orleans, where she played, wrote, and arranged music for several bands. After moving to Chicago, she played for King Oliver's Creole Jazz Band. She was married to Louis Armstrong from 1924 to 1938 and collaborated with him on a number of recordings. Williams was born in 1910 and was a composer, arranger, pianist, and bandleader whose work spanned several musical genres. During the swing era, she wrote and arranged pieces for Duke Ellington's band. Later, she worked in the style called bebop, which grew out of swing.

PRIMARY SOURCE

In a 1974 interview conducted by Canadian broadcast journalist Brian Linehan, Ella Fitzgerald was asked to explain her previous claim that she had "stolen from the horns" to create her singing style. In her reply, she spoke about the interaction between a singer and a musician, especially as she experienced it in jazz music.

You know, I think everybody steals from each other. I think that's the only way that we keep alive. As far as learning, it's just like going to school and learning history or learning anything. Actually when you're learning in school you're stealing something from another . . . from something from years back, but you add something to it, and that's the way people are.

We all learn something—the horns learn from another musician, and singers learn from another singer. And I like to try to sing like a horn sometimes in some of my songs, because to me, that's a great accomplishment, to try to feel like I'm playing what I hear a musician play.

—from Ella Fitzgerald, as interviewed by Brian Linehan on *City Lights*, a Canadian television show, 1974

The Jazz Age and Mass Culture **637**

GUIDED DISCUSSION

1. **Make Connections** How did the mixture of cultures in New Orleans influence the development of jazz there? *(The African Americans who lived in New Orleans created music based on African work songs and field hollers, and white Europeans brought classical music. The combined styles led to the development of jazz.)*

2. **Summarize** Why is the 1920s known as the Jazz Age? *(Jazz music became very popular during that decade. In major cities throughout the country, clubs played jazz music and people danced the Charleston.)*

THE WOMEN OF JAZZ

Direct students to the Primary Source feature and have a volunteer read the quotation aloud. Then share with students the following retelling, compiled from interviews with Ella Fitzgerald, of how she, an aspiring dancer, came to win a competition that set her sights in a new direction.

It was Amateur Night at the Apollo Theater in Harlem, and 15-year-old Fitzgerald took the stage and immediately came down with such a severe case of stage fright that her legs were shaking, making dancing impossible. Having to give the audience some kind of a performance, Fitzgerald decided, on the spot, to sing a song in the style of Connee Boswell, a singer whose sweet, lilting, and rhythmic voice she admired. Fitzgerald performed three encores and took home the $25 prize that night.

ASK: What connection do you find between Fitzgerald's experience in front of her first audience at the Apollo Theater and the quotation in the text? *(Possible response: Fitzgerald's natural ability to improvise and her ability to mimic sounds were evident early on. She quickly improvised and switched from dancing to singing, modeling her voice on a favorite singer, similar to how she described singing like a horn.)*

THE COTTON CLUB

Emphasize to students that the Cotton Club hired only African-American performers and workers but barred African Americans as customers. **ASK:** What effect do you think this arrangement had on the African Americans who worked at the club? *(Possible response: It must have been difficult for African Americans to work for an establishment that paid well but didn't admit African Americans as customers. The inequity of the arrangement probably put entertainers and staff in the tough position of working for whites who enjoyed more rights than they did.)*

JAZZ AND THE FLAPPER

Tell students that early in the 20th century, women were still wearing long dresses and corsets and pinning their hair into updos. Explain that styles changed drastically during the Jazz Age. **ASK:** How might the popularity of jazz music have influenced the flapper's style? *(Possible response: It would have been difficult to dance the Charleston in a long dress and corset, with hair precariously styled and pinned up. Jazz music probably influenced women's decisions to wear shorter skirts, looser and more comfortable clothes, and carefree bobbed hair.)*

SWINGING ON

A style of jazz called swing, which had a lively rhythm and was played by larger ensembles called big bands, became popular during the 1930s and 1940s. Some music scholars consider the swing era the golden age of jazz, and many would nominate Duke Ellington as the king of swing. Ellington was a bandleader, pianist, and composer. His songs, such as "It Don't Mean a Thing," are still recorded today.

During the swing era, most big bands were segregated. The white bandleader Benny Goodman was one of the few who hired both black and white musicians. Like many other successful bandleaders, Ellington was African-American. Even though his band toured nationally and played to both black and white audiences, Ellington and his musicians continually faced the possibility of being turned away from a gig because of the color of their skin.

THE COTTON CLUB

If you were trendy, fashionable, famous, or just hoping to hear some stellar jazz in 1920s New York City, the Cotton Club was the place to go. In this legendary nightclub, white audiences displayed a strange mix of admiration and disdain toward the conventionally African-American art form of jazz and those who performed it.

Located in Harlem, the Cotton Club had its heyday between 1922 and 1935. All workers and entertainers at the club were African Americans, but the clientele were exclusively white. The club's decor reflected a "stylish plantation environment," and the staff were dressed to reflect management's idea of enslaved people or plantation workers.

Despite the segregation and offensive depiction of African Americans, some of the greatest African-American jazz artists of the period played at the Cotton Club. Duke Ellington's orchestra performed as the house band between 1927 and 1931, after which the orchestra of another jazz great, Cab Calloway, took over. Cotton Club guest performers included Louis Armstrong, Ethel Waters, Lena Horne, and many other outstanding African-American musicians. Weekly radio broadcasts from the club brought their music to a national audience.

The Cotton Club moved to a new location after the Harlem riots of 1935, but it never regained its ranking as the premier New York nightclub. In 1940, it closed its doors for good.

How do you think the Cotton Club both helped and harmed the cause of African Americans?

This clapper, a percussion instrument, advertises the Cotton Club.

A Cotton Club poster from the 1930s publicizes the orchestra of Cab Calloway, a popular jazz singer and bandleader.

JAZZ AND THE FLAPPER

One popular image of the Jazz Age is the flapper, a young woman who bobbed her hair, sported a wide, lipstick-outlined smile, and wore a short, straight-waisted dress. Often, she was portrayed dancing.

Flappers were generally young white working women living in cities. As the economy improved in the 1920s, more jobs began opening up for women in offices, in department stores, and on telephone switchboards. At the same time, women had gained the right to vote. These changes helped produce a generation of newly independent-minded young women. Flappers abandoned the restrictive clothing of earlier times and adopted higher hemlines, bright colors, and cosmetics. In the evenings after work, they could be found dressed in daring new clothing styles and dancing to jazz music in nightclubs. They also engaged in smoking and drinking, activities formerly associated almost exclusively with men.

Not surprisingly, the flappers and their culture drew the condemnation of an outraged older generation. The president of the Christian Endeavor Society, for example, called jazz dancing "an offense against womanly purity." Nevertheless, even though the flappers' signature style faded away after the 1920s, their spirit of independence and youthful energy was passed on to the generations that followed.

Bobbed hair and shorter skirts were hallmarks of a flapper.

The Jazz Age and Mass Culture **639**

GUIDED DISCUSSION

3. **Analyze Language Use** Why might music scholars have considered the swing era to be "the golden age of jazz"? *(Possible response: The word* golden *suggests success and perfection, which is what band leaders and composers such as Duke Ellington and Benny Goodman achieved with their contributions to jazz. Their larger ensembles, with a greater variety of instruments and depth of sound that small jazz bands couldn't attain, allowed jazz to flourish and transform into swing.)*

4. **Compare and Contrast** What are some similarities and differences between jazz and blues music? *(Both were derived from African work songs and field hollers from the South, and both feature improvisation, especially in blues lyrics. The blues has rural roots and is characterized by a single artist playing guitar and singing about feelings and struggles. Jazz is more commonly associated with urban areas and is more popular than the blues. Ensembles of horns, drums, and basses often rely on syncopation and improvisation of musical rhythms and riffs rather than lyrics to convey feelings.)*

ACTIVE OPTIONS

On Your Feet: Write Blues Lyrics Arrange students in four or five groups and ask them to write lyrics for an original blues song using the structure in the text. Tell students to express a personal feeling or struggle and to repeat one line two or three times. Offer this example: *I woke up this mornin' / Couldn't find my phone / Ran out the house and knew I'd / Spend the day alone / Spend the day alone.* Once groups are finished, ask each group to share its blues song with the class. Encourage students to have fun with this activity.

NG Learning Framework: Compare Present-Day Music with the Past

`SKILLS` Observation, Communication

`KNOWLEDGE` Our Human Story

Instruct student groups to listen to a few jazz and blues songs recorded before 1950 and choose one to compare with a song of any genre recorded since the year 2000. Tell groups to choose songs with lyrics appropriate for a school setting. Direct groups to prepare a short presentation in which they introduce the two pieces of music (artist, title, genre, year released), play short audio clips they have prepared, and point out the similarities or influences. After all groups have completed their presentations, ask the class to discuss the music samples and identify past musicians who possibly influenced present-day artists.

JAZZ AND COMPANY

Explain to students that, in a period of less than 100 years, jazz and blues music led to the formation of diverse musical genres. **ASK:** Why do you think the blues and jazz helped create so many different genres over the course of time? *(Answers will vary. Possible response: Both genres featured improvisation, so musicians kept trying for different combinations of sounds. The most talented and innovative musicians succeeded in creating lasting music that influenced later artists.)*

WRITE ABOUT HISTORY

Examine How Jazz Reflects America This American Story describes the origins and development of jazz over the years and its effect on American culture. To help students make connections between this American Story and their own lives, ask them to write an essay about the American values or characteristics they believe jazz reflects. Remind students of where jazz originated and developed. Also have them consider which traits set jazz apart from other musical styles. Pair students to edit each other's essays and make suggestions for revision. Provide guidance about the writing process as necessary. Help students establish a style and organization that is appropriate for the task and audience.

THINK ABOUT IT

Possible response: Songs about rebellion or expressing views not accepted by parents or society in general are popular with young people. Playing this music, especially loudly, can allow young people to express their feelings and frustration about older generations' values and restrictions.

JAZZ TODAY

The popularity of jazz declined after the swing era, but the genre still has many dedicated fans and has evolved in a variety of directions. Some musicians have fused elements of jazz with the sounds of Latin and Caribbean music, while others have incorporated electronic instruments, such as synthesizers, and digital technology to move jazz into new realms. Still others continue to explore new ways to perform the classics of Duke Ellington, Louis Armstrong, Benny Goodman, and other jazz greats. Jazz in the 21st century is as diverse as those who perform it and those who listen to it.

THE EVOLUTION OF THE BLUES

Like jazz, the blues originated in the South, developing from such African roots as work songs and field hollers. The blues started out in rural areas rather than cities, sometime after the Civil War. Blues tunes principally expressed the singer's own feelings and struggles, and the instrument of choice was the guitar.

Even more than jazz, the blues featured improvisation, with singers making up both the words and melody as they played. Lyrics were often structured with one line being repeated two or three times, followed by a final line. Most of the early blues players were self-taught, and many could not read music. "The blues didn't come out of no book," the 1930s bluesman Big Bill Broonzy once remarked.

In the 1920s, blues musicians joined the northward migration to Chicago and other cities. Some of the most famous blues singers during this period were women, including Mamie Smith, who made the first blues record in 1920, and Bessie Smith, who became famous internationally. Born around 1898 to a poor family in Tennessee, Bessie Smith came to be known as the Empress of the Blues.

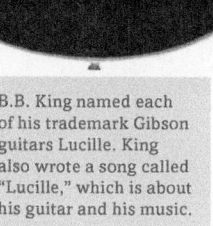

B.B. King named each of his trademark Gibson guitars Lucille. King also wrote a song called "Lucille," which is about his guitar and his music.

GREAT INFLUENCERS

Over the years, jazz and the blues would influence each other's sounds, but the two genres remained distinct. Unlike jazz, the blues never became a national craze. The blues remained popular mainly among African Americans. However, a few blues musicians, such as B.B. King, the King of the Blues, were able to cross over and appeal to a white audience.

In the 1940s, the blues branched out into rhythm and blues (R & B), and both genres influenced the development of rock and roll in the 1950s. Among the pioneers of rock and roll was the African-American singer, songwriter, and guitarist Chuck Berry, who influenced many later rock musicians. Elvis Presley recorded rock songs based on blues tunes, thrilling millions of avid young fans and scandalizing their parents with his energetic sound and his dance moves. As in the Jazz Age, parents and churches and other institutions sounded the alarm that the new music would surely warp young minds. Some of the criticisms were even racist in tone.

In later decades, rock and roll developed into rock music, which has gone in such diverse directions as heavy metal, alternative, and punk. In rap and hip-hop, listeners can trace the enduring blues elements of protest, personal expression, and irresistible rhythms. At the same time, jazz and the blues are still going strong in clubs, recording studios, and the hearts of fans.

THINK ABOUT IT

Why do you think young people turn to music to express their differences from their parents' generation?

JAZZ AND COMPANY

This chart shows the musical styles that blended to become jazz and blues, and many of the genres that evolved from jazz and blues. How many of the genres do you recognize? Which ones do you listen to?

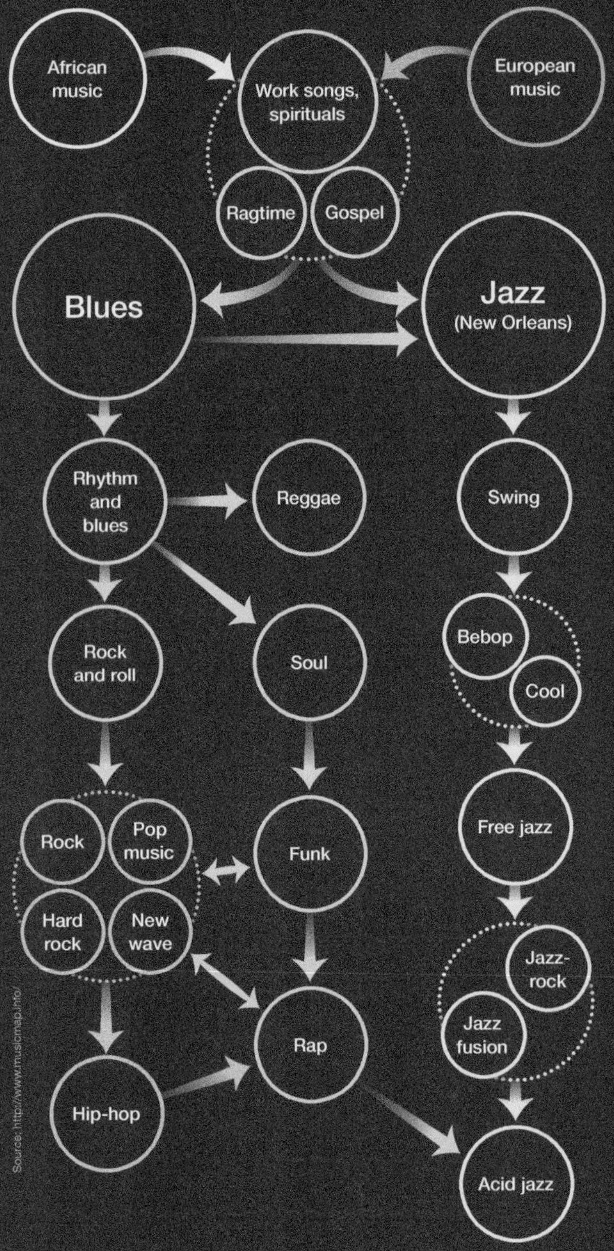

African music → Work songs, spirituals ← European music

Ragtime   Gospel

Blues ↔ Jazz (New Orleans)

Rhythm and blues → Reggae

Swing

Rock and roll   Soul

Bebop
Cool

Rock   Pop music   Funk

Free jazz

Hard rock   New wave

Jazz-rock

Rap   Jazz fusion

Hip-hop

Acid jazz

Source: http://www.musicmap.info/

The influence of a great musician often spans generations and can spark the development of new genres. Blues giant B.B. King influenced the guitar playing of hard rock musician Jimi Hendrix, who in turn influenced funk musician Prince.

B.B. King

influenced

Jimi Hendrix

influenced

Prince

The Jazz Age and Mass Culture **641**

DIFFERENTIATE

ENGLISH LANGUAGE LEARNERS

Use a Word Splash Display words from the text in a random splash arrangement. Words to display could include the following: *rhythms, melodies, syncopation, improvisation, flapper, lipstick, Harlem, Cotton Club, New Orleans, Chicago, jazz,* and *blues.* Ask students at **All Proficiencies** to choose three pairs of related words and write a sentence to show how they are related. Students can use this sentence starter: _____ and _____ are related because . . .

GIFTED & TALENTED

Create a Podcast Have students review the American Story and choose one artist to feature in a podcast. Tell students to conduct online research about the person's life and then focus on a particular aspect of the artist's music. Students should write a script for their podcast that discusses the artist's life and style and includes music clips to illustrate specific points made. Invite students to present their podcast to the class.

See the Chapter Planner for more strategies for differentiation.

HISTORICAL THINKING

Ask and have students answer the following questions.

1. **READING CHECK** How did jazz grow in popularity so rapidly?

2. **DRAW CONCLUSIONS** In what ways was the Jazz Age a liberating time for women?

3. **ANALYZE CAUSE AND EFFECT** How did racism affect African-American jazz musicians and bandleaders during this time?

ANSWERS

1. Jazz musicians moved north from New Orleans and introduced jazz to Chicago and New York City. Clubs sprang up throughout the country, and radio broadcasts from the clubs gave jazz nationwide exposure.

2. Many female composers, musicians, and vocalists had successes with jazz hits during this time. Jazz-age flappers adopted less restrictive clothing and hairstyles and became more socially liberated and independent than women of the previous generation.

3. Racism was accepted in society, and most big bands were segregated. African-American bands could be turned away from engagements based solely on their skin color. The Cotton Club, with its all-white clientele and all–African-American entertainment and service, was hugely popular and a desirable gig. Musicians who performed there were aware that they were not welcome in the audience.

MAIN IDEA In the years following World War I, a fear of communism gripped the United States and led to tensions between individual rights and the power of government.

THE RED SCARE

Think about something that scares you. What makes it so frightening? Following World War I, the threat of communism spreading to the United States frightened many Americans and put the nation on edge.

CONCERNS ABOUT COMMUNISM

The 1920s would eventually become a decade of prosperity in the United States. But as you have read, the economy stumbled right after World War I as it shifted from wartime to peacetime. Production declined as the federal government canceled war contracts for the manufacturing of defense materials, such as rifles, bullets, and bombs. These slowdowns led to large-scale layoffs just as some 4 million soldiers were returning home in need of jobs, contributing to a two-year postwar recession.

The postwar economic slowdown spurred social unrest, from racial tensions to large strikes. During these anxious times, American leaders worried that the ideas of communism might spread to the United States. As you have learned, the Russian Revolution in 1917 resulted in the formation of the Soviet Union under communist-style rule, in which the government controls all business and the distribution of goods and food. As the United States struggled economically, some Americans viewed communism as fairer and more equitable than **capitalism**, an economic system in which private individuals or groups own the resources and produce goods for a profit.

FEAR GRIPS THE NATION

The emotions sparked by postwar unrest fueled the **Red Scare** of 1919 and 1920, a time when the federal government targeted suspected communists, anarchists, and

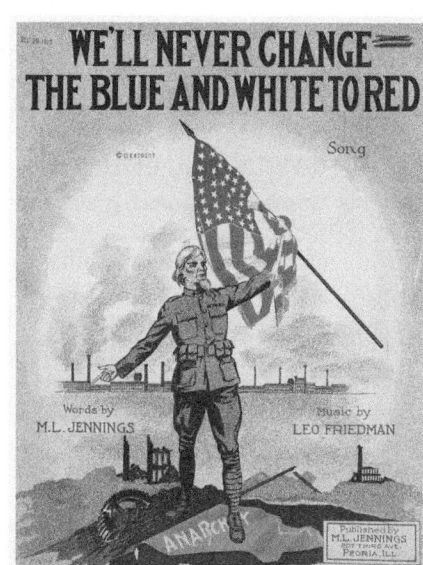

CRITICAL VIEWING Americans wrote songs such as "We'll Never Change the Blue and White to Red" after World War I amid growing fears of communism. What would "anarchy" lead to according to the cover of this sheet music?

radicals, or people who hold extreme political views. After these groups were blamed for a series of mail bombs, officials went on the offensive. Attorney General **A. Mitchell Palmer** obtained funding from Congress to establish a division in the Justice Department to hunt for radicals, naming **J. Edgar Hoover** as the head of the division. In November 1919, officials working under Palmer's direction conducted what were known as the **Palmer Raids**. Police broke into the homes and offices of suspected radicals, including labor union leaders and Russian immigrants. They made scores of arrests, often without obtaining search warrants. By January 1920, authorities had deported some 300 Russian immigrants to the Soviet Union under suspicion of communist activities.

Union leaders of the Industrial Workers of the World (IWW) "Big Bill" Haywood (seated, left) and George Speed (seated, right) appeared in court after their arrests during the Palmer Raids.

Throughout the country, Americans' civil liberties came under assault. Officials outlawed the Communist Party, and state legislatures imposed restrictions on groups and ideas they deemed radical. The Supreme Court upheld most of the laws restricting civil liberties during this time. In *Schenck* v. *United States* (1919), Charles Schenck faced espionage charges for handing out flyers encouraging citizens to resist the military draft. He claimed his arrest violated the First Amendment. However, Justice Oliver Wendell Holmes, Jr., argued that the flyers posed a "clear and present danger" to American society and were not protected by the amendment. Schenck served 10 years in prison for the flyers. In 1927, the Court reaffirmed the verdict in *Whitney* v. *California*. That case involved a Communist Party leader convicted for making a speech that some people interpreted as encouraging violence against the government.

PRIMARY SOURCE

My best judgment of America's needs is to steady down, to get squarely on our feet, to make sure of the right path. Let's get out of the fevered delirium of war, with the hallucination that all the money in the world is to be made in the madness of war and . . . its aftermath. Let us stop to consider that tranquility at home is more precious than peace abroad, and that both our good fortune and our eminence [greatness] are dependent on the normal forward stride of all the American people.

—from Warren G. Harding's campaign speech, 1920

Concern that the Red Scare was weakening freedoms protected by the Constitution led to the founding of the **American Civil Liberties Union (ACLU)** in 1920. The organization dedicated itself to defending the individual rights and freedoms of all Americans. The **Anti-Defamation League (ADL)** also worked to expose and counter the violence of extremist groups, including the Ku Klux Klan, which spread anti-Semitic and anticommunist propaganda. By late 1920, the Red Scare had lost momentum. Palmer had predicted ongoing violence, which never occurred, and his credibility was damaged.

The unrest and anxiety that immediately followed the war influenced the 1920 presidential election. Warren G. Harding easily won the election on his promise to "return to normalcy." He spoke of returning to an era of peace, wealth, and conservative values by reducing the power of government, lowering taxes, and reining in labor unions. Despite Harding's victory, the years ahead would be anything but normal. The 1920s would be a decade of extremes in the United States, combining broad cultural leaps toward modernity with deep anxiety about the country changing too fast and for the worse.

HISTORICAL THINKING

1. **READING CHECK** How did the end of World War I lead to a postwar recession?

2. **COMPARE AND CONTRAST** How was communism different from capitalism?

3. **EVALUATE** Why might the Palmer Raids be considered unconstitutional?

The Jazz Age and Mass Culture **643**

PLAN: 2-PAGE LESSON

OBJECTIVE

Analyze the effects of the Red Scare of 1919 and 1920 on civil liberties in the United States.

CRITICAL THINKING SKILLS FOR LESSON 1.1

• Compare and Contrast

• Evaluate

• Analyze Cause and Effect

• Analyze Primary Sources

HISTORICAL THINKING FOR CHAPTER 18

How did the Roaring Twenties both divide and unite Americans? Concerns in the federal government about communism becoming attractive to Americans during the economic decline of the early 1920s led to a Justice Department assault on suspected radicals. Lesson 1.1 explores the causes and consequences of government's restrictions of Americans' civil liberties.

BACKGROUND FOR THE TEACHER

A. Mitchell Palmer had a personal reason for pursuing radicals. On June 2, 1919, anarchist Carlo Valdinoci blew up the front of Palmer's house, dying in the process. Palmer was one of many politicians, judges, state and local officials, and prominent businesspeople targeted by radicals. Valdinoci was a follower of the Italian anarchist Luigi Galleani. The Galleanists were responsible for the series of mail bombs that alarmed the nation in late April 1919. Most of the mail bombs failed to reach their intended victims because the packages lacked sufficient postage, and a postal worker discovered the bombs before they could detonate. On June 2, the anarchists planted several bombs that killed two people, including Valdinoci. Palmer, who had ambitions to run for president in 1920 as a law-and-order candidate, used the Espionage Act of 1917 and the Sedition Act of 1918 to pursue the radicals.

INTRODUCE & ENGAGE

ACTIVATE PRIOR KNOWLEDGE

Invite students to share what they have learned about the Russian Revolution and communism. Record and display student responses in a Word Web for each term. Ask students to use ideas from the Word Webs to discuss why communism might have worried some Americans. Tell students that in Lesson 1.1 they will learn how fear of the spread of communism contributed to attacks on civil liberties in the United States.

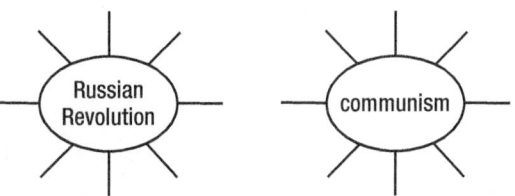

TEACH

GUIDED DISCUSSION

1. **Analyze Cause and Effect** What events and concerns led to the Palmer Raids? *(Postwar unrest and the fear of the spread of communism heightened worries about communists, anarchists, and radicals in the United States. Blame for mail bombs fell on radical groups, so Attorney General A. Mitchell Palmer created a Justice Department division to hunt for suspected radicals.)*

2. **Compare and Contrast** How were the goals of the American Civil Liberties Union and the Anti-Defamation League similar and different? *(Possible response: Both groups were concerned with protecting individuals' rights and freedoms guaranteed by the Constitution. The ACLU focused on protecting Americans' guaranteed rights, while the ADL focused on exposing radical extremist groups, such as the Ku Klux Klan.)*

ANALYZE PRIMARY SOURCES

Direct students' attention to the Primary Source feature. Have them work in groups to answer the following question: What did Warren G. Harding think was the right path for the United States? *(Possible response: Harding thought the United States should back away from its internationalist role and concentrate on achieving stability at home through normal business practices and ideals.)* Ask groups to share their ideas in a class discussion.

ACTIVE OPTIONS

On Your Feet: Discuss Supreme Court Opinions Have students form two groups. Provide one group with a copy of Oliver W. Holmes, Jr.'s majority opinion in *Schenck* v. *United States* (1919) and the other group with a copy of Louis Brandeis's concurring opinion in *Whitney* v. *California* (1927). Tell students to read the opinion provided and list the justice's main ideas and arguments. Reconvene the class and have students from the groups take turns stating one fact about the opinion from their list until all facts have been read. Guide students to discuss major similarities and differences between the two opinions and what accounts for them.

NG Learning Framework: Debate Civil Liberties Versus National Security

ATTITUDE Empowerment

KNOWLEDGE Our Human Story

Invite students to engage in a class debate. Direct half the class to argue in favor of preserving civil liberties, drawing on the views of the ACLU and ADL. The other half of the class should argue in favor of the need to protect national security, drawing on the views of A. Mitchell Palmer. Instruct groups to research their positions in context of that time period, using the text and other resources. After the debate, encourage students to discuss the strongest arguments presented by both sides.

DIFFERENTIATE

STRIVING READERS

Ready, Set, Recall After students have read the lesson, set a short time limit and tell them to write a list of facts they learned. Direct students to work in pairs to compare and combine their lists. Then ask pairs to alternately read facts from their lists until all pairs run out of new details. Keep a tally of the number of facts each pair contributes, and the one with the most facts wins.

PRE-AP

Research the Red Scare Ask students to review information they learned about the Red Scare. Tell them to use print and online resources to dig deeper and find two or three additional facts. Ask students to prepare a short oral report about their findings and present it to the whole class.

See the Chapter Planner for more strategies for differentiation.

HISTORICAL THINKING

ANSWERS

1. After the war, canceled government defense contracts caused a slowdown in manufacturing that led to massive layoffs at a time when returning soldiers were looking for work.

2. Under communism, the central government controls businesses and the distribution of goods and food. Under capitalism, private individuals or groups own the resources and produce goods for profit.

3. The Palmer Raids involved breaking into homes and offices without search warrants. The Constitution guarantees protection against wholesale searches without probable cause and warrants naming specific items and persons to be searched or seized.

CRITICAL VIEWING A pile of industrial rubble, including a partially buried cog, is labeled "Anarchy," suggesting that anarchy would lead to businesses—and therefore capitalism—being destroyed.

DIVISIONS IN SOCIETY

Sometimes it's hard to let go of old ideas, especially ideas that make you feel comfortable and secure. During the 1920s, changes in society challenged traditional ways and sparked anxiety and division.

POINTING FINGERS

After a few difficult years following World War I, the nation's economy began to recover. This triggered a wave of immigrants from around the world. More than 430,000 people sought entry to the United States in 1920, and another 805,000 immigrants came in 1921. Competition with immigrants for jobs—along with the Red Scare—contributed to a rise in nativism. This ideology favored people born in the United States over more recent immigrants. Nativists especially targeted immigrants from southern and eastern Europe, who were more willing to work for low wages. Adding to the anti-immigrant sentiment was a rise in the popularity of **eugenics**, the belief that some races are superior to others. Eugenicists thought that the more "desirable" race, which was usually western European and Protestant, should populate and grow.

The rise of nativists and eugenicists—who warned of the "degradation" of the population—prompted U.S. lawmakers to take action. Congress approved an emergency quota law in 1921 that limited immigration from Europe to 600,000 people per year. Three years later, lawmakers passed the **National Origins Act**, which reduced annual legal immigration from Europe to about 150,000 people. The act gave preference to people from western and northern European countries and blocked Asian immigrants entirely.

The courts often supported anti-immigrant legislation. One case that highlighted the courts' view involved an immigrant named Bhagat Singh Thind. Thind arrived in the United States from India in 1913 and began studying at the University of California at Berkeley. He volunteered for service in the U.S. Army during World War I. In 1920, he applied for U.S. citizenship, but he was denied under a 1917 law that barred all immigration from India. He took his case to the U.S. Supreme Court. In the 1923 case, *United States* v. *Bhagat Singh Thind*, the Court ruled that "Hindus" were "aliens ineligible to citizenship." In effect, the ruling established that the federal government could deny citizenship based merely on race or country of origin.

Concerns about immigration played into another prominent court case—a highly controversial murder trial that grabbed global headlines. In 1920, a robbery and murder took place in South Braintree, Massachusetts. Police arrested two Italian immigrants who were also known anarchists, Nicola Sacco and Bartolomeo Vanzetti. Despite claims that authorities had framed the two men, a jury found them guilty and sentenced them to death. People around the world protested against this trial, which came to be called the **Sacco-Vanzetti case**. Many believed that bias against immigrants and radical political beliefs had led to an unfair trial. During the next several years, the men's attorneys filed appeals to overturn the verdict. The American Civil Liberties Union even aided in their defense. However, by 1927, their appeals had run out, and the state of Massachusetts executed the men.

THE RISE OF THE KLAN

Nativist sentiments led to the re-emergence of the Ku Klux Klan. The Klan, as you have read, opposed Catholics, Jews, Asians, women, African Americans, and other minorities. The group, known for its white hoods, regained popularity in the 1920s and spread its beliefs of white supremacy into northern states. Its members often used violence and terrorist tactics to intimidate those they opposed. Despite its reputation for brutality, including lynching and even torture, the Klan influenced many local and state leaders. Both Democrats and Republicans adopted some of the Klan's language to appeal to voters concerned about the rise of immigration.

The Klan claimed it had 3 million members by the early 1920s, but the organization's national influence began to decline around 1925 after scandals exposed widespread corruption. Meanwhile, groups such as the NAACP fought back against Klan violence through lawsuits and efforts to pass anti-lynching legislation. Despite ongoing racism, African Americans continued to make their voices heard during the 1920s, demanding more opportunities in all aspects of American society. In particular, African-American veterans of World War I expressed their beliefs that people who had risked their lives for their country should not be discriminated against.

CRITICAL VIEWING Syracuse University is home to artist Ben Shahn's 1967 mosaic mural *The Passion of Sacco and Vanzetti* (above). The detail of the mural (right) shows the men who upheld the death sentence standing before Sacco's and Vanzetti's coffins. The trial judge is in the background. Shahn, like many people, thought the men hadn't received a fair trial. What does the artist suggest about the judge and these men by including them in this mural?

PRIMARY SOURCES

Madison Grant was a nativist and a eugenics advocate. Franz Boas was an anthropologist and an opponent of such beliefs. The two held opposite views on immigration and diversity.

These immigrants adopt the language of the native[-born] American, they wear his clothes, they steal his name and they are beginning to take his women, but they seldom adopt his religion or understand his ideals and while he is being elbowed out of his own home the American looks calmly abroad and urges on others the suicidal ethics which are exterminating his own race.

—from *The Passing of the Great Race*, by Madison Grant, 1916

The fear of continued segregation of European national groups is not founded on facts, but on vague impressions obtained from the massing of immigrants in congested city quarters. It does not take into consideration the dispersion of the second and third generation, who become so thoroughly Americanized that in many cases it is quite impossible to obtain exact information in regard to the provenience [origin] of individuals.

—from "This Nordic Nonsense," by Franz Boas in *The Forum*, 1925

The Jazz Age and Mass Culture **645**

PLAN: 4-PAGE LESSON

OBJECTIVE

Describe how clashing values divided American society in the 1920s.

CRITICAL THINKING SKILLS FOR LESSON 1.2

- Make Inferences
- Analyze Cause and Effect
- Draw Conclusions
- Make Connections
- Analyze Primary Sources
- Evaluate

HISTORICAL THINKING FOR CHAPTER 18

How did the Roaring Twenties both divide and unite Americans? Immigration, Prohibition, and new scientific theories that challenged traditional beliefs led to anxiety and unrest in the 1920s. Lesson 1.2 examines the causes and consequences of changing society.

BACKGROUND FOR THE TEACHER

Artist Ben Shahn, an immigrant from Eastern Europe, was deeply affected by the Sacco-Vanzetti case. Convinced of the men's innocence, Shahn joined protests following the pair's convictions and then created a series of 23 paintings about the case in the 1930s. The artwork shown is part of a 60-foot mosaic mural that was installed at Syracuse University in 1967. This particular mural chronicles the case in three sections—a group of men, likely immigrants, holding signs and protesting the convictions; Sacco and Vanzetti standing in heroic poses; and the two executed anarchists in their coffins being viewed by the men responsible for the deaths, including Massachusetts governor Alvan T. Fuller and his advisory committee (shown in this lesson). The symbolism in *The Passion of Sacco and Vanzetti* reflects Shahn's view of the case. He likened the executions to the crucifixion of Christ and viewed Sacco and Vanzetti as martyrs.

CONSIDER SOCIAL DIVISIONS

Guide students to suggest some issues that divide American society today, such as health care, climate change, or community policing. **ASK:** Why do you think people have such different beliefs about these issues? *(Answers will vary. Students might point out that religious beliefs could dictate peoples' values, varying levels of education among socioeconomic groups create differences in exposure to and understanding of facts, or that living in different environments, for example urban vs. rural, creates different experiences and values.)* Tell students that in this lesson they will learn about issues that divided American society during the 1920s.

TEACH

GUIDED DISCUSSION

1. **Make Connections** How is the National Origins Act connected to the social trends of nativism and eugenics? *(Warnings from nativists and eugenicists that immigration was degrading the U.S. population led Congress to pass the act, thereby reducing annual immigration, giving preference to western and northern Europeans and blocking Asian immigration.)*

2. **Make Inferences** How did the reemergence of the Ku Klux Klan contribute to the curtailing of some Americans' civil liberties? *(Possible response: The Klan spread white supremacist beliefs and violence against African Americans and other minorities into northern states, and many politicians used Klan language to appeal to voters' fears about immigration.)*

ANALYZE PRIMARY SOURCES

Direct students' attention to the Primary Sources feature. Have them work in pairs to identify and evaluate examples of bias or prejudice in Madison Grant's and Franz Boas's differing claims about immigration and diversity. Encourage students to use a table like the one shown to list and explain examples of bias. Then hold a class discussion in which pairs share their analyses. Ask students to explain the fear that specific words or phrases are playing to. *(Possible response: Students might point out that "being elbowed out" plays to the nativist fear that immigrants will come in great numbers and overwhelm cities, forcing so-called natives from their homes.)*

Language	How It Illustrates Bias

ENGLISH LANGUAGE LEARNERS

Understanding Word Roots Bring students' attention to the words *nativism* and *eugenics*. Model pronunciation and explain that both roots, *nat-* and *-gen,* relate to being born. Pair students at the **Emerging** or **Expanding** level with English-proficient students and have them make word cards with each word's definition and pronunciation and a sentence to illustrate meaning. Challenge students to find other words using these roots, such as *nation, native, genetics,* and *genocide.* Provide the following sentence frames to help students at each proficiency level explain the meaning of these words:

- **Emerging:** This root means _____. So that word means _____.
- **Expanding:** _____ is a root. It means _____. So the word _____ means _____.

GIFTED & TALENTED

Create a Science Meme Direct students to conduct online research into the scientific work and breakthroughs of Einstein, Freud, or Darwin. Then challenge them to summarize that person's mind-set or encapsulate a controversial aspect of his work in a brief phrase. Students may then find a relevant image that is available for public use or create an image of their own. Finally, direct students to use a meme-creation tool to overlay their phrase onto the image. Students may otherwise sketch the meme using pen and paper. Invite students to share their memes with the class.

See the Chapter Planner for more strategies for differentiation.

CRITICAL VIEWING Answers will vary. Possible response: Shahn seems to be implying that the men are being hypocritical by mourning the deaths of Sacco and Vanzetti since they were the individuals who upheld the pair's death sentences.

To enforce prohibition, agents, often in disguise, identified places where alcohol was being served and confiscated it. In this photo from 1921, agents pour a barrel of beer down a sewer in New York City.

MOBSTERS AND BOOTLEGGERS

As you have read, the 18th Amendment and the Volstead Act had outlawed the sale of alcohol by 1920. Many progressives believed that these laws would decrease alcohol abuse in the United States. Overall, the laws achieved this goal. National consumption of alcohol declined significantly and rates of alcoholism dropped in the first few years of Prohibition.

However, Prohibition had unintended consequences. Across the United States, **bootleggers**, or people who made, transported, or supplied alcohol illegally, sold their products to saloons or **speakeasies**, illegal drinking clubs where people secretly gathered in the evenings. Most speakeasies were tucked away in the back room or basement of a legitimate business, such as a store or a restaurant. To assure security, patrons often had to give a password at the door to be allowed in. Eventually, millions of

middle-class Americans regularly broke the law by continuing to frequent speakeasies and purchase or make alcoholic beverages. Meanwhile, mobsters and their gangs became involved in the sale of illegal liquor, leading to a wave of violence and killing among rival crime organizations. Prohibition did not create organized crime. In fact, the 1920s was not a decade of rising crime rates overall. However, the nation became more aware of crime as a social problem due to the well-publicized activities of gangsters such as **Alphonse "Al" Capone**. In the later years of the decade, Capone ran a huge and notorious organization of illegal saloons, gambling houses, and other shady businesses in Chicago.

DISCOVERIES IN SCIENCE

The anxiety and unrest that emerged during the early 1920s was also fueled by new scientific theories that challenged traditional beliefs. Scientists like **Albert Einstein** argued that space, time, and mass

Albert Einstein won the Nobel Prize for Physics in 1921 for his work on relativity. Here, he was photographed while lecturing in Vienna, Austria, in 1921. That same year, Einstein, a German, visited the United States. He was impressed during his visit by what he called Americans' "joyous, positive attitude to life."

were all relative rather than absolute. This caused people to question traditional ideas about the nature of the universe. Psychologist **Sigmund Freud** suggested that the unconscious mind controlled much of an individual's behavior, an idea that opposed established notions about the causes of mental illness and emotional distress.

These new concepts spurred passionate debates among some American Christians over the proper position to take on scientific matters. Some Christians looked for ways to incorporate new scientific and social ideas into their traditional belief systems, but conservative church leaders preached about the dangers of moving away from the strict teachings of the Bible. This led to the rise of **fundamentalism**, a movement that promoted the idea that every word of the Bible was the literal truth.

Fundamentalists criticized many aspects of modern thinking. In particular, they targeted Charles Darwin's theory of evolution, which, as you will remember, stated that diverse species originated from common ancestors and only the strongest species have adapted and changed in order to survive. Fundamentalists argued that the theory undermined the Bible's teaching that God created all life, including human life, at one fixed point in time. Lawyer and politician William Jennings Bryan emerged as a leading opponent of evolution. "It is better to trust the Rock of Ages," he said, "than to know the age of rocks." In a dozen states, lawmakers introduced bills to ban the teaching of evolution in public schools. A group called the Anti-Evolution League formed to challenge Darwin's theory. Its members hoped to ban the teaching of evolution throughout the nation.

In 1925, Tennessee passed a law that prohibited spending public money "to teach any theory that denies the story of the Divine Creation of man as taught in the Bible." That same year, authorities arrested and tried teacher **John T. Scopes** for talking about evolution in his high school classroom in Dayton, Tennessee. The Scopes trial attracted national attention, with many viewing it as a clash between traditional and modern ideas.

Bryan agreed to help prosecute Scopes. The ACLU brought in noted trial lawyer **Clarence Darrow** to defend the teacher. The judge refused to let Darrow call in scientists to defend evolution, so Darrow called Bryan as an expert witness on the Bible. Bryan defended the literal interpretation of the Bible. However, under Darrow's cross-examination, Bryan came across as contradictory and uncertain. The jury found Scopes guilty and assessed him a small fine. Although Scopes lost the trial, many Americans believed that Bryan's fundamentalism had lost the battle to science and reason.

HISTORICAL THINKING

1. **READING CHECK** What prompted the wave of immigration to the United States in the early 1920s?

2. **MAKE INFERENCES** How did nativist and eugenic beliefs fuel opposition to immigrants?

3. **ANALYZE CAUSE AND EFFECT** What effect did Prohibition have on alcohol consumption in the United States?

4. **DRAW CONCLUSIONS** Why was the Scopes trial viewed as both a victory and a defeat for fundamentalism?

BUILD BACKGROUND

TENNESSEE'S ANTI-EVOLUTION LAW

The Butler Act—the Tennessee anti-evolution law that led to the Scopes trial— represented a broad reaction against educational reforms designed to help students function in an industrial nation. By 1920, many high schools taught civic biology, an approach that sought to teach life science concepts, such as hygiene, that were critical to public health in urban areas and to provide knowledge relevant to industrialization. Farm families saw this as a threat to their way of life.

Tennessee governor Austin Peay, who had run for office on the promise of progressive educational reform, faced rural opposition when he introduced legislation to require every county to have a high school and require all state students to attend school. While the governor's legislation was tied up in committee, state senator John Washington Butler pushed through the anti-evolution bill. The bill's religious wording heightened its appeal among many rural residents.

The ACLU focused on the Butler Act as an infringement on academic freedom and free speech. The organization arranged a challenge to the law as a way to gain judicial recognition of the principle of academic freedom. After the ACLU let it be known that its attorneys would defend any Tennessee teacher charged with teaching evolution, business and political leaders in Dayton, Tennessee, asked John Scopes if he would be willing to be indicted and stand trial.

TEACH

GUIDED DISCUSSION

3. **Analyze Cause and Effect** What historical events influenced Al Capone's rise to power? *(Possible response: The continued demand for alcohol during Prohibition provided Al Capone with opportunities to meet the demand through illegal activities.)*

4. **Draw Conclusions** Why did some Americans in the 1920s find the ideas of Einstein and Freud disquieting? *(Both theorists' ideas made many Americans uncomfortable because they challenged long-held beliefs. Einstein challenged beliefs about the universe when he argued that space, time, and mass are relative. Freud challenged beliefs about mental illness and emotional distress by claiming that the unconscious mind controls much of human behavior.)*

EVALUATE

Ask students to consider whether the teaching of evolution in schools and state laws forbidding the teaching of evolution could both be considered attacks on civil liberties. **ASK**: Whose civil liberties might have been limited by teaching evolution and whose by forbidding discussion of evolution in schools? *(Answers will vary. Possible response: Fundamentalists may have felt students' right to exercise their religion was infringed by requirements to study a theory that contradicted their beliefs; teachers and other students may have felt their free speech was limited by the restriction.)*

ACTIVE OPTIONS

On Your Feet: Fishbowl Arrange students in two groups. Direct Group 1 to sit in a close circle and discuss why *United States* v. *Bhagat Singh Thind* represents an attack on civil liberties. Tell Group 2 to form a circle around Group 1 and take notes on the discussion. Then have groups switch positions and repeat the activity, with the inner circle discussing why the Sacco and Vanzetti case represents an attack on civil liberties.

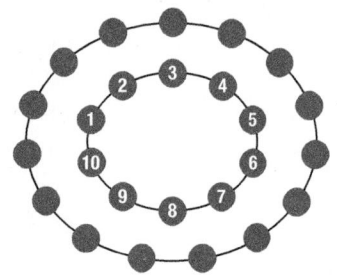

NG Learning Framework: Research Prohibition

ATTITUDE Curiosity

SKILL Communication

Direct students to work in groups to generate a question they can research about the unintended consequences of Prohibition, such as the following: How did Prohibition contribute to illegal activities in the 1920s? Tell students to research the question using both print and online sources. Then have groups use their research findings to help them hold a class discussion on why it is difficult to predict the effects of a piece of legislation.

HISTORICAL THINKING

ANSWERS

1. A wave of immigrants came to the United States in the early 1920s to take advantage of the country's improving economy.

2. Nativists believed their native-born status should give them preference over newly arrived immigrants, who often would work for less pay and compete with nativists for jobs. At the same time, promoters of eugenics were asserting that western European Protestants (whites) were superior to other races and should therefore flourish. This atmosphere of fear and rejection prompted Congress to block or limit the number of immigrants it deemed undesirable.

3. Alcohol consumption declined initially, but Americans continued to consume alcohol that they made for themselves at home or bought at speakeasies.

4. Scopes was convicted and fined for violating Tennessee law, a victory for fundamentalism. Clarence Darrow's cross-examination of William Jennings Bryan, however, revealed weaknesses and contradictions in Bryan's defense of the literal interpretation of the Bible, which many Americans noticed.

1.3 GEOLOGY IN HISTORY

MAIN IDEA Caves provided shelter for early humans and served another role thousands of years later: a place to locate speakeasies during Prohibition.

HOW GEOLOGY KEPT THE '20S ROARING
By Andrés Ruzo, National Geographic Explorer

A cave may not be where you choose to hang out with friends, but in the 1920s, caves had their attractions. For one thing, they made good hiding places. For another, in some of them, alcohol was served.

CRITICAL VIEWING The top photo shows the Longhorn Cavern in Burnet, Texas, which was converted into a speakeasy during Prohibition, complete with a wooden dance floor. The bottom photo shows the cavern today. What geologic elements shown in these pictures reveal why a cave would make an effective speakeasy?

FINDING THE PERFECT SPEAKEASY

For many people during the 1920s, hiding out and drinking were both important considerations. As you have read, the 18th Amendment, popularly known as Prohibition, had passed, making the sale, production, importation, and transportation of alcoholic beverages illegal. Household consumption of the beverages was still legal, but unless people made their own, they had no way of getting a drink—except illegally, of course.

One of the best places to buy illegal alcoholic drinks was at a speakeasy. The word *speakeasy* suggests the need to whisper, and that's just what people often had to do to get into one of these establishments. Some required a password, others a secret knock or handshake. But these precautions didn't stop the determined. People flocked to speakeasies to drink, dance, enjoy music, and just have a good time.

Still, no one wanted to be arrested, so it was important to find the right speakeasy. Privacy, comfort, seclusion, safety, and getaway routes were all factors to consider. Speakeasies promising all these things popped up everywhere: in cities and in the country as well as in homes and businesses. Some were even in caves.

HUNKERING DOWN IN CAVES

In prehistoric times, early humans took refuge from their often hostile environment in caves. Geology was also on the side of Prohibition-era Americans who sought out caves because they provided shelter from the law. Caves form over hundreds or even millions of years in rocks as water drips through their cracks, eventually hollowing out underground channels. These make for perfect hideouts and even allow for

secret passageways to be carved into the rock. And, with their thick walls, caves are insulated from the weather and so maintain near-constant temperatures all year round. As a result, speakeasies in caves were cool in the summer and relatively warm in the winter.

During Prohibition, these amenities attracted customers to the speakeasy at the Longhorn Cavern in Burnet, Texas, not far from the state capital of Austin. With its spacious dance room and dining area, the speakeasy provided a fairly respectable setting. In contrast, the speakeasy at the De Soto Cavern near Birmingham, Alabama, was known for its violence. Fights and shootings earned the speakeasy the nickname "the bloody bucket." Drunken patrons sometimes shot at the cave's **stalactites** and **stalagmites**—mineral deposits hanging from its ceiling or rising from its floor—and bullet holes can still be seen in the rock.

In 1933, Congress repealed the 18th Amendment—the only amendment to be entirely reversed—and liquor flowed freely once more. But Prohibition had forced people to think geologically and seek refuge in caves. The decade may have started on a dry note, but caves helped keep the '20s roaring.

THINK LIKE A GEOLOGIST

1. **READING CHECK** What factors did people look for in a speakeasy?

2. **ANALYZE ENVIRONMENTAL CONCEPTS** How did the formation of caves lead some people to benefit from this natural process during Prohibition?

3. **FORM AND SUPPORT OPINIONS** Would you like to explore a cave? Why or why not?

OBJECTIVE

Explain how geology helped some Americans evade Prohibition laws.

CRITICAL THINKING SKILLS FOR LESSON 1.3

• Analyze Environmental Concepts

• Form and Support Opinions

• Summarize

• Analyze Cause and Effect

• Integrate Visuals

HISTORICAL THINKING FOR CHAPTER 18

How did the Roaring Twenties both divide and unite Americans? Not all Americans agreed with Prohibition. Lesson 1.3 explores how geology helped some Americans get around the laws.

NATIONAL GEOGRAPHIC EXPLORER ANDRÉS RUZO

In this lesson, geoscientist Andrés Ruzo explains how people make use of geology for reasons other than getting the upper hand in a land battle. Longhorn Cavern began to form about 500 million years ago when limestone settled in a shallow sea that covered present-day central Texas. About 150 million years later, mountains uplifted, causing fractures that allowed water to run through the rock and dissolve some of the limestone. Formation continued as rainwater seeped from the surface. Underground water from below eroded rock and washed away stalagmites and stalactites as they formed, so Longhorn Cavern has few of either.

HISTORY NOTEBOOK

Encourage students to complete the Geology in History page for Chapter 18 in their History Notebooks as they read.

INTRODUCE & ENGAGE

DISCUSS CAVES

Ask students to recount stories they have read or legends they have heard about pirates, outlaws, and other people using caves as hiding places. **ASK:** What makes caves such good hiding places? *(Possible responses: They often have many chambers and passageways. They're dark. They're often in secluded places.)* Tell students that during Prohibition some people thought caves were an ideal location to illegally drink alcohol.

TEACH

STEM

GUIDED DISCUSSION

1. **Summarize** What was and was not allowed under the provisions of the 18th Amendment? *(It was illegal to sell, produce, import, or transport alcohol. People could legally drink alcohol at home, but they had to make their own.)*

2. **Analyze Cause and Effect** Why were speakeasies like the ones in the Longhorn and De Soto caverns no longer needed after 1933? *(Congress repealed Prohibition in 1933, allowing people once again to legally buy and drink alcohol in public.)*

GEOLOGY IN HISTORY

Integrate Visuals Have students reread the geologic information in the lesson and then examine the two photographs. **ASK:** Which geologic features mentioned in the text are missing from the photographs of the Longhorn Cavern? *(stalactites and stalagmites)* **ASK:** What is one way that the owner of the Longhorn Cavern speakeasy modified the natural processes in the cave to benefit patrons? *(Possible response: The owner added a wooden dance floor.)*

ACTIVE OPTIONS

On Your Feet: Turn and Talk Have students form small groups. Give each group this topic sentence: Geology helped to keep the '20s roaring. Tell groups to build a paragraph on the topic by having each member contribute one sentence. Suggest that students first discuss the geology of caves and then indicate how this geology benefited people seeking a place to drink and dance during Prohibition. Allow each group to present its paragraph to the class.

NG Learning Framework: Create a Presentation About Caves and Prohibition

ATTITUDE Curiosity

KNOWLEDGE Our Human Story

Instruct individual students, pairs, or small groups to use online source material to prepare a short presentation on other caves around the country that were used as speakeasies or to make alcohol during Prohibition. Presentations should include geological details about the caves and information about how the caves were modified to serve as speakeasies. Invite students to share their presentations with the class or record them on video and post them to a class blog.

DIFFERENTIATE

INCLUSION

Analyze Visuals Pair students with disabilities with students who can help them determine, through description and reading the caption, how the photos are similar (people in a large open area surrounded by stone) and different (people dressed up and drinking and dancing in the older photo). Have students work together to answer the Critical Viewing question. Give students the option of recording or typing their answers.

GIFTED & TALENTED

Create an Illustrated Time Line Direct students to conduct online research to learn more about the history and present uses of Longhorn Cavern. Tell them to gather dates, events, and relevant images. Encourage students to create their time line using an online tool. Invite students to display and discuss their time line with the whole class.

See the Chapter Planner for more strategies for differentiation.

HISTORICAL THINKING

ANSWERS

1. People wanted a private, secluded, comfortable, and secure place with easy getaway routes to avoid being arrested if police showed up.

2. Bootleggers and people who illegally operated speakeasies out of caves probably made a lot of money catering to Americans who wanted to go to a club to drink alcohol.

3. Answers will vary, but student responses should indicate specific reasons for their opinions.

CRITICAL VIEWING Answers will vary. Possible response: The cave's thick rock walls and ceiling offer seclusion and security, and its large open spaces and smaller chambers would offer areas for patrons to dance, drink, and dine and for musicians to perform. The rock walls might also provide good acoustics for music.

MAIN IDEA The postwar recession soon gave way to a prosperous economy built on consumer spending, but not all segments of society benefited from the boom.

A New Consumer Society

The camera follows a gleaming red sports car as it races down a highway. Inside, we see its slick leather interior as the driver shifts gears. Americans today are accustomed to these irresistible images, but in the 1920s this form of advertising was just developing.

Tangee lipstick—which changed color for each individual wearer—combined new technology, modern advertising, and the flapper's look to become a symbol of the Jazz Age. Young women of the 1920s carried their makeup in small compacts, like the one below, designed in the elaborate art deco style.

Art deco makeup compact

A NEW WORLD OF ADVERTISING

Despite the social anxiety and turmoil of the postwar years, the U.S. economy began to recover during the 1920s. Factory output returned to its prewar levels, and the unemployment rate fell from 12 percent of the labor force in 1922 to only 4 percent in 1927. A good portion of the recovery was stimulated by a new consumer culture, built on an expanding middle class continually encouraged to buy new products.

Advertising boomed during the 1920s. Ad agencies developed effective ways to persuade Americans to buy the many goods produced in the nation's factories. New means of communication, such as the radio, helped advertisers spread their messages and contributed to the development of **mass markets**, or large numbers of consumers to whom manufacturers can sell goods. Before World War I, about $400 million was spent on advertising annually. That number soared to $2.6 billion by 1929. "Advertising," said one industry specialist, "literally creates demand for the things of life that raise the standard of living, elevate the taste, changing luxuries into necessities."

As advertising was coming into its own, so was a new mass audience: the youth market. The growing economy made households more secure, so fewer children were expected to work to help support the family. As a result, many young people had greater freedom and more leisure time. The teen years came to be seen as a distinct phase in the development of young Americans, and the youth culture became linked with seeking fun, excitement, and novelty. Appealing images of cars, cosmetics, motion pictures, fashions, and other attractions in advertisements gave young people ideas about how to have fun and where to spend their parents' money.

Advertisers also focused on the growing number and variety of home products, including electrical appliances. The electric power industry expanded rapidly during the 1920s. By 1928, two-thirds of American families had electricity in their homes. This boosted the market for a host of appliances, from refrigerators and vacuum cleaners to electric irons and washing machines. Advertisers promised these products would make housework easier than ever and give families more time for leisure and fun.

AN AUTOMOBILE CULTURE ARISES

Among the mass consumer goods that emerged during the 1920s, none had a bigger impact on American society than the automobile. Cars became affordable to more and more Americans, thanks in large part to people like carmaker **Henry Ford**.

Ford developed a simple and affordable vehicle, the **Model T**, and he devised an efficient way to mass-produce it. In his **assembly line** system, stationary workers each added a part to a vehicle as it moved along a conveyer belt. Ford's factories were soon turning out a car every 24 seconds, and millions of Americans were getting behind the wheel of the Model T. Ford shocked industry leaders by paying his workers five dollars a day—an unusually high rate for the time. But such wages ensured loyalty and limited turnover among his employees. Higher wages also pushed his factory workers into the middle class, and they, in turn, could afford to buy his cars.

The Model T was popular, affordable, and practical, but not particularly attractive. The Ford Motor Company's lack of varied car models was an opportunity for its competitor, General Motors (GM). Under the leadership of Alfred P. Sloan, Jr., GM introduced innovations that appealed to consumers, such as self-starters, fuel gauges, and reliable headlights. The constant flow of GM's new models and features led customers to want a fresh vehicle every few years. The General Motors Acceptance Corporation made it easy to acquire a car on credit, boosting profits for GM.

As car sales increased, so did the need for good roads throughout the nation. The Federal Highway Act of 1921 left road construction to the states, but it set national standards for concrete surfaces and access to roads. Gasoline taxes brought in revenues, enabling the state governments to build roads and highways. The national network of roads grew from 7,000 miles at the end of the World War I to 50,000 miles by 1927, and more than 20 million cars drove on them. A new category of businesses popped up along the roads to cater to travelers. Motels offered overnight accommodations, roadside restaurants provided food, and gas stations sold fuel and made car repairs. Even the advertising companies got in on the scene, erecting billboards along the roadways to promote local goods and services.

Other forms of transportation expanded as well during the decade. By 1927, there were more than 3 million trucks and buses on the roads. Glenn Curtiss, a champion bicycle racer, had made tremendous advances in motorcycle technology. After one of his early models tested at more than 136.3 miles per hour, he gained a reputation as the "fastest man on earth." Curtiss wasn't content to stick with motorbikes, however. He also helped advance the field of aviation, developing airplanes that set ever-increasing distance records.

OBJECTIVE

Analyze factors leading to the emergence of a new consumer society, the plight of farmers, and scandals in the government.

CRITICAL THINKING SKILLS FOR LESSON 1.4

- Identify Main Ideas and Details
- Ask and Answer Questions
- Make Generalizations
- Analyze Cause and Effect
- Analyze Language Use
- Compare and Contrast
- Analyze Primary Sources
- Analyze Visuals

HISTORICAL THINKING FOR CHAPTER 18

How did the Roaring Twenties both divide and unite Americans? Mass marketing helped the growing middle class even as farmers struggled. Lesson 1.4 examines consumerism, aspects of the economy, and scandals in Harding's administration.

BACKGROUND FOR THE TEACHER

In the 1920s, advertisements moved from showing products to showing people enjoying products, playing on consumers' hopes of a better life and fears that they would be left behind. The subtext in advertisements was, "If you want to be seen as successful and thoroughly modern, own this product." Advertising became key in crafting mass markets, and college enrollment in advertising, marketing, consumer psychology, and retailing programs climbed, producing graduates armed with statistical and marketing strategies to measure and mold consumer demand.

HISTORY NOTEBOOK

Encourage students to complete the first Reid on the Road video series page for Chapter 18 in their History Notebooks after they view the video.

FINANCIAL LITERACY

To extend their knowledge and understanding about the concepts in this lesson, refer students to the Financial Literacy handbook.

INTRODUCE & ENGAGE

CONNECT WITH THE PAST

Distribute index cards and ask students to write one word that expresses what a car symbolizes to them. Collect the cards and read them aloud, using the words to spur comments and discussion from the class. Then ask students whether and how their lives would change if they never had access to a car. Tell them that although cars have changed a lot in the last 100 years, the way people felt about cars in the 1920s is similar to the way people feel today.

TEACH

GUIDED DISCUSSION

1. **Identify Main Ideas and Details** What economic and social developments led to the emergence of the youth market? *(A growing economy meant that fewer children needed to work to help support households, so teens had leisure time. Advertising showed young people exciting ways to spend their free time and their parents' money.)*

2. **Analyze Cause and Effect** What trends and events during the 1920s caused the U.S. economy to grow? *(Possible response: Homes across the country began to have electricity as the power industry expanded. The manufacture and advertising of electric appliances created an increasing consumer demand for products that would make people's lives easier.)*

3. **Make Generalizations** How did the popularity of automobiles change the American landscape? *(More cars led to the need for more roads and roadside places for travelers to eat and sleep.)*

ANALYZE LANGUAGE USE

Have students use a Word Web like the one shown to analyze the use of language in the Tangee lipstick ad. **ASK:** What words and phrases in the ad contribute to a central idea that the lipstick makes users attractive? *(Possible responses: "More Beautiful with Tangee," "wall-flower into the popular beauty," "blush-rose glow of nature," "alluring," "blush-rose of youth," "Be Beautiful")* **ASK:** What do these words tell you about how advertisers built mass markets for products? *(Possible response: Advertisers sent messages that particular products could transform users' lives in a positive way.)*

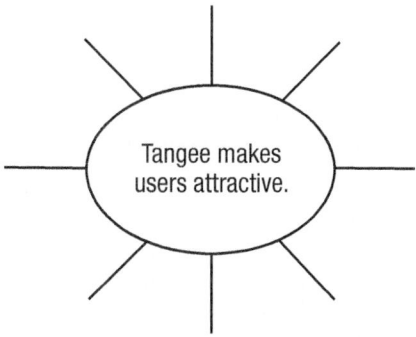

Tangee makes users attractive.

DIFFERENTIATE

STRIVING READERS

Use Reciprocal Teaching Have partners read each paragraph silently. Instruct students to quiz each other about the paragraph, asking their partners to state the main idea, identify important details that support the main idea, and then summarize the paragraph in their own words.

PRE-AP

Analyze Impacts Tell students to work alone or in pairs to conduct online research into the rise of consumerism in the 1920s. Ask them to analyze the connection between 1920s and present-day consumerism. Suggest that students use a graphic organizer to help organize their research. They might also display a graphic organizer to show the results of their investigation and explain their analysis to the class.

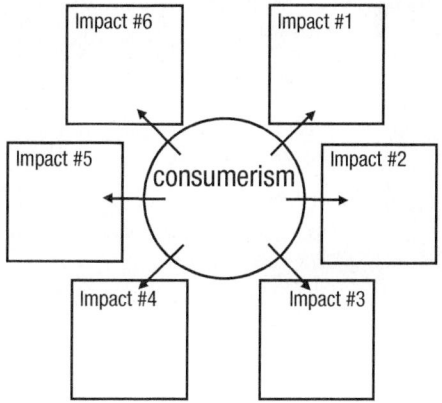

See the Chapter Planner for more strategies for differentiation.

Automakers like Henry Ford recognized that more efficient car manufacturing processes would allow them to make less expensive cars. In 1913, Ford pioneered the first large-scale moving manufacturing assembly line, and by the mid-1920s, the auto manufacturing process had achieved large-scale uniformity. In this 1914 photo, Model Ts move continuously along a Ford assembly line in Detroit, Michigan.

STRUGGLES AND SCANDALS

Even as prosperity returned, some Americans still struggled. The postwar recession continued to hit farmers hard. As European agriculture recovered from the war, many overseas markets closed for American farm products. American farmers' incomes generally leveled off after 1919, and the gap between farm earnings and urban wages widened. As a result, most farmers could not afford the modern appliances and conveniences that city dwellers enjoyed.

Not everyone in the cities flourished, either. Labor unions had lost some of their popularity during the Red Scare, and many factory workers struggled to get ahead. Increasingly, government officials and business owners, citing the cost of supporting labor, worked to weaken the power of unions.

On the positive side, some prosperous companies, such as General Electric, International Harvester, and Bethlehem Steel, offered their workers recreational facilities, benefit plans, and even profit-sharing opportunities, through which workers were paid a portion of profits when their company performed well. These extras, which would become known as **welfare capitalism**, were meant to satisfy workers' demands without relying on unions. But as the decade wore on, many of these programs stalled. The weakening of organized labor had removed the incentive for employers to make concessions to workers.

Away from the emerging mass consumerism, the nation's leadership struggled with corruption and scandal. An indecisive leader and a poor judge of people, President Warren Harding had allowed cronies and crooks to infest his administration. Attorney General Harry Daugherty was a political ally of the president, and his weak oversight of the Justice Department had allowed corruption to flourish.

The Harding administration's most serious scandal was called the **Teapot Dome scandal**. Secretary of the Interior Albert B. Fall leased federal oil reserves in Teapot Dome, Wyoming, to private oil companies. Soon after, Fall received $400,000 from his friends in the oil industry in what many taxpayers interpreted as payoffs for his leasing decisions. The Teapot Dome scandal exposed Harding's presidency as one of the more corrupt administrations in American history. The president himself did not make it to the end of his term. During a tour of the West Coast, Harding fell ill in San Francisco and died of heart disease on August 2, 1923.

Calvin Coolidge, Harding's vice president and the former governor of Massachusetts, became the nation's next president. Coolidge promised to continue growing the economy and to promote Harding's return to "normalcy." Coolidge was even more committed to conservative Republican principles than Harding had been. He proclaimed that "the chief business of the American people is business," and he endorsed policies designed to promote free enterprise. He extended tax-cutting policies and appointed pro-business individuals to head the regulatory agencies and departments that progressives had established a generation earlier.

President Coolidge used modern public relations techniques to bolster his image as the embodiment of old-time virtues of morality and frugality, or thrift. In addition, Coolidge succeeded in cleaning up much of the corruption that had plagued Harding's term in the White House.

HISTORICAL THINKING

1. **READING CHECK** How did advertising drive mass markets in the 1920s?

2. **IDENTIFY MAIN IDEAS AND DETAILS** How did Henry Ford's assembly line increase mass marketing of automobiles?

3. **ASK AND ANSWER QUESTIONS** What other questions do you have about the consequences of the new consumer economy in the 1920s, and where can you find the answers?

4. **MAKE GENERALIZATIONS** Why was the farming industry not as prosperous as other industries during the early 1920s?

BUILD BACKGROUND

HARDING ADMINISTRATION SCANDALS

Warren G. Harding was the antithesis of Woodrow Wilson—a ceremonial and custodial president rather than an activist. Unfortunately, he was not a strategic thinker, which made it easy for his Cabinet to manipulate him.

The federal oil reserves at Teapot Dome belonged to the U.S. Navy. Secretary of the Interior Albert B. Fall drafted an executive order, which Harding signed, transferring oversight of the reserves from the navy to the Department of the Interior. Fall, who had made his money as a lawyer representing oil, timber, and mining companies on the New Mexico frontier, then secretly granted the Mammoth Oil Company leases to the Teapot Dome reserves and the Pan American Petroleum Company leases to the Elk Hills and Buena Vista reserves in California. When Congress learned of the leases, members demanded that Harding revoke them. The U.S. Supreme Court then declared the leases fraudulent and the transfer of control of the reserves to Fall illegal. Fall was later convicted and jailed for accepting a bribe, the first cabinet member to be found guilty of committing a crime.

TEACH

GUIDED DISCUSSION

4. Analyze Cause and Effect What led to the emergence and the decline of welfare capitalism? *(Possible response: To keep workers from unionizing, some companies offered desirable benefits that sometimes included profit sharing. With workers feeling satisfied by their employers, the popularity of unions declined. Without unions to apply pressure, companies didn't feel the need to continue some benefits.)*

5. Compare and Contrast How were the policies of Warren G. Harding and Calvin Coolidge similar and different? *(Possible response: Both presidents were conservative Republicans who favored business and sought economic growth and a "return to normalcy." Coolidge, however, was more conservative than Harding and sought policies that supported free enterprise, hired pro-business people to head regulatory agencies, and extended tax-cutting policies.)*

6. Analyze Primary Sources Direct students' attention to the Primary Source feature and point out that the author is using figurative language when referring to prey, minnows, and whales. **ASK:** To whom is the author referring as prey, minnows, and whales, and what point does he make about truth in advertising? *(Possible response: Prey, minnows, and whales are buyers. Prey are buyers who might not question product claims and will immediately buy a product. Like minnows, there could be thousands of them, but they will not spend much or buy again if they realize they've been duped by a fraudulent claim. Telling the truth about a product will result in a satisfied customer, or whale, who may become a repeat buyer or spread the word about the product because it is exactly what the claims said it would be.)*

ANALYZE VISUALS

Direct students' attention to the photograph of the Ford assembly line. **ASK:** What details do you notice? *(Possible responses: The cars are all the same design. The section of the assembly line shown is responsible for adding the main body.)* **ASK:** What does the photo convey about Ford's mass-production techniques? *(Cars were built in stages, with workers posted at numbered stations. It's evident in the photo that the tires are not resting on the floor, so the cars are moving on a track or conveyor belt.)* **ASK:** How do you think the assembly line affected productivity? *(Possible response: Productivity increased because many workers adding parts at different stations at the same time could quickly assemble the moving cars.)*

ACTIVE OPTIONS

On Your Feet: Three Corners Post signs in three corners of the classroom: Mass-Production Techniques, Impact of New Technologies, and Effect on Landscape. Organize students into groups around each sign and ask them to discuss how their topic is connected to the rise of the automobile culture. Then have each group send students to explain the connections the group discussed to the other two groups.

NG Learning Framework: Explore 1920s Radio Advertising

ATTITUDE Curiosity

SKILL Communication

Assign students to work with partners or in small groups to research examples of radio advertisements from the 1920s. Have groups analyze the goals and techniques of each ad and the ad's contribution to building mass markets and a consumer culture. Have each group share its analysis in a multimedia presentation.

HISTORICAL THINKING

ANSWERS

1. Advertising drove mass markets by convincing consumers that their lives would improve if they bought a wide range of manufactured goods.

2. The assembly line dramatically cut production time, allowing Ford to turn out millions of cars that were affordable and available to a market convinced of the need to own them.

3. Answers will vary. Students might ask whether mass consumerism had immediate or long-term negative effects on the U.S. economy. Students might suggest that answers could be found through online research of periodicals that focus on the economy or texts about the history of advertising and mass consumerism.

4. Farmers lost European markets as European agriculture recovered after World War I, thereby driving down farm earnings.

THE BIRTH OF JAZZ

What do many of today's musicians have in common? They have been inspired by jazz artists. In fact, many rock and roll, hip-hop, and rhythm and blues musicians have been heavily influenced by jazz.

THE MUSIC OF NEW ORLEANS

After World War I, the music that came to be called **jazz** grew in popularity beyond its origins among African-American musicians in New Orleans. Jazz contains lively rhythms, sounds from a variety of instruments, and improvisation—the act of creating and playing music without prior rehearsal or reliance on a written score. Jazz is a uniquely American art form, and from its beginnings it brought together black and white musicians. The term *jazz* came into

wide use after a New Orleans group, the Original Dixieland Jazz Band, produced a best-selling record album with mass appeal.

In the 1920s, radio stations broadcast live jazz concerts almost every night, making jazz singers and bandleaders famous. A leading jazz artist, **Joe "King" Oliver**, took his band on the road to cities such as Chicago and New York. Oliver trained many new artists in jazz techniques, and these artists took what they learned and added their own variations and innovations. Jazz trumpeter **Louis** (LOO-ee) **Armstrong** was one of the musicians who worked with Oliver early in his career. Armstrong was nicknamed Satchmo, for "Satchel Mouth," because his cheeks puffed out like a bag when he played. Armstrong became one of the world's most successful musicians, and throughout his career, he helped spread American culture and goodwill through his talent.

JAZZ FROM COAST TO COAST

Modern forms of communication, such as record players and radio, helped spread the popularity of jazz from coast to coast and throughout the world. The music traveled from major American cities to smaller urban centers, such as Kansas City and Denver, and across the ocean to Britain, France, and even Russia. Part of the music's appeal lay in its fast-paced, unpredictable style. Many younger Americans looking for entertainment started attending nightclubs to dance to jazz music. The rhythms and sounds of jazz gave the 1920s its enduring title: the Jazz Age.

Jazz also helped increase the crossover appeal of other African-American musical forms, especially the blues, the roots of which reach back to slave spirituals. Unlike upbeat jazz music, blues songs speak of sadness and heartache, sometimes covering adult themes such as alcoholism and drug abuse. Blues artists **Gertrude "Ma" Rainey** and **Bessie Smith** often drew upon their personal experiences in singing their sad, soulful tunes. Early in her career, a young Bessie Smith sang with Rainey and one of her bands. Both women performed and recorded songs with Armstrong. By the end of the 1920s, Smith was the highest paid performer in the world.

Some older, more conservative Americans considered jazz shocking. They associated the music with illegal drinking and other illicit activities. Jazz and the blues became one more point of generational conflict in the divide between traditional and modern cultural norms. Eventually, jazz gained widespread appeal and respect, particularly from Armstrong's global popularity and stars such as singer and bandleader **Cab Calloway**, dancer and singer **Josephine Baker**, and pianist and bandleader **Edward Kennedy "Duke" Ellington**.

The multitalented Calloway turned down a chance to play with the famous Harlem Globetrotters basketball team and left law school to sing with a band. He became a popular bandleader at the Cotton Club in Harlem, a composer, a scat singer (someone who sings jazz using only syllables instead of words), and a Broadway and film actor. Pianist, composer, and bandleader Duke Ellington is probably the most well-known American jazz musician. He is noted particularly for writing to showcase the talent of each member of his band. In describing his inspiration to write jazz, or what he liked to call "American music," Ellington said, "My men and my race are the inspiration of my work. I try to catch the character and mood and feeling of my people."

CRITICAL VIEWING Jazz and blues artists Ma Rainey (center) and her Georgia Jazz Band (from left), Gabriel Washington, Albert Wynn, Dave Nelson, Ed Pollack, and Thomas A. Dorsey, brought old country blues and new jazz to sold-out crowds in the 1920s. The innovative Ma Rainey was the first singer to record "See See Rider," a song still popular today. What image of jazz and the blues is projected by the musicians in this photo?

Trumpeter and singer Louis Armstrong is pictured on the cover of the sheet music for "Saint Louis Blues," an iconic jazz song written in 1914 by W.C. Handy. Armstrong first recorded the song in 1929.

HISTORICAL THINKING

1. **READING CHECK** What were the origins of jazz?

2. **DESCRIBE** What are some characteristics of jazz music?

3. **FORM AND SUPPORT OPINIONS** Why do you think jazz was so popular in the 1920s?

4. **IDENTIFY** Through what methods was jazz music diffused across the United States and throughout the world?

PLAN: 2-PAGE LESSON

OBJECTIVE

Identify the factors that led to the popularity of jazz.

CRITICAL THINKING SKILLS FOR LESSON 2.1

- Describe
- Form and Support Opinions
- Identify
- Analyze Cause and Effect
- Make Connections

HISTORICAL THINKING FOR CHAPTER 18

How did the Roaring Twenties both divide and unite Americans? Jazz brought people of different races and skin colors together in the pursuit and enjoyment of music but divided the generations. Lesson 2.1 discusses the spread of jazz and early jazz and blues greats.

BACKGROUND FOR THE TEACHER

In the 1920s, radio and phonographs overtook sheet music as a medium for the spread of popular music. Record sales jumped from around 25 million in 1914 to around 110 million in 1922. The big-name companies Columbia, Edison, and Victor, as well as a host of independent producers, manufactured 78-rpm records with a three-minute song on each side. Louis Armstrong and his Hot Five and Hot Seven bands released 65 records between 1925 and 1928 on the Okeh label before going on to record with several other labels. The dance craze also helped spur record sales, as people often bought records to play while practicing the latest dance steps at home before going to dance halls.

HISTORY NOTEBOOK

Encourage students to complete the second Reid on the Road video series page for Chapter 18 in their History Notebooks after they view the video.

INTRODUCE & ENGAGE

DISCUSS GENERATIONAL DIVISIONS

Have students consider today's generational divide between young people and older adults when it comes to popular culture. **ASK:** What are some aspects of popular culture that you enjoy that older adults don't like or do not seem to understand? Write students' responses on the board and briefly discuss the reactions students have witnessed. Tell students that young people in the 1920s faced similar generational divides as older, more traditional Americans reacted negatively to the music and dance styles of the Jazz Age.

TEACH

GUIDED DISCUSSION

1. **Analyze Cause and Effect** How did cities play an important role in the spread of jazz? *(Jazz was born in New Orleans and spread to cities such as Chicago, St. Louis, and New York. Urban centers provided nightclubs and other venues where young people could gather to listen to bands and dance to music.)*

2. **Make Connections** How did radio help to spread jazz? *(Live, nightly radio broadcasts of jazz concerts enabled people outside urban centers to hear the music, making jazz music, singers, and bandleaders famous worldwide.)*

MORE INFORMATION

Attacks on Jazz Explain that Thomas Edison and Henry Ford were among prominent older Americans who opposed jazz. Edison said it would sound better played backward. Henry Ford went further, referring to jazz as "waves upon waves of musical slush that invade decent parlors" and hurling racist slurs against it. Similarly, Anne Shaw Faulkner, the president of the General Federation of Women's Clubs, declared that jazz had "a demoralizing effect upon the human brain." **ASK:** Why do you think some Americans showed such bias against jazz? *(Answers will vary. Possible response: Jazz encouraged the mixing of races and enthusiastic dancing, and many older Americans associated uninhibited dancing with illegal drinking and other illicit activities.)*

ACTIVE OPTIONS

On Your Feet: Inside-Outside Circle Use the Inside-Outside Circle strategy to check students' understanding. Direct students in the outer circle to pose questions such as the following: Which U.S. cities became jazz centers? What technologies helped jazz spread? Why did some Americans oppose jazz? Who were some of the jazz and blues greats? Direct students in the inner circle to answer the questions. Then ask students to trade inside/outside roles.

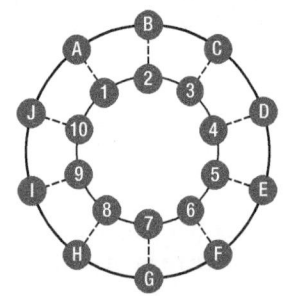

NG Learning Framework: Write a Magazine Article

| SKILL | Communication |

| KNOWLEDGE | Our Human Story |

Have each student select one of the jazz or blues artists mentioned in the lesson and then research and write a feature article on the following question: Why should this artist be included in a music Hall of Fame? Tell students to use multiple sources of information to gather information about the artist and his or her contributions to the music genre. Invite students to share their articles with the class.

For students who develop an interest in jazz music, suggest that they read the American Story at the beginning of this chapter.

DIFFERENTIATE

STRIVING READERS

Create a Word Square Ask students to write the word *Jazz* in the center oval of a Word Square and then write the definition and characteristics in the appropriate boxes. Guide them to identify examples and non-examples of jazz music and musicians. Direct students to complete another Word Square for *Blues*.

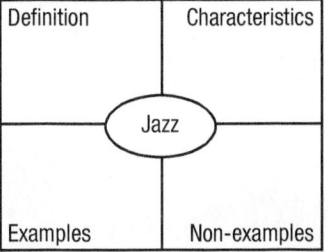

PRE-AP

Write an Online Profile Instruct students to use multiple sources to gather information about blues singer Ma Rainey and to write a profile that contains details about her life and music. Tell students to examine the lyrics of her songs and make inferences about realities for African Americans in the post-Reconstruction era. Encourage students to use words, photos, and music clips in their profiles. Invite volunteers to share their profiles with the class.

See the Chapter Planner for more strategies for differentiation.

HISTORICAL THINKING

ANSWERS

1. Jazz began among African-American communities in New Orleans.

2. Jazz is characterized by a variety of brass and percussion instruments playing lively rhythms with interludes of improvisation.

3. Answers will vary, but students should support opinions with text evidence, such as the influence of records, radio, and traveling musicians or jazz's youthful audience.

4. Musicians moved north and reached different urban audiences. People bought and shared jazz records by their favorite musicians. Radio broadcasts spread jazz around the world.

CRITICAL VIEWING Possible response: The photograph suggests that jazz and the blues are high-energy, African-American forms of music. The musicians and singer are showing their individual enjoyment while performing, suggesting freedom and exuberance.

POPULAR CULTURE AND ARTISTIC ACHIEVEMENT

Consider some of the things you like to do today, from watching videos on a computer or phone to going to movies, sporting events, or concerts. It all began in the 1920s, as mass forms of entertainment emerged and Americans began to enjoy the shared experience of popular culture.

MOVIES AND RADIO

With money to spend and more free time than ever, Americans found many ways to entertain themselves. One of the most popular activities was going to the movies. From uncertain beginnings at the turn of the century, motion picture studios had developed into large enterprises employing hundreds of people. Studio heads, including Adolph Zukor of Paramount Pictures and Louis B. Mayer of Metro-Goldwyn-Mayer (MGM), also controlled theater chains in order to show the films they had made on a tight schedule to maximize profits.

These posters, from the golden age of silent movies, advertise the films *It* (1927) with Clara Bow and *The Sheik* (1921) with Rudolph Valentino. In bright, bold colors, the posters feature the names and portraits of the stars, whose popularity drew the public into the movie "palaces," or theaters.

AN ORIGINAL AMERICAN ARCHITECTURE

During the 1920s, creative building designs flourished and became the basis of 20th century architecture. Among the most innovative architects of that time was **Frank Lloyd Wright**, who developed the Prairie style, a uniquely American design. Wright was influenced by the natural world, as represented here in his Fallingwater House, which was built in the mid-1930s in Bear Run, Pennsylvania. Today, skyscrapers and city centers throughout the world reflect aspects of Wright's distinctive Prairie style, which emphasizes geometric shapes and openness.

At the motion picture industry's peak during the 1920s, 20,000 theaters screened films attended by some 100 million people each week. Ticket prices were relatively affordable—admission was usually about 50 cents. Until the end of the decade, all the movies were silent. Live musicians in the theaters provided background music and sounds. Large urban movie palaces boasted entire orchestras to accompany silent films, but most smaller movie houses simply hired a pianist to put sound to the picture. Title cards in the films provided limited dialogue. The movie actors had to depend on their ability to convey emotions through facial expressions and actions, and actors who mastered the craft often became stars.

The movies provided a model for what young people wore, the slang they used, and even how they behaved. Women copied the fashions and bobbed haircuts of popular actresses, such as **Clara Bow**, nicknamed the "It Girl" for her on-screen appeal. Fans closely followed the personal lives of Hollywood celebrities, such as **Mary Pickford**, the biggest box office star of the decade and a leader in the film industry. Some historians consider Pickford and her husband, dashing action star **Douglas Fairbanks**, to have been the first Hollywood "supercouple." Comic actor **Charlie Chaplin** and mysterious, handsome **Rudolph Valentino** also attracted a huge following of adoring fans.

In 1926, when Valentino died suddenly at the age of 31, many of his shocked fans became hysterical. Because they had seen him on-screen and read magazine articles about him, fans felt as if they had lost someone they knew. Thousands of people paid their respects at his funeral as hundreds of thousands stood on the street outside. It was the first time a celebrity was the object of such a public outpouring of grief. The reaction to Valentino's death reflected the growing influence movie stars had on American culture.

By the end of the decade, the film industry developed the technology to synchronize sounds with the actions of actors. Sound films, or "talkies," replaced silent pictures. The first major sound film, *The Jazz Singer* (1927), starred well-known entertainer **Al Jolson**. Fans loved the possibilities sound offered to enhance the film-going experience.

Radio technology, made possible by the expansion of electricity, added to entertainment options at home. The first radio station, KDKA in Pittsburgh, went on the air in 1920. In 1923, New York station WBAY began selling airtime to advertisers, who quickly

PLAN: 4-PAGE LESSON

OBJECTIVE

Describe how movies, heroes, and writers influenced popular culture in the 1920s.

CRITICAL THINKING SKILLS FOR LESSON 2.2

- Analyze Visuals
- Compare and Contrast
- Analyze Language Use
- Draw Conclusions
- Identify Main Ideas and Details
- Synthesize
- Make Connections

HISTORICAL THINKING FOR CHAPTER 18

How did the Roaring Twenties both divide and unite Americans? Americans united around movies and national heroes, but writers of the "lost generation" felt alienated from the mainstream. Lesson 2.2 examines popular culture and literature in the 1920s.

BACKGROUND FOR THE TEACHER

As early as the 1920s, the movie industry was centered in Hollywood, California, where the climate and variation in landscape were perfect for filming. Studios turned out a steady fare of Bible epics, romances, melodramas, comedies, and Westerns, averaging about a thousand movies a year. To help generate ticket sales, publicists actively marketed each studio's stars through press releases and publicity stunts and by scheduling personal appearances and interviews. In 1929, the Academy of Motion Picture Arts and Sciences held the first Academy Awards. Although studios continued to make silent movies into the 1930s, sound was popular by the end of the 1920s. Around 300 theaters were already wired for sound only two years after the first major "talkies" appeared in 1926.

HISTORY NOTEBOOK

Encourage students to complete the American Gallery page for Chapter 18 in their History Notebooks as they read.

CONNECT WITH TODAY

Write *Popular Culture* in the center of a Concept Cluster on the board and label the other ovals *Movies, Athletes and Heroes,* and *Writers*. Ask students to suggest how movies, heroes, and writers influence popular culture today. Record and discuss student responses. Tell students that in Lesson 2.2 they will learn about how movies, heroes, and writers influenced popular culture in the 1920s.

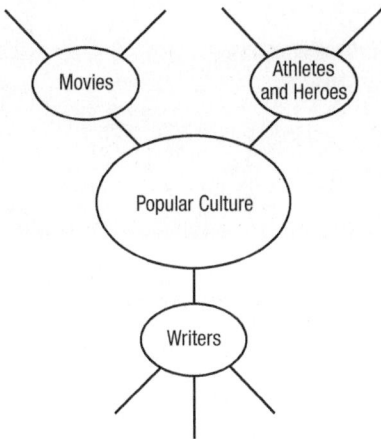

GUIDED DISCUSSION

1. **Draw Conclusions** Why might silent movies have been a good way to spread American culture around the world? *(Possible response: Silent movies relied on the actions and expressions of the actors, rather than dialogue, to get feelings and meaning across to audiences. Audiences didn't have to know a language to understand the story.)*

2. **Identify Main Ideas and Details** What evidence shows that radio technology and electricity changed home entertainment for Americans during the 1920s? *(Radios became popular consumer items, as evidenced by 400,000 households having radios by 1923.)*

MORE INFORMATION

Architecture of Frank Lloyd Wright in the 1920s Explain that Frank Lloyd Wright designed civic, commercial, and residential buildings over a career that lasted 70 years, until his death in 1959. Direct students to the Frank Lloyd Wright Foundation website and have them examine photos of Wright houses built in the 1920s, including the textile-block Ennis House and Samuel Freeman House in Los Angeles and the sprawling estate Graycliff situated on Lake Erie. **ASK:** How do the designs of these Wright buildings of the 1920s compare with Fallingwater, the Prairie-style house designed in 1935? *(Possible responses: The textile-block Ennis and Freeman houses look like fortresses and less like houses that people would live in. Graycliff, situated under trees and on a lake is more like Fallingwater, which appears to grow organically from the landscape.)* Point out that the Ennis House has been used as a location in more than 20 film and television productions, including *Blade Runner* (science fiction), *Buffy the Vampire Slayer* (fantasy), and *The House on Haunted Hill* (horror). **ASK:** What design details about Ennis House make it suitable as a film location for these three genres? *(Possible response: Ennis House is impressive in its massive size, starkness, and vaulting facade. It looks futuristic and forbidding, so it seems suitable for those genres.)*

ENGLISH LANGUAGE LEARNERS

Summarize Place students at **All Proficiencies** in pairs and assign each pair one topic—movies and radio, heroes, or writers—from the lesson. Tell partners to read their assigned section and then work together to summarize each paragraph. When all pairs are finished, have them summarize their section by reading their summary sentences to the group. Provide the following sentence frames to help students at each proficiency level create their summaries.

- **Emerging:** This paragraph is about _____.
- **Expanding:** This paragraph is about _____ and _____.
- **Bridging:** The paragraph begins by _____. It then _____ and concludes by _____.

GIFTED & TALENTED

Write an Interview Have pairs of students choose one of the heroes mentioned in the lesson and write and perform an interview. Tell students to create a list of questions that will allow the hero to reflect on significant events in his or her life. Then instruct students to conduct online research, including accessing the *Sports: Breaking Records, Breaking Barriers* exhibit on the National Museum of American History website, if relevant. Tell students to gather accurate information they can use to write answers in the voice of the chosen hero. When students have completed writing and rehearsing their interview, invite pairs to perform it for the class.

See the Chapter Planner for more strategies for differentiation.

saw the potential of radio to spread their messages. Radios soon became popular consumer items, and by 1923, they were in 400,000 households.

HEROES OF SPORT AND DARING FEATS

Another pastime that took off during the 1920s was following sports. During the decade, football grew into a national obsession. Large stadiums sprang up at colleges on the West Coast and in the Midwest. The most famous football player of the era was **Harold "Red" Grange** of the University of Illinois. When he scored 4 touchdowns in 12 minutes against the University of Michigan in 1924, his picture appeared on the cover of *Time*, a new magazine featuring news and popular culture. After he left college, Grange joined the newly formed National Professional Football League, a predecessor of today's National Football League, where he was paid $12,000 per game at the start. In contrast, the average worker in 1925 made 65 cents an hour.

Although football attracted millions of followers, baseball best captured the excitement and passion of the 1920s, especially after a phenomenal player named **George Herman "Babe" Ruth** emerged.

The National Museum of American History Washington, D.C.

Popular for his dramatic home runs and generosity to fans, Babe Ruth (1895–1948) signed this baseball for a Pennsylvania fan. The Sultan of Swat played ball at St. Mary's Industrial School for Boys before joining the Red Sox and then the Yankees, the team he led to seven American League pennants and four World Series titles.

Babe Ruth was a pitcher for the Boston Red Sox when they traded him to the New York Yankees for $400,000 in 1918. Ruth was the first of the celebrity sluggers. He belted out 54 home runs during the 1920 season alone. His team constructed Yankee Stadium ("The House That Ruth Built") to hold the growing number of fans who flocked to New York City to watch him play. Baseball fans were captivated in 1927 when Babe Ruth hit 60 home runs, helping the New York Yankees capture the American League pennant and win the World Series in four games. Other sports heroes of the time included **Gertrude Ederle**, the first woman to swim the English Channel, and heavyweight boxing champion **Jack Dempsey**.

Athletes were not the only people who gained fans through their extraordinary feats. **Charles A. Lindbergh** secured his fame and fortune by making a historic, groundbreaking flight across the Atlantic Ocean. Lindbergh, an airmail pilot for the government, took up a challenge that offered a $25,000 prize to the pilot who could make the first solo nonstop flight between New York City and Paris, France, a distance of 3,610 miles. Lindbergh raised money to have a new plane built—the *Spirit of St. Louis*. On May 10, 1927, Lindbergh took off from Roosevelt Field in New York, headed across the Atlantic Ocean to Paris. When he landed in the French capital 33 hours and 30 minutes later, he was an international celebrity. Lucky Lindy, as he came to be known, was celebrated with a parade in New York City in his honor, medals from foreign nations, and a lifetime in the public eye. To the generation growing up in the 1920s, Lindbergh's laudable feat symbolized the ability of a single person to overcome any obstacle by sheer determination.

THE "LOST GENERATION" OF WRITERS

Not all artists and entertainers tried to appeal to popular tastes. Many leading authors of this time had come of age during World War I, and the horror of that war darkened their views of society. Their writing often struck a hard and realistic tone, a style that later became known as **modernism**.

The list of influential authors of the 1920s is long and distinguished. The most popular novelist of the early 1920s was **Sinclair Lewis**, whose books *Main Street* (1920) and *Babbitt* (1922) examined small-town life in the Midwest with brutal honesty. Novelists such as **Edith Wharton**, **Willa Cather**, and **William Faulkner** produced bodies of work that examined the lives of aristocratic women (Wharton), prairie pioneers (Cather), and life in the Deep South (Faulkner) with unflinching frankness rather than rosy nostalgia.

🏛 National Air and Space Museum, Washington, D.C.

The Ryan Airlines NYP *Spirit of St. Louis* plane hangs high above visitors in a flight hall at the National Air and Space Museum. In 1927, pilot Charles Lindbergh flew the monoplane across the United States and set a transcontinental record of 21 hours and 40 minutes for the flight. Eight days later, he made the 3,610-mile flight from New York to France. His risky venture brought immediate attention and financial support to the U.S. aeronautical industry. Upon his return, Lindbergh toured the United States, Mexico, and other countries in the Americas in the *Spirit of St. Louis* and had the flags of those countries painted around the plane's nose.

Two of the most popular fiction writers of the decade were **Ernest Hemingway** and **F. Scott Fitzgerald**. World War I and its aftermath greatly shaped the works of both authors. They were among a group of artists whom fellow writer **Gertrude Stein** nicknamed the "lost generation." The phrase refers to the uncertainty and despair many artists felt after the war. Influenced by writer **Ezra Pound**, Hemingway wrote in a sharp, understated style in best sellers such as *The Sun Also Rises* (1926) and *A Farewell to Arms* (1929), which spoke of the pain and doubt suffered by those who had fought in World War I. In *The Great Gatsby* (1925), Fitzgerald told the story of young Jay Gatsby, who tried to use his wealth to impress a lost love—with tragic consequences.

PRIMARY SOURCE

Toward the end of *The Great Gatsby*, the narrator, Nick Carraway, reflects on the life of a wealthy couple with whom he had once been friends but now concludes are partly responsible for Gatsby's untimely death.

They were careless people, Tom and Daisy— they smashed up things and creatures and then retreated back into their money or their vast carelessness, or whatever it was that kept them together, and let other people clean up the mess they had made.

—from *The Great Gatsby*, by F. Scott Fitzgerald, 1925

HISTORICAL THINKING

1. **READING CHECK** How did people spend their leisure time and money in the 1920s?

2. **ANALYZE VISUALS** Based on the 1920s movie posters, what ideas do you think motion picture studios were trying to sell to their audiences?

3. **COMPARE AND CONTRAST** What was different and similar about the heroes of sports and the heroes of daring feats?

4. **ANALYZE LANGUAGE USE** What does Fitzgerald's description of his characters imply about values of the Jazz Age?

BUILD BACKGROUND

THE *SPIRIT OF ST. LOUIS*

Ryan Airlines modified their M-2 design so the *Spirit of St. Louis* could make the transatlantic flight. The designer lengthened the wingspan by 10 feet, redesigned the wing structure, and increased the length of the fuselage to allow the plane to carry more fuel. He then moved the cockpit back and the engine forward to balance the load of the fuel at the plane's center of gravity. This meant that Lindbergh had to use a periscope to see where he was going or turn the plane to look out the side window. The plane was constructed of metal tubes covered with cotton fabric. A special paint tightened the fabric and made it water and wind resistant. The plane was patched with French linen after the transatlantic flight because souvenir hunters tore off bits of the fabric when Lindbergh landed in Paris.

THE "LOST GENERATION" WRITERS

Ernest Hemingway and F. Scott Fitzgerald were not the only "lost generation" authors who dealt with their feelings of uncertainty and despair in the aftermath of World War I. Novelist John Dos Passos and poet Ezra Pound also sought solace in and used their creative work to try to make sense of the war's death and destruction and their resulting disillusionment with American idealism and materialism. Hemingway credits the term "lost generation" to eccentric American poet and avante-garde writer Gertrude Stein, who heard the French phrase *génération perdue* (lost generation) used disparagingly in reference to the younger generation while living in Paris. Stein later declared to Hemingway, "You are all a lost generation." Hemingway used the phrase in the epitaph of *The Sun Also Rises*, his novel about the post–World War I spiritual disillusionment of a group of expatriate veterans carousing in Europe.

TEACH

GUIDED DISCUSSION

3. **Synthesize** How were the spread of radio and the growth of cities related to the popularity of spectator sports in the 1920s? *(Possible response: Large cities allowed for big enough crowds to pay professional athletes and build stadiums. Radio brought the excitement of sports to people outside the cities.)*

4. **Make Connections** How did the writers of the "lost generation" react to social and political trends in the 1920s? *(Possible response: The "lost generation" writers adopted a realistic tone in their writing and examined daily life with frankness rather than nostalgia.)*

VIRTUAL MUSEUM VISIT

Charles Lindbergh's *Spirit of St. Louis* is part of the permanent collection of the Smithsonian's National Air and Space Museum. The plane has been housed in the Boeing Milestones of Flight Hall since the museum opened on the National Mall in 1976. The Boeing Milestones of Flight Hall is one of the museum's 22 galleries dedicated to memorializing, presenting, and preserving aviation and space technology and exploring planetary science. The Smithsonian began collecting aviation artifacts 100 years before the opening of the National Air and Space Museum with the 1876 acquisition of 20 kites from the Chinese Imperial Commission. Today, the National Air and Space Museum's collections include some 60,000 artifacts. The museum's Multimedia Gallery is a great resource for students, especially those who are technologically inclined. Encourage them to take a virtual visit, or do so as a class.

ACTIVE OPTIONS

Active History: Analyze Primary Sources Extend the lesson by using either the PDF or Whiteboard version of the activity. These activities take a deeper look at a topic from, or related to, the lesson. Explore the activities as a class, turn them into group assignments, or even assign them individually.

AMERICAN GALLERY ONLINE **Going to the Movies** Invite students to explore the American Gallery. Have them select one of the images and do additional research to learn more about it. Ask questions that will inspire additional inquiry about the chosen gallery image, such as: Why does this photograph belong in this chapter? How does it aid your understanding of the role of movies in mass culture? What else would you like to know about the subject of the photograph?

NG Learning Framework: Analyze a Selection by a "Lost Generation" Writer

SKILL Communication

KNOWLEDGE Our Human Story

Share the Build Background feature on the "lost generation" writers with students. Then tell them to locate and read a selection of 1920s poems, such as Ezra Pound's "These Fought in Any Case" from his larger work *Hugh Selwyn Mauberley*, or excerpts from a work by Ernest Hemingway, F. Scott Fitzgerald, John Dos Passos, or Pound. Instruct students to select and read closely one poem or excerpt that appeals to them. **ASK:** What is the historical context of the piece, and how does the language reflect the theme of disillusionment or despair? Tell students to refer to specific words, phrases, or symbols to support their statements.

HISTORICAL THINKING

ANSWERS

1. People spent their leisure time and money going to the movies, listening to the radio, and following sports and daring feats.

2. Possible response: Bare-shouldered Clara Bow is featured in *It*, suggesting a story about sex appeal. Rudolph Valentino, portrayed as a dark and brooding sheik, exudes mystery and romance. It seems that studios were selling stories that offered an escape from the mundane activities of middle-class and ordinary lives.

3. Sports heroes and heroes of daring feats faced different challenges and had different skills, but both types had to train for strength and endurance. Both types of heroes promoted their celebrity by meeting with fans and keeping in the public eye.

4. The description implies that values were absent during the Jazz Age or that the wrong things, such as thoughtless pleasure and wealth, were people's uppermost concerns.

CHANGING ROLES FOR WOMEN

Do you remember how you felt when you got your driver's license or your first job? That new sense of freedom and respect was similar to what a number of women felt in the 1920s as they gained greater independence in society.

EMBRACING NEW FREEDOMS

As it did for many people in America, World War I and its aftermath changed the lives of women. Having aided in the war effort and having won the right to vote, many younger women entered the postwar era with expectations very different from those of previous generations. Rather than moving straight from their parents' home to marriage and child-rearing, as was traditional before the war, more women sought to gain greater control over their lives by exercising personal choice in the timing of their education, career, marriage, and motherhood. After World War I, it became more common for a woman to postpone marriage or motherhood, in part because of access to new health care options, including family planning.

Standards for acceptable public behavior in the 1920s were changing for everyone, including young women. Dating young men without the presence of a chaperone and drinking in public—even though it was illegal—became commonplace. The most famous expression of these new social freedoms was conveyed through fashion. Many young women embraced a freer style of dress, and the media dubbed them "**flappers**." This name came from an illustration in a magazine showing a fashionable young woman whose rubber rain boots were open and flapping, but the real hallmarks of a flapper were her bobbed hair, her short dresses, and—perhaps most shocking of all—her use of cosmetics.

In 1925, a group of high school girls posed as flappers. The image of the flapper caught on as a symbol of a spontaneous approach to life.

AMELIA EARHART

Nicknamed Lady Lindy because she, too, was a record-breaking flier like celebrity pilot Lucky Lindy (Charles Lindbergh), aviator **Amelia Earhart** was a famous trendsetter of the 1920s. She was as skillful a flier and as knowledgeable about planes as any male pilot, and quickly established a huge fan following.

In 1928, Earhart became the first woman to fly across the Atlantic Ocean, and she was the first pilot of either gender to fly over both the Atlantic and Pacific oceans. Her dream was to become the first pilot to fly around the world. She set out on her journey in 1937, but she vanished with her navigator over the Pacific Ocean, more than 22,000 air miles into her trip. Her fate remains a mystery.

The flapper became associated with fun and fashion, and advertisers took notice. Magazines promoted this image to sell clothing and cosmetics to mass markets. As many young women looked to assert their independence, mass media pushed them to conform to the latest ideals of glamour and physical beauty. Many older suffragists scolded the younger generation for focusing on fun and glamour rather than on bringing about political and social changes. Most young women, however, were excited to break with traditional ideals, and to do it in their own ways.

ENTERING THE WORKFORCE

Women also wielded greater economic power, thanks to their increasing entry into the workforce. As the 1920s began, 8.3 million women worked outside the home, representing about 24 percent of the national workforce. Ten years later, the number of working women stood at 10.6 million, or 27 percent of the workforce. Despite this increase, the kinds of work available to women remained limited. A few occupations accounted for 85 percent of female jobs. One-third of employed women worked in clerical positions, one-fifth as domestic servants, and another third in factory jobs. And women were still paid less than men; on average, they made about half of what men earned for doing the same jobs.

In addition, not all women advanced equally. For the majority of working-class women, the barriers to opportunity remained high. Poor white women in the South often worked at dead-end jobs in textile mills or agricultural processing plants. Due to racial discrimination, African-American women found it difficult to secure nondomestic jobs in either the North or the South. Even upper- and middle-class white women faced formidable obstacles in the workplace. Many school districts forced newly married female schoolteachers to resign. The medical and legal professions employed more women than in the past, but men in power made it difficult for women to advance in these careers. In government, male employees regularly received favorable treatment. What's more, women were still expected to take care of all household duties—which made managing a full-time job all the more difficult.

HISTORICAL THINKING

1. **READING CHECK** In what ways did women's lives change in the 1920s?

2. **DESCRIBE** How did women exercise their new freedoms and increased independence after World War I?

3. **IDENTIFY MAIN IDEAS AND DETAILS** How did Amelia Earhart represent the changing roles of women in the 1920s?

4. **COMPARE AND CONTRAST** How were women's experiences in the workforce in the 1920s different from and similar to those of men and to those of women today?

PLAN: 2-PAGE LESSON

OBJECTIVE

Examine how women's roles changed in the 1920s.

CRITICAL THINKING SKILLS FOR LESSON 3.1

- Describe
- Identify Main Ideas and Details
- Compare and Contrast
- Analyze Cause and Effect

HISTORICAL THINKING FOR CHAPTER 18

How did the Roaring Twenties both divide and unite Americans? Women had won the right to vote and were ready to exercise their freedoms in postwar society. Lesson 3.1 explores the options and opportunities available to women in the 1920s.

BACKGROUND FOR THE TEACHER

As a child, Amelia Earhart was curious, adventurous, and fascinated by anything mechanical. Challenging social customs that limited the activities of girls more than those of boys, she pursued a range of sports, including tennis, bicycling, and basketball. As an adult, she argued that constraints on athletic activities in childhood caused girls to doubt their abilities, so she championed athletic training for girls. Earhart also argued that women's fashions made it difficult for women to pursue active lives. She designed her own line of more practical women's clothing that was sold at Macy's in New York City and Marshall Field's in Chicago. One of her first designs was a flying suit for the Ninety-Nines, a social and networking organization of female pilots that she helped found in 1929. The suit consisted of wide trousers and a zip-up top with large pockets.

INTRODUCE & ENGAGE

PREVIEW USING VISUALS

Draw students' attention to the photo of the high school flappers and ask them to read the caption. **ASK:** How does this photo illustrate the effects of mass media on the young women? *(Answers will vary. Possible response: The girls are all dressed similarly, likely mirroring clothing and hairstyles they see in magazines, movies, and among fashionable young adult women in society.)* Tell students that Lesson 3.1 discusses how women exercised new freedoms and expressed themselves during the 1920s.

TEACH

GUIDED DISCUSSION

1. **Analyze Cause and Effect** What historical events contributed to the social trend of women delaying motherhood in the 1920s? *(With the right to vote and feeling emboldened by having contributed to the war effort, women began to break from traditional roles of wife and mother because they had the option of family planning.)*

2. **Compare and Contrast** How were flappers and older suffragists similar and different in their views of proper female behavior? *(Both were excited about breaking with traditional ideals and behaviors, but many older suffragists thought that young women were too involved with fashion and makeup and should care more about working for political and social change.)*

MORE INFORMATION

Women's Clashing Roles and Values Remind students that women were commended as patriots for taking jobs outside the home during World War I to fill positions left vacant by men who had joined the armed services. Point out that perceptions changed once men returned home. Women in jobs traditionally held by men were accused of shirking household duties toward their children and husbands. **ASK:** How do these two different reactions illustrate that social change happens at different rates at different times and can clash with values and beliefs? *(Possible response: Women in the workforce were welcome when they were needed for the war effort and to keep the economy going. Once the soldiers returned, women were seen as obstacles to men's employment and were expected to return to their traditional roles.)*

ACTIVE OPTIONS

On Your Feet: Think, Pair, Share Give students a few minutes to think about this question: How did opportunities in the workplace differ among women of different races, social classes, and locations? Then have students choose partners and talk about the question for five minutes. Finally, ask volunteers to share their ideas with the class.

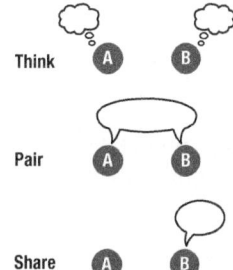

Think   A   B

Pair   A   B

Share   A   B

NG Learning Framework: Compare Women's Roles Over Time

ATTITUDE Empowerment

KNOWLEDGE Our Human Story

Have students work in groups to conduct online research to learn more about how the roles of women changed in the 1920s. Then direct students to use their research to create a chart that evaluates the long-term consequences of changes during the decade by comparing women's roles in the past and present. Invite groups to present their charts to the class and discuss the lessons they learned.

DIFFERENTIATE

STRIVING READERS

Make a List Post this heading: Five Factors That Led to New Roles for Women. After students read the lesson, ask them to copy the posted heading and add five sentences under it. Invite volunteers to share their sentences with the group.

PRE-AP

Analyze a Paradox Have students analyze the paradoxical situation that women found themselves in during the 1920s. As the lesson states, at the same time that women had more independence and freedom, they also had more pressure to conform to arbitrary standards of fashion and beauty. Direct students to conduct online research to analyze this paradox and to write an essay to explain their thoughts. Encourage them to conclude their essays by drawing parallels to similar paradoxes that exist for women today. Invite students to share their essays on a class blog or website.

See the Chapter Planner for more strategies for differentiation.

HISTORICAL THINKING

ANSWERS

1. Women had more freedom than earlier generations, and many younger women sought more control over their educations, careers, marriage, and motherhood.

2. Young women went on dates without chaperones, drank in public, and dressed in the "flapper" style.

3. With her piloting skills, Earhart proved that a woman could be as good as or better than a man at a typically male job.

4. Women today have more employment options than women in the 1920s did, but women are still often paid less for doing the same jobs that men do. In the 1920s, women were competing with men largely for manufacturing jobs, while today women and men might compete for jobs in education, law, government, and medicine. Today, the most powerful positions are still reserved for men, often restricting women's advancement.

NUMBER OF WOMEN SERVING AS GOVERNOR BETWEEN 1925 AND 2017: **37**

States that had a female governor *by* 2017: 27
States that had a female governor *in* 2017: 4

25 Were elected
9 Rose from lieutenant governor by succession
3 Replaced their husbands due to death or removal

WOMEN IN POLITICS

Hearing about women running for and being elected to prominent government positions is not uncommon today, but this is a relatively new development in the United States. It was only in the 1920s, after passage of the 19th Amendment, that women slowly began to enter politics.

WOMEN IN ELECTED OFFICE

As you have read, the 19th Amendment to the U.S. Constitution guaranteed women throughout the country the right to vote. Both supporters and opponents of women's suffrage had expected the amendment to change politics dramatically after it was ratified in 1920. It soon became apparent, however, that a majority of women tended to vote for the same candidates as the men in their lives. The notion of a unified bloc of female voters did not materialize.

Although women's suffrage did not usher in the sweeping political change some observers had predicted, increasing numbers of women served in political office in the 1920s. Two states, Wyoming and Texas, were the first to elect female governors. When Governor William Ross of Wyoming died shortly before votes were cast in his 1924 campaign for re-election, political leaders persuaded his widow, **Nellie Tayloe Ross**, to take his place on the ballot. Despite campaigning very little, Ross easily defeated her male opponent to become the United States' first female governor. She proved an excellent leader, remaining independent and refusing to bow to special interest groups. She narrowly lost her bid for re-election in 1926, after powerful business leaders backed her opponent. Ross went on to work for the federal government in Washington, D.C., as the first female director of the United States Mint, a position she held for more than 20 years.

The same year of Ross's election, **Miriam Amanda "Ma" Ferguson**, a housewife with no previous political experience, won the Texas governor's seat. The legislature had impeached and convicted her husband, the popular but corrupt James "Pa"

Ferguson, and barred him from holding state office. Ma Ferguson ran with the goal of carrying on her husband's work and clearing his name. Like Ross, she easily defeated her male opponent. Ferguson took office 15 days after Ross, making her the country's second female governor. Surrounded by the same cronies who had corrupted her husband's administration, Ferguson faced her own scandals, which kept her from winning re-election. Ferguson remained active in politics, however, and she made a comeback in 1932 when voters elected her as

Governor Nellie Tayloe Ross, c. 1925

governor again. During her second term, a much more politically experienced Ferguson proved an effective leader to her **constituency**, or those who elected her, during tough economic times.

During the 1920s, voters elected 11 women to the House of Representatives, many of them as political heirs of their husbands. Many more women won seats in state legislatures and held local offices. Other women, such as **Eleanor Roosevelt**, the wife of a rising Democratic politician in New York, built up a network of support for women's causes and careers. In 1924, Roosevelt accepted a position as chair of the National Democratic Party's platform committee on women's issues. After male party leaders refused to allow the women of the committee to participate in the final party platform decisions, Roosevelt pressed for the inclusion of more female party delegates. In 1928, she organized one of New York's most successful campaigns ever to encourage women's political participation. "Women must learn to play the game as men do," she wrote.

EQUAL RIGHTS FOR WOMEN

Having achieved the vote, a more militant, or activist, wing of the suffragists campaigned to add an **Equal Rights Amendment (ERA)** to the U.S. Constitution. The purpose of the amendment was to end gender discrimination, which primarily affected women. Examples of discrimination, according to ERA proponents, ranged from women earning less than men for the same work to being excluded from various activities and jobs. Originally proposed by Alice Paul in 1923, the amendment states, "Equality of rights under the law shall not be denied or abridged by the United States or by any state on account of sex." Paul viewed the amendment as the next logical step in bringing "equal justice under law" to all U.S. citizens.

The amendment's language seemed simple and straightforward, but in reality it left much to interpretation. Some female reformers, such as Florence Kelley and Carrie Chapman Catt, opposed

the ERA. They regarded it as a threat to hard-won laws that protected women in the workplace, such as maximum hours, minimum wage, and safe working conditions. Despite the lobbying efforts of Paul's National Woman's Party, the ERA did not gain wide support during the 1920s. Even so, the amendment was introduced in every session of Congress until it was approved in slightly modified form in the early 1970s.

A WOMAN RUNS FOR PRESIDENT

Nellie Ross and Ma Ferguson weren't the first women to run for office. At least one woman aspired to the highest position in the land decades before women were even allowed to vote. On April 2, 1870, the country's first female stockbroker, Victoria C. Woodhull, announced her candidacy for president. Her platform included an eight-hour workday, divorce laws that treated men and women equally, and support for social welfare—all issues that would come up in future decades. "I am quite well aware that in assuming this position I shall evoke more ridicule than enthusiasm at the outset," she wrote. Woodhull was disqualified for the candidacy due to her age. Presidents must be at least 35 years old; Woodhull was 34.

HISTORICAL THINKING

1. **READING CHECK** In what ways were Nellie Ross and Miriam Ferguson effective role models?

2. **MAKE INFERENCES** Why did some women see the need for an equal rights amendment?

3. **ANALYZE CAUSE AND EFFECT** Why didn't the ratification of the 19th Amendment bring about sweeping changes in American politics?

4. **INTERPRET CHARTS** Based on the chart, how many women became governor without initially running for the office?

PLAN: 2-PAGE LESSON

OBJECTIVE

Assess how women's political roles changed in the 1920s after passage of the 19th Amendment.

CRITICAL THINKING SKILLS FOR LESSON 3.2

• Make Inferences
• Analyze Cause and Effect
• Interpret Charts
• Summarize
• Draw Conclusions

HISTORICAL THINKING FOR CHAPTER 18

How did the Roaring Twenties both divide and unite Americans? The 19th Amendment did not unite women into a voting bloc even as some women sought elected office. Lesson 3.2 examines the expanding role of women in politics in the 1920s.

BACKGROUND FOR THE TEACHER

When the Equal Rights Amendment passed in 1972, Congress set a seven-year deadline for ratification, which it later extended to 1982. Thirty states quickly ratified the amendment and another five did so by 1977. After mobilization of opposition from conservative political and religious groups, however, ratification stalled, leaving the amendment three states shy of the 38 needed. Proponents of the amendment still have not given up. In 1994, supporters developed a three-state strategy aimed at getting the amendment ratified in three of the 15 states that had not done so before the 1982 deadline. On March 22, 2017, Nevada became the 36th state to ratify the amendment— exactly 35 years after the deadline. Proponents hope that Congress will reconsider the deadline if 38 states vote in favor of ratification.

INTRODUCE & ENGAGE

DISCUSS THE NEED FOR A CONSTITUTIONAL AMENDMENT

Ask students to discuss the following question: Does the U.S. Constitution need an amendment that specifically guarantees equal rights for women? Prompt students to consider areas of possible discrimination, such as wages, employment, and education, and whether existing laws offer sufficient protection. Then inform students that female activists in the 1920s debated this same issue following ratification of the 19th Amendment.

TEACH

GUIDED DISCUSSION

1. **Summarize** What are the key characteristics of Ma Ferguson's first and second terms as governor? *(In her first term as governor, Ma Ferguson had no experience and had run for governor to replace her impeached and convicted husband. Instead of clearing his name, Ma Ferguson had her own scandals as a result of keeping on her husband's corrupt associates. She lost re-election but won a second term in 1932 in which she was an effective leader.)*

2. **Make Inferences** Why did some female reformers in the 1920s oppose adding the Equal Rights Amendment to the Constitution? *(Some reformers worried that the amendment would undermine existing laws governing safety, minimum wage, and maximum hours that already protected all workers, particularly women.)*

DRAW CONCLUSIONS

Tell students to reread the paragraph about Eleanor Roosevelt. **ASK:** How does Eleanor Roosevelt's work in the 1920s exemplify the changing role of women in politics during the decade? *(Possible response: Roosevelt served as chair of the National Democratic Party's platform committee on women's issues in 1924 and pressed for more female party delegates when male party leaders refused to allow women to participate in the final platform decisions. Then in 1928, she organized a successful campaign in New York designed to encourage women to participate in politics.)*

ACTIVE OPTIONS

On Your Feet: Team Word Webbing Organize students into teams of four and have them record in a large Word Web what they know about women in politics during the 1920s. Encourage students to build on their teammates' entries as they rotate the paper from one member to the next. Then call on volunteers from each group to make statements about the ways in which women participated in politics during the decade.

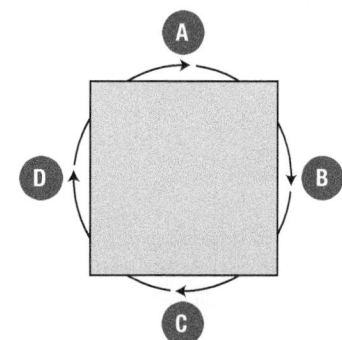

NG Learning Framework: Create a Radio Ad

`ATTITUDE` Empowerment

`KNOWLEDGE` Our Human Story

Allow students to work in pairs or small groups to learn more about one of the women mentioned in the lesson. Tell groups to use their findings to script and, if possible, record a 30-second radio advertisement for the woman's election or re-election and to focus on their subject's views on a key issue. Encourage students to find and listen to examples of radio advertisements from the 1920s online and to use a similar style. Share scripts or recordings in a class reading or audio fest.

DIFFERENTIATE

ENGLISH LANGUAGE LEARNERS `ELD`

Sound Out Words Before reading, preview with students at **All Proficiencies** the Key Vocabulary word *constituency*. You may also preview other multisyllabic words from the lesson, such as *legislature, representatives,* and *constitution*. Model the pronunciation and have students make word cards for each word, writing definitions and pronunciation hints for themselves. You may also bring students' attention to the root words *constituent, legislate, represent,* and *constitute* to help with each pronunciation and meaning.

GIFTED & TALENTED

Research and Role-Play Invite students to conduct online research about one of the female politicians in the lesson and her stance on the Equal Rights Amendment. Instruct students to use their research to create a list of reasons that support the politician's position. Tell students to use their lists to role-play for the class an interaction between the politician and a woman with the opposing view.

See the Chapter Planner for more strategies for differentiation.

HISTORICAL THINKING

ANSWERS

1. Ross and Ferguson were the first two women to be elected governor. Both were able to govern effectively, Ross in her first term and Ferguson in her second.

2. Proponents of the amendment believed that it was needed to prevent discrimination against women in areas such as employment and wages.

3. Most women voted for the same candidates as their male family members rather than voting as a unified bloc.

4. Twelve; three women replaced their husbands as governor and nine women were elected lieutenant governor and then became governor through succession.

MAIN IDEA The 1920s saw a major migration from the rural South to the urban North as African Americans sought new economic and political opportunities in large cities.

THE GREAT MIGRATION

As industry continued booming in the steel and car manufacturing cities of the North, thousands of African Americans arrived seeking better jobs and new lives. Most were not disappointed. One migrant to Chicago declared in a letter to his southern family, "Nothing here but money, and it is not hard to get."

DISCRIMINATION IN THE NORTH

During World War I, the need for northern factory workers led to the Great Migration, in which African Americans and other minority groups moved from the South to the North and West. The migration continued during the 1920s, as the economy boomed and industries expanded. In all, 1 million African Americans—about 13 percent of the South's entire black population—moved to cities such as Chicago, Detroit, New York, Los Angeles, and San Francisco.

Within their segregated neighborhoods, the migrants created vibrant communities. As African-American neighborhoods grew in the North, their residents gained greater local political influence. In addition, community magazines and newspapers, such as the *Chicago Defender*, focused on issues of local concern. Some publications gained national and international reputations, making it more difficult in some cases for political leaders to ignore the concerns of African-American citizens.

While African Americans found greater opportunity in the North and West, they still confronted racism. Whites who did not want the ethnic makeup of their cities to change or who feared economic competition, initiated conflicts with African-American migrants. In 1917, racial tensions boiled over in East

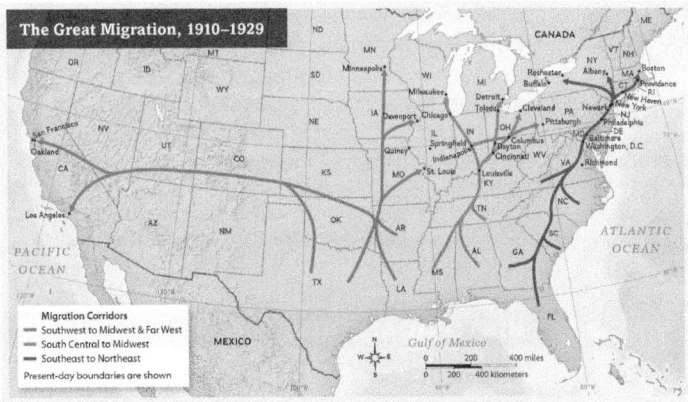

The Great Migration, 1910–1929

Migration Corridors
— Southwest to Midwest & Far West
— South Central to Midwest
— Southeast to Northeast
Present-day boundaries are shown

St. Louis, Illinois, across the Mississippi River from St. Louis, Missouri. Many migrants had moved to the area for work. Following rumors that a black man had killed a white man, roving bands of whites attacked African Americans, killing between 39 and 100 African Americans. They also destroyed $400,000 worth of property. The number of race riots increased during the postwar recession, as white workers saw African Americans as economic competitors.

In the face of growing violence and discrimination, many African Americans in the North looked to the NAACP for assistance. Since it began in 1909, the NAACP, which, as you have read, W.E.B. Du Bois helped found, had worked to build a network of local branches in cities across the country. Between 1917 and 1919 alone, the organization's membership jumped tenfold, from about 9,000 to 90,000 people.

Responding to the violence of the 1920s, civil rights leaders altered their strategies for overcoming segregation and discrimination. Focusing on the long view, the NAACP organized a team of lawyers to challenge segregationist laws in court and influence legislation. But change came slowly. It took more than 30 years for the organization to achieve one of its main goals: persuading Congress to pass a federal anti-lynching law.

A NEW HOMELAND

A number of African Americans believed the NAACP's methodical approach to combating racism and segregation was far too slow. As a result, they turned to more militant civil rights leaders who promised faster results. **Marcus Garvey**, who had immigrated to the United States from Jamaica in 1916, was among the most powerful of those leaders.

In part, Garvey followed Booker T. Washington's beliefs that African Americans should focus more on improving their personal economic conditions than on ending legal segregation. Garvey urged African Americans to support black-owned businesses and organizations to empower their communities. He also boosted the self-esteem of many followers by encouraging conversations about African pride.

The charismatic Garvey preached the doctrine of **Pan-Africanism**, a movement that sought to unify people of African descent. Many of Garvey's followers hoped to establish settlements in Africa so that African Americans could move there and live together. Garvey led this **back-to-Africa movement** and promised to "organize the 400,000,000 Negroes

At what he called the "First International Convention of the Negro Peoples of the World" in 1920, Marcus Garvey was elected the "Provisional President of Africa." This photo captured Garvey in his self-styled presidential uniform as he rode in a Harlem parade.

of the World into a vast organization to plant the banner of freedom on the great continent of Africa." He created a group called the Universal Negro Improvement Association (UNIA) to establish such settlements in areas of Africa that were not controlled by imperialist nations.

Pan-African rallies in New York and other cities often drew 25,000 people and raised funds for the UNIA. Ultimately, however, poor management caused Garvey's venture to fail. His health, finances, and political power gradually declined until his death in 1940. However, Garvey's ideas continued to influence generations of African Americans. Many civil rights groups throughout the 20th century adopted Garvey's message that urban blacks should band together to wield economic and political power.

HISTORICAL THINKING

1. **READING CHECK** Why did the Great Migration continue into the 1920s?

2. **SYNTHESIZE** What approach did the NAACP take to fight segregation and discrimination?

3. **INTERPRET MAPS** What generalization can you make about where African Americans migrated to and from?

PLAN: 2-PAGE LESSON

OBJECTIVE

Discuss discrimination and violence against African Americans and African-American responses during the Great Migration.

CRITICAL THINKING SKILLS FOR LESSON 4.1

• Synthesize
• Interpret Maps
• Draw Conclusions

HISTORICAL THINKING FOR CHAPTER 18

How did the Roaring Twenties both divide and unite Americans? The Great Migration provided African Americans with economic opportunities but not an escape from racism and discrimination. Lesson 4.1 examines the Great Migration and African-American efforts to gain equality.

BACKGROUND FOR THE TEACHER

Marcus Garvey launched the Universal Negro Improvement Association (UNIA) as a fraternal organization in Jamaica in 1914, but membership did not take off until he established chapters in the United States. As part of his message of economic independence, Garvey started several enterprises, including the Negro Factories Corporation and a shipping company, the Black Star Line. He created the Negro Factories Corporation to provide employment for African Americans and financial support for black-owned businesses, including a clothing factory, grocery stores, restaurants, and a printing press. The Black Star Line ships sailed to ports in the Caribbean and Central America where they helped recruit members for the UNIA before the line failed.

ACTIVATE PRIOR KNOWLEDGE

Ask students to tell what they recall about the Great Migration from earlier reading. *(African Americans moved from the South to cities in the North beginning around 1910.)* **ASK:** What factors contributed to the Great Migration? *(Natural disasters crippled southern agriculture, limiting jobs for black farmworkers, and World War I opened up jobs in industrial cities in the North.)* Explain to students that in this lesson they will learn how the migration continued in the 1920s.

TEACH

GUIDED DISCUSSION

1. **Draw Conclusions** How did the Great Migration change the landscape of black America? *(Possible response: Nearly 1 million African Americans left the South for cities in the North and West. In their new urban neighborhoods, African Americans gained greater political influence at the local level.)*

2. **Synthesize** What was the likely reason for Marcus Garvey's back-to-Africa movement? *(Garvey saw that people of African descent would face segregation and racism wherever they settled in the United States. A unified settlement in Africa would allow black people to live together and make successful lives for themselves without the need for laws to protect them from segregation and discrimination.)*

MORE INFORMATION

East St. Louis Race Riots Marcus Garvey condemned the riots—which began in May 1917 and ended in July—in a July 8 speech titled "The Conspiracy of the East St. Louis Riots." The NAACP investigated the riots and pushed for a congressional investigation. It also staged a silent march 10,000 people strong down Fifth Avenue in New York City on July 28. **ASK:** In what ways were the responses of Garvey and the NAACP to this historic event effective against the social trend of violence toward African Americans? *(Possible response: By voicing outrage, calling for a congressional hearing, and showing strength and unity, Garvey and the NAACP galvanized the African-American community and focused public attention on the violence.)*

ACTIVE OPTIONS

On Your Feet: Roundtable Seat students around a table in groups of four. Remind them that some African-American leaders disagreed with a long-term strategy against segregation and discrimination. **ASK:** How effective was a methodical approach to change for African Americans in the United States during the 1920s? Prompt students to answer the questions with original statements supported by facts from the lesson.

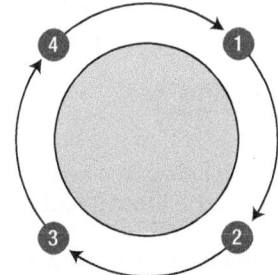

NG Learning Framework: Collaborate on a Biography

ATTITUDE Curiosity

SKILL Collaboration

Organize students into groups to research and write assigned portions of a biography of Marcus Garvey, such as early life, UNIA, back-to-Africa movement, and experiences in Europe. In chronological order, invite groups to share their portions of the biography with the class. Then discuss Garvey's long- and short-term contributions to improving the lives of African Americans in the United States.

STRIVING READERS

Analyze Main Idea and Details Direct students to read the Main Idea statement, captions, and subheadings. Then assign pairs of students to read alternating paragraphs aloud. After students read each paragraph, encourage them to make notes about details in the text that connect to the Main Idea statement. Tell them this process will help them identify and remember the most important information.

PRE-AP

Engage in a Debate Tell students to select either W.E.B. Du Bois or Marcus Garvey and research that person's strategies to improve the lives of African Americans. After students have finished gathering information, ask them to assume the role of the historical figure and participate in a debate on the best way for African Americans to achieve social, economic, and political equality. After the debate, you may ask students to discuss how Du Bois and Garvey's ideas and actions are relevant to present-day discussions about racial injustice.

See the Chapter Planner for more strategies for differentiation.

ANSWERS

1. The demand for labor in the North and West sparked by World War I continued during the economic boom and industrial expansion of the 1920s.

2. The NAACP organized a team of lawyers to fight segregation through the courts.

3. African Americans migrated from the southwestern, south central, and southeastern United States to cities in the Northeast, Midwest, and far West.

THE HARLEM RENAISSANCE

It feels good to be part of a group where everyone gets along and shares similar interests. This is how many African Americans felt as they settled in the New York City neighborhood of Harlem and built a flourishing community.

In November 1934, Zora Neale Hurston went to Chicago to give a performance of African-American stories and songs she had collected in the South. Harlem Renaissance photographer Carl van Vechten captured this shot of Hurston.

AN ERA OF CREATIVE REBIRTH

One of the vibrant communities that emerged from the Great Migration is the neighborhood of Harlem in New York City. Located on the northern part of Manhattan Island, for decades the neighborhood attracted a variety of working-class immigrants from different ethnic groups. Starting around 1904, the Afro-American Realty Company began recruiting African-American families to move to the area.

Over time, Harlem became a majority African-American neighborhood. By the 1920s, it was the premier African-American community in the United States, a place where black culture thrived. African-American writers, artists, and musicians who lived there led a wave of creativity known as the **Harlem Renaissance**, which spread across the country.

Major figures in the Harlem Renaissance included poets **Countee Cullen** ("Yet Do I Marvel," a famous sonnet) and **Claude McKay** (*Harlem Shadows*, a collection of his celebrated poetry) as well as the memoirist and songwriter **James Weldon Johnson** (*God's Trombones*). Many artists crossed over into multiple genres, such as anthropologist and writer **Zora Neale Hurston** (*Their Eyes Were Watching God*) and poet, playwright, and novelist **Langston Hughes** (*The Weary Blues*). Then as now, their work provided readers with vivid descriptions of life during segregation. "For various reasons, the average, struggling . . . Negro is the best-kept secret in America," Hurston wrote. "His revelation to the public is the thing needed to do away with the feeling of difference which inspires fear, and which ever expresses itself in dislike."

Artists of the Harlem Renaissance often joined African traditions with their American experiences. **Aaron Douglas**, an illustrator, muralist, and celebrated painter, developed a modernist style based in African and Egyptian art. **Lois Mailou Jones** called upon African and Haitian traditions for her colorful abstract oil and watercolor paintings. Sculptor **Augusta Savage** gained fame for her sculpted busts of prominent African Americans such as W.E.B. Du Bois and Marcus Garvey. Some writers and artists, such as painter **Archibald J. Motley, Jr.**, who was born in New Orleans and spent most of his life in Chicago, found inspiration in the sights and sounds of the jazz and blues scenes. The music inspired young people and artists of all ages, and the venues were places for creative thinkers to socialize and share ideas.

In 1936, artist Jacob Lawrence painted *Ice Peddlers*, a vivid portrayal of the daily journey of ice sellers on a Harlem street. Lawrence was still a teen when he created this sophisticated streetscape of the peddlers at the forefront of the bustling city that surrounds them. As one of the first young men trained by other artists in the African-American community during the Harlem Renaissance, Lawrence drew on the life around him to chronicle African-American experiences and the effects of the Great Migration.

PLAN: 4-PAGE LESSON

OBJECTIVE

Explore the Harlem Renaissance and the trends in literature, music, and art that it fostered.

CRITICAL THINKING SKILLS FOR LESSON 4.2

- Categorize
- Compare and Contrast
- Draw Conclusions
- Make Inferences
- Analyze Language Use
- Make Connections
- Analyze Primary Sources

HISTORICAL THINKING FOR CHAPTER 18

How did the Roaring Twenties both divide and unite Americans? African Americans created a vibrant multicultural community in Harlem even though racism still divided Americans. Lesson 4.2 explores the Harlem Renaissance and the prominent African Americans at the forefront of the movement.

BACKGROUND FOR THE TEACHER

Zora Neale Hurston was born in Notasulga, Alabama, in January 1891, and as a small child moved to Eatonville, Florida, the first incorporated African-American township in the United States. Shielded from discrimination, Hurston's childhood was filled with examples of black achievement. Following the death of her mother, she was forced to leave Eatonville and take menial work until 1916, when she entered Morgan Academy in Baltimore after shaving 10 years off her age to qualify for free tuition. After finishing high school, Hurston entered Howard University, where she met Alain Locke and others who would play leading roles in the Harlem Renaissance. Hurston went on to study at Barnard College, where she worked with anthropologist Franz Boas, who encouraged her to do fieldwork in Eatonville to preserve its heritage.

HISTORY NOTEBOOK

Encourage students to complete the page on the Harlem Renaissance for Chapter 18 in their History Notebooks as they read the lesson.

INTRODUCE & ENGAGE

PREVIEW USING VISUALS

Draw students' attention to the painting and have them describe details they see. *(Possible responses: All the people are African Americans. A woman is on the window sill and cleaning her apartment window. Another woman is buying something from a peddler. A boy is leaning out of his window and playing with a pet.)* **ASK:** What impression does the painting give? *(Possible response: It gives the impression that the African Americans depicted are going about their lives and engaging in activities one might see in any urban neighborhood.)* Explain that this painting depicts Harlem near the time of the Harlem Renaissance.

TEACH

GUIDED DISCUSSION

1. **Make Inferences** What was it about the sights and sounds of the jazz and blues scenes that likely influenced the paintings of Archibald J. Motley, Jr.? *(Possible response: Because he visited jazz and blues clubs in Chicago, New York, and New Orleans, Motley most likely captured the colors and moods inspired by the clothing styles, mannerisms, and popular dances of the African-American customers and musicians as they enjoyed and played music in the clubs.)*

2. **Analyze Language Use** What do you think Hurston meant by the following: "For various reasons, the average, struggling . . . Negro is the best-kept secret in America. His revelation to the public is the thing needed to do away with the feeling of difference which inspires fear, and which ever expresses itself in dislike." *(Possible response: Hurston is suggesting that whites have perpetuated the negative image of African Americans, ignorant of the average African American, who has the same struggles as the average white person. Once whites accept the similarities, their fear and dislike of African Americans will go away.)*

MORE INFORMATION

Countee Cullen Winning his first poetry awards while still in high school, Countee Cullen went on to win more literary awards than any other African-American writer of the Harlem Renaissance. Best known as a poet, Cullen was also a children's writer, a playwright, and the author of a satirical novel, *One Way to Heaven*. **ASK:** Why do you think so many writers and artists of the Harlem Renaissance might have been inspired to explore different genres? *(Possible responses: Harlem at that time was home to many writers and other artists, and they might have been inspired by the kinds of work they saw others doing in genres they had never considered before. The Harlem Renaissance offered African Americans a rare opportunity to be heard, and they probably felt so invigorated that they wanted to try everything.)*

DIFFERENTIATE

INCLUSION

Use Visuals to Make Inferences Pair students who are visually impaired with students who are not. Ask the latter to describe the photographs and painting and to read the captions and the words they can discern on the Cotton Club signs. Tell visually impaired students to ask clarifying questions as necessary. Then have the pairs work together to make inferences about different aspects of the Harlem Renaissance based on the photographs and painting. You might prompt students by reading aloud and writing these terms on the board: *visual arts, music and dance, writing and storytelling, African-American community.*

GIFTED & TALENTED

Perform a Dramatic Reading Ask students to conduct research on a few of the Harlem Renaissance writers mentioned in the text and examine some of their works. Tell students to choose one piece to perform as a dramatic reading. Encourage them to practice reading with meaningful expression, intonation, and gestures. After students have practiced, encourage them to perform their piece in front of the class. Ask students to discuss how the piece affects their understanding of the Harlem Renaissance.

See the Chapter Planner for more strategies for differentiation.

Although excluding all but white customers, the Cotton Club featured largely African-American performers. The headliners on this night in 1930 included Avis Andrews, Ann Lewis, Bill Robinson, and Cab Calloway.

The hottest nightclub in Harlem was the **Cotton Club**, originally opened as the Club Deluxe by African-American boxing champion Jack Johnson in 1920. The club featured the biggest names in jazz at the time, including Duke Ellington, Cab Calloway, and Louis Armstrong. In 1923, a white gangster named Owney Madden bought the club, expanded it, and remodeled it into a swanky, segregated venue he renamed as the Cotton Club. Although most of the Cotton Club's performers were African-American, only whites were allowed in the audience. The exclusive nature of the club enhanced its appeal among wealthy white club-goers while reinforcing racism and segregation. In many ways the Cotton Club served as a symbol of the limits of African-American success, even within black neighborhoods.

The Harlem Renaissance reached its peak in 1925. The neighborhood boasted an exciting nightlife filled with intellectuals, artists, and wealthy white patrons. A national magazine's special feature, titled "Harlem: Mecca of the New Negro," included an article describing the importance of the Harlem Renaissance for African Americans and the country:

> It has attracted the African, the West Indian, the Negro American. [Harlem] . . . has brought together the Negro of the North and the Negro of the South; the man from the city and the man from the town and village; the peasant, the student, the business man, the professional man, artist, poet, musician, adventurer and worker, preacher and criminal, exploiter and social outcast. Each group has come with its own separate motives and for its own special ends, but their greatest experience has been the finding of one another.

In the same year, Howard University professor **Alain Locke** published *The New Negro: An Interpretation*, a collection of works by Harlem Renaissance writers. The stories, essays, and poems in the book revealed a shift in how African Americans defined themselves. The work of many of the authors featured in the book has since been incorporated into American culture.

ON STAGE AND SCREEN

African Americans made advances in a variety of performing arts during the 1920s. As jazz and the blues wowed popular audiences, some African-American performers excelled in other musical forms. Opera singer **Roland Hayes** became an international star with his sensitive renditions of songs in multiple languages. He was the first African-American man to perform with a major American orchestra when he sang with the Boston Symphony.

PRIMARY SOURCE

In his introduction to *The New Negro*, Alain Locke states that his purpose was to "register the transformations of the inner and outer life of the Negro in America that have so significantly taken place in the last few years." This excerpt from an essay in the book describes life in Harlem.

[Harlem] has many unique characteristics. It has movement, color, gayety, singing, dancing, boisterous laughter and loud talk. One of its outstanding features is brass band parades. Hardly a Sunday passes but that there are several of these parades of which many are gorgeous with regalia and insignia.

—from "Harlem: The Culture Capital," an essay by James Weldon Johnson, in *The New Negro*, 1925

Actress **Ethel Waters** started her career singing the blues and jazz but soon branched out as a popular performer in Broadway and film musicals. Her signature song was the lively tune "Heat Wave." One of her occasional costars was **Paul Robeson**, the most popular African-American stage and film actor of his generation. Robeson's skills as a star student and football player in his youth led to the rare opportunity to earn college and law degrees. Discouraged by racism in the legal profession, the multitalented Robeson turned to acting. His physical stature, good looks, and booming bass voice cut an imposing figure in stage and film versions of the hit musical *Show Boat*, especially during the legendary scene in which he sang "Ol' Man River." He used his celebrity status to draw attention to human rights and civil rights concerns. In fact, the Harlem Renaissance, by fostering both self-determination and pride in African-American culture, helped set the stage for the civil rights movement to come.

HISTORICAL THINKING

1. **READING CHECK** What was the Harlem Renaissance?

2. **CATEGORIZE** Which arts did the Harlem Renaissance influence?

3. **COMPARE AND CONTRAST** How did the Cotton Club represent both opportunities and limitations for African Americans?

4. **DRAW CONCLUSIONS** Why do you think many African-American poets and other authors in the 1920s wrote about life under segregation?

BUILD BACKGROUND

THE NEW NEGRO

Alain Locke received his undergraduate and doctorate degrees from Harvard University and was the first African American to study in Europe as a Rhodes scholar. He spent his academic career teaching at Howard University. In 1925, Locke edited the "Harlem: Mecca of the New Negro" issue of *Survey Graphic,* a magazine that combined articles and graphics to explore social issues. In the edition, he contributed an essay that posited that the migration of African Americans from the rural South to the cities of the North, and Harlem in particular, marked the emergence of the New Negro, referring to people urban in outlook but grounded in optimism, self-respect, and self-dependence.

According to Locke, rather than accepting the tyranny and intimidation rooted in slavery, the Civil War, and Reconstruction, the New Negro worked to increase the prestige of African Americans through art, literature, poetry, music, scholarship, and other cultural pursuits. Locke saw the New Negro as the vanguard for elevating all people of African descent around the world. Nodding to the efforts of Marcus Garvey, Locke argued that, regardless of whether Garvey was ultimately successful, the New Negro should play a prominent role in the development of Africa. Locke saw the media as a powerful weapon in the New Negro's arsenal, pointing out that New York City was home to two African-American magazines and a newspaper that carried articles in English, French, and Spanish gathered from the United States, the Caribbean, and Africa.

TEACH

GUIDED DISCUSSION

3. **Make Connections** How does the quotation from "Harlem: Mecca of the New Negro" illustrate the impact the Great Migration had on social development during the Harlem Renaissance? *(The quotation makes the point that the Great Migration brought African Americans from the South and North together with Africans and West Indians at a place where they could experience each other and create a unique community.)* **ASK:** Why do you think the writer compares Harlem to Mecca? *(Possible response: Mecca is the birthplace of Mohammad and the center of the Muslim faith. "Mecca" can refer to a center for any specific group where one can go and gain acceptance or enlightenment.)*

4. **Draw Conclusions** Why was Alain Locke's anthology *The New Negro: An Interpretation* significant to understanding trends in the Harlem Renaissance? *(Possible response: The writings revealed that African Americans were defining themselves in new ways.)*

ANALYZE PRIMARY SOURCES

Direct students to the Primary Source feature, an excerpt from James Weldon Johnson's essay. **ASK:** According to Johnson, what unique characteristics does Harlem possess? *(It has movement, color, gaiety, singing, dancing, boisterous laughter, loud talk, and brass band parades.)* Ask students to think about this description in relation to the historical event of segregation in the South. **ASK:** Why do you think Johnson sees these characteristics as unique? *(Answers will vary. Possible response: This open, joyous behavior and free movement would not be possible in the segregated South.)*

ACTIVE OPTIONS

On Your Feet: Jigsaw Organize students into four "expert" groups. Assign each group one of the following topics: Harlem Renaissance writers, Harlem Renaissance artists, the Cotton Club, and performing arts during the Harlem Renaissance. After groups have studied their topic in depth, regroup students so that each new group has at least one member from each expert group. Then ask experts to share the results of their study.

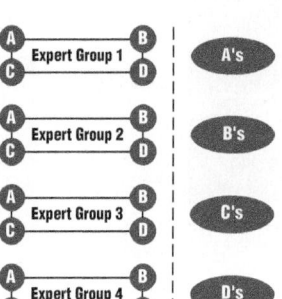

For students who develop an interest in jazz music during the Harlem Renaissance, suggest that they read the American Story at the beginning of this chapter.

NG Learning Framework: Create a Biographical Infographic

ATTITUDE Empowerment

KNOWLEDGE Our Human Story

Arrange students in groups and ask them to learn more about one of the influential African Americans discussed in the lesson or a lesser known individual of significant influence. Tell students to gather information about the individual and the influence of his or her work from the lesson and from reliable print and online sources. Tell groups to create an infographic to represent their findings. Display the infographics in the classroom or on a class blog or website. Ask students to suggest similarities among the individuals and to make other constructive comments.

HISTORICAL THINKING

ANSWERS

1. The Harlem Renaissance was an era of innovation and creativity among African-American artists, writers, and musicians that began in Harlem and spread across the country.

2. The Harlem Renaissance influenced the visual arts, such as painting; the performing arts, such as theater, film, and music; and literary arts, such as poetry, fiction, memoir writing, playwriting, and songwriting.

3. The Cotton Club showcased African-American singers and musicians, but it did not allow African-American patrons in the audience.

4. Answers will vary. Possible response: Many African-American writers wrote about life under segregation because it shaped their life experiences as well as those of many other African Americans in the 1920s.

LANGSTON HUGHES 1902–1967

"I, too, sing America. . . . I, too, am America." —Langston Hughes

Langston Hughes wasn't the first writer to "sing America" in his poetry. In fact, in the poem "I, Too," quoted above, he may have taken his cue from poet Walt Whitman, who celebrated the speech of ordinary Americans as a great symphony of song. For his part, Hughes sang about America to the strains of jazz and the blues. He infused his poetry with the rhythm and structure of these musical forms to speak to all African Americans. They, too, he affirms in his poems, are America.

YOUNG WRITER

Hughes was the first African American to make his living as a writer. But then, he came from a family of firsts. His grandmother was the first African-American woman to graduate from Oberlin College in Ohio. His great-uncle was the first African American elected to public office. Great things were expected of young Langston.

But what his father, at least, didn't expect was that his son would want to be a poet. When Hughes was a child, his parents divorced, and his father moved to Mexico. Hughes was raised first by his grandmother and then by his mother and stepfather. After Hughes graduated from high school, he spent a year with his father in Mexico. It was there that Hughes told his father he wanted to make his living as a writer.

The pair argued bitterly over Hughes's career choice. Then, a poem Hughes had written while traveling to Mexico, "The Negro Speaks of Rivers," was published in *The Crisis*, the official magazine of the NAACP. The poem connects the

This 1958 photo shows Langston Hughes on the streets of New York, a setting he often explored in his poetry.

African-American experience with the dawn of civilization ("I bathed in the Euphrates when dawns were young") and the struggle for equality in America ("I heard the singing of the Mississippi when Abe Lincoln went down to New Orleans"). Impressed, Hughes's father agreed to pay for his son's education at Columbia University in New York City—as long as he studied engineering. As fortune would have it, though, when Hughes entered Columbia in 1921, the Harlem Renaissance was in full force.

He was hooked. The writers, artists, musicians, and thinkers of the movement fueled his passion for poetry and for creating a new African-American cultural identity. As a gay man, Hughes also felt a sense of belonging in 1920s Harlem, where the rules for acceptable gendered behavior seemed more flexible for black and white Americans than in other parts of society at that time. Hughes soon became a central figure in Harlem's literary community. After just two semesters at Columbia, he dropped out.

THE VOICE OF HARLEM

Hughes solidified his reputation in the Harlem Renaissance movement with the publication of his first volume of poetry, *The Weary Blues*. It was hailed a masterpiece—even by the white press. For many, Hughes became the poetic voice of Harlem. But some African Americans criticized his work. Fearing that his poems reinforced racial stereotypes, they claimed Hughes should represent African Americans in the best possible light. Angrily, they dubbed him the "poet low-rate" of Harlem. In response to the criticism, Hughes said, "I felt that the masses of our people had as much in their lives to put into books as did those more fortunate ones."

Throughout his career, Hughes wrote poetry and prose that often angered both his black and white critics. But he continued to write about ordinary African Americans and their suffering and common experiences. These black Americans became his most devoted audience because he reflected their culture back to them through their language and music. Arguably more than any other African-American poet or writer, Hughes diligently captured the small details and frustrations of black life during the early part of the 20th century.

Hughes sang of struggles and dreams deferred, but he tempered his themes with humor, affection, and optimism. In "I, Too," Hughes writes about being denied a place at the table with white America. At the end of the poem, however, he envisions a time when there will be a place there for him and all African Americans: "They'll see how beautiful I am / And be ashamed."

HISTORICAL THINKING

1. **READING CHECK** Who was the subject of and intended audience for Hughes's poetry?

2. **MAKE INFERENCES** Why do you think Hughes often used the rhythm and structure of jazz and the blues in his poetry?

3. **FORM AND SUPPORT OPINIONS** Do you think Hughes's critics were right when they said that he should portray African Americans in the best possible light? Explain why or why not.

THE ART OF THE COVER
The books of Langston Hughes were works of art, both inside and out. For his book covers (shown from top to bottom), Hughes collaborated with the famous painters Miguel Covarrubias and Aaron Douglas and popular illustrator Cliff Roberts, all of whom conveyed the spirit of the time in stylized silhouettes.

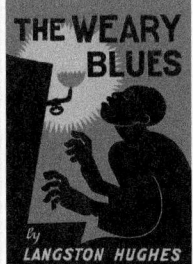

PLAN: 2-PAGE LESSON

OBJECTIVE

Examine Langston Hughes's contribution to the Harlem Renaissance.

CRITICAL THINKING SKILLS FOR LESSON 4.3

- Make Inferences
- Form and Support Opinions
- Identify
- Make Connections

HISTORICAL THINKING FOR CHAPTER 18

How did the Roaring Twenties both divide and unite Americans? While Langston Hughes gave a voice to African Americans through his poetry, he garnered criticism for not always showing African Americans in their best light. Lesson 4.3 explores the life and contributions of Langston Hughes.

BACKGROUND FOR THE TEACHER

Langston Hughes was born in Joplin, Missouri. He lived with his grandmother in Lawrence, Kansas, as a child before moving to Lincoln, Illinois. During eighth grade in Lincoln, Hughes wrote his first poems and served as class poet. His interest in poetry grew during high school in Cleveland, Ohio, where he published in and served on the editorial staff of his high school magazine, the Central High *Monthly*. An English teacher at Central High introduced Hughes to the works of Carl Sandburg and Walt Whitman, who would greatly influence his poetry. Hughes attended Columbia University for a year, then left to travel Europe and work in a series of jobs to support himself while he wrote. Later, he enrolled in Lincoln University, a historically black college in Pennsylvania, and graduated in 1929.

HISTORY NOTEBOOK

Encourage students to complete the American Voices page for Chapter 18 in their History Notebooks as they read.

INTRODUCE & ENGAGE

BRAINSTORM TRAITS

Guide students to brainstorm a list of traits a poet would need to have to become known as the voice of his or her people. Use a Word Web to record students' suggestions. Tell students that this lesson explores the works of Langston Hughes, whom the lesson describes as the poetic voice of Harlem.

TEACH

GUIDED DISCUSSION

1. **Identify** What event caused Hughes's father to change his mind about funding Hughes's college education? *(Hughes's father changed his mind after "The Negro Speaks of Rivers," a poem Hughes wrote after graduating from high school, was published in the NAACP's magazine,* The Crisis.*)*

2. **Make Connections** What factors attracted Langston Hughes to Harlem? *(The writers, artists, musicians, and thinkers who gathered in Harlem helped fuel Hughes's passion for poetry. Hughes was also attracted by the sense of belonging he got from the community that was more accepting of various lifestyles.)*

AMERICAN VOICES

Point out that the photograph of Langston Hughes was taken on the stoop of the poet's brownstone in Harlem. Although Hughes was able to support himself through his writing and lecturing, finances were often a struggle. It's not known exactly when he bought the property, but by 1948, he was living in the brownstone, located at 20 East 127th Street. The buildling currently has landmark status and is used as the headquarters of the I, Too, Arts Collective, a nonprofit that encourages Harlem's emerging writers and artists. **ASK:** How does the current use of Hughes's home honor his legacy? *(Possible response: Hughes wrote about and took pride in the ordinary people of Harlem, so nurturing today's writers and artists reflects the essence of the Harlem Renaissance and how it focused on the richness of everyday African-American culture.)*

ACTIVE OPTIONS

On Your Feet: Numbered Heads Organize students into groups of four and assign each student a number. Tell students to think about and discuss a response to this question: How did the Harlem Renaissance influence Langston Hughes's life, and what did Hughes in turn contribute to the movement? Then call a number and have the student from each group with that number report for the group.

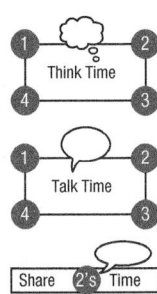

1 2
Think Time
4 3

1 2
Talk Time
4 3

Share 2's Time

NG Learning Framework: Analyze Points of View

ATTITUDE Empowerment

SKILL Problem-Solving

Arrange students in groups and direct them to locate, read, and discuss Langston Hughes's 1926 article "The Negro Artist and the Racial Mountain." If necessary, use the following questions to focus group discussions: What does Hughes mean by the "racial mountain"? What arguments do critics level against what Hughes calls "racial art"? According to Hughes, what are the artistic benefits of writing about "the low-down folks"? In their discussion, encourage students to distinguish valid arguments used by Hughes and his critics from fallacious arguments and explain their reasoning.

DIFFERENTIATE

ENGLISH LANGUAGE LEARNERS ELD

Complete Sentence Frames Use sentence frames such as those below to help students demonstrate their understanding of difficult words and ideas in the lesson. You may wish to allow students to choose words from a list on the board.

• A person who is **hooked** by something is (interested, not interested). *(interested)*

• To **reinforce** racial stereotypes is to (prove them wrong, support them). *(support them)*

• A **devoted** reader is (an opponent, a fan). *(a fan)*

• A dream **deferred** happens (immediately, later). *(later)*

PRE-AP

Perform a Hughes Poetry Slam Provide students with a sampling of Hughes's poems that are appropriate for the classroom. Allow students to read and rehearse a poem of their choice and then perform it for the class. Encourage students to use expression to lend meaning to the words. When students have completed their readings, guide a discussion of the message each poem has for the reader.

See the Chapter Planner for more strategies for differentiation.

HISTORICAL THINKING

ANSWERS

1. Hughes wrote about and for ordinary African Americans.

2. Answers will vary. Possible response: Hughes saw jazz and the blues as expressions of African-American life and wanted to incorporate that energy and rhythm into his poetry.

3. Possible responses: No. It was important to celebrate the breadth and depth of African-American culture. Yes. In a time of open discrimination, it was important to portray the strongest and most positive aspects of African-American culture.

VOCABULARY

For each pair of vocabulary words, write one sentence that explains the connection between the words.

1. capitalism; Red Scare
   During the Red Scare, many Americans were afraid of people who spoke out against capitalism.

2. stalactite; stalagmite

3. assembly line; mass market

4. jazz; flapper

5. bootlegger; speakeasy

6. Pan-Africanism; back-to-Africa movement

7. American Civil Liberties Union; Anti-Defamation League

READING STRATEGY
COMPARE AND CONTRAST

Comparing and contrasting concepts in a chart can help readers better understand the similarities and differences between people, events, and movements in history. In your chart, list traditional versus modern practices that emerged in major areas during the 1920s. Then answer the question.

Comparison Chart

	Traditional	Modern
Industry	Factories	Assembly line
Music		
Science		
Women's roles		

8. Which modern change had the most impact on a traditional practice, process, or idea? Explain your answer.

MAIN IDEAS

Answer the following questions. Support your answers with evidence from the chapter.

9. What factors led to the Palmer Raids? **LESSON 1.1**

10. What role did anti-immigration feelings play in the Sacco-Vanzetti case? **LESSON 1.2**

11. How did the Teapot Dome scandal affect Warren Harding's presidency? **LESSON 1.3**

12. How did new communications technology help popularize jazz? **LESSON 2.1**

13. What forms of entertainment grew popular during the 1920s? **LESSON 2.2**

14. How did the image of the flapper reflect the changing status of women? **LESSON 3.1**

15. Why did the passage of the 19th Amendment fail to have the immediate impact some people thought it might? **LESSON 3.2**

16. What factors made Marcus Garvey's back-to-Africa movement attractive to some African Americans? **LESSON 4.1**

17. Why did so many African Americans move to Harlem in the 1910s and 1920s? **LESSON 4.2**

HISTORICAL THINKING

Answer the following questions. Support your answers with evidence from the chapter.

18. **MAKE GENERALIZATIONS** How did culture change in the United States during the 1920s?

19. **ANALYZE CAUSE AND EFFECT** What were the main effects of the 18th Amendment and the Volstead Act?

20. **MAKE GENERALIZATIONS** What strides in politics did women make after passage of the 19th Amendment?

21. **DRAW CONCLUSIONS** Why do you think the NAACP worked to change laws even if it might take years to accomplish?

22. **FORM AND SUPPORT OPINIONS** Were the 1920s a "return to normalcy"? Support your opinion with evidence from the text.

INTERPRET VISUALS

The August 1927 cover of *McClure's* magazine features a vision of the Jazz Age by the artist John Held, Jr. Look at the cover (at right) and answer the questions that follow.

23. What do you think the portrait of the flapper symbolizes, and why?

24. In what ways does this illustration reflect the characteristics of the 1920s?

ANALYZE SOURCES

Colleen Moore was an actor during the 1920s and 1930s famous for playing flappers in numerous movies. Moore talked to author Joshua Zeitz about how she was influenced by the free-spirited young women of the 1920s during an interview for his 2006 book *Flapper: A Madcap Story of Sex, Style, Celebrity, and the Women Who Made America Modern*. Read the excerpt, which is a quotation from Moore. Then answer the question.

> They were smart and sophisticated, with an air of independence about them, and so casual about their looks and clothes and manners as to be almost slapdash. I don't know if I realized as soon as I began seeing them that they represented the wave of the future, but I do know I was drawn to them. I shared their restlessness, understood their determination to free themselves of the Victorian shackles of the pre–World War I era and find out for themselves what life was all about.

25. What were the attributes that Moore admired in flappers?

CONNECT TO YOUR LIFE

26. **ARGUMENT** Movies had a huge impact on fashion and other aspects of popular culture in the 1920s, and they still drive fashion and popular culture today. Then, as now, some people embraced this influence, and some people saw it as a threat to society and the status quo. Examine the influence of movies both now and in the 1920s, and write an argument that the art form exerts either a positive or a negative influence.

TIPS

- Use textual evidence from the chapter in your argument.
- Clearly state your point of view, briefly including the reasons for your stance.
- Acknowledge the opposite viewpoint by providing one or two valid alternative ideas.
- Provide examples from the text and your own understanding and experience to support each reason for your argument.
- Provide a conclusion that restates your argument, making your stand on the matter clear.
- Use two or three vocabulary terms from the chapter in your response.

VOCABULARY ANSWERS

1. During the Red Scare, many Americans were afraid of people who spoke out against capitalism.

2. The mineral formations called stalagmites grow from cave floors, while those called stalactites hang from cave ceilings.

3. By using an assembly line to streamline production, Henry Ford was able to produce affordable cars for a mass market.

4. The flappers' short skirts, bobbed hair, and love of jazz music often shocked older women.

5. Bootleggers supplied illegal alcohol to secret clubs known as speakeasies during Prohibition.

6. Marcus Garvey hoped to unite people of African descent through Pan-Africanism and to create settlements in Africa through the back-to-Africa movement.

7. The activities of the American Civil Liberties Union and the Anti-Defamation League included working to protect Americans' constitutional rights and to expose the violence of extremist groups.

READING STRATEGY ANSWER

	Traditional	**Modern**
Industry	Factories	Assembly line
Music	Gospel	Jazz
Science	Fundamentalism	Evolution
Women's roles	Nonvoter	Voter

8. Answers will vary. Responses should include specific impacts, such as the impact of the assembly line on mass production and the affordable price of the Model T.

MAIN IDEAS ANSWERS

9. The Red Scare and a series of bombings by radicals and anarchists led to the Palmer Raids.

10. Supporters of Sacco and Vanzetti argued that the pair received an unfair trial because they were immigrants and known anarchists, which biased the jury against them.

11. The Teapot Dome scandal resulted in the Harding presidency being seen as one of the more corrupt administrations in American history.

12. Radio stations in the 1920s broadcast live jazz concerts almost nightly, introducing jazz to a vast radio audience.

13. Movies, radio programs, football, and baseball were popular forms of entertainment in the 1920s.

14. By wearing short dresses, bobbing their hair, using cosmetics, drinking in public, and dating without chaperones, flappers reflected new freedoms women enjoyed in the 1920s.

15. Most women voted the same way the men in their lives did, rather than voting as a bloc.

16. Settlements in Africa would offer a chance for self-government and an escape from segregation and discrimination.

17. The Afro-American Realty Company began recruiting African-American families to move to Harlem around 1904, resulting in Harlem becoming the premier African-American community in the United States by the 1920s.

HISTORICAL THINKING ANSWERS

18. Possible responses: Advances in technology created mass markets for goods and spread popular culture; women gained the vote, entered the workforce in greater numbers, and enjoyed more social freedoms; the Great Migration transformed black America, helped create the Harlem Renaissance, and spread jazz and the blues; in some communities, people were less governed by the restrictive "rules" about gender and were welcomed for themselves; negative reactions to evolution led to the rise of fundamentalism; Prohibition outlawed alcohol consumption in public, leading to bootlegging and speakeasies.

19. The 18th Amendment and the Volstead Act outlawed the manufacture, transport, and sale of alcohol, resulting in the unintended consequences of bootleggers making and distributing alcohol illegally to speakeasies, where it was illegally sold to customers.

20. Women held political offices at the local, state, and national levels, including in the U.S. House of Representatives and as governors.

21. Answers will vary. Possible response: The NAACP wanted the power of the courts behind safeguards against violence, discrimination, and segregation.

22. Answers will vary. Possible response: No. Although the United States did return to peace and economic prosperity, the decade was a period of broad cultural leaps toward modernity as evidenced by the changing roles of women, the 19th Amendment, the Great Migration, and the Harlem Renaissance.

INTERPRET VISUALS ANSWERS

23. Possible response: The flapper, with her bobbed hair and revealing, short dress that shows her garters and thighs, symbolizes the shocking new trends, attitudes, and freedoms—especially for women—of the 1920s. The growth of jazz and the youth culture's enthusiasm for good times following World War I were extreme departures from the culture of 19th-century wartime America.

24. Possible response: The illustration reflects the importance of style in music, clothing, and appearance as consumers found new ways to have fun and spend money in a growing economy. The racism of the 1920s is reflected in the depiction of white rather than African-American musicians, even though jazz grew out of the African-American experience and was primarily associated with African-American musicians and composers.

ANALYZE SOURCES ANSWER

25. Moore admired the flappers' intelligence, sophistication, independence, casual approach to clothes and manners, and determination to step into the future and find their own way in life.

CONNECT TO YOUR LIFE ANSWER

26. Paragraphs will vary, but students should back up their positions with sound reasons, provide examples from the text and their own understanding to support their reasons, include at least one alternative view, incorporate two or three vocabulary terms, and end with a conclusion that restates their argument.

UNIT 6 RESOURCES

UNIT INTRODUCTION

UNIT TIME LINE

UNIT WRAP-UP

NATIONAL GEOGRAPHIC | CONNECTION

National Geographic Magazine Adapted Articles
- "The Hidden World of the Great War"
- "1918 Flu Pandemic" ONLINE

Unit 6 Inquiry: Create a Conflict Resolution Strategy

NG Learning Framework Activities
- Write a Conflict Negotiator Profile
- Settle a Dispute

Unit 6 Formal Assessment

CHAPTER 19 RESOURCES

Available at NGLSync.Cengage.com

TEACHER RESOURCES & ASSESSMENT

Reading and Note-Taking

Vocabulary Practice

Social Studies Skills Lessons
- Reading: Analyze Cause and Effect
- Writing: Explanatory

Formal Assessment
- Chapter 19 Pretest
- Chapter 19 Tests A & B
- Section Quizzes

Chapter 19 Answer Key

ExamView®
One-time Download

STUDENT DIGITAL RESOURCES

- eEdition
- Handbooks
- Online Atlas
- American Gallery Online
- History Notebook
- Active History
- American Voices (Biographies)
- Literature Analysis
- Projects for Inquiry-Based Learning

Chapter 19 Spanish Resources are available at NGLSync.Cengage.com.

AMERICAN STORIES | The Dust Bowl

- Study Primary Sources: Photographs and firsthand accounts of the Dust Bowl and an excerpt from the 1935 magazine the *New Republic*
- On Your Feet: Examine Life During the Dust Bowl

NG Learning Framework:
Analyze Land Use

SECTION 1 RESOURCES
THE STOCK MARKET CRASH

LESSON 1.1
A Deceptive Prosperity

- Active History: Graph Stock Prices
- On Your Feet: Use a Jigsaw Strategy

American Voices Biography
Herbert Hoover ONLINE

LESSON 1.2
Panic on Wall Street

- On Your Feet: Conduct a Cost-Benefit Analysis

NG Learning Framework:
Write an Article

SECTION 2 RESOURCES
THE GREAT DEPRESSION

LESSON 2.1
The Depression Begins

- On Your Feet: Fishbowl

 AMERICAN GALLERY ONLINE   The Great Depression

LESSON 2.2
THROUGH THE LENS
Jimmy Chin

- On Your Feet: Numbered Heads

NG Learning Framework:
Create a Short Documentary

LESSON 2.3
The Dust Bowl

- On Your Feet: Turn and Talk on Topic

NG Learning Framework:
Dust Bowl Then and Now

LESSON 2.4
Culture During the Depression

- On Your Feet: Four Corners

NG Learning Framework:
Analyze Lyrics and Literature

SECTION 3 RESOURCES
HOOVER'S RESPONSE

LESSON 3.1
Hoover's Initiatives

- On Your Feet: Roundtable

NG Learning Framework:
Helping Those in Need

LESSON 3.2
The Bonus Army

- On Your Feet: Inside-Outside Circle

NG Learning Framework:
Viewpoints on the Bonus Army

CHAPTER 19 REVIEW

STRATEGY 1
IDENTIFY LESSON CONTENT

Write these groups of terms on the board. Ask students to skim through the chapter and decide with which lesson each group of terms is connected. Then ask for volunteers to use each group of terms in a single sentence.

prosperity
stock market speculation
hidden economic problems
(Lesson 1.1)

Wall Street
Black Tuesday
stock market crash
(Lesson 1.2)

Great Depression
bank failures
unemployment
(Lesson 2.1)

Dust Bowl
drought
farmland
(Lesson 2.3)

Use after Lessons 1.1, 1.2, 2.1, and 2.3.

STRATEGY 2
TURN HEADINGS INTO OUTLINES

Explain to students that headings can provide a good outline of the content of a lesson. Model for students how to use a lesson title and subheadings to create a basic outline structure. Encourage students to add to their outlines as they read.

Use with All Lessons

STRATEGY 3
SEQUENCE EVENTS

Suggest that students record events in a Sequence Chain like the one shown. Tell them to add other circles and arrows as needed.

Use with All Lessons *For example, students may use the Sequence Chain to trace the events outlined in Lessons 1.1 and 1.2 that led to the Great Depression.*

STRATEGY 1
PROVIDE TERMS AND NAMES ON AUDIO

Decide which of the chapter terms and names are important for mastery. Ask a volunteer to record the pronunciations and a short sentence defining each term and name. Encourage students to listen to the recordings as often as necessary.

Use with All Lessons *You might also use the recordings to quiz students on their mastery of the terms and names. Play one definition at a time from the recording and ask students to identify the term or name.*

STRATEGY 2
USE SUPPO RTED READING

Ask students to read the chapter aloud lesson by lesson. Instruct them to stop at the end of each lesson and use these sentence frames to monitor their comprehension of the text:

- This lesson is mostly about _____.

- Other topics in this lesson are _____ and _____.

- One question I have is _____.

- One of the vocabulary words is _____, and it means _____.

- One word I don't recognize is _____.

Use with All Lessons

ENGLISH LANGUAGE LEARNERS

STRATEGY 1
PAIR PARTNERS FOR DICTATION

After reading a lesson, direct students of **All Proficiencies** levels to write a sentence in their own words that tells an important idea from the lesson. Then pair students and let them take turns dictating their sentences to each other. Encourage them to help each other with spelling and content accuracy.

Use with All Lessons *You may wish to pair students at the* **Emerging** *level with those at the* **Bridging** *level.*

STRATEGY 2
CONNECT VISUALS TO LESSON CONTENT

Direct students at the **Emerging** and **Expanding** levels to read each lesson title and study the visuals. Then ask them to explain how the visuals are related to the lesson.

Use with All Lessons *Encourage students at the* **Emerging** *level to ask questions if they have trouble connecting a visual with its lesson title. Suggest that students at the* **Bridging** *level help students at the* **Emerging** *and* **Expanding** *levels.*

STRATEGY 3
CLARIFY ENGLISH EXPRESSIONS

Pair English language learners with English-proficient students to clarify the meaning of any figurative expressions found in the chapter, such as the following:

- "make a fast buck" (Lesson 1.2)
- "drove up the price" (Lesson 2.1)
- "hitting the road" (Lesson 2.3)

Use with All Lessons

GIFTED & TALENTED

STRATEGY 1
READ A NOVEL OF THE ERA

Invite volunteers to read one of the novels mentioned in the chapter, such as John Steinbeck's *Grapes of Wrath* or Richard Wright's *Native Son*. Then ask them to deliver an oral report on their reading that includes a plot summary, character descriptions, and a discussion of major themes.

Use with Lessons 2.3 and 2.4

STRATEGY 2
CREATE A GALLERY WALK

To help them learn more about how artists, musicians, writers, filmmakers, and photographers captured aspects of the Great Depression, instruct students to locate online resources such as photographs, illustrations, song lyrics, movie posters, comic books, and quotations from key individuals. Ask students to organize their findings, either by medium or by theme, and to set up gallery-style stations around the classroom. Each station should include signage that makes connections between the artistic expressions on display and the larger social, political, and economic realities of the time period. Invite students to visit each station.

Use with Lessons 2.2–2.4

PRE-AP

STRATEGY 1
EXTEND KNOWLEDGE

Invite students to conduct research to find out more about a topic, person, or event introduced in Chapter 19. For example, students might choose to research the Kellogg-Briand Pact, the Mexican Repatriation Program, Dorothea Lange, Benny Goodman, or Richard Wright. Have students present their findings in an oral report to the class or in a digital report posted on a class blog.

Use with All Lessons

STRATEGY 2
WRITE A PROFILE

Instruct students to conduct online research about individuals who experienced unemployment, homelessness, and/or hunger during the Depression era. Then ask them to use the information to write a profile of one such person from the perspective of a Depression-era journalist reporting on the individual's challenges. Point out that they are reporting within the context of the time and should not overlay their report with present-day norms and values. Invite students to post their profiles on a class blog or publish them on a class, grade, or school website.

Use with Lessons 2.1, 2.3, 3.1, and 3.2

HISTORICAL THINKING What impact did the Great Depression have on the American people, culture, economy, and spirit?

Walker Evans's photography during the Great Depression captured the essence of Americans' despair and worry. Here, the focus of his lens lands on the plates and bowls people are holding while they stand in line at a soup kitchen in Arkansas in 1937.

674 CHAPTER 19

"**Brother,** can you spare a dime?"

—Yip Harburg, songwriter

The Great Depression 675

INTRODUCE THE PHOTOGRAPH

LINES AT SOUP KITCHENS

Ask students to study the photograph and quotation that open this chapter. Have them look closely at the people's clothing and what they're holding. **ASK:** What do these items convey about the people standing in line? *(Possible response: The clothing looks old and worn; the pie plate and chipped china bowl suggest that people have limited resources and possessions.)* Tell students that in this chapter they will learn about the lasting impact of the Great Depression on the culture, economy, and spirit of the American people.

SHARE BACKGROUND

As the Depression deepened, millions of people needed help to feed their families and themselves. Charitable organizations, such as churches, the Red Cross, and the Salvation Army, set up kitchens that offered soup, sandwiches, bread, and coffee. By 1931, New York City alone was serving 85,000 people every day. Even Chicago gangster Al Capone ran a kitchen that provided three meals a day. Photographer Walker Evans, hired by the government to document the Great Depression, took many pictures of food lines filled with hungry people. Standing in line was often deeply humiliating, especially for middle-class people thrown into poverty by the Depression. Songwriter Yip Harburg lost his own business during the Depression. When he wrote, "Brother, Can You Spare a Dime?" he knew from personal experience how quickly fortunes could fall.

For Chapter 19 Spanish Resources, visit the Resources Menu. Chapter 19 Resources are available at NGLSync.Cengage.com.

HISTORICAL THINKING QUESTION

What impact did the Great Depression have on the American people, culture, economy, and spirit?

Jigsaw Activity: Preview Content This activity will help students preview and make predictions about the topics in Chapter 19. Arrange the class into three groups and assign each group a section title. Have students discuss what they think they will learn. Ask students to consider the following clues and questions:

Group 1 Section 1 is about the hidden weaknesses in the U.S. economy in the late 1920s. What factors might have made the prosperity of the 1920s deceptive? What might have caused the stock market crash of 1929?

Group 2 Section 2 is about the beginning of the Great Depression, the Dust Bowl, and changes in American culture. How might the Depression have affected the American people, the environment, and culture? How do you think the government responded?

Group 3 Section 3 is about Hoover's initiatives to help the unemployed and his response to the Bonus Army march. How effective might the president have been in his attempts to help the unemployed?

Regroup students so that each new grouping has at least one member from each original group. Have students share their predictions about their assigned section so that other students can anticipate what might be covered in Chapter 19.

INTRODUCE THE READING STRATEGY

ANALYZE CAUSE AND EFFECT

Analyzing cause and effect can help students understand that historical events are often complex and may have multiple causes and effects. Turn to the Chapter Review and preview the Cause-and-Effect Chain with students. As they read the chapter, have students analyze the causes and effects of various events that occurred throughout the 1930s, beginning with the Great Depression.

KEY DATES FOR CHAPTER 19

1929	Stock market crashes and Great Depression begins
1930	Smoot-Hawley Tariff Act slows international trade
early 1930s	Dust storms hit the Great Plains
1931	Herbert Hoover sets up President's Organization on Unemployment Relief
1932	Revenue Act raises taxes by largest amount in nation's history during peacetime
1932	Norris-LaGuardia Act puts end to injunctions against labor and union activities
1932	Bonus Army attacked by U.S. troops in Washington, D.C.

INTRODUCE CHAPTER VOCABULARY

KEY VOCABULARY

SECTION 1

disposable income	gross national product	margin
Dow Jones Industrial Average	Kellogg-Briand Pact	speculation
Great Depression		stock market

SECTION 2

deport	mass media	trading pool
Dust Bowl	repatriation	

SECTION 3

Bonus Army	Hooverville	underwrite
fascism	injunction	

WORD WEBS

Have students complete a Word Web for each Key Vocabulary term as they read the chapter. Tell them to begin by writing each term in the center oval. Ask them to look through the chapter to find examples, characteristics, and descriptive words that may be associated with that term. At the end of the chapter, ask students what they learned about each term. Model an example for students on the board, using the graphic organizer below.

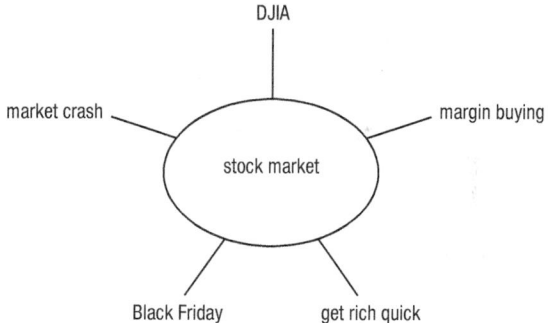

OBJECTIVES

- Analyze the causes of, and responses to, the Dust Bowl.

- Discuss the human toll of the Dust Bowl and its effects on the Great Plains region.

- Learn about Dust Bowl refugees and their social and economic impacts in California.

- Analyze the effectiveness of federal government programs in providing solutions to end the Dust Bowl.

- Study primary sources: photographs and firsthand accounts of the Dust Bowl and an excerpt from the 1935 magazine the *New Republic*.

CRITICAL THINKING SKILLS FOR "THE DUST BOWL"

- Make Connections
- Draw Conclusions
- Analyze Environmental Concepts
- Analyze Language Use
- Summarize
- Evaluate

CONNECT TO THE CHAPTER

This American Story explores the Dust Bowl, perhaps the greatest environmental disaster in U.S. history. Through the study of an interesting narrative featuring firsthand accounts, vivid photographs, and art, students will explore the causes of the "black blizzard," the ingenious solutions proposed to lessen its impact, and the ways in which it altered the lives of the many people caught in its wake.

This chapter, The Great Depression, examines the causes, effects, and early government response to the economic catastrophe that gripped the world in the 1930s. This problem was compounded in the U.S. by the concurrent environmental catastrophe known as the Dust Bowl, which ravaged American agriculture and uprooted millions. Use this American Story after reading lesson 2.3 to provide greater depth to the content.

📝 HISTORY NOTEBOOK

Encourage students to complete the American Story page for Chapter 19 in their History Notebooks as they read.

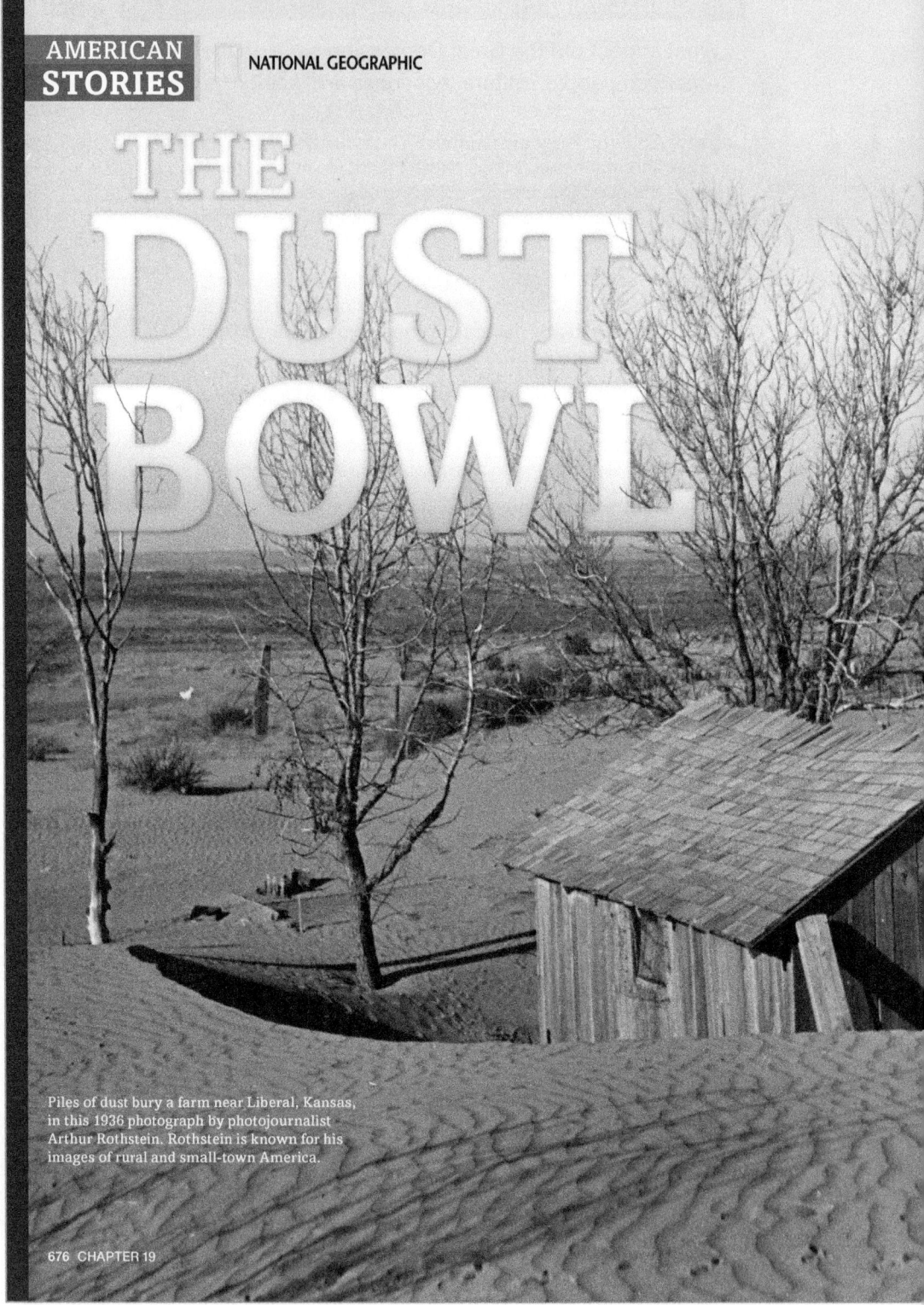

AMERICAN STORIES | NATIONAL GEOGRAPHIC

THE DUST BOWL

Piles of dust bury a farm near Liberal, Kansas, in this 1936 photograph by photojournalist Arthur Rothstein. Rothstein is known for his images of rural and small-town America.

676 CHAPTER 19

Between 1931 and 1939, so-called "black blizzards"—dangerous dust storms—were frighteningly common across the Great Plains, especially in Texas, Oklahoma, Colorado, Kansas, and New Mexico. Journalist Robert Geiger coined the nickname "Dust Bowl" for this drought-stricken region in 1935. The name stuck because it was such an apt description for a bleak time and place, and possibly the worst environmental disaster ever to strike the United States.

When a black blizzard came howling into town, it looked and felt like the end of the world. One witness described one of these traumatizing storms after it assaulted a Texas town in 1935, writing, "The front of the cloud was a rolling, bumbling, boiling mass of dust and dirt about two hundred feet high, almost vertical, and as black as an Angus bull. . . . After the front passed, the darkness rivaled the darkness inside a whale resting on the bottom of the ocean at midnight." Lorena Hickok, a newspaper reporter, was in a car when a black blizzard hit. It was "[like] driving in a fog, only worse because of the wind that seemed as if it would blow the car right off the road," she recalled. "It was as though we were picked up in a vast, impenetrable black cloud which was hurling us right off the earth."

CAUSES AND REMEDIES

To a great extent, the Dust Bowl was a human-caused catastrophe. The Great Plains region has a semiarid climate, which means it receives light annual rainfall and is prone to occasional droughts. In the 1880s and 1890s, however, when millions of European settlers were arriving on the plains, the weather was exceptionally rainy, leading the new arrivals to the comfortable assumption that the bountiful rainfall would continue.

In the decades between 1880 and 1930, agricultural technology improved, allowing farmers to plow up increasingly wide swathes of native prairie grasses in order to plant their crops. These native plants had deep roots that anchored the soil when strong winds blew across the wide-open prairies, and they were perennials, which means they would survive from year to year. In contrast, wheat and other crops had shallow roots and were annuals, or plants that die after their growing season. Thus, in 1931, when heat and drought dried up the soil, there was nothing to hold it down when the turbulent winds blew. Wendell Berry, a writer and environmental activist, observed, "We plowed the prairie and never knew what we were doing, because we did not know what we were undoing." One perceptive Texas sheepherder put it more plainly when he asserted, "Grass is what holds the earth together."

The Great Depression **677**

PREVIEW USING VISUALS

Inform students that this American Story concerns the Dust Bowl—a prolonged drought and series of dust storms that struck the Great Plains region. Direct students to view the photograph and read the caption. Prompt them to discuss why, based on the photograph, this event was named the Dust Bowl. Then tell students to review the other photos in this feature. **ASK:** Based on the photos, what effects do you think the Dust Bowl had on American people? *(Answers will vary. Possible responses: loss of property; loss of livelihood; homelessness; hunger; need to migrate)* Then tell students that in this American Story they will examine the causes and effects of this environmental disaster.

STAY OR GO?

Direct students' attention to the photograph at the beginning of this American Story. Then tell them to imagine that a disaster like this one had just taken place in their community—damaging or destroying property and crippling the ability of residents to find jobs. Draw a T-Chart on the board. Ask students the following questions: In this situation, would you stay in your community or leave it for somewhere else? Why would you make that choice? Prompt students to share their responses and write them in the T-Chart. Explain that in this American Story they will learn about the decisions made by many Americans faced with this situation during the time of the Dust Bowl.

Reasons to Stay	Reasons to Leave

A PLAGUE OF LOCUSTS

Besides the sweeping hundred-foot-high walls of dirt, there was one other menace connected to the Dust Bowl—grasshoppers. In most regions, grasshoppers are kept in check by a fungus that lives in the moist soil—a condition absent during the Dust Bowl. With no population control, grasshopper numbers exploded across America's breadbasket, destroying the few surviving plants and devouring almost anything they came across, including clothes hanging on lines.

DUST BOWL PHOTOGRAPHY

The Dust Bowl remains a powerful symbol of environmental calamity and human misery in part because of the vivid photographic record. However, these photographs were not captured by accident—they were part of a massive Depression-era government effort to put people, including artists, to work. In 1937, President Roosevelt created the Farm Security Administration (FSA) to help rehabilitate struggling rural areas. As a part of this effort, photographers were employed to document the rehabilitation and provide the public with information about this often-overlooked piece of America. The work of one of these photographers—Dorothea Lange—is featured prominently in this American Story. Photos by Lange and her contemporaries can be viewed on the Library of Congress website.

CRITICAL VIEWING The poster conveys its message by contrasting the well-maintained barn and green areas of productive farmland enclosed by bands of trees with barren fields and a dilapidated, half-buried house in a treeless area. The poster was targeting farmers and their families as its audience.

A black blizzard could carry unimaginable quantities of dirt. In 1934, one storm traveled clear across the continent, deposited 12 million tons of former prairie soil on the city of Chicago, then carried dust so far east it darkened the sky in New York City and even reached ships 300 miles from shore in the Atlantic Ocean. On what became Black Sunday, April 14, 1935, another storm ripped up an estimated 300 million tons of topsoil from the Great Plains, trapping people who were caught outside in biting winds and absolute blackness.

The end of the Dust Bowl came about through both human solutions and nature's intervention. A federal agency called the Soil Conservation Service was established to introduce new farming techniques that would help retain the soil. The agency encouraged farmers to use contour plowing, a method of plowing furrows that follow the shape of the land, rather than plowing in a straight line regardless of hills or dips in the terrain. When occasional rains did fall, the contoured furrows would catch the water as it flowed downhill rather than channeling it through the parched land. The agency also suggested planting soybeans, sweet clover, and other crops that would help anchor the soil.

President Franklin Roosevelt also promoted his own plan, known as the Shelterbelt Project. According to the plan, the government would pay farmers to plant a broad line of trees from Texas to the Canadian border. This "shelterbelt" was intended to break the momentum of winds sweeping eastward across the plains and provide cooling to

nearby areas. In the end, Roosevelt's shelterbelt was never completed, but it did help publicize the importance of taking action to reduce the negative effects of farming on the environment. By 1938, the drought continued unabated, but the tonnage of soil carried aloft by storms was reduced almost by half. In 1939, nature stepped in and rainfall resumed, putting an end to the lengthy drought.

CRITICAL VIEWING This poster from the late 1930s promotes the planting of trees on the Great Plains in order to combat wind erosion. How does the poster visually convey its message, and what audience do you think the poster was targeting?

CRITICAL VIEWING Thousands of migrant families in California carried their belongings from one farm to the next as they worked harvesting crops. How might this way of life have impacted children's social and educational lives?

TEACH

GUIDED DISCUSSION

1. **Draw Conclusions** If the weather had been more typical of the Great Plains during the 1880s and 1890s as settlers moved into the area, do you think events surrounding the Dust Bowl might have been different? Explain your reasoning. *(Answers will vary. Possible responses: Yes; the Dust Bowl might not have happened at all, because settlers might have deemed the dry land unsuitable for agriculture. Yes; it might have happened much earlier—when farmers first began plowing the dry soil. No; settlers might not have farmed the dry land at first, but they probably would have started as soon as there was a rainy year; they might have assumed that the drought years were a fluke and the rainy year was typical.)*

2. **Analyze Environmental Concepts** During the Dust Bowl, how did natural systems adjust to human-caused alterations? *(The loss of natural systems—mainly the loss of perennial natural prairie grasses that kept soil from eroding—was one of the main causes of the Dust Bowl. These systems did not fully recover until the end of drought season. However, human alterations such as contour plowing and tree planting did impact the natural process of soil erosion, lessening the effect of wind carrying away dry, loose soil.)*

CRITICAL VIEWING Children probably found it difficult to make and keep friends, because they frequently moved. They likely missed family and friends they had to leave behind. In addition, formal schooling was probably difficult without a permanent place to live. In many cases, children probably had to work in the fields instead of going to school.

THOSE WHO LEFT

When the long drought began, the United States was already in the throes of the Great Depression. Farmers were struggling to make a living after a drastic fall in crop prices. For many, the arrival of the first severe dust storms in 1933 turned a difficult situation into a desperate one. Crops and livestock were already suffering from the lack of moisture, and now the black blizzards were carrying the soil away. Homes and buildings were half buried, while animals trapped outside in the storms sickened and died

from the dirt they inhaled. One grim joke of the time told of a farmer applying for a loan to support his farm, and then looking out the window of the bank to see that same farm blowing past in the wind.

Feeling they had no options, about one quarter of the people affected by the Dust Bowl decided to abandon their homes. Many of them packed their families and belongings into their cars and headed west for California, where they believed they would find work.

The Great Depression **679**

GUIDED DISCUSSION

3. **Make Connections** Remind students that throughout American history different religious and ethnic groups, such as Catholics, Irish, Chinese, and African Americans, have experienced hardships when moving to a new place. **ASK:** How was the experience of the Okies similar to that of other migrating—and immigrating—groups in American history? *(Answers will vary. Possible response: Many groups have had similar experiences to that of the Okies. For example, many Chinese immigrants arriving in California lived in separate sections, competed with residents for jobs, and faced resentment from long-term residents.)*

4. **Analyze Language Use** Prompt students to examine the quotations found in the Those Who Stayed section. **ASK:** Based on the language used in the quotations, do you think the speakers regretted their decision to stay? Support you answer with evidence from the text. *(Answers will vary. Possible response: Judging by the first quotation, the speaker may have regretted the decision to stay, because she describes the "thick, brownish gray blanket" that overcomes her home. The second speaker, however, describes the "precious memories" she and her family associate with their home and their "faith in the future," so she probably did not regret staying.)*

SEEMS LIKE ANOTHER COUNTRY

Grant Wood and other artists who worked in the Regionalist style focused on depicting scenes they were familiar with, such as landscapes and people—real or fictitious—that one might encounter close to home. This style sharply contrasted with the more abstract cubism and surrealism popular at this time in Europe. Instead, Regionalist artists offered a glimpse of a particular time and place, and Grant Wood's region was the Midwest. Born on a farm in 1891, Wood used his early experiences as an inspiration for his paintings. Famously, he once said, "all the really good ideas I'd ever had come to me while milking a cow." His most well-known painting, *American Gothic*, depicts another regional scene: a farmhouse in Eldon, Iowa, and two stern-faced farm people whom the artist based on his sister and his dentist. **ASK:** What does Wood's painting *Young Corn* say about rural life and American identity? *(Answers will vary. Possible response: Wood's painting depicts rural life as beautiful— lush, green, and picturesque, creating an impression of the Midwest as a land of plenty. The farmers toiling in the field convey the hard work ethic characteristic of the region's people.)*

AMERICAN STORIES

SEEMS LIKE ANOTHER COUNTRY

As the black blizzards raged and bread lines stretched along city streets, some Depression-era artists sought to imagine the country in more promising times. A group of American painters known as Regionalists aimed to create a purely American style, distinct from the styles of their contemporaries in Europe, and several used the American countryside as their subject. Instead of the ravaged scenery of the Dust Bowl, they painted idealized Midwestern farms that appeared green, fertile, and prosperous. Among the most prominent Regionalists were Grant Wood, Thomas Hart Benton, and John Steuart Curry. The painting below by Grant Wood is entitled *Young Corn*.

How does the image of rural life portrayed in this painting by Grant Wood differ from the image shown in the photographs in this article?

"THE NIGHTMARE IS BECOMING LIFE"

Many people who lived through the Dust Bowl wrote horrifying accounts of black blizzards. Avis D. Carlson, of Kansas, wrote the following description in 1935 for the magazine *The New Republic*. How does the line, "It is becoming Real," contribute to the excerpt?

PRIMARY SOURCE

The impact is like a shovelful of fine sand flung against the face. People caught in their own yards grope for the doorstep. Cars come to a standstill, for no light in the world can penetrate that swirling murk. . . . The nightmare is deepest during the storms. But on the occasional bright day and the usual gray day we cannot shake from it. We live with the dust, eat it, sleep with it, watch it strip us of possessions and the hope of possessions. It is becoming Real. The poetic uplift of spring fades into a phantom of the storied past. The nightmare is becoming life.

The rich California farm fields could not have looked more different to the exhausted migrants streaming into the state. The area of California known as the Inland Empire was home to large farms growing lemons, oranges, lettuce, grapes, and many other varieties of produce. Jobs, however, were not so plentiful, and the agricultural work was back-breaking. In addition, the farm owners used the influx of migrants to force down the already low wages for all workers, including native Californians and immigrants from Mexico.

As a result, local workers intensely resented the newcomers, whom they called "Okies." The term was short for Oklahoma, although most of the migrants were not from that state. Singer Woody Guthrie, who was well acquainted with the sufferings of Dust Bowl refugees, described the connotations of the name "Okie." According to him, the term "means you ain't got no home. Sort of meant, too, that you're out of a job. Or owe more than you can rake or scrape [up]."

Many Okies were met at the state line by police officers who informed them there was no work for them in California and told them to turn back. Californians weren't very friendly towards the migrants, either—in fact some were downright hostile, likely due to differences in regional culture. As a result, thousands of Okies found themselves living in roadside camps that were collections of ramshackle huts, and in the backs of cars and trucks. There was little or no sanitation or privacy. Eventually, the federal government stepped in to help provide better conditions for the migrants, but for many, life did not noticeably improve until the end of the Great Depression.

THOSE WHO STAYED

The people who remained in the Dust Bowl learned to endure nearly unbearable heat, extreme dryness, and inescapable dust. It was impossible to keep dirt out of the houses, no matter how tightly the doors and windows were sealed. One woman described sheltering in her home during a dust storm: "All we could do was just sit in our dusty chairs, gaze at each other through the fog that filled the room and watch the fog settle slowly and silently, covering everything—including ourselves—in a thick, brownish gray blanket." At night, people slept uncomfortably on gritty sheets. When setting the table, women placed plates and glasses upside-down until it was just time to serve the food, to avoid dirt settling onto the dishes.

It was impossible to avoid breathing in some dust, which could cause a variety of illnesses. Among the worst was silicosis, nicknamed "dust pneumonia," which was caused by sharp dust particles gradually scraping the lungs until the sufferer died.

People caught outside on foot or in cars during storms were at risk of becoming lost in the darkness and being suffocated by the violently blowing dirt. Some died just a few feet away from shelter that they could not glimpse through the black blizzard. One farmer recalled stretching a wire between his house and barn so that he could navigate his way home if a dust storm hit while he was in the barn.

Asked why people stayed on their farms, one woman from Kansas replied, "In part . . . we hope for the coming of moisture, which would change conditions so we can again have bountiful harvests. And in great part, because it is home. We have reared our family here and many have precious memories of the past. We have our memories. We have faith in the future, we are here to stay."

THINK ABOUT IT

What lessons about land use or management can be drawn from the Dust Bowl?

"THE NIGHTMARE IS BECOMING LIFE"

The worst of the dust storms that Avis D. Carlson wrote about was called the Black Sunday storm. It charged across the plains seemingly out of nowhere with winds topping 60 miles per hour, temperatures plummeting, and a wall of blowing dust resembling a tsunami. Its impact was so great that songs were written about it—including by Woody Guthrie—and it was from this storm that the term *Dust Bowl* originated. The day after the storm, a reporter wrote: "Three little words . . . rule life in the dustbowl of the continent—'if it rains.'"

ASK: What words and phrases does the author use to capture the intensity of black blizzards? *(Examples include "no light in the world," "swirling murk," "nightmare," and "the poetic uplift of spring fades into a phantom of the storied past.")*

THINK ABOUT IT

The Dust Bowl teaches us about the fragility of nature and the impact of human actions and that while new technology can improve things, it can also have devastating consequences if not managed well.

ACTIVE OPTIONS

On Your Feet: Examine Life During the Dust Bowl
Direct small groups to research primary sources—excerpts found in this text, clips from documentaries, and accounts from newspapers—of people who lived through the Dust Bowl. Ask students to note details about life during the Dust Bowl, including human movement and migration patterns, and compose five main ideas about life in the Dust Bowl. Students can use the witness accounts as well as maps and other documents to support their findings. Have groups reconvene and discuss their statements.

NG Learning Framework: Analyze Land Use STEM
ATTITUDE Responsibility
KNOWLEDGE Our Living Planet

Since the Dust Bowl, the federal government has taken an active role in managing land use to prevent future disasters. For example, the U.S. Farm Bill provides funding for conservation and includes certain programs, such as incentivizing farmers to allow land to return to its natural state. Instruct student groups to investigate current land use policies—particularly those that pertain to the Great Plains, agriculture, and conservation. Prompt groups to select one specific policy and prepare a short presentation in which they explain the following: the policy, the environmental impact of the policy, and what difference—if any—such a policy would have made if it had been in place during the time of the Dust Bowl.

DUST BOWL PHOTOGRAPHER DOROTHEA LANGE

Taken in 1936, the subject of the iconic "Migrant Mother" images remained a mystery for decades. Dorothea Lange never asked the woman's name, and by the time the photographs published, the woman had moved. It wasn't until 1978 that a reporter tracked her down. Florence Owens Thompson, a Cherokee, was married at 17 and widowed at 28. During the Depression, she worked as an itinerant farmhand, following the crops that were in season. When she met Dorothea Lange, her car had broken down in Nipomo, California. She reluctantly agreed to be photographed. Ask students to study the photograph from the "Migrant Mother series." Tell them to pay particular attention to the expression on Thompson's face, the demeanor of the children, and who is—and isn't—present in the photograph. **ASK:** What does the photograph convey about the experiences of women like Thompson during the Depression? *(Answers will vary. Possible response: The worried, exhausted look on her face, as well as the fact that she is sheltering the children, seem to reflect the hardships and strain of poverty.)*

WRITE ABOUT HISTORY   STEM

Connect to the Present This American Story details the impact of environmental changes on the way in which people live. To connect this story to the present, tell students to research a current environmental change—such as rising sea levels in Bangladesh, intense heat waves in Australia, or the receding of glaciers in Alaska—and how it affects local people. Then instruct students to write an essay in which they compare the responses to environmental change in the Dust Bowl era with those in the present day. Tell students also to evaluate the consequences and present the lessons learned in their essay. Encourage students to share their finished essays with the rest of the class.

AMERICAN STORIES

To get an overview of a field or a camp that she wanted to photograph, Dorothea Lange would often climb up on the roof of her car.

DUST BOWL PHOTOGRAPHER: DOROTHEA LANGE

Dorothea Lange was not planning to become an influential documentary photographer when she moved to San Francisco. Born into a wealthy family in 1895, she studied photography at Columbia University in New York City and then worked as an apprentice to several photographers before moving west to set up a successful portrait studio.

When the Great Depression hit San Francisco, it brought the same scenes of human misery as in other cities: homelessness, unemployment, and bread lines. Disturbed by the suffering she saw daily in the streets, Lange turned her camera to the people and events outside of her studio. Soon, she was working for the federal government, tasked with a mission to document the predicaments of people forced from their land by the Dust Bowl.

From 1935 to 1939, Lange traveled throughout the western United States photographing Dust Bowl refugees in settlement camps, in their cars, and at work. She used her skills as a portrait photographer to capture faces in unguarded moments of exhaustion, worry, and occasional relaxation. Paul Taylor, who accompanied Lange on her travels, explained her technique for putting her subjects at ease. "Her method of work," he recalled, "was often to just saunter up to the people and look around,

and then when she saw something that she wanted to photograph, to quietly take her camera, look at it, and if she saw that they objected, why, she would close it up and not take a photograph, or perhaps she would wait until . . . they were used to her."

The photo on the bottom of the next page is part of a series of images that became symbolic of the Great Depression, capturing the poverty, misery, and stress endured by migratory farmworkers in the 1930s. The main subject of the "Migrant Mother" photographs was 32-year-old Florence Owens Thompson, who was the sole supporter of her seven children. Lange claimed Thompson had sold her car's tires to buy food for her children and that the family had been surviving on vegetables that had frozen in a nearby field, but Thompson's children said Lange must have confused their mother with someone else.

Lange's images from the 1930s leave an indelible impression on viewers to this day. She and other Depression-era photographers helped ensure that all Americans would know about the struggles of those impoverished and left homeless by the upheavals of the time. After the Depression ended, Lange continued her work as a documentary photographer until her death in 1965.

In these photographs taken in California in the 1930s, Dorothea Lange captured rural people at work and at rest. The photo on the top left shows two workers loading cotton. The one on the right shows Dust Bowl refugees stopped along a highway. The bottom photograph from Lange's 1936 "Migrant Mother" series features mother Florence Owens Thompson sitting in a tent with two of her seven children.

The Great Depression 683

DIFFERENTIATE

INCLUSION

Predict Using Visuals Pair special needs students with students at higher proficiency levels. Direct them to look at each photograph, poster, or painting together. Then ask partners to work together to write notes about what they think the lesson will cover. After reading, ask pairs to review their notes to see whether their predictions were confirmed.

PRE-AP

Compare Historical and Current Events Tell students that the main factors that led to the Dust Bowl, drought and farming practices, continue to be issues today. Instruct students to research the environmental and economic impacts of changing climate patterns, mechanized farming, and the planting of annual crops across vast regions of the United States. Prompt students to write a concluding statement that compares past and present needs for environmentally sound farm policy and practices and encourage them to present their findings and conclusion to the class.

See the Chapter Planner for more strategies for differentiation.

HISTORICAL THINKING

Ask and have students answer the following questions.

1. **READING CHECK** What was the Dust Bowl, and how did it come about?

2. **SUMMARIZE** Why did people leave their homes and move from the region during the Dust Bowl?

3. **EVALUATE** Which type of factors—economic, political, or cultural—do you think most motivated people to remain in their homes during the Dust Bowl? Explain your response.

ANSWERS

1. The Dust Bowl is a term used to describe the prolonged drought and dust storms that devastated the Great Plains during the 1930s. The dryness of the soil due to the drought, along with excessive plowing and the loss of natural prairie grass, created the conditions for the Dust Bowl.

2. People left their homes because of the lack of economic opportunity due to the loss of crops and livestock. Also, homes were destroyed or made unlivable, buried in dirt. These conditions forced many people to seek shelter and employment elsewhere.

3. Possible response: People who stayed behind were most motivated by cultural factors, since the first-hand accounts from people in the text cited family ties and a sense of home as reasons for staying.

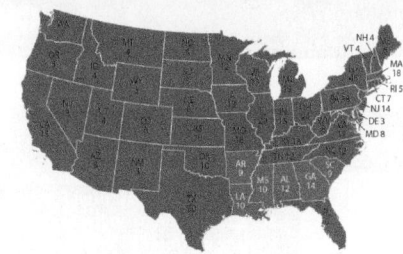

The Election of 1928

Herbert Hoover, Republican	
Electoral Vote:	444 votes, 83.6%
Popular Vote:	21,391,381 votes, 58.8%

Al Smith, Democrat	
Electoral Vote:	87 votes, 16.4%
Popular Vote:	15,016,443 votes, 41.2%

A DECEPTIVE PROSPERITY

The saying "All that glitters is not gold" is an apt description of the 1920s. When President Calvin Coolidge began his first full term in office, he believed the United States was prosperous and secure. But economic troubles lurked beneath the sparkling surface.

COOLIDGE IN THE WHITE HOUSE

In 1924, after serving out Harding's remaining term in office, Calvin Coolidge ran for and won the presidency. Strongly pro-business and against government intervention, his policy goals were modest. When Coolidge asked Congress for a cut in taxes, lawmakers responded with a measure that lowered taxes for people who made more than $100,000 a year. However, most married couples made less than $3,500 a year, so the tax cuts affected only the wealthiest Americans. The president also promoted laws to oversee the expansion of the new airline industry and to regulate the growing radio business. At the same time, Coolidge did little to help farmers and people living in rural areas. He twice vetoed a bill to aid farmers

and did not support a federal government initiative to build dams on the Tennessee River that would provide affordable electric power to that region of the country.

In foreign policy, Coolidge opposed the use of military force, but he also believed the United States had an obligation to help countries in need. In 1924, the Coolidge administration had endorsed a plan to help a struggling Germany meet its huge war reparation debt. During the next four years, Germany borrowed almost $1.5 million from the United States. Similarly, when the Soviet Union faced a famine in the early 1920s, Americans sent large amounts of food and monetary aid. But when revolution and civil war took place in China, the U.S. government did not get

involved. In fact, the State Department preferred the idea of outlawing war altogether, an idea that peace groups supported. The resulting **Kellogg-Briand Pact** was a multinational agreement in which the signing countries agreed to renounce, or reject, war. Coolidge was among those who signed the pact in 1928, and it was ratified in 1929. However, there was no way to enforce the pact worldwide.

Believing that it would be difficult for anyone to be effective in the office for more than eight years, Coolidge declined to run for a second full term. Herbert Hoover, Coolidge's secretary of commerce, beat out his political rivals to win the Republican nomination for president. Hoover faced off against the Democratic candidate, Governor Alfred E. Smith of New York, who was Roman Catholic. In the general election, Hoover benefited from the religious intolerance many Protestants held against Smith's faith. Hoover won the electoral vote in a landslide.

A TROUBLED ECONOMY

When Hoover took office, the future looked bright, but the surface prosperity of the 1920s hid some serious economic problems. The most pervasive of these was the dramatically uneven distribution of income. Agricultural overproduction had driven down crop prices throughout the decade, so farmers did not benefit from the nation's general prosperity. Furthermore, by 1929, the economy was characterized by a lopsided distribution of income. At the top level, 5 percent of Americans received 33 percent of the total annual personal income, while half of all Americans received about 16 percent of the total. More than half of American families lived near or below the poverty line even though unemployment was low. More than 21 million families, or 80 percent of the national population, did not have any savings at all. But in order to expand, the economy relied on people purchasing consumer goods. If most ordinary

Americans lacked **disposable income**—or spending money—and purchasing power, it would have a big impact on the national economy.

Other warning signs signaled the economy was in trouble, including a recession in 1927. Wholesale prices fell nearly 4.5 percent, the production of goods slowed, and consumer spending dropped. The global economy was also fragile. Germany continued to struggle with its reparation payments, even after the United States reduced the burden of German war debts in 1924. In 1929, an international committee proposed another plan that further reduced Germany's total debt and established a longer period for repayment. These concessions eased economic pressures, but only temporarily. Weakness in the German economy continued to grow as banks closed and markets disintegrated.

Yet, despite multiple national and global warning signs, the U.S. banking system continued to expand credit. Americans increasingly speculated in the **stock market**, or the buying and selling of shares in companies. Earnings from stocks could be higher than interest paid by banks, but an investor could also lose money, especially over the short term. For the average American, though, it looked like the economy would grow forever.

PRIMARY SOURCE

Coolidge focused on cutting taxes that were already low for most Americans and viewed taxation as funding "extravagance" in government.

We must have tax reform. We cannot finance the country, we cannot improve social conditions, through any system of injustice, even if we attempt to inflict it upon the rich. Those who suffer the most harm will be the poor. This country believes in prosperity. It is absurd to suppose that it is envious of those who are already personally rich. The wise and correct course to follow in taxation and all other economic legislation is not to destroy those who have already secured success but to create conditions under which everyone will have a better chance to be successful.

—from Calvin Coolidge's Inaugural Address, March 4, 1925

HISTORICAL THINKING

1. **READING CHECK** What role did religion play in the presidential race between Hoover and Smith?

2. **ANALYZE LANGUAGE USE** How did President Coolidge's use of the phrase "any system of injustice" help his argument for tax reform?

3. **IDENTIFY MAIN IDEAS AND DETAILS** What warning signs suggested that the U.S. economy was not as prosperous as it appeared?

PLAN: 2-PAGE LESSON

OBJECTIVE

Understand the principle causes, both at home and abroad, that put the U.S. economy at risk.

CRITICAL THINKING SKILLS FOR LESSON 1.1

- Analyze Language Use
- Identify Main Ideas and Details
- Make Inferences
- Analyze Cause and Effect
- Analyze Primary Sources

HISTORICAL THINKING FOR CHAPTER 19

What impact did the Great Depression have on the American people, culture, economy, and spirit? While on the surface the country's economy looked successful, warning signs arose. Lesson 1.1 discusses how unequal income distribution, international instability, falling prices, and speculation weakened the economy and set the stage for economic disaster.

BACKGROUND FOR THE TEACHER

In the 1920s, credit buying helped to fuel the deceptive prosperity. Farmers used credit to buy equipment, seed, and fertilizer, counting on crop sales to repay the loans. Because most families had little discretionary income, businesses tried to increase sales with a "buy now, pay later" policy. Installment plans enabled lower- and middle-income families to purchase items over time, such as cars, furniture, radios, vacuum cleaners, and washing machines. By the end of the decade, 75 percent of cars, 90 percent of furniture, and 75 percent of radios had been purchased on credit. Few suspected that buying on credit would have such a strong impact on the country, until people began to lose their jobs and couldn't make their payments, thus threatening the entire economy.

INTRODUCE & ENGAGE

CREATE A WORD WEB

Write the term *economic problems* in the center of the Word Web. Ask students to suggest words or phrases they associate with present-day economic problems. Then discuss what effect these problems might have on a country. Tell students that this lesson discusses how the economic troubles beneath the surface of a seemingly prosperous economy led to the Great Depression.

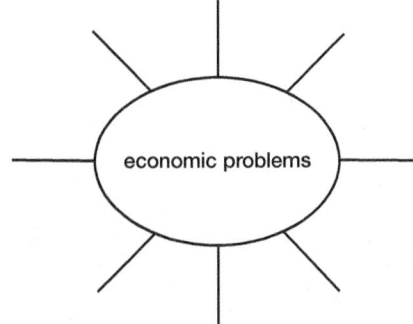

economic problems

TEACH

GUIDED DISCUSSION

1. **Make Inferences** Direct students' attention to the 1928 election map. **ASK:** Based on the results of the election, what can you infer about the attitudes of the American public toward the candidates and the economy? *(Possible responses: Most of the country appeared to prefer a Protestant president, but for people in the South, religion seemed less important than the candidates' political party. People in the South may have also wanted a change in leadership and policies. Hoover's landslide victory seems to suggest that most people approved of Republican policies and believed that the economy was sound.)*

2. **Analyze Cause and Effect** Explain how the factors that contributed to unequal income distribution led to complex effects on the U.S. economy. *(Possible response: Lack of government aid to rural people, falling crop prices, low wages, and lack of savings probably contributed to unequal income distribution. As a result, there was less disposable income, fewer goods purchased, and a slowdown in the economy.)*

ANALYZE PRIMARY SOURCES

Explain that Calvin Coolidge, the 30th president, gained popularity at a time when the economy seemed prosperous. In fact, this prosperity was referred to as "Coolidge prosperity." As president, he promised to preserve that status quo, despite growing inequities. Ask students to reread the last sentence in Coolidge's inauguration speech and then reread the first paragraph of the section "Coolidge in the White House." **ASK:** How well did Coolidge's words match his subsequent actions? *(Possible response: His actions contrasted with his words. Instead of creating conditions to help people succeed, his tax cuts and vetoes made conditions more difficult for many people.)*

ACTIVE OPTIONS

Active History: Graph Stock Prices Extend the lesson by using either the PDF or Whiteboard version of the activity. These activities take a deeper look at a topic from, or related to, the lesson. Explore the activities as a class, turn them into group assignments, or even assign them individually.

On Your Feet: Use a Jigsaw Strategy Organize students into three "expert" groups. Then assign one of the following basic economic indicators to each group: falling prices, credit buying, and disposable income. Ask each group to analyze the aggregate economic behavior of the economy in the 1920s based on their assigned indicator. Then have members of each group count off using A, B, and C. Regroup students into three new groups so that each new group has at least one member from each original group. Direct students to share their analyses, then discuss how the economic indicators might continue to influence the economy, for better or worse, in the years that followed.

DIFFERENTIATE

ENGLISH LANGUAGE LEARNERS

Identify Facts Conduct a Round Robin activity with students of mixed proficiencies to review what they learned about both domestic and foreign policy in the 1920s. Instruct them to spend three to five minutes generating facts, with all students contributing and taking notes. You may ask students at the **Expanding** and **Bridging** levels to assist students at the **Emerging** level. Invite volunteers to share responses. Write all the facts on the board.

GIFTED & TALENTED

Create Coolidge Tweets Ask students to research information about Calvin Coolidge to learn more about the man and his social, economic, and foreign policy stances. Then have students create 140-character tweets based on what they learned. Encourage them to use primary source documents as the basis of their tweets to capture both Coolidge's personality and policies. Invite students to read their tweets to the class and be prepared to answer questions.

See the Chapter Planner for more strategies for differentiation.

HISTORICAL THINKING

ANSWERS

1. Because of religious intolerance toward Roman Catholics, many Protestants voted for Hoover rather than Smith.

2. The phrase "any system of injustice" implied that Coolidge felt taxes were an unacceptable way to finance the country or improve social conditions, harming both rich and poor. Tax reform, therefore, was needed to correct this injustice.

3. Warning signs included unequal distribution of income, lack of disposable income, falling prices, global instability, credit buying, and increased speculation in the stock market.

PANIC ON WALL STREET

We all know that what goes up must eventually come down. Investors in the 1920s didn't realize that old saying also applied to the stock market. On October 29, 1929, they learned just how wrong they were.

INVESTMENT FEVER

In the 1920s, Americans pointed to the growth of the stock market as an indication of the nation's growing prosperity. The market grew so quickly that many Americans saw it as the ideal place to make a fast buck. The U.S. Treasury's sale of Liberty Bonds during World War I had shown citizens that investments could lead to wealth.

More and more, corporations offered their stocks for sale to obtain cash to finance business growth. During the prosperous Harding and Coolidge years, generous government tax policies allowed the very wealthy to pay little or no income taxes, giving them extra money to invest in the stock market.

Smaller investors often bought stocks on **margin**. That is, they purchased stocks on credit, paying only 10 or 15 percent of the actual price up front. Buying on margin is a risky strategy because the investor is betting on being able to sell the stock at a higher price, pay off the stockbroker—the person who buys and sells stocks for his or her clients—and pocket a substantial profit. The lure of making easy money in the market was so great that people borrowed money to buy on margin. Banks happily loaned American investors that money, in spite of the Federal Reserve's warnings against the practice, which consequently gave rise to the establishment of weaknesses in the economy.

When this New York investor lost everything in the 1929 stock market crash, he put his car up for sale for less than 10 percent of its value.

$100 WILL BUY THIS CAR MUST HAVE CASH LOST ALL ON THE STOCK MARKET

Buying stocks on margin is a form of **speculation**. The buyer assumes, or speculates, that stock prices will always go up, even though there is no guarantee that they will. But in the 1920s, this looked like a sure bet. On September 3, 1929, the **Dow Jones Industrial Average (DJIA)**—a leading measure of general stock market trends—hit 381.17, a high for the decade, driven up in part by speculation and margin buying. Few suspected that the weakening market was headed for collapse.

OCTOBER 29, 1929

The problem began in September 1929. At the beginning of that month, the market hit its record high, but then stock prices declined. They regained some strength but began drifting downward again. Since there had been no abrupt collapse, many on Wall Street, their confidence unshaken, saw these events as one of the normal and temporary "corrections" that typically preceded another big increase in the stock market. A few people warned that problems lay ahead, but they were dismissed as chronic naysayers who had been wrong before.

But prices did not rise. On October 24, 1929, the day that became known as **Black Thursday**, stock trading began as usual, but few investors were willing to buy. Prices collapsed as investors, many of whom had bought on margin, tried to sell their stocks before prices fell even more. Nearly 13 million stocks were traded that day, which was then an all-time record. Stockholders absorbed, by some estimates, a $9 billion loss in the value of their stocks. During the afternoon, a large banking group led by bank executive J.P. Morgan, Jr., urged investors to be calm. Morgan even purchased some stocks himself. The market seemed to settle, leading to the hope that normal trading might recover.

Recovery was not in the cards. On the following Monday, the market fell sharply—around 13 percent—and the DJIA plummeted to 260.64. Then the hammer fell on October 29, a day that is still known as **Black Tuesday**. When trading began, the sell-off continued, with more than 16 million shares changing hands in a single day. The DJIA fell to 230.07 and continued to drop for nearly three years.

The consequences of the crash were immediate and striking. The prices of individual stocks continued on their downward slide. The DJIA reached a low of 41.22 on July 8, 1932. Within a few months of the crash, General Electric's stock had dropped from $403 a share to $168, and Standard Oil shares fell from $83 to $48. During the next year, the **gross national product (GNP)**—the total goods and services produced by the nation plus the income earned by its citizens—shrank from nearly $88 billion to $76 billion. With the already existing difficulties in agriculture and the large debt crisis, the U.S. economy slumped into a long and severe decline, resulting in an economic catastrophe that became known as the **Great Depression**, the deepest and most prolonged economic downturn in American history with a substantial human toll.

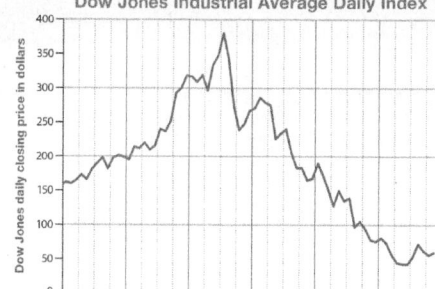

Dow Jones Industrial Average Daily Index

Source: The Dow Jones Averages (1885–1995)

PRIMARY SOURCE

Oral historian Studs Terkel interviewed people who lived through the Great Depression. In 1970, he published their stories in his book, *Hard Times*. In the following excerpt, composer Alec Wilder is speaking to Terkel of his losses in the stock market.

I knew something was terribly wrong because I heard bellboys, everybody, talking about the stock market. About six weeks before the Wall Street Crash, I persuaded my mother in Rochester to let me talk to our family adviser. I wanted to sell stock which had been left me by my father. He got very sentimental: "Oh your father wouldn't have liked you to do that." He was so persuasive, I said O.K. I could have sold it for $160,000. Four years later, I sold it for $4,000.

—from *Hard Times: An Oral History of the Great Depression*, by Studs Terkel, 1970

HISTORICAL THINKING

1. **READING CHECK** What effect did speculation and buying on margin have on stock prices?

2. **DRAW CONCLUSIONS** If trading reached record highs on October 24 and 29, why are these days called Black Thursday and Black Tuesday?

3. **INTERPRET GRAPHS** According to the graph, what were the highest and lowest averages in the DJIA in 1929, and how does the graph illustrate the cost and benefit of investing in the stock market?

PLAN: 2-PAGE LESSON

OBJECTIVE

Understand how and why the stock market crashed in 1929.

CRITICAL THINKING SKILLS FOR LESSON 1.2

- Draw Conclusions
- Interpret Graphs
- Make Generalizations
- Compare and Contrast
- Analyze Primary Sources

HISTORICAL THINKING FOR CHAPTER 19

What impact did the Great Depression have on the American people, economy, culture, and spirit? The stock market had always fluctuated, but in 1929 it went into a catastrophic decline. Lesson 1.2 discusses margin buying and the market's "corrections" and fall, signaling the start of the Great Depression.

BACKGROUND FOR THE TEACHER

The popular perception of the stock market crash of 1929 is that all investors, like the man in the photograph, lost all their money. In fact, some investors who understood the market actually made money before and after the crash. Before the crash, a savvy investor might have realized that a stock was overvalued, for instance, selling at $100 a share when it was really worth only $50 a share. He would then bet that this stock price would fall, not rise. This type of trade is called a short sale—a strategy still used today. When the crash began, these investors made a great deal of money when nearly all stock prices fell. After the crash, investors could buy undervalued stocks and wait for them to rise. When the market hit bottom in late 1929, cheap stocks were readily available to buy.

INTRODUCE & ENGAGE

FOLLOW THE CROWD?

Present a situation to students in which people must make decisions in a crisis, such as an approaching hurricane or a company filing for bankruptcy. Discuss how people might react in that situation. Would they get swept up in the emotions of others and follow the crowd? Or would they act calmly? Talk about the reasons why one course of action might be better than another. Tell students that this lesson will discuss how investors got caught up in buying and selling frenzies and how their actions affected the economy.

TEACH

GUIDED DISCUSSION

1. **Make Generalizations** How did the economic policies of the 1920s influence the stock market? *(Possible responses: Tax breaks gave the rich more money to invest, adding to the rising market. Others could purchase stock on credit. Banks could extend credit freely to anyone. With more people buying stocks, the stock market grew rapidly.)*

2. **Compare and Contrast** How were the factors that drove the stock market up and then drove it down similar and how were they different? *(Similarities: The factor of emotion influenced both actions—the desire to make money quickly drove the market up and the fear of losing money drove it down. Differences: The factor of financial institutions helped drive the market up but could do nothing when the market started falling.)*

ANALYZE PRIMARY SOURCES

Direct students' attention to the Primary Source feature. Discuss ways that Alec Wilder's story helps to make the information in the lesson more personal. Ask students to describe the toll that the stock market crash appears to have had on Wilder. Then conclude by having them list some of the reasons that documenting the human toll of historical events might be important.

ACTIVE OPTIONS

On Your Feet: Conduct a Cost-Benefit Analysis Explain that not everyone panicked during the stock market crash. Some saw opportunities in the disaster, as noted in Background for the Teacher. Divide the class into small groups and tell them they are investors thinking about investing *after* the crash in December 1929 or January 1930. Ask groups to conduct a cost-benefit analysis of investing *after* the crash. Refer them to the Financial Literacy handbook section "Using Economic Reasoning and Cost-Benefit Analysis" to guide them in their analysis. Encourage them to use the Choice and Outcome Cards in the handbook to record their findings.

NG Learning Framework: Write an Article

SKILL Communication

KNOWLEDGE Our Human Story

Encourage students to use information in the lesson and from other sources to write an article about how people reacted to the stock market crash. Have them consider the following questions for their article: What steps were taken by the Federal Reserve, Congress, and the president to combat the crisis? What toll did the market crash have on people? What part did human emotion play in the crisis? What generalizations or conclusions can they make about people's reactions? Ask volunteers to read their articles to the class.

DIFFERENTIATE

STRIVING READERS

Connect Details to a Main Idea Ask students to work in pairs to fill out a Main Idea and Details List for each section of the lesson. Model the kinds of details (facts, dates, events, descriptions) that often support a main idea. Students can share their main ideas and details with other pairs when they have finished.

Main Idea:
Detail:
Detail:
Detail:
Detail:
Detail:

PRE-AP

Compare Financial Disasters Direct students to work individually or in pairs to research and write a report comparing past and more recent financial disasters. Instruct students to use information in the lesson, plus what they learn from their research. For information on recent impacts of buying "on margin," you might suggest that they read Michael Lewis's book *The Big Short,* about the credit and housing collapse of the mid-2000s. Encourage students to share their reports with the class and answer any questions.

See the Chapter Planner for more strategies for differentiation.

HISTORICAL THINKING

ANSWERS

1. Speculation and buying on margin drove up stock prices to an artificial high.

2. The days are called Black Thursday and Black Tuesday because stock prices collapsed. The high trading volume indicated that investors were trying to sell stocks before they became worthless.

3. The highest average was slightly over 375 and the lowest about 175. These ups and downs show that as long as the stock market continued to rise, people benefited by selling stocks for more than they had bought them. The cost could be equally great if prices fell and people lost the money they had invested.

THE DEPRESSION BEGINS

The reaction in a domino chain starts with the fall of the first domino, but it's the structure of the chain that causes the other dominos to fall. That principle applied to the economy during the Great Depression.

A WEAK FOUNDATION

The stock market crash of 1929 signaled the start of the Great Depression of the 1930s, the deepest and most prolonged economic downturn in American history. But the Depression was caused by broad underlying weaknesses more deeply rooted than falling stock values. The apparent prosperity of the 1920s hid the fact that the U.S. and world economies rested on an unsound foundation. Four main factors contributed to the problem: overproduction resulting in oversaturated markets, unequal income distribution, lack of proper banking regulations, and a weak worldwide financial system.

After World War I, American farmers continued to maintain high levels of wartime production, even though Europe was once again producing its own food or buying from U.S. competitors. Soon, the surplus of American crops and meat drove down prices on the global market. In the manufacturing sector—especially in one of the nation's leading industries, the automotive industry—new machinery and assembly lines led to increased productivity, and output jumped almost 32 percent between 1923 and 1929. Similarly, the other leading U.S. industry, construction, far outpaced demand for new houses. But by 1929, growth in the auto, housing, and consumer goods industries had begun to decline. Innovations that had enabled producing those items affordably meant that many people had already purchased what they needed. As demand decreased, workers were laid off.

Income inequality, or the unequal distribution of income and wealth between the few wealthiest Americans and the rest of the population, made the problem of overproduction worse, especially in the automobile and housing construction markets.

Similarly, the uneven distribution of wealth, or the value of what a household owns minus debts, factored into an unstable economy. The small percentage of wealthy Americans purchased only so many houses, cars, and luxury goods. To keep the consumer economy growing, the majority of the population needed to purchase newly built houses and to buy cars and consumer goods. Though unemployment was low, wages did not rise as fast as production, and soon more goods existed than people could afford to buy. As businesses accumulated profits rather than increasing workers' wages, demand weakened, prices and profits actually fell, and businesses laid off workers. By 1929, more than half of American families could not meet their basic needs with their income.

A lack of regulation in the banking and financial industries was another cause of the Depression. While the Federal Reserve regulated banking, district banks often had difficulty agreeing on regulation. For example, they could not decide on how best to rein in margin buying and overspeculation. Investors formed **trading pools**, groups formed to buy and sell large amounts of stocks. They made stocks appear active by buying and selling among themselves. This drove up the price of the stock artificially, and after they had sold off their stock at high prices, other investors' shares had little value. Lack of regulation also kept the Federal Reserve from acting quickly and decisively when, as the Depression deepened, American banks began to fail.

The fragile state of the global economy also contributed to the Depression. Internationally, the world stock market, international loans, economic policies, and World War I reparations formed a web of interconnected factors that helped lead to a

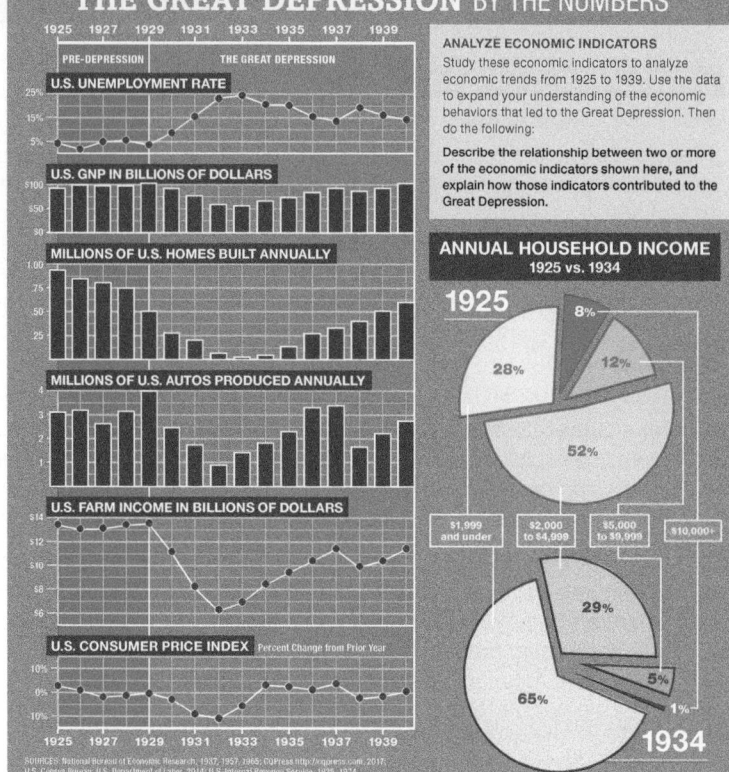

THE GREAT DEPRESSION BY THE NUMBERS

ANALYZE ECONOMIC INDICATORS
Study these economic indicators to analyze economic trends from 1925 to 1939. Use the data to expand your understanding of the economic behaviors that led to the Great Depression. Then do the following:

Describe the relationship between two or more of the economic indicators shown here, and explain how those indicators contributed to the Great Depression.

worldwide downturn. Europe was already weakened by Germany's inability to pay its war reparations. The United States had overtaken Britain after World War I as the world's financial leader and now passed protective tariffs it believed would enable American agriculture and industry to rebound. But the **Smoot-Hawley Tariff Act** of 1930, which raised customs duties to high levels, made it more difficult for European businesses to sell goods in the United States and obstructed the flow of capital, goods, and services in the world economy. Dozens of countries responded by passing retaliatory tariffs

that made it harder for the United States to export goods. International trade declined sharply, triggering international bank failures and adding to the suffering at home and abroad.

THE DEPRESSION DEEPENS

When the DJIA rose for a few months in early 1930, President Hoover told the nation, "I am convinced we have passed the worst and with continued effort shall rapidly recover." But as 1930 continued, it was clear the situation was only getting worse. Bank failures soared from 659 in 1929 to 1,350 a year later.

PLAN: 4-PAGE LESSON

OBJECTIVE

Recognize complex causes and effects that helped bring about the Great Depression.

CRITICAL THINKING SKILLS FOR LESSON 2.1

- Analyze Cause and Effect
- Synthesize
- Make Connections
- Analyze Data
- Form and Support Opinions
- Interpret Graphs
- Make Predictions
- Draw Conclusions
- Analyze Primary Sources

HISTORICAL THINKING FOR CHAPTER 19

What impact did the Great Depression have on the American people, economy, culture, and spirit? Lesson 2.1 discusses the Depression's economic and personal toll on millions of people.

BACKGROUND FOR THE TEACHER

Today, statistical data validate that it was not any one event but several factors that caused the Great Depression. But in the 1920s, officials did not gather adequate statistics. If they had, they would have realized a perfect storm was brewing. Between 1919 and 1929, workers' productivity increased by 43 percent, but their wages increased by only 8 percent. This should have alerted the government that workers were less and less able to afford the goods they were making and that too many products were flooding the markets.

FINANCIAL LITERACY

To extend their knowledge and understanding about the concepts in this lesson, refer students to the Financial Literacy handbook.

HISTORY NOTEBOOK

Encourage students to complete the Depression Begins page and the American Gallery page for Chapter 19 in their History Notebooks as they read.

INTRODUCE & ENGAGE

ACTIVATE PRIOR KNOWLEDGE

Invite students to use what they've learned thus far about the stock market crash to explain some of the principal causes of the Great Depression. Suggest that they use a Cause-and-Effect Chain to record their ideas, with *desire for wealth* written into the first box. Explain that in this lesson, they will learn about other complex causes and effects that led to the Great Depression.

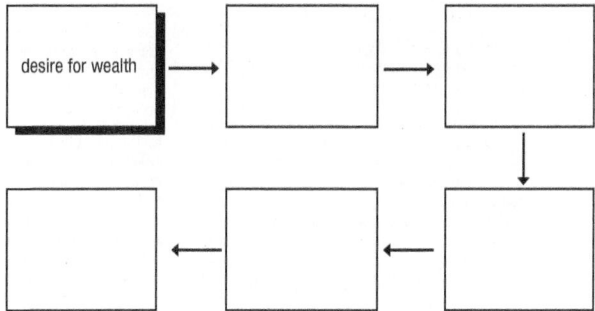

TEACH

GUIDED DISCUSSION

1. **Analyze Cause and Effect** How did the lack of regulation in banking and financial industries and the actions of the Federal Reserve affect the Depression? *(Excessive lending, unlimited margin buying, overspeculation, and manipulation of stocks by trading pools occurred as a result of banks' indecision on regulation. With little control, the Federal Reserve could not act fast enough and banks failed, making the Depression even worse.)*

2. **Analyze Data** Review the graphs shown in the infographic. How were unemployment rates influenced by the other economic indicators, and what large-scale trend can you identify from this relationship? *(As auto production, construction, and farm incomes dropped, unemployment increased. These actions indicate a severe downward economic trend.)*

3. **Form and Support Opinions** The United States adopted the Smoot-Hawley Tariff Act, which caused more damage than good in terms of international trade. What might have been a better economic policy for the country to implement when its role expanded as a world financial leader? *(Answers will vary. Possible response: The United States could have shown stronger leadership by keeping tariffs low to encourage international trade.)*

INTERPRET GRAPHS

Call attention once again to the charts and graphs shown in the infographic, and point out that the graphs run from 1925 through the 1930s. **ASK:** Why is it important to include dates beginning in the 1920s? *(Possible response: It shows the behavior of the economy during times of prosperity in contrast to the early years of the Great Depression.)* Based on the data shown for various economic indicators, what prediction might be made about the behavior of the U.S. economy going forward over the next five years? *(Answers will vary. Possible response: Because various economic indicators—GNP, homes built, autos produced, farm income, and the consumer price index—showed an increase toward the end of the 1930s, and because unemployment began to decrease, one can predict that the economy going forward will probably continue on an upward trend.)*

DIFFERENTIATE

ENGLISH LANGUAGE LEARNERS `ELD`

Analyze Word Meanings Call students' attention to the Key Vocabulary words *deport* and *repatriation*. Point out how the two words are connected yet different in meaning: *deport* means "forcibly removed from a country," while *repatriation* refers to the act of being returned to the country of one's citizenship. Ask students to discuss possible reasons behind the use of the word *repatriation* for a program that deported U.S. citizens of Mexican descent. Provide the following sentence frames to help students at each proficiency level discuss word choice.

- **Emerging:** The word _____ connotes _____. It makes me feel _____.
- **Expanding:** The word _____ connotes _____. The effect is that _____.
- **Bridging:** The word _____ has the connotation _____, and the effect is that _____.

GIFTED & TALENTED

Create a Photo Essay Ask students to choose one of the economic indicators shown in the infographic to represent in photographs. Suggest that they use online and print sources to locate photos that will bring the chosen chart or graph to life. Then have students create a photo essay. Remind them to cite the sources of their photos and to write a brief caption explaining how each photo illustrates the realities revealed in the chart or graph. Invite students to present their photo essays to the class.

See the Chapter Planner for more strategies for differentiation.

CRITICAL VIEWING In May 1933, New York City police evicted inhabitants of 80 shacks between 9th and 10th streets along the East River. What can you infer about what life was like for the people in this photo, taken shortly before their eviction?

Businesses closed, investment declined, and profits fell. Industrial production was 26 percent lower at the end of 1930 than it had been 12 months earlier. Automobile manufacturing, a prime driver of the economy in the 1920s, operated at only 20 percent of capacity. By October 1930, 4 million people were jobless (almost 9 percent of the labor force), and the trend worsened each month. Within a year, nearly 16 percent of the labor force was out of work, and by 1932, unemployment had climbed to more than 23 percent. An additional 33 percent of Americans were underemployed: they were working but not earning enough to support themselves and their families.

The stock market crash left banks in a fragile position. Rural banks were particularly vulnerable, and many failed when farmers could not repay their loans. Small local banks also shut down, leaving their communities without functioning banks. Some of these banks had contributed to their own failure by providing loans for buying stocks on margin. When stock prices fell, investors and stockbrokers could not repay their loans. In addition, some banks had placed their own assets at risk by investing their deposits directly in the stock market.

When bank failures began, the Federal Reserve took a wait-and-see attitude. Some believed the failures would weed out weaker banks and strengthen the system, helping to combat the economic crisis. By the time larger banks began to fail, it was too late for action. Bank deposits were not insured by the government, so individual banks were vulnerable when customers requested to withdraw their money. Stronger banks called in loans they had made to smaller banks to save themselves, further damaging weaker banks. When a bank failed, its customers lost their savings with no hope of recovering the funds.

ECONOMIC REALITIES

For most Americans, there was no single moment after 1929 when they knew the economy was in trouble. But in the months following October 1929, families began making lifestyle changes as workers' hours were cut and the human toll became evident. People began postponing purchases and asking their children to contribute to the household's income. Job losses had a dramatic impact on families. Savings could help tide the family over for a while, but if a family had lost its savings in a bank failure or if its savings ran out, the family would have to put its home up for sale or wait for the bank to foreclose on, or take possession of, its mortgaged property.

Some responses to the economic crisis revealed underlying ideas about civil liberties and gender in the workforce. Many female workers were pressured to give up their jobs to men in an attempt to end the unemployment crisis. Men were considered to be the main "breadwinners," or the principal sources of income for the family, and working women were accused of taking their jobs away from men. Some corporations fired all married female employees, and southern school districts dismissed married female teachers. While the Depression did hinder women's participation in the workforce and slowed their economic progress, unemployment rates were lower for women than for men because women continued to work at their clerical and domestic jobs.

For already economically vulnerable Americans, the Depression presented still greater challenges. In the South, whites seeking work forced African Americans out of the low-paying service jobs they had traditionally filled. Sometimes this process was violent. Native Americans already trapped in a life of neglect and poverty fared even worse during the Depression. The infant mortality rate among Native Americans far exceeded the rate for the white population because of poverty, lack of healthcare facilities, and inadequate sanitation. The Bureau of Indian Affairs (BIA) did not address the many social problems that the people under its jurisdiction faced.

Like African Americans and Native Americans, immigrants faced serious challenges to their civil liberties during the Depression. Theirs were in the form of backlash. In an attempt to combat economic crisis, the Hoover administration instituted immigration quotas, or limits, to reduce the number of people looking for jobs and receiving government services. While potential restrictions applied to all immigrants, these efforts targeted Mexicans and Mexican Americans. Between 1930 and 1940, in a coordinated governmental effort known as the **Mexican Repatriation Program**, about 1 million people of Mexican descent were either **deported**, or forcibly removed from the country, or pressured to leave. An estimated 400,000 of those deported had been living in California. **Repatriation** means returning or being returned to the country of one's citizenship, but an astonishing 60 percent of those who returned to Mexico were actually U.S. citizens, and their deportation violated their civil rights.

Filipinos were also pressured to leave the United States. The Filipino Repatriation Act of 1935 provided transportation funds for Filipinos who agreed to move back to their home country permanently.

On the nation's farms, where many Mexican Americans worked, produce rotted in the fields because few people could afford to buy it. The Federal Farm Board was established in 1929 to stabilize farm prices. However, when farm surpluses around the world flooded grain markets in 1930, nothing could keep crop prices from plummeting. As banks foreclosed on farm mortgages, many former landowners became tenant farmers. All economic indicators, including GNP, consumer price index, and farm income, were in decline. And now an environmental disaster was about to deliver a crushing blow.

HISTORICAL THINKING

1. **READING CHECK** How did overproduction lead to weakness in key sectors of the economy?

2. **ANALYZE CAUSE AND EFFECT** What were the unintended consequences and complexities of the Smoot-Hawley Tariff Act of 1930?

3. **SYNTHESIZE** Why was there a Great Depression? State how individuals affected the U.S. economy.

4. **MAKE CONNECTIONS** How were African Americans, married women, Mexicans, and Mexican Americans hurt by the unemployment of white male workers?

BUILD BACKGROUND

HARD TIMES FOR FAMILIES

The Great Depression had a profound effect on both working-class and middle-class families throughout the nation. During the first two years of the Depression, Herbert Hoover believed that local charity and relief programs should and would handle the crisis. However, the magnitude of the Depression soon overwhelmed the resources of towns, cities, and states. As a result, the brunt of the Depression fell on individual families.

Crime rates increased as more unemployed workers turned to theft as a means to get food. When men could no longer fulfill their role as breadwinners, some withdrew emotionally from their families. Others began drinking, while others deserted their wives and children in what became known as "a poor man's divorce." The numbers of children placed in custodial, or foster, care rose 50 percent in these years. Conditions were worse for African-American families, who experienced far higher rates of unemployment. Some families from the East Coast and the Midwest migrated west, looking for better opportunities. This migration caused depopulation in rural regions. At the same time, the Depression also brought out the resilience of families. When members of one family lost their home through foreclosure, they might move in with two or three other families to share shelter and expenses. Women started gardens, canned their own foods, and repaired and remade clothes. Board games, such as *Monopoly*, became popular during this time, as did radio shows, sports events, and other inexpensive forms of entertainment. These activities helped beleaguered families of all backgrounds survive the Great Depression.

TEACH

GUIDED DISCUSSION

4. Analyze Cause and Effect What factors could cause families to lose their incomes and savings during the Great Depression? *(Unemployment eliminated income, and families used up savings to survive; the stock market crash wiped out investments; and bank failures wiped out savings.)*

5. Make Predictions Given what happened to people's bank savings, what measures might the government have taken to prevent such losses from happening in the future? *(Answers will vary. Possible responses: The government might have decided to insure all bank holdings against future economic catastrophes. The government might have decided to prevent investors from buying stocks on margin, which had led to the failure of many banks when loans could not be repaid.)*

6. Draw Conclusions In what ways might the economic situation of the Great Depression have led to future initiatives to establish and protect the civil rights of U.S. citizens? *(Answers will vary. Possible response: As the Depression worsened, many low-paying jobs went to whites. The government's immigrant quotas impacted new arrivals as well as U.S. citizens of Mexican and Filipino descent. It is possible that such treatment could have energized future efforts at establishing and protecting civil rights.)*

ANALYZE PRIMARY SOURCES

Have students read the excerpt from *Cannery Women, Cannery Lives.* **ASK:** How does Carmen's story reflect the difficulties workers faced during the Great Depression? *(Possible response: Bosses could change working conditions, such as reducing wages, and workers could do little about it. If they spoke out, they could lose their jobs. For workers, the loss of even an hour's wage could be significant.)*

ACTIVE OPTIONS

On Your Feet: Fishbowl Direct half the class to sit in a circle facing inward and the other half to sit in a larger circle around them. Ask the inner circle to discuss this question: How did American society change in the early years of the Great Depression? Students in the outer circle should listen to the discussion and evaluate the points made. Then ask the groups to reverse positions and continue the discussion.

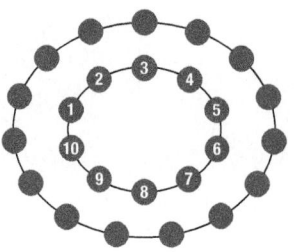

AMERICAN GALLERY
ONLINE

The Great Depression Invite students to explore the American Gallery. Have them select one of the photos and locate a sentence in the lesson that relates to the photo's content. Then ask the following question: What impact does the photo have on your understanding of the Great Depression?

HISTORICAL THINKING

ANSWERS

1. Because of agricultural overproduction, crop and meat prices decreased and farmers lost income. Manufacturing innovation had increased production of cars and housing, but by 1929, the demand for such items had begun to decrease because buyers already had what they needed. Thus, many workers were laid off.

2. Possible response: The Smoot-Hawley Tariff Act, meant to protect American agriculture and industry from foreign competition, instead caused other countries to raise their own tariffs. High taxes interfered with the flow of goods, capital, and services and weakened international trade.

3. The Great Depression occurred because of several factors acting together. The desire to share in the apparent prosperity of the country caused individuals to borrow money to invest in stock and purchase goods. Businesses and farmers flooded the markets with produce and goods. When buying slowed, prices fell, causing business owners to lay off workers. Laid-off workers couldn't make their credit payments, creating a crisis for banks. The Federal Reserve waited to intervene rather than act quickly. Tariff wars between the U.S. and Europe crippled trade among nations.

4. White workers took many of the low-level service jobs traditionally held by African Americans and demanded that African-American workers be dismissed. Some corporations and schools fired married women. Mexican immigrants and many Mexican American citizens were deported by the Hoover administration to reduce the number of people looking for work and receiving government services.

CRITICAL VIEWING One can infer that life was probably difficult for the people in the photo. The surroundings look flimsy, unkempt, and unsafe. Despite the circumstances, the group seems to have created a sense of community.

CRITICAL VIEWING Safety liaison Jamison Walsh, photographed by Chin, climbs the spire of 1 World Trade Center after leading Chin's ascent. How are New York's skyscrapers symbols of the 1920s?

THROUGH THE LENS
JIMMY CHIN

National Geographic adventure photographer Jimmy Chin is used to extreme heights. He's skied down Mount Everest, photographed free climbers on Yosemite, and conquered the granite Shark Fin's wall of Meru Peak in the Himalayas. So 1,776 feet—the height of New York's 1 World Trade Center—is no big deal. In this shoot, Chin focused on capturing the great city of New York, a city of skyscrapers, many of which rose up around the Great Depression, from the spire of the building constructed where the World Trade Center once stood.

PLAN: 2-PAGE LESSON

OBJECTIVE

Understand how modern and historic skyscrapers help define the physical and human characteristics of a major city like New York.

CRITICAL THINKING SKILLS FOR LESSON 2.2

- Analyze Visuals
- Make Connections
- Evaluate

HISTORICAL THINKING FOR CHAPTER 19

What impact did the Great Depression have on the American people, culture, economy, and spirit? New York City is defined by its skyscrapers, many of which were built during the construction boom of the prosperous 1920s. That boom ended with the onset of the Great Depression. Lesson 2.2 shows that modern skyscrapers continue to define the city's unique human landscape.

NATIONAL GEOGRAPHIC PHOTOGRAPHER
JIMMY CHIN

In this photograph, Jimmy Chin used his talent for capturing vast natural landscapes to create a striking portrait of New York City's human terrain. In addition to his work as a photographer, the Minnesota native is also a director and cinematographer and has his own production company, Camp4 Collective. Chin's main passion lies in documenting some of the most forbidding places on Earth, such as Tibet's Chang Tang Plateau. The National Geographic Society has awarded him three expedition grants. Chin hopes his work will help him reach a bigger goal: "It's about sharing stories that inspire people, highlight the infinite human spirit, and open people's eyes to a different world"—whether from the top of a skyscraper or from the tallest peak in the world.

HISTORY NOTEBOOK

Encourage students to complete the Through the Lens page for Chapter 19 in their History Notebooks as they read.

INTRODUCE & ENGAGE

CONNECT TO VISUALS

Have students study the photo, particularly the contrast between the foreground and background. **ASK:** What is the effect of making the tower and the person the dominant part of the photo? *(Possible response: It emphasizes the immense size of the tower and the challenge being faced by the person scaling the tower.)* What impression of New York City does the photo convey? *(Answers will vary. Possible response: The photo conveys the impression of pride, ingenuity, wealth, and power.)*

TEACH

GUIDED DISCUSSION

1. **Make Connections** What similar experiences might Jimmy Chin have when climbing urban skyscrapers and climbing more natural landscapes? *(Possible response: Both experiences are challenging and very dangerous. Both require tremendous concentration. Both provide Chin with spectacular views not seen by most people. Both probably give him a feeling of exhilaration.)*

2. **Evaluate** What physical or human characteristics still make New York City an attractive site for skyscraper construction? *(Possible responses: The city is a major economic hub and many companies want to be there. The only way to acquire more space in New York City is to build up. The cultural life of the city attracts many people.)*

⬙ THROUGH THE LENS

The *New York Times Magazine* hired Jimmy Chin to take a cover photo for their special 2016 issue about life in New York City at and above 800 feet. Chin saw Manhattan's skyline as an urban mountain range, with 1 World Trade Center as the tallest, most beautiful "mountain." Chin decided to climb the new skyscraper not only to take photographs but also to make a virtual reality video of his experience atop the building's 408-foot spire. On a clear April afternoon, Chin spent several hours attached to the spire, filming the city below until the sun began setting and the city's lights began to glow. The final result was this spectacular photo and a virtual reality film that offers a 360-degree view of New York City.

ACTIVE OPTIONS

On Your Feet: Numbered Heads Divide students into groups and have each group number off. Ask students to study the photograph and then discuss ways in which skyscrapers have transformed the city landscape, including what the buildings might mean to a city's identity. Call a number and have the student from each group with that number report for the group.

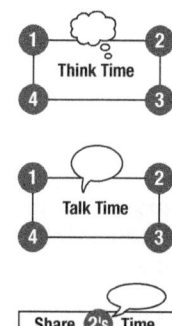

NG Learning Framework: Create a Short Documentary

SKILL Communication

KNOWLEDGE Our Human Story

Encourage students to choose an iconic U.S. skyscraper, either from the 1920s or from more modern times. Ask them to prepare a short documentary about the building, describing how it captures the physical and human characteristics of its era and of the place where it is found. Students can use video or another multimedia format to present their documentary. Invite students to share their documentary with the class.

DIFFERENTIATE

INCLUSION

Analyze Photographic Content Some students may find the photograph difficult to decipher in terms of its perspective and the contents of the background. Pair students who are visually impaired with students who are not. Have them discuss where the photographer was when he took the photo and what students can make out in the background, including buildings, street lights, and the dark water in the upper edge of the photo.

GIFTED & TALENTED

Investigate Skyscraper Photography Ask students to locate photographs showing the construction of skyscrapers during the 1920s and Depression era. Then have them present their findings to the class along with oral descriptions of what each photo depicts. Make sure that students' presentations address the fact that some photos were taken to document construction of the skyscrapers while others were publicity stunts. Hold a class discussion on why the construction of skyscrapers might have become such a popular subject for photographers to depict.

CRITICAL VIEWING

ANSWER

Possible response: Skyscrapers, with their soaring heights, artistic architecture, and advanced engineering and construction, are perfect symbols of the Roaring Twenties' optimism and prosperity. During this decade, people believed the economy would keep growing, a belief reflected in the increasing heights of the skyscrapers being built.

MAIN IDEA A lack of rain and unwise agricultural practices transformed the Great Plains into the Dust Bowl in the 1930s, forcing many farmers off their land.

THE DUST BOWL

Sometimes nature and human actions mix in deadly and destructive ways. On the Great Plains, farmers had planted millions of acres of croplands with one main crop—wheat. When prolonged drought struck in the 1930s, the golden fields of wheat turned to dust, resulting in ecological disaster and human misery.

THE DIRTY THIRTIES

Farmers, already hit hard after World War I by falling crop and livestock prices, suffered a devastating blow in the early 1930s. Record high temperatures and drought, a prolonged period of low rainfall, gripped the Great Plains. In addition to the drought, strong winds whipped through the region, causing terrifying dust storms that swept through the plains and stripped nutrients from the dry soil.

Drought is a natural occurrence on the Great Plains, as are high winds and extreme temperatures. But the dust storms that plagued the region during the 1930s were unexpected and worsened by unwise agricultural methods and human modification of the landscape. Farmers had plowed millions of acres of grasslands on the Great Plains in order to plant wheat. After the crops were harvested, farmers used new machinery, such as disc plows pulled by small gas-powered tractors, to turn up the fields again. They then left them unplanted for months. Ranchers on the plains allowed their cattle and other livestock to overgraze what grassland remained. Without the deep roots of the prairie grasses, there was nothing to keep the soil in place. The wind picked up the dry soil and carried it for hundreds of miles.

CRITICAL VIEWING On April 14, 1935, a black blizzard hit the panhandles of Texas and Oklahoma. What details in this photo convey how threatening the cloud seems as it approaches a Texas town?

John Steinbeck's novel *The Grapes of Wrath* tells the story of an "Okie" family on its way to California from Oklahoma along "Route 66." That remains the popular name for U.S. highway 66, which ran from Chicago to Los Angeles before the interstate highway system was built beginning in 1956.

[Route] 66 is the path of a people in flight, refugees from dust and shrinking land, from the thunder of tractors and shrinking ownership, from the desert's slow northward invasion, from the twisting winds that howl up out of Texas, from the floods that bring no richness to the land and steal what little richness is there.

—from *The Grapes of Wrath,* by John Steinbeck, 1939

Some of the dust storms were caused by low-level winds that blew sand into huge drifts. Others were massive storms—black blizzards—with rolling dust clouds thousands of feet high that crackled with electricity, carried precious soil away to neighboring states, and turned daylight into dark. "This is the ultimate darkness," a Kansas woman wrote in her diary. "So must come the end of the world."

The blowing dust of a black blizzard destroyed crops and sickened and killed livestock and people. Dirt permeated everything, even the inside of houses, despite people's best efforts to seal every crack, window, and door. After the storm passed and light returned, farmers found their cattle and horses buried alive. The storms turned millions of acres of cultivated land in parts of Kansas, Colorado, Oklahoma, Texas, and New Mexico into a barren desert that became known as the **Dust Bowl**. The dust storms continued as the 1930s wore on—14 in 1932, then 38 in 1933—earning the decade the nickname the "Dirty Thirties."

HITTING THE ROAD

Many people living in the Dust Bowl region stuck it out because of pride, determination, or hope. Others stayed because they were simply too poor or too beaten down to leave. But a quarter of the population fled the region, some pushed off their land as they could not pay their mortgages. In one of the largest internal migrations in the nation's history, more than 3 million "Dust Bowl refugees" in Oklahoma, Kansas, the Dakotas, and other states abandoned their farms in the 1930s. Many set out for California seeking work and opportunity. The fortunate found low-wage work there, picking fruit, boxing vegetables, and baling hay. Others went to cities to work as laborers. But few "Okies," as the Californians called them, found relief from the economic turmoil they had fled. Once in California, most lived in squatter camps along roads, often contracting diseases such as intestinal worms, typhoid, and dysentery as a result of the polluted water and lack of sanitation. The **Farm Security Administration (FSA)**, a federal agency charged with combating rural poverty, built camps to house families temporarily in somewhat improved conditions, but life was still difficult.

Okies were generally treated poorly, and they experienced discrimination at the hands of many native Californians. The Los Angeles police set up a task force called the "bum brigade" to turn Okies away at the border between California and Arizona. Residents complained about the tent communities, called "Okievilles," growing around the edges of Los Angeles, so sheriffs would ask the migrants to pack up and move on. In some towns, residents beat up the Okies and set fire to their camps.

Photographer **Dorothea Lange** documented the plight of the Okies as they traveled to California and tried to eke out a living there. Author **John Steinbeck** did the same in his 1939 novel, *The Grapes of Wrath.* His story chronicled the lives of the Joads, a fictional sharecropper family from Oklahoma, who migrated to California in search of work. Steinbeck and Lange, along with many other writers and photographers in the 1930s, captured the struggles of ordinary people weighed down by circumstances.

Once the depression lifted, some Okies returned to the plains, but many stayed in California. They infused their evangelical Protestantism, patriotic individualism, and downhome musical traditions into the culture of California's Central Valley.

HISTORICAL THINKING

1. **READING CHECK** Why did many people living in the Dust Bowl region stay during the 1930s?

2. **ANALYZE ENVIRONMENTAL CONCEPTS** How did the scale and duration of human actions, including modifying the landscape, affect the natural systems of the Great Plains during the Dust Bowl?

3. **MAKE INFERENCES** How might the social and economic impacts of the Dust Bowl refugees have influenced the reception the Okies received in California?

4. **ANALYZE LANGUAGE USE** How did Steinbeck characterize Route 66?

PLAN: 2-PAGE LESSON

OBJECTIVE

Learn how unwise agricultural practices created an environmental disaster that depopulated many rural areas.

CRITICAL THINKING SKILLS FOR LESSON 2.3

- Analyze Environmental Concepts
- Make Inferences
- Analyze Language Use
- Draw Conclusions
- Evaluate

HISTORICAL THINKING FOR CHAPTER 19

What impact did the Great Depression have on the American people, culture, economy, and spirit? New farming technology resulted in higher crop yields but also threatened the health of the land. Lesson 2.3 explores the economic, social, and cultural effects of the Dust Bowl during the Great Depression.

BACKGROUND FOR THE TEACHER

The Farm Security Administration's mission was in part to help migratory workers, including refugees from the Dust Bowl who were fleeing to California. The FSA built 95 camps in California, complete with running water and other amenities. But the camps housed only 75,000 migrants, a fraction of those in need, and people could stay only a short time. The FSA's work caused a backlash both from native Californians, who didn't want permanent camps in their midst, and federal Farm Bureau officials, who denounced the FSA as "government bureaucracy gone mad." To convince the general public that the FSA's work was needed, the agency hired photographers such as Dorothea Lange to document what was happening to people. Her photographs, capturing the suffering and resilience of the Dust Bowl refugees, helped to spur public support for relief efforts and left a lasting, visual legacy of the era.

INTRODUCE & ENGAGE

CONNECT TO TODAY

Ask students to recall a recent environmental disaster they have heard or read about, such as massive mudslides, widespread forest fires, or coastal oil spills. Discuss how human actions might have either caused the disaster or made it worse, such as stripping trees from a mountain or leaving campfires unattended. After evaluating the consequences, ask students to identify lessons learned from past disasters. Tell students that this lesson explains how human actions and nature combined to create the worst environmental disaster in U.S. history, which added to the misery of the Great Depression.

TEACH

GUIDED DISCUSSION

1. **Draw Conclusions** What lessons might people have learned from the Dust Bowl experience? *(Possible response: People need to understand the natural systems and cycles of an area and how to work with them. Then people will develop wiser practices, which will enable them to make use of the resources of the environment and protect it at the same time.)*

2. **Evaluate** How did the Dust Bowl cause a change in government policies? *(Possible response: Because of the plight of Dust Bowl refugees who migrated to California, the government switched from a "hands off" policy to a policy that tried to offer assistance through agencies like the FSA.)*

MORE INFORMATION

STEM

Desertification Explain that desertification occurs when fertile land is turned into desert-like conditions. Desertification is mainly brought on by human actions, as happened on the Great Plains. Today, deserts are the fastest growing landform, with 2.3 million square miles of cropland becoming desert each year—their fertile topsoil lost to wind and erosion. In some cases, human activity is expanding deserts that already exist. This is particularly true in developing countries that are experiencing rapid population growth. **ASK:** How might the rapid population growth on the Great Plains have helped lead to desertification? *(Possible response: Rapid population growth might have put more pressure on resources and caused a larger area to be affected.)*

ACTIVE OPTIONS

On Your Feet: Turn and Talk on Topic Arrange students in three groups. Give each group this topic sentence: Some people addressed the problem of the Dust Bowl by leaving the area, only to encounter more problems they would have to solve. Tell groups to build a paragraph on that topic by having each student contribute one sentence. Suggest that students first discuss the pros and cons of staying in the Dust Bowl versus leaving. Allow each group to present its paragraph to the class by having each student read his or her sentence.

NG Learning Framework: Dust Bowl Then and Now

ATTITUDE Curiosity

KNOWLEDGE Our Living Planet

Explain to students that they are to work in groups to create visual presentations of the Dust Bowl region, then and now. Ask them to locate online photographs of the Great Plains during the Dust Bowl and photographs of the region today to show the past and present conditions of the region. In their presentations, students should include information about how the region was restored, focusing on resulting environmental policies as well as modifications of the landscape.

For students who develop an interest in the Dust Bowl, suggest that they read the American Story at the beginning of this chapter.

DIFFERENTIATE

INCLUSION

Analyze a Photo and Primary Source Pair students who are visually impaired with students who are not. Ask the latter to describe the photograph of the dust storm and to read the Primary Source feature aloud. Tell visually impaired students to ask clarifying questions as needed. Then have pairs work together to answer the Critical Viewing question and the Historical Thinking question about Steinbeck's characterization of Route 66.

PRE-AP

Research Rail Riders Instruct students to research information about the thousands of people from the Great Plains who traveled west on freight trains, seeking work during the Dust Bowl. Ask for volunteers to share the information with the class.

See the Chapter Planner for more strategies for differentiation.

HISTORICAL THINKING

ANSWERS

1. Many people were too poor or demoralized to consider moving away. Others held a strong sense of pride, determination, and hope, which helped them tough it out.

2. For nearly 20 years, farmers used mechanized plows to tear up the deep-rooted prairie grasses, and livestock overgrazed on what remained. These practices destroyed the soil's natural protection.

3. Okies competed for jobs with native Californians and lived in squatters' camps that some Californians disliked having in their communities. As a result, native Californians tried to keep Okies out or drive them away.

4. Steinbeck characterized Route 66 as an escape route for people fleeing natural and human-made disasters.

CRITICAL VIEWING Details include the enormous size of the dust cloud enveloping the town and the absense of people, vehicles, and other signs of activity.

CULTURE DURING THE DEPRESSION

Maybe you take in a good movie or watch your favorite television show to cheer up when you're feeling down. Many people during the Great Depression tuned into their favorite radio shows, went to theaters to watch movies, and listened to music to escape reality—at least for a few minutes.

FORGETTING TROUBLES

Amid the challenges of the Depression, Americans found diversion in popular entertainment and **mass media**, or forms of communication such as radio, film, and musical recordings designed to reach large numbers of people. By the 1930s, radios had become more affordable, and they began to play a significant role in the worldwide diffusion of popular culture. Listening to a favorite radio show was a vital part of the daily lives of many families. Many listeners preferred daytime dramas such as *One Man's Family* or *Mary Noble, Backstage Wife*, which were quickly dubbed "soap operas" after the detergent companies that sponsored them.

Comic books also became popular during the Depression. The first comic books were collections of newspaper comic strips, and their heroes provided a sense that everything was going to be okay during a time of uncertainty. Among the most popular comic strip heroes were a police detective named Dick Tracy, a frontier lawman called the Lone Ranger, and Buck Rogers, a courageous space explorer living in the 25th century.

With ticket prices low and audiences hungry for a break from the stress of the Depression, movie theaters presented a wide choice of Hollywood films. Movies with sound had replaced the silent pictures of the 1920s, and people regularly went to the movies to forget their own troubles for a while.

Audiences enjoyed movie musicals and laughed at the Marx Brothers, W.C. Fields, and a new genre called screwball comedy, named for the unpredictable baseball pitch. Characterized by rapid-fire dialogue, social satire, and a blend of wacky situations and sophisticated settings, examples of screwball comedy include such hits as *It Happened One Night* (1934) and *My Man Godfrey* (1936). Not all films were pure escapism, however. Gangster films such as *The Public Enemy* and *Little Caesar* (both from 1931) were entertaining, but they also exposed viewers to the urban crime and corruption that existed in cities like Chicago and New York City.

Buck Rogers's Police Patrol Ship, a toy manufactured and sold in 1934 to accompany the Buck Rogers comic strip, is on display at the National Air and Space Museum in Washington, D.C.

The Depression was also a vibrant period for music. In Kansas City and other midwestern cities, African-American musicians developed a new jazz style known as "swing." Marked by complicated but compelling rhythms, swing was energetic and loud. As swing grew more popular, white musicians added elements of more sedate musical genres, such as classical music, to make swing more commercial. Many swing bands evolved into big bands with percussion, woodwind, and horn sections. **Benny Goodman**, from Chicago, led a big band that made swing popular with young people.

Not all music was flamboyant and brassy, however. Folk singers such as **Woody Guthrie**, Pete Seeger, and Huddie Ledbetter caught the public's attention by singing about the lives of the people hit hardest by the Dust Bowl and the Depression. Guthrie, an "Okie" who migrated to California, lived the life he sang about, riding the rails and sleeping in migrant camps. He sang on the streets for money and took whatever small jobs he could find to survive. Some of Guthrie's songs, such as "(If You Ain't Got That) Do Re Mi," describe the struggles of the Okies seeking a new beginning in California. But Guthrie also wrote the anthem "This Land Is Your Land," celebrating the beauty and diversity of the country while also commenting on the disparity between rich landowners and those who could not afford land.

Similarly, Huddie Ledbetter—nicknamed Lead Belly—chronicled the troubles of African Americans during the Depression through his songs. Lead Belly bridged a gap between folk music and the blues. He sang old folk standards of the rural South, gospel songs, the blues, and protest songs. He also composed his own music, including "Goodnight, Irene," which became a hit after his death in 1949.

CAPTURING THE DEPRESSION

Other artists joined musicians in telling Americans' stories during the Great Depression. As you have read, photographer Dorothea Lange captured images of Dust Bowl refugees. Photographer **Walker Evans** traveled throughout the South during the Depression, photographing rural life. Lange and Evans both worked for the Resettlement Administration, which later became the Farm Security Administration. Evans's photographs helped reveal the challenges faced by the rural poor. Evans also worked with

In 1943, *Life* magazine photographer Eric Schaal accompanied Woody Guthrie as he gave on-the-spot performances around New York City, where Guthrie lived from 1940 on.

writer **James Agee** to document the lives of three sharecropper families trying to farm on a dry hillside in the 1930s. In 1941, they published their text and photographs in *Let Us Now Praise Famous Men*.

Writer **John Dos Passos**, part of the "lost generation" you read about earlier, exposed the divisions in American society in his trilogy *U.S.A.*, which combined fiction, biographies of famous people, newsreels, and newspaper headlines to paint a picture of what he saw as the two halves of society: rich and poor. Novelist **Richard Wright** portrayed the discrimination and struggles faced by African Americans in his novel *Native Son*. The novel is about a young African-American man who lives in poverty on Chicago's South Side during the 1930s.

HISTORICAL THINKING

1. **READING CHECK** How did mass media trends help people cope with the Great Depression?

2. **MAKE CONNECTIONS** How did folk music, photography, and literature help recount the plight of the poor during the Great Depression?

3. **EVALUATE** Why is it important that artists document significant historical events through their art?

PLAN: 2-PAGE LESSON

OBJECTIVE

Examine how 1930s culture both distracted people from their troubles and documented their hardships.

CRITICAL THINKING SKILLS FOR LESSON 2.4

- Make Connections
- Evaluate
- Make Inferences
- Analyze Visuals

HISTORICAL THINKING FOR CHAPTER 19

What impact did the Great Depression have on the American people, culture, economy, and spirit? As the economy grew worse, American culture became more innovative and inclusive. Lesson 2.4 discusses how people turned to mass media and the arts for relief and how artists captured people's experiences.

BACKGROUND FOR THE TEACHER

Early radio broadcasts created a craze among the public. By 1939, the number of radio owners had soared from 12 million to 28 million. The country's first mass medium united communities, provided a source of entertainment and inspiration, and reinforced old-fashioned family values through its programming. But the true power of radio was its ability to communicate a single message to millions of people. While advertisers were quick to take advantage of this power, so was President Roosevelt, who recognized an opportunity to talk directly to the nation. In his 1933 inaugural address broadcast, Roosevelt firmly asserted that "The only thing we have to fear is fear itself." Using radio, he boosted the morale of millions of people.

INTRODUCE & ENGAGE

CREATE A PLAYLIST

Encourage students to think of the music, movies, television programs, or other arts that have helped them get through difficult times. Then challenge them to create a playlist for someone who needs cheering up. Ask students to share their ideas, and record their responses on the board. Tell students that this lesson discusses how people in the Great Depression used media to help them cope with discouraging times.

TEACH

GUIDED DISCUSSION

1. **Make Inferences** Why might a time of great social upheaval also be a time of great creativity in music and the arts? *(Possible response: In times of great social upheaval, normal conventions break down. This can encourage people to experiment and find new ways to express themselves.)*

2. **Evaluate** What responsibility might writers and filmmakers have felt toward the public during the Great Depression? *(Possible responses: Writers and filmmakers might have felt responsible for helping the public survive hard times by uplifting their spirits with entertainment. Many probably felt that their work had the power to actually improve people's lives by exposing the plight of the disadvantaged.)*

ANALYZE VISUALS

Direct students' attention to the photograph of the toy rocket and ask them to read the caption. **ASK:** How does this toy reflect the influence of mass media during the Depression? *(Possible response: Comic strips, like movies and radio, fed into the public's desire to escape from reality. The toy capitalized on the popularity of the comic strip hero Buck Rogers, and mass media helped advertise the product.)*

ACTIVE OPTIONS

On Your Feet: Four Corners Direct students to choose one of the following four questions about the Great Depression and American culture to discuss: (1) What themes did radio shows seem to convey to the public, and why were these themes so appealing? (2) How did the Depression impact white and black musicians and their music? (3) How was photography used in the Great Depression and why was it considered so important? (4) In what way might mass media have led to a more inclusive society? Assign each question to a corner of the room, and ask students to group into the corner of their choice to discuss the question. Then hold a class discussion to share each group's ideas.

NG Learning Framework: Analyze Lyrics and Literature

`ATTITUDE` Curiosity

`KNOWLEDGE` Our Human Story

Invite students to pick a songwriter or author mentioned in this lesson, such as Woody Guthrie, James Agee, or John Dos Passos, and select a passage from the person's work to analyze. Ask students to identify the topic of the passage and, as appropriate, the message it conveys about society, the Depression era, or human nature. Have students present the results of their analyses to the class.

DIFFERENTIATE

STRIVING READERS

Create a Concept Cluster On the board, write the words *Depression-era entertainment* in the center oval of a Concept Cluster on the board. Write *comics, movies,* and *music* in each of the other three ovals. Instruct students to review the lesson and then call out specific examples of each form of entertainment, which you can add to the board.

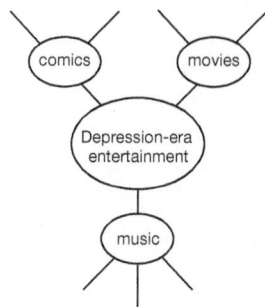

GIFTED & TALENTED

Watch a 1930s Movie Ask students to locate and watch one of the movies mentioned in the lesson and then present information about the movie to the rest of the class. Provide the following questions to help guide their presentations: What is the setting of the story? Who are the characters? What is the basic storyline? Is the movie serious or humorous or a combination of both? In what way does the movie reflect the era? Encourage students to include movie stills or posters in their presentations.

See the Chapter Planner for more strategies for differentiation.

HISTORICAL THINKING

ANSWERS

1. People escaped the hardships of the Great Depression by listening to radio programs, going to movies, reading superhero comic books, and listening to music.

2. Folk singers wrote and performed songs that expressed the struggles of the poor during the Dust Bowl and Great Depression; photographers captured the stark living conditions of the poor, while literature told their stories.

3. Answers will vary. Possible response: Facts can tell what happened and why, but artists convey what people felt, thought, and experienced during historical events.

HOOVER'S INITIATIVES

President Hoover's assumption that private citizens and businesses could work together to solve the ills created by the Great Depression reflected a faith in human decency. But the problems were too big to solve without government intervention.

CRITICAL VIEWING One of the largest and longest-lasting Hoovervilles covered 9 acres outside of Seattle, Washington, and had a population of 1,200. Based on details you see in the photo, what were living conditions like in Hoovervilles?

VOLUNTARY ACTION AND SELF-HELP

President Hoover's life experiences influenced how he handled the Great Depression. Raised as a Quaker, he believed in the power of individual effort and the obligation for all citizens to help one another. His success as a mining engineer and business leader reinforced his belief in the rewards of individual effort. His success in running relief programs during and after World War I convinced him of the effectiveness of voluntary action—private citizens and businesses working together to solve problems without government prompting or legal requirements. Hoover believed the traditional self-reliance and volunteer spirit of the American people provided the most dependable means of combating the economic crisis of the Great Depression.

Toward this end, Hoover set up presidential committees to coordinate volunteer relief efforts for the unemployed, such as the **President's Organization of Unemployment Relief (POUR)**. In an effort to keep the banking system afloat, he persuaded bankers to set up the National Credit Corporation, a private agency that would **underwrite**, or buy up the assets of, banks that had failed. That action was meant to safeguard the deposits of bank customers. Unfortunately, bank managers were reluctant to do this. Since that experiment was a failure, Hoover tried again with the Reconstruction Finance Corporation (RFC), a government agency to loan money to troubled banks that did not belong to the Federal Reserve System. During the year Hoover was to remain in office, the RFC was not particularly successful either.

Hoover's attempts to ease the misery that Americans were facing every day also failed. His programs were unable to deal with the scale of the unemployment situation. Eight million workers were jobless by 1931, a number that overwhelmed the resources of existing charitable agencies. The POUR program coordinated relief agencies and urged people to help their neighbors, but these efforts did little to alleviate the human toll of the Great Depression that gripped the country.

Millions of Americans were feeling desperate and hopeless. The homeless and unemployed took to the roads and rails, looking for work, better opportunities, or a simple meal along the way. Migrant workers moved through the farmlands of California, picking produce for whatever they could earn. Others traveled from city to city, doing their best to survive on the charity of relief stations and church groups. Homeless Americans lived in and around cities in shantytowns dubbed **Hoovervilles**. The name "Hooverville" mocked the president's failure to provide for the American people.

Yet when politicians begged the federal government to find a solution to the unemployment problem, Hoover refused to budge. His response to the drought that caused the Dust Bowl provided yet another example of the administration's failures. Congress proposed to allocate $60 million to help disaster victims buy fuel and food. Hoover offered money to feed animals, but he rejected the idea of feeding farmers and their families. This concern for animals over starving citizens conveyed a lack of empathy on the president's part, and additional derogatory references to the president circulated. A pocket turned outward to show it was empty of money was called a "Hoover flag." A newspaper unfolded and used to cover oneself for warmth was a "Hoover blanket." In 1931, in Minneapolis and Oklahoma City, crowds stormed into grocery stores and took food for themselves, and more protests against Hoover's lack of help were to come.

TURMOIL ABROAD

As the U.S. economy deteriorated, so did the international economy, inspiring some Europeans to look to strong but authoritarian leaders for relief. Such a leader had already risen to power in Europe. Playing on the social unrest and economic turmoil of the postwar years, dictator **Benito Mussolini** had seized control of Italy in 1922. Mussolini was a proponent of **fascism**, a political movement that involves extreme nationalism, militarism, and racism. As the supreme leader, or *Duce*, Mussolini destroyed Italian labor unions, censored the press, abolished all political parties but his own, and relied upon a secret police force to silence his critics. Global economic insecurity opened the door for fascism to grow in Europe. As people slid into poverty, many were willing to give up some of their rights on the basis of their authoritarian leader Mussolini's promises to bring back prosperity.

Asia was also affected. A 30 percent decrease in trade worldwide caused drops in income and productivity throughout the world. Japan, an island nation, needed raw materials for its industry and saw China as a likely source. Extreme nationalism provided a rationale for expanding its empire, and in 1931, Japan launched a war to occupy Manchuria, in China. Ultimately, Japan sought military, political, and economic control over the Pacific.

HISTORICAL THINKING

1. **READING CHECK** Why did President Hoover rely on voluntary action of citizens to try to address the economic crisis of the Great Depression?

2. **MAKE INFERENCES** Why was Hoover's response to drought victims in the Midwest unwise from a political standpoint?

3. **SYNTHESIZE** How did citizens and politicians try to deal with the effects of widespread unemployment?

OBJECTIVE

Learn how President Hoover's policies failed to combat the economic crisis and how international insecurity led to the rise of fascism.

CRITICAL THINKING SKILLS FOR LESSON 3.1

- Make Inferences
- Synthesize
- Make Connections
- Draw Conclusions
- Analyze Primary Sources

HISTORICAL THINKING FOR CHAPTER 19

What impact did the Great Depression have on the American people, culture, economy, and spirit? Principles of self-reliance and private charity failed to meet people's needs during the Great Depression. Lesson 3.1 discusses inadequate relief efforts, how citizens coped, and how international crises spurred the rise of fascism.

BACKGROUND FOR THE TEACHER

In 1932, many blamed Hoover for the severity of the Great Depression. Yet for much of his life, Hoover's conservative politics and engineering efficiency served him well. During World War I, he arranged a steady flow of food and clothing to Allied soldiers. After the war, he ran the American Relief Administration and provided food and aid to war-torn Europe, saving thousands from starvation. Europeans even called their free meals "Hoover lunches" in his honor.

Tragically, Hoover's conservative politics misled him at home. In an ironic twist, the name "Hoover," once linked to lifesaving aid, became a symbol of callous government indifference. This indifference—and perceived inaction to combat the economic crisis—would cost him re-election in the 1932 presidential election.

INTRODUCE & ENGAGE

IDENTIFY DISASTER AID

Ask students to share their opinions about the role of government during a national crisis. **ASK:** When do you think it's appropriate for the government to come to the aid of its citizens? When do you think it's not appropriate? Explain that this lesson looks at a time when the government did little to protect its citizens during a serious crisis.

TEACH

GUIDED DISCUSSION

1. **Make Connections** What facts did Hoover fail to consider as president in his efforts to help banks and the unemployed? *(Possible response: He didn't take into account that banks wouldn't want to risk their money to underwrite failing banks and that the vast number of unemployed would soon exhaust the resources of relief agencies no matter how well coordinated the agencies were.)*

2. **Draw Conclusions** During a time of historic economic instability, why might a political trend like fascism appeal to people? *(Answers will vary. Possible responses: During economic instability, people are usually frightened and want a strong, confident leader who can take charge and solve problems. People may even be willing to give up some freedoms if the leader promises to restore the country's prosperity and security.)*

ANALYZE PRIMARY SOURCES

Ask students to read Hoover's statements in the Primary Source feature. Discuss that while Hoover appeared to be insensitive to the country's problems, the situation might have looked very different from his point of view. **ASK:** How might Hoover's prior experiences with the nation's economy have shaped his opinions? *(Possible response: Hoover was used to years of economic prosperity and seemingly unlimited growth. He believed that temporary downturns were a natural part of economic cycles and the economy would rebound. From his point of view, there was no cause for alarm.)*

ACTIVE OPTIONS

On Your Feet: Roundtable Arrange students in groups of four "experts." Have each person in the group choose one of the following people to represent: a Dust Bowl farmer, an unemployed city dweller, a Hoover politician, and a radio or movie producer. Hand each group a sheet of paper containing the following question: How has the Great Depression affected you, and what do you think is the best way to help people? The first student in each group should write an answer, read it aloud, and pass the paper clockwise to the next student. Tell them to support their answers and opinions with specific details based on this lesson and on the knowledge they have acquired so far. After students have circulated the paper a few times, ask each group to share their ideas.

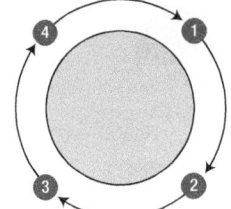

NG Learning Framework: Helping Those in Need

| ATTITUDE | Empowerment |

| KNOWLEDGE | Our Human Story |

Ask students to make a list of problems that low- and middle-income individuals and families faced during the Great Depression. Encourage them to research online several federal aid and relief programs that address these problems now and to prepare a brief "aid guidebook" for those in need. Ask students to discuss how such programs might have helped save farms, businesses, and lives during the Great Depression. Invite them to share their work with the class.

DIFFERENTIATE

ENGLISH LANGUAGE LEARNERS   ELD

Summarize Place students of **All Proficiencies** in mixed pairs. Assign each pair one or more paragraphs from the lesson. Have students read their assigned paragraphs and then work together to summarize each paragraph in one or two sentences. When all pairs have finished, have them read their summaries in the order in which the material appears to provide an oral summary of the entire lesson.

PRE-AP

Evaluate an Initiative Have students gather information from a variety of sources to create an oral or written report about the relative success or failure of one of Hoover's initiatives. Encourage students to use primary and secondary sources and to quote or paraphrase them as appropriate. Remind students to cite their sources. Invite volunteers to share their findings with the class. You may extend the activity with a discussion of how the United States has favored "big government" or "small government" at different times.

See the Chapter Planner for more strategies for differentiation.

HISTORICAL THINKING

ANSWERS

1. Hoover believed that private charity and local relief efforts could handle the crisis.

2. President Hoover's seeming indifference to people's suffering turned the voters against him.

3. Politicians pleaded for the federal government to intervene by helping the unemployed and allocating funds to provide fuel and food. Citizens tried to survive by finding work on their own, using church and private relief stations, and living in "Hoovervilles."

CRITICAL VIEWING Conditions were crowded and appear primitive, which probably contributed to the spread of diseases. The shacks were exposed to heat, cold, rain, and snow.

THE BONUS ARMY

President Hoover was quickly reminded that sometimes things go from bad to worse. As unemployment rose, Hoover's popularity with Americans plummeted. As a result, the Democrats made progress in the 1930 elections and set their sights on victory in the 1932 presidential election.

HOOVER'S WANING POPULARITY

Hoover already had a low favorability rating with his constituents because of his policies to battle unemployment. Because Hoover was a Republican, many Americans assigned blame for the nation's struggles to his party. In the 1930 election, the Democrats picked up 8 seats in the Senate and 49 in the House. Neither gave the Democrats a majority, but by the time Congress next convened, Democrats had a majority in the House due to special elections held to replace representatives who had died.

To deal with a growing budget deficit, Congress passed the **Revenue Act of 1932**, the greatest peacetime increase in taxes in the nation's history.

At a time when the economy needed Americans to have more buying power to keep factories and businesses open, the tax measure drew money out of the hands of potential consumers. Raising taxes in an election year contributed to Hoover's decreasing popularity. On the other hand, Congress also passed the **Norris-LaGuardia Act of 1932**, which extended to workers "full freedom of association" in unions and labor representation. The law restricted the use of federal **injunctions**, or court orders, to stop labor strikes, boycotts, and picketing and barred actions that prevented workers from joining unions. This legislation strengthened the power of labor, and it was popular among many American workers.

Tents and shacks burned as the U.S. Army drove the Bonus Army out of Washington, D.C., in July 1932.

To make matters worse, Congress introduced bills to provide direct assistance to the unemployed, but a coalition of Republicans and southern Democrats blocked their passage. Finally, as public pressure for action intensified, Congress passed the **Emergency Relief and Construction Act of 1932**. The act allocated federal funds to states for building public structures that could generate income, such as toll bridges, if the states proved they could not raise any money themselves. Although the law limited the kinds of construction projects that could be funded, it represented a symbolic step toward a greater federal role in combating the economic crisis and meeting the needs of desperate Americans.

THE BONUS MARCH

As the Depression worsened, economic distress triggered social protests, including one by war veterans. In 1931, a veterans organization passed a resolution demanding from Congress immediate payment of the cash bonus scheduled to be paid to World War I veterans in 1945. Veterans argued the early payment would not only help them but would also stimulate the economy. In December 1931, a bill authorizing this payment was introduced in the House. In May 1932, veterans began traveling to Washington, D.C., to show their support for the bill.

By June, more than 15,000 veterans calling themselves the Bonus Expeditionary Force, or the **Bonus Army**, had arrived in Washington to listen to Congress debate the bonus bill. While some slept in government buildings, most members of the Bonus Army camped out in makeshift tents and sheds on the banks of the Anacostia River. The Washington, D.C., police superintendent and the police captain in charge of Anacostia helped the veterans by providing food, medical care, and supplies for building their shacks. Hoover, on the other hand, ignored them. On June 17, the bill was rejected by the Senate. In July, the Hoover administration urged the Bonus Army to leave Washington and even allocated $100,000 to pay the men's transportation costs home. But many stayed on, hoping for a change in government policy.

On July 28, 1932, the secretary of war ordered the police to remove marchers from government buildings. Veterans resisted, and fighting broke out. When a police pistol went off, other officers began shooting, and soon two veterans lay dead. The president ordered the federal troops in Washington, commanded by Army Chief of Staff General **Douglas MacArthur**, to restore order. MacArthur took his

PRIMARY SOURCE

A 1932 editorial in the magazine *The New Republic* described the violence directed against the Bonus Army in Washington, D.C.

The orders which sent the soldiers to Anacostia, routing men, women and children out of bed, drenching them with tear gas, ruthlessly burning their poor shelters and whatever personal property they could not carry on their backs, then driving all of them, cripples, babies, pregnant women, up a steep hill at the point of a bayonet—these were the orders of a furious child who has been thwarted and is raging for revenge. It is profoundly humiliating to every decent American that he must see his government thus persecuting and stealing from these hungry and ragged men whom, fourteen years ago, it did not hesitate to send into the trenches at the risk of death.

—from "Bullets for the B.E.F.," *The New Republic*, August 10, 1932

men, armed with tanks and machine guns, across the Anacostia River into the Bonus Army's camp. His troops hurled tear gas canisters and burned tents and shacks as the veterans fled in terror. Documentary filmmakers captured the events, and moviegoers across the nation saw newsreels of MacArthur in full military dress directing the attack, cavalry soldiers charging veterans, and flames and smoke billowing from the camp. By the next day, the camp was a ruin and all the veterans had left. Many Americans were shocked. "If the Army must be called out to make war on unarmed citizens," wrote one newspaper editor, "this is no longer America." The public outrage spelled trouble for Hoover as the 1932 presidential election approached.

HISTORICAL THINKING

1. **READING CHECK** Why did veterans organize the Bonus Army?

2. **IDENTIFY PROBLEMS AND SOLUTIONS** What problem was the Emergency Relief and Construction Act of 1932 meant to solve?

3. **ANALYZE CAUSE AND EFFECT** How did public pressure and opinion affect the political actions of Hoover and his administration?

4. **DISTINGUISH FACT AND OPINION** Does the phrase "these were the orders of a furious child" convey a fact or an opinion? Explain your answer.

PLAN: 2-PAGE LESSON

OBJECTIVE

Analyze the actions that led to Herbert Hoover's decreasing popularity and the Democrats' increasing power.

CRITICAL THINKING SKILLS FOR LESSON 3.2

• Identify Problems and Solutions

• Analyze Cause and Effect

• Distinguish Fact and Opinion

• Synthesize

• Analyze Primary Sources

HISTORICAL THINKING FOR CHAPTER 19

What impact did the Great Depression have on the American people, culture, economy, and spirit? As high unemployment persisted, people took more direct actions in an attempt to relieve their desperate circumstances. Lesson 3.2 discusses the advances of the labor movement, the federal government's growing role, and the failed Bonus Army march.

BACKGROUND FOR THE TEACHER

The Bonus Army incident was a tragic clash between desperate citizens and a fearful government. The veterans' goal was a peaceful demonstration of their needs. Their "commander in chief," Walter Waters, insisted on military discipline and decorum in the Bonus Army encampment. He organized regular meetings, work crews, and sanitation. Supporters in Washington, D. C., kept the veterans supplied with food and clothing. The government, however, feared that communists were behind the march. After the bonus was denied, Hoover and his administration believed communist agitators were manipulating angry veterans. To them, an attempt to takeover or attack the government seemed imminent. Douglas MacArthur agreed and prepared the army to respond with force. Along with two junior officers, Dwight D. Eisenhower and George S. Patton, MacArthur led the charge that ultimately helped bring down the Hoover administration.

INTRODUCE & ENGAGE

PREVIEW USING VISUALS

Draw students' attention to the photograph and caption. Explain that the Bonus Army encampment was similar to the Dust Bowl refugee camps and Hoovervilles. **ASK:** What might have led the government to take such actions against the Bonus Army in Washington, D.C.? *(Answers will vary. Possible response: The government might have wanted to drive the Bonus Army away because the group threatened the government in some way.)*

TEACH

GUIDED DISCUSSION

1. **Synthesize** How did the government's legislation described in this lesson impact the lives of unemployed people? *(Possible response: Raising taxes made things more difficult for people with little money. The Emergency Relief and Construction Act, because of its limitations, would help only a few people hired to work on the projects. However, the Norris-LaGuardia Act gave the unemployed more power to organize as workers.)*

2. **Analyze Cause and Effect** How did the government's attack on the Bonus Army affect Hoover's reputation? *(Possible response: Hoover's popularity was already dwindling. However, the use of violent force against war veterans created widespread public outrage and seemed to confirm his lack of sympathy for those in need.)*

ANALYZE PRIMARY SOURCES

Tell students to review the excerpt from the 1932 editorial from the *New Republic*, including the citation. **ASK:** What is the author's purpose and how does his choice of language reinforce that purpose? *(Possible response: The author wanted to expose the actions of the government. He uses vivid verbs and key nouns that describe the Army "routing, burning, driving," as they attacked "pregnant women, cripples, babies, hungry and ragged men.")*

ACTIVE OPTIONS

On Your Feet: Inside-Outside Circle Arrange students in two concentric circles facing each other. Have students in the outside circle ask a question about the human toll of the Depression. Then direct each student in the inside circle to answer his or her partner's question. On your signal, students on the inside circle should rotate counterclockwise to meet new partners. On another signal, students trade inside-outside roles. For this new round, broaden the topic to include material in the rest of the chapter. Have students ask questions about how the Depression affected American culture and the international community.

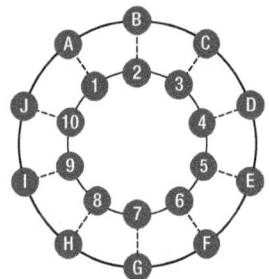

NG Learning Framework: Viewpoints on the Bonus Army

SKILL Communication

KNOWLEDGE Our Human Story

Explain to students that people had different viewpoints about the Bonus Army and the events that took place. Direct students to conduct online research about the Bonus Army, identifying different points of view about the incident. For example, the Library of Congress provides a facsimile of an argument written by a member of the Bonus Army, and a *Smithsonian* magazine article includes an argument by General MacArthur, justifying his actions. Have students choose several arguments to compare and ask them to distinguish valid arguments from fallacious arguments. They should also examine the documents to identify possible bias and prejudice in the authors' historical interpretations. Encourage students to share their results with the class.

DIFFERENTIATE

STRIVING READERS

Gather Facts After reading, ask each student to write down at least three facts they recall from the lesson. Students should then work with a partner to combine their facts into one longer list. Challenge pairs to add more facts from the lesson. Then have pairs share their lists with others and add facts they might have left out from other lists.

GIFTED & TALENTED

Write a Letter Home Instruct students to conduct online research to find out more about the veterans who were part of the Bonus Army that went to Washington D.C., in 1932. Tell them to take notes on as many specific details as possible. Then ask them to imagine that they are a member of the Bonus Army. Tell them to use their notes to write a letter home to their loved ones about what they experienced. Students may choose to write the letter before, or after, the police action that forced them out. Invite students to read their letters to the class or publish them on a school blog.

See the Chapter Planner for more strategies for differentiation.

HISTORICAL THINKING

ANSWERS

1. The Bonus Army was organized to show support for legislation that would authorize an early payment of the bonus veterans had been promised.

2. The Act was meant to provide jobs for the unemployed by giving funds to states with no money of their own to build income-producing structures such as toll bridges.

3. Public pressure and opinion forced the federal government to take a more active role in providing relief to states. But for the most part, Hoover and his administration ignored public pressure, going so far as to order armed troops to remove protesting veterans in Washington.

4. The phrase is an opinion. By using the image of a child throwing a temper tantrum, the writer strengthens the argument that the government's actions were vindictive and outrageous.

VOCABULARY

Write a paragraph about the topic using all the words in each group of words. A sentence is provided as a sample beginning.

1. Topic: the stock market crash
   Dow Jones Industrial Average
   margin   speculation
   trading pool   stock market
   Speculation was one factor impacting the Dow Jones Industrial Average.

2. Topic: effects of the Depression
   Dust Bowl   Bonus Army
   Hooverville   deportation

3. Topic: remedying the Depression
   underwrite   Smoot-Hawley   Tariff Act
   Revenue Act of 1932   injunction

READING STRATEGY
ANALYZE CAUSE AND EFFECT

Analyzing cause and effect can help you understand how situations develop throughout history. Complete the Cause-and-Effect Chain to identify the factors that led to the stock market crash in 1929 and the Great Depression that followed. Then answer the question.

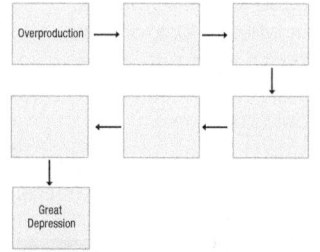

4. Describe the chain of causes and effects that resulted in the Great Depression.

MAIN IDEAS

Answer the following questions. Support your answers with evidence from the chapter.

5. What was the Kellogg-Briand Pact? **LESSON 1.1**

6. Why did intervention fail to stop the stock market slide between Black Thursday and Black Tuesday? **LESSON 1.2**

7. How did income inequality and overproduction in manufacturing work together to create problems during the 1920s? **LESSON 2.1**

8. In what ways did new farm machinery contribute to the conditions that caused the Dust Bowl? **LESSON 2.3**

9. Why was Woody Guthrie's music so important to people facing poverty during the Depression? **LESSON 2.4**

10. Why did Hoover's plan to help the banking system stay afloat fail? **LESSON 3.1**

11. How did worldwide economic problems influence the emergence of fascism? **LESSON 3.1**

12. How did the passage of the Revenue Act of 1932 hurt Hoover's popularity? **LESSON 3.2**

HISTORICAL THINKING

Answer the following questions. Support your answers with evidence from the chapter.

13. **ANALYZE CAUSE AND EFFECT** How did international loans and World War I reparations contribute to the Great Depression?

14. **MAKE CONNECTIONS** How did the Dust Bowl contribute to the depopulation of rural areas in the Great Plains?

15. **EVALUATE** In what ways did ordinary people respond to the Great Depression?

16. **ANALYZE CAUSE AND EFFECT** Did panic help cause the stock market crash, or was panic an effect of that crash? Explain your answer and describe how determining historical causes and effects can be complicated.

17. **FORM AND SUPPORT OPINIONS** How would you rate Hoover's handling of the Great Depression? Support your position with evidence from the text.

18. **ASK AND ANSWER QUESTIONS** Write a question you could ask about causes of the Great Depression, and describe how you could research the answer. Then explain the challenges of determining the causes and effects of a historical event like this.

ANALYZE VISUALS

Look closely at the political cartoon from 1929 depicting Herbert Hoover saying to a farmer, "It may not be perfect, but I'm sure it'll help quite a bit." Then answer the questions that follow.

19. What do each of the characters depicted in the cartoon represent?

20. What solution is Hoover offering the farmer, and what do the expressions of the scarecrow and crow convey about the solution?

ANALYZE SOURCES

California Industrial Scenes is a 1934 fresco by John Langley Howard depicting unemployed workers during the Great Depression.

21. How does the painting reflect the larger social and economic developments of the Depression era?

CONNECT TO YOUR LIFE

22. **EXPLANATORY** The Dust Bowl was an ecological disaster that may have been prevented if farmers had better understood the impact of their farming methods on the land. Find information about an ecological problem of today. Using the Dust Bowl as an example, write a short essay explaining why it is important that we understand problems before we can begin to solve them.

TIPS
- Think about the physical and human characteristics of the region.
- Use textual evidence from the chapter in your explanation.
- Make a connection between the Dust Bowl and the problem of today, and explain how being more informed can prevent ecological problems from turning into disasters.
- Use two or three vocabulary terms from the chapter in your response.

VOCABULARY ANSWERS

One sample paragraph is provided below, followed by topic sentences for the remaining paragraphs. Students' paragraphs should flesh out the idea stated in each topic sentence.

1. Speculation was one factor impacting the Dow Jones Industrial Average. Many people invested in the stock market, borrowing money to buy stocks on margin. Other investors formed trading pools to manipulate the prices of stocks. In 1929, the system collapsed.

2. As unemployment worsened, the homeless set up makeshift camps, called Hoovervilles, and politicians acted to deport some immigrants.

3. The Hoover administration passed the Smoot-Hawley Tariff Act to protect American industries, but it made international economic conditions worse.

READING STRATEGY ANSWER

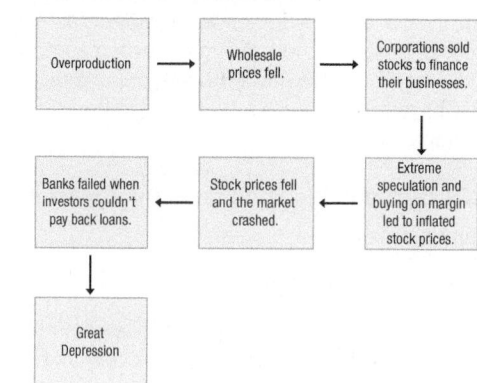

4. Overproduction reduced demand and prices fell. Corporations sold stocks to obtain cash needed for growth, which led to increased speculation and buying stocks on margin. Stock prices rose to unrealistic levels. Stock prices then fell, setting off panic selling. The stock market crashed. Banks failed when investors defaulted on margin loans. The economy slumped into a depression.

MAIN IDEAS ANSWERS

5. The Kellogg-Briand Pact was an agreement signed by many nations to renounce war.

6. When prices collapsed on Black Thursday, a banking group led by J.P. Morgan, Jr., bought stocks in an attempt to stop the collapse. Things calmed for a bit, but the slide continued on Monday. Investors panicked and resumed selling, resulting in the market collapse on Black Tuesday.

7. The unequal distribution of income meant that only a small percentage of the population was wealthy. As a result, few people could afford to buy the excess goods companies were producing.

8. New farm machinery helped farmers plant more acres of wheat on the Great Plains. The machinery cut the deep prairie grass roots and pulverized the soil into finer particles. With no grasses to hold the soil in place and more soil exposed to the sun, the land dried out, setting the stage for the Dust Bowl disaster.

9. His songs told the truth about people's lives. Like those in poverty, Guthrie rode the rails, slept in migrant camps, and sang or did odd jobs to get money for food.

10. Hoover persuaded bankers to form the National Credit Corporation to underwrite failed banks and protect their depositors. However, successful banks were reluctant to take over the assets of failed banks, so Hoover's voluntary action plan failed.

11. Economic turmoil in the postwar era helped Benito Mussolini gain power through a political movement called fascism, which merged state and business leadership under the banner of extreme nationalism.

12. The Revenue Act, the greatest peacetime increase in taxes in the nation's history, took money out of the hands of consumers at a time when the economy needed people to buy more goods.

HISTORICAL THINKING ANSWERS

13. The United States and other countries loaned money to help Germany make its reparation payments. When Germany's economy continued to weaken, the country was unable to repay its creditors, which contributed to international instability.

14. The drought and high winds destroyed crops, sickened or killed livestock and people, and caused many farm foreclosures. About one-quarter of affected farmers moved away from the Great Plains, going to California or elsewhere in search of work.

15. Men tried to find work anywhere they could, while women and children worked outside the home to earn money. Those who were employed tried to organize for better wages and conditions. Those who were homeless banded together in camps and settlements, lining up at soup kitchens for their meals.

16. The topic demonstrates the complexity of determining cause and effect, since panic was both an effect and a cause in this case. Panic resulted when stock prices started falling. However, if people had remained calm, there would have been no further slide. When people continued to panic, it caused another round of selling that finally resulted in the stock market crash.

17. Answers will vary. Students should consider such things as Hoover's slow response to the crisis, his reliance on volunteerism and charity, his rejection of congressional efforts to provide relief, and his handling of the Bonus Army march.

18. Answers will vary. Students' questions and answers should reflect the complexity of the Great Depression and the challenges of determining its causes and effects.

ANALYZE VISUALS ANSWERS

19. Possible response: The farmer represents all farmers, who is listening to Hoover explain his efforts. The scarecrow represents farm relief and is holding a rifle to scare away hard times (crows). Since a scarecrow can't shoot, the cartoonist is indicating that Hoover's farm relief will not solve farmers' problems.

20. Possible response: Hoover is offering farm relief in the form of a scarecrow with a gun. The expressions of the scarecrow and crow show disbelief in his solution.

ANALYZE SOURCES ANSWER

21. Possible response: The painting depicts a large group of people of mixed background who look serious and perhaps angry. Their expressions reflect the anguish of being unemployed. The fact that there are so many of them, crowded together, emphasizes the pervasive effects of the Depression on all of society.

CONNECT TO YOUR LIFE ANSWER

22. Essays will vary, but the ecological disaster students choose should have the same elements as the Dust Bowl: human activity that created the conditions for the disaster, what could have been done to prevent it, efforts to clearly understand the problems, and measures taken to solve the problems based on that understanding.

AMERICAN STORIES | **America's Favorite Pastime**

- Study Primary Sources: Quotations from writers, historians, journalists, and players
- On Your Feet: Conduct Baseball Interviews

NG Learning Framework:
Compare Across Time

American Voices Biographies
Jackie Robinson ONLINE

SECTION 1 RESOURCES

FRANKLIN D. ROOSEVELT'S NEW DEAL

LESSON 1.1
FDR and the 1932 Election

- On Your Feet: Inside-Outside Circle

NG Learning Framework:
Create a Collage

LESSON 1.2
An Activist Government

- On Your Feet: Fishbowl

NG Learning Framework:
Investigate a Local Legacy of the New Deal

LESSON 1.3
DOCUMENT-BASED QUESTION
The New Deal

- On Your Feet: Host a DBQ Roundtable

SECTION 2 RESOURCES

THE SECOND NEW DEAL

LESSON 2.1
The Second New Deal

AMERICAN GALLERY ONLINE Visual Arts of the New Deal

NG Learning Framework:
Investigate the Persistence of Poverty

American Voices Biographies
Huey P. Long ONLINE

LESSON 2.2
CURATING HISTORY
Milwaukee Public Museum
Milwaukee, Wisconsin

- On Your Feet: Sort the Artifacts

LESSON 2.3
Supporting Labor

- On Your Feet: Become an Expert

NG Learning Framework:
Find Parallels between Past and Present Labor Movements

LESSON 2.4
THROUGH THE LENS—AMERICAN PLACES
Golden Gate Bridge
San Francisco, California

- On Your Feet: Create an Acrostic

NG Learning Framework:
Research a Suspension Bridge

SECTION 3 RESOURCES

GROUPS STRUGGLE FOR RIGHTS

LESSON 3.1
Women During the New Deal

- On Your Feet: Identify Problems and Solutions

NG Learning Framework:
Profile the Roosevelts

LESSON 3.2
Mixed Progress on Civil Rights

- On Your Feet: Three Corners

NG Learning Framework:
Investigate the Past and Present of Mexican Americans

American Voices Biographies
Mary McLeod Bethune ONLINE

SECTION 4 RESOURCES

LEGACY OF THE NEW DEAL

LESSON 4.1
The New Deal Winds Down

- On Your Feet: Create a Problem-and-Solution Chain

NG Learning Framework:
Discover the Legacy of the FLSA

LESSON 4.2
The New Deal's Impact

- On Your Feet: Vote with Your Feet
- Active History: Analyze Primary Sources

CHAPTER 20 REVIEW

STRATEGY 1
PREVIEW THE TEXT

Work with students to preview each lesson in the chapter. For each lesson, guide them to read the lesson titles, lesson introductions, Main Idea statements, captions, and lesson headings. Then tell them to list the information they expect to find in the text. Instruct students to read a lesson and discuss with a partner what they learned and whether or not it matched their list.

Use with All Lessons

STRATEGY 2
USE RECIPROCAL TEACHING

Tell partners to take turns reading each paragraph of the lesson aloud. At the end of the paragraph, the reading student should ask the listening student questions about the paragraph. Students may ask their partners to state the main idea, identify important details that support the main idea, or summarize the paragraph in their own words. Then ask students to work together to answer the Historical Thinking questions.

Use with All Lessons

STRATEGY 3
MAKE A "TOP FIVE FACTS" LIST

Tell students to reread the lesson and any captions for visuals that it contains. Then ask students to write down five facts that they remember from the text. Instruct students to meet with a partner to compare lists and consolidate the two lists into one final list. Encourage student pairs to state facts from their lists.

Use with All Lessons

STRATEGY 1
USE MODIFIED MAIN IDEA STATEMENTS

To help students anticipate and organize content, provide modified Main Idea statements before reading. Several examples are provided below.

1.1 FDR's promise to end the Depression helped him win the presidency in 1932.

1.2 The size of government grew as FDR followed policies, called the New Deal, to help with economic problems.

2.1 FDR launched the second part of his New Deal with a new set of economic reforms.

2.3 Workers gained the right to organize into labor unions as part of the New Deal.

3.1 Eleanor Roosevelt was a strong supporter of women under the New Deal.

3.2 The lives of African Americans, Mexican Americans, and Native Americans improved in some ways under the New Deal.

Use with All Lessons

STRATEGY 2
DESCRIBE A POLITICAL CARTOON

Pair students who are visually impaired with students who are not. Ask the latter to describe the political cartoon in Lesson 1.3 in detail, including the expressions on Roosevelt's and the children's faces and the letters on the children's shirts. Prompt students to recall what federal programs the letters stand for and how those programs helped the U.S. economy. Instruct them to answer any questions their partner may have, and encourage the pair to discuss the point of view conveyed by the cartoon.

Use with Lesson 1.3

ENGLISH LANGUAGE LEARNERS ELD

STRATEGY 1
USE VISUALS TO PREDICT CONTENT

Direct students at the **Emerging** and **Expanding** levels to read the lesson title and look at the visuals. Then ask them to write a sentence for each visual, predicting how it is related to the lesson. After reading, you may wish to have students verify their predictions and reword sentences if necessary.

Use with All Lessons *Encourage students at the **Emerging** level to ask questions if they have trouble writing a prediction. Students at the **Bridging** level could help students at the **Emerging** and **Expanding** levels write their predictions.*

STRATEGY 2
COMPOSE CAPTIONS

Pair students at the **Emerging** and **Expanding** levels with English-proficient students. Direct students to work together to write original captions for the photographs in the chapter. You may want to ask pairs to compare their captions with the captions written by other pairs.

Use with Lessons 1.1, 1.2, 3.1, 3.2, 4.1, and 4.2 *For lesson 1.2, make sure students caption the photographs of FDR and of the turbine workers. You could expand this activity to include the artwork in Lesson 2.1.*

STRATEGY 3
BUILD A CONCEPT CLUSTER

Write the Key Vocabulary term "New Deal" on the board and ask students for words, phrases, or pictures that come to mind. Ask volunteers to write the words and draw simple pictures to build a Concept Cluster. Call on students to create sentences about the words and pictures. Then tell students to ask a question they would like to have answered about the Key Vocabulary term.

Use with All Lessons *You may wish to pair students at the **Emerging** level with students at the **Expanding** and **Bridging** levels.*

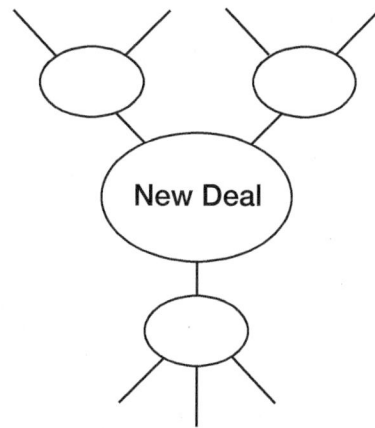

GIFTED & TALENTED

STRATEGY 1
PERFORM A SPEECH

Prompt students to conduct online research to find text and audio of various speeches given by Franklin Delano Roosevelt. Instruct students to practice a segment of one of the speeches and then perform it for the class. Remind students of the impact of rhetoric on audiences large and small. Instruct them to imitate Roosevelt's speech rhythm and intonation to achieve the same dramatic effect he had on his audiences.

Use with Lessons 1.1–1.3 and 2.3

STRATEGY 2
WRITE A LETTER

Instruct students to write a letter to Eleanor Roosevelt in the voice of a person suffering economic hardship or social injustice during the 1930s. Encourage students to conduct online research to find examples of such letters and to learn more about Eleanor Roosevelt's commitment to social justice. Invite students to post their letters on a class blog or publish them on a class, grade, or school website.

Use with Lessons 3.1 and 3.2

PRE-AP

STRATEGY 1
EVALUATE HISTORICAL INTERPRETATIONS

Direct students to conduct research using online and print sources to evaluate different historians' interpretations of Roosevelt's New Deal policies. Specifically, ask students to focus on differing views of his "big government" and "big spending" programs, which New Deal defenders acclaim and some revisionist historians criticize. Prompt students to use their research to write an essay evaluating alternative interpretations of the New Deal, including historians' use of evidence. Invite students to share their essays with the class.

Use with Lessons 1.1–1.3, 4.1, and 4.2

STRATEGY 2
CONNECT HISTORY AND LITERATURE

Instruct students to research the false accusations in the Scottsboro Boys case and the false accusations in Harper Lee's novel *To Kill a Mockingbird*. Encourage students to do a close reading of selected texts from the Scottsboro Boys case and from the novel. Prompt them to write an essay examining the similarities and differences between the novel and the court case. Ask students to conclude the essay with their thoughts on how Lee's fictional "truth" both reflects and departs from the facts that inspired it. Encourage students to share their essays with the class.

Use with Lesson 3.2

THE NEW DEAL

1933–1940

HISTORICAL THINKING In what ways were Franklin Roosevelt's policies during the Great Depression groundbreaking?

"We are helping, **and shall continue to help** the farmer."

—President Franklin D. Roosevelt

This mural, titled *Agriculture in California*, appears in Coit Tower in San Francisco. Created in 1934 by American artist Maxine Albro, it was commissioned under a federal program to fund the visual arts. In an attempt to end the Great Depression, President Franklin Roosevelt initiated programs to help workers in all occupations, including artists and farmers.

INTRODUCE THE PAINTING

AGRICULTURE IN CALIFORNIA

Direct students' attention to the *Agriculture in California* mural and have them read the caption that identifies the painting. **ASK:** Based on the artist's depiction, how would you describe California agriculture in the 1930s? *(Possible response: Farming was hard work done mostly by hand. It employed both men and women who produced a variety of crops, including flowers, fruits, and vegetables.)* Call on a volunteer to read the quotation from President Franklin Roosevelt. Point out the blue eagle and NRA (National Recovery Administration) logo on the orange crates in the painting. Tell students that in this chapter they will learn how Roosevelt's programs addressed economic and social problems.

SHARE BACKGROUND

Maxine Albro was one of 25 artists who transformed the walls of Coit Tower into an art gallery. Her work shows the influence of Diego Rivera, a renowned Mexican artist with whose assistant she studied. The 10-by-42-foot mural of California agriculture is a fresco, made by painting in wet plaster. Albro became famous for this style of art and for the Mexican influence that characterizes her work.

For Chapter 20 Spanish Resources, visit the Resources Menu. Chapter 20 Resources are available at NGLSync.Cengage.com.

HISTORICAL THINKING QUESTION

In what ways were Franklin Roosevelt's policies during the Great Depression groundbreaking?

Brainstorm Innovative Plans Organize students into groups of four and provide each group with a Word Web graphic organizer. Direct members of each group to write the word *groundbreaking* in the center circle and brainstorm associated words and phrases to complete the Web. *(Possible responses: creative, innovative, different, untried, unproven, forward-thinking, sweeping, revolutionary)* **ASK:** What kinds of policies might be considered groundbreaking? *(Possible responses: policies that tackle many problems at once; policies that approach situations in a new way)* Based on students' prior knowledge of the Great Depression, prompt them to discuss its human toll. Ask each group to make a prediction about a groundbreaking policy Roosevelt might propose to relieve the problems many Americans faced. Allow time for groups to share their ideas.

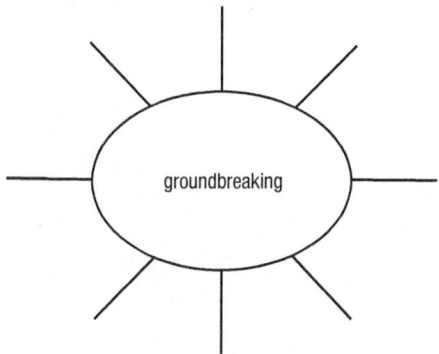

INTRODUCE THE READING STRATEGY

DETERMINE CHRONOLOGY

Explain to students that arranging events in chronological order helps readers gain historical perspective. Ask them to turn to the Chapter Review and preview the time line. As students read the chapter, encourage them to note the chronology of major events and dates.

KEY DATES FOR CHAPTER 20

1933	New Deal programs provide jobs
1934	Indian Reorganization Act
1935	WPA employs writers and artists
1936	Roosevelt elected to second term
1937	Golden Gate Bridge opens
1938	Fair Labor Standards Act passed
1939	Marian Anderson performs at Lincoln Memorial

INTRODUCE CHAPTER VOCABULARY

KEY VOCABULARY

SECTION 1

bank holiday	fireside chat	New Deal
brain trust	First Hundred Days	planned scarcity
deficit	lame duck	polio
economic planning		

SECTION 2

collective bargaining	Nazi Party	Second New Deal
court-packing plan	pension fund	sit-down strike
National Socialism	picket line	totalitarian
	populist	

SECTION 3

| breadwinner | voting bloc |

SECTION 4

| deficit spending | mobilization | welfare state |

VOCABULARY PYRAMIDS

As they read the chapter, have students complete Vocabulary Pyramids for Key Vocabulary words. Tell students to make a pyramid for each word, write what they know about each word before reading, and then add to or correct information in the pyramid after they encounter the word in the chapter. Model an example for students on the board, using the graphic organizer shown here.

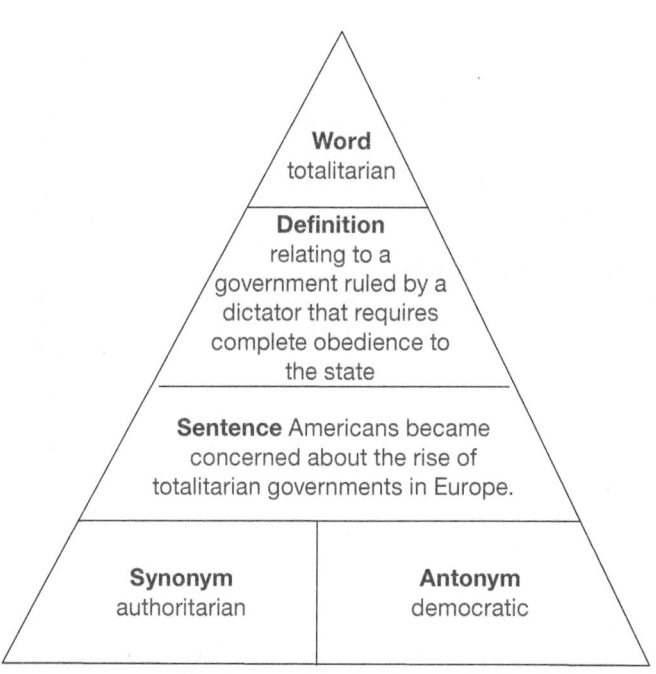

OBJECTIVES

- **Explore the significance of baseball as a unifying force in American history.**

- **Describe the role of radio in the popularity of baseball.**

- **Understand how the Great Depression affected professional baseball.**

- **Analyze how racial attitudes influenced professional baseball.**

- **Study primary sources: quotations from writers, historians, journalists, and players.**

CRITICAL THINKING SKILLS FOR "AMERICA'S FAVORITE PASTIME"

- Make Connections

- Draw Conclusions

- Evaluate

- Form and Support Opinions

- Describe

- Summarize

- Make Generalizations

CONNECT TO THE CHAPTER

This American Story explores baseball's unique place in American culture. Through the study of a narrative rife with colorful characters, interesting features, lively quotations, and historical perspective, students will explore why baseball held such an important role in 20th-century America and why it continues to hold a prominent place in the American zeitgeist.

This chapter, The New Deal, examines the Roosevelt administration's response to the Great Depression. During this crippling event, sports—and other forms of entertainment—served an important role by offering a respite and diversion from the harsh economic realities of the time. Use this American Story after reading Section 3, as that section and this American Story provide a societal counterpoint to the political focus of the chapter.

HISTORY NOTEBOOK

Encourage students to complete the American Story page for Chapter 20 in their History Notebooks as they read.

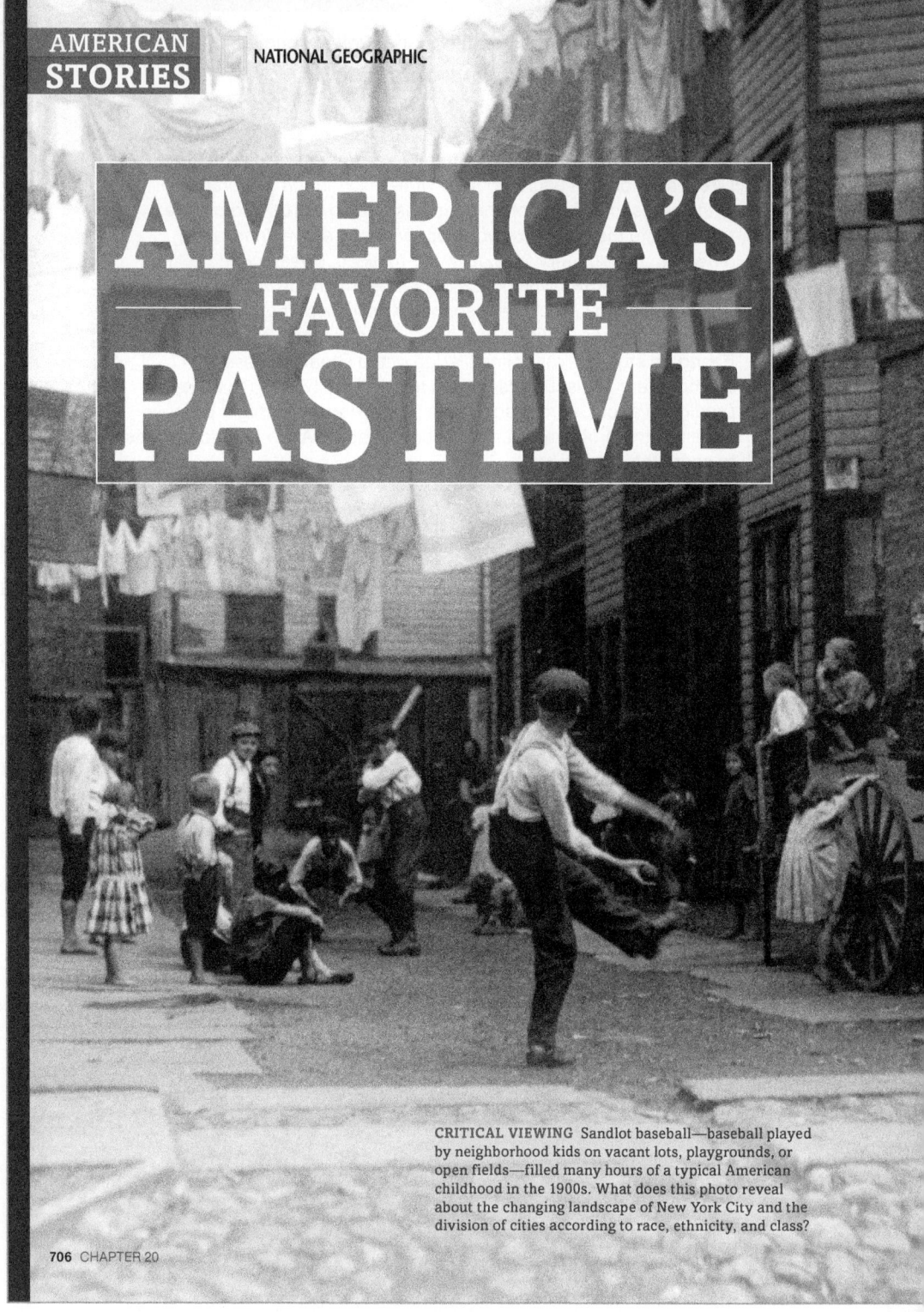

AMERICAN STORIES   NATIONAL GEOGRAPHIC

AMERICA'S FAVORITE PASTIME

CRITICAL VIEWING Sandlot baseball—baseball played by neighborhood kids on vacant lots, playgrounds, or open fields—filled many hours of a typical American childhood in the 1900s. What does this photo reveal about the changing landscape of New York City and the division of cities according to race, ethnicity, and class?

706 CHAPTER 20

In our sundown perambulations of late, through the outer parts of Brooklyn, we have observed several parties of youngsters playing "base," a certain game of ball. . . . Let us go forth awhile and get better air in our lungs. Let us leave our close rooms. . . . The game of ball is glorious.

—American poet Walt Whitman, 1846

Opening day ticket for the Cincinnati Baseball Club, April 18, 1895

When you hear the expression "America's pastime," you know the topic is baseball. Although some other popular sports, such as basketball and football, also developed in the United States, there's something about baseball that uniquely symbolizes the American identity. Russell Lewis, Chief Historian of the Chicago History Museum, has this theory about the sport in the early 1900s: "Baseball was . . . extremely popular, and I think it really cut across the ethnic groups. I think a lot of minorities found baseball one of the ways they could participate in being an American."

IN THE STADIUM AND ON THE RADIO

During the 1930s, the United States was in the grip of the Great Depression, and its human toll was widespread, touching nearly every household. Struggling to make ends meet, many Americans could not afford the cost of a ticket to the ballpark, so attendance at major league fields suffered. Between 1930 and 1933, the number of spectators at games decreased by 40 percent. Still, many people made room in their budgets for an escape to the ballpark when they could. Writer Ray Robinson, who was a child in New York City during the Depression, remembered people would "go to the ballpark to get away from the economic horrors of empty wallets and ice boxes." Children like Robinson saw "guys selling apples on street corners for a nickel. Along the Hudson River," he explains, "you had some of these guys living in ramshackle huts in rags. So going to the ballpark was a big thing."

Those who couldn't get to the ballpark could follow the games on the radio. In the 1920s, commercial radio was still a concept unfamiliar to most. The airwaves were mainly used by the military and by a handful of amateur ham radio operators. But in 1921, the World Series was first broadcast "live" by a studio announcer who read the play-by-play descriptions relayed to him from a news feed printed on a strip of paper called ticker tape. In some early radio broadcasts, a special effects operator provided sounds of an imaginary ballpark. By the 1930s, announcers were broadcasting from actual stadiums—no special effects needed. Not all team owners permitted radio coverage of the games, fearing that fans would stay home to listen and ballpark attendance would drop.

Listening to baseball on the radio in the 1930s was more challenging than it is today. Radios, cumbersome and far from portable, resided in the family living room, and often produced scratchy or static-filled sound. Sportswriter Robert Creamer wrote about listening to the World Series during the 1930s: "As a nine-year-old boy, I heard those World Series games on our living-room radio, which my mother, who was not even a fan, turned on and tuned in before I came home from school. Those old radios took a long time to warm up, and tuning to the right station took patience and a deft hand." Still, the role of radio in terms of popularizing baseball within American culture was profound.

The New Deal **707**

INTRODUCE & ENGAGE

CONNECT TO IDENTITY

Direct students' attention to the photograph and have them think about what it represents. Discuss with them why they think baseball was so popular during this period. Then display the following prompt: How does baseball symbolize the American identity? Ask students to spend two minutes writing words or sentences in response, and then invite volunteers to share what they wrote. Tell students they will read an American Story about the growth of America's favorite pastime—baseball—and how the sport became so closely linked to American culture and identity.

ANALYZE A QUOTATION

Have students read the quotation from Walt Whitman. Discuss the quotation and ask students to think about what a city like Brooklyn would have looked like in Whitman's time. **ASK:** What words from Whitman's quotation describe what it was like to live in Brooklyn at the turn of the century? *("get better air in our lungs"; "close rooms")* **ASK:** Why might baseball have been popular for people who lived in a place like this? *(Possible response: It drew people outdoors and away from cramped living conditions and stifling air.)* Inform students that this American Story will examine why baseball became known as America's favorite pastime.

DISCUSS ENTERTAINMENT

Initiate a class discussion about the role of entertainment during difficult historical times. Ask students to come up with examples—such as gladiatorial games in Rome—of people turning to popular entertainment as an escape from hardship. Then prompt them to discuss activities they engage in to distract themselves when they feel upset or disturbed. After the discussion, tell students that in this American Story they will learn that during the Great Depression baseball had an important role in boosting the spirits of the nation.

CRITICAL VIEWING The photo shows the crowded nature of a group of tenement buildings in the city. Instead of a yard, there is what looks like an alley with an outhouse. The children and adults are all white, so it appears that there is no mingling of races in this particular location. Some children are not wearing shoes and laundry is hung out to dry, suggesting a working-class neighborhood.

AMERICAN STORIES

Toward the end of the 1930s, ballpark attendance began to rebound as the Depression lifted with the start of World War II. After the war ended and the soldiers returned, game attendance would return to—and even exceed—its pre-Depression levels. In the meantime, an intriguing new way to enjoy baseball made its debut during a game between the Brooklyn Dodgers and Cincinnati Reds on August 27, 1939. That day, station W2XBS in New York City broadcast live television coverage of the game to the fortunate TV owners who lived within 50 miles of the station. A *New York Times* sportswriter reported delightedly, "At times it was possible to catch a fleeting glimpse of the ball as it sped from the pitcher's hand toward home plate."

BASEBALL LEGENDS

One name drew eager fans to the ballparks more than any other: that of legendary power hitter George Herman "Babe" Ruth of the New York Yankees. Ruth broke the single-season home run record in three consecutive seasons, hitting 29 in 1919, 54 in 1920 and 59 in 1921. In the early 1920s, he drew such a crowd that Yankees owner Jacob Ruppert built a new stadium to fit more spectators. Completed in 1923, Yankee Stadium was immediately given the nickname "The House that Ruth Built."

During the 1927 season, Ruth smashed 60 home runs, setting a record that remained unbroken until Roger Maris, who played in an era when the baseball season was 8 games longer, came along in 1961 and hit 61 home runs.

CRITICAL VIEWING Yankees hero Babe Ruth showed a group of attentive young boys in New York City how to grip a baseball bat. How might the relationship between professional athletes and their fans during the 1920s and 1930s compare to that of today?

National Baseball Hall of Fame and Museum Cooperstown, New York

Baseball legend Babe Ruth hit three home runs with this 36-inch wooden bat—a bat worthy of a museum collection—in Game Four of the 1926 World Series.

During his stellar 1927 season, Ruth hit more home runs than most major league teams—only the St. Louis Cardinals, Chicago Cubs, New York Giants, and his own team, the Yankees, managed to out homer him. To the dismay of his opponents, he hit home runs in every stadium of the American League.

In the 1930s, even though his home run stats were in decline, Ruth remained a force to be reckoned with. In the 1932 World Series, he helped the Yankees to victory over the Cubs with a three-run homer and a single in the third game of the series. Ruth hit his last major league home run at Forbes Field in Pittsburgh, Pennsylvania, on May 25, 1935. Aging and out of shape, he nonetheless hit three homers in a single game. The last of these, described by the Pittsburgh pitcher as "the longest cockeyed ball I ever saw in my life," was the first ball ever hit completely out of that park. It was Babe Ruth's 714th and final home run.

While all eyes were on Babe Ruth, his teammate Lou Gehrig was quietly setting a major league record of his own. Between May 1925 and May 1939, he played in 2,130 consecutive games, earning the nickname "The Iron Horse." When asked why he wouldn't take a rest, Gehrig replied, "There's no point to it. I like to play baseball." Gehrig's record remained unbroken for 56 years, until Cal Ripken, Jr., of the Baltimore Orioles played his 2,131st consecutive game.

Gehrig was not far behind Ruth in slugging abilities, nearly equaling Ruth's record with 47 home runs of his own in 1927. In 1932, he surpassed one of Ruth's accomplishments by hitting four home runs in a single game. Perhaps because of Ruth's fame and flamboyant personality, Gehrig spent the first half of the 1930s in Ruth's shadow, even though he was scoring runs at a faster pace than the aging star.

The 1930s saw the birth of new baseball legends as well as the passing of an earlier golden age. Center fielder Joe DiMaggio made his debut with the New York Yankees in 1936, introducing himself to the major leagues by hitting 29 home runs and batting in 125 runs during his rookie year. DiMaggio helped lead the Yankees, without Ruth, to four consecutive World Series championships between 1936 and 1939.

Also in 1939, Ted Williams, playing for the Boston Red Sox, had possibly the best major league rookie year in all of baseball: 31 home runs, 145 runs batted in, and a batting average of .327. Both DiMaggio

Ted Williams was chosen three times (in 1954, 1957, and 1958) by baseball card manufacturer Topps as the "leadoff man," meaning his was the first card in the set.

and Williams would become dominant players in the major leagues in the 1940s. In 1941, DiMaggio went on a spectacular hitting streak, racking up hits in 56 consecutive games. That same year, Williams achieved an unheard-of batting average of .406. No player since then has ever approached either of these feats.

It seems appropriate that the Baseball Hall of Fame in Cooperstown, New York, was established in 1939. That year marked the end of a decade filled with legendary players, whose names are familiar to nearly all Americans. Babe Ruth was in the first group of inductees, along with greats from earlier eras, such as Ty Cobb and Honus Wagner. Lou Gehrig was elected to the Hall of Fame later that year, even though there is normally a waiting period between a player's retirement and his induction.

THINK ABOUT IT

What connections can you make between the popularity of baseball and the Great Depression?

TEACH

GUIDED DISCUSSION

1. **Evaluate** Remind students that many owners feared that technologies such as radio would harm baseball, causing attendance to drop, but the opposite happened. **ASK:** How did the growth and effects of radio increase the popularity of baseball over time? *(Radio—and later television—made live games available to people who weren't watching the games at the stadiums. This increased baseball's exposure and helped to create more fans. In addition, television made it easier to promote stars such as Babe Ruth.)*

2. **Form and Support Opinions** Why do you think baseball, rather than another sport, like football or basketball, is dubbed "America's pastime"? *(Answers will vary. Possible responses: Baseball can be easily played in lots or streets, making it accessible to all Americans. People can enjoy baseball on many levels—some might enjoy tracking players' statistics or the social aspect of getting together to listen to or watch games. Leagues created teams all over the country, and fans and families responded by supporting their home teams.)*

VIRTUAL MUSEUM VISIT

The National Baseball Hall of Fame is one of the most popular sports destinations in the country, with nearly 300,000 people visiting it each year. Visitors can learn about baseball's history from its earliest days to the present, view plaques of the 300-plus select players officially inducted, and see thousands of artifacts, including the bat Babe Ruth used to hit his 60th home run, uniforms from Negro league players, and championship rings from every World Series winning team. Access the museum's website and point out the "Digital Collection" section. Ask groups of students to explore the collection on their own and choose one artifact that furthers their understanding of this American Story. Encourage groups to present their artifact to the class.

THINK ABOUT IT

Possible response: Although attendance at baseball games decreased during the Depression, baseball still remained popular through radio. Baseball provided people with relief through difficult economic times.

GUIDED DISCUSSION

3. **Describe** Why is it difficult to compare major league players with those in the Negro leagues? *(Negro leagues did not keep regular statistics as did the major leagues. Without consistent data, anecdotal evidence from spectators was used to draw comparisons between players in the leagues.)*

4. **Draw Conclusions** Remind students of the accomplishments of white players during the pre–World War II era of baseball, such as Ted Williams's .406 batting average, Babe Ruth's 60 home runs, and Lou Gehrig's consecutive game streak. Point out that these records have been broken only in recent years. **ASK:** What could account for the longevity of records set in this era? *(Possible responses: Some of the best players in history played in this era, thus explaining the records. Because of the racial segregation of the time, some of the best players were not allowed to compete against one another, diluting the competition.)*

ACTIVE OPTIONS

On Your Feet: Conduct Baseball Interviews Arrange students in groups of five and explain that they will conduct talk show interviews with baseball players from different eras. Student 1, the interviewer, develops a question to ask the show's "guests." Student 2, a player from the pre-World War II major leagues, Student 3, a member of the Negro leagues, and Student 4, a modern baseball player, answer the question, citing information from the American Story, as well as any additional online research. Student 5, a member of the studio audience, asks a follow-up question that the whole class can answer. Prompt participants to ask and answer several questions to adequately cover the topic.

NG Learning Framework: Compare Across Time

SKILL Communication

KNOWLEDGE Our Human Story

Divide students into small groups. Instruct groups to conduct research on Babe Ruth, focusing on topics such as evidence of his popularity, his salary relative to the national average, and his statistics compared with other players of the time. Then have groups identify another figure—either modern or historical—that they feel had a similar place in society in terms of both notoriety and skill compared with their peers. Prompt groups to prepare a presentation for the class in which they compare the two figures and present their findings.

THE NEGRO LEAGUES

Although such teams as the New York Yankees and St. Louis Cardinals dominated sports headlines throughout the 1930s, the all-white major leagues were not the only game in town. Prevented by prejudice and segregation from participating in the major leagues, African-American team owners and players formed their own leagues in the early 20th century. In 1920, Andrew "Rube" Foster, owner of the Chicago American Giants, organized the Negro National League, which consisted of eight teams in the Midwest. Other leagues soon followed, including the Negro Southern League later in 1920 and the Eastern Colored League in 1923.

Facing the same financial difficulties as the white major leagues during the Great Depression, Rube Foster's league disbanded after the 1931 season. It was soon replaced by a new Negro National League organized by Gus Greenlee, owner of the Pittsburgh Crawfords. From 1933 to 1949, Greenlee's league dominated the African-American baseball scene.

The best-known player in the Negro leagues was Leroy "Satchel" Paige, a tall, gangly pitcher with an unusual, high-legged windup and a spitfire delivery. Paige played for a number of teams, including the Pittsburgh Crawfords and the Kansas City Monarchs. There is little doubt that Satchel Paige would have been a star in the major leagues if teams had been integrated. Negro league teams did play

In a Negro league game in 1940, the Homestead Grays played the New York Black Yankees at Griffith Stadium in Washington, D.C.

The 1935 Pittsburgh Crawfords, shown here in front of their team bus, were one of the best teams in the Negro leagues.

THE NEGRO LEAGUES

As far back as the 1860s, "black-only" baseball teams traveled the country playing against whatever competition they could find. After Rube Forster consolidated the teams, players had to play frequently for the league to remain profitable. Because many black fans could afford to attend only one game a week, teams focused on Sundays—scheduling doubleheaders and using their best pitchers to increase attendance. The rest of the week was often grueling, as players traveled throughout the country, sometimes playing in as many as three games a day. One team, the Kansas City Monarchs, even traveled with portable lights—making them the first team in the country with a practical way to play night games. **ASK:** How did the existence of the Negro leagues, as well as the treatment of the players, reflect the larger social, political, and economic trends of the time? *(Segregation created the existence of the Negro leagues, reflecting discrimination toward nonwhites in American society. Popular African-American players—as well as ordinary African-American citizens—were often excluded from hotels and restaurants.)*

exhibition games against major league teams, and Paige struck out some of the toughest white hitters. Hack Wilson, a major leaguer, gave this description of Paige's fastball: "It starts out like a baseball, but when it gets to the plate it looks like a marble." Paige, known for his dazzling self-confidence and showmanship, gave this response: "You must be talking about my slowball. My fastball looks like a fish egg."

For all his brilliance, Paige may not have been the best pitcher in the Negro leagues. Some sportswriters and former players have suggested that Smokey Joe Williams or Bullet Joe Rogan may have been even better. Because the Negro leagues did not keep consistent records, it is difficult to compare players' statistics.

Despite their talent and popularity, even the top Negro league players were not allowed in most white-owned hotels and restaurants while they were on the road. However, by the end of the 1930s, some people were beginning to question the segregation of baseball. A group of African-American sportswriters was joined by the CIO labor union in calling for an end to the practice. Team owners in the major leagues ignored the calls, even though they were passing up the chance to sign extremely talented players. Over the course of the Negro leagues' existence, African-American teams played white teams in at least 438 exhibition games, and the Negro league teams won 309 times.

The racial barrier finally fell in 1947, when African-American player Jackie Robinson stepped up to the plate for the Brooklyn Dodgers. After that, the Negro leagues gradually dissolved as their best talent was hired by the now-integrated major leagues. In their later years, the Negro leagues were inclusive in a way that is not often recognized. Three women—Toni Stone, Connie Morgan, and Mamie "Peanut" Johnson—played on regular Negro league teams in the early 1950s.

This Negro leagues souvenir key chain from about 1940 features pitcher Satchel Paige.

The New Deal **711**

WORTH THE WAIT

Like the long-suffering Chicago Cubs, both the Boston Red Sox and Chicago White Sox bore some type of curse. For Boston, the hex came from perhaps the greatest player of all time—Babe Ruth. From 1914 to 1919, Ruth was a member of the Red Sox, over which time the team won three World Series championships. However, in 1919 Red Sox owner Harry Frazee sold Ruth to the Yankees for around $100,000 to fund a Broadway play, thus "cursing" the franchise for 85 years. The Red Sox remained without a championship while the Yankees won dozens. For the White Sox, who went 88 years without a World Series win, a cheating scandal where the team purposely lost the 1919 World Series at the behest of gamblers is thought by some to have set the franchise adrift. Draw students' attention to Dan Rather's thoughts about the Chicago Cubs' historic win. **ASK:** What is Dan Rather saying about the unique place of baseball in American history? *(Rather is saying that because of baseball's deep ties to American history and its slow and consistent pace, it offers a connection among different historical eras and between people from different generations.)*

WRITE ABOUT HISTORY

Identify America's Present-Day National Pastime
This American Story examines baseball, often called "America's pastime" because its popularity cuts across economic, regional, and ethnic lines. To help students think more deeply about the role of shared culture in American society, ask them to write an essay in which they consider the following question: Does present-day America have a national pastime? In their answer, students can explore issues such as the following: Is baseball still America's pastime? Is it something else? Does a national pastime even exist anymore? For this essay, students should first define in their own words what "national pastime" means and then argue whether something in our modern society fits that definition.

WORTH THE WAIT

Much of baseball history focuses on traditionally dominant teams, such as the New York Yankees and the St. Louis Cardinals. Often overlooked are the teams that struggle a little—or a lot. One of those struggling teams—the Chicago Cubs—gained the limelight in 2016. When the opening pitch of the 2016 World Series was thrown, it had been 108 years since the Cubs had won baseball's most coveted prize. Teams like the Chicago White Sox and the Boston Red Sox hadn't fared much better.

The Cubs and the Red Sox had one other quirk in common: each team carried a famous curse. In the case of the Cubs, it was the so-called Curse of the Billy Goat. The tale goes that tavern owner William Sianis tried to bring his goat, named Murphy, to Game Four of the 1945 World Series at Wrigley Field, the Cubs' ballpark. When Murphy was turned away, Sianis supposedly proclaimed that the Cubs would lose that World Series and would never win another. The Cubs did in fact lose the 1945 World Series.

For all three long-suffering teams, the World Series drought ended in the 21st century. The Red Sox took the championship in 2004, and the White Sox in 2005. And in 2016, the Cubs won the World Series in a hotly contested, seven-game series against the Cleveland Indians. Lifelong fans across the country rooted for the team to break its epic losing streak, and after what may be the greatest World Series in history, it did. The score of the final game: Cubs 8, Indians 7.

Chicagoans welcomed their beloved Cubbies home after the win with a parade and rally that drew larger crowds than the city had ever seen. And longtime journalist Dan Rather posted his thoughts on the Cubs' historic win, reflecting at the same time on what baseball means to many Americans:

In a world of nanosecond news cycles, baseball is measured in what by comparison is geologic time. It ties us to those who came before us—the many generations. And it stretches to those yet unborn. Fans of the future will hear about a curse and the 2016 Cubbies without fully understanding the full import of the moment. A cosmic quirk in the law of averages has been reconciled.

But the sun will rise tomorrow. The calendar will turn to winter and then spring. And hope on the diamond always springs eternal.

Unprecedented crowds of emotional fans took to the streets surrounding Wrigley Field after the Cubs' 2016 World Series win.

WRIGLEY FIELD HOME OF CHICAGO CUBS CUBS WIN!

TOYOTA

First baseman Anthony Rizzo leapt into the air with Kris Bryant alongside Mike Montgomery, Javier Báez, and Addison Russell seconds after the Cubs made the winning out in the 2016 World Series.

The New Deal **713**

ENGLISH LANGUAGE LEARNERS   ELD

Create a Word Web Pair students at the **Emerging** and **Expanding** levels with students at the **Bridging** level. Tell students to take turns reading paragraphs of the text, noting baseball terminology and writing terms on the spokes of a Word Web, adding additional spokes if needed. Instruct pairs to trade and compare webs, asking and answering questions about unfamiliar terms.

PRE-AP

Write a Biographical Sketch Direct students to conduct research and write a biographical sketch about one of the African-American women who played professional baseball in the Negro leagues. Encourage students to include quotations from or about the individual from primary and secondary sources. Invite students to share their biographical sketch with the class.

See the Chapter Planner for more strategies for differentiation.

HISTORICAL THINKING

Ask and have students answer the following questions.

1. **READING CHECK** How did the Great Depression and World War II influence the popularity of baseball?

2. **SUMMARIZE** What technological innovations helped boost the popularity of baseball?

3. **EVALUATE** Which player's historical accomplishments do you find most impressive in the context of his time?

4. **MAKE GENERALIZATIONS** What generalization can you make about baseball based on the fans' reaction to the historic World Series win by the 2016 Chicago Cubs?

ANSWERS

1. During the Great Depression, baseball remained popular, although attendance sagged because people could not afford to go to games. During the war, attendance rose because people had greater incomes and could afford to buy tickets.

2. Innovations such as radio and television made baseball accessible to a wide audience and increased its popularity.

3. Answers will vary. Possible response: Babe Ruth's home run record is most impressive because it dwarfed the accomplishments of other players of the era.

4. Answers will vary. Possible response: Many individuals and their families form a lifelong emotional connection with their hometown team that can span generations. The reaction of the large crowd in the photograph is an example of the celebration that can result from the culmination of 108 years of believing that the home team will again win the Series.

FDR AND THE 1932 ELECTION

When a baseball team isn't doing well, sometimes the solution is to replace the manager. That's what happened in 1932 when the country was struggling through the Great Depression. Americans decided it was time for a new leader.

NOMINATING ROOSEVELT

In the years leading up to the 1932 presidential election, Republican Herbert Hoover, who was set to run for a second term, gradually lost public support. He had failed to ease the Great Depression, and many Americans had grown to resent him and wealthy people in general. The Democrats saw an opportunity to take back the presidency and began

looking for an appealing and experienced candidate. **Franklin Delano Roosevelt**, popularly known as FDR, fit the bill. He was the distant cousin of a well-respected former president, Theodore Roosevelt, and he was married to Theodore's niece, Eleanor Roosevelt. Her political opinions and support of such causes as women's rights and labor had a great influence on her husband. Roosevelt was elected to

the New York State Senate in 1910, and he served as assistant secretary of the Navy under President Wilson. In 1920, he ran as the Democratic candidate for vice president but did not win the election.

Unfortunately, in 1921, Roosevelt contracted an infectious disease called **polio** and lost the use of his legs. The public knew about his disability, though the press did not focus on his condition. Roosevelt assumed his bout of polio and the disability it caused meant the end of his political career, but Eleanor encouraged him to carry on. After taking time off to recover, Roosevelt worked hard to reenter politics. His determination paid off in 1928 when he narrowly won the governorship of the state of New York. As governor, he earned a reputation as a strong, reform-minded leader who actively worked to address such problems as unemployment and poverty.

FDR's forceful personality and "can-do" attitude impressed many Democratic Party members. The Democrats felt Roosevelt's confidence and optimism would inspire hope in the many Americans who were struggling. They also believed his friendly, easy way of connecting with people would appeal to all Americans, rich and poor. At the party's national convention in Chicago, Roosevelt secured the presidential nomination, and John Nance Garner, a senator from Texas, was chosen as his running mate.

THE ELECTION OF 1932

The 1932 presidential race was not just a choice between Roosevelt and Hoover, however. The Socialist and Communist parties also nominated presidential candidates, hoping to appeal to Americans by proposing that their respective political systems offered the best solution to the Great Depression.

By October 1932, Hoover's public image was so unfavorable that Roosevelt's advisors assured the Democratic candidate that there was no need to campaign vigorously. FDR disagreed. Sensing that a passive campaign would not appeal to voters, he crisscrossed the country, giving speeches that convinced Americans their lives would improve if they elected him president.

On election day, November 8, 1932, Roosevelt won in a landslide, securing 57 percent of the popular vote and an overwhelming 89 percent of the electoral vote. Democratic candidates benefited from FDR's popularity, gaining 90 seats in the House and 13 in the Senate. The election proved a major

disappointment to both the Socialist and Communist parties. The Socialist candidate received fewer than 1 million votes, and the Communist candidate collected only about 100,000. Herbert Hoover was now a **lame duck**, an outgoing elected official soon to be replaced by a successor. For many Americans, his exit could not come soon enough. In fact, Congress was in the process of ratifying the **20th Amendment**, which would move up the presidential inauguration from March to January.

Meanwhile, the Great Depression continued to deepen. By the morning of Roosevelt's inauguration on March 4, 1933, many banks in New York City, the nation's financial capital, were closing. Roosevelt took the presidential oath of office in a steady, chilling rain. "Only a foolish optimist can deny the dark realities of the moment," he told the huge crowd in attendance and the millions who listened on the radio. "This nation asks for action, and action now," he declared.

Roosevelt offered few specific solutions that day. His objective was to persuade a dispirited people to have faith in him and in themselves. Standing straight in his leg braces, he stressed four major themes: sacrifice, discipline, compassion, and hope.

HISTORICAL THINKING

1. **READING CHECK** Why did Democrats believe Franklin Roosevelt was a good candidate for president?

2. **DETERMINE CHRONOLOGY** Review Roosevelt's political career before the 1932 election. How did the positions he held and the order in which he held them prepare him for the presidency?

3. **MAKE INFERENCES** Why do you think the press did not focus on FDR's disability?

4. **DRAW CONCLUSIONS** What did FDR mean when he said "the only thing we have to fear is fear itself"?

While campaigning for the presidency, Franklin Roosevelt greets a coal miner in West Virginia in this photograph from October 1932. Although he came from a wealthy, privileged background, Roosevelt was able to connect with ordinary Americans and convince them he cared.

OBJECTIVE

Explain how the Great Depression influenced the outcome of the 1932 election.

CRITICAL THINKING SKILLS FOR LESSON 1.1

- Determine Chronology
- Make Inferences
- Draw Conclusions
- Make Connections
- Make Predictions
- Analyze Primary Sources

HISTORICAL THINKING FOR CHAPTER 20

In what ways were Franklin Roosevelt's policies during the Great Depression groundbreaking? Discouraged by Herbert Hoover's inability to ease the Great Depression, American voters embraced Roosevelt's confidence. Lesson 1.1 discusses how Roosevelt inspired hope by pledging action.

BACKGROUND FOR THE TEACHER

Was Franklin Roosevelt's disability purposefully concealed from the American public? Some historians argue that voters knew about his paralysis and chose to elect him based on what he could do rather than on what he could not do. Others contend that photographers were discouraged or even forbidden to take pictures of Roosevelt in a wheelchair or being helped into a car. In 2001, a statue depicting FDR seated in a wheelchair he had designed for himself was added to the Roosevelt Memorial in Washington, D.C. The statue inspires thousands of people with disabilities who visit the site annually. However, debate continues over whether a person with Roosevelt's physical disabilities could be elected president today—he might be rejected by a society that places a high value on fitness or elected by a society that values inclusion.

INTRODUCE & ENGAGE

PREVIEW USING VISUALS

Direct students' attention to the photograph in the lesson, and call on a volunteer to read the caption aloud. **ASK:** What details in the photo support the statement that Roosevelt was able to connect with ordinary Americans? *(Possible responses: Roosevelt is giving a firm handshake to a coal miner and looking him in the eye. The presence of a child on Roosevelt's lap conveys the message that he respects families and understands the issues facing everyday people.)*

TEACH

GUIDED DISCUSSION

1. **Make Connections** How was Eleanor Roosevelt able to influence Franklin Roosevelt's political career within the context in which his candidacy for president unfolded? *(Possible response: Eleanor influenced FDR's opinions about women's rights and labor, which strengthened his voter support. She also encouraged him to continue his political career in spite of his physical disability.)*

2. **Make Predictions** How might events that occurred between Roosevelt's election and inauguration have taken a different direction if the 20th Amendment had been ratified before FDR was elected? *(Possible response: If the 20th Amendment had been ratified sooner, Roosevelt would have taken office in January instead of in March. Earlier enactment of his policies might have lessened the financial crisis that deepened in early 1933.)*

ANALYZE PRIMARY SOURCES

Direct students to look up and read FDR's entire first Inaugural Address. Challenge them to identify the sentence of the address in which Roosevelt offers his justification for seeking to expand presidential power. *("I shall ask the Congress for the one remaining instrument to meet the crisis—broad Executive power to wage a war against the emergency, as great as the power that would be given to me if we were in fact invaded by a foreign foe.")* Copy the quotation on the board. As students read about Roosevelt's presidency in this chapter, ask them to identify ways in which executive power increased.

ACTIVE OPTIONS

On Your Feet: Inside-Outside Circle Arrange students in two concentric circles facing each other. Direct students in the outside circle to interview students in the inside circle about whether they would have voted for Franklin Roosevelt in 1932 and why or why not. Students in the inside circle should justify their answer based on evidence from the lesson. At your signal, students in the outside circle should rotate to create new partnerships. Reverse roles and have students in the inside circle conduct the interviews. At the end of the exercise, ask students to summarize reasons for and against voting for Roosevelt.

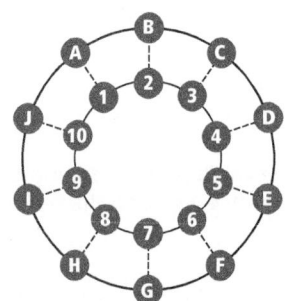

NG Learning Framework: Create a Collage

ATTITUDE Curiosity

SKILL Collaboration

Organize students in small groups and assign or let each group choose a word to describe Franklin Roosevelt. Then instruct groups to research images of Roosevelt that portray that characteristic. Direct each group to create a collage for display in the classroom. Provide time for groups to share and discuss their work.

DIFFERENTIATE

STRIVING READERS

Use Context Clues Model how to use context clues to unlock the meaning of a new word. Then ask students to write the sentences containing the terms *polio, lame duck,* and *landslide* on a piece of paper. Instruct students to underline the context clue or textual definition that provides the meaning of each word. Then have students write an original sentence using the word. Encourage students to look for context clues whenever they encounter an unfamiliar word.

GIFTED & TALENTED

Illustrate a Quotation Direct students' attention to the Primary Source feature. Challenge students to visually interpret the famous last phrase, "the only thing we have to fear is fear itself." They could create a painting, drawing, collage, or meme that incorporates the phrase. Invite students to present their work to the class.

See the Chapter Planner for more strategies for differentiation.

HISTORICAL THINKING

ANSWERS

1. Roosevelt had experience in government, a positive attitude, and the ability to relate to people from diverse backgrounds.

2. Serving as a New York state senator provided experience in running for elected office. Serving as assistant secretary of the Navy provided an understanding of the military and experience in federal government.

3. The press respected Roosevelt's desire to project a strong image, and Americans needed to focus on FDR's strengths rather than his weaknesses.

4. Roosevelt was trying to reassure people that they could solve their problems if they had the courage to overcome their fears.

AN ACTIVIST GOVERNMENT

As the old saying goes, sometimes you have to spend money to make money. Roosevelt and his advisors believed that the best way to move the United States toward economic recovery was to spend government money, so they emptied the nation's wallet and invested in the thousands of desperate Americans in need of work.

In the 1930s, President Roosevelt was photographed as he delivered one of his 30 fireside chats. He began the practice 8 days after his inauguration in 1933 and continued it until 1944.

THE FIRST HUNDRED DAYS

As soon as Roosevelt stepped into the White House, things began to change. Roosevelt asked several university professors, whom journalists called the "**brain trust**," to offer ideas on how to fix the still-floundering economy. With their help, he generated within his first few months in office 15 effective laws that fortified the nation's economy. This time of frenzied lawmaking was later dubbed the **First Hundred Days**.

The brain trust advised Roosevelt to proclaim a holiday for all the country's banks to prevent people from withdrawing their money in a panic. The **bank holiday**, which Roosevelt declared on March 6, 1933, stopped all banking operations nationwide. Roosevelt also called Congress back into a special session, so he could present laws designed to restore public confidence in the nation's banking industry. Americans were understandably anxious about the financial industry after many of them had lost their money when numerous banks closed throughout the nation. With both the House and the Senate now under firm Democratic control, Roosevelt had little trouble getting these bills passed.

The brain trust based their advice on theories developed by **John Maynard Keynes**, a leading British economist.

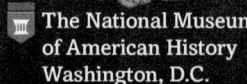

The National Museum of American History Washington, D.C.

Instead of sitting before a fire for his chats, President Roosevelt sat before an array of microphones, including the first one used for the National Broadcasting Company (NBC). Carleton Smith, who set up the RCA type 50-A microphone for NBC and introduced the radio broadcasts, donated it to the museum.

Years before, Keynes had proposed that the best way for a government to jump-start an economy was to invest all of its money back into the country, a strategy he called "priming the pump." The solution was risky because it created a **deficit**, or negative balance, in the national treasury. Basically, the idea was to print more money and give it to individual citizens, who would then stimulate the economy by spending it. The Federal Reserve Bank soon began printing more money. The brain trust also suggested a plan to regulate the banks. They called for the federal inspection of all banks, after which the banks with cash on hand would be allowed to reopen. The remaining banks would be reorganized, if possible, or closed for good.

Roosevelt then decided to address America's concerns about the banking industry directly. On March 12, 1933, he gave his first **fireside chat**, a radio broadcast that became a tradition throughout the rest of his presidency. More than 60 million Americans tuned in to listen. In the days that followed, as the stronger banks reopened, people began depositing money again. By the end of March, almost $1 billion had been returned to bank vaults. The banking crisis was over.

Roosevelt's strategy revealed his pragmatism, or practicality, and his belief in an activist government. Instead of taking a radical approach—giving the government control of all the nation's banks, for example—he demonstrated that his primary mission was to preserve capitalism. Roosevelt was willing to experiment with a wide array of ideas to save capitalism from its own excesses.

The special session of Congress continued meeting. In that time, the president established government agencies with the aim of creating jobs. One such agency was the **Civilian Conservation Corps (CCC)**, which combined the president's enthusiasm for conservation with his belief in national service. The corps provided outdoor jobs to young men ages 17 to 24. They worked on soil-erosion and flood-control projects and developed many state parks by paving roads, building cabins, and planting trees. Popular and successful, the CCC eased unemployment, lowered urban crime rates, and helped countless families.

Roosevelt chose a social worker and one of his closest advisors, **Harry Hopkins**, to help him manage the **New Deal**, a group of laws, agencies, and programs designed to combat the economic crisis. They coined the name of their plan from Theodore Roosevelt's Square Deal, and they hoped it would be as successful.

SUPPORT FOR RURAL AREAS

Roosevelt wanted to help all Americans through the Depression, including those who lived in rural areas. His New Deal featured programs designed to help poor farming families. Two major programs were in Tennessee and California.

The Tennessee River drained land in seven states. The 4 million people who lived there were some of the country's poorest farmers. Their communities were isolated and lacked doctors, proper schools, electricity, and paved roads. In May 1933, Roosevelt established a federal agency called the **Tennessee Valley Authority (TVA)** to construct dams and power plants along the river and its tributaries. Within a decade, 16 dams and hydroelectric plants operated along the river, providing thousands of jobs and bringing electrical power to residents.

In California, the New Deal funded the **Central Valley Project (CVP)**, a plan to irrigate the arid San Joaquin Valley, a portion of the state's vast Central Valley. Like the TVA, the CVP involved the construction of dams to create reservoirs for storing and delivering water.

Throughout the country, most farmers' incomes had been falling since the 1920s. In 1932, for instance,

PLAN: 4-PAGE LESSON

OBJECTIVE

Explain how Roosevelt's policies to improve the national economy expanded the role of the federal government.

CRITICAL THINKING SKILLS FOR LESSON 1.2

• Analyze Cause and Effect

• Draw Conclusions

• Determine Chronology

• Form and Support Opinions

• Make Connections

• Analyze Primary Sources

HISTORICAL THINKING FOR CHAPTER 20

In what ways were Franklin Roosevelt's policies during the Great Depression groundbreaking? Roosevelt's attempts to combat the economic crisis expanded the role of the federal government. Lesson 1.2 discusses how New Deal policies affected the economy and American life.

BACKGROUND FOR THE TEACHER

In a world with almost instantaneous video and interactive global communication, it is difficult to imagine that in the 1930s, radios—owned by almost 90 percent of American households—were an essential source of information. Franklin Roosevelt was the first president to harness the power of mass communication through radio broadcasts. His fireside chats, most of which were broadcast live from the Diplomatic Reception Room in the White House, created a direct, personal connection between the president and the listeners. Roosevelt inspired and reassured Americans during the Great Depression and World War II. His mastery of the microphone gave listeners the impression of a friendly conversation happening in their own living room.

FINANCIAL LITERACY

To extend their knowledge and understanding about the concepts in this lesson, refer students to the Financial Literacy handbook.

INTRODUCE & ENGAGE

LISTEN TO A FIRESIDE CHAT

Play a recording of Roosevelt's first fireside chat, which was about the banking crisis. Draw a T-Chart on the board like the one shown here. Ask for students' reactions to the message and the way in which the president delivered it. Prompt students to identify specific words and phrases that stood out to them in the president's speech, and record them in the first column. Then prompt students to describe the tone and style of the president's delivery, and record their responses in the second column. Discuss how Roosevelt used content and style in this broadcast to gain the support and confidence of the American people.

Words and Phrases	Tone and Style

TEACH

GUIDED DISCUSSION

1. **Determine Chronology** What does the order in which Roosevelt established programs in the first months of his presidency reveal about his priorities? *(Possible response: He first addressed the financial crisis with a bank holiday because he saw it as the most urgent problem. Then he began establishing programs to put people to work and improve their lives.)*

2. **Draw Conclusions** What does Roosevelt's collaboration with a "brain trust" indicate about his leadership? *(Possible responses: Roosevelt recognized the value of seeking input from experts to make decisions about the nation's economy. Roosevelt did not assume that he could solve the nation's economic problems on his own but instead sought guidance from others.)*

MORE INFORMATION

"Priming the Pump" The phrase used by John Maynard Keynes to describe his strategy for jump-starting an economy is based on the mechanics of pumps used to extract water from outdoor wells. A water pump that has run out of pressure will stop working and needs to have some water flushed back into it and forced through it in order to create enough pressure to begin pumping again. Share this information with students. **ASK:** How does Keynes's process for jump-starting an economy mirror the mechanics of a water pump? *(The economy is like a water pump that has run out of pressure. It needs a little bit of money to flow through it in order to regulate it enough to start a cash flow. In this instance, money is the water flowing through the pump.)*

🏛 VIRTUAL MUSEUM VISIT

Located in the nation's capital, the National Museum of American History is part of the Smithsonian Institution. Its vast collections include such diverse artifacts as the flag that inspired the national anthem and the ruby slippers from the movie *The Wizard of Oz*. In addition to information about the fireside chat microphone, the museum's searchable website provides links to resources about the New Deal, the Roosevelt family, and FDR's struggle with the effects of polio.

DIFFERENTIATE

ENGLISH LANGUAGE LEARNERS

Make Word Cards As they read the lesson, prompt students at the **Expanding** level to keep a list of any words they find that are unfamiliar or difficult, such as *generated, frenzied, pragmatism,* and *practicality*. Direct students to look up each word in a dictionary, and encourage them to make word cards to help them understand and remember the word for future use. They should write the word on one side of a card. On the other side, they should define the word and spell it phonetically. Encourage them to include a cognate or a synonym in their home language.

PRE-AP

Write About Camp Life Challenge students to investigate library or online sources, both primary and secondary, about life in a Civilian Conservation Corps camp. Suggest students look for information regarding daily routines at work and in camp, the kinds of work performed, leisure and entertainment activities, and attitudes toward the CCC program and camp life. Tell students to use what they discover to help them imagine themselves living and working in a CCC camp. Prompt them to write a letter home telling a friend or family member about their experiences in the CCC.

See the Chapter Planner for more strategies for differentiation.

The Southern Tenant Farmers' Union began during a meeting of 27 African-American and white sharecroppers held in a schoolhouse in eastern Arkansas in 1934. One man spoke up to convince the white farmers to join an integrated union.

We live under the same sun, eat the same food, wear the same kind of clothing, work on the same land, raise the same crop for the same landlord who oppresses and cheats us both. For a long time now [we] have been fighting each other and both of us has been getting whipped all the time. We don't have nothing against one another but we got plenty against the landlord.

—from a speech by African-American tenant farmer Isaac Shaw, given at an Arkansas schoolhouse, 1934

farmers were earning less than one-third of their 1929 incomes, even though the introduction of tractors and high-grade fertilizer allowed farms to produce more crops than ever.

The **Agricultural Adjustment Act (AAA)** was the New Deal's solution to declining farm incomes. Passed in 1933, the act limited the quantity of such staple crops as cotton, wheat, and corn that farmers could grow. It also paid farmers who voluntarily stopped growing crops on some of their land. The AAA was based on a theory called **planned scarcity**, in which the government lowers the supplies of certain products in order to create a high demand for them and raise their prices. The government also offered generous loans to farmers who stored their crop surpluses in government warehouses. Roosevelt funded the AAA by taxing businesses that processed farm goods, such as flour millers, cotton gin operators, and meatpackers. The plan worked. Within a year, more than 3 million farmers had signed individual contracts with the AAA. Farm incomes shot up almost 60 percent between 1932 and 1935.

In 1941, workers completed the construction of a turbine to generate hydroelectric power from water falling over the Cherokee Dam in Tennessee. The Cherokee Dam was one of 16 dams the TVA built between 1933 and 1943.

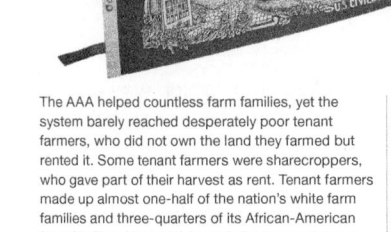

In the 1930s, members of the Civilian Conservation Corps could show their pride in the work they did for the CCC by purchasing and displaying items like this decorative pennant.

The AAA helped countless farm families, yet the system barely reached desperately poor tenant farmers, who did not own the land they farmed but rented it. Some tenant farmers were sharecroppers, who gave part of their harvest as rent. Tenant farmers made up almost one-half of the nation's white farm families and three-quarters of its African-American farm families. Under AAA regulations, tenants were supposed to get a fair share of the government payments, but this rarely occurred. Few landlords obeyed the rules, and some evicted their tenants in order to take even more land out of production.

In response, sharecroppers and other tenant farmers formed their own organization, the **Southern Tenant Farmers' Union**, to fight for their rights. But those who joined the union were evicted from their homes, ignored by potential employers, and denied credit at banks and stores. The union's organizers were beaten and jailed, and the union soon collapsed.

NATIONAL INDUSTRIAL RECOVERY ACT

The president's brain trust soon expanded to include such advisors as Eleanor Roosevelt and Harry Hopkins. The group experimented with centralized **economic planning**, or management of the economy by the federal government. The chief way Roosevelt centralized economic planning was through the **National Industrial Recovery Act (NIRA)**, enacted in June 1933. The act created two federal agencies: the **Public Works Administration (PWA)** and the **National Recovery Administration (NRA)**.

The Public Works Administration provided jobs for the unemployed and also generated new orders for factories in the steel, glass, rubber, and cement industries. It worked differently from most other New Deal agencies because it helped individual contractors hire and pay their own workers, instead of having the federal government pay the employees' wages. Roosevelt selected his Secretary of the Interior, **Harold Ickes**, to run the agency. Ickes managed hundreds of PWA projects, including the construction of the Hoover Dam in Nevada, the Golden Gate Bridge in San Francisco, the

Bonneville Dam between Washington and Oregon, and the Lincoln Tunnel in New York City.

The National Recovery Administration, led by General Hugh S. Johnson, established codes of fair business practices for individual industries. The idea was to set clear expectations for both business owners and workers in order to reduce labor strikes and allow the economy to stabilize. The NRA's main goals were to abolish child labor and give labor unions the right to organize and negotiate contracts. Johnson signed up major industries first—coal, steel, oil, automakers, and shipbuilders—and then moved on to smaller businesses. By the end of 1933, the NRA had 746 agreements in place.

But the NRA ran into trouble when small business owners complained that the codes encouraged monopolies and drowned them in paperwork. Labor leaders claimed that employers ignored the wage and hour expectations and continued to discourage union activity. To cover the cost of implementing the standards, manufacturers charged more for their products. Then consumers began to blame the NRA for rising prices.

During a court case in 1935, the Supreme Court declared the NRA unconstitutional on the grounds that Congress had delegated too much legislative authority to the president. Relieved, Roosevelt confided to an aide, "It has been an awful headache. I think perhaps NRA has done all it can do."

HISTORICAL THINKING

1. **READING CHECK** Describe the ways in which President Franklin Roosevelt used his increased presidential powers in response to the Great Depression.

2. **ANALYZE CAUSE AND EFFECT** In what ways did the expanded role of the federal government affect society and the economy in the 1930s?

3. **DRAW CONCLUSIONS** How does the Southern Tenant Farmers Union symbolize the advance and retreat of organized labor?

BUILD BACKGROUND

CIVILIAN CONSERVATION CORPS

Between 1933 and 1942, the Civilian Conservation Corps (CCC) provided jobs for more than 3 million young men. These workers lived in camps that consisted of tents or barracks for sleeping, mess halls for communal meals, and a bath house. Some camps provided classrooms, a barbershop, and even a theater. The schedule was demanding and the work was hard, but workers formed friendships, received education or job training, and earned $1 a day. They sent most of their salary home to help their families. When the CCC ended, its participants had planted more than 3 billion trees and left a legacy across the nation of forests, roads, hiking trails, and structures that still exist.

CENTRAL VALLEY PROJECT

The Central Valley Project (CVP) got underway as a state project in 1919, but the Great Depression ended California's ability to finance it. During the New Deal, the federal government built the Shasta and Friant dams and continued to finance the project after World War II. The main purpose of the CVP is to provide irrigation to California's major farming regions in the Sacramento and San Joaquin valleys, but its dams and canals also supplement urban water systems. The CVP is now one of the world's largest systems for carrying water. It stores and delivers about one-third of the state's farmland irrigation, provides water to almost 1 million households, generates enough electricity for nearly 2 million people, and supports forest and wildlife habitats.

TEACH

GUIDED DISCUSSION

3. **Form and Support Opinions** Which New Deal program do you think was most successful in addressing the problems of the Great Depression? Support your opinion with evidence from the text. *(Answers will vary. Possible response: The CCC may have been the most successful, because it not only addressed Depression-related problems such as unemployment and urban crime but also left a lasting legacy in terms of conservation and enduring structures.)*

4. **Make Connections** How did New Deal safety net programs, such as the AAA, NIRA, and CCC, establish a precedent for today's welfare programs? *(Possible response: New Deal programs established the principle followed today—that the government has a responsibility to protect disadvantaged members of society.)*

ANALYZE PRIMARY SOURCES

Direct students' attention to the Primary Source feature. **ASK:** What was the basis for Shaw's argument that African-American and white sharecroppers should join forces to fight for their rights? *(People of both races suffered the same abuses from landlords.)* Discuss why Shaw's suggestion might have been considered radical for 1930s southern society. **ASK:** How did the Southern Tenant Farmers' Union foreshadow later movements, such as the United Farm Workers of America, a labor union that exists today? *(Possible response: The Southern Tenant Farmers' Union, like organizations that came after it, emphasized the importance of workers uniting to fight for their rights. The United Farm Workers of America, in particular, shared the same goal—it, too, was formed to protect the rights of people who worked on farms but did not own the land.)*

ACTIVE OPTIONS

On Your Feet: Fishbowl Organize students so that one half of the class sits in a close circle facing inward and the other half sits in a larger circle surrounding them. Instruct students in the inner circle to identify and discuss controversies over New Deal policies and the expanded role of the federal government in society and the economy. Direct students in the outer circle to listen for new information and evaluate the discussion. Then reverse roles, and challenge students in the outer circle to provide additional insights.

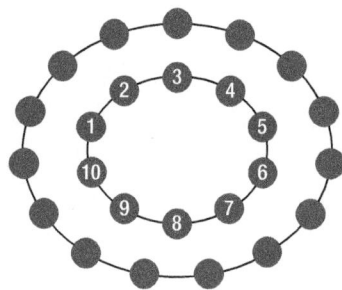

NG Learning Framework: Investigate a Local Legacy of the New Deal

ATTITUDE Curiosity

KNOWLEDGE Our Human Story

Organize students in pairs or small groups to research something in their community that was created during the New Deal through the CCC or another federal program. (You may guide students to identify appropriate artifacts, such as bridges, buildings, reservoirs, or trails in the community or in the larger region that are a legacy of the New Deal.) Direct students to tell the story of the artifact, identify the agency that worked on the project, and research individuals who worked on the project. Conclude the activity by having pairs or groups respond to the question: How is this artifact a reflection of the New Deal?

HISTORICAL THINKING

ANSWERS

1. President Roosevelt used his increased powers to give the federal government control of banks, establish agencies to create jobs, control production of certain crops, and set regulations for industries.

2. Federal policies restored public confidence in banks, reduced unemployment, and created projects that improved conservation and provided electricity to rural areas. Federal agencies centralized economic planning and improved working conditions.

3. Tenant farmers advanced organized labor by forming a union to fight for their rights. When union members suffered discrimination and violence, the union ended, a retreat for organized labor.

THE NEW DEAL

In the 1930s, the United States faced an enormous economic crisis. Many Americans, citizens and leaders alike, disagreed about how the federal government should respond to massive unemployment, business failures, labor strikes, and social unrest. It was a frightening time for the country.

Political cartoons during FDR's administration depicted Roosevelt in a variety of ways. Some painted him as strong, caring, and affable, while others characterized him as a sneaky politician, out for power. This cartoon from 1934 shows FDR surrounded by happy, dancing children who represent the various agencies established by the New Deal.

CRITICAL VIEWING Do you think this cartoon presents a positive, negative, or neutral characterization of FDR? Support your opinion with details from the cartoon.

DOCUMENT ONE

Primary Source: Speech
from Franklin D. Roosevelt's first fireside chat, March 12, 1933

In his first fireside chat to the nation, President Roosevelt outlined his plans to restore confidence in banks. He faced a daunting challenge: how to rally a downtrodden citizenry from the depths of economic despair.

CONSTRUCTED RESPONSE What challenge does FDR present Americans in place of "rumors or guesses" about the failing financial system?

After all, there is an element in the readjustment of our financial system more important than currency, more important than gold, and that is the confidence of the people themselves. Confidence and courage are the essentials of success in carrying out our plan. You people must have faith; you must not be stampeded by rumors or guesses. Let us unite in banishing fear. We have provided the machinery to restore our financial system, and it is up to you to support and make it work. It is your problem, my friends, your problem no less than it is mine. Together we cannot fail.

DOCUMENT TWO

Primary Source: Letter
from an anonymous letter to Senator Robert F. Wagner, March 7, 1934

Some Americans were wary of FDR's plans to get the country back on its feet. Many wrote letters to members of Congress and to the president himself, warning of the dire threats that the New Deal and other Roosevelt policies posed to the American social, political, and economic system.

CONSTRUCTED RESPONSE According to the author of this letter, what specific factors will lead to "disaster to all classes"?

My Dear Senator:
    It seems very apparent to me that the Administration at Washington is accelerating its pace towards socialism and communism.
    Everyone is sympathetic to the cause of creating more jobs and better wages for labor; but, a program continually promoting labor troubles, higher wages, shorter hours, and less profits for business, would seem to me to be leading us fast to a condition where the Government must more and more expand its relief activities, and will lead in the end to disaster to all classes.

DOCUMENT THREE

Primary Source: Newspaper article
from "The Roosevelt Record," *The Crisis*, November 1940

Roy Wilkins was one of the civil rights movement's most important figures. He was the editor of *The Crisis*, the official publication of the NAACP, from 1934 to 1949. From the 1940s through the 1960s, he helped organize legal efforts to overturn "separate but equal" segregation in public schools, participated in marches and protests, and served as the executive director of the NAACP.

CONSTRUCTED RESPONSE According to Wilkins, what problem could not be solved by the New Deal?

It is foolish to deny the imperfections and shortcomings of the New Deal. . . . The New Deal could not perform miracles. It could not overturn entrenched prejudices. The poor and the underprivileged, among whom are to be found most Negroes, need not look for comparison to the days of Herbert Hoover. They need only glance about them to see who is against the present administration. We are all Americans. We all seek security, justice, liberty, peace. But by what methods? And for whom?

SYNTHESIZE & WRITE

1. **REVIEW** Review what you have learned about the events surrounding the development and implementation of New Deal policies.

2. **RECALL** List the main ideas about the New Deal expressed in the three documents above.

3. **CONSTRUCT** Construct a topic sentence that answers this question: How did the federal government respond to the Great Depression, and what were the reactions to the New Deal?

4. **WRITE** Using evidence from this chapter and the documents, write an informative paragraph that supports your topic sentence in Step 3.

PLAN: 2-PAGE LESSON

OBJECTIVE
Synthesize information about the New Deal from primary source documents.

CRITICAL THINKING SKILLS FOR LESSON 1.3
- Synthesize
- Make Inferences
- Evaluate

HISTORICAL THINKING FOR CHAPTER 20
In what ways were Franklin Roosevelt's policies during the Great Depression groundbreaking? The expansion of federal power during the New Deal sparked controversy among leaders and citizens. Lesson 1.3 examines primary sources that express reactions to the New Deal.

BACKGROUND FOR THE TEACHER
Although FDR faced considerable criticism for his New Deal policies, he remained a popular president. His ability to make a personal connection with people helped him maintain public support. Roosevelt also forged good relationships with the press. He held press conferences during which reporters casually gathered around his desk in the Oval Office. Presidential approval polls, which began in 1937, rank FDR among the highest of the presidents on record, with an average approval rating of 64 percent.

INTRODUCE & ENGAGE

PREPARE FOR THE DOCUMENT-BASED QUESTION

Before students start on the activity, briefly preview the three documents. Remind students that a constructed response requires full explanations in complete sentences. Emphasize that students should use what they have learned about the New Deal in addition to the information in the documents.

TEACH

GUIDED DISCUSSION

1. **Make Inferences** Would FDR's techniques for rallying public support for his policies be as effective today as they were in the context of the 1930s? Why or why not? *(Answers will vary. Possible responses: Yes. FDR would still have a strong personality and ability to inspire confidence. No. People today have greater access to dissenting opinions and wouldn't automatically accept the word of the president.)*

2. **Synthesize** Based on the documents, what was the basis for negative reactions to the New Deal? *(Possible responses: fear that expansion of government power would infringe on individual rights; belief that relief efforts did not include all segments of the population)*

EVALUATE

After students have completed the Synthesize & Write activity, allow time for them to exchange paragraphs and read and comment on the work of their peers. Establish guidelines for comments prior to the activity so that feedback is constructive and encouraging in nature. Comments should focus on the most significant parts that address the purpose of the activity and the audience.

ACTIVE OPTION

On Your Feet: Host a DBQ Roundtable Direct students to gather in groups of four. Pose the following question: How do the effects of and the controversies arising from New Deal economic policies and the expanded role of the federal government affect society today? Instruct each student in a group to answer the question in a different way. Then ask groups to summarize their answers for the class.

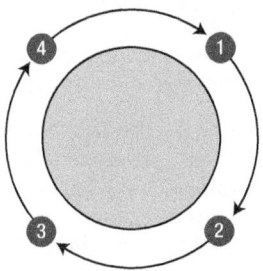

DIFFERENTIATE

INCLUSION

Use Sentence Frames Provide students with these sentence frames to help them understand the writers' main points.

- **Document 1** President Roosevelt encouraged people to have _____ *(confidence)* and _____ *(courage)* and to work together to make the financial system better.

- **Document 2** The writer objects to the New Deal policies because he thinks they will lead to _____ *(socialism)* and _____. *(communism)*

- **Document 3** Roy Wilkins acknowledges that the New Deal is not _____ *(perfect)* and that there is still much work to be done before all _____ *(Americans)* have justice, liberty, and peace.

GIFTED & TALENTED

Research and Role-Play Tell students to conduct online research in order to discover more reasons people supported or opposed the New Deal. They should find primary source documents, such as those in the lesson, as well as other information. Tell students to use what they learn to play the part of a person who is for or against the New Deal. Prompt them to create a list of points to support their position and role-play an interaction with a classmate holding the opposing view.

See the Chapter Planner for more strategies for differentiation.

SYNTHESIZE & WRITE

ANSWERS

1. Answers will vary.

2. Answers will vary. Possible response: Everyone must work together to make the New Deal work. Some people worried that government relief would negatively affect business. The New Deal could not solve the problems of racism.

3. Possible response: The federal government expanded its powers to address the problems of the Great Depression, which caused some negative reactions.

4. Students' paragraphs should include their topic sentence from Step 3 and provide several details from the documents to support the sentence.

CONSTRUCTED RESPONSE

Document 1: Possible response: FDR encourages people to have confidence and courage. He challenges them to overcome their fears and unite with him to restore the financial system.

Document 2: Possible response: The author contends that government expansion of relief activities promotes labor troubles, higher wages, and shorter hours, resulting in lower profits for business and greater expansion of government.

Document 3: Possible response: Wilkins believed the New Deal could not solve the problem of racial prejudice.

CRITICAL VIEWING Answers will vary. Students should support their opinion with details from the cartoon. Possible response: The depiction of FDR is mostly positive; the children seem happy and well-dressed, and they are looking up at him with respect.

THE SECOND NEW DEAL

In 2007, the American economy almost collapsed, and more than 8 million people lost their jobs as a result. Double that number and you have some idea of the need that overwhelmed the country during the Great Depression.

JOBS, JOBS, JOBS

The progress made by Roosevelt's administration in its first hundred days was enough for Roosevelt to earn the American voters' loyalty. The economy was rebounding, and things were looking up. But the Roosevelt administration knew that too many citizens were still dealing with the persistence of poverty. When the Democrats gained even more seats in the House and Senate after the midterm elections of 1934, Roosevelt was confident Congress would pass more relief legislation. He presented Congress with a new set of reforms, the **Second New Deal**.

Despite the progress, millions of Americans remained unemployed. Roosevelt decided once again to rely on his pragmatic and activist government to address this problem. His administration launched the **Works Progress Administration (WPA)** in 1935, which provided jobs on small construction projects in communities around the country. WPA regional development projects ranged from building new schools, bridges, and landing fields for airplanes to improving more than 650,000 miles of roads. The WPA also funded projects that employed writers, teachers, musicians, and artists. Most of the WPA jobs were temporary and relatively low-paying, so as not to compete directly with private businesses. Nonetheless, the WPA, headed by Harry Hopkins, employed more than a quarter of the entire United States' workforce by 1936.

A separate division of the WPA, inspired by Eleanor Roosevelt, provided part-time jobs specifically for high school and college students. The agency, called the **National Youth Administration (NYA)**, employed several million young people.

SOCIAL SECURITY

In addition to promoting job opportunities, Secretary of Labor **Frances Perkins** urged the government to provide for those who could not work. The war years had led Americans to value independence, hard work, and sacrifice for the sake of their country. People were expected to be financially responsible for themselves. But the Depression changed that attitude. The crash proved that even the hardest workers could face financial setbacks created by economic forces over which they had no control.

In response to Perkins's request, Roosevelt proposed the **Social Security Act**, a law that would provide old-age insurance, unemployment insurance, and financial aid to the disabled and others in need. The program established a **pension fund**, or a pool of money used to pay people a small, established income after they retire. The Social Security Act was passed in 1935 and was funded by taxes paid by both employees and employers beginning in 1937.

Although the Social Security Act provided many benefits, it had some flaws and provoked controversies. It excluded millions of people, including the self-employed, farmers, and domestic workers. Benefits were not high—between $20 and $30 a month—but they were better than what those in need had been receiving: nothing. Some retired and disabled people were literally starving.

THE FASCIST CHALLENGE

While President Roosevelt labored to right the economic ship at home, some other countries were reacting to the Great Depression in very different, and in some cases, disturbing ways.

Artists working for the Works Progress Administration Federal Art Project designed posters that publicized WPA initiatives in such areas as education, recreation, safety, and health. WPA artists created the posters shown above between 1936 and 1941.

PLAN: 4-PAGE LESSON

OBJECTIVE

Explain how the continuing economic problems in the United States and the rise of dictators in Europe affected Roosevelt's second New Deal.

CRITICAL THINKING SKILLS FOR LESSON 2.1

- Draw Conclusions
- Make Generalizations
- Compare and Contrast
- Evaluate
- Form and Support Opinions
- Analyze Visuals
- Make Inferences
- Summarize
- Synthesize

HISTORICAL THINKING FOR CHAPTER 20

In what ways were Franklin Roosevelt's policies during the Great Depression groundbreaking? Roosevelt expanded federal relief programs to provide for the poor and the unemployed. Lesson 2.1 explores support for and opposition to these programs.

BACKGROUND FOR THE TEACHER

Many WPA projects became targets for New Deal critics. At construction sites, clearly marked with the WPA logo, groups of workers did most of the backbreaking labor by hand. However, the sight of WPA workers leaning on their shovels to rest led some critics to dub the program "We Poke Along."

Federal One—the WPA's arts division—came under criticism for "make-work" projects. In the 1930s, however, the Great Depression and the popularity of phonographs, radio, and movies had put thousands of performers out of work. The Federal Theater Project employed playwrights and actors who presented shows to audiences who had never experienced live theater. The Federal Music Project sponsored local orchestras, bands, and choral groups and gave music classes in neighborhoods.

HISTORY NOTEBOOK

Encourage students to complete the American Gallery page for Chapter 20 in their History Notebooks as they read.

INTRODUCE & ENGAGE

CONSIDER OPPOSING VIEWPOINTS

Direct students' attention to the 1936 election map and data. **ASK:** After a quick glance at this map, how would you summarize the results of the election? *(Possible responses: FDR won by a landslide; only a small section of the country in the Northeast did not vote for FDR.)* **ASK:** What do these results indicate about voters' reactions to the New Deal? *(They suggest overwhelming support, but they might also indicate that the New Deal benefited people in some parts of the country more than others.)* Tell students that in this lesson they will learn about opposition to Roosevelt's policies. Provide them with a T-Chart like the one shown and instruct them to track support and opposition to the New Deal as they read the lesson.

Support	Opposition

TEACH

GUIDED DISCUSSION

1. **Evaluate** Was establishing the WPA an effective step in combating the economic crisis of the Great Depression? Why or why not? *(Answers will vary. Possible responses: yes, because it put people to work and paid them a small salary, and it provided improvements throughout the country; no, because jobs were temporary and when they ended, people were still unemployed)*

2. **Form and Support Opinions** At the time the Social Security Act was passed, did its benefits outweigh its flaws? Explain your answer. *(Answers will vary. Possible responses: yes, because it helped retired people and others in need—while it didn't offer them much money, it was more than they were getting before; no, because it excluded many groups in society, such as farmers and people who were self-employed, and the payments were not enough to meet people's needs.)*

ANALYZE VISUALS

Ask students to look at the WPA posters and read the caption. **ASK:** What was the government's purpose for commissioning these posters? *(to advertise events and promote positive behaviors; to provide jobs for unemployed artists)* **ASK:** Would the posters be as effective today as they were in the context of the time in which they were created? *(Possible responses: Yes, the messages they convey are timeless. No, people today are used to messages that incorporate action and sound.)*

As an extension to this activity, ask students to evaluate the merit of hiring artists to produce art at a time when money is tight—when that money could instead be spent to build roads or other infrastructure. Prompt students to consider the example of the WPA posters not only in the context of the time in which they were made, but also in the context of Americans today studying the artifacts of the Great Depression.

DIFFERENTIATE

ENGLISH LANGUAGE LEARNERS

Summarize Lesson 2.1 has four sections. Place students of **All Proficiencies** in pairs, and assign each pair a section. Instruct them to read the section together and then write a few sentences to summarize it. When all pairs are finished, call on them to read their summaries aloud in the order in which the material appears to provide an overview of the entire lesson.

Provide the following sentence frames to help students at each proficiency level write an effective summary.

- **Emerging:** This section is about _____. First, _____. Then, _____. At the end _____.

- **Expanding:** This section is about _____ and _____. First, _____ and then _____. Finally, _____.

- **Bridging:** The section begins by _____. It then _____ and concludes by _____. To summarize, the paragraph provides information about _____.

GIFTED & TALENTED

Create a Poster Prompt students to create a public service announcement in the style of the WPA posters of the 1930s. Point out that public service announcements are short messages conveyed in a simple yet powerful way. Tell students that their target audience is their peers, and the message should be related to an issue of concern in the school or community. Tell students to verify any facts they use and to tightly focus their message and tie it to a strong visual. Encourage students to share their posters with the class and answer any questions.

See the Chapter Planner for more strategies for differentiation.

The changing face of European politics in the 1930s would challenge the United States' foreign policy as brutal authoritarian leaders emerged in several nations, particularly in Germany and Italy.

As you have read, Benito Mussolini had risen to power in the 1920s, instituting a fascist government in Italy that was based on extreme nationalism and militarism. A few years later, **Adolf Hitler** began his rise to power in Germany when he helped form the National Socialist German Workers Party. Also known as the **Nazi Party**, this organization was one of the many extremist groups that developed after World War I. Hitler modeled himself, to some degree, on Mussolini. Both were fascist dictators who established **totalitarian** regimes, in which the government relies on force to exert complete control over a country. Hitler's philosophy of **National Socialism** promoted the superiority of Germany and the German people, rejected communism, and carried anti-Semitism—hatred of Jewish people—to extreme levels. Both Hitler and Mussolini wanted to spread their power, which stirred fears of conflict in Europe and beyond.

Some leaders with fascist tendencies also gained popularity in the United States. **Huey P. Long**, the fiery governor of Louisiana, was a champion of the poor but acted ruthlessly in gaining power in his state. He abolished local government and took control of job appointments in education, police, and fire departments throughout the state. He also controlled the state militia, the judiciary, and the election system. In 1936, shortly after he announced that he would run for the presidency, he was assassinated in Baton Rouge, Louisiana.

Father Charles E. Coughlin, a Roman Catholic priest and an influential radio host from Michigan, also gained a loyal following by championing the poor. However, he began expressing anti-democratic and anti-Semitic views, which resulted in the Catholic Church ordering him to stop broadcasting in 1942. He went on to help form a new political group called the Union Party. Both Long and Coughlin were considered **populists**, or politicians who claim to represent the concerns of ordinary people.

PRIMARY SOURCE

Out of our first century of national life we evolved the ethical principle that it was not right or just that an honest and industrious man should live and die in misery. He was entitled to some degree of sympathy and security. Our conscience declared against the honest workman's becoming a pauper, but our eyes told us that he very often did.

—from *People at Work*, by Frances Perkins, 1934

Midway into the construction of the Golden Gate Bridge in California, Frances Perkins (center) came to observe the work in March 1935.

The 1936 Election

Franklin D. Roosevelt, Democrat	
Electoral Vote:	523 votes, 98.5%
Popular Vote:	27,750,866 votes, 60.8%

Alfred M. Landon, Republican	
Electoral Vote:	8 votes, 1.5%
Popular Vote:	16,679,683 votes, 36.5%

Union and Other Parties	
Popular Vote:	1,216,442 votes, 2.7%

THE 1936 ELECTION

As the 1936 election approached, FDR had reason to be concerned about his political future. Although personal income and industrial production had risen dramatically, the country's unemployment rate was still very high. Some of his fellow Democrats argued that he needed to do more to ease Americans' suffering. In addition, more than 80 percent of the nation's newspapers and most of the business community remained loyal to the Republican Party, which meant that Roosevelt's major presidential opponent could count on strong editorial and financial support.

A coalition, or alliance, of Republican and Democratic opponents of the New Deal had formed an organization in 1934 called the **American Liberty League**. Members of the League claimed that some New Deal programs were unconstitutional because they gave increased power to the president to regulate the economy rather than to the judicial and legislative branches. League members were intent on defeating Roosevelt in the 1936 election.

But the Democrats had hope. Roosevelt's policies appealed to workers, farmers, African Americans, southern whites, and educated northerners. Many members of such religious groups as Catholics and Jews also backed the New Deal. This coalition had a good chance of keeping FDR in the White House.

The Republicans chose Kansas governor Alfred M. Landon to head their ticket, and Frank Knox, a Chicago publisher, as the vice presidential nominee. Landon, a political moderate, promised "fewer radio talks, fewer experiments, and a lot more common sense." However, Landon lacked the compassion and confidence that made Roosevelt so popular with many Americans.

Once again, Roosevelt faced presidential challenges from the Communist and Socialist parties. Both ran spirited campaigns in 1936, demanding more federal aid for the poor. Roosevelt was also opposed by the newly formed Union Party, which nominated William "Liberty Bill" Lemke, an obscure North Dakota congressman, as its presidential candidate.

Roosevelt's strategy in the 1936 election was to present himself as a champion of the common people, as opposed to the wealthy. In his final campaign speech in New York, he declared that the wealthy had "met their match" in the Roosevelt administration. If the rich and powerful hated him for that, he thundered, "I welcome their hatred."

On November 3, 1936, FDR crushed his opponents in the most one-sided election in over a century. The final totals showed Roosevelt with 27,750,866 popular votes, Landon with 16,679,683, and Lemke with about 890,000. The Socialist and Communist parties together won less than 270,000 votes. Roosevelt won every state except Maine and Vermont, securing 98.5 percent of the electoral vote. The Democratic Party added 9 seats each to its already huge majorities in the two houses of Congress.

HISTORICAL THINKING

1. **READING CHECK** In what ways did the Second New Deal improve people's lives?

2. **DRAW CONCLUSIONS** Why might people be drawn to fascist or ruthless leaders who promote extreme nationalism during difficult economic times?

3. **MAKE GENERALIZATIONS** What segments of American society did the Second New Deal target?

4. **COMPARE AND CONTRAST** How were Roosevelt's New Deal policies criticized by both Democrats and and Republicans?

BUILD BACKGROUND

FEDERAL WRITERS' PROJECT

The WPA Federal Writers' Project employed more than 6,000 writers and editors, including some of America's greatest authors, such as John Cheever, Saul Bellow, Ralph Ellison, Zora Neale Hurston, and Studs Terkel. They received only a meager salary, but these writers gained experience that influenced their later works. The Federal Writers' Project produced more than a thousand documents, including state guides, American folklore, and first-person narratives that chronicle the daily lives, feelings, and diversity of ordinary Americans. Compiled by skillful writers and editors, the works of the Federal Writers' Project provide insights into a significant period of American history.

FRANCES PERKINS

Many have called Frances Perkins "the woman behind the New Deal." Her education at Mount Holyoke and her background in public service qualified her to become the first woman cabinet member and the longest-serving secretary of labor. But Perkins called the day she witnessed the Triangle Waist Company factory fire, in which 146 workers died, the "day the New Deal was born." Perkins committed to improving working conditions and making workplaces safe. In spite of the challenge of working in a male-dominated administration, Perkins managed to achieve many of her goals. Her efforts helped abolish child labor, establish the minimum wage, and create Social Security.

TEACH

GUIDED DISCUSSION

3. Make Inferences How might the political trend of the rise of totalitarian regimes in Europe have affected Roosevelt's domestic policies? *(Possible responses: Foreign policy concerns could have interfered with Roosevelt's ability to focus on the economic crisis at home. Some U.S. leaders were influenced by fascist ideas and promoted anti-democratic policies.)*

4. Summarize How did the context of the 1936 election contribute to FDR's huge win in spite of opposition from other political parties? *(Possible response: FDR's policies had improved life for many, and he had the support of the common people whose causes he championed.)*

SYNTHESIZE

Prompt students to use the text and a brief online search to understand the views of New Deal opponents Huey P. Long, Father Charles E. Coughlin, and the American Liberty League. Instruct them to use a chart like the one shown to synthesize information and summarize why each person or group was opposed to the New Deal.

New Deal Opponent	Viewpoint

ACTIVE OPTIONS

 **Visual Arts of the New Deal** Invite students to explore the American Gallery. Have them select one of the images and do additional research to learn more about it. Ask questions that will inspire additional inquiry about the chosen gallery image, such as: What is the subject of the mural? What is the artist's background? How does the subject or artist relate to this chapter? What else would you like to know about the mural?

NG Learning Framework: Investigate the Persistence of Poverty

ATTITUDE Responsibility

KNOWLEDGE Our Human Story

Arrange students in small groups to research poverty in the United States today and identify federal welfare programs that address economic problems. Ask them to determine whether the historical events of New Deal policies and the expanded role of the federal government continue to influence trends in attitudes and policies regarding poverty today. Instruct each group to decide on an appropriate medium through which to share its findings with the class.

HISTORICAL THINKING

ANSWERS

1. The Second New Deal provided more jobs and established a safety net called Social Security to provide for people in need.

2. Possible response: People who are desperate and afraid may be drawn to strong leaders who take control of the situation and put the needs of their own people over those of people in other countries.

3. Programs of the Second New Deal targeted the unemployed—especially youth, writers, teachers, musicians, and artists—as well as people who were poor or disabled.

4. Roosevelt's Republican and Democratic opponents formed a coalition to challenge the constitutionality of New Deal programs, arguing that the executive branch of government had taken over some powers at the expense of the judicial and legislative branches. Additionally, other critics argued that more federal aid should be given to the poor.

MILWAUKEE PUBLIC MUSEUM
MILWAUKEE, WISCONSIN

The Milwaukee Public Museum is the largest natural and human history museum in the state of Wisconsin, and one of the largest in the Midwest. Chartered in 1882, its collection contains more than 4 million objects, and its exhibits feature world cultures, life-size dioramas, walk-through villages, dinosaurs, a rain forest, and a live butterfly garden.

The museum's WPA Milwaukee Handicraft Project collection (MHP) contains artifacts and photographs that tell the story of one of the first national welfare programs. During the Great Depression, it employed more than 5,000 women and minorities in Milwaukee and broke gender and color barriers, while bringing fame to the city.

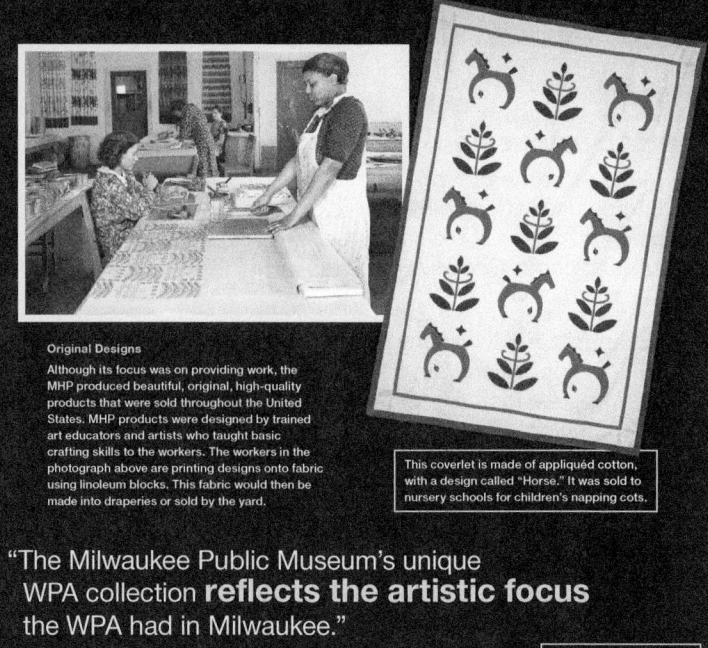

Original Designs

Although its focus was on providing work, the MHP produced beautiful, original, high-quality products that were sold throughout the United States. MHP products were designed by trained art educators and artists who taught basic crafting skills to the workers. The workers in the photograph above are printing designs onto fabric using linoleum blocks. This fabric would then be made into draperies or sold by the yard.

This coverlet is made of appliquéd cotton, with a design called "Horse." It was sold to nursery schools for children's napping cots.

Integrated Workforce

Workers on the Milwaukee Handicraft Project were paid by the federal government to create handmade goods such as toys, dolls, furniture, coverlets, and books. The products were then sold to public institutions such as schools, for the cost of the materials alone. As shown in the photo above, the MHP was racially integrated while most WPA projects were segregated. The MHP also hired women, though most WPA projects were structured to provide work for the male head of a household.

This giraffe pull-toy, which was cut from wood and painted by project workers, was sold to schools.

"The Milwaukee Public Museum's unique WPA collection **reflects the artistic focus** the WPA had in Milwaukee."

—Ellen Censky
Senior Vice President

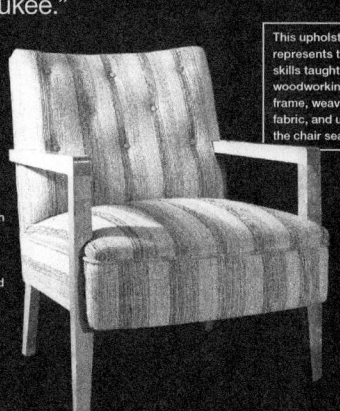

This upholstered chair represents the variety of skills taught on the MHP: woodworking for the frame, weaving for the fabric, and upholstery for the chair seat and back.

Skills Training

Many of the female workers who came to the MHP had never worked outside of their homes. The impact of the Great Depression caused many women to seek jobs for the first time to help support their families. The MHP trained the women to produce handicrafts that gave them skills they could apply to work outside of the WPA, sewing as seamstresses, repairing books, and working in factories.

PLAN: 2-PAGE LESSON

OBJECTIVE

Understand the impact of New Deal programs on the people of Milwaukee, Wisconsin.

CRITICAL THINKING SKILLS FOR LESSON 2.2

• Analyze Visuals

• Make Connections

• Describe

• Make Inferences

HISTORICAL THINKING FOR CHAPTER 20

In what ways were Franklin Roosevelt's policies during the Great Depression groundbreaking? Under Roosevelt, New Deal policies expanded the role of government in people's lives. Lesson 2.2 explores the impact of one of these policies—the WPA—on the people of Milwaukee, Wisconsin.

BACKGROUND FOR THE TEACHER

Employees of the Milwaukee Handicraft Project (MHP) often started their jobs with few relevant skills. The workers were also a diverse mixture—encompassing a range of nationalities, ages, and education levels. What they had in common, though, was a desperate need for employment. To ensure quality, workers were matched with jobs that suited their skills. For example, workers with learning disabilities performed very simple tasks, such as braiding strings for pull toys. As production picked up, a handful of older men who had been considered unemployable worked for the program as carpenters, building looms and cabinets. In the end, the MHP formed 11 production units—including areas such as rug- and doll-making, screen-printing, and bookbinding.

HISTORY NOTEBOOK

Encourage students to complete the Curating History page for Chapter 20 in their History Notebooks as they read.

INTRODUCE & ENGAGE

EXPLORE HISTORY USING PHOTOGRAPHS

Remind students that during the Great Depression, New Deal policies attempted to alleviate suffering through programs that found employment for people. Direct students' attention to the two black-and-white photographs shown in the lesson. **ASK:** What can you infer about the types of people employed and the kinds of work done in the New Deal program shown in these photographs? *(Answers will vary. Possible response: The photos show both African-American and white women employed in jobs that seem to involve making toys and working with fabric.)* Tell students that in this lesson they will explore one New Deal program—the Milwaukee Handicraft Project—through studying artifacts.

TEACH

GUIDED DISCUSSION

1. **Describe** How did the MHP differ from other WPA programs? *(Most WPA programs were designed to provide work for male heads of households and were segregated. The MHP was racially integrated and employed women.)*

2. **Make Inferences** Looking at the photographs of the pull toy, coverlet, and chair, what can you infer about the education and skills needed by the workers? *(Answers will vary. Possible response: Workers needed certain skills, such as woodworking, painting, weaving, or sewing—which they may have started out with or learned on the job—and they had to be able to follow instructions and patterns. However, there is no evidence that any specific level of education was required, and people could likely perform these jobs without needing to be able to read.)*

CURATING HISTORY

The Milwaukee Public Museum's website is a useful resource for learning more about the Milwaukee Handicraft Project. Access the website and guide students to the Milwaukee Handicraft Project online collection. Read the introduction of the accompanying essay with the class. Then organize students into three "expert" groups. Assign each group one of the three sections of the essay and have them summarize the main ideas. Then ask the members of each group to count off using the letters A, B, and C. Regroup students into three new groups so that each new group has at least one member from each expert group. Direct students in the new group to take turns sharing their summaries.

ACTIVE OPTION

On Your Feet: Sort the Artifacts Arrange students in teams of four or five to examine the museum's collection of photographs that accompany the essay about the MHP. Instruct students to use the details they see on the website and in the lesson to complete a Concept Cluster, sorting the MHP artifacts into categories. When the teams are finished, they can share their Concept Clusters with the class and note the details that most of the teams identified.

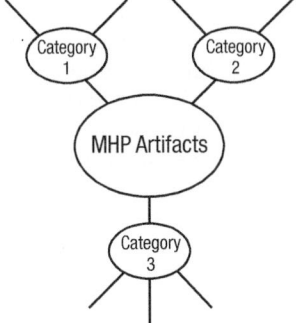

DIFFERENTIATE

INCLUSION

Describe Details in Photos Pair students who are visually impaired with students who are not. Ask the latter to describe the details in each photo in the MHP collection on the Milwaukee Public Museum's website and to answer any questions their partner might have. Then have the pairs work together to complete the Sort the Artifacts activity.

PRE-AP

Compare and Contrast Programs Assign pairs of students other programs that were part of the WPA, such as the Household Service Demonstration Project, the National Youth Administration, or the Federal Theater Project. Prompt them to construct a hypothesis, based on the name of their assigned program, about how it might be similar to and different from the Milwaukee Handicraft Project. Then give students time to research their assigned program using primary and secondary sources. Research could focus on topics such as the purpose of the program, who participated in it, and what—if anything—was created. Encourage students to find out how much (if any) previous experience, training, or education was required for participants. When finished, students should create a presentation comparing and contrasting their assigned program with the MHP and evaluating their hypothesis in light of their investigations. After the presentations, lead a class discussion synthesizing the information and evaluating the scope and impact of the WPA.

See the Chapter Planner for more strategies for differentiation.

SUPPORTING LABOR

When you are used to having no car at all, you might be thrilled to finally own an old vehicle that still runs. But once you have that, you might wish for a nicer car. As Americans' lives got better under the New Deal, their acceptance of hardship and struggle gave way to a desire for more improvements in their lives.

GAINS BY LABOR

Despite his progressive leanings, Franklin Roosevelt never fully supported organized labor. He felt uneasy when the head of the United Mine Workers, **John L. Lewis**, tripled his labor union's membership by announcing to workers, "The president wants you to join a union!" When other major labor leaders began using the same tactic to increase membership numbers, Roosevelt became irritated.

Unions needed large memberships to maintain the authority to stand up to corporate managers. As you have read, one effective labor tactic was to organize strikes to persuade management to listen to workers' demands. The more people involved in a strike, the greater the impact.

Unions used strikes to fight for the right of **collective bargaining**, or negotiation between

New laws passed during FDR's first term guaranteed workers the right to organize and strike. The practice continues today. In this photo from April 2016, members of a janitors' union march peacefully in downtown Los Angeles to publicize their campaign for higher pay and benefits.

an employer and union leaders on behalf of all union members. Union members had become aware that pay rates and benefits were not uniform for workers doing the same job. Because workers negotiated their wages and benefits individually and secretly with factory managers, two workers hired for the same position could be offered different hourly wages. Before collective bargaining, employees might complain to management, but their complaints had little effect. Union organizers used collective bargaining to negotiate employment contracts that guaranteed standard pay ranges and equal benefits for all workers.

Unfortunately, labor disputes resulted in violence on numerous occasions as scabs—workers brought in to replace those on strike—and police fought with striking workers. In 1933, for example, 60 workers at the Spang-Chalfant Seamless Tube Company, which produced steel tubing and was located near Pittsburgh, went out on strike after management increased their work hours. As the strikers were protesting on a **picket line**, 200 armed police officers arrived. A picket line is a group of strikers who form a barrier to keep scabs, or strikebreakers, from entering a building to work in their place. When the strikers refused to leave the picket line, the police began firing tear gas. When that tactic failed, the police fired bullets, killing 1 bystander and injuring 15 strikers and onlookers. The strike finally ended after three weeks when the workers agreed that the company could make changes to the work schedule. In return, the company agreed to consult union leaders about shift changes and increases or decreases in work hours.

In response to this kind of violence, Senator Robert Wagner of New York wrote a bill to protect the rights of striking workers. His legislation, later called the **Wagner Act**, passed in 1935. A portion of the act—the **National Labor Relations Act**—required employers to allow unions to collectively bargain for wages and benefits. It also prohibited employers from engaging in a wide range of "unfair labor practices," such as discriminating against a worker because of union membership and punishing workers for filing complaints against an employer. In addition, it created the **National Labor Relations Board** to supervise union elections and assign union representatives to advocate for workers. This board still meets today.

The Wagner Act made forming unions easier, but its enforcement revealed deep racial divisions when workers in non-unionized factories attempted to organize. At the 1935 convention of the American Federation of Labor (AFL), an organization of labor

unions, John Lewis pleaded with fellow union leaders to begin serious membership drives in the steel mills, automobile plants, and rubber factories. These industries employed many African Americans and immigrants from eastern and southern Europe. But most AFL leaders, who represented such skilled trade workers as masons and carpenters, had little interest in organizing such unions.

Determined, Lewis joined with like-minded labor leaders who agreed with him to form the **Congress of Industrial Organizations (CIO)**. The goal of the CIO was to create powerful unions in mass-production industries, such as auto manufacturing and steel.

CONFLICT OVER THE SUPREME COURT

In his second inaugural address, which he delivered at the Capitol on January 20, 1937, Roosevelt emphasized the New Deal's unfinished business. "I see one-third of a nation ill-housed, ill-clad, ill-nourished," he declared. His landslide election had provided him with a strong popular mandate, or authority to act. In addition, he enjoyed huge Democratic majorities in the House and Senate, enabling him to continue his political agenda.

PRIMARY SOURCE

In 1937, President Franklin Roosevelt proposed changes to the Supreme Court, which had opposed some of his New Deal legislation. In a fireside chat, he explained to the American people his view of the conflict.

Last Thursday I described the American form of Government as a three-horse team provided by the Constitution to the American people so that their field might be plowed. The three horses are, of course, the three branches of government—the Congress, the Executive and the Courts. Two of the horses are pulling in unison today; the third is not. Those who have intimated that the President of the United States is trying to drive that team, overlook the simple fact that the President, as Chief Executive, is himself one of the three horses.

It is the American people themselves who are in the driver's seat.

It is the American people themselves who want the furrow plowed.

It is the American people themselves who expect the third horse to pull in unison with the other two.

—from a fireside chat given by President Franklin Roosevelt, March 9, 1937

PLAN: 4-PAGE LESSON

OBJECTIVE

Identify rights workers gained through New Deal legislation.

CRITICAL THINKING SKILLS FOR LESSON 2.3

- Evaluate
- Form and Support Opinions
- Determine Chronology
- Identify Problems and Solutions
- Make Inferences
- Analyze Primary Sources
- Make Connections
- Analyze Visuals

HISTORICAL THINKING FOR CHAPTER 20

In what ways were Franklin Roosevelt's policies during the New Deal groundbreaking? As labor unions gained members and power, workers fought for better working conditions. Lesson 2.3 details the hard-won gains by labor during the New Deal.

BACKGROUND FOR THE TEACHER

John L. Lewis began working in a coal mine in Iowa when he was 15 years old. A few years later, he traveled the West, working in mines and gaining personal experience of the conditions in mines and the hardships of miners. He became involved with the United Mine Workers of America (UMWA) at the state level in Illinois and quickly rose to national leadership of the country's most prominent labor union. Knowing that the nation's homes and industries depended on coal, Lewis effectively organized a five-month strike to maintain the increased wages miners had gained during World War I. Lewis's political support for FDR wavered during the Great Depression, and in 1940 he backed the Republican candidate, Wendell Willkie. Similarly, Lewis ended his support of the CIO and withdrew the UMWA from the industrial union in 1942, although he always maintained his commitment to miners. He continued to work for increases in wages and benefits and succeeded in securing the Federal Mine Safety Act in 1952.

ACTIVATE PRIOR KNOWLEDGE

To preview the lesson, engage students' prior knowledge and opinions about organized labor. Post a Word Web like the one shown here. **ASK:** What are some words or phrases that spring to mind when you think of labor unions? *(Answers will vary. Possible responses: togetherness; strength in numbers; solidarity; exclusion; strikes; dues)* Prompt students to identify any current news, historical events, or personal experiences they may be familiar with regarding labor unions. After students have read the lesson, provide an opportunity for them to revisit the Word Web and change or add to their contributions.

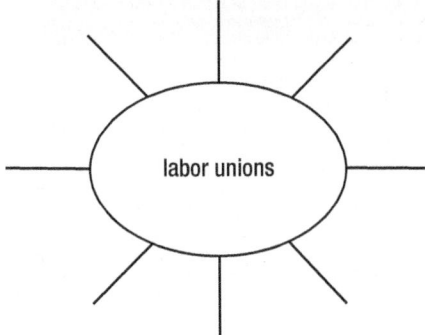

labor unions

TEACH

GUIDED DISCUSSION

1. **Identify Problems and Solutions** How did collective bargaining advance organized labor? *(Through collective bargaining, unions obtained contracts with employers that established pay ranges and equal benefits for workers.)*

2. **Make Inferences** How did social and economic trends of the 1930s necessitate both the AFL and the CIO? *(Possible response: Economic and racial segregation may have influenced the skilled-trades workers of the AFL to decline to recruit industrial laborers, among whom were more African Americans and immigrants, necessitating the creation of the CIO.)*

ANALYZE PRIMARY SOURCES

Direct students' attention to the Primary Source feature and ask them to analyze Roosevelt's use of language. **ASK:** Why do you think Roosevelt used the analogy of horses plowing a field? *(Possible response: Many of his listeners would have been familiar with the concept; Roosevelt liked to portray himself as a man of the people, so he probably wanted to make a folksy comparison.)* **ASK:** How does Roosevelt create a sense of empowerment of the people? *(Possible response: He reminds his listeners that the power of government rests in their hands, just as the power to control the horses that plow the field rests in the hands of the farmer.)*

STRIVING READERS

Complete T-Charts Instruct students to create a T-Chart. Prompt them to label the first column Spang-Chalfant Strike and the second General Motors Strike. Tell students to jot down key facts about each strike as they read the lesson. After reading, encourage students to compare their completed charts with one another, noting and discussing any differences.

Spang-Chalfant Strike	General Motors Strike

PRE-AP

Extend Knowledge Instruct students to gather information from a variety of library or online sources to learn more about how labor unions became stronger during the Roosevelt administration, especially after the U.S. Supreme Court sided with labor. When they have completed their research, ask students to share their findings with the class by giving an oral report about key factors that resulted in unions gaining strength.

See the Chapter Planner for more strategies for differentiation.

The only branch of government not on FDR's side was the judicial branch—specifically, the Supreme Court.

The Supreme Court was dominated by elderly, conservative justices who strongly opposed the New Deal legislation. Roosevelt knew that in the coming months the justices would be reviewing two of the New Deal's most important accomplishments—the National Labor Relations Act and the Social Security Act. He took action to save his programs.

In February 1937, without consulting Congress, Roosevelt ordered a complete reorganization of the federal court system. Under his plan, the Supreme Court would gain six new members, raising the total number of justices to fifteen. Roosevelt would be able to fill these new positions with judges who shared his political views. This **court-packing plan** was legal; the Constitution set no limits on the size of the Supreme Court.

Autoworkers at a General Motors plant in Flint, Michigan, staged a strike by sitting in the seats made to be installed in cars, as shown in this 1936 photograph.

Roosevelt had miscalculated the power of his mandate, however. Some politicians worried that expanding the judicial branch would throw off the balance among the three branches of government. As opposition to the plan grew stronger, aides urged Roosevelt to withdraw it. The Senate later defeated it.

As it turned out, the president did not need to pack the court. In the spring of 1937, the Supreme Court changed course. By a vote of 5 to 4, the court upheld both the National Labor Relations Act and the Social Security Act. Then, one by one, the old conservative justices decided to retire, making FDR's plan unnecessary. Roosevelt—the only president in American history to make no Supreme Court appointments during his first four-year term—filled five vacancies over the next three years. The liberal justices he chose—especially Hugo Black, Felix Frankfurter, and William O. Douglas—would steer the court for decades to come.

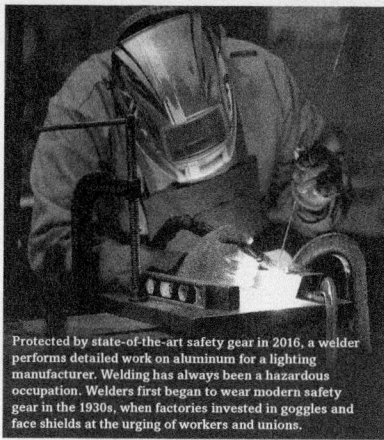

Protected by state-of-the-art safety gear in 2016, a welder performs detailed work on aluminum for a lighting manufacturer. Welding has always been a hazardous occupation. Welders first began to wear modern safety gear in the 1930s, when factories invested in goggles and face shields at the urging of workers and unions.

CONFLICT OVER UNIONS

Away from Washington, new battles raged in the automobile plants of Michigan, the textile mills of North Carolina, and the coal mines of Kentucky. Workers in such major industries demanded union recognition under the banner of the CIO, but management ignored their demand.

On November 12, 1936, a small group of autoworkers at a General Motors (GM) plant in Flint, Michigan, staged a **sit-down strike**. Instead of leaving their jobs, the workers stayed in the plant, refusing to work. They thus prevented management from bringing in scabs to continue production and shut down the plant. Unlike the Spang-Chalfant strike, the Flint strike was effective and mostly peaceful.

In addition to seeking recognition for the CIO, the sit-down strikers wanted higher wages and safer working conditions. At the time, the average autoworker earned $900 a year, far below the $1,600 the government deemed necessary to support a family of four. In addition, hundreds of workers had died in auto plants in Michigan because of dangerous working conditions. Soon, the strike spread as workers at other General Motors plants began sitting down at their jobs. Journalists called this first major labor dispute between autoworkers and management "the strike heard 'round the world."

The 44-day Flint sit-down strike ended when GM recognized the CIO's United Automobile Workers (UAW) union as the bargaining agent for its employees and raised wages. The success of the strike motivated other autoworkers to protest as well. Within a few weeks after the strike, 87 more sit-down strikes occurred in the Detroit area alone. Chrysler came to terms with strikers a few months later. Other industry leaders followed suit after the UAW victory, including Firestone, General Electric, and RCA.

Some industry leaders were not so quick to give in to unions, however. Henry Ford hired an army of thugs to rough up union organizers and disrupt strikers on picket lines. The worst violence, however, occurred outside Republic Steel's South Chicago mill on Memorial Day 1937, when heavily armed police battled rock-throwing strikers on a picket line. Casualties included 10 workers killed by gunfire, and dozens more injured. Under pressure from the National Labor Relations Board, Ford and Republic Steel gradually accepted unions as a legitimate force in American manufacturing. With a membership approaching 3 million, the CIO had come a long way since its break with the conservative, trades-oriented American Federation of Labor a few years before.

The Supreme Court battle and the sit-down strikes slowed the political momentum that followed FDR's re-election landslide in 1936. In addition, a serious recession in 1937 eroded public confidence in the New Deal. Other problems loomed in Europe, where fascism continued to gain strength. For President Roosevelt, the road ahead appeared even steeper and rockier than before.

HISTORICAL THINKING

1. **READING CHECK** What gains did American labor make during the 1930s?

2. **EVALUATE** Why were unions important to American workers in the 1930s?

3. **FORM AND SUPPORT OPINIONS** Was the Wagner Act effective? Support your opinion with evidence from the text.

4. **DETERMINE CHRONOLOGY** What sequence of events made Roosevelt's court-packing plan unnecessary?

BUILD BACKGROUND

FDR VERSUS THE SUPREME COURT

President Roosevelt's court-packing plan touched off a controversy that remains a matter of historical debate. During Roosevelt's first term, six Supreme Court justices were more than 70 years old. These so-called Four Horsemen made up a conservative bloc and voted together; they required only one other justice to provide the majority decisions that struck down several major pieces of New Deal legislation in 1935 and 1936. Fearing this precedent would continue, FDR initiated a court-packing bill that included a plan for adding a new judge to the Court for any justice who did not retire within six months after reaching the age of 70. The proposed law met strong opposition from the public, the press, and many lawmakers.

The entire issue became moot when the Court issued a ruling that reversed its earlier decision regarding a minimum-wage law. Several other decisions that upheld New Deal legislation followed. Reasons for the Court's change in direction remain unclear and have led to speculation over the years. Some attribute the pivot to Associate Justice Owen Roberts, who had often been the "swing vote" that created a majority for the Four Horsemen, but began to rule against them. Roberts's shift became known as "the switch in time that saved nine." Whatever the cause, the results of the Court's shift have been documented: The New Deal policies remained intact after the Court established support for expanded government power. Roosevelt, however, never regained the level of public support he had enjoyed during his first term in office.

TEACH

GUIDED DISCUSSION

3. **Make Connections** Do you think appointing Supreme Court justices who support a president's or a party's views is as much of a concern today as during the time of FDR's administration? Explain your answer. *(Answers will vary. Students may reference the 2016–2017 confirmation debates over Supreme Court nominees, which support the inference that appointments are still of great concern today.)*

4. **Form and Support Opinions** Which tactic for advancing the cause of organized labor do you think is more effective—a picket line or a sit-down strike? Why? *(Answers will vary. Possible responses: A picket line attracts publicity, may involve more protesters, and raises public awareness of the issues. A sit-down strike involves only the workers on the job, but it prevents production or business.)*

ANALYZE VISUALS

Direct students' attention to the photo of the welder in safety gear. Ask a volunteer to read the caption. Then challenge students to brainstorm other possible benefits for workers and for employers that might trace their origins to unions and collective bargaining in the 1930s. *(Answers will vary. Possible response: Benefits to workers might include overtime pay and limits on work hours, which could make employees more satisfied with their jobs and therefore more productive and loyal to their employers.)*

ACTIVE OPTIONS

On Your Feet: Become an Expert Organize students into four groups to study unions during the Depression. Assign one of the following topics to each group: major unions and union leaders, labor legislation, union strikes, or collective bargaining. Instruct members of each group to become experts on their assigned topic, drawing on information from the text as well as other resources. Then regroup students so that each new group has at least one member from each expert group. Allow experts to share information with their new groups.

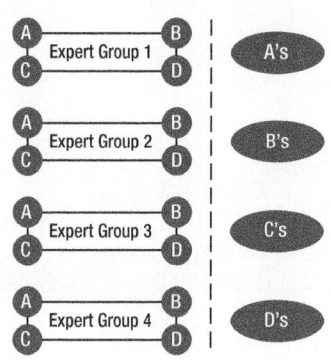

NG Learning Framework: Find Parallels between Past and Present Labor Movements

ATTITUDE Empowerment

KNOWLEDGE Our Human Story

Direct students' attention to the photograph of a 2016 janitors' union march, and call on a volunteer to read the caption. Then ask students to find parallels between the advances and retreats of organized labor in the 1930s and current labor issues. Allow them to work in pairs or teams to research the concerns and tactics of modern unions and evaluate how past events and decisions influence labor today. Challenge students to find a creative way to share the results of their research.

GOLDEN GATE BRIDGE
SAN FRANCISCO, CALIFORNIA

The iconic Golden Gate Bridge extends across the Golden Gate Strait and connects the city of San Francisco to Marin County, California. Opened in 1937, this steel suspension bridge is the product of thousands of hours of backbreaking, dangerous labor by hundreds of American workers. It was built during the Great Depression, a time when one out of four Americans were unemployed. Those who worked on it were grateful for their jobs. Bridge workers were hired through local unions, such as the Ironworkers Local Union 377, and included people from a wide range of backgrounds: farmers, lumberjacks, cowboys, and taxicab drivers. It took nerves of steel to work on the Golden Gate Bridge. Workers faced many physical challenges, including water, wind, and blinding fog. But creating this gateway to the "Golden City" during one of the lowest points in American economic history gave union workers financial stability and pride. "It was never just a job to me. I loved the work," said bridge worker Harold McClain.

CRITICAL VIEWING Measuring 1.7 miles long, the Golden Gate Bridge weighs nearly 900,000 tons. Two towers support two enormous carbon-steel cables, which are secured at each end by giant anchorages. Based on what you notice in the photograph, what challenges did workers probably face while building the bridge?

732 CHAPTER 20

The New Deal 733

PLAN: 2-PAGE LESSON

OBJECTIVE

Describe the history of San Francisco's Golden Gate Bridge and its relationship to the goals of the New Deal.

CRITICAL THINKING SKILLS FOR LESSON 2.4

- Analyze Visuals
- Make Connections
- Analyze Language Use

HISTORICAL THINKING FOR CHAPTER 20

In what ways were Franklin Roosevelt's policies during the Great Depression groundbreaking? New Deal policies created jobs for the unemployed and improvements in the nation's infrastructure. Lesson 2.4 discusses how the construction of the Golden Gate Bridge related to advances of organized labor and the goals of the New Deal.

BACKGROUND FOR THE TEACHER

Golden Gate Strait is plagued by winds, fog, and powerful tides, and it is near the San Andreas Fault. These challenges, combined with the economic crisis of the Great Depression, led many to believe the Golden Gate was "the bridge that couldn't be built." The fact that it was built testifies to the determination of chief engineer Joseph Strauss and the support of citizens in the surrounding counties who used their homes and farms as collateral for funding the project. Although WPA workers built the access roads, no federal funds were used for the bridge itself. When it was completed, the Golden Gate Bridge was the world's longest suspension bridge. On May 27, 1937, about 200,000 pedestrians walked across the bridge, which was opened to vehicles the following day.

HISTORY NOTEBOOK

Encourage students to complete the American Places page for Chapter 20 in their History Notebooks as they read.

INTRODUCE & ENGAGE
PREVIEW USING VISUALS

Direct students' attention to the photograph of the Golden Gate Bridge and elicit reactions to it. **ASK:** What makes the bridge visually interesting as well as functional? *(Possible response: Steel, concrete, and engineering make the bridge functional for carrying vehicles and pedestrians, but the color and the graceful design make it interesting to look at.)* **ASK:** What are some of the first words that come to your mind as you look at this bridge? *(Answers will vary. Possible responses: graceful, massive, scary, colorful, long, sweeping)* Discuss students' prior knowledge of the bridge. Ask those who have crossed the bridge to describe their experiences.

TEACH
GUIDED DISCUSSION

1. **Make Connections** How did building the Golden Gate Bridge help advance organized labor? *(Possible response: Workers were hired through local unions, which must have increased union membership because many workers came from other occupations—such as farming—that were not unionized.)*

2. **Analyze Language Use** How can the word *iconic* connect to both the Golden Gate Bridge's role as a famous landmark and its role in the social and economic developments of the 1930s? *(Possible response: The Golden Gate Bridge became an internationally recognized symbol, or icon, representing San Francisco. Its construction during the 1930s connects it to the economic challenges of the Great Depression and makes it an icon of the ability of ordinary Americans to work together to overcome those challenges and create a useful, lasting structure.)*

AMERICAN PLACES

From 1937 to 1938, about 3.3 million cars crossed the Golden Gate Bridge. Today, an estimated 40 million vehicles use the bridge annually. Reversible lanes facilitate morning and evening commutes, and tolls are collected for southbound (toward San Francisco) traffic only. A complex set of rules governs pedestrian and bike traffic, and animals—except service animals—are prohibited. Routinely ranked among the nation's top 10 tourist attractions, the Golden Gate Bridge hosts about 10 million visitors a year.

ACTIVE OPTIONS

On Your Feet: Create an Acrostic Write the words *Golden Gate Bridge* vertically on the board or on a large sheet of paper. Assign each letter to pairs or individual students. Instruct students to come up with a word, phrase, or sentence beginning with their assigned letter that relates the Golden Gate Bridge to the physical and human characteristics of its surroundings. Invite students to come to the board or paper and create an acrostic by writing their responses next to their assigned letter.

NG Learning Framework: Research a Suspension Bridge STEM
ATTITUDE Curiosity
SKILL Problem-Solving

Challenge students with the question: How do you build a bridge that spans more than a mile of water? Allow them to work in pairs or small groups to construct and test hypotheses and then collect information from primary and secondary sources to find out how a suspension bridge is built. Encourage them to use drawings or models to illustrate the process. After students have shared their work with the class, share the information in Background for the Teacher and discuss why the Golden Gate Bridge represents a significant achievement in American economic history.

DIFFERENTIATE
INCLUSION

Work in Pairs Allow students with disabilities to work with students who can read the lesson aloud to them. Encourage the partner without disabilities to also describe the photograph. Then have students work together to answer the Critical Viewing question.

GIFTED & TALENTED

Create a Website Tell students that many iconic buildings, roads, bridges, tunnels, and dams were built by people who were given jobs under Roosevelt's New Deal programs. Prompt students to conduct online research to identify some of these structures. Then have them choose one and create an informative website about it. Tell them to design a home page and then create a site map for the supporting pages. The website should include information about the structure itself, the people who built it, and the government programs that made it possible. Encourage students to share their website designs with the class. Some students may wish to use website templates or design software to create and publish their websites.

See the Chapter Planner for more strategies for differentiation.

CRITICAL VIEWING Possible responses: Workers faced the challenges of being injured if they fell from the towers onto the bridge or drowning if they fell in the water. In addition, it must have been hard to move materials into place. The area is wide open, and there's little to block a strong wind.

WOMEN DURING THE NEW DEAL

You probably take for granted that women hold important jobs and contribute to their families' financial security. But many jobs might still be closed to women if not for the efforts of pioneers like Eleanor Roosevelt.

OPPORTUNITIES FOR WOMEN

When the stock market crashed in 1929, men were not the only ones to lose their jobs. By 1933, about 2 million women were unemployed as well. In some families, the women were the main **breadwinners**, or contributors to a family's income. These women—in fact, all American women—had a powerful ally in Eleanor Roosevelt. The first lady was among the president's chief advisors, and her progressive beliefs strongly influenced him. An advocate for child welfare and equal rights for women and minorities, she traveled the country and reported to FDR on the social conditions she observed.

Eleanor worked to persuade those in charge of implementing the New Deal to include positions for women in their relief programs. She quoted girls and women who had written her letters telling how the Great Depression had affected them and their families. She pointed out that many women were earning their college degrees and entering the workforce with fresh ideas that the nation urgently needed. Influential leaders like Harry Hopkins listened.

Hopkins headed one of the first New Deal agencies designed to put people back to work, the Federal Emergency Relief Administration (FERA). He established a division in FERA called the Civil Works Administration (CWA), which was committed to finding jobs for women. Hopkins appointed his assistant and former Mississippi legislator, **Ellen Woodward**, to lead the CWA. Woodward required that each state hire a woman to direct the program.

As first lady of New York State, Eleanor Roosevelt took time from her political activities to serve as a volunteer. In this photo, she serves soup to unemployed women in New York in 1932.

Eleanor Roosevelt received hundreds of letters from Americans asking for help during the Great Depression. After leaving the White House in 1945, she continued to fight for social change and to champion human rights.

I hope to complete my education, but I will have to quit school I guess if there is no clothes can be bought. Mrs. Roosevelt, don't think I am just begging, but that is all you can call it I guess. There is no harm in asking I guess [either]. Do you have any old clothes you have thrown back. The clothes may be too large but I can cut them down so I can wear them. Not only clothes but old shoes, hats, hose, and under wear would be appreciated so much.

—from a letter written to Eleanor Roosevelt by a 15-year-old girl from Alabama, 1936

Where, after all, do universal human rights begin? In small places close to home—so close and so small that they cannot be seen on any map of the world. Such are the places where every man, woman, and child seeks equal justice, equal opportunity, equal dignity without discrimination. Unless these rights have meaning there, they have little meaning anywhere.

—from a speech given to the United Nations by Eleanor Roosevelt, March 27, 1958

Women were also hired to renovate buildings, conduct public surveys, help develop museums, and carry out a variety of other projects. Job opportunities were far from equal, however. Women held only 7 percent of the jobs created by the CWA, and they were paid less than their male counterparts. The situation improved when FDR established the Works Progress Administration in 1935, replacing FERA. By 1938, more than 13 percent of the people working in the agency were women.

WOMEN LEAD THE WAY

Eleanor Roosevelt and Ellen Woodward were not the only influential women in the Roosevelt administration. Others included Frances Perkins, Josephine Roche, and Hilda Smith.

Frances Perkins, a labor rights activist from New York, was appointed secretary of Labor by FDR. She was the first woman in American history to hold a cabinet-level post. As secretary, she drew on her experiences inspecting working conditions in textile mills and advocating for working-class immigrants and African Americans. She outlined her goals for the president, including a 40-hour workweek, unemployment insurance, a minimum wage, and an end to child labor. FDR incorporated so many of Perkins's ideas that she was later called "the architect of the New Deal." As a member of the Special Board for Public Works, Perkins ensured that government funds were spent on roads, schools, and post offices. As chair of the Committee on Economic Security, she helped develop the Social Security Act, which provided aid for the elderly and workers who had been laid off and grants to states for maternal and child healthcare.

Roosevelt appointed **Josephine Roche**, Colorado's first policewoman and heir to a fuel company, as the assistant secretary of the Treasury in 1934. She had previously advocated for fair wages and health benefits for Colorado mine workers and had used her own money to establish unions in her family's mines.

Before joining the Roosevelt administration as the director of Workers' Education in FERA, **Hilda Smith** was a dean at Bryn Mawr College in Pennsylvania and had been active in social work and women's suffrage. As director, Smith ran FERA and WPA camps and schools for unemployed women. The camps provided food and clothing, and the schools taught such classes as literacy and typing. Unlike the men's camps, however, the women's camps failed to provide work. The women's camps were closed down after three years when New Deal opponents began complaining about the cost. "As so often the case," Smith wrote, "the boys get the breaks, the girls are neglected."

HISTORICAL THINKING

1. **READING CHECK** How did the New Deal affect the role of women in society?

2. **IDENTIFY MAIN IDEAS AND DETAILS** Why was Frances Perkins called the "architect of the New Deal"?

3. **DESCRIBE** How did Eleanor Roosevelt influence the appointment of women to important positions in New Deal agencies?

4. **ANALYZE CAUSE AND EFFECT** Why did the camps for unemployed women fail?

PLAN: 2-PAGE LESSON

OBJECTIVE

Describe how New Deal policies affected women's benefits and opportunities.

CRITICAL THINKING SKILLS FOR LESSON 3.1

- Identify Main Ideas and Details
- Describe
- Analyze Cause and Effect
- Compare and Contrast
- Make Inferences
- Analyze Primary Sources

ESSENTIAL QUESTION FOR CHAPTER 20

In what ways were Franklin Roosevelt's policies during the Great Depression groundbreaking?
New Deal policies benefited many segments of society. Lesson 3.1 describes how opportunities for women expanded, largely through the efforts of Eleanor Roosevelt.

BACKGROUND FOR THE TEACHER

As the longest-serving first lady, Eleanor Roosevelt transformed the role and set precedents for future residents of the White House. In addition to the usual duties of entertaining diplomats and heads of state, Roosevelt became involved in the business of government. She devoted herself to becoming her husband's "legs and ears" by traveling the country and listening to the voices of Americans in need. To raise awareness of the plight of marginalized groups in society, she held press conferences, made radio broadcasts, and wrote a daily newspaper column. Eleanor Roosevelt's dedication to the rights of women and minorities continued long after her tenure as first lady ended. As U.S. delegate to the United Nations, she promoted the Universal Declaration of Human Rights that was adopted in 1948.

HISTORY NOTEBOOK

Encourage students to complete the page on Women During the New Deal in their History Notebooks as they read.

INTRODUCE & ENGAGE

CONTRAST A "HAND UP" WITH A "HANDOUT"

Ask students to brainstorm differences between the common phrases "giving a hand up" and "giving a handout." *(Possible responses: "Giving someone a hand up" means providing recipients with the means to help themselves. "Giving a handout" means giving the recipient some benefit that doesn't help that person become self-reliant. A hand up is a long-term solution to a problem. A handout is a short-term solution.)* Ask students to give examples of each kind of aid and categorize New Deal programs into the two types. Tell students that in this lesson they will learn about New Deal programs to help women. At the end of the lesson, discuss whether these programs offered a hand up or a handout.

TEACH

GUIDED DISCUSSION

1. **Compare and Contrast** How did differences in New Deal benefits for men and women indicate that values change at different rates and at different times? *(Possible response: Both men and women had more job opportunities, a relatively fast change in the value of women working. But women did not receive equal pay, a value that changed more slowly.)*

2. **Make Inferences** Based on the backgrounds, experiences, and accomplishments of influential women such as Ellen Woodward, Frances Perkins, Josephine Roche, and Hilda Smith, what inference can be made about the status of women in the 1930s? *(Answers will vary. Possible response: The status of some women was rising; those women were more likely to be highly educated and hold high-level positions. They used their roles to improve opportunities for all women.)*

ANALYZE PRIMARY SOURCES

Direct students' attention to the Primary Sources feature, and ask a volunteer to read each excerpt aloud. **ASK:** What does the letter from the 15-year-old girl suggest about Eleanor Roosevelt's character? *(Possible response: Eleanor Roosevelt must have seemed compassionate and made people feel comfortable asking for all kinds of help.)* **ASK:** What is the connection between these two documents, separated by more than 20 years? *(Possible response: Even in the context of promoting universal human rights, Roosevelt remained concerned for individuals.)*

ACTIVE OPTIONS

On Your Feet: Identify Problems and Solutions Assign students to teams and provide each team with a Problem-and-Solution graphic organizer. Instruct teams to identify a social or economic problem faced by women during the Great Depression, noting the steps the government took to solve it and summarizing the results in a conclusion. Ask teams to share their work with the class.

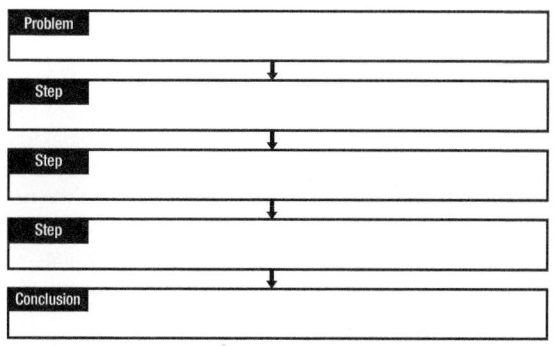

Problem

Step

Step

Step

Conclusion

NG Learning Framework: Profile the Roosevelts

ATTITUDE Curiosity

KNOWLEDGE Our Human Story

Guide students to research and create video or infographic profiles of Franklin and Eleanor Roosevelt. After students share their profiles with the class, you might show selected clips of Ken Burns's documentary *The Roosevelts*. Ask students to evaluate Burns's interpretation, including his use of evidence, and whether the documentary makes valid generalizations or includes oversimplifications about its subjects.

DIFFERENTIATE

STRIVING READERS

Write a Tweet As students read the lesson, direct them to pause after each paragraph and write a message of no more than 140 characters summarizing the paragraph's main idea in their own words. Encourage students to read their tweets aloud to a partner, alternating so that the first student reads his or her tweet about the first paragraph and the second student reads a tweet about the second paragraph. The partners continue until they reach the end of the lesson. If time permits, allow them to repeat the reading portion of the activity, this time starting with the other partner.

GIFTED & TALENTED

Perform a Dramatic Reading Prompt students to choose one of the excerpts from the Primary Sources feature and then locate and read the complete source document. Challenge students to prepare a dramatic reading of the entire document or selected portions of it. Encourage them to practice reading with expressive voice and gestures. After they have practiced, students may perform their dramatic reading for the class. Ask readers as well as listeners to discuss how the dramatic reading affected their interpretation and understanding of the document.

See the Chapter Planner for more strategies for differentiation.

HISTORICAL THINKING

ANSWERS

1. New Deal agencies provided opportunities for women to serve in leadership positions and also provided jobs for women, although women had fewer opportunities than men.

2. Perkins's progressive ideas influenced many New Deal programs and policies.

3. Eleanor Roosevelt became an advocate for women. She used her position as first lady to convince influential leaders to use women's talents and skills in New Deal agencies.

4. Women's camps failed to provide work for women. Cost-cutting measures resulted in closing the camps.

MAIN IDEA The New Deal provided varying degrees of relief for African Americans, Mexican Americans, and Native Americans.

MIXED PROGRESS ON CIVIL RIGHTS

Perhaps the greatest challenge of American democracy has been making equal rights for all a reality. Every generation has faced this challenge.

AFRICAN AMERICANS AND THE NEW DEAL

President Roosevelt crafted his New Deal policies to apply to all Americans, no matter their ethnicity. African Americans appreciated this effort, and many of them supported him at the ballot box. As you have read, the Great Migration brought many African Americans to northern cities, where they often formed a **voting bloc**, or a large group of citizens who share a common concern and tend to vote the same in elections.

Historically, most African Americans had supported the Republican Party, an allegiance that dated back to Abraham Lincoln and the Civil War. With the New Deal, however, many African Americans shifted to the Democratic Party. This massive switch occurred because the Roosevelt administration provided jobs and relief benefits to all Americans, regardless of race.

Federal assistance was especially welcome in African-American communities, where the human toll of the Great Depression was especially evident. By 1933, unemployment among African Americans had reached 50 percent. Fortunately, the two New Deal administrators most responsible for creating jobs were sympathetic to minority needs. At the

AMERICAN PLACES
Lincoln Memorial, Washington, D.C.

On a chilly Easter Sunday in 1939, world-renowned opera singer Marian Anderson performed at the Lincoln Memorial in Washington, D.C., before a crowd of about 75,000 people. Previously, the Daughters of the American Revolution had refused to allow Anderson to perform at Constitution Hall because of her skin color. Anderson began her performance with a moving rendition of "My Country 'Tis of Thee."

Public Works Administration (PWA), Harold Ickes insisted that African Americans receive equal pay on all construction projects. Although local officials often ignored this rule, the PWA provided thousands of jobs for African Americans and built African-American schools and hospitals throughout the segregated South. At the Works Progress Administration, African Americans received a share of the work in northern cities. Many African Americans welcomed an administration that showed some interest in their well-being. They particularly admired the efforts of First Lady Eleanor Roosevelt, who took strong stands in favor of equal rights for minorities and women.

Eleanor Roosevelt's interest in civil rights had been fueled in large measure by her friendship with prominent African Americans, including

THE SCOTTSBORO BOYS

In March 1931, nine young African-American men, ages 12 to 20, hopped aboard a freight train in northern Alabama to ride the rails as "hoboes," or homeless wanderers in search of work. A fight broke out between them and two white men. In the fray that followed, two white women, also riding the same train, accused the young black men of rape. Police arrested the nine African-American men and locked them up in the Scottsboro, Alabama, jail. From that point on, the nine were known as the Scottsboro Boys.

Over the course of the next seven years, the Scottsboro Boys would attend trials and retrials, which were marred by lies, bribes, and racial bias on the part of the accusers, the prosecuting attorney, and the judges. The victims gave vastly different accounts of the crime, and one even took back her accusation, admitting it was a lie. Even so, a series of all-white juries convicted and sentenced the young men to death several times. Each time, the defense appealed. The case went all the way to the U.S. Supreme Court, finally ending with five convictions and four dismissals. By 1950, all of the convicted Scottsboro Boys had been either pardoned or paroled.

Mary McLeod Bethune, founder of Bethune-Cookman College in Florida. In 1936, Eleanor Roosevelt recommended Bethune to head the National Youth Administration's Office of Negro Affairs. As the New Deal's highest-ranking African-American appointee, Bethune presided over the administration's "black cabinet," an informal group of African-American leaders who advised the White House on minority issues. Bethune went on to play an important role many years later as one of the original U.S. representatives to the United Nations and its first black female delegate.

In 1939, Eleanor Roosevelt further demonstrated her commitment to African-American rights when she resigned from a historically all-white organization called the Daughters of the American Revolution. The group had refused to allow **Marian Anderson**, a gifted African-American opera singer, to perform at Washington's Constitution Hall. A few months later, Harold Ickes arranged for Anderson to sing at the Lincoln Memorial on Easter Sunday. An integrated audience of about 75,000 gathered to hear her stirring performance.

Yet the progressive work of Eleanor Roosevelt and others could not make up for larger New Deal failures in the field of civil rights. Throughout his presidency, for example, Franklin Roosevelt made no effort to dismantle segregation or to enable African Americans to vote. He remained on the sidelines as federal anti-lynching bills were narrowly defeated in Congress. Roosevelt argued that he could not support civil rights legislation without alienating southern Democrats, who controlled the most important committees in Congress. "They will block every bill I [need] to keep America from collapsing," Roosevelt said. "I just can't take that risk." The president's position did not prevent African Americans from supporting him in 1936, however. Roosevelt received 76 percent of their votes—the same percentage that Herbert Hoover, the Republican candidate, had won four years before.

MEXICAN AMERICANS AND THE NEW DEAL

As African Americans struggled with racism and discrimination, both Mexican immigrants and American citizens of Mexican descent, or Mexican Americans, faced their own challenges during the Depression.

PLAN: 4-PAGE LESSON

OBJECTIVE

Explain and evaluate the effectiveness of New Deal relief efforts for African Americans, Mexican Americans, and Native Americans.

CRITICAL THINKING SKILLS FOR LESSON 3.2

- Compare and Contrast
- Synthesize
- Determine Chronology
- Make Inferences
- Summarize
- Identify
- Analyze Cause and Effect
- Form and Support Opinions

HISTORICAL THINKING FOR CHAPTER 20

In what ways were Franklin Roosevelt's policies during the Great Depression groundbreaking?
Roosevelt's far-reaching policies addressed the needs of all Americans, but deep-seated prejudices in American society limited benefits for certain groups. Lesson 3.2 explains the impact of inequality on New Deal programs.

BACKGROUND FOR THE TEACHER

Whether the New Deal might be considered highly beneficial to minorities or racist and ethnocentric depends on the lens through which it is viewed. Within the context of the Great Depression, the New Deal greatly expanded employment opportunities for African Americans and, for the first time in history, offered federal recognition of racial problems in the United States. However, by today's standards, federal programs in the 1930s certainly did not do much to end racial discrimination or foster integration, and FDR avoided taking actions that would alienate southern racists.

Similarly, New Deal treatment of Mexican Americans and Native Americans gets mixed reviews. The CCC and WPA employed Mexican Americans, but many did not qualify for benefits under Social Security or the National Labor Relations Act. Most Native American tribes in the 1930s approved the Indian Reorganization Act, but many Native Americans today criticize the law as a "white-imposed reform program."

INTRODUCE & ENGAGE

DISCUSS A PERFORMANCE

Play for students an audio or video recording of Marian Anderson's performance of "My Country 'Tis of Thee" at the Lincoln Memorial. Ask students to volunteer their impressions of the performance and record their responses on the board. You may wish to use a Word Web like the one shown here. Then direct students' attention to the photograph of Marian Anderson and its caption. Ask students if they wish to add new comments in light of what they now know about the circumstances of the performance. **ASK:** Why was this song especially appropriate in the context of this particular occasion? *(Possible response: The lyrics convey the irony of the situation—Marian Anderson sings about a "sweet land of liberty," when she did not have the freedom to perform at Constitution Hall simply because of her skin color.)*

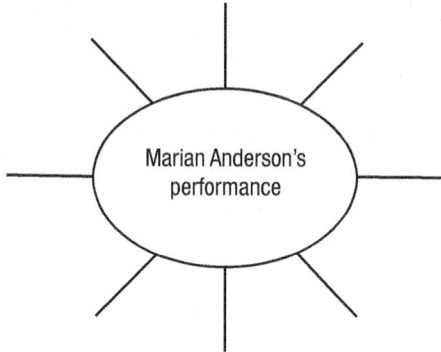

Marian Anderson's performance

TEACH

GUIDED DISCUSSION

1. **Make Inferences** What can you conclude about the diffusion of ideas about the Scottsboro case from the "Save the Scottsboro Boys" button, and how might the button affect how others felt about the Scottsboro case? *(Possible response: The button indicates that the case was publicized and that some people, both black and white, used buttons like this one to identify themselves as supporters of the Scottsboro Boys and also to advocate for their freedom. The buttons could sway public opinion about the Scottsboro Boys.)*

2. **Summarize** Within the context of the 1930s, what dilemma did FDR face in deciding whether to support civil rights legislation? *(If FDR supported equal rights for African Americans, he risked losing the votes of southern Democrats, who could then block his economic programs.)*

🧭 AMERICAN PLACES

Congress passed a bill supporting a memorial to Abraham Lincoln in 1867, but the grand structure on the mall in Washington, D.C., took years to plan and build. It was not dedicated until 1922—57 years after Lincoln's assassination. The classic design of the Lincoln Memorial resembles a Greek temple and encloses a 19-foot marble statue of the seated Lincoln. The words of the Gettysburg Address and the Second Inaugural Address are inscribed on its walls. The memorial not only honors the 16th president but also symbolizes principles of American democracy. Therefore, it has become a fitting site for historic events, including Dr. Martin Luther King, Jr.'s "I Have a Dream" speech in 1963. Encourage interested students to find out more about the design and construction of the Lincoln Memorial.

DIFFERENTIATE

ENGLISH LANGUAGE LEARNERS

Pose and Answer Questions Arrange students at the **Emerging** and **Expanding** levels in mixed pairs and ask them to reread the lesson together. Instruct them to pause after each paragraph and ask one another *who, what, when, where,* or *why* questions about what they have just read. Suggest that students use a 5Ws Chart to help organize their questions and answers. Ask students at the **Expanding** level to assist students at the **Emerging** level as needed.

PRE-AP

Form and Support a Hypothesis Challenge students to research the impact of the New Deal on one of the groups of Americans covered in the lesson. First, instruct them to develop a hypothesis regarding the predominant impact on that group. Then direct them to conduct research to find evidence that supports or refutes their hypothesis. They should use a variety of primary and secondary source materials and change their hypothesis if the evidence warrants it. Encourage students to use a graphic organizer such as the one shown here to keep track of the various impacts of the New Deal on the group they are researching. Prompt students to write an essay based on their findings. Then invite students to share their finished essays with the class.

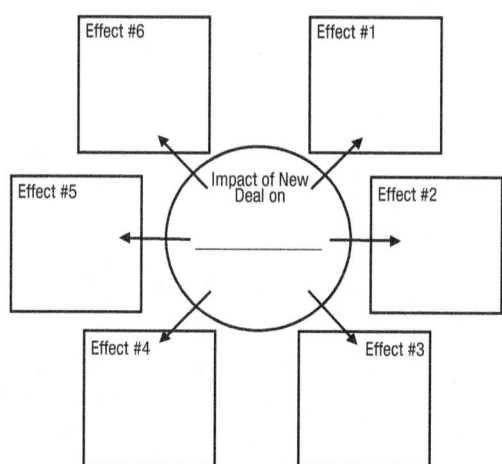

See the Chapter Planner for more strategies for differentiation.

Despite being recruited to work on American farms just 10 years before, Mexican immigrants met with deep resentment from white Americans who felt jobs were being taken away from them. In response to this resentment, in 1929, the federal government began the Mexican Repatriation Program, which, as you've read, deported hundreds of thousands of people of Mexican descent. In this context, repatriation is the act of sending an immigrant back to his or her home country to live. Some people left the United States voluntarily, accepting the government's free train fares. Others were coerced or tricked into leaving.

Many Mexican Americans were also deported to Mexico simply because authorities did not trust their claims of nationality or did not care. Of those who remained in the United States, many experienced unemployment because farm owners were hiring fewer migrant workers and giving jobs to white workers first. Farmers in various ethnic groups had begun working as migrant farm laborers after losing their farmland in bank foreclosures during the Great Depression. Many Mexican American farmers were among those who had lost their land and become migrant laborers.

Fortunately, the New Deal provided some relief. The Farm Security Administration (FSA), a New Deal agency, established camps to provide food and shelter for migrant workers and their families. Several camps were specifically for Mexican American workers. Farmworkers who lived in the camps were able to discuss labor issues among themselves. These discussions led to the formation of Mexican-American farm labor unions, which fought for higher wages and better working conditions.

In 2005, the California State Legislature passed the "Apology Act," a long-overdue response to the deportations that took place during and after the New Deal. California senator Joe Dunn wrote the act on behalf of his constituency to acknowledge the mistreatment Americans had suffered since the 1930s simply for being of Mexican descent.

However, Mexican Americans were not the only target of federal repatriation acts. In 1935, Congress passed a repatriation act targeting Filipinos. The act encouraged both Filipino immigrants and Americans of Filipino descent to return voluntarily to the Philippines, but the Filipino American community

CRITICAL VIEWING In 1930, a group of Filipino American farmworkers posed with tomatoes they harvested on California's Central Coast. The migrant workers followed the crops from the Mexican border to Alaska. Although migrant work was rough and the workers were often mistreated, why do you think these men mostly look happy in the photograph?

ENCOURAGING AN APPRECIATION OF NATIVE AMERICAN ART

As Commissioner of Indian Affairs from 1933 to 1945, John Collier worked to foster the economic independence of Native Americans, partly by promoting the work of Native American artists and craftspeople. This poster is one of a series designed by Native American artists to advertise a special exhibition held at the Museum of Modern Art in New York City from January to April of 1936. The goal of the exhibition was to expose white Americans to Native American cultures and encourage them to purchase works of art to decorate their homes.

resisted. One Filipino told an interviewer, "I would rather go hungry and die here than go home with an empty hand." At the end of the first year, only about 150 people had chosen to return to the islands, and by 1941 just 2,064 Filipinos had left the United States under the act.

NATIVE AMERICANS AND THE NEW DEAL

The New Deal brought major changes in federal policy toward Native Americans. As you have read, in 1871 the federal government had passed a law stripping Native Americans of their national sovereignty and making them wards of the state. The government had forced Native American children to attend "Indian schools," where all efforts focused on eliminating their languages and cultures. The goal was to assimilate Native Americans into mainstream American culture. The Dawes Act of 1887 attempted to turn Native Americans into farmers by dividing their reservation lands into plots intended for individual farms. However, most of the land was unsuitable for farming, and outsiders quickly bought up the best land.

When Roosevelt took office, he chose **John Collier**, a sociologist and author, as Commissioner of Indian Affairs. Collier was outraged by the effects of the Indian schools and the Dawes Act, and he set about making changes. He made sure that employers working on projects authorized by the CCC, NYA, WPA, and PWA hired Native American workers. He also encouraged Congress to authorize the **Indian Emergency Conservation Program (IECP)**. The IECP was similar to the CCC, but it employed Native Americans to work on physical improvements to reservations. Through the IECP, the government employed more than 85,000 Native Americans.

Collier worked to repeal the Dawes Act through Congressional passage of the 1934 **Indian Reorganization Act (IRA)**. The IRA provided tribes with federal funds to buy back some reservation lands. It also repealed laws that prohibited Native Americans from speaking their languages and practicing their customs. In addition, it provided for federal government recognition of tribal constitutions. Collier instituted a major shift in federal policy away from assimilation and toward autonomy.

HISTORICAL THINKING

1. **READING CHECK** How did the New Deal improve the lives of minorities in the United States?

2. **COMPARE AND CONTRAST** How did the Mexican Repatriation Program differ from the government program to repatriate Filipinos?

3. **SYNTHESIZE** What did the Scottsboro Boys case demonstrate about racism and discrimination in the United States at the time?

4. **DETERMINE CHRONOLOGY** Trace government treatment of Native Americans between 1871 and 1934. What changed and when?

BUILD BACKGROUND

LEGACY OF MARIAN ANDERSON CONCERT

Marian Anderson was internationally known, and her repertoire included traditional songs and spirituals as well as classical music and opera. The DAR's refusal to let her appear in Constitution Hall highlighted the issue of civil rights and sparked widespread controversy. As indicated by the microphone in the photograph, Anderson's performance at the Lincoln Memorial was also broadcast to a radio audience. In 1942, the DAR reversed its policies and invited Anderson to perform at Constitution Hall. On the 75th anniversary of her Lincoln Memorial performance, the DAR sponsored a concert to honor Marian Anderson's legacy.

THE SCOTTSBORO CASE

Two Supreme Court decisions in the Scottsboro case set legal precedents: *Powell* v. *Alabama* (1932) overturned the convictions because the defendants' legal counsel had been inadequate for a capital offense trial; *Norris* v. *Alabama* (1935) reversed the second conviction of one of the defendants because African Americans had been excluded from juries in the state. In 2013, Alabama legislators approved a process for granting posthumous pardons in certain felony cases. So, more than 80 years after the fact, the state of Alabama pardoned three Scottsboro Boys who had repeatedly been wrongly convicted.

TEACH

GUIDED DISCUSSION

3. **Identify** How were the FSA camps beneficial to Mexican Americans? *(Possible response: The camps provided food and shelter for workers and their families as well as a forum for discussing labor issues. As a result, farm laborers formed unions that fought for wages and benefits.)*

4. **Analyze Cause and Effect** How did the expanded role of the federal government in society affect Native Americans in the 1930s? *(Possible response: In some ways, government policies in the 1930s improved life for Native Americans by reversing earlier laws, providing jobs, and acknowledging the autonomy of tribal constitutions.)*

FORM AND SUPPORT OPINIONS

Ask students if they think the California "Apology Act" and other similar legislative actions are an effective response to racial/ethnic discrimination. Direct them to discuss their opinion with a partner, supporting their opinion with ideas based on their knowledge of human nature or on analogous situations they may have experience with or may have read about in the news. If they do not think the Apology Act was an effective response, they should identify what type of response they judge would be appropriate and effective. When pairs have finished their discussions, invite them to share their ideas with the class.

ACTIVE OPTIONS

On Your Feet: Three Corners Label three corners of the room with one of the minority groups discussed in the lesson: African Americans, Mexican Americans, and Native Americans. Instruct students to move to the corner of their choice for a focused discussion that addresses the question: What social trends did the Great Depression and New Deal bring about for this group, and how did it respond? Reconvene as a class and allow members of each group to summarize their discussions.

 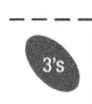

NG Learning Framework: Investigate the Past and Present of Mexican Americans

ATTITUDE Curiosity

KNOWLEDGE Our Human Story

Challenge students to investigate the status of Mexican Americans in the United States and relations between the United States and Mexico today. Ask them to draw parallels between the past and the present with regard to immigration, deportation, employment opportunities, and benefits. Encourage students to explore the consequences of past events and decisions. Direct students to share their reports in multimedia presentations, newspaper articles, interviews, or panel discussions.

HISTORICAL THINKING

ANSWERS

1. The New Deal programs provided financial relief and employment for minorities. The PWA built schools and hospitals in the South.

2. The Mexican Repatriation Program deported many Mexicans and coerced others into leaving the United States. By contrast, the Filipino repatriation program merely encouraged people to return to the Philippines voluntarily.

3. The Scottsboro Boys were convicted because they were African Americans, not because they were guilty. The case demonstrated that not all people received equal protection under the law.

4. In 1871, the government made Native Americans wards of the state and forced them to assimilate into white culture. In 1877, the Dawes Act divided Native American lands to try to turn Native Americans into farmers. John Collier made changes to ensure that federal programs hired Native American workers, and he helped establish the IECP to make improvements on reservations. In 1934, the IRA replaced the Dawes Act and allowed Native Americans to preserve their culture and have tribal constitutions.

CRITICAL VIEWING Answers will vary. Possible response: The workers may have been happy just to find work when others did not and to be in a community with other Filipino Americans.

THE NEW DEAL WINDS DOWN

The New Deal featured many ambitious, expensive programs. It had its successes and its failures; its staunch advocates and its fierce critics. By 1937, President Roosevelt had to make some hard decisions about the New Deal.

As the Fair Labor Standards Act took effect, it became the norm for teenagers to be in high school rather than in the workforce. In a 1941 photograph, energetic high school cheerleaders in Springfield, Pennsylvania, practice their routines.

THE ECONOMY STUMBLES AGAIN

As 1937 approached, the United States' national income and production rose nearly to the levels of 1929, before the stock market crash. However, the stock market itself had yet to reach its peak levels of 1929, even though stocks had enjoyed a minor boom over the preceding five years.

Roosevelt knew that government spending on programs such as the WPA had helped combat the economic crisis and fueled this recovery, and he knew that following John Maynard Keynes's economic guidance had been effective. Still, he was uncomfortable with the huge amount of government spending his programs had required. He worried that the ever-increasing national debt would cause inflation, or rising prices for goods and services,

and that federal welfare programs would diminish the recipients' initiative and self-respect. Indeed, Roosevelt had never intended for these programs to continue for the long term.

In 1937, the new Social Security payroll tax took effect, cutting into workers' take-home pay and removing billions of dollars of purchasing power from the economy. That same year, Roosevelt slashed funding for both the PWA and WPA, resulting in a loss of almost 2 million jobs. The new tax, combined with the program cuts, caused a recession. Unemployment began to rise, production plummeted, and people with no other choice began returning to breadlines and soup kitchens. The stock market fell yet again. Something had to be done, and quickly.

PRIMARY SOURCES

Elected to four terms, Franklin Roosevelt is still one of the most popular presidents in American history. But many people disagreed with his policies. For example, former president Herbert Hoover did not believe the New Deal had much chance for success.

The country is going sour on the New Deal, despite the heroic efforts of the Press. Unless there is a halt, the real question will be that, having cast off all moorings, will we swing to the "right" or to the "left." I fear first the "left," and then when the great middle class (80% of America) realizes its ruin, it will drive into some American interpretation of Hitler or Mussolini.

—from a letter written by Herbert Hoover, 1933

Four years after Hoover made his prediction, FDR was still promoting New Deal policies. In a speech to Congress, he introduced the Fair Labor Standards Act.

Our Nation so richly endowed with natural resources and with a capable and industrious population should be able to devise ways and means of insuring to all our able-bodied working men and women a fair day's pay for a fair day's work. All but the hopelessly reactionary will agree that to conserve our primary resources of man power, government must have some control over maximum hours, minimum wages, the evil of child labor and the exploitation of unorganized labor.

—from President Franklin Roosevelt's message to Congress, May 24, 1937

TRIMMING THE NEW DEAL

Starting in October of 1937, Roosevelt and Congress took steps to approve $5 billion in federal funds for relief and public works programs. The economy in crisis responded positively, but Roosevelt's public image suffered because people felt he relied on government spending to solve economic problems.

By 1938, the New Deal had clearly lost momentum. Harry Hopkins, one of the architects of the New Deal, lamented that the public was "bored with the poor, the unemployed, the insecure." Congressional Republicans and conservative Democrats—in other words, Roosevelt's political opponents—gained control of the legislature in that year's midterm elections. Without a majority in Congress supporting him, Roosevelt could not enact any more progressive programs. On top of that, Roosevelt's court-packing scheme had taken a toll on his reputation. Many members of Congress had turned against him.

The passage of the Fair Labor Standards Act was among Roosevelt's few legislative achievements in 1938. The act stipulated a minimum hourly wage and a maximum 40-hour workweek. It immediately raised the wages of almost a million American workers and shortened the work hours of millions as well. The act also finally abolished child labor in most industries. As you have read, prior to the passage of the Fair Labor Standards Act, child labor was a

common practice. In 1900, for example, 18 percent of American workers were under age 16. Now American children could concentrate on their education rather than on helping to support their families.

Without the support of Congress, most of the New Deal programs came to an end from a lack of funding in 1939. However, the nation's economic battle was not completely won. More than 8 million Americans were still unemployed. Roosevelt's critics pointed out that the New Deal strategy may have offered a measure of protection for unemployed and vulnerable workers, but it had not restored the nation to the prosperity of the 1920s. As it turned out, it would take another world war—and the full **mobilization**, or enlistment of soldiers, that followed—to bring back prosperity.

HISTORICAL THINKING

1. **READING CHECK** Why were most New Deal programs discontinued?

2. **MAKE CONNECTIONS** What types of economic indicators contributed to a recession in 1937?

3. **DRAW CONCLUSIONS** Why do you think a ban on child labor passed during the time of the New Deal?

4. **SUMMARIZE** What controversies and negative effects was Roosevelt concerned about in terms of the New Deal?

PLAN: 2-PAGE LESSON

OBJECTIVE

Analyze why the New Deal became less effective at the end of the 1930s.

CRITICAL THINKING SKILLS FOR LESSON 4.1

- Make Connections
- Draw Conclusions
- Summarize
- Generalize
- Make Inferences
- Analyze Primary Sources

ESSENTIAL QUESTION FOR CHAPTER 20

In what ways were Franklin Roosevelt's policies during the Great Depression groundbreaking? Although expansive, Roosevelt's policies were not intended to be a permanent remedy. Lesson 4.1 discusses the causes and effects of the end of New Deal programs.

BACKGROUND FOR THE TEACHER

Franklin Roosevelt made protections for workers an issue in his 1936 presidential campaign. During his second term in office, he pursued legislation for a 40-cent-per-hour minimum wage, a 40-hour workweek, and a minimum age of 16 years old for workers in certain industries, but it failed two attempts to pass the House and the Senate. The Fair Labor Standards Act succeeded only after the minimum wage was lowered to 25 cents an hour—to appease southerners who argued that 40 cents an hour would force businesses to close—and the workweek raised to 44 hours.

INTRODUCE & ENGAGE

CREATE A REPORT CARD FOR FDR

Invite students to brainstorm categories for evaluating a president's performance in office. Examples might include fulfilling promises, improving the economy, making life better for ordinary Americans, maintaining the support of the people and/or Congress. Ask students to grade FDR in each category in their final list. **ASK:** Would the grades change from his first term to his second term in office? Why or why not? *(Answers will vary. Possible response: Yes. Roosevelt won a second term by a landslide, but he lost some support due to the court-packing plan.)* Tell students that in this lesson they will learn why Roosevelt's policies began to lose momentum in the late 1930s.

TEACH

GUIDED DISCUSSION

1. **Generalize** How did the aggregate economic status of the U.S. economy coming into 1937 reflect New Deal successes and failures? *(The pre-1937 rise in income and production to 1929 levels reflected the success of New Deal programs, but they had failed to cause the stock market to rebound to its 1920s peaks.)*

2. **Make Inferences** How did the historical event of passing the Fair Labor Standards Act likely affect the overall education level in the United States? *(Possible response: More children had an opportunity to attend school longer because they were no longer part of the workforce. That would result in many more people in the United States finishing high school.)*

ANALYZE PRIMARY SOURCES

Direct students to read the Primary Sources feature and restate the arguments in their own words. **ASK:** Why do you think Hoover was so critical of the New Deal? *(Possible responses: It was more ambitious than the policies he had enacted. He feared the results of expanding government power.)* **ASK:** Why is the time difference between Hoover's letter and Roosevelt's message to Congress significant? *(Possible response: Hoover made his dire prediction near the beginning of the New Deal, when the new programs were untested. Roosevelt was able to point to the successes of previous New Deal programs when he sought support for the Fair Labor Standards Act during his second term.)*

ACTIVE OPTIONS

On Your Feet: Create a Problem-and-Solution Chain To emphasize the complexity of historical causes and effects, give small groups a Problem-and-Solution Chain like the one shown here. Instruct groups to choose one problem of the Great Depression and complete their graphic organizer, showing one step taken by the government to combat the problem, which led to another problem, which required another solution, and so on. Then have each group act out its work for the class in a human problem-and-solution chain.

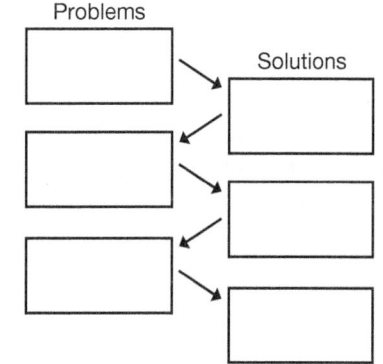

Problems

Solutions

NG Learning Framework: Discover the Legacy of the FLSA

SKILLS Collaboration, Communication

KNOWLEDGE Our Human Story

Prompt students to review the purposes of the FLSA in 1938. *(to establish a minimum wage and maximum workweek; to abolish child labor)* Direct students to investigate the issues the FLSA addresses now. Encourage them to collaborate to create posters that promote the FLSA work done by the Department of Labor today. Guide students to create a display that compares their completed posters with similar posters from 1938.

DIFFERENTIATE

STRIVING READERS

Make a List Post this heading: Five Things I Know About the New Deal. After students read the lesson, ask them to copy the posted heading and add five sentences about the topic. Remind them to include both the successes and shortcomings of the New Deal. Invite volunteers to share their sentences with the class.

GIFTED & TALENTED

Engage in a Debate Tell students to research and read the full texts of the primary source excerpts and then take Hoover's or Roosevelt's position on the success or failure of the New Deal. After students gather information and take notes, ask them to assume the role of their historical figure and participate in a debate on the value of the New Deal. After the debate, you may want to ask students to discuss how these men's opposing philosophies are relevant to today's discussions about the role of government.

See the Chapter Planner for more strategies for differentiation.

HISTORICAL THINKING

ANSWERS

1. Lack of funding due to a loss of support from Congress led to the end of most New Deal programs.

2. The Social Security payroll tax reduced purchasing power, and WPA and PWA program cuts resulted in a loss of jobs. The rise in unemployment and a decrease in production contributed to a recession.

3. Possible response: Due to increased wages, parents no longer needed children to work to help support their families. In addition, many adults were unemployed and may have needed the jobs that children had been doing for lower wages.

4. An increasing national debt could lead to inflation; federal welfare problems could make people dependent on the government and decrease their initiative.

THE NEW DEAL'S IMPACT

Without realizing it, you've probably encountered the New Deal in your everyday life. If you have a part-time job, you may be paying Social Security tax. If you have a bank account, your money is safe because it's insured by an agency that was part of the New Deal.

AMERICAN PLACES
The Hoover Dam
Arizona and Nevada

Designed to control flooding of the Colorado River and to provide water to western states, the Hoover Dam was built during the Great Depression and employed more than 21,000 workers. Its construction was a huge and dangerous undertaking, claiming more than 90 lives.

AN EXPANDED GOVERNMENT ROLE

When the Great Depression began, some people believed restricting government spending was the best way to make the economy bounce back. But President Roosevelt did just the opposite. As you have read, he took an active role in combatting the economic crisis by enacting the New Deal and following a policy of **deficit spending**, or spending more money than the government receives from taxes.

The New Deal pumped millions of dollars into the economy by creating federal jobs. It regulated banking and investment activities and increased the government's participation in the settlement of labor disputes. The New Deal also set the precedent of providing federal aid to farmers.

As you have read, the Supreme Court nullified some New Deal legislation, claiming programs were unconstitutional because they gave the executive branch of the government too much authority. Because of the new powers assumed by the executive branch, some historians have labeled the New Deal as the beginning of the **Imperial Presidency**, a presidency that exercises more power than the Constitution allows.

Some New Deal programs, such as the National Industrial Recovery Act and the WPA, reflected the principle that government has a responsibility for its citizens' welfare. Such New Deal innovations as unions' right to collective bargaining, a minimum wage, a 40-hour workweek, and Social Security also reflected that principle. Thus, the New Deal contributed to the idea of the modern **welfare state**, a system in which the government provides for the health and well-being of its citizens.

CONSERVATIVE RESPONSES

Conservatives had criticized Roosevelt's New Deal policies from the start. They believed the New Deal expanded the size and power of the federal government too much, while curbing free enterprise. They also argued that the New Deal had not reached its goals. Pointing to continuing unemployment and poverty, they claimed the New Deal had been no kind of deal at all. Some liberals, who felt the New Deal could do more to remedy social and economic problems, joined the conservatives in this criticism.

Among the New Deal's most vocal critics was Ohio senator **Robert A. Taft**, the son of former president William Howard Taft. Although he supported some New Deal programs, such as unemployment insurance, he opposed big government and thought the New Deal exhibited some of its worst aspects, from wasteful spending to excessive interference in business. The New Deal's overregulation and high taxes hurt business, Taft asserted, accusing its supporters of attacking "individual opportunity, initiative, and freedom." He continued to be a thorn in progressives' sides throughout his career.

LASTING PROGRAMS

Today, supporters and critics agree on one aspect of the New Deal: its lasting impact on the United States. Many Americans still depend on government agencies and programs that began with the New Deal. For example, most Americans take advantage of Social Security at some time. Although never intended to provide a full pension, Social Security does grant senior citizens a measure of security and a hedge against poverty. It also aids workers who have become disabled or temporarily unemployed.

The **Federal Deposit Insurance Corporation (FDIC)**, which insures the savings accounts of individual bank depositors, was part of the Glass-Steagall Banking Act of 1933. The FDIC continues to protect bank customers, insuring their deposits for up to $250,000 against loss in the event of a bank failure. After decades of urging from the big banks, Congress repealed most of the Glass-Steagall Banking Act in 1999, but it left the FDIC in place.

Another New Deal agency that still exists is the **Securities and Exchange Commission (SEC)**, created in 1934. As you have read, the economic crash in 1929 that caused the Great Depression was driven by the collapse of the stock market. Roosevelt created the SEC to protect investors in the stock market in ways similar to how the FDIC insures bank depositors. The SEC continues to oversee the stock market today, regulating stock-trading procedures and managing the nation's economic growth.

The National Labor Relations Board also continues to meet to this day. The board mediates labor disputes between unions and employers. Under the New Deal, workers gained protection of their right to organize and negotiate collectively with employers.

Thousands of bridges, dams, highways, schools, and other construction projects that remain today are another major legacy of the New Deal. Large public works projects, including the Hoover Dam, the Bonneville Dam, the California Central Valley Project, and the Tennessee Valley Authority, changed the lives of millions of Americans, providing them with flood control, irrigation, and electrical power.

HISTORICAL THINKING

1. **READING CHECK** How did the New Deal expand the role of the federal government in the nation's economy?

2. **DETERMINE CHRONOLOGY** What sequence of events led to the establishment of the Securities and Exchange Commission, and what is its function today?

3. **FORM AND SUPPORT OPINIONS** Do you agree or disagree with conservative critics of the New Deal? Give reasons for your opinion.

OBJECTIVE

Describe how certain federal programs developed during the New Deal are still in operation today.

CRITICAL THINKING SKILLS FOR LESSON 4.2

• Determine Chronology

• Form and Support Opinions

• Analyze Language Use

• Evaluate

ESSENTIAL QUESTION FOR CHAPTER 20

In what ways were Franklin Roosevelt's policies during the Great Depression groundbreaking?
The programs Roosevelt established during the New Deal greatly expanded the role of government. Lesson 4.2 discusses how some of these programs continue to affect the United States today.

BACKGROUND FOR THE TEACHER

One lasting effect of the New Deal is the Social Security number (SSN). The familiar nine-digit unique identifiers were originally created in 1936 to track workers' earnings and compute Social Security benefits. Today, the SSN has become a ubiquitous form of identification and means of tracking information about its owner. The widespread use of the SSNs have made them a principle means of identity theft. The Social Security Administration cautions people not to carry their Social Security card with them and never to disclose their SSN over the phone.

INTRODUCE & ENGAGE

REVIEW NEW DEAL ALPHABET SOUP

Because New Deal programs are known by their initials, they are sometimes referred to as "alphabet soup." Challenge students to brainstorm a list of New Deal programs. Write their responses on the board. Then call on volunteers to circle programs that they think are still in existence. At the end of the lesson, ask students to revisit the list, make additions or corrections, and judge whether each was effective.

TEACH

GUIDED DISCUSSION

1. **Analyze Language Use** Is the term *Imperial Presidency* a valid label for the New Deal? Why or why not? *(Answers will vary. Possible responses: Yes. FDR greatly expanded the role of the executive branch of government. No. The legislative and judicial branches still had the power to block or strike down executive actions.)*

2. **Evaluate** In what way do the lasting programs of the New Deal contribute to a modern welfare state? *(Possible responses: Government programs still provide for the health, safety, and well-being of citizens. Social Security helps meet the needs of seniors and people who are disabled or unemployed. The FDIC and SEC protect people's savings and investments. The NLRB protects workers' rights to negotiate with employers.)*

AMERICAN PLACES

In 1931, construction began on Hoover Dam on the Colorado River at the border of Nevada and Arizona. When completed in 1936, it was the world's tallest dam. So many people referred to the structure as Boulder Dam that in 1947 Congress officially redeclared it Hoover Dam. Managed today by the Bureau of Reclamation, Hoover Dam remains a modern engineering marvel that restrains enough water to flood the state of Pennsylvania, forming Lake Mead, the nation's biggest human-made lake. The dam has relieved Arizona and Southern California from Colorado River floods, and it generates enough hydroelectricity to meet the needs of more than a million people in Nevada, Arizona, and Southern California. It is a National Historic Landmark visited by nearly a million people each year.

ACTIVE OPTIONS

On Your Feet: Vote with Your Feet Label one side of the classroom "New Deal Supporters" and the other side "New Deal Opponents." Direct students to move to the side of the room that reflects their viewpoint. Then, alternating sides, have each student state a reason that supports his or her view. After each statement, invite students to change their allegiance by moving to the other side of the classroom, depending upon whether they found the argument valid or fallacious.

Active History: Analyze Primary Sources Extend the lesson by using either the PDF or Whiteboard version of the activity. These activities take a deeper look at a topic from, or related to, the lesson. Explore the activities as a class, turn them into group assignments, or even assign them individually.

DIFFERENTIATE

ENGLISH LANGUAGE LEARNERS   ELD

Use a Meaning Map Pair students at the **Emerging** level with students at the **Expanding** or **Bridging** levels. Tell them to use a Meaning Map to better understand the vocabulary term *Federal Deposit Insurance Corporation (FDIC)*. If time permits, instruct students to make Meaning Maps for the other lasting programs of the New Deal: Social Security, the Securities and Exchange Commission (SEC), and the National Labor Relations Board. Direct pairs to trade Meaning Maps and note similarities and differences.

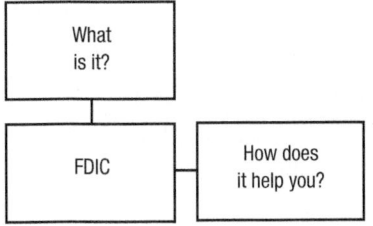

PRE-AP   STEM

Analyze Impacts Tell students that while the Hoover Dam was constructed to provide jobs, water, and electricity for people, there were many unintended consequences on the environment, particularly regarding the plants, birds, and fish that lived in or near the Colorado River. Prompt students to conduct online research into the ecological impacts of the dam, assessing the credibility of each source. Then instruct students to analyze the positive and negative impacts of the dam. Students may conclude by stating whether their research leads them to believe that the net impact of the dam has been positive or negative. Encourage students to present their findings and conclusions to the class in an oral report.

See the Chapter Planner for more strategies for differentiation.

HISTORICAL THINKING

ANSWERS

1. The federal government used deficit spending to create federal jobs for the unemployed and provide welfare to people in need.

2. The stock market crash in 1929 caused the Great Depression. To protect investors, Roosevelt created the SEC in 1934. Today, the agency regulates stock-trading procedures.

3. Answers will vary. Students should support their opinions with information from the text. Possible response: Taft's assessment was correct—businesses could thrive with lower taxes and would then be able to hire more people.

VOCABULARY

Use each of the following vocabulary words in a sentence that shows an understanding of the term's meaning.

1. **lame duck**
   Once Roosevelt won the 1932 presidential election, President Hoover was a lame duck.

2. **economic planning**

3. **First Hundred Days**

4. **New Deal**

5. **court-packing plan**

6. **voting bloc**

7. **collective bargaining**

8. **mobilization**

9. **deficit spending**

READING STRATEGY
DETERMINE CHRONOLOGY

Use a time line like the one below to organize the major events of the 1930s. Include dates and notes on the events. Then answer the question.

Time Line

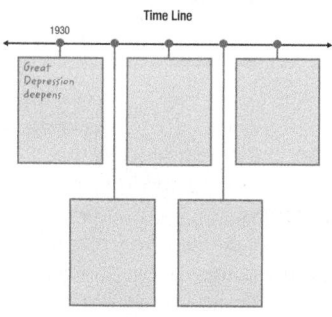

10. How did New Deal policies change the lives of ordinary Americans?

MAIN IDEAS

Answer the following questions. Support your answers with evidence from the chapter.

11. In what way did Franklin Roosevelt's 1932 election indicate a change in direction for the country? **LESSON 1.1**

12. What did President Roosevelt accomplish in the First Hundred Days? **LESSON 1.2**

13. How did planned scarcity help the nation's economy recover? **LESSON 1.2**

14. What was the purpose of the Social Security Act? **LESSON 2.1**

15. What was the main goal of the Wagner Act? **LESSON 2.3**

16. How did Eleanor Roosevelt serve as the "conscience" of the Roosevelt administration? **LESSON 3.1**

17. Who was Mary McLeod Bethune? **LESSON 3.2**

18. Why did President Roosevelt view his New Deal programs as short-term solutions? **LESSON 4.1**

19. What New Deal programs still exist today? **LESSON 4.2**

HISTORICAL THINKING

Answer the following questions. Support your answers with evidence from the chapter.

20. **SYNTHESIZE** How did the New Deal attempt to remedy problems created by the Great Depression?

21. **MAKE INFERENCES** Why do you think President Roosevelt gathered the advisers known as the brain trust around him during the beginning of his presidency?

22. **COMPARE AND CONTRAST** How were the AFL and the CIO alike and different?

23. **MAKE PREDICTIONS** What direction might the country have taken during the Depression if FDR had not been elected president?

24. **DETERMINE CHRONOLOGY** What events led to increased labor union membership and activity in the 1930s?

25. **FORM AND SUPPORT OPINIONS** Was the development of an activist government during the 1930s positive or negative? Support your opinion with evidence from the chapter.

ANALYZE VISUALS

On February 11, 1937, the *Buffalo* [New York] *Evening News* ran a cartoon by Billy Warren portraying FDR walking up some steps with a cane. Study the cartoon and answer the questions that follow.

Step by Step

26. What actions do the steps on the stairs represent?

27. What does the cartoon reveal about the artist's bias toward FDR's actions?

ANALYZE SOURCES

In 1998, the National Parks Service interviewed men about their work for the CCC during the Depression. In the transcript that follows, Reed Engle (RE) interviews Arthur Emory (AE), a former CCC worker. Read the excerpt and answer the question.

> RE: What do you think was the best thing about the CCC experience?
>
> AE: The chance for learning. You see most of the people that went in there had dropped out of school. And they were just allowed to roam the street. Which was bad—that'd get you in a heap of trouble. It kind of gave them a chance to get their feet on the ground. So they could learn if they wanted to, which most of them did. It was actually the best thing that ever happened to kids our age at that time. Because you actually earned your way in it. They learned to do so many different things. Like, nobody wants to use a shovel, I don't believe. But they had to learn to use a shovel, and everybody learned something.
>
> —from an interview with Arthur Emory, former CCC employee, 1998

28. How might this employee's experiences and personal biases have shaped his views toward the benefits of working for the CCC?

CONNECT TO YOUR LIFE

29. **INFORMATIVE** Research a New Deal artifact in your state, such as a WPA building or work of art. Write an essay describing the artifact and explaining how it reflects the New Deal.

TIPS

- Revisit the Curating History feature in this chapter. Then find more WPA artifacts at the Milwaukee Public Museum website.

- Organize your research in a two-column chart. In the first, write notes about the artifact. In the second, indicate how that information reflects the New Deal.

- Be sure to identify the New Deal agency that produced the artifact, the agency director, and who worked on the artifact, if possible. Cite information from the chapter describing the purpose of the agency.

- Conclude the essay with a paragraph that sums up what the artifact reveals about the New Deal's effects on American life.

VOCABULARY ANSWERS

1. Once Roosevelt won the 1932 presidential election, President Hoover was a lame duck.

2. Economic planning allowed the government to study economic indicators to control the nation's economy in the future.

3. In his first months in office, called the First Hundred Days, FDR launched more than a dozen new programs.

4. The New Deal refers to the programs and reforms FDR put in place to alleviate the Great Depression.

5. The court-packing plan proposed adding liberal justices to the Supreme Court to influence decisions.

6. A voting bloc of African Americans in the North helped elect Roosevelt and other Democrats who supported New Deal programs.

7. Workers gained power through collective bargaining.

8. War required the mobilization of soldiers.

9. Deficit spending grew the economy but increased the national debt.

READING STRATEGY ANSWER

Time Line

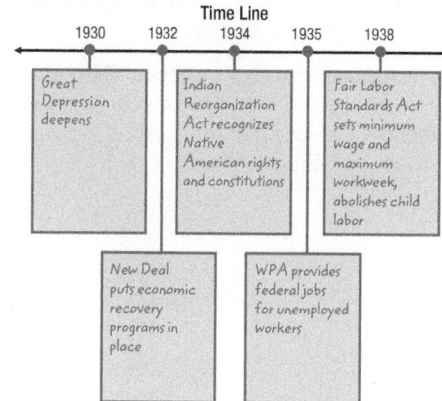

10. New Deal policies provided financial aid and employment opportunities for people in need. They protected workers' rights, abolished child labor, and created safeguards for investments and savings.

MAIN IDEAS ANSWERS

11. Roosevelt was a progressive, and his election signaled that the American people wanted a leader who would take action to end the Great Depression.

12. During the First Hundred Days, Roosevelt assembled a brain trust to advise him. He declared a bank holiday, called Congress into session, and generated 15 laws to aid the nation's economy.

13. Planned scarcity lowered the supply of certain farm products, thereby creating demand and increasing farmers' incomes.

14. The Social Security Act provided insurance for the unemployed and people in need, and it established a pension fund to provide income for retired people.

15. The Wagner Act gave workers the right to unionize without fear of retaliation from employers.

16. Eleanor Roosevelt advocated for women, children, and minorities. She worked to make sure New Deal policies addressed the needs of these segments of the population.

17. Mary McLeod Bethune was head of the National Youth Administration's Office of Negro Affairs. As the New Deal's highest ranking African-American appointee, she served as a White House advisor on minority affairs.

18. New Deal programs greatly increased government spending and diminished welfare recipients' initiative.

19. Social Security, the Federal Deposit Insurance Corporation, the Securities and Exchange Commission, and the National Labor Relations Board still exist today.

HISTORICAL THINKING ANSWERS

20. The New Deal created federal jobs to relieve unemployment; it regulated banking and investment to protect savings; it participated in settling labor disputes to protect workers' rights; and it provided federal aid to farmers.

21. The brain trust provided expert advice and a means of involving citizens in the process of fixing the economy.

22. Both organizations promoted workers' rights, but their members represented different kinds of industries. The AFL consisted of skilled workers, such as carpenters and masons. The CIO represented mass-production industries, such as auto manufacturing and steel production.

23. Answers will vary. Possible response: The Great Depression might have been longer and deeper without FDR's New Deal.

24. John L. Lewis attracted union members by indicating that FDR supported organized labor. The Wagner Act facilitated unionization. The National Labor Relations Act required employers to allow collective bargaining. The formation of the CIO created unions for workers in manufacturing.

25. Answers will vary. Possible response: It was mostly positive because many Americans were really hurt by the Great Depression, and the actions of the government helped them survive.

ANALYZE VISUALS ANSWERS

26. The first step represents FDR's expansion of the power of the executive branch of government. The second step represents FDR's proposed court-packing plan.

27. The cartoon conveys a belief that FDR's actions would make him a dictator.

ANALYZE SOURCES ANSWER

28. The employee's experiences appear to have been positive, which probably caused him to emphasize the benefits of the CCC.

CONNECT TO YOUR LIFE ANSWER

29. Answers will vary, but students' essays should clearly relate the artifact to the lasting impact of the New Deal, identify information about the New Deal agency from which the work originated, and conclude by recounting how the artifact illustrates the New Deal's continued impact on life in the United States.

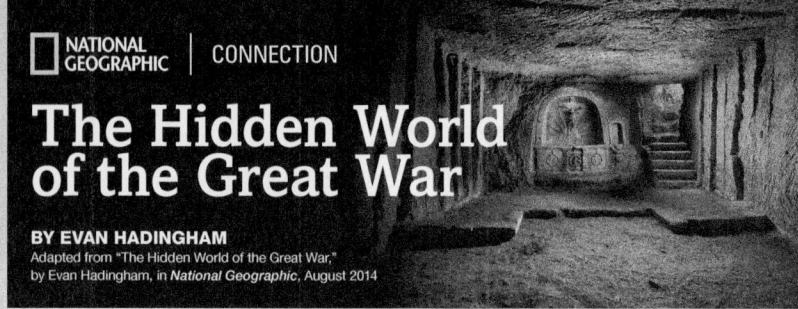

NATIONAL GEOGRAPHIC | CONNECTION

The Hidden World of the Great War

BY EVAN HADINGHAM

Adapted from "The Hidden World of the Great War,"
by Evan Hadingham, in *National Geographic*, August 2014

The entrance is a small hole in the earth in northeastern France. I'm following Jeff Gusky, a photographer and physician from Texas who has explored dozens of underground spaces like this one. Here, shortly after the outbreak of the First World War, German military engineers would take turns listening for the slightest sound of enemy tunnelers. Muffled voices or the scraping of shovels meant that a hostile mining team might be only yards away. The danger grew if the digging stopped and you heard the sounds of the enemy laying high explosives at the end of the tunnel. Most nerve-racking of all was the silence that followed. At any moment the charges might detonate and blow you apart or bury you alive.

Nearby, on one of the tunnel walls, our headlamps illuminate graffiti left by the German engineers who manned this listening post. The pencil marks appear as if they were written yesterday. The soft chalk and limestone bedrock of France's Picardy region was ideal for World War I soldiers to record their presence in penciled signatures, sketches and caricatures, carvings, and even intricate relief sculptures.

The conflict began with confidence on all sides that the fighting would be over by Christmas. By the end of 1914, the German advance had stalled, the armies had dug in, and an extensive network of trenches stretched from the North Sea coast to the Swiss border. In the grip of this deadly stalemate, the Germans, French, and British resorted to siege-warfare techniques that had changed little over the centuries. The goal was to dig under key enemy strongpoints and blow them up.

But the underground war was not confined to narrow tunnels. Beneath Picardy's fields and forests are centuries-old abandoned quarries, some of which could shelter thousands of troops. One morning, we explore one such site, led there by the owner of the property. In one cavern, we peer at an array of finely engraved badges and memorials proclaiming the French regiments that had sheltered here. Then we encounter several chapels elaborately carved and painted with religious symbols, army insignia, and the names of notable French victories.

Life in the quarries was vastly preferable to the muddy hell of the trenches above. A journalist visiting one of the caverns in 1915 noted that "a dry shelter, straw, some furniture, a fire, are great luxuries for those returning from the trenches."

The quarries kept an even temperature year-round, but as one French soldier wrote home, "vermin devour us, and it's teeming with lice, fleas, rats and mice." To pass the time, the exhausted men would daydream. Images of women proliferate on the quarry walls, including many sentimental and idealized portraits.

Both sides converted the largest quarries into underground cities, many of them remarkably intact today. Not far from the landowner's property, we find ourselves in an astonishing quarry that stretches for more than seven miles, with twisting passageways and high ceilings. In 1915, the Germans connected this network to their frontline trenches. They installed electric lights and telephones, command posts, a bakery, a butcher's shop, a machine shop, a hospital, and a chapel.

The original diesel generator and barbed wire defenses are still in place. So are dozens of street signs neatly stenciled on every corner. On the cavern walls, German troops have inscribed their names and regiments, religious and military icons, elaborately sculpted portraits and caricatures, and sketches of dogs and other cartoons.

Safe underground from the inhuman chaos of the battlefield above, the men of the First World War left these personal expressions of identity and survival. Gusky's images bring to light the subterranean world soldiers inhabited and endured while sheltering from constant shellfire.

The traces they left behind reveal a forgotten world of World War I. They also connect us to individual soldiers, many of whom would not survive the nightmare of trench warfare.

> For more from National Geographic check out "1918 Flu Pandemic" online.

UNIT INQUIRY: Create a Conflict Resolution Strategy

In this unit, you learned about conflicts the United States confronted on global, national, and local levels. From fighting in World War I to addressing political and labor unrest, embracing rights for women, and managing a massive economic downturn, American leaders and citizens alike had to navigate through new territories. Based on your understanding of the text, which conflict resolution strategies worked best? Which failed? How important were leaders' approaches in producing a positive or negative outcome?

ASSIGNMENT

Create a strategy you think could have been successful in resolving a conflict that took place in the United States between 1914 and 1940. Take into account factors that led to the conflict. Be prepared to present and defend your strategy to the class.

Plan As you create your conflict resolution strategy, think about the context in which the conflict unfolded, including the clash of old and new ideas of nationalism, government, and individual human rights. Also consider the impact of war, migration, and expanded citizenship. List the factors that sparked conflict, and address the most significant ones in your strategy. Use a graphic organizer to organize your thoughts.

Goals	Obstacles	Outcome
Summary		

Produce Use your notes to produce a detailed description of your conflict and design a solid conflict resolution strategy. Write your descriptions in outline or paragraph form.

Present Present your strategy to the class. You might consider one of these options:

- Host a debate on a conflict that you have learned about in this unit. Select volunteers to represent both sides of the conflict. Provide a short summary of the conflict to remind the audience of the main issues. Then have an appointed moderator pose prepared questions for the debaters. Allow time for the audience to pose questions as well. Conclude with a vote by the audience on which debaters proposed the best resolution to the conflict.

- Launch a campaign. Create election posters that summarize a conflict and its causes and that propose viable resolutions to the problem. Include a name for your campaign, slogans, and information that communicates the core issues.

- Write a speech that describes the origins of and proposes a resolution for the conflict through use of relevant factual evidence and sound reasoning.

NATIONAL GEOGRAPHIC | LEARNING FRAMEWORK ACTIVITIES

Write a Conflict Negotiator Profile

ATTITUDE Curiosity

KNOWLEDGE Our Human Story

Choose a historical figure you read about in this unit who demonstrated good conflict resolution skills. Research primary and secondary sources to gather evidence about his or her role in negotiating a resolution to a conflict. Note discrepancies among sources. Then write a profile for this individual or create something more visual, such as a poster or digital presentation. Your profile should include information such as birth and death dates, where the person lived, and the work she or he did. Your profile must also highlight a specific resolution to a conflict this person helped negotiate. Consider exploring what you think might have happened if she or he had not taken proactive action in negotiating a resolution.

Settle a Dispute

ATTITUDES Empowerment, Responsibility

SKILLS Collaboration, Problem Solving

Collaborate with a small group to research a dispute in your school or community. Assign roles to group members, such as researcher, interviewer, writer, and presenter. Scan the news and other diverse sources to gather evidence about the dispute, including people or groups on both (or all) sides of the conflict and important dates or events. Then, as a group, create a document or set up a poster or whiteboard on which you can chart the evidence you gather. Hold a meeting to discuss how your group might settle the dispute. Use the evidence you have gathered to put together a viable proposal. Once your group has settled on a solution, present both the dispute and your solution to the class.

NATIONAL GEOGRAPHIC CONNECTION

GUIDED DISCUSSION FOR "THE HIDDEN WORLD OF THE GREAT WAR"

1. **Compare and Contrast** How were the trenches similar to and different from the underground quarries? *(Both places were close to battlefields and full of rats, mice, fleas, and lice. While the trenches were filled with mud, narrow, and crowded, quarries were dry and spacious. Some quarries even had amenities such as electricity, furniture, a chapel for religious services, a bakery, and working telephones.)*

2. **Ask and Answer Questions** Imagine that you are able to interview one of the soldiers living in the underground quarry mentioned in the article. What questions would you have for this soldier, and how do you think the soldier might respond? *(Answers will vary. Students might suggest asking what the soldier does during cease-fire periods with the soldier replying that he writes in a journal, sketches portraits of other soldiers, or exercises by jogging throughout the quarry.)*

GUIDED DISCUSSION FOR "1918 FLU PANDEMIC"

1. **Make Connections** How might China's comparatively lower mortality rate from the 1918 flu have helped researchers? *(The lower death rate could have meant that China was exposed earlier, perhaps to a weaker strain of the virus. Researchers might have been able to develop effective vaccines from the earlier outbreak.)*

2. **Draw Conclusions** Why is it important now, many decades after the flu broke out and ran its course, to verify whether the 1918 flu pandemic began in China? *(Finding out where a specific disease, or a pandemic, may have originated could be a key factor in preventing mass disease transmission in the future.)*

 **HISTORY NOTEBOOK**

Encourage students to complete the Unit Wrap-Up page for Unit 6 in their History Notebooks.

UNIT INQUIRY PROJECT RUBRIC

ASSESS

Use the rubric to assess each student's participation and performance.

SCORE	ASSIGNMENT	PRODUCT	PRESENTATION
3 GREAT	• Student thoroughly understands the assignment. • Student participates fully in the project process. • Student using debate option works well with team members.	• Conflict strategy is well thought out. • Conflict is described in detail and resolution strategy is solid. • Descriptions are well written in outline or paragraph form.	• Presentation is clear, concise, and logical. • Presentation does a good job of creatively representing a debate, campaign, or speech. • Presentation engages the audience.
2 GOOD	• Student mostly understands the assignment. • Student participates fairly well in the project process. • Student using debate option works fairly well with team members.	• Conflict strategy is fairly well thought out. • Conflict is described with a few details and resolution strategy is evident. • Descriptions are adequately written in outline or paragraph form.	• Presentation is fairly clear, concise, and logical. • Presentation does an adequate job of creatively representing a debate, campaign, or speech. • Presentation somewhat engages the audience.
1 NEEDS WORK	• Student does not understand the assignment. • Student minimally participates or does not participate in the project process. • Student using debate option does not work well with team members.	• Conflict strategy is not well thought out. • Conflict is not clear and resolution strategy is not evident. • Descriptions are not written in outline or paragraph form.	• Presentation is not clear, concise, or logical. • Presentation does an inadequate job of representing a debate, campaign, or speech. • Presentation does not engage the audience.

NATIONAL GEOGRAPHIC LEARNING FRAMEWORK RUBRIC

ASSESS

Use the rubric to assess how each student applies the National Geographic Learning Framework.

SCORE	ASSIGNMENT	ASSIGNMENT	FINAL PRODUCTS
3 GREAT	• Profile reflects **Curiosity** well. • Profile explores **Our Human Story** well.	• Research reflects **Empowerment** and **Responsibility** well. • Research demonstrates **Collaboration** and **Problem-Solving** well.	• Final products are engaging, creative, and well presented.
2 GOOD	• Profile reflects **Curiosity**. • Profile explores **Our Human Story**.	• Research reflects **Empowerment** and **Responsibility**. • Research demonstrates **Collaboration** and **Problem-Solving**.	• Final products are interesting, logical, and complete.
1 NEEDS WORK	• Profile does not reflect **Curiosity**. • Profile does not explore **Our Human Story**.	• Research does not reflect **Empowerment** and **Responsibility**. • Research does not demonstrate **Collaboration** and **Problem-Solving**.	• Final products are not creative, complete, or interesting.

AMERICAN TROOPS ARRIVE IN PALERMO

Share with students that the following description is based on an account by John Thompson, a *Chicago Tribune* war correspondent during World War II. Thompson reported on the liberation of Palermo, having arrived in the city only a few hours after the Allies.

The final battle the Allies fought to liberate the Sicilian city of Palermo took place 33 miles from the city along a narrow pass flanked on both sides by mountain peaks, a highly strategic position for German and Italian forces. Although Axis troops received support and firepower from an aircraft battalion stationed at a nearby base, the Allies won the battle decisively after only two hours of fighting. General George Patton later claimed that the American soldier as a fighting entity had come into its own in Sicily, taking on and prevailing against the best of German and Italian soldiers.

Driving to Palermo after the battle, American troops passed through the suburbs and then the edge of the city, past well-maintained two-story stone homes and beautiful gardens full of trees and flowers. Yet as the jeeps and trucks moved into the city itself, and especially as they neared the waterfront, the streets became pocked and rutted, showing signs of heavy artillery fire. Shattered windows gave a view into bombed-out shops and gutted homes. The citizens of Palermo filled the streets to greet the incoming American forces, and many were still cheering hours later as the last of the Americans arrived. One officer likened the celebratory atmosphere to a crowd of ecstatic football fans on the day of a big win.

ASK: Based on details in the photograph and its caption, what do you think the arriving soldiers might have been feeling? *(Answers will vary. Possible response: Because of the jubilant reception from the Sicilians, the soldiers likely were happy to enter a city where residents were smiling, cheering, clapping, and reaching to shake their hands. The soldier in the foreground is smiling broadly as he shakes hands with a resident. All the soldiers might have been feeling relief and pride at having won the battle outside Palermo and hopeful about their chances of victory in the fighting to come.)*

UNIT
7

1931–1960

A NEW WORLD POWER

748

As you will learn in this unit, World War II involved countries on almost every continent. After the major Allied powers, the United States and Great Britain, liberated North Africa from the Axis powers of Italy and Germany, they set out to defeat the Italian and German forces in Europe. The Allies' Italian campaign began with the invasion in July 1943 of the island of Sicily, where they successfully drove out German and Italian troops and prepared to assault the Italian mainland. Just outside the city of Palermo, Sicilian civilians (shown below) rejoice at the sight of American troops, cheering as the soldiers' jeeps and trucks navigate the rubble of the city's streets.

THE ITALIAN CAMPAIGN

By 1943, Axis forces on the island of Sicily comprised two German divisions and 250,000 Italian troops. The Allies sent nearly 480,000 troops to Sicily, deploying about 150,000 of them during the invasion's first three days. On July 10, the Allies attacked from the sea. When they landed, they found the defending forces along the coastal area consisted of mostly Sicilians who had little interest in dying for the sake of Germany's gain. Consequently, the Sicilian troops soon surrendered, leaving the Allies with the relatively easy task of clearing the southeastern end of the island. After reaching the city of Messina, the Allied troops moved in different directions. The British headed south around Mount Etna, and the Americans moved east to take Palermo on the northern coast.

1933 EUROPE:
HITLER BECOMES CHANCELLOR

German statesman Franz von Papen was a key figure in Adolf Hitler's rise to power. Born to a privileged family in 1879, Papen began his career as a soldier, but after World War I, he moved on to politics. He belonged to the extreme right wing of the Catholic Centre Party, but he failed to become popular and was relatively unknown by the German public. So when Papen was appointed chancellor in 1932, it came as a complete surprise to most German citizens. Papen's newly established authoritarian government did not have a voting majority, so to achieve greater power, he attempted to enlist the support of the second most powerful party in the German parliament, the Nazis. Nazi leader Adolf Hitler, a man with large political aspirations of his own, had no interest in supporting Papen. **ASK:** What reasons might Hitler have had for avoiding support of Papen? *(Possible response: Hitler likely saw Papen as a political rival since he himself aspired to gaining absolute control.)*

Papen's tendency toward authoritarian rhetoric alienated several cabinet officials who had hoped to form a coalition and build a popular mandate and who routinely rejected Papen's policies. Papen resigned his chancellorship and put his support behind Hitler and the Nazis. He eventually persuaded President Carl von Hindenburg to appoint Hitler as chancellor and himself as vice chancellor. Papen hoped to improve his power base and at the same time restrict Hitler's power, but instead he soon found himself in a powerless and precarious position with Hitler actively working against him. **ASK:** What similarities do you see between Franz von Papen and Adolf Hitler? *(Possible response: Both were in favor of harsh policies that elevated one person or group over the majority, both strategized to achieve their goals, and both were appointed to the position of chancellor of Germany.)*

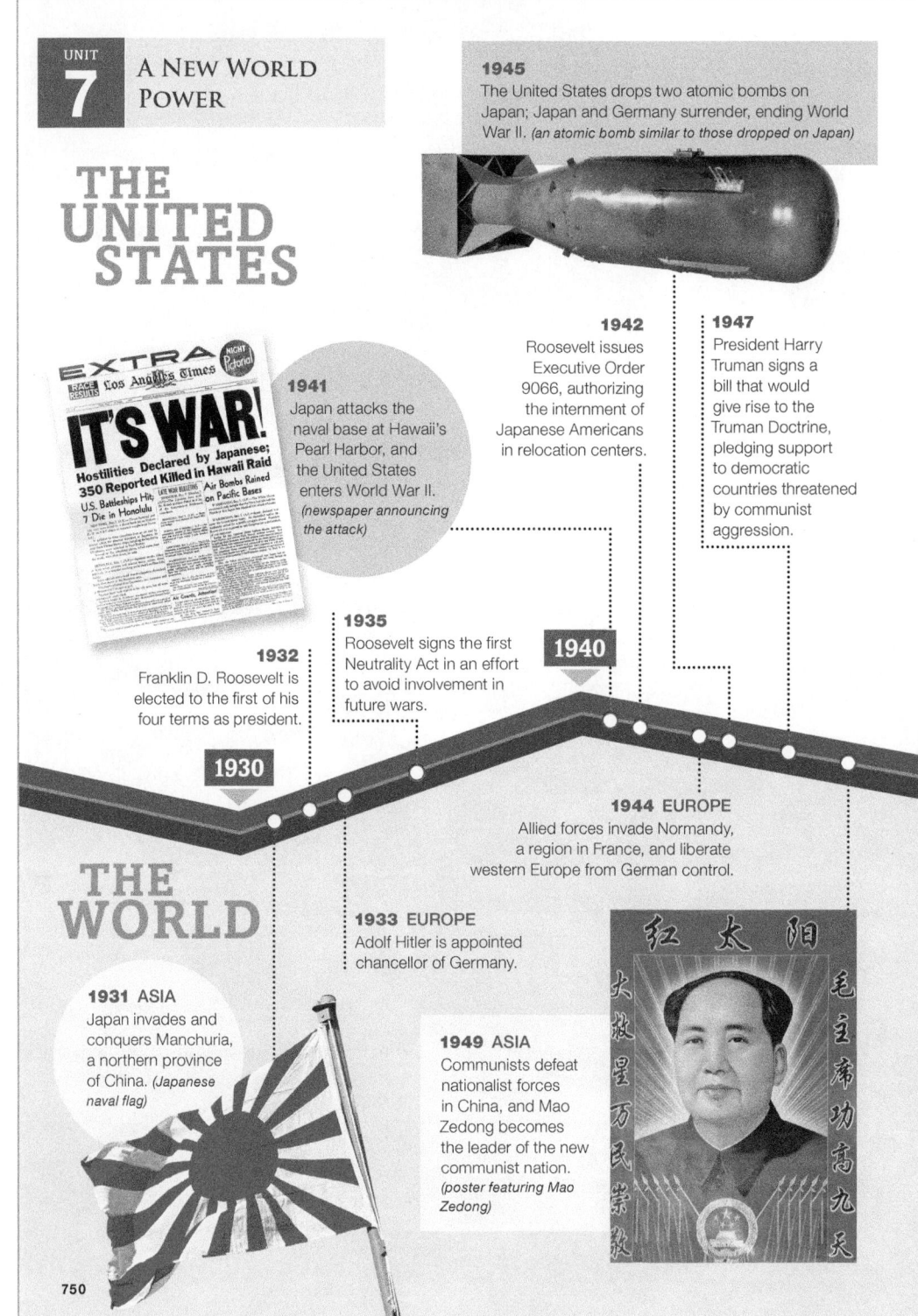

UNIT 7 A NEW WORLD POWER

1945
The United States drops two atomic bombs on Japan; Japan and Germany surrender, ending World War II. *(an atomic bomb similar to those dropped on Japan)*

THE UNITED STATES

1942
Roosevelt issues Executive Order 9066, authorizing the internment of Japanese Americans in relocation centers.

1947
President Harry Truman signs a bill that would give rise to the Truman Doctrine, pledging support to democratic countries threatened by communist aggression.

1941
Japan attacks the naval base at Hawaii's Pearl Harbor, and the United States enters World War II. *(newspaper announcing the attack)*

EXTRA Los Angeles Times
IT'S WAR!
Hostilities Declared by Japanese; 350 Reported Killed in Hawaii Raid
U.S. Battleships Hit; 7 Die in Honolulu
Air Bombs Rained on Pacific Bases

1935
Roosevelt signs the first Neutrality Act in an effort to avoid involvement in future wars.

1940

1932
Franklin D. Roosevelt is elected to the first of his four terms as president.

1930

1944 EUROPE
Allied forces invade Normandy, a region in France, and liberate western Europe from German control.

THE WORLD

1933 EUROPE
Adolf Hitler is appointed chancellor of Germany.

1931 ASIA
Japan invades and conquers Manchuria, a northern province of China. *(Japanese naval flag)*

1949 ASIA
Communists defeat nationalist forces in China, and Mao Zedong becomes the leader of the new communist nation. *(poster featuring Mao Zedong)*

750

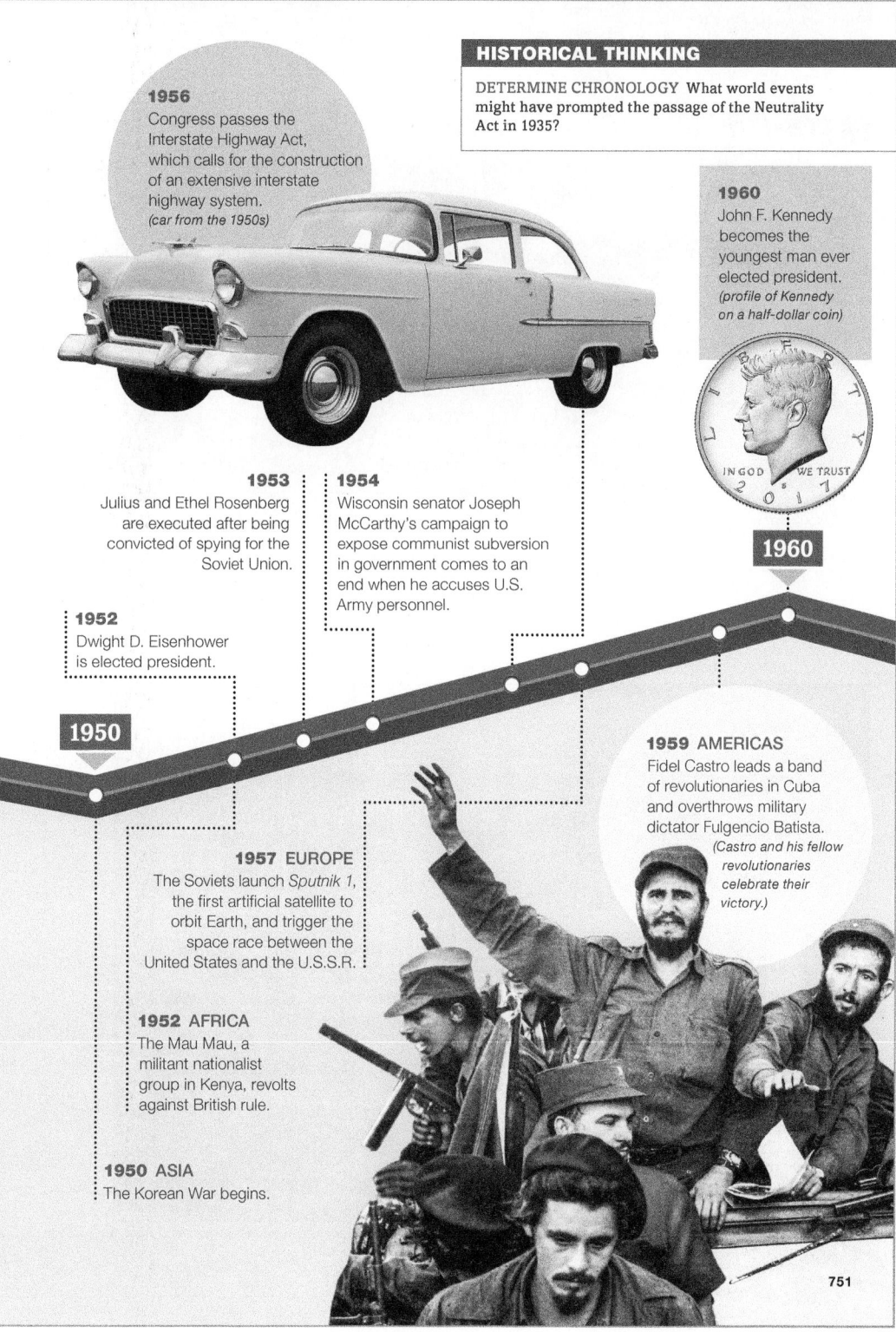

1956
Congress passes the Interstate Highway Act, which calls for the construction of an extensive interstate highway system.
(car from the 1950s)

HISTORICAL THINKING

DETERMINE CHRONOLOGY What world events might have prompted the passage of the Neutrality Act in 1935?

1960
John F. Kennedy becomes the youngest man ever elected president.
(profile of Kennedy on a half-dollar coin)

1960

1953
Julius and Ethel Rosenberg are executed after being convicted of spying for the Soviet Union.

1954
Wisconsin senator Joseph McCarthy's campaign to expose communist subversion in government comes to an end when he accuses U.S. Army personnel.

1952
Dwight D. Eisenhower is elected president.

1950

1957 EUROPE
The Soviets launch *Sputnik 1*, the first artificial satellite to orbit Earth, and trigger the space race between the United States and the U.S.S.R.

1952 AFRICA
The Mau Mau, a militant nationalist group in Kenya, revolts against British rule.

1950 ASIA
The Korean War begins.

1959 AMERICAS
Fidel Castro leads a band of revolutionaries in Cuba and overthrows military dictator Fulgencio Batista.
(Castro and his fellow revolutionaries celebrate their victory.)

INTRODUCE TIME LINE EVENT

1957 EUROPE:
SPUTNIK 1

On October 4, 1957, the Soviet Union sent the world's first artificial satellite, *Sputnik 1*, into space—an event that signaled the start of the space age and a race for space exploration dominance between the United States and the Soviet Union. *Sputnik 1* was only about 23 inches around and weighed about 184 pounds. It took 98 minutes to make a complete elliptical orbit of Earth. The launch came as a surprise to both the citizens and the government of the United States and ignited Americans' fears about the Soviets' potential for launching more satellites. Americans did not have long to ponder the next move in the Soviet space program, however. Within one month, on November 3, 1957, the Soviets launched a second satellite, *Sputnik 2*.

On January 31, 1958, the United States launched its own satellite, *Explorer 1*, which became the first in a series of successful U.S. launches. The *Sputnik* satellites changed the world and led directly to the formation of the U.S. National Aeronautics and Space Administration, or NASA. **ASK:** Why might the United States have been concerned about the Soviets' successful launches of satellites? *(Possible response: After the United States dropped an atomic bomb on the Japanese cities of Hiroshima and Nagasaki in 1945, world leaders understood how devastating such a weapon could be, even when it was used to end a war. The United States might have feared that the Soviets would wage a world war by dropping atomic bombs from satellites.)*

HISTORICAL THINKING

DETERMINE CHRONOLOGY

The Treaty of Versailles in 1919 and the 1933 appointment of Adolf Hitler as chancellor of Germany prompted the passage of the Neutrality Act. In practical terms, the act meant that U.S. ships would not sell arms to belligerents, including Germany and its new leader. Germany had already made it clear that it would not carry out its obligations under the Treaty of Versailles, which had banned German expansion efforts to rebuild its military. The United States, citing the Neutrality Act, designated all nations that engaged in violent clashes with other nations as belligerents.

751

UNIT 7 RESOURCES

UNIT INTRODUCTION

UNIT TIME LINE

UNIT WRAP-UP

NATIONAL GEOGRAPHIC | CONNECTION

National Geographic Magazine Adapted Articles
- "America's Propaganda Machine"
- "Dogs at War" ONLINE

Unit 7 Inquiry: Persuade an Audience

NG Learning Framework Activities
- Write About a Cold War Advance
- Debate the Origins of the Cold War

Unit 7 Formal Assessment

CHAPTER 21 RESOURCES

Available at NGLSync.Cengage.com

TEACHER RESOURCES & ASSESSMENT

Reading and Note-Taking

Vocabulary Practice

Social Studies Skills Lessons
- Reading: Compare and Contrast
- Writing: Narrative

Formal Assessment
- Chapter 21 Pretest
- Chapter 21 Tests A & B
- Section Quizzes

Chapter 21 Answer Key

ExamView®
  One-time Download

STUDENT DIGITAL RESOURCES

- eEdition
- Handbooks
- Online Atlas
- American Gallery Online
- History Notebook
- Active History
- Literature Analysis
- Projects for Inquiry-Based Learning

Chapter 21 Spanish Resources are available at NGLSync.Cengage.com.

AMERICAN STORIES ONLINE | **Combat Artists of World War II**

- Study Primary Sources: paintings depicting perspectives of World War II and a poem written by a soldier

- On Your Feet: Create and Visit a Museum

| **NG Learning Framework:**
Make a Recommendation

SECTION 1 RESOURCES

DICTATORS EXPAND POWER

LESSON 1.1
Fascism Spreads in Europe

- Active History: Compare and Contrast Fascism and Neo-fascism

| **NG Learning Framework:**
Compare Dictatorships

LESSON 1.2
Isolationism and Neutrality

- On Your Feet: Inside-Outside Circle

| **NG Learning Framework:**
Present a Refugee's Story

SECTION 2 RESOURCES

WAR IN EUROPE AND THE PACIFIC

LESSON 2.1
War Engulfs Europe

 The Battle of Britain

| **NG Learning Framework:**
Investigate Technologies of War

LESSON 2.2
Japan Invades China

- On Your Feet: Team Word Webbing

| **NG Learning Framework:**
Write a Biographical Sketch

SECTION 3 RESOURCES

AMERICA'S BALANCING ACT

LESSON 3.1
Supporting the Allies

- On Your Feet: Think, Pair, Share

| **NG Learning Framework:**
Evaluate a Speech

LESSON 3.2
A New Alliance

- On Your Feet: Thumbs Up/Thumbs Down

| **NG Learning Framework:**
Investigate Technology

CHAPTER 21 REVIEW

STRIVING READERS

STRATEGY 1
TURN TITLES INTO QUESTIONS

To help students set a purpose for reading, tell them to read the title of each lesson in a section and then turn that title into a question they believe will be answered in the lesson. Students can record their questions and write their own answers or they can ask each other questions.

Use with All Lessons *For example, Section 1 questions could be: How did fascism spread across Europe? and Why didn't Americans want to be involved in the conflicts in Europe?*

STRATEGY 2
IDENTIFY FACTS

Arrange students in mixed-proficiency pairs and guide them to conduct a Round Robin activity to review what they have learned. Ask pairs to generate facts for about three to five minutes and then invite one student from each pair to share their facts. Display all facts on the board and invite comments from the rest of the group.

Use with All Lessons

STRATEGY 3
CLARIFY INFORMATION

Students may have trouble understanding the complicated reasons why war engulfed much of Europe and Asia and the alliances that were formed. To help students organize their reading and clarify information in the lessons, instruct them to use a 5Ws Chart to take notes on the information under each subhead in the text.

Use with Lessons 1.1, 1.2, 2.1, and 2.2

INCLUSION

STRATEGY 1
USE ECHO READING

Point out that the Main Idea statements all relate to important aspects of the spread of war throughout Europe and Asia and the United States' position regarding neutrality or engagement. Pair each student with a proficient reader. Ask the proficient reader to read the Main Idea statement at the beginning of a lesson aloud. Tell the partner to "echo" by reading the same statement.

Use with All Lessons

STRATEGY 2
MODIFY VOCABULARY LISTS

Limit the number of Key Vocabulary terms that students will be required to master. For example, you might use language arts or history standards as a guide. As students read, instruct them to create a vocabulary card for each term in the modified list. Students may write definitions, synonyms, or examples on the back of each card. Encourage students to refer to their vocabulary cards often as they read.

Use with All Lessons

ENGLISH LANGUAGE LEARNERS   ELD

STRATEGY 1
PREP BEFORE READING

Encourage students at **All Proficiencies** to use the PREP strategy to prepare for reading. Write this acrostic on the board:

> **PREP** **P**review the title.
> **R**ead Main Idea statement.
> **E**xamine visuals.
> **P**redict what you will learn.

Use with All Lessons *Encourage students at the **Emerging** level to ask questions if they have trouble writing a prediction. Students at the **Bridging** level could help students at the **Emerging** and **Expanding** levels.*

STRATEGY 2
REVIEW TRANSITIONAL WORDS

To help students summarize what they read and put events leading to World War II in chronological order, display these transition words: *first, next, then, also, while, immediately, later, earlier, meanwhile, whenever, simultaneously, subsequently, during, following, before, afterward,* and *finally.* Direct students at the **Emerging** and **Expanding** levels to work together to write a series of sentences that tell what happens in the lesson in chronological order. Encourage them to use transition words to tell about the time order of events related to the conflicts in Europe and Asia and the reaction to them in the United States. Prompt students at the **Bridging** level to construct a paragraph that summarizes the material.

Use with All Lessons

STRATEGY 3
USE PAIRED READING

Pair students at the **Expanding** and **Bridging** levels to read passages from the text aloud.

1. Partner 1 reads a passage; partner 2 retells the passage in his or her own words.

2. Partner 2 reads a different passage; partner 1 retells it.

3. Pairs repeat the process, switching roles.

Use with All Lessons

GIFTED & TALENTED

STRATEGY 1
USE MAPS TO INTERPRET CONFLICT

Instruct students to look carefully at the legends and scales on the maps in the chapter and then write a short essay interpreting and analyzing the information that the maps convey. Have students share their essays with the class.

Use with Lessons 2.1, 2.2, and 3.2 *Invite technologically gifted students to create an animated version of the map in the lesson.*

STRATEGY 2
WRITE A HISTORICAL DIALOGUE

Tell students to write a fictional dialogue between President Roosevelt and Winston Churchill that conveys each man's personality, philosophy, and views on military strategy and alliances. Students may want to supplement their dialogues by conducting online research using primary and secondary sources. Encourage students to perform their completed dialogues for the class and answer questions.

Use with Lessons 3.1 and 3.2

PRE-AP

STRATEGY 1
CREATE AN ANNOTATED TIME LINE

Instruct students to create and annotate a time line of events leading to World War II beginning with 1931. Encourage students to illustrate their time line with flags of nations, names, or symbols. Ask students to share their completed time lines with the class and to explain in depth the connection—causal and otherwise—between one event and a larger social, economic, or political development that came later.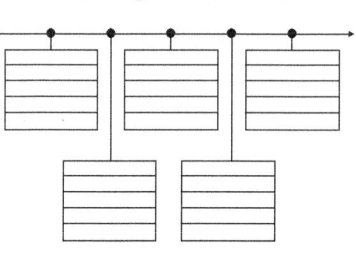

Use with All Lessons

STRATEGY 2
EXPLORE ARGUMENTS FOR AND AGAINST NEUTRALITY

Tell students that public opinion in the United States tends to swing back and forth between being more and less isolationist. Have students think about recent instances in which Americans were more or less supportive of engagements in foreign conflicts. Have students choose one of these instances and research arguments in favor of engaging or remaining neutral. Invite students to present the issue to the class, explaining the reasoning on both sides.

Use with Lesson 1.2

HISTORICAL THINKING What ideas and events brought about World War II?

The medieval cathedral and city center of Coventry, England, were leveled by German bombings on November 14, 1940. Coventry's munitions factories were a target, but the destruction of the city center, along with the killing of hundreds of civilians, was perceived as an act of terrorism to demoralize the British.

"We shall never surrender."
—Winston Churchill

752 CHAPTER 21

A Threatening World 753

INTRODUCE THE PHOTOGRAPH

THE BOMBING OF COVENTRY, ENGLAND

Have students study the photograph and the caption that open this chapter. **ASK:** Why do you think the bombing of Coventry's medieval cathedral was perceived as an act of terrorism? (Possible response: The bombing of the cathedral brought no military advantage. Instead, it caused the death of hundreds of civilians and destroyed a part of Coventry's history.) Direct students' attention to the quotation. **ASK:** What do Winston Churchill's words convey about the determination of the British while under attack? (Rather than surrender, the British will fight to the end.) Tell students that in this chapter they will learn about Germany's bombing campaign against Britain and Germany's efforts to control Europe.

SHARE BACKGROUND

More than 500 German planes dropped 30,000 bombs and 503 tons of explosives on the city of Coventry during a 12-hour period. The German onslaught killed more than 500 people and seriously wounded even more. The attack destroyed factories, homes, and the city's medieval center. The devastation was so great that the Germans used it as a benchmark level of destruction, coining the term "to Coventrate." Coventry was one of a number of industrial cities, including Manchester, Liverpool, and Birmingham, that suffered attacks from the Germans. From the German *Blitzkrieg* (lightning war), the so-called blitz attacks lasted from September 1940 until May 1941.

For Chapter 21 Spanish Resources, visit the Resources Menu. Chapter 21 Resources are available at NGLSync.Cengage.com.

HISTORICAL THINKING QUESTION

What ideas and events brought about World War II?

Roundtable Activity: Causes of Conflict Seat students around tables in groups of four. Ask groups to discuss what they have learned about other wars, such as World War I, and encourage students to consider factors that led to the wars. If students need help coming up with ideas, ask them to consider the questions below. After students have finished the activity, tell them that in this chapter they will learn about the events and ideas that led to World War II.

Question 1 What ideas of dictators or totalitarian leaders can lead to war?

Question 2 What leads countries to attempt to expand and acquire more land?

Question 3 How can economic hardship lead to conflict?

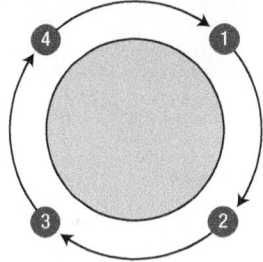

INTRODUCE THE READING STRATEGY

COMPARE AND CONTRAST

Explain to students that comparing and contrasting can help them more deeply understand concepts and events. Turn to the Chapter Review and preview the Venn Diagram with students. As they read the chapter, have students compare and contrast several topics about the events leading to World War II.

KEY DATES FOR CHAPTER 21

1933	Hitler becomes German chancellor
1934	Germany rearms
1936	Nazis occupy the Rhineland
1937	Japan invades China
1938	Munich Agreement
1939	Hitler invades Poland
1939	France and England declare war on Germany
1940	Japan joins Germany and Italy as Axis powers
1941	United States passes Lend-Lease Act

INTRODUCE CHAPTER VOCABULARY

KEY VOCABULARY

SECTION 1

Allied Powers	rearmament	Rome-Berlin Axis
Axis Powers	refugee	Third Reich
Gestapo		

SECTION 2

appeasement	Munich Agreement	purge
Long March	nonaggression pact	

SECTION 3

active defense	Atlantic Charter	belligerent

DEFINITION CHART

As they read the chapter, encourage students to complete a Definition Chart for Key Vocabulary. Ask students to list the Key Vocabulary terms in the far left column of their charts. Instruct students that as they encounter each Key Vocabulary term in the chapter, they should write its definition in the center column and what it means, using their own words, in the far right column. Model an example for students on the board, using the graphic organizer below.

Word	Definition	In My Own Words
refugee	person seeking shelter and protection from persecution	a person in need of a haven

For instructional support for the online American Story "Combat Artists of World War II," go to NGLSync.Cengage.com.

FASCISM SPREADS IN EUROPE

Would you give up any of your personal freedoms to be more economically secure or more physically safe? Some people might say they would protect freedom at all costs, but history proves that security often comes first. That was certainly true in Europe in the 1930s.

TOTALITARIANISM TIGHTENS ITS GRIP

As the United States worked to pull itself out of the Great Depression, the nations of Europe were undergoing dramatic political change. With many European economies also suffering during the 1930s, great anxiety and unrest spread across the continent. Authoritarian leaders took advantage of the turmoil and uncertainty to seize power in several countries. They took control of government, built powerful armies, and looked to expand their territory.

As you have read, Adolf Hitler and his Nazi Party seized control in Germany. Hitler had risen to power as the German economy collapsed under the weight of the global depression. Millions listened as Hitler promised to create jobs, restore what he perceived as Germany's past glory, and avenge the "humiliation" of the Treaty of Versailles, which ended World War I. Nazi representation in the Reichstag, the German parliament, rose from 12 members in 1928 to 230 by 1932. A year later, Hitler became Germany's chancellor, or the head of its government.

Hitler's regime, which the Nazi Party dubbed the **Third Reich**, suspended constitutional rights and banned all competing political parties. *Reich* means "empire," and the term Third Reich acknowledged two powerful German states of the past while envisioning a strong, prosperous state that would endure into the future. The Nazis transformed German police departments into the **Gestapo**, a brutal secret police force that went after Hitler's political opponents and anyone else whom the Nazis deemed an enemy of the Reich.

Hitler began a massive **rearmament**, a rebuilding of Germany's stockpile of weapons. By 1934, German

THE CROOKED CROSS

Before it became associated with the Nazis, the swastika (pictured on the flags in the photo on the next page) was known as an ancient symbol of good fortune. In the ancient Asian language of Sanskrit, the word *swastika* means "well-being." At the beginning of the 20th century, many in the West saw it as a good luck symbol. The Boy Scouts adopted it, and the Girls' Club of America called their official magazine *Swastika*. The Nazis interpreted the cross as a symbol of racial superiority and adopted it as their party logo. After World War II, the swastika was banned in Germany and today is almost universally seen as a symbol of hate.

factories were churning out tanks and military aircraft at an ever-increasing rate. Hitler then began building an army by instituting a draft that forced men 20 or older to join the military. In 1936, in clear violation of the Treaty of Versailles, Nazi forces marched into the Rhineland, a region of Germany that had been occupied by the French after World War I. German soldiers conquered it without firing a shot.

Meanwhile, Benito Mussolini—the fascist dictator who had risen to power in Italy in the early 1920s—had dreams of recreating the Roman Empire by conquering territory in Africa. In October 1935, Mussolini invaded Ethiopia, a nation in east-central Africa. The League of Nations condemned the act, but that did little to stop Mussolini. Italian forces took the capital, Addis Ababa, in May 1936 and annexed Ethiopia to Italy. Several months later, in October, Mussolini signed a pact of friendship with Hitler,

In 1934, Hitler walks up the steps to the speaker's platform at a harvest festival staged by the Nazis. A crowd of 700,000 attended this rally on Buckeberg, a hill in the farmland of northern Germany.

known as the **Rome-Berlin Axis**. Germany, Italy, and later Japan, would become known as the **Axis Powers**. The countries eventually opposing them would be referred to as the **Allied Powers**.

While Italy and Germany were hardening into dictatorships, **Joseph Stalin** was tightening his totalitarian grip on the Soviet Union. Stalin had come to power in 1924, and he steadily transformed his country from a peasant society into an industrial and military superpower. He ruled by terror during his brutal reign. Stalin expanded the powers of his secret police force, encouraged citizens to spy on one another, and had millions of people executed or sent to labor camps.

THE SPANISH CIVIL WAR

In 1936, civil war broke out in Spain, and Europe's dictators were eager to get involved. Spanish military officers led by **General Francisco Franco** attempted to overthrow the recently elected Spanish government, called the Republicans. Franco represented the Nationalists, a fascist group, and Hitler and Mussolini provided him with military aid, such as tanks, planes, and other weapons. Mussolini also sent 70,000 troops. Meanwhile, Stalin aided the Republicans, who represented a coalition of left wing groups, including communists, socialists, and liberal democrats, by sending weapons and money to help the government in its fight against Franco and the Nationalists.

INTRODUCE & ENGAGE

CONNECT TO THE PRESENT DAY

Ask students to imagine that the federal government passes a law revoking citizenship for blond Americans and making them enemies of the state. Soon police begin to round them up and move them to containment areas. Citizens who harbor blonds or offer assistance in any way are executed. **ASK:** If you were blond, what would you do? *(Possible responses: dye my hair and/or protest; leave the country)* **ASK:** If you were not blond, what, if anything, would you do? *(Possible responses: do nothing; harbor blond people)* Display a T-Chart and record actions that students say they would take based on whether they are blond or not. Engage students in a discussion about what they say they would do. Tell students that in this lesson they will read about how the totalitarian rule of dictators used fear of others and insecurity to build power and expand their territories.

Actions by Blond People	Actions by Others

TEACH

GUIDED DISCUSSION

1. **Analyze Cause and Effect** How did the Treaty of Versailles impact Hitler's actions as a dictator? *(Hitler viewed the harsh terms of the treaty as humiliating to Germany. As a result, he sought to build up the German military and expand Germany's territory, both of which were violations of the treaty.)*

2. **Compare and Contrast** What similarities existed in the reasons Hitler and Mussolini invaded, conquered, and annexed territory in the mid-1930s? *(Both wished to reacquire territory to revert their country's borders to an earlier historical period. Hitler wanted to restore Germany to its pre-World War I glory, and Mussolini wanted to recreate the Roman Empire.)*

ANALYZE VISUALS

Draw students' attention to the photograph. Explain that many public events, such as this one, were staged during the Nazi era. **ASK:** What aspects of the photograph emphasize Hitler's power? *(Possible response: Hitler's central place in the photo, the number of uniformed men who surround him, and the number of people attending—and being held back by police—emphasize Hitler's power.)* Remind students that nationalism was a key driver of totalitarianism. **ASK:** How is the photograph an expression of nationalism? *(Possible response: Uniforms and the display of national symbols, such as the swastika, emphasize extreme pride in country and culture—key components of nationalism.)*

DIFFERENTIATE

INCLUSION

Describe and Chart Details Pair students who are visually impaired with students who are not. Ask the latter to read the caption accompanying Picasso's *Guernica* and then provide specific details about what the painting depicts and the style of what is depicted, such as realistic or abstract. Tell visually impaired students to ask clarifying questions as necessary. Sighted students might use an Attribute Web, such as the one shown, to organize details from the caption and what the two partners discuss as they work together to answer the Critical Viewing question.

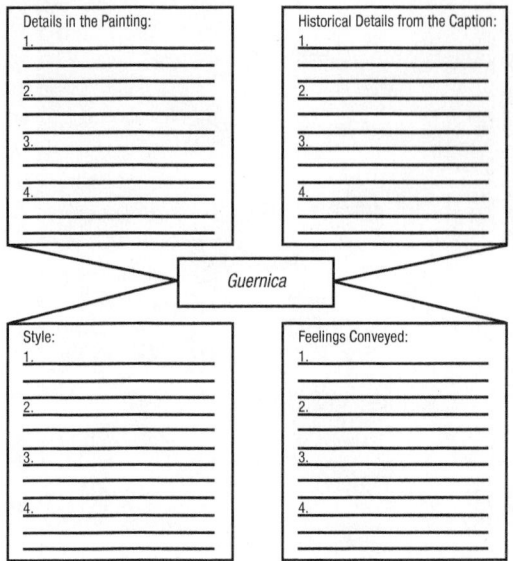

PRE-AP

Write a Report Tell students to gather information from a variety of sources about Roosevelt's denunciation of anti-Semitism and violence after Kristallnacht and to write a brief report on his reaction as reported in the press or other media. Remind students to quote or paraphrase Roosevelt from the sources they use and to cite them appropriately. Encourage students to use a graphic organizer, such as an outline, to organize their ideas. Suggest that students share and offer feedback about each other's outlines before they begin writing. Invite volunteers to read their reports to the class.

See the Chapter Planner for more strategies for differentiation.

CRITICAL VIEWING Pablo Picasso (1881–1973), born in Spain, was one of the best-known artists of the 20th century. The large painting *Guernica*, completed in 1937—two years before Franco's victory—was the artist's reaction to the bombing of a northern Spanish coastal village by the German and Italian air forces in support of Franco's Nationalists. The title of the painting is the name of the village they destroyed, including its homes and shops. Killing an estimated 1,650 people. Perhaps most disturbing, the attack was a terrorist bombing whose primary target was the civilians of the town. The first bomb fell on the center of the town on a market day.

Picasso used black, white, and gray shades of paint, depicting distorted human and animal forms and anguished facial expressions. Also shown are symbols of transition from a traditional to a modern world—a light bulb inside the sun and shapes filled with newsprint. According to Picasso's wishes, the painting was kept in New York's Museum of Modern Art until Spain restored its democracy. In 1981, the painting returned to Spain. At about 11 feet high by 25 feet wide, the painting occupies an entire wall in Madrid's Reina Sofía Museum. In applying the techniques he used, what do you think Picasso wanted visitors to feel as they viewed the painting?

Many international volunteers joined the war, including some from the United States. Some Americans praised Franco as an enemy of communism. However, many viewed him as a fascist thug trying to overthrow an elected government.

A group of several thousand Americans known as the **Abraham Lincoln Brigade** fought alongside the Spanish government. The famous American writer Ernest Hemingway, who covered the war as a reporter, summed up the anti-Franco view: "There is only one way to quell a bully and that is to thrash him." The fighting was widespread and brutal, with more than 500,000 killed. The war ended in 1939 with a complete victory for General Franco and his forces. Another dictator had taken power in Europe.

The riots of Kristallnacht, ordered indirectly by Goebbels and intended to appear as spontaneous expressions of rage, took place throughout Germany. This Jewish-owned shop in Berlin was one of more than 7,000 businesses destroyed during the two days.

PERSECUTION OF JEWS

As Europe's dictators engaged in military actions outside their borders, they also tightened their grip on the home front. Their regimes silenced critics and oppressed people whom they deemed "undesirable." In Germany, the Nazis sought to reshape society according to their vision of a pure German "master race." The Nazis believed all other races and ethnicities to be inferior, and they targeted one group in particular: Jews.

In Europe, anti-Semitism, or hostility toward and discrimination against Jewish people, had deep historical roots. Many Europeans accused Jews of working to remain a separate social and religious group that refused to adopt the values of the countries in which they lived. After Germany's defeat in World War I, many Germans believed the German Army was betrayed by politicians, especially Jewish politicians. In addition, a number of Jews worked in the banking and money-lending industries, making them easy scapegoats for Germany's financial problems.

When the Nazis gained power, the persecution of Jews became government policy. Nazis began to exclude Jews from public life. At the annual Nazi rally in 1935, Hitler announced laws denying Jewish people citizenship and prohibiting marriage between Jews and people of "German or related blood." Three years later, under Hitler's personal orders, the Nazis destroyed the Great Synagogue in Munich.

On November 7, 1938, a 17-year-old Polish Jew, Hershel Grynszpan (GRIHNZ-pan), shot and killed

Ernst vom Rath, a German diplomat in France. Joseph Goebbels (GEH-buhlz), the Nazi propaganda minister, immediately seized on the assassination to whip up rage against Jews. What followed became known as the **Kristallnacht**—the Night of Broken Glass. Between November 9 and November 10, 1938, Nazis destroyed Jewish homes, schools, and businesses, burned synagogues, and killed nearly 100 Jews. Officials arrested 30,000 Jewish men and sent them to concentration camps. Shortly after the attacks, U.S. president Franklin D. Roosevelt denounced the rising tide of anti-Semitism and violence in Germany. He also recalled Hugh Wilson, the U.S. ambassador to Germany. Nonetheless, the persecution of Jews in Germany continued.

HISTORICAL THINKING

1. **READING CHECK** What measures did Hitler take against Germany's Jews?

2. **ANALYZE CAUSE AND EFFECT** Why is it difficult to determine a single cause for four dictators all coming to power at about the same time in Europe?

3. **FORM AND SUPPORT OPINIONS** Do you think dictators and fascist regimes would have risen to power if Europe hadn't been so economically depressed after World War I? Explain your answer.

4. **MAKE CONNECTIONS** What similarities do you see among Hitler, Mussolini, and Stalin and one of today's world leaders?

BUILD BACKGROUND

THE ABRAHAM LINCOLN BRIGADE

The 2,800 Americans who fought on the side of the government in the Spanish Civil War did not have the military backgrounds one might expect. Brought to Spain by the communist organization Comintern, members of the Abraham Lincoln Brigade had little training in the military arts, and most had never fired a rifle. Their commander, Robert Hale Merriman, was a graduate student, and others had careers ranging from miners to acrobats, with the last surviving veteran having been a dishwasher. The brigade's numbers also included more than 80 African Americans and one woman, Marion Merriman, the wife of the brigade's commander, who worked as a clerk at the brigade's headquarters in Madrid.

The inexperience of the troops was tragically played out during an attack that historians assert gained no advantage and in which overall American death rates were much higher than that of the rest of the Republican Army. During the brigade's first engagement near the Jarama River, so many Americans died that their fellow soldiers were unable to bury them all. They eventually burned the remaining dead, leaving a pile of rocks, helmets, skulls, and bones. (A historian came upon this same pile when he visited the site in 1967.) American volunteers fighting and dying for a principle in another country's civil war attracted war-front visits from writers Dorothy Parker, Langston Hughes, and W. H. Auden, along with other American luminaries.

TEACH

GUIDED DISCUSSION

3. **Make Inferences** Why do you think European dictators wanted to become involved with the Spanish Civil War? *(Possible response: Franco was a fascist, so Hitler and Mussolini supported him because he shared their political philosophy. Likewise, because the Republicans were left wing, they attracted support from the communist Soviet Union.)*

4. **Analyze Cause and Effect** How did assumptions about the Jewish people lay the groundwork for their persecution by the Nazis? *(Some Germans believed that Jewish politicians had betrayed Germany during World War I and that Jews were responsible for Germany's financial problems. Such assumptions made it easier for the Nazis to target the Jews.)*

MORE INFORMATION

Art and the Spanish Civil War Although perhaps the best known, Picasso's *Guernica* is not the only work of art that depicts the horrors of the Spanish Civil War. In 1937, a number of Spain's radical artists displayed works influenced by the war at the Paris International Exposition. Among them was Joan Miró, who painted the giant anti-war mural *The Reaper* on the stairwell wall of the Exposition's Spanish pavilion. Alexander Calder, the only non-Spanish artist to participate, created *Mercury Fountain*, a sculpture that addressed the economic impact of the war and specifically the Nationalist siege of Almadén's mercury mines. To make his point, Calder built the structure over a wide pool of mercury. At the time, the toxicity of the substance was unknown, and the sculpture sat in open air. The sculpture is currently housed behind glass.

ACTIVE OPTIONS

Active History: Compare and Contrast Fascism and Neo-fascism Extend the lesson by using either the PDF or Whiteboard version of the activity. These activities take a deeper look at a topic from, or related to, the lesson. Explore the activities as a class, turn them into group assignments, or even assign them individually.

NG Learning Framework: Compare Dictatorships

SKILLS Communication, Collaboration

KNOWLEDGE Our Human Story

Break students into small groups and assign each group a different totalitarian regime, including regimes from this lesson as well as other historical examples. Have students conduct research and prepare a short presentation on the characteristics of their assigned regime, including the causes that empowered it. Ask students to divide research responsibilities equally, perhaps each student conducting research on a specific characteristic. After all groups have presented, lead a class discussion about the commonalities among these regimes and the steps that could have been taken to prevent the dictator from coming to power.

HISTORICAL THINKING

ANSWERS

1. He denied Jews German citizenship and prohibited intermarriage between Jews and non-Jews; he fomented violence against Jews that resulted in Kristallnacht; he had Jews arrested, killed, and sent to concentration camps.

2. Social, economic, and political circumstances were not identical in each country, and events unfolded differently and at different rates in what became the four dictatorships.

3. Answers will vary. Possible response: Yes. Depressed economies were not the only cause for the rise of dictatorships. For example, Hitler was in part motivated by the humiliation brought upon Germany by the Treaty of Versailles.

4. Answers will vary. Possible response: Hitler, Mussolini, and Stalin all retained dictatorial control of their countries' governments and built a military that posed a threat to surrounding countries. Kim Jong-un of North Korea is following that same path.

CRITICAL VIEWING Possible response: Picasso likely wanted visitors to have an extreme emotional response to his painting. The anguish on the faces of the human and animal victims and the grotesque portrayal of their screams are meant to evoke horror and disgust at the destruction of the village.

1.2 **MAIN IDEA** Amid the growing possibility of another large-scale war, many Americans wanted the United States to remain neutral and to isolate itself from foreign conflict.

ISOLATIONISM AND NEUTRALITY

Maybe you have been in situations where you had your own conflicting opinions about an issue. In the 1930s, many Americans did not like what was happening in Europe, but they had concerns about the United States getting involved.

A GLOBAL PERSPECTIVE Refugees still flee dangerous situations and oppressive regimes to this day. In 2016, millions of men, women, and children fled a brutal civil war in the country of Syria. Hoping to find a better life in Europe, large numbers of these refugees packed into overcrowded boats and made a dangerous voyage across the Mediterranean Sea. Many died along the way. Those who made it struggled to fit in across Europe, as many nations opposed the influx of so many immigrants. For a single day in September 2016, at Parliament Square in London, international aid organizations displayed 2,500 life jackets worn by the refugees to help bring attention to their plight.

AVOIDING INVOLVEMENT IN EUROPE

As authoritarian leaders rose to power in Europe, U.S. president Franklin Roosevelt watched with increasing alarm. Roosevelt felt very early on that Hitler posed a threat to the world unlike any other. However, a majority of Americans did not feel the same way. Many had no wish to get involved in the turmoil they saw threatening Europe.

Americans voiced many reasons for wanting to stay out of the growing conflict. In the Great Plains and Upper Midwest, some were suspicious of international bankers and arms manufacturers, believing such businesspeople were responsible for pushing the United States into World War I for their own financial gain. Americans of German descent supported isolationism because they remembered how badly German Americans were treated during World War I. Americans of Irish descent opposed any kind of aid to Great Britain because of conflicts between Ireland and Great Britain, while many Americans of Italian descent admired Mussolini, due to a propaganda campaign by the dictator meant to win over Italian Americans. Furthermore, pacifism, the belief that war is morally wrong, appealed to clergy, peace groups, and many college students.

Following the will of the American public, the U.S. Congress passed a series of Neutrality Acts. The first act, passed in 1935, banned the export of "arms, ammunition, and implements of war" from the United States to any foreign nation at war. President Roosevelt opposed the act, but bowed to pressure from Congress and the public to maintain neutrality. Congress renewed the act in 1936 and 1937, and expanded it. U.S. citizens were now forbidden from traveling on ships owned by nations at war, and the United States could bar any warring ships from entering U.S. waters.

In a compromise with Roosevelt, the act did allow the United States to sell European nations materials and supplies—just not ammunition and arms. This enabled America to provide its allies with critical resources, such as oil. In an effort to limit the interaction, European nations had to arrange to pick up the materials and pay immediately in cash. The provision thus became known as "cash-and-carry."

ROOSEVELT CHALLENGES THE NATION

Standing in direct opposition to the American people and Congress, President Roosevelt continued to push for greater American involvement in Europe. He felt the United States could not remain strictly neutral, and the time would come when the democratic countries of Europe, especially Great

---

PRIMARY SOURCE

On October 5, 1937, President Roosevelt traveled to Chicago to speak at the dedication of a bridge completed under a New Deal program. Expected to praise the accomplishment of the bridge's construction, Roosevelt instead used the occasion to make his case for opposing tyranny in Europe. His speech at the bridge dedication became known as the **Quarantine Speech.**

The political situation in the world, which of late has been growing progressively worse, is such as to cause grave concern and anxiety to all the peoples and nations. Innocent peoples, innocent nations, are being cruelly sacrificed to a greed for power and supremacy which is devoid of all sense of justice and humane considerations. If those things come to pass in other parts of the world, let no one imagine that America will escape.

—from the Quarantine Speech, by Franklin D. Roosevelt, 1937

Britain, would need help from the United States. Roosevelt gave a speech in which he compared war with a disease, saying it was the responsibility of peace-loving nations to "quarantine" countries that threatened world peace.

In that speech, Roosevelt mentioned people and nations who were being "cruelly sacrificed," referring partly to the Jews suffering under the Nazi regime. But Roosevelt's speech did not go over well with the public, and the United States refused to ease the immigration restrictions that kept large numbers of German Jews from the safety of American shores. Each year between 1935 and 1941, the United States took in an average of 8,500 Jewish **refugees**, or people seeking shelter and protection from persecution. This was far below the annual quota of 30,000 for German immigrants set by the National Origins Act of 1924. Most Americans were still feeling the sting of the Depression and did not want foreigners competing with them for jobs and resources. A combination of economics, anti-

Semitism, and isolationism in the United States kept the "golden door" shut to most Jewish refugees.

Isolationists strongly criticized the president for trying to violate neutrality, while many average Americans remained opposed to deeper U.S. involvement in Europe's troubles. As Europe moved closer to war, the United States remained neutral.

HISTORICAL THINKING

1. **READING CHECK** Why did many Americans wish to remain neutral and not take sides in the growing conflicts in Europe?

2. **COMPARE AND CONTRAST** Compare the refugee crisis described in the lesson with what you know about the status of refugees today.

3. **MAKE INFERENCES** How do you think the American experience in World War I affected the country's attitude toward international events in the 1930s?

PLAN: 2-PAGE LESSON

OBJECTIVE

Understand why Americans favored neutrality and a policy of isolationism as the threat of war in Europe grew.

CRITICAL THINKING SKILLS FOR LESSON 1.2

• Compare and Contrast

• Make Inferences

• Analyze Primary Sources

• Form and Support Opinions

HISTORICAL THINKING FOR CHAPTER 21

What ideas and events brought about World War II? Although totalitarianism continued to spread across Europe, Americans supported neutrality and isolationism. Lesson 1.2 examines the reasons why U.S. citizens opposed intervention while President Roosevelt believed the United States needed to become more involved.

BACKGROUND FOR THE TEACHER

Although the policies of isolationism and neutrality have historical roots running back to George Washington, the key to understanding the United States' anxiety in the early 1930s is the legacy of World War I. In 1934, the U.S. Senate set up a committee, chaired by isolationist Gerald P. Nye of North Dakota, to investigate the reasons for U.S. involvement in the war. The Nye committee highlighted a series of well-known facts, including that large banks and corporations had made huge profits during World War I by giving loans and selling arms to the various combatants. The press dubbed such bankers and businessmen "merchants of death," and the findings received widespread popular support. Simply blaming business interests ignored the rather tangled reality of U.S. intervention, including events such as the Zimmermann Telegram and the sinking of multiple U.S. ships.

INTRODUCE & ENGAGE

MAKE HISTORICAL CONNECTIONS

Ask students to recall the debate within the United States before entering World War I. **ASK:** Why did some Americans not want to enter World War I? *(Answers will vary. Possible response: Because of the diversity within the country, Americans had natural ties to each side of the conflict. Thus, entering the war would cause internal conflict.)* Ask students to state other reasons Americans might have for not entering a foreign war. Record, display, and discuss students' responses. Then tell students that in Lesson 1.2 they will learn about a period in history that was similar to the pre-World War I United States.

TEACH

GUIDED DISCUSSION

1. **Analyze Primary Sources** Direct students to the Primary Source feature and have them read the excerpt from Franklin Roosevelt's Quarantine Speech. **ASK:** Why do you think President Roosevelt is arguing that it is in the United States' direct interest to intervene in Europe? *(At the time, many Americans supported neutrality and isolationism, as they believed that the United States would not be affected by events in Europe if it didn't get involved. Roosevelt, however, is arguing that if totalitarianism were not actively opposed, it could spread—even to the United States.)*

2. **Form and Support Opinions** Do you think President Roosevelt was right to support greater involvement with Europe in the face of spreading totalitarianism? Explain your answer. *(Answers will vary. Possible response: Yes. Roosevelt wanted to ensure that the principles of democracy would be safeguarded at home and abroad.)*

A GLOBAL PERSPECTIVE

Direct students' attention to the photograph of Parliament Square in London. **ASK:** What connections exist between the plight of the Syrian refugees and that of German Jews who sought to escape persecution by the Nazis? *(Both groups found it difficult to find countries, including the United States, that would allow them to enter.)* **ASK:** Why do you think countries sometimes bar the entry of refugees? *(Possible response: People are afraid that refugees will take away jobs or need public assistance.)* Discuss the effectiveness of the life jacket display and whether it improved circumstances for Syrian immigrants. Then discuss measures that could be taken to address the problem of refugees worldwide.

ACTIVE OPTIONS

On Your Feet: Inside-Outside Circle Arrange students in concentric circles facing each other. Allow students time to write questions about the United States' response to events in Europe during the 1930s. Tell students in the inside circle to pose questions to students in the outside circle. Have students switch roles. Students may ask for help from other students in their circle if they are unable to answer a question.

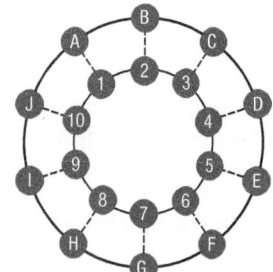

NG Learning Framework: Present a Refugee's Story

ATTITUDE Responsibility

KNOWLEDGE Our Human Story

Guide students to research and present a refugee who lived under or escaped a totalitarian regime in either the present or the past. Guide students to sources such as the U.S. Holocaust Memorial Museum's website where they can read diaries, interviews, and oral histories of Holocaust survivors; the Statue of Liberty–Ellis Island website for oral histories of immigrants by country; and reputable news sources with profiles about or interviews with refugees from present-day regimes. Suggest that students include age and gender, country of origin, reason for leaving, perils during the escape or journey, treatment upon arrival in their new country, or any other relevant information. Encourage students to provide a photo if possible and to display it as they make their presentation to the class.

DIFFERENTIATE

STRIVING READERS

Chart Isolationism in U.S. Population To help them answer the Reading Check question, instruct students to create a two-column chart such as the one shown to display reasons why segments of the U.S. population did not want the nation to become involved in conflicts in Europe. Tell students to complete the chart as they read.

Segment of Population	Reason for Isolationism

PRE-AP

Report on Public Reaction Instruct students to research and present an oral report about public reaction to Roosevelt's Quarantine Speech and whether that reaction influenced U.S. policy. Students may conclude their report by drawing parallels to other U.S. quarantine policies concerned with aggression by other nations. Have students present their oral reports to the class and answer questions.

See the Chapter Planner for more strategies for differentiation.

HISTORICAL THINKING

ANSWERS

1. Many Americans wanted to stay out of the European conflict because they had issues with the countries involved or because of their experience during World War I. For example, Irish Americans wanted to remain neutral because of the conflicts between Ireland and Great Britain. German Americans wished to remain isolationist because they had been badly treated in World War I.

2. Possible response: Large numbers of people continue to flee oppression or war-torn nations. Refugees still have difficulties finding countries that will accept them.

3. There was a strong body of opinion in the United States that the country had been drawn into World War I to benefit arms manufacturers and bankers. This made people suspicious of the motives for engaging in another war.

WAR ENGULFS EUROPE

Is it better to reason with a bully to achieve a compromise, or let the fight begin? The nations of Europe tried to compromise with Hitler as he rose to power and looked to conquer his neighbors. But in the end, they decided they had to fight.

THE MUNICH AGREEMENT

One of Adolf Hitler's main goals was to unite all German-speaking people into a "Greater Germany," or "Grossdeutschland." As you have read, Germany took its first steps toward this goal in 1936, when it reoccupied the Rhineland. In 1938, German troops marched into neighboring Austria. Hitler announced the "Anschluss" (AHN-shloos), or union, of Germany and Austria, adding six million German speakers to greater Germany.

With each aggressive step Hitler took, the nations of Western Europe made little attempt to confront him. Instead, Great Britain and France took an approach

Hitler's Advance, 1938–1940

Allied territory
Axis powers
Axis satellite
Axis-controlled by 1940
Soviet territory
Neutral nation
German troop movements

BLITZKRIEG

In invading Poland, the Germans demonstrated for the first time a new and seemingly unstoppable type of warfare—blitzkrieg (BLIHTS-kreeg), or "lightning war." Blitzkrieg was characterized first by bombing—to cripple the target's air capacity, railroads, and communication lines—followed by fast moving tanks, artillery, and waves of troops.

Using this new tactic of speed and overwhelming force, the Germans conquered Poland in a matter of weeks. In this photo, a German gunner fires from a plane attacking a Polish town.

known as **appeasement**—a policy of making political compromises in order to avoid conflict. Neither country had forgotten the horrors of World War I, and they sought to maintain peace at any price. In addition, many British politicians believed that Germany had genuine grievances, as the Treaty of Versailles had left hundreds of thousands of German-speaking people under the control of other countries in Europe. What's more, a number of Western leaders viewed communism, not fascism, as the greatest threat to Europe. Thus, they saw Hitler as a potential safeguard against Soviet expansion.

Facing little resistance, Hitler continued to invade and annex. After absorbing Austria, the German leader turned his attention to Czechoslovakia. He insisted that the Czechs surrender the Sudetenland (soo-DAY-tehn-land), a region of western Czechoslovakia where three million ethnic Germans lived. In September 1938, Hitler met with British Prime Minister Neville Chamberlain, French Premier Edouard Daladier, and Italian dictator Benito Mussolini in Munich. Under the **Munich Agreement**, the leaders agreed to Hitler's demand for the Sudetenland. In return, Hitler promised he would not occupy any more territory in Czechoslovakia. Daladier pressured the Czechs to accept the agreement and give the Sudetenland to Germany. Meanwhile, Chamberlain claimed the agreement had brought "peace in our time." Less than a year later, on March 15, 1939, Hitler violated the pact and sent German troops to seize the rest of Czechoslovakia.

GERMANY ATTACKS POLAND

In August 1939, the world was shocked to learn that two sworn enemies, fascist Nazi Germany and the communist Soviet Union, had signed a **nonaggression pact**. Under the pact, the two countries agreed to take no military action against each other for 10 years. The agreement also contained a secret section that detailed how the Soviets and Germans planned to divide up Eastern Europe. The first country targeted under their plan: Poland.

On September 1, 1939, Hitler sent the Wehrmacht—the German Army—across the German border into Poland. (The Soviets would invade weeks later and claim their share of Polish territory.) Hitler, it appeared, had finally gone too far. Two days after the German attack, Britain and France declared war on Germany. **World War II** had begun. What followed were months of quiet, known as the "phony war." During this time, the French and British hunkered down on one side of the French-German border, behind a series of fortifications known as the **Maginot** (MAJ-ih-noh) **Line**, and the Germans settled in on the other side.

GERMANY INVADES FRANCE

In April 1940, the calm came to an explosive end when German forces invaded Denmark and Norway, quickly conquering both nations and defeating British forces stationed in Norway. The defeat brought down Chamberlain's government, and he was replaced as prime minister by British statesman

---

OBJECTIVE

Understand events leading to Britain and France declaring war on Germany and Germany's response.

CRITICAL THINKING SKILLS FOR LESSON 2.1

• Interpret Maps

• Analyze Cause and Effect

• Form and Support Opinions

• Evaluate

• Compare and Contrast

• Analyze Primary Sources

HISTORICAL THINKING FOR CHAPTER 21

What ideas and events brought about World War II? Hitler's aggression in Europe was a leading cause of World War II. Lesson 2.1 describes Hitler's invasions across the continent and efforts by world powers to appease him in the interest of peace.

BACKGROUND FOR THE TEACHER

The brainchild of André Maginot (France's minister of war from 1929 to 1931), the Maginot Line was a permanent defensive barrier built in northeastern France as protection from another German attack. The fortification was a far cry from the trenches of World War I. Built of thick concrete and equipped with heavy guns, it included air-conditioning, recreation areas, and living quarters. Unfortunately, the French failed to consider the weakness of the line from a strategic point of view. The Maginot Line protected the French-German frontier but failed to extend north along the French-Belgian border. As a result, the Germans bypassed the line by marching into France from Belgium.

HISTORY NOTEBOOK

Encourage students to complete the American Gallery and the War Engulfs Europe pages for Chapter 21 in their History Notebooks as they read.

INTRODUCE & ENGAGE

K-W-L CHART

Tell students that many survivors of World War I thought that no war could be worse—but they were wrong. World War II was the deadliest war in history, with millions of fatalities. Ask students what they know about World War II. Use a K-W-L Chart like the one shown to record their answers. Then ask what they would like to know and record their responses. Allow time at the end of the lesson for students to complete the chart with information they learned in Lesson 2.1.

K What Do I Know?	W What Do I Want To Learn?	L What Did I Learn?

TEACH

GUIDED DISCUSSION

1. **Form and Support Opinions** How do you think historical events influenced the signers of the Munich Agreement and their decision to appease Hitler? *(Answers will vary. Possible response: The memory of World War I likely pushed leaders from Britain, France, and Italy to attempt to avoid war at all costs.)*

2. **Evaluate** Why did Britain and France declare war when Hitler invaded Poland but not when he invaded Czechoslovakia? *(When Hitler seized the rest of Czechoslovakia, Britain and France still hoped to avoid war. In addition, the country had many German speakers, perhaps giving some legitimacy to his action. However, when Hitler then invaded Poland, they realized there was no end to his territorial demands.)*

3. **Interpret Maps** What strategic advantage did Germany gain by invading Belgium and Luxembourg? *(These countries shared borders with both Germany and France and invading them gave Germany access to France's northeast border.)*

MORE INFORMATION

The Munich Agreement Prior to the Munich Agreement, British Prime Minister Neville Chamberlain met with Hitler on more than one occasion in an attempt to forestall German aggression toward Czechoslovakia. Various alternatives were proposed, including allowing the people of the Sudetenland to vote on the issue of joining Germany, but none was acted upon. As Hitler's demands increased, it was Chamberlain who proposed the conference that resulted in the Munich Agreement. The infamous final agreement was proposed by Mussolini but secretly written by the German Foreign Office. In the end, Czechoslovakia was given a choice: It could try to defend itself from Germany without help from its allies or submit to annexation.

DIFFERENTIATE

STRIVING READERS

Create Word Squares Ask students to write the word *appeasement* in the center oval of a Word Square. Then tell them to consult a dictionary or do online research in order to write the definition and characteristics in the appropriate boxes. Guide students to identify and write examples and non-examples.

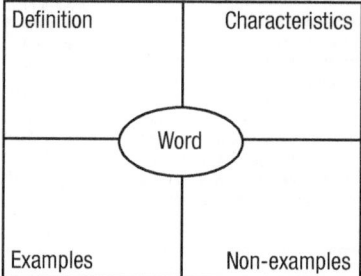

PRE-AP

Perform a Churchill Speech Tell students to conduct online research to find the full text of one of Winston Churchill's speeches quoted in the lesson and to take notes about the date and the occasion on which the speech was given. Then challenge students to prepare a dramatic reading of a section of the speech. Before performing their speech, students should explain its context, stating when, where, and what prompted it. Instruct students to be prepared to ask questions of their classmates and make comments about the words and literary devices Churchill used to add to the effectiveness of the speech.

See the Chapter Planner for more strategies for differentiation.

Winston Churchill. Meanwhile, German forces rolled on, pushing into Belgium, Holland, and Luxembourg.

Next, Germany invaded France, and German forces seized Paris in June 1940. The French signed an armistice that divided France into two regions, one under German occupation and one under French authority, with the town of Vichy (VISH-ee) as its capital. Although French leaders oversaw Vichy, the Germans controlled the region—one of the most significant strategic outcomes of the war.

Despite the German victory, some of the French decided to fight on. The French general **Charles de Gaulle** set up headquarters in Britain to allow "Free French" forces to continue fighting as a resistance force. In the autumn of 1940, a number of French colonies in Africa declared their loyalty to de Gaulle, but they were a small force compared to the German enemy. The French resistance fighters did what they could to thwart the Nazis as the war progressed.

THE NAZIS TARGET GREAT BRITAIN

The Nazis had conquered most of Western Europe in less than two months. Now they targeted Britain. Winston Churchill rallied the British to fight on against Germany's overwhelming power, despite some calls for Britain to negotiate peace with Hitler. "We shall defend our island, whatever the cost may be," Churchill declared. "We shall fight on the landing grounds, we shall fight in the fields and in the streets, we shall fight in the hills; we shall never surrender."

From June through October 1940, British and German forces fought the **Battle of Britain**. It was primarily an air war, as Britain's Royal Air Force (RAF) and Germany's air force, the Luftwaffe (LOOFT-vahf-uh), clashed over the skies of Great Britain. Germany's attempts to bomb Britain into surrender met with stiff resistance. While German attacks inflicted heavy damage on British cities, the RAF continued fighting back and eventually forced Germany's air force to retreat. Unable to achieve victory, Hitler suspended further attacks on Britain and moved on. Referring to the RAF fighters who turned back the Germans, Churchill said, "Never in the field of human conflict was so much owed by so many to so few."

The British people suffered greatly during the Battle of Britain. Families were split up, as Londoners put their children on trains for the countryside, sending them as refugees to willing rural homes in hopes of keeping them safe from the nightly bombing. All too many children never saw their parents again, as the bombing campaign known as the London Blitz claimed the

lives of nearly 17,500 civilians in London. Thousands more were killed nationwide. Relentless German raids destroyed whole neighborhoods of London and other cities as the British took cover deep beneath ground in London's Tube—or subway system—or in designated bunkers and shelters. One of the more deadly attacks toward the end of the campaign killed nearly 1,500 civilians in a single night of bombing.

Across the Atlantic Ocean, Americans watched the onset of World War II with interest and alarm. Isolationists continued to argue that the country should stay out of the conflict. Interventionists insisted the United States must enter the fight to halt Hitler's march of conquest. President Roosevelt, in particular, felt that the United States should do more to help Britain. On September 21, 1939, soon after the war had begun, Roosevelt called Congress into special session. He pressed lawmakers to amend the Neutrality Act to lift the ban on arms sales and allow the United States to provide weapons to the nations threatened by Germany, specifically Great Britain. After much debate, Congress approved the amendment. The United States was slowly moving toward greater involvement in the war.

HISTORICAL THINKING

1. **READING CHECK** Explain the theory of appeasement. Why do you think it led to war in Europe?

2. **INTERPRET MAPS** From a geographical standpoint, why was it important that Germany capture France before battling with Britain?

3. **ANALYZE CAUSE AND EFFECT** How might events have taken a different turn if the world had not underestimated Hitler's intentions?

BUILD BACKGROUND

WINSTON CHURCHILL

Winston Churchill became Britain's prime minister in 1940, largely due to his unwavering determination to defeat Hitler. Churchill had been in and out of politics for much of his adult life, having first served in Britain's House of Commons from 1901 to 1922. Appointed as head of the British Admiralty in 1939, it was as "Naval Person" that Churchill signed the first of many communications with President Roosevelt. During the war years, Churchill unrelentingly pursued an Allied victory. An orator and writer as well as a statesman, Churchill delivered a number of speeches aimed at shoring up the British during the Battle of Britain. The one ally viewed by Churchill as indispensable to victory was the United States, and he worked tirelessly to maintain its support.

THE FREE FRENCH

Refusing to accept the armistice between France and Germany, General Charles de Gaulle left France to continue the fight from London. There he broadcast an appeal to the French to continue the war with Germany. Soon recognized as the leader of the French resistance, de Gaulle began to build up Free French Forces. A few French navy units joined as well as French volunteers and soldiers living in England. Even with the added support of a number of French colonies, forces of the Free French remained small. Then in 1942, de Gaulle sent an emissary to France to unify a number of resistance groups that had sprung up. As a result, by 1943, Free French troops numbered more than 100,000 and played a significant role in bringing the war to an end.

TEACH

GUIDED DISCUSSION

4. Compare and Contrast What were the consequences of the Battle of Britain for both Britain and Germany? *(Britain sustained huge damages and casualties but resisted the Germans. Germany lost the battle and moved on.)*

5. Analyze Cause and Effects Why did the lifting of the ban on arms sales bring the United States closer to war, and what types of data could be used to verify this claim? *(Possible response: Americans were able to provide arms to Great Britain, increasing the likelihood that they eventually would support the Allies with troops as well. This also put them in clear opposition to Germany. Data that could support this claim include statistics concerning arms sent to Great Britain and speeches given by American leaders decrying German aggression.)*

ANALYZE PRIMARY SOURCES

Direct students' attention to the Primary Source feature and have them read the excerpt from Winston Churchill's speech to the House of Commons. Invite a volunteer to read the excerpt aloud. Encourage students to look up the meaning of words they do not know. **ASK:** What did Winston Churchill mean by "the lights of perverted science"? *(Churchill was likely referring to the unscientific beliefs of the Nazis, who claimed Germans were part of a master race.)* Encourage students to identify the main idea of the speech and the consequences of failure or success. Use a Main-Idea Chart like the one shown to record their responses. Guide students to discuss what might have happened if Churchill had been unsuccessful at rallying his country.

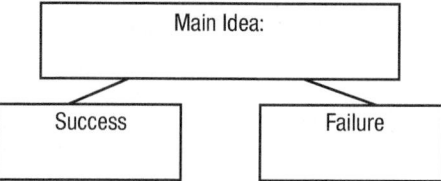

ACTIVE OPTIONS

The Battle of Britain Invite students to explore the American Gallery. Tell them to select one of the images and to do additional research to learn more about it. Ask questions that will inspire additional inquiry about the chosen gallery image, such as: Who are the children in the photo and what are they doing? Where and when was the photo taken? Who might have photographed the scene? Why do you think this photo belongs in this chapter? What else would you like to know about it?

NG Learning Framework: Investigate Technologies of War   **STEM**

ATTITUDE Curiosity

KNOWLEDGE Our Human Story

Invite students to explore the technology behind the Battle of Britain. Tell them to conduct online research to learn technical details about the airplanes, the weapons, and the ground support used on either side of the battle. Have students work in pairs to create a presentation that illustrates their findings. Encourage students to create visuals with labels to display as they speak. Call on volunteers to share their presentations with the class.

HISTORICAL THINKING

ANSWERS

1. The theory was based on compromise and letting dictators have some of what they wanted as a way of avoiding war. Rather than achieving its purpose, it allowed Hitler and Mussolini to conquer more territory with little opposition.

2. Britain is an island, which presented a host of new challenges for the Germans, as they needed to cross the English Channel or the North Sea to make an effective invasion. If Germany had not captured France first, France could have easily provided assistance to Britain because of its proximity.

3. Germany might have been contained if confronted early and aggressively. This might have prevented the devastation of the war and the deaths of millions of people.

CRITICAL VIEWING Possible responses: The children appear to be reacting in different ways. The youngest ones are smiling and looking upwards as if they're on an adventure or they're enjoying the aerial battle. The oldest girl and boy, in the foreground, look apprehensive, suggesting that they actually understand the seriousness of the battle going on above them.

JAPAN INVADES CHINA

By the time the nations of Europe went to war in the fall of 1939, another military power had risen on the other side of the globe. Japan was carving out an empire of its own, giving the world—and the United States—another serious threat to confront.

CHINA IN TURMOIL

China had been ruled as an empire for 2,000 years, and at the turn of the 20th century, it was poverty-stricken and underdeveloped. In 1911, a group of revolutionaries led by **Sun Yat-sen** overthrew the ruling Qing (CHING) Dynasty and established the Republic of China. Sun was elected China's first president, but he struggled to maintain control of the country—in reality ruled by a number of warlords, or local military leaders. After Sun's death in 1925,

power passed to **Chiang Kai-shek** (jee-AHNG ky-SHEHK). Chiang soon faced an armed resistance from the growing **Chinese Communist Party (CCP)**, led by **Mao Zedong** (MOW dzuh-DUNG).

In 1927, fearful of the CCP's increasing power, Chiang ordered a **purge**, or elimination, of CCP members in Shanghai and other Chinese cities. Chiang's troops, known as the Kuomintang, or KMT, killed tens of thousands of communists. By 1931, the KMT had

almost completely defeated Mao's forces. Some 700,000 KMT troops encircled communist positions in southeast China, preventing supplies from entering their territory. Hundreds of thousands of soldiers and peasants loyal to Mao were killed or died of starvation.

Facing almost certain defeat, the remaining Chinese communists decided to retreat to a more remote part of China. There, Mao hoped, the CCP could regroup and build its military power. In October 1934, at the beginning of what became known as the **Long March**, 86,000 communist troops and around 15,000 civilians marched out of southeast China, attempting to escape Chiang's KMT forces. They faced almost daily battles and skirmishes with KMT troops and local warlords, and they even were the targets of aerial bombardment. Many were killed in the fighting, and others died of starvation and exposure. Only 7,000 of the approximately 100,000 who had begun

the Long March the year before survived the journey. After the Long March, Chiang Kai-shek planned to wipe out the remaining communist forces, but by then a more serious threat had emerged from the neighboring nation of Japan.

JAPAN TAKES ACTION

By the early 20th century, Japan was a strong country with developed industries and a powerful military. In 1904, its forces had soundly defeated Russia in a war over several disputed territories in Asia. The easy victory had surprised observers and signaled that Japan was a rising world power. But as an island nation, it lacked the land and natural resources necessary for economic growth. Ambitious military leaders such as **Tojo Hideki** urged the young Japanese emperor **Hirohito** to seek out and conquer new land and build an empire. To achieve this goal, the Japanese turned their attention to China, their large neighbor to the west.

Mao Zedong arrives in Shaanxi Province in northern China in 1935, near the end of the Long March. Most officers rode horses, but all others walked on foot.

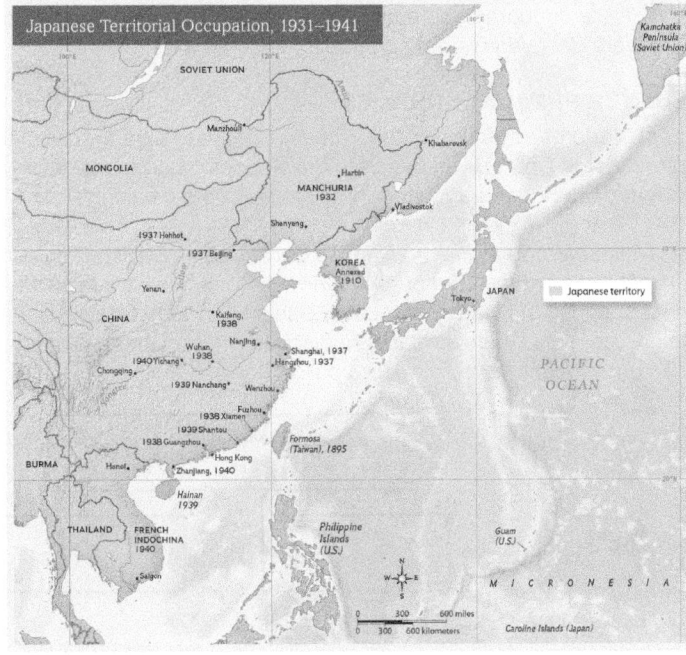

Japanese Territorial Occupation, 1931–1941

PLAN: 4-PAGE LESSON

OBJECTIVE

Understand how political developments and military actions in Asia increased tensions between the United States and Japan.

CRITICAL THINKING SKILLS FOR LESSON 2.2

- Interpret Maps
- Evaluate
- Analyze Cause and Effect
- Categorize
- Compare and Contrast
- Form and Support Opinions
- Analyze Primary Sources

HISTORICAL THINKING FOR CHAPTER 21

What ideas and events brought about World War II? Increasing tensions between Japan and the United States moved the countries closer to war. Lesson 2.2 traces Japan's rise as a military power and its changing U.S. relations.

BACKGROUND FOR THE TEACHER

During the first three months of what became known as the Long March, attacks by Chiang Kai-shek's forces reduced the 86,000 communist troops by half. The survivors—both military and civilian—traveled a total of 6,000 miles, crossing 24 rivers and 18 mountain ranges before reaching northern Shaanxi, near the border China shared with the Soviet Union. The march solidified Mao as the Communist Party leader, and stories of heroism from the journey inspired young people to join his cause. By the end of 1936, more than 30,000 troops joined the Red Army, and from their base, they were eventually able to organize and defeat the nationalists for control of China.

INTRODUCE & ENGAGE

CONSIDER A LONG MARCH

Ask students how they would feel about joining a march that would take a year to complete. Tell them that they would have to carry all their supplies and find food along the way. **ASK:** Under what circumstances would you consider participating in such a march? *(Answers will vary. Students might respond that they would undertake such a march due to imminent danger and threat to their lives or if a reward at the end would make it worthwhile.)* **ASK:** What hardships might you have to endure on a year-long march? *(Possible responses: lack of shelter; attacks from animals or other people; shortage of medicine)* Explain to students that in this lesson they will learn about a march by Chinese communists that lasted for a year.

TEACH

GUIDED DISCUSSION

1. **Analyze Cause and Effect** Why did communist troops and citizens set out on the Long March rather than fight? *(Communist troops and civilians knew that the Kuomintang was conducting purges to eliminate communists. Supplies had been cut off in the southeast, and a successful counterattack seemed impossible.)*

2. **Categorize** What economic, political, and military factors led to the turmoil experienced by China in 1911? *(Economically, China was poor, which may have motivated the Chinese to support change. Politically, warlords and military leaders ruled areas of the country, making China hard to rule as a nation. Militarily, the communists employed armed resistance against Chiang Kai-shek, who retaliated with purges.)*

MORE INFORMATION

Japanese Annexation of Korea Direct students' attention to the map. Point out that Japan annexed Korea in 1910, an early indication of Japan's desire for expansion. **ASK:** What strategic advantage did Korea's geographic location offer Japan? *(Korea provided access to Manchuria, a region in northern China.)* Explain that Korea remained under Japanese rule until 1945.

As an extension to this activity, share with students the Build Background information about the Nanjing massacre. Then direct students to conduct online research to learn more about it and to learn about the Korean independence movement in the years following annexation and how Japan responded to it. Tell students to use their findings to write an essay comparing and contrasting Japan's response to the Korean independence movement with how Japan treated the Chinese citizens of Nanjing. Encourage students to use a Venn diagram to organize their findings.

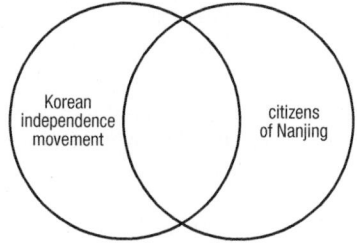

DIFFERENTIATE

ENGLISH LANGUAGE LEARNERS

Clarify Vocabulary Use the following strategies to help students at different proficiency levels clarify vocabulary.

- **Emerging**: Have students choose an unfamiliar word from the lesson. Provide these frames:
  I don't know the word _____.

  I think it means _____.

  Clues I found are _____.

  Point out any context clues and word parts and guide students to discover the word's meaning.

- **Expanding:** Have students use these frames to clarify vocabulary:
  I don't know the word _____, but I think it means _____.

  The context and word parts suggest _____. The most likely meaning is _____.

- **Bridging:** Have students draw a three-column chart with the following headings: Word/Know/Learned. Tell students to write an unfamiliar word under Word, write what they already know about the word and what the context and word parts show under Know, and explain what they learned about the word under Learned.

GIFTED & TALENTED

Interview a Historical Figure Have students work in pairs to plan, write, and perform a television interview with Chiang Kai-shek, Mao Zedong, Tojo Hideki, or Emperor Hirohito. Invite students to research their selected historical figure and focus on his motivations, actions, goals, failings, and achievements. Encourage pairs to conduct their interview in front of the class, taking turns as interviewer and subject.

See the Chapter Planner for more strategies for differentiation.

PRIMARY SOURCE

Captain Frank Roberts was aboard the *Panay* during the attack. He recalled how he narrowly escaped death.

I had only taken a couple of steps when a shower of fragments [bomb pieces] hit me in the back and knocked me to my hands and knees. At the same time, I heard the sound of a machine gun and the splatter of bullets against the ship's side. Almost simultaneously, another bomb exploded to port, knocking down some of the bunks and breaking more glass. Being dazed and dizzy, I remained on the floor for some moments while two other bombs exploded somewhere near. Later I discovered that a bullet or a metal fragment had torn a three-inch rip in my left trouser leg at the top of the pocket. Still later, I found holes in my coat, the largest at the left shoulder, and there was a severe bruise, although the bullet or fragment did not penetrate.

—from *The Panay Incident*, by Hamilton Darby Perry, 1969

China's land and resources—and its political instability—made it an attractive target to the Japanese. In 1931, as China was troubled with internal fighting, Japan invaded the Chinese province of Manchuria and made it an independent Japanese state, which it controlled completely. China turned to the League of Nations for help, and the League demanded that Japan withdraw its troops. Japan refused and withdrew from the League. By 1936, the Japanese military was in full control of Japan's government and intent on conquering new territory.

In 1937, Japan renewed its attack on China. Japanese Ambassador Hiroshi Saito defended the assault as an attempt to bring political and social order to the region. "If China's house were in order there would be no need for the presence of these foreign forces," he declared. "What our government and people want is peace and security in the Far East." Chiang reluctantly agreed to form a united front with Mao to fight the new threat, but just six

months later, Japanese forces controlled all of northern China, including Beijing, Shanghai, and the Chinese capital of Nanjing. In Nanjing, Japanese forces committed horrific war crimes, actions that violate accepted international rules of war, when they killed as many as 300,000 Chinese civilians.

In November 1937, leaders of 18 nations met in the European city of Brussels to discuss ways of ending the conflict between Japan and China. The **Brussels Conference**, as it was known, ended with a call for Japan to cease all hostilities against its neighbor. The decree had little effect, however, as Japan had refused to attend the conference and claimed that western nations had no business meddling in its affairs.

TENSIONS RISE

At first, the United States did little to contest Japan's aggression. U.S. leaders were more concerned about the rise of Nazi Germany, and they hoped to avoid

a crisis with Japan. In December 1937, Japanese warplanes sank the U.S. gunboat *Panay* on China's Yangtze (yang-tsee) River, killing 3 Americans and wounding nearly 30. President Roosevelt condemned the attack, but Japan apologized and the two nations settled the matter peacefully.

Japan, however, continued to expand its empire. In 1938, Japanese forces annexed European colonies in Southeast Asia and the Western Pacific. U.S. Secretary of State Cordell Hull warned that "Japan definitely contemplates securing domination over as many hundreds of millions of people as possible in eastern Asia." The United States responded to Japan's continued conquests by pulling back on trade. Japan purchased the bulk of its oil, steel, and machinery from America. In an effort to slow Japanese expansion, President Roosevelt declared an embargo, barring U.S. companies from selling a number of strategic industrial goods, such as oil and copper, to Japan. In May 1940, the president moved

the headquarters of the U.S. Pacific Fleet from San Diego, California, to Pearl Harbor, Hawaii. The move was intended to enable the U.S. Navy to keep a closer watch on Japan. The United States had a base in the Philippines, but it was not prepared for war.

Relations grew more strained in September 1940, when Japan signed a war agreement with Germany and Italy, forming the Axis powers. They agreed to assist one another if any one of them were attacked by a nation not already involved in the war. Roosevelt retaliated by freezing all Japanese assets in the United States and blocking shipments of scrap iron and aviation fuel to Japan. Japanese Foreign Minister Teijiro Toyoda declared, "Commercial and economic relations between Japan and third countries, led by England and the United States, are gradually becoming so horribly strained that we cannot endure it much longer." The United States and Japan were now openly at odds, and tensions were mounting.

HISTORICAL THINKING

1. **READING CHECK** Who were the opposing sides in China's civil war?

2. **INTERPRET MAPS** Based on the information on the map, why was conquering China so appealing to Japan?

3. **EVALUATE** What led to the growing tensions between Japan and the United States?

BUILD BACKGROUND

THE *PANAY* INCIDENT

Built in Shanghai, the *Panay* was an American gunboat serving with the U.S. Navy's Yangtze Patrol and charged with protecting Americans in China. On December 11, 1937, with Japanese forces moving on Nanjing, the *Panay* evacuated Americans from the city. One day later, Japanese naval aircraft attacked the *Panay* and three American oil tankers. Five U.S. civilians were among those wounded. Survivors were transferred to the U.S.S. *Oahu* and two British ships. Following the incident, the Japanese government offered a formal apology and paid the United States an indemnity of over $2 million dollars. Japanese citizens deluged the U.S. embassy in Tokyo with cards of sympathy and letters of apology.

THE NANJING MASSACRE

When the Japanese army seized Nanjing in 1937, Matsui Iwane, the army's commanding general, ordered his forces to destroy the city. What followed was one of the most infamous events of the 20th century—a series of mass executions and rapes, as well as the burning and looting of the city and nearby towns. The horrors lasted for weeks, and in the end, more than one-third of the city was destroyed. Following World War II, General Matsui Iwane and Tani Hisao, a lieutenant general who had participated in the murders and rapes, were convicted and executed for war crimes.

TEACH

GUIDED DISCUSSION

3. **Compare and Contrast** In what ways were the reasons for, and responses to, Japanese and German aggression similar at the beginning of World War II? *(Like Germany, Japan suffered from economic hardship and wanted other nations' lands and resources. Japan's leaders became very nationalistic and militaristic and, like Germany, wanted to build an empire. In both cases, world powers were reluctant to respond militarily, as they relied on appeasement, embargoes, and censure via the League of Nations.)*

4. **Form and Support Opinions** Do you think Japan's claim that it wanted peace and security in Asia was the reason for its attacks on China? Explain using text evidence. *(Answers will vary. Possible response: No. Japan committed war crimes in China, which does not indicate a desire to establish peace.)*

ANALYZE PRIMARY SOURCES

Direct students' attention to the Primary Source feature. **ASK:** What phrases does the writer use to indicate how quickly his experience occurred? *("At the same time"; "Almost simultaneously")* How does the passage describe how closely the writer came to injury or death? *(He was hit by pieces of bomb; a bullet or bomb fragments tore a hole in his trousers and made holes in his coat; he suffered a bruise but no other injuries.)* How would you describe the overall impression that the paragraph conveys? *(Answers will vary. Possible response: Ironically, the initial blast that knocked Captain Roberts to his hands and knees probably saved his life. Had he remained standing, bomb fragments and bullets might have proved fatal.)*

For students who develop an interest in how artists and writers captured the experiences of people in war and on the home front, suggest that they read the online American Story "Combat Artists of World War II."

ACTIVE OPTIONS

On Your Feet: Team Word Webbing Organize students into teams of four and have them record on a sheet of paper what they know about Japanese aggression in Asia. Encourage students to build on their teammates' entries as they rotate the paper from one member to the next. Then call on volunteers to make statements about Japanese aggression based on their Team Word Webs.

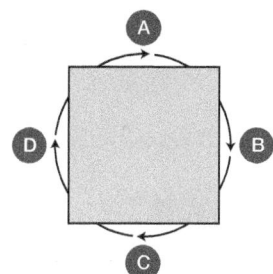

NG Learning Framework: Write a Biographical Sketch

ATTITUDE Curiosity

KNOWLEDGE Our Human Story

Have students select one of the people they are curious about after reading the lesson. Instruct students to write a biographical sketch and present it to the class. Tell students to use reliable online or print sources and to focus on life experiences or events that would help the class gain insight to the subject's actions as described in the lesson. Ask students to invite questions and comments from the class after they make their presentations.

HISTORICAL THINKING

ANSWERS

1. Mao Zedong and his Chinese Communist Party fought Chiang Kai-shek and his Nationalist Party forces.

2. China included an immense territory with natural resources that Japan wanted for further economic expansion.

3. Tensions between the United States and Japan began with Japan's invasion of China. After Japan annexed European colonies in Southeast Asia and the Western Pacific and signed a war agreement with Germany and Italy, the United States placed an embargo on Japan and froze Japanese assets in the United States.

CRITICAL VIEWING The impressionistic and vibrantly colored cress flowers stand in stark contrast to the realistic statues that comprise the other side of the memorial. The upright and angular gray wall and severe black pavement suggest oppression and despair, an impression reinforced by the representation of a man crawling, his arm extended and grotesquely exaggerated and his face sculpted in a look of disbelief and horror.

The "arsenal of democracy" included U.S.-made aircraft. In this 1940 photograph, a worker in a Los Angeles aircraft plant completes tail-fin assemblies for warplanes built for the Allies.

SUPPORTING THE ALLIES

The question on every American's mind was, "Should the United States go to war, or should it stay neutral?" Even as Americans continued to debate this issue, the nation took greater steps to support the Allies.

A THIRD TERM FOR FDR

As the 1940 presidential election approached, the leading campaign issue was the war raging in Europe. France had fallen, and Great Britain was fighting alone against the Axis Powers. In this atmosphere of turmoil, President Roosevelt took the unprecedented step of running for a third term in the White House. No American president had ever served a third term. Roosevelt felt it was his duty to continue to lead the United States through the current world crisis, so he allowed himself to be drafted by the Democratic National Convention in 1940 as their candidate. Meanwhile, the Republicans nominated lawyer and businessman Wendell Willkie of Indiana as their presidential candidate.

The 1940 presidential campaign intensified the debate over U.S. neutrality. Roosevelt favored greater intervention, while Willkie took a more isolationist stance. "The President's attacks on foreign powers have been useless and dangerous," Willkie declared. "He has courted a war for which the country is hopelessly unprepared—and which it emphatically does not want."

As you have read, Roosevelt had persuaded Congress to amend the Neutrality Act in 1939 to lift the ban on arms sales to U.S. allies and continue cash-and-carry. American ships, however, were still barred from transporting goods to ports of **belligerents**, or the countries already fighting in the war. In September 1940, at Britain's request, and without informing Congress, Roosevelt took the step of supplying the British with 50 old but usable destroyers. In return, the United States obtained the rights to establish naval bases in various British territories. The agreement outraged isolationists, who viewed it as a clear violation of American neutrality.

Nonetheless, Roosevelt easily defeated Willkie in the November election, with about 27 million votes to 22 million votes (449 electoral votes to 82 electoral votes). Although many Americans were opposed to involvement in the war, most were rooting against Germany. A national poll in 1940 found that 83 percent of U.S. citizens favored a British victory. Many Americans believed that if Britain fell to the Nazis, the United States would be on its own and potentially Germany's next target.

AN "ARSENAL OF DEMOCRACY"

After his re-election, Roosevelt continued nudging the United States toward greater involvement in the war. In December 1940, the president declared the nation must devote its industrial might to helping Britain. "We must be the great arsenal of democracy," Roosevelt proclaimed. "For us this is an emergency as serious as war itself." An arsenal is a place where weapons are stored. In his declaration, Roosevelt indicated he envisioned the United States as the major supplier of arms for its allies. He went on to say, "No dictator . . . will weaken [our] determination."

Even before Roosevelt's declaration, the nation had begun ramping up its war effort. In August 1940, Congress passed the first peacetime draft in U.S. history. Like the original Selective Service Act from World War I, the **Selective Service and Training Act** again required able-bodied young men to register for potential military service. Congress also allocated $10.5 billion for defense spending. American factories began working around the clock to build weaponry, including tanks, warplanes, and warships. Unemployment virtually disappeared. The United States' urgent push to build up its arsenal had finally ended the Great Depression.

THE LEND-LEASE ACT

As the United States increased its military production, Winston Churchill sent a plea for help to Roosevelt. Churchill told the president that Great Britain was in deep financial trouble and unable to pay for arms from the United States. Roosevelt responded by crafting the **Lend-Lease Act**, which enabled countries to receive American military aid without immediately paying for it.

Proposed in late 1940 and passed on March 11, 1941, the Lend-Lease Act allowed the president to deliver arms and other defense materials to "the government of any country whose defense the President deems vital to the defense of the United States." The act enabled the United States to more directly aid nations at war against the Axis powers, while technically remaining neutral. Isolationists, such as Republican senator Robert Taft from Ohio, strongly opposed Lend-Lease as a violation of neutrality. FDR's isolationist opponents also included Henry Ford and Charles Lindbergh, who organized the America First Committee (AFC). The AFC opposed every effort by the president to move away from neutrality, and it strongly contested Lend-Lease.

Despite Taft's and the AFC's opposition, Lend-Lease proceeded, allowing the United States to supply weapons to the Allied powers.

Lindbergh argued that by supporting one side or another, the United States was being used to aid in that country's domination of the continent. He did not evaluate the countries of Europe in terms of their ideology or aggressiveness, but viewed them all as equally seeking advantage over the others. In his mind, there was no justification for sending Americans to further those causes. Some perceived Lindbergh's position as support for the Nazis.

HISTORICAL THINKING

1. **READING CHECK** Why did Franklin Roosevelt want to run for a third term as president?

2. **COMPARE AND CONTRAST** How did cash-and-carry and Lend-Lease differ, and which was more beneficial to the Allies?

3. **ANALYZE CAUSE AND EFFECT** How did Roosevelt's push to be an "arsenal of democracy" affect technology, the U.S. economy, and people's values and beliefs?

OBJECTIVE

Analyze the reasons for, methods of, and response to President Roosevelt's increased support of Britain.

CRITICAL THINKING SKILLS FOR LESSON 3.1

• Compare and Contrast

• Analyze Cause and Effect

• Summarize

• Form and Support Opinions

HISTORICAL THINKING FOR CHAPTER 21

What ideas and events brought about World War II? Britain's solitary fight against the Axis Powers and President Roosevelt's support of Britain moved the United States closer to involvement in the war. Lesson 3.1 covers Roosevelt's aid of Britain and the subsequent objections by isolationists.

BACKGROUND FOR THE TEACHER

When President Roosevelt put out his call to transform the nation into "the great arsenal of democracy," Detroit, Michigan, rose to the challenge. Already established as a premier center of automobile manufacturing, Detroit was in an ideal position to begin producing vehicles and weapons for the war. Detroit's factories rapidly converted from the manufacture of automobiles to jeeps, bombers, and tanks. Freeways were constructed to facilitate the movement of people and war shipments, and around 350,000 workers—including women—came from the South as well as other parts of the country to contribute to Detroit's war effort by joining the ranks of factory laborers.

FINANCIAL LITERACY

To extend their knowledge and understanding about the concepts in this lesson, refer students to the Financial Literacy handbook.

INTRODUCE & ENGAGE

WORD KNOWLEDGE

Ask students if they know what the word *arsenal* means. Write students' responses on the board. Ask students what they think President Roosevelt meant by "arsenal of democracy." Tell students that in this lesson they will learn how Roosevelt's vision of the United States as an "arsenal of democracy" was realized in the production of war materials to bolster U.S. defenses and to support the Allied Powers.

TEACH

GUIDED DISCUSSION

1. **Summarize** What actions did President Roosevelt take to increase U.S. involvement in World War II? *(He supplied the British with 50 old destroyers, and in a direct response to Churchill's request for help, he created the Lend-Lease Act. He set the stage for involvement in the global war by getting rights for naval bases in British territories.)*

2. **Form and Support Opinions** Do you agree with the isolationists that the Lend-Lease Act violated U.S. neutrality? Explain your answer. *(Answers will vary. Possible response: Yes. Any aid to either side of the war would have demonstrated partiality. The Lend-Lease Act enabled the United States to directly support the Allied Powers at war against the Axis Powers, blatantly violating U.S. neutrality.)*

COMPARE AND CONTRAST

Remind students that President Roosevelt encountered both approval and opposition as the country moved toward war. **ASK:** Which actions of President Roosevelt were controversial? *(Roosevelt ran for a third term. He supplied the British with used destroyers and provided other military aid while deferring payment under the Lend-Lease Act.)* **ASK:** What evidence indicates whether Americans approved or disapproved of Roosevelt's actions? *(Roosevelt won the election by a large margin, demonstrating that the majority of Americans approved. The formation of the America First Committee, which supported neutrality, provides evidence that some Americans disapproved of Roosevelt's actions.)* Ask students to discuss whether Roosevelt's actions were justifiable within the context of the events unfolding in Europe.

ACTIVE OPTIONS

On Your Feet: Think, Pair, Share Ask students to think about whether it was better for the United States to remain neutral or to enter World War II. Tell students to form pairs in order to discuss the topic. Once pairs have completed their discussion, invite them to share their ideas with the class.

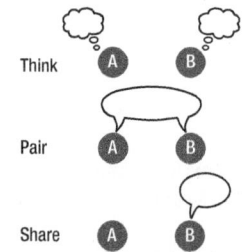

Think   A   B

Pair   A   B

Share   A   B

NG Learning Framework: Evaluate a Speech

SKILL Communication

KNOWLEDGE Our Human Story

Tell students to locate online or in print Charles Lindbergh's 1941 "America First" speech, delivered on September 11, 1941, in Des Moines, Iowa. Instruct students to work in pairs to evaluate the speech. Tell them to first identify Lindbergh's arguments for staying out of the war and then evaluate each argument in terms of whether it was based on fact or an expression of Lindbergh's point of view. Students should counter as many points as possible with interventionist arguments that appear in the lesson. Finally, have students present their conclusions to the class concerning the persuasiveness of Lindbergh's argument.

DIFFERENTIATE

ENGLISH LANGUAGE LEARNERS   ELD

Use a Main-Idea Cluster Pair students at the **Emerging** and **Expanding** levels with students at the **Bridging** level. Direct pairs to use a Main-Idea Cluster to check their understanding of each of the three sections of the lesson. Tell students to take turns reading a section of the lesson. Then have them work together to record the main idea and four details. Instruct pairs to trade and compare their Main-Idea Clusters.

PRE-AP

Write a Report Direct students to gather relevant information from several library or online sources to write a report on how increased defense spending after Roosevelt's re-election played a major role in ending the Great Depression. Encourage students to use search terms effectively, assess the credibility and accuracy of their sources, and include properly formatted citations for paraphrased data and conclusions to avoid plagiarism. Have students share their reports with the class.

See the Chapter Planner for more strategies for differentiation.

HISTORICAL THINKING

ANSWERS

1. Franklin Roosevelt felt that he should continue to lead the United States through the crisis of World War II.

2. Cash-and-carry permitted other countries to purchase supplies—but not war materials—with cash. Lend-Lease was different in that it allowed other countries to receive U.S. military goods while delaying payment. Lend-Lease required no immediate payment, so it was more beneficial to the Allies than cash-and-carry.

3. Roosevelt's push to be an "arsenal of democracy" resulted in the production of U.S. military materials, spurred economic growth, and intensified arguments by isolationists.

A NEW ALLIANCE

Sometimes no matter how much you try to stay out of a fight, circumstances force you to take action. When German warships began patrolling the Atlantic Ocean in order to stop supplies from reaching Great Britain, they targeted and tried to sink American ships. This brought the United States to the brink of battle.

THE ATLANTIC CHARTER

In the summer of 1941, the war in Europe took a dramatic turn. On June 22, Hitler pointed his army to the east and invaded the Soviet Union. The invasion was named Operation Barbarossa after the 12th-century Holy Roman Emperor, Frederick Barbarossa, and it ended the nonaggression pact between the two nations. Hitler had two objectives in mind: he wanted control of the oil supply in the Caucasus Mountains between the Black Sea and the Caspian Sea, and he wanted to conquer more territory for the expansion of Germany's population. More than 3 million German soldiers and 3,000 tanks plunged deep into Soviet territory. The German army defeated Soviet forces, captured more than 1 million prisoners, and moved toward Moscow and Leningrad.

Operation Barbarossa prompted many Americans to rethink their isolationist stance. The Nazis were becoming a true global threat. Following the German invasion, President Roosevelt offered Lend-Lease support to Soviet leader Joseph Stalin. While many Americans did not favor aiding a communist dictator, Roosevelt believed Hitler must be stopped at all costs. Over the next four years, Stalin received more than $11 billion in Lend-Lease aid from the United States to fight the Nazis.

In August 1941, two months after Germany marched on the Soviets, President Roosevelt and British prime minister Winston Churchill met aboard naval ships in Placentia Bay off the coast of Newfoundland in Canada. Even though the United States had not yet entered the war, the two leaders discussed their mutual aims and principles around fighting and winning the war. They drafted what became known as the **Atlantic Charter**. Under the eight-point charter, the two leaders agreed to such principles as freedom of the seas, greater trade among nations, and the right of people to choose the kind of government they

Operation Barbarossa, 1941

desire. The charter stated the two countries would not wage war to gain territory, and they would oppose all changes in territory brought about by any war the people who lived there opposed. They would restore self-government to any nation that had lost it in the war, they would work together with other nations to improve living and working conditions throughout the world, and—perhaps most importantly—they stated that all countries should give up the use of force against one another.

By January 1942, 26 nations of North and South America, Europe, Asia, and Africa, along with Australia and New Zealand, had allied against the Axis Powers and pledged their support to the principles of the Atlantic Charter.

HOSTILITIES INCREASE

In the fall of 1941, tensions flared between the United States and Germany over activities in the Atlantic Ocean. German U-boats, or submarines, were targeting ships on the Atlantic sea-lanes. Roosevelt responded by authorizing U.S. destroyers—a type of warship—to hunt down the German subs. This policy was called **active defense**. On September 4, 1941, Germany fired on the U.S. destroyer *Greer*. The Germans claimed it was a case of mistaken identity, as they believed the ship to be a British vessel. President Roosevelt warned that any Axis ships that attacked American vessels in the North Atlantic would "do so at their own peril."

By October, U.S. Navy ships were providing escorts for civilian cargo vessels carrying war materials to Great Britain. This angered the Germans, who clearly saw the United States as aiding and supporting their enemy. In the early morning of October 31, a German U-boat sank the U.S.S. *Reuben James*, killing 115 crewmen. Americans were outraged. The United States appeared to be on the brink of entering the war. However, it would take a shocking attack from the other side of the world to ultimately push the United States into battle.

A FRIENDSHIP THAT CHANGED HISTORY
As the world plunged into war, the personal friendship between Winston Churchill and Franklin Roosevelt helped cement the historically strong bonds between the United States and Great Britain. The friendship helped lead to the Lend-Lease Act and the Atlantic Charter. In all, the two leaders met nine times. After one of these meetings, Roosevelt wrote to Churchill, saying, "It is fun to be in the same decade with you." After Roosevelt's death, Churchill wrote, "I felt I was in contact with a very great man, who was a warm-hearted friend, and the foremost champion of the high causes which we served."

HISTORICAL THINKING

1. **READING CHECK** How did Germany's attack on the Soviet Union affect Roosevelt's foreign policy and American public opinion about the war?

2. **INTERPRET MAPS** Along which German troop path were frictions and fighting the fiercest? Why do you think this was the case?

3. **EVALUATE** How did the Atlantic Charter seek to promote global peace?

4. **DETERMINE CHRONOLOGY** What events on the Atlantic Ocean heightened U.S.-German tensions to near-conflict?

PLAN: 2-PAGE LESSON

OBJECTIVE

Understand why Germany's acts of aggression pushed the United States toward war.

CRITICAL THINKING SKILLS FOR LESSON 3.2

• Interpret Maps

• Evaluate

• Determine Chronology

• Make Inferences

• Identify Problems and Solutions

HISTORICAL THINKING FOR CHAPTER 21

What ideas and events brought about World War II? Germany's invasion of the Soviet Union and attacks on U.S. ships increased concern on the part of Americans. Lesson 3.2 describes the steps the United States took to curb Axis aggression as tensions continued to escalate.

BACKGROUND FOR THE TEACHER

The Atlantic Charter fell short of what Roosevelt and Churchill hoped to achieve—entrance of the United States into World War II. The charter also failed to address a number of other key issues. Great Britain, fearing that Japan might seize British territories in Southeast Asia, wanted the United States to issue a strong warning to Japan regarding aggression in the Pacific. Roosevelt wanted to work out a repayment plan for the money loaned through the Lend-Lease program. Despite their failure to achieve agreement on these issues, both leaders believed that the charter was necessary. The declaration raised British morale, strengthened the bonds between the United States and Britain, and defined Roosevelt's vision for a world at peace.

INTRODUCE & ENGAGE

CONNECT TO PRIOR KNOWLEDGE

Display a T-Chart labeled World War I and World War II. Tell students to think about the United States prior to entering World War I. **ASK:** What incidents moved the country closer to war? *(Possible responses: sinking of Lusitania; Zimmermann Telegram; resumption of German submarine warfare)* Note students' responses under World War I. Explain that in Lesson 3.2, students will read about incidents leading to U.S. involvement in World War II. Tell students to copy the chart and add items for World War II as they read. Students can use their charts to discuss similarities and differences in events leading to both wars.

World War I	World War II

TEACH

GUIDED DISCUSSION

1. **Make Inferences** Why do you think nations from many parts of the world pledged to support the Atlantic Charter? *(Possible response: They supported the principles it contained. For example, countries in Africa and Europe, fearing Axis invasion, supported the provision that opposed changes in territory brought about by war.)*

2. **Identify Problems and Solutions** Identify the problem that arose in the Atlantic sea-lanes, President Roosevelt's solution, and what might have been the outcome if the problem had not been solved. *(German U-boats began targeting ships in the Atlantic sea-lanes. Roosevelt's solution was to implement a policy called active defense, which authorized U.S. destroyers to actively search for German submarines. One possible alternative outcome might have been Germany taking control of Atlantic sea-lanes and preventing war supplies from reaching Britain.)*

INTERPRET MAPS

Direct students' attention to the map of Operation Barbarossa. **ASK:** In what country is the front line? *(the Soviet Union)* **ASK:** What feature of the map shows the success of the German operation? *(The legend indicates that German-controlled Soviet territory extended north almost to Leningrad and east almost to Moscow.)* **ASK:** Based on the map, what would you predict about the outcome of the war and why? *(Possible response: The Axis Powers will be victorious because they already control most of Europe and are gaining control of the Soviet Union.)*

ACTIVE OPTIONS

On Your Feet: Thumbs Up/Thumbs Down Divide the class into groups and have each group write six True-False statements about the lesson with the correct answers included. Collect the statements. Mix them up and read them aloud to the class, skipping any duplicates. Have students give a "thumbs up" for true statements and a "thumbs down" for false statements. Correct any misconceptions.

NG Learning Framework: Investigate Technology

SKILL Problem-Solving

KNOWLEDGE New Frontiers

Tell students to work in pairs or small groups to prepare a report on the technological capabilities of U.S. destroyers and German U-boats as wartime vessels in the early 1940s. Students should conduct online or library research to investigate the tactical advantages and disadvantages of each. For example, they might determine the firepower of each vessel and the speed at which each traveled. Students should conclude their presentation with an analysis of which technology was more effective during World War II. Groups should be prepared to report their findings to the class.

DIFFERENTIATE

ENGLISH LANGUAGE LEARNERS

Sequence Events To build a better understanding of the critical events in the lesson and their relationship to one another in time, instruct students to note events and dates in a Sequence Chain. You may ask students at the **Expanding** and **Bridging** levels to assist students at the **Emerging** level to make sure they understand time-order words such as *next*, *after*, and *following*.

GIFTED & TALENTED

Create Social Networking Profiles Tell students to research Franklin D. Roosevelt and Winston Churchill to learn more about each man's biographical details, accomplishments, personality, philosophy, and strategies. Then have students create social-networking profiles for each person, including photos. Invite students to share their profiles with the entire class.

See the Chapter Planner for more strategies for differentiation.

HISTORICAL THINKING

ANSWERS

1. President Roosevelt offered Lend-Lease to the Soviet Union, and many Americans reconsidered their isolationist views as they saw Nazi Germany becoming a global threat.

2. Fighting was most fierce along the path from Bialystok, Poland, to Vyaz'ma in the Soviet Union. This was likely because the Soviets hoped to repel the Germans before they reached the capital of Moscow.

3. The Atlantic Charter established a series of principles which the United States and Great Britain agreed to follow, promising, among the eight points included, not to use force against one another, to work together to restore self-government, and to work toward improving the lives of people around the globe.

4. German U-boats targeted ships in the Atlantic, and Roosevelt declared "active defense" in response. Germany fired on the U.S. destroyer *Greer.* U.S. navy ships began escorting cargo ships to Great Britain. Germany sank the U.S.S. *Reuben James.*

VOCABULARY

For each pair of vocabulary words, write a sentence that explains the connection between the words.

1. rearmament; Rome-Berlin Axis
    After Hitler's rearmament began, he joined with Mussolini to form the Rome-Berlin Axis.

2. Third Reich; Gestapo

3. Munich Agreement; appeasement

4. nonaggression pact; belligerent

5. Atlantic Charter; active defense

6. purge; Long March

READING STRATEGY
COMPARE AND CONTRAST

Comparing and contrasting can help readers form a deeper understanding of concepts and events. Both Nazi Germany and Japan disrupted world peace in the 1930s and 1940s. Complete a Venn diagram to compare and contrast Nazi Germany and Japan. Include the following features:

single charismatic leader
desire for territorial conquest
disregard for established international laws
resentment over the outcome of World War I
lack of natural resources
policy of anti-Semitism
buildup of armed forces

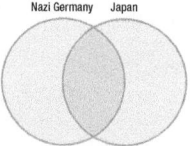

Nazi Germany   Japan

7. In what way do you think Nazi Germany and Japan were most alike? Support your opinion with details.

MAIN IDEAS

Answer the following questions. Support your answers with evidence from the chapter.

8. What complex historical causes led to the rise of Adolf Hitler in Germany during the 1930s? **LESSON 1.1**

9. How did the views of President Roosevelt and a majority of Americans differ regarding involvement in the war? **LESSON 1.2**

10. How did the German-Soviet nonaggression pact contribute to the outbreak of World War II? **LESSON 2.1**

11. Why did Japan look upon China as a desirable target for invasion? **LESSON 2.2**

12. How did President Roosevelt intend to make America an "arsenal of democracy"? **LESSON 3.1**

13. How did the breaking of the German-Soviet nonaggression pact impact the debate between isolationists and interventionists in the United States? **LESSON 3.2**

HISTORICAL THINKING

Answer the following questions. Support your answers with evidence from the chapter.

14. **DETERMINE CHRONOLOGY** What 1940 military events preceded the Battle of Britain?

15. **EVALUATE** How did changes to the Neutrality Act over the years lead to greater U.S. involvement in the war effort?

16. **SYNTHESIZE** How did the onset of World War II help bring about the Atlantic Charter?

17. **DRAW CONCLUSIONS** Why do you think so many dictators were able to rise to power during the years before World War II?

18. **FORM AND SUPPORT OPINIONS** What events helped President Roosevelt build his case that Hitler posed a threat to the world unlike any other? Support your opinion

INTERPRET VISUALS

During the Battle of Britain, many Londoners took shelter in the subway stations of the London Underground as Nazi bombs rained from the sky over their city. Study this photograph and then answer the questions.

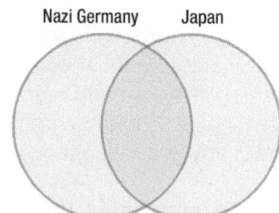

19. A slogan during the bombing of London was "Your courage, your cheerfulness . . . will bring us victory." How does this photo reflect that philosophy?

20. What potential challenges do you see in living in these conditions for an extended period?

ANALYZE SOURCES

The Atlantic Charter, drafted in 1941 by Roosevelt and Churchill, consisted of eight general principles. Read the text of the eighth principle below. Then answer the questions that follow.

> Eighth, they [President Roosevelt and Prime Minister Churchill] believe that all of the nations of the world, for realistic as well as spiritual reasons must come to the abandonment of the use of force. Since no future peace can be maintained if land, sea or air armaments continue to be employed by nations which threaten, or may threaten, aggression outside of their frontiers, they believe, pending the establishment of a wider and permanent system of general security, that the disarmament of such nations is essential. They will likewise aid and encourage all other practicable measures which will lighten for peace-loving peoples the crushing burden of armaments.

21. What does the charter argue is "essential" to helping secure world peace?

22. Describe the complex cause and effect relationships between disarmament and peace. Support your answer with evidence from the text.

CONNECT TO YOUR LIFE

23. **NARRATIVE** Reread the summary of the Atlantic Charter from the chapter. Sum up the ideals Churchill and Roosevelt expressed to the world. To what extent have those ideals become reality since the charter was written? Think of what you know about the world today. Choose one or more of the principles of the Atlantic Charter, and describe the state of that principle in the world today.

TIPS

• Read the summary of the charter's principles, and state in your own words the principles and ideals expressed there.

• State the principle or principles you will compare with today's world—for example, the principle of not expanding territory, or of open trade among nations.

• Describe some aspect of the state of the world in terms of that principle.

• Use two or three vocabulary terms from the chapter in your narrative, if possible.

• Conclude your narrative with a summary of what exists now and how it could be changed to achieve the principle or principles you named.

VOCABULARY ANSWERS

1. After Hitler's rearmament began, he joined with Mussolini to form the Rome-Berlin Axis.

2. The Gestapo were the secret police force of Hitler's Third Reich.

3. Under the Munich Agreement, leaders Chamberlain, Daladier, and Mussolini ceded the Sudetenland to Hitler, hoping that this appeasement would avoid further conflict.

4. Countries that sign a nonaggression pact are not belligerents because they are not engaging in war.

5. Although the United States supported the peaceful provisions of the Atlantic Charter, it also instituted the active defense policy, which allowed the U.S. Navy to pursue German U-boats that were attacking ships.

6. Chiang Kai-shek's purge to eliminate communists from China resulted in the Long March, in which communist troops and civilians fled to a remote part of China.

READING STRATEGY ANSWER

Nazi Germany   Japan

Students should distribute items within the Venn diagram as follows:

Nazi Germany: single charismatic leader; policy of anti-Semitism; resentment over the outcome of World War I

Both: desire for territorial conquest; disregard for established international laws; buildup of armed forces

Japan: lack of natural resources

7. Possible response: Nazi Germany and Japan were most alike in their desire for territorial conquest. Nazi Germany aimed to unite and rule all areas of German-speaking people, while Japan sought to conquer China and other nearby territories.

MAIN IDEAS ANSWERS

8. Germany was experiencing economic depression and political instability. Hitler promised to create jobs following the collapse of Germany's economy. After what Hitler considered to be the humiliating terms of the Treaty of Versailles, Hitler pledged to restore Germany to its former glory.

9. Roosevelt believed that it was important to stop Hitler even if it meant entering the war. The majority of Americans supported noninvolvement.

10. With the pact, Germany felt free to attack Poland, which was the trigger that caused Britain and France to declare war on Germany.

11. China's land and resources, as well as its political instability, made it a desirable target for invasion.

12. Roosevelt encouraged factories to produce weaponry and vehicles of war, which would be supplied to the allies.

13. The invasion of the Soviet Union caused many isolationists to rethink their views as it crystalized the danger and ambitions of Hitler's Germany.

HISTORICAL THINKING ANSWERS

14. The military events that preceded the Battle of Britain were the fall of Poland, the invasion of Denmark, the invasion of Norway, the fall of the Netherlands and Belgium, and the invasion and fall of France.

15. Over time, the Neutrality Act became less neutral. Originally, the United States was not allowed to sell war materials to any nation involved in conflict. Changes such as permitting cash-and-carry allowed the United States to sell nonmilitary materials to its allies, while the Lend-Lease Act allowed for the "loan" of military materials to countries fighting Germany.

16. The early successes of Germany, Japan, and Italy motivated Roosevelt and Churchill to boost morale by envisioning a postwar peaceful world, the principles of which were stated in the Atlantic Charter.

17. Dictators promised strong leadership and convinced people that only they could solve economic and social problems.

18. Hitler ignored international laws, invaded Poland, and broke the German-Soviet nonaggression pact by invading the Soviet Union. In addition, the Germans engaged in unrestricted submarine warfare, which included targeting U.S. cargo ships. Thus, Hitler posed an unprecedented threat to both the United States and the world.

INTERPRET VISUALS ANSWERS

19. Although cramped and uncomfortable, Londoners appear calm as they courageously huddle in the subway, some even lying on the rail tracks.

20. Answers will vary. Students may point out that Londoners had to experience prolonged and stressful periods of discomfort, lack of food, and lack of proper ventilation and sanitation.

ANALYZE SOURCES ANSWERS

21. The charter argues that disarmament of belligerent nations and abandoning the use of force by all nations is essential to securing world peace.

22. With the Atlantic Charter, Roosevelt and Churchill called for all countries to give up using force against one another. They declared that the United States and Great Britain would oppose the forceful taking of territory by an aggressor nation and would restore self-government to those who had lost it. They hoped disarmament would bring about peace. However, with Germany's aggression in Europe, the United States and Great Britain could not disarm because they would need their stockpiles of munitions to defeat Germany and restore peace.

CONNECT TO YOUR LIFE ANSWER

23. Students should clearly state in their own words the principles and ideals expressed in the charter and then describe the state of the world in terms of one or more of the stated principles. The narrative should include two or three vocabulary terms from the chapter and conclude with how the state of the world could change to meet the principles that students name.

UNIT 7 RESOURCES

UNIT INTRODUCTION

UNIT TIME LINE

UNIT WRAP-UP

NATIONAL GEOGRAPHIC | CONNECTION

National Geographic Magazine
Adapted Articles
- "America's Propaganda Machine"
- "Dogs at War" ONLINE

Unit 7 Inquiry: Persuade an Audience

NG Learning Framework Activities
- Write About a Cold War Advance
- Debate the Origins of the Cold War

Unit 7 Formal Assessment

CHAPTER 22 RESOURCES

Available at NGLSync.Cengage.com

TEACHER RESOURCES & ASSESSMENT

Reading and Note-Taking

Vocabulary Practice

Social Studies Skills Lessons
- Reading: Determine Chronology
- Writing: Argument

Formal Assessment
- Chapter 22 Pretest
- Chapter 22 Tests A & B
- Section Quizzes

Chapter 22 Answer Key

ExamView®
One-time Download

STUDENT DIGITAL RESOURCES

- eEdition
- Handbooks
- Online Atlas
- American Gallery Online
- History Notebook
- Active History
- American Voices (Biographies)
- Reid on the Road video series
- Literature Analysis
- Projects for Inquiry-Based Learning

Chapter 22 Spanish Resources are available at NGLSync.Cengage.com.

AMERICAN STORIES | The Code Talkers of World War II

- Study Primary Sources: Excerpt from a speech by President George W. Bush
- On Your Feet: Coding Roundtable

  NG Learning Framework:
  Develop a Code

SECTION 1 RESOURCES
PEARL HARBOR AND MOBILIZATION

LESSON 1.1
A Devastating Attack

- On Your Feet: Create a Quiz

  NG Learning Framework:
  Analyze Filipino Oral Histories

LESSON 1.2
Gearing Up for War

- Active History: Graph Economic Changes

  AMERICAN GALLERY ONLINE The Tuskegee Airmen

American Voices Biography
A. Philip Randolph ONLINE

American Voices Biography
The Tuskegee Airmen ONLINE

American Voices Biography
Senator Daniel Inouye ONLINE

LESSON 1.3
Women and the War Effort

- On Your Feet: Inside-Outside Circle

  NG Learning Framework:
  Explore Women in the War Oral Histories

LESSON 1.4
AMERICAN VOICES
Rosie the Riveter

- ▶ Rosie the Riveter
- On Your Feet: Sentence Chain

  NG Learning Framework:
  Investigate War Propaganda

LESSON 1.5
Japanese American Internment

- On Your Feet: Hold a Panel Discussion

  NG Learning Framework:
  Create a Virtual Museum Exhibit

American Voices Biography
Fred Korematsu ONLINE

LESSON 1.6
CURATING HISTORY
Japanese American National Museum, Los Angeles

- On Your Feet: Sort the Artifacts

SECTION 2 RESOURCES
ISLAND HOPPING IN THE PACIFIC

LESSON 2.1
Campaigns in Europe and Africa

- On Your Feet: Use a Jigsaw Strategy

  NG Learning Framework:
  Investigate Contemporary Accounts

LESSON 2.2
War in the Pacific

- On Your Feet: Tell Me More

  NG Learning Framework:
  Examine the Role of Aircraft in the Pacific Campaign

SECTION 3 RESOURCES
MARCHING TOWARD VICTORY

LESSON 3.1
Victory in Europe

- On Your Feet: Time Line

  NG Learning Framework:
  Consider Geopolitical Implications

LESSON 3.2
Victory in Asia

- On Your Feet: Fishbowl

  NG Learning Framework:
  Simulate a Cabinet Meeting

LESSON 3.3
FULBRIGHT–NATIONAL GEOGRAPHIC FELLOW: ARI BESER
Nuclear War, Nuclear Peace

- On Your Feet: Create a Quiz

  NG Learning Framework:
  Investigate Policy Issues

SECTION 4 RESOURCES
FACING THE HOLOCAUST

LESSON 4.1
The Holocaust

- On Your Feet: Think, Pair, Share

  NG Learning Framework:
  Holocaust Heroes

LESSON 4.2
Refugees and Justice

- On Your Feet: History Roundtable

  NG Learning Framework:
  Create a Time Line

CHAPTER 22 REVIEW

STRIVING READERS

STRATEGY ❶
FOCUS ON MAIN IDEAS

Tell students to locate the Main Idea statement at the beginning of each lesson. Explain that these statements summarize the important ideas of the lesson and will help them focus on what matters most in the text. Help students get in the habit of using the Main Idea statement to set a purpose for reading.

Use with All Lessons

STRATEGY ❷
USE K-W-L CHARTS

Provide each student with a K-W-L Chart. Have students brainstorm what they already know about World War II, such as its causes, participants, important events, and the multiple fronts in Europe, Africa, and Asia. Suggest that they add these ideas to the chart. Then ask students to write in the second column of the chart three questions they have, such as When did the United States enter the war? or What happened to U.S. citizens of Japanese descent? Remind students to complete their charts as they read each lesson in the chapter.

K What Do I Know?	W What Do I Want To Learn?	L What Did I Learn?

Use with All Lessons

STRATEGY ❸
TURN HEADINGS INTO OUTLINES

To help students organize and understand lesson content, explain that headings can provide a high-level outline of the lesson. Model for students how to use the lesson title and subheadings to create a basic outline structure. Encourage students to flesh out their outlines as they read.

Use with All Lessons

INCLUSION

STRATEGY ❶
DESCRIBE LESSON VISUALS

Pair visually challenged students with students who are not visually challenged. Ask the latter to describe the lesson visuals in detail and to answer any questions the visually impaired students might have.

Use with All Lessons

STRATEGY ❷
PROVIDE A SUMMARY CHART

Tell students that they will be learning about decisive battles near the end of World War II in both the European and Pacific theaters. To help students preview or understand lesson content, provide them with a summary chart of important battles, the people and places involved, and the outcomes.

Battle	People/Place	Outcomes
Operation Overlord	British, Canadian, and U.S. forces invaded Nazi-occupied France.	Heavy casualties, but ultimately successful; Allied troops took back France.
Battle of the Bulge	Allied and U.S. forces found Germans at Ardennes in southern Belgium.	Germany broke through Allied lines; heavy casualties; ultimately Allies prevailed.
Battles of Leyte Gulf	U.S. soldiers and Filipinos battled Japanese forces on Philippine island of Leyte.	Heavy casualties; U.S. forces destroyed the Japanese Navy.
Battle of Iwo Jima	U.S. soldiers fought Japanese soldiers.	Heavy casualties; U.S. forces won and used Iwo Jima as the base for bombers to attack Japan.

Use with Lessons 3.1 and 3.2 *Students can expand the chart to include the Battle of Okinawa and the atomic bombings of Hiroshima and Nagasaki.*

ENGLISH LANGUAGE LEARNERS

STRATEGY 1
CREATE SENTENCE STRIPS

Choose a paragraph from a lesson and make sentence strips from it. Read the paragraph aloud while students at **All Proficiencies** follow along in their books. Then have students close their books, and give them the set of sentence strips. Students should put the strips in order and then read the paragraph aloud.

Use with All Lessons *Before reading, you may want to ask students at the **Emerging** level to read the sentence strips aloud. Then ask them to point out meaningful words in each sentence. Repeat the exercise with another paragraph.*

STRATEGY 2
CLARIFY VOCABULARY

To help students clarify the meaning of unfamiliar words and to help you monitor their understanding, provide students at the **Emerging** and **Expanding** levels of proficiency with the following sentence frames.

Emerging:

I don't know the word _____.

I think it means _____.

Clues I found are _____.

Expanding:

I don't know the word _____, but I think it means _____.

I think this because _____.

Direct students at the **Bridging** level to create a three-column chart on which they record any unfamiliar words they encounter, what the context clues and word parts reveal about each word's meaning, and what they think each word probably means.

Use with All Lessons

GIFTED & TALENTED

STRATEGY 1
CREATE DISPLAYS

Instruct students to conduct online research to learn more about how World War II affected the lives and the public perception of African Americans, Japanese Americans, and women. Tell students to locate posters, photographs, headlines, and editorial cartoons relating to these groups of people during the war. Ask students to work together to set up displays around the classroom.

Use with Lessons 1.2, 1.3, 1.4, 1.5

STRATEGY 2
WRITE DIALOGUES

Ask students to write imaginary dialogues that might have taken place between people who played a part in the content of the lessons. For example, you might suggest the following people in Section 1:

• Franklin Roosevelt and Douglas MacArthur (Lesson 1.1)

• Roosevelt and A. Philip Randolph (Lesson 1.2)

• Head of the WACs and head of the WAVES (Lesson 1.3)

• Norman Rockwell and Westinghouse poster illustrator (Lesson 1.4)

• Roosevelt and a young Nisei serviceman (Lesson 1.5)

Use with All Lessons

PRE-AP

STRATEGY 1
WRITE NEWS REPORTS

Assign students the role of World War II-era journalists reporting on an aspect of war, either at home or abroad. Remind them that news articles begin with the most important information and usually answer most or all of the questions *who, what, where, when, why,* and *how* by the end of the article. Invite students to post their articles on a class blog or publish them on a class or school website.

Use with All Lessons

STRATEGY 2
EXTEND KNOWLEDGE

Ask students to conduct online research to find out more about a topic, a person, or an event introduced in Chapter 22. For example, students might choose to research the Bataan Death March, the Tuskegee Airmen, the Flying Tigers, women's military units, the Yalta Conference, the Nuremberg trials, Anne Frank, or Elie Wiesel. Have students present their findings in an oral report to the class or in a digital report posted on a class blog.

Use with Lessons 1.1, 1.2, 1.3, 1.4, 1.5, 3.1, 3.2, 4.1, 4.2

HISTORICAL THINKING How did World War II and the Holocaust impact Americans and the world?

"War is a grim, cruel business,

. . . justified only as a means of sustaining the forces of good against those of evil."

—General Dwight D. Eisenhower

CRITICAL VIEWING During the Battle of Iwo Jima, an island near the Japanese coast, U.S. Marines took control of Mount Suribachi, the highest point of the island. In celebration, soldiers raised the U.S. flag at the top of the peak—twice. The second time, Joseph Rosenthal captured this image of the flag-raising, which won him a Pulitzer Prize and became one of the most iconic photos of World War II. What do you think the photo symbolized to Americans on the home front?

America in World War II 775

INTRODUCE THE PHOTOGRAPH

IWO JIMA

Direct students to study the photograph and quotation that open this chapter. Have them discuss what they can tell about the location depicted and what the soldiers seem to be doing. **ASK:** How do both the debris on the ground and the action of the soldiers exemplify the quotation? *(Possible response: The area has been reduced to rubble, exemplifying the grim aspect of war. The planting of the flag suggests the sustaining of good against evil.)* Tell students that in this chapter they will learn about the United States' mobilization and participation in World War II.

For Chapter 22 Spanish Resources, visit the Resources Menu. Chapter 22 Resources are available at NGLSync.Cengage.com.

SHARE BACKGROUND

Iwo Jima was the site of a fierce battle near the end of World War II. A small island belonging to the Volcano Islands of southern Japan, Iwo Jima was strategically important. If it was captured, U.S. fighter planes could take off from the island to accompany U.S. bombers heading for Japan. The bombers were stationed on Saipan, an island farther south that the United States had captured in 1944. Three U.S. Marine divisions landed on Iwo Jima in February 1945. Battles raged for almost a month before the island was taken, mainly because the Japanese defenders had firmly entrenched themselves in caves. When Marines raised the flag on Iwo Jima's Mount Suribachi, it quickly became evident that the flag was too small to be seen by U.S. soldiers elsewhere on the island. The Marines quickly replaced the flag with a larger one.

CRITICAL VIEWING Possible response: The photo symbolized American courage, perseverance, and victory.

HISTORICAL THINKING QUESTION

How did World War II and the Holocaust impact Americans and the world?

Four Corners Activity: Activate Prior Knowledge This activity addresses four significant occurrences that happened either during or because of World War II. Post the four topics shown in the list below. Ask students to choose an occurrence that they know something about, go to that corner, and share their knowledge with other students in their group. Ask one member in each group to summarize the group's ideas.

1. **Internment of Japanese Americans** The United States imprisoned more than 100,000 Japanese Americans.

2. **The Atomic Bomb** The United States developed and deployed a new and powerful weapon.

3. **The Holocaust** The Nazis systematically exterminated millions of Jews.

4. **Shifts in Power and Geographic Boundaries** The Allies divided up Germany and determined the boundaries of Poland.

INTRODUCE THE READING STRATEGY

DETERMINE CHRONOLOGY

Explain that determining chronology means placing events in the order in which they occurred. Turn to the Chapter Review and preview the time line with students. As they read the chapter, have students order the major events of the United State's involvement in World War II. They also should note possible connections between the various events.

KEY DATES FOR CHAPTER 22

1941	Japanese attack Pearl Harbor
1941	Hitler invades Soviet Union
1942	Wannsee Conference
1942	Roosevelt signs Executive Order 9066
1942–43	United States mobilizes in Africa and Europe
1944	D-Day
1945	Germany surrenders
1945	Battle of Iwo Jima
1945	United States drops atomic bombs on Japan
1945	Japan surrenders

INTRODUCE CHAPTER VOCABULARY

KEY VOCABULARY

SECTION 1

Bracero Program	infamy	penicillin
demobilization	interned	ration
enemy alien	internment camp	wage discrimination
executive order	napalm	

SECTION 2

amphibious assault	island hopping	panzer
depth charge		

SECTION 3

amphibious landing craft	D-Day	kamikaze
atomic bomb		

SECTION 4

atrocity	crematorium	tribunal
concentration camp	Holocaust	

WORD SQUARES

As they read the chapter, encourage students to complete a Word Square for Key Vocabulary words. Ask students to enter a Key Vocabulary word in the center oval of each square. Then, as they encounter each word in the chapter, tell them to add the Key Vocabulary word's definition, as well as characteristics, examples, and non-examples of the word. Model an example for students on the board using the graphic organizer shown here.

Definition: a type of nuclear bomb	Characteristics: radioactive; explosion triggered by splitting atoms
atomic bomb	
Examples: bombs dropped on Hiroshima and Nagasaki	Non-examples: incendiary bomb; pipe bomb

OBJECTIVES

- Identify the contributions of the Navajo Code Talkers during World War II.
- Explain U.S. and Allied wartime code strategy during the war.
- Describe developments in communication and technology during the war.
- Study a primary source: excerpt from a speech.

CRITICAL THINKING SKILLS FOR "THE CODE TALKERS OF WORLD WAR II"

- Make Connections
- Draw Conclusions
- Synthesize
- Categorize
- Analyze Primary Sources
- Evaluate

CONNECT TO THE CHAPTER

This American Story reveals one of the U.S. Marines' greatest secrets during the war—and one that unfortunately remained unknown for many years. Students will learn about the vital role of Native American soldiers, specifically the Navajo and their work as Code Talkers during World War II. Photos of Code Talkers from the past and present, a chart translating Navajo words, and a general overview of coding during the war bring to life the legacy of these courageous soldiers and the significance of coding and communication.

The upcoming chapter, America in World War II, discusses the entry of the United States into the war and its subsequent growing involvement. Introduce the American Story before Lesson 1.2, which briefly touches upon the Marines' reliance on the Navajo Code Talkers.

HISTORY NOTEBOOK

Encourage students to complete the American Story page for Chapter 22 in their History Notebooks as they read.

AMERICAN STORIES · NATIONAL GEOGRAPHIC

CRITICAL VIEWING Navajo Code Talkers working with a U.S. Marine signal unit operate a portable radio in the jungles of Bougainville Island in the South Pacific. What does this photo reveal about the conditions of this military campaign?

776 CHAPTER 22

The Code Talkers of
WORLD WAR II

When U.S. Marines disembarked onto Japanese-occupied beaches in the Pacific Islands during World War II, the battle scenes were unimaginable. Fighting their way inch by inch through firestorms of artillery, the "bullets fell like deadly sleet," reported one Marine of his landing on Guam. Bombs nicknamed "daisy cutters" rained down, spraying shrapnel outward in all directions to cause maximum damage to vulnerable human bodies.

DEVELOPING THE NAVAJO CODE

Amidst the chaos, it was essential for different military units to maintain communication. Messages had to be passed quickly, accurately, cryptically, in a way the Japanese could not interpret. To do this job, the Marines relied on an elite group of fighters—the Code Talkers.

The idea of using a Native American language as a wartime code originated during World War I. By transmitting messages in Choctaw, U.S. forces were able to orchestrate a successful surprise attack against the German army. In the years following World War I, scholars from Germany, Japan, and other countries visited the United States and studied various Native American languages including Cherokee, Choctaw, and Comanche. Few people in the United States or Europe spoke or understood the Navajo language. Navajo is complex in both its structure and its pronunciation. It is a tonal language, meaning that the tone used to pronounce a word can completely change its meaning. In addition, Navajo was almost never written down—both the language and its wealth of traditional stories were passed along orally.

America in World War II **777**

K-W-L CHART

Provide students with a K-W-L Chart and have them brainstorm what they already know about the use of codes, such as Morse code, to transmit communications. Instruct students to write questions that they would like to have answered as they study this American Story, such as: What role did the Navajo play in World War II? or How did the Navajo code help the United States during the war? Then, as students read this American Story, encourage them to complete the chart with what they learn.

K What Do I Know?	W What Do I Want To Learn?	L What Did I Learn?

BACKGROUND FOR THE TEACHER

The Navajo people live primarily in New Mexico, Utah, and Arizona. Many Navajo continue to live a traditional lifestyle, speaking the native language, maintaining traditional social structures, and creating traditional works, such as woven rugs, sand paintings, and silver jewelry, some of which have ties to their spiritual beliefs. The Navajo Nation has the most sophisticated government among Native Americans, necessitated by the discovery of oil on their land in the 1920s and the need to manage the lease of land to oil companies. The nation's capital is Window Rock, Arizona, where a monument celebrates the contributions of Navajo soldiers, including the Code Talkers.

CRITICAL VIEWING Possible response: Based on the photo, military personnel would have to deal with navigating through and operating within dense jungle growth in extreme heat and at night. Leaves of a plant behind the soldiers are riddled with holes, likely left by insects, so personnel, such as the soldiers shown, probably suffered insect bites.

TEACH

GUIDED DISCUSSION

1. **Synthesize** Why was the Navajo code difficult to break? *(It's a complex, tonal language with few fluent speakers outside of Native Americans. It's almost exclusively oral, so code breakers couldn't find written definitions of word meanings.)*

2. **Categorize** What negative experiences did the Navajo Code Talkers often have after they returned home from the war? *(In the military, the Code Talkers were greatly respected for their singular role in unbreakable communications. At home, many faced the same discrimination they had experienced before their military service. Some couldn't vote, as in New Mexico, because they had not yet been granted the right. They couldn't discuss their experiences because their work was classified. As such, they didn't get public recognition.)*

ANALYZE PRIMARY SOURCES

Tell students to reread the excerpt from President Bush's speech and think about how specific words and phrases are used. **ASK:** What language does President Bush use to establish a relationship between the past and present, and what point does he convey? *(He pairs opposing ideas: "ancient people" with "modern war" and "messages traveling by field radio" with "language heard across the Colorado plateau." He emphasizes the importance of recognizing Americans throughout all of U.S. history who have made contributions and sacrifices.)*

NAVAJO CODE WORDS

Harmony is a central focus of Navajo cultural beliefs. The Navajo believe that everything in the universe is connected and that harmony must be maintained among all living creatures. **ASK:** Why do you think the Navajo words in the chart for 20th-century technology relate to animals? *(Answers will vary. Possible response: Native Americans have a strong connection to land and nature, so they apparently chose familiar animals that connected with the ideas they were encoding.)* **ASK:** Why might the Navajo Code Talkers have used their word for an owl to describe an observation plane? *(Possible response: Owls are predatory birds with the ability to zero in on prey from a distance, the same capability of an observation plane.)*

AMERICAN STORIES

NAVAJO CODE WORDS

The Navajo language did not have words for the technology of 20th-century warfare. When devising the code, the men first thought of an object that could symbolize the word they wanted to encode, then they chose the Navajo word for that object. These are some of the words for engines of war in the Navajo code.

ENGLISH	NAVAJO	MEANING
dive bomber	gini	chicken hawk
observation plane	ne-ahs-jah	owl
aircraft carrier	tsidi-ne-ye-hi	bird carrier
bombs	a-ye-shi	eggs
amphibious vehicle	chal	frog
submarine	besh-lo	iron fish

One non-native speaker who did have a basic understanding of Navajo was Philip Johnston, a civil engineer who had lived on a Navajo reservation as a child with his missionary parents. It was Johnston who suggested to the Marines that the Navajo language could form the basis of a wartime code.

In 1942, the Marines launched the Navajo code project with 29 Native American recruits. They gathered at a base in California, where they were charged with creating the code. The team devised a system of word substitutions in which a different Navajo word would stand for each letter of the English alphabet. To avoid spelling every word out, commonly used military terms were assigned their own Navajo words. For example, "fighter plane" became *da-he-tih-hi*, or "hummingbird" in Navajo. To make the code even more unbreakable, it was not written down.

The men, who came to be known as Code Talkers, memorized every single word of the code and practiced until they could quickly translate messages from English into Navajo code and back again. Chester Nez, one of the original 29, claimed that the Navajo tradition of oral storytelling helped the Code Talkers hone their memorization skills.

In an early test of the Navajo code, a message was sent over the radio from one post to another using the coding machines that were in common use. Simultaneously, one Code Talker relayed the same message orally to another. The Marine officers estimated the message would take four hours to transmit and decode using the machine method. The Code Talkers did it in under three minutes.

CODE TALKERS AT WAR

The Navajo were the largest group of Code Talkers, with around 420 members. They fought in the Pacific. Members of the Comanche, Cherokee, Chippewa, Kiowa, Pawnee, Lakota, and other tribes served as Code Talkers in Europe and other war zones. Code Talkers worked in pairs as battlefield radio officers. They carried a 30-pound radio that had to be cranked to generate electricity. As one man cranked the radio, the other transmitted coded messages to another pair of Code Talkers elsewhere on the battlefield or on a transport ship. Working under the deafening tumult of battle, the Code Talkers had to maintain enough focus to quickly translate and transmit messages, and be prepared to take part in the fighting.

The Code Talkers served with courage and distinction wherever they were assigned. In the Pacific, the Navajo Code Talkers were instrumental in several U.S. victories, including the famous battle for the island of Iwo Jima. According to one Marine officer, "The entire operation was directed by Navajo code. During the two days that followed the initial landings I had six Navajo radio nets working around the clock. They sent and received over 800 messages without an error. Were it not for the Navajo Code Talkers, the Marines never would have taken Iwo Jima."

COMING HOME

The return to civilian life after the war was difficult for many soldiers, including the Code Talkers. In their fighting units they had been respected by their fellow soldiers and treated as equals. Back in the United States, however, old prejudices were still in force. When Chester Nez returned to his home state of New Mexico after serving in the Marines, for example, he was not allowed to vote. Native Americans were not given the right to vote in that state until 1948.

Many of the returning Native American soldiers were also troubled by their experiences during the war, especially those that went against the traditions of their tribes. In his autobiography, Nez recalled being plagued with nightmares until he underwent a traditional ceremony called the Enemy Way that helped him return to the Right Way—a sense of balance between the physical and spiritual worlds.

The situation was made worse by the fact that the Code Talkers could not reveal the pivotal role they had played in so many hard-fought battles. The existence of Native American codes was kept secret until 1968, because the government did not want to reveal any possible keys to the only unbroken oral code from World War II.

After the work of the Code Talkers was declassified, or no longer declared an official secret, the soldiers were finally recognized for their true contributions to the war effort. In July 2001, the four surviving Code Talkers of the original 29 received the Congressional Gold Medal in a ceremony in Washington, D.C.

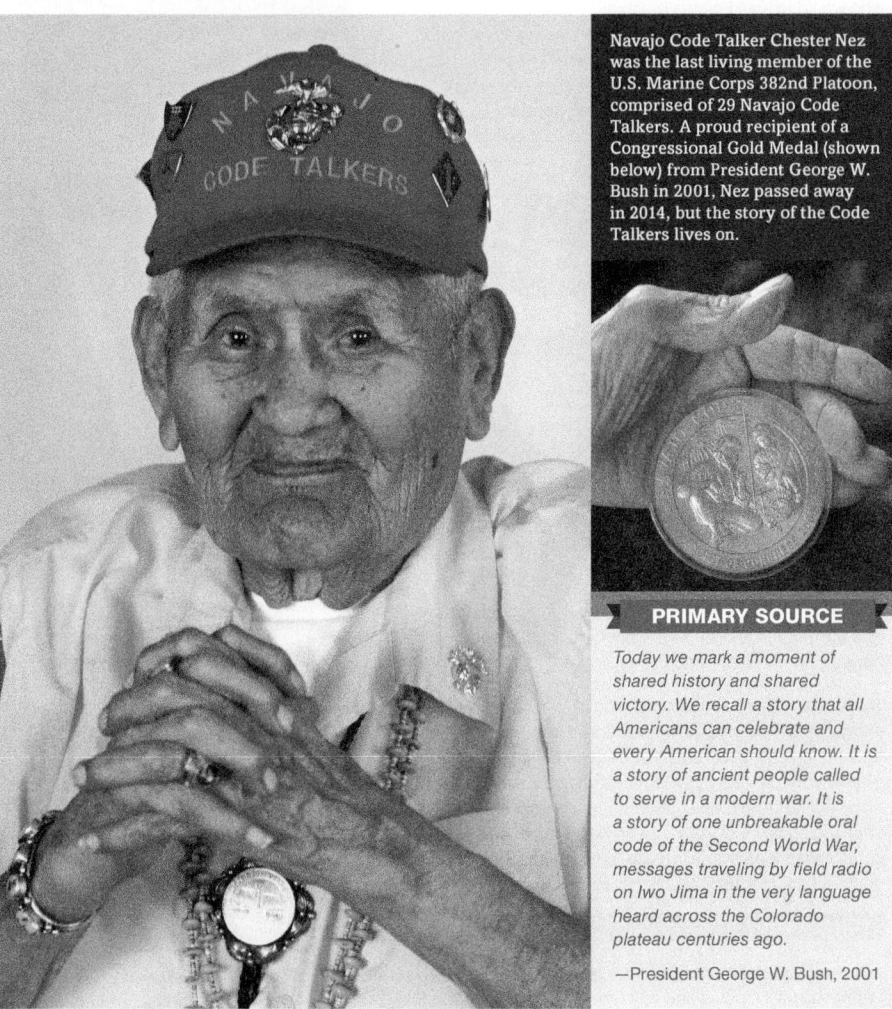

Navajo Code Talker Chester Nez was the last living member of the U.S. Marine Corps 382nd Platoon, comprised of 29 Navajo Code Talkers. A proud recipient of a Congressional Gold Medal (shown below) from President George W. Bush in 2001, Nez passed away in 2014, but the story of the Code Talkers lives on.

PRIMARY SOURCE

Today we mark a moment of shared history and shared victory. We recall a story that all Americans can celebrate and every American should know. It is a story of ancient people called to serve in a modern war. It is a story of one unbreakable oral code of the Second World War, messages traveling by field radio on Iwo Jima in the very language heard across the Colorado plateau centuries ago.

—President George W. Bush, 2001

America in World War II **779**

ACTIVE OPTIONS

On Your Feet: Coding Roundtable Divide the class into groups of four or five. Hand each group a sheet of paper with two columns labeled Navajo Code and Enigma Code. Tell students to list and compare details about the two codes. Instruct students to write a detail, read it aloud, and pass the paper clockwise to the next student. Repeat until each student has written at least two details. When students have finished, ask each group to discuss how the two codes compare.

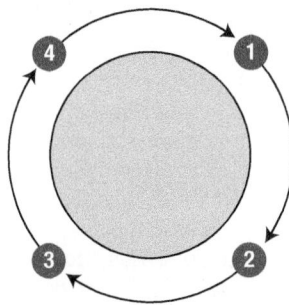

NG Learning Framework: Develop a Code

ATTITUDE Curiosity

SKILLS Communication, Collaboration

Have students work in pairs to develop their own simple coding system using sound signals, words, or numbers. Students should create a key for their code and display it as they present a coded message to the class. Challenge the class to interpret the message based on the displayed key.

FROM CODES TO COMPUTERS

Share the following information about vacuum tubes after students read the "From Codes to Computers" feature: In 1881–1882, William J. Hammer, who worked for Thomas Edison, discovered that electrical current will flow through a vacuum. This accidental discovery proved useful to British scientist John A. Fleming, who in 1904 patented a two-element vacuum tube that acted as a valve (now known as a diode), forcing current to flow exclusively in one direction. In 1907, American scientist Lee de Forest patented the Audion, a three-element electronic valve that became the key component of all broadcast and computer systems until the invention of the transistor in 1947. **ASK:** What computing technologies of the 1940s helped mathematicians and cryptanalysis personnel break codes during World War II? *(Alan Turing's electromechanical machine and the use of vacuum tubes by the British led to improved code breaking. Using a greater number of vacuum tubes, the U.S. Navy developed computers with even greater speed that could run multiple programs.)*

WRITE ABOUT HISTORY

Explore American Cultures This American Story discusses the work of Navajo Code Talkers during World War II. To help students make connections between the American Story and their own lives, ask them to write a short essay about the advantages of a multicultural society. Encourage students to provide examples of how the cultural heritage of an individual or group has enhanced the lives of others. Pair students to edit each other's essays and make suggestions for revision. Provide guidance about the writing process as necessary.

THINK ABOUT IT

Possible response: The Navajo Code Talkers provided a secure way to communicate military information, making the war effort more successful. The breaking of the Enigma code by the British and the Purple code by the United States helped the Allied Powers defeat the Axis Powers, saving lives and likely ending the war sooner.

CRITICAL VIEWING Possible response: If the Enigma code had not been broken, the Allied Powers wouldn't have had the information to avoid planned attacks against them, and Hitler's military power may have been unstoppable. Britain and France might have been defeated, and the Third Reich might have controlled all of Europe.

OTHER CODES IN WORLD WAR II

While the Navajo worked to create a unique American code, others in the U.S. military were racing to break the German and Japanese codes. Like the non-Navajo codes used by the United States, the German and Japanese forms of encryption were machine-based.

The Germans used a machine known as the Enigma to create their coded messages. An operator would type a message in plain text on the Enigma's keyboard, and a series of notched wheels, or rotors, within the machine would turn, encoding the message into a seemingly random jumble of letters. The message would then be sent via radio to another operator who would use an Enigma machine to decode it. The second operator would have to know the exact sequence of rotor settings in order to correctly decrypt the message. The rotor settings for each day—called the daily key—were listed in codebooks that each Enigma operator possessed. Not surprisingly, these codebooks were some of the most closely guarded items of the war. The Enigma code was eventually penetrated by British code breakers building on earlier work by Polish intelligence.

American code breakers focused their efforts on the Japanese code known as Purple. The Japanese had purchased an Enigma machine from the Germans in the early 1930s, then added refinements to make it easier to use and harder to decrypt. Like the Enigma, the Purple machine required a daily key. Over the course of the war, U.S. code breakers were able to identify certain patterns in the way the Japanese daily keys were determined, and by the end of the war, Purple was broken.

World War II also saw the beginning of the digital age of encryption. The Allies quickly recognized the need for a way to communicate securely via telephone between the United States, London, and other locations. In cooperation with the U.S. Army Signal Corps, Bell Laboratories devised a digital method of encoding voice signals traveling over telephone wires. The code, called Sigsaly, was in use from 1943 to 1946, but it was not declassified until 1975. It was never broken.

THINK ABOUT IT

How did developments in communication during World War II affect its participants and outcome?

CRITICAL VIEWING Introduced on German U-boats sailing in the Atlantic Ocean in February 1942, the code produced by the MK 4 Enigma was not broken until December 1942. The cracking of German cypher codes by Allied intelligence was a major achievement in cryptanalysis, or code breaking, and played an important role in the outcome of the North Atlantic U-boat engagements during World War II. How might the course of the war have been different if the Enigma's code had not been broken?

Intelligent, rebellious, and quirky, Alan Turing, represented here by actor Benedict Cumberbatch in the 2014 movie *The Imitation Game*, was also gay. British law at the time made same-sex relationships illegal, which prevented Turing from being open about his personal life. But he found social acceptance at Kings College in Cambridge. In 1952, however, Turing was arrested and charged with "indecency" after a brief relationship with a man. He did not deny the charges.

According to Andrew Hodges, a mathematician and author of the Turing biography that inspired *The Imitation Game*, "When [Turing] was arrested, the first thing he said was he thought that this shouldn't be against the law." Defiantly mocking the absurdity of his arrest, Turing traveled to Norway and the Mediterranean, where the gay rights movement was beginning to gain momentum. However, 1950s British law considered homosexuality a security risk, and Turing's arrest and conviction cost him his job and the ability to travel. Hodges believes these consequences ultimately led Turing to suicide at the age of 41.

Homosexuality was not fully decriminalized for adults in Great Britain until the 1980s. In 2009, British Prime Minister Gordon Brown publicly apologized for Turing's "utterly unfair" treatment on behalf of the British government. Four years later, Queen Elizabeth II granted him a royal pardon.

FROM CODES TO COMPUTERS

The history of code breaking is entwined with the history of computers. Alan Turing, the mathematician in charge of Britain's cryptanalysis department during World War II, is viewed by many as the father of the modern computer. He played a key role in cracking the Enigma code by helping to develop an electromechanical machine called the bombe. An improvement on a pre-war Polish machine, the bombe greatly sped up the rate at which codes could be deciphered. In 1943, British code breakers designed another machine called the Colossus, which, like early computers, used vacuum tubes to control electric current. The Colossus could do basic mathematical calculations. It could also quickly perform the repetitive operations necessary to identify the patterns found in encrypted messages.

Interest in Britain's code-breaking operation, and in Alan Turing, has been awakened in recent years by historical accounts, novels, and the popular 2014 film *The Imitation Game*. It is less well known that by the end of the war, the U.S. Navy had developed electronic machines that were similar to the Colossus but had a greater number of vacuum tubes—and thus greater computing power. Also like the Colossus, these lacked the memory of a digital computer.

Further advancements in computer technology would come as researchers developed vacuum-tube computers that could work more quickly and run a greater variety of programs. Eventually, of course, digital technology would rapidly make computers much more powerful, versatile, and accessible to users outside the military and scientific communities.

America in World War II 781

DIFFERENTIATE

ENGLISH LANGUAGE LEARNERS ELD

Use a Word Splash Display the following words and phrases in a random splash arrangement: *coding machines, Code Talkers, encryption, decryption, translate, transmit, code, decode*. Ask students at **All Proficiencies** to choose four pairs of words that are related to each other. Have students use this sentence frame to write a sentence illustrating how each pair of words is related:

_____ and _____ are related because _____.

GIFTED & TALENTED

Encode a Message Assign students the role of Code Talkers in World War II. Instruct them to find and study the Navajo Code Talkers' Dictionary at the Naval History and Heritage Command website. Challenge students to devise brief messages in English and use the dictionary to translate them to Navajo. Invite volunteers to share their English and translated messages.

See the Chapter Planner for more strategies for differentiation.

HISTORICAL THINKING

Ask and have students answer the following questions.

1. **READING CHECK** Why was code transmission—and code breaking—so important as an Allied strategy during World War II?

2. **MAKE CONNECTIONS** How did the Navajo tradition of oral storytelling help the Code Talkers learn their codes?

3. **EVALUATE** Why did the Enigma operators so carefully guard the daily key?

ANSWERS

1. Information about military operations and movements was monitored and intercepted on both sides of the war. Encoding and code breaking was crucial in sending secure messages and determining the intentions of the Axis Powers.

2. The Navajo used common words from their stories to substitute for letters and objects. To keep the code secure, the Navajo memorized it rather than writing it down, a strength they possessed due to the oral tradition of their language.

3. The daily key revealed the Enigma machine's rotor settings, which were changed each day. If the daily key fell into the wrong hands, a coded message would no longer be a secret.

A DEVASTATING ATTACK

Which of the freedoms you enjoy as an American citizen do you value the most? In 1941, President Franklin Roosevelt identified four freedoms he felt were the most essential—and worth fighting for. After an unprovoked attack, Americans would be doing just that.

FOUR FREEDOMS

In his annual address to Congress in January 1941, President Roosevelt named and discussed "four essential human freedoms" that were at stake in World War II. As a result, Roosevelt's address became known as the "Four Freedoms" speech.

In the future days, which we seek to make secure, we look forward to a world founded upon four essential human freedoms.

The first is freedom of speech and expression—everywhere in the world.

The second is freedom of every person to worship God in his own way—everywhere in the world.

The third is freedom from want—which, translated into world terms, means economic understandings which will secure to every nation a healthy peacetime life for its inhabitants—everywhere in the world.

The fourth is freedom from fear—which, translated into world terms, means a world-wide reduction of armaments to such a point and in such a thorough fashion that no nation will be in a position to commit an act of physical aggression against any neighbor—anywhere in the world.

—President Franklin D. Roosevelt, Annual Address to Congress, January 6, 1941

Roosevelt used his speech to frame the war as a conflict about fundamental values. After the United States entered the conflict, his words inspired artist Norman Rockwell to create four illustrations (at right) for the *Saturday Evening Post,* a popular weekly magazine, that translated the war aims into scenes of everyday American life.

A DAY OF INFAMY

Within a year of Roosevelt's speech, the United States would go to war against Japan to defend the freedoms he described. Relations between the two countries had long been strained. The United States had watched Japan's aggression and expansion into China with growing concern. This apprehension had increased when Japan signed the Tripartite Pact with Germany and Italy in September 1940. In an effort to put a halt to Japan's expansionism, Roosevelt froze Japanese business interests in the United States in 1941. He also established an embargo on essential goods such as oil to Japan. Many believed war between the United States and Japan was imminent. But most U.S. military analysts expected the Japanese would probably attack a European colony in the South Pacific, with an outside chance they would attack the United States in the Philippines. The U.S. military never imagined the Japanese would be bold enough to strike Hawaii.

The Japanese had planned their attack for months, and their goal was to destroy the U.S. Pacific fleet. So, in late November, a large convoy of Japanese battleships, destroyers, aircraft carriers, and cruisers headed toward the U.S. naval base at Pearl Harbor on the island of Oahu in Hawaii. On the morning of December 7, 1941, the fleet was within 200 miles of Pearl Harbor, and Japanese bomber planes took off from the aircraft carriers to launch the attack. Military personnel in Pearl Harbor had no idea they were in danger until the planes appeared on radar. And even then, they thought the planes were American fighters. In addition, the Japanese had deliberately attacked on a Sunday morning, when security at the base was likely to be more relaxed.

OURS...to fight for

Freedom of Speech

Freedom of Worship

Freedom from Want

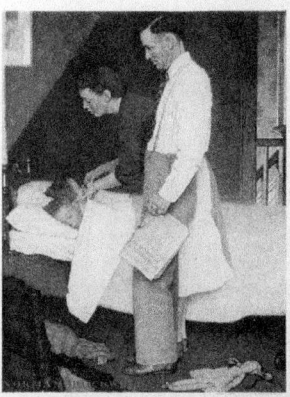

Freedom from Fear

Norman Rockwell's paintings of the Four Freedoms appeared in the *Saturday Evening Post* in March and April 1943. The U.S. government printed and sold posters of the popular paintings in a campaign that raised more than $132 million for the war effort.

PLAN: 4-PAGE LESSON

OBJECTIVE

Explore how the United States entered World War II and the early fighting in the Philippines.

CRITICAL THINKING SKILLS FOR LESSON 1.1

• Analyze Sources
• Determine Chronology
• Interpret Maps
• Evaluate
• Draw Conclusions
• Form and Support Opinions
• Analyze Primary Sources

HISTORICAL THINKING FOR CHAPTER 22

How did World War II and the Holocaust impact Americans and the world? Americans' reluctance to enter World War II ended with a surprise attack on Pearl Harbor. Lesson 1.1 examines Japan's attacks on Pearl Harbor and the Philippines.

BACKGROUND FOR THE TEACHER

Miscommunications and false assumptions helped leave Pearl Harbor open to attack. Leaders in Washington sent warnings to prepare for war with Japan but did not mention Hawaii as a likely target. Thus, Admiral Husband E. Kimmel and Lieutenant General Walter C. Short, the navy and army commanders on Oahu, took little action. They might have reacted differently if they had known that the U.S. ambassador to Japan had earlier warned of an attack against Pearl Harbor and that U.S. cryptographers had intercepted a Japanese communication asking about ship positions on Oahu. Instead, Kimmel did not institute long-range reconnaissance and failed to inform Short of this fact. Short believed that sabotage by Hawaiians of Japanese descent was the greatest threat.

INTRODUCE & ENGAGE

ACTIVATE PRIOR KNOWLEDGE

Ask students to consider this question: Why did Americans not want to join World War II before the bombing of Pearl Harbor? Begin a class K-W-L Chart, with students providing responses for the first column. Responses might include Americans' suspicions that international bankers and arms manufacturers were pushing for war for their own financial gain, German American concern that war would lead to mistreatment of people of German descent, Irish American opposition to assisting Great Britain, Italian American admiration for Mussolini, and pacifism. Then elicit and record questions in the second column that students would like to answer as they study the lesson. At the end of the lesson, provide time for a discussion to fill in the last column of the K-W-L Chart.

K What Do I Know?	W What Do I Want To Learn?	L What Did I Learn?

TEACH

GUIDED DISCUSSION

1. **Evaluate** Why was striking the naval base at Pearl Harbor a risky but strategic move for Japan? *(Possible response: It was risky for Japan to expose a large convoy of ships and aircraft to possible detection and destruction before getting close enough to attack. However, it was a strategic chance for Japan to try to destroy the U.S. Pacific fleet.)*

2. **Draw Conclusions** Why were aircraft carriers important to Japan's successful attack on Pearl Harbor? *(Possible response: Aircraft carriers enabled the Japanese to get close enough to Oahu to launch an aerial attack on Pearl Harbor, which was their best option for destroying the U.S. Pacific fleet.)*

3. **Form and Support Opinions** Share with students the information provided in Background for the Teacher. Point out that based on this information, one might conclude that Kimmel and Short could have prevented the attack on Pearl Harbor if they had been properly informed by leaders in Washington. **ASK:** Do you think this is a fair assessment? *(Possible response: Yes—the information supports this conclusion. No—in hindsight, it's easy to place blame on Washington leaders for not mentioning Hawaii as a likely target, but the situation at the time might have been more complex than this information leads us to believe.)*

ANALYZE PRIMARY SOURCES

Direct students' attention to Franklin Roosevelt's Four Freedoms speech. Have them read the excerpt to find details that explain the main idea of each freedom. **ASK:** What was required to achieve freedom from want and fear on a world level? *(Freedom from want required economic understandings that would secure a healthy peacetime. Freedom from fear required a worldwide reduction of armaments to prevent physical aggression against neighbors.)* How might Roosevelt's use of repetition in his speech have affected his listeners? *(Possible response: Roosevelt's repetition of the phrase "The ___ freedom is" to introduce each freedom helped listeners focus on the main ideas of the speech. His use of "everywhere in the world" and "anywhere in the world" helped unify his ideas and also underscored the fact that the freedoms he identified related to the entire world.)*

DIFFERENTIATE

INCLUSION

Describe Illustrations Pair students who are visually impaired with students who are not. Ask the latter to read the quotations from Roosevelt's Four Freedoms speech. After each passage about one of the freedoms, have the students who are not impaired describe Norman Rockwell's illustration of that freedom, providing specific details. Tell visually impaired students to ask clarifying questions as necessary.

PRE-AP

Investigate Historical Interpretations Explain to students that even today there is still debate among some historians over whether the United States provoked the attack on Pearl Harbor and whether the president and other officials knew about the attack before it occurred. Ask students to conduct research to find out more about these varying historical interpretations. Then, to help flesh out the complexity of these issues, suggest that students hold a panel discussion. Encourage other students to ask questions and, as appropriate, add their views to the discussion.

See the Chapter Planner for more strategies for differentiation.

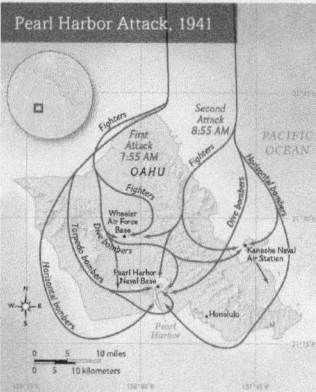

Pearl Harbor Attack, 1941

First Attack 7:55 AM
Second Attack 8:55 AM
PACIFIC OCEAN
OAHU
Fighters
Wheeler Air Force Base
Kaneohe Naval Air Station
Pearl Harbor Naval Base
Honolulu
Pearl Harbor

10 miles
10 kilometers

Smoke billows from U.S. battleships anchored in Pearl Harbor following the Japanese attack on December 7, 1941. The map on the left shows the two waves of the attack carried out by 353 fighter, dive bomber, torpedo bomber, and horizontal bomber planes. The planes launched the assault from 6 aircraft carriers north of Pearl Harbor.

The assault came in two waves, with the first bombers arriving shortly before 8 a.m., and the second wave arriving an hour later. The planes rained their bombs and bullets down on U.S. battleships anchored in the harbor and American military aircraft sitting on the ground. Battleships, including the U.S.S. *Arizona*, were completely destroyed in the attack. In the end, the Japanese demolished or damaged nearly 20 American warships and about 200 planes. Far worse, more than 2,300 Americans were killed. The Japanese lost fewer than 100 men.

Roosevelt addressed Congress and the American people by radio the next day saying, "Yesterday, December 7, 1941—a date which will live in infamy— the United States of America was suddenly and deliberately attacked by naval and air forces of the Empire of Japan." **Infamy** refers to an extremely shameful or evil act. Roosevelt called for a declaration of war, and Congress—with only one dissenting vote—agreed. On December 8, Congress declared war on Japan. Three days later, Germany and Italy honored their allegiance to Japan and declared war on the United States. As you know, many Americans had been opposed to joining the war. But the bombing of Pearl Harbor had stunned the nation and instantly turned the tide of American opinion in favor of the war. Americans took their place among the Allied powers—including Great Britain, the Soviet Union, and China—in the fight against the Axis powers Germany, Italy, and Japan.

BATAAN DEATH MARCH

Within hours of the attack on Pearl Harbor, Japanese forces struck the Philippines, which was designated a commonwealth, or territory, of the United States in 1935. The United States Armed Forces in the Far East (USAFFE) had been mobilized earlier in case of attack and headquartered in the Philippines under the command of American general Douglas MacArthur. You may remember that President Hoover called on MacArthur to restore order when World War I veterans marched on Washington, D.C., in 1932.

The majority of the forces were Filipinos, but American troops also made up the ranks. However, the troops were unprepared for the full-scale attack the Japanese had planned. The Japanese air force bombed airfields, bases, harbors, and shipyards, and approximately 56,500 soldiers from the Japanese Army came ashore at Luzon, the largest island of the Philippines. By January 2, 1942, Japanese troops had taken Manila, the country's capital. Unable to defend the territory, the USAFFE strategically retreated to the jungles of the Bataan Peninsula.

Despite suffering from disease and starvation and fighting without any air support, the USAFFE troops defended Bataan for 99 days. Then, in March 1942, Roosevelt ordered MacArthur to leave the Philippines. The official story was that Roosevelt wanted MacArthur to go to Australia to coordinate the war effort. The truth was that MacArthur was too valuable an officer for the United States to lose, especially at the beginning of a war, so he was brought to safety. The general left the Philippines but vowed, "I shall return." Despite constant bombardment, the soldiers continued to fight under General Edward P. King, Jr., the Commanding General of the Luzon Force.

Finally, on April 9, King and his 75,000 Filipino and American troops surrendered to the Japanese. The troops were forced to march some 60 miles to their prison at Camp O'Donnell with no provisions for food, water, or shelter. Those who could no longer go on were beaten, bayoneted, shot, and in some cases, beheaded by their Japanese captors. Approximately 10,000 Filipinos and 750 Americans perished in what became known as the **Bataan Death March**.

Once imprisoned in Camp O'Donnell, another 20,000 Filipinos and 1,600 Americans died. A majority of the American prisoners were later transported in the hulls of unmarked vessels, known as "Hell Ships," to Japan, China, Formosa (present-day Taiwan), and Korea, where they worked as slave laborers. Thousands died on the ships and while in servitude. U.S. involvement in World War II had just begun, but Americans quickly realized it would take a lot of strength and resources to fight their formidable enemies.

HISTORICAL THINKING

1. **READING CHECK** What events brought on Japan's attack on Pearl Harbor?

2. **ANALYZE SOURCES** In Roosevelt's Four Freedoms speech, how did he frame American beliefs on both a personal and international level?

3. **DETERMINE CHRONOLOGY** What order of events took place within days of the attack on Pearl Harbor?

4. **INTERPRET MAPS** Based on the map, what conclusions can you draw about the attack?

BUILD BACKGROUND

PHILIPPINES DEFENSE PLANS

The Washington Naval Treaty, which was agreed upon in 1921–1922, prohibited the expansion of military fortifications in U.S. possessions in the Pacific. As a result, only the islands nearest the mouth of Manila Bay were fortified against attacks. In 1941, the U.S. Army made plans to defend only Manila Bay and nearby locations in case of attack and to retreat to the Bataan Peninsula if necessary. In October 1941, however, General MacArthur convinced the War Department to expand the area of defense beyond Manila Bay. He distributed already limited equipment and supplies among strategic locations across the island of Luzon. Consequently, when the troops needed to retreat to Bataan in January 1942, a majority of their supplies were in distant locations and had to be left behind.

FILIPINO TROOPS

In July 1941, President Franklin D. Roosevelt issued an executive order calling for Filipinos to serve in the U.S. Armed Forces. More than 250,000 Filipino soldiers fought under the U.S. flag during World War II. Following the war, however, the Rescission Act of 1946, signed by President Harry S. Truman, countermanded Roosevelt's executive order and made Filipino veterans ineligible to receive the same health care, pensions, and other benefits offered to others who served. In 2009, after lobbyists had worked for decades, Congress created a fund to make one-time lump sum payments to Filipino veterans in lieu of the benefits they were denied. In 2016, Congress passed the Filipino Veterans World War II Congressional Gold Medal Act, which awarded a collective Congressional Gold Medal in recognition of Filipino service during the war.

TEACH

GUIDED DISCUSSION

4. Draw Conclusions Why did the American and Filipino forces in the Philippines have little chance of success? *(Possible response: They were unprepared for a full-scale attack. The retreat into the Bataan jungle left them with insufficient supplies and exposed them to diseases, and they lacked air support.)*

5. Determine Chronology In what order did events unfold in the Philippines? *(The Japanese attacked the Philippines within hours of bombing Pearl Harbor. By January 2, 1942, they had taken Manila, forcing the American and Filipino troops to retreat to the Bataan jungles. MacArthur left the Philippines in March, and, on April 9, 1942, General King and his troops were forced to surrender, leading to the Bataan Death March.)*

INTERPRET MAPS

Have students study the map of the attack on Pearl Harbor. **ASK:** How does the map help you understand why it was important for the Japanese to strike the air bases? *(Possible response: Since the Japanese were coming in from the north and Pearl Harbor was at the south end of Oahu, it was important to quickly knock out U.S. aircraft so they could not prevent Japanese planes from reaching Pearl Harbor.)*

ACTIVE OPTIONS

On Your Feet: Create a Quiz Organize students into two teams and have the teams move to opposite sides of the room. Instruct each team to write 10 True/False or multiple-choice questions about the Japanese attacks on Pearl Harbor and the Philippines. Have teams alternate asking one of their questions, to which the other team responds. Keep track of the number of correct answers for each team.

NG Learning Framework: Analyze Filipino Oral Histories

ATTITUDE Empowerment

KNOWLEDGE Our Human Story

Assign students to work in groups to access the Veterans History Project online at the Library of Congress website. Tell them to use the project's search tool to isolate audio or video oral histories of Filipinos who were involved in World War II. Then have each group select an oral history to analyze. Encourage them to focus on answering the following questions in their analyses: What examples of personal sacrifice or courage did the person discuss? What views did the person express about participating in the war? What comments did the person make about the aftermath of the war or about immigration to the United States? Students can share their analyses with the class.

HISTORICAL THINKING

ANSWERS

1. In response to Japan's expansion into China and its signing of the Tripartite Pact with Germany and Italy, Roosevelt froze Japanese business interests in the United States and established an embargo on essential goods to Japan.

2. Roosevelt argued that people everywhere in the world deserved the same four freedoms that Americans believed they were entitled to: freedom of speech, freedom of religion, freedom from want, and freedom from fear.

3. On December 8, the U.S. Congress declared war on Japan. Three days later, Germany and Italy honored their allegiance to Japan and declared war on the United States.

4. Possible response: Based on the map, one can conclude that the attack was very well planned and highly coordinated.

GEARING UP FOR WAR

Once the United States entered the war, the country mobilized to prepare for it. World War II would require a massive buildup of resources to fight on both the Asian and European fronts.

THE WAR EFFORT

In order to gather the materials the country would need, President Roosevelt established the **War Production Board** in 1942. He called on automobile companies, such as Ford and General Motors, to build tanks and warplanes instead of passenger cars. Roosevelt knew these large corporations could fill the military's needs quickly and gave them the bulk of the work orders. He also offered the companies low-interest loans so they could convert their factories to war production and assured factory owners they would make a profit.

To help pay for the war supplies, Congress passed the **Revenue Act of 1942**, which increased taxes on individuals and corporations. However, this measure only provided about 45 percent of the funds needed to meet expenses. So the government issued war bonds. Citizens could purchase a bond for 75 percent of its face value and later cash it in with interest. To induce Americans to buy war bonds, the government appealed to people's emotions. Remember the illustrations Norman Rockwell created after Roosevelt's Four Freedoms speech? These illustrations became a centerpiece of the bond drive. By the war's end, about half of the nation's population had purchased bonds.

New developments in various fields also aided the war effort. In aviation, the powerful B-24 bomber helped the Allies defend against German submarines. **Napalm**, a thick, flammable substance used in bombs to cause and spread fires, first appeared in World War II. Strides in medical technology and, in particular, the development of penicillin, helped save soldiers' lives. **Penicillin** is an antibiotic, or bacteria killer, made from mold and used to treat infections and disease.

Industrial demands fueled by wartime needs helped end the Depression and set a model for an expanded governmental role in regulating the economy after the war. The defense-related industries became especially critical to California's economy, helping drive other developments in the manufacturing sector and in science and technology. The state played a huge role in America's successful war effort and built more military installations than any other state. The number of military bases in California increased from 16 to 41, more than those of the next 5 states combined.

MILITARY SUPPORT

New military bases were definitely needed. Six million Americans volunteered for service between 1942 and 1945, and the country drafted another 10 million men. The draft also conscripted conscientious objectors—those who opposed the war on religious grounds. However, COs, as they were sometimes called, were allowed to participate in public works projects or serve in other nonmilitary ways.

General **George Marshall**, the chief of staff of the U.S. Army in 1939, was largely responsible for training the troops and selecting commanders for the war. He put Lesley J. McNair in charge of the Army Ground Forces once the United States entered the war. McNair dedicated himself to ensuring the troops received the most realistic combat training possible. He staged huge mock battles and simulated real wartime situations.

Though the military training the troops received was similar, men from minority groups did not fight with white soldiers. Instead they were placed in segregated troops. Nevertheless, these troops made great sacrifices and demonstrated valor and

🏛 **Tuskegee Airmen National Historical Museum Detroit, Michigan**

Toni Frissell photographed a group of Tuskegee Airmen receiving instructions for a mission at the Ramitelli airfield in Italy in 1945. Throughout the war, the Airmen played an important role, escorting allied bombers with one of the lowest loss records among escort fighter groups. They also flew about 15,500 combat missions. In recognition of their outstanding record and sacrifices, the Tuskegee Airmen received more than 150 Distinguished Flying Crosses.

distinction. The **Tuskegee Airmen** was a squadron of African-American pilots who trained in Tuskegee, Alabama, and shot down a dozen Nazi planes during an invasion of Italy in 1943. That same year saw the formation of the **442nd Infantry Regimental Combat Team**, a military unit that consisted entirely of Japanese Americans. The 442nd successfully fought in Europe in 1944 and rescued a regiment of Texas soldiers surrounded by German forces.

In April 1941, the U.S. government formed American Volunteer Groups to help the Nationalist government of China in its struggle against Japan. The "**Flying Tigers**" was the only American Volunteer Group to take part in combat. It sprang into action to help defend Burma and China against the Japanese after the attack on Pearl Harbor. Volunteer pilots from the American and Chinese air forces made up the Flying Tigers.

As you know, the Navajo provided an indispensable service to American forces during World War II. After it became clear the Japanese were intercepting and deciphering coded U.S. messages, the Marines enlisted Navajo men to transmit and translate messages using their native language. The men became known as the **Navajo Code Talkers**. The Navajo language was so difficult—and so few people spoke it—that the Japanese could not decode the messages. The Code Talkers were a major factor in the eventual Allied victory.

The military didn't welcome all Americans. Officials screened out and rejected homosexuals, though gay

---

OBJECTIVE

Analyze how the government, the military, and private citizens prepared for and contributed to the war effort.

CRITICAL THINKING SKILLS FOR LESSON 1.2

• Synthesize

• Make Inferences

• Draw Conclusions

• Summarize

• Analyze Cause and Effect

HISTORICAL THINKING FOR CHAPTER 22

How did World War II and the Holocaust impact Americans and the world? The government and civilians had to gear up for war and make sacrifices. Lesson 1.2 explores efforts and conditions on the home front.

BACKGROUND FOR THE TEACHER

The nation's entry into World War II transformed California on a scale the state had not experienced since the California Gold Rush in 1848. The population jumped from around 6.9 million in 1940 to almost 10.6 million by 1950. Before the war, California's economy was largely agrarian. While farming continued to remain important, the war also brought military bases, shipyards, and defense manufacturing plants to the state. Economic expansion continued after the war, as many defense industries retooled in order to produce consumer goods.

📄 HISTORY NOTEBOOK

Encourage students to complete the American Gallery page for Chapter 22 in their History Notebooks as they read.

FINANCIAL LITERACY

To extend their knowledge and understanding about the concepts in this lesson, refer students to the Financial Literacy handbook.

INTRODUCE & ENGAGE

BRAINSTORM IDEAS

Ask students to brainstorm things that a government might decide to do to gear up for war. Use a graphic organizer like the one shown to record ideas on the board, making sure students include ideas that relate to civilians as well as the military.

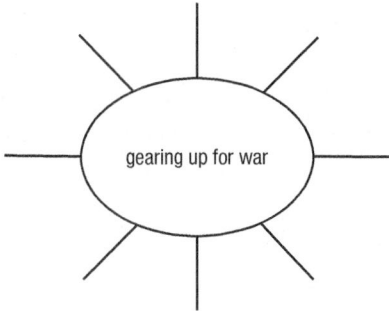

gearing up for war

TEACH

GUIDED DISCUSSION

1. **Summarize** How did President Roosevelt use the powers of the presidency to gather materials for the war effort? *(Roosevelt established the War Production Board in 1942 to gather the materials to fight the war, gave the bulk of work orders for war materials to large corporations, and offered low-interest loans to finance the retooling of factories for war.)*

2. **Draw Conclusions** What would account for the public's eagerness to purchase war bonds? *(Possible responses: The American public experienced an increased sense of patriotism after Pearl Harbor. Buying war bonds was a concrete way that civilians could participate in the war. Because the purchaser needed to pay only 75 percent of their face value, war bonds would have been considered a good personal investment.)*

3. **Analyze Cause and Effect** Share the information presented in Background for the Teacher. **ASK:** Why was World War II a watershed event for California? *(The war led to major changes, sparking immense economic and population growth by bringing military bases, shipyards, and defense manufacturing plants to the state, which in turn drew people seeking jobs in these industries.)*

🏛 VIRTUAL MUSEUM VISIT

The Tuskegee Airmen National Historical Museum was founded in 1987 to honor the Airmen and chronicle the contributions of African Americans to American aviation. The museum's online exhibits include photographs, video interviews, and historical information about the squadron. Access the museum's website and allow students to explore the online materials. Provide time for students to discuss how the information added to their understanding of the contributions made by the Airmen and the difficulties they faced.

DIFFERENTIATE

ENGLISH LANGUAGE LEARNERS

Identify Causes and Effects This lesson contains many examples of cause and effect. Provide the following sentence frames to help students at each proficiency level discuss and write about important events that occurred as the United States began gearing up for war.

Emerging:

• I read that _____ caused _____.

• _____ happened. The result was _____.

Expanding:

• I read about how _____ caused _____.

• As a result of _____, _____ happened.

Bridging:

• First the writer tells about _____. Then the writer explains how _____ resulted in _____.

• _____ happened. It may have been caused by _____ or _____. I think it was caused by _____ because _____.

GIFTED & TALENTED

Create a Multimedia Presentation Tell students to conduct online research to learn about the experiences of specific African-American or Japanese American soldiers who risked their lives fighting in World War II. Then direct them to combine their findings with those of other students to create a multimedia presentation that includes both primary and secondary sources and photos. Invite them to share the presentation with the rest of the class.

See the Chapter Planner for more strategies for differentiation.

men and women still served in the armed forces in significant numbers. Some were tolerated because of the war effort, and their fellow soldiers often came to appreciate their service. However, many other gays were imprisoned or dishonorably discharged when their sexual orientation was discovered. That persecution set the stage for increased postwar oppression and organized resistance.

ON THE HOME FRONT

At home, World War II had many long-lasting effects. Increased production made employment skyrocket, resulting in 17 million new jobs—including jobs for women and minority groups. Income for the average American nearly doubled as well, largely as a result of the overtime factory workers logged in. The new jobs drew enormous numbers of migrants from all over the country to urban areas and eventually spurred the creation of expansive suburbs, highways, and shopping complexes.

The war also drew immigrants to the United States. In 1942, the government sponsored the **Bracero Program**, which continued until 1964 and was designed primarily to import Mexican laborers to replace native-born agricultural and transportation industry workers who were mobilizing for war. California particularly benefited from the braceros, which means "strong armed ones." Importing more than 40,000 workers in 1942 alone, the state came to depend on the agricultural laborers who came through the program. By the end of the war, California had the fastest population growth of any state—and an increasingly diversified society.

Meanwhile, Americans at home faced many everyday challenges. In 1942, Roosevelt enacted the **Office of Price Administration** to help limit inflation and **ration**, or control, the supply of goods made available to the public. The military desperately needed items such as gas, rubber, and certain foods, so civilians were urged to cut back on driving and consume less sugar, coffee, and meat. To supplement their food supplies, the government encouraged people to plant victory gardens, or plots of land on which they could grow their own food. Almost 20 million Americans planted victory gardens during the war. The gardens made people on the home front feel as if they were contributing to the war effort—much as the purchase of war bonds did.

Buying war bonds and planting victory gardens made people feel patriotic, but the stress of war was hard to avoid. Popular films and radio programs provided much needed distraction from the war. Diversions such as baseball games helped take people's minds off their worries as well. Some politicians had called for the suspension of major league baseball during the war, but Roosevelt disagreed. He explained that the game helped keep up people's morale. The **Office of War Information**, formed in 1942, also boosted Americans' spirits. The agency produced posters, photos, and films that celebrated the troops and encouraged Americans' support for the war.

Dorothy Harrell of the Rockford Peaches, 1944

THE ALL-AMERICAN GIRLS PROFESSIONAL BASEBALL LEAGUE

As young men were drafted into the armed services during the war, minor league baseball lost most of its players. Philip Wrigley, owner of the Chicago Cubs, decided that a female ball league might bring fans to the parks and help keep the sport in the public eye. The result was the All-American Girls Professional Baseball League. After the athletes had been recruited and teams organized, the League first stepped up to the plate in 1943. The players were accomplished pitchers, batters, and hitters, but organizers insisted that they also be "lady-like." They attended charm school and wore make-up, even on the field. The League was an enormous success, and the women kept playing until 1954, nearly a decade after the war ended.

STRUGGLES AT HOME

As you've read, wartime factory work created new and higher-paying job opportunities for African Americans and other minorities. However, opening up the wage-labor market raised their expectations about what else they might be able to achieve. The contrast between the ideology of the war effort and the racial segregation of the armed forces sparked multiple efforts at minority equality and, in time, for civil rights activism after the war.

In 1941, a letter printed in the African-American newspaper, the *Pittsburgh Courier*, launched the "Double V" campaign. The campaign called on African Americans to fight for victory against fascism abroad and victory against racism at home. That same year, **A. Philip Randolph**, the head of the largely African-American **Brotherhood of Sleeping Car Porters** union, planned a march in Washington, D.C., to focus international attention on the hypocrisy of undemocratic practices at home while the country was poised to fight for democracy abroad. The march ultimately prompted Roosevelt to sign **Executive Order 8802** in 1941 to desegregate military-related industries.

But wartime racial discrimination went beyond the military and the workplace. In 1943, white shipyard workers attacked African-American workers in Mobile, Alabama, and a race riot between whites and blacks in Detroit resulted in more than 30 deaths and 700 injuries. That same year, Mexican Americans dressed in zoot suits also came under attack in Los Angeles, California. A zoot suit is a flamboyant man's suit that features wide-legged trousers and long jackets with wide lapels. The outfits were a fad among many African Americans and Mexican Americans. Many people considered those who wore zoot suits to be thugs.

The white American sailors who arrived in Los Angeles on leave in 1943 particularly objected to zoot suits—and the young Mexican Americans dressed in them. Tensions had long been growing between the two groups, who often fought and exchanged insults. Finally, the **Zoot Suit Riots** erupted in May when mobs of sailors attacked the zoot-suiters, beating the young men and tearing off their suits. Similar attacks continued for more than a week. During this time, the police sometimes stood by while the servicemen rampaged through the city. After the riots died down, a commission investigated the riots and identified racism as their central cause.

This photograph captured a couple of young African-American men, dressed in zoot suits, in 1943. During the war, the zoot suit became a part of the jazz world. Some people of color—including women—wore the suit to make a bold statement.

HISTORICAL THINKING

1. **READING CHECK** What measures did the U.S. government take to help pay for the war?

2. **SYNTHESIZE** What were some of the different ways in which civilians helped contribute to the war effort?

3. **MAKE INFERENCES** Why do you think African Americans, Japanese Americans, and Native Americans wanted to fight in the war?

4. **DRAW CONCLUSIONS** Why did Randolph call the treatment of African Americans at home hypocritical?

BUILD BACKGROUND

THE BRACERO PROGRAM

The Bracero Program was initiated after California farmers predicted that they would not have enough workers to harvest the fall crops in 1942. They asked for between 40,000 and 100,000 Mexican agricultural laborers. This was not the first time that the United States had instituted a guest worker program with Mexico. Between 1917 and 1921, thousands of Mexican guest workers came to the United States to offset labor shortages caused by strict immigration quotas. Mexican leaders remembered how badly the workers had been treated and required that this time the braceros be guaranteed the same wages as U.S. laborers, adequate housing, reasonably priced food, and transportation back to Mexico at the end of their contracts. However, not all farm owners lived up to these requirements.

The federal government also contracted with Mexico for railroad workers during World War II. Under the terms of the Railroad Bracero Program, approximately 6,000 workers were supposed to come to the United States to work on the railroads, primarily laying tracks and doing maintenance in the West. The number of contract workers far exceeded that estimate, as evidenced by some 50,000 workers who were sent back to Mexico in 1945 when the program ended. Like the agricultural braceros, the Mexican railroaders were promised fair working and living conditions but often lived in substandard housing, were injured or killed on the job, and faced discrimination and violence.

TEACH

GUIDED DISCUSSION

4. **Summarize** How did President Roosevelt use the powers of the presidency to face challenges on the home front and reduce discrimination in military-related industries? *(Roosevelt established the Office of Price Administration to limit inflation and ration goods, used the Office of War Information to boost morale, and issued Executive Order 8802 to desegregate military-related industries.)*

5. **Synthesize** What examples presented in this lesson point to continuing racial strife in this country despite certain efforts to the contrary? *(Possible responses: White shipyard workers in Mobile, Alabama, attacked African-American workers. Whites and blacks rioted in Detroit. Mobs of white sailors on leave rampaged through Los Angeles, attacking and beating young Mexican Americans dressed in zoot suits.)*

MORE INFORMATION

Voices from the Bracero Program Share with students the Build Background information on the Bracero Program. Then tell them that the online Bracero History Archive has collected thousands of photos, documents, and audio and video oral histories related to the experiences of agricultural and railroad workers in the Bracero Program. Have students work in groups to explore the audio and video oral histories in the archive. Ask them to find evidence of the cultural and economic effects of the programs and the reasons participants joined. Have students write and share summaries of their findings.

ACTIVE OPTIONS

Active History: Graph Economic Changes Extend the lesson by using either the PDF or Whiteboard version of the activity. These activities take a deeper look at a topic from, or related to, the lesson. Explore the activities as a class, turn them into group assignments, or even assign them individually.

AMERICAN GALLERY
ONLINE
The Tuskegee Airmen Invite students to explore the American Gallery. Have them select one of the photos and do additional research to learn more about it. Ask questions that will inspire additional inquiry about the chosen gallery photo, such as: What impressions do you have of the people portrayed in these photos? How do the photos aid your understanding of World War II? What else would you like to know about these people?

For students who develop an interest in the experiences of minority groups during the war, suggest that they read the American Story at the beginning of this chapter.

HISTORICAL THINKING

ANSWERS

1. The government raised taxes on individuals and corporations and sold war bonds.

2. Civilians bought war bonds from the government to help pay for the war. They also rationed their food, gas, and other supplies so that the military had enough, and they planted victory gardens to help grow food for themselves and others.

3. Answers will vary. Possible response: African Americans, Japanese Americans, and Native Americans wanted to prove that they were as capable of valor and honor as white troops, even in the face of discrimination.

4. The United States was fighting for democracy overseas, but the nation did not treat minorities democratically at home. In the military, African Americans were segregated from whites, and on the home front they faced racial discrimination and violence.

WOMEN AND THE WAR EFFORT

Throughout American history, women had stepped up in times of crisis but never in the numbers seen during World War II. Their reward was satisfaction in a job well done and pride in serving their country.

In 1943, the Women Airforce Service Pilots (WASP) program formed to train women to fly military aircraft for noncombat purposes. The WASP in this photo is about to take off.

NEW OPPORTUNITIES

World War II provided women with an unprecedented opportunity to enter the workforce. Many men left their jobs to fight in the war, and women filled their places in factories and offices. The defense industries, particularly in aircraft and munitions, needed workers. These businesses employed 6 million women as welders, electricians, and assembly line workers during the war.

Some women also decided to join the military and served in the few branches the military allowed women to join. The establishment of the **Women's Auxiliary Army Corps (WAAC)** in 1942 offered women a chance to participate in noncombat roles as radio operators and air-traffic controllers, for example. Women who joined the WAAC earned a salary but were not given all the benefits men in the military received. However, within just a few months of the corps's establishment, more than 25,000 women had signed up. As a result, the army dropped the "auxiliary" designation in 1943, and members of the Women's Army Corps (WAC) received full U.S. Army benefits, comparable to those of male soldiers. A total of about 150,000 women served all over the world, including in war zones.

The navy equivalent of the WAC was the **Women Accepted for Volunteer Emergency Service (WAVES)**, which was also established in 1942. About 27,000 women joined in its first year. Unlike WACs, WAVES received full benefits from the beginning as well as the same salary as men. However, WAVES were not allowed to serve abroad. Members worked in fields such as aviation, medicine, intelligence, science, and technology. About one-third of WAVES were involved with naval aviation, while others performed duties such as calculating bomb trajectories or paths, and working as meteorologists. A total of about 100,000 women served as WAVES during the war.

By enabling women to fill noncombat roles, WACs and WAVES helped free up additional men for combat duties. These branches of the service also allowed women to take on vital and complicated responsibilities in the war effort. Though male officers at first anticipated that their female counterparts would only perform clerical duties, the women's dedication and capability soon changed the male officers' minds.

UNFAIR TREATMENT

Even as women sacrificed and worked hard for the war effort, they experienced unfair treatment in their new jobs. Some employers didn't even want to hire them. They didn't believe women had the strength or ability to do the jobs. Furthermore, many employers feared the women would distract male workers and prevent them from doing their work.

Another form of unfair treatment was **wage discrimination**, or receiving lower pay for the same job based on gender, race, or ethnicity. Though women who worked in defense industries generally made more money than they did working in other jobs, they still made far less than their male coworkers. In 1945, for example, a woman working in a factory earned an average of $32 a week, while a man made an average of $55—even though a law required equal pay for equal work. Some companies dodged the law by reclassifying higher-paying jobs into a lower pay scale or assigning women to lower-level positions.

After **demobilization**, or the release of soldiers from military duty, more women remained in the workforce than had done so following World War I. Still, most were forced to leave. Employers notified women they would have to give up their jobs to the returning soldiers. Employers—and society as a whole—still believed a woman's place was in the home. Advertisers also promoted a return to traditional women's roles.

As a result, even though the majority of women wanted to keep their jobs after the war, most either had to return to their roles as homemakers or take lower-paying jobs. By 1947, women's presence in blue-collar jobs had sunk to its prewar level. Nevertheless, women had briefly enjoyed a degree of liberation and financial security in their newfound workplace roles. Unfortunately, not all segments of American society would experience as much freedom as women had.

PRIMARY SOURCE

You have just made the change from peacetime pursuits to wartime tasks— from the individualism of civilian life to the anonymity of mass military life. You have given up comfortable homes, highly paid positions, leisure. You have taken off silk and put on khaki. And all for essentially the same reason. You have a debt and a date—a debt to democracy and a date with destiny.

—from Director Oveta Culp Hobby's remarks to the first WAAC officer training class, 1942

HISTORICAL THINKING

1. **READING CHECK** What new opportunities were available to women during World War II, and how do those opportunities compare to those women have today?

2. **COMPARE AND CONTRAST** How were the jobs of WACs and WAVES alike and different?

3. **MAKE INFERENCES** Why do you think women wanted to keep their jobs in the defense industries after the war ended?

4. **EVALUATE** What tone did Hobby use in her remarks to the WAACs, and why did she use that tone?

PLAN: 2-PAGE LESSON

OBJECTIVE

Examine women's roles in the military and in industry to help the war effort.

CRITICAL THINKING SKILLS FOR LESSON 1.3

• Compare and Contrast

• Make Inferences

• Evaluate

• Draw Conclusions

• Make Generalizations

HISTORICAL THINKING FOR CHAPTER 22

How did World War II and the Holocaust impact Americans and the world? World War II provided employment opportunities for women to assist in the war effort. Lesson 1.3 explores how women served the country both in the military and in industry.

BACKGROUND FOR THE TEACHER

Soon after war broke out in Europe, pilots Jacqueline Cochran and Nancy Harkness Love had suggested using female pilots in the U.S. military. By 1942, the shortage of male pilots turned their suggestion into reality. The Air Transport Command hired Love to recruit a group of female pilots, called the Women's Auxiliary Ferrying Squadron, to transport military planes from factories to their embarkation points. Cochran was asked to direct the Army Air Force's Women's Flying Training Detachment, a program charged with training large numbers of female pilots. The two groups merged in 1943 as the Women Airforce Service Pilots (WASPs). More than 1,000 women served in the WASPs, and 38 lost their lives. The WASPs were disbanded in 1944 before they were given their promised military status. Congress belatedly granted this status in the 1970s, and in 2010, the women were awarded the Medal of Honor, the nation's highest award.

INTRODUCE & ENGAGE

THE MILITARY THEN AND NOW

Discuss with students the roles of women in the military today, including the fact that as of January 2016 all combat positions in the U.S. Armed Forces were open to women. Remind students that it took many years for such changes to evolve. **ASK:** Given what you know about the roles of women in American society prior to World War II, how surprising is it to learn that they had an important role during the war? Tell students that in this lesson they will learn about women's participation in the war effort.

TEACH

GUIDED DISCUSSION

1. **Draw Conclusions** What conclusions can be drawn about women's desires to participate in the war effort? *(Possible responses: Many women wanted to help their country. Many were eager to break into new areas of work. Some women probably viewed the war as a unique opportunity to expand their skills and knowledge.)*

2. **Evaluate** What evidence does the lesson provide that women faced unfair treatment in the defense industries? *(Possible responses: Some employers were reluctant to hire women. Women often made much less than men. Women were forced to leave their jobs after demobilization.)*

MAKE GENERALIZATIONS

Point out that the lesson discusses the WACs and WAVES but that the photograph and caption relate to yet a third military program—the WASPs—in which women were trained to fly military aircraft. Share the information provided under Background for the Teacher. **ASK:** Despite the fact that the WASPs were disbanded and their military status delayed, do you think they might have influenced future generations of women? *(Possible response: Yes—in broad terms, by showing that women could fly planes, the WASPs probably contributed to more women becoming pilots in future generations.)*

ACTIVE OPTIONS

On Your Feet: Inside-Outside Circle Use the Inside-Outside Circle strategy to check students' understanding of lesson content. Direct students in the outer circle to pose questions for students in the inner circle to answer— for example: How many women served as WACs and WAVES? What types of aviation jobs did WAVES hold? Why did some businesses not want to hire women? How did demobilization affect women in the workforce? Then ask students to trade inside/outside roles, relocate to create a new partnership, and ask new questions.

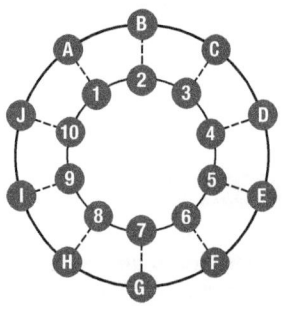

NG Learning Framework: Explore Women in the War Oral Histories

`ATTITUDE` Empowerment

`KNOWLEDGE` Our Human Story

Have students work in small groups to access the Veterans History Project online at the Library of Congress website. Tell students to use the project's search tool to isolate audio or video oral histories of women in the military and in defense industry jobs during World War II. Ask each group to select an individual and use information in the oral history to create a profile. Groups can then share their profiles with the class.

DIFFERENTIATE

STRIVING READERS

Create a Word Square Ask students to write the term *wage discrimination* in the center oval of a Word Square. Then have them work with a partner to write the definition and characteristics in the upper boxes. Guide them to identify examples and non-examples and write them in the lower boxes.

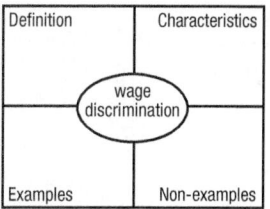

GIFTED & TALENTED

Create a Photo Essay Direct students to locate copies of photographs of women who participated in the war effort. Then, in small groups, have students combine the photos to create a photo essay titled "Women and the War Effort." Encourage them to provide captions for the photos that include any available information about the women or the circumstances depicted.

See the Chapter Planner for more strategies for differentiation.

HISTORICAL THINKING

ANSWERS

1. Vacancies resulting from men going off to war provided new, but temporary, opportunities for women to work in factories and offices and gave them temporary opportunities to serve in the military. Today, women have ongoing employment in most fields.

2. WACs and WAVES both performed noncombat military jobs, WACs with the army and WAVES with the navy. WACs could serve abroad, but WAVES could not. WACs did not immediately receive full benefits, but WAVES did.

3. Even though they earned less than men did, women still made more money in the defense industries than in other jobs. They probably wanted to keep these well-paying jobs.

4. Possible response: Hobby used a serious tone to describe how recruits' lives would change. This helped her stress the importance of their task.

ROSIE THE RIVETER 1942–1945

"She's making history, / working for victory / Rosie the Riveter."
— from "Rosie the Riveter," a song by Redd Evans and Jacob Loeb, 1943

Rosie the Riveter came to life in a song—some of its lyrics are quoted above. The song was a hit, and its title came to represent the millions of American women who took on the industrial jobs that were vacated as more and more men joined the war effort during World War II. Rosie became part of a U.S. government campaign to recruit women into the workforce. The campaign worked, and the women excelled in their new jobs. As the song says, "That little frail [woman] can do more than a male / will do."

A TALE OF TWO ROSIES

The face of Rosie the Riveter that most people were familiar with during the war was the one featured on the cover of the *Saturday Evening Post*. But this Rosie is no "little frail." In Norman Rockwell's painting, she's a muscular, monumental figure, based on the style Italian Renaissance artist Michelangelo used to depict biblical prophets in Rome's Sistine Chapel.

Apparently on her lunch break, Rosie holds a sandwich aloft and balances her riveting gun and lunchbox, etched with her name, on her lap. Her foot rests squarely on *Mein Kampf*, or *My Struggle*, Adolf Hitler's autobiography, in which he outlined his anti-Semitic views. Rosie's contempt for the German dictator and confidence that he will be defeated—with her help—are clear.

Mary Doyle Keefe, the model for Rockwell's illustration, was actually a petite young woman. Rockwell wanted to portray his Rosie as strong and powerful. Still, he apologized to Keefe for making her so brawny.

This real-life Rosie is working on an A-31 Vengeance dive bomber at a plant in Tennessee. She's adjusting the wheel well preparatory to installing the plane's landing gear, one of many tasks that made up the assembly-line production of the bombers.

Rockwell fashioned his subject after a 19-year-old neighbor named Mary Doyle Keefe. The model for another iconic image of Rosie is unknown or, at least, contested. This image was one of a series of posters created for the Westinghouse Electric Corporation in 1942 and designed to boost workers' morale. The poster of a young woman in a red-and-white bandana, flexing her arm, and exclaiming, "We can do it!" only appeared in the Westinghouse factory and only for a couple of weeks. Now fast-forward to 1982, when the poster was rediscovered and became a symbol of the movement to expand women's rights. Although the woman in the poster wasn't given a name in the 1940s, for many people today, she is Rosie the Riveter.

REAL-LIFE ROSIES

Of course, behind the song, painting, and poster were millions of women eager to do their part for the war effort. As you've read, many of these real-life Rosies worked in the aircraft and munitions industries. In some cases, they apparently did their jobs too well. A foreman in one plant told the women not to work so fast because when the war ended, the men would get their jobs back. And the men, he said, weren't nearly as productive as they were.

Many of the women came to California to find jobs during the war. One named Bettye worked the graveyard shift—which began at midnight—building B-17 bomber planes. She entered the enormous plant through a tunnel covered in camouflage. Once there, Bettye and another woman worked as a team to install rivets into the part of the plane from which the turret gun, or multishot firearm, would be fired. Her teammate stood on the outside of the compartment and drove in the rivet, which is a permanent metal fastener that looks something like a thick screw. Bettye stood on the inside and bucked the end of the rivet, pounding and flattening it. But she insisted that the process "wasn't as easy as it looked." The "skin" of the plane was fairly thin. If the operator of the rivet gun didn't hold it steady, the gun would drill a bigger-than-desired hole in the plane, and a larger rivet would have to be installed. And that, Bettye said, would weaken the whole plane.

For many of the real-life Rosies, the work provided an experience of the world they may never have had otherwise. They met and worked alongside women from many different backgrounds and ethnicities. And the work gave them independence, an income—which was certainly welcome after the deprivations of the Depression—and a sense of pride and patriotism. As one Rosie named Bonnie remarked, "I wouldn't have missed the experience for anything. And we did do good. We won the war."

HISTORICAL THINKING

1. **READING CHECK** What purpose did Rosie the Riveter serve during World War II?

2. **MAKE INFERENCES** Why do you think the women's rights movement adopted the Westinghouse Rosie poster as a symbol?

3. **DRAW CONCLUSIONS** What did Bonnie suggest when she said, "We won the war"?

PLAN: 2-PAGE LESSON

OBJECTIVE

Learn how both the fictional and real-life Rosies contributed to the war effort.

CRITICAL THINKING SKILLS FOR LESSON 1.4

- Make Inferences
- Draw Conclusions
- Make Predictions
- Evaluate

HISTORICAL THINKING FOR CHAPTER 22

How did World War II and the Holocaust impact Americans and the world? Millions of women took the places of men in U.S. aviation and munitions factories during World War II. Lesson 1.4 relates the experiences of some of these women.

BACKGROUND FOR THE TEACHER

In 2017, Representative Jared Huffman of California and Senator Bob Casey of Pennsylvania co-led a bipartisan group of lawmakers in both houses of Congress in passing a congressional resolution declaring March 21, 2017, as the first National Rosie the Riveter Day. The day honors the contributions of approximately 16 million women who filled vital work roles during World War II. Huffman noted at the time that he was inspired by a real-life Rosie, Californian Phyllis Gould, who was one of the first women to work as a navy-certified journeyman welder in the Kaiser-Richmond shipyards between 1942 and 1945. Gould, along with her fellow Rosie, Anna "Mae" Krier of Pennsylvania, spearheaded the campaign for a Rosie the Riveter Day to be made part of Women's History Month.

HISTORY NOTEBOOK

Encourage students to complete the American Voices and Reid on the Road video series pages for Chapter 22 in their History Notebooks as they read.

INTRODUCE & ENGAGE

WHAT'S IN AN IMAGE?

Have students examine Norman Rockwell's painting on the cover of *The Saturday Evening Post.* **ASK:** What do you notice about the Rosie in the painting? *(Possible responses: She is muscular in her build. She is dressed for doing hard labor. She is wearing makeup. She seems to be taking a lunch break as she sits on a piece of equipment. She has a look of confidence.)* Why do you think Rockwell painted her this way? *(Possible response: He may have wanted to characterize the Rosies as being capable and strong while remaining feminine.)*

TEACH

GUIDED DISCUSSION

1. **Make Predictions** How might Americans have reacted to Norman Rockwell's cover illustration when the magazine came out in 1943? *(Answers will vary. Possible response: In the midst of a war they didn't know if they could win, Americans would probably have been amused, inspired, and delighted to see the character of Rosie resting her foot on Hitler's autobiography.)*

2. **Evaluate** What evidence from the lesson suggests that women were sometimes better than men at the jobs they undertook? *(A foreman in one plant told the women to slow down because the men would not be as productive when they returned from war. Also, the song lyrics "That little frail [woman] can do more than a male" suggest that women were sometimes better at their jobs than men were.)*

AMERICAN VOICES

The Rosie the Riveter WWII Home Front National Historical Park opened in 2000 in Richmond, California, to document the contributions of the real-life Rosies who helped fuel the war effort. The park has partnered with the Regional Oral History Office at the University of California at Berkeley to collect oral histories from these women. **ASK:** Why is it important to record the recollections of women who worked in factories on the home front during World War II? *(Answers will vary. Possible response: The women not only helped the United States win the war but also became symbols to later generations of what women are capable of achieving.)*

ACTIVE OPTIONS

On Your Feet: Sentence Chain Organize students in small groups. Tell students to imagine that they are wartime journalists working on a feature article about the phenomenon of Rosie the Riveter and that their goal is to sell a lot of newspapers. Have groups begin the article with an attention-grabbing headline. Ask one student in each group to write the first sentence of the article. Other students can then take turns adding sentences. Groups should continue adding sentences until they feel the article is thorough. Ask groups to share the articles.

NG Learning Framework: Investigate War Propaganda

ATTITUDE Curiosity

KNOWLEDGE Our Human Story

Explain to students that the song and illustrations depicting Rosie the Riveter are examples of propaganda—forms of communication that spread information and ideas for the purpose of furthering a particular cause. Point out that both sides used propaganda of varying types during World War II—either to motivate people to believe in their cause or to instill anger toward the enemy. Ask students to conduct online research to locate several examples of World War II propaganda created by each side of the conflict. As they share their findings, have them discuss the context and purpose of each example.

DIFFERENTIATE

ENGLISH LANGUAGE LEARNERS

Identify Main Ideas and Details Pair students at the **Emerging** and **Expanding** levels with students at the **Bridging** level. Direct pairs to use two Main Idea Diagrams, one for each subsection of the lesson. Tell students to take turns reading, pausing after each paragraph to record relevant details and adding more boxes if necessary. Then have pairs work together to write a main idea statement above the details. Ask students to share and compare their diagrams.

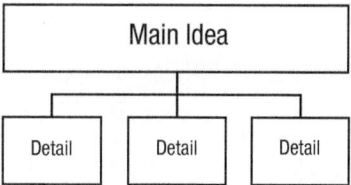

GIFTED & TALENTED

Create a Music Video Direct students to conduct online research to access the full lyrics of the 1943 song "Rosie the Riveter" and to listen to recordings of it. Then have students prepare a music video of the song, combining the music with appropriate visuals. Ask volunteers to show their videos to the class.

See the Chapter Planner for more strategies for differentiation.

HISTORICAL THINKING

ANSWERS

1. Rosie the Riveter was used as an image to recruit women into the workforce; she served as a symbol of how women could help win the war.

2. Possible response: The women's rights movement liked the slogan "We can do it!" that is shown in the poster.

3. Possible response: Bonnie suggested that women played an important part in winning the war by working in the factories that produced the aircraft and munitions needed to fight the war.

MAIN IDEA Responding to the attack on Pearl Harbor and fears of invasion from the Pacific, the U.S. government forcibly moved thousands of Japanese Americans to camps for the duration of the war.

JAPANESE AMERICAN INTERNMENT

Have you ever been unfairly accused of something? During World War II, the U.S. government viewed Japanese Americans as a threat and removed them from their homes.

EXECUTIVE ORDER 9066

Entry into the war drew most Americans together in their support for the Allied cause, but others quickly discovered their heritage marked them as objects of fear. On December 8, 1941—the day after the Pearl Harbor attack—President Roosevelt issued a series of executive orders that established the **Enemy Alien Control Program**. An **enemy alien** is someone whose loyalty to the nation is suspect. Many persons of Italian and German origin who were in the United States when World War II began were classified as enemy aliens and had their rights restricted. Thousands were **interned**, or confined in prisons or camps for military or political reasons, while many others were sent back to Germany or Italy.

Photographer Ansel Adams took this image of Japanese Americans waiting for lunch at California's Manzanar Camp in 1943.

Japanese Americans were also classified as enemy aliens and interned. Public opinion had turned sharply against Japanese Americans after the attack on Pearl Harbor. Unlike the Italians and Germans who were interned, more than 60 percent of those with Japanese ancestry who were relocated to camps were **Nisei** (nee-SAY). Nisei are people born in the United States whose parents emigrated from Japan. The general population and the military believed Japanese Americans were a threat, even though the FBI did not consider them a danger. Military leaders feared the close proximity of Japanese American communities to American military bases and aircraft plants on the West Coast, and the public associated Japanese Americans with the actions of Japan's armed forces.

In response to the perceived threat, President Roosevelt signed **Executive Order 9066** in 1942, which authorized the relocation and internment of 110,000 Japanese Americans and "resident aliens" living within 60 miles of the West Coast and in parts of Arizona on grounds of national security. An **executive order** is a directive issued by a president that has the force of law.

Nearly all Japanese Americans lived on the West Coast, in California, Washington, and Oregon. The order violated their constitutional and human rights. However, the Supreme Court, in a decision heavily criticized today, upheld its implementation in *Korematsu v. United States*, arguing that, "When under conditions of modern warfare our shores are threatened by hostile forces, the power to protect must be commensurate with [in proportion to] the threatened danger." The government removed Japanese Americans to **internment camps** in military zones, where they lived in prison-like surroundings until the war's end.

INTERNMENT

Ten internment camps were set up in California, Arizona, Wyoming, Utah, Arkansas, and Colorado. Japanese American families were forced to sell whatever belongings they could not carry and relocate to the camps. Japanese American merchants had to sell their businesses in a matter of just days or weeks. By June 1942, the government had moved 120,000 Japanese Americans into the camps. The first camp to open, in March of that year, was Manzanar in California's Owens Valley. The largest of the camps was Tule Lake, also in California, which housed more than 18,000 internees by 1944.

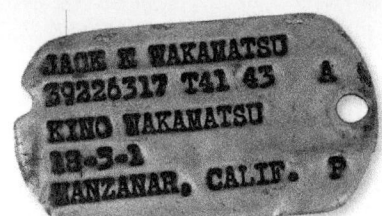

This military dog tag, or ID, belonged to Jack Wakamatsu. While his family lived behind barbed wire at Manzanar, Wakamatsu fought in the 442nd Infantry Regimental Combat Team, the all Japanese American military unit.

Families at the camps were housed in army barracks surrounded by barbed wire and towers where armed guards kept watch. The barracks themselves were not insulated, and residents had to rely on coal-burning stoves for heat. Families slept on cots and shared bathrooms with other internees. Guards were authorized to shoot residents who tried to escape. Nonetheless, Japanese Americans tried to make the camps as much like communities as possible. They established schools, churches, newspapers, and farms, and children stayed active by playing sports. And even though their government had imprisoned them, many young Japanese American men volunteered to fight for their country. They were released from the camps to do so.

After the war ended, Japanese Americans were at last allowed to return to their homes. They lost personal property, businesses, farms, and homes as a result of their forced removal. After many years of campaigning for redress, or compensation, Japanese Americans finally obtained justice. Congress formally apologized for their internment and allocated funds to compensate the survivors in 1988.

HISTORICAL THINKING

1. **READING CHECK** Why were Japanese Americans relocated to internment camps?

2. **DESCRIBE** What constitutional issues were involved in *Korematsu v. United States*, and how did the case impact events on the U.S. home front?

3. **FORM AND SUPPORT OPINIONS** Given the circumstances of the war, do you think the U.S. government was justified in interning Japanese Americans? Explain your opinion.

OBJECTIVE
Examine the causes and consequences of internment during World War II.

CRITICAL THINKING SKILLS FOR LESSON 1.5
- Describe
- Form and Support Opinions
- Evaluate
- Draw Conclusions

HISTORICAL THINKING FOR CHAPTER 22
How did World War II and the Holocaust impact Americans and the world? The United States' entry into the war led to the confinement or deportation of certain immigrant groups and to the relocation of Americans of Japanese descent. Lesson 1.5 discusses these wartime decisions.

BACKGROUND FOR THE TEACHER
Korematsu v. *United States* stemmed from the arrest of Fred Korematsu, a California-born son of Japanese immigrant parents. On May 3, 1942, Korematsu refused to go with his family when they were ordered to relocate to an internment camp. The 23-year-old was arrested on May 30, convicted of violating a military order, and sentenced to five years' probation. He and his family were later transferred to Topaz, an internment camp in Utah. After an appeals court upheld Korematsu's conviction, the Supreme Court agreed to hear his appeal. In late 1944, the Court upheld his conviction 6–3. However, Justice Robert H. Jackson, one of the three dissenting votes, argued that Korematsu had been convicted of a crime that was not usually considered a crime—being present in a state where he was born and resided.

HISTORY NOTEBOOK
Encourage students to complete the Japanese American Internment page for Chapter 22 in their History Notebooks as they read.

INTRODUCE & ENGAGE

CONSIDER THE CONSEQUENCES

Have students consider how fear during wartime can result in the public and government singling out certain groups for suspicion or ridicule. Ask students what consequences such fear could have for these groups. Record students' ideas in a Word Web. Tell them that this lesson explores how fear led to internment for people of Italian, German, and, especially, Japanese descent during World War II.

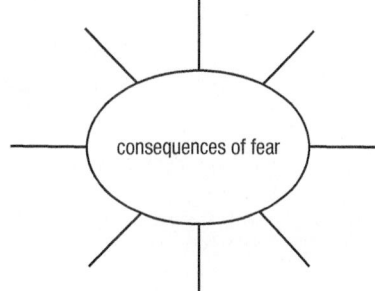

consequences of fear

TEACH

GUIDED DISCUSSION

1. **Evaluate** In what respect might the internment of Japanese Americans be viewed as an act of racial discrimination? *(Possible response: Even though people of Italian and German origin were also interned, people of Japanese ancestry were treated more harshly: More than 60 percent of interned people of Japanese ancestry had been born in the United States and were therefore American citizens.)*

2. **Draw Conclusions** Given the circumstances of internment, what would have motivated young Japanese American men to volunteer to fight? *(Answers will vary. Possible responses: They perhaps wanted to prove their loyalty to the United States. They might have wanted to serve along with their non-Japanese peers. It was a way to escape internment in the camps.)*

MORE INFORMATION

The Civil Liberties Act of 1988 Explain to students that the formal apology that Japanese Americans received from Congress was embodied in the Civil Liberties Act of 1988, which also authorized a $20,000 payment to each surviving victim of internment. Eventually, more than 82,000 individuals received compensation. **ASK:** What might be the implication of this historical event for those wronged and for future generations? *(Answers will vary. Possible response: The act acknowledged wrongdoing on the part of the government and provided compensation for victims, and it offered a hope to future generations that something like internment would not happen again.)*

ACTIVE OPTIONS

On Your Feet: Hold a Panel Discussion Have students research *Korematsu* v. *United States* to determine the particulars of the case and the views of the majority and dissenting justices. Then ask volunteers to stage a panel discussion guided by the overarching question: Which opinion in the *Korematsu* ruling is most persuasive? Why?

NG Learning Framework: Create a Virtual Museum Exhibit

SKILLS Collaboration, Communication

KNOWLEDGE Our Human Story

Arrange students in groups to construct a virtual museum exhibit on Japanese American internment during World War II. Assign groups specific topics to focus on, such as public and military reactions, *Korematsu* v. *United States*, various aspects of camp life, economic consequences for the internees, and eventual compensation. Encourage groups to include photos, audio and video oral histories, first-person accounts, and maps and diagrams to enhance the exhibit. Remind students to interpret past events and issues within the context in which they unfolded rather than solely in terms of present-day norms and values. Allow time for groups to share their portions of the exhibit with the class.

DIFFERENTIATE

ENGLISH LANGUAGE LEARNERS

Pose and Answer Questions Pair students at the **Emerging** level with students at the **Expanding** or **Bridging** level and tell them to read the lesson together. Have them pause at the end of each paragraph and ask each other a *who, what, where, when,* or *why* question about what they have just read. Allow time for partners to provide answers.

PRE-AP

Write a Biography Instruct students to conduct research to learn about the experiences of a specific American of Japanese ancestry who was interned during the war. Have students use what they learn to write a biography of the person that focuses on how Executive Order 9066 impacted the person's life. Invite volunteers to read their biographies to the class.

See the Chapter Planner for more strategies for differentiation.

HISTORICAL THINKING

ANSWERS

1. Many Americans associated Japanese Americans with the attack on Pearl Harbor; the military did not want them near West Coast naval bases and aircraft plants.

2. The *Korematsu* case weighed American citizens' constitutional rights against the government's need to protect the nation in times of war. Because the Supreme Court ruled that the internment of more than 100,000 Japanese Americans was legal, Japanese Americans remained interned for the duration of the war, and many had lost their property and businesses by the end of the war.

3. Answers will vary. Possible responses: Yes—the internment was justified, given the special circumstances of war. No—the internment went against every principle on which the United States was founded. Students should provide evidence to support their opinions.

JAPANESE AMERICAN NATIONAL MUSEUM, LOS ANGELES

The Japanese American National Museum in Los Angeles, California, presents over 150 years of Japanese American history and culture. It aims to inspire appreciation for America's ethnic and cultural diversity by sharing the struggles and triumphs of Americans of Japanese ancestry. The museum houses a permanent collection of over 60,000 items, including movies, photographs, artwork, letters, oral histories, textiles, and other artifacts that tell the stories of this group of Americans.

Many of those stories focus on the experiences of Japanese Americans whose lives were abruptly uprooted during World War II when they were relocated to internment camps. For example, the museum's collection of letters written by children in the camps to a sympathetic librarian in San Diego describe their living conditions and experiences. The museum also exhibits artwork by adults, including the pieces shown here, that document the fears and monotony of everyday life at the camps.

George Hoshida, Sketch Artist
A self-educated artist, George Hoshida (1907–1985) created a visual record of internment camp life in a series of notebooks in which he sketched portraits of inmates and painted scenes of everyday activities. In the watercolor at top right, Hoshida depicts two men playing a board game while others watch. The men in the ink drawing at bottom right are making pipes. The two ink portraits below are of internees Sawaichi Fujita (left), a tinsmith, and store owner Keizo Takata (right). Initially separated from his wife and daughters, Hoshida shared his drawing skills with other internees to pass the time and preserve history.

Hisako Hibi, Painter
In this oil painting titled *Morning*, female artist Hisako Hibi (1907–1991) depicts a scene at an internment camp in Topaz, Utah, in 1942. The painting shows U.S. soldiers marching into the camp at dawn to construct more barracks for internees. Two Japanese Americans watch the soldiers from behind a water tower.

Hibi was imprisoned at the Topaz camp along with her husband—who was also an artist—and their two young children. The Japanese Americans set up schools at the camps, and the Hibis both taught in an art school at the camp in Topaz. What does Hibi's painting suggest about the relationship between the internees and soldiers?

Jack Iwata, Photographer
Born in Seattle, Washington, professional photographer Jack Iwata (1912–1992) was forcibly relocated to an internment camp at Manzanar, California, along with his wife. Iwata and a fellow photographer established a photo lab at the camp and began documenting life there. In the photo at right, Iwata captured a group of internees arriving with their luggage at Manzanar.

In December 1944, the U.S. government announced the internment camps would be closed. Japanese Americans began leaving the camps in early 1945, and the last camp shut down in 1946. Upon release, former inmates had to rebuild their lives. In 1948, a law was passed to reimburse some of the property losses sustained by internees. And then in 1988, Congress passed the Civil Liberties Act, which awarded $20,000 to each camp survivor.

PLAN

OBJECTIVE

Identify artifacts relating to Japanese American internment during World War II.

HISTORICAL THINKING SKILLS FOR LESSON 1.6

• Analyze Visuals

• Make Connections

• Make Inferences

• Draw Conclusions

HISTORICAL THINKING FOR CHAPTER 22

How did World War II and the Holocaust impact Americans and the world? Executive Order 9066 resulted in the internment of tens of thousands of Japanese Americans. Lesson 1.6 explores the internees' experiences through artwork and photography.

BACKGROUND FOR THE TEACHER

In the mid-1980s, Japanese American businessmen and Japanese American veterans who served in the 442nd Infantry Regimental Combat Team during World War II joined forces to create the Japanese American National Museum. With support from the Japanese American community and funding from the California state legislature and the city of Los Angeles, the Japanese American National Museum opened in 1992 in Los Angeles' Little Tokyo. The museum began its existence in a 1925 building originally constructed by Japanese American immigrants to house the Nishi Hongwanji Buddhist Temple. During World War II, the building stored the belongings of Japanese Americans confined to internment camps. The museum expanded in 1999 by opening an 85,000 square-foot pavilion that is attached to the original building.

HISTORY NOTEBOOK

Encourage students to complete the Curating History page for Chapter 22 in their History Notebooks as they read.

INTRODUCE & ENGAGE

RECORDING HISTORY

Have students consider why people use art and photographs to record the activities of daily life. **ASK:** How might using art and photographs to record daily life in the internment camps help internees? *(Possible response: Creating art and photographs might give internees a feeling of control over their surroundings. In the long-term, such visual records document what people went through from the perspective of a Japanese American.)* **ASK:** Why would such a record be valuable for future generations? *(Possible response: The visual record might help prevent future generations from repeating the wrongs of the past by showing the human cost of such government actions.)* Tell students that this Curating History uses art and photographs to explore the Japanese American internment experience.

TEACH

GUIDED DISCUSSION

1. **Make Inferences** What can you infer about daily life in the internment camp from George Hoshida's sketches? *(Possible response: The activities show that people tried to maintain some sense of a normal life, such as playing games. Those who had something to share or teach set up classes to keep people busy and distract them from their circumstances.)*

2. **Draw Conclusions** What does Jack Iwata's photograph suggest about the trauma of being sent to an internment camp? *(Possible response: The fact that the new arrivals have only a few suitcases and some incongruous items like high-heeled shoes and umbrellas illustrates how quickly the internees were forced to leave much of their lives and property behind.)*

CURATING HISTORY

The Japanese American National Museum's online exhibits are a useful resource for learning more about Japanese American internment during World War II. Access the website and guide students to the Hisako Hibi collection. As a class, look at her oil painting featured in the Curating History, read the caption, and discuss the analysis, then encourage students to explore other paintings in the Hibi collection. Invite them to investigate the George Hoshida and Jack Iwata collections to learn more about life in the internment camps from the perspective of a Japanese American. Have students report their observations to the class.

ACTIVE OPTIONS

On Your Feet: Sort the Artifacts Arrange students in teams of four or five to examine the painting, drawings, and photograph in the lesson. Instruct teams to use the details they see to complete two Concept Clusters. In one cluster, have students identify details that illustrate the physical impact of internment. In the other, have them identify a different impact, such as emotional, psychological, or spiritual. When teams are finished, they can share their Concept Clusters with the class and point out what common effects all teams may have identified.

HISAKO HIBI, PAINTER

Possible response: The painting suggests a strained relationship, one of fear and distrust, between the internees and the soldiers. The woman and her child stand away from the soldiers and watch them from a distance. The soldiers march in military formation rather than entering the camp as an informal work group, which underscores their authority over the internees.

CAMPAIGNS IN EUROPE AND AFRICA

The Soviet Union received economic aid and supplies from the United States, but Stalin did not like how the war was being fought in Europe. While some of the Allies invaded Africa, Stalin's army battled the bulk of the German forces in Russia alone.

INVADING NORTH AFRICA

As the United States mobilized for war in the Pacific and in Europe, President Roosevelt and British prime minister Winston Churchill planned a course of action against Hitler in Europe and North Africa. But Soviet premier Joseph Stalin did not agree with the other two leaders on the best strategy to use against the Germans. Stalin wanted Allied help in battling the Germans and defending the Soviet Union. As you have read, Hitler's troops launched an invasion of the Soviet Union in 1941, and Stalin wanted the Allies to establish a second front, or line of battle, in western Europe to help the Soviets combat the Germans. Britain and the United States, however, preferred invading French North Africa and reclaiming Nazi-controlled areas there. The North African attack would be on a smaller, more manageable scale for the Americans, who were just entering the fight.

However, the first step toward victory in this campaign was for the United States to seize control of the Atlantic Ocean and ensure the safe mobilization of Allied troops in Africa. During the first few months of 1942, German submarines had been prowling the Atlantic, regularly sinking Allied ships. Eventually, new antisubmarine technologies and weapons such as radar and **depth charges**, underwater bombs that are programmed to explode at certain depths, enabled the Allies to strike back. By mid-1943, the German submarine threat in the Atlantic had been neutralized.

In November 1942, U.S. Army general **Dwight D. Eisenhower** led the Allied forces in an invasion of North Africa called **Operation Torch**. Eisenhower had been supreme commander of the Allied forces in Europe before taking charge of Operation Torch. By May 1943, the British and American forces had successfully recaptured Morocco and Algeria and defeated the army under German general **Edwin Rommel**, capturing more than 250,000 Nazi prisoners in Tunisia. Once they were firmly established in North Africa, the Allied forces planned to use it as a base of operations against Italy.

Germany's success in the first years of the war had been due in part to its superior fleet of tanks, known as **panzers**, which the Germans arranged in massed formations. Manufactured in Germany from the mid-1930s to the mid-1940s, the panzers were thickly armored and boasted impressive firepower, but their size and weight kept them from being speedy or easy to maneuver. The German panzers had a distinct advantage over the relatively older British tanks, but U.S. troops arrived in Europe and North Africa with American-built Sherman tanks, which could often outmaneuver the panzers. Sherman tanks had less substantial armor and firepower, but they were more agile. As a result, the British forces traded in their tanks for the Sherman tanks in 1943 and 1944.

GERMANY VERSUS THE SOVIET UNION

When Hitler's forces undertook their invasion of the Soviet Union in June 1941, they believed they could defeat the Soviet army in a matter of months. The Germans had caught the Soviets off guard, sending

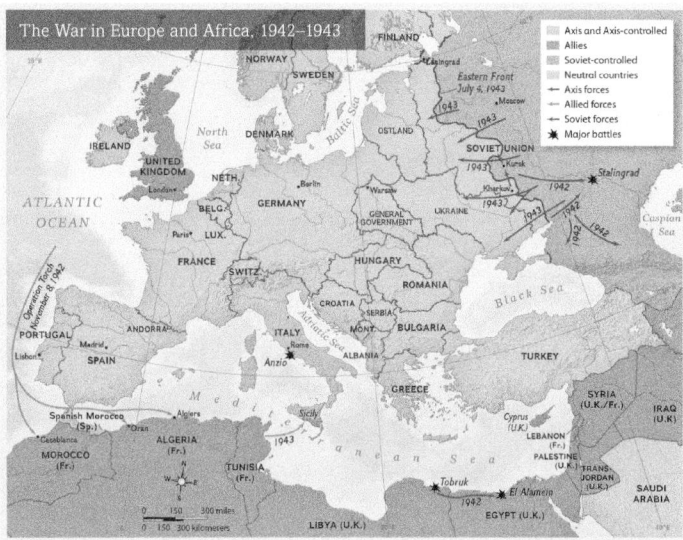

The War in Europe and Africa, 1942–1943

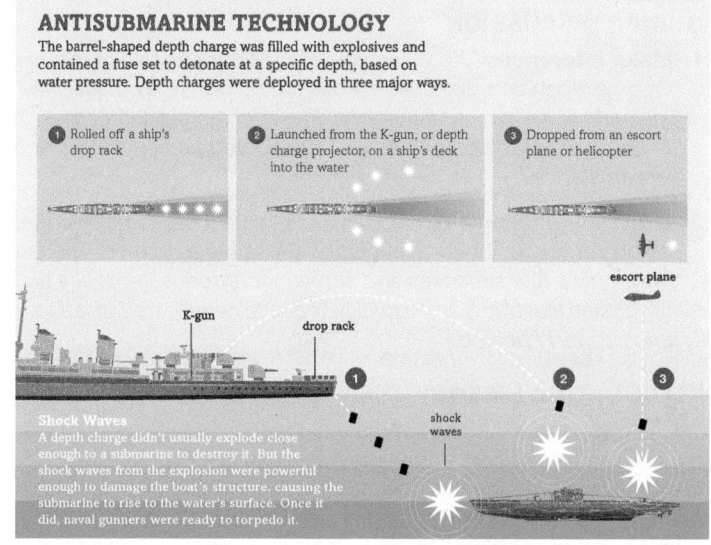

ANTISUBMARINE TECHNOLOGY
The barrel-shaped depth charge was filled with explosives and contained a fuse set to detonate at a specific depth, based on water pressure. Depth charges were deployed in three major ways.

1 Rolled off a ship's drop rack

2 Launched from the K-gun, or depth charge projector, on a ship's deck into the water

3 Dropped from an escort plane or helicopter

escort plane

K-gun   drop rack

Shock Waves
A depth charge didn't usually explode close enough to a submarine to destroy it. But the shock waves from the explosion were powerful enough to damage the boat's structure, causing the submarine to rise to the water's surface. Once it did, naval gunners were ready to torpedo it.

shock waves

OBJECTIVE

Explain how the Allied campaigns in North Africa, the Soviet Union, and Italy progressed during World War II.

CRITICAL THINKING SKILLS FOR LESSON 2.1

• Determine Chronology

• Interpret Maps

• Draw Conclusions

• Evaluate

• Analyze Visuals

• Form and Support Opinions

• Synthesize

HISTORICAL THINKING FOR CHAPTER 22

How did World War II and the Holocaust impact Americans and the world? World War II reached far beyond its starting place. Lesson 2.1 discusses the results of military campaigns in North Africa, the Soviet Union, and Italy.

BACKGROUND FOR THE TEACHER

Operation Torch was significant in its preparation, its execution, and its implication for the remainder of the war. The invasion plan represented a compromise between British and American strategists, and that compromise set the stage for future collaboration. Fighting in North Africa provided U.S. troops with valuable experience against German forces before entering the principal combat zone in Europe. Defeat of the Germans in North Africa helped shift the balance of power and eventually led to Allied victory in Europe.

KEEP TRACK OF EVENTS

Ask students to recall events that led the United States into World War II. Record answers randomly on the board. Display a Sequence Chain graphic organizer and ask students to record the events in chronological sequence. Explain that in this lesson students will learn what happened when the United States joined Allied forces in Europe and Africa.

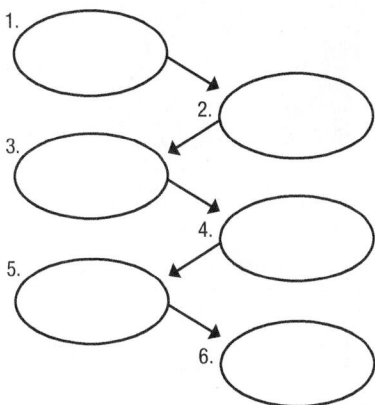

TEACH

GUIDED DISCUSSION

1. **Evaluate** How did the outcome of Operation Torch justify the decision to invade North Africa rather than establish a front in western Europe? *(Possible response: Britain and the United States succeeded in defeating the Germans in North Africa, securing a base from which the Allies could invade Italy.)*

2. **Draw Conclusions** What conclusions can you draw about the effectiveness of the Sherman tank? *(Possible response: Because the British traded their tanks for the United States' Sherman tanks, the Sherman tank's ability to outmaneuver the German panzer must have been highly desirable and effective.)*

3. **Interpret Maps** Recall the fact that when Hitler's forces first invaded the Soviet Union in June 1941, they thought they could defeat the Soviet army in a matter of months. Based on information that the map provides along the Soviet-controlled border, were Hitler's forces correct? Why or why not? *(No. The map shows extensive fighting between the German and Soviet forces in 1942 and 1943; therefore, Germany's assumption that it could defeat the Soviet Army in a few months completely wrong.)*

ANALYZE VISUALS

Direct students to examine the antisubmarine technology infographic. Discuss the problems of deploying depth charges in each of the three ways depicted. **ASK:** Based on the information shown, do you think that depth charges were an effective weapon? Explain your answer. *(Answers will vary. Possible responses: Yes. They forced enemy submarines to the surface, where they could be torpedoed. No. They allowed a large margin of error and could not destroy a submarine by themselves.)*

INCLUSION

Work in Pairs Allow students with disabilities to work with other students who can read the lesson aloud to them. Encourage the partner without disabilities to describe the map, illustration, and photographs in detail. When pairs have finished the lesson, you may want to have them work together to answer any questions that involve the map or the infographic.

PRE-AP

Write Telegrams Instruct students to conduct online research to learn more about the strategic priorities held by Joseph Stalin and Franklin Roosevelt during World War II. Challenge students to use their research to write a series of imaginary telegrams between the two men. Each message should have a date and should state the priorities and needs of the leader sending it, along with his reactions to the other leader's priorities. Encourage students to present their telegram messages to the class in a written format or through a dramatic reading with a partner.

See the Chapter Planner for more strategies for differentiation.

In October 1942, the Soviets sometimes sought defensive positions inside industrial buildings, including the Red October factory, while battling the Germans at Stalingrad. The factory protected the soldiers but was destroyed in the Battle of Stalingrad. In this photo taken by *Life* magazine photographer Thomas D. McAvoy, Soviet soldiers march German prisoners of war past the ruins of Red October.

A landing craft with General George Patton (wearing a helmet) aboard leaves the North African country of Tunisia for Sicily, in the combined British and American invasion of the island in 1943.

200 divisions with 10,000 to 20,000 soldiers each to attack along a front stretching nearly 2,000 miles from the Baltic to the Black seas. Nonetheless, the Soviet army, or Red Army, put up strong resistance. Soviet forces employed a "scorched-earth" policy, destroying crops, bridges, and railroad cars as they retreated deeper into their homeland. This strategy left the German soldiers without food or shelter as they advanced east. Still, the Germans took hundreds of thousands of prisoners along the way. By mid-July, Hitler's troops were within a couple hundred miles of Moscow.

The next few months brought unexpected hardship to the German Army. An early and severe winter settled across the Soviet Union and impeded German advances. Some Nazi generals wanted to suspend fighting until spring, but they were overruled, and the army pressed on to Moscow. Both the German troops and their machinery suffered in the cold. Because the Germans had not expected the Soviet resistance to last so long, they had not brought enough supplies to last through the winter. By November 1941, 700,000 Germans had died. The following month, the Soviets launched an organized attack on the Germans, but Hitler would not allow

his army to retreat. As a result, the Germans held on to most of the ground they had captured earlier in the year.

By the summer of 1942, Soviet casualties stood at about 4 million. German numbers were high but not nearly as staggering. In July, Hitler decided to split his forces between the Caucasus Mountains near the Turkish border and the city of Stalingrad, located about 500 miles north on the Volga River. In August, Germany began bombing the city, and the **Battle of Stalingrad** began. With residents still living in Stalingrad, the two armies fought in the streets, causing high numbers of civilian casualties.

In November 1942, the Soviets launched a counteroffensive attack against the now freezing, starving, and poorly supplied German troops. Once again, Hitler refused to allow his army to retreat from the Volga River, ordering them to fight to the death. As the Nazis weakened, the Soviets surrounded them. The German troops surrendered at the end of January 1943. But battle resumed between the two armies about six months later in Kursk, a city to the west of Stalingrad. In the largest tank battle ever fought, the German Army was dealt a crushing defeat

and suffered about 500,000 casualties. The Battle of Kursk was the last major offensive launched by the Nazis in the Soviet Union.

THE ITALIAN CAMPAIGN

In the summer of 1943, not long after the Allied victory in North Africa and the Soviet triumph in Stalingrad, the Allies turned their attention to Italy. The Soviets, still calling for a second front in Western Europe, were not happy with this turn of events, especially after the extreme losses they had suffered battling the Germans without the support of other Allied troops. Roosevelt tried to appease Stalin by promising him a second front the following year, but Stalin remained displeased.

In July 1943, Allied forces, led by American lieutenant general **George S. Patton** and British general Bernard Montgomery, began the Italian campaign by storming the island of Sicily. The invasion represented the biggest **amphibious assault** that had ever taken place. An amphibious assault uses naval support to protect military forces invading by land and air. The assault also demonstrated the cohesion of the American and British forces led by Patton and Montgomery, who successfully

worked together to secure the island. The Allies conquered Sicily in about a month, and their invasion indirectly forced a regime change in Italy. The Italian government removed, arrested, and eventually executed its leader, Benito Mussolini. Meanwhile, approximately 100,000 Axis troops retreated from Sicily and headed for Italy's mainland, having suffered many more casualties than the Allies in the battle over the island.

The Allies followed closely behind, landing on the southern coast of Italy in early September. Not long after their arrival, the new Italian government secretly agreed to sign an armistice with the Allies and help them fight against Germany. Additional Allied landings followed at Salerno and Naples along Italy's western coast, and by mid-October, Italy had officially changed sides and declared war against Germany. But Germany still occupied much of Italy. In November 1943, German troops began establishing defensive lines about halfway up the Italian peninsula to prevent the Allies from reaching Rome. Exhausting battles, the treacherous mountain terrain, and a lack of supplies slowed the Allied advance. It took four months for the Allies to move forward just 70 miles, and they were still 80 miles from Rome, Italy's capital.

For months, the Allies continued advancing up the peninsula. Then, in May 1944, they broke through one of the Germans' defensive lines and reached Rome about a month later. Fighting continued during the summer and into the fall and winter, leaving the Germans short of supplies—especially fuel. They were forced to use oxen to tow their tanks. In contrast, the Allies had received new reinforcements and weapons. German forces finally surrendered in May 1945, but the campaign had been costly on both sides. Allied casualties numbered around 300,000, while German casualties were about 434,000.

HISTORICAL THINKING

1. **READING CHECK** What strategy did Stalin want the Allies to follow against Germany?

2. **DETERMINE CHRONOLOGY** What events led to the German surrender at the Battle of Stalingrad in 1943?

3. **INTERPRET MAPS** Why did it make sense, geographically, for the Allied forces to invade Sicily and Italy's mainland after fighting in North Africa?

4. **DRAW CONCLUSIONS** Why did the Italian government switch to the Allied side during the Italian campaign?

BUILD BACKGROUND

STALINGRAD

Stalingrad's strategic location on the Volga River made it important to Soviet industry and transportation. To the Germans, Stalingrad represented a potential base of military operations in southern Russia. In 1942, the stage was set for the epic Battle of Stalingrad. Soviets considered their defeat of Hitler's forces to be the greatest battle of the war, and many historians view it as a turning point of World War II. The enormous casualties also made it one of history's bloodiest battles. After the war, Stalingrad received the title "Hero City of the Soviet Union," and a huge memorial to the heroes of the battle was constructed in a prominent location. However, the name Stalingrad does not appear on maps today. In fact, the city, which originally was called Tsaritsyn, was renamed in honor of Joseph Stalin only from 1925 to 1961. As part of Nikita Khrushchev's "de-Stalinization" effort, the name was changed to Volgograd. Recently, residents of the city have begun a movement to reinstate the name Stalingrad. The name has been used officially for certain World War II anniversaries, and many believe that someday it may reappear on Russian maps.

TEACH

GUIDED DISCUSSION

4. Form and Support Opinions Was a "scorched earth" policy an effective Soviet tactic against German troops? Consider environmental issues as you explain your answer. *(Answers will vary. Possible responses: The "scorched earth" policy was effective in that it left the advancing enemy without food or shelter. The policy was not effective because it destroyed crops and infrastructure in the Soviet Union. It was not effective because in spite of the tactic, German troops advanced almost to Moscow.)*

5. Synthesize What were the implications of the Italian campaign for postwar international relations? *(Possible response: In addition to making Italy an ally of the United States, it showed the effectiveness of cooperation between British and American forces, which foreshadowed the continued strong alliance between the countries after the war.)*

ANALYZE VISUALS

Direct students to study the photographs in this lesson and read the captions. **ASK:** In what way might the impact of the photos have changed from the time they were taken to today? *(Answers will vary. Possible response: In the 1940s, the photos would have reflected current events, and many viewers would have found them extremely compelling, especially if they had relatives or acquaintances away at war. Today, the impact of the photos has lessened because we think of them as part of history, not as reflections of unfolding events.)*

ACTIVE OPTIONS

On Your Feet: Use a Jigsaw Strategy Divide students into "expert" groups and assign each group one of the following types of military forces: land, sea, or air. Instruct members of each group to research amphibious assaults and summarize how their assigned forces support a military invasion. Then rearrange students into new groups, making sure that each new group includes members from each original group. Instruct students to share the summaries they came up with in their expert group.

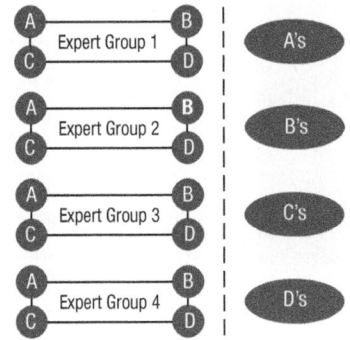

NG Learning Framework: Investigate Contemporary Accounts

SKILL Observation

KNOWLEDGE Our Human Story

Ask students to read contemporary accounts about World War II in newspapers and popular magazines. Provide the following questions to help focus their reading:

• From what point of view is the account written?

• What insights does the account provide?

• What, if any, bias or prejudice does the account express?

Invite students to share their findings. Then, as a class, discuss how World War II taught Americans to think in global terms.

HISTORICAL THINKING

ANSWERS

1. Stalin wanted the Allies to establish a second front in western Europe to help the Soviets fend off the Germans, but the Allies preferred to fight Axis forces in North Africa and Italy first.

2. The Soviets launched a counteroffensive against Germany in late 1942. Hitler refused to allow German troops to surrender, in spite of the fact that they were freezing, starving, and in need of supplies. The Soviets forced the weakened Nazis to surrender at Stalingrad in January 1943.

3. The short distance from Tunisia to Sicily made it possible for Allied troops to invade the island by crossing the Mediterranean Sea; from there, they could travel an even shorter distance to reach the mainland of Italy.

4. The successful Allied invasion of Sicily led to the downfall of Mussolini, and the new Italian government signed a secret peace agreement with the Allies and pledged to fight Germany. Additional Allied landings on the mainland prompted Italy to officially declare war against Germany.

WAR IN THE PACIFIC

If you've ever played a game of war strategy, you know that different types of battles require different plans of action. The Allies knew this as they fought Japan in the war in the Pacific.

BATTLING BY SEA AND AIR

The Americans were the primary fighting force in the Pacific and were supported by Allied troops from Australia, New Zealand, Canada, and Britain. The troops were led by General Douglas MacArthur, who, as you may recall, was ordered to leave his troops in the Philippines early in the war, and Admiral **Chester Nimitz** of the U.S. Navy. Their mission had four goals: maintain communication between the United States and Australia, where the Americans had established bases; defend North America against the Japanese; prevent the Japanese from venturing outside of the Pacific; and plan amphibious counteroffensives against them.

In spring 1942, the Japanese sought to take control of the sea north of Australia by establishing air bases in New Guinea and the Solomon Islands. From these bases, the Japanese planned to destroy U.S. naval bases along the eastern coast of Australia. However, Allied code breakers had uncovered their plan and alerted U.S. officials, who launched a preemptive attack. Over the course of several days in May, the two enemies battled by air and sea off the coast of New Guinea in what is known as the **Battle of the Coral Sea**. It was the first air-sea battle in history. Japanese forces sank one U.S. aircraft carrier and damaged another, and the Allies destroyed many Japanese planes and badly damaged a Japanese carrier.

But the Japanese remained determined. In June 1942, they tried to seize Midway Island, located 1,400 miles west of Hawaii, in an attempt to destroy a U.S. carrier fleet. Once again, the Allies had intercepted Japan's battle plans. Though the Japanese fleet far outnumbered the U.S. fleet during the three-day-long **Battle of Midway**, the Americans used the intelligence they'd received to stay one step ahead of their enemy.

On June 3, U.S. bombers attacked the Japanese fleet when it was still 500 miles from its destination. Undeterred, Japan attacked Midway the following morning, a decision it came to regret. The battle greatly reduced Japan's naval forces, including the destruction of four carriers and the loss of hundreds of planes and pilots. After its defeat at Midway, Japan canceled plans for several subsequent invasions.

ISLAND HOPPING

Having established control of the Pacific, the Allies' next move involved a two-pronged approach. Admiral Nimitz would travel west from Hawaii, and General MacArthur would travel north from Australia, carrying out a campaign of **island hopping**. This strategy was designed to capture and control islands in the Pacific one by one. The Allies planned to establish bases on the islands along a path to the Japanese homeland in preparation for an Allied attack on Japan.

The offensive began on the island of **Guadalcanal**, northeast of Australia in the Solomon Islands chain. In July 1942, the Japanese had begun constructing an air base there. A month later, the U.S. Marines were sent in to fight the Japanese and force them off Guadalcanal. As the battle dragged on, additional troops arrived to replenish both sides. By mid-October, the Japanese and the Americans each had more than 20,000 troops engaged in battle on the island. By January 1943, however, the Americans had managed to block the stream of Japanese reinforcements, while allowing the American troop strength to nearly double. The Japanese suffered many more casualties and, with their fewer numbers, soon evacuated the island. After six grueling months of battle, the Americans finally held Guadalcanal.

James Doolittle's B-25 taking off from the aircraft carrier, the U.S.S. *Hornet*

TOKYO RAIDERS

Since Japan's attack on Pearl Harbor in December 1941, the United States had wanted revenge. So in April 1942, Lieutenant Colonel James Doolittle led a squadron of B-25 bomber pilots on a surprise attack on the Japanese mainland.

As the planes flew over Tokyo, some citizens below waved to the pilots, believing the aircraft were Japanese. They were shocked when Doolittle and his raiders dropped their bombs, striking industrial and military facilities as well as civilian areas before retreating to free China, where most of them crash-landed.

Japanese casualties were relatively light, but the attack devastated Japanese morale and proved the nation was vulnerable. On the other hand, the raid gave the Americans new confidence and helped set the stage for the war in the Pacific.

More Pacific victories soon followed for the Allies. In November 1943, Nimitz led his forces west of Guadalcanal to the Gilbert Islands, where they also defeated the Japanese. Nimitz and MacArthur continued island hopping throughout 1944. MacArthur overpowered the Japanese in parts of New Guinea and the Philippines. Nimitz took control of the Marshall and Marianas islands in February and August, respectively. From there, the two commanders set their sights on the islands of Japan, only about 1,200 miles away. Meanwhile, the Allied forces in Europe were planning an invasion they hoped would turn the tide of war against Germany.

HISTORICAL THINKING

1. **READING CHECK** What was the Allied mission in the Pacific war?

2. **MAKE INFERENCES** What might have happened if the American military hadn't learned about Japan's plans for the battles of the Coral Sea and Midway?

3. **IDENTIFY PROBLEMS AND SOLUTIONS** Why was island hopping a good strategy for an Allied attack on Japan?

During the war, Allied forces used the North American Mitchell B-25 bomber, shown here, to fight battles in the Pacific and in Europe. James Doolittle flew the bomber in his raid on Tokyo. You will read about his raid and see a photo of his plane taking off for Japan later in this lesson.

PLAN: 2-PAGE LESSON

OBJECTIVE

Examine the Allied strategy in the Pacific.

CRITICAL THINKING SKILLS FOR LESSON 2.2

• Make Inferences

• Identify Problems and Solutions

• Draw Conclusions

• Identify

HISTORICAL THINKING FOR CHAPTER 22

How did World War II and the Holocaust impact Americans and the world? Fighting against both Germany and Japan put Allied troops on the front lines in several theaters of war. Lesson 2.2 focuses on Allied battle strategy in the Pacific.

BACKGROUND FOR THE TEACHER

James H. Doolittle earned a place in history for his heroism in World War II, but his impressive list of accomplishments extends long before and after the war. He served as a flight instructor in World War I, broke the record for a cross-country flight, became the first pilot to rely solely upon instruments throughout a flight, and aided in the development of aviation fuels. When Doolittle returned to active military duty in 1940, he seemed the perfect choice to lead what many considered an impossible mission. The Tokyo Raid, which involved 16 planes and 80 men, changed the balance of power in the Pacific by proving that Japan was susceptible to attack and by putting Japanese forces on the defensive. All 16 American planes were lost. Although most crew members parachuted to safety, several died in the aftermath of the raid. Doolittle received the Medal of Honor in 1942.

INTRODUCE & ENGAGE

PREDICT DIFFERENCES

Direct students to look at the maps in Lessons 2.1 and 3.2. **ASK:** How do you think differences in physical geography will make the war in the Pacific different from the war being fought in North Africa and Europe? *(Possible response: North African and European battles were being fought on land; Pacific battles will have to take the sea into account.)* What other differences do you think will make the war in the Pacific different from the war in North Africa and Europe? *(Possible responses include a different climate, a greater distance from supplies, a different enemy and way of fighting, and different objectives and tactics.)*

TEACH

GUIDED DISCUSSION

1. **Draw Conclusions** Why was the Battle of Midway a turning point in the war in the Pacific? *(Possible responses: The Japanese defeat at Midway caused Japan to alter its strategy and cancel invasions. After Midway, Allied forces began an offensive strategy, and Japan focused on defending territory it held.)*

2. **Identify** What strategy enabled American forces to defeat the Japanese at Guadalcanal? *(The Americans were able to increase their troop strength while blocking the arrival of Japanese reinforcements.)*

MORE INFORMATION

Nose Art Direct students' attention to the photograph of the Mitchell B-25 bomber. Point out that the white star in a blue circle is the standard U.S. aircraft insignia. The nose art, however—that is, the painting at the front of the plane—provided a unique identity for the crew. Popular nose art designs often included 1940s-style female "pinups" and cartoon characters. Though nose art was not sanctioned by military authority, regulations against it generally went unenforced. **ASK:** Why do you think the military allowed personalization of warplanes? *(Possible responses: The art provided relief from the horrors of war that crews faced. It provided soldiers with a connection to home. It boosted morale.)*

ACTIVE OPTIONS

On Your Feet: Tell Me More Organize students into three groups and assign each group one of the following battles: Coral Sea, Midway, or Guadalcanal. Instruct group members to research their assigned topic and complete a 5Ws Chart. Reconvene the class and ask members of the first group to present their facts one at a time. After each fact, members of the other two groups call out, "Tell me more!" until the group runs out of facts. Repeat the process with the remaining groups. Conclude by discussing how these battles helped the Allies win the war in the Pacific.

What?
Who?
Where?
When?
Why?

NG Learning Framework: Examine the Role of Aircraft in the Pacific Campaign

ATTITUDE Curiosity

KNOWLEDGE Our Human Story

Challenge students to learn more about aircraft used in World War II, particularly in the Pacific. Encourage them to research topics such as aircraft carriers, the various kinds of airplanes used, and the training of pilots. Students may choose appropriate media to share their findings with the class. Conclude by discussing how World War II changed aviation technology.

DIFFERENTIATE

STRIVING READERS

Summarize Ask students to work in pairs to read and summarize the text and photo captions. Tell students to write at least three notes for each section. After they have completed writing notes, guide students to create a summary statement for each section and then a summary statement for the whole lesson.

GIFTED & TALENTED

Map Pacific Island Hopping Instruct students to conduct online research to learn more about the Pacific war strategy of island hopping. Then have students create a map that shows the U.S. offensives in the islands of the Pacific, carried out under the leadership of Admiral Nimitz and General MacArthur. Some students may wish to use an online presentation or animation program to better convey U.S. and Japanese actions in the Pacific theater. Encourage students to present their maps to the class.

See the Chapter Planner for more strategies for differentiation.

HISTORICAL THINKING

ANSWERS

1. The Allied mission in the Pacific was to maintain communication between the United States and the U.S. bases in Australia; to defend North America against Japanese aggression; to prevent the Japanese from going outside the Pacific; and to plan amphibious counteroffensives.

2. Japan might have attacked and destroyed U.S. bases in Australia, thus weakening the Allied position in the Pacific.

3. Island hopping enabled the Allies to capture islands one by one and establish bases along a path to Japan as preparation for an attack.

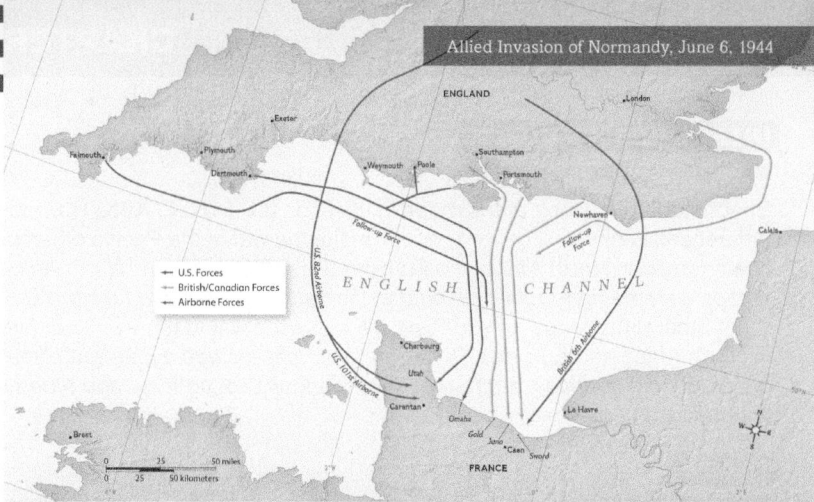

Allied Invasion of Normandy, June 6, 1944

VICTORY IN EUROPE

When faced with a daunting task, you are never sure whether you have prepared well enough, and you don't know how it will turn out. As the Allied forces advanced on Europe, they met many challenges—both expected and unexpected.

OPERATION OVERLORD

With the war in the Pacific going well, the Allies began to make plans to drive the Nazis back to Germany. In November 1943, Roosevelt, Churchill, and Stalin gathered at the **Tehran Conference** in Iran in southwest Asia. It would be the first time Roosevelt had met Stalin. At the conference, the three leaders discussed their plans to invade western Europe—the second front in the west that Stalin had been pressing for—the following spring.

The plan was for General Eisenhower to lead an Allied invasion, code-named **Operation Overlord**, from Britain. Eisenhower organized 3 million soldiers for the invasion and stockpiled plenty of supplies, including food, planes, and smaller ships. To prevent the Nazis from learning their plans, the Allies deliberately planted false information indicating they intended to invade near Calais, France, directly across the English Channel from Dover, England. In addition, in the weeks leading up to the invasion, the Allied air forces kept the Nazis distracted by dropping bombs on German airfields, military bases, and bridges over the main rivers in France. The deception ultimately helped isolate and draw the Nazis away from the invasion's actual target: the French coastal province of Normandy.

Operation Overlord was originally planned to take place in May 1944, but naval vessels called **amphibious landing craft** were not assembled until June. A departure planned for June 5 was delayed by bad weather. At last, on June 6, 1944, thousands of amphibious landing craft, airplanes, and an armada, or fleet of warships, departed from several British ports. Eisenhower's huge force headed toward five different Normandy

beaches, code-named Utah, Omaha, Gold, Juno, and Sword. By sundown that day, on what came to be known as **D-Day**, 150,000 American, British, and Canadian troops stormed the beaches.

American troops under the command of Major General **Omar Bradley** at Omaha, the largest assault area, endured some of the worst conditions. Many Americans drowned as they tried to reach the beach. The troops also faced heavy resistance from German soldiers who turned their machine-gun fire on the Americans as soon as they set foot on the beach. By the next morning, more than 2,000 American soldiers lay dead in the sand. Despite such difficult battles, the Normandy invasion was successful, and Allied forces soon began to move inland. Within two months of the initial landing, more than 1 million Allied troops were fighting to take back France.

BATTLE OF THE BULGE

It took Allied troops only about two months to reach Paris, France's capital, which was controlled by the Nazis. On August 19, 1944, Parisians—aware that the Allies would soon reach them—rose up against the occupying Germans. By the time the Allied forces arrived on August 25, the Nazis were ready to surrender. The liberation of Paris was complete. But the war was still far from over.

In early September, Allied troops advanced from northern France and captured Antwerp, Belgium, an important supply port. From there, they set out toward the German border. At this point, most people believed the end of the war was close. But as the Allies marched farther east, Nazi defenses strengthened. In mid-October, Hitler required all males between the ages of 16 and 60 to fight on behalf of the Third Reich. In mid-December,

U.S. soldiers jump off their amphibious landing craft into the water and prepare for battle on the beach at Normandy on D-Day.

OBJECTIVE

Analyze the battles and events that led to an Allied victory in Europe.

CRITICAL THINKING SKILLS FOR LESSON 3.1

• Interpret Maps

• Make Inferences

• Evaluate

• Analyze Cause and Effect

• Describe

• Interpret Visuals

• Form and Support Opinions

HISTORICAL THINKING FOR CHAPTER 22

How did World War II and the Holocaust impact Americans and the world? American forces played a key role in liberating France and defeating Germany in Europe. Lesson 3.1 explores the Allied victory in Europe.

BACKGROUND FOR THE TEACHER

Under the cover of darkness, hours before the amphibious landing at Normandy, American and British airborne divisions dropped some 13,000 American, British, and Canadian paratroopers behind the main line of German troops defending the beaches. Heavy German antiaircraft fire forced many of the more than 1,200 airplanes off course, resulting in paratroopers being dropped outside the designated target zones. To escape the antiaircraft fire, planes often failed to slow to a safe drop speed; as a result, the blasting air from the engines' propellers ripped weapons and other equipment from many of the paratroopers as they jumped. Some of the paratroopers who kept their equipment drowned when they fell into fields that the Germans had purposely flooded. Nevertheless, the scattered paratroopers did meet to form small groups and were successful in attacking the Germans. Gliders brought in more troops during daylight hours.

INTRODUCE & ENGAGE

PREVIEW USING MAPS

Direct students' attention to the map of the Normandy invasion. **ASK:** Based on the map, what can you tell about this invasion? Encourage a variety of responses based on details that catch students' attention. Record their answers on the graphic organizer shown.
ASK: What impression about the importance of this invasion do you get from this information? *(Possible response: This was a massive operation, so it must have been very important.)* Tell students that this operation was a critical moment in the war and that in this lesson they will learn more about it and the final push to an Allied victory in Europe.

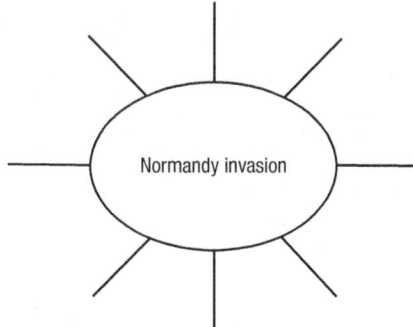

Normandy invasion

TEACH

GUIDED DISCUSSION

1. **Analyze Cause and Effect** How did the factors that delayed the departure of Allied troops add to the complexity of planning Operation Overlord? *(Possible response: The delays caused by the lateness of the amphibious landing craft and the bad weather meant that revised plans had to be coordinated among the Allied nations involved in the invasion, as well as among those directing movements of warships, planes, and landing craft.)*

2. **Describe** What military strategies did the Allies use in the weeks leading up to the Normandy invasion and on D-Day? *(Possible response: Prior to the invasion, the Allies distracted the Germans by bombing airfields, military bases, and bridges in France and spreading rumors about a planned invasion near Calais. On D-Day, the Allies launched thousands of amphibious landing craft, airplanes, and warships from England to invade five Normandy beaches code-named Utah, Omaha, Gold, Juno, and Sword, with American forces responsible for taking Utah and Omaha and the British and Canadians responsible for the rest.)*

3. **Interpret Visuals** Study the photograph of the soldiers disembarking from the landing craft. How does the impression made by the photograph differ from the typical impression of what happened on D-Day? *(Possible response: The photograph gives the impression that the soldiers were confident and had no opposition. However, the grim reality was that many soldiers drowned before reaching the beach or were shot as they came ashore.)*

MORE INFORMATION

D-Day Today, the term *D-Day* automatically makes people think of the Normandy invasion. At the most basic level, however, *D-day* simply stands for the word *day* in military lingo, just as *H-hour* stands for the word *hour*. When General Eisenhower was asked about the meaning of the term, he had his executive assistant reply that any amphibious landing has a "D-day," or launch date. When taken in this context, June 6, 1944, was just one of many D-days during the war. **ASK:** Why do you think the term is so closely associated today with the Normandy invasion? *(Possible response: People today recognize that the landing was a pivotal event in World War II.)*

DIFFERENTIATE

ENGLISH LANGUAGE LEARNERS `ELD`

Explore Cognates Point out the Spanish origin of *armada*, from the past participle of the Spanish word *armata* which comes from the Latin *armare*, meaning "to arm." Encourage students at **All Proficiencies** to think of other English words derived from this Latin root, such as *arms* (weapons), *army, armament,* and *disarm.* Then have students look for other cognates that can help them understand the meaning of words as they read the lesson. For example, students may be familiar with these Spanish cognates: *false/falso, information/información, liberation/liberación, ultimately/por último,* and *naval/naval.*

PRE-AP

Research and Write a Report Challenge students to conduct research using a variety of print and online sources to deepen their understanding of the discrepancies between the noble war aims Franklin Roosevelt articulated in his Four Freedoms speech and the discrimination African Americans faced at home and in their segregated units in the military. Encourage students to find, quote, and paraphrase primary sources from the 1940s, as well as contemporary historical analyses of the "double war" fought by African Americans. Suggest that students conclude their reports by explaining how and why African-American soldiers were allowed to fight alongside white soldiers near the end of World War II. Have students present their reports to the class and answer questions.

See the Chapter Planner for more strategies for differentiation.

reinforced with fresh soldiers, the Germans launched an unexpected attack on the Allies in southern Belgium's Ardennes region. Their goal was to split up the Allied troops and retake Antwerp.

More than 200,000 German soldiers advanced into southern Belgium, greatly outnumbering the Allied troops there, and broke through the Allied front line. This break in the front line created a "bulge," giving the battle its name: the **Battle of the Bulge**. In just one day, approximately 4,000 American soldiers surrendered. General Eisenhower called in reinforcements, eventually enlisting a half million soldiers to fight the battle and, as he hoped, move the Allies closer to victory.

Many of the soldiers Eisenhower called came directly from basic training, however, with little or no experience in combat. Also among the reinforcements called to action were about 2,500 African-American soldiers, who fought shoulder-to-shoulder with white soldiers at Ardennes. An all-black tank unit also rolled in to fight in the battle. It was the first time desegregated troops had fought in a U.S. war.

Troops fought not only the enemy but also the weather. Snow and freezing temperatures tormented the soldiers, who lacked appropriate winter clothing. Many soldiers suffered from frostbite, and some of the wounded froze to death in their foxholes, the holes they dug in the ground to shield themselves as they fired on the enemy. Thick fog also made warfare more difficult for both the troops on the ground and the pilots above—and yet, the Allies kept fighting.

The Battle of the Bulge began in mid-December, and by Christmas, the Germans were calling for the Allies to surrender. But on December 26, General Patton and his army broke through German lines to capture the strategic Belgian town of Bastogne. Then in January 1945, thousands of Allied aircraft bombed the German troops and their supply lines, forcing the Nazis to withdraw in a matter of a few weeks. About 20,000 Americans died in the Battle of the Bulge, and the Germans wounded or captured another 60,000. But that paled in comparison with the 100,000 casualties sustained by the German troops. The battle was the biggest and bloodiest the U.S. Army had fought in World War II.

General Dwight D. Eisenhower (center) and Pierre Koenig (left), leader of the French resistance, take a symbolic walk under the Arc de Triomphe in Paris on August 27, 1944, two days after the Germans surrendered the city to the Allies.

END OF THE THIRD REICH

Meanwhile, the Soviet army was advancing toward the western front. Throughout January 1945, the Soviets had moved west across Poland toward Germany. By the end of the month, they were within 40 miles of Berlin. At the same time, more Allied forces pressed east from France and Belgium, while those involved in the Italian campaign continued to push German troops north along the Italian peninsula. To prepare the way for the ground-force invasion of Germany, the Allies intensified their aerial assault on the country in February 1945. Much of this strategic bombing targeted both industrial and civilian areas.

In 1945, Churchill, Roosevelt, and Stalin (from left to right) attend the Yalta Conference.

By late March, Allied ground troops began crossing the Rhine River into western Germany. Hitler ordered his retreating troops to destroy the country's industrial plants and power and water facilities, along with any food or clothing stores. He wanted to use the scorched-earth policy, much as the Soviets had done against the Germans. But Hitler's minister of war production refused, knowing it would lead to the suffering and deaths of many German citizens—a prospect that did not concern Hitler.

On April 11, Allied troops arrived at the Elbe River, within 60 miles of Berlin. Within two weeks, the Soviet troops joined them, and together they encircled the German capital. On April 30, with the Soviets closing in on his bunker, Hitler committed suicide. With their leader gone and their cause lost, the Nazis surrendered. The war in Europe officially ended on May 8, 1945. The Third Reich had fallen.

THE YALTA CONFERENCE

Before Germany surrendered, Roosevelt, Churchill, and Stalin met at Yalta, a Russian town in the Crimea, in February 1945. With the war turning in the Allies' favor, the leaders spent a week drawing up postwar plans for Europe. The decisions they made came to be called the **Yalta Accords**. The three leaders decided to divide Germany into different occupation zones controlled by the United States, the Soviet Union, Britain, and France. They also agreed to take control of or destroy German arms industries, try German war criminals in a court of law, and establish a commission in Moscow to decide on the reparations Germany would need to make. Stalin particularly pressed for reparations. German soldiers had killed or injured about 20 million Soviet citizens during the war and destroyed many Soviet towns and businesses. Stalin wanted to ensure the Soviet Union received appropriate compensation.

In addition, the leaders discussed Poland's geographic boundaries and political future as well as the establishment of a new international body called the United Nations. At the conference, Stalin agreed to respect free elections in Poland and elsewhere in the eastern European region of the Soviet Union. However, just weeks later, he ordered the arrest of Polish anti-communist leaders and the murder of political dissidents in Romania and Bulgaria.

The war in Europe was over, but the war in the Pacific dragged on. Japan refused to quit, even after crushing defeats. Nevertheless, the Allies hoped to bring a quick end to the war in the Pacific.

HISTORICAL THINKING

1. **READING CHECK** What was Operation Overlord?

2. **INTERPRET MAPS** Why might it have made sense to the Germans that the Allied forces would stage their invasion in Calais rather than in Normandy?

3. **MAKE INFERENCES** Why do you think defeat at the Battle of the Bulge made Hitler realize he might lose the war?

4. **EVALUATE** What did Stalin's actions after the Yalta Conference reveal about the Soviet leader?

BUILD BACKGROUND

HITLER'S SUICIDE

Even at the start of the war, Hitler hinted about committing suicide should the Third Reich fail against the Allied forces. He and some other top Nazi officials likened themselves to Roman heroes, willing to take their own lives rather than surrender in defeat. Additional factors likely pushed Hitler toward suicide. Addicted to prescription drugs and basically confined to his bunker in Berlin as the Soviets moved into the city, Hitler learned on April 29 of Mussolini's execution and the public display and abuse of his corpse. In preparation for ending his life, Hitler married Eva Braun, his longtime companion, and ordered his staff to collect gasoline to burn his and Braun's bodies after death to avoid being put on public display. On April 30, Hitler and Braun committed suicide. Their bodies were burned and buried in a shallow grave.

Soviet troops found the grave and identified Hitler's remains through his unique bridgework. Rather than making the finding public, the Soviets fostered the idea that Hitler had escaped to Bavaria, which was in the U.S. occupation zone, thereby implying that the Americans were in league with the Nazis. This deception helped lead to decades of conspiracy theories claiming that Hitler was still alive.

TEACH

GUIDED DISCUSSION

4. **Describe** How did Allied and German military strategies lead to the Battle of the Bulge? *(The Allies captured Antwerp, Belgium, in early June and then headed for the German border. More than 200,000 Germans attacked the Allied troops in southern Belgium's Ardennes region, breaking through the Allied front line in hopes of splitting the troops and retaking Antwerp.)*

5. **Form and Support Opinions** Why might it be suggested that the Battle of the Bulge marked a milestone for African Americans? *(African-American soldiers fought alongside white soldiers in the battle, and an all-black tank unit participated in the battle. It was the first example of a desegregated U.S. combat force.)*

EVALUATE

Tell students to review the terms of the Yalta Accords in regard to Germany. **ASK:** Which decisions do you think would be hardest to implement, and why? *(Possible response: The decision to divide Germany into different occupation zones would probably be the hardest to implement because it would involve coordinating efforts among four nations.)*

ACTIVE OPTIONS

On Your Feet: Time Line Divide the class into four groups, and assign each group one of the subsections of the lesson. Ask each group to jot down notes that reflect important dates that are mentioned in their subsection. Then meet as a class and work together to assemble a single time line of the most significant events. Refer to the completed time lines as you discuss the cause-and-effect relationships related to the war's end in Europe.

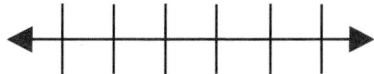

NG Learning Framework: Consider Geopolitical Implications

ATTITUDE Responsibility

SKILL Communication

Organize students into groups. Instruct them to use the lesson information and additional online research to explore the impact of the Allied victory in Europe on postwar international relations. In their research, groups should consider the following:

• Allied military strategies and operations in Europe

• the Yalta Accords

• Poland

• the United Nations

Ask groups to use their findings to summarize the geopolitical implications for postwar Europe. Work with groups to create a format for sharing their summaries with the class.

HISTORICAL THINKING

ANSWERS

1. Operation Overlord was the code name of the Allied invasion of Normandy, the beginning of a major push to win Europe back from the Nazis.

2. Calais would have seemed like a sensible place for the Allies to stage their invasion because the English Channel is narrow there.

3. Possible response: The battle had been intended to make quick work of the Allies, but instead it raged on until the Allies won. Tens of thousands of Germans died or were captured or wounded. The battle was so bloody and the loss to Germany so great that it caused Hitler to face the prospect of losing the war.

4. Possible response: Stalin's broken promise to respect free elections in Poland revealed that he had little trouble being untruthful and that he therefore was untrustworthy.

VICTORY IN ASIA

The Allies found themselves up against a determined and relentless enemy in the Japanese. A strong sense of honor prevented Japanese soldiers from surrendering, even when the odds were heavily stacked against them. Faced with defeat, some even chose suicide.

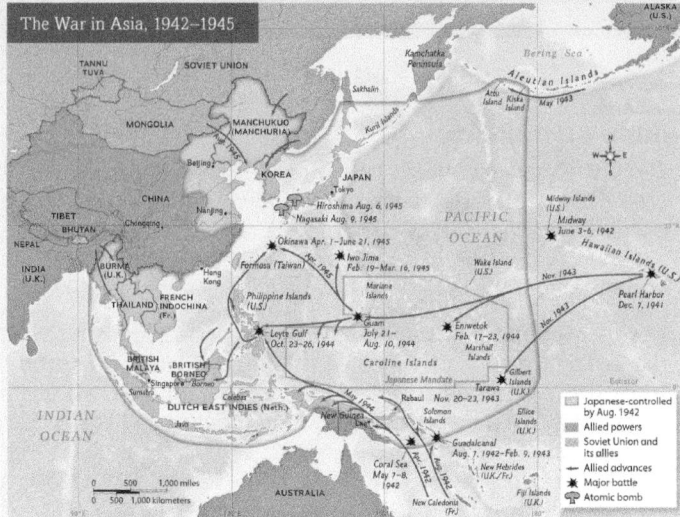

The War in Asia, 1942–1945

LIBERATING THE PHILIPPINES

As the Allies gained ground and fought to secure victory in Europe, war continued to rage in the Pacific. In mid-September 1944, President Roosevelt and General MacArthur decided that the Philippines—which Japan had seized early in 1942—should be the next target of an Allied invasion, with American naval forces taking the lead. In preparation for the liberation, Filipino and American troops had formed guerrilla groups on the ground.

On October 20, 1944, General MacArthur led an amphibious landing on the island of Leyte, southeast of Luzon, where the Philippine capital, Manila, is located. The Allies had judged correctly that the Japanese did not have a strong defense on Leyte. In fact, the Japanese used a decoy ship to draw some of the U.S. naval fleet away from the island. They also sent forces to attack the American fleet at the landing. But the U.S. Navy had anticipated Japan's strategy and, on October 23, used submarines to sink two Japanese cruisers as they approached Leyte. The next day, American aerial attacks sank a Japanese battleship, and the fighting began in earnest.

The **Battles of Leyte Gulf** took place between October 23 and October 26, 1944, during which time the Japanese suffered heavy losses—far more than the Americans. Japanese losses were due, in part, to Japan's decision to deploy suicide bomber pilots called **kamikaze**, meaning "divine wind." These Japanese pilots volunteered to crash their planes, loaded with explosives, into American ships. Over the course of the rest of the war, the kamikaze destroyed 34 U.S. ships, but about 2,800 Japanese pilots sacrificed their lives in the process.

Though the United States did not achieve total control over Leyte until the end of December, the battles destroyed the Imperial Japanese Navy. The United States finally liberated the Philippines in March 1945. Filipino soldiers played an important role in the war effort, but the conflict had taken a terrible toll on their island nation. Manila became the second most devastated city in the world after Warsaw, Poland. By the end of the war, as many as 1 million civilians in the Philippines had died.

CLOSING IN ON JAPAN

Once the Philippines was under American control, the Allies turned their attention to Japan itself. The Allied forces wanted to establish a base for their B-29 bombers close to the Japanese mainland to conduct aerial attacks. They chose the Japanese island of Iwo Jima, located 760 miles southeast of Tokyo.

On February 19, 1945, the Allies, made up mostly of U.S. Marines, landed on Iwo Jima to confront the roughly 20,000 Japanese troops they believed were stationed there. Before the landing, however, the Allies had bombarded the island with napalm bombs and rockets. When the Marines set foot on the devastated island, they saw no sign of life and thought, for a moment at least, that they were going to take the island without a fight. Then suddenly, machine-gun fire erupted, seemingly out of nowhere. The Japanese were firing from a network of hidden natural caves and tunnels they had carved out all over Iwo Jima. And once again, they used kamikaze air raids, crashing their planes into American vessels, sinking one U.S. carrier and damaging many other ships. Fighting was intense, but eventually the Allies prevailed. About 6,000 Americans died while fighting

the **Battle of Iwo Jima**, and nearly all the Japanese soldiers and civilians on the island perished. The Marines took Iwo Jima on March 16, and the United States staged about 2,000 B-29 bombers there.

That same month, just before the Marines secured Iwo Jima, the Allies used a new bombing technique on Tokyo, Japan: nighttime napalm firebombs. The first drop destroyed 25 percent of Tokyo's buildings and killed tens of thousands of people—most of them civilians. The Allies then used a similar technique on several other Japanese cities, hoping that the bombing campaigns would avoid the necessity of sending ground troops into Japan and force the Japanese to surrender.

On April 1, Allied troops landed on the island of Okinawa, located about 400 miles south of Honshu, Japan's main island, where Tokyo is located. Admiral Nimitz and 180,000 troops, most of his carriers, and 18 battleships faced off against 110,000 Japanese soldiers in the **Battle of Okinawa**. Nimitz's troops captured Okinawa's airfields, but the Japanese refused to back down. A few days later, Japan launched a counterattack that involved hundreds of kamikaze raids against the Allied fleet and a successful attack on a U.S. destroyer.

As a result of the kamikaze strategy, American casualty rates skyrocketed. And as on Iwo Jima, a maze of natural caves lay beneath the surface of Okinawa. Japanese soldiers hunkered down in the caves and in pillboxes, small concrete fortifications used to house weapons. American troops were forced to go from one hiding place to another and destroy them with dynamite. Fighting did not officially end on Okinawa until July 2. By then, 7,000 U.S. troops had died on land, and 5,000 more had died at sea. In addition, 40,000 American troops had sustained injuries. More than 100,000 Japanese died in the battle. The overwhelming losses on both sides would play a big role in the U.S. government's decision to use a new strategy to end the war.

A NEW PRESIDENT

Meanwhile, back on the home front, Roosevelt won an unprecedented fourth term in office. During his campaign, Roosevelt chose a new running mate for vice president, Senator **Harry S. Truman** of Missouri. When Roosevelt suddenly died of a massive stroke on April 12, 1945, just a few weeks after his inauguration, Truman became president. Truman was born in Missouri and had fought in World War I. He was an experienced politician, having served

OBJECTIVE

Analyze the battles and events that led to an Allied victory in Asia.

CRITICAL THINKING SKILLS FOR LESSON 3.2

• Compare and Contrast

• Determine Chronology

• Form and Support Opinions

• Make Connections

• Identify Main Ideas and Details

• Analyze Cause and Effect

• Evaluate

HISTORICAL THINKING FOR CHAPTER 22

How did World War II and the Holocaust impact Americans and the world? Despite Germany's surrender, the war with Japan continued. Lesson 3.2 examines the hard-fought road to an Allied victory in the Pacific.

BACKGROUND FOR THE TEACHER

In the wake of Japan's occupation of the Philippines, American and Filipino soldiers who had not surrendered joined with citizens to form small guerrilla groups around the islands. Although these groups harassed the Japanese, their scattered nature limited their effectiveness. General MacArthur became aware of their activities toward the end of 1942 when two U.S. officers—William L. Osbourne and Damon J. Gause—and other military personnel escaped the Philippines and made their way to Australia. MacArthur decided to provide funding and strategic support to help mold the guerrillas into an effective insurgent force, for he believed that they could provide valuable intelligence information to help with a future Allied invasion. Toward that end, MacArthur set up supply and communication lines between Australia and the Philippines and coordinated activities across the groups.

DISCUSS THE SACRIFICES OF WAR

Briefly discuss what students recall from Lesson 1.1 about the hardships that American and Filipino military personnel and civilians suffered during the Allied surrender of the Philippines. Use a Concept Cluster to record students' responses. Then ask students to build upon those responses by thinking about the following questions as they read Lesson 3.2:

• What sacrifices did military personnel and civilians make?

• Why was visionary and courageous leadership necessary?

• What examples of brutality were evident in the conflict?

• Why was logistical support necessary for victory?

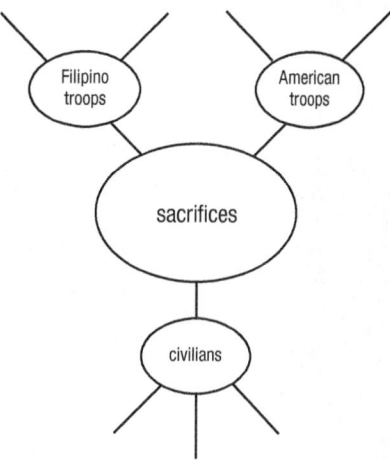

GUIDED DISCUSSION

1. **Make Connections** What evidence indicates that the Japanese takeover of the Philippines and the eventual Allied liberation of that nation were difficult on civilians as well as on troops? *(More than 1 million civilians died in the Philippines during the war, and Manila was the second most devastated city in the world by the end of the war.)*

2. **Identify Main Ideas and Details** Why was capturing Iwo Jima an important part of the Allied plan for defeating Japan, and what was the ultimate goal of this strategy? *(The Allies wanted to take control of Iwo Jima in order to establish a B-29 bomber base from which they could conduct aerial raids on Japan. The Allies hoped that the raids would help push Japan to surrender and thus keep Allied ground troops from having to invade.)*

3. **Determine Chronology** Look closely at the map. In what order did the major battles in the Pacific occur? *(Pearl Harbor, December 7, 1941; Coral Sea, May 7–8, 1942; Midway, June 3–6, 1942; Guadalcanal, August 7, 1942–February 9, 1943; Tarawa, November 20–23, 1943; Eniwetok, February 17–23, 1944; Guam, July 20–August 10, 1944; Leyte Gulf, October 23–26, 1944; Iwo Jima, February 19–March 16, 1945; Okinawa, April 1– June 21, 1945)*

COMPARE AND CONTRAST

Direct students to think about the United States' need to mobilize for a two-front war. **ASK:** How did the United States fight differently on the Pacific front versus the North African/European front? *(Possible response: The Pacific was much more of a sea war, as the Allies hopped from island to island toward Japan. In North Africa and Europe, naval operations often involved antisubmarine warfare and troop transport, since fighting there was predominately a ground war with air support.)*

STRIVING READERS

Make a List Post this heading: Five Things I Know About the Atomic Bombs Dropped on Japan. After students read the lesson, ask them to copy the posted heading and add five or more sentences about the topic. Remind them to include both the immediate and subsequent consequences of the atomic bombs. Invite volunteers to share their sentences with the class.

GIFTED & TALENTED

Investigate News of the Day Instruct students to conduct online research to locate American newspaper headlines, editorials, and political cartoons from the final year of the war. Have students work together to create a display of their findings. Challenge the class to make connections between items on display and particular events mentioned in the lesson.

See the Chapter Planner for more strategies for differentiation.

The atomic bomb explodes over Hiroshima on August 6, 1945. In addition to the deaths caused by the explosion, tens of thousands of Japanese in both Hiroshima and Nagasaki died from radiation sickness.

first as a county judge and later as U.S. senator. But as the new president, he struggled to manage operations during the war.

President Truman was receiving conflicting advice about how to end the war and how to deal with Stalin, who was going back on promises he made at the Yalta Conference. Roosevelt's former vice president, Henry Wallace, encouraged Truman to negotiate with Stalin. The U.S. ambassador to the Soviet Union, however, urged the president to demand Stalin's compliance with the Yalta Accords. Truman took the ambassador's advice and pressed the Soviet foreign minister to convince Stalin to comply with the agreements, threatening that the United States would otherwise withdraw economic aid.

In mid-July 1945, Truman met with Churchill and Stalin in Potsdam, Germany, near Berlin. At the **Potsdam Conference**, the leaders agreed to the terms of peace for Germany and the procedure for bringing Nazi war criminals to trial, among other issues. The defeat of Churchill's Conservative Party interrupted the conference, as Churchill had to return to Britain to pass on his role as prime minister to a new leader. When the Potsdam Conference resumed, the friction between Truman and Stalin was apparent. Stalin brushed aside Truman's concerns about Poland and Eastern Europe, while Truman opposed Stalin's demand for reparations from Germany.

THE ATOMIC BOMB

Another talking point the leaders discussed at the Potsdam Conference was the possibility of using an **atomic bomb**, a type of nuclear bomb whose violent explosion is triggered by splitting atoms, which releases intense heat and radioactivity. Armed with this powerful weapon, Truman warned Japan about the disaster that would befall if the nation refused to surrender without conditions. But for the Japanese, any surrender would be a great dishonor to their country and to their emperor, Hirohito.

Truman had only learned of the atomic bomb's existence after he took office in April 1945. Roosevelt had decided to build the bomb after he was advised the Nazis were taking steps to build one themselves. The U.S. effort, known as the **Manhattan Project**, included top-secret facilities in Washington state, New Mexico, and Tennessee, where scientists designed, built, and tested the new weapon.

Truman formed committees to advise him on how best to deploy the atomic bomb. One of the committees recommended that the United States drop the bomb on four Japanese cities: Kokura, Niigata, **Hiroshima**, and **Nagasaki**. The president decided that although using atomic weapons would cause horrendous loss of life, it would also end the war more quickly, saving more lives in the long run.

In the end, Truman had two Japanese cities bombed. On August 6, 1945, a B-29 bomber called the *Enola Gay* dropped an atomic bomb on Hiroshima. At least 100,000 civilians died in the explosion and the firestorm that followed. A second atomic bomb was dropped on Nagasaki on August 9. Between 35,000 and 40,000 people died, and a similar number of Japanese were injured.

On August 15, Japan accepted the terms of surrender. World War II officially ended on September 2, 1945, when the Japanese signed the formal document of surrender aboard the battleship U.S.S. *Missouri* in Tokyo Bay. After the Japanese surrendered, the Allies occupied Japan, but they allowed the emperor to remain in power to restore order to the country. The Allies also conducted trials against Japanese military and government officials accused of war crimes.

Although American war casualties were small in comparison with those suffered by other nations, more than 400,000 Americans lost their lives. But in Europe as well as Japan, not only soldiers died in the war. The Allies would soon confront murder of civilians on a scale never seen before.

Photographer Alfred Eisenstaedt captured this moment of celebration in Times Square, New York, on August 14, 1945, the day the Japanese surrendered.

HISTORICAL THINKING

1. **READING CHECK** What strategies did the Americans and the Japanese use in the Battles of Leyte Gulf?

2. **COMPARE AND CONTRAST** In what ways were the Battles of Iwo Jima and Okinawa similar, and how did they differ?

3. **DETERMINE CHRONOLOGY** How soon after the Potsdam Conference were atomic bombs deployed over Japan?

4. **FORM AND SUPPORT OPINIONS** Do you think Truman was justified in dropping the atomic bomb on Hiroshima and Nagasaki? Explain your answer.

BUILD BACKGROUND

HIROSHIMA AND NAGASAKI

"Little Boy," the 9,700-pound bomb dropped on Hiroshima, had the estimated power of 15,000 tons of TNT—a big enough blast to destroy almost all the structures within a mile of ground zero and to damage nearly every structure within a three-mile radius. People and animals at ground zero were immediately incinerated, and 9 out of 10 people within half a mile died within minutes. The firestorm that followed the blast consumed more than four square miles of the city, killing those who had escaped the initial blast.

Kokura, not Nagasaki, was the intended target for the second bomb, but weather prevented the drop. A slight clearing over Nagasaki enabled the second B-29 to drop "Fat Boy" on that city instead. "Fat Boy" was 40 percent stronger than "Little Boy," but it resulted in less devastation. In the wake of earlier air raids, some people, including many schoolchildren, had evacuated the city for the countryside. In addition, the bomb hit an industrial area rather than a residential or commercial area, and the surrounding hills helped contain the blast.

TEACH

GUIDED DISCUSSION

4. **Compare and Contrast** How did the tone of the Potsdam Conference differ from that of the Yalta Conference six months earlier, and how do you explain the difference? *(Possible response: At Yalta, there was a general sense of cooperation among the three Allied nations. Shortly after that conference ended, however, Stalin broke his promise to respect free elections in eastern Europe. That fact led to greater distrust, and, along with Stalin's demands for reparations from Germany, it made the Potsdam Conference a more tense meeting.)*

5. **Analyze Cause and Effect** What made President Truman decide to drop atomic bombs on Japan despite his knowing the horrendous consequences? *(After warnings did not persuade Japan to surrender, Truman decided that it was better to use atomic bombs to end the war more quickly, thus ultimately saving more lives.)*

EVALUATE

With the class, create a list of the political consequences of surrender for Japan. **ASK:** Which consequence do you think would be the most controversial, and why? *(The consequences were that the Allies occupied Japan after the surrender, that the emperor was allowed to remain in power to restore order, and that the Allies put members of the Japanese military and government on trial for war crimes. Students may feel that the decision to leave the emperor in power would be the most controversial because it seems to excuse him from responsibility for the death and destruction caused by Japanese forces.)*

ACTIVE OPTIONS

On Your Feet: Fishbowl Share the Background for the Teacher information with the class. Then tell part of the class to sit in a close circle facing inward and the other part to sit in a larger circle around them. Ask students on the inside to discuss what they have learned about the sacrifices of military personnel and civilians during the Pacific. As those on the outside listen for new information, ask them to decide what might have been omitted from the discussion. Then have groups reverse positions, with students in the new inner circle discussing what they have learned and those on the outside listening.

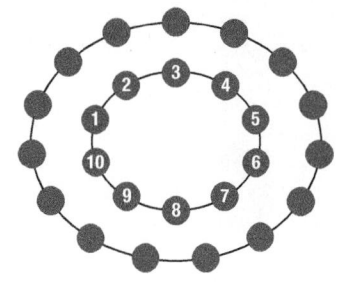

NG Learning Framework: Simulate a Cabinet Meeting

ATTITUDE Responsibility

SKILL Collaboration

Instruct small groups of students to research President Truman's decision to drop two atomic bombs on Japan to end the war. In their research, ask groups to use multiple primary and secondary sources to collect information that supports arguments both for and against the bombing. Ask them also to consider both Truman's rationale and differing historical judgments about dropping the bombs. Direct the groups to use their research to simulate the decision-making process Truman's cabinet used to evaluate the then-available evidence about the condition of Japan and the probable effects of using nuclear weapons. Based on their evaluation, ask each group to make a reasoned recommendation. As a class, compare the recommendations and the thinking that led to them.

HISTORICAL THINKING

ANSWERS

1. In the Battles of Leyte, the Allies used the element of surprise by targeting an island that the Japanese had poorly defended. They used both naval and air power to overwhelm and disable the Japanese fleet. The Japanese tried to use a decoy ship to draw the Allies away from Leyte, but their most devastating tactic was the use of kamikaze to dive-bomb Allied ships.

2. The Allies bombarded Iwo Jima with napalm and rockets before landing. Both Iwo Jima and Okinawa were riddled with natural caves, where the Japanese hid to stage surprise attacks on the Allies. Kamakaze fought in both battles, crashing their planes into American vessels.

3. The United States deployed atomic bombs in Japan less than a month after the Potsdam Conference.

4. Answers will vary. Possible positive responses could note that Truman saved many thousands of Allied lives by forcing an end to the war; negative responses might note that he unleashed a supremely dangerous weapon on the world and that the bombs slaughtered thousands of innocent Japanese civilians in one of the most horrific ways possible.

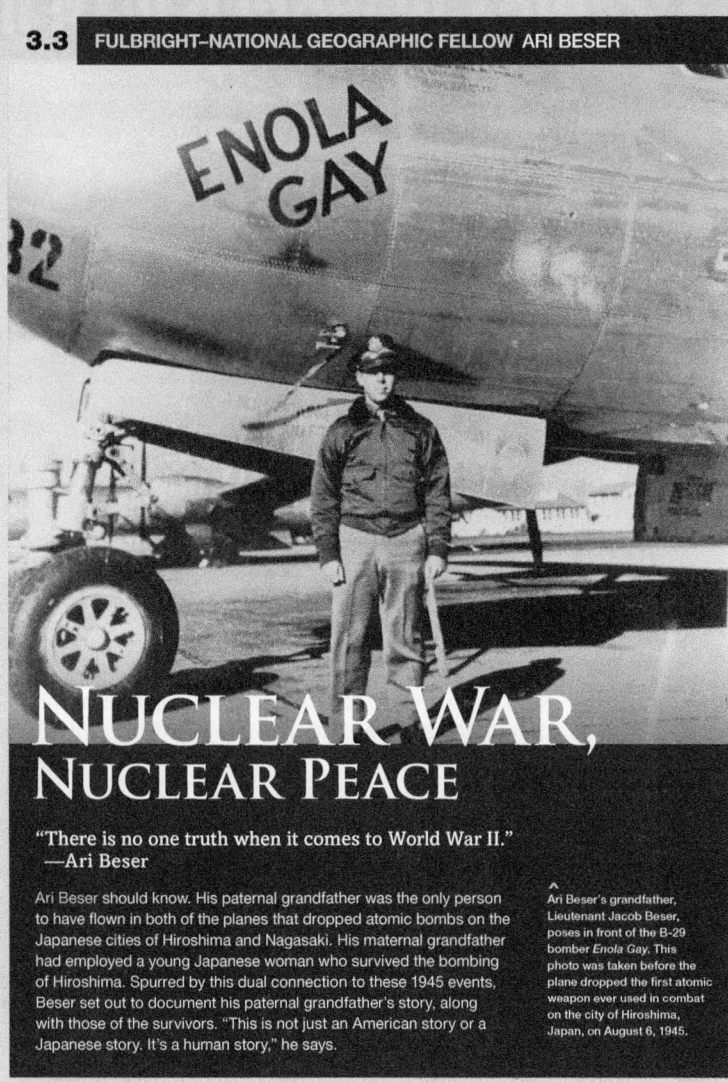

NUCLEAR WAR, NUCLEAR PEACE

"There is no one truth when it comes to World War II."
—Ari Beser

Ari Beser should know. His paternal grandfather was the only person to have flown in both of the planes that dropped atomic bombs on the Japanese cities of Hiroshima and Nagasaki. His maternal grandfather had employed a young Japanese woman who survived the bombing of Hiroshima. Spurred by this dual connection to these 1945 events, Beser set out to document his paternal grandfather's story, along with those of the survivors. "This is not just an American story or a Japanese story. It's a human story," he says.

^ Ari Beser's grandfather, Lieutenant Jacob Beser, poses in front of the B-29 bomber *Enola Gay*. This photo was taken before the plane dropped the first atomic weapon ever used in combat on the city of Hiroshima, Japan, on August 6, 1945.

MAIN IDEA American scholar Ari Beser investigates the stories of atomic bomb survivors to promote peace and reconciliation.

Ari Beser (left) poses with Clifton Truman Daniel (right), grandson of President Harry Truman, who ordered the use of atomic weapons against Japan in 1945. They are joined by survivors of the bombs and their family members in Hiroshima.

ATOMIC HERITAGE

Growing up, Ari Beser had long heard tales of his grandfather's crucial role in the most historic of events. An engineer, Lieutenant (Lt.) Jacob Beser modified radar systems to suit the unique needs of the bombing mission. He was unapologetic about his part. He viewed the bombings as a necessary step in ending the war with Japan. Nonetheless, he expressed the wish that no such tragedy should ever happen again and made a point of ensuring that his grandchildren were aware of his story.

Lt. Beser left behind a technical memoir about his time on the Manhattan Project, the research and development initiative during World War II that produced the first atomic weapons. From the memoir, Ari Beser gained a wealth of firsthand information about his grandfather and his perspective on World War II. To better understand the perspective of the Japanese impacted by the bombing, Beser set out to talk to some of the remaining *hibakusha*—survivors of the bombs.

TRUTH AND RECONCILIATION

Through projects that aimed to raise awareness of the events at Hiroshima and Nagasaki, Beser did just that. A Fulbright–National Geographic Digital Storytelling Fellowship allowed him to travel to Japan in 2015 for the 70th anniversary of the bombings. The bombs together had killed some 200,000 people. Thousands more suffered radiation sickness. Beser has interviewed more than 50 *hibakusha* about their experiences during and in the wake of the bombings.

Despite the horrors they experienced, many *hibakusha* were eager to talk to Lt. Beser's grandson. The survivors bore no ill will toward the family of the man who had participated in the bombing missions. Ari Beser's frank but respectful approach gained him the trust of his interviewees. "How do you always get me to say things I've never said before?" asked a relative of Sadako Sasaki, who gained international renown for folding over 1,000 paper cranes as she battled leukemia caused by radiation exposure.

Gaining that trust was a necessary step. The accounts of the *hibakusha* are universally awful. They recount vividly the bright flash, the heat, and the wind generated by the bomb. And they all have tales of the carnage they witnessed in the aftermath. The rivers were choked with human remains, and horribly injured survivors wandered in search of help. Many were burned and stripped of skin. Even those who recovered endured years of chronic pain and wounds that wouldn't heal. As painful as reliving these memories is, the *hibakusha* insist that recording them is essential. Remarkably, many suspend judgment of the actions taken by the United States. Beser concurs. "We are each other's history," he says. "We all have a relative somewhere that fought in some war. This just happens to be my family's story."

It is his hope—and the hope of the *hibakusha*—that the exchange of these stories will put an end to nuclear warfare once and for all.

HISTORICAL THINKING

1. **READING CHECK** What does Beser hope to accomplish by talking to bomb survivors?

2. **EVALUATE** Compare the 1945 bombing of Japan to a similar recent event. What were the consequences of both events? What lessons were learned from them?

3. **MAKE GENERALIZATIONS** How do most survivors view the bombings?

PLAN: 2-PAGE LESSON

OBJECTIVE

Learn about Ari Beser's experiences interviewing Japanese survivors of the Hiroshima and Nagasaki bombings.

CRITICAL THINKING SKILLS FOR LESSON 3.3

- Evaluate
- Make Generalizations
- Make Inferences
- Identify Problems and Solutions

HISTORICAL THINKING FOR CHAPTER 22

How did World War II and the Holocaust impact Americans and the world? The bombing of Hiroshima and Nagasaki had a lasting effect on Japanese survivors and the Americans involved in the missions. Lesson 3.3 examines Ari Beser's journey to understand events from both sides.

FULBRIGHT–NATIONAL GEOGRAPHIC FELLOW ARI BESER

Ari Beser first went to Japan in 2011 in preparation for writing *The Nuclear Family*, a book about his grandfather and the effects of the Hiroshima and Nagasaki bombings on the Japanese. In addition to his work interviewing the *hibakusha*, Beser has related the experiences of Japanese citizens affected by the meltdown of the three nuclear reactors in Fukushima following the 2011 Great East Japan earthquake and tsunami. Arriving in Japan not long after the disaster occurred, he volunteered his time and effort to help clean up the destruction. As a Fulbright–National Geographic Fellow digital storyteller, Beser uses photographs, video, online blogs, and news articles to tell his stories.

HISTORY NOTEBOOK

Encourage students to complete the Explorer page for Chapter 22 in their History Notebooks as they read.

INTRODUCE & ENGAGE

DISCUSS RESEARCH SOURCES

Point out that Ari Beser's goal was to interview survivors of the bombing of Hiroshima and Nagasaki. **ASK:** Would his interviews produce primary-source information or secondary-source information? *(primary-source information)* Why would primary-source information be valuable—and what challenges might be involved in obtaining it? *(Possible response: Primary-source information makes historical events relevant and personal; it is more immediate than secondary-source information. In this case, the main challenge might be the traumatic memories that the survivors experience.)* Tell students that in this lesson they will learn how Ari Beser handled the delicate task of collecting survivors' stories.

TEACH

GUIDED DISCUSSION

1. **Make Inferences** Why was Lieutenant Jacob Beser most likely included on both bombing missions? *(Jacob Beser probably was needed aboard for his technical expertise because he had modified the radar systems to meet the needs of these missions.)*

2. **Identify Problems and Solutions** Why would it have been a problem for Ari Beser to gain the trust of the *hibakusha*, and how did Beser overcome that problem? *(Possible response: The problem was that the* hibakusha *were being asked to open up about very painful experiences to the grandson of one of the people responsible for their pain. To overcome that problem, Beser was honest in his questions and respectful toward the* hibakusha, *showing them that his motives were sincere.)*

MORE INFORMATION

Environmental Effects of the Bombings Tell students that the bombs that dropped on Hiroshima and Nagasaki leveled or burned approximately 70 percent of the buildings in Hiroshima and leveled more than 2.5 square miles of Nagasaki. The blasts raised temperatures to 7,200°F (4,000°C), killing plants, animals, and humans near ground zero. They were followed by a black rain filled with radioactive fallout, which blanketed the cities. Have students locate photographs of the cities taken before and after the bombings. Then, as a class, use the photographs to discuss how the bombings modified the landscape and environment.

ACTIVE OPTIONS

On Your Feet: Create a Quiz Have students work in small groups to create a fill-in-the-blank quiz based on the content of the lesson. Then direct each group to ask another group their questions. Encourage students to use the text to confirm their answers.

NG Learning Framework: Investigate Policy Issues

ATTITUDE Responsibility

KNOWLEDGE Our Living Planet

Point out that scientists postulate that the environmental destruction that the two atomic bombs caused in Japan pales in comparison to what would happen today if nations were to deploy stockpiled nuclear weapons in a war. Have students work in groups to research the scientific views of the potential destruction and the ways in which scientists try to inform environmental and political policies concerning the use of nuclear weapons. Invite groups to share their findings with the class.

DIFFERENTIATE

STRIVING READERS

Use Context Clues Help students use textual definitions and context clues to understand challenging words in the lesson. Call attention to the Japanese word *hibakusha* and the definition that follows the word. Assist them in unlocking the meaning of other potentially difficult words, such as *crucial, unapologetic, perspective,* and *reconciliation.*

PRE-AP

Write a Compare-and-Contrast Essay Ask students to conduct online research on organizations dedicated to collecting testimonies of survivors of war and injustice, from the Armenian genocide to the internment of Japanese Americans to the Holocaust to the Rwandan genocide. Have students choose one of these organizations and read about its mission and work. Then instruct students to compare and contrast that organization's work with Ari Beser's project about Japanese survivors of the atomic bomb. Encourage students to use a Venn Diagram to keep track of the similarities and differences. Tell them to use their research to write a compare-and-contrast essay that they can share with the class.

See the Chapter Planner for more strategies for differentiation.

HISTORICAL THINKING

ANSWERS

1. Beser hopes to better understand the Japanese perspective. He also hopes that by exchanging stories, he can help put an end to nuclear warfare.

2. Answers will vary, but students should compare both consequences and lessons learned.

3. Possible response: Despite the horrors they experienced and remember, most survivors hold no ill will toward American participants and their families or toward the United States. They do believe, however, that it is important to record their memories.

THE HOLOCAUST

In the haze of war, Americans knew about Hitler's hatred of the Jews, but few allowed themselves to imagine the full extent of his anti-Semitic fervor. After the war in Europe was over, the world learned what the Nazis were capable of.

After putting up a fight in 1943, the Jews in Poland's Warsaw ghetto who survived were captured and deported to concentration camps. The Nazis systematically destroyed the city and blew up Warsaw's Great Synagogue. This photo is one of many taken by a Nazi photographer to document the Jews' removal.

NAZI PERSECUTION OF JEWS

When the Allies invaded Germany and Poland in the spring of 1945, they encountered scenes of horror: **concentration camps** full of starving and dying prisoners. Most were Jews, but there were also non-Jewish Poles; Roma, or Gypsies; homosexuals; and political dissidents.

The nightmare began when Hitler became Germany's chancellor in January 1933. You've learned that Hitler considered Jews an inferior race, and he began almost immediately to devise a plan for their extermination. On Hitler's command, the Nazis began to systematically restrict the civil and political rights of Jews. They removed Jews from German schools and universities and banned them from many public areas. Businesses were taken away from their Jewish owners, and Jewish doctors and lawyers were not allowed to practice. In time, the Jewish people lost their right to vote.

Persecution of the Jews escalated with Kristallnacht on November 9, 1938, when, as you have read, rioters attacked and killed about 100 Jews and destroyed Jewish shops and synagogues. Many German Jews sought refuge in other countries, but the Nazis made travel outside of Germany difficult. Soon, Jews were forbidden to leave the country at all.

Germany invaded Poland in 1939, and the Nazis subjected both Jewish and non-Jewish Poles to brutal treatment. They made Poles perform hard labor and seized their property. They also created about 400 confined areas in Polish cities, called ghettos, forcing huge numbers of Jews to live in them. Barbed wire, thick walls, and armed guards surrounded the ghettos to prevent residents from escaping. Jews older than the age of six in Poland and in all German-occupied territories eventually were forced to wear a yellow Star of David with *Jew* written in the region's

Jews in the Netherlands were forced to wear a Star of David, like this one, with the Dutch word *Jood*, meaning "Jew." Any Jew in a German-occupied territory who refused to wear a star faced severe punishment or even death.

language on it. With so many people living in such tight quarters, food was scarce, and disease spread quickly. In 1941, the Nazis rounded up others they had imprisoned as "undesirables" and sent them to the Polish ghettos. But the ghettos were just holding places until the Nazis came up with a plan to solve what they called "the Jewish question."

"THE FINAL SOLUTION"

When Germany invaded the Soviet Union, special military units accompanied the German Army. Their sole responsibility was to kill Jews, Gypsies, and Soviet heads of government departments. By 1943, these mobile killing units had executed an estimated 1 million Jews. This was the first step in what the Nazis called the "final solution." "Final solution" was code for the plan to murder all the Jews in Europe—approximately 11 million in all. Hitler had made

it known that this was his goal. In January 1942, **Reinhard Heydrich**, head of the Gestapo, called a meeting of high-ranking Nazis in Wannsee, a suburb of Berlin. Heydrich had gathered the men together at the **Wannsee Conference** to explain how the rest of the plan would be carried out.

Heydrich told the men that concentration camps would be constructed in eastern Europe. Jews would be sent to the camps, where the able-bodied among them would build roads and do other work. The work would be so hard that many Jews would die due to "natural reduction." Those who put up any resistance would be executed. But Jewish genocide, or the systematic destruction of a racial, cultural, or ethnic group and its culture, was the real purpose of the camps. The Nazis equipped most of the camps with facilities for carrying out the killings. The camps became known as extermination or death camps.

OBJECTIVE

Examine Hitler's plan for exterminating Jews and other minorities.

CRITICAL THINKING SKILLS FOR LESSON 4.1

- Make Inferences
- Draw Conclusions
- Summarize
- Analyze Cause and Effect
- Make Connections
- Analyze Visuals
- Form and Support Opinions
- Evaluate
- Analyze Primary Sources

HISTORICAL THINKING FOR CHAPTER 22

How did World War II and the Holocaust impact Americans and the world? World War II resulted in immense loss of life through both military action and the Holocaust. Lesson 4.1 describes the brutality of the Holocaust.

BACKGROUND FOR THE TEACHER

The people who ran the death camps were referred to as "SS soldiers," from the German word *Schutzstaffel*, meaning "Protective Echelon," a group that was started to protect Hitler himself. This elite group of soldiers expanded from more than 250,000 at the war's beginning to more than 900,000 as the war progressed. Many were recruited from outside Germany and had to prove they had no Jewish ancestry. Unlike German soldiers fighting on the fronts, these soldiers specialized in finding and exterminating the Jews and their sympathizers. They were known for their cruelty and brutality and committed most of the war crimes.

HISTORY NOTEBOOK

Encourage students to complete the Holocaust page for Chapter 22 in their History Notebooks as they read.

INTRODUCE & ENGAGE

PREVIEW USING VISUALS

Instruct students to look at the images as well as the title and subheadings in the lesson. Point out the Star of David and the crowded wooden "beds." **ASK:** What does *anti-Semitism* mean? *(hatred against Jews)* Tell students that in this lesson they will read about one of the most brutal, inhuman actions in history.

TEACH

GUIDED DISCUSSION

1. **Summarize** How would you describe the plight of Jews living in Germany in the 1930s? *(Possible response: Jews faced ever-increasing threats to most aspects of their lives, including their ability to earn a living, go to school, vote, practice their religion, and, ultimately, stay alive.)*

2. **Analyze Cause and Effect** Why might the German people have turned a blind eye to the persecution of Jews and the events of the Holocaust? *(Answers will vary. Possible responses: People wanted someone to blame for their problems, and Hitler stirred them to extreme hatred of the Jews. People were afraid of the Nazis. Many Germans did not know about the concentration camps.)*

3. **Make Connections** What similarities existed between Hitler's treatment of Jews and the treatment of African Americans in the United States before and after the Civil War? *(Answers will vary. Possible responses: Both groups were treated as inferior races. Both were intimidated and abused physically and psychologically. Both were denied the right to vote. Both were deprived of or limited in their ability to make a living or go to school.)*

4. **Analyze Visuals** Have students examine the photo of the Jews being removed from Warsaw and sent to concentration camps. **ASK:** What might be in their bags? *(their few possessions)* How old are the people in the photograph? *(They vary in age from children to adults.)* Do you think the people know where they are going? *(Possible responses: No—they would look more desperate if they knew what was going to happen. Yes—they look worried and defeated.)*

MORE INFORMATION

The Armenian Genocide Often referred to as the first genocide of the 20th century, the Armenian genocide, which started in the spring of 1915 and continued through the fall of 1916, involved the annihilation of Armenian Christians living in the Ottoman Empire. Of the estimated 1.7 to 2.1 million Armenians living in the Ottoman Empire, as many as 1.2 million died during the genocide. Henry Morgenthau, Sr., the U.S. ambassador to Constantinople, was gravely concerned about the atrocities and, along with others, sought to raise the world's awareness of the Armenians' plight. During the Holocaust era, Ambassador Morgenthau's son, Henry Morgenthau, Jr., was Franklin Roosevelt's treasury secretary and, with fresh memories of the Armenian genocide, became a main advocate for the establishment of the War Refugee Board, which rescued as many as 200,000 Jews from German-occupied Europe.

DIFFERENTIATE

STRIVING READERS

Determine Chronology Assign students to work in pairs. Explain that they are to determine the chronology of events presented in the lesson. Suggest that they first scan the lesson and write the dates mentioned in chronological order in a Sequence Chain, adding more squares as needed. Then ask students to read the lesson more carefully, pausing to jot down notes in their Sequence Chain about significant events that happened on various dates. When they have finished, instruct students to take turns reading the notes in their Sequence Chain aloud, using transitional phrases such as *and then* or *after that* to show connections between events.

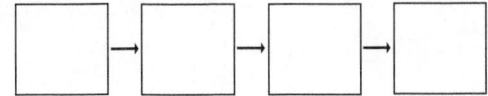

PRE-AP

Write a Report on Resistance Tell students that in addition to the Jewish uprising in Warsaw, people in other places came together to resist Nazism and fascism even as they overwhelmed Europe. Instruct students to conduct preliminary research about the resistance groups that emerged in occupied France, Italy, and Yugoslavia, as well as in Germany itself. Then have students choose a specific instance of resistance on which to conduct in-depth research. Tell students to use relevant information from several library or online sources to write a report on the actions of the resistance group. Encourage students to share their findings with the class.

See the Chapter Planner for more strategies for differentiation.

CRITICAL VIEWING These survivors of Buchenwald, one of the largest concentration camps inside Germany, were photographed as U.S. forces arrived at the camp in April 1945. Among them is Elie Wiesel, whose face appears farthest to the right in the second bunk from the bottom. Wiesel would describe his experiences in concentration camps in his memoir *Night*. What does the survivors' appearance suggest about their treatment in the camp?

Anne Frank, 1942

PRIMARY SOURCE

The most famous Jew who went into hiding from the Nazis is Anne Frank, a young girl who hid with her family in a secret attic apartment in Amsterdam, the Netherlands. Not long before the Nazis found the Franks and deported Anne to Auschwitz, she wrote the following in her famous diary. She died in Bergen-Belsen in 1945.

In spite of everything I still believe that people are really good at heart. I simply can't build up my hopes on a foundation consisting of confusion, misery, and death. I see the world gradually being turned into a wilderness, I hear the ever approaching thunder, which will destroy us too, I can feel the sufferings of millions and yet, if I look up into the heavens, I think that it will all come right, that this cruelty too will end, and that peace and tranquility will return again.

—from *The Diary of a Young Girl*, by Anne Frank, published in 1947

From 1942 until early 1945, the Nazis rounded up millions of Jews all across Europe. Jews were often ordered to gather in a town square, where Nazi officers terrorized them and then packed them into trains for "deportation," or transport, to the death camps. The overcrowded train cars were hot in the summer and freezing in the winter, and passengers did not receive food or water during the journey. Some died before they reached their destinations.

A number of Jews went into hiding or resisted rather than board the trains. The most famous example of resistance took place in 1943, when Jews in the Polish ghetto of Warsaw fought back against the Nazis. Armed with weapons they had managed to smuggle into the ghetto, the group held off the Nazis for a time. But in the end, the far better-equipped German troops overpowered the Jews. About 7,000 of those in the Warsaw ghetto were shot immediately. The rest—about 50,000—were sent to the camps.

DEATH CAMPS

The most notorious death camps were located in Poland and included Chelmno, Treblinka, and **Auschwitz** (OWSH-vits), the largest of the camps. Auschwitz consisted of three main camps. All were labor camps, and one included a killing center. Because Auschwitz was at a junction where several railways converged, the camp served as a convenient place for the Nazis to transport prisoners from all across Europe. In 1944, for example, Nazis transferred more than 400,000 Hungarian Jews there.

When prisoners first arrived, a doctor would review them, sending certain groups of people to their death, including pregnant women, young children, the elderly, the disabled, and the ill. Most of these people were killed immediately in specially prepared gas chambers, where they were told they would simply be taking a shower. Then the victims' bodies were burned in **crematoria**, or ovens. Those who were in good physical shape were put to work, often in factories in the area. When the laborers could no longer work due to malnutrition, illness, or exhaustion, the Nazis sent them to the gas chambers. An estimated 1.1 million Jews died at Auschwitz, including those who had been subjected to terrible medical "experiments" performed by the camp's chief doctor, Josef Mengele.

Even when the end of the war in Europe—and the end of the Third Reich—was in sight, the killings at Auschwitz and other death camps continued. But as the Soviets and other Allies advanced across eastern Europe, the Nazis who ran the camps abandoned them and fled. First, however, they tried to destroy any evidence of what had happened in the camps. They dismantled the barracks where prisoners had lived, burned down buildings that housed crematoria, and destroyed warehouses containing prisoners' clothing and personal items. Nonetheless, plenty of evidence remained of the murders that had been committed in the camps. In all, about 6 million Jews died in the **Holocaust**, which is what the systematic genocide carried out by the Nazis came to be called.

HISTORICAL THINKING

1. **READING CHECK** What was the "final solution"?

2. **MAKE INFERENCES** Why do you think the Nazis forced Jews to wear a yellow Star of David?

3. **DRAW CONCLUSIONS** In what ways did the initial restrictions placed on the civil and political rights of the Jews impact the events of the holocaust?

BUILD BACKGROUND

THE WARSAW GHETTO

Once imprisoned in the ghetto, the Jews of Warsaw did what they could to make life bearable and to preserve their culture. One woman organized an underground children's school. Musicians performed as choirs or chamber groups. These details and many more have been recorded thanks to an archive initiated by Emanuel Ringelblum, a historian and resident of the ghetto. Ringelblum began chronicling daily life in the ghetto and soon invited others to participate in the creation of what became a secret archive known as the *Oyneg Shabbes*, or "Joy of the Sabbath." By 1942, Ringelblum and his collaborators had amassed thousands of documents, including diaries, poems, essays, and reports. The collection further included paintings, sketches, and more mundane items, such as food coupons. To keep the archive from the German soldiers, the collaborators buried parts of it in three separate locations. Shortly thereafter, the Germans reduced much of the ghetto to rubble. Nevertheless, the three Oyneg Shabbes collaborators who survived the war managed to determine one of the locations and, in 1946, succeeded in unearthing 10 boxes filled with documents. In 1950, workers stumbled upon a second cache in a couple of metal milk cans. Some 35,000 documents have been recovered, a testament to how those in the Warsaw Ghetto lived and what they had to endure.

TEACH

GUIDED DISCUSSION

5. Form and Support Opinions Do you think it would have been better for the Warsaw Jews if they had not chosen to fight the Nazis? Explain your answer. *(Possible response: No—the Nazis would have tried to kill them one way or another, and there was always a chance their efforts would succeed.)*

6. Evaluate How might an earlier discovery of the death camps have changed the fate of European Jews? *(Possible response: An earlier discovery might have led to greater efforts of rescue and offers of sanctuary from the Allies and neutral nations.)*

ANALYZE PRIMARY SOURCES

Ask students to read the paragraph from Anne Frank's diary. **ASK:** What words does she use to describe the present and to describe the future? *(present: confusion, misery, death, wilderness, thunder, destroy, sufferings, cruelty; future: peace, tranquility)* On what does she base her hopes for the future? *(She believes that people are really good at heart.)* Have students discuss whether they agree with her that people are good at heart. Encourage them to support their opinions with real-life examples.

ACTIVE OPTIONS

On Your Feet: Think, Pair, Share Give students a few minutes to think about the following question: Why should everyone learn about the Holocaust? Then have students choose partners and discuss the question for several minutes. Finally, allow volunteers to share their ideas with the class.

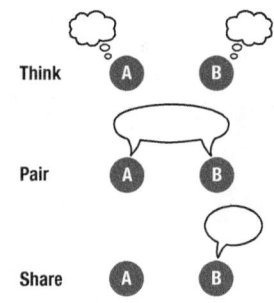

Think A B

Pair A B

Share A B

NG Learning Framework: Holocaust Heroes

ATTITUDE Responsibility

KNOWLEDGE Our Human Story

During World War II, thousands of non-Jews in Europe did what they could to save Jews from the Nazis. Years later, many were honored by the Israeli Parliament for their heroic deeds. Ask students to conduct online research to learn about one of these individuals. Have them share the specifics of the person's story with the class.

HISTORICAL THINKING

ANSWERS

1. The "final solution" was Hitler's plan to murder all Jews in Europe.

2. The Star of David could help the Nazis identify Jews and distinguish them from other people.

3. Initial civil, economic, and political restrictions, in addition to travel restrictions, made it close to impossible for Jews to resist or escape Nazi efforts, thus making the Holocaust more inevitable.

CRITICAL VIEWING The survivors' emaciated appearance makes it clear that they were given very little food. Some look as though they could do nothing but lie there because they are too weak or ill to move.

REFUGEES AND JUSTICE

When American troops discovered the concentration camps and their starved, tortured inmates, they could scarcely believe what they saw. For the first time, many of the soldiers understood what they'd been fighting for.

PLIGHT OF THE REFUGEES

While most Americans were unaware of the existence of the Nazi concentration camps, the Allied leaders of the United States, Britain, and the Soviet Union did know about them. In December 1942, Roosevelt, Churchill, and Stalin issued a declaration officially recognizing the mass murder of European Jews and vowing to bring those responsible to justice. Even so, the Allies did not make bombing death camps and the railroad tracks that carried the prisoners a priority. Thousands of Jews fleeing Europe were admitted to the United States, but many thousands

more were turned away. The U.S. State Department claimed that some of the refugees could be spies and therefore posed a national security risk.

Finally, pressured by American Jewish organizations and officials in his own government, President Roosevelt created the **War Refugee Board** in January 1944 to rescue Jews. In its most ambitious effort, the board helped finance the work of Swedish diplomat **Raoul Wallenberg** to save tens of

United States Holocaust Memorial Museum Washington, D.C.

When Masha Kessler and her 17-year-old daughter, Esther, arrived at the Kaiserwald concentration camp in the northern European country of Latvia, one of the two Polish women was issued this striped uniform coat. The rectangular patch at the top of the coat once contained the prisoner's ID number, and the yellow triangle beneath the patch indicated the prisoner was Jewish. Prior to their transfer to Kaiserwald, the mother and daughter had been forced to live in a Jewish ghetto. The pair worked as slave laborers in several concentration camps before Soviet troops liberated them in January 1945. Masha or Esther continued to wear the coat throughout their imprisonment in the camps. The Holocaust Memorial Museum displays this coat and other artifacts worn by Holocaust victims in their permanent collection.

thousands of Hungarian Jews from the death camps. Wallenberg traveled to Nazi-occupied Hungary and set up hospitals, soup kitchens, and safe houses for Jews in Budapest. He and his colleagues also distributed certificates of protection and Swedish passports to the Jews. During World War II, Sweden remained neutral, which meant the Nazis could not legally harm citizens holding a Swedish passport.

THE NUREMBERG TRIALS

The world learned about the extent of Nazi **atrocities**, or extremely cruel and shocking acts of violence, when the International Military Tribunal charged and tried former Nazi officials, military officers, industrialists, and others as war criminals. A **tribunal** is a court with authority over a specific matter. The series of trials, known as the **Nuremberg trials**, took place in Nuremberg, Germany, beginning in 1945. The tribunal determined that defendants could be charged with any of the following: crimes against peace, for having waged a war of aggression; crimes against humanity, for having exterminated groups of people; and war crimes, for having violated common and agreed-upon laws of war. Members of the tribunal represented the United States, Great Britain, the Soviet Union, and France and had the authority to determine the guilt of any individual or group. As evidence, the prosecution presented Nazi propaganda films, footage filmed at concentration camps by Allied troops, and ghastly artifacts taken from the camps. Survivors of the camps also testified, describing what they had witnessed and experienced.

Trials for 22 major Nazi war criminals were held in 1945 and 1946. Several of the leading figures in the party could not be tried, however. Hitler and two of his top officers, Heinrich Himmler and Joseph Goebbels, committed suicide before they could be brought to justice. Most of those charged did not deny or apologize for their actions. In their defense, many said they were "just following orders." On October 1, 1946, the tribunals issued their verdicts. While the tribunals acquitted some of the major war criminals and sent others to prison, they sentenced 12 to death by hanging. One of the 12 was Hermann Goering, whom Hitler had designated as his successor. However, Goering evaded execution by committing suicide. He swallowed a tablet of cyanide, which he had hidden in his cell, the day before he was to hang.

The Nuremberg trials attempted to bring Nazi war criminals to justice. But for many of those who

PRIMARY SOURCE

In 1986, Elie Wiesel was awarded the Nobel Peace Prize. In this excerpt from his acceptance speech, Wiesel explains our role in the face of suffering and oppression.

There is much to be done, there is much that can be done. One person—a Raoul Wallenberg . . . one person of integrity, can make a difference, a difference of life and death. As long as one dissident is in prison, our freedom will not be true. As long as one child is hungry, our lives will be filled with anguish and shame. What all these victims need above all is to know that they are not alone; that we are not forgetting them, that when their voices are stifled we shall lend them ours, that while their freedom depends on ours, the quality of our freedom depends on theirs.

—from Elie Wiesel's Nobel Peace Prize acceptance speech, December 10, 1986

survived the Nazi atrocities, their experiences would continue to haunt them throughout their lives. Some survivors, including the Romanian-born writer **Elie Wiesel**, wanted to bring the horrors of the Holocaust to the world's attention. Wiesel was 15 years old when he was sent to Auschwitz along with his parents and sister. He was later transferred to Buchenwald. After the war, Wiesel wrote *Night*, an account of the violence and abuse he experienced and witnessed in the camps. He did not want the world to forget what happened.

Holocaust museums created after the war have the same mission. By telling the stories of the victims and survivors, these museums show that those affected were not numbers but real people. The museums also stress the responsibility of citizens to speak out against hatred and prejudice to help prevent genocide from happening again.

HISTORICAL THINKING

1. **READING CHECK** What did Raoul Wallenberg do to try to save Hungarian Jews in Budapest?

2. **MAKE INFERENCES** Why do you think it was important to bring Nazi war criminals to trial instead of simply executing them?

3. **DRAW CONCLUSIONS** What did Wiesel mean when he said, "their [the victims'] freedom depends on ours, the quality of our freedom depends on theirs"?

PLAN: 2-PAGE LESSON

OBJECTIVE

Learn about the U.S. response to the mass murder of European Jews and the Nuremberg trials of former Nazi officials.

CRITICAL THINKING SKILLS FOR LESSON 4.2

- Make Inferences
- Draw Conclusions
- Evaluate
- Determine Chronology

HISTORICAL THINKING FOR CHAPTER 22

How did World War II and the Holocaust impact Americans and the world? The United States did little to assist European Jews until 1944. Lesson 4.2 discusses the establishment of the War Refugee Board and the Nuremberg trials.

BACKGROUND FOR THE TEACHER

The U.S. State Department, well known for its anti-Semitism in the World War II era, made it virtually impossible for Jewish refugees fleeing the Nazis to enter the United States. An applicant for a wartime visa had to provide the names of two American sponsors before submitting six copies of a form that measured four feet in length. As a result, only 10 percent of America's immigration quotas were met during World War II, leaving almost 200,000 slots unfilled. In addition, the War Department claimed that rail lines leading to the death camps were targets too dangerous and too far away to bomb. Yet in 1944, Allied bombers flew hundreds of missions within a 35-mile radius of Auschwitz. The government's lack of action cost thousands of lives.

INTRODUCE & ENGAGE

CONNECT TO TODAY

On the board, write the word *refugee* in the center of a Word Web. **ASK:** What words and phrases come to mind when you hear this word? As students offer their ideas, add them to the web. Explain that in this lesson they will learn how the United States handled the issue of European refugees during World War II.

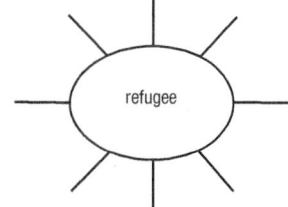

TEACH

GUIDED DISCUSSION

1. **Evaluate** Do you think claims that they might be spies was a valid reason for denying refugees entry into the United States during World War II and that it continues to be valid today? Explain your reasoning. *(Answers will vary. Possible response: No—during World War II, the government knew that most refugees had endured suffering and were seeking safety, a situation that also applies to many refugees seeking asylum today.)*

2. **Determine Chronology** How much time elapsed between the Allies' declaration recognizing the genocide of European Jews and the creation of Roosevelt's War Refuge Board? *(official declaration: December 1942; War Refugee Board: January 1944 = 13 months)*

VIRTUAL MUSEUM VISIT

The United States Holocaust Memorial Museum in Washington, D.C., is "a living memorial to the Holocaust." Its mission is the prevention of genocide. The museum works with professionals in many segments of society to provide insight into how to protect democratic values and confront hate. Access the museum's website and find "The Holocaust: A Learning Site for Students." Suggest that students browse the ID cards and discuss how receiving such a card would personalize the events of the Holocaust for a visitor. Then access the "Voyage of the *St. Louis*" feature and have students read it. **ASK:** What does this incident reveal about the U.S. response to the plight of the refugees?

ACTIVE OPTIONS

On Your Feet: History Roundtable Divide the class into groups of four. Tell each group to move desks together to form a table where they can all sit. Hand each group a sheet of paper containing the following question: What social and political impacts did the Holocaust have? The first student in each group should write an answer, read it aloud, and pass the paper clockwise to the next student. The paper should circulate around the table until students run out of answers.

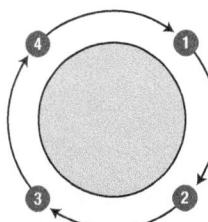

NG Learning Framework: Create a Time Line

| ATTITUDE | Responsibility |
| KNOWLEDGE | Our Human Story |

Ask students to conduct research to determine the Roosevelt administration's response to the plight of European Jews and the response of Jewish organizations that were trying to help. Instruct students to work in pairs to create an annotated time line, beginning when the administration first learned of the Holocaust and ending with the trials at Nuremberg. Students can then compare their time lines.

DIFFERENTIATE

ENGLISH LANGUAGE LEARNERS `ELD`

Use Terms in Sentences Pair students at the **Emerging** level with those at the **Bridging** or **Expanding** level. Direct partners to take turns creating sentences for the Key Vocabulary terms *atrocities* and *tribunal*. You may want to expand the exercise to other words from the lesson, such as *defendants, aggression, exterminated, guilt, propaganda, ghastly,* and *witnessed.* Invite pairs to share their sentences and discuss different ways to use each word.

GIFTED & TALENTED

Create a Multimedia Presentation Direct students to create a multimedia presentation using first-person accounts of life before, during, and after the Holocaust. Instruct students to find and use written, audio, and video testimonies collected by organizations such as the World Holocaust Remembrance Center (Yad Vashem), the United States Holocaust Memorial Museum, and the Illinois Holocaust Museum and Education Center. If possible, have students find first-person accounts that establish what life was like (1) in a Jewish community before the Holocaust, (2) in Jewish ghettos during the war, (3) in concentration camps, and (4) during and after liberation. Invite students to share their finished multimedia presentations with the class.

See the Chapter Planner for more strategies for differentiation.

HISTORICAL THINKING

ANSWERS

1. Wallenberg set up hospitals, soup kitchens, and safe houses and also issued certificates of protection and Swedish passports to keep Hungarian Jews safe.

2. Possible response: It showed that the Allies were nations that relied on justice and that even those accused of the most heinous crimes deserve a fair trial to determine true guilt or innocence.

3. Possible response: He meant that we can take steps to free the victims of oppression and that if we do not, our own experience of freedom will be less for it.

VOCABULARY

Use each of the following vocabulary words in a sentence that shows an understanding of the term's meaning.

1. **atomic bomb**
   The atomic bomb caused firestorms and released radioactivity in Hiroshima and Nagasaki, resulting in thousands of casualties.

2. **wage discrimination**

3. **Holocaust**

4. **infamy**

5. **ration**

6. **concentration camp**

7. **kamikaze**

8. **internment camp**

READING STRATEGY
DETERMINE CHRONOLOGY

When you determine chronology, you place events in the order in which they occurred and note correlations between events. Use a time line like this one to order the key events in America's involvement in World War II. Then answer the question.

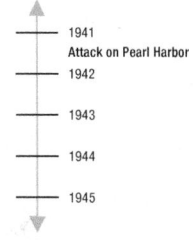

— 1941
Attack on Pearl Harbor

— 1942

— 1943

— 1944

— 1945

9. What events in 1945 led the United States to drop two atomic bombs on Japan?

MAIN IDEAS

Answer the following questions. Support your answers with evidence from the chapter.

10. Why did President Roosevelt order General MacArthur to leave the Philippines? **LESSON 1.1**

11. How did the experience of war impact California demographically, economically, socially, and politically? **LESSON 1.2**

12. What advantages did American-built Sherman tanks have over German panzers? **LESSON 2.1**

13. What unique impact did James Doolittle's raid on Tokyo have on Americans and the Japanese? **LESSON 2.2**

14. What postwar plans for Europe did Roosevelt, Churchill, and Stalin draw up at the Yalta Conference? **LESSON 3.1**

15. How did America win the war in the Pacific? **LESSON 3.2**

16. How did Roosevelt respond to Hitler's atrocities against Jewish people? **LESSON 4.2**

HISTORICAL THINKING

Answer the following questions. Support your answers with evidence from the chapter.

17. **MAKE INFERENCES** Why do you think Norman Rockwell chose to illustrate the four freedoms from Roosevelt's speech as scenes from everyday life?

18. **SYNTHESIZE** How did World War II serve to advance movements for equality at home and abroad?

19. **DRAW CONCLUSIONS** How did the American government change because of World War II?

20. **COMPARE AND CONTRAST** How was the war mobilized and fought differently in the Atlantic versus the Pacific?

21. **FORM AND SUPPORT OPINIONS** Do you think President Roosevelt and the Allies should have bombed death camps and railroads in Poland, or were they right to prioritize ending the war quickly? Explain your answer.

INTERPRET VISUALS

In 1942, the U.S. War Production Board published this poster to encourage Americans to contribute scrap—in this case, discarded pieces of metal, rubber, and clothing—to the war effort. Study the poster, and then answer the questions that follow.

YOUR SCRAP
...brought it down

KEEP SCRAPPING
Rubber · Metal · Rags

GIVE TO A COLLECTOR,
SALVAGE DEPOT OR SELL TO A DEALER

22. According to the poster, what did contributions of scrap bring down?

23. Why might the poster have inspired Americans to contribute scrap?

ANALYZE SOURCES

Lawson Inada's collection *Only What We Could Carry* provides firsthand accounts of the Japanese American experience during World War II, including oral histories of Japanese servicemen. The collection includes *Citizen 13660* by Miné Okubo, a Japanese American who was relocated during the war. In this excerpt from *Citizen 13660*, Okubo describes the train ride from the assembly center near San Francisco to the internment camp.

> The trip was a nightmare that lasted two nights and a day. The train creaked with age. It was covered with dust, and as the gaslights failed to function properly we traveled in complete darkness most of the night. All the shades were drawn and we were not allowed to look out of the windows. Many became train sick and vomited. The children cried from restlessness.

24. What details does Okubo use to convey the frightening journey?

CONNECT TO YOUR LIFE

25. **ARGUMENT** Before the attack on Pearl Harbor, many Americans did not want to get involved in World War II. Do you think the United States was ultimately right to go to war? Or do you believe that war is never justified? Write a paragraph in which you make an argument for or against going to war.

TIPS

- State your position about whether the country was right to go to war.
- Explain what, if any, circumstances make war justifiable.
- Use information from the chapter to help support your ideas.
- Address any counterarguments.
- Conclude your argument with a sentence summarizing your position.

VOCABULARY ANSWERS

1. The atomic bomb caused firestorms and released radioactivity in Hiroshima and Nagasaki, resulting in thousands of casualties.

2. Despite their contributions to the defense industries, women still suffered from wage discrimination.

3. Many wondered why the U.S. government had not done more to stop Nazi atrocities during the Holocaust.

4. Bombings, genocide, and terrorism are acts of infamy that have led to international condemnation, war, and criminal trials.

5. The government's decision to ration gas caused people to cut back on driving.

6. Until the Nuremberg trials, many people had no idea of the horrors that took place in concentration camps.

7. Japanese kamikaze destroyed more than 30 U.S. ships by crashing their planes into them.

8. Following Pearl Harbor, many Japanese Americans on the West Coast were confined to internment camps.

READING STRATEGY ANSWER

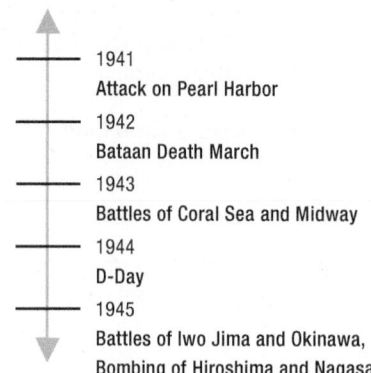

— 1941
Attack on Pearl Harbor

— 1942
Bataan Death March

— 1943
Battles of Coral Sea and Midway

— 1944
D-Day

— 1945
Battles of Iwo Jima and Okinawa, Bombing of Hiroshima and Nagasaki

9. Possible response: Heavy losses in the battles of Iwo Jima and Okinawa led President Truman to worry about the additional loss of American lives that would result from an invasion of Japan. When Japan refused to surrender unconditionally, Truman decided to drop atomic bombs on two Japanese cities to force a surrender.

MAIN IDEAS ANSWERS

10. President Roosevelt wanted to ensure General MacArthur was safe as Japanese troops continued to attack the U.S. Armed Forces in the Far East.

11. California benefited economically and politically from the defense-related industries and military bases located in the state. This, in turn, led to social and demographic changes as people moved to the state to find employment or came from Mexico through the Bracero Program.

12. Though Sherman tanks had less substantial armor than panzers, they were more agile in battle conditions.

13. The raid gave Americans new confidence and helped set the stage for the war in the Pacific. It also damaged Japanese morale by proving the nation was vulnerable.

14. The three leaders agreed to divide Germany into different occupational zones, take control of or destroy German arms industries, try German war criminals, and establish a reparations commission. They also began talks on setting Poland's geographic boundaries, holding free elections, and establishing the United Nations.

15. The Allies closed in on Japan by liberating the Philippines and winning the battles of Iwo Jima and Okinawa. Ultimately America won the war by dropping atomic bombs on Hiroshima and Nagasaki, thus forcing Japan to surrender.

16. After being pressured by government officials and American Jewish organizations, President Roosevelt created the War Refugee Board, which helped finance the rescue of Jews in Europe.

HISTORICAL THINKING ANSWERS

17. Possible response: Rockwell selected images that Americans could relate to on a personal level. This made it easier for people to empathize with others around the world who were seeking the same freedoms.

18. Possible response: The war gave women the opportunity to work in industries they had never worked in before, such as the defense industry. Also, many women began working outside of the home for the first time in their lives. Women also entered the military as WACs, WAVES, and WASPs. African Americans, Japanese Americans, and Native Americans had their own roles in the military, fighting in special squadrons in Europe and Asia and serving as Code Talkers to transmit secret information.

19. Possible response: The American government took a much more active role in shaping the economy and society. For example, it established the War Production Board, created the Office of Price Administration, and sponsored the Bracero Program. The president also issued executive orders to enhance public safety and security, often at the expense of the rights and freedoms of some groups of Americans and immigrants.

20. In Europe, the troops mainly fought a ground war using armor and artillery in battle. The war in the Pacific relied heavily on aircraft carriers, battleships, submarines, and air support to island hop as the Allies closed in on Japan.

21. Answers will vary, but students should cite text evidence to support their opinions. Supporters of prioritizing the war's end might argue that bombing the death camps would have put prisoners in danger. Conversely, those opposed to this strategy might argue that waiting enabled the Nazis to kill more prisoners and to destroy evidence.

INTERPRET VISUALS ANSWERS

22. Scrap contributions brought down German war planes.

23. Because the poster illustrates a direct tie between donated scrap and the downing of a German war plane, it would have made Americans feel inspired to contribute scrap to help win the war.

ANALYZE SOURCES ANSWER

24. Possible response: Okubo details the creaking, dusty train cloaked in darkness; the drawn shades; people's sickness; and children's fear and restlessness.

CONNECT TO YOUR LIFE ANSWER

25. Answers will vary but should include a clear position, use at least two vocabulary words from the chapter, and address any counterarguments.

UNIT 7 RESOURCES

UNIT INTRODUCTION

UNIT TIME LINE

UNIT WRAP-UP

NATIONAL GEOGRAPHIC | CONNECTION

National Geographic Magazine
Adapted Articles
- "America's Propaganda Machine"
- "Dogs at War" ONLINE

Unit 7 Inquiry: Persuade an Audience

NG Learning Framework Activities
- Write About a Cold War Advance
- Debate the Origins of the Cold War

Unit 7 Formal Assessment

CHAPTER 23 RESOURCES

Available at NGLSync.Cengage.com

TEACHER RESOURCES & ASSESSMENT

Reading and Note-Taking

Vocabulary Practice

Document-Based Question Template

Social Studies Skills Lessons
- Reading: Synthesize
- Writing: Narrative

Formal Assessment
- Chapter 23 Pretest
- Chapter 23 Tests A & B
- Section Quizzes

Chapter 23 Answer Key

ExamView®
  One-time Download

STUDENT DIGITAL RESOURCES

- eEdition
- Handbooks
- Online Atlas
- American Gallery Online
- History Notebook
- Active History
- American Voices (Biographies)
- Literature Analysis
- Projects for Inquiry-Based Learning

Chapter 23 Spanish Resources are available at NGLSync.Cengage.com.

AMERICAN STORIES ONLINE — Cold War Spy Technology

- Study Primary Sources: Excerpt of a Report to President Eisenhower, 1954
- On Your Feet: Create a Diagram

NG Learning Framework:
Design Spy Technology

SECTION 1 RESOURCES
THE IRON CURTAIN

LESSON 1.1
Europe Rebuilds

- On Your Feet: Word Chain

NG Learning Framework:
Explore the Geneva Conventions

LESSON 1.2
The Soviet Threat

- Active History: Compare Cold War Enemies

NG Learning Framework:
Examine Life in East and West Berlin

LESSON 1.3
DOCUMENT-BASED QUESTION
The Cold War Begins

- On Your Feet: Use a Jigsaw Strategy

LESSON 1.4
Truman's Fair Deal

- On Your Feet: Inside-Outside Circle

NG Learning Framework:
Examine Desegregation of the Armed Forces

SECTION 2 RESOURCES
CONFRONTING COMMUNISM

LESSON 2.1
Escalating Tensions

- On Your Feet: Question and Answer

NG Learning Framework:
Investigate Weapons Development

LESSON 2.2
Cold War Around the Globe

- On Your Feet: Rotating Discussion

NG Learning Framework:
Compare Declarations of Independence

LESSON 2.3
The Korean War

AMERICAN GALLERY ONLINE — The Korean War

NG Learning Framework:
Review Personal Stories

SECTION 3 RESOURCES
McCARTHY AND DOMESTIC TENSION

LESSON 3.1
The Red Scare Continues

- On Your Feet: Three-Step Interview

NG Learning Framework:
Research Loyalty Oaths

LESSON 3.2
The Rise of McCarthyism

- On Your Feet: Turn and Talk on Topic

NG Learning Framework:
Evaluate Points of View

American Voices Biography
Dalton Trumbo and Joseph McCarthy
ONLINE

CHAPTER 23 REVIEW

STRIVING READERS

STRATEGY 1
CREATE IDEA WEBS

Have students summarize the chapter by creating three Idea Webs. They should write *Iron Curtain* in the center of the first Idea Web, *Communism* in the second one, and *McCarthyism* in the third. Ask students to complete each Idea Web with relevant information from each lesson.

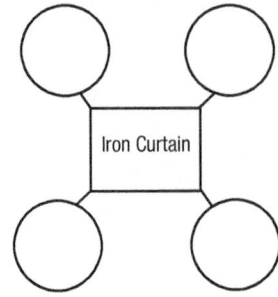

Use with All Lessons *For example, for the Iron Curtain web, students could add information about occupation zones, containment, the Soviet threat, the Cold War, and the Berlin airlift.*

STRATEGY 2
MAKE A TOP FIVE FACTS LIST

Assign a lesson to be read. After reading, have students write in their own words five important facts that they have learned. Tell students to meet with a partner to compare lists and consolidate the two lists into one final list. Call on students to offer facts from their lists.

Use with All Lessons *Throughout the chapter, help students get in the habit of making lists of facts as they read.*

STRATEGY 3
USE A TASKS APPROACH

Help students get information from visuals by using the following TASKS strategy.

    T Look for a **title** that may give the main idea.

    A **Ask** yourself what the visual is trying to show.

    S Determine how any **symbols** are used.

    K Look for a **key** or legend

    S **Summarize** what you learned.

Use with Lessons 1.1, 1.2, 1.4, 2.1–2.3, and 3.1 *Suggest that students use the TASKS strategy to analyze the graphs in Lessons 1.1 and 2.1, the maps in Lessons 1.2 and 2.1–2.3, and the posters in Lessons 1.4 and 3.1.*

INCLUSION

STRATEGY 1
USE SUPPORTED READING

Arrange students in pairs and have them read the chapter aloud lesson by lesson. Instruct them to stop at the end of each lesson and use these sentence frames to monitor their comprehension of the text:

- This lesson is mostly about _____.
- Other topics in this lesson are _____.
- One question I have about the lesson is _____.
- One of the vocabulary words is _____. It means _____.
- One word I do not recognize is _____.
- I don't think I understand _____.

Use with All Lessons

STRATEGY 2
PROVIDE AUDIO SUPPORT

Decide which of the terms and names are important for mastery and ask a volunteer to record the pronunciation and a short sentence defining each. Encourage students to listen to the recording as often as necessary.

Use with All Lessons *You might also use the recordings to quiz students on their mastery of terms and names. Play one definition at a time from the recording and ask students to identify the term or name described.*

ENGLISH LANGUAGE LEARNERS

STRATEGY 1
USE KEY VOCABULARY IN A SENTENCE

Pair students at the **Emerging** level with students at the **Expanding** or **Bridging** levels and tell them to work together to compose a sentence using selected Key Vocabulary words. Have the more proficient students assist the others in checking the accuracy of their sentences. Invite pairs to share their sentences and discuss different ways to use each word.

Use with All Lessons

STRATEGY 2
COMPOSE CAPTIONS

Pair students at the **Emerging** and **Expanding** levels with English-proficient students. Have students cover the photograph captions and work together to write an original and accurate caption for each.

Use with Lessons 1.1, 1.2, 2.1, 3.1, and 3.2 *You may wish to invite pairs to compare their captions with those in the lesson and with those written by other pairs.*

STRATEGY 3
ASK EITHER/OR QUESTIONS

Monitor students' comprehension of the lesson by asking them to answer Either/Or questions. After students have answered the questions, pair students at the **Emerging** level with students at the **Bridging** level and ask them to work together to check their answers.

- To defeat Nazi Germany and Imperial Japan, did the United States and the Soviet Union fight with or against each other? *(with)*

- After World War II ended, did the Soviet army withdraw from or stay in Eastern European countries? *(stay in)*

- Was Berlin in the Soviet-controlled or the Western-controlled part of Germany? *(Soviet-controlled)*

- Did President Truman act upon the policy of containment to fight communism in the Soviet Union or in the Mediterranean? *(the Mediterranean)*

Use with Lesson 1.2

GIFTED & TALENTED

STRATEGY 1
DESIGN AN INFOGRAPHIC

Guide students to conduct additional research about the impact of the United Nations and its programs after World War II to the present day. Then instruct students to use what they learn to create an infographic that uses data and other visual information to show the impact of several United Nations programs over time. Invite students to compare their infographics and generate a master list of programs and their impacts.

Use with Lesson 1.1

STRATEGY 2
WRITE AND PERFORM A SKIT

Invite students to use a variety of documents to deepen their understanding of the frictions that developed between communist nations in the Soviet bloc and capitalist nations in the Western bloc. Have students choose one event to illustrate such frictions and use it as the basis for a short skit. Allow time for students to prepare and practice before performing their skit for the class.

Use with Lessons 1.2, 1.3, and 2.1–2.3

PRE-AP

STRATEGY 1
TEACH A CLASS

Before beginning the chapter, allow students to choose one of the lessons listed below and prepare to teach the content to the class. Give them a set amount of time in which to present their lesson. Suggest that students think about any visuals or activities they will want to use when they teach.

Use with Lessons 1.4, 3.1, and 3.2

STRATEGY 2
ANALYZE EFFECTS

Tell students to work individually or in pairs to research and analyze ways that McCarthyism impacted American society, politics, and culture during the 1940s and 1950s. After students do preliminary research, instruct them to narrow the scope of their analysis. You may suggest that they focus on one of the following aspects of McCarthyism:

- political impact (Communists and people on the left)

- social impact (homosexuals)

- cultural impact (writers, artists, and filmmakers)

Suggest that students use a Cause-Effect Organizer to display the results of their investigation and analysis.

Use with Lessons 3.1 and 3.2

THE COLD WAR AND KOREA 1945–1960

HISTORICAL THINKING What impact did communism have on the United States and the rest of the world?

"Peace must be built upon **power.**"

—President Harry S. Truman

CRITICAL VIEWING The Korean War Veterans Memorial on the National Mall in Washington, D.C., dedicated in 1995, includes 19 stainless steel figures representing all branches of the U.S. armed forces. The ponchos they are wearing indicate the extreme weather conditions the soldiers faced in Korea. How do the statues convey the tension and uncertainty the soldiers experienced?

822 CHAPTER 23

The Cold War and Korea 823

INTRODUCE THE PHOTOGRAPH

THE KOREAN WAR VETERANS MEMORIAL

Have students read the quotation from President Truman. **ASK:** What do you think President Truman meant by peace being built upon power? *(Possible response: Truman meant that a nation must have military power to help keep the peace.)* Tell students to examine the photograph. **ASK:** How does the quotation from President Truman connect to the figures in the photograph of the Korean War Veterans Memorial? *(Possible response: The figures of the soldiers represent a strong military, the means by which a nation demonstrates its power.)*

SHARE BACKGROUND

In 1986, Congress authorized a memorial to honor veterans of the Korean War. Sculptor Frank C. Gaylord II spent five years creating the work he called "The Column." In addition to the realistic figures of steel with wind-blown ponchos frozen in motion, the memorial includes a highly reflective granite slab that displays 2,400 images of military equipment and service men and women culled from actual photos taken during the war. A reflecting pool—the "Pool of Remembrance"—includes a stone wall jutting into the water to represent the peninsula of Korea. A poignant quotation is inscribed on the wall: "Freedom is not free."

CRITICAL VIEWING The tension in the faces of the figures ranges from impassive disbelief (slack jaw and staring eyes on face in the foreground) to weariness (expressionless profile in middle ground). Uncertainty is conveyed through the posture of the figures, each head turned watchfully in a different direction, suggesting danger on all sides.

For Chapter 23 Spanish Resources, visit the Resources Menu. Chapter 23 Resources are available at NGLSync.Cengage.com.

What impact did communism have on the United States and the rest of the world?

Jigsaw Activity: Preview Content This activity will help students preview and make predictions about the topics covered in Chapter 23. Divide the class into three groups. Assign one of the section titles to each group and have them discuss what they think they will learn. Ask students to consider the following questions:

Group 1 Section 1 is about the United States and the Soviet Union facing off after World War II. Why might two allies who worked together to defeat Germany become adversaries so quickly?

Group 2 Section 2 is about the escalation of the arms race between the United States and the Soviets, China's turn to communism, and the Korean War. Why might the United States and the Soviet Union choose to confront each other in a foreign war?

Group 3 Section 3 is about the growing fear of communist influence in the United States. What could have caused Americans to be susceptible to overblown claims of communism infiltrating U.S. culture and government after World War II?

Regroup students so each new grouping has at least one member from each original group. Have students share what they predicted about their assigned section so that the other students in the new group can learn what they might expect from reading Chapter 23.

INTRODUCE THE READING STRATEGY

SYNTHESIZE

Explain that synthesizing information involves reading and absorbing facts and evidence, making connections with what is already known, and arriving at a new idea or understanding. Turn to the Chapter Review and preview the chart with students. As they read the chapter, have students use the chart to gain a clearer understanding of the Cold War and the Korean War.

KEY DATES FOR CHAPTER 23

1945	World War II ends
1946	George F. Kennan lays out containment doctrine
1947	Truman proposes Truman Doctrine
1948	Soviets begin Berlin blockade
1949	Germany divided and Cold War begins
1949	Truman introduces Fair Deal agenda
1949	NATO formed
1950	North Korea invades South Korea
1950–1954	Era of McCarthyism
1953	Korean War ends with a truce

INTRODUCE CHAPTER VOCABULARY

KEY VOCABULARY

SECTION 1

containment	liberal consensus	rural electrification
GI Bill	Marshall Plan	white-collar
iron curtain	occupation zone	

SECTION 2

aerospace industry	domino theory	military-industrial complex
arms race	government-in-exile	proxy war
demilitarized zone	hydrogen bomb	

SECTION 3

loyalty oath	McCarthyism	subversion

DEFINITION CHART

As they read the chapter, have students complete a Definition Chart for Key Vocabulary. Ask students to list the Key Vocabulary terms in the far left column of their chart. Then, as they encounter each term in the chapter, tell them to write its definition in the center column and what it means using their own words in the far right column. Model an example for students on the board using the graphic organizer below.

Word	Definition	In My Own Words
subversion	the act of secretly undermining something in an attempt to destroy it	when a person or a group of people plot to ruin something without anyone else knowing about it

AMERICAN STORIES ONLINE

For instructional support for the online American Story "Cold War Spy Technology," go to NGLSync.Cengage.com.

EUROPE REBUILDS

When a powerful storm destroys buildings, people rebuild and try to make them stronger. Following the war, the United States and its allies worked to rebuild war-torn Europe and to strengthen international cooperation in order to keep the horrors of World War II from happening again.

THE UNITED NATIONS

In the autumn of 1945, the world sighed with relief. The guns were silent. Peace had arrived. As World War II ended, the Allies turned their attention to building a lasting peace. As you have read, early in the war, a number of nations signed on to the Atlantic Charter, which promoted the ideals of democracy and mutual respect among nations. The Allies acted on these ideals to create the **United Nations (UN)**, a global organization promoting cooperation among nations and working together to resolve conflicts peacefully. On October 24, 1945, the required 28 nations had ratified the organization's charter, and the United Nations became a reality. By the end of the year, it had a total of 52 member nations.

While the main focus of the United Nations was to promote international peace, it also worked proactively to help promote economic development, social progress, and human rights around the world. Officials created a number of smaller organizations within the UN to support these goals. The **United Nations Educational, Scientific, and Cultural Organization (UNESCO)** was created in 1945 to rebuild schools, libraries, and museums that had been destroyed during World War II. The **UN Commission on Human Rights**, established in 1946, aimed to protect fundamental human rights and freedoms around the world. And in 1948, the United Nations established the **World Health Organization (WHO)** to promote health worldwide.

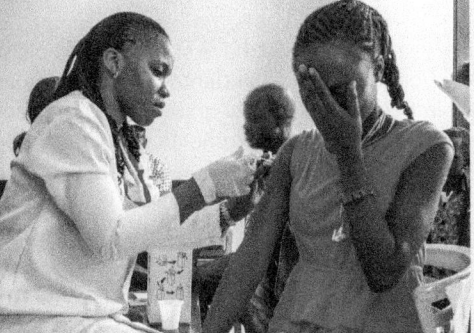

A GLOBAL PERSPECTIVE
In 2016, the World Health Organization worked with local authorities in Angola and the Democratic Republic of the Congo (DRC) to vaccinate 30 million citizens against yellow fever.

In this photo, a nurse vaccinates a young woman at a clinic in Kinshasa, the capital of the DRC. Yellow fever causes severe flu symptoms and in some cases can be fatal. Nearly 1,000 cases of the disease had been confirmed in the 2 countries before the end of the outbreak was declared in July 2016.

In addition to establishing a much-needed structure of organizations to rebuild and promote peace, the United Nations also formally documented basic human rights. In 1948, the UN adopted its **Universal Declaration of Human Rights**, which set out the fundamental rights of all people of all nations. These rights include freedom of thought and religion as well as freedom of expression and the right to assemble peacefully.

Several other organizations were created after the war to help battle-scarred nations recover economically. Proposed in 1944, the **International Monetary Fund** was officially established in 1945 to standardize worldwide financial relations and rates of exchange between countries. Its purpose is to safeguard and stabilize the global monetary system. The **World Bank** was founded in 1944 to provide financial support to countries that needed to rebuild after World War II. The **General Agreement on Tariffs and Trade (GATT)** was launched in 1947 and created rules for world trade.

In addition to working toward a lasting peace, the United States and its allies also sought to make any future wars more humane and just. In 1949, a number of nations agreed to the **Geneva Conventions**. This was the collective name of a revised set of three earlier treaties establishing rules for the humane treatment of prisoners of war as well as wounded or sick soldiers. Nations created and agreed to a fourth treaty that called for fair treatment and protection of civilians living in and around war zones.

THE MARSHALL PLAN

Across Europe, from Germany to Poland and the Soviet Union, the destruction from World War II was immense. Rail lines lay in ruin, roads were impassable, and major parts of cities were piles of rubble. Economies were no longer functioning, and the threat of mass starvation hung over the continent. In contrast, the United States had emerged from the war as the world's strongest economic and military power. The United States was determined to rebuild Europe and keep its economy from collapsing.

In June 1947, U.S. Secretary of State George C. Marshall proposed a massive financial aid plan he called the **European Recovery Program**. Marshall assured Europeans that it was a helping hand and not a way for the United States to control the continent. "Our policy is not directed against any country or doctrine," Marshall said, "but against hunger, poverty, desperation, and fear." Most Americans agreed and broke from their isolationist past. As citizens of the

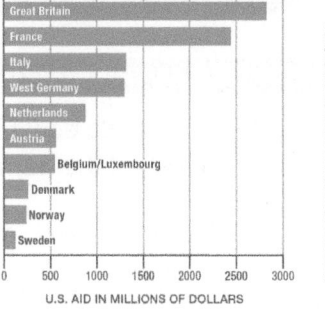

The Marshall Plan

[Bar chart titled "The Marshall Plan" showing U.S. aid in millions of dollars for: Great Britain, France, Italy, West Germany, Netherlands, Austria, Belgium/Luxembourg, Denmark, Norway, Sweden. X-axis: 0, 500, 1000, 1500, 2000, 2500, 3000]

U.S. AID IN MILLIONS OF DOLLARS

Source: Nicholas Crafts (2011), "The Marshall Plan: A Reality Check"

wealthiest and most powerful nation, they accepted the idea that they had some responsibility to keep the peace and help countries rebuild. Congress granted the billions of dollars needed to fund the proposal, which became known as the "**Marshall Plan**," and committed more than 10 percent of the U.S. federal budget to restore Europe's economic health.

As the Marshall Plan came together, the nations of Europe, including the Soviet Union, met to assess their common needs. But the Soviets soon walked out. They objected to giving critical Soviet economic information to outsiders. The Soviets also believed that accepting aid from capitalist countries might undermine their communist system. With the Soviets out, the Marshall Plan targeted mainly Western Europe. In the end, the program proved to be a tremendous success. It helped to rebuild Britain, Germany, and France and restore economic confidence to many European nations. Helping rebuild Europe also increased American trade and investment in Europe, creating new markets for U.S. goods.

HISTORICAL THINKING

1. **READING CHECK** What are the main goals of the United Nations?

2. **DRAW CONCLUSIONS** What might the Soviet Union's response to the Marshall Plan meeting have indicated about the potential for tension with the United States?

3. **INTERPRET GRAPHS** In total, how much did the Marshall Plan give to the top three aid recipients?

PLAN: 2-PAGE LESSON

OBJECTIVE

Analyze efforts to rebuild Europe and create a framework for diplomacy and peace after World War II.

CRITICAL THINKING SKILLS FOR LESSON 1.1

- Draw Conclusions
- Interpret Graphs
- Form and Support Opinions
- Make Connections

HISTORICAL THINKING FOR CHAPTER 23

What impact did communism have on the United States and the rest of the world? The growth of communism after the war altered East-West relationships forever. Lesson 1.1 looks at the rebuilding of Europe via the Marshall Plan and the creation of international diplomatic organizations, such as the United Nations, that were intended to reduce the risk of another world war.

BACKGROUND FOR THE TEACHER

General George Marshall became Secretary of State in 1947 after a highly distinguished career in the U.S. Army. Many members of Congress initially opposed the $27 billion budget that Marshall requested for his European Recovery Program, but a reduced budget of under $13 billion was passed in 1948. The economic benefits Marshall predicted soon bore fruit. As countries rebuilt their war-torn cities and economies, the standard of living began to rise, economic confidence throughout Europe grew stronger, and the United States gained more stable and wealthy trading partners for American goods. These strengthened trade markets helped fuel America's increasingly robust postwar economy. As demand for products grew at home and abroad, more Americans found work and saw their own standard of living increase.

INTRODUCE & ENGAGE

CREATE A PRIORITY LIST

Print and display photographs of destroyed areas of London, Berlin, and Dresden, or have students locate photographs online. Discuss the level of destruction evidenced in them. Explain that after the war ended, many local governments had to organize the rebuilding of their towns, homes, economies, and infrastructure. Ask students the following questions: What would your priorities be to help your town get back to normal? What would you want to do first? Whose help might you enlist? Call on volunteers and write their responses on the board. Ask each student the rationale for his or her suggestion. Then have the class prioritize the first 10 things a town would need to do. After reading the lesson, revisit students' responses and ask what changes, if any, they would make to the list.

TEACH

GUIDED DISCUSSION

1. **Form and Support Opinions** Do you think the Marshall Plan was a successful investment for the United States to make after World War II? Explain your answer. *(Answers will vary. Possible response: Even though it was expensive, the Marshall Plan was a good investment because it helped European countries severely damaged in the war get back on their feet quickly. It also helped create additional trade markets for U.S. goods, which helped America's economy after the war.)*

2. **Make Connections** How have the combined efforts of United Nations institutions, such as the International Monetary Fund (IMF) and the World Bank, and agreements, such as the General Agreement on Tariffs and Trade (GATT) and the Universal Declaration of Human Rights, worked to maintain peace and international order since the end of World War II? *(Answers will vary. Possible response: The IMF, the World Bank, and GATT make it easier for countries around the world to do business under some clear rules and guidelines, thus diminishing the potential for conflict.)*

GLOBAL PERSPECTIVE

Direct students' attention to the photograph of the nurse vaccinating the young woman. **ASK:** Based on the photograph, how does the World Health Organization reflect the mission of the United Nations? *(By addressing health issues on a global scale, the UN supports human rights and social progress.)* Why do you think the WHO continues to be one of the most positive and respected UN programs? *(The WHO helps people across the planet by bringing medical and health professionals together from around the world to work on causes beneficial to all people.)* Discuss with the class other international humanitarian organizations they may know of and explore why such organizations are able to cross physical and political borders.

ACTIVE OPTIONS

On Your Feet: Word Chain Arrange students in three lines. Hand a piece of paper to the first person in each line with one of these terms from the text: Geneva Conventions, Declaration of Human Rights, UNESCO. The first student in line adds a word to the list that relates to the original word or term. Students pass the paper from person to person, each one adding a word or phrase they associate with the term from the text. Ask a volunteer from each group to read the Word Chain. Ask the rest of the class to listen for any words that were used in more than one chain or that may not connect to the original word or term.

NG Learning Framework: Explore the Geneva Conventions

ATTITUDE Curiosity

SKILL Observation

Divide the class into small groups and tell students to research the specific protections described in the Geneva Conventions of 1949 and to explain specific wartime actions on which the protection is based. Have one member from each group share the findings with the class. Then discuss with the whole class why they think the United States continues to support the Geneva Conventions.

DIFFERENTIATE

STRIVING READERS

Chart UN Organizations Tell students to create a chart with the headings Cultural Programs, Human Health and Human Rights Programs, and Economic Programs and to write the names of UN programs under the correct heading. Tell students to add a sentence about each program's purpose. Encourage students to compare charts and sentences with each other.

PRE-AP

Write a Problem-Solution Essay Have students conduct research in order to write an essay about one of the postwar problems that the United Nations or the United States sought to solve as they aided in efforts to rebuild cities in Europe. Encourage students to keep track of what they learn through their research by taking notes in a Problem-and-Solution Organizer. Remind students to cite their sources. Invite volunteers to share their essays with the class.

See the Chapter Planner for more strategies for differentiation.

HISTORICAL THINKING

ANSWERS

1. The main goals of the United Nations are to support international peace and provide a system for nations to resolve disputes without warfare. In addition, the UN also promotes economic development, social progress, and human rights around the world.

2. The Soviets walked out on the Marshall Plan meeting because they did not want to reveal information about their economy, and they didn't want to take money from capitalist nations. This might have indicated that tensions going forward might result from the dichotomy of capitalist and communist policies that divide the Soviets from Western Europe and the United States.

3. The Marshall Plan gave the top three aid recipients approximately $6.5 billion dollars.

MAIN IDEA Sharp divisions between Western capitalist countries, led by the United States, and communist countries, led by the Soviet Union, created a new threat to world peace.

THE SOVIET THREAT

Did you ever work with someone you didn't like in order to win a game or complete a project? The United States and the Soviet Union put aside their differences to help win World War II—but then their differences re-emerged and ushered in a new struggle.

THE DIVISION OF EUROPE

The Allies had fought hard together to defeat Nazi Germany and Imperial Japan, and the Soviet Union had been essential to that effort. Soon, however, relations between the Soviets and the West began to decline. As you have read, President Franklin Roosevelt, Soviet Premier Joseph Stalin, and British Prime Minister Winston Churchill met at Yalta in 1945 to make plans for postwar Europe. The leaders had difficulty reaching any agreements. Underlying the rift was a vast difference between the political and economic structures of the United States and Soviet Union.

The disagreement was based on differing visions of government and economic policy. The United States and Great Britain wanted capitalist democratic governments established throughout Europe. Capitalism is an economic system in which private individuals or groups own the resources and produce goods for a profit. In contrast, Stalin wanted the Soviet Union to dominate the internal affairs of its Eastern European neighbors, controlling them under a communist regime, where all economic resources are owned by the state. In addition, the Soviets wanted to spread communism to other nations. The fundamental differences between communism and capitalism would shape the relationship between the United States and the Soviet Union for decades to come.

By the war's end, Soviet forces had occupied much of Eastern Europe, creating suspicion of communism among Western countries. Instead of withdrawing, the Soviet Army stayed, and Stalin installed communist rule throughout the region.

"Glory to the Russian people—the *bogatyr* people, the creator people!" is the message on this Soviet propaganda poster created by Viktor Ivanov in 1947. The man in front is a Russian engineer, a symbol of Soviet postwar industrial growth, and the towering figure standing behind him is a *bogatyr*, a Russian medieval hero. The intention of the poster is to motivate the working masses, the new "heroes" of Soviet nationalism.

By 1947, Stalin had created a ring of communist "satellite states" around the Soviet Union that became known as the **Eastern Bloc**. These Soviet-style communist governments suppressed political opposition, using the brutal methods employed by Stalin and his Soviet secret police. When the slightest stirrings of political independence arose in Eastern Europe, Soviet officials removed key people from power, imprisoned opponents, and in some instances, executed perceived "rebels."

The defeated nation of Germany was a special case. In the summer of 1945, the victors—the United States, Great Britain, France, and the Soviet Union—split Germany into four allied **occupation zones**. The eastern part of Germany became an occupation zone ruled by the Soviet Union. The western part was split into three occupation zones, with the United States, Great Britain, and France each controlling a zone. Berlin, Germany's capital, was entirely within the Soviet occupation zone, but it was governed by a joint agency of all four nations.

In 1946, the Americans and British combined their two sections of Berlin into a single section: West Berlin. In May 1949, the occupation zones of Germany controlled by the United States, Britain, and France merged into a single zone and, on May 23, this zone became the sovereign nation of the **Federal Republic of Germany**, or West Germany. The Soviets reacted to the formation of West Germany by creating the **German Democratic Republic**, or East Germany, in October 1949.

CONTAINMENT AND THE TRUMAN DOCTRINE

While visiting the United States in 1946, former British prime minister Winston Churchill addressed the growing concern over Soviet expansion. Speaking at Westminster College in Missouri, Churchill summed up the division of Europe. "From Stettin in the Baltic to Trieste in the Adriatic," he declared, "an **iron curtain** has descended across the Continent." The term "iron curtain" became shorthand for the divide in Europe between Western capitalist and Eastern communist countries. Churchill insisted the Soviets must be dealt with from a position of strength, and the United States must take a leading role in preventing the further expansion of communism.

By the time Churchill had spoken, the United States was already mapping out a plan for confronting the Soviets. The plan's architect was George F. Kennan, a foreign service officer stationed at the U.S. embassy in Moscow. In early 1946, Kennan laid out the doctrine of **containment**, or control of Soviet influence, that would shape American foreign policy for the next 40 years. Under containment, the

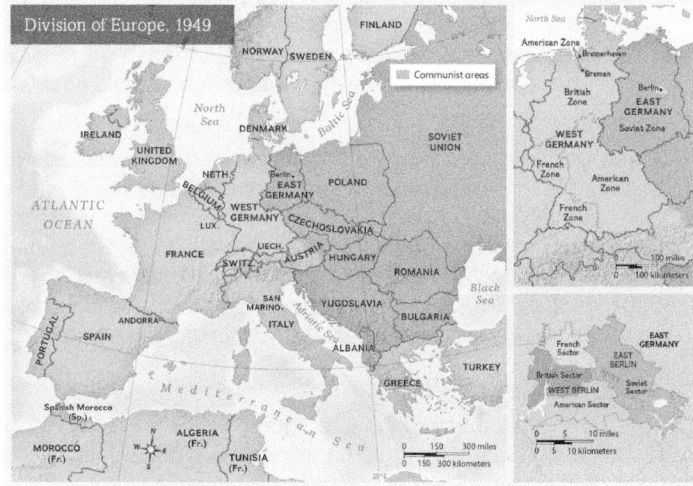

Division of Europe, 1949

PLAN: 4-PAGE LESSON

OBJECTIVE

Learn how political ideologies clashed after the war and established two opposing economic and geopolitical factions.

CRITICAL THINKING SKILLS FOR LESSON 1.2

- Interpret Maps
- Compare and Contrast
- Make Connections
- Synthesize
- Draw Conclusions
- Analyze Visuals
- Summarize
- Evaluate

HISTORICAL THINKING FOR CHAPTER 23

What impact did communism have on the United States and the rest of the world? By helping in the Allied war effort against Germany, the Soviet Union occupied much of Eastern Europe. After the war, the Soviets stayed in Eastern Europe, creating a bloc of countries under communist rule. Lesson 1.2 examines the growing role of the United States as the leader of Western opposition to the spread of communism.

BACKGROUND FOR THE TEACHER

After World War II, the federal government actively helped to transition the nation back to a peacetime economy. The Employment Act of 1946 promoted hiring and increased factory production. Veterans got affordable loans for education and homes through the GI Bill, and the number of homeowners soared. Construction boomed and suburbs grew—a trend that lasted into the 1960s.

The American auto industry ramped up mass-market production. Televisions appeared in living rooms. In 1946, there were 17,000 TVs in homes nationwide; by 1950, Americans were buying 250,000 TVs per month. The average median family income grew from $4,300 to $6,000 in the decade following the war. With rising wages and low unemployment, capitalism in the United States was thriving. By 1955, the United States was the dominant economic world power.

INTRODUCE & ENGAGE

CONNECT TO TODAY

Create a Word Web with *Relations Between United States and Russia* in the center. Remind students that present-day Russia was once part of the Soviet Union and was an ally during World War II. Ask students to suggest words they associate with the current relationship and conflicts between the two countries. Tell students that this lesson examines the post-World War II conflict between the former allies.

Relations Between
United States
and Russia

TEACH

GUIDED DISCUSSION

1. **Synthesize** Ask students to consider what they have read in this lesson about post-World War II relations between the United States and the Soviet Union. **ASK:** How did the political actions of Stalin and the Soviets determine the United States' response to rebuilding Europe? Explain your response using your prior knowledge and evidence from the text. *(Answers will vary. Possible response: Because the Soviets aggressively asserted power over Eastern European countries after the war and installed communist governments in many, the U.S. approach to rebuilding Europe became somewhat defensive in an effort to prevent Soviet expansion. The Allies consolidated their areas of divided Germany into one democratic West Germany, and the United States adopted policies such as containment and the Truman Doctrine in response to Soviet aggression.)*

2. **Make Connections** How might have the U.S. effort in ending World War II and funding the rebuilding of postwar Germany influenced the roles that the United States and Great Britain played in the world? *(Answers will vary. Possible response: After the war, the United States had the most powerful military in the world, a position Great Britain had maintained for decades and from which it was retreating. Since Great Britain had its own economic recovery and rebuilding to deal with, the United States assumed the task of defending the free world and helping to rebuild Europe.)*

DRAW CONCLUSIONS

Explain that after the war the differences between communist and capitalist economies could not have been more distinct. **ASK:** Why did capitalist economies flourish after World War II and communist economies did not? *(Possible response: Communist economies were strictly controlled by the state, which minimized personal profit and limited innovation. Capitalist economies allowed individuals and private companies to innovate and create goods and services for their own profit. Innovators created new businesses, and, along with existing businesses, they had a vast pool of potential workers in men returning from the armed forces. Postwar consumers probably wanted to buy more products that might improve their lives, so their purchases helped to boost the economy. Capitalism apparently allows an economy to expand more efficiently than communist economic policies.)*

DIFFERENTIATE

ENGLISH LANGUAGE LEARNERS **ELD**

Summarize After students of **All Proficiencies** read the lesson, have them write a sentence summarizing the main idea. Ask pairs to dictate their sentences to each other. Then have them work together to check the sentences for accuracy and spelling. Provide the following sentence frames for students according to their proficiency level.

- **Emerging:** The lesson is about _____.
- **Expanding:** The main idea in this lesson is _____. I know that because _____.
- **Bridging:** The main idea is _____, which is related to the details _____ and _____.

GIFTED & TALENTED

Illustrate a Metaphor Bring students' attention to the metaphors "iron curtain" and "iron fist" used by Winston Churchill and President Truman, respectively. Have students draw a picture or use computer software to create artwork to render the metaphor graphically in any artistic style, from realistic to impressionistic to cartoon style. Have students share their pictures with the class and explain why they chose the style and images they did.

See the Chapter Planner for more strategies for differentiation.

United States would focus on keeping communism from expanding. American forces, Kennan said, would employ "the adroit [skillful] and vigilant [watchful] application of counterforce at a series of constantly shifting geographical and political points, corresponding to the shift and maneuvers of Soviet policy." President Truman firmly supported the policy of containment and its goal of blocking the Soviets from spreading communism to other countries. "Unless Russia is faced with an iron fist and strong language, another war is in the making," Truman predicted. "I am tired of babying the Soviets."

In 1947, the United States acted on its containment policy as it entered a conflict in the Mediterranean region. The Soviet Union was threatening to take land in Turkey, while in Greece, communist-led guerrillas were battling the government in a bloody civil war. Great Britain, which controlled the area, warned the United States that Britain could no longer afford to offer military and economic aid to Greece and Turkey. In response, Truman told Congress that "Great Britain finds itself under the necessity of reducing or liquidating its commitments in several parts of the world." He then proposed that the United States provide economic and military aid to all countries threatened by a communist takeover. This proposal became known as the **Truman Doctrine**. The president asked for and received from Congress $400 million in aid for Greece and Turkey.

The world had now entered an era of U.S.-Soviet conflict known as the **Cold War** that would last from the late 1940s to 1991. It was termed the "cold" war because the United States and Soviet Union would never engage in open warfare against each other. Instead, each country would try to weaken the other's influence around the world, and each country would take sides in a number of smaller wars. In the end, the Cold War would be a massive ideological and geopolitical struggle with consequences rippling across the globe.

HISTORICAL THINKING

1. **READING CHECK** Why is the decades-long struggle between the United States and Soviet Union referred to as the "Cold War"?

2. **INTERPRET MAPS** What does the map show about Berlin in 1949?

3. **COMPARE AND CONTRAST** Following WW II, how did the economic policies of Western capitalist and Soviet communist countries differ from each other?

4. **MAKE CONNECTIONS** What is the doctrine of containment, and how was it applied?

THE BERLIN AIRLIFT

The Soviet Union resented having a democratic West Berlin in the middle of its occupation zone. In June 1948, the Soviets began a blockade of the city, cutting off land access and hoping to starve out the British and Americans. Unwilling to use military force to end the blockade, the Western allies devised another way to get food, fuel, and other supplies to West Berlin.

In what became known as the Berlin Airlift, allied cargo planes used open air corridors over the Soviet occupation zone to drop the supplies into West Berlin. By the spring of 1949, it was clear that the Soviet blockade had failed, and it was lifted by the middle of May.

While on their way to school in 1948, West Berlin children and adults turned to watch an inbound U.S. C-47 cargo plane heading for Tempelhof Airport with food and other supplies.

BUILD BACKGROUND

THE BERLIN CRISIS

After the war, the city of Berlin became the rope in the tug of war between the Allies and the Soviet Union. This struggle led to the Berlin Airlift. As the division of Germany took place, the United States, Great Britain, and France introduced the Deutschmark in West Germany to prevent Soviet control of the markets in the divided city of Berlin. The Soviets responded by creating the Ostmark. But they did something else as well: They cut off all major roads, railways, and canals between West Berlin and West Germany, which severely limited supplies of food, electricity, and coal. The only access available to the United States and its allies was by air. Beginning on June 26, 1948, the United States launched "Operation Vittles," a program that delivered food, fuel, and other essentials into West Berlin. Great Britain joined in with their campaign called "Operation Plainfare."

The German Communist party marched in protest in Berlin—and so did the West Berliners, with approximately 300,000 supporters of the airlift taking to the city streets. The Berlin Airlift continued, and the number of aircraft increased, with supply planes landing at an estimated one plane every 45 seconds. After the Soviets lifted their blockade in 1949, the states of West Germany and East Germany were officially established.

TEACH

GUIDED DISCUSSION

3. **Analyze Visuals** Based on the details in the photograph, what must life have been like in Berlin after the war? *(Possible response: It must have been stressful. Trying to go to school or work would've been challenging because of the rubble and obstacles. Trying to rebuild the city would have been slow and complicated. People were probably worried about finding housing, clothing, and food every day.)*

4. **Summarize** How did the policy of containment, the Truman Doctrine, and the Marshall Plan contribute to creating the Cold War? *(Possible response: All three policies contributed to isolating the Soviet Union from Western alliances. The Marshall Plan was viewed by the Soviets as a way to expand the influence of Western capitalism; both containment and the Truman Doctrine were directed at preventing Soviet influence and the spread of communism. The Cold War became the proxy war for the United States and the Soviet Union in their attempt to prevent the spread and influence of each other's ideas and economic systems.)*

EVALUATE

Explain that U.S. policy was intended to promote democracy, capitalism, and open markets in other countries across the globe using positive economic interactions and encouraging values like self-determination. After World War II, the United States instituted the policy of containment to limit Soviet influence and the spread of communism. **ASK:** How did the United States' approach to international policy change after the war? *(Possible response: Before the war, the United States didn't call for military aggression in its foreign policy. After Germany was defeated, the Soviets used military force to control Eastern Europe and move into Turkey. The United States realized such aggression could lead to the further spread of communism. By instituting the policy of containment, the United States changed its approach to foreign policy to use its military might to help secure and protect democracies and capitalist economies.)*

ACTIVE OPTIONS

Active History: Compare Cold War Enemies Extend the lesson by using either the PDF or Whiteboard version of the activity. These activities take a deeper look at a topic from, or related to, the lesson. Explore activities as a class, turn them into group assignments, or even assign them individually.

NG Learning Framework: Examine Life in East and West Berlin

SKILL Communication

KNOWLEDGE Our Human Story

Have students work in small groups to research life in East Berlin and West Berlin between 1948 and 1950. Allow groups to select which city they want to research and create a presentation about the business climate, hospitals, schools, and the availability and condition of utilities such as water and electricity. Encourage students to use visuals, such as maps, photographs, and charts. Once completed, invite each group to share its presentation.

HISTORICAL THINKING

ANSWERS

1. The conflict was a "cold" war because it never escalated into open warfare between countries. Instead, each country tried to weaken the other's influence around the world.

2. The map shows the original Berlin occupation zone divisions among the United States, France, Great Britain, and the Soviet Union. By 1949, the city was divided into two areas—East Berlin (controlled by the Soviets) and West Berlin (controlled by the Allies).

3. Western capitalism was based on private individuals and groups owning their own resources to produce goods and sell them in an open and free marketplace. Soviet communism was based on state control of resources with little incentive for individuals or groups to produce anything but what was necessary and allowed by the state.

4. The doctrine of containment was a plan to limit Soviet influence. It was tested when the Soviet Union threatened to take control of Turkey and Greece. Under the policy, the United States instituted the Truman Doctrine, which provided economic and military aid to any nation threatened by communism.

THE COLD WAR BEGINS

The years following the end of World War II saw the onset of the Cold War, as the United States and the Soviet Union battled each other for global dominance.

The notion of an "Iron Curtain" across Europe symbolized the Cold War and the deep division between the free West and the communist world. Not surprisingly, it was a favorite subject of cartoonists. British cartoonist Leslie Illingworth sketched this cartoon the day after Winston Churchill's famous speech in Missouri in 1946. He depicts Churchill peeking under a curtain that carries a message signed by "Joe," a reference to Soviet leader Joseph Stalin. The cartoon also features several symbols of the division of Europe.

CRITICAL VIEWING Look closely at the cartoon. Which symbols of the division of East and West does the cartoonist include?

DOCUMENT ONE

Primary Source: Speech
from Winston Churchill's speech, delivered at Westminster College in Fulton, Missouri, March 5, 1946

In this famous speech, Churchill condemned the Soviet Union's policies in Europe and coined the phrase "Iron Curtain." The speech ends with a strong plea for a unified international front against communist expansion.

CONSTRUCTED RESPONSE A metaphor is a figure of speech that directly compares two unlike things. What does the metaphor "iron curtain" help you understand about the situation Churchill describes in his speech?

An *iron curtain* has descended across the Continent. Behind that line lie all the capitals of the ancient states of Central and Eastern Europe. Warsaw, Berlin, Prague, Vienna, Budapest, Belgrade, Bucharest and Sofia, all these famous cities and the populations around them lie in what I must call the Soviet sphere, and all are subject . . . not only to Soviet influence but to a very high and, in some cases, increasing measure of control from Moscow.

DOCUMENT TWO

Primary Source: Speech
from President Harry S. Truman's speech, delivered March 12, 1947, before a joint session of Congress

How should the United States react to the advance of communism in Europe? In a dramatic speech to a joint session of Congress, President Truman asked Congress to appropriate money to stop communist aggression in Greece and Turkey. The president first articulated the Truman Doctrine in this speech.

CONSTRUCTED RESPONSE Truman's speech is considered the opening "shot" of the Cold War. Why do you think it is regarded as such?

At the present moment in world history nearly every nation must choose between alternative ways of life. The choice is too often not a free one. . . . I believe that it must be the policy of the United States to support free peoples who are resisting attempted subjugation (control) by armed minorities or by outside pressures. I believe that we must assist free peoples to work out their own destinies in their own way. I believe that our help should be primarily through economic and financial aid which is essential to economic stability and orderly political processes.

DOCUMENT THREE

Secondary Source: Newspaper Article
from "Truman Acts to Save Nations From Red Rule," by Felix Belair, Jr., March 12, 1947, the *New York Times*

The *New York Times* journalist Felix Belair covered the speech in which President Truman announced the Truman Doctrine.

CONSTRUCTED RESPONSE What are two important points the newspaper reporter has gathered from Truman's speech?

President Truman outlined a new foreign policy for the United States. He proposed that this country intervene wherever necessary throughout the world to prevent the subjection of free peoples to Communist-inspired totalitarian regimes. . . . Although the President refrained from mentioning the Soviet Union by name, there could be no mistaking his identification of the Communist state as the source of much of the unrest throughout the world.

SYNTHESIZE & WRITE

1. **REVIEW** Review what you have learned about the events that led to the Cold War and the division of Europe.

2. **RECALL** On your own paper, write the main differences between the views of Stalin and other Soviet leaders and the views of Western leaders toward the postwar situation.

3. **CONSTRUCT** Construct a topic sentence that answers this question: How did President Truman respond to the advance of communism in Europe?

4. **WRITE** Using evidence from this chapter and the documents, write an informative paragraph that supports your topic sentence in Step 3. Include information about Truman's and Churchill's views of the Soviet Union.

PLAN: 2-PAGE LESSON

OBJECTIVE

Synthesize information about the start of the Cold War based on primary source documents.

CRITICAL THINKING SKILLS FOR LESSON 1.3

- Synthesize
- Compare and Contrast
- Make Inferences
- Evaluate

HISTORICAL THINKING FOR CHAPTER 23

What impact did communism have on the United States and the rest of the world? The relationship between the Soviet Union and the Western Allies began to show strain soon after World War II ended. Lesson 1.3 includes excerpts of speeches and news articles that provide perspective on the growing conflict between the United States and the Soviet Union.

BACKGROUND FOR THE TEACHER

The cost of winning World War II devastated the Soviet Union's economy. Stalin demanded that Soviet-controlled Eastern European countries provide raw materials and machinery to aid in the Soviet recovery. Stalin also used the threat of war with the West—specifically the United States—as a way to tighten economic control. Though Stalin gained power over many Eastern European nations by military force during the war, he also promoted local communist parties so they could gain political power to maintain communist control in the region. By 1948, seven of these countries were under the control of communist governments. This allowed the Soviet Union to exploit resources that would be needed to aid in Stalin's confrontation with the Western Allies after World War II.

INTRODUCE & ENGAGE

PREPARE FOR THE DOCUMENT-BASED QUESTION

Before students start on the activity, briefly preview the three documents. Remind students that a constructed response requires a full explanation in complete sentences. Emphasize that students should use what they have learned about post-World War II Europe and the decisions that led to the Cold War in addition to the information presented in the documents.

TEACH

GUIDED DISCUSSION

1. **Compare and Contrast** How would you characterize the differences between the excerpts from Churchill's and Truman's speeches? *(Possible response: Churchill's speech uses the metaphor of the "iron curtain" and casts the Soviet Union's actions in a broader historical context. Truman's speech is much more direct—he enumerates a number of actions he feels the United States should undertake in its response to Soviet aggression.)*

2. **Make Inferences** Journalist Feliz Belair, Jr.'s coverage of Truman's speech is a summary of what the President said. Why do you think he connects Truman's words directly to the Soviet Union and communism? *(Answers will vary. Possible response: His role as a journalist is to explain and interpret Truman's speech for the public. Even though Truman doesn't specifically mention the Soviet Union or communism, Belair makes it clear that the Truman Doctrine is aimed at stopping Soviet aggression and the spread of communism.)*

EVALUATE

After students have completed the Synthesize & Write activity, allow time for them to exchange paragraphs and read and comment on the work of their peers. Establish guidelines for comments prior to this activity so that feedback is constructive and encouraging in nature. Comments should focus on the most significant parts that address the purpose of the activity and the audience.

ACTIVE OPTION

On Your Feet: Use a Jigsaw Strategy Organize students into "expert" groups and have students from each group analyze one of the documents and summarize its main ideas in their own words. Then have members of each group count off using the letters A, B, C, and so on. Regroup students into new groups so that each new group has at least one member from each expert group. Have students in the new groups take turns sharing the simplified summaries they came up with in their expert groups.

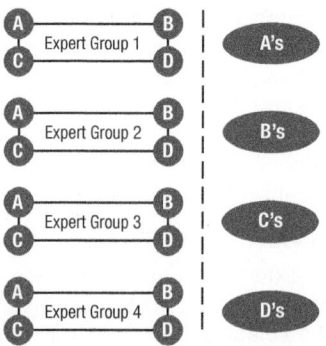

DIFFERENTIATE

INCLUSION

Highlight and Summarize Help students minimize distractions by creating a handout that includes only the three document excerpts. Give a copy to each student along with a highlighter. Tell students to highlight important words and ideas. Then have them write a summary sentence for each excerpt, using several of the words and phrases they highlighted.

PRE-AP

Form and Support a Thesis Challenge students to find and read the full texts of the documents excerpted in the lesson. Then have students conduct further online research into the early stages of the Cold War in order to develop a thesis regarding what started it. Have them write an essay supporting their thesis with a variety of primary and secondary source material, plus their own analysis. Encourage students to share their essays on a class or school blog.

See the Chapter Planner for more strategies for differentiation.

SYNTHESIZE & WRITE

ANSWERS

1. Answers will vary.

2. Answers will vary.

3. Answers will vary. Possible response: President Truman responded to the advance of communism in Europe by implementing containment, the Marshall Plan, and the Truman Doctrine.

4. Answers will vary. Students' paragraphs should include their topic sentence from Step 3 and provide several details from the documents to support the sentence.

CONSTRUCTED RESPONSE

Document 1: Possible response. The metaphor helps describe the unyielding (iron) attitude of the Soviet Union toward the West and a world divided (curtain) by the ideologies of capitalism and communism.

Document 2: Possible response. Truman's speech set the tone for U.S. foreign policy with the Soviet Union by making it clear that countries would have to choose between communism and democracy. He praised the tenets of democracy and made it clear that the United States would support "free peoples" financially and economically if they chose to resist subjugation.

Document 3: Possible response. The two important points in the newspaper article are that Truman proposed that the United States intervene in the world when free people are threatened by communist totalitarianism and that Truman identified the communist state as the source of much unrest in the world.

CRITICAL VIEWING The cartoonist includes symbols of the division between East and West such as the iron wall, the Soviet flag on one side of the wall, the dead-end railroad tracks (suggesting the Berlin blockade), the word "Europe" cut off by the wall, and a sign labeled "Russia" pointing toward the wall.

TRUMAN'S FAIR DEAL

Imagine being a soldier returning home after fighting on the front lines of World War II. You have no job waiting for you. What do you do? Can you count on the government to help you?

THE POSTWAR ECONOMY

In addition to the foreign policy challenges of the impending Cold War, President Truman's domestic challenges proved demanding as well. When millions of soldiers came back from overseas, ready to resume their lives as civilians, the U.S. economy struggled to accommodate them. With no more military orders to fill, factories closed, causing widespread layoffs. There was little work for returning soldiers. In addition, home construction had been on hold during the war, which caused a major housing shortage for veterans and their families. Homelessness spiked in major cities—Chicago had more than 100,000 homeless veterans and Washington, D.C., had 25,000.

Fortunately, the United States was entering a period where both the Democrats and Republicans saw the benefit of working together to solve many of the nation's problems. They agreed that the welfare state that began during the New Deal should be continued and even expanded. Legislators supported the development of a national security system to fight communism within the country. And they believed a strong central government with a powerful executive branch could help achieve these goals. Historian Godfrey Hodgson called this agreement between parties the **liberal consensus**.

VETERANS if buying a Farm, Home or Business, learn about **GUARANTEED LOANS**

CONSULT YOUR NEAREST OFFICE OF THE **VETERANS ADMINISTRATION**

CRITICAL VIEWING The longest lasting and most popular feature of the GI Bill was the guaranteed loan for veterans. How might the poster above encourage a World War II veteran and his family to apply for a loan?

For example, in 1944 both parties in Congress worked together to pass the Servicemen's Readjustment Act, commonly known as the **GI Bill**. "GI," short for "Government Issue," is a military term that refers to U.S. armed forces. The GI Bill provided long-term, low-interest loans to veterans; funds to help pay college tuition; and a $2,000 bonus toward the purchase of a new home. As a result, millions of new homes popped up around the country, and newly educated veterans joined the nation's growing **white-collar**, or professional, workforce.

Not all domestic efforts went so smoothly. In June 1946, Truman lifted the price controls on consumer goods previously imposed during the war to prevent inflation, even though he feared the cost of food and other necessities would skyrocket without the controls. They did. In just weeks, the cost of meat doubled. Faced with higher prices and no increase in wages, unions across the country began to strike.

The United Auto Workers went on strike for 113 days, demanding a pay increase. Large railroad and mine workers' unions also went on strike for higher pay, bringing U.S. transportation and energy industries to a standstill. Although the strikes were resolved, Congress passed the **Taft-Hartley Act** in 1947 to limit strikes in the future. The act allowed the president to impose an 80-day federal injunction to temporarily stop strikes that threatened national safety or health and required unions to give their employers a 60-day notice before staging a strike. Truman vetoed it, but Congress overrode his veto.

TRUMAN'S PLAN

Truman also faced the problem of racial conflict in the United States after the war, and he took a strong stand for civil rights. He authorized a special task force to investigate racial discrimination in the country. The task force recommended the desegregation of the armed forces, the creation of a civil rights division in the federal government, and the end of segregation and lynching in the United States. After Congress failed to pass any civil rights laws, Truman ordered the armed forces to be desegregated in 1948.

As the 1948 election approached, President Truman was on shaky ground. His stance on racial equality had caused a group of southern Democrats to split from the party, demanding "complete segregation of the races." He had a rocky relationship with other members of Congress as well, some of whom urged him not to run for re-election. And he faced a strong Republican opponent, New York Governor **Thomas E. Dewey**.

PRIMARY SOURCE

We cannot afford to float along ceaselessly on a postwar boom until it collapses. It is not enough merely to prepare to weather a recession if it comes. Instead, government and business must work together constantly to achieve more and more jobs and more and more production—which mean more and more prosperity for all the people.

—from President Harry Truman's State of the Union speech in reference to the "Fair Deal," 1949

As the election neared, Dewey held the lead in opinion polls and was widely predicted to become the next president. However, Truman launched a vigorous campaign, traveling by train across the country attacking the "do-nothing" Congress. In a surprising upset, Truman won the election. The *Chicago Tribune* newspaper even ran the mistaken headline "Dewey Defeats Truman."

At his inauguration on January 20, 1949, Truman introduced a plan he called the **Fair Deal**, after Roosevelt's New Deal. The Fair Deal included such progressive ideas as expanding Social Security, increasing the minimum wage, continuing subsidies to support crop prices, instituting national health care, and passing an anti-discrimination law. He also called for expanding the Tennessee Valley Authority and providing funds for **rural electrification** in farm communities that did not yet have electricity.

The Fair Deal was a mixed success. By the end of his term, Truman had managed to expand Social Security and raise the minimum wage, but many of his other proposals were blocked by a conservative Congress. Also, the national debt grew in order to cover the government programs that boosted the postwar economy. In turn, the federal government had to pay higher interest rates on that debt, although neither the vital programs nor the nation's economy were in jeopardy. Still, the Fair Deal set the stage for future administrations to push a progressive agenda with the help of the liberal consensus.

HISTORICAL THINKING

1. **READING CHECK** What did Truman propose in the Fair Deal, and how did Congress respond?

2. **MAKE GENERALIZATIONS** How did the GI Bill improve the lives of soldiers returning from the war?

3. **IDENTIFY MAIN IDEAS AND DETAILS** What were the goals of the liberal consensus?

PLAN: 2-PAGE LESSON

OBJECTIVE

Examine President Truman's efforts to transform the U.S. wartime economy to a progressive peacetime economy.

CRITICAL THINKING SKILLS FOR LESSON 1.4

• Make Generalizations

• Identify Main Ideas and Details

• Make Inferences

• Analyze Primary Sources

HISTORICAL THINKING FOR CHAPTER 23

What impact did communism have on the United States and the rest of the world? As countries affected by World War II began repairing their economies, the United States encountered a variety of challenges. Lesson 1.4 describes programs and legislative efforts that President Truman and Congress enacted to revitalize the postwar economy.

BACKGROUND FOR THE TEACHER

In 1946, the Republican Party won both houses of Congress. While Congress agreed with Democratic President Truman on some legislation to aid the U.S. economic recovery, the opposition party and southern conservative Democrats had their own agenda, which included opposition to labor unions. Unions had expanded greatly since the 1920s, aided by pro-labor federal laws passed after the Great Depression and endorsed by President Roosevelt. Because of the union strikes by auto, railroad, and mine workers in 1946, public support for the Taft-Hartley Act was strong. The bill outlawed forcing workers to join unions that were already established at their workplaces, restricted the political contributions unions could make, and encouraged states to pass laws making union organizing more difficult.

FINANCIAL LITERACY

To extend their knowledge and understanding about the concepts in this lesson, refer students to the Financial Literacy handbook.

INTRODUCE & ENGAGE

CONSIDER POSTWAR PERSPECTIVES

Explain that when World War II ended, millions of American soldiers returned home to a peacetime economy with high unemployment. Ask students to imagine that they are one of the following after the war ended: a soldier returning home, a returning soldier's spouse who has been working full-time at a factory, a family member of a returning soldier, or a member of Congress. Tell students to consider the following questions and write a few sentences from the point of view of the person they chose: What is the first thing you want to do? What fears do you have? How can you get back to a normal life? How can you help yourself or others affected by the war? Ask volunteers to read their responses aloud to the class and use them as a basis for discussion.

TEACH

GUIDED DISCUSSION

1. **Make Inferences** How did Congress intend the Taft-Hartley Act to spur economic growth? *(Possible response: By reducing the power of the unions in workplaces, the act was intended to make it easier for employers and businesses to hire people.)*

2. **Analyze Primary Sources** How does the excerpt from President Truman's speech reflect the legislation he worked to pass after the war? *(Possible response: The excerpt reflects Truman's desire to be proactive and try to create "more and more prosperity for all the people." Legislation like the GI Bill, expanding social security, and increasing the minimum wage aided in avoiding a recession, one of Truman's major concerns.)*

MORE INFORMATION

Truman's Civil Rights Agenda Share the Background for the Teacher information with students. Explain that Truman advocated equal rights for African Americans and wanted to create a permanent Fair Employment Practices Committee (FEPC) that would continue to investigate discrimination against African Americans. This and other social reforms did not make it through Congress. **ASK:** Why do you think only a few of Truman's progressive measures were passed? *(Possible response: Republicans controlled Congress, and, while they passed measures to spur economic growth and aid returning soldiers, Republicans' and some southern Democrats' conservative agendas prevented the passage of many social reforms.)*

ACTIVE OPTIONS

On Your Feet: Inside-Outside Circle Arrange students in concentric circles facing each other. Tell students in the outer circle to pose questions about Truman's Fair Deal, such as the following: Which ideas in the Fair Deal were most important for postwar America? For the ensuing decades? Direct students in the inner circle to answer questions. Then ask students to trade inside/outside roles and relocate to create a new partnership.

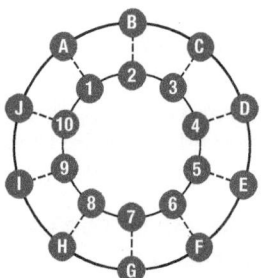

NG Learning Framework: Examine Desegregation of the Armed Forces

ATTITUDE Responsibility

KNOWLEDGE Our Human Story

Organize students into small groups. Direct them to research and write a short analysis of the effects of Truman's executive order to desegregate the armed forces. They should include the effect on soldiers and commanding officers, the response from the public, and effectiveness of the order in changing attitudes. Tell students to provide details to support their analysis. Have one member from each group share their findings with the class.

DIFFERENTIATE

ENGLISH LANGUAGE LEARNERS

Sequence Events Arrange students of **All Proficiencies** in pairs. Instruct them to note key events that caused Truman to implement his Fair Deal in a Sequence Chain. You may ask students at the **Expanding** and **Bridging** levels to assist students at the **Emerging** level. Invite pairs to share their Sequence Chains.

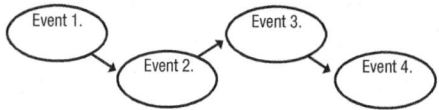

GIFTED & TALENTED

Write Diary Entries Instruct students to conduct online research about President Truman's stand on racial injustice and then write a series of dated diary entries that Truman might have written on the subject. Students might investigate reasons for the task force to end racial discrimination or Truman's order to desegregate the U.S. Armed Forces. Ask volunteers to share their diary entries by posting them in order by date online or by reading them aloud.

See the Chapter Planner for more strategies for differentiation.

HISTORICAL THINKING

ANSWERS

1. Truman proposed an extension of Social Security, a minimum wage increase, a permanent Fair Employment Practices Act, and rural electrification. Congress blocked all but the extension of Social Security and the minimum wage increase.

2. With the GI Bill, veterans received affordable loans and bonuses for buying homes and the opportunity to attend college, which provided the education and skills needed for civilian professions.

3. The goals of the liberal consensus were to fight communism and expand welfare state programs begun under the New Deal.

CRITICAL VIEWING The word *guaranteed* might encourage veterans to apply because it suggests that they're certain to get a loan. The well-dressed couple looks confident as they view their prospective farm, an image that might make a veteran see the process as enjoyable and without difficulty.

ESCALATING TENSIONS

One of the benefits of being part of a group of friends is a feeling of security and knowing that people "have your back." As the Cold War began, nations joined sides with either the United States or the Soviet Union, seeking that same feeling of protection in a world of new dangers.

THE SOVIETS UNVEIL THE BOMB

On August 29, 1949, a little more than four years after the United States dropped the first atomic bomb on Hiroshima, the Soviet Union stunned the world by conducting a test explosion of its own atomic bomb. Americans were shocked. Few believed the Soviets could have developed such a weapon. After all, the Soviet Union was considered a backward nation struggling to rebuild its destroyed infrastructure—roads, buildings, and public utilities—after the war. A number of officials accused the Soviets of espionage, or obtaining the bomb plans through theft or spying.

The development of the Soviet bomb set off a nuclear **arms race** between the United States and

the Soviet Union that would last for decades. As the two countries continued their competitive buildup of nuclear weapons, the odds that they might use them kept rising. However, the complete destructive potential of both stockpiles ultimately acted as a deterrent to using them.

The onset of the arms race led to rapid growth for the U.S. defense industry. Factories geared up to design and build planes, rockets, and satellites. Southern California, in particular, became the booming center of the U.S. **aerospace industry**. The availability of land and a favorable climate made southern California an attractive location, and more than half of the nation's 25 largest aerospace companies would

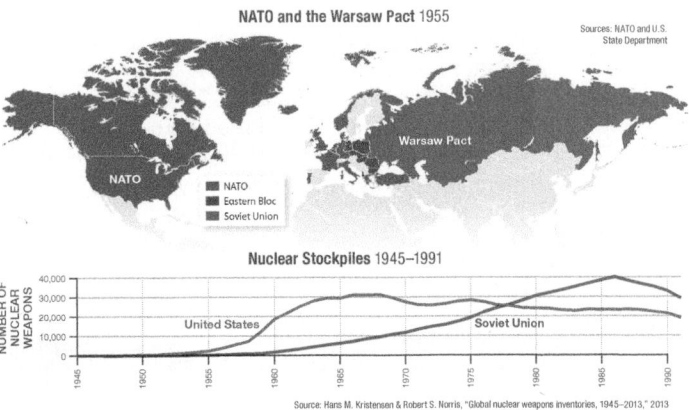

NATO and the Warsaw Pact 1955

Sources: NATO and U.S.
State Department

- ■ NATO
- ■ Eastern Bloc
- ■ Soviet Union

NATO

Warsaw Pact

Nuclear Stockpiles 1945–1991

NUMBER OF NUCLEAR WEAPONS

United States

Soviet Union

Source: Hans M. Kristensen & Robert S. Norris, "Global nuclear weapons inventories, 1945–2013," 2013

Rows of new F-4 Phantom fighter jets designated for the U.S. Navy and Air Force in the 1960s

PRIMARY SOURCE

Many years after the arms race began, President Dwight D. Eisenhower (elected in 1952) gave a speech in which he warned against the close relationship that had grown between the military and the aerospace industry, a relationship he called the **military-industrial complex**.

In the councils of government, we must guard against the acquisition of unwarranted influence, whether sought or unsought, by the military-industrial complex. The potential for the disastrous rise of misplaced power exists and will persist. . . . Only an alert and knowledgeable citizenry can compel the proper meshing of the huge industrial and military machinery of defense with our peaceful methods and goals, so that security and liberty may prosper together.

—from President Dwight D. Eisenhower's Farewell Address, 1961

come to reside there. Between 1952 and 1962, the U.S. government funneled more than $50 billion into California, twice the amount received by any other state. For decades, the aerospace industry would be a major driving force of the California economy.

CREATING ALLIANCES

In addition to stockpiling arms, the United States and the Soviet Union formed alliances to keep each other in check. In 1949, the United States, Canada, and 10 Western European nations formed the **North Atlantic Treaty Organization (NATO)**. Member nations agreed to aid each other should one of the countries be attacked. To counter NATO, the Soviets created the **Warsaw Pact**, a collective defense treaty of communist countries that included the Soviet Union, Albania, Poland, Romania, Hungary, East Germany, Czechoslovakia, and Bulgaria. Similar to NATO, the Warsaw Pact stated that the member countries would defend each other against attack. Several years later, the United States would help establish a similar alliance among Asian countries, known as the **Southeast Asia Treaty Organization (SEATO)**.

As the United States built global alliances, the nation also moved to strengthen its own security and defense. In 1947, lawmakers passed the National Security Act, which unified all of the armed forces under a single **Department of Defense**. The act also created the **National Security Council (NSC)**

to gather and provide foreign policy information to the president. In addition, the act established the **Central Intelligence Agency (CIA)** to collect classified information overseas and uncover what other nations were doing behind the scenes. The CIA was similar to wartime intelligence agencies that had since been disbanded.

In 1950, Secretary of State Dean Acheson wrote a secret document known as National Security Council Paper 68 (NSC68), which called for a steep increase in peacetime military spending—from $13 billion to $50 billion per year. It also called for the construction of a "thermonuclear device," a **hydrogen bomb**, that would be even more powerful than the atomic bomb. Truman never showed NSC68 to Congress, but when the document was declassified, or made public, in 1975, it provided a look at how U.S. defense policy was shaped.

HISTORICAL THINKING

1. **READING CHECK** How was the establishment of international alliances in the 1950s tied to the arms race?

2. **ANALYZE CAUSE AND EFFECT** How did the development of a Soviet atomic bomb affect the economy of southern California?

3. **INTERPRET GRAPHS** During which decade did the Soviets begin to surpass the United States in number of nuclear weapons?

INTRODUCE & ENGAGE

CONSIDER ESCALATING TENSIONS

Have students think about how and why tensions escalated between groups of people they've heard about in the news. Suggest that gang rivalries, political differences among relatives, or even something as explosive as the relationship between some African-American communities and the local police are examples of escalating tensions. **ASK:** Why do you think conflicts between groups can so easily escalate? What might be reasonable solutions to such escalating tensions? After students read the lesson, have them identify the important events that lead to the escalation of tensions between the United States and the Soviet Union and ask them to predict what they think the outcome might be if the tensions go unchecked.

TEACH

GUIDED DISCUSSION

1. **Draw Conclusions** What effect did NATO and the Warsaw Pact have on the Northern Hemisphere? Explain. *(Possible response: They officially split the Northern Hemisphere in two—Western U.S.-led allies and Eastern Soviet-led allies. While trade and communication remained between the two blocs, both alliances limited their economic and social interactions.)*

2. **Make Connections** How did the creation of the Department of Defense and the National Security Council strengthen the powers of the president? *(Possible response: The creation of the NSC and the Defense Department consolidated much of the nation's military and foreign policy concerns under the president's control.)*

ANALYZE PRIMARY SOURCES

Direct students' attention to President Eisenhower's Farewell Address. **ASK:** Why might Eisenhower, a four-star general who commanded the Allied troops' victory over the Germans in WWII, make such a powerful warning about the military-industrial complex? *(Possible response: Eisenhower was a soldier who, as president, learned how politics, the economy, war, and the military become intertwined. He knew that the military would always look for battles to fight and weapons producers would look to create more weapons. If they were to influence government, they could wield a terrible power.)*

ACTIVE OPTIONS

On Your Feet: Question and Answer Tell half the class to write 10 True/False questions based on what they learned in the lesson. Ask the other half of the class to create answer cards, writing "true" on one side of the card and "false" on the other side. Instruct students from the question group to take turns asking their questions. Students in the answer group should respond by holding up either "true" or "false." Have students keep track of their correct answers and help clarify students' understanding when answers are incorrect.

NG Learning Framework: Investigate Weapons Development

| ATTITUDE | Curiosity |

| SKILLS | Communication, Collaboration |

Divide the class into small groups and have each group research weapons development in the United States and the Soviet Union/present-day Russia. Tell them to identify the prominent developments between 1950 and 2010. Remind students that there have been diplomatic as well as technological developments over the past 60 years. Ask a volunteer from each group to read their list. Then work with the class as a whole to compile and discuss a list of the most important developments.

For students who develop an interest in Cold War technology, suggest that they read the online American Story for this chapter.

DIFFERENTIATE

STRIVING READERS

Create Word Squares Ask students to write *Arms Race* in the center oval of a Word Square and to write the definition and characteristics in the appropriate boxes. Guide them to identify examples and non-examples.

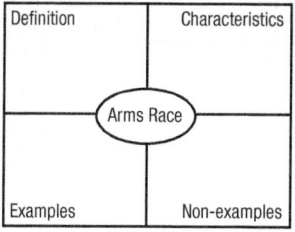

PRE-AP

Write a Report Direct students to gather relevant information from several library or online sources to write a report on the military-industrial complex that emerged during the Cold War. Encourage students to conclude the report with an assessment of the current state of U.S. military spending and the ease or difficulty of controlling the military-industrial complex today. Have students share their reports with the class.

See the Chapter Planner for more strategies for differentiation.

HISTORICAL THINKING

ANSWERS

1. As each side built and improved their arsenal, the threat that those weapons would be put to use increased. Nations on both side banded together for mutual support and defense.

2. The development of the Soviet bomb led to a build up of the defense and aerospace industries. Many companies chose locations in southern California due to the available land and cooperative weather and employed thousands of Californians who pumped their income back into the consumer economy.

3. The Soviets surpassed the United States in number of nuclear weapons during the middle-to-late 1970s.

COLD WAR AROUND THE GLOBE

Have you ever seen a video of hundreds of dominoes falling in a chain reaction? During the Cold War, some feared that might happen with countries: if one became communist, its neighbors might quickly follow.

THE CHINESE REVOLUTION

As the United States and its allies confronted the Soviet Union, another communist power was emerging—China. As you have read, communist forces had been active in China since the 1920s. By the 1930s, the Chinese Communist Party (CCP), led by Mao Zedong, was battling Chiang Kai-shek and his Chinese Nationalist Party, which ruled the country.

When World War II broke out, the two sides joined together to help defeat Japan. After the war, however, their civil war resumed. On paper, Chiang and his forces had better resources. But Chiang's government had grown increasingly corrupt, ineffective, and unpopular during World War II. Meanwhile, Mao had become an inspiring leader. He attracted many people, and his Communist Party gained a reputation for supporting the common man. Chiang responded to communist attacks with increased violence and repression, which only made him more unpopular.

Despite strong U.S. support for Chiang in the Chinese civil war, the tide turned in favor of Mao's communist army, now called the People's Liberation Army (PLA). The PLA captured the city of Beijing in January 1949 and occupied, or took over, Nanjing and Shanghai soon after. In late 1949, Mao claimed victory. He announced the formation of the **People's Republic of China** and declared his communist solidarity with the Soviet Union.

Chiang and his remaining forces fled to the island of Taiwan, where they set up a **government-in-exile**, or a government that has been deposed and attempts to rule from another land. Chiang claimed to lead the only legitimate Chinese government. The United States strongly backed this claim. Now, mainland China, once a loyal U.S. ally, had become a clear enemy to the United States. With the world starkly divided into American and Soviet spheres of influence, or areas

🏛 **The Andy Warhol Museum
Pittsburgh, Pennsylvania**

The 5-foot wide by 7-foot tall image of Mao by artist Andy Warhol suggests the enormous scale of the images of communist leaders publicly displayed in their countries. Warhol made hundreds of silk screens of Mao, each altered in a different way by adding paint. The Mao series of work comments on communist propaganda and popular culture in the United States. Warhol was a leading practitioner of pop art.

Andy Warhol, "Mao", © 2017 The Andy Warhol Foundation for the Visual Arts, Inc. / Artists Rights Society (ARS), New York

In 1945, Ho Chi Minh declared Vietnam's independence from France using rhetoric from the French Declaration of the Rights of Man and the Citizen and from the American Declaration of Independence.

The Declaration of the French Revolution made in 1791 on the Rights of Man and the Citizen also states: 'All men are born free and with equal rights, and must always remain free and have equal rights.' Nevertheless for more than 80 years, the French imperialists . . . have built more prisons than schools. They have mercilessly slain our patriots; they have drowned our uprisings in rivers of blood. They have . . . impoverished our people, and devastated our land. They have robbed us of our rice fields, our mines, our forests.

—from Declaration of Independence of the Democratic Republic of Vietnam, by Ho Chi Minh, 1945

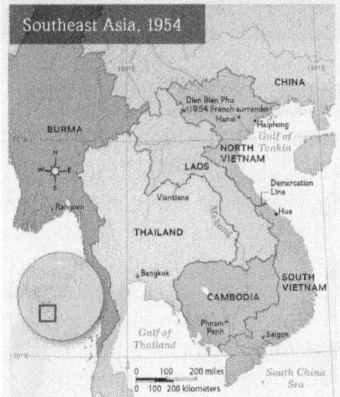

Southeast Asia, 1954

of authority, China's shift was seen as a serious loss for the West. A debate raged in Washington about who was to blame for "losing China" to communism. Opponents of President Truman portrayed Mao's victory as an "avoidable catastrophe" that the president failed to prevent by focusing too much on Eastern Europe and not enough on China.

FROM CHINA TO SOUTHEAST ASIA

The policy of containment, as you have read, was based on a fear that communism would spread. Western leaders reinforced this idea with the **domino theory**. They argued that just like rows of dominoes knocking each other down, communist countries—especially those in Asia—would "knock over" their neighbors and make them communist as well.

After World War II, the French controlled much of Southeast Asia, including Vietnam, Laos, and Cambodia, a region known as Indochina. In Vietnam, France soon faced a revolt led by communist leader **Ho Chi Minh**. Ho led a group known as the Viet Minh. In September 1945, the Viet Minh announced their independence from France, seized control of the northern part of the country, and declared the **Democratic Republic of Vietnam (North Vietnam)** with Ho as president.

Financial backing and military supplies from the United States helped France secure control of the southern region and set up the **State of Vietnam (South Vietnam)**. For the next five years, France fought the

Viet Minh, who were supported by the Soviet Union and China, for control of Vietnam. Ho and his troops realized it was impossible to win large-scale battles against the French. Instead, they conducted a guerrilla war in the countryside, attacking the French and then retreating into Vietnam's mountains and jungles.

In March 1954, the Viet Minh defeated a large French force at the **Battle of Dien Bien Phu**. The two sides negotiated a peace agreement that officially divided Vietnam into two countries: communist North Vietnam and democratic South Vietnam. However, the situation remained unstable and battles continued to erupt. By the end of the 1950s, the United States would increase its direct involvement in the Vietnam conflict. But before that, the United States focused on stopping the spread of communism in another Asian country—Korea.

HISTORICAL THINKING

1. **READING CHECK** Why did the United States support Chiang's Chinese government-in-exile?

2. **INTERPRET MAPS** What war advantage did North Vietnam have, considering its location next to China?

3. **DRAW CONCLUSIONS** How might breaking Vietnam into two separate countries lead to conflict later on? Use evidence from the text to support your prediction.

4. **FORM AND SUPPORT OPINIONS** Does it make sense to compare countries to game pieces that might fall in a chain reaction as the domino theory did? Why or why not?

OBJECTIVE

Trace the spread of communism into Asia after the Chinese Revolution.

CRITICAL THINKING SKILLS FOR LESSON 2.2

- Interpret Maps
- Draw Conclusions
- Form and Support Opinions
- Make Connections
- Evaluate

HISTORICAL THINKING FOR CHAPTER 23

What impact did communism have on the United States and the rest of the world? As the United States and the Soviet Union settled into a defensive Cold War, many Asian countries—most prominently China—turned to communism as their form of government. Lesson 2.2 examines China's influence in the spread of communism in Southeast Asia and the response of Western leaders.

BACKGROUND FOR THE TEACHER

Born in rural China to a peasant family that gained modest wealth, Mao was educated as a youth and pursued some higher education as a young man. He served as a soldier in 1911 in a revolt against the Qing Dynasty and as a youth considered Napoleon Bonaparte and George Washington as heroes. Mao took on leadership roles in organizing anti-government groups as a young man, and his small groups of revolutionaries used guerilla warfare tactics to successfully attack government forces.

Like many intellectual aspiring revolutionaries, Mao considered the peasants of rural China to be ignorant. But during an extended stay in his home province in 1925, his attitude changed when he saw small local peasant groups protesting against the repressive government. As a Marxist, Mao saw the revolutionary potential of the rural peasantry, which in time was an important part of his ultimately successful defeat of Chiang Kai-shek's Chinese Nationalist government.

INTRODUCE & ENGAGE

CREATE A WORD WEB

Create a Word Web like the one shown, with *domino theory* in the center. Ask students what the phrase means and add their ideas to the web. If possible, set a row of dominoes in motion to demonstrate the idea of a political event in one nation causing similar events to happen in nearby nations. Tell students that this lesson examines the United States' and Western allies' fear that if one country fell to communist rule, others in the region would do the same.

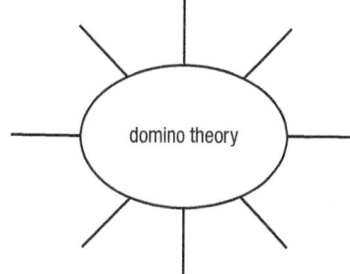

domino theory

TEACH

GUIDED DISCUSSION

1. **Make Connections** How effective was the U.S. policy of containment in the political development of communism in China? *(Possible response: The fact that the country with the largest population in the world aligned itself with communism and the Soviet Union reveals that the U.S. policy of containment was inadequate and ineffectual.)*

2. **Evaluate** How do you think events influenced the United States' decision to support France in its conflict in Vietnam? *(Possible response: After the victory of the communists in China and its solidarity with the Soviet Union, the United States supported France to keep Vietnam from falling to a communist regime.)*

🏛 VIRTUAL MUSEUM VISIT

Located only a few miles from the home where Warhol grew up, Pittsburgh's Andy Warhol Museum houses the largest collection of the artist's work in the world. Dabbling in painting, sculpture, and photography, Warhol is best known for pop art, a post-World War II art movement that incorporated common items and cultural elements such as advertising, TV, and cartoons. Some of Warhol's most well-known pop-art paintings include his series of Campbell's Soup cans, Marilyn Monroe screenprints, and the Mao series, one of which is 15 feet tall. **ASK:** What effect could Warhol have been trying to create with these colorful, oversized depictions of Mao? *(Possible response: Warhol may have painted Mao large and colorful to acknowledge or poke fun at his importance on the world stage and in the lives of hundreds of millions of followers.)*

ACTIVE OPTIONS

On Your Feet: Rotating Discussion Divide the class into four groups and assign each group a corner of the room. Ask each group to prepare four questions about how containment and the domino theory affected the Cold War superpowers in post-World War II Asia. Begin the discussion by asking Group 1 a question about the topic. After Group 1 answers, they ask one of the other groups a question they have prepared. Continue until all groups have exhausted their questions.

NG Learning Framework: Compare Declarations of Independence

ATTITUDE Responsibility

SKILLS Observation, Communication

Divide the class into small groups and have groups read both the American Declaration of Independence and Ho Chi Minh's Declaration of Independence of the Democratic Republic of Vietnam. Instruct students to look for and take notes on the connections and similarities between the two documents. Ask each group to write a short response describing the similarities between them. Then discuss with the class as a whole the differences (and ironies) between a democratic nation's declaration and a communist nation's declaration, using evidence and reasoning from both documents.

DIFFERENTIATE

ENGLISH LANGUAGE LEARNERS

Pose and Answer Questions Arrange students at the **Emerging** and **Expanding** levels in mixed pairs and ask them to reread the lesson together. Instruct them to pause after each paragraph and ask one another *who, what, when, where,* or *why* questions about what they have just read. Suggest students use a 5Ws Chart to organize their questions and answers. Tell students at the **Expanding** level to assist students at the **Emerging** level as needed.

GIFTED & TALENTED

Host a Talk Show Arrange students in pairs and direct them to locate an online transcript of Ho Chi Minh's speech proclaiming the independent Democratic Republic of Vietnam in 1945. Tell students to assume the roles of a talk show host and Ho Chi Minh, and to plan, write, and perform an interview focusing on the views and reasoning expressed in the speech. The student playing Ho Chi Minh should use as many direct quotes from the speech as possible in answering the host's questions. Invite pairs to present their talk show to the class.

See the Chapter Planner for more strategies for differentiation.

HISTORICAL THINKING

ANSWERS

1. Although it was increasingly corrupt, Chiang's Nationalist Party was not communist.

2. North Vietnam borders China, so the North Vietnamese could easily receive military support from China in the fight against the French and the South Vietnamese.

3. Answers will vary. Possible response: Since France retained control of South Vietnam, Ho's forces in the North might continue to try to reunite the two nations under a communist government.

4. Answers will vary. Possible response: The domino comparison makes sense because it illustrates the precariousness of countries that are surrounded by other countries that have fallen to communism.

THE KOREAN WAR

Did you ever become involved in an argument or debate between two people because you wanted to support a friend or because you strongly supported one side? As the Cold War heated up, the United States became involved in a far-off civil war in order to halt the spread of communism.

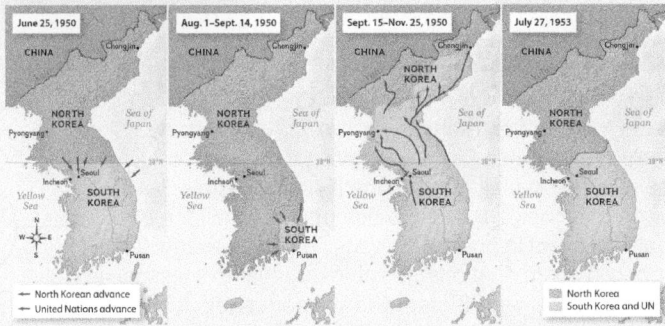

The Korean War, 1950–1954

June 25, 1950 | Aug. 1–Sept. 14, 1950 | Sept. 15–Nov. 25, 1950 | July 27, 1953

— North Korean advance
-- United Nations advance

☐ North Korea
☐ South Korea and UN

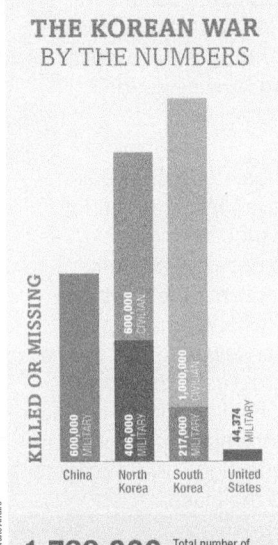

THE KOREAN WAR BY THE NUMBERS

KILLED OR MISSING

China — 600,000 MILITARY
North Korea — 406,000 MILITARY, 600,000 CIVILIAN
South Korea — 217,000 MILITARY, 1,000,000 CIVILIAN
United States — 44,374 MILITARY

Sources: CNN and the Department of Veterans Affairs

1,789,000 Total number of U.S. troops serving

36,574 U.S. soldiers killed in action

>7,800 American soldiers still unaccounted for as of June 2016

WAR ERUPTS IN KOREA

The nation of Korea lies on a peninsula that borders northeastern China. Japan had ruled the land since the late 1800s. In 1945, after Japan's defeat in World War II, the Allies took control. They divided the Korean Peninsula roughly in half at the **38th parallel**, which is 38 degrees latitude north of the equator. Soviet troops controlled North Korea, while American-backed troops controlled the Republic of Korea, also called South Korea. With Soviet backing, a communist government was set up in North Korea, while the United States helped establish democratic rule in the south. Both sides claimed to be the legitimate ruler of the entire peninsula, and skirmishes along the border were common. In 1948, the United Nations moved to unify the country through national elections. But the Soviets refused to let UN officials into North Korea, preventing the elections from taking place.

On June 25, 1950, North Korean troops crossed the 38th parallel and invaded South Korea, taking everyone by surprise. It was clear that, although North Korea was the immediate aggressor, it attacked with the approval of the Soviet Union. This situation—where a major power starts a war in which it does not become directly involved—is called a **proxy war**. A proxy is a person or nation that acts as a substitute for or on behalf of another.

President Truman viewed the invasion as a test of his containment policy aimed at preventing the Soviets from spreading communism further. At Truman's urging, the United Nations condemned the attack and ordered North Korea to withdraw. North Korea refused, and the UN dispatched a multinational military force to South Korea. Meanwhile, Truman ordered additional American troops stationed in Japan to provide additional military support to the UN forces, including those U.S. troops already stationed on the Korean peninsula. He also sent an American naval fleet into the waters between China and Taiwan.

A BACK-AND-FORTH BATTLE

North Korean forces had moved swiftly, and within weeks they had captured the South Korean capital of Seoul (sohl). The army continued to push south. By the end of July 1950, North Korea had pushed UN troops to the southern tip of the peninsula, into a small region around the city of Pusan. The defenders, however, dug in and fought off one furious attack after another as they waited for reinforcements.

As North Korea seemed poised to win, U.S. commander General Douglas MacArthur executed a bold plan. He sent UN and U.S. troops by sea to the port of **Incheon**, 150 miles behind North Korean lines. MacArthur intended to surprise and overwhelm the enemy by attacking from the rear. It worked. With their communications cut and under heavy bombardment, the North Koreans fled back north across the 38th parallel. Sensing an opening, MacArthur chased the enemy over the border, deep into North Korea. Surrounded and under siege, the North Koreans pressed for peace and a return to the old border at the 38th parallel. The United States and South Korea, however, had set their sights on controlling all of Korea. Then China stepped in.

CHINA JOINS THE WAR

In November 1950, China staged a massive attack across its border into Korea. While the Chinese had initially stayed out of the conflict, they were not about to let their fellow communists in North Korea suffer a defeat. More than 300,000 Chinese troops overwhelmed American and South Korean forces.

MacArthur, who had assured President Truman the Chinese would not enter the fight, now admitted, "We face an entirely new war." Scores of troops retreated to the south by sea. Meanwhile, several U.S. Marine and Army divisions trapped inland battled ferociously to escape. U.S. and UN forces withdrew south of the 38th parallel, and in January 1951, abandoned Seoul for a second time. After several months of intense fighting, the retreating forces held their ground just south of Seoul along the 37th parallel. MacArthur launched attack after attack, slowly pushing the Chinese and North Koreans back up the peninsula and eventually back over the 38th parallel.

TRUMAN FIRES MACARTHUR

China's entry into the war caused tensions between Truman and MacArthur. The general wanted to strike China with nuclear weapons, but President Truman strongly rejected the idea. Any attempt to widen the war, Truman reasoned, would alarm other UN partners and perhaps provoke the Soviets into starting a larger, more deadly war.

MacArthur, however, refused to be silent. He sent a letter to Congress criticizing Truman's refusal to meet force "with maximum counterforce" and ended with his oft-quoted phrase: "There is no substitute for victory." MacArthur also leaked information to the press, warning of a crushing defeat for UN forces if nuclear bombs were not used. On his own, MacArthur issued a warning to China, threatening to expand the war into Chinese territory. Truman was furious. In April 1951, the President

---

INTRODUCE & ENGAGE

MAKE A CHOICE

Explain to students that after World War II, the Allies divided Korea into two sections, with communist North Korea supported by the Soviet Union and democratic South Korea supported by the United States. Tell students that, without provocation, North Korea invaded South Korea. Ask students how they would react to the invasion. If they were members of the U.S. Congress, would they choose to intervene or stay out of the conflict? What would be their reasons? Display an Argument Chart with the labels Intervene, Reasons, and Do Not Intervene, as shown. Poll students, adding their names and stated reasons to the chart. Generate a discussion about intervening in international conflicts, referring to reasons noted on the chart. Tell students that in this lesson, they will learn why the United States chose to intervene in Korea.

Intervene	Reasons	Do Not Intervene

TEACH

GUIDED DISCUSSION

1. **Make Inferences** Why might President Truman have felt so strongly that the United States needed to intervene when North Korea invaded South Korea? *(Possible response: North Korea's invasion—backed by the Soviets—violated the Truman Doctrine and the United States' containment policy. Truman wanted the world to see that the United States would support democratic nations under attack.)*

2. **Identify** Why was General MacArthur's strategy in North Korea so effective? *(Possible response: MacArthur caught the North Koreans completely off guard. By severing the North Korean army's supply and communications lines to the North Korean capital, the army was unable to continue fighting effectively and retreated.)*

3. **Analyze Language Use** What did General MacArthur mean when, after China attacked Korea, he admitted to President Truman that "We face an entirely new war"? *(He meant that the battlefield changed drastically with the arrival of Chinese troops and that the U.S. military strategy would have to be rethought.)*

INTEGRATE VISUALS

Tell students to examine the Korean War By the Numbers infographic and the maps, noting the changes in territory over time. **ASK:** How does the information on the infographic connect to the maps? *(Possible response: The infographic shows that North Korea and South Korea experienced the most casualties, which corresponds to the back-and-forth gains and losses in territory as shown on the maps.)*

DIFFERENTIATE

INCLUSION

Use Clarifying Questions Pair inclusion students with students who can read the lesson aloud to them. Ask the inclusion students' partners to describe the infographic and maps. Encourage inclusion students to ask clarifying questions as needed.

GIFTED & TALENTED

Engage in a Debate Tell students they will assume the role of either President Truman or General MacArthur and debate that person's position regarding the best military strategy for the Korean War. Tell students to decide which person they will play and then conduct online research to learn more about that person's military and diplomatic strategies. Students should take detailed notes and use their notes to practice and role-play the debate in front of their classmates.

See the Chapter Planner for more strategies for differentiation.

North Korea today remains a communist-ruled country and is isolated from much of the rest of the world. In this 2012 photo, North Korean soldiers carry a large portrait of late leader Kim Il Sung in a military parade in Kim Il Sung square in Pyongyang, the capital city of North Korea. North Korea follows a policy of "Songun Chong'chi," or "Military First," and its army of more than 1 million is one of the largest in the world.

removed MacArthur from his post, accusing him of insubordination, or refusal to obey orders. Truman replaced MacArthur with General Matthew Ridgway.

MacArthur returned to the United States to public acclaim as a hero who symbolized old military values in a world complicated by the threat of nuclear war. Letters poured into the White House, and the vast majority—21 to 1—were against his firing. Angry groups of citizens even burned President Truman in effigy. An effigy is a crude model of a person, made to be damaged in protest. MacArthur gave a farewell address to a joint session of Congress. His closing words were: "Old soldiers never die; they just fade away. And like the old soldier of that ballad, I now close my military career and just fade away—an old soldier who tried to do his duty as God gave him the light to see that duty."

THE KOREAN WAR ENDS

As the Truman-MacArthur drama unfolded on the home front, the war in Korea settled into a standoff. By spring of 1951, both sides seemed willing to accept the prewar border of the 38th parallel. Truce talks began that summer but dragged on for two more years due to continuous disagreements. In July 1953, both sides finally signed a truce that stopped the fighting without formally ending the war.

The truce called for both sides to pull back from the battle line and designated the space between them along the 38th parallel as a **demilitarized zone**. No army could enter the zone without breaking the truce. The demilitarized zone, often referred to as the DMZ, still stretches across the entire width of the Korean Peninsula—a 148-mile border—from which hundreds

of thousands of troops remain ready for conflict to erupt. South Korean troops, joined by U.S. troops, face North Korean troops across this fenced and guarded wasteland, which has now become a haven for vegetation and wildlife.

The toll from the first "hot" conflict of the Cold War was high, resulting in hundreds of thousands of lives lost, hundreds of cities and villages destroyed, and a ruined countryside, but it did not change the postwar division of Korea into two countries. War is always brutal, but the devastation of the

Korean War is unparalleled. The demilitarized zone continues to separate families and stifle the culture of a once united nation. But in defining their Korean identity, many South Koreans see themselves as a united community. North Korea presents itself as a united country, but its people have experienced long famines and much poverty. The armies still poised on either side of the DMZ ready to fight at any moment keep the two countries and the rest of the world on edge. After the North Korean government tested nuclear missiles in March 2013, South Korean officials called the act "an unforgiveable threat to the Korean peninsula's peace and safety."

HISTORICAL THINKING

1. **READING CHECK** What were the two major turning points in the Korean War?

2. **EVALUATE** North Korea was the Soviet Union's proxy in the Korean War. Was South Korea a proxy for the United States? Explain your answer.

3. **INTERPRET MAPS** According to the map, how did the war affect territory controlled by each side?

4. **FORM AND SUPPORT OPINIONS** Was President Truman right to fire MacArthur? Explain your opinion.

BUILD BACKGROUND

GENERAL DOUGLAS MACARTHUR

Although a distinguished leader, General MacArthur had a career that was not without controversy. In 1932, when veterans of World War I marched into Washington, D.C., during the Depression to demand bonus payments for their service, MacArthur sent current enlisted soldiers to break up their fellow veterans' protests. He retired from the army in 1937 but was recalled to serve during World War II, where he led the U.S. effort against Japan in the Philippines, New Guinea, and the Solomon Islands. After Japan surrendered, MacArthur oversaw the disassembly of the Japanese military and the creation of a new constitution. MacArthur, described as egotistical and aloof by some, warm and humble by others, was an inscrutable man who spent nearly 50 years serving in the U.S. Army.

PRESIDENT DWIGHT DAVID EISENHOWER

President Eisenhower served as Commanding General of Europe during World War II and ran for President in 1952, winning in a landslide. Eisenhower had served as an aide to General MacArthur during the 1930s and was quoted as saying he "studied dramatics under [MacArthur] for seven years." As president, Eisenhower was determined to end the lingering Korean War truce talks. He appointed John Foster Dulles as his Secretary of State. Dulles made it clear to the Chinese that the United States would consider using atomic bombs to end the ongoing conflict if a truce wasn't reached soon. In July 1953, a truce was signed, though it did not formally end the Korean War. While Eisenhower continued President Truman's policy of containment, his "New Look" approach focused on nuclear weapons and long-range missile technology. The Cold War between the United States and the Soviet Union would march on.

TEACH

GUIDED DISCUSSION

4. Draw Conclusions How would you characterize the first proxy war in the Cold War between the United States and the Soviet Union? *(Possible response: After North Korea—backed by the Soviets—invaded South Korea, the UN—at Truman's request—ordered North Korea to withdraw but to no avail. U.S. and multinational troops clashed, and eventually China entered to support its fellow communists in the north. Over the course of the war, hundreds of thousands of lives were lost, cities and countrysides were destroyed, and millions of dollars were spent, yet neither the United States nor the Soviets gained any real advantage because Korea remained divided.)*

5. Make Generalizations How did their alliances support North Korea and South Korea? *(Possible response: South Korea has been served best by its alliances because it is a democracy and the country has been an active participant in the world economy. North Korea's alliances have not been as beneficial, as it has experienced famine and severe poverty and has been isolated from the world economy.)*

ANALYZE PRIMARY SOURCES

Direct students' attention to the Primary Source feature. Point out that President Truman refers to "specific responsibilities . . . imposed by the Constitution." **ASK:** What responsibilities does President Truman refer to and why does he point to them in his speech? *(Truman makes it clear that the Constitution stipulates that the Commander in Chief has the final word in military policy and can make changes in military command. He wants Americans to understand that he had the right to fire General MacArthur.)* Review with students the events leading to Truman firing MacArthur. Then discuss the idea of the military chain of command, posing questions such as the following to prompt discussion: Should a civilian, such as a president, be the highest level of command for a military organization? Is it ever acceptable for a lower-ranked person to disobey a superior? Why might it be important for military personnel to follow the orders of a superior?

ACTIVE OPTIONS

AMERICAN GALLERY ONLINE

The Korean War Invite students to explore the American Gallery. Have them select one of the images and do additional research to learn more about it. Ask questions that will inspire additional inquiry about the chosen gallery image, such as: At what point in the war was this photograph taken? Where is this? Who took this photograph? Where was this photograph published and for what purpose? Why does this photograph belong in this chapter? What else would you like to know about it?

NG Learning Framework: Review Personal Stories

ATTITUDE Curiosity

KNOWLEDGE Our Human Story

Have students read and evaluate excerpts from *I Remember Korea* by Linda Granfield or *The Coldest Winter* by David Halberstam. Suggest that each student read a section of five to ten pages from one of the books. Explain that the writers use personal accounts, research, and interviews to convey the experiences of soldiers and refugees involved in the Korean War. Organize students into small groups to discuss what they learned from their readings, noting what people endured during the war. Have each group present a summary of their findings to the class.

HISTORICAL THINKING

ANSWERS

1. MacArthur's decision to attack Inchon by sea and China's decision to enter the war were the major turning points in the war.

2. Possible responses: No. The United States played an active role in the war, sending U.S. troops to support the UN forces and battle the North Koreans. Yes. Although the United States was more directly involved in the war, the fight between North and South Korea was clearly a proxy for the larger fight between the competing ideologies of the Soviet Union and the United States.

3. Both sides were able to push their enemies to the brink of their borders, getting them in a position where victory seemed inevitable, only to be pushed back to the other side of the country. The war went back and forth between North Korea and South Korea, with neither side able to keep the ground they gained.

4. Answers will vary. Possible responses: Truman was right to fire MacArthur since the general disobeyed orders and wanted to use nuclear weapons against China, which would have expanded the war. Truman should not have fired MacArthur since the general was on the ground and knew firsthand what needed to be done to win back lost territory and bring the war to an end.

THE RED SCARE CONTINUES

Everyone knows fear can be contagious, and there was plenty of fear to go around in the years following World War II. Many people were afraid communism could gain a foothold in the United States, and that fear led to a period of suspicion and accusations, some of which implicated ordinary, innocent Americans.

A SECOND RED SCARE

As you have read, fear of communism seized America following World War I in what became known as the Red Scare. After World War II, a second Red Scare swept the nation. Americans watched with alarm as the Soviet Union imposed its communist rule across Eastern Europe and successfully tested an atomic bomb. In Asia, Mao Zedong's communist army toppled the pro-American government of Chiang Kai-shek in China, and the United States sent troops overseas to battle communist forces in Korea. As communism appeared to be on the march everywhere, Americans started to look for signs of the enemy at home, even among their friends and neighbors.

Congress led the attack on suspected communists through its **House Un-American Activities Committee (HUAC)**. The committee had originally been established to investigate Nazi propaganda in the United States in the 1930s. After World War II, HUAC began targeting suspected communists. Officials used the **Alien Registration Act**, also called the Smith Act, to prosecute alleged communist activity. The 1940 act, written in part by Democratic congressman Howard W. Smith, made it illegal to discuss overthrowing the government and required immigrants to register with authorities. Fewer than 200 people were charged under the legislation. When civil rights organizations spoke out against such practices, they too were targeted as possible communist sympathizers.

The 1956 Hollywood movie *Invasion of the Body Snatchers* tells the story of aliens who take over the bodies of humans. Many viewed the film as a commentary on the nation's postwar, anticommunist hysteria. The official movie poster released by the studio, Allied Artists Pictures, highlights the fear of the postwar years.

THE HOLLYWOOD TEN

In 1947, HUAC launched a highly publicized anticommunist investigation into the American motion picture industry. The committee accused ten screenwriters and film directors of creating pro-communist films and materials. Committee members issued the writers and directors a subpoena, or formal request to appear before them. During their hearings, the writers and directors refused to answer questions about their political beliefs and associations. Judges charged the **"Hollywood Ten,"** as they became known, with contempt of Congress and sent them to jail. In addition, the group was blacklisted in the entertainment industry, which meant no one was willing to do any further work with them.

In the years that followed, many people found themselves in communism-related Supreme Court cases. The film industry became so linked to communism that its labor union, the Screen Actors Guild (SAG), required its members to take a **loyalty oath**, a sworn statement that they did not belong to various organizations including those identified as communist. Some universities, school districts, and school boards also started requiring their members to take loyalty oaths. In 1950, as part of a newly enacted state law, leaders of the University of California required its employees to take a loyalty oath and reject radical beliefs. A number of university professors lost their positions when they refused to sign loyalty oaths. In 1952, the California Supreme Court ruled in favor of the professors, but not until 1967 did federal courts rule the law unconstitutional.

SPY CASES GRIP THE NATION

The growing fear of communism at home sparked two prominent spy cases that captivated Americans. In 1948, American writer **Whittaker Chambers** testified before HUAC and claimed to have once been part of a "communist cell" in Washington, D.C. Chambers added that the cell included **Alger Hiss**, a former government official who had advised President Roosevelt in foreign affairs. Hiss denied the allegations in testimony before HUAC. When Chambers repeated the charge on a national radio broadcast, Hiss sued him for libel, the crime of making unsubstantiated negative claims about someone.

Chambers struck back by producing dozens of classified State Department documents from the 1930s that suggested Hiss was a spy for the Russians. The evidence included photographs and summaries of confidential reports Hiss had written in longhand

or typed on a unique typewriter he once owned. **Richard M. Nixon**, a young California congressman, made a name for himself by pushing hard for Hiss's indictment, or formal charge of a criminal offense. Hiss could not be charged with espionage, as the alleged crime occurred too long ago. Instead, a federal grand jury indicted him for perjury, or lying, before HUAC. Hiss's first trial ended in a hung jury, or a jury that can't agree on a verdict. His second trial ended with a guilty verdict and a jail sentence for Hiss.

Another stunning trial involved **Julius and Ethel Rosenberg**, a New York couple who were active in the Communist Party. The case began in 1950, when the FBI discovered a spy network of American and British communists who were passing the Soviets information about U.S. atomic bomb development. After authorities arrested a German-born nuclear physicist for espionage, they discovered that Julius and Ethel Rosenberg were part of the same network of spies.

The Rosenbergs were arrested and convicted, in part on the testimony of Ethel Rosenberg's brother, David Greenglass, an engineer working on the Manhattan Project, which developed the American atomic bomb. A number of people viewed the Rosenbergs as innocent victims of anticommunist hysteria. However, numerous appeals and pleas for clemency, or mercy, failed. In 1953, the Rosenbergs were executed for treason.

Decades later, after the fall of the Soviet Union, information concerning the case was made public, including a number of radio messages. These messages were gathered and decrypted by the Venona Project, a code-breaking operation run by the U.S. Army. The messages, known as the Venona Papers, bolstered HUAC's claims of a communist threat in the United States. For years, the Rosenbergs' sons worked to prove their parents' innocence. By 2016, new evidence confirmed their father's guilt, but cast doubt on their mother's involvement.

HISTORICAL THINKING

1. **READING CHECK** What international events sparked the second Red Scare?

2. **DESCRIBE** Who were the prime targets of the House Un-American Activities Committee, and why were they targeted?

3. **MAKE INFERENCES** Why do you think the Screen Actors Guild agreed to blacklist members of its own union?

PLAN: 2-PAGE LESSON

OBJECTIVE

Learn how the spread of communism in Eastern Europe and Asia created fear at home in the United States.

CRITICAL THINKING SKILLS FOR LESSON 3.1

- Describe
- Make Inferences
- Analyze Cause and Effect
- Analyze Visuals

HISTORICAL THINKING FOR CHAPTER 23

What impact did communism have on the United States and the rest of the world? The Soviet Union's success in spreading communism was met with both a U.S. military response and an internal response at home that was more insidious. Lesson 3.1 examines how fear of communist influence affected American citizens as well as government employees and turned some citizens against each other.

BACKGROUND FOR THE TEACHER

T-10 was the identification code for one of the FBI's Hollywood informants during the Red Scare, but most people know him as Ronald Reagan, who became America's 40th president. As a member of the Screen Actors Guild Board of Directors in the 1940s, Reagan and his then-wife, actress Jane Wyman, provided the FBI with the names of actors whom they knew were involved with various communist organizations. Although Reagan testified before the House Un-American Activities Committee in 1947 while serving as President of the Screen Actors Guild, his attitude toward HUAC was complicated. In his closing remarks to the committee, Reagan expressed his distaste for the communist philosophy, but he also stated, ". . . at the same time I never as a citizen want to see our country become urged, by either fear or resentment of [communists], that we ever compromise with any of our democratic principles through that fear or resentment. I still think that democracy can do it."

INTRODUCE & ENGAGE

INVESTIGATE SUSPICIONS

Before starting, look for a small number of students who are wearing something unique that can be singled out (item of clothing, glasses, etc.). Then pull aside four or five other students and tell them quietly that they need to round up the unique group and conduct interviews to find out why they are wearing the unique item. Instruct them not to believe any reasons—legitimate or not—that the interrogated students give. After a few minutes of interrogation, engage the whole class in a discussion about suspicion and how targets feel and act when singled out and the role of interrogators when investigating suspicious acts. Tell students that in this lesson they will learn about a similar event that happened in the United States as a result of a widespread fear of communism.

TEACH

GUIDED DISCUSSION

1. **Make Inferences** Why do you think that HUAC specifically investigated the American motion picture industry? *(Possible response: Movies were popular with the public, and HUAC may have been afraid that Hollywood filmmakers would try to convey communist messages in movies that could influence millions of Americans.)*

2. **Analyze Cause and Effect** How did the Cold War and fear of communism affect the American public? *(Institutions such as universities and schools interrogated people and created blacklists, making the accused outcasts. Spy cases involving Whittaker Chambers and Alger Hiss and the trial of the Rosenbergs fueled Americans' anticommunist fears and concerns about national security, creating an atmosphere of distrust.)*

ANALYZE VISUALS

Direct students' attention to the 1956 movie poster. **ASK:** How does the poster convey the fears people felt during the postwar years? *(The red and yellow colors of the poster mimic the Soviet Union's flag, a possible reference to communism. The grasping hand suggests a horror that the terrified man and woman are running from.)* Ask students to find online a poster for the 1978 remake of *Invasion of the Body Snatchers* and compare it to the 1956 poster. **ASK:** What might account for the differences between the two posters? *(Possible response: The 1978 version shows tendrils and the words "From deep space." Outer space may have been more popular and communism considered less of a threat in the 1970s.)*

ACTIVE OPTIONS

On Your Feet: Three-Step Interview Have students work in pairs. One student should interview the other student using these questions: Would you give names of people you know to a government committee investigating the politics of American citizens? Why or why not? Then students should reverse roles. Ask students to share their responses and reasons in a class discussion.

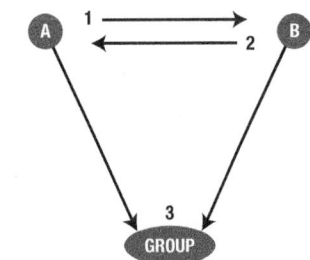

NG Learning Framework: Research Loyalty Oaths

| ATTITUDE | Responsibility |

| SKILL | Collaboration |

Organize students into three groups. Group 1 will research the loyalty oaths that the state of California required university employees to take in the 1950s. Group 2 will research the position of professors who refused to take the oaths. Group 3 will research the rulings of the courts. Ask groups to report the exact wording of oaths, positions, and rulings in addition to other pertinent details. Have student groups report their findings from both primary and secondary sources to the class. Then guide a discussion in which students state whether they agree with the courts' rulings and why.

DIFFERENTIATE

ENGLISH LANGUAGE LEARNERS `ELD`

Use a Meaning Map Pair students at the **Emerging** level with students at the **Expanding** or **Bridging** levels. Have them complete a Meaning Map for *loyalty oath*. Encourage students to use a dictionary to understand both of the words in the term. Direct pairs to share their Meaning Maps and make revisions that aid in their understanding of the term.

PRE-AP

Write a Biographical Article Direct students to conduct online research to learn about the Hollywood Ten. Have students choose one of the men and write a biographical article for a class blog, including information on why the person refused to answer questions and how the decision affected his life. Ask students to post their articles on a class blog or the school website. Invite the class to read the articles and comment on what the subject of the article lost or gained by his actions.

See the Chapter Planner for more strategies for differentiation.

HISTORICAL THINKING

ANSWERS

1. Americans were alarmed by the spread of communism around the world, such as the Soviets having control over much of Eastern Europe, Mao Zedong's communist takeover of China, and the standoff between North and South Korea.

2. Immigrants, civil rights organizations, writers, and Hollywood filmmakers were among those targeted. Some viewed immigrants with suspicion and questioned their allegiance to the United States, thinking they might be spies. When civil rights organizers spoke out, they too were accused. Writers, entertainers, and members of the film industry were suspected of promoting communist and anti-American ideas in their productions.

3. Answers will vary. Possible response: SAG leaders might have feared the consequences of associating with known communists, such as the government exerting control over the film industry.

Senator Joseph McCarthy points to a map while questioning Joseph Welch, the lawyer for the army in Senate committee hearings in 1954. McCarthy's accusations of communist infiltration of the army led to diminishing support for his investigations.

THE RISE OF MCCARTHYISM

Have you ever been afraid to speak your mind out of fear that others will attack you or accuse you of something? That is the way many people felt during Senator Joseph McCarthy's hunt for communists within the U.S. government during the early 1950s.

McCARTHY'S LIST OF COMMUNISTS

On a bleak February evening in 1950, Senator **Joseph R. McCarthy**, a little-known politician from Wisconsin, delivered a speech to a Republican women's club in Wheeling, West Virginia. The topic of the speech was communist subversion in the federal government. **Subversion** is the act of secretly undermining something in an attempt to destroy it. "I have here in my hand," McCarthy told his audience, "a list of 205 Communists that were made known to the secretary of state and who are still working and shaping the policy of the State Department." The message was clear. The United States was losing the Cold War to the evil forces of communism because the U.S. government was filled with "traitors."

Among the politicians who targeted suspected communists at home during the Cold War, none stood out more than Joe McCarthy. Wisconsin's junior senator was an erratic, or unpredictable, politician, known for his reckless ambition and rowdy behavior. He knew little about communists in government or anywhere else. But as he spoke out about alleged sympathizers of communism within the U.S. government, the public listened. McCarthy had struck a nerve in a country growing more anxious about Soviet aggression and communist expansion. As the nation searched for explanations, McCarthy provided a simple answer. Disloyal Americans, especially those working in Washington, D.C., were the real enemy.

PRIMARY SOURCES

In an attack on President Truman's foreign policy in February 1950, Senator Joseph McCarthy claimed to have a list of hundreds of communists employed by the federal government, but he never publicly revealed any of those names. In June 1950, Senator Margaret Chase Smith went before the Senate to deliver a personal rebuttal to McCarthyism in her "Declaration of Conscience."

While I cannot take the time to name [them], I have in my hand 205 cases of individuals who would appear to be either card carrying members or certainly loyal to the Communist Party, but who nevertheless are still helping to shape our foreign policy.

One thing to remember in discussing the Communists in our government is that we are not dealing with spies who get thirty pieces of silver to steal the blueprints of a new weapon. We are dealing with a far more sinister type of activity because it permits the enemy to guide and shape our policy.

—from a speech in West Virginia by Senator Joseph R. McCarthy, 1950

The United States Senate has long enjoyed worldwide respect as the greatest deliberative body in the world. But recently that deliberative character has too often been debased to the level of a forum of hate and character assassination sheltered by the shield of congressional immunity.

The American people are sick and tired of being afraid to speak their minds lest they be politically smeared as "Communists" or "Fascists" by their opponents. Freedom of speech is not what it used to be in America. It has been so abused by some that it is not exercised by others.

—from a speech in the Senate by Senator Margaret Chase Smith, 1950

RECKLESS ACCUSATIONS

McCarthy's charges of treason in high places made him an instant celebrity. Prominent Republicans, sensing the political benefits of the "communist issue," embraced his attacks, which became known as **McCarthyism**. As he gained fame, McCarthy's assertions grew bolder. He called former secretary of state George C. Marshall a traitor, mocked the current secretary of state, Dean Acheson, as the "Red Dean of fashion," and described President Truman as a drunkard, saying that he should be impeached. Yet Republican colleagues continued to encourage McCarthy, who they thought could turn public distrust into votes for their party.

During the 1952 national elections, Republicans won control of Congress. McCarthy became chairman of the Senate Subcommittee of Investigations. He used the power of his committee to force government officials to testify and defend their loyalty. Among those he targeted were homosexuals in government positions who might have access to classified information, whom he claimed were vulnerable to blackmail. In what became known as the Lavender Scare, federal agencies fired many employees suspected of being homosexuals. The wave of discrimination didn't end there. Throughout the nation, suspected lesbians and gay men were targeted for surveillance and persecution, and many were forced out of career positions in state and local government, education, and even private industry.

Academics—specifically, faculty members at the nation's most prestigious colleges and universities—were also targeted as dangerous communist influences by McCarthy and his fellow committee members. Professors at Harvard, the University of Chicago, Johns Hopkins, Sarah Lawrence College, and other centers of higher learning were called to testify before the committee. Fortunately, most of these schools supported their faculty and refused to take action against any accused employees.

MCCARTHY'S FALL

Eventually, McCarthy went too far. In 1954, his committee attempted to uncover suspected communists within the ranks of the army. During televised hearings, the senator repeatedly bullied respected army officials, including General Ralph W. Zwicker, whom McCarthy declared was "unfit to wear the uniform" of the U.S. Army. Even President Eisenhower had seen enough. McCarthy quickly lost his credibility. The public turned away from him, and the Senate openly criticized him for bringing it into "dishonor and disrepute." The darkest days of McCarthyism soon ended, but the effects of the "witch hunts" and the alarm over communism followed the country into the next decade.

HISTORICAL THINKING

1. **READING CHECK** How did Joseph McCarthy increase suspicion of government officials?

2. **SYNTHESIZE** How might McCarthy's investigations have affected academic freedom in U.S. colleges?

3. **ANALYZE LANGUAGE USE** What did Senator Smith mean when she said that freedom of speech had "been so abused by some that it is not exercised by others"?

PLAN: 2-PAGE LESSON

OBJECTIVE

Examine how U.S. Senator Joseph McCarthy fueled Americans' fear of communism through accusations and congressional investigations.

CRITICAL THINKING SKILLS FOR LESSON 3.2

- Synthesize
- Analyze Language Use
- Make Inferences
- Form and Support Opinions
- Analyze Primary Sources

HISTORICAL THINKING FOR CHAPTER 23

What impact did communism have on the United States and the rest of the world?
Americans' fear of communism turned toward possible communist influences in government. Lesson 3.2 examines how McCarthyism infected the nation, damaging some politicians' reputations and fomenting fear and paranoia.

BACKGROUND FOR THE TEACHER

Edward R. Murrow became a household name in America during World War II. Broadcasting for CBS radio from Europe during the war, Murrow and his team of reporters brought the drama and tragedy of the war into U.S. homes. Murrow flew on multiple bombing missions and was one of the first reporters to cover the horrific revelations of the Nazi death camps. After the war, he created and hosted "See It Now," a television news show. As Senator Joe McCarthy's witch hunt for communists gained national prominence, Murrow used his popular TV show to combat McCarthyism. While clearly anti-communist, Murrow believed deeply in political and civil liberties, and he didn't hesitate to call out McCarthy's destructive tactics. In March 1954, Murrow broadcast "A Report on Senator Joseph R. McCarthy," an exposé that revealed McCarthy to be an extremist. The show made a huge impact on the public and contributed to the downfall of the junior senator from Wisconsin.

INTRODUCE & ENGAGE

ACTIVATE PRIOR KNOWLEDGE

Ask students to recall injustices that have occurred throughout U.S. history. Pose the following question: When have groups of people been targeted and mistreated because of race, religion, nationality, or politics? Discuss occurrences with students such as the Japanese internment camps during World War II, attacks on African Americans by the Ku Klux Klan, and the plight of Muslims after September 11, and ask students to identify why the perpetrators of the injustices believed they were right. After students share their ideas, explain that this lesson examines how fear of communism affected the American public in the 1950s.

TEACH

GUIDED DISCUSSION

1. **Make Inferences** Why do you think Senator McCarthy was so successful in creating an atmosphere of fear about potential communist influence in the United States? *(Answers will vary. Possible responses: Americans were genuinely concerned about the spread of communism, and the arms race that began during the Cold War fueled their concern. McCarthy's assertions that communism was rampant in the government resonated with an already fearful population.)*

2. **Form and Support Opinions** Do you think the actions of Senator McCarthy and Congress served national security and the public interest? Explain why or why not and support your answer with evidence. *(Answers will vary. Possible response: They did not. McCarthy and Congress created fear and paranoia, violated peoples' right to free speech, and made unfounded accusations, fostering fear and suspicion. They were catering to a fearful public in order to garner votes for their party.)*

ANALYZE PRIMARY SOURCES

Direct students' attention to the Primary Sources feature. Have them work in pairs to evaluate the two points of view on the threat of communism. Encourage students to identify each senator's claims and reasons. Then hold a class discussion in which pairs share their evaluations. Take time to clarify any discrepancies so students clearly understand each point of view.

ACTIVE OPTIONS

On Your Feet: Turn and Talk on Topic Arrange students in three groups. Give each group this topic sentence: Senator McCarthy created an atmosphere of fear and paranoia in the United States. Tell students to build a paragraph on the topic by having each student contribute one sentence. Suggest that the groups first discuss why the American public was so susceptible to fear-based ideas. Ask a volunteer from each group to present the group's paragraph to the class.

NG Learning Framework: Evaluate Points of View

ATTITUDE Responsibility

SKILLS Observation, Communication

Place students in groups or pairs and ask them to further research the Lavender Scare. Have students evaluate different primary and secondary sources and different authors' points of view and use evidence and claims to construct a hypothesis about how the Lavender Scare shaped attitudes and/or policies related to the lesbian and gay community from the 1950s to the present. Tell each group to write a short report stating their hypothesis and supporting it with evidence and claims from their sources. Ask groups to present their reports to the class as a panel, with individuals reading a section to the class.

DIFFERENTIATE

STRIVING READERS

Record Details Instruct students to use a Main-Idea and Details Chart to record details about how McCarthyism impacted different groups of people. Tell students to reread the lesson to identify which groups were targeted and to note why McCarthy decided they posed a threat. Encourage students to compare their completed charts.

GIFTED & TALENTED

Create Social Networking Profiles Tell students to research Joseph McCarthy and Margaret Chase Smith to learn more about their character, philosophies, and thoughts about communism, democracy, and First Amendment freedoms. Then have students create social networking profiles for each, providing a brief summary and one or two photos. Ask students to end each profile with a statement that sums up that senator's career. Invite students to share their profiles with the rest of the class.

See the Chapter Planner for more strategies for differentiation.

HISTORICAL THINKING

ANSWERS

1. Joseph McCarthy made unsupported accusations about communists in the State Department and the security threat resulting from the government employment of homosexuals.

2. Possible response: McCarthy's investigations might have hindered or stopped academics from researching and expressing certain ideas in class or in publications. Discussing ideas that were believed to support communism may harm a professor's reputation or career, so he or she may have censored his or her own work.

3. Senator Smith was making the point that accusers had used their right of free speech to make accusations that cast suspicion on groups of individuals. As a result, members of a targeted group would not exercise their right to speak up for fear of having accusations turned upon them.

VOCABULARY

Write a paragraph to answer each question. Use all the words that appear below each question in your paragraph.

1. How were American politics and culture shaped by the Cold War?

   subversion   hydrogen bomb
   domino theory   containment
   McCarthyism

2. What effect did the Cold War have on jobs in business and government sectors?

   aerospace industry   white-collar
   arms race   GI Bill

READING STRATEGY
SYNTHESIZE

When you synthesize, you identify the most important information in a text, look for evidence that connects the facts, and think about what you already know about the topic. Then you use the evidence, explanations, and your prior knowledge to form an overall understanding of what you have read. Use the chart below to help you synthesize the information presented in this chapter. Then answer the question.

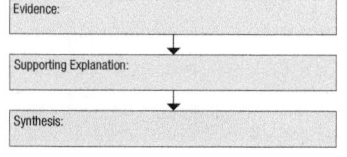

The Roots of McCarthyism

Evidence:

↓

Supporting Explanation:

↓

Synthesis:

3. How did world events following the Allied victory in World War II lead to distrust and suspicion within the United States?

MAIN IDEAS

Answer the following questions. Support your answers with evidence from the chapter.

4. Name two organizations formed by the United Nations in the 1940s and the purposes of those organizations. LESSON 1.1

5. How did American foreign policy shift after World War II? LESSON 1.2

6. What caused the arms race between the United States and the Soviet Union? LESSON 2.1

7. How was the Chinese Communist Party able to win the support of the Chinese people following World War II? LESSON 2.2

8. Why did President Truman remove General Douglas MacArthur from command of the American troops in Korea? LESSON 2.3

9. How were the Alger Hiss and the Rosenberg spy cases similar and different? LESSON 3.1

10. What brought about the end of Joseph McCarthy's investigation of communist influence in the U.S. government? LESSON 3.2

HISTORICAL THINKING

Answer the following questions. Support your answers with evidence from the chapter.

11. IDENTIFY MAIN IDEAS AND DETAILS How did the United Nations originate, and what purpose was it intended to serve?

12. DRAW CONCLUSIONS How did the Cold War and fear of communism affect ordinary Americans?

13. ANALYZE CAUSE AND EFFECT What triggered the larger conflict in Korea?

14. ANALYZE LANGUAGE USE Why did the historian Godfrey Hodgson refer to the postwar interaction of Republicans and Democrats as a "liberal consensus"?

15. SUMMARIZE What threats did the United States face from the expansion of communism throughout Eastern Europe and parts of Asia?

16. MAKE INFERENCES Why do you think the National Security Council Paper 68 called for an increase in military spending?

17. FORM AND SUPPORT OPINIONS How did the Cold War affect American politics?

INTERPRET VISUALS

Look carefully at this comic book cover created during the Cold War. Then answer the questions that follow.

IS THIS TOMORROW
AMERICA UNDER COMMUNISM!

18. What elements in the image convey the fear that arose from the Cold War?

19. Is the message of this image based on opinion or fact? Explain your response.

ANALYZE SOURCES

Not everyone trusted Senator Joseph McCarthy or believed his accusations. The excerpt below is from a letter President Truman wrote in 1950, but never sent, in response to a telegram he had received from the senator.

This is the first time in my experience . . . that I ever heard of a Senator trying to discredit his own Government before the world. Your telegram is not only not true and an insolent approach to a situation that should have been worked out between man and man—but it shows conclusively that you are not even fit to have a hand in the operation of the Government of the United States.

20. Based on the excerpt, how would you describe the president's attitude toward McCarthy's accusations?

CONNECT TO YOUR LIFE

21. NARRATIVE You have considered how the Cold War affected ordinary American citizens between 1945 and 1960. Judging a person's response to historical events is often easier than knowing how you might behave in the same situation without the advantage of hindsight. Write a story in which you are a main character and explore what you may have thought or done in the midst of the Cold War as events occurred.

TIPS

- Focus on one or two historical events that present a conflict for you and describe them.

- Identify your character's thoughts and feelings as world events unfolded.

- Use vivid language to describe the location of the story and the other characters in it.

- Include realistic dialogue in your story.

- Use two or three vocabulary terms from the chapter in your narrative.

- End the narrative by stating a moral, or a lesson one or more of the characters learned.

VOCABULARY ANSWERS

1. Possible response: The Cold War shaped American politics and culture in multiple ways. The United States was concerned about the domino theory playing out as countries in Eastern Europe and Asia fell to communist rule. As a result, the United States officially adopted a policy of containment to try to limit the spread of Soviet communist influence and to support democracies with financial and military aid. After the Soviets tested their own atom bomb, the United States devoted great resources to developing the more powerful hydrogen bomb, thereby escalating the arms race between the two countries. In the United States, the fear of communist subversion and infiltration resulted in McCarthyism, the widespread accusations of treason named after Wisconsin Senator Joseph McCarthy, who heightened fears across the nation.

2. Possible response: The arms race was a boon to the U.S. economy with the government pouring money and resources into building weapons and developing the aerospace industry to compete with the Soviets. Large investments in defense-related businesses created millions of new jobs that also fueled the economy. The GI Bill gave returning soldiers access to affordable tuition loans that could help them get required education for government or defense-related jobs. All businesses require management, so as companies were created and grew, white-collar jobs increased as well.

READING STRATEGY ANSWER

The Roots of McCarthyism

Evidence: The Soviet Union installed communist governments in Eastern Europe and aided communist revolutions in China, Korea, and Vietnam. The Soviet Union had nuclear weapons.

↓

Supporting Explanation: Americans worried that the Soviet Union had spies in the United States. Joseph McCarthy led investigations into communists in the government and the motion picture industry.

↓

Synthesis: World events created an atmosphere in which a determined Joseph McCarthy led investigations into suspected communists and homosexuals, ruining careers and lives. This demonstrated that fear and prejudice in Americans can be inflamed to destructive ends.

3. Possible response: Soviet domination of Eastern Europe and Soviet influence in communist revolutions made the Soviet Union a threat to the West. Fear of spies in the government, promoted by Joseph McCarthy, made American citizens suspicious of each other.

MAIN IDEAS ANSWERS

4. Possible response: The purpose of the United Nations Educational, Scientific, and Cultural Organization (UNESCO) was to rebuild schools, libraries, and museums that had been destroyed during World War II. The purpose of the International Monetary Fund was to safeguard the stability of the international monetary system.

5. Almost immediately following the war, the Soviet Union began occupying Eastern European countries and spreading communism. The United States took a lead role in fighting the further spread of communism by giving aid to countries that were being threatened by the Soviet Union.

6. The United States and the Soviet Union both thought they needed to protect themselves by having a larger stockpile of weapons than the other.

7. Many Chinese remembered how corrupt, ineffective, and unpopular the nationalists had been during World War II and thought that Mao Zedong and the communists were on the side of the common man. When the two parties clashed, the nationalist government became violent and repressive.

8. MacArthur wanted to use nuclear force against China, but Truman refused. MacArthur leaked information to the press about Truman's refusal and sent a threatening message to China. Truman removed MacArthur for insubordination.

9. Both cases involved Americans accused of spying. Their charges and sentencing were different. Hiss was jailed for lying, and the Rosenbergs were executed for treason.

10. When McCarthy and his committee tried to uncover suspected communists within the ranks of the U.S. Army, McCarthy lost all credibility and the investigations soon ended.

HISTORICAL THINKING ANSWERS

11. Towards the end of World War II, representatives of "the Big Four"—the United States, Great Britain, the Soviet Union, and China—decided that the world needed an international organization to negotiate conflicts before they erupted into war. Representatives from 50 countries worked on the charter of the United Nations. They pledged to work together to prevent wars and resolve conflicts peacefully.

12. Americans were fearful and suspicious of the Soviets and the possibility that some Americans were helping them. Americans began attacking and accusing each other. Suspicions of communist spying made people distrustful, afraid to speak their minds, and afraid of unfounded accusations that could ruin their lives.

13. When the United Nations tried to hold elections in Korea to choose a government for the whole country, the Soviets prevented the elections north of the 38th parallel. The two sides threatened each other repeatedly and then, in 1950, North Korea invaded South Korea.

14. The term refers to Democrats and Republicans working together to achieve largely progressive ends, such as expanding the welfare state, creating a national security system to fight communism, and passing the GI Bill.

15. The United States faced the threat that communism would continue to spread and capitalism and democracy would be destroyed.

16. National Security Council Paper 68 called for increased military spending in order to fund organizations like the newly formed CIA and to invest in the U.S. hydrogen bomb program as a response to the arms race with the Soviet Union.

17. Possible response: The Cold War created an atmosphere of fear and suspicion that largely overshadowed party politics in America. Congress became obsessed with alleged communist activity in the United States. Prominent Republicans, emboldened by the acceptance of McCarthyism, focused on American citizens' associations with socialist or communist organizations. Republicans and Democrats alike seemed to disregard the freedoms of speech and assembly in an effort to convince the nation that they were keeping the country safe from the spread of communism.

INTERPRET VISUALS ANSWERS

18. The image shows what some Americans feared would happen under communism: Soviet soldiers attacking Americans, American ideals destroyed as evidenced by the flag in flames, and society in chaos with whites and African Americans fighting one another.

19. The message is based on opinion since the Soviet Union never attempted to invade the United States.

ANALYZE SOURCES ANSWER

20. The president suggests that McCarthy's accusations are absurd and unfounded. The wording of the letter suggests that Truman is extremely angry at McCarthy's insolence and arrogance.

CONNECT TO YOUR LIFE ANSWER

21. Students' stories should include themselves as a main character during the Cold War and reveal their thoughts and feelings as events unfold. Students should use vivid language to describe the setting and other characters, use realistic dialogue, include two or three vocabulary terms from the chapter, and conclude with a moral or lesson learned by one of the characters.

UNIT 7 RESOURCES

UNIT INTRODUCTION

UNIT TIME LINE

UNIT WRAP-UP

NATIONAL GEOGRAPHIC | **CONNECTION**

National Geographic Magazine Adapted Articles

- "America's Propaganda Machine"
- "Dogs at War" ONLINE

Unit 7 Inquiry: Persuade an Audience

NG Learning Framework Activities

- Write About a Cold War Advance
- Debate the Origins of the Cold War

Unit 7 Formal Assessment

CHAPTER 24 RESOURCES

Available at NGLSync.Cengage.com

TEACHER RESOURCES & ASSESSMENT

Reading and Note-Taking

Vocabulary Practice

Social Studies Skills Lessons
- Reading: Make Inferences
- Writing: Explanatory

Formal Assessment
- Chapter 24 Pretest
- Chapter 24 Tests A & B
- Section Quizzes

Chapter 24 Answer Key

ExamView®
  One-time Download

STUDENT DIGITAL RESOURCES

- eEdition
- Handbooks
- Online Atlas
- American Gallery Online
- History Notebook
- Active History
- Reid on the Road video series
- Literature Analysis
- Projects for Inquiry-Based Learning

Chapter 24 Spanish Resources are available at NGLSync.Cengage.com.

AMERICAN STORIES | The Birth of Rock and Roll

- Study Primary Sources: Perspectives about rock and roll and excerpts from publications
- ▶ The Motown Sound
- On Your Feet: Debate Contributions to Rock and Roll

NG Learning Framework: Study Cultural Change

SECTION 1 RESOURCES

THE POSTWAR BOOM

LESSON 1.1
Eisenhower as President

- On Your Feet: Question That Answer!

NG Learning Framework: Explore the 1956 Presidential Race

LESSON 1.2
American Society

 Consumer America

NG Learning Framework: Weigh Pros and Cons

LESSON 1.3
Suburbs Surround Cities

- On Your Feet: Turn and Talk on Topic

NG Learning Framework: Explore a Local Suburb

SECTION 2 RESOURCES

NEW MEDIA AND TECHNOLOGIES

LESSON 2.1
Automobile Mania

- On Your Feet: Identify Car Culture Startups

NG Learning Framework: Research the Oil Industry

LESSON 2.2
THROUGH THE LENS
Cars & American Culture

- On Your Feet: Analyze a Photograph

NG Learning Framework: Engage in an Online Discussion

LESSON 2.3
Culture of the Fifties

- On Your Feet: One-on-One Interviews

NG Learning Framework: Analyze the Beat Generation

LESSON 2.4
CURATING HISTORY
National Baseball Hall of Fame and Museum Cooperstown, New York

- Active History: Major League Baseball Attendance
- On Your Feet: Sort the Artifacts

SECTION 3 RESOURCES

POVERTY AND DISCRIMINATION

LESSON 3.1
Urban and Rural Poverty

- On Your Feet: Jigsaw

NG Learning Framework: Research Attempts at Reform

LESSON 3.2
Native Americans and Mexican Americans

- On Your Feet: Four Corners

NG Learning Framework: Explore Organizations

CHAPTER 24 REVIEW

STRATEGY ❶

READ AND RECALL

Invite students to work in groups of two to four. First have each student read the lesson independently. After reading, instruct students to meet without the book and share ideas and facts they recall. One student takes notes. As a group, students then review the lesson and decide what to add or change in the notes.

Use with All Lessons *Suggest that students use an outline, a Main Idea and Details Chart, or another graphic organizer to help them organize their ideas and cover the entire lesson.*

STRATEGY ❷

PREVIEW THE TEXT

Work with students to preview each lesson in the chapter. Guide them to read each lesson's title, introduction, Main Idea statement, captions, and lesson headings. Then tell them to list the information they expect to find in the text. Instruct students to read the lesson and then discuss with a partner what they learned and whether or not the information matches the ideas on their list.

Use with All Lessons

STRATEGY ❸

USE RECIPROCAL TEACHING

Tell partners to take turns reading each paragraph of the lesson aloud. At the end of the paragraph, the reading student should ask the listening student questions about the paragraph. Students may ask their partners to state the main idea, identify important details that support the main idea, or summarize the paragraph in their own words. Then prompt students to work together to answer the Historical Thinking questions.

Use with All Lessons

INCLUSION

STRATEGY ❶

MODIFY MAIN IDEA STATEMENTS

To help students anticipate and organize content, provide modified Main Idea statements before reading. Several examples are provided below.

1.1 Although President Eisenhower was a Republican, he maintained many of Democratic President Truman's domestic policies while changing foreign policies.

1.2 As the United States moved into the Cold War, ordinary citizens' lives changed in many ways both positive and negative.

1.3 A combination of factors led to a large population shift from cities to suburbs during the Cold War.

3.1 While many Americans' lives improved economically in the 1950s, other Americans struggled with poverty.

3.2 Mexican Americans and Native Americans suffered from poverty and discrimination in the 1950s.

Use with All Lessons

STRATEGY ❷

USE CLARIFYING QUESTIONS

Allow students with disabilities to work with other students who can read the lesson aloud to them and describe the photographs if necessary. Instruct students to ask and answer clarifying questions. Encourage them to discuss the point of view conveyed by Jeff Idelson's quotation and whether they agree or disagree with his opinion.

Use with Lesson 2.4

ENGLISH LANGUAGE LEARNERS ELD

STRATEGY ❶
USE VISUALS TO PREDICT CONTENT

Direct students at the **Emerging** and **Expanding** levels to read the lesson title and look at the visuals. Then ask them to write a sentence predicting how the visuals are related to the lesson. After they finish reading the lesson, you may wish to have students review their predictions and revise them if necessary.

Use with All Lessons *Encourage students at the Emerging level to ask questions if they have trouble writing a prediction. Students at the Bridging level could help students at the Emerging and Expanding levels write their predictions.*

STRATEGY ❷
SUMMARIZE

Place students of **All Proficiencies** in pairs and assign partners one or more paragraphs from the lesson. Instruct students to read their assigned paragraphs and then work together to summarize each paragraph in one or two sentences. When all pairs are finished, ask them to read their summaries in the order in which the material appears in the lesson.

Use with All Lessons

STRATEGY ❸
USE A MAIN IDEA CLUSTER

Pair students at the **Emerging** and **Expanding** levels with students at the **Bridging** level. Direct pairs to use a Main Idea Cluster to check their understanding of the lesson. Tell students to take turns reading a section of the lesson. Then have them work together to record the main idea and four details. Instruct pairs to trade and compare clusters.

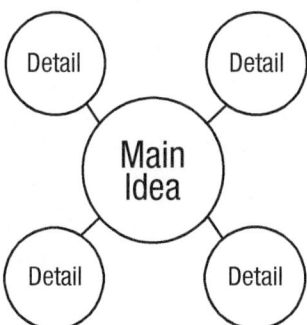

Use with All Lessons

GIFTED & TALENTED

STRATEGY ❶
RESEARCH AND PERFORM A SPEECH

Have students conduct online research to find the text of Eisenhower's "Atoms for Peace" speech, as well as audio and video. Instruct students to choose a segment of the speech and practice it, trying to capture Eisenhower's cadence. Then ask students to perform their speech excerpts for the class.

Use with Lesson 1.1

STRATEGY ❷
CREATE AND ILLUSTRATE A TOURIST MAP

Instruct students to create an illustrated map of Route 66 for tourists, using either paper and markers or online mapping or presentation software. Students may choose to map and illustrate the entire route or a segment of it, perhaps a portion that passes near where they live. Once students have created the basic map of Route 66, tell them to research tourist attractions along the route and illustrate selected points of interest. Invite students to share their maps with the class and answer questions about the tourist destinations they illustrated.

Use with Lesson 2.1

PRE-AP

STRATEGY ❶
WRITE AN ANALYSIS ESSAY

Direct students to conduct research using online and print sources—including maps, charts, U.S. census data, and other documents—to analyze internal migration in the postwar decades. Students could focus on topics such as the migration patterns of Native Americans, Mexican Americans, African Americans, or Caucasian Americans from rural to urban or urban to suburban areas. Prompt students to write an essay analyzing a migration pattern and whether it was or was not part of postwar economic expansion. Invite students to share their essays with the class.

Use with Lessons 1.3 and 3.1

STRATEGY ❷
FORM AND SUPPORT A THESIS

Ask students to choose one of the major changes in U.S. society that took place in the Cold War era, such as a social, political, economic, medical, or technological change. Then instruct students to develop a thesis regarding the factors that contributed to the change and how that change affects or does not affect people's lives today. Direct students to conduct online research to find source materials that support or refute their thesis. Then have students prepare an oral report to present their findings to the class.

Use with Lesson 1.2

HISTORICAL THINKING How did the prosperity of the post–World War II period shape American society?

"I don't care what people say, **rock and roll is here to stay.**"
—Danny and the Juniors

Young couples dance to music at the Harlem Cafe in Greenville, South Carolina, in 1956, while others look over the song list in the coin-operated jukebox. American photographer Margaret Bourke-White took this photo as she traveled through the South.

Postwar Prosperity 849

INTRODUCE THE PHOTOGRAPH

ROCK AND ROLL IS HERE TO STAY

Direct students to study the photograph and caption and read the quotation that opens this chapter. Students should focus on the energy in the photo and music technology of the time. **ASK:** What type of technology is shown in the photograph? How do you think technological developments affected social interactions in the context of the 1950s? *(Students should recognize the jukebox and share what they know about jukeboxes. Possible response: The ability to listen to and share music without needing a live band allowed social gatherings to occur easily.)* Tell students that in this chapter they will learn how changes in technology and increased prosperity after World War II affected the American landscape in the 1950s.

SHARE BACKGROUND

Jukeboxes, such as the one in the photo, were a common sight in the 1950s. Credit for the invention goes to Louis Glass and William S. Arnold, who installed the first coin-operated device that played a musical recording (on a wax cylinder) in 1889. Jukeboxes with disc recordings appeared in the early 1900s and became very popular once amplifiers were invented and then added in the late 1920s. It is estimated that 400,000 jukeboxes could be found in the United States in 1940. By the mid-1950s—due in part to the introduction of jukeboxes that could play as many as 200 songs—the number rose to about to 750,000. Early jukeboxes were designed to resemble radios, but designers for jukebox manufacturers later gave the jukebox the colorful art deco styling that is common today.

For Chapter 24 Spanish Resources, visit the Resources Menu. Chapter 24 Resources are available at NGLSync.Cengage.com.

HISTORICAL THINKING QUESTION

How did the prosperity of the post–World War II period shape American society?

Host a Roundtable Discussion Divide the class into groups of four. Prompt them to name several aspects of society (for example, family life, employment, relationships among various groups). Tell them to imagine that they live in a society that has just gone through a long, traumatic experience. That bleak time has finally passed, and the coming days look brighter. **ASK:** How do you think this new time would affect various aspects of your society? Encourage each student to contribute ideas. Tell students that in Chapter 24 they will learn about ways in which American society—and the United States as a world power—changed following World War II.

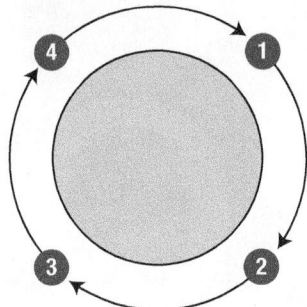

INTRODUCE THE READING STRATEGY

MAKE INFERENCES

Explain to students that by pairing information they read with what they already know and have experienced, they can make inferences—"educated guesses"—about events. Turn to the Chapter Review and preview the graphic organizer with students. As they read the chapter, have students use the text and the primary sources to help them make inferences about political, social, and economic issues of the 1950s.

KEY DATES FOR CHAPTER 24

1953	Dwight D. Eisenhower sworn in as president
1953	United States helps restore the shah of Iran to power
1955	Chuck Berry records "Maybelline"
1955	Jonas Salk introduces the polio vaccine
1956	Federal-Aid Highway Act signed
1957	First large-scale nuclear power plant starts in Pennsylvania
1957	Soviet Union launches *Sputnik 1*
1957	NASA established
1958	National Defense Education Act passed
1960	California Master Plan adopted

INTRODUCE CHAPTER VOCABULARY

KEY VOCABULARY

SECTION 1

agribusiness	covert action	nuclear power
baby boom	Frostbelt	smog
brinkmanship	homogeneity	subdivision
bulwark	Interstate Highway System	suburbanization
consumerism		Sunbelt
consumer society	nuclear deterrence	transistor

SECTION 2

rock and roll	situation comedy	suburban sprawl

SECTION 3

poverty rate	termination policy	urban renewal

WORD WEBS

As they read the chapter, encourage students to complete Word Webs for Key Vocabulary words. Ask them to write each word in the center of an oval. Instruct students to look through the chapter to find examples, characteristics, and descriptive words that may be associated with the vocabulary word. Model a partial example on the board. At the end of the chapter, ask students what they learned about each word.

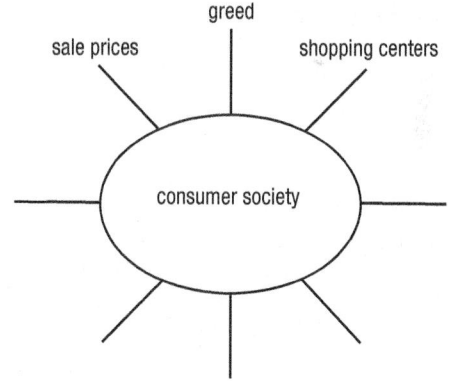

OBJECTIVES

- **Describe the beginnings of rock and roll music and the role it plays in American culture.**
- **Understand how radio and other technology contributed to the nationwide spread of rock and roll.**
- **Learn how the early legends of rock and roll influenced a generation.**
- **Study primary sources: perspectives about rock and roll and excerpts from publications.**

CRITICAL THINKING SKILLS FOR "THE BIRTH OF ROCK AND ROLL"

- Make Connections
- Draw Conclusions
- Summarize
- Analyze Primary Sources
- Form and Support Opinions
- Synthesize

CONNECT TO THE CHAPTER

This American Story explores the birth of rock and roll, a form of music that enthralled teenagers and worried many adults, beginning in the postwar 1950s. Through the study of a narrative featuring quotations, photographs, and an overview of key innovators, students will explore the multiethnic beginnings of the genre and its significance within the changing societal landscape of the United States.

This chapter, Postwar Prosperity, examines American society during the Eisenhower presidency. This time is often noted for the economic growth following World War II and for conformity, as many middle-class white Americans moved to suburbs and participated in traditional domestic roles. Beneath this facade of normalcy, a new, vibrant, and rebellious culture was emerging, and rock and roll was at its center. Use this American Story after reading Lesson 2.3.

HISTORY NOTEBOOK

Encourage students to complete the American Story page for Chapter 24 in their History Notebooks as they read and the Reid on the Road video series page after they view the video.

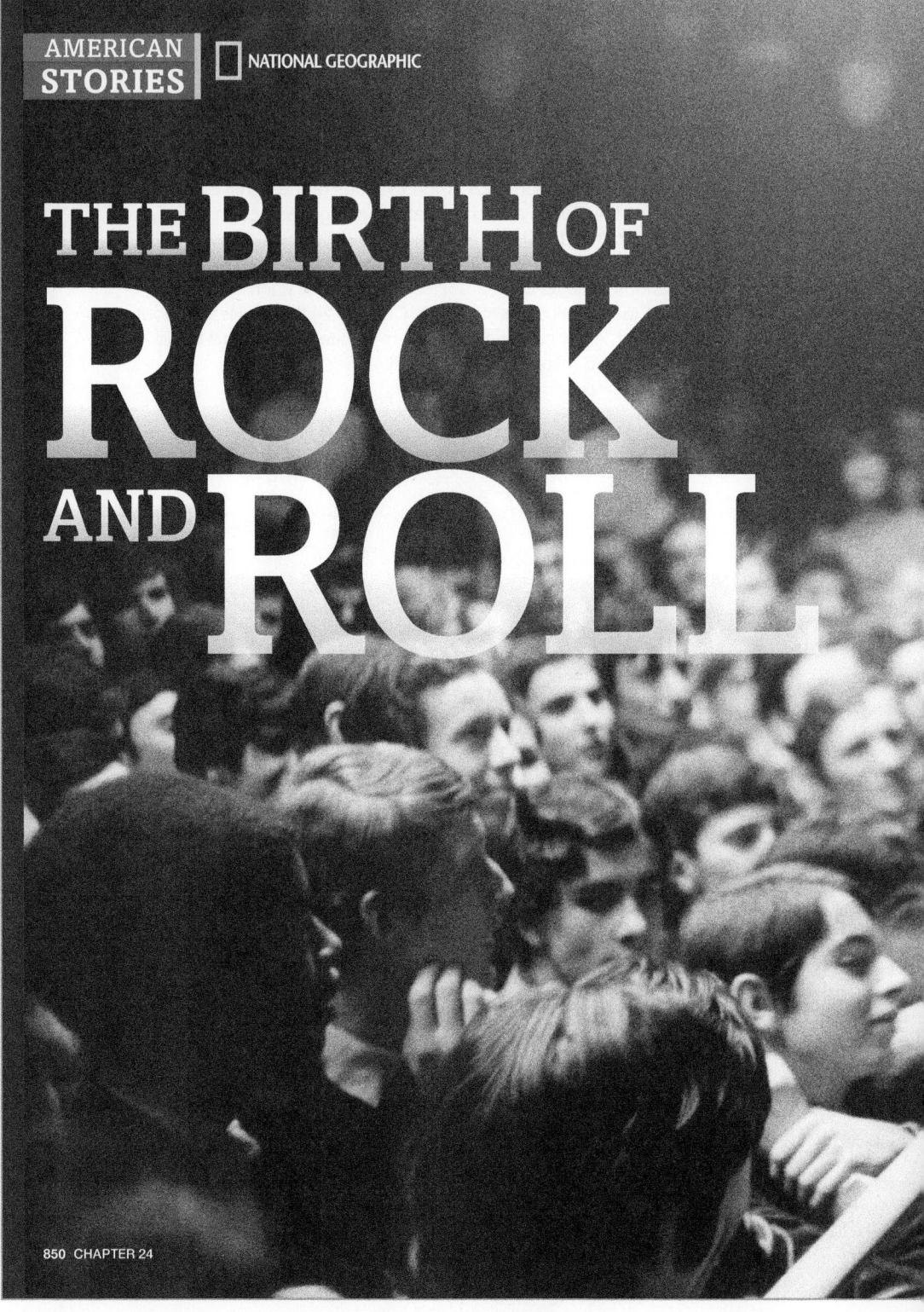

AMERICAN STORIES | NATIONAL GEOGRAPHIC

THE BIRTH OF ROCK AND ROLL

850 CHAPTER 24

CRITICAL VIEWING Rock and roll pioneer Chuck Berry performs before an enthusiastic audience in 1966. What do you observe about the demographics of the crowd?

Postwar Prosperity **851**

INTRODUCE & ENGAGE

REVIEW MUSIC STYLES

Play excerpts of different styles of music for the class. First play an excerpt from a song by Frank Sinatra or Bing Crosby. Have students describe what they hear and describe the style of music. Next play an excerpt from a song by Chuck Berry or Little Richard. Discuss the song and style of music from the second excerpt. **ASK:** How do the two songs differ? *(Possible response: The second was faster, easier to dance to, and features a guitar.)* Then ask students to think about popular music today. Discuss with students what style of music they think is most popular today and why. Include in the discussion what this style of music sounds like and how it is different from the two excerpts they just heard.

SURVEY AND WRITE

Conduct an informal survey among students to establish how many students listen to rock and roll music, how many listen to country music, and so on, naming different genres. If needed, prompt a short discussion about the different genres of music today. Then display the following prompt: How does music define identity? Ask students to spend two minutes freewriting in response to the prompt. Encourage volunteers to share what they have written, and invite comments from the class. Then tell students they are going to read an American Story about how rock and roll defined the identity of a generation.

EXPLORE A CONCEPT

Display the phrase Music and Controversy. Prompt students to discuss the topic and identify current controversies in music as you record their responses on the board. Then have students locate the Frank Sinatra quotation near the end of this American Story. **ASK:** Why do you think Frank Sinatra made this statement about rock and roll? *(Possible response: Frank Sinatra probably felt threatened by the popularity of this new style of music. He may have been concerned that young people would spend their money on rock and roll recordings rather than on his.)* **ASK:** Why might adults outside the music industry have opposed rock and roll? *(Possible response: They may have felt that the music evoked a style of dancing and emotions that threatened societal standards of morality.)* Tell students that in this American Story they will learn about the beginnings of rock and roll music and some controversies during the early years.

CRITICAL VIEWING Except for one African-American young man in the foreground, the crowd appears to be made up of young white males, a demographic quite different from that of the middle-aged African-American performer, Chuck Berry. In spite of this difference, Chuck Berry's music held an appeal that captivated these young men and made them appreciate and respect his talent.

CHUCK BERRY

Rock and roll pioneer Chuck Berry was raised in a segregated neighborhood in St. Louis, Missouri, enmeshed in the sounds of gospel, blues, country, and R & B music. By the early 1950s, he was playing in local bands, focusing mainly on blues, pop, and country. It was in the mid-1950s that he changed music forever. From another guitarist, T-Bone Walker, Berry learned to bend—and rough up—two strings at once. This sound became known as the "Chuck Berry lick" and has been copied countless times by other bands, including the Rolling Stones. Despite his popularity, musical hits, and influence on rock and roll, he never won a Grammy Award until he was given a lifetime achievement award in 1984. In 1986, Berry was inducted into the Rock and Roll Hall of Fame.

ROCK AND ROLL SONGWRITERS

Although performers like Elvis Presley and Jerry Lee Lewis are the most famous names from the beginnings of rock and roll, their success relied on an important group that is often overlooked—songwriters. Many early performers did not write their own music and depended on composers to write the memorable hits of the era. For example, Jerry Leiber and Mike Stoller penned the Elvis hits "Jailhouse Rock" and "Hound Dog." Doc Pomus and Mort Shuman also wrote some of Elvis's hits, including "Viva Las Vegas," as well as some of the greatest songs in rock history, including the Drifters' hit song "This Magic Moment." Phil Spector wrote and produced a flurry of hits for Ben E. King, Gene Pitney, Curtis Lee, and—later—the Beatles.

AMERICAN STORIES

Transistor radio c. 1960

It's the rhythm that gets to the kids— they're starved for music they can dance to, after all those years of crooners.

—disc jockey Alan Freed, 1956

Since the dawn of humanity,

there have been teenagers. The word *teenager*, however, didn't come into existence until sometime during World War II. At the time, there was nothing new about young people coming of age and seeking ways to rebel against society's norms. In the 1920s' Jazz Age, youths in their twenties defined themselves through music, clothing, and behavior that their elders found scandalous. In the 1940s and 1950s, the rebels were a little younger—high-school age—but they too sought their own social identity. And, like the jazz fans of the 1920s, they were looking for a new kind of music to serve as the soundtrack to their rebellion.

As the 1950s dawned, the tunes playing on America's pop radio stations weren't exactly exciting to a teenage audience. A record producer of the era later recalled, "Big fiddle-faddle orchestras . . . played lush mood music for relaxing, cocktails, and vacationing in far-away places." Such singers as Frank Sinatra and Bing Crosby—known as "crooners" because of their deep voices and smooth, romantic styles—dominated the airwaves, appealing to mainly white audiences.

American teenagers, however, were looking for something different in the way of entertainment, and they had the money to spend on it in the prosperous postwar economy. Teens also had access to new technology that made it easier to buy and listen to music independently from their parents.

Transistor radios like the one shown above were small, portable units, unlike the large console radios that squatted somberly in a family's living room. Advancements in recording technology allowed teens to buy inexpensive "singles," small vinyl records that featured just one song on each side.

While the crooners serenaded white listeners, many African Americans were drawn to "race records," songs with strong, syncopated beats and a sound directly derived from jazz and the blues. Around 1950, the term *race records* was replaced by the more accurate—and less offensive—*rhythm and blues*, or R & B.

One record store owner in Cleveland, Ohio, noticed his white teenage customers purchasing R & B records in large numbers. When he shared this information with local disc jockey Alan Freed, a rock and roll phenomenon was born. Freed debuted *The Moondog Show* on WJW radio in June 1951 in an exuberant, unheard-of style. As the records spun, Freed would leave his microphone on and accompany the music with cries of "Ho, now!" and "Go! Go! Gogogogogogogo!" while pounding madly on a phone book he kept in the studio. Music critic Ed Ward later wrote, "It was just what a very large number of teenagers had been waiting all their lives to hear." Freed is credited with first using the term *rock and roll* to describe the music that was emerging from R & B in the 1950s.

Guitar wizard Les Paul plays in the New York City nightclub called Fat Tuesday's.

LES PAUL

New technologies helped create the distinctive sounds of rock and roll both onstage and in the recording studios. One of rock's most influential early innovators was Les Paul, an inventor and popular, well-respected guitarist.

Paul was a pioneer in the use of overdubbing—recording a performance, and then replaying it and layering additional instruments or voices onto the recording. Using overdubbing, Paul sped up the sound of his guitar to create new and unusual effects. In 1952, he invented the eight-track tape recorder, which facilitated overdubbing and became standard in the recording industry. Today, music recording has gone digital, but the complex, layered sounds listeners are accustomed to hearing owe much to Paul's experiments.

Paul is perhaps best known for the solid-body electric guitar he designed, which was also released in 1952. He had worked for years to perfect an electric guitar that could sound and sustain a note without distortions. Paul's was not the first solid-body guitar on the market; the Fender Broadcaster had been introduced in 1948. However, the Les Paul Standard, sold by the Gibson guitar company, quickly rose in popularity and was adopted by many legendary rock guitarists.

Throughout his inventing career, Paul remained an accomplished, Grammy-winning performer. He was inducted into the Rock and Roll Hall of Fame in 1988 and continued both tinkering and performing until his death in 2009.

1968 Prototype Gibson Les Paul Custom Recording Model

1952 Gibson Les Paul Goldtop

GUIDED DISCUSSION

1. **Summarize** How did technological developments contribute to the popularity of rock and roll in the 1950s? *(Technological innovations like the transistor radio made listening to music without parental supervision easier. Also, the introduction of vinyl singles allowed fans to purchase songs. Processes such as overdubbing gave rock and roll recordings a unique and exciting sound.)*

2. **Analyze Primary Sources** Direct students' attention to the Alan Freed quotation. **ASK:** What criticism does Freed offer concerning previous genres of music? *(Freed suggests they lacked rhythm, were hard to dance to, and didn't appeal to younger audiences.)*

LES PAUL

Prior to overdubbing, recording music was a slow and arduous process. For mono and early stereo recordings, all members of a band were in the same room and recorded a song on a single track. With this method, however, if one performance was off—such as the vocals or drums—the entire recording needed to be redone. Overdubbing solved this by allowing different performers to perform separately. Individual performances could then be edited and perfected before the entire song was put together. Thus if the guitar was out of tune but the rest of the song was perfect, only the guitar player had more work to do. **ASK:** How did Les Paul's innovations change music? *(Through overdubbing, Les Paul gave music a complex and more polished sound. The electric guitar he designed sustained notes without distortion and became hugely popular with many rock guitarists.)*

TOP OF THE LIST

In existence for more than 120 years, *Billboard* is one of the oldest continuous publications in the United States. Beginning in 1894, *Billboard* was originally conceived to cover the outdoor advertising industry—hence its name. Over the years, its focus changed to entertainment, as it covered circuses, fairs, vaudeville acts, minstrel shows, movies, and television. The first regular column on music began in 1905, but it wasn't until 1940 that the famous charts first appeared.

Changes in the music industry have not negatively affected the publication. Historically, the charts have adapted to reflect new technologies, such as singles, CDs, digital downloads, and streaming music. In 1958, *Billboard* introduced its "Hot 100" list, which tracks the popularity of songs based on sales and airplay. According to this measure, as of 2013, "The Twist" by Chubby Checker was the most popular song of all time. **ASK:** How can historians use publications like *Billboard* to understand social trends and developments? *(Because of its long history,* Billboard *offers information about changes in the social aspect of entertainment across American history. For example, historians could study the charts to understand when new genres, such as rock and roll or rap, became popular, which may indicate larger societal trends and developments.)*

Freed moved to New York in 1954 and began to organize R & B concerts that drew enthusiastic audiences of both white and African-American teens. He drew criticism from those who considered rock and roll obscene and from those who objected to people of different races mixing socially, but his popularity expanded throughout the 1950s.

Who were the artists making the new music that enthralled American teens and horrified many of their elders? In the early 1950s, most of the hit-makers were male, with roots in R & B or country and western music. Bill Haley, for example, started his career playing in a country band called the Saddlemen, but he loved the blues and experimented with combining many musical traditions. In 1953, the Saddlemen became Bill Haley & His Comets. In 1954, they released the single "Rock Around the Clock," which was featured in the 1955 film *Blackboard Jungle* and became a wildly successful anthem for the new rock generation, selling a record-setting 6 million copies.

Meanwhile, in Memphis, Tennessee, record producer Sam Phillips was frustrated because he was recording tracks by talented black musicians, but white radio stations would not give them airtime.

"If I could find a white man with the Negro sound and Negro feel, I could make a million dollars," he told his assistant. Enter Elvis Presley, soon to become a rock star of unprecedented fame and teen idol to millions worldwide.

Presley's signature sound was strongly influenced by the African-American blues and gospel singers he had listened to in his youth, and he gratefully acknowledged their contributions throughout his career. In addition to having a versatile singing voice, Presley was handsome and charismatic, had a dazzling smile, and performed energetic, provocative dance moves. Presley once remarked, "Rock and roll music, if you like it, if you feel it, you can't help but move to it. That's what happens to me. I can't help it." Not everyone agreed that Presley's way of moving was a good thing. When he appeared on a popular television variety show, he was filmed from the waist up because his hip shimmy was considered too suggestive for viewers. One Catholic cardinal accused Presley of promoting a "creed of dishonesty, violence, lust, and degeneration" among teens. Presley's best-selling singles of the 1950s include "Hound Dog," "Jailhouse Rock," "Heartbreak Hotel," "Love Me Tender," and "Don't Be Cruel."

Rock and roll singer Elvis Presley leans toward his screaming fans during an outdoor concert around 1957.

TOP OF THE LIST

In the 1950s, *Billboard* was a magazine that tracked the popularity of individual musicians and songs, publishing weekly charts of top sellers. From 1950 through 1954, the number one songs on the *Billboard* charts were mostly swing songs and ballads, with frequent appearances by such crooners as Tony Bennett and Frank Sinatra. Les Paul and his wife Mary Ford appeared on the 1953 list with a slow song called "Vaya Con Dios" (May God Be With You).

In July 1955, "Rock Around the Clock" by Bill Haley and His Comets took the number one spot, opening the door for rock and roll to dominate the charts. Chuck Berry and Little Richard also had hit records in 1955, and by 1957, rock and roll musicians were regular top sellers.

Excerpt from *Billboard*'s Top 50 Best Sellers in Stores, November 18, 1957

Position In List	TITLE	ARTIST
1	JAILHOUSE ROCK	Elvis Presley
2	WAKE UP LITTLE SUSIE	The Everly Brothers
3	YOU SEND ME	Sam Cooke
4	SILHOUETTES	The Rays
5	BE-BOP BABY	Ricky Nelson
6	LITTLE BITTY PRETTY ONE	Thurston Harris
7	MY SPECIAL ANGEL	Bobby Helms
8	APRIL LOVE	Pat Boone
9	CHANCES ARE	Johnny Mathis
10	HONEYCOMB	Jimmie Rodgers
15	KEEP A KNOCKIN'	Little Richard
19	ROCK AND ROLL MUSIC	Chuck Berry
25	PEGGY SUE	Buddy Holly
30	WAIT AND SEE	Fats Domino
39	WHOLE LOTTA SHAKIN' GOIN' ON	Jerry Lee Lewis
40	THAT'LL BE THE DAY	The Crickets (Buddy Holly)

Joel Whitburn's Top Pop Playlists 1955–1969, 2014

Postwar Prosperity **855**

GUIDED DISCUSSION

3. **Draw Conclusions** How did racial attitudes during the 1950s contribute to the rise of Elvis Presley? Use primary source evidence from the text to support your answer. *(Possible response: Because of racial prejudice, it was difficult for African-American musicians to get airtime even though their music was popular. Elvis benefited from this dynamic, as he was a white artist whose style was influenced by and similar to that of African-American singers. Sam Phillips describes this issue in his quotation, explaining that a white man performing the "Negro sound" would "make a million dollars.")*

4. **Form and Support Opinions** Remind students that rock and roll is an art form that originated within the United States. **ASK:** Could rock and roll have developed in a different society? Explain your reasoning. *(Answers will vary. Possible response: the unique cultural makeup of the United States—particularly with the contributions of African-American musical traditions—was vital to rock and roll's development. It's unlikely that a similar sound would have developed in a different country.)*

ACTIVE OPTIONS

On Your Feet: Debate Contributions to Rock and Roll Divide the class into multiple teams and assign each team one of the rock and roll legends—such as Alan Freed, Elvis Presley, or Chuck Berry—featured in this American Story. Give teams time to form an argument for why their individual was the most important person in the rise of rock and roll. Have teams present their arguments and respond to their classmates' questions and comments.

NG Learning Framework: Study Cultural Change

ATTITUDE Curiosity

KNOWLEDGE Our Human Story

Locate online a *Billboard* top sellers chart from 1950 and one from 1957 and display them for the class. Explain that historians can use documents like the *Billboard* charts to help them understand cultural identity by examining specific preferences of a group for a specific time. Arrange students in groups and instruct them to research a few songs from each chart to determine the ethnicity of the artist, genre, and likely audience. Then have students prepare a short presentation in which they identify and explain the cultural identity of 1950 versus 1957 based on the type of music that was most popular. After each presentation, prompt the class to make comments and ask questions about larger social, economic, and political trends that might account for differences between the two cultural identities.

COVERING UP

Since the advent of radio entertainment, controversy has continually brewed over what is appropriate to play over the air. In the 1960s, the Rolling Stones' song "(I Can't Get No) Satisfaction" received limited airtime due to its suggestive lyrics. In 1981, Olivia Newton-John's "Physical" was barred from two Utah stations because of the sexual connotations of the word *physical*. **ASK:** Do cover artists deserve credit for increasing the popularity of rock and roll by "cleaning it up"? Why or why not? *(Answers will vary. Some students may argue that covers promoted the music to a larger audience, increasing rock and roll's popularity. Others may claim that sanitized versions were lesser imitations of the real thing.)*

THE DAY THE MUSIC DIED

Ritchie Valens's seat on the plane ride that claimed his life came down to chance. Valens and Tommy Allsup, a member of Buddy Holly's band, had flipped a coin to see who would ride on the plane instead of the bus to the next tour stop. Valens correctly called heads. **ASK:** What evidence from the front page of the *Mason City Globe-Gazette* can be used to make an argument concerning the significance of the plane crash and the popularity of the musicians involved? *(Possible response: It can be argued this was a very significant event since it is the subject of the headline and the front-page article. The word* idols *shows the popularity of the musicians.)*

THINK ABOUT IT

By exposing people to new ideas, rock and roll can be seen as a precursor to changes in the 1960s, such as the sexual revolution and the civil rights movement.

AMERICAN STORIES

While performing with his band in 1956, rock and roll star Little Richard props his foot on top of the piano, a signature move.

COVERING UP

Today, when a song has potentially offensive lyrics, radio stations play it with the problematic words edited out. In the 1950s, a cover artist would record the song with alterations to make it appealing to different markets. Many R & B hits, for example, were recorded in "sanitized" versions that were more acceptable to the decision-makers at pop radio stations. It was not uncommon for several versions of a hit song to be in circulation at the same time.

Pat Boone was one of the most successful of the cover artists, with an enthusiastic following of mostly white teenagers and a string of hit songs. His clean-cut, wholesome image presented a contrast to the raucous and raw performances of Elvis Presley, Little Richard, and other early rockers. In 1956, rock and roll music reached a milestone when Little Richard's sensual recordings of "Long Tall Sally" and "Rip It Up" outsold Pat Boone's covers of the same tunes. Parents and conservative radio station owners may have preferred the white cover artist's cleaned-up version, but the younger generation had voted with their dollars.

> **Rock and roll is the most brutal, ugly, degenerate, vicious form of expression—lewd, sly, in plain fact, dirt.** —singer Frank Sinatra, 1957

Several African-American stars also rose to fame on the rock and roll tide. Little Richard burst onto the scene with a flamboyant splash and was one of the first African-American rock and roll musicians to play to integrated audiences. A brilliant pianist, Little Richard fixed his audiences with an intense, wide-eyed gaze and astonished them with irrepressible dance moves, sometimes planting a foot on top of the piano as he played. In the words of music writer Donald Clarke, "In two minutes [Little Richard] used as much energy as an all-night party." Little Richard's hit songs "Tutti Frutti" and "Good Golly Miss Molly" were hugely popular, but because his lyrics were suggestive, he received relatively little airplay.

Chuck Berry, another African-American musician, was an early master of the instrument that came to define the sound of rock and roll—the electric guitar. His dexterous playing and unforgettable guitar licks, or short patterns of notes, influenced generations of players. Berry engaged his listeners with songs that told a story. His first hit, "Maybellene," narrated the comic miseries of a man chasing after his unfaithful girlfriend. "Sweet Little Sixteen" spoke directly to the teenagers in his audience.

By the end of the 1950s, some people felt, and perhaps hoped, rock and roll was a fad that would quickly fade away. Instead, it not only endured but evolved into a musical scene more diverse than even Alan Freed might have imagined. Later rock stars have acknowledged the debt they owe to the musicians who pioneered the genre. In fact, singer-songwriter John Lennon of the Beatles, one of the best-selling rock bands of all time, introduced Chuck Berry on a 1972 television show by saying, "If you had to give rock and roll another name, you might call it Chuck Berry."

THINK ABOUT IT

How did the introduction of rock and roll serve as a means for social change?

THE DAY THE MUSIC DIED

Ritchie Valens, the first Latino rock and roll star, added a distinctive Mexican flavor to the R & B beat of his songs. Born in California, the Mexican American singer had a number of hits in his short career, including "Donna," which reached number two on the pop charts in 1959. Today, he is best remembered for "La Bamba," a Mexican folk tune with a rock and roll beat. Since its first release in 1958, the song has been recorded by several bands, including Los Lobos.

While still a teenager, Valens appeared on national television and on Alan Freed's radio show. In 1959, Valens went on tour with a group of fellow rock sensations, including Buddy Holly, whose 1957 song "That'll Be the Day" had reached number one on the charts in both the United States and Great Britain. On February 3, Valens, Holly, and J. P. "the Big Bopper" Richardson boarded a small plane for their next stop on the tour. The plane crashed near Clear Lake, Iowa, killing everyone aboard. Valens was just 17 years old, and Holly just 22. In 1971, singer Don McLean wrote a popular song about the crash and called it "American Pie." In the song, McLean referred to the tragedy as "the day the music died."

A self-taught musician, Ritchie Valens joined his first band at age 16.

MASON CITY GLOBE-GAZETTE
"The Newspaper That Makes All North Iowans Neighbors"

Rock 'n' Roll Idols Among Lake Crash Dead

Plane Piloted by Clear Lake Man Plows Into Field

Bodies of two victims (arrows) lie near the demolished plane in stubble field

Russ Hold ... Iowa's Right-to-Work Law ... '3 Reasons'

An Iowa newspaper reports the plane crash that killed a local pilot and musicians Ritchie Valens, Buddy Holly, and J. P. Richardson on February 3, 1959.

ENGLISH LANGUAGE LEARNERS

Create a Word Web Pair students at the **Emerging** and **Expanding** levels with students at the **Bridging** level. Tell students to take turns reading paragraphs aloud, noting words related to rock and roll music. Instruct students to write words they note on the spokes of a Word Web, adding more spokes if necessary. Ask pairs to trade and compare their webs.

GIFTED & TALENTED

Create a Multimedia Newscast Challenge students to conduct online research to find archival news reports, photographs, and footage of early rock and roll artists and performances. Then have students write a script in the form of a contemporary newscast, incorporating the information, images, and film clips they discovered. Instruct students to assemble their script and materials into a multimedia newscast about the birth of rock and roll music and present it to the class.

See the Chapter Planner for more strategies for differentiation.

HISTORICAL THINKING

Ask and have students answer the following questions.

1. **READING CHECK** What events contributed to rock and roll's initial popularity?

2. **SUMMARIZE** Why was rock and roll controversial?

3. **SYNTHESIZE** How did African Americans contribute to the rise of rock and roll music?

4. **FORM AND SUPPORT OPINIONS** Does rock and roll still hold the same cultural significance it did in the 1950s?

ANSWERS

1. Possible response: Music combining jazz and blues emerged, relying on syncopated beats and guitar sounds. Alan Freed played this new music and stirred enthusiasm with his exuberant commentary. Teenagers loved the music and bought the records.

2. Some adults reacted negatively to suggestive song lyrics and dance moves. Some associated the genre with African Americans and the mixing of black and white cultures, which went against the prevailing racial attitudes.

3. Rock and roll grew out of African-American musical styles, such as gospel, jazz, and blues, and many of the earliest stars were African Americans.

4. Answers will vary. Possible response: No. While rock and roll is still popular, other forms of music, such as rap, are now more important to understanding current culture.

MAIN IDEA As a moderate Republican, President Eisenhower continued many of Truman's domestic policies but introduced a new approach in foreign policy.

EISENHOWER AS PRESIDENT

Have you ever found it hard to choose sides in a political debate? Dwight D. Eisenhower didn't fit neatly on either the Democratic or the Republican side. But when he ran for president, he had to choose.

THE ELECTION OF EISENHOWER

The Cold War affected not only the nation's foreign policy but also the lives of everyday Americans. The United States enjoyed great prosperity and stability in the post–World War II period, made possible in part by the growth of industries that provided the technology needed to fight the Cold War. Not all Americans shared in the general prosperity, however. Minorities continued to face discrimination that made it more difficult to achieve the American dream of a secure job, a comfortable home, and a healthy family.

As the Cold War continued, Americans turned to a strong general to lead the country's government and maintain stability.

In preparation for the 1952 presidential election, Democrats and Republicans searched for candidates to nominate. Both parties approached the same person—General Dwight D. Eisenhower, a celebrated World War II general and former commander of NATO forces. Until this time, Eisenhower had never declared allegiance to a particular political party.

In this photograph from September 1956, President Eisenhower (left) escorts Vice President Nixon (right) to the airplane that would take Nixon on a campaign tour for their re-election.

In January 1952, he chose to run for president as a Republican, probably to distance himself from Truman and the Democratic Party, which had been losing popularity.

The Republican Party had problems as well. The party was split between moderates and conservatives, who fought each other for control. Eisenhower, a moderate, had to face off against a conservative Republican leader, Ohio senator Robert A. Taft. Eisenhower's fame as a dynamic leader won him the nomination and unified the party. The Democrats nominated the governor of Illinois, **Adlai Stevenson**. While Stevenson was a distinguished diplomat and had helped found the United Nations, he lacked the popularity that bolstered Eisenhower's election campaign.

Eisenhower did not wage a typical Republican campaign. He supported many of Truman's Fair Deal programs, which conservative Republicans threatened to revoke, and he vowed to support the U.S. soldiers who were fighting in the Korean War. But he purposefully left out specific details about his goals as president. He stated he was "pro-business" and practiced "modern Republicanism," which he defined as economic conservatism paired with social liberalism. Eisenhower and his running mate, Richard Nixon, beat Stevenson in a landslide, 442 electoral votes to 89.

Eisenhower immediately assigned several business leaders to his Cabinet. He chose the former president of General Motors, Charles E. Wilson, to serve as secretary of defense and a former steel company president, George Humphrey, to serve as secretary of the treasury. In 1953, he appointed Oveta Culp Hobby, the first commander of the Woman's Army Corps (WACs), to run the newly created Department of Health, Education, and Welfare. Eisenhower took measures to continue Social Security and unemployment insurance but otherwise cut government spending whenever he could. And due to the liberal consensus, which you have read about, Congress was usually willing to follow his lead.

PROSPERITY UNDER EISENHOWER

Postwar prosperity continued through the 1950s for the majority of Americans. This ongoing economic success was due largely to the position of the United States as a dominant world power, which enabled the nation to negotiate advantageous trade deals worldwide, and its embrace of **consumerism**. According to the theory of consumerism, the economy flourishes when people buy, or consume, a lot of goods and services.

The country's new role as a world leader meant the United States had to be on the cutting edge of technology. Military defense, electronics, and aerospace industries, essential to fighting the Cold War, flourished. Many of these industries were located in the **Sunbelt**, the southern region of the country that enjoys warm weather year-round. As a result, people from the **Frostbelt**, the north-central and northeastern region that has cold winters, migrated to Georgia, Florida, Texas, and California, where manufacturing jobs were on the rise.

Labor unions grew stronger and helped expand the middle class by ensuring that their members, who worked in these booming industries, received competitive pay, health insurance, paid vacations, and retirement benefits. Additionally, the number of service-sector, white-collar, and professional-sector jobs in business and government increased.

The growing middle class had more money to spend on consumer goods, such as food and automobiles. New industries developed to meet consumers' demands. Railroad, bank, and meatpacking companies created **agribusiness**—or the commercial business of agriculture—by buying up small family farms and creating huge, efficient factory farms. The companies converted the relatively humble occupation of farming into lucrative businesses. They opened supermarkets that offered middle-class shoppers a much wider variety of foods than was available at small corner markets.

As more people bought cars, the demand for highways and gasoline grew. Oil companies expanded their exploration programs and refineries and quickly became dominant businesses. Gas stations and auto repair shops flourished.

The growth of industries had some negative effects, however. Throughout the 1950s and into the 1960s, industrial waste products polluted the air and the lakes and rivers of major cities. **Smog**, a noxious combination of fog and smoke from factories, began to blanket such cities as Gary, Indiana, and Pittsburgh, Pennsylvania. The beaches of Lake Erie, the smallest and shallowest of the Great Lakes, were often covered in dead fish, killed by industrial pollutants that poisoned the water.

COLD WAR DEVELOPMENTS

Just as he supported many of Truman's domestic policies, Eisenhower also supported Truman's containment policy, aimed at preventing the spread of communism in the world. However, Eisenhower believed he could prevent any communist advance

OBJECTIVE

Analyze how the Cold War affected foreign policy and the lives of everyday Americans.

CRITICAL THINKING SKILLS FOR LESSON 1.1

- Describe
- Interpret Time Lines
- Evaluate
- Make Inferences
- Analyze Environmental Concepts
- Make Connections
- Synthesize
- Compare and Contrast
- Analyze Primary Sources

HISTORICAL THINKING FOR CHAPTER 24

How did the prosperity of the post–World War II period shape American society? President Eisenhower's "pro-business" stance helped new industries develop to meet the needs of a growing middle class. Lesson 1.1 discusses the effects of domestic prosperity and the development of new industries needed to fight the Cold War.

BACKGROUND FOR THE TEACHER

Because of health concerns following two dangerous illnesses, there was early doubt that President Eisenhower would run for a second term. However, Eisenhower announced his willingness to return to office. Eisenhower and Nixon easily won the nomination at the Republican National Convention and ran on the slogan "We like and we'll stick with Ike and Dick." The Democrats once again nominated Adlai Stevenson. Both the Republicans and Democrats relied on the new popularity of television for their campaigns. Eisenhower was endorsed by three-fifths of the country's newspapers and went on to win the election; in fact, he bettered his 1952 results, receiving 57.4 percent of the popular vote and 457 electoral votes.

INTRODUCE & ENGAGE

DISCUSS POSTWAR PROMISES

Write the title Peace, Progress, and Prosperity on the board, followed by the headings National Economy, Foreign Policy, and Domestic Tranquility. Direct students' attention to the 1953 campaign button shown on the time line. Ask students to suggest postwar aspirations that Americans may have had as they left the war years behind them and looked to the future. Add students' ideas under each heading.

ASK: How might Americans have interpreted the promise of peace, progress, and prosperity in the context of the postwar years? (*Possible responses: greater job opportunities, more personal income, fewer foreign involvements, a focus on expanding America's infrastructure*)

Peace, Progress, and Prosperity		
National Economy	Foreign Policy	Domestic Tranquility

TEACH

GUIDED DISCUSSION

1. **Make Inferences** How did the position of the United States as a dominant world power encourage American consumerism? (*The United States could negotiate advantageous trade deals worldwide, reducing the price of goods and providing an incentive for Americans to purchase more items.*)

2. **Analyze Environmental Concepts** How were natural systems affected by the growth of industry in places like Gary, Indiana, and Pittsburgh, Pennsylvania? (*Industrial waste products polluted the air, lakes, and rivers of major cities. Smog blanketed cities, and beaches along the Great Lakes were sometimes covered by dead fish killed by industrial pollutants.*)

3. **Make Connections** In matters of foreign policy, how did the powers of the presidency increase in response to the Cold War, and in what way was the exercise of those increased powers integral to the Cold War policies of Eisenhower's administration? (*Eisenhower authorized the CIA to become involved in covert actions as part of his foreign policy. These actions included interference in the politics of foreign governments that Eisenhower viewed as communist threats.*)

MORE INFORMATION

The Sunbelt Explain that the term *Sunbelt* refers to the warm, sunny region across the southern and southwestern portion of the United States, which experienced rapid postwar economic and population growth. Point out that thousands of people migrated from colder Frostbelt states to Phoenix, Arizona, in the late 1950s—not only for its climate but also for the region's economic focus on technology used by the military. The city's quick growth was assisted by investments from the federal, state, and local governments and encouraged through efforts of the Phoenix Chamber of Commerce and the state tourist industry. In one such case in 1946, the federal government passed the Federal Airport Act. Monies from this grant combined with funds from the city of Phoenix to expand the regional airport. The growth of highways and railroads, including the Southern Pacific and the Santa Fe, connected Phoenix with cities across the nation. The state provided tax incentives to bring businesses to the region, and the military attracted such growing electronics firms as Motorola and General Electric due to the presence of Fort Huachuca.

ASK: Based on the example of Phoenix, what effect do you think the rapid growth of the Sunbelt had on the region's infrastructure? (*Possible response: With so many people moving to the Sunbelt, the region needed to expand its infrastructure to serve the increased population. The newly expanded infrastructure made travel to and from the region easier and probably encouraged even more people to migrate.*)

DIFFERENTIATE

STRIVING READERS

Understand Main Ideas Check students' understanding of the main ideas by asking them to correctly complete either/or statements such as the following:

- Eisenhower was a(n) [usual or unusual] Republican candidate who [supported or did not support] many policies of Truman's Democratic administration.

- Labor unions grew [stronger or weaker] during the Eisenhower presidency.

- The rise of large agribusiness led to [more or fewer] farmers.

- Under Eisenhower's policy of nuclear deterrence, defense spending [increased or decreased].

PRE-AP

Connect Past to Present Challenge students to conduct research about the environmental impacts that accompanied the growth of industry in the Eisenhower years. Then have them research current environmental impacts of an industry in their area. Tell students to utilize multiple print and digital sources and to combine their research into past and present to write a report on the environmental impacts of industry. As students do their research, remind them to evaluate the credibility and accuracy of each source. Instruct students to document data that they quote or paraphrase and to follow a standard format for citation. Invite students to share their reports with the class.

See the Chapter Planner for more strategies for differentiation.

February 1953
President Eisenhower appoints Allen Dulles, the brother of Secretary of State John Foster Dulles, to head the CIA.

July 27, 1953
China signs a truce establishing North and South Korea, thus ending the Korean War.

June 18, 1954
The CIA stages a coup in Guatemala, replacing the recently elected president with a military dictator who supports United States' interests.

July 26, 1956
President Nasser takes control of the Suez Canal in Egypt. (Container ship in the modern Suez Canal)

November 4, 1956
Soviets crush the Hungarian revolt.

November 6, 1956
Eisenhower is re-elected to a second term as president.

1953   1954   1955   1956

January 20, 1953
Dwight D. Eisenhower is sworn in as the 34th president of the United States. (Campaign button of Dwight "Ike" Eisenhower, 1952)

August 19, 1953
The United States restores the shah of Iran to power after his prime minister had successfully overthrown him a few days before. (Reza Shah Pahlavi's honor guard salutes him upon his return to Iran in 1953.)

October 23, 1956
Hungarian citizens revolt against Soviet troops in Budapest. (Hungarians burn a portrait of Stalin in 1956.)

November 6, 1956
Egypt, Israel, Britain, and France sign a cease-fire in the Suez Canal conflict. (United Nations peacekeeping troops in Port Said, Egypt, in 1956)

PRIMARY SOURCE

As the threat of nuclear war loomed in 1953, President Eisenhower addressed the United Nations about his nuclear deterrence policy.

I know that the American people share my deep belief that if a danger exists in the world, it is a danger shared by all—and equally, that if hope exists in the mind of one nation, that hope should be shared by all. . . . Atomic bombs today are more than 25 times as powerful as the weapons with which the atomic age dawned, while hydrogen weapons are in the ranges of millions of tons of TNT equivalent. . . . But the dread secret, and the fearful engines of atomic might, are not ours alone.

—from President Eisenhower's "Atoms for Peace" address to the United Nations, December 8, 1953

by using the threat of a nuclear attack rather than by mobilizing an army. Eisenhower's plan was called **nuclear deterrence**. It involved placing enough nuclear weapons in numerous safe places to guarantee that an enemy could not destroy all the weapons at once. Supposedly, nations would not risk war because both sides would be annihilated. Nuclear deterrence resulted in a world constantly on the brink, or the edge, of nuclear war. Secretary of State **John Foster Dulles** called this tension "**brinkmanship**," claiming that "the ability to get to the verge without getting into the war is the necessary art." Critics of nuclear deterrence claimed it was too dangerous. Still, the production of nuclear warheads increased, while the number of soldiers in service decreased and overall defense spending was actually cut by 20 percent between 1953 and 1955.

Meanwhile, the importance of strategic military bases in Hawaii and Alaska helped move these two U.S. territories toward full statehood. Near the end of Eisenhower's terms of office, in 1959, first Alaska and then Hawaii became the 49th and 50th states.

U.S. INVOLVEMENT OVERSEAS

As part of his containment program, Eisenhower gave the Central Intelligence Agency (CIA) new authority to investigate communism in other countries. In 1953, Eisenhower appointed **Allen Dulles** to head the CIA. Under Dulles, the CIA practiced **covert action**, gathering intelligence and secretly getting involved in the politics and internal affairs of other nations. In opposing communism, the United States came to support some authoritarian and corrupt governments.

For example, in 1953 in Iran, a new, duly elected government led by Prime Minister **Mohammad Mossadegh** (MOH-sah-dehk) deposed

the shah, or king, named **Reza Shah Pahlavi** (rih-ZAH shah PAH-luh-vee). The U.S. government feared Mossadegh was a communist. Eisenhower did not want a communist heading the country from which the United States received most of its oil, so he commanded the CIA to work with the secret services of other nations to topple Mossadegh and return the shah to power. In exchange, the shah's government granted American companies 40 percent of Iran's oil production. Reacting to similar communist suspicions, in 1954 the CIA ousted the newly elected president of Guatemala, **Jacobo Árbenz Guzmán**, and replaced him with a military dictator who protected American business interests in that Central American nation.

In 1956, two major world events captured Americans' attention. In Budapest, Hungary, citizens revolted against the communists that governed their country. Street battles soon escalated into all-out war. The Soviet Union sent troops to help the Hungarian government. Eisenhower refused to send American troops for fear of triggering a war between the United States and the Soviet Union. Soviet troops crushed the revolt within a month.

In Egypt, President **Gamal Abdel Nasser** seized control of the **Suez Canal**, the British-controlled waterway that lay between Africa and Asia, connecting the Red and Mediterranean seas. Two months later, Israeli troops advanced on Egypt,

followed by French and British paratroopers who worked together to retake the canal. Tensions heightened when the Soviet Union threatened nuclear war on Western Europe if Israel, Britain, and France did not withdraw from Egypt. A cease-fire resolved the situation, but the canal remained a source of conflict.

Meanwhile, the Cold War continued. As you've read, the Truman Doctrine supported free people and nations resisting communist takeovers. Although Eisenhower had failed to live up to this doctrine in Hungary, he continued to funnel money and American soldiers to Turkey and Greece, the **bulwarks**, or protective defenses, against Soviet expansion into the Middle East and Africa.

HISTORICAL THINKING

1. **READING CHECK** Which of Truman's domestic policies did President Eisenhower continue?

2. **DESCRIBE** How did technological development affect society and the economy in the United States during the 1950s?

3. **INTERPRET TIME LINES** How did the United States interfere in foreign governments during Eisenhower's first term in office?

4. **EVALUATE** What were some advantages of Eisenhower's nuclear deterrence plan?

BUILD BACKGROUND

MISSILE GAP

Government officials in the late 1950s and early 1960s used the term *missile gap* to refer to a perceived United States lag behind the Soviet Union in ballistic missile technology. Fears heightened following the Soviet testing of an intercontinental ballistic missile (ICBM) in August 1957. The U.S. military expressed concern that the Soviet Union had the capability to both improve its missile technology and increase its numbers of nuclear missiles, endangering the security of the United States. The November 1957 Gaither Report encouraged President Eisenhower to significantly increase weapons production, antiballistic missile defenses, and the defense budget in order to maintain a U.S. nuclear deterrent and be prepared for strong retaliation against any attempted Soviet use of ballistic missiles against the United States. Eisenhower resisted the advice (and later addressed the danger of allowing the military-industrial complex to influence foreign policy in his January 1961 Farewell Address). Military intelligence officials later informed him that the missile gap, in fact, did not exist. A National Intelligence Estimate briefing in September 1961 confirmed this information, stating that the Soviet Union had some 10–25 missile launchers while the United States had more than 100 land- and sea-based missiles deployed both in foreign countries and on U.S. submarines.

TEACH

GUIDED DISCUSSION

3. **Synthesize** How did a belief in nuclear deterrence combined with the principle of brinkmanship shape President Eisenhower's Cold War policy? *(Eisenhower believed that the increased production and strategic placement of nuclear warheads combined with the ever-present threat of nuclear war was enough to deter the Soviet Union from launching a nuclear attack.)*

4. **Compare and Contrast** Why do you think President Eisenhower chose not to send American troops to Hungary when he was willing to interfere in Iran and Guatemala? *(Possible response: Iran and Guatemala were not nuclear powers, so interference there would not have resulted in nuclear conflict. Hungary, however, was backed by the Soviet Union's nuclear capabilities, and interfering there presented the risk of starting a nuclear war if the Soviets felt threatened.)*

ANALYZE PRIMARY SOURCES

Direct students' attention to the Primary Source feature. Instruct them to work in pairs to analyze Eisenhower's argument in support of his nuclear deterrence policy. They then should write a statement that summarizes what Eisenhower believed was the greatest deterrent to nuclear war. Encourage students to use a graphic organizer like the one shown here to organize their thoughts. Then hold a class discussion in which students compare their summary statements, comment upon Eisenhower's reasoning, and consider how his response to the threat of nuclear conflict might have taken a different direction.

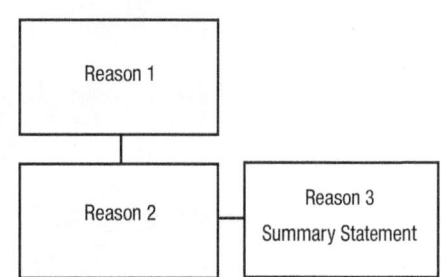

ACTIVE OPTIONS

On Your Feet: Question That Answer! Instruct each student to write an answer to a question that historians might ask about U.S. involvement overseas in the 1950s. Divide the class in half. Ask students in one group to provide one of the answers and students in the other group to formulate a question prompted by the answer. Then have the groups switch roles. To wrap up, work with the class to prepare a summary statement of U.S. involvement overseas during Eisenhower's tenure as president.

NG Learning Framework: Explore the 1956 Presidential Race

`ATTITUDE` Curiosity

`SKILLS` Communication, Collaboration

Divide the class into two groups to explore the 1956 presidential campaign, with one group researching the campaign promises and platform of Dwight D. Eisenhower and the other group researching the campaign promises and platform of Adlai Stevenson. Encourage students to use both primary and secondary sources in their research and to keep in mind the norms, values, and attitudes of Americans in the postwar era. Instruct each group to create and display a campaign poster for their candidate and then to present the candidate's bid for the presidency in a campaign speech.

HISTORICAL THINKING

ANSWERS

1. Eisenhower sought to maintain the successful programs of the Fair Deal while cutting government spending and empowering private businesses.

2. Technology drove the U.S. economy as growth in military defense and the aerospace industries created employment opportunities across the country and as the demand by consumers for new electronics and other new products increased consumer spending.

3. The United States worked covertly to influence the politics and internal affairs of foreign governments, including replacing a recently elected president with a military dictator in Guatemala and restoring the shah of Iran to power after he had been deposed.

4. Eisenhower's nuclear deterrence plan had several advantages. First, it put nuclear warheads in numerous safe places so that an enemy could not destroy all the weapons at once. Second, it enabled the United States to avoid mobilizing an army. Third, it presented the threat of war so clearly that, in theory, other nations would dare not risk a nuclear strike against the United States.

AMERICAN SOCIETY

If you had more money than you needed, what would you do with it? Would you save it? Spend it? Share it? Many Americans had this choice to make as they confronted social changes during the Cold War years.

THE COLD WAR'S EFFECTS

The Cold War shaped the daily lives of Americans in numerous ways. Its economic effects were especially significant. To fight the Cold War, the government made heavy investments in the defense and aerospace industries, which became major American employers in such states as California and Missouri. In addition, millions of veterans took advantage of the GI Bill of Rights and received a college education. Many of them then contributed to building the nation's technology industries. Thus, the livelihoods of many Americans depended on Cold War government investments and goals.

A growing group of educated, white-collar Americans strengthened the nation's industrial base, earned more money, and enjoyed a steady increase in their standard of living. With their new affluence, these Americans began to consume more goods and services, adding to the general prosperity.

PRESSURES ON AMERICAN WOMEN

It happened after World War I, and again after World War II. After each war, employers pressured the women who had stepped in to keep industries and businesses running during the wars, to leave their jobs and make room for the returning soldiers. Between 1945 and 1947, more than 2 million women dropped out of the workforce, either by choice or by force. Women were also pressured to drop out of college to make room for men. The graduation rate for college women fell from 40 percent during the war to 25 percent by 1950.

Married and single women generally returned to domesticity, or home life. Many women, especially those who enjoyed working or were college-educated, found the transition from self-sufficiency to dependence on male breadwinners difficult and disappointing. Those who remained in the workforce, often out of financial necessity, were typically paid 53 percent less than men performing similar tasks.

The return of soldiers after World War II brought other changes as well. Americans were longing for life to return to normal after years of war. As you have read, the GI Bill helped many veterans of the war obtain college educations, improving their career prospects and earning potential. Provisions of the law also encouraged home-ownership, another cornerstone of increasing affluence and financial stability, through downpayment and mortage rate assistance. And as families were being reunited, many more couples were marrying and starting new families.

Immediately following World War II, the U.S. marriage rate spiked dramatically before leveling off slightly, which you can see in the graph on the next page. Americans were also entering into marriage at younger ages than prior to the war. The high marriage rate, in turn, led to a situation that changed the nation in profound ways.

THE BABY BOOM

More marriages, paired with increased economic optimism, led to a 20-year surge in the number of babies born in the United States, a phenomenon called the **baby boom**. American birth rates began to climb following the war, reaching more than 4 million births in 1954, a figure that held relatively steady until the mid-1960s.

It wasn't only that there were more couples having children during the baby-boom years; perhaps due to confidence in the economy and their ability to provide for their families, couples were having more children as well. An estimated 75 million Americans were born between 1946 and 1964, and by 1965, around 40 percent of Americans were younger than 20 years old.

Manufacturers and advertisers zeroed in on the growing market in children's products. Clothing, specialized foods, and toys were promoted directly to children during televised cartoons and other programming. Baby boomers, as this generation came to be called, are still a prime target of advertisers nearly a lifetime later.

Due to their sheer numbers, baby boomers have affected the national culture throughout their lives. They spearheaded the social changes and antiwar activism of the 1960s. Today, as they move into retirement, they are putting a strain on the Social Security system. Perhaps the baby boom's major impact, however, has been to spur on consumerism in every decade from the 1950s to the present.

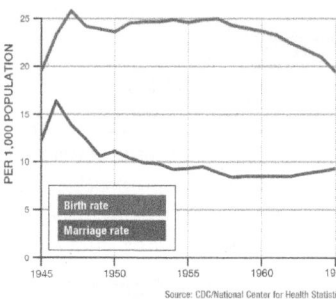

Birth and Marriage Rates in the Baby Boom Era (1945–1965)

Source: CDC/National Center for Health Statistics

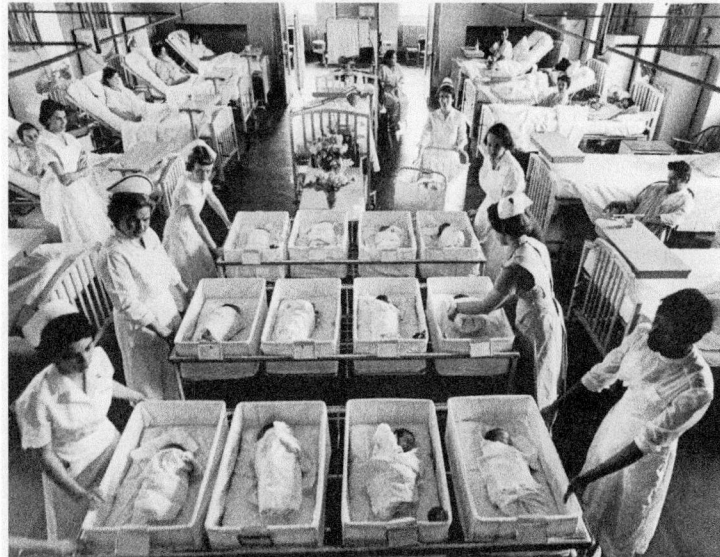

In 1958, nurses deliver a group of infants to their mothers in a hospital dormitory room. During the baby boom, a shortage of rooms for mothers and babies overwhelmed hospitals, which were designed for fewer births. In addition, home births declined and hospital births rose from 37 percent of all births in 1935 to 88 percent in 1950. The baby boom led to a growth in hospitals and a dramatic increase in the demand for many products and services.

PLAN: 4-PAGE LESSON

OBJECTIVE

Describe the 1950s in terms of changes in family life, advances in many fields, and a rise in consumerism.

CRITICAL THINKING SKILLS FOR LESSON 1.2

- Analyze Cause and Effect
- Identify Main Ideas and Details
- Make Predictions
- Make Generalizations
- Make Inferences
- Form and Support Opinions
- Analyze Visuals

HISTORICAL THINKING FOR CHAPTER 24

How did the prosperity of the post–World War II period shape American society? With a postwar focus on growing families, Americans looked to improve their lives. Lesson 1.2 explains how the return to a peacetime economy and the rise of the Cold War drove scientific advances and increased the marriage rate.

BACKGROUND FOR THE TEACHER

Baby boomers exert an outsize influence on the U.S. economy—not only as consumers but also as workers. When baby boomers delay retirement, they leave fewer job openings for new college graduates. Some employers worry that once baby boomers retire in greater numbers, they'll cause a "brain drain," removing a large body of knowledge and experience from the workforce. In addition, funds for retirement programs such as pensions and Social Security come from the paychecks of current workers. The census bureau reports that the U.S. birthrate is at a historic low, and that by 2030 one in five Americans will be 65 or older. With more retirees and fewer active workers, younger people in the near future may have to pay a greater percentage of their wages to support retired workers.

HISTORY NOTEBOOK

Encourage students to complete the American Gallery page for Chapter 24 in their History Notebooks as they read.

INTRODUCE & ENGAGE

USE A KWL CHART

Provide each student with a KWL Chart. Then ask students to consider what they think they know about everyday life in the United States in the 1950s from TV, movies, and stories told by relatives and neighbors. Suggest that students focus on family life, the workplace, and the technology of the era. Then ask students to write some questions that they would like to have answered as they study this lesson, such as: What kinds of products did most Americans want to have in their homes? How much did everyday Americans think about the Cold War? Allow time at the end of the lesson for students to fill in what they have learned and to discuss how the information either confirms or reshapes their vision of that era.

K What Do I Know?	W What Do I Want To Learn?	L What Did I Learn?

TEACH

GUIDED DISCUSSION

1. **Make Predictions** What trends in service sector and professional sector jobs might the GI Bill have sparked? *(Possible responses: growth in jobs in the construction of houses, schools, and commercial properties as well as in accounting, teaching, and repair and medical services)*

2. **Make Generalizations** What was the overall perspective of veterans returning to civilian life in the late 1940s and early 1950s? Include a detail about how that perspective affected the role of women in society. *(Possible response: Veterans hoped to get married, raise a family, and enjoy the prosperity that the country was experiencing by returning to the workforce, which meant replacing women in the workplace.)*

3. **Make Inferences** Given the buying power and the shifting needs of baby boomers over time, what changes would you expect to see in the marketing geared to this important consumer group? *(Possible response: At first there were a lot of toys and children's products aimed at baby boomers, but later there was probably an increase in products related to home and car ownership and careers, then items related to aging, such as hearing aids and plans for retirement.)*

MORE INFORMATION

GI Bill of Rights Explain to students that the GI Bill of Rights, officially called the Servicemen's Readjustment Act of 1944, provided an array of benefits for veterans of World War II, including tuition and expenses for veterans who attended trade schools and universities, low-interest mortgages for homes and businesses, and unemployment compensation. From 1944 to 1956, some 7.8 million veterans took advantage of the educational benefits offered through the GI Bill. In 1947, veterans made up 49 percent of college enrollments. Veterans hoping to return to the farm learned about new agriculture technologies and research in farming techniques. Veterans invested in new farming equipment that enabled farming to take place on a large scale. Other veterans trained for jobs in the energy industry to meet increased demands for electricity, including installing electric lines across rural America. **ASK:** How did the GI Bill encourage returning veterans to be part of the postwar economic boom and the social transformation that accompanied it? *(Possible response: By paying educational and training expenses for returning soldiers, the GI Bill offered veterans the financial means to pursue new opportunities in changing fields. With this training, they could help usher in social transformations resulting from the growth of the nation's technology industry.)*

DIFFERENTIATE

STRIVING READERS

Write Tweets As students read the lesson, direct them to pause after each paragraph and write a tweet—a 140-character message summarizing the paragraph's main idea in their own words. Have students read their tweets aloud to the class or a partner one at a time, with the first student reading his or her tweet about the first paragraph, the second student reading a tweet about the second paragraph, and so forth.

PRE-AP

Use Statistics Challenge students to find statistics that could be used to demonstrate the complex effects that veterans returning from World War II had on women in the workforce. For example, students might research such statistics as the rates of marriage and childbirth before and during the war, extending the range of the graph shown in the text. They could expand their research to include the number of women in the workforce and of women enrolled in or graduating from college in the years before, during, and after the war. Students should then graph their data to show changes over time. When they have finished their graphs, invite them to present their results to the class. They should point out the trends shown in the graphs and explain how those trends relate to the effects of returning veterans on women in the workforce.

See the Chapter Planner for more strategies for differentiation.

Customers listen as a salesperson points out the new features of a television set at an appliance store in Silver Spring, Maryland, in 1950.

A young girl looks apprehensively at the needle before receiving a lifesaving Salk polio vaccine in the 1950s. Health departments and schools vigorously publicized the free vaccination program with public service posters, newspaper ads, and radio announcements. An oral vaccine developed by Alfred Sabin was also developed in the 1950s and given in drops placed on a sugar cube.

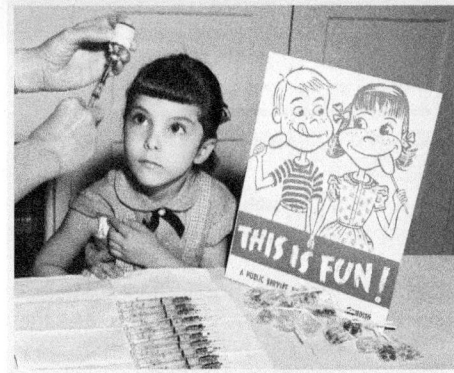

THE CONSUMER SOCIETY

During the Cold War years, many Americans had more money to spend and more goods to buy. Thanks to strong labor unions negotiating for regular working hours and personal time off, they also had more free time in which to shop. Consumer spending was now considered a patriotic way to build the nation's economy. Between 1946 and 1950, this new **consumer society** purchased over 21 million automobiles, 20 million refrigerators, 5.5 million electric stoves, and more than 2 million dishwashers. Shopping became an important part of the American lifestyle.

The consumer society was supported by easy access to credit—buying now and paying later, in installments. In 1950, a financial company called Diners Club issued the first credit cards in the United States. Department stores soon followed, offering charge accounts with easy payment plans.

Televisions became a popular item to charge to credit accounts. By the 1950s, televisions were no longer a luxury item that only upper-class families could afford. Most American homes had a TV; in fact, stores were selling millions of televisions every year.

Television provided advertisers easy access to millions of consumers. Enticing television commercials promoted shiny new appliances and unique gadgets guaranteed to make life easier for Americans. Much of this advertising was directed specifically at women. Commercials told women they could be more efficient and effective wives and mothers if they owned the newest washing machine, dishwasher, and vacuum. In addition to encouraging consumer spending, these advertisements also reinforced women's traditional domestic roles.

MEDICINE, SCIENCE, AND EDUCATION

The Cold War years also featured major advances in medicine, science, and education. One of the most important medical breakthroughs was the development of a vaccine against polio, an infectious, crippling disease. Between the late 1940s and early 1950s, doctors had reported 35,000 new cases of the disease in the United States. In 1952, the nation experienced its worst polio outbreak—58,000 cases. Three years later, in 1955, **Jonas Salk**, an American physician and medical researcher, introduced the **Salk vaccine**. The incidence of polio quickly fell, and the disease is no longer a threat in the United States.

In the late 1940s, three American physicists invented the **transistor**, an electronic device used to control the flow of electricity in electronic equipment. Transistors became available for public purchase during the 1950s and were commonly used in small, portable radios and hearing aids. Today, transistors are components of the microchips found in computers and many other electronic devices.

One of the first commercial computers designed for processing business data was the **Universal Automatic Computer (UNIVAC)**. Developed in the late 1940s, the room-size UNIVAC was put into use by various businesses and organizations. For example, the **Bureau of the Census**, the government agency that counts the nation's population, used the UNIVAC to count and record part of the 1950 population.

Scientists also explored ways to produce cheaper energy to meet the nation's growing energy demands. Using the same science behind the atomic bomb, scientists working in the United States developed a way to capture the heat released during nuclear fission, which is the reaction that occurs when atoms split apart. The steam from this heat can be used to turn turbine blades to power generators and make electricity. The energy created from this process is called **nuclear power**. In 1957, the first large-scale American nuclear power plant started operating in Shippingport, Pennsylvania.

Advances in the sciences were not limited to earthbound endeavors. Scientists studied planetary satellites, or bodies in space that orbit other bodies of a larger size. On October 4, 1957, the Soviet Union sent the first mechanical, or human-made, satellite, called *Sputnik 1*, into space to orbit Earth. Americans worried that such satellites might enable the Soviets

to direct nuclear missiles toward the United States. President Eisenhower responded by establishing the **National Aeronautics and Space Administration (NASA)**, which oversees the U.S. space program. NASA worked to match and exceed the Soviets' accomplishments in space exploration.

After being caught off guard by *Sputnik*, the American public demanded improvements to their educational systems. Eisenhower responded by signing the National Defense Education Act (NDEA) into law on September 2, 1958. The purpose of NDEA was to improve schools through government funding, encourage students to attend college, and promote education in science, engineering, math, and foreign languages. In California, educators used NDEA funding to reorganize the state's higher education system. The **California Master Plan**, adopted in 1960, joined the state's universities and community colleges into one accessible and affordable system governed by a framework that promoted academic excellence.

HISTORICAL THINKING

1. **READING CHECK** How did the Cold War affect the lives of ordinary Americans?

2. **ANALYZE CAUSE AND EFFECT** Explain how the return of World War II veterans had complex effects on women in the workforce, and identify the types of data that could be used in determining these effects.

3. **IDENTIFY MAIN IDEAS AND DETAILS** What factors contributed to the development of a consumer society in the United States?

BUILD BACKGROUND

A WAVE OF INNOVATION

Many items that got their start in the wave of 1950s American consumerism are still popular today. Super Glue was invented in 1951, and the first diet soda sold in 1952. Children today still play with Mr. Potato Head (1952), Hula Hoops (1958), and Barbie dolls (1959). Future consumer use of computers took a giant step forward in the 1950s with the introduction of the first computer hard disk in 1956 (replacing punch cards and magnetic tape as the media for storage of information), followed by Fortran (a computer language) in 1957, and the invention of the modem in 1958. Drivers enjoyed the benefits of power steering in 1951, and some made their first stop at McDonalds in 1955 for a 15-cent hamburger. Bar codes, patented in 1952 by Joseph Woodland and Bernard Silver, are essential to retail sales today. Of importance to all consumers were advances in medicine, including clinical trials of oral contraceptives in 1954 and a patent for tetracycline in 1955.

TEACH

GUIDED DISCUSSION

4. **Form and Support Opinions** Imagine yourself as an adult in the 1950s. In the context of that time, why would you probably believe that credit cards and charge accounts are good things? *(They allow people to increase their consumer spending and buy the things they want.)* **ASK:** In retrospect, what argument could be made against them? *(Possible response: The concept of "buy now, pay later" encourages people to spend more than they can afford and become burdened by debt.)*

5. **Analyze Cause and Effect** How did advances in technology after 1945 transform both energy production and the way people communicated? *(Scientists learned how to use nuclear power to produce energy to meet the country's growing energy needs. Meanwhile, the invention of the transistor was used in portable radios, hearing aids, and the microchips found in computers, increasing opportunities for people to communicate.)*

ANALYZE VISUALS

Direct students' attention to the photograph of the child who will soon receive a dose of the polio vaccine and to the poster beside her. **ASK:** Who was the intended audience of the poster, and do you think it was effective? Why or why not? *(Possible response: It was directed at children with the intention of making the prospect of a vaccine less scary. It was probably effective in helping to put kids at ease in a setting populated by doctors and nurses.)*

ACTIVE OPTIONS

AMERICAN GALLERY ONLINE **Consumer America** Invite students to explore the American Gallery. Have them select one of the images and do additional research to learn more about it. Ask questions that will inspire additional inquiry about the chosen gallery image, such as these: What is this? Why was it created? What is it made of? Why does it belong in this chapter? What else would you like to know about it?

NG Learning Framework: Weigh Pros and Cons

ATTITUDE Responsibility

KNOWLEDGE Our Living Planet

Divide the class into groups and instruct them to research the effects of nuclear power and how it has altered the environment. Groups should examine both the positive and negative effects of nuclear energy, comparing and contrasting the environmental consequences of nuclear energy with those associated with other forms of energy. Students should also investigate how people's knowledge of and ideas about the environmental effects of nuclear energy have changed over time and have influenced local economies. Have groups report back to the class on what they have learned.

HISTORICAL THINKING

ANSWERS

1. The government's efforts to fight the Cold War created jobs in the defense and aerospace industries for ordinary Americans. Education for such jobs created an overall rise in college education, too.

2. During the war, women were strongly encouraged to fill the positions men left behind. Once the war was over, women were pressured to leave those jobs so that men could reclaim them, while women were expected to return to their roles as homemakers. These effects could be shown by changes over time in statistics such as the following: birth rate, marriage rate, women in the workplace, women enrolled in college, women graduating from college, and men's pay versus women's pay.

3. The United States became a consumer society because Americans had more money after the war. Many families had been frugal for a long time and had saved a large amount of money. Jobs were plentiful after the war and paid higher wages. Freed from the hardships of the war years, Americans were eager to spend their money.

SUBURBS SURROUND CITIES

Where would you most like to live—in a city, suburb, small town, or rural area? During the Cold War years, many Americans chose to move to suburbs. Why might the suburbs have appealed to them?

MOVING TO THE SUBURBS

As populations were increasing in Sunbelt states in response to the expansion of aerospace and other industries in the region, another major demographic change was also taking place. **Suburbanization**, or a population shift from cities to outlying communities, was rapidly transforming the American landscape.

In 1950, about 1.7 million new houses were built in the United States, and more than 80 percent were built in suburbs. A home in the suburbs offered relief from crowded cities. Suburbs often had larger homes, better schools, and lower crime rates. By 1950, more than 18 million people, or 1 in every 8 Americans, had moved from cities to suburbs.

The GI Bill, which offered loans to World War II veterans to purchase houses, helped make suburbanization possible. So did two federal government agencies. The **Veterans Administration (VA)**, which serves the needs of veterans, and the **Federal Housing Administration (FHA)**, which provides financing for housing, worked together to manage the GI Bill program. From 1944 to 1952, the government issued nearly 2.4 million low-interest home loans as a benefit of the GI Bill, accelerating the movement of families to the suburbs.

All over the country, veterans paid building contractors to construct affordable, single-family homes. **William Levitt**, a New York contractor, purchased several thousand acres of farmland in Hempstead, New York, 25 miles east of Manhattan, for the mass production of private homes. Levitt based his building operation on Henry Ford's assembly lines. His company manufactured precut building materials in his factories, delivered them using his trucking company, and assembled the homes using his builders. On the construction site, each worker performed a single task, such as framing or pouring concrete, to complete each house. Levitt's builders constructed as many as 180 houses in a week. When completed in 1951, **Levittown, Long Island**, boasted 17,000 houses plus dozens of parks, ball fields, swimming pools, churches, and shopping areas for its 82,000 residents.

Levitt's system of mass-produced neighborhoods was duplicated across the country. Linking Cold War thinking and home ownership, Levitt declared, "No man who owns his own house and lot can be a communist."

Meanwhile, new expressways improved access between suburbs and cities. President Eisenhower viewed road improvement as vital to the national defense during the Cold War. When he signed the **Federal-Aid Highway Act of 1956**, launching one of the greatest public works projects in history, he stated, "In case of atomic attack on our key cities, the road net must permit quick evacuation of target areas." Better roads would also benefit the economy by creating jobs, making it easier and cheaper for industries to transport goods, and allowing Americans to live farther away from their workplaces. In fact, state and local governments often covered the entire cost of highway segments in response to local commuting demand. The resulting **Interstate Highway System** linked towns, cities, and suburbs nationwide with limited access, multilane highways.

IMPACT OF SUBURBANIZATION

Suburbanization dramatically transformed American culture. The American dream of owning one's home became a reality for millions. The first house sold in Levittown, Long Island, came with a free television and appliances, prompting Levitt to call it "the best house in the U.S."

But social observers criticized these developments, mocking the uniform design of the "little boxes." Far more troubling was the **homogeneity**, or sameness, of the residents. Many mass-produced neighborhoods, or **subdivisions**, refused to admit minorities, especially African Americans. Levittown's standard sales contract stated that homes could not be "used or occupied by any person other than members of the Caucasian race." Nearly 10 years after the U.S. Supreme Court ruled in 1948 against such discrimination, not a single African American lived in Levittown. Social observers also deplored the homogeneity of the suburbanites' lives. The men commuted from their uniformly designed houses to work in offices that were also mostly alike, and the women cleaned house, cooked, and raised children.

Suburbanization and discrimination changed the makeup of American cities. African Americans and the less wealthy remained in the cities, where making a living became more difficult. Many businesses and factories also moved to the suburbs, taking jobs and services with them. Fewer residents and businesses meant lower revenues for city or local governments, but as taxes were raised to cover the shortfall, even more people moved to the suburbs. In just a few years, many American cities lost a large portion of their upper- and middle-class residents.

Suburbanization also affected rural communities and natural environments. The relentless demand for subdivisions and the expansion of interstate highways pressured farmers near cities to sell their land. In 1930, more than 30 million Americans lived on farms. By 1960, that number had fallen to 15.6 million, and nearly one in three Americans lived in a suburb. Suburbs and highways also disrupted wildlife habitats, a process that continues to this day.

HISTORICAL THINKING

1. **READING CHECK** What motivated many Americans to move to suburbs during the Cold War years?

2. **MAKE INFERENCES** What did William Levitt mean when he said "No man who owns his own house and lot can be a communist"?

3. **IDENTIFY PROBLEMS AND SOLUTIONS** What do you consider the greatest problem to have resulted from the growth of suburbs?

CRITICAL VIEWING An aerial photograph taken in 1954 reveals the sprawling Levittown, Long Island, suburb that had once been farmland. What elements in this photograph support the criticism that suburban developments featured too much uniformity, or sameness?

OBJECTIVE

Identify how government programs directed at public works and new housing technologies encouraged the growth of suburbs.

CRITICAL THINKING SKILLS FOR LESSON 1.3

- Make Inferences
- Identify Problems and Solutions
- Analyze Cause and Effect
- Make Connections

HISTORICAL THINKING FOR CHAPTER 24

How did the prosperity of the post–World War II period shape American society? The appeal of life in the suburbs resulted in the loss of farmland and a shift of population and business away from American cities. Lesson 1.3 discusses the programs that promoted the growth of suburbs and details the consequences of suburbanization.

BACKGROUND FOR THE TEACHER

William Levitt and his brother, Alfred, got their start in housing construction when they landed a government contract in 1941 to build 2,350 housing units in Norfolk, Virginia, for defense workers. In 1947, with the purchase of 1,000 acres of potato farms on Long Island, they began construction of Levittown. Ever conscious of costs, William Levitt built homes with lumber harvested from his own forests in Oregon and even used nails made by his company. The typical Levittown house sat on one-seventh of an acre. Each house had 750 square feet of space and included two bedrooms, a living room and kitchen, and an unfinished second floor, but not a garage. Setting the sale price at $7,990, the Levitt brothers made a profit of about $1,000 on every house they built and sold. William Levitt sold his company, Levitt & Sons, to ITT Corp in 1968 for $92 million in stock. However, he was barred from building homes in the United States for 10 years as part of the deal.

DESIGN AN IDEAL COMMUNITY

Invite students to share their vision of an ideal community, one that they could design from start to finish. Suggest that students consider the types of housing they would build, landscaping and community green space, businesses, schools, parks, and other things that make a community an enjoyable place to live. Ask them whether their community would appeal to a broad range of residents or to a limited group. Use a graphic organizer to record ideas. Tell students that in this lesson they will learn how this kind of thinking began to reshape American society.

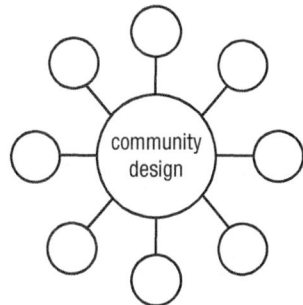

TEACH

GUIDED DISCUSSION

1. **Analyze Cause and Effect** How did legislation for new federal spending on infrastructure influence trends in the American workforce and the beginnings of suburbanization? *(The Federal-Aid Highway Act of 1956 funded the building of local roads and led to the Interstate Highway System. This public works project created jobs; eventually, it also helped people realize that they could live in more pleasant suburban surroundings and commute to work.)*

2. **Make Connections** In what ways did subdivisions such as Levittown affect American culture and demographics? *(Possible response: As suburbs grew, Americans began to view the ideal life as a house in the suburbs, with homes that were uniformly designed in areas that included families of similar demographics. People moved from cities and from farms to suburbs, causing changes in demographics to urban and rural areas.)*

MORE INFORMATION

Education in California California's population grew by 5 million people from 1950 to 1960, creating new demands for the state. California's investment in its California Master Plan expanded educational opportunities for millions of Californians with the promise of tuition-free education to residents of the state, along with a tiered university system that allowed wide access to a postsecondary education. Because of the California Master Plan, some 2.5 million students graduated from the University of California system; furthermore, three-fourths of California's veterans attended community colleges on the GI Bill. **ASK:** How do you think these policies helped industries in Silicon Valley and Central Valley to become important to California's growth and economy? *(Possible response: These policies resulted in a large pool of well-educated adults to work in high-tech industries. Those industries thrived, and the region became a major center for the high-tech industry.)*

ACTIVE OPTIONS

On Your Feet: Turn and Talk on Topic Organize students into three to five groups. Give each group this topic sentence: Government programs encouraged many Americans to move out of crowded cities and into suburbs. Tell students to build an essay on that topic by having each student in the group contribute one paragraph. Allow time for each group to present its essay to the class. Follow up with a discussion of the key supporting details.

NG Learning Framework: Explore a Local Suburb

| **ATTITUDE** | Curiosity |
| **KNOWLEDGE** | Our Human Story |

Direct students to use diverse primary and secondary sources, including maps, to research how a selected suburb in their area has grown since the 1950s. Instruct students to focus not only on the history of the suburb and the way in which it is perceived today but also on ways in which its expansion influenced the natural systems of the area—and how the human modification of the landscape influenced subsequent environmental policies. Encourage students to share their information visually, as in an infographic or a multimedia presentation.

INCLUSION

Work in Pairs Instruct visually impaired students to work with sighted partners. Tell the partner without disabilities to describe the aerial photo of Levittown in detail and read the captions. Have the pair work together to answer the Critical Viewing question.

GIFTED & TALENTED

Write a Monologue Tell students to imagine they are living during the period of rapid suburbanization in the 1950s. Instruct them to access primary and secondary source documents that describe people's experiences. Ask students to choose one of the following: a former city dweller or someone from a rural area who has moved to the suburbs; someone who has stayed behind in the city, in a small town, or on a farm. Then prompt students to write and perform a monologue from that person's perspective. Invite the class to reflect on differences they note among the experiences of different characters.

See the Chapter Planner for more strategies for differentiation.

ANSWERS

1. Postwar confidence, increased prosperity, a desire for better living conditions, and more affordable housing motivated Americans to move to the suburbs.

2. Possible response: Levitt meant that by owning a house and lot, people participate in growing their personal wealth and enjoy the ability to make the kinds of personal decisions that are possible only in a democracy.

3. Responses will vary but may include any of the following: housing discrimination against African Americans, worsening circumstances for the urban poor, the loss of family farmland, the conformity of suburban culture, the isolation of communities from the city, the growing obsession with consumer goods.

CRITICAL VIEWING Possible response: The photo shows a uniformity of housing, with all houses equally spaced and placed to maximize the number of houses in an area. It doesn't appear that any trees line the perfectly spaced and defined roads, nor that different areas have their own character through the addition of green space or unique landscaping features.

AUTOMOBILE MANIA

Can you imagine never using a car? If not, you're in step with the majority of Americans who rely on cars for transportation at least part, if not most, of the time. That dependence developed during the 1950s.

CRITICAL VIEWING In 1948, The Track, an innovative drive-in restaurant in Los Angeles, used technology to entice hungry drivers. Instead of employing carhops, or waiters, to serve people at their cars, The Track installed a conveyor belt. How do you think this system worked, and to whom might it appeal?

GROWING RELIANCE ON AUTOMOBILES

The growth of suburbs during the Cold War years made Americans more dependent on automobiles. Many workers had to commute from the suburbs to jobs in the city each day. As the demand for automobiles increased, American production quadrupled from 2 million cars in 1946 to 8 million in 1955. Between 1945 and 1960, new technologies cut by half the time it took to manufacture a car. As a result, the nation's gross national product (GNP), the total value of goods and services produced during a year, skyrocketed from $212 billion to $503 billion. The business of making cars became the most important contributor to the U.S. economy.

During the Cold War years, the automobile industry employed a large percentage of the country's population. By 1960, one out of six Americans earned paychecks by contributing to the production of cars, either directly by assembling vehicles or indirectly by working for a company that supplied automotive parts and equipment. Factory employees rolled out close to 58 million new cars during the 1950s.

The United Automobile Workers (UAW), an industrial union representing automotive workers, had grown in size and become a powerful force in the automotive industry by the 1950s. The UAW, in partnership with other labor unions, successfully organized strikes for better wages and benefits and negotiated paid vacation days, pensions, and medical care for union members.

A CAR CULTURE

The growth of the car culture rapidly transformed the American landscape. Entire industries blossomed along the increasing network of roads and highways lined with gas stations. Restaurants adjusted their operations so drivers could buy food "to go" or even eat meals without leaving their cars. One of the first restaurant owners to adopt this "fast food" model was Ray Kroc. He opened the first McDonald's restaurant in 1955 in Des Plaines, Illinois, a suburb of Chicago. Motor hotels, or motels, were built along busy roads to accommodate the growing number of travelers taking road trips. The American car culture also prompted the development of drive-in movie theaters and shopping malls. All these businesses added to **suburban sprawl**, or the spread of suburban developments over more and more land.

As the car culture spread, the economies of the United States and other Western nations became increasingly dependent on oil, which is the source of gasoline, diesel fuel, and many other products.

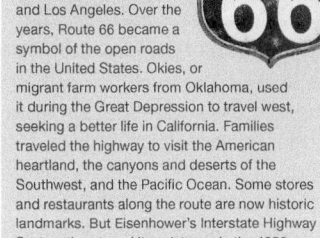

ROUTE 66

Completed in 1926, this famous highway ran 2,448 miles between Chicago and Los Angeles. Over the years, Route 66 became a symbol of the open roads in the United States. Okies, or migrant farm workers from Oklahoma, used it during the Great Depression to travel west, seeking a better life in California. Families traveled the highway to visit the American heartland, the canyons and deserts of the Southwest, and the Pacific Ocean. Some stores and restaurants along the route are now historic landmarks. But Eisenhower's Interstate Highway System threatened its existence in the 1950s. Many travelers chose the newer, more direct highways over the often meandering Route 66.

Between 1945 and 1960, U.S. oil production rose by nearly 50 percent, and annual oil imports increased from 74 million to 371 million barrels. The need for oil—not only to power automobiles but also to meet other energy needs—would affect American foreign and domestic policy for decades to come.

The large number of gas-guzzling cars on American roads led to rising air pollution in cities. By 1966, motor vehicles contributed more than 60 percent of the pollutants discharged into the nation's air, amounting to 86 million tons out of 146 million tons. In 1955, the U.S. Congress passed the Air Pollution Control Act, the first law to address air pollution. The act was amended in 1963 to provide funding to study the effects of automobile exhaust on people's health.

Other environmental problems resulted from the extraction, refining, and transportation of oil. During the 1960s and beyond, oil spills and the dumping of oil wastes damaged wildlife habitats and polluted streams, lakes, and other bodies of water.

HISTORICAL THINKING

1. **READING CHECK** Why did many Americans become dependent on automobiles during the Cold War years?

2. **MAKE INFERENCES** How might the need for oil affect American foreign policy?

3. **ANALYZE ENVIRONMENTAL CONCEPTS** How did its increased oil production help the United States, and what environmental problems were caused by Americans' growing dependence on oil?

PLAN: 2-PAGE LESSON

OBJECTIVE

Analyze the impact of the auto industry on the American economy and changing lifestyle.

CRITICAL THINKING SKILLS FOR LESSON 2.1

• Make Inferences

• Analyze Environmental Concepts

• Analyze Data

• Determine Word Meaning

• Analyze Cause and Effect

HISTORICAL THINKING FOR CHAPTER 24

How did the prosperity of the post–World War II period shape American society? The auto industry transformed the American economy with new jobs, new services related to the auto industry, and a new "on the go" lifestyle. Lesson 2.1 discusses the role of the auto industry in a changing American landscape.

BACKGROUND FOR THE TEACHER

The United Automobile Workers, organized in 1935 in Detroit, Michigan, was already an integral part of the automobile industry as the United States rolled into the car culture of the 1950s. The UAW launched its first employee strike in 1936, forcing General Motors to negotiate with the union. In 1937 it staged another strike at nine Chrysler plants that resulted in union recognition for those workers, and in 1941 it lodged a strike against Ford. In 1944 the UAW called for equal pay for women, and in 1946 it established the first agricultural implement department. By 1961 it had established the first employer-paid pension program at Ford, had worked for a guaranteed annual wage, and had won fully paid hospitalization benefits from General Motors and a nondiscrimination agreement that disallowed discrimination on the basis of race, creed, color, or national origin.

INTRODUCE & ENGAGE

DISCUSS A "DRIVE-THROUGH" ECONOMY

Draw a Concept Cluster on the board. Ask students to think about businesses that offer "drive-through" services and identify three kinds of drive-through businesses to discuss. **ASK:** Why do you think people like to frequent these businesses? *(Possible responses: They are convenient. Customers don't have to get out of their cars, which is especially attractive during bad weather.)* **ASK:** How do you think these businesses affect the local economy? *(Possible responses: They employ a lot of people, which boosts the local economy. They could take customers away from businesses that offer good products but are not as speedy.)* Explain that in Lesson 2.1, students will learn how Americans' love for automobiles in the 1950s laid the groundwork for today's drive-throughs.

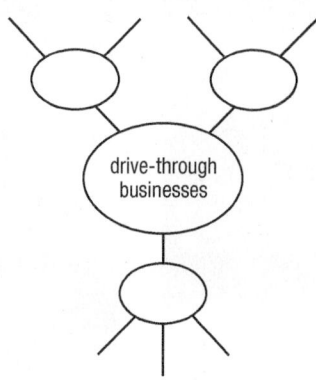

drive-through businesses

TEACH

GUIDED DISCUSSION

1. **Analyze Data** Statistically speaking, what was the effect of the automobile industry on the health of the American economy? *(Demand for automobiles quadrupled between 1946 and 1955, with the result that the gross national product more than doubled, making car-related goods and services the most important contributor to the U.S. economy.)*

2. **Determine Word Meaning** What new attitudes are embodied in the term *car culture*? *(Car culture embodies attitudes such as the desire to own and operate a car, the tendency to value a faster pace of life that includes drive-in restaurants and movies, trips to shopping malls, and the appeal of taking road trips and living farther from work.)*

ANALYZE CAUSE AND EFFECT

Direct students' attention to the Route 66 highway sign. Ask students to read the caption, share how Route 66 was used, and speculate on the types of businesses that sprang up along it. **ASK:** How did Eisenhower's Interstate Highway System affect local economies along Route 66? *(As people traveled along Route 66, they stopped at restaurants, motels, grocery and other stores, gas stations, and repair shops. Once the Interstate Highway System was built, however, many travelers chose the faster route. Local economies suffered as fewer people frequented the once-thriving small businesses along Route 66.)*

ACTIVE OPTIONS

On Your Feet: Identify Car Culture Startups Arrange students in three lines. Hand a piece of paper with *1950s automobile industry* written on it to the first student in each line. Instruct that student to add a type of business startup that grew from the 1950s car culture (for example, auto repair shops). Students pass the paper from person to person, each one adding a new type of business. Ask a volunteer from each group to read its completed list as the rest of the class listens for any type of business that was not previously mentioned. Compile a master list on the board. Finally, review the master list and work with students to create a statement that summarizes how the auto industry changed this aspect of the American landscape in the 1950s.

NG Learning Framework: Research the Oil Industry

ATTITUDE Curiosity

KNOWLEDGE Our Living Planet

Divide the class into small groups. Instruct the groups to learn more about the growth of the oil industry from 1945 to 1960, with a special focus on the political, economic, and environmental consequences of that growth. Prompt students to create an infographic that details their research. Encourage groups to share their research and compare their infographics.

DIFFERENTIATE

ENGLISH LANGUAGE LEARNERS ELD

Look for Cognates Suggest that as students read they look for words that are similar in spelling and meaning to words in their home language. For example, the words *automobile, commute,* and *quadruple* have cognates in Spanish: *automóvil, conmutar,* and *cuadruplicar.* For each word they identify, students of **All Proficiencies** should make a vocabulary card with the English word and definition on one side. On the other side, have them write the word and its definition in their home language.

PRE-AP

Analyze Impact Have students conduct research on the impact of "automobile mania," from economic and environmental to physical and psychological effects. Instruct students to gather information from a variety of sources, organize that information in a logical way, and then write an essay analyzing some of the positive and negative effects of car culture. Challenge students to conclude their essay with a recommendation to their city council that would reduce negative impacts of car use. Invite students to share their analyses and recommendations with the class.

See the Chapter Planner for more strategies for differentiation.

HISTORICAL THINKING

ANSWERS

1. During the Cold War years, many middle-class Americans were newly prosperous and living in suburbs, where cars were necessary for transportation.

2. Possible response: Since the United States needed to import oil to meet its needs, the government might have worked to stay on friendly terms with oil-producing nations and perhaps offered incentives to ensure that the United States would be favored in sales of oil.

3. Increased oil production allowed the United States to meet its energy needs and provided an ample supply of gasoline for gas-guzzling cars, but Americans' dependence on oil also contributed to air pollution, oil spills, and environmental damage from oil waste.

CRITICAL VIEWING Possible response: It appears that the conveyor belt brought food to cars parked by the restaurant. The system most likely appealed to younger people who enjoyed the novelty of food coming to them on a conveyor belt or to anyone who appreciated technological innovation.

1950s hot rod

Music fan driving to Woodstock, 1969

Dressed in their Sunday best, boys strike a serious pose on the hood of a car in a Chicago South Side neighborhood, 1941.

2.2

THROUGH THE LENS

CARS & AMERICAN CULTURE

It's surprising that a brutish industrial-age machine has maintained its status as a cultural icon amid the buzz of technology in the digital age. Decades ago, owning a car was about horsepower, status, and youthful rebellion. Cars inspired movies, songs, and literature. They were a driver's ticket to the freedom and glory of the open road. Do you think concerns about pollution, gridlock, and gas prices will cause the American car obsession to subside?

American World War II soldier in a seagoing Jeep, Europe, c. 1946

Tail fins on a 1959 Cadillac Eldorado

Architect Frank Lloyd Wright's 1930 Cord L-29

American actor and car enthusiast James Dean pushes his cousin in a homemade roadster in Indiana, 1955.

In 1977, Janet Guthrie was the first woman to drive in the Indianapolis 500 and the Daytona 500.

Electric vehicle charging at a Detroit, Michigan, auto show

870

Postwar Prosperity 871

PLAN: 2-PAGE LESSON

OBJECTIVE

Study photographs of automobiles and understand how these vehicles offer a window into the historical realities of the time.

CRITICAL THINKING SKILLS FOR LESSON 2.2

- Analyze Visuals
- Make Connections
- Form and Support Opinions

HISTORICAL THINKING FOR CHAPTER 24

How did the prosperity of the post–World War II period shape American society? The rise of the automobile was a symbol of postwar America. Lesson 2.2 examines the history of America's car obsession through the study of photographs.

BACKGROUND FOR THE TEACHER

While car ownership has long been a hallmark of American culture, that may be starting to change. Since 1960, the United States Census Bureau has tracked the number of carless homes in the country, and the number had steadily decreased over the decades. In 2012, for the first time, there was an increase in the percentage of Americans who chose not to own an automobile. While it's hard to pinpoint a specific cause for this trend, many have pointed to the rejection by millennials of car culture and to the popularity of ride-sharing apps. However, this change is not confined to coastal states like New York and California with high-density cities and easy access to ride-sharing. More rural states like Maine, Nevada, and Indiana also saw significant decreases in car ownership.

HISTORY NOTEBOOK

Encourage students to complete the Through the Lens page for Chapter 24 in their History Notebooks as they read.

INTRODUCE & ENGAGE

PREDICT THE TOPIC

Direct students to examine the photographs in the lesson. Call on volunteers to identify the topic of the lesson based on the images. **ASK:** Why do you think an entire lesson is devoted to automobiles? *(Answers will vary. Possible response: Automobiles have played an important cultural and economic role in American history.)* Inform students that in this lesson they will examine the importance of cars in American culture.

TEACH

GUIDED DISCUSSION

1. **Analyze Visuals** Have students examine the photographs. Note that some are in color and some are black and white. **ASK:** How does color—or lack thereof—change how the viewer experiences and interprets the image? *(Answers will vary. Possible response: In the color photographs, the viewer's eye is drawn to the machines, as they are colorful, detailed, and vivid. However, in the black-and-white photographs—such as the photograph of African-American children in 1941—the viewer focuses on the people rather than on the cars.)*

2. **Form and Support Opinions** How do the designs of cars in previous eras compare with those seen today, and what historical or technological events do you think account for changing trends? *(Answers will vary. Possible response: Older cars appear larger, with more prominent details, like grills and fenders, than the sleeker models of today. The trend toward smaller, more aerodynamic cars was probably pushed by historical events that limited Americans' access to fuel or drove up the price, making people value fuel efficiency—paired with advances in aerodynamic design.)*

THROUGH THE LENS

The freedom provided by the automobile had a transformative effect on American culture as it opened up seemingly unlimited possibilities for recreation outside the workplace. Where previous generations were tethered to the dueling locations of work and home, cars gave people more freedom and mobility. This allowed Americans to move from cities to the suburbs and, for fun, to pack the family in the car for extended vacations across the country. In addition, this new freedom deeply changed the lives of young people, as they increasingly escaped the watchful eyes of their parents by participating in activities outside the home. These changes also impacted the economy and physical landscape of the nation. Demand for manufacturing materials like steel and glass—along with roadside services like restaurants, gas stations, and motels—skyrocketed, while older industries like commuter rails and animal-powered transit disappeared.

ACTIVE OPTIONS

On Your Feet: Analyze a Photograph Divide the class into small groups and assign each group a different photograph from the lesson. Ask the groups to discuss the details they see in the photograph. Prompt them to talk about what each photograph conveys about the nation during that particular time. For example, what personality traits did people value? What design styles were considered desirable? When they have finished, invite groups to present their ideas to the class.

NG Learning Framework: Engage in an Online Discussion

SKILL Communication

KNOWLEDGE Our Human Story

Remind students of the question presented at the beginning of this lesson: Do you think concerns about pollution, gridlock, and gas prices will cause the American obsession with cars to subside? Ask students to take a position on this question and participate in an online discussion defending their point of view. Students should conduct research to find factual evidence—such as car sales data, opinions about pollution, or historical gas prices—to support their arguments. Direct them to post their opinions in an online class discussion board. After posting their work, students should read and respond to their classmates' comments.

DIFFERENTIATE

INCLUSION

Describe Details in Photos Pair students who have visual impairments with students who do not. Ask the students without visual impairments to describe the details in the photos. Prompt partners to discuss the differences between both the vehicles and the people in each image. Consider incorporating the discussion into the Analyze a Photograph activity.

PRE-AP

Research a Best Seller Assign pairs of students a particular year and have them identify the best-selling vehicle of that year. Then ask them to prepare a short presentation on that vehicle in which they analyze why the vehicle was a best seller and what this suggests about the historical conditions of the time. Ask pairs to present their work in chronological order. At the end, have a class discussion about how consumer goods offer a window into cultural conditions of a specific time period.

Wearing a TV-inspired Davy Crockett T-shirt, cowboy boots, and coonskin cap, a young boy reads about the legendary American frontiersman at his school desk in the 1950s. The 1950s pin-back button shown below pictures Crockett carrying his rifle and wearing a deerskin shirt and coonskin cap.

CULTURE OF THE FIFTIES

The next time you're watching your favorite TV show or listening to your favorite music, consider that much of what we now consider American pop culture came into being during the 1950s.

THE GOLDEN AGE OF TELEVISION

You have read about the important role television played in American consumer culture, both as an item for consumers to purchase and as a way for advertisers to sell their products. In 1948, less than one percent of American households could boast of owning a TV set. Back then, television's fuzzy black-and-white images were anything but "must-see." The first televised baseball game was filmed using only one camera. The first TV actors sweated under hot lights and wore black lipstick and green makeup just to show up on screen. But by 1959, more than 83 percent of homes in the United States had one or more televisions.

Television evolved by modeling itself on another medium—radio. In the 1930s and 1940s, radio offered a variety of entertainment to more than 60 percent of U.S. households and was available in nearly 2 million cars. Some radio programs were so popular that many movie theaters did not bother opening for the evening until after the top programs had aired. Early television programs just couldn't compete with the witty dialogue and skillfully achieved sound effects of radio, but television continued to improve.

Among the major changes in television technology was the introduction of color in 1950. In the early 1950s, special cables were used to link both coasts, marking a significant change in communication and allowing millions of viewers to watch the same program simultaneously. In 1949, a TV set appeared for the first time in the Sears department store catalog. Its price was $149.95. Only a year later, Americans were buying 20,000 television sets a day.

By 1954, three national television networks—ABC, CBS, and NBC—were broadcasting regularly. These networks were also the major radio broadcasters, and they boasted better technology and greater talent than their competitors. They also had two other advantages. Their profits from radio broadcasting enabled them to invest in new television programming. They could also move their most popular radio programs, including *Jack Benny, Burns & Allen*, and *Amos 'n' Andy*, over to television.

Television in the 1950s introduced or reinvented many genres, including variety shows, quiz shows, informational programming, and high-quality dramas. Among the most popular genres was the **situation comedy**, or sitcom, a weekly series that featured a familiar setting and a group of characters who faced amusing problems. These shows reflected traditional elements of American society, often with a twist. For example, on the popular sitcom *I Love Lucy*, the title character was a woman who stayed at home while her husband, Ricky, worked as a musician. Money was never an issue for the couple and their young son, and no one stayed angry for long. The show's humor came from crazy schemes Lucy developed to make her life more interesting. *I Love Lucy* introduced techniques that revolutionized the television industry, including taping in front of a live studio audience and using multiple cameras to film scenes from different angles. The show became so popular that more people tuned in to watch *I Love Lucy* on January 19, 1953—a staggering 44 million—than would watch President Eisenhower's inauguration the following day.

Though racial minorities rarely appeared in the 1950s sitcoms, they did play major—if stereotypical—roles in several popular shows. The most popular was *Amos 'n' Andy*, an adaptation of a radio comedy created by two white men and featuring an all-black cast. The NAACP angrily denounced *Amos 'n' Andy* for portraying blacks as "clowns" and "crooks," but others praised the performers for transforming racist stereotypes into humor that authentically portrayed the African-American experience.

By the mid-1950s, TV networks were mining the riches of children's programming. American film producer Walt Disney struck gold with his three-part series about the historical American frontiersman Davy Crockett, which aired nationally in December 1954. In the months that followed, millions of schoolchildren began wearing coonskin caps just like the one Crockett wore on the program. Stores soon began selling other Davy Crockett merchandise, including shirts, blankets, toothbrushes, and lunch boxes. One department store chain sold 20,000 surplus tents in less than a week simply by printing "Davy Crockett" on a flap.

Television and marketing businesspeople noted the new media's power to sell products. Important advertisers started sponsoring entire programs. The television industry expanded with each new program, providing work for hundreds of performers and technicians at a time and taking business away from the motion picture industry. By the mid-1950s, the "golden age" of television was in full swing.

A NEW KIND OF MUSIC

In the 1950s, a distinctive teenage culture emerged, rooted in the prosperity and population boom that followed World War II. While the threat of nuclear war was ever-present, teenagers had little experience of the grim events of the previous two decades. They were raised in relative affluence, surrounded by ads that ignored the traditional value of thrift. Fewer were employed than in prewar years, but close to half had summer jobs, and many had their own money. By 1956, teenagers bought $9 billion worth of products a year; a typical teen spent as much on entertainment as the average family had spent in 1941.

Many teens chose to spend their money on the popular music of the time. Known as **rock and roll**, this musical genre grew out of rhythm and blues, the music brought north by African-American musicians during the Great Migration. Most rock and roll songs were originally written or performed by African-American artists. Because African-American music was not considered appropriate for white audiences, music studio executives rerecorded versions of these songs using white "cover artists" so that white radio stations would play them.

PLAN: 4-PAGE LESSON

OBJECTIVE

Identify new forms of cultural expression from the 1950s and understand how they changed American society.

CRITICAL THINKING SKILLS FOR LESSON 2.3

- Analyze Cause and Effect
- Make Connections
- Make Inferences
- Determine Chronology
- Compare and Contrast
- Draw Conclusions
- Analyze Primary Sources

HISTORICAL THINKING FOR CHAPTER 24

How did the prosperity of the post–World War II period shape American society? Even as many Americans enjoyed new forms of entertainment, consumerism became a target for protest. Lesson 2.3 describes how television, rock and roll, and Beat literature changed the American landscape.

BACKGROUND FOR THE TEACHER

Children during the 1950s watched a variety of programs aimed at educating and entertaining. *Wallace and Ladmo*, which premiered in 1954, introduced young viewers in Arizona to characters such as Aunt Maud and a clown named Boffo. *Romper Room*, aimed at a preschool audience, was a combination of songs, moral lessons, and games. It ran on local channels, but all of its hosts received the same training. One of the most loved characters on children's TV was Bozo the Clown, who entertained with high-energy slapstick. Bozo became extremely popular in personal appearances, too; in fact, an appearance at a Washington, D.C., McDonald's became the inspiration for Ronald McDonald.

HISTORY NOTEBOOK

Encourage students to complete the Culture of the Fifties page for Chapter 24 in their History Notebooks as they read the lesson.

INTRODUCE & ENGAGE

PREVIEW USING VISUALS

Direct students' attention to the photograph of the boy reading a book about Davy Crockett and the photograph of Elvis Presley. Call on volunteers to generate questions they would like to ask about popular things in the 1950s, based on what they see in the photos. *(Responses might include questions about topics such as popular books, children's toys, foods, and music. Possible responses: What kinds of books did young people read? How were children's toys different from the toys of today? What did 1950s parents think of music that was popular with young people?)* Use a graphic organizer like the one shown here to keep track of the suggested questions. Return to the questions at the end of the lesson to see if all have been answered or if students would like to pursue answers through research. Invite comparisons to parallel elements in popular culture today.

What Was Popular in the 1950s?
Question
Question
Question
Question
Question

TEACH

GUIDED DISCUSSION

1. **Make Inferences** How do you think the rise of television affected the American family? *(Possible response: Families began watching TV shows together, became connected to other parts of the country in a more immediate way, started looking to TV as a source of news, and were influenced politically and socially by the programs they watched.)*

2. **Make Connections** How might television have affected family purchases and the national economy? *(Possible response: Families would probably be influenced by the programs they watched and desire many of the products seen on television. Their television-inspired purchases would strengthen the national economy.)*

3. **Determine Chronology** How would you describe the transition from radio to the "golden age" of television? Explain your answer. *(Possible response: The transition was rapid. In 1948, less than 1 percent of American homes had a television; by 1959, more than 83 percent had at least one television.)*

MORE INFORMATION

Color Television Explain to students that color television became a reality in the early 1950s, but consumers bought few of them at first. Later models built on a different technology went on sale in 1954 and had more success. Westinghouse sold a color TV for $1,295—the equivalent of about $11,800 in 2017 dollars. Soon after, RCA introduced one for $1,000. Emerson rented color television sets. However, the price and the screen size (only 15 to 19 inches) made color televisions less desirable than black-and-white sets, and only 150,000 color television sets had been sold by 1957. Improved technology and lower prices made color sets more popular in the 1960s. The sale of color television sets finally exceeded black-and-white sets in 1970. **ASK:** What other improvements have been made to televisions since the 1950s? *(Answers will vary. Possible responses: Technological advances have made it possible to make larger, lighter, flat-screen televisions with high definition. Televisions can be used to stream programs whenever you wish to see them.)*

DIFFERENTIATE

STRIVING READERS

Create a Concept Cluster Write the words *Culture of the Fifties* in the center oval of a Concept Cluster, and then write *Television, Music,* and *Literature* in each of the other three ovals. Ask students to copy the graphic organizer. Instruct them to reread the lesson and write specific examples of 1950s culture on the spokes. Tell students to share their Concept Cluster with a partner, noting similarities and differences.

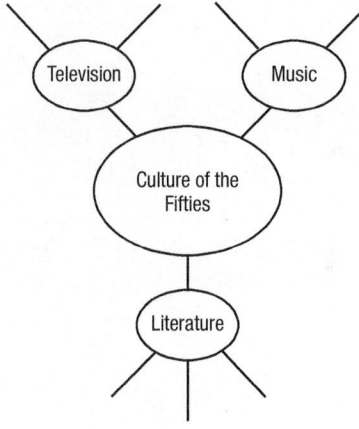

PRE-AP

Create a Social Media Profile Ask students to choose one of the Beat Generation writers mentioned in this lesson. Instruct them to conduct research using a variety of print and online sources to learn more about the person's background, philosophy, and writing. Then prompt students to create a social media profile for their writer and compose social media posts in that person's style. Invite students to share their profile and posts with the class.

See the Chapter Planner for more strategies for differentiation.

The wildly popular Elvis Presley (1935–1977) sings and dances at the Olympia Theater in Miami, Florida, in 1956. Presley had an exceptional vocal range.

That situation began to change in 1951, after an American disc jockey named **Alan Freed** learned that white teens in Cleveland were buying up records featuring African-American rhythm and blues artists. Freed began playing the hard-edged music on the air. Suddenly, teens could discover new music just by turning a radio dial.

In 1955, African-American rhythm and blues artist **Chuck Berry** (1926–2017) recorded one of the first rock and roll songs, "Maybellene," which quickly became a hit. Berry followed up with "Roll Over Beethoven" (1956), "Rock and Roll Music" (1957), and "Johnny B. Goode" (1958). A rock and roll pioneer, Berry played guitar in an infectious, rhythmic style and wrote songs about cool cars and dances to appeal to teenagers. Berry's showmanship on stage—playing guitar between his legs and behind his head and performing a movement called the "duckwalk"—influenced many rock and roll guitarists.

In 1955, a 21-year-old truck driver from Memphis named **Elvis Presley** exploded onto the popular music scene. Born in rural Mississippi, Presley grew up singing country music, gospel, and blues. Tall and handsome with long sideburns and slicked-back hair, he was a riveting performer. His music was strongly rooted in the southern music of his childhood.

Presley quickly became a national sensation. In less than a year, he recorded 8 number one songs and 6 of the all-time top 25 records of music company RCA. However, Presley had many critics, including teachers and members of the clergy, who complained that his unique way of dancing and shaking his hips proved that rock and roll posed a moral danger to the country's youth. This criticism only increased Presley's popularity among young people.

In 1956, rock and roll reached a milestone when an African-American singer named **Little Richard**

outsold tamer versions of his songs that had been rerecorded by Pat Boone, a leading white cover artist. The success of Little Richard and other rock and roll musicians led major record companies to start recording more of the genre, performed by both black and white musicians. Music sales tripled during the 1950s, aided by such technological advances as portable transistor radios and vinyl records.

THE BEAT GENERATION

While rock and roll was changing the American music scene, another youth rebellion transformed American writing. The **Beat Generation** was a group of young writers and poets in San Francisco and New York City who attacked the values and beliefs of mainstream American society. They called themselves "beat" because they were tired of living in the homogenous, or uniform, society they felt was taking hold in the United States. They despised politics, consumerism, and technology, and they valued creative expression.

Poet **Allen Ginsberg** expressed the Beats' disgust for the conventions of the time in his long, free verse poem "Howl" (1955). Its opening line—"I saw the best minds of my generation destroyed by madness"—sets a mood of anger and despair. Ginsberg's work demonstrated his belief that a mass audience could relate to an individual's thoughts and experiences, no matter how outside the norm they might be.

The Beats equated happiness and creativity with total freedom of expression. Their model of authentic living was Dean Moriarty, the hero of *On the Road* (1957) by Beat author **Jack Kerouac**. Loosely based on an actual road trip that Kerouac and some friends took, the book tells of the cross-country adventures of a group of young Americans trying to escape from middle-class life. *On the Road* became a national best seller and a cult book on college campuses. Like Presley, Little Richard, and Ginsberg, Kerouac appealed to the young people dissatisfied with conventional American culture of the 1950s.

HISTORICAL THINKING

1. **READING CHECK** What forms of entertainment that developed in the 1950s became part of mainstream American culture?

2. **ANALYZE CAUSE AND EFFECT** How did racism affect television programming in the 1950s?

3. **MAKE CONNECTIONS** How do you think the historical story of rock and roll influenced social trends in today's popular music?

BUILD BACKGROUND

VINYL RECORDS

Rock and roll music played over and over again in the homes of Americans, thanks to the technology of vinyl records. Records designed to spin at 78 revolutions per minute (rpm) had been around for a long time, but the technology got a boost in 1948 when Columbia Records introduced the 12-inch Long Play (LP) 33⅓ rpm vinyl record; soon afterward, rival RCA Victor released the 7-inch 45 rpm Extended Play (EP) vinyl record. LPs offered up to 30 minutes of music per side; EPs, also known as "singles," had a much shorter playing time and usually held just one song per side. With a growing interest in stereo sound, record companies in 1955 sought to record stereo sound on a 12-inch LP, and they succeeded by 1957. Sales of LPs grew during the early 1960s. By 1968, nearly all LPs were produced in stereo. Individual record companies tracked record sales in the 1950s until 1958, when the Recording Industry Association of America began offering Gold Record awards for singles and albums that reached $1 million in sales (later changing the award to recognize 500,000 records sold). The first Gold Record award went to Perry Como for "Catch a Falling Star," followed by Laurie London for "He's Got the Whole World in His Hands," and then to rock and roll star Elvis Presley in August 1958 for "Hard Headed Woman."

TEACH

GUIDED DISCUSSION

4. **Compare and Contrast** How did the culture of the Beat Generation differ from conventional American culture? *(Members of the Beat Generation believed that happiness and creativity came from total freedom of expression. Unlike conventional Americans, those who identified as part of the Beat Generation viewed politics, consumerism, and technology as constraints on free expression.)*

5. **Draw Conclusions** Why did rock and roll gain such popularity among young people in the context of the 1950s, and how did technology accelerate its popularity? *(Answers will vary. Possible response: Rock and roll was seen as rebellious and new at a time when teenagers began to develop a culture of their own, and it was easy to listen to on new transistor radios and vinyl records.)*

For students who develop an interest in the history of rock and roll, suggest that they read the American Story located at the beginning of this chapter.

ANALYZE PRIMARY SOURCES

Review what is said about Jack Kerouac and *On the Road* in the lesson. Then direct students' attention to the Primary Source feature and have them read the quotation together, pausing briefly after each comma. (You may also want to invite volunteers to interpret it as a dramatic reading.) **ASK:** What do you think Kerouac means by his use of the word *mad* in this passage? *(Possible response: He is talking about having great passion for living as an individual, unbound by convention and wanting to experience as much of life as possible.)* Point out that the passage is a single sentence, symbolic of Kerouac's desire to pack as much living as possible into a single moment.

ACTIVE OPTIONS

On Your Feet: One-on-One Interviews Ask pairs of students to write three questions and detailed answers about popular culture in the 1950s based on the information in the lesson. Instruct one student to interview the other as if they are on a news talk show and then to take questions from the "audience." Students' answers should demonstrate an understanding of the early days of television, the beginnings of rock and roll, and the Beat Generation. Partners may want to use a graphic organizer to write their questions and detailed answers to prepare for the talk show.

Questions	Answers

NG Learning Framework: Analyze the Beat Generation

ATTITUDE Curiosity

KNOWLEDGE Our Human Story

Direct students to select one of the Beat Generation artists who sparks their curiosity. Instruct them to research various sources and write a short paper about the significance of the Beat Generation and the artist's role in the movement. In particular, encourage students to analyze the claims of any critics of the artist or the movement by corroborating or challenging their claims with other information. Have students share their analyses in a panel discussion or a whole-class discussion.

HISTORICAL THINKING

ANSWERS

1. The two most influential forms of entertainment that developed during the 1950s were television and rock and roll music.

2. Racial minorities rarely appeared in most TV shows, and the shows in which they did appear, such as *Amos 'n' Andy*, tended to present them as laughable stereotypes.

3. Answers will vary. Students may point to the humble beginnings of some of today's top popular musicians, to the way that some musicians challenge tradition, or to the way that some musicians have inspired a particular subculture.

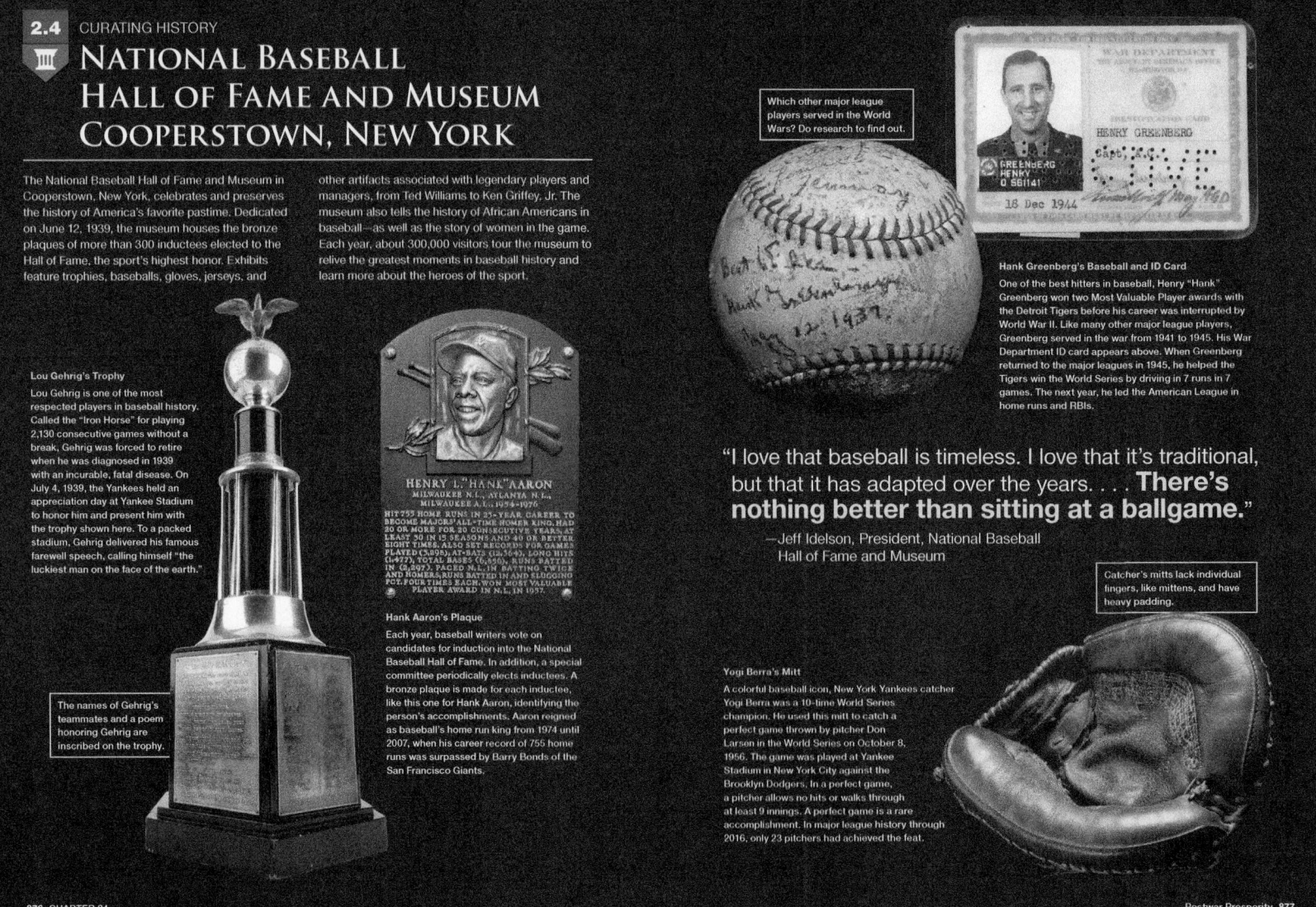

NATIONAL BASEBALL HALL OF FAME AND MUSEUM
COOPERSTOWN, NEW YORK

The National Baseball Hall of Fame and Museum in Cooperstown, New York, celebrates and preserves the history of America's favorite pastime. Dedicated on June 12, 1939, the museum houses the bronze plaques of more than 300 inductees elected to the Hall of Fame, the sport's highest honor. Exhibits feature trophies, baseballs, gloves, jerseys, and other artifacts associated with legendary players and managers, from Ted Williams to Ken Griffey, Jr. The museum also tells the history of African Americans in baseball—as well as the story of women in the game. Each year, about 300,000 visitors tour the museum to relive the greatest moments in baseball history and learn more about the heroes of the sport.

Which other major league players served in the World Wars? Do research to find out.

Lou Gehrig's Trophy
Lou Gehrig is one of the most respected players in baseball history. Called the "Iron Horse" for playing 2,130 consecutive games without a break, Gehrig was forced to retire when he was diagnosed in 1939 with an incurable, fatal disease. On July 4, 1939, the Yankees held an appreciation day at Yankee Stadium to honor him and present him with the trophy shown here. To a packed stadium, Gehrig delivered his famous farewell speech, calling himself "the luckiest man on the face of the earth."

The names of Gehrig's teammates and a poem honoring Gehrig are inscribed on the trophy.

Hank Aaron's Plaque
Each year, baseball writers vote on candidates for induction into the National Baseball Hall of Fame. In addition, a special committee periodically elects inductees. A bronze plaque is made for each inductee, like this one for Hank Aaron, identifying the person's accomplishments. Aaron reigned as baseball's home run king from 1974 until 2007, when his career record of 755 home runs was surpassed by Barry Bonds of the San Francisco Giants.

Hank Greenberg's Baseball and ID Card
One of the best hitters in baseball, Henry "Hank" Greenberg won two Most Valuable Player awards with the Detroit Tigers before his career was interrupted by World War II. Like many other major league players, Greenberg served in the war from 1941 to 1945. His War Department ID card appears above. When Greenberg returned to the major leagues in 1945, he helped the Tigers win the World Series by driving in 7 runs in 7 games. The next year, he led the American League in home runs and RBIs.

"I love that baseball is timeless. I love that it's traditional, but that it has adapted over the years. . . . **There's nothing better than sitting at a ballgame.**"

—Jeff Idelson, President, National Baseball Hall of Fame and Museum

Catcher's mitts lack individual fingers, like mittens, and have heavy padding.

Yogi Berra's Mitt
A colorful baseball icon, New York Yankees catcher Yogi Berra was a 10-time World Series champion. He used this mitt to catch a perfect game thrown by pitcher Don Larsen in the World Series on October 8, 1956. The game was played at Yankee Stadium in New York City against the Brooklyn Dodgers. In a perfect game, a pitcher allows no hits or walks through at least 9 innings. A perfect game is a rare accomplishment. In major league history through 2016, only 23 pitchers had achieved the feat.

PLAN: 2-PAGE LESSON

OBJECTIVE

Explore artifacts in the National Baseball Hall of Fame and consider the role of baseball in American popular culture.

CRITICAL THINKING SKILLS FOR LESSON 2.4

• Analyze Visuals
• Make Connections
• Identify
• Draw Conclusions

HISTORICAL THINKING FOR CHAPTER 24

How did the prosperity of the post–World War II period shape American society? In the years after World War II, Americans embraced popular culture and entertainment in many forms, including baseball. Lesson 2.4 illustrates how baseball produced American sports heroes and both challenged and broke down class, gender, and racial barriers.

BACKGROUND FOR THE TEACHER

In 1905 the Mills Commission was given the task of determining the official origins of baseball. In its final report, issued in 1908, the commission asserted that Abner Doubleday, a Civil War hero, invented baseball in Cooperstown, New York, in 1839. In 1935, a baseball with a stitched cover that was discovered in a farmhouse near Cooperstown was to be declared the first modern baseball. It was dubbed the "Doubleday baseball." Cooperstown philanthropist Stephen C. Clark purchased the Doubleday baseball for $5 and displayed it at a local club, setting the future location and purpose for the Baseball Hall of Fame. In 1962, Jackie Robinson became the first African American inducted into the Baseball Hall of Fame; in 1973, Roberto Clemente became the first Latino inductee.

HISTORY NOTEBOOK

Encourage students to complete the Curating History page for Chapter 24 in their History Notebooks as they read.

INTRODUCE & ENGAGE

EXPLORE HISTORY THROUGH ARTIFACTS

Remind students that examining objects is one way that historians understand the past. Invite students to name types of artifacts they think should be displayed in a baseball museum. Direct students' attention to the baseball in the photograph—especially its inscription. **ASK:** What can you infer about the significance of this baseball? *(Possible response: The date on the baseball suggests that it was perhaps a winning pitch or a home run ball from the game played on the recorded date.)*

TEACH

GUIDED DISCUSSION

1. **Identify** How are players chosen for induction into the Hall of Fame, and what does it mean to be an inductee? *(Baseball writers, and at times a special committee, vote on who will be inducted into the Hall of Fame. The induction signifies that the inductee is among the great players in the history of baseball.)*

2. **Draw Conclusions** Why do you think people continue to honor the history and players of professional baseball? *(Possible response: Baseball is part of the American identity. Players who have distinguished themselves are respected for their accomplishments.)*

🏛 CURATING HISTORY

The website of the National Baseball Hall of Fame and Museum is a useful resource for learning more about the history of baseball. Access the website and guide students to the Digital Collection section, where they can find oral histories from baseball's greatest players. Prompt students to access and listen to an oral history of their choosing and prepare a summary of its contents.

ACTIVE OPTIONS

Active History: Major League Baseball Attendance Extend the lesson by using either the PDF or Whiteboard version of the activity. These activities take a deeper look at a topic from, or related to, the lesson. Explore the activities as a class, turn them into group assignments, or even assign them individually.

On Your Feet: Sort the Artifacts Direct students to work in teams of four to examine both the artifacts in the lesson and images related to the history of baseball that are available at the National Baseball Hall of Fame and Museum's website. Then have students complete two Concept Clusters like those shown below. In one cluster, students should identify artifacts and photographs that reveal information about baseball's best players. In the other, have them identify a different class or genre of artifacts and/or photographs to be determined by them. When teams are finished, they can share their Concept Clusters with the class and note details that most of the teams identified.

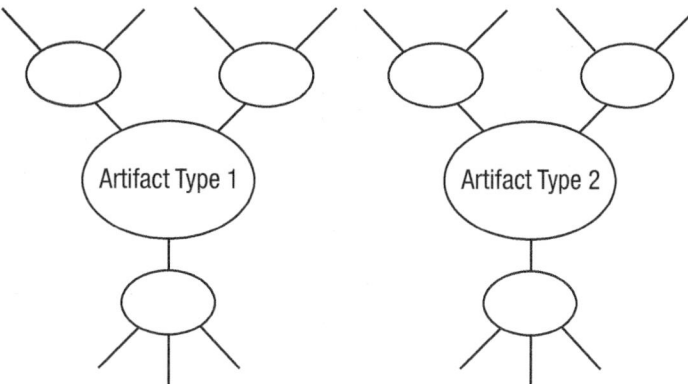

DIFFERENTIATE

ENGLISH LANGUAGE LEARNERS `ELD`

Pose and Answer Questions Arrange students at the **Emerging** and **Expanding** levels in mixed pairs and ask them to reread the lesson together. Instruct them to pause after each paragraph, caption, or quotation and ask one another *who, what, when, where,* or *why* questions about what they have just read. Tell students at the **Expanding** level to assist students at the **Emerging** level as needed.

GIFTED & TALENTED

Create an Annotated Time Line Instruct students to create and annotate a time line incorporating the information presented in this lesson. Tell students that their time lines should include dates and a brief description of the person, item, place, and/or actions associated with each event. Students may also use photographs, newspaper headlines, or other images to add further information and visual appeal to the time line. Encourage students to present their time lines to the class and discuss how the events in the time line have influenced events in the present day.

See the Chapter Planner for more strategies for differentiation.

HANK GREENBERG'S BASEBALL AND ID CARD

Answers will vary. Provide time for students to research major-league players who served in World War II, such as Yogi Berra and Ted Williams.

URBAN AND RURAL POVERTY

If you don't experience something yourself, you may find it hard to imagine it even exists. In the 1950s, middle-class suburbanites lived sheltered from the poverty that plagued inner cities and rural areas.

American photographer Wayne Miller took this photograph of tenements in Chicago in 1948 as part of a project documenting the lives of African Americans who were left out of the postwar economic boom.

PERSISTENT POVERTY

The 1950s were a prosperous time for the United States as a whole, but the nation's wealth was not distributed equally. While the total amount of wealth in the country increased, the economic gap between the wealthy and the poor remained the same. In the late 1950s, the **poverty rate**, or the percentage of the population living in poverty, was 22.4 percent, which amounted to about 39.5 million people.

American journalists and writers of the early 1960s worked to expose the pervasive poverty in the United States. In 1960, journalist Edward R. Murrow revealed the harsh living conditions of migrant farm workers in a nationally aired documentary for CBS, *Harvest of Shame*. Television viewers witnessed families who could barely afford food for themselves as they harvested crops for the wealthiest, best-fed

country in the world. In the book *The Other America*, published in 1962, author Michael Harrington portrayed the persistence of poverty among such groups as the working poor, the elderly, and the mentally ill. The book became required reading in college courses and prompted government officials to address some of the problems it had exposed.

URBAN POVERTY

As you have read, many middle-class Americans and businesses moved to the suburbs in the 1950s. This population shift lowered the taxes collected by cities, decreased municipal budgets, and influenced the racial concentrations in cities. Those departing for new homes in the suburbs were mostly white, while those who remained in the cities were more often members of minority groups. This difference was due both to economic factors and to discriminatory practices that prevented members of minorities from moving to largely white suburban neighborhoods.

President Truman's Fair Deal had included the American Housing Act of 1949. The act provided mortgage assistance for Americans buying homes and began the process of **urban renewal**, which involved clearing slums to replace them with large, publicly funded housing projects. Federal and state government urban renewal programs continued into the 1960s. Although the original intent of the plan was good, the huge projects destroyed existing communities, were too large to manage efficiently, and often isolated the residents from affordable services. Instead of alleviating problems, many of the housing projects became centers of despair and unemployment. Out-of-wedlock births increased, as did criminal activity and drug abuse. By the late 1960s, the urban renewal effort was largely deemed a failure.

> **PRIMARY SOURCE**
>
> *The American city has been transformed. The poor still inhabit the miserable housing in the central area, but they are increasingly isolated from contact with, or sight of, anybody else. Middle-class women coming in from Suburbia on a rare trip may catch the merest glimpse of the other America on the way to an evening at the theater, but their children are segregated in suburban schools. The business or professional man may drive along the fringes of slums in a car or bus, but it is not an important experience to him. The failures, the unskilled, the disabled, the aged, and the minorities are right there, across the tracks, where they have always been. But hardly anyone else is.*
>
> — from *The Other America*, by Michael Harrington, 1962

RURAL POVERTY

Poverty in the United States was not confined to the inner cities in the 1950s. As you have read, suburbanization affected rural areas as well. The loss of farmland, the rise of agribusiness, and increased mechanization meant fewer farming jobs. Many rural communities slowly declined, especially as young people left in search of job opportunities.

Some rural areas were extremely poor. **Appalachia**, a part of the Appalachian Mountain region that stretches from northern Alabama to southern New York, had one of the most severe poverty rates in the United States in the late 1950s and early 1960s. In 1960, when the overall United States poverty rate was 22 percent, the poverty rate in Appalachia averaged more than 31 percent.

Appalachia was mountainous and hard to farm, but it had an abundance of coal. With little else to sustain the local economy, the region became dependent on coal mining. But mining was hard, dirty, and dangerous work. It stripped forests and polluted the air, land, and water, contributing to a variety of environmental problems. By the mid-20th century, the introduction of machinery that could do the

work of many miners in a much shorter time frame put many miners out of work. Logging provided some temporary jobs, but the process scarred the Appalachian landscape.

Over time, efforts to reduce poverty in many places in the United States were successful, but Appalachia saw little economic improvement. In a decade, the region had lost 1.5 percent of its jobs, even as the nation's total employment grew by 17 percent. Its rugged landscape was unattractive to most industries, and re-education and job training programs were well intentioned but ineffective. Between 1945 and 1965, approximately 3.5 million people left Appalachia, seeking better lives and work opportunities in larger cities in the Midwest.

HISTORICAL THINKING

1. **READING CHECK** How did suburbanization contribute to urban and rural poverty in the 1950s?

2. **ANALYZE CAUSE AND EFFECT** Why did many urban renewal projects of the 1950s and 1960s fail?

3. **IDENTIFY PROBLEMS AND SOLUTIONS** Why did attempts to reverse Appalachian poverty fail?

PLAN: 2-PAGE LESSON

OBJECTIVE

Examine the reasons for and identify the consequences of urban and rural poverty in the United States during the 1950s.

CRITICAL THINKING SKILLS FOR LESSON 3.1

- Analyze Cause and Effect
- Identify Problems and Solutions
- Evaluate
- Make Connections
- Analyze Primary Sources

HISTORICAL THINKING FOR CHAPTER 24

How did the prosperity of the post–World War II period shape American society? While wealth increased during the 1950s, the gap between rich and poor remained the same. Lesson 3.1 compares urban poverty with rural poverty, explaining the causes and the government's attempts to remedy the problem.

BACKGROUND FOR THE TEACHER

The Housing Act of 1949, whose goal was to ensure that every American family lived in a "decent environment," made funds available for the building of 810,000 units of housing over a six-year period. The Housing Act of 1954 continued the federal government's efforts to address problems with housing and urban development by expanding urban renewal efforts and calling for the rehabilitation of blighted areas. As a stipulation for receiving urban renewal funding, the law required communities to establish a program to eliminate and prevent slums. In particular, the Housing Act of 1954 provided new assistance for housing programs for low-income families. The Housing Act of 1956 provided relocation payments for individuals and families displaced by urban renewal efforts.

FINANCIAL LITERACY

To extend their knowledge and understanding about the concepts in this lesson, refer students to the Financial Literacy handbook.

INTRODUCE & ENGAGE

DISCUSS THE EFFECTS OF POVERTY

Draw a Detail Web on the board. Using the Chicago tenements photograph as a prompt, encourage students to consider the social and emotional effects of poverty. **ASK:** How does poverty affect individuals and families? *(Possible responses: Individuals may have limited educational and employment opportunities. Families may have limited access to food or medical services.)* Prompt students to generate ideas on how poverty affects the family unit, communities, and people's general health and welfare. Tell students that in this lesson they will learn how poverty shaped life in some urban and rural communities in the 1950s.

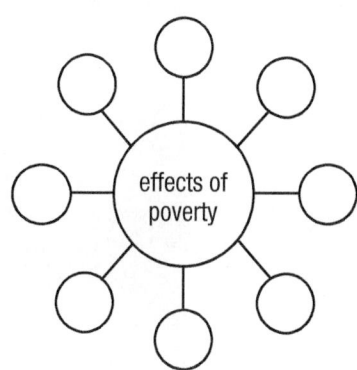

TEACH

GUIDED DISCUSSION

1. **Evaluate** Would you characterize the intent and effect of federal urban renewal efforts as positive, negative, or both? Explain your evaluation. *(Possible response: The intent of urban renewal was positive and laudable because the goal was to improve the lives of city dwellers. However, the efforts ended negatively, disrupting communities and creating despair and social detachment.)*

2. **Make Connections** In what ways did the use of new technology contribute to the trend toward rural poverty and negatively affect the environment of the Appalachia region? *(Because machines could do the work miners did—but much more quickly—many miners lost their jobs. Moreover, the machines that mined and cleared the land of trees destroyed landscapes and polluted the air, water, and land.)*

ANALYZE PRIMARY SOURCES

Direct students' attention to the Primary Source feature. Hand out two sticky notes to each student. Ask students to read the excerpt from *The Other America* and to write on each sticky note a word or phrase that relates to the picture of urban poverty described by Michael Harrington. Instruct students to place their sticky notes on a common area on the board or wall. Then ask them to work together to group all the notes to create categories that broadly identify the effects of urban poverty. Guide a general discussion about how the responses were grouped and about how poverty affects urban individuals and families.

ACTIVE OPTIONS

On Your Feet: Jigsaw Organize students into three "expert" groups and assign each group one of the following topics: urban renewal; rural poverty; the working poor. Students should discuss their assigned topic in depth. Then reorganize the groups so that each new group includes at least one member from each expert group. Ask students in each new group to share what they learned about their topic.

NG Learning Framework: Research Attempts at Reform

SKILL Communication

KNOWLEDGE Our Human Story

Direct students to find out more about the human toll of urban renewal policies. Encourage students to research trends in out-of-wedlock births, criminal behavior, and drug use. Each student should evaluate the various explanations for each of these trends and determine which explanation best accords with textual evidence. Prompt them to learn more about what happened to displaced residents. Ask students to present their research and participate in a discussion about what actually happened to affected individuals as a result of urban renewal.

DIFFERENTIATE

ENGLISH LANGUAGE LEARNERS

Use Word Maps Pair students at the **Emerging** level with students at the **Expanding** or **Bridging** level. Have them use Word Maps to better understand the vocabulary terms *poverty rate* and *urban renewal*. Direct pairs to trade Word Maps and note similarities and differences.

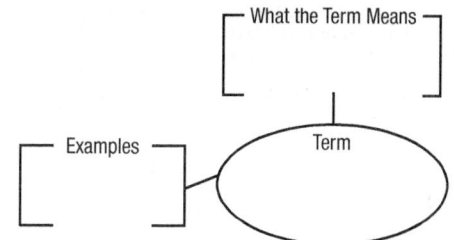

PRE-AP

Write a Comparison-Contrast Essay Instruct students to learn more about urban and rural poverty in the 1950s by conducting online research. Suggest students use a Venn Diagram to keep track of the similarities and differences between the causes, effects, locations, and other aspects of rural and urban poverty. Direct students to use their research to write a comparison-contrast essay and to share their essay with the class.

See the Chapter Planner for more strategies for differentiation.

HISTORICAL THINKING

ANSWERS

1. As city dwellers moved to the suburbs, cities lost tax revenue, while rural areas lost young farmers to job opportunities and homes in the suburbs. The result was the increase of areas, both urban and rural, in which the poverty level was high and opportunities for improvement were low.

2. The replacing of slums with large, publicly funded housing projects failed for several reasons. It destroyed neighborhoods and a sense of pride in one's community, replacing those neighborhoods with large, hard-to-manage buildings that often were isolated from affordable services. In addition, the social problems that gained traction in those areas were not well addressed.

3. Efforts to alleviate Appalachian poverty failed because the programs established to retrain and educate the people of Appalachia were inadequate and because people simply left the area in search of better job opportunities outside of the region.

NATIVE AMERICANS AND MEXICAN AMERICANS

The 1950s were great years to be a white, middle-class American. But if you were Native American or Mexican American, it was a different story.

DEMANDING A PLACE AS CITIZENS

In the years following World War II, Native Americans, many of whom had volunteered and fought bravely during the war, found themselves shut out of both the postwar economic boom and the political system. On reservations, they faced high rates of poverty and unemployment, poor access to government assistance and services, and inadequate schools. Many Native Americans did not even have the right to vote, despite the fact that, in 1924, Congress had granted citizenship to all Native Americans born within the United States. In addition, for decades, the federal government's policy toward Native Americans' sovereignty, or self-government, was inconsistent.

Some states refused to grant suffrage to Native Americans. The states took the position that Native Americans living on reservations were not citizens of the state, but rather citizens of their individual tribes or nations. Native Americans turned to the courts.

In 1948, Miguel Trujillo, a U.S. Marine war veteran and member of the Isleta Pueblo in New Mexico, was denied when he attempted to register to vote. He filed suit against the registrar and the state. A panel of three federal judges ruled in *Trujillo* v. *Garley* that the portion of New Mexico's constitution that prohibited Native American reservation residents from voting violated the 14th and 15th amendments of the U.S. Constitution.

Their decision backed up a similar case, *Harrison and Austin* v. *Laveen*, which had been brought by two Mojave-Apache men in Arizona that same year. These two cases effectively granted all Native American citizens the right to vote throughout the United States; however, Maine did not officially grant this right until 1953, and Utah held out until 1957.

Another major issue in the postwar era was poor government management of reservations. The Meriam Report, a government study released in 1928, had documented the problems and suggested specific reforms. The Indian Reorganization Act, passed in 1934, was an attempt to address the problems. The act sought to decrease federal control of Native American affairs and to encourage Native American self-government. It ended the government practice—adopted with the Dawes Act in 1887—of selling off the best reservation lands to white land speculators and homesteaders. It recognized the authority of tribal governments and promoted their self-government by urging them to adopt constitutions drafted by the Bureau of Indian Affairs.

But the reorganization was not a success. The act did not give Native Americans full control over their lands and governments. Instead, the reservations remained under the management of the Bureau of Indian Affairs, and little progress was made in solving the problems detailed in the Meriam Report.

Hoping to restore their tribal sovereignty and take control of their own future, Native Americans from 50 tribes and associations met in Denver, Colorado, to establish the National Congress of American Indians in 1944. In one year, membership rose to about 800 tribes and nations, representing nearly every Native American group in the United States. The organization began working to protect treaty rights, maintain Native American traditions, and push for self-determination and self-government.

Protester George Pletnikoff, Jr., a member of the Unangax (Aleut) tribe, helps train protesters in nonviolent methods.

Krystal Two Bulls, a member of the Northern Cheyenne and Oglala Lakota tribes, raises her fist in protest at right.

Nailed to a signpost at the main protest camp are the names of participating tribes and the distances to their homelands.

Protester Ray Curtis Yazzie, a member of the Blackfeet tribe, displays a Blackfeet Nation flag.

STANDING ROCK PROTEST

The struggle by Native Americans to protect their rights has continued into the 21st century. Beginning in April 2016, the Standing Rock Sioux led a 10-month protest in North Dakota against construction of the Dakota Access oil pipeline, designed to travel along the Missouri River and connect North Dakota oil fields with pipeline networks in Illinois. Seeking to protect their freshwater source and the diverse environmental regions crossed by the pipeline from potential oil leaks, the Standing Rock Sioux were joined by people from hundreds of indigenous tribes, including those shown above. In late February 2017, police cleared the main protest camp, following an executive order by President Donald Trump to advance approval of the pipeline's construction.

PLAN: 4-PAGE LESSON

OBJECTIVE

Evaluate the government's response to poverty and civil rights issues among Native Americans and Mexican Americans in the 1950s.

CRITICAL THINKING SKILLS FOR LESSON 3.2

- Identify Main Ideas and Details
- Identify Problems and Solutions
- Make Inferences
- Draw Conclusions
- Synthesize
- Analyze Visuals
- Form and Support Opinions

HISTORICAL THINKING FOR CHAPTER 24

How did the prosperity of the post–World War II period shape American society? While suburbanites enjoyed the benefits of greater prosperity, other Americans suffered. Lesson 3.2 explains how failed government programs and discrimination led to poverty and other problems for Native Americans and Mexican Americans.

BACKGROUND FOR THE TEACHER

The Bureau of Indian Affairs (BIA) oversees the policies governing Native American lands and educational programs. Established in 1824 as part of the War Department, it was moved to the newly established Department of the Interior in 1849. Its mission includes promoting economic opportunity and protecting Native American assets, but this has not always been its role. Beginning in 1887, the BIA oversaw the reduction of around 90 million acres of Native American lands. As part of the federal government's termination policy, the BIA ended its responsibility for more than 100 Native American tribes and bands. Today there are 567 federally recognized tribes. The BIA currently oversees management of 55 million surface acres and 57 million acres of subsurface mineral estates.

EXPLORE SELF-IDENTITY

Draw the Idea Web shown on the board and write *self-identity* in the circle. Guide students in discussing what the term means in relation to groups of individuals, such as Native Americans or Mexican Americans. **ASK:** What does it take for a group to maintain its self-identity? *(Possible responses: freedom to speak one's own language; access to appropriate food and clothing; ability to maintain customs; knowledge of history and traditions; a community of others who share a common history and identity)* Students should consider such factors as religion, land, language, clothing, and traditions. Review the completed web. Then tell students that in this lesson they will learn how Native Americans and Mexican Americans fought to maintain their self-identity in the 1950s.

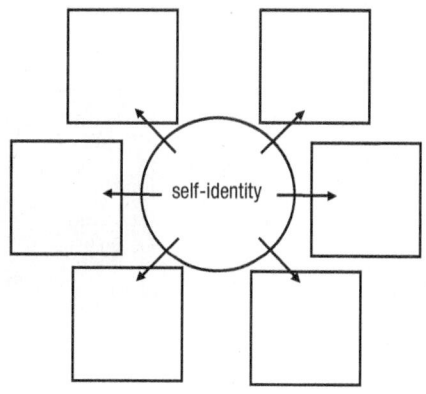

TEACH

GUIDED DISCUSSION

1. **Make Inferences** Why do you think two cases needed to go before the United States Supreme Court before all Native Americans gained suffrage? *(Possible response: Although Native Americans were granted the right to vote in 1924 and were protected by the 14th and 15th Amendments, Native Americans in New Mexico and Arizona were affected by discriminatory practices that had been in place for years, and the government had little interest in changing those practices.)*

2. **Draw Conclusions** How did the issue of Native American suffrage highlight an ongoing clash between federal authority and states' rights? *(Even though federal law mandated that all Native Americans be allowed to vote, some states—for example, New Mexico, Maine, and Utah—claimed the power to deny them that right.)*

3. **Synthesize** Consider why the Indian Reorganization Act failed. What do you think could have been done differently to make success more likely? *(Possible response: The act could have given Native Americans full control over their lands and could have assisted them in learning how to govern themselves. In addition, more could have been done to address the problems identified years earlier in the Meriam Report.)*

ANALYZE VISUALS

Direct students' attention to the images of Native Americans participating in the Standing Rock protest against the Dakota Access oil pipeline. Have them read and briefly discuss the caption. **ASK:** What word or phrase comes to mind as you look at the photo of the raised fist? Explain your response. *(Possible responses: The word* determination *comes to mind because a raised fist usually suggests a powerful desire to take a stand. The tattoo suggests the word* selflessness *because it shows a willingness to put a cause before one's personal well-being.)* Ask pairs of students to analyze the other photos in a similar way. Invite pairs to share and compare their responses.

STRIVING READERS

Complete a T-Chart Instruct students to create a T-Chart to keep track of the types and examples of discrimination described in the lesson. Have students label the first column Native Americans and the second column Mexican Americans. As they read, prompt students to complete the chart with details. After reading, encourage them to compare their completed charts.

Native Americans	Mexican Americans

GIFTED & TALENTED

Write and Deliver a Monologue Instruct students to choose one of the Native American or Mexican American people mentioned in the lesson. Then have them conduct online research in order to gather information to write a dramatic monologue. The monologue should focus on a particularly important event in the person's life. Ask volunteers to perform their monologues and respond to questions from their classmates.

See the Chapter Planner for more strategies for differentiation.

MORE FAILED POLICIES

In 1943, a year before the National Congress of American Indians began to organize, the U.S. Senate decided to investigate living conditions on Native American reservations. They found serious problems: poverty, racism, abuse by police officers, and alarming rates of alcoholism and suicide.

Under President Eisenhower, the federal government decided to remove Native Americans from reservations and encourage them to assimilate into mainstream society. And so began the disastrous government program known as the **termination policy**. In 1953, Congress set a goal to "as rapidly as possible make Indians within the territorial limits of the United States subject to the same laws and entitled to the same privileges and responsibilities as are applicable to other citizens of the United States." Under this policy, the government terminated all benefits and services to reservations, withdrawing its responsibility to maintain reservations and ending the limited sovereignty of individual tribes and nations.

Among the first tribes to be terminated were the Agua Caliente, who owned the land around Palm Springs, California, and the Klamath, whose land in Oregon was rich in lumber. The federal government took over their lands, as well as the land belonging to 107 other tribes between 1953 and 1964. Much of the land was sold to non-Native Americans.

Under this policy, Native Americans were expected to assimilate quickly into the mainstream of American society. To aid in this process, the Bureau of Indian Affairs set up a relocation program to move Native Americans from reservations to cities, where they were expected to find higher-paying jobs. The bureau set up relocation centers in Los Angeles, San Francisco, San Jose, Denver, Dallas, Cincinnati, Cleveland, St. Louis, and Chicago to help Native Americans find work, housing, and community resources. But not everyone found employment, and adjustment was difficult. Families were often separated, and tribal affiliations severed. In addition, a large number of Native Americans remained in poverty, and alcoholism continued to be a problem among many relocated populations.

Ultimately, the termination policy and the relocation program were failures. Federal termination efforts ended in 1963, and some of the affected tribes have been successful in regaining their lands through a number of lawsuits. The relocation era lasted for nearly two more decades, with as many as 750,000 Native Americans migrating to cities between 1950 and 1980.

THE THREAT OF DEPORTATION

During President Truman's eight years in office, from 1945 to 1953, about 127,000 undocumented immigrants were deported and more than 3.2 million left in fear of deportation. In 1954, under President Eisenhower, the government responded to an economic recession and a large U.S. labor pool with a program called "Operation Wetback," a reference to an offensive name for Mexicans who crossed the Rio Grande illegally. Intended to deport undocumented workers, the program mistreated many Mexicans and indiscriminately deported U.S. citizens as well. Officially, 2.1 million people of Mexican descent were deported through this aggressive, military-like campaign between 1954 and 1958.

MEXICAN AMERICAN WORKERS

In the 1950s and 1960s, the Latino population in the United States was relatively small. In 1960, about 6 million Latinos lived in the country. Many had first entered the United States to take part in the Bracero Program, an organized labor program that invited Mexican agricultural workers to replace U.S. farmworkers who were serving in World War II.

The government extended the Bracero Program after the war, and the number of braceros entering the United States increased. Most of the workers arrived from Mexico, but some came from Jamaica and the Bahamas. When the program was terminated in 1964, nearly 5 million worker contracts had been issued. Although President Truman had signed legislation to protect the rights of legal migrant workers in the United States, he also proposed legislation to stop employers from hiring undocumented immigrants. Congress did not approve it.

After the Bracero Program ended, many workers maintained connections with friends and families by continuing to cross the border informally and to return at will. Still others, knowing they would find fewer opportunities back at home, remained in the United States illegally after they were no longer in the program. Businesses were happy to hire these workers, paying them even lower wages than other migrant laborers. These low-paid workers contributed much to the economy of California and the Southwest, yet they lived in poverty and faced the constant threat of deportation.

THE LONGORIA INCIDENT

Even though they aided the United States during World War II, Mexican Americans faced

Braceros registering to enter the United States to work are fingerprinted and given documents at the Monterrey Processing Center in Mexico in 1956.

discrimination in the Southwest and elsewhere in the nation, whether they were citizens or undocumented immigrants. The Longoria incident was a prime example. Felix Longoria, a Mexican American war hero, was killed in the Philippines during World War II. When his body was returned to his family in 1948, his widow attempted to hold a wake in his honor at the only funeral home in Three Rivers, Texas. The owner of the funeral home refused her, saying, "The whites wouldn't like it."

The incident became front-page news across the country. **Dr. Hector P. Garcia**, a Mexican American and the president of the American GI Forum, a Latino veterans' civil rights organization, gathered more than 1,000 people to protest. He also sent a telegram directly to influential Texas senator **Lyndon B. Johnson**, who would later rise to the presidency. By the next afternoon, Johnson replied with an offer to bury Private Longoria at Arlington National Cemetery. The funeral was held there on February 16, 1949. The incident inspired many Mexican Americans to unify in their quest for civil rights and equal opportunities.

As early as the 1920s, Mexican Americans had organized to address discrimination. The **League of United Latin American Citizens (LULAC)**, formed in 1929, was one such organization. In 1945, LULAC sued the segregated Orange County, California, school system for openly discriminating against

Latino children. LULAC also protested the Longoria incident. In the 1960s, the organization actively supported the United Farm Workers, a labor union representing California farmworkers, most of whom were Latino. LULAC grew in the following decades, and today it provides college scholarships and other kinds of support to the Latino community.

Inspired by the agendas, strategies, and effectiveness of the civil rights movement elsewhere in the country, another Mexican American organization, the **Unity League,** was launched in California in 1947. The league campaigned against blatant acts of discrimination in housing, cemeteries, theaters, schools, and public administration. The league won lawsuits in the 1950s in cases involving segregation in schools and public swimming pools.

HISTORICAL THINKING

1. **READING CHECK** What kinds of discrimination did Native Americans and Mexican Americans face during the 1950s?

2. **IDENTIFY MAIN IDEAS AND DETAILS** Why did the United States open its borders to Mexican workers during World War II?

3. **IDENTIFY PROBLEMS AND SOLUTIONS** What actions did Mexican Americans take to gain civil rights during the 1950s?

BUILD BACKGROUND

AGUA CALIENTE BAND OF THE CAHUILLA INDIANS

The Agua Caliente have called Tahquitz Canyon, in the Palm Springs area of southern California, home since the Cahuilla settled there at least 5,000 years ago. It is a culturally rich area. Evidence of Cahuilla settlement includes rock art, irrigation ditches, and areas where food was preserved. The Cahuilla named the region *Sec-he*, meaning "boiling water." With the arrival of the Spanish, the region became known as *Agua Caliente*, the Spanish phrase for "hot water." The hot springs of the region were considered to be a spiritual connection to an underworld where sacred beings, called *nukatem*, lived. The springs also were used for healing purposes. The Agua Caliente traded food and seashells with neighboring tribes. Women gathered plants, including acorns and mesquite beans. Water from nearby streams irrigated crops. In 1876, by executive order, President Grant set aside a portion of the Tahquitz Canyon as reservation land for the Agua Caliente. In 1891, the government determined that the land should be broken into allotments and, in 1959, finalized a plan for individual ownership. Today, the Agua Caliente collectively remain the largest landowner in Palm Springs.

TEACH

GUIDED DISCUSSION

4. **Form and Support Opinions** How would you characterize both the intent of the termination policy and its results in the context of larger social developments? *(Possible response: On the surface, the intent of the termination policy seemed noble because it ensured that Native Americans were entitled to the same privileges and rights as other citizens; in reality, however, it was very punishing in that it also ended the limited sovereignty of individual tribes and halted all benefits and services to reservations.)*

5. **Draw Conclusions** How did Lyndon B. Johnson's response to the Longoria incident empower the Mexican American community? *(Possible response: Mexican Americans were glad to know that someone in the federal government supported their cause. They also were bolstered politically because they saw that speaking up for what is right and just can result in positive change.)*

MORE INFORMATION

Paying the Braceros Explain to students that, with a labor shortage predicted in the spring of 1942, the call went out to allow between 40,000 and 100,000 Mexicans into the United States to work the farm fields of California. Admissions for Mexican laborers peaked in 1944 with 62,000 being allowed to work on U.S. farms. Farmers employing Braceros between 1942 and 1949 withheld about 10 percent of their wages and gave the money to banks in the United States, which then sent it to Mexican banks. The intent was to place the money into savings accounts for the workers, but the money often disappeared once it reached the Mexican banks. As the result of lawsuits filed against the banks and both the U.S. and Mexican governments, some Braceros and their survivors were able to recoup their forced savings. **ASK:** Might such a forced savings plan ever be a good idea? Why or why not? *(Answers will vary. Possible responses: Yes. It would be a good idea if run fairly because it might keep vulnerable migrant workers from being robbed or cheated of their money. No. It would never be a good idea because there is always a likelihood of corruption or fraud somewhere in the transfer, and the worker might not even discover it until much later.)*

ACTIVE OPTIONS

On Your Feet: Four Corners Make a sign for each of these policies and programs: termination policy, relocation program, Bracero Program, deportation. Place one sign in each corner of the room. Instruct students to go to the corner with the sign of the policy or program they think most unified people and influenced future events or social, economic, and political trends. Give groups time to discuss the reasons for their choice, considering the context in which the policies and programs unfolded; then have a representative from each group present the group's ideas to the class.

NG Learning Framework: Explore Organizations

ATTITUDE Curiosity

KNOWLEDGE Our Human Story

Tell students to select an organization that piques their curiosity after reading this lesson. Instruct them to research the organization and create a fact sheet about it, using information from the chapter and from additional source material. Each fact sheet should include the purpose of the organization and the event or policy that prompted its beginning. Invite students to post their fact sheets in the classroom.

HISTORICAL THINKING

ANSWERS

1. Native Americans were not allowed to exercise their right to vote or to have full control over their lands and governments. The Native American termination policy also can be seen as discriminatory. Mexican Americans suffered from racial prejudice and from discrimination regarding employment (as in the Bracero Program).

2. There was a shortage of people working on farms during World War II. Opening the borders to Mexican workers was a way of alleviating this shortage.

3. Mexican Americans united and formed organizations, including the United Farm Workers, the League of United Latin American Citizens, and the Unity League, to protest injustices and work to end discrimination.

VOCABULARY

Use each of the following vocabulary terms in a sentence that shows an understanding of the term's meaning.

1. suburbanization
   As a result of suburbanization, subdivisions replaced large tracts of land.
2. nuclear deterrence
3. brinkmanship
4. consumer society
5. suburban sprawl
6. situation comedy
7. urban renewal
8. poverty rate
9. termination policy

READING STRATEGY
MAKE INFERENCES

Complete a graphic organizer like the one below to make an inference about the postwar effects of the GI Bill of Rights. Tell what you know about the subject in the "I Know" section. Write your inference in the "And So" section. Then answer the question that follows the graphic organizer.

Make Inferences

I Read
Millions of veterans gained a college education through the GI Bill of Rights, and many became employed in technology industries.

I Know	And So

10. Why might some Americans today idealize the 1950s?

MAIN IDEAS

Answer the following questions. Support your answers with evidence from the chapter.

11. How did Eisenhower present his political ideas during his campaign for president in 1952? LESSON 1.1
12. How did women's wages compare with men's wages after the end of World War II and during the 1950s? LESSON 1.2
13. How was the system used to build houses in Levittown similar to production on an assembly line? LESSON 1.3
14. In what ways did Americans' obsession with cars affect other industries during the 1950s? LESSON 2.1
15. What aspects of American life did the Beat poets rebel against? LESSON 2.3
16. Why did Appalachia suffer from a high poverty rate in the 1950s? LESSON 3.1
17. How did Dr. Hector P. Garcia help resolve the Longoria incident? LESSON 3.2

HISTORICAL THINKING

Answer the following questions. Support your answers with evidence from the chapter.

18. EVALUATE What were some drawbacks of Eisenhower's nuclear deterrence plan?
19. MAKE CONNECTIONS What effects of the suburbanization of the 1950s do you notice in your life today?
20. IDENTIFY What were some long-lasting effects of the Bracero Program?
21. FORM AND SUPPORT OPINIONS Based on the results of the urban renewal projects of the 1950s and 1960s, what advice would you give an urban planner who wants to replace decaying neighborhoods in a city?

22. MAKE INFERENCES How do you think voters in Guatemala reacted when the United States ousted their elected president in 1954?
23. DETERMINE CHRONOLOGY What sequence of events led the federal government to establish the termination policy and relocation programs for Native Americans?

INTERPRET VISUALS

With the baby boom in full swing in the 1950s, toy manufacturers had a ready market for their products. Study the toy advertisement and answer the questions that follow.

24. What is the manufacturer's purpose in offering a space man and jet rocket for free?
25. What does it tell you about the growing consumer society that the manufacturers chose a space rocket as the perfect toy to offer kids?

ANALYZE SOURCES

In the 1950s, William H. Whyte, a magazine editor, wrote a book about the culture of large corporate organizations and the suburbs where the employees—the "organization men"—lived. He found the suburbs alarming rather than blissful.

> At Levittown, Pennsylvania, residents are very much aware of who has what "modification" of the basic ranch-house design, and one house on which the owner mounted a small gargoyle became so famous a sight that many residents used to drive out of their way to show it to visitors. People have a sharp eye for interior amenities also, and the acquisition of an automatic dryer . . . or any other divergence from the norm is always cause for notice. Those who lack such amenities, conversely, are also noted.
>
> —from *The Organization Man*, by William Whyte, 1956

26. What is Whyte implying about people's values and attitudes in the suburbs?

CONNECT TO YOUR LIFE

27. EXPLANATORY You have read about American life and culture during the 1950s. Some historians think the postwar era laid the foundation for our current American identity. Review the chapter and research the lives of teenagers in the 1950s. Then write a short essay comparing their lives and experiences with yours.

TIPS

- Use a Venn Diagram or a T-Chart to make notes about similarities and differences between your experiences and those of a teenager in the 1950s.
- Choose two or three of the most interesting items on your chart to write about.
- Conduct an Internet or library search to find more information on the topic.
- Use two or three vocabulary words from the chapter in your essay.
- End the essay with a generalization about the similarities and differences.

VOCABULARY ANSWERS

1. As a result of suburbanization, subdivisions replaced large tracts of land.
2. The United States focused on nuclear deterrence as a means to prepare for any outside attack.
3. John Foster Dulles helped promote a policy of brinkmanship in dealing with potentially hostile nations.
4. Desire for new gadgets propelled the consumer society.
5. Suburban sprawl resulted when people leaving the cities caused outlying communities to spread farther.
6. Situation comedies are TV shows that reflect some aspect of life using humorous story lines.
7. Cities planned urban renewal projects as a way to improve their inner impoverished areas.
8. As the poverty rate rises, a greater number of people face financial hardship.
9. The United States adopted a termination policy for Native Americans, removing their identity as members of tribes.

READING STRATEGY ANSWER

Make Inferences

I Read
Millions of veterans gained a college education through the GI Bill of Rights, and many became employed in technology industries.

I Know	And So
Many veterans needed to learn new skills once World War II ended. Veterans wanted to become part of the consumer society. The GI Bill paid for the cost of college.	The GI Bill improved the quality of life for veterans.

10. For many, the 1950s was a time of prosperity, where life in the suburbs, family rides in the car, a new TV, and rock and roll music made life seem worry free and fun.

MAIN IDEAS ANSWERS

11. Eisenhower described his political stance as "modern Republicanism." During the campaign, he said that the welfare programs of the New Deal were social rights, not social issues, and he vowed to help Americans fighting in Korea.

12. Wages that women received were only 53 percent of what men were paid for similar work.

13. The two systems were similar because the processes were broken down into single, specialized tasks. Workers in the factory precut the manufactured pieces of the homes, deliverymen trucked the materials and equipment to the building site, and many workers assembled the house.

14. Because cars were so valued and necessary in the suburbs, businesses adjusted to accommodate drivers. Restaurants added drive-through service and car service, for example, and theater owners developed drive-in movies.

15. Believing that America was turning into a bland society that did not encourage individual expression, the Beat poets rebelled against politics, consumerism, and technology.

16. New technology took over many of the coal mining jobs once filled by the people of Appalachia. Training and educational programs to help unemployed miners prepare for other jobs were inadequate.

17. Garcia, a Mexican American veteran, helped the Longoria family by contacting the president directly. He also organized protesters.

HISTORICAL THINKING ANSWERS

18. Possible response: Eisenhower's nuclear deterrence plan hinged on the belief that the ability of the United States to launch a nuclear attack would deter other countries from launching a first strike. It was risky and created a world that was less safe.

19. Student responses might address areas of development outside a main city where houses go up in uniform developments, green space becomes roadways, concentrated business areas are created, and consumerism is noticeable.

20. The Bracero Program was a guest worker program between the United States and Mexico. Once it ended, its lasting effects included a continued flow of people who worked in the United States but then returned to Mexico, as well as workers who lived in the United States illegally. These workers usually filled jobs that paid lower wages, reducing job opportunities for migrant workers.

21. Answers will vary. Possible response: I would advise urban planners to find ways to minimize the disruption of the community by meeting with the residents of the area, ensuring they have alternative housing options, and designing housing that meets the needs of different income groups.

22. The people of Guatemala most likely resented American interference in their government and elections.

23. Students should share details covering the Indian Removal Act of 1830, the Indian Wars of the late 1800s, the Dawes Act and allotments of 1887, the Indian Reorganization Act of 1934, and then the termination era beginning in 1953.

INTERPRET VISUALS ANSWERS

24. The space man and jet rocket are offered for free as an incentive to purchase Kolynos toothpaste.

25. A space rocket was appealing because Americans were fast becoming interested in NASA and the federal government's plans for sending rockets into space.

ANALYZE SOURCES ANSWER

26. Whyte is implying that people who live in the suburbs think alike and live in similar ways—so much so that even a minor change in how things look or what people do attracts attention.

CONNECT TO YOUR LIFE ANSWER

27. Students' essays should present information gained from reading the chapter and from researching the lives of teenagers in the 1950s, incorporate vocabulary words from the chapter, and explain how the experiences of teenagers in the 1950s were both similar to and different from those of teenagers today.

National Geographic | CONNECTION

America's Propaganda Machine

BY BECKY LITTLE

Adapted from "Inside America's Shocking WWII Propaganda Machine," by Becky Little, news.nationalgeographic.com, December 2016

The United States was about six months into World War II when it founded the Office of War Information (OWI). Its mission: to disseminate political propaganda. The office spread its messages through print, radio, and film. But perhaps its most striking legacy is its posters with bright colors and sensational language. They encouraged Americans to ration their food, buy war bonds, and basically perform everyday tasks in support of the war effort. In one, a woman carrying her groceries is compared to soldiers carrying weapons. The poster implies that by walking instead of driving she is doing her patriotic duty. By not driving, people extended the lives of their cars and reduced the use of rubber and metal, which were instead needed to make tanks and weapons for the war.

LOOSE LIPS SINK SHIPS

Both the Allies and the Axis powers feared that leaked information could undermine their troops. With that in mind, the OWI produced posters urging people to keep sensitive information to themselves so enemies wouldn't overhear it. According to Stephen G. Hyslop, co-author of the National Geographic book *The Secret History of World War II*, the OWI struggled to find the best way to convey this message. As an example, he points to a poster that depicts a mysterious figure in a German helmet and warns "He's Watching You."

"The point of the poster is it's a German soldier" who could overhear what you say, Hyslop explains, but its message was too subtle. Consequently, the United States began to favor posters that got right to the point. In one of these, a woman's image appears alongside the words "WANTED! FOR MURDER. Her careless talk costs lives." This very clear message was still a bit strange. Most civilians didn't have access to sensitive military information, yet the images telling them to zip their lips were pretty aggressive and sometimes created the feeling of "Are the authorities on my side or are they after me?"

The OWI's propaganda was made for people at home and abroad, and it was always clear that these messages came from the U.S. government. However, the United States had another propaganda arm that produced messages specifically for the enemy and made it look like this propaganda was coming from inside the enemy's country.

ATTACKING ENEMY MORALE

Creating propaganda that hid or misrepresented its source wasn't only done by the United States. Germany transmitted radio messages to France, Britain, and other countries that appeared to originate from inside those nations.

The American Office of Strategic Services (OSS) responded with its own "black propaganda," as the practice was known. One mission, called Operation Cornflakes, involved dropping mailbags into Germany containing fake newspapers that looked as if they were made by Nazi resisters. Some of the mail had stamps with a picture of a deathly, skeletal-looking Hitler with the words *Futsches Reich* ("Ruined Empire").

The Allies also transmitted radio messages that appeared to come from inside Germany. This was an easier way to get information into the country than by dropping mailbags, Hyslop says.

Three-quarters of a century later, technological advances have made it even easier to sneak information into a country. As an example, Hyslop points to Russia's use of the Internet to spread propaganda during the 2016 U.S. election. Could future history books about our current era be illustrated with Internet political memes, just as today's history books are with propaganda posters? It's not unthinkable.

For more from National Geographic, check out "Dogs at War" online.

UNIT INQUIRY: Persuade an Audience

In this unit, you learned about a watershed event in which the United States became a major actor on the global stage: World War II. The Second World War placed tremendous demands on Americans, both those who fought abroad and those who remained at home. In public speeches and informal talks, Franklin Roosevelt and other leaders of the time worked to inspire citizens to make huge personal sacrifices in support of the war effort. How important were the rhetorical skills of the major leaders of this period? What kinds of persuasive language and appeals did they use? As you read quotes from their addresses, think about the way in which they crafted their messages to reach people's minds and hearts.

ASSIGNMENT

Choose an audience of the World War II era—such as newly enlisted soldiers, factory workers, farmers, or high school students—and write a speech persuading them to contribute to the war effort in a specific way. For example, you might research victory gardens and encourage high school students to plant one at their school to supplement the nation's food supply. Be prepared to present your speech to the class.

Plan Think about the reasons that success in World War II was vital to Americans and the way that Allied leaders like Roosevelt and Churchill inspired people to go all out to win the war. Then consider your audience and the contribution you're asking them to make. You might want to use a graphic organizer to outline your argument.

```
I.  _____
    A. _____
    B. _____
II. _____
    A. _____
    B. _____
III. _____
    A. _____
    B. _____
```

Produce Use your outline to write a persuasive speech that will inspire your audience to support the war effort in the way you've identified. Incorporate persuasive language and appeals directed specifically to your audience. Use words and phrases that clarify the relationship between your reasons and evidence. Provide a concluding statement that supports your argument.

Present Share your speech with the class. You might consider one of these options:

- Record a "fireside chat" audiotape. Play the audiotape in class, and then play a portion of one of Roosevelt's fireside chats. Invite students to compare and contrast your oratory style with Roosevelt's style.

- Create notes of your speech, then practice the speech and deliver it to the class. Ask students to identify the persuasive techniques you used and rate their effectiveness.

National Geographic | LEARNING FRAMEWORK ACTIVITY

Write About a Cold War Advance

SKILLS Observation, Communication
KNOWLEDGE Our Human Story

Major advances in medicine, science, and technology occurred during the Cold War years. Identify and research a Cold War development that improved Americans' lives, like the use of nuclear power as an energy source, or the development of new vaccines or commercial computers. Write a narrative incorporating real or imagined experiences during the Cold War, focusing on how the advancement affected a particular character's life. Use dialogue, description, and reflection to express the importance of the advancement on society.

Debate the Origins of the Cold War

ATTITUDE Curiosity
SKILL Collaboration

Work with a small group to research the major debates among historians concerning the origins of the Cold War. Read excerpts from *Origins of the Cold War* by Arthur M. Schlesinger, Jr., and excerpts from *The Tragedy of American Diplomacy* by William A. Williams. Evaluate each historian's use of evidence, looking for sound generalizations or misleading oversimplifications. Choose a creative way to present both sides of the argument, and have a class debate about the roles the United States and the Soviet Union played in the start of the Cold War.

NATIONAL GEOGRAPHIC CONNECTION

GUIDED DISCUSSION FOR "AMERICA'S PROPAGANDA MACHINE"

1. **Summarize** What purpose did propaganda in the war effort serve in the United States and abroad during World War II? *(In the United States, propaganda spurred American citizens to make sacrifices and not discuss information that might be used by the enemy. Abroad, U.S. propaganda stirred up enemy fears with fake newspapers and radio messages.)*

2. **Make Connections** What are some means by which propaganda can affect the world today? *(Answers will vary. Possible response: Users of social media can spread opinions and preferences that pressure others to feel or respond in particular ways. Realistic-sounding but untrue news stories in print, on television, or in digital media can influence people's thinking and incite them to take political action for or against important issues.)*

GUIDED DISCUSSION FOR "DOGS AT WAR"

1. **Compare and Contrast** How do Smoky's actions compare with service dogs you know of? *(Possible response: Smoky was small and able to run the telephone wires underground. Unlike rescue, therapy, or bomb-sniffing dogs, Smoky had no rigorous training. Instead, she performed a crucial task that relied on her size, instincts as a terrier, and willingness to please her master.)*

2. **Cause and Effect** What might explain the powerful effect of dogs on wounded veterans and soldiers in war zones? *(Answers will vary. Possible response: Dogs elicit feelings of care and normalcy. Their presence can create a pleasant mood and relieve the boredom felt by patients or the stress felt by active soldiers.)*

HISTORY NOTEBOOK

Encourage students to complete the Unit Wrap-Up page for Unit 7 in their History Notebooks.

UNIT INQUIRY PROJECT RUBRIC

ASSESS

Use the rubric to assess each student's participation and performance.

SCORE	ASSIGNMENT	PRODUCT	PRESENTATION
3 GREAT	• Student thoroughly understands the assignment. • Student participates fully in the project process.	• Speech is well thought out. • Speech offers a number of persuasive examples of how to contribute to the war effort. • Speech contains all of the key elements listed in the assignment.	• Presentation is clear, concise, and logical. • Presentation does a good job of creatively persuading the audience. • Presentation engages the audience.
2 GOOD	• Student mostly understands the assignment. • Student participates fairly well in the project process.	• Speech is fairly well thought out. • Speech offers at least one persuasive example of how to contribute to the war effort. • Speech contains most of the key elements listed in the assignment.	• Presentation is fairly clear, concise, and logical. • Presentation does an adequate job of creatively persuading the audience. • Presentation somewhat engages the audience.
1 NEEDS WORK	• Student does not understand the assignment. • Student minimally participates or does not participate in the project process.	• Speech is not well thought out. • Speech does not offer persuasive examples of how to contribute to the war effort. • Speech contains few or none of the key elements listed in the assignment.	• Presentation is not clear, concise, or logical. • Presentation does an inadequate job of creatively persuading readers. • Presentation does not engage the audience.

NATIONAL GEOGRAPHIC LEARNING FRAMEWORK RUBRIC

ASSESS

Use the rubric to assess how each student applies the National Geographic Learning Framework.

SCORE	ASSIGNMENT	ASSIGNMENT	FINAL PRODUCTS
3 GREAT	• Narrative demonstrates **Observation** and **Communication** well. • Narrative explores **Our Human Story** well.	• Project reflects **Curiosity** well. • Project demonstrates **Collaboration** well.	• Final products are engaging, creative, and well presented.
2 GOOD	• Narrative demonstrates **Observation** and **Communication**. • Narrative explores **Our Human Story**.	• Project reflects **Curiosity**. • Project demonstrates **Collaboration**.	• Final products are interesting, logical, and complete.
1 NEEDS WORK	• Narrative does not demonstrate **Observation** and **Communication**. • Narrative does not explore **Our Human Story**.	• Project does not reflect **Curiosity**. • Project does not demonstrate **Collaboration**.	• Final products are not creative, complete, or interesting.

MEMPHIS SANITATION WORKERS STRIKE

By 1968, tensions between African-American sanitation workers and Memphis city officials had been brewing for years. On February 12, those tensions came to a head, with more than 1,000 dissatisfied workers staging a strike. Their demands included better wages and working conditions, and people all over the city marched in support of the workers. But the city would not bend. Civil rights leader Martin Luther King, Jr., traveled to Memphis to support the workers' cause through a peaceful demonstration, and 5,000 people showed up on March 29 to join his march.

The march was peaceful at first, but violence broke out when a small contingent of demonstrators shattered windows and began looting stores. The city requested reinforcements, and 4,000 National Guard troops were called in. King left town, but he promised to return at a later date to try again for a peaceful demonstration. He did so on April 3, 1968. The following evening, King was assassinated outside his Memphis motel room. The sanitation workers' strike ended two weeks later, when the city granted the workers both higher pay and union recognition.

Direct students' attention to the photograph. **ASK:** What details do you notice about the soldiers and the marchers that suggest their intentions? *(Possible response: The National Guard troops are holding their rifles, with bayonets mounted, in a threatening stance, looking as if they intend to charge or shoot if the men make a wrong move. The men are marching single file a few feet apart from each other—perhaps to avoid looking at all like a mob—only a few feet from the guardsmen. They do not appear to be shouting or chanting or doing anything to provoke attack. The signs hanging from the men's necks speak for them, declaring, "I Am A Man." Their intent appears to be a peaceful, nonviolent protest. They know violence and property damage would hurt their cause and bring them harm if the guardsmen use their rifles.)*

Ask students to look closely at the faces of the men in the photograph. **ASK:** How would you describe the expressions on the faces of the marchers? *(Possible responses: Most of the African-American men are expressionless or look stern and are looking away from the guardsmen. The man at the front has an understandably angry look. The white man in the photo, who is not wearing a sign, is looking directly at the guardsmen. He has a bemused expression, as if wondering why they are pointing their guns at peaceful protesters.)* Guide students in a discussion about the use or show of force when protests are planned. Ask students to discuss the balance that protesters and law or military enforcement must maintain so as not to incite the opposing side to acts of violence.

UNIT
8 1954–1975
YEARS OF TURBULENCE

CRITICAL VIEWING U.S. National Guard troops block Beale Street in Memphis, Tennessee, on March 29, 1968, as civil rights marchers pass by. The activists held a number of marches over several days. Martin Luther King, Jr., participated in one of them. It was one of the last public appearances he would make before he was assassinated on April 4. What message are the protesters trying to convey with their signs?

888

SEEDS OF THE STRIKE

The incident that sparked the Memphis sanitation workers' strike took place during a rainstorm on February 1, 1968, when two African-American workers were accidentally crushed to death by their truck's garbage compactor. That same day, due to the poor weather, the city dismissed nearly two dozen African-American city sewer workers from work without pay, even as the white supervisors were kept on through the day at full pay.

Because the city did not officially recognize the sanitation workers' union, the workers had little recourse when they encountered unfair labor practices. Even when most of the city's 1,300 African-American sanitation workers went out on strike, Mayor Henry Loeb remained unmoved. As civic advocacy groups stepped in to try to solve the crisis, the mayor held fast to his anti-union stance. Nevertheless, support for the workers continued to grow, as organizations contributed money, time, and personnel to support the workers' cause.

CRITICAL VIEWING Answers will vary. Possible response: The signs bear a simple message that reflects a complex idea. By asserting that they are men—human beings—first, the marchers focus on their right as free people to equal treatment and basic dignity, as guaranteed by the Declaration of Independence. The fact that the marchers were declaring themselves to be what should have been obvious emphasized the inequality that African Americans were experiencing in Memphis.

1959 AMERICAS:
FIDEL CASTRO BECOMES LEADER OF CUBA

When Fidel Castro died in 2016 at the age of 90, his legacy included responsibility for creating the first communist state in the Western Hemisphere. Castro's political activity began when he was a young student at the University of Havana, and he later joined the reform-oriented Cuban People's Party, a party he hoped to represent in the Cuban elections slated for June 1952. In March 1952, however, Fulgencio Batista overthrew the Cuban government, established himself as dictator, and canceled the national elections. Castro organized a resistance force against Batista to instigate a revolution that would oust the new leader. **ASK:** Why might Castro have opposed Batista's dictatorship in Cuba? *(Possible response: Batista held all the power, but Castro believed in communism, an ideology structured on common ownership and minimal distinction among social classes. In its ideal form, communism cannot exist under a dictatorship.)*

The resistance was small at first. Castro's forces fought Batista's soldiers using daring guerrilla tactics, which proved surprisingly effective. As Castro's resistance grew, his guerrilla fighters scored several important victories against much larger numbers. **ASK:** Why might Castro's forces have been able to overpower a much larger army? *(Possible response: Like the colonists fighting the British in the American Revolution, Castro's guerrilla troops likely used the element of surprise.)* By January 1959, Batista had abdicated and fled Cuba, and his 30,000 troops had surrendered to a mere 800 of Castro's guerrilla fighters. The defeat made Castro a legend, and the new interim government put him in control of Cuba's military. But when the interim government was ousted in February, Castro quickly took power, becoming Cuba's premier and, by 1976, its president. He headed the Cuban government until 2008, when he stepped down because of ill health.

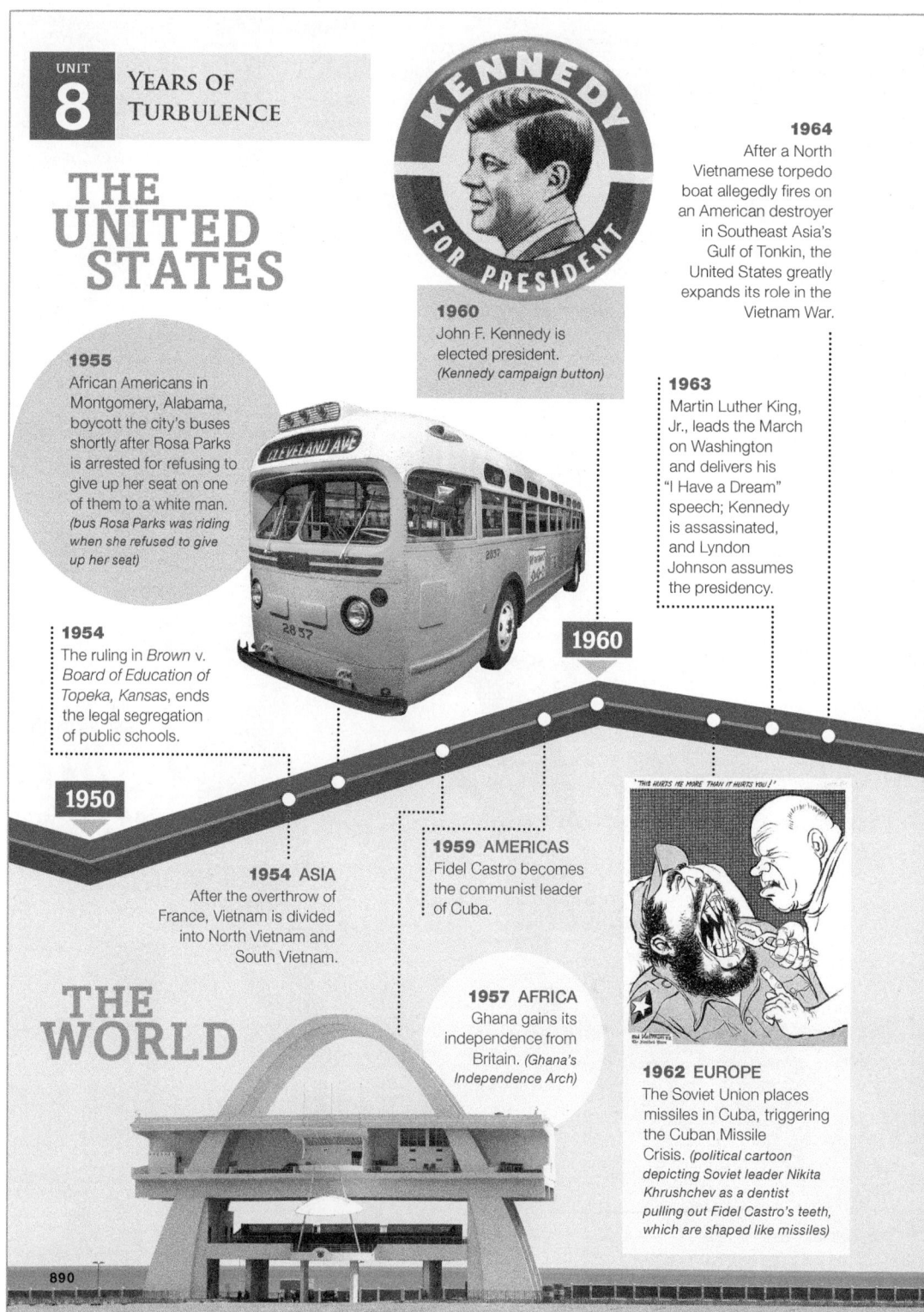

UNIT **8** YEARS OF TURBULENCE

KENNEDY FOR PRESIDENT

THE UNITED STATES

1964
After a North Vietnamese torpedo boat allegedly fires on an American destroyer in Southeast Asia's Gulf of Tonkin, the United States greatly expands its role in the Vietnam War.

1960
John F. Kennedy is elected president. *(Kennedy campaign button)*

1955
African Americans in Montgomery, Alabama, boycott the city's buses shortly after Rosa Parks is arrested for refusing to give up her seat on one of them to a white man. *(bus Rosa Parks was riding when she refused to give up her seat)*

1963
Martin Luther King, Jr., leads the March on Washington and delivers his "I Have a Dream" speech; Kennedy is assassinated, and Lyndon Johnson assumes the presidency.

CLEVELAND AVE

1960

1954
The ruling in *Brown v. Board of Education of Topeka, Kansas*, ends the legal segregation of public schools.

1950

THE WORLD

1954 ASIA
After the overthrow of France, Vietnam is divided into North Vietnam and South Vietnam.

1959 AMERICAS
Fidel Castro becomes the communist leader of Cuba.

1957 AFRICA
Ghana gains its independence from Britain. *(Ghana's Independence Arch)*

"THIS HURTS ME MORE THAN IT HURTS YOU!"

1962 EUROPE
The Soviet Union places missiles in Cuba, triggering the Cuban Missile Crisis. *(political cartoon depicting Soviet leader Nikita Khrushchev as a dentist pulling out Fidel Castro's teeth, which are shaped like missiles)*

890

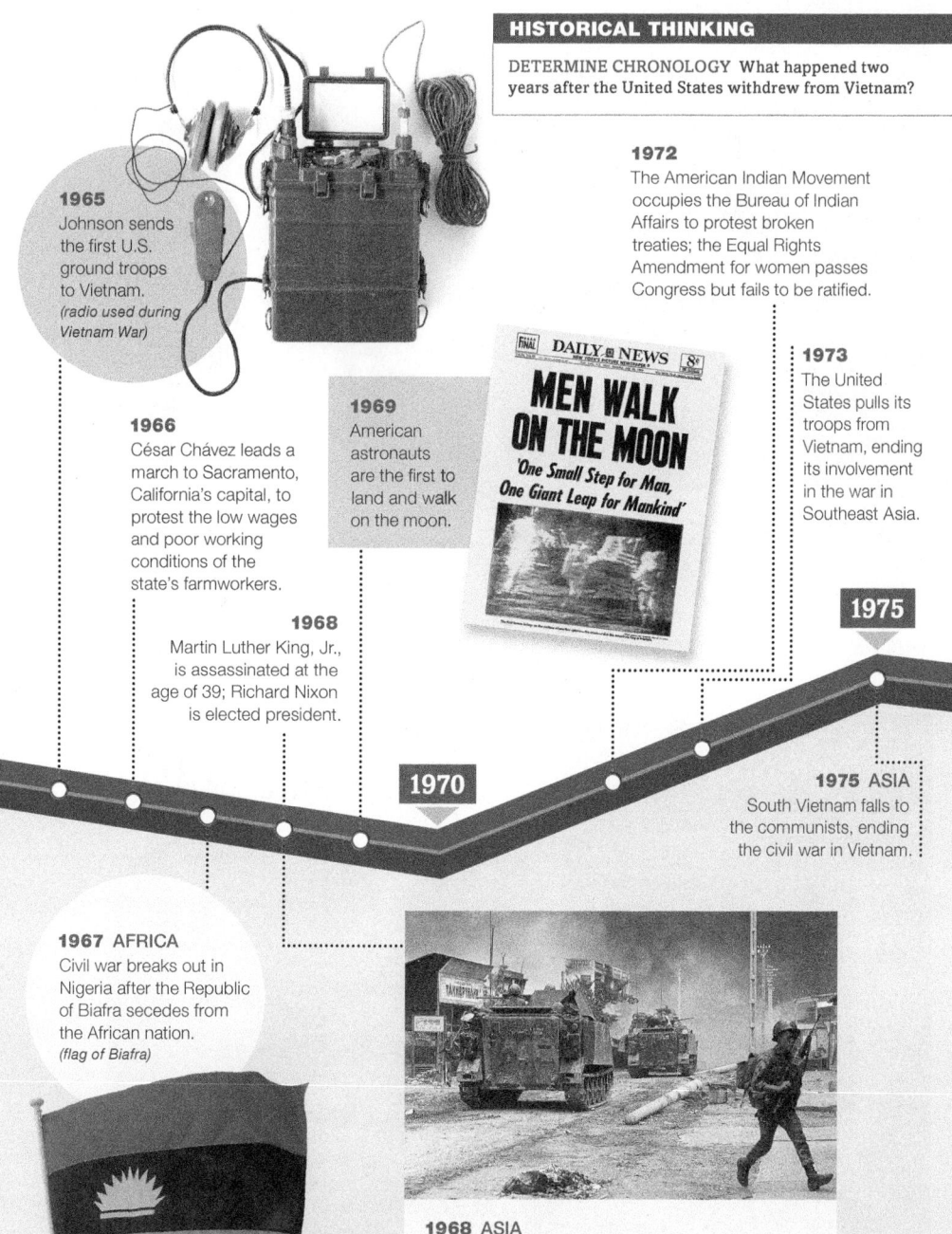

HISTORICAL THINKING

DETERMINE CHRONOLOGY What happened two years after the United States withdrew from Vietnam?

1965
Johnson sends the first U.S. ground troops to Vietnam.
(radio used during Vietnam War)

1966
César Chávez leads a march to Sacramento, California's capital, to protest the low wages and poor working conditions of the state's farmworkers.

1968
Martin Luther King, Jr., is assassinated at the age of 39; Richard Nixon is elected president.

1969
American astronauts are the first to land and walk on the moon.

1972
The American Indian Movement occupies the Bureau of Indian Affairs to protest broken treaties; the Equal Rights Amendment for women passes Congress but fails to be ratified.

1973
The United States pulls its troops from Vietnam, ending its involvement in the war in Southeast Asia.

DAILY NEWS

MEN WALK ON THE MOON
'One Small Step for Man, One Giant Leap for Mankind'

1975

1970

1975 ASIA
South Vietnam falls to the communists, ending the civil war in Vietnam.

1967 AFRICA
Civil war breaks out in Nigeria after the Republic of Biafra secedes from the African nation.
(flag of Biafra)

1968 ASIA
North Vietnamese forces launch the Tet Offensive and attack many cities and towns in South Vietnam.
(Troops battle in Saigon following the Tet Offensive.)

891

INTRODUCE TIME LINE EVENT

1967 AFRICA: CIVIL WAR IN NIGERIA

In May 1967, the eastern region of the West African nation of Nigeria declared its independence. The population of the eastern region was made up mostly of a people known as the Igbo. The years leading up to secession were full of turmoil across Nigeria, which had long struggled from political instability. Ethnic resentments divided much of the population, including a long-standing feud in the northern region between the majority Hausa people and the Igbo minority. **ASK:** What can you infer about the population of West Africa in the 1960s? *(Answers will vary. Possible response: West Africa was made up of various ethnic groups that were at odds with each other.)*

The feud between the Hausa and the Igbo turned violent in 1966. Thousands of Igbo were killed, and 1 million more fled, heading for the Igbo-dominated eastern region. With this massive influx of population, the eastern region barred non-Igbo from entry and expelled non-Igbo already living in the area. In May 1967, the leader of the eastern region declared independence from Nigeria and renamed the eastern region the Republic of Biafra. Nigeria's federal government seized control of Biafra's ports, greatly reducing the new state's access to needed supplies. France and the Soviet Union supplied arms and food to the fledgling state, but Biafra soon fell into famine. In early 1970, Biafra collapsed and ceased to exist as an independent republic. **ASK:** What could have caused famine in Biafra? *(Possible response: The Nigerian government took control of Biafra's ports, which limited access to supplies. In addition, the displacement of people could have led to disruption in food production because farmers may have been forced off their lands.)*

HISTORICAL THINKING

DETERMINE CHRONOLOGY

Two years after the United States withdrew from Vietnam, the civil war in Vietnam ended, with communist North Vietnam defeating South Vietnam.

CRITICAL VIEWING: U.S. National Guard troops block Beale Street in Memphis, Tennessee, on March 29, 1968, as civil rights marchers pass by. The activists held a number of marches over several days. Martin Luther King, Jr., participated in one of them. It was one of the last public appearances he would make before he was assassinated on April 4. What message are the protesters trying to convey with their signs?

888

AMERICAN STORIES Civil Rights Stories

- Study Primary Sources: Excerpt from a speech by President Barack Obama
- On Your Feet: Fishbowl

NG Learning Framework:
Plan a Movement

SECTION 1 RESOURCES
ROOTS OF THE MOVEMENT

LESSON 1.1
Progress After the War

- On Your Feet: Hold a Roundtable Discussion

NG Learning Framework:
Examine the Roles of Civil Rights Advocates

American Voices Biography
Bayard Rustin ONLINE

LESSON 1.2
Resistance Through the Arts

- On Your Feet: Create a Concept Cluster

NG Learning Framework:
Research African-American Artists

LESSON 1.3
Challenging School Segregation

- On Your Feet: Evaluate Authors' Claims

NG Learning Framework:
Investigate the Diffusion of the Civil Rights Movement

LESSON 1.4
AMERICAN VOICES
Thurgood Marshall

- On Your Feet: Fishbowl

NG Learning Framework:
Assess the Validity of a Claim

SECTION 2 RESOURCES
THE MOVEMENT GATHERS FORCE

LESSON 2.1
Women Take a Stand

- On Your Feet: Create a Cause-and-Effect Chain

NG Learning Framework:
Trace the Influence of the Civil Rights Movement

LESSON 2.2
Martin Luther King, Jr., and a Growing Movement

- Active History: Research Leaders in Nonviolent Civil Disobedience

AMERICAN GALLERY ONLINE The Freedom Riders

American Voices Biography
Fannie Lou Hamer ONLINE

American Voices Biography
Martin Luther King, Jr. ONLINE

American Voices Biography
The Freedom Riders ONLINE

LESSON 2.3
Protests in Birmingham

- On Your Feet: Think, Talk, and Share

NG Learning Framework:
Write a News Article

LESSON 2.4
DOCUMENT-BASED QUESTION
Demanding Reform

- On Your Feet: Use a Jigsaw Strategy

LESSON 2.5
The March on Washington

- Active History: Hold a Fishbowl Discussion

NG Learning Framework:
Advertise the March on Washington

CHAPTER 25 REVIEW

STRIVING READERS

STRATEGY ❶
MAKE A LIST

Post this heading: *What I Know About the Civil Rights Movement*. Instruct students to copy the heading into their notebooks. After students read each lesson, challenge them to add at least three sentences under the heading. Invite volunteers to share their sentences with the class. Encourage students to add sentences from their peers to create a comprehensive list.

Use with All Lessons *Throughout the chapter, help students get in the habit of adding to their lists as they read.*

STRATEGY ❷
TURN HEADINGS INTO OUTLINES

Explain that lesson and section headings can be turned into a good outline of the lesson and chapter. Model for students how to begin a basic outline structure. Encourage students to flesh out their outlines as they read.

Use with All Lessons

STRATEGY ❸
ANALYZE MAIN IDEAS

Direct students to read the Main Idea statements aloud for each lesson. Explain that these statements identify and summarize the key idea for each lesson. As students read the lessons, encourage them to make notes about details they find in the text that connect to the Main Idea statements. Explain that this process will help them identify and remember the most important information.

Use with All Lessons

INCLUSION

STRATEGY ❶
BUILD A TIME LINE

Instruct students to identify key events of the civil rights movement in each lesson and then add them to a time line. To expand the time line, guide students to add more key events as they read each lesson in the chapter.

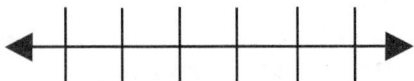

Use with All Lessons *For example, key events from Lesson 1.1 might include the founding of the NAACP (1909) and its 1,000-fold increase in membership by 1946; Lesson 1.2 might include Marian Anderson's performance at the Metropolitan Opera; and students can add the many important dates in Martin Luther King's life found in Lessons 2.2, 2.3, 2.4, and 2.5.*

STRATEGY ❷
USE SUPPORTED READING

Assign pairs of students paragraphs to read aloud together. At the end of each paragraph, have them use the following sentence frames to identify what they do and do not understand:

• This paragraph is about _____.

• One fact that stood out to me was _____.

• I had trouble understanding _____, so I figured it out by _____.

Use with All Lessons

ENGLISH LANGUAGE LEARNERS

STRATEGY 1
PREP BEFORE READING

Encourage students at **All Proficiencies** to use the PREP strategy to prepare for reading. Write this acrostic on the board:

> **PREP** **P**review the title.
> **R**ead the Main Idea statement.
> **E**xamine visuals.
> **P**redict what you will learn.

Use with All Lessons *Encourage students at the Emerging level to ask questions if they have trouble writing a prediction. Students at the Bridging level could help students at the Emerging and Expanding levels write their predictions.*

STRATEGY 2
USE PAIRED READING

Pair students at the **Expanding** and **Bridging** levels to read passages from the text aloud.

1. Partner 1 reads a passage; Partner 2 retells the passage in his or her own words.

2. Partner 2 reads a different passage; Partner 1 retells it.

3. Pairs repeat the process, switching roles.

Use with All Lessons

STRATEGY 3
CREATE SENTENCE STRIPS

Choose a paragraph from the lesson and make sentence strips from it. Read the paragraph aloud while students follow along in their books. Have students close their books and give them the set of sentence strips. Students should put the strips in order and then read the paragraph aloud.

Use with All Lessons *Before reading, ask students at the Emerging level to read the sentence strips aloud. Then ask them to point out important words in each sentence. Repeat the exercise with another paragraph.*

GIFTED & TALENTED

STRATEGY 1
REPORT ON KEY EVENTS

Invite students to choose an event in the struggle to end segregation—for example, an event related to school desegregation (Lessons 1.3 and 1.4), bus desegregation (Lesson 2.1), or restaurant desegregation (Lesson 2.2). Instruct students to conduct online research to deepen their understanding of that event and what it revealed about societal divisions concerning race. Then have students assume the role of either a newspaper or television reporter and report on the event in the context of the time in which the event occurred.

Use with Lessons 1.3, 1.4, 2.1, and 2.2

STRATEGY 2
CREATE A GRAPHIC BIOGRAPHY

Tell students to conduct research to learn more about one of the writers, artists, singers, or musicians whose work advanced the civil rights movement. Students will use what they learn to create a graphic biography in the style of a comic book or graphic novel. Encourage students to interpret the person's thoughts and actions within the context of their own time. Students may include quotations and visuals illustrating that individual's personality and achievements.

Use with Lesson 1.2 *As subjects for research and biography, you might suggest Jacob Lawrence, Charles Henry Alston, Elizabeth Catlett, Billie Holiday, Nina Simone, Harry Belafonte, Odetta, Pete Seeger, Richard Wright, Ralph Ellison, Lorraine Hansberry, or James Baldwin.*

PRE-AP

STRATEGY 1
TEACH A CLASS

Before beginning the chapter, allow volunteers to choose one of the lessons and prepare to teach the content to the class. Give them a set amount of time in which to present their lesson. Suggest that students plan ahead for any visuals or activities they want to use when they teach.

Use with Lessons 1.1–1.3 and 2.1–2.3

STRATEGY 2
WRITE AN EDITORIAL

Encourage students to expand upon the lesson's coverage of the NAACP by doing research into that organization's current work. Challenge students to find present-day statistics and opinions related to the organization. Then have them write an editorial that either commends the NAACP or recommends some change in its practices.

Use with Lessons 1.1, 1.4, and 2.1

THE CIVIL RIGHTS MOVEMENT
1954–1964

HISTORICAL THINKING How did the civil rights movement redefine American identity?

AMERICAN STORIES | Civil Rights Stories

SECTION 1 **Roots of the Movement**
SECTION 2 **The Movement Gathers Force**

AMERICAN GALLERY ONLINE | The Freedom Riders

"Nobody's free until **everybody's free.**"
—Fannie Lou Hamer, civil rights leader

In 1963, the African American Student Nonviolent Coordinating Committee (SNCC) staged a sit-in to protest racial segregation at two Toddle House restaurants in Atlanta, Georgia.

The Civil Rights Movement 893

INTRODUCE THE PHOTOGRAPH

SECOND-CLASS CITIZENS

The Toddle House chain of restaurants, begun in the 1930s, was located primarily in the South. The restaurant exteriors resembled cozy cottages, but their interiors featured a no-frills counter with backless stools. Their 24-hour menu offered hamburgers and breakfast fare. In some locations, the chain provided restaurants called Harlem Houses for African-American patrons. The Atlanta locations, however, did not welcome African Americans. This situation was addressed in 1963.

Direct students' attention to the photograph that opens this chapter and its accompanying caption. **ASK:** What do the photo and caption reveal about the status of civil rights in 1963? *(Possible responses: Segregation was a major part of life in the South. Protestors felt the need to stage sit-ins in defiance of forced segregation.)* Tell students that in this chapter they will learn how these kinds of protests influenced the civil rights movement.

SHARE BACKGROUND

Even after slavery was abolished and the 13th, 14th, and 15th amendments were added to the Constitution, inequality persisted. Supreme Court decisions, such as *Plessy* v. *Ferguson*, reinforced the segregation mandated by Jim Crow laws. In the early 20th century, lynching remained a common form of punishment and intimidation against African Americans in the South. In the North, African Americans faced discrimination in housing, employment, and education. The NAACP emerged as a dominant force in challenging these firmly entrenched societal norms. During World War II, African-American soldiers experienced greater equality and social acceptance in other countries than at home. Meanwhile, African-American workers at home experienced discrimination in defense industries. These conditions fueled the fight for civil rights after the war.

For Chapter 25 Spanish Resources, visit the Resources Menu. Chapter 25 Resources are available at NGLSync.Cengage.com.

HISTORICAL THINKING QUESTION

How did the civil rights movement redefine American identity?

Roundtable Discussion: Define Equal Rights This activity will help acquaint students with the central issues of the civil rights movement of the 1950s and 1960s, which they will learn about in Chapter 25. Divide the class into small groups. **ASK:** What does the term *equal rights* mean? Ask groups to explore the question by completing a Word Square like the one shown. Reconvene the class and have a volunteer from each group share the definitions, characteristics, examples, and non-examples they recorded. Then **ASK:** What is the difference between equal rights and equal opportunity? *(Possible response: Equal rights are rights usually guaranteed by law that all people are acknowledged to be the same and should be granted the same treatment. Equal opportunity is the chance to have the experiences that any and all people have.)* Is it possible to have equal rights without equal opportunity? *(Possible response: No. Without everyone having access to the same opportunities, equality is impossible.)*

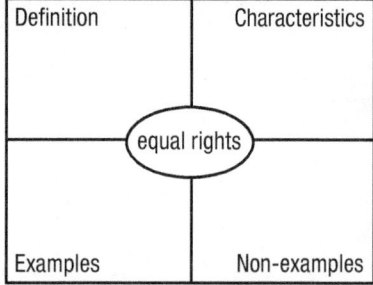

INTRODUCE THE READING STRATEGY

MAKE INFERENCES

Remind students that inferences are not stated in the text. Explain that to make inferences, they will need to dig deeper into the significance of and connections between historical events they read about in this chapter. Ask them to turn to the Chapter Review and preview the chart. As students read the chapter, encourage them to list key events and American reactions. Guide them to use reasoning to make inferences based on the information they have listed.

KEY DATES FOR CHAPTER 25

1954	*Brown v. Board of Education of Topeka*
1955	Montgomery Bus Boycott starts
1957	Little Rock Nine integrate Central High School
1960	Greensboro sit-in succeeds
1961	Freedom Riders test desegregation laws
1963	Violence erupts in Birmingham
1963	March on Washington for Jobs and Freedom
1967	Thurgood Marshall appointed to Supreme Court

INTRODUCE CHAPTER VOCABULARY

KEY VOCABULARY

SECTION 1

| dehumanize | desegregation | grassroots activism |

SECTION 2

| Freedom Riders | sit-in | voter registration drive |
| Montgomery Bus Boycott | solitary confinement | |

WORD WEBS

As students read the chapter, encourage them to complete Word Webs for Key Vocabulary terms. Instruct students to list each Key Vocabulary term in the center of a Word Web. Then, as they encounter a term in the chapter, students should complete the Web by adding words or phrases related to the term and its meaning. Model an example for students using the graphic organizer shown.

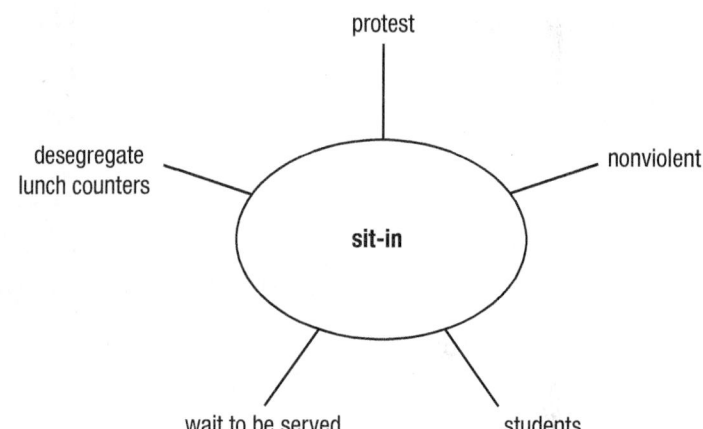

OBJECTIVES

- **Learn about key people and specific groups fighting for civil rights.**
- **Analyze the methods used by groups to gain civil rights.**
- **Compare civil rights issues and the strategies used to gain rights today with those in the past.**
- **Study a primary source: excerpt from a speech by President Barack Obama.**

CRITICAL THINKING SKILLS FOR "CIVIL RIGHTS STORIES"

- Make Connections
- Draw Conclusions
- Analyze Visuals
- Describe
- Form and Support Opinions
- Compare and Contrast
- Evaluate
- Identify

CONNECT TO THE CHAPTER

This American Story explores civil rights by examining different groups who have fought for equality throughout U.S. history. Through the study of distinct and fascinating stories—interesting narratives, vivid photographs, and a primary source—students will learn about the arguments and strategies employed to gain civil rights.

This chapter, The Civil Rights Movement, examines the push for equality by African Americans during the 1950s and 1960s. While this is certainly the most famous—and studied—civil rights movement in U.S. history, it is not the only one. In our recent history other marginalized groups, such as those with disabilities and members of the lesbian, gay, bisexual, transgender, and queer (LGBTQ, or sometimes referred to as LGBT) community, have fought for equal protection under the law. This American Story connects the historical thread of the early civil rights movement to the present day. It can be used after completing the chapter to provide a historical link from the past to our present.

HISTORY NOTEBOOK

Encourage students to complete the American Story page for Chapter 25 in their History Notebooks as they read.

AMERICAN STORIES | NATIONAL GEOGRAPHIC

CIVIL RIGHTS STORIES

On June 26, 2015, the White House was lit with rainbow colors to mark a civil rights milestone: the U.S. Supreme Court's ruling to legalize same-sex marriage.

894 CHAPTER 25

The struggle for civil rights in the 1950s and 1960s evokes powerful images in the minds of Americans: Dr. Martin Luther King, Jr., delivering his "I Have a Dream" speech; young African-American children facing angry crowds of protesters trying to keep them out of school; citizens marching to demand equal voting rights or school desegregation. These images represent the long and ongoing process of establishing and defending civil rights for all citizens. This American Story highlights the stories of some of the key people, places, and events in the civil rights movements, from the 1930s to the present day.

THE MARCH ON WASHINGTON

One familiar image from the civil rights movement shows Dr. Martin Luther King, Jr., standing on the steps of the Lincoln Memorial in Washington, D.C., delivering his most famous speech to a crowd of more than 200,000 people. It was a day of true unity—civil rights organizations, religious leaders, and men and women of all races came together to protest the inequalities African Americans still faced even 100 years after Abraham Lincoln's Emancipation Proclamation.

The 1963 March on Washington for Jobs and Freedom was not the first-ever march to the capital planned to support the rights of African Americans. You may recall that in 1941, A. Philip Randolph proposed a march on Washington to protest racial discrimination in the context of federal jobs. Randolph canceled the march, however, when President Franklin D. Roosevelt issued an executive order barring discrimination in the growing defense industry.

In 1963, President John F. Kennedy proposed a sweeping civil rights bill, but it was mired in a divided Congress. In an attempt to demonstrate public support for the bill and encourage Congress to act, Randolph and other civil rights leaders decided it was time to organize an even larger march on Washington. About 100,000 participants were expected to flood the city. Organizations such as the National Association for the Advancement of Colored People (NAACP) and the Southern Christian Leadership Conference planned the event, encouraging African Americans and whites from all states to come to Washington in a display of unified support for equal rights. And on August 28, 1963, around 200,000 people gathered peacefully in front of the Lincoln Memorial.

At the 1963 march, a multiracial crowd listened to songs by popular performers, prayers by prominent clergymen, and speeches by activists, including Dr. Martin Luther King, Jr.

The Civil Rights Movement **895**

COMPARE THE PAST TO THE PRESENT

Display a Comparison Chart on the board with the title Civil Rights. Write the term *Issue* in the first column, *Past* in the second column, and *Present* in the last column. **ASK:** What issues do you think of when you hear the term *civil rights*? *(Answers will vary. Possible responses: segregation in schools; racial discrimination; marriage legislation)* Ask students to identify civil rights issues from both the past and present and record students' responses in the first column of the chart. Discuss the list as a class, asking students which issues they think are relevant today. Place a checkmark in the relevant column to indicate past and present issues. Inform students that this American Story discusses the civil rights movement from the 1960s to the present. After students have read the text, go back to the chart and ask students to add or change anything based on what they have learned. Conclude by guiding a discussion about why continuing issues have not yet been resolved.

Issue	Past	Present

THE MARCH ON WASHINGTON

Organized in less than two months, the March on Washington was a highly coordinated and an extensively planned political protest. Leaders of the march knew that nonviolence and organization were critical, as the mere appearance of a problem could torpedo the chance for civil rights legislation. A. Philip Randolph's partner Bayard Rustin meticulously planned every detail of the event. With a staff of over 200 civil rights activists, he trained individuals to act as marshals to control the crowd nonviolently; provided talking points to keep participants on message; and coordinated an effort to publicize the march, recruit volunteers, raise money, and provide transportation. The efforts paid off. The crowds were calm, and no incidents were reported to police. **ASK:** How did A. Philip Randolph's past experiences during the Great Depression and 1940s influence his decision to call for a March on Washington in 1963? *(Randolph was successful in leading the movement to desegregate the defense industry in the 1940s. This was accomplished by the threat of a march on Washington, which President Roosevelt avoided. Randolph used a similar technique in 1963 to push for equal rights.)*

Present-day civil rights groups work to continue the efforts of Martin Luther King, Jr., and other civil rights heroes of our past. One of these groups, the Southern Poverty Law Center (SPLC), uses the courts to advocate for children's rights, economic equality for those on the lower tiers of society, justice for immigrants, gender equality, and criminal justice reform. In addition, the SPLC monitors hate and extremist groups throughout the country, publishing data concerning each group's goals, locations, and numbers. The work of the American Civil Liberties Union (ACLU) focuses on using the courts to defend liberties granted by the Constitution. Past historic court cases include the Scopes "monkey" trial, *Brown* v. *Board of Education*, and *Roe* v. *Wade*. In recent times, the ACLU has brought to court cases against the Trump administration's travel ban on immigrants from several Muslim majority countries.

COLLABORATING TO DESEGREGATE EDUCATION

Today, American public schools are more racially segregated than in the 1970s. Across the country, more than one-third of African-American and Latino students attend schools that are upwards of 90 percent non-white. Conversely, more than one-third of white students go to schools that are 90 to 100 percent white. The reason for this is tied to economics and class. Schools with a majority of minority students are located in overwhelmingly low-income areas creating a situation in which minorities are increasingly stuck in high poverty areas with poorly performing schools. This factor—added to decreased efforts by schools to promote diversity through the use of busing or efforts to actively enroll a diverse population—has been the driving force behind the resegregation of American education. **ASK:** What do you think can be done to promote further integration of public schools? *(Answers will vary. Students could discuss ideas such as an increase in charter schools that draw students from a greater geographic area, redistricting efforts to promote greater diversity, or reinstatement of busing programs.)*

AMERICAN STORIES

EDMUND PETTUS BRIDGE

CRITICAL VIEWING The Obama family, members of Congress, former President George W. Bush, and civil rights leaders cross the bridge in Selma to commemorate the 50th anniversary of Bloody Sunday, a 1965 civil rights march that turned violent. How might this photo reflect the progress of the civil rights movement in the United States?

COLLABORATING TO DESEGREGATE EDUCATION

As you will read in greater detail later in this chapter, well into the 1950s, many parts of the United States, especially the South, had racially segregated schools. School segregation had been made legal in 1896 by the *Plessy* v. *Ferguson* court case, which held that having separate public facilities for African Americans and whites was constitutional as long as the facilities were equal to each other.

For many decades, African-American and white civil rights lawyers worked together to challenge this "separate but equal" ruling. In 1930, the NAACP hired Nathan Margold, a white lawyer from New York. Margold conducted a study and found that African-American and white schools were not funded equally. This violated the equal protection rights provided for by the 14th Amendment. He recommended suing segregated public schools.

In 1934, Charles H. Houston, a prominent African-American lawyer, began directing the NAACP's

legal campaign against segregation and focused on higher education programs. One case involved African-American student Lloyd Gaines who was denied admission to the University of Missouri's law school because of his race. At the time, no law school in the state accepted African-American students. Although Gaines was offered a scholarship to attend a school out of state, he sued the university with the help of Houston, who argued that the state must either admit Gaines or provide an equal facility in Missouri. The courts agreed.

Through numerous other cases and victories, the NAACP's lawyers worked to protect civil rights. By the 1950s, a young African-American lawyer named Thurgood Marshall made it his mission to end segregation. He won many cases, preparing him for a historic legal battle in Topeka, Kansas.

In Kansas, segregation still existed in public schools. Linda Brown was denied enrollment in

AMERICAN PLACES
The Edmund Pettus Bridge

Some places will forever remain in the national consciousness as symbols of the fight for African-American civil rights in the 1950s and 1960s. One such place is the Edmund Pettus Bridge in Selma, Alabama. Completed in 1940, the bridge was named after a Confederate general and leader of the racist Ku Klux Klan in Alabama.

On March 7, 1965, a group of 600 protesters set out from Selma on a march to the state capital of Montgomery, to protest restrictions on voting rights for African Americans. On the Edmund Pettus Bridge just outside of town, local law enforcement officers waited with clubs and tear gas. They attacked the demonstrators and forced them back into Selma in an outbreak of violence that came to be known as Bloody Sunday. The marchers tried again on March 9 and were again turned away at the bridge. On March 21, after a federal judge had ruled in favor of the protesters' right to march along a public highway in order to "petition . . . government for redress of grievances," a new Selma-to-Montgomery march began. This time, 3,200 people set out from Selma and 25,000 arrived in the state capital. You will read more about these three marches in the next chapter.

Today, the Edmund Pettus Bridge is part of the Selma to Montgomery National Historic Trail administered by the National Park Service. On March 7, 2015, President Barack Obama and his family joined thousands of Americans at the bridge to commemorate the courage of the Bloody Sunday protesters. Among the 2015 marchers were some who had been present on Bloody Sunday, including Representative John Lewis of Georgia and Amelia Boynton Robinson, one of the original march's organizers.

the all-white school in her neighborhood. She had to walk more than a mile, cross a dangerous railroad yard, and then take a bus, to attend a school that accepted African Americans. Represented by Thurgood Marshall, the Brown family and other families decided to sue the school system, and in 1954, they won what would become one of the most important Supreme Court cases of all time, *Brown* v. *Board of Education of Topeka*.

While the landmark Brown ruling legally ended segregation, it did not erase it from the United States. Today, few schools and neighborhoods are truly racially integrated.

THINK ABOUT IT

Why might it have been advantageous for African-American and white lawyers to collaborate on cases to end racial discrimination in schools?

Linda Brown, shown here in front of the all-white Sumner Elementary School in 1953, lived only a few blocks away from this school but couldn't attend it.

The Civil Rights Movement **897**

TEACH

GUIDED DISCUSSION

1. **Analyze Visuals** Have students review the photographs accompanying the March on Washington and the Edmund Pettus Bridge features. **ASK:** What similarities do you see in the photographs regarding the methods used to raise public awareness about civil rights? *(Possible response: The photographs depict diverse and peaceful crowds. Well-known people, such as Martin Luther King, Jr., President Obama, clergymen, and performers in attendance heightened the importance of the events.)*

2. **Describe** How did individuals and the courts work in tandem on issues such as the right to march in Selma and the desegregation of schools? *(Possible response: Individuals such as Lloyd Gaines, Linda Brown, and the protestors on the Edmund Pettus Bridge challenged unconstitutional norms. Eventually, in each of these cases, the courts agreed with their arguments about the need to change the laws.)*

AMERICAN PLACES

The 1940 naming of the bridge in Selma, Alabama, after Edmund Pettus was a particularly flagrant example of the racial hostility of the time. Pettus was a renowned figure in Alabama, known for his proslavery views and opposition to Reconstruction. Pettus came from a family that profited immensely from slaveholding. Following the Civil War, he settled in Selma amid a system that attempted to roll back the rights granted to newly freed African Americans. Pettus participated in this process as a U.S. senator from 1897 to 1907, campaigning against the constitutional amendments passed following the Civil War. Today, the controversial Edmund Pettus Bridge, and other landmarks named after divisive figures, serve as stark reminders of the United States' racially divided past and present.

CRITICAL VIEWING The election of Barack Obama as the first African-American president of the United States is an indicator of the progress made by the civil rights movement. In addition, the diversity among the marchers and the bipartisan support of the march—as seen by the participation of President George W. Bush—shows the respect that civil rights heroes have in the nation.

THINK ABOUT IT

Possible response: Because of the racial segregation and discrimination of the time, white lawyers likely had an easier time getting cases to court than African-American lawyers did.

THE RIGHTS OF THE DISABLED

The disability rights movement got its start following World War I and World War II when disabled veterans demanded that the government provide rehabilitation and training. It wasn't until the civil rights movement of the 1960s, however, that calls for equal rights for the disabled gained momentum. Many early disabled-rights advocates were parents who demanded better conditions for their children, who were often institutionalized, placed in asylums, or put in schools cut off from the larger student body. These efforts culminated in the 1970s with a march on Washington and the passage of the Rehabilitation Act, which, for the first time in U.S. history, provided equal opportunities for the disabled and prohibited discrimination in employment for the federal government and in federally funded programs. **ASK:** Why do you think it has taken so long for Americans with disabilities to see progress toward equal rights? *(Answers will vary. Students could argue that because the ADA requires businesses, schools, and communities to make modifications to existing structures—such as ramps or larger parking spaces—it is difficult to get organizations to comply, thus slowing progress.)*

MARRIAGE LEGISLATION

The Supreme Court case that established same-sex marriage—*Obergefell* v. *Hodges*—found its constitutional basis in the 14th Amendment. Section 1 states, in part, that *"No state shall make or enforce any law which shall abridge the privileges or immunities of citizens of the United States; nor shall any state deprive any person of life, liberty, or property, without due process of law; nor deny to any person within its jurisdiction the equal protection of the laws."* Previous court cases had established that marriage was a fundamental liberty, as it supplied protection for children and families and was seen as a cornerstone to social order. In the *Obergefell* decision, the Supreme Court found there was no difference between opposite-sex and same-sex marriage regarding its ability to provide protection and stability. Therefore, denying same-sex couples the ability to marry violated the idea of equal protection of the law because it was treating different people unequally for no valid reason. **ASK:** What strategies did gay activists and supporters use to reverse the decision on same-sex marriage? *(They fought to reverse the decision through advertising campaigns, working with lobbyists in Washington, and voting in elections.)*

THE RIGHTS OF THE DISABLED

In 1990, the Americans With Disabilities Act (ADA), a bipartisan effort, was passed by Congress and signed into law by President George H. W. Bush. It banned job discrimination against people with disabilities and required buildings, businesses, and public transportation to be accessible to all. "The ADA was a response to an appalling problem: widespread, systemic, inhumane discrimination against people with disabilities," explains Robert Burgdorf, Jr., a disability rights legal advocate.

Ehlena Fry, 12, of Michigan, sits with her service dog Wonder outside the Supreme Court in Washington, D.C. Fry, who has cerebral palsy, is fighting to bring Wonder to school with her for assistance.

In 1971, according to Burgdorf, a "judge described people with disabilities as 'the most discriminated [against] minority in our nation.'" He was not alone in believing this. State-run residential treatment centers were "primitive and often unsanitary, dangerous, overcrowded and inhumane," states Burgdorf. Many children with disabilities were routinely prevented from attending public schools and therefore did not have access to an adequate education. Very few public transportation systems or private vehicles accommodated the disabled, making taxis, buses, trains, and ferries virtually unusable by people with physical impairments. Accessibility aids, such as flat entrances, ramps, sidewalk curb cuts, or Braille elevator signs, were not included in parks, stores, and office buildings.

Additionally, individuals with disabilities were often excluded from rights most Americans count on, from applying for a driver's license, to voting, to running for public office. In some states, people with developmental disabilities could not legally marry or enter into a contract. Even cities, such as Columbus, Ohio, and Chicago, practiced discrimination by enacting "ugly laws" to keep people whose physical conditions were perceived as "unpleasant" from public places.

Crucial victories in the courts during the 1970s and 1980s led to gains for people with disabilities in the fight for equal access to public schools and improved conditions in live-in facilities. As activists and protesters tackled the unfair treatment of individuals with disabilities, the courts ruled against discrimination in housing, transportation, voting, contracts, and medical services.

Since its passage, the ADA has had a positive impact on the lives of people with disabilities and their families. Accessible entrances, now the norm rather than the exception, assist those with mobility limitations as they enter buildings, cross streets, and visit public parks. Conveniently located parking spaces for people with disabilities are set aside in garages and parking lots to give people better access to public and private buildings. Mass transit accessibility in cities has also progressed, even if improvements to public transportation systems under the ADA have occurred more slowly and less consistently than many would like.

Yet not all equality issues for people with disabilities have been resolved, and people see tremendous disparities in how the ADA is enforced among business owners, school districts, and communities. In fact, according to Burgdorf, "Some . . . have taken an I-won't-do-anything-until-I'm-sued attitude toward the obligations imposed on them" by the act. Although there are many battles yet to be fought, the passing of the ADA was an inarguably significant milestone for ensuring equal rights for the disabled.

MARRIAGE LEGISLATION

The question of marriage as a civil rights issue for same-sex couples garnered much attention in the 2010s, but the legal struggle began decades earlier. In 1970, Jack Baker and Michael McConnell applied for a marriage license in Minneapolis, Minnesota. When the men were refused a license, they took the case to court. Baker, a lawyer, made the case that prohibiting same-sex marriage was unconstitutional and a form of discrimination. He drew parallels to the 1967 case *Loving v. Virginia*, in which the Supreme Court ruled that it was unconstitutional to forbid interracial marriage. When Baker and McConnell's case was sent to the Supreme Court in 1972, however, the court refused to hear it.

The next legal test for same-sex marriage rights took place in Hawaii in 1996. There, a judge ruled that the state had no reason to prevent same-sex couples from marrying. A national backlash soon followed. Congress passed and President Bill Clinton signed the Defense of Marriage Act (DOMA), which defined marriage as existing solely between a man and a woman in federal law. Several states, Hawaii among them, enacted constitutional amendments prohibiting same-sex marriage.

With the majority of both legislators and public opinion against same-sex marriage, gay activists and their supporters began a long campaign to change the minds of individual Americans. They also worked to bring the question to courtrooms and ballot boxes throughout the country. Gay marriage advocacy groups launched extensive advertising campaigns and engaged lobbyists to meet with lawmakers. Over time and despite staunch opposition, their efforts began to pay off. In 2004, the Massachusetts Supreme Court ruled in favor of same-sex marriage, and this time, the ruling was not reversed by a constitutional amendment. By 2011, the majority of the public supported same-sex marriage.

In 2015, when the United States Supreme Court agreed to rule on the issue it had turned down in 1972, gay marriage was legal in 36 states. On June 26, 2015, the nation's highest court ruled that the Constitution guarantees the right to marriage for same-sex couples in all 50 states. In the decision, Justice Anthony Kennedy wrote, "Their hope is not to be condemned to live in loneliness, excluded from one of civilization's oldest institutions. They ask for equal dignity in the eyes of the law. The Constitution grants them that right."

In what ways were the campaigns for same-sex marriage and other civil rights campaigns similar and different?

Legislation aside, same-sex marriage remains a hotly debated topic. Some believe all individuals deserve the right to be married, regardless of gender or sexual orientation (above). Others only support marriages between a man and a woman (below). The issue has become highly politicized in the United States.

TEACH

GUIDED DISCUSSION

3. **Draw Conclusions** Have students read the feature titled "The Civil Rights Movement's New Era." **ASK:** What does the existence of the Black Lives Matter protests tell us about the conditions faced by many African Americans today? *(Although much progress has been made, issues of inequality, such as poverty, inadequate schools, and unfair treatment by law enforcement, still exist for African Americans.)*

4. **Form and Support Opinions** Explain to students that throughout U.S. history the umbrella of civil rights has gradually expanded to include more and more people. **ASK:** What groups within the country have not yet achieved true equal protection under the law, and what still needs to be done? *(Answers will vary. Students might state that people in the LGBTQ community still do not have equal rights or that African Americans still face discrimination. Students could also discuss other groups such as felons, who are often not allowed to vote, or minors who are not afforded the same rights as adults.)*

ACTIVE OPTIONS

On Your Feet: Fishbowl Direct half the class to sit in a small circle, facing inward. Tell the other half of the class to sit in a larger circle around them. Pose the following question: How did various movements for equality build upon one another? Ask students to identify commonalities in goals, organizational structures, forms of resistance, and members. Students can note major events in the development of these movements and their consequences. Have students in the inner circle discuss the question while those in the outer circle listen to the discussion and evaluate the points made. Instruct the groups to reverse roles and continue the discussion.

NG Learning Framework: Plan a Movement

ATTITUDES Responsibility; Empowerment

SKILL Collaboration

Divide the class into small groups. Instruct them to plan a peaceful protest, social media campaign, or other movement in support of a current civil rights issue. Examples could include transgender rights, issues of religious freedom, or the rights of people convicted of a crime. Have groups identify and research an issue and make a plan that includes a description of the issue, the goals of the movement, supporting arguments, the targeted audience, proposed solutions, and the next course of action. Ask groups to designate a group member to present the group's plan to the class.

THE NATIONAL MUSEUM OF AFRICAN AMERICAN HISTORY AND CULTURE

The architectural design of the museum is an inverted pyramid. Beginning on the lower-levels and traveling upwards, the museum traces the progression of African-American experiences, from the first arrival of enslaved Africans up through the civil rights movement. On the upper floors, visitors learn about the accomplishments of modern African Americans, including artists and pop culture icons. Another design element is the filigree patterns that cover the outside of the building. This represents the ironwork of enslaved craftspeople that adorns cities such as New Orleans. **ASK:** How does the Museum of African American History and Culture help accomplish the goals articulated by President Obama in the Primary Source feature? *(By showing the artifacts of slavery, the museum helps visitors better appreciate the experiences of Americans.)*

THE CIVIL RIGHTS MOVEMENT'S NEW ERA

Technology has played an important role in the civil rights movement since the 1960s, when activists used a Wide Area Telephone Service (WATS) line to report abuses directly to civil rights organizations, who then cataloged the events and alerted the media. Today's technology includes text messaging, online video platforms, and Apps such as Twitter to rapidly relay information and images. **ASK:** How have technological changes affected the modern civil rights movement? *(Possible response: Modern civil rights protesters can organize more quickly than in earlier decades by using social media platforms. Messaging and posts enable protesters to take immediate action, as people did in Ferguson, Missouri.)*

WRITE ABOUT HISTORY

Explore Civil Rights in Your Own Life To help students make connections between the American Story and their own lives, have them write a short essay about a time in which they personally experienced—or witnessed—a violation of civil rights. In their essays, have students describe the incident, the rights that were violated, and the recourse that was, or could have been, taken to remedy the situation. If students prefer, they can write about a violation they heard of in the news. Provide guidance about the writing process as needed.

THE NATIONAL MUSEUM OF AFRICAN AMERICAN HISTORY AND CULTURE

On September 24, 2016, the Smithsonian Institution in Washington, D.C., opened a new museum. Standing alongside the other Smithsonian buildings on the National Mall, the National Museum of African American History and Culture (NMAAHC) offers a unique perspective on U.S. history, civil rights, and national identity. "This museum will tell the American story through the lens of African-American history and culture," explained Lonnie G. Bunch, III, the NMAAHC's Founding Director. "This is America's Story and this museum is for all Americans."

The galleries on the lower levels of the NMAAHC display collections of original artifacts that recount African-American history from the earliest years of the country to the present day. The dark times of slavery are represented by the manacles, whips, and other items used by slaveholders to control the enslaved. The museum also gives a voice to enslaved Americans by displaying items they created to express themselves. One such object is an embroidered pillowcase given by an enslaved mother to her nine-year-old daughter when the girl was sold. The pre-emancipation collection also includes Harriet Tubman's hymn book and Frederick Douglass's cane.

> ### PRIMARY SOURCE
>
> At the opening of the National Museum of African American History and Culture in Washington, D.C., President Barack Obama struck a hopeful note in a speech about the need for continuing progress on civil rights and the museum's role in the quest for equality.
>
> *This national museum helps to tell a richer and fuller story of who we are. . . . Hopefully this museum can help us talk to each other. And more importantly, listen to each other. And most importantly, see each other—Black and White and Latino and Native American, and Asian American—see how our stories are bound together. And bound together with women in America, and workers in America, and entrepreneurs in America, and LGBT Americans.*
>
> —President Barack Obama, September 24, 2016

CRITICAL VIEWING At the 2016 museum dedication, President Barack Obama praised the coexistence of "protest and love of country" and referenced recent examples of racial tension in the U.S. Which other individuals do you recognize in the photo below, and why might it have been significant that they attended this event?

CRITICAL VIEWING Students may recognize First Lady Michelle Obama, former president and first lady George W. and Laura Bush, and Congressman John Lewis, who was active in the Civil Rights movement throughout his life. The presence of President Bush signifies the bipartisan support for the museum.

Other collections in the historical galleries illustrate Reconstruction and the civil rights movement. More recent events such as the 2008 election of the first African-American president of the United States and the 2012 Olympic successes of African-American gymnast Gabby Douglas are also celebrated.

The Culture and Community galleries of the museum focus on the diverse African-American communities within the United States. Exhibits highlight achievements in the arts and sports, and ongoing efforts to bring about positive social change.

In 1963, a bomb exploded at the predominantly African-American 16th Street Baptist Church in Birmingham, Alabama, killing four young girls. This stained glass rosette from that church is part of the NMAAHC collection.

THE CIVIL RIGHTS MOVEMENT'S NEW ERA

The civil rights movement of the 1950s and 1960s achieved notable advancements for African Americans, such as desegregation and bans on many forms of discrimination. Yet many issues remain, such as poverty and lack of jobs in African-American neighborhoods, and the disproportionate numbers of African Americans who are jailed.

Present-day organizations such as Black Lives Matter (BLM) utilize social media and public protests to make their voices heard. BLM began in July 2013, after a white man named George Zimmerman was acquitted of the shooting death of black teenager Trayvon Martin. Alicia Garza wrote in a Facebook post, "I continue to be surprised at how little Black lives matter." Patrice Cullors, a friend of Garza's, was struck by that sentence and created the hashtag #BlackLivesMatter. Another friend built a social-media platform around the hashtag.

Many Americans became aware of Black Lives Matter in 2014, after a black teenager named Michael Brown was shot and killed by a white police officer in Ferguson, Missouri. People from all parts of the country used the platform to express their outrage and to plan protests in Ferguson and other cities. BLM groups continue to stage protests following other police shootings of African Americans and to strongly advocate for reform.

Black Lives Matter is sometimes described as "not your grandfather's civil rights movement." For one thing, social media was not an option years ago. And unlike groups such as the Student Nonviolent Coordinating Committee, which had centralized leadership, Black Lives Matter chapters operate independently to plan local events. BLM also pursues civil rights for women and the LGBTQ community, while earlier civil rights groups often marginalized female leaders and put men at the forefront.

Some believe that Black Lives Matter's methods are most effective for today's civil rights issues. Others feel modern civil rights groups should more closely follow the structures and techniques that succeeded in the 1950s and 1960s.

Photojournalist Eli Reed's book *Black in America* includes this 1999 photo of members of the Minority Achievement Committee at Shaker Heights High School in Ohio. Reed captures the diversity of the African-American experience, the consequences of prejudice, and the continuing efforts to secure a better life for all.

The Civil Rights Movement **901**

PROGRESS AFTER THE WAR

The struggle for civil rights in America spans many decades, many presidents, and across many states, and it continues today. Change has come slowly. But with each court ruling and protest, more people have seen the need for all Americans to have the same rights. This chapter highlights some of the key events and people who have inspired racially based social changes throughout the mid-20th century in America.

At a press conference in New York City in 1964 (from left) Norman Hill, Frederick D. Jones, and Bayard Rustin called for New York City to desegregate its public schools or face a series of coordinated boycotts. The three civil rights leaders were lifelong anti-violence activists who orchestrated demonstrations and boycotts and negotiated with government officials.

CHANGE DRIVEN BY THE PEOPLE

In many ways, World War II changed race relations in the United States and gave momentum to the civil rights movement. Millions of African Americans, Native Americans, and Mexican Americans had contributed to the U.S. war effort through military service or work in the defense industry. Having served their country in a war often framed as being against two racist empires (Germany and Japan), they were determined to claim their rights as guaranteed by the Constitution. Minority groups began fighting against laws that prevented them from voting and kept their children from attending public schools. Some Native American veterans filed lawsuits challenging these practices. Furthermore, many minorities did not want to lose the economic foothold they had gained from their wartime jobs.

Individuals engaged in **grassroots activism** to bring about the equality they desired. Grassroots activism refers to political movements driven by people who individually do not have much power, but who, working together, can be very effective. Churches in the rural South and urban North played important roles in the grassroots diffusion of the civil rights movement. Church leaders stressed the value of equality and communal support, which inspired church members to make sacrifices for racial justice. Groups also used churches as meeting places. The NAACP, a grassroots group, began with 60 members in 1909. By 1946, it had 600,000 members and was working to persuade Congress to pass federal anti-lynching laws. NAACP leaders, including **Walter White**, **Thurgood Marshall**, and the writer James Weldon Johnson, organized lawsuits against people accused of civil rights violations and used those cases to command the public's attention.

A. Philip Randolph and **Bayard Rustin** were also notable civil rights leaders. As you've read, Randolph, a journalist and labor organizer, established the country's first African-American trade union, the Brotherhood of Sleeping Car

Porters. Rustin became a leader in movements for civil rights and nonviolence beginning in the 1940s and for gay rights in the 1950s. He would eventually become a close advisor to Dr. Martin Luther King, Jr. In 1941, Randolph and Rustin threatened to lead tens of thousands of people in a march on Washington, D.C., to protest employment discrimination in the federal government. President Franklin D. Roosevelt averted the march by issuing an executive order prohibiting discriminatory hiring in government jobs. The order also established the Fair Employment Practices Committee, whose mission was to investigate violations of the new policy.

In 1942, civil rights activist **James Farmer** helped to found the interracial **Congress of Racial Equality (CORE)**. The organization fought discrimination through nonviolent acts of protest. It would play a crucial role in future decades of the civil rights movement. Activist and NAACP member **Mary Church Terrell** led the antidiscrimination struggle in deeply segregated Washington, D.C. In 1950, she entered a restaurant and ordered lunch, knowing the owners would refuse to serve her. In a lawsuit, she cited laws from the 1870s that guaranteed equal rights to African Americans in all "places of public accommodation." Her case reached the Supreme Court, which ruled unanimously in her favor.

TRUMAN'S SUPPORT FOR CIVIL RIGHTS

After Franklin D. Roosevelt's death in 1945, his vice president Harry Truman became the 33rd president. Truman was the grandchild of slave owners and had grown up in a segregated town in Missouri. But Truman proved to be a strong supporter of civil rights. In 1946, he established the **President's Committee on Civil Rights (PCCR)**. Its mission was to protect all Americans' civil rights. The PCCR report, "To Secure These Rights," detailed widespread discrimination and recommended 34 immediate actions, including desegregating the U.S. military. Truman sent to Congress a plan for stronger civil rights statutes, better protection of the right to vote, and federal protection against lynching. But Republicans and conservative southern Democrats blocked the plan.

At the 1948 Democratic National Convention, Senate candidate Hubert Humphrey implored his fellow Democrats to strongly support the civil rights movement. Moderates, including aides to Truman, favored a weaker stance on civil rights, fearing the loss of votes in the South. In the end, Humphrey got his way. Shortly after the convention, Truman abolished segregation in the U.S. military and prohibited discriminatory hiring practices in the federal civil service. When Americans cast their ballots in 1948, Truman won re-election, thanks in part to the support of African-American voters.

HISTORICAL THINKING

1. **READING CHECK** How did World War II stimulate the civil rights movement?

2. **DRAW CONCLUSIONS** How can grassroots activism cause change? Use examples from the text.

3. **SYNTHESIZE** How does Truman's message to Congress and William Colmer's response reflect the idea that change is complicated?

OBJECTIVE

Examine post-World War II efforts to raise awareness of civil rights.

CRITICAL THINKING SKILLS FOR LESSON 1.1

- Draw Conclusions
- Synthesize
- Make Inferences
- Compare and Contrast
- Analyze Primary Sources

HISTORICAL THINKING FOR CHAPTER 25

How did the civil rights movement redefine American identity? The contributions of minorities in World War II brought attention to civil rights. Lesson 1.1 discusses social changes that began after the war.

BACKGROUND FOR THE TEACHER

The struggle for African-American civil rights dates back to the 19th century, when abolitionists such as William Lloyd Garrison, Harriet Tubman, John Brown, and Frederick Douglass pushed for an end to slavery. In the post-Civil War era, civil rights advocates such as Booker T. Washington and W.E.B. Du Bois attempted to better the lives of African Americans amid rampant discrimination. Later, progressive era reformers, including Jane Addams, and Florence Kelley, advocated for the rights of women and minorities. During the New Deal in the 1930s, Eleanor Roosevelt and Mary McLeod Bethune became staunch supporters of African-American rights. More than 100 years of civil rights activism, however, had not achieved equal rights and equal opportunities for African Americans. Legal statutes still prevented many from voting. Jim Crow laws and intimidation preserved the status quo.

INTRODUCE & ENGAGE

PREDICT THE NEXT STEPS

Share and discuss the information in Background for the Teacher with students. **ASK:** Why do you think Americans have struggled with civil rights? *(Possible response: Because some Americans do not view all citizens as being equal.)* Given all of the past attempts to address African-American civil rights, what do you think might have been different in the civil rights movement that came about after World War II? *(Answers will vary. Possible responses: People were tired of living under the weight of discrimination. The war had highlighted the inconsistency between American democratic ideals and the treatment of minorities in the United States. These contradictions changed how people felt about their own rights and the rights of others.)* Explain to students that in this lesson they will learn why and how the struggle for civil rights gained momentum after World War II.

TEACH

GUIDED DISCUSSION

1. **Make Inferences** Why do you think churches were effective in promoting grassroots activism? *(Possible response: Churches are places where like-minded people gather, and they are usually well organized. Thus, parishioners and church leaders have the opportunity to influence people to act in support of a cause.)*

2. **Compare and Contrast** How did historical events influence the differences in Truman and Roosevelt's support for civil rights? *(Both presidents promoted desegregation. However, Roosevelt acted because of external events—namely the threatened march on Washington—while Truman's order was more proactive, as he was a strong supporter of civil rights.)*

ANALYZE PRIMARY SOURCES

Direct students' attention to the Primary Sources feature and call on volunteers to read each quotation aloud. **ASK:** How does each speaker draw on history to support his argument? *(Truman refers to "the ideals for which this Nation was founded" to support his argument in favor of civil rights. Colmer refers to "the first gun fired on Fort Sumter" to support his argument in favor of states' rights against a federal mandate to abolish segregation.)* Discuss how both historical references appeal to their audiences on an emotional level.

ACTIVE OPTIONS

On Your Feet: Hold a Roundtable Discussion Direct students to gather in groups of four. Pose the following question for discussion: Given the context in which the events in this lesson took place, what was the most effective strategy for raising awareness about the need for social change? Have each student answer the question within the group and explain his or her answer based on what they learned in the lesson. Allow time for groups to share the different answers with the class.

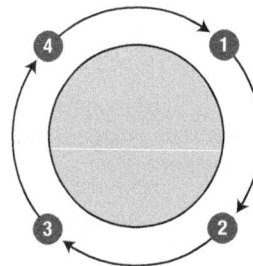

NG Learning Framework: Examine the Roles of Civil Rights Advocates

`ATTITUDE` Curiosity

`KNOWLEDGE` Our Human Story

Invite students to choose one of the civil rights advocates referenced in this lesson and write a short biography of the activist, examining his or her role in shaping the movement. Encourage students to use specific events in the activist's life to convey how they contributed to the civil rights effort. Ask volunteers to read their biographies to the class.

DIFFERENTIATE

STRIVING READERS

Write a Tweet As students read the lesson, direct them to pause after each paragraph and write a tweet, a 140-character message, summarizing the paragraph's main idea in their own words. Have students do alternate reading of their tweets aloud to a partner, with the first student reading a tweet about the first paragraph, the second student reading a tweet about the second paragraph, and so on.

PRE-AP

Write a Comparison-Contrast Essay Instruct students to conduct online research to learn more about grassroots activism in the post-World War II years and also about "astroturfing" (which creates the impression of widespread grassroots support for something) in recent decades. Encourage students to use a Venn diagram to keep track of the similarities and differences between the two forms of activism. Instruct students to use their research to write a comparison-and-contrast essay and to share their essays with the class.

See the Chapter Planner for more strategies for differentiation.

HISTORICAL THINKING

ANSWERS

1. Minorities contributed to the war effort. After the war, these minority groups began to fight against laws that denied them equal rights in the country they had defended.

2. People who do not have power individually can achieve change by working together. Examples include the NAACP, the Brotherhood of Sleeping Car Porters, and the Congress of Racial Equality.

3. Possible response: Both show how change is complicated. Truman's message asserts the civil rights of all Americans, while Colmer's response argues that the federal government cannot override states' rights, thus federal effort to enforce equality is not valid.

RESISTANCE THROUGH THE ARTS

Looking at a painting, listening to a song from another culture, and reading a book can help us understand how another person views the world. With that idea in mind, artists, musicians, and writers use their art to influence public opinion.

FREEDOM THROUGH ART AND SONG

The civil rights movement wasn't limited to nonviolent student and political organizations or the leadership of individual activists, such as Martin Luther King, Jr. Other forms of social advocacy sprang up around the country, notably in its art and music scenes. Activists took ideas from earlier artists and musicians and incorporated them into their own works as a way to express the connections between generations of African-American creativity.

The folk-inspired style of artist **William H. Johnson**, who painted from roughly 1920 to 1945, showed scenes of African-American soldiers and people doing everyday activities. His expressionistic subjects and use of bright colors are reflected in the paintings of **Jacob Lawrence** and **Charles Henry Alston**, artists working at the beginning of the civil rights movement.

Some artists working in the 1960s saw the civil unrest happening around them and found ways to incorporate their passion and solidarity with the protesters into their art. The subject matter of many African-American artists became more political. For example, artist **Norman Lewis** chose to use red, white, and blue in his work. Sculptor **Elizabeth Catlett** posed her figures in defiant positions, with crossed arms or a fist to the sky.

Billie Holiday, shown here performing in New York City in 1947, is considered by many to be the best jazz vocalist of all time. She sought inspiration from such artists as Louis Armstrong and Bessie Smith, and flatly refused to be silent about racism, using music as a way to explore the issue.

Musicians also built public awareness about civil rights. In 1939, jazz singer **Billie Holiday** recorded "Strange Fruit," a song about lynching in the South. It was the first time a popular African-American singer had spoken out against racism through music. She inspired other singers to do so as well. Throughout her career, jazz singer **Nina Simone** performed songs protesting lynching, segregation, and the Vietnam War. **Harry Belafonte**, a singer famous for a style of Caribbean music called calypso, was a social activist who donated time and money to civil rights efforts.

Many African-American musicians incorporated the spirituals and gospel songs that arose out of the slavery era to help fuel the civil rights movement. African-American folk singer **Odetta** taught her audiences the lyrics to spirituals as a way to unite the protesters. Odetta knew the old work songs, such as "We Shall Overcome" and "Go Tell It on the Mountain," from her childhood in Birmingham, Alabama. The spirituals inspired white folk singers, including Pete Seeger, **Bob Dylan**, and **Joan Baez**, to perform them at concerts and raise money and popular support for the civil rights cause.

Other activist musicians fought racism not with the words they sang but through the concert halls where they performed. In 1955, Marian Anderson became the first African-American opera singer to perform at New York's Metropolitan Opera. People flocked to hear the well-respected artist. "Men as well as women were dabbing at their eyes," reported the *New York Times*. Anderson's success at the Met was considered an important step toward racial equality because she proved African-American artists could draw large and diverse crowds.

THE POWER OF THE WRITTEN WORD

African-American authors bolstered the civil rights movement with words. In his 1940 novel *Native Son*, **Richard Wright** explored poverty and oppression in the lives of African Americans. Another novel, *Invisible Man* by **Ralph Ellison**, told of an unnamed African-American civil rights worker who moves from the South to New York City to escape segregation. The civil rights worker in the novel feels **dehumanized**, no longer regarded as a person, after he encounters racism in the city.

Playwright **Lorraine Hansberry** examined racial harassment as experienced by a working-class African-American family in the groundbreaking 1959 play *A Raisin in the Sun*. The character Beneatha decides to wear her hair in the natural style of people living in Africa, instead of in the straightened style of white women. Her decision symbolized a shift in African-American identity because Beneatha embraced her African heritage.

Civil-rights activist and influential African-American author **James Baldwin** released a book of two essays in 1963 called *The Fire Next Time*. In the book, he uses his personal experiences to explain what it was like to live in the United States as an African American. "[White people] have had to believe for many years, and for innumerable reasons, that black men are inferior to white men," he wrote. "Many of them, indeed, know better, but, as you will discover, people find it very difficult to act on what they know."

INVISIBLE MAN

A NOVEL

BY RALPH ELLISON

A RANDOM HOUSE BOOK

PRIMARY SOURCE

Recipient of the 1953 National Book Award for fiction, Ralph Ellison wrote *Invisible Man* in an experimental style, hoping to portray a truth about the human condition, race, and identity.

I am an invisible man. No, I am not a spook like those who haunted Edgar Allan Poe; nor am I one of your Hollywood-movie ectoplasms [ghosts]. I am a man of substance, of flesh and bone, fiber and liquids—and I might even be said to possess a mind. I am invisible, understand, simply because people refuse to see me.

—from *Invisible Man* by Ralph Ellison, 1952

HISTORICAL THINKING

1. **READING CHECK** How did artists raise awareness of the civil rights movement among the public?

2. **ANALYZE LANGUAGE USE** What does Ralph Ellison mean when he writes, "I am an invisible man"?

3. **MAKE INFERENCES** How might spirituals and gospel songs from the slavery era help fuel the civil rights movement?

PLAN: 2-PAGE LESSON

OBJECTIVE

Understand the role of artists in raising public awareness of long-standing inequality during the civil rights movement.

CRITICAL THINKING SKILLS FOR LESSON 1.2

• Analyze Language Use

• Make Inferences

• Evaluate

HISTORICAL THINKING FOR CHAPTER 25

How did the civil rights movement redefine American identity? Activists worked to make the country more inclusive. Lesson 1.2 explains how artists, musicians, and writers used their work to help focus the public's attention on racial injustices in American society.

BACKGROUND FOR THE TEACHER

The song "We Shall Overcome" had its beginning as a 19th-century hymn titled "I'll Overcome Someday." In 1945, African-American tobacco workers on strike in South Carolina adapted the song and gave it the present title. Its lyrics were changed, often spontaneously, to reflect the struggle for equal rights. Pete Seeger, a white folk singer and activist of the civil rights era, added the words "black and white together." Mary Ethel Dozier, an African-American high school student, added the verse "We are not afraid" during a police raid at a school. As a result, "We Shall Overcome" combines influences of religious songs, white American folk songs, African-American work songs, and protest events to capture the essence of the civil rights movement.

INTRODUCE & ENGAGE

EXAMINE SOCIAL CHANGE AND THE ARTS

Invite students to discuss how literature, music, and visual art can affect people. Guide them to consider the personal as well as the societal influences of the arts. **ASK:** How effective can the arts be in changing public opinion about an important social issue? *(Possible response: Very effective. Literature can dramatize stories of important issues, music can popularize and unite people around an issue, and visual art can express issues in posters, films, and videos.)* Tell students that in this lesson they will explore how writers, singers, painters, and other artists used their works to draw attention to civil rights.

TEACH

GUIDED DISCUSSION

1. **Evaluate** Why was it important that both African-American and white singers performed during the civil rights movement? *(Possible response: African-American artists inspired others to protest and make their stories known. White singers introduced music inspired by African Americans to a larger audience, and they raised awareness as well as money to support civil rights.)*

2. **Make Inferences** What does James Baldwin mean when he says "[White people] have had to believe for many years . . . that black men are inferior to white men"? *(Possible response: The idea that African Americans are inferior is irrational, but society—and people—believed it in order to sustain an unjust system.)*

VIRTUAL MUSEUM VISIT

The Smithsonian's National Museum of African American History and Culture in Washington, D.C., opened on September 24, 2016. The museum focuses on the themes of history, culture, and community and features more than 35,000 artifacts, including Civil War photographs, a recording of blues singer Bessie Smith, and the dress sophomore Carlotta Walls wore on her first day at Little Rock High School in 1957. Invite students to explore the museum's interactive website. Have them visit the online collection and locate an artifact related to the civil rights movement. Allow volunteers to share their artifact and explain how it helps them better understand the era.

ACTIVE OPTIONS

On Your Feet: Create a Concept Cluster Arrange students in three groups and assign one of the following forms of popular culture to each group: art, music, or literature. Instruct the groups to gather in separate areas of the room to discuss how their assigned form addressed civil rights—through subject matter and/or theme, through subtle or demonstrative expression, and so forth. Allow time for them to locate specific examples of their medium through online research. Reconvene as a class and invite a volunteer from each group to add information to a large version of a Concept Cluster.

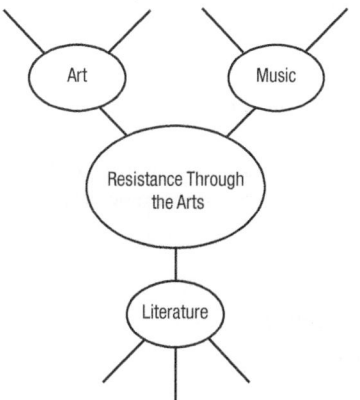

NG Learning Framework: Research African-American Artists

ATTITUDE Curiosity

KNOWLEDGE Our Human Story

Allow students to work in pairs or small groups to research one of the African-American artists, musicians, or writers mentioned in this lesson. Encourage them to become "experts" on the artist's life and work. Then have students create a media presentation that analyzes the connection between their artist and the civil rights movement. Ask students to share their completed presentations with the class.

DIFFERENTIATE

ENGLISH LANGUAGE LEARNERS

Pose and Answer Questions Arrange students at the **Emerging** and **Expanding** levels in mixed pairs and ask them to reread the lesson together. Instruct them to pause after each paragraph and ask one another *who, what, when, where,* or *why* questions about what they have just read. Suggest that students use a 5Ws Chart to help organize their questions and answers. Ask students at the **Expanding** level to assist students at the **Emerging** level as needed.

What?
Who?
Where?
When?
Why?

GIFTED & TALENTED

Create a Multimedia Presentation Challenge students to conduct research using print and online sources to learn about Abel Meeropol, the teacher who wrote the poem that would become the lyrics to the protest song "Strange Fruit." Have students assemble their findings in a compelling multimedia presentation that gives the backstory of the song's lyrics and includes a recording of the song. Invite students to share their presentation with the class.

See the Chapter Planner for more strategies for differentiation.

HISTORICAL THINKING

ANSWERS

1. Artists' paintings, music, and writings helped the public understand African-American experiences and feelings, which provided a better understanding of the reasons for and goals of the civil rights movement.

2. Ellison is saying in his writing that white people ignored African Americans and still pretend they don't exist.

3. Songs from the slavery era express the sufferings of enslaved people and their hopes for a better future. By using these songs, a direct connection between the two eras was established, thus giving the civil rights movement the goal of rectifying longstanding inequalities in American history.

CHALLENGING SCHOOL SEGREGATION

Third-grader Linda Brown lived just a short walk from an elementary school in Topeka, Kansas. But because she was an African American, she was forced to walk to a school farther from her home. This injustice became the focus of a landmark civil rights case.

CHALLENGING "SEPARATE BUT EQUAL"

In the 1940s, civil rights activists such as Thurgood Marshall and **William Hastie** began to mount legal attacks on *Plessy v. Ferguson*, the 1896 case that established the doctrine of "separate but equal." Marshall was chief of the NAACP's Legal Defense and Education Fund, a group of lawyers who pursued inequality and segregation lawsuits against educational institutions. In 1946, a federal lawsuit known as *Mendez v. Westminster* successfully challenged "separate but equal." Five Mexican American families sued their local school board in California for forcing their children to attend schools for Mexican students only. The court ruled in favor of the families, declaring that the segregation of Mexican American, Native American, and Asian American students was unconstitutional. This case provided a basis for further challenges.

On September 4, 1957, 15-year-old Elizabeth Eckford was followed by an angry mob as she tried to enter Central High School. Eckford was one of the Little Rock Nine, a group of African-American students who desegregated the school in Little Rock, Arkansas.

In 1946, Thurgood Marshall took the case of Heman Marion Sweatt, an African American seeking admission to the University of Texas School of Law. The university rejected Sweatt because of his race, but to comply with the "separate but equal" doctrine, it established a law school solely for African Americans. In 1950, the U.S. Supreme Court ruled in *Sweatt v. Painter* that the university must admit Sweatt to the original law school under the 14th Amendment. That same day, the Supreme Court ruled against segregation in *McLaurin v. Oklahoma State Regents*. Because of these decisions, college classes throughout the nation were to be integrated, meaning they would have to allow the free association of people of all races and ethnicities.

By 1953, five civil rights lawsuits had reached the Supreme Court, including *Brown v. Board of Education of Topeka*. That year, President Eisenhower had appointed **Earl Warren** as the court's Chief Justice, even though Warren's political views were more liberal than his own.

BROWN v. BOARD OF EDUCATION

Remember that *Brown v. Board of Education* centered on a Kansas law permitting cities to segregate their public schools. The case began when a team of six NAACP lawyers—five black, one white—represented the Reverend Oliver Brown in suing the Topeka school board. The lawyers argued that Brown's 8-year-old daughter should not have to attend a segregated school 21 blocks from her home when a white public school was much closer. One of the lawyers' strategies was to present social science studies showing that segregated schools had a negative effect on the self-esteem of African-American children, especially that of girls.

Eventually, the Supreme Court agreed to hear the case. The African-American and white lawyers collaborated on finding documented evidence of unequal education in several states. In a unanimous decision delivered on May 17, 1954, the Supreme Court ruled that the doctrine of "separate but equal" had no place in public education. Chief Justice Warren wrote, "Separate educational facilities are inherently [essentially] unequal." The court ordered the speedy integration of the nation's public schools. Because of the decision, the definition of *equal rights* included the equal opportunity for education and inspired a new generation of civil rights activists.

Many white southerners were outraged and reacted violently to **desegregation** efforts, or stopping the practice of separating groups of people in public spaces. To them, the ruling was an example of the federal government misusing its power. President Eisenhower was quiet about the issue. When asked directly about the *Brown* decision, he replied: "The Supreme Court has spoken . . . and I will obey."

In 1956, about 100 members of Congress from former Confederate states issued a document called "The Southern Manifesto on Integration." Vowing to use "all lawful means" to resist the *Brown* decision and court-ordered integration, they claimed *Brown* was a misinterpretation of the 14th Amendment and that the government was forcing states to carry out a law no one had voted for.

In 1957, this conflict over federal authority and states' rights erupted in Little Rock, Arkansas, when nine African-American students who tried to integrate a local high school were denied access to the school by the governor, the National Guard, and local citizens. President Eisenhower finally sent federal troops to escort the **Little Rock Nine** to their classes and to restore order. That month, he signed the **Civil Rights Act of 1957**, which protected the voting rights of African Americans. To remedy the act's shortcomings, he later signed the **Civil Rights Act of 1960**. Neither act proved to be effective.

PRIMARY SOURCE

Segregation of white and colored children in public schools has a detrimental effect upon the colored children. The impact is greater when it has the sanction of the law, for the policy of separating the races is usually interpreted as denoting the inferiority of the negro group. A sense of inferiority affects the motivation of a child to learn. Segregation with the sanction of law, therefore, has a tendency to [retard] the educational and mental development of negro children and to deprive them of some of the benefits they would receive in a racial[ly] integrated school system.

—from *Brown v. Board of Education of Topeka,* Supreme Court Decision, May 17, 1954

HISTORICAL THINKING

1. **READING CHECK** How did many white southerners, including those in Congress, react to desegregation?

2. **ANALYZE CAUSE AND EFFECT** How did the court decisions in *Mendez, Sweatt,* and *McLaurin* affect the Brown ruling?

PLAN: 2-PAGE LESSON

OBJECTIVE

Learn how years of legal cases resulted in the Supreme Court decision that desegregated public schools.

CRITICAL THINKING SKILLS FOR LESSON 1.3

- Analyze Cause and Effect
- Draw Conclusions
- Evaluate
- Analyze Primary Sources

HISTORICAL THINKING FOR CHAPTER 25

How did the civil rights movement redefine American identity? Segregated education was one of the defining inequalities in American life. Lesson 1.3 examines how the civil rights movement worked to begin to overturn the doctrine of "separate but equal."

BACKGROUND FOR THE TEACHER

In 1949, at the age of 25, Jack Greenberg joined Thurgood Marshall's Legal Defense and Education Fund (LDF). He quickly established himself as a valuable member of the team and was the youngest lawyer to help argue *Brown* v. *Board of Education*. As a Jewish man who grew up in the Bronx, Greenberg understood the connection between anti-Semitism and discrimination against African Americans—a topic he felt especially close to as the son of immigrants who had fled the pogroms (violent riots against Jews) of Eastern Europe. His dedication to the civil rights struggle, despite some resistance from African Americans, prompted Marshall to comment that Greenberg was "about as Negro as a white man can get." When Marshall became a federal appellate judge in 1961, Greenberg succeeded him as director of the LDF, a job he held for 23 years.

INTRODUCE & ENGAGE

INTERPRET A HISTORICAL EVENT

Direct students' attention to the photograph of Elizabeth Eckford and ask a volunteer to read the caption. **ASK:** What insights does the photograph provide about the struggle to desegregate schools? *(Possible response: It shows the determination and courage of African-American students as well as the intense opposition exhibited by whites.)* Tell them that in this lesson they will examine the struggle for equal educational opportunities.

TEACH

GUIDED DISCUSSION

1. **Draw Conclusions** Why was overturning the *Plessy* v. *Ferguson* decision of 1896 central to the civil rights struggle of the 1940s and 1950s? *(Plessy had established the "separate but equal" doctrine, which was the basis for the system of segregation that civil rights activists fought to overturn.)*

2. **Evaluate** How did the resistance to desegregation in Little Rock influence the political response to civil rights? *(The Little Rock resistance caused an increase in political support of civil rights. It prompted President Eisenhower to use federal troops to restore order in the state of Arkansas. It led to the Civil Rights acts of 1957 and 1960. However, the political response to the resistance did not prove to be very effective.)*

ANALYZE PRIMARY SOURCES

Direct students' attention to the Primary Source feature. **ASK:** What evidence does the decision provide that supports Chief Justice Warren's statement, "Separate educational facilities are inherently unequal"? *(Possible response: The decision gives evidence that separate schools lower the self-esteem and motivation of African-American students and can slow their development.)* As a class, discuss whether students think the argument presented is valid and convincing.

ACTIVE OPTIONS

On Your Feet: Evaluate Authors' Claims Provide a copy of "The Southern Manifesto on Integration" for students to analyze. Work as a class to identify at least three claims the authors make to support the states' right to uphold segregation. Record the claims on a chart like the one shown. Then provide the text of the Supreme Court decision in *Brown* v. *Board of Education*. Have students work in groups to identify evidence in the decision to challenge the claims of the manifesto. Ask groups to come to the board and record the evidence on the chart. Then ask students to synthesize the information in the chart to build a case for integration.

Claims: "The Southern Manifesto on Integration"	Challenge: *Brown* v. *Board of Education of Topeka*

NG Learning Framework: Investigate the Diffusion of the Civil Rights Movement

ATTITUDE Curiosity

KNOWLEDGE Our Human Story

Have groups of students do further research to investigate the civil rights movement in Little Rock, Arkansas. Direct them to focus on answering this question: What led to the civil rights movement coming to Little Rock, and what inspired the students to take action? Ask each group to locate one primary source—such as a first-person account from one of the participants—to help answer the question. Then tell groups to share their primary source with the class.

DIFFERENTIATE

STRIVING READERS

Read and Recall Invite students to work in groups of two to four. First have each student read the lesson independently. After reading, students should meet without the book and share information they recall. One student should take notes. As a group, students should then review the lesson and decide what to add or change in their notes.

GIFTED & TALENTED

Write Diary Entries Instruct students to conduct preliminary research to discover details about the experiences of the Little Rock Nine. Then have students choose one of the students and write a series of diary entries that he or she might have created. The entries should capture what it was like to be denied access to the all-white school and then escorted by federal troops sent by President Eisenhower. Encourage volunteers to perform readings of their diary entries.

See the Chapter Planner for more strategies for differentiation.

HISTORICAL THINKING

ANSWERS

1. Many white southerners and white southern Congress members did not want schools or their states desegregated; they protested and vowed to fight the *Brown* decision in court.

2. All three court decisions ruled against school segregation and opened the door to desegregation. *Sweatt* and *McLaurin* were U.S. Supreme Court decisions that helped pave the way for the *Brown* v. *Board of Education* decision.

THURGOOD MARSHALL 1908–1993

"To protest against injustice is the foundation of all our American democracy."—Thurgood Marshall

Fighting for justice and the rights of others became Thurgood Marshall's life's work. In his first case as a lawyer, he helped defend Donald Murray, a young African American who had been denied admission to the University of Maryland School of Law in 1935 because of his race. The case hit home. In 1930, Marshall himself had been refused entry to the school because he was black. He took on the Murray case to battle against the school's blatant discrimination and won. The young man became the first African American admitted to the law school.

CIVIL RIGHTS LAWYER

Instead of Maryland's law school, Marshall attended the Howard University School of Law in Washington, D.C., the oldest historically black law school in the United States. There he found a mentor in Charles Hamilton Houston, the school's vice-dean from 1929 to 1935 and an early civil rights lawyer. After graduating in 1933 from Howard—*cum laude*, or "with distinction"—Marshall eventually followed Houston to New York City. In time, Marshall became the chief counsel of the NAACP Legal Defense and Education Fund, a position he held for 21 years.

During his career at the NAACP, Marshall took on cases involving segregation and discrimination and, as you know, helped to successfully overturn the entire legal basis of "separate but equal." Sometimes his work took him to the Deep South where he experienced firsthand the racism his clients suffered. After winning one case in Tennessee, Marshall was nearly lynched. Many of his cases went to the Supreme Court, including the one for which he is

In his early years as chief counsel of the NAACP, Marshall successfully challenged the practice in several southern states of holding "white primaries" and preventing African Americans from voting.

most famous, *Brown v. Board of Education*. Of the 32 cases he argued before the Court, Marshall won 29. In fact, over his career, he won more Supreme Court cases than any other lawyer in American history.

Those who witnessed him in action said that Marshall's oratorical style was not flowery and emotional. Rather, he spoke eloquently and with great dignity, often addressing the moral and social implications of a case. Most of all, he conveyed his deep respect for the law and the Constitution, which he had been forced to memorize as punishment for

Marshall is sworn in as U.S. solicitor general while his family (front left) and Johnson (behind left) look on. The solicitor general is often called the 10th justice because he or she works closely with Supreme Court justices.

misbehaving when he was a high school student in Baltimore. When asked by a journalist why he had become a lawyer, Marshall (who had once wanted to be a dentist) replied that he didn't know. "The nearest I can get," he said, "is that my dad, my brother, and I had the most violent arguments you ever heard about anything. I guess we argued five out of seven nights at the dinner table."

JUDGE AND JUSTICE

In recognition of his brilliance, Marshall was appointed to high-level judicial positions during the 1960s. In 1961, President John Kennedy nominated him to the U.S. Court of Appeals. Four years later, President Lyndon Johnson made Marshall the first African-American U.S. solicitor general, the lawyer representing the federal government before the Supreme Court. Finally, in 1967, Johnson appointed Marshall as a justice on the Court, claiming that it was "the right thing to do, the right time to do it, the right man and the right place." And so the great-grandson of a slave became the first African American on the Supreme Court.

During Marshall's first years there, the Court, headed by Chief Justice Earl Warren, was decidedly liberal. Most of the justices agreed on such issues as racial discrimination and immigration. However, after Johnson, a Democrat, left the White House, Republican presidents picked the next eight justices. When President Richard Nixon made Warren Burger

chief justice in 1969, the Court became more ideologically conservative, and Marshall grew more and more marginalized. As the Court's rulings chipped away at abortion rights, limited affirmative action laws, and reinstated the death penalty, Marshall voiced his disagreement with these decisions in forceful dissents.

Marshall retired from the Supreme Court in 1991 and was replaced by Clarence Thomas, a conservative African American. Though Marshall was less celebrated than Martin Luther King, Jr., and Malcolm X—an African-American civil rights activist in the 1960s—he arguably had the greatest impact on the civil rights movement of the three. As one obituary declared after Marshall died in 1993, "We make movies about Malcolm X, we get a holiday to honor Dr. Martin Luther King, but every day we live with the legacy of Justice Thurgood Marshall."

HISTORICAL THINKING

1. **READING CHECK** What was particularly meaningful about Marshall's first case?

2. **MAKE INFERENCES** Why do you think it was important to Marshall to express his disagreement with some of the Supreme Court decisions made under Warren Burger?

3. **DRAW CONCLUSIONS** What did the writer of the obituary mean by the statement: "every day we live with the legacy of Justice Thurgood Marshall"?

PLAN: 2-PAGE LESSON

OBJECTIVE

Explore Thurgood Marshall's contributions to the civil rights movement.

CRITICAL THINKING SKILLS FOR LESSON 1.4

- Make Inferences
- Draw Conclusions
- Form and Support Opinions

HISTORICAL THINKING FOR CHAPTER 25

How did the civil rights movement redefine American identity? The goal of the civil rights movement was to expand the rights of marginalized Americans. Lesson 1.4 discusses the role of Thurgood Marshall in challenging injustice through the courts.

BACKGROUND FOR THE TEACHER

Thurgood Marshall was named after his grandfather, Thoroughgood, but he shortened the spelling when he was in grade school. Born and raised in Baltimore, Marshall witnessed racial discrimination firsthand as the city was highly segregated. His father, a steward at an all-white club, sometimes took Marshall and his brother to court to observe legal procedures and then prompted them to debate the issues. This experience, along with his time as a member of the high school debate team, honed the skills he used as a lawyer. Marshall's mother sold her wedding and engagement rings to help pay his law school expenses. His success at Howard University School of Law, and his subsequent career, justified her faith in him.

HISTORY NOTEBOOK

Encourage students to complete the American Voices page for Chapter 25 in their History Notebooks as they read.

INTRODUCE & ENGAGE

CREATE A LIST OF SUPERLATIVES

Invite students to brainstorm a list of superlatives that might be used to describe a hero or significant historical figure. List responses on the board. *(Possible responses: first, greatest, best, most successful, most respected, most influential)* Discuss which claims can be substantiated and which are based only on opinion. Explain to students that many superlatives have been used to describe Thurgood Marshall, whom they will learn about in this lesson. As students read the text, have them evaluate which superlatives could be used to describe Marshall's life and accomplishments.

TEACH

GUIDED DISCUSSION

1. **Make Inferences** How might Marshall's style as a lawyer arguing in court have helped him win the *Brown* v. *Board of Education* case before the Supreme Court? *(Possible response: His eloquent style would have probably conveyed a tone of sincerity and legitimacy, which would have helped persuade the Court.)*

2. **Form and Support Opinions** Do you think Marshall was more effective as a lawyer or as a Supreme Court justice? Explain. *(Answers will vary. Possible response: He was more effective as a lawyer because he won most of the cases he argued before the Supreme Court. As a justice, Marshall collaborated on liberal decisions, but he was limited to writing dissenting opinions when the Court became more conservative.)*

🔲 AMERICAN VOICES

In addition to his efforts to get the first African American admitted to the University of Maryland School of Law in 1935, lawyer Thurgood Marshall was successful in bringing many lawsuits against other state universities. As the dissenting voice during his tenure on the Supreme Court, he often expressed anger and disappointment when affirmative action was challenged. In the *Regents of the University of California* v. *Bakke* case of 1978, in which the court found it unconstitutional for a state medical school to hold 16 out of 100 openings for black and other minority students, Marshall wrote: "In light of the sorry history of discrimination and its devastating impact on the lives of Negroes, bringing the Negro into the mainstream of American life should be a state interest of the highest order. To fail to do so is to insure that America will forever remain a divided society." Ask students to discuss whether they agree or disagree with Marshall's dissenting opinion.

ACTIVE OPTIONS

On Your Feet: Fishbowl Arrange students in two concentric circles facing inward. Pose the following question for discussion: How was Thurgood Marshall uniquely qualified for his roles as legal activist, appellate judge, and Supreme Court justice? Instruct students in the inner circle to discuss the question, while those in the outer circle listen and evaluate. Have the groups reverse roles and continue the discussion. Provide time for each group to share their evaluations and synthesize the main points of both discussions.

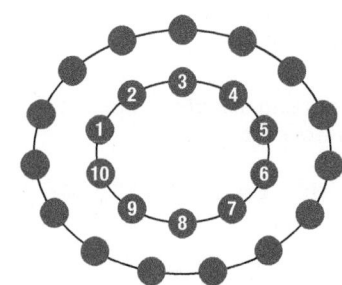

NG Learning Framework: Assess the Validity of a Claim

SKILL Collaboration

KNOWLEDGE Our Human Story

Guide students to test the validity of the following claim: "Every day we live with the legacy of Justice Thurgood Marshall." Instruct students to work in pairs or small groups to collect information about Marshall's legacy, including primary and secondary sources, such as court decisions and biographies, to support their argument. Remind them they must express a clear opinion of whether they think the claim is valid. Provide an opportunity for students to share their findings in oral or written presentations.

DIFFERENTIATE

ENGLISH LANGUAGE LEARNERS ELD

Summarize Place students of **All Proficiencies** in pairs or groups, and assign each group one or more paragraphs from the lesson. Instruct students to read their assigned paragraphs and then work together to summarize each paragraph in one or two sentences. When all pairs or groups are finished, have them create a mini-biography of Thurgood Marshall by reading their summaries in the order in which the material appears in the lesson.

PRE-AP

Investigate Court Cases In light of Marshall's legacy as a crusader for justice, direct students to hold a panel discussion that addresses the continuing controversy between group rights to equality of opportunity as opposed to individual rights to equal treatment. In preparation for the panel, suggest that students investigate various court cases, such as *Plyler* v. *Doe*, which addressed education for undocumented children; *Fisher* v. *University of Texas*, regarding affirmative action; and *Shelby County* v. *Holder*, which dealt with the Voting Rights Act. As students share their findings about these cases, encourage them to consider the influence of the past on the present.

See the Chapter Planner for more strategies for differentiation.

HISTORICAL THINKING

ANSWERS

1. Marshall had been denied entry to the University of Maryland School of Law because of his race. In his first law case, Marshall fought that same school's discrimination policy and won, making it possible for an African American to be admitted.

2. Marshall remained true to his ideals by dissenting from conservative Supreme Court decisions that he believed would have the effect of limiting personal freedoms.

3. Marshall won court cases—such as ending segregation in education—that continue to impact life in the United States.

WOMEN TAKE A STAND

Sometimes people have to break the rules to prove a point. A woman stepped onto a city bus in Montgomery, Alabama, one fateful evening in 1955 to do just that. Her action sparked a national debate over civil rights.

A BOYCOTT BEGINS

A year and a half after the Supreme Court's ruling in *Brown* v. *Board of Education*, its decision continued to rock the nation. Meanwhile, in Montgomery, Alabama, another major civil rights development was taking shape.

Segregation and discrimination were firmly established and strictly enforced in Montgomery, "the cradle of the Confederacy." African Americans were expected to tip their hats to whites, stand in the presence of whites unless told to sit, and address whites with titles of respect. City buses were segregated, and the first four rows of seats were reserved for whites, according to a Montgomery ordinance. African Americans had to pay their fares in the front, then get off the bus and enter the designated "colored section" through the rear door. They could also sit in the middle rows of the bus, but they had to relinquish their seat to white passengers when the front section filled up.

One regular bus rider was **Rosa Parks**, an African-American woman and longtime civil rights activist who worked as an assistant tailor at a downtown Montgomery department store. She also served as secretary for the Montgomery chapter of the NAACP, which she had joined in 1943. In the summer of 1955, the 42-year-old Parks traveled to the Highlander Folk School in Tennessee for a two-week interracial conference focused on leadership in the struggle against segregation. She later revealed that through this experience, she "gained strength to persevere in my work for freedom, not just for [African Americans] but for all oppressed people."

Rosa Parks holds up the identification number in her booking photo after being arrested during the Montgomery Bus Boycott in 1956.

PRIMARY SOURCE

Four months after refusing to give up her bus seat, Rosa Parks spoke to an interviewer about that fateful evening.

I felt that I was not being treated right, and that I had a right to retain the seat that I had taken as a passenger on the bus. The time had just come when I had been pushed as far as I could stand to be pushed, I suppose. They placed me under arrest. No, I wasn't frightened at all. I don't know why I wasn't, but I didn't feel afraid. I had decided that I would have to know once and for all what rights I had as a human being and a citizen, even in Montgomery, Alabama.

—from a transcript of a radio interview with Rosa Parks, April 1956

During the Montgomery Bus Boycott, many people chose to carpool rather than take the bus, as shown in this 1956 photo. The empty bus in the background is a sign of the boycott's success.

Earlier in 1955, other African-American women had refused to give up their bus seats in Montgomery. In March, 15-year-old Claudette Colvin was arrested after refusing to give up her seat in the black section of the bus for a white woman. "It's my constitutional right to sit here as much as that lady. I paid my fare!" she yelled as the policemen dragged her off the bus. Rosa Parks was one of the volunteers who raised money for Colvin's court hearing, but in addition to segregation violations, police charged Colvin with assaulting the officers, so civil rights activists decided not to pursue her case. In October, police arrested 18-year-old Mary Louise Smith for violating the same segregation policies. Civil rights leaders deemed Smith an unsympathetic plaintiff because she was poor and young.

Knowing that the NAACP was looking for a lead plaintiff in a case to test Montgomery's segregated bus law, Parks boarded a bus on December 1, 1955. She took a seat in the middle section of the mostly empty bus, but after a few stops, the white section of the bus filled up. When more white passengers stepped aboard, the driver asked Parks and three

other African-American passengers sitting in the same row to move to the back of the bus, where they would have had to stand. The others reluctantly complied, but Parks refused to give up her seat. The driver called the police, who arrested Parks for violating the ordinance.

Parks's civil disobedience, or act of purposely breaking a law in protest, and her arrest galvanized Montgomery's African-American community. **Jo Ann Robinson**, the president of a local political group called the Women's Political Council, organized volunteers who distributed 50,000 flyers declaring a one-day boycott of the city's buses. The initial **Montgomery Bus Boycott** was so successful that Robinson and other civil rights leaders decided to extend it to a long-term campaign. Activists, including Robinson's Women's Political Council and members of the NAACP, joined with a group of local ministers at the Holy Street Baptist Church to form the Montgomery Improvement Association (MIA). For its president, the MIA chose an eloquent, energetic young minister named **Martin Luther King, Jr.**, who had just arrived in Montgomery the previous year.

PLAN: 4-PAGE LESSON

OBJECTIVE

Examine the causes and effects of the Montgomery Bus Boycott.

CRITICAL THINKING SKILLS FOR LESSON 2.1

- Describe
- Make Inferences
- Draw Conclusions
- Compare and Contrast
- Interpret Visuals
- Analyze Primary Sources
- Synthesize
- Make Connections

HISTORICAL THINKING FOR CHAPTER 25

How did the civil rights movement redefine American identity? Lesson 2.1 explains how African-American women in the South combatted segregation and asserted their civil rights.

BACKGROUND FOR THE TEACHER

In 1954 and again after Rosa Parks's arrest in 1955, African-American leaders in Montgomery issued a list of demands that would modify segregation policies on city buses. The demands included courteous treatment for African-American passengers; seating on a first-come, first-served basis; and African-American drivers on predominately African-American routes. When these demands were not met, leaders of the Montgomery Improvement Association (MIA) changed their goals from reforming segregation to abolishing it by filing a federal lawsuit to challenge the constitutionality of segregation on public buses. This shift in purpose set the stage for activism and established a precedent for future strategies of the civil rights movement.

HISTORY NOTEBOOK

Encourage students to complete the Women Take a Stand page for Chapter 25 in their History Notebooks as they read the lesson.

INTRODUCE & ENGAGE

EXPLORE A DEFINITION

Share the following story with students: When Thurgood Marshall argued *Brown* v. *Board of Education* before the Supreme Court, Justice Frankfurter asked him what he meant by "equal." Marshall responded, "Equal means getting the same thing, at the same time, and in the same place." **ASK:** Why do you think Marshall made the three distinctions in his answer? (*Possible response: Without all three distinctions, true equality is not possible.*) Then have students think about how this quote can be applied to areas such as education or transportation. **ASK:** In these areas, how was it possible that some of these distinctions were fulfilled but not others? (*Possible response: In education, white and African-American students were technically getting the "same thing," but they were not in the "same place." This led to unequal outcomes.*) Tell students that in this lesson they will learn how civil rights activists fought to bring Marshall's definition of equality to Montgomery, Alabama.

TEACH

GUIDED DISCUSSION

1. **Draw Conclusions** How did discrimination and segregation affect the economic and social status of African Americans in the South? (*Possible response: The "rules" by which African Americans were expected to live made them second-class citizens. Thus, it was impossible for them to be seen as social equals to whites and to have equal opportunity to secure well-paying jobs.*)

2. **Compare and Contrast** Why was Rosa Parks's protest more successful than those of Colvin and Smith? (*Possible response: Colvin and Smith were teenagers whose protests were dismissed by civil rights leaders. Parks was a respected member of the African-American community and a civil rights activist whose arrest prompted widespread attention.*)

3. **Interpret Visuals** What qualities of civil rights activists do the photos of Rosa Parks and the Montgomery Bus Boycott demonstrate? (*Possible response: Activists were vigilant in that they were willing to go to jail to bring about social change. They stayed true to their cause, despite being greatly inconvenienced by the boycott of public transportation. They were unified, as the organized carpooling reveals.*)

ANALYZE PRIMARY SOURCES

Direct students to read the Primary Source feature and identify the feelings expressed by Rosa Parks. **ASK:** How did Parks's attitudes and demeanor qualify her to become the lead plaintiff in the NAACP case against Montgomery's segregated bus law? (*Possible response: Parks had the courage to stand up for her rights, and she did not react to her arrest with fear or violence. She believed the fight for African-American civil rights had broad applications for other people whose rights had been denied.*)

DIFFERENTIATE

ENGLISH LANGUAGE LEARNERS `ELD`

Create a Word Web Pair students at the **Emerging** and **Expanding** levels with students at the **Bridging** level. Tell them to take turns reading paragraphs in the lesson, noting any legal terms. After each paragraph, instruct students to write those terms on the spokes of a Word Web like the one shown. Then have student pairs trade and compare their Word Webs, looking up unfamiliar words in a dictionary. The completed Word Webs might include the following terms: *ruling, ordinance, unsympathetic plaintiff, lead plaintiff, accusation, precedent,* and *unconstitutional.*

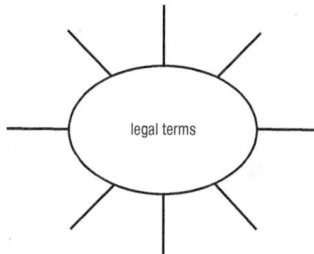

PRE-AP

Connect Past and Present Instruct students to utilize online materials from the Rosa Parks Collection at the Library of Congress to learn more about the motivations behind Parks's activism. In particular, challenge students to learn about Parks's knowledge of the murder of Emmett Till and similar murders in which the white defendants were not convicted. Then have students research the Black Lives Matter movement and the murders of African Americans that sparked it. Tell students to use their research to write a report on the persistence of racial injustice in the United States. Invite students to share their reports with the class.

See the Chapter Planner for more strategies for differentiation.

THE MURDER OF EMMETT TILL

While some women fought for civil rights through activism, staging and engaging in boycotts and marches, others took very personal stands that led to national action. In August of 1955, Mamie Till-Mobley sent her 14-year-old son Emmett on a train to visit relatives in Mississippi. A few days after Emmett had left his home in Chicago, Mrs. Till-Mobley received a phone call. Two white men had killed her child. The men claimed Emmett had flirted with a white woman in a local grocery store. They beat Till, shot him, and hung a 75-pound metal fan around his neck to keep his body hidden at the bottom of the Tallahatchie River.

A jury quickly released the white men. It wasn't until 2008 that the woman who claimed Till had physically and verbally attacked her admitted that she had made up those accusations.

Mrs. Till-Mobley brought Emmett's body back home to Chicago. The condition of Emmett's maimed body would usually call for a closed casket, but Mrs. Till-Mobley insisted on keeping his casket open during the funeral. "Let the people see what I've seen," she said. *Jet* magazine published photos of Mrs. Till-Mobley mourning over her son's body and forced the American public to witness the glaring brutality of racism in their country. Till's casket is now at the Smithsonian National Museum of African American History and Culture in Washington, D.C.

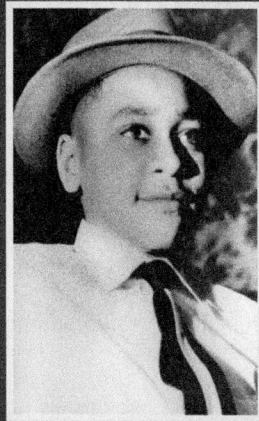

An undated photograph shows the young Emmett Till before his murder in 1955.

Mamie Till-Mobley mourns for her son as she leans against his glass-covered coffin. Following Emmett's funeral, she helped form a campaign for justice and civil rights.

THE BOYCOTT GAINS MOMENTUM

Boycott organizers knew their protest would be effective because African Americans accounted for roughly three-quarters of Montgomery's bus ridership. Losing most of these riders would have harsh economic consequences for the city's bus company. The organizers also knew that since few African Americans owned cars, the boycott would be difficult to sustain. However, the community was determined to keep the protest going. Friends, coworkers, and neighbors formed carpools to get people to their jobs and other destinations. Churches hosted boycott-related meetings and raised money for fuel, and African-American-owned garages did auto repair work free of charge. Many people rode bicycles or simply walked.

Days stretched into weeks, weeks into months, and still the boycott continued. It pushed the bus company to the brink of bankruptcy and dealt a severe financial blow to white-owned businesses in downtown Montgomery. Some whites retaliated by firing or threatening to fire African-American workers, and others threw bombs into churches and homes, including King's home.

On June 5, 1956, a federal district court, citing the *Brown v. Board of Education* decision as precedent, ruled that Alabama state statutes and Montgomery city ordinances requiring segregation on buses were unconstitutional. The Supreme Court affirmed this ruling on November 13 of that year, and on December 20, a U.S. marshal delivered a court order to Montgomery City Hall requiring the integration of the city's buses. King immediately called off the boycott and urged African Americans to begin riding the buses again the following day. The 381-day boycott had demonstrated both the power of collective action and the possibility of social change.

Coretta and Martin Luther King, Jr., leave the courthouse after his arrest for conspiring to boycott Montgomery city buses in 1956.

HISTORICAL THINKING

1. **READING CHECK** How did the African-American community work together to sustain the bus boycott?

2. **DESCRIBE** How might historical events have taken a different direction if Claudette Colvin, Mary Louise Smith, and Rosa Parks had not taken a stand?

3. **MAKE INFERENCES** What personal traits do you think Rosa Parks and other civil rights activists must have had in order to work for the freedom of all people?

BUILD BACKGROUND

THE ROLE OF CHURCHES

As mentioned earlier, the civil rights movement was closely tied to religion through its grassroots leadership and strategies. Churches provided safe places where African Americans could worship and gain support from people who shared their beliefs and hopes. In many parts of the South, the church was the center of community life. Naturally, this led churches to become centers for the strategic planning of civil rights protests. For example, Martin Luther King, Jr., planned the Montgomery Bus Boycott in the basement of Dexter Avenue Baptist Church. African-American churches in the North also played an important role in the civil rights movement. Members of Siloam Presbyterian Church in Brooklyn, New York, took part in protests at construction sites to force unions to hire minority workers. In addition, churches in the North contributed money, which the Southern Christian Leadership Conference used to fund protests and training in the South.

Unfortunately, as African-American churches became symbols of the civil rights movement in the 1950s and 1960s, they also became targets of violence. For many years, church bombings persisted throughout the country. These actions, while destroying buildings and sometimes killing or injuring innocent people, did not destroy the spirit of the civil rights movement.

TEACH

GUIDED DISCUSSION

4. **Synthesize** Share the information in Build Background. **ASK:** How did churches in both the North and the South aid the diffusion of the civil rights movement? *(Possible response: Churches in the South provided meeting places for strategic planning. Northern Churches supporting civil rights also engaged in protests and raised money.)*

5. **Make Connections** How was the decision about segregation on city buses related to the decision in *Brown* v. *Board of Education*? *(The federal district court cited* Brown v. Board of Education *as a precedent for its ruling that segregation of city buses was unconstitutional. Both decisions mandated integration in public places.)*

MORE INFORMATION

The Emmett Till Case In a 1956 *Look* magazine interview, Roy Bryant and J.W. Milam admitted that they had murdered Emmett Till, but they could not be retried after their acquittal. Later, after Carolyn Bryant, the white woman whose accusations resulted in Emmett Till's death, recanted her story, a grand jury decided not to indict her. **ASK:** Do you think it's important that Bryant finally told the truth? Explain. *(Possible responses: No. Her admission did not result in anyone being punished for Till's murder. Yes. She confirmed Till's innocence and provided closure for his family.)*

ACTIVE OPTIONS

On Your Feet: Create a Cause-and-Effect Chain Arrange students in groups. Instruct each group to create a Cause-and-Effect Chain for the events in this lesson. Then have each group share their work. Discuss the complexity of historical causes and effects, including the limitations on determining cause and effect.

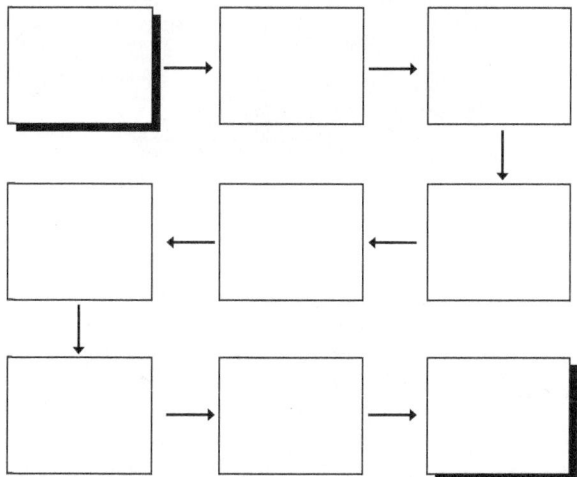

NG Learning Framework: Trace the Influence of the Civil Rights Movement

ATTITUDE Curiosity

KNOWLEDGE Our Human Story

Challenge students to investigate how advances in the African-American struggle for equality influenced similar movements for American Indians, Asian Americans, and Hispanic Americans. Ask them to discuss what similar civil rights methods and techniques these groups used to attain their goals. Allow students to choose an appropriate medium to share their information with the class.

ANSWERS

1. Instead of taking buses, people walked, rode bikes, or carpooled to get to work or other places. Churches raised funds for fuel, and African-American garage owners did repairs for free.

2. Possible responses: Segregation in the South might have lasted longer if Colvin, Smith, and Parks had not taken a stand. Their actions drew attention to inequality and inspired others to work for civil rights.

3. Possible responses: Civil rights activists had courage because they put themselves in danger to stand up for justice. They had determination and a strong sense of values.

MARTIN LUTHER KING, JR., AND A GROWING MOVEMENT

When he was 15 years old, Martin Luther King, Jr., left the segregated South for the first time and spent the summer in Connecticut. Seeing African Americans and whites eating in the same restaurants, shopping in the same stores, and worshiping in the same churches shaped his vision of what the United States could be: a multiracial, peaceful society.

THE EMERGENCE OF DR. KING

King was born on January 15, 1929, in Atlanta, Georgia. His parents were college educated, and the family lived in a middle-class neighborhood known for its thriving African-American businesses and churches. His father was a pastor at the highly regarded Ebenezer Baptist Church, a position his maternal grandfather had also held.

In 1944, King graduated from high school and entered Atlanta's Morehouse College. His studies there focused on medicine and law, but by the time of his graduation, he had decided to follow the example of his father and join the ministry. His spiritual and intellectual mentor, Morehouse president Benjamin Mays, also influenced his decision. Mays was not only an influential educator and minister, but also a strong voice for racial equality. King enrolled at the liberal-leaning Crozer Theological Seminary in Pennsylvania and graduated three years later with a bachelor's degree in divinity. He then earned a doctoral degree in theology from Boston University.

While completing his studies, King accepted a position in Montgomery, Alabama, as pastor at Dexter Avenue

WAITING ROOM FOR WHITES ONLY BY ORDER OF POLICE DEPT.

Official signs enforcing segregated seating were common, particularly across the South, during the first half of the 20th century.

Baptist Church. The following year, in 1955, he led the Montgomery Bus Boycott, which helped bring an end to segregation on the city's buses. In the wake of that successful protest, King joined with other African-American ministers and civil rights activists to form the **Southern Christian Leadership Conference (SCLC)** in 1957. This organization, whose strength came from the leadership of African-American churches, promoted racial justice through peaceful means and provided assistance and guidance to local protest groups.

King was convinced that nonviolent civil disobedience was the best way for African Americans to fight injustice and bring about social change. His philosophical and religious dedication to nonviolence took shape while he was in the seminary where his studies exposed him to the teachings of **Mohandas Gandhi**. A lawyer, politician, writer, and civil rights activist, Gandhi advocated peaceful protest and noncooperation in the struggle against colonial injustice in India. Through this approach, Gandhi had helped free his country from British imperial rule. King applied Gandhi's use of nonviolent methods throughout his career as a civil rights activist.

A MASS MOVEMENT FORMS

The Supreme Court's *Brown* v. *Board of Education* decision and the success of the Montgomery Bus Boycott profoundly altered race relations in the United States. Thanks to the extraordinary courage of ordinary African-American men, women, and children who joined the battle, the call for civil rights transformed into a mass movement that included Americans of all races.

Developments in North Carolina in 1960 ushered in a new phase in the movement. On February 1, four African-American college students entered a Woolworth's store and restaurant in Greensboro, took seats at the lunch counter marked "For Whites Only," and politely attempted to order lunch. The waitstaff refused to serve them and the manager asked them to leave, but they stayed until closing time. The next day, they returned with 25 fellow students. On the third day, the number of student protesters rose to 63, and by the fifth day it exceeded 300.

News outlets around the country reported the story, and soon more people in many other cities were staging **sit-ins**, coordinated protests in which people occupy seats or floor space in places that are the targets of protest. There also were other "ins." African-American churches organized kneel-ins at segregated churches and wade-ins at segregated pools. These protests were remarkably effective. In the following months, segregation began to yield to integration in cities across the South. On July 25, nearly six months after the first day of the Greensboro sit-in, the four original protesters were finally served at the Woolworth's lunch counter.

The success of the sit-ins and similar nonviolent protests inspired a group of African-American students to create their own political organization, the **Student Nonviolent Coordinating Committee (SNCC)**. A cofounder of SCLC, **Ella Baker**, had become frustrated with its cautious approach and hierarchical nature, so she left that organization to become an advisor to SNCC. Baker had also served as a national director for the NAACP and had co-founded an organization called In Friendship, which raised money to fight Jim Crow laws in the South. While serving at SCLC, Baker helped to organize a "prayer pilgrimage" to Washington, D.C., and an ambitious voter registration campaign called the Crusade for Citizenship.

North Carolina A&T College students (left to right) Ronald Martin, Robert Patterson, and Mark Martin joined the second day of the sit-in at the Greensboro lunch counter.

PLAN: 4-PAGE LESSON

OBJECTIVE

Examine the development of the civil rights movement and the leadership of Martin Luther King, Jr.

CRITICAL THINKING SKILLS FOR LESSON 2.2

- Form and Support Opinions
- Make Inferences
- Analyze Cause and Effect
- Make Connections
- Draw Conclusions
- Identify Problems and Solutions
- Evaluate

HISTORICAL THINKING FOR CHAPTER 25

How did the civil rights movement redefine American identity? The civil rights movement began with the courageous efforts of individual Americans. Lesson 2.2 describes how the struggle developed into a mass movement.

BACKGROUND FOR THE TEACHER

African-American ministers served as media spokespeople, strategists for organized protests, and motivators for their congregations. Martin Luther King, Jr., and other clergy, such as Andrew Young, Jesse Jackson, Fred Shuttlesworth, Wyatt T. Walker, and Joseph Lowery, were charismatic leaders and gifted orators who gave a religious significance to the struggle for equality. Their emotionally charged speeches inspired people to participate in the movement and to make personal sacrifices for the cause.

HISTORY NOTEBOOK

Encourage students to complete the American Gallery page for Chapter 25 in their History Notebooks.

INTRODUCE & ENGAGE

ASSOCIATE A WORD WITH A MOVEMENT

Write the word *nonviolence* on the board. **ASK:** In what way might this word be associated with the civil rights movement? *(Possible response: Activists used nonviolence as a strategy to protest injustice.)* Encourage students to analyze the word by completing a Word Square like the one shown. Provide time for them to share their responses. Then read aloud the following quotation from Mohandas Gandhi: "Nonviolence is the greatest force at the disposal of mankind. It is mightier than the mightiest weapon of destruction devised by the ingenuity of man." Ask students whether they agree or disagree with the statement and why. Then tell them that in this lesson they will learn how the philosophy of Mohandas Gandhi influenced the civil rights movement.

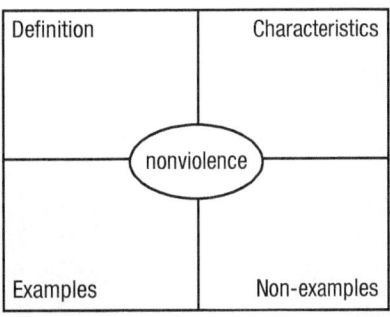

TEACH

GUIDED DISCUSSION

1. **Make Connections** How did Martin Luther King, Jr.'s background prepare him for his leadership role in the civil rights movement? *(Possible response: His family and education provided him with examples of leadership and a belief in racial equality. His studies introduced him to the nonviolent philosophy that became the hallmark of his civil rights strategy.)*

2. **Draw Conclusions** In what way did the Greensboro sit-in represent a new phase in the civil rights movement? *(Possible response: It inspired coordinated protests in other cities and led to greater involvement of students in the struggle for civil rights.)*

MORE INFORMATION

SCLC and SNCC The Student Nonviolent Coordinating Committee (SNCC) was founded in 1960 with the hope of advancing the idea of using sit-ins for protest. Martin Luther King, Jr., had hoped that SNCC would become the student branch of the Southern Christian Leadership Conference (SCLC), but the students wanted to remain independent in order to develop their own projects and protest approaches. During the 1960s, SNCC grew in size and impact. As the civil rights movement evolved over the next several years, ideological conflicts often arose both between the two organizations and within SNCC's own membership as students grew impatient for change. Many began to debate the effectiveness of the nonviolent approach to social change.

After students have read "A Mass Movement Forms" in their text, share this additional information. Then have them use both sources to analyze how SCLC and SNCC are different and similar. Students can complete a Venn diagram to help them organize their information about the two organizations.

DIFFERENTIATE

STRIVING READERS

Complete a T-Chart Instruct students to create a T-Chart, labelling the first column Mohandas Gandhi and the second column Martin Luther King, Jr. As students read the lesson, have them complete the chart with details about each person. Encourage them to compare their completed charts.

Mohandas Gandhi	Martin Luther King, Jr.

GIFTED & TALENTED

Write an Online Profile Have students gather information about one of the Freedom Riders in order to write a profile about that person. Encourage students to use multiple print and digital sources, and to cite both primary and secondary sources. The profile should explore the person's background, motivations, and goals, as well as their experiences as they traveled south from Washington D.C. Invite volunteers to share their profiles with the class.

See the Chapter Planner for more strategies for differentiation.

Barely escaping alive from their burning bus, a group of Freedom Riders waits on the roadside outside Anniston, Alabama. The 13 men and women who set out on an interstate trip to test desegregation laws were assaulted by Ku Klux Klan members before they were rescued several hours later. News of this and other vicious attacks led hundreds of people to join the Freedom Riders throughout 1961.

Another prominent leader of SNCC was a woman named **Fannie Lou Hamer**. Hamer had been born into poverty and oppression in the Mississippi Delta, the 20th child of sharecropper parents, and her education had ended at the 6th-grade level. Her background made her later accomplishments all the more remarkable.

As a SNCC field secretary whose job was to assist in building membership, Hamer fought to end segregation and protect the rights of African Americans. Angered that Mississippi's conservative, white-dominated Democratic Party did not allow African Americans to participate in meetings, she helped to establish the **Mississippi Freedom Democratic Party**, a grassroots political group established as an alternative to the larger, more conservative state arm of the Democratic Party. The Mississippi Freedom Democratic Party was dedicated to encouraging African-American voter registration. Hamer earned the respect of many, and in 1964, she delivered a powerful speech at a Democratic National Convention about the

intimidation and violence that African Americans in her state faced when they attempted to register to vote. Because of their strong leadership, Baker and Hamer joined Rosa Parks as influential women in the civil rights movement.

THE FREEDOM RIDERS

In November 1960, **John F. Kennedy** was elected president of the United States. (Read more about Kennedy's election and presidency in the next chapter.) Although he was more sympathetic to the civil rights cause than Eisenhower had been, Kennedy wanted change to come slowly, without the mass protests and violent incidents that had made headlines around the world. He worried, too, that White House support for immediate desegregation would cost him the goodwill of powerful southern Democrats in Congress.

In December 1960, the Supreme Court had ruled in a case called *Boynton v. Virginia*, finding that racial segregation was illegal in bus terminals, restrooms, and other facilities serving passengers traveling

across state lines. Shortly thereafter, CORE, which you read about earlier in this chapter, announced plans to test that court decision to see if local police were upholding the law. CORE's stated objective was "to provoke the southern authorities into arresting us and thereby prod the Justice Department into enforcing the law of the land."

In May 1961, seven African-American and six white "**Freedom Riders**" left Washington, D.C., on two buses bound for New Orleans. At stops along the way, they ignored "white" and "colored" signs that hung by the restrooms, lunch counters, and waiting rooms in defiance of federal law. Trouble erupted in Anniston, Alabama, when white segregationists firebombed one of the buses. As the passengers

THE GREEN BOOK
In 1936, publisher Victor Green saw the need for a national guide for African-American travelers. Titled *The Negro Motorist Green Book*, the book listed restaurants, rooming houses, barbers, and tourist activities that welcomed African Americans in the time of segregation, particularly in areas with strict Jim Crow laws. Unlike most book publishers, Green looked forward to the time when his Green Book was not necessary. "That is when we as a race will have equal opportunities and privileges in the United States," he wrote in an introduction to his book.

escaped, a mob beat them with fists and clubs. Riders on the second bus suffered a similar attack in Birmingham. Local police in these and other cities made little effort to stop the attacks. The continuing violence finally compelled Attorney General **Robert F. Kennedy**, who was President Kennedy's younger brother and close aide, to send U.S. marshals to protect the riders. CORE, with assistance from SNCC, continued to organize freedom rides until September of that year, when the federal government banned interstate buses and trains from using any terminal that segregated people by race.

Meanwhile, another key development in the civil rights movement unfolded in Mississippi. After repeatedly being denied admission to the all-white University of Mississippi, an African-American student named James Meredith filed a discrimination lawsuit against the university. Supported by the NAACP, Meredith took his case all the way to the Supreme Court, which ruled in his favor. When he attempted to register at the university, however, state troopers, acting on the orders of Mississippi governor Ross Barnett, turned him away. U.S. marshals accompanied Meredith during several more attempts to register, but large numbers of protesters and state troopers blocked him. Riots broke out as the situation escalated. After the federal government sent hundreds of agents to the scene, Meredith was finally able to register and attend classes as the university's first African-American student.

This period in Mississippi's civil rights movement is memorably captured in *Coming of Age in Mississippi*, an autobiography by activist and writer Anne Moody. With bracing honesty, she tells of growing up desperately poor in rural southern Mississippi, of the brutal racism that she and her family faced, and of fighting for the rights of African Americans.

HISTORICAL THINKING

1. **READING CHECK** What legal action did the federal government take in response to the Freedom Rides?

2. **FORM AND SUPPORT OPINIONS** Do you think nonviolent civil disobedience proved to be a good strategy for bringing about social change? Support your opinion with evidence from the text.

3. **MAKE INFERENCES** Why do you think Fannie Lou Hamer focused her efforts on African-American voter registration?

4. **ANALYZE CAUSE AND EFFECT** What caused the sit-in protest in Greensboro, and what effect did the protest have on the larger civil rights movement?

BUILD BACKGROUND

STUDENT PARTICIPATION

Sit-ins and freedom rides highlighted student participation in the civil rights movement and demonstrated the courage required by nonviolent protests. Those who took part in lunch counter sit-ins received specific instructions about how to behave. They were told to wear their best clothes, sit quietly at the counter, and wait for service. If they were threatened through intimidation—such as name-calling or having food or drink poured on them—they were told not to respond. If the worst happened and they were physically attacked, protestors were taught to curl up in a ball on the floor and not retaliate. Leaders stressed that segregationist violence must be met with nonviolence to create a clear distinction for observers. When participants were arrested, they cooperated peacefully, knowing that others would take their place.

While sit-in participants faced harassment, beatings, and arrests, Freedom Riders— most of whom were college students—faced far worse. In Anniston, Alabama, a bus driver delivered his passengers to the Ku Klux Klan, who were given permission by local authorities to attack the Freedom Riders. In Birmingham, the Freedom Riders' bus was attacked, and the riders were beaten. In Montgomery, some riders suffered permanent injuries when local police refused to protect them against a white mob. In Jackson, Mississippi, riders spent six weeks in jail cells under inhumane conditions. Fifty years later, many of the Freedom Riders participated in interviews about their experiences. None expressed any reservations or regrets for their roles in opposing segregation and supporting civil rights.

TEACH

GUIDED DISCUSSION

3. **Make Inferences** Based on the information provided about Fannie Lou Hamer, what can you infer about the Mississippi Democratic party in relation to African Americans? *(Possible response: The party did little to represent or protect African-American voters, as evidenced by Hamer's efforts to form an alternative political group and her moving speech at the 1964 Democratic National Convention.)*

4. **Identify Problems and Solutions** What problem did the Freedom Riders address and how did they intend to solve it? *(Possible response: Southern communities had ignored federal law by maintaining segregated restrooms and waiting rooms along interstate routes. Freedom Riders defied segregation policies in order to test whether local governments would enforce the court's ruling.)*

5. **Evaluate** Despite the undeniable importance of Martin Luther King, Jr., and other famous leaders in the civil rights movement, some historians think that their portrayal as heroes of the movement obscures the invaluable contributions of ordinary individuals. Research the various arguments made by historians, evaluating the authors' use of evidence. Based on the information in this lesson and your additional research, would you agree? Why or why not? *(Possible responses: Yes. It's obvious that the contributions of many ordinary individuals must be acknowledged if this historic movement is to be understood. No. Though ordinary people made tremendous contributions, it would be wrong to downplay the outstanding work of leaders such as Martin Luther King, Jr.)*

MORE INFORMATION

Desegregating the University of Mississippi James Meredith's admission to the University of Mississippi resulted in a violent protest that caused two deaths and hundreds of injuries. It also provoked a confrontation between Governor Ross Barnett and President John Kennedy. Barnett was caught between his allegiance to Mississippi segregationists and his responsibility to uphold a federal court order. Kennedy attempted to reach a peaceful resolution, but he was determined to enforce the law. Some historians believe the violence that accompanied the desegregation of Ole Miss marked a turning point in the struggle for civil rights.

Have students examine the photographs found in this lesson. **ASK:** Why do you think the desegregation of the University of Mississippi, along with the sit-ins and freedom rides, were pivotal in gaining support for civil rights? *(Answers will vary. Possible response: By contrasting peaceful protestors with violent proponents of segregation, these events gave the moral high ground to the movement and began to sway public opinion.)*

ACTIVE OPTIONS

Active History: Research Leaders in Nonviolent Civil Disobedience Extend the lesson by using either the PDF or Whiteboard version of the activity. These activities take a deeper look at a topic from, or related to, the lesson. Explore the activities as a class, turn them into group assignments, or even assign them individually.

 **The Freedom Riders** Invite students to explore the American Gallery. Have them select one of the images and do additional research to learn more about it. Ask questions that will inspire additional inquiry about the chosen gallery image, such as: Why did you choose this particular image? How does it aid your understanding of the Freedom Riders? What else would you like to know about the subjects depicted in the images?

HISTORICAL THINKING

ANSWERS

1. The government prohibited interstate transportation companies from using segregated terminals.

2. Answers will vary. Possible responses: Yes. Nonviolent disobedience accomplished its goals in places like Greensboro. No. Those who participated in protests such as the freedom rides were viciously attacked by Ku Klux Klan members.

3. Possible response: Registering people to vote enabled them to participate in democracy and advocate for their civil rights.

4. Racial discrimination at Woolworth's lunch counter caused the sit-in. It inspired other groups such as the Student Nonviolent Coordinating Committee to take action.

PROTESTS IN BIRMINGHAM

In Kelly Ingram Park in Birmingham, Alabama, vicious police dogs lunge at peaceful protesters. Children cower before a powerful water cannon. Church ministers kneel in prayer. These scenes, depicted in sculptures, tell of a dark time in the city's history.

By 1963, major news media sent reporters and photographers to cover the unfolding civil rights demonstrations that targeted the segregated city of Birmingham, Alabama. As the Birmingham fire department turned high velocity water hoses on peaceful demonstrators, a photographer recorded one of the assaults that shocked Americans.

CONFRONTATION IN BIRMINGHAM

In December 1962, three months after James Meredith's lawsuit to be admitted into the University of Mississippi was successful, President Kennedy received a telegram from Dr. Martin Luther King, Jr., with this message: "A virtual reign of terror is still alive in Birmingham, Alabama. It is by far the worst big city in race relations in the United States."

The previous day, Birmingham's Bethel Baptist Church had been bombed for the third time in 6 years. For 15 years, white segregationists had committed numerous other acts of intimidation and violence against African Americans, including the 1961 attack on the Freedom Riders. The police, under the command of **Eugene T. "Bull" Connor**, the Commissioner of Public Safety, strictly enforced segregation ordinances. Connor was an active white segregationist with close ties to the Ku Klux Klan.

The following spring, King and other leaders of SCLC developed plans for an all-out campaign to confront segregation in Birmingham. They scheduled the campaign to coincide with the busy Easter shopping season. The organizers kicked off the campaign in early April 1963 with mass meetings, lunch-counter sit-ins, a boycott of downtown merchants, and marches, each intended to provoke confrontation and sympathy for the civil rights cause. As days passed, more people joined in the protests, and the police made more arrests.

"LETTER FROM BIRMINGHAM CITY JAIL"

On April 12, 1963, King himself was arrested. That same day, the *Birmingham News* published a letter from eight white ministers titled "A Call for Unity." The ministers appealed to African Americans to withdraw their support for the demonstrations, and they denounced King and others for inciting hatred and violence. From his jail cell, King responded with what would become known as his "Letter from Birmingham City Jail." The letter eloquently rebutted the ministers' arguments and defended the morality of nonviolent civil disobedience. King was released from jail after eight days of **solitary confinement**, being locked in an enclosed cell alone.

As support for the protests began to fade, King and the other organizers seized upon the idea of bringing local students into the campaign in order to re-energize it. On May 2, more than 1,000 students, some as young as 6, marched from the 16th Street Baptist Church to City Hall. Police arrested and held 969 students, among others, packing the city's jails.

Abandoning restraint, Bull Connor ordered the police and fire departments to use police dogs and high-pressure fire hoses to break up the protest. News outlets across the United States and around the world carried shocking images of Birmingham police officers striking peaceful protestors with batons, vicious dogs attacking children and adults alike, and officials blasting people with powerful fire hoses.

On May 10, the campaign's organizers announced that they had worked out an agreement with Birmingham city leaders to end the public demonstrations. The agreement established specific steps and a timetable for ending segregation in Birmingham's public facilities and for creating an employment program for African Americans.

Once again Alabama was headlined in national newspapers when, on June 11, 1963, its segregationist governor **George Wallace**, flanked by state troopers, physically blocked two African-American students from registering at the University of Alabama in Tuscaloosa. President Kennedy and Attorney General Robert Kennedy responded to Wallace's symbolic action by authorizing the Alabama National Guard to physically remove the governor and by allowing the students to register.

On national television that evening, President Kennedy delivered an impassioned speech on civil rights. He spoke of the "moral crisis" facing the country and declared that "The events in Birmingham . . . have so increased the cries for equality that no city or state or legislative body can prudently choose to ignore them." Just hours after the broadcast, a white segregationist in Mississippi shot and killed civil rights activist **Medgar Evers** in front of his home.

The following week, Kennedy expanded the role of the federal government as a guarantor of civil rights by sending Congress a proposal for a civil rights bill that was far stronger than the civil rights bills that had passed in 1957 and 1960. In fact, it was the most sweeping civil rights bill since Reconstruction.

The turmoil in Alabama had a powerful impact on race relations in the United States, as well as on the perception of how protesters were being treated. Many white Americans had been indifferent to the plight of African Americans. But because the violence and brutality in Birmingham was widely televised, most Americans, no matter what their backgrounds, were horrified by the violence. They began to pay attention to and support the civil rights movement.

HISTORICAL THINKING

1. **READING CHECK** What was the goal of the Birmingham campaign, and what caused the organizers to end the campaign?

2. **EXPLAIN** How did the television footage of police officers attacking protesters contribute to the diffusion of the civil rights movement?

3. **FORM AND SUPPORT OPINIONS** What effect do you think President Kennedy's address about the events in Birmingham had on the nation?

4. **IDENTIFY** What was the role of Martin Luther King, Jr., in the Birmingham protests?

OBJECTIVE

Examine how events in Birmingham in 1963 resulted in proposed civil rights legislation.

CRITICAL THINKING SKILLS FOR LESSON 2.3

- Explain
- Form and Support Opinions
- Identify
- Draw Conclusions
- Evaluate
- Analyze Language Use

HISTORICAL THINKING FOR CHAPTER 25

How did the civil rights movement redefine American identity? The civil rights movement had made progress, but challenges remained. Lesson 2.3 describes how confrontations in Birmingham, Alabama, impacted the fight for equality.

BACKGROUND FOR THE TEACHER

In 1963, civil rights activists in Birmingham—with some hesitation—enlisted children into the struggle for civil rights, a tactic now known as the Children's Crusade. Leaders rationalized that children suffered the effects of segregation and were therefore an untapped source of potential protestors. They also hoped the children's involvement would gain support for the cause. To prepare, young people attended workshops where they were trained in nonviolent approaches to protest. But few of the young people who marched on May 2 succeeded in completing the half-mile walk to City Hall. Many were arrested and spent several days in jail. Hundreds of others who marched on the second day of the crusade were subjected to violent abuse. Fifty years later, one of the participants recalled, "I don't think I will ever forget that water and when you would run they had the dogs waiting." Through international news coverage, the sacrifices of Birmingham children did much to raise public awareness.

INTRODUCE & ENGAGE

SHARE REACTIONS

Read aloud the introductory paragraph about Kelly Ingram Park. Invite students to share their reactions. **ASK:** What emotions does this paragraph evoke? *(Possible response: sadness, anxiety, admiration for protestors' courage)* Why do you think this dark time in Birmingham's history is memorialized with sculptures? *(Possible responses: It honors the sacrifices people made in the struggle for freedom. It is necessary to remember the past.)* Tell students that in this lesson they will learn how the violence depicted in these statues changed the way people thought about the civil rights movement.

TEACH

GUIDED DISCUSSION

1. **Draw Conclusions** Why was the timing of the Birmingham campaign significant? *(The protests were timed to disrupt Easter shopping, which would have an economic impact on Birmingham businesses.)*

2. **Evaluate** How did events in Birmingham lead to an expansion of the role of the federal government in the civil rights movement? *(Possible response: President Kennedy authorized the National Guard to force Governor Wallace to obey the law, and Kennedy sent Congress a proposal for the strongest civil rights legislation in decades.)*

ANALYZE LANGUAGE USE

Provide an opportunity for students to listen to an excerpt from President Kennedy's speech in which he refers to the events in Birmingham (Report to the American People on Civil Rights, June 11, 1963). Discuss how Kennedy's use of language influenced his television and radio audience. **ASK:** How did Kennedy engage the American people in the struggle for equality? *(He appealed to their sense of history and their moral character.)*

ACTIVE OPTIONS

On Your Feet: Think, Talk, and Share Arrange students in groups of four to meet in separate areas of the classroom. Pose the following question: Why is the Birmingham campaign considered one of the turning points of the civil rights movement? Instruct students to think about the topic individually and then discuss it within their group. After students have discussed the topic, ask them to count off within their group. Call a number, and have the student from each group with that number share the group's answers with the rest of the class.

NG Learning Framework: Write a News Article

SKILL Communication

KNOWLEDGE Our Human Story

Guide students to provide insights into the events in Birmingham by writing a news article from the viewpoint of a reporter on the scene. Encourage them to choose one of the incidents discussed in the lesson and to provide accurate details about it. Post the following graphic organizer as a model for how students might organize their ideas. Encourage the class to develop an online newspaper by combining their articles.

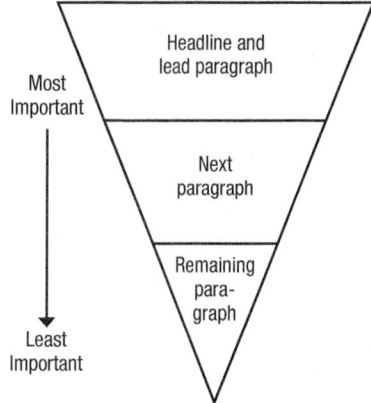

DIFFERENTIATE

ENGLISH LANGUAGE LEARNERS

Use a Term in a Sentence Pair students at the **Emerging** level with those at the **Bridging** or **Expanding** level. Bring students' attention to the terms *reign of terror, solitary confinement,* and *moral crisis.* Have students take turns reading each term in the context of the paragraph in which it appears. Then challenge pairs to compose their own sentence for each term. Invite pairs to share their sentences.

GIFTED & TALENTED

Create a Podcast Direct students to conduct online research to find news coverage of the Birmingham protests in newspapers, as well as on radio and television. Encourage students to note any discrepencies among the sources. Then have students write a script in the form of a contemporary podcast, incorporating the 1962 news coverage and sound clips. Instruct students to assemble their script and research materials into a podcast to share with the class.

See the Chapter Planner for more strategies for differentiation.

HISTORICAL THINKING

ANSWERS

1. The goal was to end segregation and gain public support for civil rights. The campaign ended when city leaders agreed to end segregation and create an employment program for African Americans.

2. Television coverage raised awareness of the harsh realities of segregation. This led to increased public support for civil rights for African Americans.

3. Possible response: As the president, Kennedy made civil rights and the treatment of African Americans a national issue rather than merely a local problem confined to the South.

4. King developed plans for mass meetings, lunch-counter sit-ins, a boycott of downtown merchants, and marches.

DEMANDING REFORM

African-American civil rights activists worked through the nation's judicial and legislative systems to win the rights of full citizenship, but they also turned to nonviolent protest to raise awareness of their cause and win support for their movement. Sometimes that meant paying a legal cost.

CRITICAL VIEWING In 1967, four years after he wrote "Letter from Birmingham City Jail," Martin Luther King, Jr., returned to the Alabama jail to complete serving his sentence for participating in the 1963 civil rights demonstration. In 10 years, King was arrested more than 10 times for conducting peaceful protests. Why do you think this photo of King in an Alabama jail cell has become a symbol of the civil rights movement?

DOCUMENT ONE

Primary Source: Speech
from *Speech at the March on Washington*, by John Lewis, August 28, 1963

John Lewis, the son of Alabama sharecroppers, helped organize the March on Washington for Jobs and Freedom and was its youngest speaker. His speech focused on the need for civil rights legislation that would address how the economy affected African Americans and the nation's poor and homeless.

CONSTRUCTED RESPONSE What does Lewis mean when he says "we will not and cannot be patient"?

We march today for jobs and freedom, but we have nothing to be proud of. While we stand here, there are sharecroppers in the Delta of Mississippi who are out in the fields working for less than three dollars a day, twelve hours a day.

We must have legislation that will protect the Mississippi sharecropper who is put off of his farm because he dares to register to vote. We need a bill that will ensure the equality of a maid who earns five dollars a week in a home of a family whose total income is $100,000 a year. . . . For we cannot stop, and we will not and cannot be patient.

DOCUMENT TWO

Primary Source: Newspaper Article
from "A Call for Unity," by eight Alabama clergymen, April 12, 1963

During the campaign in Birmingham, as you have learned, local newspapers printed a letter titled "A Call for Unity," which was signed by eight white religious leaders. The men agreed that segregation was wrong, but believed King's tactics were "unwise and untimely."

CONSTRUCTED RESPONSE What evidence in the text suggests the clergymen are sympathetic to the protesters?

We are now confronted by a series of demonstrations by some of our Negro citizens, directed and led in part by outsiders. We recognize the natural impatience of people who feel that their hopes are slow in being realized. But we are convinced that these demonstrations are unwise and untimely.

DOCUMENT THREE

Primary Source: Letter
from "Letter from Birmingham City Jail," by Martin Luther King, Jr., April 16, 1963

In this excerpt from the letter he wrote in response to "A Call for Unity," King addresses the ministers' assertion that the demonstrations were "directed and led in part by outsiders."

CONSTRUCTED RESPONSE What is King's response to the label of "outsider"?

I cannot sit idly by in Atlanta and not be concerned about what happens in Birmingham. Injustice anywhere is a threat to justice everywhere. We are caught in an inescapable network of mutuality, tied in a single garment of destiny. Whatever affects one directly affects all indirectly. Never again can we afford to live with the narrow, provincial "outside agitator" idea. Anyone who lives inside the United States can never be considered an outsider anywhere in this country.

SYNTHESIZE & WRITE

1. **REVIEW** Review what you have learned about the civil rights movement from the *Speech at the March on Washington*, the Birmingham campaign, and other strategies.

2. **RECALL** On your own paper, write the main idea expressed in each of these documents: John Lewis's speech, the "A Call for Unity" letter, and the "Letter from Birmingham City Jail."

3. **CONSTRUCT** Construct a topic sentence that supports this question: In what ways did the different forms of protest work together to bring about change?

4. **WRITE** Using evidence from this chapter and the documents, write an informative paragraph that supports your topic sentence in Step 3.

PLAN: 2-PAGE LESSON

OBJECTIVE

Synthesize information about civil rights activists from primary source documents.

CRITICAL THINKING SKILLS FOR LESSON 2.4

• Synthesize
• Analyze Language Use
• Make Predictions
• Evaluate

HISTORICAL THINKING FOR CHAPTER 25

How did the civil rights movement redefine American identity? Nonviolent protestors were often arrested and subjected to harsh treatment. Lesson 2.4 provides excerpts from documents that show different perspectives on the protests and those who took part in them.

BACKGROUND FOR THE TEACHER

John Lewis participated in the freedom rides in 1961, and in 1963, he became chairman of SNCC. At the age of 23, Lewis was one of the Big Six leaders who planned a national march on Washington, D.C. The other members of that elite group were Whitney Young, A. Philip Randolph, James Farmer, Roy Wilkins, and Martin Luther King, Jr. On the night before the march, a copy of Lewis's speech circulated among the event's leaders, who requested changes to the fiery rhetoric. They encouraged Lewis to tone down his criticism of President Kennedy's civil rights bill, which he called "too little and too late." Lewis also changed the wording of a threat to "march through the heart of Dixie, the way Sherman did." In the final speech, Lewis said, "We will march with the spirit of love and with the spirit of dignity that we have shown here today."

INTRODUCE & ENGAGE

PREPARE FOR THE DOCUMENT-BASED QUESTION

Before students start on the activity, briefly preview the three documents. Remind students that a constructed response requires full explanations in complete sentences. Emphasize that students should use what they have learned about civil rights activism in addition to the information in the documents.

TEACH

GUIDED DISCUSSION

1. **Analyze Language Use** What is the purpose of the specific examples Lewis uses in his speech? *(Possible response: The examples illustrate real-life situations in which African Americans suffered economic and political inequality.)*

2. **Make Predictions** How do you think the "Letter from Birmingham City Jail" affected the future of the civil rights movement? *(Possible response: By reinforcing the universal cause of civil rights, King's letter likely encouraged activists nationwide and challenged others to examine their own responsibility to support civil rights.)*

EVALUATE

After students have completed the Synthesize & Write activity, allow time for them to exchange paragraphs and read and comment on the work of their peers. Establish guidelines for comments prior to this activity so that feedback is constructive and encouraging in nature. Comments should focus on the most significant parts that address the purpose of the activity and the audience.

ACTIVE OPTION

On Your Feet: Use a Jigsaw Strategy As a class, analyze the full text of "A Call for Unity" and identify four arguments that the Alabama clergymen make. Then organize students in four "expert" groups and assign one of the arguments to each group. Instruct members of each group to analyze the full text of "Letter from Birmingham City Jail" and summarize King's response to their assigned argument. Have members of each group count off, using the letters A, B, C, and D. Regroup students so that each new group has at least one member from each expert group. Direct students in the new groups to share the clergymen's arguments and King's responses.

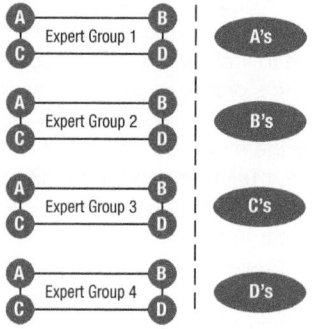

DIFFERENTIATE

INCLUSION

Analyze the Photograph and Primary Sources Pair students who are visually impaired with students who are not. Ask the latter to describe not only the subject of the photograph of Martin Luther King, Jr., but also the mood it conveys. Ask these students to then read each of the primary source documents aloud. Encourage visually impaired students to ask clarifying questions whenever they need to. Then have the pairs work together to answer the Constructed Response questions.

GIFTED & TALENTED

Role-Play Historical Figures Direct students to find and read the full texts of the primary source excerpts. Have them choose to role-play either one of the eight clergymen in "A Call for Unity," John Lewis, or Dr. King by introducing and delivering the person's speech or written document. After they deliver the speeches, have students speculate on what these historical figures might feel about the status of civil rights and current civil rights activism in the United States and in the world today. What progress might they acknowledge, and what challenges might they still see ahead?

See the Chapter Planner for more strategies for differentiation.

SYNTHESIZE & WRITE

ANSWERS

1. Answers will vary.

2. Possible response: Immediate legislation is required to achieve equality (John Lewis's speech); change must not be rushed ("A Call for Unity"); civil rights must be the concern of all Americans (Martin Luther King, Jr.'s letter).

3. Possible response: Speeches, letters, and nonviolent activism called attention to inequality and prompted government response.

4. Answers will vary. Students' paragraphs should include their topic sentence from Step 3 and provide several details from the documents to support the sentence.

CONSTRUCTED RESPONSE

Document 1: Possible response: Lewis expresses frustration that civil rights activism has not produced the desired results, and he demands immediate action from legislators.

Document 2: Possible response: The clergymen recognize that people are impatient with the lack of progress in realizing their hopes.

Document 3: Possible response: King argues that no one living in the United States can be considered an outsider because anything that affects one American affects all Americans.

THE MARCH ON WASHINGTON

Important speeches tend to include memorable and often-quoted words. Take, for example, Patrick Henry's "Give me liberty or give me death!" Without question, the most famous speech of Martin Luther King, Jr., became a rallying point for justice, freedom, and a better world.

CRITICAL VIEWING Martin Luther King, Jr., waves to the diverse crowd following the March on Washington for Jobs and Freedom. From the Lincoln Memorial, King began what became known as his "I Have a Dream" speech. As he spoke, his friend, gospel singer Mahalia Jackson, eagerly called out to him "Tell them about the dream." From your view of King and the crowd in the photograph, what do you think was the effect of King's message about his dream?

JOBS AND FREEDOM

As you have read, in July 1963 President Kennedy sent Congress a proposal for a sweeping civil rights bill. Recent events in Birmingham and Tuscaloosa, Alabama, had convinced him of the urgent need for strong legislation protecting the rights of African Americans. The legislation faced stiff opposition in Congress, and the bill stalled there.

Meanwhile, plans were underway for a major rally in the nation's capital in support of civil rights and the civil rights bill. The demonstration took place on August 28, 1963, and was called the **March on Washington for Jobs and Freedom**. Its chief organizer was Bayard Rustin. Starting in 1941, Rustin and A. Philip Randolph had built an alliance of civil rights, labor, and religious organizations, bringing unity to the movement.

Rustin expected 100,000 people to take part in the 1963 March on Washington, but more than twice that number arrived. They came from every region of the country and every walk of life. Most were African American, but roughly one-fourth were white. After assembling on the grounds of the Washington Monument, the participants sang "We Shall Overcome" and marched down Constitution and Independence avenues. They ended at the Lincoln Memorial for the day's main program. It featured prayers, a performance by gospel singer **Mahalia Jackson**, and speeches by civil rights leaders.

DR. KING'S DREAM

The last and most highly anticipated speaker at the March on Washington was King. The eloquent and uplifting speech he delivered that afternoon is considered one of the greatest orations in American history. King began by reminding his listeners that although almost 100 years had passed since President Lincoln emancipated enslaved people, "the Negro is still sadly crippled by the manacles of segregation and the chains of discrimination. Now is the time," he proclaimed, "to rise from the dark and desolate valley of segregation to the sunlit path of racial justice." Putting aside his prepared notes, King spoke of his dream for a brighter future:

I have a dream that one day this nation will rise up and live out the true meaning of its creed: "We hold these truths to be self-evident, that all men are created equal."

I have a dream that my four little children will one day live in a nation where they will not be judged by the color of their skin but by the content of their character.

The March on Washington demonstrated the growing power and unity of the civil rights movement. Just weeks later, however, a horrific event in Alabama was a reminder of the gulf between King's dream and the harsh reality that African Americans still faced. On Sunday morning, September 15, a bomb planted by the Ku Klux Klan killed four young African-American girls at Birmingham's 16th Street Baptist Church.

In the fall of 1963, SNCC and CORE launched a **voter registration drive** in Mississippi to sign up as many eligible African-American voters as possible. Expanded in 1964, the program was called the Mississippi Summer Project, or **Freedom Summer**. More than 700 student volunteers, most of whom were white, came from colleges in the North to work with local civil rights organizations in Mississippi. On June 21, 1964, two white workers, Andrew Goodman and Michael Schwerner from New York, and one local African-American worker, James Chaney, disappeared after investigating the burning of an African-American church. Six weeks later, acting on a tip, authorities uncovered the bodies of the workers. All three had been shot at close range. It was clear that the nonviolent civil rights movement still faced dangerous opposition.

HISTORICAL THINKING

1. **READING CHECK** In what ways did the March on Washington demonstrate the power and unity of the civil rights movement?

2. **MAKE GENERALIZATIONS** How does the fact that students volunteered to travel to Mississippi after the violence of the Birmingham campaign speak to larger developments in the civil rights movement?

3. **ANALYZE LANGUAGE USE** What was the impact of King's deliberate repetition of the phrase "I have a dream" in his speech?

OBJECTIVE

Understand the reasons for the March on Washington and the cultural and political environment in which it took place.

CRITICAL THINKING SKILLS FOR LESSON 2.5

• Make Generalizations

• Analyze Language Use

• Make Inferences

• Evaluate

HISTORICAL THINKING FOR CHAPTER 25

How did the civil rights movement redefine American identity? To push forward political and economic goals, civil rights activists in 1963 planned a mass demonstration in the nation's capital. Lesson 2.5 describes how the March on Washington was organized and carried out.

BACKGROUND FOR THE TEACHER

Martin Luther King, Jr.'s "I Have a Dream" speech is one of the most famous and recognizable in our nation's history. Ironically, King did not intend to deliver the parts of the speech that are most often quoted. He had used the "I have a dream" refrain in previous speeches and had decided not to include it at the Lincoln Memorial. Though King's prepared speech was well received by his listeners, it seemed to lack the power required by the moment. Then Mahalia Jackson called out, "Tell them about the dream, Martin." As King departed from his script, his voice and demeanor became more animated, and the crowd responded enthusiastically. Fifty years later, people continue to be inspired by his speech and view it as a quintessential example of rhetorical excellence.

HISTORY NOTEBOOK

Encourage students to complete the page on the March on Washington for Chapter 25 in their History Notebooks as they read the lesson.

INTRODUCE & ENGAGE

REVIEW THE FACTS

Post a large version of a chart like the one shown and have students use it to review what they have learned about the civil rights movement. Call on volunteers to add information without looking back at previous lessons. Then challenge the class to synthesize the information and discuss the following question: Why was there a civil rights movement? Their answers should include the hurdles minorities faced in the mid-20th century and the role of activists.

What?
Who?
Where?
When?

TEACH

GUIDED DISCUSSION

1. **Make Inferences** Why might President Kennedy's proposed civil rights legislation have faced opposition in Congress? *(Possible response: Southern members of Congress included segregationists who were opposed to equal rights for African Americans.)*

2. **Evaluate** What impact do you think the murders of white volunteers from the North had on the civil rights movement? *(Possible responses: The murders may have made volunteers realize how serious things were. They may have made people feel more determined to get involved. They may have discouraged some from volunteering.)*

MORE INFORMATION

Voter Registration In 1962, less than 7 percent of eligible African Americans in Mississippi were registered voters because state and local officials had denied African-American voting rights by charging poll taxes, requiring literacy tests, and using intimidation tactics. Civil rights activists believed that voting was essential to bringing about equality, as it would enable African Americans to influence social and political changes through the ballot box. In 1964, thousands of African Americans in Mississippi attempted to register to vote, but only a small percentage were successful. This failure led to an increased effort to pass voting rights legislation. **ASK:** Why do you think the Freedom Summer project focused on voter registration in Mississippi? *(Possible responses: Mississippi had a very low percentage of African-American voters. A key activist, Fanny Lou Hamer, was from Mississippi and had helped establish the Mississippi Freedom Democratic Party, whose goal was to encourage African-American voter registration.)*

ACTIVE OPTIONS

On Your Feet: Hold a Fishbowl Discussion Pose the question: Did the March on Washington in 1963 accomplish its purpose? Arrange students in two concentric circles facing inward. Instruct students in the inner circle to discuss the question while students in the outer circle listen and take notes. Reverse roles. At the end of the discussion, allow groups to synthesize their ideas and share their evaluations of the discussions.

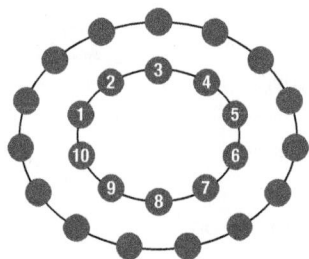

NG Learning Framework: Advertise the March on Washington

ATTITUDE Empowerment

KNOWLEDGE Our Human Story

Guide students to learn more about the March on Washington by researching the day's activities, the speakers, and the entertainers who participated. Ask them to create posters or flyers advertising the march and encouraging people to attend. Direct students to read eyewitness accounts to discover why 200,000 people marched on Washington. Provide time for students to share their work and discuss their research.

For students who develop an interest in the March on Washington, suggest that they read the American Story at the beginning of this chapter.

DIFFERENTIATE

ENGLISH LANGUAGE LEARNERS

Understand Imagery Pair students at the **Emerging** and **Expanding** levels with those at the **Bridging** level. Explain that Martin Luther King, Jr., was a master of rhetorical devices, including the use of vivid imagery to create strong mental pictures. Call students' attention to the phrases *manacles of segregation, chains of discrimination, valley of segregation,* and *sunlit path of racial justice* that appear in the lesson's text. Ask pairs to discuss the mental images created by these words.

PRE-AP

Form and Support a Thesis Challenge students to research the alliances that strengthened the civil rights movement. After students conduct preliminary research using a variety of print and online sources, instruct them to develop a thesis regarding what they consider the most important alliance among, for example, religious, labor, women, or other groups. Then have students continue to conduct research in order to support their thesis. Finally, instruct them to write an essay about the alliance. Invite students to share their essays on a class or school blog.

See the Chapter Planner for more strategies for differentiation.

HISTORICAL THINKING

ANSWERS

1. The march showed that thousands of African Americans and whites were united in support of civil rights.

2. The struggle for civil rights had evolved into a mass movement in which volunteers were willing to risk injury or even death for a cause in which they believed.

3. Repetition of the phrase emphasized that the goals of the civil rights movement had not yet been achieved and that continued efforts were needed.

CRITICAL VIEWING Possible responses: King's speech likely energized the crowd and renewed people's determination to realize the dream of achieving equality.

VOCABULARY

Use each of the following vocabulary terms in a sentence that shows an understanding of the term's meaning.

1. desegregation

   The Supreme Court ruled against "separate but equal" education, which led to the desegregation of public schools.

2. Freedom Riders

3. sit-in

4. grassroots activism

5. dehumanize

6. solitary confinement

READING STRATEGY
MAKE INFERENCES

Texts don't always spell out exactly how an event affected the lives of those who lived through it or the outcomes of other related events. Sometimes a reader needs to evaluate the information in the text to infer these effects and outcomes. Use a chart like the one below to make inferences about ways Americans reacted to key events in the civil rights movement. Then answer the question.

The Civil Rights Movement

Key Events	American Reactions	Inferences

7. How did the civil rights movement redefine American identity?

MAIN IDEAS

Answer the following questions. Support your answers with evidence from the chapter.

8. How did the issue of civil rights divide Democrats at their 1948 convention? **LESSON 1.1**

9. By writing about his own experience of living in the United States as an African-American man, what did James Baldwin hope to accomplish? **LESSON 1.2**

10. How did the definition of equal rights change after the Supreme Court issued the *Brown* decision? **LESSON 1.3**

11. How did the Montgomery African-American community react to the arrest of Rosa Parks, and what was the arrest's effect? **LESSON 2.1**

12. In what ways do the teachings of Gandhi still affect the civil rights movement today? **LESSON 2.2**

13. What impact did the Greensboro sit-in have across the South? **LESSON 2.2**

14. How did Dr. King respond to the letter titled "A Call for Unity" written by white ministers in Birmingham? **LESSON 2.3**

15. How was the March on Washington a key event in the evolution of the civil rights movement? **LESSON 2.5**

HISTORICAL THINKING

Answer the following questions. Support your answers with evidence from the chapter.

16. **IDENTIFY PROBLEMS AND SOLUTIONS** What was the role of various civil rights organizations in influencing public opinion and achieving civil rights legislation?

17. **DESCRIBE** Who were some of the leaders of the civil rights movement, and what were their contributions?

18. **SYNTHESIZE** Why was the civil rights movement able to gain momentum during the 1950s and into the 1960s?

19. **EVALUATE** What were the goals and strategies of the civil rights movement, and how did change affect those goals?

20. **DRAW CONCLUSIONS** Describe the strategy civil rights lawyers used to end segregation in education.

INTERPRET VISUALS

Pulitzer Prize-winning cartoonist Bill Mauldin drew this cartoon in 1960, six years after the Supreme Court's *Brown* v. *Board of Education* decision and five years after the court ordered that desegregation of public schools should proceed "with all deliberate speed."

21. What point is the cartoonist making about segregation in schools?

22. What details from the cartoon support this point of view?

ANALYZE SOURCES

In his January 1963 inaugural speech, Alabama governor George Wallace defied the civil rights movement and federal efforts to end discrimination and segregation in his state.

> Today I have stood, where once Jefferson Davis stood, and took an oath to my people. It is very appropriate then that from this Cradle of the Confederacy, this very Heart of the Great Anglo-Saxon Southland, that today we sound the drum for freedom as have our generations of forebears before us done, time and time again down through history. Let us rise to the call of freedom-loving blood that is in us and send our answer to the tyranny that clanks its chains upon the South. In the name of the greatest people that have ever trod this earth, I draw the line in the dust and toss the gauntlet before the feet of tyranny and I say: segregation today, segregation tomorrow, segregation forever.

23. What is Wallace referring to when he says "the tyranny that clanks its chains upon the South," and does this statement show bias?

CONNECT TO YOUR LIFE

24. **EXPOSITORY** The civil rights protesters you've read about risked their safety to achieve equal rights. Write a short paragraph describing a cause you would march for, and explain why the cause is important.

- List causes that are important to you, and if necessary, research them online.

- Decide which cause you listed is most important by evaluating how society would be affected if the cause were not supported.

- State your main idea clearly at the beginning of the paragraph.

- Provide a concluding sentence that summarizes the importance of the cause.

VOCABULARY ANSWERS

1. The Supreme Court ruled against "separate but equal" education, which led to the desegregation of public schools.

2. In 1961, a group known as the Freedom Riders challenged segregation in public facilities in the South.

3. Students staged a lunch counter sit-in and refused to give up their seats until they were served.

4. People who have little power individually can enact change together through grassroots activism.

5. Constant denial of their rights made African Americans feel dehumanized.

6. Solitary confinement punishes prisoners by denying them all human contact.

READING STRATEGY ANSWER

The Civil Rights Movement

Key Events	American Reactions	Inferences
Rosa Parks refused to give up her seat on a bus.	African Americans boycotted city buses in Montgomery.	Individual actions can have significant impact.
Students staged a sit-in in Greensboro.	Students formed SNCC.	Social activism can inspire national organizations.
Birmingham officials used violence against protestors.	News coverage resulted in public outrage.	The media can have an impact on society.

7. Answers will vary. Possible response: Prior to the civil rights movement, American identity—and the rights associated with it—applied mostly to whites. As a result of the civil rights movement, American identify became more diverse and inclusive.

MAIN IDEAS ANSWERS

8. Hubert Humphrey strongly supported civil rights, but Truman favored a more moderate approach in order to avoid the loss of southern votes.

9. Baldwin hoped to show what life was like for African Americans and to convince white people to acknowledge that blacks are not inferior to whites.

10. The *Brown* decision found that the doctrine of "separate but equal" had no place in public education, thus chipping away at one of the lynchpins of segregation.

11. The African-American community boycotted Montgomery's city buses, which eventually ended segregation on buses.

12. Gandhi's teachings inspired King's philosophy of nonviolent civil disobedience, which is still used in protests today.

13. The Greensboro sit-in inspired African Americans in other cities to conduct similar protests and helped end segregation throughout the South.

14. King wrote a letter in which he refuted the ministers' claims and defended nonviolent civil disobedience as a means of achieving equality.

15. The March on Washington was an attempt to pressure Congress to pass legislation to address inequality, a key issue in the civil rights movement.

HISTORICAL THINKING ANSWERS

16. Possible response: CORE fought discrimination through nonviolent protests. The NAACP sponsored many programs to support the political, economic, and social equality of African Americans. SCLC worked through churches to assist local protest groups. SNCC promoted student involvement in the fight for civil rights.

17. Possible response: Martin Luther King, Jr., who was the most prominent leader of the civil rights movement, provided the movement with its philosophy and strategies. Rosa Parks inspired the Montgomery Bus Boycott by refusing to give up her seat on a city bus. Ella Baker and Fannie Lou Hamer cofounded organizations that mobilized citizens to action. Bayard Rustin helped organize the March on Washington.

18. Organizations such as the NAACP, SNCC, and CORE organized protests and marches and filed lawsuits that influenced public opinion, changed laws, and prompted the federal government to defend equal rights and opportunities.

19. The original goals of the civil rights movement were to end segregation and provide equal rights for African Americans. Legal victories, such as the *Brown* decision, expanded civil rights goals to include equal opportunities.

20. Civil rights lawyers used the decision in *Mendez* v. *Westminster* to argue that "separate but equal" in education had already been declared unconstitutional in 1946. From there, lawyers were able to argue several other cases that challenged segregation in education and win, including the famous *Brown* decision.

INTERPRET VISUALS ANSWERS

21. Possible response: The cartoonist is making the point that school segregation is a very big problem that will require a lot of effort to solve, but progress is slowly being made.

22. The door marked "school segregation" is huge, and students are trying to push it open. They have opened the door slightly, so they are making progress "inch by inch."

ANALYZE SOURCES ANSWER

23. Wallace is referring to the federal government, which he considers tyrannical because it is enforcing desegregation. This statement definitely shows bias against the federal government because Wallace was strongly opposed to desegregation.

CONNECT TO YOUR LIFE ANSWER

24. Answers will vary, but students' paragraphs should address all bullet points and clearly explain why their cause is important.

UNIT 8 RESOURCES

UNIT INTRODUCTION

UNIT TIME LINE

UNIT WRAP-UP

NATIONAL GEOGRAPHIC | CONNECTION

National Geographic Magazine Adapted Articles
- "Who Was Jim Crow?"
- "Before Stonewall" ONLINE

Unit 8 Inquiry: Design a Museum Exhibit

NG Learning Framework Activities
- Write a Letter
- Create a Song

Unit 8 Formal Assessment

UNIT 8 1954–1975
YEARS OF TURBULENCE

CRITICAL VIEWING U.S. National Guard troops block Beale Street in Memphis, Tennessee, on March 28, 1968, as civil rights marchers pass by. The activists held a number of marches over several days. Martin Luther King, Jr., participated in one of them. It was one of the last public appearances he would make before he was assassinated on April 4. What message are the protesters trying to convey with their signs?

CHAPTER 26 RESOURCES

Available at NGLSync.Cengage.com

TEACHER RESOURCES & ASSESSMENT

Reading and Note-Taking

Vocabulary Practice

Social Studies Skills Lessons
- Reading: Draw Conclusions
- Writing: Argument

Formal Assessment
- Chapter 26 Pretest
- Chapter 26 Tests A & B
- Section Quizzes

Chapter 26 Answer Key

ExamView®
One-time Download

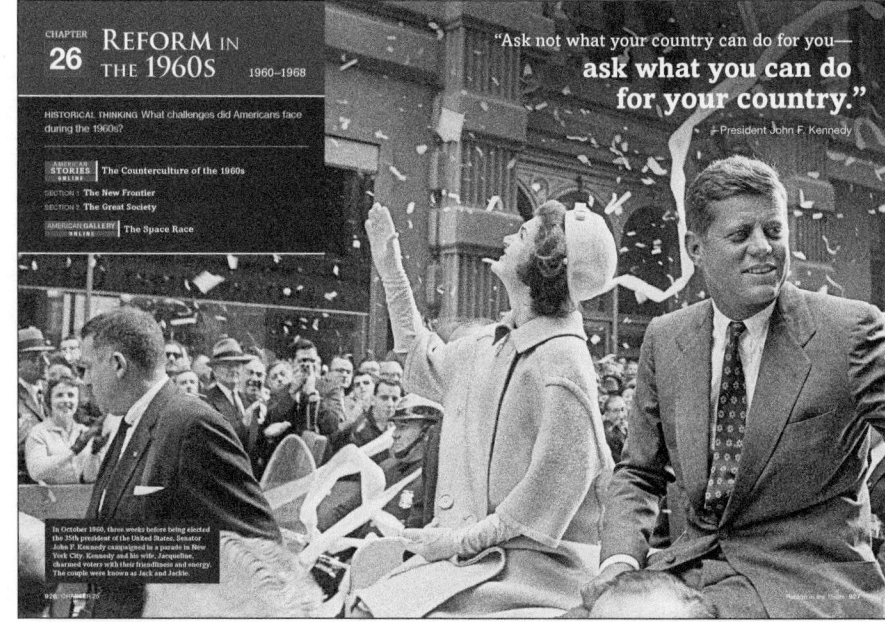

CHAPTER 26 REFORM IN THE 1960s 1960–1968

HISTORICAL THINKING What challenges did Americans face during the 1960s?

AMERICAN STORIES ONLINE The Counterculture of the 1960s
SECTION 1 The New Frontier
SECTION 2 The Great Society
AMERICAN GALLERY ONLINE The Space Race

"Ask not what your country can do for you—**ask what you can do for your country.**"
—President John F. Kennedy

In October 1960, three weeks before being elected the 35th president of the United States, Senator John F. Kennedy campaigned in a parade in New York City. Kennedy and his wife, Jacqueline, charmed voters with their friendliness and energy. The couple were known as Jack and Jackie.

STUDENT DIGITAL RESOURCES

- eEdition
- Handbooks
- Online Atlas
- American Gallery Online
- History Notebook
- Active History
- Literature Analysis
- Projects for Inquiry-Based Learning

Chapter 26 Spanish Resources are available at NGLSync.Cengage.com.

The Counterculture of the 1960s

- Study Primary Sources: Music festival posters and a statement about the 1960s counterculture

- On Your Feet: View Historic Festivals

  NG Learning Framework:
  Write a Folk Song

SECTION 1 RESOURCES

THE NEW FRONTIER

LESSON 1.1
Kennedy's Early Challenges

- Active History: Analyze Cold War Berlin

  NG Learning Framework:
  Evaluate Historic Decisions

LESSON 1.2
Kennedy Embraces Progress

 **AMERICAN GALLERY ONLINE** The Space Race

  NG Learning Framework:
  Explore the New Frontier

LESSON 1.3
The Cuban Missile Crisis

- On Your Feet: Fishbowl

  NG Learning Framework:
  Evaluate Authors' Interpretations

LESSON 1.4
AMERICAN VOICES
John Fitzgerald Kennedy

- On Your Feet: History Roundtable

  NG Learning Framework:
  Craft a Speech

LESSON 1.5
NATIONAL GEOGRAPHIC EXPLORER
LESLIE DEWAN
Reinventing Clean Energy

- On Your Feet: Debate

  NG Learning Framework:
  Investigate Changing Natural Systems

LESSON 1.6
THROUGH THE LENS
David Guttenfelder

- On Your Feet: Numbered Heads

  NG Learning Framework:
  Create a Virtual Tour

SECTION 2 RESOURCES

THE GREAT SOCIETY

LESSON 2.1
Johnson's Strong Start

- On Your Feet: Compare Civil Rights Acts

  NG Learning Framework:
  Evaluate Arguments

LESSON 2.2
The Great Society

- On Your Feet: Immigration Criteria Roundtable

  NG Learning Framework:
  Conduct a Cost-Benefit Analysis

LESSON 2.3
Selma to Montgomery

- On Your Feet: Voting Rights Today

  NG Learning Framework:
  Create Line Graphs

LESSON 2.4
New Leaders and Challenges

- On Your Feet: Analyze the Kerner Commission Report

  NG Learning Framework:
  Explore the Legacy of Civil Rights

LESSON 2.5
CURATING HISTORY
National Civil Rights Museum Memphis, Tennessee

- On Your Feet: Examine Permanent Exhibitions

CHAPTER 26 REVIEW

STRIVING READERS

STRATEGY ❶
USE K-W-L CHARTS

Provide each student with a K-W-L Chart. Have students brainstorm what they already know about historical events of the 1960s, such as Kennedy's presidency and assassination, Johnson's presidency and Great Society initiatives, both leaders' commitments to civil rights, and the push for racial equality under the leadership of Martin Luther King, Jr., Malcolm X, and others. Tell students to add these ideas to the chart. Then ask students to write in the second column of the chart three questions they have, such as the following: What were Kennedy's most important achievements? or How did the civil rights movement impact racism? Remind students to complete their charts as they read each lesson in the chapter.

K What Do I Know?	W What Do I Want To Learn?	L What Did I Learn?

Use with All Lessons

STRATEGY ❷
CREATE IDEA WEBS

Instruct students to summarize the chapter by creating three Idea Webs. They should write *Kennedy* in the center of the first Idea Web, *Johnson* in the second one, and *African-American Fight for Justice* in the third. Ask students to complete each web with relevant information as they read the lessons.

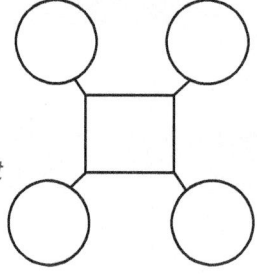

Use with All Lessons *For example, for the Kennedy Idea Web, students could add* Cuban missile crisis, space race, arms race, *and* Peace Corps.

STRATEGY ❸
SUMMARIZE A LESSON

Read the lesson aloud while students follow along in the text. At the end of each paragraph, ask students to write a sentence on their own paper to summarize the content. Invite volunteers to write their summary sentences on the board in the order in which they appear in the lesson. Point out to students that taken together, the sentences represent a summary of the whole lesson.

Use with All Lessons *Throughout the chapter, help students get in the habit of summarizing paragraphs and sections as they read.*

INCLUSION

STRATEGY ❶
WORK IN PAIRS

Allow students with disabilities to work with students who can read the lesson aloud to them. Encourage the partner without disabilities to describe any photographs, maps, graphs, or other visuals in detail after reading the text related to them. When pairs have finished the lesson, you may want to have them work together to answer the Historical Thinking questions.

Use with All Lessons

STRATEGY ❷
PROVIDE A SUMMARY CHART

Tell students that they will be learning about dramatic events leading up to the passage of the Voting Rights Act. To help them understand lesson content, provide them with a summary of important dates, the people and places involved, and the outcomes. For example, you might provide students with the following chart as they preview and read Lesson 2.3.

Date/Event	People/Place	Outcomes
March 7, 1965 "Bloody Sunday"	John Lewis and 500 peaceful demonstrators begin a march from Selma to Montgomery, Alabama, for voting rights and are beaten by local law enforcement.	Assaults are broadcast on television, causing greater support for demonstrators.
March 9, 1965 Second attempt to march from Selma to Montgomery	Martin Luther King, Jr., other clergy, and 2,000 people begin to march but retreat in face of armed officials.	More publicity and support are granted to demonstrators seeking justice and equality for African Americans.
March 21, 1965 Successful march to Montgomery	Martin Luther King and 3,200 people begin the march with federal protection.	Many others join along the way, and 25,000 rally for voting rights in Montgomery.
August 6, 1965	President Johnson signs the Voting Rights Act.	Literacy tests and other barriers to voting are prohibited.

Use with Lesson 2.3

ENGLISH LANGUAGE LEARNERS ELD

STRATEGY 1
COMPILE SENTENCE STRIPS

Choose a key paragraph from the lesson and make sentence strips from it. Read the paragraph aloud while students at **All Proficiencies** follow along in their books. Have students close their books and give them the set of sentence strips. Students should put the strips in order and then read the paragraph aloud.

Use with All Lessons *Before reading, you may want to ask students at the Emerging level to read sentence strips aloud. Then ask them to point out meaningful words in each sentence. Repeat the exercise with another paragraph.*

STRATEGY 2
USE PAIRED READING

Pair students at the **Expanding** and **Bridging** levels to read passages from the text aloud.

1. Partner 1 reads a passage; Partner 2 retells the passage in his or her own words.

2. Partner 2 reads a different passage; Partner 1 retells it.

3. Pairs repeat the process, switching roles.

Use with All Lessons

STRATEGY 3
USE DEFINITION MAPS

Pair students at the **Emerging** level with those at the **Expanding** and **Bridging** levels. Have them use a Definition Map for each of the Key Vocabulary words. As students work, they can discuss the words and clear up any misunderstandings. You may want pairs to compare their responses with those of other pairs.

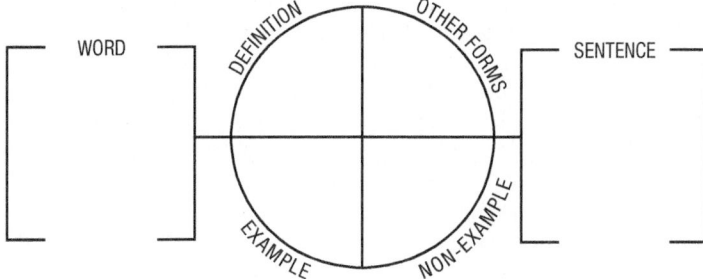

Use with All Lessons

GIFTED & TALENTED

STRATEGY 1
CREATE A GALLERY WALK

Instruct students to conduct online research to learn more about connections between the arms race and civil defense preparedness and how they impacted social and political trends. Suggest that students access newspaper headlines, newsreels, and quotations from key individuals and civil defense posters. Ask students to work together to group their findings and to set up stations around the classroom. Then hold a gallery walk, inviting students to stop at each station.

Use with Lessons 1.2 and 1.3

STRATEGY 2
HOLD A DEBATE

Pair students and have them flip a coin to decide who will take a position supporting the philosophy of Martin Luther King, Jr., or that of Malcolm X. Tell students to use primary and secondary source materials for information on the men's philosophies and actions regarding racial injustice. Then hold a debate in front of the class that explores which philosophy was most effective in the fight for racial justice. At the end of the debate, discuss the reasoning used on each side.

Use with Lesson 2.4

PRE-AP

STRATEGY 1
ANALYZE EFFECTS

Tell students that when the Watts Riots and other race riots happened in the 1960s, nearly all journalists were white, which led to bias in the immediate reporting and in historical interpretation. One recommendation of President Johnson's National Advisory Commission on Civil Disorders (the Kerner report) was that news organizations should hire more African-American journalists. Instruct students to research coverage of a riot in the 1960s and coverage of a riot in the 21st century. Have students report to the class about whether the racial and ethnic make-up of journalists in mainstream media has changed over time and whether changes have affected bias and prejudice in news coverage of such events.

Use with Lesson 2.4

STRATEGY 2
DESIGN AN INFOGRAPHIC

Guide students to conduct research about the Peace Corps from the time Kennedy created it until the present day. Have them create an infographic that uses statistics, facts, and visual information to show the impact of the Peace Corps in the past and the present. Invite students to share their infographics with the class.

Use with Lesson 1.2

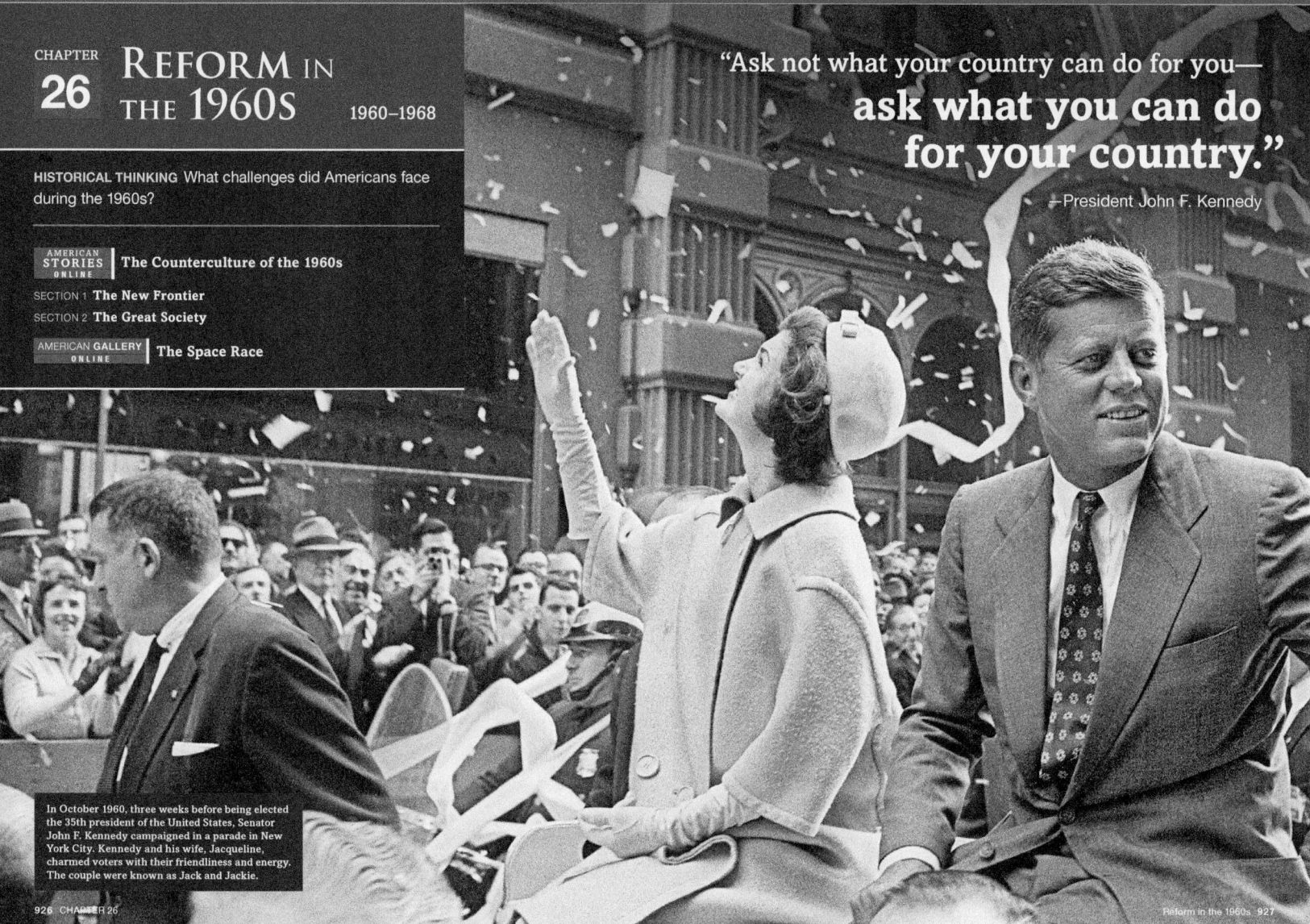

REFORM IN THE 1960S

1960–1968

HISTORICAL THINKING What challenges did Americans face during the 1960s?

AMERICAN STORIES ONLINE | The Counterculture of the 1960s

SECTION 1 **The New Frontier**

SECTION 2 **The Great Society**

AMERICAN GALLERY ONLINE | The Space Race

"Ask not what your country can do for you—
ask what you can do for your country."

—President John F. Kennedy

In October 1960, three weeks before being elected the 35th president of the United States, Senator John F. Kennedy campaigned in a parade in New York City. Kennedy and his wife, Jacqueline, charmed voters with their friendliness and energy. The couple were known as Jack and Jackie.

926 CHAPTER 26

Reform in the 1960s 927

INTRODUCE THE PHOTOGRAPH

JOHN AND JACKIE KENNEDY

Have students study the photograph and quotation that open this chapter. Instruct them to look closely at what is going on in the photograph. **ASK:** What response do people in the crowd seem to be having toward the Kennedys? *(Possible response: Most are enthusiastic, and others seem to be more neutral or skeptical.)* What attitudes or emotions does Kennedy's quotation evoke? *(empowerment, service, responsibility, dedication)* What kind of president does the quotation suggest that Kennedy will be? *(Possible response: a forceful president who will probably use his presidential powers to get the public involved in his goals)* Tell students that in this chapter they will learn about the challenges that the United States faced in the 1960s and how attempts to meet those challenges changed the nation.

SHARE BACKGROUND

In 1960, the U.S. political scene was dominated by the Cold War and by a growing civil rights movement. The battle over school desegregation in Arkansas and other areas of the South foreshadowed even larger battles ahead. The Soviet Union and the United States were engaged in a nuclear arms race that by 1961 would give both sides the ability to destroy the world. The clash between communism and capitalism now had global life-and-death consequences. In such dangerous times, many considered Kennedy to be too young and inexperienced to be president. But in his inaugural address on January 20, 1961, Kennedy challenged people at home and abroad to take action on humanity's pressing problems. His famous words to his "fellow Americans" were followed by the quotation on this page.

For Chapter 26 Spanish Resources, visit the Resources Menu. Chapter 26 Resources are available at NGLSync.Cengage.com.

HISTORICAL THINKING QUESTION

What challenges did Americans face during the 1960s?

Jigsaw Activity: Activate Prior Knowledge This activity will help students access prior knowledge and make predictions about the topics covered in Chapter 26. Divide the class into two groups and assign each group a section title. Have students discuss what they know about the topic and what they think they will learn. Ask students to consider the following clues and questions:

Group 1 Section 1 is about the many challenges facing the country on the domestic and international fronts during the early 1960s. What events led up to the election of John F. Kennedy? How did the Cold War influence U.S. and Soviet actions in Berlin, Cuba, and space? Why were New Frontier programs such as the Peace Corps and Alliance for Progress so important?

Group 2 Section 2 is about the social and political changes that transformed the United States. How did the Civil Rights Act and Voting Rights Act affect American society? What programs did President Johnson establish that still exist today? How did the civil rights movement evolve in the later 1960s?

Regroup students so that half of each new group is composed of members from the original two groups. Have students share their prior knowledge and their predictions about their assigned section so that other students can anticipate what might be covered as they read Chapter 26.

INTRODUCE THE READING STRATEGY

DRAW CONCLUSIONS

Explain that drawing conclusions can help a reader make connections and better understand history. Turn to the Chapter Review and preview with students the chart about drawing conclusions. As they read the chapter, encourage them to draw conclusions about the different events, leaders, and policies produced by the challenges of the 1960s.

KEY DATES FOR CHAPTER 26

1960	John F. Kennedy is elected president
1961	Bay of Pigs invasion takes place; Berlin Wall is built
1962	John Glenn is first American to orbit Earth; Cuban Missile Crisis takes place
1963	Kennedy is assassinated; Johnson becomes president
1964	Civil Rights Act passes
1964	Johnson launches War on Poverty, Great Society
1965	Immigration Act and Voting Rights Act pass
1965	Malcolm X is assassinated
1966	Black Panthers are established
1968	Martin Luther King, Jr., is assassinated

INTRODUCE CHAPTER VOCABULARY

KEY VOCABULARY

SECTION 1

ballistic missile	naval quarantine	space race
Cuban Missile Crisis	New Frontier	voter fraud

SECTION 2

affirmative action	*de jure* segregation	landmark legislation
bipartisan	demographic composition	Medicaid
black separatist		Medicare
busing	disenfranchise	miscegenation
de facto segregation	filibuster	

WORD MAPS

Instruct students to complete Word Maps for Key Vocabulary words as they read the chapter. Ask them to write each word in the center oval. Have them look through the chapter to find examples, characteristics, and descriptive words that may be associated with the vocabulary word. At the end of the chapter, ask students what they learned about each word. Model an example for students on the board, using the graphic organizer below.

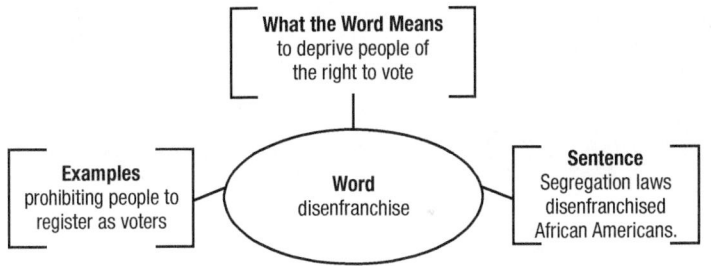

 For instructional support for the online American Story "The Counterculture of the 1960s," go to NGLSync.Cengage.com.

The 1960 Election

John F. Kennedy, Democrat
Electoral Vote: 303 votes, 56.5%
Popular Vote: 34,227,096, 49.7%

Richard M. Nixon, Republican
Electoral Vote: 219 votes, 40.75%
Popular Vote: 34,107,646, 49.6%

Harry Byrd, Democrat*
Electoral Vote: 15 votes, 2.75%
Popular Vote: 0, 0%

*Although he was not formally a candidate, electors in three states cast votes for Democratic Senator Harry Byrd.

KENNEDY'S EARLY CHALLENGES

When you commit to something, you know how important it is to follow through. In 1960, both presidential candidates promised to fight communism aggressively. John Kennedy won the election and had to act quickly on his commitment.

THE 1960 ELECTION

In the previous chapter, you read about John F. Kennedy's fight for the civil rights movement. Before that battle, he had fought hard to become president. In the 1960 election, both presidential candidates were tough, hard-driving campaigners. The Republicans ran Eisenhower's vice president Richard M. Nixon against then-Senator John Kennedy, the Democratic candidate. The men were the first two presidential candidates born in the 20th century, and both had entered Congress in 1946 after serving as junior naval officers during World War II.

But that was where the similarities ended. Nixon, 47, had grown up in modest circumstances. His Quaker parents ran a grocery store in Whittier, California,

near Los Angeles, where Nixon worked as a boy. After his service in the Navy, Nixon's political rise was swift, helped by his strong stance against communism. Nixon then went on to win a U.S. Senate seat in 1950 after accusing his Democratic opponent, Helen Gahagan Douglas, of being "soft on communism." From 1953 to 1960, Nixon served as vice president, where he emerged as a vocal leader of the Republican Party.

John Kennedy, on the other hand, grew up in Boston, a child of wealth and privilege. A Catholic, Kennedy attended the finest private schools and graduated from Harvard University. Though he was elected to Congress in 1946 and to the Senate in 1952, Kennedy did not really stand out as a legislator. Nonetheless,

CRITICAL VIEWING On September 26, 1960, Kennedy and Nixon met in the first-ever televised presidential debate. What details in the photos convey how the two men might have come across to voters watching on television?

he showed a desire to run for higher office. In 1956, he was nearly chosen to be the Democratic vice presidential candidate. Over the next four years, Kennedy traveled the country with his wife, Jacqueline, to build support for a 1960 presidential run. The couple drew crowds wherever they went.

For his running mate, Nixon chose Henry Cabot Lodge, Jr., a respected politician who served in the Senate and as U.S. ambassador to the United Nations. Like Kennedy, Lodge was from Massachusetts, and Nixon hoped his roots in the Northeast would help make the Republican ticket competitive in Kennedy's home region. Meanwhile, Kennedy surprised almost everyone by selecting Senator Lyndon Johnson, a longtime rival, as his running mate. Johnson was a Texan who held liberal political views. Kennedy felt Johnson, as a Texan, could help win votes in the conservative South without losing votes in the more liberal North.

Nixon campaigned largely on Eisenhower's record, reminding Americans that the United States was prosperous and at peace. Kennedy attacked that record without criticizing the popular Eisenhower directly. He portrayed the United States as reacting too slowly to a changing world and promised new leadership "to get the country moving once again." Kennedy had two main obstacles to overcome: a prejudice against Catholics that ran through U.S. history, and his inexperience—he was 43 years old. Kennedy addressed the religion issue in a powerful speech in the fall of 1960 in which he vowed to uphold the constitutional separation of church and state. He dispelled much doubt about his inexperience during a series of debates with Nixon.

For the first time in a presidential election, the debates were televised, which benefited Kennedy.

The first debate had the greatest impact, as more than 80 million Americans watched on television or listened by radio. Though both candidates spoke well, the handsome, well-groomed Kennedy radiated confidence and charm on the TV screen, while Nixon appeared awkward and ill at ease.

Kennedy won the election, but the popular vote was the closest since the presidential election of 1888. A difference of several thousand votes in Texas and Illinois, where there were charges of **voter fraud**, or illegal manipulation of ballots, would have given the election to Nixon.

TROUBLE IN CUBA

President Kennedy charged into office in 1961 with ambitious plans both at home and abroad, and with increased powers in response to the Cold War. He immediately had to focus on a growing foreign policy crisis. The threat of communism had emerged on the small island nation of Cuba, just 90 miles south of Florida. In 1959, a year before Kennedy's election, communist revolutionaries led by **Fidel Castro** had overthrown Fulgencio Batista, the dictator of Cuba. Castro seized control of most of the country's industries and drove out foreign investors. Those investors, many of whom were Americans, lost millions of dollars. Thousands of Cubans who had supported Batista fled to the United States, mostly to Florida. They settled largely around Miami, where they would help shape the culture and politics of the region for years to come.

Castro quickly joined the Soviet bloc, establishing economic and military ties with the Soviet Union. Americans responded with alarm, as they now faced an ally of the Soviet Union located just off their shores. Soviet leader **Nikita Khrushchev** (nih-KEE-tuh KROOsh-chehf) warned the United

---

OBJECTIVE

Learn how John F. Kennedy won the 1960 election and how he used his presidential powers to contain communism during the Cold War.

CRITICAL THINKING SKILLS FOR LESSON 1.1

- Evaluate
- Draw Conclusions
- Interpret Maps
- Make Connections
- Make Predictions
- Analyze Cause and Effect
- Analyze Primary Sources

HISTORICAL THINKING FOR CHAPTER 26

What challenges did Americans face during the 1960s? After a close election, President Kennedy faced immediate tests to his power. Lesson 1.1 discusses the presidential campaign and Cold War crises of 1960.

BACKGROUND FOR THE TEACHER

The Kennedy-Nixon debates fundamentally changed the course of political campaigns—and how candidates were selected. In the first of four televised debates, the sharp contrast between Kennedy's appearance and that of Nixon made a deep impression on viewers. Kennedy seemed calm and confident, while Nixon looked sweaty and sallow. Nixon had recently been hospitalized due to a knee injury and was also recovering from the flu. At the time of the debate, he was tired, frail, and 20 pounds underweight. Those who listened to the debates on radio thought Nixon won, but those who watched on television gave the victory to Kennedy. The debates marked a turning point not only in Kennedy's favor but also in American political campaigns. Since 1960, television has become a powerful factor in American politics. Political parties have had to consider how potential candidates present themselves, what they look like, and how they sound. For better or worse, television has allowed the public to judge candidates on a different basis than before the 1960 election.

INTRODUCE & ENGAGE
CONNECT TO TODAY

Write the term *presidential candidate* in the center of a Word Web. Ask students what qualities they would look for in a candidate for president, given the current problems in the country and in the world. Record their responses on the Word Web. Tell students that in this chapter they will learn about the 1960 presidential race between Richard M. Nixon and John F. Kennedy and the challenges the winner of that election faced.

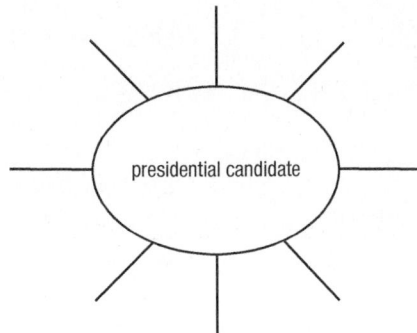

TEACH
GUIDED DISCUSSION

1. **Evaluate** What was the basis for each candidate's claim that he would be the strongest president for the country? *(Nixon based his claim on his political experience, achievements, and strong stand against communism. Kennedy based his claim on his portrayal of the United States as reacting too slowly to world events and on his promise to get the country moving again.)*

2. **Draw Conclusions** What lessons might other presidential candidates have learned from the televised Kennedy-Nixon debates? *(Possible responses: Television is a powerful campaign tool. A candidate's appearance and demeanor are as important as his or her policies and experience. Candidates must learn how to present themselves on television.)*

3. **Make Connections** How did Cuba's change in leadership from Fulgencio Batista to Fidel Castro affect the development of the Cold War? *(After taking over Cuba, Castro established military and economic ties with the Soviet Union, giving the Soviets a base close to U.S. shores. This proximity increased the threat of communism and raised security concerns for the United States.)*

MAKE PREDICTIONS

Direct students' attention to the 1960 election map. Point out that a third candidate, Senator Henry Byrd, won the Democratic vote in Mississippi and gained electoral votes in Oklahoma and Louisiana. **ASK:** What might have happened in the 1960 election if Kennedy had chosen a running mate from the Northeast or Midwest? *(Possible response: Nixon also had a running mate who could appeal to the Northeast and Midwest. If Kennedy had done the same, he might have lost more states in the South to Byrd, which could have cost him the election.)*

DIFFERENTIATE
ENGLISH LANGUAGE LEARNERS

Use Definition Maps Pair students at the **Emerging** level with students at the **Expanding** and **Bridging** levels. Have them create a Definition Map for three words they are struggling with in the lesson. Direct pairs to trade Definition Maps, review them, and then write another sentence using the word. You may also have students discuss how the word helps them understand the main ideas in the lesson.

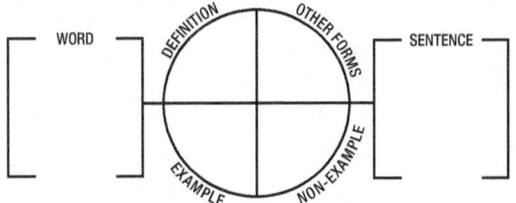

PRE-AP

Analyze a Debate Instruct students to watch and analyze the first Kennedy-Nixon debate, focusing on both the candidates' words and their body language. Then have students conduct online research using a variety of sources to gather information about the impact of this first televised debate and narrow or broaden the research when appropriate. Ask students to present their findings in an oral or written report that describes the many ways voters are persuaded to support a particular candidate. Encourage students to explore how those ways change according to technology, such as television and the Internet. Invite volunteers to share their analytical reports with the class.

See the Chapter Planner for more strategies for differentiation.

CRITICAL VIEWING Possible responses: Kennedy, with his hand outstretched, might have come across as more welcoming and more animated, while Nixon appears more reserved and stiff. Kennedy looks younger and has a thoughtful expression on his face, while Nixon looks older and has a somewhat dazed expression. Kennedy is wearing a darker suit, which gives him a formal, professional demeanor, while Nixon's lighter suit looks less pulled together and impressive.

States not to interfere with Cuba, promising to defend his new ally with nuclear weapons, if necessary. In response, the United States issued a trade embargo against Cuba.

THE BAY OF PIGS

As tensions grew between the United States and Cuba, Kennedy put into action a plan developed by the Eisenhower administration to overthrow Castro's government. The covert, or secret, plan called for anti-Castro exiles, trained and equipped by the CIA, to invade Cuba and trigger an anticommunist revolution. On April 17, 1961, 1,500 exiles waded ashore at the **Bay of Pigs**, on Cuba's southern coast. The attack fell apart almost immediately. The landing site contained sharp coral reefs and swampy terrain, making it hard to unload supplies and move out from the beaches. In addition, Cuban intelligence already knew of the plan from gossip among Cuban exiles in Miami. Cuban forces fired on the invaders as they came ashore. More than 100 of the anti-Castro exiles were killed, and most of the rest were captured.

The invasion was a humiliating defeat for the United States. American aggression in the region angered Cubans and other Latin Americans and drove Castro even closer to the Soviet Union. After reviewing the events with his advisors, Kennedy took a walk on the White House lawn. It was "the first time in my life," a friend recalled, "that I ever saw tears come to his eyes." Nonetheless, the president continued trying to overthrow Castro. During his administration, he approved a top-secret program, code-named Operation Mongoose, intended to topple the Cuban government and assassinate its leaders. U.S. officials also devised plans to destroy Cuba's vital sugar crop and even send a box of exploding cigars to Castro. The plans never materialized. In hindsight, one Kennedy aide called the overall effort against Cuba "an expensive and embarrassing failure."

THE BERLIN WALL

Shortly after the Bay of Pigs, Kennedy faced another communist challenge, this time in Europe. As you have read, following World War II, Germany was divided into democratic West Germany and communist East Germany. Berlin, the capital of Germany and its largest city, was located entirely within East Germany and itself was divided into three Western-occupied zones that made up West Berlin, and East Berlin, a Soviet-occupied zone. By the early 1960s, the division of Berlin was proving an embarrassment to Khrushchev. West Berlin thrived as a model of democracy and capitalism, while East

Berlin was communist. Each day, more than 1,000 refugees from East Berlin poured into West Berlin seeking a better life. As a result, East Germany was losing many skilled workers to the West.

In August 1961, East German officials constructed a wall of concrete that encircled West Berlin. Intended to stop the migration from East Berlin and from surrounding East Germany to West Berlin, the **Berlin Wall** stretched 27 miles and divided the city in two. It stopped the flow of refugees across the border and for decades would stand as a symbol of the division between the **Western bloc** and the **Soviet bloc** nations of Europe. The presence of the wall heightened the anxiety of the Cold War.

Kennedy chose not to challenge the building of the Berlin Wall, but he did make a historic visit to the site in June 1963. Thousands of West Berliners greeted him with flowers and confetti. In a brief speech to a crowd of 120,000 people, Kennedy praised the city and declared his solidarity with its citizens. "Today," he declared, "Ich bin ein Berliner (I am a Berliner)!"

HISTORICAL THINKING

1. **READING CHECK** Why did the United States launch the Bay of Pigs invasion? Why did the mission fail?

2. **EVALUATE** Using text evidence, explain how you think historical events influenced Kennedy's decision not to challenge the building of the Berlin Wall.

3. **DRAW CONCLUSIONS** What did the Berlin Wall seem to say about life under communism?

4. **INTERPRET MAPS** Examine the 1960 election map. Why would Nixon have won the election if he had won Illinois and Texas?

CRITICAL VIEWING Built around 1790, the Brandenburg Gate served as a monument at an entry point to the city of Berlin. When Berlin was divided, the gate was on the border, barely within East Berlin, as shown in the top photo from around 1965. In the 1981 photo below, a West Berlin policeman patrols in front of a sign that reads, "Caution: You are leaving West Berlin." What do the photos reveal about people's feelings about the division of East and West Berlin?

BUILD BACKGROUND

THE AMERICAN-CUBAN RELATIONSHIP

Fidel Castro did not start out as a communist ruler in Cuba. At first, he allowed many U.S. companies, including oil refineries and sugar plantations, to remain in American hands. However, when Castro signed an oil deal with the Soviets, U.S. refineries in Cuba refused to process the oil. In response, Castro seized their operations, expelled many company personnel, and eventually declared himself as a communist ally of the Soviet Union. The United States' actions against Cuba rallied the Cubans to support Castro. Ironically, the failed actions of the United States ensured that Castro would remain in power as a Soviet ally for decades.

WHY THE WEST STOOD BY

West Berliners were outraged by the failure of the West to stop construction of the Berlin Wall. Why didn't the United States and its allies simply knock the wall down? The complex Cold War politics of the 1950s and 1960s may have made military intervention impossible. The Soviets had massed their troops near Berlin, and the mere threat of armed conflict between the Soviet bloc and Western allies raised the specter of nuclear war. No one wanted to fire the first shot that might set off World War III. The West also reasoned that if people kept leaving East Germany, that nation might become unstable, threatening the fragile status quo in Europe. Although President Kennedy and Nikita Khrushchev traded threats and warnings about the wall, Khrushchev rightly guessed the West would not stop its construction.

TEACH

GUIDED DISCUSSION

4. Evaluate How did historical events impact Kennedy's powers of the presidency during his first months in office? *(Possible response: Kennedy initially diminished the powers of the presidency; he tried to be a strong civilian and military leader but failed to overthrow Castro or prevent construction of the Berlin Wall.)*

5. Analyze Cause and Effect What effect might the events of 1960 have had on the political development of the Cold War between the Soviet Union and the United States? *(Possible response: From Castro's leadership in Cuba to the Berlin Wall, the events of 1960 caused an increase in tensions between the Soviet Union and the United States. Khrushchev and the Soviet Union appeared stronger and more aggressive.)*

ANALYZE PRIMARY SOURCES

Direct students' attention to the Primary Source feature. **ASK:** What effect does Kennedy achieve in his speech by repeating the phrase "Let them come to Berlin" in English and finally in German? *(Possible response: The effect is to underscore the fact that coming to Berlin would dispel any doubts about the harsh realities of communism versus the success of democracy.)*

ACTIVE OPTIONS

Active History: Analyze Cold War Berlin Extend the lesson by using either the PDF or Whiteboard version of the activity. These activities take a deeper look at a topic from, or related to, the lesson. Explore the activities as a class, turn them into group assignments, or even assign them individually.

NG Learning Framework: Evaluate Historic Decisions

SKILL Communication

KNOWLEDGE Our Human Story

West Berliners felt abandoned by the West, and particularly the United States, when the Soviets began building the Berlin Wall. Have students investigate the Cold War context behind the decision made by the United States, France, and Great Britain not to stop the Soviets. Encourage students to put themselves in the position of Kennedy and other Western leaders as they do their research. Ask students to share their work with the class, explaining the context and political bases for the decision about the Berlin Wall.

HISTORICAL THINKING

ANSWERS

1. The United States wanted to trigger an uprising among the Cuban people and overthrow Castro. The invasion force was ill prepared, and Castro knew about the invasion in advance.

2. Kennedy had suffered "a humiliating defeat" in the Bay of Pigs and may not have wanted to test his power against the Soviet Union so soon afterward.

3. The wall seemed to say that life under communism was such an economic and political failure that people had to be forced to stay in East Germany.

4. Victories in Illinois and Texas would have given Nixon enough electoral votes to win.

CRITICAL VIEWING Possible responses: The division is heightened by the fact that the wall is on the border of both East and West Germany, at the point of the Brandenburg Gate. The area around the wall is bleak and empty; the signs, streetlights, and border guards make it clear you are leaving one area for another. The top photo shows there are two walls encircling the Brandenburg Gate area, possibly to make escape from East Berlin even more difficult.

KENNEDY EMBRACES PROGRESS

"The Best and the Brightest" was the nickname some observers gave to John Fitzgerald Kennedy's administration. Young, well-educated, and full of new ideas, his team was eager to make its mark and continue moving the nation forward.

THE NEW FRONTIER

Kennedy's ambitious presidential agenda became known as the **New Frontier**, a reference to a new decade and new opportunities awaiting the nation. Kennedy believed that creative problem solving could help the United States win friends overseas, resolve economic challenges at home and abroad, and achieve scientific and technological feats only imagined by others.

Kennedy's administration shared the president's optimism and confidence in problem solving. The new secretary of state, Dean Rusk, came from the Rockefeller Foundation, while the new defense secretary, Robert McNamara, had resigned as president of the Ford Motor Company so he could help restructure the nation's armed forces. You might recall that Kennedy chose his younger brother Robert Kennedy to serve as his attorney general.

SUCCESS AND SETBACK

A key domestic priority for Kennedy and his team was re-energizing the U.S. economy. Economic growth in the Eisenhower years had been steady but increasingly slow. Real wages for an average family rose a remarkable 20 percent in the 1950s. However, a series of recessions toward the end of Eisenhower's second term prompted a drop in factory production and a rise in unemployment. By the time Kennedy took office, more Americans were out of work than at any other time since the end of World War II. In 1961, Kennedy devised an economic plan that called for a major tax cut for consumers and businesses. He hoped the tax cut would boost the economy by encouraging both individuals and businesses to spend more. The plan successfully achieved low unemployment, stable prices, and

steady growth. He pushed through Congress increases in various Social Security benefits, including an increase in the minimum monthly retirement benefit from $33 to $40. Kennedy also asked for and received a raise in the minimum wage, from $1 to $1.25 an hour.

Congress did not support all of Kennedy's plans, however. It defeated a number of the president's proposals, including an effort to increase education spending for school construction and higher teacher salaries. For the most part, Kennedy moved cautiously in pushing his domestic agenda, including the push for civil rights, as you have read. Since he had won the election by a slim margin, he lacked the widespread popularity that might have enabled him to do more.

In addition, Republicans and conservative southern Democrats in Congress were largely opposed to expanding the power and reach of the federal government. Kennedy understood this, so he picked his battles carefully and only pushed on those proposals he thought were most critical. One of them was a civil rights bill designed to strengthen the weak bills that had passed in 1957 and 1960. The new bill would eventually pass and would become an important step toward achieving equal rights for all.

STRENGTHENING FRIENDSHIPS

President Kennedy bypassed Congress to implement one of his most famous and lasting programs. On March 1, 1961, Kennedy issued an executive order, or a legally binding directive from a president, to create the **Peace Corps** and named R. Sargent Shriver, the husband of Kennedy's sister Eunice, as its director. The first group of 51 Peace Corps volunteers arrived

A GLOBAL PERSPECTIVE The Peace Corps proved to be one of Kennedy's most successful and long-lasting endeavors. By 2016, the Peace Corps had sent more than 220,000 volunteers to 140 nations throughout the world. In Cambodia in 2014, a volunteer helps villagers develop safe and nutritious food practices, including managing gardens and preparing healthy meals.

in Accra, the capital of the African nation of Ghana, in August 1961, to serve as teachers. Within 6 years, the Peace Corps sent thousands of American volunteers to 55 underdeveloped nations, or nations with a low standard of living compared with other nations, to provide educational and technical assistance.

With a tiny budget, the Peace Corps became one of Kennedy's great triumphs, showcasing American idealism and know-how throughout the world. A geopolitical consequence of the Cold War, American leaders viewed the Peace Corps as not only a humanitarian program, but also a vital tool in the fight against communism. By spreading American goodwill and improving living conditions in underdeveloped nations, the president and others hoped the Peace Corps would help prevent countries from embracing communism.

With this same goal in mind—winning more allies and undermining communism—the Kennedy administration worked to strengthen its Latin American policy. During the 1940s and 1950s, the United States had focused primarily on assisting Europe and confronting the Soviet Union, resulting in a weakening of relationships with Latin American countries. After seeing Cuba turn communist, however, American leaders moved to improve relations with the larger Latin American world. In 1961, Kennedy persuaded Congress

---

PLAN: 4-PAGE LESSON

OBJECTIVE

Learn about President Kennedy's achievements and setbacks as he set his New Frontier agenda.

CRITICAL THINKING SKILLS FOR LESSON 1.2

- Draw Conclusions
- Form and Support Opinions
- Make Connections
- Summarize
- Analyze Cause and Effect
- Analyze Primary Sources
- Evaluate
- Interpret Time Lines

HISTORICAL THINKING FOR CHAPTER 26

What challenges did Americans face during the 1960s? By the time Kennedy took office, the economy had slowed down and there was a rise in unemployment. Kennedy acted quickly to implement his agenda, known as the New Frontier. Lesson 1.2 discusses the push toward progress through Kennedy's domestic and foreign programs.

BACKGROUND FOR THE TEACHER

The highly successful Peace Corps had a rocky beginning. Sergeant Shriver had doubts that the program would work. But a tour of eight nations requesting U.S. aid convinced him otherwise. During the Cold War and Vietnam War, the Peace Corps drew criticism at home and abroad. At home, it was criticized as an "escape" for draft dodgers. Overseas, volunteers were often accused of being CIA spies, despite a strict separation between the two agencies. Yet 50 years later, 82 percent of the program's alumni say their service helped people have a better understanding of the United States. Today, the Peace Corps allows people to choose the country in which they will serve, sharply increasing the number of applicants.

HISTORY NOTEBOOK

Encourage students to complete the American Gallery page for Chapter 26 in their History Notebooks as they read.

INTRODUCE & ENGAGE

TRACK GOALS AND OUTCOMES

Explain to students that when Kennedy took office, he had an agenda that included scientific and technological goals in order to keep moving the nation forward. Discuss with students the current state of the nation and the issues they think need to be addressed. Ask students to consider the top three goals they think should be the focus for the United States today. Encourage students with different viewpoints to explain their opinion. As students read the lesson, suggest that they use a Goal-and-Outcome Chart to record the goals and outcomes of Kennedy's agenda. At the end of the lesson, provide time for students to share their charts.

Goals	Obstacles	Outcome

Summary

TEACH

GUIDED DISCUSSION

1. **Summarize** How did Kennedy use his presidential power to fulfill his promise to "get the country moving again"? *(Possible response: He persuaded Congress to accept his tax cuts and increases in Social Security and the minimum wage. This stimulated the economy, reduced unemployment, and stabilized prices. He also used the power of an executive order to create the Peace Corps.)*

2. **Analyze Cause and Effect** How might Kennedy's international goals, such as the Peace Corps program, have affected U.S. efforts to contain the political development of communism? *(Possible response: Kennedy hoped that promoting American ideals abroad and winning more allies in Latin America would undermine and contain communism, preventing more "Cubas.")*

3. **Analyze Primary Sources** What message was Kennedy conveying when he said that he sought to help the poor "not because the communists may be doing it, not because we seek their votes, but because it is right"? *(Possible response: He was conveying that he placed helping the poor above his concerns about the Cold War and above politics. Instead, it was "right"; that is, a matter of ethics and morality.)*

A GLOBAL PERSPECTIVE

Direct students' attention to the photograph of the Peace Corps volunteer and caption. **ASK:** How does the activity in the photo appear to carry out Kennedy's original goals for the Peace Corps? *(The volunteer appears to be sharing her expertise and helping to prepare a meal with the community, thus creating goodwill for the United States.)* **ASK:** What impression might the children have of this Peace Corps volunteer? *(Possible response: They probably have a favorable impression not only because of the volunteer's skills but also because they see a teacher from an important country who looks a lot like them.)* Discuss other volunteer programs that help people abroad, such as Habitat for Humanity or Heifer International. Ask students what they think motivates people to volunteer for these types of programs and whether such programs today reflect Kennedy's original goals.

DIFFERENTIATE

ENGLISH LANGUAGE LEARNERS

Create a Word Web Pair students at the **Emerging** and **Expanding** levels with students at the **Bridging** level. Tell students to take turns reading paragraphs of the lesson, noting any economic terms related to Kennedy's domestic agenda. Ask them to write those terms on the spokes of a Word Web. Then have pairs trade and compare clusters, looking up unfamiliar words in a dictionary. Final clusters may include: wages, recessions, unemployment, tax cut, stable prices, steady growth, retirement benefit, and minimum wage.

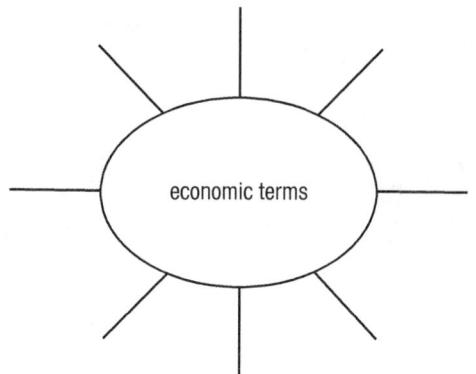

economic terms

PRE-AP

Write a Comparison-Contrast Essay Instruct students to conduct online research to learn how the arms race and space race each played an important role in the Cold War and how they related to one another. Encourage students to use a Venn diagram to keep track of the similarities and differences between the arms race and the space race. Then have them write a comparison-contrast essay. Call on volunteers to share their essays with the class.

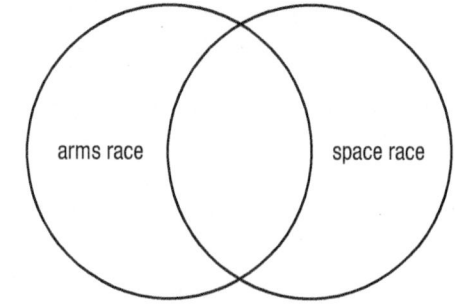

arms race   space race

With John Glenn standing beside him, President Kennedy (left) looks inside *Friendship 7* in 1962, after Glenn's historic mission to orbit the earth.

to fund the **Alliance for Progress**, an aid program to improve education, health, and economic conditions in Latin America. During its first year alone, the program provided more than $1 billion in aid to various countries. The effort achieved mixed results. Some corrupt leaders misspent the money, and communism ultimately gained a foothold in some Latin American countries. In the end, however, houses, schools, electrical grids, roads, and hospitals were built, and children fed.

THE SPACE RACE

One of Kennedy's boldest proposals involved expansion of the space program. Shortly after taking office, the president declared the United States would put a man on the moon before the end of the decade, and he persuaded Congress to allocate between $7 billion and $9 billion for space research.

As with many of his other initiatives, the Cold War drove Kennedy's push for technological development in space travel. In addition to their arms race, the United States and Soviet Union engaged in a **space race**, or the Cold War rivalry between the United States and the Soviet Union to see who would dominate in its ability to travel in and collect data from space.

The competition had begun in the late 1950s, after the Soviets launched the first satellite, *Sputnik 1*, and President Eisenhower responded with the creation of NASA to advance space exploration. In 1959, NASA

carefully selected seven men for the first class of American astronauts, or space travelers. These astronauts trained for nearly two years as part of Project Mercury. The scientists' primary goal for Project Mercury was to send a manned spacecraft into orbit around the earth. Doing so naturally entailed the astronauts returning to Earth unharmed, with their spacecraft intact. While in space and afterward, scientists closely monitored the physical effects of space travel on the astronauts' bodies, gathering data to improve safety and technology for future launches.

By the time Kennedy took office, both countries were making bold advances into space—and captivating the world. In April 1961, Soviet cosmonaut—the Russian term for *astronaut*—Yuri Gagarin orbited Earth in less than two hours. A month later, American Alan Shepard rocketed 300 miles from Cape Canaveral into space. In February 1962, American John Glenn achieved the historic feat of orbiting Earth three times aboard *Friendship 7* before splashing down in the Caribbean Sea. Glenn became a national hero, celebrated with ticker-tape parades and a televised address before a joint session of Congress.

Throughout the 1960s, astronauts were cheered as heroes and celebrities as the media closely followed space-race developments. The space race would have a huge impact on the world, producing dramatic scientific and technological advances with far-reaching applications in a surprisingly short amount of time.

HISTORICAL THINKING

1. **READING CHECK** What important roles did the Peace Corps serve in the context of the Cold War?

2. **DRAW CONCLUSIONS** Why might some people consider the Alliance for Progress a failure despite its successes?

3. **FORM AND SUPPORT OPINIONS** How was Kennedy both bold and cautious in promoting his presidential agenda? Support your opinion with evidence from the text.

4. **MAKE CONNECTIONS** What effects did the space race have on society and the economy?

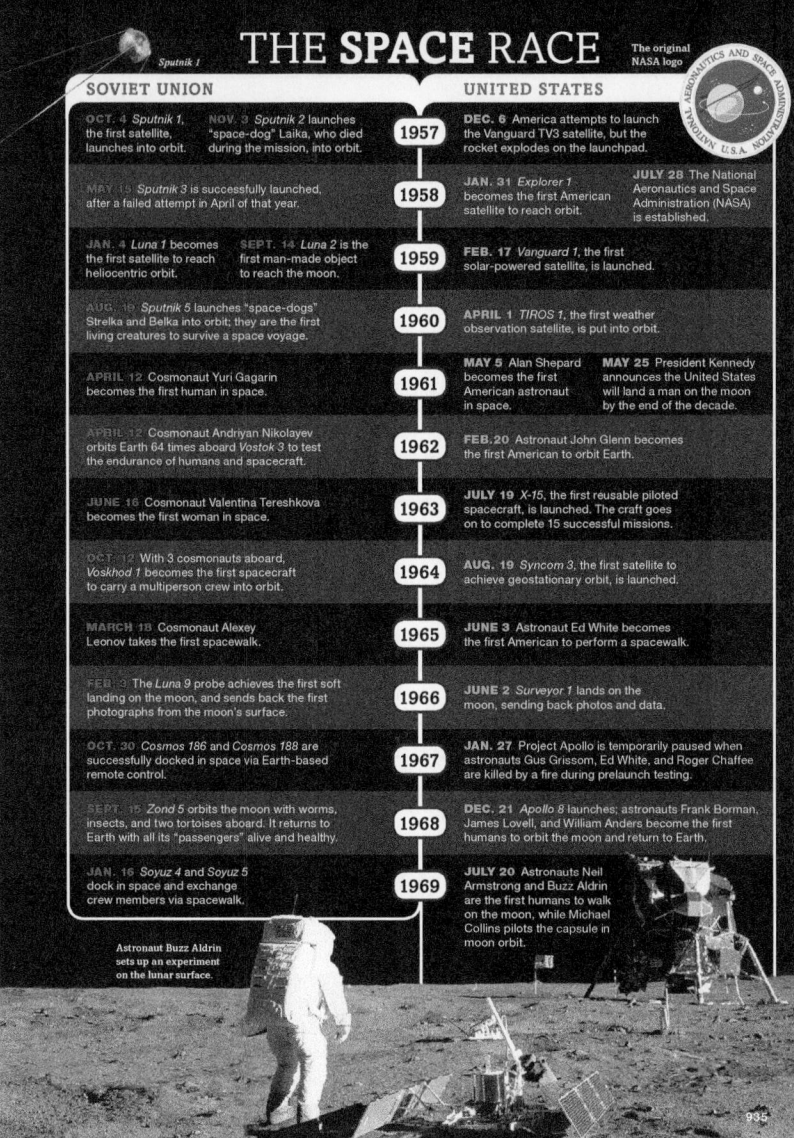

THE **SPACE** RACE

Sputnik 1

The original NASA logo

SOVIET UNION		UNITED STATES	
OCT. 4 *Sputnik 1*, the first satellite, launches into orbit.	**NOV. 3** *Sputnik 2* launches "space-dog" Laika, who died during the mission, into orbit.	**1957**	**DEC. 6** America attempts to launch the Vanguard TV3 satellite, but the rocket explodes on the launchpad.
MAY 15 *Sputnik 3* is successfully launched, after a failed attempt in April of that year.		**1958**	**JAN. 31** *Explorer 1* becomes the first American satellite to reach orbit. **JULY 28** The National Aeronautics and Space Administration (NASA) is established.
JAN. 4 *Luna 1* becomes the first satellite to reach heliocentric orbit.	**SEPT. 14** *Luna 2* is the first man-made object to reach the moon.	**1959**	**FEB. 17** *Vanguard 1*, the first solar-powered satellite, is launched.
AUG. 19 *Sputnik 5* launches "space-dogs" Strelka and Belka into orbit; they are the first living creatures to survive a space voyage.		**1960**	**APRIL 1** *TIROS 1*, the first weather observation satellite, is put into orbit.
APRIL 12 Cosmonaut Yuri Gagarin becomes the first human in space.		**1961**	**MAY 5** Alan Shepard becomes the first American astronaut in space. **MAY 25** President Kennedy announces the United States will land a man on the moon by the end of the decade.
APRIL 12 Cosmonaut Andriyan Nikolayev orbits Earth 64 times aboard *Vostok 3* to test the endurance of humans and spacecraft.		**1962**	**FEB. 20** Astronaut John Glenn becomes the first American to orbit Earth.
JUNE 16 Cosmonaut Valentina Tereshkova becomes the first woman in space.		**1963**	**JULY 19** *X-15*, the first reusable piloted spacecraft, is launched. The craft goes on to complete 15 successful missions.
OCT. 12 With 3 cosmonauts aboard, *Voskhod 1* becomes the first spacecraft to carry a multiperson crew into orbit.		**1964**	**AUG. 19** *Syncom 3*, the first satellite to achieve geostationary orbit, is launched.
MARCH 18 Cosmonaut Alexey Leonov takes the first spacewalk.		**1965**	**JUNE 3** Astronaut Ed White becomes the first American to perform a spacewalk.
FEB. 3 The *Luna 9* probe achieves the first soft landing on the moon, and sends back the first photographs from the moon's surface.		**1966**	**JUNE 2** *Surveyor 1* lands on the moon, sending back photos and data.
OCT. 30 *Cosmos 186* and *Cosmos 188* are successfully docked in space via Earth-based remote control.		**1967**	**JAN. 27** Project Apollo is temporarily paused when astronauts Gus Grissom, Ed White, and Roger Chaffee are killed by a fire during prelaunch testing.
SEPT. 15 *Zond 5* orbits the moon with worms, insects, and two tortoises aboard. It returns to Earth with all its "passengers" alive and healthy.		**1968**	**DEC. 21** *Apollo 8* launches; astronauts Frank Borman, James Lovell, and William Anders become the first humans to orbit the moon and return to Earth.
JAN. 16 *Soyuz 4* and *Soyuz 5* dock in space and exchange crew members via spacewalk.		**1969**	**JULY 20** Astronauts Neil Armstrong and Buzz Aldrin are the first humans to walk on the moon, while Michael Collins pilots the capsule in moon orbit.

Astronaut Buzz Aldrin sets up an experiment on the lunar surface.

935

BUILD BACKGROUND

SPACE RACE TECHNOLOGY

Although driven by Cold War politics and fear of nuclear war, the space race ended up providing almost 2,000 technological spin-offs that changed the way we live. A few of the more notable ones include the following:

- Satellite television was created based on NASA's need to communicate with astronauts in space.

- The laptop computer came from a need to have a compact way for astronauts to perform navigation and other calculations within the cramped space capsules.

- The cordless portable vacuum was a by-product of a battery-powered drill that NASA asked a power tool manufacturer to develop.

- The joystick, well known to gamers, began its life as a steering mechanism for the Apollo lunar rover, or moon buggy.

- Telemedicine equipment was developed to monitor the astronauts' health remotely when they were in space.

- Virtual reality (VR) was originally developed to provide simulations to train astronauts for a moon landing.

Since 1958, every dollar spent on space exploration has returned $8 to $10 in economic benefits.

TEACH

GUIDED DISCUSSION

4. Draw Conclusions How did Kennedy's New Frontier affect the rate of technological and social change in the early 1960s? *(Possible response: His programs accelerated the pace of change through diplomatic and scientific programs that harnessed American ingenuity and resources.)*

5. Evaluate Why did the space race become an important part of the Cold War between the United States and the Soviet Union? *(Possible response: Once the Soviets began to develop long-range, high-altitude rockets and put satellites in space, the United States couldn't allow the Soviets to maintain their technological advantage. Such rockets or satellites could be used to threaten U.S. security and had to be countered by the United States developing its own.)*

INTERPRET TIME LINES

Have students study the space race time line, comparing the achievements of the Soviet Union and the United States. **ASK:** At what point did the United States take the lead in the space race? *(Possible response: With Apollo 8 in December 1968, the United States took the lead in the space race with a successful three-man orbital mission to the moon and back. In July 1969, the historic moon landing solidified the U.S. lead and fulfilled President Kennedy's promise to land a man on the moon by the end of the decade.)*

ACTIVE OPTIONS

AMERICAN GALLERY ONLINE **The Space Race** Invite students to explore the American Gallery. Have them select one of the images and do additional research to learn more about it. Ask questions that will inspire additional inquiry about the chosen gallery image, such as: What is this? What is it designed to do? Why was it created? What is it made of? Why does it belong in this chapter? What else would you like to know about it?

NG Learning Framework: Explore the New Frontier

ATTITUDE Curiosity

KNOWLEDGE Our Human Story

Discuss with students the meaning of the word *frontier* and why Kennedy might have used the term in reference to his ambitious presidential agenda. Then instruct groups of students to each choose one of Kennedy's "frontiers," such as space, international relations, domestic programs, and so on. Ask groups to list the main achievements accomplished in their frontier area, citing examples from the text or from other sources. Then have group members discuss the connections they can see between their frontier area and larger social, economic, and political developments of the 1960s.

HISTORICAL THINKING

ANSWERS

1. It provided humanitarian assistance and helped fight communism by promoting American goodwill and values. The work done by Peace Corps volunteers gave people a good impression of the United States.

2. Some corrupt Latin American leaders misspent the money meant to aid their countries. In addition, communism gained a foothold in several Latin American countries despite U.S. aid.

3. Kennedy pushed boldly in areas such as space exploration, global assistance, and economic stimulus incentives but moved cautiously on legislation dealing with civil rights and spending on education. Without a strong voter mandate, he had to carefully choose the battles he could fight.

4. At first, Americans felt that the Soviets were winning the space race, but as NASA began to achieve success, the race became a source of national pride and worldwide attention. It made interest in outer space a permanent feature of U.S. culture. In addition, many of the technological innovations turned out to have commercial applications, which was a boon to the economy.

Cuban Missile Crisis, 1962

Range of medium-range ballistic missiles (1,000 miles)
Range of intermediate-range ballistic missiles (2,000 miles)
◆ Soviet missile sites
---- U.S. naval blockade
← Approaching Soviet ships

THE CUBAN MISSILE CRISIS

Do you remember a time when you were involved in a compromise—when each side gave up something to avoid a fight or some other negative outcome? In 1962, the United States and the Soviet Union engaged in a tense standoff, and only a compromise would be able to save the world from an impending nuclear war.

THE MISSILES OF OCTOBER

By 1962, Americans were in good spirits. A growing economy and Kennedy's optimism were inspiring the nation. But ongoing Cold War tensions between the United States and the Soviet Union continued to be a threat. In October 1962, those tensions erupted and would put the world at the brink of nuclear war.

The trouble began with rumors, confirmed by American U-2 spy plane photos, that the Soviets were establishing intermediate-range **ballistic missiles**, or rocket-propelled, self-guiding nuclear weapons, in Cuba. In the eyes of Cuban leader Fidel Castro, this was simply a means of defending his nation. As a communist country in the middle of the Western Hemisphere, Cuba felt increasingly isolated and under siege. The Kennedy administration had imposed an economic embargo on Cuba and arranged for Cuba's expulsion from the **Organization of American States (OAS)**, an alliance of Western Hemisphere nations established in 1948, whose purpose is to keep peace among the nations of North and South America. What's more, the United States had already attacked Cuba at the Bay of Pigs in early 1961. Whatever his reasons, Castro was stockpiling nuclear weapons capable of reaching dozens of American cities. U.S. leaders would not stand for such a threat.

A TENSE STANDOFF

Kennedy demanded the Soviets remove the missiles in Cuba. In addition, the president ordered a **naval quarantine**, or blockade of ports, of Cuba to stop the Soviets from delivering more missiles. On October 22, 1962, the president went on television to reassure an increasingly tense nation. The entire world watched anxiously as Soviet ships headed

toward Cuba and the U.S. warships enforcing the quarantine. On October 26, Kennedy received a note from Soviet leader Nikita Khrushchev suggesting a settlement. "There is no intention to . . . doom the world to the catastrophe of thermonuclear war," he wrote. "Let us take measures to untie [the] knot."

Khrushchev promised to remove his missiles if the United States pledged never to invade Cuba. Before Kennedy could respond, he received a second note, demanding the United States also remove its missiles on the Soviet border with Turkey. Attorney General Robert Kennedy advised his brother to respond to the first note and ignore the second. On October 27, the president vowed not to invade Cuba if the Soviets removed the missiles. In private, Robert Kennedy assured the Soviets the United States would remove its missiles from Turkey in the near future.

On October 28, Khrushchev accepted the deal. In the end, he had miscalculated the stern American response to the placement of offensive missiles so close to U.S. shores. In fact, many of the president's advisors had recommended a military strike, but Kennedy rejected their advice. Secretary of State Dean Rusk summed up the feelings of everyone in the Kennedy administration: "We [were] eyeball to eyeball, and I think the other fellow just blinked." The **Cuban Missile Crisis**, as it came to be known, had ended, but it left a deep impression. For those two weeks, the world had seemed headed for nuclear war and the real possibility of annihilation for both sides.

PEACEFUL RESOLUTION

Throughout the 1950s, the U.S. government developed a civil defense system to keep American

A year before the Cuban Missile Crisis, President Kennedy urged Americans to build fallout shelters for their homes. Promotional photos show the features of one model available commercially in 1955.

937

OBJECTIVE

Understand the geopolitical consequences of the Cuban Missile Crisis and the effects of John F. Kennedy's assassination.

CRITICAL THINKING SKILLS FOR LESSON 1.3

- Determine Chronology
- Summarize
- Interpret Maps
- Make Connections
- Analyze Cause and Effect
- Analyze Language Use

HISTORICAL THINKING FOR CHAPTER 26

What challenges did Americans face during the 1960s? Cold War tensions between the United States and the Soviet Union continued in the 1960s, with the threat of nuclear war hanging in the balance. Lesson 1.3 explains how that tension developed into the Cuban Missile Crisis and describes the effects of Kennedy's assassination.

BACKGROUND FOR THE TEACHER

Unknown to the country, President Kennedy tape-recorded all White House discussions during the Cuban Missile Crisis. The tapes reveal that Kennedy's fears of nuclear war were divided between Cuba and the tense situation in West Berlin. The missiles in Cuba, Kennedy believed, were preliminary to an assault on West Berlin. Nikita Khrushchev had been trying for a decade to make the entire city part of East Germany. As a result, Kennedy faced a terrible dilemma. If the Soviets moved against Berlin, the only way to protect West Berliners would be to launch a nuclear strike against the Soviet Union, which would retaliate. Both nations had enough nuclear warheads to destroy each other several times over. While the world's attention was riveted on the Soviet ships heading for Cuba, Kennedy was putting the military on alert to strike the Soviet Union if troops moved toward West Berlin. Fortunately, Khrushchev backed down, and Kennedy never had to make that terrible decision.

INTRODUCE & ENGAGE

DISCUSS CONFRONTATION AND COMPROMISE

Ask students to recall a time from their own lives or from history when there was a serious argument or confrontation that ended in a compromise. Have them discuss the issues that were at stake and then use a Sequence Chart to diagram the steps that led to a compromise, thus resolving the situation. Tell students that Lesson 1.3 discusses a U.S.-Soviet confrontation that brought the world to the brink of nuclear war until a compromise allowed both countries to step back.

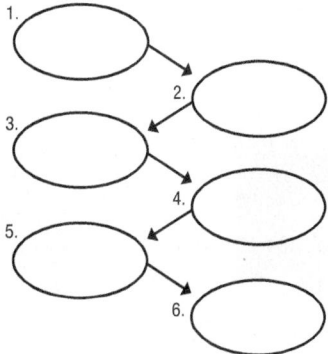

TEACH

GUIDED DISCUSSION

1. **Analyze Cause and Effect** What complex causes led to Fidel Castro's decision to build up a supply of nuclear weapons? *(While the exact reasons are unknown, Castro may have wanted to protect his isolated country from attack since the United States had attacked Cuba once before.)*

2. **Summarize** What compromises did Kennedy and Khrushchev make to resolve the Cuban Missile Crisis, and how did relations between the United States and the Soviet Union change? *(Possible response: Khrushchev agreed to remove the missiles from Cuba. Kennedy agreed never to invade Cuba and privately promised to remove U.S. missiles from Turkey in the near future. Relations improved as the two countries set up a hotline and later signed a treaty agreeing to limit the development of nuclear weapons.)*

3. **Make Connections** In what ways did U.S. foreign policy regarding the Soviets affect U.S. domestic policy? *(Conflicts with the Soviets and the threat of nuclear war led the federal government to create a bomb shelter program and civil defense system. Although bomb shelters are no longer used, the civil defense system is still in use to alert people during natural disasters.)*

ANALYZE LANGUAGE USE

Direct students' attention to Secretary of State Dean Rusk's quotation and point out that the phrase "eyeball to eyeball" is an idiom. **ASK:** What did Rusk mean by his statement? *(He meant that it was as if two people were in a standoff face-to-face with each other to see who would blink first. In this case, the Soviets blinked first, meaning they stepped down from the standoff.)* **ASK:** What does his statement convey about the attitude or feelings of the Kennedy administration? *(Leaders in the administration held strong but they were nervous, waiting to see what would happen.)*

DIFFERENTIATE

INCLUSION

Analyze a Map Pair students who are strong readers with students who have reading or perception issues. Instruct pairs to study the information presented in the Cuban Missile Crisis map. Students should first place a finger on Cuba and then count the number of diamonds dotting the island. Then they should use their fingers to trace the perimeter of the smaller, blue-tinted area and move on to trace the larger, orange-tinted area. Make sure students study the map legend and are able to explain the significance of the diamonds and the tinted areas. You may want to ask students to imagine what might have happened in their state if the crisis had not been averted.

GIFTED & TALENTED

Create an Annotated Time Line Instruct students to use the Russian archives on the Library of Congress website, as well as other print and online sources, to learn more about communications and actions during the Cuban Missile Crisis. Encourage students to find formal public communications and private back-channel ones. Then tell students to create an annotated time line of the most important events, including private communications between Khrushchev and the pope and between Soviet ambassador Anatoly Dobrynin and Robert Kennedy. Have students compare time lines and discuss the risks and benefits of secret back-channel communications.

See the Chapter Planner for more strategies for differentiation.

CRITICAL VIEWING Attorney General Robert Kennedy was one of the closest advisors to his brother, President John F. Kennedy. Here the two meet in the Oval Office of the White House in October 1962, during the Cuban Missile Crisis. What feelings are conveyed by the two men?

THE SECOND VATICAN COUNCIL

On October 11, 1962, 10 days before President Kennedy went on television to explain to the nation the crisis around the presence of Soviet missiles in Cuba, Pope John XXIII (the 23rd) announced the principles of the Second Vatican Council in Rome. The Council called for a new openness in the Catholic Church and for the Church to take a role in promoting peace and social justice worldwide.

As news of the crisis became known, a priest from the Vatican attending a conference on peace in Massachusetts suggested asking the pope to intervene. The White House approved the suggestion, and the pope broadcast a message on Vatican radio begging the two leaders to consider all of humanity and find a peaceful solution to the crisis.

The pope also sent a message personally to Khrushchev asking him to be "the man of peace." Khrushchev agreed to do so and ordered the missiles withdrawn. The Soviet leader was reported to say the pope's message was the only "gleam of hope" in the crisis. In 1963, partly in response to the crisis now past, the pope issued a statement calling for "Peace on Earth," reinforcing that principle of what came to be called Vatican II (2).

leaders and as many American civilians as possible safe in case of nuclear war. Civil defense plans were communicated throughout the nation, through signs in public places and a broadcast communications network that was established to keep people informed should an attack occur. Plans to build large-scale public shelters, however, were put forth and rejected. In their place were signs in public buildings indicating evacuation areas.

But the Cuban Missile Crisis frightened U.S. and Soviet leaders into changing their relationship from brinkmanship to one in which they would work together to manage tensions. The reality of mutual assured destruction seemed to inspire the leaders to consider more peaceful options. In July 1963, officials installed a direct telephone link, known as the "hotline," between the White House and the Kremlin, the residence and office of the Soviet leader. Shortly after, the United States and the Soviet Union joined other nations in agreeing to limits on future development of nuclear weapons. The United States and the Soviet Union began seeking ways to coexist peacefully. While no one denied that significant differences existed between them, the countries both mutually recognized that they could not risk the type of confrontation that could destroy civilization.

Nonetheless, the nation's civil defense system remains active in protecting citizens. When natural disasters such as hurricanes and floods strike, the people affected depend on clear communication and effective evacuation plans and routes. In addition, since the early years of

the 21st century, concerns about terrorism have emerged, and civil defense practices appropriate to the new types of threats have been developed.

TRAGEDY IN DALLAS

By 1963, President Kennedy had positioned himself well to run for re-election. He had moved the country forward economically and had proved himself on the world stage. However, not all Americans were behind him. Kennedy's support for the growing civil rights movement particularly angered white southern Democrats. In an attempt to win southern votes, President and Jacqueline Kennedy traveled to Texas—the southern state with the most electoral votes—to campaign in late November 1963. On November 22, as the Kennedys' motorcade passed through Dealey Plaza in Dallas, shots rang out from a window on the sixth floor of a nearby building—a textbook depository, or warehouse, near the motorcade route. Kennedy suddenly slumped in his seat, shot in the head. The motorcade raced to Parkland Hospital, where doctors pronounced the president dead.

Within hours, the police arrested a 24-year-old suspect named **Lee Harvey Oswald**, whom witnesses identified as fleeing the book depository after Kennedy's assassination. Two days later, on November 24, as law enforcement officers were moving Oswald between jails, Dallas nightclub owner Jack Ruby stepped forward and shot and killed him. Ruby claimed he killed Oswald out of a sense of patriotism and extreme distress over Kennedy's death. Ruby died in prison four years later.

With the murder of the prime suspect in Kennedy's assassination, many people suspected the events were all part of a larger conspiracy. The federal government immediately assembled a special group led by Chief Justice Earl Warren to investigate. After spending almost a year sifting through every bit of evidence available on the murders, the **Warren Commission** report concluded that both Oswald and Ruby had acted alone. Despite this conclusion, alternative interpretations of this event are still debated as various theories of the assassination have been proposed. Some blame Fidel Castro, others the Mafia, the Ku Klux Klan, or the CIA. To some, the simple explanation that a deranged man had committed a senseless act of violence and met a violent end himself did not explain sufficiently the death of a president so young and full of life.

Such doubts reflected the depth of shock over Kennedy's assassination. Few other events in the

Three-year-old John Kennedy, Jr., salutes his father, President Kennedy, one last time at the president's funeral, November 25, 1963.

nation's history produced so much bewilderment and grief. Even Khrushchev felt a deep loss, calling Kennedy's death "a heavy blow to all people who hold dear the cause of peace and Soviet-American cooperation." Kennedy had seemed an ideal president: a charming, handsome war hero with a glamorous wife. The reality was different, of course. Kennedy's three years in office saw failures as well as successes, and after his death, evidence emerged of personal shortcomings that raised questions about his character. Still, Kennedy's final months were his most productive, and many supporters felt he would have accomplished even more in a second term.

HISTORICAL THINKING

1. **READING CHECK** What were the origins and geopolitical consequences of the Cuban Missile Crisis?

2. **DETERMINE CHRONOLOGY** Identify in order three major events that occurred between November 22 and November 24, 1963.

3. **INTERPRET MAPS** Based on the map, what part of the United States would be safe from a missile attack from Cuba?

BUILD BACKGROUND

THE POPE AND VATICAN II

Pope John XXIII, the man who announced the Second Vatican Council, or Vatican II, had a deep concern for the world as well as for the Catholic Church. He had served as a chaplain in World War I, helped locate prisoners of war in Turkey, and in 1944 went to France to assist in postwar efforts. He was elected pope in 1958. Before the council, the Church had been viewed as mainly concerned with its own inner stability and its missionary activity. During Vatican II, the pope urged the Church to reconsider its practices. He encouraged members to engage with all aspects of the outside world and establish friendship with other faiths, laying the groundwork for the modern Catholic Church. He believed firmly that human dignity and freedom were the foundation for world order and peace.

LEE HARVEY OSWALD

Born in New Orleans, Louisiana, Lee Harvey Oswald developed an early interest in socialism and communism. He joined the Marines at age 17, became an above-average sharpshooter, and was court-martialed twice for violent behavior and owning an illegal weapon. Oswald moved to Russia, where he married Marina Prusakova in 1961, but returned with his family to the United States and became a supporter of communist Cuba. In early 1963, he began working at the Texas School Book Depository, from which the fatal shots were fired. Questions about his motive for killing President Kennedy and whether he acted alone still remain. Contrary to the Warren Commission, a 1979 independent report from the House of Representatives Assassination Committee stated that another shooter might have been involved.

TEACH

GUIDED DISCUSSION

4. Make Connections How did the Second Vatican Council help the pope influence President Kennedy and Nikita Khrushchev during the Cuban Missile Crisis? *(Possible response: The Second Vatican Council urged the Catholic Church to promote peace and justice in the world. This gave the pope more authority to plead with both Kennedy and Khrushchev to end the crisis peacefully.)*

5. Analyze Cause and Effect What impact did the assassination of Kennedy have on the country and on the world? *(Possible response: Kennedy's assassination produced not only national grief but also public distrust of the official investigation into the event, a distrust that continues today. Worldwide, as Khrushchev expressed, Kennedy's death was felt as the loss of someone who worked toward peace and improvement of U.S.-Soviet relations.)*

MORE INFORMATION

Irony and Chance Two factors—irony and chance—make Kennedy's assassination at Dealy Plaza unusually inauspicious. First, the plaza was named after the Dealy family, publishers of an anti-Kennedy newspaper. The morning of Kennedy's visit, the paper published a full-page attack ad accusing him of being a communist. Second, because the weather had been rainy, a bubble top was set to be put on the limousine. While not bulletproof, the bubble top might have affected the accuracy of the shooter. But by the time of the motorcade, the weather had cleared, and the limousine entered Dealy Plaza with its top removed.

ACTIVE OPTIONS

On Your Feet: Fishbowl Have one group of students sit in a circle facing each other while a second group sits in another circle around them. Ask the inner circle to think about the information about the Second Vatican Council and the principles it expressed. Tell students to discuss this question: What methods might Pope John XXIII use today to influence world leaders, and what responses might he receive? Ask the outer circle to listen carefully to the ideas expressed. After a time, direct the two circles to switch places and continue the discussion. Encourage students to draw conclusions about how Pope John XXIII might reach out to present-day world leaders and how world leaders might respond.

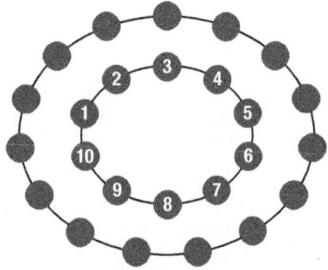

NG Learning Framework: Evaluate Authors' Interpretations

SKILLS Observation, Communication

KNOWLEDGE Our Human Story

Have students do research online to find two different historical interpretations of either the Cuban Missile Crisis or Kennedy's assassination. Invite them to evaluate each author's interpretation of the past events, analyze the authors' use of evidence and primary sources, and determine whether they provide sound generalizations or misleading oversimplifications. As part of their evaluations, students should distinguish valid arguments from fallacious arguments in the authors' interpretations. Encourage students to share their analyses with the class.

HISTORICAL THINKING

ANSWERS

1. Cuba's fear of another U.S. invasion prompted the Soviet Union to send arms, including nuclear missiles, to its ally. The United States could not tolerate the threat of Soviet missiles so close to its borders. As a result, the two rivals became locked in a confrontation over the missiles, with the possibility of nuclear war looming. The United States sent ships to block Cuban ports as Soviet ships headed to Cuba. After a tense standoff, a compromise was reached.

2. President Kennedy was assassinated. Lee Harvey Oswald was arrested. Jack Ruby killed Oswald.

3. Hawaii, Alaska, California, Nevada, the northwestern states, and most of Montana would be safe from a Cuban missile attack.

CRITICAL VIEWING Possible response: Robert Kennedy appears deep in thought, while President Kennedy seems to be looking to his brother—perhaps for help or advice. Given the situation, both men convey a feeling of deep concern.

JOHN FITZGERALD KENNEDY 1917–1963

"Let the word go forth from this time and place, to friend and foe alike, that the torch has been passed to a new generation of Americans."—John F. Kennedy

The entire Kennedy clan gathered for this 1935 photo taken at Hyannis Port. Seated from left to right: Patricia, Robert, Rose, John, Joseph, Sr., with Edward on his lap; standing from left to right: Joseph, Jr., Kathleen, Rosemary, Eunice (rear), Jean

John F. Kennedy, who is often referred to by his initials, JFK, spoke these words at his inaugural address on January 20, 1961. The words were probably meant to energize his supporters and send a warning to his enemies. JFK heralded a new era of youth, vigor—one of his favorite words—and confidence. He embodied all three. Kennedy was the youngest U.S. president ever elected, and he seemed the picture of health. (He wasn't; more on that later.) His confidence was very likely a quality instilled by his family.

THE KENNEDY CLAN

Kennedy, as you know, grew up amid great wealth in Boston, Massachusetts. His father, Joseph (Joe) Kennedy, Sr., was a highly successful businessman and held several political positions, including U.S. ambassador to Great Britain. However, Joe, Sr., always felt he had been prevented from achieving higher office as a result of the anti-Catholic animosity in the United States. He vowed his children would overcome that prejudice. Rose Kennedy, the family matriarch, was "the glue that always held the family together," as John once said about his mother. She devoted herself to her brood of four boys and five girls.

The brothers and sisters were close-knit but extremely competitive, especially in sports. Any visitor to the family's summer home in Hyannis Port on Cape Cod had to be ready to take part in a game

In September 1962, JFK addressed a crowd of 40,000 at Rice University in Houston, Texas, with his now-famous speech in which he boldly announced, "We choose to go to the moon."

of touch football. And the game could get rough. John's wife, Jacqueline (Jackie), once broke her ankle while playing—and she was pregnant at the time. After that, she refused to play touch football again. John threw himself into the family games, but the physical activity was often hard on him. He had been a sickly child and suffered from ill health all his life. Nevertheless, Joe, Sr., liked to pit John and his older brother, Joe, Jr., against each other. On a bicycle race organized by their father, the brothers collided, and John had to have 28 stitches. Joe, Sr., wanted his boys to be tough.

During World War II, both brothers served in the U.S. Navy. As a lieutenant, John commanded a patrol torpedo boat, PT-109. One night, a Japanese destroyer rammed into the boat in the Pacific Ocean. Two crew members were killed, but 11 others survived the collision, including John. Despite suffering from a bad back, he swam for 4 hours to an island while tugging an injured man with him. They ending up swimming to yet another island in search of food and fresh water. There, John carved a message on a coconut shell and sent it with two scouts in a canoe to the Australian Coast Guard. John was awarded a medal for gallantry. Later, when someone asked Kennedy how he came to be a hero, he replied, "It was involuntary. They sank my boat."

Joe, Jr., flew combat missions over Europe in the war. Then he volunteered to take part in a secret and highly dangerous mission that involved flying a drone loaded with explosives to Normandy, France. The explosives unexpectedly detonated before Joe, Jr., could parachute out of the plane. His death at age 29 was the first in a series of tragedies that plagued the Kennedy family. Some called it a curse. Kathleen, the second-eldest daughter of the clan, died in a plane crash three years later. Before his son's death, Joe, Sr., had hoped to fulfill his political ambitions through Joe, Jr. Now he pinned his hopes on John.

THE CAMELOT PRESIDENCY

John Kennedy may have succeeded beyond his father's wildest dreams. During the 1,037 days of his presidency, as you know, JFK experienced both successes and failures. But he remained a charismatic leader throughout his time in office. His idealism inspired people to believe they really could make their country and the world a better place. The handsome president and his beautiful wife enchanted Americans, who followed their trips and social engagements on television and in the news with avid interest. Women admired Jackie and tried to imitate her sophisticated taste in fashion. When the first lady gave the first-ever televised tour of the White House in 1962 to show the restorations she'd had done, a record 56 million people tuned in to watch.

Americans were also charmed by JFK's wit, which he often directed toward himself. After naming his inexperienced 36-year-old brother, Robert, as attorney general, JFK joked, "I don't see anything wrong with giving Bobby a little legal experience before he goes out on his own to practice law." On a visit to Paris in 1961, as it became clear Jackie was the one the crowds had come out to see, he said, "I do not think it altogether inappropriate to introduce myself. I am the man who accompanied Jacqueline Kennedy to Paris, and I have enjoyed it."

PLAN: 4-PAGE LESSON

OBJECTIVE

Understand how the family and early life of John F. Kennedy shaped the man who would be president.

CRITICAL THINKING SKILLS FOR LESSON 1.4

• Make Inferences

• Analyze Cause and Effect

• Evaluate

• Draw Conclusions

• Make Connections

• Form and Support Opinions

HISTORICAL THINKING FOR CHAPTER 26

What challenges did Americans face during the 1960s? The challenges of the 1960s—both global and domestic—were ones with roots deep in the past. Lesson 1.4 examines President Kennedy, how he was shaped by this past, and what his election symbolized for the era.

BACKGROUND FOR THE TEACHER

Though John F. Kennedy was the only Kennedy to attain the office of president, many other members of the family have served in government. John's two brothers, Robert and Ted, both served as U.S. senators. Robert was elected in New York following his brother's assassination, and he held the post until his own assassination in 1968. Ted was one of the longest-serving senators in U.S. history, representing Massachusetts for almost 47 years. Robert's oldest son, Joseph, served five terms in Congress from 1987 to 1999, and Ted's son Patrick was an eight-term congressman. This pattern has continued with the latest generation. In 2012, Robert's grandson Joseph III was elected to the U.S. House of Representatives after serving two years in the Peace Corps—an organization founded by his presidential great-uncle.

HISTORY NOTEBOOK

Encourage students to complete the American Voices page for Chapter 26 in their History Notebooks as they read.

INTRODUCE & ENGAGE
DISCUSS MEANING THROUGH WORDS

Inform students that John F. Kennedy's inaugural address is one of the most famous in American history. Play a recording—either a portion or the entirety—of this speech. If pressed for time, start at the latter half, the section beginning with "In your hands." **ASK:** What does Kennedy think about the relationship between citizens and the country? *(Kennedy thinks citizens should work to better the country rather than wait for the country to benefit them.)* Why might this idea have been exciting to many people? *(It gave them the opportunity to become active in their government and the world.)* Tell students that in this lesson they will learn more about the upbringing of John F. Kennedy and how it shaped his views toward government and the world.

TEACH
GUIDED DISCUSSION

1. **Draw Conclusions** How did Joe, Sr.'s style of parenting influence his children? Cite evidence from the text. *(Possible response: Joe, Sr., taught his children to be highly competitive and not to back down. This was exemplified in the PT-109 incident where John swam for hours to save a fellow soldier.)*

2. **Make Connections** What social and economic trends contributed to the popularity of Jackie Kennedy? *(Her popularity was aided by the rise of mass media, such as television, which increased her exposure. In addition, rising postwar consumerism allowed people to shop for—and purchase—products that enabled them to emulate the first lady.)*

AMERICAN VOICES
The image and accessibility of John Kennedy was crucial to his popularity. People had greater access to Kennedy—and his family—than perhaps any other president in history. He came along in the era of color magazine photography and live television. In fact, his debate with Richard Nixon was the first ever televised.

Have students examine the photograph of the Kennedy clan. **ASK:** What words can be used to describe the family, based on this image? *(Answers will vary. Possible response: well mannered, wealthy, polite, happy)* Why do you think a photograph like this, taken in 1935, would appeal to people of the era? *(After decades of economic depression and war, the Kennedy family appeared to represent a new and better beginning.)* Then instruct students to study the photograph of Kennedy giving a speech as president. Allow time for them to locate photographs of other presidents from the postwar period, such as Truman, Eisenhower, Roosevelt, or Nixon. **ASK:** How does Kennedy's appearance contrast with these other leaders? *(Answers will vary. Students might point out that Kennedy appears younger and more vibrant than previous presidents.)*

DIFFERENTIATE
STRIVING READERS

Tweet a Biography As students read the lesson, direct them to pause after each paragraph and write a tweet, a 140-character message, summarizing the paragraph's main idea in their own words. Then have students create a condensed biography by reading their tweets aloud to the class one at a time, with the first student reading his or her tweet about the first paragraph, the second student reading a tweet about the second paragraph, and so on.

GIFTED & TALENTED

Write and Deliver a Monologue Instruct students to research the life of John Fitzgerald Kennedy in order to write a first-person monologue in his voice. (Some students may wish to read portions of the many biographies of JFK for more information.) Tell students that their monologue may focus on JFK's role in a particular event, such as World War II or the Cuban Missile Crisis, or it may deal with the high and low points of his entire life. Have students incorporate quotations by or about JFK in their monologues. Ask volunteers to perform their monologues for the class and respond to any questions asked.

See the Chapter Planner for more strategies for differentiation.

Kennedy commanded PT-109, which was split in two by a Japanese destroyer on August 1, 1943. He and his crew salvaged what they could from the boat, including a wood plank they used to tow two men—who couldn't swim—to safety.

JFK's children, Caroline and John Jr., often had the run of the White House. Here, John Jr. peeks out from what he called the "secret door" of his father's desk in the Oval Office.

Kennedy's presidency would come to be called "Camelot," suggesting that it brought the romantic legend of King Arthur to life. But this characterization masks the anguish that lay beneath the surface. JFK had chronic back pain and suffered from a rare disorder called Addison's disease, which causes severe fatigue and muscle weakness. Jackie had her own pain while she endured her husband's unfaithfulness. Most tragically of all, they both mourned the death of their infant son, Patrick, who died 39 hours after his birth in August 1963.

TRAGEDY AND LOSS

Of course, just a few months later, John Kennedy himself would be dead. Widowed at 34, Jackie planned her late husband's funeral and modeled it on that of Abraham Lincoln. She had a horse-drawn wagon carry Kennedy's flag-draped casket to the White House. Then the mourners followed a riderless horse, with boots symbolically reversed in the stirrups, to the church where the service was to be held. Jackie's strength and dignity throughout the funeral helped the nation cope with its own sorrow.

At the Democratic National Convention held in August 1964, Robert Kennedy took the floor to introduce a short film on his brother's legacy.

But every time he tried to speak, the delegates erupted into applause. This went on for more than 20 minutes. Just about 4 years later, Robert would be cut down by an assassin's bullet, too. John Kennedy's son, John F. Kennedy, Jr., died in 1999 at age 38 in a plane crash. To many, the Kennedy family certainly seemed to be cursed.

In defiance of the curse, however, more than 50 years after his death, John Kennedy remained the most popular president of the post–World War II era. The young president's ideals still capture people's imaginations and hearts. As JFK once said, "A man may die, nations may rise and fall, but an idea lives on."

HISTORICAL THINKING

1. **READING CHECK** How was John Kennedy shaped by his early years?

2. **MAKE INFERENCES** What do the quotations by JFK in this lesson reveal about the man?

3. **ANALYZE CAUSE AND EFFECT** Describe the complex effects the death of Joseph Kennedy, Jr., had on JFK and the country.

4. **EVALUATE** What limitations might prevent you from determining the effects referred to in question 3?

People thronged the streets of Dallas to see JFK and Jackie riding in this limousine on November 22, 1963. John Connally, Jr., the governor of Texas, and his wife, Nellie, rode in the seat in front of them. Moments before JFK was shot, she said to Kennedy, "Mr. President, you certainly cannot say that Dallas does not love you."

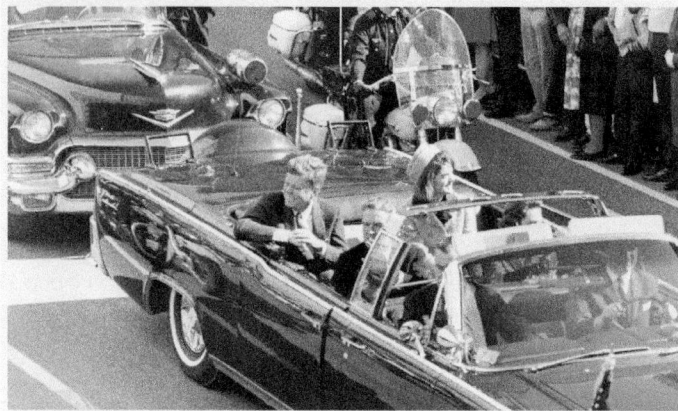

President Kennedy's flag-draped coffin moves slowly past mourners on November 25, 1963. The president was buried in Arlington Cemetery, where an eternal flame marks his grave.

BUILD BACKGROUND

JACKIE KENNEDY

Jackie Kennedy was born in 1929 as Jacqueline Lee Bouvier. Raised in a well-to-do New York family, she attended prestigious boarding schools, was an accomplished equestrian, and took ballet lessons at the old Metropolitan Opera House. After high school in Connecticut, she attended Vassar College and George Washington University, where she studied history, art, and French.

After graduating, Jackie worked for a newspaper as the "Inquiring Camera Girl," where she took photographs of people and interviewed them about the issues of the day. It was here that she gained access to the political world; one of her interviewees was Richard Nixon, and she covered Dwight Eisenhower's inauguration. It was also at this time that she met her future husband, who was then a congressman and soon to be a senator from Massachusetts.

In 1960, when John ran for president, Jackie accompanied him on the campaign trail. However, after learning she was pregnant with their second child, she remained home where she personally responded to campaign letters, taped commercials, gave interviews, and got back to her early roots by writing a weekly newspaper column.

After John won the election, Jackie became first lady at the age of only 31. While living in the White House, her first priorities were always her young children, but she also spent time restoring and updating the grounds, including adding a kindergarten, pool, and playground. She also updated all the public rooms with examples of historical American art and furniture.

TEACH

GUIDED DISCUSSION

3. **Evaluate** How does the fact that Kennedy had Addison's disease contrast with the public image of the man? *(In the public eye, he was an athletic, youthful, and vigorous war hero. However, because of his condition, the reality was different from the image; he had chronic back pain, fatigue, and muscle weakness.)*

4. **Form and Support Opinions** Why do you think Kennedy is still one of the most popular presidents in history? *(Answers will vary. Possible response: Kennedy's message of hope and idealism will always resonate, and, because of his short time in office, he is remembered most for his successes and the possibility of what might have been.)*

MAKE CONNECTIONS

Inform students that Kennedy's Roman Catholicism was a major issue in the campaign of 1960, as there was genuine belief that—as a Roman Catholic—Kennedy would put religious belief over the laws of the country. In fact, late in the contest, he gave an entire speech reaffirming his belief in the separation of church and state. **ASK:** How have our ideas about religious beliefs and politics changed from those during the time of Kennedy, and how have those aspects remained the same? *(Answers will vary. Possible response: In today's United States, a Roman Catholic running for office would not seem controversial, thus some progress has been made. However, religious bigotry is still present in our politics as evidenced by the rumors that Barack Obama was a Muslim or Mitt Romney's reluctance to speak about his Mormonism during the 2012 campaign.)*

ACTIVE OPTIONS

On Your Feet: History Roundtable Arrange students around tables or in circles in groups of four or five. Hand each group a sheet of paper containing the following question: How did his family and early life shape John F. Kennedy? The first student in each group should write an answer, read it aloud, and pass the paper clockwise to the next student. Each student in the group should add at least one answer. Students should circulate the paper around the table until they run out of answers. Call on volunteers from each group to share their ideas.

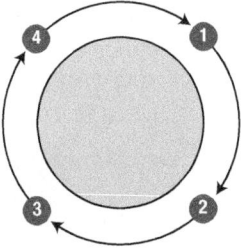

NG Learning Framework: Craft a Speech

SKILLS Communication, Collaboration

KNOWLEDGE Our Human Story

Divide the class into small groups. Tell the groups to imagine that the year is 1959 and the upstart Kennedy campaign has hired them all as speechwriters. Their job is to craft a speech for Kennedy in which he introduces himself to the country and explains why he wants to be president. Groups should use the information from the lesson and examples of Kennedy's actual speeches for inspiration. When finished, have groups present their speeches to the class.

HISTORICAL THINKING

ANSWERS

1. Kennedy's competitive upbringing, his time in the military, and the tragic loss of his brother may have influenced his motivations for seeking political office and his hopes to affect the course of history.

2. Answers will vary. Possible response: They show his optimism and eloquence with words.

3. The death of Joseph, Jr., put pressure on John to enter politics, which eventually led to his becoming leader of the country.

4. There is no firsthand account from John describing how this incident affected him, which makes any speculation merely that.

REINVENTING
CLEAN ENERGY

"I think I can save the world with nuclear power."
—Leslie Dewan

Leslie Dewan stands out from the crowd—a visionary woman in a male-dominated field. With guidance and input from her female teachers and mentors, and with a nod to history and its lessons, Dewan is determined to develop a cleaner form of nuclear power that will reinvent the definition of clean energy. This carbon-free energy will power the world, and—as a side note—will greatly decrease the production of nuclear waste. It's ambitious, but if it can be done, this National Geographic Explorer will figure out how.

^
As one of the only women in her graduate school classes at the Massachusetts Institute of Technology (MIT), Leslie Dewan, shown here on the MIT campus, learned to take the lead.

MAIN IDEA Leslie Dewan is developing a safer, cleaner alternative to traditional nuclear power.

A NEW SOURCE OF ENERGY

From the beginning of history, humans have used fire to generate power. In fact, as early as 2000 B.C., people burned coal for energy. They later discovered the usefulness of natural gas and petroleum. But as you know, fossil fuels like coal, oil, and natural gas are nonrenewable energy sources. Burning them is believed to have negative impacts on our planet, including air, land, and water pollution. Utilizing cleaner energy sources is a must for the environment.

Although fossil fuels are still widely in use, we now harness the power of the sun, wind, water, and geothermal sources more than ever before to generate power and electricity. Leslie Dewan, an MIT-trained nuclear engineer, National Geographic Explorer, and environmentalist, would like to add nuclear power to that list, but others disagree. The impact on people and the environment that resulted from nuclear disasters at power plants, including Three Mile Island in the United States, Chernobyl in the Ukraine, and Fukushima in Japan, leaves many uneasy. They feel nuclear power is just too dangerous.

Scientists first figured out how to generate nuclear power about 70 years ago. It was exciting at first, imagining nuclear-powered cars, planes, and weapons, and nuclear reactors to generate electricity. At that time, the focus was not on reducing carbon dioxide emissions, but on gaining energy independence from other countries.

As you have read, nuclear technology was used during the Cold War to create weapons of mass destruction. The Cuban Missile Crisis brought the world to the brink of nuclear war. After World War II, Americans were acutely aware of the destructive power of nuclear weapons, so the fear of "being nuked" during the Cold War led people to build bomb shelters and practice nuclear attack drills.

Decades later, highly publicized nuclear disasters gave people the impression that nuclear power was more dangerous than useful. Serious failures did occur, and they were disastrous—in the case of Chernobyl, a whole continent was affected. There were also serious concerns about technology and safety. In its rush to develop reactors, the United States built reactors similar to those designed for

In 1979, the Three Mile Island nuclear power station in Pennsylvania had the most serious accident in U.S. history. Luckily, the small amount of radioactive material released had no health effects on plant workers or the public.

nuclear submarines instead of developing ones better suited for land. Nearly all of the reactors still in use in this country today are submarine-style reactors.

SAFER NUCLEAR REACTORS

That's where Dewan comes in. She's designing a safer, more efficient alternative to today's nuclear reactors, and says, "I want to come up with new technology that keeps the good elements of nuclear power but solves the bad aspects." Dewan and her colleague, Mark Massie, developed a new design for a molten salt reactor, initially intended for nuclear-powered airplanes. Ideally, their reactors would leave behind less than half as much nuclear waste as existing reactors, and produce enough energy to power the world for decades. Dewan hopes to develop a prototype by 2020 and a commercial reactor by the 2030s.

Currently, nuclear power provides 10 percent of the world's electricity and 45 percent of the world's fossil-free electricity. Dewan believes nuclear energy will move the world away from fossil fuels and offer dramatic reductions in carbon dioxide emissions. She notes, "I think the world needs nuclear power, alongside solar, wind, hydro, and geothermal, if we want to have any hope of reducing fossil fuel emissions and preventing global climate change."

HISTORICAL THINKING

1. **READING CHECK** What problem is Dewan attempting to solve with her development of new nuclear reactor technology?

2. **ANALYZE ENVIRONMENTAL CONCEPTS** How might nuclear technology affect the environment in both positive and negative ways?

PLAN: 2-PAGE LESSON

OBJECTIVE

Learn about the history of nuclear energy and how Leslie Dewan is developing a way to harness this technology in the modern age.

CRITICAL THINKING SKILLS FOR LESSON 1.5

• Analyze Environmental Concepts

• Make Inferences

• Form and Support Opinions

• Make Connections

HISTORICAL THINKING FOR CHAPTER 26

What challenges did Americans face during the 1960s? Both the threat and opportunity resulting from the development of nuclear energy were defining aspects of the 1960s. Lesson 1.5 explores the history of nuclear power and describes nuclear engineer Leslie Dewan's work in creating safer nuclear reactors.

NATIONAL GEOGRAPHIC EXPLORER
LESLIE DEWAN

Leslie Dewan's company—Transatomic Power—is attempting to solve two problems that have long plagued the nuclear power industry: how to make a safer plant and what to do with the waste. During a power outage, Dewan's molten salt reactors automatically shut off and drain the hazardous fuel into a tank, which is then frozen solid—preventing the possibility of a meltdown. In addition, most traditional reactors only use a small portion of the energy in the uranium, which leads to the need to store vast amounts of radioactive fuel rods, or nuclear waste. Dewan's reactor, however, uses this waste as its source of fuel, thus potentially reducing the 300,000 metric tons of nuclear waste currently stored across the world.

HISTORY NOTEBOOK

Encourage students to complete the Explorer page for Chapter 26 in their History Notebooks as they read.

INTRODUCE & ENGAGE

BRAINSTORM POSITIVE AND NEGATIVE ASSOCIATIONS

Write the term *nuclear energy* on the board. Have students brainstorm the words, phrases, or events they associate with the term. Record their ideas on the board. Then ask students to examine the results and group them into two categories: positive and negative. Discuss which of the categories is typically more closely associated with the term *nuclear energy*, and why. Explain to students that in this lesson they will learn about a National Geographic Explorer who is creating a new technology that focuses on the positive characteristics of nuclear energy.

TEACH

GUIDED DISCUSSION

1. **Make Inferences** What does Leslie Dewan's comment "I think I can save the world with nuclear power" reveal about her opinion of different energy sources? *(Possible response: Dewan is confident that nuclear energy can be produced safely and cleanly. She also implies that other widely used ways of generating power will lead to environmental issues.)*

2. **Form and Support Opinions** Do you agree that Dewan's safer reactors could affect the amount of fossil fuels and other resources used to create energy? Support your response. *(Answers will vary. Possible responses: Yes. If nuclear energy becomes safer and cleaner, it could eliminate the use of fossil fuels to generate energy and provide much of the world's electricity. No. Even a "safer" type of nuclear reactor would present health and safety problems related to nuclear fuel, so people might still prefer alternative fuel sources.)*

MAKE CONNECTIONS

Reread the short biography of Leslie Dewan and the accompanying caption under the photograph. **ASK:** What role do you think gender played in Leslie's drive and success? *(Answers will vary. Possible response: As a female in a male-dominated field, Leslie may have had to work harder to prove her worth, thus pushing her to succeed.)* **ASK:** What other examples of women succeeding in male-dominated fields can be found throughout history and in present day? *(Answers will vary. Examples include Marie Curie, Amelia Earhart, Sheryl Sandberg, and Hillary Clinton.)* As a class, discuss the characteristics these women have in common.

ACTIVE OPTIONS

On Your Feet: Debate Pose the following question to the class: Should the United States expand its use of nuclear energy? Divide the class into two groups and assign one to argue for expansion and the other to argue against it. Have each group use the information in the lesson—as well as outside research—to organize and write the strongest arguments to support their position. Each group should also generate some suggestions to address the possible concerns of the other group. Then give the groups a chance to debate the topic by taking turns presenting their arguments and suggestions. Encourage the class to reach consensus on one or two suggestions.

NG Learning Framework: Investigate Changing Natural Systems

ATTITUDE Curiosity

KNOWLEDGE Our Living Planet

Inform students that the human practices of using nuclear technology, and the resulting disasters, have had severe impacts on the natural systems of given environments. Assign groups of students to conduct research on different nuclear disasters, such as Chernobyl, Three-Mile Island, and Fukushima. Have groups prepare a presentation in which they evaluate the impact of the nuclear disaster. Students should examine conditions both before and after the accident and assess the changes that took place. Invite groups to share their presentations with the class.

DIFFERENTIATE

STRIVING READERS

Create a Word Square Have students write the term *clean energy* in the center oval of a Word Square. Explain that the term has different meanings to different people, but ask them to use what they learn in the lesson to write a definition and characteristics in the appropriate boxes. Guide them to identify and write examples and non-examples. Then hold a class discussion on the meanings of and issues surrounding clean energy.

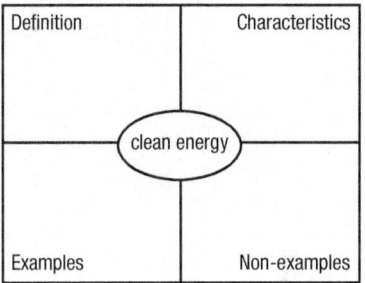

PRE-AP

Research and Write an Essay Instruct students to choose an energy source (nuclear, fossil fuel, geothermal, solar, or wind) and learn about its pros and cons by conducting research using online and print sources. Encourage students to use reliable sources and to quote or paraphrase them as appropriate. Invite volunteers to share their findings with the class.

See the Chapter Planner for more strategies for differentiation

HISTORICAL THINKING

ANSWERS

1. She is attempting to create a safer nuclear reactor that produces less waste.

2. Nuclear technology can benefit the environment because it offers the potential for cleaner energy; however, if accidents occur, this technology can have devastating effects on the surrounding ecosystem because of radioactive emissions.

CRITICAL VIEWING How does Cuba's history with the United States relate to the abundance of classic American cars on the historic streets of Havana?

EDIFICIO CORTINA

In May 2016, National Geographic photographer David Guttenfelder set sail from Miami, Florida, on the first cruise ship to sail from the United States to Havana, Cuba, in nearly 50 years. His images capture Cuba's colorful culture and identity, but also its infrastructure, much of which hasn't been updated since the 1960s when the United States cut off ties. Guttenfelder's photos reveal how, in many ways, time has stood still on this island country until recently.

PLAN: 2-PAGE LESSON

OBJECTIVE

Understand how the United States' relationship with Cuba changed and the effects of that change.

CRITICAL THINKING SKILLS FOR LESSON 1.6

- Analyze Visuals
- Make Connections
- Evaluate
- Compare and Contrast

HISTORICAL THINKING FOR CHAPTER 26

What challenges did Americans face during the 1960s? U.S.-Cuban relations changed once the United States placed a trade embargo on Cuba in the early 1960s. Lesson 1.6 shows some of the effects of Cuba's isolation.

NATIONAL GEOGRAPHIC PHOTOGRAPHER DAVID GUTTENFELDER

David Guttenfelder has spent his entire career as a photojournalist working and living in more than 75 countries, including Tanzania, Kenya, Japan, and India. His award-winning stories range from opium wars in Afghanistan to Japan's Fukushima nuclear refugees, and his photographs have been published in *National Geographic* magazine on topics such as the slaughter of migratory birds, the hidden aspects of North Korea, and the greater Yellowstone ecosystem. Guttenfelder's decade-long coverage of the U.S.-led war in Afghanistan was part of the exhibit "War/Photography: Images of Armed Conflict and Its Aftermath" at Houston's Museum of Fine Arts. He has also been an industry leader in smartphone photography.

HISTORY NOTEBOOK

Encourage students to complete the Through the Lens page for Chapter 26 in their History Notebooks as they read.

INTRODUCE & ENGAGE

ACTIVATE PRIOR KNOWLEDGE

Discuss with students what they already know about the history of Cuba. Remind them that the island nation was ruled first by Spain and then by the United States before Fidel Castro took over. Ask students to speculate about how the combination of the U.S. embargo, communist rule, and the loss of Soviet economic aid might have affected the Cuban way of life. Explain that in this lesson they will see what National Geographic photographer David Guttenfelder witnessed firsthand when he visited Cuba.

TEACH

GUIDED DISCUSSION

1. **Evaluate** What impression do the building's physical characteristics convey in terms of its architecture and condition? *(Possible response: The older, Spanish-style architecture and the poor condition of the building convey an impression of European influence, times of former wealth, and years of neglect and hardship.)*

2. **Compare and Contrast** Why might the photographer have contrasted the 1950s American cars with the building? *(Possible responses: to show images of a more prosperous time before the United States cut off ties with Cuba; to reflect Cuba's history of Spanish and U.S. rule; to show that Cuba has been cut off from much of the world since the 1960s)*

THROUGH THE LENS

On the historic trip described in the text, David Guttenfelder and the rest of the National Geographic team were able to photograph Havana and other locations around the island. The building in this photo, with its arched entryways on the first floor, elaborate facades, and balconies on the second and third floors, is typical of Cuba's colonial architecture. The 1950s American convertible is reminiscent of a time when the United States and Cuba were trading partners. Over the decades, some of Cuba's classic architecture has deteriorated, as shown here in this photograph.

ACTIVE OPTIONS

On Your Feet: Numbered Heads Organize students into groups of four and have each group member number off. Instruct groups to research how the U.S. trade embargo influenced the social and economic development of Cuba. Then call a number and have the student with that number in each group report for the group.

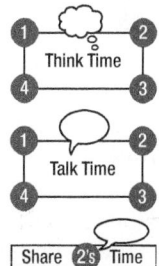

NG Learning Framework: Create a Virtual Tour

| ATTITUDE | Curiosity |

| KNOWLEDGE | Our Human Story |

Invite students to locate other photographs taken by David Guttenfelder during his Cuban visit in 2016, as well as information about the Photo Camp in Havana that National Geographic sponsors for young people. Have students build a web page that showcases these photographs to create a virtual tour of the physical and human characteristics of Havana. Encourage students to present their virtual tour to the class and discuss what they learned about present-day Cuba from the photos.

DIFFERENTIATE

INCLUSION

Analyze a Photograph Pair students who are visually impaired with students who are not. Ask the latter to describe the photograph in detail, including evidence of both neglect and preservation. Tell visually impaired students to ask clarifying questions as necessary. Then have the pairs work together to answer the Critical Viewing question.

GIFTED & TALENTED

Write Captions Instruct students to write captions for the photograph from three perspectives: that of a Cuban auto mechanic, that of a Cuban-American family in the United States and that of a U.S. diplomat. Tell students to conduct online research to learn more about what each person would "see" in the photograph. For example, a Cuban immigrant in the United States might see evidence of Cuba's stagnation and poverty, while a Cuban mechanic might see the ingenuity and skill that has kept classic American cars looking good and running well. Have students share their captions and discuss the different interpretations.

See the Chapter Planner for more strategies for differentiation.

CRITICAL VIEWING Possible response: After President Kennedy initiated an economic embargo on Cuba, that country could no longer acquire U.S. cars. Without access to new imports, Cubans relied on the "classic" American cars that are still found on Havana's streets.

PRIMARY SOURCES

Senator Richard Russell, Jr., a Democrat from Georgia, opposed civil rights legislation for decades and joined the Senate filibuster against the civil rights bill. Illinois senator Everett M. Dirksen, a Republican and a strong supporter of the bill, spoke out to end the long filibuster and debate and move it to a vote.

We will resist to the bitter end any measure or any movement which would have a tendency to bring about social equality and intermingling and amalgamation [mixture] of the races in our [Southern] states.

—from a speech by Senator Richard Russell, Jr., during the Senate filibuster, March 30, 1964

There is another reason why we dare not temporize with [delay] the issue which is before us. It is essentially moral in character. It must be resolved. It will not go away. Its time has come.

—from a speech in the Senate by minority leader Everett M. Dirksen, June 10, 1964

JOHNSON'S STRONG START

"All I have, I would gladly have given not to be standing here today," Lyndon Johnson said in his first address to Congress. But the job was his, and, while determined to carry on the work started by Kennedy, he still blazed his own path forward.

A SMOOTH TRANSITION

On the night of November 22, 1963, just hours after President Kennedy's assassination, Vice President Lyndon Johnson took the presidential oath of office aboard Air Force One. Lyndon Baines Johnson—popularly called LBJ—was born in a small house in the hills of south-central Texas in 1908. He belonged to a lower social class and an older political generation than Kennedy. And with his down-home style and earthy language, he seemed rather crude to the East Coast newscasters and journalists compared with the media-savvy Kennedy. Yet few people knew more than LBJ about how to get things done in Washington.

Lyndon Johnson was sworn in as president aboard Air Force One before it left Dallas, only 90 minutes after Kennedy was pronounced dead. Crowded into the plane's stateroom, and photographed by White House photographer Cecil Stoughton, were Johnson, Judge Sara Hughes, Jacqueline Kennedy, Johnson's wife Lady Bird, reporters, and Kennedy's staff.

THE CIVIL RIGHTS ACT

With his political expertise, Johnson was able to win early legislative victories. One of his first presidential acts was to work for the stalled tax cut Kennedy had supported. Like Kennedy, Johnson believed lower taxes would encourage economic growth and reduce unemployment. In February 1964, he signed a measure that cut taxes by $10 billion over the following two years. The economy responded. The GNP rose by 7 percent in 1964 and 8 percent in 1965. Unemployment fell below 5 percent for the first time since World War II. As Johnson predicted, the resulting economic growth also generated greater federal revenues.

Johnson entered the White House with three decades of political experience in hand. After running the Texas division of the National Youth Administration, a New Deal program, he won a seat in Congress in 1937. By 1949, Johnson had become a master of Texas politics, and used all his savvy to win election to the U.S. Senate. Elected Senate majority leader in the 1950s, he worked with the Eisenhower White House to craft important legislation on defense spending, highway construction, and civil rights. Johnson proved to be such an effective Senate majority leader that some even referred to him as the "Master of the Senate."

He became president under tragic circumstances but moved quickly to restore public confidence through a smooth transition of power. Johnson told Congress, "The ideas and ideals which [Kennedy] so nobly represented must and will be translated into effective action." To provide continuity, he kept Kennedy's team largely intact, persuading Secretary of State Dean Rusk, Secretary of Defense Robert McNamara, and other key cabinet members to stay on.

Johnson also set about achieving some of Kennedy's civil rights goals. Both Kennedy and Johnson were supporters of civil rights and believed the federal government needed to create laws to help promote greater equality in the United States. As Senate majority leader, Johnson had steered the Civil Rights Acts of 1957 and 1960 through Congress. Just weeks after taking office, Johnson met with Martin Luther King, Jr., and other African-American leaders to assure them of his commitment to a stronger civil rights act—the one Kennedy had proposed in 1963.

At great political risk, Johnson immediately took up the battle for Kennedy's stalled bill. "No memorial oration or eulogy," Johnson said in a speech to Congress on November 27, 1963, "could more eloquently honor President Kennedy's memory than the earliest possible passage of the civil rights bill for which he fought so long." Johnson then successfully persuaded Congress to enact federal programs in civil rights, education, and social welfare.

In early 1964, the House of Representatives, by a vote of 290 to 130, approved Kennedy's civil rights bill, but it hit a wall in the Senate. Southern senators had formed a bloc to oppose the bill. They used the **filibuster**—a strategy in which a small group of senators take turns speaking and refuse to stop the debate or allow the bill to come to a vote—against it. A number of Democratic and Republican senators gathered **bipartisan** support to ultimately end what had grown to an 83-day filibuster. The Senate passed the bill, proving Congress's commitment to civil rights.

On July 2, President Johnson signed the **Civil Rights Act of 1964** into law. The seven-part act was one of the most comprehensive civil rights laws Congress

---

PLAN: 4-PAGE LESSON

OBJECTIVE

Analyze Lyndon Johnson's transition to president and the passage—and effects—of key civil rights legislation in the country.

CRITICAL THINKING SKILLS FOR LESSON 2.1

- Compare and Contrast
- Draw Conclusions
- Determine Chronology
- Summarize
- Make Inferences
- Analyze Primary Sources
- Describe
- Evaluate

HISTORICAL THINKING FOR CHAPTER 26

What challenges did Americans face during the 1960s? As Lyndon Johnson began his presidency, the country still mourned the loss of President Kennedy and the civil rights movement was in full swing. Lesson 2.1 discusses how Johnson moved forward during this time of transition.

BACKGROUND FOR THE TEACHER

An unusual set of circumstances enabled the Civil Rights Act of 1964 to pass, despite strong opposition. Televised news of the fight against segregation had mobilized public opinion, and Kennedy's death had created support in Congress to continue his progressive agenda. In addition, Texas-born Lyndon Johnson, who had seen as a young teacher how prejudice and poverty restricted the lives of minorities, was determined to change these conditions. Johnson seized his chance when he became president, although he would lose southern votes. When the Senate filibuster threatened to kill the Civil Rights Act, he turned to an unlikely ally—conservative Republican Everett Dirksen, who ordinarily championed the rights of states over the federal government. This time, however, Dirksen understood that the public and a majority of legislators strongly favored the act. He agreed to help end the filibuster, quoting French author Victor Hugo: "Stronger than all the armies is an idea whose time has come."

INTRODUCE & ENGAGE

IDENTIFY PRESIDENT KENNEDY'S LEGACY

Ask students to recall proposals that President Kennedy had been successful and unsuccessful at getting through Congress. Draw a T-Chart with the headings Successful Proposals and Unsuccessful Proposals and record students' responses. Responses under Successful Proposals might include a tax cut for consumers that resulted in low unemployment and stable prices, an increase in Social Security benefits, an increase in minimum wage, the Peace Corps (by executive action), and the space program. Responses under Unsuccessful Proposals might include an increase in spending for construction of schools and teacher salaries, the expansion of the power of federal government, and a civil rights bill. Point out that after President Kennedy was assassinated, Lyndon Johnson had a number of issues to deal with as he assumed the presidency. Then tell students that Lesson 2.1 describes how President Johnson used federal power to address Kennedy's unresolved civil rights agenda.

Successful Proposals	Unsuccessful Proposals

TEACH

GUIDED DISCUSSION

1. **Summarize** How might events have taken a different direction if, in his first four months in office, Johnson had not carried out Kennedy's initiatives? *(Possible response: Johnson managed to pass tax-cut legislation, which stimulated the economy, and continued work on civil rights legislation. If he hadn't passed that legislation, economic growth would have stalled. The GNP would not have risen but unemployment would have.)*

2. **Draw Conclusions** Why might civil rights leaders have expected Johnson, who was from the South, to maintain Kennedy's civil rights agenda? *(Possible response: Johnson had been working on civil rights legislation since the Eisenhower years and had helped pass two previous civil rights bills. He also met with Martin Luther King, Jr., and others to pledge his support.)*

3. **Make Inferences** What did the southern senators hope to accomplish by conducting such a long filibuster of the Civil Rights Act? *(Possible response: They probably hoped they could force the government to drop its efforts to pass the bill, since the filibuster prevented anything else from getting done in the Senate.)*

ANALYZE PRIMARY SOURCES

Tell students that both Richard Russell, Jr., and Everett M. Dirksen were considered articulate, skilled orators. They were recognized as leaders in the Senate and, through their eloquence, often rallied other senators to their causes. **ASK:** What language does Russell use that shows he will not tolerate any kind of civil rights changes? *(Possible response: He says he will resist "any measure and any movement" that would even have a "tendency" to let the races be equal or mix together.)* What effect might this excerpt from Dirksen's speech have had on his listeners? *(Possible responses: The short sentence structure is direct and creates a feeling of urgency regarding civil rights. Dirksen's statement that the issue is "moral in character" makes any rebuttal of the cause seem morally and ethically wrong, so listeners would have found it emotionally compelling.)*

DIFFERENTIATE

ENGLISH LANGUAGE LEARNERS

Understanding a Loan Word Have students at **All Proficiencies** review how the word *savvy* is used in the lesson to describe both Kennedy and Johnson. Explain that the word came from the Portuguese term *sabe*, meaning "he or she knows," which then became part of English-based Creole languages of the West Indies, and finally entered English as *savvy*. (Spanish and French speakers will recognize *sabe/savez* because all three languages share the word's Latin root *sapere*.) Tell students to explore the meaning of *savvy* in a dictionary and then create at least two original sentences using the word. Invite students to share their sentences with the class.

GIFTED & TALENTED

Write Diary Entries Instruct students to conduct online research to learn more about Johnson's words and actions in the 100 days following Kennedy's assassination. Based on their research, challenge students to write a series of diary entries that Johnson might have written. Each entry should have a date and include legislative priorities and strategies as well as personal thoughts and feelings. Encourage students to quote LBJ and also touch upon possible reasons Johnson may have had for pursuing Kennedy's agenda—not only to honor the murdered president but also to ensure his own influence and legacy. Invite students to share their diary entries with the class as dramatic readings.

See the Chapter Planner for more strategies for differentiation.

had ever enacted. It expanded the role of the federal government in the fight for civil rights by enforcing desegregation in public schools and prohibiting discrimination in federally funded public programs and in such facilities as restaurants, parks, libraries, and movie theaters. The new law made discrimination in the workplace based on gender illegal, and it created the **Equal Employment Opportunity Commission (EEOC)** to monitor and protect workplace rights. The act prohibited employment discrimination based on race, creed, national origin, and gender. As a result of the Civil Rights Act, women and minorities who faced workplace discrimination could seek assistance from the EEOC.

RESISTANCE IN THE SOUTH

The Civil Rights Act of 1964 met with stiff resistance in the South. One of the most notable examples occurred in Atlanta, Georgia, within a few days of the act's signing. A segregationist restaurant owner named Lester Maddox refused to serve food to three African-American college students, calling them "dirty devils" and "dirty communists" and pointing a gun at them. Some of the white customers in the restaurant threatened the students with ax handles that Maddox kept on hand. A month later, Maddox decided to close his restaurant rather than obey a court order to desegregate it. Maddox went on to become governor of Georgia in 1966.

Dr. Martin Luther King, Jr., stands behind President Lyndon Johnson (seated) to witness the signing of the Civil Rights Act of 1964. Others in the room include Republican and Democratic representatives who voted for the most far-reaching civil rights legislation enacted since Reconstruction.

CRITICAL VIEWING In the South, African Americans were still being kept from voting even after the Civil Rights Act was passed. On September 7, 1963, SNCC organized more than 350 African Americans to come to register to vote at the county courthouse in Selma, Alabama. What appears to be taking place on the courthouse steps?

Voting rights gained additional protection in August 1964 when the states ratified the **24th Amendment**, which banned poll taxes. Southern states had required citizens to pay fixed voter registration fees, a strategy used to discourage African Americans from voting. With these landmark laws, the federal government re-established a commitment to providing people of all races, ethnicities, religious groups, and sexes with the rights of full citizenship.

December 1964 brought yet another victory for the civil rights movement. Dr. Martin Luther King, Jr., was awarded the Nobel Peace Prize for his leadership in the movement against discrimination and segregation and his commitment to nonviolence in the effort. In his acceptance speech, he said, "I refuse to accept the view that mankind is so tragically bound to the starless midnight of racism and war that the bright daybreak of peace and brotherhood can never become a reality."

King celebrated the 1964 Civil Rights Act as a tremendous advance in the struggle for racial equality, but believed it fell short in some areas, especially voting rights. The act restricted, but did not prohibit, literacy tests and other tricks white segregationists used to **disenfranchise** African Americans, or take away their right to vote. The tricks proved effective: in many areas of the Deep South, only a small percentage of the African-American population was registered to vote. King and other civil rights leaders chose establishing hard and fast voting rights as their next battle, while Johnson turned to other social and international issues.

HISTORICAL THINKING

1. **READING CHECK** Why did Johnson want members of Kennedy's Cabinet to stay in their current roles?

2. **COMPARE AND CONTRAST** Examine the primary source excerpts in this lesson. How do the senators' points of view differ on the issue of civil rights?

3. **DRAW CONCLUSIONS** How do you think Johnson's experiences in Congress may have helped him get legislation passed as president?

4. **DETERMINE CHRONOLOGY** How did the Civil Rights Act of 1964 build on previous legislation and civil rights activism?

BUILD BACKGROUND

NEED FOR FEDERAL POWER

When schools first became desegregated in the 1950s and 1960s, people saw whites blocking school doorways, attacking desegregation buses, and resisting federal orders. Why was federal power needed to help integrate schools? Surprisingly, the answer dates back to the 1600s and 1700s, when the Atlantic slave trade began. To justify slavery, some Europeans and Americans developed the theory that human beings were divided into races, with the white race superior to them all. Various "scientific" measures were used to bolster this theory, but its main purpose was to show that those being enslaved could never achieve the same intellectual, moral, or spiritual levels as whites. Over time, the false idea of racial superiority became institutionalized in many states as segregation laws. With whites firmly in control of life in the states, any change to segregation had to come from the federal level of government. A federal civil rights act would supersede all segregation laws and finally give African Americans and others access to a better education, employment opportunities, and the voting booth. To this day, federal laws guarantee equal rights and protections for all citizens.

TEACH

GUIDED DISCUSSION

4. **Describe** How was the federal government involved in the civil rights movement? *(It passed the Civil Rights Act, which expanded the power of the federal government to enforce school desegregation and prohibit discrimination. The new law also created the Equal Employment Opportunity Commission (EEOC), which protects workplace rights. With the 24th Amendment, the federal government re-established full rights for all citizens.)*

5. **Evaluate** How did the 24th Amendment affect the voting process in the South for white southerners and African Americans? *(Possible response: White southerners lost a valuable weapon in the poll tax, but they still had ways to deny people the vote. For African Americans, removal of the poll tax was only a first step; stronger measures were needed to significantly change restrictions on voting.)*

MORE INFORMATION

African Americans' Civil Rights Prior to the 1960s Explain to students that African Americans had achieved full civil rights under two acts passed in 1866 and 1875. Among other rights, these acts granted freed slaves all the rights and privileges given to white citizens, particularly in the judicial process, and prohibited discrimination in housing, transportation, and public facilities. By the early 1900s, however, nearly all provisions of the acts had been nullified by the courts, including the U.S. Supreme Court. These rights would not be restored until the 1960s.

ACTIVE OPTIONS

On Your Feet: Compare Civil Rights Acts Have students work in groups to obtain and read copies of the Civil Rights Acts of 1875 and 1964. These documents are available online or in most libraries. Ask students to fill out a Venn diagram to compare and contrast the provisions of the two acts. Instruct groups to discuss the expanding role of the federal government as a political development in promoting civil rights and then share their ideas as a class.

Civil Rights Acts

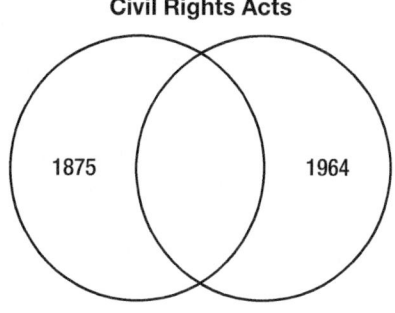

1875   1964

NG Learning Framework: Evaluate Arguments

SKILL Communication

KNOWLEDGE Our Human Story

Encourage students to read Senator Richard Russell's "Southern Manifesto" or a 1960s speech by Governor Maddox or Governor Wallace. These documents are available online or in the public library. Ask students to evaluate their chosen politician's premises, claims, and evidence by corroborating or challenging them with other information. Tell students to consider the following questions when conducting their evaluations: What underlying assumptions does the person make? How does he develop his argument or opinion, and what are his conclusions? Which arguments are valid and which ones are fallacious or misleading? Invite students to share their work with the class.

HISTORICAL THINKING

ANSWERS

1. He wanted to reassure the nation that there would be a smooth transition of power after Kennedy's assassination and that Kennedy's programs would go forward.

2. Their views are completely opposite. Russell will fight to maintain separation of the races "to the bitter end." Dirksen believes integration is a moral issue whose time has come and that it should be implemented without delay.

3. Johnson's experience in Congress was invaluable. He could use his knowledge, relationships, and influence to get bipartisan support for his legislation.

4. Johnson had helped Congress pass Civil Rights Acts in 1957 and 1960, which both had weaknesses. This realization, in addition to activists' grassroots efforts to register people to vote and organize protests against segregation, provided a strong foundation for what became the Civil Rights Act of 1964.

CRITICAL VIEWING Possible response: There appears to be a confrontation occurring between the white policemen and the African-American men urging others to register to vote. The officer on the left is showing one of the African-American men some kind of document, perhaps an order to leave the courthouse steps. The officer in the center has his baton out and seems ready to use it. The three other men are watching the confrontation, waiting to see what will happen.

THE GREAT SOCIETY

Do you know someone who can walk into a room and make his or her presence felt right away? To many people, that was President Lyndon Johnson. The president had energy and determination to spare, and he relied on it to work toward many lofty goals.

LANDSLIDE IN 1964

Lyndon Johnson achieved legislative success early on as he worked to accomplish some of Kennedy's goals. Johnson hoped to build on this momentum and enact his own sweeping presidential agenda. First, he would have to hold on to the presidency by winning the 1964 election. Johnson chose as his running mate Senator Hubert H. Humphrey of Minnesota, a likable leader nicknamed "the Happy Warrior," who shared Johnson's goals.

For Republicans, things did not line up so easily. By 1964, the party was facing deep divisions between moderates, who supported the civil rights movement and agreed with a limited expansion of government, and conservatives, who favored smaller government and the use of force to stop communism.

PRIMARY SOURCE

The Great Society is a place where every child can find knowledge to enrich his mind and to enlarge his talents. It is a place where the city of man serves not only the needs of the body and the demands of commerce but the desire for beauty and the hunger for community.

But most of all, the Great Society is not a safe harbor, a resting place, a final objective, a finished work. It is a challenge constantly renewed, beckoning us toward a destiny where the meaning of our lives matches the marvelous products of our labor.

—from a speech at the University of Michigan by President Lyndon B. Johnson, May 22, 1964

After intense debate, Republicans nominated conservative senator **Barry Goldwater** of Arizona for president and Representative William Miller of New York as his running mate. Goldwater's vision for the country couldn't have been further from those of Johnson and Kennedy. In the Senate, he had voted against Social Security increases, the Nuclear Test Ban Treaty of 1963, and the Civil Rights Act of 1964. In accepting the nomination, Goldwater promised a "spiritual awakening" for the United States. He declared: "Extremism in the defense of liberty is no vice. Moderation in the pursuit of justice is no virtue."

The Johnson campaign focused on some of Goldwater's most extreme views to portray him as a dangerous and unpredictable candidate. In one of the most famous television campaign commercials ever, a three-year-old child was shown counting the petals of a daisy, out of order. Her counting turned into an ominous male voice counting down to a launch. The girl disappeared as the viewer saw a missile being launched, followed by the blast and mushroom cloud of a nuclear explosion. The "Daisy" ad, the name by which it became known, implied that Goldwater would destroy innocent lives by leading the nation into a nuclear war. Viewers found the commercial so disturbing that it ran only once.

On Election Day, Johnson won 61 percent of the popular vote and 44 of the 50 states, which translated to 486 electoral votes. Johnson's lopsided margin of victory helped the Democrats increase their substantial majorities in both houses of Congress. Although the Republicans lost ground, the election returns showed that a new coalition was forming in their ranks. The party was gaining strength among middle-class white voters in the South and Southwest. Furthermore, Goldwater attracted thousands of young recruits determined to reshape the Republican Party along more conservative lines. For the growing number of Republicans, 1964 was a beginning rather than the end.

WAR ON POVERTY

President Johnson viewed his landslide victory as a mandate for change. He spoke of creating "a great society" for Americans, one free of poverty, ignorance, and discrimination, where the spirit of "true community" would prevail. Together, his sweeping set of programs became known as the **Great Society**. The centerpiece of Johnson's agenda was what he called his **War on Poverty**—an all-out effort to address the persistence of poverty and create a decent standard of living for all Americans. Despite a strong economy, about 20 percent of the nation still lived in poverty in 1964. "We shall not rest until [this] war is won," Johnson insisted. "The richest nation on Earth can afford to win it. We cannot afford to lose it."

Some War on Poverty programs aimed to help children. **Head Start**, for example, was an educational program designed to better prepare low-income preschoolers for primary school. Title I of the

Federal spending on education in 1966 funded this Head Start program in Clarksdale, Mississippi, providing both jobs for teachers and learning opportunities for children.

PLAN: 4-PAGE LESSON

OBJECTIVE

Learn about the government programs Lyndon Johnson enacted to help improve people's lives.

CRITICAL THINKING SKILLS FOR LESSON 2.2

- Ask and Answer Questions
- Interpret Graphs
- Evaluate
- Analyze Language Use
- Make Connections
- Analyze Primary Sources
- Synthesize

HISTORICAL THINKING FOR CHAPTER 26

What challenges did Americans face during the 1960s? While the U.S. economy was strong, many people still lived in poverty. To address the issue of poverty—as well as health care and immigration—President Johnson initiated the Great Society. Lesson 2.2 discusses the impact of his programs on the nation.

BACKGROUND FOR THE TEACHER

As a young teacher in Cotulla, Texas, Lyndon Johnson saw his students regularly going through the garbage for something to eat. This gave him a lifelong desire to create a better society. Johnson's vision focused on equal opportunity and job creation. Johnson realized he would need bipartisan support to put his ideas into action. Rather than pit rich against poor, liberal against conservative, he focused on the common enemies of society—poverty, ignorance, ill health, and discrimination. For example, Head Start, based on the latest research on poverty in the 1960s, was designed to help low-income families not only with their educational needs but also with their emotional, social, health, nutritional, and psychological needs. Today, Head Start still enjoys strong bipartisan support.

HISTORY NOTEBOOK

Encourage students to complete the Great Society page for Chapter 26 in their History Notebooks as they read.

INTRODUCE & ENGAGE

EXPLORE THE WAR ON POVERTY

Write *War on Poverty* in the center circle of a Concept Cluster and discuss with students what that concept might mean. Then have them study the black-and-white photograph and read the caption about Head Start. Explain that Head Start was one of President Johnson's programs to fight the war on poverty. Ask students to think of other programs the government might create to eliminate poverty. Record their suggestions in the outer circles of the Concept Cluster. After students have made suggestions, discuss the following questions: What groups of people might need such programs the most? How might the government measure the programs' success or failure? Write students' answers on the lines extending out from the outer circles. Tell students that in this lesson they will learn about Johnson's sweeping set of programs to improve the standard of living in the United States.

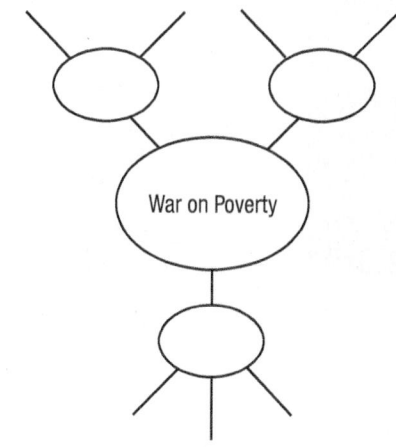

War on Poverty

TEACH

GUIDED DISCUSSION

1. **Evaluate** Why were the outcomes of the 1964 election so important for Johnson in terms of his agenda? *(Possible response: In winning by a landslide, he felt he had a mandate from the people to enact change in the country. The election also gave Democrats greater control of Congress, which meant he had a better chance of getting his legislation passed.)*

2. **Analyze Language Use** What might Johnson have meant when he said that the richest nation on Earth could afford to win but not afford to lose the war on poverty? *(Possible response: "War" implies an all-out effort by government and industry to defeat an enemy—in this case, poverty. He uses two meanings of "afford": The United States has the resources to afford, or pay for, the War on Poverty programs, but it cannot afford, or risk, to lose the war and leave so many people in poverty.)*

3. **Make Connections** How does the photograph of the Head Start classroom demonstrate ways in which programs like Head Start influenced economic and social development for low-income families? *(Possible response: The photo shows children receiving early education, which could help them catch up to more affluent students; it also shows the employment opportunities for adults that Head Start created.)*

ANALYZE PRIMARY SOURCES

Have students read the excerpt from Johnson's speech, noticing how he describes the Great Society. **ASK:** What human needs does Johnson believe are important for a Great Society to meet? *(Possible response: the human needs for knowledge, physical health, economic opportunities, beauty, and community)* According to Johnson, how does the Great Society exemplify the purpose of American society? *(Possible response: He says that the purpose is not to create a "safe harbor" or "finished work" but to help the country achieve a society in which meaningful lives are as important as productive achievements.)*

DIFFERENTIATE

STRIVING READERS

Predict Using Visuals Guide students to predict how the two photographs and the chart in this lesson are related to President Johnson's philosophy, legislative achievements, and lasting impact. First have students read the lesson title and Main Idea statement. Then ask them to examine the visuals and read the captions, using that information to write predictions. After students read the lesson, tell them to discuss with a partner what they learned and whether or not it matched their predictions.

PRE-AP

Report on a Presidential Plan Instruct students to research and write a report on Johnson's relative success or failure to reach his stated goal to build a Great Society that would, among other things, "end poverty and racial injustice." Have students complete a Goal-and-Outcome Chart to keep track of their research and organize their report. Encourage students to explore why achieving the Great Society was important to Johnson and to offer insights about why his plans did or did not result in the changes he hoped for.

Goals	Obstacles	Outcome

Summary

See the Chapter Planner for more strategies for differentiation.

Food stamps help people pay for meals, but low-income neighborhoods often lack supermarkets with affordable healthy foods. In response, a nonprofit organization in Chicago has pioneered the use of buses to bring fresh produce to communities where there are no markets residents can reach easily.

IMMIGRATION AND CITIZENSHIP, 1960–2015

Source: Migration Policy Institute

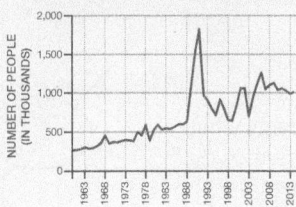

Non-U.S. Citizens Granted Permanent-Resident Status by Year, 1963–2013

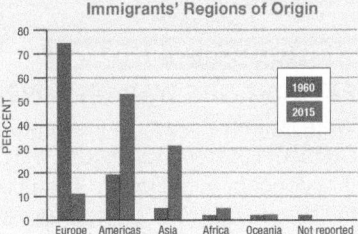

Immigrants' Regions of Origin

Elementary and Secondary Education Act of 1965 provided extra federal funding to public schools that served a high percentage of low-income students. In addition, the Food Stamp program helped families afford nutritional meals. Johnson himself had experienced poverty and hunger as a child, and those memories drove his desire to help relieve the suffering of others.

As another part of his antipoverty effort, Johnson pushed the **Economic Opportunity Act** through Congress in 1964. The act established a range of programs aimed at creating jobs and battling poverty. The War on Poverty focused attention on community action, which led to an increase of minority participation in local affairs. Johnson named Peace Corps director R. Sargent Shriver to coordinate the numerous work programs created by the act. These work programs included the Job Corps, an education and training program for young people; the Neighborhood Youth Corps, which provided employment, job counseling, and additional education to low-income youth; and Volunteers in Service to America (VISTA), a domestic service program modeled on the Peace Corps.

Overall, the War on Poverty achieved considerable success. It did not eradicate poverty, and some critics have argued that it made impoverished people dependent on the federal government. Nonetheless, poverty declined dramatically in the late 1960s—the result of both the expanding economy and the federal programs aimed directly at alleviating poverty. By 1970, the number of Americans living below the poverty line had dropped from more than 40 million (about 20 percent of the population) to around 24 million (about 12 percent). Over the years, Congress continued to renew many of these anti-poverty programs, most of which are still in place today.

HEALTH CARE AND IMMIGRATION

In addition to tackling the issue of poverty, Johnson believed medical care for all was an essential part of the Great Society. When Johnson took office in 1963, a majority of older Americans, as well as the one-fifth of the nation living below the poverty line, were without health insurance. The American Medical Association (AMA) and private insurers strongly opposed the idea of lower-cost or even free health care, calling it "socialized medicine." The president, however, was determined. After months of intense lobbying, Congress passed landmark legislation that Johnson had requested to fund medical insurance for the neediest Americans. The legislation created two federal programs. **Medicare** provided federal health care assistance to the elderly. **Medicaid** extended medical coverage to welfare recipients.

Both programs grew rapidly, reaching as many as 40 million Americans by 1970. Supporters pointed to statistics showing an increase in life expectancy and a drop in infant mortality as a result of the programs. However, opponents argued the programs led to high costs and gaps in coverage, while the quality of care patients received through the programs was low.

The Great Society also included an important new immigration law that went largely unnoticed at the time. In one bold sweep, the **Immigration Act of 1965** removed the national origins quotas as well as the ban on Asians, which dated back to 1924. Although it capped the number of immigrants allowed into the country at about 300,000 per year, the law permitted many foreign family members of American citizens to enter the United States without limit. Immigration from Asia and Latin America grew rapidly. By the mid-1970s, the majority of legal immigrants came from seven Asian and Latin American countries: Korea, Taiwan, India, the Philippines, Cuba, the Dominican Republic, and Mexico. The law had a dramatic impact on the **demographic composition** of the United States, which refers to the number and concentration of a variety of ethnic groups within the nation.

THE DOMINICAN INTERVENTION

The challenges faced by President Johnson and his administration were not confined to domestic issues, however. In 1965, the United States intervened in a civil war in the nearby **Dominican Republic**. The Dominican Republic lies slightly southeast of Cuba and shares the island of Hispaniola with the nation of Haiti.

Until he was assassinated in 1961, General **Rafael Trujillo** (troo-HEE-yoh) had ruled over the Dominican Republic as a dictator for more than 30 years. Although a brutal leader, he opposed communism, earning U.S. support. His death created a power vacuum, and the government was unstable for several years. In 1965, civil war broke out. In April of that year, Johnson sent in thousands of U.S. Marines, who joined troops from the Organization of American States in an attempt to bring the chaotic situation under control. The official reason for Johnson's action, which became known as the **Dominican Intervention**, was to rescue Americans on the island. However, the actual reason for the intervention was to keep communism from spreading to other Caribbean nations.

The strategy worked. The troops put down the rebellion within a few weeks, and the OAS restored a democratically elected government to the Dominican Republic. While the outcome was positive, Johnson was widely criticized for using American military might to interfere in the government of another nation. This criticism grew as the United States became involved even more deeply in a fight against communism in Vietnam, half a world away.

HISTORICAL THINKING

1. **READING CHECK** What was the Great Society?

2. **ASK AND ANSWER QUESTIONS** Read about cost-benefit analysis in the online Financial Literacy Handbook. Generate a list of questions you could ask to help determine how society benefits economically from the reduction of poverty.

3. **INTERPRET GRAPHS** Which region of the world experienced the largest decrease in immigration to the United States from 1960 to 2015?

BUILD BACKGROUND

IMMIGRATION REFORM IN 1965

The Immigration Act of 1965 was considered landmark legislation in establishing a new egalitarian basis for immigration. The prior immigration quotas had been based on the same type of racial hierarchy as the one used to justify slavery. The earlier law clearly stated that white people from Scandinavia and western Europe were superior to people from southern Europe, the Mediterranean area, and all other regions of the world. During the early 1960s, people from Portugal, Italy, Greece, and other countries protested against such discrimination. In an era when civil rights and equality had become a national priority, the old racially based policy was an embarrassment. The Democratic Party, led by Kennedy and Johnson, pledged to address the issue. Symbolically, the 1965 Immigration Act was signed in a ceremony held at the foot of the Statue of Liberty. Yet very few officials and experts believed that the law would significantly change the nation's demographic composition. President Johnson and Secretary of State Dean Rusk estimated that only a few thousand people would take advantage of the new immigration policy since its main purpose was to reunite families. Officials at the Customs and Immigration Services (CIS), however, understood the implications. The new law would not only cause a sharp increase in applications, they contended, but also cause foreign-born minorities to flood the system with petitions for their relatives to immigrate. The CIS predictions turned out to be true. The government had badly underestimated how many people wanted to come to the United States.

TEACH

GUIDED DISCUSSION

4. **Synthesize** What general needs of the poor did the War on Poverty programs address, and what was the overall result of these programs? *(Possible response: The programs addressed the needs for education, nutrition, jobs, community action, and health care. The programs appeared to have an overall positive result; in only five years, the number of people living in poverty was reduced, infant mortality declined, and life expectancy increased.)*

5. **Make Connections** How do you think the nation's focus on equality and the Great Society affected the transformation of the American demographic composition, as shown in the graphs? *(Possible response: The Immigration Act of 1965 removed the national origin quotas, which favored Europeans, and gave people from all nations an equal opportunity to immigrate to the United States. Thus, thousands of people from around the world came to this country, particularly Asians, who had been barred for many years. Also, the movement to unite families probably added to the number of immigrants from Asia and Latin America.)*

EVALUATE

Ask students to think about the various programs and the international policy implemented during the Johnson administration. **ASK:** How well did Johnson maintain Kennedy's domestic and international agenda? *(Possible response: Johnson followed through on Kennedy's concerns with equality and civil rights, including reforming immigration, and also continued efforts to contain communism abroad by intervening in the Dominican Republic.)*

ACTIVE OPTIONS

On Your Feet: Immigration Criteria Roundtable
Explain to students that setting criteria for numbers and categories of people who can enter the United States each year has always been a subject of debate. Discuss with them the kinds of criteria for immigration they may already have heard about. Arrange students in groups of four and tell them to imagine that they are part of an immigration committee advising the president. Have each student around the table provide an immigration criterion he or she believes would be fair and realistic to recommend. Ask students to provide reasons for their criteria. Afterward, invite groups to share their criteria.

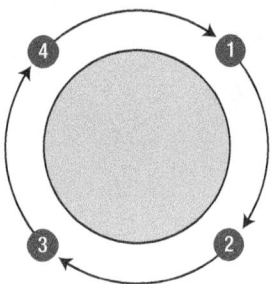

NG Learning Framework: Conduct a Cost-Benefit Analysis   STEM

SKILL Communication

KNOWLEDGE Our Human Story

Explain to students that to determine the effectiveness of social programs, economists often do cost-benefit analyses and use measures of aggregate economic behaviors, such as increases or decreases in tax revenues, employment figures, number of people living in poverty, and number of children served by programs. Have students choose a War on Poverty program, such as Head Start or Job Corps, and research data on the program to conduct a cost-benefit analysis, using aggregate economic indicators (e.g., number of families lifted out of poverty, number of people employed, and so on). Direct students to the Financial Literacy handbook, Lesson 3, for help in constructing a cost-benefit analysis. Have them share their analyses with the class.

For students who develop an interest in the genesis of social change in the United States, suggest that they read the online American Story "The Counterculture of the 1960s."

HISTORICAL THINKING

ANSWERS

1. Johnson envisioned the Great Society as one free of poverty, ignorance, and discrimination, thus creating a spirit of true community. The Great Society consisted of a set of programs, with the key program being the War on Poverty.

2. Answers will vary. Possible responses: Can the Great Society programs actually reduce the number of people living in poverty? How would money spent on nutritional programs reduce child mortality? Can job-training programs increase the number of people employed? How can assistance to low-income people raise their overall standard of living?

3. Europe experienced the largest decrease in immigration from 1960 to 2015.

SELMA TO MONTGOMERY

For centuries, African Americans suffered cruel and violent oppression. That treatment continued as they marched for voting rights, but as support grew from around the country, glimmers of hope appeared.

MARCHING FOR EQUALITY

As you have read, Dr. Martin Luther King, Jr., viewed the 1964 Civil Rights Act as a victory for racial equality, but he felt it fell short in terms of voting rights. Securing equal voting rights for all, King and other civil rights leaders believed, was the next battle to wage. One place where the fight was already underway was Selma, Alabama, where in 1963 SNCC and other local activists had organized a "Freedom Day." Lines formed around the block as 350 African-American people appeared at the courthouse to register to vote. Facing strong white resistance, the activists asked King and SCLC for support.

In the first of a series of 1965 voting rights marches, Alabama police gave demonstrators two minutes to turn around at the Edmund Pettus Bridge. The marchers paused, but the police advanced anyway and beat the demonstrators, sending more than 50 people to the hospital on what became known as Bloody Sunday.

Freedom Day led to the Selma voting rights campaign that began early in 1965. Local African Americans marched daily to the courthouse, where Sheriff Jim Clark—wearing a huge button bearing the single word *NEVER*—turned them away with force. Thousands were beaten with clubs, shocked with cattle prods, and arrested for attempting to register with the local election board.

On March 7, a day that would be remembered as **Bloody Sunday**, 700 people set out to walk 50 miles to the state capital on the first of 3 **Selma-to-Montgomery marches**. Leading the procession was a key organizer of the march, **John Lewis**, a representative of SNCC. Upon crossing the Edmund Pettus Bridge at the edge of Selma, Lewis and the marchers found their way blocked by a large contingent of Sheriff Clark's deputies and Alabama state police. When the peaceful marchers refused orders to disperse, the police attacked them with clubs, whips, and tear gas. The police officers forced the marchers to retreat while white onlookers cheered. Dozens of marchers were injured, and some required hospitalization. News crews captured the assault on film. That evening, television stations aired the shocking footage into millions of American homes, sparking national outrage and calls for government action to protect voting rights.

On March 9, a crowd of 2,000 people gathered with King for the second march. Roughly a third were religious leaders who had rushed to Selma to show their support. When they crossed the Edmund Pettus Bridge and again faced a roadblock, the marchers knelt in prayer. Then, instead of attempting to continue on to Montgomery, they turned back. That night in Selma, a group of white segregationists attacked three white Unitarian Universalist ministers who had participated in the march. One of the ministers, James Reeb, died from his injuries two days later.

On March 21, a third attempt at the march to Montgomery got underway, with King leading roughly 3,200 marchers out of Selma. Under the terms of a ruling by a federal judge, more than 1,800 members of the Alabama National Guard under federal command, as well as roughly 2,000 U.S. soldiers, federal marshals, and FBI agents, protected the marchers. The protesters walked about 12 miles each day and slept in fields along the highway at night. Their numbers grew along the way, and on the fifth day, 25,000 marchers arrived at the steps of the state capitol for a final rally.

VOTING RIGHTS ACT OF 1965

In early August 1965, less than five months after the Selma-to-Montgomery marches, Congress passed the **Voting Rights Act of 1965**, and President Johnson signed it into law. The act outlawed literacy tests and other discriminatory tactics used by segregationists to deny African Americans and other minorities the right to vote. It also required states with a history of voting discrimination to obtain approval from federal authorities for any changes, even minor ones, to their voting laws or practices. The act did not ban poll taxes, but it directed the U.S. attorney general to challenge their constitutionality wherever they were found to be in use in local and state elections.

It did not take long for the impact of this **landmark legislation**, or important and historic law, to be felt. By the end of 1965, as many as 250,000 new African-American voters had been registered, and within three years, the registration rate of African Americans in the South had climbed to more than 60 percent. Although challenged in the courts because it changed the relationship of the federal and state governments, the Supreme Court upheld the act's constitutionality in 1966 and in 1968. With the Civil Rights Act of 1964 and the Voting Rights Act of 1965, the civil rights movement had been the most important stimulus in moving the federal government to ensure and protect African-American civil rights, including voting rights.

The movement used grassroots activism to mobilize the government into defending those rights for all citizens. Through the efforts of grassroots organizations and the leadership of presidents Kennedy and Johnson, the civil rights movement made great strides in the 1960s in the South. Discrimination was most visible and dramatic there, but African Americans also faced obstacles in the North, where there was still much work to be done.

HISTORICAL THINKING

1. **READING CHECK** How did the passage of the Civil Rights Act of 1964 and the Voting Rights Act of 1965 affect the nation?

2. **MAKE CONNECTIONS** Describe the role of the government, citizens, and religious leaders in the civil rights movement.

3. **SYNTHESIZE** How did the Selma marches represent the role of civil rights advocates in ensuring the ability of African Americans to vote in elections?

PLAN: 2-PAGE LESSON

OBJECTIVE

Learn about the role of African-American civil rights leaders in the passage of the Voting Rights Act of 1965.

CRITICAL THINKING SKILLS FOR LESSON 2.3

• Make Connections

• Synthesize

• Identify Problems and Solutions

• Make Predictions

HISTORICAL THINKING FOR CHAPTER 26

What challenges did Americans face during the 1960s? During the early 1960s, African Americans still did not have equal voting rights. As peaceful protesters marched in Alabama for the right to vote, state police blocked and attacked the marchers. Lesson 2.3 discusses how the work of civil rights advocates led to the passing of the Voting Rights Act of 1965.

BACKGROUND FOR THE TEACHER

On March 7, 2015, thousands of marchers gathered on the Edmund Pettus Bridge to mark the 50th anniversary of Bloody Sunday. The crowd included not only some of the same civil rights advocates, such as John Lewis, who played a role in the first march but also Barack Obama, the first African-American president of the United States. His presence signified, more than anything else, the far-reaching effects of the Voting Rights Act. The peaceful, racially mixed scene on the bridge that day was in marked contrast to the confrontation shown in the lesson's photograph. Even though the bridge still carries the name of two-term U.S. senator and Alabama Ku Klux Klan leader Edmund Pettus, people of both races have resisted efforts to rename the bridge. They believe that if the name were changed, the memory of the history they lived through would also be forgotten. With its mixed heritage, the bridge remains a monument to the civil rights struggle.

INTRODUCE & ENGAGE

DISCUSS VOTING RIGHTS

Have students discuss why a group might want to deny others the right to vote. As a class, complete a Cause-and-Effect Chart for each of the following questions:

- What effects would restricting the vote have on the dominant group?
- What effects would it have on those denied the right to vote?

Encourage students to consider effects such as legislative representation, education, and housing. Tell students that Lesson 2.3 discusses the struggle of African Americans to gain full voting rights.

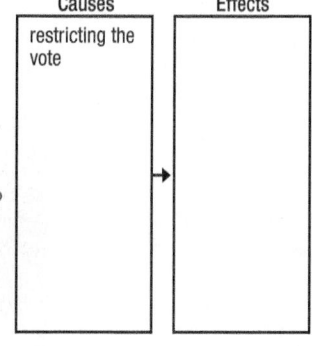

TEACH

GUIDED DISCUSSION

1. **Identify Problems and Solutions** What problems did civil rights advocates face in the voting rights struggle, and how did they resolve them? *(Possible response: They faced violent opposition to registration in Selma, and when repeated efforts to register failed, they decided to march to Montgomery. Attacked on the bridge, they tried marching twice more until, with federal help, they finally succeeded.)*

2. **Make Predictions** How do you think the Voting Rights Act will affect the balance of political power in the southern states? *(Possible response: Because African Americans, who make up a significant percentage of the population in these states, will now be able to register and vote, political power may become more balanced between the races.)*

MORE INFORMATION

Voting Rights Act, Section 4 In 2013, the Supreme Court ruled that states with a history of racial discrimination no longer need federal approval to make changes to their voting laws. Several states quickly initiated narrow "voter ID" laws and redrew their legislative districts in a way that discriminated against African Americans. When these measures were challenged in court, several were struck down as unconstitutional. Other voter suppression measures include reducing the number of early voting days and eliminating early voting on weekends, which disproportionately affect minority voters. **ASK:** How do these actions exemplify the need for federal government action and continued grassroots activism? *(Discrimination measures are still taking place today to deny equal voting rights for African Americans.)*

ACTIVE OPTIONS

On Your Feet: Voting Rights Today Share a copy of the 2013 Supreme Court decision striking down Section 4 of the Voting Rights Act and discuss it with students. Arrange students in three groups and tell them to investigate how states have responded to the decision in terms of changes in their voting laws and legislative districts. Have groups write a paragraph to compare present and past voting rights issues and evaluate any lessons advocates learned that might be applied today.

NG Learning Framework: Create Line Graphs

ATTITUDE Curiosity

KNOWLEDGE Our Human Story

Invite students to show the effects of the Voting Rights Act by creating line graphs that track the number of African Americans registered to vote before and after the act passed. Discuss with students the time frame they might cover and then have them conduct online research to find the statistics needed to create the graphs. Suggest they do one line graph showing the aggregate number of voters from all states and then create separate line graphs for regions: South, Northeast, Midwest, and West. Encourage students to share their line graphs with the class and discuss the connection between the passage of the Voting Rights Act and political trends in the country.

DIFFERENTIATE

ENGLISH LANGUAGE LEARNERS ELD

Examine Word Meaning Over Time Explain to students at **All Proficiencies** that word usage changes over time and that some words take on figurative meanings in addition to their literal meanings. Bring students' attention to the Key Vocabulary term *landmark legislation*. Have them look up *landmark* in a print or online dictionary and write down what they think was its original, or literal, meaning. Then ask a volunteer to read its other more figurative definition, which reflects its use in this lesson. Instruct pairs to create sentences for each meaning.

PRE-AP

Extend Knowledge Tell students that although many presidents extended the 1965 Voting Rights Act over time, the Supreme Court struck down an important provision of the act in 2013 in *Shelby* v. *Holder*. Challenge students to conduct research across multiple print and online sources and then write a report on a modern effort to limit or deny voting rights, such as one of the specific voting restrictions introduced in state legislatures. As students do their research, remind them to evaluate the credibility and accuracy of each source. Invite students to share their reports with the class.

See the Chapter Planner for more strategies for differentiation.

HISTORICAL THINKING

ANSWERS

1. Possible response: With the passage of these acts, the rights of African Americans were made more secure and resulted in major changes to their participation in educational, political, economic, and civic pursuits.

2. Citizens and religious leaders raised the issues of discrimination and voter rights and brought the struggle for equality before the government and the public. Some of them even lost their lives in the struggle. State governments resisted the movement, but the federal government supported it with troops and civil rights legislation.

3. The Selma marches represented the role of civil rights advocates by showing that leaders could conduct nonviolent actions whose purpose was to change the laws disenfranchising them. By putting their lives at risk on the marches, civil rights advocates and their followers gained national support for their cause, which helped ensure passage of the voting rights laws.

NEW LEADERS AND CHALLENGES

By the mid-1960s, many African Americans were growing increasingly impatient with the slow pace of racial progress in the United States. Was it time to abandon the nonviolent tactics preached by King in favor of a more militant approach?

SEGREGATION OUTSIDE THE SOUTH

From its beginnings in the early 20th century, the civil rights movement had focused on the South, where African Americans faced blatant discrimination and *de jure* **segregation**—separation enforced by law. In other regions of the country, however, African Americans and other minorities also confronted discrimination, though it was perhaps less extreme than in the South. Northern states had not passed laws mandating racial separation, but it existed anyway. *De facto* **segregation**, or segregation that is present in society despite there being no laws to enforce it, greatly affected urban areas. Many African Americans lived in public housing where crime was rampant, public services were poor, and schools were inferior. Banks often refused home loans to African Americans who sought to buy houses outside their traditional neighborhoods. Many people self-segregated simply to avoid ugly conflicts. And yet conflicts arose and anger was building.

One catalyst for frustration was police targeting of and violence against African Americans. For instance, in August 1965, a white police officer pulled an African-American motorist over on suspicion of impaired driving in the predominantly African-American section of south central Los Angeles known as Watts. African-American drivers were often pulled over and cited for traffic infractions, founded or not. The incident escalated into an argument, which in turn sparked a riot. Rioters looted stores and burned down hundreds of buildings. When police officers clashed with the rioters, at least 34 people died and more than 1,000 were injured. The violent clashes between residents and police, which became known as the **Watts Riots**, continued for 6 days. The following year, similar conflicts rocked Chicago, Detroit, Cleveland, Newark, and other U.S. cities.

THE BLACK POWER MOVEMENT

At the time of these riots, King's leadership in the civil rights movement was coming under increasing criticism due to a split between generations. On one side were "old" civil rights groups, such as King's and the NAACP, which saw racial integration and nonviolent resistance as the keys to African-American advancement. On the other side were "new" movement groups, such as SNCC, who embraced more forceful and even violent strategies.

At a 1966 rally in Mississippi, an activist named **Stokely Carmichael** who had just served time in jail for peacefully protesting, set out to fire up the crowd by yelling about "Black Power." The phrase became a rallying cry for many younger African Americans. To some, it meant group strength and independent action. To the more radical **black separatists**—those like Carmichael who believed in the political and cultural division of African Americans and whites—it meant taking extreme measures to claim their rights and maintain their freedoms. The radicals felt that African Americans should work together to gain economic power in order to create a separate nation within the United States. As you have read, these ideas were central to black nationalism, a movement Marcus Garvey originally embraced in the early 20th century.

One of the most extreme of the "new" movement groups was the **Black Panther Party**, founded in Oakland, California, in 1966 by **Huey Newton** and **Bobby Seale**. Its original mission was to conduct heavily armed patrols to protect African-American neighborhoods from police brutality and harassment. It also began an effective free-lunch program for children, but as the party grew, it evolved into a revolutionary movement that fiercely opposed

CRITICAL VIEWING Black Panther Party members hold a vigil outside a New York City courthouse on April 11, 1969, to protest the arrest of party members accused of criminal activities related to terrorism. The arrested men were acquitted more than one year later. Why do you think the photographer included the Abraham Lincoln quote "the ultimate justice of the people" in the photograph of the Black Panthers?

American society. The Black Panthers demanded that the government release all African Americans from prison and pay reparations for slavery. They won modest support for their community work but lost influence when a few members were jailed for committing crimes such as extortion, or obtaining money through forceful coercion, and drug-dealing. The Panthers became a feared enemy and primary target of local, state, and federal law enforcement. While they never received the mainstream support that the general civil rights movement did, their emphasis on racial pride, their celebration of black culture, and their powerful criticisms of racism continue to influence American culture today.

MALCOLM X AND THE NATION OF ISLAM

Newton and Seale had been strongly influenced by **Malcolm X**, one of the most controversial African-American activists of the 1960s. Malcolm X, born Malcolm Little and later known as el-Hajj Malik el-Shabazz, adopted the "X" to replace Little, the slave name imposed on his ancestors by their slave master. In the late 1940s, while serving in prison for robbery, Malcolm X became a member of the **Nation of Islam**, a religious black nationalist movement founded in Detroit in 1930. The organization preached a doctrine of self-help, moral discipline, and complete separation of the races. Members of the Nation of Islam, also called Black Muslims, were forbidden to smoke, drink alcohol, or eat pork.

PLAN: 4-PAGE LESSON

OBJECTIVE

Learn about the emergence of militant civil rights advocates and the diffusion of the civil rights movement to the North.

CRITICAL THINKING SKILLS FOR LESSON 2.4

- Compare and Contrast
- Interpret Visuals
- Identify Main Ideas and Details
- Draw Conclusions
- Synthesize
- Describe
- Analyze Visuals
- Make Connections

HISTORICAL THINKING FOR CHAPTER 26

What challenges did Americans face during the 1960s? The slow pace of racial integration frustrated many African Americans. Despite some progress, segregation and discrimination still persisted not only in the southern states but also in the North. Lesson 2.4 discusses changes in the civil rights movement.

BACKGROUND FOR THE TEACHER

Martin Luther King, Jr., and his Chicago Freedom Movement (CFM) focused on Chicago as part of their effort to end *de facto segregation* in the North. After marching in Marquette Park on Chicago's southwest side, CFM leaders planned to march in Cicero, an all-white suburb with a history of racial violence. In 1951, an African-American family had rented an apartment there, and thousands of angry whites had burned down the entire building. Since then, nothing had changed. Threats of violence against CFM marchers in Cicero were so high that leaders called off the march. In return, Chicago officials agreed to enforce open housing laws and desegregation of public housing. However, a more militant faction of the civil rights movement, influenced by Malcolm X, decided to march anyway. Rejecting a pledge to nonviolent resistance, they flung back the bricks and bottles hurled at them by whites, signaling a change in the civil rights movement.

INTRODUCE & ENGAGE

CONSIDER HUMAN RIGHTS MOVEMENTS

Provide each student with a K-W-L Chart. Lead students in a discussion to brainstorm what they already know about human rights movements. Ask students to record the rights specific groups have fought for or the violations groups have fought against and the means that they used to bring attention to their cause or achieve results. Then ask students to write questions that they would like to have answered as they study Lesson 2.4, which discusses civil rights leaders and the challenges they faced while trying to achieve integration on a national level. Allow time at the end of the lesson for students to complete the K-W-L Chart with what they have learned.

K What Do I Know?	W What Do I Want To Learn?	L What Did I Learn?

TEACH

GUIDED DISCUSSION

1. **Draw Conclusions** Why might Martin Luther King, Jr., and other civil rights leaders have found *de facto* segregation in the North harder to fight than *de jure* segregation in the South? *(Possible response: De jure segregation is enforced by laws that can be changed by Congress and the courts to create a more equitable society. De facto segregation consists more of attitudes, practices, and customs, which are far more difficult to change through legal or legislative means.)*

2. **Synthesize** Despite the passage of civil rights legislation, why did advocates such as Huey Newton and Malcolm X believe that more militant action or complete racial separation was necessary? *(Possible response: They believed that change was too slow and that nonviolence wouldn't be enough to change continued discrimination and white violence. They thought that the only solution was to use more forceful means or even create a separate nation within the United States.)*

3. **Describe** How did groups like the Black Panthers and the Nation of Islam develop a separate African-American identity within traditional American society? *(Possible response: The two groups made skin color a point of pride and strength, called people to reject "slave" names and choose their own names, and encouraged people to embrace a sense of identity separate from their history with white people.)*

ANALYZE VISUALS

Direct students' attention to the black-and-white photograph of the Black Panthers. **ASK:** What details do you notice in the photograph? *(Possible response: The people are dressed in military-style clothing, and they are standing in military-like poses. The expressions on their faces indicate strength and determination.)* How does the photograph of the Black Panthers exemplify the ideals of black nationalism? *(Possible response: Their military-style clothing and postures show the Black Panthers as a strong group, unified in protecting African Americans as their own police force.)*

DIFFERENTIATE

STRIVING READERS

Compare and Contrast Movements Instruct students to label the first column of a T-Chart Older Civil Rights Movement and the second column Newer Civil Rights Movement. As students read, have them complete the chart with details about the leadership, strategies, and desired outcomes for the old and new movements. After students finish reading the lesson, encourage them to compare their completed charts.

Older Civil Rights Movement	Newer Civil Rights Movement

GIFTED & TALENTED

Connect Past and Present Tell students to research and write an oral report connecting past and present protests against racial injustice. As part of their research, encourage students to refer to the Kerner report commissioned by President Johnson, noting its rebuke of the dominant media's framing of the uprisings as riots rather than as expressions of legitimate grievances. Ask students to present their oral reports to the class or to record and post them online.

See the Chapter Planner for more strategies for differentiation.

CRITICAL VIEWING Answers will vary. Possible response: The photographer wanted to emphasize that the people—like the group shown here—bring about justice.

While at a New York City rally, Malcolm X held up the *Muhammad Speaks* newspaper, emphasizing his consistent message: "Our Freedom Can't Wait!"

This iconic photograph by South African photographer Joseph Louw was taken immediately after Martin Luther King, Jr.'s assassination on April 4, 1968. King lies on the hotel balcony, bleeding from a neck wound, while aides point to the opposite rooftop where they had seen the shooter, James Earl Ray, fleeing after firing at King.

Malcolm X quickly rose to a position of prominence within the Nation of Islam and helped it to achieve explosive growth. In fiery speeches, he denounced white American society for the injustices it inflicted on African Americans. He also scorned King's tactics of nonviolence and civil disobedience. He preached self-defense, saying that African Americans must protect themselves "by any means necessary" and that "killing is a two-way street." Malcolm X's intense philosophy made it easy to interpret the Nation of Islam's message as one of violence and hate.

In 1963, tensions developed between Malcolm X and **Elijah Muhammad**, the leader of the Nation of Islam, and in early 1964 Muhammad expelled Malcolm from the religion. After making a pilgrimage to the Muslim holy city of Mecca, Malcolm renounced some of the more extreme ideas he had espoused in the past, including racial separatism. Upon returning to the United States, Malcolm continued to speak out against racism and work for change, despite threats against his life from members of the Nation of Islam. In February 1965, they followed through with their threats, assassinating Malcolm X as he gave a speech in Harlem.

THE MOVEMENT MOVES NORTH

As rioting shook northern cities and the Black Power movement grew, Dr. King decided to take the civil rights movement to the North and broaden its scope. He focused his efforts on fighting poverty among African Americans and on opposing U.S. military involvement in the Vietnam War. Speaking in New York City in April 1967, he pointed out the contradiction of sending young African-American men 8,000 miles away "to guarantee liberties in Southeast Asia which they had not found in southwest Georgia and East Harlem."

On April 3, 1968, King led a peaceful march in Memphis in support of a strike by sanitation workers. The following day, while King was standing on the balcony of the Lorraine Motel, a white segregationist named James Earl Ray shot and killed him. The nation mourned the assassination of the civil rights movement's most famous leader. But King's words would have enduring effects on American life as his legacy continued with the work of other supporters, including President Johnson.

The rioting and segregation that had troubled King also troubled President Johnson. Johnson had established the National Advisory Commission on Civil Disorders in 1967, also known as the Kerner Commission, to study the causes of urban riots. He appointed Illinois governor Otto Kerner to lead it. In its report, the commission concluded that the United States was "moving toward two societies, one black, one white—separate and unequal." The report criticized the media for failing to cover the violent protests from the rioters' perspective and concluded by stating "the press has too long basked in a white world, looking out of it, if at all, with white men's eyes and a white perspective."

As you have read, Johnson's administration developed strategies for expanding the welfare state and providing a broader safety net for vulnerable Americans as part of his Great Society program. One of these strategies demonstrated the government's commitment to providing education to all Americans. You have read about the Elementary and Secondary Education Act, which Johnson signed into law in 1965. This act provided federal funding to ensure that all children regardless of race, ethnicity, religion, or sex received equal educational opportunities.

Still, schools remained unequal because of *de facto* segregation, so courts ordered **busing**, or transporting students of all races to schools outside their school districts or neighborhoods to assure integration and therefore equal opportunity. Busing sparked controversy and legal challenges. In the 1971 case *Swann v. Charlotte-Mecklenburg Board of Education*, the Supreme Court unanimously upheld busing programs. Three years later, however, in *Milliken v. Bradley* (1974), the Court struck down a plan to desegregate schools in Detroit by busing students between the predominantly African-American city and its predominantly white suburbs.

Supreme Court rulings continued to expand the government's role in supporting civil rights. In the 1967 case *Loving v. Virginia*, the Court cited a violation of the 14th Amendment when it overturned Virginia state laws prohibiting **miscegenation**, or marriage between people of different races. The Court's decision abolished anti-miscegenation laws around the country.

Another strategy of the Johnson administration was **affirmative action**, a government policy that institutes racial quotas to favor groups that suffer from discrimination. The goal of supporters of affirmative action was to improve educational and employment opportunities for all Americans. Like school busing, affirmative action ignited controversy and was challenged in court. In the 1978 case, *Regents of the University of California v. Bakke*, the Supreme Court ruled that affirmative action programs were constitutional in some circumstances but that quotas based solely on race were not.

HISTORICAL THINKING

1. **READING CHECK** In the 1960s, what were some of the challenges African Americans faced in the North?

2. **COMPARE AND CONTRAST** On which issues did the "old" and "new" civil rights activists disagree?

3. **INTERPRET VISUALS** In addition to the headline, what message do you think Malcolm X wanted to convey when he held up the newspaper?

4. **IDENTIFY MAIN IDEAS AND DETAILS** What were the Johnson administration's strategies for fighting segregation and poverty?

BUILD BACKGROUND

SUNDOWN TOWNS

Civil rights legislation had little initial effect on many all-white "sundown towns" outside the South. Between the 1890s and 1960s, thousands of these towns and suburbs in the West, Midwest, and Northeast had either driven out their African-American populations or prevented them from living there in the first place. Signs posted at their city limits warned African Americans not to be caught in town "after sundown," hence the term "sundown towns." These *de facto* segregation communities were difficult to integrate. There were few segregation laws to challenge, and few African Americans wanted to live in such hostile environments. Today, however, many former sundown towns and suburbs have more diverse populations. But their history remains a little-known chapter in American race relations.

MILLIKEN V. BRADLEY

By 1970, most of Detroit was populated by African Americans, and efforts to desegregate the schools would have to involve the white suburbs. Thus, the NAACP stepped in and filed suit against the state of Michigan to desegregate Detroit's schools. After reviewing the system of drawing school district boundaries that kept white and African-American districts segregated, a federal judge ruled that school district lines should not be the basis for denying students their constitutional rights. It was the first time that city-suburb borders were recognized as a tool of maintaining school segregation, similar to gerrymandering in legislative districts. On appeal, however, the Supreme Court overturned the lower court decision, even though the effect would maintain a segregated city-suburb school system.

TEACH

GUIDED DISCUSSION

4. Compare and Contrast What were the similarities and differences between the goals of Martin Luther King, Jr., Malcolm X, and Elijah Mohammad? *(Possible response: Martin Luther King, Jr., wanted whites and blacks to live in equality side by side; Malcolm X at first wanted two separate societies but then came to adopt a vision of wider unity among all races; Elijah Mohammad, as head of the Nation of Islam, wanted two nations—one white and one black.)*

5. Make Connections As one of the new groups involved in the civil rights movement, how did the Nation of Islam help diffuse the civil rights movement among the younger generation? *(Possible response: Its message drew those who were impatient with the slow progress being made and who were angered by violence from the white majority.)*

DRAW CONCLUSIONS

Review with students the court cases described in the lesson. **ASK:** In what ways did the University of California case and the *Loving* v. *Virginia* case affect the evolution of civil rights? *(Possible response: The California case made quotas based solely on race unconstitutional but upheld affirmative action; the Virginia case eliminated all state laws prohibiting marriage between the races.)*

ACTIVE OPTIONS

On Your Feet: Analyze the Kerner Commission Report Tell students to find copies online of the Kerner Commission report and read its findings. Have them form groups of four and number off within each group. Ask students to discuss the following question: What evidence does the commission cite that led to the conclusion there was media bias in covering urban riots? After groups have discussed the question, call a number and have the student with that number from each group provide a summary of the group's discussion. Then discuss as a class the commission's findings on media perspectives of race relations.

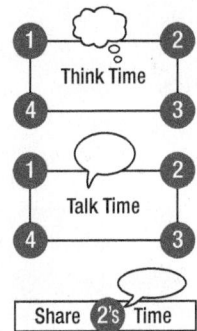

NG Learning Framework: Explore the Legacy of Civil Rights

ATTITUDE Empowerment

KNOWLEDGE Our Human Story

Draw a Detail Web on the board and write the term *civil rights legacy* in the center. Have students think about the topics discussed in this lesson: education, voting rights, race relations, housing, employment, civil rights leaders, and court cases. Ask students what they think are some of the lasting effects of the key events, policies, and court cases covered in the lesson. Encourage students to consider how the country is different now than it was in the 1960s. Complete the Detail Web as students share their ideas.

HISTORICAL THINKING

ANSWERS

1. While the North did not have laws enforcing racial segregation, discrimination and segregation remained issues. African Americans had poor housing, public services, and schools. Banks would not loan African Americans money to buy homes in better areas. Whether warranted or not, African-American drivers were often pulled over by white police for traffic citations.

2. The "old" and "new" civil rights activists disagreed on the pace of change that was occurring and on the pledge of nonviolent resistance. Younger activists wanted a more militant response to attacks.

3. Possible response: Malcolm X was demanding that change happen more quickly. He believed that African Americans deserved their full rights and freedoms, if not through the courts, then through more aggressive, militant action.

4. Strategies used by the Johnson administration to fight segregation and poverty included legislation such as the Elementary and Secondary Education Act, busing, and affirmative action.

NATIONAL CIVIL RIGHTS MUSEUM
MEMPHIS, TENNESSEE

The National Civil Rights Museum has a fascinating location: the grounds of the Lorraine Motel, where Dr. Martin Luther King, Jr., was assassinated in 1968 while staying in Memphis, Tennessee. Visitors reflect upon this important historical site while viewing the museum's impressive collection of historic objects, documents, and photographs spanning five centuries of African-American history—from the beginning of the resistance to slavery through the Civil War, Reconstruction, the rise of Jim Crow, and the civil rights movement. The National Civil Rights Museum's exhibits center around African-American history and the quest for racial equality in the United States, but also feature the culture of slavery and international human rights. The museum's mission is clear: to educate, inform, and inspire.

The museum's four-acre site includes the Lorraine Motel (shown below) and its related buildings and the nearby Young and Morrow Building, from which James Earl Ray fired the shot that killed Dr. King.

Room 306
Dr. Martin Luther King, Jr., was a frequent guest at the Lorraine Motel in downtown Memphis. He stayed there in April 1968 while in town to support a strike by sanitation workers. On April 4, he spent the day at the motel with his brother and aides. When Dr. King stepped onto the balcony outside his room to talk to friends, he was shot in the neck from across the street. Motel owner Walter Bailey never rented room 306 again, turning it instead into a memorial. As part of the museum's collection, room 306 has been preserved exactly as it looked on that tragic night.

Protest signs from the museum's 1963 March on Washington exhibit

"I Am a Man" Exhibit
This museum exhibit tells the story of the 1968 sanitation strike that drew Dr. King to Memphis during what would become his final days. Represented in bronze statues, strikers holding iconic "I am a man" signs—designed to humanize the protesters—appear in front of National Guard troops, while footage from the strike is projected onto a garbage truck. The exhibit also features footage from Dr. King's famous "I've Been to the Mountaintop" speech, which he gave in Memphis the day before his assassination.

Black Panther Jacket
The museum's Black Power exhibit highlights the rise and fall of one of the most influential movements in civil rights history: the Black Panther Party.

The black leather jacket shown here was worn in the late 1960s by Cyril Innis, Jr., of the Corona, New York, chapter of the Black Panthers. The museum's collection also includes a beret and a crossed fist necklace worn by party members. Black Panther Party founders Huey P. Newton and Bobby Seale encouraged members to dress neatly in a uniform consisting of a light blue shirt under a black leather jacket, black pants and shoes, a black beret, and black gloves.

What impact do you think historical events such as the assassination of Dr. King and the fall of the Black Power movement had on the civil rights movement?

PLAN: 2-PAGE LESSON

OBJECTIVE
Study artifacts and exhibitions related to the civil rights movement and African-American history.

CRITICAL THINKING SKILLS FOR LESSON 2.5
- Analyze Visuals
- Make Connections
- Identify
- Make Inferences

HISTORICAL THINKING FOR CHAPTER 26
What challenges did Americans face during the 1960s? The 1960s saw the strengthening of the civil rights movement—the decades-long struggle for African-American equality. Lesson 2.5 allows students to examine artifacts from, and draw conclusions about, this era.

BACKGROUND FOR THE TEACHER
During the era of segregation, the Lorraine Motel was one of the few establishments that accepted African-American guests. The building was purchased in 1945 by Walter Bailey, who added a second floor and converted it from a hotel to a motel to accommodate highway travelers. At its height, the Lorraine was known for its upscale atmosphere, home-cooked meals, affordable prices, and its acceptance of both blacks and whites. Famous African-American performers, including Ray Charles, Aretha Franklin, and Otis Redding, were frequent guests. Unfortunately, by the mid-1970s, the motel and its surrounding neighborhood had slid into decay. The creation of the museum was the culmination of an effort beginning in the 1980s to resurrect the motel and preserve this important American landmark.

HISTORY NOTEBOOK
Encourage students to complete the Curating History page for Chapter 26 in their History Notebooks as they read.

INTRODUCE & ENGAGE
DISCUSS THE SIGNIFICANCE OF HISTORIC BUILDINGS

Ask students to describe historic or impressive buildings that they have seen or visited. Discuss characteristics that make these buildings impressive, such as their size or architectural style. Then direct students' attention to the photograph of the Lorraine Motel. **ASK:** Are there reasons, in addition to architecture and appearance, that a building might be important? *(Possible response: Yes. A building can be important because it's where a significant event took place.)* Inform students that in this lesson they will learn about the National Civil Rights Museum, located in a motel that is the site of the assassination of Martin Luther King, Jr.

TEACH
GUIDED DISCUSSION

1. **Identify** What do the protest signs from the 1963 March on Washington exhibit reveal about the goals of the march and who participated? *(The goals of the march went beyond simply ending segregation, as they included fair employment and housing. In addition, the participants of the march were diverse, including people of various races and religions.)*

2. **Make Inferences** Why do you think Huey P. Newton and Bobby Seale encouraged Black Panthers to dress neatly and in uniform? *(Answers will vary. Possible response: Dressing neatly and in uniform helped establish an air of respectability and solidarity. It also made it easy to identify members.)*

CURATING HISTORY

The National Civil Rights Museum's website is a useful resource for studying the African-American experience across American history. Access the website and guide students to the photograph from the exhibition called "King's Last Hours," which features his motel room. Have the class study the photograph of the room and read the accompanying text. **ASK:** Why do you think museum curators chose to re-create King's motel room so exactly? What is the purpose they had in mind?

ACTIVE OPTION

On Your Feet: Examine Permanent Exhibitions Arrange students in teams of four or five to examine photographs of the museum's other permanent exhibitions. Ask each team to choose three exhibitions that they think are the most interesting and use the details they see in the photographs to complete a Concept Cluster. When the teams are finished, have them compare their Concept Clusters.

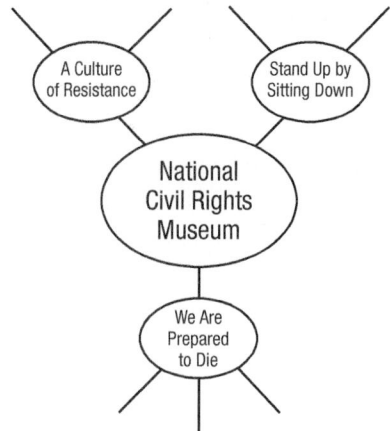

DIFFERENTIATE
STRIVING READERS

Use Context Clues Ask pairs of students to look for context clues to help them define any challenging words in the lesson, such as *reflect, impressive, spanning, resistance, humanize,* and *influential.* If students have difficulty unlocking meaning, refer them to an online dictionary for assistance. Then ask pairs to use each word in a sentence.

GIFTED & TALENTED

Propose an Exhibition Ask small groups of students to plan their own exhibition that might be added to the National Civil Rights Museum offerings. After students agree on an idea, encourage them to jot down notes about the contents of their display—the artifacts and photographs they might include, the historic places they might want to re-create, and so on. Suggest that they then write a proposal, stating the purpose and goals of the exhibition. Invite a volunteer from each group to read the proposal. As a class, discuss which ideas seem the most interesting, educational, and inspiring.

See the Chapter Planner for more strategies for differentiation.

BLACK PANTHER JACKET

Answers will vary. Possible response: These historical events became temporary setbacks for the civil rights movement. The movement eventually recovered and, particularly because of King's death, gained momentum and focus.

VOCABULARY

Use each of the terms below in a sentence that expresses an understanding about an event or topic from the chapter.

1. affirmative action
2. ballistic missiles
3. bipartisan
4. disenfranchise
5. *de facto* segregation
6. miscegenation
7. Medicare
8. New Frontier
9. space race

READING STRATEGY
DRAW CONCLUSIONS

Drawing conclusions can help a reader make connections and better understand the text. Complete the following chart to draw conclusions about how the domestic policies of Kennedy and Johnson affected the United States.

Text Clues	What I Know	My Conclusions
"optimism and confidence in problem solving"	Kennedy developed new programs and approaches.	Kennedy looked forward to the future in responding to problems.

10. How did Kennedy's and Johnson's domestic policies impact the United States?

MAIN IDEAS

Answer the following questions. Support your answers with evidence from the chapter.

11. What were Kennedy's first two challenges? **LESSON 1.1**

12. Why did the Soviet Union build the Berlin Wall? **LESSON 1.1**

13. What was the purpose of the international treaty the United States and the Soviet Union signed in 1963? **LESSON 1.2**

14. What event sparked the Cuban Missile Crisis? **LESSON 1.3**

15. What is the main function of the Equal Employment Opportunity Commission? **LESSON 2.1**

16. How did southern members of Congress try to kill the Civil Rights Act? **LESSON 2.1**

17. What was the collective name of Johnson's reform policies designed to relieve economic inequality in the United States? **LESSON 2.2**

18. What did the Immigration Act of 1965 eliminate? **LESSON 2.2**

19. How was the Civil Rights Act of 1964 different from previous civil rights legislation? **LESSON 2.3**

20. What was the goal of the Selma-to-Montgomery marches? **LESSON 2.3**

21. In what ways did Stokely Carmichael's phrase "Black Power" divide the civil rights movement? **LESSON 2.4**

HISTORICAL THINKING

Answer the following questions. Support your answers with evidence from the chapter.

22. **FORM AND SUPPORT OPINIONS** Using information from the chapter, explain whether and why you think a cost-benefit analysis would have supported continuing the Alliance for Progress program.

23. **ANALYZE CAUSE AND EFFECT** How did the Cuban Missile Crisis ultimately make the world safer, and how could events surrounding it have taken a different direction?

24. **FORM AND SUPPORT OPINIONS** Would you have agreed with senators supporting the Immigration Act of 1965 or with those opposing the bill? Write a brief paragraph explaining your response.

25. **COMPARE AND CONTRAST** How were the presidencies of Kennedy and Johnson similar and different in terms of their accomplishments, problems, and impact on larger social, economic, and political trends?

INTERPRET GRAPHS

Look closely at the graph below. Use information from the chapter and in the graph to answer the questions that follow.

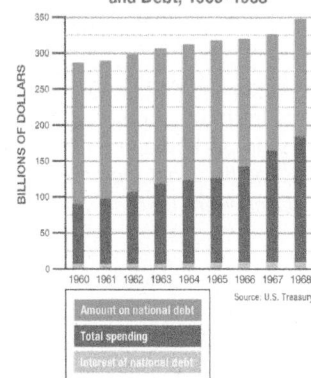

U.S. National Spending and Debt, 1960–1968

BILLIONS OF DOLLARS

1960 1961 1962 1963 1964 1965 1966 1967 1968

Source: U.S. Treasury

Amount on national debt
Total spending
Interest of national debt

26. Based on what you know about programs and issues during the Kennedy and Johnson administrations, how would you explain the trend in government spending shown in the graph?

27. According to the graph, how are changes in spending reflected in changes in the national debt, or the amount of money the government has borrowed, and in the interest on that debt?

ANALYZE SOURCES

The space race was both an idealistic vision and important to national security. Here, in interviews, two of the seven Mercury astronauts, Wally Schirra and Scott Carpenter, express different thoughts about the meaning of the effort.

> The challenge was that Kennedy had made a mess in Cuba at the Bay of Pigs, and he had to do something to look good. The . . . concept of going to the moon and back before the decade was out was quite a goal, which we all accepted, because we loved the man. —Wally Schirra, 2007
>
> I am so overjoyed that the competition has now [changed] into cooperation. Space is not an enterprise that belongs to the United States or to Russia or to China—it is a human endeavor. —Scott Carpenter, 2012

28. What different messages do Schirra and Carpenter convey about the American space program, and what evidence do you see of bias and prejudice in the historical interpretations of these individuals?

CONNECT TO YOUR LIFE

29. **ARGUMENT** Many people questioned President Kennedy's proposal to spend billions of dollars to put a man on the moon within 10 years. Suppose a president of the United States proposed to commit trillions of dollars to colonizing Mars within 10 years. Write a short argument stating reasons why you would or would not support such an endeavor.

TIPS

• Evaluate the consequences of Kennedy's plan and determine the lessons that were learned.

• Summarize your viewpoint and your reasoning clearly before you present your points in more depth.

• Use textual evidence from the chapter in supporting your argument.

• Include reasons why the United States should or should not invest in such a goal.

• Counter the strengths of the opposing viewpoint with your own position.

VOCABULARY ANSWERS

1. Affirmative action redressed past discrimination.

2. Far-reaching ballistic missiles could hit any target in the world.

3. The Voting Rights Act required bipartisan support in order to pass.

4. Poll taxes and literacy tests were put in place to disenfranchise minorities.

5. *De facto* segregation was harder to fight since it wasn't segregation by law.

6. Miscegenation laws prevented mixed marriages.

7. Elderly people were given health care under Medicare.

8. Kennedy's agenda was known as the New Frontier and focused on new opportunities for the nation.

9. The space race helped put a man on the moon.

READING STRATEGY ANSWER

Text Clues	What I Know	My Conclusions
"optimism and confidence in problem solving"	Kennedy developed new programs and approaches.	Kennedy looked forward to the future in responding to problems.
Joseph Kennedy, Sr., "vowed his children would overcome" prejudice against Catholics.	JFK was elected president.	The Kennedys broke through religious barriers in politics.
"At great political risk, Johnson immediately took up the battle for Kennedy's stalled bill."	JFK was assassinated, and Johnson assumed the presidency as an experienced politician.	Johnson used his experience and savvy as a politician to convince Congress to honor the memory of President Kennedy by enacting the civil rights bill and federal education and social welfare programs.

10. Answers will vary but should note that Kennedy and Johnson tried to expand opportunities for all Americans and aid the most vulnerable groups.

MAIN IDEAS ANSWERS

11. Kennedy's first two challenges were the Bay of Pigs invasion and the Berlin Wall built by the Soviets.

12. The Soviets wanted to prevent East Germans from leaving the country for better jobs and opportunities in West Germany.

13. The purpose was to limit the spread of nuclear weapons and stop atomic weapons testing.

14. An American U-2 spy plane spotted Soviet missiles in Cuba.

15. Its main function is to monitor and protect workplace rights. Women and minorities facing discrimination can seek help from this commission.

16. They attempted to filibuster the act so it could not come to a vote.

17. It was the War on Poverty, a war Johnson said the United States could not afford to lose.

18. The Immigration Act eliminated national quotas and the ban on Asian immigration.

19. The 1964 Civil Rights Act expanded the federal government's role by enforcing desegregation in public schools and prohibiting discrimination based on race, gender, creed, and national origin in federally funded programs and in many public facilities. It also outlawed such discrimination in the workplace.

20. The goal was to gain voting rights for African Americans. The marches helped to pass federal voting rights legislation.

21. The idea of "Black Power" split the civil rights movement into those who remained committed to steady progress and nonviolent resistance and those who wanted faster results and were willing to use militant means or even separate completely from white culture.

HISTORICAL THINKING ANSWERS

22. Students' answers should weigh the funds misspent by corrupt officials against the benefits that people received.

23. The crisis made both leaders realize they needed to reduce tensions between their nations. They established a hotline and signed a nuclear test ban treaty. Had the crisis not been resolved, there could have been a nuclear war.

24. Answers will vary but should cover such points as equality regarding national origin versus the numbers of immigrants likely to enter the United States and the consequences of the demographic shift. Students should support their answers with evidence from the text.

25. Students' answers will vary but should include that the two presidents were similar in their domestic agenda and programs and their overall impact on the larger social, economic, and political trends. Differences included Kennedy's focus on international outreach and Johnson's ability to get legislation through Congress.

INTERPRET GRAPHS ANSWERS

STEM

26. Possible response: The programs of both presidents required federal expenditures. As the programs expanded and their costs rose, federal spending steadily increased.

27. Possible response: The graph shows that federal spending has become a larger share of the national debt, with a corresponding increase in interest on that debt.

ANALYZE SOURCES ANSWER

28. Possible response: Schirra's message about the space program is more nationalistic and personal, including the observation that Kennedy used the program partly to redeem himself. Carpenter's message is more universal, saying space belongs to everyone and not to any one nation.

CONNECT TO YOUR LIFE ANSWER

29. Essays will vary. The pro argument should include the technological, social, and economic benefits produced by colonizing Mars. The con argument should include the other earthbound needs the money could be used to address.

UNIT 8 YEARS OF TURBULENCE (1954–1975)

UNIT 8 RESOURCES

UNIT INTRODUCTION

UNIT TIME LINE

UNIT WRAP-UP

 **NATIONAL GEOGRAPHIC** | CONNECTION

National Geographic Magazine
Adapted Articles
- "Who Was Jim Crow?"
- "Before Stonewall" ONLINE

Unit 8 Inquiry: Design a Museum Exhibit

NG Learning Framework Activities
- Write a Letter
- Create a Song

Unit 8 Formal Assessment

CHAPTER 27 RESOURCES

Available at NGLSync.Cengage.com

TEACHER RESOURCES & ASSESSMENT

Reading and Note-Taking

Vocabulary Practice

Social Studies Skills Lessons
- Reading: Form and Support Opinions
- Writing: Argument

Formal Assessment
- Chapter 27 Pretest
- Chapter 27 Tests A & B
- Section Quizzes

Chapter 27 Answer Key

ExamView®
One-time Download

STUDENT DIGITAL RESOURCES

- eEdition
- Handbooks
- Online Atlas
- American Gallery Online
- History Notebook
- Active History
- Reid on the Road video series
- Literature Analysis
- Projects for Inquiry-Based Learning

Chapter 27 Spanish Resources are available at NGLSync.Cengage.com.

AMERICAN STORIES ONLINE | The Vietnam Wall

- Study Primary Sources: Excerpt from Maya Lin's design submission
- On Your Feet: Write a Review

NG Learning Framework:
Explore Artists

SECTION 1 RESOURCES
U.S. INVOLVEMENT IN VIETNAM

LESSON 1.1
The Cold War in the Third World

- On Your Feet: Create a Quiz

NG Learning Framework:
Analyze a Memoir

LESSON 1.2
Gulf of Tonkin

- On Your Feet: Conduct Talk-Show Interviews

NG Learning Framework:
Research the Gulf of Tonkin Resolution

SECTION 2 RESOURCES
A DIFFICULT WAR

LESSON 2.1
War Strategies

- On Your Feet: Team Word Webbing

NG Learning Framework:
Evaluate an Article

LESSON 2.2
Growing Opposition to the War

AMERICAN GALLERY ONLINE | Reporters Go to War

NG Learning Framework:
Write a News Story

SECTION 3 RESOURCES
1968: A TURNING POINT

LESSON 3.1
The Tet Offensive

- On Your Feet: Numbered Heads

NG Learning Framework:
Create a Tet Offensive Infographic

LESSON 3.2
1968: Violence and Division

- On Your Feet: Turn and Talk on Topic

NG Learning Framework:
Debate Events at the 1968 DNC

LESSON 3.3
The Counterculture

 Haight-Ashbury

- On Your Feet: Just the Facts

NG Learning Framework:
Create a Social Media Page

SECTION 4 RESOURCES
ENDING THE WAR

LESSON 4.1
Vietnamization Under Nixon

- Active History: Compare the Korean and Vietnam Wars

NG Learning Framework:
Create an Annotated Time Line

LESSON 4.2
Legacy of the War

- On Your Feet: Inside-Outside Circle

NG Learning Framework:
Develop a Multimedia Presentation

CHAPTER 27 REVIEW

STRIVING READERS

STRATEGY ❶
READ AND RECALL

Arrange students in pairs. First have each student read the lesson independently. After reading, direct students to meet without the text, share ideas they recall, and take notes. Then tell students to use the text to review the lesson and decide what to add or change in their notes.

Use with All Lessons

STRATEGY ❷
USE A SORTING ACTIVITY

Write the following terms on the board and tell students to sort them into three groups of four related terms. Then instruct students to write a paragraph that shows how each set of terms are related.

selective service	mortars
hippies	psychedelic drugs
guns	deferment
draft	conscription
grenades	counterculture
communes	weaponry

Use with Lessons 2.1, 2.2, and 3.3 *You may use this activity before and again after students study each of these lessons.*

STRATEGY ❸
CREATE IDEA WEBS

Have students summarize the chapter by creating three Idea Webs, one for each of the following topics: U.S. Involvement in Vietnam, Turning Point (1968), and Ending the War. Tell students to complete each web with relevant information as they read the lessons.

Use with All Lessons *For example, for U.S. Involvement, students could add the following:* U.S. support for autocratic Vietnamese president, escalation after Gulf of Tonkin Resolution, guerrilla warfare difficult for U.S. troops, and opposition increases as war continues with no end in sight.

INCLUSION

STRATEGY ❶
USE SUPPORTED READING

Tell students to work in pairs and read the chapter aloud lesson by lesson. Instruct them to stop at the end of each lesson and use these sentence frames to monitor their comprehension of the text:

- This lesson is mostly about _____.
- Other topics in this lesson are _____.
- One question I have about the lesson is _____.
- One of the vocabulary words is _____. It means _____.
- One word I do not recognize is _____.
- I don't think I understand _____.

Use with All Lessons

STRATEGY ❷
PREVIEW USING A MAP

To help students comprehend lesson text, preview the Tet Offensive, 1968 map. Tell students to place a finger on the blue line marked Ho Chi Minh Trail and trace that line from North Vietnam, through parts of Laos and Cambodia, and into South Vietnam. Explain that the line shows how North Vietnamese and Viet Cong soldiers were able to enter South Vietnam and attack many locations. Instruct students to point to and count each of the black markers indicating major battles. Then have students trace the blue lines with arrows showing the routes that about 80,000 North Vietnamese troops took to fight these major battles of the Tet Offensive.

Use with Lesson 3.1

ENGLISH LANGUAGE LEARNERS

STRATEGY ❶
UNDERSTAND LOAN WORDS

Instruct students at **All Proficiencies** to review how the French loan words *coup* and *impasse* are used in Lessons 1.1 and 3.2, respectively. Tell students that *coup* has a silent *p* (the word rhymes with *blue* and *chew*) and that its original French meaning was "strong hit or blow." The French word *impasse* originally meant "dead end or a place through which one cannot pass." Encourage students to look the words up in a dictionary to understand their usage and meanings (*coup*: a sudden, violent, illegal seizing of power; *impasse*: a deadlock or situation in which there's no apparent way out). Tell students to create at least two original sentences using each word.

Use with Lessons 1.1 and 3.2

STRATEGY ❷
PAIR PARTNERS FOR DICTATION

After reading a lesson, direct students at **All Proficiencies** to write an original sentence telling an important idea from the reading. Pair students and let them take turns dictating their sentences to each other. Then allow them to work together to check spelling and accuracy.

Use with All Lessons *You may wish to pair students at the* ***Emerging*** *level with those at the* ***Bridging*** *level.*

STRATEGY ❸
PREP BEFORE READING

Encourage students at **All Proficiencies** to use the PREP strategy to prepare for reading. Write this acrostic on the board:

> **PREP** **P**review the title.
> **R**ead the Main Idea statement.
> **E**xamine visuals.
> **P**redict what you will learn.

Use with All Lessons *Encourage students at the* ***Emerging*** *level to ask questions if they have trouble writing a prediction. Encourage students at the* ***Bridging*** *level to help students at the* ***Emerging*** *and* ***Expanding*** *levels write their predictions.*

GIFTED & TALENTED

STRATEGY ❶
CREATE A PODCAST

Before beginning the chapter, allow students to choose one lesson and use the information in that lesson to prepare an episode of a history podcast. Tell students that their podcast should establish a point of view that is both informative and entertaining. Invite students to present their podcast live or record it and play it for the class.

Use with All Lessons

STRATEGY ❷
REPORT ON A DOCUMENTARY

Invite students to watch brief segments of some of the many documentaries about the Vietnam War. Then have them choose one documentary to research and watch in its entirety. Tell students to gather information about the documentarians and analyze their motivations, their filmmaking process, and style. Instruct students to write a report about the documentary, including clips to illustrate the points they make. Encourage students to share their reports with the class.

Use with All Lessons

PRE-AP

STRATEGY ❶
WRITE A PROFILE

Have students conduct online research about specific Vietnamese, Laotian, or Cambodian refugees who came to the United States during the 1960s and 1970s. Tell students to assume the role of a journalist reporting on the plight of refugees during this time period and write a profile of one refugee. Remind students to report within the context of the time and not to overlay their report with present-day values. Invite students to post their articles on a class blog or school website.

Use with Lesson 4.2

STRATEGY ❷
EXTEND KNOWLEDGE

Invite students to conduct research about a person, event, or topic introduced in the chapter and to connect their subject to larger social, economic, environmental, or political trends. For example, students might choose to investigate the use of Agent Orange and its impact on both human and environmental health or research an aspect of the counterculture that emerged in the 1960s. Have students present their findings in an oral report to the class or in a digital report posted on a class blog.

Use with All Lessons

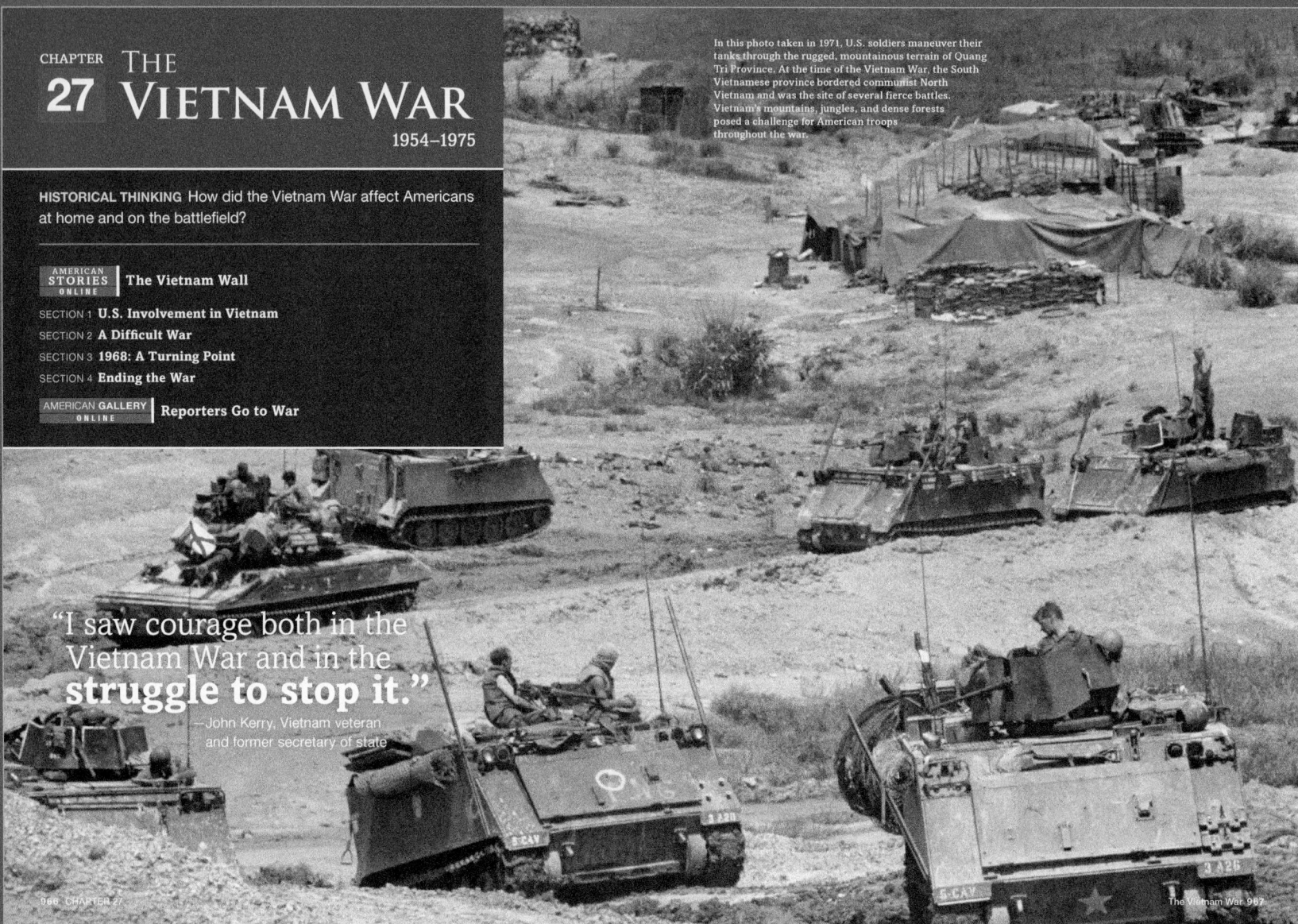

27 THE VIETNAM WAR

1954–1975

HISTORICAL THINKING How did the Vietnam War affect Americans at home and on the battlefield?

AMERICAN STORIES ONLINE | The Vietnam Wall

SECTION 1 **U.S. Involvement in Vietnam**

SECTION 2 **A Difficult War**

SECTION 3 **1968: A Turning Point**

SECTION 4 **Ending the War**

AMERICAN GALLERY ONLINE | Reporters Go to War

"I saw courage both in the Vietnam War and in the **struggle to stop it.**"

—John Kerry, Vietnam veteran and former secretary of state

In this photo taken in 1971, U.S. soldiers maneuver their tanks through the rugged, mountainous terrain of Quang Tri Province. At the time of the Vietnam War, the South Vietnamese province bordered communist North Vietnam and was the site of several fierce battles. Vietnam's mountains, jungles, and dense forests posed a challenge for American troops throughout the war.

966 CHAPTER 27

The Vietnam War 967

INTRODUCE THE PHOTOGRAPH

WAGING WAR

Invite students to study the photograph that opens this chapter. Direct them to focus on the terrain in the photograph and to read the caption. **ASK:** Based on the photograph and caption, what were some of the challenges U.S. troops faced while using conventional military tactics in Vietnam? *(Possible response: Because of the rugged and mountainous terrain, jungles, and dense forests, conventional tactics must have been difficult to use. Tanks, for instance, might not have been effective in jungle locations.)* Tell students that in this chapter they will learn how the Vietnam War affected not only American soldiers fighting a difficult and unconventional war, but also civilians at home.

For Chapter 27 Spanish Resources, visit the Resources Menu. Chapter 27 Resources are available at NGLSync.Cengage.com.

SHARE BACKGROUND

The Quang Tri Province, referenced in the caption of the photograph, was the site of some of the fiercest fighting and bombing during the Vietnam War. More bombs and other ordnance were dropped on the province than were dropped on Germany during World War II. The U.S. Department of Defense estimates that approximately 10 percent of the ordnance used in Vietnam failed to detonate, and decades after the war's end, the Vietnamese are still dealing with unexploded ordnance (UXO). Since 1975, nearly 105,000 Vietnamese have been unintentionally killed or wounded by UXO left over from the war. More than 8,500 residents of the Quang Tri Province have been killed or wounded, with children accounting for nearly one third of the victims. The Vietnam-based Project RENEW is working to remove the ordnance and educate the public about the dangers of UXO.

HISTORICAL THINKING QUESTION

How did the Vietnam War affect Americans at home and on the battlefield?

Roundtable Activity: A Divisive War Arrange students into an even number of small groups and number each group. Assign odd-numbered groups this question: How might an unpopular war divide a society? Assign even-numbered groups this question: How might an unpopular war affect the soldiers fighting it? Have the first student in each group write an answer on a sheet of paper and pass the paper clockwise to the next student, who adds an answer, and so on, until students are out of ideas. Compile a master list of answers for each question. Then tell students that in Chapter 27 they will learn how the Vietnam War divided Americans, producing both societal and military effects.

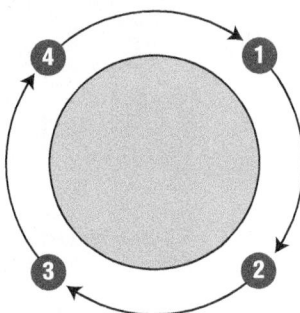

INTRODUCE THE READING STRATEGY

FORM AND SUPPORT OPINIONS

Explain that if students want their opinions to be considered valid, they need to support them with examples and facts. Turn to the Chapter Review and preview the chart showing how to organize examples and facts with students. As they read the chapter, have students collect examples and facts to support the opinions they form about various aspects of the Vietnam War.

KEY DATES FOR CHAPTER 27

1955	U.S. aid to South Vietnam begins
1963	Ngo Dinh Diem assassinated in coup
1964	Congress passes Gulf of Tonkin Resolution
1967	March on the Pentagon
1968	Communists launch Tet Offensive
1968	Riots at Democratic National Convention
1969	Secret bombings of Cambodia and Laos begin
1971	Pentagon Papers released
1973	Peace agreement signed
1975	South Vietnam falls to communists

INTRODUCE CHAPTER VOCABULARY

KEY VOCABULARY

SECTION 1

autocrat	escalation	third world
coup	insurgent	

SECTION 2

Agent Orange	dove	mortar
credibility gap	hawk	war of attrition
deferment		

SECTION 3

counterculture	impasse

SECTION 4

induction	post-traumatic stress disorder (PTSD)	Vietnamization

DEFINITION CHART

As they read the chapter, encourage students to complete a Definition Chart for Key Vocabulary terms. Instruct students to list the Key Vocabulary terms in the first column of the chart. They should add each term's definition in the center column as they encounter the term in the chapter and then restate the definition in their own words in the third column. Model an example on the board, using the graphic organizer shown.

Word	Definition	In My Own Words
autocrat	a tyrant with absolute power	a leader who rules with complete authority

For instructional support for the online American Story "The Vietnam Wall," go to NGLSync.Cengage.com.

MAIN IDEA The United States supported the anticommunist government that arose in South Vietnam, but the South Vietnamese leader proved to be a tyrant.

THE COLD WAR IN THE THIRD WORLD

If you've ever fought for a cause you believed was just, you probably encountered some obstacles along the way. The United States would run into quite a few as it tried to halt the spread of communism in Southeast Asia.

After Ngo Dinh Diem formed South Vietnam and made himself its president in 1955, tribesmen from the country's mountains and plateaus came to pledge their loyalty to him. Here, President Diem (seated) receives gifts from the tribesmen.

CONFRONTING COMMUNISM IN ASIA

In the 1950s and 1960s, the U.S. government focused to a large extent on domestic policy, particularly on civil rights for African Americans. But foreign policy and events in Southeast Asia also claimed the attention of several presidents during this period, beginning with Dwight Eisenhower. Remember reading about the victory of Ho Chi Minh's communist forces against the French in the Southeast Asian country of Vietnam? After the decisive Battle of Dien Bien Phu in 1954, a peace agreement negotiated in Geneva, Switzerland, temporarily divided the country roughly in half.

According to the **Geneva Accords**, which detailed the terms of the agreement, Vietnam was split along the 17th parallel. Ho and the Viet Minh governed the northern part of the country, while the French colonial government remained in the south. The accords also called for free democratic elections in 1956, the withdrawal of the French from Indochina, and the reunification of Vietnam under a national government. In 1955, however, **Ngo Dinh Diem** (ungh-oh dihn zih-EHM), the prime minister of the southern part of the country, founded the Republic of Vietnam, or South Vietnam, and proclaimed himself its president. During Ho's anti-imperialist revolution against the French, Diem had lived for a time in the United States.

The United States fully backed Diem and his new government. Eisenhower embraced President Harry Truman's containment policy to prevent the spread of communism throughout Asia. To achieve that goal, Eisenhower believed that an anticommunist government had to be established in South Vietnam, which was considered a "third world" country. During the Cold War, a country that was not aligned with either the United States or the Soviet Union was called a **third world** country. Communist and democratic forces struggled to gain influence over third world countries. The United States used the Southeast Asia

Treaty Organization (SEATO) to justify its increasing involvement in Southeast Asia after the French conceded to the Vietnamese in 1956. You may recall that the United States and other countries, including France, Great Britain, Thailand, and the Philippines, formed SEATO in 1955 to help prevent communist expansion in Southeast Asia. The United States claimed Vietnam as a whole to be a territory that fell under SEATO protection.

DIEM'S GOVERNMENT

Diem had declared that he would uphold democratic principles as stipulated by the Geneva Accords. However, with Eisenhower's support and encouragement, he refused to allow free elections to take place in 1956. Instead, he ruled

HAM RỒNG CHIẾN THẮNG

This North Vietnamese poster shows two soldiers and a worker standing in front of the Thang Hoa Bridge. In 1945, the Viet Minh destroyed the bridge (nicknamed Ham Rong, or "Dragon's Jaw") to prevent the French from transporting arms across it. The bridge was rebuilt in 1957.

PLAN: 4-PAGE LESSON

OBJECTIVE

Examine the United States' early involvement in South Vietnam's unstable political scene.

CRITICAL THINKING SKILLS FOR LESSON 1.1

- Draw Conclusions
- Make Inferences
- Analyze Cause and Effect
- Identify Main Ideas and Details
- Make Connections
- Integrate Visuals
- Form and Support Opinions

HISTORICAL THINKING FOR CHAPTER 27

How did the Vietnam War affect Americans at home and on the battlefield? Attempts to contain communism in Southeast Asia led the United States to support the Diem regime. Lesson 1.1 examines the causes and consequences of U.S. foreign policy in South Vietnam.

BACKGROUND FOR THE TEACHER

The Eisenhower administration's positive view of Ngo Dinh Diem was colored by American religious and cultural views of the 1950s. American supporters of Diem, including much of the media, were comforted by the fact that Diem was a Roman Catholic and assumed that meant he would favor democracy, oppose communism, and champion capitalism. At the same time, the Eisenhower administration accepted Diem's more authoritarian approach to governing because the administration believed that a firm hand would help the predominantly peasant population grow into democratic participation. Supporters also touted the fact that the Republic of Vietnam operated under a constitution. However, they failed to realize or just ignored the fact that the constitution provided Diem with almost unlimited power to change laws, control the military, declare states of emergency, and suspend civil liberties.

INTRODUCE & ENGAGE

ACTIVATE PRIOR KNOWLEDGE

Ask students to recall events in Vietnam following World War II. *(The French gained control of much of Indochina after World War II. Ho Chi Minh led a revolt against the French in Vietnam, seizing control of the north and establishing the Democratic Republic of Vietnam. The United States provided money and supplies to help France take control of the southern region of Vietnam and establish the State of Vietnam. The French fought Ho's Viet Minh, who were backed by the Soviet Union and China, for control of Vietnam until the French defeat at the Battle of Dien Bien Phu. The two sides negotiated a peace agreement that divided Vietnam into communist North Vietnam and democratic South Vietnam.)* Use a Sequence Chain to record the events. Then tell students that Lesson 1.1 picks up with events in Vietnam following France's defeat, as the United States increases its involvement in South Vietnam.

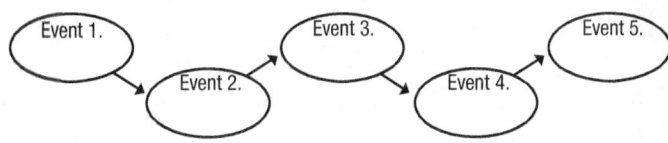

TEACH

GUIDED DISCUSSION

1. **Identify Main Ideas and Details** In what sense were the Geneva Accords an attempt to shape the future of Vietnam? *(The Geneva Accords temporarily split Vietnam along the 17th parallel, with Ho in control in the north and the French colonial government in control in the south. The Accords required the French to withdraw from Indochina and called for free democratic elections in 1956 and the eventual reunification of Vietnam under a national government.)*

2. **Make Connections** What role did SEATO play in U.S. attempts to deter communist expansion in Southeast Asia? *(The United States used its membership in SEATO, an organization formed to help prevent communist expansion in Southeast Asia, to justify increased American involvement in Vietnam.)*

3. **Draw Conclusions** What evidence is there that Diem and Eisenhower failed to uphold the Geneva Accords? *(Diem ultimately refused to hold free elections in 1956. Eisenhower encouraged and supported that decision.)*

INTEGRATE VISUALS

Have students read the caption and study the photograph of Diem's meeting with the tribesmen. **ASK:** How do the photograph and caption reinforce the idea that Diem ruled as an autocrat? *(Possible response: The caption indicates that Diem made himself president, which means the people did not elect him. The caption also indicates that the tribesmen are there to pledge loyalty to Diem. In a democracy, loyalty is to the office of president and not to the individual holding the office. In addition, the tribesmen look worried and apprehensive, suggesting they may feel obligated to be there.)*

DIFFERENTIATE

STRIVING READERS

Understand Compound Words Pair students and bring their attention to the two parts of the word *autocrat*. Tell students to brainstorm and write words beginning with *auto-* (e.g., *automobile, automatic, autograph, autofocus*) and to do the same with words ending in *-crat* (e.g., *Democrat, plutocrat, bureaucrat, technocrat*). Ask students to deduce the meaning of *auto-* (self) and *-crat* (member or supporter of a form of government or rule). Instruct students to write their own definition of *autocrat* and to then compare it to a dictionary definition.

PRE-AP

Analyze a Theory Instruct students to conduct research about the domino theory, using multiple online and print sources. Then tell students to write a paper analyzing the theory's historical and intellectual underpinnings and validity (or lack thereof), quoting or paraphrasing historians and other experts. Encourage students to first define the theory and then relate it to the history, culture, and politics of Vietnam and neighboring countries. Students should conclude their analyses by stating whether the events in Southeast Asia proved or disproved the domino theory. Invite volunteers to share their analyses with the class.

On July 17, 1963, police set up barbed wire to block a demonstration at the Giac Minh pagoda in Saigon during the Buddhist crisis. In this photo, demonstrators try to pull down the barbed wire. The police beat and arrested some of the protesters.

THE BUDDHIST CRISIS

Eisenhower began to send military personnel and aid to South Vietnam in 1955. By the time Kennedy became president in January 1961, however, this aid effort had decreased. An anticommunist, Kennedy revitalized the effort and sent 500 Special Forces troops as military advisors to South Vietnam in May. Kennedy ignored the advice of French general Charles de Gaulle, who warned him that war in Vietnam would drag the United States into "a bottomless military and political swamp." The American president continued to send military advisors to South Vietnam until their numbers totaled about 16,000 in 1963.

Meanwhile, Diem's discrimination against Buddhists reached a critical point. On May 7, 1963, government forces angered Buddhists by tearing down the religious flags they hung on homes and buildings in the city of Hue (HWAY). Diem had passed a law against such displays, but up to that point, the law had not been enforced. In protest, a crowd of more than 3,000 Buddhists gathered the next day—on the Buddha's birthday—and marched to the center of town. Later that evening, as the protests continued, soldiers fired bullets and tossed grenades at the crowd, killing 8 people and seriously injuring another 4. Diem blamed the Buddhists for the violence.

Seeking nonviolent solutions, Buddhist clergy presented a list of demands to the government. They asked the government to grant Buddhists the right to display their flags, worship freely, and enjoy the same rights as Catholics. Some Buddhists also staged hunger strikes. Kennedy encouraged Diem to reform his policy toward the Buddhists, but Diem ignored his advice. Finally, in June, 500 monks and nuns gathered in Saigon, South Vietnam's capital. They watched while a monk immolated himself, or burned himself to death, to protest Diem's treatment of Buddhists. A photographer captured the event, drawing worldwide attention to the Buddhists' plight in South Vietnam.

Protests continued throughout the summer, and more Buddhist monks and nuns immolated themselves. Then, on August 21, Diem declared martial law, giving military forces, rather than the police, the authority to enforce order. That night, the military raided Buddhist pagodas in cities throughout South Vietnam. When monks and nuns used sticks and stones to resist the soldiers, many were arrested on charges of possessing weapons.

As the Buddhist crisis continued, the United States began to distance itself from Diem and withdraw its support from his government. When officers in the South Vietnamese Army approached U.S. officials about staging a **coup** (KOO), or an illegal overthrow of the government, the Americans stated they would do nothing to prevent it. According to some accounts, in fact, the U.S. officials even encouraged the action. As a result, Diem was arrested on November 1, 1963, and assassinated the next day.

Diem's death caused political instability in South Vietnam. A series of military leaders followed who, like Diem, never actually instituted a democratic government. As you know, President Kennedy was also assassinated in November 1963. Under President Johnson, U.S. engagement in South Vietnam increased. As in Korea, the United States conducted a proxy war in Vietnam.

PRIMARY SOURCE

For Lam Quang Thi, the years from 1950 to 1975 were the most important of the 20th century. He spent that time serving in South Vietnam's army. Thi wrote about his experiences as a soldier and general in his memoir, *The Twenty-Five Year Century*. In this excerpt from the memoir, Thi recalls the pagoda raids in August 1963.

We heard the news of the raids on the pagodas in Saigon by armed troops. More than 1,400 monks had been arrested and some of them had been beaten. This brutal act of repression . . . sealed the fate of the regime and marked the beginning of its downfall. Washington . . . was stunned by the pagoda raids. President Kennedy . . . authorized the suspension of economic subsidies for South Vietnam's commercial imports and a cutoff of financial aid to the Vietnamese Special Forces. The financial assistance would resume only under the specific condition that the Special Forces be put under the control of the Joint General Staff . . . who were plotting against the regime.

—from *The Twenty-Five Year Century*, by Lam Quang Thi, 2001

as an **autocrat**, a tyrant with absolute power, and appointed members of his own wealthy family to serve in the highest levels of his government. For example, Diem's younger brother was his chief advisor.

Furthermore, even though the majority of Vietnamese people were Buddhist, Diem, a Roman Catholic, strongly favored those of his own faith. He filled his government with Catholics and retained the anti-Buddhist laws the French had put in place. On the positive side, Diem provided refuge in his country for the hundreds of thousands of Vietnamese fleeing communist rule in the north. However, he dealt harshly with **insurgents**, or rebels, within his country who belonged to the National Liberation Front, or **Viet Cong**. These insurgents tried to spread communism among the South Vietnamese and wage war against Diem's government. Diem put his

younger brother in charge of a special army unit that tracked down communists and imprisoned or killed them. Even those who were only suspected of aiding the rebels—often with little or no evidence—were likely to meet the same fate.

Diem's heavy-handed tactics against the insurgents and his treatment of Buddhists made him increasingly unpopular among the people of South Vietnam. Nonetheless, presidents John Kennedy and Lyndon Johnson continued to support President Eisenhower's domino theory, formulated in 1954. As you may recall, this theory states that if one Southeast Asian country were to become communist, all the rest would follow like falling dominoes. Kennedy and Johnson used the domino theory to explain the presence of the U.S. military in South Vietnam.

HISTORICAL THINKING

1. **READING CHECK** Why did the United States back Ngo Dinh Diem's government?

2. **DRAW CONCLUSIONS** Why did Kennedy suspend financial aid to South Vietnam after the Buddhist pagoda raids?

3. **MAKE INFERENCES** Why do you think the U.S. government did nothing to prevent the coup against Diem?

4. **ANALYZE CAUSE AND EFFECT** What complex string of events led to the assassination of Diem?

BUILD BACKGROUND

THE BUDDHIST CRISIS

As the Buddhist crisis grew, the Kennedy administration pressed Diem to make concessions toward greater religious freedom and reconciliation. Diem made only half-hearted overtures at reform, however, largely because he and his advisor brother, Ngo Dinh Nhu, believed that Buddhists were willing to side with the Viet Cong. Nhu's wife, Madame Nhu, complicated the situation further by referring to the Buddhist acts of self-immolation as "barbecues," branding the protesting Buddhists as communists, and calling on the South Vietnamese government to expel Buddhist monks and anyone else considered to be a foreign agitator. Diem and Ngo Dinh Nhu also argued that the United States was too heavily involved in South Vietnamese government and military affairs, and Nhu called for a cut in U.S. military forces.

With public, media, and congressional pressure mounting against Diem in the United States and Nhu undermining U.S. strategic goals, the Kennedy administration demanded that Diem oust his brother from the South Vietnamese government and work more closely with the Americans. When Diem refused, his fate was sealed. The Kennedy administration allowed the coup to proceed in order to replace his regime.

TEACH

GUIDED DISCUSSION

4. **Draw Conclusions** Which of Diem's actions benefited containment? *(Possible response: Diem welcomed refugees who were fleeing communism in the north and had Viet Cong insurgents in the south tracked down, imprisoned, and killed.)*

5. **Make Inferences** How were the domino theory and the policy of containment related in the context of Vietnam? *(Possible response: The domino theory held that if one country fell to communism, neighboring countries also would fall. Thus, communism needed to be contained in Vietnam to prevent all of Indochina from falling under communist rule.)*

FORM AND SUPPORT OPINIONS

Direct students' attention to the Primary Source feature and have them read the excerpt from Lam Quang Thi's memoir. **ASK:** Do you think Thi was correct in claiming that the raids on the pagodas in Saigon sealed the fate of Diem's regime, or could the outcome have been different? Cite evidence from the text to support your opinion. *(Possible responses: Yes. The raids led President Kennedy to suspend financial aid to Vietnam and tie its resumption to Diem's placing the Vietnamese Special Forces under the control of the Joint General Staff. The raids forced the United States to distance itself from Diem, making the Kennedy administration more likely to support the coup. No. Even after the raids, the United States might have continued to support Diem's government and prevented the coup if Diem had reformed his policies toward Buddhists.)*

ACTIVE OPTIONS

On Your Feet: Create a Quiz Organize students into two teams and have the teams move to opposite sides of the room. Instruct each team to write 10 true-false statements or multiple-choice questions about the rise and fall of Ngo Dinh Diem. Encourage teams to include questions that reflect viewpoints of the time and that show connections among events. Have teams alternate reading a statement or asking a question to which the other team will respond. Clarify incorrect answers and keep track of the number of correct answers for each team.

NG Learning Framework: Analyze a Memoir

SKILLS Communication, Collaboration

KNOWLEDGE Our Human Story

Tell students to work in groups to examine and summarize Lam Quang Thi's views on the Diem regime, the Buddhist crisis, and the 1963 coup as presented in his memoir, *The Twenty-Five Year Century.* Relevant pages of the memoir are available online. Then have groups use their summaries to hold a class discussion on Thi's perspective on this phase of U.S. involvement in Vietnam. In particular, ask students to include in their discussion how they distinguished valid arguments from fallacious arguments in Thi's historical interpretation of events.

HISTORICAL THINKING

ANSWERS

1. The United States backed Diem because he was anticommunist, and the United States wanted to prevent the spread of communism.

2. Kennedy suspended financial aid to South Vietnam after the Buddhist pagoda raids because Diem continued to ignore U.S. requests to reform his government's policies toward the Buddhists.

3. Possible response: The Buddhist crisis had drawn worldwide attention, and Diem's autocratic policies had turned many South Vietnamese against him. These events reflected badly on the United States and threatened American objectives, so the United States had little reason to prevent the coup.

4. Diem, who was Roman Catholic, dealt harshly with Buddhists and ran the country with the aid of family members in an autocratic fashion, even declaring martial law. As head of a special army unit, his younger brother imprisoned or killed insurgents and those suspected of assisting the rebels. Diem became so unpopular with his people that South Vietnamese military officers approached the United States with plans for a coup, and the administration did not intervene. Diem was arrested and then assassinated during the coup.

On March 8, 1965, about 3,500 Marines landed in Da Nang to protect its airbase. They were the first U.S. combat troops in South Vietnam. Although both the United States and South Vietnam had wanted the troops to come ashore without fanfare, the Marines were greeted by a cheering crowd.

GULF OF TONKIN

A challenge by one side in wartime often results in an increase in hostilities by the other side. That's exactly what happened when a perceived threat occurred in the waters off the coast of Vietnam.

Vietnam, 1964

UNOFFICIAL DECLARATION OF WAR

When Lyndon Johnson assumed the presidency after John Kennedy's assassination in 1963, he had little foreign policy experience. As a result, he chose to continue the former president's course of action in Southeast Asia. But he also decided to make Vietnam a priority. Determined not to lose South Vietnam to the communists, Johnson intensified the effort there. For example, he authorized the U.S. military to carry out covert operations in North Vietnam and gather information on communist activity. However, Johnson was opposed to sending American ground forces to Vietnam. As he said, "We are not about to send American boys nine or ten thousand miles away from home to do what Asian boys ought to be doing for themselves." Johnson insisted the ultimate responsibility for resolving the conflict lay with the Vietnamese.

Soon, though, several events made him re-evaluate his position. On August 2, 1964, the USS *Maddox* reported that it had been attacked by a North Vietnamese torpedo boat while patrolling off the coast of northern Vietnam in the Gulf of Tonkin. The U.S. destroyer fought off the attack, and the torpedo boat retreated. Then, on August 4, the *Maddox* and another destroyer, the USS *C. Turner Joy*, reported renewed unprovoked attacks. In response, Johnson ordered an air attack on North Vietnamese naval bases and put the **Gulf of Tonkin Resolution** before Congress. The resolution would give the president the power to take any action necessary to repel armed aggression and defend South Vietnam.

Congress passed the resolution within days. Although the resolution was not an official declaration of war against North Vietnam, it came to be considered as such. Almost immediately, however, some people questioned whether the second attack had actually occurred. After reviewing the often contradictory tape recordings from the incident, even Johnson said that the Vietnamese in the boats were probably just "sailors shooting at flying fish!" Others even believed the attack had been provoked by American forces. Nevertheless, the Johnson administration publicly stuck to its official line, claiming the Vietnamese had been the aggressors.

WAR EXPANDS

Johnson's secretary of defense, Robert McNamara, who strongly championed war, made many of the decisions related to the conflict in Vietnam. In fact, over the next few years, the war would come to be called "McNamara's War." As you may remember, McNamara had been part of Kennedy's Cabinet and continued to serve Johnson after the latter won re-election in November 1964. The secretary favored **escalation**, or

an increase in intensity, of the war. Under McNamara's advice, Johnson increased the number of military advisors in Vietnam to 23,000 and ordered limited air raids on the Ho Chi Minh Trail, a series of connected paths linking North Vietnam with South Vietnam by way of neighboring Laos and Cambodia.

The war escalated further in February 1965. The Viet Cong attacked a U.S. air base at Pleiku (PLAY-koo), South Vietnam, killing eight Americans. Johnson

countered by initiating a sustained air bombing campaign of North Vietnam, known as Operation Rolling Thunder. The campaign involved a series of gradually intensified bombings designed to decrease the flow of supplies from North Vietnam to the Viet Cong and force the communists to negotiate a lasting peace. Operation Rolling Thunder would continue for more than three years. During this period, bombs dropped by air strikes on the Ho Chi Minh Trail and other targets in Southeast Asia would be twice the number of those dropped during World War II.

Soon after Rolling Thunder began, Johnson sent the first ground troops to South Vietnam—even though, as you know, he had vowed he would not do so. In the beginning, the troops were instructed to protect U.S. air bases, not to fight. But before long, American soldiers would be drawn into combat as the U.S. military embarked on an air and ground war that aimed to eliminate the communist threat from South Vietnam.

PRIMARY SOURCE

In a televised address on August 4, 1964, Johnson informed the nation about the attacks in the Gulf of Tonkin and the retaliation that would be taken against North Vietnam. In this excerpt from the address, the president paints a frightening picture of the situation.

Aggression by terror against the peaceful villagers of South Vietnam has now been joined by open aggression on the high seas against the United States of America. The determination of all Americans to carry out our full commitment to the people and to the government of South Vietnam will be redoubled [increased all the more] by this outrage. Yet our response, for the present, will be limited and fitting. We Americans know, although others appear to forget, the risks of spreading conflict. We still seek no wider war.

—from President Lyndon B. Johnson's report on the Gulf of Tonkin Incident, August 4, 1964

HISTORICAL THINKING

1. **READING CHECK** What authority did the Gulf of Tonkin Resolution give Johnson?

2. **EVALUATE** Identify examples of bias in Johnson's televised address used to sway the American people into thinking that retaliation against North Vietnam was justified.

3. **FORM AND SUPPORT OPINIONS** Do you think Johnson was right to escalate the war? Cite evidence from the text to support your opinion.

OBJECTIVE

Discuss the events that led to President Johnson's escalation of U.S. involvement in Vietnam.

CRITICAL THINKING SKILLS FOR LESSON 1.2

• Evaluate

• Form and Support Opinions

• Summarize

• Make Connections

• Interpret Maps

HISTORICAL THINKING FOR CHAPTER 27

How did the Vietnam War affect Americans at home and on the battlefield? Although at first President Johnson was reluctant to send more U.S. troops to South Vietnam, subsequent events and Robert McNamara's counsel changed his mind. Lesson 1.2 explores how U.S. involvement in Vietnam expanded in the mid-1960s.

BACKGROUND FOR THE TEACHER

Lyndon Johnson's initial reluctance to expand the war was due in part to concerns over the upcoming presidential election. To appease the widest range of voters, Johnson wanted to strike a careful balance between bold action and restraint in Vietnam. The U.S.S. *Maddox* attack enabled him to do that. Johnson satisfied conservatives who wanted more U.S. intervention by calling for bombing. With the conservatives satisfied that he was sufficiently bullish on the war, the president then could appeal to voters who were less supportive of U.S. involvement in Vietnam by stressing moderation. The incident also helped Johnson push through the Gulf of Tonkin Resolution. Because the election was so near, most members of Congress—even those uneasy with the U.S. presence in Vietnam—backed the resolution rather than have voters question their commitment to fighting communism.

INTRODUCE & ENGAGE

CONSIDER MILITARY STRATEGY

Introduce the term *escalation*. Then direct students' attention to the map in this lesson and ask them to locate the Gulf of Tonkin. **ASK:** Why might an event in the Gulf of Tonkin create a challenge for U.S. involvement in Vietnam? *(Possible response: The gulf is located off North Vietnam, which was under the control of the communists.)* Tell students that Lesson 1.2 explores what role the Gulf of Tonkin played in the expansion of U.S. involvement in the Vietnam War.

TEACH

GUIDED DISCUSSION

1. **Summarize** How did August 1964 mark a turning point in U.S. involvement in Vietnam? *(Attacks on two U.S. ships off the coast of North Vietnam that month quickly resulted in the Gulf of Tonkin Resolution, which gave the president authority to take any action deemed necessary with regard to Vietnam.)*

2. **Make Connections** What text evidence helps you understand why some people referred to the Vietnam War as "McNamara's War"? *(McNamara made many of the decisions concerning the war. He also influenced President Johnson's decisions, such as the president's decision to increase the number of military advisors to 23,000.)*

INTERPRET MAPS

Ask students to locate the Ho Chi Minh Trail on the map of Vietnam in 1964. **ASK:** How does the map help explain why Operation Rolling Thunder targeted the Ho Chi Minh Trail? *(The map shows that the Ho Chi Minh Trail provided the Viet Cong with access to Pleiku, where the U.S. had an air base, and to many other locations in South Vietnam. By bombing the trail, Operation Rolling Thunder made the South less accessible to the Viet Cong.)*

ACTIVE OPTIONS

On Your Feet: Conduct Talk-Show Interviews Group students into teams of three and tell them to prepare questions to conduct talk show interviews on President Johnson's escalation of U.S. involvement in Vietnam. Student 1, the interviewer, develops a question to ask the show's "guest." Student 2, an "expert" on the war, answers the question, citing information from the lesson. Student 3, a member of the studio audience, asks a spin-off question for the whole class to answer. Encourage participants to ask and answer several questions to ensure a solid review of the topic. Students may want to use a graphic organizer to prepare their questions.

NG Learning Framework: Research the Gulf of Tonkin Resolution

| ATTITUDE | Empowerment |
| KNOWLEDGE | Our Human Story |

Assign groups of students to research the Gulf of Tonkin Resolution. Instruct them to find out about Robert McNamara's testimony, the congressional debate involved in passing the resolution, the resolution's stipulations, and the refusal by senators Wayne Morse and Ernest Gruening to support it. Once groups have finished researching and recording their notes, have the groups use their notes to hold a class discussion about the resolution. Encourage students to identify signs of bias and prejudice in the congressional testimony and debate.

DIFFERENTIATE

ENGLISH LANGUAGE LEARNERS

Use a Main-Idea Diagram Pair students at the **Emerging** and **Expanding** levels with students at the **Bridging** level. Direct pairs to complete two Main-Idea Diagrams, one for each section of the lesson. Direct students to take turns reading the lesson, pausing after each paragraph to record relevant details, adding more boxes if necessary. Then have pairs work together to write a main-idea statement for each section of the lesson.

GIFTED & TALENTED

Write a Narrative Tell pairs of students to research Johnson's Gulf of Tonkin Resolution, including its reasons and consequences. Then instruct students to write a realistic narrative incorporating dialogue between President Johnson and Secretary of Defense McNamara as they react to what happened in the Gulf of Tonkin in August 1964. Encourage pairs to write one ending that reflects the historical events and one that imagines another outcome. Ask students to post their narratives on a class blog or website. Invite them to comment on both endings and their implications.

See the Chapter Planner for more strategies for differentiation.

HISTORICAL THINKING

ANSWERS

1. The resolution gave President Johnson the authority to take any action necessary to repel military aggression from North Vietnam and to defend South Vietnam.

2. Possible response: Johnson portrays North Vietnamese attacks as "aggression by terror" against "peaceful" South Vietnamese villagers and "open aggression on the high seas" against the United States. He suggests that "all Americans" support South Vietnam and that the United States best knows the risks of spreading conflict, while other nations "appear to forget."

3. Possible responses: Yes. Johnson was right to escalate the war because of the attacks on U.S. ships and the air base at Pleiku and because Secretary of Defense McNamara recommended attacking the Ho Chi Minh Trail. No. Johnson should not have committed U.S. troops after discovering the second Gulf of Tonkin attack was probably not intentional. Also, bombing the Ho Chi Minh Trail likely contributed to further escalation, such as the attack on the U.S. air base at Pleiku.

WAR STRATEGIES

Imagine running onto a field with a game plan in hand for playing a soccer match only to find you're actually playing baseball. Something like that happened to the U.S. military forces when they came to fight in Vietnam.

HEARTS AND MINDS

The United States employed two key strategies to win the war in Vietnam. First, it planned to use its superior military technology and weaponry to defeat the enemy through both air strikes and ground force operations. Second, it set out to gain the complete support of the South Vietnamese people—to win their hearts and minds. The United States particularly

wanted their help in defeating the Viet Cong. But many South Vietnamese believed life under their U.S.-supported government was no better than life under the North Vietnamese communists.

The increasing influx of American troops arriving in South Vietnam did not help win the people's hearts and minds. General **William Westmoreland**,

who had begun commanding the American forces in Vietnam in June 1964, persuaded leaders in Washington to increase the number of ground troops in Vietnam. By the end of 1965, nearly 185,000 American troops had landed. The American soldiers were originally supposed to train the South Vietnamese troops of the Army of the Republic of Vietnam (ARVN). The idea was that, once they were transformed into a strong fighting force, the ARVN would be equipped to combat the communists from the north. Unfortunately, many of the South Vietnamese troops—and their generals—were ineffectual. While some ARVN soldiers were well trained, disciplined, and dedicated to the cause, others were not. In some cases, they were reluctant to fight against those they considered their countrymen. As a result, American troops soon found themselves engaged in actual combat.

Still, Westmoreland hoped to weaken and wear down the North Vietnamese and Viet Cong through a **war of attrition**. The American general thought he could win the war by inflicting heavy losses on the enemy through fighting many small battles that would add up, ultimately, to victory. But the communists refused

to back down, no matter how many casualties they suffered. They were engaged in what they considered a national struggle for independence. Men from the North and the South were willing to take the place of fallen soldiers and reoccupy areas that the Americans and ARVN had cleared. The communist forces in Vietnam also benefited from the weapons and other supplies they received from the Soviet Union and China.

A GUERRILLA WAR

General Westmoreland underestimated his enemy's determination. He and other military leaders were also not prepared for the type of war the Vietnamese fought. The United States was supremely ready to fight a conventional war against another industrialized country. But Vietnam was not industrialized, and the Viet Cong and others opposing U.S. forces engaged in unconventional warfare. Bands of trained and untrained Viet Cong soldiers fought a guerrilla war against the ARVN and the U.S. military. Their arsenal included guns, grenades, and **mortars**, or short range, muzzle-loaded cannons. They also manufactured their own bombs and set booby traps.

CRITICAL VIEWING U.S. Army paratroopers wade across a river in the rain, searching for Viet Cong in a jungle area of South Vietnam in September 1965. Paratroopers are military personnel who parachute into a war zone. What details in the photo convey the conditions the soldiers had to deal with?

974

Helicopters like this one, nicknamed "Huey" for their early "HU-1" designation, were used to transport soldiers to and from war zones and airlift the wounded in Vietnam. Hueys carried U.S. troops to South Vietnam's Ia Drang Valley in November 1965, where the American soldiers engaged in the first major battle of the war with North Vietnamese forces.

The Vietnam War **975**

PLAN: 4-PAGE LESSON

OBJECTIVE

Assess the military strategies used by both sides in the Vietnam War.

CRITICAL THINKING SKILLS FOR LESSON 2.1

- Make Inferences
- Analyze Environmental Concepts
- Draw Conclusions
- Describe
- Compare and Contrast
- Integrate Visuals
- Analyze Visuals

HISTORICAL THINKING FOR CHAPTER 27

How did the Vietnam War affect Americans at home and on the battlefield? American soldiers faced a very different kind of war in Vietnam. Lesson 2.1 examines military strategies used in the war and some of their consequences.

BACKGROUND FOR THE TEACHER

Many historians are critical of Westmoreland's handling of the Vietnam War. Some of the most serious criticisms relate to his focus on fighting a war of attrition, which many argue was destined to fail, given the resolve and tactics of the Viet Cong. Critics also note that the strategy relied on body counts as the measure of success. Consequently, high counts gave Westmoreland—along with the Johnson administration, Congress, and the public—the impression that anticommunist forces were making progress when, in reality, the Viet Cong were constantly replenishing their ranks. Critics also argue that the focus on attrition caused Westmoreland to neglect two other important military objectives: countering insurgency in the rural villages of South Vietnam and building up the Army of the Republic of Vietnam so that it eventually could take over the fighting.

INTRODUCE & ENGAGE

PREVIEW USING TEXT FEATURES

Have students preview the lesson's introductory note, the three subheadings, and the photograph of the Ca Mau Peninsula and its caption. **ASK:** Based on these text features, what questions do you expect this lesson to answer? *(Answers will vary. Possible responses: What did the United States hope to accomplish with its military strategy? What is meant by "hearts and minds" in this context? Who waged a guerrilla war? Who carried out search-and-destroy missions and where? When did the first major battle of the Vietnam War take place? Why were Agent Orange and other defoliants used?)* Use a Five-Ws chart to categorize the questions. After students have read and discussed the lesson, ask them to add answers that they found. Urge students to research unanswered questions and report the answers to the class.

What?
Who?
Where?
When?
Why?

TEACH

GUIDED DISCUSSION

1. **Describe** How did the introduction of U.S. ground troops not go as planned? *(U.S. ground troops were supposed to train the ARVN to take over combat operations, but many of the ARVN troops and generals were ineffectual or reluctant to fight, so U.S. troops were pulled into combat.)*

2. **Compare and Contrast** Why do you think the North Vietnamese and Viet Cong were willing to keep fighting in the face of high casualties, while the South Vietnamese were sometimes reluctant to fight? *(The communists believed that they were fighting for independence and a united Vietnam. Many South Vietnamese were unwilling to fight or kill people whom they considered fellow countrymen.)*

3. **Make Inferences** Why might a nation that is not industrialized need to fight an unconventional war? *(Possible response: Without industries of their own to manufacture airplanes, tanks, and massive amounts of artillery, a nation would need to buy supplies from industrialized nations—an expensive plan. Unconventional warfare would require less massive and less expensive equipment.)*

INTEGRATE VISUALS

Direct students' attention to the photograph of the helicopter and tell them to read the caption. **ASK:** How might helicopters be useful in a combat terrain like Vietnam's? *(Possible response: Helicopters could be used for dropping supplies, transporting soldiers to and from combat, retrieving the wounded, and flying low to strafe enemy targets.)*

DIFFERENTIATE

INCLUSION

Work in Pairs Allow students with disabilities to work with other students who can read the lesson aloud to them or otherwise make the lesson accessible. Encourage the partner without disabilities to describe the photographs and illustration in detail after reading the text. When pairs have finished the lesson, instruct them to work together to answer the Critical Viewing question.

PRE-AP

Write a Letter Home Tell students to conduct online research to learn about the experiences of U.S. soldiers in Vietnam. Encourage them to find and read actual letters from soldiers in online archives and in nonfiction books about the Vietnam War. Then have students imagine themselves to be soldiers who were trained to fight a conventional war but are now fighting a guerrilla war in Vietnam. Have them write a letter to a friend or family member about what they see, hear, feel, and think. Invite volunteers to post their letters on a class blog or read them aloud to the class.

See the Chapter Planner for more strategies for differentiation.

CRITICAL VIEWING Possible response: Soldiers had to deal with muddy rivers, rain, and dense jungles that could hide the enemy. The constant dampness could cause medical issues for soldiers, such as fungal infections. In the photograph, soldiers are holding their rifles above the water to avoid getting them wet, which could cause the weapons to malfunction.

The war in Vietnam did not have official fronts and battles like conventional wars. More often, the Viet Cong launched ambushes and carried out hit-and-run attacks against the U.S. troops and the ARVN, taking off before they could be captured. And American soldiers couldn't always tell enemies apart from friends. The Vietnamese villagers who smiled in welcome when the soldiers arrived were sometimes hiding hand grenades ready to be tossed.

Fighting often took place in jungle terrain, where the dense foliage made it easy for the Viet Cong to camouflage both themselves and their bases. Often soldiers on both sides had to slog through swamps, submerged up to their waists in the mosquito-infested waters. In areas closer to Saigon, where the terrain provided less cover, the Viet Cong traveled through an extensive system of underground tunnels. Local villagers had helped build the tunnels, which

stretched for thousands of miles and served not only as shelters where soldiers could retreat, but also as bases of operation.

As they launched their surprise attacks—sometimes firing from concealed bunkers within the tunnels—the Viet Cong entered and exited through well-hidden entryways. The tunnels contained chambers where the Viet Cong stored their weapons, water, and food, and even housed sleeping chambers and kitchens, enabling the soldiers to live in the tunnels for weeks at a time. American and South Vietnamese troops known as "tunnel rats" crawled through the narrow passages, searching for Viet Cong and setting off explosives in an attempt to collapse the tunnels. In the process, however, they had to be careful not to trigger any of the booby traps planted by the Viet Cong, such as bamboo spikes or trip wires that set off grenades.

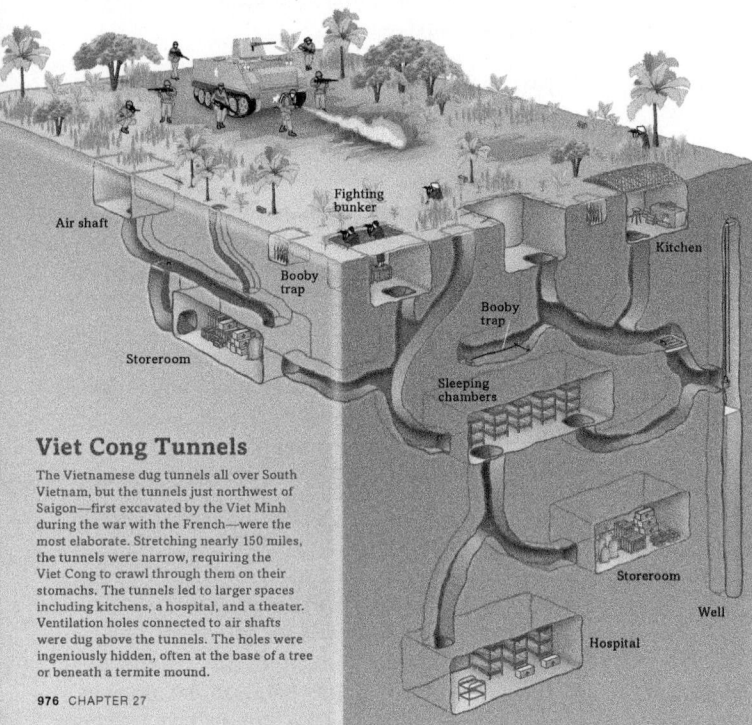

Viet Cong Tunnels

The Vietnamese dug tunnels all over South Vietnam, but the tunnels just northwest of Saigon—first excavated by the Viet Minh during the war with the French—were the most elaborate. Stretching nearly 150 miles, the tunnels were narrow, requiring the Viet Cong to crawl through them on their stomachs. The tunnels led to larger spaces including kitchens, a hospital, and a theater. Ventilation holes connected to air shafts were dug above the tunnels. The holes were ingeniously hidden, often at the base of a tree or beneath a termite mound.

SEARCH-AND-DESTROY MISSIONS

To combat the Viet Cong and North Vietnamese Army, General Westmoreland used search-and-destroy missions in villages and along the Ho Chi Minh Trail. First, low-flying helicopters sprayed an area with gunfire, and then ground troops moved in to search out enemies, destroy them, and get away quickly. Though these missions often resulted in the eradication of Viet Cong bases and the confiscation of their arms and supplies, such attacks could also devastate entire villages and kill hundreds of civilians.

To deal with the thick growth in the jungles that so effectively concealed the Viet Cong, the U.S. Air Force began spraying **Agent Orange**, a potent herbicide, or chemical substance used to kill vegetation. Agent Orange destroyed foliage, but doctors discovered later that the herbicide caused serious health issues, for both the Vietnamese and U.S. soldiers. American troops also frequently used napalm, a flammable jellied gasoline that, like Agent Orange, helped clear foliage and undergrowth. When it came into contact with skin, however, napalm caused severe burns, leaving some people with long-lasting injuries. Together, the search-and-destroy missions and use of chemical agents did little to win the hearts and minds of the South Vietnamese or turn them against the communists. The chemicals harmed many South Vietnamese civilians and burned their villages and farms.

The American cause wasn't helped by the rise to power of **Nguyen Cao Ky** (NWIHN KOW KAY), who became prime minister of South Vietnam following a military coup in 1965. The Vietnamese people viewed Ky, who prohibited criticism of his government and imprisoned his opponents, as an autocrat similar to Diem. The United States supported Ky, even though his corrupt regime was anything but democratic.

Meanwhile, by the end of 1965, great numbers of soldiers had deserted the ARVN, with many joining the North Vietnamese army. The Viet Cong had gained control, to some degree, of about 50 percent of the countryside in South Vietnam. As Westmoreland's war of attrition failed to discourage the communist forces in Vietnam, American casualties started to mount over the course of that first year of the war. Progress seemed elusive, and methods of calculating success were muddled and hard to measure. American troops fought bravely, but the stress of combat in Vietnam led many soldiers to suffer from low morale and depression. As the war dragged on, the conflict also became the subject of growing criticism at home.

In 1963, the Ca Mau Peninsula at the southern tip of South Vietnam was almost completely covered with forests. As a stronghold of the Viet Cong, this stretch of Ca Mau was heavily sprayed with Agent Orange and defoliated in 1968. This photo was taken four years later and, as you can see, the forests showed no signs of recovery.

HISTORICAL THINKING

1. **READING CHECK** How did the U.S. military hope to win the war in Vietnam?

2. **MAKE INFERENCES** Why do you think guerrilla warfare was so effective against American troops?

3. **ANALYZE ENVIRONMENTAL CONCEPTS** How did Agent Orange and napalm affect the natural systems and resources in the jungles of South Vietnam?

4. **DRAW CONCLUSIONS** How did the U.S. military strategy undermine the campaign to win the hearts and minds of the South Vietnamese?

BUILD BACKGROUND

VIET CONG TUNNELS

The Viet Cong adopted the practice of using tunnels as base camps from Chinese guerrilla fighters and perfected their tunnel-building techniques while fighting the French. There were three basic types of tunnels, ranging in size and depth depending on the number of troops in the base camp. A typical squad tunnel might be only 6 feet deep and 100 feet long. Those for a company were wider and had a limited number of chambers. The tunnels for a battalion, however, could burrow 50 feet deep and include multiple levels and chambers. The Viet Cong base camp near Saigon at Cu Chi had multiple levels and some 130 miles of tunnels. Conditions in the tunnels were challenging. Diseases, such as malaria, were common, and the air was thin. Some Viet Cong spent months in the tunnels, sometimes in blackout conditions, and entire villages retreated to the tunnels during periods of heavy fighting.

The U.S. military used dogs to locate the tunnels by sniffing out the airshafts and cooking chimneys, but the Viet Cong developed techniques to thwart detection. In some instances, they placed strong spices, such as chili peppers and garlic, near the openings to repel the dogs or deaden their sense of smell. At other times, they placed American soldiers' clothing near the openings or bathed in American GI soap so that the dogs would sense a familiar smell and not signal a place of interest.

TEACH

GUIDED DISCUSSION

4. Make Inferences Why might being proficient at fighting conventional wars make a military force less successful against unconventional tactics such as guerrilla warfare? *(Possible response: In conventional wars, there are front lines and massive troop movements. Opposing forces can identify enemy troop and supply movements by the use of large equipment for air and ground support. In guerrilla warfare, however, the enemy uses smaller fighting units, the element of surprise, and easily portable weaponry such as guns, grenades, mortars, and booby traps.)*

5. Compare and Contrast In what ways was Nguyen Cao Ky's regime similar to Diem's? *(Both regimes were autocratic, ruthless in their treatment of those who opposed or criticized their government, and deeply unpopular with the Vietnamese people. In addition, both were backed by the United States, even though their regimes were undemocratic.)*

ANALYZE VISUALS

Have students examine the Viet Cong tunnel diagram. **ASK:** What do you notice about the angles of the tunnels between levels, and what might be the advantage of this design? *(The tunnels are often slanted or curved, rather than straight up and down. The slant might make it more difficult for enemy troops to drop explosives between levels.)* **ASK:** Why do you think the Viet Cong dug wells underground? *(Possible response: Underground wells kept the water from being poisoned by enemy troops and made water readily available within the tunnels.)* **ASK:** How are bunkers attached to tunnels an advantage? *(Bunkers gave soldiers a quick avenue of escape; also, soldiers could fire at the enemy from the bunker, then quickly retreat into the tunnels.)*

ACTIVE OPTIONS

On Your Feet: Team Word Webbing Gather students in small groups and provide each group with a single large sheet of paper. Give each student a different colored marker. Ask students to create a web or cluster diagram to brainstorm words and phrases that come to mind for the following topics: U.S. military strategy and North Vietnamese military strategy. Each student should add to the part of the web closest to him or her. After a minute, signal to the groups to rotate their paper and repeat. Continue until all students have contributed. Use the web to guide a discussion about the effectiveness of the strategies of the opposing forces.

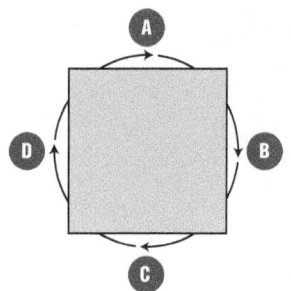

NG Learning Framework: Evaluate an Article

ATTITUDE Responsibility

KNOWLEDGE Our Human Story

Share the information in the Background for the Teacher feature with students. Then instruct groups of students to locate articles in which historians critique General Westmoreland's strategy in Vietnam. Ask each group to select one article to evaluate. Remind groups to consider the validity of the author's premise, claim, and argument and either corroborate or challenge the author with information from other historians. Encourage students to make distinctions between sound generalizations and misleading oversimplifications in the author's critique. Work with groups to select a format for sharing their evaluations with the class.

HISTORICAL THINKING

ANSWERS

1. The U.S. military hoped to win by using air strikes and ground forces equipped with superior weaponry and military technology and also by winning the support of the South Vietnamese people.

2. Answers will vary. Possible response: American military forces were trained to fight conventional wars with designated front lines. Guerrilla warfare took advantage of the jungle terrain and tunnels to ambush U.S. forces.

3. Both were detrimental to the area's natural systems and resources. The herbicide Agent Orange destroyed jungle foliage, while napalm burned away foliage and undergrowth.

4. Possible response: Search-and-destroy missions—which often involved the use of Agent Orange, napalm, and sprays of gunfire—sickened, burned, and killed villagers and destroyed their homes and farms. Such devastation made winning the hearts and minds of the South Vietnamese difficult, if not impossible.

GROWING OPPOSITION TO THE WAR

You're no doubt used to the 24/7 coverage of world events available on TV, the Internet, and social media. But in the 1960s, information wasn't so easily accessed. So when reports on the Vietnam War filled the television airwaves, people watched—and thought about what they saw.

THE TELEVISION WAR

The Vietnam War became the first in the nation's history to be broadcast regularly on television. Journalists and photographers covered the war from the jungles and battlefields of Vietnam and brought it into people's homes, night after night. As a result, the Vietnam War became known as the "television war" or "living-room war." Recording their accounts in the haze of war, American journalists reported on television what urban warfare and guerrilla fighting entailed. Film clips of fighting, bombings, and dead or wounded soldiers appeared on nightly newscasts. The public's daily exposure to the horrors of war kept people informed about events. In time, it would also begin to influence their opinion of the war.

However, despite what television reports revealed about casualties and conditions in Vietnam, government and military officials made announcements about the war's progress. The Johnson administration launched a "success offensive," a campaign to convince the public that the United States was defeating the communists in Vietnam.

In 1967, General Westmoreland made three trips to the United States to promote this idea, appearing before Congress to present his positive assessments of the war. But Westmoreland manipulated the numbers of enemy losses and claimed that U.S. forces had won every battle. He told Congress that "your continued strong support is vital to the success of our mission . . . over the communist aggressor!" In truth, neither the bombing campaign nor the ground war in Vietnam was having any measurable effect on the enemy.

Americans became increasingly aware of the difference between the optimistic reports they heard from the government and what they saw for themselves on television. This contrast resulted in a **credibility gap**, an increasing skepticism about what the government told them about the war. In this context, Americans eventually started to call into question the principles upon which the war was being fought. Why, many wondered, was the United States involved in Vietnam at all?

Some members of Congress also began to take issue with the U.S. involvement in Vietnam. Senator George McGovern of South Dakota expressed his opposition in 1963. In 1966, Arkansas senator J. William Fulbright, chairman of the Senate Foreign Relations Committee, also voiced his opposition to the bombing of North Vietnam. That same year, Fulbright published a book called *The Arrogance of Power* in which he criticized the government's goal in Vietnam. He wrote, "We are trying to remake Vietnamese society, a task which certainly cannot be accomplished by force and which probably cannot be accomplished by any means available to outsiders. The objective may be desirable, but it is not feasible [practical]."

An American television news crew interviews U.S. soldiers in South Vietnam in 1967. The Vietnam War was a dangerous assignment. During the course of the war, nine television personnel were killed, and many more were wounded.

AMERICAN WOMEN IN VIETNAM

Women could not serve in combat during the conflict, but thousands of female members of the military took on other roles in Vietnam. The vast majority worked as nurses. The number and severity of war casualties—and the rate at which the wounded arrived to be treated—meant that the nurses had to make quick decisions about whom to treat first. They also had to determine the treatment on their own, without much advice from doctors, who were often busy with their own patients. Thousands of civilian women also worked in Vietnam, many of them serving with the American Red Cross or working as journalists, like the woman in this photo.

CONTROVERSY OVER THE DRAFT

While some people voiced their objection to the war, many others opposed the idea of conscription, commonly known as the draft. With the escalation of the war, more young men were needed to fight it. Hundreds of thousands of American men volunteered for or were drafted to serve in the war, which government and military leaders portrayed as an extension of broader Cold War struggles. The Selective Service System, a federal agency, administered the draft. On turning 18 years old, all young men were required to register with their local draft board, but some could be granted

OBJECTIVE

Explain how media coverage and protests affected public perceptions of the Vietnam War.

CRITICAL THINKING SKILLS FOR LESSON 2.2

- Draw Conclusions
- Make Inferences
- Form and Support Opinions
- Make Connections
- Make Generalizations
- Analyze Primary Sources

HISTORICAL THINKING FOR CHAPTER 27

How did the Vietnam War affect Americans at home and on the battlefield? As the news media reported mounting casualties, opposition to the war grew on the home front. Lesson 2.2 examines media coverage and protests.

BACKGROUND FOR THE TEACHER

More than 5,000 Army nurses, both male and female, served in Vietnam over the course of the war. In January 1965, the army had 15 nurses stationed in Vietnam and only 113 hospital beds for sick or wounded soldiers. By December 1968, the number of nurses had grown to 900, and the total number of beds stood at 5,283, located in 23 army hospitals. The average nurse was in his or her early-to-mid 20s and had fewer than 2 years of nursing experience. Each nurse's tour of duty in Vietnam lasted 12 months. In the early years of the war, nurses lived in tents, but from 1967 on, most lived in tropical buildings. Sleep was a rare commodity, though, since nurses worked 12-hour shifts, 6 days a week, and were on call for emergencies.

HISTORY NOTEBOOK

Encourage students to complete the American Gallery page for Chapter 27 in their History Notebooks as they read.

INTRODUCE & ENGAGE

CONNECT TO TODAY

Preview the photograph of the March on the Pentagon with students. Discuss the significance of protests. **ASK:** Why do individuals or groups protest? *(Possible responses: to bring attention to something they feel isn't right; to inform the greater public)* **ASK:** What is an example of a recent protest that you feel was successful in informing the public about a situation that the protesters considered unfair? Tell students to use a graphic organizer like the one shown to note the topic of the protest, the means by which the protesters presented their views, and the outcome of the protest. *(Answers will vary. Students may reflect on a local, state, or national protest event.)* Ask students to share details from their graphic organizers. Guide a discussion in which students begin to discuss why and how a protest takes shape. Tell students that Lesson 2.2 examines the causes of protests during the Vietnam War and how these protests were conducted.

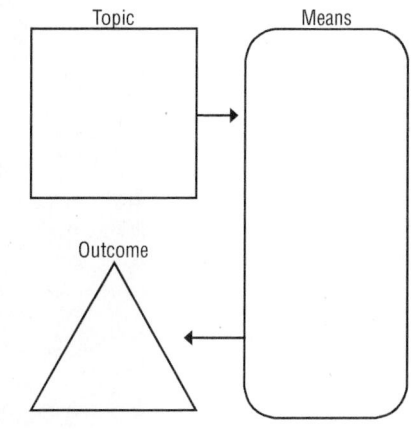

TEACH

GUIDED DISCUSSION

1. **Make Connections** How did General Westmoreland and news reports contribute to the credibility gap regarding the Vietnam War, and what lesson might be learned from the existence of a credibility gap? *(Westmoreland regularly provided overly optimistic assessments of the war to Congress by exaggerating the number of enemy dead and the number of U.S. victories. By closely covering the Vietnam War from the battlefields, the news media made it clear that Westmoreland's optimistic descriptions did not match what was actually happening. Noticing the disparity between the two, Americans grew skeptical about the government's position and truthfulness. Lesson learned: Government and military leaders best serve the public by being honest and sharing accurate information.)*

2. **Form and Support Opinions** Do you agree with Senator Fulbright's criticism of the government's approach to the Vietnam War? Why or why not? *(Answers will vary. Possible responses: Yes. A society cannot be remade through force and likely cannot be remade by outsiders. Change has to come from within a society. No. Spreading democracy is a worthwhile goal, even if the task is difficult.)*

3. **Make Generalizations** How did women in the military show their leadership qualities in the Vietnam War? *(Possible response: Most military women in Vietnam served as nurses. Because of the high numbers of wounded, nurses often had to evaluate injuries and decide how to treat patients with little assistance from doctors.)*

MORE INFORMATION

Female Journalists in Vietnam Draw students' attention to the photograph of the female journalist. Explain that unlike today, when every major news outlet employs women reporters, not many women covered the Vietnam War. Explain that those who did, such as Tad Bartimus, Dickey Chapelle, Gloria Emerson, Denby Fawcett, Jurate Kazickas, Edith Lederer, Laura Palmer, Elizabeth Pond, and Kate Webb (some of whom paid the cost of travel to Vietnam themselves), proved that women could cover wars as effectively and bravely as men. Further explain that these journalists flew on bombers and in helicopters, encamped with special forces units, parachuted into danger zones, were captured by the enemy (as Pond and Webb were), and even died (as Chapelle did) while covering the war. Assign students to work in groups to investigate online one of the female journalists named above and to write a brief report about her accomplishments as a journalist.

DIFFERENTIATE

STRIVING READERS

Summarize Have students work in pairs to read and summarize the lesson text and photograph captions. Tell students to write at least three notes for each of the lesson's sections. After they have completed taking notes, guide students to create a summary statement for each section and then a summary statement for the whole lesson.

GIFTED & TALENTED

Create a Playlist Instruct students to conduct online research to discover the musical soundscape of the Vietnam War, what Americans were listening to during the years that this chapter focuses on. Then have students create a playlist that conveys some of the empathy, concern, anger, sadness, and other emotions related to the war. While there are many anti-war songs (for example, Bob Dylan's "Blowin' in the Wind," Creedence Clearwater Revival's "Fortunate Son," Marvin Gaye's, "What's Going On," or Jimi Hendrex's performance of the "Star Spangled Banner"), students may also find patriotic songs, such as Barry Sadler's "Ballad of the Green Berets" and Merle Haggard's "Okie from Muskogee." Encourage students to play excerpts of each song on their playlist to the class, giving background information about the artists and songs, as well as explaining why they chose the songs they did.

See the Chapter Planner for more strategies for differentiation.

a **deferment**, or official permission to delay conscription. For example, men enrolled full-time in college could claim a student deferment for as long as they remained in school.

However, the agency did not always act fairly in its selection process. Draft board members could show favoritism to friends, family members, and others by granting their sons special deferments. Many of the men who received deferments also came from wealthy and educated families. As a result, most of the draftees came from poor and working-class families. A substantial percentage of these men belonged to minority groups. In the first few years of the war, once it became clear that American minorities were fighting and dying in numbers that were disproportionate to their representation in the country, many activist rights groups loudly protested the war. They objected to the war on the grounds that, to them, it represented one more form of oppression—oppression for minorities at home and abroad.

More moderate voices also spoke out against the war, including civil rights leader Martin Luther King, Jr., who called it "a white man's war, a black man's fight." Most famously, in a 1967 speech, King criticized the war both for its expense and for the large number of poor men of all races who were fighting it. He pointed out that the money the government spent on the war could have been used to fight poverty in the United States. He also objected to the devastation the war was bringing to the Vietnamese people and their land. The response to King's speech was largely negative. Newspaper editorials attacked him for his stance on the war. And even the NAACP criticized King for linking what the organization considered two separate issues: civil rights and the Vietnam War. However, King did not back down and continued to speak out against the war and the draft.

INCREASING PROTESTS

In 1964, other civil rights advocates began the **Free Speech Movement** in response to a ban on distributing political flyers at the University of California at Berkeley campus. When police arrested a student for handing out civil rights pamphlets and put him in their patrol car, other students sat down around the car to prevent it from being driven away. A young man named Mario Savio jumped on top of the car and addressed the crowd. Savio emerged as the movement's leader, and the students sitting around the police car passed around a hat to collect money to repair the vehicle. They wanted to show that they were good citizens. The protest continued for more than 30 hours until authorities dropped the charges, and the student was released.

Then, on December 1, 1964, Savio and other movement leaders led a rally, exhorting students to take part in a sit-in at Sproul Hall, Berkeley's administration building. As a result, thousands of students occupied the building and remained there for many hours. Finally, the police moved in and arrested about 800 people. As the police ushered them away, some of the officers physically assaulted the students. Eventually, the university lifted its ban on on-campus political activity, and the Free Speech Movement declared victory.

The Free Speech Movement soon turned its focus on the Vietnam War. Students at Berkeley and other college campuses throughout the country organized protests against the war. These antiwar protests, provoked by the expansion of the war in Vietnam, reflected and contributed to a deep rift within American society and culture. Americans became divided into **hawks**, who supported the war, and **doves**, who opposed it.

Another movement, called the **New Left**, arose out of student activism. One New Left group, the **Students for a Democratic Society (SDS)**, originated at the University of Michigan at Ann Arbor in the early 1960s and soon spread to other colleges. The SDS promoted socialist principles and denounced racism, militarism, and in time, U.S. involvement in Vietnam. In April 1965, the SDS sponsored the first major antiwar rally in Washington, D.C.

During the March on the Pentagon, this young woman offered a flower to the soldiers guarding the building with bayoneted M-14 rifles. At one point, a group of demonstrators tried to levitate, or lift, the Pentagon and used spells to drive "the evil war spirits" out of the Defense Department headquarters.

About two weeks earlier, President Johnson had pledged to continue military operations in Vietnam. The event drew tens of thousands of people calling for U.S. withdrawal from South Vietnam. Protesters picketed the White House and carried signs saying "No more war." At the Capitol, people delivered speeches, and performers such as activist and folk-singer Joan Baez (BY-ehz) led the crowd in song.

While the 1965 protest rally was largely peaceful, the March on the Pentagon, which took place in the capital in October 1967, was far more confrontational. The demonstration, organized by the National Mobilization Committee to End the War in Vietnam—a coalition of antiwar groups—sought to shut down the Pentagon. By this point in the war, about 13,000 Americans had died in Vietnam, and more than half of the population disapproved of the president's handling of the war. An estimated 100,000 people rallied first at the Lincoln Memorial and then marched to the Pentagon. When the protesters arrived, they found about 2,500 troops and U.S. marshals guarding the Pentagon. Some of the protesters placed flowers in the barrels of the soldiers' rifles, but a small group of demonstrators managed to gain access to the building. Soldiers and marshals used tear gas and force to clear them out. In the end, nearly 700 people were arrested.

Despite the protests at home, the war in Vietnam continued. But in 1968, a military campaign launched by North Vietnam and the Viet Cong would mark a turning point in the war and the beginning of American withdrawal from the conflict.

HISTORICAL THINKING

1. **READING CHECK** Why was the Vietnam War called the "television war"?

2. **DRAW CONCLUSIONS** How did the war in Vietnam affect the larger trend toward equality at home?

3. **MAKE INFERENCES** Why did Mario Savio compare the University of California at Berkeley to a machine?

4. **FORM AND SUPPORT OPINIONS** Do you think peaceful antiwar protests in the 1960s were more effective than more confrontational protests? Why or why not?

BUILD BACKGROUND

THE FREE SPEECH MOVEMENT

Like other students at Berkeley, Mario Savio had spent the summer of 1964 working on voter registration drives in the South. When he returned to Berkeley for classes, he was fired up about what he had experienced in Mississippi, and he wanted to recruit other students to help in the civil rights movement. The first student arrested for distributing civil rights literature was Jack Weinberg, a former graduate student in mathematics. As thousands of students stood around the police car watching the arrest, someone shouted, "Sit down," and the crowd complied. Consequently, the police car could not move.

Both Savio and Weinberg continued their interest in civil rights and social justice after their graduation. When Savio died in 1996, he was working to curb university fee hikes that burdened working-class students. Weinberg went on to become an environmental activist. Berkeley honored Weinberg and other former student activists at a 50th-anniversary gathering in 2014, which included speeches, lectures, exhibits, concerts, and a rally. And earlier, following Savio's death, the university named the front steps of Sproul Hall after him. It was on those steps that Savio delivered his speech on stopping the Berkeley machine, leading up to the administration building sit-in.

TEACH

GUIDED DISCUSSION

4. Make Inferences Based on Martin Luther King, Jr.'s 1967 speech criticizing the Vietnam War, how do you think King would have felt about the way draft deferments were granted? Explain your reasoning. *(Possible response: The fact that King believed that too many poor men of all races were fighting a "white man's war" suggests that he would have been troubled by the fact that most deferments went to men in college and men from wealthy and educated families. These were men who represented white America far more than they represented minority groups.)*

5. Make Connections How did the division of society into doves and hawks reflect changing attitudes toward the war? *(Possible response: As protests against the war gained more supporters, the American public became more polarized. People participating in or swayed by protests against the war identified themselves as doves. Americans who continued to believe that the war was necessary for containing communism in Southeast Asia identified themselves as hawks.)*

ANALYZE PRIMARY SOURCES

Direct students' attention to the Primary Source feature and tell students to read the excerpt from Mario Savio's speech. **ASK:** What problem does Savio identify, and what does he want his listeners to do to solve it? *(Savio contends that the university is unfair in its restrictions upon student freedoms. He wants his listeners to do whatever they can to show their opposition to the restrictions, even if their protests bring the day-to-day workings of the university to a halt.)*

ACTIVE OPTIONS

AMERICAN GALLERY ONLINE

Reporters Go to War Invite students to explore the American Gallery. Have them select one of the images and do additional research to learn more about it. Ask questions that will inspire additional inquiry about the chosen gallery image, such as: What is the reporter doing? What aspect of Vietnam or the Vietnam War does it reflect? How does it help you understand the experiences of war? How does it reflect the impact of the war on soldiers, civilians, or the environment?

NG Learning Framework: Write a News Story

ATTITUDE Curiosity

KNOWLEDGE Our Human Story

Instruct students to work in pairs to learn more about the Free Speech Movement, Students for a Democratic Society (SDS), or the National Mobilization Committee to End the War in Vietnam. Ask them to choose one organization, frame a list of questions they have about it, and then use library resources or conduct online research to find answers to their questions. Instruct students to use their research to collaborate on a short news article reporting on the beliefs and goals of the organization. Invite pairs who chose the same organization to compare their findings. Then ask one student from each pair to read their article to the class.

HISTORICAL THINKING

ANSWERS

1. The Vietnam War was the first war to be broadcast on American television on a regular basis. Reporters, photographers, and film crews documented the war directly from the jungles and battlefields of Vietnam.

2. Answers will vary. Possible response: The war highlighted the issue of the oppression of minority groups, since men from minority groups were fighting and dying in disproportionately higher numbers than white men were.

3. Possible response: By comparing the university to a machine, Savio underscored his view that those who ran the university were unfeeling and did not care about individual freedoms, preferring to treat students—and the entire university system—impersonally and restrictively.

4. Answers will vary. Possible responses: Yes. Peaceful protests kept people focused on the message of the group, and the issues it raised, rather than on the confrontation. No. The more confrontational protests received more media attention and illustrated the urgency of the message and the determination of the protesters.

MAIN IDEA In 1968, the North Vietnamese and Viet Cong launched a series of attacks in South Vietnam, hoping to provoke a popular uprising among its people.

THE TET OFFENSIVE

The element of surprise can be key in a battle. An attack by communist forces in South Vietnam surprised the U.S. military and stunned the American people, who began to cry "Enough!" in ever greater numbers.

A SURPRISE ATTACK

It all began on Tet, the celebration of the Lunar New Year and the most important holiday in Vietnam. In other years, hostilities on both sides of the war had been suspended during the holiday. But early on the morning of January 31, 1968, about 80,000 North Vietnamese and Viet Cong forces initiated a coordinated and unexpected attack on dozens of locations throughout South Vietnam. The sites of the **Tet Offensive** included cities and towns, military bases, General Westmoreland's headquarters, and even the U.S. embassy in Saigon. In launching their attack, communist forces hoped to provoke a popular uprising against U.S. and ARVN troops and persuade the United States to pull out of Vietnam.

A few months before the Tet Offensive, the communists had begun a campaign to distract the Americans and ARVN from the real targets. First, the communists attacked a couple of towns in South Vietnam, and then a U.S. Marine base located in the northwest corner of the country. Johnson and Westmoreland sent 50,000 troops to protect the besieged Marine base as well as other bases in the country. Once the troops had been diverted and the communists' true targets stood nearly undefended, the Tet Offensive began.

Initially, the communist forces scored a few successes, including invading the embassy grounds in Saigon, but the U.S. and ARVN troops soon defeated the communists there and managed to retake most of the other targeted locations. However, fighting in the city of Hue raged on for nearly a month. As you may remember, Hue was the site of a major Buddhist protest against Diem in 1963. Hue was also once the capital of Vietnam and the

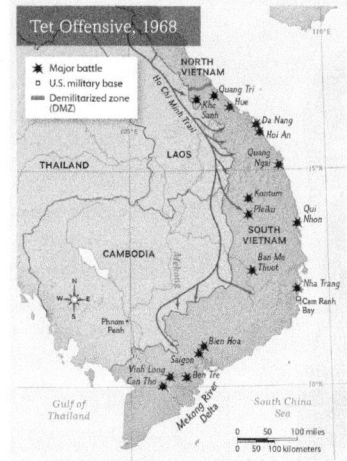

Tet Offensive, 1968

★ Major battle
□ U.S. military base
━ Demilitarized zone (DMZ)

home of its emperor. It was a symbolic target for the communists and poorly defended. On the morning of the Tet Offensive, communist forces quickly seized control of the city. The U.S. and ARVN troops fought fiercely, going from house to house in the city to root out the communist occupiers before finally winning the Battle of Hue.

It would be one of the longest and bloodiest battles of the war. After taking control of the city, the Americans discovered mass graves filled

Journalist Walter Cronkite, popularly called "the most trusted man in America" for the integrity of his reporting, went to Vietnam to cover the aftermath of the Tet Offensive. For two weeks, he reported from battle sites, and his commentary influenced public opinion.

with thousands of Hue civilians murdered by the communists. Before the battle, the North Vietnamese and Viet Cong had executed those they believed were sympathetic to the American cause. The Battle of Hue also resulted in heavy losses, with about 5,000 dead on the communist side and around 500 on the American and South Vietnamese side. Thousands more died or were wounded in other battles of the Tet Offensive. The communists were defeated militarily, and they didn't win more South Vietnamese to their side, but they did score a strategic victory. Television crews had captured scenes of the fighting. To many viewers, it didn't look as though the United States was about to win the war, as the government had led them to believe.

DISILLUSIONMENT WITH THE WAR

After the Tet Offensive, an overwhelming number of Americans called for an end to the war. Few now really believed the United States was winning the

conflict. From Saigon, American broadcast journalist Walter Cronkite reported that the Tet Offensive made "more certain than ever that the bloody experience of Vietnam is to end in a stalemate." In other words, Cronkite believed neither side would be able to claim a clear victory.

In February 1968, Secretary of Defense Robert McNamara resigned from his position. He, too, had become disillusioned with the war and realized he had misjudged the resolve of the North Vietnamese. Like McNamara, the American public had grown weary of the war. They no longer believed the government's positive assessment of it or Westmoreland's optimistic claim after the Tet Offensive that there was now "light at the end of the tunnel."

Just a few weeks after Tet, General Westmoreland requested an additional 206,000 troops in Vietnam. About 550,000 American troops were already stationed there. Clark Clifford, who replaced McNamara as secretary of defense, advised Johnson to deny the request. He also recommended that the United States reduce its bombing raids over North Vietnam and take steps to end the war.

Johnson took Clifford's advice and refused to send Westmoreland all the troops he'd requested, approving only an additional 13,500 soldiers. The president also informed the South Vietnamese leadership that its army would have to assume a greater role in the fight. But to many Americans, Johnson's actions were too little, too late. After the Tet Offensive, his approval ratings dropped by more than 10 percentage points. The unpopular war had taken a severe toll on Johnson's presidency.

HISTORICAL THINKING

1. **READING CHECK** How did the communists devise and carry out their surprise attack?

2. **ANALYZE CAUSE AND EFFECT** What does the Tet Offensive—which North Vietnam lost—suggest about the complexity of historical causes and effects?

3. **DRAW CONCLUSIONS** Why was the Tet Offensive a major turning point in the war?

PLAN: 2-PAGE LESSON

OBJECTIVE

Analyze the Tet Offensive as a turning point in the Vietnam War.

CRITICAL THINKING SKILLS FOR LESSON 3.1

- Analyze Cause and Effect
- Draw Conclusions
- Evaluate
- Identify Main Ideas and Details
- Interpret Maps

HISTORICAL THINKING FOR CHAPTER 27

How did the Vietnam War affect Americans at home and on the battlefield? The communists' massive Tet Offensive caught the United States off guard, both in Vietnam and at home. Lesson 3.1 examines the Tet Offensive and its consequences.

BACKGROUND FOR THE TEACHER

The aftermath of the Tet Offensive shows an important disconnect between General Westmoreland and both the American public and the federal government. Westmoreland felt some degree of optimism following the Tet Offensive. The North Vietnamese had abandoned guerrilla warfare for a widespread traditional military campaign, and Westmoreland believed that such an offensive played to the strength of the U.S. military. He and other U.S. military leaders believed that they could break the stalemate by pressing on with their own aggressive offensive, which is why he requested a large number of additional troops. Reacting to negative public and media pressure, however, Congress balked and called for a congressional review of Vietnam War policies. Similarly worried, President Johnson ordered his own policy review.

INTRODUCE & ENGAGE

CREATE A WORD WEB

Display a Word Web with the term *turning point* in the center. **ASK:** What do we mean when we speak of a turning point? *(It refers to a moment in time at which a significant change occurs in a situation or process.)* **ASK:** What kinds of things might be a turning point in a war? Add students' suggestions to the Word Web. Tell students that in this lesson, they will learn why the Tet Offensive is seen as a turning point in the Vietnam War. After students have completed the lesson, allow time for them to add details about the Tet Offensive to the Word Web.

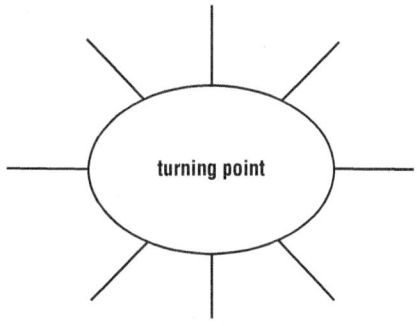

TEACH

GUIDED DISCUSSION

1. **Evaluate** Explain that in a Pyrrhic victory, the side that wins does so at great cost. **ASK:** In what sense did the Tet Offensive present the United States with a Pyrrhic victory? *(Although the United States ultimately won on the battlefield, thousands of American and South Vietnamese soldiers and civilians died. Furthermore, the offensive created such negative feeling among Americans that protesters pushed harder for the war to end, even if there wouldn't be a decisive victory.)*

2. **Identify Main Ideas and Details** What events in the Johnson administration signaled that the federal government's attitude toward the war was changing? *(Secretary of Defense Robert McNamara resigned in disillusionment after realizing that he had misjudged North Vietnam's resolve. Clifford Clark, McNamara's replacement, urged President Johnson to reduce bombing raids over the North, to deny Westmoreland's request for 206,000 additional troops, and to take steps toward ending the war. Johnson authorized only 13,500 new troops and told South Vietnamese leadership that its army would need to increase its participation in the fighting.)*

INTERPRET MAPS

Ask students to examine the map of the Tet Offensive. **ASK:** What can you conclude about the nature of the Tet Offensive, based on the map? *(Possible response: The offensive was well organized and widespread, with communist forces attacking locations throughout South Vietnam. This fact indicates a high level of long-term planning and effective execution on the part of the communist forces.)*

ACTIVE OPTIONS

On Your Feet: Numbered Heads Count off students in groups of four and instruct them to discuss the news media's reaction to the Tet Offensive and the significance of that reaction. Then choose a number and ask the student with that number in each group to share something from the group's discussion with the class. Continue to choose numbers until all students have had the chance to contribute or until students have nothing more to share.

NG Learning Framework: Create a Tet Offensive Infographic

SKILLS Collaboration, Communication

KNOWLEDGE Our Human Story

Invite students to work together in groups to learn more about the Tet Offensive, such as factors leading up to it, key events during its duration, and comprehensive statistics about its results. Remind students that an event may have multiple and complex causes and effects. Then instruct students to prepare an infographic that presents their findings. Work with groups to present a gallery of the finished infographics, with one or two representatives from each group providing commentary.

DIFFERENTIATE

STRIVING READERS

Sequence Events Have students work in pairs to determine the sequence of events leading up to, and then following, the Tet Offensive. Encourage students to add more circles to the Sequence Chain as needed. For each event, students should include the date and a summary of what took place. Invite students to share their Sequence Chains with other pairs and to discuss and reconcile any differences.

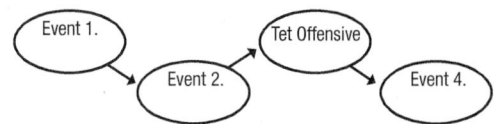

PRE-AP

Analyze Televised War Coverage Challenge students to find online archival television reports made during the Vietnam War and to choose one or two to analyze. You may bring students' attention to Walter Cronkite's reports from Vietnam, as well as his analysis in a CBS Special Report on February 27, 1968. Tell students to analyze the television images and reporting and to explain how it changed Americans' perceptions of the war. Invite volunteers to share their analytical reports with the class.

See the Chapter Planner for more strategies for differentiation.

HISTORICAL THINKING

ANSWERS

1. Perhaps most importantly, communist forces attacked on Tet instead of observing the traditional holiday cease-fire. The communists diverted the attention of U.S. and ARVN troops away from intended targets by attacking a few towns and a U.S. Marine base in the northwest corner of South Vietnam. The diversion left the actual targets vulnerable.

2. Possible response: Even though the communists ultimately lost the offensive, the scope and duration of the fighting convinced the American media and public that the war would end in a stalemate, thus the offensive had the unintended effect of increasing opposition to the war on the home front.

3. Possible response: In addition to increasing public opposition to the war, the Tet Offensive lessened the Johnson administration's commitment to the war.

1968: VIOLENCE AND DIVISION

When Walter Cronkite said after the Tet Offensive that the war was mired in stalemate, Johnson reportedly said, "If I've lost Cronkite, I've lost Middle America." Soon, Johnson would make a decision that would rock the nation.

A DIVIDED DEMOCRATIC PARTY

Johnson's unpopularity among Middle America, or average middle-class Americans, weakened his chances in the 1968 presidential race. At the end of November 1967, Senator **Eugene McCarthy** of Minnesota announced he would seek the nomination of the Democratic Party. McCarthy opposed the Vietnam War and won strong support for his position, especially among young people. He also performed surprisingly well against Johnson in the first Democratic primary election in New Hampshire

in March 1968. Johnson won the primary with 49 percent of the vote—but McCarthy was a close runner-up. He captured 42 percent of the vote. As you may know, in a primary election, voters in a particular state choose the candidate they'd like to see on the ballot in the general election.

Just a few days after the primary, John Kennedy's brother and former attorney general, Senator Robert Kennedy of New York, also joined the race. Kennedy had stated before that he would not run, but McCarthy's success in New Hampshire made

A protester in Chicago bends to pick up a tear gas canister and throw it back at the police during the Democratic National Convention. Nearly 600 people were arrested in the riots, and more than 200 were injured, including both police and protesters.

him change his mind. Like McCarthy, Kennedy ran as an antiwar candidate. Kennedy's decision to run upset some voters because they believed his candidacy might undermine McCarthy's campaign. Others, however, acknowledged that Kennedy, with his money and connections, had a better prospect of winning the Democratic nomination.

On March 31, faced with the likelihood of losing the primary in Wisconsin, Johnson dropped a bombshell by announcing that he would not seek a second term as president. During his televised address, Johnson also revealed his intentions to scale back the bombings in North Vietnam and engage in peace talks with the North Vietnamese. A few weeks later, Johnson's vice president, Hubert Humphrey, joined the race for president. Humphrey, who received Johnson's endorsement, decided against directly campaigning or running in the state primaries against McCarthy and Kennedy. Instead, he hoped to receive enough votes from the state delegations to win the nomination at the Democratic National Convention.

Meanwhile, peace talks began with the North Vietnamese in Paris, but negotiations were short-lived. The North Vietnamese demanded that Johnson scale back the bombing everywhere, not just in North Vietnam, but Johnson resisted. With the talks at an **impasse**, or standstill, heavy combat continued in South Vietnam throughout the spring of 1968. And American troops continued to fight and die in Southeast Asia.

VIOLENCE AND CHAOS

Less than a week after Johnson's startling announcement, Martin Luther King, Jr., was assassinated in Memphis, Tennessee. His violent death touched off a series of riots in more than 100 cities across the country, including Washington, D.C., Baltimore, San Francisco, and Chicago. Rioters set fires and looted stores. In some cities, officials called in the military to establish order. The police made thousands of arrests across the country, and dozens of people died. And the violence was just beginning. In fact, 1968 would become one of the most chaotic years in American history.

Throughout the turbulent spring, McCarthy and Kennedy continued battling in the primaries. Kennedy drew greater support from African Americans and Latinos, while McCarthy had more success with white college students. But on June 5, the contest between the two came to an abrupt and horrifying

end. Only moments after Kennedy delivered a victory speech in Los Angeles celebrating his California primary win, an assassin shot him. Kennedy died the following day. For the second time in just two months, the nation was shocked and heartbroken over the death of a major national leader.

McCarthy remained in the race after Kennedy's assassination, but Hubert Humphrey was the strong favorite going into the Democratic National Convention, which was held in Chicago during the last week of August. Chicago mayor Richard J. Daley had prepared for the internal divisions among delegates inside the convention hall. He was also ready for any confrontations that might take place outside the hall. Daley had turned the convention center into a fortress, bulletproofing its doors and surrounding it with fencing and barbed wire. Police patrolled the area inside the fence, poised for the worst. And that's just what happened.

As many as 15,000 antiwar protesters flooded the city, intent on making their voices heard. The plan was for their protest to be peaceful but loud. Instead, violence erupted when protesters refused to leave a nearby park. The mayor sent about 27,000 police officers and members of the National Guard into the park to confront the crowds. There, the officers lobbed tear gas at the protesters and beat them with clubs. Clashes continued as protesters tried to approach the convention site. Innocent bystanders, including doctors and reporters, got caught in the mayhem. And once again, America watched the violence on television.

In the end, the delegates nominated Humphrey, who was backed by moderates in the Democratic Party. The young people who supported McCarthy felt betrayed. And they saw Humphrey's candidacy as a continuation of Johnson's pro-war policies. Disillusioned with American values, some young people would simply withdraw from traditional society and adopt an unconventional lifestyle.

HISTORICAL THINKING

1. **READING CHECK** What divided the Democratic Party in 1968?

2. **EVALUATE** How did the protests against the Vietnam War affect domestic issues and policies?

3. **MAKE INFERENCES** Given the social and political climate of 1968, how do you think Americans reacted to the images of the Democratic National Convention they saw on television?

PLAN: 2-PAGE LESSON

OBJECTIVE

Describe how events in Vietnam and on the home front affected the 1968 Democratic primaries and nominating convention.

CRITICAL THINKING SKILLS FOR LESSON 3.2

- Evaluate
- Make Inferences
- Compare and Contrast
- Form and Support Opinions

HISTORICAL THINKING FOR CHAPTER 27

How did the Vietnam War affect Americans at home and on the battlefield? Divisions over the war and two political assassinations in the United States rocked Americans in 1968. Lesson 3.2 examines this tumultuous year.

BACKGROUND FOR THE TEACHER

Many of the protesters at the Democratic National Convention hoped that there would be no violence, but the cards were stacked in favor of confrontation and overreaction. The Republican National Convention in Miami had been marred by violence, so Mayor Richard J. Daley was determined to keep order in Chicago. He established a curfew, denied the protesters permits to march or to sleep in the city parks, and gave law enforcement "shoot to kill" orders in certain cases. The situation was so tense that the SDS and other antiwar groups urged their members to stay away. The warnings reduced the number of protesters coming to the city, but not the likelihood of violence.

HISTORY NOTEBOOK

Encourage students to complete the 1968: Violence and Division page for Chapter 27 in their History Notebooks as they read the lesson.

DISCUSS ELECTION INFLUENCES

As a class, discuss the following question: How can news events and the mood of the electorate affect preparations for a presidential election? To encourage discussion, tell students to think about recent elections—local, state, or national—and invite them to share their responses. Tell students that in this lesson they will learn how deep divisions over the Vietnam War and shock over events on the home front affected the Democratic Party as members prepared for the 1968 presidential race.

GUIDED DISCUSSION

1. **Compare and Contrast** How did supporters of Eugene McCarthy, Robert Kennedy, and Hubert Humphrey differ in their view of U.S. involvement in Vietnam? *(Possible response: Supporters of McCarthy and Kennedy appreciated the candidates' opposition to U.S. involvement in Vietnam. Supporters of Humphrey may have varied in their commitment to the war, but it's likely that they generally felt that Humphrey would continue to support Johnson's policies in Vietnam until peace could be achieved.)*

2. **Form and Support Opinions** Do you think violence was inevitable at the Democratic National Convention? Why or why not? *(Answers will vary. Possible responses: Yes. Deep divisions over the war and the atmosphere of fear in Chicago created by Mayor Richard J. Daley's tactics made violence inevitable. No. The protesters came to Chicago with the intention of being loud but peaceful. However, if they had left the park when ordered to do so, violence may have been avoided.)*

MORE INFORMATION

The Paris Peace Talks Representatives of South Vietnam unexpectedly walked away from the Paris peace talks just before the presidential election. It was later revealed that Richard Nixon's presidential campaign staff had encouraged them to walk by telling them that a Nixon presidency would better protect their interests. There is evidence that President Johnson knew about the campaign's interference but decided not to make the information public because he lacked solid proof that Nixon was directly involved. **ASK:** How might the Nixon campaign's action and Johnson's failure to act have influenced the election's outcome? *(Possible response: The sudden collapse of peace talks likely hurt Hubert Humphrey's chances of winning the election. Had Johnson revealed what he knew, the information might have cost Nixon the election.)*

ACTIVE OPTIONS

On Your Feet: Turn and Talk on Topic Arrange students into four lines. Give each group the following topic sentence: The Vietnam War shaped the Democratic presidential primaries in 1968. Instruct groups to create a paragraph by having each student in the line add a sentence that supports the topic. Direct groups to present their completed paragraph to the class by having each student in line read his or her sentence in a logical order.

NG Learning Framework: Debate Events at the 1968 DNC

ATTITUDE Responsibility

KNOWLEDGE Our Human Story

Direct students to work in groups to conduct additional research about the 1968 Democratic Convention and then stage a debate about whether the actions of Mayor Daley and the police against protesters were warranted. Allow groups to pick the members who will debate and the members who will serve as debate judges. Encourage students to debate the issues within the context of that era and not refer to police clashes with protesters that occurred in later years.

ENGLISH LANGUAGE LEARNERS ELD

Use an Idiom Pair students at the **Emerging** level with students at the **Expanding** or **Bridging** levels. Tell students to find and read the sentence that uses the idiom "dropped a bombshell." Instruct pairs to discuss the literal and figurative meaning of the idiom and to discuss why Johnson's decision not to run for re-election was considered a bombshell. Have students work together to write two original sentences using the phrase. Encourage students to share their sentences with another pair.

GIFTED & TALENTED

Create a Multimedia Presentation Challenge students to create a multimedia presentation that illustrates and explains the events leading up to the 1968 Democratic Nation Convention in Chicago. Instruct students to conduct online research to find archival photographs, video footage, and news reports of the chaotic and confusing spring and summer of 1968 and to select events that best represent contributing factors. Tell students to conclude their presentations by showing how the events of 1968 led to Democrats being divided in the presidential campaign and election that followed. Invite students to share their multimedia presentation with the class.

See the Chapter Planner for more strategies for differentiation.

ANSWERS

1. The Democratic Party was divided over the Vietnam War. Two of the party's candidates opposed the war; the third represented the Johnson administration's policy of continuing the fighting while trying to negotiate peace.

2. Opposition to the war made Johnson so unpopular with Middle America that he decided not to run for another term. The prospect of antiwar protests at the 1968 Democratic National Convention led Chicago Mayor Richard J. Daley to prepare for violence with his own strong show of force.

3. Possible response: Given the unsettled climate in the United States, marked by antiwar protests and two political assassinations, Americans probably were alarmed by the violent actions of the protesters and those of the Chicago police and the National Guard.

THE COUNTERCULTURE

"Power to the people." "Don't trust anyone over 30." "Flower power." These are just a few of the slogans adopted by groups of young people who rejected middle-class values, the war, and what came to be called "the establishment."

ANTIESTABLISHMENT

From within the antiwar and rights protest movements of the New Left, a **counterculture** emerged, promoting a way of life that was in opposition with American society's established rules and behavior. Those who participated in the counterculture, often called "hippies," were frustrated with the war, politics, and discrimination in America. They believed that true equality and peace could only be realized through a revolution of cultural values.

Thus, hippies decided to "check out" from mainstream society as a way of rebelling against middle-class American values and seeking true happiness. They embraced pacifism and demonstrated against the conflict in Vietnam, declaring that waging war anywhere in the world was wrong. "Make love, not war" and "Give peace a chance" were popular hippie slogans. These members of the counterculture rebelled by calling into question Cold War values and even long-standing American principles.

The counterculture had its own distinctive style of music, dress, language, and films, all of which influenced mainstream social and cultural sensibilities. Both men and women in the counterculture typically let their hair grow long, dressed in tie-dyed shirts and bell-bottom pants, and adorned themselves with strings of beads.

They also had liberated attitudes toward sexuality and the use of psychedelic drugs, which produced hallucinations and an altered state of consciousness. In 1960, Harvard psychologist and researcher Timothy Leary had begun studying the effects of psychedelic drugs and became a folk hero of the counterculture. Leary promoted the use of such drugs with his slogan "Tune in, Turn On, Drop Out." Counterculture music used electronically distorted

sounds to try to reproduce the experience of using these drugs. And films about the counterculture, such as *Easy Rider* and *Wild in the Streets*, were shown in theaters across the country.

To create a sense of family, some hippies formed communes, where they shared living arrangements, food, and possessions. Communes were often founded in rural areas where members longed to get "back to the land." They rejected the consumerism of modern life, grew their own food, and reconnected with nature. Many other members of the counterculture settled in urban areas, such as San Francisco's Haight-Ashbury neighborhood, where they lived in the company of like-minded hippies. More than 75,000 young people migrated to the neighborhood in 1967 alone.

WOODSTOCK NATION

Perhaps the high point of the counterculture came in August 1969 when the Woodstock Music Festival took place on a farm in Bethel, New York. Billed as "Three Days of Peace and Music," Woodstock drew a crowd of about 400,000 people—twice the number expected. They came to see some of the biggest musical acts of the day, including Jimi Hendrix, Janis Joplin, the Grateful Dead, and the Who. Many of these singers performed songs that were critical of the Vietnam War—to the delight of their audience.

The organizers of the festival had planned to use the profits from it to build a recording studio, but they were unprepared for the masses that thronged the festival. Unable to handle the crowds, the organizers let everyone in for free. Though plagued by rain, mud, and inadequate facilities for the audience, Woodstock was a great success and, remarkably, largely peaceful. Only two deaths occurred at the festival: one from an accident involving a tractor

In this photo, audience members at the Woodstock festival stand and perch on top of cars and buses to watch the show. The enormous crowds created a food shortage. When people in the area heard about the situation, they donated food, including 10,000 sandwiches. Others served rice, vegetables, and granola, which came to be associated with hippies. In an effort to feed everyone, thousands of cups of granola were passed through the audience.

and the other from a drug overdose. The term "Woodstock Nation" would be used to describe the youth counterculture of the 1960s.

By the end of the decade, however, the hippies' hopes for a world filled with peace and love were fading. The rampant drug use was taking its toll. Some of the musicians who had performed at the Woodstock festival had died from drug overdoses. Partly in response to the counterculture's drug abuse, the federal government declared a "war on drugs" in the early 1970s. Agencies were created to provide treatment for drug abusers and to establish federal and local task forces to fight the drug trade.

Meanwhile, many mainstream Americans, who had been scandalized by the counterculture and troubled by the protests, longed for an end to the unrest. They saw the counterculture's emphasis on "free love" and rejection of consumerism as a threat to the American

way of life. They feared that the drug culture was increasing crime in their communities. They wanted the nation to return to the way it was in the years of social conformity that followed World War II. They wanted a leader who could re-establish order and end the war in Vietnam. They believed they had found such a leader in former vice president Richard Nixon.

HISTORICAL THINKING

1. **READING CHECK** What values set members of the counterculture apart from members of traditional American society?

2. **MAKE INFERENCES** Why did the emergence of the counterculture coincide with the Vietnam War?

3. **MAKE CONNECTIONS** What characteristics of the counterculture described in the lesson do you see around you today? Explain the similarities.

PLAN: 2-PAGE LESSON

OBJECTIVE

Examine the values and characteristics of the 1960s counterculture.

CRITICAL THINKING SKILLS FOR LESSON 3.3

- Make Inferences
- Make Connections
- Analyze Cause and Effect

HISTORICAL THINKING FOR CHAPTER 27

How did the Vietnam War affect Americans at home and on the battlefield? The antiwar and civil rights movements helped give rise to an American counterculture, with young people rejecting traditional and Cold War values. Lesson 3.3 provides insight into the rise of this counterculture.

BACKGROUND FOR THE TEACHER

Some of the young people who flocked to Haight-Ashbury in 1967 came to take part in the Gathering of the Tribes, or Human Be-In, on January 14, 1967. The San Francisco counterculture organized the event to draw together the different wings of the movement. Held at Golden Gate Park, the event included antiwar speeches and music by such Haight-Ashbury residents as Jefferson Airplane and the Grateful Dead. Timothy Leary launched the festivities with his famous "Tune In, Turn On, Drop Out," and poet Allen Ginsberg, comedian Dick Gregory, and many other counterculture icons entertained a crowd of more than 20,000. Tens of thousands more young people came to San Francisco during that year's "Summer of Love," drawn by the attention the national media gave to Haight-Ashbury and the counterculture movement.

HISTORY NOTEBOOK

Encourage students to complete the Reid on the Road video series page for Chapter 27 in their History Notebooks after they view the video.

INTRODUCE & ENGAGE
PREVIEW USING VISUALS

Direct students' attention to the photograph of the audience at Woodstock and ask them to read the caption. **ASK:** Why have these young people gathered? *(to enjoy a music festival)* **ASK:** How would you describe the setting? *(Possible responses: extremely crowded; relaxed; filled with laid-back young people and vehicles, including painted buses)* Explain that in this lesson, students will see how the Woodstock music festival reflected a set of ideals that were opposed to much of American politics and life in the 1960s.

TEACH
GUIDED DISCUSSION

1. **Analyze Cause and Effect** What impact did psychedelic drugs have on the counterculture and on federal, state, and local government programs? *(The use of psychedelic drugs influenced individuals of the counterculture who attempted to alter their consciousness. It also influenced the music of the counterculture, as musicians tried to re-create the experience of using drugs by electronically distorting sounds. Rampant drug use, however, took a heavy toll on its users, leading the government to declare a "war on drugs." Agencies to treat drug abusers were created, as were federal and local task forces to fight the drug trade.)*

2. **Make Connections** How did the counterculture influence the migration of people within the United States? *(Possible response: Some members of the counterculture moved to rural areas to form communes or to urban areas, such as Haight-Ashbury, to be with people with the same values. In 1967, more than 75,000 young people moved to Haight-Ashbury.)*

MORE INFORMATION

Preserving Haight-Ashbury Tell students that the San Francisco Planning Department has designated some buildings in Haight-Ashbury as cultural landmarks in recognition of the counterculture's role in American social history. One such building is 557 Ashbury, at the corner of Haight and Ashbury streets. In the 1960s, the first floor housed one of the first hippie stores in San Francisco. The upstairs was used for living quarters. **ASK:** Why might a city want to preserve such a building? *(Possible response: Preserving buildings in the area underscores the historic importance of the 1960s and provides landmarks for visitors interested in this era. The buildings hold nostalgic value for those who took part in the movement and will help future generations understand what happened there in the 1960s.)*

ACTIVE OPTIONS

On Your Feet: Just the Facts Divide students into Teams A and B, one to focus on the anti-establishment counterculture and the other to focus on Woodstock. Direct teams to write a list of facts about their topic and to include three likely but false statements as well. Explain that teams will take turns stating their facts and false statements to each other. When a team member presents a false statement, members of the other team should call out, "Just the facts!" Teams get a point when they correctly identify a false statement made by the opposing team, when the opposing team fails to identify one of their false statements, or when the opposing team incorrectly identifies a fact as false. Continue until teams run out of statements. The team with the most points wins.

NG Learning Framework: Create a Social Media Page

SKILL Communication

KNOWLEDGE Our Human Story

Direct students to work in groups to research Woodstock and create a social media page that chronicles the three-day event as if such technology had been available during the festival. Instruct groups to include information about the music, location, weather, size of the crowd, food distribution, and other matters of interest. Encourage students to include maps, photographs, or other media to illustrate the physical and human characteristics of Woodstock. Invite groups to print and share or post their social media page.

DIFFERENTIATE
STRIVING READERS

Complete a T-Chart Instruct students to create a T-Chart listing what members of the counterculture stood for and against. They should label the first column For and the second column Against. As students read, tell them to complete the T-Chart with details. Encourage students to compare their completed T-Charts and revise them as necessary.

GIFTED & TALENTED

Present a Song Direct students to conduct online research to locate an iconic song of the 1960s counterculture that was performed at Woodstock. Tell them to access the full lyrics and listen to recordings of it and research information about the writer, original and cover artists, and the song's significance. Students should perform or play the song for the class and then present the information they gathered about the role the song played in the 1960s counterculture.

See the Chapter Planner for more strategies for differentiation.

HISTORICAL THINKING
ANSWERS

1. Members of the counterculture were pacifists and against war anywhere for any reason. They rebelled against mainstream values and appearance, rejecting traditional family structures and forming their own families, sometimes living in communes and away from city life. They were sexually liberated and experimented with drugs to achieve altered states of consciousness, looking for a higher sense of being rather than accumulating wealth and status.

2. Possible response: Many young people were angry about the war and blamed the established political and social order for U.S. involvement in Vietnam. They wanted to create their own culture that opposed war, discrimination, consumerism, and mainstream politics.

3. Answers will vary. Possible response: Like the counterculture of the 1960s, today's youth adopt distinctive language and styles of dress, enjoy specific genres of music and movies, question established values, and experiment with nontraditional behaviors and lifestyles.

VIETNAMIZATION UNDER NIXON

Many Americans wanted peace in Vietnam and on their streets. They thought Republican Richard Nixon could deliver on both.

Some men, like these protesters in New York's Central Park in 1967, publicly burned their draft classification cards to protest the draft and the Vietnam War.

AN HONORABLE PEACE

Republican Richard Nixon narrowly beat Democrat Hubert Humphrey in the presidential election, winning the popular vote by less than one percent. You may remember that Nixon was involved in the campaign against communism when he was a congressman in the 1940s. He also served for eight years as Dwight Eisenhower's vice president. To sway voters, Nixon had appealed to more conservative Americans—those who conformed to social norms, unlike the members of the counterculture. The social unrest the country had experienced made many people long for law and order. Nixon would later refer to these Americans as "the silent majority."

During his campaign, Nixon had promised he could bring about a quick victory in Vietnam, but he didn't provide any details. He also referred to seeking "an honorable peace." A reporter called this vague promise Nixon's "secret plan." Once Nixon assumed the presidency in January 1969, he and his National Security Advisor **Henry Kissinger** discussed what to do about Vietnam. They knew the United States could not win the war, but they didn't want to pull their forces out of South Vietnam, leaving it vulnerable to invasion from communist North Vietnam. And Nixon didn't want the war to destroy his presidency as it had Lyndon Johnson's. Soon he came up with a plan to end the war.

Nixon proposed a strategy called **Vietnamization**, which allowed for the gradual replacement of U.S. troops with ARVN troops. Under this plan, all American troops would be out of Vietnam by 1972. Nixon began the process of Vietnamization in June 1969 with the withdrawal of 25,000 U.S. troops. He announced more withdrawals that September. In April 1970, Nixon expressed his intention of pulling an additional 150,000 troops out of Vietnam within a year. General Creighton Abrams, who had replaced General Westmoreland as commander in Vietnam, expressed concern about the American troops' ability to train additional ARVN troops in such a short time, but Nixon was determined to follow through with his Vietnamization plan.

Nixon also proposed a change to the conscription process. During the early years of the war, the Selective Service had drafted any eligible man between the ages of 18 and 26, with the oldest men drafted first. This system was replaced with a draft lottery, which had last been used in 1942. On December 1, 1969, the Selective Service placed 366 plastic capsules—one for every day of the year, including February 29—into a

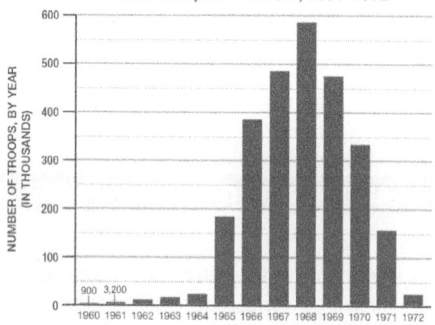

U.S. Troops in Vietnam, 1960–1972

Source: U.S. Department of Defense

jar and drew them out by hand. The first capsule drawn was September 14. This meant that all men born between 1944 and 1950 on that date were assigned the number 1 and would be the first to be considered for the draft. The drawing continued until all the dates had been assigned numbers. The higher your number, the less likely you would be chosen for **induction**, or being drafted into the military.

COVERUPS AND SECRETS

In the midst of what appeared to be positive news about the war, Americans learned about an incident in South Vietnam that had occurred the year before. In March 1968, U.S. troops led by Lieutenant William Calley entered the tiny village of My Lai (MEE LYE) in search of Viet Cong. The troops didn't find any Viet Cong, but they rounded up the unarmed civilians—mostly women, children, and elderly men—and brutally murdered them. Approximately 500 people died in the **My Lai Massacre**, almost the entire population of the village.

The U.S. Army covered up the mass killing, but a soldier who had heard of the massacre eventually spoke to the press, which broke the story to the public in November 1969. Outraged people from around the world demanded justice. In the end, only Calley was punished for the incident. He was put under house arrest and released within four years.

Nixon also tried to keep some secrets of his own. The United States had suspected Vietnam's neighbors, Cambodia and Laos, of sheltering Vietnamese communists. The government also knew that communists transported supplies along the Ho Chi Minh Trail, which passed through those countries. General Abrams suggested carrying out heavy bombing raids on Cambodia and Laos to root out the communist forces, and Nixon and Kissinger agreed to the plan. The United States had conducted air attacks over Cambodia and Laos for several years, but Nixon chose to "carpet bomb" the countries, or attack them with large numbers of missiles.

By showing the communists in Vietnam the lengths to which he was willing to go, Nixon hoped to force them into negotiations. The secret bombing of Cambodia and Laos began in March 1969—not even Congress knew about it. But in May 1969, the *New York Times* reported on the attacks. Furious with the newspaper's revelation, Nixon had the FBI discover the source of the leak in the name of national security. In spite of the leak, the president continued carpet bombing Cambodia and Laos until 1973.

PLAN: 4-PAGE LESSON

OBJECTIVE

Understand the factors that brought the Vietnam War to an end in 1973.

CRITICAL THINKING SKILLS FOR LESSON 4.1

- Analyze Cause and Effect
- Draw Conclusions
- Form and Support Opinions
- Summarize
- Make Inferences
- Make Connections
- Analyze Primary Sources

HISTORICAL THINKING FOR CHAPTER 27

How did the Vietnam War affect Americans at home and on the battlefield? President Nixon's secrecy about the war heightened antiwar tensions. Lesson 4.1 examines the consequences of Vietnamization and the withdrawal of U.S. forces at the war's end.

BACKGROUND FOR THE TEACHER

The My Lai Massacre happened in the wake of the Tet Offensive and in an area known to be a Viet Cong stronghold. Lieutenant Calley's troops, already emotionally on edge from a memorial service for one of their fallen, were told that My Lai would be clear of civilians by the time of the attack and that only Viet Cong would remain. The soldiers were given free-fire orders and told to destroy the village's buildings, crops, and livestock. Once on the ground, the Americans encountered hundreds of civilians. Some leaders, like Calley, failed to adjust their orders and began to attack. Over 500 civilians were killed before a helicopter pilot, Warant Officer Hugh Thompson, stopped the massacre by landing his helicopter between civilians and U.S. troops. The My Lai Massacre divided Americans even further. Many supporters of the war believed in the military and felt that Calley was being used as a scapegoat. Opponents of the war seized on the horror of the event and its subsequent cover-up as proof the United States should pull out of Vietnam.

INTRODUCE & ENGAGE

PREVIEW USING A GRAPH

Direct students' attention to the graph of U.S. troops in Vietnam. **ASK:** What can you infer about the progress of the war, based on the graph? *(The war was getting more intense from 1965 to 1968, requiring more and more U.S. troops to fight the Viet Cong. Then things began to change around 1969, and the number of troops began to fall.)* Ask students to recall what they read earlier in the chapter. **ASK:** What happened early in 1968 to account for the surge in the number of troops? *(the Tet Offensive)* Tell students Lesson 4.1 reveals how the decline in the number of troops is related to Richard Nixon's war policy.

TEACH

GUIDED DISCUSSION

1. **Summarize** How and why did Richard Nixon appeal to "the silent majority" in 1968? *(Nixon appealed to "the silent majority" by promising law and order and "an honorable peace" in Vietnam, outcomes that he assumed conservative Americans wanted based on the lack of protests from this segment of the population.)*

2. **Form and Support Opinions** Do you think Nixon's move to a lottery system for the draft was a wise decision? Why or why not? *(Answers will vary. Possible responses: Yes. It allowed young men to plan for their future, based on their position in the lottery. It also meant that older men would not necessarily be the first to be drafted. No. It ran the risk of encouraging only those individuals with low draft numbers to join the military to avoid being drafted, thereby shrinking the pool of qualified recruits.)*

3. **Analyze Cause and Effect** Why did General Creighton Abrams have concerns about Vietnamization but favor bombing Cambodia? *(Abrams felt that the Vietnamization timetable for pulling out U.S. troops was too rapid to allow for adequate training of additional ARVN troops. However, he also believed that carpet bombing Cambodia would disrupt supply lines along the Ho Chi Minh Trail and root out communist forces.)*

MORE INFORMATION

Nixon's Secret Bombings Tell students that President Nixon kept the bombing of Cambodia a secret from the American people, and he authorized the Air Force to falsify records of the bombings. When the *New York Times* reported the bombings and cited well-placed sources, Nixon ordered the FBI to wiretap several of Henry Kissinger's aides, assuming that the leak came from the National Security Council. Then Nixon extended the wiretaps to include journalists. Years later, Nixon said that he had wanted to keep the bombings quiet because his administration was only a few months old, and he did not want to generate antiwar protests. Have the class discuss whether Nixon's actions seem like an abuse of power under the circumstances. Use a T-Chart to record students' responses and reasons.

Abuse of Power	No Abuse of Power

DIFFERENTIATE

INCLUSION

Summarize Lesson Content Place students in a Fishbowl arrangement to review the lesson. Place students of mixed ability levels in each circle. Call on more advanced students to take turns summarizing the lesson content. Encourage students to take notes, recording key events and dates. When the first group of students has concluded its summary, switch positions and have the second group do the same. Then have inclusion students review the lesson content using their notes. Clarify inaccuracies.

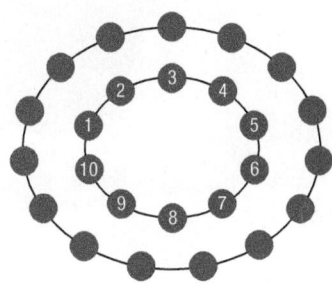

GIFTED & TALENTED

Write Diary Entries Instruct students to conduct research using online and print sources to learn more about the draft lottery begun in 1969. Ask students to imagine that they are watching the live television broadcast of the draft lottery, and they discover they have a low draft number and will almost certainly be sent to fight in Vietnam. Instruct students to write three or four diary entries about their thoughts, feelings, and plans regarding fighting in Vietnam. Encourage students to share their diary entries with the class.

See the Chapter Planner for more strategies for differentiation.

Then in April 1970, Nixon sent 20,000 U.S. and ARVN ground troops into Cambodia to find and destroy what he and the military thought were secret Viet Cong headquarters there. When the White House announced the Cambodian ground invasion, protests broke out. Some of the protests turned violent. On May 4, the National Guard shot into a crowd of student demonstrators at Kent State University in Ohio, killing four students and injuring several others. On May 15, at Jackson State, a predominantly black university in Mississippi, two African-American students were killed and 12 were injured following protests of U.S. policy in Cambodia and Vietnam and demonstrations against racial discrimination. Nixon pulled ground troops out of Cambodia in June.

The release in 1971 of what came to be known as the **Pentagon Papers** revealed more embarrassing secrets. In 1967, then Secretary of Defense Robert McNamara commissioned a study on U.S. activities and policies in Vietnam between 1947 and 1967. The 7,000-page work was never meant for the public eye. Daniel Ellsberg worked on the study and, at that time, was a strong supporter of the Vietnam War. As the war escalated, however, Ellsberg came to oppose it, and he turned the classified document over to the *New York Times*.

The Pentagon Papers revealed that U.S. involvement in Vietnam during the administrations of Truman, Eisenhower, Kennedy, and Johnson had been far greater than the American public had been led to believe. Although Nixon wasn't mentioned in the study, he was enraged by its publication. He considered the Pentagon Papers an attack on his presidency and his handling of the war. Nixon unsuccessfully used both legal and illegal means to incriminate Ellsberg.

THE END OF THE WAR

By 1972, only about 24,000 American troops remained in Vietnam as Nixon continued his gradual withdrawal plan. However, that spring, North Vietnam launched attacks on South Vietnam, prompting Nixon to bomb North Vietnam. Once again, he was trying to force North Vietnam to negotiate a peace agreement. The bombing continued into the next presidential election, which Nixon won in a landslide. In December, one month after Nixon's re-election, the United States dropped more bombs on the North Vietnamese cities of Hanoi and Haiphong than they had dropped in the previous two years. The bombing devastated North Vietnam, destroying harbors, railway lines, and factories.

PRIMARY SOURCE

On January 23, 1973, Nixon addressed the nation on television and radio, announcing an agreement to bring an end to the war in Vietnam. In this excerpt from his address, Nixon echoes the "honorable peace" he'd promised.

Your steadfastness in supporting our insistence on peace with honor has made peace with honor possible. Now that we have achieved an honorable agreement, let us be proud that America did not settle for a peace that would have betrayed our allies, that would have abandoned our prisoners of war, or that would have ended the war for us but would have continued the war for the 50 million people of Indochina. Let us be proud of . . . those who sacrificed, who gave their lives so that the people of South Vietnam might live in freedom and so that the world might live in peace.

—from an address by President Nixon, 1973

On January 27, 1973, North Vietnam, South Vietnam, and the United States negotiated an agreement calling for U.S. troop withdrawal from South Vietnam in exchange for the release of prisoners of war. But Nixon declared the United States would attack North Vietnam again if it committed acts of aggression against South Vietnam. About two months after the signing, the last American troops departed South Vietnam: U.S. involvement in the war was over.

In direct violation of the agreement they signed, the communists began planning their attack on South Vietnam in October 1974. North Vietnamese troops moved into the nation in March 1975. Congress denied requests to send emergency aid to South Vietnam. In late April, Saigon fell to the communists. With the communist victory, the Vietnam War was finally over, but its memory and legacy would haunt the United States for years to come.

HISTORICAL THINKING

1. **READING CHECK** What was Vietnamization?

2. **ANALYZE CAUSE AND EFFECT** What social and political developments occurred as a result of the Cambodian ground invasion?

3. **DRAW CONCLUSIONS** In his 1973 address, what did Nixon mean by "peace with honor"?

4. **FORM AND SUPPORT OPINIONS** Do you think the U.S. involvement in Vietnam was justified? Explain why or why not.

TRAGEDY AT KENT STATE

After several days of student protest at Kent State, classes resumed on May 4. When students gathered for an unauthorized demonstration that day, the National Guard fired tear gas canisters into the crowd to disperse it. Some students picked up the canisters and other items and threw them back at the soldiers, who responded by firing their guns into the crowd. Two of the students killed were walking to class, including Jeffrey Miller, shown lying on the ground in this photo. The image, taken by photojournalism student John Filo, shows Mary Ann Vecchio kneeling by Miller, screaming in anguish. The photo won the Pulitzer Prize and became a symbol of the protest movement.

BUILD BACKGROUND

THE KENT STATE SHOOTINGS

Tensions mounted at Ohio's Kent State University in the days leading up to the shootings on May 4, 1970. On May 1, the day after President Nixon announced U.S. ground troops had invaded Cambodia, protests broke out on college campuses across the nation, including Kent State. That night, protesters clashed with police and lit bonfires in the streets of downtown Kent. Alarmed at the prospect of continued violence, the mayor declared a state of emergency and requested that Governor James Rhodes send Ohio National Guard troops. When the National Guard arrived at the university, the guardsmen found the ROTC building on fire and ringed by protesters.

On Sunday, Governor Rhodes arrived in Kent. He further heightened tensions by suggesting that he would declare a state of emergency and use every force of law against the protesters. Although he never declared a state of emergency, the university and the National Guard assumed they were operating under martial law with the Guard in authority. The school banned protests, but on Monday students gathered on the school Commons where a protest had been planned. Now students had two targets of protest—the war and the presence of the National Guard. When ordered to disperse, students responded by shouting and throwing rocks. Finally, students began to disperse, and the National Guard followed them as they moved over a steep hill into a parking lot. As the guardsmen were moving back up the hill, several of them suddenly turned and fired their weapons. Most fired at the ground or into the air, but a few guardsmen fired into the crowd, killing and injuring the students.

TEACH

GUIDED DISCUSSION

4. Make Inferences Why was the publication of the Pentagon Papers embarrassing for the United States? *(Possible response: The 7,000-page document was an internal study, never meant for publication. It revealed that the American public had been misled—that U.S. involvement in Vietnam between 1947 and 1967 had taken place at a far higher level than the public had been told.)*

5. Make Connections Why did Nixon resume bombing of North Vietnam in the spring of 1972? *(That spring, North Vietnam attacked South Vietnam. Nixon hoped that intense bombing of North Vietnam would force its leaders to negotiate a peace treaty.)*

ANALYZE PRIMARY SOURCES

Direct students' attention to the Primary Source feature and ask students to read the excerpt from Nixon's January 23 address to the nation. Tell students to recall what they read about the outcome of the war. **ASK:** Why might a historian have a valid argument that President Nixon was being overly optimistic in his speech? *(Possible response: Nixon calls the peace agreement "honorable" and says that soldiers died "so that the people of South Vietnam might live in freedom." A historian could argue that Nixon was overly optimistic in assuming that South Vietnam would remain free. However, the withdrawal of U.S. troops left South Vietnam vulnerable to communist attacks. Nixon probably did not expect Congress to end U.S. involvement entirely by denying aid to South Vietnam.)*

ACTIVE OPTIONS

Active History: Compare the Korean and Vietnam Wars Extend the lesson by using either the PDF or Whiteboard version of the activity. These activities take a deeper look at a topic from, or related to, the lesson. Explore the activities as a class, turn them into group assignments, or even assign them individually.

NG Learning Framework: Create an Annotated Time Line

`ATTITUDE` Responsibility

`KNOWLEDGE` Our Human Story

Direct students to work in small groups to research the cover-up of the My Lai Massacre. Ask them to consider the roles of Hugh Thompson, Ron Ridenhour, Seymour Hersch, and Ron Haeberle in bringing the massacre and its cover-up to public attention, the subsequent trials, and Lieutenant Calley's eventual pardon. Assign groups different topics to research. Then ask students to use their research to create an annotated time line of the events. Discuss the time line as a class.

HISTORICAL THINKING

ANSWERS

1. Vietnamization was Nixon's exit strategy from Vietnam. It involved the gradual replacement of U.S. troops with ARVN troops and having all U.S. troops out of Vietnam by 1972.

2. Nixon's decision to send ground troops into Cambodia in April 1970 sparked protests, some violent. Four students were killed at Kent State University in Ohio and two at Jackson State in Mississippi in May. In June, Nixon pulled the troops out of Cambodia.

3. By "peace with honor," Nixon meant exiting Vietnam without betraying U.S. allies, specifically the South Vietnamese. It was a justification for withdrawing from Vietnam without admitting defeat.

4. Answers will vary. Possible responses: Yes. Although the war did not end in victory, it did send a message to communist countries that the United States would aggressively pursue containment. No. Given that the war ended without a victory and that Vietnam was eventually united under the communists, the cost in lives, money, and social unrest was not worth U. S. involvement.

LEGACY OF THE WAR

Many American veterans came home to a country they hardly recognized and where they seemed to be regarded as living symbols of an unpopular war. It would be difficult for everyone to adjust to the post-war world.

CASUALTIES OF WAR

Before 2010, the Vietnam War was the longest conflict in U.S. history. It claimed the lives of almost 60,000 Americans and about 2 million Vietnamese. As agreed, about two weeks after they signed the January 1973 peace agreement, the North Vietnamese began releasing American prisoners of war, or POWs. The POW camps freed 120 prisoners every two weeks, with the sick and injured leaving first, followed by those who had been imprisoned the longest. Some soldiers had been prisoners for more than 8 years, during which time many endured torture and isolation. Prisoners referred to one of the worst prison camps as the "Hanoi Hilton," a sarcastic reference to a famous hotel chain. At this camp in North Vietnam's capital, American soldiers were tortured and interrogated for information. It took about two months for all of the nearly 600 POWs to return home.

In 1973, about 2,500 American troops remained missing in action, or MIA. The Vietnamese landscape, with its thick jungles and swamps, made it difficult to locate the soldiers' remains. The military could not search the area for missing or dead soldiers because the United States never occupied North Vietnam. Though some of those who were MIA later returned to the United States and others were discovered to have died in POW camps, 1,600 men were still designated MIA in 2015.

Once veterans returned from Vietnam, they faced a new set of problems. Unlike soldiers of other wars, Vietnam veterans were not given a hero's welcome when they came home. No parades or celebrations awaited them. The country was still deeply divided over the war. For the most part, Americans didn't want to hear about the veterans' experiences in the war. At best, the returning soldiers were ignored; at worst, they were despised. While most veterans made a successful return to civilian life, some struggled with physical injuries, mental health problems, and drug addictions that had begun while they were in Vietnam.

Some of the physical problems veterans suffered from were due to exposure to Agent Orange. The herbicide contained dioxin, a toxic compound that could cause a host of problems, such as cancer and birth defects. The government was slow to acknowledge the relationship between exposure to Agent Orange and the various health problems soldiers reported.

Other veterans experienced **post-traumatic stress disorder (PTSD)**, a condition brought on by injury or psychological trauma. Symptoms of PTSD can include flashbacks—vivid, realistic memories of horrific events—sleeping disorders, and sudden, often irrational bursts of anger. When they didn't receive adequate support or treatment for their physical and emotional problems, many veterans turned to substance abuse, and some committed suicide. Long after the troops had returned home, the effects of their time in Vietnam lingered, sometimes for many years.

LESSONS OF WAR

Attitudes at home about the war often reflected peoples' political viewpoints. Conservatives fumed because the United States had lost the war, while liberals thought the country should never have waged the war. As one veteran said, "The left hated us for killing, and the right hated us for not killing enough." Over time, though, conservatives learned that Vietnam veterans had fought valiantly under very challenging circumstances, and liberals learned that the veterans, too, were victims of the war.

The American public also collectively realized that forcing democracy on an unstable country such as Vietnam was a recipe for disaster. As a result of the war, Americans became more critical of their government. In fact, the escalation of the Vietnam War and the secret bombings of Laos and Cambodia proved to be the culmination, or conclusion, of Cold War strategies. Ultimately, Vietnam caused Americans to question the underlying assumptions of the Cold War era and protest against their government's policies abroad.

In the 1990s, the United States began to normalize relations with Vietnam. In 1994, President William Clinton lifted a trade embargo that the United States had imposed on North Vietnam in 1964 and on the newly reunited Vietnam in 1975. Veterans' groups

🏛 Vietnam Veterans Memorial Washington, D.C.

The Vietnam Veterans Memorial consists of three parts: The Three Soldiers statue, the Vietnam Women's Memorial, and the Vietnam Veterans Memorial Wall, which lists the names of all the servicemen and women who died in the war. Men and women who served in Vietnam sometimes leave mementos of their war experience in front of the three memorials—especially boots. The National Park Service collects these items and stores them. Many are put on display at the Smithsonian Museum of American History.

After Saigon fell to North Vietnam in April 1975, the United States evacuated Americans and many South Vietnamese by helicopter. In this photo, U.S. Marines help a long line of South Vietnamese board a helicopter on a lawn near the U.S. Embassy, seen in the background at the left. The helicopters made many trips, but not all those desperate to leave could be evacuated.

PLAN: 4-PAGE LESSON

OBJECTIVE

Evaluate the consequences of the Vietnam War in terms of human costs and political and social change.

CRITICAL THINKING SKILLS FOR LESSON 4.2

- Form and Support Opinions
- Identify
- Make Inferences
- Analyze Cause and Effect
- Evaluate
- Describe
- Summarize
- Draw Conclusions
- Analyze Primary Sources

HISTORICAL THINKING FOR CHAPTER 27

How did the Vietnam War affect Americans at home and on the battlefield? The war's legacy left veterans struggling to adjust, a Congress determined to reassert its control over war policy, and an influx of refugees. Lesson 4.2 explores the war's long-term consequences.

BACKGROUND FOR THE TEACHER

The U.S. military used Agent Orange and other defoliants in the demilitarized zones of both Korea and Vietnam. Over time, the U.S. government realized that ground troops exposed to the defoliants, along with Air Force and Air Force Reserve members who worked on or flew in the planes used to drop Agent Orange, tended to suffer from certain cancers, heart conditions, nervous system disorders, and other diseases. The government now compensates veterans who have these diseases if they served in Vietnam between January 9, 1962, and May 7, 1975, or in or near the demilitarized zone in Korea between April 1, 1968, and August 31, 1971. Veterans who meet the time-frame requirements need not prove that they were directly exposed to Agent Orange. Any of their children born with birth defects associated with Agent Orange may be eligible for compensation as well.

INTRODUCE & ENGAGE

EXPLORE LEGACY AS A CONCEPT

Direct students' attention to the lesson title. Explain that while the word *legacy* often has positive connotations, it can refer to negative aspects that are left by a person or a historical event. Discuss the concept of legacy with the class. Invite students to suggest the legacies that a war like Vietnam might produce. Use a Detail Web to record their responses. As students read Lesson 4.2, encourage them to add to the web.

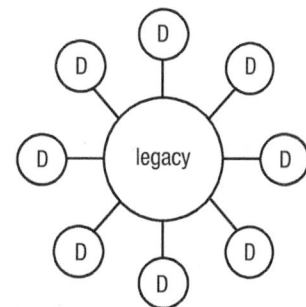

TEACH

GUIDED DISCUSSION

1. **Analyze Cause and Effect** What factors affected the release of U.S. POWs and the search for MIAs, and how? *(Possible response: The 1973 peace agreement set in motion the release of U.S. POWs. The North Vietnamese released the sick and injured first, followed by the longest imprisoned. Vietnam's challenging terrain and the inability of the United States to search North Vietnam complicated the effort to find soldiers missing in action.)*

2. **Evaluate** Share the information in Background for the Teacher with students. **ASK:** Why was it important for the U.S. government to change its position on the health hazards of Agent Orange? *(Possible response: Agent Orange is associated with several illnesses and birth defects. Once the government recognized the link between Agent Orange and these medical conditions, it had a responsibility to compensate veterans who fell ill after exposure to the defoliant during their military service.)*

3. **Describe** How did post-traumatic stress disorder change the lives of some returning veterans? *(Possible response: PTSD took a heavy toll because it produced severe symptoms, such as flashbacks, sleeping disorders, and irrational bursts of anger. These symptoms would have disrupted a veteran's family and work life and could possibly have contributed to drug abuse and suicide among veterans.)*

VIRTUAL MUSEUM VISIT

The Vietnam Veterans Memorial, dominated by the v-shaped Vietnam Wall, was designed by Maya Lin, a 21-year-old architecture student at Yale University and the daughter of Chinese immigrants. Lin had designed the memorial as an assignment in an architecture seminar and then entered her design in the national competition for the Vietnam Veterans Memorial to be built on the National Mall. Out of the nearly 1,400 submissions, Lin's received first place with a $20,000 prize. Since the submissions were anonymous, judges had no idea that the design they chose belonged to an undergraduate student who had earned a B in her class. Encourage students to learn more about the Vietnam Veterans Memorial and its legacy at the memorial's website.

For students who develop an interest in the memorial, suggest that they read the online American Story "The Vietnam Wall."

DIFFERENTIATE

ENGLISH LANGUAGE LEARNERS

Determine Word Meanings Use the following strategies to help students at different proficiency levels determine the meaning of unfamiliar words.

- **Emerging:** Have students choose an unfamiliar word from the lesson. Provide these frames:

  I don't know the word _____.

  I think it means _____.

  Clues I found are _____.

  Point out any context clues and word parts and guide students to discover the word's meaning.

- **Expanding:** Have students use these frames to clarify vocabulary.

  I don't know the word _____, but I think it means _____.

  The context and word parts suggest _____.

  The most likely meaning is _____.

- **Bridging:** Have students draw a three-column chart with the following headings: Word/Know/Learned. Tell students to write an unfamiliar word under Word, write what they already know about the word and what the context and word parts show under Know, and explain what they learned about the word under Learned.

PRE-AP

Explore Outcomes Direct students to conduct online research to learn more about who the "winners" and "losers" were in the Vietnam War. Encourage students to explore the nuances of what it meant to win or lose for different people involved in the war and how a communist victory ultimately led to a capitalist economy. Invite students to share their findings with the class in a written or oral report.

See the Chapter Planner for more strategies for differentiation.

initially opposed this decision. However, Clinton lifted the embargo largely due to Vietnam's cooperation in tracking down and supplying information about American MIAs. Finally, in 1995, Clinton re-established diplomatic relations with Vietnam. In 1997, he named Douglas Peterson, a former American POW who had been imprisoned in Vietnam for six years, as the country's ambassador from the United States. Today, Vietnam is still a communist nation, but it has also embraced elements of capitalism and has a growing economy.

POLITICAL AND SOCIAL CHANGE

The impact of the Vietnam War extended to the U.S. Constitution. The document mandated that citizens had to be 21 years old to vote. But during the war, some people began to support lowering the voting age to 18. Arguing in favor of the age reduction in 1970, Senator Edward Kennedy of Massachusetts pointed out that about one-third of the troops fighting in Vietnam—and about one-half of those who died—were under the age of 21. Kennedy said, "At the very least, the opportunity to vote should be granted in recognition of the risks an 18-year-old is obliged to assume when he is sent off to fight and perhaps die for his country." Senator Kennedy also pointed out that many other countries, including South Vietnam, gave 18-year-olds suffrage. The **26th Amendment**, which reduced the voting age to 18, was ratified in 1971.

Another important political change took place a couple of years later. In 1973, Congress passed the War Powers Resolution, also known as the War

Powers Act. The act required the president to notify Congress about any American troops sent overseas within 48 hours of their deployment. After 60 days, the president had to obtain congressional approval for the troops to remain in a state of armed conflict or make a formal declaration of war. Legislators intended the act as a check on the president's power to send troops into battle without the consent of Congress. Many believed the act was also passed to avoid future Vietnams.

The reunification of Vietnam brought about social change to the United States in the form of a significant influx of Southeast Asian immigrants. When Saigon fell to the North Vietnamese in April 1975, crowds of South Vietnamese fled to the U.S. Embassy and other buildings in the city, hoping to escape the communist invasion. Though U.S. pilots managed to evacuate 7,000 South Vietnamese in less than 24 hours—making the effort the largest

helicopter airlift in history—hundreds more were left behind in the embassy. About one month before the fall of Saigon, however, the U.S. government had ordered Operation Babylift. The government airlifted about 3,000 Vietnamese orphans from Saigon to the United States throughout April and placed them with adoptive parents.

Many Vietnamese, Cambodian, and Laotian refugees would arrive as immigrants to the United States in

the coming decades, however. The greatest numbers of immigrants arrived between 1980 and 2000. Though the immigrant flow has since decreased, the Vietnamese still made up the sixth largest immigrant population in the United States as of 2014. Most settled in California, Texas, Washington, and Florida. Like other groups that have immigrated to the United States, the Vietnamese have become part of the country's rich diversity, and they now embrace their own American identities.

HISTORICAL THINKING

1. **READING CHECK** What problems did Vietnam veterans face when they returned home from the war?

2. **FORM AND SUPPORT OPINIONS** What do you think is the most important legacy of the Vietnam War? Support your opinion with evidence from the text.

3. **IDENTIFY** What domestic policies changed as a result of the Vietnam War?

4. **MAKE INFERENCES** Explain the meaning behind the Vietnam veteran's statement, "The left hated us for killing, and the right hated us for not killing enough," and describe how people's viewpoints toward Vietnam veterans could be so different.

In 1975, John Tenhula began interviewing refugees from Vietnam, Cambodia, and Laos who immigrated to the United States. In this excerpt from an interview, Heng Mui, a South Vietnamese woman, talks about becoming an American citizen.

I became a citizen last year; I am now an American. I do not especially feel like an American, but I don't know if there is any special way I should feel. For some refugees, becoming an American is not an easy thing to do. It means you give up that final thing that is yours, your nationality. But after it happened, I never thought about it. There is something exciting about holding my new blue passport and knowing that I will vote next year for the president.

—from *Voices from Southeast Asia*, by John Tenhula, 1991

National Geographic photographer Michael S. Lewis captured the lights and activity of Lam Son Square in modern Ho Chi Minh City, formerly known as Saigon. Today, Vietnam's economy is one of the fastest-growing in the world, and the country boasts a developing middle class.

BUILD BACKGROUND

OPERATION BABYLIFT

Operation Babylift, like many things associated with the Vietnam War, was controversial. Proponents of the program saw it as a humanitarian effort designed to save children who faced an uncertain future in a communist-controlled Vietnam. This was particularly true of children fathered by U.S. soldiers. Critics of the program argued that it was akin to baby snatching, since many of the airlifted children were not actually orphans. Desperate mothers of mixed-race children and parents who had cooperated with the Americans sometimes gave up their children out of fear for their safety. Some parents hoped to immigrate to the United States and reunite their families. Unfortunately, these parents often had no paper trail to follow, and few of the airlifted children were ever reunited with their birth families.

NATIONAL GEOGRAPHIC PHOTOGRAPHER
MICHAEL S. LEWIS

Michael S. Lewis grew up in Missouri but has lived in Colorado since 1986. He credits his small-town upbringing for his honest respect for the people and places he photographs. Lewis started with National Geographic in 1995, photographing the Rocky Mountains and Canada, and has since traveled on assignment to such places as Africa and Vietnam. For his work on the National Geographic book *Africa*, Lewis shot photographs of people and their environment in eight different regions of the continent.

TEACH

GUIDED DISCUSSION

4. **Summarize** How and why did President Clinton normalize relations with Vietnam? *(President Clinton lifted a trade embargo on Vietnam in 1994 in return for Vietnam's help in tracking down and supplying information about MIAs. He then re-established diplomatic relations in 1997.)*

5. **Draw Conclusions** From what evidence can you conclude that immigrants from Vietnam have had a significant impact on the United States? *(Answers will vary. Possible response: Immigration from Vietnam continued after the fall of Saigon, peaking in the years between 1980 and 2000. Today, the Vietnamese make up the sixth largest immigrant group in the United States, adding to the country's cultural diversity.)*

ANALYZE PRIMARY SOURCES

Direct students' attention to the Primary Source feature and ask a volunteer to read aloud the comment from Heng Mui. **ASK:** What do you think the legacy of the Vietnam War was for her? Explain your answer. *(Answers will vary. Possible response: The legacy of the war for Heng Mui is good and bad. She is sad to have lost part of her identity, but—as a new citizen—she is excited about being able to take part in an election for the president.)*

ACTIVE OPTIONS

On Your Feet: Inside-Outside Circle Arrange students in concentric circles facing each other. Tell students in the outside circle to ask students in the inside circle a question about the lesson. After students answer, have the outside circle rotate one position to the right to create new pairings. After five questions, tell students to switch roles and continue.

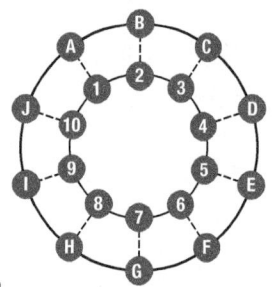

NG Learning Framework: Develop a Multimedia Presentation

SKILLS Communication, Collaboration

KNOWLEDGE Our Human Story

Arrange students in groups and ask them to research the impact of Vietnamese refugees on American society after the Vietnam War, including the influence of their food, clothing, and culture. Instruct groups to use their research to develop a multimedia presentation that includes historical and current statistics, background information, and first-person accounts. Encourage students to include photographs and video segments. Allow time for groups to share their presentation with the class.

HISTORICAL THINKING

ANSWERS

1. Vietnam veterans were not welcomed home with parades or celebrations as veterans of earlier wars had been. Some people saw them as failures for not winning the war or as killers for having fought in the war. Some returning veterans struggled with drug addiction, mental health problems (including PTSD and suicidal tendencies), physical injuries, and health problems associated with exposure to Agent Orange.

2. Answers will vary. Students might focus on the long-term plight of returning soldiers, the realization that democracy cannot be forced on a country, the end of Cold War strategies, or the curtailing of presidential power. Students should support their answers with evidence from the text.

3. The 26th Amendment, which lowered the voting age to 18, was ratified in recognition of the fact that soldiers who were too young to vote were fighting and dying in the war. Congress passed the War Powers Resolution to use the authority of Congress to check the power of the presidency regarding troop deployment and duration.

4. Possible response: At least initially, the left blamed soldiers for going to Vietnam and fighting at all, while the right held soldiers responsible for administration policies that didn't execute the war more forcefully.

VOCABULARY

Use each of the following vocabulary words in a sentence that shows an understanding of the term's meaning.

1. **impasse**
   Since neither side was willing to compromise, the negotiations reached an impasse.

2. **hawk**

3. **post-traumatic stress disorder**

4. **coup**

5. **induction**

6. **escalation**

7. **deferment**

8. **counterculture**

READING STRATEGY
FORM AND SUPPORT OPINIONS

When you form an opinion, you determine and assess the importance and significance of something. Your opinion is your personal judgment, not a fact, so you should support your opinion with examples and facts. Use a chart like this one to form and support an opinion about protesters during the Vietnam War. Then answer the question.

Role of Protesters		
Example/Fact	Example/Fact	Example/Fact

Opinion

9. Do you think Vietnam War protesters played a positive or a negative role in the conflict?

MAIN IDEAS

Answer the following questions. Support your answers with evidence from the chapter.

10. Who were the Viet Cong? **LESSON 1.1**

11. Why was President Johnson initially opposed to sending American ground troops to Vietnam? **LESSON 1.2**

12. What was the purpose of General Westmoreland's war of attrition? **LESSON 2.1**

13. How did hawks and doves differ in their views of the war in Vietnam? **LESSON 2.2**

14. Why did the communists choose to begin their offensive on Tet? **LESSON 3.1**

15. Why did Johnson choose not to run for a second term as president? **LESSON 3.2**

16. What happened at My Lai? **LESSON 4.1**

17. What right did the 26th Amendment guarantee? **LESSON 4.2**

HISTORICAL THINKING

Answer the following questions. Support your answers with evidence from the chapter.

18. **ANALYZE CAUSE AND EFFECT** How did American journalists affect the war in Vietnam?

19. **EVALUATE** What did Martin Luther King, Jr., mean when he called the Vietnam War "a white man's war, a black man's fight"?

20. **MAKE INFERENCES** Why did the U.S. government present positive assessments of the war, even when it was going badly?

21. **DRAW CONCLUSIONS** How was the Tet Offensive a strategic victory for the communists in Vietnam?

22. **COMPARE AND CONTRAST** How was the war in Vietnam similar to and different from other Cold War struggles?

23. **ANALYZE CAUSE AND EFFECT** How did the Vietnam War cause Americans to question the assumptions behind Cold War policy?

24. **SUMMARIZE** What turned American public opinion against U.S. involvement in Vietnam?

25. **FORM AND SUPPORT OPINIONS** How do you think American society changed as a result of the Vietnam War?

26. **SYNTHESIZE** What combination of factors caused the United States to end its involvement in the Vietnam War?

27. **MAKE CONNECTIONS** What similarities do you detect between the Vietnam War and more recent conflicts in Southwest Asia?

INTERPRET GRAPHS

Study the graph below, which shows the Vietnamese immigrant populations in the United States between 1980 and 2010. Then answer the questions that follow.

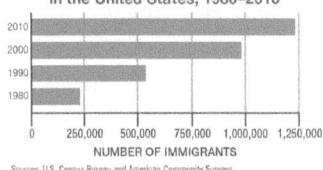

Vietnamese Immigrant Population in the United States, 1980–2010

NUMBER OF IMMIGRANTS

Sources: U.S. Census Bureau and American Community Surveys

28. Why do you think the number of Vietnamese immigrants more than quadrupled between 1980 and 2000?

29. How might Vietnam's growing economy explain why the number of immigrants coming to the United States had tapered off by 2010?

ANALYZE SOURCES

Tim O'Brien wrote about his experiences as a soldier in the Vietnam War. In this excerpt from his 1973 autobiographical story "If I Die in a Combat Zone," which appears in *The Vietnam Reader*, O'Brien discusses the summer he was drafted.

> The summer of 1968, the summer I turned into a soldier, was a good time for talking about war and peace. Eugene McCarthy was bringing quiet thought to the subject. Lyndon Johnson was almost forgotten. Robert Kennedy was dead but not quite forgotten; Richard Nixon looked like a loser. With all the tragedy and change that summer, it was fine weather for discussion. And, with all of this, there was an induction notice tucked into a corner of my billfold.

30. What details in the excerpt convey O'Brien's bias toward the politicians he names?

CONNECT TO YOUR LIFE

31. **ARGUMENT** Service in the armed forces today is voluntary. Do you think the draft should be reinstated? If so, do you think it should apply to both men and women? Write a paragraph in which you make an argument for or against the draft.

TIPS

- State your position on the draft.

- List arguments for and against the draft.

- Explain why you think either voluntary or required military service is more fair or just.

- Use information from the chapter to help support your ideas.

- Address the counterarguments you listed.

- Conclude your argument with a sentence summarizing your position.

VOCABULARY ANSWERS

1. Since neither side was willing to compromise, the negotiations reached an impasse.

2. Robert McNamara began as a hawk, favoring aggressive tactics, but he later became disillusioned with the war.

3. Post-traumatic stress disorder caused some veterans to experience uncontrollable outbursts of anger and flashbacks of horrific wartime memories.

4. The United States supported the coup that removed Ngo Dinh Diem from office in 1963.

5. Getting a high number in the draft lottery meant that a person had little chance of being inducted into the army.

6. McNamara's advice to President Johnson led to an escalation of the war, with more military advisors sent overseas and more air attacks.

7. During the war, some college students received a deferment from military service so they could continue their studies.

8. The counterculture of the 1960s practiced alternative lifestyles and held values that differed from the traditions of older generations.

READING STRATEGY ANSWER

Role of Protesters		
Example/Fact	Example/Fact	Example/Fact
questioned principles of the war	argued that the poor and minorities did most of the fighting and dying	pushed back on secret actions, such as bombing Cambodia

Opinion
Vietnam War protesters played a positive role.

9. Answers will vary. Possible responses: The protestors played a positive role. They questioned the principles of the war, such as containing communism. Protesters argued that the war represented forms of oppression and racism because the poor and minorities were doing most of the fighting and dying in Vietnam. Protesters also brought attention to deceptive government actions, like the secret bombing of Cambodia. The protestors played a negative role. They incited rioting and broke the law, weakened the morale of soldiers, and pushed the government to abandon Vietnam before achieving a military victory.

MAIN IDEAS ANSWERS

10. The Viet Cong were members of the National Liberation Front, an insurgent group trying to spread communism among the South Vietnamese and bring down the Diem government.

11. President Johnson initially opposed sending ground troops to Vietnam because he believed that the South Vietnamese should fight their own war.

12. General Westmoreland believed that he could defeat the communists through attrition by winning many smaller battles, eventually wearing down the enemy.

13. Hawks supported the war in Vietnam, while doves opposed it.

14. As a holiday, Tet was usually marked by a suspension of fighting, so the Americans were not expecting an attack.

15. Johnson believed that the war had made him so unpopular with Middle America that he could not win.

16. In March 1968, American troops massacred almost the entire village of My Lai—including unarmed women, children, and elderly men—during their search for Viet Cong.

17. The 26th Amendment gave 18-year-olds the right to vote by lowering the voting age from 21.

HISTORICAL THINKING ANSWERS

18. Journalists helped end the Vietnam War by reporting on conditions in the war and policies at home, calling into question the optimistic portrayal of the war offered by the military and the administration.

19. King was referring to the fact that while minorities had no say in war policy, African Americans were dying and fighting in disproportionate numbers in Vietnam.

20. The government presented a positive assessment of the war in order to maintain public support for the war effort and to curb protests.

21. Although the communists were defeated in the Tet Offensive, they gained a strategic victory because the length and violence of the offensive strengthened many Americans' opposition to the war and the United States began to scale back involvement.

22. Possible response: Vietnam was similar to other Cold War struggles in that its purpose was to contain communism. It was different because of the use of guerrilla tactics and widespread public opposition in the United States.

23. The Vietnam War caused people to question Cold War policy by showing that military action was not an effective way to contain communism and spread democracy.

24. One factor that turned the American public against the Vietnam War was television coverage. What people saw from the war zone didn't match what the military and the administration said about the war's progress, thereby creating a credibility gap. Antiwar protests also helped turn the public against the war.

25. Answers will vary. Possible response: The Vietnam War changed American society by making people question the actions of the government and the powers of the president, by lowering the voting age, and by increasing immigration from Southeast Asia.

26. Possible response: The United States ended its involvement for reasons that included ongoing losing strategies against guerrilla tactics, the instability of and corruption of the South Vietnamese government, the inherent difficulties of involvement in a civil war and a war of communist containment, and the unpopularity of the war among U.S. citizens.

27. Answers will vary. Possible response: In Vietnam, U.S. forces fought insurgents who used guerrilla tactics in a war that dragged on. In recent conflicts, U.S. forces have been involved in ground wars, such as in Afghanistan, where mountainous terrain makes ground fighting difficult in a war that has also dragged on. Terrorist tactics, such as bombings, armed assaults, hijackings, kidnappings, and assassinations under the direction of ISIS, continue without real progress toward a victory over radical factions.

INTERPRET GRAPHS ANSWERS

28. An increased number of Vietnamese immigrants came to the United States to escape communist rule following the war and for economic opportunites.

29. As Vietnam's economy grew, people had more opportunities for economic success and didn't feel the need to leave Vietnam to improve their lives.

ANALYZE SOURCES ANSWER

30. Possible responses: O'Brien credits McCarthy with "quiet thought," which implies a positive view. He indicates his negative view of Nixon by noting that he "looked like a loser."

CONNECT TO YOUR LIFE ANSWER

31. Responses will vary. Students should state their position, list arguments either for or against the draft, explain the fairness of voluntary or required military service, use evidence from the chapter as support, address counterarguments, and conclude with a sentence summarizing their position.

UNIT 8 RESOURCES

UNIT INTRODUCTION

UNIT TIME LINE

UNIT WRAP-UP

 | CONNECTION

National Geographic Magazine Adapted Articles
• "Who Was Jim Crow?"
• "Before Stonewall" ONLINE

Unit 8 Inquiry: Design a Museum Exhibit

NG Learning Framework Activities
• Write a Letter
• Create a Song

Unit 8 Formal Assessment

CHAPTER 28 RESOURCES

Available at NGLSync.Cengage.com

TEACHER RESOURCES & ASSESSMENT

Reading and Note-Taking

Vocabulary Practice

Social Studies Skills Lessons
• Reading: Analyze Cause and Effect
• Writing: Expository

Formal Assessment
• Chapter 28 Pretest
• Chapter 28 Tests A & B
• Section Quizzes

Chapter 28 Answer Key

ExamView®
  One-time Download

STUDENT DIGITAL RESOURCES

• eEdition
• Handbooks
• Online Atlas

• American Gallery Online
• History Notebook
• Active History

• American Voices (Biographies)
• Literature Analysis

• Projects for Inquiry-Based Learning

Chapter 28 Spanish Resources are available at NGLSync.Cengage.com.

AMERICAN STORIES One Giant Leap

- Study Primary Source: Excerpt from a speech by President John F. Kennedy
- On Your Feet: Roundtable

NG Learning Framework:
Research Apollo 11 Moon Experiments

SECTION 1 RESOURCES
LATINOS ORGANIZE

LESSON 1.1
Latino Lives in the United States

- On Your Feet: Four Corners

NG Learning Framework:
Investigate Court Decisions

LESSON 1.2
THROUGH THE LENS
Angélica Dass

- On Your Feet: The Meaning of Color

NG Learning Framework:
Discuss Race

LESSON 1.3
Minority Workers Fight for Equality

- On Your Feet: Investigate Issues

NG Learning Framework:
Research Activists

American Voices Biography
César Chávez ONLINE

American Voices Biography
Dolores Huerta ONLINE

SECTION 2 RESOURCES
NATIVE AMERICANS AND ASIAN AMERICANS

LESSON 2.1
Native Americans Mobilize

- On Your Feet: Think-Pair-Share

NG Learning Framework:
Create a Poster

LESSON 2.2
Native American Activism

- On Your Feet: Numbered Heads

NG Learning Framework:
Create a News Broadcast

American Voices Biography
Russell Means ONLINE

LESSON 2.3
Asian American Civil Rights

- On Your Feet: Fishbowl

NG Learning Framework:
Research Apologies and Reparations

SECTION 3 RESOURCES
MOVEMENTS FOR EQUALITY

LESSON 3.1
New Voices for Women

AMERICAN GALLERY ONLINE The Women's Movement

NG Learning Framework:
Write an Analytical Essay

LESSON 3.2
Women Seek Equality

- Active History: Analyze Charts and Graphs
- On Your Feet: Debate the ERA

LESSON 3.3
THROUGH THE LENS—AMERICAN PLACES
Stonewall National Monument, New York City

- On Your Feet: Turn and Talk on Topic

NG Learning Framework:
Develop a Class Presentation

American Voices Biography
Sylvia Rivera ONLINE

SECTION 4 RESOURCES
FROM EARTH TO THE MOON

LESSON 4.1
The Space Race Continues

- On Your Feet: Fishbowl

NG Learning Framework:
Create a Storyboard

LESSON 4.2
"One Giant Leap for Mankind"

- On Your Feet: Show Stages

NG Learning Framework:
Devise an Experiment

CHAPTER 28 REVIEW

STRIVING READERS

STRATEGY 1
PREVIEW THE TEXT

Work with students to preview each lesson in the chapter. Guide them to read each lesson's title, introduction, Main Idea statement, captions, and lesson headings. Then tell them to list the information they expect to find in the text. Instruct students to read the lesson and then discuss with a partner what they learned and whether or not it matches the information on their list.

Use with All Lessons

STRATEGY 2
TURN HEADINGS INTO OUTLINES

To help students organize and understand lesson content, explain that headings can provide a high-level outline of the lesson. Model for students how to use the lesson title and subheadings to create a basic outline structure. Encourage students to add to their outlines as they read.

Use with All Lessons *Suggest that students keep their lesson outlines together and use them for review at the end of the chapter.*

STRATEGY 3
USE RECIPROCAL TEACHING

Tell partners to take turns reading each paragraph of the lesson aloud. At the end of the paragraph, the reading student should ask the listening student questions about the paragraph. Students may ask their partners to state the main idea, identify important details that support the main idea, or summarize the paragraph in their own words. Then have students work together to answer the Historical Thinking questions.

Use with All Lessons

INCLUSION

STRATEGY 1
MODIFY MAIN IDEA STATEMENTS

To help students anticipate and organize content, provide modified Main Idea statements before reading. Several examples are provided below.

2.1 In the 1960s, Native Americans protested against assimilation and stood up for their cultures and traditions.

2.2 Because Native Americans' complaints were largely ignored, some activist groups took stronger action.

2.3 After a long history of discrimination, Asian Americans demanded equal rights.

Use with All Lessons

STRATEGY 2
USE CLARIFYING QUESTIONS

Allow students with disabilities to work with students who can read the lesson aloud to them and describe the photographs. Instruct students to ask and answer clarifying questions. Encourage them to discuss the point of view conveyed by the quotation from *The Feminine Mystique* and tell whether they agree or disagree with Betty Friedan's viewpoint.

Use with Lesson 3.1

ENGLISH LANGUAGE LEARNERS

STRATEGY 1
USE VISUALS TO PREDICT CONTENT

Direct students at the **Emerging** and **Expanding** levels to read the lesson title and look at the visuals. Then ask them to write a sentence predicting how the visuals will relate to the lesson. After they finish reading the lesson, you may wish to have students review their predictions and revise them if necessary.

Use with All Lessons *Encourage students at the **Emerging** level to ask questions if they have trouble writing a prediction. Students at the **Bridging** level could help students at the **Emerging** and **Expanding** levels compose their predictions.*

STRATEGY 2
PAIR PARTNERS FOR DICTATION

After reading a lesson, direct students at **All Proficiencies** to write in their own words a sentence telling an important idea from the lesson. Pair students and let them take turns dictating their sentences to each other. Then allow them to work together to check spelling and accuracy.

Use with All Lessons

STRATEGY 3
USE A TERM IN A SENTENCE

Pair English language learners at **All Proficiencies** with English-proficient students. Provide pairs with a list of important words and terms from the lesson. Then have each pair work together to use each word in a written sentence. Invite pairs to share their sentences and discuss different ways to use each word. The list might include these terms:

- boycott
- mobilize
- charter
- self-determination
- "zone of privacy"
- misogyny

Use with All Lessons

GIFTED & TALENTED

STRATEGY 1
RESEARCH AND PERFORM PRESIDENTIAL REMARKS

Instruct students to conduct online research to find the text as well as a video of President Kennedy's remarks to representatives of Native American tribes at the White House on August 15, 1962. Ask students to perform the speech for the class. Discuss how specific parts of the speech reveal Kennedy's support of Native Americans' rights and his respect for their self-determination.

Use with Lesson 2.1

STRATEGY 2
CREATE A BIOGRAPHICAL PODCAST

Direct students to research one of the people mentioned in the chapter and profile that person in a podcast. For example, they might profile a Mexican American Nobel Prize winner, an interned Japanese American, a Native American activist, an African-American "computer" at NASA, or a female astronaut. Suggest that students include interviews and other sound clips in their podcast. Tell students that their podcast should be factually correct and tell an engaging story of the person's life, conveying values, struggles, and achievements. Invite students to play the podcast for the class.

Use with All Lessons

PRE-AP

STRATEGY 1
WRITE AN ANALYSIS ESSAY

Prompt students to learn more about the struggle for farmworkers' rights from the 1960s to the present day, comparing present and past struggles. You could suggest that students read *Tomatoland* and watch the documentary *Food Chains*. Have students use their research to write an essay analyzing past and present problems of farmworkers and some successful tactics organizers have used to improve the lives of the people who bring food to American tables.

Use with Lesson 1.3

STRATEGY 2
FORM AND SUPPORT A THESIS

Instruct students to form and support a thesis about why, many decades after the Equal Pay Act of 1963 was passed, women continue to be paid less than men doing the same job. Direct students to find research data that support their thesis. Then have students write a report that includes charts, statistics, and expert analyses of why the gender pay gap continues today. Students may conclude their report with suggestions as to how their generation could work to end pay disparity.

Use with Lesson 3.1

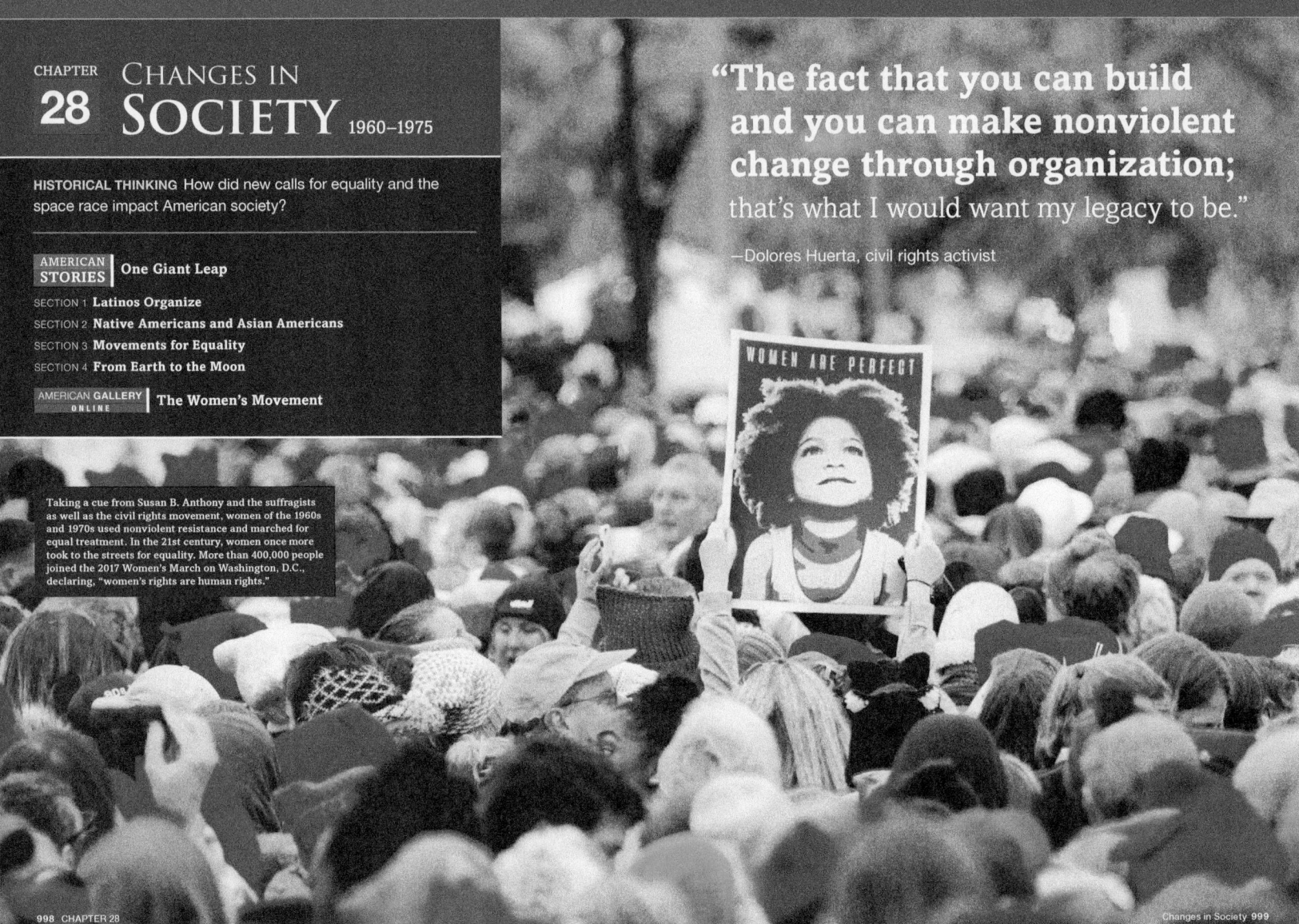

HISTORICAL THINKING How did new calls for equality and the space race impact American society?

Taking a cue from Susan B. Anthony and the suffragists as well as the civil rights movement, women of the 1960s and 1970s used nonviolent resistance and marched for equal treatment. In the 21st century, women once more took to the streets for equality. More than 400,000 people joined the 2017 Women's March on Washington, D.C., declaring, "women's rights are human rights."

WOMEN ARE PERFECT

"The fact that you can build and you can make nonviolent change through organization; that's what I would want my legacy to be."

—Dolores Huerta, civil rights activist

INTRODUCE THE PHOTOGRAPH

THE WOMEN'S MARCH

Have students examine the photograph and quotation that open this chapter. **ASK:** How does the 2017 Women's March exemplify the comment by Dolores Huerta? *(Possible response: The Women's March was an organized, nonviolent action aimed at protecting not only women's rights but also the rights of all people.)* **ASK:** What kind of statement do you think the "Women Are Perfect" poster makes about the marcher, and why do you think the photographer chose to showcase it? *(Possible response: The marcher believes that women should not be made to feel inferior. The poster offers a visual counterpoint to the crowd and makes a statement about why people—men as well as women—are marching.)*

SHARE BACKGROUND

The idea for the 2017 Women's March on Washington, D.C., started as a post on social media as a way to show politicians in the seat of the federal government the strength of public support for issues important to women. However, the demonstrations soon spread to hundreds of other cities and towns across the United States and around the world, with participation swelling far beyond what organizers had expected. Hundreds of thousands of marchers attended "sister" marches in New York, Chicago, and Los Angeles. Marches small and large took place on all seven continents and ultimately included some 5 million supporters. Protesters marched in support of such diverse issues as women's rights, health care, immigration, and racial justice.

For Chapter 28 Spanish Resources, visit the Resources Menu. Chapter 28 Resources are available at NGLSync.Cengage.com.

HISTORICAL THINKING QUESTION

How did new calls for equality and the space race impact American society?

Think, Pair, Share Activity: Calls for Change Invite pairs of students to preview the chapter and to discuss possible answers to the Historical Thinking question. Tell students to focus on the following aspects of the topic:

• How might minority workers fight to overcome unfair or discriminatory working conditions?

• What wrongs might Native Americans and Asian Americans work to overturn?

• What equal rights might women and members of the LGBTQ community try to attain?

• How might the space race change the lives and attitudes of everyday Americans?

Finally, call on volunteers to share their ideas with the rest of the class.

INTRODUCE THE READING STRATEGY

ANALYZE CAUSE AND EFFECT

Explain that historical events rarely, if ever, happen in a vacuum. They are related to some previous events, and they influence some events that follow. The effects of some of these events are seen right away, while others might not be apparent for a long time. Turn to the Chapter Review and preview the graphic organizer with students. As they read the chapter, have students analyze causes of calls for equality and the effects of these calls on American society.

KEY DATES FOR CHAPTER 28

1963	Equal Pay Act signed into law
1963	*The Feminine Mystique* published
1965	Immigration Act signed into law
1966	National Organization for Women founded
1968	MALDEF founded to promote Latino civil rights
1968	American Indian Movement founded
1969	Apollo 11 becomes first manned moon landing
1972	Congress passes Title IX
1973	*Roe* v. *Wade* decision legalizes abortion
1973	Homosexuality declassified as mental illness

INTRODUCE CHAPTER VOCABULARY

KEY VOCABULARY

SECTION 1

manifesto   peer

SECTION 2

militant

SECTION 3

feminism   gender bias   misogyny

SECTION 4

module   spacewalk

WORD WEBS

Encourage students to complete Word Webs for Key Vocabulary words as they read the chapter. Ask them to write each word in the center of the oval. Have them look through the chapter to find examples, characteristics, and descriptive words that may be associated with the vocabulary word. At the end of the chapter, ask students what they learned about each word. Model an example for students on the board, using the graphic organizer shown.

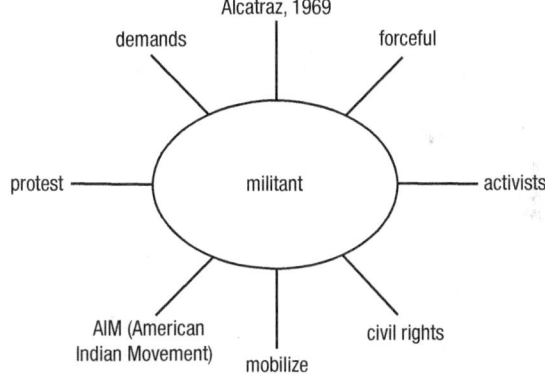

OBJECTIVES

- Describe the effects the space program has had on society and the economy.
- Learn about the Apollo 11 mission and the race to get a man on the moon.
- Understand the roles of mathematicians, engineers, and specialists involved in the space program.
- Distinguish valid arguments from fallacious arguments as well as sound generalizations and misleading oversimplifications in interpretations of the lunar landing.
- Study a primary source: excerpt from a speech by President John F. Kennedy.

CRITICAL THINKING SKILLS FOR "ONE GIANT LEAP"

- Make Connections
- Draw Conclusions
- Summarize
- Identify Problems and Solutions
- Analyze Primary Sources
- Distinguish Fact and Opinion
- Describe

CONNECT TO THE CHAPTER

In this American Story, students learn about one of the most monumental events of the 20th century: the 1969 Apollo 11 moon landing. Enhancing the discussion are photos of the landing, an excerpt from a speech by John F. Kennedy about space exploration, and a diagram detailing the complex layering that goes into space suit construction.

The upcoming chapter, Changes in Society, explores the tumultuous social upheaval that took place in the United States during the 1960s and 1970s. This American Story provides students with an understanding of how the moon landing united a nation and raised morale during a period of social and political struggles. Introduce the American Story after students have read about the Apollo 11 mission in Lesson 4.2.

HISTORY NOTEBOOK

Encourage students to complete the American Story page for Chapter 28 in their History Notebooks as they read.

AMERICAN STORIES — NATIONAL GEOGRAPHIC

ONE GIANT LEAP

Astronauts Buzz Aldrin (shown here) and Neil Armstrong set up scientific experiments near their landing site on the moon. One of the experiments used seismometers powered by solar panels to measure lunar shock waves caused by seismic activity—moonquakes. It also measured the impact of meteoroids or other objects on the lunar surface.

1000 CHAPTER 28

On the evening of July 20, 1969, most Americans were fixated on a television screen, witnessing one of the greatest feats of engineering and technology in history: the first landing of a human on the moon. Years later in an interview, Neil Armstrong shared the credit for his lunar landing with a team of hundreds of thousands of men and women whose feet never left Earth, remarking, "Every guy that's setting up the tests, cranking the torque wrench, and so on, is saying—man or woman—'if anything goes wrong here, it's not going to be my fault.'"

Apollo 11
mission patch

THE SPACE RACE

Much of the technology needed to put Neil Armstrong and Buzz Aldrin on the moon was developed in a remarkably short span of time. One of the motivations for inventing that technology—competition—is as old as humanity.

As you have read, in 1957, the United States and the Soviet Union were engaged in a period of mutual distrust and hostility—the Cold War. Each country worried about the other developing more advanced weaponry or spying capabilities. When the Soviet Union launched *Sputnik* on October 4 of that year, Americans fretted that if the Soviets were more advanced in space technology, they might be ahead in weapons technology as well.

The American public was not reassured when, in December 1957, the U.S. Navy attempted to launch a satellite aboard a Vanguard rocket that caught fire upon take–off and crashed, earning the nickname "flopnik" from the press. A month later, however, the first U.S. satellite reached space atop a Jupiter rocket launched by the army. The space race between the Americans and Soviets was on.

HUMAN COMPUTERS

In May 1961, President Kennedy set out an ambitious goal in a speech before Congress, telling legislators, "I believe that this nation should commit itself to achieving the goal, before this decade is out, of landing a man on the moon and returning him safely to the earth." It was time to get to work.

Neil Armstrong's estimate of "hundreds of thousands" of people needed to place him on the moon was not an exaggeration. By one account, around 36,000 employees from NASA and 376,700 from universities or private industry worked on aspects of the lunar landing.

Armstrong was also correct to note that both men and women were involved in the massive effort. During the early years of space exploration, digital computers were not very advanced and could not perform the complex mathematics of placing a satellite, or a human being, in orbit or on the moon. That job fell to humans who held the job title of "computer" at NASA facilities such as Jet Propulsion Laboratory (JPL) in California and the Langley Research Center in Virginia. Most of the human computers were women.

COMPARE PAST AND PRESENT

Provide students with a blank Comparison Chart and instruct them to label the middle column 1960s Space Program and the right column Present-Day Space Program. Ask students to consider topics such as mission destination and purpose, whether the mission was an international effort, the type of craft used, and crew members and tasks. Tell students to write the topics in the left column and check off or record information as appropriate in the other columns. Then tell students they will read about one of the greatest achievements of the 20th century: a safe landing on the moon.

	1960s Space Program	Present-Day Space Program
Year; Mission purpose		
Destination		
International effort		
Type of craft		

BACKGROUND FOR THE TEACHER

Neil Armstrong became commander of the Apollo 11 mission largely as a result of his ability to remain calm under pressure. Before he, Buzz Aldrin, and Michael Collins served together as astronauts on the mission, Armstrong had already survived being shot down as a pilot during the Korean War. And not long before the Apollo 11 mission, Armstrong had managed to eject from his moon-landing trainer just seconds before it crashed. Buzz Aldrin joined the Apollo 11 crew after successfully working on Project Gemini for NASA. As part of that project, Aldrin helped on the rendezvous of spacecraft—a crucial element of the Apollo 11 mission. Like Armstrong, Aldrin had been a pilot during the Korean War. The third crew member of Apollo 11, Michael Collins, had also worked on Gemini prior to Apollo 11. As part of the Gemini mission, Collins became the country's third spacewalker.

GUIDED DISCUSSION

1. **Summarize** What role did women play in the success of NASA's missions? *(Women were the primary human computers at NASA, plotting trajectories and calculating fuel loads for rockets. Women were also the first programmers at NASA.)*

2. **Identify Problems and Solutions** What challenges did the astronauts face on the Apollo 11 spacecraft? *(They had to rely on the lunar module properly detaching from the command module and then docking again. They had to plant the flag on the moon wearing gloves that provided a limited range of motion. They also had limited food choices since they could only eat specially prepared food that was compact, lightweight, and produced no debris that could get into and damage equipment.)*

ANALYZE PRIMARY SOURCES

Direct students' attention to the Primary Source feature. Discuss with students President Kennedy's reasons for the United States to lead the quest for the moon. **ASK:** Why does President Kennedy think it is so important that the United States become the world leader in space exploration? *(He says that the United States will ensure that space remains a peaceful place by being the first to explore it instead of a nation who might see it as a conquest.)* **ASK:** What implications does he make about the consequences if the United States is not first? *(He implies that the moon could be used as a platform from which to launch weapons of mass destruction.)*

AMERICAN STORIES

Both Langley and JPL had started hiring female computers in the 1940s, before they became part of NASA, to calculate the trajectories of rockets and missiles being developed for World War II. Later, the women turned their superb math skills to plotting trajectories and calculating fuel loads for rockets that would carry satellites and humans into space.

The computers were a diverse group. At JPL, Helen Ling was an immigrant from China, and Janez Lawson was the first African American hired for a professional position at the laboratory. At Langley, many of the computers were African-American women who were forced to use a separate workspace and bathroom until the facility was officially desegregated in 1958.

As digital computers began to outpace humans' ability to perform calculations, the human computers became NASA's first programmers. In 1962, however, when preparing for his orbital flight, astronaut John Glenn was not ready to trust the new machines. He wanted Katherine Johnson, one of the African-American computers at Langley, to do the math. "Get the girl to do it," he said. "I want this human computer to check the output of the electronic computer, and if she says they're good, you know, I'm good to go."

On September 12, 1962, President John F. Kennedy gave a speech at Rice University about the quest for the moon. In it, he expressed his optimism and enthusiasm for the space program.

PRIMARY SOURCE

The exploration of space will go ahead, whether we join in it or not, and it is one of the great adventures of all time, and no nation which expects to be the leader of other nations can expect to stay behind in the race for space.

We mean to be a part of it—we mean to lead it. For the eyes of the world now look into space, to the moon and to the planets beyond, and we have vowed that we shall not see it governed by a hostile flag of conquest, but by a banner of freedom and peace. We have vowed that we shall not see space filled with weapons of mass destruction, but with instruments of knowledge and understanding.

Yet the vows of this Nation can only be fulfilled if we in this Nation are first, and, therefore, we intend to be first. In short, our leadership in science and in industry, our hopes for peace and security, our obligations to ourselves as well as others, all require us to make this effort, to solve these mysteries, to solve them for the good of all men, and to become the world's leading space-faring nation.

—from President John F. Kennedy's speech at Rice University, September 12, 1962

The 2016 film *Hidden Figures* tells the story of the African-American "computers" at Langley who helped put astronauts on the moon. Here, actor Taraji P. Henson (right), in the role of Katherine Johnson, does mathematical calculations in front of an impressed audience.

1002 CHAPTER 28

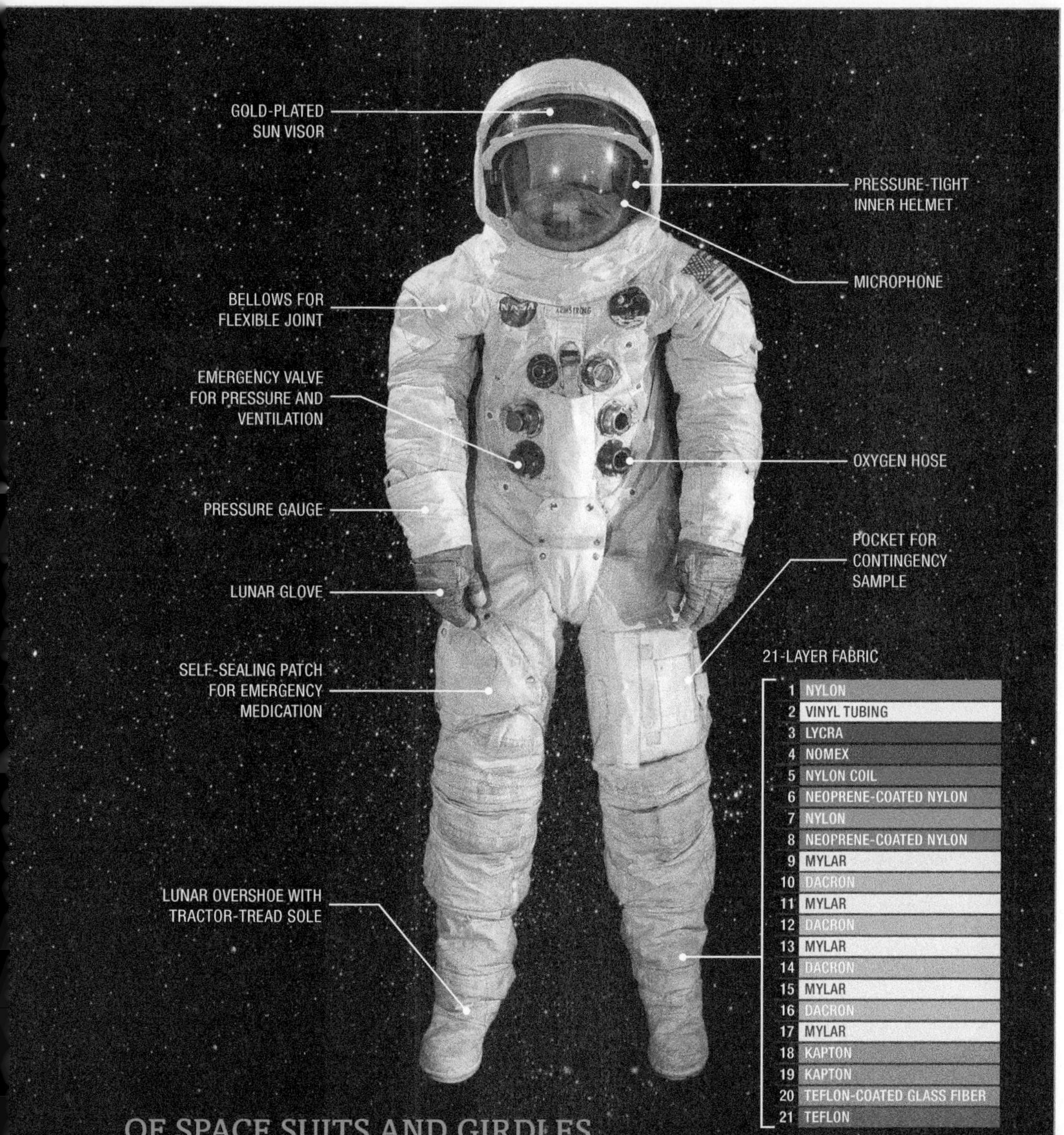

GOLD-PLATED SUN VISOR

PRESSURE-TIGHT INNER HELMET

MICROPHONE

BELLOWS FOR FLEXIBLE JOINT

EMERGENCY VALVE FOR PRESSURE AND VENTILATION

OXYGEN HOSE

PRESSURE GAUGE

LUNAR GLOVE

POCKET FOR CONTINGENCY SAMPLE

SELF-SEALING PATCH FOR EMERGENCY MEDICATION

LUNAR OVERSHOE WITH TRACTOR-TREAD SOLE

21-LAYER FABRIC

1	NYLON
2	VINYL TUBING
3	LYCRA
4	NOMEX
5	NYLON COIL
6	NEOPRENE-COATED NYLON
7	NYLON
8	NEOPRENE-COATED NYLON
9	MYLAR
10	DACRON
11	MYLAR
12	DACRON
13	MYLAR
14	DACRON
15	MYLAR
16	DACRON
17	MYLAR
18	KAPTON
19	KAPTON
20	TEFLON-COATED GLASS FIBER
21	TEFLON

OF SPACE SUITS AND GIRDLES

Before Sally Ride went into space aboard NASA's space shuttle in 1983, all American astronauts were men. And yet, the maker of the first space suits was best known for its popular lines of bras and girdles—attire not commonly associated with male pilots. The International Latex Corporation, known as Playtex, had experience and expertise in working with latex and other tough, stretchy fabrics—just the materials needed to make a space suit.

Skilled Playtex seamstresses had to meticulously assemble 21 layers of material into a space suit tailored to fit each astronaut. Neil Armstrong described the suit he wore on the moon as a "spacecraft," and it did indeed have to function as a one-man habitat, providing air and a constant temperature as he walked on the moon's inhospitable surface. In the 1970s, the division of Playtex that designed and made space suits split off to become a separate company called ILC Dover that continues to make space suits today.

How were the 1960s a period of rapid change? Explain your answer in the context of space technology, social values and norms, and politics.

Changes in Society **1003**

OF SPACE SUITS AND GIRDLES

Each member of the Apollo 11 crew had three space suits made for him: a training suit, a flight suit, and a backup flight suit. This made the workload for seamstresses even greater, given that each space suit had 21 layers. Today, space suits have far fewer layers than those worn by the Apollo 11 crew. **ASK:** Why were the Apollo 11 crew's space suits more complicated than the current ones are? *(Possible response: Materials and processes are more advanced now than they were in the 1960s. Back then it was probably more necessary to have different materials for different purposes, such as temperature control and flame resistance.)*

ACTIVE OPTIONS

On Your Feet: Roundtable Divide the class into groups of four or five. Hand each group a sheet of paper containing the following question: In what ways has the space program captured the imagination of the American public? The first student in each group should write an answer, read it aloud, and pass the paper clockwise to the next student. Have students circulate the paper until they run out of answers or the time is up.

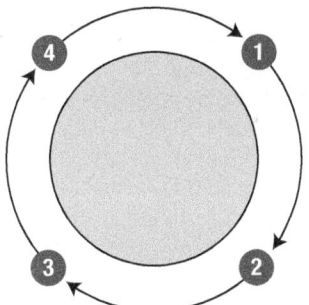

NG Learning Framework: Research Apollo 11 Moon Experiments

ATTITUDE Curiosity

SKILLS Communication, Collaboration

Have students work with a partner to conduct online research about the experiments the Apollo 11 astronauts completed on the moon. Instruct pairs to determine the conclusions NASA was able to draw about the moon as a result of these experiments. Then have students write a short summary of their findings. Call on pairs to present their research to the class.

Kevin Hand grew up in Vermont in an environment that enabled effortless stargazing. Obsessed with aliens and science fiction as a child, Hand now hopes to penetrate the thick ice of Europa to collect organic material that may lie underneath. According to Hand, Europa likely offers scientists the best chance of discovering extraterrestrial life. Hand reminds us of the vastness of space: "Our complex industrial, technological society has really disconnected us from the stars above. We need to remember to stop, look up, and let the wonder take over."

MISSIONS TO MARS

Students may know Elon Musk as CEO of Tesla Inc., the manufacturer of all-electric cars and solar panels. Explain that Tesla's mission is "to accelerate the world's transition to sustainable energy." In June 2017, Musk's SpaceX launched a geostationary communications satellite, BulgariaSat-1, from NASA's Kennedy Space Center that will provide television and data communications to European locations. SpaceX is also developing reusable rockets. **ASK:** Do you think it likely that Elon Musk's ventures will contribute to making humanity a multiplanetary species? *(Answers will vary. Possible responses: Yes. Musk has ventures that are dedicated to using solar power, enhanced data communications, and reusable rockets, all of which would facilitate planetary space exploration. No. Musk's products may enhance the experience of humans on Earth, but they wouldn't help humans live on a planet without oxygen and abundant water.)*

WRITE ABOUT HISTORY

Take a Stand for Space Exploration This American Story discusses one of the country's greatest achievements—sending astronauts to the moon. To help students make connections between the American Story and their own lives, ask them to write a short essay about why they think space travel should remain a priority for the United States. Pair students to edit each other's arguments and make suggestions for revision. Provide guidance about the writing process as necessary.

THINK ABOUT IT

Possible response: The space program led to advances in computer technology, rocket science, fireproof clothing, and navigation systems for airplanes. Jobs in related fields were created, and schools and universities added curricula and training.

AMERICAN STORIES

TO THE MOON AND BACK

While the computers worked on the math, engineers and other specialists were laboring to develop the technology that could carry humans into space, keep them alive there, and bring them back to Earth. They invented a spacecraft called a command module that would launch atop a powerful Saturn V rocket, which would place it in orbit around the moon. A lunar module would detach from this spacecraft to land on the moon. For the return trip, the lunar module would blast off from the moon's surface to dock with the command module for the return to Earth. Every part of the rocket and modules had to be engineered to perfection. There would be no rescue if a key component malfunctioned in the airless cold of space.

Even packing food for the trip required enormous amounts of planning. NASA researchers had to consider what would happen to a sandwich in orbit. As author Mary Roach noted, "A crumb in zero gravity does not drop to the floor where it can be ignored and ground into the flooring until the janitor comes around." Instead, it can float into delicate equipment and cause real damage. Foods had to be devised that would be light, easily packed into tight spaces, and neat to eat. Sadly for the early astronauts, deliciousness wasn't a top requirement of space food.

When Neil Armstrong set foot on the moon, the United States won the space race. The prizes for winning, however, included benefits for all countries. Between 1969 and 1972, 12 astronauts walked on the lunar surface, gathering evidence that advanced our understanding of the solar system. These missions also spurred the growth of computer technology and led to numerous product advancements, from fireproof clothing to better navigation systems for airplanes.

THINK ABOUT IT

How did the space program affect the U.S. economy and society?

HOW TO PLANT A FLAG ON THE MOON

The American flag that was planted on the moon by the Apollo 11 astronauts symbolizes both a victory for the United States and the complexity of performing simple tasks without Earth's gravity.

Because there is no wind on the moon, but just enough gravity to pull a flag down into a droop, a special flagpole had to be designed with a hinged crossbar at the top from which the flag would hang. Next came the problem of how to transport the flagpole, as there was not enough room inside the lunar module. It had to be mounted on the outside of the vehicle in a specially engineered case that could withstand the 2,000-degree Fahrenheit heat produced by the module's descent engine.

Setting up the flag wearing gloves that limited their range of motion would be tricky for the astronauts once they reached the moon, so they conducted several practice sessions on Earth to make sure they could plant the flag while wearing space suits. As this photo reveals, all their planning and practice paid off.

EXPLORING ALTERNATIVE VIEWS

After the lunar landing, conspiracy theorists insisted the event was actually an elaborate hoax created by the U.S. government to appear to have beaten the Soviets to the moon. They claimed Armstrong and Aldrin acted out their space mission on a secret film set, citing evidence to support their theories.

One piece of so-called evidence is video footage of Aldrin planting a waving American flag on the moon. Conspiracy theorists claimed the moving flag reveals the presence of wind, which is impossible in space. NASA says Aldrin was twisting the flagpole to penetrate the lunar soil, causing the flag to wave.

Decades later, some still support the lunar landing conspiracy theory. Conduct research about the conspiracy theorists' alternative interpretation of the historic event. Analyze their evidence and consider why many experts and historians dispute it. **As you research, do the following:**

• Distinguish valid arguments from fallacious ones in the conspiracy theorists' historical interpretation.

• Identify any evidence of bias and/or prejudice in the conspiracy theorists' historical interpretation.

• Distinguish between sound generalizations and misleading oversimplifications in both the conspiracy theory and in the more widely accepted account of the lunar landing.

NATIONAL GEOGRAPHIC

LIFE BEYOND EARTH?

National Geographic Explorer Kevin Hand wants to know if there is life beyond Earth. Working at JPL, the astrobiologist is helping to plan a NASA mission to Europa, a moon of Jupiter located about 600 million miles from Earth. In the 1990s, NASA's Galileo probe flew past the ice-covered moon and detected hints of a vast subsurface ocean. This led researchers to speculate about the possibility of life there. In 2013 and 2016, scientific teams using NASA's Hubble Space Telescope spotted what they believed were plumes of water erupting from beneath Europa's surface, raising hopes that a Europa probe might fly through a plume and analyze its chemistry.

To gain an understanding of the extreme conditions that might be found on other planets and their moons, Kevin Hand has explored such remote Earth locations as Alaska's north slope, Antarctica, and the depths of the ocean. "I'm trying to understand extremes of life here, so we can better assess and investigate habitable environments on alien worlds like Europa," he says.

Hand is as concerned about life on Earth as he is about possible life on a distant moon. He founded Cosmos Education, a foundation that helps educate and empower some of Africa's poorest children through science, health, and environmental education. "When I think about the desire to connect with life elsewhere in the universe," he reflects, "it gives me an incredible sense of the fragility of life here on Earth and how crucial it is to protect our collective home."

National Geographic's Kevin Hand prepares to deploy a rover beneath the ice of Alaska's Sukok Lake.

MISSIONS TO MARS

For some, the obvious next step in space exploration is Mars. NASA is exploring the possibility of sending astronauts to Mars and has already landed several unmanned vehicles on the planet. In September 2016, Elon Musk, owner of the private space contractor SpaceX, announced his goal to land a spaceship with humans aboard on Mars within a decade, establish a colony there, and ensure that humanity becomes a "multiplanetary species." Many are skeptical Musk can make this dream a reality in the foreseeable future, but his goals prove Mars exerts a strong pull on human imagination.

SpaceX's Falcon 9 rocket makes its first successful upright landing on a droneship in April 2016, 200 miles offshore in the Atlantic Ocean after launching from Cape Canaveral, Florida.

In the meantime, NASA missions are studying the sun and our solar system, expanding our understanding of the universe, and developing technology that also benefits humans on Earth. Whether we reach Mars in a decade or a century, it seems certain that our drive to explore space will continue to expand human knowledge and lead to new technologies we can only imagine today.

ENGLISH LANGUAGE LEARNERS   ELD

Create a Word Web Pair students at the **Emerging** and **Expanding** levels with students at the **Bridging** level. Display a Word Web and write *space travel* in the center. Tell students to take turns reading paragraphs of the American Story, noting any words relating to space travel. After each paragraph, instruct students to write related words on the spokes of the Word Web, adding more spokes as necessary. Instruct pairs to trade and compare webs.

PRE-AP

Write a Report Prompt students to conduct online research about some of the implications—historical, political, legal, and symbolic—of planting a flag on the moon, many of which were addressed by NASA's Committee on Symbolic Activities for the First Lunar Landing. Instruct students to use their research to write a report providing a brief history of flag-planting as a way to claim ownership, an overview of the deliberations of the NASA committee, and an explanation of the decision to plant a U.S. flag on the moon. Invite students to post their reports on a class blog or publish them on a school website.

See the Chapter Planner for more strategies for differentiation.

HISTORICAL THINKING

Ask and have students answer the following questions.

1. **READING CHECK** Why was sending astronauts to the moon such a challenge for NASA?

2. **DISTINGUISH FACT AND OPINION** Is the evidence people cite when questioning whether the moon landing happened based on fact or opinion? Why? Explain NASA's response.

3. **DESCRIBE** What do scientists hope to learn by studying places like Europa and Mars?

ANSWERS

1. NASA had to build a craft, construct suits, formulate food and fuel, and make all the correct calculations to safely land and return the astronauts.

2. It is based on opinion. People who don't understand the science behind a moon landing may not be able to picture how such a feat could happen. Some people questioned how a flag could wave on the moon without wind, but NASA explained that Aldrin twisted the flag into the surface, making it seem to wave.

3. Scientists want to investigate whether life is sustainable on other planets, and the discovery of past or present water may hint at the possibility.

LATINO LIVES IN THE UNITED STATES

Once an idea takes hold, it tends to spread. The advances of the African-American civil rights movement encouraged other minority groups to mount their own campaigns for legislative and judicial recognition of their civil rights.

The *Arte de las Americas* mural runs along busy Calle Ocho, or Southwest 8th Street, in the Little Havana neighborhood, the heart of Cuban American life in Miami, Florida. Among the cultural icons portrayed on the wall are musicians, including world-famous salsa singer Celia Cruz.

LATINOS IN THE 1950s AND 1960s

As you have read, the term *Latino* refers to someone whose heritage is Latin American. In the mid-20th century, the Latino population of the United States consisted of three main groups. The largest group of Latinos were Mexican Americans, who began coming to the United States in significant numbers during World War II as part of the Bracero Program, a government program created to fill the nation's need for agricultural workers. Most Mexican Americans settled in California and the Southwest. Cuban Americans, many of whom fled Cuba after communist leader Fidel Castro seized power, settled mainly in Florida. And about 900,000 Puerto Ricans lived in the United States at that time, the vast majority of them in New York City.

By 1960, almost 6 million Latinos lived in the United States. Within the next 10 years, the population had increased to over 9 million Latinos. Immigration rose largely because of the Immigration Act of 1965, which raised immigration quotas and eased restrictions on settling in the United States.

World War II generated opportunities for Mexican Americans, along with others, to serve on the battlefield and to support the war effort in a variety of ways. However, in the years following the war, Mexican Americans, like other minority groups, continued to face discrimination and bias. In 1948, the **American GI Forum (AGIF)**, a newly formed Hispanic veterans' group, and other Mexican American organizations, such as the Unity League and the League of United Latin American Citizens (LULAC), mobilized during the postwar years to fight for Latinos' civil rights.

Aided by these organizations, Latinos pushed for greater equality in education. In 1948, organizers challenged the segregation of Latino children in Bastrop, Texas, and three other Texas school districts in the case *Delgado* v. *Bastrop Independent School District*. The suit maintained that the children were being separated and provided with substandard facilities because of their race and without any legal or educational basis. The court agreed and ordered an end to the segregation. This case was similar to *Mendez* v. *Westminster*, which, as you have read, preceded *Brown* v. *Board of Education* and paved the way to ending public school segregation nationwide.

Latinos also succeeded in advancing their legal rights, including a significant victory in the 1954 case *Hernandez* v. *Texas*. Supporters of farmworker Pete Hernandez sued the state of Texas after Hernandez was convicted of murder by an all-white jury. For many years, counties in Texas—including the county where Hernandez was tried—systematically kept Mexican Americans from serving as jurors. The Latino attorneys representing Hernandez argued that, because the jury had not been made up of Hernandez's **peers**, or equals, their client had been denied equal protection under the law as guaranteed by the 14th Amendment. The case, *Hernandez* v. *Texas*, went all the way to the U.S. Supreme Court. The Court ruled unanimously in favor of Hernandez, stating that the 14th Amendment guaranteed protection not only on the basis of race, but also on the basis of ethnicity. *Hernandez* v. *Texas* set a precedent, or a basic legal standard, for many of the civil rights cases that followed.

A STRUGGLE FOR MANY

As Latinos pushed for greater civil rights, some made strides in achieving success. A number of Latinos joined the middle class. They also made notable achievements in the scientific fields. Latino biochemist Severo Ochoa received the Nobel Prize in medicine in 1959 for his research into the enzymes associated with DNA and RNA. Luis Alvarez received the Nobel Prize in physics in 1968 for his research into the basics of particle physics. Baseball star Roberto Clemente thrilled fans throughout the 1960s, while Cuban-born Desi Arnaz earned fame on the hit show *I Love Lucy* and became a successful television actor and producer.

For the vast majority of Latinos, however, success was a distant dream. In fact, life for the many Mexican American migrant workers was a struggle. Although migrant farm labor was vital to the success of the agricultural economy, in the mid-20th century migrant workers were not treated as the important human resource they were. They were paid poorly, earning an average of about $1,500 a year when the median U.S. income was about $6,200. They worked long hours with few breaks, and most lived in shacks, if they had housing at all. Because migrants continuously moved from farm to farm, most migrant children only occasionally attended school, and some received no education at all. And because they were poor and not well represented, farmworkers had been unable to organize or form a union, although they had been trying to improve their conditions since the end of World War II. Building upon the civil rights efforts of African Americans, a new generation of Latino leaders began an organized campaign to achieve greater equality and rights for farmworkers.

HISTORICAL THINKING

1. **READING CHECK** How did the Immigration Act of 1965 change the process for immigrating to the United States and transform American society?

2. **MAKE INFERENCES** How would serving in World War II affect the expectations of Latinos returning to the United States after the war?

3. **EVALUATE** How did the living and working conditions of migrant farmworkers make it difficult for them to demand greater equality and rights?

PLAN: 2-PAGE LESSON

OBJECTIVE

Analyze the problems faced by the growing Latino community in the 1950s and 1960s and ways in which Latinos began to seek solutions.

CRITICAL THINKING SKILLS FOR LESSON 1.1

• Make Inferences

• Evaluate

• Analyze Cause and Effect

HISTORICAL THINKING FOR CHAPTER 28

How did new calls for equality and the space race impact American society? The Latino population of the United States grew in the 1950s and 1960s. Lesson 1.1 describes the discrimination directed at the Latino community and ways in which Latinos began to mobilize and campaign for greater civil rights.

BACKGROUND FOR THE TEACHER

The intent of the Immigration Act of 1965 was to provide greater equality in immigration by getting rid of the "national origins" quota system. As originally written, the law favored immigrants whose skills were especially sought by the United States. Conservatives, however, changed the law's priorities to give preference to foreigners seeking to join family members already in the United States. In this way, conservatives believed that the U.S. population would remain primarily of European ancestry. That plan backfired because the new law led to chain immigration. For example, a Latino immigrant could settle in the United States and then sponsor family members—who in turn would sponsor others from their homeland.

HISTORY NOTEBOOK

Encourage students to complete the Latino Lives in the United States page for Chapter 28 in their History Notebooks as they read.

INTRODUCE & ENGAGE

PREVIEW USING VISUALS

Direct students' attention to the photograph of the mural (which is a detail from a larger work). Invite students to point out details that catch their eye. **ASK:** In what ways does this work of art signify both the migration of people and the diffusion of ideas? *(Possible response: The mural features elements of Cuban culture, but it is located in Miami, where many Cuban immigrants to the United States have settled. It suggests that this Cuban community wishes to celebrate its musical heritage and share it with Americans who have no Cuban ties.)* Tell students that this lesson will trace the growth and the hardships of America's Latino community in the years following World War II.

TEACH

GUIDED DISCUSSION

1. **Analyze Cause and Effect** What relationship do you see between the formation of organizations such as the American GI Forum and improved education for Latino children? *(These organizations supported Latinos who pushed for greater equality in education and filed lawsuits that ultimately ended segregation of Latino children.)*

2. **Evaluate** How would you evaluate the progress made by Latinos as individuals and as a group in the United States during the 1950s and 1960s? *(Possible response: A subset of Latinos joined the middle class, and some individuals, such as Severo Ochoa and Desi Arnaz, gained prominence in their professions, but as a group, Latinos—especially migrant workers—still struggled.)*

MORE INFORMATION

Muralist Archie Nica Point out "ARCHIE NICA 2009" and "PINTOR MURALISTA" (muralist painter) on the far right of the detail from the mural. Explain that *Nica* is short for Nicaragua, the artist's birthplace. The artist, whose given name is Luis Manuel Cuadra Peralta, has been painting for some 50 years and pioneered the graffiti movement in his homeland. Archie Nica combines a number of media, including ink, watercolor, and oil, to create his large works. The United States, Panama, and Costa Rica are among the countries where the artist has showcased his work. **ASK:** Have you seen large outdoor murals like this one? If so, how were they similar to or different from this one? *(Answers will vary. Possible response: They were colorful like this one, but they focused on other subjects, such as flowers or geometric patterns.)*

ACTIVE OPTIONS

On Your Feet: Four Corners Place one of the following signs in each corner of the classroom: Immigration Act of 1965; *Delgado* v. *Bastrop Independent School District*; *Hernandez* v. *Texas*; Ochoa and Alvarez awarded Nobel Prizes. Ask students to choose the event that they think was of greatest benefit to Latinos and go to that corner. Tell each group to discuss the event and its significance to the Latino community. Then invite group representatives to report on the discussions.

NG Learning Framework: Investigate Court Decisions

ATTITUDE Curiosity

KNOWLEDGE Our Human Story

Review with students the court decisions made in *Delgado* v. *Bastrop Independent School District* and in *Hernandez* v. *Texas*. Then divide the class into two groups and have each group research one of these decisions—each side's arguments, the court's explanation of its decision, and commentary (past or present) on the decision. After each group presents its findings, invite comparisons and other comments.

DIFFERENTIATE

INCLUSION

Describe Details in Artwork Pair students who are visually impaired with students who are not. Ask the latter to describe the section of the *Arte de Las Americas* mural, providing specific details about each person represented, as well as giving an overall impression of the style of the painting and the emotions conveyed. Prompt visually impaired students to ask clarifying questions as necessary.

PRE-AP

Analyze Legal Precedents Tell students to research the Latino legal precedents that paved the way for desegregation of schools in *Brown* v. *Board of Education* and other important civil rights legal cases and legislation. In addition to the *Delgado* v. *Balstrop* and *Mendez* v. *Westminster* cases mentioned in the lesson, you may want to encourage students to investigate *Alvarez* v. *Board of Trustees of the Lemon Grove School District* (1931), the first successful desegregation case in U.S. history. Instruct students to write a report analyzing the Latino legal precedents in the fight for equal rights, concluding with a statement about the importance of legal precedents. Invite students to share their reports with the class by reading them aloud or posting them online.

See the Chapter Planner for more strategies for differentiation.

HISTORICAL THINKING

ANSWERS

1. The act raised immigration quotas and eased restrictions on settling in the United States, which led to an increase in the number of Latinos living in the United States. Their numbers and their culture brought many changes to American society.

2. Because Latinos had fought during the war, they probably expected to be appreciated back home, not discriminated against.

3. Migrant farmworkers experienced poor living and working conditions, which made it difficult for them to organize and form unions through which to demand greater equality and rights.

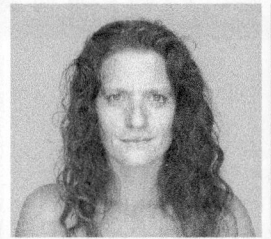
PANTONE® 58-7 C

PANTONE® 323-1 C

PANTONE® 51-6 C

PANTONE® 99-9 C

PANTONE® 321-6 C

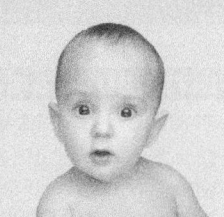
PANTONE® 95-9 C

1.2 THROUGH THE LENS

ANGÉLICA DASS

Humanæ, by the Brazilian artist Angélica Dass, is a photographic work intended to illustrate our similarities as global citizens. By identifying people with a Pantone color based on the actual color of their skin rather than by their nationality, gender, race, social class, or religion, Dass challenges us to think about how we see one another. Her portraits have been exhibited worldwide in museums and as public art installations.

PANTONE® 62-6 C

PANTONE® 116-5 C

PANTONE® 7522 C

PANTONE® 77-9 C

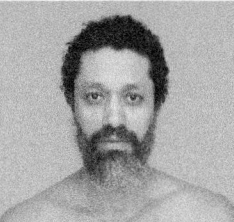
PANTONE® 58-6 C

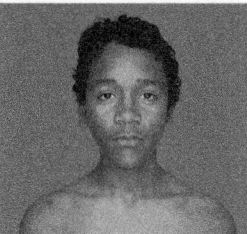
PANTONE® 66-5 C

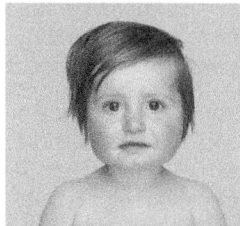
PANTONE® 92-9 C

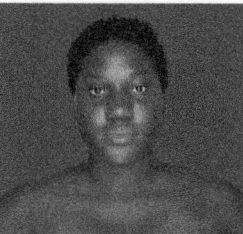
PANTONE® 319-2 C

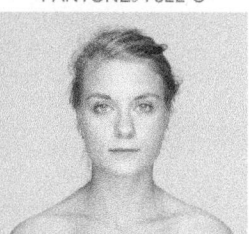
PANTONE® 57-7 C

PANTONE® 97-7 C

PANTONE® 317-5 C

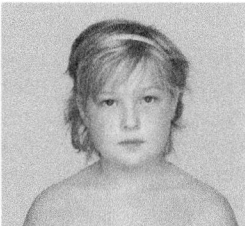
PANTONE® 58-7 C

PANTONE® 322-1 C

PANTONE® 71-5 C

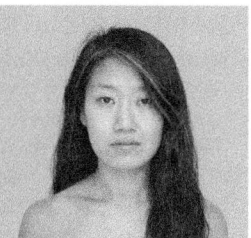
PANTONE® 53-7 C

PLAN: 2-PAGE LESSON

OBJECTIVE

Learn how one artist uses photography to showcase shared human identity.

CRITICAL THINKING SKILLS FOR LESSON 1.2

• Analyze Visuals

• Make Connections

• Form and Support Opinions

HISTORICAL THINKING FOR CHAPTER 28

How did new calls for equality and the space race impact American society? As the push for civil rights expanded in the United States, diverse and historically marginalized groups began to demand greater equality. Lesson 1.2 examines how an artist documents human diversity and commonality by exploring skin tones.

BACKGROUND FOR THE TEACHER

Pantone, a printing company, created the Pantone Matching System in 1963 as a way to standardize, catalog, and label available colors. Before this system, it was difficult for different businesses and agencies—such as designers, advertisers, and printers—to communicate exact colors to one another, since people can picture a range of different colors when they hear terms such as "dark red." To accomplish this standardization, Pantone produced books with chips of colors, each individually labeled with numbers and letters like those seen in Angélica Dass's work. By the 1970s, more than 100,000 of the books had been sold, and Pantone had a firm grasp on defining specific colors. Today the Pantone system includes more than 2,000 different colors—with new ones added regularly—and is used widely throughout the world.

📄 HISTORY NOTEBOOK

Encourage students to complete the Through the Lens page for Chapter 28 in their History Notebooks as they read.

INTRODUCE & ENGAGE

CONSIDER THE CONTEXT

Direct students' attention to the photographs in the lesson. Ask students to think about why the artist posed the subjects and arranged the photographs as she did. **ASK:** How do these photographs of people differ from those you're used to seeing? *(Possible response: In these photos, the background is the same color as the subjects' skin, which is unusual because artists often pose subjects against a contrasting background.)* Point out that the images are labeled by skin color, using a system called Pantone. Discuss with students why they think the artist used this approach. Then inform students they will learn about the artist Angélica Dass's globe-spanning Humanæ work and its message of shared global humanity.

TEACH

GUIDED DISCUSSION

1. **Form and Support Opinions** What do you think Angélica Dass is trying to say with this work of art? *(Answers will vary. Possible response: By showing people only through skin, hair, and eye color—without clothing, jewelry, and other indicators of social class or economic wealth—Dass is illustrating the similarities between all people in an attempt to upend prejudice.)*

2. **Make Connections** What relevance does this international work of art have for Americans, and what does it say about issues like immigration, voting rights, and citizenship? *(Answers will vary. Possible response: Because the United States is a very diverse place, Dass's central message of shared identity is uniquely relevant in this country. Thus, this work could be used to make arguments supporting issues like civil rights and increased immigration or to suggest that it's impossible to tell from looking at someone whether that person is a citizen.)*

THROUGH THE LENS

Angélica Dass began the Humanæ project in 2012 as part of her master's program. Growing up in Brazil—a country that did not abolish slavery until 1888 and in which poverty and race are strongly connected—Dass was always keenly aware that the color of her skin played a role in how she was perceived. But in her mind, these distinctions were arbitrary. Springing from this belief, the project began with two photographs—Dass and her husband—and now includes more than 3,000 images, with subjects ranging in age from 7 months to 70 years and from cities and countries throughout the world. The Humanæ project is currently classified as a work in progress—soliciting volunteers across racial, national, gender, and economic lines—with no set end date.

ACTIVE OPTIONS

On Your Feet: The Meaning of Color Arrange students into two groups. Give one group the color version of Humanæ and the other a black-and-white copy. Then provide each group with a large sheet of paper. Prompt groups to discuss the meaning and emotions elicited by the work of art and record their ideas on the paper. Next have the groups post their sheets of paper at the front of the classroom. As a class, note any similarities and differences in the two sets of conclusions. Finally, discuss why Dass used color the way she did and how that choice impacted the meaning of the work.

NG Learning Framework: Discuss Race

SKILL Communication

KNOWLEDGE Our Human Story

Guide students to Angélica Dass's website, where they can learn more about the artist and Humanæ. Then conduct a class discussion about the importance of race in our current world society. Topics could include: What is Dass trying to say about race? Why does race remain an issue in the world today? What are the historical reasons for racial prejudice having continued across the globe? Do you think worldwide racial relations are getting better or worse? After the discussion, have students write a short response to the following question: In 100 years, will Dass's work have the same meaning as today? Why or why not?

DIFFERENTIATE

STRIVING READERS

Answer Questions Post the following questions on the board:

• What is Humanæ?

• What does Humanæ say about the world?

After students explore the lesson, have them work in pairs to write sentences that answer each question. Call on volunteers to share their sentences with the class.

GIFTED & TALENTED

Create a Work of Art Remind students that Angélica Dass's subjects come from across the globe. However, it would be possible to do a similar project using only citizens of the United States because of the broad diversity in this country. First have students use online resources to learn more about the Humanæ project. As they explore, ask them to think about Dass's message and how she expresses it through art. Then task students with creating a work of art that illustrates both the diversity and shared identity of Americans. The work can take many forms, such as a multimedia presentation, video, collage, or photograph. When students have finished, ask them to share their works of art and explain the reasons for their choices.

See the Chapter Planner for more strategies for differentiation.

MINORITY WORKERS FIGHT FOR EQUALITY

Do you remember a time you felt ignored or treated unfairly? This was how a large number of Mexican American and Filipino American farmworkers felt during the 1960s. Latino and Filipino leaders joined forces to organize a historic campaign to win more rights for workers by drawing on strategies diffused from the African-American civil rights movement.

ORGANIZING FARMWORKERS

César Chávez was born in Yuma, Arizona, in 1927. His family owned a ranch and a grocery store, but they lost their property during the Great Depression. They moved to California, where they became migrant farmworkers. After serving two years in the U.S. Navy during World War II, Chávez returned to the fields. In 1952, Chávez became involved in the **Community Service Organization (CSO)**, a Latino civil rights group. He spoke on behalf of workers' rights and helped organize Latinos to register and vote in their local elections. In 1958, Chávez became director of the CSO.

During his time at the CSO, Chávez met **Dolores Huerta**. Huerta was born in New Mexico and moved at the age of three with her mother to Stockton, California, soon after her parents divorced. Growing up, Huerta was bright, talented, and a good student, but she often experienced discrimination because she was a Latina. After college, she became a teacher in an impoverished farming community. The difficult living situations of so many of her students—the children of migrant workers—inspired her to become an activist.

Chávez and Huerta quickly realized that they shared a common goal of helping better the lives and wages of farmworkers. Chávez left the CSO and formed the Farm Workers Association (FWA) while Huerta left to form the Agricultural Workers Association (AWA). In 1962, they merged their organizations to form the **National Farm Workers Association (NFWA)**. Their goal was to unionize farmworkers and help them seek better wages and more rights. The two activists were a powerful combination—Huerta was usually the negotiator and Chávez, an inspirational speaker and recruiter.

THE GRAPE BOYCOTT

Chávez and Huerta were dedicated to nonviolent protest. Chávez admired the work of Mohandas Gandhi and Martin Luther King, Jr., both of whom used nonviolent means—including boycotts and marches—to protest prejudice and injustice. These methods took time to deliver results, and Chávez knew that patience and cooperation were essential to success. In September 1965, Chávez and the NFWA joined a strike started by the **Agricultural Workers Organizing Committee (AWOC)**, made up largely of Filipino American grape packers in Delano, California. These farmworkers, led by labor leader **Larry Itliong**, were protesting a pay cut and demanding to be paid the legal minimum wage. On September 16, Mexican Independence Day, NFWA grape pickers walked out in solidarity with the AWOC strikers. It would be the beginning of *La Causa*, a five-year struggle to win a fair wage for the farm laborers.

Chávez organized a nationwide boycott of any grapes that did not bear a union label. To help build recognition for the strikers and the boycott, Chávez and Huerta led a peaceful 340-mile march from Delano, California, to the state capitol at Sacramento in March 1966. They began with only 100 people.

THE GREAT GRAPE STRIKE

For years, attempts to organize farmworkers were defeated, often by growers who had played one race against the other. But change began in 1965, when Larry Itliong and 1,000 mostly Filipino grape laborers walked off their jobs, demanding better pay. Within days, Itliong asked Dolores Huerta and César Chávez of the NFWA to join the strike. Dismayed at some growers' brutal treatment of the strikers, Chávez, Huerta, and 1,200 Latino farmworkers joined the strike. By working together, these three leaders brought new life to the nonviolent fight to gain equality for all farmworkers.

Dolores Huerta

César Chávez

Larry Itliong

A boycott poster depicts farm-labor families gathered before a lettuce field as the setting sun displays the United Farm Workers symbol and its motto in Spanish and English. Immediately after the grape strike settlement, the UFW led a nationwide boycott of non-union lettuce to help improve lettuce pickers' wages and living conditions.

"We, as Filipinos, are not alone anymore. We have brothers among the Mexicans and the Blacks and in the conscience of the American people." —Larry Itliong

---

PLAN 4-PAGE LESSON

OBJECTIVE

Learn how Mexican American and Filipino American farmworkers mobilized to improve working conditions and fight for civil rights.

CRITICAL THINKING SKILLS FOR LESSON 1.3

- Draw Conclusions
- Analyze Cause and Effect
- Make Generalizations
- Make Connections
- Analyze Language Use
- Analyze Visuals
- Make Inferences

HISTORICAL THINKING FOR CHAPTER 28

How did new calls for equality and the space race impact American society? Latinos and Filipino Americans mobilized to improve the lives of farmworkers. Lesson 1.3 discusses various techniques that helped minority farmworkers gain fair wages and civil rights.

BACKGROUND FOR THE TEACHER

Larry Itliong is an unsung hero of the farm labor movement. While César Chávez is well known for his work on behalf of farmworkers, Itliong's contribution has been largely overlooked. Yet it was Filipino workers led by Itliong who first walked off the vineyards, touching off the Delano grape strike of 1965. In the face of threatened pay cuts, Itliong—a seasoned labor leader—urged workers to strike. To honor Itliong, in 2015 California governor Jerry Brown signed legislation recognizing October 25, Itliong's birthday, as Larry Itliong Day and requiring public schools in California to teach Itliong's story.

BUILD A TIME LINE

Draw a long time line on the board. Ask students to identify important events they recall from the history of organized labor, such as the creation of the American Federation of Labor and the Congress of Industrial Organizations and any recent labor strikes or court rulings they know of. Place these events in their relative positions on the line, leaving room to add events from the lesson. Tell students that in this lesson they will learn about important labor events related to minority workers in the 1960s. After reading the lesson, prompt students to add more events to the time line and use it to trace the advances and retreats of organized labor, such as the formation of the United Farm Workers union.

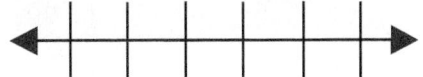

TEACH

GUIDED DISCUSSION

1. **Analyze Cause and Effect** How did the personal experiences of César Chávez and Dolores Huerta influence them to become activists? *(Chávez worked in the fields, so he knew the hardships that workers faced. As a Latina, Huerta experienced discrimination, and as a teacher in a poor farming community, she saw that the children of migrant workers led hard lives and wanted to advocate for them.)*

2. **Make Connections** How did the strike of 1965 and the boycott of 1966 reflect the ideals of Mohandas Gandhi and Martin Luther King, Jr.? *(Gandhi and King were pacifists who championed nonviolent means of protest. Under the leadership of Chávez and Huerta, the strike of 1965 and the boycott of 1966 were executed peacefully, gaining support for the movement from people who may have objected to violent means of protest.)*

3. **Analyze Language Use** What does Itliong mean when he says that "we have brothers . . . in the conscience of the American people"? *(Possible response: He means that other Americans believe that Filipino workers have the right to decent working conditions and a living wage.)*

ANALYZE VISUALS

Draw students' attention to the poster with the motto of the United Farm Workers, "Sí se puede—It can be done." **ASK:** Why do you think the United Farm Workers chose that motto? *(Possible responses: The organization believed that through the unity of its members it could affect change. The UFW wanted to express hope and optimism that their work would produce positive results.)* **ASK:** What other impressions do you get from this poster? *(Possible responses: The people are still working hard even as the sun sets. The workers are all dark-skinned people. The inclusion of children suggests that even children have to work hard or that these workers want a better life for their children.)*

STRIVING READERS

Write a Tweet As students read the lesson, direct them to pause after each paragraph and write a tweet, a 140-character message, summarizing the paragraph's main idea in their own words. Prompt students to read their tweets aloud to the class or to a partner one at a time, with the first student reading a tweet about the first paragraph, the second student reading a tweet about the second paragraph, and so forth.

GIFTED & TALENTED

Present a Chicana Activist Instruct students to research a Chicana who was in the labor movement, such as Gloria Arellanes, Helen Chávez, Juanita Dominguez, Luz Gutierrez, or Rosie Castro. Then have them use what they have learned to present their subject to the class in a format of their choosing, such as: writing a dramatic monologue that focuses tightly on the person's role in a particular event or gives an overview of the person's life; creating a painting or mural about the person's life and work; writing and illustrating a graphic novel about that person and her role in the labor movement. After students present their work to the class, prompt them to discuss what they learned.

See the Chapter Planner for more strategies for differentiation.

They finished the trek with more than 1,000. The pilgrimage drew national attention to the situation farmworkers faced. A few months later, in August, the NFWA and AWOC merged and became the United Farm Workers Organizing Committee, which later became the **United Farm Workers (UFW)**, a full-fledged union.

The union's combined strength enabled it to expand its protest movement and target all California grape growers. The UFW organized strikes and picket lines at farms across the state. Other unions offered their support. In the San Francisco Bay Area, for example, longshoremen refused to load grapes onto ships, instead leaving tons of grapes to rot on the docks. Meanwhile, a growing number of consumers in North America supported the workers by refusing to buy grapes. The campaign did not always go smoothly, and at one point Chávez went on a 24-day water-only fast to protest against some of his own union members who were advocating more violent forms of opposition. As grape growers watched their profits decline, they eventually gave in to the UFW. In 1970, the boycott ended as growers agreed to a collective bargaining agreement with at least 10,000 laborers, as well as better wages, union recognition, a health clinic, a health plan, and a credit union.

FIGHTING FOR CHICANO RIGHTS

As Latino civil rights efforts gained greater attention, a growing number of Mexican Americans in California and the Southwest began raising their voices. Throughout the 1960s, scores of activists and young people mobilized to protest a variety of issues—including the Vietnam War, police brutality,

and economic and social inequalities—as well as to promote cultural pride. Many activists began identifying with the term "Chicano," another name for Mexican American, and their different protests and campaigns became known collectively as the **Chicano Civil Rights Movement**, or "El Movimiento."

A leading voice in the movement was **Rodolfo "Corky" Gonzales**, a poet and activist in Denver who called on Chicanos to take greater control over their own destinies. He argued that the white establishment could not provide adequate education, economic stability, or social acceptance, and that Chicanos should look for alternatives. Under his leadership, Denver's Chicano community developed its own school, newspaper, and credit bureau, and it continued to fight for better economic and housing opportunities. Gonzales became the voice of the Chicano movement when his epic poem *I Am Joaquín* became widely read. It is an elegant statement of the complex history of Mexican Americans and their lives in the United States.

Gonzales also convened the first Chicano Youth Liberation Conference in Denver in 1969, which was attended by many activists and artists. At the conference, attendees drafted the *El Plan Espiritual de Aztlán*, more commonly known as **El Plan de Aztlán**. This **manifesto**, or declaration, called for a new nationalism among Chicanos. It spoke to the dream of gaining back the land Mexico surrendered to the United States—including California and much of the Southwest—in the Treaty of Guadalupe Hidalgo in 1848.

In California, Chicano students became increasingly engaged in El Movimiento. In 1968, approximately 15,000 high school students protested racial discrimination and low-quality education by walking out of their classrooms in five East Los Angeles high schools in a series of protests they called "blowouts." At that time, schools in Los Angeles received funding based on how many students attended per day. By walking out of their homerooms before attendance was taken, the students made their point both actively and financially. Although the blowouts did not bring about immediate change, they empowered the Chicano community and built unity and solidarity for the cause. Chicano activists also drafted the **El Plan de Santa Bárbara: A Chicano Plan for Higher Education**, a document that called for the creation of Chicano Studies programs throughout the California state college system. In a victory for the Chicano movement, state officials adopted the plan in April 1969.

© Herald-Examiner Collection/Los Angeles Public Library

As part of their fight for greater equality and rights, some Chicano activists publicly protested the Vietnam War, claiming that a disproportionately high number of Mexican Americans were being drafted, wounded, and killed in the conflict. Across the country, Chicanos engaged in a series of antiwar protests, which became known as the Chicano Moratorium. This movement culminated in a major protest in Los Angeles in August 1970. The protest proceeded peacefully enough, as more than 30,000 people marched through East Los Angeles. Although it inspired more Hispanics to become involved in the movement for Chicano rights, it ended in tragedy as protesters were met with a heavy-handed police response. In the resulting violence, three people were killed.

In Texas in 1968, the **Mexican American Legal Defense Education Fund (MALDEF)** was founded specifically to protect and promote Latino civil rights. Modeled on the NAACP's Legal Defense Fund and LULAC, the organization's role was to provide the legal expertise for the grassroots Latino community. Throughout the 1960s, Chicanos increased their political activity, and by the end of the decade they had organized their own political party. José Angel Gutiérrez, later an attorney and college professor,

founded the **La Raza Unida Party** in response to many Chicanos' dissatisfaction with the mainstream political parties. La Raza Unida promoted Chicano nationalism and was most influential in Texas and southern California. The party experienced its greatest successes at the local level in southwest Texas, where its members won seats on a number of city councils and school boards. But the party failed to gain widespread support, and by the late 1970s, it had faded away. However, Hispanic Americans around the country would continue to organize politically and work to promote their causes at the local, state, and national levels of government.

BUILD BACKGROUND

THE DELANO-TO-SACRAMENTO MARCH

César Chávez organized the 340-mile march after angry growers sprayed strikers with pesticides. Fifty years later, Dolores Huerta recalled that police tried to block the marchers, who left by using the sidewalks rather than the street. The marchers carried a banner that bore an image of the Virgin of Guadalupe, a symbol of hope and of Mexican nationalism. One "first" that occurred during the march was the signing of the first labor contract in farmworker history, a contract with the wine-grape company Schenley Industries. Protester and writer Terence Cannon climbed onto a truck to announce the news. After the march, work conditions improved. For example, workers were no longer required to drink water from a shared cup; instead, they were allowed to have their own cups.

THE MEXICAN AMERICAN LEGAL DEFENSE AND EDUCATION FUND

More than 40 years after its founding, the Mexican American Legal Defense and Education Fund (MALDEF) continues to play a major role in the defense and advancement of Latino civil rights. The organization is headquartered in Los Angeles, but it maintains regional offices in San Antonio, Chicago, and Washington, D.C. Known as the "law firm of the Latino community," MALDEF encourages partnerships with other law firms in order to increase advocacy and legal representation for the millions of Latinos living in the United States. Each year MALDEF holds a policy roundtable, called the Latino State of the Union, to identify upcoming issues. MALDEF is particularly active with regard to voting rights and the rights of Latino immigrants.

TEACH

GUIDED DISCUSSION

4. **Make Inferences** Why do you think the 1848 Treaty of Guadalupe Hidalgo increased nationalism among Chicano youth in the context of the late 1960s? *(Possible response: Chicanos considered the land ceded to the United States by the treaty to be rightly their own. They dreamed of enjoying their culture in a Chicano homeland.)*

5. **Draw Conclusions** How did Corky Gonzales contribute to El Movimiento as both an activist and a poet? *(Gonzales led Denver's Chicano community in its fight for better economic and housing opportunities. His poetry inspired Chicanos and reinforced their cultural identity.)*

6. **Analyze Cause and Effect** Share the Build Background on the Mexican American Legal Defense and Education Fund. **ASK:** Why do you think the founders of MALDEF felt the need to create a legal group specifically to help the Latino community? *(Answers will vary. Possible response: While Latinos may face some of the same kinds of discrimination as African Americans and other groups, many also face additional obstacles, such as a language barrier or the danger of deportation, and would be best served by lawyers very familiar with those issues.)*

MORE INFORMATION

The Women of El Movimiento Mexican American women, or Chicanas, had long worked to change educational inequalities for Mexican American children, mostly working behind the scenes in their communities. High school girls became particularly active in voicing opposition to the practice of funneling Mexican American girls into educational tracks that prepared them for little more than low-paying domestic work. Following the "blowouts," many young girls and women joined El Movimiento, often focusing their activities on local issues. Women, however, struggled against gender biases within some of those groups, and rarely obtained leadership roles. Among those who did was Gloria Arellanes, who joined the Brown Berets. Arellanes served as minister of finance and correspondence and edited *La Causa*, the Brown Berets' newspaper. **ASK:** What perspective do you think female leaders brought to the Brown Berets and other El Movimiento groups? *(Possible response: They represented women and mothers, who make up much of the workforce. They likely brought a female perspective to discussions about childcare and women's educational opportunities and wages.)* Invite students to research and report more information about Arellanes and other women who were active in El Movimiento, such as Helen Chávez, Juanita Dominguez, Luz Gutierrez, and Rosie Castro).

ACTIVE OPTIONS

On Your Feet: Investigate Issues Divide the class into small groups. Instruct half the groups to research the topic of Latinos in politics, including those elected to Congress. Direct the other groups to research affirmative action as it relates to the Latino community. When all groups have finished, prompt a representative of each group to summarize the group's findings.

NG Learning Framework: Research Activists

SKILL Collaboration

KNOWLEDGE Our Human Story

Divide the class into groups. Explain that half the members of each group will research Larry Itliong while the other half researches César Chávez. Direct the groups to use online sources to find information about each man's role as a labor activist, his involvement in the grape boycott and the United Farm Workers, and how each is honored at the local, state, or national level. When group members have finished, ask them to meet as a group to compare and contrast the information they have found about each man. Then convene as a class and offer groups the opportunity to share any surprising facts they learned.

HISTORICAL THINKING

ANSWERS

1. The goals of the National Farm Workers Association were to unionize farmworkers and to work to attain higher wages and more rights.

2. These leaders were all trying to help minority farmworkers. Cooperation was vital because it brought together a bigger group of people to put pressure on growers to improve conditions for workers.

3. Student responses may include the following: The UFW organized strikes and picket lines at farms across California. In Los Angeles, longshoremen refused to load grapes onto ships, causing tons of grapes to spoil on the docks. A growing number of consumers around the United States and Canada started refusing to buy grapes.

4. Chicanos protested the fact that the war was being fought by a disproportionate number of Mexican Americans.

PRIMARY SOURCE

Possible response: Earlier generations of Chicanos had succeeded in preserving their culture but had failed to improve Chicanos' economic prospects in the United States.

Native Americans Mobilize

What are the things you like most about where you live? Why do you consider your neighborhood a special place? Many Native Americans considered their ancient homelands special and sacred. They did not want to move from their lands. Instead, they wanted greater rights and opportunities to improve their living conditions.

THE DECLARATION OF PURPOSE

In the 1960s, Native Americans were one of the nation's smallest minority groups, but collectively, they continued to suffer greatly. Many lived in poverty and faced discrimination and neglect from the nation at large.

As you have read, the U.S. government enacted the termination policy in the early 1950s in an effort to better assimilate Native Americans into mainstream society. Officials ended federal support for reservations—many of which had become isolated, poverty-stricken places—and tried to urge Native American families to move to the cities, where more jobs were available. The effort was largely a failure.

Many Native Americans did not wish to assimilate. Instead, they began to seek greater rights and opportunities as they insisted on preserving their distinct culture and staying on their land. **Ben Nighthorse Campbell**, a member of the Northern Cheyenne tribe and later a U.S. senator from Colorado, spoke for many Native Americans in criticizing the

PRIMARY SOURCE

After the American Indian Chicago Conference, President Kennedy met with delegates from 90 Native American tribes, including (from left) Eleanor Red Fawn Smooth, Mohawk and Cherokee Nations, Connecticut; Calvin W. McGhee, Atmore, Alabama, representing the Creek Nation east of the Mississippi; and Kathitha Addison, of the Narragansett Nation. They spoke on the lawn of the White House, where Kennedy acknowledged the plight of Native Americans and promised his support.

I hope that this visit here, which is more than ceremonial, will be a reminder to all Americans of the number of Indians whose housing is inadequate, whose education is inadequate, whose employment is inadequate, whose health is inadequate, whose security and old age is inadequate—a very useful reminder that there is still a good deal of unfinished business.

—John F. Kennedy, August 15, 1962

termination policy. "If you can't change them [Native Americans], absorb them until they simply disappear into the mainstream culture," he declared with irony. "In Washington's infinite wisdom, it was decided that tribes should no longer be tribes, never mind that they had been tribes for thousands of years."

Rather than assimilate, Native Americans pushed to preserve their identity and demanded greater support from the federal government in helping them improve their lives. In 1961, some 700 Native Americans from 64 tribes met in Chicago to draft a common agenda and call to action. During the weeklong conference, the group created the **Declaration of Indian Purpose**, a document listing the major issues facing Native Americans and calling for a policy of greater self-determination. "We, the Indian People, must be governed in a democratic manner with a right to choose our own way of life," the statement declared. "We believe we have the responsibility of preserving our precious heritage." The declaration urged the federal government to move away from its termination policy and instead help Native Americans to better thrive on their own. "What we ask of America," the declaration stated, "is that the nature of our situation be recognized and made the basis of policy and action."

SLOW PROGRESS

By the early 1960s, U.S. officials began pulling back from the termination policy and instead promoted greater self-determination for Native Americans. Activists found sympathetic supporters in both President Kennedy and President Johnson. Kennedy secured funding to build adequate public housing on a prominent Native American reservation, and he worked during his short time as president to set the groundwork for later legislation promoting greater rights and federal support for Native Americans.

When Lyndon Johnson assumed the presidency after Kennedy's death, he pledged to help Native Americans as part of his War on Poverty. As you have read, this program sought to create a decent standard of living for all Americans. Early in his term Johnson stated, "Both in terms of statistics and in terms of human welfare, it is a fact that America's first citizens, our Indian people, suffer more from poverty than any other group in America." In 1968, Johnson gave a speech titled "The Forgotten American" to Congress, in which he stressed the need to raise Native American living standards to the same level as that of other American citizens. He said that Native Americans should be able to

live wherever they pleased, whether it was on a reservation or in a city, and that any Native American policy should stress self-help, self-development, and self-determination for the minority group. "For two centuries," Johnson told Congress, "he [the Native American] has been an alien in his own land."

Despite such commitment at the highest level, progress proved slow. Among Native Americans, younger activists began to express frustration—both with the federal government and their own tribal leaders—over what they viewed as too little action and too few results. A group of younger leaders eventually broke away and formed the **National Indian Youth Council (NIYC)**. The NIYC included members of diverse tribes, yet they shared the same agenda: to draw greater attention to the cause of Native Americans through stronger mobilization and protest. The NIYC charter, or founding document, declared, "We, the younger generation, at this time in the history of the American Indian, find it expedient [practical] to band together on a national scale in meeting the challenges facing our Indian people."

NIYC priorities included reclaiming Native American hunting and fishing rights on their traditional lands. Diffusing the African-American civil rights movement model of sit-ins, NIYC held "fish-ins" by occupying areas around rivers and disrupting the commercial fishing activity there. Members of the group also protested at museums that displayed sacred artifacts taken from their tribes. They challenged movies and other media to present more honest portrayals of Native Americans and asked colleges and universities to create Indian Studies programs. These efforts revealed a younger generation of Native Americans ready to advance its agenda through bolder protest strategies. In the years ahead, they would engage in even more disruptive and confrontational tactics in their quest to gain greater rights.

HISTORICAL THINKING

1. **READING CHECK** What was the thinking behind the Declaration of Purpose?

2. **ANALYZE LANGUAGE USE** Why do you think President Kennedy kept repeating the word "inadequate" in the primary source quotation?

3. **EVALUATE** Why did young Native American leaders start the National Indian Youth Council?

4. **COMPARE AND CONTRAST** How were the federal policies and actions toward Native Americans in the 1960s different from those of the past, and why?

PLAN: 2-PAGE LESSON

OBJECTIVE

Understand how Native Americans sought greater opportunities and self-determination.

CRITICAL THINKING SKILLS FOR LESSON 2.1

• Analyze Language Use

• Evaluate

• Compare and Contrast

HISTORICAL THINKING FOR CHAPTER 28

How did new calls for equality and the space race impact American society? Native Americans demanded greater support from the government in helping them to improve their lives without giving up their heritage. Lesson 2.1 explains how Native Americans drafted a common agenda and call to action in the 1960s.

BACKGROUND FOR THE TEACHER

Founded in 1961, the National Indian Youth Council (NIYC) promotes its mission to improve the welfare of Native Americans economically, educationally, and socially. It continues a variety of campaigns to show that "All Native American Lives Matter." NIYC works both nationally and internationally. Funding by the U.S. Department of Labor supports its job training and placement program in the United States. Internationally, the NIYC works within the framework of the United Nations to advocate for urban native issues and for the UN Declaration on the Rights of Indigenous Peoples. Health care, education, and homelessness define the organization's current priorities.

INTRODUCE & ENGAGE

PREVIEW USING VISUALS

Direct students' attention to the Primary Source feature. **ASK:** What general term would you use to describe the occasion shown in the photograph, and why would you choose that term? *(Possible response: Fitting terms to use might be* important, official, *or* symbolic, *because it shows Native Americans in traditional dress meeting the president of the United States, John F. Kennedy.)* **ASK:** Why do you think the Native Americans are wearing traditional clothing? *(Possible response: They are proud of their culture and/or are attending an event that focuses on their traditions.)* Have students read the John F. Kennedy quotation and predict what the lesson will be about.

TEACH

GUIDED DISCUSSION

1. **Analyze Language Use** How did Ben Whitehorse Campbell use irony in his criticism of the federal government's policy toward Native Americans? *(Possible response: Campbell describes the U.S. policy of encouraging assimilation as wanting Native Americans to "simply disappear" when they can't be changed, but that is a way of changing them. He also calls it an example of "infinite wisdom" when he clearly thinks it is the opposite—the height of folly.)*

2. **Evaluate** How effective do you think the NIYC's "fish-ins" were as a protest? Explain. *(Possible response: Fish-ins were probably effective because threatening the viability of an economic enterprise, such as commercial fishing, generally gets attention.)*

MORE INFORMATION

Native American Testimony Explain that readers can get a different perspective on Native American issues by reading Native American literature or personal histories. *Native American Testimony: A Chronicle of Indian and White Relations from Prophecy to the Present, 1492–1992,* edited by Peter Nabokov, for example, is an anthology that presents testimony on confrontations with settlers, missionaries, and traders as well as testimony focusing on reservation life. **ASK:** Why might it be valuable to read fiction written by Native Americans or nonfiction accounts in a Native American's own words? *(Possible response: It could help the reader see issues through the eyes of the people they affect rather than through the assumptions of outsiders.)* Invite interested students to explore *Native American Testimony* or other such primary sources and to report on their findings.

ACTIVE OPTIONS

On Your Feet: Think-Pair-Share Present students with this question: What lessons were learned from the termination policy of the 1950s, and how did federal government policy change as a result? Direct pairs to discuss the question and share an answer with the class. Then discuss the following question as a class: How is the present different from the past regarding Native Americans in society?

NG Learning Framework: Create a Poster

ATTITUDE Responsibility

SKILL Communication

Invite students to create posters in support of Native American self-determination. They might devise a slogan or rely on a visual to convey their message. Display the posters around the room and discuss the variety of techniques used to convey a single message.

DIFFERENTIATE

ENGLISH LANGUAGE LEARNERS ELD

Create a Word Square Tell students of **All Proficiencies** to write the word *assimilation* in the center oval of a Word Square. Instruct them to consult a dictionary and write the definition and characteristics in the appropriate boxes. Then prompt students to review the lesson text to find and write examples and non-examples of assimilation.

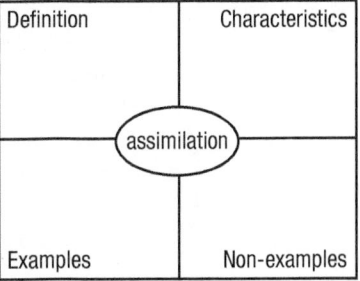

GIFTED & TALENTED

Illustrate a Phrase Direct students' attention to President Johnson's characterization of Native Americans as "America's first citizens," "the forgotten American," and "an alien in his own land." Challenge students to visually interpret one of these phrases. For example, students may create a drawing, painting, editorial cartoon, or meme that incorporates the phrase. Have students present their visual interpretations to the class.

See the Chapter Planner for more strategies for differentiation.

HISTORICAL THINKING

ANSWERS

1. The Declaration of Purpose listed major problems facing Native Americans and called for a policy of self-determination.

2. Kennedy repeated *inadequate* to stress just how many aspects of Native Americans' lives were not up to the standards that most Americans enjoyed.

3. The leaders felt that the federal government and tribal leaders were moving too slowly and were not producing much in the way of desired change.

4. The federal government began pulling back on the termination policy because it was a failure and instead began promoting greater self-determination for Native Americans.

CRITICAL VIEWING In 1969, the members of various Native American tribes held a vigil, or watchful protest, on the dock at Alcatraz Island as other members negotiated with the U.S. government over the island's fate. What alterations were made to the sign behind the occupiers, and what do you think was the purpose of the alterations?

NATIVE AMERICAN ACTIVISM

The advances of the African-American civil rights movement helped breathe new life into Native Americans' fight for their own rights, but the way forward proved to be more difficult. Native Americans were few in number and saw little public attention paid to their cause. As a result, they began taking more extreme measures to make their voices heard.

THE AMERICAN INDIAN MOVEMENT

In 1968, a group of Native American activists in Minneapolis founded the **American Indian Movement (AIM)**. The group's founders, including **George Mitchell, Dennis Banks,** and others, were members of the Ojibwe (oh-JIHB-way) tribe. Their goal was to help fellow Native Americans displaced during the years of the termination policy and to call attention to their substandard living conditions. AIM established urban centers where Native Americans could meet to give and receive help finding jobs, housing, and transportation. The organization grew and set up chapters in Cleveland, Chicago, Milwaukee, Denver, and San Francisco.

As AIM expanded, its leaders' strategies took an increasingly active and **militant**, or forceful, turn in promoting Native American rights. In November 1969, AIM members occupied the abandoned federal prison on Alcatraz Island in San Francisco Bay as a protest against the city's refusal to let Native Americans use the site as a cultural and heritage center. AIM initially received an outpouring of support in the form of donated funds, food, and clothing, but the protest eventually lost momentum and effectiveness. The occupiers included a number of local college students who returned to school and were replaced by people less interested in the cause than in living rent-free. By June 1971, the number of occupiers had dwindled, and U.S. marshals removed them from the island.

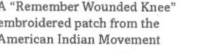

A "Remember Wounded Knee" embroidered patch from the American Indian Movement

A year later, a week before the 1972 presidential election, AIM organized the "Trail of Broken Treaties," a march on Washington, D.C., involving about 1,000 protesters. It ended with the occupation of the **Bureau of Indian Affairs (BIA)** headquarters. AIM protesters seized large numbers of files from the BIA offices and caused more than $2 million in damage to the building. They also presented President Nixon with 20 demands for immediate action. Government officials eventually negotiated a peaceful end to the occupation.

Meanwhile, in Minnesota, AIM leaders helped parents establish Native American "survival schools" to avoid the biases of local child welfare and legal systems. As the schools multiplied, they engaged adults and students with issues of Native American language, culture, spirituality, and identity.

PROTESTS AT WOUNDED KNEE

In February 1973, AIM engaged in what would become one of its best-known and most violent protests. About 200 members of the Oglala Lakota tribe along with AIM leaders seized and occupied the town of Wounded Knee, South Dakota, on the Pine Ridge Reservation. The occupiers were protesting the failure to impeach tribal president Richard Wilson, whom they accused of corruption and abuse of opponents. They were also protesting the U.S. government's failure to fulfill promises made in treaties with Native Americans, and they

demanded the reopening of treaty negotiations. The activists chose the site of the 1890 Wounded Knee Massacre, where federal troops had killed more than 150 Lakota. A tense standoff ensued for 71 days, in which two AIM members were shot and killed and a U.S. marshal was shot and paralyzed. Ultimately, a truce was negotiated and federal officers agreed to review a number of treaties made with Native Americans. Dennis Banks and another prominent AIM leader, **Russell Means**, were charged with crimes for their role in the event, but the charges were later dismissed.

Despite their largely symbolic protests, the strategies and effectiveness of Native Americans led to some gains. In 1975, Congress passed the **Indian Self-Determination and Educational Assistance Act**, which boosted funds for Native American education and gave Native Americans greater control in administering local programs. In 1978, Congress passed the **Indian Religious Freedom Act**, which allowed Native Americans to practice their traditional religions freely. Native Americans also gained greater representation within the Bureau of Indian Affairs, a federal organization they had long criticized for not being fully attentive to their needs.

In addition, Native Americans used the courts to accomplish what protests could not. They sued state and federal governments to force compliance with old treaties that had been ignored and took legal action to win back numerous land and water rights. The Pueblo in New Mexico, for example, regained rights to their land, as did several tribes in Maine. Court decisions also enabled Native Americans to receive millions of dollars for their land claims, while other rulings allowed Native Americans to impose taxes on businesses on their reservations and take greater control of their economic futures.

HISTORICAL THINKING

1. **READING CHECK** Why did the American Indian Movement take more drastic actions than other civil rights movements?

2. **ANALYZE CAUSE AND EFFECT** What effect did the passage of the Indian Self-Determination and Education Assistance Act have on the Native American community?

3. **DRAW CONCLUSIONS** How effective were the lawsuits brought by Native Americans to establish their basic civil rights? Support your response with evidence from the text.

OBJECTIVE

Analyze why and how some Native Americans adopted more aggressive tactics in campaigning for Native Americans' civil rights.

CRITICAL THINKING SKILLS FOR LESSON 2.2

- Analyze Cause and Effect
- Draw Conclusions
- Identify Problems and Solutions
- Analyze Visuals

HISTORICAL THINKING FOR CHAPTER 28

How did new calls for equality and the space race impact American society? In the late 1960s, Native Americans stepped up the fight for their rights. Lesson 2.2 discusses the goals, leaders, and accomplishments of the American Indian Movement.

BACKGROUND FOR THE TEACHER

Heart of the Earth Survival School in Minneapolis and Red School House in St. Paul were the first Native American "survival schools," so named because they were established to provide basic education and life skills to Native American children unlikely to go to college. At least a dozen additional survival schools followed in California, Oklahoma, South Dakota, Wisconsin, and Canada. The schools emphasized the cultural backgrounds of the students, who studied native languages as well as English. Because understanding the law would be an important life skill for Native American groups, organizers held workshops and seminars for teachers in several states. Subjects included juvenile law and Indian law.

INTRODUCE & ENGAGE

ACTIVATE PRIOR KNOWLEDGE

Ask students to recall what they know about the treatment of Native Americans since settlers began to arrive in what is now the United States. **ASK:** What are some ways in which Native Americans were poorly treated, and how did they respond? *(Possible response: Native Americans were pushed off their land, disrespected, and subjected to broken treaties. They sometimes responded with violence, but they were forced into submission for many years. In the 1960s, however, they began to mobilize and campaign for civil rights.)* Explain that in this lesson students will read about some actions taken by Native Americans in the late 1960s and early 1970s as they continued to fight for their rights.

TEACH

GUIDED DISCUSSION

1. **Identify Problems and Solutions** How did AIM address some of the problems resulting from the termination policy? *(AIM set up centers in urban areas where many Native Americans moved after the government closed their reservations. The centers offered assistance with housing, job searches, and transportation. AIM leaders in Minnesota helped set up "survival schools" to help students preserve their culture. They also staged protests to draw attention to the need for government help.)*

2. **Analyze Cause and Effect** In what way did the Bureau of Indian Affairs change in response to the more aggressive campaigns by Native American activists? *(More Native Americans were brought into the organization to better represent the people who were most affected by BIA policies.)*

ANALYZE VISUALS

Point out the embroidered AIM patch. **ASK:** What happened on the two dates shown on the patch? *(More than 150 Lakota were killed by U.S. soldiers at Wounded Knee in 1890. In 1973, AIM engaged in a protest at Wounded Knee.)* **ASK:** Why do you think AIM used the slogan "Remember Wounded Knee," recalling a historical event nearly 100 years in the past, as a way to influence trends in the present? *(Possible response: Wounded Knee is a strong reminder of the wrongs endured by Native Americans and could be an effective rallying cry to fight for justice and self-determination.)*

ACTIVE OPTIONS

On Your Feet: Numbered Heads Arrange students in groups of four and have students within each group number off. Tell students to consider this question: How effective was the American Indian Movement? Allow students to think individually about the question and then discuss it as a group, citing evidence from the lesson. Then call a number and ask the students with that number to report for their group.

NG Learning Framework: Create a News Broadcast

ATTITUDE Empowerment

KNOWLEDGE Our Human Story

Direct students to learn about another Native American protest (by AIM or another organization involved in Native American activism) between 1961 and 1975, such as the 1970 National Day of Mourning, the 1971 occupation of Mount Rushmore, or the 1972 "Trail of Broken Treaties" march and the Twenty Points Position Paper that accompanied it. Students should shape their research into a news report that covers the organization responsible, the goal of the protest, when and where the protest occurred, and the protest's outcome. Allow students time to broadcast their reports to the class.

DIFFERENTIATE

STRIVING READERS

Read and Recall Invite students to work in groups of two to four. First ask each student to read the lesson independently. After reading, tell groups to meet without the book and share ideas they recall. One student should take notes. As a group, students then review the lesson and decide what to add or change in the notes.

PRE-AP

Analyze the Twenty Points Position Paper Instruct students to use online or library sources to locate the Twenty Points Position Paper drafted by Native American activist Hank Adams for the "Trail of Broken Treaties" cross-country protest. Prompt students to extract examples of the demands made in the proposal. Then tell them to conduct further research to find concessions offered by the federal government in response to the protest. Have students present their findings to the class in an oral report or multimedia presentation.

See the Chapter Planner for more strategies for differentiation.

HISTORICAL THINKING

ANSWERS

1. AIM was a relatively small group, which made it more difficult to gain attention.

2. The act boosted funds for Native American education and gave Native Americans greater control in administering local programs.

3. The lawsuits were effective. They resulted in land and water rights returned to some tribes, enabled Native Americans to impose taxes on reservation businesses, and paid awards of millions of dollars for land claims.

CRITICAL VIEWING The sign reads "United Indian Property" and "Indians Welcome" as a way of saying that the United States was actually the land of Native Americans.

ASIAN AMERICAN CIVIL RIGHTS

Asia, the world's largest continent, encompasses many diverse countries and cultures. As a result, the term "Asian American" refers to all Americans of Asian origin. They share a desire for equal opportunities in the United States.

DISCRIMINATION AGAINST ASIAN AMERICANS

Like other groups seeking equal civil rights, the story of Asian Americans has been one of exclusion, discrimination, and the gradual gaining of rights and respect. The decision by Congress to pass the Chinese Exclusion Act in 1882 was based largely on complaints that Chinese immigrants were taking labor union jobs. The measure denied any Chinese person the opportunity to immigrate to the United States. The Immigration Act of 1924 expanded the law and excluded all Asians. It wasn't until World War II, when the United States and China became allies, that restrictions against Chinese immigration were eased. During the war, as you learned, it was

Japanese Americans who suffered discrimination, and worse. Thousands of Japanese Americans were confined to internment camps based on fears they were disloyal and dangerous.

Internment robbed many Japanese Americans of their homes, land, and livelihoods, and racist discrimination made it hard for many of them to recover their property. For example, in California, an Alien Land Law passed in 1913 prohibited Asian immigrants who were noncitizens—usually because of immigration restrictions—from owning agricultural land. Kajiro Oyama had moved to the United States as a teenager. In 1934, he bought six acres of farmland, registering the property in the name of his son, Fred,

who had been born in the United States and thus was an American citizen. During World War II, the Oyama family took part in a "voluntary evacuation," relocating to Utah rather than being forced into an internment camp. When they returned to California after the war, they found that their farm had been seized. With the help of the **Japanese American Citizens League**, Kajiro sued to get his land back. *Oyama v. California* reached the U.S. Supreme Court, which ruled in 1948 that Fred Oyama's rights as an American citizen had been violated. The Oyama family retained ownership of the land, but the Court did not overturn the Alien Land Law until 1952.

Other Asian American groups also endured discrimination. As you have read, Filipino Americans worked largely as farm laborers and collaborated with Latino workers to push for better pay and more rights. Pacific Islanders struggled in their relations with the United States. The natives of Guam became Americans overnight when the United States acquired their island after winning the Spanish-American War in 1898. But Americans did little to acknowledge and support the island's culture. Similarly, when the United States annexed the Hawaiian Islands in 1898, land was taken from native Hawaiians and their culture suffered from the imposition of American values in the territory.

PROGRESS ON CIVIL RIGHTS

As a result of the Immigration Act of 1965, which raised quotas on immigrants from outside Europe, the number of Asian Americans grew steadily through the second half of the 20th century. In the 1950s, Asians represented 6 percent of all immigrants to the United States, and by 1980, that number had climbed to 42 percent. Like other groups that had to fight for their civil rights, Asian Americans and Pacific Islanders also vary widely in their backgrounds and cultures, and as they grew in numbers, they united to fight for greater rights and recognition.

In 1968, students at the University of California, Berkeley, started the **Asian American Political Alliance (AAPA)** to advocate on behalf of Asian Americans. The group fought for many issues, from improved housing for poor Asians to use of the term "Asian American" rather than widely used derogatory terms. That same year, Asian American students went on strike at San Francisco State College (renamed San Francisco State University in 1974). Forming a coalition with other student groups, including the Black Student Union and the Third World Liberation Front (a group that included Native Americans, African Americans, and Latinos),

the students demanded establishment of an Ethnic Studies program. The strike lasted five months until the university acquiesced, agreeing to add the program. In 1969, students and activists in Seattle, Washington, founded the **Asian Coalition for Equality (ACE)**, which protested police brutality and worked to desegregate the region's industries and open up clubs and organizations to minorities.

Meanwhile, Japanese Americans began pressuring the federal government to issue an apology for the World War II internment camps. In 1976, the government responded. President Gerald Ford signed **Proclamation 4417**, formally apologizing for the internment program. Twelve years later, President Reagan signed the **Civil Liberties Act of 1988**, which paid each living internee $20,000 in reparations for what they had experienced in the camps. Today, some 18 million Asian Americans and Pacific Islanders live in the United States. That is about 5.8 percent of the country's population. Their population continues to grow, and while they continue to face prejudice, they also continue to achieve success and help to shape and build the American identity.

HISTORICAL THINKING

1. **READING CHECK** What kinds of discrimination have Asian Americans faced?

2. **IDENTIFY** What were the reasons given for American immigration policies, and how did bias or prejudice contribute to the policies' transformation of society?

3. **COMPARE AND CONTRAST** How are Asian Americans similar to and different from other groups seeking equal rights?

Protesters surrounded the San Francisco State College administration building, demonstrating against alleged racism and political harassment by college administrators.

PLAN: 2-PAGE LESSON

OBJECTIVE

Understand how Asian Americans faced discrimination but achieved some reforms in the 1960s and 1970s.

CRITICAL THINKING SKILLS FOR LESSON 2.3

- Identify
- Compare and Contrast
- Analyze Cause and Effect
- Make Connections
- Analyze Primary Sources

HISTORICAL THINKING FOR CHAPTER 28

How did new calls for equality and the space race impact American society? Decades of restrictions on immigration from Asia and discrimination toward Asian Americans began to reverse in the 1960s. Lesson 2.3 discusses Asian American activism and key responses from the federal government.

BACKGROUND FOR THE TEACHER

The Immigration Act of 1965 went largely unnoticed at the time of its passage. Those who did note it tended to view it as a natural progression of the 1964 Civil Rights Act. However, in one bold sweep, the Immigration Act removed the "national origins" quotas, as well as the ban on Asian immigration. Although it set a ceiling of about 300,000 immigrants per year, the law permitted the family members of American citizens—both naturalized and native born—to enter the United States without limit. By the mid-1970s, a majority of legal immigrants came from Korea, Taiwan (which is a province of China), India, the Philippines, Cuba, the Dominican Republic, and Mexico.

HISTORY NOTEBOOK

Encourage students to complete the Asian American Civil Rights page for Chapter 28 in their History Notebooks as they read.

INTRODUCE & ENGAGE

REVIEW AND PREVIEW

Tell students to review with a classmate previous lessons concerning civil rights movements. Pairs should then preview this lesson by looking at the photo, headings, and Key Vocabulary words. Suggest that students think about how this lesson might be similar to and different from previous lessons about civil rights. Prompt pairs to write down three things they would like to know about Asian American civil rights. At the end of the lesson, ask them whether they have found answers to their questions. If not, urge them to do independent research to find the answers.

TEACH

GUIDED DISCUSSION

1. **Analyze Cause and Effect** How did the political alliances of World War II contribute to changing trends in the way the federal government treated different groups of Asian Americans? *(When China and the United States became allies, the United States eased its restrictive immigration policies toward the Chinese. However, because Japan was allied with the Axis Powers, Japanese Americans suffered discrimination, and the government sent thousands to internment camps.)*

2. **Make Connections** How did both Proclamation 4417 and the Civil Liberties Act of 1988 respond to the Japanese American fight for civil rights? *(The proclamation apologized for the internment program, thereby acknowledging that the civil rights of Japanese Americans had been denied; the Civil Liberties Act went a step further by offering reparations.)*

ANALYZE PRIMARY SOURCES

Direct students' attention to the Primary Source feature and have students read it. **ASK:** Why do you think the writer used quotation marks around the word *voluntarily* in describing her father's evacuation of his family to Utah? *(The quotation marks express sarcasm or irony. They indicate that the evacuation was not voluntary but may have been called such to gloss over a forced relocation.)*

ACTIVE OPTIONS

On Your Feet: Fishbowl Divide the class in half, with one half sitting in a circle facing inward and the other half sitting in a larger circle around them. Tell students in the inside circle to discuss the following question: How have the Immigration Act of 1965 and subsequent acts transformed American society? Ask students on the outside circle to listen for new information. Then tell students to reverse positions. Once students have completed the exercise, call on volunteers to name key points from their discussion and to categorize each point as transforming culture, demographics, or civil rights.

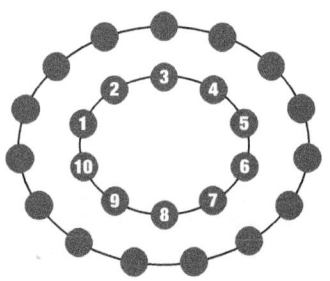

NG Learning Framework: Research Apologies and Reparations

ATTITUDE Empowerment

KNOWLEDGE Our Human Story

Prompt small groups of students to use online resources to locate and read the text of Proclamation 4417 and the Civil Liberties Act of 1988. Then have them research further issues of interest surrounding the documents, such as: For what purpose were these documents created? How did the American public feel about these governmental actions? How were individuals and families affected by each? Why were some members of Congress opposed to the Civil Liberties Act of 1988? Who was entitled to reparations and who was not? Did these actions live up to their intentions? Instruct groups to summarize their findings in a list of bullet points. Encourage them to share the list with the class.

DIFFERENTIATE

ENGLISH LANGUAGE LEARNERS

Look for Cognates Suggest that as students read they look for words that are similar in spelling and meaning to words in their home language. For example, the words *evacuation, coalition, proclamation,* and *reparations* have cognates in Spanish: *evacuación, coalición, proclamación,* and *reparaciones.* For each word they identify, have students of **All Proficiencies** make a vocabulary card with the English word and definition on one side. On the other side, ask them to write the word and its definition in their home language, using a bilingual dictionary if necessary. Encourage them to note any differences in the meanings of the two words.

PRE-AP

Write a Biographical Sketch Instruct students to choose one Asian American group (Chinese American, Japanese American, Filipino American, or other) to focus on. Then have them conduct research using online and print sources to find a specific person from that group who suffered discrimination in the 20th century. Encourage students to find first-person written or oral histories and to quote or paraphrase those sources as they write their biographical sketches. Invite students to post their biographical sketches online or read them to the class.

See the Chapter Planner for more strategies for differentiation.

HISTORICAL THINKING

ANSWERS

1. Asian Americans have faced discrimination such as immigration restrictions and a prohibition against owning land, and some Japanese Americans were sent to internment camps during World War II.

2. One reason given for American immigration policies was that immigrants were taking labor union jobs. Bias or prejudice contributed to keeping Asian Americans a small minority in American society until the second half of the 20th century.

3. Like other groups, Asian Americans have experienced discrimination and prejudice for years and vary widely in their backgrounds and experiences. Unlike other groups, Asian Americans faced quite different circumstances depending on their specific heritage or country of origin.

NEW VOICES FOR WOMEN

Did you ever expect a streak of good fortune to continue, and then it didn't? After World War II, the professional opportunities American women had grown accustomed to decreased, and women were strongly discouraged from working outside the home.

THE WOMEN'S MOVEMENT REAWAKENS

Like other groups, women had done their fair share during World War II. They worked in factories and served in the military, although they were not officially allowed to fight in combat. Yet, as you have read, after the war many women found themselves back in the midst of domestic life. They were often discouraged from pursuing careers, and those still in the workforce generally received lower pay than men doing the same jobs.

Even so, in the post-war years the nation made some attempts to address the problem of limited opportunities for women. In 1961, President Kennedy created the **President's Commission on the Status of Women**, a 20-member committee chaired by Eleanor Roosevelt, that developed recommendations for overcoming employment discrimination and establishing services "which will enable women to continue their role as wives and mothers while making a maximum contribution to the world around them." The committee recommended paid maternity leave, affordable child care, and equal employment opportunities. Its report led to the **Equal Pay Act of 1963**, which prohibited wage discrimination based on sex. Two years later, in 1965, President Johnson established the Equal Employment Opportunity Commission (EEOC) to help give women greater security in the workplace.

The EEOC, for example, declared that employers who fired a woman for such acts as getting married or having a baby were in violation of federal law.

Despite these actions, progress for women was slow. Just like other groups, women realized they could not rely solely on the federal government. They would have to push for greater equality themselves. Like their predecessors in the early 1900s, women in the 1960s began to mobilize. In the eyes of many, the effort began with the publication of a groundbreaking book.

A National Organization for Women pin-back button from the 1970s

In 1970s' New York City, three young women donned Equal Rights Amendment (ERA) buttons to march for the ERA and celebrate a day for women's rights.

Its author was **Betty Friedan**, a graduate of Smith College who worked as a reporter. When Friedan and her husband Carl were expecting their second child, she lost her job, so she stayed home to raise her children. But she experienced a growing sense of restlessness and frustration with the limits imposed on her by society. She talked to other Smith graduates and discovered that many felt the same way.

Friedan compiled what she learned into a book called *The Feminine Mystique*. The word *mystique* means "an air of mystery," and in this context, referred to the silent unhappiness, or "problem that had no name," that many women dealt with. Published in 1963, *The Feminine Mystique* challenged the assumption that all women wanted to be mothers and homemakers. The book encouraged women to seek their own paths.

Response to the book was overwhelming, and it became a bestseller. Women across the country began voicing their dissatisfaction and their demands. The idea of "choice," implicit in the book, captured what many women wanted: the opportunity to make choices that weren't limited to domestic roles or by other people. While the book's ideas may seem less controversial now than they did in 1963, *The Feminine Mystique* is still considered one of the most influential books of its time. Inspired, women wanted their contributions and importance acknowledged, and began working to promote the ideals of **feminism**, or greater political, economic, social, and cultural rights for women. **Gloria Steinem** was another writer and feminist who used communication to unite women in the fight for equality. In 1971, she and several other feminists founded *Ms.*, a successful magazine that focused on life and politics from women's perspectives.

FEMINISM IN ACTION

The civil rights movements of the 1960s helped fuel women's push for greater equality. Women were obviously inspired by the efforts of African Americans and other minorities in their quest for equality, and many women became part of and worked hard for civil rights causes. Ironically, however, many women who joined the larger civil rights movements reported feeling like second-class citizens, restricted to unimportant tasks and largely kept out of any policy decisions. Just as in their personal lives, women found that their contributions were not as highly valued as those of men. It was clear that in order to achieve success in their quest for equality, women needed to form their own movement and promote their agenda.

In 1966, Friedan and other women leaders gathered together to form the **National Organization for**

PRIMARY SOURCE

The problem lay buried, unspoken, for many years in the minds of American women. It was a strange stirring, a sense of dissatisfaction, a yearning that women suffered in the middle of the twentieth century in the United States. Each suburban wife struggled with it alone. As she made the beds, shopped for groceries, matched slipcover material, ate peanut butter sandwiches with her children, chauffeured Cub Scouts and Brownies, lay beside her husband at night—she was afraid to ask even of herself the silent question—"Is this all?"

—from *The Feminine Mystique*, by Betty Friedan, 1963

What information in the source leads you to understand why Friedan and others decided to form a women's rights organization?

Women (NOW). This grassroots association of activist feminists included not only straight women and lesbians, but also men. NOW's goals extended beyond fair pay: it wanted to guarantee women's access to health care, including reproductive rights, affordable child care, and the passage of equal rights legislation at the state and national levels. Similar to the NAACP, NOW pursued legal equality for women in the public sphere. The group lobbied Congress to pass laws emphasizing equality for women, raised awareness about women's issues, and reached out to women in all walks of life to promote feminism.

Led by NOW, feminists pushed for significant changes in society, and while their fight ahead would be a difficult one, they would achieve a number of groundbreaking victories. A major victory for women occurred in 1968 when **Shirley Chisholm** was elected the first African-American Congresswoman. She represented her Brooklyn, New York, district for seven terms, building a reputation as a "people's politician" and "Fighting Shirley" from her advocacy for inner-city poor people.

HISTORICAL THINKING

1. **READING CHECK** Why did women want a larger role in society?

2. **DRAW CONCLUSIONS** Why was *The Feminine Mystique* so much more controversial when it first appeared than it is today?

3. **ANALYZE CAUSE AND EFFECT** What lesson did women learn from their early participation in the civil rights movements of the 1960s?

PLAN: 2-PAGE LESSON

OBJECTIVE

Explore the reawakening of the women's movement—its supporters' beliefs and the actions they took—in the 1960s.

CRITICAL THINKING SKILLS FOR LESSON 3.1

- Draw Conclusions
- Analyze Cause and Effect
- Compare and Contrast
- Analyze Primary Sources

HISTORICAL THINKING FOR CHAPTER 28

How did new calls for equality and the space race impact American society? In the 1960s, a growing number of women promoted the ideals of feminism. Lesson 3.1 discusses the rise of the women's movement and the equality-related goals for which its adherents campaigned.

BACKGROUND FOR THE TEACHER

In the 1960s, more than four decades after gaining the vote, American women still played a minor role in government affairs. In 1963, there were no female governors, cabinet officers, or Supreme Court justices. The U.S. Senate contained one female member, Margaret Chase Smith of Maine. In some states, laws prevented women from sitting on juries or making wills. Discrimination also pervaded the workplace. Women were increasingly concentrated in low-paying service and clerical jobs despite their rising level of education. Full-time working women earned about 60 percent of the income of men.

HISTORY NOTEBOOK

Encourage students to complete the American Gallery page for Chapter 28 in their History Notebooks as they read.

INTRODUCE & ENGAGE

DISCUSS CHARACTERISTICS OF MOVEMENTS

Ask students to name some social or political movements they know about. Examples may be historical (such as abolitionism and women's suffrage) or recent (such as Occupy and fair trade). **ASK:** What characteristics do you think these movements have in common? *(Answers will vary. Possible responses: Their members work to make change. They have grassroots beginnings. They use various tactics, such as boycotts, strikes, and marches, to influence public opinion.)* Discuss differences as well, such as who participates and whether they use violent or nonviolent tactics. Tell students that in Lesson 3.1 they will read about the women's movement.

TEACH

GUIDED DISCUSSION

1. **Analyze Cause and Effect** In what sense did Betty Friedan's experience in the workforce contribute to the development of the women's movement? *(After Friedan lost her job, she became frustrated with the limitations imposed on working women and wrote about them. The resulting book,* The Feminine Mystique, *encouraged women to be more aggressive in seeking greater recognition and better opportunities.)*

2. **Compare and Contrast** How did NOW mark a change in the women's movement from the efforts that had preceded it earlier in the 1960s? *(Earlier efforts had focused on wage equity and other workplace matters. NOW pushed for women to have legally reinforced equality in all areas of public life.)*

ANALYZE PRIMARY SOURCES

Direct students' attention to the Primary Source feature. Ask students to identify words and phrases in the passage that support Friedan's claim that American women had an "unspoken problem." *(Possible responses: strange stirring; sense of dissatisfaction; yearning; struggled . . . alone; afraid to ask)* **ASK:** According to Friedan, why were American women dissatisfied? *(Possible response: They wanted something beyond being housewives and mothers.)* Encourage interested students to read and discuss selections from the writings of other leading feminists and their opponents, tracing gains in women's access to education, politics, and the workforce and obstacles to representation at the highest levels of business and politics.

ACTIVE OPTIONS

AMERICAN GALLERY
ONLINE

The Women's Movement Invite students to explore the American Gallery. Tell them to select one of the images and to do additional research to learn more about it. Ask questions such as these to inspire additional inquiry about the chosen gallery image: What does the image show? Who might have created it? Why does it belong in this chapter? What else would you like to know about it?

NG Learning Framework: Write an Analytical Essay

ATTITUDE Curiosity

KNOWLEDGE Our Human Story

Prompt students to make connections between women's suffrage and later events of the women's movement. Direct them to write a brief essay in which they answer this question: How do you think the work of Elizabeth Stanton and Susan B. Anthony in the 19th century influenced the women's movement of the 1960s? Students should consider differing perspectives on the roles of women and should support their response with information gleaned from a study of primary and secondary sources. Ask students to read their essays aloud to the class. Invite comparisons and constructive comments.

DIFFERENTIATE

STRIVING READERS

Use a Main Idea Cluster Direct pairs of students to use a Main Idea Cluster to check their understanding of each section in the lesson. First tell students to take turns reading the paragraphs in a section of the lesson. Then have partners work together to record the main idea of the section and four details that support the main idea. Instruct pairs to trade and compare clusters.

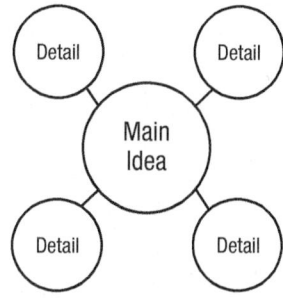

GIFTED & TALENTED

Create Social Networking Profiles Tell students to conduct online research to learn more about the early feminists Betty Friedan and Gloria Steinem. Instruct them to focus on each woman's biographical details, accomplishments, personality, philosophy, strategies, successes, and failures. Have students use what they learn to create social networking profiles for each woman, including photographs. Invite students to share their profiles with the rest of the class.

See the Chapter Planner for more strategies for differentiation.

HISTORICAL THINKING

ANSWERS

1. During World War II, women contributed to the war effort. After the war, they did not want to lose the feeling of making a difference.

2. The book inspired women to fight for equality, a decades-long fight that is no longer new.

3. Women found inspiration in the civil rights movement; however, because they were not treated as the equals of men even there, they formed their own movement and campaigned for their own agenda.

PRIMARY SOURCE

The belief that many women were dissatisfied with their role in society but struggled alone led to the idea of organizing.

WOMEN SEEK EQUALITY

The fight for equality sometimes proceeds at an uneven rate, with breakthroughs and advances alternating with long periods where progress is difficult or impossible. Half a century after securing the right to vote, women were still struggling for fair wages, attention to women's health issues, and an end to discrimination based on gender.

University of Tennessee Head Coach Pat Summitt (left) and guard Shanna Zolman (5) evaluate the play during a basketball game in 2004. Summitt retired from coaching at Tennessee having achieved the highest National Collegiate Athletic Association (NCCA) overall win record at that time of 1,098–208. The passage of Title IX gave many hardworking and talented women like Coach Summitt and her players the opportunity to compete at exceptionally high levels.

BATTLES FOR GENDER EQUALITY

NOW leaders and women activists pushed for a number of reforms. One area they focused on was long-standing **gender bias**, or the preference for one gender over another, against women in education. In particular, activists targeted the area of women's sports, which schools and colleges viewed as an afterthought. Women's teams often received little funding and support. As a result, women had fewer opportunities to earn scholarships or play collegiate sports. Feminists pushed for federal legislation banning gender discrimination in education. In 1972, Congress passed a law known collectively as the **Education Amendments**. One section, **Title IX**, prohibited federally funded schools from discriminating against girls and women in nearly all areas, from admissions to athletics. Title IX helped to bolster women's athletics as well as to give women and girls the chance to obtain athletic and academic scholarships formerly reserved only for men.

Women also made advances on social and cultural fronts. Throughout the 1970s, feminists promoted women's health clinics and opened shelters for victims of domestic abuse. They tackled day-to-day sexism with the mantra "the personal is political"— meaning they were willing to fight against laws that restricted their personal and private lives.

One such area was women's health, particularly reproductive rights. When the Food and Drug Administration approved the use of an oral birth control pill in 1960, women finally had access to a discreet, extremely effective contraceptive, or means of preventing pregnancy. But some states still made it difficult for women to use birth control. In Connecticut, birth control had been outlawed in 1879. Women's groups claimed the law unconstitutionally denied women a right to privacy. The case, *Griswold v. Connecticut*, went to the U.S. Supreme Court. In a victory for women, the Court agreed, ruling in 1965 that a ban on contraceptives violated privacy rights. The debate over forms of birth control continued, especially among Catholics. In the Second Vatican Council (Vatican II), held in 1962, the Church had an impact on civil rights and other human rights movements by encouraging its members to participate in them. But the Church was less supportive of women's rights when, in 1968, it condemned "artificial" birth control, defying a growing consensus among its parishioners.

In 1973, feminists achieved victory for a woman's right to make personal choices again, in a landmark case that remains controversial even today: *Roe v. Wade*. During the 1950s and 1960s, abortion, or the purposeful termination of a pregnancy, was illegal in most states. Two Texas attorneys sued on behalf of "Jane Roe," an unnamed defendant, arguing that the inability to obtain a safe abortion violated Roe's constitutional right to privacy. The Supreme Court agreed, saying that a woman's decision to end her pregnancy lay within the "zone of privacy" that is protected by the Constitution. Since this decision, *Roe v. Wade* has been a target of conservatives, who argue against it on religious and moral grounds. For those who agree with the Court's decision, it supports a woman's right to make choices about her own reproductive health and to choose when and if to have children.

EQUAL RIGHTS AMENDMENT

Another primary goal of the women's movement was the long-overdue passage of the Equal Rights Amendment (ERA) to the Constitution, which would guarantee protection from gender-based discrimination or even from **misogyny**, a hatred of women. As you learned, the ERA was proposed in 1923, three years after the 19th Amendment granted women the right to vote. The ERA lacked support among several groups and stalled for years on Capitol Hill. Finally, in 1972, Congress passed the ERA and sent it to the states for ratification, with 38 states (three-quarters) needed to ratify, or vote "yes," and make the amendment part of the Constitution.

A coalition of fundamentalist religious groups, states' rights advocates, and political conservatives opposed the ERA. They claimed that it would have unintended consequences, such as forcing women into combat and destroying conventional marriage. Among women leaders opposing the ERA was **Phyllis Schlafly**, a lawyer and activist, who argued that the ERA would subject women to the military draft and force them to lose federal benefits they received as "dependents." The ERA's opponents eventually helped to defeat the measure and keep it from becoming law. It had been ratified by 35 states—3 states short of approval.

By the end of the 1970s, women's lives had changed dramatically. Their career options had grown and were no longer limited to traditional professions, such as nurse, secretary, or teacher. More women's health-care clinics, rape crisis centers, and shelters for domestic abuse victims were available. More women enrolled in medical and law schools. Colleges once closed to women, including the U.S. military academies, opened their doors to female students. The changing roles of women in society, especially as more women entered the labor force, were accompanied by changing family structures.

HISTORICAL THINKING

1. **READING CHECK** How did Title IX benefit college-bound women?

2. **ANALYZE LANGUAGE USE** What did feminists mean by the phrase "the personal is political"?

3. **MAKE GENERALIZATIONS** In what ways did the legal cases won by feminists help change the roles of women in society?

PLAN: 2-PAGE LESSON

OBJECTIVE

Learn about legal decisions in the 1960s and 1970s that increased equality for women in a number of areas of life.

CRITICAL THINKING SKILLS FOR LESSON 3.2

- Analyze Language Use
- Make Generalizations
- Determine Chronology
- Analyze Cause and Effect

HISTORICAL THINKING FOR CHAPTER 28

How did new calls for equality and the space race impact American society? As the 1960s progressed, women began seeking legal remedies to battle discrimination and obtain the rights they sought. Lesson 3.2 discusses several court cases that strengthened women's rights and chronicles the history of the ERA.

BACKGROUND FOR THE TEACHER

On August 26, 1970, feminist leaders organized a nationwide rally to mark the 50th anniversary of the 19th Amendment. Thousands showed up for the rally, many carrying signs that ranged from "Sisterhood Is Powerful" to "Don't Cook Dinner— Starve a Rat Today." The speeches focused on equality for women in education and employment, the importance of reproductive freedom, and passage of the Equal Rights Amendment. Handbooks written in the 1970s, such as *Our Bodies, Ourselves* (1971) and *The New Woman's Survival Catalogue* (1972), sold millions of copies by combining a new feminist ideology based on professional achievement and personal freedom with medical and psychological strategies for good health.

INTRODUCE & ENGAGE

CONNECT TO TODAY

Write the term *gender bias* on the board and invite students to define it. Lead a brief discussion about whether women or men in the United States currently experience gender bias. Consider situations such as the workplace, pay, health issues, and child care. Tell students that in this lesson they will see how women fought against gender bias in the 1970s.

TEACH

GUIDED DISCUSSION

1. **Determine Chronology** Identify, in sequence, three victories for the women's movement in the area of reproductive rights. *(the approval of the first oral contraceptive, 1960; the lifting of a ban on contraception in* Griswold *v.* Connecticut, *1965; the legalization of abortion in* Roe *v.* Wade, *1973)*

2. **Analyze Cause and Effect** What historic decision regarding a women's issue did the Catholic Church make in 1968, and why did it create a dilemma for some Catholic women? *(The Church condemned the use of "artificial" birth control. The decision forced Catholic women to either forgo contraceptives or defy a Church ruling.)*

MORE INFORMATION

Explain that because of Vatican II, women and girls began to assist in Catholic Church services (a change that was reinforced in 1994). Nuns were encouraged to work among the people in their communities rather than spend all their time in convents and to exchange their long black habits for more modern clothing. Prompt students to compare these decisions with the Church's 1968 decision about birth control, pointing out that all three decisions were controversial. **ASK:** Why do you think the 1968 decision resulted in more widespread controversy than the two Vatican II decisions? *(Possible response: The 1968 decision disempowered women, whereas the two Vatican II decisions empowered them. Furthermore, the 1968 decision affected all Catholic women, not just those closely tied to the work of the Church.)*

ACTIVE OPTIONS

Active History: Analyze Charts and Graphs
Extend the lesson by using either the PDF or Whiteboard version of the activity. These activities take a deeper look at a topic from, or related to, the lesson. Explore the activities as a class, turn them into group assignments, or even assign them individually.

On Your Feet: Debate the ERA Arrange students into an even number of small groups and direct them to prepare to debate the ERA. Assign half the groups to defend the ERA and the other half to oppose it. Group members should research and discuss the issue among themselves and then choose a representative to present the group's ideas. After students have debated the pros and cons of the issue, explain that 38 states were needed to pass the ERA and make it part of the Constitution, but only 35 states ratified it by the deadline. Then ask students to discuss why they think the ERA failed and whether they think it would pass today. Point out to students that Nevada ratified the ERA in 2017 and Illinois ratified it in 2018. Ask students what these actions signify.

DIFFERENTIATE

ENGLISH LANGUAGE LEARNERS ELD

Use Meaning Maps Pair students at the **Emerging** level with students at the **Expanding** or **Bridging** level. Have them complete a Meaning Map for the term *gender bias*. Have students look up the word *gender* and the word *bias* in a dictionary. Prompt them to make Meaning Maps for other terms using *bias*, such as *racial bias*, *linguistic bias*, and *confirmation bias*. Direct pairs to trade Meaning Maps and note similarities and differences.

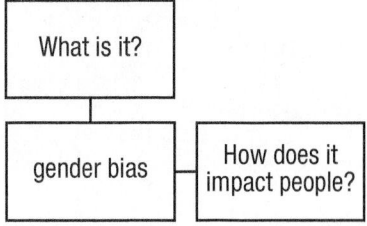

GIFTED & TALENTED

Create a Campaign Tell students to conduct online research to find out why people have supported or opposed the Equal Rights Amendment. Then prompt students to develop a campaign for or against the ERA—in the context of the 1970s or today. They could create a poster or mailer or write and deliver a speech addressing issues such as women's wages, health care, or workplace experiences. Students might also address the role that gender imbalance in legislatures has played in the defeat of the ERA and other women's issues.

See the Chapter Planner for more strategies for differentiation.

HISTORICAL THINKING

ANSWERS

1. Title IX prevented federally funded schools from discriminating against girls and women in admissions, athletics, and other areas. It made athletic and academic scholarships available to women as well as to men.

2. Feminists meant that they would fight against laws that restricted women's personal lives.

3. Legal victories in court (*Griswold* v. *Connecticut* and *Roe* v. *Wade*) offered women greater access to birth control and abortions, and the passage of Title IX expanded women's opportunities for a college education and scholarship money. Together, they helped promote societal roles for women beyond the traditional roles of wives and mothers.

STONEWALL NATIONAL MONUMENT NEW YORK CITY

The mid-20th century saw the beginning of a broader struggle for equal rights for the **lesbian, gay, bisexual, transgender, and queer (LGBTQ)** community, which endured prejudice and discrimination. Not only was homosexuality against the law at that time, it was also classified as a mental illness. Emboldened by the civil rights movements, members of the LGBTQ community began seeking legal and political changes. By the mid-1970s, laws criminalizing homosexuality were repealed by 17 states.

The Stonewall Inn was a popular gathering place for LGBTQ individuals in the 1960s. On June 28, 1969, police raided Stonewall. Patrons refused to line up and show their identification, sparking several days of rioting in the New York neighborhood of Greenwich Village. This event, which is now known as the Stonewall Uprising, became the first major step in the modern LGBTQ rights movement. On June 24, 2016, President Barack Obama announced the Stonewall National Monument at this historic site. This American Place represents the first national monument focused on LGBTQ history.

CRITICAL VIEWING Designated the birthplace of the modern LGBTQ rights movement, the Stonewall Inn still maintains its local neighborhood identity. By the mid-1970s, the LGBTQ community had gained momentum in its quest for equality, but discrimination based on sexual orientation and gender identity continues today. Examine this photograph of the Stonewall Inn. How does a gathering place such as this one help unify a cause or community?

PLAN: 2-PAGE LESSON

OBJECTIVE
Learn about how the LGBTQ community joined the campaign for civil rights and equal treatment under the laws of the United States.

CRITICAL THINKING SKILLS FOR LESSON 3.3
- Analyze Visuals
- Make Connections
- Compare and Contrast

HISTORICAL THINKING FOR CHAPTER 28
How did new calls for equality and the space race impact American society? After years of enduring prejudice and discrimination, the LGBTQ community began to fight for their civil rights. Lesson 3.3 discusses discrimination experienced by homosexual men and women and focuses on the Stonewall Uprising, the first major step in the LGBTQ rights movement.

BACKGROUND FOR THE TEACHER
The United States lagged behind Canada and some European countries in granting civil rights to the LGBTQ community. Religious conservatives regarded homosexuality as a violation of divine law and opposed legislation or court decisions that would include homosexuals in marriage law. However, younger Americans—many of whom were familiar with gay and lesbian people in their everyday lives or as characters on television shows—tended to be more open to same-sex unions. Massachusetts was the first state to legalize gay marriage in 2004. In June 2015, after more than a decade of legal battles, the U.S. Supreme Court ruled that same-sex marriages were legal in all states. According to Justice Anthony Kennedy, the plaintiffs asked for "equal dignity in the eyes of the law. The Constitution grants them that right."

HISTORY NOTEBOOK
Encourage students to complete the American Places page for Chapter 28 in their History Notebooks as they read.

INTRODUCE & ENGAGE
PREVIEW USING VISUALS

Direct students' attention to the photograph and ask them to examine all of its elements. **Ask:** What details in the photograph suggest the historic importance of this place? *(Possible responses: The arrangement of symbolic flags on the edifice of Stonewall Inn, a banner that identifies Stonewall Inn as the place "where pride took off," the word PRIDE on the door, the large rainbow banner)* What other impressions do you have of the street scene? *(Possible responses: Adjoining the Stonewall Inn are other businesses that are typical of an urban street, such as a nail salon and spa and a real estate office. Young people are engaging in everyday activities.)* Tell students that Lesson 3.3 explains why the Stonewall Inn became a national monument honoring the LGBTQ community's struggle to gain their civil rights.

TEACH
GUIDED DISCUSSION

1. **Compare and Contrast** How were the civil rights issues faced by the LGBTQ community similar to and different from those encountered by other groups? *(Possible response: The LGBTQ community faced prejudice and discrimination, as other groups did; but homosexuality had been declared illegal and, in some states, a mental illness. This created unique obstacles the LGBTQ community had to overcome to gain their civil rights.)*

2. **Make Connections** Explain how the movements for equality you've been reading about have built upon one another. Give examples. *(Possible response: Success in one civil rights movement inspired other such movements. For example, the African-American civil rights movement showed women that they needed to organize to fight for equality, and earlier movements influenced the movement for LGBTQ rights.)*

AMERICAN PLACES

In 2016, President Obama designated Stonewall Inn, Christopher Park across the street, and other parts of the surrounding neighborhood as a National Monument in honor of the LGBTQ civil rights movement. The open space known as Christopher Park was included because it served for years as a refuge and gathering place for the LGBTQ community to hold parades, protests, and demonstrations. The Stonewall National Monument has special meaning not only for LGBTQ people in the United States but also for those around the world.

ACTIVE OPTIONS

On Your Feet: Turn and Talk on Topic Organize students into three groups. Give each group this topic sentence: American society's current view of the LGBTQ community differs from social attitudes during the 1960s, and several factors led to that change. Tell groups to build a paragraph on that topic by having each member contribute one sentence. Suggest that students first compare current attitudes with 1960s attitudes and then identify the social and historical events that helped bring about changes.

NG Learning Framework: Develop a Class Presentation

SKILLS Observation, Collaboration

KNOWLEDGE Our Human Story

Arrange students into groups. Remind them that the civil rights movement includes many different communities: African Americans, Native Americans, Asian Americans, Latinos and Hispanics, women, and LGBTQ people. Instruct students to conduct outside research to answer this question: Did the civil rights movement succeed? Ask groups to report their conclusions and evidence as part of a class presentation. You could allow students to select one specific community to research or assign each group a different community. To support their answer, students should gather evidence from this chapter and from outside sources.

DIFFERENTIATE
STRIVING READERS

Review Facts Post this heading: Five Things I Know About the Stonewall Uprising and LGBTQ Rights. After students read the lesson, ask them to copy the heading and add five sentences about the topic. Encourage students to include both successes and setbacks in the struggle for equal treatment for LGBTQ people. Invite volunteers to share their sentences.

PRE-AP

Research LGBTQ Symbols Tell students to use information from several library or online sources to write a report on who designed the rainbow flag and how and why it became a global symbol of the LGBTQ community. You may suggest that students explore the symbolism of the rainbow as a whole, as well as its individual colors, and how the flag and its symbolism continue to evolve. As an alternative or additional activity, students can investigate and report on the evolution of the pink triangle symbol, gay pride parades, and/or *The Advocate*, an LGBTQ magazine. Ask students to share their reports with the class.

See the Chapter Planner for more strategies for differentiation.

CRITICAL VIEWING A place such as Stonewall Inn can help unify a cause or community by giving people a sense of pride, identity, and history and by serving as a focal point for community events, political action, and cultural affairs.

THE SPACE RACE CONTINUES

As the United States grappled with civil unrest and struggles for equality at home, the Cold War with the Soviet Union continued. Throughout the 1960s, the two nations battled for supremacy in space. During a time of turmoil, Americans found common ground in cheering on the U.S. space program's goal of putting a man on the moon.

THE DREAM OF SPACE TRAVEL

Life in the United States during the 1950s and 1960s came with an undercurrent of fear. The United States was at odds with the world's only other superpower, the Soviet Union. The two nations struggled with an uneasy and fragile peace. As you have read, one night in 1957, Americans got a fright: orbiting over their heads was a piece of Soviet machinery called *Sputnik 1*, the first artificial satellite ever launched into orbit. It was not just the satellite orbiting over their heads that concerned Americans. It was also the fact that *Sputnik* had been launched into orbit by a powerful rocket.

Rockets had been invented by the Chinese in the 13th century, and they have been used for fireworks and in warfare ever since. But modern rocket science really began in Germany during World War II. After the war, some of Germany's leading scientists surrendered to American forces and were brought to the United States, while others were recruited into the Soviet Union's rocket program. Among those who immigrated to the United States was **Wernher von Braun**, who had developed the powerful V-2 rocket for Hitler. Although his role in producing this rocket during the war is controversial, Von Braun's real desire

The 363-foot-tall Saturn V rocket launches the Apollo 11 spacecraft toward the moon in 1969.

was to design a rocket that would travel into space, and working for the United States gave him that opportunity.

When NASA was set up in 1958, it combined a number of different, individual organizations that had been working on space-age rocket research, including von Braun's team at the Army Ballistic Missile Agency in Huntsville, Alabama. The United States was not about to allow the Soviet Union to gain an advantage in rocket research, so the new agency had 8,000 employees and a budget of $100 million. The space race had begun, and, as you have read, in 1961 President Kennedy set a remarkable goal: the United States would land a man on the moon by the end of the decade.

With this ambitious challenge, NASA got to work. The location of many NASA facilities was determined by political influence. For example, Houston, Texas, was chosen as the location for the Johnson Space Center largely because Lyndon Johnson, then vice president, was from Texas. NASA's first major launch site, however, was in **Cape Canaveral**, Florida, and it offered two chief advantages, neither of them political. First, all rocket launches would be directed eastward, over the Atlantic Ocean, which was a safety precaution in case of any rocket malfunction. Second, Cape Canaveral was closer to the Equator than other possible launch sites. By launching rockets eastward from a site near the Equator, NASA could take advantage of Earth's eastward rotation in lifting the rocket into orbit.

FROM GEMINI TO APOLLO

The early efforts in the space race focused on sending astronauts deeper and deeper into orbit and safely bringing them back. The first manned space flights were known as Project Mercury. They culminated with American astronaut John Glenn orbiting Earth three times before touching down in the Caribbean Sea. A second astronaut program, Project Gemini, built on what NASA had learned during Mercury's six flights. In a significant step forward, the Gemini space capsules carried two astronauts instead of one. A highlight of the Gemini mission was the first successful American **spacewalk**, in which an astronaut, Edward H. White, ventured outside the spacecraft on June 3, 1965.

From there, NASA initiated its Apollo program, which set its sights on taking the final crucial steps to achieving a moon landing. The earlier Mercury and Gemini programs had solved many of the major

Edward H. White was the first American to take a spacewalk.

challenges involved with launching humans safely into space, from surviving in extreme conditions to returning safely to Earth. NASA now focused its efforts on developing the procedures and equipment that would make a moon orbit and landing possible.

Early on in the Apollo program, however, tragedy struck. On January 27, 1967, during a launch pad test, the Apollo 1 capsule caught fire, trapping three astronauts inside. Virgil "Gus" Grissom, Roger Chaffee, and Edward H. White—the first American to ever walk in space—died in the accident. In the aftermath of this tragedy, NASA conducted an investigation to discover the cause of the fire. The recommendations the investigators made in their report led to engineering and design improvements to the space capsule as well as advances in quality control, manufacturing, and testing procedures. Despite the horrific event, the space program pushed on.

HISTORICAL THINKING

1. **READING CHECK** What were Wernher von Braun's qualifications for working on the American space program?

2. **COMPARE AND CONTRAST** How were the goals of the Mercury and Gemini programs different from those of Apollo?

3. **DESCRIBE** Describe the effects of America's space program on society and the economy. Use evidence from the text to support your response.

4. **ANALYZE CAUSE AND EFFECT** How did NASA respond to the launch pad tragedy that killed three Apollo astronauts?

PLAN: 2-PAGE LESSON

OBJECTIVE

Understand how the Soviet Union's successful launch of *Sputnik 1* in 1957 challenged the United States to push its own space program.

CRITICAL THINKING SKILLS FOR LESSON 4.1

• Compare and Contrast

• Describe

• Analyze Cause and Effect

• Make Inferences

HISTORICAL THINKING FOR CHAPTER 28

How did new calls for equality and the space race impact American society? NASA, with 8,000 employees and a budget of $100 million, contributed to the U.S. economy as its space endeavors captured the attention of the public. Lesson 4.1 describes NASA's first manned space flights in preparation for a moon landing.

BACKGROUND FOR THE TEACHER

Astronaut Edward H. White was the first American to participate in an extravehicular activity (EVA), soon to become known as a spacewalk. White's EVA during Gemini 4 followed Soviet cosmonaut Alexei Leonov's spacewalk on March 18 by a matter of months. White was tethered to the spacecraft by a 25-foot umbilical line that provided him with oxygen and also enabled him to communicate with the spacecraft. He wore an emergency oxygen pack on his chest and carried a Hand-Held Self-Maneuvering Unit. By expelling oxygen, the unit provided thrust, which enabled White to control his movements. White's walk lasted 20 minutes, during which he did some long-distance sightseeing over Houston. As the U.S. space program moved forward, spacewalking proved essential for landing on the moon and building the International Space Station.

INTRODUCE & ENGAGE

ACTIVATE PRIOR KNOWLEDGE

Ask students to recall what they know about *Sputnik 1*. Remind them that it was the first artificial satellite to be launched into orbit around Earth. **ASK:** What effect did *Sputnik 1* have on American society? *(Americans were concerned that the Soviet Union now had the means to spy on them and the capability to launch powerful rockets.)* Tell students that in this lesson they will read about how the space race continued in response to *Sputnik 1*.

TEACH

GUIDED DISCUSSION

1. **Analyze Cause and Effect** How did the physical characteristics of Cape Canaveral influence NASA's choice of a launch site during the early days of the space program? *(Cape Canaveral was located by the ocean, so a malfunctioning rocket would likely drop into the water instead of onto a populated area. It also was close enough to the Equator that Earth's eastward rotation would help lift a rocket into orbit.)*

2. **Make Inferences** Why do you think astronauts needed to perform spacewalks? *(Possible response: A spacewalk would be the only way to perform repairs to the outside of a spacecraft. It also might be useful for observation or for performing experiments in space.)*

MORE INFORMATION

Wernher von Braun Explain that to understand the science of rocketry, Wernher von Braun taught himself calculus and trigonometry while still a teenager. He wanted to build large rockets, which led him to work for the German Army, developing ballistic missiles. Although he developed the V-2 rocket for the Nazis, in 1945 von Braun persuaded some 500 of his top scientists to surrender to the Americans. From then on, he worked with the U.S. Army to develop ballistic missiles and became a well-known spokesperson for the exploration of space. **ASK:** Why do you think von Braun gained such a prominent position instead of being punished for his role in developing weapons for the Nazis? *(Possible response: U.S. officials probably believed that his help in developing American rocket technology outweighed his role in the war.)*

ACTIVE OPTIONS

On Your Feet: Fishbowl Arrange the class so that half the students sit in a circle facing inward and the other half sit in a larger circle around them. Students on the inside should discuss what they have learned about the space race during the 1960s. Those on the outside should listen for new information and decide what might have been omitted from the discussion. Then have groups switch positions, with the new inner circle discussing the same topic.

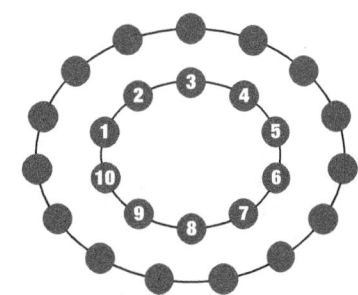

NG Learning Framework: Create a Storyboard

SKILL Communication

KNOWLEDGE New Frontiers

Direct students to learn more about how the space race of the 1960s affected society and to create a storyboard that illustrates their findings. Students may choose a series of events or a single program or mission. Invite students to display the storyboards in the classroom and to narrate their work, perhaps in the format of a gallery walk.

DIFFERENTIATE

STRIVING READERS

Summarize Have students work in pairs to read and summarize the lesson. Tell students to write at least three notes for each of the lesson's sections. After they have completed taking notes, guide students to create a summary statement for each section and then a summary statement for the whole lesson.

GIFTED & TALENTED

Create an Annotated Time Line Instruct students to create and annotate a time line of the most significant programs and events that led to the successful lunar landing. Students should supplement information from the lesson with online research. Tell students to add relevant photographs, news headlines, statistics, and facts to the time line. Allow them to use an online graphics program, if available, to create the time line. Have students share their finished time lines with the class, explain the significance of each item on the time line, and answer questions.

See the Chapter Planner for more strategies for differentiation.

HISTORICAL THINKING

ANSWERS

1. Von Braun was a scientist who had developed the powerful V-2 rocket.

2. The goal of Mercury and Gemini was to put astronauts into orbit and return them safely to Earth; Apollo's goal was to reach the moon.

3. America's space program caught the public's imagination, giving Americans something to cheer about after Russia launched *Sputnik 1*. As NASA ramped up, it employed 8,000 people and had a budget of $100 million, which helped the U.S. economy.

4. NASA introduced design and engineering improvements and improved its quality control, manufacturing, and testing procedures to prevent a recurrence.

"ONE GIANT LEAP FOR MANKIND"

Have you ever looked up at the moon and imagined what it would be like to walk on its surface, gazing back at Earth? People had been wondering about this for thousands of years, but it wasn't until 1969 that the technology, and the will to attempt such a challenge, allowed it to become reality.

THE U.S. MOON MISSION

In the years after the tragic loss of the Apollo 1 crew, the United States continued making steady progress toward its moon landing goal. NASA developed a rocket, the Saturn V, which officials believed would be powerful enough to set the astronauts on a course that would send them all the way to the moon. It also developed a command **module**, or unit, called *Columbia*, and a lunar module, nicknamed *Eagle*, that astronaut Michael Collins later described as "the weirdest looking contraption I have ever seen in the sky." Collins was one of the three men chosen as the crew of **Apollo 11**, the mission that would shoot for the moon. Collins piloted *Columbia*. **Neil Armstrong** was mission commander, and **Edwin "Buzz" Aldrin** was *Eagle's* pilot.

Dawn on July 16, 1969, was clear and sunny at Cape Kennedy. (Cape Canaveral's name was changed to Cape Kennedy in 1963 after the president's assassination, but it would revert to its original name in 1973.) At 9:32 a.m., Armstrong, Aldrin, and Collins took off in the nose of a massive Saturn V rocket. Spectators cheered as the rocket, wreathed in fire and smoke, rose into the sky. Twelve minutes later, the crew was in orbit and headed toward the moon. The trip took three days. As they approached the moon, Armstrong and Aldrin climbed into *Eagle*, disengaged from *Columbia*,

and headed for the moon's surface. Collins stayed behind, piloting *Columbia*. At 4:18 p.m. eastern daylight time on July 20, with just 30 seconds' worth of fuel left, *Eagle* landed on the moon. Armstrong radioed the news back to Earth: "Houston, Tranquility Base here. The *Eagle* has landed."

People at Mission Control in Houston roared in glee and applauded as they watched the landing. For the first time, human beings were on the surface of another celestial body. Kennedy's dream had been realized: Americans were on the moon before any other nation. Armstrong exited *Eagle*, climbed down its ladder, and

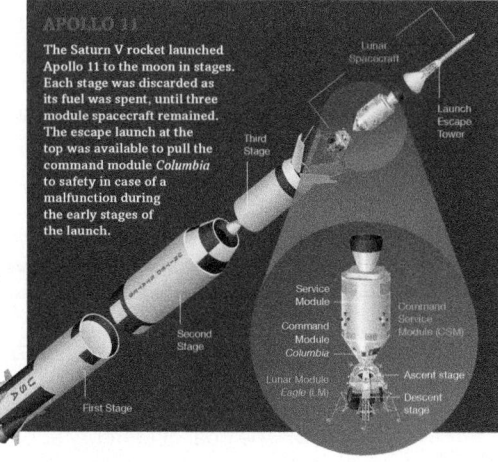

APOLLO 11

The Saturn V rocket launched Apollo 11 to the moon in stages. Each stage was discarded as its fuel was spent, until three module spacecraft remained. The escape launch at the top was available to pull the command module *Columbia* to safety in case of a malfunction during the early stages of the launch.

Lunar Spacecraft
Launch Escape Tower
Third Stage
Second Stage
First Stage
Service Module
Command Module *Columbia*
Command Service Module (CSM)
Lunar Module *Eagle* (LM)
Ascent stage
Descent stage

The National Air and Space Museum, Washington, D.C.

The *Columbia*, the Apollo 11 command module, was the living quarters of the three-person crew during the first manned lunar landing mission in July 1969. This command module, no. 107, was one of three parts of the complete Apollo spacecraft and was the only part of the spacecraft to return to Earth, transporting the three astronauts aboard. Its furnishings included a heating unit, water supply, pressure-suit connectors, scientific equipment, and even a vacuum cleaner! The module and its travel ring, or transporting cradle, weighs over 13,600 pounds.

became the first person to walk on the moon. "That's one small step for [a] man, one giant leap for mankind," he radioed back to Earth, where 500 million people—about 14 percent of the world's population—received his words and images broadcast from 238,900 miles away. Together, Aldrin and Armstrong explored and collected samples. "Magnificent desolation" is how Aldrin described the lunar surface.

After two and a half hours, they placed a plaque on the moon memorializing their visit, which described them not as Americans, but as "men of Earth" who came in peace. They also left an American flag, medallions in memory of the Apollo 1 crew and for 2 Russian cosmonauts, and a silicon disk engraved with goodwill wishes from 78 nations. Then they returned to *Eagle,* which was a two-part module: one for descending to the lunar surface, and one for taking off from the surface. Each part of the module had its own fuel supply. The ascent module blasted off, using the descent module as a launching pad, to meet up with Collins and *Columbia*. Upon their return to Earth (after a few days in quarantine), the astronauts were given a huge parade in New York City and were celebrated around the world.

OTHER LUNAR LANDINGS

Five more Apollo missions landed astronauts on the moon between 1969 and 1972. The soil and rock samples the Apollo astronauts brought back from the moon were a treasure trove of information. Scientists confirmed that no life existed on the moon and that its mineral composition was similar to Earth's. The moon is very ancient; its youngest rocks are about the same age as the oldest Earth rocks. These lunar rocks are still being studied.

One of the later Apollo missions, Apollo 13, never reached the moon. Launched on April 11, 1970, it was

200,000 miles from Earth when all water, electrical power, propulsion, and oxygen in the command module were lost. The crew retreated to the lunar module, which kept them alive while the damaged ship did a lunar flyby and headed back to Earth. The men drank only six ounces of water a day as Apollo 13 limped home. All three crewmembers survived. Investigators eventually determined that exposed wires on a fan shorted out, setting the insulation on fire, and causing an oxygen tank to explode.

After the Apollo program ended, NASA's focus shifted away from the moon. Starting in the 1980s, it developed the space shuttle, an orbiter that could be used repeatedly for missions. NASA also began admitting women to the astronaut program. On June 18, 1983, **Sally Ride** became the first American woman to fly in space on a space shuttle mission.

Together, the nations of the world, led by the United States and Russia (the former Soviet Union), began building the International Space Station. Scientists on the space station conduct experiments to learn about how outer space affects living things and study the cosmos without visual interference from Earth's atmosphere. NASA continues to send unmanned probes to explore Mars, Jupiter, Saturn, their moons, and the outer reaches of our solar system.

HISTORICAL THINKING

1. **READING CHECK** What was the major accomplishment of NASA's Apollo program?

2. **ANALYZE CAUSE AND EFFECT** Why do you think NASA has moved away from manned space missions?

3. **ASK AND ANSWER QUESTIONS** What questions do you still have about NASA's technological developments, and where can you find the answers?

PLAN: 2-PAGE LESSON

OBJECTIVE

Discuss the Apollo 11 mission and ways in which NASA has explored space since the first manned moon landing.

CRITICAL THINKING SKILLS FOR LESSON 4.2

- Analyze Cause and Effect
- Ask and Answer Questions
- Make Connections
- Draw Conclusions

HISTORICAL THINKING FOR CHAPTER 28

How did new calls for equality and the space race impact American society? The United States continued to pursue its goal of landing humans on the moon. Lesson 4.2 describes how the Apollo 11 mission achieved that goal and how the United States has participated in space exploration since then.

BACKGROUND FOR THE TEACHER

The schematic of Apollo 11 shows the three stages of Saturn V and the spacecraft's modules. After the spacecraft left Earth's orbit, a reaction control thruster separated the command module (which stayed attached to the service module until just before re-entering Earth's atmosphere at the mission's end) and the lunar module from the rocket's third stage. The command module pilot then turned the spacecraft around, thereby lining up the command module's docking probe with the lunar module's drogue, a funnel-shaped receptacle. This maneuver linked the two modules. When the spacecraft reached the moon, the lunar module separated from the command module in order to transport Neil Armstrong and Buzz Aldrin to the moon's surface. You may wish to search online for videos that show this procedure, known as transposition and docking.

INTRODUCE & ENGAGE

BRAINSTORM ABOUT LUNAR MISSIONS

Invite students to brainstorm a list of the challenges involved in sending humans to the moon and returning them safely. Students' responses may be based on what they have learned about space flight in previous lessons, on what they know from other sources, and even on conjecture. Discuss why the United States accepted those challenges, pointing out not only the desire for scientific knowledge but also the goal of beating the Soviet Union in the context of the space race. Then tell students that they are about to read how the United States met the challenges in Apollo 11—and what happened afterward.

TEACH

GUIDED DISCUSSION

1. **Make Connections** What roles did Saturn V, *Columbia*, and *Eagle* play in placing astronauts on the moon? *(Saturn V was the rocket that provided the power to set the astronauts' course;* Columbia *was the command module, used as living quarters; the lunar module* Eagle *enabled the astronauts to land on the moon and then return to* Columbia.*)*

2. **Draw Conclusions** What lesson did the malfunction during the Apollo 13 mission provide about the importance of reliable technology and the risks that astronauts take? *(Possible response: Even minor parts of a mission's systems, such as the wires on a fan, can pose life-threatening consequences if they malfunction.)*

🏛 VIRTUAL MUSEUM VISIT

The National Air and Space Museum is home to more than 60,000 artifacts, including 9,000 space objects—the world's largest collection of space and aviation artifacts. Access the museum's website, go to the Topics menu, and select "Apollo Program." As a class, read an article or two and discuss how the information helps readers better understand space exploration. Then ask groups of students to explore the website on their own and to choose an artifact related to the Apollo program or to previous programs. Invite students to present the artifact and explain how it works, if applicable, and why they find it of interest.

ACTIVE OPTIONS

On Your Feet: Show Stages Arrange students in small groups. Share with them the specifics of the Apollo 11 stages outlined in Background for the Teacher. If time allows, show students an online video (or give them time to search for one) detailing how the modules and rocket parts fit together and how the different stages functioned during a space flight. Then prompt them to work together to create a flip book, storyboard, or mural depicting the process.

NG Learning Framework: Devise an Experiment `STEM`

`SKILL` Collaboration

`KNOWLEDGE` New Frontiers

Explain to students that while on the moon, the astronauts of the six Apollo lunar landings performed activities aimed at learning more about the moon. Ask students to work with a partner to design an activity or experiment aimed at increasing our knowledge about the moon. Students should be prepared to explain their experiment and its purpose, using visual support as appropriate.

For students who develop an interest in the Apollo 11 mission, suggest that they read the American Story *at the beginning of this chapter.*

DIFFERENTIATE

INCLUSION

Work in Pairs Pair students who are visually impaired with students who are not. Ask the latter to describe the illustration of the Apollo 11 rocket components and lunar spacecraft components, as well as the photograph of the Apollo 11 command module. Tell visually impaired students to ask clarifying questions as necessary. The partner without disabilities may be able to answer some of the questions by reading the captions.

GIFTED & TALENTED

Create a Multimedia Newscast Challenge students to conduct online research to find video footage of the moon landing, as well as newspaper articles and photographs. Then prompt students to write a script in the form of a contemporary newscast, incorporating the information, images, and video clips they discovered. Instruct students to assemble their script and research materials into a multimedia newscast about the moon landing and present it to the class.

See the Chapter Planner for more strategies for differentiation.

HISTORICAL THINKING

ANSWERS

1. The Apollo program ultimately transported astronauts to the moon and back.

2. Missions that have human crews are very expensive and logistically more difficult, and they put human lives at risk. Probes can gather information more economically.

3. Students' questions will vary. Information on NASA's technological developments can be found on NASA's website.

VOCABULARY

Use each of the following vocabulary words in a sentence that shows an understanding of the term's meaning.

1. **peer**
   His new teammates considered him a peer because his skills were equal to theirs.

2. misogyny

3. manifesto

4. militant

5. module

6. feminism

7. gender bias

8. spacewalk

READING STRATEGY
ANALYZE CAUSE AND EFFECT

Use a graphic organizer like the one below to describe the civil rights movements, their effect on American society, and how they were influenced by the African-American civil rights movement.

Cause and Effect

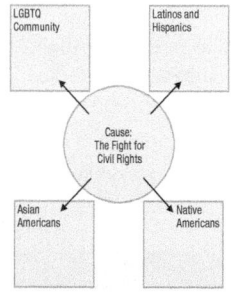

9. How did various groups experiencing discrimination fight for equality and civil rights in the 1960s?

MAIN IDEAS

Answer the following questions. Support your answers with evidence from the chapter.

10. What factors led to the Latino rights movement? **LESSON 1.1**

11. Why did Larry Itliong ask the Mexican American farmworkers to join the Filipino grape laborers' strike? **LESSON 1.3**

12. What governmental decision made the creation of the Native American Declaration of Purpose necessary? **LESSON 2.1**

13. What was the American Indian Movement (AIM)? **LESSON 2.2**

14. What were the goals of the National Organization for Women (NOW)? **LESSON 3.1**

15. How did Title IX make schools and sports more fair for women? **LESSON 3.2**

16. How did the technology NASA developed for the Apollo program build on lessons learned from Project Gemini? **LESSON 4.1**

17. What did Neil Armstrong mean when he said, "That's one small step for [a] man, one giant leap for mankind"? **LESSON 4.2**

HISTORICAL THINKING

Answer the following questions. Support your answers with evidence from the chapter.

18. **ANALYZE CAUSE AND EFFECT** Was *The Feminine Mystique* a cause or an effect of the women's movement, or both, and what limitations might prevent you from determining this?

19. **MAKE GENERALIZATIONS** Why is the designation of the Stonewall Inn as a National Monument important for the LGBTQ community?

20. **DRAW CONCLUSIONS** Which strategies undertaken by Native Americans in pursuit of their civil rights were similar to those strategies undertaken by African Americans, and how effective were they?

21. **FORM AND SUPPORT OPINIONS** Which civil rights movement in this chapter do you think made the greatest strides during this time period?

INTERPRET VISUALS

Physicist and astronaut Sally Ride monitors the control panel from the pilot's seat on the space shuttle. Ride took her first space flight in 1983 as a mission specialist.

22. **DRAW CONCLUSIONS** What kind of training do you think Ride, or any other astronaut, would need to perform this job in the space shuttle?

23. **MAKE INFERENCES** Why would an astronaut need the large windows shown here, rather than the smaller ones in early capsules?

ANALYZE SOURCES

César Chávez led farmworkers in many protests.

"The consumer boycott is the only open door in the dark corridor of nothingness down which farm workers have had to walk for many years. It is a gate of hope through which they expect to find the sunlight of a better life for themselves and their families."

—César Chávez, as quoted in *Why We Fight: The Origins, Nature, and Management of Human Conflict*, by David Churchman, 2013

24. Based on the quotation, why do you think Chávez chose boycotts as an effective strategy for achieving equality?

CONNECT TO YOUR LIFE

25. **EXPOSITORY** Talk to family members or other adults you know about one of the civil rights movements described in this chapter. What does the adult remember about it? Ask him or her to explain in what ways civil rights for different groups of Americans have changed or remained unchanged over time. Have these movements made your life today different from what it would have been in the 1960s or 1970s? In a paragraph explain how these movements have affected your life today.

TIPS

- Use information from the chapter to craft your questions before you conduct any of your interviews.

- Ask the people you interview for concrete details from their memories and experiences.

- Compare your life today with the life described by the adults in your interviews.

- Conclude by drawing from your experiences and feelings to explain why you think these movements had an overall positive or negative impact on American society.

- Use two or three vocabulary terms from the chapter in your response.

VOCABULARY ANSWERS

1. His new teammates considered him a peer because his skills were equal to theirs.

2. One of the goals of the ERA was to protect women from abuse and other forms of misogyny.

3. The manifesto was a written declaration of the group's goals.

4. AIM was militant in its promotion of Native American rights.

5. The astronauts used the lunar module to land on the moon's surface and later return to the command module that orbited the moon.

6. Feminism seeks to establish greater rights for women.

7. Gender bias can lead to discrimination against people of one sex.

8. Edward H. White was the first astronaut to participate in a spacewalk.

READING STRATEGY ANSWER

Cause and Effect

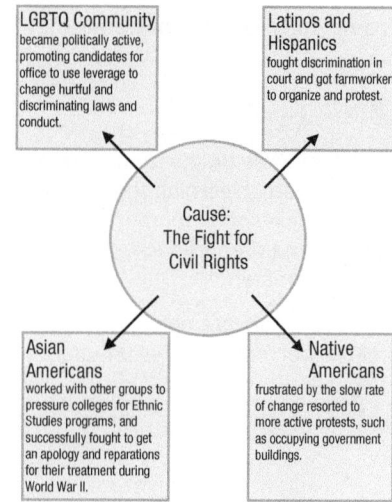

9. They brought lawsuits, organized strikes and boycotts, occupied government buildings, and became politically active.

MAIN IDEAS ANSWERS

10. The demand for rights grew because Latinos had made important contributions to the war effort, some Latinos were well respected and successful, and more immigrants were coming to the United States from Mexico and Latin American nations that had struggling economies.

11. Larry Itliong wanted to achieve greater solidarity with other minority workers.

12. The termination policy of the 1950s had a big negative effect on Native Americans, increasing poverty and prejudice. The Declaration of Purpose listed the major issues facing Native Americans and called for a policy of self-determination.

13. AIM was a Native American rights movement that took a more active and militant approach to protest than other groups.

14. The goals of NOW were to advocate for women's rights, particularly in the workplace, and for women's health care.

15. Title IX required any organization that received federal funding to provide equal opportunities for women and men.

16. Project Gemini featured a capsule that held a crew of two astronauts. With each mission, NASA learned more about navigating in space and returning safely, including how people could walk in space outside the capsule. Apollo, with a crew of three, built on that knowledge and added to it.

17. Armstrong meant that reaching the moon was a triumph for every person, not just for Americans and not just for him.

HISTORICAL THINKING ANSWERS

18. *The Feminine Mystique* was a cause of the women's movement because it inspired women to organize in order to demand greater civil rights, but it could also be seen as an outgrowth of earlier ideas about women's roles. Some women might have read it because they were already influenced by the women's movement.

19. Possible response: Designation of the Stonewall Inn is an important recognition of the individuals who stood up to prejudice and the impact their actions had on the LGBTQ community and the nation.

20. Similar to sit-ins held by African Americans, Native Americans launched "fish-ins" to cause economic disruption. They also called attention to offensive depictions in the media and pushed for Indian Studies programs. These strategies did not bring change quickly enough in the eyes of many Native Americans.

21. Students' answers will vary. Accept any reasonable responses that are supported with text evidence.

INTERPRET VISUALS ANSWERS

22. An astronaut would need training to operate complicated controls and to learn how to stay safe and healthy aboard a spacecraft.

23. An astronaut might need large windows to help navigate, to observe spacewalk activity, or to observe Earth or other bodies in space.

ANALYZE SOURCES ANSWER

24. Chávez chose boycotts as the only means available to farmworkers to affect change.

CONNECT TO YOUR LIFE ANSWER

25. Essays will vary but should describe how the 1960s and 1970s were important decades of change for many groups that found inspiration in the civil rights movement, including, but not limited to, women, Latinos and Hispanics, Asian Americans, Native Americans, and the LGBT community.

NATIONAL GEOGRAPHIC | CONNECTION

HERE LIES JIM CROW

Who Was Jim Crow?

BY BECKY LITTLE

Adapted from "Who Was Jim Crow?" by Becky Little. news.nationalgeographic.com, August 2016.

In 1944, the Detroit chapter of the National Association for the Advancement of Colored People (NAACP) held a mock funeral for him. In 1963, participants in the March on Washington for Jobs and Freedom symbolically buried him. Racial discrimination existed all over the United States in the 20th century, but it had a special name in the South—Jim Crow.

President Lyndon B. Johnson tried to bury Jim Crow by signing the Voting Rights Act of 1965 into law. The Voting Rights Act and its predecessor, the Civil Rights Act of 1964, fought racial discrimination by banning segregation in public accommodations and outlawing the poll taxes and tests that were used to stop African Americans from voting.

Today, we still use "Jim Crow" to describe that system of segregation and discrimination in the South. But the system's namesake isn't actually Southern. Jim Crow came from the North.

Thomas Dartmouth Rice, a white man, was born in New York City in 1808. He devoted himself to the theater in his 20s. In the early 1830s, he began performing the act that would make him famous: He painted his face black and did a song and dance he claimed were inspired by an African-American slave. The act was called "Jump, Jim Crow" (or "Jumping Jim Crow").

Rice's routine was a hit in New York City, one of many places in the North where working-class whites could see blackface minstrelsy, which was quickly becoming a dominant form of theater and a leading source for popular music in America. Rice took his act on tour. As his popularity grew, his stage name seeped into the culture. Jim Crow became a name that was applied to African Americans in general. "So much so," says Eric Lott, professor at the City University of New York Graduate Center, "that by the time of Harriet Beecher Stowe's *Uncle Tom's Cabin*, which was 20 years later in 1852," one character refers to another as Jim Crow.

Regardless of whether the term Jim Crow existed before Rice took it to the stage, his act helped popularize it as a derogatory term for African Americans. To call someone Jim Crow wasn't just to point out his or her skin color: it was to reduce that person to the kind of caricature that Rice performed on stage.

After the Civil War, southern states passed laws that discriminated against newly freed African Americans. As early as the 1890s, these laws had gained a nickname. In 1899, a North Carolina newspaper published an article subtitled "How 'Capt. Tilley' of the A. & N.C. Road Enforces the Jim Crow Law."

Experts aren't sure how a racist show in the North came to embody racist laws in the South. But they can speculate. Since the term originated in blackface minstrelsy, Lott says that it's almost "perversely accurate . . . that it should come to be the name for official segregation and state-sponsored racism."

"I think probably in the popular white mind, it was just used because that's just how they referred to black people," he says.

"Sometimes in history a movie comes out or a book comes out and it just changes the language . . . and you can point at it," says David Pilgrim, director of the Jim Crow Museum and vice president for Diversity and Inclusion at Ferris State University.

"And in just this case," he says, "I think it just evolved. And I think it was from many sources."

However it happened, the new meaning stuck. Blackface minstrelsy's popularity faded, and Thomas Rice is barely remembered. Most people today don't know his name. But everybody knows the name Jim Crow.

For more from National Geographic, check out "Before Stonewall" online.

UNIT INQUIRY: Design a Museum Exhibit

In this unit, you learned about a turbulent period in American life. The assassinations of three national leaders and a divisive war shattered the hopeful visions of progress proposed in the New Frontier and the Great Society. Protest movements by numerous groups—African Americans, Native Americans, Latinos, women, and antiwar activists—divided the nation and often turned violent. How did the popular culture of the time reflect this great turmoil? Which songs best express the mood of the time? What works of art and literature capture the confusion of those years? How did clothing and hairstyles become protest statements?

ASSIGNMENT

Design a museum exhibit that answers this question: How did popular culture reflect the turbulence of the time period? You might explore popular culture in general or focus on a particular aspect of it, such as music, art, literature, movies, or fashion. Be prepared to present your design to the class.

Plan First choose the subject of your exhibit and identify its main idea or theme. Then research your subject and compile a list of primary sources in diverse formats, such as songs, photographs, works of art, or newspaper articles, that will form your exhibit. You'll use these objects to tell your story. You might use a graphic organizer to outline your theme and arrange your primary sources.

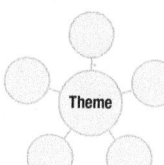

Theme

Produce Create a title for your exhibit and write an introduction of one or more paragraphs. Then write a caption for each primary source in your exhibit, providing identifying information and explaining the object's significance.

Present Share your exhibit design with the class. You might consider one of these options:

- Use a computer program to create a virtual museum exhibit and post it on a website that your classmates can access. Invite viewers to share their reactions to the exhibit.

- Create a museum board model for display in the classroom. After viewing one another's displays, hold a class discussion comparing the popular culture of the period with the popular culture of the current time. Discuss how you would characterize the contemporary culture.

NATIONAL GEOGRAPHIC | LEARNING FRAMEWORK ACTIVITIES

Write a Letter

ATTITUDE Responsibility
KNOWLEDGE New Frontiers

Write a letter, addressed to your classmates or to the president of the United States, outlining a "New Frontier" or "Great Society" challenge that you think your generation should tackle. Explain your vision of progress, how you would implement it, and how it will improve people's lives. Compare your ideas with those of either President Kennedy or President Johnson. Share your letter with your classmates, and discuss the ideas and visions presented for the future.

Create a Song

KNOWLEDGE Our Human Story
SKILLS Collaboration, Communication

If you have musical skills, collaborate with one or more partners to compose a song that captures a current conflict in American society, perhaps in the lives of American youth. Consider various styles of music, such as rap, pop, country, folk, and rock. Choose a style and a theme, and play around with lyrics and melody until a song develops. Practice the song and perform it for the class. Discuss how it relates to the conflict. Ask for feedback, inviting suggestions for changes to the lyrics or music.

NATIONAL GEOGRAPHIC CONNECTION

GUIDED DISCUSSION FOR "WHO WAS JIM CROW?"

1. **Analyze Language Use** How did the term *Jim Crow* become associated with segregation laws in the South? (*A white entertainer performed a song-and-dance act in blackface called "Jump, Jim Crow" in New York City, claiming it was inspired by an African-American slave. Racist attitudes led to the popularity of blackface minstrelsy, and the derogatory name was in common enough usage to become the term used for segregation laws in the South.*)

2. **Identify** In what way did President Johnson try to "bury Jim Crow"? (*Johnson actively pushed Congress to pass the Civil Rights Act of 1964 and the Voting Rights Act of 1965 in an effort to stop racial segregation in places open to the public and ban poll taxes that inhibited African Americans from voting.*)

GUIDED DISCUSSION FOR "BEFORE STONEWALL"

1. **Make Generalizations** What generalizations can you make about the LGBT sites in the article? (*Possible response: All are places where police violated human rights, such as Henry Gerber's home, where police stole personal property. It was "common practice" for police to raid gay bars and hangouts and beat patrons who were dancing or drinking alcohol, a legal activity for the general population.*)

2. **Form and Support Opinions** Why do you think Stonewall became the touchpoint event of the LGBT resistance movement? (*Possible response: After years of raids, the LGBT community had had enough, and the three-day protest brought national attention to the issue of LGBT rights.*)

HISTORY NOTEBOOK

Encourage students to complete the Unit Wrap-Up page for Unit 8 in their History Notebooks.

UNIT INQUIRY PROJECT RUBRIC

ASSESS

Use the rubric to assess each student's participation and performance.

SCORE	ASSIGNMENT	PRODUCT	PRESENTATION
3 GREAT	• Student thoroughly understands the assignment. • Student participates fully in the project process.	• Exhibit design is well thought out. • Exhibit design offers multiple examples that reflect the turbulence of the period. • Exhibit design contains all of the key elements listed in the assignment.	• Presentation is clear, concise, and logical. • Presentation does a good job of sharing the exhibit design. • Presentation engages the audience.
2 GOOD	• Student mostly understands the assignment. • Student participates fairly well in the project process.	• Exhibit design is fairly well thought out. • Exhibit design offers at least two examples that reflect the turbulence of the period. • Exhibit design contains most of the key elements listed in the assignment.	• Presentation is fairly clear, concise, and logical. • Presentation does an adequate job of sharing the exhibit design. • Presentation somewhat engages the audience.
1 NEEDS WORK	• Student does not understand the assignment. • Student minimally participates or does not participate in the project process.	• Exhibit design is not well thought out. • Exhibit design does not offer examples that reflect the turbulence of the period. • Exhibit design contains few or none of the key elements listed in the assignment.	• Presentation is not clear, concise, or logical. • Presentation does an inadequate job of sharing the exhibit design. • Presentation does not engage the audience.

NATIONAL GEOGRAPHIC LEARNING FRAMEWORK RUBRIC

ASSESS

Use the rubric to assess how each student applies the National Geographic Learning Framework.

SCORE	ASSIGNMENT	ASSIGNMENT	FINAL PRODUCTS
3 GREAT	• Letter reflects **Responsibility** well. • Letter explores **New Frontiers** well.	• Song demonstrates **Collaboration** and **Communication** well. • Song explores **Our Human Story** well.	• Final products are engaging, creative, and well presented.
2 GOOD	• Letter reflects **Responsibility**. • Letter explores **New Frontiers**.	• Song demonstrates **Collaboration** and **Communication**. • Song explores **Our Human Story**.	• Final products are interesting, logical, and complete.
1 NEEDS WORK	• Letter does not reflect **Responsibility**. • Letter does not explore **New Frontiers**.	• Song does not demonstrate **Collaboration** and **Communication**. • Song does not explore **Our Human Story**.	• Final products are not creative, complete, or interesting.

THE HIGH LINE

Until recently, Manhattan's High Line, or High Line Park, was a crumbling relic of a rail line that had been inactive since 1980. When Peter Obletz bought the line from Conrail in the 1980s, he planned to reopen it for rail use. But that didn't happen, and when Obletz died in 1996, New York City officials were eager to tear down the old railway. They failed to get their way, thanks in large part to a grassroots organization called Friends of the High Line, whose efforts eventually resulted in procurement of a team of architectural designers to concoct a visually stunning plan for remodeling the site. **ASK:** Why might members of Friends of the High Line have believed it was important to preserve the old rail line? *(Possible response: With technological advances pressing to replace the old with the new, people might have felt the need to keep a bit of old New York and to rehabilitate and repurpose part of the city's history into something beautiful and useful.)*

The designers' concept was to keep a sense of the old rail line but to combine it with more sophisticated visual elements. To accomplish this, they kept the original tracks, embedding them into the elevated walkway's pavement and integrating them into a landscape thruway lined with greenery, wildflowers, and wooden benches. The High Line opened to the public in June 2009 and draws between 4 and 5 million visitors annually. **ASK:** Why do you think the High Line's designers wanted to retain the railroad tracks from the old line? *(Possible responses: Keeping the tracks in place would serve as a reminder of the High Line's original use. By merging the old with the new, the designers could create something unique among the city's public spaces. The cost of labor can be significant, especially in Manhattan, so it may have been less costly to keep the tracks than tear them out.)*

UNIT
9

1968–Present

CHALLENGES OF A NEW CENTURY

1034

CRITICAL VIEWING The High Line, an elevated public park built on an old, unused freight rail line, extends between the buildings of Manhattan's West Side. Benches give visitors a peaceful place to rest above the busy New York City streets, and plants, grasses, and trees recall the wild landscape that once ran along the abandoned railway. How might the High Line serve as an example of a solution to a modern urban challenge?

1035

CENTRAL PARK, NEW YORK CITY

New York City has a long and proud tradition of incorporating nature in its cityscape. In 1853, the state of New York set aside 750 acres of Manhattan real estate to make way for an enormous landscaped public park. The state ended up spending about $7.4 million for 843 acres, more than the United States paid to Russia for the entire state of Alaska in 1867. Historians disagree as to the reasons behind the park's creation. Some claim it was a way for New York City to compete with world-class European cities. Others believe the primary intention was to drive up property values for the wealthy homeowners who lived near the planned site. The designers' vision for Central Park included creating a space in an urban location with a countryside appearance, much in the tradition of European public grounds. **ASK:** What other reasons can you think of for creating a large public park in a crowded urban setting? *(Possible response: A park would provide people with a pleasant place to walk, run, or bike and would provide eye-catching natural vistas and respite from the concrete and cars so prevalent in crowded urban areas.)*

Central Park, designed by Frederick Law Olmsted and Calvert Vaux, has become a must-see destination with more than 40 million visitors annually. The park's design and layout reveal Olmsted and Vaux's intention to create a microcosm of New York State, reflecting the state's diverse landscapes and vistas. Hills and forest areas with towering trees, lakes, and fountains surround walkways shared by pedestrians and cyclists, gardens and gazebos, sunken roads and bridges, a skating rink, and a bridle path. Park visitors can even see a sheep pasture—something Olmsted insisted upon—although sheep are no longer allowed in the park. In addition to enjoying nature, the public can visit a world-class art museum, attend a play at an outdoor theater, or wander through the park's zoo.

CRITICAL VIEWING One challenge for many urban areas is that few places exist in which people can escape the noise, car exhaust, crowds, and traffic. The elevated High Line offers a quiet, calm oasis from the noise and frenzy of the city below. Because of the green plants that line much of the High Line, the area also serves as an antidote to toxic levels of pollution that can build up from the city's heat and traffic.

1989 EUROPE:
THE FALL OF THE BERLIN WALL

In 1961, the East German government built the Berlin Wall to limit (and ultimately prevent) access to West Germany. From 1949 until 1961, 2.5 million East Germans fled to West Germany, many of whom were skilled workers and members of the professional class. The loss of these workers greatly threatened East Germany's economic future. The Berlin Wall was part of East Germany's strategy to stave off an economic disaster. The barrier was 15 feet high, built of concrete, surrounded by live mines, and guarded by armed sentinels. These measures failed to keep East Germans from attempting to reach West Berlin, and over the years, nearly 5,000 people made it to West Germany. Another 5,000 were captured, and close to 200 were killed as they tried to escape East Berlin.

The Berlin Wall fell in 1989 along with the hard-line communist government of East Germany as democratic sentiment began to reach a critical mass throughout Eastern Europe. For the first time in decades, free movement between East Germany and West Germany was possible. **ASK:** Why do you think so many East Germans wanted to cross into West Berlin? *(Possible response: Many probably did not want to live in a communist state because they believed they would have more freedom and economic opportunity on the western side of the Berlin Wall. Others may have wanted to join family and loved ones in West Berlin.)*

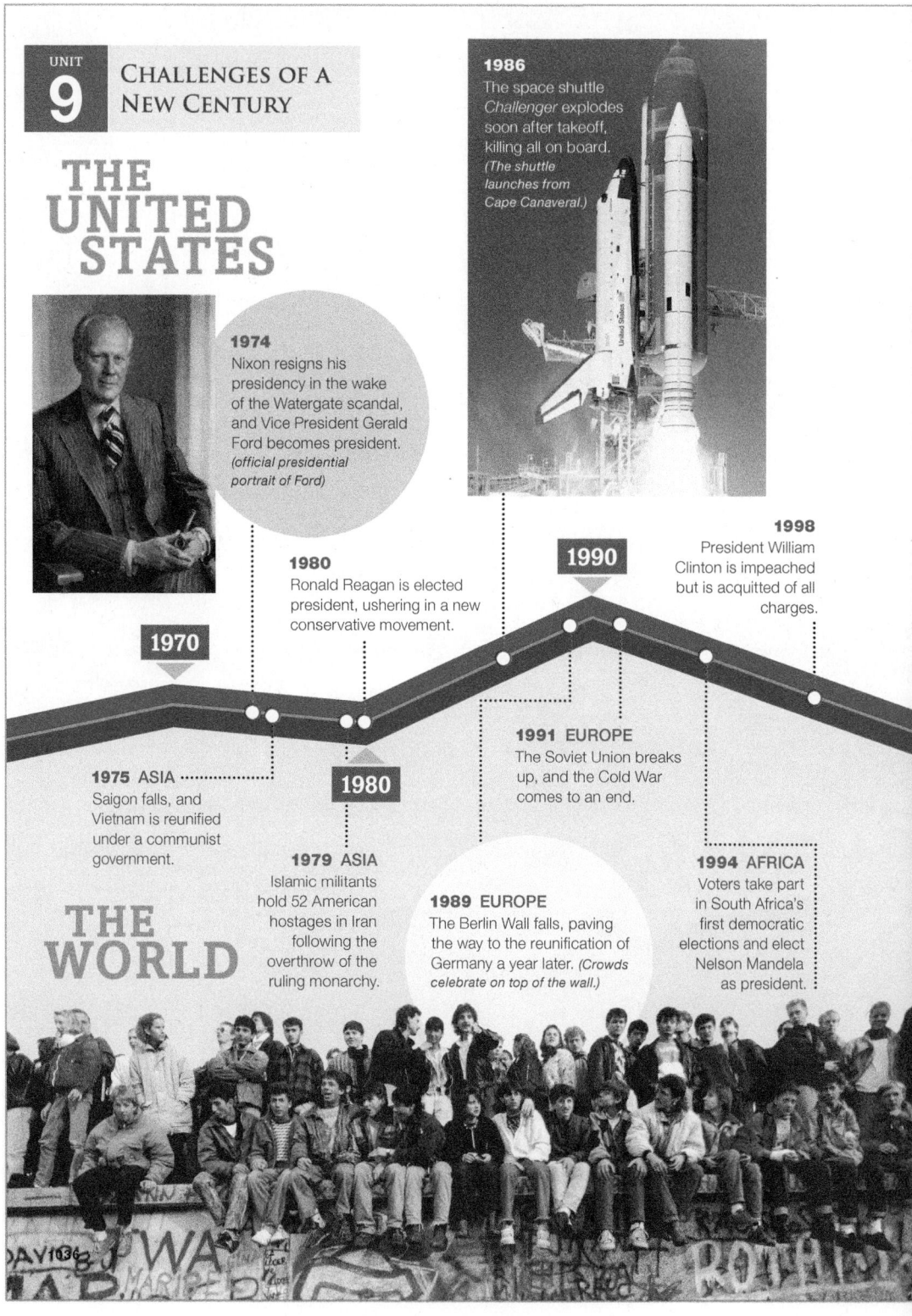

UNIT **9** CHALLENGES OF A NEW CENTURY

THE UNITED STATES

1986
The space shuttle *Challenger* explodes soon after takeoff, killing all on board. *(The shuttle launches from Cape Canaveral.)*

1974
Nixon resigns his presidency in the wake of the Watergate scandal, and Vice President Gerald Ford becomes president. *(official presidential portrait of Ford)*

1980
Ronald Reagan is elected president, ushering in a new conservative movement.

1998
President William Clinton is impeached but is acquitted of all charges.

1970

1990

1975 ASIA
Saigon falls, and Vietnam is reunified under a communist government.

1980

1979 ASIA
Islamic militants hold 52 American hostages in Iran following the overthrow of the ruling monarchy.

1989 EUROPE
The Berlin Wall falls, paving the way to the reunification of Germany a year later. *(Crowds celebrate on top of the wall.)*

1991 EUROPE
The Soviet Union breaks up, and the Cold War comes to an end.

1994 AFRICA
Voters take part in South Africa's first democratic elections and elect Nelson Mandela as president.

THE WORLD

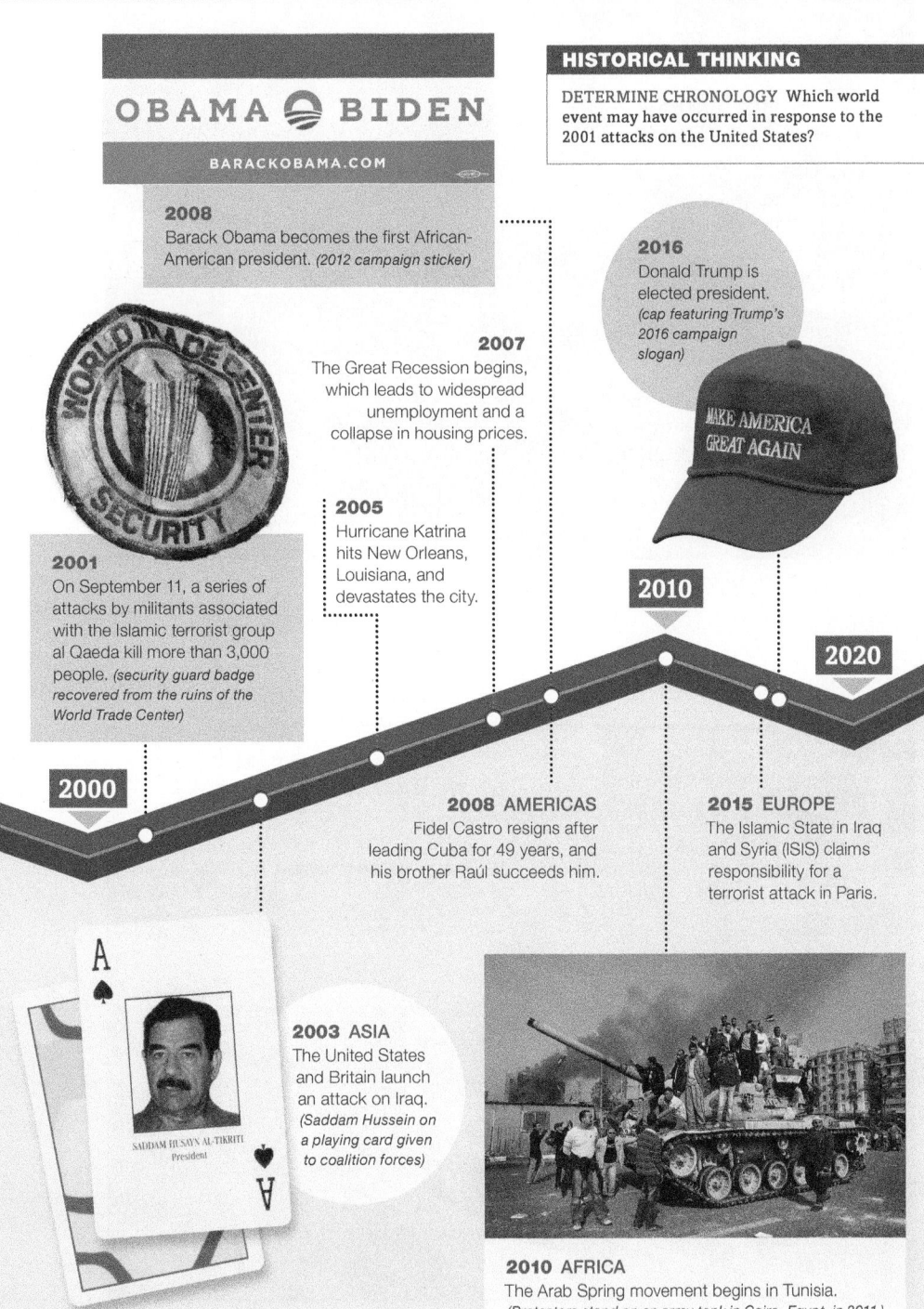

OBAMA BIDEN
BARACKOBAMA.COM

2008
Barack Obama becomes the first African-American president. *(2012 campaign sticker)*

2007
The Great Recession begins, which leads to widespread unemployment and a collapse in housing prices.

2005
Hurricane Katrina hits New Orleans, Louisiana, and devastates the city.

2001
On September 11, a series of attacks by militants associated with the Islamic terrorist group al Qaeda kill more than 3,000 people. *(security guard badge recovered from the ruins of the World Trade Center)*

2000

2003 ASIA
The United States and Britain launch an attack on Iraq. *(Saddam Hussein on a playing card given to coalition forces)*

SADDAM HUSAYN AL-TIKRITI
President

HISTORICAL THINKING

DETERMINE CHRONOLOGY Which world event may have occurred in response to the 2001 attacks on the United States?

2016
Donald Trump is elected president. *(cap featuring Trump's 2016 campaign slogan)*

MAKE AMERICA GREAT AGAIN

2010

2020

2008 AMERICAS
Fidel Castro resigns after leading Cuba for 49 years, and his brother Raúl succeeds him.

2015 EUROPE
The Islamic State in Iraq and Syria (ISIS) claims responsibility for a terrorist attack in Paris.

2010 AFRICA
The Arab Spring movement begins in Tunisia.
(Protesters stand on an army tank in Cairo, Egypt, in 2011.)

1037

INTRODUCE TIME LINE EVENT

2010 AFRICA: THE ARAB SPRING BEGINS

In 2010, in a small town in Tunisia, local police demanded that a young fruit and vegetable peddler named Mohamed Bouazizi show them a permit for his cart. The young man had no such permit. When the police went to take the cart from Bouazizi, he refused to give it up. A police officer slapped him across the face, and the public humiliation enraged the young man. A short time later, Bouazizi stepped in front of a government building and set himself on fire. This act of suicidal protest struck a chord with many in the town, engendering other protests. The demonstrators used cell phones to record the protests and posted the videos to the Internet and shared them on social media. Many of the videos went viral, and soon demonstrations against the authoritarian government were taking place across the country.

As protests for democracy and against authoritarian rule grew, Tunisians began to call for their president to step down. He did so a month later and escaped from the country. The success of the protest movement in Tunisia sparked similar movements all over the Middle East, including in Egypt, Libya, Syria, and Yemen. Together, the international protest movements became known as the Arab Spring. **ASK:** What role did technology play in the Arab Spring? *(Possible response: Without cell phone technology, protesters could not have recorded and immediately posted photographs and videos to the Internet and shared their plight with like-minded people in other Arab countries.)*

HISTORICAL THINKING

DETERMINE CHRONOLOGY

In 2003, as a response to the attacks of September 11, 2001, the United States and Great Britain launched an attack on Iraq.

AMERICAN STORIES ONLINE | **The Iran Hostage Crisis**

- Study Primary Sources: A hostage's comments about the experience of returning home after the crisis ended
- On Your Feet: Numbered Heads

NG Learning Framework:
Negotiate a Deal

SECTION 1 RESOURCES

NIXON'S PRESIDENCY

LESSON 1.1
Nixon's Comeback

- On Your Feet: Take a Stand

NG Learning Framework:
Analyze the Influence of Television

LESSON 1.2
Nixon's New Federalism

- On Your Feet: Rank the Accomplishments

NG Learning Framework:
Understand School Integration

LESSON 1.3
Protecting the Environment

 **AMERICAN GALLERY ONLINE** Saving the Earth

NG Learning Framework:
Research and Debate Environmental Issues

American Voices Biography
Rachel Carson ONLINE

LESSON 1.4
THROUGH THE LENS
Paul Nicklen

- On Your Feet: Compare Viewpoints

NG Learning Framework:
Explore the Impact of an Image

LESSON 1.5
The Watergate Scandal

- On Your Feet: Create a Sequence Chain

NG Learning Framework:
Discuss the Power of the Presidency

SECTION 2 RESOURCES

FORD, CARTER, AND ECONOMIC BLUES

LESSON 2.1
Ford Succeeds Nixon

- On Your Feet: Identify Problems and Solutions

NG Learning Framework:
Construct and Test a Hypothesis

LESSON 2.2
Carter and the Energy Crisis

- Active History: Analyze Steps to Peace

NG Learning Framework:
Conduct a Cost-Benefit Analysis

LESSON 2.3
Hostages in Iran

- On Your Feet: Create an Annotated Time Line

NG Learning Framework:
Connect Past and Present

CHAPTER 29 REVIEW

STRIVING READERS

STRATEGY ①
SEQUENCE EVENTS

Encourage students to note critical events and their relationship to one another in time in a Sequence Chain like the one shown. Arrange students in pairs and ask them to tell their partner about each event, why it is important, and how it had an impact on the next event in the chain.

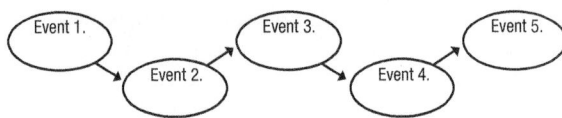

Use with Lessons 1.3, 1.5, 2.2, and 2.3 *Suggest that students use the Sequence Chain to trace the sequence of events leading to the modern environmental movement (1.3), to Nixon's resignation (1.5), to the Camp David Peace Accords (2.2), and to the Iran hostage crisis (2.3).*

STRATEGY ②
ANALYZE MAIN IDEAS

Direct students to read the Main Idea statements for each lesson aloud and explain that they identify and summarize the key idea for each lesson. Encourage students to write the Main Idea statements in their notebooks and, as they read the lessons, to make notes about details in the text that connect to the statements. Tell students that this process will help them identify and remember the most important information in each lesson.

Use with All Lessons

STRATEGY ③
CREATE IDEA WEBS

Have students summarize the chapter by creating three Idea Webs, one each for Nixon's, Ford's, and Carter's presidencies. As they read the lessons, instruct students to complete each Idea Web with relevant information about the president and his domestic and foreign accomplishments and challenges.

Use with All Lessons *For example, for Nixon's presidency, students could add the following: enacts progressive civil rights, welfare, environment, and workplace safety reforms; opens relationship with China; signs Strategic Arms Limitation Talks; resigns as a result of the Watergate scandal.*

INCLUSION

STRATEGY ①
PROVIDE TERMS AND NAMES ON AUDIO

Decide which of the terms and names are important for mastery and ask a volunteer to record the pronunciations and a short sentence defining each one. Encourage students to listen to the recording as often as necessary.

Use with All Lessons *You might also use the recordings to quiz students on their mastery of the terms. Play one definition at a time from the recording and ask students to identify the term or name described.*

STRATEGY ②
DESCRIBE LESSON VISUALS

Pair students who are visually impaired with students who are not. Ask the latter to describe the visuals in the lesson, read the captions, and answer questions their partner may have. Students might capture information about each photograph in a graphic organizer like the one below. Then have students work together to answer any Critical Viewing questions in the lesson.

Photograph		
Detail	**Detail**	**Detail**

Use with All Lessons *In addition to the photographs in each lesson, inclusion students may need assistance with the maps in Lessons 1.1 and 2.2 and the charts in Lessons 1.2 and 2.1.*

ENGLISH LANGUAGE LEARNERS ELD

STRATEGY ❶
USE DEFINITION MAPS

Pair students at the **Emerging** level with those at the **Expanding** and **Bridging** levels. Have them use a Definition Map, such as the one shown, to help them understand unfamiliar words and terms in the lesson. Encourage students to discuss the words and terms and clear up any misunderstandings. Encourage pairs to exchange and compare their responses and to use a dictionary to resolve discrepancies.

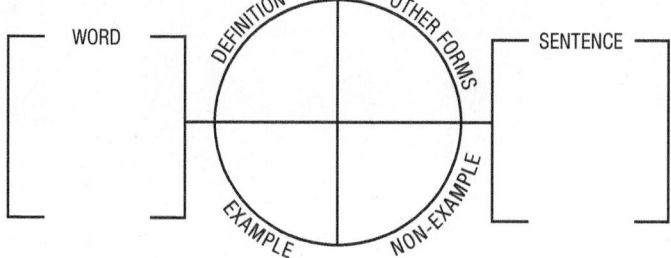

Use with All Lessons

STRATEGY ❷
CREATE SENTENCE STRIPS

Choose a paragraph from the lesson and make sentence strips from it. Read the paragraph aloud while students follow along in their books. Tell students to close their books and give them the set of sentence strips. Students should put the strips in order and then read the paragraph aloud.

Use with All Lessons *Before reading, ask students at the* ***Emerging*** *level to read sentence strips aloud. Then ask them to point out meaningful words in each sentence.*

STRATEGY ❸
USE PAIRED READING

Pair students at the **Expanding** and **Bridging** levels to read passages from the text aloud.

1. Partner 1 reads a passage; Partner 2 retells the passage in his or her own words.

2. Partner 2 reads a different passage; Partner 1 retells it.

3. Pairs repeat the process, switching roles.

Use with All Lessons

GIFTED & TALENTED

STRATEGY ❶
CREATE A MULTIMEDIA PRESENTATION

Instruct students to use multiple online sources to access historians' analyses of the legacy of President Nixon, Ford, or Carter. Tell students to focus on lasting impacts, such as Nixon's environmental and workplace protections, Ford's plan to fight stagflation, and Carter's pursuit of peace and human rights through the Carter Center. Students should use an online presentation tool, relevant photographs, videos, charts, and other visuals. Invite students to share their presentations with the class and answer questions.

Use with Lessons 1.2, 1.5, and 2.1–2.3

STRATEGY ❷
TEACH A CLASS

Before beginning the chapter, allow students to choose one of the lessons and prepare to teach the content to the class. Give them a set amount of time in which to present their lesson. Suggest that students think about any visuals or activities they will want to use when they teach.

Use with All Lessons

PRE-AP

STRATEGY ❶
WRITE AN EDITORIAL

Encourage students to write an editorial in which they comment on a connection between an event in this chapter and a current or recent event in U.S. domestic or foreign affairs. Students could connect Nixon's abuses of power with a distrusted politician or Carter's support of renewable energy with current climate change concerns and energy policies. Tell students to locate present-day statistics and expert opinions to reference in their editorials. Instruct students to post their editorials on a school website and to submit them to local newspapers for publication.

Use with All Lessons

STRATEGY ❷
EXPLORE LONG-TERM CONSEQUENCES

Direct students to research and evaluate various historians' analyses of the consequences and repercussions of past U.S.-Iran policies. Tell students to use the analyses to write an essay on the long-term impacts of the U.S. support of the shah of Iran, focusing on the Iran hostage crisis and the relationship between the two nations since then. Instruct students to conclude their essay with what they consider to be the most important lessons learned. Invite students to share their research essays with the class.

Use with Lesson 2.3

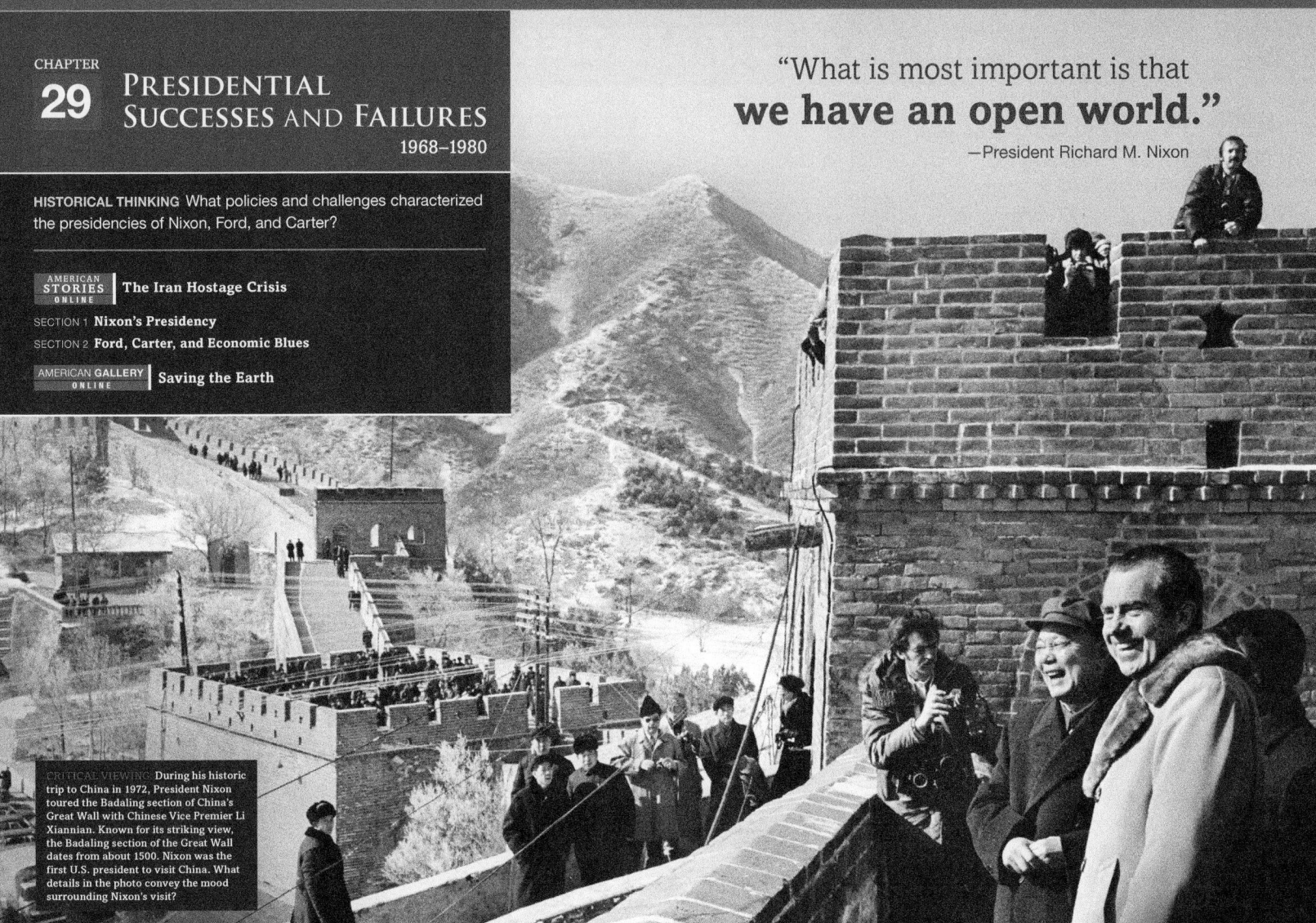

HISTORICAL THINKING What policies and challenges characterized the presidencies of Nixon, Ford, and Carter?

AMERICAN STORIES ONLINE **The Iran Hostage Crisis**

SECTION 1 **Nixon's Presidency**

SECTION 2 **Ford, Carter, and Economic Blues**

AMERICAN GALLERY ONLINE **Saving the Earth**

"What is most important is that **we have an open world.**"
—President Richard M. Nixon

CRITICAL VIEWING During his historic trip to China in 1972, President Nixon toured the Badaling section of China's Great Wall with Chinese Vice Premier Li Xiannian. Known for its striking view, the Badaling section of the Great Wall dates from about 1500. Nixon was the first U.S. president to visit China. What details in the photo convey the mood surrounding Nixon's visit?

1038 CHAPTER 29

Presidential Successes and Failures 1039

INTRODUCE THE PHOTOGRAPH

A WORLD WITHOUT WALLS

Nixon's visit to the Great Wall occurred on the fourth day of his historic visit to China. The president and first lady, accompanied by the secretary of state and a few Chinese officials, spent an hour at the site. In an exchange with reporters, Nixon praised the Great Wall and those who built it, but he expressed the hope that walls, whether physical or ideological, would not divide the world's peoples. **ASK:** Based on the photograph, how did the setting enhance Nixon's message? *(Possible response: The Great Wall is a magnificent structure, which Nixon acknowledged by praising Chinese achievements and culture. However, he also used the wall as a symbol of something that divides people. Nixon then invited the Chinese to engage in his political mission of establishing an open world.)*

SHARE BACKGROUND

The media played a major role in Nixon's visit to China. The president strongly preferred television coverage over print because it would give American audiences a window into the sites on the itinerary. TV cameras followed Mrs. Nixon as she visited schools, workplaces, and medical facilities, and both American and Chinese media provided extensive footage of Nixon shaking hands with Chinese leaders and toasting his hosts at formal banquets. As Nixon hoped, criticism of the visit was drowned out as the television coverage projected a clear message that a cordial relationship had been forged between China and the United States.

CRITICAL VIEWING Possible response: President Nixon and the Chinese vice premier appear relaxed and pleased with the visit. The Chinese and American onlookers seem curious, and many have cameras to capture the historic event. Overall, the mood is positive and optimistic.

For Chapter 29 Spanish Resources, visit the Resources Menu. Chapter 29 Resources are available at NGLSync.Cengage.com.

HISTORICAL THINKING QUESTION

What policies and challenges characterized the presidencies of Nixon, Ford, and Carter?

Think, Pair, Share Activity: Predict Challenges and Policies Divide the class into groups of four and have them count off within each group. Pose the following question: What challenges of the 1960s caused Americans to be concerned about the future of the country? Instruct group members to think about the question and then discuss their answers. Then tell groups to propose a presidential policy to address one of the challenges. Call out a number and have the person with that number in each group summarize the group's discussion for the class. Create a chart on the board on which students list the challenges and proposed policies. As students read Chapter 29, have them revisit their chart and revise it to reflect the challenges and policies that characterized the presidencies of Nixon, Ford, and Carter.

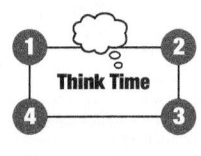
Think Time

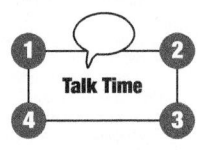
Talk Time

Share 2's Time

INTRODUCE THE READING STRATEGY

IDENTIFY MAIN IDEAS AND DETAILS

Explain that identifying main ideas and details helps students recognize important concepts and enables them to locate supporting evidence for answers or arguments. Ask them to turn to the Chapter Review and preview the graphic organizer. As students read the chapter, encourage them to identify main ideas and supporting details about the topics.

KEY DATES FOR CHAPTER 29

1968	Richard Nixon elected president
1970	First Earth Day celebration; EPA created
1972	President Nixon visits China
1973	United States withdraws troops from Vietnam
1973	OPEC oil embargo begins
1974	Nixon resigns; Gerald R. Ford becomes president
1975	Ford signs Helsinki Accords
1976	Jimmy Carter elected president
1978	Camp David Accords
1979	Americans taken hostage in Iran

INTRODUCE CHAPTER VOCABULARY

KEY VOCABULARY

SECTION 1

antiballistic missile (ABM)	détente	silent majority
	executive privilege	Watergate break-in
cover-up	New Federalism	wiretapping
DDT	overregulation	

SECTION 2

economic stagnation	malaise	stagflation
Islamic republic		

DEFINITION CHART

As they read the chapter, have students complete a Definition Chart for Key Vocabulary terms. Tell students to list Key Vocabulary in the left column and, as they encounter each term in the chapter, write the definition in the center column. In the right column they can write an explanation of the definition in their own words. Model an example for students on the board using the graphic organizer below.

Word	Definition	In My Own Words
détente	an easing of tensions and an improvement in relations between countries	establishing friendlier relations between two or more nations

AMERICAN STORIES ONLINE

For instructional support for the online American Story "The Iran Hostage Crisis," go to NGLSync. Cengage.com.

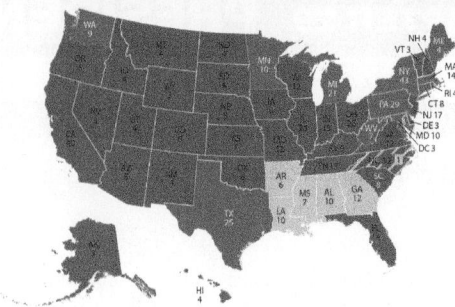

The 1968 Election

Richard Nixon, Republican
Electoral Vote: 301 votes, 55.9%
Popular Vote: 31,785,480 votes, 43.4%

Hubert Humphrey, Democrat
Electoral Vote: 191 votes, 35.5%
Popular Vote: 31,275,166 votes, 42.7%

George Wallace, Independent
Electoral Vote: 46 votes, 8.4%
Popular Vote: 9,906,473 votes, 13.5%

NIXON'S COMEBACK

Have you ever achieved something important because you refused to give up and simply kept trying? Despite setbacks, Richard Nixon did not give up his quest for the presidency, and in 1968, his perseverance paid off.

NIXON'S RISE, FALL, AND RISE

In the months leading up to the 1968 election, many Americans were anxious about the state of the country. The assassinations of Martin Luther King, Jr., and Robert Kennedy, ongoing demonstrations against the Vietnam War, and changing cultural values left people feeling the country was out of control.

Richard Nixon was a familiar name to most Americans, having served as President Eisenhower's vice president from 1953 to 1961. The son of Quaker parents living in California, Nixon had excelled in academics and debate. After law school, he took a government job, which he left to serve in the U.S. Navy during World War II. After the war, Republican Party leaders suggested he run for a Congressional seat in California, which he won. Nixon appeared to be a rising star in the party.

As a member of Congress, Nixon gained a reputation for being tough on communism. His participation in the trial of Alger Hiss, a suspected Russian spy, in 1949 helped him win a seat in the U.S. Senate in 1950. Just two years later, Dwight Eisenhower chose Nixon as his vice-presidential running mate. However, trouble emerged during the campaign when some critics accused Nixon of accepting an $18,000 campaign contribution and using it for his personal benefit. To silence these critics, Nixon went on national television and admitted to accepting one personal gift from a supporter—a dog, whom his young daughter named Checkers. The speech won over the public.

After serving eight years as Eisenhower's loyal vice president, Nixon seemed destined to win the White House in 1960. As you have read, however, he narrowly lost that election to John F. Kennedy. Two years later, he lost the California governor's race. Many observers thought Nixon's political career was over. In fact, after his defeat, a bitter Nixon told reporters, "You won't have Nixon to kick around anymore."

PRIMARY SOURCE

After being accused of spending campaign money on private expenses, Richard Nixon addressed the nation, claiming that the only gift he had received was a dog named Checkers.

We did get something, a gift, after the election. A man down in Texas heard . . . that our two youngsters would like to have a dog, and, believe it or not . . . we got a message from Union Station in Baltimore, saying they had a package for us. It was a little cocker spaniel dog . . . black and white, spotted, and our little girl Tricia, the six year old, named it Checkers. And you know, the kids, like all kids, loved the dog, and . . . we are going to keep it.

—from Richard Nixon's "Checkers" speech, September 23, 1952

With no political office to keep him in California, Nixon moved to New York City, where he practiced law and successfully rebuilt his reputation by assisting Republican candidates in their campaigns. Despite his election failures, he was regarded as a knowledgeable and experienced politician. After the Republicans lost the 1964 national election, their leaders turned to Nixon, hoping he could regain the White House in 1968. They felt voters were dissatisfied with reform-minded Democrats. Nixon chose Quaker Governor **Spiro T. Agnew** of Maryland as his running mate. Agnew was a moderate who supported civil rights but advocated a tough stance on crime. Nixon hoped Agnew would increase the ticket's appeal to both moderate and conservative voters.

THE 1968 ELECTION

The year 1968 marked the beginning of a swing toward conservatism that would last for several decades. Many Americans were upset with the excesses of the 1960s, including the counterculture, illegal drug use, and rising crime rates in cities. In his campaign, Nixon tapped into these feelings of insecurity and appealed to what he called the **silent majority**, those who are not actively involved in politics and do not voice their political opinions publicly. At this time, the silent majority consisted of moderate voters who wanted the United States to take a more stable and conservative course.

At the Republican National Convention, Nixon promised to make law and order his top priority at home and to bring "peace with honor" to Vietnam. The Democrats, on the other hand, were divided over the war in Vietnam, and antiwar protesters were upset with the nomination of Vice President Hubert Humphrey as the Democratic candidate. Demonstrations turned violent outside the

Democratic National Convention in Chicago when police officers clashed with protesters. The clashes gave Nixon an advantage with voters who wanted a more peaceful country.

To attract even more voters, Nixon's campaign also targeted people in the southern states who historically voted for Democrats. His southern strategy appealed to white southerners who were disappointed with Democratic support of the civil rights movement. If Nixon could turn these southern states Republican, he stood an excellent chance of winning the election.

However, for the first time since 1948, there was a serious third-party candidate: former Alabama governor George Wallace. Wallace was a segregationist, and now he based his platform on his opposition to civil rights. Wallace proved popular among the white southern voters Nixon had hoped to attract. While these voters rejected Humphrey's support of civil rights, they also did not favor Nixon, who was neither pro-civil rights nor a segregationist. Wallace ended up winning five southern states, but Nixon still won the election.

HISTORICAL THINKING

1. **READING CHECK** Why did some experts believe that Richard Nixon's political career was over by the early 1960s?

2. **ANALYZE CAUSE AND EFFECT** Describe the complex cause-and-effect relationship between the political situation in the country, Nixon's campaign platform, and his victory in the 1968 presidential election.

3. **INTERPRET MAPS** What effect did Wallace's third-party candidacy have on the 1968 election?

PLAN: 2-PAGE LESSON

OBJECTIVE

Understand the events and strategies that contributed to Richard Nixon's political reemergence and winning of the presidency.

CRITICAL THINKING SKILLS FOR LESSON 1.1

- Analyze Cause and Effect
- Interpret Maps
- Identify Main Ideas and Details
- Synthesize
- Analyze Primary Sources

HISTORICAL THINKING FOR CHAPTER 29

What policies and challenges characterized the presidencies of Ford, Nixon, and Carter? The 1968 election signaled a shift in American politics. Lesson 1.1 explores Richard Nixon's background, campaign strategy, and governmental philosophy— all of which influenced how he confronted the challenges of his presidency.

BACKGROUND FOR THE TEACHER

Nixon referred to his televised address as the "Fund Speech" because he considered the "Checkers" title demeaning to his message. Yet, his remarks about the little black and white spotted dog became the most memorable part of the 30-minute speech. Viewed by 60 million people, the "Checkers" speech, which some have called one of the most significant of the 20th century, was remarkable for several reasons. The setting, with Mrs. Nixon seated in an armchair while her husband spoke to the nation, made it seem as if the Nixons were visiting viewers' homes. The speech also incorporated middle-class values that helped change the elitist image of Republicans. Finally, it ushered in an era in American politics in which television became an important medium that provided voters with a new perspective on candidates and elected officials.

INTRODUCE & ENGAGE

CREATE A QUESTIONNAIRE

Challenge students to create a questionnaire to determine the qualifications of a potential presidential candidate. First, direct students to determine categories, such as background, education, experience, attitudes, or stances on specific issues. Then have volunteers develop questions for each category. Post the questions on the board. After students have read the lesson, ask them to revisit the questionnaire and determine Richard Nixon's qualifications for the presidency.

TEACH

GUIDED DISCUSSION

1. **Identify Main Ideas and Details** What details support the following main idea: Nixon experienced success and failures in his political life? *(Nixon successfully served as a congressman, senator, and vice president. However, before being elected as president in 1968, Nixon was accused of using campaign funds inappropriately, lost the presidential election of 1960, and lost his bid for governor of California.)*

2. **Synthesize** How did views on civil rights influence the 1968 election? *(Possible responses: Democratic candidate Hubert Humphrey supported civil rights, and third-party candidate George Wallace was a segregationist. Nixon took the middle ground and won the election, with white southerners supporting Wallace and depriving the Democrats of a needed constituency.)*

ANALYZE PRIMARY SOURCES

Direct students' attention to the Primary Source feature and ask them to read Nixon's speech. **ASK:** What personal characteristics does Nixon portray in the excerpt from the "Checkers" speech? *(Possible response: He presents himself as a humble, honest man and a caring, loving father.)* **ASK:** Why do you think the speech won over the American public? *(Possible responses: Nixon connected with the audience on a personal level. He spoke of topics with universal appeal, such as the kindness of providing a gift to his children, the bond between children and pets, and the determination of a parent to protect his or her child from pain or heartache.)*

ACTIVE OPTIONS

On Your Feet: Take a Stand Label the four corners of the room with one of the following topics: Appeal to the silent majority; Promise to end Vietnam War with "peace and honor"; Influence of Wallace's third-party candidacy; Clashes between police and protesters at Democratic Convention. Ask students which factor had the greatest influence on Nixon's election in 1968. Instruct them to gather in the corner of their choice and to discuss their reasons. Then invite one member from each group to summarize the group's discussion for the class.

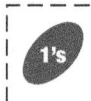

NG Learning Framework: Analyze the Influence of Television

SKILL Communication

KNOWLEDGE Our Human Story

Provide an opportunity for students to watch a video of Nixon's televised "Checkers" speech. Remind students that television was a relatively new medium in 1952. Ask them to pay attention to Nixon's use of the medium to influence the audience. Divide students into small groups and ask them to discuss the following questions: What techniques did Nixon use to convince viewers that he was not guilty of misusing campaign funds? Do you think television saved Nixon's career in 1952? Do you think Nixon's televised speech would be as effective today as it was when it was delivered? Provide an opportunity for representatives of each group to share their group's analysis with the class.

DIFFERENTIATE

STRIVING READERS

Create and Annotate a Time Line To help students understand the path that brought Nixon to the presidency, instruct them to note important dates on a time line as they read the lesson. (You may provide them with the dates 1949, 1950, 1953–60, 1960, 1962, and 1968, if needed.) Then have students reread the text, inserting dates and adding details into the time line. Suggest that students use a highlighter to make an upward or downward slanting arrow over particular date ranges to indicate the time periods corresponding to Nixon's rise, fall, and subsequent rise. Invite students to compare their time lines and make changes or additions.

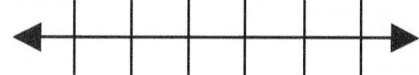

PRE-AP

Analyze Rhetorical Devices Instruct students to find the complete text of Nixon's "Checkers" speech. Tell them to read it closely a number of times and analyze Nixon's use of rhetorical devices and appeals. Ask students to note Nixon's appeal to facts and data as well as emotion. Tell students to conclude their analysis by stating how the public reacted to the speech, how it impacted Nixon's career, and how it marked a turning point in the way politicians use television. Invite volunteers to share their analytical reports with the class.

See the Chapter Planner for more strategies for differentiation.

HISTORICAL THINKING

ANSWERS

1. Nixon had lost the presidential election in 1960 and the election for California governor in 1962.

2. Americans' dissatisfaction with the liberal politics and culture of the 1960s opened the door for a conservative. Nixon capitalized by downplaying civil rights, promising to bring law and order, and pledging to end the Vietnam War.

3. Wallace's third-party candidacy split the Democratic vote, allowing Nixon to win some traditionally Democratic states, such as North and South Carolina.

Nixon's New Federalism

Some presidents are easy to categorize as being either conservative, moderate, or liberal. But Richard Nixon is difficult to pigeonhole. His actions covered the entire political spectrum.

NIXON'S DOMESTIC POLICIES

President Nixon advocated a number of reforms in welfare policy, civil rights, and other areas. In 1970, he requested a bill be introduced in Congress called the **Family Assistance Plan (FAP)**. The plan provided direct cash payments to those in need, while requiring participants to work or receive job training. Conservative members of Congress opposed the idea of the government supporting unemployed people. Liberal Congress members thought the minimum household income in order to qualify for Nixon's plan was too low. Because of these and other dissenting views, Congress never passed the FAP.

Also in 1970, Nixon signed amendments that renewed the Voting Rights Act of 1965, which protected African-American voters at the polls by prohibiting literacy tests. Even though African Americans had the right to vote, many still experienced discrimination and intimidation at polling stations, which kept a number of them away from the polls. After Nixon's renewal of the act, the number

of African-American voters fully participating in the election process increased. Nixon also issued an executive order supporting affirmative action, which aimed to improve job opportunities for minorities. However, many white citizens opposed the order, believing it was a form of reverse racism, or prejudice against white people.

Nixon supported other progressive reforms. For example, he approved legislation that provided automatic cost-of-living adjustments for Social Security recipients. He also signed the bill that established the **Occupational Safety and Health Administration (OSHA)**, which enforces workplace safety standards.

Although he supported some progressive measures, Nixon believed the federal government had assumed too much responsibility for social problems. In 1972, Nixon signed legislation to return some of the authority of the federal government to state and local governments. He created a five-year revenue sharing plan, which required the federal government to collect taxes and then distribute the money directly to state and local governments. The system allowed those governments to allocate, or give out, money to the programs that benefited their constituents most. Nixon called his tax plan the **New Federalism**.

SCHOOL DESEGREGATION

By 1971, Nixon had the rare opportunity to appoint four Supreme Court justices. In 1969, he chose **Warren E. Burger**, a moderate Republican, as chief justice. His other three appointees were conservatives. Some politicians were concerned that Nixon's conservative appointments would shift the Supreme Court radically to the right, but the Burger Court proved more independent than expected.

PRIMARY SOURCE

The Voting Rights Act of 1965 has opened participation in the political process. In the 5 years since its enactment, close to 1 million Negroes have been registered to vote for the first time and more than 400 Negro officials have been elected to local and State offices. These are more than election statistics; they are statistics of hope and dramatic evidence that the American system works. They stand as an answer to those who claim that there is no recourse except to the streets.

—from Richard Nixon's Voting Rights Act Amendments signing speech, 1970

In 1970, two Cincinnati school districts agreed to a busing plan in which African-American children from one district would attend the predominantly white schools of the other. Second graders in one of the newly merged schools say the Pledge of Allegiance together to begin their school day.

Nixon stated that he opposed school segregation, which the Court had found unconstitutional in 1954. However, in one case, his administration won a request in a lower court to allow 33 Mississippi school districts to postpone their school desegregation plans. In a 1969 ruling, the Burger Court overturned the lower court ruling and ordered the immediate desegregation of the Mississippi school districts.

However, the Burger Court went on to issue mixed decisions on the use of forced busing to eliminate *de facto* segregation. *De facto* segregation of schools still existed because children attended neighborhood schools, and neighborhoods were not integrated. In 1964, an African-American couple in Charlotte, North Carolina, Vera and Darius Swann, tried to enroll their son in an integrated public school. The Swanns lived in the attendance area of a school in which all the students were African American, but the integrated school was actually closer to their home. The Swanns' request was denied, and the NAACP brought the case to a federal court on their behalf.

In 1969, the court ruled in favor of the Swanns and went further by requiring the Charlotte-Mecklenburg school district to implement a busing program to integrate its schools. As you have read, in the landmark case of *Swann* v. *Charlotte-Mecklenburg Board of Education*, the Supreme Court upheld the lower court's ruling. The ruling also granted the federal courts broad powers in ordering and overseeing school desegregation.

The *Swann* ruling changed, however, in 1974 after the Court's decision on *Milliken* v. *Bradley*. In that case, the NAACP had sued the state of Michigan for failure to desegregate Detroit-area schools. Most African-American families lived in the city, so a desegregation plan would require busing students to suburban areas, which would be similar to the plan in Charlotte. In *Milliken*, however, the Court ruled that the federal government could not force the local government to bus students across school districts' boundaries. The decision shifted most of the responsibility for carrying out integration back to local communities.

OBJECTIVE

Describe the domestic reforms and foreign policy of the Nixon administration.

CRITICAL THINKING SKILLS FOR LESSON 1.2

- Synthesize
- Make Inferences
- Interpret Graphs
- Compare and Contrast
- Make Connections
- Analyze Primary Sources
- Draw Conclusions
- Categorize

HISTORICAL THINKING FOR CHAPTER 29

What policies and challenges characterized the presidencies of Nixon, Ford, and Carter? Nixon faced social and economic challenges as well as foreign policy concerns. Lesson 1.2 discusses how he initiated reforms at home and worked on issues in China, the Soviet Union, and the Middle East.

BACKGROUND FOR THE TEACHER

The Yom Kippur War—which resulted in tense relationships and boundary disputes between Israel and its neighbors—provided the United States with an opportunity to negotiate peace in the Middle East. While Nixon was preoccupied with matters at home, Secretary of State Kissinger embarked on multiple short trips among capitals in the Middle East (a technique dubbed "shuttle diplomacy") in an attempt to broker a deal between Egypt, Syria, and Israel. Quickly, the U.S. secretary of state successfully negotiated an agreement between Egypt and Israel. However, finding common ground between Israel and Syria proved much more difficult. Separate prenegotiation meetings with both sides took place in Washington for several weeks. Then Kissinger traveled to Israel for almost a month of tense negotiations before Syria and Israel finally signed an agreement. In the end, shuttle diplomacy had established a reasonable stability among Israel and its neighbors.

INTRODUCE & ENGAGE

GRAPH THE POLITICAL SPECTRUM

Draw an arrow on the board and ask students to review the political spectrum. Label the arrow with conservatives on the right, liberals on the left, and moderates in the middle. **ASK:** What are the characteristics of each political ideology? *(Possible response: Conservatives favor tradition, less government, and a free market. Liberals favor progress, a government that takes responsibility for citizens' welfare, and a regulated market. Moderates favor a mix of ideas from both sides.)* List students' responses on the scale, making clarifications or corrections as necessary. Tell students that in this lesson they will examine how Nixon straddled the lines among these ideologies.

TEACH

GUIDED DISCUSSION

1. **Compare and Contrast** How was Nixon's New Federalism similar and different from previous programs such as the New Deal or the Great Society? *(Possible response: While all three of these programs attempted to offer direct relief to people in need, Nixon's program gave the states the ability to decide how to allocate and distribute funds, which previously had been handled by the federal government.)*

2. **Make Inferences** What reason might Nixon's administration have had for requesting that some Mississippi school districts be allowed to postpone desegregation plans? *(Answers will vary. Possible responses: Nixon won the election in part due to support from states in the south. The request for postponement may have been a gesture of gratitude, since it's likely that Mississippi school districts did not want to desegregate. Nixon's administration may have feared violent resistance to desegregating schools in those districts and wanted to let surrounding areas desegregate their schools first.)*

3. **Make Connections** How were the *Swann* and *Milliken* decisions connected to *Brown* v. *Board of Education*? *(While* Brown *declared segregated schools unconstitutional, it did not specifically explain how to desegregate. This issue was taken up both controversially and contradictorily in subsequent rulings.)*

ANALYZE PRIMARY SOURCES

Direct students' attention to the Primary Source feature. **ASK:** What evidence does Nixon use to argue the success of the Voting Rights Act and how does it speak to members of the silent majority? *(Nixon offers statistics to show that the Voting Rights Act has increased African-American voting numbers and representation in government. He also argues that the act offers an alternative to people taking recourse "to the streets"—the sort of action Nixon stood against and that was opposed by the silent majority.)*

DIFFERENTIATE

ENGLISH LANGUAGE LEARNERS ELD

Complete Sentence Frames Before students read the lesson, provide them with the sentence frames below. Then pair students at the **Emerging** level with those at the **Bridging** level and instruct them to take turns reading paragraphs of the lesson, using what they read to complete the sentence frames. After students have completed the sentence frames, have them compare their answers with another pair.

- Nixon's renewal of the Voting Rights Act increased _____ participation in elections. *(African-American)*

- Although Nixon appointed four Supreme Court justices, the court was more _____ than many people expected. *(independent)*

- Nixon wanted a closer relationship with China to _____. *(promote trade; achieve an alliance and a better bargaining position with the Soviet Union)*

- The Strategic Arms Limitation Talks eased the tension between the U.S. and _____ when both agreed to _____. *(the Soviet Union; limit their possession of long-range missiles)*

GIFTED & TALENTED

Create an Infographic Tell students that Nixon was a complicated person who did not fit into conventional categories of conservatism or liberalism. To illustrate this, have students conduct online research to learn more about Nixon's conservative and more liberal or progressive ideas and actions. Then have them illustrate these by creating a vertical or horizontal infographic, labeling one end conservative initiative, and the other liberal initiative, and placing Nixon's initiatives in the appropriate place. Students should use words and images to briefly annotate each initiative. Invite volunteers to post their infographics online or on the class bulletin board.

See the Chapter Planner for more strategies for differentiation.

NIXON'S FOREIGN POLICY

Nixon preferred to focus on foreign policy, where presidents sometimes have a more immediate and direct impact than they do on domestic affairs. As you have learned, Henry Kissinger was Nixon's national security advisor and secretary of state, and he aided the president in many diplomatic achievements. Nixon and Kissinger believed in a foreign policy based on realism, as opposed to idealism. They thought national interests, rather than such ideals as freedom and human rights, should dictate foreign policy. In Latin America and the Middle East, for example, they supported dictatorships that furthered U.S. interests.

One of Nixon's first moves as president was to take advantage of the growing divide between communist China and the Soviet Union. Nixon wanted a closer relationship with China for several reasons. He wanted to promote trade with China. He also hoped China, as an ally of North Vietnam, would help the United States achieve a peace settlement in Vietnam. In addition, a close relationship with China would strengthen the United States' bargaining position with the Soviet Union, who feared any alliance between the United States and China.

No American president had visited China or even officially talked with Chinese leaders since China became a communist state in 1949, partly because Nixon and other anti-communist leaders had opposed any contact. Nixon broke this taboo on February 22, 1972, becoming the first American president to visit China. The trip ended with a joint statement that promised closer relations between the two countries in trade, travel, and cultural exchange. Three months later, the president traveled to Moscow for a summit meeting with Soviet leader Leonid Brezhnev (LEHY-uh-nihd BREZH-nehf). Nixon believed that his successful trip to China, coupled with a declining Soviet economy, would make the Soviets more likely to strike serious deals with the United States on arms control and trade. Both countries possessed huge numbers of nuclear weapons that cost billions of dollars and increased the chances of nuclear war. In addition, the Soviets desperately needed grain, heavy equipment, and technical assistance. American farmers and manufacturers were eager to market these goods and services to the Soviet Union.

On May 22, 1972, the United States and the Soviet Union signed an agreement arising out of the **Strategic Arms Limitation Talks**. The agreement

President Nixon (center) already knew how to use chopsticks when he sat down with Premier Chou En-Lai (left) and Communist Party leader Chang Chun-Chiao (right) at a banquet in honor of his visit to China in 1972. Before the trip, Nixon had taken lessons on how to properly use chopsticks, hoping to make a good impression on his hosts.

TOWARD ENERGY INDEPENDENCE

Americans were already aware of the benefits of using less petroleum before the 1973 war between Israel and Egypt and Syria. Although the oil embargo of 1973 was short-lived, it served as a wakeup call that the United States was in a vulnerable position regarding its energy needs.

The Arab countries in OPEC that participated in the embargo provided only a small percentage of all the oil imported, but a decrease in supply of more than a million barrels a day still made a difference. Spurred on by the environmental movement and the development of new technologies, the United States began to work toward energy independence. While petroleum imports increased through the 1980s and 1990s, new sources of energy were being developed. These energy sources included shale oil, natural gas, and such renewables as wind and solar power. Experts think energy independence by 2035 may be an attainable goal for the United States.

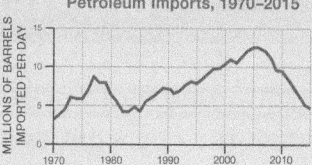

Petroleum Imports, 1970–2015

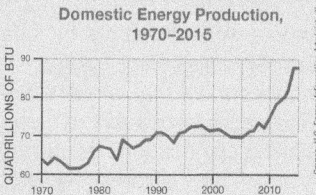

Domestic Energy Production, 1970–2015

Source: U.S. Energy Information Administration

became known as **SALT I**, and it limited the number of long-range offensive missiles both countries could possess. The two countries also signed an agreement to stop the production of **antiballistic missiles (ABMs)**—missiles designed to destroy other bomb-carrying missiles before they hit the ground—for the next five years. ABMs were a problem because their possession by one side or the other provided an advantage and increased the temptation for those owning them to attack first with their own weapons. Henry Kissinger helped negotiate these treaties, which taken together represented a breakthrough in Soviet-American relations. The Moscow summit provided a solid foundation for **détente** (day-TAHNT), or an easing of tension between countries.

Despite these successes, Nixon continued to face foreign policy challenges in the Middle East. War broke out in the Middle East on the Jewish holiday of Yom Kippur, October 6, 1973. Egypt and Syria attacked the predominantly Jewish country of Israel on two fronts. The United States supported Israel, a longtime ally, by airlifting vital military supplies. These supplies proved essential in helping Israel drive back the attack. The Yom Kippur War lasted less than three weeks and ended when United Nations officials negotiated a cease-fire.

To protest American support of Israel, certain Middle Eastern countries in the **Organization of**

Petroleum Exporting Countries (OPEC), a multinational organization that sets petroleum prices and policies, began an embargo, or official ban, on exports of oil to the United States. While Americans accounted for barely 6 percent of the world's population in 1974, they used more than 30 percent of the world's oil. Between 1968 and 1973, the United States' consumption of imported oil had tripled. The embargo created an immediate panic. It forced Americans to reduce their energy use and wait in long lines to buy high-priced gas for their cars. The oil embargo ended in April 1974, but oil costs continued to rise because OPEC had tripled its prices.

HISTORICAL THINKING

1. **READING CHECK** What was the New Federalism?

2. **SYNTHESIZE** Explain the connections between Nixon's trip to China and larger political and economic developments during his administration.

3. **MAKE INFERENCES** What did Nixon mean when he said that the increase in the number of African-American elected officials and registered voters was evidence that the American system worked?

4. **INTERPRET GRAPHS** How does the overall trend in petroleum imports from 1970 to 2015 compare with that of domestic energy production, and what significant change in the relationship between the two occurred in 2005?

BUILD BACKGROUND

PING-PONG AND PANDAS

In April 1971, while the U.S. Ping-Pong team was competing in the World Table Tennis Championship in Japan, members of the Chinese team extended an invitation to the Americans to visit their country. Thus, a group of Ping-Pong players, officials, and journalists became the first Americans permitted in China since the beginning of the communist regime in 1949. Premier Chou En-Lai welcomed the visitors with a banquet and provided them with opportunities to tour the Great Wall and other sites. Media coverage enabled the American public to share the visitors' experiences. The United States reciprocated with an invitation for the Chinese table-tennis team to visit and tour American cities. Ping-Pong diplomacy forged cultural ties between China and the United States and paved the way for President Nixon's visit in 1972.

Another cultural tie resulted when Mrs. Nixon told the Chinese premier how much she liked pandas, to which Chou En-Lai replied, "I'll give you some." The first pair of giant pandas arrived at the Smithsonian National Zoo in Washington, D.C., in April 1972. Ling-Ling and Hsing-Hsing became a popular attraction, drawing millions of visitors. That initial gift from China gave American scientists an opportunity to study pandas and made the United States a leader in their conservation. Through a series of agreements, the United States and China have continued to participate in "panda diplomacy." China now loans pandas to the United States in exchange for funds and expertise, which are used to conserve the animals' natural habitat.

TEACH

GUIDED DISCUSSION

4. Compare and Contrast What were the similarities and differences between Nixon's goals in China and in the Soviet Union? *(Possible response: Nixon wanted to improve relations and develop trade with both countries. However, he believed a better relationship with China would strengthen the U.S. throughout the region, specifically in dealing with Vietnam and the Soviet Union. A better relationship with the Soviet Union would not give the U.S. a specific advantage over another country, but it would lessen the possibility of nuclear war.)*

5. Draw Conclusions How did U.S. support for Israel in the Yom Kippur War impact the American economy? *(Middle Eastern opponents of Israel formed OPEC, which raised prices on oil exports to the United States.)*

CATEGORIZE

After students have read the lesson, have them revisit the political-spectrum scale they created. **ASK:** Why is it difficult to categorize Richard Nixon's political ideology? *(Some of his policies were conservative, and others were moderate or liberal.)* Invite students to complete a Venn diagram by listing Nixon's liberal policies on the left, his conservative policies on the right, and his moderate policies in the middle. Discuss differences of opinion about the categorization.

ACTIVE OPTIONS

On Your Feet: Rank the Accomplishments Write the following questions on the board: What was Nixon's most important domestic policy? What was Nixon's most important foreign policy? Arrange students in groups of four in separate areas of the classroom and assign one of the questions to each group. Instruct members of each group to answer the question and provide an explanation for their answer. Tell groups to record their various responses. Conclude the activity by asking groups to evaluate their discussions by creating a list in which they rank the accomplishments from most important to least. Have groups share their lists. Discuss similarities and differences between the groups' answers.

NG Learning Framework: Understand School Integration

ATTITUDE Curiosity

SKILL Collaboration

Remind students that in the wake of *Brown* v. *Board of Education*, the task of desegregating public schools was presented to the country. However, this task was massively complex, especially since most of the country was segregated by neighborhood. Divide the class into small groups. Tell students to research school integration with the purpose of forming an opinion about how the federal or local government should have accomplished it. First have groups review the relevant court cases, including those found in this lesson. Then have students research some of the effects of school integration, such as the Boston busing crisis. Ask groups to respond to the following questions: Given that most neighborhoods were not integrated, whose responsibility was it to ensure school integration? What might be the best way to integrate schools? Why is it difficult to determine the best methods for school integration and its effects on students, communities, and the country? Lead a class discussion in which groups share their findings.

HISTORICAL THINKING

ANSWERS

1. The New Federalism was Nixon's plan to return power to the states. It consisted of a tax plan in which the federal government gave money directly to state and municipal governments to use as needed.

2. Nixon hoped to establish ties with China to strengthen the economy via trade. In addition, he hoped to address two problem areas internationally by getting a peace agreement with Vietnam and forcing the Soviet Union into an arms agreement.

3. Nixon meant that civil rights legislation had provided opportunities for African Americans to take part in government.

4. The overall trend of domestic energy production was roughly in line with petroleum imports from 1985 to 2005. Then in 2005, domestic energy production rose and petroleum imports began to decline, indicating a trend toward reliance on domestic energy production.

Protecting the Environment

Consider what you do each day to protect the environment. Perhaps you recycle old school papers or drink from a reusable water bottle. The idea of taking responsibility for how your everyday behavior affects the environment gained traction during the late 1960s and the early 1970s.

THE ENVIRONMENTAL MOVEMENT

Americans have long been concerned about the negative effects of human activities on the environment. Near the beginning of the 20th century, conservationists such as John Muir and Theodore Roosevelt took action to protect natural places from human destruction. In the 1950s, activists protested the negative environmental effects of nuclear weapons development and testing and of nuclear energy production.

In the 1960s, American scientists published environmental articles and books that raised public awareness and gave rise to the modern environmental movement. American marine biologist **Rachel Carson** published *Silent Spring* in 1962, bringing concerns about pollution into the spotlight. After years of research, Carson showed how a common pesticide called **DDT** entered the food chain. Farmers sprayed DDT on their crops to kill insects, but the contaminated food ended up killing animals, especially birds, and harming people. If the contamination of the food supply continued, Carson warned, it could lead to a world in which all life would be endangered.

Stanford University biologist **Paul Ehrlich** warned about the global consequences of human population growth in *The Population Bomb* (1968). Ehrlich argued that the global food supply would not be able to support the increasing number of people on Earth. He predicted that the world would experience wide-scale hunger by the 1970s. Ehrlich's predictions did not come true, partly because of a dramatic increase in agricultural production, but he continued to promote the need to curb global population growth.

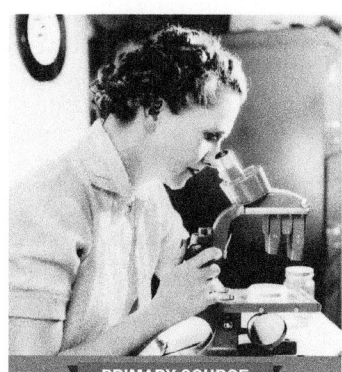

PRIMARY SOURCE

Rachel Carson (above) was a biologist whose gift for writing enabled her to explain environmental science to the public. She sounded an alarm about environmental pollution in her book *Silent Spring*.

The most alarming of all man's assaults upon the environment is the contamination of air, earth, rivers, and sea with dangerous and even lethal materials. This pollution is for the most part irrecoverable; the chain of evil it initiates not only in the world that must support life but in living tissues is for the most part irreversible. In this now universal contamination of the environment, chemicals are the sinister and little-recognized partners of radiation in changing the very nature of the world—the very nature of its life.

—from *Silent Spring*, by Rachel Carson, 1962

CRITICAL VIEWING In the 1940s, cities began to spray DDT in residential neighborhoods to kill mosquitoes. This photo shows a fogger for spraying DDT being tested in Long Island, New York. What details in the photo indicate a lack of public awareness about the dangers of DDT?

During Nixon's presidency, environmental problems often covered the front pages of newspapers. In June 1969, the Cuyahoga River in Cleveland, Ohio, caught fire due to the dumping of industrial waste. Lake Erie was declared "dead," or lacking in any aquatic life, due to pollution. Smog blanketed major cities, such as New York City and Los Angeles. Biologists warned that the national symbol of the United States, the bald eagle, faced extinction due to habitat destruction, illegal hunting, and DDT contamination. The environmental problems were so severe that people around the country began to push for more effective conservation measures.

On April 22, 1970, U.S. Senator Gaylord Nelson and Harvard graduate student Denis Hayes organized the first Earth Day, a celebration to raise awareness about the environmental movement and to educate people on the importance of conservation. Around the country, nearly 20 million people participated. The largest gatherings were in Washington, D.C., and New York City, where conservationists took to the streets to show their support of the movement.

LEGISLATION AND ORGANIZATIONS

Responding to these growing concerns, President Nixon worked with Congress to pass laws to preserve and protect the environment. The **National Environmental Policy Act (NEPA)** was the first law of its kind when it was enacted on January 1, 1970. It required the federal government to consider the environmental impact of any new federally funded construction project. The following year, Nixon created the **Environmental Protection Agency (EPA)** to ensure enforcement of environmental laws. The **Clean Air Act** of 1970 set strict national guidelines to reduce emissions from vehicles and factories and help curb smog. In 1972, Congress passed amendments to the 1948 Federal Water Pollution Control Act, which then became known as the **Clean Water Act**. The amendments allotted $25 billion for the cleanup of polluted lakes and rivers. This costly effort proved effective in bringing polluted waters, such as the Cuyahoga River, back to life. In 1973, Congress passed the **Endangered Species Act** to keep rare plant and animal species from dying out.

The courts also played a role as environmental groups brought lawsuits against various businesses to stop them from polluting. In a 1966 case brought on behalf of all the citizens of Suffolk County in Long Island, New York, the Suffolk County Supreme Court awarded relief in the form of a ban on DDT use in the county. The case was supported by scientists who documented for the court the nearly irreparable environmental damage resulting from use of the pesticide. Interest in the group's success arose across the nation, and in 1967, Charles Wurster and nine other scientists involved in the suit formed the **Environmental Defense Fund (EDF)** to work on a variety of environmental issues. The EDF's efforts led to a New York statewide ban on DDT in 1971 and a nationwide ban by the EPA in 1972. In 1970, a group of law students and attorneys founded the **National Resources Defense Council (NRDC)**.

PLAN: 4-PAGE LESSON

OBJECTIVE

Explore the people, events, and legislation that shaped the environmental movement.

CRITICAL THINKING SKILLS FOR LESSON 1.3

• Compare and Contrast

• Form and Support Opinions

• Analyze Environmental Concepts

• Analyze Language Use

• Evaluate

• Synthesize

HISTORICAL THINKING FOR CHAPTER 29

What policies and challenges characterized the presidencies of Nixon, Ford, and Carter?
Environmental issues arose during Nixon's presidency. Lesson 1.3 discusses the response to concerns about the environment.

BACKGROUND FOR THE TEACHER

Lake Erie impacts about 12 million people who live in its watershed as well as the numerous aquatic species who inhabit it. Industries, agriculture, commercial fishers, recreational facilities, and tourism all rely on the health of the lake. The "death" of Lake Erie in the 1960s resulted from decades of pollution which created high levels of phosphorus that promoted the growth of plants and algae. The warm, relatively shallow waters aided algae growth, which in turn led to a lack of oxygen, killing aquatic life. The coordinated efforts of U.S. and Canadian environmental agencies succeeded in reducing phosphorus levels and improving the health of the lake. Through the Lake Erie Management Plan, the two governments continue to cooperate in preserving the ecosystem they share.

HISTORY NOTEBOOK

Encourage students to complete the Protecting the Environment page and the American Gallery page for Chapter 29 in their History Notebooks as they read.

INTRODUCE & ENGAGE

REVISIT THE THREE *R*'s

Ask students to think about something they have done recently to protect the environment. Display a large version of the graphic organizer shown here and invite students to add examples of individual behaviors that reduce, reuse, and recycle. Explain to students that although these activities are a familiar part of their lives, people have not always been concerned about the environment. In Lesson 1.3, they will learn how the modern environmental movement started.

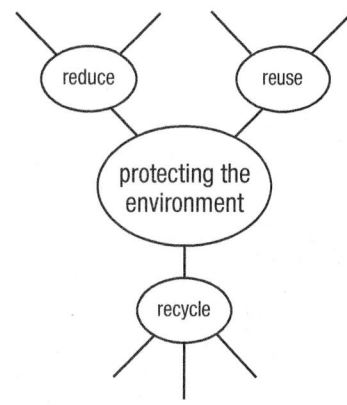

TEACH

GUIDED DISCUSSION

1. **Analyze Language Use** What words does Rachel Carson use to indicate the seriousness of the problem of contamination of the environment? *(Possible response: Words like "irrecoverable," "irreversible," and "universal" indicate the seriousness and widespread nature of the problem.)*

2. **Analyze Environmental Concepts** How did the pollution of natural systems, such as the Cuyahoga River and Lake Erie, impact the quality, quantity, and reliability of services provided by those systems? *(Possible response: Pollution destroyed fish and plants and contaminated the water supply. This affected the quality of life and the economy of those who depended on the services provided by these natural systems.)*

3. **Evaluate** How were courts important to the environmental movement? *(Possible response: Courts enforced environmental legislation by prosecuting businesses that violated the laws.)*

MORE INFORMATION

The DDT Controversy DDT was first widely used during World War II to control insects that caused malaria and other diseases among military personnel overseas. However, during the 1950s and 1960s, the pesticide became widely used within the United States to combat insects in residential areas as well as on farms. Largely thanks to the meticulous research and documentation of Rachel Carson, DDT was banned due to its deleterious effects on wildlife and its classification as a probable carcinogen. Even after its ban, however, controversy over the use of DDT has continued, as current proponents argue that the pesticide's effectiveness in controlling mosquitoes could potentially save millions of lives in areas plagued by malaria.

Ask students to examine past examples of pro-DDT propaganda. Hold a class discussion in which students summarize the arguments made for the pesticides and what they reveal about the scientific knowledge and values of the time.

DIFFERENTIATE

INCLUSION

Work in Pairs Allow students with disabilities to work with students who can make the lesson more accessible to them. Encourage the partner without disabilities to describe in detail the photographs of Carson at her microscope, DDT being sprayed, and Minerva Terrace in Yellowstone National Park. Suggest that students use a graphic organizer such as the one shown to work together to answer the Critical Viewing question.

Truck spraying DDT
Detail:
Detail:
Detail:
Detail:
Detail:

GIFTED & TALENTED

Research Environmental Degradation Tell students to conduct online research about one of the environmental issues raised during the 1960s and 1970s, such as nuclear proliferation, consequences of human population growth, or the effects of pollution on natural systems including the Cuyahoga River or Love Canal, and the environmental protection laws that were passed as a result in the 1970s. Ask students to present their findings to the entire class. Encourage a class discussion in which students note similarities and differences between environmentalism and other forms of social or political activism of the decade, such as the civil rights movement, antiwar protests, or women's liberation.

See the Chapter Planner for more strategies for differentiation.

CRITICAL VIEWING Possible responses: The sign on the truck says: "Harmless to Humans," indicating that while insects are the target, other animal life, including humans and birds, were not considered to be at risk. The men who are using the fogger are not wearing any protective gear, such as respirators, goggles, or hazmat suits, and a boy in a bathing suit is standing directly in the spray.

AMERICAN PLACES

📍 **Yellowstone National Park, Wyoming**

Minerva Terrace, part of Mammoth Hot Springs in Yellowstone National Park, consists of a series of multi-colored terraces composed of calcium carbonate deposited by hot springs. Microorganisms tint the terrace rock various colors. Minerva Terrace is one of the many spectacular natural features of Yellowstone, the world's first national park.

This stunning photograph of Minerva Terrace was taken by National Geographic photographer Frans Lanting. By capturing the magnificence of the natural world, National Geographic photographers help people understand the importance of protecting Earth and its diversity.

The EDF and the NRDC were the first nonprofit environmental groups focused initially on bringing about environmental change by filing research-based lawsuits against polluting companies and agencies.

Some conservation organizations that had existed for many years experienced a newfound popularity and purpose as a result of the environmental movement of the late 1960s and the 1970s. The **Sierra Club**, founded in 1892 by naturalist John Muir, was largely responsible for the preservation of lands in the West, including Yosemite National Park in California. By the 1970s, the Sierra Club had become a leading lobbyist group and environmental protection advocate, fighting to protect natural areas from industrial and agricultural development. The club helped protect California's redwood forests as well as wilderness areas in Alaska.

The Sierra Club often joined with other environmental groups to achieve common goals. One of these groups was the **Wilderness Society**, which was founded in 1935 to fight for the protection of America's wild natural areas. Since its founding, the Wilderness Society has succeeded in preserving some 110 million acres of land across 44 states. In 1969, David Brower, a former leader of the Sierra Club, formed the **League of Conservation Voters** to organize support for pro-environmental political candidates and policies.

CONTROVERSY ON REGULATION

The new environmental laws passed in the 1970s restricted business operations and land use. Some corporations and conservative politicians began to criticize what they viewed as **overregulation**, or excessive control and oversight, by the EPA and other federal agencies. They claimed that the regulations limited profits, job creation, and economic progress.

In the early 1970s, for example, officials with the Tennessee Valley Authority (TVA) were attempting to expand construction of a dam along the Little Tennessee River. The dam promised to extend hydroelectric power over a large region. In 1973, researchers discovered a previously unknown species of fish, called the snail darter, in the Little Tennessee River area. Scientists warned that the dam could destroy the snail darter's natural habitat, and thus potentially destroy the entire population of this rare creature. In 1975, government officials listed the snail darter as protected under the Endangered Species Act. After several years of back and forth decisions in the courts, the U.S. Supreme Court ruled in 1978 that the dam would violate the law protecting the snail darter. The Court ordered a halt to construction of the dam. Eventually, Tennessee officials persuaded Congress to pass a law specifically allowing completion of the dam. As a result, the snail darter became extinct in the Little Tennessee River region. However, thanks to relocation efforts, the snail darter was able to survive in other areas.

Meanwhile, the amount of federally protected land was growing. In 1978, Congress passed a law expanding the size of California's Redwood National and State Parks, much to the disappointment of some leaders in the logging industry. Federal officials also expanded the protection of lands in Alaska, where many oil companies wanted to drill in such wilderness areas as the Arctic National Wildlife Range. The range was renamed the **Arctic National Wildlife Refuge** to highlight its protected status. By the end of the 1970s, new legislation more than doubled the size of the national park system, protecting millions of acres of land and thousands of plant and animal species, but at the same time upsetting some business leaders.

The mid-1970s saw the rise of a movement called the **Sagebrush Rebellion**, led by a group of landowners, miners, loggers, and ranchers in certain western states who resented federal laws limiting the extraction of natural resources on federally protected lands. As supporters of property rights, or the right to use property as the owner sees fit, they wanted more local control and even ownership of federal lands so they could use the lands for their benefit. The rebellion continued into the early 1980s and inspired similar movements in later years to reclaim western lands from federal control.

HISTORICAL THINKING

1. **READING CHECK** What environmental problems resulted from human modifications of landscapes in the 1960s and 1970s?

2. **COMPARE AND CONTRAST** How was the environmental movement similar to and different from other activist movements of the 1960s and 1970s?

3. **FORM AND SUPPORT OPINIONS** Do you think the U.S. government should own land and control how it is used? Give reasons for your opinion.

4. **ANALYZE ENVIRONMENTAL CONCEPTS** How might the quality of life in the United States be different today if the modern environmental movement had not developed?

BUILD BACKGROUND
EARTH DAY

April 22, 1970, marked the first Earth Day—a grassroots movement with a lasting legacy. The event came about from the combined efforts of students, environmentalists, concerned citizens, and politicians who wished to create a "national teach-in for the environment." This public protest achieved bipartisan support in Congress and led to the passage of the major environmental legislation discussed in this lesson, which still remains in effect. In 1990, another campaign was planned, and Earth Day became a global event celebrated in 141 countries with 200 million people working toward a sustainable environment. The movement has continued to grow, focusing the power of the people on issues such as global warming and clean energy alternatives. By 2017, the Earth Day Network consisted of organizations in roughly 195 countries, and more than a billion people took part in celebrations around the world.

NATIONAL GEOGRAPHIC PHOTOGRAPHER FRANS LANTING

For several decades, National Geographic photographer Frans Lanting has raised public awareness of environmental issues through his work. His photographs capture the relationship between humans and nature, and his stunning images of wild creatures provide motivation for the protection of Earth's delicate ecosystems. Lanting's books and exhibitions promote a sense of awe about the planet and fulfill his goal to "inspire people to help achieve a sustainable future for all life on Earth." Encourage students to visit the National Geographic website to learn more about Frans Lanting and view some of his unique work.

TEACH

GUIDED DISCUSSION

4. **Synthesize** How have environmental groups created both progress and backlash? *(Possible response: Environmental groups have succeeded in protecting millions of acres of forests and wilderness areas across the United States through lobbying Congress and supporting candidates and policies that favor environmental preservation. However, their success has also created a backlash, as evidenced by the property rights movement.)*

5. **Analyze Environmental Concepts** What competing factors were weighed by Congress when it allowed the TVA to build a dam on the Little Tennessee River? *(The dam would improve life for people by providing hydroelectric power to a large area. However, its creation would also destroy the natural habitat of the snail darter, which was native to the area.)*

AMERICAN PLACES

Yellowstone is the oldest of the 59 national parks in the United States, and its 2.2 million acres spread across Wyoming, Montana, and Idaho. The park offers approximately 1,000 miles of hiking trails, but many of the park's attractions can be seen by driving Grand Loop Road, where visitors can look for wild inhabitants including grizzly bears, gray wolves, bison, and moose as well as many other species. Yellowstone remains a unique ecological marvel where people witness the volcanic power of geysers, the hypothermal activity of hot springs, and the constantly changing formations of travertine terraces. Guide students to the park's website, where they can take virtual tours of Yellowstone's nature sites, including Mammoth Hot Springs where Minerva Terrace is located.

ACTIVE OPTIONS

AMERICAN GALLERY ONLINE **Saving the Earth** Invite students to explore the American Gallery. Have them select one of the photographs and do additional research to learn more about it. Ask questions that will inspire additional inquiry about the chosen photograph, such as: What is this? How does the subject of the photo connect to Earth Day or the topic of conservation? What else would you like to know about it?

NG Learning Framework: Research and Debate Environmental Issues

ATTITUDE Responsibility

KNOWLEDGE Our Living Planet

Guide students to research environmental case studies—such as the controversial expansion of Redwood National and State Parks in 1978 and oil drilling in the Arctic National Wildlife Refuge—as background for a debate. Encourage students to evaluate the consequences of these past events and decisions and to determine the lessons that were learned. Then arrange students in teams to debate the appropriate role of government in dealing with present-day environmental issues, such as climate change.

HISTORICAL THINKING

ANSWERS

1. Water pollution resulted from the dumping of industrial waste and habitat destruction, and the use of pesticides threatened animal species and contaminated the food supply.

2. Like other movements, the environmental movement began at the grassroots level with concerned individuals who effected change through protest, legislation, and court filings. However, the environmental movement was more global in scale, had less of a constitutional basis, and relied more on scientific research.

3. Answers will vary. Students' responses should be based on information in the lesson, such as environmental laws or the Sagebrush Rebellion.

4. Answers will vary. Possible response: Without the protections created through the environmental movement, the environment would likely be more polluted, diminishing the quality of human life and possibly threatening many plant and animal species.

CRITICAL VIEWING Alaska's Denali National Park and Preserve is home to North America's highest mountain as well as these Dall sheep. The park's strict rules protect wildlife habitats and ecosystems, keeping its 6 million acres of land as they have been for thousands of years. Paul Nicklen believes sea ice and polar ecosystems like those found in the park play an important role in our current climate era. What types of controversies currently exist between environmental protection advocates like Nicklen and property rights activists? Whose views do you support?

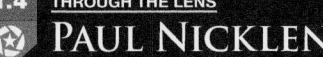

1.4 THROUGH THE LENS

PAUL NICKLEN

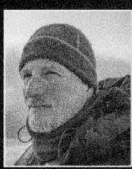

Canadian-born National Geographic photographer and marine biologist Paul Nicklen documents both the beauty and the plight of the world's oceans and Arctic regions for a global audience. His personal mission is to use his emotional, evocative, and inspiring photographs to ignite conversations about the future of our planet's natural wonders and to promote conservation.

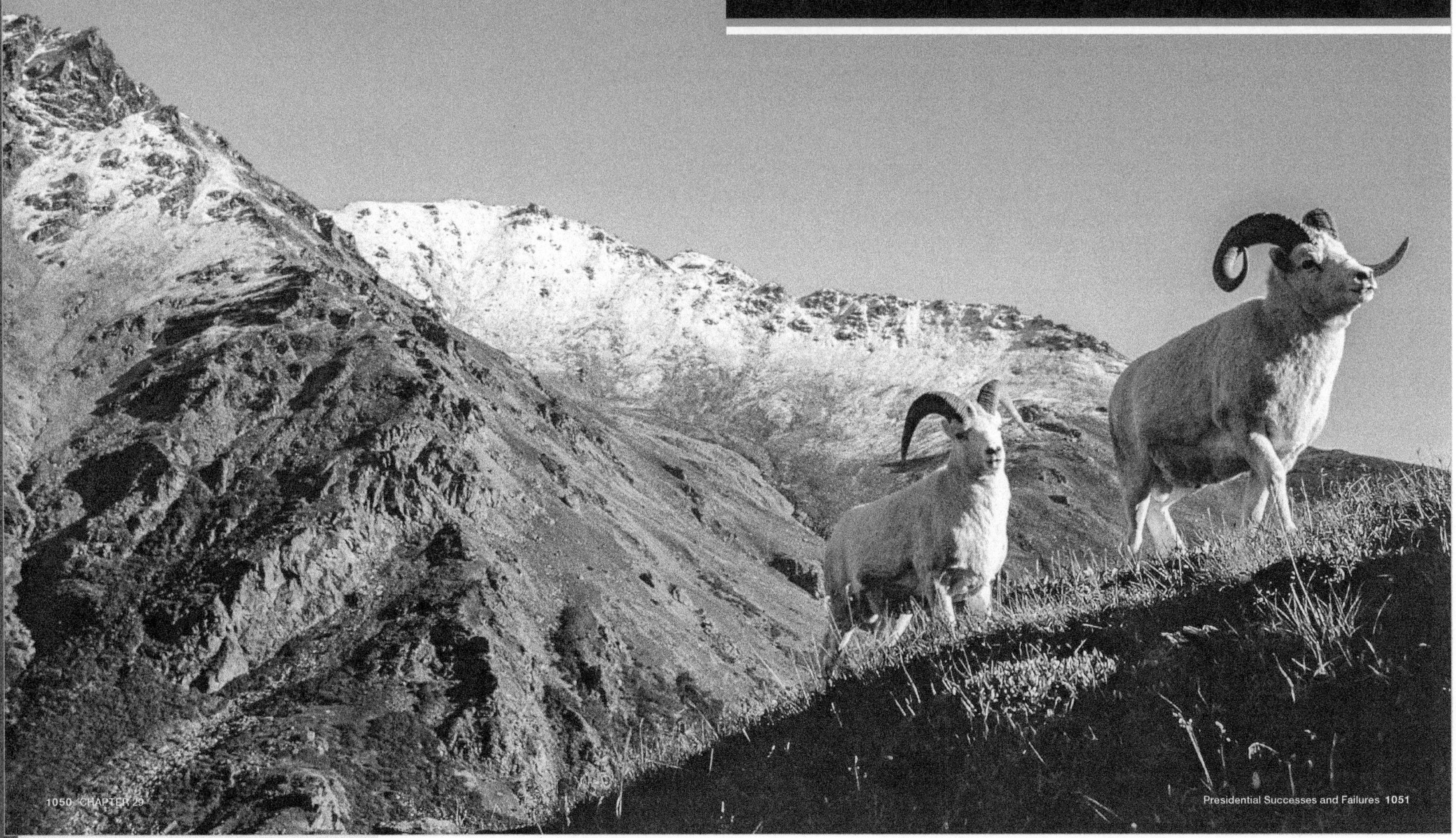

1050 CHAPTER 29

Presidential Successes and Failures 1051

PLAN: 2-PAGE LESSON

OBJECTIVE

Discuss issues regarding the preservation and protection of ecosystems like those found in Denali National Park.

CRITICAL THINKING SKILLS FOR LESSON 1.4

- Analyze Visuals
- Make Connections
- Make Inferences
- Evaluate

HISTORICAL THINKING FOR CHAPTER 29

What policies and challenges characterized the presidencies of Nixon, Ford, and Carter? The environmental movement promoted concern for the future of Earth's ecosystems. Lesson 1.4 features the work of a photographer who promotes awareness of environmental issues.

NATIONAL GEOGRAPHIC PHOTOGRAPHER PAUL NICKLEN

Having grown up among the Inuit in the Canadian Arctic and having worked as a biologist in the Northwest Territories, Paul Nicklen possesses a unique perspective on environmental issues. His work takes him to many parts of the world, but Nicklen specializes in polar regions, especially the impact of global warming on species that depend on icy environments. Nicklen considers himself an interpreter of scientific knowledge and is a popular public speaker. More so than words, he relies on the power of his photographs to get his message across, showing how species are interconnected with their environment. Nicklen also helped to found SeaLegacy, an organization that works for the conservation of oceanic environments threatened by climate change.

HISTORY NOTEBOOK

Encourage students to complete the Through the Lens page for Chapter 29 in their History Notebooks as they read.

INTRODUCE & ENGAGE

COMPOSE A CAPTION

Challenge students to compose a one-sentence caption that expresses the feelings inspired by the photograph. Invite students to share their captions by posting them on the board. Then ask the group to categorize the captions as expressions of awe, respect, concern, conflict, or other feelings. Point out that environmental issues provoke a range of responses similar to the range of captions that the class produced.

TEACH

GUIDED DISCUSSION

1. **Make Inferences** Why do you think the photographer chose to include Dall sheep in the image of Denali National Park? *(Answers will vary. Possible responses: The sheep are interconnected with the environment. They are examples of animals that contribute to the diversity of the ecosystem. The sheep provide incentive for conservation.)*

2. **Evaluate** How does this photograph relate to Paul Nicklen's personal mission? *(Possible response: Nicklen's mission is to promote concern for the future of Earth's natural wonders. This photo inspires viewers' interest in animals and the environment in which they live.)*

THROUGH THE LENS

Explain to students that the name *Denali*, meaning "Tall One" or "Great One" in the language of the native Athabaskan-speaking people, was restored in 2015 by executive order of President Barack Obama. The peak had borne the name *Mount McKinley* since 1896, named for President William McKinley by a gold prospector. The park was dedicated in 1917 as a preserve for Dall sheep and other animals. As with present-day struggles between conservationists and private interests, early park rangers were tasked with protecting the animals from poachers who provided meat to railroad workers and miners.

ACTIVE OPTIONS

On Your Feet: Compare Viewpoints Divide the class into two groups and assign one of the following topics to each group: environmental protection or property rights. Display an Argument Chart such as the one shown. Instruct group members to collaborate on researching their topic and completing the column that corresponds to their topic and the Support column. Then have students pair up with someone from the other group. Students should discuss their opposing views and complete the final column of their chart. Have students use the completed organizers as the basis for a discussion of the viewpoints of environmental protection advocates and property rights advocates. Encourage students to refer to their Argument Chart to help them respond to the Critical Viewing question.

Environmental Protection Advocates	Support	Property Rights Advocates

NG Learning Framework: Explore the Impact of an Image

SKILL Communication

KNOWLEDGE Critical Species

Share with students the Paul Nicklen quotation, "It just takes one image to get someone's attention." Invite them to explore Nicklen's photographs online and to choose one photograph of a species that gets their attention. Then have the class collaborate on an exhibition of their chosen images and a discussion of how the photographs relate to current environmental issues.

DIFFERENTIATE

ENGLISH LANGUAGE LEARNERS `ELD`

Use Meaning Maps Pair students at the **Emerging** level with students at the **Expanding** or **Bridging** levels. Instruct students to use a dictionary and print or online images to complete Meaning Maps for the terms *wildlife habitat*, *sea ice*, and *polar ecosystem*. Direct pairs to trade Meaning Maps and note similarities and differences. Pairs should also discuss how the terms help them understand Paul Nicklen's mission.

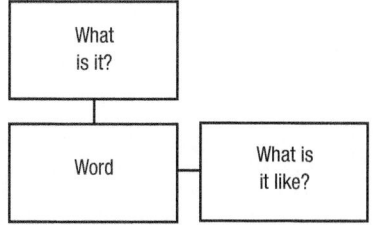

GIFTED & TALENTED

Watch and Report on a TED Talk Direct students to watch one of Paul Nicklen's TED Talks online. Then have them analyze his presentation and its effectiveness by noting how he gets the audience's attention, organizes the content of the talk, and uses visual aids. Students should also analyze how Nicklen uses appeals to emotion, rationality, and his own credibility. Encourage students to present their analysis to the class, utilizing clips from the talk to illustrate their points, and ending with their conclusion about the overall effectiveness of Nicklen's talk. Encourage the class to discuss whether Nicklen's talk might influence people's attitudes and actions.

See the Chapter Planner for more strategies for differentiation.

CRITICAL VIEWING Answers will vary. Students might support the views of environmental protectionists because they advocate preserving natural environments for people to enjoy and to provide natural habitats for wildlife. Students might support the views of property rights advocates because they believe the federal government has overregulated and overcontrolled property that is legally owned by individuals.

THE WATERGATE SCANDAL

Have you ever wanted something so badly you were willing to do almost anything to get it? Unfortunately, Richard Nixon wanted to remain president so badly that he was willing to break the law and compromise his entire administration.

NIXON'S BID FOR RE-ELECTION

By the end of his first term, President Nixon had built a strong record, especially in foreign affairs. He had successfully negotiated foreign policy agreements with China and the Soviet Union. He also had made progress in the Vietnam War peace talks.

The Republican Party nominated Nixon and his vice president, Spiro Agnew, for re-election, and they did so enthusiastically. Statisticians and journalists favored Nixon to win handily against any of the 11 Democratic primary candidates who were vying for their party's nomination.

Despite all his accomplishments, Nixon worried about the election. Not only did he want to maintain the presidency, he wanted his party to take control of Congress. To this end, some of his supporters founded a political action group called the **Committee to Re-Elect the President (CRP)** in the

Washington Post reporters Carl Bernstein (left) and Bob Woodward received anonymous tips linking the Watergate break-in to the White House. In 2005, it was revealed that the source had been a deputy director of the FBI.

spring of 1971. Nixon's opponents mocked him by referring to the CRP as "CREEP." Attorney General **John Mitchell** resigned his cabinet position to lead the committee.

Mitchell and other CRP members resorted to what came to be known as "dirty tricks" to ruin the chances of the strongest contenders for the Democratic presidential nomination. For example, one CRP member sent a forged letter to a newspaper in New Hampshire that accused the Democratic primary favorite, Senator Edmund Muskie of Maine, of using an ethnic slur to refer to French Canadians.

CRP's dirty tricks may have worked. In July 1972, the Democratic Party chose an underdog as its nominee, South Dakota Senator **George McGovern**. McGovern was a staunch opponent of the Vietnam War, but otherwise his platform was vague. His relative inexperience in politics, compared to Nixon's broad experience, made him a weak candidate.

THE WATERGATE BREAK-IN

On June 17, 1972, just weeks before McGovern won the Democratic nomination, a security guard on his rounds of the Watergate building complex in Washington, D.C., noticed a piece of tape that prevented a door from locking. That door was the entrance to the Democratic National Headquarters. The security guard called the police, who surprised and arrested five men in possession of burglary tools, cameras, film, tear gas guns, and surveillance equipment. Among the burglars was **James W. McCord, Jr.**, the security director for CRP. The next day a second CRP member and a former presidential aide were named as accomplices in the burglary. Journalists called the incident the **Watergate break-in**.

In response to news of the break-in, President Nixon assured the public that no one "presently employed" in his administration was involved "in this very bizarre incident." At first, few people paid much attention to the crime. But over the next several months, *Washington Post* reporters **Bob Woodward** and **Carl Bernstein** slowly began to uncover the connection between the break-in and top government officials closely connected to the White House.

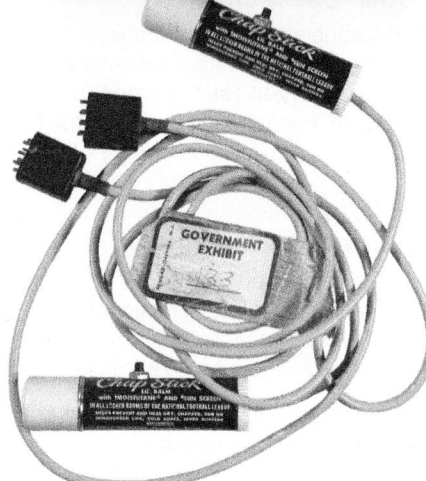

CRITICAL VIEWING Radio microphones hidden in lip balm containers were found in the White House office safe of one of the leaders of the Watergate break-in team. They were displayed, along with many other listening devices, at the trial of the Watergate burglars. What does evidence like this suggest about the nature of the trial?

Months passed, and the election campaigns continued. The Watergate break-in had little effect on the outcome of the November 1972 election because the journalists were still investigating the incident. Nixon won the presidency by a landslide, but the Democratic Party, much to Nixon's disappointment, kept control of Congress.

THE WATERGATE TRIALS

Woodward and Bernstein continued to publish reports through the end of 1972 describing the dirty tricks that CRP members had played to sabotage Nixon's opponents. In January 1973, the same month as Nixon's inauguration, the trial of the Watergate burglars began with Judge **John Sirica** presiding.

At the time, Nixon's public approval rating was very high, at 68 percent, but it fell sharply as the journalists continued to uncover information about the break-in. The *Post's* reports led Judge Sirica

---

PLAN: 4-PAGE LESSON

OBJECTIVE
Understand why Richard Nixon resigned from office.

CRITICAL THINKING SKILLS FOR LESSON 1.5
- Draw Conclusions
- Synthesize
- Evaluate
- Make Predictions
- Describe
- Make Inferences
- Analyze Primary Sources

HISTORICAL THINKING FOR CHAPTER 29
What policies and challenges characterized the presidencies of Nixon, Ford, and Carter? Based on his strong record, Nixon easily won re-election in 1972. Lesson 1.5 explains how the Watergate scandal became an insurmountable challenge that led to Nixon's downfall.

BACKGROUND FOR THE TEACHER

In his resignation speech on August 8, 1974, Richard Nixon admitted that some of his judgments had been wrong, but he asserted ". . . they were made in what I believed at the time to be the best interest of the nation." In May 1977, Nixon participated in a series of television interviews with David Frost, a popular talk-show host. In one of the interviews, Nixon acknowledged, "I let down our system of government, and the dreams of all those young people that ought to get into government but now think it is too corrupt." This is perhaps the enduring legacy of the ordeal—a lingering distrust of government.

INTRODUCE & ENGAGE

GRAPH APPROVAL RATINGS

Remind students that presidential approval ratings are based on public opinion polls. Display a graph, such as the one here, and label the x-axis to represent the period from January 1973 to August 1974 and the y-axis to represent approval ratings from 20 percent to 70 percent. Tell students in January 1973, President Nixon's approval rating was 68 percent. Ask a student to place that rating on the graph. **ASK:** Why do you think Nixon had strong public support at the beginning of his second term? *(Possible responses: He had a strong record in foreign policy, and his domestic policies had initiated welfare reforms, supported civil rights, and improved safety in the workplace. He was working on a peaceful resolution in Vietnam.)* Place a mark on the graph to represent a 27 percent approval rating in July 1974. Tell students that they will examine the reasons why Nixon's approval rating plummeted.

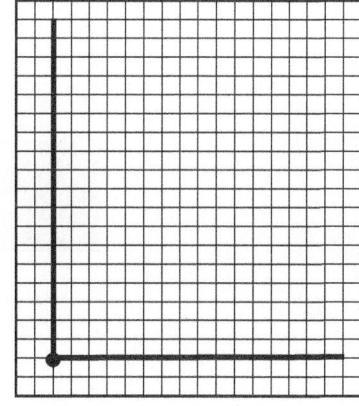

TEACH

GUIDED DISCUSSION

1. **Evaluate** Were the CRP's dirty tricks successful in influencing the outcome of the 1972 presidential election, and what types of evidence could be used to support your answer? *(Possible response: CRP's tactics influenced the choice of a Democratic candidate by ruining the chances of the leading contenders. George McGovern lacked the experience of Richard Nixon, thereby enhancing Nixon's chances for re-election. Data such as approval ratings for Edmund Muskie before and after the supposed slur would help support this argument.)*

2. **Make Predictions** How might Nixon's second term have been different if Bob Woodward and Carl Bernstein had not investigated the Watergate break-in? *(Possible response: Nixon likely would have served out his term without scandal because people generally dismissed the Watergate break-in. Woodward and Bernstein's investigation revealed a connection between Nixon and the scandal that led to his downfall. In addition, public respect for, and confidence in, the presidency might not have eroded as it did.)*

MORE INFORMATION

The Legacy of Watergate Share with students the information in Background for the Teacher. **ASK:** What is your attitude toward people in elected government offices? *(Possible responses: Negative. People in elected office are corrupt and in it for their own gain. Positive. Elected officials have the opportunity to improve people's lives.)* Divide the class into two groups based on their responses and have them form a fishbowl grouping, with two concentric circles facing inward. Instruct students in the inside circle to discuss reasons for their response while students in the outside circle listen and evaluate their discussion. Then reverse roles. Conclude by having each group share its assessment of the discussions.

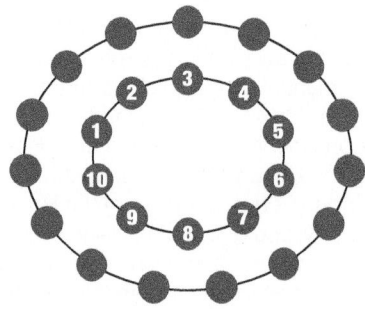

DIFFERENTIATE

ENGLISH LANGUAGE LEARNERS

Write an Original Sentence Pair students at the **Emerging** level with students at the **Expanding** or **Bridging** levels. Instruct pairs to work together to write an original sentence using selected words and terms. Have the more English-proficient partner assist in checking the accuracy of the sentences. Invite pairs to share their sentences and discuss ways to use each word or term. Suggest the following terms:

forged	contempt of Congress
accomplice	impeachment
staunch	

GIFTED & TALENTED

Write a Film Treatment Tell students that the Watergate scandal has been the basis of many books and movies, partly because of its compelling characters and strong narrative arc. Instruct students to conduct research using online and print sources to learn more about Watergate in order to write a film treatment (or short narrative synopsis of a film). Students may choose one character or incident to focus on or they may take a wider view. Encourage students to take notes in a Story Map, such as the one shown, before writing their film treatment. Invite students to read their treatments to the class.

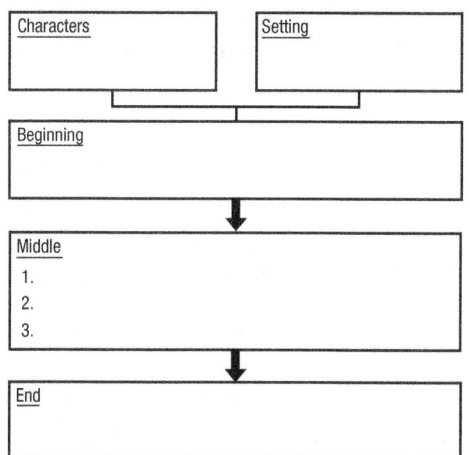

See the Chapter Planner for more strategies for differentiation.

CRITICAL VIEWING This evidence suggests that in addition to obtaining the tapes, prosecutors did not shrink from obtaining a wide range of evidence from inside the White House. Faced with a historic task, prosecutors may have wanted the court to understand that the possession of many listening devices suggests that the burglars routinely illegally monitored DNC activities.

to suspect a **cover-up**, or an attempt to hide the truth. He did not believe that the burglars had acted without the knowledge of either the CRP or the president. In January, four of the Watergate burglars pled guilty to minor charges of theft and **wiretapping**, or placing a device on a telephone in order to secretly listen to conversations. McCord, who had pled not guilty, was convicted of conspiracy along with the other two offenses.

In March 1973, McCord wrote a letter to Judge Sirica implicating Nixon in the cover-up of the Watergate burglary. McCord's letter resulted in the dismissal or the resignation of several of Nixon's chief advisors, including White House counsel John Dean, chief of staff H. R. Haldeman, and chief domestic advisor John Ehrlichman. Nixon continued to deny any involvement in Watergate. He claimed that he had been too busy running the nation to keep up with the activities of his re-election campaign staff. Many Americans—and most Republican leaders—believed Nixon. Representative **Gerald R. Ford** of Michigan declared, "I have the greatest confidence in the president and am absolutely positive he had nothing to do with this mess."

Nonetheless, the Senate formed the **Watergate Committee** in May 1973. The special committee, chaired by North Carolina senator **Sam Ervin**, heard sworn testimonies from present and former Nixon aides. The aides described crimes committed before the 1972 election that were intended to undermine the president's opponents. Additionally, a former aide to the president revealed that Nixon had been secretly tape-recording his conversations in the White House's Oval Office since 1971.

In May 1973, Attorney General **Elliot Richardson** appointed Harvard Law School professor **Archibald Cox** as a special prosecutor in the Watergate case. Cox, Judge Sirica, and committee chairman Ervin demanded to hear the relevant Oval Office tapes. However, Nixon withheld them, claiming **executive privilege**, the principle that the president may withhold certain information from Congress in the nation's interest. Cox presented the White House with a subpoena demanding the tapes, which Nixon's lawyers asked Sirica to block. Sirica ordered the tapes to be turned over. Now the White House was in a battle with the courts as well as with the Watergate Committee, provoking a constitutional crisis.

At the same time, Vice President Spiro Agnew was enmeshed in his own separate scandal. Beginning in April 1973, the U.S. Justice Department had been investigating allegations that Agnew had accepted

illegal payoffs from building contractors while he was governor of Maryland from 1967 to 1969. Initially, Agnew denied the charges. Then, on October 10, 1973, he pleaded no contest in court to income tax evasion, and he resigned as vice president.

On October 20, Nixon ordered Attorney General Richardson to fire Cox, but Richardson refused. Nixon retaliated by firing Richardson. With Richardson gone, the attorney general's second-in-command, Solicitor General Robert Bork, fired Cox and replaced him with a lawyer named Leon Jaworski. These dramatic developments, known as the "Saturday Night Massacre," prompted the House Judiciary Committee to consider hearings for impeachment, or formal charges brought against a public official for misconduct while in office. At this point, the White House turned over some, but not all, of the tapes. In December 1973, Congress confirmed Nixon's choice of Gerald Ford to replace Agnew as vice president.

THE TAPES AND THE RESIGNATION

In March 1974, Nixon's chief advisors, who had resigned or were dismissed as a result of McCord's letter to Judge Sirica, were indicted for crimes. In July, prosecutor Jaworski ordered Nixon to release 64 additional tapes of his conversations in the Oval Office. Rather than release the tapes, Nixon handed over more than 1,000 pages of edited transcripts. Jaworski appealed to the Supreme Court. In *United States* v. *Nixon*, the Supreme Court ruled unanimously that the tapes did not fall under the

protection of executive privilege and that Nixon must surrender them. By this point, Nixon had lost the trust of most American citizens. A Gallup poll taken just months earlier showed Nixon's public approval rating had dropped from 68 to 27 percent.

Also in July 1974, the House Judiciary Committee began debating charges of presidential impeachment before a national television audience. One member of the committee was Representative **Barbara Jordan** of Texas, who became famous for her powerful speeches. Three days after the Supreme Court ordered Nixon to hand over the Oval Office tapes, the committee approved three charges: obstruction of justice, abuse of power, and contempt of Congress. On August 5, the president released the tapes, one of which had an 18-minute gap of silence. The gap led many people to believe that something may have been erased. Although investigators could not prove Nixon knew of the burglary before it occurred, the tapes confirmed that he played an active role in the attempt to cover up the burglary. He offered money to the burglars to keep quiet about their role in the crime. He developed a plan for the CIA to block the FBI's investigation. Ultimately, Nixon was charged with obstruction of justice and abuse of power.

Nixon's impeachment seemed certain. Rather than risk further disgrace, on August 8, 1974, Nixon resigned, becoming the first president to do so. In a tearful farewell to his staff the next morning, he offered advice he himself had ignored. "Always

remember," he said, "those who hate you don't win unless you hate them. And then you destroy yourself." Vice President Gerald Ford was sworn in as president shortly after noon on the same day.

Nixon's involvement in Watergate deepened a public distrust of government that had grown during the Vietnam War years. The scandal also demonstrated the dangers of an imperial, or overly powerful, presidency and sent the Congress into constitutional crisis mode. Fortunately, the Constitution's system of checks and balances allowed the judicial and legislative branches to rein in the executive branch. For his part, however, Nixon, who died in 1994 at the age of 81, never directly admitted his guilt in the matter.

HISTORICAL THINKING

1. **READING CHECK** What was Nixon's involvement in the Watergate scandal?

2. **DRAW CONCLUSIONS** Do Representative Jordan's comments indicate bias on her part, or does she present valid arguments? Explain your answer.

3. **SYNTHESIZE** What role did the characteristics of power in Washington, D.C., play in the actions and resignation of Nixon?

4. **EVALUATE** Within the context of the Watergate scandal, identify what you believe to be a valid argument that was used as well as a fallacious argument used to analyze events. Explain your choices.

> BUILD BACKGROUND

THE IMPEACHMENT PROCESS

The Constitution provides a mechanism for removing from office a president who has committed "treason, bribery, or other high crimes and misdemeanors." Based on the recommendation of the House Judiciary Committee and approved by a majority vote, the House of Representatives impeaches, or brings formal charges against, a president. The Senate then conducts a trial presided over by the Chief Justice of the United States. During the trial, the accused president has defense lawyers, and selected members of the House play the role of prosecutors. Senators act as the jury, and guilt is determined by a two-thirds majority vote. A president who is convicted at an impeachment trial is removed from office, and the vice president becomes president. An impeachment trial is a political process rather than a criminal proceeding, so no sentencing or fines are imposed.

Richard Nixon resigned to avoid impeachment and probable conviction. Only two other presidents have been impeached—Andrew Johnson in 1868 and Bill Clinton in 1998. Both were acquitted.

TEACH

GUIDED DISCUSSION

3. **Describe** What was the purpose and significance of the Watergate Committee? *(It was a special committee formed by the Senate to make inquiries and hear testimonies about the break-in at the DNC Headquarters, also known as the Watergate burglary. It was significant in that a former aide of Nixon, while giving sworn testimony, revealed the existence of tapes made during conversations in the Oval Office.)*

4. **Make Inferences** How did Nixon perceive the power of the president? *(Possible response: Based on his actions, Nixon considered the president to be above the law and the other branches of government. He claimed executive privilege to cover his knowledge of the Watergate break-in and refused to comply with the legal process.)*

ANALYZE PRIMARY SOURCES

Direct students' attention to the Primary Source feature and ask them to read it within the context of the Watergate hearings. **ASK:** Do you think Jordan's speech represented the opinions of the majority of the House Judiciary Committee? *(Answers will vary. Possible response: The committee considered impeachment hearings, and Nixon resigned to avoid conviction, so Jordan's sentiments seem to have been shared by other committee members.)*

ACTIVE OPTIONS

On Your Feet: Create a Sequence Chain Divide students in groups of five and provide each group with five sheets of paper. Instruct group members to collaborate in choosing five events from the lesson that they consider to be the most significant. Have them write each event on a separate sheet of paper. On the back of each paper, they should write a brief description of why they consider the event to be significant. Take turns calling groups to the front of the class and ask members to display their events in random order. Challenge the class to sequence the events chronologically by rearranging the group members. Then have the group share the significance of its events.

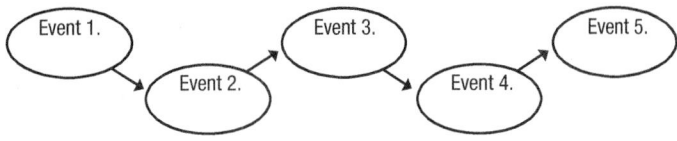

NG Learning Framework: Discuss the Power of the Presidency

ATTITUDE Responsibility

SKILL Communication

Write the term *imperial presidency* on the board and discuss how it relates to the Nixon administration. **ASK:** Were Nixon and his staff above the law? *(Possible response: Nixon acted as if he were above the law by refusing to comply with a court order. However, the Constitution has checks and balances that keep one branch of the government from being more powerful than the others.)* Engage in a class discussion about the power of the president today. Pose questions such as the following: How is the issue of presidential power relevant today? Is the president more powerful than other branches of the government? Do you think the president has too much or too little power? In what areas should the president be given more or less power? At the conclusion, write the following on the board: The president has (too much, the right amount of, too little) power. Have students vote their opinions and tally the results for the class.

ANSWERS

1. Based on testimony and the Oval Office tapes, Nixon likely knew of and possibly authorized the Watergate burglary. Nixon was charged with abuse of power and obstruction of justice for his attempt to cover up his involvement.

2. Answers will vary. Possible response: Jordan presents valid arguments that she bases on evidence and the impeachment provision in the Constitution.

3. Nixon resigned because the House had the power to impeach him, and the Senate had the power to convict him.

4. Answers will vary. Possible response: The argument that Watergate deepened distrust in government is valid. Prior to Nixon, presidents like Roosevelt, Eisenhower, and Kennedy were widely admired and trusted. After Nixon, this was not the case. The argument that the 18-minute gap on one tape was an intentional erasure to remove incriminating evidence is fallacious because there is no proof that the gap was created intentionally.

CRITICAL VIEWING Nixon is smiling and giving a "V" for victory sign, suggesting that he did not feel defeated. He may have been relieved that the ordeal was finally over.

FORD SUCCEEDS NIXON

Americans felt betrayed by the Watergate scandal. Their president left office barely apologizing for the chaos he had caused and without admitting his guilt. They hoped the man who took his place would prove more trustworthy.

THE WATERGATE LEGACY

When Vice President Agnew resigned in 1973, Gerald Ford rose from Congressional representative to vice president—the first selected under the **25th Amendment**. Ratified under President Johnson in 1967, the amendment calls for the president to nominate and Congress to approve a replacement for the vice president when necessary. On August 9, 1974, the day after President Nixon resigned and less than a year after being confirmed as vice president, Ford became the 38th president of the United States. The American people had a president they had never voted for—another first.

In his 25 years in Congress, Ford had developed a reputation for honesty and openness, traits Americans were looking for in their president. During his vice-presidential confirmation hearing in 1973, Ford had stated he would not give Nixon a presidential pardon. A president has the constitutional right to grant a pardon to anyone. A pardon excuses a person from punishment for a crime. In September 1974, Ford reversed his position and pardoned Nixon for all crimes he "may have committed" during his term in office. Ford's pardon ended any further criminal investigation into Nixon's actions as president.

Ford hoped the pardon would finally allow Americans to move forward and put the Watergate scandal behind them. However, many Americans wanted justice and felt that Ford had betrayed them. As a result, Ford's public approval rating plummeted from 72 percent to 49 percent.

ECONOMIC TROUBLES

Ford inherited an ailing economy that worsened over the course of his presidency. The economy slowed almost to a standstill, a situation called **economic stagnation**. The stagnation was due to years of slow economic growth and high unemployment rates. At the same time, energy costs kept rising, pushing up the inflation rate, or the annual percent increase in the prices of goods and services. Economists called this unusual combination of stagnation and inflation "**stagflation**."

Ford was at odds with the Democratic Congress over economic policies. He did not want to increase the federal deficit, and so he defied Congress's plan to lower taxes and increase government spending. Instead, in October 1974, Ford proposed a plan that involved a tax hike and a reduction in government spending. To get Americans on board with his plan, he initiated a campaign called Whip Inflation Now (WIN), in which he asked citizens to voluntarily limit their spending and consumption through thriftiness.

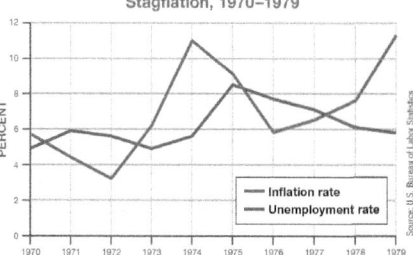

Stagflation, 1970–1979

PERCENT (y-axis: 0, 2, 4, 6, 8, 10, 12)

x-axis: 1970 1971 1972 1973 1974 1975 1976 1977 1978 1979

— Inflation rate
— Unemployment rate

Source: U.S. Bureau of Labor Statistics

In January 1975, he offered a new plan that called for a modest tax cut and a reduction in government spending. Congress approved this plan, but only after adding more tax cuts and raising government spending. In his battle with Congress, Ford vetoed more than 60 bills. Congress overrode the president's veto on several bills, increasing Social Security benefits, funding public works projects, and raising the minimum wage. Ford also battled Congress over energy policy, which had arisen as an issue under Nixon.

FOREIGN POLICY

In addition to an ailing economy, Ford also inherited the ongoing conflict in Vietnam and its many geopolitical consequences. As you have read, the United States withdrew combat troops from Vietnam in 1973 but kept an embassy in South Vietnam. However, fighting between the North and South Vietnamese had continued. The South Vietnamese army was no match for the combined North Vietnamese and Viet Cong forces. In October 1974, the leaders of communist North Vietnam prepared their final plans for the conquest of South Vietnam.

In March 1975, the North Vietnamese launched a massive assault, overwhelming South Vietnamese forces near the demilitarized zone (DMZ). As North Vietnamese troops rapidly advanced toward Saigon, the capital of South Vietnam, chaos and panic gripped the city. Thousands of soldiers left their units, and masses of civilians crowded the highways, trying to flee. Ignoring a plea from President Ford, the U.S. Congress refused to extend emergency aid to South Vietnam. A few U.S. forces remained in the city, and they worked to evacuate as many Americans and South Vietnamese as they could. On April 30, 1975, the North Vietnamese took control of Saigon and reunited North and South Vietnam into one communist-led nation. With the fall of Saigon, American efforts to stop the spread of communism in Southeast Asia failed, raising concerns about the limits of U.S. military power.

Communism also spread to neighboring Cambodia with the rise of a rebel guerilla force called the **Khmer Rouge** (kuh-MEHR ROOZH). After a civil war, a brutal communist regime took over Cambodia in 1975. The Khmer Rouge carried out a massive genocide against the Cambodian people. Not wanting to become involved in another war in Southeast Asia, the United States took no military action. By the time the regime was overthrown four years later, the Khmer Rouge had killed almost 2 million people—one-fourth of the nation's population.

Ford continued Nixon's policy of détente with the Soviet Union and signed the Helsinki Accords, or the Helsinki Final Act, in 1975. In this agreement, the 35 signing nations, including the United States and the Soviet Union, agreed to resolve conflicts peacefully, cooperate economically and scientifically, and respect human rights.

President Ford inherited from his predecessor the issue of U.S. dependence on foreign oil. In 1975, to promote conservation and energy independence, Ford imposed an import fee on oil. He hoped the fee would spur consumers to use less energy and so decrease demand for OPEC oil. Here Ford discusses his plan with the press outside the White House.

HISTORICAL THINKING

1. **READING CHECK** What challenges did President Ford inherit from President Nixon?

2. **ASK AND ANSWER QUESTIONS** What questions do you have about the fall of Saigon, and how can you find the answers to your questions?

3. **INTERPRET GRAPHS** In terms of the economic behavior of the United States, what was the trend in inflation while unemployment was falling from 1975 to 1979?

PLAN: 2-PAGE LESSON

OBJECTIVE

Explain how President Ford addressed the problems inherited from Nixon's administration.

CRITICAL THINKING SKILLS FOR LESSON 2.1

• Ask and Answer Questions

• Interpret Graphs

• Form and Support Opinions

• Make Connections

• Evaluate

HISTORICAL THINKING FOR CHAPTER 29

What policies and challenges characterized the presidencies of Nixon, Ford, and Carter? When Nixon resigned, the foreign and domestic challenges of his presidency became the responsibility of Gerald Ford. Lesson 2.1 discusses Ford's response to these challenges.

BACKGROUND FOR THE TEACHER

When President Ford signed the Helsinki Accords, he was harshly criticized for seemingly accepting Soviet control of Eastern Europe. When viewed from a historical perspective, however, it was a milestone in the protection of human rights. Prior to the agreement, pointing out human rights violations was not seen as an effective tool to use against powerful and oppressive regimes. However, the agreement included language that emphasized human rights, including freedom of movement, thought, conscience, belief, and the press. To verify compliance, the accords set up monitoring groups which tracked violations and brought them to the attention of the international community. Human Rights Watch—presently the best known human rights organization—originated as one of these groups.

FINANCIAL LITERACY

To extend their knowledge and understanding about the concepts in this lesson, refer students to the Financial Literacy handbook.

INTRODUCE & ENGAGE

REVIEW THE PATH TO THE PRESIDENCY

Invite students to complete a sequence of steps to the presidency. *(declare candidacy → campaign → win party nomination → choose running mate → campaign → general election → electoral college vote → inauguration)* **ASK:** Did Gerald Ford follow this path? *(No. When Vice President Agnew resigned, Nixon nominated Ford for vice president and Congress confirmed the nomination. When Nixon resigned, Ford became president.)* Ask students to volunteer what Gerald Ford may have been feeling and thinking on August 9, 1974. Tell students that Lesson 2.1 describes the challenges of Ford's presidency.

TEACH

GUIDED DISCUSSION

1. **Form and Support Opinions** What is your opinion of Ford's pardon of Nixon? Explain your answer. *(Answers will vary. Possible responses: The pardon was the right thing to do because it allowed the country to move forward. Punishing Nixon for criminal offenses would not have served any useful purpose. The pardon was a betrayal of the American people, who deserved to see justice carried out. Additionally, Ford had promised not to pardon Nixon, but he broke his word.)*

2. **Make Connections** How did the Helsinki Accords build on the policy of détente between the United States and the Soviet Union? *(Possible response: Détente reduced tension between the United States and the Soviet Union. By signing the Helsinki Accords, the United States, the Soviet Union, and other countries agreed to peaceful resolution of conflicts and international cooperation regarding science and economics.)*

EVALUATE

Healing the Nation Read the following quotations or post them for students to read:

I assume the Presidency under extraordinary circumstances . . . This is an hour of history that troubles our minds and hurts our hearts. —Gerald Ford, August 9, 1974

For myself and for our Nation, I want to thank my predecessor for all he has done to heal our land. —Jimmy Carter, Inaugural Address, 1975

Discuss each president's quotation within the context in which it was made. Ask students to write and share a paragraph that evaluates the extraordinary circumstances under which Ford assumed the presidency and the ways in which he healed the nation.

ACTIVE OPTIONS

On Your Feet: Identify Problems and Solutions Arrange students in small groups and provide each group with a Problem-and-Solution Organizer like the one shown. Instruct group members to choose an economic problem or foreign-policy problem that President Ford faced. Then have them complete the Problem-and-Solution Organizer to indicate how Ford addressed the problem. Allow time for groups to share their work with the class.

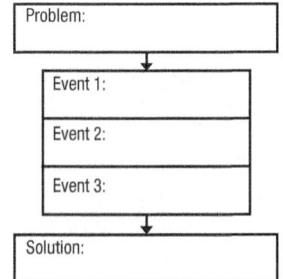

NG Learning Framework: Construct and Test a Hypothesis

ATTITUDE Curiosity

SKILLS Observation, Problem-Solving

Guide students to use the economic data from this lesson to construct and test a hypothesis concerning why stagflation is an unusual economic situation. Encourage them to collect and evaluate information from multiple primary and secondary sources about the causes and whether the stagflation that occurred in the 1970s could happen again. Then invite students to share the information in an appropriate oral or written presentation with the class.

DIFFERENTIATE

ENGLISH LANGUAGE LEARNERS ELD

Understand Portmanteau Words Inform students at **All Proficiencies** that portmanteau words are those, such as *stagflation*, that combine the sounds and meanings of two other words to create a new word. Tell students that they can often deduce the meaning from one or both of the original words. Put students into mixed-proficiency pairs and have them make a list of portmanteau words they know, and the two words they are made from, such as *podcast* (iPod + broadcast), *motel* (motor + hotel), *brunch* (breakfast + lunch), and *intercom* (internal + communication). Invite pairs to share their lists and create a master list of portmanteau words.

PRE-AP

Write a Report Instruct students to choose one of the problems that President Gerald Ford inherited and conduct online research into its origins, how Ford dealt with it, and to what degree he succeeded or failed. Students may choose domestic economic issues such as inflation, unemployment, or the energy crisis, or foreign policy issues with Vietnam, Cambodia, or the Soviet Union. Encourage students to report their findings and conclusions in writing or orally to the class.

See the Chapter Planner for more strategies for differentiation.

HISTORICAL THINKING

ANSWERS

1. President Ford had to deal with the distrust of the American people, a stagnant economy, and the ongoing conflict in Vietnam.

2. Answers will vary. Students may want to know what happened in Vietnam between the pullout of American troops and the North Vietnamese capture of Saigon. Students may suggest finding answers to their questions in print and online resources, such as texts written about the war or archival news stories.

3. As the unemployment rate began to decline, inflation rose dramatically.

CARTER AND THE ENERGY CRISIS

If you're like most people, you probably wouldn't want to be considered an "outsider." But for a presidential candidate, it's sometimes an advantage, particularly if voters don't trust the "insiders."

Rising prices and declining supplies of oil in the 1970s resulted in long lines and rationing at gas stations such as this one in Connecticut. States, cities, and individual gas stations themselves imposed limits on gas purchases.

THE OUTSIDER PRESIDENT

Gerald Ford dreamed of winning the White House in his own right, but he faced a serious challenge in 1976—conservative California governor **Ronald Reagan**. In his primary campaign, Reagan portrayed Ford as a weak president who was unable to control a Democratic Congress or to confront the Soviet Union. Reagan campaigned effectively, but Ford managed a narrow primary victory and became the Republican presidential nominee.

Because Ford appeared vulnerable in 1976, the Democratic race for president attracted a number of candidates. Among them was a little-known politician named **James Earl (Jimmy) Carter, Jr.** Although he was not taken seriously at first, Carter presented the right image for the post-Watergate era. He was a deeply religious man who promised voters, "I will never lie to you." And he was not part of the Washington political establishment, which many Americans had come to distrust.

Born in Plains, Georgia, in 1924, Carter graduated from the U.S. Naval Academy and spent seven years as a naval officer. He returned to Plains to run the family's farm supply and peanut business. As his company prospered, he turned to politics, becoming the governor of Georgia in 1970. Known as a "new South" politician, Carter supported progressive causes and civil rights, which appealed to African-American voters. At the Democratic National Convention, delegates chose Carter as their presidential nominee, and he went on to win the 1976 presidential race against Ford.

Carter won praise for some of his early actions in office, including the appointment of popular civil rights leader **Andrew Young, Jr.**, as U.S.

ambassador to the United Nations. Young had been a close associate of Dr. Martin Luther King, Jr., and was elected to Congress in 1972. Carter also supported the creation of the **Department of Education** to coordinate federal education policy. Previously, numerous federal offices had handled education-related issues. Through Carter's efforts, Congress approved the consolidation of these efforts into one cabinet-level department in 1979. Carter was also a strong supporter of affirmative action in federal government hiring. As you have read, affirmative action was challenged and upheld by the Supreme Court in the 1978 case of *Regents of the University of California* v. *Bakke*.

Carter often found himself at odds with Congress, however. Many Congressional representatives considered Carter difficult to work with. A relationship of dislike and distrust developed as Congress voted down bill after bill that Carter proposed. In return, Carter vetoed many of the bills that Congress had approved.

THE ENERGY CRISIS

Like Presidents Nixon and Ford, Carter had to battle an ongoing energy crisis. Since the 1973 oil embargo, the United States had faced rising prices for oil, declining domestic supplies, and growing energy needs. To address the crisis, Carter presented Congress with his plan for the National Energy Program in April 1977. This environmental policy emphasized reducing the demand for energy through conservation. It also called for decreased dependence on foreign oil and increased use of domestic coal as well as the development of alternative energy sources, such as solar, wind, and nuclear power. In promoting his program, Carter appealed to Americans to reduce their consumption of oil and gas.

Carter's plan ran into immediate opposition from oil companies, the auto industry, and others who supported the increased production of oil and the removal of restrictions on oil pricing. Nonetheless, in October 1977, President Carter established the **Department of Energy** to oversee federal energy policy and programs. In November 1978, he signed five energy bills into law.

Carter's push for alternative energy sources experienced a setback in 1979. A mechanical failure at the Three Mile Island nuclear power plant in Pennsylvania threatened the East Coast with a possible radiation leak. Even though power plant workers avoided a crisis, the incident raised awareness of the great risks associated with nuclear power.

In early 1979, a public uprising in Iran, as well as a strike by oilfield workers, disrupted the oil supply from that country. In late 1979, two OPEC nations decided to raise oil prices. The oil shortage and price increases led to a high rate of inflation in the United States. The events underscored the need for new sources of energy to build energy independence. But in the meantime, angry and frustrated Americans blamed Carter.

In a nationally televised speech, Carter prefaced his proposals for solving the energy crisis by describing a "crisis of confidence" gripping the nation. He claimed that many Americans no longer believed in a great future for the nation. In what came to be called the "malaise" (muh-LAYZ) speech, Carter portrayed Americans as suffering from low morale. The word *malaise* means "a general feeling of illness or unease." In the days following his speech, Carter's approval rating increased, but then negative reviews came out in the press. Carter's speech ultimately undermined confidence in his leadership. Many Americans felt that Carter blamed them, instead of his own lack of leadership, for the state of the country.

OBJECTIVE

Describe President Carter's domestic and foreign policies and accomplishments.

CRITICAL THINKING SKILLS FOR LESSON 2.2

- Identify Main Ideas and Details
- Make Inferences
- Interpret Maps
- Synthesize
- Draw Conclusions
- Identify Problems and Solutions
- Evaluate
- Form and Support Opinions
- Analyze Primary Sources

HISTORICAL THINKING FOR CHAPTER 29

What policies and challenges characterized the presidencies of Nixon, Ford, and Carter? The energy crisis and foreign affairs continued to challenge presidents in the 1970s. Lesson 2.2 discusses how Jimmy Carter addressed these pressing issues.

BACKGROUND FOR THE TEACHER

Jimmy Carter did not have a good relationship with the media. Some reporters interpreted his manner as arrogant and unfriendly. Others poked fun at his informal style and lack of pretension. Accordingly, the media portrayed Carter as inept. The so-called killer rabbit story is an example of the media's portrait of Carter. On a vacation, Carter was fishing when a rabbit swam toward him and the president used an oar to splash water on the animal to deter it from jumping in the boat. The story became national news—with articles and cartoons depicting the incident—and reinforced the image of Carter as a lightweight, trying—and failing—to defend himself against a hardly ferocious opponent.

INTRODUCE & ENGAGE

DISCUSS POLITICAL INSIDERS AND OUTSIDERS

Tell students the labels *insider* and *outsider* are relative terms, but in national politics, an insider is generally someone who has experience in federal government. For example, Gerald Ford was an insider because he had served in Congress and as vice president. **ASK:** Would you be more likely to vote for a presidential candidate who is an insider or an outsider? Why? Display a T-Chart on the board and invite students to list their reasons. *(Possible responses: An insider would know how to get things done within the system. An outsider may bring new perspectives to government.)* Tell students that in this lesson they will learn about the presidency of Jimmy Carter—an outsider.

Insider	Outsider

TEACH

GUIDED DISCUSSION

1. **Synthesize** What were President Carter's strengths and weaknesses? *(Possible response: Carter's strengths were his principles, his trustworthiness, and his support of civil rights and affirmative action. His weaknesses were his inability to work with Congress and his lack of experience in federal government.)*

2. **Draw Conclusions** How did the energy crisis raise awareness of the dependence of the U.S. economy on energy consumption? *(Answers will vary. Possible responses: Rising prices for a decreasing supply of gasoline made Americans aware of how much they depended on energy in their lives. This made some argue for the need for alternative forms of energy, which would transform the economy.)*

IDENTIFY PROBLEMS AND SOLUTIONS

Direct students' attention to the photograph of the car at a gas station. **ASK:** How does the photo illustrate a solution to the gas shortage? *(The station owner had limited the amount of gas each customer could buy.)* **ASK:** What problem might that limitation have caused if all gas stations had adopted this policy? *(Possible responses: People would have had to spend more of their time making trips to a number of gas stations to get the amount of gas they wanted or needed. Longer lines at gas stations might have resulted, causing traffic jams and increased tension in motorists.)* Challenge students to complete a Problem-and-Solution Chain to show the multiple ramifications of the energy crisis.

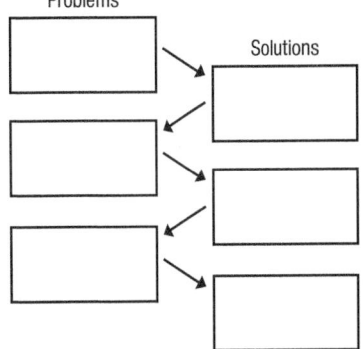

DIFFERENTIATE

STRIVING READERS

Use Either/Or Questions Monitor students' comprehension of the lesson by asking them to answer Either/Or questions independently. Then arrange them in pairs to use the text to confirm or revise their answers.

- In the 1976 general election, did Gerald Ford run against Ronald Reagan or Jimmy Carter? *(Carter)*

- Did Carter support progressive or conservative issues such as affirmative action? *(progressive)*

- Was Carter's call to conserve oil and gas supported or opposed by energy companies and the auto industry? *(opposed)*

- Do most historians consider Carter's most significant accomplishment to be the Middle East peace treaty or the return of the Panama Canal? *(Middle East peace treaty)*

GIFTED & TALENTED

Write a Historical Dialogue Instruct students to conduct online research to learn more about the peace negotiations that President Carter facilitated between Anwar Sadat and Menachem Begin at Camp David. Students should use what they learn to write dialogues that could have taken place between the leaders. The dialogues may address such topics as establishing diplomatic relations after centuries of distrust, unrest, and war in the Middle East; Israel's capture of and possible withdrawal from particular territories—including the Sinai; or the question regarding the right of Israelis and Palestinians to exist as people of independent nations. Invite students to post their dialogues online. Challenge students to rehearse and perform their dialogues for the class.

See the Chapter Planner for more strategies for differentiation.

PRIMARY SOURCE

It's clear that the true problems of our nation are much deeper— deeper than gasoline lines or energy shortages, deeper even than inflation or recession.

The threat is nearly invisible in ordinary ways. It is a crisis of confidence. It is a crisis that strikes at the very heart and soul and spirit of our national will. We can see this crisis in the growing doubt about the meaning of our own lives and in the loss of a unity of purpose for our nation.

The erosion of our confidence in the future is threatening to destroy the social and the political fabric of America.

—from the "malaise" speech by President Carter, July 15, 1979

In foreign affairs, Carter centered his policies on human rights. He believed the United States should promote human rights throughout the world, including rights to food, housing, and education as well as civil and political rights. He also believed all people had the right to bodily integrity, or ownership of one's self, which provides freedom from slavery, torture, and unlawful imprisonment. Addressing human rights violations in Latin America, Carter withdrew American support for a military dictatorship in Chile, cut off aid to a repressive regime in Nicaragua, and encouraged the governments of Brazil and Argentina to take steps toward establishing democracy.

Despite having little previous experience in foreign affairs, President Carter proved to be a successful diplomat. Shortly after taking office, he prioritized resolving a long-standing issue with the country of Panama. As you've read, Theodore Roosevelt negotiated for the United States to have control of the Panama Canal Zone in 1904. Over the years, tension grew between the United States and Panama over the issue of canal ownership. In 1977, President Carter and Omar Torrijos (OH-mahr toh-REE-hohs), the dictator of Panama, negotiated two treaties. The first treaty allowed the U.S. military to use the canal for defense. The second treaty outlined the

process of transferring ownership of the Panama Canal Zone from the United States back to Panama. Both treaties provoked fierce national debate in the Senate for more than six months, but they were eventually ratified. The treaties greatly improved relations between the United States and Latin America.

Carter's greatest foreign policy achievement involved the Middle East, however. In 1977, Egyptian President **Anwar Sadat** (AHN-wahr suh-DAHT) stunned the Arab world by visiting Israel to explore the possibility of peace talks with Prime Minister **Menachem Begin** (muh-NAH-khuhm BAY-gihn). Egypt and Israel had been enemies for many years and seemed at an impasse. Their discussions were friendly but unproductive, as neither man seemed willing to take the political risks that peace demanded.

Carter invited Sadat and Begin to join him at the presidential retreat at Camp David in Maryland in September 1978 to negotiate a peace agreement. The **Camp David Accords** led to a historic treaty the following year. Egypt agreed to recognize the state of Israel, previously unthinkable for an Arab nation. Israel agreed to return the Sinai Peninsula, which it had acquired in the 1967 Six-Day War, to Egypt.

Carter also worked to improve foreign relations with the Soviet Union by building upon the SALT I treaty you have read about. A new round of talks, **SALT II**, had begun in 1972 when Nixon was president. For seven years, negotiators refined the language of the treaty. In 1979, President Carter and General Secretary Leonid Brezhnev of the Soviet Union signed the SALT II Treaty, which limited the number of weapons each nation could have and restricted their deployment. When the U.S. Senate received the treaty for ratification, Republicans and conservative Democrats opposed the deal and wrote a letter to Carter in December 1979 explaining, "Ratification of a SALT II Treaty will not reverse trends in the military balance adverse to the United States." Days later, the Soviets invaded neighboring Afghanistan, which resulted in Carter withdrawing the

CRITICAL VIEWING President Carter (center), Egyptian president Anwar Sadat (left), and Israeli prime minister Mehanchem Begin shake hands together to celebrate the signing of the 1979 treaty that ended 31 years of war between Egypt and Israel. What does the photo convey about the mood of this moment?

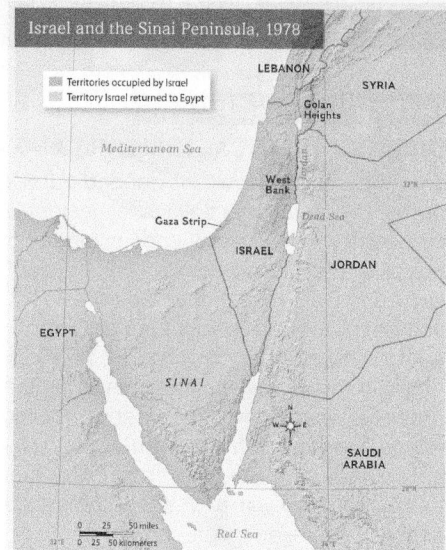

Israel and the Sinai Peninsula, 1978

- Territories occupied by Israel
- Territory Israel returned to Egypt

Mediterranean Sea · LEBANON · SYRIA · Golan Heights · West Bank · Gaza Strip · Dead Sea · ISRAEL · JORDAN · EGYPT · SINAI · SAUDI ARABIA · Red Sea

0   25   50 miles
0   25   50 kilometers

SALT II treaty from consideration and organizing an international boycott of the 1980 Summer Olympics to be held in Moscow. The Soviet invasion was intended to stop a revolt by Islamic fundamentalists against the pro-Soviet regime that ruled the country. The United States then supported and equipped the Afghan fighters, contributing to massive casualties for the Soviet troops. The invasion worsened the tensions between the United States and the Soviet Union.

HISTORICAL THINKING

1. **READING CHECK** How did President Carter plan to address the energy crisis?

2. **IDENTIFY MAIN IDEAS AND DETAILS** Describe the main features of U.S. Middle East policy and outline its strategic, political, and economic objectives.

3. **MAKE INFERENCES** Why were the Camp David Accords historically important?

4. **INTERPRET MAPS** After returning the Sinai Peninsula to Egypt, what territories did Israel still occupy?

BUILD BACKGROUND

NATIONAL ENERGY PROGRAM

After the 1973 oil embargo, U.S. oil imports increased 65 percent annually. By 1976, per capita energy use in the United States was more than twice the average in Japan and the European Economic Community. The United States also consumed 25 percent of OPEC oil production, and when OPEC increased oil prices from $13 to more than $34 per barrel, the United States experienced inflation. As a result, rising gas prices impacted consumers' budgets and reduced their income.

President Carter's strategies to reach national and personal goals for reducing energy consumption included requiring automobile manufacturers to produce more efficient cars and asking consumers to cut their use of gasoline. He also proposed insulating federal buildings and improving the efficiency of their heating and cooling systems. He asked Americans to do the same with their homes and argued for a tax incentive that would reduce the cost.

An analysis of the proposed plan by Congress ominously stated, "If the United States acts now, it may be able to . . . prevent serious economic, social, and environmental impacts. To postpone decisions . . . could mean severe hardships for all Americans within the next 10 years." Carter's plan succeeded initially. When he left office, the United States had stockpiled supplies of oil and natural gas and, by the early 1980s, increased domestic production, which decreased oil imports from 8.2 to 4.5 million barrels a day.

TEACH

GUIDED DISCUSSION

3. **Evaluate** How did Carter's position on human rights influence his foreign policy in Latin America? *(Possible response: Carter encouraged democracy in Latin American countries and withdrew American support from governments that denied human rights.)*

4. **Form and Support Opinions** Did Carter make the correct decision when he withdrew the SALT II treaty? *(Answers will vary. Possible response: Yes. The treaty was doomed in the Senate, and Soviet actions in Afghanistan proved the Soviets did not intend to honor the agreement.)*

ANALYZE PRIMARY SOURCES

Direct students' attention to the Primary Source feature. **ASK:** Why is this called the "malaise" speech even though President Carter did not use that word? *(Carter describes a general lack of confidence and feelings of lack of purpose among the American people, which could be considered malaise.)* **ASK:** Why do you think Americans initially had a positive reaction to the speech? *(Answers will vary. Possible response: People may have agreed with the president and felt that his pointing out that many felt a lack of purpose provided an opportunity to solve the problem.)* Invite students to read or listen to the entire speech and ask them to discuss their reactions.

ACTIVE OPTIONS

Active History: Analyze Steps to Peace Extend the lesson by using either the PDF or Whiteboard version of the activity. These activities take a deeper look at a topic from, or related to, the lesson. Explore the activities as a class, turn them into group assignments, or even assign them individually.

NG Learning Framework: Conduct a Cost-Benefit Analysis

ATTITUDES Curiosity, Responsibility

SKILLS Collaboration, Communication

Share with students the information from Build Background. Discuss how the energy crisis impacted the aggregate economic behavior of the U.S. economy. Then direct students to research the National Energy Program of 1977. Have students choose one aspect of the plan—such as limiting energy use, using alternative fuels, or taxing fuel inefficient vehicles—and conduct a cost-benefit analysis. After students share their analyses with the class, discuss how Carter's proposed program would impact the economy.

HISTORICAL THINKING

ANSWERS

1. Carter planned to reduce the demand for energy by appealing to Americans to cut back their consumption of oil and gas. He also proposed the use of domestic coal and the development of alternative sources of energy to decrease U.S. dependence on foreign oil.

2. Carter's strategic objective was to broker peace between Egypt and Israel. This allowed for formal recognition of the state of Israel and the return of the Sinai Peninsula to Egypt. Peaceful relations generally allow for greater economic ties between nations.

3. Egypt and Israel had been enemies of long standing, and Sadat and Begin were actually broaching a peace agreement. The Camp David Accords provided a means for the countries to peacefully negotiate their differences.

4. Israel occupied the Golan Heights, the West Bank, and the Gaza Strip.

CRITICAL VIEWING Possible responses: All three leaders are smiling, appearing to be pleased with the agreement. The celebratory triple handshake conveys friendship among the nations and optimism for the future.

HOSTAGES IN IRAN

On a visit to Iran in 1977, President Carter described the Middle Eastern nation as "an island of stability in one of the most troubled areas in the world." He did not know that within two years upheaval in Iran would threaten his own presidency.

TURMOIL IN THE PERSIAN GULF

Today, the United States and the world face an ongoing threat to peace due to uprisings and violent unrest in the Middle East, but the anti-American, anti-Western sentiments of many people in the region are nothing new. In the 1970s, Iran was vital to American interests as both an oil supplier and a political ally against communist influences in the Middle East. But the United States' relationship with Iran changed dramatically in 1979.

In 1953, President Eisenhower approved a CIA operation to return the shah of Iran, Reza Shah Pahlavi, to power by overthrowing the democratically elected prime minister Mohammed Mossadegh.

Eisenhower feared that Mossadegh's rise to power would affect American access to oil supplies in the Middle East.

Many Iranians resented the United States for directly interfering with their government by returning the shah to power. They also opposed the shah's dictatorial rule. In January 1979, protesters launched the Iranian Revolution, also referred to as the Islamic Revolution, under the leadership of **Ayatollah Ruhollah Khomeini** (ah-yuh-TOH-luh roo-HOH-luh koh-MAY-nee). An exiled religious leader, Khomeini aimed to turn Iran into an **Islamic republic**, or a state governed by Islamic law. The shah fled Iran, initially for Egypt, as Khomeini returned to the

country and took power. As a result of perceived corruption in the shah's relationship with the United States, the new leadership opposed Western influence. One of Khomeini's first moves was to end oil shipments to the United States, which he called "the Great Satan." Then other OPEC countries raised their oil prices. In the United States, long lines reappeared at gas stations, and the price of gas reached a dollar per gallon—the most expensive it had ever been.

THE HOSTAGE CRISIS

In October 1979, President Carter allowed the deposed shah to enter the United States to receive cancer treatments. This decision, which Carter viewed as a simple humanitarian gesture, angered many Iranians. On November 4, militant students in **Tehran**, the capital of Iran, stormed the American embassy and took 66 Americans as hostages, or prisoners held to force another party to do what the holder of the prisoners wants. The world watched as the blindfolded hostages were paraded before television cameras. The militants demanded the United States return the shah to Iran for trial in exchange for the release of the American hostages. Otherwise, the prisoners would be tried and possibly executed as spies.

Carter refused to return the shah to Iran. Diplomats from the United States and other countries tried to negotiate the release of the hostages but failed. The militants ignored Carter's attempts to settle the crisis through the United Nations. A painful standoff ensued.

Many Americans believed the Iran hostage crisis demonstrated that the United States' prestige and power were declining in the world. Television networks flashed nightly pictures of the hostages on humiliating public display in Tehran while crowds shouted "Death to Carter" and "Down with the United States." Americans appeared helpless and discouraged as they faced daunting challenges abroad.

DEATH IN THE DESERT

As the hostage crisis continued, President Carter consulted with the families of the hostages and mobilized his administration to find a diplomatic solution. Finally, desperate to save the Americans, Carter ordered a secret military mission to free them

The wreckage of an American helicopter and the plane it crashed into lie in the Iranian desert. The collision occurred during a failed mission in April 1980 to rescue American hostages held in Iran.

by force. The result was disastrous. In April 1980, two American helicopters involved in the secret rescue mission were disabled by mechanical problems in the Iranian desert. Another helicopter hit a U.S. cargo plane, killing eight members of the mission. Not only did the soldiers fail to free the hostages, they never even made it to Tehran. The Iranians proudly displayed the burned corpses of the helicopter crash victims before the television cameras.

Carter's credibility as a leader plummeted because most Americans blamed him for the failed mission. The 1980 presidential election was approaching, and Carter's chances for re-election did not look good.

HISTORICAL THINKING

1. **READING CHECK** What was the purpose of the Iranian Revolution of 1979?

2. **SYNTHESIZE** Describe the strategies President Carter used to address the hostage crisis in the Middle East, and explain how they related to political and economic interests.

3. **MAKE PREDICTIONS** If President Carter had made different choices during the hostage crisis, how might they have led to an alternative outcome to this historical event?

4. **ANALYZE VISUALS** What message about American power do the two photos on these pages convey?

On November 4, 1979, Iranian militants captured American embassy workers, blindfolded them, and paraded the hostages before television cameras for the world to see.

OBJECTIVE

Explain why President Carter lost the support of the American people.

CRITICAL THINKING SKILLS FOR LESSON 2.3

- Synthesize
- Make Predictions
- Analyze Visuals
- Analyze Cause and Effect
- Make Inferences

HISTORICAL THINKING FOR CHAPTER 29

What policies and challenges characterized the presidencies of Nixon, Ford, and Carter? One of Carter's major accomplishments was aiding in negotiating peace between Israel and Egypt. Lesson 2.3 explains how another Middle Eastern nation created his greatest challenge.

BACKGROUND FOR THE TEACHER

Carter's decision in October 1979 to allow the shah to undergo surgery in a New York City hospital was motivated by multiple factors. Reportedly, the president was misinformed about the seriousness of the shah's medical condition, as he had been told the shah was near death and that the only medical facility that could save his life was in New York. In addition, powerful forces inside the country—such as Henry Kissinger—heavily lobbied the administration for the shah's admittance. Finally, the president had received assurances that Iranian officials would protect Americans in Iran. Carter believed these assurances even though the existence of the new government made the promises likely moot. In the end, while the shah was recuperating in the United States, American hostages were taken in Tehran, where they remained after the shah's death in July 1980.

INTRODUCE & ENGAGE

EXPLORE THE POWER OF AN IMAGE

Before students view the lesson, read aloud the caption for the photograph of the blindfolded hostages. Invite students to share their reactions. Then have them examine the photograph. **ASK:** What details in the photo add to your understanding of the situation? *(Possible response: The hostages are blindfolded and their hands are tied behind them, which makes them appear humiliated and helpless.)* Tell students that in Lesson 2.3 they will learn how images like this influenced public opinion.

TEACH

GUIDED DISCUSSION

1. **Analyze Cause and Effect** Why did Khomeini cut off oil shipments to the United States, and what were the economic effects of this action? *(Possible response: Khomeini stopped the oil shipments because he resented historical U.S. interference in Iran. As a result, OPEC raised oil prices, which affected the cost of gasoline for Americans.)*

2. **Make Inferences** What impact did media coverage have during the Iranian hostage crisis? *(Possible response: By airing humiliating images of hostages and showing the disastrous results of a failed attempt to rescue them, the media portrayed the United States as a weakened power. Consequently, public opinion turned against Carter's leadership.)*

MORE INFORMATION

Nightly News Coverage For months, the Iranian hostage crisis dominated American news. ABC began a nightly program entitled *Iran Crisis: America Held Hostage*, hosted by Ted Koppel, which provided viewers with updates on the developments in Iran. On the CBS Evening News, revered anchor Walter Cronkite chronicled the crisis's long duration during his familiar sign-off when he intoned: "That's the way it is, Thursday, June 12, 1980, the 222nd day of captivity for the hostages in Iran." **ASK:** Why do you think American news continued to cover the story daily over such a long period of time? *(Possible response: Reporters felt the issue was critically important, and reporting on it daily ensured the public would not forget about it.)*

ACTIVE OPTIONS

On Your Feet: Create an Annotated Time Line Ask students to develop a list of events in U.S.–Iran relations from 1953 to 1980. Write the events on the board. Then divide students into groups and assign one event to each. Provide a large sheet of paper to each group and tell members to work together to label and annotate their event. Annotations should indicate the significance of the event to the political and economic relationship between the United States and Iran. Direct groups to create a time line by arranging the events in order. Invite groups to discuss their event with the class.

NG Learning Framework: Connect Past and Present

ATTITUDE Curiosity

KNOWLEDGE Our Human Story

Divide the class into three groups to gather facts about Iran's government under Reza Shah Pahlavi, the government under Ayatollah Ruhollah Khomeini, and the current relationship between the United States and Iran. Invite each group to choose an appropriate means of sharing information with the class. Then discuss how the content of the three presentations are related—focusing specifically on how events of the past influence current realities.

For students who develop an interest in the causes and resolution of the hostage crisis, suggest that they read the online American Story "The Iran Hostage Crisis."

DIFFERENTIATE

STRIVING READERS

Summarize Direct students to work in pairs to read and summarize the text and photograph captions. Tell students to write at least two notes for each of the sections. After they have completed their notes, guide students to create a summary statement for each section followed by a summary statement for the whole lesson.

PRE-AP

Write a Comparison-Contrast Essay Instruct students to conduct online research to learn how the United States' relationship with Iran changed after the Islamic Revolution in 1979 and how events following the revolution have continued to impact the two countries' relationship. Encourage students to use a Venn diagram or Comparison Chart to note the similarities and differences of the relationship between the nations before and after 1979. Instruct students to use their research to write a comparison-contrast essay. Invite students to share their essays with the class.

See the Chapter Planner for more strategies for differentiation.

HISTORICAL THINKING

ANSWERS

1. The purpose of the Iranian Revolution was to remove the shah from power and to create an Islamic republic.

2. Iran was a political ally in the Middle East and economically valuable as an oil supplier, so Carter tried diplomatic means to free the hostages and not sour the relationship between the two countries. However, he ordered a secret military mission to rescue them when other means failed.

3. If Carter had used effective military intervention, the hostages might have been freed. However, effective military intervention might have led to war.

4. The photos send the message that the United States was weak and unable to effectively respond to a crisis.

CHAPTER 29 REVIEW
PRESIDENTIAL SUCCESSES AND FAILURES

VOCABULARY

Use each of the following vocabulary words in a sentence that shows an understanding of the term's meaning.

1. silent majority

   Nixon hoped to appeal to the silent majority, rather than to those Americans protesting on the streets.

2. détente
3. DDT
4. overregulation
5. wiretapping
6. stagflation
7. malaise
8. Islamic republic

READING STRATEGY
IDENTIFY MAIN IDEAS AND DETAILS

Use a graphic organizer like the one below to identify the supporting details about the impact of the Watergate scandal. Then answer the question.

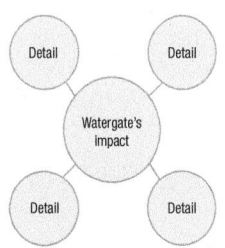

9. What impact did the Watergate scandal have on Nixon's presidency?

MAIN IDEAS

Answer the following questions. Support your answers with evidence from the chapter.

10. What group of Americans made up Nixon's silent majority? **LESSON 1.1**

11. What were some of the Burger Court's rulings on forced busing to achieve integration? **LESSON 1.2**

12. Why did Nixon create the Environmental Protection Agency? **LESSON 1.3**

13. What conflict arose between environmentalists and property rights advocates in the 1970s? **LESSON 1.3**

14. How did the Watergate scandal provoke a constitutional crisis? **LESSON 1.5**

15. How did the Vietnam War come to an end, and what were the results? **LESSON 2.1**

16. What were the results of the Camp David Accords? **LESSON 2.2**

17. What event initiated the Iran hostage crisis? **LESSON 2.3**

HISTORICAL THINKING

Answer the following questions. Support your answers with evidence from the chapter.

18. **DRAW CONCLUSIONS** What did George Wallace's presidential campaign reveal about changing voting patterns in the United States?

19. **MAKE CONNECTIONS** What aspects of Carter's energy policy are still emphasized today?

20. **EVALUATE** What were some of Nixon's notable achievements as president?

21. **FORM AND SUPPORT OPINIONS** What is your opinion of President Ford's pardon of Richard Nixon? Give reasons for your answer.

22. **SYNTHESIZE** How did events in the 1970s reflect a more global and interconnected economy?

23. **COMPARE AND CONTRAST** How did national policies on integration in public schools change during the 1970s?

INTERPRET GRAPHS

This graph shows the percent change in world oil prices, U.S. gas prices, sales of Japanese-made cars in the United States, and all car sales in the United States from 1978 to 1982. The base year is 1978. A positive percent change represents an increase from the base, while a negative percent change represents a decrease. Study the graph and answer the questions that follow.

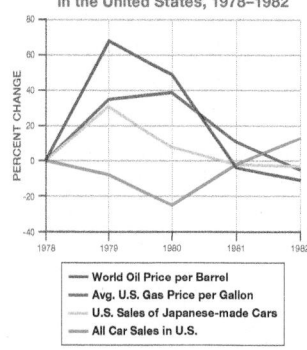

Gas Prices and Car Sales
in the United States, 1978–1982

- World Oil Price per Barrel
- Avg. U.S. Gas Price per Gallon
- U.S. Sales of Japanese-made Cars
- All Car Sales in U.S.

Sources: Inflationdata.com, CQPress, U.S. International Trade Commission

24. Based on the graph and what you know about Japanese-made cars, what is a possible cause of the increase in the sales of these cars in 1979?

25. What limitations exist in assigning exact cause-and-effect relationships to the factors shown on the graph? In other words, why is it difficult to say for sure that one factor causes another?

ANALYZE SOURCES

American nature writer Edward Abbey based his book *Desert Solitaire* (1968) on his experiences working as a park ranger in Utah. Abbey's writing, though sometimes controversial, expressed his deep-seated love of the American West. Read this excerpt from *Desert Solitaire* and answer the question that follows.

No, wilderness is not a luxury but a necessity of the human spirit, and as vital to our lives as water and good bread. A civilization which destroys what little remains of the wild, the spare, the original, is cutting itself off from its origins and betraying the principle of civilization itself.

26. What is your opinion of the reasons Abbey gives for the need to practice environmental conservation?

CONNECT TO YOUR LIFE

27. **EXPLANATORY** President Nixon enacted various measures to address environmental problems in the United States. Choose a region of the United States and identify an environmental issue there. Write an essay in which you describe the policies that address that issue, and explain how these policies affect your life.

TIPS

- Research the physical and human characteristics of the region you've chosen as well as policies that address the environmental issue you've identified.
- Create a topic sentence that introduces the region and issue you've chosen.
- Develop your topic by describing relevant policies on this issue and explaining their effects on your life.
- Use two or three vocabulary words from the chapter in your essay.
- End your essay with a general statement about the impact of environmental protections.

VOCABULARY ANSWERS

1. Nixon hoped to appeal to the silent majority, rather than to those Americans protesting on the streets.

2. Jimmy Carter's negotiations with Israeli and Egyptian leaders led to a period of détente between those countries.

3. Rachel Carson warned of the effects of the pesticide DDT entering the food chain.

4. Restrictive environmental laws led some corporations and politicians to criticize the government for overregulation.

5. The Watergate burglars pled guilty to wiretapping phones, which allowed them to secretly listen to conversations.

6. Slow economic growth, high unemployment rates, and rising inflation led to a period of stagflation during the 1970s.

7. Carter's address to the nation in 1979 was called the malaise speech because he accused Americans of losing confidence in the future.

8. The Iranian Revolution placed religious leader Ayatollah Khomeini in power with the rule of law based on Islam, turning Iran into an Islamic republic.

READING STRATEGY ANSWER

9. Americans lost trust in Nixon, his approval rating dropped, and he resigned in order to avoid impeachment and removal from office.

MAIN IDEAS ANSWERS

10. Nixon's silent majority consisted of conservative Americans who wanted the country to be more stable but did not voice their concerns publicly.

11. In *Swann* v. *Mecklenburg Board of Education*, the Burger Court forced the school district to integrate schools through busing. Later, the *Milliken* v. *Bradley* decision put the responsibility for integration on local communities.

12. Nixon created the Environmental Protection Agency (EPA) to enforce laws such as the Clean Air Act, the Clean Water Act, and the Endangered Species Act.

13. Environmentalists supported the expansion of public lands, but property rights advocates argued that limiting their use of natural resources on protected lands interfered with economic progress.

14. Judge John Sirica ordered President Nixon to release potentially incriminating tapes that were recorded in the Oval Office. Nixon refused, claiming executive privilege. Special Prosecutor Leon Jaworski appealed to the Supreme Court, and the Court ruled that Nixon's tapes were not protected by executive privilege and that Nixon must hand them over.

15. The Vietnam War ended when the United States withdrew its troops and the North Vietnamese took over Saigon, reuniting North and South Vietnam into one communist nation. The inability of American efforts to stop the spread of communism raised doubts about U.S. military power.

16. The Camp David Accords led to a treaty in which Egypt recognized the state of Israel and Israel returned the Sinai Peninsula to Egypt.

17. Iranian militants took American hostages in retaliation for President Carter's decision to allow the shah to undergo medical treatment in the United States.

HISTORICAL THINKING ANSWERS

18. Wallace's campaign revealed that the South was moving away from the Democratic Party.

19. The expansion of alternative energy sources and the decreased dependence on foreign oil are aspects of Carter's energy policy still emphasized today.

20. Nixon's achievements include establishing relations with China, negotiating nuclear arms restrictions with the Soviet Union, enacting legislation to ensure workplace safety, and providing protection for the environment.

21. Answers will vary. Possible responses: The pardon allowed the country to focus on other matters. The pardon betrayed Americans who wanted Nixon punished.

22. Answers will vary. Possible response: Events like the 1973 oil embargo showed how events in one nation could directly impact conditions in another. During this event, OPEC's decision led to soaring gas prices in America.

23. The Supreme Court first ruled that the federal government could force school districts to integrate via busing but later ruled that the federal government could not force local governments to bus students, thus leaving it to local communities to determine how to integrate their schools.

INTERPRET GRAPHS ANSWERS

24. Japanese-made cars were more fuel-efficient than American-made cars, which appealed to consumers in view of rising gas prices.

25. Answers will vary. Possible response: Other factors not shown on the table, such as price and car size may have influenced car sales.

ANALYZE SOURCES ANSWER

26. Answers will vary. Possible response: Edward Abbey's argument that a civilization must keep in touch with its origins is thoughtful and a conclusion that a civilized society should agree with. Abbey makes a good case that the wild is landscape unmodified by humans and a place to be preserved and appreciated.

CONNECT TO YOUR LIFE ANSWER

27. Answers will vary. Students should create a topic sentence that introduces the region and environmental issue associated with it. Students should specify policies that address the issue and describe how the policies affect their lives. Essays should reflect relevant research and accurate reporting of environmental policies, include two or three vocabulary words from the chapter, and conclude with a general statement about the impact of environmental protections.

UNIT 9 RESOURCES

UNIT INTRODUCTION

UNIT TIME LINE

UNIT WRAP-UP

CONNECTION

National Geographic Magazine Adapted Articles

- "U.S. Climate Refugees Race Against Time"
- "Shell Shock" ONLINE

Unit 9 Inquiry: Conduct Oral History Interviews

NG Learning Framework Activities

- Create a History Game
- Form a Political Party

Unit 9 Formal Assessment

CHAPTER 30 RESOURCES

Available at NGLSync.Cengage.com

TEACHER RESOURCES & ASSESSMENT

Reading and Note-Taking

Vocabulary Practice

Document-Based Question Template

Social Studies Skills Lessons

- Reading: Analyze Cause and Effect
- Writing: Explanatory

Formal Assessment

- Chapter 30 Pretest
- Chapter 30 Tests A & B
- Section Quizzes

Chapter 30 Answer Key

ExamView®
One-time Download

STUDENT DIGITAL RESOURCES

- eEdition
- Handbooks
- Online Atlas

- American Gallery Online
- History Notebook
- Active History

- American Voices (Biographies)
- Reid on the Road video series
- Literature Analysis

- Projects for Inquiry-Based Learning

Chapter 30 Spanish Resources are available at NGLSync.Cengage.com.

AMERICAN STORIES ONLINE | The Gulf Wars

- Study Primary Sources: Speech by President George H.W. Bush
- On Your Feet: Conduct an Interview

NG Learning Framework:
Report on an Environmental Disaster

SECTION 1 RESOURCES
THE CONSERVATIVE MOVEMENT

LESSON 1.1
Roots of the Conservative Movement

- On Your Feet: Word Chain

NG Learning Framework:
Write a Biography

LESSON 1.2
Growth of the Sunbelt

- On Your Feet: Team Word Webbing

NG Learning Framework:
Draft a City Plan

LESSON 1.3
Election of Ronald Reagan

- On Your Feet: Create a Visual Time Line

NG Learning Framework:
Analyze Speeches

American Voices Biography
Ronald Reagan ONLINE

SECTION 2 RESOURCES
REAGAN'S REVOLUTION

LESSON 2.1
Reducing Government

- On Your Feet: Three-Step Interview

NG Learning Framework:
Compare Past and Present Policies

LESSON 2.2
Reagan's Foreign Policy

- On Your Feet: Jigsaw Strategy

NG Learning Framework:
Investigate Iran-Contra Scandal

LESSON 2.3
Social Changes and Tensions

- ▶ Internet Research
- Active History: Evaluate the Impact of Technology

NG Learning Framework:
Map Activism in History

American Voices Biography
Ellen Ochoa ONLINE

SECTION 3 RESOURCES
THE COLD WAR ENDS

LESSON 3.1
Collapse of the Soviet Union

AMERICAN GALLERY ONLINE | The Fall of the Berlin Wall

NG Learning Framework:
Report on Tiananmen Square

LESSON 3.2
CURATING HISTORY
The Newseum, Washington, D.C.

- On Your Feet: Be a Journalist

LESSON 3.3
DOCUMENT-BASED QUESTION
The End of the Cold War

- On Your Feet: Jigsaw Strategy

LESSON 3.4
George H.W. Bush and the Persian Gulf War

- On Your Feet: Create a Fact Chart

NG Learning Framework:
Research the Gulf War

CHAPTER 30 REVIEW

STRIVING READERS

STRATEGY ❶
USE K-W-L CHARTS

Provide each student with a K-W-L Chart. Work with students to brainstorm what they already know about historical events of the 1980s and early 1990s, such as Ronald Reagan's election, the end of the Cold War, George H.W. Bush's election, and the Persian Gulf War. Have students add these ideas to the first column of the chart. In the second column, tell them to write three questions they want to know the answers to, such as "How did a movie star become president?" or "What were the effects of deregulation?" Encourage students to complete their charts as they read each lesson.

K What Do I Know?	W What Do I Want To Learn?	L What Did I Learn?

Use with All Lessons

STRATEGY ❷
USE A TASKS APPROACH

Help students get information from visuals by using the following TASKS strategy.

T Look for a **title** that may give the main idea.

A **Ask** yourself what a visual is trying to show.

S Determine how any **symbols** are used.

K Look for a **key** or legend.

S **Summarize** what you learned.

Use with Lessons 1.2 and 3.4 *Suggest that students use the TASKS strategy to analyze the maps and photographs in these lessons.*

STRATEGY ❸
MAKE A TOP FIVE FACTS LIST

Tell students to reread the lesson and all captions for visuals that it contains. Then ask students to write down five facts they remember from the text. Have students work with a partner to compare lists and then to consolidate their lists into one final top five facts list. Encourage pairs to read facts from their lists aloud.

Use with All Lessons

INCLUSION

STRATEGY ❶
BUILD A TIME LINE

After students read each lesson, instruct them to identify key events of the conservative revolution and of the Reagan and Bush presidencies. Help students add these events to a time line on the board. You may expand and extend the time line as you guide students to add more key events from each lesson in the chapter.

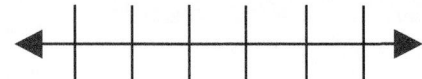

Use with All Lessons *For example, key events from Lesson 1.1 might include the founding of conservative organizations and think tanks (late 1960s) and reaction against* Roe v. Wade *(1973).*

STRATEGY ❷
USE ECHO READING

Point out that the Main Idea statements all relate to important aspects of renewed conservatism in the United States during the 1980s. Pair each inclusion student with a proficient reader. Ask the proficient reader to read aloud the Main Idea statement at the beginning of a lesson. The less proficient partner will "echo" by reading the same statement.

Use with All Lessons

ENGLISH LANGUAGE LEARNERS

STRATEGY 1
USE VISUALS TO PREDICT CONTENT

Direct students at the **Emerging** and **Expanding** levels to read the lesson title and look at the visuals. Then ask them to write a sentence predicting how the visuals will relate to the lesson. After reading, you may wish to have students verify their predictions and reword sentences if necessary.

Use with All Lessons *Encourage students at the **Emerging** level to ask questions if they have trouble writing a prediction. Students at the **Bridging** level could help students at the **Emerging** and **Expanding** levels write their predictions.*

STRATEGY 2
COMPOSE CAPTIONS

Pair students at the **Emerging** and **Expanding** levels with English-proficient students. Have students work together to write original captions for the photographs in the chapter. You might ask pairs to compare their captions with the captions written by other pairs.

Use with All Lessons *For lessons with more than one photograph, make sure students write original captions for all photographs. You might also expand this activity to include the painting of Sandra Day O'Connor in Lesson 2.1.*

STRATEGY 3
PAIR PARTNERS FOR DICTATION

After reading a lesson, direct students at **All Proficiencies** levels to write in their own words a sentence expressing an important idea from the lesson. Pair students and let them take turns dictating their sentences to each other. Then encourage them to work together to check spelling and accuracy.

Use with All Lessons

GIFTED & TALENTED

STRATEGY 1
CREATE A GRAPHIC BIOGRAPHY

Tell students to conduct online research about one of the important conservative figures in the Reagan presidency and then create a graphic-style biography. Encourage students to interpret the person's thoughts and actions within the context of the 1980s. Students may include direct or indirect quotations and visuals illustrating that individual's role in the conservative revolution. Invite students to share their completed graphic biographies and answer any questions.

Use with Lessons 1.1, 2.1, 2.2, and 3.4 *You might suggest students choose one of the prominent people mentioned in the lessons as a subject for their biography.*

STRATEGY 2
TWEET THE FALL OF THE WALL

Have students conduct online research to find firsthand acounts of the Berlin Wall falling. Instruct students to take on the identity of a real or imagined person and create the person's Twitter handle and online profile. Then ask students to compose a series of tweets about what is going on as the wall comes down, complete with hashtags. Discuss with the class how the tweets brought the historical event to life.

Use with Lessons 3.1 and 3.3

PRE-AP

STRATEGY 1
WRITE A LETTER HOME

Instruct students to conduct online research to learn more about the migration of people from the Frostbelt to the Sunbelt. Tell students to suppose they were part of that migration and are writing a letter back home describing their new city and the reasons they migrated. Contrast their new life with their previous one, addressing both positive and negative aspects. Invite students to read their letters to the class.

Use with Lesson 1.2

STRATEGY 2
CREATE A GALLERY WALK

Have students locate online resources, such as editorial cartoons, photographs, illustrations, song lyrics, and quotations from key individuals, to learn more about the conservative revolution. Students can work together to group their findings by medium or by theme and set up stations with signs to connect items they have for display with the larger social, political, and economic developments of the 1980s. Ask students to discuss the impact the displayed items might have had on the present. Then conduct a gallery walk.

Use with All Lessons

HISTORICAL THINKING What major changes occurred in the United States during Ronald Reagan's presidency?

CRITICAL VIEWING *Portrait of President Ronald Reagan in the Oval Office* was taken by American photographer Arnold Newman in 1981, the year Reagan took office. What does the photo convey about the former actor and California governor's attitude toward his new job?

"**The business of our nation goes forward.**"

—President Ronald Reagan

1066 CHAPTER 30

The Conservative Revolution 1067

INTRODUCE THE PHOTOGRAPH

PRESIDENT REAGAN AT THE WHITE HOUSE

Have students study the photograph and quotation that open this chapter. Explain that the photographer wanted to convey a message about President Reagan through his photograph. Tell students to focus on how President Reagan is standing, the position of his arms, and the look on his face. **ASK:** Why might the photographer have wanted to portray President Reagan as determined, tough, and in command? *(Possible response: Reagan was still viewed by many people in the country as an actor, not a serious politician. The photographer may have wanted to make him appear more presidential.)*

SHARE BACKGROUND

The Oval Office is located in the southeast corner of the West Wing of the White House and is the president's main office. The room is 35 feet long, 29 feet wide, and 18 feet high at its highest point. Doors along the walls open to different places in the White House, including the Rose Garden, a private smaller study, and the president's personal dining room. Every incoming president is allowed to personalize the Oval Office, including new furniture, artwork, historic pieces, drapes, upholstery colors, and the presidential rug. Several presidents, including President Reagan, have chosen to use the historic Resolute desk, made from wood once part of a British ship, the H.M.S. *Resolute*. The presidential flag stands to the left of the president's desk, with the United States flag to the right.

CRITICAL VIEWING Possible response: With a close-up of President Reagan in the foreground and the Oval Office in the background, the photograph conveys the idea that Reagan is an imposing leader.

For Chapter 30 Spanish Resources, visit the Resources Menu. Chapter 30 Resources are available at NGLSync.Cengage.com.

HISTORICAL THINKING QUESTION

What major changes occurred in the United States during Ronald Reagan's presidency?

Jigsaw Activity: Preview Content This activity will help students preview and make predictions about the topics covered in Chapter 30. Divide the class into three groups. Assign one of the section titles to each group and have them discuss what they think they will learn. Ask students to consider the following cues and questions:

Group 1: Section 1 is about the roots and beliefs of the conservative movement and the election of Ronald Reagan as president of the United States. What factors contributed to the growth of the conservative movement in the United States? Why was Ronald Reagan a popular figure in the conservative movement?

Group 2: Section 2 is about the domestic and foreign policies that framed the Reagan presidency and the social and technological changes during the 1980s. How did conservative beliefs affect policy decisions made by the Reagan administration? What social changes and challenges in space exploration did the country face?

Group 3: Section 3 is about how the collapse of the Soviet Union and the end of the Cold War ushered in new political and military challenges caused by tensions in the Middle East. What caused the collapse of the Soviet Union? What new challenges and conflicts did the United States experience in the Middle East?

Regroup students so each new grouping has at least one member from each original group. Have students share what they predicted about their assigned section so that other students can learn what to expect from their reading in Chapter 30.

INTRODUCE THE READING STRATEGY

ANALYZE CAUSE AND EFFECT

Explain that identifying the cause of an event can help students understand how one event affects later events. Turn to the Chapter Review and preview the Cause-and-Effect Chart with students. As they read the chapter, have students analyze how one event affected succeeding events and created new challenges and opportunities for Americans.

KEY DATES FOR CHAPTER 30

1980	Ronald Reagan elected president
1981	Attempted assassination of President Reagan
1981	Sandra Day O'Connor is first woman on Supreme Court
1983	Invasion of Grenada
1986	Explosion of the *Challenger* space shuttle
1986	Iran-Contra scandal
1987	Intermediate-Range Nuclear Forces Treaty
1988	George H.W. Bush elected president
1990	Persian Gulf War
1991	Collapse of the Soviet Union

INTRODUCE CHAPTER VOCABULARY

KEY VOCABULARY

SECTION 1

conservative	safety-net programs	think tank
Rustbelt		

SECTION 2

acquired immunodeficiency syndrome (AIDS)	human immunodeficiency virus (HIV)	originalism
		personal computer
apartheid	income inequality	static
cultural advocacy	Internet	supply-side economics
deregulation		

SECTION 3

deficit reduction	hardliner	Politburo
glasnost	*perestroika*	theocracy

WORD MAP

As they read the chapter, have students complete a Word Map for each Key Vocabulary word. Have them write the term in the center oval and then, as they encounter the term in the chapter, complete as much of the Word Map for that term as they can. Model an example for students on the board, using the graphic organizer below.

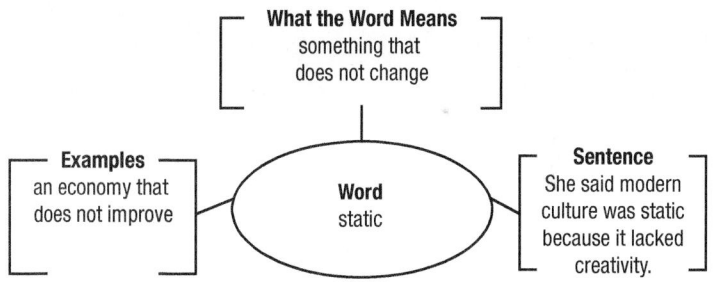

What the Word Means
something that does not change

Examples
an economy that does not improve

Word
static

Sentence
She said modern culture was static because it lacked creativity.

AMERICAN STORIES ONLINE

For instructional support for the online American Story "The Gulf Wars," go to NGLSync.Cengage.com.

ROOTS OF THE CONSERVATIVE MOVEMENT

The Republican Party had suffered two major blows in the 1960s and 1970s: the failed 1964 candidacy of Barry Goldwater and Richard Nixon's Watergate scandal. For the 1980 election, the party was looking for an upbeat nominee with the charisma to charm both Republicans and Democrats dissatisfied with Carter's presidency.

A CONSERVATIVE MOVEMENT ARISES

With the nation enduring economic and foreign policy difficulties, Jimmy Carter faced a difficult bid for re-election in 1980. Carter and his fellow Democrats faced another challenge as well—the steady rise of a conservative movement in the country. Several Republican presidential candidates competed for the nomination in 1980. Two notable politicians in the running were former CIA director **George H.W. Bush** and moderate Republican congressman **John B. Anderson** from Illinois. But the favorite to win the nomination was Ronald Reagan, the popular California governor and former movie star. Since delivering a well-received speech endorsing Barry Goldwater for president in 1964, Reagan had emerged as a conservative leader.

The conservative movement began in the late 1960s when numerous grassroots organizations, such as the American Conservative Union (ACU) and Young Americans for Freedom, began working together to promote their ideals. **Conservatives** support traditional policies in economic and social legislation and are more likely to favor established systems of government over progressive ideas

Three teleprompters broadcast Pastor Joel Osteen's Sunday service to about 25,000 people at the Lakewood Church in Houston, Texas. The rise in religious fundamentalism during the 1980s led to the creation of today's megachurches, or very large non-Catholic Christian churches.

or radical changes. During this time, a number of conservative **think tanks** emerged: groups of experts who conduct research and discuss issues in order to craft potential solutions to social and economic problems. Conservative politicians used the data that think tanks generated to inform their decisions about legislation. Prominent conservative think tanks still active today include the **American Enterprise Institute** and the **Heritage Foundation**. Conservative think tanks, lobbyists, and politicians shared the goal of shaping a compelling message to attract voter support. They hoped to gain more influence throughout the nation and in Washington.

CONSERVATIVE BELIEFS

In general, conservatives favored making the government smaller, decreasing taxes, and deregulating industries. They opposed greater federal regulation of the economy. They argued that if people and businesses had more freedom to make their own economic choices, their purchasing power would stimulate greater growth and a better standard of living for all. Conservatives favored less taxation, arguing that allowing consumers and businesses to keep more of their wages and profits would spur greater investment and growth. In addition, because of their belief that individualism is superior to government action, conservatives opposed government social programs, including many of President Johnson's Great Society welfare reforms, claiming they required high taxation and massive spending by the federal government. As American patriots, however, they did believe in government spending to support a robust, well-funded military.

Many conservatives, but not all, drove a large social agenda that was deeply rooted in religion. This agenda was hotly debated by those who felt that allowing religious views to shape political policies violated the separation of church and state. Still, the 1970s and 1980s were a time of renewed interest in Christian values, much like the First and Second Great Awakenings of the 18th and 19th centuries. Instead of giving powerful sermons in tents, however, the conservative movement built part of its base and conveyed its message through evangelical churches, televangelism, and other media outlets. The Reverend **Jerry Falwell**, a Baptist minister from Virginia, started a grassroots organization called the **Moral Majority**. The organization was made up of Christian fundamentalists, or people who believe in the literal interpretation of the Bible, and evangelists, or people who believe it is their duty to spread their religious faith and win converts. According to Falwell,

the purpose of the Moral Majority was to press the government into supporting social programs that promoted what they termed "traditional family values." Falwell and his followers spoke out against what they saw as the evils of society: abortion, out-of-wedlock births, homosexuality, the teaching of evolution in schools, and increased drug use among Americans. They also condemned what they perceived as the resulting breakdown of the American family.

Television programs, magazines, and newspapers featured Falwell regularly. The organization's message became so popular that Pat Robertson, one of Falwell's supporters and a fundamentalist Christian preacher, created a television network to feature the views of prominent members of the Moral Majority. The ideas of the Moral Majority spread throughout American politics as well. Conservative politicians spoke out against abortion and the *Roe v. Wade* decision (1973), which made abortion legal under certain circumstances. They demanded that Congress restrict access to abortion, publicly protesting outside abortion clinics and organizing large "Right to Life" demonstrations.

Many religious conservatives also spoke out against Darwin's theory of evolution, an idea they deemed blasphemous, or ungodly, because it contradicted the creation account in the Bible. The growing gay rights and feminist movements as well as the rise in out-of-wedlock births received criticism because the Moral Majority believed these things threatened the traditional definition of family—a married man and woman, and their children. Throughout the late 1970s, and especially in the South and the West, conservatives were becoming a growing and powerful political force.

HISTORICAL THINKING

1. **READING CHECK** What were the conservatives' views on the federal government?

2. **DESCRIBE** What was the main goal of the conservative movement?

3. **MAKE GENERALIZATIONS** The Moral Majority was concerned about the effects of which social changes and movements on the American family, and why?

PLAN: 2-PAGE LESSON

OBJECTIVE

Analyze the emergence of the conservative movement in the 1970s and 1980s and how it affected American life.

CRITICAL THINKING SKILLS FOR LESSON 1.1

- Describe
- Make Generalizations
- Make Connections
- Determine Word Meaning
- Analyze Primary Sources

HISTORICAL THINKING FOR CHAPTER 30

What major changes occurred in the United States during Ronald Reagan's presidency?
The 1960s conservative movement focused on smaller government, reduced taxes, deregulation, and conservative religious beliefs. Lesson 1.1 describes the growth of the conservative movement, including fundamentalist Christian values.

BACKGROUND FOR THE TEACHER

Christian fundamentalism arose in the late 19th century and continued to grow as a movement over the next two centuries. Fundamentalism started out as a response to the theory of biological evolution, which many church leaders believed was in opposition to biblical teachings. Instead, they supported creationism, based on the creation story in Genesis, and intelligent design, a belief that biological diversity could be explained only through the existence of an intelligent Creator. In the early 20th century, fundamentalists worked to ban the teaching of evolution in public schools. In 1950, the Baptist Bible Fellowship formed and became one of the largest Christian fundamentalist organizations in the country. From its teachings emerged Liberty University, founded in 1971 by Jerry Falwell, and Regent University, founded in 1978 by Pat Robertson. Through the end of the 20th century and into the 21st century, Christian fundamentalists have continued to fight against the teaching of evolution in schools.

INTRODUCE & ENGAGE

ANALYZE THE FIRST AMENDMENT

Review with students the First Amendment and the Establishment Clause, which states, "Congress shall make no law respecting an establishment of religion." Discuss with students the intent and function of the Establishment Clause. Then write the term "separation of church and state" on the board. Ask students what they think the term means and how it relates to the First Amendment. Tell students they will learn about the conservative movement of the 1980s and how it led to the rise of Christian fundamentalism and its influence on politics.

TEACH

GUIDED DISCUSSION

1. **Make Connections** How might religious conservatives interpret the First Amendment clause regarding the debate over the separation of church and state? (*Possible response: Religious conservatives might say the First Amendment clause is about treating all religions equally and that any political intentions that do not favor one religion over another are legal under the Constitution.*)

2. **Determine Word Meaning** How did the Moral Majority define "traditional family values," and does that definition still apply today? (*Possible response: The Moral Majority described "traditional family values" as supportive of heterosexual marriages, against abortion, and promoting fundamentalist teachings. Today the term "traditional family values" is far less meaningful, as the word* family *now includes heterosexual, same-sex, and single-parent families with diverse religious and social beliefs.*)

ANALYZE PRIMARY SOURCES

Direct students' attention to the Primary Source feature. Have them work in pairs to interpret the meaning of Jerry Falwell's 1980 statement. Encourage students to use a graphic organizer like the Problem-and-Solution diagram shown here to record their thoughts. Students should identify the "internal problems" Falwell is referring to and then note his solution. Invite pairs to share their ideas with the class.

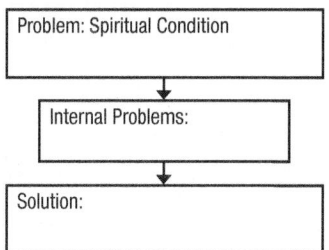

Problem: Spiritual Condition

↓

Internal Problems:

↓

Solution:

ACTIVE OPTIONS

On Your Feet: Word Chain Arrange students in three lines. Hand a piece of paper to the first person in each line with one of these words or terms from the text: *conservatives, Moral Majority, Christian fundamentalists*. The first student in line adds a word that relates to the original word or term. Students pass the paper from person to person, each one adding a word or phrase they associate with the previously written word. Ask a volunteer from each group to read the word chain, and have the rest of the class listen for any words that were used in more than one chain or that may not connect to the original word or term.

NG Learning Framework: Write a Biography

ATTITUDE Curiosity

KNOWLEDGE Our Human Story

Guide students to learn more about one of the religious leaders featured in this lesson. Instruct them to write a short biography or profile about the religious leader, using information from the chapter and additional source materials. Encourage students to make the connection between the leader's beliefs and his role in politics. Students should include in their biography the rise of Christian fundamentalism and its connection to the debate over the separation of church and state. Invite students to share their biography or profile with the class.

DIFFERENTIATE

ENGLISH LANGUAGE LEARNERS `ELD`

Create a Word Web Pair students at the **Emerging** and **Expanding** levels with students at the **Bridging** level. Tell partners to take turns reading paragraphs in the lesson, noting characteristics of the conservative movement. After each paragraph, instruct students to write the characteristics on the spokes of the Word Web. Direct pairs to trade and compare webs, looking up unfamiliar terms. Final webs may include *smaller government, larger military, industry deregulation, lower taxes, fewer social programs,* and *social agenda rooted in fundamentalist Christian principles.*

PRE-AP

Research and Write a Report Tell students that before the 1970s, think tanks used objective research to educate politicians and influence government policies. Instruct students to conduct online research to learn more about how 1970s conservative think tanks began to influence the political world in new ways. Have students report on the general goals and methods of think tanks and analyze the impact of conservative think tanks, providing examples from the 1970s and recent years. Remind students to assess the credibility of each source they find and to cite any source they quote or paraphrase. Invite students to present their reports to the class.

See the Chapter Planner for more strategies for differentiation.

HISTORICAL THINKING

ANSWERS

1. Conservatives believed in limited government, decreased taxes, deregulation of industries, and reduced regulation of the economy. They believed that businesses flourish when government intervention is minimal and individuals make their own economic choices.

2. The main goal of the conservative movement was to convince politicians and American voters to start adopting more traditional stances on economic and social issues.

3. The Moral Majority was concerned with the breakdown of traditional family values due to the Supreme Court decision in *Roe* v. *Wade*, the growing feminist and gay rights movements, and an increase in both out-of-wedlock births and the use of illegal drugs.

GROWTH OF THE SUNBELT

Have you ever moved from one part of the country to another, or do you know friends or family members who have? In the decades following World War II, many Americans migrated from the northern part of the country to the South and West—a demographic shift that changed the nation's political landscape.

DEMOGRAPHIC SHIFTS

As you have read, after World War II, the United States experienced a widespread demographic shift as families moved from cities and farms to suburbs. In addition, a large number of Americans began moving from the nation's Frostbelt—the Northeast, the Great Lakes region, and the Midwest—to the nation's southern and western states, a region that became known as the Sunbelt. Population booms occurred in states such as Texas, Florida, and California. In fact, migration to the Sunbelt helped California become the most populous state in the country by 1962. And the migration continued for the next few decades.

Low taxes were one of the primary draws to the Sunbelt for both people and businesses. Taxes had steadily increased in the large cities of the North to help support aging infrastructure and social programs, such as the War on Poverty. In contrast, there were smaller populations and less infrastructure to support across the Sunbelt. Furthermore, land in the Sunbelt states cost a fraction of what it did in the crowded Northeast. Businesses could build

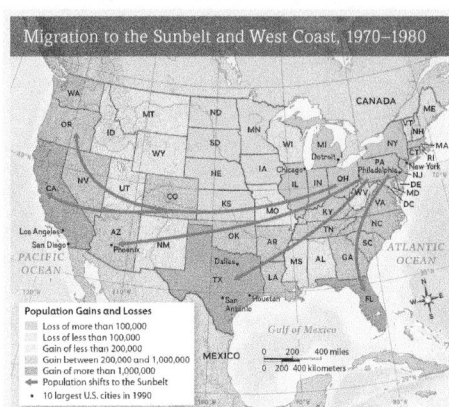

Migration to the Sunbelt and West Coast, 1970–1980

Population Gains and Losses
- Loss of more than 100,000
- Loss of less than 100,000
- Gain of less than 200,000
- Gain between 200,000 and 1,000,000
- Gain of more than 1,000,000
- → Population shifts to the Sunbelt
- • 10 largest U.S. cities in 1990

AIR-CONDITIONING AND THE SUNBELT

People first started using mechanical air conditioners in the early 20th century, but air-conditioning units did not become a practical appliance in most homes until after World War II. Innovations during the war made them more portable and less expensive. Air conditioners made it possible for people living in the American South and West to escape the dangerous summer heat. As a result, more people moved to the Sunbelt. With the increased population came increased political representation for Sunbelt states, including Florida, Georgia, Texas, California, Arizona, and New Mexico.

new factories for much less than it cost to update their old facilities in the North. And the warmer weather meant less wear-and-tear on buildings and equipment—another cost saver for businesses. As a result, a number of companies closed their Frostbelt factories and moved south or west. Soon some northern industrial cities became known collectively as the **Rustbelt**, a reference to the way that abandoned tools and machines corrode and rust.

In addition to attracting businesses, the Sunbelt drew many senior citizens. Due to improvements in medicine, life spans in the United States were steadily increasing. Payouts from pensions and Social Security also gave people greater financial security later in life. Healthier and more secure, many elderly Americans chose to enjoy their retirement years in warmer climates.

In 1970, active retirees enjoyed the mild winter weather as they pedaled their bikes around Sun City, Arizona, the first planned retirement community built in the Sunbelt.

POLITICAL IMPACT OF THE SUNBELT

Traditionally, the southern and western regions of the United States have been more politically conservative than the Northeast and upper Midwest. As you have read, the South became even more conservative following the Civil Rights Act of 1964. Many southern Democrats were opposed to civil rights legislation. In the wake of the historic act, a number of southern Democrats switched to the Republican Party as a protest against their more progressive northern counterparts. The influx of new residents strengthened the region's conservatism. Business owners and workers, especially those who flocked to the defense and energy industries in the Sunbelt, tended to be politically conservative. So did many senior citizens. As a result, cities and towns across the Sunbelt grew increasingly conservative during the 1960s and 1970s.

Places such as Orange County, California, located just south of Los Angeles, became centers of conservative thought. In the years leading up to the 1980 election, residents of Orange County sponsored anticommunism events for school students and eagerly backed conservative presidential candidate Barry Goldwater in his 1964 bid. They also spearheaded local and state initiatives against women's reproductive rights, public obscenity, and taxation. In particular, they targeted rising property taxes. Much like the people involved in the Sagebrush Rebellion, Orange County residents and other Sunbelt conservatives distrusted big government and liberal legislators.

With every new resident who migrated to the region, the Sunbelt's political power expanded. As you have learned, a state's population determines the number of representatives it sends to the House of Representatives. The migration to the South and West helped the Sunbelt states gain seats in Congress even as the Rustbelt states were losing them. The shift in population also affected each state's designated number of electoral votes, or votes cast by the representatives who elect the president and the vice president. The combination of conservative northerners' migration to the Sunbelt and southern politicians moving away from the Democratic Party eventually made the South and West strongholds for the Republican Party. The phenomenon became a significant factor in the 1980 presidential election.

HISTORICAL THINKING

1. **READING CHECK** What is the connection between the Sunbelt migration and the rise of the conservative movement?

2. **DESCRIBE** What government and economic factors drew businesses to the Sunbelt?

3. **ANALYZE CAUSE AND EFFECT** How did the Sunbelt migration affect northeastern and upper midwestern states both politically and economically?

4. **INTERPRET MAPS** Which areas of the country experienced the least significant population shift?

PLAN: 2-PAGE LESSON

OBJECTIVE

Explain how the conservative movement gained momentum in the fast-growing southern and western regions of the country.

CRITICAL THINKING SKILLS FOR LESSON 1.2

- Describe
- Analyze Cause and Effect
- Interpret Maps
- Make Generalizations
- Make Connections

HISTORICAL THINKING FOR CHAPTER 30

What major changes occurred in the United States during Ronald Reagan's presidency?
Businesses and older Americans were drawn to the South and West. They brought with them conservative ideas and a distrust of big government. Lesson 1.2 describes how this demographic shift changed the political landscape of the nation.

BACKGROUND FOR THE TEACHER

Migration to America's Sunbelt continues today, particularly to the Southeast, Texas, and mountainous areas of the West. Population estimates from 2015 indicated that over 50 of the nation's major cities gained more people, with the majority of those growing cities located in the South and West. Thirteen of the 15 biggest gainers in population were part of the Sunbelt. While growth of the suburbs slowed during the depressed housing market in the first decade of the 21st century, the current trend shows a resurgence of suburban growth, with migration from urban areas to lower density developing suburbs within the Sunbelt. Data indicate that the greatest suburban growth is occurring in the Texas metropolitan areas of San Antonio, Austin, and Houston, and in Orlando, Florida. Conversely, trends show that population losses continue to impact the Frostbelt, with the greatest migration from New York in the Northeast and from Chicago in the Midwest.

INTRODUCE & ENGAGE

IDENTIFY ADVANTAGES AND DISADVANTAGES

Draw a T-Chart on the board. Title one column Advantages and the other column Disadvantages. Invite students to recall what they already know about the Sunbelt region. Then discuss with them the reasons why people would or would not want to move there. **ASK:** What might be the advantages and disadvantages of living in the Sunbelt? *(Possible responses: Advantages include a warmer climate, more job opportunities, a growing urban environment, beautiful landscapes, and like-minded individuals. Disadvantages include the lack of seasons, constant heat and/or humidity, adapting to a new region, changing jobs, and finding housing.)* Add students' ideas to the chart as they are generated.

TEACH

GUIDED DISCUSSION

1. **Make Generalizations** What types of problems did fast-growing Sunbelt regions experience during the 1970s, and were those problems similar to ones previously faced by fast-growing urban areas in the Frostbelt? *(Possible response: Like the Frostbelt, the Sunbelt needed to ensure available housing and jobs for those migrating south. Unlike the Frostbelt, however, the Sunbelt had ample land for growth, and many of the people moving to the Sunbelt were retiring seniors. As a result, the pressure for housing and employment was much less than it had been in the fast-growing urban areas in the Frostbelt.)*

2. **Make Connections** How does migration such as Frostbelt to Sunbelt affect the demographics of a region, and how would that migration affect political development? *(Possible response: As a region becomes populated with people of similar political beliefs and party affiliation, the region can shift from one party to another. Thus, people are able to elect more of their party's representatives to Congress. Those representatives, in turn, can pass laws that not only satisfy their constituents but also may have a larger impact on the nation, as conservatives did in the 1970s and in the 1980 election.)*

INTERPRET MAPS

Direct students' attention to the map. Point out that the map shows the migration from 1970 to 1980. Have students review the information about population gains and losses, and then tell students to find the 10 largest U.S. cities in 1990 on the map. **ASK:** How many of the 10 largest cities in 1990 are in the Sunbelt? *(6)* What influence did the migration have on city size in 1990? *(As some northern cities lost population, the southern and western cities gained population.)*

ACTIVE OPTIONS

On Your Feet: Team Word Webbing Arrange teams of students around a large piece of paper. Give each team member a different colored marker. Pose the following question: How does the Sunbelt influence the rest of the country? Have students write their answer on the part of the web nearest to them. On your signal, students rotate the paper, and each student writes on the nearest part again. When finished, tell the groups to compare their answers and to share their answers with the class.

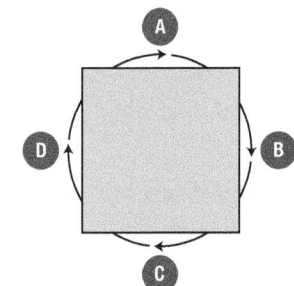

NG Learning Framework: Draft a City Plan

SKILL Collaboration

KNOWLEDGE Our Human Story

Divide the class into groups of three. Have groups conduct online research to investigate some of the major cities located in the Rustbelt, focusing on their current issues and any innovative solutions developed to deal with changes the region has experienced. Once each group completes their initial research, tell them to choose one city in the Rustbelt and create a city plan showing what it will take for the city to attract more people and businesses. Encourage groups to share their city plans with the class.

DIFFERENTIATE

INCLUSION

Understand a Map Pair students of different proficiency levels and ask more proficient students to assist their partners in understanding the information on the map. Instruct pairs first to read each line in the legend and then use a finger to trace the corresponding colored area of the map and the arrows showing where the greatest number of people migrated from and to. Ask students to make predictions about why so many people would migrate to the Sunbelt, and then check their predictions after they read, revising them if necessary.

PRE-AP

Present Information Graphically Challenge students to conduct online research to find statistical data on the population shift to southern and western states and the corresponding shift in political power, reflected in congressional seats lost or gained. Students may focus on their own state or on a group of states that experienced the most population loss or gain. Students can experiment with different ways to display the information graphically—in a line chart, bar graph, or more creative infographic. Invite students to display their work on a class bulletin board, website, or blog.

See the Chapter Planner for more strategies for differentiation.

HISTORICAL THINKING

ANSWERS

1. Individuals looking for employment and senior citizens who migrated to the Sunbelt tended to be conservative. As a result, the conservative movement gained members throughout the region.

2. Businesses could build new factories for less cost in the Sunbelt; warmer temperatures meant less wear and tear on the buildings and equipment; and low taxes made it more profitable to run a business in this region.

3. As populations moved from the Frostbelt to the Sunbelt, Frostbelt cities struggled economically, and the region became less politically diverse. In contrast, states in the Sunbelt gained more seats in Congress and more electoral votes.

4. The upper Midwest region, including North Dakota, South Dakota, Nebraska, Kansas, Minnesota, and Iowa, experienced the least significant shift.

ELECTION OF RONALD REAGAN

Can a movie actor or entertainer be a good president? What traits and experiences would work in his or her favor, and which ones would work against such a candidate? During the late 1970s, former actor Ronald Reagan leveraged his strong communication skills and his conservative beliefs to reach the highest office in the land.

CRITICAL VIEWING In the 1953 Western movie *Law and Order,* Ronald Reagan played a sheriff who rids a small town of outlaws. How might this photo and the movie itself connect to the conservative trends discussed in previous lessons?

THE RISE OF REAGAN

As the 1980 election loomed, the conservative movement found a strong messenger for their cause in California politician Ronald Reagan. Reagan grew up in Illinois and moved to Iowa shortly after graduating from college to work as a sports broadcaster. While on a business trip to California, he auditioned for Hollywood producers, who liked his presence on camera and hired him to act in films. Reagan was cast in 53 roles and, in 1947, became president of the Screen Actors Guild, the union for film actors. During his leadership of the union, his political views shifted. Reagan had been a New Deal Democrat, but the FBI investigations of communist activity in the movie industry led him to adopt more conservative beliefs. During this time, he met Nancy Davis, a film actor whom he would marry in 1952.

From 1954 to 1962, Reagan was a spokesman for the General Electric (GE) company. He was charismatic, and his years in front of the camera had made him a seasoned communicator. Reagan hosted GE's television program, *General Electric Theater,* and toured the country for the company, giving speeches about the dangers of communism, big government, and high taxes. The job prepared him for a televised speech he gave in support of Republican leader Barry Goldwater in 1964. As you've read, that speech caught the attention of California politicians, who later asked Reagan if he was interested in being governor. He ran for governor in 1966 and won. After serving two terms, Reagan moved on to the national scene. In 1976, he challenged incumbent president Gerald Ford in the Republican presidential primary. Reagan narrowly lost, but his strong national showing positioned him well for the future.

THE ELECTION OF 1980

That future came four years later, when Reagan became the Republican candidate in the 1980 presidential election. His opponent, President Jimmy Carter, was seeking a second term. With the ongoing hostage crisis in Iran, a gas shortage, and a struggling economy, many voters in both parties saw President Carter as an ineffective leader. Carter won the Democratic nomination, but only after a strong challenge from U.S. Senator Ted Kennedy of Massachusetts. The race also featured a third-party candidate, Congressman John B. Anderson, a Republican from Illinois, who had run in the Republican primaries in the hope of securing the party's nomination. Arguing that Reagan was too conservative, Anderson ran as an independent candidate and promoted himself as an alternative to the two traditional parties.

PRIMARY SOURCE

We must increase productivity . . . making it possible for industry to modernize . . . bringing government spending back within government revenues. I've already placed a freeze on [government] hiring. I've put a freeze on pending regulations . . . [and] decontrolled oil. We cannot delay in implementing an economic program aimed at both reducing tax rates to stimulate productivity and reducing the growth in government spending to reduce unemployment and inflation.

—from Ronald Reagan's address to the nation on the economy, February 5, 1981

The campaign, however, ultimately pitted Reagan against Carter. As the two candidates prepared for their single televised debate, popularity polls had them tied. During the debate in late October 1980, Carter described Reagan as a dangerous and unreliable political extremist, citing Reagan's plans to repeal the minimum wage, gut social **safety-net programs** that were helping people in poverty, and promote a nuclear arms buildup in the Middle East. Reagan focused on the nation's faltering economy, asking viewers: "Are you better off now than you were four years ago?" referring to when Carter took office. Reagan bet that when Americans thought about gas shortages and rising unemployment, most would answer, "No."

He was right. In November 1980, Reagan won the election in a landslide. Voters cast nearly 44 million ballots for Reagan and 35 million for Carter. John Anderson received 5.7 million votes, a strong showing for a third-party candidate. The Republicans also regained control of the Senate, picking up 12 seats from the Democrats. Reagan won by uniting the growing population of fiscal and social conservatives and by winning over a number of working-class Democrats worried about the economy and jobs. With Ronald Reagan's victory, a new era of conservatism was about to begin.

HISTORICAL THINKING

1. **READING CHECK** What made Ronald Reagan a good choice to lead the conservative movement of the 1980s?

2. **FORM AND SUPPORT OPINIONS** Was President Carter's warning about Ronald Reagan a good argument in support of his re-election? Support your opinion with evidence from the text.

3. **IDENTIFY** In his address to the nation on the economy, how did President Reagan propose to reduce unemployment and inflation?

PLAN: 2-PAGE LESSON

OBJECTIVE

Identify the conservative principles that won the vote and resulted in the election of Ronald Reagan as president of the United States in 1980.

CRITICAL THINKING SKILLS FOR LESSON 1.3

• Form and Support Opinions

• Identify

• Determine Chronology

• Analyze Primary Sources

HISTORICAL THINKING FOR CHAPTER 30

What major changes occurred in the United States during Ronald Reagan's presidency?

With the election of Ronald Reagan as president of the United States, and with Republicans picking up 12 Senate seats from the Democrats, the country moved toward an era of conservatism. Lesson 1.3 describes Ronald Reagan's political rise and the election of 1980.

BACKGROUND FOR THE TEACHER

John Anderson was a moderate Republican and a well-respected, 10-term U.S. congressman when he decided to run for president as an independent. He was at odds with conservative Republicans on most issues, including Watergate, Vietnam, abortion rights, and gun control. Many of his stands were unpopular among the moderate Republican base as well. Anderson also committed several mistakes as a politician that did not help his candidacy. At a debate in Iowa, a state that exported tons of agricultural products, he urged farmers to support a grain embargo against the Soviet Union in response to the Soviet invasion of Afghanistan. At another campaign stop in New Hampshire, he asked gun enthusiasts to support a gun registration program. President Carter refused to debate Anderson. When Ronald Reagan debated Anderson without Carter present, the debate did more for Reagan than for Anderson. In the election, Anderson gained a respectable 7 percent of the national vote. He retired from public life following the election.

INTRODUCE & ENGAGE

NAME A POLITICAL LEADER'S QUALITIES

Have students think about political leaders and identify the key qualities they think a political leader should have. Explain that Ronald Reagan was known for his charisma, or a charming personality that attracted supporters and admirers. Discuss the value of charisma as a quality within the political arena. Direct students' attention to the 1953 photograph of Reagan. **ASK:** What about Reagan made him a charismatic figure during his early acting days, and how might charisma have helped him in politics? *(Possible response: He was handsome, projected a sense of strength and leadership, and seemed like someone others could easily like and respect. All of these qualities are valued in politics.)*

TEACH

GUIDED DISCUSSION

1. **Determine Chronology** What events led to Ronald Reagan's political rise from his start in Illinois to the highest office in the nation? *(Reagan began his career as a sports broadcaster. Later, he became a successful actor, and in 1947 he was elected president of the Screen Actors Guild. He went on to became a spokesman for GE, promoting conservative values in his speeches. In 1964, he gave a speech in support of Republican Barry Goldwater that inspired Republicans in California to ask Reagan to run for governor. He won in 1966 and ended up serving two terms. In 1976, he made a bid for the Republican nomination but lost. Finally, in 1980, he became the Republican candidate for president and won the election in a landslide.)*

2. **Form and Support Opinions** If two presidential candidates today took the same stance on issues as Carter and Reagan did in 1980, which candidate do you think would win and why? *(Answers will vary: Students should give reasons for their opinions, such as people today believe in government's role to serve and protect the most vulnerable, or people today believe that government should interfere much less in people's lives.)*

ANALYZE PRIMARY SOURCES

Have students read the excerpt from Ronald Reagan's 1981 address to the nation. **ASK:** What economic problems does Reagan identify? *(unemployment, inflation, excessive government spending, high tax rates)* What goals does Reagan identify? *(increase productivity, modernize industry, reduce tax rates, reduce growth in government spending)* Then discuss with students President Reagan's domestic policies. **ASK:** What strategy did Reagan use to achieve his goals? *(Possible response: His strategy was to regard the problems as interrelated and identify ways to address all of them instead of one at a time.)*

ACTIVE OPTIONS

On Your Feet: Create a Visual Time Line Provide students with banner or chart paper. Have students form teams of four. Tell them that they are going to create a visual time line of Ronald Reagan's presidency. They will need to collect photos that show events from the beginning of his presidency until he left office and place them on a time line. Instruct teams to research and discuss the key events, policy issues, and speeches during Reagan's administration. Then, as a group, they will decide what to feature on the time line. Along with visuals, students should include captions detailing the past events and issues within the specific time context. Have teams present their completed time lines to the class.

NG Learning Framework: Analyze Speeches

ATTITUDE Empowerment

SKILL Communication

Remind students that Ronald Reagan was known for his ability to communicate. Discuss the qualities a good communicator should have, including effective writing and good delivery. Divide the class into small groups. Students should research and listen to at least three of Reagan's speeches, paying close attention to what he says and how he says it. Then have groups identify aspects of those speeches that made them effective. Ask each group to present one of Reagan's selected speeches and to share their analysis.

DIFFERENTIATE

STRIVING READERS

Connect Details to a Main Idea Instruct students to work in pairs to fill out a Main Idea and Details List, pointing out the kinds of details (facts, dates, events, reasons) that often support a main idea. Have students share their lists with other pairs, noting similarities and differences.

GIFTED & TALENTED

Write Diary Entries Direct students to watch the Carter-Reagan debate online and conduct further research about each candidate and about historians' opinions of the debate. Students can use what they learn to write journal entries that each candidate might have written after the debate. Students should consider each candidate's personality, experience, and debate performance. Invite students to present their research findings in an oral report and then perform a dramatic reading of their journal entries.

See the Chapter Planner for more strategies for differentiation.

HISTORICAL THINKING

ANSWERS

1. As president of the Screen Actors Guild, Reagan shifted his political viewpoint and championed more conservative beliefs. His engaging style and skills as a communicator made him a good choice for conservative Republicans, who urged him to serve as governor of California. He had a natural charisma that made his conservative beliefs appealing to the public at a time when Carter's popularity was plummeting.

2. Possible response: While Carter's warning about Reagan may have been accurate in the eyes of many, it was not an effective argument in support of his re-election. The economy was struggling, and people wanted someone who had solutions to their problems, not just warnings about an opponent.

3. President Reagan placed freezes on government hiring and on pending regulations, decontrolled oil, lowered taxes, reduced government spending—all in an effort to stimulate the economy and reduce unemployment and inflation.

CRITICAL VIEWING Possible response: The photo and the movie both give the impression of a strong and independent American, upholding law and order, who can take on a difficult situation and resolve it through his own efforts.

REDUCING GOVERNMENT

Change is hard—especially when you're in the habit of doing things a certain way. The United States had spent four years under Democratic leadership and was now facing the challenge of shifting to a conservative Republican administration.

RECOVERING WITH HUMOR
During President Reagan's recovery from the attempt on his life, he and his wife Nancy enthusiastically greeted well-wishers gathered below his hospital room window. Reagan was known for his sense of humor, which was often revealed in short, witty remarks, and for his love of his wife, two traits that endeared him to many of his supporters. Although seriously injured, Reagan still managed to joke with Nancy as he was taken to surgery, saying, "Honey, I forgot to duck."

THE REAGAN ERA BEGINS

The Reagan administration led a resurgence of the Republican Party with a focus on three key areas that restructured the scope of the federal government. The first was to establish a smaller government by decreasing taxes on individuals and businesses and deregulating industries. The second was to advocate conservative social values, including supporting legislation to outlaw abortion, promoting heterosexual marriage, opposing ratification of the Equal Rights Amendment, and championing individual accomplishment as opposed to funding social safety-net programs.

Also troubled by a rise in out-of-wedlock births and drug abuse, conservatives hoped to affect these and their other social concerns by supporting faith-based **cultural advocacy**, or exerting influence on politicians and social institutions to advance a particular religious belief system—in this case, conservative Christianity. The third area of the administration's focus was to expand the military while managing the Cold War. In all of these areas, the Reagan administration achieved both successes and setbacks.

The first months of Reagan's term were eventful and established the new president as a strong leader. After 444 days in captivity, the U.S. hostages in Iran were released as Reagan took office, a significant victory for the president. In February, his proposed economic program of tax and spending cuts was well received. Then, on March 30, 1981, a would-be assassin named John W. Hinckley, Jr., shot Reagan and his press secretary, James Brady, as the president and his advisors were leaving the Washington Hilton Hotel in Washington, D.C. The president recovered completely, and his courage and good humor during the crisis increased his popularity.

That summer, Reagan took decisive action during a strike by some 13,000 members of the Professional Air Traffic Controllers Organization (PATCO). As government employees, the controllers could not legally strike, and Reagan gave them 48 hours to return to work or lose their jobs. Most of them refused, and they were fired. While some citizens considered Reagan's actions to be extreme, much of the public backed the president. A Gallup poll taken shortly afterward showed that 59 percent of the American people supported firing the striking air traffic controllers.

The risk Reagan took in breaking the PATCO strike paid off for his administration immediately: he achieved a reputation for being a tough negotiator, both domestically and internationally, and particularly with the Soviet Union. The long-term consequences were less positive, though. To restore the air traffic control system to its pre-strike condition cost billions of dollars (an amount much higher than that requested from the strikers for pay increases and revised safety procedures) and took several years. In addition, air travel decreased during that time, thus affecting the earnings of airlines and related travel industries as well.

REAGANOMICS

An urgent focus for the Reagan administration was reviving the stalled U.S. economy and addressing the persistence of poverty. Reagan called for decreasing taxes on individuals and corporations, a strategy his administration termed **supply-side economics**.

Reagan administration officials believed that lower taxes would encourage consumers and businesses to spend and invest the money they kept, thus stimulating the economy and leading to job growth. Critics referred to the plan as "trickle-down economics," arguing that it aided the wealthiest Americans most, while only a small amount of job growth and wealth would "trickle down" to the neediest groups. In addition to tax cuts, Reagan called for an increase in military spending. To offset the loss of tax revenue and cover those increases in spending, Reagan proposed significant cuts to social programs, including public education, low-income housing, and Medicaid.

As Reagan worked to implement his policies, the economy worsened. During the early 1980s, unemployment rose to nine million, while thousands of businesses failed and many people lost their homes. The president's popularity plummeted, and Republicans lost seats in the House in the 1982 midterm elections. By the end of 1983, however, the economy began to turn around. Unemployment dropped and so did inflation. The economic growth continued, and Reagan's supporters would eventually cheer what they called "the longest peacetime expansion in American history."

Critics, however, argued that tax cuts continued to benefit mainly the rich and that under Reagan, **income inequality**, or a large gap between what the poorest and the richest citizens earn, had grown wider. Opponents also criticized the administration's continued military spending. While many of Reagan's supporters credited his increased defense spending as part of the reason for the eventual collapse of the Soviet Union, military spending played a big role in tripling the national debt by the end of Reagan's second term.

DEREGULATION

Another campaign promise Reagan sought to fulfill was his pledge to reduce government regulations on American industry. The Carter administration had already begun to eliminate government regulations on the airlines, as well as on the railroad and trucking industries. Reagan, however, felt that these moves didn't go far enough. He initiated a program of **deregulation**, or removing rules and limitations, on a large scale. Among his first targets were environmental regulations.

His choice for secretary of the interior, **James Watt**, was a fierce opponent of environmental protection. Watt proposed a number of changes that outraged environmentalists, including leasing federal lands for oil and gas exploration and reducing funding to national parks. Watt was one of Reagan's most controversial cabinet appointees, and his brief tenure as secretary of the interior was marked not only by his environmentally damaging proposals but also by his frequent insulting remarks, which did not endear him either to Congress or the American people. Watt resigned in October 1983, just as the Senate was drafting a resolution to have him removed from office.

Anne Gorsuch, tapped to direct the Environmental Protection Agency (EPA), was another of Reagan's controversial cabinet picks. During her two years as EPA director, she cut the EPA budget by 22 percent and made moves that critics claimed weakened the Clean Air and Clean Water Acts. In 1982, Congress

OBJECTIVE

Describe the economic principles President Reagan put into place to encourage economic growth and evaluate their effectiveness.

CRITICAL THINKING SKILLS FOR LESSON 2.1

- Analyze Environmental Concepts
- Make Generalizations
- Analyze Language Use
- Analyze Cause and Effect
- Summarize
- Identify
- Evaluate
- Analyze Primary Sources
- Identify Problems and Solutions

HISTORICAL THINKING FOR CHAPTER 30

What major changes occurred in the United States during Ronald Reagan's presidency?
Reagan focused on restructuring the federal government, promoting conservative social values, and funding military expansion. Lesson 2.1 discusses Reagan's successes and setbacks.

BACKGROUND FOR THE TEACHER

During the attempted assassination of President Reagan, his press secretary, James Brady (1940–2014), received a gunshot wound to the head that left him partially paralyzed. After the attack, Congress passed the Brady Handgun Violence Prevention Act in 1993 against strong opposition from the National Rifle Association. Signed into law by President Clinton, the act required a five-day waiting period and a background check before a buyer could purchase a gun. The United States Supreme Court struck down the act in 1997. In 1998, the National Instant Criminal Background Check System (NICS) was established so federally licensed dealers could quickly perform background checks. Brady was awarded the Presidential Medal of Freedom in 1996. The White House briefing room was renamed to honor him in 2000.

FINANCIAL LITERACY

To extend their knowledge and understanding about the concepts in this lesson, refer students to the Financial Literacy handbook.

INTRODUCE & ENGAGE
RANK GOVERNMENT SPENDING

Write the term "Government Spending" in the center of a Word Web on the board. Ask students to name areas of government spending, such as national defense, social programs, and health care. Then discuss with students the areas of spending they think are the most critical today and why. Have them rank the importance of each area and, as a class, come to a consensus on the top three. Talk about where they would cut funding in order to add funding to the top three. Tell students that in this lesson they will learn about the Reagan administration's actions to reduce government spending.

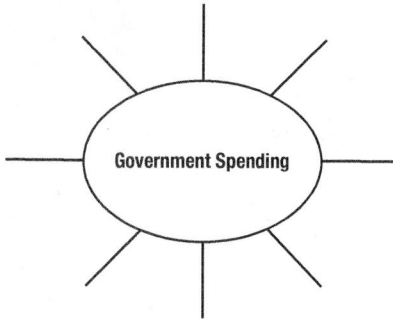

Government Spending

TEACH
GUIDED DISCUSSION

1. **Analyze Cause and Effect** How did President Reagan's firing of PATCO striking members affect the economy in the long run? *(It had a negative effect in the long run. It took billions of dollars and several years to restore the air traffic control system to its pre-strike levels. Also, the airlines lost earnings due to reduced air travel.)*

2. **Summarize** What was the most prevalent criticism of Reaganomics? *(Many criticized Reaganomics as tax cuts that benefited the rich while decreasing the wealth of working- and middle-class Americans.)*

3. **Identify** What policy decisions by James Watt resulted in the Senate drafting a resolution to remove him as secretary of the interior? *(James Watt's policies included leasing federal lands for oil and gas exploration and reducing funds for national parks.)*

MORE INFORMATION

Tax Reform Act of 1986 Tax reform was at the top of President Reagan's agenda, and he achieved a major victory in that area. Congress passed the biggest tax system overhaul in the nation's history—the Tax Reform Act of 1986. This law created three main changes to the tax code. First, it lowered the tax rate for those with high incomes from 50 percent to 28 percent while raising the tax rate for those with low incomes from 11 percent to 15 percent. Second, it required Social Security numbers for all individuals claimed as dependents on tax returns. Third, it increased the deduction for interest paid on home mortgages in an effort to increase home ownership. **ASK:** How did the Tax Reform Act of 1986 affect the income gap between wealthy and working-class Americans? *(Possible response: It increased the gap because the wealthy paid fewer taxes on their income, and working-class individuals paid more.)*

DIFFERENTIATE
ENGLISH LANGUAGE LEARNERS ELD

Make Word Cards Have students at the **Expanding** level make word cards for words and terms associated with Reaganomics, including *supply-side economics, deregulation,* and *trickle-down economics.* You may want to add additional important terms from the lesson, such as *resurgence, stalled, mortgages,* and *income inequality.* Tell students to write the word or term on one side of a card and define it on the opposite side, either in English or in their first language. Students then work in pairs, asking a partner what each word or term means. Each pair continues until all cards are shared.

PRE-AP

Research the Strike Invite students to research the air traffic control workers' strike and determine its impact on labor unions and strikes in the following decades. Encourage students to read various historians' explanations or claims regarding the strike and to corroborate or challenge their work with other information. Have students consider questions such as the following: What are historians' beliefs and opinions about the strike? Was the firing of the workers inevitable or could the strike have had another outcome? Ask students to present their reports to the class and initiate a class discussion of this historical event.

See the Chapter Planner for more strategies for differentiation.

demanded that the EPA turn over records for the Superfund program, which was responsible for the cleanup of toxic waste sites. Few of the sites designated for cleanup were actually being cleaned up, and Gorsuch and her agency were accused of mismanagement. When she refused to turn over the records, she was forced to resign.

Of President Reagan's efforts at deregulation, the one that may have had the most long-lasting impact was the lifting of regulations on the savings and loan (S&L) industry. The original S&Ls were small banks designed to help people buy homes at a time when most banks did not issue relatively small loans and mortgages. By the early 1980s, inflation and interest rates were high enough that S&Ls were hurting, and

TROUBLE AT THE EPA
The federal Superfund program was established within the EPA to protect the public and the country's natural resources by cleaning up large contaminated toxic waste sites. In 1982, however, the agency's regulatory actions dropped by about 60 percent, and few highly polluted sites were added to the Superfund list. Of the $700 million in fines owed by corporate polluters of water, land, and air, only $40 million was collected, which left the Superfund budget more reliant on taxpayer funds than on fines collected from polluters during the 1980s.

the mortgages they held began to lose value. The government's reaction was to deregulate the S&L industry, which then expanded rapidly.

At the same time, the Reagan administration reduced the number of bank examiners, which contributed to less oversight and fewer inspections of the S&L industry. In addition, the S&Ls carried federal deposit insurance that guaranteed they would be bailed out if they lost money. Those two conditions gave S&L operators a false sense of security and led many of them to plunge into risky and often illegal ventures. In 1983 and 1984, banks and S&L businesses made bad loans, created poorly financed companies, and hired corrupt employees who looted their firms. The reckoning for these actions would not come until 1989, after Reagan had left office, when the S&L industry suffered a catastrophic collapse, leaving taxpayers with the $500 billion bill for reimbursing depositors at the failed institutions. In all, over 1,000 people involved in the banking scandal were prosecuted, and many went to jail.

RESHAPING THE SUPREME COURT
President Reagan also moved the Supreme Court in a more conservative direction. Upon the retirement of Justice Potter Stewart in 1981, Reagan nominated **Sandra Day O'Connor** as his replacement. A moderate conservative, her nomination had

widespread support from both conservatives and liberals. She made history as the first woman justice to serve on the Supreme Court, a symbol of the changing roles of women in society.

The president would not have another opportunity to appoint a justice until Chief Justice Warren Burger resigned in 1986. Reagan elevated Justice William Rehnquist, a conservative, to replace Burger as Chief Justice and named a conservative federal appeals court judge, Antonin Scalia, to fill the seat Rehnquist had vacated. Scalia was a strong proponent of **originalism**, the belief that when interpreting the Constitution, the courts should refer to what it meant when it was originally adopted, not to what it might mean from a present-day perspective. If people wanted to change the law, he thought, they should use the democratic process and do so through legislation. Scholars and justices who disagreed with Scalia categorized originalism as a **static**, or unchanging, doctrine that does not allow the law to change with the times. While Justice Scalia helped to make the idea of originalism more widespread within academic and popular culture, he was often unable to get other justices to agree in applying it to court cases.

In 1987, after the Democrats had regained control of the Senate, Justice Lewis Powell resigned, and President Reagan nominated Robert Bork, another conservative appeals court judge, to replace him. Bork had written extensively on many divisive legal issues before becoming a judge, and Senate Democrats and many women and civil rights organizations opposed him. They said he was outside the mainstream of American judicial thinking. The Senate rejected Bork's nomination, but the contentious process had a lasting impact on future Supreme Court nominations. Anthony Kennedy was nominated for the seat and confirmed to the Court early in 1988. Perceived as being balanced and fair in his judicial rulings and writings, he received bipartisan support.

An oil painting of Associate Justice of the Supreme Court Sandra Day O'Connor dressed in her judicial robes hangs in the National Portrait Gallery, Washington, D.C. The painting is by Jean Marcellino.

Yes, I will bring the understanding of a woman to the Court, but I doubt that alone will affect my decisions. I think the important thing about my appointment is not that I will decide cases as a woman, but that I am a woman who will get to decide cases.

—Sandra Day O'Connor, quoted in "Sandra Day O'Connor, Warm, Witty, and Wise," by Pam Hait, *Ladies' Home Journal*, 1982

HISTORICAL THINKING

1. **READING CHECK** How was supply-side economics supposed to revive the economy and decrease poverty?

2. **ANALYZE ENVIRONMENTAL CONCEPTS** What human practices of the past led to the designation of Superfund sites for cleanup processes?

3. **MAKE GENERALIZATIONS** What were some of the consequences of President Reagan's deregulation of the savings and loan industry?

4. **ANALYZE LANGUAGE USE** Why did Sandra Day O'Connor make the distinction that it was important that she was "a woman who will get to decide cases"?

The site of a Superfund slag heap, or a hill made from industrial or mining waste material, has become a bird haven at the Ormond Beach Wetlands near Oxnard, California. The EPA is working with the local community and the site owners to remove toxic materials, but the entire process will take many years to complete.

BUILD BACKGROUND

SANDRA DAY O'CONNOR
Sandra Day O'Connor (b. 1930) received unanimous Senate approval when nominated to the U.S. Supreme Court and served for 24 years until her retirement in 2006. While she often voted in line with the conservative platform, she was a key swing vote in several significant cases, including upholding *Roe* v. *Wade* in the 1992 decision in *Planned Parenthood of Southeastern Pennsylvania* v. *Casey*. In 2000, she would be the key again in another controversial case, *Bush* v. *Gore,* which contested the results of the 2000 presidential election. Her deciding vote upheld Florida's electoral votes and ended the recount. After leaving the Supreme Court, she helped launch *iCivics*, an online civics education program aimed at teaching students about the federal government. In 2009, President Obama awarded O'Connor the Presidential Medal of Freedom.

ANTHONY KENNEDY
Anthony Kennedy (b. 1936) began his activism in the Republican Party as a lawyer and a lobbyist. In 1975, on Governor Reagan's recommendation, President Ford nominated Kennedy to a seat on the U.S. Court of Appeals for the Ninth Circuit. When Reagan became president, he eventually chose Kennedy as a candidate to fill a vacancy on the U.S. Supreme Court. Unanimously confirmed by the Senate, Kennedy joined the Supreme Court as a recognized conservative voice. However, in 2015, when it came time to rule on same-sex marriage, Kennedy surprised nearly everyone. He ended up writing the majority opinion for the Supreme Court's 5-to-4 ruling that guaranteed the right of same-sex couples to marry. Later, with the American Bar Association, Kennedy helped to design *Dialogues on Freedom*, an online civics education program that is used today in high schools across the country.

TEACH

GUIDED DISCUSSION

4. Evaluate What did Reagan fail to realize about the American public's attitude toward environmental protection policies? *(Possible response: He failed to realize that the public overall was strongly committed to environmental protection and would fight any efforts to weaken the EPA and the Superfund.)*

5. Analyze Primary Sources What do both the painting of Sandra Day O'Connor and her quotation convey about her character that would seem to make her a good candidate for the first woman justice on the Supreme Court? *(Possible response: The painting shows her in a judge's robe, not in a dress or suit, underscoring her dedication to the law. Her face looks serious and attentive, as if she were considering legal arguments. O'Connor's quotation shows that she will be fair and unbiased in her decisions.)*

IDENTIFY PROBLEMS AND SOLUTIONS

Have students review the text about the EPA and the Superfund as well as the photograph and caption. Instruct students to work with a partner to identify the chain of problems that unfolded and the solutions put in place to address each problem involved with the Superfund. Encourage students to use a graphic organizer like the Problem-and-Solution Chain shown here to organize their thoughts. Then hold a class discussion in which pairs share their findings about the Superfund.

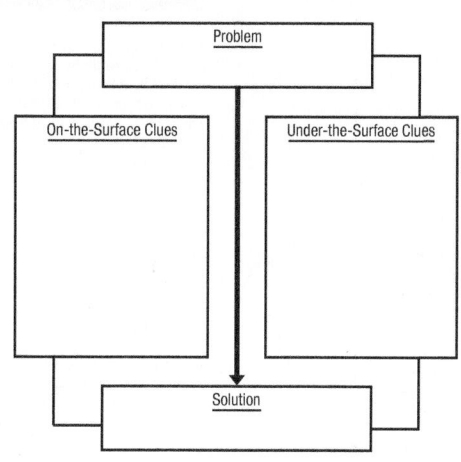

ACTIVE OPTIONS

On Your Feet: Three-Step Interview Tell students to work in pairs. One student should interview the other using these questions: How did deregulation of the Superfund affect the economy? Do you think regulations are needed or not needed? Why are some people today against too much regulation? Then have students reverse roles. Finally, invite each student to share with the class the results of his or her interview.

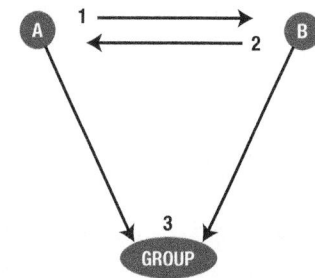

NG Learning Framework: Compare Past and Present Policies

SKILLS Observation, Communication

KNOWLEDGE Our Human Story

Have students work in pairs to create a list of the policy changes that occurred during the Reagan presidency. Students should then pick one policy change to research, identifying the issue and how the policy change addressed the issue. Then instruct pairs to compare the policy change with the policy on the same issue today. They should note any consequences of past decisions, determine what lessons were learned, and identify how the federal government has responded to the policy change. Ask students to create a three-minute multimedia presentation to share their comparisons of past and present policies with the class.

HISTORICAL THINKING

ANSWERS

1. Reagan believed supply-side economics would lower taxes, encouraging people and businesses to spend the money they saved, which would then stimulate the economy. Businesses would grow and more jobs would be created.

2. The Superfund was established to clean up large areas that had been contaminated by toxic waste from industry.

3. Deregulation of the savings and loan industry led to its 1989 collapse, requiring taxpayers to pay a total of $500 billion to reimburse depositors for money held by failed financial institutions.

4. Possible response: While Sandra Day O'Connor was the first woman to be appointed to the United States Supreme Court, she wanted the focus to be on her ability to decide cases and not on her gender.

REAGAN'S FOREIGN POLICY

Think of something you strongly believe in. President Reagan was a strong anticommunist who believed in standing up to the Soviets around the world. This belief would serve as the foundation of U.S. foreign policy during the 1980s.

ANTICOMMUNIST POLICIES

Ronald Reagan's tough stance against communism had long been a part of his image. As president, he vowed to fight the spread of communism around the world. He increased military spending, advocating a policy of "peace through strength."

The Reagan administration put its anticommunist stance into action around the world with results of success as well as failure. When the Soviet Union invaded Afghanistan in 1979 to support a Soviet-backed government, the Carter administration had sent military aid to the anti-Soviet guerillas. Reagan increased the aid, hoping the guerillas could use it to force a Soviet withdrawal.

Reagan also moved against communism in Latin America. The United States invaded the small Caribbean island of Grenada in 1983 after a communist government seized power. Within two days, the Marines had subdued the communist forces and helped establish a new anticommunist government. The United States also took action in Nicaragua after a pro-Soviet group known as the **Sandinistas** seized power and attempted to shape Nicaragua's government along communist lines. In response, the Reagan administration began secretly arming an anti-Sandinista guerilla force known as the **Contras**. The Contras waged a civil war with the Sandinistas throughout the 1980s from the headquarters they established in Honduras, directly north of Nicaragua.

Two days before the invasion of Grenada, tragedy struck the American military half a world away. On October 23, 1983, a suicide bomber drove a truck bomb into a barracks, or sleeping quarters, for marines in Beirut, Lebanon. The tremendous

explosion had the force of 12,000 pounds of TNT. It destroyed the barracks and killed 241 marines. They had been deployed as peacekeepers during a cease-fire in the hostilities between Lebanese Christians and Muslims, a move that was controversial among Reagan's military advisors, who believed the situation was too unstable to be contained.

Back home, some people accused the president of using the invasion of a tiny, nonthreatening Caribbean country as a distraction from the reckless political blunders that had put those 241 marines in Lebanon in harm's way. The planning done before the October 23 bombing proved that the invasion wasn't merely a reaction to the event. When Reagan ran for re-election in 1984, however, it was clear that the invasion of Grenada had offered the president a public relations boost that helped to distract voters from the Beirut bombing.

IRAN AND SOUTH AFRICA

Congress eventually learned of the secret funding of the Contras and banned further aid to the group in 1984. Two years later, a news story reported that the United States had sold military equipment to Iran—a country that supported international terrorism—as part of an effort to gain the release of the American hostages taken prisoner there in the late 1970s. This contradicted Reagan's claim that the United States would never negotiate with terrorists, but the Reagan administration was afraid of political fallout from another hostage situation. Less than a month later, a follow-up news story revealed that $48 million from the weapons sale to Iran had been turned over to the Contras, which became known as the **Iran-Contra scandal**. Reagan fired the two men most responsible for the scandal: head of the National Security Council

Lieutenant Colonel Oliver North took an oath to tell the truth during the congressional hearings convened to investigate the Iran-Contra scandal.

John Poindexter and one of his aides, Lieutenant Colonel Oliver North of the U.S. Marine Corps. The president appointed John Tower, a former Texas senator, to head a commission to investigate the scandal. Poindexter and North were tried and convicted of lying to Congress and obstruction of justice, among other charges.

President Reagan took full responsibility for the arms-for-hostages deal, but he claimed he knew nothing about the diversion of funds to the Contras. Still, a number of people, including some members of Congress, doubted him. Reagan's popularity declined, but only temporarily. A federal appeals court eventually overturned the convictions of Poindexter and North.

Reagan's strong anticommunist policy also became controversial when he allied the United States with the government of South African prime minister P. W. Botha. The repressive South African regime supported a system of **apartheid**, or extreme official racial segregation. Seeing Botha as a leader who would join him in preventing the spread of communism, Reagan proposed that moderates in the South African government would eventually end apartheid. He vetoed sanctions the U.S. Congress wanted to place on South Africa for its apartheid.

But Reagan's policy led South Africa to continue its segregation, and violence erupted. Ironically, Reagan's policy also tarnished American ideals and, ironically, hampered U.S. efforts abroad as the "good guy" in its competition with the Soviet Union. Finally, in 1986, the Senate overrode Reagan's veto of sanctions against South Africa.

THE STRATEGIC DEFENSE INITIATIVE

Meanwhile, tension between the Soviet Union and the United States continued to escalate. In 1983, several false alarms about imminent missile strikes by both sides cast doubt on the effectiveness of the doctrine of mutual assured destruction. And, while neither side overreacted, the arms race between the Soviet Union and the United States had reached its highest point, with the accumulation of more than 69,000 global nuclear weapons.

In this atmosphere, Reagan proposed his most ambitious plan for addressing Soviet power: to put a missile defense system in orbit around Earth. Dubbed the **Strategic Defense Initiative (SDI)**, it would use lasers and other technologies to destroy Soviet missiles before they reached their targets. Popularly referred to as "Star Wars," after the movie series, this idea met with many critics who argued that the "other technologies" used to blow the missiles out of the sky didn't even exist yet. They feared that the technical challenges of such a project might swallow the entire defense budget. Ultimately, the proposed SDI technology became too complex and expensive, and the program was never realized.

HISTORICAL THINKING

1. **READING CHECK** How did President Reagan try to achieve his policy of "peace through strength"?

2. **DRAW CONCLUSIONS** Why did some people believe that the invasion of Grenada was a distraction from the bombing in Lebanon?

3. **COMPARE AND CONTRAST** How was U.S. involvement in Nicaragua different from U.S. involvement in Grenada?

4. **MAKE INFERENCES** Why did no president after Reagan continue the Strategic Defense Initiative?

OBJECTIVE

Learn how President Reagan's support of U.S. Cold War and containment policies became a strong focus of his administration.

CRITICAL THINKING SKILLS FOR LESSON 2.2

- Draw Conclusions
- Compare and Contrast
- Make Inferences
- Evaluate

HISTORICAL THINKING FOR CHAPTER 30

What major changes occurred in the United States during Ronald Reagan's presidency?
The Reagan administration enforced its anticommunist agenda around the world. Lesson 2.2 explains how taking a strong stand against the Soviet Union and communism worldwide became the focus of President Reagan's foreign policy and his interactions with foreign governments.

BACKGROUND FOR THE TEACHER

The Iran-Contra scandal violated the Boland Amendment, which restricted assistance to Nicaragua from the CIA and Department of Defense. The Reagan administration found a way around the amendment to continue supplying the Contras with aid by setting up an illegal deal with Iran. In 1985, Iranian terrorists were holding seven Americans hostage. When Iran made a secret request to buy weapons from the United States, despite an arms embargo, Reagan agreed to an arms-for-hostages exchange. Iran had received more than 1,500 missiles by the time the sales were discovered, but only three hostages had been released. The initial investigation revealed that only some of the money paid by Iran was received. Lieutenant Colonel Oliver North had been redirecting the funds to the Contras, with the knowledge of the national security advisor, Admiral John Poindexter. Following an eight-year investigation, 14 people were charged with involvement in the Iran-Contra scandal.

INTRODUCE & ENGAGE

ACTIVATE PRIOR KNOWLEDGE

Invite students to share what they know about communism, anticommunism, and the Cold War. Record their ideas in a three-column chart. Discuss with them the lessons learned from past foreign policies on communism. Explain that Lesson 2.2 shows how anticommunism shaped Reagan's foreign policy.

Communism	Anticommunism	Cold War

TEACH

GUIDED DISCUSSION

1. **Make Inferences** Why do you think the Iran-Contra scandal only temporarily hurt President Reagan's popularity as a leader in the Cold War? *(Possible response: Reagan was a charismatic president who had taken popular stands against communism and didn't hesitate to use military action. For many people, his overall record outweighed the scandal.)*

2. **Evaluate** Which of the foreign policy decisions made by the Reagan administration were the most beneficial in countering the spread of communism and why? *(Possible response: Support for Afghan guerillas against Soviet invaders and the invasion of Grenada proved that the United States was willing to use military force when required. This sent a message that the nation would not hesitate to act when communist governments seized power.)*

DRAW CONCLUSIONS

Remind students that when they draw conclusions, they are making judgments based on evidence. **ASK:** What evidence can you find to support the conclusion that the Strategic Defense Initiative was likely to fail? *(lack of technology, significant expense, and complexity of the project)* If SDI had succeeded, what effect might it have had on the U.S.-Soviet rivalry? *(Possible response: The Soviet Union, in response, might have built more weapons, escalating the Cold War and worsening relations with the United States.)*

ACTIVE OPTIONS

On Your Feet: Jigsaw Strategy Organize students into four "expert" groups and have each group analyze the Reagan administration's Cold War or containment policies in one of these areas: Sandinistas, Contras, South Africa, SDI. Tell groups to research their chosen policy using the following steps: 1. Define the policy. 2. Find out the rationale behind it and how it was carried out. 3. Determine whether the policy reflected American democratic ideals. Ask group members to summarize their analysis in their own words. Then re-form the groups so that each new group has at least one member from each expert group. Have students in new groups take turns sharing their summaries.

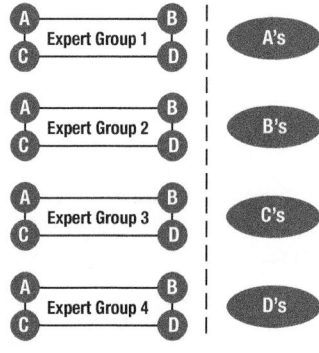

NG Learning Framework: Investigate Iran-Contra Scandal

ATTITUDE Curiosity

KNOWLEDGE Our Human Story

Instruct groups of students to work together to investigate the Iran-Contra scandall. They should research questions such as: Who were the individuals involved in the Iran-Contra scandal? What roles did they play? How were they caught, and what happened to them as a result? What role do you think President Reagan played in the scandal? How did the Iran-Contra scandal affect U.S. foreign policies? Then have groups write a report of their investigation. Students should include in their report why the Iran-Contra scandal was a significant event and how events could have taken a different direction. Encourage groups to present their reports to the class.

DIFFERENTIATE

INCLUSION

Use Supported Reading Assign pairs of students selected paragraphs to read aloud together. At the end of each paragraph, ask them to use the following sentence frames to identify what they do and do not understand:

• This paragraph is about _____.

• One fact that stood out to me was _____.

• I had trouble understanding _____, so I tried to figure it out by _____.

Be sure all students understand the content before moving on to the next paragraph.

PRE-AP

Extend Knowledge Instruct students to gather information from a variety of sources to learn more about the complicated covert activities that became known as the Iran-Contra scandal. Encourage them to investigate who first came up with the idea of diverting funds to the Contras, who knew about the illegal dealings, and how the conspirators were caught. Ask them to use primary and secondary sources and quote or paraphrase them as appropriate. Remind students to cite their sources for all facts and claims. Invite volunteers to share their findings with the class.

See the Chapter Planner for more strategies for differentiation.

HISTORICAL THINKING

ANSWERS

1. Reagan increased military spending and stood up to communism around the world, using military force when he thought it was necessary to fight Soviet influence.

2. The invasion occurred right after the bombing in Beirut, Lebanon, that killed 214 U.S. Marines, so critics thought Reagan was trying to divert attention away from the bombing.

3. The United States invaded Grenada, but in Nicaragua, it financed the Contras, who were fighting the Nicaraguan government. The public knew about the invasion of Grenada, but the Contras funding was kept secret.

4. Possible response: There was still too much uncertainty about the technology and cost of funding the SDI. Later presidents might also have questioned whether it was even the best way to handle the Soviet threat.

SOCIAL CHANGES AND TENSIONS

Consider how much computers, smartphones, and tablets are part of your daily life. The 1980s saw a wave of advances in technology—including computer technology—that began to change many aspects of how people lived.

NEW TECHNOLOGIES

Away from the political arena, the 1980s was a time of significant technological progress. In 1981, a communications company called International Business Machines (IBM) announced its plan to sell **personal computers**, small computers for home use. The announcement caused two computer software writers, Bill Gates and Paul Allen, to develop their own graphical user interface system, or GUI, that would appeal to a wide audience by helping people understand how to use the computer. They built their system using a simpler version of a computer language called BASIC. From there, Gates and Allen developed other software programs for their Microsoft company, such as spreadsheets and Microsoft Windows, an operating system that manages computer memory and function.

Apple, a competing company founded in 1976 by Steve Jobs and Steve Wozniak in a garage in Cupertino, California, also developed a GUI and, eventually, a version of a personal computer, named the Apple Macintosh, now known as the Mac. These innovations quickly transformed the personal computer from a novelty item to a common household device. Soon, people would be able to use their computers to publish books, track finances, make travel reservations, and play games.

CRITICAL VIEWING Desktop computers like the one below were among the earliest computers sold in the 1970s in America. This one came with a cassette drive and a tape player attached. It was popular in schools that had just begun teaching computer technology. Although the screen looks like a movable monitor, it was actually an attached built-in display. The computer sold new for about $700. Which of its elements can you identify, and how is the computer similar to or different from the computers you use?

After January 1983, sales of personal computers rose to more than half a million per year. New software companies sprang up all over the country, especially in California and Massachusetts. The California tech corridor would become known as "Silicon Valley" for the local resource, silica, used to make silicon computer chips.

Massachusetts companies were able to recruit computer talent from the pool of expertise at MIT, the Massachusetts Institute of Technology. Eventually computers needed to be connected so that people in different cities could collaborate on the same projects. The Pentagon offered its network of computers to computer users and researchers to exchange messages. Other networks in the United States and around the world connected throughout the late 1970s and early 1980s, and this supernetwork became known as the **Internet**, the global system of interconnected computer networks.

At the same time, television technology was expanding. Cable television, a system in which televisions receive transmissions through wires instead of air waves like radios do, had been around since the late 1940s. Its original purpose was to provide television reception to people who lived in geographically isolated communities. By the early 1980s, cable television could provide improved picture and sound quality and offer viewers throughout the whole nation a wide variety of channels. Suddenly every American with cable access could tune in to the same television networks, which contributed to shared cultural experiences. Teenagers watched their favorite bands play in music videos broadcast by MTV. Cable News Network (CNN) reported national news all day, every day.

Meanwhile, NASA continued to make strides with its shuttle program in the 1980s. Unfortunately, a catastrophe temporarily set back its efforts. On January 28, 1986, NASA launched the spacecraft *Challenger* from its facility at Cape Canaveral, Florida. Seconds later, however, it disintegrated in midair in a fiery explosion, killing the seven astronauts onboard. One of the astronauts was Christa McAuliffe, a high school teacher from Concord, New Hampshire, who had been selected from thousands of applicants to be the first private citizen in space. An investigation later determined

TEACHER AND ASTRONAUT
Christa McAuliffe was the first candidate accepted for the NASA Teacher in Space Project in 1985. She received her astronaut training and became a payload specialist on board the orbiter *Challenger* when it launched on January 28, 1986. McAuliffe had prepared a science lesson plan for students who would have tuned in to the *Challenger* for the live and taped lessons. After McAuliffe died in the *Challenger* explosion, many of her students told how she had challenged them and inspired them to enter the field of education.

that a damaged rocket booster was to blame for the tragedy. After the investigation, NASA scientists made changes to space shuttles to improve safety conditions, but the shock of the tragedy temporarily stopped work on the space program.

CHANGES IN THE AMERICAN FAMILY

Technology wasn't the only thing changing in the 1980s. The decade saw dramatic shifts in the dynamics of American families. For instance, the number of women giving birth out of wedlock had risen steadily since the 1970s, a social trend that contributed to the 6.7 million increase of single-parent households in the country from 1970 to 1992.

PLAN: 4-PAGE LESSON

OBJECTIVE

Describe the effects on American society of new technologies, a health epidemic, and a shift in demographics.

CRITICAL THINKING SKILLS FOR LESSON 2.3

- Identify
- Make Predictions
- Describe
- Determine Chronology
- Evaluate
- Draw Conclusions
- Identify Problems and Solutions
- Make Connections

HISTORICAL THINKING FOR CHAPTER 30

What major changes occurred in the United States during Ronald Reagan's presidency?
Computer technology and the Internet dramatically changed the way people lived and communicated, while demographic changes and a health epidemic increased social strains. Lesson 2.3 describes the effects of major technological and social changes on American society.

BACKGROUND FOR THE TEACHER

In 1972, President Nixon annouced that NASA would build a reusable space shuttle that would go into orbit and return to Earth. Five years later, the space shuttle, *Columbia*, successfully launched into outer space and returned safely. *Challenger* completed nine missions before its tragic end on January 28, 1986. The night before the final launch, the weather turned unseasonably cold for Florida. NASA engineers warned officials that the O-rings, which sealed the shuttle's solid rocket boosters, could fail at such low temperatures. Their warnings went unheeded. The space shuttle exploded shortly after launch, killing *Challenger*'s crew. An investigation showed that the O-ring seals on the rocket boosters had failed and allowed fuel to leak. As the shuttle gained altitude, the fuel ignited and caused the disastrous explosion.

📄 HISTORY NOTEBOOK

Encourage students to complete the Reid on the Road video series page for Chapter 30 in their History Notebooks.

INTRODUCE & ENGAGE

TECHNOLOGY THEN AND NOW

Direct students' attention to the photograph of the computer. Point out that before the computer was invented, information could be spread only by word of mouth, handwritten texts, telegraph, or messenger. Discuss with students other technologies that allow news to reach a wide audience rapidly, much like the Internet does today. Show students photographs of a computer from the 1990s, one of the first laptops, and an old cell phone. Ask students to comment on how these items and the computer in the lesson's photograph each represented a major advance in information technology.

TEACH

GUIDED DISCUSSION

1. **Determine Chronology** How did personal computers move from concept to the retail shelf, and how quickly did this happen? *(To go from concept to retail shelf, computer developers had to invent the hardware and the GUI software systems to run the computers and provide functions for users. Apple began its computer development in 1976, followed by IBM in 1981. By 1983, more than 500,000 personal computers had been sold.)*

2. **Evaluate** Why did cable television gain in popularity, and how did it contribute to social trends? *(Cable television was popular because it provided improved picture and sound quality and a wide variety of channels. Viewers across the country could watch programs at the same time, which provided a shared cultural experience. New channels, such as MTV with its music videos, rapidly spread new trends in popular culture.)*

3. **Draw Conclusions** How might the *Challenger* tragedy have been prevented? *(Possible response: All parts of the space shuttle should have been checked carefully, and any damaged parts should have been repaired before the shuttle launch, or the mission should have been canceled until all parts were verified as secure.)*

MORE INFORMATION

***Challenger*'s Lost Lessons** As America's first teacher in space, Christa McAuliffe planned to conduct eight science lessons aboard the *Challenger*. Included in the lessons was an experiment on whether plants could grow in space without soil by spraying them with a coat of nutrient-rich water. If plants didn't need soil, it could lighten the weight load for future missions. Other planned lessons would have tested the effects of space on magnetism and on Newton's laws of motion, including whether a billiard ball or a ball with half the mass accelerates faster in microgravity. Another experiment involved dropping an antacid tablet in water to show how bubbles act in space (antacids fizz and bubble with much more intensity in space). McAuliffe had also planned "The Ultimate Field Trip"—a live tour of the *Challenger*. **ASK:** Why are McAuliffe's lessons significant? *(Possible response: The lessons would have helped students learn about space experientially, which may have engaged them more in science. They would also have seen how certain physical properties and laws acted differently in space than on Earth.)*

DIFFERENTIATE

STRIVING READERS

Complete a T-Chart Instruct students to create a T-Chart and label the first column Technological Changes and the second column Social Changes. Explain, if necessary, that social changes include changes relating to marriage and families, religious beliefs, lifestyle, education, and health. Tell students as they read the lesson to jot down key facts under Technological Changes or Social Changes. At the end, encourage students to compare their completed charts and fill in any facts they might have missed.

Technological Changes	Social Changes

GIFTED & TALENTED

Research and Perform an Oral History Have students access AIDS oral histories, available online at the National Institutes of Health, University of California San Francisco, or other websites. Encourage students to find oral histories of doctors, nurses, scientists, activists, and others who played important roles in helping AIDS patients and in discovering what caused the disease and how best to treat it. Instruct students to select a portion of an oral history that they can read aloud in four to five minutes. Invite them to share their selections with the class. Discuss how the oral histories reinforce or supplement the information in the lesson.

See the Chapter Planner for more strategies for differentiation.

CRITICAL VIEWING Possible response: The basic design of a computer keyboard and screen are similar, but they are built into one unit instead of being separate. There is no mouse or speakers, and the only means of recording data is on cassettes. The monotone color of the screen and the lack of images are definitely different from computers today.

CRITICAL VIEWING In 1996, the AIDS Memorial Quilt (left) made its fifth appearance on the National Mall in Washington, D.C. The quilt held 37,440 panels, or blocks, covering the entire grassy stretch of lawn on the Mall. What do the individual panels (above) tell you about the people they memorialize and the people who made them?

AMERICAN PLACES
The National Mall, Washington, D.C.

The most familiar part of the National Mall is a broad grassy area stretching for almost two miles between the U.S. Capitol Building and the Lincoln Memorial. Americans have historically held rallies and protests here, watched presidential inaugurations, and displayed challenging exhibits, such as the AIDS Memorial Quilt. The Mall is also the gateway to presidential and American memorials and a growing number of museums that house art, cultural artifacts, and unique architecture. An estimated 25 million people visit the Mall each year, free of charge.

Nearly 2,300 American elm trees line the Mall, and more than 26 miles of sidewalks and 8 miles of bike trails extend throughout the surrounding area, officially called the National Mall and Memorial

Parks. This larger area encompasses the White House, museums, lush gardens, and the Tidal Basin, where the Cherry Blossom Festival is held each spring. The more than 9,000 trees that cover the larger Mall area not only provide shade and landscaped scenery but also remove about 492 tons of air pollution from Washington, D.C.

The National Mall was originally designed in 1791 by Pierre L'Enfant to be the city's grandest avenue. But it wasn't until 1902 that a commissioned report to Congress advised a restoration, development, and extension of L'Enfant's proposal. The result, with continued modern, sustainable alterations, is the National Mall of today.

Divorce rates reached their highest levels ever in the early 1980s. And women were entering the workforce in record numbers: 67 percent of married women were working in 1986 compared with 26 percent in 1950.

American families were also facing challenges in education. In 1983, a government committee released a document called *A Nation at Risk* on the status of public schools in the United States. The committee's findings were grim. American schools were experiencing low state test scores and high turnover rates among teachers. As many as 23 million American adults could not read or write. The report stated, "If an unfriendly foreign power had attempted to impose on America the mediocre educational performance that exists today, we might well have viewed it as an act of war." *A Nation at Risk* called for massive reform to retain the best teachers and to raise students' academic performances.

One of the most famous educational reforms of the 1980s began in a school in Oakland, California. First Lady Nancy Reagan was addressing an elementary school about the perils of drug use and abuse. A student stood up and asked Mrs. Reagan what students should say if someone asks them to try drugs or alcohol. Mrs. Reagan responded, "Just say no." That advice became a national catchphrase, and schools around the country formed clubs that aimed to teach students how to resist peer pressure. Ultimately, data showed that the programs were not successful.

THE CHALLENGE OF HIV/AIDS

Beginning in the early 1980s, a new disease caused by the **human immunodeficiency virus (HIV)** was attacking its victims' immune systems. In the United States, most of the first victims of HIV were members of the gay community, where the incidence of infection was particularly high. In some patients, the virus destroyed so much of the immune system, the infected person's body could no longer fight off the most common ailments. The last stage of HIV was known as **acquired immunodeficiency syndrome (AIDS)**. Not all HIV patients advanced to this often-deadly stage.

As the 1980s progressed, more HIV/AIDS patients were identified, mostly in large American cities such as New York City and San Francisco. Little was known about the disease then, so panic and confusion rose in the nation and around the world.

In 1985, after the New York City school system reported a child with AIDS attending one of its 622 elementary schools, a large number of parents kept their children home out of fear of the virus. This made the gay community and especially those who contracted the virus an even greater target for discrimination.

Eventually, scientists determined that the virus spread through the exchange of certain body fluids, including fluids exchanged during sexual contact. Infected pregnant mothers could pass the disease to their children in the womb. Drug users contracted the virus if they shared contaminated needles, and some hospital patients were stricken after receiving infected blood during transfusions.

In an effort to stop the epidemic, many HIV/AIDS activists promoted safer sex practices, provided clean needles to intravenous drug users, and generated greater awareness about the disease. The Reagan administration as well as leading conservatives resisted such actions. They argued that poor "lifestyle" choices put people at risk for the disease, and they urged a greater adherence to "traditional family values." By 1989, at least 100,000 Americans had contracted HIV/AIDS and thousands of people had died from the disease. The number of deaths rose until the mid-1990s when new drugs were introduced to manage the virus's symptoms.

In 1985, activist Cleve Jones launched the Names Project, enlisting families and friends of people with AIDS to create quilted panels in an effort to keep alive the memory of the thousands who had died. When first displayed in 1987, the quilt covered an area larger than a football field. Since the disease first appeared, 600,000 to 700,000 Americans have died from AIDS.

HISTORICAL THINKING

1. **READING CHECK** What social tensions were caused by changing demographics in the United States during the 1980s?

2. **IDENTIFY** How have personal computers changed the lives of Americans?

3. **MAKE PREDICTIONS** What might have happened if the Reagan administration had chosen to support the educational programs HIV/AIDS activists had suggested?

4. **DESCRIBE** In what ways did women's roles change in society during the 1980s?

BUILD BACKGROUND

FACTS ABOUT AIDS

HIV/AIDS is still a global health risk. The disease AIDS, caused by a retrovirus (HIV), takes approximately 2 to 15 years to develop, depending on the individual. The virus is transmitted only through the exchange of body fluids from infected individuals and not through normal everyday contact, which includes hugging, shaking hands, or sharing personal objects.

According to the World Health Organization, AIDS has claimed more than 35 million lives around the globe, with one million dying from it in 2015 alone. Approximately 37 million people worldwide are infected with HIV. A concentration of cases in the Sub-Saharan Africa region accounts for approximately two-thirds of all infected patients.

Advances in HIV treatments hold promise for many with the infection. Antiretroviral (ARV) drugs appear to both control the virus and prevent its transmission. However, only approximately 19 million people currently receive ARV drugs. Equally troublesome is the fact that only about 70 percent of individuals with HIV know the status of their illness, with another 30 percent needing access to HIV testing services.

The good news is that HIV infections fell by about 35 percent between 2000 and 2016, and HIV-related deaths fell by about 33 percent. This resulted in 13.1 million lives saved through preventive measures, ARV drugs, and medical advances.

TEACH

GUIDED DISCUSSION

4. Identify Problems and Solutions What problems in education did the government uncover, and how did it address these challenges? *(A Nation at Risk documented the nation's low state test scores, high rate of teacher turnover, and poor literacy rates. Some reforms were made to retain the best teachers and to raise students' academic performance. Also, Nancy Reagan started a "Just say no" antidrug campaign.)*

5. Make Connections In the 1980s no one knew how HIV was spread. What impact did this have on the public's reaction to the disease? *(Possible response: The fact that the origin and spread of HIV was a mystery increased people's fear and prejudice toward the gay community, since the virus seemed to originate among this group.)*

AMERICAN PLACES

The National Mall, the most visited of all national parks, almost didn't happen. In the late 1700s, French engineer Pierre L'Enfant drew up plans for a mall, but they were never implemented. In 1850 President Millard Fillmore commissioned another architect to create a landscape design, but these plans were also dropped. In 1854, the Baltimore & Ohio Railroad Company build a rail line and terrminal on the mall (the site of President Garfield's assassination in 1881). During the Civil War, the Mall was used to house soldiers in temporary camps. Eventually, L'Enfant's original plans were resurrected and his design was finally adopted. Today, the Mall stretches two miles between the Capitol steps and the Lincoln Memorial and is lined with world-class museums, including the National Museum of African American History and Culture, the National Gallery of Art. and the National Air and Space Museum, which houses the Wright brothers' Kitty Hawk plane. A second air museum location in Chantilly, Virginia, houses the Apollo 11 Command Module *Columbia*.

ACTIVE OPTIONS

Active History: Evaluate the Impact of Technology Extend the lesson by using either the PDF or Whiteboard version of the activity. These activities take a deeper look at a topic from, or related to, the lesson. Explore the activities as a class, turn them into assignments, or even assign them individually.

NG Learning Framework: Map Activism in History

ATTITUDES Responsibility, Empowerment

KNOWLEDGE Our Human Story

Remind students that in the early history of the AIDS epidemic, much of the American public reacted with fear and hostility, as it has with other incidents or movements that have been perceived as threats. Divide the class into groups, and instruct each group to track the initial reactions and resulting activism for three social issues: the AIDS epidemic and two other issues, such as civil rights, the women's movement, or the gay rights movement. Groups can use a graphic organizer, such as the cause-and-effect one shown here, to map the details of their research. Once their maps are completed, groups should answer this question: How did reactions and activism related to other movements in history compare with the initial reactions and subsequent activism of the AIDS epidemic? Have each group present their completed map to the class.

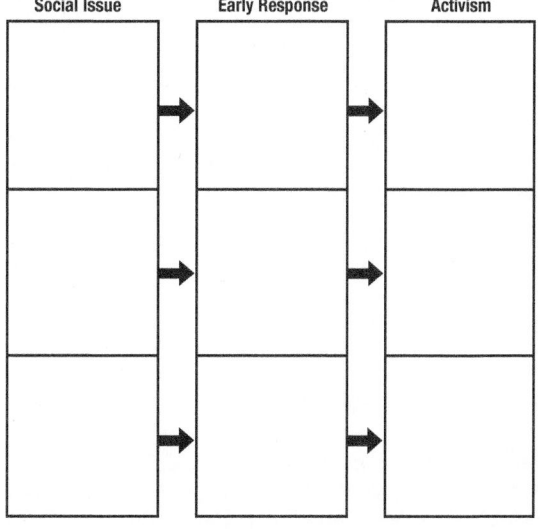

Social Issue | Early Response | Activism

HISTORICAL THINKING

ANSWERS

1. High divorce rates and an increase in single-parent households made the conservative movement fear there was a decline in the country's morals.

2. Possible response: Personal computers now make it easy for people to do personal and business tasks online, work remotely, and communicate with anyone in any part of the world in real time.

3. Possible response: Had the Reagan administration supported preventive measures, fewer people may have become infected, slowing or even halting the epidemic. Also, people may have shown more compassion for those with the disease.

4. Record numbers of women were having children on their own, getting divorced, and entering the workforce in the 1980s.

CRITICAL VIEWING Possible response: The panels put a name and sometimes a face to the person who died, while also sharing something about who that person was. The people who made the quilt were dedicated to keeping the memory of their loved ones alive and to communicating to the public the human impact of the disease on family and friends.

COLLAPSE OF THE SOVIET UNION

The fall of the Soviet Union and the end of communism in Eastern Europe was surely something people believed they would never witness in their lifetimes. And then it happened.

A WEAKENED SOVIET EMPIRE

Since the aftermath of World War II, the opposing doctrines of the capitalist United States and the communist Soviet Union had generated conflicts that had an impact on the entire world. In 1980, Ronald Reagan took office as president, hoping to promote free-market relations and anticommunist policies throughout the world.

By 1984, the U.S. economy had revived and was growing. This helped Ronald Reagan win a convincing re-election. What also helped was Reagan's strong anticommunist stance, which a majority of Americans favored. As Reagan pursued his anticommunist foreign policy into his second term, the Soviet Union was experiencing a period of inner turmoil. By the mid-1980s, the Soviet Union was struggling with a deteriorating economy and an unpopular war against anticommunist rebels in Afghanistan.

In 1985, the Soviet **Politburo**, the ruling committee of the Communist Party and thus the nation, agreed on a new leader, **Mikhail Gorbachev** (mih-KYL GOR-buh-chof). Younger than most of the aging Communist Party leaders, Gorbachev brought energy and new ideas to the nation. Hoping that increasing freedom of ideas and speech would lead to a stronger nation, he instituted the policy of *glasnost*, or "openness." For the first time in decades, churches were allowed to open, some political prisoners were released, and journalists were given some freedom to criticize officials.

Central planning, which directed all aspects of Soviet business, farming, and manufacturing, continued to be an inefficient way to govern such a massive country, and people had no economic incentive to pursue innovation. The Soviet Union's economy had stagnated. In addition, in 1979, the Soviet Union had invaded Afghanistan, hoping to intervene on behalf of the country's communist government against anticommunist Muslim rebels. This decision led to a decade-long hostile occupation of Afghanistan, in which thousands of Soviet soldiers died. The conflict drained an enormous amount of money from the Soviet treasury.

Gorbachev reformed the economy more directly through his policy of *perestroika* (peh-ruh-STROY-kuh), or economic restructuring. Loosening the nation's strict control over the economy, he gave more freedom to local officials to make decisions. Some people were even allowed to open small businesses. Gorbachev was not trying to overturn communism with his reforms. Rather, he hoped that these changes would lead to a more efficient, more innovative, and wealthier nation. The country's economy remained stalled, however. And the people used their increased freedom to speak up about their dissatisfactions.

Meanwhile, President Reagan had been building a massive military program, the largest in U.S. peacetime history. He also took an aggressive position against the Soviets' hold on Eastern Bloc countries. On June 12, 1987, he delivered a speech in West Berlin about the evils of communism. He stood not far from the Berlin Wall, a symbol of communist rule. He declared, "Mr. Gorbachev, tear down this wall!" That admonition became an iconic moment, marking the peak of the conflict between the two nations. The Soviet Union's economy was too weak to compete with a U.S. military buildup, so Gorbachev began working on a diplomatic program aimed at controlling nuclear arms.

On December 9, 1987, he met with Reagan to sign the Intermediate-Range Nuclear Forces (INF) Treaty, which banned both nations from owning certain kinds of nuclear missiles.

As Soviet power dwindled, Reagan reached the end of his second presidential term. His vice president, George H.W. Bush, ran against Michael Dukakis, the former Democratic governor of Massachusetts. Bush was elected president in 1988 by a large margin of electoral and popular votes. Formerly ambassador to the United Nations and director of the Central Intelligence Agency, Bush had extensive foreign policy experience and was poised to continue the nation's strong stance against the Soviet Union.

END OF THE SOVIET UNION

Gorbachev's economic policies had not energized the Soviet Union as much as he had hoped. He withdrew troops from Afghanistan in 1989, but the Soviet intervention there had been costly and damaging for national morale. *Glasnost*, which had been meant to spur innovation, had encouraged rebellious voices. While Russia was the largest republic in the Soviet Union, non-Russians held the ethnic majority in many of the other Soviet republics, and they wanted freedom from Soviet rule. In 1990, the Baltic republic of Lithuania declared its independence from the union. Worried that other republics would follow its lead, Gorbachev ordered a military assault in 1991 on unarmed citizens in Lithuania's capital.

This assault further damaged Gorbachev's reputation in the Soviet Union. **Boris Yeltsin**, a member of parliament and the newly elected president of the Russian Republic, emerged as a rival to Gorbachev's overarching power. Though he assisted Gorbachev in leading the country, he was a vocal critic of Gorbachev's policies.

On August 18, 1991, conservative members of the Communist Party attempted a coup to overthrow Gorbachev, fearing that their power was diminishing. Tanks and other military vehicles rolled into Moscow, but the party **hardliners**, or staunch Soviet communists, were shocked to find that the people no longer feared such shows of government force.

Soviet General Secretary Mikhail Gorbachev and President Ronald Reagan strolled on the South Lawn of the White House during the Washington Summit on December 10, 1987. Two days before, they had signed the Intermediate-Range Nuclear Forces Treaty.

Despite his disagreements with Gorbachev, Yeltsin jumped onto a tank and rejected the coup, to cheers from the crowd and support from President Bush and other world leaders. Shortly after, the hardliners ordered the military to attack the Soviet parliament, but military leaders refused. The Communist Party and the Politburo had lost. The Russian parliament voted to dissolve them completely. As communist rule collapsed, many of the Soviet republics, such as Estonia and Latvia, declared their independence. Though Gorbachev pushed for unity, the momentum for independence was too great. On December 25, 1991, the Soviet Union ceased to exist, and the former republics of the Union of Soviet Socialist Republics (U.S.S.R.) became independent countries.

OBJECTIVE

Analyze how Reagan's policies and other world factors led to the West's Cold War victory.

CRITICAL THINKING SKILLS FOR LESSON 3.1

- Make Connections
- Analyze Cause and Effect
- Make Inferences
- Identify Main Ideas and Details
- Draw Conclusions
- Make Generalizations
- Compare and Contrast
- Integrate Visuals

HISTORICAL THINKING FOR CHAPTER 30

What major changes occurred in the United States during Ronald Reagan's presidency?
The 1980s saw the end of the Cold War. Lesson 3.1 explores the fall of the Soviet Union and the rise of freedom movements around the world.

BACKGROUND FOR THE TEACHER

The high-ranking Soviet leaders who attempted the August coup called themselves the State Emergency Committee, and they included the Politburo's vice-president and prime minister. Coup leaders wanted to prevent ratification of a treaty restructuring the government. They confined Gorbachev to his countryside house in Crimea and announced that Vice President Gennady Yanayev would assume presidential powers. But the coup leaders failed to shut down broadcasts of the event on Russian TV, which led thousands of people who were against the coup to protest in Moscow. The people responded to President Boris Yeltsin's call to unite and keep the coup leaders from entering government offices. On the fourth day of the attempted government takeover, the coup leaders surrendered.

HISTORY NOTEBOOK

Encourage students to complete the Collapse of the Soviet Union page and American Gallery page for Chapter 30 in their History Notebooks as they read.

INTRODUCE & ENGAGE

REBUILD A GOVERNMENT

Discuss with students what they think happens when a government collapses. **ASK:** What factors might lead to a government collapse? *(economic depression, protests for freedoms and civil rights, too much government control)* Have students identify the consequences of a government collapse, such as the fall of leadership and the undoing of laws that governed the country. Then have students consider ways to rebuild the government, such as restructuring international agreements. Draw a Cause-and-Effect Chart on the board and list ideas as students generate them.

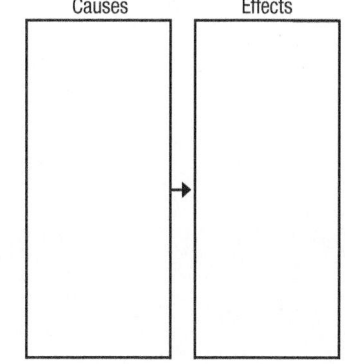

TEACH

GUIDED DISCUSSION

1. **Identify Main Ideas and Details** What political factors in the Soviet Union contributed to the West's victory in the Cold War? *(Possible response: Mikhail Gorbachev's policies of* glasnost *and* perestroika, *which relaxed some of the Politburo's controls; demands among Russians for more freedoms; and the rising independence movements in Soviet satellite countries)*

2. **Analyze Cause and Effect** What was the impact of the Soviet Union's involvement in Afghanistan, and what international consequences did it have? *(The occupation in Afghanistan drained the Soviet economy, making the Soviets unable to compete with the U.S. military buildup. Eventually, the Soviet Union and the United States signed the Intermediate-Range Nuclear Forces (INF) Treaty, which restricted ownership of certain kinds of nuclear missiles.)*

3. **Make Connections** Which Baltic republic was first to declare its independence, and how did its action affect Gorbachev's rule? *(Lithuania was first to declare its independence. Gorbachev, worried that other republics would follow, launched a military assault, which weakened his leadership at home and abroad and led to the emergence of Boris Yeltsin as a rival leader.)*

DRAW CONCLUSIONS

Divide the class into three groups and have each group examine the consequences of the end of the Cold War. Ask groups to draw conclusions about how the end of the Cold War affected the Soviet Union and its republics and what developments came out of it. Groups should draw from text evidence and their own knowledge to support their conclusions. Once groups have examined the consequences, discuss them as a class. Use a Concept Cluster to record their conclusions.

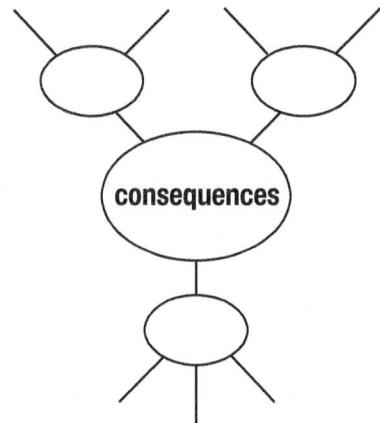

DIFFERENTIATE

ENGLISH LANGUAGE LEARNERS

Pose and Answer Questions Arrange students at the **Emerging** and **Expanding** levels in mixed pairs and ask them to reread the text together. Instruct them to pause after each paragraph and ask one another *who, what, when, where,* or *why* questions about what they have just read. Suggest that students use a 5Ws Chart to help organize their questions and answers. Ask students at the **Expanding** level to assist students at the **Emerging** level as needed.

What?
Who?
Where?
When?
Why?

GIFTED & TALENTED

Perform a Dramatic Reading Have students find online text and video of Reagan's speech at the Berlin Wall in 1987. Then challenge students to prepare a dramatic reading of one or more excerpts from the speech. Encourage them to imitate Reagan's delivery style. After they have practiced, invite students to perform their dramatic reading in front of the class. Ask the class to discuss how the reading affected their interpretation and understanding of the speech and its impact on the United States, the Soviet Union, West Germany, and East Germany.

See the Chapter Planner for more strategies for differentiation.

As in the Soviet Union, democratic movements arose across the globe during the late 1980s and early 1990s. In China, a solitary demonstrator stands in the way of Chinese army tanks as they roll along the Avenue of Eternal Peace in Beijing. For weeks during the spring of 1989, people had demonstrated in the nearby Tiananmen Square (below) for freedom of speech and the press.

FREEDOM IN CENTRAL AND EASTERN EUROPE

Even before the Soviet Union collapsed, communist rule had fallen throughout Eastern Europe. The reforms instituted by Gorbachev had included granting greater freedom to the Soviet-controlled Eastern Bloc countries. This inspired those countries, starting with Poland, to push for even greater control of their economic and political futures. In 1988, Polish workers, angry at a faltering economy, went on a countrywide strike. Poland's military leaders agreed to legalize a workers' union and cooperate with them, which eventually led to other national reforms and the country's first free elections in 1989 and 1990. The Polish people voted union leader Lech Walesa (LEHK vuh-WEHN-suh) the country's new president in 1990.

In Hungary, reformers were inspired by Poland's drastic transformation. Hungarian leaders adopted policies that moved the country toward a free-market economy and free elections. In 1989, radical reformers took over the Communist Party congress and voted to dissolve the party itself. Czechoslovakia also enjoyed a peaceful transition to democracy. Watching the developments elsewhere, the Czech public marched peacefully against the nation's Communist Party. Massive protests forced the dissolution of the party in 1989. A newly formed parliament elected playwright and activist Václav Havel (VAHT-slav HAH-vehl) president. Romania also saw the fall of communism in 1989, though not without bloodshed. After dictator Nicolae Ceausescu (NIHK-oh-ly chow-CHEHS-kew) ordered the killing of hundreds of peaceful protestors, the Romanian army sided with the uprising against him. Ceausescu and his wife were arrested and executed, and Romania started to hold free elections in 1990.

Meanwhile, people in East Germany organized massive protests for greater freedom. Then, on November 9, 1989, the Berlin Wall was opened. An East German official had mistakenly issued an order to let people cross to West Germany. A series of contradictory instructions followed. Meanwhile, East German crowds at the wall grew by thousands. In an attempt to restore stability, the government first let a few people cross the border and then more. Soon, thousands of people from East and West Germany descended on the scene in joyous celebration. East Germans made it clear that they rejected the Communist Party and wanted reunification with West Germany. About a year later, Germany became one country again, and the Berlin Wall was torn down.

FREEDOM SPREADS

In addition to the spectacular fall of the Soviet Union, the world witnessed other successful freedom movements during this time. In 1989, the newly elected president of South Africa, F. W. de Klerk, began to dismantle apartheid. He lifted restrictions on the media and civil rights groups and ended the plan to force black people to live in separate homelands. In 1990, he freed civil rights leader Nelson Mandela, who had spent 27 years in prison for anti-apartheid activities. The following few years were filled with negotiations led by Mandela and de Klerk to finally end the practice of apartheid and establish the country's first multi-ethnic government. In 1994, Mandela was elected president of South Africa.

Free elections were held in Chile in 1989, ending the military dictatorship that had ruled since 1973. In Nicaragua, the long conflict between the ruling Sandinistas and the rebel Contras, which had sparked the Iran-Contra scandal in the United States, ended when a coalition of anti-Sandinista political parties finally won the national election.

As a wave of activism for democracy rose in China, the nation's communist government stood firm. In 1987, Chinese Communist Party general secretary Hu Yaobang was forced to resign largely for encouraging democratic reforms. When Hu died in 1989, he became a symbol of political democracy. That spring, students demonstrated against the government in **Tiananmen Square**, a large public space in Beijing. Thousands of students protested peacefully and started a hunger strike, gaining support from around the world. On June 4, the military rolled tanks into the square, opening fire and killing hundreds. Despite the democratic movements across the globe, repressive regimes still prevailed in a number of countries, and international tensions still ran high.

HISTORICAL THINKING

1. **READING CHECK** What were Mikhail Gorbachev's policies of *glasnost* and *perestroika*?

2. **MAKE CONNECTIONS** What larger political trends in Eastern Europe were reflected in the opening of the Berlin Wall?

3. **ANALYZE CAUSE AND EFFECT** How did changes in the Soviet Union lead to the fall of communism in other Eastern Bloc countries?

4. **MAKE INFERENCES** How did Mikhail Gorbachev's policies hurt his own reputation after the Soviet invasion of Lithuania in 1989?

BUILD BACKGROUND

APARTHEID

Apartheid is an Afrikaans word whose literal meaning is "separateness." As a political structure, apartheid was meant to keep races rigidly separated. In 1950, South Africa passed the Population Registration Act, which classified all South Africans by race: Bantu, or all black Africans; colored, or mixed race; and white. Later, a fourth category was added: Asian, or Indian and Pakistani. The Group Areas Act, also passed in 1950, created residential and business areas based solely on race. Individuals from another race were barred from owning land or having a residence or business in an area designated for a specific race. As a direct result of the Group Areas Act, 80 percent of South Africa's land was designated as "white," even though whites were a minority.

Laws passed later restricted social contact between races, created separate educational standards, segregated jobs along racial lines, and prevented nonwhites from participating in government. Individuals who ventured into restricted areas were required to carry documents authorizing their presence or face arrest. In 1959, the Promotion of Bantu Self-Government Act created 10 African homelands, all of which were politically and economically dependent on South Africa.

Criticism of government policies was brutally suppressed. Nonetheless, antigovernment demonstrations persisted, some of them quite violent. In March 1960, police opened fire on protesters in Sharpeville, killing some 69 black Africans. The 1976 Soweto riots were even more violent and resulted in worldwide demands for political reforms in South Africa.

TEACH

GUIDED DISCUSSION

4. Make Generalizations What statement could be made about the transitions from communist governments to democracies in Eastern Europe? *(Possible response: Although most transitions were peaceful, such as the one in Hungary, some transitions were violent, as in Romania, where hundreds of peaceful protesters were killed.)*

5. Compare and Contrast Why were pro-democracy protests in China unsuccessful, whereas similar protests had led to change in Eastern Europe and in some Latin American countries? *(Possible response: The will of the people can be more easily suppressed in tightly controlled governments such as China, whereas in smaller countries, the government is much more vulnerable to pressures for change from mass protests and other forms of civil disobedience.)*

INTEGRATE VISUALS

Direct students' attention to the two photographs and have them read the caption. Draw attention to the body language of protesters in both photographs. Have students speculate on what they may be responding to and what their body language communicates. **ASK:** What personal characteristics do the individuals in these photographs convey? *(Possible responses: courage, hope, defiance, determination, anger, confusion, fear)*

ACTIVE OPTIONS

The Fall of the Berlin Wall Encourage students to explore the American Gallery. Invite them to select one of the photographs and do research to learn more about the story behind the photo. Ask questions that can help guide their research, such as: What connection does the subject matter in this photo have with the Berlin Wall? Where was this photo taken, and what does it show about life in East and West Berlin? What else would you like to know about the Berlin Wall and why it eventually fell?

NG Learning Framework: Report on Tiananmen Square

SKILL Observation

KNOWLEDGE Our Human Story

Organize students into pairs and ask them to research the student protest at Tiananmen Square in 1989 to create a news report about the event. Have half of the pairs write the report from the perspective of a Chinese journalist in 1989 communist China. The other half will prepare a report from the perspective of a U.S. journalist today. Encourage students to consider whether the historic event influenced subsequent political developments in China. Invite pairs to present their news reports to the class. Ask the class to compare the past account of the event with the present account, evaluating the consequences and determining lessons learned from the event.

HISTORICAL THINKING

ANSWERS

1. Gorbachev introduced the policy of *glasnost*, or "openness," to let information and ideas move freely. This meant that churches could open, some political prisoners were released, and authors and reporters could criticize politicians. *Perestroika*, or economic restructuring, allowed the Soviet Union to move away from a completely centralized, government-controlled economy. Local officials had more freedom to make decisions, and some small businesses started up.

2. The opening of the Berlin Wall began when an East German official mistakenly issued an order to open the wall and allow people to cross into West Germany. As additional confusing instructions came across, East German crowds gathered near the wall. The government then allowed a few people to cross the border, and slowly others were let through as well.

3. Gorbachev's reforms allowed for greater freedoms not only in the Soviet Union but also in the Soviet-controlled Eastern Bloc countries. People in Eastern Europe were inspired to take control of their own economies and governments.

4. Possible response: When Lithuania declared its independence, Gorbachev ordered a military assault on unarmed citizens in the country's capital city. Gorbachev had been seen as a reformer, but his actions in Lithuania made him seem like a communist leader determined to control the people.

THE NEWSEUM
WASHINGTON, D.C.

Located between the White House and the U.S. Capitol, the interactive Newseum promotes, explains, and defends free expression and the five freedoms of the First Amendment: religion, speech, press, assembly, and petition. The museum's goal is to serve as a neutral forum for fostering open discussions. It engages visitors in the central debates of our time, including the future of investigative journalism, the tensions between national security and privacy, and the role of religious freedom.

The Newseum's 7 levels of interactive exhibits include 15 galleries and 15 theaters. Among the most memorable exhibits are the 9/11 Gallery, which features the broadcast antenna from the top of the World Trade Center and the Pulitzer Prize Photographs Gallery, displaying photographs from every Pulitzer Prize-winning entry since 1942. The Newseum also traces the evolution of electronic communication from the birth of radio to the technologies of the present and the future.

Documenting the Kennedy Assassination

Before President John F. Kennedy even reached the Dallas hospital after being shot on November 22, 1963, 58-year-old Russian immigrant Abraham Zapruder knew the president was dead. He had watched the assassination unfold through the viewfinder of his 8-millimeter Bell and Howell home movie camera and had unknowingly created one of history's most famous films.

Abraham Zapruder's camera as well as an ID belonging to White House correspondent Sid Davis are part of the Newseum's traveling exhibit devoted to the assassination of President Kennedy.

How does a museum like the Newseum show the connections between historical events and larger social and political trends and developments?

The Berlin Wall Gallery

At the center of the Newseum's Berlin Wall Gallery stand eight 12-foot-high concrete sections of the Berlin Wall—the largest display of unaltered portions of the wall outside of Germany. A three-story East German guard tower that stood near

Checkpoint Charlie, Berlin's best-known East-West crossing point, stands nearby. The gallery tells the story of how news and information helped topple a closed and oppressive society, signaling the end of the Cold War.

"I am dedicated to keeping the Newseum at the cutting edge of national and international conversations about **the meaning of—and threats to—freedom.**"
—Jeffrey Herbst, Newseum President and CEO

The 9/11 Gallery

Exploring an event like 9/11 through artifacts, such as the newspaper headlines shown here, documentary films, and first-person accounts from journalists who covered the story, has a profound impact on Newseum visitors in this gallery.

Along with police and firefighters, journalists ran toward danger on September 11, 2001. Among the 2,749 people who lost their lives in New York City that day were photojournalist Bill Biggart, who was killed in the collapse of one of the World Trade Center towers, and 6 broadcast engineers who died at their posts at the top of the 110-story complex.

News organizations faced extraordinary challenges that day. From the Pentagon to New York City to Shanksville, Pennsylvania, shocking news broke minute by minute, and journalists scrambled to cover the stories.

PLAN: 2-PAGE LESSON

OBJECTIVE

Trace the role of media in the diffusion of popular culture and in reporting historical events in the United States and worldwide.

CRITICAL THINKING SKILLS FOR LESSON 3.2

- Analyze Visuals
- Make Connections
- Describe
- Evaluate

HISTORICAL THINKING FOR CHAPTER 30

What major changes occurred in the United States during Ronald Reagan's presidency?
The main goal of the Reagan presidency was to end the Cold War, which included tearing down the Berlin Wall and reuniting Germany under a democratic government. Lesson 3.2 explores the artifacts and exhibits, such as the Berlin Wall Gallery, found at the Newseum that tell the story of these historic events.

BACKGROUND FOR THE TEACHER

The First Amendment Center, founded by John Seigenthaler in 1991, is an integral part of the Newseum. With a mission to create a dialogue on the rights and values inherent in the First Amendment, the center offers a library of First Amendment research articles, FAQs, and cases brought before the U.S. Supreme Court. The center reports on challenges to First Amendment freedoms, on the meaning of the amendment's rights, and on surveys of citizens' views regarding First Amendment issues. The center also offers podcasts that focus on how a free press can foster change, along with publications and articles on current First Amendment debates. Together with the Newseum's online access to daily newspaper headlines from around the world, the First Amendment Center provides a rich resource for students and teachers.

HISTORY NOTEBOOK

Encourage students to complete the Curating History page for Chapter 30 in their History Notebooks as they read.

INTRODUCE & ENGAGE

PREVIEW USING VISUALS

Point out the sections of the Berlin Wall found in the Berlin Wall Gallery. Discuss with students how graffiti is a form of expression, and encourage them to look at the details of the graffiti. **ASK:** What messages are expressed in the art shown on the sections of the Berlin Wall? *(Possible response: There is a message to "act up," and another message that says, "You are the power." These empowering messages are a call for people to take action.)* Tell students that in this lesson they will explore forms of freedom of expression by studying artifacts and exhibits.

TEACH

GUIDED DISCUSSION

1. **Describe** In what way was the 8-millimeter Bell and Howell home movie camera a significant tool in accurate news reporting, and why is it a highly valued artifact at the Newseum? *(The camera captured the assassination of President Kennedy and provided visual evidence of the accuracy of news being reported in newspapers. It is highly valued not only for capturing a historic event but also for helping to verify actual events.)*

2. **Evaluate** What role did news reporting play in future political debates regarding the terrorist attack on September 11, 2001? *(Possible response: Journalism played a significant role in accurately reporting the news and firsthand accounts of the 9/11 terrorist attack, which provided information for later debates on laws and policies in an effort to prevent another terrorist attack from happening.)*

CURATING HISTORY

The Newseum website is a useful resource for learning more about the role of journalism in documenting U.S. history and in securing the rights guaranteed by the First Amendment. Have groups of students visit the online collection of exhibits and look through the headlines of the more than 800 newspapers that each day submit their front pages to the Newseum. Then ask each group to report on the exhibit or collection of headlines they found most interesting.

ACTIVE OPTION

On Your Feet: Be a Journalist Divide the class into small groups, and tell students that each group is a team of journalists. As a class, decide on a recent school activity or community event to report about. Each team should develop a set of questions to be answered in the story, interview individuals who were part of the school activity or community event, and gather relevant facts related to the story. Suggest that teams use the News Article Organizer to plan and write their story. Have teams share their news articles, compare and contrast their headlines, and evaluate the effectiveness of how each story is presented.

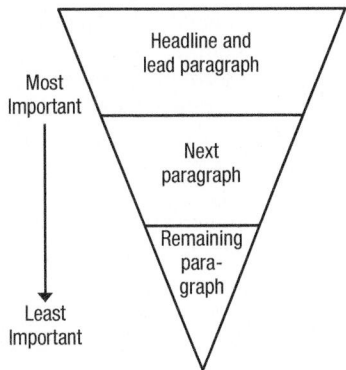

DIFFERENTIATE

STRIVING READERS

Preview and Review the Text Have students preview the lesson by reading the title and introductory text and examining the photographs. Instruct them to write questions about the photos that might be answered in the captions. Then have them read the captions and quotation. After students read the lesson, have them discuss what they learned, review the text, and find answers to their preview questions.

PRE-AP

Write a Compare-and-Contrast Essay Direct students to conduct online research to find out more about the Newseum, especially how it differs from a more traditional museum, such as Chicago's Field Museum of Natural History or the Smithsonian Institution. Tell students to choose another museum and encourage students to use a Venn diagram to keep track of the similarities and differences between the Newseum and the museum they have chosen. Instruct students to use their research and their graphic organizer to write a compare-and-contrast essay about the two museums. Invite volunteers to read their essays to the class.

See the Chapter Planner for more strategies for differentiation.

CURATING HISTORY

Possible response: By connecting artifacts with stories, the Newseum is able to show the human impact and social and political importance of events, create a time line of trends and stories depicting how an event unfolded, and present the effects or consequences of the event.

THE END OF THE COLD WAR

As the general secretary of the Communist Party of the U.S.S.R., Mikhail Gorbachev took office in 1985 with ideas for reform. U.S. President Ronald Reagan had had a few years to develop his foreign policy plan by then, and he had made a commitment to fighting communist forces around the world. Though the two leaders had competing ideologies, they were willing to work with each other to decrease tensions between their countries.

On November 9, 1989, East German officials opened the border between East and West Berlin. That weekend, more than 2 million Berliners flowed across the border, breaking down the concrete and barbed wire barrier that had divided them for 28 years. This photo was taken from the West Berlin side of the wall.

CRITICAL VIEWING Examine the scene in the photo and compare the activity in the foreground on the west side of the Berlin Wall to that in the background on the east side of the wall. How would you describe the scene on both sides of the wall?

DOCUMENT ONE

Primary Source: Article
from *Pravda*, April 24, 1985, by Mikhail Gorbachev

Soon after being appointed general secretary of the Communist Party, Mikhail Gorbachev wrote a newspaper article addressing the country's economic problems. Here, he explains his new ideas of *glasnost* and *perestroika* and how he thinks that restructuring the economy can help the Soviet Union become stronger.

CONSTRUCTED RESPONSE How did Gorbachev's ideas for reform signal a move toward free-market economics?

The main question now is: How, and at what cost, will the country be able to achieve accelerated economic development? Examining this question in the Politburo [a committee made up of the Soviet Union's main policy makers], we have unanimously reached the conclusion that there are real possibilities for this. The task of accelerating growth rates, substantially accelerating them, is completely feasible. We must more boldly advance along the path of expanding the rights of enterprises and their independence, introduce economic accountability and, on this basis, increase the responsibility and stake of labor collectives in the final results of work.

DOCUMENT TWO

Primary Source: Speech
from President Ronald Reagan's speech in West Berlin, June 12, 1987

President Reagan's speech at the Berlin Wall was amplified so that people in East Berlin could hear it as well. He addressed the recent changes in the Soviet Union and wondered where they would lead.

CONSTRUCTED RESPONSE Why did Reagan use the Berlin Wall as a symbol as he addressed changes in the Soviet Union?

Now the Soviets themselves may, in a limited way, be coming to understand the importance of freedom. Are these the beginnings of profound changes in the Soviet state? Or are they token gestures, intended to raise false hopes in the West, or to strengthen the Soviet system without changing it? There is one sign the Soviets can make that would be unmistakable, that would advance dramatically the cause of freedom and peace. General Secretary Gorbachev, if you seek peace, if you seek prosperity for the Soviet Union and Eastern Europe, if you seek liberalization: Come here to this gate! Mr. Gorbachev, open this gate! Mr. Gorbachev, tear down this wall!

DOCUMENT THREE

Primary Source: Speech
from President George H.W. Bush's address to the nation, December 25, 1991

President George H.W. Bush addressed the citizens of the United States on Christmas, announcing the resignation of Mikhail Gorbachev and, essentially, the end of the Cold War.

CONSTRUCTED RESPONSE How did President Bush view Gorbachev's role in the dissolution of the Cold War?

New, independent nations have emerged out of the wreckage of the Soviet empire. Last weekend, these former republics formed a Commonwealth of Independent States. This act marks the end of the old Soviet Union, signified today by Mikhail Gorbachev's decision to resign. Mikhail Gorbachev's revolutionary policies transformed the Soviet Union. His policies permitted the peoples of Russia and the other republics to cast aside decades of oppression and establish the foundations of freedom. The United States applauds and supports the historic choice for freedom by the new states of the Commonwealth. We congratulate them on the peaceful and democratic path they have chosen, and for their careful attention to nuclear control and safety during this transition.

SYNTHESIZE & WRITE

1. **REVIEW** Review what you have learned about the events that led to the end of the Cold War.

2. **RECALL** On your own paper, write details about American and Soviet leaders' actions during the 1980s.

3. **CONSTRUCT** Construct a topic sentence that explains President Reagan's and Mikhail Gorbachev's roles in ending the Cold War.

4. **WRITE** Using evidence from the chapter and these documents, write an informative paragraph that supports your topic sentence in Step 3.

PLAN: 2-PAGE LESSON

OBJECTIVE

Synthesize information from primary sources about the role of the Reagan administration and other factors in ending the Cold War.

CRITICAL THINKING SKILLS FOR LESSON 3.3

• Synthesize

• Make Connections

• Compare and Contrast

• Evaluate

HISTORICAL THINKING FOR CHAPTER 30

What major changes occurred in the United States during Ronald Reagan's presidency?
Despite ideological differences, Ronald Reagan and Mikhail Gorbachev worked together to decrease Cold War tensions between their two countries. Lesson 3.3 features the words of U.S. and Soviet leaders regarding the Cold War and its end.

BACKGROUND FOR THE TEACHER

The photograph in this lesson shows young East German soldiers looking through a gap in the Berlin Wall at the crowd of civilians in West Germany. Since there was no need to absorb the entire East German army into a reunified German army, the question became what to do with 170,000 East German soldiers. As plans moved forward for Germany's reunification, part of the problem solved itself when many of the 92,500 East German army conscripts simply blended into the crowd after the border was opened. However, high-ranking officers in the East German army, all of whom had been members of the Communist Party, were not considered fit for duty in the new German military. East German soldiers age 25 or younger, on the other hand, were regarded as the best candidates for continued military service under the new German government.

INTRODUCE & ENGAGE

PREPARE FOR THE DOCUMENT-BASED QUESTION

Before students start on the activity, briefly preview the three documents. Remind students that a constructed response requires full explanations in complete sentences. In addition to information in the documents, emphasize that students should use what they have learned about the Cold War and U.S. foreign policy during the 1980s.

TEACH

GUIDED DISCUSSION

1. **Make Connections** How does Gorbachev's article convey a change in attitude about the Soviet Union's communist economy? *(He talks about accelerating growth in the economy and says that to do so, they must "boldly advance" and expand rights and allow more independence, which is in marked contrast to the previously closed and limited economy.)*

2. **Compare and Contrast** How would you compare the tone of President Reagan's and President Bush's speeches, and what bias do they both show? *(President Reagan's tone is cautiously optimistic but ends with a challenge to Gorbachev, revealing Reagan's bias toward Western values. President Bush's tone is congratulatory and supportive but also shows bias toward Western forms of democracy. The speeches of both men show their assumptions that the former Soviet Union countries will follow a Western democratic model.)*

EVALUATE

After students have completed the Synthesize & Write activity, allow time for them to exchange paragraphs and read and comment on the work of their peers. Establish guidelines for comments prior to this activity so that feedback is constructive and encouraging. Comments should focus on the most significant parts that address the purpose of the activity and the audience.

ACTIVE OPTIONS

On Your Feet: Jigsaw Strategy Organize students into "expert" groups and have students from each group analyze one of the documents and summarize its main ideas in their own words. Then tell the members of each group to count off using the letters A, B, C, and so on. Regroup students into new groups so that each new group has at least one member from each expert group. Students in the new groups should take turns sharing the simplified summaries they developed in their expert groups.

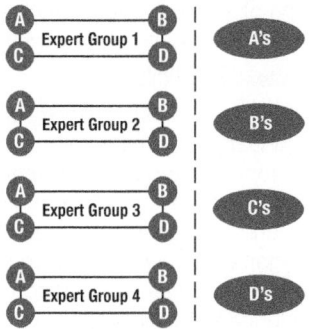

DIFFERENTIATE

INCLUSION

Work in Pairs Pair students who are visually impaired with students who are not. Ask the latter to describe the photograph of the section of the Berlin Wall coming down and to read aloud the photo caption and each of the Primary Sources. Tell visually impaired students to ask clarifying questions as necessary. Then have the pairs work together to answer the Critical Viewing and the Constructed Response questions.

PRE-AP

Analyze a Leader's Role Have students gather information in order to write an essay about one of the leaders who played an important role in ending the Cold War. Instruct students to use multiple print and online sources and to cite both primary and secondary sources in their essay. Encourage them to elucidate the key communications and events, as well as the individual's personality, in analyzing the leader's role in ending the Cold War. Invite volunteers to share their essays with the class.

See the Chapter Planner for more strategies for differentiation.

SYNTHESIZE & WRITE

ANSWERS

1. Answers will vary.

2. Answers will vary.

3. Possible response: Mikhail Gorbachev's reforms of *glasnost* and *perestroika*, economic problems in the Soviet Union, and Ronald Reagan's increased military spending and pressure against the Soviets led to the end of the Cold War.

4. Answers will vary. Students' paragraphs should include their topic sentence from Step 3 and provide several details from the documents to support their sentence.

CONSTRUCTED RESPONSE

Document 1: Gorbachev's ideas for reform focused on expanding the rights of business enterprises and allowing them more freedom to act, as well as establishing economic accountability. All these elements would give companies more flexibility to conduct business and more investment in their work.

Document 2: The Berlin Wall was a barrier the Soviets erected to separate capitalist West Berlin from communist East Berlin. Reagan used the challenge of Gorbachev tearing down the wall as a symbol that the Soviets were serious about change.

Document 3: Bush views Gorbachev as being instrumental in ending the Cold War because the policies Gorbachev instituted broke the hold of communism in the Soviet Union and established the basis for greater freedom.

CRITICAL VIEWING Possible response: The two scenes offer a stark contrast. On the East German side of the wall, four young soldiers stare at the crowd, while behind them are construction cranes and the bleak, empty streets of East Berlin. In contrast, on the West German side, citizens of all walks of life, including a few soldiers, are crowded around the wall as if wanting to pull it down themselves.

GEORGE H.W. BUSH AND THE PERSIAN GULF WAR

Have you ever had to challenge assumptions that you have held for a long time? What was difficult about it? After decades of sparring with the Soviet Union during the Cold War, the United States faced threats from a new location, which required very different strategies.

An F-14A Tomcat flies over Kuwait where oil well fires set by the Iraqis burned for months after Operation Desert Storm ended.

CONFLICT IN THE MIDDLE EAST

After the Soviet Union collapsed, President Bush was in the position to use his years of experience handling international conflict to assist the former Warsaw Pact countries as they adjusted to democracy. While hope grew in Europe, tensions were about to boil over in Southwest Asia, more commonly known as the Middle East.

In the 1980s, the Southwest Asian countries of Iran and Iraq both had authoritarian governments. Since the Iranian Revolution of 1979, Iran had operated as a **theocracy**, or a nation governed by the principles of a single religion. Its leaders were fundamentalist Muslim clerics, or religious leaders. Meanwhile, in Iraq, a member of the Ba'th political party, **Saddam Hussein**, helped his party orchestrate a coup against the country's prime minister. By 1979, Hussein had forced out Iraq's sick and aging president, Ahmad Hasan al-Bakr, and he began a long, tyrannical reign. A brutal dictator, Hussein extinguished any voices of dissent, operating a secret police force that arrested and tortured his enemies.

In 1980, Iran and Iraq went to war. Hussein's goal was to conquer the other countries around the Persian Gulf and preside as the leader over a single, oil-rich Arab nation. In 1980, he attempted an invasion of neighboring Iran's oil fields, leading to the Iran-Iraq War. Religious tensions also played a role in the conflict. Dominated by different branches of Islam, the two countries were often at odds with each other over their beliefs and traditions, especially as they intersected with political and government practices and goals. Hussein was a member of the **Sunni** (SOO-nee) denomination, while Iran was controlled by the **Shi'ite** (SHE-ite) sect. The war between the two countries raged until 1988, when both sides, depleted of funds and resources, agreed to a hostile ceasefire, or an agreement in which the problems being fought over remain unchanged or unresolved, but the parties to the conflict agree to stop fighting while peace plans are made.

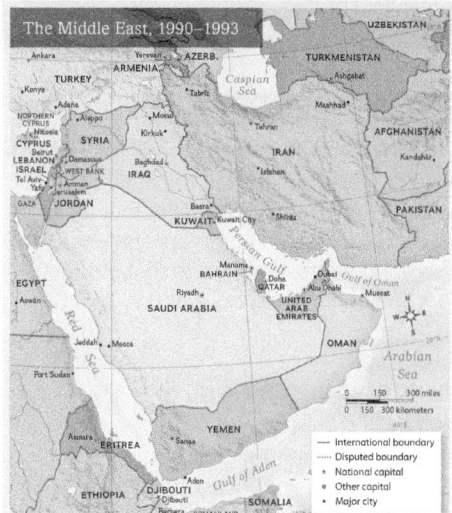

The Middle East, 1990–1993

International boundary
Disputed boundary
● National capital
○ Other capital
● Major city

OPERATION DESERT STORM

In August 1990, Hussein ordered Iraqi troops to invade another neighboring country, **Kuwait**, in order to take over the small nation's vast oil resources. The conflict, which later became known as the **Persian Gulf War**, expanded to include a buildup of international troops in nearby countries. The presence of Iraq in Kuwait was a major concern for the rest of the world, especially since world leaders suspected that Hussein planned next to attack Saudi Arabia, the world's largest oil producer.

In response, President Bush increased the number of American troops stationed in Saudi Arabia to 400,000, hoping to deter Iraq with a show of force. In addition, the United Nations called for an international ban on trade with Iraq, but neither action deterred Hussein. President Bush then worked with other NATO countries to form a military coalition against Hussein. On January 16, 1991, the coalition moved into Kuwait to force Iraqi troops out.

The coalition effort, called **Operation Desert Storm**, ended quickly. In six weeks it drove Iraq out of Kuwait. The coalition's success was partly owed to modern technology that was used for the first

INTRODUCE & ENGAGE

DETERMINE THE CONSEQUENCES OF WAR

Direct students' attention to the photograph of the F-14A Tomcat flying over Kuwait and have students read the caption. Draw a Venn diagram on the board. Discuss the possible environmental and economic consequences of the oil well fires to Kuwait and other countries. List students' ideas on the diagram as they are generated, recording the environmental effects in one circle and the economic effects in the other circle. **ASK:** What might the economic and environmental consequences be for Kuwait as a result of its oil fields being set on fire, and how would those consequences also impact the international community? *(Possible responses: The air would be polluted at the ground level in Kuwait and then would pollute upper levels as it traveled around the globe. From an economic standpoint, with a reduction in oil reserves, gas and oil prices would rise.)*

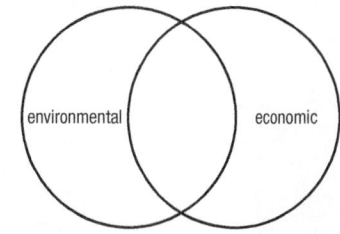

GUIDED DISCUSSION

1. **Draw Conclusions** What threat did Saddam Hussein's military ambitions pose to the U.S. and world economy? *(If Saddam Hussein had gained control of the oil-rich areas of the Middle East, he would have been able to control vast supplies of oil and dictate its price to oil-dependent countries, such as the United States.)*

2. **Analyze Cause and Effect** What was President Bush's initial response in 1990 to Saddam Hussein's attack on Kuwait, and what effect did it have? *(President Bush sent more troops to Saudi Arabia in a show of force, but it did not deter Hussein from his invasion of Kuwait.)*

3. **Ask and Answer Questions** Think up a series of questions about Hussein's invasion of Kuwait and the battles fought there, and explain how you would answer those questions. *(Answers will vary: Students might ask questions about how the oil fires were extinguished, what Kuwait is like now, and so on. They may explain that they would need to research official and personal accounts of the war to answer their questions.)*

INTERPRET MAPS

Direct students' attention to the map of the Middle East. Discuss with students their initial observations about the location of each country, its relative size, and its proximity to water, required for the transport of oil. **ASK:** What strategic advantage would Iraq have gained by conquering Kuwait? *(Possible response: Iraq would have gained additional access to the Persian Gulf for transport of oil and to launch military actions against Saudi Arabia.)*

DIFFERENTIATE

ENGLISH LANGUAGE LEARNERS

Use Main Idea Clusters Pair students at the **Emerging** and **Expanding** levels with students at the **Bridging** level. Direct pairs to use Main Idea Clusters to check their understanding of each of the four sections of the lesson. Tell students to take turns reading a section of the lesson. Instruct them to work together to record the main idea and four details for that section and then move on to the next section. After they have completed the lesson, instruct pairs to trade and compare clusters.

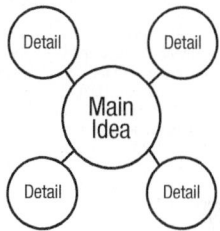

PRE-AP

Research Judicial Appointees' Impacts Have students conduct online research into presidential judicial appointees in order to write an essay about the long-term impact of such appointments. Remind students that presidents continue to influence society long after leaving office because federal judges and Supreme Court justices hold lifetime appointments. While the Supreme Court usually decides fewer than 100 cases a year, federal appellate circuit courts have the final say on thousands of cases. Challenge students to find out who the judges are in the federal circuit court in their area and which president appointed what percentage of them. Encourage students to analyze some of those judges' rulings and the impact particular presidents' judicial appointees continue to have.

See the Chapter Planner for more strategies for differentiation.

time in a war. Microchips and digital advances were used in precision-guided munitions that relied on laser guidance systems to increase the effectiveness of aerial bombings. On the ground, microcomputers, laser rangefinders, and guided-missile systems were incorporated in new tanks, helicopters, and weapons.

Bush did not pursue Hussein to remove him from power. The goal of Operation Desert Storm had been to drive the Iraqis out of a country they had invaded. To send military troops into Iraq itself would be considered an act of aggression and would put NATO troops at risk. Allowing Hussein to stay in power, however, set the stage for later conflict.

THE CHALLENGE OF ACHIEVING PEACE

Much like Saddam Hussein, **Manuel Noriega** of Panama had developed a troubled relationship with the United States as he turned from a CIA informer to a criminal liability. Noriega had brutally gained control of Panama and engaged in drug trafficking and racketeering throughout the 1980s. In 1988, the Senate subcommittee on terrorism, narcotics, and international operations declared that Noriega "represents one of the most serious foreign policy failures for the United States."

Americans intervened in Panama in 1989, when President Bush ordered an invasion to depose and capture the dictator. Though the United States was successful, many people around the world criticized its involvement in foreign governments. President Bush was aware of this growing criticism, and during the conflict with Iraq, he presented to Congress and the nation his ideas for achieving peace through cooperation, in what he called a **New World Order**. His emphasis was on ensuring that nations relied on the rule of law, multinational cooperation, and collective security through the United Nations as the Cold War ended.

BUSH'S DOMESTIC POLICIES

President Bush's four years in office were heavily associated with the intervention of the United States in the Persian Gulf. Many items on his domestic agenda still managed to stand out, however. When the liberal-leaning Supreme Court justice William J. Brennan announced his retirement in 1990, President Bush appointed the little-known New Hampshire judge David H. Souter to replace him.

During Souter's first year on the Court, he joined Justice William Rehnquist in several conservative rulings. Then, in 1991, the retirement of Supreme Court justice Thurgood Marshall allowed President Bush to appoint a new justice to the high Court. He nominated **Clarence Thomas**, a federal judge who had held several offices under the Reagan administration. Senate hearings for his appointment to the Court erupted in controversy, however, when law professor Anita Hill testified that Thomas had sexually harassed her when she had worked for him. Despite the contentious hearings, which the nation watched live on television, the Senate eventually approved Thomas's appointment with a vote of 52 to 48.

Republican appointees to the Court held eight seats and seemed ready to move the Court to the right, rolling back rulings on civil rights, abortion, and religion. But Justice Souter surprised conservatives by often voting with the Democrats' appointees and liberal justices. Souter's record on the Court

Two hours after U.S. and Allied jets attacked Iraqi military defenses, President George H.W. Bush announced the beginning of Operation Desert Storm on January 16, 1991. During his televised speech, Bush explained that a coalition of 28 nations had "exhausted all reasonable efforts to reach a peaceful resolution."

In the following remarks, President Bush introduced the Americans with Disabilities Act that guaranteed civil rights to people with disabilities.

This act is powerful in its simplicity. It will ensure that people with disabilities are given the basic guarantees for which they have worked so long and so hard . . . specifically, first the ADA ensures that employers covered by the act cannot discriminate against qualified individuals with disabilities. Second, the ADA ensures access to public accommodations such as restaurants, hotels, shopping centers, and offices. And third, the ADA ensures expanded access to transportation services. And fourth, the ADA ensures equivalent telephone services for people with speech or hearing impediments.

—from George H.W. Bush's remarks on the signing of the Americans with Disabilities Act, July 26, 1990

disappointed many conservatives and contributed to their growing dissatisfaction with President Bush.

However, President Bush kept a campaign promise and signed significant civil rights legislation for people with disabilities. For years, the disability rights movement had been working to show that the exclusion and segregation of people with disabilities was discrimination. Following the example of the civil rights movement, activists conducted sit-ins at federal buildings, obstructed public transportation, marched in the streets, and took their case to the courts and Congress. Legal changes began in the 1970s, but the most comprehensive civil rights legislation wasn't passed until 1990 when President Bush signed the **Americans with Disabilities Act**, which had passed Congress with bipartisan support.

Another major piece of legislation signed by President Bush was also the result of activism that began in the mid-20th century. In the 1980s, Americans became aware that rainfall made acidic by industrial pollution could travel from the pollution source to other areas, often damaging forests and lakes. In 1989, Bush proposed revisions to the Clean Air Act, specifically targeting acid rain, urban air pollution, and toxic air emissions. The revisions also improved pollution enforcement authority. The bill passed by large votes in both the House of Representatives and the Senate in 1990.

The United States had stopped developing and testing nuclear weapons by the early 1990s. Growing efforts made throughout the 1980s by activists as part of the "nuclear freeze" movement had brought attention and pressure to both the Reagan and Bush administrations to change U.S. nuclear policies. Though complete nuclear disarmament was not achieved, the United States significantly reduced its nuclear weapons. President Bush also signed the Radiation Exposure Compensation Act, which gave partial restitution to people, mostly in western states, who contracted cancer and other diseases as a result of their exposure to atmospheric nuclear testing undertaken during the Cold War or from their employment in the uranium industry.

Bush ran for re-election in 1992, but he was haunted by a campaign promise he had made four years earlier. In 1988, during his speech at the Republican National Convention, he had declared, "Read my lips: no new taxes." His words proved memorable to the American people. But when he took office in 1989, the federal budget debt was about $2.8 trillion, almost three times what it had been in 1980. Unemployment rose, and gas prices spiked during the Gulf War conflicts. Ultimately, the United States faced a recession. The budget deficit was quickly growing, and it limited the president's ability to increase domestic spending. In 1990, President Bush found that he needed to compromise with Congress on a plan of **deficit reduction** that included budget cuts and tax increases to rein in spending and improve the economy.

As Bush explained to the nation why he felt this plan was necessary, people were reminded of his famous pledge to avoid new taxes. Even other Republicans were quick to bring up the broken promise. Despite bipartisan attempts at deficit reduction, people were dissatisfied with the economy by the end of Bush's term. A moderate Democrat, **William Jefferson "Bill" Clinton**, was readying himself to take on the challenge of running for the presidency.

HISTORICAL THINKING

1. **READING CHECK** What were the main criticisms of George H.W. Bush's economic policies?

2. **IDENTIFY MAIN IDEAS AND DETAILS** How did the United States government have to shift its foreign policy during Bush's presidency?

3. **ANALYZE CAUSE AND EFFECT** What was the main cause of the Persian Gulf War?

4. **SUMMARIZE** What impact did President Bush's revisions to the Clean Air Act have on protecting the environment?

BUILD BACKGROUND

NUCLEAR FREEZE

More than 35 years ago, Dr. Randall Caroline Forsberg launched the Nuclear Weapons Freeze Campaign to stop the proliferation of nuclear weapons. The campaign quickly became a mass movement among peace activists, religious groups, and labor organizations. The manifesto "Call to Halt the Nuclear Arms Race," drafted by Dr. Forsberg, gained widespread public support. In the early 1980s, a referendum for a nuclear freeze was placed on ballots in cities, counties, and states across the country, especially in northern and western states.

On June 12, 1982, an antinuclear demonstration in New York City attracted nearly a million participants, one of the largest political rallies to date in the United States. Soon after, a nuclear freeze petition signed by 2,300,000 Americans was delivered to the U.S. and Soviet offices at the United Nations. By 1983, the nuclear freeze initiative had been endorsed by a wide range of local and state governments and became part of the 1984 Democratic presidential campaign platform.

Although neither President Reagan nor President Bush embraced the initiative, President Bush did ask Dr. Forsberg to serve as a consultant to his administration. Eventually the nuclear freeze campaign merged with the National Committee for a Sane Nuclear Policy to become a single nuclear freeze organization called Peace Action.

TEACH

GUIDED DISCUSSION

4. **Identify** What was the political significance of the Supreme Court appointments made by President Bush? *(Possible response: President Bush was able to nominate conservative justices to the U.S. Supreme Court, including David H. Souter and Clarence Thomas, sending a clear message to the nation that he hoped the court would move to the right in its decisions.)*

5. **Make Connections** How did the nuclear freeze movement influence foreign and domestic politics? *(Possible response: Because of its broad support, the nuclear freeze movement succeeded in fostering important nuclear disarmament conversations between the United States and the Soviet Union. It also addressed the medical needs of people in the United States who had been sickened by their exposure to radioactive fallout from atmospheric nuclear testing or by working in the uranium industry during the Cold War.)*

ANALYZE PRIMARY SOURCES

Direct students' attention to the Primary Source feature. Have students work in pairs to study the remarks and understand the provisions of the Americans with Disabilities Act as explained by President Bush. Encourage students to use a graphic organizer like the Main Idea Diagram shown below to organize their thoughts. Then hold a class discussion in which pairs share their notes. Discuss how the Americans with Disabilities Act continues to secure the civil rights of individuals with disabilities. You may wish to invite a panel of business people to speak to the class on how the ADA is enforced in their business.

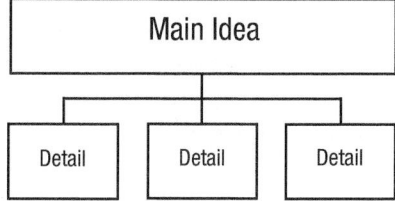

ACTIVE OPTIONS

On Your Feet: Create a Fact Chart Organize students into small groups. Assign each group a Middle Eastern country. Title a separate sheet of chart paper with the name of each country and post the sheets. Ask students to research their assigned country and add three bullet points describing the structure of the country's government to the chart paper. Tell students that bullet points cannot be repeated among countries, so they may need to do additional research on their particular nation. Discuss the results and encourage students to show the connections between particular events discussed in the chapter and the different governments in the Middle East.

NG Learning Framework: Research the Gulf War

SKILLS Observation, Communication

KNOWLEDGE Our Human Story

Have students work in groups to conduct online research about the United States' involvement in the Persian Gulf War. Groups should access a transcript of President Bush's 1991 televised speech announcing the beginning of Operation Desert Storm. Instruct groups to identify President Bush's justification for joining the coalition of nations in attacking Iraq's military forces. Students can investigate questions such as the following: What interests did NATO have in the Middle East, and which nations put troops in the field? What military innovations were used in the war? What goals did Operation Desert Storm seek to achieve, and what were the results? Invite students to share with the class what they learned.

For students who develop an interest in the Gulf War, suggest that they read the online American Story "The Gulf Wars."

HISTORICAL THINKING

ANSWERS

1. Critics pointed out that Bush broke his promise about taxes and that the economy was stalling due to rising unemployment, high gas prices, and a huge budget deficit.

2. The Soviet Union's collapse at the beginning of Bush's presidency meant that tensions with Eastern Europe were no longer the focus of U.S. foreign policy. Instead, attention shifted to the Middle East in response to conflicts in Iran and Iraq.

3. Iraq, led by Saddam Hussein, invaded Kuwait to take control of its oil resources. Worried about a threat to other oil-producing nations, especially Saudi Arabia, NATO nations formed a coalition to drive Iraq out of Kuwait.

4. The revisions to the Clean Air Act improved pollution enforcement, specifically targeting the negative effects of acid rain, urban air pollution, and toxic air emissions on the surrounding environment.

VOCABULARY

Use each of the following vocabulary words in a sentence that shows an understanding of the term's meaning.

1. conservative

   A person who supports traditional social or economic policies is a conservative.

2. think tank

3. safety net

4. supply-side economics

5. deregulation

6. originalism

7. income inequality

8. apartheid

9. deficit reduction

READING STRATEGY
ANALYZE CAUSE AND EFFECT

When you identify causes and effects, you determine how events affect later events. Complete the following chart to identify causes and effects related to Ronald Reagan's presidency. Then answer the question.

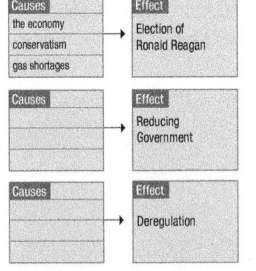

10. What were some of the most influential policies enacted during Reagan's presidency, and how did they affect the nation?

MAIN IDEAS

Answer the following questions. Support your answers with evidence from the chapter.

11. How did the conservative movement respond to Johnson's Great Society programs? **LESSON 1.1**

12. What aspects of post–World War II life in the United States contributed to Sunbelt migration? **LESSON 1.2**

13. What was the significance of Reagan asking the American people if they were better off under Carter's presidency? **LESSON 1.3**

14. Why did the government deregulate the savings and loan industry? **LESSON 2.1**

15. What was the Iran-Contra scandal? **LESSON 2.2**

16. How did the Reagan administration address the increased use of drugs in the United States? **LESSON 2.3**

17. How did the collapse of communism after the fall of the Soviet Union affect countries in Central and Eastern Europe? **LESSON 3.1**

18. What international challenges did President George H.W. Bush face during his term? **LESSON 3.4**

HISTORICAL THINKING

Answer the following questions. Support your answers with evidence from the chapter.

19. **COMPARE AND CONTRAST** In what ways did President Reagan's position on the size of government differ from President Carter's?

20. **MAKE CONNECTIONS** The early years of the HIV/AIDS epidemic were confusing and people were fearful. What other events in American history caused similar anxiety?

21. **DETERMINE CHRONOLOGY** What evidence reveals that the invasion of Grenada was not planned as a distraction from the bombing in Beirut, Lebanon, that killed 241 U.S. marines?

22. **ANALYZE CAUSE AND EFFECT** Why did the Soviet Politburo select Mikhail Gorbachev to become general secretary in 1985?

23. **FORM AND SUPPORT OPINIONS** Do you think President Reagan was right to fire air traffic controllers during the PATCO strike? Support your opinion with evidence from the text.

24. **IDENTIFY PROBLEMS AND SOLUTIONS** What regional environmental problems did President George H.W. Bush address in legislation?

INTERPRET VISUALS

Look closely at this photo of American medical students who were studying at a university in Grenada when the U.S. military invaded to oust the communist government. Then answer the questions that follow.

25. Why do you think the expressions of the students and that of the soldier appear to convey different emotional states?

26. What details in the photograph help you understand how U.S. intervention in Grenada increased Reagan's popularity among American voters?

ANALYZE SOURCES

Read the excerpt from Ronald Reagan's Farewell Address, January 11, 1989, at the end of his presidency. Then answer the question that follows.

> And in all of that time I won a nickname, "The Great Communicator." I wasn't a great communicator, but I communicated great things, and they didn't spring full bloom from my brow, they came from the heart of a great nation—from our experience, our wisdom, and our belief in the principles that have guided us for two centuries. They called it the Reagan revolution. Well, I'll accept that, but for me it always seemed more like the great rediscovery, a rediscovery of our values and our common sense.

27. How does the excerpt above help demonstrate why President Reagan was considered "The Great Communicator"?

CONNECT TO YOUR LIFE

28. **EXPLANATORY** Think about the challenges, achievements, and shortcomings faced by President Ronald Reagan. Then consider the challenges, achievements, and shortcomings of the current U.S. president. In a short essay, explain how the role of president has changed and stayed the same from Ronald Reagan's two terms to the present day.

TIPS

- Research legitimate biographical and news sources about the current president. List the challenges, accomplishments, and missteps, if any, faced by the president while in office.

- Read through the chapter for text evidence of Reagan's accomplishments, challenges, and missteps, and list them.

- Chart similarities and differences in a Venn diagram or another graphic organizer.

- Use your findings to craft a solid thesis statement. Write a paragraph containing at least three sentences and three vocabulary words from the chapter in your response.

VOCABULARY ANSWERS

1. A person who supports traditional social or economic policies is called a conservative.

2. A think tank is a group of experts who conduct research and discuss issues in order to craft potential solutions to social and economic problems.

3. Safety-net programs help individuals who live in poverty and need special services.

4. Supply-side economics advocates decreasing taxes on individuals and corporations to encourage consumers and businesses to spend money and to enable businesses to invest in the economy.

5. Deregulation is the removal of government rules and limitations on an industry.

6. If you advocate originalism, you believe that the U.S. Constitution should be interpreted only in terms of how it was intended or applied when first written.

7. Income inequality is the gap between the earnings of the poorest individuals and those of the richest.

8. Apartheid is a rigid segregation of the races, imposed through laws and enforced by the courts and police/military forces.

9. President Bush compromised with Congress on deficit reduction by agreeing to budget cuts and tax increases to balance the budget and improve the economy.

READING STRATEGY ANSWER

10. Among Reagan's most influential policies were supply-side economics as a way to stimulate the economy; anticommunism, exemplified by his invasion of Grenada and improved relations with the Soviet Union, capped by a nuclear missile reduction agreement; and deregulation of the savings and loan industry, which ended in a disastrous collapse of the industry and a huge financial bill paid by U.S. taxpayers.

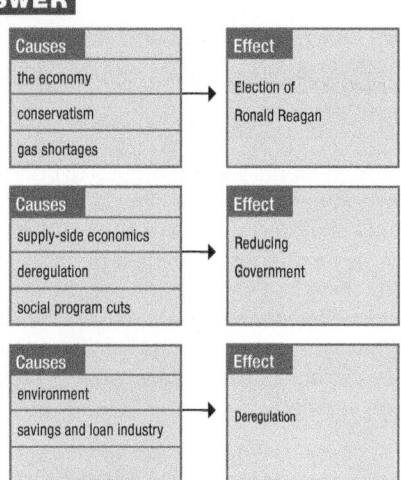

MAIN IDEAS ANSWERS

11. Conservatives wanted to cut Johnson's social programs as part of their strategy to reduce the size of the federal government.

12. In contrast to the Frostbelt, the Sunbelt offered low taxes for individuals and businesses, a less expensive lifestyle, cheaper land for building business, and less costly equipment repair, plus the development of communities that served the needs of seniors who received pensions and Social Security.

13. Because of gas shortages and a struggling economy, Reagan's question made Americans reflect on Carter's failures as president. The question resonated with the public and helped him win the election by a landslide.

14. In the early 1980s, inflation and interest rates were so high that mortgages the S&Ls held on peoples' homes started to lose value.

15. The United States sold military equipment to Iran as part of an effort to get the release of American hostages. This went against President Reagan's claim that he would not negotiate with terrorists. Then it was discovered that some of the money from Iran had been turned over to the Contras to help topple the government of Nicaragua, even though Congress had passed a law forbidding any military aid to the Contras.

16. Nancy Reagan adopted the issue as a project and came up with the slogan, "Just say no." She started youth groups that taught schoolchildren the dangers of drinking and drugs.

17. Eastern European countries such as Poland, Czechoslovakia, East Germany, and Romania abandoned their communist governments and moved towards democracy. The Soviet republics, such as Estonia and Latvia, declared their independence from Russia for the first time in 70 years.

18. Possible response: Iraq invaded Kuwait, forcing the United States and other NATO countries to go to war in the Persian Gulf. After campaigning for president by declaring, "Read my lips: no new taxes," Bush was forced to create a deficit reduction plan that included budget cuts and tax increases.

HISTORICAL THINKING ANSWERS

19. Reagan believed in minimizing the size of the federal government by decreasing taxes and deregulating industries. Carter supported Johnson's Great Society programs, which expanded the government and kept many regulations in place.

20. Answers will vary. Possible responses may address the civil rights movement, drug culture, women's movement, gay rights movement, Vietnam War, and U.S. military involvement in the Persian Gulf.

21. The U.S. military planned to invade the island on October 25, 1983, two days before a suicide bomber blew up the Marine barracks in Beirut.

22. Central planning proved to be an inefficient way to run such a big country, stifling innovation and stagnating the economy. The invasion of Afghanistan only made the economy worse. The Politburo selected Gorbachev, hoping that his new ideas about how to run the government would help the economy and make the country stronger.

23. Possible responses: Yes. It was a good move because it showed the country that Reagan was a strong leader and would not back down in a fight. No. It was not a good move because air traffic controllers have huge responsibilities in maintaining air safety, it cost billions to replace them, and the air travel industry suffered economically from reduced flights.

24. President Bush proposed revisions to the Clear Air Act that targeted urban pollution, acid rain, and toxic air emissions. The legislation permitted stricter enforcement of the provisions of the law.

INTERPRET VISUALS ANSWERS

25. Possible response: The students seem pleased that the communist government has been ousted and welcome the American soldier. But for the soldier, the moment is about the seriousness of his military mission and the possibility of further fighting.

26. Possible response: The soldier in the photograph represents the military strength of the United States and the successful fight against communism, while the medical students represent hope for the future. Both symbols played well with American voters, particularly at election time.

ANALYZE SOURCES ANSWER

27. Even though Reagan acknowledges the great praise he has received, he is modest enough to give the credit for his successes to the experience, wisdom, and principles of the American people. He uses colorful imagery, such as "spring full bloom," and "the heart of a great nation," to appeal to the emotions and patriotism of his audience.

CONNECT TO YOUR LIFE ANSWER

28. Answers will vary but should highlight examples of how national and world conditions have changed since Reagan's presidency and how the role of president has evolved in response.

UNIT 9 RESOURCES

UNIT INTRODUCTION

UNIT TIME LINE

UNIT WRAP-UP

NATIONAL GEOGRAPHIC | **CONNECTION**

National Geographic **Magazine Adapted Articles**
- "U.S. Climate Refugees Race Against Time"
- "Shell Shock" ONLINE

Unit 9 Inquiry: Conduct Oral History Interviews

NG Learning Framework Activities
- Create a History Game
- Form a Political Party

Unit 9 Formal Assessment

CHAPTER 31 RESOURCES

Available at NGLSync.Cengage.com

TEACHER RESOURCES & ASSESSMENT

Reading and Note-Taking

Vocabulary Practice

Social Studies Skills Lessons
- Reading: Form and Support Opinions
- Writing: Explanatory

Formal Assessment
- Chapter 31 Pretest
- Chapter 31 Tests A & B
- Section Quizzes

Chapter 31 Answer Key

ExamView®
  One-time Download

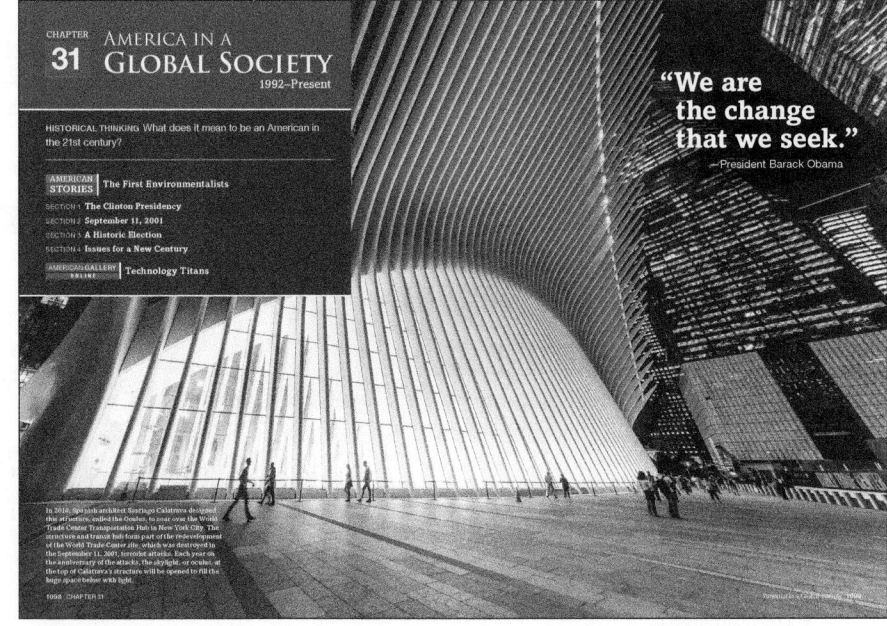

STUDENT DIGITAL RESOURCES

- **eEdition**
- **Handbooks**
- **Online Atlas**
- **American Gallery Online**
- **History Notebook**
- **Active History**
- **American Voices (Biographies)**
- **Reid on the Road video series**
- **Literature Analysis**
- **Projects for Inquiry-Based Learning**

Chapter 31 Spanish Resources are available at NGLSync.Cengage.com.

AMERICAN STORIES | **The First Environmentalists**

- Study Primary Sources: Excerpt from the Constitution of the Iroquois Nations
- On Your Feet: Inside-Outside Circle

NG Learning Framework:
Write About Rivers

SECTION 1 RESOURCES
THE CLINTON PRESIDENCY

LESSON 1.1
Moderate Reform Under Bill Clinton

- On Your Feet: Host a Quiz Show

NG Learning Framework:
Research LGBTQ Activism

American Voices Biography
Ruth Bader Ginsburg ONLINE

American Voices Biography
Harvey Milk ONLINE

LESSON 1.2
Globalization and Immigration

- Active History: Diagram Economic Interdependence

NG Learning Framework:
Immigration Factors

LESSON 1.3
Economic Boom and Scandals

AMERICAN **GALLERY** ONLINE   Technology Titans

NG Learning Framework:
Compare Booms

SECTION 2 RESOURCES
SEPTEMBER 11, 2001

LESSON 2.1
The Contested Election of 2000

- On Your Feet: Fishbowl

NG Learning Framework:
Evaluate Conservatism: 1980s versus 2000

LESSON 2.2
September 11, 2001

- On Your Feet: Presidential Power After 9/11

NG Learning Framework:
Construct and Test Hypotheses

LESSON 2.3
The War on Terror

- On Your Feet: Roundtable

NG Learning Framework:
Construct a Time Line

LESSON 2.4
THROUGH THE LENS—AMERICAN PLACES
New Orleans, Louisiana

- On Your Feet: Three-Step Interview

NG Learning Framework:
Investigate New Orleans' Levees

SECTION 3 RESOURCES
A HISTORIC ELECTION

LESSON 3.1
The Great Recession

- On Your Feet: Play a Recession Word Game

NG Learning Framework:
Write a News Article

LESSON 3.2
The Election of 2008

- On Your Feet: Jigsaw

NG Learning Framework:
Track the Evolution of the Presidency

LESSON 3.3
AMERICAN VOICES
Barack Hussein Obama II, 1961–Michelle LaVaughn Robinson Obama, 1964–

- On Your Feet: Two Options

NG Learning Framework:
Analyze an Obama Speech

SECTION 4 RESOURCES
ISSUES FOR A NEW CENTURY

LESSON 4.1
Civil Rights in the 21st Century

- On Your Feet: Inside-Outside Circle

NG Learning Framework:
Research Continuity and Change

LESSON 4.2
Environmental Challenges

- On Your Feet: Ready, Set, Recall

NG Learning Framework:
Evaluate Climate Change Explanations

American Voices Biography
Steven Chu ONLINE

LESSON 4.3
Globalizing American Society

- On Your Feet: History Relay

NG Learning Framework:
Research De-industrialization

LESSON 4.4
NATIONAL GEOGRAPHIC EXPLORER
TRISTRAM STUART
Using Food Waste to Feed the World

- On Your Feet: Think, Pair, Share

NG Learning Framework:
Create a Food Waste Reduction Plan

LESSON 4.5
An Interconnected World

- ▶ The Statue of Liberty
- On Your Feet: Rotating Discussion

NG Learning Framework:
Explore Global Terrorism

LESSON 4.6
The Election of 2016

- On Your Feet: Debate the Electoral College

NG Learning Framework:
Write About the Paris Agreement

LESSON 4.7
THROUGH THE LENS
Lynsey Addario

- On Your Feet: Descriptive Words

NG Learning Framework:
Investigate the Lives of Syrian Refugees

CHAPTER 31 REVIEW

STRIVING READERS

STRATEGY 1
TURN HEADINGS INTO OUTLINES

To help students understand lesson content, explain that headings can provide a high-level outline of the lesson. Model for students how to use the lesson title and subheadings to create a basic outline structure. Encourage students to add to their outlines as they read.

Use with All Lessons

STRATEGY 2
SEQUENCE EVENTS

To build understanding of the critical events in a section and their relationship to one another in time, encourage students to note them in a Sequence Chain like the one shown. Encourage students to add circles and arrows as necessary to show the multiplicity and complexity of the causes of historical events.

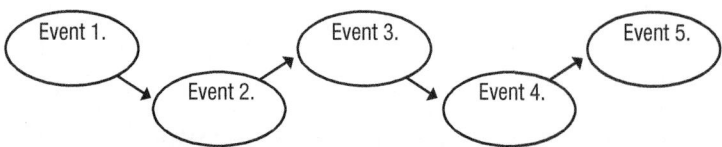

Use with All Lessons *You may suggest students use the Sequence Chain to trace the major events of the Clinton administration in Lessons 1.1 and 1.3, the events of the contested election of 2000 in Lesson 2.1, and the events leading to and following 9/11 in Lessons 2.2 and 2.3.*

STRATEGY 3
CLARIFY INFORMATION

Students may have trouble understanding the complicated reasons for the collapse of the housing market and the subsequent recession. To help students clarify the information in the lesson, instruct them to take notes on the information in each paragraph using a 5Ws Chart.

Use with Lesson 3.1

INCLUSION

STRATEGY 1
PROVIDE TERMS AND NAMES ON AUDIO

Decide which of the terms and names are important for mastery and ask a volunteer to record the pronunciations and a short sentence defining each term or name. Encourage students to listen to the recording as often as necessary.

Use with All Lessons *You might also use the recordings to quiz students on their mastery of the terms. Play one definition at a time from the recording and ask students to identify the term or name described.*

STRATEGY 2
USE SUPPORTED READING

Arrange students in pairs and tell them to read each lesson aloud to each other. Instruct them to stop at the end of each lesson and use these sentence frames to monitor their comprehension of the text:

- This lesson is mostly about _____ .
- Other topics in this lesson are _____ and _____ .
- One question I have is _____ .
- One of the vocabulary words is _____ , and it means _____ .
- One word I don't recognize is _____ .

Use with All Lessons

ENGLISH LANGUAGE LEARNERS

STRATEGY ➊
CREATE SENTENCE STRIPS

Choose a key paragraph from the lesson and make sentence strips from it. Read the paragraph aloud while students at **All Proficiencies** follow along in their books. Have students close their books and give them the set of sentence strips. Tell students to put the strips in order and read the paragraph aloud. Correct any inaccuracies.

Use with All Lessons *Before reading, you might ask students at the **Emerging** level to read the sentence strips aloud. Then ask them to point out meaningful words in each sentence. Repeat the exercise with another paragraph.*

STRATEGY ➋
USE PAIRED READING

Pair students at the **Expanding** and **Bridging** levels to read passages from the text aloud.

1. Partner 1 reads a passage; Partner 2 retells the passage in his or her own words.

2. Partner 2 reads a different passage; Partner 1 retells it.

3. Pairs repeat the process, switching roles.

Use with All Lessons

STRATEGY ➌
USE DEFINITION MAPS

Pair students at the **Emerging** level with those at the **Expanding** and **Bridging** levels. Have them use a graphic organizer, such as the Definition Map shown, for Key Vocabulary or other important terms. After they complete their graphic organizers, ask students to compare their responses with a partner's. Encourage students to discuss the terms and clear up any misunderstandings.

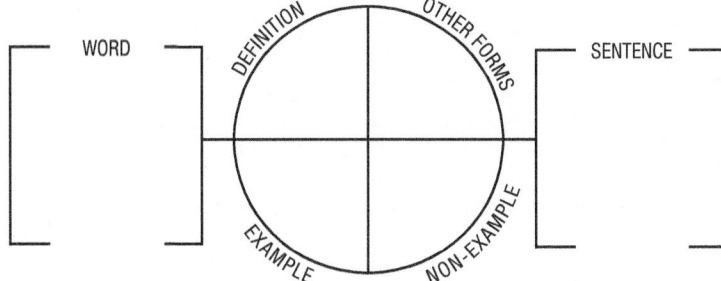

Use with All Lessons

GIFTED & TALENTED

STRATEGY ➊
PERFORM A SPEECH

Direct students to conduct online research to find the complete text and video of the presidents' speeches excerpted in the lessons: Clinton's remarks on NAFTA, Bush's address to Congress after 9/11, and Obama's victory speech. Instruct students to select a segment of one of the speeches that they find particularly powerful or meaningful and to practice delivering the segment. Then have students perform the speech for the class. Invite listeners to discuss which aspects of the speech they found memorable and why.

Use with Lessons 1.2, 2.2, and 3.2

STRATEGY ➋
CREATE AN INFOGRAPHIC

Allow students to choose one of the lessons listed and conduct online research to gather additional information about the impact of human modifications on Earth's atmosphere, water, or a specific environment. Tell students to create an infographic based on their findings. Challenge students to include powerful visuals and supporting data. Invite students to present their completed infographics to the class. Encourage feedback from students about how environmental policies impact life on Earth.

Use with Lessons 4.2 and 4.3

PRE-AP

STRATEGY ➊
USE MAPS TO INTERPRET CONFLICT

Invite students to look carefully at the legends and color-coding of the maps in Lessons 2.3 and 4.5. Then tell students to learn more about how one of the conflicts arose and evolved by conducting research using multiple print and online sources. Instruct students to write an essay interpreting and analyzing the conflict. Have students share their essays with the class.

Use with Lessons 2.3 and 4.5

STRATEGY ➋
WRITE AN ALTERNATIVE HISTORY

Instruct students to write an alternative history in which they imagine that the manual recount in Florida showed a victory for Al Gore. Challenge students to consider specific ways in which U.S. military engagements and environmental policies would have unfolded under a Gore administration. Invite students to read their alternative histories to the class and answer questions from their classmates.

Use with Lessons 2.1–2.4

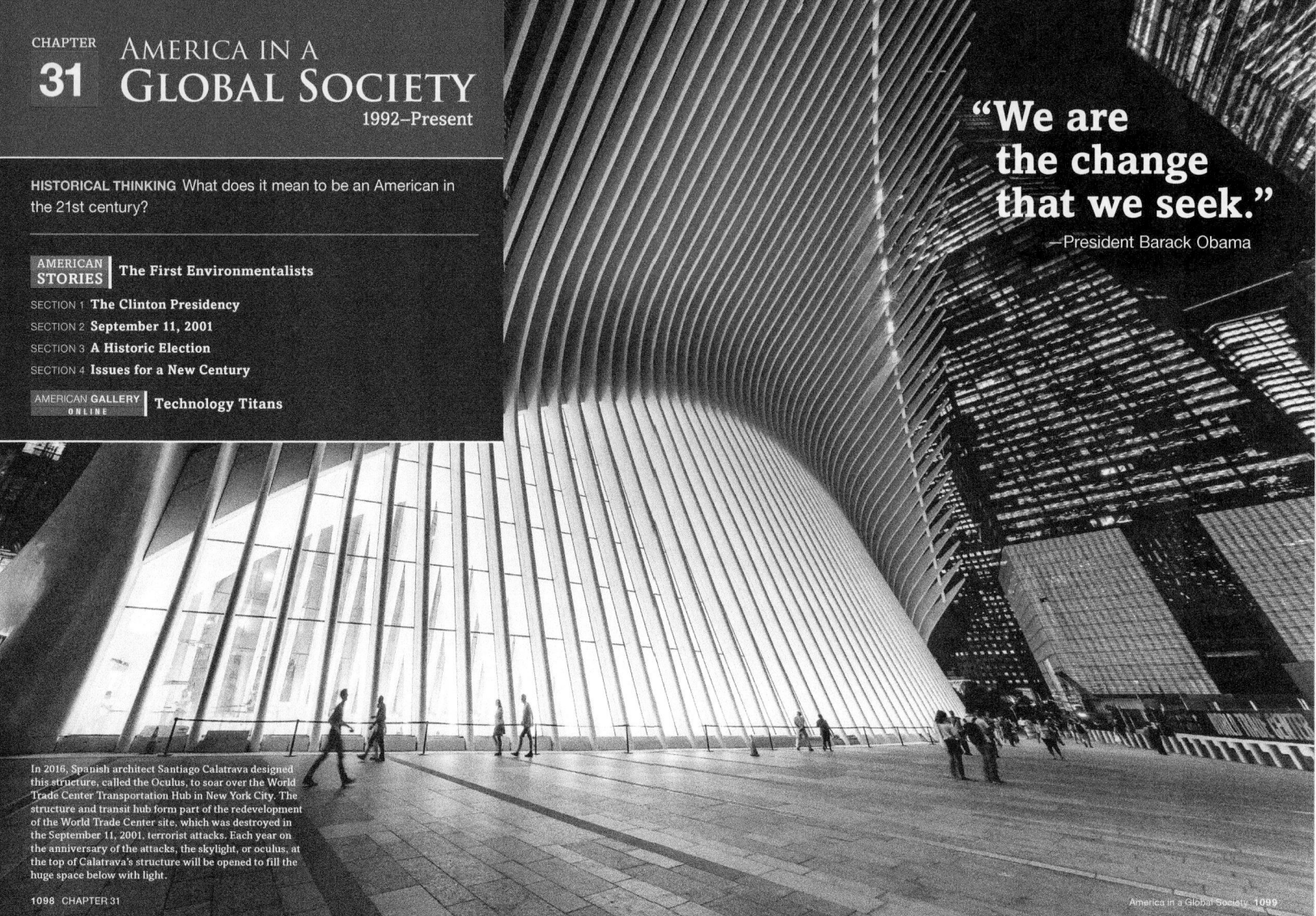

HISTORICAL THINKING What does it mean to be an American in the 21st century?

AMERICAN
STORIES | The First Environmentalists

SECTION 1 **The Clinton Presidency**

SECTION 2 **September 11, 2001**

SECTION 3 **A Historic Election**

SECTION 4 **Issues for a New Century**

AMERICAN GALLERY
ONLINE | Technology Titans

"We are
the change
that we seek."
—President Barack Obama

In 2016, Spanish architect Santiago Calatrava designed this structure, called the Oculus, to soar over the World Trade Center Transportation Hub in New York City. The structure and transit hub form part of the redevelopment of the World Trade Center site, which was destroyed in the September 11, 2001, terrorist attacks. Each year on the anniversary of the attacks, the skylight, or oculus, at the top of Calatrava's structure will be opened to fill the huge space below with light.

INTRODUCE THE PHOTOGRAPH

THE OCULUS

Have students study the photograph. Point out that people are walking along the outside of the structure. Note the upward sweep of the building's "ribs." Tell students that when people view the building from the front, they often remark that it looks like a dove in flight. **ASK:** Why might it be fitting to incorporate the shape of a dove into the design? (*Possible response: Doves represent peace and love and thus would be a healing counterpoint to the violence and tragedy of September 11, 2001.*) **ASK:** Why do you think the architect chose to include an oculus that can be opened? (*Possible response: An eye must open and let in light to see. Maybe he is using the oculus as a symbol of understanding and clarity.*) Tell students that in this chapter they will learn about the 9/11 terrorist attack on the World Trade Center.

SHARE BACKGROUND

The Oculus is reminiscent of other birdlike buildings by architect Santiago Calatrava. The steel-ribbed walls of the Oculus soar 160 feet high, and the skylight stretches along the center length of the 355-foot building. The 224 glass panels in the skylight fully retract to open the interior of the building to the sky. Each year on September 11, the panels will be opened for 102 minutes—the number of minutes between the first plane striking the first World Trade Center tower and the collapse of the second tower. For the remainder of the year, the closed panels will help light the interior of the building. The building is not without critics, in part because of the $4 billion price tag. Critics also argue that the need to strengthen the bones of the structure for security reasons have detracted from its design, making it look more like a dinosaur than a soaring bird.

For Chapter 31 Spanish Resources, visit the Resources Menu. Chapter 31 Resources are available at NGLSync.Cengage.com.

HISTORICAL THINKING QUESTION

What does it mean to be an American in the 21st century?

Jigsaw Activity: Preview Content This activity will help students preview and make predictions about the topics covered in this chapter. Divide the class into four groups. Assign one section title to each group and have them discuss what they think they'll learn in that section. Have them consider the following clues and questions:

Group 1 Section 1 is about the Clinton presidency. What challenges might a president face while in office? What types of things might a president want to accomplish?

Group 2 Section 2 is about the September 11, 2001, terror attack and the resulting war on terror. Why might such an attack have been a surprise? In what ways might the United States respond to it?

Group 3 Section 3 is about the Obama presidency. What made the Obama presidency historic? How might a president set priorities?

Group 4 Section 4 is about social issues in the 21st century and the 2016 presidential election. What are some major social issues facing the United States today? How might people address these issues?

Regroup students so each new grouping has at least one member from each original group. Have students share what they predicted about their assigned section so that other students can learn what to expect from their reading in Chapter 31.

INTRODUCE THE READING STRATEGY

FORM AND SUPPORT OPINIONS

Remind students that if they want their opinions to be considered valid, they need to support them with verifiable examples and facts. Turn to the Chapter Review and preview the chart showing how to organize examples and facts with students. As they read the chapter, have students collect examples and facts to support the opinions they form about issues facing Americans in the 21st century.

KEY DATES FOR CHAPTER 31

1992	Bill Clinton elected president
1995	Alfred P. Murrah Federal Building bombed
1999	Clinton acquitted of impeachment charges
2000	George W. Bush elected president
2001	Al-Qaeda launches terror attacks on U.S. soil
2001	Operation Enduring Freedom begins
2007	Fall of housing prices launches Great Recession
2008	Barack Obama elected president
2015	U.S. Supreme Court legalizes same-sex marriage
2016	President Obama visits Cuba
2016	Donald Trump elected president

INTRODUCE CHAPTER VOCABULARY

KEY VOCABULARY

SECTION 1

disintegration	integration	perjury
free-enterprise zone	job dislocation	task force
globalization	maquiladora	

SECTION 2

American exceptionalism	neoconservative	terrorism
compassionate conservatism	rogue state	weapons of mass destruction (WMD)
	surge	

SECTION 3

bailout	investment bank	subprime mortgage
economic stimulus		

SECTION 4

colluded	greenhouse gas	new media
genetically modified food	marriage equality	service sector
greenhouse effect	multinational corporation	swing state

DEFINITION CHART

As they read the chapter, encourage students to complete a Definition Chart for Key Vocabulary terms. Ask students to list the Key Vocabulary terms in the far left column of their chart. Instruct students that as they encounter each term in the chapter, they should write its definition in the center column and what it means, using their own words, in the far right column. Model an example for students on the board, using the graphic organizer below.

Word	Definition	In My Own Words
job dislocation	the movement of jobs to other places	when businesses move jobs from one place to another

OBJECTIVES

- **Discuss environmental problems in regions of North America.**

- **Examine the impact of the use of natural resources and the need for and controversies associated with environmental conservation.**

- **Relate current events to the physical and human characteristics of places and regions.**

- **Study a primary source: excerpt from the Constitution of the Iroquois Nations.**

CRITICAL THINKING SKILLS FOR "THE FIRST ENVIRONMENTALISTS"

- Make Connections
- Draw Conclusions
- Identify Problems and Solutions
- Analyze Environmental Concepts
- Analyze Primary Sources

CONNECT TO THE CHAPTER

This American Story teaches students about the balance between environmental conservation and the use of natural resources in Native American communities. Photographs and other images of Native American environmental activists support the content, and an excerpt from the Iroquois Nations' Constitution outlines the sustainable environmental practices members must follow.

The upcoming chapter, America in a Global Society, details the environmental, social, political, and economic changes that have taken place in the United States since the 1990s. This American Story will expand students' understanding of the concept of environmental justice that Native Americans have promoted for hundreds of years. Introduce the American Story after students have read about environmental challenges facing the planet in Lesson 4.2.

HISTORY NOTEBOOK

Encourage students to complete the American Story page for Chapter 31 in their History Notebooks as they read.

AMERICAN STORIES   NATIONAL GEOGRAPHIC

THE FIRST ENVIRONMENTALISTS

Protesters march on the Standing Rock Indian Reservation in North Dakota in 2016, attempting to halt the construction of a pipeline along the northern edge of the reservation.

1100 CHAPTER 31

In 1971, an organization called Keep America Beautiful launched an anti-pollution advertising campaign that quickly went viral. Billboards, magazine ads, and television commercials featured a solemn-faced Native American man in traditional clothing. As he regarded a landscape littered with garbage, a single tear trickled down his weathered cheek. The image (right), accompanied by slogans such as "Pollution hurts all of us," became instantly recognizable. The "Crying Indian" campaign was hugely successful in enlisting Americans to join the crusade against pollution.

This signature image also effectively illustrates a long-held stereotype of Native Americans as simple hunters or farmers living in harmony with nature, leaving no trace—the first American environmentalists. While some may consider this portrayal as flattering, it may also be an oversimplification. Native Americans have been using natural resources in a variety of sophisticated, evolving ways since long before the first Europeans arrived. Native American groups are as diverse as the nationalities found on any continent, and their complex relationships with nature reflect that diversity.

PRE-CONTACT

The term "pre-contact" is sometimes used to refer to Native Americans during the time before their first encounters with European explorers and settlers. Scholars believe that most pre-contact groups shared a broadly similar worldview incorporating the ideas that animals, plants, and the earth itself harbored sacred spirits, and that humans could ask the spirits to influence the weather, harvests, or the results of an upcoming battle. However, the cultures and survival practices of the tribes varied widely to suit the diverse North American geography. Some groups did indeed leave little trace on the land, while others took an active role in molding the ecosystems that surrounded them. Historian Louis S. Warren wrote, "To claim that Indians lived without affecting nature is akin to saying that they lived without touching anything, that they were a people without a history."

Different groups manipulated their environments in different ways to suit their needs. The Choctaw, Iroquois, and Pawnee, for example, cleared forests to create fields for farming. When those fields were no longer fertile, the tribes would abandon them and clear new land. When land was abundant, this practice could continue for a long time but led to deforestation

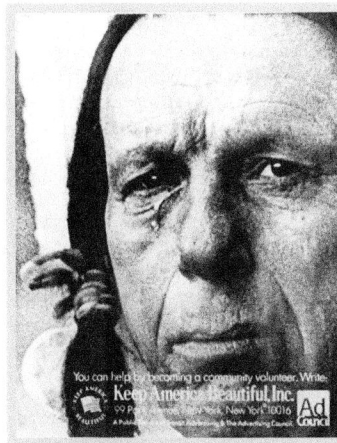

IRON EYES CODY

The story of the "Crying Indian" from the Keep America Beautiful ad campaign contains some curious twists relating to perceptions of Native American identity. The craggy-faced man featured in the ads was an actor named Iron Eyes Cody who had played Native Americans in movies since the 1920s. Sometime after the famous ad campaign, however, it was revealed that Iron Eyes Cody was not of Cherokee and Cree ancestry, as he claimed. In fact, he was a Sicilian American, born in Louisiana with the name Espera Oscar de Corti.

It would be easy to dismiss Cody as a mockery or cheap fake, but he took his pseudo-Native American identity very seriously. He married a Native American woman, adopted two Native American sons, and followed Native American practices and beliefs during his entire adult life. He also vigorously supported numerous Native American causes. In 1995, the Hollywood Native American community honored him for his work, although some were angered by Cody's very public appropriation of Native American identity through actions and beliefs rather than birth.

Ask students to examine the photograph of the protesters and the accompanying caption. **ASK:** What struggles have Native Americans undergone in the United States? *(Possible response: The U.S. government has forced Native Americans onto reservations and taken a vast amount of their land.)* **ASK:** What do the photograph, title, and caption help you understand about the specific struggles that this American Story will address? *(Possible response: Native Americans are still struggling to hold and control their land. Apparently government or private interests are building a pipeline in spite of Native Americans owning the land and their concern about the pipeline's potential to pollute and contaminate the environment.)*

IRON EYES CODY

Over the course of many years, non-Native American actors have played Native American characters in movies, on television, and on radio broadcasts. One example of such a character is Tonto, companion to the Lone Ranger, whom white actors portrayed both on the original radio show of the 1930s and more recently in film. (Jay Silverheels, a Native American actor, played Tonto on the long-running television series.) The character of Tonto has long been thought to perpetuate Hollywood stereotypes of Native Americans, particularly through his monosyllabic speech. **ASK:** How did the hiring of a non-Native American actor for the "Crying Indian" campaign affect Native American identity? *(It caused confusion because people believed he was a Native American. Then it was revealed he was a Sicilian American.)* **ASK:** Why have so many non-Native American actors, like Iron Eyes Cody, been hired to portray Native Americans? *(Possible responses: Some actors might have misled casting directors about their backgrounds or had facial features of stereotypical Native Americans that were perpetuated in cartoons and on television. Iron Eyes Cody, for example, falsely claimed to be a Native American, which probably helped him get roles he might not have otherwise gotten.)*

In 1851, the Treaty of Fort Laramie—agreed to by the Sioux, other Great Plains Native Americans, and the U.S. government—relinquished Sioux land in Minnesota to the U.S. government in exchange for money. As part of the treaty, the U.S. government forced the Sioux onto a reservation and persuaded them to adopt an agricultural lifestyle. By the early 1860s, the Sioux began to suffer from starvation as a result of a lack of funds and food sources. In 1862, they launched the Sioux Uprising to try to rid the region of outsiders. As a result of these actions, the U.S. government executed 38 Santee Sioux in the country's largest mass execution ever to take place. The government also forced the remaining Santee Sioux to relocate to reservations in the Dakota Territory and Nebraska. It is against this backdrop that the Dakota Access Pipeline protests took place in 2016. Arguing that the Treaty of Fort Laramie guaranteed to them land that the pipeline ran through, the Sioux of North Dakota's Standing Rock Reservation fought its construction and what they saw as yet another example of encroachment on their land.

THE GREAT LAW OF PEACE

The Iroquois Confederacy originally consisted of the Mohawk, Oneida, Onondaga, Cayuga, and Seneca tribes. These tribes first banded together to protect their lands and prevent invasions. A council of clan and village chiefs representing each tribe came together to vote on civil affairs. Each tribe had one vote, and all decisions needed to be unanimous in order to pass. **ASK:** How might the confederacy's concept of seven-generation sustainability also have benefited the tribes and their lands? *(Possible response: It would have ensured that enough natural resources were available for future generations. In doing so, it would have enabled the continuation of the tribes themselves since people's survival depends on access to adequate resources.)*

CRITICAL VIEWING Possible response: By creating national parks, the land and habitats are protected from destruction and development. Wildlife populations are also protected.

AMERICAN STORIES

and stress on local species. There is evidence that certain tribes may have even caused their own downfall by overusing local resources. Some researchers believe the Ancestral Puebloans who once lived in southeastern Utah disappeared from their villages in the 13th century because they had depleted the wood in the region by burning it for fuel.

Fire was a powerful tool groups used to shape an ecosystem to their advantage. For example, some groups used fire to help create open prairies where large game animals such as bison, deer, elk, and antelope could graze. Fires were sometimes used in hunts to force animals into small open areas where they could be easily hunted. Burning was also used to clear ground for crops or drive out pests.

But many pre-contact groups actively practiced conservation techniques to protect the species they relied upon. The Algonquian lived along the Atlantic Coast and divided hunting territories among families. Each family would hunt its land according to systems the group had developed to maintain the game supply. In the Pacific Northwest, some Native American tribes trapped salmon swimming up rivers to spawn, but were also careful to let enough fish escape and lay their eggs so that the supply would be maintained from year to year.

THE PRESENT DAY

For years after European settlers arrived, Native Americans continued to use many of their pre-contact techniques for living within and managing ecosystems. As the groups were relocated and pushed onto reservations in the 19th century, however, most of these systems were disrupted. In the centuries since the first European contact, Native Americans have faced the challenge of adapting to new environments and maintaining their cultures in a changing, sometimes hostile world. Climate change may pose one of the most severe threats to some groups, particularly in Alaska, where melting ice and permafrost are profoundly affecting species including polar bears and caribou.

Native American groups remain at the forefront of conservation efforts, and many tribes are uniquely positioned to protect wild lands. According to one study, "many tribal lands still represent some of the largest intact habitats . . . in North America," and more than 81,236 square miles of land in the lower 48 states and 62,500 square miles of land in Alaska are controlled by Native American tribes. "Much of this land is relatively undisturbed, providing a significant amount of rare and important fish and wildlife habitat," the authors of the study claim.

CRITICAL VIEWING A grizzly bear fishes for salmon in Alaska's Katmai National Park. To what extent do national parks like this one help reduce the effects of human activities on natural systems and habitats?

Examples abound of Native American tribes working to restore habitats and species. One of the most publicly recognized Native American conservation efforts is the fight to restore the American bison. Historically, the bison had provided a living for numerous tribes on the Great Plains and was important to the tribes' cultural and religious lives. By 1884, as a result of overhunting, only 325 wild bison remained in the United States. Today, organizations such as the Intertribal Buffalo Council (ITBC) work to reintroduce American bison to tribal lands in South Dakota, Montana, Oklahoma, and New Mexico. Currently, the ITBC has 58 member tribes, including the Lakota, Crow, Blackfeet, Ho Chunk, and Choctaw. In 2016, ITBC controlled a herd of more than 15,000 bison spread across 19 states. Emphasizing the cultural and environmental importance of bison, the ITBC asserts, "To re-establish healthy buffalo populations on tribal lands is to re-establish hope for Indian people."

Still, it would be shortsighted to view Native Americans' relationship with the environment as one-dimensional. Like all Americans, Native Americans need to make a living, coping with the demands of modern life while maintaining cultural traditions. In some cases, that means balancing conservation with the use of natural resources to earn money. Members of the Hoopa Valley Tribe in California, for example, have a strong belief in conservation and powerful cultural and religious ties to the species that populate their wooded land. At the same time, cutting and selling trees for timber is necessary for the tribe's economy. Thus, the Hoopa have developed ways to maintain a sustainable logging industry while protecting the forest habitat. Similarly, on the Great Plains, some groups harvest and sell bison meat as a healthier alternative to beef and also work to preserve the wild herds.

Occasionally, tribes' traditional practices bring them into conflict with environmental organizations. The Makah Indians in Washington State had been whaling for more than 1,000 years when they stopped in 1929, in the face of a declining whale population. In 1999, they resumed hunting, having been authorized by the government to take five whales a year. The Makah argue that whaling is central to their culture and traditions. They also point to the Treaty of Neah Bay, signed in 1855, which granted whaling rights to the Makah in exchange for tribal lands.

THE GREAT LAW OF PEACE

The Iroquois Confederacy was bound by a constitution that had existed for centuries before the first Europeans arrived. In the present day, it is known by different names, including the Great Law of Peace. In pre-contact times, the constitution was transmitted by oral tradition.

One passage in the constitution has, in recent years, been used to form the basis of an idea called seven-generation sustainability, or the seventh-generation principle. The concept, supported by many environmentalists and other scientists, is that humans should make decisions about natural resources with the fate of our seventh-generation descendants in mind. Today's decisions, in other words, should lead to healthy, sustainable ecosystems for many generations to come.

PRIMARY SOURCE

In all of your deliberations in the Confederate Council, in your efforts at lawmaking, in all your official acts, self-interest shall be cast into oblivion. Cast not over your shoulder behind you the warnings of the nephews and nieces should they chide you for any error or wrong you may do, but return to the way of the Great Law which is just and right. Look and listen for the welfare of the whole people and have always in view not only the present but also the coming generations, even those whose faces are yet beneath the surface of the ground—the unborn of the future Nation.

—from the Constitution of the Iroquois Nations

Environmentalists argue that certain gray whale groups are nearly depleted, and whaling by the Makah could threaten their dwindling numbers. Some also criticize the Makah for using modern technology, in addition to traditional tools, to kill whales.

In 2000, former Tribal Council Chairman Ben Johnson summed up the frustration many Native Americans feel about stereotypes that would simplify Native American culture and freeze it in time. "Times change and we have to change with the times," he said. "[People] want us to be back in the primitive times. We just want to practice our culture."

TEACH

GUIDED DISCUSSION

1. **Identify Problems and Solutions** In what ways did some pre-contact Native American groups overuse natural resources? *(Some groups cleared excessive amounts of forest for farming, leading to deforestation. Other groups, like the Ancestral Puebloans, burned all the trees for fuel and eventually left their villages as a result.)*

2. **Analyze Environmental Concepts** What are some arguments for and against the Dakota Access Pipeline? *(Some people supported the construction of the pipeline, arguing that it created jobs and offered a safer method for transporting oil than other methods. But the Standing Rock Sioux tribe saw the pipeline as both an environmental threat and an invasion of their land. They were concerned that a possible oil spill could contaminate their water supply.)*

ACTIVE OPTIONS

On Your Feet: Inside-Outside Circle Divide the class into two groups. Instruct one group to form an inside circle and the other group to form an outside circle, facing each other. Ask student pairs from the two circles to discuss their opinions of the Dakota Access Pipeline with each other for a few minutes. Then instruct the outside circle to move one spot over so that a new pair can share ideas. Continue the rotation until each student has paired up with several different partners.

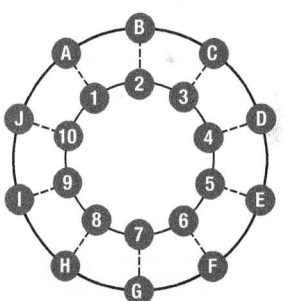

NG Learning Framework: Write About Rivers

SKILLS Observation, Communication

KNOWLEDGE Our Living Planet

Encourage students to investigate conservation or clean-up efforts related to a river in the United States, such as the Rio Grande, the Colorado, or the Mississippi. Instruct students to conduct online research of specific environmental issues related to the river and the efforts that organizations or individuals are making to resolve issues. Students should identify the specific issue, the cause of the issue, and how it affects the natural water cycle. After students have completed their research, ask them to write a report that describes the issue and their findings and present it to the class.

Conservationist Sandra Postel serves as director of the Global Water Policy Project and is co-creator of Change the Course, an initiative that works to restore water to rivers and wetlands. Postel's work focuses on the geography of water stress and how it affects natural resources, regional peace, and security. One of the foremost experts on freshwater issues, she is dedicated to water conservation and protecting animal life. Postel has served as an environmental studies lecturer and has written dozens of articles and opinion pieces for a variety of publications.

Have students read the National Geographic feature. Explain that New Mexico's summer temperature can exceed 100 degrees Fahrenheit below 5,000 feet, but with relatively low humidity, the state experiences a mild arid or semiarid climate. In addition, the Rio Grande Valley, which the Rio Grande flows through, receives little annual rainfall. **ASK:** How do you think the valley's climate exacerbates the issues with the river's water levels? *(Possible response: High temperatures would cause evaporation, lowering water levels in the river. With little rainfall in the area, diverting water from the river for irrigation purposes must be crucial.)*

WRITE ABOUT HISTORY

Compare Past and Present This American Story focuses on the efforts of Native Americans to protect their culture and the environment in the face of internal and external struggles. Ask students to write a short essay comparing the pre-contact factors and the present-day factors that affect native tribes' efforts to maintain their culture, the environment, and their own economic stability. Pair students to edit each other's essays and make suggestions for revision. Provide guidance about the writing process as necessary.

ANALYZE ENVIRONMENTAL CONCEPTS

Possible response: Native Americans have had to balance the need to survive and make a living with their duty to protect and preserve the environment. For example, the Intertribal Buffalo Council has worked to reintroduce American bison after the depletion of the animal's numbers in the 1800s. Also, though the Hoopa depend on the lumber industry for their livelihood, they also practice sustainable logging.

CRITICAL VIEWING Possible response: Cooperation is going to have better results and avoid conflicts. More can be achieved if tribes and outside agencies work together to understand what is needed while also protecting the environment.

THE DAKOTA ACCESS PIPELINE

In 2016, an environmental protest placed the Standing Rock Sioux tribe in headlines across the country. The Sioux were fighting the construction of the Dakota Access Pipeline (DAPL) beneath the Missouri River on land that is adjacent to the Standing Rock Reservation in North Dakota. The DAPL is a 1,170-mile-long underground pipeline intended to transport oil from fields in North Dakota to southern Illinois, where it can be shipped to refineries. The $3.7 billion project is financed by a private company.

The Standing Rock Sioux object to the pipeline on both cultural and environmental grounds. They claim construction will disrupt sacred tribal burial sites and believe that if the DAPL suffers an oil spill, it will permanently contaminate the Missouri River, the reservation's principal source of water. Protesters claim the land through which the pipeline runs is in fact Sioux land, deeded to them in the Treaty of Fort Laramie in 1851. Since 1851, the government has taken much of the land, but the treaty was never nullified.

In 2016, artist-activists collaborated with photographers to create a series of images, including this one by Ernesto Yerena, that capture the shared humanity of our diverse America.

In spring of 2016, tribe members set up a camp on the reservation in North Dakota and publicized their mission statement, stating: "Our goal is to peacefully and prayerfully defend our rights, and rise up as one to sustain Mother Earth and her inhabitants." Protests staged from the camp were largely peaceful, although some clashes with police did occur. Environmentalists, celebrities, and others joined the Standing Rock Sioux in their protests. Many others used donations or social media to express their support. For example, in November 2016, when the rumor circulated that police officers were using Facebook check-ins to track the locations of protesters, more than 1 million people across the United States "checked in" at the Standing Rock Reservation.

On the other side of the issue, many Americans favor the construction of the DAPL, which some claim has created thousands of jobs—the reason the pipeline is supported by several labor unions. Others believe transporting oil through a pipeline is much safer than using trucks, tankers, and trains.

Experts debate the relative safety of moving oil through pipelines, and a major leak discovered in 2016 in an older North Dakota pipeline added to safety concerns about the new one.

At the end of 2016, the matter of the Dakota Access Pipeline was still unsettled. In November 2016, the Army Corps of Engineers, which must approve the project, determined "additional discussion and analysis are warranted in light of the history of the Great Sioux Nation's dispossessions of lands, the importance of Lake Oahe to the Tribe, our government-to-government relationship, and the statute governing easements through government property." In December, the Army denied a permit to complete the project and said it would continue its environmental impact study.

ANALYZE ENVIRONMENTAL CONCEPTS

What decisions have Native American groups faced in terms of resources and natural systems, and how did those factors influence the groups' actions?

NATIONAL GEOGRAPHIC

RESTORING THE RIO GRANDE

In September 2016, National Geographic Freshwater Fellow Sandra Postel reported on an innovative collaboration between Native American tribes and Audubon New Mexico, a conservation society, to restore flow to the Rio Grande. Even though the Rio Grande is the second largest river in the Southwest, parts of it dry up in the summer as water is diverted for irrigation and other purposes. This is alarming to water conservationists like Postel because the Rio Grande supports numerous native fish and birds, including some listed as threatened or endangered.

Seeking to restore some of the river's flow, Audubon New Mexico asked Native American groups in the Middle Rio Grande Valley to contribute a portion of the water they receive from the river through allocations. In exchange, Audubon committed to use the water for the river's benefit and to seek funding to restore river habitats on tribal lands. The Sandia, Isleta, Santa Ana, and Cochiti Pueblos agreed, transferring over 130 million gallons of water to Audubon New Mexico. With contributions from another user, the total water donation came to more than 260 million gallons.

National Geographic Freshwater Fellow (2009–2015) Sandra Postel

The water was stored in a reservoir and released at strategic locations during the summer of 2016. At the same time, the Pueblos and Audubon New Mexico worked to plant trees and restore habitats along the river's banks. Postel praised the partnership between Native American groups and an environmental organization to save the threatened Rio Grande. "River by river," she wrote, "the movement of water stewardship and restoration we are working to build is growing."

CRITICAL VIEWING Why is cooperation among tribes and outside agencies important in achieving environmental goals such as the restoration of the Rio Grande, shown below?

America in a Global Society 1105

INCLUSION

Predict Using Photographs and Captions Pair special needs students with students who can assist in making the text more accessible. Ask pairs to look at each photograph and take turns reading its caption. Instruct students to predict what they will learn based on what they read and see. Encourage students who are assisting to aid in taking notes.

PRE-AP

Examine the Approval of the Dakota Access Pipeline Tell students that the Dakota Access Pipeline, first proposed in 2014, went through a regulatory process for approval before and during construction. Direct students to conduct online research about the decision-making process and the government agencies involved. Have students create a time line of the major assessments, approvals, and court decisions made, including a caption about how each affected the construction and operation of the pipeline. Lead the class in a discussion about how the process of making decisions about natural systems and resources has changed over time.

See the Chapter Planner for more strategies for differentiation.

HISTORICAL THINKING

Ask and have students answer the following questions.

1. **READING CHECK** How have Native Americans sometimes had complicated relationships with environmental groups?

2. **ANALYZE PRIMARY SOURCES** What does the Constitution of the Iroquois Confederacy imply might happen if the current generation does not consider future generations?

3. **ANALYZE ENVIRONMENTAL CONCEPTS** How did the Standing Rock protesters' mission statement reflect their commitment to the environment?

ANSWERS

1. Native Americans sometimes feel as if environmental groups don't respect their traditions, such as whale hunting. Other times, the groups work well together, as when conserving water from the Rio Grande River.

2. It says not to ignore the warnings of "nieces and nephews" because they will chide current people for errors that will affect future generations.

3. By mentioning "Mother Earth," the mission statement made it clear that the protesters considered the pipeline a direct threat to the land as well as themselves.

MODERATE REFORM UNDER BILL CLINTON

In 1963, a 16-year-old boy named Bill Clinton visited the White House and shook hands with President John F. Kennedy. Afterward, the boy told his friends that he would have Kennedy's job someday. Three decades later, Clinton became the country's 42nd president.

THE 1992 ELECTION

In February of 1992, President George H.W. Bush announced plans to run for a second term on the Republican Party ticket. A year earlier, he might have seemed unbeatable. However, as you have read, his approval rating had dropped sharply as the result of an economic recession.

Arkansas governor Bill Clinton emerged on the Democratic side as Bush's challenger in the presidential election. For his vice-presidential running mate, Clinton went against political wisdom by selecting another southerner: Senator Al Gore of Tennessee, who had championed many environmental issues in Congress. Clinton campaigned as a "New Democrat," or a moderate member of the party who supported more conservative economic policies than many other Democrats.

As governor, Clinton boasted a strong record in education, civil rights, and economic growth in Arkansas. His critics attacked his character, however, claiming that Clinton, a married man, had had extramarital affairs and

Clinton addresses a rally in front of the courthouse in Carthage, Tennessee, during the 1992 campaign. Gore, along with his wife and children, stand behind Clinton. Growing up, Gore spent his summers working on his family's farm in Carthage.

evaded the draft during the Vietnam War. The legality of some of his business dealings was also questioned.

Disappointed by the Bush-Clinton matchup, many voters—especially Republicans—wanted an alternative. They got one when a Texas computer billionaire named **H. Ross Perot** threw his hat into the ring. Plainspoken and tough-talking, Perot argued that professional politicians lacked the will to tackle the country's most difficult problems. His popularity soared, and he briefly moved ahead of Bush and Clinton in the polls. However, with the Republican base split between Bush and Perot, Clinton won on election day.

DOMESTIC REFORMS

Upon taking office, President Clinton focused on domestic policy. To slash the massive federal budget deficit he had inherited from his predecessor, Clinton proposed an economic package that combined tax increases and spending cuts. He lobbied hard to win support for the plan, and in August 1993, it squeaked through Congress. Other initiatives of the early Clinton administration included the expansion of federal support for housing and nutritional programs aimed at assisting low-income families and addressing the persistence of poverty.

Clinton's most ambitious domestic goal was to overhaul the country's health care system to ensure that all Americans had access to quality, affordable care. Nearly 40 million Americans at that time lacked health insurance, and the costs of medical care were rising at an alarming rate. Just days into his presidency, Clinton created a **task force**, or group organized for a special mission, to reform the health care system. He appointed his wife, Hillary Clinton, to lead it. Mrs. Clinton, an accomplished lawyer, had advocated for children and education as first lady of Arkansas. During the 1992 campaign, Clinton had told the public that, with his election, they would get "two for the price of one," meaning that his wife would play an active role in his administration.

By September 1993, Mrs. Clinton and the task force had developed a proposal called the Health Security Act, which called for universal health coverage, managed care, and a restructured health insurance industry. The proposal met with fierce opposition from insurance companies, small-business organizations, the American Medical Association, and Congress. The "Clinton Health Plan," as it was known, failed to be adopted.

Among Clinton's domestic reforms was the Brady Handgun Violence Prevention Act, passed by Congress in 1993. James Brady (left), President Ronald Reagan's press secretary, was shot in the head and left partially paralyzed in the assassination attempt against the president in 1981. After the shooting, Brady and his wife worked tirelessly to promote handgun legislation. The act helped block the sale of an estimated one million guns to dangerous criminals.

SOCIAL CHANGES

President Clinton also dealt with important social issues. In fact, the first bill he signed into law was the Family and Medical Leave Act, which Bush had vetoed twice. Designed to help employees balance work and family life, the act allowed workers to take up to 12 weeks of unpaid, job-protected leave each year to care for newborn or newly adopted children or seriously ill family members.

The growing activism and prominence of LGBTQ (lesbian, gay, bisexual, transgender, and queer) groups resulted in further social change. In 1974, a politician and LGBTQ activist named Elaine Noble had won election to the Massachusetts House of Representatives, becoming the first openly lesbian or gay person ever elected to a state legislature. Three years later, voters in San Francisco elected a popular community leader and openly gay activist named **Harvey Milk** to the city's Board of Supervisors.

In 1992, the year Clinton was elected, the AIDS epidemic remained one of the most critical issues affecting the LGBT community. That year, AIDS became the number one cause of death for

---

INTRODUCE & ENGAGE

DISCUSS APPROVAL RATINGS

Ask a volunteer to read the first paragraph of the lesson aloud. Then, as a class, briefly discuss what students recall from the previous chapter about George H.W. Bush's low approval ratings in the lead-up to the 1992 presidential election. **ASK:** What caused George H.W. Bush's popularity to plunge toward the end of his presidency? *(Bush had promised no new taxes but was forced to agree with Congress to raise taxes and cut spending in an effort to reverse the budget deficit that was sparking a recession.)* **ASK:** Why would a plunge in popularity at the end of a term be particularly bad for a president seeking re-election? *(Answers will vary. Possible response: Voters tend to cast votes based on their immediate concerns.)* Tell students that this lesson looks at Bush's loss in the 1992 presidential election and Bill Clinton's first term in office.

TEACH

GUIDED DISCUSSION

1. **Analyze Cause and Effect** How do you think Bill Clinton's chances of winning the 1992 presidential election were affected by his campaigning as a "New Democrat"? Explain your answer. *(Possible response: Campaigning as a "New Democrat" improved his chances of victory because his more conservative economic policies appealed to some moderate Republicans, while his pro-social issues record in Arkansas and his selection of environmentalist Al Gore as his running mate appealed to Democrats.)*

2. **Form and Support Opinions** Do you think the failure of the Clinton administration's proposed overhaul of the health care system was a positive or a negative development? Support your opinion with text evidence. *(Answers will vary. Possible responses: It was a positive development because the proposal called for universal health care, which would have placed a burden on small business and likely raised insurance rates, and the restructuring of the insurance market would have hurt insurance companies. It was a negative development because nearly 40 million Americans had no health insurance and costs of medical care were climbing; the proposal supported universal health care and a restructuring of the insurance market, which might have curbed costs and increased access for the poor.)*

3. **Draw Conclusions** Why might the Family and Medical Leave Act have been popular among working families across the socioeconomic spectrum? *(The law enabled all workers to take up to 12 weeks of unpaid leave to care for seriously ill family members or for newborns or newly adopted children without losing their jobs.)*

MORE INFORMATION

H. Ross Perot Explain to students that the third presidential candidate in the 1992 election, H. Ross Perot, operated outside the established political order. He announced his independent campaign on cable news, used his own money to finance getting on the ballot on all 50 states, and chose to campaign in only 16 states. Instead, Perot used his wealth to buy half-hour slots on national television to talk about issues. Although he ran an erratic campaign, dropping out for several months at one point, he managed to garner about 19 percent of the vote, the best showing of an independent candidate since Teddy Roosevelt. His support came primarily from white small-business owners who were distrustful of politicians. **ASK:** Why might a third-party candidate appeal to voters dissatisfied with current social or economic trends? *(Answers will vary. Possible response: Dissatisfied voters might believe that an outsider could bring about change by taking actions that someone entrenched in the political system would be unwilling to take.)*

DIFFERENTIATE

STRIVING READERS

Read and Recall Arrange students in mixed-proficiency pairs. After students have read the lesson, tell them to close their books and share ideas and facts that they recall from the lesson. Ask one student in each pair to take notes. Then invite pairs to share their notes and create a master list of ideas and facts.

PRE-AP

Analyze a Failed Proposal Have students conduct online research to learn the main reasons why the Health Security Act of 1993 failed. Direct students to use their research to write an analysis essay, citing their sources. Encourage students to conclude with a paragraph that hypothesizes how life would be different for many Americans today if the act had passed.

See the Chapter Planner for more strategies for differentiation.

The worst act of domestic terrorism in American history occurred during Clinton's presidency. On the morning of April 19, 1995, a truck bomb exploded at the Alfred P. Murrah Federal Building in Oklahoma City, Oklahoma, killing 168 people, including 19 children, and injuring more than 500. The bombing was carried out by Timothy McVeigh, an antigovernment activist and Persian Gulf War veteran. He was convicted and executed for the crime in 2001.

The Outdoor Symbolic Memorial, part of the Oklahoma City National Memorial, is located where the Murrah Federal Building once stood. Symbolic elements in the memorial include the Field of Empty Chairs, shown here, which contains 168 chairs, one for each victim. Two gates at the entrance to the memorial are carved with the times 9:01 and 9:03, indicating the minute before and after the attack.

American men between the ages of 25 and 44. A disproportionate number of the disease's victims were gay men. The Clinton administration responded to the crisis by establishing the Presidential Advisory Council on HIV/AIDS and by dramatically increasing government funding for AIDS research, prevention, and treatment.

Clinton was the first major presidential candidate to court the gay vote. Shortly after taking office, he reaffirmed a controversial campaign vow to overturn the U.S. military's longstanding ban on homosexuals. Top military leaders wanted to keep the ban, as did many members of Congress, including Senator Sam Nunn of Georgia, the powerful chairman of the Senate Armed Services Committee.

In July 1993, Clinton announced a compromise policy that came to be known as "Don't Ask, Don't Tell." Under the new policy, homosexuals would be allowed to serve in the military as long as they kept their sexual orientation to themselves. But Clinton's support for gay rights had limits. In 1996, he took a stand against same-sex marriage by signing the **Defense of Marriage Act (DOMA)**. This law defined marriage as "a legal union between one man and one woman," and it denied same-sex couples the federal benefits, privileges, and recognition that opposite-sex couples received. Clinton's stand left many of his gay supporters feeling betrayed.

THE REPUBLICAN REVOLUTION

Meanwhile, Republican opponents began to investigate the Clintons' purchase in the late 1970s of a real estate development in Arkansas known as **Whitewater** and charged the couple with financial wrongdoing. In early 1994, the U.S. attorney general appointed a special prosecutor to look into their role in what came to be known as the Whitewater scandal. The resulting inquiry spanned about 6 years and cost more than $50 million, but investigators failed to find sufficient evidence to charge the Clintons with any crime.

The president's rivals had greater success when they challenged him politically. In the 1992 election, Democrats had retained their majorities in both houses of Congress. This political landscape shifted dramatically in 1994, however, after the midterm congressional elections. The Republicans won a sweeping victory, gaining control of both the Senate and the House of Representatives for the first time in four decades. **Newton "Newt" Gingrich**, a congressman from Georgia, became Speaker

of the House. Before the elections, Gingrich had co-authored a document called a **Contract with America**, which promised tax cuts for the middle class, strong anticrime legislation, and constitutional amendments requiring a balanced budget and term limits for members of Congress.

When Congress reconvened in January 1995, the House Republicans immediately began to push the legislation detailed in the contract through Congress. Some of the measures eventually passed into law, including a major welfare reform law called the Personal Responsibility and Work Opportunity Reconciliation Act of 1996. This legislation required welfare recipients to work after receiving benefits for two years, limited the time they could stay on welfare, and shifted much of the responsibility for social welfare administration from the federal government to the states. Critics argued that the act destroyed the safety net that protected the country's neediest and most vulnerable citizens. Still, many of the measures proposed by the House were rejected by the Senate or vetoed by Clinton.

The 1994 midterm elections seemed to make Clinton's re-election in 1996 unlikely, but missteps on the part of Republicans in 1995 helped the president regain popularity. One of these errors occurred toward the end of the year when the White House and Congress became deadlocked over the federal budget. Rather than negotiate, Gingrich and other members of the GOP majority in the House shut down the government. They hoped this action would pressure the White House into agreeing with their position. The strategy backfired when the public blamed the Republicans for the budget impasse. By early January 1996, the government had resumed normal operations.

HISTORICAL THINKING

1. **READING CHECK** How did H. Ross Perot's candidacy affect the 1992 presidential election?

2. **ANALYZE CAUSE AND EFFECT** Describe the causes that may have led to the Republicans gaining control of both the Senate and House of Representatives in 1994.

3. **EXPLAIN** How did the government respond to social changes during the Clinton administration? Provide examples from the text.

4. **DRAW CONCLUSIONS** How did the persistence of poverty influence the social policies of President Clinton?

BUILD BACKGROUND

CLINTON'S COMEBACK

Numerous factors helped Bill Clinton repair his prospects for a second term, even though his presidency had taken a hit in the 1994 midterm elections and his popularity had been eroded by scandals and the defeat of his health care proposal. Clinton's ability to calm and reassure Americans after the Oklahoma City bombing showcased Clinton at his most presidential. Voters remembered that. The timing of the two government shutdowns at the end of 1995 also worked to the advantage of the president and against the Republicans, particularly the 21-day shutdown in December, which forced national parks and government offices to close and left some 750,000 federal employees unsure if they would be paid during the holiday season. Added to this, the House Republicans, armed with the Contract with America, set their sights on gutting environmental protection programs, providing tax breaks for the wealthy, and cutting Medicare spending. These actions alarmed many voters, including moderate Republicans. They saw Clinton as a protection against the overreach of the Republicans. Clinton reinforced this view by emphasizing his support for social reforms that benefited the middle class. Clinton also repositioned himself as a moderate on such issues as welfare reform, crime, and affirmative action, thus separating himself from the Gingrich Republicans on the right and liberal Democrats on the left. Finally, the economy improved, which enabled Clinton to take credit for low unemployment and interest rates and a decline in the federal deficit.

TEACH

GUIDED DISCUSSION

4. Analyze Cause and Effect Why might Clinton's gay supporters have felt betrayed by some of the president's actions? *(Possible response: Although the president responded to the HIV/AIDS crisis by establishing the Presidential Advisory Council on HIV/AIDS and attempted to keep his campaign promise of overturning the U.S. military's longstanding ban on homosexuals, Clinton signed the Defense of Marriage Act (DOMA), which denied same-sex couples the federal benefits, privileges, and recognition afforded opposite-sex married couples.)*

5. Draw Conclusions Why do you think critics of the Personal Responsibility and Work Opportunity Reconciliation Act of 1996 argued that the act destroyed the safety net that protected the country's neediest and most vulnerable citizens and contributed to the persistence of poverty? *(Possible response: The act required that those on welfare work after receiving benefits for two years. This would have put single mothers at risk of increased poverty because of the need to obtain work-related childcare. Moving the administration of social welfare from the federal government to the states also ran the risk of uneven coverage from state to state.)*

INTEGRATE VISUALS

Direct students to examine the photographs and captions related to the bombing of the Alfred P. Murrah Federal Building in Oklahoma City, Oklahoma. Check students' reading by asking detailed questions concerning the date and human toll of the bombing. *(April 19, 1995; 168 dead, including 19 children, and 500 injured)* **ASK:** Who committed the act? *(Timothy McVeigh, an antigovernment activist and Persian Gulf War veteran)* Prompt students to conduct research about the immediate assumption by the press and others that the bombing was the work of Muslim extremists. Ask volunteers to report their findings to the class.

ACTIVE OPTIONS

On Your Feet: Host a Quiz Show Ask each student to write one question about the 1992 presidential election or Clinton's first term as president. Then bring teams of five students to the front of the class to take part in a quiz show. Ask for volunteers to alternate acting as quiz show hosts. Instruct hosts to pose student questions. Keep track of questions that stumped players and go over the answers to those questions as a class.

NG Learning Framework: Research LGBTQ Activism

SKILLS Communication, Collaboration

KNOWLEDGE Our Human Story

Instruct students to work in groups to research how the activism of the LGBTQ rights movement, Elaine Noble, and Harvey Milk impacted the history of the HIV/AIDS epidemic in the United States. Encourage groups to tap into local resources, if possible, to explore how the epidemic related to a retreat from some areas of the civil rights, women's liberation, and sexual liberation movements. Groups can use their research to hold a class discussion.

HISTORICAL THINKING

ANSWERS

1. Perot split the Republican vote, which enabled Clinton, a Democrat, to win the presidential election in 1992.

2. Possible response: Voter opposition to Democratic initiatives, such as Clinton's tax increases and spending cuts to balance the budget, health care reform, the Brady Handgun Violence Prevention Act, increased rights for the LGBTQ community, and strengthening of social programs for low-income families, coupled with Clinton's legal troubles, may have contributed to a conservative Republican backlash.

3. Possible responses: The government's response to social change can be seen in Clinton's signing of the Family and Medical Leave Act, the establishment of the Presidential Advisory Council on HIV/AIDS, and the "Don't Ask, Don't Tell" policy, which allowed homosexuals to serve in the military as long as they remained quiet about their sexual orientation.

4. Clinton expanded federal support for housing and nutritional programs to help the poor.

GLOBALIZATION AND IMMIGRATION

"Nothing is permanent except change." In the 1990s, this saying might have rung truer than ever. The world was shrinking, and everything seemed to be in a state of flux. What would all this change mean for Americans?

Many American workers and labor unions united in their opposition to NAFTA. When a bill was proposed in 1997 that would require Congress to vote yes or no on a trade agreement submitted by a president within 90 days, these Maryland steelworkers protested. The legislation was defeated.

GLOBALIZED BUSINESS

During the Clinton presidency, **globalization**, or the faster and freer flow of people, resources, goods, and ideas across national borders, had a powerful effect on the United States. Through trade, investments, migration, and the rapid sharing of information, countries and people around the world became increasingly interconnected.

Globalization had a profound impact on U.S. manufacturing. Many American companies began moving their operations to Mexico, where lower labor costs meant they could produce goods for less money. In time, some companies moved their operations from Mexico to China and then to smaller nations such as Bangladesh, to take advantage of even lower labor costs. These shifts resulted in falling prices for many goods that Americans consumed. However, producing these goods outside of the United States also led to **job dislocations**, or the movement of jobs to other places. These dislocations caused many Americans to lose their jobs.

Some American businesses, including computer software, retail, and automobile companies, have fared well in the globalized world. These industries established research centers and factories abroad and expanded their businesses in European, Asian, and African markets. American industrial leaders also recruited the best and the brightest from around the world to work in their companies.

THE UNITED STATES AND MEXICO

The growth of world trade in the second half of the 20th century came largely as a result of international trade agreements. In 1947, as you may recall,

23 countries signed the General Agreement on Tariffs and Trade (GATT), whose purpose was to reduce tariffs and other trade barriers so that countries could trade more freely with one another. In 1994, the World Trade Organization (WTO) replaced GATT. The WTO strives to set and enforce rules for trade, resolve trade disputes, ensure that developing countries benefit from the growth in international trade, and continue to support free trade.

The success of the European Economic Community—which, as you know, formed in 1958—prompted leaders in North America to consider creating a similar union. In 1988, the United States and Canada signed a free-trade pact that called for the elimination of most trade barriers. Then, in 1992, the United States, Canada, and Mexico ceremonially signed the **North American Free Trade Agreement (NAFTA)**. In the United States, George H.W. Bush had proposed and led the fight for the agreement during his presidency. NAFTA played a central role in fostering close relationships among the three countries and created the world's largest trading bloc.

The economic ties between the United States and Mexico had begun to deepen after the Cold War ended. These ties were strengthened by manufacturing plants called *maquiladoras* (mah-kee-luh-DOOR-uhz), which were established along the border between the United States and Mexico in the 1960s. A **maquiladora** is a plant located in an export-processing zone. A plant in this zone imports materials and then uses them to manufacture products for export. The plants allow

U.S. companies to take advantage of low labor costs in Mexico. In addition, maquiladoras operate as **free-enterprise zones**, which allow the suspension of both Mexican and U.S. tax and custom laws. As a result, goods flowed between the two countries at freer and faster rates from the 1980s through the 2000s.

In the early 1990s, Mexico prepared for **integration**, or the process of joining economic forces, with the United States and Canada under NAFTA by instituting a series of economic reforms. One of these called for communally owned farms in the southern Mexico state of Chiapas to be privatized, or transferred from public to private ownership. In response, an armed uprising called the **Chiapas Rebellion** took place in 1994. The rebellion was launched by a revolutionary force made up of local, rural people called Zapatistas (zah-puh-TEES-tuhz). They called for "a world in which many worlds fit," not a mono, or single, world with no space for them. Their response was an example of **disintegration**, or the endurance of nationalist, tribalist, and separatist alternatives to globalization.

Implementation of NAFTA was and continues to be controversial on both sides of the border. In the United States, critics feared the agreement would cause the country to lose even more manufacturing jobs to Mexico. And although it is true that the United States did lose some jobs, the loss was not as large as

PLAN: 4-PAGE LESSON

OBJECTIVE

Analyze the social and economic effects of globalization and immigration on the United States and Mexico.

CRITICAL THINKING SKILLS FOR LESSON 1.2

- Compare and Contrast
- Form and Support Opinions
- Summarize
- Make Connections
- Analyze Primary Sources
- Analyze Cause and Effect
- Analyze Data

HISTORICAL THINKING FOR CHAPTER 31

What does it mean to be an American in the 21st century? Globalization and free trade affected American businesses and workers, and immigration changed America's social fabric in the late 20th century. Lesson 1.2 explores these changes.

BACKGROUND FOR THE TEACHER

Critics note that the North American Free Trade Agreement hurt Mexican workers. Before NAFTA, all of Mexico's maquiladoras were located along the border. NAFTA enabled foreign companies to open free-enterprise zone factories in other areas of Mexico as easily as they could along the border. The growth of maquiladoras since NAFTA is fueled, in part, by low wages. Mexican workers' hourly wages have stagnated, while wages in countries like China have risen; China's average hourly wage topped Mexico's in 2011, and today it's 40 percent higher. Wages are particularly low for maquiladora workers along the border. Critics argue that low wages, long hours, and poor working conditions encourage Mexican workers to cross the U.S. border to find better opportunities.

INTRODUCE & ENGAGE

CONNECT TO TODAY

Direct students' attention to the photograph and caption of the steelworkers protesting the North American Free Trade Agreement. **ASK:** Why might labor unions oppose an agreement that opened markets between countries by lowering barriers to trade? *(Possible responses: A free trade agreement might make it hard for American workers to compete against cheap foreign workers and might drive down U.S. wages and/or lead to job loss. Such an agreement would likely bring more benefits to business owners than to workers.)* Use a Cause-and-Effect Web like the one shown to record students' ideas. Remind students that NAFTA is still controversial today by pointing out that one of Donald Trump's campaign promises during the 2016 presidential election was to renegotiate or scrap NAFTA. Tell students that Lesson 2.1 looks at the origin of NAFTA and other issues related to globalization.

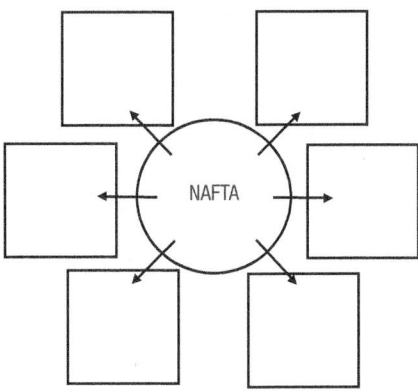

TEACH

GUIDED DISCUSSION

1. **Make Connections** In what ways is NAFTA a continuation of an economic postwar trend? *(Possible response: NAFTA represents a trend toward free trade that began with the 1947 General Agreement on Tariffs and Trade (GATT), which reduced tariffs and other trade barriers, and the success of the European Economic Community, which formed in 1958.)*

2. **Compare and Contrast** Share the information provided in Background for the Teacher with students. **ASK:** Why might some workers in the United States and Mexico share similar views of NAFTA? *(Possible response: Some American workers might oppose NAFTA because it resulted in job losses when manufacturing was moved to Mexico. Similarly, some Mexican workers might oppose NAFTA because it lowered wages as maquiladoras spread across Mexico.)*

3. **Analyze Primary Sources** According to the Primary Source feature, how did President Clinton think NAFTA would benefit the United States and the world? *(Clinton thought NAFTA would promote economic growth and equality, help preserve the environment, and possibly help bring about world peace.)*

MORE INFORMATION

The Zapatistas Tell students that the Chiapas Rebellion began on January 1, 1994, the same day NAFTA went into effect. Some 3,000 Zapatistas joined the rebellion, capturing six towns in Chiapas. The rebels argued that NAFTA would make Mexico more dependent on imported crops and hurt indigenous farmers. When the Mexican army attempted to put down the rebellion, student protests in Mexico City in support of the Zapatistas turned into riots. The government and the Zapatistas declared a ceasefire and entered peace talks, but the issues of contention still remain.

DIFFERENTIATE

ENGLISH LANGUAGE LEARNERS

Make Word Cards Have students at the **Expanding** level make word cards for the terms *globalization, job dislocation, maquiladora, integrate,* and *disintegrate.* Tell them to write a term on one side of a card and define it in their own language on the other side, using a bilingual dictionary if necessary. Then have students write a sentence in English using the term. Encourage students to read their sentences to one another.

GIFTED & TALENTED

Interpret a Slogan Bring students' attention to the slogan used by many of the Zapatista communities involved in the Chiapas Rebellion: "A world in which many worlds fit." (You may ask Spanish-speaking students to state the slogan in its original language.) Challenge students to interpret the slogan artistically—in a painting, drawing, or other art form. Invite students to display their interpretations and answer questions from their classmates.

See the Chapter Planner for more strategies for differentiation.

some critics had predicted. Still, tensions remain on issues related to economic regulation, labor conditions, increased immigration from Mexico, and damage to the environment. However, on the plus side, trade between the United States and Mexico has grown dramatically since NAFTA. A huge increase in exports bolstered Mexico's economy, and a similar increase in imports gave Mexican consumers access to lower-priced, better-quality goods. The borderland between the United States and Mexico is the scene of dynamic interactions in work, commerce, and culture.

NEW IMMIGRATION PATTERNS

As you've read, many critics of NAFTA were concerned that the agreement would result in a rise in the number of Mexican immigrants. The Immigration Act of 1965 had already liberalized country-of-origin policies by opening the United States to people of all nationalities. The act emphasized family reunification by giving special preference to relatives of immigrants who were already citizens of the United States. The new policy soon brought about major demographic and social changes. The U.S. population became increasingly

diverse as immigration increased and newcomers arrived from all parts of the world. Immigration from Mexico jumped dramatically, from approximately 575,000 Mexicans in 1960 to more than 4 million in 1990.

As legal immigration to the United States increased, so did illegal immigration. Many of the people who crossed the border illegally—without proper documentation—came from Mexico or Central America in search of work and a better future. Illegal immigration emerged as a major issue in the 1990s, especially in states along the U.S.-Mexico border. Many people felt that these undocumented immigrants took jobs away from Americans, caused crime rates to rise, and took advantage of the country's social services without paying taxes. In 1996, Congress addressed the flood of illegal immigrants by allocating funds for increased border security.

People in some states bordering Mexico also took steps against illegal immigration. For example, in 1994, California voters approved **Proposition 187**, a controversial ballot measure that denied illegal immigrants state services such as public education

Vendors at the Little Saigon Night Market in Westminster, California, grill fresh fish and other street food in this 2015 photo. These open-air stalls are common in Vietnam, and immigrants brought the tradition to the United States. Night markets have sprung up across the country.

During the 1994 Chiapas Rebellion against NAFTA, a man known as "Subcomandante Marcos" (shown below wearing a black mask) led the Zapatistas. His army, consisting mostly of poor Maya farmers, briefly occupied several towns before agreeing to a truce with the Mexican government.

and health care. All but one provision of Proposition 187 was blocked by federal courts throughout the 1990s, but other anti-immigrant measures soon followed. **Proposition 209**, which won approval in 1996, prohibited state-supported affirmative action that was intended to help minority groups suffering from discrimination. Two years later came **Proposition 227**, which banned bilingual education in California's public schools.

Major world events also affected immigration patterns in the last decades of the 20th century. As you've learned, the end of the Vietnam War in 1975 brought hundreds of thousands of refugees from Vietnam and neighboring Southeast Asian countries to the United States. Immigration from Vietnam continued to grow as relatives sought to join family members who had arrived earlier. Similarly, the 1979 Islamic Revolution in Iran drove a large influx of Iranians to U.S. shores.

The United States has always been made up of people from many different cultures. However, the growing diversity of the U.S. population led to debate over the concept of multiculturalism. In the early 1990s, conservatives accused liberals of using multiculturalism to divide society into

conflicting groups, limit free speech on campuses by suppressing conservative views, and reject traditional Western culture. Liberals countered that multiculturalism was necessary to tackle problems that arise as our society becomes more diverse.

As Clinton dealt with globalization and immigration, he also concentrated on seeking a second term as president. He would be aided in achieving this goal by the country's strong economy. Clinton's second four years, however, would not be smooth sailing.

HISTORICAL THINKING

1. **READING CHECK** Why did some American companies move to Mexico, China, and Bangladesh?

2. **COMPARE AND CONTRAST** What have been some of the advantages and disadvantages of NAFTA?

3. **FORM AND SUPPORT OPINIONS** Based on what you have read in this lesson, do you think globalization is a good thing? Support your opinion with evidence from the text.

4. **SUMMARIZE** How did the federal government and California voters respond to international migration in the 1990s?

BUILD BACKGROUND

PROPOSITION 209

More than 20 years after passage of Proposition 209, its effect on African-American and Latino enrollment in California universities is still debated. The proposition had a chilling effect on minority enrollment when it went into effect in 1998, particularly in schools such as UC Berkeley and UCLA. First-year African-American enrollment at UCLA, for instance, dropped from 264 students in 1995 to 144 in 1998. Today, UCLA's African-American enrollment is near pre-proposition levels in absolute numbers, although the percentage of African-American first-year students is still lower than it was in 1995. Other schools in the system have also shown improvement. In 2016, African Americans and Latinos accounted for 39 percent of California high-school seniors accepted to one of the nine UC undergraduate campuses. This is a dramatic improvement from the 16 percent in 1998.

UCLA credits its improved numbers to an aggressive program designed to recruit promising minority high-school students. The university uses college fairs, community events, information sessions in neighborhoods, and campus tours to entice students to apply. Recruiters keep in touch with promising students to form bonds. The university also mentors minority high-school students. UCLA's Black Male Institute, for example, mentors students at Washington Prep in the Westmont area of Los Angeles County.

TEACH

GUIDED DISCUSSION

4. Summarize Share information from Build Background with students. **ASK:** How has UCLA tried to compensate for the impact of Proposition 209 on minority enrollment? *(UCLA has recruited minority students through college fairs, community events, information sessions in neighborhoods, and campus tours. It has also kept in touch with promising students to form bonds and has established mentoring programs.)*

5. Analyze Cause and Effect How did major world events affect trends in immigration to the United States during the last quarter of the 20th century? *(The end of the Vietnam War increased immigration from Southeast Asia, and the 1979 Islamic Revolution in Iran caused a large number of Iranians to immigrate to the United States.)*

ANALYZE DATA

As mentioned in the lesson, both the Immigration Act of 1965 and NAFTA brought about major changes in the U.S. immigrant population. Have students examine online census data to identify basic immigrant demographic shifts from 1950 to today. Arrange for students to work in groups to collect the census data and to look for information that helps them answer the following questions: What significant changes do you see in immigrants' countries of origin? *(Possible responses: The number of European immigrants declined between 1960 and 1990, then leveled off. Immigration to the United States from Latin America, Asia, and other sources steadily climbed after 1970.)* How might the Immigration Act of 1965 have influenced this trend? *(The act opened U.S. immigration to all nationalities.)* What indication is there that NAFTA had an impact on immigration to the United States from Latin America? *(Immigration from Latin American countries has increased sharply since the 1990s.)*

ACTIVE OPTIONS

Active History: Diagram Economic Interdependence Extend the lesson by using either the PDF or Whiteboard version of the activity. These activities take a deeper look at a topic from, or related to, the lesson. Explore the activities as a class, turn them into group assignments, or even assign them individually.

NG Learning Framework: Immigration Factors

ATTITUDE Curiosity

KNOWLEDGE Our Human Story

Have students work in groups to research and analyze the push and pull factors that have contributed to shifting immigration patterns in the United States in the late 20th and early 21st centuries. As part of their analysis of pull factors, tell students to consider the United States' changing immigration policies, starting with the Immigration Act of 1965. Students can then use their research and analysis to hold a class discussion on how these policies have affected American society.

HISTORICAL THINKING

ANSWERS

1. Some companies moved to lower labor costs so they could produce goods more cheaply.

2. Advantages: NAFTA created the world's largest trading bloc; strengthened economic ties between the United States and Mexico; led to economic reforms in Mexico; resulted in lower-priced, better-quality goods for Mexican consumers; and led to dynamic cultural and economic interactions in the borderlands. Disadvantages: NAFTA resulted in some U.S. job losses; led to the Chiapas Rebellion in Mexico; and gave rise to American concerns over economic regulations, immigration to the United States from Mexico, and the environment.

3. Answers will vary. Possible responses: Yes. Globalization provides a broader pool of qualified workers, expands markets, lowers the cost of making and buying goods, and speeds distribution. No. Globalization threatens manufacturing in the United States and increases immigration.

4. Congress increased funds for border security in 1996 to help stem the tide of immigrants crossing the Mexican border illegally. California passed a series of propositions: Proposition 187, which was primarily blocked by federal courts, sought to deny public education, health care, and other state services to illegal immigrants; Proposition 209 outlawed state-supported affirmative action; and Proposition 227 banned bilingual education in California public schools.

ECONOMIC BOOM AND SCANDALS

Websites, blogs, Wi-Fi, and social media are part of everyday life today, but before the technology boom of the 1990s, they were all but unknown. They all have to do with the Internet, which fueled major cultural changes and big economic growth.

SECOND-TERM ACCOMPLISHMENTS

After Clinton defeated Republican candidate Robert Dole and Reform Party candidate H. Ross Perot in the 1996 election, the nation's economy continued to improve. Unemployment fell from 5.4 to 4.9 percent in 1997, and by 2000, it had dropped to 4 percent—the lowest level in three decades. The stock market soared to record levels, and inflation fell. In 1998, the president presented the first balanced budget since 1969. The federal government took in more money than it spent in 1998 and in each of the next three years, allowing for a rare budget surplus. With Americans enjoying plentiful jobs and stable prices, a sense of optimism swept the nation and kept Clinton's job approval ratings around 60 percent.

One of the main forces driving this strong economic growth was the rise of the Internet and the rapid development of companies that took advantage of this revolutionary new mode of information-sharing. The result was a "dot-com" boom in the stock market, named for the suffix of most corporate web pages. Investors poured money into the stocks of Internet-related companies, and entrepreneurs who started popular social media and commercial websites became millionaires almost overnight. The center of this rapid growth in technology was California's Silicon Valley where, as you know, the personal computer was developed.

In his second term, as in his first, Clinton pursued an agenda of moderate domestic reforms. Addressing Americans' concerns about the soaring costs of higher education, for example, he proposed and signed a bill calling for tax breaks, tuition grants, and scholarships to help working-

and middle-class families pay for college. In foreign policy matters, Clinton led efforts to expand the North Atlantic Treaty Organization (NATO) by bringing in former communist countries in Eastern Europe. In 1995, during his first term, Clinton had worked to bring about a cease-fire among warring Serbs, Croats, and Bosnians in the Balkans, a mountainous region in Eastern Europe that was once part of Yugoslavia. In 1999, Clinton authorized NATO to carry out air strikes against Serbia to end its mass killing of ethnic Albanians in the Serbian province of Kosovo. Clinton's administration also played an important role in implementing the **Oslo Accords**, which were aimed at ending the decades-long conflict between the Israelis and Palestinians.

The Dot-Com Boom, 1995–2004

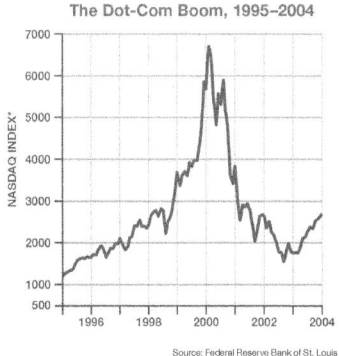

Source: Federal Reserve Bank of St. Louis

* The NASDAQ is a stock market of stocks that are traded electronically. The index expresses stocks' values with respect to a 1971 base index of 100.

CLINTON'S IMPEACHMENT

While Clinton achieved many political successes during his second term, a serious scandal arose that threatened to end his presidency. In 1994, a former Arkansas state employee named Paula Jones had filed a sexual harassment suit against Clinton, accusing him of unwanted sexual advances. Kenneth Starr, the special prosecutor in charge of the Whitewater inquiry, expanded his investigation to include the Paula Jones case, even though there was no connection between the two. In late 1997, stories began to surface about another sexual relationship, this one between Clinton and a young female White House intern named Monica Lewinsky. Lawyers for Jones subpoenaed Lewinsky as a witness, but in a sworn statement, she denied any relationship with the president. When Clinton testified under oath in the case, he, too, denied the relationship.

However, Starr eventually uncovered strong evidence of sexual encounters between Clinton and Lewinsky. Faced with this evidence, the president testified before a grand jury in August 1998 and admitted to having had "inappropriate intimate contact" with her. The following month, Starr submitted a report to Congress that identified 11 possible grounds on which the president could be impeached, or formally charged with "treason, bribery, or other high crimes and misdemeanors." Impeachment is limited to the president, vice president, and other civil officers of the United States. An official convicted of the charge is removed from office.

According to the Constitution, the House of Representatives votes to impeach an official, while the Senate tries the case. In December 1998, the Republican-controlled House voted largely along party lines to bring two charges against Clinton. The first alleged the president had committed **perjury**, or had lied under oath. The second claimed he had obstructed justice by attempting to hide his relationship with the intern and encouraging her to lie in her sworn statement. The only other president ever to be impeached was Andrew Johnson in 1868.

In January 1999, Clinton's impeachment trial began. After just four weeks of testimony, the Senate voted to acquit Clinton of both charges, having failed to obtain the two-thirds majority needed for conviction. He remained in office, but the scandals and trial damaged his reputation with the American people. As a result, concern over candidates' moral character would have a big impact on the election of 2000.

The *New York Daily News* ran this special edition of its newspaper on December 20 1998, the day after the House voted to impeach Clinton. Before his acquittal, the president told the American people that he was "profoundly sorry for all I have done wrong in words and deeds."

HISTORICAL THINKING

1. **READING CHECK** What were some of the indicators of the strong economy during Clinton's second term, and how did the Internet play a role?

2. **MAKE INFERENCES** What might the Republicans in Congress have hoped to gain by impeaching President Clinton?

3. **FORM AND SUPPORT OPINIONS** Do you think Clinton's presidency was a success or a failure? Explain your opinion.

4. **INTERPRET GRAPHS** What stock market trend began just after 2000, and what impact did this probably have on Internet-related companies?

OBJECTIVE

Examine President Clinton's second term in office and the technology boom.

CRITICAL THINKING SKILLS FOR LESSON 1.3

• Make Inferences

• Form and Support Opinions

• Interpret Graphs

• Draw Conclusions

• Analyze Cause and Effect

HISTORICAL THINKING FOR CHAPTER 31

What does it mean to be an American in the 21st century? For Americans, Clinton's second term was a study in contrasts—the U.S. economy flourished, but the president faced impeachment. Lesson 1.3 examines these historic events and their effects.

BACKGROUND FOR THE TEACHER

With hindsight, analysts point out that the dot-com boom of the 1990s was destined to go bust. Technology stocks were wildly overvalued, even though many start-up companies made no profits. Stock values for these companies were primarily based on demand for the stocks themselves rather than on the value of the companies' products or services. This was true even for e-commerce companies that had products to sell. Nevertheless, stock prices kept climbing. On March 10, 2000, the NASDAQ reached a high of 5,048.62. The next day, it began to crash. By the time the tech bubble completely burst, the NASDAQ had lost 75 percent of its peak value of $6.71 trillion. The technology sector rebounded, however, leading to a second tech boom in the 2010s that sent the NASDAQ soaring past its old record high.

HISTORY NOTEBOOK

Encourage students to complete the American Gallery page for Chapter 31 in their History Notebooks as they read.

INTRODUCE & ENGAGE

CONSIDER THE CONSEQUENCES

Begin a class discussion about how episodes of bad judgment can overshadow a person's accomplishments. Have students brainstorm a list of famous people who are remembered more for an action that brought legal or social recrimination than for their accomplishments. Tell students that Lesson 1.3 discusses Clinton's impeachment and his accomplishments.

TEACH

GUIDED DISCUSSION

1. **Draw Conclusions** How did President Clinton's second-term accomplishments help contribute to international peace efforts? *(Clinton led efforts to admit former communist countries in Eastern Europe to NATO, helped negotiate a cease-fire among Croats, Serbs, and Bosnians in the Balkans, and helped implement the Oslo Accords aimed at ending the Israeli–Palestinian conflict.)*

2. **Analyze Cause and Effect** Upon what basis did the House of Representatives charge President Clinton with obstruction of justice and perjury in the historic vote to impeach him? *(The House charged that Clinton lied under oath when he claimed that he had not had a sexual relationship with Monica Lewinsky and obstructed justice by attempting to hide the relationship and encouraging Lewinsky to lie in her sworn testimony.)*

INTERPRET GRAPHS

Direct students' attention to the graph. Clarify that most technology stocks are traded through the NASDAQ stock exchange. **ASK:** How do the graph and text of the lesson work together to help you understand the dot-com boom? *(Possible response: The graph provides numeric information showing that the price of tech stocks increased by around 600 percent between 1995 and 2000, and the text explains that the rise of Internet-related companies was the cause of the increase.)*

ACTIVE OPTIONS

AMERICAN GALLERY ONLINE

Technology Titans Invite students to explore the American Gallery. Have them select one of the photographs and do additional research to learn more about it. Ask questions that will inspire additional inquiry about the chosen gallery photograph, such as: Who and/or what does it show? How does it reflect the technology boom of the 1990s? What impression do you have of the person depicted?

NG Learning Framework: Compare Booms

SKILL Communication

KNOWLEDGE New Frontiers

Have students work in groups to find out more about the dot-com boom of the 1990s, its bust in 2000, and the second technology boom in the 2010s. Assign groups to focus on one of the following topics for the two time frames: causes of the boom, effects on the stock market, and economic risks. Ask groups to use their research to create a Venn diagram to compare the two booms. Then hold a class discussion on how evaluating the consequences of past events and determining the lessons learned can inform current events.

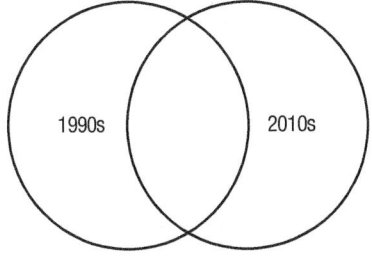

DIFFERENTIATE

STRIVING READERS

Connect Details to a Main Idea Challenge students to identify the two main ideas of the lesson, the strong economy and the scandals. Then have students work in pairs to complete a Main-Idea and Details List for each of the two main ideas. Model the kinds of details (facts, dates, events, descriptions) that can often support a main idea. Students can then share their diagrams with other pairs.

Main Idea:
Detail:
Detail:
Detail:
Detail:
Detail:

PRE-AP

Extend Knowledge Instruct students to gather information from a variety of sources to write an essay about the many ways in which the U.S. economy improved during the Clinton administration. Tell them to explain the reasons behind the various improvements and their impacts on average citizens. Invite volunteers to share their essays with the class.

See the Chapter Planner for more strategies for differentiation.

HISTORICAL THINKING

ANSWERS

1. Indicators included low unemployment, a soaring stock market, falling inflation, and a balanced budget. The development of the Internet played a role in boosting the stock market, as investors aggressively pursued stocks in Internet-related companies.

2. Answers will vary. Possible response: Even if Clinton was not convicted, Republicans hoped to tarnish Clinton's name and slow his and other Democrats' political agenda.

3. Answers will vary. Possible responses: Yes. Clinton's presidency was a success because it improved the economy and contributed to world peace. No. Despite his economic and international achievements, Clinton's personal behavior made his presidency a failure.

4. In 2000, stock prices dropped sharply. The impact on Internet-related companies was probably negative, making it harder for them to raise money.

The 2000 Election

Al Gore, Democrat		
Electoral Vote: 266 votes, 49.4%		
Popular Vote: 50,992,335 votes, 48.4%		

George W. Bush, Republican		
Electoral Vote: 271 votes, 50.4%		
Popular Vote: 50,455,156 votes, 47.9%		

Ralph Nader, Green		
Popular Vote: 2,882,738 votes, 2.7%		

The 2000 election was one of the closest in modern U.S. history. In this photo, candidate Bush shakes hands with supporters at a campaign rally.

THE CONTESTED ELECTION OF 2000

Most elections are decided easily: the candidate receiving the most votes is the winner. But as Americans learned in 2000, sometimes U.S. presidential elections are not so straightforward.

THE 2000 CAMPAIGN

During Clinton's impeachment trial, many leading political figures were already looking ahead to the 2000 presidential election—particularly among Republicans. They knew Clinton's scandals had weakened the Democratic Party. By early July 1999, nine Republicans had announced their candidacy. After a long primary battle, the Republican Party nominated Texas governor **George W. Bush**, the eldest son of former president George H.W. Bush.

HANGING CHADS
Many Florida voters used punch-card ballots in the 2000 presidential election. However, a number of voters failed to punch a hole in their card, leaving a fragment of paper, called a "hanging chad," attached. Election officials, like the one shown here, studied the ballots, trying to determine the voter's intent in each instance.

Bush embraced what he called **compassionate conservatism**, a political philosophy that blended traditional conservative ideas about economic policies with a concern for disadvantaged people. He echoed Ronald Reagan's populist stand in the 1980s. Like Reagan, Bush criticized establishment elites and supported a smaller, contracted government and advocated for social programs that promoted traditional family values. He also vowed to restore executive power, which he felt Congress had weakened.

As his vice president, Bush chose Richard Cheney, who had served as secretary of defense under George H.W. Bush. Politically, Cheney was a neoconservative. A **neoconservative**, or "neocon," is someone who strongly supports a free-market economy with few regulations and believes the United States should use its influence and military power to actively promote its ideals and national interests around the world. For example, neocons shared the view that Saddam Hussein, the autocratic president of Iraq, was a destabilizing influence in Southwest Asia (often referred to as the Middle East), one of the world's most troubled regions. Neocons regretted that George H.W. Bush had not removed Hussein from power during the 1990–91 Persian Gulf War. They also believed strongly in what they called **American exceptionalism**—the idea that the United States is superior to other nations due to its history and ideology. As such, neocons claimed the country had a mission to spread democracy and change the world.

On the Democratic side, Vice President Al Gore easily won his party's nomination. In the minds of many Americans, however, Gore had been tarnished by the scandals of the Clinton presidency, and many

voters thought he was arrogant. In televised debates with Bush, Gore sighed, rolled his eyes, and seemed to talk down to his opponent. Ralph Nader ran as the candidate of the Green Party, which supported nonviolence, environmentalism, and social justice. During his candidacy, Nader promoted universal health care and spoke out against the power of big business. Because he drew much of his support from young, liberal, politically independent voters, some people would later claim that Nader took votes away from Gore and cost the vice president the election.

BUSH v. GORE

On election day, the voting was very close in many states. By the end of the night, with final and projected counts still being reported, Gore led in the popular vote. Still, neither candidate had yet gained the 270 electoral votes needed to win the election. It became clear that Florida, with 25 electoral votes, would determine the next president.

Shortly after 2 a.m., news outlets began declaring that Bush had won Florida and, therefore, the election. Gore called Bush to concede, or accept, defeat but soon took back his concession when he learned the count in Florida was much closer than had been previously reported. Bush led by fewer than 600 votes, and the gap continued to narrow as the counting continued. Furthermore, Gore's aides had noted irregularities and compromised ballots at polling places in several Democratic counties.

The slimness of the margin called for the application of a Florida law, which required a statewide recount by machine. The recount reduced Bush's

lead to 327. Some counties then initiated manual recounts, although the legality of these recounts was challenged in court. The Gore and Bush camps exchanged charges of fraud, manipulation, and the exercise of excessive political pressure throughout November.

In early December, the Florida Supreme Court ordered a manual statewide recount of the roughly 45,000 undervotes—ballots that had not been counted by the voting machines because the voter's intent was unclear. Days later, lawyers for both sides argued the **Bush v. Gore** case before the U.S. Supreme Court. In a decision that many commentators considered both hasty and biased toward Republicans, the Court declared the Florida Supreme Court's recount order unconstitutional. As a result, Bush became the president-elect. Although Gore had won the nationwide popular vote by more than 500,000 votes, he accepted the outcome as final and conceded the election.

HISTORICAL THINKING

1. **READING CHECK** How could the election of 2000 have taken other directions?

2. **ANALYZE CAUSE AND EFFECT** What impact did the closeness of the election and its controversial results have on the American people and on Bush's authority as president?

3. **FORM AND SUPPORT OPINIONS** Based on past elections, including the 2000 election, do you think American voters should directly elect the president, or do you think the current system is fine as it is? Explain your answer.

PLAN: 2-PAGE LESSON

OBJECTIVE

Understand the outcome and impact of the 2000 election and how events might have taken a different direction.

CRITICAL THINKING SKILLS FOR LESSON 2.1

• Analyze Cause and Effect

• Form and Support Opinions

• Make Connections

• Determine Chronology

HISTORICAL THINKING FOR CHAPTER 31

What does it mean to be an American in the 21st century? In 2000, George W. Bush ran against Vice President Al Gore for president. Lesson 2.1 discusses the neoconservatives who supported Bush and the disputed election of 2000.

BACKGROUND FOR THE TEACHER

Some neocons, including Richard Cheney, Donald Rumsfeld, and Paul Wolfowitz, had once served as advisors to Ronald Reagan but differed sharply with him on foreign policy. Reagan built a strong U.S. military, but he used diplomacy to achieve most of his ends, particularly when Mikhail Gorbachev assumed power in the Soviet Union in 1985. Although Reagan's neocon advisors believed the Soviets were preparing a pre-emptive strike against the United States and urged him to use military force to win the Cold War, Reagan rejected their advice. Instead, even as he issued his famous 1987 challenge, "Mr. Gorbachev, tear down this wall," Reagan engaged in personal diplomacy with Gorbachev and other Soviet leaders, assuring them the United States would not attack. Soon after, the Russians withdrew from their satellite countries, and the Soviet Union collapsed. In George W. Bush, however, the neocons found a president more willing to embrace their militaristic, nation-building approach.

INTRODUCE & ENGAGE

DISCUSS THE MEANING OF *NEOCONSERVATIVE*

Ask students to recall what they learned about Reagan-era conservatism. List key aspects on the board. Display the word *neoconservative* and ask a volunteer to define the prefix *neo- (new)*. Explain that this lesson describes the neoconservative movement in the 2000s. Ask students to make predictions about what principles might be associated with neoconservatism. Record students' responses to display and review at the end of the lesson.

TEACH

GUIDED DISCUSSION

1. **Make Connections** What lessons did the neocons believe George W. Bush could learn from the consequences of George H.W. Bush's actions in the Middle East? *(Possible responses: Neocons believed it was a mistake to let Saddam Hussein become a destabilizing force in the Middle East. The lesson they embraced was that using U.S. military force was necessary to remove Hussein and spread democracy in the Middle East.)*

2. **Determine Chronology** What series of events led to the outcome of the 2000 presidential election? *(On election night, neither candidate had 270 electoral votes. The next day, media outlets reported that Bush had won. Gore conceded and then retracted his concession. Throughout November, Florida recounted votes by machine and manually in some counties. In early December, the Florida Supreme Court ordered a statewide manual recount. A few days later, the U.S. Supreme Court ruled against the Florida manual recount. Bush was declared the winner.)*

MORE INFORMATION

Voter ID Requirement Tell students that after the 2001 election, Congress created the U.S. Election Assistance Commission to provide federal funding to states to upgrade voting equipment and improve the process of voter registration. Many states also began requiring IDs from voters. Present-day debates continue about the most accurate type of voting equipment, the need for paper backups of electronic ballots, and the fairness of voter ID requirements. **ASK:** Why might people support or oppose voter ID requirements and paper backups? *(Possible response: Requiring IDs might reduce voting fraud, but it might also prevent some citizens from voting. Paper backups can counter vote tampering, but they would make elections more expensive.)*

ACTIVE OPTIONS

On Your Feet: Fishbowl Arrange students in two concentric circles, with both circles facing inward. Ask students in the inner circle to discuss possible roots of American exceptionalism in earlier concepts such as manifest destiny, Theodore Roosevelt's big stick diplomacy, or the Monroe Doctrine, and how American exceptionalism has influenced U.S. policies since 2000. Direct students in the outer circle to evaluate the discussion. Have students reverse roles to provide additional insights.

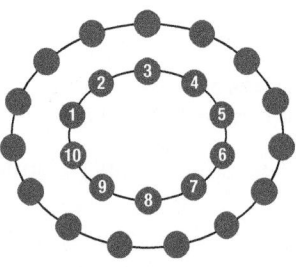

NG Learning Framework: Evaluate Conservatism: 1980s versus 2000

SKILL Communication

KNOWLEDGE Our Human Story

Have students extend and use their knowledge of Ronald Reagan's policies by evaluating how conservative principles influenced the nation in the early 2000s. Share information from the Background for the Teacher and then assign students to work in groups to research and further compare the principles and practices of Reagan and the neocons. Assign each group a topic, such as views on the role of the federal government, economic policies, or foreign relations. Instruct groups to prepare a chart showing their findings. Use the charts to guide a class discussion about which conservative principles from the 1980s influenced American society in the 2000s and in what ways they were manifested.

DIFFERENTIATE

ENGLISH LANGUAGE LEARNERS

Use Verb and Noun Forms Pair students at the **Emerging** and **Expanding** levels with students at the **Bridging** level. Point out the verb *concede* and the noun *concession* in the lesson. Discuss the meanings of the words and identify clues to determining parts of speech, such as that the ending *-ion* signals a noun. Provide students with other verb/noun pairs, such as: *secede/secession, recede/recession, proceed/procession, confess/confession,* and *succeed/succession*. Encourage students to use a dictionary to look up definitions, if necessary. Instruct students to work together to write an original sentence for each word in each word pair. Encourage pairs to exchange and read each other's sentences.

PRE-AP

Engage in a Debate Tell students that they will research and then debate the validity of the idea of American exceptionalism. Have students research its origins and the assumptions behind it, and let them decide whether to debate in favor of or opposition to American exceptionalism. Instruct students to prepare their debate notes using a variety of unbiased sources to find strong support for their position and to prepare counterarguments. Ask students to cite sources from their research and to include historical or present-day examples of the impact of American exceptionalism for good or for ill. Arrange for students to debate in front of the class.

See the Chapter Planner for more strategies for differentiation.

HISTORICAL THINKING

ANSWERS

1. Possible response: Had the Supreme Court refused to hear *Bush* v. *Gore,* Gore might have won Florida in a manual recount. Had those who voted for Nader voted for Gore, Gore might have had enough electoral votes to win the election.

2. Possible response: The outcome might have weakened Bush's authority because many felt the election result was based on the ruling of the Supreme Court and biased in favor of Republicans.

3. Answers will vary. Possible responses: Americans should directly elect the president. The use of electoral votes should be abandoned because it can contradict the will of the people. The current system is fine and should be followed because using electoral votes serves the interests of all states.

SEPTEMBER 11, 2001

A list of the darkest dates in U.S. history would certainly include April 12, 1861, the day the Civil War broke out, and December 7, 1941, when Japanese warplanes attacked Pearl Harbor. It would also include September 11, 2001, the day of the deadliest terrorist attacks ever on American soil.

UNDER ATTACK

As Americans went about their normal routines on the morning of Tuesday, September 11, 2001, news outlets reported an odd event in New York City. At 8:46 a.m., an airplane crashed into one of the twin 110-story towers of the World Trade Center in the city's downtown financial district. Smoke and flames billowed out of a gaping hole near the top of the north tower, and firefighters and police officers rushed to the scene. At first, many people assumed the crash had been an accident. Seventeen minutes later, however, people around the country looked on in disbelief as news cameras filmed another large jetliner slamming into the south tower. There could no longer be any question: the United States was under attack by terrorists.

The Federal Aviation Administration (FAA) immediately ordered all takeoffs to be halted at U.S. airports. Airplanes in the air were directed to land at the nearest airport. Minutes after the FAA issued this order, another plane crashed into the Pentagon, the headquarters of the U.S. Department of Defense, near Washington, D.C. Soon news came that a fourth airplane had crashed. This one was not flown into a building, however. It plunged into a field in a rural area of southwestern Pennsylvania. Passengers onboard the plane had struggled with the terrorists and prevented the aircraft from hitting its intended target, believed to have been the White House or the U.S. Capitol Building.

The attacks ended with the fourth crash, but there were more horrors to come. Around 10 a.m., as emergency responders worked desperately to evacuate the World Trade Center and battle the fires that engulfed it, the south tower collapsed. The collapse created a thick cloud of dust in the air that spread outward in every direction. Less than a half hour later, the north tower collapsed. The site of the collapsed towers became known as Ground Zero. In the hours after the attack, people with missing loved ones began gathering at the site, hoping desperately for good news. "Missing" posters soon covered walls, lampposts, and store windows in the area.

Over the next few days, authorities pieced together the story of the attacks. Nineteen terrorists, divided into groups of four or five, had boarded four

🏛 National September 11 Memorial Museum, New York City

The New York firefighter who wore this helmet on 9/11 was last seen carrying a woman from the north tower lobby when the building collapsed on top of them. His helmet, partially melted by the heat in the tower after it was hit, is one of thousands of artifacts on display in the museum.

The day after the attack on the World Trade Center, firefighters, city workers, members of the National Guard, and others began searching the wreckage for the bodies of victims, as well as any possible survivors.

1119

PLAN: 4-PAGE LESSON

OBJECTIVE

Summarize the effects of the 9/11 attacks on U.S. domestic and Middle East policies.

CRITICAL THINKING SKILLS FOR LESSON 2.2

- Make Inferences
- Form and Support Opinions
- Make Connections
- Compare and Contrast
- Analyze Visuals
- Summarize
- Analyze Cause and Effect
- Analyze Primary Sources

HISTORICAL THINKING FOR CHAPTER 31

What does it mean to be an American in the 21st century? In 2001, Saudi Arabian terrorists struck the United States. Lesson 2.2 discusses the worst terrorist attack on U.S. soil and its aftermath.

BACKGROUND FOR THE TEACHER

When the first plane struck the North Tower, Rick Rescorla, security chief of banking company Morgan Stanley Dean Witter, located in the South Tower, was not surprised. A military veteran born in Britain, Rescorla was in the World Trade Center when it was bombed in 1993. Although the bomb did little damage, Rescorla realized the vulnerability of the Twin Towers to an air attack. He warned bank management and began holding escape drills, in which company employees practiced walking as quickly as possible down the long tower stairs. As a result, when the second plane struck the South Tower everyone knew exactly what to do. Rescorla escorted 21 floors of bank employees out of the South Tower, singing patriotic songs to keep them calm. He then went back in to search for stragglers and died when the tower collapsed. His remarkable foresight and discipline saved 2,700 lives that day.

SECURITY VERSUS CIVIL LIBERTIES

Tell students to imagine that their school had been the target of serious vandalism committed by unknown parties. Discuss what security measures students would suggest to catch the suspects and to keep the building and the student body safe. Encourage students to voice opinions on how much access to students' belongings and information security personnel should have as they investigate. Tell students that this lesson discusses the 9/11 attacks—a crime much more serious than vandalism—and the federal government's foreign and domestic responses.

TEACH

GUIDED DISCUSSION

1. **Compare and Contrast** How were the 9/11 attacks similar to and different from the attack on Pearl Harbor? *(Possible response: Like Pearl Harbor, the attack occurred when the United States was at peace, the enemy struck various targets from the air, and the United States was caught unprepared. Unlike Pearl Harbor, the attackers used passenger planes, conducted the strikes as a suicide mission, and lost control of one airplane to its passengers.)*

2. **Make Connections** What message might the attackers have intended to send by targeting the Pentagon and the White House or U.S. Capitol building? *(Possible response: The Pentagon symbolizes the military power of the United States, and the White House and U.S. Capitol building, believed to have been targets, symbolize government power. The attackers might have wanted to show that the United States, despite the global power of its military and government, was vulnerable to a small, dedicated force.)*

3. **Analyze Visuals** Why might the physical details and location in the large photograph of Ground Zero provoke strong feelings? *(Possible response: Details such as the rubble, smoking ruins, and rescue workers searching for survivors emphasize the complete destruction of buildings and high death toll from the attack. The location, in one of the most famous cities in the nation, might provoke patriotic outrage in viewers.)*

🏛 VIRTUAL MUSEUM VISIT

New York City's National September 11 Memorial Museum is part of the rebuilt World Trade Center complex. Access the museum's website and demonstrate the Virtual Museum Tour. Display a sampling of the photographs and artifacts, such as the firefighter's helmet. **ASK:** In what ways are the first responders and the nearly 3,000 victims remembered? *(They are remembered with photographs in the Memorial Exhibition and plaques around the Memorial Pools.)* Allow groups of students to explore the site on their own. Ask groups to select an object or video clip that students feel best represents the main purpose of the museum and then present their selection to the class and explain the reasons for their choice.

STRIVING READERS

Understand Main Ideas Check students' understanding of the main ideas in the lesson by asking them to correctly complete Either/Or statements such as the following:

- Osama bin Laden was the leader of [the Taliban or al Qaeda]. *(al Qaeda)*
- Americans were deeply divided [before or after] the terrorist attacks of 9/11. *(before)*
- The collapse of the twin towers released large amounts of [harmless or toxic] substances into the air. *(toxic)*
- The federal government [gained or lost] power to conduct surveillance on U.S. citizens after the attacks. *(gained)*
- Because some Americans blamed [al Qaeda or Muslims] for the 9/11 attacks, there was an increase in hate crimes. *(Muslims)*
- The English word *God* and the Arabic word *Allah* refer to [the same or very different] things. *(the same)*

GIFTED & TALENTED

Create a Multimedia Presentation Challenge students to find a variety of first-person accounts of the terrorist attacks of 9/11 using print and online sources. Instruct students to choose one person's account and use it as the basis of a multimedia presentation that conveys that person's story in the larger historical context of the terrorist attacks. Encourage students to use photographs, news headlines, video clips, and other media to enhance their presentation. Invite students to share their presentations with the class and to lead a follow-up discussion about how first-person accounts affect our perception of historical events.

See the Chapter Planner for more strategies for differentiation.

commercial airplanes—two in Boston, one in Newark, New Jersey, and one in Washington, D.C. All four planes were originally scheduled to fly to the West Coast, so they were carrying full fuel tanks. After takeoff, the terrorists seized control of each airplane, perhaps using box cutters as weapons. They then piloted the planes toward targets selected for their symbolic significance. On the fourth airplane, however, the passengers and crew had learned about the other plane crashes and, as you've read, fought back.

Authorities believed the terrorists were linked to **al Qaeda** (al KY-duh), an Islamic extremist organization founded in the late 1980s. A Saudi Arabian militant named **Osama bin Laden** led this group from his base in Afghanistan. There, al Qaeda was protected and supported by the **Taliban**, an ultraconservative Islamic group that had gained control of much of the country. Determined to bring an end to U.S. influence in Southwest Asia, bin Laden employed **terrorism**, or the use of violent acts and threats to achieve a political goal, as his principal tactic. He had masterminded other attacks against the United States, including the 1998 bombing of U.S. embassies in Kenya and Tanzania, which left 224 people dead, and the 2000 bombing in Yemen of a U.S. warship called the U.S.S. *Cole*, which killed 17 sailors. The September 11, 2001, attacks were far deadlier. About 2,750 people were killed in New York City alone. The death toll at the Pentagon was 184, and the plane crash in Pennsylvania claimed 40 lives.

THE NATION UNITES

The September 11 attacks left Americans feeling profoundly sad, angry, and vulnerable. But the attacks also drew Americans together. In his first months in office, George W. Bush had governed a deeply divided populace. Increasingly, Americans saw their country as split between Democrats and Republicans. The public was also divided over the tax cuts passed by the president and the Republican-controlled Congress. Democrats claimed the tax cuts mainly benefited the wealthy.

However, 9/11, as the day of the terrorist attacks came to be called, inspired strong feelings of patriotism that united all Americans. The night of the attacks, Bush addressed the country saying, "These [terrorist] acts shattered steel, but they cannot dent the steel of American resolve." Many Americans displayed the flag or wore flag pins. People in countries around the world also condemned the attacks and expressed their solidarity with the United States. On September 12, a French newspaper declared, "We are all Americans."

AMERICAN PLACES
The Freedom Tower New York City

The Freedom Tower, also known as One World Trade Center, is the main building of the rebuilt World Trade Center complex and opened in 2014. At a symbolic 1,776 feet tall, the office building is the tallest in the Western Hemisphere. The tower stands before the 9/11 Memorial, shown in the foreground of this photo. Bronze panels inscribed with the names of the terrorists' victims edge two reflecting pools that sit within the footprints of the original twin towers.

Stories of heroism, sacrifice, and resilience during and after the attacks also drew people together. Many of the stories involved firefighters, police, and other first responders who had rushed bravely into the burning towers of the World Trade Center and led countless people to safety. But when the towers collapsed, more than 400 of the responders lost their own lives. Thousands more later developed severe health problems related to the smoke and toxic dust they inhaled. The collapse of the twin towers released dust containing high levels of lead, mercury, asbestos, and other harmful substances.

The mayor of New York City, Rudy Giuliani, also emerged as a hero. The calm, courage, and humanity he showed after the attacks helped comfort distressed New Yorkers. He spoke with many rescue workers and grieving families and, as victims were buried, attended as many as five funerals a day.

THE AFTERMATH

In the wake of the attacks, U.S. foreign policy, especially on the Middle East, underwent great change. The Bush administration shifted its focus from rival superpowers Russia and China to the connections between terrorist groups such as al Qaeda and **rogue states**. These states included countries, such as Iraq, Iran, and North Korea, that were perceived to violate international law and threaten world peace. Government officials suspected some rogue states of possessing **weapons of mass destruction (WMD)**, or weapons that use nuclear, chemical, or biological substances to harm large numbers of people.

Domestically, the attacks led to a dramatic increase in governmental vigilance. New laws passed during the Bush administration strengthened border and airport security and tightened screening of international travelers. The **USA Patriot Act** greatly expanded the government's powers to conduct surveillance on its own citizens. The act allowed federal agencies to tap the phones of those suspected of terrorist activity. Critics argued that the new policies focusing on national security and defense impinged upon Americans' civil liberties, especially freedom of speech and protection from unreasonable search and seizure.

The attacks also resulted in a rise in hate crimes against Muslims. Although the attacks had been carried out by an Islamic extremist group, some Americans blamed all Muslims for 9/11. Hate crimes were also carried out against those believed to be Muslims—notably Sikhs. Within days of the attacks,

a Sikh gas station owner in Arizona, who had just donated $75 to help 9/11 victims, was shot by a man who had announced his intention to kill Muslims.

Following September 11, the Bush administration embraced the idea of taking pre-emptive, or preventive, military action against countries that harbored or actively supported terrorist groups. In a nationally broadcast speech before Congress 10 days after the attacks, Bush promised a "war on terror." Addressing the leaders of the Taliban, he made a non-negotiable demand: "Deliver to United States authorities all the leaders of al Qaeda who hide in your land." Bush went on to say that if the Taliban refused to hand over the terrorists, the Islamic group would "share in their fate." The president soon took steps to make good on this threat.

HISTORICAL THINKING

1. **READING CHECK** How did foreign and domestic policies change after the 9/11 attacks?

2. **MAKE INFERENCES** Al Qaeda chose its targets for their symbolic value. What do you think the World Trade Center symbolized?

3. **FORM AND SUPPORT OPINIONS** Does the Patriot Act protect U.S. citizens or violate their civil liberties? Research both arguments to formulate a response.

4. **MAKE CONNECTIONS** How do the events leading up to and following 9/11 relate to the U.S. Middle East policy at the time? Use information from this chapter and other sources to explain.

BUILD BACKGROUND

WHY DID THE 9/11 ATTACKS HAPPEN?

After the 9/11 attacks, Americans wanted to know who the attackers were and why they had such anger against the United States. The fact that 15 of the 19 men were from Saudi Arabia, a strategic partner of the United States, and led by Saudi radical Osama bin Laden, was even more mystifying. Reasons for the attacks turned out to be complex, including Cold War politics, U.S. interference in Arab states' affairs, and Israel-Palestine conflicts. The United States entered the Middle East after WWII to help the Persian Gulf states develop their oil resources. As U.S. dependence on this oil grew, U.S. leaders came to regard a steady flow of oil as critical to U.S. national security in the Cold War. The United States began to take a more active role in Middle Eastern affairs, even deposing the elected leaders of some nations to put into place repressive rulers who would support American interests.

Such American actions left many in the Middle East angry and disillusioned about U.S. promises to foster democracy. The 1970s, 1980s, and 1990s saw tensions increase between the United States and the Gulf states as U.S. support for Israel grew and U.S. military bases became permanent fixtures in several states, a fact Saudi Arabia and others resented. From the Arab perspective, U.S. officials failed to understand the religious, cultural, and ethnic complexities of the region. Factions within these countries began funding or harboring radical groups that wanted to form Islamic states and reject all Western interference. The United States became a prime target of this rising militancy.

TEACH

GUIDED DISCUSSION

4. **Summarize** What evidence helped U.S. authorities conclude quickly that al Qaeda and the Taliban were connected to the 9/11 attacks? *(Possible response: Al Qaeda was led by Osama bin Laden, who had stated he wanted end to U.S. influence in the Middle East and had initiated previous attacks on U.S. targets. Authorities also knew that the Taliban supported and sheltered al Qaeda in Afghanistan.)*

5. **Analyze Cause and Effect** What effects did the 9/11 attacks and their aftermath have on the American public? *(Possible response: The attacks briefly helped unite the country. The aftermath sparked a debate about the security measures the government put in place. Hate crimes directed toward Muslims also rose in the aftermath.)*

6. **Analyze Primary Sources** What strategic message might President Bush have wanted his speech to send to U.S. allies in the Middle East and around the world? *(Possible response: Bush may have wanted the world to know he distinguished America's friends from its enemies based on their actions, not on their religion. The true enemies were a network of terrorists and the governments supporting them.)*

AMERICAN PLACES

The Freedom Tower stands 69 stories tall with eight walls—each an isosceles triangle—that create an octagon at the building's vertical center, while the top and bottom are square. Glass prisms that coat the exterior of the tower reflect changing colors of light as the sun moves. A beacon of light shines from the 408-foot spire atop the tower at night as a symbol of the nation's spirit. Visitors can buy tickets to view the city from the enclosed One World Observatory deck on the roof.

ACTIVE OPTIONS

On Your Feet: Presidential Power After 9/11 Direct students to research governmental actions after 9/11 that reflected expansions of presidential powers, such as increasing domestic surveillance. Tell students to analyze debates among historians and commentators regarding whether such acts violate Americans' civil liberties and/or overstep the Constitutional powers of the executive branch of the government. Have students evaluate how the authors of their sources use evidence, distinguishing between sound generalizations and misleading oversimplifications. Then have students use sound evidence from their research to support a position in a debate about whether—and under what conditions—the president has the right to implement measures that might violate civil liberties.

NG Learning Framework: Construct and Test Hypotheses

ATTITUDE Empowerment

KNOWLEDGE Our Human Story

Ask students to generate a hypothesis to explain an aspect of the 9/11 attacks, such as why the attacks happened or why the towers collapsed as they did. Ask students to conduct research using primary and secondary sources to help them construct and find evidence that supports or refutes their hypotheses. Invite students to share their findings in a written or oral presentation.

HISTORICAL THINKING

ANSWERS

1. The focus of U.S. foreign policy shifted from Russia and China to terrorist groups and rogue states. Domestically, the U.S. government enacted policies that strengthened border security, expanded screening of international travelers, and dramatically increased domestic surveillance.

2. Al Qaeda probably chose the Twin Towers as a symbol of American economic power.

3. Answers will vary. Students should support their opinions with evidence and sound reasoning. Possible responses: The USA Patriot Act protects citizens by helping to identify potential terrorists and their plans. The USA Patriot Act goes too far and violates the constitutional protection of freedom of speech and prohibition of unreasonable search and seizure.

4. Answers will vary. Students should include the fact that the U.S. Middle East policy before 9/11, though it included military intervention against Hussein, was subordinate to U.S. concerns about China and Russia. After 9/11, Middle East policy shifted to defeating terrorist networks, a policy that included pre-emptive strikes and implementing the neocons' mission for America in the world.

THE WAR ON TERROR

It was a high-stakes game of hide-and-seek. Osama bin Laden, leader of al Qaeda, was believed to be hiding out somewhere in the mountains of Afghanistan. The U.S. government was determined to find him.

WAR AGAINST THE TALIBAN

Less than a month after September 11, President Bush put his war on terror in motion. The first phase of the war focused on the Southwest Asian country of Afghanistan, which, as you know, was largely controlled by the Taliban. Since the mid-1990s, the group had instituted policies based on a strict interpretation of *shari'a*, or Islamic law, over the Afghani people. These laws enforced the unequal treatment of women and harsh punishments for crimes such as theft. When the Taliban refused to hand over suspected terrorists—and, in particular, Osama bin Laden—the United States initiated Operation Enduring Freedom on October 7, 2001.

The war began with U.S. and British air strikes launched against Taliban and al Qaeda targets in Afghanistan. Within weeks, both the United States and Britain also began sending ground troops to Afghanistan. Soon, other countries, including France and Germany, joined the coalition, while other allies provided intelligence and the use of their military bases. These nations believed the United States had the right to strike those who had supported and sheltered the 9/11 terrorists. By December, the multinational coalition had driven the Taliban out of power. U.S. intelligence services then began an exhaustive but unsuccessful search for bin Laden.

Afghanistan held democratic elections and passed a new constitution, but fighting in the country continued. Taliban insurgents, or rebels, reorganized and took up arms against the coalition forces. More troops went to fight in Afghanistan as the war dragged on and crossed into neighboring Pakistan. Finally, in May 2011, the U.S. military located bin Laden in a compound in Pakistan and killed the al Qaeda leader. Major U.S. combat operations in Afghanistan officially ended in December 2014. It became the longest war the United States had ever fought.

WAR IN IRAQ

While U.S. troops were engaged in Afghanistan, the Bush administration also focused its efforts on Iraq and ousting its brutal president, Saddam Hussein. The Bush administration claimed that Hussein's regime was linked to al Qaeda. Officials also believed Iraq possessed weapons of mass destruction (WMD)

Following the invasion of Iraq and capture of Saddam Hussein, U.S. forces remained in the country to keep order. The U.S. troops shown here are accompanying Iraqi school children in 2009 after attending the reopening of a Baghdad elementary school that had been damaged during the war.

that could be used against the United States. In November 2002, the United Nations demanded that Iraq allow weapons inspectors to search for WMD. The inspectors failed to find any such weapons, but the Bush administration remained skeptical. Vice President Cheney and other neocons didn't trust the Iraqi government. They had called for Hussein's elimination since the Persian Gulf War in 1990.

On March 19, 2003, coalition forces, again led by the United States and Britain, launched strikes against government and military targets in Iraq. This time, though, few other countries joined the coalition. Days later, ground troops invaded the country. Within a few weeks, they had defeated the Iraqi army and brought an end to Saddam Hussein's rule. Hussein himself went into hiding, but he was eventually captured, tried in an Iraqi court, and executed.

After Iraq's defeat, inspectors continued to search for WMD, but none were ever found. Further, no links were uncovered between Hussein's regime and al Qaeda. Many Americans became angry after learning the Bush administration had led the United States into war based on faulty intelligence.

Meanwhile, the United States and Britain occupied Iraq and began rebuilding the country and preparing its people for a democratic form of government. But democracy never really took hold in Iraq. Government corruption and a civil war between the country's two main religious groups, the Sunni Muslims and the Shi'ite Muslims, prevented Iraq from becoming the stable state the United States had envisioned.

The war in Iraq was a major issue in the 2004 presidential election. Bush faced a strong challenge from the Democratic Party's nominee, Senator John Kerry of Massachusetts. Bush won a narrow victory, but his second term got off to a rocky start. As the violence continued in Iraq and more American soldiers died, Bush's approval rating fell. It dropped even further following his mismanagement of the Hurricane Katrina relief effort in August 2005, when the storm flooded low-lying areas of New Orleans where the city's poor and minority populations lived. Tens of thousands of people were left stranded on the tops of buildings, and more than 1,500 died. These factors helped the Democrats gain control of both houses of Congress in the 2006 elections and allowed Democrat Nancy Pelosi of California to become the first female Speaker of the House.

In January 2007, President Bush announced plans for a **surge**, or quick increase, in the number of U.S. troops in Iraq to halt the ongoing fighting and restore security. The United States sent roughly 30,000 additional troops to Iraq, bringing total troop strength to about 170,000, but still the war continued. Soon, however, Bush was forced to shift his focus from Iraq to a crisis at home that threatened the United States with economic collapse.

HISTORICAL THINKING

1. **READING CHECK** What U.S. interests led to the war in Afghanistan?

2. **SYNTHESIZE** How did U.S. involvement in the wars in Afghanistan and Iraq demonstrate neoconservative views?

3. **INTERPRET MAPS** Why were some of the U.S. military bases for operations in Afghanistan located outside of that country?

The War in Afghanistan and the War in Iraq, 2001–2003

Overthrow of Saddam Hussein in Iraq
- Coalition ground forces, March–April 2003
- Special operations forces and airborne forces, March–April 2003

Movement against Taliban in Afghanistan
- Moderate Taliban control, Sept. 2001
- Heavy Taliban control, Sept. 2001
- Northern Alliance control, 2001
- Northern Alliance and U.S. military operations, Oct.–Dec. 2001
- U.S. military bases for operation in Afghanistan

CONNECT TO THE PAST

Discuss with students questions that people in the United States might have wanted the government to answer and what they might have wanted the government to do after 9/11. Ask students to consider the difficulty of setting and executing a course of action on foreign soil. Tell students that in this lesson they will learn about the Bush administration's response to 9/11 and the aftermath of that response.

GUIDED DISCUSSION

1. **Make Connections** How were U.S. actions and outcomes in the war in Afghanistan similar to and different from those of the 1990–1991 Persian Gulf War? *(Possible response: Like the 1990–1991 Persian Gulf War, the United States formed a coalition to defeat an enemy and gained a decisive victory. However, in Afghanistan, the United States was caught in a long-term conflict.)*

2. **Analyze Cause and Effect** What were the likely long-term consequences of the wars for Iraq, Afghanistan, and the United States? *(Possible response: The wars caused destruction, killed citizens, and created the conditions for ongoing civil wars in Iraq and Afghanistan. Mistakes on the part of the United States, such as poor intelligence about WMDs in Iraq, damaged U.S. credibility and influence in the Middle East.)*

INTERPRET MAPS

Direct students' attention to the map in the lesson. Explain that the single-color shading of Iraq indicates control by a single leader, Saddam Hussein. **ASK:** How did the political situation of Afghanistan differ from that of Iraq at the start of each war? *(Possible response: In Afghanistan, the country was divided into different sectors under control of the Taliban and Northern Alliance.)* **ASK:** How might the terrain in Iraq have assisted U.S.-British military operations? *(Possible response: The country is relatively flat, so transport of troops and supplies may have been easier than in mountainous Afghanistan.)*

ACTIVE OPTIONS

On Your Feet: Roundtable Arrange students in groups of four. Assign one student in each group the role of a reporter, a U.S. government official, a coalition military leader, and an Iraqi or Afghani citizen. Instruct students to think about how a person in their assigned role might have experienced one of the wars. Then ask students to answer the following question from their assigned perspective: What did the war on terror accomplish in Iraq and Afghanistan? Encourage students to conduct their own research and draw on information from the lesson to help them answer the question.

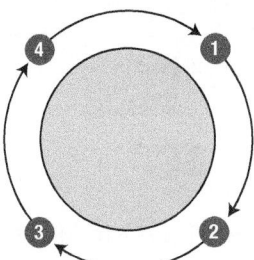

NG Learning Framework: Construct a Time Line

SKILLS Collaboration, Communication

KNOWLEDGE Our Human Story

Have groups of students construct two time lines, one for the war in Iraq and one for the war in Afghanistan, showing major events in the wars from beginning to the present. Then ask students how their time lines reflect changing goals of U.S. Middle East policy—such as nation building, intervention in the government of another country, or fighting terrorist networks—at different points of the conflicts. Invite students to present their time lines to the class.

INCLUSION

Understand a Map Pair inclusion students with partners who can aid in making the text accessible. More proficient students might assist their partners by magnifying or explaining the legend in the map or by pointing out topographical symbols and explaining the information that they indicate. Ask pairs to then work together to answer the Interpret Maps question.

PRE-AP

Write an Explanatory Essay Have students gather information from a variety of primary and secondary sources to write an explanatory essay that summarizes the anticipated and actual course of the Iraq War. Guide students in using unbiased news and fact-based sources to gather information about how top officials imagined the war would proceed and what they imagined a post-war Iraq would look like. Invite volunteers to share their essays with the class.

See the Chapter Planner for more strategies for differentiation.

ANSWERS

1. The United States had strategic and political interests in closing al Qaeda bases, capturing Osama bin Laden, and replacing the repressive Taliban regime with a democracy.

2. Neocons were willing to use military force to spread democratic values and to protect U.S. interests, such as stopping terrorists. They had also wanted to eliminate Saddam Hussein as a destabilizing force in the region since the 1990–1991 Persian Gulf War.

3. U.S. forces launched attacks from bases in Pakistan and Uzbekistan because they were near heavily Taliban-controlled areas of Afghanistan.

NEW ORLEANS, LOUISIANA

Built in a bowl-shaped geographic depression, much of New Orleans lies below sea level. When Hurricane Katrina, the most destructive storm in U.S. history, struck the Gulf Coast on August 29, 2005, it sent a storm surge barreling toward the low-lying city. The floodwaters demolished New Orleans' ineffective levee system, flooding the streets and leaving most of the city underwater. Nearly 2,000 people died in the city and along the Gulf Coast, and more than 1 million lost their homes.

Stranded and desperate for aid that was slow to come, the people of New Orleans felt abandoned by President George W. Bush and the government agencies tasked with providing support during disasters. According to the *New York Times*, "New Orleans became a global symbol of American dysfunction and government negligence. At every level and in every duty, from engineering to social policy to basic logistics, there were revelations of malfunction and failure before, during and after Katrina."

Fortunately, New Orleans has slowly rebounded. Neighborhoods destroyed by flooding, like the Lower Ninth Ward (opposite page), are being rebuilt, and billions of dollars in federal aid have funded new schools and hospitals, replacing some that were in dire need of an overhaul before Katrina even hit. Many residents have also returned—although local demographics have changed dramatically. In 2013, nearly 100,000 fewer African Americans lived in New Orleans than in 2000. Population shifts are common in port towns, but for a city challenged by racial and class inequalities throughout history, the fallout from Katrina has been especially hard to overcome.

While the economic and social impact of the hurricane may affect New Orleans long after the restoration of the city is complete, its music, culture, and character remain strong and dynamic. The bustling, vibrant French Quarter (shown below), filled with music and colorful historic buildings, celebrates the city's distinctive Creole culture and is as unique, diverse, and rich in history as ever. Hundreds of thousands of people flock to New Orleans' legendary Mardi Gras festivities, boosting the city's continued rebuilding efforts with tourism dollars and establishing New Orleans as an example of the strength and resilience of great American cities.

CRITICAL VIEWING What does this 2015 photo of New Orleans' Lower Ninth Ward reveal about its recovery from Katrina and the neighborhood's relationship with the Mississippi River?

CRITICAL VIEWING On Bourbon Street in New Orleans' French Quarter, you might suddenly find yourself marching in a second line parade, made up of people who follow the band just to enjoy the music. What do you observe about the physical and human characteristics of the city from the photos in this lesson, and how might those characteristics have been impacted by Hurricane Katrina?

1125

PLAN: 2-PAGE LESSON

OBJECTIVE

Describe how New Orleans was affected by Hurricane Katrina.

CRITICAL THINKING SKILLS FOR LESSON 2.4

- Analyze Visuals
- Make Connections
- Draw Conclusions
- Synthesize

HISTORICAL THINKING FOR CHAPTER 31

What does it mean to be an American in the 21st century? When Hurricane Katrina flooded New Orleans in 2005, the nation was caught unprepared. Lesson 2.4 discusses how New Orleans has recovered from this natural catastrophe and inadequate government response.

BACKGROUND FOR THE TEACHER

New Orleans is one of the few cities in the United States with mixed French, Spanish, and American heritage, evident in its architecture and culture. It was founded by the French in 1718 and ceded to the Spanish in 1763. Spanish law allowed free African Americans to live and prosper in the city, where they remained free after Louisiana was sold to the United States in 1803. By the 1850s, New Orleans was the wealthiest city in the United States, important in U.S. shipping to the Caribbean, South America, and Europe. In the 20th century, new pump technology, levees, and canals allowed New Orleans to expand into areas below sea level. After World War II, racial conflicts drove many whites to the suburbs, leaving a large African-American population in the core area that was most vulnerable to Hurricane Katrina.

HISTORY NOTEBOOK

Encourage students to complete the American Places page for Chapter 31 in their History Notebooks as they read.

INTRODUCE & ENGAGE

BEFORE AND AFTER PHOTOS

Have students look at photographs online of the Ninth Ward of New Orleans before Hurricane Katrina and during the flooding, and compare them with the photograph in this lesson. Discuss with students what the "before" and "after" photos show about changes in the Ninth Ward's population and economic conditions. Explain that this lesson describes New Orleans' experience during and after Katrina.

TEACH

GUIDED DISCUSSION

1. **Draw Conclusions** What natural and human-made physical characteristics of New Orleans made the hurricane such a disaster? *(Possible response: A combination of being below sea level, the Mississippi River, which provided a waterway for storm surges, and the ineffective levee system meant that a powerful hurricane would be a disaster for New Orleans.)*

2. **Synthesize** How did federal government responses to Katrina affect the population of New Orleans? *(Possible responses: Federal agencies were slow in providing help, which probably increased the storm's death toll. Federal aid after the storm helped slowly rebuild the city, but by that time, 100,000 African Americans had permanently left the city, changing its demographics.)*

AMERICAN PLACES

One of the lowest parts of the city, the Lower Ninth Ward is cut off from the rest of New Orleans by a shipping channel of the Mississippi River, shown in the photograph. When Katrina hit, the wall of the shipping canal burst and inundated the neighborhood for weeks. While most of New Orleans has recovered since 2005, the Ninth Ward has not. Some lots where buildings once stood are now vacant, and some homes are only partially rebuilt, consequences of federal money proving inadequate for current construction costs and unscrupulous contractors who defrauded some residents. Many small businesses permanently left the ward. Some recovery has taken place, with a drugstore, a new high school, and a new community center now serving the area.

ACTIVE OPTIONS

On Your Feet: Three-Step Interview Organize students into two groups to investigate how the human characteristics of New Orleans have changed since Katrina. Assign one group to research what role federal, state, and local governments played in New Orleans' population shift. Assign the other group to research elements of the city's culture that have been lost and gained in the population shift. Then ask students to form pairs to interview each other about their assigned topics. At the end, each pair will share with the class what they learned from their partners.

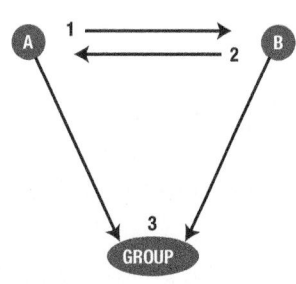

NG Learning Framework: Investigate New Orleans' Levees STEM

SKILL Communication

KNOWLEDGE Our Human Story

Tell students to research the Army Corps of Engineers' levee systems used in New Orleans. Ask students to describe the engineering design of the old system and why it failed and the new levee system and how it changed the physical characteristics of New Orleans. Ask students to explore how local, state, and federal governments were involved in levee design and repairs, and whether people think the city is safer than before Katrina. Have them share their work with the class.

DIFFERENTIATE

ENGLISH LANGUAGE LEARNERS ELD

Create a Word Web Pair students at the **Emerging** and **Expanding** levels with students at the **Bridging** level. Tell students to take turns reading sentences in the first paragraph of the lesson, noting words and terms referring to the geographic location of New Orleans and writing them on the spokes of a Word Web. Tell students to look up unfamiliar words and terms in a dictionary or encyclopedia and to add notes and illustrations that aid their understanding. Have pairs trade and compare Word Webs.

PRE-AP

Connect Past, Present, and Future Instruct students to use online sources to learn more about the unique geography of New Orleans, focusing on both its geologic history and its history as a U.S. city. Ask students to consider the city's possible future, given that it is located below sea level and surrounded by water. Tell students to use their research to write a report that connects the geography and history to a possible future for New Orleans. Invite students to share their reports with the class. Use students' reports to spur discussion of the increasing threat to coastal communities around the world.

See the Chapter Planner for more strategies for differentiation.

CRITICAL VIEWING Possible responses: All the houses look new, indicating that all the old ones were destroyed. Some plots of land are still vacant, showing recovery is not complete. The Mississippi is close, constituting both a shipping channel and a flood threat.

CRITICAL VIEWING Possible responses: Physical characteristics include the Spanish and French architecture and the openness of Bourbon Street to pedestrians. Human characteristics include music, spontaneity, celebration, and diversity of people. Katrina impacted both types by damaging the buildings and changing the city's population.

THE GREAT RECESSION

We all know that bubbles burst pretty quickly. In the first years of the 21st century, a housing bubble developed, fueled by the high demand for new homes. When the bubble burst, it had terrible consequences for the country's economy.

In 2009, a woman in San Antonio, Texas, wrote these words on her house to announce she was facing foreclosure. She had recently lost her job and could no longer make her mortgage payments.

HOUSING MARKET RISE AND FALL

The housing market crash was many years in the making. Banks and other lenders had begun to adopt unwise economic policies and lending strategies—mostly related to home-buying—in the 1980s and 1990s. These practices continued into the first decade of the 2000s, setting the stage for the economic problems that developed in 2007, toward the end of George W. Bush's second term.

Owning a home is a big part of the American dream, but rates of homeownership are usually significantly lower among minorities and people with low incomes. Spurred by their own business interests and by affordable-housing goals established by the federal government, lenders took steps to increase the pool of potential home buyers. They relaxed down-payment and employment-history requirements and began to offer more **subprime mortgages**, or home loans to buyers with poor credit history. To entice people to buy, banks also offered loans with low initial interest rates, called adjustable-rate mortgages. After a certain period of time, though, the interest rates on these loans would be raised, increasing the borrowers' payments—often to amounts few could afford.

Although subprime mortgages were risky, banks felt comfortable offering them because they could sell many of the mortgages to two government-sponsored enterprises: Fannie Mae (the Federal National Mortgage Association) and Freddie Mac (the Federal Home Loan Mortgage Corporation). Wall Street investment banks bundled groups of mortgages into what they called "managed packages" and sold them on the international financial market as profitable but highly unstable investments. An **investment bank** is a financial institution that purchases and sells stocks and bonds and helps other companies raise capital and manage their assets.

As demand for housing increased, prices rose dramatically. The widespread belief was that rising prices would cause the real estate to increase significantly in value. But then the bubble burst in 2007, and housing prices fell. Increasing numbers of subprime mortgage holders found they could not afford their loan payments. To make matters worse, they could not sell their homes. There were too many homes up for sale at the same time, and demand was low. Housing prices tumbled. Many of these homes went into foreclosure—that is, the banks took possession of them because the buyers could no longer make their house payments. Millions of families lost their homes to foreclosure. The housing market crash triggered a severe recession that, because of globalization, spread quickly around the world. Japan and many countries in Europe were hit especially hard due to their strong financial and trade ties to the United States. Echoing the Great Depression of the 1930s, the downturn became known as the **Great Recession**.

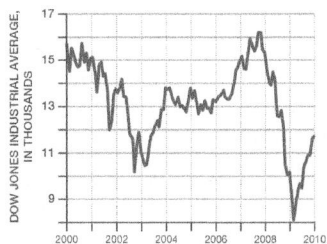

Stock Market Index, 2000–2010

DOW JONES INDUSTRIAL AVERAGE, IN THOUSANDS

17
15
13
11
9

2000   2002   2004   2006   2008   2010

Source: Federal Reserve Bank of St. Louis

LOOMING ECONOMIC COLLAPSE

The Great Recession grew steadily worse in 2008. Many small banks went bankrupt, and other banks severely limited their lending. Wall Street financial institutions that had invested heavily in managed packages tied to subprime mortgages suffered huge losses. Plunging real estate prices meant that Americans could no longer finance major purchases such as cars by borrowing against the value of their homes. As a result, the recession also devastated the American automobile industry. A reduction in spending by wary consumers hurt many other industries, including those related to travel, construction, and home furnishings. Many companies were forced to make cuts, and millions of people lost their jobs. As government revenues shrank, cities and states also cut their budgets and laid off workers. As a result, the unemployment rate climbed to around 10 percent.

The terrible state of the economy raised the concern that some investment banks were "too big to fail." And if they did, many economists believed the country's entire financial system would collapse. But after some powerful firms did go bankrupt, Congress passed the Emergency Economic Stabilization Act (EESA) of 2008. This act, which Bush signed into law in October, provided the Treasury Department with up to $700 billion to buy mortgages and other "troubled assets," or unstable investments, from banks. The legislation also established the Troubled Asset Relief Program (TARP), designed to help individuals and businesses secure bank loans. But much of this money was used to save large investment banks. The costly **bailout** spurred widespread resentment. Some critics blamed the recession on the greed of the banks and argued that the government should have let them fail.

While the bailout was being debated, the stock market plunged on September 29. The crash erased much of the savings ordinary Americans had been counting on. The recession affected almost everyone. And with so many people unemployed and in debt, the recession and the persistence of poverty became the main issues of the 2008 presidential election.

HISTORICAL THINKING

1. **READING CHECK** Why were lenders eager to offer subprime mortgages to potential buyers?

2. **FORM AND SUPPORT OPINIONS** Who do you think played the biggest role in the housing market crash: home buyers, mortgage companies, or investment banks? Explain.

3. **INTERPRET GRAPHS** How many points did the stock market plunge between 2008 and 2009?

PLAN: 2-PAGE LESSON

OBJECTIVE

Understand the causes and effects of the Great Recession.

CRITICAL THINKING SKILLS FOR LESSON 3.1

- Form and Support Opinions
- Interpret Graphs
- Ask and Answer Questions
- Evaluate

HISTORICAL THINKING FOR CHAPTER 31

What does it mean to be an American in the 21st century? Americans experienced an economic downturn in the beginning of the 21st century. Lesson 3.1 discusses the causes of the Great Recession and its effects on Americans.

BACKGROUND FOR THE TEACHER

California played a central role in the housing bubble. The state ended up with more foreclosures and bad loans than any other state, in part because it has the largest housing sector in the country. California lenders also issued more than half of all subprime mortgages from 2005 to 2007, spurred in part by the exceptionally high price of California housing. A single California-based financial institution, Countrywide Savings, issued more mortgages than any other U.S. lender. Many Californians bought homes with no down payment or with adjustable mortgages that increased during the life of the mortgage. Any downturn in income was likely to result in foreclosure. When the bubble burst, the majority of the top 10 bank failures in the United States were California mortgage banks.

FINANCIAL LITERACY

To extend their knowledge and understanding about the concepts in this lesson, refer students to the Financial Literacy handbook.

INTRODUCE & ENGAGE

ACTIVATE PRIOR KNOWLEDGE

Ask students what they know about the Great Depression. *(At 12 years, it was the world's longest and deepest economic downturn, resulting from the stock market crash in October 1929.)* Invite students to name some of the causes and effects of the Great Depression that they learned about in earlier lessons. Use a Cause-and-Effect Chart like the one shown to record their responses. Then tell students that they will read about the Great Recession, a more recent economic downturn that was similar in many ways to the Great Depression.

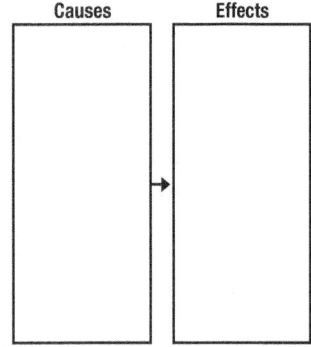

Causes | Effects

TEACH

GUIDED DISCUSSION

1. **Ask and Answer Questions** Read about cost-benefit analysis in the Financial Literacy handbook. List questions you could ask to help gather the information needed to make a sound decision when buying a house. *(Answers will vary but should reflect the process of making economic choices.)*

2. **Evaluate** Do you think the bailout benefited average Americans during the Great Recession? Support your answer with information from the text. *(Possible responses: No. Many average- to low-income Americans lost their jobs, their savings, or both, while large investment banks were rescued. Yes. The bailout kept the recession from getting worse.)*

INTERPRET GRAPHS

Point out the graph showing the average stock market prices during the first decade of the 21st century. **ASK:** When were stocks at their highest and their lowest? *(highest in 2008 and lowest in 2009)* **ASK:** How does the graph reflect the Great Recession? *(Stock prices fell sharply when the recession was at its worst.)*

ACTIVE OPTIONS

On Your Feet: Play a Recession Word Game Arrange students in small groups. Give each group nine sheets of paper and tell them to mark each with a letter in the word *recession* so that the sheets, when placed in order, will spell out the word. Explain that on each sheet, teams should write a sentence or phrase about the Great Recession that begins with the letter on the sheet. For example, they might write on the *O* sheet, "Owners of homes experienced foreclosure." (Allow students to use this sentence if they wish.) Announce a time limit for teams to write their sentences, and when time is up, tell each team to line up and display their sheets in the proper order. Teams missing sentences for one or more letters should note what other teams used.

NG Learning Framework: Write a News Article

ATTITUDE Curiosity

KNOWLEDGE Our Human Story

Encourage students to learn more about the Great Recession. Tell students to work in pairs to frame a list of questions they have about how the recession affected Americans from both low-income and high-income households. Encourage pairs to use library resources or conduct online research from multiple sources to find answers to their questions. Have pairs synthesize the information into a short news article and share their article in a class blog or live presentation.

DIFFERENTIATE

STRIVING READERS

Understand Cause and Effect Provide pairs with a Cause-and-Effect Chain to complete as they reread the lesson. Tell students to note specific practices and events that caused the collapse of the housing market and subsequent high unemployment rate. Invite students to share their Cause-and-Effect Chains with other pairs and discuss any differences.

GIFTED & TALENTED

Create an Editorial Cartoon Tell students that the phrase "too big to fail" was often used during the economic crisis of 2008 and is still used when referring to the bailout of large companies, a process that often involves taxpayer money. Instruct students to research the phrase and find examples of specific businesses that the government rescued from their own mistakes. Prompt students to think about the reasons large companies should or should not be considered "too big to fail" and how a small business owner might feel about large businesses being rescued from their own mistakes. Then challenge students to draw an editorial cartoon that conveys their point of view. They might incorporate the phrase in the cartoon or use it as a caption. You might then have students collaborate on creating a format to present their cartoons to the class.

See the Chapter Planner for more strategies for differentiation.

HISTORICAL THINKING

ANSWERS

1. Lenders were eager to sell those managed packages of bundled subprime mortgages to investment banks to make a profit.

2. Answers will vary. Possible response: Mortgage companies were the most responsible because they created the terms of the adjustable-rate loans that proved disastrous to many home buyers. They were more concerned with making a profit and helping investment banks grow their assets.

3. The stock market plunged 6,000 points between 2008 and 2009.

THE ELECTION OF 2008

At the beginning of 2008, an atmosphere of gloom hung over the United States. The Great Recession was worsening, and the war in Iraq was dragging into its sixth year. As the 2008 election approached, many Americans were ready for a change.

HISTORY IS MADE

With George W. Bush's approval rating around 30 percent, Democrats felt they had the advantage over Republicans in 2008. The early Democratic favorite was New York senator Hillary Clinton, wife of former president William Clinton. She faced a strong challenge, however, from Senator **Barack Obama** of Illinois. A historic outcome was guaranteed. If Clinton won, she would become the first female nominated for president by a major party. If Obama won, he would become the first African American nominated by a major party.

On election night, November 4, 2008, President-elect Barack Obama delivered his victory speech before 240,000 people gathered in Chicago's Grant Park. With his family beside him, Obama said, "If there is anyone out there who still doubts that America is a place where all things are possible; who still wonders if the dream of our founders is alive in our time; who still questions the power of our democracy, tonight is your answer."

Ceding many of the most populated states to Clinton, Obama focused his efforts on winning as many convention delegates as he could in less populous states. The strategy worked. Even though Clinton won the popular vote in the primaries, Obama secured more convention delegates and thus became the Democratic nominee. For his vice-presidential running mate, he chose Senator Joe Biden of Delaware.

On the Republican side, the leading candidates in the primary elections included former Massachusetts governor Mitt Romney, former Arkansas governor Mike Huckabee, and Senator John McCain of Arizona. McCain eventually secured the Republican nomination, winning all but one of the final 21 primaries. For his running mate, he chose Alaska governor Sarah Palin, who was not well known outside her home state. Her controversial remarks, however, quickly brought her a great deal of public attention. The outspoken Palin drew large crowds to her campaign speeches.

Both presidential candidates addressed the financial crisis facing the nation. But while McCain seemed uncertain about what measures he would take, Obama's focused, confident response to the crisis won over many voters. With his message of hope and change, Obama won the election in November with relative ease and became the first African-American president in the country's 232-year history.

OBAMA'S PRIORITIES

One of Obama's top priorities as president was to lead the country out of the Great Recession. Soon after taking office, he signed into law the American Recovery and Reinvestment Act, which authorized $787 billion in government spending as an **economic stimulus**, or a measure aimed at promoting and enabling financial recovery and growth. The act was designed to save existing jobs and to create new ones. Obama and the federal government also bailed out the auto industry, providing $80 billion to the three major U.S. automakers to prevent them from failing. By the end of Obama's two terms as president, the unemployment rate had dropped to 5 percent, and the auto industry had recovered—and repaid the bailout money.

Initiating comprehensive health care reform was another of Obama's goals. Like Bill Clinton, the new president sought to extend the scope of the government and provide health care insurance for all U.S. citizens. In a speech to Congress in September 2009, he pointed out that more than

30 million Americans lacked health insurance. He also spoke of rising health care costs, unethical insurance practices and claims, and the heavy burden government programs such as Medicare and Medicaid put on taxpayers. The House passed a health care bill in early November, and on Christmas Eve, the Senate passed its own version of the bill.

A development in Massachusetts, however, threatened to doom the legislation. Scott Brown, a conservative Republican, won a special election to fill the vacancy created by the death of Democratic Senator Edward Kennedy, the brother of John and Robert Kennedy. By picking up a seat in the Senate, Republicans gained the ability to block legislation through the use of filibusters. Congressional Democrats, meanwhile, retreated from their commitment to health care reform.

Prospects for passage of the president's initiative seemed bleak. However, the determination of Speaker of the House Nancy Pelosi and Obama's persistence helped secure the passage of a health care package in March 2010. The bill that Obama signed into law was called the **Patient Protection and Affordable Care Act (PPACA)**, but it became popularly known as Obamacare. Although Republicans tried to block it through legislation and in the federal courts, the act had provided health insurance coverage to nearly 20 million Americans by 2016.

Passage of the Affordable Care Act and other progressive bills inspired the rise of a conservative populist movement known as the **Tea Party**. It was not a formal organization but rather a loose confederation of individuals and groups united by their antigovernment, antitax, and anti-immigration views. Most of those in the grassroots movement were Republicans who hoped to influence the direction of the party. Energized by the fast-growing Tea Party, Republicans gained 6 seats in the Senate and took control of the House by picking up 63 seats there in the 2010 midterm elections. As a result, Obama would face strong opposition to many of his initiatives during the rest of his time in office.

HISTORICAL THINKING

1. **READING CHECK** What factors helped Obama win the 2008 presidential election?

2. **EVALUATE** How did President Obama seek to address U.S. poverty and economic problems?

3. **MAKE INFERENCES** How do you think most members of the Tea Party felt about the economic stimulus legislation and Obamacare?

PLAN: 2-PAGE LESSON

OBJECTIVE

Examine how Barack Obama became the first African-American president and what his priorities were following his election.

CRITICAL THINKING SKILLS FOR LESSON 3.2

- Evaluate
- Make Inferences
- Identify Problems and Solutions

HISTORICAL THINKING FOR CHAPTER 31

What does it mean to be an American in the 21st century? In 2008, the United States elected its first African-American president. Lesson 3.2 discusses the historic election of Barack Obama and the two priorities of President Obama's first term.

BACKGROUND FOR THE TEACHER

With Republicans in control of Congress after 2010, President Obama relied on executive orders to move his initiatives forward. In his first term alone, the president issued 147 executive orders. Among these orders, his "Mini-Dream Act" addressed the deportation of immigrants, and his "We Can't Wait" action (an obvious reference to a dysfunctional Congress), raised automotive fuel efficiency standards and placed a cap on student loans. When Congress refused to confirm the president's appointments, Obama made several while Congress was in recess. Three of the recess appointments breathed new life into the National Labor Relations Board, which had been inactive due to unfilled positions. In addition, Obama utilized the Antiquities Act of 1906 to name as a national monument the Chimney Rock Archaeological Area in Colorado and to dedicate the César E. Chávez National Monument in California.

INTRODUCE & ENGAGE

ASSESS NATIONAL PRIORITIES

Engage students in a brief discussion of national priorities. **ASK:** If you were to become president tomorrow, what would your priorities be for the United States, and why? *(Answers will vary but should reflect current issues and reasonable goals.)* Following the discussion, tell students that they will read about President Obama's priorities following his election in 2008.

TEACH

GUIDED DISCUSSION

1. **Identify Problems and Solutions** What problem did Obama face while running in the Democratic presidential primary, and how did he solve it? *(Obama had to figure out how to win the nomination when running against Hillary Clinton, who was the Democratic favorite. Obama acknowledged that Clinton would win several large states, so he focused on winning enough convention delegates from the states with smaller populations to secure the nomination.)*

2. **Make Inferences** What do you think were some of the causes that contributed to nearly 30 million Americans having no health insurance coverage prior to the passage of the Affordable Care Act? *(Possible response: They may not have been able to obtain coverage due to insurance industry restrictions, because they were unemployed as a result of the Great Recession, or because they were not covered by employers and could not afford private insurance.)*

MORE INFORMATION

American Recovery and Reinvestment Act Share details about the results of the American Recovery and Reinvestment Act. Five years after it was signed, the stimulus had achieved the following:

- created or saved 1.6 million jobs annually through 2012
- upgraded infrastructure, including more than 40,000 miles of roads and 2,700 bridges
- brought almost 700 potable water systems into compliance with federal standards for clean water
- introduced high-speed Internet to institutions in approximately 20,000 communities
- provided tax cuts to families and unemployment benefits to people who needed help due to the poor economy

Challenge students to further research the act and to conduct a cost-benefit analysis of one aspect of it. Remind students that they may wish to reread the section on cost-benefit analysis in the Financial Literacy handbook.

ACTIVE OPTIONS

On Your Feet: Jigsaw Group students evenly into "expert" groups. Assign each group one of Obama's first-term priorities to research in depth. Regroup students so that each new group has at least one member from each expert group. Invite experts to report on their assigned priority.

NG Learning Framework: Track the Evolution of the Presidency

SKILLS Observation, Communication

KNOWLEDGE Our Human Story

Have students work in pairs or groups to view online video clips or excerpts from notable convention or inaugural addresses of presidents Nixon, Carter, Reagan, George H.W. Bush, Clinton, George W. Bush, Obama, and Trump. Tell groups to develop a tally sheet to track continuity and change over time in the tone, goals, and problems that each president identifies in his address. Instruct students to use the information to create digital or large paper graphs or infographics accompanied by text that address the following question: How has the presidency changed, and how has it stayed the same? Share groups' digital work in a class website or blog or display print infographics in the classroom.

DIFFERENTIATE

ENGLISH LANGUAGE LEARNERS

Understand Homophones Instruct students at **All Proficiencies** to keep a chart of homophones in their notebook, noting the meaning of each of the two or more words that sound the same. Bring students' attention to the sentence in the lesson beginning with the word *ceding*, and ask them to think of any words that sound the same. *(seeding)* Tell students to add these words to their charts. Point out that they can determine the meaning of *ceding* (to yield or give up) from the context and from the Latin root *cede*, which is the root of other words they may be familiar with, such as *recede/recession* and *concede/concession*.

GIFTED & TALENTED

Interpret a Quotation Direct students' attention to the quotation from President Obama's victory speech in the photograph caption. Challenge students to interpret the quotation with a drawing, collage, meme, or other visual. Alternatively, they could adapt the quotation and use it in an original poem, song, or rap. Encourage students to present their interpretations to the class. Discuss how the different interpretations enhance and extend the meaning of Obama's words.

See the Chapter Planner for more strategies for differentiation.

HISTORICAL THINKING

ANSWERS

1. Obama's confidence and reasonable plans for solutions to the nation's economic problems appealed to many voters.

2. Obama authorized an economic stimulus package to promote financial recovery and growth. The package was designed to save existing jobs and create new ones. Providing health care to all U.S. citizens constituted a way to alleviate the burden of the cost of health care for the poor.

3. Possible response: Since members of the Tea Party believed in smaller government and lower taxes, most would not have been happy that the government had authorized a stimulus package and taken on the responsibility of insuring most Americans.

BARACK HUSSEIN OBAMA II 1961–
MICHELLE LAVAUGHN ROBINSON OBAMA 1964–

"If you were going to list the 100 most popular things that I have done as president, being married to Michelle Obama is number one."—Barack Obama

The president probably wasn't exaggerating. When Barack Obama's approval numbers were at their lowest in 2013—due to controversies over both his domestic and foreign policies—his wife, Michelle, still drew adoring crowds wherever she appeared in public. Initially reluctant to embrace Washington and relinquish her own career, Michelle threw her full support behind her husband when he first ran for the presidency. Barack and Michelle entered the White House as a team, but their path to its door could hardly have been more different.

EARLY LIVES
Barack Obama had an unsettled childhood. His parents met as students at the University of Hawaii. His mother, Ann Dunham, was a white American from Kansas. His father, Barack Obama, Sr., was a black African from Kenya. The couple divorced when their child was two years old, and Barack had very little contact with his father after that. His mother later married an Indonesian, and the family lived in Indonesia for a time. Then, when Barack was 10, his mother sent him to live with his grandparents in Hawaii. She eventually returned to Hawaii and her parents' home after divorcing her second husband. Barack's parents died when he was a young man: his father in 1982, his mother in 1995.

By contrast, Michelle Obama grew up in a stable, close-knit family. Her parents, Marian and Fraser

The Obamas stroll along the Colonnade of the White House in 2010. In his final speech, the president told his wife, "You have made me proud, and you have made the country proud."

Robinson, raised their children in a small house in Chicago. Michelle and her brother, Craig, slept in the living room and strung up a sheet to divide the space and provide some privacy. Education was a priority in the Robinson home, and both children did well in school. Michelle would later say, "I liked being smart. I thought being smart was cooler than anything in the world."

Barack Obama pursued education as well. After graduating from Columbia University in New York City and working as a community organizer in Chicago, he enrolled in Harvard Law School in 1988. After his first year at Harvard, he interned at a law firm in Chicago. His supervisor was Michelle Robinson, and he was immediately attracted to her. At first, Michelle resisted his advances, but eventually the pair fell in love. They married in 1992. Meanwhile, Barack completed his law degree at Harvard. Soon he decided to enter politics.

POTUS and FLOTUS
Running as a Democrat, Obama won an Illinois state senate seat in 1996. Then, in 2004, he was elected to the U.S. Senate representing Illinois. That same year he gave the keynote speech at the Democratic National Convention to endorse presidential candidate John Kerry. However, the speech is best remembered for launching Obama onto the national stage and paving the way for his successful presidential run in 2008. In his speech, he delivered a message of unity that resonated with many Americans: "There's not a liberal America and a conservative America—there's the United States of America. There's not a black America and white America and Latino America and Asian America; there's the United States of America." Because of speeches like this, Obama is considered one of the most powerful orators of his generation.

As you know, Obama faced a host of political issues when he became president of the United States (POTUS), but he also endured challenges to the legitimacy of his presidency. Members of the so-called "birther movement" claimed the president had not been born in the United States and so was ineligible to hold the office. Some birthers also asserted that Obama was Muslim, a charge designed to suggest the president was somehow "un-American." Despite concrete evidence disproving birther allegations—his Hawaiian birth certificate, for example—the contentions dogged Obama throughout his presidency.

While lies swirled during his presidency, Obama depended on Michelle—his "rock," as he called her—to help keep him grounded. Levelheaded and funny, Michelle was not part of what Obama called the

Michelle often accompanied her husband on state visits, including this trip in March 2011 to the Central American country of El Salvador. Here, shortly after their arrival in the country's capital of San Salvador, the POTUS and FLOTUS greet school children waving American flags.

"silliness of Washington." As first lady of the United States (FLOTUS), Michelle undertook an initiative called "Let's Move" to get kids to exercise and eat healthy foods. She and the POTUS also protected the privacy of their daughters, Malia and Sasha, as they grew up in the White House.

At the end of his second term, Obama delivered a farewell address in Chicago. After encouraging Americans not to take their democracy for granted, he said: "I do have one final ask of you as your president—the same thing I asked when you took a chance on me eight years ago. I am asking you to believe. Not in my ability to bring about change—but in yours." And in her final speech, Michelle Obama had a special message, based on her own experience, for young Americans: "Empower yourself with a good education. Then get out there and use that education to build a country worthy of your boundless promise. Lead by example with hope: never fear."

HISTORICAL THINKING

1. **READING CHECK** How did Barack and Michelle Obama's early lives differ?

2. **MAKE INFERENCES** What does Barack Obama's speech at the Democratic National Convention suggest about politics in the country at that time?

3. **EVALUATE** What false charges were leveled against President Obama, and what did those who alleged them hope to accomplish?

PLAN: 2-PAGE LESSON

OBJECTIVE
Recount how Barack and Michelle Obama used their voices to inspire Americans.

CRITICAL THINKING SKILLS FOR LESSON 3.3
- Make Inferences
- Evaluate
- Identify
- Synthesize

HISTORICAL THINKING FOR CHAPTER 31
What does it mean to be an American in the 21st century? Americans often say that any child could grow up to be president, and Barack and Michele Obama's childhoods suggest the aphorism is true. Lesson 3.3 describes the Obamas' backgrounds and their work as president and first lady of the United States.

BACKGROUND FOR THE TEACHER
While American presidents are elected to lead, first ladies receive no such mandate. Nevertheless, these high-profile women have a unique opportunity to initiate programs of their own, and they have often used their energy and their voices to do so. First Lady Dolley Madison set a precedent for dedication to America's youth with her support of the Washington City Orphan Asylum during the presidency of her husband, James Madison (1809–1817). Many first ladies followed suit, including Michelle Obama. Her initiatives aimed at improving the lives of young people include *Let's Move!, Reach Higher,* and, in conjunction with the president, *Let Girls Learn.* Mrs. Obama also worked with the vice president's wife, Dr. Jill Biden, to launch *Joining Forces* in support of service members and veterans.

HISTORY NOTEBOOK
Encourage students to complete the American Voices page for Chapter 31 in their History Notebooks as they read.

PREVIEW USING VISUALS

Ask students to examine the photographs that accompany the lesson. **ASK:** What do the two photos suggest about the Obamas' relationship? *(Possible responses: They have a fondness for and feel close to one another. They work as a team.)* **ASK:** How do you think Michelle's presence enhanced her husband's initiatives during state visits such as the one shown here? *(Possible response: It appears that she engaged well with young people and created goodwill.)*

TEACH

GUIDED DISCUSSION

1. **Identify** As young people, what was important to both Barack and Michelle, and how was that priority expressed after Obama was elected? Support your answer with information from the text. *(They both valued education. Michelle thought that being smart was cool. Both studied law, which helped Obama become a legislator and president. As first lady, Michelle Obama promoted the importance of education.)*

2. **Synthesize** How did the Obamas express optimism in their final speeches as POTUS and FLOTUS? *(Possible response: Barack Obama expressed belief in the ability of Americans to effect change. Michelle Obama expressed belief that a good education is the key to building a great country.)*

AMERICAN VOICES

American presidents have long used their voices to persuade, to educate, and to move the country forward. For example, on March 12, 1933, Franklin Delano Roosevelt broadcast the first of his "fireside chats" to inform and rally Americans during the Great Depression. Abraham Lincoln's 1863 Gettysburg Address, which dedicated the Soldiers' National Cemetery, resonates to this day. **ASK:** What makes a speech great? *(Answers will vary but may include subject, organization, clarity, choice of words, or emotional appeal.)* List the characteristics and qualities students name on the board as a basis for discussion. **ASK:** Do you think Barack Obama will take his place in history as one of America's great orators? *(Answers will vary. Students should support their opinions with information from the text.)*

ACTIVE OPTIONS

On Your Feet: Two Options Label one location in the room with the following quotation from Barack Obama: "I am asking you to believe. Not in my ability to bring about change— but in yours." Label another area with this quotation from Michelle Obama: "Lead by example with hope: never fear." Invite students to walk to the corner of the room with the quotation they would most like to discuss. Arrange students in each corner into small groups. Tell them to discuss how they might apply the quote to their own lives, either in the present or in the future. For example, they might launch a school initiative or run for a position in local government. Have a student from each small group share a summary of the group's ideas with the class.

NG Learning Framework: Analyze an Obama Speech

SKILL Communication

KNOWLEDGE Our Human Story

Tell students to read and/or watch a video of one of the speeches Obama made during his years as president. For example, students might choose Obama's First Inaugural Address or a speech on national security, the Affordable Care Act, or immigration reform. Prompt students to write a short essay citing the purpose of the speech they chose and explaining why the speech is effective. Students should also select an excerpt from the speech that illustrates Obama's skill as an orator, read the excerpt to the class, and explain why they chose it.

DIFFERENTIATE
STRIVING READERS

Summarize Instruct students to work in pairs to read and summarize the text and captions. Tell students to write at least three notes for each of the two sections of the lesson. Guide students to first create a summary statement for each section and then a summary statement for the entire lesson. Invite pairs to compare their summary statements and note any similarities and differences.

PRE-AP

Research and Report on Impacts After they read the lesson, have students write three questions they have about the impact that Barack or Michelle Obama had on the United States. The questions should seek a deeper understanding of the priorities and motivations of the president or first lady. Then have students conduct online research to answer their questions. Direct students to summarize their findings in a report that analyzes the impact of the president or first lady during the Obama administration (2008–2016) or explores their continuing impact.

See the Chapter Planner for more strategies for differentiation.

HISTORICAL THINKING

ANSWERS

1. The son of divorced parents, Barack hardly saw his father and lived for several years with his grandparents. Michelle came from a stable, close-knit family and grew up in Chicago.

2. Obama's speech suggests that the country was divided by politics and race.

3. Some people falsely claimed that Obama had not been born in the United States and therefore was ineligible to serve as president. Another false claim was that Obama was Muslim. Accusers wanted to make his presidency illegitimate and paint him as un-American.

CIVIL RIGHTS IN THE 21ST CENTURY

To oppressed people around the world, the United States symbolizes freedom and opportunity. Some Americans, however, are still denied their full rights as citizens. The fight for these rights goes on.

ADVANCES AND SETBACKS FOR WOMEN

Women have made great strides in gaining their civil rights in recent decades. In business, some have broken through the "glass ceiling"—an invisible barrier of attitudes and prejudices that prevents women and minorities from advancing to high-level positions. In 1998, for instance, Meg Whitman was named president and chief executive officer of a major online auction company. The following year, Carly Fiorina was appointed head of a giant software and computer services company. Women continue to increase their representation in politics as well. Since 1990, about half of the 50 states have elected female governors. In 2007, as you've learned, Congresswoman Nancy Pelosi became the first female Speaker of the House. And in 2016, women held about 20 percent of the seats in Congress.

Nevertheless, little progress has been made in other areas. For decades, women have been demanding equal pay for equal work. They make up about half of the American workforce and are the main wage-earners in roughly 4 of every 10 families. Yet white women are paid about 20 percent less than men, African-American women earn around 35 percent less, and Latinas make about 40 percent less.

As more women have moved into the workforce, access to affordable, quality childcare has also posed a significant problem, especially for low-income women. Although traditional ideas about the family structure and gender roles in society are changing, the primary responsibility for taking care of children is still more often assumed by women than by men. This means that women face a greater challenge in balancing work and family commitments. In a 2015 survey, the majority of women said that being a working parent made it harder for them to advance in their career.

Legal access to abortion was one of the most divisive issues in the United States in the second half of the 20th century, and it remains so in the 21st. Despite being challenged many times, the landmark 1973 Supreme Court ruling in *Roe* v. *Wade*, which legalized abortion nationwide, has never been overturned. The Department of Health and Human Services, at both the federal and state levels, has provided family planning and pregnancy prevention and care programs. However, some lawmakers have tried to cut off the funding for such programs. In addition, many states have passed laws restricting women's access to abortion.

THE AMERICANS WITH DISABILITIES ACT

In 1990, President George H.W. Bush signed the Americans with Disabilities Act (ADA), which granted civil rights for Americans with a disability, defined as "a physical or mental impairment that substantially limits one or more major life activities." Amendments were added to the ADA in 2008 that broadened the definition of "disability" and protected more people. Considered one of America's most comprehensive pieces of civil rights legislation, the ADA prevents discrimination in employment and guarantees access to public services, accommodations, and transportation.

JUSTICE FOR ALL

As you know, the civil rights movement of the 1950s and 1960s achieved major breakthroughs in the struggle to end segregation and discrimination against African Americans. Activists have continued to fight for further progress, but full racial equality has remained elusive. Many African Americans continue to live in segregated city neighborhoods where schools, housing, and public services are inferior. Public housing funded by federal and state governments has contributed to keeping these neighborhoods segregated. In addition, federal, state, and local laws that had ended in the late 20th century still impact racial segregation today. These laws include those that designated white neighborhoods as residential areas and black neighborhoods as commercial areas, and those that prohibited the sale of property to African Americans.

Crime rates in segregated neighborhoods are higher, and drug abuse and out-of-wedlock births are more prevalent. Prison sentences for many of the crimes are also longer. For example, blacks convicted of drug offenses serve substantially more time in prison than do whites convicted of similar offenses. Local law enforcement often focuses on urban areas and, in particular, low-income communities. Blacks are also less likely than whites to graduate from high school and attend college. They suffer higher rates of unemployment and poverty. And although their incomes have risen, their pay is still, on average, far below those of whites.

In the 21st century, increasing charges of local police brutality against African Americans have been leveled. In some instances, police officers have used excessive force and sometimes shot and killed unarmed African Americans. One of the most widely publicized of these shootings occurred in Ferguson, Missouri, a predominantly African-American suburb of St. Louis. As you read in the American Story on civil rights, in 2014, a white Ferguson police officer shot and killed an unarmed black teenager named Michael Brown, touching off angry protests that continued for weeks. Remember that in the wake of this event and others like it, **Black Lives Matter** rose to national prominence. Activists in the movement organized protests to draw attention to unwarranted police violence toward African Americans and to demand justice for victims of this violence.

The movement polarized Americans. Some people believed it increased the violence. At a Black Lives Matter protest in Dallas, Texas, in July 2016, a sniper opened fire on police officers, killing five of them. A week and a half later, another gunman ambushed and killed three police officers in Baton Rouge, Louisiana. The African-American men who carried out the shootings were killed by the police.

In December 2014, Black Lives Matter supporters marched in New York City to take part in a "Justice for All" demonstration. A similar march took place in Washington, D.C. Protesters called for an end to racial profiling and police violence and demanded change in the justice system.

PLAN: 4-PAGE LESSON

OBJECTIVE

Analyze how the quest for civil rights and the debate over immigration shaped attitudes and events in the early 21st century.

CRITICAL THINKING SKILLS FOR LESSON 4.1

- Form and Support Opinions
- Make Inferences
- Interpret Maps
- Draw Conclusions
- Make Connections
- Analyze Cause and Effect
- Summarize

HISTORICAL THINKING FOR CHAPTER 31

What does it mean to be an American in the 21st century? Issues surrounding civil rights and immigration were at the center of social and political life in the United States in the early 21st century. Lesson 4.1 looks at these issues in relation to different groups of people.

BACKGROUND FOR THE TEACHER

In 2017, the Republican-controlled Congress passed and President Donald Trump signed into law legislation giving states permission to cut off funds to Planned Parenthood and other health providers that perform abortions. The law reversed a rule put into place by the Obama administration that kept state and local governments from withholding federal funds earmarked for contraceptive services, sexually transmitted infection testing and treatment, fertility and pregnancy care, and women's cancer screenings from qualified health-care providers, such as Planned Parenthood, that also offer abortion services. The 2017 law, therefore, jeopardizes a wide range of health services by defunding Planned Parenthood and other providers that also perform abortions.

HISTORY NOTEBOOK

Encourage students to complete the Civil Rights in the 21st Century page for Chapter 31 in their History Notebooks as they read.

INTRODUCE & ENGAGE

GIVE IT A TWIRL

Tell students that, in this lesson, they will learn about civil rights and immigration in the 21st century. Copy the following mnemonic on the board and tell students to use the TWIRL strategy to prepare for the lesson.

Think of a question you would like to ask about civil rights or immigration.

Write your question on a piece of paper.

Interact with a partner by discussing your questions and possible answers.

Report details about your discussion to the class.

Listen politely as other students talk about their discussions.

TEACH

GUIDED DISCUSSION

1. **Draw Conclusions** What evidence in the lesson supports the conclusion that minority women have made less progress in the workplace than white women? *(Possible response: While white women make about 20 percent less than men, African-American women make about 35 percent less, and Latina women make about 40 percent less.)*

2. **Make Connections** Why is the Americans with Disabilities Act (ADA) considered one of the most comprehensive civil rights legislations? *(The law is comprehensive because it applies to people with a wide range of physical or mental impairments that limit life activities and because it not only protects them from discrimination in employment, but also guarantees them access to public services, transportation, and accommodations.)*

3. **Analyze Cause and Effect** How did issues regarding local police responses in communities with concentrations of African Americans contribute to an increase in African-American activism? *(Possible response: Anger and frustration over the apparent use of excessive force by police in predominantly African-American communities—such as the killing of Michael Brown, an unarmed African-American teenager, in Ferguson, Missouri—spurred protests and fueled the Black Lives Matter movement. Such activism aims to draw attention to and demand justice for African Americans subjected to racial profiling and unwarranted violence by police.)*

MORE INFORMATION

Women Governors Remind students that Nellie Taloe Ross in Wyoming and Miriam "Ma" Ferguson in Texas were the first women to serve as governors. They both entered office in 1925. Ferguson again served as governor in the mid 1930s. It was not until the late 1960s that another woman became governor, when Lurleen Wallace served as governor of Alabama. Thirty-six more women joined the ranks of governor between 1975 and 2017, including Nikki Haley of South Carolina and Susana Martinez of New Mexico, the first two women of color to be elected governor. As a class, access a list of women governors and highlight their terms in office. **ASK:** What conclusions can you draw about the pace of women's political gains from this list? *(Answers will vary. Possible response: Women have made the greatest gains in the 21st century.)* Use the list as a springboard for discussion about ways in which the status of women in general and minority women in particular in the United States has changed or remained unchanged over time.

DIFFERENTIATE

STRIVING READERS

Use a Sorting Activity Write the following terms on the board:

racial equality
border enforcement
gay
glass ceiling
police brutality
marriage equality
Latino community
equal pay for equal work
prison sentences
childcare
Black Lives Matter
transgender discrimination
comprehensive immigration legislation
LGBTQ community
without documentation

Instruct pairs to work together to sort them into four groups of related terms, one for each section of the lesson. Then challenge students to write a paragraph that shows how each set of terms are related.

(Possible response: Women's rights: glass ceiling, equal pay for equal work, childcare; African-American rights: racial equality, prison sentences, police brutality, Black Lives Matter; LGBTQ rights: LGBTQ community, gay, marriage equality, transgender discrimination; Immigration: without documentation, border enforcement, Latino community, comprehensive immigration legislation)

PRE-AP

Research Civil Rights Progress Prompt students to choose one of the groups of people that continues to struggle for civil rights. Challenge students to conduct research using multiple print and online sources to learn more about the progress the group has made and how far they have yet to go to gain full civil rights. Students should then present what they have learned in a written or oral report. Encourage students to use both statistics and stories to illustrate the group's civil rights achievements and struggles. Ask students to conclude their report with their personal thoughts about whether or not full civil rights and justice for all is an attainable goal.

See the Chapter Planner for more strategies for differentiation.

The incidents increased racial tensions and led some to accuse Black Lives Matter of encouraging violence against police. However, white citizens also directed racially charged violence against African Americans. In June 2015, Dylann Roof, a self-proclaimed white supremacist, massacred nine African-American worshipers attending a prayer meeting at the Emanuel African Methodist Episcopal Church in Charleston, South Carolina. When arrested, Roof claimed he wanted to start a race war.

SOCIAL LEGISLATION

In the American Story on civil rights, you also read about the LGBT community's struggle to achieve marriage equality. **Marriage equality** is the legal right of gays and lesbians to marry their partners and have the same privileges that married heterosexual couples enjoy. However, even after same-sex marriage became legal in 2015, other issues arose that challenged the LGBTQ community's civil rights. One of these involved the right of transgender individuals to use the public restroom that corresponds to their gender identity rather than their gender at birth. In 2013, California became the first state to pass a law guaranteeing this right for transgender students in public schools. The law allowed them to use whichever restroom they wanted. Over the next few years, other states passed similar laws. Then, in 2016, President Obama issued guidelines to all school districts in the country, detailing the steps they should take to make sure their students were not discriminated against. The guidelines included allowing students to use the restroom of their choice.

Supporters of transgender laws suffered a number of setbacks in 2017. The federal government withdrew its position on bathroom protections for transgender students and declared the issue was one of states' rights. Soon after this declaration, North Carolina, which had passed a bathroom bill in 2016, repealed the measure after just a year. In Virginia, a transgender high school student named Gavin Grimm sought to ban discrimination based on gender identity at his school, where separate facilities had been set aside for him alone. Grimm took his case to the Supreme Court, but it would not hear the case.

MEXICAN IMMIGRATION

American civil rights leaders in the 21st century consider immigration a civil rights issue because they claim that many immigrants are not given a chance to succeed economically—especially those from Mexico. By the 2000s, the status of Mexican Americans and Mexican immigrants became a national political discussion. The wave of immigration from Mexico—in particular, the estimated 6 million who entered the United States illegally, or without documentation—worried and angered many Americans. Some claimed these immigrants hurt the economy by taking jobs from American citizens, driving down wages, avoiding paying taxes, and putting pressure on social service agencies. Many economists dismissed such claims, stating that immigrants actually benefit the economy by taking jobs Americans don't want, paying their share of taxes, and buying products and services.

After the September 11, 2001, terrorist attacks, fear for national security led Congress to provide for increased border enforcement. And so, in 2006, President George W. Bush signed into law the Secure Fence Act, authorizing the construction of 700 miles of fencing along the U.S.-Mexico border. Still, the influx of immigrants continued. Meanwhile, a bill called the Development, Relief, and Education for Alien Minors (Dream) Act was proposed by a coalition of both Democrats and Republicans in 2001 but failed to pass. The act would have provided children brought to the United States illegally the opportunity to seek legal residency in the country. Proponents continued to urge passage of the act, but time and again the legislation died in Congress due to a lack of consensus, or agreement. Finally, President Obama created the **Deferred Action for Childhood Arrivals (DACA)** program in 2012. The program allowed the children of illegal immigrants who came to the United States before 2007 to defer deportation and apply for work permits in the country for a two-year renewable period. Applicants had to undergo a thorough background check every two years. In 2012, about 800,000 young people—who came to be known as "Dreamers"—enrolled in DACA.

Obama also sought to enforce border security. In 2014, he issued an executive order that strengthened the border between Texas and Mexico. However, the order also offered temporary legal status to millions of illegal immigrants. After issuing the order, Obama emphasized that the efforts of immigration authorities would be focused on punishing "Felons, not families. Criminals, not children. Gang members, not a mom who's working hard to provide for her kids." Republican leaders and many American citizens were angered by the order, claiming that the president's actions would lead to more illegal immigration, not less. During his presidency, Obama wrestled with many other issues that divided Americans, including one that scientists said affected the entire planet: climate change.

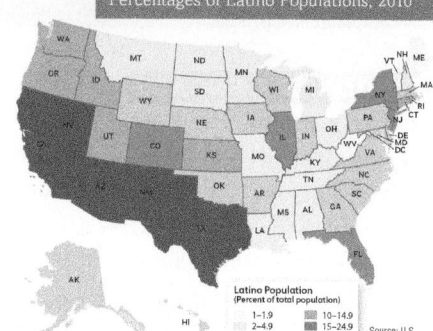

Percentages of Latino Populations, 2010

Latino Population
(Percent of total population)
1–1.9 10–14.9
2–4.9 15–24.9
5–9.9 25–50

Source: U.S. Census Bureau

HISTORICAL THINKING

1. **READING CHECK** How have beliefs about women's roles changed, and how have they stayed the same?

2. **FORM AND SUPPORT OPINIONS** Since the civil rights movement, do you think African Americans have continued to make significant gains in achieving equality? Explain your answer.

3. **MAKE INFERENCES** Why do you think DACA applicants were called "Dreamers"?

4. **INTERPRET MAPS** Which states had the largest percentages of Latino populations in the country in 2010, and why do you think that was so?

The U.S. Border Patrol apprehended these Central American women and children after they crossed the Rio Grande and illegally entered Texas in 2014. The law at that time required such refugees to appear at a hearing before an immigration judge.

BUILD BACKGROUND

MEXICAN IMMIGRATION FLOWS

The Pew Research Center estimates that between 2009 and 2014, more Mexicans left the United States than entered, either legally or illegally. Although the movement of undocumented workers is difficult to track with precision, Pew used U.S. and Mexican census data to measure the flow of people back and forth across the border. During that time period, Pew estimates that 1 million Mexican families living in the United States returned to Mexico. The returning family members often included children born in the United States. During this same time period, Pew estimates that around 870,000 Mexican nationals came to the United States.

Pew posits several reasons for this phenomenon, including the slow economic recovery in the United States following the recession, which may have discouraged Mexicans from coming to the United States and encouraged families in the United States to return to Mexico. Stricter border security may also have reduced the flow of Mexicans to the United States, while increases in deportations upped the flow in the opposite direction. According to Mexican census information, however, most of the 1 million Mexicans who returned did so out of the desire to reunite with family members in Mexico.

TEACH

GUIDED DISCUSSION

1. Summarize What gains and setbacks has the LGBTQ community experienced in the 21st century? *(Gains: The U.S. Supreme Court legalized same-sex marriage. New laws guaranteed restroom choice for transgender students in California and other states. Setbacks: In 2017, the federal government abandoned support for bathroom protections, declaring it a states' rights issue, and North Carolina repealed its protections.)*

2. Form and Support Opinions Do you agree or disagree with civil rights leaders who see immigration as a civil rights issue? Explain your answer. *(Answers will vary. Possible responses: I agree, because many immigrants are not given a chance to succeed economically, particularly undocumented ones who take on jobs that Americans do not want. I disagree, because immigration, particularly the flow of undocumented immigrants over the Mexico-U.S. border, is a security issue, not a civil rights issue.)*

ANALYZE CAUSE AND EFFECT

Prompt students to think about U.S. immigration policy in relation to Mexico during the 21st century. **ASK:** What steps did presidents Bush and Obama take to strengthen border security? *(In 2006, President Bush signed the Secure Fence Act, authorizing 700 miles of fencing along the Mexico-U.S. border. President Obama signed an executive order in 2014 that strengthened the border between Texas and Mexico. He also directed immigration authorities to focus on felons, criminals, and gang members.)*

ACTIVE OPTIONS

On Your Feet: Inside-Outside Circle Assign half the students in class to write questions about civil rights in the 21st century and half to write questions about immigration. Then have students form two concentric circles facing each other. Students in the inside circle pose questions about civil rights to students in the outside circle, who answer the questions. Then the students switch roles and students in the outside circle ask questions about immigration. If students cannot answer a question, they may ask others in their circle for help.

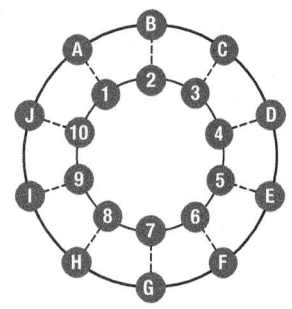

NG Learning Framework: Research Continuity and Change

`ATTITUDE` Responsibility

`KNOWLEDGE` Our Human Story

Have students work in groups to research one of the following questions: In what ways have the civil rights of immigrants, people of color, disabled Americans, and lesbian, gay, bisexual, and transgender Americans changed over time, and how have these rights remained the same? How is the life of a new immigrant to the United States today the same as the life of a new immigrant in 1900, and how is it different? As part of the last question, have students consider the impact of globalization on immigrant communities today. Have groups share their research with the class.

HISTORICAL THINKING

ANSWERS

1. Possible response: Women are now viewed as capable of serving at high levels of government and business, as evidenced by the number of female governors and other politicians, and chief executives in business. However, women, on average, still make less money than men and assume the majority of childcare duties.

2. Answers will vary. Possible responses: Yes. African Americans have made progress, and Barack Obama's presidency is a clear indication that Americans' ideas about race are changing. No. The rise of movements such as Black Lives Matter and the fact that so many African Americans are still struggling in poverty, living in crime-ridden neighborhoods, and subject to police brutality show that, though some progress has been made, African Americans are far from achieving equality.

3. Possible response: Those who enrolled in DACA were called "Dreamers" because they sought the protections afforded in the failed Dream Act, named from the initials of the bill: Development, Relief, and Education for Alien Minors. The name "Dreamers" also refers to the hope of DACA recipients that they will be able to fulfill their personal dreams if they gain U.S. residency status.

4. California, Nevada, Arizona, New Mexico, and Texas had the largest percentages of Latinos. All of these states were once Mexican territory, so they have a core Latino population and culture that encourages further immigration from Mexico. In addition, all share a border or are close to the U.S. border with Mexico.

ENVIRONMENTAL CHALLENGES

You've probably heard scientists and politicians talk about climate change and global warming. They're not the same thing, but the two terms are related. The vast majority of scientists believe global warming is driving climate change.

CLIMATE CHANGE OR GLOBAL WARMING?

Climate change is a gradual shift in Earth's overall climate. Throughout its history, Earth has undergone many climate changes. Global warming, on the other hand, is a term used by many scientists to describe the rapid warming of Earth's surface observed over the last century. These scientists believe this warming is causing climate change and is largely due to human activities. Experts say that the heavy use of nonrenewable fossil fuels, including coal, oil, and natural gas, contributes to rising temperatures. Burning these energy sources releases **greenhouse gases**, such as carbon dioxide and methane. The greenhouse gas emissions trap the sun's heat and warm Earth's surface, causing its temperature to rise. This warming is called the **greenhouse effect**.

Scientists believe the greenhouse effect began to significantly increase around 1750 with the Industrial Revolution, when people began burning more fossil fuels to run factories. Consumption of these fuels has intensified during the last 250 years or so, with the introduction of trains, automobiles, and airplanes. As a result, since the beginning of the 20th century, the average temperature of the globe has risen 1.4° F. That number may seem small, but a change of even one degree is cause for concern.

Researchers believe they have already detected evidence of the impact of this seemingly small rise in global temperature. The vast ice sheets that cover Antarctica and Greenland, for example, have begun to melt and shrink. And oceans are warming, causing sea ice to melt and sea levels to rise. Scientists say these changes are already destroying habitats and changing ecosystems. Earth's warming may also result in more intense hurricanes and typhoons, which in turn could lead to high casualty tolls and damage to coastlines and other geographic features.

COMBATING GLOBAL WARMING

The majority of scientists believe that global warming will continue unless greenhouse gas emissions are dramatically reduced. Such a reduction will not be easy to achieve, however. In 1988, as concern about global warming was growing, the United Nations and the World Meteorological Organization took a step toward addressing the problem by creating the **Intergovernmental Panel on Climate Change (IPCC)**. The panel is made up of top climate experts from around the world. Its mission is to assess "the scientific, technical, and socioeconomic information relevant to understanding the scientific basis of risk of human-induced climate change." The panel's reports help world leaders set climate policies.

International action on climate change was undertaken in 1997 with a treaty called the **Kyoto Protocol**, which committed countries to reducing greenhouse gas emissions to below 1990 levels. Eventually, nearly 200 countries implemented the treaty, but the United States—which at the time was the world's largest emitter of these gases—was not among them. President George W. Bush, who was skeptical about what caused climate change, opposed the treaty, arguing that it would "harm our economy and hurt our workers." He also objected to the fact that developing countries were exempt from complying with the treaty.

Since then, however, the United States has made efforts to reduce emissions by moving toward the use of more renewable energy sources, such as solar, wind, and geothermal power. In 2009, President Obama allocated billions of dollars to promote renewable and clean energy programs. In 2016, the country's first offshore wind farm was completed in the Atlantic Ocean near Rhode Island's Block Island, and federal agencies announced a plan to accelerate the development of additional offshore wind energy.

Obama and the U.S. Environmental Protection Agency unveiled the Clean Power Plan in 2015. The president called the plan "the single most important step America has ever taken in the fight against global climate change." It established nationwide standards aimed at greatly reducing carbon dioxide emissions from power plants.

In 2016, the United States made its most ambitious commitment to date toward dealing with global warming by ratifying the Kyoto Protocol's successor, a climate treaty known as the **Paris Agreement**. The goal of the agreement was to prevent Earth from warming more than 2° C, or approximately 3.6° F. Scientists believe that allowing Earth to warm beyond that limit would result in destructive and dangerous climate change. It remains to be seen whether the countries that signed the agreement will meet the pledge—and even if they do, whether their efforts will help protect the environment.

AN INCONVENIENT TRUTH

In this 2006 documentary film, former vice president Al Gore seeks to educate the public about global warming. Throughout the film, Gore uses photos, graphs, and flow charts to make his case that global warming is real and caused by human activities. Stressing that global warming is a moral issue rather than a political one, Gore encourages his audience to take steps to combat it. He says, "We have everything that we need to reduce carbon emissions, everything but political will. But in America, the will to act is a renewable resource."

HISTORICAL THINKING

1. **READING CHECK** What controversies are associated with the concept of climate change and with environmental conservation?

2. **ANALYZE ENVIRONMENTAL CONCEPTS** How might our consumption of natural resources, such as coal, oil, and natural gas, influence the geographic extent, composition, biological diversity, and viability of natural systems?

3. **DESCRIBE** How has the human modification of landscapes contributed to global warming, and what types of environmental policies have resulted from it?

OBJECTIVE

Assess the challenges of and viewpoints about climate change and global warming.

CRITICAL THINKING SKILLS FOR LESSON 4.2

• Analyze Environmental Concepts

• Describe

• Analyze Cause and Effect

HISTORICAL THINKING FOR CHAPTER 31

What does it mean to be an American in the 21st century? When it comes to climate change and global warming, Americans are affected by U.S. policies as well as by those of other nations. Lesson 4.2 examines the scientific evidence of and policy issues surrounding climate change and global warming.

NATIONAL GEOGRAPHIC PHOTOGRAPHER PETER MCBRIDE

Peter McBride is an award-winning photographer, writer, and filmmaker who specializes in water-related stories. He has traveled to more than 75 nations on assignment for a host of magazines, including *National Geographic Traveler*. In recognition of his environmental advocacy and concerns about water conservation, National Geographic has named him a "freshwater hero." Raised on a cattle ranch in Colorado, McBride takes a special interest in the Colorado River. The river is the focus of his 2011 short film *Chasing Water*. In the film, McBride satisfies a childhood curiosity about where the water his family used to irrigate their ranch went after it drained into the watershed. On a 1,500-mile journey by raft and aircraft, McBride follows the Colorado River from its source to the sea. What he discovers sheds light on the toll that the overuse of water can take on a river.

INTRODUCE & ENGAGE

TAKE A POLL

Poll students about their current views on the environment by asking them how worried they are about climate change and global warming, to what extent they agree that humans play a role in global warming, and whether students believe governments need to act to halt or reverse global climate change. Discuss student responses. Then tell students that this lesson discusses issues related to climate change and global warming.

TEACH

GUIDED DISCUSSION

1. **Analyze Environmental Concepts** What evidence does the text provide linking the quantities of resources humans consume and its effect on the planet? *(The burning of fossil fuels beginning with the Industrial Revolution around 1750 led to an increase in the greenhouse effect, and the temperature of the globe has risen 1.4°F since the beginning of the 20th century, when humans began burning fossil fuels for transportation.)*

2. **Analyze Cause and Effect** Why do many countries believe it is important to achieve the Paris Agreement's goal to prevent Earth from warming more than 2°C, or about 3.6°F? *(The goal is important because scientists believe that warming past this point would result in harmful climate change.)*

MORE INFORMATION

Tijuana River Pollution Point out to students that the borderland between the United States and Mexico is a dynamic region in which cultures merge and environmental issues cross political boundaries. For example, in early 2017, a collapse of a sewer line in Tijuana dumped raw sewage into the Tijuana River, which carried it to the U.S. side of the border. The lack of notification from Mexico alarmed U.S. officials and highlighted the need for renewed cooperation. Direct students to work in groups to investigate steps the United States and Mexico took in response to the incident. Prompt students to use information from their research in a class discussion on the following question: What considerations were involved in making decisions about the resources and natural systems in the Tijuana River, and how did those factors influence international decisions?

ACTIVE OPTIONS

On Your Feet: Ready, Set, Recall Tell students to work in small groups to write down all the details they recall from their reading of the lesson. Then have groups take turns sharing with the class one fact at a time from their lists. Write each group's contributions on the board. When a group runs out of items, it must drop out of the game but can rejoin if members recall a new fact that no other group has mentioned. Continue until time is up. The group with the most facts is the winner.

NG Learning Framework: Evaluate Climate Change Explanations

ATTITUDE Responsibility

KNOWLEDGE Our Living Planet

STEM

Instruct students to work in groups to research the different explanations for climate change and to evaluate how well the various texts and arguments they find support different explanations, including the ideas that climate change is part of a natural cycle or caused by human activity. Have groups share their evaluations with the class and discuss which explanation best accords with textual evidence and where texts leave some matters uncertain.

For students who develop an interest in preserving the environment, suggest that they read the American Story at the beginning of this chapter.

DIFFERENTIATE

ENGLISH LANGUAGE LEARNERS ELD

Preview and Review the Text Prompt students at the **Emerging** and **Expanding** levels to preview the lesson. First have them read the title, Main Idea, subheadings, captions, and questions. Then ask them to write questions that they expect to be answered in the text. After students read the lesson, have them work with a partner to discuss answers to their questions.

GIFTED & TALENTED

Write a Proposal Challenge students to find out where the energy that powers the school's computers, lights, heating, and cooling comes from. Then have them conduct research into ways the school might integrate one or more forms of clean, renewable energy: solar, wind, geothermal, hydroelectric, or hydrokinetic. Instruct students to use what they learn to write a proposal to their school board that includes an examination of the costs, benefits, and impacts of fossil fuel versus renewable energy.

See the Chapter Planner for more strategies for differentiation.

HISTORICAL THINKING

ANSWERS

1. Some Americans disagree with scientists who say human activity contributes to climate change and that cutting greenhouse gas emissions can help conserve the environment. They also argue that curbing emissions would harm the U.S. economy.

2. Acquiring nonrenewable fossil fuels, such as drilling for oil or mining for coal, alters the landscape and its composition, and affects local biological diversity by affecting habitats. Burning fossil fuels contributes to a greenhouse effect that alters and can threaten natural systems by warming the Earth's climate.

3. Humans have modified the landscape by mining for fossil fuels and building factories and cars that burn fossil fuels, which emit greenhouse gases. International agreements, such as the Kyoto Protocol and the Paris Agreement, and U.S. regulations have aimed to slow global warming by reducing fossil fuel emissions and promoting clean energy.

CRITICAL VIEWING Possible response: Heavy irrigation demands, coupled with drought, have caused the Colorado River to shrink, leaving the land dry and seemingly unable to support plant and animal life along the waterway.

In January 2013, Beijing, China's capital, registered a near record level of air pollution. The dense smog is visible over the city as these tourists, wearing masks to protect them from the polluted air, visit the Temple of Heaven, a complex of religious buildings.

GLOBALIZING AMERICAN SOCIETY

Not so long ago, Americans found satisfying, well-paid work in automobile plants and steel factories. In our global economy, those days seem to be over.

ECONOMY AND ENVIRONMENT

Beginning in the 1970s and continuing through recent times, U.S. economic production has shifted away from heavy industry and toward the service sector. The **service sector** provides services rather than goods and includes jobs in banking, education, retail, and health care. This de-industrialization has altered the daily lives of many working- and middle-class American families.

Over the past 30 years, the gaps in income between top earners and middle- and working-class earners have become wider and more pronounced. Working-class wages have stagnated as higher-paying unionized blue collar factory jobs have been outsourced and replaced with minimum-wage paying service sector jobs. The stagnant or decreasing wealth of working- and middle-class Americans has been compounded by changes in tax structures and safety-net programs. It has also been amplified by higher costs for education, child care, and housing. In the early 2010s, a populist movement called Occupy Wall Street sought to bring attention to the income gap through protests and demonstrations. Some members of the movement tried to provide solutions through education or organization.

Part of the reason for the decreasing income of many Americans is globalization and the rise of **multinational corporations**, or companies that have offices and factories in multiple countries. In the first 15 years of the 21st century, the United States lost an estimated 5 million manufacturing jobs. Many of these jobs were outsourced to Mexico or China, where wages are much lower than in the United States.

In many ways, the globalized economy has had a broad, negative impact on the environment. The rapid industrialization of countries with lax environmental standards, such as China, Mexico,

and India, has resulted in severe air, water, and soil pollution. Globalization has also led to a tremendous increase in deforestation. Around the world, people have cleared vast tracts of forest so that the land can be developed for homes or factories or used as farmland or pasture for grazing cattle. Because trees absorb carbon dioxide through the process of photosynthesis, the loss of immense numbers of them is a major factor in global warming. Even the use of large, standardized containers to ship goods all over the world has played a role in increasing the levels of carbon dioxide released into the air.

SOCIAL IMPACT

The way we work has become globalized, and so has the way we communicate, thanks to new media. **New media** refers to digital products and services that provide content through the Internet, and it has fundamentally changed the way people work, learn, interact socially, and spend their leisure time. Today, texting, instant messaging, and social networking allow fast and easy communication among people around the world. Much of this is done with smartphones, which combine communication and software applications into one handheld device. The technology enables people all over the world to connect with one another and share ideas and information instantaneously. As a result, culture sometimes forms around shared ideas or interests, rather than in a physical location.

Globalization has even affected what the world eats. Multinational fast food chains have popped up all over the planet. In just about any country, you can find some of your favorite restaurants. Some fear this will create a universal food culture, one in which people in all parts of the world eat the same things rather than the traditional foods of their culture. A universal food culture could result in the loss of regional cuisines and a wide range of crop varieties.

Foods from other countries are also imported to the United States. But because food production in some of these countries lacks safety standards, some Americans worry about possible contamination and public health issues. Many are also concerned about the explosion of genetically modified (GM) foods. **Genetically modified foods** are grown from plants that have been changed in a way that does not occur naturally, often through the introduction of a gene from a different organism. Plants are sometimes modified in this way to make them disease-resistant and to increase crop yields. While the practice is controversial, GM foods may provide a sustainable way to feed the world's population.

HISTORICAL THINKING

1. **READING CHECK** Why did the wealth gap between top earners and the majority of Americans grow between the 1970s and 2010s?

2. **ANALYZE ENVIRONMENTAL CONCEPTS** How have global industrialization and the modification of landscapes affected natural systems around the world?

3. **ANALYZE CAUSE AND EFFECT** How do you think the aspects of globalization discussed in the lesson might define U.S. environmental policy issues?

4. **EVALUATE** What are some of the advantages and disadvantages of new media?

PLAN: 2-PAGE LESSON

OBJECTIVE

Analyze the economic, social, and environmental effects of globalization.

CRITICAL THINKING SKILLS FOR LESSON 4.3

• Analyze Environmental Concepts

• Analyze Cause and Effect

• Evaluate

HISTORICAL THINKING FOR CHAPTER 31

What does it mean to be an American in the 21st century? Globalization has contributed to a decrease in manufacturing jobs in the United States and to the growth of the service sector. Lesson 4.3 examines the causes and consequences of globalization.

BACKGROUND FOR THE TEACHER

Some social scientists see multinational companies as a driving force behind de-industrialization. They argue that the corporations find it more profitable to move production to modern foreign plants than to invest in upgrading aging plants in the United States. Others point to the globalization of markets and to trade between developed and developing nations. Still others see it more as a consequence of increased productivity that reduces the need for workers or factories. When looking at the consequences, social scientists argue that the focus needs to be at the regional and local levels to capture the impact on individuals and communities. In regions that are hit particularly hard, such as the Midwest, people cannot always retrain for higher-paying service jobs, and communities are often ravaged by abandoned buildings, lack of community services, and an atmosphere of despair.

INTRODUCE & ENGAGE

INVITE AN EXPERT

Bring in an expert from the community who is versed in the impact of globalization on the state or local economy or on the environment. Prompt students to prepare questions to ask the expert about the social and political challenges associated with globalization. To help them formulate questions, encourage students to consider issues they have seen in the news or the personal experiences of friends and family members.

TEACH

GUIDED DISCUSSION

1. **Analyze Environmental Concepts** How might deforestation cause opposition between environmental advocates and property rights advocates? *(Possible response: Property rights advocates support the right of farmers to clear vast tracts of privately owned forests to raise crops and graze livestock. Environmental advocates oppose the clearing of large tracts of forests for private gain because trees absorb carbon dioxide through photosynthesis. Clearing the trees contributes to global warming by disrupting this process.)*

2. **Analyze Cause and Effect** How has globalization affected social trends involving food? *(Possible response: The growth of multinational fast food chains is changing food culture by introducing the same cuisine around the world. This runs the risk of crowding out regional cuisines.)*

MORE INFORMATION

GMOs Remind students that new technologies often lead to social debate. Tell students that this is certainly true in the case of GMOs. Scientists, large corporations, and environmentalists square off in the debate over the health, safety, and economics of GMOs. Proponents of GMOs argue that genetic engineering protects and improves the global food supply by making vital crops disease and herbicide resistant and engineering foods to combat nutrition-related diseases. Opponents argue that GMOs selectively benefit large corporations, interfere with good farming practices, and endanger global health. Have students work in groups to research the environmental impact of GMOs on the global food supply. Then guide students to use their research to hold a class discussion on how new technologies influence environmental policy.

ACTIVE OPTIONS

On Your Feet: History Relay Divide the class into two teams. Allow time for each student to think of a question about the lesson. Tell students from each team to take turns asking a question to students on the other team. If a student answers incorrectly, that student must switch to the other team. If a student answers correctly, the asker must switch teams. Continue until each student has asked a question or time is up. The team with the most students at the end of the game is the winner.

NG Learning Framework: Research De-industrialization

ATTITUDE Curiosity

KNOWLEDGE Our Human Story

Instruct students to work in groups to research the causes and consequences of de-industrialization in the United States. When considering the causes, encourage students to explore the effects of factors mentioned in Background for the Teacher: globalization, multinational corporations, trade, and increased productivity due to technology. When researching the consequences, encourage students to consider the impact on workers and communities—including areas such as Silicon Valley. Have groups share their findings with the class.

DIFFERENTIATE

STRIVING READERS

Use a Concept Cluster Tell students they can keep track of main ideas and supporting details by creating a Concept Cluster. Have students label the center oval Impacts of Globalization on . . . and label the other ovals Economy, Environment, and Society/Culture. As students read the lesson, have them work together to enter key facts and ideas on the spokes of the diagram, drawing more spokes as necessary.

PRE-AP

Research Occupy Wall Street Challenge students to use online sources to learn more about the Occupy Wall Street movement, such as: What were the group's goals and methods? Which institutions and practices did it target for reform? What solutions did it propose? What offshoot protests sprang from the Occupy Wall Street movement? Instruct students to summarize their findings for the class in multimedia presentations.

See the Chapter Planner for more strategies for differentiation.

HISTORICAL THINKING

ANSWERS

1. De-industrialization resulted in a shift from higher-paying unionized factory jobs to service-sector jobs. This caused the wealth of the working and middle classes to stagnate or decrease, while the wealth of the top earners grew.

2. Possible response: Landscapes in rapidly industrializing countries have suffered deforestation; the lack of trees leaves more carbon dioxide in the air, contributing to global warming.

3. Possible response: Globalization might affect how the United States views environmental treaties and controversial practices such as genetically modifying food crops.

4. Possible response: Advantages include fast, easy communication, social networking, working remotely, and educational opportunities. Disadvantages include loss of face-to-face contact, cyberbullying, and providing a platform for propaganda, hate groups, and terrorists.

USING FOOD WASTE TO FEED THE WORLD

"We want to catalyze a food-waste revolution one person, one town, one country at a time."—Tristram Stuart

Tristram Stuart has an ambitious goal in mind: to create a healthy planet with zero hunger. He knows it can be done. After all, one-third of all food produced on Earth ends up in landfills and garbage heaps, and the impact extends far beyond the dinner plate. Growing food and raising animals takes its toll on the land. Water and other precious resources are wasted, trees are cut down. Pollution is greatly increased. Stuart is starting a food-waste revolution, and he urges you to join him: to eat less, buy less, waste less.

National Geographic Explorer, author, and campaigner Tristram Stuart is also a renowned activist fighting against worldwide food waste at a farmer's market near you.

MAIN IDEA Tristram Stuart is creating a food-waste revolution to stop hunger and save our planet.

WASTED FOOD

For thousands of years, pigs have been fed what their human owners didn't need. In fact, National Geographic Explorer Tristram Stuart says that's the exact reason pigs were domesticated—to recycle human food scraps. So when Stuart raised pigs as a teen, he fed them leftovers from his school cafeteria and local stores—good-quality leftovers that would otherwise have been discarded. But most pigs are now fed soy, wheat, and corn—foods that could nourish hungry people.

Food waste is a big problem, and it goes well beyond the pigs. As Stuart attests, "About a third of all food globally is wasted in the same world in which 1 billion people don't have enough to eat." From the moment he became aware of this global epidemic, Stuart hasn't looked back. He has written two best-selling books and has spoken to people around the world about curbing food waste. "I'd seen bins full of food being trucked off to landfill sites. And I thought, surely there is something more sensible to do with food than waste it."

What's unfortunate is that the food being thrown away is not rotten at all—it's good, fresh food that may not meet strict grocery store regulations of size, shape, or appearance. Before Stuart intervened, as much as 40 percent of these "ugly" fruits and vegetables were left in fields to rot around the world—even in countries where millions suffer from malnutrition.

This immense waste extends beyond produce. Bakeries throw away the ends of bread, edible parts of animals are discarded, fish that are too small are dumped back in the sea. In addition, harvesting food that ends up getting thrown away creates pollution, wastes water, and greatly impacts the land.

ADDRESSING A GLOBAL ISSUE

To demonstrate just how much actually gets wasted, Stuart and his organization, Feedback, set up an initiative called Feeding the 5,000. Food that would have been discarded is cooked up by local chefs and served to the community—for free. This public event first took place in London in 2009 and has since expanded to many locations around the world, including New York City in 2016. The goal is to create awareness while calling on individuals and

CRITICAL VIEWING Imperfect yet edible produce like this typically gets rejected by stores and consumers. Why might shoppers pass up food like this, contributing to potential food waste?

companies to strategize more responsible ways to waste less—whether by buying less or by planning better—so that everything purchased is consumed.

Food waste is a global issue, and its solution is one that we must all take part in. Stuart recognizes that it is nearly impossible to have a world with zero waste. However, he draws attention to the burdens that our wastefulness is putting on Earth. "We are reaching the ecological limits that our planet can bear. And when we chop down forests—as we are every day to grow more and more food—when we extract water from depleting water reserves, when we emit fossil fuel emissions in the quest to grow more and more food and then we throw away so much of it—we have to start thinking about what we can start saving."

Through his books and public campaigns—including Gleaning Network, which coordinates the collection of produce that would normally have been left to rot—Tristram Stuart is on a mission to end food waste and save the world, 5,000 meals at a time.

HISTORICAL THINKING

1. **READING CHECK** What do Tristram Stuart's Feeding the 5,000 events aim to accomplish and inspire among their participants?

2. **ANALYZE CAUSE AND EFFECT** How does a global issue like hunger relate to the physical and human characteristics of places and regions?

3. **DRAW CONCLUSIONS** How can you and your family contribute to Stuart's mission to end food waste and improve the world?

OBJECTIVE

Explain how food waste impacts the planet and people around the world.

CRITICAL THINKING SKILLS FOR LESSON 4.4

- Analyze Cause and Effect
- Draw Conclusions
- Identify Problems and Solutions

HISTORICAL THINKING FOR CHAPTER 31

What does it mean to be an American in the 21st century? Many poor Americans fall victim to hunger. Large amounts of food are also wasted in the United States. Lesson 4.4 explores Tristram Stuart's efforts to impact food waste and help the hungry.

NATIONAL GEOGRAPHIC EXPLORER TRISTRAM STUART

Tristram Stuart, a Briton, notes that his country throws away enough grain products yearly to feed 30 million of the world's hungry. He also notes that the water wasted on irrigating food that people worldwide eventually discard could meet the drinking and household needs of 9 billion people. Stuart helped pass laws in the United Kingdom that require grocery stores to share with farmers the financial burden of reducing orders at the last minute. The goal is to get grocers to plan better so food is not wasted when farmers can't sell it after short-notice cancellations. Farmers have also benefited from Stuart's efforts to get grocers to accept less-than-perfect produce. Some farmers have seen a 20 percent yearly sales bump since grocery stores began to accept "ugly" produce.

HISTORY NOTEBOOK

Encourage students to complete the National Geographic Explorer page for Chapter 31 in their History Notebooks as they read.

INTRODUCE & ENGAGE

BRAINSTORM LISTS

Create a T-Chart on the board like the one shown here. Prompt students to brainstorm a list of ways in which people waste food. Write students' suggestions in the left column of the chart. Then have students brainstorm ways in which people might waste less food. Write those suggestions in the right column. Tell students that in this lesson they are going to learn why food waste is a serious problem for people and the environment and what National Geographic Explorer Tristram Stuart is doing to help solve the problem.

Food Waste	Less Waste

TEACH

GUIDED DISCUSSION

1. **Analyze Cause and Effect** In what way is world hunger today related to the way we currently feed pigs? *(Possible response: Pigs used to eat food waste. Now they eat soy, wheat, and corn that could be used to feed the world's hungry.)*

2. **Identify Problems and Solutions** How do initiatives such as Feedback and the Gleaning Network address the current problem of world hunger as well as the problems of farmers? *(Possible response: These initiatives take food that would be wasted—for example, because it doesn't look perfect—and use it to feed people who otherwise might not have enough food. The Gleaning Network coordinates the collection of food that would normally be left in fields to rot. It therefore aids farmers by clearing fields of unwanted produce and helps poor people avoid going hungry by giving them the produce. Feedback transforms food that would otherwise be discarded into free meals for the public.)*

MORE INFORMATION

Grain Demand Tell students that one of Tristram Stuart's primary concerns is the impact upon poor countries of the waste of grain products by wealthier nations. Stuart argues that, because grain is traded worldwide, a high demand in wealthy countries drives up prices globally by limiting the overall supply. **ASK:** Suppose that in a changing climate, many heavy storms arise and destroy much of the world's crop of a key grain. Based on Stuart's analysis, how would global hunger be affected? *(Possible response: A shortage in grain would likely increase the price. If the price of grain increased, hunger would increase worldwide, particularly in poorer countries because poor people would not be able to afford to buy enough grain.)*

ACTIVE OPTIONS

On Your Feet: Think, Pair, Share Give students a few minutes to think about these questions: How is food waste an environmental problem? How it a social problem? An economic problem? A political problem? Then have students choose partners and talk about the questions for five minutes. Finally, ask pairs to share their ideas with the class.

NG Learning Framework: Create a Food Waste Reduction Plan

`ATTITUDE` Responsibility

`KNOWLEDGE` Our Human Story

Divide the class into three groups to research grocery store food waste in the United States and in the community. Assign each group one of the following topics to research:

• grocery store practices that encourage food waste;

• laws that encourage food donations;

• charities and organizations that collect and distribute food.

Instruct groups to develop a list of practical suggestions related to their research topic for reducing grocery store food waste. Allow each group to share its research findings and suggestions with the class. Use the groups' suggestions as the basis for a class discussion on the implications of grocery store food waste for combating hunger in the United States.

DIFFERENTIATE

INCLUSION

Work in Pairs Allow students with disabilities to work with other students who can read the lesson aloud to them. Tell the reading partners to describe the photographs in detail, including all the odd-looking carrots, peppers, squash, and sweet potatoes. Then have students work together to answer the Critical Viewing question. Give students the option of recording their answers rather than writing them out.

GIFTED & TALENTED

Create a Public Service Announcement Guide students to conduct research using a variety of online sources to learn more about the problem of food waste. Tell students to look for especially startling facts and images, and to use what they learn to create a public service announcement for print, radio, television, or social media. The announcement should raise public awareness of the problem and suggest one or more actions people can take to waste less food. Invite students to present their public service announcements to the class. Then have the class brainstorm how some of the announcements could reach a wider audience in their community.

See the Chapter Planner for more strategies for differentiation.

HISTORICAL THINKING

ANSWERS

1. Through its events, Feeding the 5,000 aims to raise awareness of food waste and encourage people and businesses to waste less food.

2. Possible response: Today, instead of food waste, livestock are fed grains people could eat. In addition, edible food is thrown away, creating more landfills and perpetuating hunger. To try to feed hungry people, more forests are cut to make room for fields and pastureland and more water is diverted for irrigation.

3. Answers will vary. Possible response: My family could do more meal planning, eat leftovers, and not buy in bulk.

CRITICAL VIEWING Possible response: Consumers might assume that the food is diseased in some way and therefore dangerous to eat, or they might think it will not make an attractive display on the dinner table.

AN INTERCONNECTED WORLD

During the 20th century, the United States became so powerful and dominant that historians began speaking of "the American century." How will the country's role change in the interconnected world of the 21st century?

PURSUING A MORE HOPEFUL WORLD

During his terms in office, President Obama favored a diplomatic approach in shaping U.S. relations with other countries. In 2009, the president began working to improve relations with Cuba. The two countries had been at odds since Fidel Castro seized power in Cuba in 1959 and established a communist dictatorship there. Then in 2008, with his health declining, Castro handed over power to his brother Raúl, who soon began to institute reforms. The following year, Obama lifted restrictions on travel to Cuba from the United States, and in 2015, the two countries restored diplomatic ties. In March 2016, Obama became the first sitting U.S. president to visit Cuba in nearly 90 years. Fidel Castro died at the age of 90 in November 2016.

Obama also attempted to improve relations between the United States and Iran. The two countries had been adversaries since the 1979 Iranian Revolution, which brought an anti-American Muslim cleric, or religious leader, to power. Tensions between the two countries increased early in the 21st century when the United States accused Iran of secretly developing a nuclear weapons program. As a result, the United States imposed harsh economic sanctions on Iran. In 2012, diplomats representing the two nations began discussing the nuclear issue and struck a deal in 2015. Iran promised to use its nuclear research for peaceful purposes and to provide inspectors greater access to the program, and the United States agreed to lift its sanctions. Obama said the agreement marked "one more chapter in our pursuit of a safer, more helpful and more hopeful world." However, the deal drew criticism from many Americans who did not believe Iran would keep its promise.

GLOBAL TERRORISM

No deals can be made with terrorists, however. Terrorist groups have emerged as major threats to world security. Foremost among these groups is al Qaeda, which you have read about. During the ongoing war on terror, President Obama ordered American soldiers to hunt down and kill al Qaeda leaders, including Osama bin Laden, the mastermind of the September 11, 2001, terror attacks. Nevertheless, the group has survived and continues to commit acts of terrorism.

Another terrorist organization called the **Islamic State in Iraq and Syria (ISIS)** may be more dangerous than al Qaeda. ISIS is a militant extremist group that has taken control of large areas of Syria and Iraq. The group first gained widespread attention in early 2014 when its forces seized control of cities and territories in Iraq and Syria, which was being torn apart by a bloody civil war. In the summer of 2015, ISIS destroyed ancient buildings and artifacts in and around the Syrian city of Palmyra. Leaders of the group claimed the ancient Greek and Roman ruins had no value because they weren't made by Muslims. The rest of the world condemned this misguided attack on our common heritage. In the end, however, terrorism can't destroy the enduring record of human life on Earth.

Europe also came under attack. In November 2015, ISIS members carried out terrorist attacks in Paris, killing roughly 130 people. Five months later, the militant Muslim group claimed credit for killing more than 30 people in Brussels, Belgium. Some of the men who carried out the attacks were born and raised in Europe. ISIS and other terrorist groups have been able to recruit new members through the Internet. Their message of inclusion appeals to many economically disadvantaged and alienated people—particularly young men—around the world.

The fighting in Syria and Iraq displaced millions of people and contributed to a worldwide refugee crisis. By 2015, about 4 million refugees had fled from Syria. In the United States, the question of whether or not to accept Syrian refugees sparked intense debate. Opponents expressed fear that some of the refugees might carry out terrorist attacks on U.S. soil.

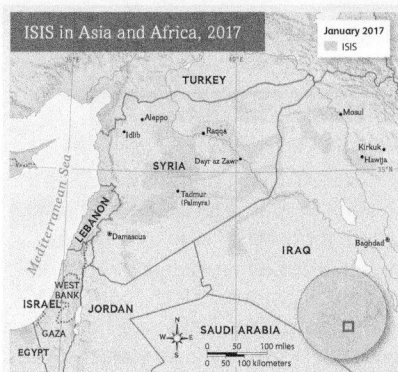

ISIS in Asia and Africa, 2017

Yet as the leader of the world's democratic societies, the United States has long been a magnet for people all over the world who yearn for a life of freedom and opportunity—and political stability. Under our democratic political system, the United States has achieved a level of freedom and economic prosperity that has made it a model for other nations.

As you know, Americans' rights and freedoms are the result of a carefully defined set of political principles embodied in the Constitution. But these freedoms are imperfect. For example, even though Americans elected an African-American president in 2008, poverty, incarceration, and lower life-expectancy rates continue to afflict communities of color at rates that are far higher than those of white communities. Still, the enduring significance of the United States lies in its free political system, its pluralistic nature, and its promise of opportunity. The country has demonstrated the strength and dynamism of a racially, religiously, and culturally diverse people. Our democratic political system depends on them—as educated citizens—to survive and prosper.

National Geographic photographer David Guttenfelder took this photo of a passenger waving the American and Cuban flags as his ship arrived in Havana, Cuba's capital, in May 2016. The vessel was one of the first cruise ships to travel from the United States to Cuba in decades.

HISTORICAL THINKING

1. **READING CHECK** What steps did President Obama take to improve relations with Cuba?

2. **SYNTHESIZE** How has globalization helped encourage the rise of terrorist groups?

3. **FORM AND SUPPORT OPINIONS** Do you think the United States should pursue diplomatic solutions to problems with other countries, or use force? Explain your answer.

PLAN: 2-PAGE LESSON

OBJECTIVE

Analyze how U.S. foreign policy has improved international relations and been affected by global terrorism.

CRITICAL THINKING SKILLS FOR LESSON 4.5

- Synthesize
- Form and Support Opinions
- Analyze Cause and Effect
- Make Connections
- Interpret Maps

HISTORICAL THINKING FOR CHAPTER 31

What does it mean to be an American in the 21st century? In the early 21st century, American foreign policy reflected the challenges of living in an interconnected world. Lesson 4.5 explores the impact of global terrorism and other challenges.

NATIONAL GEOGRAPHIC PHOTOGRAPHER DAVID GUTTENFELDER

Photojournalist David Guttenfelder spent 20 years covering news stories for the Associated Press. During that time, he traveled to more than 75 countries, including North Korea. Geopolitics is one of his main interests. His first article for *National Geographic*, "Afghanistan's Opium Wars," appeared in 2011. Over the years, Guttenfelder has won many awards for his photojournalism, including seven World Press Photo Awards and a variety of awards from the Overseas Press Club of the United States. In addition, he has been a finalist for a Pulitzer Prize multiple times and won awards for his smartphone photography, including being named *TIME* magazine's 2014 Instagram Photographer of the Year.

HISTORY NOTEBOOK

Encourage students to complete the Reid on the Road video series page for Chapter 31 in their History Notebooks after they view the video.

INTRODUCE & ENGAGE

DISCUSS THE IMPACT OF FOREIGN POLICY

Ask students to examine the photograph of the cruise ship arriving in Cuba. Read aloud the caption. **ASK:** Why do you think the man might be holding both the American and the Cuban flags? *(Answers will vary. Possible responses: The man or his family may have lived in Cuba before Castro seized power, but he may currently be a resident of the United States. He is proud of both countries and is excited to be in Cuba. He might want to celebrate a new era of friendship between the two countries.)* Briefly discuss how changes in foreign policy can affect average Americans in an interconnected world.

TEACH

GUIDED DISCUSSION

1. **Analyze Cause and Effect** What complex factors might have influenced President Obama's decision to restore diplomatic ties with Cuba and reach out to Iran? *(Answers will vary. Possible response: In 2008, Raúl Castro took power and began instituting reforms, and Obama may have hoped that restoring diplomatic ties with Cuba would encourage further reforms. In the case of Iran, Obama may have hoped to curb the power of an adversary in a volatile area of the world or even to shift the relationship away from an adversarial one.)*

2. **Make Connections** How does ISIS illustrate the trend of the globalization of terrorism? *(Possible responses: In addition to seizing large territories in Syria and Iraq, ISIS also claimed responsibility for attacks in Europe, including the November 2015 attack in Paris and the 2016 attack in Brussels, Belgium. The group recruits members worldwide via the Internet.)*

INTERPRET MAPS

Direct students' attention to the map of ISIS in Asia and Africa. **ASK:** In which country did ISIS have the strongest presence in 2017? *(Syria)* **ASK:** In what other countries did ISIS have a presence? *(Iraq and Egypt)* **ASK:** Based on the text discussion, why might ISIS have been successful in these areas? *(Possible response: Both Syria and Iraq were being torn apart by civil war in 2017, which would have made these countries vulnerable.)*

ACTIVE OPTIONS

On Your Feet: Rotating Discussion Arrange students in a large circle, facing inward. Ask a question about the lesson and toss a beanbag to a student, who must answer the question. After answering, the student tosses the beanbag to another student, who may choose to add information to the first answer or to ask his or her own question of a different student, tossing the beanbag to that student. Continue until all students have either asked or answered a question. If students get stuck on a question, prompt them to toss the beanbag to you to request clarification.

NG Learning Framework: Explore Global Terrorism

SKILL Communication

KNOWLEDGE Our Human Story

Instruct students to work in groups to explore the complex effects of globalization on terrorism and the U.S. military's response to it by researching the following questions:

• How might the trend of globalization lead to a clash of cultures that fuels terrorism? Consider the impact of both economic and cultural globalization.

• How does globalization affect the U.S. military actions in the war on terror? Consider both the impact on military alliances and tactics and on Americans serving in the military.

Have groups share their research in a roundtable discussion.

DIFFERENTIATE

ENGLISH LANGUAGE LEARNERS

Pose and Answer Questions Arrange students at the **Emerging** and **Expanding** levels in mixed pairs and ask them to read the lesson together. Instruct students to pause after each paragraph and ask one another *who, what, when, where,* or *why* questions about what they have just read. Suggest students use a 5Ws Chart to help organize their questions and answers. Ask students at the **Expanding** level to assist students at the **Emerging** level as needed.

GIFTED & TALENTED

Profile a Diplomat Tell students that thousands of diplomats work for the Foreign Service, part of the U.S. Department of State. Challenge students to conduct research using a variety of online sources to find out more about the work of a specific U.S. diplomat. (You may wish to suggest Wendy Sherman or Stephen Bosworth.) Then have students write a profile of that person, describing how he or she became a diplomat, where that person served, and one diplomatic success. Suggest that students conclude their profile by discussing the advantages of using the "soft power" of negotiating versus the "hard power" of military force.

See the Chapter Planner for more strategies for differentiation.

HISTORICAL THINKING

ANSWERS

1. He lifted a ban on travel to Cuba, rekindled diplomacy, and visited Cuba.

2. Possible responses: Global access to the Internet and social media help terrorist groups organize, recruit, and spread propaganda. Easy global transportation of people and goods (including weapons) enables terrorists to carry out attacks around the world.

3. Possible responses: Diplomatic solutions hold the most promise for lasting peace, since they provide an avenue for discussion and compromise. A show of force is better than diplomacy when dealing with countries that sponsor terrorism or have poor records of upholding agreements.

The 2016 Election

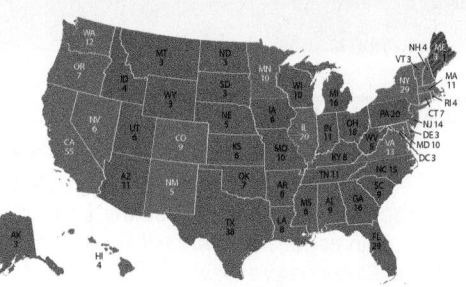

Donald J. Trump, Republican		
Electoral Vote: 306 votes, 56.9%		
Popular Vote: 62,979,636 votes, 46.1%		

Hillary Rodham Clinton, Democrat		
Electoral Vote: 232 votes, 43.1%		
Popular Vote: 65,844,610 votes, 48.2%		

Write-Ins & Others		
7,804,213 votes, 5.7%		

THE ELECTION OF 2016

In 2016, American voters were presented with two historic major party candidates. One was a wealthy businessman and TV personality with no political experience. The other was a woman with more than a decade of experience in both the legislative and executive branches. The outcome surprised many.

A POPULIST PREVAILS

As you have read, populists such as William Jennings Bryan and H. Ross Perot launched unsuccessful presidential bids in the past. In 2016, after emerging from a crowded field of candidates to become the Republican nominee, **Donald J. Trump** ran a populist campaign in which he claimed that only he, with his business expertise, could solve the nation's problems. Unlike his populist predecessors, Trump won the 2016 election, defeating Democratic nominee Hillary Rodham Clinton.

Clinton had served as U.S. Senator from New York and as President Obama's secretary of state. She was the wife of former president Bill Clinton. Trump, on the other hand, had never run for or served in public office prior to 2016. A real-estate developer and reality TV celebrity, Trump was extremely outspoken in his views, political and otherwise. He chose **Mike Pence**, the governor of Indiana, as his running mate. Clinton's running mate was Tim Kaine, a senator from Virginia.

While Clinton ran a traditional campaign based on issues and proposed solutions, Trump's populist campaign was fueled by his message: The interests of the United States should be placed above those of other nations. His lively rallies attracted the support of traditional Republicans and a number of independent voters. His promises to build a wall along the entire length of the border with Mexico, deport undocumented immigrants, and ban foreign Muslims from entering the United States appealed to nativists. He pledged to repeal the Affordable Care Act, put an end to NAFTA, and bring a quick end to international terrorism.

During the campaign, U.S. intelligence agencies and the Department of Justice gathered evidence that Russia had engaged in a complex, high-tech effort to disrupt the nation's electoral process. According to the Department of Homeland Security, Russian hackers attempted to access voter databases in 21 states and succeeded in breaching the systems of three states. There was no evidence these efforts affected the actual vote. Russian operatives also spread misinformation and negative "news" about Clinton on social media and hacked into both parties' email systems, leaking information that tended to be primarily unfavorable to Clinton and the Democrats.

On Election Day, Trump won a narrow majority of voters in a number of **swing states**, or states where

Donald Trump and Hillary Clinton take the stage for their second of three 2016 presidential debates. The debate was held at Washington University in St. Louis, Missouri, on October 9.

the election might go to either party. Even though almost 3 million more Americans cast their votes for Clinton, Trump won the electoral vote 306 to 232.

In 2017, Congress overwhelmingly voted to add new sanctions to those already in place to address Russia's cyberattacks during the election. The unusual election also raised suspicion that Trump's campaign had **colluded**, or conspired, with the Russians. Even though Trump denied the allegations, the Department of Justice appointed a special prosecutor, **Robert Mueller**, to investigate. As of early 2018, the investigation was still ongoing, while Trump declined to impose the additional sanctions on Russia. He claimed existing sanctions were effective enough.

TRUMP'S FIRST YEAR

Trump began his presidency by issuing a number of executive orders, including a controversial directive banning people from seven specific, primarily Muslim, nations from entering the United States. Enforcement of the order began as many travelers were already on their way to the United States, causing widespread confusion at airports. Federal courts initially blocked this order, stating it was unconstitutional. Parts of the ban were reinstated and the government issued new versions of the ban in 2017. These were also contested in federal courts.

Trump attempted to secure funding for the construction of a border wall early in his term, but Congress approved only a small portion of the money required. He also ordered a sharp increase in the number of **Immigration and Customs Enforcement (ICE)** agents, raising the deportation rate of undocumented immigrants. In September 2017, President Trump chose to end the DACA program,

handing Congress the responsibility of passing an act to protect the Dreamers. Otherwise, these immigrants would face deportation to the place of their birth. Trump also insisted that Congress should pass tougher immigration laws and fund the border wall.

Congress failed to repeal the Affordable Care Act, but a clause in its Tax Cuts and Jobs Act, which passed in December 2017, ended the individual mandate, an important funding measure requiring Americans not covered by an insurance plan to pay a tax. This threatened the affordability and the future of the ACA. The tax bill lowered tax rates for individuals temporarily and corporations permanently but took no steps to make up the lost revenue caused by these cuts. Some economists believed this new tax plan would result in a sharp rise to the national debt.

On the international front, Trump ended U.S. involvement in the **Trans-Pacific Partnership (TPP)**, a trade agreement with Asia. He also threatened to leave NAFTA, although he ultimately decided to try to renegotiate it. To the dismay of many nations, Trump withdrew the United States from the Paris Agreement on climate change. Together with his pledge to promote the use of coal and other fossil fuels, as opposed to cleaner energy sources, Trump's actions have put the United States at odds with many of its allies.

HISTORICAL THINKING

1. **READING CHECK** How did the swing states affect the 2016 election?

2. **DETERMINE WORD MEANINGS** How did Trump fit the definition of a populist?

3. **EVALUATE** How effective was Trump in meeting his campaign promises during his first year as president?

PLAN: 2-PAGE LESSON

OBJECTIVE

Examine the reasons for Donald Trump's successful presidential election and the controversies that surrounded his first year in office.

CRITICAL THINKING SKILLS FOR LESSON 4.6

- Determine Word Meanings
- Evaluate
- Compare and Contrast
- Analyze Cause and Effect
- Analyze Language Use

HISTORICAL THINKING FOR CHAPTER 31

What does it mean to be an American in the 21st century? Core American values, such as liberty and democracy, continue to face challenges in the 21st century. Lesson 4.6 examines how the 2016 presidential election heightened debates about immigration and raised concerns about the integrity of the election system.

BACKGROUND FOR THE TEACHER

President Trump's Executive Order 13769, banning residents of seven majority-Muslim countries from entering the United States, was controversial from the start. Critics of the ban pointed out that many of the countries on the list were experiencing humanitarian crises—people were fleeing calamities such as famine, war, or drought—circumstances that should allow them to seek refuge in the United States. Others noted that none of the countries on the list had harbored the terrorists who attacked the United States on September 11, 2001, calling into question how effective the travel ban would be in making the country safer—its stated goal. The lower federal courts ruled that parts of the ban were unconstitutional and motivated more by partisan politics than by national security threats. In response, the White House submitted modified versions of the ban. However, the final decision on the constitutionality of any presidential order rests with the U.S. Supreme Court.

INTRODUCE & ENGAGE
PREVIEW THE ELECTION MAP
Direct students' attention to the map, The 2016 Election, and have them cover the legend with their hand. **ASK:** What does the map show about the "red" and "blue" candidates in the 2016 presidential election? *(Possible responses: The "red" candidate has won most of the states and must be popular in most of the country. The "blue" candidate seems to appeal mainly to states along the western and northeastern coasts, capturing only five states in the West and Midwest and none in the South.)* Then direct students to read the legend, noting that the "blue" candidate actually received more popular votes. Tell students that this lesson explains the complex story of the 2016 presidential election and describes the controversial actions of President Trump during his first year in office.

TEACH
GUIDED DISCUSSION
1. **Compare and Contrast** How did Donald Trump's and Hillary Clinton's campaigns differ in the 2016 election? *(Clinton ran a more traditional campaign, focusing on major issues and her solutions, while Trump ran a more populist campaign, focusing on putting America's interests first and on some people's fears about immigration and border security.)*

2. **Analyze Cause and Effect** What initially caused the United States to investigate Russian activities during the election, and what were some of the effects of this investigation? *(The United States had evidence that Russian hackers had tried to access the voter databases in some states, had hacked into the email systems of both the Republican and Democratic parties, and had spread misinformation on social media. In response, the United States issued new sanctions against Russia and also began investigations into possible ties between the Trump campaign and the Russians. This created an ongoing controversy during Trump's early administration.)*

ANALYZE LANGUAGE USE
Prompt students to review the meaning of the word *colluded* in the lesson. Give them time to consider what this word suggests about possible connections between Trump's campaign and the Russians. **ASK:** Why is the charge of colluding with a foreign power considered so serious? *(Possible response: Colluding with a foreign power to gain an elected position would undermine the democratic election process and call into question his or her allegiances and priorities while in office.)*

ACTIVE OPTIONS
On Your Feet: Debate the Electoral College Divide the class into two groups. Direct both groups to conduct additional research about the electoral college, including why it was created, and how it works. Then assign one group the position of supporting the role of the electoral college in electing the president and the other group the position of using the popular vote to elect the president. Organize the two groups so that all students research and contribute to their teams' arguments. Then have each group select four members to formally debate the issue, providing reasons and examples for why their method for electing the president is best.

NG Learning Framework: Write About the Paris Agreement
ATTITUDES Responsibility, Empowerment
KNOWLEDGE Our Living Planet

Direct students to learn more about the Paris Agreement, such as what the pact says, which countries signed it, and what its goals are. Then ask students to explain in a brief report how the United States' withdrawal from the agreement caused tensions with allies. Allow time for volunteers to present their reports to the class.

DIFFERENTIATE
STRIVING READERS
Review Facts Post this heading: Five Facts About President Trump. After students read the lesson, ask them to copy the posted heading and add five sentences under it. Invite volunteers to share their sentences with the group.

PRE-AP
Create a Report Inform students that Donald Trump's election, leadership style, and policies are considered by some to be unprecedented departures from those of previous presidents. Challenge students to compare and contrast the views held and actions taken by Trump and his predecessors on topics such as foreign policy, economic policy, immigration, and communication/leadership style. Encourage students to use primary and secondary sources to create an oral or written report presenting their evaluation. Invite volunteers to share their findings with the class.

See the Chapter Planner for more strategies for differentiation.

HISTORICAL THINKING
ANSWERS
1. Because Trump won the electoral votes in a number of swing states, he won the election, despite losing the overall popular vote. If Clinton had narrowly won those swing states, Trump would have lost the election.

2. Trump ran as a nontraditional candidate who focused on his business expertise and issues affecting ordinary people rather than following the traditional beliefs and political leaders of the Republican Party.

3. Possible response: He was partially effective. For example, parts of his Muslim ban were challenged in the courts, though others were eventually reinstated. Also, Trump got some funding for a border wall, but not the amount he sought. Finally, the Affordable Care Act was weakened, but not repealed.

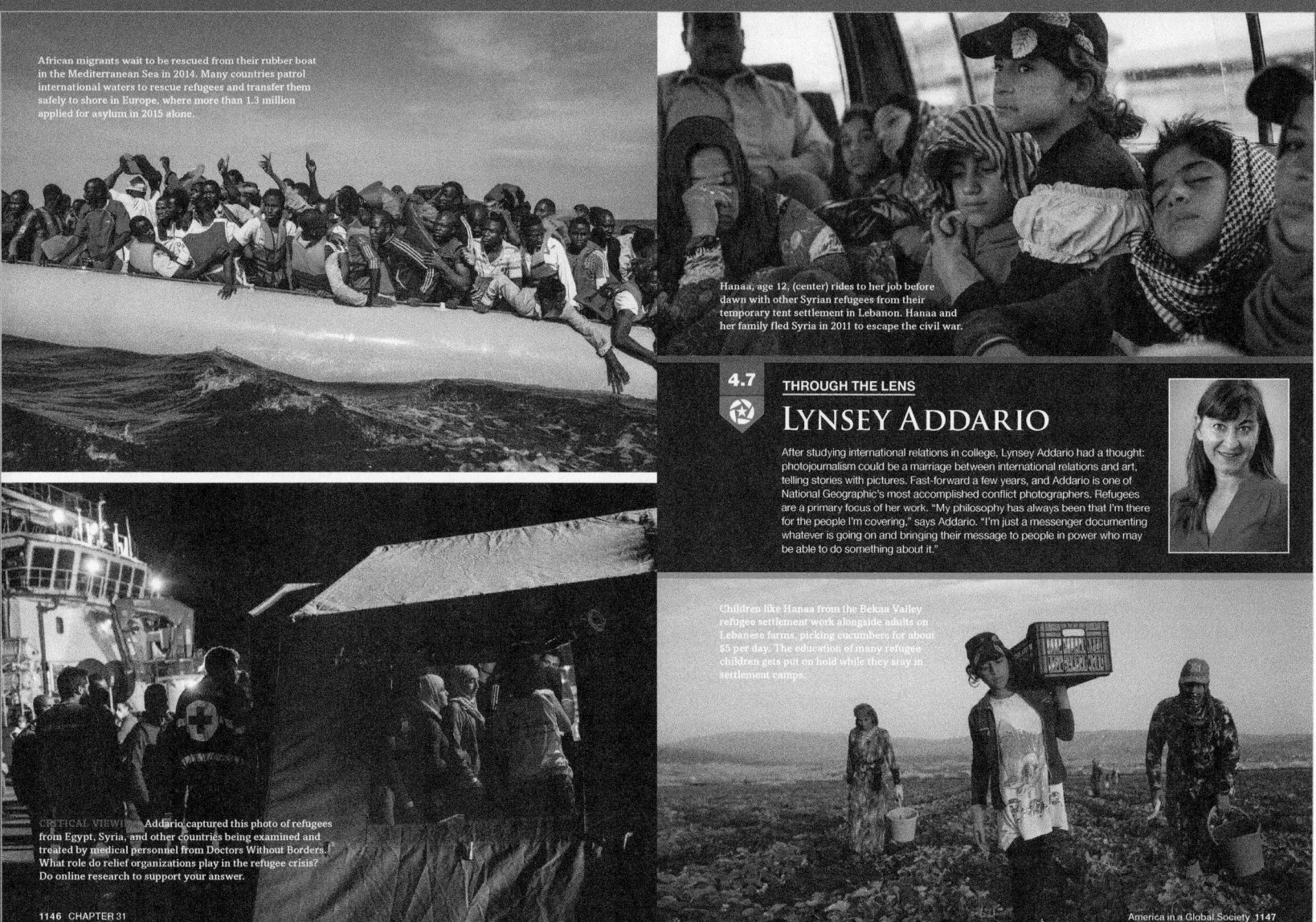

African migrants wait to be rescued from their rubber boat in the Mediterranean Sea in 2014. Many countries patrol international waters to rescue refugees and transfer them safely to shore in Europe, where more than 1.3 million applied for asylum in 2015 alone.

Hanaa, age 12, (center) rides to her job before dawn with other Syrian refugees from their temporary tent settlement in Lebanon. Hanaa and her family fled Syria in 2011 to escape the civil war.

4.7

THROUGH THE LENS

LYNSEY ADDARIO

After studying international relations in college, Lynsey Addario had a thought: photojournalism could be a marriage between international relations and art, telling stories with pictures. Fast-forward a few years, and Addario is one of National Geographic's most accomplished conflict photographers. Refugees are a primary focus of her work. "My philosophy has always been that I'm there for the people I'm covering," says Addario. "I'm just a messenger documenting whatever is going on and bringing their message to people in power who may be able to do something about it."

Children like Hanaa from the Bekaa Valley refugee settlement work alongside adults on Lebanese farms, picking cucumbers for about $5 per day. The education of many refugee children gets put on hold while they stay in settlement camps.

CRITICAL VIEWING Addario captured this photo of refugees from Egypt, Syria, and other countries being examined and treated by medical personnel from Doctors Without Borders. What role do relief organizations play in the refugee crisis? Do online research to support your answer.

PLAN: 2-PAGE LESSON

OBJECTIVE

Describe the circumstances of refugees shown in the photographs of Lynsey Addario.

CRITICAL THINKING SKILLS FOR LESSON 4.7

- Analyze Visuals
- Make Connections
- Draw Conclusions
- Compare and Contrast

HISTORICAL THINKING FOR CHAPTER 31

What does it mean to be an American in the 21st century? Millions of refugees from Syria, Egypt, and other countries have fled their homeland, some reaching Europe and others living in refugee camps. Lesson 4.7 explores the lives of refugees through the photographs of Lynsey Addario.

NATIONAL GEOGRAPHIC PHOTOGRAPHER LYNSEY ADDARIO

Photojournalist Lynsey Addario has covered conflicts, human rights, women's issues, and the plight of refugees and people displaced within their own nations in war zones, including Iraq, Afghanistan, and Sudan. Addario has been kidnapped twice while covering conflicts. The first time was in 2004 in Iraq while photographing fighting in Fallujah. In 2011, she was kidnapped in Libya while covering fighting between rebels and government forces for the *New York Times.* Since her second kidnapping, Addario has focused more on the effects of war on civilians and refugees, while avoiding front lines. She has received many awards for her work, including the Award of Excellence from Pictures of the Year in 1999.

HISTORY NOTEBOOK

Encourage students to complete the Through the Lens page for Chapter 31 in their History Notebooks as they read.

INTRODUCE & ENGAGE

PREVIEW USING VISUALS

Direct students to the photographs in the lesson. Ask students what the photographs show. *(events in the lives of refugees)* Point out that photojournalist Lynsey Addario sees herself as a messenger. Discuss with students what message they think she or the people in the photographs might be conveying.

TEACH

GUIDED DISCUSSION

1. **Draw Conclusions** What can you conclude from Addario's photograph of African migrants about conditions in the homelands of the people shown? *(Possible response: Conditions in their home countries must be extremely difficult, because the migrants are so desperate to flee their homes for Europe that they are willing to leave behind most of their possessions and risk their lives in overcrowded boats.)*

2. **Compare and Contrast** How is the situation of Hanaa, shown working on a farm in Lebanon, similar to and different from the conditions faced by migrant workers from Mexico in the United States? *(Possible response: Like Hanaa, migrant workers from Mexico are providing labor in exchange for low wages in order to help their families economically. Most Mexican migrant workers, however, have the option to return home. Hanaa and her family have no place to go while civil war rages in Syria.)*

THROUGH THE LENS

Since civil war broke out in 2011, more than 5 million Syrians have fled their country. Over 6 million are categorized as internally displaced, or refugees who have stayed in Syria. Many refugees have fled to nearby Lebanon, where they live in informal refugee camps, since there are no formal, government-sponsored ones. These camps are spread around Lebanon in both urban and rural areas. The Bekaa Valley, where Hanaa and her family settled, has the largest concentration of Syrians, with some 300,000 refugees. The United Nations estimates that about 70 percent of the more than 1 million registered Syrian refugees in Lebanon live in poverty. Because the camps are informal, life is especially precarious. In May 2017, the Lebanese army issued eviction notices to 86 tent settlements in the Bekka Valley, citing the settlements as too close to a Lebanese military airport. This left some families homeless as they scrambled to find new locations that would allow them to set up camps.

ACTIVE OPTIONS

On Your Feet: Descriptive Words Distribute four sticky notes to each student. Then have students closely examine each photograph. Direct students to write a single word or a short phrase to describe each photograph, one per sticky note. Tell students to place their notes on the board or a wall. As a class, discuss the posted descriptions and implications for U.S. foreign policy.

NG Learning Framework: Investigate the Lives of Syrian Refugees

SKILL Observation

KNOWLEDGE Our Human Story

Prompt small groups of students to use online sources to learn more about the experiences of Syrian refugees fleeing the civil war in their homeland. Groups might focus on different topics relating to refugees, such as: when and why particular individuals and families decided to leave; dangers and hardships of the journey; life in refugee camps; making a home in a foreign land; legal and other obstacles to immigration; discrimination refugees face in their new surroundings. Hold a class discussion in which students present their findings.

DIFFERENTIATE

INCLUSION

Describe Details Pair students who are visually impaired with students who are not. Ask the latter to describe each photograph in detail, including the expressions on people's faces, and to read the captions. Encourage visually impaired students to ask clarifying questions as necessary.

PRE-AP

Summarize a Health Care Strategy Explain that Lynsey Addario took photographs for an article in the *New York Times Magazine*, "What Can Mississippi's Health Care System Learn from Iran" (July 27, 2012), that examines how replicating aspects of Iran's health care system could benefit people in a high-poverty area of the United States. Prompt students to find and read this article. Then have them create a multimedia presentation to summarize the article for the class.

See the Chapter Planner for more strategies for differentiation.

CRITICAL VIEWING Students should support their answers with findings from online research. Possible response: Relief organizations provide essential goods and services, such as medical, dental, and psychiatric care; food assistance; household items and clothing, water and sanitation; child protection; and education.

VOCABULARY

For each of the following vocabulary terms, write a sentence in which you use the term correctly.

1. globalization
   Globalization, which has allowed for the faster and freer flow of people and goods across national borders, has powerfully affected the United States.

2. free-enterprise zone

3. compassionate conservatism

4. neoconservative

5. rogue state

6. bailout

7. service sector

8. marriage equality

9. greenhouse gas

10. new media

READING STRATEGY
FORM AND SUPPORT OPINIONS

When you form an opinion, you determine and assess the importance and significance of an issue. Your opinion is your personal judgment, not a fact, so you should support your opinion with examples and facts. Use a chart like this one to form and support an opinion about issues in the 21st century. Then answer the question.

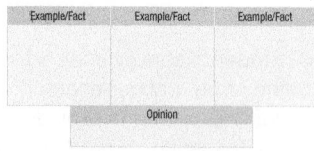

Example/Fact	Example/Fact	Example/Fact

Opinion

11. What do you think is the most critical issue facing the United States in the 21st century?

MAIN IDEAS

Answer the following questions. Support your answers with evidence from the chapter.

12. What was the Contract with America? **LESSON 1.1**

13. How did globalization affect U.S. manufacturing jobs during the 1990s? **LESSON 1.2**

14. How might bias have played into the outcome of the 2000 presidential election? **LESSON 2.1**

15. Why did President George W. Bush order the invasion of Iraq? **LESSON 2.3**

16. What impact did the Great Recession have on American industries and the employment rate? **LESSON 3.1**

17. What were Obama's priorities when he became president? **LESSON 3.2**

18. What evidence of global warming have scientists detected? **LESSON 4.2**

19. What are genetically modified foods? **LESSON 4.3**

20. Why were many voters surprised by the outcome of the 2016 election? **LESSON 4.6**

HISTORICAL THINKING

Answer the following questions. Support your answers with evidence from the chapter.

21. **COMPARE AND CONTRAST** Why is the United States more diverse now than it was in the middle of the 20th century?

22. **DRAW CONCLUSIONS** How have shifts in foreign policy and immigration affected America's national identity from the 1980s through recent times?

23. **MAKE INFERENCES** How do you think Muslims in the United States may have been regarded by some other Americans after September 11, 2001?

24. **EVALUATE** How has the role of the federal government—and especially the presidency—changed from the 1970s through more recent times?

25. **SYNTHESIZE** What does globalization mean, and how has it affected Americans?

26. **FORM AND SUPPORT OPINIONS** Do you think groups such as Black Lives Matter and Occupy Wall Street are ultimately effective? Why or why not?

27. **ANALYZE ENVIRONMENTAL CONCEPTS** How has deforestation affected the natural system of photosynthesis and increased global warming?

INTERPRET GRAPHS

Study the graphs below, which show the relative populations of ethnic groups in the United States between 1950 and 2010. Then answer the questions that follow.

U.S. Ethnic Population, 1950–2010

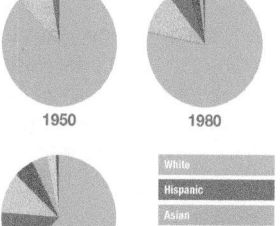

1950   1980

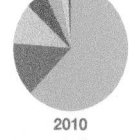

2010

| White |
| Hispanic |
| Asian |
| African American |
| Native American |
| Two or more ethnicities |
| Other |

Source: U.S. Census Bureau

28. How did the composition of the United States shift between 1950 and 1980?

29. What additional shifts occurred between 1980 and 2010?

ANALYZE SOURCES

In this excerpt from an address to the nation on immigration that President Obama delivered on November 20, 2014, he explains why he welcomes immigrants to the United States.

> My fellow Americans, we are and always will be a nation of immigrants. We were strangers once, too. And whether our forebears were strangers who crossed the Atlantic, or the Pacific, or the Rio Grande, we are here only because this country welcomed them in, and taught them that to be an American is about something more than what we look like, or what our last names are, or how we worship. What makes us Americans is our shared commitment to an ideal—that all of us are created equal, and all of us have the chance to make of our lives what we will.

30. What vision of the United States does Obama describe in his address?

CONNECT TO YOUR LIFE

31. **EXPLANATORY** Grassroots movements such as the Tea Party, Occupy Wall Street, and Black Lives Matter formed in the early 21st century. Why do you think such movements form, and why are people drawn to them? Write a paragraph in which you explain the connection between such groups and larger issues.

TIPS

- State the purpose of grassroots movements in a main idea statement.

- Describe the social, economic, and political factors that may be involved in the movements' formation.

- Explain what people who join the movements hope to get out of them.

- Use information from the chapter to help support your ideas.

- Conclude your paragraph with a sentence summarizing your ideas.

VOCABULARY ANSWERS

1. Globalization, which has allowed for the faster and freer flow of people and goods across national borders, has powerfully affected the United States.

2. Free-enterprise zones make it easier to trade goods between Mexico and the United States.

3. Compassionate conservatism promotes services for the disadvantaged as well as cutting taxes.

4. Neoconservatives support using military force to achieve goals.

5. Iran is a rogue state that threatens world peace.

6. The federal government saved banks via a bailout.

7. Teachers and bankers work in the service sector.

8. Gay and lesbian couples fought for marriage equality to win the legal benefits afforded opposite-sex couples.

9. Greenhouse gases are linked to global warming.

10. Many people rely on new media conveyed by the Internet.

READING STRATEGY ANSWER

Example/Fact	Example/Fact	Example/Fact
Greenhouse gases cause temperatures to rise.	Average temperatures have risen 1.4°F.	Ice sheets in Antarctica and Greenland have begun to melt.

Opinion
Global warming is the most critical issue facing the United States in the 21st century.

11. Answers will vary. Possible response: Global warming is the most critical issue facing the United States in the 21st century. The greenhouse effect, which began during the Industrial Revolution around 1750, has resulted in an increase in average temperature. Scientists have registered an increase of 1.4° F since the beginning of the 20th century, beginning with the advent of trains, cars, and airplanes. Greenhouse gases warm Earth's surface by capturing the sun's heat, resulting in serious consequences. The gradual melting of the vast ice sheets in Antarctica and Greenland destroys habitats, changes ecosystems, and affects weather.

MAIN IDEAS ANSWERS

12. The Contract with America was a document co-authored by Newt Gingrich that promised tax cuts for the middle class, strong anti-crime legislation, and constitutional amendments requiring a balanced budget and term limits.

13. Globalization diminished U.S. manufacturing jobs in the 1990s when companies moved their operations to countries with lower labor costs.

14. The U.S. Supreme Court ruling against the Florida recount might have been biased toward the Republicans because it was hasty and reversed the ruling of the Florida Supreme Court.

15. Bush ordered the invasion of Iraq on the false premise that Saddam Hussein's government possessed weapons of mass destruction.

16. The Great Recession hurt industries because consumers could no longer afford or finance big-ticket items such as automobiles, travel, home furnishings, and construction. The unemployment rate increased as companies cut jobs when sales plummeted.

17. When President Obama took office, his top priority was to lead the country out of recession. He also wanted to initiate comprehensive health care reform to provide health insurance for more Americans.

18. Scientists have detected an average global temperature increase of 1.4° F since the beginning of the 20th century and melting and shrinkage of the Antarctica and Greenland ice sheets.

19. Genetically modified foods are foods grown from plants into which genes from different organisms have been introduced.

20. Possible response: Voters could have been surprised by the outcome of the election because Donald Trump lacked the experience and qualifications that Hillary Clinton possessed to become president of the United States, and Trump's campaign promises would have alienated the majority of voters who had previously elected President Obama for two terms.

HISTORICAL THINKING ANSWERS

21. The Immigration Act of 1965 opened the United States to immigrants from all countries and gave preference to immigrants who already had relatives in the United States who were U.S. citizens. The end of the Vietnam War increased immigration from Southeast Asia, and the Islamic Revolution brought an influx of Iranians.

22. As the United States became more diverse, some Americans began to resent multiculturalism. In California, citizens voted for propositions that would have denied illegal immigrants state services such as public education, ended state-sponsored affirmative action, and banned bilingual education.

23. Possible response: Some Americans treated Muslims with suspicion after the terrorist attacks on September 11, 2011, and some blamed all Muslims for the terrorism of one extremist group, which led to a rise in hate crimes against Muslims.

24. The power of the federal government and the presidency has increased since the 1970s. In the wake of September 11, 2001, the USA Patriot Act greatly expanded the government's power to conduct surveillance on its own citizens. Another example is the degree to which the federal government stepped in to bail out banks and the automobile industry during the Great Recession.

25. Globalization is the faster and freer flow of people, resources, goods, and ideas across national borders. It has positively affected Americans by making consumer goods more affordable, increasing the pool of talented workers, and spurring economic expansion for multinational companies, including computer software, retail, and automobile companies. Some American workers have experienced unemployment because of job dislocation.

26. Answers will vary. Possible responses: Yes. These groups bring issues to the forefront, leading to investigations and possible policy changes. No. These groups polarize Americans and have the potential to incite violence.

27. Deforestation has eliminated trees, which absorb carbon dioxide as part of photosynthesis. The loss of trees results in higher levels of carbon dioxide, thereby increasing global temperatures.

INTERPRET GRAPHS ANSWERS

28. The percentage of whites in the population decreased between 1950 and 1980, while the percentage of Hispanics, Asians, and Others increased. The percentage of African Americans remained relatively constant.

29. Between 1980 and 2010, the trend continued for Hispanics, Asians, and Others. In addition, the percentage of the population that reported two or more ethnicities increased.

ANALYZE SOURCES ANSWER

30. Possible response: President Obama presents a vision of the United States made stronger by its diverse immigrant roots and united by the ideals of freedom and equality.

CONNECT TO YOUR LIFE ANSWER

31. Answers will vary but should include the purpose of grassroots movements; describe the social, economic, and political factors that contribute to their formation; explain what the people in the movements hope to accomplish; use information from the text; and conclude with a sentence that summarizes ideas.

U.S. Climate Refugees Race Against Time

BY CAROLYN VAN HOUTEN
Adapted from "The First Official Climate Refugees in the U.S. Race Against Time," by Carolyn van Houten, news.nationalgeographic.com, May 2016

A shot rings out across what remains of Isle de Jean Charles as the sun drops behind the gnarled skeletons of what once were massive oak trees. Rifle in hand, Howard Brunet, 14, looks down at the rabbit he shot. His sister Juliette, 13, leaps down the stairs to retrieve the body. Next comes rabbit stew. It's a normal evening at the Brunet household. The kids are tough. The water forces them to be.

Since 1955, the Isle de Jean Charles band of the Biloxi-Chitimacha-Choctaw tribe has lost 98 percent of its land to the encroaching Gulf waters. Of the 22,400-acre island that stood at that time, only several hundred acres remain. The island is located deep in the southern bayous of Louisiana, about 15 miles (24 kilometers) from the Gulf of Mexico. As the land has eroded, the tribe's identity, food, and culture have slowly eroded with it.

In response, in 2016, the Department of Housing and Urban Development awarded the tribe $48 million to relocate. But moving isn't a simple solution. The tribe is receiving funding, but the fight to save their culture is not over. The federal grant will help save the tribe from the eroding landscape, but addressing the effects of cultural erosion is far more difficult. "Once our island goes, the core of our tribe is lost," says Chantel Comardelle, the deputy tribal chief's daughter. "We've lost our whole culture—that is what is on the line."

For generations, the Biloxi-Chitimacha-Choctaw have sustained themselves off the island's natural resources. But today, residents say the land loss has made that untenable. The land is disappearing into the Gulf of Mexico because of a combination of coastal erosion, rising sea levels, lack of soil renewal, and shifting soil due to dredging for oil and gas pipeline placement. The soil that remains is nutrient depleted due to saltwater intrusion enabled by eroding marshes.

As the effects of climate change transform coastal communities around the world, the people of Isle de Jean Charles will be only 60 of the estimated 200 million people globally who could be displaced by 2050 because of climate change.

The only way into or out of Isle de Jean Charles is on Island Road. In 1953, the year the road was built, land and thick marsh surrounded the road. But erosion is eating away at it. Every time a strong storm heads toward the island, residents have to decide whether they will evacuate. Once the storm arrives, the road out of the island will be flooded. The water has overtaken many structures that were once a part of the community. Many of the tribal members who remain on the island can't afford any other option. Most of those who have left the island remain in the tribe but are spread throughout Louisiana.

"The tribe has physically and culturally been torn apart with the scattering of members," states the resettlement proposal submitted to the Department of Housing and Urban Development. "A new settlement offers an opportunity for the tribe to rebuild their homes and secure their culture on safe ground."

The resettlement proposal argues that Isle de Jean Charles is an excellent test case for deciding how to best relocate people threatened by climate change. The plan aims to move families to a culturally appropriate community. Because tribe members have already lost so much of their land and their tribal heritage to the water, relocation is crucial not just for their personal safety but also for the longevity of their culture and traditions.

"At one time, water was our life, and now it's almost our enemy because it is driving us out, but it still gives us life," Comardelle says. "It's a double-edged sword. It's our life and our death."

For more from National Geographic, check out "Shell Shock" online.

In this unit, you learned about recent American history, which includes events that your parents and many adults alive today have witnessed. You'll have no difficulty finding adults who watched TV news reports of the Watergate investigation and of President Nixon leaving the White House after resigning. These adults have vivid, emotional memories of the 9/11 terrorist attacks on the World Trade Center in New York City and on the Pentagon in Washington, D.C. What can you learn from these adults about the way average Americans reacted to such events? How has life in the United States changed over the course of their lives? What is better about life today? What is worse?

ASSIGNMENT

Conduct oral history interviews with people who were adults in the years after 1970. Find out how they and other Americans reacted to major events that occurred between 1970 and 2010. Be prepared to present your findings to the class.

Plan Review the major events covered in this unit and choose a couple to focus on. Compose a list of questions about those events and about changes in the United States between 1970 and 2010. You might use a graphic organizer to help you formulate your questions or to take notes. Then identify three adults and ask if they would be willing to be interviewed.

Produce Decide if you want to take notes during your interviews or make an audio or video recording. Then schedule and conduct the interviews. In your notes or at the beginning of a recording, be sure to identify each interviewee by name and birthdate.

Present Share your interviews with the class. You might consider one of these options:

- If you made audio or video recordings, write and record an introduction to them. Then edit your recordings and produce a final version to play for the class. (You have created your own primary source.)

- Either transcribe your interviews or write a summary of what you learned from them and distribute your written account to the class.

- Prepare and deliver an oral report of the highlights of your interviews.

Check out the History Notebook for another oral history project.

Who? _____

What? _____

Where? _____

When? _____

Why? _____

NATIONAL GEOGRAPHIC | **LEARNING FRAMEWORK ACTIVITIES**

Create a History Game

ATTITUDE Curiosity

SKILLS Communication, Collaboration

Perhaps you've played board games that require you to answer questions about literature, science, popular culture, and other subjects. Work with a partner to create a history game modeled on such board games. Using the information in this unit, write 50 questions that can be answered in a word or phrase. Use the questions as the basis of a board game, and play the game with a group of classmates. As an alternative, create a crossword puzzle using key words and names from the unit. Give the puzzle to a classmate to solve.

Form a Political Party

ATTITUDES Responsibility, Empowerment

KNOWLEDGE Our Human Story

You've read about the beliefs, policies, and agendas of a number of American political parties during this course. Now form a political party that represents your beliefs. Decide on a name for your party, and write a platform and a description of the programs you'd like to institute. Tell how your party differs from the Democratic and Republican parties in the United States. Identify groups of Americans who would be likely to support your party. Give an oral presentation in which you describe your political party to the class.

NATIONAL GEOGRAPHIC CONNECTION

GUIDED DISCUSSION FOR "U.S. CLIMATE REFUGEES RACE AGAINST TIME"

1. **Compare and Contrast** How has the Biloxi-Chitimacha-Choctaw tribe's island environment changed since 1955? *(While some members of the tribe remain on Isle de Jean Charles, living off the natural resources available to them, many have left. The usable area of the island is shrinking due to rising water and erosion from climate change. What was once fresh water is now salt water, and the soil is depleted of nutrients from pipeline drilling.)*

2. **Make Inferences** What did Chantel Comardelle mean when she said, "Once our island goes, the core of our tribe is lost"? *(Comardelle is suggesting that the life and history of the tribe are inseparable from the land they occupy. Loss of the island and relocation means the loss of their culture—the way they farm, hunt, feed themselves, and practice traditions as a group.)*

GUIDED DISCUSSION FOR "SHELL SHOCK"

1. **Identify Main Ideas and Details** How do data and implications for treatment differ between blast-force brain injuries and concussions? *(Blast-force pattern of scarring in the brain is different from that of concussions. Researchers believe that some standard treatments may be missing the mark for blast-force brain trauma.)*

2. **Draw Conclusions** How does the treatment for shell shock during World War I serve as warning for treatment of blast-force brain injury? *(New findings indicate that many blast-force brain injuries during World War I may have been misdiagnosed as mental health problems, so doctors may need a different starting point for diagnoses and treatments involving the brain.)*

HISTORY NOTEBOOK

Encourage students to complete the Unit Wrap-Up page for Unit 9 in their History Notebooks.

UNIT INQUIRY PROJECT RUBRIC

ASSESS
Use the rubric to assess each student's participation and performance.

SCORE	ASSIGNMENT	PRODUCT	PRESENTATION
3 GREAT	• Student thoroughly understands the assignment. • Student participates fully in the project process.	• Oral history interviews are well thought out. • Oral history interviews offer three adults' perspectives. • Oral history interviews contain all of the key elements listed in the assignment.	• Presentation is clear, concise, and logical. • Presentation does a good job of creatively sharing the interviews. • Presentation engages the audience.
2 GOOD	• Student mostly understands the assignment. • Student participates fairly well in the project process.	• Oral history interviews are fairly well thought out. • Oral history interviews offer two or three adults' perspectives. • Oral history interviews contain most of the key elements listed in the assignment.	• Presentation is fairly clear, concise, and logical. • Presentation does an adequate job of creatively sharing the interviews. • Presentation somewhat engages the audience.
1 NEEDS WORK	• Student does not understand the assignment. • Student minimally participates or does not participate in the project process.	• Oral history interviews are not well thought out. • Oral history interviews offer one or no adults' perspectives. • Oral history interviews contain few or none of the key elements listed in the assignment.	• Presentation is not clear, concise, or logical. • Presentation does an inadequate job of sharing the interviews. • Presentation does not engage the audience.

NATIONAL GEOGRAPHIC LEARNING FRAMEWORK RUBRIC

ASSESS
Use the rubric to assess how each student applies the National Geographic Learning Framework.

SCORE	ASSIGNMENT	ASSIGNMENT	FINAL PRODUCTS
3 GREAT	• Game or puzzle reflects **Curiosity** well. • Game or puzzle demonstrates **Communication** and **Collaboration** well.	• Oral presentation reflects **Responsibility** and **Empowerment** well. • Oral presentation explores **Our Human Story** well.	• Final products are engaging, creative, and well presented.
2 GOOD	• Game or puzzle reflects **Curiosity**. • Game or puzzle demonstrates **Communication** and **Collaboration**.	• Oral presentation reflects **Responsibility** and **Empowerment**. • Oral presentation explores **Our Human Story**.	• Final products are interesting, logical, and complete.
1 NEEDS WORK	• Game or puzzle does not reflect **Curiosity**. • Game or puzzle does not demonstrate **Communication** or **Collaboration**.	• Presentation does not reflect **Responsibility** and **Empowerment**. • Oral presentation does not explore **Our Human Story**.	• Final products are not creative, complete, or interesting.

AMERICA THROUGH THE DECADES

A picture is worth a thousand words. You've probably heard that before—now see if you agree. Each image in this photo essay represents one of the decades you have learned about, starting with the 1900s and going through the 2010s. Test your knowledge of American history by identifying each photograph according to its decade while you consider the historical events, important people, and social and cultural movements you have studied.

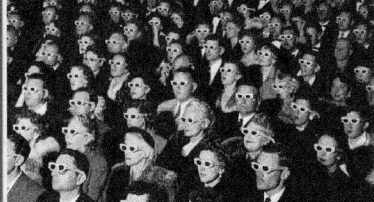

1152

PLAN: 2-PAGE LESSON

OBJECTIVE

Study photographs and place them in their proper historical context.

CRITICAL THINKING SKILLS FOR THROUGH THE LENS

- Analyze Visuals
- Make Connections
- Synthesize

BACKGROUND FOR THE TEACHER

Photographers have played a crucial role—sometimes deliberately and sometimes accidentally—in documenting American history. The photograph of the 1920s jazz band, identified as the St. Louis Cotton Club Band, was certainly planned. The musicians' poses capture the improvisational energy and rule-breaking spirit of jazz at a time when the art was new and, in many places, socially unacceptable. The photo of the World Trade Center was taken only moments after the second plane crashed into the south tower during the terrorist attacks on September 11, 2001. The first plane had struck the north tower 17 minutes earlier in what many assumed was an accident. This photograph, however, captures the exact moment Americans realized the United States was under attack.

HISTORY NOTEBOOK

Encourage students to complete the Through the Lens page for America Through the Decades in their History Notebooks as they read.

INTRODUCE & ENGAGE

IDENTIFY VISUAL CLUES

Direct students to examine the photographs in the lesson. Then prompt them to think about the eras from which the photos came. **ASK:** What are some of the visual clues we can use to distinguish the older photos from the newer ones? *(Answers will vary. Possible response: the clothes people wear, the design of the automobiles, the quality of the photographs)* Tell students that in this lesson they will further explore photographs to identify the stories they tell and their significance.

TEACH

GUIDED DISCUSSION

1. **Analyze Visuals** What decade does each photograph depict? Explain using evidence from the photographs. *(Answers will vary, but students should use historical indicators, such as President Nixon or the bombing of the World Trade Center, to justify their response. Answers for photographs are: page 786 clockwise from upper left: 1960s, 1920s, 1910s, 1940s, 1950s; page 787 clockwise from the upper left: 1990s, 1970s, 2000s, 1900s, 2010s, 1980s, 1930s)*

2. **Synthesize** How does this collection of photographs tell a story about American social, economic, or political trends over the past century? *(Answers will vary. Possible response: This collection of photos shows us the social changes of the last century— including the struggle for women's suffrage, the conformity of the 1950s, the civil rights movement, and the current Black Lives Matter protests.)*

THROUGH THE LENS

Our relationship to history has changed since the invention of photography. While the events of our nation's founding, such as the Boston Tea Party, exist today as only words on a page or in other mediums, such as paintings, many important events over the past 100 years have been exhaustively documented through photography. Sometimes these photos become iconic, representing not just a single event but an entire period in history. The photograph of Martin Luther King, Jr., speaking to the crowd near the Washington Monument reminds us not only of the "I Have a Dream" speech but also of the entire struggle for civil rights in this country. Likewise, although the photo of the construction workers having lunch on the beam may have been staged, it conveys a bigger truth: Modern America was built by a steady and fearless generation who were undefeated by the Great Depression and emerged victors in World War II.

ACTIVE OPTIONS

On Your Feet: Research a Photograph Invite students to form small groups. Assign each group one of the photographs featured in the lesson and ask groups to summarize the story behind the photo. Summaries can include identifying the people in the photograph, the place and time in which the photograph was taken, and the background of the event. Then ask each group to write a caption for their photograph. When they have finished, encourage groups to share their summaries and captions with the class.

NG Learning Framework: Create a Photographic Feature

SKILL Communication

KNOWLEDGE Our Human Story

Ask students to examine the photographs in this lesson and discuss why they think these specific photos were chosen. Then pair students and instruct them to conduct research to collect more photographs that represent each of the decades in this lesson. Tell them to print their choices, arrange them on a larger sheet of paper, and write a few sentences that explain the common theme expressed by the photos. Invite volunteers to present and explain their choices to the class.

DIFFERENTIATE

ENGLISH LANGUAGE LEARNERS

Use Sentence Frames To help promote discussion about the photographs in this lesson, provide students at the **Emerging** level with sentence frames, such as:

The photo of _____ and the photo of _____ are similar because _____.

The _____ in this photo leads me to conclude that _____.

This photo tells about _____.

PRE-AP

Build a Time Line Provide small groups of students with copies of the photographs from this lesson and a large sheet of paper. Ask them to place the photographs in chronological order. Instruct them to annotate the time line by noting causes and effects of—as well as any significant connections between—the events depicted in the photos. Then ask students to write a short paragraph on one of the connections they made.

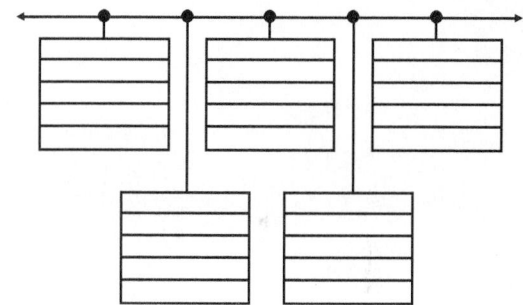

STUDENT REFERENCES

CITIZENSHIP HANDBOOK ...R2

U.S. CAPITOL, WASHINGTON, D.C.

R1

Drafting the Declaration The Declaration of Independence with which we are familiar today is not, in fact, the original draft that Thomas Jefferson wrote. After meeting with the "Committee of Five" several times, Jefferson spent two and a half weeks drafting the Declaration. He rose before dawn each day, sat down at his personally designed desk, wrote down his ideas, and often ripped up drafts that did not satisfy him.

Once he had a draft of the Declaration that did satisfy him, Jefferson showed it to both Benjamin Franklin and John Adams. They were delighted by his wording and suggested only minor revisions. On June 28, 1776, Jefferson submitted the draft to the Continental Congress. Delegates debated it for days and had many criticisms. The most controversial passage offered a fierce condemnation of slavery, in which Jefferson accused King George of "wag[ing] cruel war against human nature itself, violating it's [sic] most sacred rights of life & liberty in the persons of a distant people who never offended him, captivating & carrying them into slavery." However, delegates from Georgia and South Carolina objected strenuously to the passage because their economies relied heavily upon the slave trade. In the end, the passage was removed, and no mention of slavery was made in the Declaration. By the time the debates were over, delegates had deleted about a quarter of Jefferson's submitted text.

CITIZENSHIP
HANDBOOK

This Citizenship Handbook will help you take an in-depth look at our nation's two most important documents: the Declaration of Independence and the U.S. Constitution, which contains the Bill of Rights. The handbook includes notes to help you understand the formal language and difficult concepts contained in the more than 225-year-old documents. The handbook also provides background information and historical context to better help you understand the thinking and motivations of the Framers. At the end of the handbook, you will read about citizenship and the rights and responsibilities that come along with it. You will also find out how you can build and practice citizenship skills in the classroom and beyond.

The Charters of Freedom, as the Declaration of Independence, U.S. Constitution, and Bill of Rights are collectively known, are housed in the National Archives Museum in Washington, D.C.

DECLARATION OF INDEPENDENCE

Introduction

The American colonists wrote the Declaration of Independence in 1776 to formally call for their separation and independence from Britain. Up until then, colonists who were legally British citizens had lived in relative isolation from the king's authority and largely governed themselves. They modeled their colonial governments on Parliament, Britain's legislative body, by forming elected assemblies similar to the House of Commons. Unlike the British legislature, however, elected officials in colonial assemblies lived in the areas they represented. The colonists believed representatives who lived among those who elected them would better understand local interests and needs. At the same time, the colonists had no representatives in Parliament and sometimes resented what they felt to be unfair treatment by Britain.

ROAD TO REVOLUTION

The colonists' resentment grew after they fought alongside the British in the French and Indian War. The Americans had joined the fight so they could expand their settlements westward into Native American territory. But after Britain won the war against the French in 1763, British king George III wanted to keep the peace. To do so, he believed he needed to limit contact between the Native Americans and the colonists. As a result, the British government issued the Proclamation of 1763, which stated that colonists could not settle west of the Appalachian Mountains.

Furthermore, victory in the war had left Britain with overwhelming debt. To help pay it down, King George introduced a series of taxes against the colonists, including customs duties, the Sugar Act of 1764, and the Stamp Act of 1765, which taxed printed materials in the colonies. The Stamp Act was the first direct tax Britain had imposed on the colonists.

The American colonists protested the British legislation with shouts of "No taxation without representation." Angry colonists formed secret groups, such as the Sons of Liberty, and organized demonstrations and boycotts of British goods. As tensions continued to rise, violence erupted. In 1770, the Boston Massacre resulted in the deaths of five colonists at the hands of British soldiers. Three years later, colonists demonstrated their anger over a law on the sale of tea by staging the Boston Tea Party in Boston Harbor.

Finally, in 1775, feelings on both sides reached the boiling point. After British troops learned the colonists had stored weapons in Concord, Massachusetts, the troops marched to the town.

Colonial militiamen rushed to face down the British soldiers in nearby Lexington. During the clash, shots rang out at what would later be called the first battle of the American Revolution.

BREAK WITH BRITAIN

American leaders had convened a conference of colonial delegates to respond to British taxation in 1774. At this conference in Philadelphia, known as the First Continental Congress, some delegates had called for the colonies to separate completely from Britain. By 1775, the Second Continental Congress was prepared to take action. The Congress raised an army and formed a committee to write an official document to declare independence from Britain. This "Committee of Five" included Thomas Jefferson, John Adams, Benjamin Franklin, Roger Sherman, and Robert Livingston. Jefferson, the youngest member of the Congress at 33, was chosen to be the principal author of the Declaration of Independence.

Enlightenment thinkers such as John Locke influenced the ideological origins of the American Revolution and the Declaration. Locke argued that humans were born free and equal and that a leader could rule only with the consent of the people. Jefferson was also inspired by the Enlightenment philosophy of unalienable, or natural, rights. The Founding Fathers considered that these rights were "divinely bestowed," or God-given. Unalienable rights, Jefferson insisted, could not be taken away.

On July 4, 1776, the delegates to the Continental Congress adopted the Declaration of Independence. In 1782, seven years after the first shots were fired, the American Revolution officially ended. The American colonists had fought for and won their freedom and independence from Britain.

Citizenship Handbook **R3**

GUIDED DISCUSSION

1. **Analyze Cause and Effect** Why is it difficult to determine one specific cause for the writing of the Declaration of Independence? *(Prior to the drafting of the document, the colonies and Britain experienced a series of incidents—such as the Proclamation of 1763, increased taxation, colonial demonstrations and boycotts, the Boston Massacre, and the armed confrontation in Lexington—that slowly soured the relationship. Thus, the Declaration was not the product of a specific event but the result of a complex historical process that took several years to unfold.)*

2. **Make Inferences** Consider the ideas about government expressed by Enlightenment thinkers like John Locke and Thomas Jefferson. Since these ideas were considered revolutionary in the 1700s, what can you assume about the general view of government in most other countries at that time? *(Locke argued that leaders ruled only because of the consent of the people; Jefferson argued that people had "natural rights," which a ruler could not infringe upon. If these were revolutionary ideas, it can be assumed that in other countries, leaders ruled without much thought to the will of the people and that any rights people did have would be based on the will of their ruler, not on "nature.")*

MORE INFORMATION

News Travels Slowly With the signing of the Declaration of Independence on July 4, 1776, the colonies formally declared independence from Britain. However, it took some time for the people in the colonies—and in the world—to learn about that decision. Because most people in 1776 received their information from newspapers, printed broadsides, and public readings, news generally traveled slowly.

People living in Philadelphia learned of independence quickly, because on July 6, the text of the Declaration was published in local papers. Four days later, word reached New York City; two weeks later, Boston got the news. On July 20, the Declaration was published in Virginia, the largest colony and the home of Jefferson. It wasn't until August 2 that South Carolina learned the news—almost a full month after the event. It took even longer for this monumental announcement to appear overseas. Britain learned of its colonies' attempted separation in mid-August. The news reached other parts of Europe over the next several months.

Discuss with students the technological changes that enable nearly instantaneous communication today. Challenge students to consider how these changes affect the ways in which the population receives and interprets news. **ASK:** In our modern information age, do you think citizens make better political or worse political decisions? Explain. *(Answers will vary. Students could argue that in modern times, access to information allows citizens to stay informed, read diverse viewpoints, and thus make more rational decisions. Other students may claim that because of the vast and sometimes biased array of news sources, citizens become overwhelmed with information. As a result, they fail to make informed decisions, or they choose whatever "news" best supports their personal opinions.)*

HISTORICAL THINKING

ANSWER

Jefferson is constructing a logical argument about why the colonies have a right to declare independence. The grievances against the king supply evidence for Jefferson's argument.

THE DECLARATION OF INDEPENDENCE

IN CONGRESS, JULY 4, 1776

The Declaration of Independence begins by explaining why the colonists at the Continental Congress want to break away from Britain and become independent. Jefferson and the other Founding Fathers believed it was necessary to explain their motivations.

The unanimous Declaration of the thirteen united States of America, When in the Course of human events, it becomes necessary for one people to dissolve the political bands which have connected them with another, and to assume among the powers of the earth, the separate and equal station to which the Laws of Nature and of Nature's God entitle them, a decent respect to the opinions of mankind requires that they should declare the causes which impel them to the separation.

Here, Jefferson states that people are born equal and have rights, including life, liberty, and the pursuit of happiness, that should be safeguarded by the government. John Locke's idea that government is based on the consent of the people is also established. Jefferson claims that when a government takes away the people's rights, they must overthrow the government. But this step should not be taken lightly.

We hold these truths to be self-evident, that all men are created equal, that they are endowed by their Creator with certain unalienable Rights, that among these are Life, Liberty and the pursuit of Happiness.—That to secure these rights, Governments are instituted among Men, deriving their just powers from the consent of the governed, —That whenever any Form of Government becomes destructive of these ends, it is the Right of the People to alter or to abolish it, and to institute new Government, laying its foundation on such principles and organizing its powers in such form, as to them shall seem most likely to effect their Safety and Happiness. Prudence, indeed, will dictate that Governments long established should not be changed for light and transient causes; and accordingly all experience hath shown, that mankind are more disposed to suffer, while evils are sufferable, than to right themselves by abolishing the forms to which they are accustomed. But when a long train of abuses and usurpations, pursuing invariably the same Object evinces a design to reduce them under absolute Despotism, it is their right, it is their duty, to throw off such Government, and to provide new Guards for their future security.—Such has been the patient sufferance of these Colonies; and such is now the necessity which constrains them to alter their former Systems of Government. The history of the present King of Great Britain is a history of repeated injuries and usurpations, all having in direct object the establishment of an absolute Tyranny over these States. To prove this, let Facts be submitted to a candid world.

The Declaration goes on to explain exactly what King George has done by listing the colonists' grievances against him.

HISTORICAL THINKING Why do you think Jefferson lists the colonists' grievances against the king?

The king has failed to approve or disapprove laws needed by the people. At the time, colonial laws had to be approved by the king. Britain could also veto colonial legislation.

He has refused his Assent to Laws, the most wholesome and necessary for the public good.

He has forbidden his Governors to pass Laws of immediate and pressing importance, unless suspended in their operation till his Assent should be obtained; and when so suspended, he has utterly neglected to attend to them. He has refused to pass other Laws for the accommodation of large districts of people, unless those people would relinquish the right of Representation in the Legislature, a right inestimable to them and formidable to tyrants only.

He has called together legislative bodies at places unusual, uncomfortable, and distant from the depository of their public Records, for the sole purpose of fatiguing them into compliance with his measures.

He has dissolved Representative Houses repeatedly, for opposing with manly firmness his invasions on the rights of the people.

He has refused for a long time, after such dissolutions, to cause others to be elected; whereby the Legislative powers, incapable of Annihilation, have returned to the People at large for their exercise; the State remaining in the mean time exposed to all the dangers of invasion from without, and convulsions within.

He has endeavored to prevent the population of these States; for that purpose obstructing the Laws for Naturalization of Foreigners; refusing to pass others to encourage their migrations hither, and raising the conditions of new Appropriations of Lands.

He has obstructed the Administration of Justice, by refusing his Assent to Laws for establishing Judiciary powers.

He has made Judges dependent on his Will alone, for the tenure of their offices, and the amount and payment of their salaries.

He has erected a multitude of New Offices, and sent hither swarms of Officers to harass our people, and eat out their substance.

He has kept among us, in times of peace, Standing Armies without the Consent of our legislatures.

He has affected to render the Military independent of and superior to the Civil power.

The king has ordered his royal governors to block colonial legislation. He has claimed that unless people in the colonies give up the right to have representatives in their own government in America, he will not pass laws those people need.

The king has dissolved many colonial lawmaking bodies because they stood up against laws that threatened the rights of Americans. By 1776, many colonial assemblies had been dissolved.

After the legislatures were dissolved, some colonies had no laws to protect them. Citizens often created special assemblies to maintain some form of government.

Some colonial legislatures tried to establish courts, but the king dismissed them. Judges have also been appointed who favored the king's interests.

The king has sent soldiers to America without the consent of colonial legislatures. He has made his soldiers more powerful than the colonists.

GUIDED DISCUSSION

1. **Form and Support Opinions** Do you think that it is fair to criticize Jefferson's view of equality, which did not extend to African Americans, women, and even men who did not own property? *(Answers will vary. Possible responses: No. Jefferson was a product of his era, and his views were not generally considered prejudicial. For its time, the Declaration extended equality to more people than other nations did. Yes. Even in the Framers' time, slavery was controversial. Not extending rights to African Americans was a deliberate decision based primarily on economics.)*

2. **Analyze Language Use** What words or phrases in the Declaration of Independence suggest that Jefferson believed his argument to be universal—not just applicable to the American colonies—and what does this language imply about the political trends of the era? *(Possible response: Phrases such as "unalienable rights" imply that the rights are universal. Also, in the second paragraph, Jefferson uses terms such as "Governments" and "their" instead of "Britain" and "colonists." This language implies that Jefferson believed that other nations were ready to overthrow monarchy and that his ideas would appeal to them.)*

MORE INFORMATION

The Declaration Heard 'Round the World The Declaration of Independence was meant, in part, as a biting criticism of the British monarchy, but its effect was felt across Europe and the world. At the time of its publication, most European countries were ruled by monarchs whose power was absolute. Thus, a document that denied the legitimacy of such a government was not warmly received.

In Austria, news of the Declaration was heavily censored. The empress was outraged when a newspaper described the American Revolution as a clash between monarchy and self-rule rather than as an unlawful rebellion. In Russia, the colonists were described in print as "rebels" rather than "revolutionaries" or "freedom fighters." The British government published a response to the Declaration that forcibly argued against the document's reasoning.

In other countries, news of the Declaration and the American Revolution was received more positively. For example, the people of Belgium, a country under the control of Austria, closely followed news of the Declaration. By 1787, the Belgians had begun their own movement for independence.

DECLARATION OF INDEPENDENCE

The king has allowed others to pass and enforce new laws in the colonies that the colonists consider to be invalid ("pretended").

He has combined with others to subject us to a jurisdiction foreign to our constitution, and unacknowledged by our laws; giving his Assent to their Acts of pretended Legislation:

For Quartering large bodies of armed troops among us:

For protecting them, by a mock Trial, from punishment for any Murders which they should commit on the Inhabitants of these States:

Jefferson introduces acts of Parliament the colonists considered to be unconstitutional. For example:

- making sure that soldiers who kill colonists are given a fake trial and not held accountable for murder;
- stopping American trade with other countries;
- taxing without permission;
- often refusing the right of trial by jury;
- sending colonists far away to be tried in courts for things they have not done;
- abolishing laws made by the colonies;
- stopping lawmaking groups in America and declaring that only the British government can make laws for people in America.

For cutting off our Trade with all parts of the world:

For imposing Taxes on us without our Consent:

For depriving us in many cases, of the benefits of Trial by Jury:

For transporting us beyond Seas to be tried for pretended offences

For abolishing the free System of English Laws in a neighboring Province, establishing therein an Arbitrary government, and enlarging its Boundaries so as to render it at once an example and fit instrument for introducing the same absolute rule into these Colonies:

For taking away our Charters, abolishing our most valuable Laws, and altering fundamentally the Forms of our Governments:

For suspending our own Legislatures, and declaring themselves invested with power to legislate for us in all cases whatsoever.

The colonists claim that the king has essentially given up, or abdicated, his power to govern them. Now the king refuses to protect the colonists and has started a war against them.

He has abdicated Government here, by declaring us out of his Protection and waging War against us.

He has plundered our seas, ravaged our Coasts, burnt our towns, and destroyed the lives of our people.

The king is sending foreign soldiers to fight and suppress the colonists—an act of barbarism unworthy of a civilized nation.

He is at this time transporting large Armies of foreign Mercenaries to complete the works of death, desolation and tyranny, already begun with circumstances of Cruelty & perfidy scarcely paralleled in the most barbarous ages, and totally unworthy the Head of a civilized nation.

DECLARATION OF INDEPENDENCE

He has constrained our fellow Citizens taken Captive on the high Seas to bear Arms against their Country, to become the executioners of their friends and Brethren, or to fall themselves by their Hands.

He has excited domestic insurrections amongst us, and has endeavored to bring on the inhabitants of our frontiers, the merciless Indian Savages, whose known rule of warfare, is an undistinguished destruction of all ages, sexes and conditions.

> He has encouraged Native Americans to attack the colonists.

In every stage of these Oppressions We have Petitioned for Redress in the most humble terms: Our repeated Petitions have been answered only by repeated injury. A Prince whose character is thus marked by every act which may define a Tyrant, is unfit to be the ruler of a free people.

> The colonists have repeatedly and unsuccessfully made formal requests for this behavior to stop. However, the king has become a tyrant.

Nor have We been wanting in attentions to our British brethren. We have warned them from time to time of attempts by their legislature to extend an unwarrantable jurisdiction over us. We have reminded them of the circumstances of our emigration and settlement here. We have appealed to their native justice and magnanimity, and we have conjured them by the ties of our common kindred to disavow these usurpations, which, would inevitably interrupt our connections and correspondence. They too have been deaf to the voice of justice and of consanguinity. We must, therefore, acquiesce in the necessity, which denounces our Separation, and hold them, as we hold the rest of mankind, Enemies in War, in Peace Friends.

> We have appealed to the British people, pointing out the injustice of our treatment and our close ties to them ("consanguinity"), but they have ignored us. We have no choice but to consider them our enemies.

We, therefore, the Representatives of the united States of America, in General Congress, Assembled, appealing to the Supreme Judge of the world for the rectitude of our intentions, do, in the Name, and by Authority of the good People of these Colonies, solemnly publish and declare, That these United Colonies are, and of Right ought to be Free and Independent States; that they are Absolved from all Allegiance to the British Crown, and that all political connection between them and the State of Great Britain, is and ought to be totally dissolved; and that as Free and Independent States, they have full Power to levy War, conclude Peace, contract Alliances, establish Commerce, and to do all other Acts and Things which Independent States may of right do. And for the support of this Declaration, with a firm reliance on the protection of divine Providence, we mutually pledge to each other our Lives, our Fortunes and our sacred Honor.

> For all these reasons, Jefferson declares that the United Colonies are free and independent states with no further allegiance to Britain. As free and independent states, they can declare war, negotiate peace, make agreements to work with other countries, establish commerce, and participate in all other activities allowed by independent states.

Citizenship Handbook **R7**

GUIDED DISCUSSION

1. **Evaluate** Which of Jefferson's grievances do you think have merit, and which do not? Explain. *(Answers will vary. Possible response: Jefferson makes a valid argument when he complains that the colonists were not afforded the right to a fair trial, because this is a clear attack on liberty. However, other complaints—such as the regulation of trade and the use of troops—might have less merit, because they would fall under the normal powers of a leader and would not necessarily violate specific rights.)*

2. **Form and Support Opinions** How do you think your life would be different if the Declaration of Independence had never been written? *(Answers will vary. Possible response: If the Declaration had never been written, history would have taken a different direction. The colonies might have remained part of Britain for a longer period of time. In fact, today's Americans might still be considered "British." Perhaps more important, many of the principles outlined in the Declaration—such as "unalienable rights" and "all men are created equal"—might not have spread ideas of self-determination and democracy so widely among the world's people.)*

MORE INFORMATION

The People's House According to Article I, Section 2.1, members of the House of Representatives are to be chosen by "the People." While this phrasing may seem unnecessary today—who else would choose their representatives in a democratic republic?—at the time of the nation's founding, this was the only part of the legislative branch in which "the People" had a direct say. As students will read in Section 3.1, senators originally were selected by state legislatures and not by "the People." This exclusion can be said to extend to the judicial branch, because Supreme Court justices are appointed by the president (with congressional approval; see Article II, Section 2.2). Similarly, although "the People" can vote for president, the official choice is made by the electoral college and not by the voters (Article II, Sections 1.1–1.4).

To make the House of Representatives the part of government most responsive to the needs of "the People," the bar for becoming a representative was set purposely low. The House has the least restrictive qualifications in terms of age and citizenship. In addition, representatives go up for reelection more frequently than do senators or the president, making it easier for citizens to exert influence on their elected politicians.

Have students identify the specific qualifications a person must meet in order to become a member of the House of Representatives. Then discuss aspects of our modern lives—such as life expectancy—that differ from those in the time of the Framers. **ASK:** If you were writing the Constitution today, would you change the qualifications for becoming a representative? Why or why not? *(Answers will vary. Some students might consider lowering the age requirement from 25 to 18. At 18, today's Americans are considered mature enough to vote, so they also should be considered mature enough to serve in the government. Other students might feel there should be more requirements to run for office, such as having to pass literacy tests or civic tests on how the government actually works.)*

CONSTITUTION OF THE UNITED STATES

Introduction

In 1787, delegates at the Constitutional Convention in Philadelphia engaged in debates for four months as they drafted the Constitution. Among other issues, they debated how the legislative branch should work, how to elect the president, and whether enslaved people should be included in a state's population. After agreeing to a series of compromises, the Framers signed the U.S. Constitution, which, once ratified by the states, became the supreme law of the land in the United States. Considering the size and complexity of the United States today and its position as a world power, the U.S. Constitution is relatively simple. It consists of a Preamble, 7 articles, and currently 27 amendments, based on the 7 key principles below.

1. Popular Sovereignty The phrase means "the authority of the people." The opening words of the Constitution, "We the people" emphasize the idea that people together create a social contract in which they agree to be governed. Government authority is derived from the citizens, who determine how much power the government should have and what rules it must follow.

2. Republicanism This is a form of representational democracy. In a republic, citizens have the power and authority to make decisions as to how they are governed. Citizens elect representatives, who then have the power to write and enforce laws. Most Americans today use the terms *representational democracy* and *republicanism* interchangeably.

3. Federalism Federalism is a form of government in which power is distributed among several levels of government. A federalist system features a strong central government, but states do not lose all rights and power. States pursue and protect their interests as they see fit, while working together as a nation. In American federalism, the federal government's powers are enumerated, or listed. The states have powers that are reserved, or unwritten. Concurrent powers are powers shared by the federal and state governments.

4. Separation of Powers To reduce the potential for abuse of power and to prevent one branch from becoming too powerful, government was divided into three branches: the legislative branch (Congress, consisting of the Senate and the House of Representatives), which writes laws; the executive branch (led by the president), which enforces the laws written by Congress; and the judicial branch (made up of the U.S. Supreme Court and additional lower federal courts), which interprets and applies the laws.

5. Checks and Balances Each branch of government can limit the power of the other two, and so exert a check on the others. As with separation of powers, a system of checks and balances helps prevent one branch from becoming too powerful. For example, the judicial branch can declare a law passed by Congress to be unconstitutional. The president can veto a law written by Congress, but Congress can override the presidential veto. Congress can confirm or reject the president's nominees to his cabinet and the courts.

6. Limited Government The Articles of Confederation had failed because the central government was too weak and lacked the authority to tax or regulate trade. A stronger, stable central government was needed, but the Framers did not want to give it too much power or allow it to abuse what power it had. This principle of limited government seeks to protect rights by restricting the power of the central government. The Framers explicitly outlined the powers of the federal government and set additional limits in the Bill of Rights and other amendments.

7. Individual Rights Amendments, or changes and additions to the Constitution, have become part of the U.S. Constitution over the years. The first 10 amendments, known as the Bill of Rights, were added in 1791. These amendments address many individual rights, such as freedom of religion, freedom of speech, and the right to trial by jury. The Bill of Rights also places strict limits on what the federal government can do. The Bill of Rights was added to the Constitution to ensure that all states would accept and ratify this new plan for government.

THE CONSTITUTION

Preamble We the People of the United States, in Order to form a more perfect Union, establish Justice, insure domestic Tranquility, provide for the common defense, promote the general Welfare, and secure the Blessings of Liberty to ourselves and our Posterity, do ordain and establish this Constitution for the United States of America.

Article I Legislative Branch

SECTION 1: CONGRESS

All legislative Powers herein granted shall be vested in a Congress of the United States, which shall consist of a Senate and House of Representatives.

SECTION 2: THE HOUSE OF REPRESENTATIVES

1 The House of Representatives shall be composed of Members chosen every second Year by the People of the several States, and the Electors in each State shall have the Qualifications requisite for Electors of the most numerous Branch of the State Legislature.

2 No Person shall be a Representative who shall not have attained to the Age of twenty five Years, and been seven Years a Citizen of the United States, and who shall not, when elected, be an Inhabitant of that State in which he shall be chosen.

3 *Representatives and direct Taxes shall be apportioned among the several States which may be included within this Union, according to their respective Numbers, which shall be determined by adding to the whole Number of free Persons, including those bound to Service for a Term of Years, and excluding Indians not taxed, three fifths of all other Persons.* The actual Enumeration shall be made within three Years after the first Meeting of the Congress of the United States, and within every subsequent Term of ten Years, in such Manner as they shall by Law direct. The Number of Representatives shall not exceed one for every thirty Thousand, but each State shall have at Least one Representative; and until such enumeration shall be made, the State of New Hampshire shall be entitled to choose three, Massachusetts eight, Rhode-Island and Providence Plantations one, Connecticut five, New-York six, New Jersey four, Pennsylvania eight, Delaware one, Maryland six, Virginia ten, North Carolina five, South Carolina five, and Georgia three.

4 When vacancies happen in the Representation from any State, the Executive Authority thereof shall issue Writs of Election to fill such Vacancies.

5 The House of Representatives shall choose their Speaker and other Officers; and shall have the sole Power of Impeachment.

NOTE Boldfaced headings, section numbers, margin notes, and questions have been inserted to help you understand and interpret this rich and evolving document. Passages that are no longer part of the Constitution have been printed in italic type.

PREAMBLE
UNDERSTANDING THE CONSTITUTION The Preamble to the Constitution outlines the goals of the U.S. government. With the words, "We the People," the Framers establish that the Constitution's authority comes from the people of the United States.

ARTICLE I
UNDERSTANDING THE CONSTITUTION Sections 1 and 2 The Constitution establishes a bicameral, or two-house, Congress. Representatives in the House serve the members of their districts and are elected every two years. The House provides one of the most direct and effective ways in which citizens can participate in the political process. Constituents can contact their representatives by mail, email, and phone, and by visiting their lawmakers' offices. Representatives must be responsive to the needs and interests of their constituents or face losing their seats.

UNDERSTANDING THE CONSTITUTION 2.3 The number of seats in the House is based on each state's population. Populous states have more representatives than less-populated states.

HISTORICAL THINKING How might changes in a state's population affect its political power?

UNDERSTANDING THE CONSTITUTION 2.5 The Speaker of the House presides over sessions of Congress, but the Constitution says nothing about further responsibilities of the Speaker or those of other officers.

GUIDED DISCUSSION

1. **Synthesize** Considering the steps the Framers took to limit the powers of the federal government, what conditions made them feel that each of these steps was necessary? *(Possible response: In monarchies of the time, the government had almost unlimited power. In order to avoid this fate, the Framers proposed principles such as "separation of powers" and "checks and balances," which were meant to ensure that no one branch of the government could hold too much power.)*

2. **Make Inferences** In Section 2.3, the italicized phrase "three fifths of all other Persons" refers to enslaved people. Why do you think slaves were not counted in the same way as free persons? *(Enslaved people were considered property, not citizens; thus, they could not vote nor did they pay taxes. However, southern states wanted slaves included in their population so their states would have more representation. Northern states objected to this ploy. The "three fifths of all other Persons" phrasing is a compromise reached by the Framers.)*

HISTORICAL THINKING

ANSWER

Because population determines the number of representatives in the House, a rise in population would cause a state to gain representatives—and thus political power. A decrease in population would cause a state to lose both representatives and political power.

MORE INFORMATION

Power of the Purse The issue of taxation was important to the Framers, and they addressed it in the Constitution. In the years leading up to the American Revolution, the cry "no taxation without representation" was a crucial rallying point for colonists. It referred to the British government's levying of taxes on the colonists without their input—a practice that colonists interpreted as a violation of their rights as British citizens.

Article I, Section 7.1, addresses the "power of the purse"—the ability to levy taxes and spend revenue. The Framers debated who should have this authority. In Britain, the king had power over spending decisions. The Framers, however, were adamant that in the United States, the people should control public financing. Thus, the president was unanimously disqualified for the role. Some argued that the Senate should take this responsibility—but since the makeup of the Senate favored small states, and thus their interests, the Senate was given limited power as well. As a result, all taxation and spending decisions would begin in the House, as it was this chamber that more clearly reflected the wishes of the people.

HISTORICAL THINKING

ANSWER

Possible responses: Yes. Without an impeachment process in place, the only way to remove a president who posed a serious threat to the nation would be by force. No. Impeachment might be initiated for purely partisan reasons, thus undermining the integrity of the federal government.

CONSTITUTION OF THE UNITED STATES

UNDERSTANDING THE CONSTITUTION 3.1 Section 3 describes the Senate. Originally, state legislatures chose the senators. With the passage of the 17th Amendment in 1913, senators were elected by voters, which made the process of selecting these federal officials more democratic.

UNDERSTANDING THE CONSTITUTION 3.2 The terms of senators are staggered. One class of senators begins its term in an even-numbered year, the next class begins two years later, and the third class begins two years after that.

As president of the Senate, Vice President Richard Cheney is shown here presiding over the daily proceedings of the legislative body in 2009. House Speaker Nancy Pelosi stands beside him.

UNDERSTANDING THE CONSTITUTION 3.6 The House of Representatives has the power to bring impeachment charges, but the Senate conducts the trial and determines if the individual is to be removed from office. The president, vice president, all civil officers, and federal judges can be impeached.

HISTORICAL THINKING Do you think the power to impeach is essential to the system of checks and balances? Explain why or why not.

SECTION 3: THE SENATE

1 The Senate of the United States shall be composed of two Senators from each State, chosen by the Legislature thereof, for six Years; and each Senator shall have one Vote.

2 Immediately after they shall be assembled in Consequence of the first Election, they shall be divided as equally as may be into three Classes. The Seats of the Senators of the first Class shall be vacated at the Expiration of the second Year, of the second Class at the Expiration of the fourth Year, and of the third Class at the Expiration of the sixth Year, so that one third may be chosen every second Year; and if Vacancies happen by Resignation, or otherwise, during the Recess of the Legislature of any State, the Executive thereof may make temporary Appointments until the next Meeting of the Legislature, which shall then fill such Vacancies.

3 No Person shall be a Senator who shall not have attained to the Age of thirty Years, and been nine Years a Citizen of the United States, and who shall not, when elected, be an Inhabitant of that State for which he shall be chosen.

4 The Vice President of the United States shall be President of the Senate, but shall have no Vote, unless they be equally divided.

5 The Senate shall choose their other Officers, and also a President pro tempore, in the Absence of the Vice President, or when he shall exercise the Office of President of the United States.

6 The Senate shall have the sole Power to try all Impeachments. When sitting for that Purpose, they shall be on Oath or Affirmation. When the President of the United States is tried, the Chief Justice shall preside: And no Person shall be convicted without the Concurrence of two thirds of the Members present.

7 Judgment in Cases of Impeachment shall not extend further than to removal from Office, and disqualification to hold and enjoy any Office of honor, Trust or Profit under the United States: but the Party convicted shall nevertheless be liable and subject to Indictment, Trial, Judgment and Punishment, according to Law.

SECTION 4: CONGRESSIONAL ELECTIONS

1 The Times, Places and Manner of holding Elections for Senators and Representatives, shall be prescribed in each State by the Legislature thereof; but the Congress may at any time by Law make or alter such Regulations, except as to the Places of choosing Senators.

2 *The Congress shall assemble at least once in every Year, and such Meeting shall be on the first Monday in December, unless they shall by Law appoint a different Day.*

CONSTITUTION OF THE UNITED STATES

SECTION 5: RULES

1 Each House shall be the Judge of the Elections, Returns and Qualifications of its own Members, and a Majority of each shall constitute a Quorum to do Business; but a smaller Number may adjourn from day to day, and may be authorized to compel the Attendance of absent Members, in such Manner, and under such Penalties as each House may provide.

2 Each House may determine the Rules of its Proceedings, punish its Members for disorderly Behavior, and, with the Concurrence of two thirds, expel a Member.

3 Each House shall keep a Journal of its Proceedings, and from time to time publish the same, excepting such Parts as may in their Judgment require Secrecy; and the Yeas and Nays of the Members of either House on any question shall, at the Desire of one fifth of those Present, be entered on the Journal.

4 Neither House, during the Session of Congress, shall, without the Consent of the other, adjourn for more than three days, nor to any other Place than that in which the two Houses shall be sitting.

SECTION 6: PAY AND EXPENSES

1 The Senators and Representatives shall receive a Compensation for their Services, to be ascertained by Law, and paid out of the Treasury of the United States. They shall in all Cases, except Treason, Felony and Breach of the Peace, be privileged from Arrest during their Attendance at the Session of their respective Houses, and in going to and returning from the same; and for any Speech or Debate in either House, they shall not be questioned in any other Place.

2 No Senator or Representative shall, during the Time for which he was elected, be appointed to any civil Office under the Authority of the United States, which shall have been created, or the Emoluments whereof shall have been increased during such time; and no Person holding any Office under the United States, shall be a Member of either House during his Continuance in Office.

SECTION 7: PASSING LAWS

1 All Bills for raising Revenue shall originate in the House of Representatives; but the Senate may propose or concur with Amendments as on other Bills.

2 Every Bill which shall have passed the House of Representatives and the Senate, shall, before it become a Law, be presented to the President of the United States; If he approve he shall sign it, but if not he shall return it, with his Objections to that House in which it shall have originated, who shall enter the Objections at large on their Journal, and proceed to reconsider it. If after such Reconsideration two thirds of that House shall agree to pass the Bill, it shall be sent, together with

UNDERSTANDING THE CONSTITUTION Section 5 This section empowers each house of Congress to make its own rules. The House and Senate have developed different rules over the years that affect how they operate. For example, only members of the Senate can engage in a filibuster, which allows a senator to speak in the chamber as long as it may take to block a piece of legislation. The filibuster gives the minority party in the Senate some power to block or slow the passage of legislation.

UNDERSTANDING THE CONSTITUTION 7.2

How a Bill Becomes a Law in Congress

(A) The first step in the legislative process is the introduction of a bill to Congress. Although anyone can write a bill or request certain legislation, only a member of Congress can introduce a bill.

(B) The bill is debated and usually revised. Congressional committees and their subcommittees are the key groups that move bills through the process. Once out of committee, the full House or Senate votes on the bill.

(C) Each house reviews, debates, and amends the bill, often resulting in different versions. A committee made up of members from both houses then works to resolve differences and create one final version of the bill.

(D) If both houses accept the compromises, Congress sends the bill to the president.

(E) The president can either sign the bill—and it becomes law—or veto the bill, which prevents the bill from becoming law. Congress can, however, override the veto with a vote of two-thirds of the members present in each house, in which case the bill becomes law.

Citizenship Handbook **R11**

GUIDED DISCUSSION

1. Make Inferences Review the requirements to be a senator and those to be a representative. Why do you think potential senators face stricter requirements? *(Possible response: Senators serve longer terms, represent more people, and have greater powers— such as the ability to impeach the president—than members of the House do. Given these facts, the Framers probably thought higher standards were required for those who wanted to be senators.)*

2. Form and Support Opinions What impact has awarding each state two senators had on our modern political environment? *(Answers will vary. Students may point out that larger states—and thus the majority of the people—are not given a proportional voice concerning the Senate's decisions. On the other hand, students may argue that smaller states and their concerns would be ignored if not for the makeup of the Senate. Students might note that in recent times this formula has favored the Republican Party, which tends to dominate smaller states, enabling Republicans to control the Senate. In 2016, for example, Republicans kept control of the Senate despite the fact their presidential candidate received fewer votes in the national election.)*

MORE INFORMATION

Suspension of *Habeus Corpus* *Habeus corpus*, a foundational part of American law that originated in England, was designed to protect people from illegal imprisonment. A writ of *habeus corpus* requires law enforcement to give legal justification for a person's detainment, such as the specific law that the person broke. If no justification can be given, the person must be released.

Article I, Section 9.2, gives the government the ability to suspend *habeus corpus* in times of rebellion or to protect public safety during an invasion. The suspension allows law enforcement to imprison people without having a specific legal reason. This section of the Constitution has been invoked on a few occasions. During the Civil War, for example, President Lincoln suspended *habeus corpus* in Maryland to silence protesters, crack down on riots, and prevent the movement of Confederate troops. In 1871, President Grant suspended *habeus corpus* across South Carolina to combat the violence being perpetrated by the Ku Klux Klan.

In recent years, suspension has been rare. However, following the terrorist attacks of September 11, 2001, Congress passed—and the president signed—a law banning detainees at the American naval base in Guantanamo Bay, Cuba, from invoking this right, thus allowing for their prolonged imprisonment. **ASK:** Why might the Framers have thought that suspending *habeus corpus* was a necessary tool during times of rebellion and invasion? *(Possible response: During times of imminent threat, finding a specific legal reason to detain someone may be too time consuming, thus endangering "the public Safety.")*

HISTORICAL THINKING

ANSWER

The collection of taxes is vital for keeping the government and all its activities funded.

ANSWER

Possible response: Without the commerce clause, states would be able to make laws that would promote their own economy but put other states at an economic disadvantage. For example, California could tax fruit imported from Florida and levy a tariff on steel made in Pennsylvania, making fruit and steel produced in California a "better buy." These laws would benefit California's economy while hurting the economies of Florida and Pennsylvania.

CONSTITUTION OF THE UNITED STATES

the Objections, to the other House, by which it shall likewise be reconsidered, and if approved by two thirds of that House, it shall become a Law. But in all such Cases the Votes of both Houses shall be determined by yeas and Nays, and the Names of the Persons voting for and against the Bill shall be entered on the Journal of each House respectively. If any Bill shall not be returned by the President within ten Days (Sundays excepted) after it shall have been presented to him, the Same shall be a Law, in like Manner as if he had signed it, unless the Congress by their Adjournment prevent its Return, in which Case it shall not be a Law.

3 Every Order, Resolution, or Vote to which the Concurrence of the Senate and House of Representatives may be necessary (except on a question of Adjournment) shall be presented to the President of the United States; and before the Same shall take Effect, shall be approved by him, or being disapproved by him, shall be re-passed by two thirds of the Senate and House of Representatives, according to the Rules and Limitations prescribed in the Case of a Bill.

UNDERSTANDING THE CONSTITUTION Section 8 Section 8 begins with a list of 17 enumerated powers given to Congress, which cannot be modified by the states. The Constitution includes little detail as to how some of these powers should be carried out. The authority to collect taxes—perhaps the most important power granted to Congress—is often referred to as the "power of the purse."

HISTORICAL THINKING Why do you think the authority to collect taxes is an important power?

UNDERSTANDING THE CONSTITUTION 8.3 This clause is generally referred to as the commerce clause. Regulating commerce with foreign nations means controlling imports and exports to provide maximum benefit for U.S. businesses and consumers. Regulating commerce between states means maintaining a common market among the states, with no restrictions.

HISTORICAL THINKING Without the commerce clause, what kinds of disputes might arise between states engaged in interstate commerce?

SECTION 8: POWERS OF CONGRESS

1 The Congress shall have Power To lay and collect Taxes, Duties, Imposts and Excises, to pay the Debts and provide for the common Defense and general Welfare of the United States; but all Duties, Imposts and Excises shall be uniform throughout the United States;

2 To borrow Money on the credit of the United States;

3 To regulate Commerce with foreign Nations, and among the several States, and with the Indian Tribes;

4 To establish an uniform Rule of Naturalization, and uniform Laws on the subject of Bankruptcies throughout the United States;

5 To coin Money, regulate the Value thereof, and of foreign Coin, and fix the Standard of Weights and Measures;

6 To provide for the Punishment of counterfeiting the Securities and current Coin of the United States;

7 To establish Post Offices and post Roads;

8 To promote the Progress of Science and useful Arts, by securing for limited Times to Authors and Inventors the exclusive Right to their respective Writings and Discoveries;

9 To constitute Tribunals inferior to the supreme Court;

10 To define and punish Piracies and Felonies committed on the high Seas, and Offences against the Law of Nations;

11 To declare War, grant Letters of Marque and Reprisal, and make Rules concerning Captures on Land and Water;

CONSTITUTION OF THE UNITED STATES

12 To raise and support Armies, but no Appropriation of Money to that Use shall be for a longer Term than two Years;

13 To provide and maintain a Navy;

14 To make Rules for the Government and Regulation of the land and naval Forces;

15 To provide for calling forth the Militia to execute the Laws of the Union, suppress Insurrections and repel Invasions;

16 To provide for organizing, arming, and disciplining, the Militia, and for governing such Part of them as may be employed in the Service of the United States, reserving to the States respectively, the Appointment of the Officers, and the Authority of training the Militia according to the discipline prescribed by Congress;

17 To exercise exclusive Legislation in all Cases whatsoever, over such District (not exceeding ten Miles square) as may, by Cession of particular States, and the Acceptance of Congress, become the Seat of the Government of the United States, and to exercise like Authority over all Places purchased by the Consent of the Legislature of the State in which the Same shall be, for the Erection of Forts, Magazines, Arsenals, dock-Yards, and other needful Buildings;—And

18 To make all Laws which shall be necessary and proper for carrying into Execution the foregoing Powers, and all other Powers vested by this Constitution in the Government of the United States, or in any Department or Officer thereof.

SECTION 9: RESTRICTIONS ON CONGRESS

1 *The Migration or Importation of such Persons as any of the States now existing shall think proper to admit, shall not be prohibited by the Congress prior to the Year one thousand eight hundred and eight, but a Tax or duty may be imposed on such Importation, not exceeding ten dollars for each Person.*

2 The Privilege of the Writ of Habeas Corpus shall not be suspended, unless when in Cases of Rebellion or Invasion the public Safety may require it.

3 No Bill of Attainder or ex post facto Law shall be passed.

4 *No Capitation, or other direct, Tax shall be laid, unless in Proportion to the Census or Enumeration herein before directed to be taken.*

5 No Tax or Duty shall be laid on Articles exported from any State.

6 No Preference shall be given by any Regulation of Commerce or Revenue to the Ports of one State over those of another: nor shall Vessels bound to, or from, one State, be obliged to enter, clear, or pay Duties in another.

UNDERSTANDING THE CONSTITUTION Section 8 The last of the enumerated powers has been referred to as the "elastic clause" or the "necessary and proper clause." This clause allows Congress "to make all laws which shall be necessary and proper" to support its duties and responsibilities. It is called the "elastic clause" because it allows Congress to expand its authority and handle issues that might not have been anticipated. The vagueness of the phrase "necessary and proper" has created controversy. The Supreme Court provided some guidance in the 1819 case of *McCulloch* v. *Maryland* when it gave Congress wide authority to determine what is "necessary and proper."

UNDERSTANDING THE CONSTITUTION Section 9 Section 9 lists specific areas in which Congress may not legislate.

UNDERSTANDING THE CONSTITUTION 9.4 A "capitation tax" is a tax charged on an individual.

UNDERSTANDING THE CONSTITUTION 9.6 Congress cannot pass laws that favor commerce in one state over that in another. For example, Congress cannot pass a law requiring shipping to go through a particular state's port.

Citizenship Handbook **R13**

GUIDED DISCUSSION

1. **Describe** How does the Constitution balance the power of Congress to raise and support armies? *(Congress has the ability to raise and support armies, while the president is charged with commanding the armies. This balance of power ensures that one branch of the government does not have too much control over the military.)*

2. **Draw Conclusions** Consider conditions at the time when the Constitution was written. Why do you think this document has a specific provision for the establishment of post offices and post roads? *(Possible response: At that time, sending letters through the mail was the primary form of long-distance communication. To ensure the continuation of lines of communication, a functioning postal system and network of roads had to be established and funded.)*

MORE INFORMATION

The Electoral College Article II of the Constitution includes the establishment of the electoral college, an institution that has been controversial since the nation's beginnings. Originally, the electoral college functioned as a mechanism to allow citizens to vote, but with the safeguard of having knowledgeable electors make the final decision about who would actually serve as the chief executive.

It may be surprising for modern readers to learn that the electoral college was closely linked to slavery. At the time of its creation, most Americans lived in the North. Thus, an election by popular vote alone would guarantee free states a firm grip on the presidency. However, the three-fifths clause counted a fraction of enslaved people (who could not vote) when determining representation in the House of Representatives. Thus, by using the number of representatives in its determination of electors, the electoral college gave southern states a voice in deciding the presidency that was disproportionate to their voting population.

In modern times, the electoral college has remained controversial. Although electors now—with rare exceptions—follow the wishes of the voting public and the three-fifths clause is gone, critics argue that the electoral college makes some people's votes more important than others. Thus, in states where votes tend to be close in presidential elections—such as Florida or New Hampshire—a person's vote is far more important than in more politically polarized larger states, such as California or Alabama. In addition, the elections of 2000 and 2016, in which the winner of the electoral college did not win the popular vote, heightened calls to reform the system.

Divide the class into small groups and present this question: How would presidential campaigns and elections be different if presidents were elected by popular vote? Ask groups to construct a hypothesis that addresses the question. The hypothesis could touch on many aspects—for example, which political party would do better or worse, what the impact on voter turnout might be, or how the situation would affect candidates' campaign strategies. Have groups employ information from multiple primary and secondary sources and share their findings in an oral or written presentation.

HISTORICAL THINKING

ANSWER

Possible response: Federal officials who receive payments or other types of presents from foreign governments may allow these emoluments to influence the decisions they make. These decisions might be against the best interests of the United States and benefit a foreign power.

CONSTITUTION OF THE UNITED STATES

UNDERSTANDING THE CONSTITUTION 9.8 This provision, known as the "emoluments clause," is a commitment to transparency and to the prevention of corruption. The clause prohibits federal government officials from benefiting financially from the office they hold by receiving payments from foreign governments.

HISTORICAL THINKING Why might a violation of the emoluments clause by a federal government official have significant consequences?

UNDERSTANDING THE CONSTITUTION Section 10 Section 10 limits the power of the states by preventing them from entering into a treaty, coining money, or passing laws that interfere with contracts.

ARTICLE II
UNDERSTANDING THE CONSTITUTION Section 1 Article II establishes an executive branch of government to carry out the laws passed by Congress. Section 1 describes a detailed process for choosing the president, although this process was replaced in 1804 by the 12th Amendment.

HISTORICAL THINKING Why might some Americans object to the electoral college?

7 No Money shall be drawn from the Treasury, but in Consequence of Appropriations made by Law; and a regular Statement and Account of the Receipts and Expenditures of all public Money shall be published from time to time.

8 No Title of Nobility shall be granted by the United States: And no Person holding any Office of Profit or Trust under them, shall, without the Consent of the Congress, accept of any present, Emolument, Office, or Title, of any kind whatever, from any King, Prince, or foreign State.

SECTION 10: LIMITING THE AUTHORITY OF STATES

1 No State shall enter into any Treaty, Alliance, or Confederation; grant Letters of Marque and Reprisal; coin Money; emit Bills of Credit; make any Thing but gold and silver Coin a Tender in Payment of Debts; pass any Bill of Attainder, ex post facto Law, or Law impairing the Obligation of Contracts, or grant any Title of Nobility.

2 No State shall, without the Consent of the Congress, lay any Imposts or Duties on Imports or Exports, except what may be absolutely necessary for executing its inspection Laws: and the net Produce of all Duties and Imposts, laid by any State on Imports or Exports, shall be for the Use of the Treasury of the United States; and all such Laws shall be subject to the Revision and Control of the Congress.

3 No State shall, without the Consent of Congress, lay any Duty of Tonnage, keep Troops, or Ships of War in time of Peace, enter into any Agreement or Compact with another State, or with a foreign Power, or engage in War, unless actually invaded, or in such imminent Danger as will not admit of delay.

Article II The Executive Branch

SECTION 1: ELECTING THE PRESIDENT

1 The executive Power shall be vested in a President of the United States of America. He shall hold his Office during the Term of four Years, and, together with the Vice President, chosen for the same Term, be elected, as follows

2 Each State shall appoint, in such Manner as the Legislature thereof may direct, a Number of Electors, equal to the whole Number of Senators and Representatives to which the State may be entitled in the Congress: but no Senator or Representative, or Person holding an Office of Trust or Profit under the United States, shall be appointed an Elector.

CONSTITUTION OF THE UNITED STATES

3 *The Electors shall meet in their respective States, and vote by Ballot for two Persons, of whom one at least shall not be an Inhabitant of the same State with themselves. And they shall make a List of all the Persons voted for, and of the Number of Votes for each; which List they shall sign and certify, and transmit sealed to the Seat of the Government of the United States, directed to the President of the Senate. The President of the Senate shall, in the Presence of the Senate and House of Representatives, open all the Certificates, and the Votes shall then be counted. The Person having the greatest Number of Votes shall be the President, if such Number be a Majority of the whole Number of Electors appointed; and if there be more than one who have such Majority, and have an equal Number of Votes, then the House of Representatives shall immediately choose by Ballot one of them for President; and if no Person have a Majority, then from the five highest on the List the said House shall in like Manner choose the President. But in choosing the President, the Votes shall be taken by States, the Representation from each State having one Vote; A quorum for this Purpose shall consist of a Member or Members from two thirds of the States, and a Majority of all the States shall be necessary to a Choice. In every Case, after the Choice of the President, the Person having the greatest Number of Votes of the Electors shall be the Vice President. But if there should remain two or more who have equal Votes, the Senate shall choose from them by Ballot the Vice President.*

4 The Congress may determine the Time of choosing the Electors, and the Day on which they shall give their Votes; which Day shall be the same throughout the United States.

5 No Person except a natural born Citizen, or a Citizen of the United States, at the time of the Adoption of this Constitution, shall be eligible to the Office of President; neither shall any Person be eligible to that Office who shall not have attained to the Age of thirty five Years, and been fourteen Years a Resident within the United States.

6 *In Case of the Removal of the President from Office, or of his Death, Resignation, or Inability to discharge the Powers and Duties of the said Office, the Same shall devolve on the Vice President, and the Congress may by Law provide for the Case of Removal, Death, Resignation or Inability, both of the President and Vice President, declaring what Officer shall then act as President, and such Officer shall act accordingly, until the Disability be removed, or a President shall be elected.*

7 The President shall, at stated Times, receive for his Services, a Compensation, which shall neither be increased nor diminished during the Period for which he shall have been elected, and he shall not receive within that Period any other Emolument from the United States, or any of them.

UNDERSTANDING THE CONSTITUTION 1.3 The italicized text refers to how vice presidents were originally elected. In the presidential election of 1800, the top two vote winners (Thomas Jefferson and Aaron Burr) received the same number of electoral votes. The selection of the president then fell to the House of Representatives, which chose Jefferson. Today, presidential candidates select a running mate, and voters cast a single vote for the entire ticket.

UNDERSTANDING THE CONSTITUTION 1.4 The Constitution does not stipulate when federal elections are to be held. Congress determined in 1792 that federal elections should be held in November. In 1845, it established election day as the Tuesday following the first Monday in November in years divisible by four.

GUIDED DISCUSSION

1. **Make Inferences** What political trends or developments do you think led to the changes made in Section 1.3 of Article II? *(Possible response: Originally, after votes were counted, the person with the most electoral votes became president, and the runner-up became vice president. But with the rise of political parties—a phenomenon the Framers didn't anticipate—these two people were often rivals and could not work together effectively. Having both officials come from the same party, therefore, helped the executive branch run more smoothly.)*

2. **Evaluate** Is the Constitution clear about whether a future president must be born on American soil? Explain using text evidence. *(Section 1.5 of Article II states that a president must be a "natural born Citizen." However, this term is not defined in the Constitution nor has it been clarified by the Supreme Court. Thus, there is no definitive answer.)*

HISTORICAL THINKING

ANSWER

Possible response: Students may argue that the electoral college is objectionable because it can allow someone who has not won the popular vote to become president, thus failing to reflect the true will of the people.

MORE INFORMATION

The Constitution and the Court The Constitution has surprisingly little to say about the makeup and specific powers of the Supreme Court. Today, the Court consists of eight associate justices and one Chief Justice, but that has not always been the case. Because the Constitution is not specific about the number of justices, several laws over time have addressed this issue. The Judiciary Act of 1789 called for five associate justices and one Chief Justice. Later, Congress passed various laws changing the number, which varied from as many as 10 to as few as 5. In 1869, another Judiciary Act set the number at nine—a standard kept ever since.

The most important job of the Court is determining whether laws and presidential actions are in line with the Constitution. However, this responsibility—known as judicial review—is not explicitly granted in the Constitution. Some Framers, such as Alexander Hamilton and James Madison, argued that the Court should take the role of interpreter of the Constitution. Others, however, including Thomas Jefferson, were convinced that judicial review would make the Court too powerful. They argued that all three branches should have equal say over constitutionality.

It wasn't until 1803 that the argument was settled in *Marbury* v. *Madison*. In this case, the Court affirmed its responsibility for judicial review when Chief Justice John Marshall wrote, "It is emphatically the province of the judicial department to say what the law is."

HISTORICAL THINKING

ANSWER

Answers will vary. Possible responses: No. The risk of having a president gain too much power, and thus undermining the balance of powers in the federal government, is never justified. Yes. In times of attack or other widespread threat, the president must be able to act quickly and unilaterally to ensure the nation's safety, as Lincoln and Roosevelt did in the past.

CONSTITUTION OF THE UNITED STATES

UNDERSTANDING THE CONSTITUTION 1.8 Beginning with George Washington, every president has taken the oath of office as it appears in the Constitution.

UNDERSTANDING THE CONSTITUTION Section 2 Section 2 outlines the president's authority. Among other duties, the president serves as commander in chief of the armed forces, has the power to make treaties, and can appoint ambassadors and Supreme Court justices. However, the powers of the presidency increased during the Great Depression, World War II, and the Cold War. For example, although the Constitution states that only Congress can declare war, President Harry Truman began an undeclared war against North Korea in the Cold War.

HISTORICAL THINKING Do you think a president is justified to exceed constitutional powers in some situations? Why or why not?

In this photo, President Barack Obama delivers his annual State of the Union address to Congress in 2016. To fulfill the rule in Section 3 on keeping Congress informed "from time to time," presidents present this address every year except in the first year of a new president's term.

UNDERSTANDING THE CONSTITUTION Section 4 In the phrase "high crimes and misdemeanors," the word *high* does not mean "more serious" but rather refers to highly placed public officials.

8 Before he enter on the Execution of his Office, he shall take the following Oath or Affirmation:—"I do solemnly swear (or affirm) that I will faithfully execute the Office of President of the United States, and will to the best of my Ability, preserve, protect and defend the Constitution of the United States."

SECTION 2: EXECUTIVE POWERS

1 The President shall be Commander in Chief of the Army and Navy of the United States, and of the Militia of the several States, when called into the actual Service of the United States; he may require the Opinion, in writing, of the principal Officer in each of the executive Departments, upon any Subject relating to the Duties of their respective Offices, and he shall have Power to grant Reprieves and Pardons for Offences against the United States, except in Cases of Impeachment.

2 He shall have Power, by and with the Advice and Consent of the Senate, to make Treaties, provided two thirds of the Senators present concur; and he shall nominate, and by and with the Advice and Consent of the Senate, shall appoint Ambassadors, other public Ministers and Consuls, Judges of the supreme Court, and all other Officers of the United States, whose Appointments are not herein otherwise provided for, and which shall be established by Law: but the Congress may by Law vest the Appointment of such inferior Officers, as they think proper, in the President alone, in the Courts of Law, or in the Heads of Departments.

3 The President shall have Power to fill up all Vacancies that may happen during the Recess of the Senate, by granting Commissions which shall expire at the End of their next Session.

SECTION 3: THE PRESIDENT AND CONGRESS

He shall from time to time give to the Congress Information of the State of the Union, and recommend to their Consideration such Measures as he shall judge necessary and expedient; he may, on extraordinary Occasions, convene both Houses, or either of them, and in Case of Disagreement between them, with Respect to the Time of Adjournment, he may adjourn them to such Time as he shall think proper; he shall receive Ambassadors and other public Ministers; he shall take Care that the Laws be faithfully executed, and shall Commission all the Officers of the United States.

SECTION 4: IMPEACHMENT

The President, Vice President and all civil Officers of the United States, shall be removed from Office on Impeachment for, and Conviction of, Treason, Bribery, or other high Crimes and Misdemeanors.

CONSTITUTION OF THE UNITED STATES

Article III The Judiciary Branch

SECTION 1: SUPREME COURT AND LOWER COURTS

The judicial Power of the United States, shall be vested in one supreme Court, and in such inferior Courts as the Congress may from time to time ordain and establish. The Judges, both of the supreme and inferior Courts, shall hold their Offices during good Behavior, and shall, at stated Times, receive for their Services, a Compensation, which shall not be diminished during their Continuance in Office.

SECTION 2: AUTHORITY OF THE SUPREME COURT

1 The judicial Power shall extend to all Cases, in Law and Equity, arising under this Constitution, the Laws of the United States, and Treaties made, or which shall be made, under their Authority;—to all Cases affecting Ambassadors, other public Ministers and Consuls;—to all Cases of admiralty and maritime Jurisdiction;—to Controversies to which the United States shall be a Party;—*to Controversies between two or more States;—between a State and Citizens of another State;—between Citizens of different States;—between Citizens of the same State claiming Lands under Grants of different States, and between a State, or the Citizens thereof, and foreign States, Citizens or Subjects.*

2 In all Cases affecting Ambassadors, other public Ministers and Consuls, and those in which a State shall be Party, the supreme Court shall have original Jurisdiction. In all the other Cases before mentioned, the supreme Court shall have appellate Jurisdiction, both as to Law and Fact, with such Exceptions, and under such Regulations as the Congress shall make.

3 The Trial of all Crimes, except in Cases of Impeachment, shall be by Jury; and such Trial shall be held in the State where the said Crimes shall have been committed; but when not committed within any State, the Trial shall be at such Place or Places as the Congress may by Law have directed.

SECTION 3: TREASON

1 Treason against the United States, shall consist only in levying War against them, or in adhering to their Enemies, giving them Aid and Comfort. No Person shall be convicted of Treason unless on the Testimony of two Witnesses to the same overt Act, or on Confession in open Court.

2 The Congress shall have Power to declare the Punishment of Treason, but no Attainder of Treason shall work Corruption of Blood, or Forfeiture except during the Life of the Person attainted.

The Supreme Court justices posed for this photo in 2017. In the top row, from left to right, are Elena Kagan, Samuel Alito, Jr., Sonia Sotomayor, and Neil Gorsuch. In the bottom row, from left to right, are Ruth Bader Ginsburg, Anthony Kennedy, John Roberts, Jr. (chief justice), Clarence Thomas, and Stephen Breyer.

ARTICLE III
UNDERSTANDING THE CONSTITUTION Section 1 Article III Section 1 establishes the federal court system. The Supreme Court of the United States is the highest court in the land and the only part of the federal judiciary specifically required by the Constitution. Lower courts were established by Congress by the Judiciary Act of 1789.

UNDERSTANDING THE CONSTITUTION Section 2 The italicized portion in 2.1 was changed in 1795 by the 11th Amendment. The last part of 2.2 describes the Supreme Court as the final appeals court. As a result of the landmark 1803 case *Marbury* v. *Madison*, the Court is often asked to rule on the constitutionality of a law.

UNDERSTANDING THE CONSTITUTION Section 3
Treason is the only crime specifically defined in the Constitution. Between 1954 and 2016, one person was charged with treason for collaborating in the production of propaganda videos for the terrorist group al Qaeda. Protesting or opposing U.S. government actions or policies, however, is protected by the free speech clause in Amendment 1.

GUIDED DISCUSSION

1. **Analyze Cause and Effect** What would be the effect of requiring two-thirds of the Senate to approve of a treaty? *(Possible response: Such a provision would require senators on both sides of the aisle to vote their approval. Thus, treaties of necessity would become more bipartisan.)*

2. **Form and Support Opinions** Reread the explanation of how the powers of the presidency have expanded since the Great Depression. Do you think that Article II, Section 2, of the Constitution is still adequate, or should it be amended to address modern historical realities? Explain. *(Answers will vary. Some students may feel that the Constitution needs to be amended in this regard. For example, the president's ability to unilaterally send military troops without technically declaring war seems to violate the principles of the Framers. Other students may feel the president needs such flexibility of powers to meet the fast-moving conditions and challenges of today's world.)*

MORE INFORMATION

Religion and the Constitution The only overt mention of religion in the original, unamended Constitution is found in Article VI, Section 3. This portion, known as the "no religious test" clause, forbids requiring federal office holders to be of a specific religion to serve. Thus, anyone—Muslim, Jew, Christian, Sikh, or follower of any other belief (or having no belief at all)—theoretically could be elected to Congress or become president. The Framers inserted this provision because they believed that singling out certain religions would inevitably lead to discrimination. They also believed that religious requirements might prohibit some of the best people from serving the national interests.

In the nation's early days, however, this clause did not apply to state officeholders. Every state required local officeholders to be Christian; in some cases, only Protestants could hold office. This interpretation lasted until 1961 when, in the case *Torasco* v. *Watkins*, the Supreme Court ruled that all religious tests—even at the local level—were unconstitutional.

After sharing the More Information note with students, hold a class discussion about the role of religion in American politics. Include questions such as these:

- Even though the Constitution prohibits a religious test for office, do you think that public life is truly open to people of all faiths and beliefs?

- What types of beliefs would seemingly disqualify a person from being elected? For example, could an atheist realistically become president?

- Which religions do you think are the most represented among members of Congress? Which do you think are the least represented? After students give their opinions, have them do online research to find the answers.

HISTORICAL THINKING

ANSWER

Possible response: The Framers might have purposely avoided the mention of slavery to gain the cooperation of the southern states in ratifying the Constitution. Also, by not mentioning slavery, they avoid institutionalizing it in the Constitution, something the northern states would have strongly rejected.

CONSTITUTION OF THE UNITED STATES

ARTICLE IV
UNDERSTANDING THE CONSTITUTION Section 1 "Full faith and credit" means that states agree to respect and honor each other's laws, court decisions, and documents. For example, a driver's license issued by one state must be honored by all other states. Section 1 was included as a way to create cohesiveness among individual states.

UNDERSTANDING THE CONSTITUTION 2.3 The text in italics is known as the fugitive slave clause, which barred people who had escaped slavery in the South from living as free people in northern states. It became obsolete with the abolition of slavery. It is interesting to note that the words *slave* and *slavery* do not appear in the Constitution.

HISTORICAL THINKING Why might the Framers have chosen not to mention slavery in the Constitution?

UNDERSTANDING THE CONSTITUTION Section 4 In the "guarantee clause," the Constitution commits the U.S. government to protecting the people of a state from attack by a foreign government as well as from domestic violence or terrorism.

Article IV States and Citizens

SECTION 1: MUTUAL RESPECT AMONG STATES

Full Faith and Credit shall be given in each State to the public Acts, Records, and judicial Proceedings of every other State. And the Congress may by general Laws prescribe the Manner in which such Acts, Records and Proceedings shall be proved, and the Effect thereof.

SECTION 2: CITIZENS OF STATES AND OF THE UNITED STATES

1 The Citizens of each State shall be entitled to all Privileges and Immunities of Citizens in the several States.

2 A Person charged in any State with Treason, Felony, or other Crime, who shall flee from Justice, and be found in another State, shall on Demand of the executive Authority of the State from which he fled, be delivered up, to be removed to the State having Jurisdiction of the Crime.

3 *No Person held to Service or Labor in one State, under the Laws thereof, escaping into another, shall, in Consequence of any Law or Regulation therein, be discharged from such Service or Labor, but shall be delivered up on Claim of the Party to whom such Service or Labor may be due.*

SECTION 3: NEW STATES

1 New States may be admitted by the Congress into this Union; but no new State shall be formed or erected within the Jurisdiction of any other State; nor any State be formed by the Junction of two or more States, or Parts of States, without the Consent of the Legislatures of the States concerned as well as of the Congress.

2 The Congress shall have Power to dispose of and make all needful Rules and Regulations respecting the Territory or other Property belonging to the United States; and nothing in this Constitution shall be so construed as to Prejudice any Claims of the United States, or of any particular State.

SECTION 4: PROTECTION OF STATES BY THE UNITED STATES

The United States shall guarantee to every State in this Union a Republican Form of Government, and shall protect each of them against Invasion; and on Application of the Legislature, or of the Executive (when the Legislature cannot be convened), against domestic Violence.

CONSTITUTION OF THE UNITED STATES

Article V Amending the Constitution

1 The Congress, whenever two thirds of both Houses shall deem it necessary, shall propose Amendments to this Constitution, or, on the Application of the Legislatures of two thirds of the several States, shall call a Convention for proposing Amendments, which, in either Case, shall be valid to all Intents and Purposes, as Part of this Constitution, when ratified by the Legislatures of three fourths of the several States, or by Conventions in three fourths thereof, as the one or the other Mode of Ratification may be proposed by the Congress.

2 Provided that no Amendment which may be made prior to the Year One thousand eight hundred and eight shall in any Manner affect the first and fourth Clauses in the Ninth Section of the first Article; and that no State, without its Consent, shall be deprived of its equal Suffrage in the Senate.

Article VI The Supreme Law of the Land

1 All Debts contracted and Engagements entered into, before the Adoption of this Constitution, shall be as valid against the United States under this Constitution, as under the Confederation.

2 This Constitution, and the Laws of the United States which shall be made in Pursuance thereof; and all Treaties made, or which shall be made, under the Authority of the United States, shall be the supreme Law of the Land; and the Judges in every State shall be bound thereby, any Thing in the Constitution or Laws of any State to the Contrary notwithstanding.

3 The Senators and Representatives before mentioned, and the Members of the several State Legislatures, and all executive and judicial Officers, both of the United States and of the several States, shall be bound by Oath or Affirmation, to support this Constitution; but no religious Test shall ever be required as a Qualification to any Office or public Trust under the United States.

ARTICLE V
UNDERSTANDING THE CONSTITUTION Article V This article describes the process for amending the Constitution but states that the first and fourth clauses in Article 1's ninth section cannot be amended before 1808. These clauses refer to the importation of slaves and to a tax charged on an individual. The Framers realized that the Constitution would need to be amended at some point, but they made the amendment process extremely difficult. According to U.S. Senate records, approximately 11,699 bills have been proposed as amendments to the Constitution. However, as of 2017, only 27 amendments had been added to the Constitution.

HISTORICAL THINKING Do you think the amendment process should be made easier? Explain why or why not.

ARTICLE VI
UNDERSTANDING THE CONSTITUTION Article VI Paragraph 2 is known as the "supremacy clause." The clause establishes the Constitution and all federal laws and treaties as the supreme law of the land. When state law is in conflict with federal law, federal law prevails. The Supreme Court has used the supremacy clause to ensure that federal law pre-empts, or takes priority over, state law. This is known as the doctrine of pre-emption.

Today, "the people" referred to in the Constitution includes all adult U.S. citizens.

GUIDED DISCUSSION

1. **Identify Problems and Solutions** Reread Article IV, Section 2.2. What problem was this provision in the Constitution intended to solve, and what was the solution? *(Possible response: It can be inferred that prior to the Constitution, some people had committed a crime in one state and then fled to another state to avoid prosecution. This provision makes that option impossible by mandating extradition—that is, requiring states to return a fugitive to the state in which the crime had been committed.)*

2. **Form and Support Opinions** Do you think that the effect of Article VI on the present-day relationship between the states and the federal government is what the Framers intended? Explain your answer. *(Possible response: Article VI has made the power of the federal government greater than that of the states. For example, state laws cannot contradict or supersede federal laws. Whether the Framers intended this is debatable. It can be argued that many Framers, such as Jefferson, were wary of excessive federal power and favored states' rights. Others, such as Hamilton, favored a strong federal government to avoid the chaos of contradictory interstate laws.)*

HISTORICAL THINKING

ANSWER

Answers will vary. Students may argue that by making the amendment process so difficult, the Framers wanted to avoid too-rapid and upsetting changes to the Constitution. However, students may also claim that because of the strict requirements, amendments have become nearly impossible to pass, undermining the intent of the Framers to keep the Constitution relevant to changing times.

MORE INFORMATION

Stubborn Rhode Island Rhode Island's reluctance to ratify the Constitution stemmed from its citizens' fear that a strong central government would become too powerful, stifling Rhode Island's tradition of individualism, self-reliance, and abolitionism. Members of the colony's ruling rural party were so opposed to becoming part of the United States, in fact, that they refused to send delegates to the Philadelphia Convention of 1787.

The Framers wanted each state to hold its own local conventions to debate the ratification of the Constitution. However, from 1787 to 1790, the leaders of Rhode Island refused to do so. Instead, they put the choice to popular vote, allowing the citizens to choose for themselves. The results were overwhelming: Rhode Islanders voted to reject the Constitution by a vote of 2,708 to 243. It wasn't until eight months after George Washington's inauguration that a local convention was finally called. Even so, it took two attempts and the narrowest vote of any state (34 to 32) before Rhode Island joined the United States.

HISTORICAL THINKING

ANSWER

Possible response: The ratification conventions allowed states to debate the issues about the new government that concerned them, argue for and against ratification, and then take a vote on whether to accept the Constitution and become part of the United States. In effect, they were using the very processes outlined in the Constitution for democratic rule.

CONSTITUTION OF THE UNITED STATES

ARTICLE VII
UNDERSTANDING THE CONSTITUTION Article 7 The Framers clearly stated in Article 7 that the Constitution required the approval of only 9 states, not the entire 13. This contrasted with the Articles of Confederation, which required the consent of all 13 states. In addition, the Framers decided to hold a special ratification convention in each state. Delegates to these conventions were chosen by the state's citizens.

On June 21, 1788, New Hampshire became the 9th state to ratify the Constitution and make it the law of the United States. However, the Framers knew that the new nation's survival depended on the populous and wealthy states of Virginia and New York, which were slow to ratify. After lengthy debates, first Virginia and then New York approved the measure, becoming the 11th and 12th states to ratify the Constitution. Rhode Island was the only obstacle to unanimous approval. It officially joined the United States only after being warned that it would be treated like a foreign government if it did not.

HISTORICAL THINKING Why did the Framers call for ratification conventions in the 13 states?

Article VII Ratification

The Ratification of the Conventions of nine States, shall be sufficient for the Establishment of this Constitution between the States so ratifying the Same.

[Here appears some text noting corrections that were made on the original copy of the document.]

Done in Convention by the Unanimous Consent of the States present the Seventeenth Day of September in the Year of our Lord one thousand seven hundred and Eighty seven and of the Independence of the United States of America the Twelfth In witness whereof We have hereunto subscribed our Names,

G°. Washington
President and deputy from Virginia

Massachusetts
Nathaniel Gorham
Rufus King

New York
Alexander Hamilton

Delaware
George Read
Gunning Bedford, Jr.
John Dickinson
Richard Bassett
Jacob Broom

Virginia
John Blair
James Madison, Jr.

Pennsylvania
Benjamin Franklin
Thomas Mifflin
Robert Morris
George Clymer
Thomas Fitzsimons
Jared Ingersoll
James Wilson
Gouverneur Morris

New Hampshire
John Langdon
Nicholas Gilman

New Jersey
William Livingston
David Brearley
William Paterson
Jonathan Dayton

Connecticut
William Samuel Johnson
Roger Sherman

North Carolina
William Blount
Richard Dobbs Spaight
Hugh Williamson

South Carolina
John Rutledge
Charles Cotesworth Pinckney
Charles Pinckney
Pierce Butler

Maryland
James McHenry
Daniel of St. Thomas Jenifer
Daniel Carroll

Georgia
William Few
Abraham Baldwin

THE BILL OF RIGHTS AND AMENDMENTS 11–27

Introduction

Individual rights are fundamental to liberty. The Magna Carta, the charter of English liberties granted in 1215, helped inspire the Bill of Rights. Those who sailed to North America from Britain had enjoyed the freedoms granted to them under both the Magna Carta and the English Bill of Rights. They believed they were entitled to these same rights when they settled their colonies.

No one argued whether Americans should have these rights, but there was debate as to whether it was necessary and advisable to include them in the Constitution. At first, James Madison didn't believe the rights needed to be included. He argued that state constitutions already offered the explicit protection of individual liberties. Stating the rights in the Constitution might actually have the effect of limiting them. However, in 1787, Thomas Jefferson wrote to Madison, "[A] bill of rights is what the people are entitled to against every government on earth, general or particular, and what no just government should refuse." After long discussion among the Framers, Madison changed his mind. He drafted 19 amendments. On December 15, 1791, 10 of them were ratified, and the Bill of Rights was added to the Constitution.

The following is a transcription of the Bill of Rights. Over time, as you'll see, more amendments were added to the Constitution to address issues that arose as the nation grew and changed.

The Preamble to the Bill of Rights

Congress of the United States begun and held at the City of New York, on Wednesday the fourth of March, one thousand seven hundred and eighty nine.

THE Conventions of a number of the States, having at the time of their adopting the Constitution, expressed a desire, in order to prevent misconstruction or abuse of its powers, that further declaratory and restrictive clauses should be added: And as extending the ground of public confidence in the Government, will best ensure the beneficent ends of its institution.

RESOLVED by the Senate and House of Representatives of the United States of America, in Congress assembled, two thirds of both Houses concurring, that the following Articles be proposed to the Legislatures of the several States, as amendments to the Constitution of the United States, all, or any of which Articles, when ratified by three fourths of the said Legislatures, to be valid to all intents and purposes, as part of the said Constitution; viz.

UNDERSTANDING THE PREAMBLE *Viz* is Latin for "that is to say" or "namely."

Bills of Rights Over the years, nations as diverse as South Africa, the Philippines, Canada, France, and India have incorporated a bill, charter, or declaration of human rights into their constitutions. Often, these documents protect many of the same freedoms guaranteed by the U.S. Bill of Rights—speech, assembly, religion, and freedom from unlawful imprisonment. Like the Bill of Rights, which includes a prohibition on forcing citizens to quarter soldiers, these documents can also address other, more specific concerns of a nation's citizens.

For example, India's Fundamental Rights (Article III of its constitution) guarantees citizens the freedom to practice any profession they choose and prohibits a form of discrimination called "untouchability." South Africa's Bill of Rights protects the rights of citizens to form and join labor unions. In France, the Declaration of the Rights of Man and the Citizen, written in 1789, specifically prohibited certain actions that the monarchy had taken before the French Revolution. **ASK:** Why might people who are forming a new government consider a specific list of protected rights to be important? *(Possible responses: People forming a new government might have recent memories of times when their rights, or the rights of others, were violated. People might not want to assume that everyone who leads the government will share their opinions about human rights.)* If the Constitution were being written today, what specific rights would you want to add and protect? *(Answers will vary. In addition to the rights already included, students might suggest the right to basic health care or a right to free and open Internet access.)*

MORE INFORMATION

Miranda Rights In the decision *Miranda* v. *Arizona* (1966), the Supreme Court considered four cases in which people had been convicted of crimes on the basis, or partial basis, of their own confession. In some cases, people had been interrogated several times, or over many days, and at no time had anyone told them of their right to remain silent. The Court debated whether, given the stress and isolation of the interrogations these people had experienced, they might have been "compelled" to be witnesses against themselves, in violation of Amendment 5. The Court concluded that "without proper safeguards, the . . . inherently compelling pressures" of being interrogated could "compel" people to speak, when otherwise they would not. To prevent this issue, persons being arrested must be informed of their rights. In 2000, the Supreme Court upheld this decision.

Since the decision, the Miranda Warning (named for Ernesto Miranda, the plaintiff in the case) has become well known, partially due to its ubiquity in popular culture. Its text states: "You have the right to remain silent. Anything you say can and will be used against you as evidence in a court of law. You have the right to an attorney. If you cannot afford an attorney, one will be appointed for you. Do you understand these rights as they have been read to you?"

HISTORICAL THINKING

ANSWER

Possible responses: No. The right to bear arms is clearly stated in the Constitution and should not be restricted by the federal government. Yes. The context of Amendment 2 applies specifically to self-defense. Today guns are being used in mass shootings and other crimes, so there needs to be some kind of gun control.

AMENDMENTS

UNDERSTANDING AMENDMENT 1
Amendment 1 protects the free exercise of religious liberty by prohibiting the government from establishing a church, endorsing a particular religion, or favoring one set of religious beliefs over another. Thomas Jefferson's 1786 Statute for Religious Freedom, which he wrote for the Virginia legislature, influenced the protection of religious freedom. In his statute, Jefferson also called for the separation of church and state. This idea is contained—although not explicitly—in the "establishment" clause. The Framers debated the wording of the clause and finally adopted that shown here.

UNDERSTANDING AMENDMENT 2
This amendment has been debated for decades. Many Americans believe the amendment ensures the right to possess guns. Others think gun ownership should be controlled. In 2008, the Supreme Court ruled in *District of Columbia* v. *Heller* that Amendment 2 guarantees the right to possess a firearm for self-defense and hunting. There has been debate as to whether the amendment protects ownership of any type of weapon, however.

HISTORICAL THINKING Do you think gun ownership should be controlled? Why or why not?

ARTICLES in addition to, and Amendment of the Constitution of the United States of America, proposed by Congress, and ratified by the Legislatures of the several States, pursuant to the fifth Article of the original Constitution.

Amendment 1 (1791)

Congress shall make no law respecting an establishment of religion, or prohibiting the free exercise thereof; or abridging the freedom of speech, or of the press; or the right of the people peaceably to assemble, and to petition the Government for a redress of grievances.

Amendment 2 (1791)

A well regulated Militia, being necessary to the security of a free State, the right of the people to keep and bear Arms, shall not be infringed.

Amendment 3 (1791)

No Soldier shall, in time of peace be quartered in any house, without the consent of the Owner, nor in time of war, but in a manner to be prescribed by law.

Amendment 4 (1791)

The right of the people to be secure in their persons, houses, papers, and effects, against unreasonable searches and seizures, shall not be violated, and no Warrants shall issue, but upon probable cause, supported by Oath or affirmation, and particularly describing the place to be searched, and the persons or things to be seized.

AMENDMENTS

Amendment 5 (1791)

No person shall be held to answer for a capital, or otherwise infamous crime, unless on a presentment or indictment of a Grand Jury, except in cases arising in the land or naval forces, or in the Militia, when in actual service in time of War or public danger; nor shall any person be subject for the same offence to be twice put in jeopardy of life or limb; nor shall be compelled in any criminal case to be a witness against himself, nor be deprived of life, liberty, or property, without due process of law; nor shall private property be taken for public use, without just compensation.

Amendment 6 (1791)

In all criminal prosecutions, the accused shall enjoy the right to a speedy and public trial, by an impartial jury of the State and district wherein the crime shall have been committed, which district shall have been previously ascertained by law, and to be informed of the nature and cause of the accusation; to be confronted with the witnesses against him; to have compulsory process for obtaining witnesses in his favor, and to have the Assistance of Counsel for his defence.

Amendment 7 (1791)

In Suits at common law, where the value in controversy shall exceed twenty dollars, the right of trial by jury shall be preserved, and no fact tried by a jury, shall be otherwise re-examined in any Court of the United States, than according to the rules of the common law.

Amendment 8 (1791)

Excessive bail shall not be required, nor excessive fines imposed, nor cruel and unusual punishments inflicted.

Amendment 9 (1791)

The enumeration in the Constitution, of certain rights, shall not be construed to deny or disparage others retained by the people.

Amendment 10 (1791)

The powers not delegated to the United States by the Constitution, nor prohibited by it to the States, are reserved to the States respectively, or to the people.

UNDERSTANDING AMENDMENTS 4–6 These three amendments protect people who are suspected of a crime or are being tried for one.

Amendment 4 says that police must have "probable cause" (a good reason) before they can seize someone's possessions. It also protects people from unreasonable searches by government officials.

Amendment 5 protects those accused of crimes. The Due Process Clause was the basis for the defense of Fred Korematsu, an American citizen and the son of Japanese parents, who refused to obey President Franklin Roosevelt's executive order and report to an internment camp during World War II. Under Roosevelt's order, Korematsu's lawyers argued, Japanese Americans were "deprived of life, liberty, or property, without due process of law." The case, *Fred Korematsu* v. *United States of America*, finally went to the Supreme Court, which upheld Korematsu's removal to an internment camp.

Amendment 6 guarantees a speedy public trial to those accused of a crime.

HISTORICAL THINKING Why do you suppose the Supreme Court upheld Roosevelt's executive order?

UNDERSTANDING AMENDMENTS 9 and 10 Amendment 9 prevents the government from denying rights that are not listed in the Bill of Rights. These are called "unenumerated" rights and include the right to travel and to vote.

The Framers added Amendment 10 to better define the balance of power between the states and the federal government. Each state is given the power to make laws that are not covered by the Constitution.

GUIDED DISCUSSION

1. **Make Connections** How do you think historical events influenced the Framers' decision to insist that there should be "no law respecting the establishment of religion"? *(Possible response: Religious freedom was one of the most basic principles and motivating factors for the settlement of the colonies. For example, Puritans came to North America to flee religious persecution, and colonies such as Rhode Island and Pennsylvania explicitly guaranteed religious freedom. Thus, for the Framers, religious freedom was philosophically in line with the history and values of the country.)*

2. **Categorize** Which amendment could opponents of the death penalty use to argue that the practice is unconstitutional? Use text evidence to explain. *(Amendment 8 could be used because it outlaws "cruel and unusual punishment." In fact, this is the argument often used by opponents of the death penalty.)*

HISTORICAL THINKING

ANSWER

Possible response: The United States was at war with Japan, and Roosevelt believed that to prevent Japanese spies from operating in this country, the government needed to move all Japanese people, whether U.S. citizens or not, to internment camps. The Court upheld Roosevelt's order probably because they agreed with the argument that the Japanese as a group were a threat to the security of the United States.

MORE INFORMATION

The 2000 Presidential Election The race between Republican George W. Bush and Democrat Al Gore was close in many states, with one candidate or the other holding a lead of just a few thousand—or in some cases, a few hundred—votes. Bush needed only Florida's electoral votes to win. Initially, he had enough of a lead in the state that Gore conceded the election. As vote counting continued, however, Bush's Florida lead shrank to fewer than 600 votes and then to fewer than 400. Gore took back his concession. Over the next several weeks, election officials in Florida held recounts and examined whether issues with some of Florida's ballots might have affected the totals.

Eventually, the Florida Supreme Court called for a manual recount, which the Bush campaign appealed. In deciding *Bush* v. *Gore*, the United States Supreme Court overturned the recount decision, which meant that Bush's narrow Florida victory stood. As a result, Bush won the electoral college vote by a single digit and became the nation's 44th president. He had lost the popular vote by about half a million votes. **ASK:** Why might an election like this one prompt people to challenge the role of the electoral college in presidential elections? *(Possible response: When the electoral college makes an election decision that seems to go against the decision made by voters, people may question whether their votes really count or even whether the electoral college is necessary.)*

HISTORICAL THINKING

ANSWER

Possible responses: Yes. The electoral college does not accurately reflect the will of the people and should be eliminated. No. The Framers had good reasons for establishing the electoral college, and it should be maintained as part of the Constitution.

AMENDMENTS

UNDERSTANDING AMENDMENT 12
Amendment 12 established the electoral college. As you know, prior to its passage, the presidential candidate who received the most electoral votes won the presidency. The candidate with the second most votes became the vice president. The amendment changed this system by allowing the delegates of each party to choose its nominees for both president and vice president.

The electoral college was challenged in 2000 and 2016, when the candidates who won the popular vote (Al Gore in 2000 and Hillary Clinton in 2016) lost the elections to George W. Bush and Donald Trump, respectively.

HISTORICAL THINKING Do you think the electoral college should be abolished? Why or why not?

Amendment 11 (1798)

[**Note:** Article 3, Section 2, of the Constitution was modified by the 11th Amendment.]

The Judicial power of the United States shall not be construed to extend to any suit in law or equity, commenced or prosecuted against one of the United States by Citizens of another State, or by Citizens or Subjects of any Foreign State.

Amendment 12 (1804)

[**Note:** Part of Article 2, Section 1, of the Constitution was replaced by the 12th Amendment.]

The Electors shall meet in their respective states and vote by ballot for President and Vice-President, one of whom, at least, shall not be an inhabitant of the same state with themselves; they shall name in their ballots the person voted for as President, and in distinct ballots the person voted for as Vice-President, and they shall make distinct lists of all persons voted for as President, and of all persons voted for as Vice-President, and of the number of votes for each, which lists they shall sign and certify, and transmit sealed to the seat of the government of the United States, directed to the President of the Senate; —the President of the Senate shall, in the presence of the Senate and House of Representatives, open all the certificates and the votes shall then be counted; —The person having the greatest number of votes for President, shall be the President, if such number be a majority of the whole number of Electors appointed; and if no person have such majority, then from the persons having the highest numbers not exceeding three on the list of those voted for as President, the House of Representatives shall choose immediately, by ballot, the President. But in choosing the President, the votes shall be taken by states, the representation from each state having one vote; a quorum for this purpose shall consist of a member or members from two-thirds of the states, and a majority of all the states shall be necessary to a choice. *And if the House of Representatives shall not choose a President whenever the right of choice shall devolve upon them, before the fourth day of March next following, then the Vice-President shall act as President, as in case of the death or other constitutional disability of the President.* The person having the greatest number of votes as Vice-President, shall be the Vice-President, if such number be a majority of the whole number of Electors appointed, and if no person have a majority, then from the two highest numbers on the list, the Senate shall choose the Vice-President; a quorum for the purpose shall consist of two-thirds of the whole number of Senators, and a majority of the whole number shall be necessary to a choice. But no person constitutionally ineligible to the office of President shall be eligible to that of Vice-President of the United States.

AMENDMENTS

Amendment 13 (1865)

[Note: A portion of Article 4, Section 2, of the Constitution was superseded by the 13th Amendment.]

SECTION 1: Neither slavery nor involuntary servitude, except as a punishment for crime whereof the party shall have been duly convicted, shall exist within the United States, or any place subject to their jurisdiction.

SECTION 2: Congress shall have power to enforce this article by appropriate legislation.

Amendment 14 (1868)

[Note: Article 1, Section 2, of the Constitution was modified by Section 2 of the 14th Amendment.]

SECTION 1: All persons born or naturalized in the United States, and subject to the jurisdiction thereof, are citizens of the United States and of the State wherein they reside. No State shall make or enforce any law which shall abridge the privileges or immunities of citizens of the United States; nor shall any State deprive any person of life, liberty, or property, without due process of law; nor deny to any person within its jurisdiction the equal protection of the laws.

SECTION 2: Representatives shall be apportioned among the several States according to their respective numbers, counting the whole number of persons in each State, excluding Indians not taxed. But when the right to vote at any election for the choice of electors for President and Vice-President of the United States, Representatives in Congress, the Executive and Judicial officers of a State, or the members of the *Legislature thereof, is denied to any of the male inhabitants of such State, being twenty-one years of age, and citizens of the United States,* or in any way abridged, except for participation in rebellion, or other crime, the basis of representation therein shall be reduced in the proportion which the number of such male citizens shall bear to the whole number of male citizens twenty-one years of age in such State.

SECTION 3: No person shall be a Senator or Representative in Congress, or elector of President and Vice-President, or hold any office, civil or military, under the United States, or under any State, who, having previously taken an oath, as a member of Congress, or as an officer of the United States, or as a member of any State legislature, or as an executive or judicial officer of any State, to support the Constitution of the United States, shall have engaged in insurrection or rebellion against the same, or given aid or comfort to the enemies thereof. But Congress may by a vote of two-thirds of each House, remove such disability.

**UNDERSTANDING AMENDMENTS
13–15** Amendments 13–15 are often referred to as the "civil war" or "reconstruction" amendments because they were created in the aftermath of the war. These post-Civil War amendments laid the foundation for the legal phase of the 20th-century civil rights movement.

UNDERSTANDING AMENDMENT 13
This amendment outlawed slavery.

**UNDERSTANDING AMENDMENT
14 Section 1** This section defines citizenship and ensures that all citizens enjoy the same rights and the same protections by the law. The amendment has been continually reinterpreted and applied to different contexts by the courts. For example, sometimes it has been employed as a protection for workers and other times as a protection for corporations. In the 1877 case, *Munn v. Illinois*, the Supreme Court upheld the idea that a corporation and its business activities were protected by the 14th Amendment.

**UNDERSTANDING AMENDMENT 14
Section 2** This section overrides the three-fifths clause in Article I. As a result of this amendment, each citizen is counted as a whole person. Section 2 also calls for reducing the number of representatives of a state if it denies some citizens the right to vote.

GUIDED DISCUSSION

1. **Make Connections** Why do you think Section 1 of Amendment 14 remains relevant in court cases heard today? *(Answers will vary. Possible response: The section gives people "equal protection of the laws." Over time, as various groups have fought for equality—such as African Americans, women, and the LGBT community—they have used this section to fight discrimination.)*

2. **Identify Problems and Solutions** What problem-solving ideas appear in Section 2 of Amendment 14, and what problems were left to be solved at a later time? *(Section 2 overturned the three-fifths clause and granted voting rights to African-American men. However, it continued to exclude women from voting, and it stated that Native Americans were not counted in congressional representation as they were not citizens of the country. Making those changes would have to wait.)*

MORE INFORMATION

The Equal Rights Amendment Three years after Amendment 19 granted women the right to vote, former suffrage activist Alice Paul introduced a potential Amendment 20 to Congress, one that would grant equal rights in all areas to women who were citizens of the United States. The Equal Rights Amendment, or ERA, did not pass in 1923; it languished in committee in the House, appearing at each session but never getting approval.

Finally, in 1970, Representative Martha Griffiths petitioned to have the ERA brought out for House approval. It won House approval in 1971 and Senate approval the following year. The ERA faced strong public and political opposition, however. Although a majority of states (35) ratified it, it did not reach the number needed to pass (38). Had it passed, it would have become Amendment 27. Efforts to pass the ERA still continue, and the amendment has been reintroduced periodically. To date, however, it remains stuck in Congress.

ASK: Do you think that a new constitutional amendment would be an effective way to achieve widespread equal rights for all people? *(Answers will vary. Students should support their opinions with evidence from history, their own experiences, and their understanding of existing constitutional amendments.)*

HISTORICAL THINKING

ANSWER

Possible response: After the Civil War, some states wished to return to the status quo, which was based upon white supremacy. Yet in some areas in the South, African Americans were in the majority and would have acquired considerable political power had they been able to vote. Prohibiting African-American men from voting was a way to help achieve the goal of allowing whites to dominate the political system once again.

AMENDMENTS

SECTION 4: The validity of the public debt of the United States, authorized by law, including debts incurred for payment of pensions and bounties for services in suppressing insurrection or rebellion, shall not be questioned. But neither the United States nor any State shall assume or pay any debt or obligation incurred in aid of insurrection or rebellion against the United States, or any claim for the loss or emancipation of any slave; but all such debts, obligations and claims shall be held illegal and void.

SECTION 5: The Congress shall have the power to enforce, by appropriate legislation, the provisions of this article.

Amendment 15 (1870)

SECTION 1: The right of citizens of the United States to vote shall not be denied or abridged by the United States or by any State on account of race, color, or previous condition of servitude—

SECTION 2: The Congress shall have the power to enforce this article by appropriate legislation.

UNDERSTANDING AMENDMENT 15
The 15th Amendment prohibits federal and state governments from limiting or denying an individual's ability to vote because of "race, color, or previous conditions of servitude." Section 2 of the amendment gives Congress the authority to enforce the amendment by passing federal laws that guarantee voting rights. Note that the amendment granted African-American men voting rights but not women of any race. In addition, some states imposed literacy tests, white primaries, poll taxes, and other barriers to keep African Americans from voting. Almost 100 years would pass before African Americans secured stronger protections through federal legislation and the 24th Amendment.

HISTORICAL THINKING Why might some states have made it difficult for African-American men to vote?

In this illustration, a group of men who helped bring about the 15th Amendment, including Abraham Lincoln, Hiram Revels, and Frederick Douglass, watch as President Ulysses S. Grant signs the amendment.

UNDERSTANDING AMENDMENT 16
The 16th Amendment was the first of four "Progressive" amendments. During the Progressive Era (1890–1920), many Americans worked to reform government. Seeking to reduce tariffs and still provide revenue for the federal government, progressives pushed for this amendment, which established an income tax.

Amendment 16 (1913)

[**Note:** Article 1, Section 9, of the Constitution was modified by the 16th Amendment.]

The Congress shall have power to lay and collect taxes on incomes, from whatever source derived, without apportionment among the several States, and without regard to any census or enumeration.

AMENDMENTS

Amendment 17 (1913)

[Note: Article 1, Section 3, of the Constitution was modified by the 17th Amendment.]

The Senate of the United States shall be composed of two Senators from each State, elected by the people thereof, for six years; and each Senator shall have one vote. The electors in each State shall have the qualifications requisite for electors of the most numerous branch of the State legislatures.

When vacancies happen in the representation of any State in the Senate, the executive authority of such State shall issue writs of election to fill such vacancies: Provided, That the legislature of any State may empower the executive thereof to make temporary appointments until the people fill the vacancies by election as the legislature may direct.

This amendment shall not be so construed as to affect the election or term of any Senator chosen before it becomes valid as part of the Constitution.

Amendment 18 (1919)

Repealed by the 21st Amendment.

SECTION 1: *After one year from the ratification of this article the manufacture, sale, or transportation of intoxicating liquors within, the importation thereof into, or the exportation thereof from the United States and all territory subject to the jurisdiction thereof for beverage purposes is hereby prohibited.*

SECTION 2: *The Congress and the several States shall have concurrent power to enforce this article by appropriate legislation.*

SECTION 3: *This article shall be inoperative unless it shall have been ratified as an amendment to the Constitution by the legislatures of the several States, as provided in the Constitution, within seven years from the date of the submission hereof to the States by the Congress.*

Philadelphia's Director of Public Safety, Smedley Butler, smashes casks of beer in 1924 to enforce Prohibition.

UNDERSTANDING AMENDMENT 17
The 17th Amendment changed the process by which Senators are elected. Through the popular election of senators, the amendment made the process more democratic.

UNDERSTANDING AMENDMENT 18
Known as the Prohibition Amendment, the 18th Amendment prohibited the production, sale, or transportation of alcoholic beverages in the United States. Many of those who supported the amendment also supported the temperance movement, which advocated for the control of alcohol consumption. Many progressives viewed alcohol abuse as a significant social problem. Congress passed the Volstead Act in 1919, which gave the U.S. Treasury Department the power to enforce Prohibition.

HISTORICAL THINKING In what way was Amendment 18 different from the preceding amendments?

GUIDED DISCUSSION

1. **Describe** How did Amendment 16 make the United States a more democratic nation? *(Possible response: Prior to the amendment, senators were not required to be elected by popular vote; instead, they could be appointed by high-ranking officials. As a result, they often did not work in the interests of the people of their state, and there was no way for the people to hold them accountable. Directly electing senators by popular vote gave citizens the ability to choose senators who best reflected their interests. The people's power to vote senators out of office was a check on politicians' activities.)*

2. **Analyze Visuals** What do the images around the edges of the print suggest about the illustrator's thoughts on the effect of Amendment 15? *(Possible response: The images show African Americans getting married, attending school, serving in the government and military, and waiting to vote. These images suggest that the right to vote will lead to more opportunities for African Americans and their descendents in all areas of society.)*

HISTORICAL THINKING

ANSWER

Possible response: Previous amendments expanded the rights of people or explicitly forbade the government from taking certain actions, Amendment 18 took away something that people had been doing for centuries—making, buying and selling, and consuming alcoholic drinks. These activities were made illegal after the ratification of Amendment 18.

Citizenship Handbook **R27**

MORE INFORMATION

Presidential Term Limits Students may be surprised to learn that the two-term limit on the presidency was only tradition, not law, prior to 1951. Like several other presidential traditions—such as the form of address "Mr. President" or the wording and public delivery of the inaugural oath of office—the two-term presidency began with George Washington's administration. As Washington's second term came to a close, many people pressured him to continue in the office. (Some people encouraged it even after his retirement.) Although he had been unanimously elected to both of his terms, Washington had never been eager for the position. Additionally, he felt that the rise of political parties meant that he would no longer have the full support of the people.

This precedent held until the election of 1940. President Franklin D. Roosevelt also claimed reluctance to serve more than two terms, but he felt that the looming international crisis—the Second World War—justified his run for re-election. By a constitutional coincidence, in addition to inspiring Amendment 22 with his four-term presidency, Roosevelt was also the first president to be inaugurated under the requirements outlined by Amendment 20.

HISTORICAL THINKING

ANSWER

Possible response: The wording mirrors the language of Amendment 15, which granted suffrage to African-American men. This leaves no doubt that the amendment's purpose was to grant universal suffrage to women and that no local, state, or federal government could prohibit or interfere with that right.

AMENDMENTS

Following the passage of the 19th Amendment, the women shown here voted for the first time in a 1920 election in New York City.

UNDERSTANDING AMENDMENT 19
Although many states had granted some voting privileges to women before 1920, the 19th Amendment extended equal voting rights to all women in the country. In the 1800s, women's rights leaders such as Elizabeth Cady Stanton and Susan B. Anthony dedicated their lives to securing political and social equality for women. Their actions helped inspire and launch another movement in the 1960s, which called for further rights for women and offered differing perspectives on the roles of women.

HISTORICAL THINKING Why does the amendment specify that women's right to vote "shall not be denied or abridged by the United States or by any state"?

UNDERSTANDING AMENDMENT 20
This amendment is often called the "Lame Duck Amendment." In government, a lame duck is an elected official whose term in office is about to end. So, for instance, a president who has already served two terms is a lame duck. Officials who have not won re-election are also considered lame ducks. Congress has little incentive to work with a lame duck president.

Amendment 19 (1920)

The right of citizens of the United States to vote shall not be denied or abridged by the United States or by any State on account of sex.

Congress shall have power to enforce this article by appropriate legislation.

Amendment 20 (1933)

[**Note:** Article 1, Section 4, of the Constitution was modified by Section 2 of the 20th Amendment. In addition, a portion of the 12th Amendment was superseded by Section 3.]

SECTION 1: The terms of the President and the Vice President shall end at noon on the 20th day of January, and the terms of Senators and Representatives at noon on the 3d day of January, of the years in which such terms would have ended if this article had not been ratified; and the terms of their successors shall then begin.

SECTION 2: The Congress shall assemble at least once in every year, and such meeting shall begin at noon on the 3d day of January, unless they shall by law appoint a different day.

SECTION 3: If, at the time fixed for the beginning of the term of the President, the President elect shall have died, the Vice President elect shall become President. If a President shall not have been chosen before the time fixed for the beginning of his term, or if the President elect shall have failed to qualify, then the Vice President elect shall act as President until a President shall have qualified; and the Congress may by law provide for the case wherein neither a President elect nor a Vice President elect

AMENDMENTS

shall have qualified, declaring who shall then act as President, or the manner in which one who is to act shall be selected, and such person shall act accordingly until a President or Vice President shall have qualified.

SECTION 4: The Congress may by law provide for the case of the death of any of the persons from whom the House of Representatives may choose a President whenever the right of choice shall have devolved upon them, and for the case of the death of any of the persons from whom the Senate may choose a Vice President whenever the right of choice shall have devolved upon them.

SECTION 5: Sections 1 and 2 shall take effect on the 15th day of October following the ratification of this article.

SECTION 6: This article shall be inoperative unless it shall have been ratified as an amendment to the Constitution by the legislatures of three-fourths of the several States within seven years from the date of its submission.

Amendment 21 (1933)

SECTION 1: The eighteenth article of amendment to the Constitution of the United States is hereby repealed.

SECTION 2: The transportation or importation into any State, Territory, or possession of the United States for delivery or use therein of intoxicating liquors, in violation of the laws thereof, is hereby prohibited.

SECTION 3: This article shall be inoperative unless it shall have been ratified as an amendment to the Constitution by conventions in the several States, as provided in the Constitution, within seven years from the date of the submission hereof to the States by the Congress.

Amendment 22 (1951)

SECTION 1: No person shall be elected to the office of the President more than twice, and no person who has held the office of President, or acted as President, for more than two years of a term to which some other person was elected President shall be elected to the office of the President more than once. But this Article shall not apply to any person holding the office of President when this Article was proposed by the Congress, and shall not prevent any person who may be holding the office of President, or acting as President, during the term within which this Article becomes operative from holding the office of President or acting as President during the remainder of such term.

SECTION 2: This article shall be inoperative unless it shall have been ratified as an amendment to the Constitution by the legislatures of three-fourths of the several States within seven years from the date of its submission to the States by the Congress.

UNDERSTANDING AMENDMENT 21
Amendment 21 repealed Amendment 18 and ended Prohibition. Amendment 21 is the only amendment that was ratified by state conventions rather than state legislatures. Section 2 of the amendment returned the regulation of alcohol to the states, giving them significant control of alcohol within and across their borders. Consequently, alcohol laws vary throughout the states. States also have the power to establish the legal drinking age within their borders. In an effort to prohibit the sale of alcohol to minors, the federal government provides federal funds only to states who set the legal drinking age at 21. All 50 states have done so.

HISTORICAL THINKING What potential problems or issues might arise when states have different laws regulating people of the same age?

UNDERSTANDING AMENDMENT 22
Democrat Franklin D. Roosevelt served three terms as president of the United States and was elected to a fourth term shortly before he died in 1945. George Washington had declined to run for a third term. All presidents before Roosevelt followed this unwritten custom and served no more than two terms. Within months of Roosevelt's death, Republicans in Congress presented the 22nd Amendment for consideration.

HISTORICAL THINKING Do you think a president should be able to serve for more than two terms? Explain your answer.

GUIDED DISCUSSION

1. **Identify Problems and Solutions** Why did the authors of Amendment 20 consider extended lame duck sessions a problem? *(During a lame duck session, many members of the government may no longer be supported by the people. Thus, the decisions they make do not necessarily reflect the public's wishes. In addition, if a crisis is unfolding at the same time, the president and Congress are hampered in their ability to respond.)*

2. **Form and Support Opinions** Considering its repeal only 14 years later, was the original passage of Amendment 18 a mistake? Explain. *(Possible responses: No. Prohibition was an attempt to address the considerable societal problems of alcoholism. Yes. Regulating personal morality is difficult and probably against the intentions of the Framers.)*

HISTORICAL THINKING

ANSWER

Possible response: Such a difference in states' laws may cause conflict and legal confusion between states because an action that is illegal in one—such as drinking alcohol or driving a car at age 18—may be legal in another. This would encourage young people to cross state lines to engage in a behavior where it is legal. Should they have an accident or commit a crime as a result, conflicting state laws would only add to the legal confusion about where and under what laws people should be held accountable.

ANSWER

Possible responses: Yes. Limiting a president to two terms is inherently undemocratic, because popular leaders who are supported by the people would not be able to continue in office. No. Term limits are a safeguard against possible dictators, because leaders would be prevented from governing for extended periods of time.

MORE INFORMATION

Washington D.C.'s Statehood Movement Amendment 23 gave residents of the nation's capital a say in choosing the president and vice president, but residents have not stopped fighting for full representation in Congress. Organizations supporting full statehood, such as the New Columbia Statehood Commission, have pushed to reclassify the district's residential areas and have them admitted to the union as the 51st state. Opponents to statehood argue that the move would drastically shift the balance of power in Congress because the district is heavily Democratic.

In 2016, a referendum calling for a congressional petition for D.C.'s statehood passed with 79 percent of the vote. This meant that the mayor could then petition Congress for admission on the grounds that the voters had approved a state constitution drafted and made available for citizens to review. If admitted, the new state would be called New Columbia. **ASK:** In your opinion, would full statehood for the residents of the District of Columbia be a good idea? *(Answers will vary. Students should support their opinions with evidence and sound reasoning.)*

HISTORICAL THINKING

ANSWER

Possible response: Amendment 24 applies to the voting rights of all citizens and not just those in minority groups. If specific minority groups were named, it is conceivable that poll taxes could still be used against unnamed groups.

AMENDMENTS

UNDERSTANDING AMENDMENT 23
The District of Columbia is the official seat of the U.S. government, but it is a federal territory, not a state, and has only a nonvoting representative in Congress. Washington, D.C., began as a small community, but by 1960, more than 760,000 people who paid federal taxes and could be drafted into the military lived there. The states ratified Amendment 23 in 1961 to allow residents of the District to vote in presidential elections. The District of Columbia has three electoral votes.

UNDERSTANDING AMENDMENT 24
This amendment abolished poll taxes and election fees charged by states to keep low-income and mostly African-American citizens from voting. The successful push to get the amendment passed was in part based on the support and demands of the civil rights movement. The amendment gave African Americans greater access to the political process. As written, Amendment 24 prohibits poll taxes only in federal elections. The Voting Rights Act of 1965 and a 1966 Supreme Court decision banned poll taxes in state elections as well.

HISTORICAL THINKING Why do you think the amendment refers to the "right of citizens of the United States to vote," rather than name specific minority groups?

Amendment 23 (1961)

SECTION 1: The District constituting the seat of Government of the United States shall appoint in such manner as the Congress may direct:

A number of electors of President and Vice President equal to the whole number of Senators and Representatives in Congress to which the District would be entitled if it were a State, but in no event more than the least populous State; they shall be in addition to those appointed by the States, but they shall be considered, for the purposes of the election of President and Vice President, to be electors appointed by a State; and they shall meet in the District and perform such duties as provided by the twelfth article of amendment.

SECTION 2: The Congress shall have power to enforce this article by appropriate legislation.

Amendment 24 (1964)

SECTION 1: The right of citizens of the United States to vote in any primary or other election for President or Vice President, for electors for President or Vice President, or for Senator or Representative in Congress, shall not be denied or abridged by the United States or any State by reason of failure to pay any poll tax or other tax.

SECTION 2: The Congress shall have power to enforce this article by appropriate legislation.

AMENDMENTS

Amendment 25 (1967)

[**Note:** Article 2, Section 1, of the Constitution was affected by the 25th Amendment.]

SECTION 1: In case of the removal of the President from office or of his death or resignation, the Vice President shall become President.

SECTION 2: Whenever there is a vacancy in the office of the Vice President, the President shall nominate a Vice President who shall take office upon confirmation by a majority vote of both Houses of Congress.

SECTION 3: Whenever the President transmits to the President pro tempore of the Senate and the Speaker of the House of Representatives his written declaration that he is unable to discharge the powers and duties of his office, and until he transmits to them a written declaration to the contrary, such powers and duties shall be discharged by the Vice President as Acting President.

SECTION 4: Whenever the Vice President and a majority of either the principal officers of the executive departments or of such other body as Congress may by law provide, transmit to the President pro tempore of the Senate and the Speaker of the House of Representatives their written declaration that the President is unable to discharge the powers and duties of his office, the Vice President shall immediately assume the powers and duties of the office as Acting President.

Thereafter, when the President transmits to the President pro tempore of the Senate and the Speaker of the House of Representatives his written declaration that no inability exists, he shall resume the powers and duties of his office unless the Vice President and a majority of either the principal officers of the executive department or of such other body as Congress may by law provide, transmit within four days to the President pro tempore of the Senate and the Speaker of the House of Representatives their written declaration that the President is unable to discharge the powers and duties of his office. Thereupon Congress shall decide the issue, assembling within forty-eight hours for that purpose if not in session. If the Congress, within twenty-one days after receipt of the latter written declaration, or, if Congress is not in session, within twenty-one days after Congress is required to assemble, determines by two-thirds vote of both Houses that the President is unable to discharge the powers and duties of his office, the Vice President shall continue to discharge the same as Acting President; otherwise, the President shall resume the powers and duties of his office.

UNDERSTANDING AMENDMENT 25
The 25th Amendment was ratified in 1967 to establish procedures to follow if a president becomes disabled while in office. The amendment was proposed after the assassination of President John F. Kennedy in 1963. Following his death, many questioned what would have happened if he had survived the shooting but been unable to govern. Eight presidents have died and one resigned while in office. In addition, seven vice presidents have died while in office and two have resigned. This amendment provides for an orderly transfer of power.

HISTORICAL THINKING Why is there a plan of succession for the presidency?

GUIDED DISCUSSION

1. **Evaluate** Considering the climate of the 1950s and 1960s, why might civil rights activists have considered a constitutional amendment, rather than individual state laws, a more effective way to influence state governments and address the issue of poll taxes? *(Possible response: An amendment would apply to all states at once. However, only three-fourths of the states would have to ratify it, so it could become the law of the land even if a few states objected. As proof of this strategy, of the 38 states needed to ratify the amendment, only two from the former Confederacy—where poll taxes posed the biggest issue—voted to approve it.)*

2. **Make Connections** How do amendments prompted by specific historical events, such as Amendment 25, illustrate the importance of the amendment process in ensuring an effective Constitution? *(Possible response: Such amendments illustrate how the process enables the Constitution to change in order to address issues that were not considered or never envisioned by the Framers.)*

HISTORICAL THINKING

ANSWER

The presidential succession plan ensures that the government always has executive leadership and helps guarantee a peaceful transition of power should something happen to the president, vice president, or other top leaders.

MORE INFORMATION

Amendment 27 In 1789, James Madison suggested 12 amendments to the Constitution (whittled down from his original 19)—but only 10 of them were approved and ratified. Amendment 27, which would give the people a way to vote on any pay raises Congress might try to give itself, was one of the two that failed.

During Madison's time, the issue of congressional pay was not a pressing one. After all, the country had yet to truly begin, so politicians enriching themselves from the nation's coffers was not on people's minds. However, a series of unpopular actions by Congress brought the issue into the limelight. In 1978, Congress voted to give itself a pay raise, despite the measure's unpopularity. In 1981, a special congressional tax break was inserted into a bill covering black lung disease. These actions were followed by a series of scandals, including congressional members not paying for meals in the Capitol cafeteria, and by the House raising members' salaries again in 1989. As a result, momentum for the amendment grew, and it was ratified in 1992.

ASK: Why might Madison have thought it important to give voters a chance to respond before Congress gives itself a pay raise? *(Possible response: Madison might have thought that since congressional salaries are paid by tax dollars, voters should be be able to approve or disapprove of how those dollars are being spent.)*

HISTORICAL THINKING

ANSWER

Answers will vary. Possible responses: No. Lowering the voting age to 18 was based on the fact that people of this age could serve in the military and thus deserved to have a voice in government. Also, Americans under 18 generally do not have the maturity to vote wisely. Yes. Many decisions made by the federal government affect people under the age of 18. For example, policies about education affect students of all ages. In addition, many young people have more maturity than many adults. Thus, the voting age should be lowered again.

AMENDMENTS

Pat Keefer, a leader in advocating for the youth vote in the early 1970s, holds signs urging 18-year olds to vote.

UNDERSTANDING AMENDMENT 26
Amendment 26 continued the Constitution's expansion of voting rights. In 1954, President Dwight Eisenhower proposed lowering the voting age to 18 years. The movement acquired new momentum in the late 1960s during the Vietnam War. People began to question why 18-year-old men could be drafted to serve in the military but could not vote.

HISTORICAL THINKING Do you think the voting age should be reduced even more? Explain your answer.

UNDERSTANDING AMENDMENT 27
Amendment 27 defers any congressional pay raise to the next election cycle. The amendment was first proposed in 1789 by James Madison. However, it was ratified more than 200 years later, thanks to a college student's research project. In his research, the student found that a proposed amendment remains pending, no matter how much time passes before action is taken on it. The student decided to see if he could get the amendment passed and found that he was able to gather enough support to do so.

Amendment 26 (1971)

[**Note:** Amendment 14, Section 2, of the Constitution was modified by Section 1 of the 26th Amendment.]

SECTION 1: The right of citizens of the United States, who are eighteen years of age or older, to vote shall not be denied or abridged by the United States or by any State on account of age.

SECTION 2: The Congress shall have power to enforce this article by appropriate legislation.

Amendment 27 (1992)

No law, varying the compensation for the services of the Senators and Representatives, shall take effect, until an election of Representatives shall have intervened.

Citizenship and You

For many high school students, getting to a job, meeting with friends, and participating in activities require some source of transportation. Many young adults borrow a car from their parents to get around. To continue to enjoy this privilege, you have to handle responsibilities and prove you are dependable. You have to obey the rules of the road and be a careful, alert driver. Similarly, our responsibilities to our communities, states, and nation balance the rights we receive as citizens. Let's examine some aspects of American citizenship—of being a full member of a country in exchange for certain responsibilities.

STRUGGLE FOR EQUAL RIGHTS

As you have learned by studying the U.S. Constitution and Bill of Rights, privileges and rights such as citizenship and voting have been contested, reshaped, and amended during our country's history. Beginning with freedoms and rights cherished and protected in the Constitution by the Framers, Americans from all walks of life have struggled to expand their own rights and those of others. People gained rights they had been denied through the efforts of the civil rights movement, including the right to participate in government, the right to free expression—in all its forms—and the right to equal treatment under the law. Federal, state, and local governments have responded to these social changes with more equitable laws. For example, in response to demands by the LGBT community, the

Individuals act as participatory citizens by exercising their right to vote in local, state, and federal elections.

Supreme Court legalized same-sex marriage in 2015. The efforts and sacrifices of rights activists have helped move all Americans forward in our continuing struggle to become a more perfect union—a struggle that continues today.

WE THE PEOPLE

What role do rules play in your life? Have you ever considered what your life would be like if there were no rules? Imagine arriving at school on the first day of your senior year of high school. You discover that there are no schedules. No one knows where to go, what classes to attend, which locker to use. No one understands the processes and procedures that allow a school to operate efficiently.

This is similar to what would happen in a government without clear rules—or laws—that define the rights and responsibilities of citizens. Order, organization, equality, and safety would all be threatened without laws and established procedures and processes. The most concrete example of our society's rules are our laws, and the most fundamental duty of an American citizen is to obey them.

Is it fair that a government makes laws that people must follow? As you learned while studying the Constitution, the United States is a representative democracy, as demonstrated by the phrase "We the people." Your exploration of the Constitution has revealed that the American people hold the power to shape the government and determine its practices. When our government and representatives act in ways that oppose our rules and ideals, we have the means to point the country in the right direction. Americans work to be *good citizens* by obeying laws, *participatory citizens* by voting and serving on juries, and *socially-just citizens* by standing up for the rights of others.

THINK ABOUT IT

SUMMARIZE Why are rules and laws important, and what would happen without them?

Citizenship Handbook **R33**

GUIDED DISCUSSION

1. **Evaluate** Do you consider the textbook's view of American history as one in which "activists have helped move all Americans forward in our continuing struggle to become a more perfect union" to be a fair interpretation? *(Answers will vary. Some students could argue that the textbook is biased toward the view that peoples' rights have continuously expanded across American history. Other students might point to evidence that contradicts this interpretation by citing the recent rollback of voting rights in some states or the government's infringement upon religious freedom described by some conservatives.)*

2. **Form and Support Opinions** Is obeying the law always a requirement for being a good citizen? Support your opinion with examples from history or your own experience. *(Answers will vary, but students should support their opinions with sound reasoning and examples from experience or history. Students may note that there have been times when laws contradicted the word or spirit of the Constitution. For example, Rosa Parks technically disobeyed a law. Yet, because of the nature of that law, it would be difficult to conclude from her actions that she was not a good citizen.)*

THINK ABOUT IT

Possible response: Rules and laws help establish stability, protection, and fairness for citizens in a society. Without laws, society would become chaotic, subject to a leader's or ruling party's whims, and might cease to function altogether.

MORE INFORMATION

First Amendment Cases Point out to students that the text's example of "crying 'Fire!' in a crowded theater when there is no fire" comes directly from a Supreme Court decision. In the case of *Schenck* v. *United States* (1919), the defendant, Charles T. Schenck, had been convicted of espionage for distributing a leaflet that discouraged people from obeying the draft during World War I. The Court ruled that while "ordinarily" the First Amendment would protect someone's right to oppose a military draft, in wartime such activity could "create a clear and present danger." "The most stringent protection of free speech," Justice Oliver Wendell Holmes, Jr., wrote, "would not protect a man in falsely shouting fire in a theatre and causing a panic." With this reasoning, the Court upheld Schenck's conviction.

Many other landmark Supreme Court cases have outlined the specific limits and protections of the First Amendment. For example, in *Tinker* v. *Des Moines Independent Community School District* (1969), the Court extended First Amendment protection to students expressing political opinions in schools unless the school officials could prove that the expression violated other students' rights or interfered with the educational process. **ASK:** Do you agree with the Supreme Court's opinion that free speech can be restricted under some circumstances? *(Possible responses: Yes. There must be a balance between defending the Constitution and preserving people's safety and general order. If, for example, a person's speech causes clear and immediate harm to others, the person is infringing upon the rights of people in his audience. No. It may be too easy to claim that a person's speech is meant to harm others when the real reason may be a desire to silence that person. Censorship in the name of security or safety can erode First Amendment rights of free speech.)*

The Rights and Responsibilities of Citizens

Our Constitution defines many of the rights we enjoy as Americans. These rights apply to all citizens, regardless of whether they were born here or immigrated from another country. Knowing your rights can help you better understand the responsibilities that come with being a citizen, and help you determine what you must do to support and protect those rights. Responsibilities include doing what is right, showing good character, and acting in an ethical manner. As you read, think about specific actions you already perform and other steps you might take to be a good, participatory, and socially just citizen.

AMERICAN CITIZENSHIP

Some residents of the United States are citizens because they were born in the country. They are native-born citizens. Others came legally from foreign countries to live in the United States. Our democratic principles have fostered high levels of freedom, political stability, and economic prosperity. These features have attracted people to our nation for hundreds of years. In addition, our political and economic systems have become models for other nations throughout the world. People looking for opportunity and freedom are drawn to our country.

A person who has immigrated to the United States and desires to become a legal citizen goes through a process called **naturalization**. Individuals may qualify for naturalization if they are at least 18 years old and have been a permanent resident in the United States for at least 5 years (or 3 years if they are married to a U.S. citizen). They must learn the laws, rights, and responsibilities of American citizenship.

Following a successful interview with government officials, a prospective citizen must pass a citizenship test. After completing all the steps in this process, a new citizen is sworn in during a naturalization ceremony. As you know, the United States is a country of immigrants. Throughout our country's history, immigrants have helped build our nation, strengthen our economy, and enhance our society. It is a proud day when they become U.S. citizens.

For both native and naturalized citizens, being an American means much more than just living in the United States. After all, Americans living in foreign countries are still citizens of the United States. They are always connected to the United States and other Americans because of their citizenship. Citizenship also encompasses elements of the American tradition, which includes a shared history, customs, and political and cultural beliefs and values. These values include freedom, liberty, and equality—those principles Thomas Jefferson described in the Declaration of Independence.

Rights of Citizens
Right to freedom of religion
Right to freedom of speech (with some limits)
Right to freedom of the press
Right to assemble
Right to trial by jury (in specific types of cases)
Right to vote
Right to buy and sell property
Right to freely travel across the country and to leave and return to the country

RESTRICTIONS ON RIGHTS

By now, you're probably familiar with the basic rights of citizens as guaranteed in the Constitution. These rights also carry responsibilities and are subject to interpretation by the courts. For example, Amendment 1 guarantees the right to free speech—to state one's views or ideas without fear of punishment. Nonetheless, an employer or teacher, for example, can limit speech to what is appropriate in the circumstances. Speech intended to cause harm to others is not protected. For example, crying "Fire!" in a crowded theater when there is no fire is not protected by the right to free speech. The person's "speech" could cause harm to others. The Supreme Court has also placed limits on speech intended to motivate an individual to break the law. Threats of violence are also restricted.

New citizens are sworn in at a naturalization ceremony on July 4, 2016, in Seattle, Washington.

TWO TYPES OF RESPONSIBILITIES

American citizens have two different types of responsibilities: civic and personal. **Civic responsibilities** include voting, paying taxes, and serving on juries. Some of these responsibilities are duties: actions required by law. For example, all citizens must obey laws, pay taxes, and perform jury duty when notified. Neglecting these duties may result in legal penalties. Males over the age of 18 must register with the government in case they are needed for military service.

Personal responsibilities are not required, but they contribute to a more civil society. These include respecting others and their rights, helping in the community, standing up for others, and staying informed about important issues. Personal responsibilities are not as clearly defined as civic duties. They are, however, vital to maintaining an effective government and just society.

All American citizens over the age of 18 have the right to vote. Many people take that right for granted but don't bother to exercise it. Perhaps they don't consider the fact that the right to vote is a privilege that is not granted to people in some countries. These people have no say in how they are governed. Voters also have a responsibility to become informed about issues. They have an obligation to use reliable sources to learn about candidates and their positions on issues. Informed voters can then analyze the credibility of a candidate's claims.

BEING A RESPONSIBLE CITIZEN

When you think of your personal responsibilities as a citizen, consider the choices you make in terms of your actions. Being a responsible citizen means behaving in ways that are right, moral, and just, and acting in a way that benefits you and those around you. Considering the rights of all people, not just the rights of a select few, will help you be a personally responsible citizen.

Citizens have many personal responsibilities, such as being open-minded, respecting the opinions of others, and showing respect for the beliefs and individuality of people with different backgrounds. People of any age can take on personal responsibilities by doing community service projects, standing up for the rights of others, and respecting all people regardless of ethnicity, nationality, gender identity, sexual orientation, or beliefs. Tolerance for others is an important part of being an American citizen.

Tolerance of differences is essential in a democracy, especially one that is as diverse as the United States. Responsible citizens are also willing to give time, effort, and money to improve their communities. Living up to these personal responsibilities helps citizens contribute to an environment of respect and caring and one that protects and promotes the health and welfare of everyone. Responsible citizens work to contribute to the common good.

THINK ABOUT IT

EXPLAIN How does taking on personal responsibilities as a citizen contribute to the common good?

Citizenship Handbook **R35**

GUIDED DISCUSSION

1. **Summarize** Why must new citizens go through a naturalization process? *(To be an effective citizen, a person needs to understand the laws, rights, and citizen responsibilities of the nation. Thus, the naturalization process helps ensure that new citizens can function and thrive in American society.)*

2. **Make Predictions** What consequences might occur if people do not work to become informed voters before they cast their vote? *(Possible responses: People might elect unqualified or dishonest officials. They might fail to vote for someone who best represents their political beliefs. They might inadvertently contribute to the implementation of laws or policies with which they disagree or that might even be harmful.)*

THINK ABOUT IT

Possible response: People who take on personal responsibilities as citizens reinforce the institutions of democracy and show they are willing to work with others to safeguard personal rights and liberties and to create strong communities.

MORE INFORMATION

National History Day As the text suggests, one way to become more involved in the democratic process is to participate in National History Day. Despite its name, National History Day is not a holiday or even a single day. Rather, it is a national competition in which students create in-depth presentations on the history-related theme announced for that year. Students initially compete in their local regions, with winners going on to the state level. Winners of the state competitions advance to the national NHD event. Once there, they are eligible for a number of prizes.

The approximately 500,000 students who participate each year develop papers, documentaries, online presentations, artistic performances, or exhibits that engage with the announced theme for that year. The use of sound research methods, such as conducting interviews, primary and secondary source research, and on-site visits, is strongly encouraged. Students not only learn more about their nation's history but can also teach others the stories they uncover.

THINK ABOUT IT

Answers will vary, but students should clearly describe at least one active citizenship project that they find interesting. In addition, students should describe the specific steps they could take to become involved in their community, including who they would like to serve and the outcome or results they would hope to produce by participating.

Building and Practicing Citizenship Skills

Building citizenship skills is like learning to play an instrument. It takes hard work and repetition, but the rewards make the effort worth it. Some citizenship skills, such as helping raise voter participation, will require you to seek out specific opportunities. Others, such as refusing to tolerate unjust behavior, can be exercised whenever appropriate situations arise. Citizenship affords many rights and requires many responsibilities. Enjoying these rights and responsibilities is the reward of being a good citizen.

The following chart includes ways you can build and apply citizenship skills in the classroom and in your community to become an active participant in our democracy. Study the chart and check out the Active Citizenship for the Environment Activities in this program's online resources. Then brainstorm more ways you can be a good, participatory, and socially just citizen and put them to practice.

After a gunman terrorized her Parkland, Florida high school on February 14, 2018, killing 17 people and injuring many others, Emma González transformed from a high school student into an activist and gun control advocate. As an engaged citizen, González lobbies for changes to gun legislation, and participates in peaceful protests such as the March For Our Lives, which was held on March 24, 2018, in hundreds of U.S. cities.

THINK ABOUT IT

DESCRIBE What opportunities for active citizenship appeal to you? Explain what you could do to be involved and engaged in your community and country.

ACTIVE CITIZENSHIP

Responsibilities	Citizenship Projects: Ways to Promote Civic Engagement
Become engaged.	• Get information from reliable, unbiased sources. • Ask questions of others who are well informed. • Attend or organize peaceful public demonstrations about issues important to you. • Register to vote, encourage others to vote, and consider becoming an election judge or poll watcher. • Serve your country and your fellow citizens through the military or by participating in organizations such as AmeriCorps, AmeriCorps VISTA, and the Peace Corps. • Participate in citizen journalism by reporting information accurately through blogs, news sites, and social media.

Responsibilities	Citizenship Projects: Ways to Promote Civic Engagement
Do historical research.	• Conduct oral histories with family or community members to better understand historical trends. • Interview citizens who served in the military, took part in social justice movements, or were involved in bringing about social change in schools or the workplace. • Research how you and your classmates can participate in National History Day at a state or national level.
Participate in the democratic process.	• Ask a teacher to organize a trip to a local courtroom to see the legal system in action. • Contact a local political candidate whose ideas you support to see how you might help with his or her campaign. • With the help of a parent or teacher, seek opportunities to witness a naturalization ceremony.
Lobby for change.	• Form a lobbying committee with other students to influence legislation or public policy. • Establish a goal for your lobbying campaign. • Identify whom to lobby. (Who are the people who can help you accomplish your goal?) • Find information and statistics to support your goal. • Get public support for your cause. You might consider gathering signatures on a petition or creating flyers to publicize your campaign. • Present your case to the appropriate individuals.
Volunteer in your community.	• Determine how your skills and interests could help someone else. • Talk with your parents, teachers, and friends to learn what types of volunteer services your community needs. • Make volunteering a regular part of your life. You could consider serving food to the homeless, collecting clothing or canned goods to help a local shelter, cleaning or restoring a local park or playground, or tutoring students who are struggling with their school work.
Pay taxes.	• Read more about your local and state taxes, and what the revenue is used for. • Recognize that you are already paying sales taxes when you purchase many items.
Express political opinions.	• Write a letter or an email to a newspaper editor about an issue that concerns you.
Obey the law.	• Become familiar with the laws in your state, city, and town that apply to people your age.
Stand up for the rights of others.	• Work to stop the discrimination of all people. • Write articles and blog posts about the importance of protecting and supporting the rights of people of different races, religions, and sexual orientations.
Listen to the opinions of others. Discuss differences of opinion in a kind and civil manner.	• When friends or acquaintances express opinions that differ from yours, politely explain why you disagree, if you do.
Respect the value of individuals. Respect differences among people.	• Enjoy and appreciate the differences among people from various backgrounds. • Make friends with people who are different from you. • Volunteer in your community to interact with and help others.
Accept responsibility for your actions.	• If someone asks about a mistake you have made, tell the truth. • Ask what you might do to make up for the mistake.

Citizenship Handbook **R37**

GUIDED DISCUSSION

1. **Ask and Answer Questions** One responsibility noted in the chart is the responsibility to pay taxes. What kinds of questions might a citizen have about taxes, and how could he or she find answers for them? *(Possible responses: How much of my income goes to pay taxes? What kinds of taxes do I need to pay? What things are paid for by my taxes? How do current taxes compare with past taxes? A citizen could find answers by researching online or by contacting a city, state, or federal tax office or qualified tax preparer.)*

2. **Make Inferences** Why is locating reliable sources an important citizenship skill? *(Possible response: With the advent of the Internet and the increase in partisan journalism and cable news, much of the available information is tilted toward a specific point of view. People who do not know how to locate reliable sources, or who do not examine the reliability of their sources, risk creating a society in which people are unable to identify objective, verifiable facts about issues; unable to debate issues on their merits rather than on personal opinions; or unable to work with others who have opposing views to solve problems.)*

VOCABULARY WORDS BY CHAPTER

VOCABULARY WORDS BY CHAPTER

sit-down strike (page 731)
totalitarian (page 724)
voting bloc (page 736)
welfare state (page 742)

Chapter 21
A THREATENING WORLD
active defense (page 771)
Allied Powers (page 755)
appeasement (page 761)
Atlantic Charter (page 770)
Axis Powers (page 755)
belligerent (page 768)
Gestapo (page 754)
Long March (page 765)
Munich Agreement (page 761)
nonaggression pact (page 761)
purge (page 764)
rearmament (page 754)
refugee (page 759)
Rome-Berlin Axis (page 755)
Third Reich (page 754)

Chapter 22
AMERICA IN
WORLD WAR II
amphibious assault (page 801)
amphibious landing
  craft (page 804)
atomic bomb (page 810)
atrocity (page 819)
Bracero Program (page 788)
concentration camp (page 814)
crematorium (page 817)
D-day (page 804)
demobilization (page 791)
depth charge (page 799)
enemy alien (page 794)
executive order (page 795)
Holocaust (page 817)
infamy (page 784)
interned (page 794)
internment camp (page 795)
island hopping (page 803)
kamikaze (page 808)
napalm (page 786)
panzer (page 799)
penicillin (page 786)
ration (page 788)
tribunal (page 819)
wage discrimination (page 790)

Chapter 23
THE COLD WAR AND
KOREA
aerospace industry (page 834)
arms race (page 834)
containment (page 827)
demilitarized zone (page 840)
domino theory (page 837)
GI Bill (page 833)
government-in-exile (page 836)
hydrogen bomb (page 835)
iron curtain (page 827)
liberal consensus (page 832)
loyalty oath (page 843)
Marshall Plan (page 825)
McCarthyism (page 845)
military-industrial
  complex (page 835)
occupation zone (page 827)
proxy war (page 838)

rural electrification (page 833)
subversion (page 844)
white-collar (page 833)

Chapter 24
POSTWAR PROSPERITY
agribusiness (page 859)
baby boom (page 862)
brinkmanship (page 860)
bulwark (page 861)
consumer society (page 864)
consumerism (page 859)
covert action (page 860)
Frostbelt (page 859)
homogeneity (page 867)
Interstate Highway
  System (page 866)
nuclear deterrence (page 860)
nuclear power (page 865)
poverty rate (page 878)
rock and roll (page 873)
situation comedy (page 872)
smog (page 859)
subdivision (page 867)
suburban sprawl (page 869)
suburbanization (page 866)
Sunbelt (page 859)
termination policy (page 882)
transistor (page 865)
urban renewal (page 878)

Chapter 25
THE CIVIL RIGHTS
MOVEMENT
dehumanize (page 905)
desegregation (page 907)
Freedom Riders (page 917)
grassroots activism (page 902)
Montgomery Bus
  Boycott (page 911)
sit-in (page 915)
solitary confinement (page 918)
voter registration
  drive (page 922)

Chapter 26
REFORM IN THE 1960S
affirmative action (page 961)
ballistic missile (page 936)
bipartisan (page 949)
black separatist (page 958)
busing (page 961)
Cuban Missile Crisis (page 936)
de facto segregation (page 958)
de jure segregation (page 958)
demographic
  composition (page 955)
disenfranchise (page 951)
filibuster (page 949)
landmark legislation (page 957)
Medicaid (page 954)
Medicare (page 954)
miscegenation (page 961)
naval quarantine (page 936)
New Frontier (page 932)
space race (page 934)
voter fraud (page 929)

Chapter 27
THE VIETNAM WAR
Agent Orange (page 977)
autocrat (page 970)
counterculture (page 986)

coup (page 971)
credibility gap (page 979)
deferment (page 980)
dove (page 980)
escalation (page 972)
hawk (page 980)
impasse (page 985)
induction (page 989)
insurgent (page 970)
mortar (page 975)
post-traumatic stress disorder
  (PTSD) (page 993)
third world (page 969)
Vietnamization (page 988)
war of attrition (page 975)

Chapter 28
CHANGES IN SOCIETY
feminism (page 1021)
gender bias (page 1022)
manifesto (page 1012)
militant (page 1016)
misogyny (page 1023)
module (page 1028)
peer (page 1006)
spacewalk (page 1027)

Chapter 29
PRESIDENTIAL
SUCCESSES AND
FAILURES
antiballistic missile
  (ABM) (page 1045)
cover-up (page 1054)
DDT (page 1046)
détente (page 1045)
economic
  stagnation (page 1056)
executive privilege (page 1054)
Islamic republic (page 1062)
malaise (page 1059)
New Federalism (page 1042)
overregulation (page 1049)
silent majority (page 1041)
stagflation (page 1056)
Watergate break-in (page 1053)
wiretapping (page 1054)

Chapter 30
THE CONSERVATIVE
REVOLUTION
acquired immunodeficiency
  syndrome (AIDS) (page 1083)
apartheid (page 1079)
conservative (page 1068)
cultural advocacy (page 1074)
deficit reduction (page 1095)
deregulation (page 1075)
glasnost (page 1084)
hardliner (page 1085)
human immunodeficiency
  virus (HIV) (page 1083)
income inequality (page 1075)
Internet (page 1081)
originalism (page 1077)
perestroika (page 1084)
personal computer (page 1080)
Politburo (page 1084)
Rustbelt (page 1071)
safety-net
  programs (page 1073)
static (page 1077)
supply-side
  economics (page 1074)

theocracy (page 1093)
think tank (page 1069)

Chapter 31
AMERICA IN A GLOBAL
SOCIETY
American
  exceptionalism (page 1116)
bailout (page 1127)
collude (page 1145)
compassionate
  conservatism (page 1116)
disintegration (page 1111)
economic stimulus (page 1129)
free-enterprise
  zone (page 1111)
genetically modified
  food (page 1139)
globalization (page 1110)
greenhouse effect (page 1136)
greenhouse gas (page 1136)
integration (page 1111)
investment bank (page 1126)
job dislocation (page 1110)
maquiladora (page 1110)
marriage equality (page 1134)
multinational
  corporation (page 1138)
neoconservative (page 1116)
new media (page 1138)
perjury (page 1115)
rogue state (page 1121)
service sector (page 1138)
subprime mortgage (page 1126)
surge (page 1123)
swing state (page 1144)
task force (page 1107)
terrorism (page 1120)
weapons of mass destruction
  (WMD) (page 1121)

ARCHAEOLOGY AND
U.S. HISTORY
artifact (page 342)
context (page 342)
material record (page 342)

CITIZENSHIP
HANDBOOK
civic responsibility (page R35)
naturalization (page R34)
personal
  responsibility (page R35)

STORY OF A CONTINENT
Agricultural Revolution (page 4)
Bering Land Bridge (page 2)
chiefdom (page 4)
domestication (page 4)
glacial period (page 1)
hunter-gatherer (page 3)
ice age (page 1)
Pleistocene epoch (page 1)

GLOSSARY

A

49th parallel *n.* (for-tee-NYNTH PAIR-uh-lehl) the line of latitude established at 49 degrees north latitude; the fixed border between the United States and Canada established with Britain in 1818 (page 236)

abolitionist *n.* (a-buh-LIH-shuhn-ihst) a person who wants to end slavery (page 223)

acquired immunodeficiency syndrome (AIDS) *n.* (uh-KWYRD ih-MYOO-noh-dih-FIH-shun-see SIHN-drohm) the final stage of a virus that attacks the system in the human body that fights off illnesses (page 1083)

active defense *n.* (ACK-tihv DEE-fehns) a policy allowing U.S. warships to defend against attacks by German submarines on ships in shipping traffic lanes in the Atlantic Ocean (page 771)

adversary *n.* (AD-vur-sehr-ee) an enemy, an opponent (page 145)

aerospace industry *n.* (AIR-oh-spayss IHN-duhs-tree) the business of building airplanes, spacecraft, and other vehicles that travel in the air (page 834)

affirmative action *n.* (uh-FUR-muh-tihv AK-shuhn) a government policy that institutes racial quotas to favor groups that suffer from discrimination (page 961)

African diaspora *n.* (A-frih-kuhn dy-AS-puh-ruh) the removal of Africans from their homelands to the Americas (page 49)

Agent Orange *n.* (AY-juhnt OR-ihnj) a potent herbicide used to kill vegetation (page 977)

agrarian *adj.* (ah-GRAIR-ee-ehn) related to agriculture or farming (page 182)

agribusiness *n.* (A-gruh-bihz-nuhs) the commercial business of agriculture (page 859)

Agricultural Revolution *n.* (AHG-rih-kuhl-chuhr-uhl REV-oh-luh-shuhn) the transition in human history from hunting and gathering food to planting crops and raising animals (page 4)

Allied Powers *n.* (AHL-ayhd POHW-uhrs) Several countries, including France and Great Britain, working together to oppose the Axis Powers of Germany, Italy, and Japan during World War II (page 755)

allotment *n.* (uh-LOT-muhnt) a portion; specifically, a piece of land given to a Native American for farming (page 484)

American Anti-Imperialist League *n.* (uh-MAIR-uh-kuhn AN-ty ihm-PIHR-ee-uhl-ist LEEG) an organization that formed in 1898 to oppose the United States' annexation of the Philippines (page 581)

American Civil Liberties Union (ACLU) *n.* (uh-MAIR-uh-kuhn SIH-vuhl LIH-bur-teez YOON-yuhn) an organization, formed in 1920, dedicated to defending the individual rights and freedoms of all Americans (page 643)

American exceptionalism *n.* (uh-MAIR-uh-kuhn ek-SEHP-shuhn-uh-lih-zuhm) the idea that the United States is superior to other countries due to its history and ideology (page 1116)

American Expeditionary Forces (AEF) *n.* (uh-MAIR-uh-kuhn ehk-spuh-DIH-shuhn-air-ee FORS-uhz) the corps of American soldiers sent to fight in Europe during World War I (page 608)

American System *n.* (uh-MAIR-uh-kuhn SIHS-tuhm) a policy of promoting the U.S. industrial system through the use of tariffs, federal subsidies to build roads and other public works, and a national bank to control currency (page 227)

Americanization *n.* (uh-mair-uh-kan-ih-ZAY-shuhn) an effort to immerse immigrants in what some people defined as American culture and transform them into "true" Americans (page 518)

amnesty *n.* (AM-nuh-stee) the pardon of a large group of individuals by a government or other authority (page 434)

amphibious assault *n.* (am-FIH-bee-uhs uh-SAWLT) an attack that uses naval support to protect military forces invading by land and air (page 801)

amphibious force *n.* (am-FIH-bee-uhs FAWRS) a military unit consisting of troops attacking from both land and sea or air simultaneously (page 331)

amphibious landing craft *n.* (am-FIH-bee-uhs LAN-ding KRAFT) boats used to convey soldiers and equipment from the sea to the shore during military attacks (page 804)

Anaconda Plan *n.* (a-nuh-KAHN-duh PLAN) a military strategy during the Civil War in which the North planned to set up a blockade around the southern coast to ruin the South's economy and secure ports on the Mississippi River; much as a huge snake, such as an anaconda, crushes its prey (page 393)

anarchism *n.* (AN-ahr-kih-zuhm) the idea that governments are not necessary and that all social and political cooperation should be voluntary (page 515)

annexation *n.* (a-nehk-SAY-shuhn) the adding of a territory to a country (page 323)

Anti-Defamation League (ADL) *n.* (AN-ty deh-fuh-MAY-shun LEEG) an international Jewish service organization founded to combat anti-Semitism, religious and racial intolerance, and all forms of organized discrimination based on stereotypical beliefs (page 643)

anti-Semitism *n.* (AN-ty SEHM-ih-tih-zuhm) discrimination, prejudice, and hostility against the Jewish people (page 524)

antiaircraft gun *n.* (AN-ty-AIR-kraft GUHN) a piece of heavy artillery modified so that it can be pointed skyward at enemy planes (page 612)

antiballistic missile (ABM) *n.* (AN-ty-buh-LIHS-tihk MIH-suhl) a missile designed to destroy a bomb-carrying missile before it hits its target (page 1045)

antifederalist *n.* (an-tee-FEH-duh-ruh-lihst) a person who opposed the U.S. Constitution of 1787 because of its emphasis on a strong national government (page 162)

apartheid *n.* (uh-PAHR-tayt) the legal separation of the races in South Africa (page 1079)

appeasement *n.* (uh-PEEZ-muhnt) a policy of making political compromises in order to avoid conflict (page 761)

aqueduct *n.* (A-kwuh-duhkt) a structure that carries a canal or water system over a river or ravine; a water bridge (page 228)

aquifer *n.* (AH-kwuh-fur) a geologic formation below Earth's surface that can hold a large groundwater reservoir (page 474)

archipelago *n.* (ahr-kuh-PEH-luh-go) a chain of islands (page 572)

armistice *n.* (AHR-muh-stuhss) an agreement between opposing sides in a conflict to stop fighting (page 625)

arms race *n.* (AHRMZ RAYSS) a political situation in which rival countries try to gather or produce the most military weapons (page 834)

arsenal *n.* (AHRS-uh-nuhl) a place where weapons and other military equipment are stored (page 117)

Articles of Confederation *n.* (AHR-TIH-kuhls UHV kuhn-feh-duh-RAY-shuhn) a set of laws adopted by the United States in 1777 that established each state in the Union as a republic; replaced by the U.S. Constitution in 1789 (page 126)

artifact *n.* (AHR-tif-ackt) an item made by a human that has historical or cultural meaning (page 342)

assassination *n.* (uh-SA-suh-nay-shuhn) an act of murder committed for political reasons (page 427)

assembly line *n.* (uh-SEHM-blee LYN) a method of manufacturing in which the work passes from one worker to another, each of whom has a specific, specialized task (page 651)

assimilate *v.* (uh-SIHM-uhl-ate) to take on the qualities and similarities and way of life of another culture (page 260)

Atlantic Charter *n.* (aht-LAHN-tick CHAHR-tuhr) a charter that lists eight principles for a better world, composed during a meeting between President Franklin Roosevelt and British Prime Minister Winston Churchill in August 1941 (page 770)

atomic bomb *n.* (uh-TAH-mihk BAHM) a type of nuclear bomb whose violent explosion is triggered by splitting atoms, which releases intense heat and radioactivity (page 810)

atrocity *n.* (uh-TRAH-suh-tee) an extremely cruel and shocking act of violence (page 819)

attorney general *n.* (uh-TUR-NEE JEN-ruhl) a member of the president's Cabinet, whose primary roles are to represent the United States before the Supreme Court and act as head of the Department of Justice (page 179)

autocrat *n.* (AW-tuh-krat) a tyrant with absolute power (page 970)

Axis Powers *n.* (ACK-sihs POHW-uhrs) Germany, Italy, and Japan, which formed an alliance together at the start of World War II (page 755)

B

baby boom *n.* (BAY-bee BOOM) a significant increase in the birthrate (page 862)

back-to-Africa movement *n.* (BAK TOO A-frih-kuh MOOV-muhnt) a movement headed by Marcus Garvey that encouraged African Americans to leave the United States and return to Africa (page 665)

backcountry *n.* (BAK-kuhn-tree) the western part of the Southern Colonies just east of the Appalachian Mountains (page 78)

bailout *n.* (BAYL-owt) during the Great Recession, the act of buying mortgages and unstable investments from banks (page 1127)

ballistic missile *n.* (buh-LIHS-tihk MIH-suhl) a nuclear weapon that is propelled by a rocket and guided using a GPS system (page 936)

bank holiday *n.* (BANGK HAH-luh-day) a day or period when banks are closed by government order (page 716)

bankruptcy *n.* (BANGK-ruhpt-see) the state of lacking sufficient funds to pay one's debts; business failure (page 229)

barrage *n.* (buh-RAHJ) heavy artillery fire concentrated on a single line or area (page 416)

battery *n.* (BA-tuh-ree) a group of artillery pieces such as cannons (page 410)

belligerent *n.* (buh-LIH-juh-ruhnt) a country fighting in a war (page 768)

GLOSSARY

Bering Land Bridge *n.* (BAIR-ingh LAND BRIJ) a piece of land between Alaska and Siberia that was above sea level 13,000 years ago, allowing early humans to cross into North America (page 2)

besiege *v.* (bih-SEEZH) to surround using military force (page 45)

Bessemer process *n.* (BEH-seh-mur PRAH-sehs) a process in which workers use forced air to remove impurities such as carbon from iron, which transforms the iron into steel (page 503)

bicameral legislature *n.* (BY-KA-muh-ruhl LEH-jeh-slay-chur) a government body responsible for making laws, made up of two separate houses (e.g. the Senate and the House of Representatives of the U.S. Congress) (page 158)

Bill of Rights *n.* (BIHL UHV RYTS) the first 10 amendments to the U.S. Constitution; a list of guarantees to which every person in a country is entitled (page 165)

bipartisan *adj.* (by-PAHR-tuh-zuhn) relating to both parties in a two-party system (page 949)

black separatist *n.* (BLAK SEH-puh-ruh-tihst) a radical African-American activist who believes the only way to achieve equality and justice in the United States is to separate culturally and economically from whites (page 958)

Bleeding Kansas *n.* (BLEE-dihng KAN-zuhs) the nickname given to the Kansas Territory in the wake of a number of clashes between proslavery and antislavery supporters in 1856 (page 371)

Bonus Army *n.* (BOH-nuhs AHR-mee) the thousands of veterans, determined to collect promised cash bonuses early, who came to Washington during the summer of 1932 to listen to Congress debate the bonus proposal (page 701)

boomtown *n.* (BOOM-town) a town that experiences a great population increase in only a short time period (page 335)

bootlegger *n.* (BOOT-leh-gur) an individual who made, transported, or supplied alcohol illegally to saloons or "speakeasies" where city dwellers congregated in the evenings (page 646)

border state *n.* (BOR-dur STAYT) at the time of the Civil War, a state that bordered both Union and Confederate states, namely Maryland, Kentucky, Delaware, Missouri, and West Virginia (page 391)

Boston Massacre *n.* (BAW-stuhn MA-sih-kur) the 1770 incident in which British soldiers fired on locals who had been taunting them (page 114)

Boston Tea Party *n.* (BAW-stuhn TEE PAHR-tee) the 1773 incident in which the Sons of Liberty boarded British ships and dumped their cargo of tea in protest of British taxes on the colonists (page 114)

Boxer Rebellion *n.* (BAHK-sur rih-BEL-yuhn) a 1900 political uprising in northern China against foreigners in the country (page 574)

boycott *n.* (BOY-kaht) a form of protest that involves refusing to puchase goods or services (page 111)

Bracero Program *n.* (brah-SEH-roh PROH-gram) a program designed to import Mexican laborers to replace native-born agricultural and transportation industry workers who were mobilizing for World War II (page 788)

brain trust *n.* (BRAYN TRUHST) a group of experts who advised President Franklin Roosevelt during the Great Depression (page 716)

breadwinner *n.* (BREHD-wih-nur) a member of a household who contributes to the family's income (page 734)

brinkmanship *n.* (BRIHNGK-muhn-ship) the practice of pushing a conflict to the edge of violence without getting into a war, usually as a tactic to gain a favorable outcome (page 860)

broadside *n.* (BRAWD-syd) a single sheet of printed information (page 139)

bulwark *n.* (BUHL-wurk) something that provides protection or defense (page 861)

busing *n.* (BUH-sing) transporting students of all races to schools outside their neighborhoods or school districts to assure integration and provide equal opportunities in education (page 961)

C

Cabinet *n.* (KAB-niht) the heads of the departments that assist the U.S. president (page 178)

capital *n.* (KA-puh-tuhl) money and other assets needed to start and fund a business (page 219)

capitalism *n.* (KAP-ih-tuh-lih-zuhm) an economic system in which private individuals or groups own the resources and produce goods for a profit (page 642)

caravan *n.* (KEHR-uh-van) a group of people and animals traveling together, usually for trade (page 25)

caravel *n.* (KEHR-ah-vehl) a small, fast ship used by Spanish and Portuguese explorers (page 28)

carpetbagger *n* (KAHR-puht-ba-gur) a northerner who went South after the Civil War, often looking to make a living from the Reconstruction government or to gain power through involvement in the politics of the South (page 439)

cartographer *n.* (kahr-TAH-gruh-fuhr) a mapmaker (page 28)

cavalry *n.* (KA-vuhl-ree) army troops who fight on horseback (page 395)

census *n.* (SEHN-suhs) a formal count of the population of a country (page 179)

charter *n.* (CHAHR-tur) a document that establishes the main goal of an endeavor (page 50)

chattel slavery *n.* (CHA-tuhl SLAY-veh-ree) a system of permanent bondage in which enslaved people have no human rights and are classified as goods (page 30)

checks and balances *n.* (CHEHKS AND BA-luhn-suhz) the system established by the U.S. Constitution that gives each of the branches of government the power to limit the power of the other two (page 160)

chiefdom *n.* (CHEEF-duhm) a large community of people ruled by a chief (page 4)

Children's Bureau *n.* (CHIHL-druhnz BYUR-oh) a U.S. government agency that was created in 1912 and is focused on improving the lives of children and families (page 554)

circumnavigate *v.* (sur-cuhm-NA-vuh-gayt) to go around something instead of through it (page 30)

civic republicanism *n.* (SIH-vihk rih-PUH-blih-kuh-nih-zuhm) the tradition of political thought that stresses individual freedom, active citizenship, and support for the common good (page 180)

civic responsibility *n.* (SIH-vihk rih-SPAWN-suh-BIHL-uh-tee) responsibility that is either required or essential that people perform, such as voting, paying taxes, and serving on juries (page R35)

civil case *n.* (SIH-vuhl KAYS) a legal dispute between two or more individuals or organizations, often involving contract issues or other business problems (page 179)

civil disobedience *n.* (SIH-vuhl dihs-uh-BEE-dee-uhnts) the nonviolent disobeying of laws as a form of protest (page 282)

civil liberties *n.* (SIH-vuhl LIH-bur-teez) individual rights protected by law from government interference (page 610)

coalition *n.* (koh-uh-LIH-shuhn) an alliance of people, parties, or states focused on a common goal (page 241)

collateral *n.* (kuh-LA-tuh-ruhl) secondary property pledged by a borrower as security to protect the lender's interests (page 435)

collective bargaining *n.* (kuh-LEHK-tihv BAHR-guhn-ihng) negotiation between an employer and union leaders on behalf of all union members (page 728)

collude *v.* (kuh-LOOD) to conspire (page 1145)

Columbian Exchange *n.* (kuh-LUM-bee-uhn ehks-CHAYNJ) the exchange of plants, animals, microbes, people, and ideas between the Americas, Europe, and Africa that began after Columbus's first voyage to the Western Hemisphere (page 31)

commission government *n.* (kuh-MIH-shuhn GUH-vur-muhnt) a form of city government in which voters elect a small number of officials called commissioners, each of whom heads a city department (page 560)

committee of correspondence *n.* (kuh-MIH-tee UHV KAWR-uh-spahn-duhnts) in the Revolutionary era, a group of colonists whose duty it was to spread news about protests against the British (page 114)

Committee on Public Information (CPI) *n.* (kuh-MIH-tee ON PUH-blihk ihn-fur-MAY-shuhn) a committee established during World War I to counter possible dissent and raise the country's enthusiasm for the war (page 610)

commodity *n.* (kuh-MAH-duh-tee) a trade good (page 48)

common school *n.* (KAH-muhn SKOOL) a colonial elementary school (page 74)

common school movement *n.* (KAH-muhn SKOOL MOOV-mehnt) an educational reform movement in the 1830s that promoted free public schools funded by property taxes and managed by local governments (page 278)

communism *n.* (KAHM-yuh-nih-zuhm) a form of government in which all the means of production and transportation are owned by the state (page 625)

compassionate conservatism *n.* (kuhm-PAH-shuh-nuht kuhn-SUR-vuh-tih-zuhm) a political philosophy that blends traditional conservative ideas about economic policies with a concern for disadvantaged people (page 1116)

Compromise of 1877 *n.* (KAHM-pruh-myz UHV 1877) a deal in which Democrats agreed to make Rutherford B. Hayes president if Republicans ended Reconstruction and pulled federal troops out of the South (page 453)

concentration camp *n.* (kahnt-suhn-TRAY-shuhn KAMP) a place where prisoners of war or members of persecuted minorities are confined; in World War II, the camps where Jews and others were held and murdered by the Nazis (page 814)

Conestoga wagon *n.* (kah-nuh-STOH-guh WA-guhn) a kind of wagon, made by German settlers in North America, that could carry heavy loads (page 78)

Confederacy *n.* (kon-FED-ur-uh-see) the 11 southern states that seceded from the Union to form their own nation, the Confederate States of America (page 379)

confiscate *v.* (KON-fuh-skayt) to take by governmental act (page 408)

conquistador *n.* (kon-KEES-tuh-dohr) a Spanish conqueror who sought gold and other riches in the Americas (page 44)

conscientious objector *n.* (KAHN-shee-ehnt-shuhs ahb-JEHK-tur) a person who refuses to fight in a war for religious reasons (page 610)

conscription *n.* (kuhn-SKRIHP-shuhn) the requirement to enlist for service in a country's armed forces (page 407)

conservation *n.* (kahn-sur-VAY-shuhn) the management and protection of natural resources (page 562)

conservative *n.* (kuhn-SUR-vuh-tihv) a member of a political party who believes in traditional values, social structure, and gradual change in policies (page 1068)

constituency *n.* (kuhn-STIH-chu-uhn-see) a group of citizens who has elected, or is entitled to elect, a representative to the government (page 663)

constitutional republic *n.* (kahn-stuh-TOO-shuh-nuhl rih-PUH-blihk) a government in which the representatives gain their authority from the consent of the governed as determined by a written constitution (page 158)

consumer society *n.* (kuhn-SOO-mur suh-SY-uh-tee) a society in which shopping and buying goods has become an important part of people's lifestyles (page 864)

consumerism *n.* (kuhn-SOO-muh-rih-zuhm) a theory stating that the economy flourishes when people buy, or consume, a lot of goods and services (page 859)

containment *n.* (kuhn-TAYN-muhnt) a U.S. security policy during the Cold War in which military action was used to stop the Soviet Union from spreading communism (page 827)

context *n.* (KAHN-text) the circumstances and setting in which an object is located, which gives an understanding of how an object is used (page 342)

contiguous *adj.* (kuhn-TIH-gyuh-wuhs) connected (page 331)

contingent *n.* (kuhn-TIHN-juhnt) a small group that represents a larger group (page 415)

contraband *n.* (KON-truh-band) during the Civil War, an enslaved African American living in the South who was captured by Union troops and treated as enemy property during the U.S. Civil War (page 404)

cooperative *n.* (koh-AH-pruh-tihv) an organization run and funded by its members (page 477)

Copperhead *n.* (KAH-pur-hehd) a negative nickname for Democrats who opposed emancipation of enslaved people and the draft (page 404)

corporation *n.* (kor-puh-RAY-shuhn) a company or group that acts legally as a single unit to run a business (page 227)

cotton gin *n.* (KAH-tuhn JIHN) a machine that separates the cotton seeds and hulls from the cotton boll (tuft of cotton) (page 222)

counterculture *n.* (kown-tur-KUHL-chur) a movement in the 1960s that promoted a way of life in opposition to American society's established rules and behavior (page 986)

coup *n.* (KOO) an illegal overthrow of the government (page 971)

court-packing plan *n.* (KORT PA-king PLAN) President Franklin Roosevelt's controversial plan to increase the number of justices on the Supreme Court from nine to fifteen by adding six justices who shared his progressive views (page 730)

cover-up *n.* (KUH-vur UHP) an attempt to hide the truth from the public (page 1054)

covert action *n.* (KOH-vurt AK-shuhn) an activity performed secretly to influence the political, economic, or military situation in another country (page 860)

credibility gap *n.* (kreh-dih-BIHL-uh-tee GAP) an increasing skepticism among Americans about government reports on the Vietnam War (page 979)

credit *n.* (KREH-diht) the privilege of purchasing something or borrowing money and paying the purchase price or money back over time (page 156)

crematorium *n.* (kree-muh-TOR-ee-uhm) a furnace or oven used to burn human or animal remains; in World War II, the ovens used by Nazis to burn their victims' bodies (page 817)

criminal case *n.* (KRIH-muh-nuhl KAYS) a legal dispute in which the government accuses a person or group of breaking the law and endangering society (page 179)

Crittenden Plan *n.* (KRIHT-uhn-duhn PLAN) a proposal that stated the federal government would have no power to abolish slavery in the states where it already existed; it proposed reestablishing and extending the Missouri Compromise line to the Pacific Ocean (page 378)

Crusades *n.* (kroo-SAYDZ) military expeditions of the Roman Catholic Church to take back holy lands in the Middle East from Muslim control, 1096–1291 (page 21)

Cuban Missile Crisis *n.* (KYOO-buhn MIH-suhl CRY-suhs) a political showdown in 1962 between the United States and the Soviet Union caused by the presence of Soviet nuclear weapons in Cuba (page 936)

cult of domesticity *n.* (KUHLT UHV doh-mehs-TIH-suh-tee) an opinion about women common during the 19th century in the middle and upper classes that women should marry, stay at home to care for the family household and children, and act as the moral center of the household (page 292)

cultural advocacy *n.* (KUHLCH-ruhl AD-vuh-kuh-see) a political strategy in which members of a religion influence politicians and social institutions in an effort to promote their beliefs (page 1074)

cultural diffusion *n.* (KUHLCH-ruhl di-FYOO-zhuhn) the spreading of traditions and ways of living from one place to another (page 49)

currency *n.* (KUR-uhn-see) money that is in circulation to be used for buying and selling goods and services; paper money (page 156)

D

D-day *n.* (DEE DAY) the day, June 6, 1944, in World War II when Allied forces invaded northern France by landing on beaches at Normandy (page 804)

dark horse *n.* (DARK HAWRS) a little-known candidate whose nomination is unexpected and usually the result of a compromise between factions (page 326)

DDT *n.* (DEE-DEE-TEE) a pesticide, now banned in the United States and many other countries, that was found to be harmful to animals and to cause long-term contamination of the environment (page 1046)

de facto segregation *n.* (dih FAK-toh seh-grih-GAY-shuhn) segregation that is present in society even though no laws enforce it (page 958)

de jure segregation *n.* (dee JUR-ee seh-grih-GAY-shuhn) segregation enforced by law (page 958)

debt peonage *n.* (DEHT PEE-uh-nihj) a form of labor in which a person works just to pay off a debt (page 444)

Declaration of Independence *n.* (deh-kluh-RAY-shun UHV ihn-duh-PEHN-duhns) the document declaring U.S. independence from Great Britain, adopted July 4, 1776 (page 125)

defensive war *n.* (dih-FEHN-sihv WOR) a war to protect one's own land, on familiar ground, from outside attackers (page 391)

deferment *n.* (dih-FUR-muhnt) an official permission to delay conscription (page 980)

deficit *n.* (DEH-fuh-suht) a negative monetary balance that occurs when expenditures exceed income (page 716)

deficit reduction *n.* (DEH-fuh-suht rih-DUHK-shun) the steps taken by a government to pay off debt (page 1095)

deficit spending *n.* (DEH-fuh-suht SPEHND-ihng) the act of spending more money than the government receives from taxes (page 742)

deflation *n.* (dee-FLAY-shuhn) a decrease in the prices of goods and services (page 513)

dehumanize *v.* (dee-HYOO-mahn-ize) to treat people as if they are not human beings (page 905)

demilitarized zone *n.* (dee-MIH-luh-tuh-ryzd ZOHN) an area in which military personel and weapons are not allowed (page 840)

demobilization *n.* (dih-moh-buh-ly-ZAY-shuhn) the release of soldiers from military duty (page 791)

demographic composition *n.* (dem-uh-GRA-fihk kahm-puh-ZIH-shuhn) the make-up of the population of a specific area based on ethnicity (page 955)

department store *n.* (dee-PAHRT-mehnt STOHR) large store that provides a wide variety of merchandise organized into different departments but all under one roof (page 531)

deploy *v.* (dih-PLOY) to send into military action (page 131)

deport *v.* (dih-PORT) to forcibly remove from the country, or to pressure to leave (page 691)

depression *n.* (dee-PREH-shuhn) a severe and longterm economic decline characterized by a number of business failures, reduced industrial output, and high unemployment (page 152)

depth charge *n.* (DEHPTH CHAHRJ) an underwater bomb that is programmed to explode at a certain depth (page 799)

deregulation *n.* (dee-reh-gyuh-LAY-shun) the act of repealing laws on a large scale; usually related to a particular industry (page 1075)

desegregation *n.* (dee-seh-grih-GAY-shuhn) the process of ending a policy that forces the separation of groups of people in public spaces (page 907)

détente *n.* (day-TAHNT) an easing of tensions and an improvement in relations between countries (page 1045)

dime novel *n.* (DYM NAH-vuhl) popular fiction that sold for 10 cents a book in the late 18th and early 19th centuries (page 489)

direct primary *n.* (duh-REKT PRY-mair-ee) a preliminary election in which voters choose the party candidates to run in a later election for public office (page 561)

GLOSSARY

disenfranchise *v.* (dihs-ihn-FRAN-chyz) to deprive someone of a legal right or privilege, such as the right to vote (page 951)

disintegration *n.* (dihs-ihn-tuh-GRAY-shuhn) the endurance of nationalist, tribalist, and separatist alternatives to globalization (page 1111)

disposable income *n.* (dih-SPOH-zuh-buhl IHN-kuhm) spending money (page 685)

dissenter *n.* (dih-SEHN-tur) a person who disagrees with a majority belief or position (page 56)

dividend *n.* (DIH-vuh-dehnd) money paid regularly to shareholders of a company from the company's profits or reserves (page 183)

doctrine of nullification *n.* (DAHK-truhn UHV nuh-luh-fuh-KAY-shuhn) a doctrine that said a state could nullify, or reject, a federal law they felt was unconstitutional, held by some southern politicians before the Civil War (page 258)

domesticate *v.* (duh-MEHS-tih-kayt) to raise plants and animals for human benefit and consumption (page 15)

domestication *n.* (duh-mehs-TIH-kay-shuhn) the practice of raising animals and growing plants for human benefit (page 4)

domino theory *n.* (DAH-muh-noh THEER-ee) an idea during the Cold War that countries that neighbor communist countries are more likely to fall to communism (page 837)

dove *n.* (DUHV) a person who opposes war (page 980)

Dow Jones Industrial Average *n.* (DAU JOHNZ ihn-DUH-stree-uhl A-vuh-rihj) an index of the stock of leading companies, tracked daily and used as a measure of general stock market trends (page 686)

draft *n.* (DRAFT) a mandatory term of military service (page 407)

Dred Scott decision *n.* (DRED SKAHT dih-SIH-zhuhn) a Supreme Court decision that African Americans held no rights as citizens and that the Missouri Compromise of 1820 was unconstitutional; Dred Scott, the escaped slave at the center of the case, was returned to slavery (page 372)

dry farming *n.* (DRY FAHR-mihng) agricultural techniques used in areas with little rainfall (page 471)

dual sovereignty *n.* (DOO-uhl SAH-vuh-ruhn-tee) the concept that state governments have certain powers the federal government cannot overrule (page 158)

Dust Bowl *n.* (DUHST BOHL) areas of Kansas, Colorado, Oklahoma, Texas, and New Mexico that, during the 1930s, suffered ecological devastation and turned into a barren desert (page 695)

duty *n.* (DOO-tee) a tax on imports (page 110)

E

earthworks *n.* (URTH-wurks) human-made land modifications (page 122)

economic planning *n.* (eh-kuh-NAH-mihk PLAN-ihng) management of the economy by the federal government (page 719)

economic stagnation *n.* (eh-kuh-NAH-mihk stahg-NAY-shuhn) a period of little or no economic growth (page 1056)

economic stimulus *n.* (eh-kuh-NAH-mihk STIHM-yuh-luhs) a measure aimed at promoting and enabling financial recovery and growth (page 1129)

egalitarianism *n.* (ih-gal-uh-TAIR-ee-uhn-ih-zuhm) a belief in the equality of all people, especially in their political, economic, and social concerns (page 152)

electoral college *n.* (ee-lehk-TAWR-uhl KAH-lihj) the group that elects the U.S. president; each state receives as many electors as it has congressional representatives and senators combined (page 160)

emancipation *n.* (ih-man-suh-PAY-shuhn) the act of freeing the enslaved (page 288)

Emancipation Proclamation *n.* (ih-man-suh-PAY-shuhn prah-kluh-MAY-shuhn) an 1863 document issued by Abraham Lincoln that declared all slaves living in Confederate-held territory during the American Civil War to be free (page 405)

embargo *n.* (ihm-BAHR-goh) a ban against engaging in commerce with specified countries (page 198)

empresario *n.* (ehm-pruh-SAH-ree-oh) an agent who entered into a contract with New Spain or, later, the Mexican government, to recruit Americans to settle the land that is now Texas (page 321)

encomienda *n.* (ehn-koh-mee-EHN-duh) a system in Spain's American colonies in which wealthy settlers were given plots of land and allowed to enslave the people who lived there (page 47)

enemy alien *n.* (EH-nuh-mee AY-lyuhn) someone whose loyalty to the nation in which the person lives is suspect (page 794)

enfranchisement *n.* (ihn-FRAN-chyz-muhnt) the granting of the rights of citizenship, especially the right to vote (page 555)

Enlightenment *n.* (ihn-LY-tuhn-muhnt) an intellectual movement that emphasized the use of reason to examine previously accepted beliefs (page 88)

entrepreneur *n.* (ahn-truh-pruh-NUR) a person who starts, manages, and is responsible for a business (page 335)

envoy *n.* (AHN-voy) an ambassador (page 187)

escalation *n.* (ehs-kuh-LAY-shuhn) an increase in intensity (page 972)

espionage *n.* (EH-spee-uh-nahj) the practice of spying to obtain information (page 139)

estuary *n.* (EHS-chuh-wair-ee) the area at the mouth of a river where fresh water and sea water mix (page 194)

eugenics *n.* (yoo-JEH-nihks) the belief that some races were superior to others and that breeding should be controlled so that populations of superior races increase (page 644)

evangelist *n.* (ih-VAN-juh-lihst) a preacher who enthusiastically urges believers to experience a spiritual rebirth and accept Jesus as their personal savior (page 277)

excise tax *n.* (EHK-syz TAKS) a tax levied on one particular product (page 182)

executive branch *n.* (ihg-ZEH-kyuh-tihv BRANCH) the section of the U.S. government headed by the president; responsible for enforcing the law (page 158)

executive order *n.* (ihg-ZEH-kyuh-tihv OR-dur) a directive issued by a president that has the force of law (page 795)

executive privilege *n.* (ihg-ZEH-kyuh-tihv PRIHV-lij) the principle that in the nation's interest, the president may withhold certain information from Congress (page 1054)

exemption *n.* (ihg-ZEHMP-shuhn) a release from obligations (page 408)

Exoduster *n.* (EKS-oh-duhs-tur) an African American who migrated from the South to the Great Plains after Reconstruction had failed (page 470)

expansionism *n.* (ihk-SPAN-shuh-nih-zuhm) a policy or practice of increasing a country's territory (page 572)

exploitative *adj.* (ehks-PLOY-tuh-tihv) unfairly and often abusively using people for profit or other advantage (page 221)

exposé *n.* (ehk-spoh-ZAY) a work of writing that publicizes a scandal or injustice (page 553)

F

fascism *n.* (FA-shih-zuhm) a political movement based on extreme nationalism, militarism, and racism promoting the superiority of a particular people over all others (page 699)

federalism *n.* (FEH-duh-ruh-lih-zuhm) a system of government in which power is shared between national and state or provincial governments (page 158)

federalist *n.* (FEH-duh-ruh-lihst) a person who supported the U.S. Constitution of 1787 as it was written during the process of ratification (page 162)

feminism *n.* (FEH-muh-nih-zuhm) the idea that women are equal to men socially and politically (page 1021)

feudalism *n.* (FEW-dahl-izm) a political and social system in which a vassal receives protection from a lord in exchange for obedience and service (page 20)

filibuster *n.* (FIH-luh-buhs-tur) a political strategy in which a small group of legislators take turns speaking and refuse to stop the debate or allow a bill to come to a vote (page 949)

financier *n.* (fih-nuhn-SIHR) a person who lends or manages money for a business or undertaking (page 137)

fireside chat *n.* (FY-ur-syd CHAT) one of a series of radio broadcasts that President Franklin Roosevelt made to the nation throughout his presidency (page 716)

First Hundred Days *n.* (FURST HUHN-druhd DAYZ) President Franklin Roosevelt's first 100 days in office, during which he produced 15 laws that formed the basis of the New Deal (page 716)

flanking maneuver *n.* (FLAYNG-kihng muh-NOO-vuhr) a military movement of troops around the side of an enemy line in the hope of gaining an advantage (page 411)

flapper *n.* (FLA-pur) a young woman in the 1920s who embraced a freer style of dress and the use of cosmetics (page 660)

forage *v.* (FOR-ihj) to search for plants (page 480)

foreclosure *n.* (fohr-KLOH-zhur) the action of a bank taking possession of a property because the buyer can no longer make payments (page 156)

forty-niner *n.* (FAWR-tee-NY-nur) one of the thousands of prospective miners who traveled to California seeking gold in 1849 (page 335)

Fourteen Points *n.* (FOR-teen PAWIHNTS) President Woodrow Wilson's proposed program for peace at the end of World War I (page 623)

Framer *n.* (FRAYM-ur) one of the delegates sent by the states to create the Constitution of the United States (page 157)

franchise *n.* (FRAN-chyz) a constitutional right, especially the right to vote (page 555)

free silver movement *n.* (FREE SIHL-vur MOOV-mehnt) a monetary system that would allow private citizens to mint their silver into U.S. coins (page 477)

free-enterprise zone *n.* (FREE EHN-tur-pryz ZOHN) an area that allows the suspension of both tax and custom laws (page 1111)

freedman *n.* (FREED-man) a formerly enslaved person (page 404)

Freedmen's Bureau *n.* (FREED-muhns BYOOR-oh) the Bureau of Refugees, Freedmen, and Abandoned Lands, created by Congress in 1865 to help former slaves, as well as poor white southerners (page 446)

Freedom Riders *n.* (FREE-duhm RY-durz) interracial groups who rode buses in the South and ignored "white" and "colored" signs when they stopped at restrooms and lunch counters so that a series of federal court decisions declaring segregation illegal in facilities serving travelers would not be ignored by white officials (page 917)

front *n.* (FRUHNT) a battle line between armies (page 401)

Frostbelt *n.* (FRAHST-behlt) the north-central and northeastern regions of the United States, which have cold winters (page 859)

fugitive slave clause *n.* (FYOO-juh-tihv SLAYV KLAWZ) a provision in Article 4 of the U.S. Constitution that prevented free states from emancipating enslaved workers who had escaped from their masters in other states (page 161)

fundamentalism *n.* (FUHN-duh-mehn-tah-lih-zuhm) a movement that promoted the idea that every word of the Bible was the literal truth (page 647)

G

gag rule *n.* (GAG ROOL) a series of regulations adopted by Congress in the 1830s and 1840s to prevent the discussion or consideration of antislavery petitions brought to Congress; any regulation that prohibits legislative or public discussion of a specific subject (page 291)

garrison *n.* (GAIR-uh-suhn) a defense force of soldiers (page 132)

gender bias *n.* (JEHN-dur BY-uhs) the preference for one gender over another (page 1022)

genetically modified food *n.* (juh-NEH-tik-lee MAH-duh-fyd FOOD) food grown from plants that have been changed in a way that does not occur naturally (page 1139)

genocide *n.* (JEH-nuh-syd) the deliberate murder of a large number of people belonging to a specific racial, cultural, or political group (page 483)

Gestapo *n.* (guh-SHTAH-poh) Nazi secret police force (page 754)

Ghost Dance *n.* (GOHST DANSS) a ceremonial dance performed by some Native Americans who believed the dance would summon a deliverer who would restore their world (page 484)

GI Bill *n.* (JEE I BIHL) a government program started in 1944 that helped veterans returning from World War II buy homes and attend college (page 833)

glacial period *n.* (GLAY-shuhl PEER-ee-uhd) a period of time in history during which huge sheets of ice covered much of Earth (page 1)

glacial till *n.* (GLAY-shuhl TIHL) a deposit of unsorted sediment that may include silt, sand, clay, rock, and other materials dropped and left behind by retreating glaciers (page 238)

glasnost *n.* (GLAZ-nohst) a government policy of open communication in the former Soviet Union (page 1084)

globalization *n.* (gloh-buh-luh-ZAY-shuhn) the faster and freer flow of people, resources, goods, and ideas across national borders (page 1110)

gold standard *n.* (GOHLD STAN-durd) a monetary system in which a nation's currency is backed by gold (page 477)

government-in-exile *n.* (GUH-vur-muhnt IHN EHG-zyl) a government that has been deposed and attempts to rule from another land (page 836)

grandfather clause *n.* (GRAHND-fah-thur KLAWZ) a part of a law that excludes certain people and things because of conditions that existed before the law was passed (page 535)

grassroots activism *n.* (GRAS-roots AK-tih-vih-zuhm) political movements driven by people who individually do not have much power, but who, working together, can be very effective (page 902)

Great Awakening *n.* (GRAYT uh-WAY-kuhn-ing) a series of Protestant religious revivals that swept across the American colonies (page 90)

Great Depression *n.* (GRAYT dee-PREH-shuhn) a worldwide economic downturn in the 1930s, marked by poverty and high unemployment (page 687)

Great Migration *n.* (GRAYT my-GRAY-shuhn) a massive movement of African Americans who left the South for cities in the North, beginning in 1910 (page 619)

greenback *n.* (GREEN-bak) paper currency issued by the Union, replacing the notes of individual banks (page 393)

greenhouse effect *n.* (GREEN-hows uh-FEHKT) the warming of Earth's surface caused when greenhouse gas emissions trap the sun's heat (page 1136)

greenhouse gas *n.* (GREEN-hows GAS) a gas such as carbon dioxide or methane (page 1136)

gross national product (GNP) *n.* (GROHS NA-shuh-nuhl PRAH-duhkt) the total goods and services produced by the nation plus the income earned by its citizens (page 687)

guerrilla tactic *n.* (guh-RIH-luh TAK-tihk) an unconventional method of warfare, such as sneak attacks and sabotage, used by independent military groups (page 117)

H

hacienda *n.* (hah-see-EHN-duh) a large plantation in a Spanish-speaking colony (page 47)

hardliner *n.* (HAHRD-ly-nur) a person, usually within a political or special-interest group, who strictly supports a set of ideas or policies (page 1085)

Harlem Renaissance *n.* (HAHR-luhm reh-nuh-SAHNTS) a cultural movement that originated in Harlem in the 1920s and promoted African-American writers, artists, and musicians (page 666)

hawk *n.* (HAWK) a person who supports war (page 980)

Haymarket Riot *n.* (HAY-mahr-kuht RY-uht) a violent confrontation between workers and police on May 4, 1886, which began as a protest against police conduct during a strike at a factory of the McCormick Company in Chicago, Illinois (page 515)

heretic *n.* (HAIR-uh-tihk) a person who holds beliefs different from the teachings of the Catholic Church (page 54)

Hessian *n.* (HEH-shuhn) a German soldier hired by the British to fight during the American Revolution (page 123)

Holocaust *n.* (HOH-luh-cawst) the mass slaughter by the Nazis of six million Jews and others during World War II (page 817)

homogeneity *n.* (hoh-muh-juh-NAY-uh-tee) the state of being the same or similar (page 867)

Hooverville *n.* (HOO-vur-vil) a makeshift village for homeless Americans, usually at the edge of a city with shelters made of cardboard, scrap metal, or whatever was cheap and available (page 698)

horizontal integration *n.* (hor-uh-ZAHN-tuhl ihn-tuh-GRAY-shuhn) purchasing other companies that offer the same goods and services in order to reduce the number of competitors and achieve control within an industry (page 503)

human immunodeficiency virus (HIV) *n.* (HYOO-muhn ih-MYOO-noh-dih-FIH-shun-see VY-ruhs) a virus that attacks the system in the human body that fights off illnesses (page 1083)

humanism *n.* (HYOO-muh-nih-zhum) a movement that focuses on the importance of the individual (page 21)

hunter-gatherer *n.* (HUHN-tuhr GAHTH-uhr-uhr) a human who hunts animals and gathers wild plants to eat (page 3)

hydraulic mining *n.* (hy-DRAW-lik MY-nihng) a process of uncovering precious minerals by using pressurized water to remove soil (page 472)

hydrogen bomb *n.* (HY-druh-juhn BAHM) a nuclear weapon that explodes due to compacted gases inside (page 835)

I

ice age *n.* (AISS AJ) a period of time in history during which huge sheets of ice covered much of Earth (page 1)

impasse *n.* (IHM-pass) a situation in which no progress is possible (page 985)

impeachment *n.* (ihm-PEECH-muhnt) formal charges brought against a public official for misconduct in office (page 160)

imperialism *n.* (ihm-PIHR-ee-uh-lih-zuhm) a policy or practice of exerting control over weaker nations or territories (page 572)

impressment *n.* (ihm-PREHS-muhnt) the act of forcing people into military or naval service (page 186)

inauguration *n.* (uh-NAW-gyuh-ray-shun) the swearing-in ceremony that marks the beginning of a presidency (page 178)

income inequality *n.* (IHN-kuhm ih-nih-KWAH-luh-tee) an economic phenomenon in which a large gap exists between what the poorest and the richest citizens in a nation earn (page 1075)

income tax *n.* (IHN-kuhm TAKS) a tax that is based on the amount a person earns (page 571)

indentured servant *n.* (ihn-DEHN-churd SUR-vuhnt) a person under contract to work, usually without pay, in exchange for free passage to the colonies (page 51)

Indian Removal Act *n.* (IHN-dee-uhn rih-MOO-vuhl AKT) a law that ended the U.S. government's earlier policy of respecting the rights of Native Americans to remain on their land (page 260)

Indian Territory *n.* (IHN-dee-uhn TAIR-uh-tawr-ee) the area of land in present-day Oklahoma and parts of Kansas and Nebraska to which Native Americans were forced to migrate (page 260)

induction *n.* (ihn-DUHK-shun) the act of being drafted into the military (page 989)

indulgence *n.* (in-DUHL-juhnts) the release from punishment for sins, sold by papal officials (page 22)

Industrial Revolution *n.* (ihn-DUH-stree-uhl rehv-uh-LOO-shuhn) an era in which widespread production by machinery replaced goods made by hand (page 219)

infamy *n.* (IHN-fuh-me) the state of being known for committing an extremely shameful or evil act (page 784)

infantry *n.* (IHN-fuhn-tree) foot soldiers (page 395)

GLOSSARY

inflation *n.* (ihn-FLAY-shuhn) a decrease in the value of money that causes an increase in the price of goods and services (page 137)

influenza *n.* (ihn-floo-EHN-zuh) an acute and highly contagious illness commonly called "the flu" (page 621)

infrastructure *n.* (IHN-fruh-struhk-chur) the basic systems of a society including roads, bridges, sewers, and electricity (page 17)

initiative *n.* (ih-NIH-shuh-tihv) a procedure by which citizens can propose new laws to be voted on by the public or by the legislature (page 561)

injunction *n.* (ihn-JUHNGK-shuhn) court orders that demand or forbid certain actions (page 700)

insurgent *n.* (ihn-SUR-juhnt) a rebel or revolutionary (page 970)

insurrection *n.* (ihn-suh-REHK-shuhn) a violent rebellion against a government or political authority (page 330)

integrate *v.* (IHN-tuh-grayt) to bring into society as equals (page 435)

integration *n.* (ihn-tuh-GRAY-shuhn) the process of joining economic forces (page 1111)

interchangeable part *n.* (ihn-tur-CHAYN-juh-buhl PAHRT) a part of a mechanism that can be substituted for another identical one (page 219)

intermediary *n.* (ihn-tur-MEE-dee-ehr-ee) someone who helps disputing sides negotiate and come to an agreement (page 187)

interned *v.* (ihn-TURND) confined in prisons or camps for military or political reasons during wartime (page 794)

Internet *n.* (IHN-tur-neht) the worldwide network of computers (page 1081)

internment camp *n.* (ihn-TURN-muhnt KAMP) a prison camp to hold enemy aliens and other prisoners of war during wartime (page 795)

interstate commerce *n.* (IHN-tur-stayt KAH-murs) the sale, purchase, or trade of goods; transportation of people, money, or goods; and navigation of waters between different states (page 161)

Interstate Highway System *n.* (IHN-tur-stayt HY-way SIHS-tuhm) the network of highways launched by President Eisenhower in 1956 to span the United States and connect states and major cities (page 866)

investment bank *n.* (ihn-VEHST-muhnt BANK) a financial institution that purchases and sells stocks and bonds and helps companies raise capital and manage their assets (page 1126)

iron curtain *n.* (I-urn KUR-tuhn) the military and political divide in Europe between Western capitalist and Eastern communist countries (page 827)

ironclad *n.* (I-urn-klahd) a ship armored with iron plates to protect it from cannon fire (page 399)

irregular *n.* (ih-REH-gyuh-lur) a soldier who fights for an army on and off instead of committing to a set length of time of military service (page 142)

Islamic republic *n.* (IZ-lahm-ik RE-puhb-lik) a state either incorporating or based entirely on Islamic law (page 1062)

island hopping *n.* (I-luhnd HAH-pihng) a strategy that involves capturing and setting up military bases on island groups one island at a time (page 803)

isolationism *n.* (I-soh-LAY-shuh-nih-zuhm) a policy in which a nation stays out of the affairs of other nations (page 572)

isthmus *n.* (IHS-muhs) a narrow strip of land connecting two larger land areas (page 583)

J

Jacksonian democracy *n.* (jak-SOH-nee-uhn dih-MAH-kruh-see) a political movement that celebrated the common man and defended the will of the people, named for President Andrew Jackson (page 253)

jazz *n.* (JAZ) a style of music originating among African-American musicians that contains lively rhythms, sounds from a variety of instruments, and improvisation (page 654)

Jim Crow laws *n.* (JIHM KROH LAWZ) laws established after the Reconstruction period that enforced racial segregation across the southern states (page 535)

job dislocation *n.* JAHB dihs-loh-KAY-shuhn) the movement of jobs to other places (page 1110)

joint-stock company *n.* (JOYNT STAHK KUHM-puh-nee) a company whose shareholders own stock in the company (page 50)

judicial branch *n.* (joo-DIH-shuhl BRANCH) the section of the U.S. government that includes the courts and legal system, led by the Supreme Court; responsible for interpreting the law (page 158)

judicial review *n.* (joo-DIH-shuhl rih-VYOO) the power to invalidate any law the Supreme Court deems unconstitutional, even if it has been passed by Congress and signed into law by the president (page 189)

K

kamikaze *n.* (kah-mih-KAH-zee) one of a group of Japanese suicide bomber pilots who crashed their planes, loaded with explosives, into American ships (page 808)

Kellogg-Briand Pact *n.* (KEH-lawg bree-AHN PAKT) a multinational agreement from 1928 in which the signing countries agreed to reject war (page 685)

kitchen cabinet *n.* (KIH-chuhn KAB-niht) a group of unofficial advisors to Andrew Jackson (page 255)

L

labor union *n.* (LAY-bur YOON-yuhn) groups of workers who band together to achieve better pay, safer working conditions, and other benefits (page 279)

laissez-faire economics *n.* (leh-say FAIR eh-kuh-NAH-mihks) a policy that calls for less government involvement in economic affairs, so that businesses choose how they will operate, with little or no oversight (page 513)

lame duck *n.* (LAYM DUHK) an outgoing elected official soon to be replaced by a successor (page 715)

landmark decision *n.* (lahnd-MARK dih-SIH-zhuhn) a legal case that settles important questions about new or existing laws (page 235)

landmark legislation *n.* (lahnd-MARK lehj-iss-LAY-shun) an important and historic law (page 957)

League of Nations *n.* (LEEG UHV NAY-shuhnz) President Woodrow Wilson's plan proposed after World War I for a general assembly of countries that would stabilize relations among countries and help preserve peace (page 626)

legislative branch *n.* (LEH-jeh-slay-tihv BRANCH) the section of the U.S. government led by Congress; responsible for making the law (page 158)

libel *n.* (LY-buhl) the crime of publishing negative claims about someone without evidence (page 93)

liberal consensus *n.* (LIH-buh-ruhl kuhn-SEHN-suhs) the agreement between the Democrats and Republicans in Congress made after World War II to continue welfare, develop a national security system, and strengthen the executive branch of government (page 832)

Liberty Bond *n.* (LIH-bur-tee BAHND) a government bond sold to individuals to help support U.S. involvement in World War I (page 608)

lien *n.* (LEEN) a legal claim to a person's property and income if debts aren't paid (page 443)

literacy test *n.* (LIH-tur-uh-see TEST) a test of one's ability to read and write (page 451)

local color *n.* (LOH-kuhl KUH-lur) a writing style that expresses the style and characteristics of a region (page 490)

lock *n.* (LAHK) a confined section of water used to raise or lower ships (page 227)

lode *n.* (LOHD) vein of ore (page 472)

Long March *n.* (LOHNGH MAHRCH) a 6,000-mile journey by Chinese communists to relocate the communist revolutionary base from southeast China to central China (page 765)

long-staple cotton *n.* (LAWNG STAY-puhl KAH-tuhn) a type of cotton that produces long fibers suitable for the manufacture of fine cloth and lace; it grows best in just a few climates and soils (page 222)

loose constructionist *n.* (LOOS kuhn-STRUHK-shuh-nihst) someone who interprets the U.S. Constitution as giving expansive powers to Congress and the president (page 182)

Louisiana Purchase *n.* (loo-ee-zee-A-nuh PUR-chuhs) an 1803 treaty in which the United States purchased a large area of land between the Mississippi River and the Rocky Mountains from France (page 190)

Loyalist *n.* (LOY-uh-lihst) an American colonist who supported Britain during the American Revolution (page 111)

loyalty oath *n.* (LOY-uhl-tee OHTH) a sworn statement confirming a person does not belong and has never belonged to various organizations including those identified as communist (page 843)

lynch *v.* (LIHNCH) to hang someone illegally by mob action (page 409)

M

machine gun *n.* (muh-SHEEN GUHN) a gun designed to fire hundreds of bullets per minute (page 612)

malaise *n.* (muh-LAYZ) a general feeling of illness or unease (page 1059)

mandate *n.* (MAN-dayt) the authority to carry out a course of action, given to a representative by voters (page 269)

manifest destiny *n.* (MAN-uh-fehst DEHS-tuh-nee) the belief that Americans were intended to settle all the land between the Atlantic and Pacific coasts (page 314)

manifesto *n.* (man-uh-FEHS-toh) a written declaration of intent (page 1012)

manor system *n.* (MA-nur SIHS-tuhm) an economic system in which peasants are bound to a lord and work his land, or manor, in exchange for food and shelter (page 20)

maquiladora *n.* (mah-kee-luh-DOR-uh) a manufacturing plant located in an export-processing zone (page 1110)

margin *n.* (MAHR-juhn) money borrowed from a bank in order to pay for an investment, such as stocks (page 686)

maritime *adj.* (MAR-uh-tym) related to the sea (page 72)

market revolution *n.* (MAHR-kuht rehv-uh-LOO-shuhn) the transition from a pre-industrial economy to a market-oriented, capitalist economy (page 226)

marriage equality *n.* (MEHR-ihj ih-KWAH-luh-tee) the legal right of gays and lesbians to marry their partners and have the same privileges that married heterosexual couples enjoy (page 1134)

Marshall Plan *n.* (MAHR-shuhl PLAN) a U.S. economic aid program to restore economic stability to Western Europe after World War II (page 825)

martial law *n.* (MAHR-shuhl LAW) law applied to an occupied society and enforced by the military (page 117)

mass market *n.* (MAS MAHR-kuht) a large number of consumers to whom manufacturers can sell goods that are manufactured in mass quantities (page 651)

mass media *n.* (MAS MEE-dee-uh) forms of communication such as radio, film, and musical recordings with the potential to reach large audiences (page 696)

mass production *n.* (MAS pruh-DUHK-shuhn) the use of machinery to make goods in large quantities (page 219)

material record *n.* (muh-TEEHR-ee-uhl REK-uhrd) the buildings and objects that survive from a previous era (page 342)

McCarthyism *n.* (muh-KAHR-thee-ih-zuhm) the practice of accusing people of being traitors to their country without offering proof (page 845)

Medicaid *n.* (MEH-dih-kayd) a U.S. government program started in 1965 that gives medical insurance to impoverished people (page 954)

Medicare *n.* (MEH-dih-kair) a U.S. government program started in 1965 that gives medical insurance to elderly people (page 954)

mercantilism *n.* (MUHR-kuhn-teel-ih-zuhm) an economic policy that gives a country sole ownership of the trade occurring in its colonies (page 23)

mercenary *n.* (MUR-suh-nair-ee) a soldier who is paid to fight for a country other than his or her own (page 123)

merger *n.* (MUR-jur) the act of incorporating two or more businesses into one (page 563)

Middle Passage *n.* (MIH-duhl PA-sihj) the long trip across the Atlantic Ocean in which enslaved Africans were brought to the Americas; the second leg of the triangular trade route (page 49)

midnight judge *n.* (MIHD-nyt JUHJ) one of a group of judges commissioned by President John Adams the night before he left office (page 189)

militant *adj.* (MIH-luh-tuhnt) overly aggressive in achieving a goal (page 1016)

militarism *n.* (MIH-luh-tuh-rih-zuhm) the belief that a government must create a strong military and be prepared to use it to achieve the country's goals (page 600)

military-industrial complex *n.* (mih-luh-tair-EE ihn-DUS-tree-uhl CAHM-plehks) a country's military establishment and industries producing arms or other military materials (page 835)

minuteman *n.* (MIH-nuht-man) an American colonial militia member who was ready to join in combat at a moment's notice (page 117)

miscegenation *n.* (MIH-sehj-ehn-a-shuhn) marriage between people of different races (page 961)

misogyny *n.* (MISS-ah-jihn-ee) a dislike, contempt for, or hatred of women; prejudice against women (page 1023)

Missouri Compromise *n.* (mih-ZUR-ee KAHM-pruh-myz) an agreement that stated the people of Missouri could own slaves and be admitted to the Union along with Maine, a free state (page 240)

mobilization *n.* (moh-buh-luh-ZAY-shuhn) the act of assembling and organizing military forces (page 741)

mobilize *v.* (MOH-buh-lyz) to organize and prepare troops for war (page 125)

modernism *n.* (MAH-dur-nih-zuhm) a modern artistic and literary style, featuring a hard, realistic tone and a tendency to reject or avoid artistic and literary practices of the past (page 658)

module *n.* (MAH-jool) a segment of a spacecraft that can function on its own (page 1028)

monoculture *n.* (mahn-oh-KUHL-chuhr) the practice of growing a single crop (page 509)

monopoly *n.* (muh-NAH-puh-lee) the complete and exclusive control of an industry by one company (page 226)

Montgomery Bus Boycott *n.* (mahnt-GUH-muh-ree BUHS BOY-kaht) a mass protest, sparked by the arrest of Rosa Parks, against the racial segregation practices of the public bus system in Montgomery, Alabama (page 911)

moral diplomacy *n.* (MOR-uhl duh-PLOH-muh-see) the concept that the United States should drastically reduce its intervention in the affairs of other countries (page 604)

morphine *n.* (MOR-feen) a powerful painkiller (page 429)

mortar *n.* (MOR-tur) a short-range, muzzle-loaded cannon (page 975)

mountain men *n.* (MOWN-tuhn MEHN) the American trappers, fur traders, and explorers who began to explore and move west (page 314)

mountain pass *n.* (MOWN-tuhn PAS) a passageway through a mountain range that is lower than the surrounding peaks (page 337)

muckrakers *n.* (MUHK-ray-kurs) investigative journalists of the early 1900s who exposed misconduct by powerful organizations or people (page 505)

multinational corporation *n.* (muhl-tee-NA-shuh-nuhl kor-puh-RAY-shuhn) a company that has offices and factories in multiple countries (page 1138)

Munich Agreement *n.* (MYOO-nihk uh-GREE-muhnt) an agreement Hitler made with the rulers of Great Britain, France, and Italy, declaring that Germany had the right to seize the Sudetenland, a portion of Czechoslovakia (page 761)

N

napalm *n.* (NAY-pahlm) a thick flammable, jellylike substance used in bombs to cause and spread fires (page 786)

nation-state *n.* (NAY-shuhn STAYT) a country with an independent government and a population united by a shared culture, language, and national pride; a political unit in which people have a common culture and identity (page 23)

National Socialism *n.* (NA-shuh-nuhl SOH-shuh-lih-zuhm) the political doctrine of the Nazi Party in Germany, which promoted the superiority of Germany and the German people, rejected communism, and carried anti-Semitism—hatred of Jewish people—to extreme levels (page 724)

nationalism *n.* (NA-shuh-nuh-lih-zuhm) a strong sense of loyalty to one's country and belief in its superiority to others (page 145)

nativist *n.* (NAY-tih-vihst) someone who opposes immigration and favors the interests of native-born citizens (page 369)

naturalization *n.* (NACH-uh-ruh-lih-ZAY-shuhn) the process of becoming a U.S. citizen for people who are not native-born citizens (page R34)

naval quarantine *n.* (NAY-vuhl KWAWR-uhn-teen) a blockade imposed on the ports of another country (page 936)

Nazi Party *n.* (NAHT-see PAHR-tee) a political party that was led by Adolf Hitler and used force to exert complete control over Germany from 1933 to 1945 (page 724)

neoconservative *n.* (nee-oh-kuhn-SUR-vuh-tihv) a person who strongly supports a free-market economy and believes the United States should actively promote its ideals around the world (page 1116)

New Deal *n.* (NOO DEEL) the laws, agencies, and programs initiated by President Franklin Roosevelt and his administration in response to the Great Depression of the 1930s (page 717)

New Federalism *n.* (NOO FEH-duh-ruh-lih-zuhm) a plan by President Richard Nixon to turn the control of some federal programs over to the states (page 1042)

New Frontier *n.* (NOO fruhn-TEER) a U.S. political strategy in 1960 in which President Kennedy stressed creative problem solving, foreign diplomacy, and technological advancements to overcome the country's problems (page 932)

new media *n.* (NOO MEE-dee-uh) digital products and services that provide content through the Internet (page 1138)

nomadic *adj.* (noh-MA-dihk) roaming across land without a fixed pattern of movement, sometimes following animal herds (page 16)

nonaggression pact *n.* (nahn-uh-GREH-shuhn PAKT) an agreement made in 1939 between Nazi Germany and the Soviet Union, declaring that they would not take military action against each other for the next 10 years (page 761)

nuclear deterrence *n.* (NOO-klee-ur dih-TUR-unts) a strategy of using nuclear weapons as a threat to ward off an enemy attack (page 860)

nuclear power *n.* (NOO-klee-ur POW-ur) energy that is created by either splitting or fusing the nuclei of atoms (page 865)

nullification *n.* (nuh-luh-fuh-KAY-shuhn) the act of taking away legal or binding force; in the case of American history, the attempt of a state government to veto a federal law that it deems unconstitutional (page 187)

O

occupation zone *n.* (AH-kyoo-pay-shuhn ZOHN) an area of a country in which a foreign military takes control (page 827)

offensive war *n.* (uh-FEHN-sihv WOR) a war fought mostly on the enemy's land (page 391)

omnibus bill *n.* (AHM-nih-buhs BIHL) a proposed law within one bill that may address many unrelated topics (page 362)

GLOSSARY

Open Door Policy *n.* (OH-puhn DOHR PAH-luh-see) an American proposal that aimed to establish equal access to ports among countries trading with China in 1900 (page 574)

ordinance *n.* (AWR-duh-nuhns) a law or authoritative regulation (page 154)

originalism *n.* (OH-rihj-ihn-uh-lih-zuhm) a belief system used to interpret the U.S. Constitution from the point of view of the intent of the document when it was originally written (page 1077)

overregulation *n.* (oh-vur-reh-gyuh-LAY-shuhn) excessive rules and regulations (page 1049)

overseer *n.* (OH-vur-see-ur) a supervisor (page 81)

P

pacifism *n.* (PA-suh-fih-zuhm) the belief that war is morally wrong (page 60)

Pan-Africanism *n.* (PAN A-frih-kuh-nih-zuhm) a movement in the early 1900s that sought to unify people of African descent (page 665)

pandemic *n.* (pan-DEH-mihk) the sudden outbreak of a disease that spreads over a wide geographic area (page 621)

Panic of 1837 *n.* (PA-nihk UHV 1837) the widespread fear of a failing economy that caused the beginning of a U.S. economic recession that lasted until 1840 (page 270)

Panic of 1873 *n.* (PA-nihk UHV 1873) an economic crisis triggered by bank and railroad failures (page 453)

panzer *n.* (PAHN-zur) a thickly armored German tank with impressive firepower used during World War II (page 799)

parent company *n.* (PAIR-uhnt KUHM-puh-nee) a company that controls all or part of other, smaller companies (page 509)

Parliament *n.* (PAHR-luh-muhnt) the legislative body of England, and, later, Great Britain (page 93)

patent *n.* (PA-tuhnt) a document that gives the bearer exclusive rights to make and sell an invention (page 226)

Patriot *n.* (PAY-tree-uht) an American colonist who supported the right of the American colonies to govern themselves (page 111)

peer *n.* (PEER) a person of the same age, rank, or social status as another (page 1006)

penicillin *n.* (peh-nuh-SIH-luhn) an antibiotic, or bacteria killer, made from mold and used to treat infections and disease (page 786)

penitentiary *n.* (peh-nuh-TEHN-chuh-ree) a state or federal prison whose stated goal was to rehabilitate criminals (page 278)

pension fund *n.* (PEHN-shuhn FUHND) a pool of money used to pay people a small, established income after they retire (page 722)

perestroika *n.* (peh-ruh-STROY-kuh) a government policy of reform in the former Soviet Union (page 1084)

perjury *n.* (PUR-juh-ree) the act of lying under oath (page 1115)

personal computer *n.* (PURS-uh-nuhl kuhm-PYOO-tur) an electronic device that processes data and is specifically designed for home use (page 1080)

personal responsibility *n.* (PURS-uh-nuhl rih-SPAWN-suh-BIHL-uh-tee) responsibility that is not required but that contributes to a more civil society, such as respecting and standing up for others' rights, helping in the community, and staying informed (page R35)

phonograph *n.* (FOH-nuh-graf) a machine that reproduces sounds from a record (page 509)

picket line *n.* (PIH-kuht LYN) a group of strikers who form a barrier to keep scabs, or strikebreakers, from entering a building to work in their place (page 729)

Piedmont *n.* (PEED-mont) a relatively flat area between the Appalachian Mountains and the coastal plain (page 78)

placer mining *n.* (PLAH-sur MY-nihng) mining techniques involving the use of lightweight tools to pan for gold in rivers and streams (page 472)

planned scarcity *n.* (PLAND SKEHR-suh-tee) the economic theory that lowering the supply of a product will increase demand for it and raise its price (page 718)

Pleistocene epoch *n.* (PLEIS-to-seen EH-puhk) a period in the history of Earth in which large animals and plants existed and glaciers covered Earth (page 1)

polio *n.* (POH-lee-oh) an infectious disease that sometimes causes muscle weakness or paralysis (page 715)

Politburo *n.* (PAW-luht-byoor-oh) the main ruling government committee that made policy decisions in the Communist Party; often refers to those of China or the former Soviet Union (page 1084)

political machine *n.* (poh-LIH-tih-kuhl muh-SHEEN) a political organization in which one person or a small group is able to maintain control over a city or a state (page 532)

poll tax *n.* (POHL TAKS) a fee charged when people register to vote (page 451)

pontoon *n.* (pahn-TOON) a portable, cylindrical float used to build a temporary bridge (page 403)

popular sovereignty *n.* (PAH-pyuh-lur SAHV-run-tee) the idea that the residents of a region or nation decide an issue by voting (page 362)

populism *n.* (PAH-pyuh-lih-zuhm) the belief that ordinary people should control government (page 477)

populist *n.* (PAH-pyuh-lihst) a politician who claims to represent the concerns of ordinary people (page 724)

portage *n.* (POHR-tihj) the act of carrying boats or goods between bodies of water or around obstructions on a waterway (page 193)

posse *n.* (PAH-see) group of armed men formed to capture an outlaw (page 488)

post-traumatic stress disorder (PTSD) *n.* (POHST truh-MAH-tihk STREHS dihs-AWR-dur) a condition brought on by injury or psychological trauma (page 993)

potlatch *n.* (PAHT-lach) a gift-giving ceremony practiced by the Kwakiutl and Haida Native American tribes (page 15)

poverty rate *n.* (PAH-vur-tee RAYT) the percentage of the population living in poverty (page 878)

prairie schooner *n.* (PRAIR-ee SKOO-nur) a horse-drawn wagon with a white canvas cover; used for traveling long distances in the early 19th century (page 319)

preamble *n.* (PREE-am-buhl) a short written introduction before a constitution or statute (page 125)

precedent *n.* (PREH-suh-duhnt) an example; a previous determination in a court case that sets a standard for comparison with similar new cases (page 154)

Presidential Reconstruction *n.* (preh-zuh-DEHN-shuhl ree-kuhn-STRUHK-shuhn) a policy that stated Confederate states must take loyalty oaths to the Union, ratify the 13th Amendment, and create new governments with new constitutions before they could rejoin the Union (page 436)

presidio *n.* (prih-SEE-dee-oh) a military post or settlement (page 330)

privateer *n.* (pry-vuh-TEER) an armed but privately owned ship that acts under the authority of a government to participate in warfare; or a sailor on such a ship (page 137)

Proclamation of 1763 *n.* (prah-kluh-MAY-shuhn UHV 1763) a law requiring colonists to stay east of a line drawn on a map along the crest of the Appalachian Mountains (page 99)

profiteering *n.* (prah-fih-TEER-ihng) the act of charging high prices for items in high demand and short supply to make more money (page 137)

Progressive Era *n.* (pruh-GREH-sihv EHR-uh) a period from about 1890 to 1920 in which reformers sought to correct many social, economic, and political inequalities and injustices in the United States (page 552)

progressivism *n.* (pruh-GREH-sih-vih-zuhm) reform movement from 1890 to 1920 that sought to make state and national politics more democratic and government more efficient (page 533)

prohibition *n.* (proh-uh-BIH-shuhn) the act of outlawing the production, distribution, and sale of alcohol (page 557)

Prohibition *n.* (proh-uh-BIH-shuhn) the constitutional ban on the sale of alcoholic beverages that was in effect between 1920 and 1933 (page 619)

promissory note *n.* (PRAH-muh-sawr-ee NOHT) a written agreement to pay a person or business back by a specified date (page 393)

propaganda *n.* (prah-puh-GAN-duh) misleading ideas and information that are spread in order to influence people's opinions or advance an organization or party's ideas (page 526)

proprietor *n.* (pruh-PRY-uh-tuhr) a person with ownership of a colony, including the right to manage and distribute land and to establish government (page 62)

prospector *n.* (PRAH-spek-tur) a person who searches in the earth for valuable resources, such as gems or precious metals (page 334)

protectorate *n.* (pruh-TEHK-tuh-ruht) a country that is partly governed by a more powerful country (page 572)

Protestant Reformation *n.* (PRAH-tuh-stuhnt reh-fuhr-MAY-shuhn) the religious movement to reform Christianity that occurred in Western Europe in the 1500s (page 23)

provision *n.* (pruh-VIH-zhuhn) a legal condition that anticipates a future need (page 145)

proviso *n.* (pruh-VY-zoh) a condition attached to a legal document or legislation (page 360)

proxy war *n.* (PRAHK-see WOR) a series of battles that are provoked by a nation that does not participate in the fighting (page 838)

purge *n.* (PUHRJ) removing or eliminating something (page 764)

push-pull factor *n.* (PUSH PUL FAK-tur) a reason why people migrate; "push" factors cause them to leave; "pull" factors make them come to a place (page 518)

Q

quinine *n.* (KWHY-nyn) a substance made from the bark of a tree that is an effective remedy for malaria (page 31)

R

radical *n.* (RA-dih-kuhl) a person who wants an extreme change or holds an extreme political position (page 185)

Radical Reconstruction *n.* (RA-dih-kuhl ree-kuhn-STRUHK-shuhn) the name given to the Republicans' plan in passing the Reconstruction Acts of 1867 (page 439)

Radical Republican *n.* (RA-dih-kuhl rih-PUH-blih-kuhn) an abolitionist member of the U.S. Congress who supported African-American rights (page 404)

rancho *n.* (RAN-choh) land granted by Mexico to settlers in the form of a large estate in what is now California (page 333)

ratify *v.* (RA-tuh-fy) to approve, formally, by vote (page 127)

ration *v.* (RA-shuhn) to control the supply of goods made available to the public, especially in wartime (page 788)

rearmament *n.* (ree-AHR-muh-muhnt) the effort of a nation to rebuild a stockpile of weapons to replace those that are out-of-date or have been taken away (page 754)

recall *n.* (REE-kawl) a procedure by which citizens can vote to remove an elected public official from office (page 561)

recession *n.* (rih-SEH-shuhn) a relatively short-lasting slowdown in economic growth, often part of a normal business cycle (page 359)

Reconstruction *n.* (ree-kuhn-STRUHK-shuhn) the effort to rebuild and reunite the United States following the Civil War (page 427)

Red Scare *n.* (REHD SKAIR) a period in 1919 and 1920 when the federal government targeted suspected communists, anarchists, and radicals (page 642)

referendum *n.* (reh-fuh-REN-duhm) an election where the people vote directly on specific measures (page 533)

refugee *n.* (REH-fyoo-jee) a person seeking shelter and protection from political persecution (page 759)

Renaissance *n.* (reh-nuh-SAHNTS) meaning "rebirth," a period in the 1300–1500s in which culture and the arts flourished (page 21)

reparations *n.* (reh-puh-RAY-shunz) money paid to the victors by the losing side in a war (page 575)

repatriation *n.* (ree-PAY-tree-ay-shuhn) returning or being returned to the country of one's origin or citizenship (page 691)

republican motherhood *n.* (rih-PUH-blih-kuhn MUH-thur-hud) the idea that women should raise their children to be good citizens who participate actively in the government (page 180)

republicanism *n.* (rih-PUH-blih-kuh-nih-zuhm) the belief that a government's power comes from its citizens and the representatives they choose to make their laws (page 152)

reservation *n.* (reh-zur-VAY-shuhn) an area of land designated for and managed by a particular Native American tribe (page 480)

reservoir *n.* (REH-zuh-vwahr) a large, contained body of water that can be tapped (page 474)

robber barons *n.* (RAHB-ur BA-ruhns) railroad industry leaders such as Cornelius Vanderbilt and Jay Gould who became renowned for their ruthless methods against competitors (page 503)

rock and roll *n.* (RAHK AND ROHL) a form of music, derived from rhythm and blues, that became popular in the 1950s (page 873)

rogue state *n.* (ROHG STAYT) a country perceived to violate international law and threaten world peace (page 1121)

Romanticism *n.* (roh-MAN-tuh-sih-zuhm) a philosophical, literary, and artistic movement in the 19th century that emphasized imagination, emotion, and action (page 281)

Rome-Berlin Axis *n.* (ROHM-burh-LIHN ACK-sihs) an agreement formed between Germany and Italy in 1936 (page 755)

rule of law *n.* (ROOL UHV LAW) the idea that people and institutions are required to follow the regulations set forth by the government (page 120)

rural electrification *n.* (RUR-uhl ih-LEHK-truh-fuh-kay-shuhn) a government program that ran power lines through rural communities (page 833)

Rustbelt *n.* (RUHST-behlt) the area in the northeastern and midwestern United States in which manufacturing has diminished significantly (page 1071)

S

sack of Lawrence *n.* (SAK UHV LAWR-uhns) a term describing a violent attack in May 1856 in Lawrence, Kansas, in which proslavery advocates ransacked the town and destroyed homes and businesses (page 371)

safety-net programs *n.* (SAFE-tee NEHT PROH-grams) a collection of programs provided by the state or federal government designed to prevent people from falling deeper into poverty (page 1073)

salutary neglect *n.* (SAL-yuh-tair-ee nih-GLEKT) the policy of the British government to not strictly enforce its colonial policies (page 93)

salvation *n.* (sal-VAY-shuhn) the act of being forgiven by one's deity (god) for one's wrongdoings or sins (page 90)

sanitation *n.* (sa-nuh-TAY-shuhn) measures such as sewers to protect public health (page 532)

savanna *n.* (su-VA-nuh) an area of lush tropical grasslands (page 26)

scabs *n.* (SKABS) nonunion workers willing to cross strike lines in order to work (page 515)

scalawag *n.* (SKA-lih-wag) an unworthy person; term used to refer to white southerners who acted to support Reconstruction for personal gain after the Civil War (page 440)

scapegoat *n.* (SKAYP-goht) an individual or group blamed for the mistakes or faults of others (page 409)

Schlieffen Plan *n.* (SHLEE-fuhn PLAN) a German plan (1905–1906) to make a rapid conquest of France, followed by a march on Russia (page 602)

scientific management *n.* (sy-uhn-TIH-fihk MA-nihj-muhnt) a management method that relies on experimental studies to identify the most efficient way to execute tasks in a factory or other workplace (page 570)

secession *n.* (seh-SEH-shuhn) the act of formally withdrawing from an organization, a nation, or any other group in order to be independent (page 191)

Second Great Awakening *n.* (SEHKund GRAYT uh-WAYK-ning) an American Protestant movement based on revival meetings and a direct and emotional relationship with God (page 276)

Second New Deal *n.* (SEHK-und NOO DEEL) a second set of New Deal programs, which President Franklin Roosevelt presented to Congress after the 1934 midterm elections (page 722)

sectionalism *n.* (SEHK-shuh-nuh-lih-zuhm) a loyalty to whichever section or region of the country one is from, rather than to the nation as a whole (page 239)

sedition *n.* (sih-DIH-shuhn) the criminal act of trying to persuade individuals to undermine the government (page 187)

segregation *n.* (seh-grih-GAY-shuhn) the separation of different groups of people, usually based on race (page 535)

Seneca Falls Convention *n.* (SEH-nihkuh FAWLS kuhn-VEHN-shuhn) an 1848 women's rights convention organized by Elizabeth Cady Stanton and Lucretia Mott in Seneca Falls, New York (page 294)

separate but equal *n.* (SEHP-uh-reht BUHT EE-kwuhl) a policy that allowed businesses and institutions to segregate African Americans from whites as long as the facilities or services provided were about equal (page 536)

separation of powers *n.* (seh-puh-RAY-shuhn UHV POW-urz) the division of governmental power among the three branches of U.S. government: the executive branch, the judicial branch, and the legislative branch (page 158)

separatist *n.* (SEH-prah-tihst) a person who wished to leave the Church of England (page 56)

service sector *n.* (SUR-vuhss SEHK-tur) the part of the economy that provides services rather than goods (page 1138)

shaft mining *n.* (SHAFT MY-nihng) mining technique in which a vertical channel is blasted into a mountain and people are lowered down the shaft to mine (page 472)

sharecropping *n.* (SHAIR-krahp-ihng) an agricultural system in which a farmer raises crops for a landowner in return for part of the money made from selling the crops (page 443)

short-staple cotton *n.* (SHORT STAY-puhl KAH-tuhn) a coarse, easy-to-cultivate type of cotton with short fibers; it is suited for growing in a wide range of climates and soils (page 222)

silent majority *n.* (SY-luhnt muh-JOR-uh-tee) a term used by Richard Nixon in the late 1960s to describe a large group of moderate voters who did not publicly express their political opinions (page 1041)

sit-down strike *n.* (SIHT DAUN STRYK) a strike in which the workers do not walk out, but rather stay at their place of employment and refuse to do any work (page 731)

sit-in *n.* (SIHT IHN) an organized protest where people sit down and refuse to leave (page 915)

situation comedy *n.* (sih-chuh-WAY-shuhn KAH-muh-dee) a weekly series that features a familiar setting and a group of characters who face amusing problems (page 872)

slash-and-burn agriculture *n.* (SLASH AND BURN A-grih-kuhl-chur) a method of clearing fields for planting that involves cutting and setting fire to existing trees and plants (page 16)

slave codes *n.* (BLAK KOHDZ) laws adopted by the colonies beginning in 1660 that limited the rights of enslaved African Americans with varying degrees of severity, depending on the colony (page 67)

sluice *n.* (SLOOS) an inclined wooden trough used in mining to strain water from gold (page 472)

smallpox *n.* (SMAWL-pawks) a deadly virus that causes a high fever and small blisters on the skin (page 45)

smog *n.* (SMAHG) a noxious combination of fog and smoke from factories (page 859)

GLOSSARY

Social Darwinism *n.* (SOH-shuhl DAHR-wuh-nih-zuhm) 19th-century philosophy that argued that human social history could be understood as a struggle between the wealthy and poor, with the strongest and the fittest invariably triumphing (page 503)

social justice *n.* (SOH-shuhl JUH-stuhs) the fair distribution of opportunities and privileges, including for racial equality (page 448)

Social Security *n.* (SOH-shuhl sih-KYOOR-ih-tee) a government program that provides income to the elderly, disabled, and unemployed (page 570)

socialism *n.* (SOH-shuh-lih-zuhm) a system of government in which the community or government controls economic resources (page 517)

solitary confinement *n.* (SAHL-it-tar-ee cuhn-FINE-ment) a form of punishment, isolating a prisoner from contact with other people (page 918)

sovereignty *n.* (SAH-vuh-ruhn-tee) the power to govern (page 152)

space race *n.* (SPAYS RAYS) the competition between the United States and the Soviet Union to be the first to travel outside Earth's atmosphere (page 934)

spacewalk *n.* (SPAYS-wawk) any period of time when an astronaut ventures outside the spacecraft (page 1027)

speakeasy *n.* (SPEEK-ee-zee) an illegal drinking club where people secretly gathered in the evenings during Prohibition (page 646)

specie *n.* (SPEE-shee) coined money; often refers to silver or gold coins (page 156)

speculation *n.* (speh-kyuh-LAY-shuhn) taking on a business risk, such as buying stocks on margin even though there is no guarantee that they will increase in value (page 686)

speculator *n.* (SPEH-kyuh-lay-tur) someone who invests in property or stocks, hoping to make a profit (page 155)

sphere of influence *n.* (SFEER UHV IHN-floo-ents) the claim by a country to exclusive control over a foreign area or territory (page 574)

spoils system *n.* (SPOY-uhlz SIHS-tuhm) the practice of rewarding political backers with government jobs; also known as the patronage system (page 241)

stagflation *n.* (stag-FLAY-shuhn) an economic condition in which stagnation, or slow economic growth, is accompanied by inflation, or rising prices (page 1056)

stalactite *n.* (stuh-LAK-tyt) a column of minerals that hangs from the roof of a cave (page 648)

stalagmite *n.* (stuh-LAG-myt) a column of minerals that form upward from the floor of a cave (page 648)

stalemate *n.* (STAYL-mayt) a situation in which neither side in a conflict can claim victory (page 141)

static *adj.* (stat-IK) having the quality of not moving or changing (page 1077)

steppe *n.* (STEP) a vast, grassy plain (page 24)

stewardship *n.* (STOO-uhrd-shihp) the responsible management of someone or something entrusted to one's care (page 287)

stock market *n.* (STAHK MAHR-kuht) the buying and selling of shares in companies (page 685)

Stono Rebellion *n.* (STOH-noh rih-BEL-yuhn) a 1739 revolt by enslaved Africans against their owners (page 83)

streetcar *n.* (STREET-kahr) a vehicle that runs on rails through city streets and carries passengers (page 531)

strict constructionist *n.* (STRIHKT kuhn-STRUHK-shuh-nihst) someone who interprets the U.S. Constitution as honoring the rights of states over federal power (page 182)

subdivision *n.* (SUHB-duh-vih-zhuhn) a tract of land that has been divided into smaller lots on which houses are built (page 867)

subprime mortgage *n.* (SUHB-prym MOR-gihj) home loan issued to buyers with poor credit history (page 1126)

subsidiary *n.* (suhb-SIH-dee-ehr-ee) a secondary business (page 509)

subsidy *n.* (SUHB-suh-dee) a government grant for improvements or support of commerce (page 227)

subsistence farming *n.* (suhb-SIHS-tuhnts FAHR-ming) the practice of producing enough food for a farmer and his or her family but not enough to sell for profit (page 72)

subtreasury system *n.* (suhb-TREH-zhuh-ree SIHS-tuhm) a system proposed by which farmers would store their crops in silos until prices rose and the government would lend the farmer money to buy new seeds for the next year's crops (page 477)

suburb *n.* (SUH-burb) a community near or on the outskirts of a city (page 531)

suburban sprawl *n.* (suh-BUR-buhn SPRAWL) the spread of housing developments over more and more suburban and rural land (page 869)

suburbanization *n.* (suh-bur-buh-nuh-ZAY-shuhn) a population shift from cities to outlying communities (page 866)

subversion *n.* (suhb-VUR-zhuhn) an act of destabilizing a major social or political system in an attempt to destroy it (page 844)

suffrage *n.* (SUH-frihj) the right to vote (page 152)

suffragist *n.* (SUHF-rih-jihst) a person who supports women's right to vote (page 295)

Sunbelt *n.* (SUHN-behlt) the southern and southwestern regions of the United States, which have mild winters (page 859)

supply-side economics *n.* (suh-PLY SYD eh-kuh-NAH-mihks) a financial theory in which tax rates are lowered for businesses and investors in the hope of boosting production and trade in the country (page 1074)

surge *n.* (SURJ) a sudden increase (page 1123)

swing state *n.* (SWIHNGH STAYT) a state where the election may be won by either party (page 1144)

syllabary *n.* (SIH-luh-bair-ee) a set of written symbols or characters used to represent a word's syllables (page 260)

syndicate *n.* (SIHN-dih-kuht) a group of criminals who control organized criminal activities (page 568)

T

tank *n.* (TANGK) an armored, heavily armed vehicle that uses treads instead of wheels (page 612)

tariff *n.* (TAIR-uhf) a tax on imports and exports (page 227)

Tariff of Abominations *n.* (TAIR-uhf UHV uh-bah-muh-NAY-shuhns) the term used by southerners to refer to the Tariff of 1828 because it stirred feelings of disgust and hatred (page 256)

task force *n.* (TASK FORS) a group of people organized for a special mission (page 1107)

telegraph *n.* (TEHL-uh-graf) a device that transmits messages along connected wires to communicate over long distances (page 508)

temperance movement *n.* (TEHM-pur-uhns MOOV-mehnt) a 19th-century reform movement that encouraged the reduction or elimination of alcoholic beverage consumption (page 277)

tenant farmer *n.* (TEH-nuhnt FAHR-muhr) a farmer who works land owned by someone else and who pays rent for it either in cash or with produce (page 443)

tenement *n.* (TEH-nuh-muhnt) a large building that rents rooms and apartments, and which is usually overcrowded and badly maintained (page 524)

termination policy *n.* (tur-muh-NAY-shuhn PAH-luh-see) a policy enacted under President Eisenhower that removed Native Americans from reservations, while the government ended the limited sovereignty of individual tribes and nations (page 882)

terrorism *n.* (TEHR-ur-ih-zuhm) the use of violent acts and threats to achieve a political goal (page 1120)

theocracy *n.* (thee-AH-kruh-see) a government ruled by a religious leader or religious leaders (page 1093)

think tank *n.* (THIHNK TAYNK) a group of experts who conduct research and discuss issues in order to craft potential solutions to social and economic problems (page 1069)

Third Reich *n.* (THURD RYK) name used by the Nazi party to describe the time when Adolph Hitler believed he was creating a third German empire (page 754)

third world *adj.* (THURD WURLD) during the Cold War, a country that was not aligned with either the United States or the Soviet Union (page 969)

topography *n.* (tuh-PAH-gruh-fee) the arrangement of the physical features of a landscape (page 336)

total war *n.* (TOH-tuhl WOR) a war in which all rules and laws of war are ignored and all resources are used for defeating the enemy (page 422)

totalitarian *adj.* (toh-ta-luh-TAIR-ee-uhn) relating to a government that is headed by a dictator and requires complete obedience to the state (page 724)

trading pool *n.* (TRAYD-ihng POOL) groups formed to buy and sell large amounts of stocks (page 688)

Trail of Tears *n.* (TRAYL UHV TEERS) the route the Cherokee and other Native Americans took during their forced migration from the southeastern United States to Oklahoma (page 265)

trans-Saharan *adj.* (tran-suh-HAHR-uhn) across the Sahara (page 25)

transcendentalism *n.* (tran-sehn-DEHN-tuh-li-zuhm) an intellectual and social movement of the 1830s and 1840s that called for rising above society's expectations (page 281)

transcontinental railroad *n.* (trans-kahn-tuh-NEHN-tuhl RAYL-rohd) a railroad that runs across a continent (page 336)

transistor *n.* (tran-ZIHS-tur) an electronic device used to control the flow of electricity in electronic equipment (page 865)

Treaty of Versailles *n.* TREE-tee UHV vur-SY) the treaty that officially brought World War I to a close (page 626)

trench warfare *n.* (TREHNCH WOR-fair) a type of warfare in which long ditches dug deep in the ground provide protection for soldiers (page 407)

triangular trade *n.* (try-ANG-yuh-lur TRAYD) a transatlantic trade network formed by Europe, West Africa, and the Americas (page 48)

tribunal *n.* (try-BYOO-nuhl) a court of justice with authority over a specific matter (page 819)

trust *n.* (TRUHST) a company managed by members of a board rather than by owners or stockholders (page 505)

trustbuster *n.* (TRUHST-buhst-ur) a person who seeks to break up business trusts, or monopolies, especially a federal official who enforces antitrust laws (page 564)

trustee *n.* (truhs-TEE) a person who has powers to administer a colony or other institution for the purpose of supporting that institution, and not for personal gain (page 65)

tundra *n.* (TUHN-druh) the flat treeless land found in arctic and subarctic regions (page 14)

turnpike *n.* (TURN-pyk) a road on which tolls are charged to allow travelers to pass (page 227)

U

U-boat *n.* (YOO BOHT) a German submarine (page 606)

Underground Railroad *n.* (uhn-dur-GROWND RAYL-rohd) a network of people who worked together to help African Americans escape from slavery from the southern United States to the northern states or to Canada before the Civil War (page 364)

underwrite *v.* (UHN-dur-ryt) to take on the financial responsibilities—including the risks—of a set of assets (page 698)

unorganized territory *n.* (uhn-AWR-guh-nyzd TAIR-uh-tawr-ee) lands governed by the federal government but not belonging to any state (page 240)

urban renewal *n.* (UR-buhn rih-NOO-uhl) a program that involves clearing slums and replacing them with large, publicly funded housing projects (page 878)

utopian community *n.* (yu-TOH-pee-uhn kuh-MYOO-nuh-nee) a group of people who live together cooperatively to form an ideal society (page 282)

V

vaquero *n.* (vah-KAIR-oh) a cowboy, especially in Spanish-settled North America (page 320)

vaudeville *n.* (VAWD-vihl) theatrical show that involved singing and dancing acts (page 530)

vertical integration *n.* (VUR-tih-kuhl ihn-tuh-GRAY-shuhn) a procedure in which a company takes control of all phases of production from start to finish (page 503)

veteran *n.* (VEH-tuh-ruhn) a person who has served in the military (page 429)

viceroyalty *n.* (VYS-roy-uhl-tee) a territory governed by a governor of Spain's colonies in the Americas who represented the Spanish king and queen (page 47)

Vietnamization *n.* (vee-eht-nuh-muh-ZAY-shun) a military strategy that allowed for the gradual replacement of U.S. troops with South Vietnamese troops during the Vietnam War (page 988)

voter fraud *n.* (VOH-tur FRAWD) illegal manipulation of ballots to help win an election (page 929)

voter intimidation *n.* (VOH-tur ihn-tih-muh-DAY-shuhn) actions, often violent, taken to frighten and deter people from voting and often specifically aimed at African Americans, immigrants, or people a powerful group does not agree with. (page 445)

voter registration drive *n.* (VOH-tur reh-juh-STRAY-shuhn DRYV) an effort by groups or government to sign up as many eligible voters in a targeted area as possible (page 922)

voting bloc *n.* (VOHT-ihng BLOK) a large group of citizens who share a common concern and tend to vote the same in elections (page 736)

W

wage discrimination *n.* (WAYJ dihs-krih-muh-NAY-shuhn) the act of lowering pay for the same job based on gender, race, or ethnicity (page 790)

wage economy *n.* (WAYJ ih-KAH-nuhmee) an economy in which people are paid for their work (page 447)

war bond *n.* (WOR BAHND) a debt security issued by the government to help finance military expenses during wartime (page 153)

War Hawk *n.* (WOR HAWK) a person who approves of and encourages war; an American who favored war with Great Britain in 1812 (page 199)

War Industries Board (WIB) *n.* (WOR IHN-duh-streez BAWRD) a board that oversaw manufacturing in the United States during World War I (page 608)

war of attrition *n.* (WOR UHV uh-TRIH-shun) a military strategy in which an army wears another down by conducting many small battles over a long period of time (page 975)

Watergate break-in *n.* (WAH-tur-gayt BRAYK IHN) a break-in at the Democratic National Headquarters in the Watergate complex in Washington, D.C., in 1972 by burglars associated with President Richard Nixon's re-election committee (page 1053)

weapons of mass destruction (WMD) *n.* (WEH-puhnz UHV MAS dih-STRUHK-shuhn) weapons that use nuclear, chemical, or biological substances to harm large numbers of people (page 1121)

welfare capitalism *n.* (WEHL-fair KA-puh-tuh-lih-zuhm) a business practice in which companies offer workers extra benefits, including recreational facilities, benefit plans, and profit-sharing opportunities (page 653)

welfare state *n.* (WEHL-fair STAYT) a system in which the government provides for the health and well-being of its citizens (page 742)

Whig Party *n.* (WIHG PAHR-tee) a political party formed to oppose the policies of Andrew Jackson, who the party believed had exceeded his power as president (page 269)

white-collar *adj.* (HWYT-KAH-lur) relating to the class of people whose jobs typically take place in an office or professional environment and don't involve manual labor (page 833)

wiretapping *v.* (WY-urh-tap-ihng) placing a device on a telephone in order to secretly listen to conversations (page 1054)

workers' compensation *n.* (WUR-kurz kahm-puhn-SAY-shuhn) insurance for employees injured while on the job, providing assistance for medical care and loss of income (page 513)

writ of assistance *n.* (RIHT UHV uh-SIHS-tuhns) a legal document giving authorities the right to enter and search a home or business (page 112)

writ of *habeus corpus* *n.* (RIHT UHV HAY-bee-uhs COR-puhs) a law that allows prisoners to petition to a judge if they believe they have been arrested unlawfully (page 391)

Y

yellow journalism *n.* (YEH-loh JUR-nuh-lih-zuhm) a type of journalism that stresses sensationalism over facts (page 577)

Z

Zimmermann Telegram *n.* (ZIH-mur-muhn TEH-luh-gram) a secret German telegram sent to the German ambassador in Mexico laying out a plan to ally with Mexico (page 607)

ACADEMIC VOCABULARY

acquiesce *v.* (a-kwee-EHS) to agree, especially after an argument (page 1019)

affluence *n.* (A-floo-ehns) wealth, prosperity (page 862)

agitator *n.* (A-juh-TAY-tuhr) someone who stirs up anger and rebellion (page 484)

allegory *n.* (A-luh-gawr-ee) a story in which objects or people stand for abstract or spiritual ideas (page 21)

allocate *v.* (A-luh-kayt) to give out, to distribute (page 1042)

amenity *n.* (uh-MEH-nih-tee) a benefit that promotes comfort and ease of use or lifestyle (page 516)

arable *adj.* (A-ruh-buhl) fertile, as soil for agriculture (page 78)

artisan *n.* (AHR-tuh-zuhn) craftsperson (page 27)

autonomy *n.* (aw-TAH-nuh-mee) independence; freedom to act on one's own (page 167)

blacklist *v.* (BLAK-lihst) to put one or more people on a list indicating they are to be shunned or punished (page 843)

blasphemous *adj.* (BLAS-fuh-muhs) ungodly, sacrilegious (page 1069)

boll *n.* (BOHL) cotton seed pod (page 222)

brackish *adj.* (BRA-kihsh) partially salty (page 50)

brevity *n.* (BRE-vuh-tee) shortness; the quality of being quick and to the point (page 425)

burgeon *v.* (BUR-juhn) to expand; to grow (page 79)

card *v.* (KARD) to prepare cotton fibers for spinning by cleaning, combing out tangles, and gathering fibers together (page 220)

charisma *n.* (kuh-RIHZ-muh) charm, often connected with magnetic leadership ability (page 187)

clandestine *adj.* (klan-DEHS-tuhn) secret (page 330)

clemency *n.* (KLEH-mehn-see) mercy, leniency (page 843)

coerce *v.* (coh-URS) to make someone do something by use of force, threat, or trickery (page 738)

cohesion *n.* (coh-HEE-zhuhn) unity, tight organization (page 801)

comply *v.* (uhm-PLY) to meet the terms of, to obey (page 907)

conclusive *adj.* (kuhn-KLOO-sihv) final (page 401)

contraband *n.* KAHN-truh-band smuggled goods (page 112)

covenant *n.* (KUHV-nuhnt) binding promise (page 95)

culmination *n.* (kuhl-muh-NAY-shuhn) the conclusion, the finale (page 993)

default *v.* (dee-FAWLT) to fail to pay, as a debt (page 152)

depository *n.* (dih-PAH-suh-tor-ee) a warehouse, a place where items are stored (page 939)

devout *adj.* (dih-VOWT) religiously faithful (page 277)

disproportionate *adj.* (dihs-pruh-POR-shuh-nuht) unequal, unbalanced, usually weighed to the larger part (page 1109)

diversify *v.* (dih-VUR-sih-fy) to expand one's options (page 476)

diversity *n.* (duh-VUR-suh-tee) variety (page 77)

domestic *adj.* (duh-MEHS-tihk) household (as type of chores or duties) (page 67)

effigy *n.* (EH-fuh-jee) a dummy representing a person, particularly a famous person (often a politician) who is hated or reviled (page 111)

eke *v.* (eek) to obtain with great effort (page 472)

empathize *v.* (EM-puh-thyz) to feel an emotional connection with another (page 365)

eradicate *v.* (ih-RA-duh-kayt) to wipe out, to destroy utterly (page 562)

erratic *adj.* (ih-RA-tihk) unpredictable, inconsistent (page 844)

exodus *n.* (EHK-suh-duhs) departure (usually of many people at once) (page 21)

exorbitant *adj.* (ihg-ZOR-buh-tuhnt) excessive, overpriced (page 472)

expedient *adj.* (ehk-SPEE-dee-uhnt) convenient, practical (page 1015)

extortion *n.* (ecks-TOR-shuhn) the act of obtaining something—usually money or information—through forceful coercion; blackmail (page 959)

frugality *n.* (froo-GA-luh-tee) thriftiness (page 189)

ghetto *n.* (GEH-toh) a section of a city in which certain groups, usually Jews, are required to live; more recently, a section of a city where certain minority groups live, usually due to poverty (page 815)

herbicide *n.* (UR-buh-syd) a chemical substance used to kill plants (page 977)

hieroglyphic *adj.* (hy-uh-ruh-GLIH-fihk) picture-based (as in a writing form) (page 17)

homogenous *adj.* (hoh-MAH-juh-nuhs) uniform, equal, consistent, standardized (page 875)

hostage *n.* (HAH-stihj) someone who is held prisoner to force another party to follow the demands of those who hold him or her (page 1062)

hypothesis *n.* (hy-PAH-thuh-suhs) specific idea to be tested through the scientific method (page 88)

illicit *adj.* (ih-LIH-suht) illegal, unlawful (page 655)

immolate *v.* (IH-muh-layt) to destroy by setting on fire (page 971)

incorporate *v.* (ihn-COR-puh-rayt) to blend, to unite (page 905)

influx *n.* (IHN-fluhks) an arrival, an entry (as of immigrants) (page 518)

insubordination *n.* (ihn-suh-bor-dih-NAY-shuhn) disobedience, rebelliousness (page 568)

interventionist *n.* (ihn-tur-VEHN-shuh-nishst) someone who supports getting involved, as in a war (page 762)

invincible *adj.* (ihn-VIHN-suh-buhl) impossible to conquer, indestructible (page 557)

jurisdiction *n.* (jur-uhs-DIHK-shuhn) legal power (page 364)

laudable *adj.* (LAW-duh-buhl) praiseworthy (page 658)

lease *v.* (lees) to either sign or provide a contract that gives rights to land or facilities for a certain amount of time at an agreed upon rent (page 579)

lucrative *adj.* (LOO-kruh-tihv) moneymaking, profitable, well-paid (page 76)

mudslinging *n.* (MUHD-slihng-ing) nasty personal attacks (usually on a political opponent) (page 253)

mystique *n.* (mih-STEEK) an air of mystery, or the unknown, that surrounds a person, thing, or idea (page 1021)

normalcy *n.* (NOR-muhl-see) a condition or situation that is typical, usual, or expected, such as the general social, political, and economic conditions of a nation (page 629)

notorious *adj.* (noh-TOR-ee-uhs) famous for having a bad reputation, dishonorable (page 646)

noxious *adj.* (NAHK-zhuhs) foul, offensive, digusting (page 532)

obstruction *n.* (uhb-STRUHK-shuhn) something that blocks a path or an action (page 1055)

oratorical *adj.* (or-uh-TOR-ih-kuhl) having to do with speechmaking (page 908)

philanthropic *adj.* (fih-lahn-THRAW-pihk) charitable (page 505)

pluralism *n.* (PLUR-uh-lih-zuhm) the coexistence of different cultural groups within a single larger civilization (page 518)

pragmatism *n.* (PRAG-muh-tihzm) practicality, rationality (page 716)

pre-emptive *adj.* (pree-EHMP-tihv) preventive, defensive (page 1121)

privatize *v.* (PRY-vuh-tyz) to transfer from public to private control (page 111)

prominence *n.* (PRAH-muh-nuhnts) the state of being important or noticeable (page 253)

proponent *n.* (pruh-POH-nuhnt) a supporter, an advocate (page 518)

protagonist *n.* (proh-TA-guh-nihst) the main character of a work of fiction (page 489)

quota *n.* (KWOH-tuh) a proportional amount, percentage, or share, often in reference to proportion of members of minority or gender groups allotted for a particular benefit (page 691)

redress *n.* (rih-DREHS) compensation for wrongdoing (page 795)

relinquish *v.* (rih-LIHNG-kwihsh) to give up; to surrender (page 327)

renounce *v.* (rih-NOWNTS) to reject, to give up (page 685)

repressive *adj.* (rih-PREH-sihv) oppressive, brutally authoritarian (page 1079)

rescind *v.* (ree-SIHND) to withdraw; to take back (page 113)

scurrilous *adj.* (SKUR-uh-luhs) insulting, slanderous, scandalous (page 610)

solidarity *n.* (saw-luh-DAIR-uh-tee) unity of purpose (page 516)

subjugation *n.* (suhb-jih-GAY-shuhn) the act of bringing a group of people under control by force (page 831)

subordinate *adj.* (suh-BAWR-duh-nuht) lesser (page 298)

subpoena *n.* (suh-PEE-nuh) a legal demand to appear before a court, judge, or government committee (page 843)

subversive *adj.* (suhb-VUR-sihv) rebellious (page 58)

superfluous *adj.* (suh-PUR-floo-uhs) unnecessary (page 164)

unanimous *adj.* (yoo-NA-nuh-muhs) undisputed, with all votes the same (page 907)

unicameral *adj.* (yoo-nih-KA-mur-uhl) having one chamber, as a legislature with only one house of lawmakers (page 158)

warlord *n.* (WOR-lord) a local military leader who holds great power in his limited region (page 765)

GLOSARIO

A

abolicionista *s.* persona que quiere acabar con la esclavitud (página 223)

acción afirmativa *s.* política gubernamental que establece cuotas raciales para favorecer a los grupos que han sufrido discriminación (página 961)

activismo comunitario *s.* movimiento político impulsado por personas que individualmente no tienen mucho poder, pero que trabajando juntos logran obtener resultados (página 902)

acto de hábeas corpus *s.* ley que permite a los prisioneros reclamar una audiencia ante un juez si consideran que han sido arrestados ilegalmente (página 391)

acueducto *s.* estructura que transporta agua o un sistema de aguas (página 228)

Acuerdos de Múnich *s.* acuerdos que realizó Hitler con los gobernantes de Gran Bretaña, Francia e Italia, declarando que Alemania tenía el derecho de apoderarse de la región de los Sudetes, que formaba parte de Checoslovaquia (página 761)

acuífero *s.* formación geológica debajo de la superficie de la tierra que puede albergar un gran depósito de agua subterránea (página 474)

adjudicación *s.* lote de tierra entregado a un indígena para su cultivo (página 484)

administración *s.* manejo responsable de alguien o algo confiado a nuestro cuidado (página 287)

administrador *s.* persona con el poder de administrar una colonia o una institución con el único propósito de ayudar y sin recibir retribución (página 65)

adversario *s.* enemigo; oponente (página 145)

Agente Naranja *s.* herbicida potente usado para matar la vegetación (página 977)

agrario *adj.* relativo a la agricultura y siembra (página 182)

agricultura de subsistencia *s.* modo de producir suficientes alimentos para el granjero y su familia, pero no para la venta (página 72)

agricultura de tala y quema *s.* método de despejar los campos para sembrar cultivos que consiste en cortar y quemar los árboles y las plantas existentes (página 16)

agroindustria *s.* el negocio comercial de la agricultura (página 859)

aislacionismo *s.* política en la cual una nación permanece fuera de los asuntos de otras naciones (página 572)

algodón de punta corta *s.* tipo de algodón grueso de fibras cortas y fácil de cultivar que se podía cultivar en una amplia variedad de climas y suelos (página 222)

algodón de punta larga *s.* tipo de algodón que produce fibras largas útiles en la producción de prendas finas; crece en pocos climas y suelos (página 222)

Aliados *s.* varios países, entre ellos Francia y gran Bretaña, que lucharon juntos para oponerse a las Potencias del Eje de Alemania, Italia y Japón (página 755)

alimentos genéticamente modificados *s.* alimentos producidos a partir de plantas que han sido modificadas de una manera que no ocurre naturalmente (página 1139)

allanamiento de Watergate *s.* allanamiento en la sede nacional del Partido Demócrata dentro del complejo de Watergate en Washington, D.C., en 1972 por ladrones asociados con el comité para la reelección del presidente Richard Nixon (página 1053)

amarillismo *s.* tipo de periodismo que hace hincapié en el sensacionalismo en lugar de los hechos (página 577)

americanización *s.* proceso de inmersión dirigido hacia los inmigrantes para que aprendieran lo que algunos definen como la cultura estadounidense y así transformarlos en "verdaderos" estadounidenses (página 518)

ametralladora *s.* pistola diseñada para disparar cientos de balas por minuto (página 612)

amnistía *s.* perdón que concede un gobierno u otra autoridad a un grupo de personas (página 434)

anarquía *s.* concepto que postula que los gobiernos no son necesarios y que toda la cooperación social y política debe ser voluntaria (página 515)

anexionarse *v.* tomar posesión de un territorio o país (página 323)

antifederalista *s.* persona que se oponía a la Constitución de EE. UU. de 1787 porque el énfasis de esta era un gobierno nacional poderoso (página 162)

antisemitismo *s.* discriminación, prejuicio y hostilidad contra el pueblo judío (página 524)

apaciguamiento *s.* política de hacer compromisos para evitar conflictos (página 761)

aparcería *s.* sistema agrícola en donde los jornaleros levantan la cosecha de un terrateniente a cambio de recibir una parte de la venta de dichas cosechas (página 443)

aparcero *s.* agricultor que trabaja la tierra de un terrateniente y, a cambio de provisiones y refugio, entrega la mayor parte de sus cultivos al terrateniente (página 443)

apartheid *s.* separación legal entre las razas en Sudáfrica (página 1079)

aplazamiento *s.* permiso oficial para demorar el reclutamiento (página 980)

arancel de las abominaciones *s.* término usado por los sureños para referirse al arancel de 1828 porque lo consideraban odioso y opresivo (página 256)

archipiélago *s.* conjunto de islas (página 572)

armas de destrucción masiva (ADM) *s.* armas que usan material nuclear, químico o biológico para causar un inmenso daño a un gran número de personas (página 1121)

armisticio *s.* acuerdo entre dos fuerzas en conflicto para detener el combate (página 625)

arsenal *s.* lugar donde se almacenan armas y otros equipos militares (página 117)

artefacto *s.* artículo hecho por un ser humano que tiene un significado histórico o cultural (página 342)

artículo investigativo *s.* escrito que revela un escándalo o una injusticia (página 553)

Artículos de la Confederación *s.* conjunto de leyes adoptado por los Estados Unidos en 1777, que establecía cada estado de la Unión como una república, reemplazado por la Constitución en 1789 (página 126)

artillería antiaérea *s.* arma pesada modificada para poder ser dirigida hacia el cielo y disparar contra aviones enemigos (página 612)

asegurar *v.* asumir las responsabilidades financieras, incluidos los riesgos, de un conjunto de activos (página 698)

asimilar *v.* asumir las cualidades de otra cultura, así como su modo de vida (página 260)

atrocidad *s.* acto de crueldad y violencia extremas (página 819)

autócrata *s.* gobernante que tiene poder absoluto; tirano (página 970)

B

backcountry *s.* la zona oeste de las Colonias del Sur justo al este de los montes Apalaches (página 78)

baluarte *s.* algo que proporciona protección o defensa (página 861)

bancarrota *s.* estado en cual se carece de fondos para asumir las deudas; fracaso empresarial (página 229)

banco de inversión *s.* institución financiera que compra y vende acciones y bonos y ayuda a las empresas a recaudar capital y administrar sus activos (página 1126)

bar clandestino *s.* un local ilegal donde las personas se reunían en secreto para consumir alcohol durante la Prohibición (página 646)

batería *s.* grupo de piezas de artillería, como cañones (página 410)

beligerante *s.* país que está en guerra (página 768)

bimetalismo *s.* sistema monetario que permitiría a los ciudadanos acuñar moneda estadounidense con plata de su propiedad (página 477)

bipartidista *adj.* relativo a ambas partes en un sistema de dos partidos políticos (página 949)

bloque electoral *s.* grupo grande de ciudadanos que comparten ideologías y tienden a votar por igual en las elecciones (página 736)

boicot *s.* forma de protesta que rechaza la compra de bienes o servicios (página 111)

boicot de autobuses de Montgomery *s.* protesta masiva, provocada por el arresto de Rosa Parks, en contra de las prácticas de segregación racial del sistema de autobuses públicos en Montgomery, Alabama (página 911)

bolsa de valores *s.* marco en el cual se realiza la compra y venta de acciones de sociedades y empresas (página 685)

bomba atómica *s.* un tipo de bomba cuya violenta explosión es provocada por la división de los átomos, lo cual libera un intenso calor y radioactividad (página 810)

bomba de hidrógeno *s.* arma nuclear que explota debido a los gases compactados dentro (página 835)

bombardeo *s.* fuego de artillería pesada dirigido hacia un objetivo o área específicos (página 416)

bono de guerra *s.* título de deuda emitido por el gobierno para ayudar a financiar los gastos militares durante una guerra (página 153)

bono de la libertad *s.* bono del gobierno vendido a ciudadanos para ayudar a apoyar la participación de los Estados Unidos en la Primera Guerra Mundial (página 608)

GLOSARIO

Brain Trust *s.* grupo de expertos que asesoró al presidente Franklin Roosevelt durante la Gran Depresión (página 716)

brecha de credibilidad *s.* creciente escepticismo de los estadounidenses acerca de los informes gubernamentales sobre la guerra de Vietnam (página 979)

bribones *(scalawags) s.* término para describir después de la Guerra Civil, a aquellos blancos sureños que apoyaron la Reconstrucción únicamente por intereses económicos (página 440)

C

caballería *s.* tropas de un ejército que luchan montadas a caballo (página 395)

caballo negro *s.* candidato poco conocido cuya nominación inesperada es usualmente el resultado de un compromiso entre facciones (página 326)

Cabeza de Cobre *s.* apodo peyorativo para designar a los miembros del Partido Demócrata que en los estados de la Unión se oponían a la emancipación de los esclavos y al reclutamiento (página 404)

cacicazgo *s.* comunidad de personas regida por un cacique o jefe (página 4)

callejón sin salida *s.* situación en la que no es posible progresar (página 985)

caminata espacial *s.* cualquier período de tiempo en el que un astronauta sale de la nave espacial (página 1027)

Camino de Lágrimas *s.* ruta que los cheroquis y otras tribus norteamericanas tomaron durante su migración forzada desde el sureste de los Estados Unidos hacia Oklahoma (página 265)

campaña de registro electoral *s.* esfuerzo realizado por grupos independientes o por el gobierno para inscribir la mayor cantidad posible de votantes en un área determinada (página 922)

campo de concentración *s.* lugar donde se encuentran confinados prisioneros de guerra o miembros de minorías perseguidas; en la Segunda Guerra Mundial, los campos donde judíos y otros fueron detenidos y asesinados por los nazis (página 814)

campo de internamiento *s.* campo de prisioneros para detener a extranjeros enemigos y otros prisioneros de guerra durante la guerra (página 795)

capataz *s.* supervisor (página 81)

capital *s.* dinero y otros bienes necesarios para fundar y emprender una empresa (página 219)

capitalismo benefactor *s.* práctica empresarial en la que las empresas ofrecen a los trabajadores beneficios adicionales, incluyendo instalaciones recreativas, cobertura médica y oportunidades de participación en las ganancias (página 653)

capitalismo *s.* sistema económico donde las entidades privadas, por oposición al gobierno, son propietarias de negocios que administran con fines de lucro (página 642)

carabela *s.* barco pequeño y rápido usado por los exploradores españoles y portugueses (página 28)

caravana *s.* grupo de personas y animales que viajan juntos, usualmente para comerciar (página 25)

carga de profundidad *s.* bomba submarina que está programada para explotar a cierta profundidad (página 799)

carrera de armamentos *s.* situación política en la que países rivales tratan de acumular o producir la mayor cantidad de armas militares (página 834)

carrera espacial *s.* competencia entre los Estados Unidos y la Unión Soviética para ser el primero en realizar un viaje fuera de la atmósfera terrestre (página 934)

carreta Conestoga *s.* tipo de carreta diseñada por colonos alemanes en Norteamérica para llevar cargas pesadas (página 78)

carreta cubierta *s.* vehículo cubierto con una lona blanca y tirado por caballos que se usó para recorrer grandes distancias en el siglo XIX (página 319)

Carta del Atlántico *s.* un documento que enlista ocho principios para un mundo mejor, redactado durante la reunión entre el presidente Franklin Roosevelt y el primer ministro británico Winston Churchill en 1941 (página 770)

Carta *s.* documento de tipo histórico en el cual se establece el objetivo principal de un proyecto o un empeño (página 50)

cartógrafo *s.* persona que hace mapas (página 28)

casa de vecindad *s.* edificio grande que alquila habitaciones y apartamentos, y que suele estar abarrotado y mal mantenido (página 524)

caso civil *s.* disputa legal entre dos o más individuos u organizaciones que involucra a menudo asuntos contractuales o de negocios (página 179)

caso criminal *s.* disputa legal en la cual el gobierno acusa a una persona o grupo de romper la ley y ser una amenaza para la sociedad (página 179)

caso Dred Scott *s.* decisión de la Corte Suprema que dictaminó que los afroamericanos no tenían derechos como ciudadanos y que invalidó el Compromiso de Missouri de 1820; Dred Scott, el esclavo en cuestión, fue devuelto a la esclavitud (página 372)

caso histórico *s.* caso legal que sienta un precedente para leyes nuevas o ya existentes (página 235)

cateador *s.* persona que busca en la tierra recursos minerales valiosos, especialmente piedras y metales preciosos (página 334)

Catorce Puntos *s.* programa propuesto por el presidente Woodrow Wilson para establecer la paz al final de la Primera Guerra Mundial (página 623)

cazador y recolector *s.* ser humano que caza animales y recolecta plantas silvestres para alimentarse (página 3)

censo *s.* conteo formal de la población de un país o una región (página 179)

chivo expiatorio *s.* individuo o grupo culpado por los errores o las faltas de otros (página 409)

circunnavegar *v.* viajar por completo alrededor de la Tierra (página 30)

ciudad en auge *s.* ciudad cuya población aumenta repentinamente y en grandes cantidades (página 335)

cláusula de esclavo fugitivo *s.* disposición del Artículo 4 de la Constitución de EE. UU. que prohíbe a los estados libres la liberación de trabajadores esclavos que se hayan escapado de sus amos en otros estados (página 161)

cláusula de exención *s.* parte de una ley que excluye a ciertas personas y cosas debido a condiciones previas a su promulgación (página 535)

cláusula *s.* condición adjunta a un documento legal o ley (página 360)

clientelismo *s.* práctica que recompensa a los partidarios políticos con puestos en el gobierno (página 241)

coalición *s.* alianza de personas, partidos o estados centrada en un objetivo común (página 241)

códigos de esclavos *s.* leyes adoptadas en las colonias a principios de 1600 que regían los derechos de los esclavos afroamericanos con diferentes grados de severidad según la colonia (página 67)

colateral *s.* segunda propiedad ofrecida como seguro al solicitar un préstamo, y que protege los intereses del prestamista (página 435)

colega *s.* persona de la misma edad, rango o estatus social que otra (página 1006)

Colegio electoral *s.* grupo que elige al presidente de los EE. UU.; cada estado tiene un número de electores igual al número de sus representantes y senadores en el Congreso (página 160)

coludir *v.* conspirar o armar un complot para hacer daño a otros (página 1145)

combativo *adj.* extremadamente agresivo en la búsqueda de un objetivo (página 1016)

comercio interestatal *s.* la compra, venta o intercambio de bienes; transporte de personas, dinero o bienes entre los diferentes estados (página 161)

comercio triangular *s.* red transatlántica de comercio formada por Europa, África Occidental y las Américas (página 48)

comité de correspondencia *s.* en la época de la independencia, grupo de colonos cuyo deber era hacer correr la voz para la organización de protestas contra los británicos (página 114)

Comité de Información Pública (CPI) *s.* comité establecido durante la Primera Guerra Mundial para contrarrestar la posible disensión y estimular el entusiasmo del país por la guerra (página 610)

comité de vigilancia *s.* grupo de hombres armados reunidos para capturar a un proscrito (página 488)

complejo industrial-militar *s.* dirigencia militar de un país y las industrias que producen armas u otros materiales bélicos (página 835)

composición demográfica *s.* composición de la población de un área específica basada en la etnicidad (página 955)

Compra de Louisiana *s.* tratado entre Francia y los Estados Unidos, por el cual fue comprada una gran extensión de tierras entre el río Mississippi y las montañas Rocosas (página 190)

Compromiso de 1877 *s.* acuerdo mediante el cual el Partido Demócrata se comprometió a reconocer a Rutherford B. Hayes como presidente a cambio de que los Republicanos concluyeran la Reconstrucción y retiraran a las tropas federales del Sur (página 453)

Compromiso de Missouri *s.* acuerdo que estableció que Missouri podía tener esclavos y a su vez ser admitido a la Unión junto con Maine, un estado libre (página 240)

computadora personal *s.* dispositivo electrónico que procesa datos y está específicamente diseñado para el uso doméstico (página 1080)

comunidad utópica *s.* grupo de personas que viven juntas y cooperan para formar una sociedad ideal (página 282)

comunismo *s.* forma de gobierno en la que todos los medios de producción y transporte son propiedad del estado (página 625)

Confederación *s.* los 11 estados que se separaron de la Unión para formar su propia nación: los Estados Confederados de América (página 379)

confinamiento solitario *s.* forma de castigo en la que se aísla a un prisionero del contacto con otras personas (página 918)

confiscar *v.* acto de tomar posesión de una propiedad por parte del gobierno (página 408)

conquistador *s.* explorador español que buscaba oro y otras riquezas en las Américas (página 44)

consenso liberal *s.* acuerdo entre demócratas y republicanos en el Congreso, pactado después de la Segunda Guerra Mundial, para continuar las prestaciones sociales, desarrollar un sistema de seguridad nacional y fortalecer el poder ejecutivo (página 832)

conservador *s.* miembro de un partido político que cree en los valores tradicionales, la estructura social y el cambio gradual en las políticas (página 1068)

conservadurismo compasivo *s.* filosofía política que combinaba las ideas conservadoras tradicionales sobre las políticas económicas con una preocupación por las personas desfavorecidas (página 1116)

consumismo *s.* teoría que sostiene que la economía florece cuando la gente compra o consume muchos bienes y servicios (página 859)

contención nuclear *s.* estrategia de usar las armas nucleares como amenaza para evitar un ataque enemigo (página 860)

contención *s.* política de seguridad estadounidense durante la Guerra Fría en la que se utilizó la acción militar para impedir que la unión soviética propagara el comunismo (página 827)

contexto *s.* las circunstancias y el entorno en el que se encuentra un objeto que ayudan a comprender cómo se utiliza un objeto (página 342)

contiguo *adj.* conectado; junto (página 331)

contingente *s.* pequeño grupo de personas que representa a uno más grande (página 415)

contrabandista *s.* individuo que fabricaba, transportaba o suministraba alcohol ilegalmente a tabernas o "bares clandestinos" donde los habitantes se congregaban por las tardes (página 646)

contracultura *s.* movimiento de los años sesenta que promovió un modo de vida que estaba en oposición a las reglas y el comportamiento establecidos por la sociedad estadounidense (página 986)

contrato colectivo *s.* negociación entre un empleador y un sindicato (página 728)

Convención de Seneca Falls *s.* convención por los derechos de la mujer, organizada por Elizabeth Cady Stanton y Lucretia Mott en Seneca Falls, Nueva York, en 1848 (página 294)

Conversación junto a la chimenea *s.* serie de emisiones de radio que el presidente Franklin Roosevelt hizo a la nación durante su presidencia (página 716)

cooperativa *s.* organización dirigida y financiada por sus miembros (página 477)

corporación *s.* empresas o grupos de personas que invierten en un negocio y luego comparten sus beneficios (página 227)

corsario *s.* buque mercante privado autorizado por un gobierno para perseguir a las embarcaciones enemigas siguiendo las leyes de guerra, o un marinero a bordo ese tipo de barco (página 137)

cortina de hierro *s.* división militar y política en Europa entre los países capitalistas occidentales y los países comunistas orientales (página 827)

crédito *s.* privilegio para comprar algo o pedir prestado dinero, devolviendo el dinero con el tiempo (página 156)

crematorio *s.* horno utilizado para quemar restos humanos o animales; en la Segunda Guerra Mundial , los hornos utilizados por los nazis para quemar los cuerpos de sus víctimas (página 817)

Crisis de los Misiles en Cuba *s.* enfrentamiento político de 1962 entre los Estados Unidos y la Unión Soviética causado por la presencia de armas nucleares en Cuba (página 936)

Crusadas *s.* expediciones militares patrocinadas por la Iglesia Católica para recuperar la llamada "tierra santa" del dominio musulmán en Oriente Medio, 1096–1291 (página 21)

cuarentena naval *s.* un bloqueo impuesto a los puertos de otro país (página 936)

cuartel *s.* edificio militar utilizado para alojar a los soldados (página 132)

cuerpo especial *s.* un grupo de personas organizadas para una misión especial (página 1107)

cultivo en seco *s.* conjunto de técnicas agrícolas utilizadas en zonas con escasa precipitación (página 471)

culto a la domesticidad *s.* concepto que durante el siglo XIX planteaba que las mujeres de clases media y alta debían casarse y permanecer en la casa al cuidado de los hijos, y el deber de constituirse en el eje moral del hogar (página 292)

D

Danza de los Espíritus *s.* danza ceremonial realizada por algunos indígenas con la esperanza de que esta convocaría a un libertador que restauraría su mundo (página 484)

darwinismo social *s.* filosofía del siglo XIX que sostenía que la historia social humana podía entenderse como una lucha entre los ricos y los pobres, con los más fuertes y los más aptos invariablemente triunfando (página 503)

DDT *s.* insecticida, actualmente prohibido en los Estados Unidos y muchos otros países, que resultó ser perjudicial para los animales

y causar contaminación a largo plazo del medio ambiente (página 1046)

de cuello blanco *adj.* relacionado con la clase de personas cuyos trabajos suelen tener lugar en una oficina o entorno profesional y no implican trabajo manual (página 833)

Declaración de Derechos *s.* las diez primeras enmiendas a la Constitución de EE. UU.; lista de garantías a las que tienen derecho todas las personas del país (página 165)

Declaración de Independencia *s.* documento que declara la independencia de los Estados Unidos de Gran Bretaña, emitido el 4 de julio de 1776 (página 125)

defensa activa *s.* política que permite a los buques de guerra de los Estados Unidos defenderse contra los ataques de submarinos alemanes sobre buques en tránsito dentro del océano Atlántico (página 771)

déficit *s.* saldo monetario negativo que ocurre cuando los gastos exceden los ingresos (página 716)

deflación *s.* disminución en los precios de bienes y servicios (página 513)

democracia jacksoniana *s.* movimiento político que honraba al hombre común y defendía la voluntad del pueblo; su nombre deriva de Andrew Jackson (página 253)

deportar *v.* expulsar por la fuerza del país, o presionar para que esto se haga (página 691)

depresión *s.* deterioro económico severo y a largo plazo, caracterizado por una serie de fracasos empresariales, reducción de la producción industrial y elevado desempleo (página 152)

derechos civiles *s.* derechos individuales protegidos por la ley contra el abuso gubernamental (página 610)

desagravio *s.* dinero pagado para compensar por daños hechos (página 575)

desegregación *s.* proceso mediante el cual se pone fin a una política que obliga a la separación de grupos de personas en espacios públicos (página 907)

deshumanizar *v.* tratar a las personas como si no fueran seres humanos (página 905)

desigualdad económica *s.* fenómeno económico en el que existe una gran brecha entre lo que ganan los ciudadanos más pobres y los más ricos de una nación (página 1075)

desintegración *s.* resistencia por parte de alternativas nacionalistas, tribales y separatistas a la globalización (página 1111)

desmotadora de algodón *s.* máquina que separa las fibras de algodón de sus semillas y vainas (página 222)

desmovilización *s.* liberación de soldados del servicio militar (página 791)

desobediencia civil *s.* desobediencia no violenta de las leyes como forma de protesta (página 282)

desplegar *v.* el envío de tropas en una operación militar (página 131)

desregulación *s.* acto de derogar a gran escala algunas leyes, generalmente relacionadas con una industria en particular (página 1075)

destino manifiesto *s.* creencia de que era el destino de los estadounidenses colonizar toda la tierra entre las costas atlántica y pacífica (página 314)

GLOSARIO

détente *s.* distención y mejoramiento de relaciones entre dos países (página 1045)

Día-D *s.* 6 de junio de 1944, día en el que los Aliados invadieron el norte de Francia durante la Segunda Guerra Mundial, desembarcando en las playas de Normandía (página 804)

diáspora africana *s.* el traslado de africanos de su lugar natal a las Américas (página 49)

difusión cultural *s.* la propagación de las tradiciones y maneras de vivir de un lugar a otro (página 49)

diplomacia moral *s.* concepto de que los Estados Unidos debería reducir drásticamente su intervención en los asuntos de otros países (página 604)

discriminación salarial *s.* el acto de recibir un sueldo más bajo por el mismo trabajo debido al género, la raza o el origen étnico (página 790)

discriminación sexual *s.* preferencia por un género sobre otro (página 1022)

disidente *s.* persona que está en desacuerdo con la mayoría de una posición o creencia (página 56)

dislocación de empleo *s.* movimiento de los trabajos a otros lugares (página 1110)

dividendo *s.* dinero pagado con regularidad a los accionistas de una compañía y que proviene de los ingresos y reservas de la misma compañía (página 183)

doble soberanía *s.* sistema en el cual los gobiernos de los estados tienen ciertos poderes que el gobierno federal no puede desautorizar (página 158)

doctrina de anulación *s.* doctrina que decía que un estado podía anular o rechazar una ley federal si creía que era inconstitucional, apoyada por un político sureño antes de la Guerra Civil (página 258)

domesticación *s.* práctica de criar animales y cultivar plantas para el beneficio humano (página 4)

domesticar *v.* criar animales y cultivar plantas para el beneficio humano (página 15)

Dust Bowl *s.* áreas de Kansas, Colorado, Oklahoma, Texas y Nuevo México que, durante la década de 1930, sufrieron devastación ecológica y se convirtieron en un desierto árido (página 695)

E

ecologismo *s.* gestión y protección de los recursos naturales (página 562)

economía de la oferta *s.* teoría financiera en la que las tasas de impuestos se reducen para las empresas y los inversionistas con la esperanza de impulsar la producción y el comercio en el país (página 1074)

economía *laissez-faire* *s.* política que exige menos participación del gobierno en los asuntos económicos, para que las empresas escojan cómo operar, con poca o ninguna supervisión (página 513)

economía salarial *s.* economía en la que una persona recibe un pago regular por su trabajo (página 447)

efecto invernadero *s.* calentamiento de la superficie de la Tierra que ocurre cuando las emisiones de gases de efecto invernadero atrapan el calor del Sol (página 1136)

Eje Roma-Berlín *s.* acuerdo entre Alemania e Italia firmado en 1936 (página 755)

ejecución hipotecaria *s.* acción que realiza un banco para tomar posesión de una propiedad porque el comprador ya no puede hacer los pagos de la hipoteca (página 156)

Ejército del Bono *s.* grupo de miles de veteranos de guerra, decididos a cobrar los bonos en efectivo que les habían sido prometidos, que acudieron a Washington, D.C., durante el verano de 1932 para escuchar el debate del Congreso sobre la propuesta de bonificación (página 701)

el Sangriento Kansas *s.* nombre dado en 1856 al Territorio de Kansas debido al gran número de enfrentamientos entre tropas antiesclavistas y esclavistas (página 371)

elección primaria directa *s.* elección preliminar en la cual los votantes eligen a los candidatos de su partido que luego se postularán a elecciones para cargos públicos (página 561)

electorado *s.* grupo de ciudadanos que ha elegido o tiene derecho a elegir un representante para el gobierno (página 663)

electrificación rural *s.* programa gubernamental que trajo electricidad a las comunidades rurales (página 833)

emancipación *s.* fin de la esclavitud (página 288)

embalse *s.* gran cuerpo de agua que puede ser aprovechada (página 474)

embarcaciones de desembarco anfibio *s.* botes o barcazas usadas para transportar soldados y equipamiento militar desde el mar a la costa durante ataques militares (página 804)

embargo *s.* prohibición de comerciar con determinados países (página 198)

empoderamiento *s.* concesión de derechos de ciudadanía, especialmente del derecho al voto (página 555)

emprendedor *s.* persona que inicia, administra y es responsable de un negocio (página 335)

empresario *s.* agente que tenía un contrato con el gobierno mexicano para reclutar Americanos y poblar los territorios de Nueva España, antes de que fueran parte de los EE.UU. (página 321)

encomienda *s.* sistema de España en sus colonias en América, en el cual colonos ricos recibían terrenos y se les permitía esclavizar a las personas que allí vivían (página 47)

encubrimiento *s.* intento de esconder la verdad del público (página 1054)

energía nuclear *s.* energía que se crea dividiendo o fusionando los núcleos de átomos (página 865)

era glacial *s.* período de tiempo en la historia durante el cual enormes capas de hielo cubrieron gran parte de la Tierra (página 1)

Era Progresista *s.* período de 1890 a 1920 en el que los reformadores trataron de corregir muchas desigualdades e injusticias sociales, económicas y políticas en los Estados Unidos (página 552)

escasez planificada *s.* teoría económica de que bajar la oferta de un producto aumentará su demanda y por lo tanto su precio (página 718)

esclavitud como propiedad personal *s.* sistema según el cual las personas esclavizadas no tienen ningún derecho humano y se clasifican como bienes (página 30)

esclavos de contrabando *s.* esclavos afroamericanos del Sur que durante la Guerra Civil eran capturados por tropas de la Unión y tratados como propiedad enemiga (página 404)

escuela común *s.* escuela colonial (página 74)

esfera de influencia *s.* afirmación de un país al control exclusivo de una zona o territorio extranjero (página 574)

esmog *s.* combinación nociva de niebla y humo de fábricas (página 859)

especulación *s.* asumir un riesgo empresarial, como comprar acciones con reserva, sin garantía de que aumenten en valor (página 686)

especulación *s.* aumento en los precios de los artículos escasos y de gran demanda con la intención de ganar más dinero (página 137)

especulador *s.* alguien que invierte en propiedades y acciones para obtener ganancias (página 155)

espionaje *s.* la actividad de espiar (página 139)

estado benefactor *s.* sistema en el que el gobierno proporciona los servicios de salud y beneficios a sus ciudadanos (página 742)

estado bisagra *s.* estado en el que puede triunfar cualquier partido político (página 1144)

Estado de derecho (rule of law) *s.* concepto según el cual las personas e instituciones deben acatar las regulaciones establecidas por el gobierno (página 120)

estado fronterizo *s.* estado que durante la Guerra Civil limitaba tanto con los estados de la Unión como con los estados Confederados, específicamente Maryland, Kentucky, Delaware, Missouri y Virginia Occidental (página 391)

estado paria *s.* país percibido como violador del derecho internacional y que amenaza la paz mundial (página 1121)

estalactita *s.* columna de minerales que cuelga del techo de una cueva (página 648)

estalagmita *s.* columna de minerales que se forma hacia arriba desde el suelo de una cueva (página 648)

estancamiento económico *s.* período de poco o ningún crecimiento económico (página 1056)

estanflación *s.* condición económica con estancamiento, o crecimiento económico lento, acompañado de inflación, o aumento de los precios (página 1056)

estático *adj.* tener la cualidad que no moverse ni cambiar (página 1077)

estepa *s.* planicie amplia y cubierta de hierbas (página 24)

estímulo económico *s.* medida destinada a promover y permitir la recuperación y el crecimiento financieros (página 1129)

estuario *s.* lugar donde un río se junta en su desembocadura con el agua salada del mar (página 194)

eugenesia *s.* creencia de que algunas razas son superiores a otras y que la reproducción humana debe ser controlada para que aumenten las poblaciones de razas superiores (página 644)

evangelista *s.* predicador entusiasta que urge a los creyentes a aceptar a Jesús como su salvador (página 277)

excavaciones *s.* modificaciones a la tierra hechas por la mano del hombre (página 122)

exceso de regulación *s.* conjunto de reglas excesivas (página 1049)

exclusa *s.* espacio cerrado de agua que se usa para subir o bajar embarcaciones (página 227)

exención *s.* librar de obligaciones a alguien (página 408)

exoduster *s.* afroamericano que emigró del Sur a las Grandes Llanuras después de que la Reconstrucción había fracasado (página 470)

expansión urbana *s.* desarrollo de proyectos de vivienda en áreas cada vez más suburbanas y rurales (página 869)

expansionismo *s.* política o práctica de ampliar el territorio de un país (página 572)

explosión de natalidad *s.* aumento significativo en la tasa de natalidad (página 862)

explotar *v.* aprovecharse de personas o recursos, por lo general con fines de lucro (página 221)

extranjero enemigo *adj.* persona cuya lealtad a la nación en la que vive es poco fiable (página 794)

F

factor de expulsión o atracción *s.* una razón por la cual las personas emigran; los factores de "expulsión" hace que se vayan; los factores de "atracción" hace que vengan de un lugar (página 518)

fascismo *s.* movimiento político basado en el nacionalismo extremo, el militarismo y el racismo, que promueve la superioridad de un pueblo en particular sobre todos los demás (página 699)

federalismo *s.* apoyo al gobierno en el cual el poder es compartido entre el gobierno nacional central y los estados o provincias (página 158)

federalista *s.* persona que apoyaba la Constitución de EE. UU. de 1787 según se redactó durante el proceso de ratificación (página 162)

feminismo *s.* principio de que las mujeres son iguales a los hombres social y políticamente (página 1021)

feriado bancario *s.* día o período de tiempo en el que los bancos están cerrados por orden del gobierno (página 716)

ferrocarril transcontinental *s.* ferrocarril que opera a lo largo de un continente (página 336)

feudalismo *s.* sistema político y social en el que un vasallo recibe protección de un señor feudal a cambio de prestarle obediencia y servicio (página 20)

financista *s.* persona que presta o maneja dinero para un negocio u emprendimiento (página 137)

fiscal general *s.* miembro del Gabinete del presidente, cuyo papel principal es representar a los EE. UU. ante la Corte Suprema (página 179)

flanquear *s.* movimiento de tropas hacia un lado de la línea enemiga para tomar ventaja (página 411)

flapper *s.* mujer joven en la década de 1920 que adoptó un estilo más libre de vestir y el uso de cosméticos (página 660)

fondo de pensiones *s.* reserva de dinero usada para pagar a una persona un pequeño ingreso establecido después de jubilarse (página 722)

fonógrafo *s.* máquina que reproduce sonidos de un disco (página 509)

forrajear *v.* buscar plantas para comer (página 480)

forty-niner **(buscador de oro)** *s.* uno de los miles de futuros mineros que viajaron a California a buscar oro en 1849 (página 335)

Framers **(autores de la Constitución)** *s.* término histórico para los delegados en la Convención Constitucional de 1787, quienes ayudaron a crear y redactar la Constitución de los Estados Unidos (página 157)

fraude electoral *s.* manipulación ilegal de boletas para ganar una elección (página 929)

frente *s.* línea de batalla entre dos ejércitos (página 401)

Frostbelt *s.* región del centro-norte y noreste de los Estados Unidos, que tiene inviernos fríos (página 859)

fuerza anfibia *s.* unidad militar compuesta por aviones y barcos que atacan simultáneamente (página 331)

Fuerzas Expedicionarias Estadounidenses (AEF) *s.* cuerpo de soldados estadounidenses enviados a luchar en Europa durante la Primera Guerra Mundial (página 608)

fundamentalismo *s.* movimiento que promulgó la idea de que cada palabra de la Biblia debía ser tomada literalmente (página 647)

fusión *s.* acto de incorporar dos o más negocios en uno (página 563)

G

G.I. Bill *s.* programa del gobierno iniciado en 1944 que ayudó a los veteranos que regresaban de la Segunda Guerra Mundial a comprar casas y asistir a la universidad (página 833)

Gabinete *s.* los jefes de los departamentos que asisten al presidente de los EE. UU. (página 178)

gas de efecto invernadero *s.* gas como el dióxido de carbono o metano (página 1136)

gastar públicamente déficit *v.* gastar más dinero del que el gobierno recibe por impuestos (página 742)

genocidio *s.* asesinato intencional de un gran número de personas pertenecientes a determinado grupo racial, cultural o político (página 483)

Gestapo *s.* policía secreta nazi (página 754)

glasnost *s.* política gubernamental de comunicación abierta en la ex Unión Soviética (página 1084)

globalización *s.* flujo más rápido y libre de personas, recursos, bienes e ideas a lo largo de las fronteras entre países (página 1110)

gobierno en exilio *s.* gobierno que ha sido depuesto e intenta gobernar desde otro país (página 836)

gobierno por comisión *s.* forma de gobierno citadino en la que los votantes eligen un pequeño número de funcionarios llamados comisionados, cada uno de los cuales dirige un departamento de la ciudad (página 560)

golpe de estadp0 *s.* derrocamiento ilegal del gobierno (página 971)

Gran Depresión *s.* una recesión económica mundial en la década de 1930, marcada por la pobreza y el alto desempleo (página 687)

Gran Despertar *s.* serie de avivamientos religiosos protestantes que se extendieron por las colonias en Norteamérica (página 90)

Gran Migración *s.* movimiento masivo de afroamericanos que se fueron del Sur para las ciudades del norte, comenzando en 1910 (página 619)

gravamen *s.* reclamación legal sobre los bienes e ingresos de una persona si no se pagan deudas (página 443)

grupo de comercio *s.* grupo formado para comprar y vender grandes cantidades de acciones

grupo de comercio *s.* grupos que se forman para manipular la compra y venta de acciones (página 688)

guerra de desgaste *s.* una estrategia militar en la que un ejército lleva a otro abajo conduciendo muchas pequeñas batallas durante un largo período de tiempo (página 975)

guerra de guerrillas *s.* guerra en la que pequeños grupos móviles de fuerzas anómalas usan tácticas de ataque y huida para luchar contra fuerzas militares convencionales (página 117)

guerra de trincheras *s.* tipo de guerra en la que se excavan largas y profundas zanjas en el suelo para proteger a los soldados (página 407)

guerra defensiva *s.* guerra que se libra en terreno conocido para defender la tierra propia de un ataque externo (página 391)

guerra ofensiva *s.* guerra que se libra principalmente en terreno enemigo (página 391)

guerra sin cuartel *s.* guerra en la cual se ignoran todos los convenios bélicos y se usan todos los recursos para vencer al enemigo (página 422)

guerra subsidiaria *s.* conjunto de batallas provocadas por una nación que luego no participa en la lucha (página 838)

H

hacienda *s.* plantación grande en una colonia española (página 47)

Halcón de Guerra *s.* persona partidaria de la guerra; estadounidense que estaba a favor de la guerra contra Gran Bretaña en 1812 (página 199)

halcón *s.* persona que apoya la guerra (página 980)

helero *s.* depósito de una mezcla de sedimentos que puede incluir cieno, arcilla, arena, rocas y otros materiales que dejan los glaciares en retroceso (página 238)

hereje *s.* persona que tiene creencias diferentes a las enseñanzas de la Iglesia Católica (página 54)

hesianos *s.* soldados alemanes contratados por los británicos para luchar durante la Guerra de Independencia (página 123)

hipotecas de alto riesgo *s.* préstamos hipotecarios otorgados a compradores que tenían un historial de crédito pobre (página 1126)

hito legislativo *s.* una legislación importante e histórica (página 957)

GLOSARIO

Holocausto *s.* la matanza masiva por parte de los nazis de seis millones de judíos y otros durante la Segunda Guerra Mundial (página 817)

hombre de paja *s.* funcionario electo que está por finalizar su mandado y será reemplazado por un sucesor (página 715)

hombres de montaña *s.* cazadores y comerciantes de pieles conocidos como tramperos que contribuyeron con la exploración del Oeste (página 314)

homogeneidad *s.* estado de similitud o igualdad (página 867)

Hooverville *s.* un grupo de viviendas improvisadas para dar albergue a gente sin techo, hechas con restos de cartón, placas metálicas u otros materiales baratos, que se construyeron durante la Gran Depresión y fueron bautizadas con el nombre del presidente Herbert Hoover (página 698)

huelga de brazos caídos *s.* huelga en la que los trabajadores no se van del lugar trabajo, sino que permanecen ahí sin realizar labor alguna (página 731)

humanismo *s.* movimiento basado en la importancia del individuo (página 21)

I

igualdad matrimonial *s.* derecho legal de las personas homosexuales a casarse con sus parejas y tener los mismos privilegios que disfrutan las parejas heterosexuales casadas (página 1134)

igualitarismo *s.* creencia de que todas las personas son iguales, especialmente en sus interese políticos, económicos y sociales (página 152)

Ilustración *s.* movimiento intelectual caracterizado por el uso de la razón para revisar creencias aceptadas anteriormente (página 88)

imperialismo *s.* política o práctica de ejercer control sobre naciones o territorios más débiles (página 572)

impuesto electoral *s.* impuesto cobrado en el momento de registrarse para votar (página 451)

impuesto sobre la renta *s.* impuesto que se basa en la cantidad de dinero que gana una persona (página 571)

impuesto sobre ventas *s.* impuesto que grava un artículo en particular (página 182)

inauguración *s.* ceremonia de juramento que enmarca el comienzo de un periodo presidencial (página 178)

indemnización laboral *s.* seguro que cubre a los empleados lesionados en el trabajo y que ofrece asistencia médica y compensación por la falta de ingresos (página 513)

índice bursátil Dow Jones *s.* índice de las acciones de empresas líderes, que tiene seguimiento diario y es utilizado como medida de las tendencias generales del mercado bursátil (página 686)

índice de pobreza *s.* porcentaje de la población que vive en la pobreza (página 878)

indiferencia saludable *s.* política del gobierno británico que evitaba que sus leyes en las colonias se cumplieran estrictamente (página 93)

indulgencia *s.* perdón de los pecados que vendían los oficiales papales (página 22)

industria aeroespacial *s.* negocio comercial relacionado a la construcción de aviones, naves espaciales y otros vehículos que vuelan (página 834)

infamia *s.* acción de maldad o vileza extrema (página 784)

infantería *s.* tropas de soldados a pie (página 395)

inflación *s.* disminución en el valor de una moneda que causa el aumento en el precio de bienes y servicios (página 137)

influenza *s.* enfermedad aguda y altamente contagiosa comúnmente llamada "gripe" (página 621)

infraestructura *s.* sistemas físicos básicos de una sociedad, incluyendo carreteras, puentes, alcantarillas y electricidad (página 17)

iniciativa *s.* procedimiento mediante el cual los ciudadanos pueden proponer nuevas leyes para ser votadas por el público o por los legisladores (página 561)

injuria *s.* delito de hacer declaraciones negativas verbales o escritas sobre alguien sin evidencia (página 93)

insurgente *s.* rebelde o revolucionario (página 970)

insurrección *s.* rebelión violenta contra un gobierno o una autoridad política (página 330)

integración horizontal *s.* compra por parte de una compañía de otras que ofrecen los mismos bienes y servicios para reducir el número de competidores y lograr el dominio de una industria (página 503)

integración *s.* proceso mediante el cual se juntan recursos económicos (página 1111)

integración vertical *s.* procedimiento en el que una empresa toma el control de todas las etapas de producción (página 503)

integrado *adj.* que permite la libre asociación de personas de diferentes razas o grupos étnicos (página 435)

intensificación *s.* aumento en la intensidad durante una guerra (página 972)

intercambio colombino *s.* intercambio de plantas, animales, microbios, personas e ideas entre Europa y las Américas después del primer viaje de Colón al Hemisferio Occidental (página 31)

interdicto *s.* orden judicial que exige o prohíbe ciertas acciones (página 700)

intermediario *s.* alguien que ayuda a dos partes en disputa a llegar a un acuerdo (página 187)

internar *v.* confinar a una prisión o campo por razones militares o políticas durante la guerra (página 794)

Internet *s.* red mundial de ordenadores (página 1081)

interpretación estricta *s.* un entendimiento de la Constitución en el cual la Constitución debe ser seguida estrictamente como fue redactada (página 182)

interpretación flexible *s.* un entendimiento de la Constitución que le da al Congreso y al presidente amplios poderes (página 182)

intervención telefónica *s.* la colocación de un dispositivo en un teléfono para poder escuchar en secreto las conversaciones ajenas (página 1054)

intimidación del votante *s.* acciones a menudo violentas con la intención de atemorizar a los votantes; con frecuencia dirigidas a afroamericanos, inmigrantes o a personas con quienes un grupo de poder no está de acuerdo (página 445)

intransigente *s.* persona que generalmente pertenece a un grupo político o de intereses especiales y que apoya de manera estricta y dura un conjunto de ideas o políticas (página 1085)

ironclad **(barco blindado)** *s.* barco revestido con planchas de hierro para protegerlo del fuego de los cañones (página 399)

irregular *s.* soldado que combate intermitentemente en un ej (página 142)

istmo *s.* estrecha franja de tierra que conecta dos áreas de tierra más grandes (página 583)

J

jazz *s.* estilo de música que se originó entre los músicos afroamericanos y que contiene ritmos vivos, sonidos de una variedad de instrumentos y mucha improvisación (página 654)

jueces de medianoche *s.* grupo de jueces nombrados por el presidente John Adams una noche antes de terminar su mandato de gobierno (página 189)

juicio político *s.* cargos formales presentados contra un funcionario público por mala conducta en el cargo (página 160)

Junta Militar de Industrias (WIB) *s.* consejo que supervisó la industria de manufactura dentro de los Estados Unidos durante la Primera Guerra Mundial (página 608)

juramento de lealtad *s.* declaración jurada que confirma que una persona no pertenece y nunca ha pertenecido a determinadas organizaciones, por ejemplo, aquellas identificadas como comunistas (página 843)

justicia social *s.* régimen caracterizado por una justa distribución de las oportunidades y los privilegios, incluyendo la igualdad racial (página 448)

K

kamikaze *s.* miembro de un grupo de pilotos japoneses que estrellaban su avión, cargado con explosivos, en los barcos estadounidenses (página 808)

kitchen cabinet *s.* grupo de asesores no oficiales de Andrew Jackson (página 255)

L

la Reforma *s.* movimiento religioso protestante basado en la necesidad de reformar la cristiandad en Europa Oriental en el siglo XVI (página 23)

laboratorio de ideas *s.* grupo de expertos que realizan investigaciones y discuten temas para elaborar soluciones potenciales a problemas sociales y económicos (página 1069)

Larga Marcha *s.* viaje de 6.000 millas realizado por los comunistas chinos para trasladar la base revolucionaria comunista del sureste al centro de China (página 765)

leal a Gran Bretaña *s.* colono que apoyaba a Gran Bretaña en la Guerra de Independencia (página 111)

legislatura bicameral *s.* órgano del gobierno conformado por dos cámaras separadas que tiene la facultad de hacer leyes (ej. el Senado y la Cámara de Representantes) (página 158)

leva *s.* reclutamiento forzoso en las fuerzas militares (página 186)

Ley de Desalojo de los Indígenas *s.* ley que terminó con una ley anterior de los EE. UU. que respetaba los derechos de los indígenas norteamericanos a permanecer en sus tierras (página 260)

ley marcial *s.* ley que se impone a un país ocupado por parte de las fuerzas al mando (página 117)

ley mordaza *s.* serie de medidas adoptadas por el Congreso entre 1830 y 1840 para evitar la discusión y consideración de políticas antiesclavistas; cualquier medida que prohíbe discusión legal o pública sobre un tema específico (página 291)

Leyes de Jim Crow *s.* leyes establecidas después de la Reconstrucción que imponían la segregación racial a lo largo de los estados sureños (página 535)

liberto *s.* condición del esclavo liberado (página 404)

Liga antidifamación (ADL) *s.* organización judía internacional de servicio fundada para combatir el antisemitismo, la intolerancia religiosa y racial, y todas las formas de discriminación organizada basadas en estereotipos (página 643)

Liga estadounidense antiimperialista *s.* organización formada en 1898 para oponerse a la anexión de las Filipinas por los Estados Unidos (página 581)

linchar *v.* ejecución ilegal por parte de una turba (página 409)

línea de ensamblaje *s.* sistema en el cual cada trabajador se coloca en determinado lugar, y el proceso de producción pasa de una función a otra, en línea recta, hasta que un producto se ensambla por completo (página 651)

M

macartismo *s.* la práctica de acusar a la gente de ser traidores a su país sin ofrecer pruebas (página 845)

mafia *s.* grupo de delincuentes que controlan actividades criminales organizadas (página 568)

magnates ladrones *s.* líderes de la industria ferroviaria, como Cornelius Vanderbilt y Jay Gould, que se hicieron famosos por sus métodos despiadados en contra de sus competidores (página 503)

magnicidio *v.* el asesinato de una persona muy importante por su cargo o poder (página 427)

malestar *s.* sensación general de enfermedad (página 1059)

mandato *s.* autoridad para llevar a cabo alguna acción, otorgado a un representante por los votantes (página 269)

manejo científico *s.* gestión basada en estudios experimentales para identificar la forma más eficiente de ejecutar tareas en una fábrica u otro lugar de trabajo (página 570)

manifiesto *s.* declaración de intenciones por escrito (página 1012)

maquiladora *s.* planta de manufactura ubicada en una zona de exportación (página 1110)

maquinaria política *s.* organización política en la que una persona o un grupo pequeño es capaz de mantener el control sobre una ciudad o un estado (página 532)

margen *s.* diferencia que representa el porcentaje por el cual se gana o se pierde algo, como en una elección (página 686)

marítimo *adj.* relativo al mar (página 72)

Masacre de Boston *s.* incidente en 1779, en el cual soldados británicos dispararon contra personas locales que los estaban insultando (página 114)

maternidad republicana *s.* la idea de que las mujeres debían criar a los hijos para ser buenos ciudadanos que participaran activamente en el gobierno (página 180)

mayoría silenciosa *s.* término usado por Richard Nixon a finales de los años sesenta para describir a un gran grupo de votantes moderados que no expresaban públicamente sus opiniones políticas (página 1041)

Medicaid *s.* programa del gobierno de los Estados unidos iniciado en 1965 para ofrecer cobertura médica a la gente pobre (página 954)

Medicare *s.* programa del gobierno de los Estados Unidos iniciado en 1965 para ofrecer cobertura médica a personas de edad avanzada (página 954)

medios de comunicación de masas *s.* formas de comunicación como la radio, el cine y las grabaciones musicales que tienen el potencial de alcanzar grandes audiencias (página 696)

medios de comunicación modernos *s.* productos y servicios digitales que proporcionan contenido a través de internet (página 1138)

mercado masivo *s.* enorme número de consumidores a quienes los fabricantes venden mercancías producidas en cantidades industriales (página 651)

mercantilismo *s.* política económica que le da a un país la propiedad exclusiva del comercio en sus colonias (página 23)

mercenario *s.* soldado al que se le paga para luchar por un país que no es el suyo (página 123)

mestizaje *s.* matrimonio entre personas de diferentes razas (página 961)

militarismo *s.* creencia de que un gobierno debe desarrollar un ejército fuerte y estar preparado para usarlo para alcanzar sus objetivos (página 600)

minería aluvial *s.* técnicas mineras que incluyen el uso de herramientas ligeras para encontrar oro en ríos y arroyos (página 472)

minería hidráulica *s.* proceso de descubrimiento de minerales preciosos mediante el uso de agua a presión para eliminar el suelo (página 472)

minería subterránea *s.* técnica minera en la que se abre un túnel vertical en una montaña para que los mineros bajen hacia la mina (página 472)

minuteman *s.* miliciano colonial listo para entrar en combate al instante (página 117)

misil antibalístico (ABM) *s.* misil diseñado para destruir un misil portador de bomba antes de que este alcance su objetivo (página 1045)

misil balístico *s.* arma nuclear propulsada por un cohete y guiada por un sistema GPS (página 936)

misoginia *s.* aversión, desprecio u odio hacia las mujeres; prejuicio contra las mujeres (página 1023)

modernismo *s.* estilo artístico y literario moderno, con tono duro y realista y una tendencia a rechazar o evitar las prácticas artísticas y literarias del pasado (página 658)

módulo *s.* segmento de una nave espacial que puede funcionar de manera independiente (página 1028)

moneda *s.* dinero en circulación para la compra de bienes y servicios (página 156)

monedas *s.* cambio; relacionado a menudo con monedas de plata y oro (página 156)

monocultivo *s.* la práctica de cultivo único de una especie vegetal (página 509)

monopolio *s.* control total de una industria o el mercado de un servicio o producto (página 226)

morfina *s.* potente analgésico (página 429)

mortero *s.* cañón de corto alcance cuya carga se inserta por la boca (página 975)

Motín del Té *s.* incidente en 1773, en el cual los Hijos de la Libertad subieron a bordo de barcos británicos y botaron al mar los cargamentos de té en protesta por los impuestos británicos a los colonos (página 114)

movilización militar *s.* acto de reunir y organizar fuerzas militares (página 741)

movilizar *v.* organizar y preparar tropas para la guerra (página 125)

movimiento de escuelas comunes *s.* movimiento de reforma a la educación en la década de 1830 para promover escuelas públicas gratuitas financiadas por la recolección de impuestos a la propiedad y manejadas por los gobiernos locales (página 278)

movimiento de retorno a África *s.* movimiento encabezado por Marcus Garvey, quien alentó a los afroamericanos a abandonar los Estados Unidos y regresar a África (página 665)

movimiento por la moderación *s.* movimiento social y político del siglo XIX y principios del siglo XX que animaba a las personas a limitar su consumo de alcohol o abstenerse del alcohol por completo (página 277)

muckrakers *s.* periodistas de investigación de principios del siglo XX que revelaron las conductas indebidas de organizaciones o personas poderosas (página 505)

multinacional *s.* empresa que tiene oficinas y fábricas en varios países (página 1138)

N

nación-estado *s.* país con un gobierno independiente cuyos habitantes comparten cultura, lenguaje y orgullo nacional; unidad política con una cultura e identidad en común (página 23)

nacionalismo *s.* fuerte sentido de lealtad al país al que uno pertenece y la creencia en la superioridad del mismo los demás países (página 145)

nacionalsocialismo *s.* doctrina política del partido nazi en Alemania, que promovió la superioridad de Alemania y del pueblo alemán, rechazó el comunismo y llevó el antisemitismo (el odio al del pueblo judío) a niveles extremos (página 724)

napalm *s.* substancia espesa, inflamable y gelatinosa usada en bombas para causar y propagar incendios (página 786)

nativista *s.* persona que se opone a la inmigración y quiere proteger los intereses de la población nativa (página 369)

naturalización *s.* proceso mediante el cual una persona que no nació en los Estados Unidos se convierte en ciudadana (página R34)

GLOSARIO

neoconservador *s.* persona que apoya firmemente una economía de libre mercado y cree que los Estados Unidos debe promover activamente sus ideales en todo el mundo (página 1116)

New Deal *s.* leyes, organismos y programas iniciados por el presidente Franklin Roosevelt y su administración en respuesta a la Gran Depresión de la década de 1930 (página 717)

nómada *adj.* persona que recorre una extensión de tierra sin un patrón fijo de movimiento, algunas veces siguiendo las manadas de animales (página 16)

novela de diez centavos *s.* publicación de literatura popular que se vendía por 10 centavos a finales del siglo XVIII y principios del XIX (página 489)

Nueva Frontera *s.* estrategia política de los Estados Unidos en 1960, en la que el presidente Kennedy enfatizó la resolución creativa de problemas, la diplomacia extranjera y los avances tecnológicos para superar los problemas del país (página 932)

Nuevo Federalismo *s.* plan del presidente Richard Nixon para transferir el control de algunos programas federales a los estados (página 1042)

nulificar *s.* anular o negar algo, especialmente en términos legales; en la historia de EE. UU. se entiende como el intento del gobierno estatal de vetar una ley federal que considera inconstitucional (página 187)

O

objetor de conciencia *s.* persona que se niega a luchar en una guerra por razones religiosas (página 610)

obstrucción *s.* estrategia política en la que un pequeño grupo de legisladores se turnan para hablar y evitar así que finalice un debate o que un proyecto de ley sea sometido a votación (página 949)

Oficina de Libertos *s.* Oficina para Refugiados, Hombres Libres y Tierras Abandonadas, creada por el Congreso en 1865 para brindar ayuda a los afroamericanos que habían sido esclavos, así como a los sureños blancos más pobres (página 446)

Oficina de Protección al Menor *s.* agencia gubernamental estadounidense creada en 1912 para mejorar la vida de los niños y sus familias (página 554)

oleada *s.* aumento repentino (página 1123)

operación anfibia *s.* ataque que utiliza el apoyo naval para proteger a las fuerzas militares que invaden por tierra y por aire (página 801)

operación encubierta *s.* actividad realizada secretamente para influir en la situación política, económica o militar en otro país (página 860)

orden de asistencia *s.* documento legal que daba a las autoridades el derecho de entrar y registrar una casa o negocio (página 112)

orden ejecutiva *s.* directiva emitida por un presidente que tiene fuerza de ley (página 795)

ordenanza *s.* mandato, decreto o ley oficial (página 154)

originalismo *s.* sistema de creencias utilizado para interpretar la constitución de los Estados Unidos desde el punto de vista de la intención del documento cuando fue escrito originalmente (página 1077)

P

pacifismo *s.* creencia de que la guerra es moralmente incorrecta (página 60)

Pacto de Briand-Kellogg *s.* acuerdo multinacional de 1928 en el que los países firmantes aceptaron rechazar la guerra (página 685)

pagaré *s.* acuerdo por escrito que especifica una fecha de pago (página 393)

país de tercer mundo *s.* durante la Guerra Fría, cualquier país que no estaba alineado ni con los Estados Unidos ni con la Unión Soviética (página 969)

paloma *s.* persona que se opone a la guerra (página 980)

pan-africanismo *s.* movimiento de principios del siglo XX que procuró unificar a la gente de ascendencia africana (página 665)

pandemia *s.* el brote repentino de una enfermedad que se extiende sobre una amplia área geográfica (página 621)

Pánico de 1837 *s.* episodio de temor por una caída de la economía, que causó el comienzo de una recesión económica en los EE. UU. hasta 1840 (página 270)

Pánico de 1873 *s.* crisis económica desencadenada por la quiebra de algunos bancos y empresas ferroviarias (página 453)

panzer *s.* tanque alemán fuertemente blindado y que poseía gran potencia de fuego, utilizado durante la Segunda Guerra Mundial (página 799)

paralelo 49 *s.* línea de latitud establecida a los 49 grados de latitud norte; frontera entre los EE. UU. y Canadá demarcada por los británicos en 1888 (página 236)

Parlamento *s.* cámara legislativa de Inglaterra, y después de Gran Bretaña (página 93)

parte intercambiable *s.* parte de un mecanismo que puede ser sustituida por otra (página 219)

Partido de los Whigs *s.* partido político que se opuso a las políticas de Andrew Jackson, de quien consideraban que tenía demasiado poder (página 269)

Partido Nazi *s.* partido político dirigido por Adolfo Hitler y que mediante la fuerza ejerció control total sobre Alemania de 1933 a 1945 (página 724)

pasaje medio *s.* el largo viaje a través del océano Atlántico durante el cual los africanos esclavizados eran llevados a las Américas; segunda etapa de la ruta del comercio triangular (página 49)

Pasajeros de la libertad *s.* grupos interraciales que viajaban en autobuses por el Sur, haciendo caso omiso a las leyes de segregación cuando usaban los baños públicos y los cafés, para así asegurar que las decisiones judiciales federales que habían establecido como ilegal la segregación en lugares de atención públicos para viajeros fuesen cumplidas por los funcionarios blancos (página 917)

paso de montaña *s.* ruta para atravesar una montaña que evita escalar los picos altos (página 337)

patente *s.* licencia que otorga a un inventor derechos exclusivos para usar, vender o

hacer una invención durante un número específico de años (página 226)

patriota *s.* colono que apoyaba el derecho de las colonias en Norteamérica a gobernarse a sí mismas (página 111)

patrón oro *s.* sistema monetario en el que la moneda de una nación está respaldada por oro (página 477)

penicilina *s.* antibiótico hecho de moho y utilizado para tratar infecciones y enfermedades (página 786)

penitenciaría *s.* prisión federal o estatal cuyo objetivo es la rehabilitación de los criminales (página 278)

perestroika *s.* política gubernamental de reforma en la antigua Unión Soviética (página 1084)

período glacial *s.* período de tiempo en la historia durante el cual enormes capas de hielo cubrieron gran parte de la Tierra (página 1)

perjurio *s.* acto de mentir bajo juramento (página 1115)

pesos y contrapesos *s.* sistema establecido en la Constitución de EE. UU. que da a cada una de las ramas del gobierno el poder para controlar a las otras dos (página 160)

piedemonte *s.* área relativamente plana entre los montes Apalaches y la planicie costera (página 78)

piquete *s.* grupo de huelguistas que forman una barrera para evitar que los rompehuelgas entren en un edificio para trabajar en su lugar (página 729)

Plan Anaconda *s.* estrategia militar durante la Guerra Civil, en la cual el Norte planeó un bloqueo alrededor de las costas sureñas para arruinar la economía del Sur y tomar los puertos en el Mississippi; al igual que una enorme serpiente, como la anaconda, estrangula a su presa (página 393)

Plan de Crittenden *s.* propuesta que establecía que el gobierno federal no tuviera poderes para abolir la esclavitud en los estados donde ya existía; reestablecía y extendía el límite del Compromiso de Missouri hasta el océano Pacífico (página 378)

Plan de desbordamiento de la corte *s.* controvertido plan del presidente Franklin Roosevelt para aumentar el número de jueces de la Corte Suprema de nueve a quince, sumando seis jueces que compartían sus valores progresistas (página 730)

Plan Marshall *s.* programa de ayuda económica de los Estados Unidos para restablecer la estabilidad económica en Europa occidental después de la Segunda Guerra Mundial (página 825)

Plan Schlieffen *s.* plan alemán para conquistar rápidamente a Francia entre 1905 y 1906, seguido por un ataque a Rusia (página 602)

planificación económica *s.* administración de la economía por el gobierno federal (página 719)

Pleistoceno *s.* era de la historia de la Tierra en la que vivieron grandes animales y plantas y los glaciares cubrieron la tierra (página 1)

poder ejecutivo *s.* rama del gobierno de EE. UU. presidida por el presidente; responsable de que se cumpla la ley (página 158)

poder judicial *s.* rama del gobierno de EE. UU., que incluye las cortes o tribunales y el sistema legal, presidida por la Corte Suprema; responsable de interpretar las leyes (página 158)

poder legislativo *s.* rama del gobierno de EE. UU. presidida por el Congreso; responsable de hacer las leyes (página 158)

polio *s.* enfermedad infecciosa que a veces causa debilidad muscular o parálisis (página 715)

politburó *s.* principal comité gubernamental que tomó decisiones políticas en el partido comunista; a menudo se refiere al comité de China o la antigua Unión Soviética (página 1084)

Política De Puertas Abiertas *s.* propuesta estadounidense que pretendía establecer la igualdad de acceso a los puertos de los países que comerciaban con china en 1900 (página 574)

política de riesgo calculado *s.* la práctica de llevar un conflicto hasta el borde de la violencia sin caer en una guerra, usualmente una táctica para obtener un resultado favorable (página 860)

política de terminación *s.* política promulgada bajo el presidente Eisenhower que sacó a los indígenas de sus reservas a la vez que el gobierno ponía fin a la limitada soberanía de las tribus y pueblos (página 882)

pontón *s.* flotador cilíndrico portable, que se usaba para construir un puente temporal (página 403)

populismo *s.* creencia de que la gente común debe controlar el gobierno (página 477)

populista *s.* político que dice representar las preocupaciones de la gente común (página 724)

portear *v.* acto de cargar embarcaciones o bienes entre cuerpos de agua o alrededor de obstrucciones en una vía fluvial (página 193)

Potencias del Eje *s.* Alemania, Italia y Japón, que formaron una alianza a comienzos de la Segunda Guerra Mundial (página 755)

potlatch *s.* ceremonia de entrega de obsequios practicada por las tribus indígenas norteamericanas kwakiutl y haida (página 15)

preámbulo *s.* texto corto que se escribe como introducción a una constitución o un estatuto (página 125)

precedente *s.* determinación previa en un caso judicial para establecer una comparación con casos nuevos similares (página 154)

presidio *s.* cárcel o asentamiento militar (página 330)

presión cultural *s.* estrategia política en la que los miembros de una religión influyen en los políticos y las instituciones sociales en un esfuerzo por promover sus creencias (página 1074)

Primeros Cien Días *s.* los primeros 100 días del presidente Franklin Roosevelt en el gobierno, durante los cuales promulgó 15 leyes que formaron la base del New Deal (página 716)

privación *v.* acción de negar a alguien un derecho legal o un privilegio (página 951)

privilegio ejecutivo *s.* principio que sostiene que, para proteger los intereses de la nación, el Presidente puede no

divulgar cierta información al Congreso (página 1054)

privilegio estadounidense *s.* la idea de que los Estados Unidos es superior a otros países debido a su historia e ideología (página 1116)

Procedimiento Bessemer *s.* proceso en el que se utiliza aire forzado para eliminar impurezas del hierro, como el carbono, transformando así el hierro en acero (página 503)

Proclamación de 1763 *s.* ley que establecía que los colonos debían mantenerse al este de una línea dibujada en un mapa, a lo largo de la cima de los montes Apalaches (página 99)

Proclamación de Emancipación *s.* documento de 1863, emitido por Abraham Lincoln, que abolió la esclavitud en los estados gobernados por la Confederación durante la Guerra Civil de los Estados Unidos (página 405)

producción masiva *s.* uso de maquinaria para producir mercancías en grandes cantidades (página 219)

producto básico *s.* un bien de intercambio; mercancía (página 48)

producto nacional bruto (PNB) *s.* total de bienes y servicios producidos por un país, más los ingresos obtenidos por sus ciudadanos (página 687)

Programa Bracero *s.* programa diseñado para importar obreros mexicanos para reemplazar a los trabajadores agrícolas y de transporte estadounidenses que eran reclutados para la Segunda Guerra Mundial (página 788)

progresismo *s.* reforma entre 1890 y 1920 que buscaba hacer más democráticas las políticas estatales y nacionales y hacer más eficiente el gobierno (página 533)

prohibición *s.* el acto de prohibir la producción, distribución y venta de alcohol (página 557)

Prohibición *s.* prohibición constitucional de la venta de bebidas alcohólicas, vigente entre 1920 y 1933 (página 619)

propaganda *s.* información difundida para influenciar las opiniones o promover la ideas de un partido o una organización (página 526)

propietario *s.* dueño de una colonia, que tenía el derecho a manejar y distribuir tierras y a establecer un gobierno (página 62)

protectorado *s.* país que es gobernado en parte por un país más poderoso (página 572)

provisión legal *s.* condición legal que establece una necesidad a futuro (página 145)

Proyecto de ley sobre ajustes distintos *s.* propuesta dentro de un proyecto de ley que podría abarcar temas no relacionados (página 362)

prueba de alfabetización *s.* un examen mediante el cual se mide la capacidad de leer y escribir (página 451)

puente de Beringia *s.* pedazo de tierra entre Alaska y Siberia que estaba por encima del nivel del mar hace 13.000 años y que permitió a los primeros humanos cruzar hacia Norteamérica (página 2)

punto muerto *s.* situación en la que ninguna de las partes en un conflicto puede afirmar la victoria (página 141)

purga *s.* eliminación de algo (página 764)

Q

quinina *s.* sustancia hecha de la corteza de un árbol que es un remedio eficaz contra la malaria (página 31)

R

racionar *v.* control de los suministros a la población, especialmente en tiempos de guerra (página 788)

radical *s.* persona que quiere un cambio extremo o tiene una posición política extrema (página 185)

rancho *s.* terreno cedido por México a los colonos, en forma de grandes fincas, en lo que hoy es California (página 333)

ratificar *v.* aprobar formalmente mediante el voto (página 127)

rearmamento *s.* el esfuerzo de una nación para reaprovisionar su arsenal y reemplazar aquellas que están desfasadas o han sido eliminadas (página 754)

rebelión de los bóxer *s.* levantamiento político de 1900 en el norte de China contra los extranjeros en el país (página 574)

rebelión del Stono *s.* revuelta de esclavos africanos en contra de sus dueños ocurrida en 1793 (página 83)

recesión *s.* desaceleración relativamente breve del crecimiento económico, a menudo parte de un ciclo económico normal (página 359)

reclutamiento *s.* acto de ser ingresado en el ejército (página 407)

reclutamiento *s.* acto de ser llamado a prestar servicio militar (página 989)

Reconstrucción Presidencial *s.* política impulsada para obligar a los estados confederados a ratificar la Decimotercera Enmienda y a formar nuevos gobiernos, regidos por nuevas constituciones, como condición para poder reintegrarse a la Unión (página 436)

Reconstrucción Radical *s.* nombre dado al plan del Partido Republicano que buscaba aprobar las Leyes de Reconstrucción de 1867 (página 439)

Reconstrucción *s.* etapa posterior a la Guerra de Secesión caracterizada por el anhelo de reunificar a los Estados Unidos de América (página 427)

redes de seguridad *s.* conjunto de programas proporcionados por el gobierno estatal o federal diseñados para evitar que la gente permanezca en la pobreza (página 1073)

reducción del déficit *s.* medidas adoptadas por un gobierno para pagar una deuda (página 1095)

referendo *s.* una elección donde el pueblo vota directamente sobre medidas específicas (página 533)

refugiado *s.* persona que huye a otro país para escapar de un peligro o una persecución (página 759)

regionalismo *s.* lealtad a cualquier sección o región del país de donde una persona es, en vez de a la nación como tal (página 239)

registro material *s.* edificaciones y objetos que sobreviven de épocas anteriores (página 342)

Renacimiento *s.* período entre 1300 y 1500 en que florecieron la cultura y las artes (página 21)

GLOSARIO

Renacimiento de Harlem *s.* movimiento cultural que se originó en Harlem en la década de 1920 y dio a conocer a muchos escritores, artistas y músicos afroamericanos (página 666)

renovación urbana *s.* programa que consiste en rehabilitar los barrios pobres y construir grandes proyectos de vivienda financiados con fondos públicos (página 878)

renta disponible *s.* dinero del que se dispone para gastos (página 685)

repatriación *s.* el acto de devolver a un ciudadano a su país de origen (página 691)

república constitucional *s.* gobierno en el cual los gobernantes obtienen el poder de parte de sus gobernados según lo determina una Constitución escrita (página 158)

República islámica *s.* estado o país que incorpora o se basa enteramente en la ley islámica (página 1062)

republicanismo cívico *s.* pensamiento político que enfatiza la libertad individual, el activismo ciudadano y el respeto del bien común (página 180)

republicanismo *s.* gobierno en el que la gente elige a sus representantes para crear las leyes (página 152)

republicano radical *s.* miembro del Congreso de los Estados Unidos que apoyaba los derechos de los afroamericanos (página 404)

rescate financiero *s.* durante la Gran Recesión, el acto de comprar hipotecas e inversiones inestables de los bancos (página 1127)

reserva *s.* área de tierra designada y administrada por una tribu indígena (página 480)

responsabilidad cívica *s.* obligación requerida o necesaria por parte de la población, como votar, pagar impuestos y formar parte de los jurados (página R35)

responsabilidad personal *s.* responsabilidad que no es regulada pero que contribuye a una sociedad más civil, como respetar y defender los derechos de los demás, ayudar en la comunidad y mantenerse informado (página R35)

reverso verde *(greenback)* *s.* papel moneda emitido por la Unión para crear una moneda nacional (página 393)

revisión judicial *s.* poder de la Corte Suprema para invalidar cualquier ley que considere inconstitucional, incluso si fue aprobada por el Congreso o firmada por el presidente (página 189)

revocatoria *s.* proceso mediante el cual los ciudadanos pueden votar para sacar del poder a un funcionario público (página 561)

Revolución agrícola *s.* transición en la historia humana de la caza y la recolección de alimentos a la siembra de cultivos y la cría de animales (página 4)

revolución del mercado *s.* transición de una economía preindustrial a una economía capitalista, o sea orientada hacia el mercado (página 226)

Revolución industrial *s.* época en que la producción de bienes hechos con máquinas reemplazó de manera generalizada a los productos hechos a mano (página 219)

Revuelta de Haymarket *s.* enfrentamiento violento entre los trabajadores y la policía el 4 de mayo de 1886, que comenzó como una protesta contra la conducta policial durante una huelga en una fábrica de la compañía McCormick, en Chicago, Illinois (página 515)

rock and roll *s.* estilo musical derivado del rhythm and blues, que se popularizó en la década de 1950 (página 873)

Romanticismo *s.* movimiento artístico, literario y filosófico del siglo XIX que enfatizaba en la imaginación, la emoción y la acción (página 281)

rompehuelgas *s.* trabajadores no sindicalizados dispuestos a desafiar los piquetes para trabajar (página 515)

rustbelt *s.* el área en el Noreste y Medio Oeste de los Estados Unidos en la que la industria manufacturera ha disminuido significativamente (página 1071)

S

sabana *s.* área de praderas tropicales exuberantes (página 26)

saetín *s.* canal de madera inclinado utilizado en la minería para separar el agua del oro (página 472)

salto de rana *s.* estrategia en la que se capturan grupos de islas una por una para establecer en ellas bases militares (página 803)

salvación *s.* acto de ser perdonado por una deidad (Dios) por los pecados cometidos (página 90)

saneamiento *s.* medidas como las alcantarillas para proteger la salud pública (página 532)

saqueo de Lawrence *s.* término para describir el violento ataque de 1856 a Lawrence, Kansas, en el cual personas a favor del esclavismo arrasaron la ciudad destruyendo casas y negocios (página 371)

secesión *s.* acto de separación formal de una nación o de un territorio para ser independiente (página 191)

sector de servicios *s.* parte de la economía que proporciona servicios en lugar de bienes (página 1138)

sedición *s.* acto criminal de tratar de persuadir a las personas para rebelarse o menoscabar el gobierno (página 187)

segregación *de facto* *s.* segregación presente en la sociedad a pesar de que no hay leyes que la impongan (página 958)

segregación *de jure* *s.* segregación impuesta por la ley (página 958)

segregación *s.* separación de diferentes grupos de personas, generalmente basada en la raza (página 535)

Segundo Gran Despertar *s.* movimiento protestante estadounidense basado en las reuniones de reavivamiento y en una relación directa y emocional con Dios (página 276)

Segundo *New Deal* *s.* segundo conjunto de programas del New Deal, que el presidente Franklin Roosevelt presentó al Congreso después de las elecciones del Congreso de 1934 (página 722)

seguridad social *s.* programa gubernamental que proporciona ingresos a los ancianos, discapacitados y desempleados (página 570)

sentada *s.* protesta organizada donde la gente se sienta y se niega a irse (página 915)

separación de poderes *s.* división de poderes gubernamentales entre las tres ramas del gobierno de los EE. UU.: el poder ejecutivo, el poder judicial y el poder legislativo (página 158)

separados pero iguales *s.* política que permitió a las empresas e instituciones segregar a los afroamericanos de los blancos, siempre y cuando las instalaciones o servicios proporcionados fueran casi iguales (página 536)

separatista negro *s.* activista afroamericano radical que creía que la única manera de lograr la igualdad y la justicia en los Estados Unidos era separarse cultural y económicamente de los blancos (página 958)

separatista *s.* persona que quería dejar la Iglesia de Inglaterra (página 56)

servicio militar *s.* obligación de alistarse para el servicio en las fuerzas armadas de un país (página 407)

servidumbre por mora *s.* tipo de servidumbre en la cual una persona trabaja únicamente para pagar una deuda (página 444)

silabario *s.* grupo de símbolos o caracteres usados para representar las sílabas de una palabra (página 260)

sindicato de trabajadores *s.* grupos de trabajadores que se unen para lograr mejores salarios, condiciones de trabajo más seguras y otros beneficios (página 279)

síndrome de inmunodeficiencia adquirida (SIDA) *s.* etapa final de un virus que ataca al sistema del cuerpo humano que combate las enfermedades (página 1083)

sirviente ligado por contrato *s.* persona obligada por contrato a trabajar, generalmente sin paga, a cambio de un boleto gratis a las colonias (página 51)

Sistema americano *s.* política para promover el sistema industrial de los EE. UU. mediante aranceles, subsidios federales para construir carreteras y otras obras públicas y un banco nacional para controlar la moneda (página 227)

Sistema de carreteras interestatales *s.* red de autopistas inaugurada por el presidente Eisenhower en 1956 para poder atravesar los Estados Unidos y conectar entre sí estados y grandes ciudades (página 866)

sistema de señorío *s.* sistema que consistía en que los campesinos trabajaban la tierra de un señor feudal a cambio de protección militar (página 20)

sistema de sub-tesorería *s.* propuesta mediante la cual los agricultores almacenarían sus cultivos en silos hasta que los precios subieran, mientras que el gobierno les prestaría dinero para comprar semillas para los cultivos del siguiente año (página 477)

sitio *s.* táctica militar que consiste en rodear una ciudad (página 45)

soberanía popular *s.* idea de que los residentes de una región o país deciden sobre un tema mediante el voto (página 362)

soberanía *s.* libertad de control por parte de potencias externas (página 152)

socialismo *s.* sistema de gobierno en el que la comunidad o el gobierno controla los recursos económicos (página 517)

sociedad de consumo *s.* sociedad en la que la comprar de bienes y productos se ha convertido en una parte muy importante del estilo de vida de las personas (página 864)

Sociedad de las Naciones *s.* plan que propuso el presidente Woodrow Wilson después de la Primera Guerra Mundial, en el que habría una asamblea general de países para estabilizar las relaciones entre sí y ayudar a preservar la paz (página 626)

sociedad fiduciaria *s.* empresa administrada por miembros de una junta directiva en lugar de por propietarios o accionistas (página 505)

sociedad mayor *s.* compañía que tiene el control total o parcial de otras empresas más pequeñas (página 509)

sociedad por acciones *s.* compañía cuyos accionistas poseen un número determinado de acciones (página 50)

sostén de familia *s.* miembro de la familia que contribuye más a los ingresos del hogar (página 734)

subdivisión *s.* parcela de terreno que ha sido dividida en lotes más pequeños en los que se construyen casas (página 867)

subsidio *s.* fondo del gobierno para mejoras y apoyo al comercio (página 227)

suburbanización *s.* asentamiento de la población de las ciudades en comunidades de la periferia (página 866)

suburbio *s.* comunidad cerca o en las afueras de una ciudad (página 531)

subversión *s.* acto de desestabilización de un sistema social o político importante en un intento por destruirlo (página 844)

sucursal *s.* negocio secundario (página 509)

sufragio femenino *s.* derecho de las mujeres al voto (página 152)

sufragio *s.* derecho constitucional, especialmente el derecho al voto (página 555)

sufragista *s.* persona que apoya el derecho de las mujeres a votar (página 295)

sunbelt *s.* las regiones del sur y suroeste de los Estados Unidos, que tienen inviernos templados (página 859)

T

tanque *s.* vehículo blindado y fuertemente armado que usaba bandas de rodadura en lugar de ruedas (página 612)

tarifa arancelaria *s.* impuesto a las importaciones y exportaciones (página 227)

telecomedia *s.* serie televisiva semanal que cuenta con un entorno familiar y un grupo de personajes que se enfrentan a problemas divertidos (página 872)

telégrafo *s.* dispositivo que transmite mensajes a lo largo de cables conectados, para comunicarse a largas distancias (página 508)

telegrama Zimmermann *s.* un telegrama secreto alemán enviado al embajador alemán en México, exponiendo un plan para la alianza con México (página 607)

Temor Rojo *s.* período en 1919 y 1920 en el que el gobierno federal acosó a presuntos comunistas, anarquistas y radicales (página 642)

teocracia *s.* gobierno liderado por uno o más líderes religiosos (página 1093)

teoría del dominó *s.* una idea de la Guerra Fría que sostenía que los países cercanos a un vecino comunista son más propensos a adoptar ese régimen (página 837)

Tercer Reich *s.* nombre utilizado por el Partido Nazi para describir la época en que Adolf Hitler creía que estaba creando un tercer imperio alemán (página 754)

Territorio Indígena *s.* área de tierra, en lo que hoy es Oklahoma y parte de Kansas y Nebraska, a la cual fueron obligados a migrar los indígenas norteamericanos (página 260)

territorio no organizado *s.* tierras bajo el gobierno federal pero que no le pertenecían a ningún estado (página 240)

terrorismo *s.* el uso de actos violentos y amenazas para lograr un objetivo político (página 1120)

tienda por departamentos *s.* tienda grande que ofrece una amplia variedad de mercancías, organizadas en diferentes departamentos, pero todos bajo un mismo techo (página 531)

topografía *s.* el estudio y reconocimiento de las características físicas de un terreno (página 336)

totalitario *adj.* relativo a un gobierno que está encabezado por un dictador y que requiere completa obediencia al estado (página 724)

transahariano *adj.* que cruza el Sahara (página 25)

transistor *s.* dispositivo electrónico utilizado para controlar el flujo de electricidad en equipos electrónicos (página 865)

transporte escolar de minorías *s.* transporte de estudiantes de diferentes razas a escuelas fuera de sus vecindarios o distritos escolares para asegurar la integración y proporcionar igualdad de oportunidades en la educación (página 961)

tranvía *s.* vehículo que corre sobre rieles por las calles de la ciudad y transporta pasajeros (página 531)

trascendentalismo *s.* movimiento intelectual y social en las décadas de 1830 y 1840 que pedía ir más allá de lo que la sociedad esperaba de cada uno (página 281)

trastorno por estrés postraumático (TEPT) *s.* condición causada por lesión o trauma psicológico (página 993)

Tratado de no Agresión *s.* acuerdo hecho en 1939 entre la Alemania nazi y la Unión Soviética, declarando que no tomarían acción militar el uno contra el otro durante los siguientes 10 años (página 761)

Tratado de Versalles *s.* tratado que oficialmente puso fin a la Primera Guerra Mundial (página 626)

Tren Clandestino *s.* red de personas que trabajaron juntas para ayudar a los afroamericanos a escapar de la esclavitud en los estados sureños de los EE. UU. hacia los estados del Norte y Canadá antes de la Guerra Civil (página 364)

tribunal *s.* corte de justicia con autoridad sobre un asunto específico (página 819)

trustbuster *s.* persona que busca deshacer las sociedades fiduciarias o los monopolios, especialmente un funcionario federal que hace cumplir las leyes antimonopolio (página 564)

tundra *s.* terreno plano y sin árboles de las regiones ártica y subártica (página 14)

turnpike *s.* carretera en la que se pagan peajes para transitar (página 227)

U

U-boat *s.* submarino alemán (página 606)

Unión Estadounidense por las Libertades Civiles (ACLU) *s.* organización formada en 1920, dedicada a defender los derechos y las libertades individuales de todos los estadounidenses (página 643)

V

valijeros *s.* blancos norteños que se desplazaron al sur tras la Guerra Civil, a menudo buscando oportunidades durante el periodo de Reconstrucción o en busca de poder político (página 439)

vaquero *s.* nombre dado al trabajador de las haciendas ganaderas en tierras de los EE. UU. colonizadas por españoles (página 320)

veta *s.* filón mineral (página 472)

veterano *s.* persona que sirvió en el ejército (página 429)

vietnamización *s.* estrategia militar que permitió la sustitución gradual de tropas estadounidenses por tropas sur vietnamitas durante la guerra de Vietnam (página 988)

virrey *s.* gobernador de las colonias españolas en las Américas que representaba al Rey y la Reina de España (página 47)

viruela *s.* virus mortal que causa fiebre alta y pequeñas ampollas en la piel (página 45)

virus de la inmunodeficiencia humana (VIH) *s.* virus que ataca al sistema del cuerpo humano que combate las enfermedades (página 1083)

visión regional *s.* estilo de escritura que expresa las características de una región (página 490)

vodevil *s.* espectáculo teatral que incluía canto y danza (página 530)

volante *s.* hoja o pedazo de papel con información que se reparte en la calle (página 139)

Z

zona de libre empresa *s.* área que permite la suspensión de leyes fiscales y de aduanas (página 1111)

zona de ocupación *s.* área de un país en la que el ejército de otro país toma el control (página 827)

zona desmilitarizada *s.* área en la que se prohíbe la presencia de personal y armas militares (página 840)

VOCABULARIO ACADÉMICO

afluencia *s.* arribo, entrada en masa (de inmigrantes) (página 518)

agitador *s.* alguien que llama a la rebelión o la desobediencia (página 484)

alegoría *s.* una historia en la que personas y objetos representan ideas abstractas o espirituales (página 21)

arable *adj.* fértil, como el suelo para la agricultura (página 78)

arrendar *v.* firmar o proporcionar un contrato que otorgue derechos a tierras o a propiedades por un tiempo en base a un alquiler acordado (página 579)

artesano *s.* persona que fabrica objetos manualmente (página 27)

asentir *v.* consentir, estar de acuerdo con alguien luego de un debate o discusión (página 1019)

autonomía *s.* independencia; libertad de actuar según sus propios principios (página 167)

blasfemo *adj.* que va contra Dios, sacrílego (página 1069)

bolita de algodón *s.* cápsula que contiene la semilla del algodón (página 222)

brevedad *s.* corta extensión o duración de una cosa (página 425)

cardar *v.* preparar las fibras del algodón para su limpieza, peinando los nudos y juntando las fibras sueltas (página 220)

carisma *s.* agradable y de carácter atractivo, frecuentemente relacionado con la capacidad de atracción de un líder (página 187)

citación *s.* exigencia legal de presentarse a corte, ante un juez o comité del gobierno (página 843)

clandestino *adj.* secreto (página 330)

clemencia *s.* misericordia, capacidad de perdonar (página 843)

coerción *s.* presión ejercida sobre alguien mediante la amenaza o el engaño (página 738)

cohesión *s.* que muestra unidad y buena organización (página 801)

comodidad *s.* un beneficio generado a partir de servicios para mejorar la forma de vida (página 516)

cumplir *v.* satisfacer los términos de un acuerdo, obedecer (página 907)

conclusivo *adj.* final (página 401)

contrabando *s.* bienes que se comercian de manera ilegal (página 112)

conveniente *adj.* oportuno (página 1015)

culminación *s.* la conclusión, el final de algo (página 993)

cuota *s.* proporción, porcentaje o participación, a menudo en referencia a la proporción de grupos minoritarios o de género que obtienen algún beneficio en particular (página 691)

depósito *s.* un almacén, lugar donde se guardan cosas (página 939)

desistir *v.* ceder; renunciar (página 327)

desproporcionado *adj.* desigual, desequilibrado, generalmente en comparación a la mayoría (página 1109)

devoto *adj.* entregado a su fe religiosa (página 277)

difamación *s.* ataque al carácter de otra persona (generalmente un rival político) (página 253)

distribuir *v.* repartir (página 1042)

diversidad *s.* variedad (página 77)

diversificar *v.* ampliar las opciones (página 476)

doméstico *adj.* relativo a las tareas del hogar (página 67)

efigie *s.* imagen o representación de una persona (por lo general un político) odiado o repudiado por el pueblo (página 111)

erradicar *v.* eliminar, destruir por completo (página 562)

errático *adj.* impredecible, inconsistente (página 844)

éxodo *s.* emigración (generalmente de muchas personas a la vez) (página 21)

exorbitante *adj.* excesivo, caro (página 472)

extorsión *s.* acto de obtener algo, generalmente dinero o información, mediante el uso de coacción; chantaje (página 959)

filantrópico *adj.* caritativo, bondadoso (página 505)

florecer *v.* expandirse; crecer (página 79)

frugalidad *s.* templanza, moderación en algo (página 189)

gueto *s.* sección de una ciudad en la cual ciertos grupos, generalmente judíos, estaban obligados a vivir; en uso moderno se refiere a la sección de una ciudad donde viven ciertos grupos minoritarios, generalmente debido a la pobreza (página 815)

herbicida *s.* sustancia química que se usa para matar plantas (página 977)

hipótesis *s.* idea específica que debe ser comprobada a través del método científico (página 88)

homogéneo *adj* uniforme, igual, coherente, estandarizado (página 875)

ilícito *adj.* ilegal (página 655)

incorporar *v.* unir (página 905)

incumplimiento de pago *s.* que se ha dejado de pagar una deuda, moroso (página 152)

injurioso *adj.* insultante, calumnioso, escandaloso (página 610)

inmolar *v.* destruir mediante el fuego (página 971)

insubordinación *s.* desobediencia, rebeldía (página 568)

intervencionista *adj.* persona cuya tendencia es involucrarse en algo, como en una guerra (página 762)

invencible *adj.* imposible de vencer, indestructible (página 557)

jeroglífico *adj.* representación pictórica de una historia (página 17)

jurisdicción *s.* que tiene poder legal sobre algo (página 364)

laudable *adj.* meritorio, digno de reconocimiento (página 658)

lucrativo *adj.* que genera ganancia, bien remunerado o pagado (página 76)

mística *s.* aire de misterio que rodea a una persona, cosa o idea (página 1021)

nocivo *adj.* ofensivo, desagradable (página 532)

normalidad *s.* condición o situación típica, usual o esperada, como las condiciones sociales, políticas y económicas generales de una nación (página 629)

notorio *adj.* famoso por tener mala reputación (página 646)

obstrución *s.* estrategia política en la que un pequeño grupo de legisladores se turnan para hablar y evitar así que finalice un debate o que un proyecto de ley sea sometido a votación (página 1055)

opulencia *s.* riqueza, prosperidad (página 862)

oratoria *s.* relacionado al discurso (página 908)

partidario *s.* defensor, seguidor de una causa o idea (página 518)

pluralismo *s.* coexistencia de diferentes grupos culturales dentro de una civilización (página 518)

poner en la lista negra *v.* poner a una o más personas en una lista indicando que deben ser rechazadas o castigadas (página 843)

pragmatismo *s.* utilidad, sentido práctico (página 716)

preventivo *adj.* prioritario, defensivo (página 1121)

privatizar *v.* transferir del control público al privado (página 111)

prominente *s.* cualidad de ser importante o notable (página 253)

protagonista *s.* personaje principal de una obra de ficción (página 489)

rectificar *v.* compensar por un daño (página 795)

rehén *s.* persona detenida para obligar a alguien a cumplir las demandas de quienes han detenido a esa persona (página 1062)

represivo *adj.* opresivo, cruelmente autoritario (página 1079)

rescindir *v.* anular (página 113)

salobre *adj.* un poco salado (página 50)

señor de la guerra *s.* líder de una milicia local que ejerce un gran poder en esa limitada región (página 765)

simpatizar *v.* sentir una conexión emocional con otra persona (página 365)

solidaridad *s.* unidad por una causa (página 516)

subordinado *adj.* que pertenece a algo mayor (página 298)

subsistir a duras penas *v.* obtener algo luego de un gran esfuerzo (página 472)

subversivo *adj.* rebelde (página 58)

subyugación *s.* acto de controlar a un grupo de personas mediante el uso de la fuerza (página 831)

superfluo *adj.* innecesario (página 164)

tratado *s.* promesa vinculante (página 95)

unánime *adj.* indiscutible, que ha obtenido todos los votos (página 907)

unicameral *adj.* formado por una sola cámara, como el poder legislativo que solo tiene una cámara de representantes (página 158)

INDEX

INDEX

INDEX

INDEX

INDEX

INDEX

INDEX

INDEX

INDEX

INDEX

SKILLS INDEX

ACKNOWLEDGMENTS

NATIONAL GEOGRAPHIC LEARNING | CENGAGE

National Geographic Learning gratefully acknowledges the contributions of the following National Geographic Explorers and affiliates to our program:

Sam Abell, National Geographic Photographer
Lynsey Addario, National Geographic Photographer
Robert Ballard, National Geographic Explorer-in-Residence
Ari Beser, Fulbright-National Geographic Fellow
Jimmy Chin, National Geographic Photographer
Kevin Crisman, National Geographic Explorer
Jason De León, National Geographic Explorer
Leslie Dewan, National Geographic Explorer
Jeffrey Gusky, National Geographic Photographer
David Guttenfelder, National Geographic Photographer
Kevin Hand, National Geographic Explorer
Fredrik Hiebert, National Geographic Archaeologist-in-Residence
Kathryn Keane, Vice President, National Geographic Exhibitions
Bill Kelso, National Geographic Explorer
Michael Nichols, National Geographic Photographer
Paul Nicklen, National Geographic Photographer
Sarah Parcak, National Geographic Fellow
William Parkinson, National Geographic Explorer
Sandra Postel, National Geographic Freshwater Fellow (2009–2015)
Robert Reid, National Geographic Digital Nomad
Andrés Ruzo, National Geographic Explorer
Tristram Stuart, National Geographic Explorer

Photographic Credits

Front cover, Title, Copyright (tl) Tetra Images/Getty Images. (tr) Andy Sacks/Getty Images. (cl) ©Rosalia Torres/Brandon Torres-Weiner. (c) ©Bettmann/Getty Images. (cr) pidjoe/Getty Images. (bl1) Joel Sartore/National Geographic Creative. (bl2) David Hiser/National Geographic Creative. (bc) Amos Chapple/Getty Images. (br) Library of Congress, LC-DIG-ds-07422. **Back Cover** SpaceX.

T3 (bl) Mark Thiessen/National Geographic. (bc) Mary Lynne Ashley Photography/National Geographic Learning. (br) National Geographic Learning. **T4**(tl) KMK/National Geographic Creative. (tr) Robert Reid/National Geographic Creative. (cl) Brian Nelson/National Geographic Learning. (cr) Courtesy of Andres Ruzo/National Geographic Learning. **T5** (t1) ©Kari Wehrs. (t2) MARK THIESSEN/National Geographic Creative. (t3) Ari Beser. (t4) ©Kevin Crisman/National Geographic. (t5) ©Jason DeLeon. (t6) ©Lynn Johnson/National Geographic Creative. (c1) ©Mark Thiessen/National Geographic Creative. (c2) MLADEN ANTONOV/Getty Images. (c3) ©freddieclaire. (c4) ©Mark Thiessen/National Geographic Creative. (c5) HOGUE KAT KEENE /National Geographic Creative. (b1) Roberto Ricciuti/Getty Images. (b2) MIKEY SCHAEFER/National Geographic Creative. (b3) ©Jeff Gusky. (b4) DAVID GUTTENFELDER /National Geographic Creative. (b5) Nick Nichols/National Geographic Creative. (b6) Christina Mitermeier/National Geographic Creative. **T7** ©Cory Richards/National Geographic Creative. **T8** ©KMK/National Geogrpahic Learning. **T9** ©George Ohrstrom/Kenneth Garrett Photography. **T10** (t) ©Robert Reid/National Geographic Creative. (b) ©Marcie Goodale/National Geographic Creative. **T28** (spread) Paul Chesley/National Geographic Creative. **T29** (tl) Michael Marquand/Getty Images. (tr) ©Daniella Nowitz/National Geographic Creative. (c) ©US Capitol. **T30** ©Jez Coulson/Insight-Visual. **T31** (tl) debra millet/Alamy Stock Photo. (tr) aimintang/Getty Images. (c) Richard Wong/Alamy Stock Photo. **T32** The Oregon Trail, 1869 (oil on canvas)/Bierstadt, Albert (1830-1902)/BUTLER INSTITUTE OF AMERICAN ART/Butler Institute of American Art, Youngstown, OH, USA/Bridgeman Images. **T33** (t) joe daniel price/Getty Images. (cl) Nativestock.com/Marilyn Angel Wynn/Alamy Stock Photo. (cr) JamesTung/Getty Images. **T34** (spread) Library of Congress, Prints & Photographs Division, LC-DIG-ds-05505. **T35** (tl) Hulton Archive/Getty Images. (tr) Marc Hoberman/Getty Images. (cl) ©Jason Demek/500px. (cr) Library of Congress Prints and Photographs Division[LC-DIG-cwpb-02660]. **T36** (spread) Library of Congress, Prints & Photographs Division, LC-D401-13643. **T37** (tl) ©The Field Museum, Image No. GN91795_07Ad. (tr) Library of Congress, Prints & Photographs Division, LC-DIG-ppmsca-24362. (cl) ©Anthony Barboza/Getty Images. (cr) PETE MCBRIDE/National Geographic Creative. **T38** (spread) Allentown Art Museum; Purchase: Leigh Schadt and Edwin Schadt Art Museum Trust, 2012. (2012.09). **T39** (tl) swim ink 2 llc/Getty Images. (tr) Buyenlarge/Getty Images. (cl) New York Times Co./Getty Images. (cr) New York Times Co./Getty Images. **T40** (spread)©Robert Capa/International Center of Photography/Magnum Photos. **T41** (tl) Library of Congress, Prints & Photographs Division, Reproduction number LC-DIG-fsac-1a35369 (digital file from original transparency) LC-USW361-137 (color film copy slide). (tr) ANDREW CABALLERO-REYNOLDS/Getty Images. (cr) Yale Joel/Getty Images. **T42** (spread) Bettmann/Getty Images. **T43** (tl) Courtesy of NASA. (tr) ©NASA. (cl) Keystone-France/Getty Images. (cr) ZUMA Press, Inc./Alamy Stock Photo. **T44** (spread) DIANE COOK, LEN JENSHEL/National Geographic Creative. **T45** (tl) ©Lynsey Addario/Reportage/Getty Images. (cl) Wathiq Khuzaie/Getty Images. (tr) PETE MCBRIDE / National Geographic Creative. **T47** (tr) ©freddieclaire. (b) ©Danny Lyon/Magnum Photos. **T48** (tl) Buyenlarge/Getty Images. **T49** (tr) MICHAEL NICHOLS/National Geographic Creative. (bl) Source: Library of Congress, Prints & Photographs Division, LC-DIG-ppmsca-54230. **T50** (spread) ©Mapping Specialists/National Geographic Learning. (background) Daniel Gomes Lacerda / EyeEm/Getty Images. **T52** ©Levi Stroud/Michigan News. **T53** ©David Coventry/National Geographic Creative. **T54** IRA BLOCK/National Geographic Creative. **T55** (tl) Philippe Psaila/Science Source. (t) Nicolle Rager Fuller, National Science Foundation. **T56** (tr) Werner Forman/Getty Images. (cr) IRA BLOCK/National Geographic Creative. (cr) Paul Chesley/National Geographic Creative. (br) ©Werner Forman Archive/Heritage Image Partnership Ltd/Alamy Stock Photo. **T57** (tr) ©National Museum of the American Indian, Smithsonian Institution 5/4385. (cr) Werner Forman/Getty Images. (bc) ©musée du quai Branly - Jacques Chirac, Dist. RMN-Grand Palais/Art Resource, NY. (br) Human effigy vessel, Late Mississippian period, 1300-1500 (ceramic)/Mississippian culture (c.800-1500)/DIRK BAKKER PHOTOGRAPHY/Private Collection/Bridgeman Images. (bl) IRA BLOCK/National Geographic Creative. **8-9** Paul Chesley/National Geographic Creative. **10** (c) Science & Society Picture Library/Getty Images. (tr) Robert Clark/National Geographic Creative. (b) Alexanderclayton/Getty Images. **11** (tl) Kean Collection/Getty Images. (cr) Scottish pistol marked to the 1st Battalion of the 42nd Regiment of Foot/DON TROIANI COLLECTION/Private Collection/Bridgeman Images. (bl) John Warburton Lee/SuperStock. (br) Imagno/Getty Images. **12-13** (spread) Richard Ellis/Alamy Stock Photo. **14** (b) Peter Horree/Alamy Stock Photo. **16** (b) Michael Marquand/Getty Images. **17** (tr) Kenneth Garrett/National Geographic Society/BANCO CENTRAL DE RESERVA DEL PERÚ, Lima, Perú. **18** (t) ©freddieclaire. **19** (tr) ©Sarah Parcak/Digital Globe. **20** (b) Science Source. **21** (t) Woman Holding a Balance, c.1664 (oil on canvas)/Vermeer, Jan (Johannes) (1632-75)/National Gallery of Art, Washington DC, USA/Bridgeman Images. **22** (b) Two folios from the Gutenberg Bible, printed in the workshop of Johannes Gutenberg, 1455 (parchment)/German School, (15th century)/BILDARCHIV STEFFENS (FIRST ACCOUNT)/Universitatsbibliothek, Gottingen, Germany/Bridgeman Images. **25** (t) Jorge Santos/Getty Images. **26** (t) ©Jimmy Chin/National Geographic. **28** (b) DEA/W. BUSS/Getty Images. **30** (tr) Erich Lessing/Art Resource, NY. **32** (b) Glasshouse Images/Alamy Stock Photo. **35** (tr) Abraham Cresques/Getty Images. **36-37** (spread) Kevin Fleming/Getty Images. **38-39** (spread) Ira Block/National Geographic. **40** (b) MANNIE GARCIA/Getty Images. **41** (cr) ©Ira Block/National Geographic Creative. **42** (tr) ©Ira Block/National Geographic Creative. (bl) john norman/Alamy Stock Photo. **43** (tr) ©Historic Jamestowne. (cl) IRA BLOCK/National Geographic. (cr) ©Historic Jamestowne. (br) Pamphlet encouraging colonists to go to Virginia in America, published in 1609 (colour litho)/English School/PETER NEWARK'S PICTURES/Private Collection/Bridgeman Images. **44** (b) Lebrecht Music and Arts Photo Library/Alamy Stock Photo. **47** (t) canimag/AGE Fotostock. **48** (b) Library of Congress Prints and Photographs Division [LC-USZ62-44000]. **50** (b) ©Daniella Nowitz/National Geographic Creative. **51** (tr) Pocahontas (c.1595-1617) 1616 (oil on canvas)/English School, (17th century)/PETER NEWARK'S PICTURES/Private Collection/Bridgeman Images. **52** (t) MLADEN ANTONOV/Getty Images. **53** (tl) ©Art Resource, NY. (tr) ©National Geographic. **55** (t) Bildarchiv Preussischer Kulturbesitz/Art Resource, NY. **56** (b) Tom Croke/Alamy Stock Photo. **57** (tr) Head of Squanto (wood)/

American School, (17th century)/Private Collection/Bridgeman Images. **59** (t) North Wind Picture Archives/Alamy Stock Photo. **61** (t) US Capitol. **63** (t) ©2010 robinharrison. **64** (bl) Indigo (colour litho)/PURIX VERLAG/Bridgeman Images. (br) American Folk Art Museum/Art Resource, NY. **65** (tr) Richard Ellis/Alamy Stock Photo. **66** (bl) Collection of the Smithsonian National Museum of African American History and Culture, Gift of Oprah Winfrey. (br) ©Courtesy, Georgia Archives, Vanishing Georgia Collection, sap093. **70-71** (spread) Sean Pavone/Alamy Stock Photo. **72** (br) Hemis/Alamy Stock Photo. **73** (t) Richard Cavalleri/Shutterstock.com. **74** (c) Pictorial Press Ltd/Alamy Stock Photo. **75** (t) ©Chris Randall. **77** (t) Everett - Art/Shutterstock.com. **78** (b) National Museum of American History, Kenneth E. Behring Center. **80** (b) Bloomberg/Getty Images. **81** (tr) Bloomberg/Getty Images. **83** (t) The Trustees of the British Museum/Art Resource. (b) USA: 'The Old Plantation' (Slaves Dancing on a South Carolina Plantation), watercolour on paper, attributed to John Rose, c. 1785-95. Abby Aldrich Rockefeller Folk Art Museum, Williamsburg, Virginia, USA/PICTURES FROM HISTORY/Bridgeman Images. **84** (c) British Library Board / Robana/Art Resource, NY. **85** (tr) British Library Board/Robana/Art Resource, NY. **86** (c) (b) ©2015 Elsa Hahne/Whitney Plantation. **87** (t) (c) (b) ©2015 Elsa Hahne/Whitney Plantation. **88** (c) Print Collector/Getty Images. **89** (tr) Barry Winiker/Getty Images. **91** (t) George Whitefield preaching/Collet, John (c.1725-80)/Private Collection/Bridgeman Images. **92** (b) AP Images/Dan Kitwood. **94** (b) Philip Scalia / Alamy Stock Photo. **95** (t) Library of Congress Prints and Photographs Division. **97** (tl) Library of Congress Prints & Photographs Division, [LC-USZC4-5315]. **99** (tr) Pontiac (1720-69) 1763 (oil on canvas)/Stanley, John Mix (1814-72)/PETER NEWARK'S PICTURES/Private Collection/Bridgeman Images. **102** NYC Department of Records. **104-105** ©Jez Coulson/Insight-Visual. **106** (tl) Boston Tea Party tea leaves in a glass bottle, collected by T.M. Harris, Dorchester Neck, December 1773/American School, (18th century)/ MASSACHUSETTS HISTORICAL SOCIETY/Massachusetts Historical Society, Boston, MA, USA/Bridgeman Images. (tr) George Ostertag/AGE Fotostock. (b) Best View Stock/Alamy Stock Photo. **107** (tl) George Washington Inaugural button circa 1789/ DON TROIANI COLLECTION/Private Collection/Bridgeman Images. (tr) Ira Block/National geographic. (b) DEA/A. DAGLI ORTI/Getty Images. **108-109** (spread) ©Brian Jannsen Photography. **110** (b) Teapot 'Stamp Act Repeal'd', Cockhill Pit Factory, 1766 (lead-glazed earthenware)/English School, (18th century)/ PEABODY ESSEX MUSEUM/Peabody Essex Museum, Salem, Massachusetts, USA/Bridgeman Images. **111** (tl) Colonists under Liberty Tree (colour litho)/American School, (18th century)/PETER NEWARK'S PICTURES/Private Collection/Bridgeman Images. **112** (b) Mrs James Warren (Mercy Otis) c.1763 (oil on canvas)/Copley, John Singleton (1738-1815)/MUSEUM OF FINE ARTS, BOSTON/ Museum of Fine Arts, Boston, Massachusetts, USA/Bridgeman Images. **113** (t) Art Resource, NY. **115** (t) Michael Blanchard Photography/Boston Tea Party Ships & Museum. **116** (b) The Metropolitan Museum of Art. Image source: Art Resource, NY. **118-119** (spread) Steve Dunwell/age fotostock/Superstock. **121** (t) Library and Archive of Quebec. (b) debra millet/Alamy Stock Photo. **123** (t) Brunswick drum captured at the Battle of Bennington/DON TROIANI COLLECTION/Massachusetts State Archives, Boston, MA., USA/Bridgeman Images. **124** (cr) DEA PICTURE LIBRARY/Getty Images. **125** (br) Drafting the Declaration of Independence (oil on canvas)/Chappel, Alonzo (1828-87)/HECKSCHER MUSEUM OF ART/The Heckscher Museum of Art, Huntington, NY, USA/Bridgeman Images. **126-127** (t) Drafting the Declaration of Independence (oil on canvas)/ Chappel, Alonzo (1828-87)/HECKSCHER MUSEUM OF ART/The Heckscher Museum of Art, Huntington, NY, USA/Bridgeman Images. **128** (b) Buyenlarge/Getty Images. **130** (bl) (br) Museum of the American Revolution. **133** (b) Washington Crossing the Delaware River, 25th December 1776, 1851 (oil on canvas) (copy of an original painted in 1848)/Leutze, Emanuel Gottlieb (1816-68)/ Metropolitan Museum of Art, New York, USA/Bridgeman Images. **135** (t) Battle of Saratoga, the British General John Burgoyne surrendering to the American General, Horatio Gates, October 17, 1777, c.1822-32 (oil on canvas)/Trumbull, John (1756-1843)/Yale University Art Gallery, New Haven, CT, USA/Bridgeman Images. **136** (t) aimintang/Getty Images. (b) The New York Historical Society/Getty Images. **139** (tr) Universal History Archive/Getty Images. **140** (c) RMN-Grand Palais/Art Resource, NY. **141** (tr) Smith Collection/Gado/Getty Images. **142-143** (t) ©Swamp Fox Murals Trail Society, Manning, Clarendon County, SC, www. swampfoxtrail.com. **144** (b) Architect of the Capitol. **146** (bl)

©Mount Vernon Ladie's Association. (br) Courtesy of Mount Vernon Ladies' Association. Photograph by Mark Finkenstaedt. **147** (t) ©Mount Vernon Ladie's Association. (cr) Courtesy of Mount Vernon Ladies' Association. Photograph by Gavin Ashworth. (bl) ©Mount Vernon Ladie's Association. **150-151** (spread) kickstand/ Getty Images. **152** (c) Everett Collection Inc/Alamy Stock Photo. **153** (tl) Fine Art/Getty Images. **155** (t) N.C. Wyeth's painting Daniel Boone—The Home Seeker: Cumberland Val ley (c. 1940) ©Copyright 2018 National Museum of American Illustration™, Newport RI Photos courtesy Archives of the American Illustrators Gallery™ NYC. **156** (c) IllustratedHistory/Alamy Stock Photo. **157** (t) Library of Congress. Exchange and Gift Division/Smithsonian. **159** (l) Library of Congress, Prints & Photographs Division, Reproduction number LC-DIG-det-4a26389 (digital file from original). (c) Classic Image/Alamy Stock Photo. (r) Everett Collection Historical/Alamy Stock Photo. **160** (b) A Slave Sale notice published in a newspaper in Charleston, South Carolina, 1766 (print)/American School, (18th century)/PETER NEWARK'S PICTURES/Private Collection/Bridgeman Images. **162** (bl) John Jay, 1786 (oil on canvas)/Wright of Derby, Joseph (1734-97)/NEW YORK HISTORICAL SOCIETY/Collection of the New-York Historical Society, USA/Bridgeman Images. (br) Patrick Henry, 1851 (oil on canvas)/Sully, Thomas (1783-1872)/VIRGINIA HISTORICAL SOCIETY/Virginia Historical Society, Richmond, Virginia, USA/ Bridgeman Images. **165** (t) The Signing of the Constitution of the United States in 1787, 1940 (oil on canvas)/Christy, Howard Chandler (1873-1952)/Hall of Representatives, Washington D.C., USA/Bridgeman Images. **166** (b) UniversalImagesGroup/Getty Images. **169** (bl) Bequest of Susan W. Tyler, 1979/The Metropolitan Museum of Art. **170-171** (spread) ©Cameron Davidson. **172** ©Courtesy National Gallery of Art, Washington. **174** (tr) Portrait of Thomas Jefferson, 1805 (oil on canvas)/Peale, Rembrandt (1778-1860)/NEW YORK HISTORICAL SOCIETY/Collection of the New-York Historical Society, USA/Bridgeman Images. (bl) Fine Art/Getty Images. **175** (c) Cephas Picture Library/Alamy Stock Photo. **176** (tr) Benjamin Franklin (1706-1790), c.1779 (oil on canvas)/Duplessis, Joseph Siffred (1725-1802)/NORTH CAROLINA MUSEUM OF ART/North Carolina Museum of Art, Raleigh, USA/ Bridgeman Images. **177** (tr) Science & Society Picture Library/Getty Images. (cl) Library of CongressCover page o/CQ/Roll Call/ Washington D.C. USA. (cr) Benjamin Franklin Drawing Electricity from the Sky, c.1816 (oil on canvas)/West, Benjamin (1738-1820)/ PHILADELPHIA MUSEUM OF ART/Philadelphia Museum of Art, Pennsylvania, PA, USA/Bridgeman Images. (br) Photo by Peter Harholdt, 2004. **178** (br) First in War, First in Peace and First in the Hearts of His Countrymen (colour litho)/American School, (19th century)/NEW YORK HISTORICAL SOCIETY/Collection of the New-York Historical Society, USA/Bridgeman Images. **180** (br) The Copley Family, 1776/77 (oil on canvas)/Copley, John Singleton (1738-1815)/National Gallery of Art, Washington DC, USA/ Bridgeman Images. **183** (t) Sara Krulwich/The New York Times/ Redux. **185** (b) DEA/G. DAGLI ORTI/Getty Images. **186** (b) Justin Sullivan/Getty Images. **188** (b) Rudy Sulgan/Getty Images. **191** (tr) "A Deed of the Pen", Louisiana Purchase Exposition, March-Two-Step by the Composer of "Hiawatha" Whitney-Warner Pub-Co. Detroit, New York, 1904 (colour litho)/American School, (20th century)/SMITHSONIAN INSTITUTION/Smithsonian Libraries, Washington DC, USA/Bridgeman Images. **192** (cl) (cr) James E. Russell/National Geographic Creative. **193** (t) Richard Wong/ Alamy Stock Photo. **194** (tl) ©American Philosophical Society. **195** (tr) Division of Political History, National Museum of American History, Smithsonian Institution. **196** (c) GROVE, DAVID (ARTIST)/ National Geographic Creative. **197** (tr) Sacagawea with Lewis and Clark during their expedition of 1804-06 (colour litho)/ Wyeth, Newell Convers (1882-1945)/PETER NEWARK'S PICTURES/Private Collection/Bridgeman Images. **199** (t) Library of congress Prints and Photographs Division [LC-DIG-pga-01891]. **200** (br) Smithsonian's National Museum of American History. **201** (tr) ©2004 White House Historical Association. **203** (bl) The Miriam and Ira D. Wallach Division of Art, Prints and Photographs: Photography Collection, The New York Public Library. "Repairing the Star Spangled Banner" The New York Public Library Digital Collections. 1860 - 1920. **204-205** National Geographic. **206-207** The Oregon Trail, 1869 (oil on canvas)/Bierstadt, Albert (1830-1902)/BUTLER INSTITUTE OF AMERICAN ART/Butler Institute of American Art, Youngstown, OH, USA/Bridgeman Images. **208** (tr) Dorling Kindersley ltd/Alamy Stock Photo. (tl) Cream Jug, 1825-1840 (lead glass)/Boston & Sandwich Glass Company (fl.1825-1888) (attr.to)/MUSEUM OF FINE ARTS, HOUSTON/ Museum of Fine Arts, Houston, Texas, USA/Bridgeman Images. (b)

litho)/American School, (19th century)/PETER NEWARK'S PICTURES/Private Collection/Bridgeman Images. **389** ©Ira Block/National Geographic Creative. **392** Scott's Great Snake, 1861 (hand-coloured engraving), Elliott, J. B. (fl.1861)/Collection of the New-York Historical Society, USA/Bridgeman Images. (tl) WorldPhotos/Alamy Stock Photo. (tr) US Ten Dollar note known as a greenback 1863/DON TROIANI COLLECTION/Museum of Connecticut History, Hartford, CT., USA/Bridgeman Images. **394** Kenneth Garrett Photography. **396-397** (spread) ©Kenneth Garrett. **398** Library of Congress Prints and Photographs Division Washington, D.C.[LC-USZ62-1770]. **399** Buyenlarge/Superstock. **401** ©Confederate Memorial Hall Museum. **402** Source: Library of Congress Prints and Photographs Division/LC-DIG-ppmsca-33279. **403** IanDagnall Computing/Alamy Stock Photo. **405** (tl) MPI/Getty Images. (tr) National Museum of African American History and Culture, Smithsonian Institution. **406** Kenneth Garrett. **407** MPI/Getty Images. **408** Fotosearch/Getty Images. **409** Moviestore/REX/Shutterstock.com. **411** MPI/Archive Photos/Getty Images. **412** (t) Sam Abell/National Geographic Creative. (bl) ©Kari Wehrs. **413** Sam Abell/National Geographic Creative. **414** Source: The Library of Congress- Prints & Photographs/LC-USZ62-3794. **415** Maurice Savage/Alamy Stock Photo. **416** David Monette/Alamy Stock Photo. **418** (c) (b) National Civil War Museum. **419** (tl) (cl) (br) National Civil War Museum. **420** Justin Sullivan/Getty Images. **421** National Museum of American History. **422** GL Archive/Alamy Stock Photo. **423** The Protected Art Archive/Alamy Stock Photo. **424** Abraham Lincoln, Proclamation of Freedom, 1863/UNIVERSAL IMAGES GROUP/Bridgeman Images. **427** TOM LOVELL/National Geographic Creative. **428** (t) Bettmann/Getty Images. (b) Library of Congress Prints and Photographs Division [LC-USZC4-5341]. **432-433** Howard University. **434** GL Archive/Alamy Stock Photo. **435** Arlington National Cemetery. **436** ©CORBIS/Corbis via Getty Images. **440** Bettmann/Getty Images. **441** JUNG YEON-JE/Getty Images. **442** Library of Congress Prints and Photographs Division[LC-DIG-cwpb-02660]. **443** Lightfoot/Getty Images. **444** Source: Detroit Publishing Company LC-DIG-det-4a13398. **445** MPI/Getty Images. **446** ©The Art Archive/REX/National Archives Washington DC/Mathew Brady. **447** Sunday morning in Virginia, 1877 (oil on canvas)/Homer, Winslow (1836-1910)/CINCINNATI ART MUSEUM/Cincinnati Art Museum, Ohio, USA/Bridgeman Images. **448** 'The First Vote' for black voters in the South during state elections of 1867 (colour litho)/Waud, Alfred Rudolph (1828-91) (after)/PETER NEWARK'S PICTURES/Private Collection/Bridgeman Images. **449** Library of Congress, Prints & Photographs Division [LC-DIG-ppmsca-17564]. **450** National Museum of American History. **451** Library of Congress Prints and Photographs Division[LC-DIG-ppmsca-34808]. **452** The Rush from the New York Stock Exchange on September 18, 1873, from 'A History of the Last Quarter Century' by E. Benjamin Andrews, published in Scribner's Magazine, July 1895 (oil on canvas)/Pyle, Howard (1853-1911)/DELAWARE ART MUSEUM/Delaware Art Museum, Wilmington, USA/Bridgeman Images. **454** National Geographic Learning. **456** Library of Congress, Prints & Photographs Division, LC-DIG-ppmsca-21452. **458-459** (spread) The Library of Congress. **460** (tr) Collection of the Smithsonian National Museum of African American History and Culture; Gift of the Descendants of Garfield Logan, In Honor of Philip Henry Logan. (cl) DEA PICTURE LIBRARY/Getty Images. (br) Nick Norman/National Geographic Creative. **461** (tl) Gift of Mr. James Harvey Young, Division of Medicine & Science, National Museum of American History, Smithsonian Institution. (c) David Frent/Getty Images. (br) Steve Speller/Alamy Stock Photo. **462-463** (spread) Jim Brandenberg/Minden/SuperStock. **464-465** (spread) Columbia Pictures/Courtesy Everett Co/Everett Collection. **466** Transcendental Graphics/Getty Images. **467** The Library of Congress. **468** Silver Screen Collection/Getty Images. **469** (tr) AF archive/Alamy Stock Photo. (br) ©National Museum of American History/Smithsonian Institution. **471** Pioneer Family Portrait, Custer County, Nebraska, 1888 (b/w photo)/UNIVERSAL IMAGES GROUP/Bridgeman Images. **473** A Mexican Vaquero, 1890 (oil on canvas)/Remington, Frederic (1861-1909)/ART INSTITUTE OF CHICAGO/The Art Institute of Chicago, IL, USA/Bridgeman Images. **474** Library of Congress, Prints & Photographs Division, LC-DIG-fsa-8b27566. **475** Randy Olson/National Geographic Creative. **476** Jake Lyell/Alamy Stock Photo. **478-479** (spread) Rick Herrmann/500px. **482** ANAND VARMA/National Geographic Creative. **483** Library of Congress, Prints & Photographs Division, Reproduction number LC-USZ62-49148. **485** (t) ©National Museum of the American Indian/Smithsonian Institution. (cr) ©National Museum of the American Indian/Smithsonian Institution. **486** (cr)

©The Field Museum, Image No. GN91795_07Ad. (b) ©The Field Museum, Image No. GN91795_07Ad, Photographer John Weinstein. **487** (tl) ©The Field Museum, Image No. A114986d_009B, Cat. No. 15781, PhotographerJohn Weinstein. (cr) ©The Field Museum, Image No. A108351c, Cat. No. 19166, Photographer Ron Testa. (bl) ©The Field Museum, Image No. A110026c, Cat. No. 56174, Photographer Ron Testa. **489** Library of Congress Prints and Photographs Division [LC-DIG-ppmsca-24362]. **490** Pictorial Press Ltd/Alamy Stock Photo. **491** This image was obtained from the Smithsonian Institution. The image or its contents may be protected by international copyright laws. **493** Library of Congress Printed Ephemera Collection. **494-495** (spread) Bettmann/Getty Images. **496-497** (spread) Bill Pugliano/Getty Images. **498** The Library of Congress. **499** Everett Collection Inc/Alamy Stock Photo. **500** STEVE RAYMER/National Geographic Creative. **501** Marcie Goodale/National Geographic Learning. **504** Keith Levit/Axiom Photographic/Design Pics/Superstock. **506** (cr) ©California State Railroad Museum Library. (bl) ©California State Railroad Museum Library. **507** (tr) LeighSmithImages/Alamy Stock Photo. (cl) ©California State Railroad Museum Library. (br) ©California State Railroad Museum Library. **508** ullstein bild/Getty Images. **511** (t) Anthony Barboza/Getty Images. (br) Graphic Arts Collection, National Museum of American History, Smithsonian Institution. **512** National Archives and Records Administration. **515** Front cover of booklet entitled' The Chicago Riot: A record of the terrible scenes of May 4', 1886 by Paul C. Hull, 1886 (colour litho)/Williams, True (19th Century)/CHICAGO HISTORY MUSEUM/©Chicago History Museum, USA/Bridgeman Images. **517** ©Lorenzo Dow Turner papers, Anacostia Community MuseumArchives, Smithsonian Institution, gift of Lois Turner Williams. **519** (tl) (tr)(bl) (br) ©Jordan J. Lloyd/Dynamichrome. **520** National Geographic Learning. **521** ©Courtesy of California State Parks. Image 231-18-9. **522** (tl) Courtesy of California State Parks, Image 231-18-87. (tc) Courtesy of California State Parks, Image 231-18-76. (tr) (b) The Library of Congress. **523** (t) The Library of Congress. (cl) DAVID BOWMAN/National Geographic Creative. (br) The Library of Congress. (bl)Jose Azel/Aurora Photos. **525** (t) Lewis W. Hine/George Eastman House/Getty Images. (br) ©The University of Chicago Map Collection. **526** ©The Ohio State University Billy Ireland Cartoon Library & Museum. **527** ©Riverside Metropolitan Museum, Harada Family Archival Collection. **528** Bettmann/Getty Images. **529** (tc) Wallace Kirkland/Getty Images. (tr) ©Courtesy of Jane Addams Hull-House Museum. **530** Library of Congress, Prints & Photographs Division, Reproduction number LC-USZC4-6075. **531** Museum of the City of New York/The Art Archive at Art Resource, NY. **532** Chicago History Museum/Archive Photos/Getty Images. **534** Courtesy Sal Bigone/McIntyre-Sullivan Family History Site. **535** Universal Images Group/Art Resource, NY. **536** Library of Congress, Prints and Photographs Division [LC-USZC2-1058]. **538** Smithsonian American Art Museum, Washington, DC/Art Resource, NY. **541** National Geographic Learning. **542-543** (spread) Gary Crabbe/Enlightened Images/Alamy Stock Photo. **545** National Archives and Records Administration. **547** (br) ©From the Collections of The Henry Ford. (bl) ©The New York Public Library Digital Collections. **548** (t) National Archives and Records Administration. (b) National Geographic Learning. **549** INTERFOTO/Alamy Stock Photo. **550** The Library of Congress. **551** AFP/Getty Images. **552** George Rinhart/Getty Images. **555** AP Images. **556** Library of Congress, Prints & Photographs Division, Reproduction number LC-USZ62-683. **558** (br1) "Votes for Men", cover of 'Life' magazine, 15 September 1910 (litho)/O'Malley, Power (b.1909)/TOPHAM PICTURE SOURCE/Private Collection/Bridgeman Images. (br2) NEW YORK HISTORICAL SOCIETY/Collection of the New-York Historical Society, USA/Bridgeman Images. **559** ©From the Collections of The Henry Ford. **560** Niday Picture Library/Alamy Stock Photo. **562** ©Division of Political History/National Museum of American History. **563** Bettmann/Getty Images. **564** Library of Congress, Prints & Photographs Division, Reproduction number LC-DIG-ppmsca-36413. **566-567** (spread)PETE MCBRIDE/National Geographic Creative. **569** Everett Collection Inc /Alamy Stock Photo. **570** ullstein bild/Getty Images. **573** DESIGN PICS INC/National Geographic Creative. **575** China: Official portrait of Empress Dowager Cixi (1835-1908) by court photographer Yu Xunling, c. 1895/Yu Xunling (c.1880–1943)/PICTURES FROM HISTORY/Bridgeman Images. **576** Destruction of the U.S. Battleship Maine in Havana Harbor, February 15th, 1898 (colour litho)/Kurz and Allison (fl.1880-98)/NEW YORK HISTORICAL SOCIETY/Collection of the New-York Historical Society, USA/Bridgeman Images. **578** Buyenlarge/Getty Images.

580 Damir Sagol/Reuters. 582 Bettmann/Getty Images. 585 ©National Geographic Learning. 586 Michael & Patricia Fogden/Minden Pictures/Superstock. 588-589 (spread) Allentown Art Museum; Purchase: Leigh Schadt and Edwin Schadt Art Museum Trust, 2012. (2012.09). 590 (tr) Car Culture/Getty Images. (cl) Library of Congress, Prints & Photographs Division, LC-DIG-ppmsc-03521 . (bc) Akademie/Alamy Stock Photo. 591 (tl) Fotosearch/Getty Images. (tr) Carol Highsmith Library of Congress, Prints & Photographs Division, LC-DIG-ppmsc-03521. (br) Eddie Gerald/Alamy Stock Photo. 592-593 (spread) Buyenlarge/UIG/AGE Fotostock. 594 Bettmann/Getty Images. 595 National Geographic Learning. 596 MPI/Getty Images. 597 DeAgostini/ Superstock. 599 (tr) MARK THIESSEN/National Geographic Creative. (b) ©Ken Marschall. 602 Precision Graphics/National Geographic Learning. 603 Popperfoto/Getty Images. 604 Bettmann/Getty Images. 605 National Geographic Learning. 606 Bygone Collection/Alamy Stock Photo. 609 (tl) FPG/Getty Images. (tr) Bettmann/Getty Images. 611 (cr) ©The National World War I Museum. (bl) Library of Congress, Prints & Photographs Division, Reproduction number LC-USZCN4-4455 (color film copy transparency) LC-USZCN4-25 (color film copy neg.). (br) swim ink 2 llc/Getty Images. 612 PhotoDisc. 613 (tl) (tr) (cl) (cr) Lachina/National Geographic Learning. (b) Artville. 614 ©National Portrait Gallery, Smithsonian Institution. 615 Buyenlarge/Getty Images. 616 (tc)(bl)(br) ©Jeffrey Gusky. 617 (tl) (tr) (cr) (b) ©Jeffrey Gusky. 618 The Migration Series, Panel No. 1: During World War I there was a great migration north by southern African Americans, 1940-41 (casein tempera on hardboard)/Lawrence, Jacob (1917-2000)/PHILLIPS COLLECTION/The Phillips Collection, Washington, D.C., USA/Bridgeman Images. 619 David Frent/Getty Images. 620 Bettmann/Getty Images. 621 National Geographic Learning. 624 (t) Rick Herrmann/500px. (b) Neil Hall/Reuters. 626 Hulton Archive/Getty Images. 628 Bettmann/Getty Images. 629 ©University of Washington Libraries, Special Collections, [A. Curtis 37055]. (tc) ©University of Washington. 631 PARIS PIERCE/Alamy Stock Photo. 632-633 (spread) AF archive/Alamy Stock Photo. 634-635 Robert Holmes/Alamy Stock Photo. 636 Nightlife, 1943 (oil on canvas)/Motley Jr., Archibald J. (1891-1981)/ART INSTITUTE OF CHICAGO/The Art Institute of Chicago, IL, USA/Bridgeman Images. 637 (t)The Estate of David Gahr/Premium Archive/Getty Images. (bl) INTERFOTO/Alamy Stock Photo. 638 (bl) ©National Museum of African American History and Culture. (br) ©National Geographic Learning. 639 ClassicStock/Alamy Stock Photo. 640 Dosfotos/Getty Images. 641 (tr) Everett Collection Historical/Alamy Stock Photo. (cr) EVERETT COLLECTION, INC. (br) Michael Ochs Archives/Getty Images. 642 Library of Congress Prints and Photographs Division Washington, D.C. 643 National Geographic Learning. 645 (t)(cr) ©Courtesy of the Syracuse University Art Collection. 646 Image Asset Management/AGE Fotostock. 647 GL Archive/Alamy Stock Photo. 649 (tl) National Geographic Learning. (b) National Geographic Learning. 650 (l) Mary Evans/Jazz Age Club Collection/AGE Fotostock. (br)Mary Evans Picture Li/AGE Fotostock. 652 Bettmann/Getty Images. 654 Pictorial Press Ltd/ AlamyStock Photo. 655 Blank Archives/Getty Images. 656 (bl) Glasshouse Images/Alamy Stock Photo. (br) Herbert Dorfman/Getty Images. 657 Richard T. Nowitz/Getty Images. 658 Division of Culture & the Arts, National Museum of American History, Behring Center, Smithsonian Institution. 659 Photo by Eric Long, Smithsonian National Air and Space Museum. 660 Kirn Vintage Stock/Getty Images. 661 Hulton Deutsch/Corbis Premium Historical/Getty Images. 662 Governor Nellie Ross, c. 1925 (b/w photo)/Bain, George Grantham (1865-1944)/Private Collection/Bridgeman Images. 665 Bettmann/Getty Images. 666 State Archives of Florida/Florida Memory/Alamy Stock Photo. 667 The Jacob and Gwendolyn Lawrence Foundation/Art Resource, NY. 668 Photo Researchers, Inc/Alamy Stock Photo. 670 Robert W. Kelley/Getty Images. 671 (tr) (cr) (br) ©National Geographic Learning. 673Universal History Archive/Getty Images. 674-675 (spread) Library of Congress, Prints & Photographs Division, Reproduction number LC-DIG-ppmsca-15611. 676-677 (spread) The Library of Congress. 678 The Library of Congress. 679 Library of Congress Prints and Photographs Division Washington, D.C. 680 Artepics/Alamy Stock Photo. 682 The Library of Congress. 683 (tl) (tr) (b) The Library of Congress. 684 Everett Collection Inc/Alamy Stock Photo. 686 Everett Collection Inc/Alamy Stock Photo. 690 New York Times Co./Getty Images. 692-693 (spread) ©Jimmy Chin Photography. 693 (tr) MIKEY SCHAEFER/National Geographic Creative. 694 Everett Collection Inc/Alamy Stock Photo. 696 National Air and Space Museum. 697 Eric Schaal/Getty Images. 699 Bettmann/Getty Images. 700 Everett Collection Inc/Alamy Stock Photo. 703 (bl) Photo Researchers/Getty Images. (tr) California Industrial Scenes fresco Image Missing in RP. 704-705 (spread)FrancoisGalland/Getty Images. 706 Universal History Archive/Getty Images. 707 ©National Baseball Hall of Fame Library. 708 (bl)PhotoQuest/Getty Images. (b) ©National Baseball Hall of Fame. 709 ©Ronald Gabriel Baseball Memorabilia Collection, 1912-2009, Archives Center, National Museum of American History. 710 Transcendental Graphics/Getty Images. 711 (t) National Baseball Hall of Fame Library/MLB Photos/Getty Images. (br) Transcendental Graphics/Getty Images. 712 TASOS KATOPODIS/Getty Images. 713 Ron Vesely/Getty Images. 714 (bc) Bettmann/Getty Images. (br) Blank Archives/Getty Images. 716 ©Division of Political History, National Museum of American History, Smithsonian Institution. 717 Stock Montage/Getty Images. 718 AP Images. 719 David Frent/Getty Images. 720 Historical/Getty Images. 723 (tl) Library of Congress, Prints & Photographs Division, Reproduction number LC-USZC2-854. (tr) Library of Congress, Prints & Photographs Division, Reproduction number LC-USZC2-987. (bl) Library of Congress, Prints & Photographs Division, Reproduction number LC-USZC2-1174. (br) Library of Congress, Prints & Photographs Division, Reproduction number LC-USZC2-5653. 724 Bettmann/Getty Images. 726 (cr) ©Image Courtesy of Milwaukee Public Museum, negative number #H49639-34a. (bl) ©Image Courtesy of Milwaukee Public Museum. 727 (tl) ©Image Courtesy of Milwaukee Public Museum, negative number #H49624-24a. (tr) ©Image Courtesy of Milwaukee Public Museum. (b) ©Image Courtesy of Milwaukee Public Museum, negative number #H49629-35a. 727 MARK RALSTON/Getty Images. 730 Bettmann/Getty Images. 731 Bloomberg/Getty Images. 732-733 (spread) Tom Till/SuperStock. 734 Bettmann/Getty Images. 736 Bettmann/Getty Images. 737 David Frent/Getty Images. 738 National Geographic Learning. 739 Library of Congress, Prints & Photographs Division, Reproduction number LC-USZC2-936. 741 Bettmann/Getty Images. 743 Kerrick James/Getty Images. 745 ©Billy Warren/The Buffalo News. 746 ©Jeffrey Gusky. 748-749 Robert Capa/International Center of Photography/Magnum Photos. 750 (tr) LOS ALAMOS NATIONAL LABORATORY/SCIENCE PHOTO LIBRARY/Getty Images. (cl) American Stock Archive/Getty Images. (bl) 7maru/Getty Images. (br) Keren Su/Getty Images. 751 (tc) schlol/Getty Images. (cr) United States coin image from the United States Mint. (br) Everett Collection Historical/Alamy Stock Photo. 752-753 (spread) Hulton Deutsch/Getty Images. 755 Print Collector/Getty Images. 756 Guernica, 1937 (oil on canvas)/Picasso, Pablo (1881-1973)/MuseoNacional Centro de Arte Reina Sofia, Madrid, Spain/Bridgeman Images. 757 Universal ImagesGroup/Getty Images. 759 Eric TSCHAEN/REA/Redux. 761 SZ Photo/Scherl/The Image Works. 763 Paul Popper/Popperfoto/Getty Images. 764 FototecaStoricaNazionale./Getty Images. 766-767 (spread) VCG/Getty Images. 769 Fox Photos/Getty Images. 771 Franklin D. Roosevelt Presidential Library & Museum/National Archives. 773 Bettmann/Getty Images. 774-775 Everett Collection Inc/Alamy Stock Photo. 776-777 Everett Collection Inc/Alamy Stock Photo. 779 (bl) AP Images/Dean Hanson. (br) Lyn Alweis/Getty Images. 780 Science & Society Pictures Library/Getty Images. 781 Weinstein Company/Everett Collection. 783 Pictorial Press Ltd/Alamy Stock Photo. 784-785 Library of Congress, Prints & Photographs Division, Reproduction number LC-USW33-038539-ZC. 787 Library of Congress, Prints & Photographs Division, Reproduction number LC-DIG-ppmsca-13259 (digital file from original neg.). 788 Bettmann/Getty Images. 789 Bettmann/Getty Images. 791 Peter Stackpole/Getty Images. 792 Photo 12/Alamy Stock Photo. ©Printed by permission of the Norman Rockwell Family AgencyCopyright ©1942 the Norman Rockwell Family Entities. 793 Library of Congress. 794 Library of Congress, Prints & Photographs Division, Reproduction number LC-DIG-ppprs-00368. 795 Manzanar National Historic Site/NPS. 796 ©Japanese American National Museum, Gift of IbukiHibi Lee (96. 601. 8). 797 (cl) Japanese American National Museum, Gift of June HoshidaHonma, Sandra Hoshida and Carole HoshidaKanada (97. 106. 1EN). (tr) Japanese American National Museum, Gift of June HoshidaHonma, Sandra Hoshida and Carole HoshidaKanada (97. 106. 1EN). (br) Japanese American National Museum, Gift of Jack and Peggy Iwata (93. 102. 127). (tc) Japanese American National Museum, Gift of June HoshidaHonma, Sandra Hoshida and Carole HoshidaKanada (97. 106. 1EN). (cr) Japanese American National Museum, Gift of June HoshidaHonma, Sandra Hoshida and Carole HoshidaKanada (97. 106. 2CA). 800 Thomas D. McAvoy/Getty Images. 801 Historical/Getty Images. 802 ANDREW CABALLERO-REYNOLDS/Getty Images. 803 ©Aviation History Collection/

Alamy Stock Photo. **805** Hulton Archive/Getty Images. **806** LAPI/Getty Images. **807** Library of Congress, Prints & Photographs Division, Reproduction number LC-USZ62-7449. **810** Photo Researchers, Inc/Alamy Stock Photo. **811** Alfred Eisenstaedt/Pix Inc./Time & Life Pictures/Masters/Getty Images. **812** (tc) ©Courtesy of the Beser family. **813** KIMIMASA MAYAMA/Newscom/European Pressphoto Agency/HIROSHIMA/HIROSHIMA/JAPAN. **814** ©United States Holocaust Memorial Museum. **815** National Archives/Getty Images. **816** Historical/Getty Images. **817** Anne Frank Fonds Basel/Premium Archive/Getty Images. **818** ©United States Holocaust Memorial Museum. **821** GalerieBilderwelt/Hulton Archive/Getty Images. **823-824** (spread) Cameron Davidson/Getty Images. **824** ©WHO/E. Soteras Jalil. **826** Heritage Images/Getty Images. **828-829** (spread) Walter Sanders/Getty Images. **830** ©Leslie Illingworth Associated Newspaper/Solo Syndication, London. **832** National Archives. **835** BRUCE DALE/National Geographic Creative. **836** ©The Andy Warhol Museum, Pittsburgh; Founding Collection, Contribution Dia Center for the Arts©The Andy Warhol Foundation for the Visual Arts, Inc. **840-841** (spread) Bobby Yip/REUTERS. **840-841** (spread) AFP/Getty Images. **842** Movie Poster Image Art/Getty Images. **845** (tc) Everett Collection Inc/Alamy Stock Photo. **847** Universal History Archive/Getty Images. **848-849** (spread) Margaret Bourke-White/Getty Images. **850-851** Tony Frank/Sygma/Getty Images. **852** INTERFOTO/Alamy Stock Photo. **853** (r) KevorkDjansezian/Getty Images. (tl) New York Daily News Archive/Getty Images. **854** Hulton Archive/Getty Images. **855** (tl) The Advertising Archives/Alamy Stock Photo. (cl) Apic/Getty Images. (c) C12/Corbis. (cl) CBW/Alamy Stock Photo. (bl) Marc Tielemans/Alamy Stock Photo. **856** Michael Ochs Archives/Getty Images. **857** (tr) RB/Getty Images. (b) ZUMA Press, Inc./Alamy Stock Photo. **858** Everett Collection/AGE Fotostock. **860** (tl) ©Collection of the New-York Historical Society. (tr) Bettmann/Getty Images. **861** (tl) Frederic Neema/Getty Images. (cl) Hulton Deutsch/Getty Images. (cr) Popperfoto/Getty Images. **863** Yale Joel/Getty Images. **864** PhotoQuest/Getty Images. **865** ClassicStock/AlamyStock Photo. **867** Everett Collection Inc/Alamy Stock Photo. **868** Bettmann/Getty Images. **869** vincent noel/Shutterstock.com. **870** (tl) Wayne Miller/Magnum Photos. (tr) Three Lions/Getty Images. (cl) Thomas D. McAvoy/Getty Images. (cr) Car Culture/Getty Images. (bl) Carol M. Highsmith/The Library of Congress. (br) Dennis Stock/Magnum Photos. **871** (t) Corbis Premium Historical/Getty Images. (bl) ZUMA Press, Inc./Alamy Stock Photo. (br) Bryan Mitchell/Getty Images. **873** (tl) Bettmann/Getty Images. (tr) Blank Archives/Getty Images. **874** Charles Trainor/Getty Images. **876** (b) (cr) ©National Baseball Hall of Fame. **877** (tl)(tr)(br) ©National Baseball Hall of Fame. **879** ©Wayne Miller/Magnum Photos. **881** (tl)(tc) (tr) (bl) (br) Erika Larsen/National Geographic Creative. **883** ©Leonard Nadel/National Museum of American History/Kenneth E. Behring Center. **885** Buyenlarge/Getty Images. **886** Bettmann/Getty Images. **888-889** (spread) Bettmann/Getty Images. **890** (t) Independent Picture Service/Alamy Stock Photo. (c) Ian Dagnall/Alamy Stock Photo. (bl) Ulrich Doering/Alamy Stock Photo. (br) Library of Congress, Prints & Photographs Division, Reproduction number LC-DIG-ppmsc-07978. **891** (t) Gary Ombler/Getty Images. (c) New York Daily News Archive/Getty Images. (bl) Pacific Press/Getty Images. (br) Bettmann/Getty Images. **892-893** (spread) Danny Lyon/Magnum Photos. **894-895** AP Images/Pablo Martinez Monsivais. **895** Leonard Freed/Magnum Photos. **896-897** AP Images/Jacquelyn Martin. **897** (br) Carl Iwasaki/Getty Images. **898** AP Images/Molly Riley. **899** (t) Jim West/Alamy Stock Photo. (b) B Christopher/Alamy stock photo. **900** David Hume Kennerly/Getty Images. **901** (t) ©National Museum of African American History and Culture, Gift of the Family of Rev. Norman C. "Jim" Jimerson and Melva Brooks Jimerson. (b) Eli Reed/Magnum Photos. **903** Arthur Brower/Getty Images. **904** The Library of Congress- Prints & Photographs Online Catalog. **905** 'Invisible Man' by Ralph Ellison (1914-94) published by Random House, New York, 1952/American School, (20th century)/CHRISTIES IMAGES/Private Collection/Bridgeman Images. **906** Bettmann/Getty Images. **908** Cornell Capa/Getty Images. **909** Bettmann/Getty Images. **910** UniversalImagesGroup/Getty Images. **911** Don Cravens/Getty Images. **912** (t) (b) AP Images. **913** Bettmann/Getty Images. **914** ©Smithsonian National Museum of African American History and Culture. **915** Bettmann/Getty Images. **916** Underwood Archives/Getty Images. **917** ©**Collection of the Smithsonian National Museum of** African American History and Culture. **919** AP Images/BILL HUDSON. **920** Wyatt Tee Walker/CSU Archives/Everett Collection. **923** Francis Miller/Getty Images. **925** Copyright 1960, St. Louis Post-Dispatch/Library of Congress [LC-DIG-

ppmsca-05522]. **926-927** (spread) Bettmann/Getty Images. **928** (bl) (br) Bettmann/Getty Images. **931** (t) Historical/Getty Images. (b) Ulrich Baumgarten/Getty Images. **933** Photo Courtesy of Peace Corps. **934** Everett Collection Inc/Alamy Stock Photo. **935** (t) (b) NASA. **937** (bl) Underwood Archives/Getty Images. (br) Bettmann/Getty Images. **938** Art Rickerby/Getty Images. **939** Bettmann/Getty Images. **940** Bettmann/Getty Images. **941** Bachrach/Getty Images. **942** (tl) Historical/Getty Images. (tr) Bettmann/Getty Images. **943** (t) Bettmann/Getty Images. (b) Everett Collection Historical/Alamy Stock Photo. **944** Lynn Johnson/National Geographic Creative. **945** Phil Degginger/Alamy Stock Photo. **946-947** (spread) DAVID GUTTENFELDER/National Geographic Creative. **948** Keystone-France/Getty Images. **950** UniversalImagesGroup/Getty Images. **951** Danny Lyon/Magnum Photos. **953** AP Images/Charles Kelly. **954** ©Bob Stefko. **956** ©Copyright held by Spider Martin/The Spider Martin Civil Rights Collection. NARA. **959** David Fenton/Getty Images. **960** AP Images/Anonymous. **961** Joseph Louw/Getty Images. **962** (cr) Brooks Kraft/Getty Images. (br) National Geographic Learning. **963** (tr) National Geographic Learning. (tcr) Ian Dagnall/Alamy Stock Photo. (cl) Paul Briden/Alamy Stock Photo. (br) Raymond Boyd/Getty Images. **966-967** (spread) BrunoBarbey/Magnum Photos. **968** AP Images. **969** Vietnam: Communist propaganda poster: 'Victorious Ham Rong'/PICTURES FROM HISTORY/Bridgeman Images. **970** AP Images/HORST FAAS. **973** AP Images. **974** AP Images/HENRI HUET. **975** ©National Air and Space Museum. **977** Ian Berry/Magnum Photos. **978** tim page/Getty Images. **979** AP Images/Anonymous. **981** Marc Riboud/Magnum Photos. **983** CBS Photo Archive/Getty Images. **984** Julian Wasser/Getty Images. **987** John Dominis/Getty Images. **989** BurtGlinn/Magnum Photos. **990** John Filo/Getty Images. **992** Photograph courtesy of the National Mall and Memorial Parks, National Park Service. **993** Juan Valdez/National GEOGRAPHIC Learning. **994-995** (spread) MICHAEL S. LEWIS/National Geographic Creative. **998-999** (spread) ©Aaron Huey. **1000-1001** Courtesy of NASA. **1001** ©Smithsonian National Air and Space Museum. **1002** EVERETT COLLECTION, INC. **1003** ©Smithsonian National Air and Space Museum. **1004** NASA. **1005** (t) MARK THIESSEN/National Geographic Creative. (b) NASA/Getty Images. **1007** ZUMA Press, Inc./Alamy Stock Photo. **1008** (bg) ©AngélicaDass. (c) ©KattiaZanetta. **1009** ©AngélicaDass. **1011** (tl) Cathy Murphy/Getty Images. (cl) Tim Graham/Getty Images. (r) Library of Congress Prints and Photographs Division Washington [LC-DIG-ds-03091] With permission from CWLU Herstory Project. (bl) National Geographic Learning. **1013** ©Los Angeles Public Library. **1014** Bettmann/Getty Images. **1016** ©Minnesota Historical Society. **1017** Bob Kreisel / Alamy Stock Photo. **1018** Bettmann/Getty Images. **1020** (cr) Blank Archives/Getty Images. (br) ©Library of Congress Prints and Photographs Division Washington, D.C. (br) Blank Archives/Getty Images. **1023** NCAA Photos/Getty Images. **1024-1025** istock.com/jcarillet. **1026** Ralph Morse/The LIFE Picture Collection/Getty Images. **1027** Science & Society Picture Library/Getty Images. **1028** Kenneth Batelman/National Geographic Learning. **1029** ©National Air and Space Museum. **1031** NASA. **1032** Historical/Getty Images. **1034-1035** DIANE COOK, LEN JENSHEL/National Geographic Creative. **1036** (tr) Bettmann/Getty Images. (cl) Universal History Archive/Getty Images. (b) Tom Stoddart Archive/Contributor. **1037** (tl)Universal History Archive/Getty Images. (tr) Bettmann/Getty Images. (b) Tom Stoddart Archive/Contributor. (br) Dennis Tarnay, Jr./Alamy Stock Photo. (cl) MICKE Sebastien/Getty Images. (cr) JEFF KOWALSKY/European Pressphoto Agency/Newscom. (bl)Mark Stewart/Camera Press/Redux. (br) Peter Macdiarmid/Getty Images. **1039-1040** (spread)Bettmann/Getty Images. **1040** George Silk/Getty Images. **1043** Bettmann/Getty Images. **1044** Bettmann/Getty Images. **1046** George Rinhart/Getty Images. **1047** Bettmann/Getty Images. **1048** FransLanting/FransLanting Stock/National Geographic Creative. **1050-1051** (spread) PAUL NICKLEN/National Geographic Creative. **1051** Christina Mitermeier/National Geographic Creative. **1052** AP Images. **1053** ©National Archives. **1055** Bettmann/Getty Images. **1057** Library of Congress Prints and Photographs Division Washington, D.C. **1059** Owen Franken/Getty Images. **1060** Government Press Office. **1062** Bettmann/Getty Images. **1063** Bettmann/Getty Images. **1066-1067** (spread) Arnold Newman/Getty Images. **1068** Timothy Fadek/Getty Images. **1071** Ralph Crane/Getty Images. **1072** Entertainment Pictures/Alamy Stock Photo. **1075** Diana Walker/Getty Images. **1076** Al Seib/Getty Images. **1077** National Portrait Gallery, Smithsonian Institution/Art Resource, NY. **1079** Terry Ashe/Getty Images. **1080** Retro Ark/Alamy Stock Photo. **1081** Encyclopaedia Britannica/Getty Images. **1082** (tl) ZUMA Press, Inc./Alamy Stock Photo. (tr)Richard Ellis/

Illustration and Map Credits

Unless otherwise indicated, all illustrations were created by Lachina and all maps were created by Mapping Specialists.

Text Credits